CANADIAN
GLOBAL
ALMANAC
2005

CANADIAN
GLOBAL
ALMANAC
2005

All the facts you need
about Canada and the World

Economic News | Entertainment | Famous Canadians |
Geography | Government and Politics | Population |
Science | Sports | World Events | World Statistics

John Wiley and Sons Canada
Toronto

Contents

LANDFORMS

Canada is the largest country in the Western Hemisphere and the second largest in the world, with a total area of 9,970,610 sq. km. It stretches north to south from Cape Columbia on Ellesmere Island to Middle Island in Lake Erie, a distance of 4,634 km. The greatest east-west distance is 5,514 km from Cape Spear, Newfoundland, to the Yukon–Alaska border. Within this vast expanse, Canada contains an extremely wide variety of geographical features: the towering peaks of the Rockies, the flat Prairies, the rugged north and the gently rolling landscape of the east. But within this seemingly wide range of features, five areas with common characteristics are found. These physiographic regions are generally used to describe Canada and form the basis of Canada's geographical landforms and geological regions.

■ The Canadian Shield

Also known as the Precambrian Shield, this area is located in the central part of the continent. Viewed from the air it is a vast, inhospitable land of rocks, lakes and trees. It makes up roughly half of Canada's surface area, sweeping around Hudson Bay like a giant horseshoe, but also is the foundation for the rest of the continent.

The Canadian Shield has not always looked as it does today. Early in the Earth's history this area was the site of towering mountains, deep valleys and mighty rivers. The mountains were thrust up by volcanic activity as long as 3.8 billion years ago, during the Precambrian era. Over time, the forces of erosion—wind, water, freezing temperatures, ice—wore down the rocks that formed the mountain peaks and carried the materials away. Now all that remains are the roots of the once-mighty mountains.

The processes of volcanism present at the time of mountain-building caused minerals to form in the cooling rock of the Precambrian mountains. Deep inside the mountains, minerals such as gold, silver, copper and nickel came together into veins of ore. These ore bodies make the Shield a rich storehouse of mineral wealth.

■ The Appalachian Region

To the east of the Shield, this region was also once the site of massive mountain peaks. The rock that forms these peaks is not as old as the rock of the Shield, and is of a type that is more easily eroded. The Appalachian Region runs in a northeasterly direction from the southern United States to Newfoundland.

The mineral deposits found in the region reflect the complexity of the geology, and include gypsum, barite, salt, copper, zinc, lead, gold and silver. Since the end of the mountain-building period, erosion has worn off the tops of the mountains and filled the valleys with sediments, which gives the area its present-day less rugged appearance.

■ The Interior Plains

West of the Shield, rock which formed at the bottom of ancient lakes and seas gives the Prairies their distinctive flatness.

The Interior Plains occupy the central portion of the continent. Minerals found in the Interior Plains include potash, a substance produced when lakes and shallow seas evaporate, leaving deposits. Potash deposits in Saskatchewan are among the largest in the world. Coal, oil and natural gas were formed from organic materials trapped by the sedimentary layers during Palaeozoic times. An extension of the Interior Plains thrusts up between the Canadian Shield and the Appalachian Region, forming the Great Lakes–St. Lawrence Lowlands landform area. Soils throughout the Interior Plains are fertile, since the sedimentary materials that are found in the Plains break down easily.

Other lowland areas were formed during the Palaeozoic era as a result of the deposit of sediment which created the Interior Plains. The Hudson Bay Lowlands on the southwestern edge of Hudson Bay are relatively thin layers of sedimentary rock on top of the Precambrian Shield. The Arctic Lowlands, between the Shield and the Innuition Mountains of the high Arctic, are similar in age and characteristics to the material of the Interior Plains.

■ The Western Cordillera

As the Precambrian mountains eroded, the sedimentary layers were deposited over a great distance and formed the Appalachian Region to the east. These deposits also provided the material from which future landforms would be built to the west. These landforms are now known as the Western Cordillera.

When the continent started its westward movement about 200 million years ago, its leading edge was forced against the adjacent oceanic plate and the land moved overtop the ocean. Geologists speculate that the tremendous pressure exerted during this process caused the sedimentary layers of the plate's edge to buckle into a massive dome. Magma, the hot fluid substance below the Earth's crust, flowed into the dome and formed a core which eventually collapsed between 65 and 160 million years ago, breaking the rock layers. This core stretches along the edge of the continental plate and absorbs the pressure of the two plates as they press upon each other.

The Western Cordillera is an area of great complexity; rocks composed of different materials and through different processes are thoroughly mixed. The Coast Ranges which form the leading western edge of the continent are composed of both igneous and metamorphic rock. The interior of the Cordillera is a jumble of plateaus, folded and broken rock layers and recent volcanoes. The sedimentary materials of the Rockies on the eastern edge of the Cordillera were folded and broken during a period of mountain-building in Eocene times, some 40-65 million years ago.

The Cordillera contains minerals associated with all the processes involved in its creation. The igneous rocks of the western part of the Cordillera are a major source of minerals including lead, zinc, silver, copper and gold. The sedimentary deposits of the eastern Cordillera are responsible for the coal and petroleum found there.

■ Innuitian Region

Mountain-building shaped the landforms of the high Arctic during the Devonian period (about 405 million years ago). The most recent activities appear to have occurred about 30 million years ago, which was long after the mountain-building period that thrust up the Rocky Mountains in the Cordillera.

Little detail is known about this region because research is so difficult in the inhospitable climate, but some geologists have suggested mountain-building is the result of the North American plate advancing on the Eurasian plate.

The topography of this region is characterized by low plateau mountains, with ridges as high as 3,000 m. The area is composed mainly of sedimentary rocks but includes some metamorphic and volcanic rocks.

For more information on geological time periods, see the chart in the Science and Nature section.

Highest Point in Each Province and Territory

Province/Territory	Highest Point	Elev. (m)
Newfoundland & Labrador	Mt. Caubvick[1]	1 652
Prince Edward Island	46° 20'—63° 25' (Queen's County)	142
Nova Scotia	46° 42'—60° 36' (Cape Breton Highlands)	532
New Brunswick	Mt. Carleton	817
Quebec	Mont D'Iberville[2]	1 652
Ontario	Ishpatina Ridge	693
Manitoba	Baldy Mtn.	832
Saskatchewan	Cypress Hills	1 468
Alberta	Mt. Columbia	3 747
British Columbia	Fairweather Mtn.	4 663
Yukon Territory	Mt. Logan	5 959
Northwest Territories	61° 52'—127° 42' (unnamed peak, Mackenzie Mtns.)	2 773
Nunavut	Barbeau Peak (Ellesmere Island)	2 616

Source: *Natural Resources Canada*

(1) On the Nfld & Lab./Que. border; also known as Mt. D'Iberville in Quebec; next highest point in Nfld & Lab. is Cirque Mt. at 1,568 m. (2) On the Nfld & Lab./ Que. border; also known as Mt. Caubvick in Nfld & Lab.; next highest point in Que. is Mont Jacques-Cartier at 1,268 m.

Largest Lakes in Canada

Lake	Area[1] (sq. km)	Lake	Area[1] (sq. km)
Superior, Ont.[2]	82 100	Nettilling, NT*	5 542
Huron, Ont.[3]	59 600	Winnipegosis, Man.	5 374
Great Bear, NWT	31 328	Nipigon, Ont.	4 848
Great Slave, NWT	28 568	Manitoba, Man.	4 624
Erie, Ont.[4]	25 700	Dubawnt, NT*	3 833
Winnipeg, Man.	24 387	Lake of the Woods, Ont./Man.[6]	4 472
Ontario, Ont.[5]	18 960	Amadjuak, NT*	3 115
Athabasca, Sask.	7 935	Melville, Nfld/Lab.	3 069
Reindeer, Sask./Man.	6 650	Wollaston, Sask.	2 681
Smallwood Reservoir, Nfld/Lab.	6 527	Lac Mistassini, Que.	2 335

Source: *Natural Resources Canada*   *Nunavut

(1) Total area, including islands except for the Great Lakes, where area does not include islands larger than 0.052 sq. km. (2) Includes 53,400 sq. km in US. (3) Includes 23,600 sq. km in US. (4) Includes 12,900 sq. km in US. (5) Includes 8,960 sq. km in US. (6) Includes 1,322 sq. km in US.

The Great Lakes

The Great Lakes form the largest body of fresh water in the world and with their connecting waterways are the largest inland water transportation unit. They enable shipping to reach the Atlantic via the St. Lawrence River; the Gulf of Mexico via the Illinois Waterway, from Lake Michigan to the Mississippi River; a third outlet connects with the Hudson River and thence the Atlantic via the New York State Barge Canal System.

	Superior	Michigan	Huron	Erie	Ontario
Length in km	563	494	332	388	311
Breadth in km	257	190	295	92	85
Deepest soundings in metres	405	281	229	64	244
Volume of water in cubic km	12 100	4 920	3 540	484	1 640
Area[1] (sq. km) in US	53 400	57 800	23 600	12 900	8 960
Area[1] (sq. km) in Canada	28 700	0	36 000	12 800	10 000
Total Area[1] (sq. km) US and Canada	**82 100**	**57 800**	**59 600**	**25 700**	**18 960**
National boundary line in km	430	0	446	404	281

Source: *Natural Resources Canada*   (1) Does not include islands larger than 0.052 sq. km.

Longest Rivers in Canada

River	Length (km)	Flows Into	River	Length (km)	Flows Into
Mackenzie	4 241	Arctic Ocean	North Saskatchewan	1 287	Saskatchewan R.
Yukon	3 185	Bering Sea	Ottawa	1 271	St. Lawrence R.
St. Lawrence	3 058	Gulf of St. Lawrence	Athabasca	1 231	Lake Athabasca
Nelson	2 575	Hudson Bay	Liard	1 115	Mackenzie R.
Columbia	2 000	Pacific Ocean	Assiniboine	1 070	Red R.
Saskatchewan	1 939	Lake Winnipeg (via Cedar Lake)	Severn	982	Hudson Bay
			Albany	982	James Bay
Peace	1 923	Lake Athabasca	Back	974	Arctic Ocean
Churchill (Man.)	1 609	Hudson Bay	Thelon	904	Hudson Bay
South Saskatchewan	1 392	Saskatchewan R.	La Grande Rivière	893	James Bay
Fraser	1 370	Pacific Ocean			

Source: *Natural Resources Canada*

Canadian Heritage Rivers System (CHRS)

It's not quite a national holiday, but the second Sunday in June is now Canadian Rivers Day, which was celebrated for the first time **June 8, 2003**. Heritage Minister Sheila Copps proclaimed the special day in mid-2002. Among the groups calling for the special day was the Canadian Heritage Rivers System board, which was established in 1984 as part of a federal-provincial plan to manage Canada's rivers. Individual rivers are administered by the government responsible for the land each flows through. However, the CHRS assists by supporting a management plan with funding and policy initiatives. No management plan is put forward until after public consultation is complete and a consensus has been reached.

The Heritage Rivers System is overseen by a fourteen member board made up of a representative appointed by each of the provincial and territorial governments, plus a federal appointee from the Department of Indian Affairs and Northern Development and another from Canadian Heritage's Parks Canada. This board meets at least once a year to designate funding and program priorities, and to review and approve new guidelines and policies. Thirty-one rivers have been designated for special management and conservation attention; 8 have been nominated for CHRS status (Bay du Nord, Newfoundland; Churchill, Saskatchewan; Coppermine, NWT; Hayes, Manitoba; Jacques-Cartier, Quebec; Missinaibi, Ontario; Montague-Three Rivers, P.E.I.; Tatshenshini, Yukon). More are under study, including the Mackenzie.

For information about the CHRS and detailed fact sheets on each river, visit www.chrs.ca.

Designated Rivers	Location	Length
Alsek River	Kluane National Park Reserve, Yukon	90 km section
Arctic Red River	Arctic Red River (Tsiigèhnjik), Northwest Territories	450 km
Athabasca River	Canadian Rocky Mountains National Parks, Alberta and BC	1 538 km
Bloodvein River	Woodland Caribou Provincial Park/Atikaki Wilderness Park, Ontario/Manitoba	306 km section
Bonnet Plume River	Yukon	350 km
Boundary Waters-Voyageur Waterway	Quetico, Middle Falls and Voyageur Provincial Parks, Ontario	250 km section
Clearwater River	Alberta and Saskatchewan	295 km
Cowichan River	British Columbia	47 km
Detroit River	Ontario	51 km
Fraser River	British Columbia	1 375 km
French River	French River Provincial Park, Ontario	110 km
Grand River	Ontario	627 km
Hillsborough River	Prince Edward Island	45 km
Humber River	Ontario	100 km
Kazan River	Nunavut	850 km
Kicking Horse	Canadian Rocky Mountains National Parks, Alberta and BC	68 km section
Main River	Newfoundland and Labrador	57 km
Margaree-Lake Ainslie River System	Nova Scotia	120 km
Mattawa River	Mattawa River Provincial Park, Ontario	65 km section
North Saskatchewan River	Canadian Rocky Mountains National Parks, Alberta and BC	48.5 headwater section
Rideau Waterway	Ontario	202 km
Seal River	Manitoba	260 km section
Shelburne River	Nova Scotia	53 km
Soper River	Nunavut	248 km
South Nahanni River	Nahanni National Park Reserve, Northwest Territories	540 km
St. Croix	New Brunswick	185 km
St. Marys River	Ontario	125 km
Thames River	Ontario	273 km
Thelon River	Nunavut	545 km section
Upper Restigouche	New Brunswick	55 km section
Yukon River	Yukon	Thirty Mile Section 48 km

Source: *Parks Canada*

VEGETATION

Coniferous forests dominated by spruce, fir and pine cover much of the Canadian landscape, sweeping across the continent in a broad band. Through the rest of the country there is a range of forest conditions. To the north, cold temperatures limit growth and the trees become small and fewer in number. At the tree line, trees grow only in sheltered river valleys. The tree line marks the northern extent of forests and the beginning of tundra conditions (moss, lichens and dwarf vegetation with permanent frozen subsoil).

The massive spruce, fir and pine of the forests along the coast of British Columbia are encouraged by a friendly climate. The moisture-laden winds from the Pacific Ocean keep the land well-supplied with rain. Under these conditions tree growth is rapid: the soils are constantly being replenished with minerals by the rains, and plant decay is also rapid in the damp conditions, thereby releasing more minerals for tree growth. With average monthly temperatures seldom going below freezing, the growing season is long. Coniferous trees thrive under such conditions.

The Interior Plains is one region of Canada that is not covered by forests because there is not enough precipitation, or available moisture, to sustain tree growth. In Alberta, Saskatchewan and Manitoba, forests gradually give way from north to south through a transitional area called the park belt, which contains both trees and grassland, before yielding to grasslands. Within these provinces, there are areas where moisture levels are insufficient to support grasslands and even hardy grasses have difficulty growing. During the 1930s, the lack of rainfall in the Interior Plains led to "dust bowl" conditions because vegetation could not grow enough to anchor the soil.

The forests of southeastern Canada are mixed, containing both coniferous and deciduous trees. Adequate rainfall and warm temperatures allow the less hardy species such as oak, maple, hickory and walnut to flourish in southern Ontario and Quebec and the Maritime provinces.

The Arctic tundra is so very dry and cold that the growing season is extremely limited. The vegetation of the tundra consists of mosses, lichen, dwarf bushes and heather. These plants are able to grow because they have adapted to the difficult conditions through characteristics such as small size and slow growth. Some shrubs and lichen grow so slowly that their development must be measured in centimetres per century.

AGRICULTURE

There are four main types of farms in Canada: livestock farms, grain farms producing such crops as wheat and oats, mixed farms producing both grain and livestock, and special crop farms producing vegetables, fruits, tobacco and other products. Both the type and amount of farming within Canada are affected by climate and location.

■ The Atlantic Region

The Atlantic region is an area of diverse agricultural activity. Newfoundland, because of poorly developed soils and a difficult climate, has a limited agricultural industry supplying only local markets. Encouraged by a moist climate and silty, stone-free soils, farming is the leading industry on Prince Edward Island; potatoes are the main crop. The land also supports mixed grains and dairy farms.

Nova Scotia's main agricultural areas surround the Bay of Fundy and Northumberland Strait where they are protected from Atlantic gales; dairy farming and poultry production are common. Nova Scotia's Annapolis Valley is famous for fruit, mainly apples. In New Brunswick, potatoes and livestock are produced in the Saint John River valley, and there is mixed farming in the northwest of the province.

■ The Central Region

In Canada's central region, the fertile soils and moist climate of southern Ontario and Quebec support a thriving agricultural industry. Although these growing conditions allow a variety of crops, the population concentration in this area encourages specialization in products with high transportation costs. Dairy farms are concentrated around Montreal and in southwestern Ontario, supplying milk, butter and cheese to the major centres such as London, Hamilton, Toronto, Kingston,

Montreal and Quebec City. Vegetable crops are also grown near these centres. Farms specializing in poultry and egg production, sheep and hogs are also common.

The Niagara Peninsula, between lakes Ontario and Erie, is a major fruit-growing centre. The moderating effects of the lakes delay the growth of the fruit trees in the spring until the danger of frost is past. Tender fruit crops—peaches, pears, plums and cherries—as well as grapes thrive in these conditions. Tobacco (and now ginseng) grow well on the glacially created sand plains of southwestern Ontario.

■ The Prairie Provinces

Manitoba, Saskatchewan and Alberta contain 80 percent of Canada's farmland. Here, a combination of flat, easily worked land, fertile soils, long sunny summer days and sufficient precipitation encourages the healthy growth of high-quality grains. This area grows most of Canada's wheat, about 90 percent of its barley and rye, and more than 75 percent of its oats.

Manitoba grows canola and flax in addition to wheat and other grains. Mixed farming in the province emphasizes beef cattle. Dairy farms are common around Winnipeg. Saskatchewan grows about 60 percent of Canada's wheat and large quantities of other grains. Mixed farming, poultry, egg and livestock production contribute to the provincial economy. Alberta, also a major grain producer, has more beef cattle ranches than any other province. They are located mainly in the south

of the province and in the foothills of the Rocky Mountains where the steep slopes and dry land is unsuited to growing crops.

■ The Pacific Region

In the Pacific region, only 2 percent of British Columbia is agricultural land. But the pockets of farmland are extremely productive. The lower mainland and the southern tip of Vancouver Island comprise the Georgia Strait agricultural region, an area concentrating on dairy farming and poultry raising to supply the province's population centres. Other crops include raspberries, strawberries, peas, tomatoes and flowers.

The Okanagan Valley contains 90 percent of British Columbia's orchards, producing grapes, apples and tender fruit such as peaches, plums, apricots and cherries. Here, local climatic and physiographic characteristics have resulted in conditions suitable for the orchard industry, although irrigation is often necessary and frost damage is a hazard. Beef cattle and sheep are raised in the interior of the province, where growing conditions are not suitable for crops requiring cultivation, but grazing can be carried out.

■ The North

Canada's North generally has soil and climatic conditions unsuited to agriculture. A small number of farms produce some dairy products, beef cattle and vegetables for the local market.

How's the Weather In Space?

*W*e all talk about the weather on Earth, but what about the weather in space? Sure, there are no rainstorms, no snow, no balmy blue skies. But over the past few years, "space weather" has become the accepted term for a collection of physical processes, beginning at the sun and ultimately affecting human activities on Earth and in space. The sun emits energy, in the form of radio waves, infra-red light, ultraviolet light and X-rays, as well as energetic electrically charged particles, such as electrons. The radiation, moving at the speed of light, takes about 8 minutes to get to Earth; the charged particles travel more slowly, taking from a few hours to several days to cover the distance.

These radiation and particles cause concentrations of energetic particles to collect and electric currents to flow in the outer atmosphere, which can have a variety of effects on human technology. The high-energy particles can put the satellites out of operation. Radio waves are affected by the increased ionization, potentially disrupting satellite communications or GPS navigation systems. Disturbances in Earth's magnetic field directly affect such things as magnetic surveys, directional drilling, or the use of compasses. Magnetic disturbances also induce electric currents in power lines and pipelines, causing outages or corrosion.

Source: *Geological Survey of Canada*

CLIMATE

Within Canada, climate is primarily affected by surrounding landforms, proximity to large bodies of water and the degree of latitude.

Landforms Air masses are forced to rise over mountains which lie in their path. As this happens, the air cools and its ability to retain moisture is reduced. Condensation then occurs and precipitation falls in the form of snow or rain. For instance, Prince Rupert on the western side (windward) of the Coastal Mountains receives over 2,500 mm of precipitation annually.

On the leeward side of the mountains (the side away from the wind), the air mass descends, warms and is able to once again retain moisture. Moreover, there may be little moisture left in the air mass. Thus precipitation is light and a rain-shadow effect is created. In a rain-shadow area, such as near Kamloops, B.C., desert-like conditions exist.

Water Parts of Canada near large bodies of water have more moderate climates due to the differing abilities of land and water to gain or lose heat. Whereas water can act like a heat bank, releasing accumulated heat through the fall and early winter and warming the land nearby, the reverse is also true. In the spring and early summer, the water is cooler than the land and can keep the land temperature lower.

Wind direction also determines the degree to which this influence is felt. On the Pacific coast the prevailing westerlies blow off the water onto the land and the influence of the Pacific Ocean is keenly felt. On the Atlantic coast, the westerlies blow off the land onto the water so the effect of the Atlantic Ocean is not as pronounced. Victoria's lowest monthly average temperature is 4.6°C in January with an annual range of only 11°C between the warmest and coldest months while Halifax's lowest monthly average is –4.8°C in February with an annual range of 22.7°C.

Latitude Latitude is the distance north or south of the equator and is expressed in degrees. Its effects on climate are twofold. Firstly, the further north the location, the more the curvature of the earth results in the sunlight spreading over a greater surface area. This decreases the solar radiation per unit area of ground so that less warmth from the sun is felt. Secondly, solar radiation has to travel a greater distance through the atmosphere at higher latitudes which again reduces the amount of energy reaching the earth.

Other Factors Because the prevailing wind direction is from west to east, the air masses move eastward across the continent picking up moisture from lakes and rivers and releasing it further along. Therefore, generally, precipitation increases with greater distance eastward from the central continent: the average precipitation in Winnipeg is 504 mm, Toronto 781 mm, Montreal 940 mm and Halifax 1,474 mm.

Also, the Labrador Current affects climate on the Atlantic coast. This cold current within the Atlantic Ocean flows south along the coast of Newfoundland and Labrador and reduces the moderating effect of the ocean on the land. It also causes the thick Newfoundland fog when relatively warm air is cooled from below on contact with the cold waters.

Smog Can Be Hazardous To Your Health

*T*he word "smog" is a combination of the words smoke and fog, but it's used today to describe a mixture of air pollutants, including gases and fine particles, that can be seen as a haze in urban centres, although it can be carried by the wind to rural areas as well. Smog is made up of airborne particles and ground-level ozone. The particles are solid or tiny drops of liquid, small enough to remain suspended in the air. The smallest particles, those less than 2.5 micrometres across, are of particular concern because they can penetrate deep within the lungs.

The ozone molecule, a variant of normal oxygen that has three oxygen atoms instead of two, forms a colourless and highly irritating gas. Studies show that every major Canadian city has enough ground-level ozone to pose a health risk. The gas is also known to damage vegetation and cause the deterioration of some natural and synthetic materials, including paints and dyes.

Source: *Environment Canada*

Average Weather Data for Selected Airports in Canada

	Temperature °C				Precipitation	
	Winter		Summer		Annual Snowfall cm	Total Precipitation mm
Airport	High	Low	High	Low		
Vancouver...............	6.1	0.5	21.7	13.2	48.2	119.0
Calgary	-2.8	-15.1	22.9	9.4	126.7	412.6
Edmonton................	-7.3	-16.0	22.8	12.1	123.5	476.9
Regina..................	-10.7	-21.6	25.7	11.8	105.9	388.1
Winnipeg................	-12.7	-22.8	25.8	13.3	110.6	513.7
Toronto.................	-2.1	-10.5	26.8	14.8	115.4	792.7
Ottawa..................	-6.1	-15.3	26.5	15.4	235.7	943.5
Montreal................	-5.8	-14.9	26.3	15.5	214.2	966.8
Saint John..............	-2.7	-13.6	22.4	11.7	256.9	1390.3
Halifax.................	-0.2	-9.2	22.1	13.5	176.4	1421.4
Charlottetown	-3.3	-12.6	23.2	13.8	311.9	1173.3
St. John's	-0.9	-8.6	20.3	10.5	322.3	1513.7
Iqaluit	-22.5	-30.6	11.6	3.7	235.8	412.0
Yellowknife	-22.7	-30.9	21.1	12.4	151.8	280.7
Whitehorse	-13.3	-22.0	20.5	7.7	145.0	267.4

	Wind			Sunshine	
Airport	Average Speed km/hr	Prevailing Direction	Peak Wind km/hr	Bright Sunshine hours	Possible Sunshine hours
Vancouver...............	11.8	E	129	1928	4781
Calgary	14.8	N	127	2405	4585
Edmonton.................	12.1	NW	117	2299	4693
Regina..................	18.6	SE	153	2338	4679
Winnipeg................	16.9	S	129	2372	4646
Toronto.................	14.7	N	135	2038	4653
Ottawa..................	12.9	W	135	2061	4631
Montreal	14.3	W	161	2029	4627
Saint John..............	16.1	SW	146	1950	4515
Halifax.................	15.1	NW	150	1965	4525
Charlottetown	17.4	SW	177	1859	4610
St. John's	23.3	W	193	1512	4629
Iqaluit	15.4	NW	156	1506	4934
Yellowknife	14.0	E	113	2265	5234
Whitehorse	12.7	S	106	1855	4979

	Annual Number of Days						
Airport	Frost	Wet Weather	Thunder-storms	Freezing Precipitation	Smoke/ Haze	Blowing Snow	Fog
Vancouver...............	46	166	6	1	48	0	23
Calgary	196	114	27	6	14	7	21
Edmonton.................	179	126	19	7	17	3	10
Regina..................	200	115	22	13	4	24	27
Winnipeg................	194	124	27	12	11	22	16
Toronto.................	146	146	28	9	83	8	27
Ottawa..................	159	163	24	17	64	12	34
Montreal	155	165	24	13	51	11	17
Saint John..............	169	162	11	12	14	10	98
Halifax.................	142	166	11	13	16	11	100
Charlottetown	166	184	10	18	16	22	44
St. John's	174	216	5	39	11	25	119
Iqaluit	272	155	0	6	0	58	14
Yellowknife	222	119	5	12	9	9	18
Whitehorse	225	122	7	2	2	2	14

Source: Environment Canada

CANADA

Canada at-a-Glance

■ LAND

Area	9 976 140 sq. km
Length of coastline	202 080 km (longest in the world)
Length of border with U.S. inc. Alaska	8 890 km
Longitudinal centre of Canada	97°W (close to Winnipeg)
Latitudinal centre of Canada	62°N (close to Yellowknife, Northwest Territories)
Geographic centre of Canada	Arviat, Nunavut (60°06'30"N, 94°03'30"W)
Greatest distance east to west	5 514 km (Cape Spear, Newfoundland, to the Yukon/Alaska border)
Greatest distance north to south	4 634 km (Cape Columbia, Ellesmere Island, to Middle Island, Lake Erie)
Largest island	Baffin Island, Nunavut, 507 451 sq. km
Northernmost point	Cape Columbia, Ellesmere Island, Nunavut, 83°06'N–69°57'W
Southernmost point	Middle Island, Lake Erie, Ontario, 41°41'N–82°40'W
Easternmost point	Cape Spear, Newfoundland, 47°31'N–52°37'W
Westernmost point	Yukon/Alaska boundary, 141°00'W
Northernmost community	Grise Fiord, Ellesmere Island, Nunavut, 76°25'N–82°54'W
Southernmost community	Pelee Island South, Ontario, 41°45'N–82°38'W
Easternmost community	Blackhead, Newfoundland, 47°32'N–52°39'W
Westernmost community	Beaver Creek, Yukon Territory, 62°23'N–140°52'W
Longest river	Mackenzie River, Northwest Territories, 4 241 km
Largest lake (entirely) in Canada	Great Bear Lake, Northwest Territories, 31 328 sq. km
Highest waterfall	Della Falls, Della Lake, B.C., 440 metres (more than one drop)

■ PEOPLE

Population (July 2004 est.)	31 946 316
Population growth rate (2004)	0.92%
Life expectancy at birth (2004 est.)	79.9; men: 76.6; women: 83.5
Age structure of the population (2003)	0–19 years: 25.0%; 20–64: 62.2%; 65+: 12.8%
Official language	English and French

■ NATION

Confederation	July 1, 1867
Governor General	Her Excellency, the Right Honourable Adrienne Clarkson
Prime Minister	The Right Honourable Paul Martin
Motto	*A Mari usque ad Mare* (From Sea to Sea)
National symbols	the Maple Leaf and the Beaver (both official)
National game	lacrosse (summer), hockey (winter)
Anthem	"O Canada" (National), "God Save the Queen" (Royal)
National capital	Ottawa, Ontario
Date of the last general election	June 28, 2004
Largest province	Quebec, 1 542 056 sq. km
Smallest province	Prince Edward Island, 5 660 sq. km

■ ECONOMY

GDP at market prices (July 2004)	$1 044.7 billion
Rate of inflation (August 2004)	1.9%
Rate of unemployment (August 2004)	7.2%

Source: *Canadian Heritage; Natural Resources Canada; Statistics Canada*

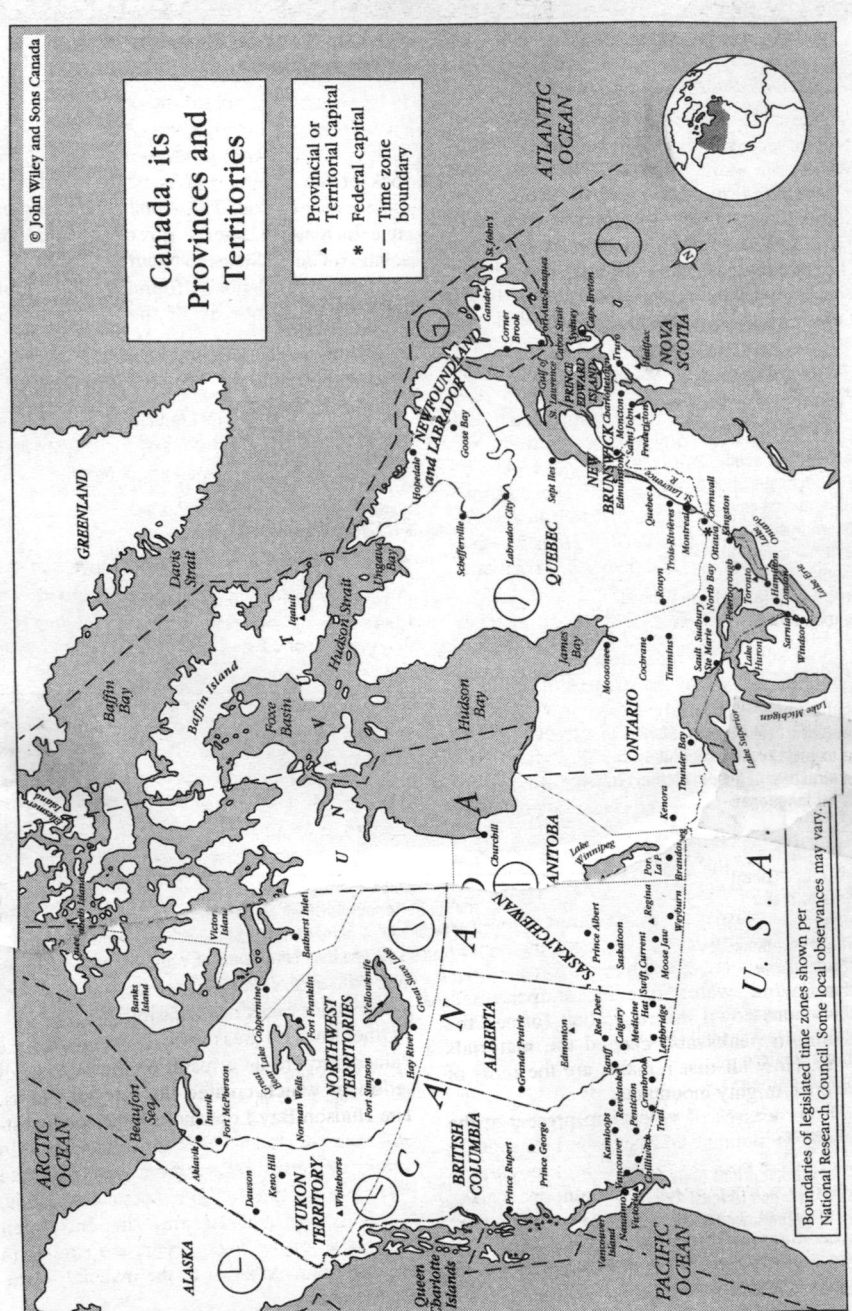

Canada, its Provinces and Territories

▲ Provincial or Territorial capital
✴ Federal capital
— — Time zone boundary

© John Wiley and Sons Canada

Boundaries of legislated time zones shown per National Research Council. Some local observances may vary.

2

Some of the information in this publication is made available through the cooperation of Statistics Canada. Any items credited to Statistics Canada are copyright of Statistics Canada; integral and/or adapted reproductions are published with permission of the Minister of Industry, Science and Technology. Readers wishing further information on any of the subjects credited to Statistics Canada may obtain copies of related publications by contacting Publications Sales, Statistics Canada, Ottawa, Ontario, Canada KIA 0T6, or by calling 1-613-951-7277 or 1-800-267-6677 (toll free in Canada and the United States). Readers may also fax orders by dialing 1-613-951-1584 or fax order line 1-877-287-4369 (toll free in Canada and the United States).

Researchers, editors, contributors and Publisher have used their best efforts in preparing this book. John Wiley and Sons Canada, the researchers, editors, and contributors make no representations or warranties with respect to the accuracy or completeness of the contents of this book and specifically disclaim any implied warranties of merchantability or fitness for a particular purpose. There are no warranties that extend beyond the descriptions contained in this paragraph. No warranty may be created or extended by sales representatives or written sales materials. The accuracy and completeness of the information provided herein and the opinions stated herein are not guaranteed or warranted to produce any specific results, and the advice and strategies contained herein may not be suitable for every individual. Neither John Wiley and Sons Canada, the researchers, editors, nor the contributors shall be liable for any loss of profit or any other commercial damages including but not limited to special, incidental, consequential or other damages.

Cover photographs used by permission of The Canadian Press, Toronto.

National Library of Canada Cataloguing in Publication Data

The National Library of Canada has catalogued this publication as follows:

The Canadian global almanac.

Annual.
1992-
Imprint varies.
Continues: Canadian world almanac and book of facts, ISSN 0833-532X.
ISSN 1187-4570
ISBN 0-470-83523-0 (2005 edition)

1. Almanacs, Canadian (English). 2. Almanacs.

AY414.C36 1992-   031.02   C92-031173-3

Printed in Canada

CANADIAN
GLOBAL
ALMANAC
2005

Managing Editor	**NICOLE LANGLOIS**
Contributing Editors	**ANDREW BORKOWSKI** *(Arts and Media)*
	FRANKLIN CARTER *(Politics and History)*
	PETER HAMMERSCHMIDT *(News Events)*
	MICHAEL KELLY *(Sports)*
	DAVID PHILLIPS *(Climate)*
	MICHAEL SMITH *(Geography, Science)*
	DONNA WILLIAMS *(Hall of Fame, Obituaries)*
Typesetter	**BETH CRANE,** *Heidy Lawrance Associates*
Researchers	**SONJA RUTHARD**
	ANN McILWRAITH
	BOB BALL
Indexer	**CHRISTINE DUDGEON**
Cover Designer	**IAN KOO**

Ocean Currents

Oceans or large bodies of water such as the Great Lakes affect the climate of the land nearby because they act as heat reservoirs and heat exchangers. Water heats up more slowly than land, and it holds that heat for a longer time. Because of this, the climate in the areas closest to water is more moderate than the climate inland: even though the air over the coastal land is warmer in summer and colder in winter than the air over water at the same latitude, it won't be as hot (or as cold) as the air over land that is far away from the coast.

These water bodies also affect rainfall, wind and clouds: when the water is warmer than the air above it, it generates clouds, rain and wind; when the water is colder than the air above, the opposite happens—there is likely to be fog, less rain, and winds are reduced.

As the ocean currents move heat and cold around the world, Canada is affected by the warm Gulf Stream on the Atlantic coast and the weaker but still warm Alaska Current on the Pacific side; both of these flow northward. Cold currents such as the West Greenland Current and the Labrador Current flow south from the Arctic on the east side; the banks of fog off the southeast coast of Newfoundland mark the spot where the Labrador Current meets the Gulf Stream. In general, however, because our weather flows from west to east, it is the currents on the Pacific side that have the greatest effect on Canada's climate.

Inland, the Great Lakes and Hudson Bay are two vast areas of water that affect the climate around them: the Great Lakes act as a huge heat reservoir that moderates the weather in southern Ontario and Quebec, while Hudson Bay is frozen over for six months, and even during the summer months melting ice keeps the surface water temperature close to freezing. Hudson Bay's most common effect is fog in summer and precipitation, cloud and strong winds during the rest of the year.

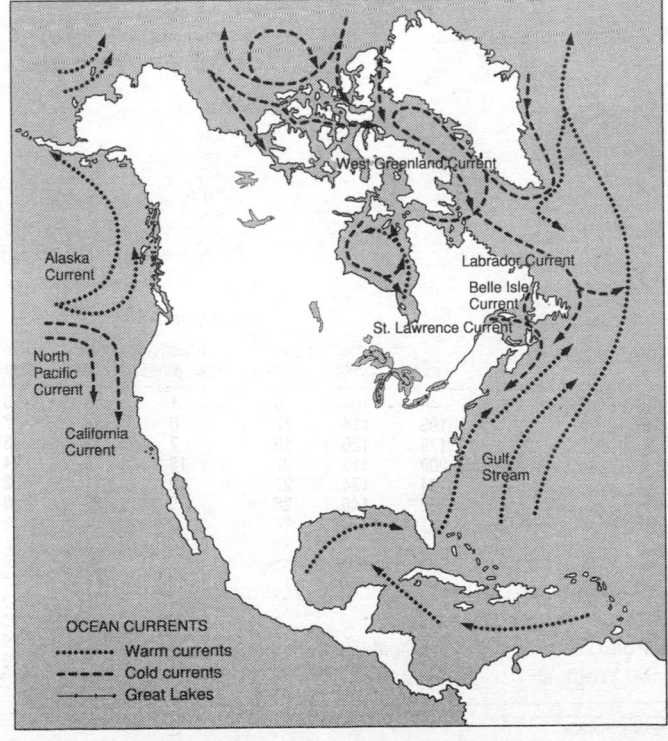

SUMMER AIR MASSES AND CIRCULATION

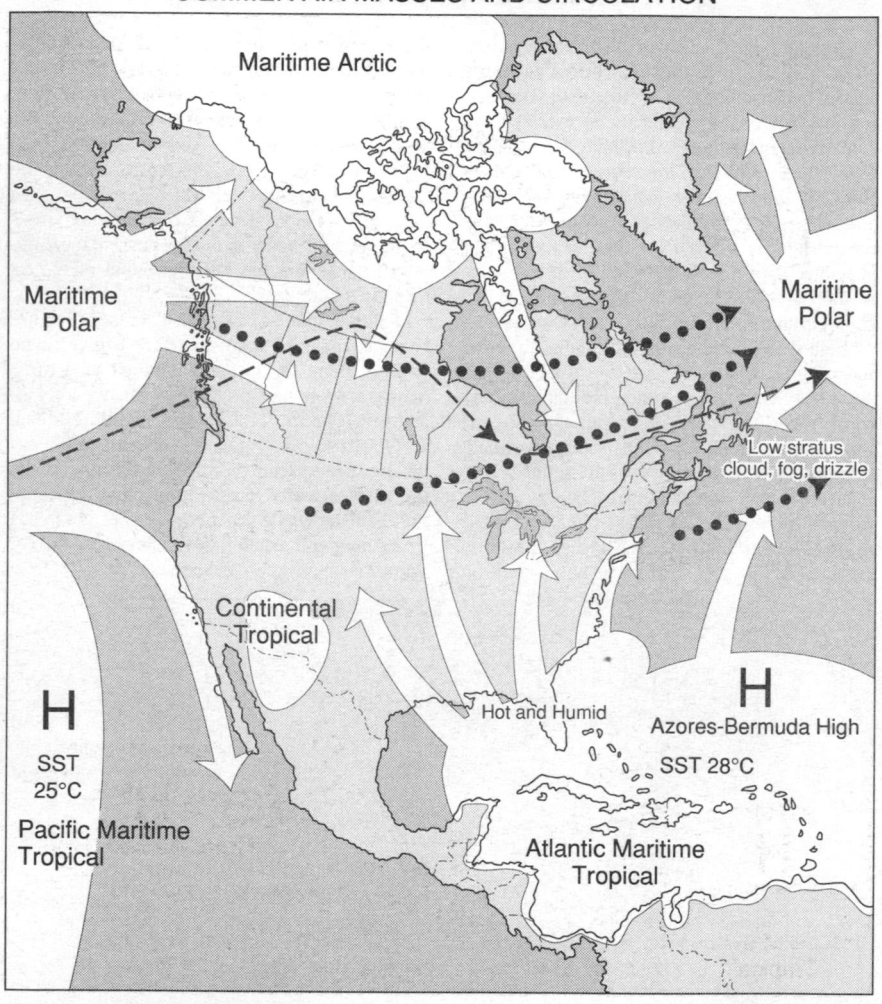

Maritime Arctic

Maritime Polar

Maritime Polar

Low stratus cloud, fog, drizzle

Continental Tropical

H
SST 25°C

H
Azores-Bermuda High
SST 28°C

Hot and Humid

Pacific Maritime Tropical

Atlantic Maritime Tropical

– – – Polar jet stream

● ● ● ● Primary storm tracks

SST   Sea Surface Temperature

Pacific Maritime Tropical: high pressure precludes moist air
Atlantic Maritime Tropical: very hot, humid, unstable
Maritime Arctic: modified by water
Maritime Polar: warmer, more stable than Maritime Arctic air
Continental Tropical: hot, dry, unstable

WINTER AIR MASSES AND CIRCULATION

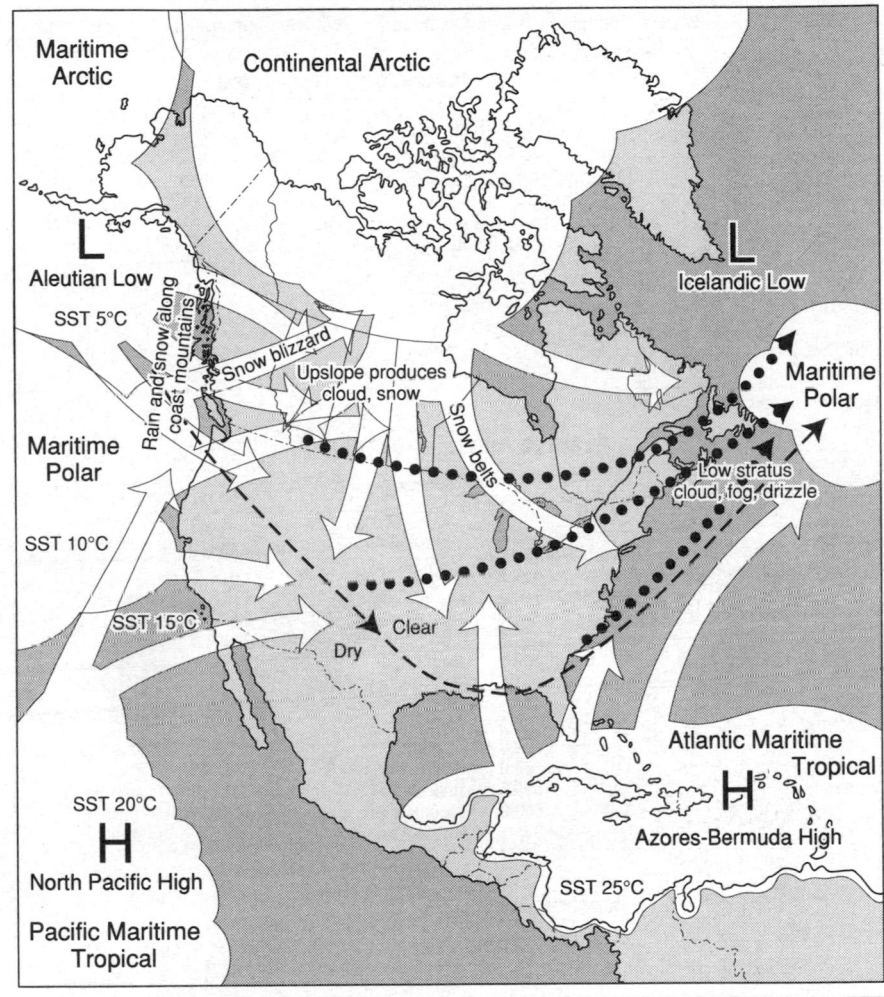

— — — —   Polar jet stream
● ● ● ● ●   Primary storm tracks
SST   Sea Surface Temperature

Continental Arctic: very cold, dry, stable
Maritime Arctic: very unstable, clouds, frequent showers or flurries
Maritime Polar: milder, more stable than Arctic air
Pacific Maritime Tropical: stable in lower 1000m
Atlantic Maritime Tropical: warm and humid

Provincial Weather Facts

Province	Warmest Temperature Ever Recorded °C	Date	Station	Coldest Temperature Ever Recorded °C	Date	Station
Newfoundland & Labrador	41.7	Aug. 11, 1914	Northwest River	-51.1	Feb. 17, 1973	Esker 2
P.E.I.	36.7	Aug. 19, 1935	Charlottetown	-37.2	Jan. 26, 1884	Kilmahumaig
New Brunswick	39.4	Aug. 18, 1935	Nepisiguit Falls	-47.2	Feb. 1, 1955	Sisson Dam
Nova Scotia	38.3	Aug. 19, 1935	Collegeville	-41.1	Jan. 31, 1920	Upper Stewiacke
Quebec	40.0	July 6, 1921	Ville Marie	-54.4	Feb. 5, 1923	Doucet
Ontario	42.2	July 20, 1919	Biscotasing	-58.3	Jan. 23, 1935	Iroquois Falls
Manitoba	44.4	July 11, 1936	St. Albans	-52.8	Jan. 9, 1899	Norway House
Saskatchewan	45.0	July 5, 1937	Midale	-56.7	Feb. 1, 1893	Prince Albert
Alberta	43.3	July 21, 1931	Bassano Dam	-61.1	Jan. 11, 1911	Fort Vermilion
British Columbia	44.4	July 16, 1941	Lillooet	-58.9	Jan. 31, 1947	Smith River
Yukon	36.1	June 14, 1969	Mayo	-63.0	Feb. 3, 1947	Snag
Northwest Territories	39.4	July 18, 1941	Fort Smith	-57.2	Dec. 26, 1917	Fort Smith
Nunavut	33.9	July 22, 1973	Arviat	-57.8	Feb. 13, 1973	Shepherd Bay

Source: *Environment Canada*

Average Annual Precipitation

Province	Greatest mm	Station	Least mm	Station
Newfoundland & Labrador	1 699.7	Burgeo	739.8	Nain
Prince Edward Island	1 169.4	Charlottetown A	921.0	Montague
New Brunswick	1 444.4	Saint John A	909.6	Upsalquitch Lake
Nova Scotia	1 630.7	Ingonish Beach	973.7	Pugwash
Quebec	1 559.8	Mont Logan	295.9	Cape Hopes Advance
Ontario	1 191.1	West Guilford	569.0	Kenora TCPL
Manitoba	696.1	Peace Gardens	402.3	Churchill A
Saskatchewan	530.1	Brabant Lake	287.9	Nashlyn
Alberta	1 072.0	Waterton Park HQ	270.8	Empress
British Columbia	6 655.0	Henderson Lake	205.6	Ashcroft
Yukon	590.6	Tuchitua	135.9	Komakuk Beach A
Northwest Territories	663.2	Cape Dyer A	137.6	Tuktoyaktuk
Nunavut	355.1	Fort Simpson	61.0	Rea Point

Source: *Environment Canada*

Average Annual Bright Sunshine

Province	Greatest Hrs	Station	Least Hrs	Station
Newfoundland & Labrador	1 572	Churchill Falls A	1 303	St. Shotts
Prince Edward Island	1 967	Tignish	1 817	East Baltic
New Brunswick	2 010	Chatham A	1 373	Summit Depot
Nova Scotia	1 969	Shearwater A	1 449	Sable Island
Quebec	2 054	Montreal Int'l. A	1 158	Mont Logan
Ontario	2 203	Thunder Bay A	1 635	New Liskeard
Manitoba	2 460	Delta U	1 828	Churchill A
Saskatchewan	2 537	Estevan A	2 073	Cree Lake
Alberta	2 490	Coronation A	1 724	Banff
British Columbia	2 244	Cranbrook A	949	Stewart A
Yukon	1 844	Whitehorse A	1 789	Watson Lake A
Northwest Territories	2 277	Yellowknife A	1 899	Inuvik
Nunavut	2 091	Eureka	1 443	Mould Bay A

Source: *Environment Canada*

Average Annual Snowfall

Province	Greatest cm	Station	Least cm	Station
Newfoundland & Labrador	322.8	Woody Point	91.6	St. Shotts
Prince Edward Island	330.6	Charlottetown A	173.3	Montague
New Brunswick	448.8	Dawson Settlement	176.2	Southwest Head
Nova Scotia	406.7	Cheticamp	104.1	Baccaro
Quebec	648.4	Mont Logan	161.6	Havre aux Maisons
Ontario	430.0	Searchmount	74.0	Lakeview MOE
Manitoba........................	332.7	Island Lake	94.9	Lundar
Saskatchewan	348.6	Collins Bay	58.0	Aylesbury
Alberta	642.9	Columbia Icefield	59.9	Empress
British Columbia	1 433.0	Glacier NP Mt. Fidelity	20.4	Carnation Creek
Yukon	365.7	Keno Hill	60.1	Komakuk Beach A
Northwest Territories..............	234.5	Fort McPherson	65.2	Tuktoyaktuk
Nunavut	602.4	Cape Dyer A	28.6	Rea Point

Source: *Environment Canada*

Wind

Province	Highest Average Annual Wind Speed km/hr		Station	Highest % of Calms %	Station
Newfoundland & Labrador	28.0	(W)	Bonavista	17.1	Wabush Lake A
Prince Edward Island	22.4	(SSW)	Summerside A	4.4	Summerside A
New Brunswick	22.4	(W)	Miscou Island (AUT)	11.8	Fredericton A
Nova Scotia	25.7	(W)	Sable Island	16.9	Greenwood A
Quebec	32.0	(NW)	Grindstone Island	20.4	Gaspé A
Ontario	21.0	(SW)	Bruce Ontario Hydro	30.2	White River
Manitoba	22.7	(WNW)	Churchill A	21.0	Norway House A
Saskatchewan	22.9	(W)	Swift Current A	12.8	La Ronge A
Alberta	21.5	(W)	Pincher Creek	39.7	High Level A
British Columbia	33.7	(NW)	Cape St. James	48.5	Quesnel A
Yukon	14.1	(SSE)	Whitehorse A	57.5	Dawson A
Northwest Territories	19.9	(E)	Nicholson Peninsula	18.9	Fort Simpson
Nunavut	35.3	(NW)	Resolution Island	35.1	Eureka

Source: *Environment Canada*

"Coldest Days" (Wind Chill)

Province	ET/WCF[1]	Location	Date	Temp (°C)	Wind (km/hr)
Newfoundland & Labrador	-71/2814	Wabush Lake	Jan. 20, 1975	-41	40
Prince Edward Island	-57/2450	Charlottetown	Jan. 18, 1982	-32	37
Nova Scotia	-53/2309	Sydney	Jan. 18, 1982	-25	59
New Brunswick	-61/2547	Charlo	Jan. 18, 1982	-31	54
Quebec	-77/3001	Nitchequon	Jan. 20, 1975	-42	56
Ontario	-70/2753	Thunder Bay	Jan. 10, 1982	-36	54
Manitoba	-76/2938	Churchill	Jan. 18, 1975	-41	56
Saskatchewan	-70/2757	Swift Current	Dec. 15, 1964	-34	89
Alberta	-68/2740	Red Deer	Dec. 15, 1964	-35	61
British Columbia	-69/2749	Old Glory Mtn.	Dec. 15, 1964	-36	58
Yukon	-83/3152	Komakuk Beach	Feb. 12, 1975	-50	40
NWT/Nunavut	-92/3357	Pelly Bay	Jan. 13, 1975	-51	56

Source: *Environment Canada*

(1) ET is equivalent wind chill temperature in °C. WCF is wind chill factor in watts/square metre

Weather Highlights July 2003 to June 2004

JULY 2003: During most of the summer, a large Pacific high pressure area anchored near the coast kept rainy weather away from B.C. In the Interior, temperatures soared as high as 40°C. Kamloops had 19 days with temperatures above 30°C; normal in July is 11. Kelowna, with 44 consecutive rainless days, recorded its driest summer since recordkeeping began in 1899. On the coast, Victoria received a paltry 8.2 mm of rain—its driest summer since 1914. The forests in the south were tinder-dry and the forest floor volatile. It was the most terrifying fire season in memory and the most expensive natural disaster in BC history: not counting lost timber, the cost of firefighting alone approached $500 million. In total, nearly 2,500 forest fires charred 2,650 square kilometres of land, bush and residential areas—11 times the annual average area burned over the last 10 years.

In Alberta, a fire in Crowsnest Pass burned for most of the summer. Fires also blackened huge chunks of Manitoba's forests, making it the province's third worst forest fire season on record.

On July 2, a tornado with winds above 180 km/h ripped through Narrow Hills Provincial Park northeast of Prince Albert. It was a massive funnel—1.4 km wide with a path 26.5 km long—that mowed down 11 square kilometres of forest, stripped pavement from highways, rolled a transport truck, and destroyed a logging camp. On July 12, lightning struck and killed a 14-year-old female soccer player from Maine during a tournament in Fredericton.

AUGUST 2003: Almost all of Canada recorded warmer-than-normal temperatures in August. In B.C., the heat, drought and extreme forest fire conditions of July continued. On August 22, a wildfire burned 248 houses in a suburb of Kelowna; insurers called it the costliest wildfire in Canadian history.

Early in August, a weather system entrenched over the Maritimes brought near-continuous showers to the region. Halifax and Saint John received more rain in the first week of August than they would usually get in an entire month. Farmers couldn't harvest their second crop of hay. On August 4, the Appalachian region of Quebec got 160 mm of rain in just five hours.

However, a hot spell rewrote records across the eastern Prairies. Winnipeg had 10 days above 30°C, and Val Marie, near the Canadian-USA border, endured 16 consecutive days above 30°C. Following soaking rains during the 2002 harvest and normal to above-normal winter and spring precipitation, Prairie soil at the start of the growing season was in the best shape it had been in 15 years. But the southern Prairies received less than 38 percent of the normal summer rainfall; the hot dry weather brought hordes of grasshoppers. Harvest time was warm, dry, sunny and frost-free; the perfect weather meant that more than 90 percent of the spring wheat crop reached the top two grades, ranking it among the best-quality crops in recent history.

SEPTEMBER 2003: On September 16, Calgarians woke up to about 3 cm of wet snow on the ground and temperatures 17 degrees cooler than normal. Jasper and Banff got the heaviest snowfall—up to 25 cm. However, the late summer snowfall helped to cool the still smoldering fire in the Crowsnest Pass.

Residents of southern Ontario prepared anxiously for the coming of Hurricane Isabel, reminded often by the media of Hurricane Hazel in 1954. But on September 19, Isabel entered the province as a much weaker storm than it had been days earlier. In Ontario, rainfalls from Isabel totaled 30 to 50 mm; winds gusted to 73 km/h; and wave heights reached 4 m in the western end of Lake Ontario.

Tropical storm Juan was the most damaging cyclone to hit Halifax in modern history; losses across Nova Scotia and Prince Edward Island totaled more than $200 million. The storm, arriving September 28, tore down power lines, flooded waterfront properties, sank dozens of yachts, heaved sidewalks and damaged stately downtown homes in Halifax and Charlottetown. Even more tragic was the irreplaceable loss of 100 million trees, some of them century-old. Eight people died from the storm and its after-effects. Juan was a Category 2 hurricane when it hit Nova Scotia with sustained winds at 158 km/h gusting over 185 km/h. Maximum wave heights outside the harbour were measured at nearly 20 m.

OCTOBER 2003: Hurricane Kate skirted Cape Race, Newfoundland, on October 6. The storm's remnants packed maximum sustained winds of 120 km/h and generated waves 10 m high. Rains soaked St. John's with 45.2 mm, setting a single-day October record for rainfall.

Around mid-month, a huge storm, dubbed the Pineapple Express, carried moisture from the tropical Pacific near Hawaii into British Columbia. The system brought record rainfalls—a steady, intense downpour that was perhaps the heaviest in 200 years. Slopes left bare by earlier wildfires couldn't hold back the raging waters as they washed soil and trees down mountains and took out bridges and highways. The week-long rains left three dead and forced 1,200 to flee mud-filled homes. Victoria had its rainiest day on record on October 16 with 136 mm. Squamish set several rainfall records, including 239 mm in two days. In the Elaho Valley, up to 600 mm fell over a four-day period.

Hurricane Juan aside, Atlantic Canada had a pleasant fall, with temperatures between 1 and 3 degrees warmer than normal and rainfall ranging from 20 to 80 percent of normal. It was the warmest fall since 1961. In Newfoundland and Labrador, October was the second consecutive month with record warmth.

On October 28, fierce winds swept through parts of southern and central British Columbia, uprooting trees and causing widespread power outages. Sustained winds reached 81 km/h at Vancouver Airport, breaking the previous record for October.

NOVEMBER 2003: Across B.C., floods gave way to frost in early November; dozens of low temperature records were shattered. In Kelowna, it was minus 13°C on November 5—about five degrees colder than it gets in January, the coldest time of the year. In Victoria, freezing temperatures turned many flowers to pulp and worried fruit growers. Vancouver set low temperature records three days running, dipping to minus 4.6°C, colder than all of the previous winter. On November 28, a storm dropped more than 100 mm of rain on the Lower Mainland in 24 hours. The same storm triggered a landslide that severed a natural gas pipeline to Prince Rupert, cutting some residents' fuel supply for a week.

A fierce windstorm on November 12 and 13 blew across southern Ontario, felling trees and cutting power to 100,000 customers. The Georgian Bay-Muskoka area was hit with lake snow squalls that produced zero visibility in whiteouts. In London, the storm kept thousands of children out of school, uprooted trees and peeled the roofs from several buildings.

On November 22, a Pacific disturbance moved through central and southern Yukon, dumping a record amount of snow. Mayo Airport reported 21 cm of snow—the greatest daily November snowfall since records began in 1926 and the fourth snowiest day ever. On November 22, Edmonton's Commonwealth Stadium was the scene of the largest professional hockey game ever played outdoors: 57,167 fans were on hand to watch. Temperatures at game time were around minus 16°C and later dropped to minus 20°C at rink-side, some 12 degrees colder than normal, with a wind chill of minus 28.

DECEMBER 2003: The year was the 11th consecutive with above-normal temperatures in Canada; it was also the sixth warmest in 56 years of national records. It was especially warm in the Arctic, where temperatures averaged 2 degrees above normal. Nationally, all four seasons had above-normal temperatures making an unprecedented stretch of 25 of the last 26 seasons in Canada warmer than normal.

Two early winter storms a week apart clobbered parts of Atlantic Canada with snow and blustery winds. The first rolled into New Brunswick on December 8 with freezing rain, heavy snowfall and strong winds; five people died. Moncton was hardest hit, getting up to 70 cm of snow; its airport was closed for almost two full days. Winds reached close to 100 km/h, causing whiteouts and hefty drifts.

The storm also walloped central Newfoundland with 25 to 45 cm of snow, disrupting schools, shopping and travel, and creating scattered power outages. Charlottetown got 40 cm of snow, forcing many schools and businesses to close. A week later, before snow removal and recovery had been completed, there was a repeat nor'easter across the Maritimes. Sloppy, slushy roads were made more treacherous by powerful winds gusting over 100 km/h.

JANUARY 2004: Balmy temperatures of 12°C across Ontario and Quebec on January 3 brought out golfers and joggers in droves—but it would be the last warm day for nearly eight weeks. A brutal cold snap gripped most of Canada throughout the month. On January 28, Key Lake in northern Saskatchewan recorded the coldest temperature of the winter at minus 52.6°C—the coldest place on Earth for two days. Toronto issued its first cold-weather alert of the winter by the end of the first week of January, urging the homeless to seek shelter from frigid overnight temperatures, which on January 10 dipped to minus 23°. In parts of New Brunswick, wind chills approached minus 50. On January 15, more than 30 schools in Halifax were closed, after buses wouldn't start. In St. John's, fire fighters had to de-ice the fire trucks.

Near Evangeline, P.E.I., a storm surge at high tide on January 19 carried tonnes of sea ice across cliffs and dunes, and into beachfront cottages and summer homes. The ice floes were 50 cm thick and from 3 to 4 m long.

On January 25 and 26, a blizzard brought western and northern Newfoundland to a standstill. Corner Brook was hard-hit with 30 cm of snow, northwesterly winds gusting to 110 km/h, and temperatures of minus 10°C. A couple from Quebec survived for 21 hours in a snow-buried car in southern Labrador by tearing the car seats apart for insulation and pushing springs up through the roof to attract searchers.

On January 26 and 27, southern Ontario had its biggest storm of the winter. Blustery winds and upwards of 40 cm of snow delayed planes, cancelled trains, and spun automobiles into ditches and guardrails.

FEBRUARY 2004: In contrast to a wintry January, February was milder than normal across most of the country. However, on February 10, 2004, a 10-cm snowfall, icy cold temperatures, and vicious winds generated blizzard conditions and icy roads across most of Saskatchewan, the second major blizzard in two weeks. The storm caused a 50-vehicle pile-up, described as the worst chain-reaction accident in the province's history, although no one was killed.

An exploding nor'easter—dubbed a white weather bomb by meteorologists—hammered parts of the Maritimes on February 19. Heavy snow and winds up to 100 km/h shut down highways and knocked out power to thousands in P.E.I. and Nova Scotia, where officials declared province-wide states of emergency for the first time. Halifax got a record 88 cm of snow in one day, and 95 cm over 30 hours. In downtown Halifax, a travel ban was implemented to help crews rid blocked streets of towering snow banks. The western side of Newfoundland was also hammered by the storm.

On February 25, dense fog snarled air transportation in Edmonton; nearly 80 flights were held up over 24 hours. The only plane that managed to land was a chartered First Air 737, which missed the runway and landed on a snow-covered, grassy infield.

At the end of February, a powerful blizzard battered parts of eastern Labrador for three days. An extraordinary 121 cm of snow fell at Cartwright, Newfoundland. The last time the area had received such a huge snow dump from a single storm was 19 years ago.

MARCH 2003: Mild and rainy weather in southern Quebec during the first week of March was responsible for at least two major ice jams on the Chateauguay River near Lac St. Louis, causing major flooding.

On March 10, strong winds and blowing snow caused a flurry of accidents in and around Regina, including a fatal five-car pile-up northwest of the city. All highways in and out of Regina were closed in the morning due to slippery roads and near-zero visibility.

On March 16, a storm hammered parts of southern Ontario. Hamilton got 32 cm of snow over two days. Port Colborne got 25 cm in just six hours and close to 40 in total.

On March 18, a snow storm packing winds up to 90 km/h wreaked havoc on southern

Vancouver Island, toppling trees that smashed a power transmission tower and left the town of Ladysmith and 30,000 customers without power for several hours. The snow blocked the Trans-Canada Highway north of Victoria and prevented thousands of commuters from getting home.

A rainstorm saturated parts of Winnipeg on March 27 and 28. An all-time March record rainfall of 45 mm on melted snow submerged sections of the city in huge puddles on still frozen ground.

At the end of March, Albertans shed their parkas for a few days as July-like temperatures smashed records. The nation's hot spot was Drumheller at 28°C—warmer than Hawaii.

APRIL 2004: Ice jams north of Winnipeg broke about a month earlier than normal, swamped swollen rivers, and caused extensive flooding in the Red River watershed. At Selkirk, the rising water threw truck-sized hunks of ice over a highway and left land under a metre of cold water.

Vancouver had its second sunniest and third driest April on record and temperatures hovered a full two degrees warmer than normal. The month had 270 hours of sunlight, second only to 1951 with 294 hours. Just 15 mm of rain fell at the airport. Victoria got 300 hours of sunshine up from a normal of 187 hours—the second warmest and second driest on record. Precipitation was a scant 10 percent of normal—4.4 mm compared to 44 mm. Of concern, it was the second driest December-to-April period on record, with 322 mm of precipitation compared to the normal 518 mm. Only 1941-42, with 319.7 mm, was drier.

MAY 2004: A spring snowstorm from Montana swept across the southern half of the Prairies on May 11, dumping mounds of wet snow from Calgary to Kenora. It was Winnipeg's largest single daily May snowfall on record—30 cm. In the Kenora and Dryden areas, highways closed and ditches filled with cars after more than 80 mm of water-equivalent precipitation accumulated.

On May 13, Ontario issued its first smog advisory of the season with much of south-central Ontario blanketed in polluted air. Hot, sunny weather created the perfect conditions for high levels of ozone and particulates in the air.

Across most of Canada during summer's first long weekend, the weather featured copious rain and weather that was cool, dull, and violent in places. Unsettled conditions throughout much of southern B.C. meant showers most of the holiday. Rain and snow across Alberta put a damper on camping and hiking. In Manitoba, temperatures at times were single digits, in snow flurries. In Ontario, unsettled weather—severe thunderstorms, hail, winds and tornadoes—made it a busy weekend for meteorologists. More than 125 mm of rain fell in the Windsor area.

On May 23-24, two tornadoes stuck southwestern Ontario near Stratford and Mitchell within minutes—one of them thought to be the fiercest to hit the province in eight years. Winnipeg experienced one of its coldest and wettest Mays on record; it was only the sixth coldest but none of those colder were as wet. London had double the usual monthly May rainfall at 176.6 mm. In Hamilton, May had 137.6 mm of rain, breaking the rainfall record established just last year.

JUNE 2004: On June 9, a violent storm packing heavy rain, fierce lightning, high winds and a tornado wreaked havoc across southwestern Ontario. Up to 100 mm of rain fell in 90 minutes between Strathroy and London. In eastern Ontario, just east of Gananoque, a man was killed when a downburst felled a tree onto his porch as he was watching the storm.

It was the third coldest spring on record in Winnipeg. A low pressure system hovering over the eastern Prairies and Ontario on and off since February diverted cold air from the Arctic. With loads of sunshine, excessive dryness, and frequent plus-30°C days, parts of the Yukon and the northern Mackenzie region became bone-dry and ready to erupt in flames. On June 17, Inuvik, north of the Arctic Circle, reached 30.9°C—warmer than any place in southern Ontario so far this summer.

On June 21, record warm temperatures prevailed across B.C. Osoyoos reached a scorching 40.5°C on June 20, and Terrace reached a sizzling 36.5°C. Nearby, forests erupted in flames, prompting hundreds of residents to evacuate their homes. Lightning sparked fires in the Kamloops and Tweedsmuir Park areas.

Seasonal Temperature and Precipitation in Canada

All figures are based on the thirty-year period 1961 to 1990 inclusive.
Airport station unless * designates city office station.

	January			April		
	Average Temperature (°C)		Total	Average Temperature (°C)		Total
Station	Mid Afternoon	Early Morning	Precipitation (mm)	Mid Afternoon	Early Morning	Precipitation (mm)
Calgary, Alta..........	-2.8	-15.1	11.6	11.3	-2.1	23.9
Charlottetown, P.E.I.	-3.3	-12.6	106.4	6.7	-1.4	87.8
Churchill, Man.........	-22.7	-30.7	16.9	-5.0	-14.5	19.0
Dawson, Yk...........	-22.5	-30.9	19.2	7.6	-7.5	8.0
Edmonton, Alta	-7.3	-16.0	22.5	11.3	-0.3	26.0
Fredericton, N.B.	-4.0	-15.5	109.6	9.7	-1.1	87.4
Halifax, N.S...........	-0.2	-9.2	134.7	8.1	0.2	114.3
Hamilton, Ont.	-2.2	-9.7	65.8	11.2	1.2	78.0
Iqaluit, Nvt	-22.5	-30.6	21.1	-9.9	-19.6	28.2
Kitchener, Ont.........	-3.1	-11.0	64.4	11.1	0.4	76.9
London, Ont.	-2.4	-10.1	74.2	11.6	1.0	82.2
Moncton, N.B.	-3.6	-14.3	119.2	8.0	-1.7	99.3
Montreal, Que.........	-5.8	-14.9	70.4	10.7	0.7	76.1
Ottawa, Ont...........	-6.1	-15.3	70.2	10.8	0.6	72.4
Quebec, Que.	-7.9	-17.6	89.8	7.8	-1.3	81.2
Regina, Sask..........	-10.7	-21.6	14.9	10.9	-2.0	23.5
Saint John, N.B........	-2.7	-13.6	139.4	8.3	-1.2	104.2
St. John's, Nfld	-0.9	-8.6	150.0	5.2	-2.0	121.8
Saskatoon, Sask.......	-11.8	-22.3	15.2	10.6	-1.9	23.9
Sault Ste. Marie, Ont....	-5.5	-15.5	71.3	8.4	-2.2	68.5
Toronto, Ont..........	-2.1	-10.5	52.2	11.5	1.0	68.4
Vancouver, B.C........	6.1	0.5	153.6	13.1	5.3	84.0
Victoria, B.C.	6.9	0.7	136.6	13.4	4.1	44.5
Whitehorse, Yk........	-13.3	-22.0	16.7	6.4	-4.6	7.0
Windsor, Ont..........	-0.9	-8.1	57.6	13.4	3.0	85.1
Winnipeg, Man.	-12.7	-22.8	19.7	10.3	-2.4	31.9
Yellowknife, NWT......	-22.7	-30.9	14.1	0.4	-11.0	10.8

▶

A Question of Waterfall Volume

*W*hat makes a major waterfall? Height is one factor, but so is the volume of water that goes over the falls. So Niagara Falls, at 57 metres, is justly regarded as one of the world's great waterfalls, because it is estimated that about 6,000 cubic metres of water flows over it every second on average. On the other hand, Niagara is dwarfed in height by almost a dozen other waterfalls in Canada, including Della Falls, flowing into Della Lake, B.C., which at 440 metres is the highest in the country.

Reversing falls result from the tides. At low tide, inland waters flow into the sea over a shallow waterfall. But as the tide rises above the falls, the sea forces its way back, creating whirlpools, eddies and rapids that make the falls appear to have reversed. In Canada, reversing falls are found on the Saint John River, in New Brunswick, at Wager Bay, in Nunavut, and at Barrier Inlet, also in Nunavut.

Source: *Atlas of Canada*

Station	July Average Temperature (°C) Mid Afternoon	July Average Temperature (°C) Early Morning	July Total Precipitation (mm)	October Average Temperature (°C) Mid Afternoon	October Average Temperature (°C) Early Morning	October Total Precipitation (mm)
Calgary, Alta..........	22.9	9.4	67.9	12.1	-1.4	13.9
Charlottetown, P.E.I.	23.2	13.8	85.8	11.8	3.8	108.6
Churchill, Man.........	17.3	6.8	56.0	1.1	-4.5	46.9
Dawson, Yk...........	23.1	8.1	48.4	-0.5	-9.4	31.6
Edmonton, Alta	22.8	12.1	91.7	10.9	0.3	17.9
Fredericton, N.B.	25.6	13.0	87.1	12.8	1.2	97.7
Halifax, N.S...........	22.1	13.5	107.4	13.1	5.1	126.6
Hamilton, Ont.	26.3	15.1	86.5	13.8	4.4	72.5
Iqaluit, Nvt	11.6	3.7	59.4	-2.0	-7.7	36.7
Kitchener, Ont.........	25.9	13.7	91.8	13.4	2.9	65.6
London, Ont.	26.3	14.6	82.2	14.0	4.0	97.7
Moncton, N.B.	24.5	12.6	103.3	12.4	1.8	103.8
Montreal, Que.........	26.3	15.5	90.1	12.5	3.1	77.6
Ottawa, Ont...........	26.5	15.4	90.6	12.5	3.0	79.4
Quebec, Que..........	25.0	13.4	127.8	10.7	1.7	101.7
Regina, Sask..........	25.7	11.8	64.4	11.5	-2.0	21.8
Saint John, N.B........	22.4	11.7	101.5	11.9	2.7	124.8
St. John's, Nfld	20.3	10.5	89.4	10.5	3.3	161.9
Saskatoon, Sask.......	24.9	11.4	60.1	10.8	-1.9	16.7
Sault Ste. Marie, Ont....	24.0	11.3	76.8	11.5	2.5	86.7
Toronto, Ont..........	26.8	14.8	74.4	13.9	3.9	64.1
Vancouver, B.C........	21.7	13.2	39.6	13.5	6.6	112.6
Victoria, B.C.	21.9	10.8	19.5	14.2	5.3	75.7
Whitehorse, Yk........	20.5	7.7	41.4	4.3	-3.1	23.8
Windsor, Ont..........	27.9	17.4	81.8	15.6	6.2	64.9
Winnipeg, Man.	25.8	13.3	70.6	10.8	-0.3	36.0
Yellowknife, NWT......	21.1	12.4	35.0	1.0	-4.4	35.0

Source: *Environment Canada*

How Many Glaciers in Canada?

*T*he short answer is that no one really knows. The National Hydrology Research Institute of Environment Canada is currently trying to identify and measure all Canada's glaciers. But some estimates exist, especially for our Arctic islands. So, for instance, Baffin Island is thought to have 10,224 glaciers, with a total ice area of 35,900 square kilometres. Ellesmere Island has more ice area—77,600 square kilometres—but the exact number of individual glaciers isn't known yet. On the mainland, the Nelson River drainage area in British Columbia is thought to have 1,616 glaciers, but the total ice area is only 320 square kilometres. On the other hand, the Pacific Ocean drainage basin has 36,350 square kilometres of ice, but an exact count of glaciers doesn't exist.

Source: *Atlas of Canada*

Spring and Fall Frost Dates in Canada

Frost occurs whenever temperatures fall to 0°C or lower. All frost dates and values are based on the available data during the period 1951–80. Growing degree-day data are from the period 1961–90. Data reported from airport stations unless * designates city office station.

	1 in 10 Chance Last Spring Frost After Date	1 in 10 Chance First Fall Frost Before Date	Frost-free Period (days)	Growing Degree-Days Above 5°C[1]
Newfoundland & Labrador				
Corner Brook*	June 10	Sept. 8	139	1 432
St. John's*	June 24	Sept. 19	131	1 262
Prince Edward Island				
Charlottetown	May 27	Oct. 6	151	1 636
Nova Scotia				
Halifax	May 28	Sept. 30	155	1 707
New Brunswick				
Fredericton	June 10	Sept. 13	126	1 760
Moncton	June 10	Sept. 14	124	1 649
Saint John	June 10	Sept. 18	139	1 499
Quebec				
Chicoutimi*	June 4	Sept. 18	135	1 575
Gaspé*	June 12	Sept. 11	123	1 336
Montreal	May 19	Sept. 26	157	2 079
Quebec	May 28	Sept. 14	137	1 688
Schefferville	June 27	Aug. 22	77	604
Ontario				
Kitchener*	May 25	Sept. 17	151	1 992
London	May 25	Sept. 23	147	2 121
Moosonee*	July 6	July 30	70	1 078
Ottawa	May 25	Sept. 21	147	2 045
St. Catharines*	May 18	Oct. 5	173	2 451
Sudbury	June 11	Sept. 11	128	1 680
Thunder Bay	June 13	Aug. 29	104	1 427
Timmins	June 23	Aug. 19	91	1 395
Toronto	May 25	Sept. 18	149	2 090
Windsor	May 10	Oct. 3	177	2 544
Manitoba				
Brandon	June 9	Aug. 31	108	1 652
Churchill	July 7	Aug. 20	76	562
Flin Flon	June 10	Sept. 2	115	1 379
Winnipeg	June 10	Sept. 11	121	1 802
Saskatchewan				
Prince Albert	June 21	Aug. 17	95	1 455
Regina	June 14	Aug. 27	109	1 723
Saskatoon	June 10	Sept. 1	117	1 658
Alberta				
Banff*	June 30	Aug. 6	89	1 124
Calgary	June 10	Aug. 27	112	1 435
Edmonton	June 14	Aug. 13	105	1 352
Fort McMurray	June 30	Aug. 2	84	1 352
Lethbridge	May 31	Sept. 2	124	1 779
Medicine Hat	May 27	Sept. 8	129	1 971
Peace River	June 23	Aug. 13	93	1 276
British Columbia				
Fort Nelson	June 7	Aug. 14	106	1 289
Kamloops	May 18	Sept. 19	149	2 259
Penticton	May 23	Sept. 14	148	2 163
Prince George	July 1	Aug. 11	85	1 238
Prince Rupert	May 25	Sept. 28	156	1 181
Vancouver	Apr. 21	Oct. 13	216	2 018
Victoria	Apr. 30	Oct. 17	201	1 864

▶

	1 in 10 Chance Last Spring Frost After Date	1 in 10 Chance First Fall Frost Before Date	Frost-free Period (days)	Growing Degree-Days Above 5°C[1]
▶ **Yukon**				
Dawson*	June 16	Aug. 6	91	1 015
Whitehorse	June 24	Aug. 13	82	871
Northwest Territories				
Yellowknife	June 9	Sept. 3	111	1 039
Nunavut				
Alert*	July 15	July 16	4	30
Iqaluit	July 12	July 26	59	177
Resolute	July 15	July 16	9	29

Source: *Environment Canada*
(1) Growing degree days represent the average total number of heat units (daily mean temp. –5°C) during the growing season

Plant Hardiness Zones in Canada

A plant's hardiness rating is related to its ability to survive in specific climate conditions. Plant hardiness zones were originally based on average minimum winter temperatures in a location, and first developed by the U.S. Department of Agriculture (USDA).

The USDA created 11 zones, each of which have since been split into subzones a and b. Canada's Department of Agriculture took the concept of hardiness further by including other factors besides minimum temperature in designating Canada's plant hardiness zones. They created a weighted equation that took into account such factors as the average minimum temperature of the coldest month; the average length of the frost-free period; average rainfall between June and November; the average maximum temperature in the hottest month; the amount of snow; and the maximum windspeeds in the last 30 years in any given area.

Canada's zones range from 0a in our coldest regions to 9a in our most temperate locations, and the minimum temperature equivalents are shown below. Canadian gardeners may find themselves in micro-climates that differ from the conditions the zone map indicates; however most should choose perennials based on the zone the garden is in and the hardiness rating of the plant. (A plant can survive in the zone it's rated for or a higher/warmer one.)

To find out what zone you're in, consult a local nursery or visit the map at http://res.agr.ca/ CANSIS/SYSTEMS/online_maps.html

Hardiness Zone	Average Minimum Temperature (°C)	Hardiness Zone	Average Minimum Temperature (°C)
0a – 0b	–46 or colder	5a – 5b	–20 to –15
1a – 1b	–46 to –37	6a – 6b	–15 to –12
2a – 2b	–37 to –29	7a – 7b	–12 to –6
3a – 3b	–29 to –23	8a – 8b	–6 to –1
4a – 4b	–23 to –20	9a	–1 to 4 or warmer

Source: *Agriculture Canada*

Farms and Farmers Declining

*T*he number of farms and farmers in Canada is falling, according to Statistics Canada, but the acreage of crops is increasing and so are the numbers of livestock. The 2001 Census of Agriculture reports 346,200 farm operators, 10 percent fewer than the 385,600 reported in 1996. On May 15, 2001, they were operating 246,923 farms, down 10.7 percent from 1996.

On the other hand, the census found, the farmers reported they were cultivating 89.9 million acres of crops, up 4.2 percent from 1996. As well, livestock numbers increased: cattle were up by 4.4 percent, pigs by 26.4 percent, and sheep by 46 percent.

There are fewer young farmers: Those under 35 represented 11.5 percent of all farmers in 2001, compared with 15.8 percent in 1996 and 19.9 percent in 1991. Both men and women have increased their rate of working off the farm since 1990, and roughly equal proportions of women farm operators (45.6 percent) and men (44.2 percent) worked at non-farm jobs in 2000.

There were 2,230 farms producing organic crops, mostly field crops, such as wheat, alfalfa, canola and barley.

PROVINCES AND TERRITORIES

Latitude, Longitude, Elevation of Canadian Cities

City	Lat. N °	Lat. N '	Long.W °	Long.W '	Elev. (m)	City	Lat. N °	Lat. N '	Long.W °	Long.W '	Elev. (m)
Alert, NT*	82	30	62	22	31	Moose Jaw, Sask.	50	23	105	32	544
Brandon, Man.	49	51	99	57	409	Niagara Falls, Ont.	43	06	79	03	180
Brantford, Ont.	43	08	80	15	215	North Bay, Ont.	46	18	79	27	204
Burlington, Ont.	43	19	79	47	87	Ottawa, Ont.	45	26	75	41	56
Calgary, Alta.	51	02	114	03	1 045	Peterborough, Ont.	44	18	78	19	205
Charlottetown, PEI	46	14	63	07	9	Prince Rupert, BC	54	19	130	19	38
Churchill, Man.	58	45	94	10	29	Quebec, Que.	46	48	71	12	50
Dartmouth, NS	44	39	63	34	7	Regina, Sask.	50	27	104	36	577
Dawson, Yukon	64	03	139	26	369	Saint John, NB	45	16	66	03	8
Edmonton, Alta.	53	32	113	29	666	St. John's, Nfld & Lab.	47	34	52	43	61
Fredericton, NB	45	57	66	38	9	Saskatoon, Sask.	52	07	106	39	484
Guelph, Ont.	43	32	80	14	325	Sault Ste. Marie, Ont.	46	30	84	20	180
Halifax, NS	44	38	63	34	18	Sherbrooke, Que.	45	24	71	53	191
Hamilton, Ont.	43	15	79	52	100	Sudbury, Ont.	46	29	80	59	347
Hull, Que.	45	25	75	42	56	Sydney, NS	46	08	60	11	62
Iqaluit, NT*	63	45	68	31	34	Thunder Bay, Ont.	48	22	89	14	188
Kingston, Ont.	44	13	76	28	80	Toronto, Ont.	43	39	79	23	91
Kitchener, Ont.	43	26	80	29	335	Trois-Rivières, Que.	46	21	72	33	35
LaSalle, Que.	45	25	73	39	34	Vancouver, BC	49	18	123	04	43
Laval, Que.	45	33	73	44	43	Victoria, BC	48	25	123	21	17
Lethbridge, Alta.	49	41	112	49	910	Whitehorse, Yukon	60	43	135	03	703
London, Ont.	42	59	81	14	251	Winnipeg, Man.	49	53	97	08	232
Moncton, NB	46	05	64	46	12	Yellowknife, NWT	62	28	114	22	205
Montreal, Que.	45	30	73	33	27						

Source: *Natural Resources Canada*

*Nunavut

Area¹ of Canadian Provinces and Territories

(sq. km)

	Land	Water	Total	% of Total Area of Canada
Newfoundland and Labrador	373 872	31 340	405 212	4.06
Prince Edward Island	5 660	—	5 660	0.06
Nova Scotia	53 338	1 946	55 284	0.55
New Brunswick	71 450	1 458	72 908	0.73
Quebec	1 365 128	176 928	1 542 056	15.44
Ontario	917 741	158 654	1 076 395	10.78
Manitoba	553 556	94 241	647 797	6.49
Saskatchewan	591 670	59 366	651 036	6.52
Alberta	642 317	19 531	661 848	6.63
British Columbia	925 186	19 549	944 735	9.46
Yukon	474 391	8 052	482 443	4.83
Northwest Territories	1 183 085	163 021	1 346 106	13.48
Nunavut	1 936 113	157 077	2 093 190	20.96
Canada	**9 093 507**	**891 163**	**9 984 670**	**100.00**

Source: *Natural Resources Canada*

(1) Calculated from the National Atlas of Canada 1:1000000 scale hydrology base. (—) = zero

Newfoundland & Labrador

□ **CAPITAL:** St. John's, CMA pop. (2003) 177,775. **Date entered Confederation:** Mar. 31, 1949.

□ **POPULATION (2003):** 520,170; Pop. density: 1.26 per sq. km. **Pop. growth** (2002–03): 0.1%. **Pop. urban** (2001): 57%. **Age structure** (2001): 25% under 19; 62.7% 20-64; 12% over 65. **Median age** (2001): 38.4. **Net interprovincial migration** (2000-01): -3 541.

□ **VITAL STATISTICS: Rates** (per 1 000 pop., 2001): birth: 8.8; death: 8.4. **Life expectancy at birth** (1999): 77.7.

□ **GEOGRAPHY: Total area** 405 212 sq. km; **Land area** 373 872 sq. km; **Forested land** 142 000 sq. km; **Length of coastline** 23 232 km. **Climate:** ranges from subarctic in Labrador and northern tip of island to humid continental with cool summers and heavy precipitation. **Topography:** Island of Newfoundland: highlands of the Long Range Mtns. (elev. 900 m) along W coast; barren and rocky central plateau descends to lowlands towards the N east; coast is deeply indented with bays and fjords. Labrador: mountainous in the N; rugged coast and interior plateau.

□ **ECONOMY: Gross Domestic Product** at market prices (2003): $18,015 million; **% change GDP** (2002–03): 8.8%; **Per capita GDP** (2003): $34,632. **Employment distrib.** (2000): goods-producing industries (agriculture, primary ind., mfg, construction) 22%; service-producing industries (transpt., trade, finance, service, pub. admin, unclassified) 78%. **Unemployment rate** (2003): 16.7%. **Principal industries:** mining, manufacturing, fishing, logging and forestry, electricity production, tourism.

□ **EDUCATION: Elem. enrolment** (2001–02): 82,656. **Spending** per full-time equiv. student (1999): $5,841. **Post-sec. degrees** granted (1998): 2 999.

□ **INTERNATIONAL AIRPORTS:** Gander.

□ **NATIONAL PARKS:** Gros Morne, Terra Nova.

□ **PROVINCIAL DATA: Motto:** *Quaerite Prime Regnum Dei:* "Seek Ye First the Kingdom of God." **Flower:** Pitcher plant. **Bird:** Atlantic Puffin (unofficial). **Anthem:** Ode to Newfoundland. **Tartan:** Newfoundland Tartan.

□ **POLITICS: Premier:** Danny Williams (Prog. Cons.). **Leaders, opposition parties:** Jack Harris (NDP), Roger Grimes (Lib.). **Date of last general election:** Oct. 21, 2003. **Lt. Governor:** Hon. Edward M. Roberts.

Prince Edward Island

□ **CAPITAL:** Charlottetown, CMA pop. (2004) 65,000. **Date entered Confederation:** July 1, 1873.

□ **POPULATION (2003):** 137,941. Pop. density: 23.9 per sq. km. **Pop. growth** (2002–03): 0.1%. **Pop. urban** (2001): 44.0%. **Age structure** (2001): 27.3% under 19; 59.0% 20-64; 13.7% over 65. **Median age** (2001): 37.7. **Net interprovincial migration** (2000–01): 71.

□ **VITAL STATISTICS: Rates** (per 1 000 pop., 2001): birth: 10.8; death: 9.4. **Life expectancy at birth (1999):** 78.4.

□ **GEOGRAPHY: Total area** 5 660 sq. km; **Land area** 5 660 sq. km; **Forested land** 3 000 sq. km; **Length of coastline** 1 076 km. **Climate:** humid continental with temperatures moderated by maritime location. **Topography:** flat through gently rolling hills; sharply indented coastline; many streams but only small rivers and lakes.

□ **ECONOMY: Gross Domestic Product** at market prices (2003): $3,500 million; **% change GDP** (2002–03): 4.9%; **Per capita GDP** (2001): $23,460. **Employment distrib.** (2000): goods-producing industries (agriculture, primary ind., mfg, construction) 27%; service-producing industries (transpt., trade, finance, service, pub. admin, unclassified) 73%. **Unemployment rate** (2003): 11.1%. **Principal industries:** agriculture, tourism, fishing, manufacturing.

□ **EDUCATION: Elem. enrolment** (2001–2): 24,327. **Spending** per full-time equiv. student (1999): $5,677. **Post-sec. degrees** granted (1998): 407.

□ **INTERNATIONAL AIRPORTS:** none.

□ **NATIONAL PARKS:** Prince Edward Island (north shore).

□ **PROVINCIAL DATA: Motto:** *Parva Sub Ingenti:* "The small under the protection of the great." **Flower:** Lady's slipper. **Bird:** Blue Jay. **Tree:** Red Oak.

□ **POLITICS: Premier:** Pat Binns (Prog. Cons.). **Leaders, opposition parties:** Robert Ghiz (Lib.), Gary Robichaud (NDP). **Date of last general election:** Sept. 29, 2003. **Lt. Governor:** Hon. J. Léonce Bernard.

Nova Scotia

☐ **CAPITAL:** Halifax, Reg. CMA. pop. (2001) 359 183. **Date entered Confederation:** July 1, 1867.

☐ **POPULATION (2003):** 936,878 **Pop. density:** 16.42 per sq. km. **Pop. growth** (2002–03): 0.1%. **Pop. urban** (2001): 55.0%. **Age structure** (2001): 25.0% under 19; 61.1% 20–64; 13.9% over 65. **Median age** (2001): 38.8. **Net interprovincial migration** (2000–01): -824.

☐ **VITAL STATISTICS: Rates** (per 1 000 pop., 2001): birth: 9.9; death: 9.0. **Life expectancy at birth** (1999): 78.7.

☐ **GEOGRAPHY: Total area** 55 284 sq. km; **Land area** 53 338 sq. km; **Forested land** 41,000 sq. km; **Length of coastline** 6 014 km. **Climate**: humid continental with some moderating effects due to maritime location. **Topography**: Atlantic Uplands are segmented by river valleys; Cape Breton Is. rises from lowland in the S to a high plateau; many rivers, lakes and jagged coastline.

☐ **ECONOMY: Gross Domestic Product at market prices (2001):** $23,368 million; **% change GDP** (2000–01): 2.4%; **Per capita GDP** (2001): $25 735. **Employment distrib.** (2000): goods-producing industries (agriculture, primary ind., mfg, construction) 22%; service-producing industries (transpt., trade, finance, service, pub. admin, unclassified) 78%. **Unemployment rate** (2002): 9.8%. **Principal industries:** manufacturing, fishing and trapping, mining, agriculture, pulp and paper.

☐ **EDUCATION: Elem. enrolment** (2001–2): 149,111. **Spending** per full-time equiv. student (1999): $5 642. **Post-sec. degrees** granted (1998): 7 811.

☐ **INTERNATIONAL AIRPORTS:** Halifax

☐ **NATIONAL PARKS:** Cape Breton Highlands, Kejimkujik.

☐ **PROVINCIAL DATA: Motto:** *Munit Haec et Altera Vincit:* "One defends and the other conquers." **Flower:** Mayflower. **Bird:** Osprey. **Tree:** Red Spruce. **Gem:** Agate.

☐ **POLITICS: Premier:** Dr. John Hamm (Prog. Cons.). **Leaders, opposition parties:** Wayne Gaudet (Lib.), Darrel Dexter (NDP). **Date of last general election:** Aug. 5, 2003. **Lt. Governor:** Hon. Myra A. Freeman.

New Brunswick

☐ **CAPITAL:** Fredericton, metro pop. (2001) 47,560. **Date entered Confederation:** July 1, 1867.

☐ **POPULATION (2003):** 750,460. **Pop. density:** 10.0 per sq. km. **Pop. growth** (2002–03): 0%. **Pop. urban** (2001): 50.0%. **Age structure** (2001): 24.8% under 19; 61.7% 20–64; 13.6% over 65. **Median age** (2001): 38.6. **Net interprovincial migration** (2000–01): -81.

☐ **VITAL STATISTICS: Rates** (per 1 000 pop., 2001): birth: 10.2; death: 8.9. **Life expectancy at birth** (1999): 78.4.

☐ **GEOGRAPHY: Total area** 72 908 sq. km; **Land area** 71 450 sq. km; **Forested land** 61,000 sq. km; **Length of coastline** 2 298 km. **Climate**: humid continental climate except along the shores where there is a marked maritime effect. **Topography:** northern upland; rolling central plateau; southern lowland plain with many rivers.

☐ **ECONOMY: Gross Domestic Product at market prices** (2003): $22,358 million; **% change GDP** (2002–03): 0.6%; **Per capita GDP** (2003): $29,792. **Employment distrib.** (2000): goods-producing industries (agriculture, primary ind., mfg, construction) 25%; service-producing industries (transpt., trade, finance, service, pub. admin, unclassified) 75%. **Unemployment rate** (2002): 10.1%. **Principal industries:** manufacturing, fishing, mining, forestry, pulp and paper, agriculture.

☐ **EDUCATION: Elem. enrolment** (2001–02): 116,713. **Spending** per full-time equiv. student (1999): $6 433. **Post-sec. degrees** granted (1998): 4,030.

☐ **INTERNATIONAL AIRPORTS:** none.

☐ **NATIONAL PARKS:** Fundy, Kouchibouguac.

☐ **PROVINCIAL DATA: Motto:** *Spem Reduxit:* "Hope was restored." **Flower:** Purple Violet. **Bird:** Black-capped Chickadee. **Tree:** Balsam Fir.

☐ **POLITICS: Premier:** Bernard Lord (Prog. Cons.). **Leaders, opposition parties:** Shawn Graham (Lib.), Elizabeth Weir (NDP). **Date of last general election:** June 9, 2003. **Lt. Governor:** Hon. Herménégilde Chiasson.

Quebec

☐ **CAPITAL:** Quebec, CMA pop. (2001) 682 757. **Date entered Confederation:** July 1, 1867.

☐ **POPULATION (2003):** 7,503,502. **Pop. density:** 4.69 per sq. km. **Pop. growth** (2002–03): 0.2%. **Pop. urban** (2001): 80.0%. **Age structure** (2001): 24.2% under 19; 62.5% 20-64; 13.3% over 65. **Median age** (2001): 38.8. **Net interprovincial migration** (2000-01): -11 782.

☐ **VITAL STATISTICS: Rates** (per 1000 pop., 2001): birth: 9.7; death: 7.2. **Life expectancy at birth** (1999): 78.5.

☐ **GEOGRAPHY: Total area** 1 542 056 sq. km; **Land area** 1 356 128 sq. km; **Forested land** 940 000 sq. km; **Length of coastline** 15 208 km. Climate: varies from subarctic to continental. **Topography:** lowlands along the St. Lawrence R. valley separate the Laurentian Mtns. to the N and the Appalachian Mtns. to the S; Canadian Shield landscape dominates north.

☐ **ECONOMY: Gross Domestic Product at market prices** (2003): $276,657 million; **% change GDP** (2002–03): 1.6%; **Per capita GDP** (2003): $36,870. **Employment distrib.** (2000): goods-producing industries (agriculture, primary ind., mfg, construction) 26%; service-producing industries (transpt., trade, finance, service, pub. admin, unclassified) 74%. **Unemployment rate** (2002): 8.6%. **Principal industries:** manufacturing, electric power, mining, pulp and paper, transportation equipment.

☐ **EDUCATION: Elem. enrolment** (2001–2): 1,022,209. **Spending** per full-time equiv. student (1999): $7,097. **Post-sec. degrees** granted (1998): 51,066.

☐ **INTERNATIONAL AIRPORTS:** Trudeau; Mirabel.

☐ **NATIONAL PARKS:** Forillon, La Mauricie, Mingan Archipelago, Saguenay-St. Lawrence Marine Park.

☐ **PROVINCIAL DATA: Motto:** *Je me souviens:* "I remember." **Flower:** Lys blanc de jardin (White Garden (Madonna) Lily). **Bird:** Harfang des neiges (Snowy Owl).

☐ **POLITICS: Premier:** Jean Charest (Lib.). **Leader, opposition parties:** Bernard Landry (Parti Québécois), Mario Dumont (A.D.). **Date of last general election:** April 14, 2003. **Lt. Governor:** Hon. Lise Thibault.

Ontario

☐ **CAPITAL:** Toronto, CMA pop. (2003) 5,101,610. **Date entered Confederation:** July 1, 1867.

☐ **POPULATION (2003):** 12,280,731. **Pop. density:** 10.6 per sq. km. **Pop. growth** (2002–03): 0.3%. **Pop. urban** (2001): 84.0%. **Age structure** (2001): 26.3% under 19; 60.8% 20-64; 12.9% over 65. **Median age** (2001): 37.2. **Net interprovincial migration** (2000-01): 17 877.

☐ **VITAL STATISTICS: Rates** (per 1 000 pop., 2001): birth: 11.1; death. 7.4; **Life expectancy at birth** (1999): 79.4.

☐ **GEOGRAPHY: Total area** 1 076 395 sq. km; **Land area** 917 741 sq. km; **Forested land** 807 000 sq. km; **Length of coastline** 1 324 km. Climate: ranges from humid continental in south to subarctic in far north; westerly winds bring winter storms; the Great Lakes moderate winter temperatures. **Topography:** Rugged, rocky Canadian Shield plateau is broken by lowlands around Great Lakes, St. Lawrence R. and Hudson Bay.

☐ **ECONOMY: Gross Domestic Product at market prices** (2003): $494,229 million; **% change GDP** (2002–03): 2.2%; **Per capita GDP** (2003): $40,244. **Employment distrib.** (2000): goods-producing industries (agriculture, primary ind., mfg, construction) 27%; service-producing industries (transpt., trade, finance, service, pub. admin, unclassified) 73%. **Unemployment rate** (2002): 7.0%. **Principal industries:** manufacturing, construction, agriculture, forestry, mining.

☐ **EDUCATION: Elem. enrolment** (2001–2): 1,848,807. **Spending** per full-time equiv. student (1999): $7 554. **Post-sec. degrees** granted (1998): 65 899.

☐ **INTERNATIONAL AIRPORTS:** Pearson (Toronto); Ottawa.

☐ **NATIONAL PARKS:** Bruce Peninsula, Fathom Five Marine Park, Georgian Bay Islands, Point Pelee, Pukaskwa, St. Lawrence Islands.

☐ **PROVINCIAL DATA: Motto:** *Ut Incepit Fidelis Sic Permanet:* "Loyal she began, loyal she remains." **Flower:** White trillium. **Bird:** Common Loon. **Tree:** Eastern White Pine. **Gem:** Amethyst.

☐ **POLITICS: Premier:** Dalton McGuinty (Lib.). **Leaders, opposition parties:** Ernie Eves (Prog. Cons.); Howard Hampton (NDP). **Date of last general election:** October 2, 2003. **Lt. Governor:** Hon. James K. Bartleman.

Manitoba

☐ **CAPITAL:** Winnipeg, CMA pop. (2001) 671 274. **Date entered Confederation:** July 15, 1870.

☐ **POPULATION (2003):** 1,164,135. **Pop. density:** 1.72 per sq. km. **Pop. growth** (2002–03): 0.1%. **Pop. urban** (2001): 71.0%. **Age structure** (2001): 28.1% under 19; 58.0% 20-64; 14.0% over 65. **Median age** (2001): 36.8. **Net interprovincial migration** (2000-01): -3 094.

☐ **VITAL STATISTICS: Rates** (per 1 000 pop., 2001): birth: 12.4; death: 9.0. **Life expectancy at birth** (1999): 78.0.

☐ **GEOGRAPHY: Total area** 647 797 sq. km; **Land area** 553 556 sq. km; **Forested land** 349 000 sq. km; **Length of coastline** 990 km. **Climate:** continental with seasonal extremes. **Topography:** the land rises gradually south and west from Hudson Bay; flat plateau through south central region; countless lakes, streams and bogs.

☐ **ECONOMY: Gross Domestic Product** at market prices (2003): $34,676 million; **% change GDP** (2002–03): 1.9%; **Per capita GDP** (2003): $29,786. **Employment distrib.** (2000): goods-producing industries (agriculture, primary ind., mfg, construction) 26%; service-producing industries (transpt., trade, finance, service, pub. admin, unclassified) 74%. **Unemployment rate** (2002): 5.5%. **Principal industries:** manufacturing, agriculture, food industry, mining, construction.

☐ **EDUCATION: Elem. enrolment** (2001–2): 207,368. **Spending** per full-time equiv. student (1999): $7,432. **Post-sec. degrees** granted (1998): 5 639.

☐ **INTERNATIONAL AIRPORTS:** Winnipeg.

☐ **NATIONAL PARKS:** Riding Mountain, Wapusk.

☐ **PROVINCIAL DATA: Motto:** Glorious and Free. **Flower:** Prairie Crocus. **Bird:** Great Grey Owl. **Tartan:** Manitoba Tartan.

☐ **POLITICS: Premier:** Gary Doer (NDP). **Leaders, opposition parties:** Stuart Murray (Prog. Cons.), Jon Gerrard (Lib.). **Date of last general election:** June 3, 2003. **Lt. Governor:** Hon. John Harvard.

Saskatchewan

☐ **CAPITAL:** Regina, CMA pop. (2001) 192 800. **Date entered Confederation:** Sept. 1, 1905.

☐ **POPULATION (2003):** 995,003. **Pop. density:** 1.5 per sq. km. **Pop. growth** (2002–03): 0%. **Pop. urban** (2001): 64.0%. **Age structure** (2001): 29.2% under 19; 55.8% 20-64; 15.1% over 65. **Median age** (2001): 36.7. **Net interprovincial migration** (2000–01): -10 453.

☐ **VITAL STATISTICS: Rates** (per 1 000 pop., 2001): birth: 12.3; death: 9.1. **Life expectancy at birth** (1999): 78.5.

☐ **GEOGRAPHY: Total area** 651 036 sq. km; **Land area** 591 670 sq. km; **Forested land** 178 000 sq. km; **Climate:** continental, with cold winters and hot summers. **Topography:** gently rolling plains through south; higher, hilly plateaus in the SW; north is rugged Canadian Shield.

☐ **ECONOMY: Gross Domestic Product** at market prices (2003): $32,100 million; **% change GDP** (2002–03): 4.7%; **Per capita GDP** (2003): $32,261. **Employment distrib.** (2000): goods-producing industries (agriculture, primary ind., mfg, construction) 28%; service-producing industries (transpt., trade, finance, service, pub. admin, unclassified) 72%. **Unemployment rate** (2002): 5.9%. **Principal industries:** agriculture, mining, manufacturing, electric power, construction, chemical prod.

☐ **EDUCATION: Elem. enrolment** (2001-2): 192 920. **Spending** per full-time equiv. student (1999): $6 277. **Post-sec. degrees** granted (1998): 5 443.

☐ **INTERNATIONAL AIRPORTS:** Saskatoon.

☐ **NATIONAL PARKS:** Grasslands, Prince Albert.

☐ **PROVINCIAL DATA: Motto:** *Multis E Gentibus Vires:* "from many peoples strength." **Flower:** Western Red Lily. **Bird:** Prairie sharp-tailed grouse. **Tree:** White Birch. **Tartan:** Saskatchewan Tartan.

☐ **POLITICS: Premier:** Lorne Calvert (NDP). **Leaders, opposition parties:** Brad Wall (Sask.), David Karwacki (Lib.). **Date of last general election:** Nov. 5, 2003. **Lt. Governor:** Hon. Lynda M. Haverstock.

Alberta

☐ **CAPITAL:** Edmonton, CMA pop. (2001) 937 854. **Date entered Confederation:** Sept. 1, 1905.

☐ **POPULATION (2003):** 3,164,400. **Pop. density:** 4.49 per sq. km. **Pop. growth** (2002–03): 0.3%. **Pop. urban** (2001): 80.0%. **Age structure** (2001): 28.3% under 19; 61.4% 20-64; 10.4% over 65. **Median age** (2001): 35.0. **Net interprovincial migration** (2000–01): 25 748.

☐ **VITAL STATISTICS: Rates** (per 1 000 pop., 2001): birth: 11.8; death: 5.7. **Life expectancy at birth** (1999): 79.2.

☐ **GEOGRAPHY: Total area** 661 848 sq. km; **Land area** 642 317 sq. km; **Forested land** 349 000 sq. km. Climate: great variance in temperatures between regions and seasons; summer highs between 16°C and 32°C; winters as low as -45°C. Topography: Rocky Mtns. in SW to rolling prairie throughout southern region; far north is a forested plateau.

☐ **ECONOMY: Gross Domestic Product** at market prices (2003): $129,532 million; **% change GDP** (2002–03): 3.6%; **Per capita GDP** (2003): $40,934. **Employment distrib.** (2000): goods-producing industries (agriculture, primary ind., mfg, construction) 27%; service-producing industries (transpt., trade, finance, service, pub. admin, unclassified) 73%. **Unemployment rate** (2002): 5.3%. **Principal industries:** chemical products, mining, agriculture, food, manufacturing, construction, oil prod. and refinement.

☐ **EDUCATION: Elem. enrolment** (2001–2): 541,596. **Spending** per full-time equiv. student (1999): $6,871. **Post-sec. degrees** granted (1998): 13 003.

☐ **INTERNATIONAL AIRPORTS:** Edmonton; Calgary.

☐ **NATIONAL PARKS:** Banff, Elk Island, Jasper, Waterton Lakes, Wood Buffalo (shared with Northwest Territories).

☐ **PROVINCIAL DATA: Motto:** *Fortis et Liber:* "Strong and free." **Flower:** Wild Rose. **Bird:** Great horned owl. **Tree:** Lodge pole pine. **Tartan:** Alberta Tartan. **Stone:** Petrified wood.

☐ **POLITICS: Premier:** Ralph Klein (Prog. Cons.). **Leaders, opposition parties:** Kevin Taft (Lib.), Raj Pannu (NDP). **Date of last general election:** March 12, 2001. **Lt. Governor:** Hon. Lois E. Hole.

British Columbia

☐ **CAPITAL:** Victoria, CMA pop. (2001) 311 902. **Date entered Confederation:** July 20, 1871.

☐ **POPULATION (2003):** 4,158,649. **Pop. density:** 4.13 per sq. km. **Pop. growth** (2002–03): 0.3%. **Pop. urban** (2001): 84.0%. **Age structure** (2001): 25.0% under 19; 61.4% 20–64; 13.6% over 65. **Median age** (2001): 38.4. **Net interprovincial migration** (2000–01): -12 689.

☐ **VITAL STATISTICS: Rates** (per 1 000 pop., 2001): birth: 9.8; death: 6.8. **Life expectancy at birth** (1999): 80.0.

☐ **GEOGRAPHY: Total area** 944 735 sq. km; **Land area** 925 186 sq. km; **Forested land** 633 000 sq. km; **Length of coastline** 22 898 km. Climate: maritime with mild temperatures and abundant rainfall in the coastal areas; continental climate with temperature extremes in the interior and northeast. Topography: mostly mountainous; deep river valleys and gorges, except for the NE area which is an extension of the Great Plains; indented coast with numerous bays and islands.

☐ **ECONOMY: Gross Domestic Product** at market prices (2003): $142,418 million; **% change GDP** (2002–03): 5.1%; **Per capita GDP** (2003): $34,246. Employment distrib. (2000): goods-producing industries (agriculture, primary ind., mfg, construction) 21%; service-producing industries (transpt., trade, finance, service, pub. admin, unclassified) 79%. **Unemployment rate** (2002): 8.7%. **Principal industries:** forestry, wood and paper, mining, tourism, agriculture, fishing, manufacturing.

☐ **EDUCATION: Elem. enrolment** (2001–2): 655,100. **Spending** per full-time equiv. student (1999): $6 985. **Post-sec. degrees** granted (1998): 15 779.

☐ **INTERNATIONAL AIRPORTS:** Vancouver; Victoria.

☐ **NATIONAL PARKS:** Glacier, Kootenay, Mount Revelstoke, Pacific Rim, Gwaii Haanas (South Moresby), Yoho.

☐ **PROVINCIAL DATA: Motto:** *Splendor Sine Occasu:* "Splendor without Diminishment." **Flower:** Dogwood. **Bird:** Stellar's Jay.

☐ **POLITICS: Premier:** Gordon Campbell (Lib). **Leader, opposition parties:** Carole James (NDP). **Date of last general election:** May 16, 2001. **Lt. Governor:** Hon. Iona Campagnolo.

Yukon Territory

☐ **CAPITAL:** Whitehorse, metro pop. (2001) 19 058. **Date entered Confederation:** June 13, 1898.

☐ **POPULATION (2003):** 31,371. **Pop. density:** 0.05 per sq. km. **Pop. growth** (2002–03): 1.0%. **Pop. urban** (2001): 58.0%. Age structure (2001): 29.0% under 19; 64.9% 20–64; 6.0% over 65. **Median age** (2001): 36.1. **Net interprovincial migration** (2000–01): -846.

☐ **VITAL STATISTICS: Rates** (per 1 000 pop., 2001): birth: 13.3; death: 4.8. **Life expectancy at birth** (1999): 76.9.

☐ **GEOGRAPHY: Total area** 482 443 sq. km; **Land area** 474 391 sq. km; **Forested land** 242 000 sq. km; **Length of coastline** 418 km. **Climate**: great variance in temperatures; warm summers, very cold winters; low precipitation. **Topography**: main feature is the Yukon plateau with 21 peaks exceeding 3 300 m; open tundra in the far north.

☐ **ECONOMY: Gross Domestic Product** at market prices (2002): $1,211 million; **% change GDP** (2001–02): 1.5%; **Per capita GDP** (2002): $38,602. **Unemployment rate** (2000): n.a. **Principal industries:** mining, tourism.

☐ **EDUCATION: Elem. enrolment** (May 31, 2002): 5 432. **Spending** per full-time equiv. student (1999): $12 392.

☐ **INTERNATIONAL AIRPORTS:** Whitehorse.

☐ **NATIONAL PARKS:** Ivvavik, Kluane, Vuntut.

☐ **PROVINCIAL DATA: Flower:** Fireweed. **Bird:** Common Raven.

☐ **POLITICS: Govt. Leader:** Dennis Fentie (Yukon Party), **Leaders, opposition parties:** Pat Duncan (Lib.), Todd Hardy (NDP). **Date of last general election:** Nov. 4, 2002. **Commissioner:** Hon. Jack Cable.

Northwest Territories

☐ **CAPITAL:** Yellowknife, metro pop. (2001) 16 541. **Date entered Confederation:** July 15, 1870.

☐ **POPULATION (2003):** 42,040; **Pop. density:** 0.02 per sq. km.; **Pop. growth** (2002–2003): 0.4%; **Pop. urban (2001):** 58%; **Age structure** (2001): 35.0% under 19; 60.7% 20–64; 4.4% over 65; **Median age** (2001): 30.1; **Net interprovincial migration** (2000–01): -606.

☐ **VITAL STATISTICS: Rates** (per 1 000 pop., 2001): birth: 17.1; death: 3.8. **Life expectancy at birth** (1999): 75.3.

☐ **GEOGRAPHY: Total area** 1 346 106 sq. km; **Land area** 1 183 085 sq. km; **Forested land** 615 000 sq. km; **Length of coastline** 14 734 km. **Climate**: extreme temperatures and low precipitation; arctic and sub-arctic. **Topography**: mostly tundra plains formed on the rocks of the Canadian Shield; the Mackenzie Lowland is a continuation of the Great Plains; the Mackenzie River Valley is forested.

☐ **ECONOMY: Gross Domestic Product** at market prices (2003): $3,332 million; **% change GDP** (2002–03): 1.3%; **Per capita GDP** (2003): $79,257. **Unemployment rate** (2000): n.a. **Principal industries:** construction, mining, utilities, services, tourism.

☐ **EDUCATION: Elem. enrolment** (2001-2): 7 944. **Spending** per full-time equiv. student (1999): $11 261 (incl. Nunavut).

☐ **INTERNATIONAL AIRPORTS:** none.

☐ **NATIONAL PARKS:** Aulavik, Nahanni, Tuktut Nogait, Wood Buffalo (shared with Alberta).

☐ **PROVINCIAL DATA: Flower:** Mountain Avens. **Bird:** Gyrfalcon. **Tree:** Jack pine.

☐ **POLITICS: Premier:** Joe Handley. **Date of last general election:** Nov. 24, 2003. **Commissioner:** Hon. Glenna F. Hansen.

Provinces on the Web

Newfoundland & Labrador: www.gov.nf.ca
Prince Edward Island: www.gov.pe.ca
Nova Scotia: www.gov.ns.ca
New Brunswick: www.gnb.ca
Quebec: www.gouv.qc.ca
Ontario: www.gov.on.ca
Manitoba: www.gov.mb.ca

Saskatchewan: www.gov.sk.ca
Alberta: www.gov.ab.ca
British Columbia: www.gov.bc.ca
Nunavut: www.gov.nu.ca
Northwest Territories: www.gov.nt.ca
Yukon Territory: www.gov.yk.ca

Nunavut

☐ **CAPITAL:** Iqaluit, metro pop. (2001): 5 236. **Date became territory:** April 1, 1999.

☐ **POPULATION (2003):** 29,357. Pop. density: 0.01 per sq. km. **Pop. growth** (2002–03): -0.1%. **Pop. urban** (2001): 32%. **Age structure** (2001): 46.5% under 19; 51.2% 20–64; 2.2% over 65. **Median age** (2001): 22.1. **Net interprovincial migration** (2000–01): 220.

☐ **VITAL STATISTICS: Rates** (per 1 000 pop., 2001): birth: 25.3; death: 5.5. **Life expectancy at birth** (1999): 68.9.

☐ **GEOGRAPHY: Total area**: 2 093 190 sq. km; **Land area**: 1 936 113 sq. km. **Length of coastline:** 114 920 km. **Climate**: extreme temperatures and low precipitation; arctic. **Topography**: rocky tundra with stunted vegetation located above the tree line; snow-covered most of the year.

☐ **ECONOMY: Gross Domestic Product** at market prices (2001): 941 million; **% change GDP** (2000-01): 3.7%; **Per capita GDP** (2001): $35 184. **Unemployment rate** (1996): 15.4. **Principal industries:** mining, tourism, shrimp and scallop fishing, hunting and trapping, arts and crafts production.

☐ **EDUCATION (1999–2000 est.): No.** of schools: 42 elem. and sec.; 1 post-sec. **Enrolment:** 7 462 elem. and sec.; 167 post-sec.

☐ **INTERNATIONAL AIRPORTS:** Iqaluit.

☐ **NATIONAL PARKS:** Auyuittuq, Quttinirpaaq (Ellesmere Island), Sirmilik.

☐ **PROVINCIAL DATA:** n.a.

☐ **POLITICS: Premier:** Paul Okalik. **Date of last general election:** Feb. 16, 2004. **Commissioner:** Hon. Peter Irniq.

CANADIAN CITIES

A census metropolitan area (CMA) is a very large urban area (known as the urban core) together with adjacent urban and rural areas (known as urban and rural fringes) which have a high degree of social and economic integration with the urban core. A CMA has an urban core population of at least 100 000 based on the previous census. Once an area becomes a CMA, it is retained as a CMA even if the population of its urban core declines below 100 000. All CMAs are subdivided into census tracts. A CMA may be consolidated with adjacent census agglomerations (CAs) if they are socially and economically integrated. This new grouping is known as a consolidated CMA and the component CMA and CA(s) are known as the primary census metropolitan area (PCMA) and primary census agglomeration(s) [PCA(s)]. A CMA may not be consolidated with another CMA.

The following information is based on the 2001 Census, for which Abbotsford, B.C., and Kingston, Ont., were added to the list of CMAs. For more recent population data on capital cities, where it is available, see the Province and Territories section, pages 25–31.

Abbotsford, B.C.

Year Incorporated: 1995 Area: 626 sq. km.

☐ **DEMOGRAPHICS: CMA Population** (2001): 147 370 Pop. density: 235 per sq. km. **Pop. growth** (1996–2001): 7%. **Immigrant pop.** (1996): n.a. **Age Structure** (2001): Male pop.: under 25: 38%, over 65: 12%; Female pop.: under 25: 35%, over 65: 15%.

☐ **OFFICIAL LANGUAGES (1996):** n.a.

☐ **FAMILIES (1996):** n.a.

☐ **FAMILY INCOME (2000): Median Family Income:** n.a. **Median Income for Husband-Wife Families:** n.a. **Median Income for Lone-parent families:** n.a.

☐ **LABOUR FORCE (2001): Labour Force (000s):** n.a. **Employed Full-time (000s):** n.a. **Employment rate:** n.a. **Unemployed (000s):** n.a. **Unemployment rate:** n.a. **Participation rate:** n.a.

☐ **CLIMATE: Avg. day/night temps.:** 5.8°/-0.6° (Jan.); 23.4°/11.5° (July) **Avg. annual sunshine:** 1 866 h **Avg. annual precip.:** 1 573.2 mm **Avg. annual snowfall:** 63.5 cm.

Calgary, Alta

Year Incorporated: 1893. **Area:** 5 083 sq. km.

☐ **DEMOGRAPHICS: CMA Population** (2001): 951 395. Pop. density: 187 per sq. km. **Pop. growth** (1996–2001): 15%. **Immigrant pop.** (1996): 20.8%. **Age Structure** (2001): Male pop.: under 25: 35%, over 65: 8%; Female pop.: under 25: 33%, over 65: 10%.

☐ **OFFICIAL LANGUAGES (1996):** 90.7% English; 0.1% French; 7.3% bilingual; 1.9% neither.

☐ **FAMILIES (1996): Avg. family size:** 3.2. **Lone-parent families:** 13.2% of families.

☐ **FAMILY INCOME (2000):** Median Family Income: $60 700. Median Income for Husband-Wife Families: $66 500. Median Income for Lone-parent families: $30 400.

☐ **LABOUR FORCE (2001):** Labour Force (000s): 596.3. Employed Full-time (000s): 477.7. Employment rate: 72.1. Unemployed (000s): 26.8. Unemployment rate: 4.5. Participation rate: 75.5.

☐ **CLIMATE:** Avg. day/night temps.: -2.8°/-15.1° (Jan.) 22.9°/9.4° (July) **Avg. annual sunshine:** 2 405 h **Avg. annual precip.:** 412.6 mm **Avg. annual snowfall:** 126.7 cm

Chicoutimi–Jonquière, Que.

Year Incorporated: 1976. Area: 1 754 sq. km.

☐ **DEMOGRAPHICS: CMA Population** (2001): 154 938. Pop. density: 88 per sq. km. **Pop. growth** (1996–2001): -3%. **Immigrant pop.** (1996): 0.7%. **Age Structure** (2001): Male pop.: under 25: 33%, over 65: 11%; Female pop.: under 25: 30%, over 65: 15%.

☐ **OFFICIAL LANGUAGES (1996):** 0.1% English; 82.5% French; 17.4% bilingual.

☐ **FAMILIES (1996):** Avg. family size: 3.1. Lone-parent families: 15.0% of families.

☐ **FAMILY INCOME (2000):** Median Family Income: $50 900. Median Income for Husband-Wife Families: $55 700. Median Income for Lone-parent families: $25 200.

☐ **LABOUR FORCE (2001):** Labour Force (000s): 78.9. Employed Full-time (000s): 56.5. Employment rate: 52.9. Unemployed (000s): 8.8. Unemployment rate: 11.2. Participation rate: 59.6.

☐ **CLIMATE:** Avg. day/night temps.: -10.3°/-21.7° (Jan.) 24.2°/12.0° (July) **Avg. annual sunshine:** 1 873 h **Avg. annual precip.:** 950.8 mm **Avg. annual snowfall:** 341.6 cm.

Edmonton, Alta

Year Incorporated: 1904. Area: 9 419 sq. km.

☐ **DEMOGRAPHICS: CMA Population** (2001): 937 845. Pop. density: 100 per sq. km. **Pop. growth** (1996–2001): 8%. **Immigrant pop.** (1996): 18.4%. **Age Structure** (2001): Male pop.: under 25: 36%, over 65: 9%; Female pop.: under 25: 34%, over 65: 12%.

☐ **OFFICIAL LANGUAGES (1996):** 90.9% English; 0.1% French; 7.5% bilingual; 1.6% neither.

☐ **FAMILIES (1996):** Avg. family size: 3.2. Lone-parent families: 15.0% of families.

☐ **FAMILY INCOME (2000):** Median Family

Income: $56 300. Median Income for Husband-Wife Families: $62 700. Median Income for Lone-parent families: $26 800.

☐ **LABOUR FORCE (2001):** Labour Force (000s): 531.1. Employed Full-time (000s): 408.1. Employment rate: 67.1. Unemployed (000s): 26.2. Unemployment rate: 4.9. Participation rate: 70.6.

☐ **CLIMATE:** Avg. day/night temps.: -7.3°/-16° (Jan.) 22.8°/12.1° (July) **Avg. annual sunshine:** 2 299 h **Avg. annual precip.:** 476.9 mm **Avg. annual snowfall:** 123.5 cm.

Halifax, N.S.

Year Incorporated: 1841. Area: 5 496 sq. km.

☐ **DEMOGRAPHICS: CMA Population** (2001): 359 183. Pop. density: 65 per sq. km. **Pop. growth** (1996–2001): 4%. **Immigrant pop.** (1996): 7.1%. **Age Structure** (2001): Male pop.: under 25: 33%, over 65: 9%; Female pop.: under 25: 31%, over 65: 12%.

☐ **OFFICIAL LANGUAGES (1996):** 88.9% English; 0.1% French; 10.7% bilingual; 0.3% neither.

☐ **FAMILIES (1996):** Avg. family size: 3.1. Lone-parent families: 15.9% of families.

☐ **FAMILY INCOME (2000):** Median Family Income: $53 400. Median Income for Husband-Wife Families: $60 200. Median Income for Lone-parent families: $23 500.

☐ **LABOUR FORCE (2001):** Labour Force (000s): 197.5. Employed Full-time (000s): 152.5. Employment rate: 65.5. Unemployed (000s): 13.9. Unemployment rate: 7.0. Participation rate: 70.5.

☐ **CLIMATE:** Avg. day/night temps.: -0.2°/-9.2° (Jan.) 22.1°/13.5° (July) **Avg. annual sunshine:** 1 965 h **Avg. annual precip.:** 1421.4 mm **Avg. annual snowfall:** 176.4 cm

Hamilton, Ont.

Year Incorporated: 1846. Area: 1 372 sq. km.

☐ **DEMOGRAPHICS: CMA Population** (2001): 662 401. Pop. density: 483 per sq. km. **Pop. growth** (1996–2001): 6%. **Immigrant pop.** (1996): 23.3%. **Age Structure** (2001): Male pop.: under 25: 34%, over 65: 12%; Female pop.: under 25: 31%, over 65: 16%.

☐ **OFFICIAL LANGUAGES (1996):** 91.7% English; 0.1% French; 6.8% bilingual; 1.5% neither.

☐ **FAMILIES (1996):** Avg. family size: 3.1. Lone-parent families: 14.3% of families.

☐ **FAMILY INCOME (2000):** Median Family Income: $59 700. Median Income for Husband-

Wife Families: $65 900. Median Income for Lone-parent families: $28 000.

☐ **LABOUR FORCE (2001):** Labour Force (000s): 371.1. Employed Full-time (000s): 281.6. Employment rate: 63.2. Unemployed (000s): 22.8. Unemployment rate: 6.1. Participation rate: 67.4.

☐ **CLIMATE:** Avg. day/night temps.: -2.2°/–9.7° (Jan.) 26.3°/15.1° (July) Avg. annual sunshine: 2 088 h Avg. annual precip.: 910.1 mm Avg. annual snowfall: 161.8 cm

Kingston, Ont.

Year Incorporated: 1998. Area: 1 907 sq. km.

☐ **DEMOGRAPHICS: CMA Population** (2001): 146 838 Pop. density: 77 per sq. km. **Pop. growth** (1996–2001): 1%. **Immigrant pop.:** n.a. **Age Structure** (2001): Male pop.: under 25: 33%, over 65: 12%; Female pop.: under 25: 31%, over 65: 16%.

☐ **OFFICIAL LANGUAGES:** n.a.

☐ **FAMILIES:** n.a.

☐ **FAMILY INCOME (2000):** Median Family Income: n.a. Median Income for Husband-Wife Families: n.a. Median Income for Lone-parent families: n.a.

☐ **LABOUR FORCE (2001):** Labour Force (000s): n.a. Employed Full-time (000s): n.a. **Employment rate:** n.a. **Unemployed (000s):** n.a. **Unemployment rate:** n.a. **Participation rate:** n.a.

☐ **CLIMATE:** Avg. day/night temps.: -3.2°/–12.2° (Jan.) 24.8°/15.7° (July) Avg. annual sunshine: 1 992 h Avg. annual precip.: 968.2 mm Avg. annual snowfall: 180.9 cm.

Kitchener, Ont.

Year Incorporated: 1912. Area: 827 sq. km.

☐ **DEMOGRAPHICS: CMA Population** (2001): 414 284. Pop. density: 501 per sq. km. **Pop. growth** (1996–2001): 8%. **Immigrant pop.** (1996): 21.6%. **Age Structure** (2001): Male pop.: under 25: 36%, over 65: 9%; Female pop.: under 25: 33%, over 65: 13%.

☐ **OFFICIAL LANGUAGES (1996):** 91.4% English; 0.1% French; 6.9% bilingual; 1.6% neither.

☐ **FAMILIES (1996):** Avg. family size: 3.2. Lone-parent families: 13.7% of families.

☐ **FAMILY INCOME (2000):** Median Family Income: $60 700. Median Income for Husband-Wife Families: $66 200. Median Income for Lone-parent families: $28 700.

☐ **LABOUR FORCE (2001):** Labour Force (000s): 240.5. Employed Full-time (000s): 186.3. Employment rate: 66.0. Unemployed (000s): 14.8. Unemployment rate: 6.2. Participation rate: 70.3.

☐ **CLIMATE:** Avg. day/night temps.: -3.1°/–11° (Jan.) 25.9°/13.7° (July) Avg. annual sunshine: 1 920 h Avg. annual precip.: 907.9 mm Avg. annual snowfall: 159.5 cm.

London, Ont.

Year Incorporated: 1855. Area: 2 333 sq. km.

☐ **DEMOGRAPHICS: CMA Population** (2001): 432 451. Pop. density: 185 per sq. km. **Pop. growth** (1996–2001): 3%. **Immigrant pop.** (1996): 19.1%. **Age Structure** (2001): Male pop.: under 25: 35%, over 65: 11%; Female pop.: under 25: 32%, over 65: 15%.

☐ **OFFICIAL LANGUAGES (1996):** 92.2% English; 6.6% bilingual; 1.1% neither.

☐ **FAMILIES (1996):** Avg. family size: 3.1. Lone-parent families: 15.5% of families.

☐ **FAMILY INCOME (2000):** Median Family Income: $56 200. Median Income for Husband-Wife Families: $63 000. Median Income for Lone-parent families: $26 300.

☐ **LABOUR FORCE (2001):** Labour Force (000s): 230.7. Employed Full-time (000s): 171.1. Employment rate: 63.3. Unemployed (000s): 14.7. Unemployment rate: 6.4. Participation rate: 67.6.

☐ **CLIMATE:** Avg. day/night temps.: -2.4°/–10.1° (Jan.) 26.3°/14.6° (July) Avg. annual sunshine: 1 800 h Avg. annual precip.: 987.1 mm Avg. annual snowfall: 202.4 cm.

Montreal, Que.

Year Incorporated: 1832. Area: 4 047 sq. km.

☐ **DEMOGRAPHICS: CMA Population** (2001): 3 426 350. Pop. density: 847 per sq. km. **Pop. growth** (1996–2001): 3%. **Immigrant pop.** (1996): 17.6%. **Age Structure** (2001): Male pop.: under 25: 33%, over 65: 11%; Female pop.: under 25: 30%, over 65: 15%.

☐ **OFFICIAL LANGUAGES (1996):** 8.5% English; 39.8% French; 49.7% bilingual; 1.9% neither.

☐ **FAMILIES (1996):** Avg. family size: 3.1. Lone-parent families: 17.4% of families.

☐ **FAMILY INCOME (2000):** Median Family Income: $50 000. Median Income for Husband-Wife Families: $56 000. Median Income for Lone-parent families: $26 600.

☐ **LABOUR FORCE (2001): Labour Force (000s):** 1 857.7. Employed Full-time (000s): 1 426.7. **Employment rate:** 60.4. **Unemployed (000s):** 152.0. **Unemployment rate: 8.2. Participation rate:** 65.7.

☐ **CLIMATE:** Avg. day/night temps.: -5.8°/–14.9° (Jan.) 26.3°/15.5° (July) **Avg. annual sunshine:** 2 029 h **Avg. annual precip.:** 966.8 mm **Avg. annual snowfall:** 214.2 cm.

Oshawa, Ont.

Year Incorporated: 1924. Area: 903 sq. km.

☐ **DEMOGRAPHICS: CMA Population** (2001): 296 298. Pop. density: 328 per sq. km. **Pop. growth** (1996–2001): 10%. **Immigrant pop.** (1996) 16.4%. **Age Structure** (2001): Male pop.: under 25: 37%, over 65: 9%; Female pop.: under 25: 34%, over 65: 12%.

☐ **OFFICIAL LANGUAGES (1996):** 92.8% English; 0.1% French; 6.7% bilingual; 0.5% neither.

☐ **FAMILIES (1996): Avg. family size:** 3.2. **Lone-parent families:** 14.1% of families.

☐ **FAMILY INCOME (2000): Median Family Income:** $64 700. **Median Income for Husband-Wife Families:** $71 800. **Median Income for Lone-parent families:** $28 900.

☐ **LABOUR FORCE (2001): Labour Force (000s):** 163.4. Employed Full-time (000s): 127.5. **Employment rate:** 65.2. **Unemployed (000s):** 9.2. **Unemployment rate:** 5.6. **Participation rate:** 69.0.

☐ **CLIMATE:** Avg. day/night temps.: -1.4°/-9.2° (Jan.) 25°/15.5° (July) **Avg. annual sunshine:** 1 893 h **Avg. annual precip.:** 877.9 mm **Avg. annual snowfall:** 118.4 cm.

Ottawa-Hull, Ont./Que.

Year Incorporated: 1854 (Ottawa). Area: 5 318 sq. km.

☐ **DEMOGRAPHICS: CMA Population** (2001): 1 063 664. Pop. density: 200 per sq. km. **Pop. growth** (1996–2001): 6%. **Immigrant pop.** (1996): 16.0%. **Age Structure** (2001): Male pop.: under 25: 34%, over 65: 9%; Female pop.: under 25: 31%, over 65: 12%.

☐ **OFFICIAL LANGUAGES (1996):** 45.8% English; 9.0% French; 44.0% bilingual.

☐ **FAMILIES (1996): Avg. family size:** 3.1. **Lone-parent families:** 15.6% of families.

☐ **FAMILY INCOME (2000): Median Family Income:** $65 500. **Median Income for Husband-Wife Families:** $72 900. **Median Income for Lone-parent families:** $30 500.

☐ **LABOUR FORCE (2001): Labour Force (000s):** 615.0. Employed Full-time (000s): 477.0. **Employment rate:** 65.8. **Unemployed (000s):** 39.0. **Unemployment rate: 6.3. Participation rate:** 70.3.

☐ **CLIMATE: CLIMATE: Avg. day/night temps.:** -6.1°/–15.3° (Jan.) 26.5°/15.4° (July) **Avg. annual sunshine:** 2 061 h **Avg. annual precip.:** 943.5 mm **Avg. annual snowfall:** 235.7 cm.

Quebec, Que.

Year Incorporated: 1832. Area: 3 154 sq. km.

☐ **DEMOGRAPHICS: CMA Population** (2001): 682 757. Pop. density: 216 per sq. km. **Pop. growth** (1996–2001): 1%. **Immigrant pop.** (1996): 2.6%. **Age Structure** (2001): Male pop.: under 25: 31%, over 65: 11%; Female pop.: under 25: 28%, over 65: 15%.

☐ **OFFICIAL LANGUAGES (1996):** 0.2% English; 69.6% French; 30.0% bilingual; 0.2% neither.

☐ **FAMILIES (1996): Avg. family size:** 3.0. **Lone-parent families:** 16.1% of families.

☐ **FAMILY INCOME (2000): Median Family Income:** $53 300. **Median Income for Husband-Wife Families:** $58 200. **Median Income for Lone-parent families:** $29 800.

☐ **LABOUR FORCE (2001): Labour Force (000s):** 367.8. Employed Full-time (000s): 270.0. **Employment rate:** 59.7. **Unemployed (000s):** 28.8. **Unemployment rate: 7.8. Participation rate:** 64.8.

☐ **CLIMATE:** Avg. day/night temps.: -7.9°/–17.6° (Jan.) 25.0°/13.4° (July) **Avg. annual sunshine:** 1 905 h **Avg. annual precip.:** 1230.3 mm **Avg. annual snowfall:** 315.9 cm.

Regina, Sask.

Year Incorporated: 1903. Area: 3 408 sq. km.

☐ **DEMOGRAPHICS: CMA Population** (2001): 192 800. Pop. density: 57 per sq. km. **Pop. growth** (1996–2001): -1%. **Immigrant pop.** (1996): 7.9%. **Age Structure** (2001): Male pop.: under 25: 37%, over 65: 11%; Female pop.: under 25: 34%, over 65: 14%.

☐ **OFFICIAL LANGUAGES (1996):** 93.9% English; 0.1% French; 5.6% bilingual; 0.4% neither.

☐ **FAMILIES (1996): Avg. family size:** 3.2. **Lone-parent families:** 16.6% of families.

☐ **FAMILY INCOME (2000): Median Family Income:** $56 600. **Median Income for Husband-Wife Families:** $64 700. **Median Income for Lone-parent families:** $25 600.

☐ **LABOUR FORCE (2001): Labour Force (000s):** 111.3. Employed Full-time (000s): 86.6.

Employment rate: 67.4. Unemployed (000s): 6.1. Unemployment rate: 5.5. Participation rate: 71.3.

☐ CLIMATE: Avg. day/night temps.: -10.7°/–21.6° (Jan.) 25.7°/11.8° (July) Avg. annual sunshine: 2 338 h Avg. annual precip.: 388.1 mm Avg. annual snowfall: 105.9 cm.

St. Catharines–Niagara, Ont.

Year Incorporated: 1876. Area: 1 406 sq. km.

☐ DEMOGRAPHICS: CMA Population (2001): 377 009. Pop. density: 268 per sq. km. Pop. growth (1996–2001): 1%. Immigrant pop. (1996): 18.1%. Age Structure (2001): Male pop.: under 25: 32%, over 65: 15%; Female pop.: under 25: 29%, over 65: 19%.

☐ OFFICIAL LANGUAGES (1996): 90.8% English; 0.2% French; 8.3% bilingual; 0.7% neither.

☐ FAMILIES (1996): Avg. family size: 3.0. Lone-parent families: 14.8% of families.

☐ FAMILY INCOME (2000): Median Family Income: $53 300. Median Income for Husband-Wife Families: $59 100. Median Income for Lone-parent families: $26 200.

☐ LABOUR FORCE (2001): Labour Force (000s): 202.7. Employed Full-time (000s): 150.0. Employment rate: 59.0. Unemployed (000s): 12.7. Unemployment rate: 6.3. Participation rate: 63.0.

☐ CLIMATE: Avg. day/night temps.: -0.5°/–7.7° (Jan.) 27.1°/16.4° (July) Avg. annual sunshine: 2 005 h Avg. annual precip.: 873.6 mm Avg. annual snowfall: 136.6 cm.

Saint John, N.B.

Year Incorporated: 1785. Area: 3 360 sq. km.

☐ DEMOGRAPHICS: CMA Population (2001): 122 678. Pop. density: 37 per sq. km. Pop. growth (1996–2001): -3%. Immigrant pop. (1996): 3.9%. Age Structure (2001): Male pop.: under 25: 34%, over 65: 11%; Female pop.: under 25: 31%, over 65: 15%.

☐ OFFICIAL LANGUAGES (1996): 87.5% English; 0.1% French; 12.3% bilingual; 0.1% neither.

☐ FAMILIES (1996): Avg. family size: 3.1. Lone-parent families: 16.9% of families.

☐ FAMILY INCOME (2000): Median Family Income: $47 800. Median Income for Husband-Wife Families: $55 200. Median Income for Lone-parent families: $20 800.

☐ LABOUR FORCE (2001): Labour Force (000s): 64.2. Employed Full-time (000s): 48.6. Employment rate: 57.8. Unemployed (000s): 6.1. Unemployment

rate: 9.5. Participation rate: 63.8.

☐ CLIMATE: Avg. day/night temps.: -2.7°/–13.6° (Jan.) 22.4°/11.7° (July) Avg. annual sunshine: 1 950 h Avg. annual precip.: 1 390.3 mm Avg. annual snowfall: 256.9 cm.

St. John's, Nfld and Labrador

Year Incorporated: 1888. Area: 805 sq. km.

☐ DEMOGRAPHICS: CMA Population (2001): 176 918. Pop. density: 215 per sq. km. Pop. growth (1996–2001): -1%. Immigrant pop. (1996): 2.9%. Age Structure (2001): Male pop.: under 25: 35%, over 65: 9%; Female pop.: under 25: 32%, over 65: 12%.

☐ OFFICIAL LANGUAGES (1996): 94.5% English; 0% French; 5.4% bilingual; 0.1% neither.

☐ FAMILIES (1996): Avg. family size: 3.2. Lone-parent families: 16.8% of families.

☐ FAMILY INCOME (2000): Median Family Income: $48 800. Median Income for Husband-Wife Families: $56 300. Median Income for Lone-parent families: $21 200.

☐ LABOUR FORCE (2001): Labour Force (000s): 94.5. Employed Full-time (000s): 73.4. Employment rate: 60.5. Unemployed (000s): 8.6. Unemployment rate: 9.1. Participation rate: 66.6.

☐ CLIMATE: Avg. day/night temps.: -0.9°/–1.5° (Jan.) 20.3°/10.5° (July) Avg. annual sunshine: 1 512 h Avg. annual precip.: 1 513.7 mm Avg. annual snowfall: 322.3 cm.

Saskatoon, Sask.

Year Incorporated: 1906. Area: 5 192 sq. km.

☐ DEMOGRAPHICS: CMA Population (2001): 225 927. Pop. density: 44 per sq. km. Pop. growth (1996–2001): 3%. Immigrant pop. (1996): 7.5%. Age Structure (2001): Male pop.: under 25: 38%, over 65: 10%; Female pop.: under 25: 36%, over 65: 13%.

☐ OFFICIAL LANGUAGES (1996): 92.9% English; 0.0% French; 6.5% bilingual; 0.5% neither.

☐ FAMILIES (1996): Avg. family size: 3.2. Lone-parent families: 15.9% of families.

☐ FAMILY INCOME (2000): Median Family Income: $51 600. Median Income for Husband-Wife Families: $58 300. Median Income for Lone-parent families: $22 600.

☐ LABOUR FORCE (2001): Labour Force (000s): 123.2. Employed Full-time (000s): 91.8. Employment rate: 63.7. Unemployed (000s): 7.6. Unemployment rate: 6.2. Participation rate: 67.8.

☐ **CLIMATE:** Avg. day/night temps.: -11.8/–22.3° (Jan) 24.9°/11.4° (July) **Avg. annual sunshine:** 2 328 h **Avg. annual precip.:** 350.0 mm **Avg. annual snowfall:** 97.2 cm.

Sherbrooke, Que.

Year Incorporated: 1875. Area: 1 108 sq. km.

☐ **DEMOGRAPHICS:** CMA Population (2001): 153 811. Pop. density: 139 per sq. km. **Pop. growth** (1996–2001): 2%. **Immigrant pop.** (1996): 4.2%. **Age Structure** (2001): Male pop.: under 25: 34%, over 65: 10%; Female pop.: under 25: 31%, over 65: 16%.

☐ **OFFICIAL LANGUAGES (1996):** 1.9% English; 58.8% French; 39.1% bilingual; 0.3% neither.

☐ **FAMILIES (1996):** Avg. family size: 3.0. Lone-parent families: 17.0% of families.

☐ **FAMILY INCOME (2000):** Median Family Income: $47 600. **Median Income for Husband-Wife Families:** $52 900. **Median Income for Lone-parent families:** $26 300.

☐ **LABOUR FORCE (2001):** Labour Force (000s): 80.7 Employed Full-time (000s): 61.4. **Employment rate:** 59.2. **Unemployed (000s):** 6.3. **Unemployment rate:** 7.8. **Participation rate:** 64.2.

☐ **CLIMATE:** Avg. day/night temps.: -5.7°/–18.0° (Jan.) 24.7°/11.4° (July) **Avg. annual sunshine:** 1 850 h **Avg. annual precip.:** 1 144.1 mm **Avg. annual snowfall:** 294.3 cm.

Sudbury, Ont.

Year Incorporated: 1930. Area: 3 536 sq. km.

☐ **DEMOGRAPHICS:** CMA Population (2001): 155 601. Pop. density: 44 per sq. km. **Pop. growth** (1996–2001): -7%. **Immigrant pop.** (1991): 8.1%. **Age Structure** (2001): Male pop.: under 25: 33%, over 65: 12%; Female pop.: under 25: 31%, over 65: 15%.

☐ **OFFICIAL LANGUAGES (1996):** 58.0% English; 1.5% French; 40.1% bilingual; 0.3% neither.

☐ **FAMILIES (1996):** Avg. family size: 3.1. Lone-parent families: 15.2% of families.

☐ **FAMILY INCOME (2000):** Median Family Income: $54 400. **Median Income for Husband-Wife Families:** $61 300. **Median Income for Lone-parent families:** $23 100.

☐ **LABOUR FORCE (2001):** Labour Force (000s): 79.4. Employed Full-time (000s): 57.5. **Employment rate:** 56.2. **Unemployed (000s):** 6.9. **Unemployment rate:** 8.7. **Participation rate:** 61.6.

☐ **CLIMATE:** Avg. day/night temps.: -8.4°/–18.6° (Jan.) 24.8°/13.3° (July) **Avg. annual sunshine:** 1 989 h **Avg. annual precip.:** 899.3 mm **Avg. annual snowfall:** 274.4 cm

Thunder Bay, Ont.

Year Incorporated: 1970. Area: 2 548 sq. km.

☐ **DEMOGRAPHICS:** CMA Population (2001): 121 986. Pop. density: 48 per sq. km. **Pop. growth** (1996–2001): -4%. **Immigrant pop.** (1996): 12.2%. **Age Structure** (2001): Male pop.: under 25: 33%, over 65: 13%; Female pop.: under 25: 30%, over 65: 17%.

☐ **OFFICIAL LANGUAGES (1996):** 91.7% English; 0.1% French; 7.4% bilingual; 0.7% neither.

☐ **FAMILIES (1996):** Avg. family size: 3.1. Lone-parent families: 16.0% of families.

☐ **FAMILY INCOME (2000):** Median Family Income: $57 100. **Median Income for Husband-Wife Families:** $63 800. **Median Income for Lone-parent families:** $24 500.

☐ **LABOUR FORCE (2001):** Labour Force (000s): 67.5. Employed Full-time (000s): 48.5. **Employment rate:** 61.0. **Unemployed (000s):** 5.4. **Unemployment rate:** 8.0. **Participation rate:** 66.3.

☐ **CLIMATE:** Avg. day/night temps.: -8.6°/–21.1° (Jan.) 24.2°/11.0° (July) **Avg. annual sunshine:** 2 168 h **Avg. annual precip.:** 711.6 mm **Avg. annual snowfall:** 187.6 cm.

Toronto, Ont.

Year Incorporated: 1834. Area: 5 903 sq. km.

☐ **DEMOGRAPHICS:** CMA Population (2001): 4 682 897. Pop. density: 793 per sq. km. **Pop. growth** (1996–2001): 9%. **Immigrant pop.** (1996): 41.6%. **Age Structure** (2001): Male pop.: under 25: 34%, over 65: 10%; Female pop.: under 25: 31%, over 65: 13%.

☐ **OFFICIAL LANGUAGES (1996):** 87.4% English; 0.1% French; 8.0% bilingual; 4.5% neither.

☐ **FAMILIES (1996):** Avg. family size: 3.3. Lone-parent families: 15.5% of families.

☐ **FAMILY INCOME (2000):** Median Family Income: $55 000. **Median Income for Husband-Wife Families:** $61 400. **Median Income for Lone-parent families:** $29 400.

☐ **LABOUR FORCE (2001):** Labour Force (000s): 2 745.7. Employed Full-time (000s): 2 177.0. **Employment rate:** 65.1. **Unemployed (000s):** 173.8. **Unemployment rate:** 6.3. **Participation rate:** 69.5.

☐ **CLIMATE:** Avg. day/night temps.: -2.1°/–10.5° (Jan.) 26.8°/14.8° (July) **Avg. annual sunshine:** 2

038 h **Avg. annual precip.:** 792.7 mm **Avg. annual snowfall:** 115.4 cm.

Trois–Rivières, Que.

Year Incorporated: 1857. Area: 880 sq. km.

☐ **DEMOGRAPHICS: CMA Population** (2001): 137 507. Pop. density: 156 per sq. km. **Pop. growth** (1996–2001): -2%. **Immigrant pop.** (1996): 1.6%. **Age Structure** (2001): Male pop.: under 25: 31%, over 65: 13%; Female pop.: under 25: 28%, over 65: 18%.

☐ **OFFICIAL LANGUAGES (1996):** 0.1% English; 75.4% French; 24.4% bilingual.

☐ **FAMILIES (1996):** Avg. family size: 3.0. Lone-parent families: 16.1% of families.

☐ **FAMILY INCOME (2000):** Median Family Income: $45 900. Median Income for Husband-Wife Families: $51 700. Median Income for Lone-parent families: $23 800.

☐ **LABOUR FORCE (2001):** Labour Force (000s): 72.5. Employed Full-time (000s): 53.5. **Employment rate:** 56.1. **Unemployed (000s):** 7.0. Unemployment rate: 9.7. Participation rate: 62.1.

☐ **CLIMATE:** Avg. day/night temps.: -7.3°/–17.6° (Jan.) 25.5°/14.1° (July) **Avg. annual sunshine:** 1 967 h **Avg. annual precip.:** 1 099.8 mm **Avg. annual snowfall:** 241.3 cm.

Vancouver, B.C.

Year Incorporated: 1886. Area: 2 879 sq. km.

☐ **DEMOGRAPHICS: CMA Population** (2001): 1 986 965. Pop. density: 690 per sq. km. **Pop. growth** (1996–2001): 8%. **Immigrant pop.** (1996) 34.6%. **Age Structure** (2001): Male pop.: under 25: 32%, over 65: 11%; Female pop.: under 25: 30%, over 65: 14%.

☐ **OFFICIAL LANGUAGES (1996):** 87.9% English; 0.1% French; 7.4% bilingual; 4.7% neither.

☐ **FAMILIES (1996):** Avg. family size: 3.2. Lone-parent families: 13.9% of families.

☐ **FAMILY INCOME (2000):** Median Family Income: $50 100. Median Income for Husband-Wife Families: $55 200. Median Income for Lone-parent families: $26 900.

☐ **LABOUR FORCE (2001):** Labour Force (000s): 1 125.1. Employed Full-time (000s): 843.2. **Employment rate:** 61.4. **Unemployed (000s):** 74.0. **Unemployment rate:** 6.6. **Participation rate:** 65.7.

☐ **CLIMATE:** Avg. day/night temps.: 6.1°/0.5° (Jan.) 21.7°/13.2° (July) **Avg. annual sunshine:** 1 928 h **Avg. annual precip.:** 1 199.0 mm **Avg. annual snowfall:** 48.2 cm

Victoria, B.C.

Year Incorporated: 1862. Area: 695 sq. km.

☐ **DEMOGRAPHICS: CMA Population** (2001): 311 902. Pop. density: 449 per sq. km. **Pop. growth** (1996–2001): 2%. **Immigrant pop.** (1996): 19.0%. **Age Structure** (2001): Male pop.: under 25: 30%, over 65: 15%; Female pop.: under 25: 27%, over 65: 20%.

☐ **OFFICIAL LANGUAGES (1996):** 90.6% English; 0.0% French; 8.6% bilingual; 0.7% neither.

☐ **FAMILIES (1996):** Avg. family size: 2.9. Lone-parent families: 14.1% of families.

☐ **FAMILY INCOME (2000):** Median Family Income: $55 200. Median Income for Husband-Wife Families: $60 800. Median Income for Lone-parent families: $28 100.

☐ **LABOUR FORCE (2001):** Labour Force (000s): 158.5. Employed Full-time (000s): 113.3. **Employment rate:** 57.7. **Unemployed (000s):** 9.6. Unemployment rate: 6.1. Participation rate: 61.4.

☐ **CLIMATE:** Avg. day/night temps.: 6.9°/0.7° (Jan.) 21.9°/10.8° (July) **Avg. annual sunshine:** 2 086 h **Avg. annual precip.:** 883.3 mm **Avg. annual snowfall:** 43.8 cm

Windsor, Ont.

Year Incorporated: 1892. Area: 1 023 sq. km.

☐ **DEMOGRAPHICS: CMA Population** (2001): 307 877. Pop. density: 301 per sq. km. **Pop. growth** (1996–2001): 7%. **Immigrant pop.** (1996): 20.4%. **Age Structure** (2001): Male pop.: under 25: 35%, over 65: 11%; Female pop.: under 25: 32%, over 65: 14%.

☐ **OFFICIAL LANGUAGES (1996):** 87.8% English; 0.2% French; 10.5% bilingual; 1.5% neither.

☐ **FAMILIES (1996):** Avg. family size: 3.2. Lone-parent families: 16.0% of families.

☐ **FAMILY INCOME (2000):** Median Family Income: $64 200. Median Income for Husband-Wife Families: $72 000. Median Income for Lone-parent families: $28 200.

☐ **LABOUR FORCE (2001):** Labour Force (000s): 165.7. Employed Full-time (000s): 124.7. **Employment rate:** 61.9. **Unemployed (000s):** 11.1. Unemployment rate: 6.7. Participation rate: 66.3.

☐ **CLIMATE:** Avg. day/night temps.: -0.9°/–8.1° (Jan.) 27.9°/17.4° (July) **Avg. annual sunshine:** 2 027 h **Avg. annual precip.:** 918.3 mm **Avg. annual snowfall:** 126.6 cm

Winnipeg, Man.

Year Incorporated: 1873. Area: 4 151 sq. km.

☐ **DEMOGRAPHICS: CMA Population** (2001): 671 274. Pop. density: 162 per sq. km. **Pop. growth** (1996–2001): 0.6%. **Immigrant pop.** (1996): 16.7%. **Age Structure** (2001): Male pop.: under 25: 34%, over 65: 11%; Female pop.: under 25: 31%, over 65: 16%.

☐ **OFFICIAL LANGUAGES (1996):** 87.9% English; 0.1% French; 10.9% bilingual; 1.1% neither.

☐ **FAMILIES (1996): Avg. family size:** 3.1. Lone-parent families: 15.8% of families.

☐ **FAMILY INCOME (2000): Median Family Income:** $52 500. **Median Income for Husband-Wife Families:** $58 400. **Median Income for Lone-parent families:** $25 500.

☐ **LABOUR FORCE (2001): Labour Force (000s):** 377.6. Employed Full-time (000s): 290.7. **Employment rate:** 66.7. **Unemployed (000s):** 19.4. **Unemployment rate:** 5.1. **Participation rate:** 70.3.

☐ **CLIMATE:** Avg. day/night temps.: -12.7°/–22.8° (Jan.) 25.8°/13.3° (July) **Avg. annual sunshine:** 2 372 h **Avg. annual precip.:** 513.7 mm **Avg. annual snowfall:** 110.6 cm.

Where Do We Live?

*I*n the cities—51 percent of us (15.3 million strong) live in four highly urbanized regions: metropolitan Montreal; the Golden Horseshoe in Ontario; the Calgary–Edmonton corridor in Alberta; and the Lower Mainland–south Vancouver Island portion of British Columbia. The other 49 percent of Canada's citizens are scattered across our vast geography—and many of them also live in smaller urban centres.

While the census of 1871 showed a nation with 19.6 percent of Canadians living in urban areas and 80.4 percent living in rural areas, the 2001 census makes it clear how much times have changed: 79.7 percent of us now live in urban areas and 20.3 percent live in rural areas. As planners at all levels of government begin to work with the new census data, it's clear that the needs of the urban areas, be they social or economic, may necessitate some structural changes to a governing system that was created to serve the rural population of 1871.

The census data also showed that we've continued to move to Ontario and Alberta, as the Atlantic provinces (with the exception of PEI, which held steady), Quebec, Manitoba, Saskatchewan and B.C. experienced a net loss of people through emigration during each of the last five years. The northern territories of Yukon and the Northwest Territories also experienced net losses, while Nunavut has seen very modest net population gains through inter-provincial migration in the last two years.

Growth in some municipalities was explosive: in five years, Cochrane, Alberta, grew by 58.9 percent; Sylvan Lake, Alberta, by 44.5 percent and Strathmore, Alberta, by 43.4 percent. Still in Alberta, Calgary grew by 15 percent, Red Deer by 13 percent and Grande Prairie by 18 percent. In contrast, the CMA of Toronto grew only by 9.8 percent; the outlying area of Richmond Hill, Ontario, grew by 29.8 percent. In Toronto's case, however, the relatively modest percentage of growth resulted in absorbing 419,000 newcomers.

In several areas, the population in the core municipality is growing more slowly than in the areas around it, forming a doughnut. The larger the difference in the growth between the two, the more pronounced the "doughnut effect." This phenomenon was particularly prominent in areas such as Saskatoon and Regina.

Globalization may be making urban economies the new focus of attention. The health of urban centres is becoming a hot topic among planners and Canada's cities are ready for a new deal that will give them a better chance to manage their infrastructure (development, transportation and primary services) to build prosperity.

Source: *Statistics Canada*

NATIONAL PARKS

Canada's national parks are protected by law to preserve representative natural areas throughout the country. The parks are maintained to enhance public understanding, appreciation and enjoyment of the country's natural heritage, and increasingly, park management efforts are being directed to protect Canada's wide variety of ecosystems for the long term.

In 1988, the National Parks Act was amended to ensure that each park's management plan would maintain the ecological integrity of the area, that is, that the structure and function of the existing ecosystem would not be harmed by human activity. This amendment was made as it became increasingly clear that many ecological features, such as grizzly bear populations, require very large areas and very long time lines if they are to survive, if not thrive. The host of modern environmental stresses also affect protected areas and their inhabitants, and mere protection is not enough; a co-operative parks management structure— including public, corporate, environmental and Aboriginal interest groups—and an ecosystem management approach is the preferred management model to minimize damage.

The goal of the national parks policy is to create at least one national park in each of Canada's 39 natural regions. Forty national parks and national park reserves currently exist; however, more national parks are needed. Once completed, the parks system will preserve just over 3 percent of the country's land mass. For more information, visit www.parkscanada.ca

Park	Location	Size (sq. km)	Year est.	Description
Aulavik	northern portion of Banks Is., NWT	12 200	(1992)[1]	Thomsen River forms core of a park marked by deep river canyons and desert-like badlands. Area supports high concentration of musk oxen. The Thomsen River is Canada's most northerly navigable river.
Auyuittuq[2]	Cumberland Peninsula, Baffin Is., NT	21 469	1976	Located on the Arctic Circle; this is an isolated and very rugged wilderness area with mountains, fjords, tundra and permafrost. Park protects part of Northern Davis Strait Natural Region and portions of Baffin Island Shelf Marine region. Contains prehistoric and historic resources from ancient Thule settlements.
Banff	Banff, Alta.	6 641	1885	Our first national park is noted for ice-capped peaks, canyons, glaciers, hot springs, and hoodoos (rock pillars, often in fantastic shapes). Wildlife includes bighorn sheep, black and grizzly bears, elk and caribou. Banff is part of UNESCO's Rocky Mountain Parks World Heritage Site.
Bruce Peninsula, including Fathom Five National Marine Park	299 km northwest of Toronto, between Lake Huron and Georgian Bay	154	(1987)[1]	This park was created to protect the Niagara Escarpment and the limestone cliffs on Georgian Bay; contains mixed forests, wetlands and limestone cliffs. Fathom Five National Marine Park includes 19 islands, over 20 shipwrecks, clear water and distinctive underwater geological features.
Cape Breton Highlands	across northern Cape Breton Is., N.S.	948	1936	The scenic Cabot Trail is characterized by a rugged shoreline with plunging cliffs.
Elk Island	45 km east of Edmonton, Alta.	194	1913	A large population of plains and wood bison, elk and moose inhabit the rolling woodlands and lakes. Other wildlife include bear, beaver and coyote.

▶

▶ Park	Location	Size (sq. km)	Year est.	Description
Forillon	northeast tip of Gaspé Peninsula, Que.	244	1970	Protects parts of the Notre-Dame and Mégantic mountains and some of the Gulf of St. Lawrence marine area. Features a rich variety of seabirds and animals, limestone cliffs, Arctic-alpine plants and the highest mountains in eastern Canada.
Fundy	southeastern shore on the Bay of Fundy, N.B.	206	1948	The giant tides of the Bay of Fundy, among the highest in the world, and a bold, irregular coastline.
Georgian Bay Islands	160 km northwest of Toronto, Ont.	25	1929	59 glacier swept islands are home to endangered species, limestone cliffs, caves and archaeological sites. This area was the inspiration for many of the Group of Seven artists.
Glacier	45 km east of Revelstoke, B.C.	1 349	1886	Protects a section of the Columbia Mountains Natural Region that includes habitats for grizzly bear and mountain caribou. Steep angular mountains, deep valleys, icefields, glaciers, waterfalls, avalanche paths and high precipitation characterise the area.
Grasslands	100 km south of Swift Current, Sask.	906	(1975)[1]	Unique natural habitat of short-grass prairie; blacktailed prairie dogs, pronghorn antelope and the prairie falcon are found.
Gros Morne	west coast of Nfld	1 805	(1970)[1]	Park is dominated by a coastal lowland and an alpine plateau that each boast a variety of land mammals, bird species, fish and trees, ferns and flowers. The park has been declared a UNESCO World Heritage Site because of its spectacular geology.
Gulf Islands	Georgia Strait, B.C.	33	2003	Canada's 5th smallest national park consists of 16 islands and numerous small islets and reef areas in British Columbia's southern Gulf Islands. The waters surrounding or adjacent to park lands, extending 200 metres seaward from the natural boundary of the lands, are also protected
Gwaii Haanas (South Moresby)[2] including Gwaii Haanas, National Marine Conservation Area	southern part of Queen Charlotte Islands, B.C.	1 495	(1987)[1]	Canada's "Galapagos," home to 39 unique plants, an estimated 750,000 seabirds come to nest, and animals such as black bear, pine marten, deer mice, shrews and weasels. Geography features deep fjords, rugged mountains, and one of the finest old-growth temperate rainforest left on Pacific coast.
Ivvavik	northern tip of Yukon	10 168	1984	Migration route for Porcupine caribou herd; major North American waterfowl area; home to grizzly, black and polar bears. Contains unique non-glaciated landscape.
Jasper	340 km west of Edmonton, Alta.	10 878	1907	Contains the largest icefield in the Canadian Rockies—Columbia Icefield—and preserves the headwaters of major rivers, particularly the Athabasca.
Kejimkujik	central southwestern N.S.	404	1974	Gently rolling country with many lakes and rivers. The earliest inhabitants—Maritime Archaic Indians—arrived about 4,500 years ago. ▶

Park	Location	Size (sq. km)	Year est.	Description
▶ Kluane[2]	southwest corner of Yukon	22 013	1976	Features Mount Logan, Canada's highest peak, Kluane Lake (Yukon's largest), grizzly bears, dall sheep and whitewater rivers.
Kootenay	1 km east of Radium Hot Springs, B.C.	1 406	1920	The park contains Rocky Mountain wilderness and is part of UNESCO's Rocky Mountain Parks World Heritage Site. Hot springs, alpine lakes, canyons, glaciers, home to bighorn sheep, mountain goats.
Kouchibouguac	eastern N.B.	239	1979	Swimming, sunbathing on the beaches and dunes; cycling, hiking trails; windsurfing.
La Mauricie	55 km north of Trois-Rivières, Que.	536	1977	Hilly terrain at the edge of the Canadian Shield with transitional forest vegetation from evergreens to deciduous. Beaver, moose and the common loon; an area filled with brooks, lakes and waterfalls.
Mingan Archipelago[2]	N of Anticosti Is. along the St. Lawrence shore, Que.	151	1984	This is a limestone environment that is home to diversified plant species, nesting seabirds and whales, seals and porpoises.
Mount Revelstoke	Revelstoke, B.C.	260	1914	Columbia Mountain ranges. Park is characterised by deep snow accumulation and high annual precipitation. Contains three ecoregions: Interior Alpine Tundra, Interior Sub-alpine Tundra and Interior Cedar Hemlock.
Nahanni[2]	southwestern NWT	4 765	1976	The wild and spectacular South Nahanni river passes through this long, narrow park. The route contains four canyons; the river plunges from twice the height of Niagara Falls at Virginia Falls. Park contains sulphur hotsprings, alpine tundra and vast forests, plus numerous species of birds, mammals and fish.
Pacific Rim [2]	west coast of Vancouver Island, B.C.	500	(1970)[1]	3 sections—Long Beach, Broken Group Islands and West Coast Trail—offer rainforest, beaches and scenic, rugged hiking. Park contains native archaeological sites that indicate settlement for at least 4,300 years.
Point Pelee	southernmost point of Ont.	15	1918	Extensive marshlands and beaches provide refuge for many migratory birds and butterflies. The temperate climate allows over 70 species of tree to survive, as well as a huge variety of reptiles, birds, amphibians, insects and spiders.
Prince Albert	200 km north of Saskatoon, Sask.	3 875	1927	Mixture of forest land and lakes, home to woodland caribou, bison and a pelican colony. Archaeological digs indicate that the area has been inhabited by Aboriginal cultures for at least 6,000 years.
Prince Edward Island	north shore of P.E.I.	22	1937	40 km of fine saltwater beaches, sand dunes, high coastal cliffs, marshes, ponds and woodlands. Green Gables in located in this park.
Pukaskwa	northeastern shore of Lake Superior	1 878	(1971)[1]	Hilly terrain is characterised by ridges and cliffs, and lakes on rocky shores with shallow soil. Park interior features spruce, fir, cedar, aspen and birch. Wildlife includes moose, wolves, black bears and woodland caribou. This park is also the site of rare Arctic plants. ▶

Park	Location	Size (sq. km)	Year est.	Description
Quttinirpaaq **(Ellesmere Island)**	northern tip of Canada	37 775	1988	Vast isolated high Arctic wilderness park. Mountains, glaciers, musk-oxen, Peary's caribou. Fragile permafrost environments. Historic sites and artifacts from early Arctic explorers.
Riding Mountain	270 km northwest of Winnipeg, Man.	2 973	1929	Wildlife—wolf, elk, moose, black bear and beaver—abound.
Saguenay- St. Lawrence Marine Park	At the confluence of the Saguenay Fjord and St. Lawrence estuary; access through L'Anse-Saint-Jean, on the north shore of the St. Lawrence near Tadoussac		1988	A rich diversity of marine life; whales, seals, plants and birds of all kinds.
Sirmilik[2]	northern Baffin Is., incl Bylot Is. and Borden Penin	22 200	(1992)	Mountains, snowfields, glaciers, tundra. Sparse vegetation: 50 bird species incl. murres, kittiwakes, snow geese. Caribou, wolf, Artic fox, lemming, seals, whales, walrus, polar bear
St. Lawrence Islands	Thousand Islands	8	1904	Park includes over 21 islands and 90 islets between Kingston and Brockville, with 100 acres on the mainland at Mallorytown Landing. The area features Thousand Islands landscape and the St. Lawrence River. The Great Lakes moderate the climate, allowing many animals and plants to exist further north than might otherwise be possible.
Terra Nova	east coast of Nfld on Bonavista Bay	400	1957	Rolling forested hills are remnants of the ancient Appalachian Mountains. Rugged cliffs and sheltered inlets are featured on the coast; the interior has spongy bogs, rolling hills covered with forest and inland ponds.
Tuktut Nogait	east of Inuvik in NWT	16 340	1996	Spectacular river canyons and cliffs dotted by hundreds of archaeological sites. Park protects calving grounds of Bluenose caribou and one of the highest concentrations of birds of prey in North America.
Vuntut	Old Crow Flats, northern Yukon	4 345	(1993)[1]	Yukon's most important waterfowl habitat and home to porcupine caribou, grizzly bear, moose, muskrat and several species of fish. Vertebrate fossils found at over 56 sites within park
Wapusk	northeast corner of Manitoba	11 475	1996	This region of flat inland expanse of tundra, eskers and permafrost includes one of the world's largest known polar bear denning areas.
Waterton Lakes	southwest corner of Alta.	505	1895	Officially renamed the Waterton-Glacier International Peace Park in 1932; the world's first park established by two governments.
Wood Buffalo	straddles the Alta.-NWT border	44 802	1922	Canada's largest national park is also a UNESCO World Heritage Site. Home to the largest free-roaming herd of bison; only site of naturally nesting whooping cranes, peregrine falcons and red-sided garter snakes.
Yoho	25 km east of Golden, BC	1 313	1886	Contains several of the highest peaks in the Rocky Mountains, icefields, waterfalls and a varied plant and animal life.

Source: *Canadian Heritage, Parks Canada*   (1) Park created by federal/provincial/territorial agreement rather than federal enactment and administered by special legislation. (2) Park reserve, set aside for national park and under jurisdiction of National Parks Act, but lands, fish and wildlife are subject to future settlement of native land claims.

Canadian World Heritage Sites

World Heritage sites are designated around the world by UNESCO to raise local and international awareness of indigenous cultural and natural treasures. "Cultural heritage" consists of monuments, groups of buildings or sites of historical, aesthetic, archaeological, scientific, ethnological or anthropological value. "Natural heritage" refers to outstanding physical, biological and geological features; habitats of threatened plants or animal species and areas of value on scientific or aesthetic grounds or from the point of view of conservation. Thirteen of the organization's World Heritage sites are in Canada. The majority of these sites relate to Canada's natural heritage.

UNESCO has created a World Heritage Educational Resource Kit. Based on an interactive and interdisciplinary approach, the kit invites teachers and students to explore aspects of heritage conservation in the form of a journey through the world's magnificent cultural and natural heritage. More information about the kit can be found at www.whc.unesco.org.

	Province or Territory	Area	Year Designated	Criteria N:Natural C:Cultural
Nahanni National Park	Northwest Territories	4 766 km^2	1978	N
L'Anse aux Meadows Archaeological Site	Newfoundland & Labrador		1978	C
Kluane /Wrangell-St. Elias / Glacier Bay / Tatshenshini—Alsek Park	Canada/US	97 303 km^2 9 850 km^2	1979 Added in 1994	N
Dinosaur Provincial Park	Alberta	7 492 km^2	1979	N
Head-Smashed-In Buffalo Jump Provincial Historic Site	Alberta		1982	C
SGaang Gwaii (Anthony Island)	British Columbia		1981	C
Wood Buffalo National Park	Alberta/Northwest Territories	44 807 km^2	1983	N
CANADIAN ROCKY MOUNTAIN PARKS Banff National Park Jasper National Park Kootenay National Park Yoho National Park Mount Robson Provincial Park Mount Assiniboine Provincial Park Hamber Provincial Park	Alberta/British Columbia	22 990 km^2	1984 and 1990	N
THE HISTORIC DISTRICT OF QUEBEC Fortifications of Quebec National Historic Site Artillery Park National Historic Site	Quebec		1985.	C
Gros Morne National Park	Newfoundland & Labrador	1 805 km^2	1987	N
WATERTON—GLACIER INTERNATIONAL PEACE PARK Waterton Lakes National Park (Canada) Glacier National Park (U.S.)	Canada/U.S.	4 600 km^2	1995	N
The Old Town Lunenburg	Nova Scotia		1995	C
Miguasha Park	Quebec	873 km^2	2000	N

Source: *Canadian Heritage, Parks Canada*

THE PEOPLE

POPULATION

Population of Provinces and Territories[1]
(thousands)

	Canada	N&L	PEI	NS	NB	Que	Ont	Man	Sask	Alta	BC	YT	NWT	NVT
1861[2]...	3 230	n.a.	81	331	252	1 112	1 396	*	n.a.	n.a.	52	*	7	n.a.
1871....	3 689	n.a.	94	388	286	1 192	1 621	25	n.a.	n.a.	36	*	48	n.a.
1881....	4 325	n.a.	109	441	321	1 360	1 927	62	n.a.	n.a.	49	*	56	n.a.
1891....	4 833	n.a.	109	450	321	1 489	2 114	153	*	*	98	*	99	n.a.
1901....	5 371	n.a.	103	460	331	1 649	2 183	255	91	73	179	27	20	n.a.
1911....	7 207	n.a.	94	492	352	2 006	2 527	461	492	374	393	9	7	n.a.
1921....	8 788	n.a.	89	524	388	2 361	2 934	610	758	588	525	4	8	n.a.
1931....	10 377	n.a.	88	513	408	2 875	3 432	700	922	732	694	4	9	n.a.
1941....	11 507	n.a.	95	578	457	3 332	3 788	730	896	796	818	5	12	*
1951....	14 009	361	98	643	516	4 056	4 598	777	832	940	1 165	9	16	*
1961....	18 238	458	105	737	598	5 259	6 236	922	925	1 332	1 629	15	23	*
1971....	21 962	531	113	797	643	6 137	7 849	999	932	1 666	2 241	19	36	*
1981....	24 820	575	124	855	706	6 548	8 811	1 036	976	2 294	2 824	24	48	*
1986....	26 101	577	128	889	725	6 708	9 438	1 092	1 029	2 431	3 004	25	55	*
1991....	28 031	580	130	915	746	7 065	10 428	1 110	1 003	2 593	3 373	29	39	22
1996 ...	29 611	560	136	931	752	7 247	11 083	1 134	1 019	2 775	3 874	31	42	26
2001 ...	31 021	522	137	932	750	7 397	11 898	1 151	1 000	3 057	4 078	30	41	28
2002[3] ..	31 362	519	137	934	750	7 443	12 097	1 155	995	3 114	4 115	30	41	29
2002[3] ..	31 630	520	138	936	751	7 487	12 238	1 163	995	3 154	4 147	31	42	29

Source: © *Census of Canada, Statistics Canada*
(n.a.) Not applicable (*) Included with the Northwest Territories. (1) As of July 1 in non-census years. Totals may not add due to rounding. (2) Pre-Confederation (3) Post-censal Estimates based on 2001 Census data adjusted for undercount.

Age Structure of the Population[1]

	Total (000s)	% Under 5 Years	% 5–19 Years	% 20–44 Years	% 45–64 Years	% 65+ Years
1851	2 436	18.51	37.81	31.65	9.40	2.67
1861	3 230	16.81	37.21	32.66	10.15	3.03
1871	3 689	14.67	38.03	32.58	11.14	3.66
1881	4 325	13.85	36.02	33.94	12.14	4.12
1891	4 833	12.64	34.49	35.40	12.91	4.55
1901	5 371	12.03	32.73	36.19	14.00	5.05
1911	7 207	12.35	30.15	38.81	14.06	4.66
1921	8 788	12.05	31.51	36.63	15.02	4.78
1931	10 377	10.36	31.29	36.07	16.74	5.55
1941	11 507	9.14	28.39	37.19	18.61	6.67
1951	14 009	12.29	25.60	36.63	17.74	7.75
1961	18 238	12.37	29.44	33.19	17.37	7.63
1971	21 568	8.42	30.97	33.87	18.66	8.09
1981	24 343	7.32	24.70	39.14	19.13	9.70
1991	27 297	6.99	20.42	41.33	19.66	11.61
1996	29 672	6.62	20.35	39.63	21.32	12.07
2001	31 021	5.67	20.03	37.77	23.89	12.6
2003	31 630	5.42	19.56	37.10	25.08	12.8

Source: © *Census of Canada, Statistics Canada*
(1) As of July 1 each year. Percentages may not add to 100 due to rounding.

Male and Female Population by Age Group
(thousands)

		Total Population	Under 5 Years	5–9 Years	10–14 Years	15–24 Years	25–34 Years	35–44 Years	45–54 Years	55–64 Years	65 Years and Over
1851	MALE	1 250	233	173	152	248	168	116	78	46	35
	FEMALE ...	1 186	218	173	146	252	161	103	67	38	30
1861	MALE	1 660	277	218	203	341	232	156	107	70	54
	FEMALE ...	1 570	266	211	196	337	222	141	92	59	44
1871	MALE	1 869	276	264	243	374	249	175	132	86	74
	FEMALE ...	1 820	265	255	233	385	256	171	120	73	61
1881	MALE	2 189	304	284	262	455	302	217	161	111	94
	FEMALE ...	2 136	295	278	251	464	301	212	153	100	84
1891	MALE	2 460	309	300	282	504	366	263	191	131	115
	FEMALE ...	2 373	302	292	272	499	354	246	180	122	105
1901	MALE	2 752	326	313	297	543	412	331	234	157	139
	FEMALE ...	2 620	320	306	285	530	386	299	214	148	133
1911	MALE	3 822	450	396	356	745	687	475	334	209	171
	FEMALE ...	3 385	440	389	346	653	535	388	286	184	165
1921	MALE	4 530	534	529	462	757	693	630	434	276	215
	FEMALE ...	4 258	525	521	452	761	650	532	366	246	206
1931	MALE	5 375	543	573	543	990	778	707	590	356	295
	FEMALE ...	5 002	531	560	531	962	717	627	485	306	281
1941	MALE	5 901	534	529	556	1 083	920	745	649	494	391
	FEMALE ...	5 606	518	517	545	1 069	891	691	579	421	377
1951	MALE	7 089	879	714	575	1 070	1 066	950	728	557	551
	FEMALE ...	6 921	843	684	556	1 077	1 108	919	679	520	535
1961	MALE	9 219	1 154	1 064	948	1 316	1 258	1 191	959	655	674
	FEMALE ...	9 019	1 102	1 016	908	1 301	1 222	1 199	920	635	717
1971	MALE	10 795	930	1 152	1 181	2 016	1 462	1 286	1 132	854	782
	FEMALE ...	10 773	887	1 102	1 129	1 988	1 428	1 241	1 160	877	963
1981	MALE	12 068	914	912	985	2 356	2 106	1 497	1 256	1 031	1 011
	FEMALE ...	12 275	869	865	936	2 303	2 110	1 471	1 242	1 128	1 350
1991	MALE	13 455	976	978	963	1 944	2 420	2 176	1 487	1 180	1 330
	FEMALE ...	13 842	931	930	915	1 887	2 446	2 196	1 479	1 220	1 840
1996	MALE	14 692	1 007	1 033	1 031	2 059	2 400	2 502	1 891	1 253	1 515
	FEMALE ...	14 980	958	984	978	1 965	2 346	2 499	1 897	1 286	2 067
2001[1]	MALE	14 707	868	1 011	1 051	2 034	1 967	2 517	2 185	1 411	1 663
	FEMALE ...	15 300	828	965	1 002	1 975	2 028	2 585	2 235	1 457	2 226

Source: © *Census of Canada, Statistics Canada*   (1) Unadjusted census count.

Canadian Population Projections[1] by Age Group
(thousands)

	Total Population	Under 5 Years	5–9 Years	10–14 Years	15–24 Years	25–34 Years	35–44 Years	45–54 Years	55–64 Years	65 Yrs and Over
2006										
MALE	15 947.4	841.4	918.4	1 075.8	2 213.4	2 228.3	2 519.7	2 509.1	1 796.5	1 844.8
FEMALE ...	16 281.2	798.8	872.0	1 020.6	2 109.6	2 167.4	2 482.9	2 517.5	1 855.3	2 457.3
2011										
MALE	16 511.6	855.1	880.0	957.7	2 261.3	2 311.7	2 343.3	2 667.9	2 129.3	2 105.4
FEMALE ...	16 850.2	811.3	835.9	905.9	2 155.0	2 244.8	2 305.2	2 651.2	2 200.4	2 740.6
2016										
MALE	17 044.8	877.0	893.6	919.8	2 155.4	2 383.3	2 369.6	2 536.7	2 388.1	2 521.0
FEMALE ...	17 375.0	831.7	848.2	870.3	2 051.3	2 313.1	2 321.5	2 505.9	2 451.9	3 181.1
2021										
MALE	17 531.4	890.6	915.2	933.2	2 003.3	2 430.3	2 449.2	2 374.1	2 545.9	2 989.7
FEMALE ...	17 850.4	844.3	868.4	882.4	1 904.5	2 356.1	2 394.2	2 337.4	2 582.0	3 681.1
2026										
MALE	17 939.6	880.9	928.6	954.5	1 979.9	2 327.9	2 517.4	2 403.3	2 431.6	3 515.5
FEMALE ...	18 250.9	834.9	880.8	902.2	1 881.7	2 254.8	2 458.2	2 354.3	2 446.4	4 237.5

Source: © *Statistics Canada*   (1) Figures represent the medium-growth projection and are based on 2000 population estimates. Due to rounding, the totals may not always add up to the sum of the figures.

Canada's Changing Population

The release of data from the 2001 census gave Canadians a look at how the country is changing. One notable change is visible in the statistics on the age of our citizens.

CANADIANS ARE GETTING OLDER
In 1966, the median age of Canada's population—the age where half the population is older and half is younger—was 25.4 years. In 2001, the median age was 37.6, a gain of 2.3 years from the previous high of 35.3 in the 1996 census. The estimated median age for 2003 was 37.9 years. This information has implications for social planners, particularly those who are forecasting the futures of our labour force and our economy, and demands on social services and healthcare systems.

The population age group 45 to 64 increased to 24.3 per cent of the total population; planners forecast that by 2011, nearly one-third of the population will be in that bracket. As increasing numbers of the labour force near age 65, there will be more competition for workers, which could mean higher wages (and higher prices). There may even be a need to change the age for mandatory retirement, particularly in light of the better levels of health and fitness of older Canadians.

While 37.9 was the median age for the country, age distribution varies. As the table below shows, Nova Scotia and Quebec are the "oldest" provinces, with median ages of over 39. Nunavut is the youngest, by a wide margin.

Age Distribution, Canada, Provinces and Territories, 2003

	Median Age (years)	Age Group Distribution		
		0–19	20–64 (percent)	65+
Canada	37.9	25.0	62.2	12.8
Newfoundland and Labrador	39.3	23.5	64.0	12.6
Prince Edward Island	38.6	26.1	60.0	13.9
Nova Scotia	39.5	23.8	62.3	13.9
New Brunswick	39.2	23.5	62.9	13.5
Quebec	39.4	23.2	63.4	13.4
Ontario	37.4	25.6	61.8	12.6
Manitoba	36.8	27.4	59.0	13.6
Saskatchewan	36.9	28.2	57.0	14.8
Alberta	35.1	27.1	62.6	10.3
British Columbia	38.8	23.8	62.7	13.5
Yukon Territory	36.3	27.4	66.2	6.4
Northwest Territories	30.4	33.4	62.4	4.2
Nunavut	22.9	45.2	52.5	2.3

Ten Youngest Municipalities with Population More Than 5,000

	Median Age
Mackenzie No. 23, Alberta	22.0
Stanley, Manitoba	25.2
Lloydminster, Saskatchewan	26.8
Hanover, Manitoba	27.8
Slave Lake, Alberta	28.1
Taber, Alberta	28.3
Iqaluit, Nunavut	28.3
Wellesley, Ontario	28.7
Mapleton, Ontario	29.2
Oromocto, New Brunswick	29.3

Ten Oldest Municipalities with Population More Than 5,000

	Median Age
Qualicum Beach, B.C.	58.1
White Rock, B.C.	50.9
Sidney, B.C.	50.7
Cote-Saint-Luc, Quebec	50.5
Parksville, B.C.	49.6
Nanaimo G, B.C.	49.5
Elliot Lake, Ontario	49.4
Columbia-Shuswap C, B.C.	48.8
North Saanich, B.C.	47.8
Oak Bay, B.C.	47.8

Source: *2001 Census, Annual Demographic Estimates 2003,* © *Statistics Canada*

Canadian Urban and Rural Population

(thousands)

Year	Urban Total	%	Rural Non-Farm	%	+	Farm	%	=	Total	%
1871	722	19.6	n.a.	n.a.		n.a.	n.a.		2 967	80.4
1881	1 110	25.7	n.a.	n.a.		n.a.	n.a.		3 215	74.3
1891	1 537	31.8	n.a.	n.a.		n.a.	n.a.		3 296	68.2
1901	2 014	37.5	n.a.	n.a.		n.a.	n.a.		3 357	62.5
1911	3 273	45.4	n.a.	n.a.		n.a.	n.a.		3 934	54.6
1921	4 352	49.5	n.a.	n.a.		n.a.	n.a.		4 436	50.5
1931	5 469	52.7	1 670	16.1		3 238	31.2		4 908	47.3
1941	6 271	54.5	2 123	18.4		3 113	27.1		5 236	45.5
1951	8 817	62.9	2 423	17.3		2 769	19.8		5 192	37.1
1956	10 715	66.6	2 734	17.0		2 632	16.4		5 366	33.4
1961	12 700	69.6	3 465	19.0		2 073	11.4		5 538	30.4
1966	14 727	73.6	3 374	16.9		1 914	9.6		5 288	26.4
1971	16 410	76.1	3 738	17.3		1 420	6.6		5 158	23.9
1976	17 367	75.5	4 591	20.0		1 035	4.5		5 626	24.5
1981	18 436	75.7	4 867	20.0		1 040	4.3		5 907	24.3
1986	19 352	76.5	5 067	20.0		890	3.5		5 957	23.5
1991	20 907	76.6	5 583	20.5		807	3.0		6 390	23.4
1996	22 415	77.9	5 485	19.1		851	3.0		6 336	22.1
2001	23 908	79.7	n.a.	n.a.		n.a.	n.a.		6 099	20.3

Source: © *Census of Canada, Statistics Canada*   (n.a.) Not available.

Definitions: Urban: persons living in a built-up area having a population of 1 000 or more, and a population density of 400 or more per sq. km; **Rural:** persons living outside "urban areas"; **Rural Farm:** persons living in rural areas who are members of households of farm operators; **Rural Non-Farm:** persons living in rural areas who are not members of households of farm operators.

Urban and Rural Population by Province

Province	1951 Rural	1951 Urban	1991 Rural	1991 Urban	2001[3] Rural	2001[3] Urban
Canada	**5 174 555**	**8 473 458**	**6 389 724**	**20 907 135**	**6 098 883**	**23 908 211**
Nfld and Labrador[1]	n.a.	n.a.	264 023	304 451	216 734	296 196
Prince Edward Island	73 744	24 685	77 952	51 813	74 619	60 675
Nova Scotia	297 753	344 831	418 434	481 508	400 998	507 009
New Brunswick	300 686	215 011	378 686	345 214	361 596	367 902
Quebec	1 358 363	2 697 318	1 544 752	5 351 211	1 420 330	5 817 149
Ontario	1 346 443	3 251 099	1 831 043	8 253 842	1 747 499	9 662 547
Manitoba	336 961	439 580	304 767	787 175	314 262	805 321
Saskatchewan	579 258	252 470	365 531	623 397	349 897	629 036
Alberta	489 826	449 675	514 660	2 030 893	569 647	2 405 160
British Columbia	371 739	793 471	641 922	2 640 139	597 885	3 309 853
Yukon Territory	6 502	2 594	11 462	16 335	11 831	16 843
Northwest Territories	13 280[2]	2 724[2]	36 492[2]	21 157[2]	15 529	21 831
Nunavut[3]	n.a.	n.a.	n.a.	n.a.	18 056	8 689

Source: © *Census of Canada, Statistics Canada*
(1) Newfoundland joined confederation in 1949, and urban/rural split in population was not included in 1951 census data. (2) Includes Nunavut. (3) Unadjusted census count.

Population of Canadian Towns and Cities

(more than 5,000 inhabitants)

Town or city classification is made according to the official designations adopted by provincial or federal authority.

	POPULATION		AREA 2001
	1996	2001	(sq. km)
■ NEWFOUNDLAND AND LABRADOR			
Bay Roberts	5 472	**5 237**	23.92
Clarenville	5 335	**5 104**	140.73
Conception Bay South	19 265	**19 772**	59.27
Corner Brook*	21 893	**20 103**	148.27
Gander	10 364	**9 651**	104.25
Grand Falls-Windsor	14 160	**13 340**	54.48
Happy Valley-Goose Bay	8 655	**7 969**	305.87
Labrador City	8 455	**7 744**	10.02
Marystown	6 742	**5 908**	61.97
Mount Pearl*	25 531	**24 964**	15.74
Paradise	7 948	**9 598**	29.24
Portugal Cove-St. Philip's	5 773	**5 866**	57.35
St. John's*	101 936	**99 182**	446.04
Stephenville	7 764	**7 109**	35.50
Torbay	5 230	**5 474**	34.88
■ PRINCE EDWARD ISLAND			
Charlottetown*	32 531	**32 245**	44.33
Stratford	5 869	**6 314**	22.48
Summerside*	14 525	**14 654**	28.36
■ NOVA SCOTIA			
Amherst	9 669	**9 470**	12.02
Bridgewater	7 351	**7 621**	13.61
Halifax (Regional. Mun.)	342 851	**359 111**	5 490.90
Kentville	5 551	**5 610**	17.35
New Glasgow	9 812	**9 432**	9.93
Truro	11 938	**11 457**	37.62
Yarmouth	7 568	**7 561**	10.56
■ NEW BRUNSWICK			
Bathurst*	13 815	**12 924**	91.55
Campbellton*	8 404	**7 798**	18.66
Dieppe	12 497	**14 951**	51.16
Edmundston*	17 876	**17 373**	106.90
Fredericton*	46 507	**47 560**	131.23
Grand Falls (Grand-Sault)	6 133	**5 858**	18.06
Miramichi*	19 241	**18 508**	179.83
Moncton*	59 313	**61 046**	141.15
Oromocto	9 194	**8 843**	22.37
Quispamsis	13 579	**13 757**	57.12
Riverview	16 684	**17 010**	33.88
Rothesay	11 470	**11 505**	34.13
Sackville	5 393	**5 361**	74.32

	POPULATION		AREA 2001
	1996	2001	(sq. km)
Saint John*	72 494	**69 661**	316.31
Woodstock	5 092	**5 198**	13.26
■ QUEBEC			
Acton Vale	7 172	**7 299**	90.74
Alma	26 121	**25 918**	109.28
Amos	13 632	**13 044**	430.27
Amqui	6 800	**6 473**	120.81
Anjou	37 308	**38 015**	13.62
Asbestos	6 793	**6 580**	29.67
Aylmer	34 901	**36 085**	88.96
Baie-Comeau	25 554	**23 079**	338.87
Baie-Saint-Paul	7 366	**7 290**	546.28
Beaconsfield	19 414	**19 310**	11.01
Beauceville	6 371	**6 261**	167.54
Beauharnois	6 435	**6 387**	40.94
Beauport	72 920	**72 813**	74.37
Bécancour	11 489	**11 051**	441.00
Bellefeuille	12 803	**14 066**	49.99
Beloeil	19 294	**19 053**	24.09
Blainville	29 603	**36 029**	55.10
Boisbriand	25 227	**26 729**	27.76
Bois-des-Filion	7 124	**7 712**	4.28
Boucherville	34 989	**36 253**	70.80
Bromptonville	5 583	**5 571**	76.78
Brossard	65 927	**65 026**	45.74
Buckingham	11 678	**11 668**	15.11
Candiac	11 805	**12 675**	17.51
Cap-de-la-Madeleine	33 438	**32 534**	18.25
Cap-Rouge	14 163	**13 700**	6.80
Carignan	5 614	**5 915**	62.42
Chambly	19 716	**20 342**	25.23
Charlemagne	5 739	**5 662**	2.17
Charlesbourg	70 942	**70 310**	66.28
Charny	10 661	**10 507**	8.07
Châteauguay	41 423	**41 003**	35.89
Chibougamau	8 664	**7 922**	699.16
Chicoutimi	63 061	**60 008**	156.11
Coaticook	8 809	**8 988**	218.55
Contrecoeur	5 331	**5 222**	61.19
Côte-Saint-Luc*	29 705	**30 244**	6.94
Cowansville	12 051	**12 032**	46.09
Delson	6 703	**7 024**	7.13
Deux-Montagnes	15 953	**17 080**	6.16
Dolbeau-Mistassini	15 214	**14 879**	295.67 ▶

	POPULATION		AREA 2001		POPULATION		AREA 2001
	1996	2001	(sq. km)		1996	2001	(sq. km)
Dollard-des-Ormeaux ...	47 826	**48 206**	15.10	Mont-Laurier	8 007	**7 365**	79.59
Donnacona	5 739	**5 479**	20.01	Montmagny	11 885	**11 654**	126.07
Dorval*	17 572	**17 706**	20.87	Montréal 1 016 376		**1 039 534**	185.94
Drummondville	44 882	**46 599**	71.44	Montréal-Nord	81 581	**83 600**	11.07
Farnham	7 899	**7 747**	92.04	Montréal-Ouest	5 254	**5 172**	1.41
Fleurimont	16 262	**16 521**	35.47	Mont-Royal	18 282	**18 682**	7.66
Gaspé	16 517	**14 932**	1 120.63	Mont-Saint-Hilaire	13 064	**14 270**	44.29
Gatineau	100 684	**102 898**	146.78	Mont-Tremblant	7 298	**8 352**	255.23
Granby	43 316	**44 121**	72.04	Nicolet	7 795	**7 928**	96.11
Grand-Mère	14 223	**13 179**	62.95	Otterburn Park	7 320	**7 866**	5.35
Greenfield Park	17 337	**16 978**	4.78	Outremont	22 571	**22 933**	3.83
Hampstead	6 986	**6 974**	1.79	Pierrefonds	53 151	**54 963**	24.90
Hull	62 339	**66 246**	36.49	Pincourt	10 023	**10 107**	7.54
Iberville	9 635	**9 424**	5.21	Plessisville	6 810	**6 756**	4.30
Joliette	17 541	**17 837**	22.81	Pointe-Claire	28 435	**29 286**	18.87
Jonquière	56 503	**54 842**	216.04	Pont-Rouge	6 821	**7 146**	121.22
Kirkland	18 678	**20 434**	9.64	Port-Cartier	7 070	**6 412**	292.86
La Baie	21 057	**19 940**	262.67	Prévost	7 308	**8 280**	35.00
La Malbaie	9 274	**9 143**	459.35	Princeville	5 750	**5 703**	195.53
La Plaine	14 413	**15 673**	40.19	Québec	167 264	**169 076**	92.93
La Prairie	17 128	**18 896**	43.69	Repentigny	53 824	**54 550**	24.48
La Sarre	8 345	**7 728**	148.69	Rimouski	31 773	**31 305**	76.18
La Tuque	12 102	**11 298**	579.46	Rivière-du-Loup	17 801	**17 772**	84.23
Lac-Brome	5 073	**5 444**	205.13	Roberval	11 640	**10 906**	152.99
Lachenaie	18 489	**21 709**	42.07	Rock Forest	16 604	**18 667**	48.22
Lachine	39 910	**40 222**	17.83	Rosemère	12 025	**13 391**	10.77
Lachute	11 556	**11 628**	108.65	Rouyn-Noranda	30 936	**28 270**	348.07
Lac-Mégantic	5 864	**5 897**	21.76	Roxboro	5 785	**5 642**	2.22
Lac-Saint-Charles	8 540	**8 912**	34.07	Saint-Antoine	10 806	**11 488**	9.93
Lafontaine	9 008	**9 477**	14.36	Saint-Basile-le-Grand ...	11 771	**12 385**	36.10
L'Ancienne-Lorette	15 895	**15 929**	7.63	Saint-Bruno-de-Montarville	23 714	**23 843**	43.28
LaSalle	72 029	**73 983**	16.75	Saint-Constant	21 933	**22 577**	57.30
L'Assomption	15 573	**15 615**	98.91	Sainte-Adèle	8 719	**9 215**	119.98
Laval	330 393	**343 005**	247.07	Sainte-Agathe-des-Monts	7 878	**7 116**	41.01
Le Gardeur	16 853	**17 668**	37.29	Sainte-Anne-de-Bellevue .	4 700	**5 062**	10.57
Lévis	40 407	**40 926**	43.55	Sainte-Anne-des-Monts			
L'Île-Bizard	13 038	**13 861**	22.77	-Tourelle	7 183	**6 835**	263.31
L'Île-Perrot	9 178	**9 375**	5.56	Sainte-Anne-des-Plaines .	12 908	**12 908**	92.79
Longueuil	127 977	**128 016**	44.00	Sainte-Catherine	13 724	**15 953**	10.19
Loretteville	14 168	**13 737**	6.37	Sainte-Foy	72 330	**72 547**	83.85
Lorraine	8 876	**9 476**	6.04	Sainte-Julie	24 030	**26 580**	49.52
Louiseville	7 911	**7 622**	62.59	Sainte-Marie	10 966	**11 320**	107.20
Magog	14 050	**14 283**	13.94	Sainte-Marthe-du-Cap ...	6 150	**6 162**	39.89
Marieville	7 636	**7 240**	62.78	Sainte-Marthe-sur-le-Lac	8 295	**8 742**	9.31
Mascouche	28 097	**29 556**	106.63	Saint-Émile	9 889	**10 940**	8.36
Masson-Angers	7 989	**9 799**	54.97	Sainte-Thérèse	23 477	**24 269**	9.58
Matane	12 364	**11 635**	24.80	Saint-Eustache	39 848	**40 378**	69.42
Mercier	9 059	**9 442**	45.95	Saint-Félicien	10 797	**10 622**	363.57
Mirabel	22 626	**27 330**	485.41	Saint-Georges	20 057	**20 787**	25.33
Mont-Joli	6 267	**5 886**	9.95	Saint-Hubert	77 042	**75 912**	65.98 ▶

	POPULATION		AREA 2001
	1996	2001	(sq. km)
Saint-Hyacinthe	38 995	**38 739**	37.46
Saint-Jean-Chrysostome	16 161	**17 089**	85.80
Saint-Jean-sur-Richelieu	36 435	**37 386**	47.06
Saint-Jérôme	23 916	**24 583**	16.23
Saint-Lambert	20 971	**21 051**	8.15
Saint-Laurent	74 240	**77 391**	42.88
Saint-Léonard	71 327	**69 604**	13.52
Saint-Lin – Laurentides	12 039	**12 384**	118.68
Saint-Louis-de-France	7 327	**7 246**	60.55
Saint-Luc	18 371	**20 573**	51.51
Saint-Nicéphore	9 251	**9 966**	95.80
Saint-Nicolas	15 594	**16 645**	95.09
Saint-Raymond	8 733	**8 836**	670.58
Saint-Rédempteur	6 358	**6 349**	3.71
Saint-Rémi	5 707	**5 736**	78.79
Saint-Romuald	10 604	**10 825**	17.94
Saint-Timothée	8 495	**8 299**	69.49
Salaberry-de-Valleyfield	26 600	**26 170**	27.45
Sept-Îles	25 224	**23 791**	294.20
Shawinigan	18 943	**17 535**	28.15
Shawinigan-Sud	11 804	**11 544**	48.97
Sherbrooke	76 786	**75 916**	58.15
Sillery	12 003	**11 909**	6.70
Sorel-Tracy	36 021	**34 194**	58.07
Terrebonne	42 214	**43 149**	72.15
Thetford Mines	17 635	**16 628**	36.95
Trois-Rivières	48 419	**46 264**	77.83
Trois-Rivières-Ouest	22 886	**23 287**	29.73
Val-Bélair	20 176	**21 332**	69.88
Val-d'Or	24 479	**22 748**	2 889.53
Vanier	11 174	**11 054**	4.59
Varennes	18 842	**19 653**	92.53
Vaudreuil-Dorion	18 466	**19 920**	72.47
Verdun	59 714	**60 564**	9.82
Victoriaville	38 174	**38 841**	82.65
Westmount	20 420	**19 727**	4.02
Windsor	5 515	**5 321**	14.28

■ ONTARIO

	1996	2001	(sq. km)
Ajax	64 430	**73 753**	67.09
Amherstburg	19 273	**20 339**	185.67
Arnprior	7 113	**7 192**	13.03
Aurora	34 857	**40 167**	49.61
Aylmer	7 022	**7 126**	6.05
Barrie*	79 191	**103 710**	76.98
Belleville*	46 195	**45 986**	241.79
Blue Mountains	5 667	**6 116**	286.77
Bluewater	6 874	**6 919**	416.99
Bracebridge	13 223	**13 751**	617.47
Bradford West Gwillimbury	20 213	**22 228**	201.03
Brampton*	268 251	**325 428**	266.53

	POPULATION		AREA 2001
	1996	2001	(sq. km)
Brant*	29 800	**31 669**	845.49
Brantford*	84 764	**86 417**	71.56
Brighton	9 022	**9 449**	222.57
Brockville*	21 752	**21 375**	20.73
Burlington*	136 976	**150 836**	185.71
Caledon	39 893	**50 595**	687.04
Cambridge*	101 429	**110 372**	112.82
Campbellford/Seymour, Percy, Hastings	**12 437**	12 569	511.10
Carleton Place	8 483	**9 083**	8.83
Chatham-Kent*	109 350	**107 341**	2 457.97
Clarence-Rockland*	18 633	**19 612**	296.53
Clarington	60 615	**69 834**	611.06
Cobourg	16 185	**17 172**	22.37
Cochrane	5 955	**5 690**	538.74
Collingwood	15 596	**16 039**	33.46
Cornwall*	47 403	**45 640**	61.83
Dryden*	8 289	**8 198**	65.31
East Gwillimbury	19 770	**20 555**	245.06
Elliot Lake*	13 588	**11 956**	698.12
Erin	10 657	**11 052**	296.98
Espanola	5 796	**5 449**	82.37
Essex	19 437	**20 085**	277.95
Fort Erie	27 183	**28 143**	167.42
Fort Frances	8 790	**8 315**	26.09
Gananoque	5 217	**5 167**	7.29
Georgian Highlands	10 497	**10 381**	589.03
Georgina	34 777	**39 263**	287.72
Goderich	7 553	**7 604**	7.91
Gravenhurst	10 030	**10 899**	517.94
Greater Napanee	14 994	**15 132**	459.71
Greater Sudbury*	165 336	**155 219**	3354.34
Greenstone	6 530	**5 662**	2 780.56
Grimsby	19 585	**21 297**	68.94
Guelph*	95 821	**106 170**	86.66
Haldimand*	42 041	**43 728**	1 252.37
Halton Hills	42 390	**48 184**	276.35
Hamilton*	467 799	**490 268**	1 117.11
Hanover	6 965	**6 869**	9.81
Hawkesbury	10 162	**10 314**	9.45
Hearst	6 049	**5 825**	98.67
Huntsville	15 918	**17 338**	703.29
Huron East	9 937	**9 680**	669.16
Ingersoll	10 502	**10 977**	12.90
Innisfil	24 711	**28 666**	284.18
Iroquois Falls	5 714	**5 217**	599.42
Kapuskasing	10 036	**9 238**	83.98
Kawartha Lakes*	67 926	**69 179**	3 059.22
Kenora*	16 365	**15 838**	211.08
Kingston*	112 605	**114 195**	450.39 ▶

	POPULATION		AREA 2001
	1996	2001	(sq. km)
Kingsville	18 409	**19 619**	246.83
Kirkland Lake	9 905	**8 616**	262.24
Kitchener*	178 420	**190 399**	136.86
Lakeshore	26 127	**28 746**	530.67
Lambton Shores*	10 874	**10 571**	331.92
LaSalle	20 566	**25 285**	65.25
Leamington	25 389	**27 138**	262.45
Lincoln	18 801	**20 612**	162.86
London*	325 669	**336 539**	421.77
Markham	173 383	**208 615**	212.47
Midland	16 347	**16 214**	29.09
Milton	32 104	**31 471**	366.46
Minto	7 854	**8 164**	300.37
Mississauga*	544 382	**612 925**	288.42
Mississippi Mills	11 069	**11 647**	509.05
Mono	6 552	**6 922**	277.77
New Tecumseth	22 904	**26 141**	274.18
Newmarket	57 125	**65 788**	38.07
Niagara Falls*	76 917	**78 815**	209.99
Niagara-on-the-Lake	13 238	**13 839**	133.67
Norfolk*	60 534	**60 847**	1 606.95
North Bay*	54 332	**52 771**	314.92
North Perth	11 808	**12 055**	493.18
Oakville	128 405	**144 738**	138.51
Orangeville	21 498	**25 248**	15.57
Orillia*	27 846	**29 121**	28.61
Oshawa*	134 364	**139 051**	145.65
Ottawa*	721 136	**774 072**	2 778.64
Owen Sound*	21 390	**21 431**	23.51
Parry Sound	6 326	**6 124**	13.33
Pelham	14 343	**15 272**	126.42
Pembroke*	14 177	**13 490**	14.35
Penetanguishene	7 900	**8 316**	25.36
Perth	5 902	**6 003**	10.36
Petawawa	15 304	**14 398**	164.68
Peterborough*	69 742	**71446**	58.61
Pickering*	78 989	**87 139**	231.58
Plympton-Wyoming	7 344	**7 359**	318.76
Port Colborne*	18 451	**18 450**	123.37
Port Hope and Hope	15 446	**15 605**	278.99
Prince Edward*	25 046	**24 901**	1 049.99
Quinte West*	41 676	**41 409**	499.14
Renfrew	8 125	**7 942**	12.77
Richmond Hill	101 725	**132 030**	100.89
Sarnia*	72 738	**70 876**	164.62
Saugeen Shores	12 084	**11 388**	170.58
Sault Ste. Marie*	80 054	**74 566**	223.45
Sioux Lookout	5 165	**5 336**	378.64
Smiths Falls	9 131	**9 140**	8.21
South Bruce Peninsula . .	8 004	**8 090**	531.92

	POPULATION		AREA 2001
	1996	2001	(sq. km)
South Huron	10 229	**10 019**	425.35
St. Catharines*	130 926	**129 170**	97.11
St. Marys	5 952	**6 293**	12.48
St. Thomas*	31 407	**33 236**	32.24
Stratford*	29 007	**29 676**	21.92
Tecumseh	23 151	**25 105**	120.31
Thorold*	17 883	**18 048**	84.82
Thunder Bay*	113 662	**109 016**	328.47
Tillsonburg	13 211	**14 052**	22.34
Timmins	47 499	**43 686**	2961.52
Toronto*	2 385 421	**2 481 494**	629.91
Vaughan*	132 549	**182 022**	273.50
Wasaga Beach	8 698	**12 419**	58.45
Waterloo*	77 949	**86 543**	64.09
Welland*	48 411	**48 402**	83.47
West Nipissing	13 481	**13 114**	1 909.67
Whitby	73 794	**87 413**	146.52
Whitchurch-Stouffville . .	19 835	**22 008**	206.74
Windsor*	197 694	**208 402**	120.63
Woodstock*	32 253	**33 061**	30.44

■ MANITOBA

Brandon*	39 175	**39 716**	74.53
Dauphin*	8 266	**8 085**	12.65
Flin Flon (Part)*	6 572	**6 000**	13.88
Morden	5 689	**6 142**	12.86
Portage la Prairie*	13 077	**12 976**	24.68
Selkirk*	9 881	**9 752**	24.87
Steinbach*	8 478	**9 227**	25.57
The Pas	5 945	**5 795**	34.74
Thompson*	14 385	**13 256**	17.18
Winkler	7 241	**7 943**	17.02
Winnipeg*	618 477	**619 544**	465.16

■ SASKATCHEWAN

Estevan*	10 752	**10 242**	17.53
Humboldt*	5 074	**5 161**	11.66
Lloydminster (Part)*	7 636	**7 840**	17.34
Melfort*	5 759	**5 559**	14.78
Moose Jaw*	32 973	**32 131**	46.81
North Battleford*	14 051	**13 692**	33.51
Prince Albert*	34 777	**34 291**	65.76
Regina*	180 404	**178 225**	118.66
Saskatoon*	193 653	**196 811**	148.34
Swift Current*	14 890	**14 821**	24.03
Weyburn*	9 723	**9 534**	15.72
Yorkton*	15 154	**15 107**	24.02

■ ALBERTA

Airdrie*	15 946	**20 382**	21.48
Banff	6 098	**7 135**	4.85 ▶

	POPULATION		AREA 2001
	1996	2001	(sq. km)
Beaumont	5 838	7 006	10.50
Bonnyville	5 100	5 709	14.09
Brooks	10 093	11 604	17.46
Calgary*	768 082	878 866	701.79
Camrose*	13 728	14 854	25.85
Canmore	8 354	10 792	68.80
Coaldale	5 770	6 008	7.92
Cochrane	7 424	11 798	16.51
Cold Lake*	11 791	11 520	59.30
Crowsnest Pass	6 356	6 262	373.04
Drayton Valley	5 883	5 801	7.96
Drumheller	7 833	7 785	107.93
Edmonton*	616 306	666 104	683.88
Edson	7 399	7 585	29.54
Fort Saskatchewan*	12 408	13 121	45.30
Grande Prairie*	31 353	36 983	60.42
High River	7 359	9 345	11.43
Hinton	9 961	9 405	25.76
Innisfail	6 116	6 928	9.80
Lacombe	8 330	9 384	18.05
Leduc*	14 346	15 032	36.97
Lethbridge*	63 053	67 374	121.83
Lloydminster (Part)*	11 317	13 148	24.19
Medicine Hat*	46 783	51 249	111.99
Morinville	6 226	6 540	11.34
Okotoks	8 528	11 664	17.91
Olds	5 815	6 607	11.05
Peace River	6 536	6 240	24.87
Ponoka	6 152	6 330	10.67
Red Deer*	60 080	67 707	60.90
Rocky Mountain House	5 809	6 208	12.44
Slave Lake	6 553	6 600	14.24
Spruce Grove*	14 271	15 983	26.40
St. Albert*	46 888	53 081	34.61
St. Paul	4 880	5 061	6.85
Stettler	5 228	5 215	9.52
Stony Plain	8 274	9 589	27.07
Strathmore	5 314	7 621	15.59
Sylvan Lake	5 184	7 493	9.48
Taber	7 214	7 671	15.09
Vegreville	5 337	5 376	13.47
Wainwright	5 079	5 117	8.24
Wetaskiwin*	10 959	11 154	15.83
Whitecourt	7 783	8 334	26.14

■ **BRITISH COLUMBIA**

	1996	2001	(sq. km)
Abbotsford*	105 403	115 463	359.18
Burnaby*	179 209	193 954	90.09
Castlegar*	7 030	7 002	18.00
Chilliwack*	60 186	62 927	257.96

	POPULATION		AREA 2001
	1996	2001	(sq. km)
Colwood*	13 848	13 745	17.76
Comox	11 069	11 172	14.20
Coquitlam*	101 820	112 890	121.68
Courtenay*	17 404	18 304	17.02
Cranbrook*	18 329	18 476	17.80
Dawson Creek*	11 125	10 754	20.66
Fort St. John*	15 021	16 034	21.54
Kamloops*	76 394	77 281	297.57
Kelowna*	89 442	96 288	211.22
Kimberley*	6 738	6 484	58.31
Ladysmith	6 456	6 587	8.43
Langley*	22 523	23 643	10.22
Merritt*	7 631	7 088	24.90
Nanaimo*	70 130	73 000	89.17
Nelson*	9 585	9 298	7.27
New Westminster*	49 350	54 656	15.40
North Vancouver*	41 475	44 303	11.95
Parksville*	9 472	10 323	14.60
Penticton*	30 987	30 985	42.42
Port Alberni*	18 782	17 743	19.87
Port Coquitlam*	46 682	51 257	28.79
Port Moody*	20 847	23 816	25.62
Prince George*	75 150	72 406	315.99
Prince Rupert*	16 714	14 643	54.90
Qualicum Beach	6 734	6 921	12.45
Quesnel*	10 532	10 044	35.34
Revelstoke*	8 047	7 500	30.72
Richmond*	148 867	164 345	128.69
Sidney	10 701	10 929	5.04
Smithers	5 624	5 414	15.55
Surrey*	304 477	347 825	317.40
Terrace*	12 783	12 109	41.45
Trail*	7 874	7 575	34.78
Vancouver*	514 008	545 671	114.67
Vernon*	32 165	33 494	77.92
Victoria*	73 504	74 125	19.68
View Royal	6 441	7 271	14.48
White Rock*	17 210	18 250	5.28
Williams Lake*	11 235	11 153	33.03

■ **YUKON TERRITORY**

	1996	2001	(sq. km)
Whitehorse*	19 157	19 058	416.44

■ **NORTHWEST TERRITORIES**

	1996	2001	(sq. km)
Yellowknife*	17 275	16 541	105.20

■ **NUNAVUT**

	1996	2001	(sq. km)
Iqaluit	4 220	5 236	52.34

Source: © *Census of Canada, Statistics Canada*

*Indicates a city or *ville* in Quebec; all others are towns.

Population of Census Metropolitan Areas[1] in Canada

Statistics Canada defines a census metropolitan area (CMA) as a very large urban area, together with neighbouring urban and rural areas that have a high degree of economic and social integration with that large urban area. The urban area itself (or urbanized core) must have a population of at least 100,000 based on the previous census. For a more detailed look at these cities, see "Canadian Cities" pages 31–38.

| CMA | Population | | | | Land Area (sq. km) |
	1976	1986	1996	2001[2]	2001
Abbotsford, B.C.[3]	n.a	n.a.	136 480	147 370	625.94
Calgary, Alta.	469 917	671 453	821 628	951 395	5 083.00
Chicoutimi, Que.	128 643	158 468	160 454	154 938	1 753.67
Edmonton, Alta.	554 228	774 026	862 597	937 845	9 418.62
Halifax, N.S.	267 991	295 922	342 966	359 183	5 495.54
Hamilton, Ont.	529 371	557 029	624 360	662 401	1 371.76
Kingston, Ont.[3]	114 069	122 350	144 528	146 838	1 906.82
Kitchener, Ont.	272 158	311 195	382 940	414 284	826.98
London, Ont.	270 383	342 302	416 546	432 451	2 333.37
Montreal, Que.	2 802 485	2 921 357	3 326 447	3 426 350	4 047.35
Oshawa, Ont.	135 196	203 543	268 773	296 298	903.23
Ottawa-Hull, Ont.-Que.	693 288	819 263	998 718	1 063 664	5 318.36
Quebec, Que.	542 158	603 267	671 889	682 757	3 154.35
Regina, Sask.	151 191	186 521	193 652	192 800	3 407.84
St. Catharines-Niagara, Ont.	301 921	343 258	372 406	377 009	1 406.42
St. John's, Nfld and Lab.	143 390	161 901	174 051	172 918	804.63
Saint John, N.B.	112 974	121 265	125 705	122 678	3 359.61
Saskatoon, Sask.	133 750	200 665	219 056	225 927	5 192.22
Sherbrooke, Que.	104 505	129 960	149 569	153 811	1 108.16
Sudbury, Ont.	157 030	148 877	165 618	155 601	3 536.10
Thunder Bay, Ont.	119 253	122 217	126 643	121 986	2 548.16
Toronto, Ont.	2 803 101	3 431 981	4 263 759	4 682 897	5 902.74
Trois Rivières, Que.	98 583	128 888	139 956	137 507	880.47
Vancouver, B.C.	1 166 348	1 380 729	1 831 665	1 986 965	2 878.52
Victoria, B.C.	218 250	255 225	304 287	311 902	695.34
Windsor, Ont.	247 582	253 988	286 811	307 877	1 022.53
Winnipeg, Man.	578 217	625 304	667 093	671 274	4 151.48

Source: © *Census of Canada, Statistics Canada*
(1) Total land area considered to be part of CMA varied from census to census. (2) Unadjusted census count. (3) Abbotsford, B.C., and Kingston, Ont., were reclassified as Census Metropolitan Areas for the 2001 census. Data for previous years shows Census Agglomeration population, where appropriate.

VITAL STATISTICS

Births in Canada

Births	Birth Rate[1]		Births	Birth Rate[1]		Births	Birth Rate[1]
1971–1972.... 351 256	15.8		1982–1983.... 373 594	14.7		1993–1994.... 386 159	13.3
1972–1973.... 345 815	15.4		1983–1984.... 374 533	14.6		1994–1995.... 381 998	13
1973–1974.... 342 446	15		1984–1985.... 376 265	14.6		1995–1996.... 372 453	12.6
1974–1975.... 355 960	15.4		1985–1986.... 375 381	14.4		1996–1997.... 357 313	11.9
1975–1976.... 364 278	15.5		1986–1987.... 373 022	14.1		1997–1998.... 345 123	11.4
1976–1977.... 357 850	15.1		1987–1988.... 370 033	13.8		1998–1999.... 338 295	11.1
1977–1978.... 359 793	15		1988–1989.... 384 035	14.1		1999–2000.... 336 912	11
1978–1979.... 362 432	15		1989–1990.... 403 280	14.6		2000–2001.... 327 107	10.5
1979–1980.... 367 286	15		1990–1991.... 402 929	14.4		2001–2002.... 332 806	10.6
1980–1981.... 372 139	15		1991–1992.... 403 107	14.2		2002–2003.... 331 522	10.5
1981–1982.... 372 472	14.8		1992–1993.... 392 181	13.7			

Source: © *Statistics Canada*
(1) Calculated per 1,000 population, each period covers from July 1 of one year to June 30 of the next year.

Births by Province, 2002–03[1]

	Births	Birth Rate[2]		Births	Birth Rate[2]
Canada.................	**331 522**	**10.5**	Manitoba................	13 834	11.9
Newfoundland & Labrador ..	4 573	8.8	Saskatchewan............	12 123	12.2
Prince Edward Island	1 384	10.0	Alberta	38 163	12.1
Nova Scotia	8 710	9.3	British Columbia..........	40 134	9.7
New Brunswick...........	7 050	9.4	Yukon	333	10.7
Quebec.................	71 964	9.6	Northwest Territories	606	14.5
Ontario	131 921	10.8	Nunavut	727	24.7

Source: © *Statistics Canada*   (1) Period covers July 1, 2002, to June 30, 2003. (2) Rate is calculated per 1,000 population.

Age-specific Fertility Rates

(per 1,000 women)

Age-specific fertility rates are calculated by dividing the number of live births in each age group by the total female population (in thousands) in each age group. Trends in the last ten years indicate that while women aged 25-29 are the most likely to give birth (although at a declining rate), births in the younger age groups are generally declining, while the fertility rates among women 30 and over hold steady or show modest increases.

	1986	1991	1996	1997	1999	2002
15-19 years[1]	23.01	25.98	22.34	20.19	18.70	15.0
20-24 years	78.74	77.50	67.28	64.07	60.90	54.0
25-29 years	119.01	120.33	105.82	103.88	100.00	97.5
30-34 years	72.52	83.63	85.51	84.44	85.80	90.9
35-39 years	22.30	28.27	32.22	32.52	33.60	36.4
40-44 years	3.15	3.88	5.06	5.19	5.50	6.2
45-49 years[2]	0.13	0.17	0.20	0.20	0.20	0.2

Source: © *Statistics Canada*
(1) Live births to women under 20 years of age per 1,000 women aged 15 to 19.
(2) Live births to women aged 45 years and over per 1,000 women aged 45 to 49.

Birth by Age of Mother, by Province, 2002

In 1999, despite 337,249 births, Canadian fertility hit a then record low of 1.52 children per woman—since surpassed by a rate of 1.49 in 2000. A comparison with the US revealed the US fertility rate for 1999 was 2.08. Canada's population growth is now only about three-quarters of the growth south of the border. Projections indicate that the growth rate in the US will continue to be higher in the coming years.

Where's the difference? The fertility rate among women aged 30 and over has increased at the same rate on both sides of the border. The fertility difference shows up in the women in their 20s and younger. In Canada, fertility among women aged 20

to 24 has decreased by nearly 40 per cent in the last 20 years; fertility among women aged 25 to 29 has dropped by 25 per cent. An additional factor: American teenage fertility rates continue to be relatively high compared to other industrialized countries. Why the difference? Researchers have suggested everything from the use of more effective birth control methods in Canada to Canadians' relative difficulty in establishing themselves in the work force.

Low fertility means that immigration is the main contributor to population growth. Within 20 years it's likely that deaths will exceed births, and immigration will be the only source of population growth.

Age	Canada	N&L	PEI	NS	NB	Que	Ont	Man	Sask	Alta	BC	YT	NWT	NVT
under 15 .	120	4		5	3	20	20	19	11	18	14			6
15-19	15 413	304	89	512	455	2 775	4 755	1 281	1 159	2 225	1 603	25	72	158
20-24	56 729	988	260	1 759	1 586	13 877	17 744	3 114	2 877	7 885	6 186	68	145	237
25-29	100 646	1 452	422	2 599	2 356	24 945	37 256	4 080	3 793	11 992	11 298	101	185	167
30-34	100 768	1 325	372	2 453	1 878	20 798	43 383	3 602	2 711	10 995	12 904	84	159	103
35-39	46 468	510	158	1 136	662	8 553	21 337	1 499	1 039	4 746	6 672	48	62	46
40-44	8 354	68	27	193	102	1 455	3 884	287	165	800	1 341	12	11	9
45-49	286			5	4	53	138	6	6	29	43	1	1	
not stated .	18			1		1	11			1	4			
Total	328 802	4 651	1 328	8 663	7 046	72 477	128 528	13 888	11 761	38 691	40 065	339	635	726

Source: © *Statistics Canada*
Please note that the data reflects the province of residence of the mother, not the actual location of the birth.

The 2001 Census Teacher's Kit

*S*tatistics Canada has developed a teacher's kit of materials related to the census for use in elementary, intermediate and secondary schools across the country. The activities have been classroom tested and meet curriculum requirements. There is a on-line teacher's guide (including 156 lesson plans by grade level and subject) plus activities that can be applied to subjects as varied as English, economics, mathematics, art, social studies, geography, history, family studies, theatre arts, science and phys ed. There are also materials that can be used in an ESL setting in the form of a literacy kit.

All materials can be downloaded from Statistics Canada's web site. They are in PDF format and require Adobe Acrobat Reader to access them at www.statcan.ca/english/kits/2001/tkit.htm (The material is also available in French.)

Life Expectancy

Life expectancy is the number of years a person would be expected to live, starting from birth (for life expectancy at birth) or at age 65 (for life expectancy at age 65), on the basis of the mortality statistics for a given observation period.

Disability-free life expectancy is a more comprehensive indicator than that of life expectancy because it introduces the concept of quality of life. It is used to distinguish between years of life free of any activity limitation and years experienced with at least one activity limitation. To that end, disability-free life expectancy establishes a threshold based on the nature of such limitations. Years of life lived in conditions above this threshold are counted in full. Those lived in conditions below the threshold are not counted. Thus, the emphasis is not exclusively on the length of life, as is the case for life expectancy, but also on the quality of life.

Life Expectancy, 2001

	At birth			At age 65		
	Both sexes	Males	Females	Both sexes	Males	Females
Canada	**79.6**	**77.0**	**82.1**	**19.0**	**17.1**	**20.6**
Newfoundland and Labrador	78.1	75.6	80.8	17.4	15.2	19.5
Prince Edward Island	78.9	75.2	82.6	18.8	16.4	21.0
Nova Scotia	78.9	76.3	81.5	18.3	16.4	19.8
New Brunswick	79.0	76.1	81.9	18.5	16.4	20.3
Quebec	79.4	76.5	82.0	18.7	16.6	20.4
Ontario	79.9	77.5	82.1	19.0	17.3	20.4
Manitoba	78.6	75.7	81.6	18.8	16.8	20.6
Saskatchewan	79.2	76.3	82.2	19.1	17.1	21.0
Alberta	79.7	77.0	82.3	19.4	17.5	21.1
British Columbia	80.4	78.0	82.9	19.7	17.9	21.2
Yukon Territory	77.5	76.6	80.1	16.8	17.0	18.3
Northwest Territories	75.9	73.5	78.8	16.4	16.0	16.8
Nunavut	69.4	66.3	70.3	15.5	16.3	11.4

Source: © *Statistics Canada*

Disability-free Life Expectancy, 1996

	At birth			At age 65		
	Both sexes	Males	Females	Both sexes	Males	Females
Canada	**68.6**	**66.9**	**70.2**	**11.7**	**10.9**	**12.4**
Newfoundland and Labrador	68.1	65.9	70.4	11.1	10.2	12.0
Prince Edward Island	67.6	65.3	70.0	11.1	9.8	12.4
Nova Scotia	65.5	63.5	67.4	10.2	9.0	11.2
New Brunswick	66.6	64.5	68.8	10.7	9.6	11.6
Quebec	70.2	68.1	72.3	12.5	11.5	13.4
Ontario	68.0	66.6	69.4	11.3	10.6	11.9
Manitoba	67.9	66.4	69.5	11.4	10.6	12.2
Saskatchewan	68.3	66.6	70.0	12.0	11.2	12.7
Alberta	68.0	66.8	69.3	11.3	10.8	11.7
British Columbia	68.9	67.3	70.5	12.1	11.5	12.6
Yukon Territory	66.9	64.9	68.8	10.3	8.8	11.6
Northwest Territories	67.0	66.2	67.8	10.4	10.6	10.3
Nunavut	62.9	61.7	64.1	9.2	9.3	9.2

Source: © *Statistics Canada*

Expected Years of Life Remaining by Sex

	At Birth		At Age 20		At Age 40		At Age 60		At Age 80	
	Male	Female	Male	Female	Male	Female	Male	Female	Male	Female
1921[1]	n.a.	n.a.	49.1	49.2	32.2	33.0	16.6	17.1	6.0	6.1
1931	60.0	62.1	49.1	49.8	32.0	33.0	16.3	17.2	5.6	5.9
1941	63.0	66.3	49.6	51.8	31.9	34.0	16.1	17.6	5.5	6.0
1951	66.3	70.8	50.8	54.4	32.5	35.6	16.5	18.6	5.8	6.4
1956	67.6	72.9	51.2	55.8	32.7	36.7	16.5	19.3	5.9	6.8
1961	68.4	74.2	51.5	56.7	33.0	37.5	16.7	19.9	6.1	6.9
1966	68.8	75.2	51.5	57.4	33.0	38.2	16.8	20.6	6.4	7.3
1971	69.3	76.4	51.7	58.2	33.2	39.0	17.0	21.4	6.4	7.9
1976	70.2	77.5	52.1	59.0	33.6	39.7	17.2	22.0	6.4	8.2
1981	71.9	79.0	53.4	60.1	34.7	40.7	18.0	22.9	6.9	8.8
1986	73.0	79.7	54.3	60.7	35.5	41.2	18.4	23.2	6.9	8.9
1991	74.6	80.9	55.6	61.7	36.8	42.2	19.4	24.0	7.2	9.4
1997	75.4	81.1	56.3	61.9	37.4	42.4	19.8	24.1	7.2	9.3

Source: © *Census Canada, Statistics Canada*   (n.a.) Not available. (1) Excludes Quebec.

Deaths in Canada

	Deaths	Death Rates[1]		Deaths	Death Rates[1]		Deaths	Death Rates[1]
1921[2]	104 531	11.6	**1976**	166 428	7.1	**1990**	192 608	7.0
1926[2]	111 055	11.4	**1977**	165 747	7.0	**1991**	192 439	6.9
1931[3]	108 446	10.2	**1978**	169 030	7.1	**1992**	196 967	6.9
1936[3]	111 111	9.9	**1979**	165 805	6.9	**1993**	201 808	7.0
1941[3]	118 797	10.1	**1980**	171 460	7.0	**1994**	206 464	7.1
1946	118 785	9.4	**1981**	170 535	6.9	**1995**	209 389	7.1
1951	125 823	9.0	**1982**	172 352	6.9	**1996**	209 766	7.1
1956	131 961	8.2	**1983**	176 522	7.0	**1997**	217 221	7.3
1961	140 985	7.7	**1984**	174 159	6.8	**1998**	217 688	7.2
1966	149 863	7.5	**1985**	179 085	6.9	**1999**	217 632	7.2
1972	159 533	7.2	**1986**	183 353	7.0	**2000**	217 229	7.1
1973	162 618	7.2	**1987**	182 599	6.9	**2001**	219 114	7.1
1974	166 284 —	7.3	**1988**	189 917	7.1	**2002**	222 833	7.1
1975	168 751	7.3	**1989**	188 408	6.9	**2003**	227 630	7.2

Source: © *Statistics Canada*
(1) Per 1,000 population. (2) Excludes Que., Nfld. & Lab., Yukon and N.W.T. (3) Excludes Nfld. & Lab., Yukon and N.W.T. From 1972 onwards, each year listed represents the period from July 1 of the previous year to June 30th of the next year. For example, 1972 represents the period from July 1, 1971, to June 30, 1972.

Deaths by Province, 2002–2003

	Deaths	Death Rate[1]		Deaths	Death Rate[1]
Canada	227 630	7.2	Manitoba	10 050	8.6
Newfoundland & Labrador	4 350	8.4	Saskatchewan	8 965	9.0
Prince Edward Island	1 213	8.8	Alberta	18 732	5.9
Nova Scotia	8 243	8.8	British Columbia	28 757	6.9
New Brunswick	6 335	8.4	Yukon	145	4.7
Quebec	54 585	7.3	Northwest Territories	175	4.2
Ontario	85 950	7.0	Nunavut	130	4.4

Source: © *Statistics Canada*   (1) Per 1,000 population.

Selected Causes of Death

	2000		2001	
	Males	**Females**	**Males**	**Females**
Neoplasms (cancer)	34 096	30 015	34 736	30 469
Hodgkin's disease.	78	50	72	59
Sudden infant death syndrome.	71	50	69	44
Iron deficiency anaemia	6	9	7	12
Sickle-cell disorders	6	0	4	7
Schizophrenia.	44	59	33	56
Eating disorders	5	14	7	20
Anorexia nervosa	0	1	0	5
Bulimia nervosa	1	2	0	0
Diabetes mellitus	3 322	3 392	3 440	3 657
Insulin-dependent diabetes mellitus	278	278	304	289
Non-insulin-dependent diabetes mellitus	644	705	669	772
Obesity	83	104	89	128
Cystic fibrosis.	22	27	35	31
Bacterial meningitis, not elsewhere classified. . . .	15	14	17	12
Meningitis due to other and unspecified causes. . .	18	9	20	11
Huntington's disease	34	35	37	43
Parkinson's disease	803	668	869	731
Alzheimer's disease	1 548	3 459	1 708	3 769
Ischaemic heart diseases	23 354	19 063	22 579	18 802
Influenza and pneumonia	2 238	2 728	2 139	2 637
Emphysema	507	325	492	297
Asthma.	109	183	109	177
Crohn's disease (regional enteritis)	23	52	26	45
Osteoporosis	23	176	33	178
Enterocolitis due to Clostridium difficile	74	117	106	149
Tuberculosis.	52	29	65	43
Legionnaires' disease	6	3	1	1
Toxic shock syndrome	2	3	6	2
Creutzfeldt-Jakob disease.	11	25	18	26
Viral hepatitis	96	42	196	124
Human immunodeficiency virus [HIV] disease. . . .	429	82	369	66
Traffic accidents	2 079	911	2 028	849
Water transport accidents	64	8	82	10
Air and space transport accidents	54	3	55	7
Falls	827	735	881	846
Accidental drowning and submersion.	229	58	231	47
Choking	144	127	144	99
Exposure to electric current, radiation and extreme ambient air temperature and pressure. .	18	3	27	2
Exposure to smoke, fire and flames	150	92	144	99
Contact with hornets, wasps and bees	1	1	2	0
Exposure to excessive natural heat.	3	0	8	9
Exposure to excessive natural cold.	65	27	60	28
Accidental poisoning by and exposure to noxious substances.	679	281	670	285
Intentional self-harm	2 798	807	2 869	819
Complications of medical and surgical care	84	83	85	72

Source: © *Statistics Canada*

MIGRATION

How to Become a Canadian Citizen

To become a Canadian citizen, you must be at least 18 years of age, a permanent resident and in Canada legally.

If you are a permanent resident, you must have lived in Canada for at least three of the four years before the date of your application. If you lived in Canada before becoming a permanent resident, that time is counted at half the rate if it was during the four years before your application date.

You must be able to speak and understand spoken English or French, or be able to read and write in simple English or French.

If you are between 18 and 59 years of age, you must learn about Canada before becoming a citizen. When you apply for citizenship, you'll be sent a free publication called *A Look at Canada* on which your citizenship test will be based. You can also find this publication online at the Web site for Citizenship and Immigration Canada: www.cic.gc.ca.

Children under 18 don't need to meet the three-year residency requirement; however, you must already be a Canadian citizen or be applying to become one. Children don't write a citizenship test.

Who Doesn't Qualify

Not everyone can become a Canadian citizen. You cannot become a citizen if:

- you were convicted of an indictable offence in the past three years;
- you are under a deportation order;
- you were in prison, on parole or on probation in the past four years;
- you have been charged with an indictable offence;
- you are now charged with an offence under the Citizenship Act;
- your Canadian citizenship has been revoked in the past five years;
- you are under investigation for war crimes or crimes against humanity.

Applying

1. **Get the correct application form.** It should be the "Application for Citizenship." Each child for whom you are applying needs a separate form.

2. **Read the form.** The cost to process your forms isn't refundable, so be sure you are ready to become a citizen and fill the form out carefully. The current fee for citizenship is $100.

3. **Complete the application and attach necessary documents.** Photocopies of documents are acceptable, but you may need to bring the original when you take the test. The application form comes with detailed instructions.

4. **Mail the completed application.** Check that you have included all documentation and filled in the application completely.

5. **Prepare for your test.** Read the book *A Look at Canada* that will be sent to you. You may want to take a citizenship class if one is being held near you. A notice detailing the date and time of your citizenship test will be sent to you. The test may be oral or written.

6. **Take the oath.** Once you have met all the requirements, you will receive a notice detailing when and where the citizenship ceremony will take place.

Call Centres and Citizenship Offices

You can get more information on any of the topics discussed here by contacting one of the call centres listed below.

Montreal: (514) 496-1010
Toronto: (416) 973-4444
Vancouver: (604) 666-2171
Toll-free: 1-888-242-2100

Case Processing Centre

P.O. Box 7000
Sydney, NS B1P 6V6

Source: *Citizenship and Immigration Canada*

Canadian Immigration Totals

Year	Total	Year	Total	Year	Total	Year	Total
1855*	25 296	1924	124 164	1950	73 912	1976	149 429
1860*	6 276	1925	84 907	1951	194 391	1977	114 914
1865*	18 958	1926	135 982	1952	164 498	1978	86 313
1870	24 706	1927	158 886	1953	168 868	1979	112 093
1875	27 382	1928	166 783	1954	154 227	1980	143 136
1880	38 505	1929	164 993	1955	109 946	1981	128 639
1885	79 169	1930	104 806	1956	164 857	1982	121 176
1890	75 067	1931	27 530	1957	282 164	1983	89 188
1895	18 790	1932	20 591	1958	124 851	1984	88 273
1900	41 681	1933	14 382	1959	106 928	1985	84 333
1905	141 465	1934	12 476	1960	104 111	1986	99 326
		1935	11 277	1961	71 689	1987	152 001
1910	286 839	1936	11 643	1962	74 586	1988	161 500
1911	331 288	1937	15 101	1963	93 151	1989	191 497
1912	375 756	1938	17 244	1964	112 606	1990	216 398
1913	400 870	1939	16 994	1965	146 758	1991	232 751
1914	150 484	1940	11 324	1966	194 743	1992	254 820
1915	36 665	1941	9 329	1967	222 876	1993	256 739
1916	55 914	1942	7 576	1968	183 974	1994	224 373
1917	72 910	1943	8 504	1969	164 531	1995	212 860
1918	41 845	1944	12 801	1970	147 713	1996	226 044
1919	107 698	1945	22 722	1971	121 900	1997	216 024
1920	138 824	1946	71 719	1972	122 006	1998	174 191
1921	91 728	1947	64 127	1973	184 200	1999	189 922
1922	64 224	1948	125 414	1974	218 465	2000	227 346
1923	133 729	1949	95 217	1975	187 881	2001	250 484
						2002[1]	229 091

Source: *Citizenship and Immigration Canada*   (*) Pre-Confederation. (1) Preliminary figure.

Persons Granted Canadian Citizenship[1]

Year	Number	Year	Number	Year	Number	Year	Number
1920	3 004	1961	56 476	1975	137 507	1989	87 478
1925	13 288	1962	72 082	1976	117 276	1990	104 267
1930	21 221	1963	69 468	1977	123 655	1991	118 630
1935	20 903	1964	64 334	1978	223 214	1992	115 757
1940	18 207	1965	63 844	1979	156 699	1993	150 543
1941	15 594	1966	60 852	1980	118 590	1994	217 320
1942	14 213	1967	59 968	1981	94 457	1995	227 720
1943	12 533	1968	60 055	1982	87 468	1996	166 627
1944	12 827	1969	59 900	1983	90 328	1997	154 624
1945	13 562	1970	57 556	1984	109 504	1998	134 485
1950	10 441	1971	63 669	1985	126 466	1999	189 945
1955	58 711	1972	80 866	1986	103 800	2000	214 568
		1973	104 697	1987	73 638	2001	167 353
1960	62 378	1974	130 278	1988	58 810	2002	141 588

Source: *Citizenship and Immigration Canada*   (1) For fiscal year ending Mar 31 for 1920 to 1951; calendar years 1952 onwards.

Dual Citizenship for Canadians

*C*anada's Citizenship Act allows a Canadian citizen to acquire a foreign nationality without automatically losing Canadian citizenship. Since 1977, a Canadian citizen acquiring citizenship rights elsewhere may retain Canadian citizenship—unless he or she voluntarily applies to renounce it and that application gets approval from a citizenship judge.

Two or more citizenships and allegiances can be held at the same time for an indefinite period. This means an individual may have the citizen's rights and obligations of each country—when present in that country. When travelling outside both countries, a passport from one of them will be necessary.

Immigration to Canada[1]

	Total Immigrants	United States	Asia[2]	Europe	Caribbean[3]	South America	Africa	Oceania
1956	164 857	9 777	3 537	145 554	1 351	1 551	1 079	1 924
1960	104 111	11 247	4 002	82 922	1 542	1 823	833	1 657
1965	146 758	15 143	11 215	108 285	3 420	2 471	3 196	2 711
1966	194 743	17 514	13 835	148 410	4 357	2 604	3 661	4 057
1967	222 876	19 038	20 740	159 979	9 004	3 090	4 608	6 168
1968	183 974	20 422	21 686	120 702	8 129	2 693	5 204	4 815
1969	161 531	22 785	23 319	88 363	13 908	4 767	3 297	4 411
1970	147 713	24 424	21 170	75 609	13 371	4 943	2 863	4 385
1971	121 900	24 366	22 171	52 031	11 653	5 058	2 841	2 902
1972	122 006	22 618	23 325	51 293	9 218	4 309	8 308	2 143
1973	184 200	25 242	43 193	71 883	20 704	11 057	8 307	2 671
1974	218 465	26 541	50 566	88 694	25 276	12 528	10 450	2 594
1975	187 881	20 155	47 382	72 898	19 483	13 270	9 867	2 174
1976	149 429	17 315	44 328	49 903	16 198	10 628	7 752	1 886
1977	114 914	12 888	31 368	40 748	13 187	7 840	6 372	1 545
1978	86 313	9 945	24 007	30 075	9 240	6 782	4 261	1 233
1979	112 096	9 617	50 540	32 858	7 060	5 898	3 958	1 395
1980	143 117	9 926	71 602	41 168	8 141	5 433	4 330	2 497
1981	128 618	10 559	48 831	46 299	9 625	6 163	4 889	2 253
1982	121 147	9 360	41 686	46 156	10 317	6 871	4 513	2 119
1983	89 157	7 381	36 906	24 312	10 864	4 816	3 659	1 213
1984	88 239	6 922	41 920	20 901	9 706	4 085	3 552	1 151
1985	84 302	6 669	38 597	18 859	11 143	4 356	3 545	1 128
1986	99 219	7 275	41 600	22 709	14 947	6 686	4 770	1 227
1987	152 098	7 967	67 337	37 563	18 100	10 801	8 501	1 827
1988	161 929	6 537	81 136	40 689	15 108	7 255	9 380	1 822
1989	192 001	6 931	93 261	52 105	16 764	8 685	12 199	2 041
1990	213 334	6 057	111 195	51 667	19 459	8 888	13 426	2 642
1991	232 020	20 122[4]	120 736	48 232	12 978	10 632	16 175	3 145[5]
1992	253 345	20 123[4]	139 546	44 933	14 993	10 415	19 669	3 666[5]
1993	255 935	8 025	147 378	46 622	24 315	9 588	16 922	3 085[5]
1994	223 912	6 242	141 600	38 652	13 486	7 919	13 708	2 305[5]
1995	212 463[6]	5 199	128 534	41 127	13 352	7 485	14 560	1 873[5]
1996	226 050[6]	5 896	143 956	40 009	12 958	6 115	14 836	2 058[5]
1997	216 050	5 053	138 018	38 580	8 195	5 682	14 473	2 024
1998	174 162	4 781	101 297	38 482	6 341	4 964	13 672	1 639
1999	189 922[8]	5 528	113 934	38 990	6 758	5 609	15 695	532
2000[7]	227 346[8]	5 814	140 988	42 950	7 149	6 784	19 828	696
2001	250 484[8]	5 894	132 711	43 204	—[10]	20 129	48 278[11]	—[9]
2002	229 091	5 288	118 899	38 841	—[10]	19 417	46 113[11]	—[9]

Source: *Citizenship and Immigration Canada*
(1) By country of last permanent residence. (2) Includes China and Hong Kong. (3) Includes Central America, Greenland and St. Pierre & Miquelon for 1956–76; except for 1991, 1992 when North and Central America were included with U.S. figures (4) Includes North and Central America. (5) Includes Australia and other islands. (6) Includes those whose country of last permanent residence was not stated. (7) Preliminary numbers. (8) Includes those whose last permanent residence was North and Central America and those not stated. (9) Included in Asia. (10) Included in South America. (11) Includes Middle East.

Dual Citizenship for Immigrants

*I*mmigrants to Canada may have several citizenships: if born in a country other than Canada, naturalized in Canada (without the loss of citizenship in the birth country), and naturalized in a third country, an individual may be a citizen of all three. Cases of dual citizenship are most common.

Dual citizenship may carry benefits, but it may bring difficulties—legal proceedings, taxation or financial responsibilities, military service, emigration problems, even imprisonment for failure to comply with citizenship obligations. Canadian officials will not be able to help if a Canadian citizen who is also a citizen elsewhere has difficulties while in their other homeland.

Immigration by Province of Intended Destination

	Totals[1]	N&L	PEI	NS	NB	Que	Ont	Man	Sask	Alta	BC	YT	NWT	NVT
1956	**164 857**	426	112	1 639	852	31 396	90 662	5 796	2 202	9 959	17 812	n.a.	n.a.	n.a.
1960	**104 111**	306	83	1 210	634	23 774	54 491	4 337	2 087	6 949	10 120	n.a.	n.a.	n.a.
1965	**146 758**	604	137	1 612	1 074	30 346	79 702	3 948	2 649	8 049	18 502	n.a.	n.a.	n.a.
1970	**147 713**	630	185	2 007	1 070	23 261	80 732	5 826	1 709	10 405	21 683	n.a.	n.a.	n.a.
1975	**187 881**	1106	235	2 124	2 093	28 042	98 471	7 134	2 837	16 277	29 272	n.a.	n.a.	n.a.
1980	**143 117**	541	190	1 616	1 207	22 538	62 257	7 683	3 603	18 839	24 437	n.a.	n.a.	n.a.
1985	**84 302**	325	113	974	609	14 884	40 730	3 415	1 905	9 001	12 239	n.a.	n.a.	n.a.
1990	**214 230**	546	176	1 563	842	40 842	113 438	6 637	2 361	18 994	28 723	83	75	n.a.
1991	**232 020**	641	150	1 504	685	52 155	119 257	5 659	2 455	17 043	32 263	84	124	n.a.
1992	**253 345**	787	151	2 359	754	48 597	138 453	5 084	2 511	17 696	36 709	133	111	n.a.
1993	**255 935**	807	165	3 021	702	44 964	134 420	4 874	2 403	18 580	45 724	104	171	n.a.
1995	**212 463**	585	167	3 581	639	27 182	115 681	3 603	1 949	14 329	44 541	108	91	n.a.
1996	**226 072**	585	154	3 225	717	29 802	119 072	3 928	1 824	13 896	52 026	87	92	n.a.
1997	**216 048**	431	150	2 873	631	27 905	117 431	3 799	1 759	12 976	47 880	86	101	n.a.
1998	**174 190**	412	136	2 059	750	26 645	92 220	3 015	1 578	11 214	35 998	62	63	n.a.
1999	**189 922**	415	125	1 601	663	29 085	104 010	3 701	1 725	12 059	36 076	79	54	10
2000	**227 346**	415	191	1 607	761	32 489	133 440	4 644	1 891	14 332	37 409	60	82	12
2001	**250 484**	402	135	1 711	809	37 523	148 571	4 588	1 708	16 377	38 352	67	93	12
2002	**229 091**	405	110	1 419	710	37 627	133 641	4 621	1 665	14 729	34 000	49	61	12

Source: _Citizenship and Immigration Canada_   (1) Includes those whose destination was not stated.

Top Five Provincial Destinations for Immigration

	2000		2001		2002	
	#	%	#	%	#	%
Total Number of Immigrants	**227 346**	**100**	**250 484**	**100**	**229 091**	**100**
Destination:						
Ontario	133 440	58.69	148 571	59.31	133 641	58.34
British Columbia	37 409	16.45	38 352	15.31	34 000	14.84
Quebec	32 489	14.29	37 523	14.98	37 627	16.43
Alberta	14 332	6.31	16 377	6.54	14 729	6.43
Manitoba	4 644	2.05	4 588	1.83	4 621	2.01

Source: _Citizenship and Immigration Canada_

Top Ten CMA Destinations for Immigration

	2000		2001		2002	
	#	%	#	%	#	%
Total Number of Immigrants	**227 346**	**100**	**250 484**	**100**	**229 091**	**100**
Toronto	110 069	48.41	125 114	49.95	111 580	48.71
Vancouver	33 289	14.64	34 234	13.67	29 922	13.06
Montreal	28 138	12.38	32 377	12.93	33 004	14.41
Calgary	8 478	3.73	10 166	4.06	9 038	3.95
Ottawa–Hull (ON)	7 774	3.42	8 441	3.37	7 156	3.12
Edmonton	4 313	1.90	4 588	1.83	4 225	1.84
Winnipeg	3 700	1.63	3 750	1.50	3 810	1.66
Hamilton	3 166	1.39	2 779	1.11	3 079	1.34
London	1 978	0.87	1 963	0.78	1 710	0.75
Quebec City	1 405	0.62	1 836	0.73	1 335	0.58

Source: _Citizenship and Immigration Canada_

Immigrants in Canada: Census 2001 Highlights

The Immigrant Population

The 2001 census has provided important new information on Canada's immigrant population. Immigrants formed a significant, and increasing, proportion of the country's population, reaching 5.4 million in 2001. Immigrants have accounted for the highest recorded share of Canada's population (18.4 percent) since 1931. More than one-third arrived in Canada in the 1991-2001 decade and over 80 percent chose to become Canadian citizens.

Sixty percent of recent immigrants (those who arrived between 1991 and 2001) came from Asia and the Middle East. Not surprisingly, a growing proportion of Canada's newest immigrants (61 percent in 2001, compared to 55 percent in 1991) reported speaking a language other than English or French most often at home, with Chinese spoken in a third of these households. Religious affiliations have also changed: the number of recent immigrants who identified themselves as one of Muslim, Hindu, Sikh or Buddhist has almost doubled.

Immigrants were much more likely to be among the working-age population. Sixty-seven percent were between 25 and 64 years old, compared to only 52 percent of the non-immigrant population. The remaining 33 percent were more likely to be over 65 years but less likely to be under 24. Immigrants were also increasingly well educated. Among working-age immigrants who arrived in the 1990s, 41 percent were university-trained, 13 percent had a college diploma and eight percent had a trade certificate.

Recent immigrants are much more likely than the Canadian-born population to live in a census metropolitan area. Ninety-four percent of immigrants who arrived in the 1990s settled in an urban area compared to 64 percent of the overall population. Taken together, Toronto, Vancouver and Montreal were home to 80 percent of recent immigrant city-dwellers.

■ Employment

Immigrant landings accounted for almost 70 percent of labour force growth between 1991 and 2001, adding about 965,000 people to the work force. Despite comprising only seven percent of the working-age population, recent immigrants aged 25 to 64 constituted an impressive 24 percent of the work force for higher skilled occupations in 2001.

Immigrants accounted for 20 percent of the labour force, an increase of one percent compared to 1996. The employment rates (see note) for immigrants and very recent immigrants (those who arrived in the last five years) were 77.4 percent and 69.4 percent respectively. These percentages represent an improvement over the 1996 figures (72.3 percent and 62.2 percent respectively), but are still below 1991 levels (78.5 percent and 71.7 percent respectively). A significant gap in employment rates, larger for females than males, remained between very recent immigrants and the Canadian-born.

■ Earnings

Male immigrants aged 25 to 54 who arrived in Canada in the 1990s earned $33,900 in 2000, an average of 25 percent less than their Canadian-born counterparts. Similarly, female immigrants aged 25 to 54 earned 24 percent less than their Canadian-born counterparts, their yearly earnings averaging $21,959.

The income of recent arrivals tended to increase the longer they remained in Canada. After ten years, a male immigrant earned an average of 80 percent of his Canadian-born counterpart's salary, compared to only 63 percent after one year in Canada. Despite this improvement, the relative gap between recent immigrants and the Canadian-born widened. Whereas in 1980, a male immigrant who had been in Canada ten years earned an average of $1.04 for every dollar earned by his Canadian-born counterpart, the figure had dropped to $0.90 by 1990 and $0.80 by 2000.

The average real family income for immigrants has increased by 12 percent, from $59,016 in 1995 to $65,825 in 2000, while the increase for non-immigrant families was 11 percent. The distribution of income also changed for the better. In all income groups, there were relatively fewer people with lower incomes in 2000 than in 1995. For example, 46.7 percent of immigrant families earned less than $50,000 in 2000 compared to 51.2 percent in 1995.

■ Children Living in Poverty

Despite these gains, there are a significant number of children in poor immigrant families. Thirty-three percent of children whose parents have been in Canada for less than ten years come from low-income families. This compares to 15.5 percent of children living with Canadian-born parents and 15 percent of children living with immigrant parents who have been in Canada for more than ten years. There were relatively more children from poor immigrant families in 2000 (33 percent) than

there were either in 1980 (20 percent) or 1990 (27 percent).

What conclusions can be drawn from these findings? The gap in financial well-being between Canadian-born and immigrant families may be attributed to a number of factors, including the language barrier many immigrants face when they arrive on Canadian soil, and the fact that Canadian educational institutions or business organizations may not recognize the qualifications an immigrant brings from his or her home country. Unfortunately, it is also likely that, in spite of Canada's reputation for tolerance, many immigrants (especially those from visible minorities) experience intolerant attitudes that limit their employment potential and success.

Note: The employment rate as defined here is the product of the proportion of the labour force that is employed and the labour force participation rate.

Immigrant Earnings (10 Years after Arrival in Canada) as a Percentage of Canadian-born Earnings

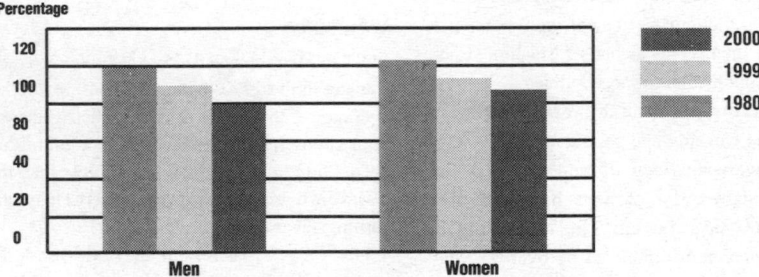

Children Living in Low Income Families, by the Parents' Immigration Status

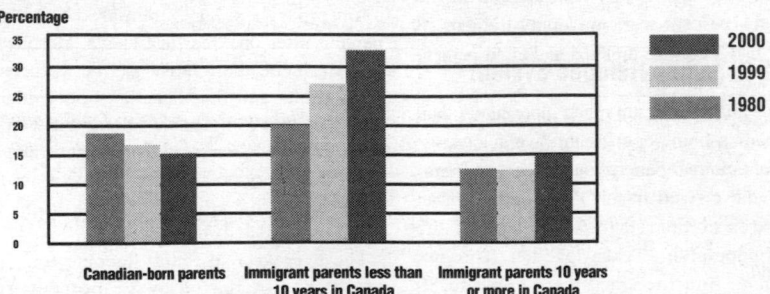

Source: *Citizenship and Immigration Canada*

Refugees to Canada[1]

1962	1 733	1973	2 381	1983	14 062	1993	24 835
1963	2 024	1974	1 656	1984	15 553	1994	19 739
1964	2 279	1975	6 109	1985	17 000	1995	27 753
1965	2 131	1976	5 576	1986	19 485	1996	28 352
1966	2 058	1977	3 670	1987	21 950	1997	24 221
1967	1 499	1978	3 038	1988	27 230	1998	22 787
1968	9 971	1979	27 894	1989	37 361	1999	24 393
1969	3 604	1980	40 638	1990	36 093	2000	30 072
1970	1 361	1981	15 058	1991	35 891	2001	27 899
1971	614	1982	17 000	1992	36 943	2002	25 111
1972	5 204						

Source: *Refugees Branch, Citizenship and Immigration Canada*
(1) Includes persons admitted from abroad as Convention Refugees or members of Designated Classes, as well as persons recognized in Canada as Convention Refugees or members of the special Backlog Clearance Designated Class. Does not include special humanitarian movements of other persons.

Refugees by Province of Destination[1]

	Total[2]	N&L	PEI	NS	NB	Que	Ont	Man	Sask	Alta	BC	YT	NWT
1981	14 997	28	11	119	76	3 257	5 544	822	657	2 751	1 722	6	4
1982	16 991	40	28	161	47	3 200	7 013	1 031	644	3 112	1 706	7	2
1983	14 062	11	17	89	61	2 184	6 100	844	574	2 488	1 692	0	2
1984	15 553	40	20	175	85	2 228	6 900	1 032	773	2 446	1 848	1	5
1985	17 000	55	33	206	165	1 906	8 301	1 131	749	2 529	1 919	1	5
1986	19 485	77	43	253	170	2 530	9 580	1 350	777	2 677	2 018	5	5
1987	21 921	87	45	241	192	3 216	11 026	1 366	791	2 673	2 277	3	4
1988	27 230	93	18	290	208	3 690	14 716	1 653	806	3 265	2 453	7	1
1989	37 361	94	49	329	194	5 137	21 585	1 929	815	4 535	2 679	9	6
1990	36 093	94	50	361	182	5 085	20 644	2 325	776	4 118	2 447	6	5
1991	35 891	265	40	337	211	6 284	21 342	1 579	706	2 738	2 382	4	3
1992	36 943	220	28	176	95	7 111	22 894	1 048	568	2 428	2 374	1	0
1993	24 835	243	41	189	100	5 776	14 433	692	375	1 649	1 325	1	11
1994	19 739	225	64	173	137	4 430	10 485	582	515	1 606	1 520	2	0
1995	27 753	208	61	223	179	6 122	16 413	663	575	1 447	1 854	8	0
1996	28 352	173	72	232	189	8 909	13 937	683	547	1 341	2 264	2	3
1997	24 221	133	63	211	150	7 686	11 646	621	558	1 156	1 996	1	0
1998	22 787	113	58	235	162	6 227	11 496	655	532	1 275	2 033	0	1
1999	24 393	148	66	258	149	7 333	11 961	779	509	1 281	1 892	0	0
2000	30 072	140	109	269	267	8 044	15 114	1 016	649	1 871	2 578	0	1
2001	27 899	157	50	265	230	7 147	14 226	1 161	595	1 875	2 189	0	1
2002	25 122	135	50	225	159	6 438	12 618	982	602	1 786	2 113	3	10

Source: *Refugees Branch, Citizenship and Immigration Canada*   (1) Includes Refugees Resettled from Abroad, their Dependants and inland Determination where destination is known. (2) Shows only those whose destination was identified.

The Canadian Refugee System

*R*efugees are people in or outside Canada who fear returning to their country of nationality or habitual residence. In keeping with its humanitarian tradition and international obligations, Canada offers safe haven to thousands of persons every year who have a well-founded fear of persecution, torture, or cruel and unusual treatment or punishment.

Canada has signed the United Nations 1951 Geneva Convention Relating to the Status of Refugees and its 1967 Protocol. This Convention protects refugees from being returned to a country where they would face persecution. To find out about claiming refugee status, contact the nearest Citizenship and Immigration Canada office, or consult their Web site at www.cic.gc.ca.   **Source:** *Citizenship and Immigration Canada*

Where Canadians Move Within Canada

When Canadians move from one province to another, it tends to be related to economic conditions. During 1977–81 the resource boom in Alberta caused an influx from other provinces. Falling oil prices in the early 1980s led to a reversal as Canadians moved east, especially to Ontario.

By the late 1980s, BC was the choice location. For the latter part of the 1990s, up to the present, Ontario and Alberta were on top again. The table shows net interprovincial migration—the number of persons moving into a province minus the number of persons moving out.

	N&L	PEI	NS	NB	Que	Ont	Man	Sask	Alta	BC	YK	NWT	NVT[1]
1982–86	-14 117	811	7 442	835	-67 235	165 460	-2 395	-7 057	-82 737	3 226	-2 393	-1 840	n.a.
1987–91	-11 355	-65	-607	-2 063	-45 406	28 876	-39 533	-69 397	-13 198	154 126	871	-2 249	n.a.
1992–95	-18 730	1 826	-5 454	-3 015	-37 711	-32 592	-18 977	-19 418	242	135 036	-129	-1 078	n.a.
1996–97[2]	-8 134	136	-1 648	-1 263	-17 436	1 977	-5 873	-2 794	26 282	9 880	-54	-696	-377
1997–98[2]	-9 490	-416	-2 569	-3 192	-16 958	9 231	-5 276	-1 940	43 089	-10 029	-1 024	-1 316	-110
1998–99[2]	-5 695	193	201	-1 244	-13 065	16 706	-2 113	-4 333	25 191	-14 484	-747	-555	-55
1999–00[2]	-4 263	104	-270	-1 183	-12 146	22 369	-3 456	-7 947	22 674	-14 610	-691	-651	70
2000–01	-4 493	165	-2 077	-1 530	-9 442	18 623	-4 323	-8 410	20 457	-8 286	-572	-160	48
2001–02[2]	-3 352	62	-898	-1 218	-4 350	5 354	-4 344	-8 820	26 235	-8 556	-221	84	24
2002–03[2,3]	-14	571	777	-628	-1 722	-1 814	-1 189	-4 223	12 081	-4 591	686	10	56

Source: © *Statistics Canada* n.a. not applicable (1) Nunavut became a territory in 1999. (2) Year ends June 30. (3) Preliminary data.

Population Growth Components

(thousands)

Population growth is made up of natural increase (births minus deaths) plus net migration (immigration minus emigration). As the birth rate in Canada falls and the death rate continues to rise, the role of immigration becomes an increasingly important factor in population growth. By 2030, natural increase is expected to be close to zero, and immigration will become our sole source of population growth.

	Total Population Growth	Natural Increase		Net Migration	
		Births	**Deaths**	**Immigration**	**Emigration**
1851–1861	793	1 281	670	352	170
1861–1871	459	1 370	760	260	411
1871–1881	636	1 480	790	350	404
1881–1891	508	1 524	870	680	826
1891–1901	538	1 548	880	250	380
1901–1911	1 836	1 925	900	1 550	739
1911–1921	1 581	2 340	1 070	1 400	1 089
1921–1931	1 589	2 415	1 055	1 200	971
1931–1941	1 130	2 294	1 072	149	241
1941–1951	2 141	3 186	1 214	548	379
1951–1956	2 071	2 106	633	783	185
1956–1961	2 157	2 362	687	760	278
1961–1966	1 777	2 249	731	539	280
1966–1971[1]	1 553	1 856	766	890	427
1971–1976	1 626	1 755	824	1 053	358
1976–1981	1 470	1 820	843	771	278
1981–1986	1 386	1 872	885	677	278
1986–1991	1 973	1 933	946	1 199	213
1991–1996	1 848	1 936	1 024	1 137	229
1996–2001	1 114	1 705	1 089	1 051	248
2000–01	320	326	224	252	67
2001–02	340	333	223	256	48
2002–03[2]	268	332	228	199	48

Source: © *Statistics Canada*   (1) Updated data. Year ends June 30th. (2) Preliminary data.

SOCIAL TRENDS

Marriages by Province

	1999	2000	2001	2002	Rate (%)
Canada	155 742	157 395	146 618	147 634	4.7
Newfoundland and Labrador	3 400	3 412	2 964	2 910	5.6
Prince Edward Island	932	962	901	899	6.6
Nova Scotia	5 481	5 517	4 903	4 870	5.2
New Brunswick	4 147	4 447	3 906	3 874	5.2
Quebec	22 910	24 912	21 961	22 045	3.0
Ontario	66 110	65 426	62 574	63 262	5.2
Manitoba	6 627	6 471	5 968	5 962	5.2
Saskatchewan	5 919	5 717	5 060	5 034	5.1
Alberta	18 223	18 063	17 433	17 770	5.7
British Columbia	21 622	22 086	20 558	20 616	5.0
Yukon	161	155	147	147	4.9
Northwest Territories	117	138	142	143	3.5
Nunavut	93	89	101	102	3.5

Source: © *Statistics Canada*

Divorces by Province

	1999	2000	2001	2002	Rate (%)
Canada	70 910	71 144	71 769	72 347	2.3
Newfoundland and Labrador	892	913	904	897	1.7
Prince Edward Island	291	272	272	274	2.0
Nova Scotia	1 954	2 054	2 047	2 045	2.2
New Brunswick	1 671	1 717	1 713	1 707	2.3
Quebec	17 144	17 054	17 090	17 120	2.3
Ontario	26 088	26 148	26 574	26 946	2.2
Manitoba	2 572	2 430	2 431	2 428	2.1
Saskatchewan	2 237	2 194	2 178	2 167	2.2
Alberta	7 931	8 176	8 308	8 444	2.7
British Columbia	9 935	10 017	10 083	10 148	2.5
Yukon	112	68	68	67	2.2
Northwest Territories	48	61	59	57	1.4
Nunavut	35	40	42	47	1.6

Source: © *Statistics Canada*

Defining Marriage and Family

A family portrait taken by the census at the outset of the 21st century shows a continuation of many of the changes in families over the last 20 years. The proportion of "traditional" families—mom, dad and the kids—continues to decline, while families with no children at home are on the increase.

As of May 15, 2001, married or common-law couples with children aged 24 and under living at home represented only 44 percent of all families in Canada. In 1991, they accounted for 49 percent of all families, and in 1981 they represented more than one-half (55 percent).

At the same time, couples with no children living at home accounted for 41 percent of all families in 2001, up from 38 percent in 1991 and 34 percent in 1981.

Behind this shift in living arrangements are diverse factors, such as lower fertility rates, couples who are delaying having children or who choose to remain childless. In addition, life expectancy is increasing, with one result being that couples have more of their lives to spend together as "empty-nesters" after their children have grown up and left home.

Some couples with children consist of step families. According to the 2001 General Social Survey, Canada had 503,100 step families in 2001. This represents almost 12 percent of all Canadian couples with children in 2001, compared to 10 percent in 1995.

The 2001 census showed that an increasing proportion of couples choose to live common-law. The proportion of married-couple families was 70 percent in 2001, down from 83 percent in 1981. At the same time, the proportion of common-law families increased from 5.6 percent to 14 percent.

The census counted 5,901,420 married families and 1,158,410 common-law families in 2001. The 1,311,190 lone-parent families represented 16 percent of families in Canada. The trend toward common-law relationship continued to be strongest in Quebec, where 508,520 common-law families represented 30 percent of all couple families in that province.

A recent study based on Statistics Canada's General Social Survey showed that common-law unions have become more and more popular in Quebec, and that trend has started to take hold among younger people in other provinces.

Still, while younger Canadian men and women are more likely to start their conjugal life through a common-law relationship (about 40 percent of men and women aged 30 to 39), most will eventually marry (roughly 75 percent) if trends observed in 2001 continue.

■ Same-sex partnerships in the 2001 census

For the first time, the 2001 census provides data on same-sex partnerships.

Changes in the legal status of same-sex common-law couples was the primary reason for collecting data on same-sex partnerships in the 2001 census. The number of same-sex couples in the census reflects people who identified themselves as living in a same-sex common-law relationship.

The 2001 census did not ask about sexual orientation. Therefore, the data on same-sex partnerships should not be interpreted as an estimation of the number of gays and lesbians in Canada, some of whom may be living alone or with parents or friends.

A total of 34,200 same-sex common-law couples were counted in Canada in 2001, representing 0.5 percent of all couples.

There were 10,360 couples in Quebec and 5,790 couples in British Columbia who identified themselves as same-sex common-law couples, accounting for 0.6 percent of all couples living in each province. Ontario had the largest number of same-sex couples (12,505), representing 0.5 percent of all couples.

Although the actual numbers are small, same sex couples also represented 0.6 percent of all couples (married and common-law) in the Yukon.

Newfoundland and Labrador had the lowest proportion of same-sex couples (0.1 percent of all couples).

There were slightly more male same-sex common-law couples than female. The census counted about 19,000 male same-sex couples, 55 percent of the total.

More female same-sex couples have children living with them. About 15 percent of the 15,200 female same-sex couples are living with children, compared to only 3 percent of male same-sex couples. Less than 10 percent of male and female same-sex couples live with other household members (other than children). The majority of same-sex couples (88 percent of male couples and 77 percent of female couples) had no other people living in their household.

Male couples were more likely to live in census metropolitan areas. Eighty-five percent live in the larger urban areas of Canada, compared with 76 percent of female couples.

The metropolitan areas of Ottawa-Hull (now known as Ottawa-Gatineau) and Vancouver had the highest proportions of same-sex common-law couples (about 0.9 percent of all couples). Close to 4,000 same-sex couples were counted in Vancouver, and 2,170 couples identified themselves as same-sex couples in Ottawa-Hull.

Same-sex common-law couples represented 0.8 percent of all couples in the metropolitan areas of Montreal and Victoria.

Source: © *Census of Canada, Statistics Canada*

Marital Status of the Canadian Population, 2003[1]

	Total Population		Single		Married[2]		Widowed		Divorced	
	Male (000s)	Female (000s)	Male (%)	Female (%)	Male (%)	Female (%)	Male (%)	Female (%)	Male (%)	Female (%)
Total	12 701 126	13 146 934	32.3	25.3	60.5	58.8	2.3	9.5	4.9	6.5
15-19.	1 088 772	1 031 773	99.0	97.0	0.9	2.9	0.0	0.0	0.1	0.1
20-24.	1 119 035	1 069 466	86.9	75.0	12.8	24.5	0.0	0.0	0.2	0.4
25-29.	1 073 969	1 044 163	57.9	42.1	40.9	56.1	0.1	0.1	1.1	1.6
30-34.	1 124 790	1 103 923	34.9	23.3	62.3	72.8	0.1	0.2	2.7	3.7
35-39.	1 247 414	1 233 785	24.0	15.9	71.2	77.5	0.1	0.5	4.7	6.2
40-44.	1 364 310	1 355 014	18.2	12.6	75.0	78.2	0.3	0.9	6.5	8.3
45-49.	1 251 593	1 264 150	13.6	10.1	77.8	77.6	0.5	1.7	8.1	10.5
50-54.	1 078 752	1 097 745	9.9	8.1	80.0	76.2	1.0	3.5	9.1	12.2
55-59.	913 922	928 537	7.4	6.4	81.8	74.3	1.7	6.6	9.1	12.7
60-64.	684 822	711 978	6.2	5.6	82.6	70.5	2.9	12.5	8.3	11.4
65-69.	552 166	595 736	5.8	5.3	81.8	64.2	5.3	21.1	7.1	9.4
70-74.	484 186	554 927	5.7	5.4	79.3	54.2	9.3	33.2	5.7	7.2
75-79.	358 752	480 675	5.8	5.7	75.1	41.4	14.9	47.9	4.2	5.0
80-84.	221 629	362 027	5.3	6.2	69.7	27.8	22.2	62.6	2.9	3.4
85-89.	97 229	199 724	5.3	7.6	59.3	14.7	33.3	75.6	2.1	2.1
90+	39 785	113 311	6.6	9.0	44.1	6.7	47.9	83.3	1.4	1.0

Source: © *Statistics Canada*   (. . .) Less than 0.1 percent. (1) As of July 1. (2) Includes common-law.

Composition of Canadian Families

(thousands)

	1971		1981		1991		2001	
	No. of Families	%	No. of Families	%	No. of Families	%	No. of Families	%
Total families[1]	5 071	100.0	6 325	100.0	7 356	100.0	8 371	100.0
Without children at home	1 545	30.5	2 013	31.8	2 580	35.1	3 059	36.5
With children at home	3 526	69.5	4 312	68.2	4 776	64.9	5 311	63.4
With one child	1 045	20.6	1 580	25.0	1 945	26.4	2 285	27.2
two children	1 077	21.2	1 648	26.1	1 927	26.2	2 087	24.9
three children[2]	677	13.4	730	11.5	691	9.4	939	11.2
four children	367	7.2	243	3.8	165	2.2	n.a.	n.a.
five children or more	360	7.1	112	1.8	48	0.5	n.a.	n.a.
Lone parent families	471	9.3	653	10.3	955	13.0	1 311	15.6
lone female parent	371	7.3	541	8.6	786	10.7	1 065	12.7
lone male parent	100	2.0	112	1.8	168	2.3	246	2.9

Source: © *Census of Canada, Statistics Canada*   (n.a.) Not available.

(1) Based on the census family definition: a husband and wife (without children or with children who never married) or a parent with one or more children who never married, living together in the same home. (2) The 2001 census grouped all families of 3 or more children into the "three children" category.

Size of Families in Canada

(thousands)

	1971		1981		1991		2001	
	No. of Families	Avg. Size	No. of Families	Avg. Size	No. of Families	Avg. Size	No. of Families	Avg. Size
Canada	5 071	3.7	6 325	3.3	7 356	3.1	8 371	3
Newfoundland and Labrador	108	4.4	135	3.8	151	3.3	154	2.9
Prince Edward Island	24	4.0	30	3.5	34	3.2	38	3
Nova Scotia	181	3.8	216	3.3	245	3.1	263	2.9
New Brunswick	140	4.0	177	3.4	198	3.1	215	2.9
Quebec	1 357	3.9	1 672	3.3	1 883	3.0	2 020	2.9
Ontario	1 882	3.6	2 279	3.2	2 727	3.1	3 191	3
Manitoba	236	3.6	262	3.2	286	3.1	303	3
Saskatchewan	216	3.7	246	3.3	258	3.2	266	3
Alberta	382	3.7	566	3.3	668	3.1	811	3
British Columbia	534	3.5	728	3.1	888	3.0	1 086	2.9
Yukon	11[1]	4.3[1]	6	3.3	7	3.1	8	3
Northwest Territories	11[1]	4.3[1]	9	4.0	13	3.7	10	3.3
Nunavut	—	—	—	—	—	—	6	3.8

Source: © *Census of Canada, Statistics Canada*   (1) Includes both the Yukon and Northwest Territories.

Lone-Parent Families by Province, 2001

Province	Lone-Parent Families	Average Family Size	Male Parent	Average Family Size	Female Parent	Average Family Size
Canada	1 369 157	2.5	224 220	2.4	1 144 937	2.6
Newfoundland & Labrador	23 297	2.4	3 260	2.4	20 037	2.4
Prince Edward Island. . . .	6 471	2.6	1 143	2.6	5 328	2.6
Nova Scotia	47 218	2.5	6 893	2.3	40 325	2.6
New Brunswick	33 316	2.4	5 357	2.3	27 959	2.5
Quebec	359 700	2.5	67 403	2.3	292 297	2.5
Ontario	530 652	2.6	77 552	2.4	453 100	2.6
Manitoba	48 068	2.6	7 364	2.5	38 722	2.7
Saskatchewan	41 044	2.7	6 211	2.6	34 833	2.7
Alberta.	111 605	2.6	20 625	2.4	90 980	2.6
British Columbia	169 768	2.6	28 412	2.4	141 356	2.6

Source: © *Statistics Canada*

Lone-Parent Families by Age, 2001

	Total Families	Size of Families		
		2 Members	3 Members	4 or more Members
Headed by Male Parent	**224 220**	**154 934**	**54 623**	**14 663**
Age 15-24	1 924	1 665	188	71
25-34	20 552	14 613	4 782	1 157
35-44	71 229	43 758	21 583	5 888
45-54	76 627	51 139	20 100	5 388
55-64	25 557	19 528	4 873	1 156
65+	28 331	24 231	3 097	1 003
Headed by Female Parent	**1 144 937**	**662 512**	**347 330**	**135 095**
Age 15-24	70 005	51 068	15 959	2 978
25-34	237 167	115 823	82 756	38 588
35-44	374 674	164 575	144 887	65 212
45-54	255 151	155 244	77 379	22 528
55-64	77 506	62 410	12 459	2 637
65+	130 434	113 392	13 890	3 152

Source: © *Statistics Canada*

Census Families by Size and Structure, 2001

Two-parent Families	Total Families	Families by Size				Average Family Size
		2 members	3 members	4 members	5 members	
Canada	6 988 831	2 875 942	1 468 415	1 776 542	659 058	3.1
Newfoundland & Labrador .	133 551	50 772	36 904	35 380	8 908	3.1
Prince Edward Island	32 120	12 330	7 196	7 685	3 485	3.2
Nova Scotia	212 610	93 696	47 917	50 292	16 463	3.0
New Brunswick	183 979	77 144	46 027	44 206	13 475	3.0
Quebec.	1 660 021	684 583	377 224	419 586	140 352	3.1
Ontario.	2 671 937	1 048 980	556 540	715 873	265 043	3.2
Manitoba	253 874	104 977	50 966	60 613	26 845	3.2
Saskatchewan	224 390	100 325	38 658	49 129	25 681	3.2
Alberta	714 030	297 172	134 928	178 663	76 303	3.2
British Columbia	902 319	405 963	172 055	215 115	82 503	3.1

Source: © *Statistics Canada*

Average Household Expenditure, including Budget Share

(dollars)

	2000		2001		2002	
	Average expenditure ($ current[1])	Share of budget (%)	Average expenditure ($ current[1])	Share of budget (%)	Average expenditure ($ current[1])	Share of budget (%)
Total Expenditure	55 614	100.0	57 496	100.0	60 090	100.0
Personal taxes	12 012	21.6	12 218	21.3	12 025	20.0
Shelter	10 278	18.5	10 738	18.7	11 204	18.6
Transportation	7 576	13.6	7 596	13.2	8 431	14.0
Food........................	6 217	11.2	6 438	11.2	6 684	11.1
Recreation	3 165	5.7	3 453	6.0	3 537	5.9
Personal insurance payments and pension contributions	3 135	5.6	3 125	5.4	3 415	5.7
Household operation	2 516	4.5	2 619	4.6	2 783	4.6
Clothing	2 351	4.2	2 398	4.2	2 450	4.1
Household furnishings and equipment	1 557	2.8	1 655	2.9	1 793	3.0
Health Care..................	1 357	2.4	1 420	2.5	1 590	2.6
Gifts of money and contributions.	1 302	2.3	1 259	2.2	1 444	2.4
Tobacco products and alcoholic beverages	1 218	2.2	1 313	2.3	1 478	2.5
Miscellaneous expenditure......	827	1.5	865	1.5	901	1.5
Education...................	826	1.5	898	1.6	926	1.5
Personal care	740	1.3	960	1.7	829	1.4
Reading material and other printed matter	275	0.5	276	0.5	285	0.5
Games of chance expense (net) ..	261	0.5	267	0.5	313	0.5

Source: © *Statistics Canada*   (1) Not adjusted for inflation.

Kids count when it comes to recreational spending

*O*ver the past two decades, spending on recreation by households with children grew faster than that of others. Two-parent households saw their recreational spending increase by 50 percent and lone-parent households by 57 percent. Couples without children recorded a 36 percent growth in expenditures and one-person households a 17 percent rise.

Purchases of cable television represented the largest single increase in recreational spending for all types of households. The home recreation equipment category also recorded large increases, mainly because this category includes computer equipment and supplies. Sixty-seven percent of two-parent and 44 percent of lone-parent households spent money on computers in 1999, compared with 34 percent of couples only and 19 percent of one-person households. Many parents now feel that owning a computer is no longer a luxury but a necessity to help their children succeed academically.

Source: *Statistics Canada, Canadian Social Trends, 11-008 (Spring 2002)*

Average Household Expenditure by Province

(dollars)

Ontario and Alberta remained the most expensive provinces when it came to maintaining a household in 2001, with householders in Ontario, Alberta, Manitoba and Saskatchewan seeing significant increases in their spending as compared to the previous year. Households in Newfoundland and Labrador once again had the lowest average household spending.

	1999 ($ current[1])	2000 ($ current[1])	2001 ($ current[1])	2002 ($ current[1])
Newfoundland and Labrador	$ 42 510	$ 43 085	$ 46 448	$ 47 965
Prince Edward Island	45 400	44 848	46 756	48 065
Nova Scotia	45 850	48 289	48 686	51 243
New Brunswick	44 730	46 857	47 396	50 039
Quebec	46 870	48 129	49 977	51 213
Ontario	58 780	62 499	64 092	67 538
Manitoba	49 410	50 117	51 587	53 129
Saskatchewan	46 900	46 685	48 260	51 365
Alberta	59 210	61 844	65 516	67 727
British Columbia	54 970	55 498	57 138	60 596

Source: © *Statistics Canada*   (1) Not adjusted for inflation.

Average Household Expenditure by Metropolitan Area, by Province

(dollars)

Given the statistics above on household spending by province, it is no surprise that households in CMAs in Ontario and Alberta once again captured the top four spots as most expensive cities to live in in 2001.

2001 Rank	2002 Rank		2000 ($ current[1])	2001 ($ current[1])	2003 ($ current[1])
2	1	Calgary, Alta.	$ 67 727	$ 73 584	$ 76 541
3	2	Toronto, Ont.	76 379	69 940	76 029
1	3	Ottawa, Ont.	68 559	82 736	73 698
5	4	Vancouver, B.C.	61 687	64 734	66 809
4	5	Edmonton, Alta.	66 091	65 735	65 314
8	6	Regina, Sask.	61 641	56 368	61 746
7	7	Halifax, N.S.	56 508	57 189	61 664
6	8	St. John's, Nfld and Lab.	51 080	59 667	61 128
10	9	Winnipeg, Man.	52 614	55 721	58 817
13	10	Victoria, B.C.	52 417	50 618	57 419
9	11	Saskatoon, Sask.	53 390	56 002	57 415
11	12	Montreal, Que.	53 134	54 116	56 462
14	13	Saint John, N.B.	53 086	49 268	53 445
12	14	Québec, Que.	42 117	52 680	49 381
15	15	Charlottetown-Summerside, P.E.I.	43 986	45 322	45 057

Source: © *Statistics Canada*   (1) Not adjusted for inflation.

Body Mass Index of the Canadian Population, % by Age and Sex

Body mass index (BMI) is a measure of weight relative to height. It is a good indicator of possible health concerns that can be obtained without special equipment and can be taken from fairly accessible measures. The table below shows the values for normal, overweight and obesity. Find your height in inches in the left column; find your body weight in pounds along that row. The weight value should fall into one of three categories (underweight is not shown, nor is highly obese). The number at the top of the column where your weight is listed gives a BMI rating.

Why does this matter? Overweight and obesity are linked to the development of a variety of serious health problems, including heart disease, some forms of cancer and diabetes. A BMI in the normal range will give you a better chance of avoiding those (and other) ailments, and give you a much better chance of fighting them successfully if they develop.

How do Canadians rate? The next page shows a comparison of men and women by age, over an 8-year period: our weight is slowly creeping up. (Internationally, the proportion of Canadians who are definitely overweight is higher than that in Australia or Scotland.)

Body Mass Index Table

	Normal						Overweight					Obese									
BMI	19	20	21	22	23	24	25	26	27	28	29	30	31	32	33	34	35	36	37	38	39
Height (Inches)												Body Weight (pounds)									
58	91	96	100	105	110	115	119	124	129	134	138	143	148	153	158	162	167	172	177	181	186
59	94	99	104	109	114	119	124	128	133	138	143	148	153	158	163	168	173	178	183	188	193
60	97	102	107	112	118	123	128	133	138	143	148	153	158	163	168	174	179	184	189	194	199
61	100	106	111	116	122	127	132	137	143	148	153	158	164	169	174	180	185	190	195	201	206
62	104	109	115	120	126	131	136	142	147	153	158	164	169	175	180	186	191	196	202	207	213
63	107	113	118	124	130	135	141	146	152	158	163	169	175	180	186	191	197	203	208	214	220
64	110	116	122	128	134	140	145	151	157	163	169	174	180	186	192	197	204	209	215	221	227
65	114	120	126	132	138	144	150	156	162	168	174	180	186	192	198	204	210	216	222	228	234
66	118	124	130	136	142	148	155	161	167	173	179	186	192	198	204	210	216	223	229	235	241
67	121	127	134	140	146	153	159	166	172	178	185	191	198	204	211	217	223	230	236	242	249
68	125	131	138	144	151	158	164	171	177	184	190	197	203	210	216	223	230	236	243	249	256
69	128	135	142	149	155	162	169	176	182	189	196	203	209	216	223	230	236	243	250	257	263
70	132	139	146	153	160	167	174	181	188	195	202	209	216	222	229	236	243	250	257	264	271
71	136	143	150	157	165	172	179	186	193	200	208	215	222	229	236	243	250	257	265	272	279
72	140	147	154	162	169	177	184	191	199	206	213	221	228	235	242	250	258	265	272	279	287
73	144	151	159	166	174	182	189	197	204	212	219	227	235	242	250	257	265	272	280	288	295
74	148	155	163	171	179	186	194	202	210	218	225	233	241	249	256	264	272	280	287	295	303
75	152	160	168	176	184	192	200	208	216	224	232	240	248	256	264	272	279	287	295	303	311
76	156	164	172	180	189	197	205	213	221	230	238	246	254	263	271	279	287	295	304	312	320

Source: *National Heart, Lung and Blood Institute*

Body Mass Index[1] of the Canadian Population[2], % by Age and Sex, 2003

	Number of persons	Underweight[3] BMI under 18.5	Normal weight BMI 18.5–24.9	Overweight BMI 25.0–29.9	Obese BMI 30.0 or higher
■ 18 years and over					
Males	11 794 013	1.2	41.2	41.0	15.9
Females.	12 043 745	4.1	52.1	25.7	13.9
■ 18–24 years					
Males	1 516 347	2.7	60.8	26.2	9.2
Females.	1 406 375	10.6	66.7	12.3	6.3
■ 25–34 years					
Males	2 054 636	1.1	45.0	37.3	15.9
Females.	1 954 117	5.3	57.6	20.3	12.0
■ 35–44 years					
Males	2 671 810	0.8	38.2	44.6	15.9
Females.	2 590 519	3.1	56.9	22.7	13.1
■ 45–54 years					
Males	2 240 920	0.7	35.4	44.7	18.7
Females.	2 327 258	2.0	48.0	29.0	16.0
■ 55–64 years					
Males	1 650 676	0.7	33.0	45.5	20.3
Females.	1 639 957	1.7	41.7	33.3	19.7
■ 65 years and over					
Males	1 659 626	1.3	39.6	43.8	14.0
Females.	2 125 520	4.0	44.2	33.5	14.7

Source: © _Statistics Canada_
(1) Body mass index (BMI) is calculated by dividing the respondent's body weight (in kilograms) by their height (in metres) squared. (2) Population aged 18 and over, excluding pregnant women and persons less than 3 feet (0.914 metres) tall or greater than 6 feet 11 inches (2.108 metres). (3) Use any data less than 1.0% with caution.

Findings of the Canadian Community Health Survey, 2003

_M_ore than 1.2 million Canadians were unable to find a regular doctor in 2003, and more than twice as many didn't have one because they hadn't looked for one, according to new results from the Canadian Community Health Survey (CCHS). The results are part of a comprehensive survey of more than 135,000 Canadians conducted between January and December 2003.

Eighty-six percent of Canadians reported that they had a regular medical doctor in 2003. This proportion was virtually unchanged from 1994, when the National Population Health Survey examined the same issue. However, for the first time, the CCHS asked those who did not have a regular medical doctor to report why not. About 5% of Canadians, an estimated 1.2 million people, could not find a regular doctor; an additional 9%, or about 2.4 million, had not looked for one.

The survey also asked a variety of questions on health issues, ranging from smoking habits to obesity and self-perceived health. For the first time in a Statistics Canada survey, information on sexual orientation was also collected to improve the understanding of health issues specific to the homosexual and bisexual populations. The goal was to provide a statistical snapshot of the health of Canadians at the national, provincial and sub-provincial health-region level.

Data showed, for example, that smoking has decreased substantially during the past 10 years, and that the decline was particularly dramatic among teenagers and young adults. Also, obesity rates were highest among men and those aged 45 to 64. In addition, fewer individuals considered their health to be excellent or very good compared with 10 years ago.

Another goal of the survey was to produce health information for 126 health regions in Canada. These areas are defined by the provinces and generally represent districts of responsibility for regional health boards. **Source:** _The Daily, June 15, 2004 © Statistics Canada_

Dietary Practices by Age and Sex,[1] 2003

	Total Number 2003	Consume fruits and vegetables less than 5 times per day		**Consume fruits and vegetables 5 to 10 times per day**		Consume fruits and vegetables more than 10 times per day		Fruit and vegetable consumption not stated	
		Number	%	**Number**	**%**	Number	%	Number	%
Total, 12 years and over	26 578 125	14 668 191	55.2	**9 369 778**	**35.3**	980 031	3.7	1 560 124	5.9
Males	13 090 299	8 025 140	61.3	**3 816 954**	**29.2**	402 195	3.1	846 010	6.5
Females	13 487 826	6 643 051	49.3	**5 552 824**	**41.2**	577 837	4.3	714 115	5.3
12–19 years	3 316 567	1 686 079	50.8	**1 199 952**	**36.2**	194 933	5.9	235 604	7.1
Males	1 700 772	899 150	52.9	**558 124**	**32.8**	104 227	6.1	139 271	8.2
Females	1 615 795	786 929	48.7	**641 827**	**39.7**	90 706	5.6	96 333	6.0
20–24 years	2 166 912	1 256 173	58.0	**701 638**	**32.4**	114 784	5.3	94 317	4.4
Males	1 111 860	692 938	62.3	**307 997**	**27.7**	53 264	4.8	57 661	5.2
Females	1 055 052	563 235	53.4	**393 640**	**37.3**	61 520	5.8	36 656	3.5
25–34 years	4 150 865	2 431 894	58.6	**1 413 302**	**34.0**	167 653	4.0	138 016	3.3
Males	2 054 636	1 335 564	65.0	**572 224**	**27.9**	69 277	3.4	77 571	3.8
Females	2 096 229	1 096 330	52.3	**841 078**	**40.1**	98 376	4.7	60 445	2.9
35–44 years	5 296 597	3 184 513	60.1	**1 743 674**	**32.9**	173 399	3.3	195 011	3.7
Males	2 671 810	1 787 692	66.9	**702 320**	**26.3**	59 964	2.2	121 834	4.6
Females	2 024 787	1 396 821	53.2	**1 041 354**	**39.7**	113 435	4.3	73 177	2.8
45–54 years	4 571 406	2 655 184	58.1	**1 593 717**	**34.9**	123 711	2.7	198 794	4.3
Males	2 240 920	1 476 517	65.9	**617 697**	**27.6**	44 261	2.0	102 445	4.6
Females	2 330 486	1 178 667	50.6	**976 020**	**41.9**	79 450	3.4	96 349	4.1
55–64 years	3 290 633	1 756 331	53.4	**1 239 535**	**37.7**	106 203	3.2	188 564	5.7
Males	1 650 676	1 009 674	61.2	**503 845**	**30.5**	37 208	2.3	99 949	6.1
Females	1 639 957	746 657	45.5	**735 690**	**44.9**	68 995	4.2	88 615	5.4
65–74 years	2 182 159	1 036 901	47.5	**873 384**	**40.0**	63 986	2.9	207 889	9.5
Males	1 030 238	549 213	53.3	**344 863**	**33.5**	23 109	2.2	113 052	11.0
Females	1 151 922	487 688	42.3	**528 520**	**45.9**	40 876	3.5	94 837	8.2
75 years +	1 602 986	661 116	41.2	**604 577**	**37.7**	35 363	2.2	301 930	18.8
Males	629 388	274 392	43.6	**209 884**	**33.3**	10 885	1.7	134 227	21.3
Females	973 598	386 724	39.7	**394 693**	**40.5**	24 478	2.5	167 702	17.2

Source: © *Statistics Canada*
(1) Population aged 12 and over by the average number of times per day that they consume fruit and vegetables.

Canadians with Diabetes[1] by Age Group and Sex, 2003

Statistics Canada has been tracking the number of Canadians diagnosed by a health professional as having diabetes since 1994. In 2003, an average of 4.6 percent of Canadians aged 12 or older had developed diabetes. The figure varies with age and gender: 2.1 percent of those 35 to 44 had been diagnosed with diabetes, while 12.7 percent of seniors 75 and over had the disease. Between men and women, 5.2 percent of men aged 45 to 54 had diabetes, compared to only 4.1 percent of women, and 14 percent of men over 75 had diabetes, compared to 11.8 percent of women.

There were no big provincial differences among the population with diabetes. The prevalence of diabetes for all provinces ranged between 3 and 5 percent.

Age Group & Sex	Total population[2]	With diabetes[3]		Without diabetes	
		Number	%[3]	Number	%
Total, 12 years and over	26 578 125	1 222 882	4.6	25 331 210	95.3
Males	13 090 299	645 215	4.9	12 431 966	95.0
Females	13 487 826	577 666	4.3	12 899 244	95.6
■ 12–19 years	3 316 567	11 262	0.3	3 303 619	99.6
Males	1 700 772	6 562	0.4	1 693 249	99.6
Females	1 615 795	4 700	0.3	1 610 370	99.7
■ 12–14 years	1 275 076	3 132	0.2	1 271 217	99.7
Males	664 241	2 057	0.3	661 828	99.6
Females	610 835	...	...	609 389	99.8
■ 15–19 years	2 041 491	8 130	0.4	2 032 402	99.6
Males	1 036 531	4 505	0.4	1 031 422	99.5
Females	1 004 960	3 625	0.4	1 000 981	99.6
■ 20–34 years	6 317 776	51 633	0.8	6 261 249	99.1
Males	3 166 496	23 176	0.7	3 140 703	99.2
Females	3 151 281	28 457	0.9	3 120 547	99.0
■ 20–24 years	2 166 912	11 768	0.5	2 152 740	99.3
Males	1 111 860	...	...	1 103 411	99.2
Females	1 055 052	5 377	0.5	1 049 330	99.5
■ 25–34 years	4 150 865	39 865	1.0	4 108 509	99.0
Males	2 054 636	16 785	0.8	2 037 292	99.2
Females	2 096 229	23 080	1.1	2 071 217	98.8
■ 35–44 years	5 296 597	112 782	2.1	5 180 297	97.8
Males	2 671 810	48 397	1.8	2 621 825	98.1
Females	2 624 787	64 385	2.5	2 558 472	97.5
■ 45–64 years	7 862 039	536 813	6.8	7 315 640	93.1
Males	3 891 595	309 469	8.0	3 577 251	91.9
Females	3 970 443	227 344	5.7	3 738 389	94.2
■ 45–54 years	4 571 406	210 234	4.6	4 355 188	95.3
Males	2 240 920	115 527	5.2	2 122 751	94.7
Females	2 330 486	94 707	4.1	2 232 437	95.8
■ 55–64 years	3 290 633	326 579	9.9	2 960 452	90.0
Males	1 650 676	193 942	11.7	1 454 500	88.1
Females	1 639 957	132 636	8.1	1 505 952	91.8
■ 65 years and over	3 785 145	510 392	13.5	3 270 404	86.4
Males	1 659 626	257 612	15.5	1 398 937	84.3
Females	2 125 520	252 780	11.9	1 871 467	88.0
■ 65–74 years	2 182 159	307 612	14.1	1 871 813	85.8
Males	1 030 238	169 283	16.4	858 839	83.4
Females	1 151 922	138 328	12.0	1 012 974	87.9
■ 75 years and over	1 602 986	202 780	12.7	1 398 591	87.2
Males	629 388	88 329	14.0	540 098	85.8
Females	973 598	114 451	11.8	858 493	88.2

Source: © *Statistics Canada*
(1) Population aged 12 and over who report that they have been diagnosed by a health professional as having diabetes.
(2) Includes non-responses. (3) Includes data deemed unreliable.

Canadians with Low Incomes,[1] 1998

Statistics Canada defines the "low-income cut off" as spending 20 percent more of income on food, shelter and clothing than the average Canadian (see Average Household Expenditure on pages 71 and 72). In general, families and individuals with low incomes spend more than 55 percent of their income on those three items. While these are not official poverty lines and have no status as such, they do indicate the number of Canadians living in less than affluent circumstances.

Low incomes are not spread evenly across the country: in PEI, 12.7 percent of the popula-tion is below the low-income cut-off; the number is 22.1 percent in Quebec. The rest of the provinces fall in between. Children and seniors are more likely to live in low-income situations; mother-led, lone-parent families are much more likely to fall below the low-income cut-offs than almost any other group. The level of educational attainment (not shown here) also plays a role in determining income. Families headed by people who did not graduate from high school are twice as likely to fall below the low-income cut-offs.

	Canada	N&L	PEI	NS	NB	Que	Ont	Man	Sask	Alta	BC
POPULATION WITH LOW INCOMES (000s)	5 055.9	108.7	17.2	168.3	117.3	1 620.1	1 603.7	218.3	160.0	458.1	584.2
As a % of total population	16.9	20.0	12.7	18.2	15.8	22.1	14.0	20.0	16.3	15.9	15.0
% of Population with Low Income by age											
Under 18	19.2	25.3	n.a.	19.3	18.1	24.0	17.7	23.6	18.8	17.3	14.9
18-64	15.5	18.7	n.a.	18.1	15.0	20.0	12.6	17.4	14.8	15.2	14.3
65 and over	19.7	n.a	n.a.	17.0	15.4	29.9	14.4	25.4	18.3	16.8	18.7
% of Population with Low Income by sex											
Men	15.3	18.7	n.a.	14.5	14.2	20.1	12.7	17.3	13.9	15.1	14.0
Women	18.4	21.3	n.a.	21.8	17.2	24.1	15.3	22.6	18.7	16.7	15.9
% of Population with Low Income											
Aboriginal peoples	28.9	n.a.	n.a.	n.a.	n.a.	36.3	22.1	41.6	27.4	25.7	27.8
Immigrants	18.6	n.a.	n.a.	n.a.	n.a.	44.0	13.3	19.7	n.a.	17.6	16.4
People in a visible minority	24.3	n.a.	n.a.	n.a.	n.a.	56.1	16.7	n.a.	n.a.	27.0	18.1
FAMILIES WITH LOW INCOME											
% of two-parent families with children	10.7	16.2	n.a.	7.6	9.5	13.8	9.3	13.2	10.8	11.3	8.2
% of lone-parent families, male head	23.1	n.a.	n.a.	n.a.	n.a.	n.a.	n.a.	36.5	n.a.	n.a.	n.a.
% of lone-parent families, female head	52.9	68.6	n.a.	74.3	59.8	56.6	50.5	66.6	40.1	46.5	49.4
% of families with head aged 65 and over	9.7	n.a.	n.a.	n.a.	n.a.	15.6	6.9	14.4	6.3	n.a.	9.5
UNATTACHED INDIVIDUALS WITH LOW INCOME											
Men under 65	33.0	44.9	35.7	34.3	41.2	39.3	30.1	37.6	32.9	32.6	25.8
Women under 65	43.6	66.5	45.9	58.5	44.7	48.6	36.3	53.1	42.6	45.3	41.4
Men over 65	35.1	n.a.	n.a.	n.a.	n.a.	44.3	32.3	39.5	30.1	28.3	36.5
Women over 65	47.9	66.5	38.0	50.4	49.4	63.0	38.4	51.6	41.0	46.2	42.8

Source: © *Statistics Canada*
(1) Statistics Canada defines those with Low Income as those who usually spend more than 55% of their income on food, shelter and clothing. Base year is 1992.

EDUCATION

Canadian Population[1] by Highest Level of Schooling, 2001

(percentage)

	Elementary–Secondary Schooling Only	Post secondary, Non-university Education	University Without a Degree	University With a Degree
Canada..........................	**41.8**	**34.3**	**11.3**	**19.6**
Newfoundland & Labrador..............	48.7	34.4	10.9	12.4
Prince Edward Island..................	45.2	34.8	12.3	15.1
Nova Scotia........................	41.5	35.3	13.3	18.0
New Brunswick......................	49.1	31.7	11.7	14.4
Quebec............................	46.9	32.8	6.8	18.6
Ontario............................	39.9	33.9	12.0	21.4
Manitoba..........................	45.8	31.7	14.0	16.7
Saskatchewan......................	46.0	32.5	15.2	15.4
Alberta............................	37.7	38.3	12.5	18.8
British Columbia....................	36.6	36.7	15.0	20.9
Yukon Territory.....................	29.0	45.7	2.4	26.7
Northwest Territories................	38.3	40.6	10.1	17.0
Nunavut..........................	48.5	39.7	4.8	10.0

Source: © *Census of Canada, Statistics Canada*   (1) Population aged 20 years and over only.

Labour Force[1] by Highest Level of Schooling

	2002			2003		
	Population[2] (000s)	% of Pop. by educational attainment	Participation rate[3]	Population[2] (000s)	% of Pop. by educational attainment	Participation rate[3]
Total, all education levels ..	24 945.1	100	66.9	25 250.7	100.0	67.5
0–8 years.............	2 361.4	9.5	25.1	2 305.9	9.1	26.0
Some high school	4 228.4	17.0	52.3	4 038.5	16.0	52.9
High school diploma.....	4 862.6	19.5	71.7	4 857.6	19.2	71.0
Some post-secondary ...	2 278.1	9.1	69.3	2 446.2	9.7	69.6
Post-secondary certificate or diploma	7 150.8	28.7	77.2	7 277.0	28.8	78.0
University degree.......	4 063.8	16.3	81.2	4 325.7	17.1	80.5
Bachelor's degree.....	2 794.4	11.2	81.4	2 983.6	11.8	80.6
Above bachelor's degree	1 269.4	5.1	80.7	1 342.1	5.3	80.4

Source: *copyright Statistics Canada*
(1) Employed workers and those who are unemployed but actively seeking work. (2) Age 15 years and over. (3) Participation rate is the percent of that population segment that has been able to find work.

Elementary-Secondary Enrolment[1] by Province

(thousands)

	Canada	N&L	PEI	NS	NB	Que	Ont	Man	Sask	Alta	BC	YT	NWT	NVT
1999-2000..	4 862.8	88.9	24.4	150.5	120.0	1 027.1	1 862.8	205.4	193.6	530.9	636.2	5.8	9.4	7.7
2000-01....	4 867.3	85.7	24.4	149.7	118.3	1 024.4	1 858.9	206.4	193.3	536.1	646.2	6.0	9.6	7.9
2001-02....	4 864.9	82.7	24.3	149.1	116.7	1 022.2	1 848.8	207.4	192.9	541.6	655.1	6.0	9.8	7.9

Source: © *Statistics Canada*   (1) Estimates, including public, private, federal and overseas schools.

University Qualifications Granted by Field of Study[1], by Sex

	1995–96	1996–97	1997–98	1998–99	1999–2000
Canada.	178 120	173 935	172 075	173 575	175 555
Male.	75 110	73 045	71 940	72 200	72 765
Female.	103 010	100 890	100 135	101 375	102 790
Social sciences	67 860	66 665	67 020	66 990	67 775
Male.	29 030	28 420	27 990	28 300	28 245
Female.	38 830	38 245	39 030	38 690	39 530
Education.	29 790	27 810	25 955	26 765	27 015
Male.	8 695	8 040	7 565	7 740	7 735
Female.	21 095	19 770	18 390	19 025	19 280
Humanities.	22 355	21 370	20 815	20 445	20 150
Male.	8 275	8 035	7 590	7 420	7 315
Female.	14 080	13 335	13 225	13 025	12 835
Health professions and occupations	12 900	13 075	12 660	12 705	11 935
Male.	3 520	3 460	3 515	3 295	3 210
Female.	9 380	9 615	9 145	9 410	8 725
Engineering and applied sciences	13 065	12 765	12 830	12 685	13 235
Male.	10 445	10 125	10 120	9 905	10 045
Female.	2 620	2 640	2 710	2 780	3 190
Agricultural and biological sciences	11 400	11 775	12 205	12 535	12 435
Male.	4 755	4 780	4 775	4 810	4 770
Female.	6 645	6 995	7 430	7 725	7 665
Mathematics and physical sciences	9 785	9 740	9 990	10 460	11 250
Male.	6 725	6 750	6 875	7 200	7 595
Female.	3 060	2 990	3 115	3 260	3 655
Fine and applied arts	5 205	5 205	5 260	5 200	5 335
Male.	1 780	1 705	1 735	1 740	1 715
Female.	3 425	3 500	3 525	3 460	3 620
Arts and sciences.	5 760	5 530	5 340	5 790	6 425
Male.	1 885	1 730	1 775	1 790	2 135
Female.	3 875	3 800	3 565	4 000	4 290

Source: © *Statistics Canada*
(1) Includes bachelor's and first professional degrees, undergraduate diplomas and certificates, other undergraduate qualifications, master's degrees, doctoral degrees, and graduate diplomas and certificates.

Community College Diplomas in Career Programs[1], by Sex

	1994–95	1995–96	1996–97	1997–98	1998–99
Canada.	72 520	79 545	85 910	91 345	88 415
Male.	30 275	33 835	36 310	38 445	37 230
Female.	42 245	45 710	49 600	52 900	51 185
Business and commerce	20 980	22 055	23 325	24 475	22 760
Male.	6 600	7 285	7 725	8 150	7 550
Female.	14 380	14 770	15 600	16 325	15 210
Engineering and applied sciences	14 720	16 245	18 280	20 095	21 255
Male.	12 150	13 510	14 975	16 160	16 965
Female.	2 570	2 735	3 305	3 935	4 290
Social sciences and services	14 290	15 565	16 780	17 720	18 655
Male.	3 940	4 070	4 120	4 230	4 195
Female.	10 350	11 495	12 660	13 490	14 460
Health sciences	11 025	11 625	11 620	11 575	10 980
Male.	2 045	2 275	2 165	1 985	1 745
Female.	8 980	9 350	9 455	9 590	9 235
Arts	5 965	6 375	7 190	7 475	7 815
Male.	2 515	2 765	2 965	3 110	3 240
Female.	3 450	3 610	4 225	4 365	4 575
Natural sciences & primary industries	3 705	4 225	4 820	5 005	4 795
Male.	2 365	2 570	2 880	2 890	2 705
Female.	1 340	1 655	1 940	2 115	2 090
Humanities.	1 160	1 175	1 235	1 395	995
Male.	350	385	375	380	300
Female.	810	790	860	1 015	695
Arts and sciences.	540	1 805	2 530	3 350	800
Male.	240	785	1 055	1 385	330
Female.	300	1 020	1 475	1 965	470
Discipline not known	55	110	80	145	115
Male.	55	70	40	95	55
Female.	40	40	50	60	
Not reported.	80	365	50	110	245
Male.	15	120	10	60	145
Female.	65	245	40	50	100

Source: © *Statistics Canada*   (1) Includes related institutions such as hospital schools, agricultural colleges and other specialized colleges and other specialized colleges.

Expenditures on Education, by Education Level, 1999–2000

($ millions)

	Canada	N&L	PEI	Nova Scotia	New Brunswick	Quebec	Ontario
All expenditures[1]	67 696.7	1 116.4	267.8	1 963.6	1 602.5	15 953.7	25 429.8
LEVEL							
Elementary and secondary	39 309.4	569.3	142.3	1 079.6	885.9	8 530.3	15 773.0
Community college	5 467.9	34.2	21.0	102.7	63.9	2 020.0	1 923.2
University	14 549.0	271.7	57.8	605.8	340.7	3 516.8	5 364.2
Vocational training	8 370.4	241.2	46.7	175.4	312.0	1 886.6	2 369.4
DIRECT SOURCE OF FUNDS							
Federal government[2]	5 567.6	149.1	31.3	172.4	136.9	1 264.5	1 536.5
Provincial governments	39 502.8	807.0	187.7	1 244.1	1 256.4	11 017.9	13 634.1
Municipal governments[3]	10 800.0	0.1	0.0	147.6	0.0	1 023.8	5 825.3
Fees and other sources	11 826.3	160.2	48.8	399.5	209.2	2 647.6	4 433.9

	Manitoba	Saskatchewan	Alberta	British Columbia	Yukon	Northwest Territories	Nunavut
All expenditures[1]	2 694.1	2 419.2	6 918.5	8 702.3	122.0	167.1	175.9
LEVEL							
Elementary & secondary	1 751.2	1 383.4	3 891.4	4 994.4	80.4	85.4	118.2
Community college	104.9	61.2	550.1	521.5	7.6	33.8	20.5
University	540.3	591.7	1 379.8	1 790.9	3.7	4.9	0.8
Vocational training	297.7	382.8	1 097.1	1 395.4	30.4	43.1	36.3
DIRECT SOURCE OF FUNDS							
Federal government[2]	405.4	426.3	573.0	663.7	14.5	15.2	15.9
Provincial governments	1 309.3	1 109.0	3 515.1	5 034.4	100.7	139.2	148.1
Municipal governments[3]	602.1	597.3	1 301.9	1 291.4	0.4	0.9	9.1
Fees and other sources	377.3	286.6	1 528.4	1 712.7	6.5	11.8	2.7

Source: © Statistics Canada

((1) Includes operating, capital, student aid and all departmental expenditures. (2) In addition to the direct funding reported here, the federal government also provides indirect support in respect of post secondary education to provinces and territories under the Federal-Provincial Fiscal Arrangements and Federal Post-secondary Education and Health Contributions Act, 1977 and under the Official Languages in Education Program. (3) Includes local school taxation.

Education Spending: Where the Money Goes

*T*otal *school board expenditures and expenditures per student in public elementary-secondary education rose 2.1 percent in 1999 (in current dollars). This was the largest annual increase in school board expenditures and expenditures per student since 1992. (In comparison, the Consumer Price Index (CPI) rose only 1.8 percent in 1999.) School boards spent $32.3 billion in 1999, representing 3.3 percent of the gross domestic product (GDP). This continued a downward trend that started after 1992, when spending by school boards peaked at 4.3 percent of GDP.*

From 1994 to 1997, expenditures per full-time equivalent student remained relatively stable at about $6,850 in current dollars. In 1998, they started to rise, reaching over $7,100 in 1999. Expenditures per student increased in 1999 in every jurisdiction except Ontario, British Columbia and the Northwest Territories. For Canada as a whole, average expenditures per student increased about 4 percent in the last five years, compared with an increase of 6 percent in the CPI for the same period. (The expenditures per pupil include all public elementary and secondary education-related expenditures.)

Expenditures by school boards account for about 80 percent of total elementary and secondary education spending. (And teachers' salaries make up over 60 percent of those expenditures.) Other categories of elementary and secondary expenditures include private schools, federal schools, special education schools and departmental expenditures by the ministries of education. About 95 percent of school board revenues come from provincial or territorial governments and local taxation.

School board expenditures include both operating and capital spending. Operating expenditures are salaries, benefits, supplies and services, fees and contractual services, and other operating costs. These expenses can be further broken down by function (instruction, administration, transportation, school facilities and other categories). **Source:** *The Daily, July 23, 2002 © Statistics Canada*

RELIGION

Major Religious Groups in Canada, 1991 and 2001[1]

	1991		2001		Percentage change
	Number	%	Number	%	1991–2001
Roman Catholic	12 203 625	45.2	12 793 125	43.2	4.8
Protestant	9 427 675	34.9	8 654 845	29.2	-8.2
Christian Orthodox	387 395	1.4	479 620	1.6	23.8
Christian, not included elsewhere[2]	353 040	1.3	780 450	2.6	121.1
Muslim	253 265	0.9	579 640	2	128.9
Jewish	318 185	1.2	329 995	1.1	3.7
Buddhist	163 415	0.6	300 345	1	83.8
Hindu	157 015	0.6	297 200	1	89.3
Sikh	147 440	0.5	278 415	0.9	88.8
No religion	3 333 245	12.3	4 796 325	16.2	43.9

Source: © *Statistics Canada*
(1) For comparability purposes, 1991 data are presented according to 2001 boundaries.
(2) Includes persons who report Christian, as well as those who report Apostolic, Born-again Christian and Evangelical.

Changes in Religious Practice

■ Canada still predominantly Roman Catholic and Protestant

Seven out of every ten Canadians identify themselves as either Roman Catholic or Protestant, according to new data from the 2001 census.

The census showed a continuation of a long-term downward trend in the population who report Protestant denominations. The number of Roman Catholics increased slightly during the 1990s, but their share of the total population fell marginally.

At the same time, the number of Canadians who reported religions such as Islam, Hinduism, Sikhism and Buddhism has increased substantially.

Much of the shift in the nation's religious make-up during the past several decades is the result of the changing sources of immigrants, which has contributed to a more diverse religious profile. As well, many major Protestant denominations that were dominant in the country 70 years ago, such as Anglican and United Church, are declining in numbers, in part because their members are aging and fewer young people are identifying with these denominations.

In 2001, Roman Catholics were still the largest religious group, drawing the faith of just under 12.8 million people, or 43 percent of the population, down from 45 percent in 1991. The proportion of Protestants, the second largest group, declined from 35 percent of the population to 29 percent, or about 8.7 million people.

Combined, the two groups represented 72 percent of the total population in 2001, compared with 80 percent a decade earlier.

The 2001 census also recorded an increase in those reporting simply that they were "Christian," without specifying a Catholic, Protestant or Christian Orthodox faith. This group more than doubled (+121 percent) during the decade to 780,400, representing 2.6 percent of the population in 2001. This was one of the largest percentage increases among all major religious groups.

In addition, far more Canadians reported in the 2001 census that they had no religion. This group accounted for 16 percent of the population in 2001, compared with 12 percent a decade earlier.

Respondents in the 2001 census were instructed to report a specific denomination or group, even if they were not practising members of their group. Consequently, these data indicate only religious affiliation. Other data sources, principally Statistics Canada's General Social Survey, are available as measures of attendance at religious services.

The census collects information on religious affiliation only, regardless of whether respondents actually practice their religion. Data on the frequency of attendance at religious services have been collected by Statistics Canada's General Social Survey since 1986. The survey samples adults aged 15 and over living in private households in the ten provinces.

According to GSS data, attendance at religious services has fallen dramatically across the country over the past 15 years. Nationally, only one-fifth (20 percent) of individuals aged 15 and over attended religious services on a weekly basis in 2001, compared with 28 percent in 1986. In 2001, four in ten adults (43 percent) reported that they had not attended religious services during the 12 months prior to the survey, compared with only 26 percent in 1986.

GSS data showed that religious attendance is influenced by factors including demographics, immigration patterns and cultural background.

■ Roman Catholics: the largest religious group in Canada

Between 1991 and 2001, the number of Roman Catholics in Canada increased slightly, while the number adhering to Protestant denominations continued a long-term decline. The census enumerated just under 12.8 million Roman Catholics, up 4.8 percent, while the number of Protestants fell 8.2 percent to about 8.7 million.

For more than 100 years in Canada, Protestants outnumbered Catholics. In 1901, Protestant faiths accounted for well over one-half (56 percent) of the total population, compared with 42 percent for Roman Catholics.

This reflected immigration patterns at the time. Prior to 1961, most European immigrants came from the United Kingdom, Italy, Germany and the Netherlands.

However, by 1971, for the first time since Confederation, Catholics outnumbered Protestants as the sources of immigration to Canada began to change. In 1971, Roman Catholics represented 46 percent of the population, and Protestants 44 percent.

The proportion of Protestant faiths in the population has been declining since it peaked at 56 percent in 1921. The proportion of Roman Catholics peaked in 1971.

One reason for the recent growth among Roman Catholics was immigration. Of the 1.8 million immigrants who came to Canada between 1991 and 2001, Roman Catholics accounted for nearly one-quarter (23 percent) of this total, the highest proportion for any major religion among these recent arrivals.

While the proportion of immigrants of Roman Catholic faith entering Canada in the past 40 years has declined, they nevertheless have remained the largest religious denomination within each new wave of immigrants since the 1960s. Roman Catholics represented 39 percent of immigrants who came to Canada before 1961, increasing to 43 percent of those who arrived between 1961 and 1970. Immigrants of Roman Catholic faith represented about one-third of those who came during both the 1970s and 1980s.

■ Protestants still second largest major religion

Protestant denominations still comprised the second largest major religious group in 2001.

Most of the decline in Protestant denominations during the 1990s occurred within the six largest denominations. Only one of these groups recorded growth during the 1990s: Baptist, which increased 10 percent to 729,500.

The two major influences in the declines among the largest Protestant denominations have been immigration and the fact that there are fewer young people reporting these denominations. Many adherents of these faiths are descendants of European immigrants who arrived in Canada prior to 1961.

Since 1961, the proportion of immigrants entering Canada who were Protestant has declined steadily. Protestants represented four out of every 10 immigrants (39 percent) who came to Canada prior to 1961. This ratio declined to one in 10 (11 percent) among those who arrived during the 1990s.

Contributing to the decline of those reporting Protestant denominations was the increase during the decade among those reporting simply "Christian," as well as the increase in those reporting no religion.

■ Growth in Islam, Hinduism, Sikhism and Buddhism

The largest gains in religious affiliations occurred among faiths consistent with changing immigration patterns toward more immigrants from regions outside of Europe, in particular Asia and the Middle East.

Among this group, those who identified themselves as Muslim recorded the biggest increase, more than doubling from 253,300 in 1991 to 579,600 in 2001. These individuals represented 2 percent of the total population in 2001, up from under 1 percent a decade earlier.

The number of people who identified themselves as Hindu increased 89 percent to 297,200. Those who identified themselves as Sikh rose 89 percent to 278,400, while the number of Buddhists increased 84 percent to about 300,300. Each represented around 1 percent of the total population.

Immigration was a key factor in the increases for all these groups. The proportion of immigrants entering Canada with these religions increased with each new wave of arrivals since the 1960s. Of the 1.8 million new immigrants who came during the 1990s, Muslims accounted for 15 percent, Hindus almost 7 percent and Buddhists and Sikhs each about 5 percent.

In terms of age, each of these religions had relatively young populations. The median age of Muslims was 28 years, Sikhs 30, and Hindus 32, all well below the median of 37 for the overall population.

Ontario was home to 73 percent of the Hindu population in 2001, 61 percent of all Muslims, and 38 percent of all Sikhs. Nearly one-half of the Sikh population lived in British Columbia.

■ An increase among Orthodox Christians

Just over 479,600 people identified themselves as members of a Christian Orthodox religion in the 2001 census, a 24 percent increase from 1991. They represented 1.6 percent of the total population, up slightly from 1.4 percent in 1991.

About 215,200 people identified themselves as members of the Greek Orthodox Church, a 7 percent decline from 1991. At the same time, the number of Ukrainian Orthodox adherents declined 5 percent to 32,700. The median age for both groups was older than for the total population, 41 years for Greek Orthodox and 46 years for Ukrainian Orthodox.

The census enumerated just over 20,500 members of the Serbian Orthodox faith, up from just under 10,000 in 1991, and about 15,600 members of the Russian Orthodox, up from 6,600 in 1991. These increases are likely a result of increased immigration to Canada over the past decade from countries of the former Yugoslavian and Soviet republics.

In addition, the number of people reporting their religion as simply "Orthodox" increased during the past decade, contributing to the overall increase in the number of people of Orthodox faith in 2001.

■ Slight increase in Jewish faith

The number of individuals who identified themselves as Jewish increased 3.7 percent during the 1990s to nearly 330,000.

They accounted for 1.1 percent of the population in 2001, virtually unchanged during the decade. Well over one-half of these individuals, about 190,800, lived in Ontario.

According to the census, nearly one-third (31 percent) of people of Jewish faith in 2001 were born outside Canada. However, Jewish people accounted for only 1 percent of the 1.8 million immigrants who came to Canada during the 1990s.

CRIME AND JUSTICE

Selected Criminal Code Incidents by Province, 2002

	Canada	N&L	PEI	NS	NB	Que	Ont
Population[1]	31 629 677	519 570	137 781	936 025	750 594	7 487 169	12 238 300
Homicide *Actual incidents*	548	5	1	8	8	100	178
Rate per 100,000 population	1.7	1.0	0.7	0.9	1.1	1.3	1.5
Percentage change in rates[2]	-6.6	149.9	-0.6	-11.3	-11.2	-15.8	-1.2
Sexual Assault *Actual incidents*	23 425	496	142	889	645	4 326	7 682
Rate per 100,000 population	74.1	95.5	103.1	95.0	85.9	57.8	62.8
Percentage change in rates[2]	-5.2	-10.2	-4.0	-4.2	-13.6	3.8	-9.2
Assault, levels 1 to 3 *Actual incidents*	236 103	4 098	1 020	9 304	6 079	37 657	73 246
Rate per 100,000 population	746.5	788.7	740.3	994.0	809.9	503.0	598.5
Percentage change in rates[2]	-0.7	2.8	2.1	8.7	2.6	-1.0	-6.4
Robbery *Actual incidents*	28 332	64	18	623	206	6 952	9 567
Rate per 100,000 population	89.6	12.3	13.1	66.6	27.4	92.9	78.2
Percentage change in rates[2]	5.4	-20.1	-0.6	11.1	-9.7	0.7	6.0
Total, crimes of violence							
Actual incidents	304 515	4 845	1 236	11 220	7 442	53 373	95 948
Rate per 100,000 population	962.8	932.5	897.1	1 198.7	991.5	712.9	784.0
Percentage change in rates[2]	-0.7	1.3	1.2	7.3	0.3	-0.7	-5.4
Breaking and Entering *Actual incidents*	284 496	3 824	1 033	7 665	5 337	67 346	81 661
Rate per 100,000 population	899.5	736.0	749.7	818.9	711.0	899.5	667.3
Percentage change in rates[2]	2.4	10.0	5.2	16.2	10.7	-4.8	-1.1
Motor Vehicle Theft *Actual incidents*	171 017	656	273	2 709	1 761	36 981	46 549
Rate per 100,000 population	540.7	126.3	198.1	289.4	234.6	493.9	380.4
Percentage change in rates[2]	4.7	11.9	11.3	3.1	12.4	-0.5	-0.4
Frauds *Actual incidents*	92 838	1 166	393	2 698	2 532	17 198	33 038
Rate per 100,000 population	293.5	224.4	285.2	288.2	337.3	229.7	270.0
Percentage change in rates[2]	0.3	1.4	-10.6	11.0	6.9	-7.3	-2.8
Property crimes *Actual incidents*	1 303 569	13 565	4 957	34 206	22 770	244 757	396 655
Rate per 100,000 population	4 121.4	2 610.8	3 597.7	3 654.4	3 033.6	3 269.0	3 241.1
Percentage change in rates[2]	3.7	4.9	9.0	8.1	6.8	-2.1	0.2
Impaired operation of motor vehicle, boat or aircraft *Actual incidents*	77 038	950	607	2 447	2 104	18 373	19 056
Rate per 100,000 population	243.6	182.8	440.6	261.4	280.3	245.4	155.7
Percentage change in rates[2]	4.6	-4.0	10.7	3.5	-10.7	-6.9	-8.6
Total drug offenses *Actual incidents*	85 953	819	264	2 266	2 290	19 417	22 475
Rate per 100,000 population	271.8	157.6	191.6	242.1	305.1	259.3	183.6
Percentage change in rates[2]	-8.1	-9.2	-23.3	-4.4	-12.6	-3.4	-24.1
Total, all Criminal Code offences, including traffic *Actual incidents*	2 688 097	33 631	12 593	82 953	56 307	508 516	779 619
Rate per 100,000 population	8 498.7	6 472.9	9 139.9	8 862.3	7 501.7	6 791.8	6 370.3
Percentage change in rates[2]	5.1	3.3	9.8	10.3	5.9	6.2	0.4 ▶

▶	Man	Sask	Alta	BC	YK	NWT	NVT
Population[1]	1 162 776	994 843	3 153 723	4 146 580	31 060	41 872	29 384
Homicide *Actual incidents*	43	41	63	93	1	4	3
Rate per 100,000 population ...	3.7	4.1	2.0	2.2	3.2	9.6	10.2
Percentage change in rates[2]	18.7	52.0	-11.1	-26.8	0.0	-1.1	46.7
Sexual Assault *Actual incidents* .	1 504	1 381	2 405	3 424	65	176	290
Rate per 100,000 population ...	129.4	138.8	76.3	82.6	209.3	420.3	986.9
Percentage change in rates[2]	0.6	-7.6	-8.5	-2.0	-31.5	-3.3	-7.9
Assault, levels 1 to 3 *Actual incidents*	14 829	16 678	27 227	40 481	1 028	2 532	1 924
Rate per 100,000 population ...	1 275.3	1 676.5	863.3	976.3	3 309.7	6 047.0	6 547.8
Percentage change in rates[2]	-1.7	12.0	1.6	0.4	3.9	19.9	11.2
Robbery *Actual incidents*	1 753	1 427	3 210	4 443	33	27	9
Rate per 100,000 population ...	150.8	143.4	101.8	107.2	106.3	64.5	30.6
Percentage change in rates[2]	6.7	33.3	20.7	-4.2	10.4	27.2	-2.2
Total, crimes of violence							
Actual incidents...............	18 906	20 466	34 696	50 025	1 180	2 844	2 334
Rate per 100,000 population ...	1 625.9	2 057.2	1 100.2	1 206.4	3 799.1	6 792.1	7 943.1
Percentage change in rates[2]	-0.7	11.0	2.0	-0.3	1.3	18.5	9.0
Breaking and Entering *Actual incidents*	14 122	17 279	30 692	52 949	565	1 003	1 020
Rate per 100,000 population ...	1 214.5	1 736.9	973.2	1 276.9	1 819.1	2 395.4	3 471.3
Percentage change in rates[2]	11.3	14.2	11.1	4.3	2.6	9.2	16.1
Motor Vehicle Theft *Actual incidents*	12 913	7 763	20 868	39 729	190	381	244
Rate per 100,000 population ...	1 110.5	780.3	661.7	958.1	611.7	909.9	830.4
Percentage change in rates[2]	5.9	12.2	14.7	9.5	-17.4	11.5	17.6
Frauds *Actual incidents*	2 447	4 216	13 846	14 905	130	188	81
Rate per 100,000 population ...	210.4	423.8	439.0	359.5	418.5	449.0	275.7
Percentage change in rates[2]	-6.2	0.9	3.6	13.2	-5.9	44.2	-11.0
Property crimes *Actual incidents* ..	64 899	65 784	161 490	287 036	2 305	3 023	2 122
Rate per 100,000 population ...	5 581.4	6 612.5	5 120.6	6 922.2	7 421.1	7 219.6	7 221.6
Percentage change in rates[2]	12.4	14.1	9.5	5.9	0.6	18.4	15.2
Impaired operation of motor vehicle,							
boat or aircraft *Actual incidents* .	3 001	5 508	12 310	11 719	263	520	180
Rate per 100,000 population ...	258.1	553.7	390.3	282.6	846.8	1 241.9	612.6
Percentage change in rates[2]	-8.2	-7.3	-0.2	3.0	-18.5	14.1	35.4
Total drug offences *Actual incidents*	2 619	3 214	7 496	24 199	288	355	251
Rate per 100,000 population ...	225.2	323.1	237.7	583.6	927.2	847.8	854.2
Percentage change in rates[2]	-3.1	-7.6	-1.7	6.3	-27.5	-6.3	-3.7
Total, all Criminal Code offences,							
including traffic *Actual incidents*	148 722	162 850	339 579	528 441	8 380	16 067	10 439
Rate per 100,000 population ...	12 790.3	16 369.4	10 767.6	12 744.0	26 980.0	38 371.7	35 526.1
Percentage change in rates[2]	10.2	11.2	7.2	6.0	-2.8	13.4	18.5

Source: *copyright Statistics Canada, Uniform Crime Reporting Survey, Canadian Centre for Justice Statistics*
(1) Population estimates as of July 1, 2003. (2) In comparison to the previous year.

Rates of Criminal Code Incidents in Canada[1]

	1992	1993	1994	1995	1996	1997
Population[2] (000)................	28 366.7	28 681.7	28 999.0	29 302.1	29 610.8	29 907.2
Violent Crime Rate...............	1084.06	1081.52	1047.43	1009.15	1002.16	992.71
Annual % change	2.33	-0.23	-3.15	-3.65	-0.69	-0.94
Property Crime Rate	5904	5575.12	5257.14	5292.2	5274.47	4880.22
Annual % change	-4.16	-5.57	-5.57	0.67	-0.33	-7.47
Other Criminal Code Rate	3051.8	2881.24	2820.6	2707.07	2655.58	2602.52
Annual % change	-2.26	-5.59	-2.1	-4.03	-1.9	-2
Total Criminal Code Rate[3]	10039.86	9537.88	9125.17	9008.42	8932.2	8475.45
Annual % change	-2.92	-5	-4.33	-1.28	-0.85	-5.11

	1998	1999	2000	2001	2002	2003
Population[2] (000)................	30 157.1	30 403.9	30 689.0	31 021.3	31 361.6	31 629.7
Violent Crime Rate...............	982.08	958.19	984.38	983.8	969.17	962.75
Annual % change	-1.07	-2.43	2.73	-0.06	-1.49	-0.66
Property Crime Rate	4569.08	4275.71	4080.89	4003.5	3974.54	4121.35
Annual % change	-6.38	-6.42	-4.56	-1.9	-0.72	3.69
Other Criminal Code Rate	2609.96	2517.85	2601.2	2668.14	2764.58	3048.27
Annual % change	0.29	-3.53	3.31	2.57	3.61	10.26
Total Criminal Code Rate[3]	8161.12	7751.74	7666.48	7655.43	7708.29	8132.37
Annual % change	-3.71	-5.02	-1.1	-0.14	0.69	5.5

Source: *Uniform Crime Reporting Survey, Canadian Centre for Justice Statistics © Statistics Canada*
(1) Rates are calculated per 100,000 people. (2) Population estimates as of July 1. (3) Does not include traffic violations.

Persons Charged, by Age

	Adults charged		Youths charged	
	2002	2003	2002	2003
Homicide	443	421	42	56
Attempted murder	499	524	59	69
Sexual assault..............	7 547	6 954	1 620	1 450
Assault, levels 1 to 3.........	96 598	94 472	16 876	14 731
Other sexual offences........	656	626	157	133
Abduction.................	131	108	5	1
Robbery	6 900	7 004	3 292	3 127
Total, crimes of violence	**121 130**	**118 415**	**23 153**	**20 664**
Breaking and entering........	19 702	19 788	11 327	11 158
Motor Vehicle Theft	8 280	8 558	5 536	4 949
Theft over $5,000...........	1 999	1 990	292	284
Theft under $5,000..........	54 280	56 493	18 617	12 307
Total, property crimes......	**123 006**	**126 922**	**43 177**	**35 092**
Fraud	20 781	20 731	1 719	1 409
Prostitution................	3 583	3 441	41	40
Offensive weapons	6 340	6 567	1 558	1 506
Arson	819	782	556	576
Counterfeiting currency	810	1 165	179	285
Mischief	14 263	13 783	7 050	5 561
Impaired operation of motor vehicle, causing death.............	98	137	n/a	n/a
Impaired operation of motor vehicle, causing bodily harm........	931	885	n/a	n/a
Cocaine...................	10 015	11 332	489	500
Cannabis..................	33 681	25 983	7 447	4 463
Total, drug offences	**48 301**	**41 922**	**8 510**	**5 533**
Total, Criminal Code, excluding traffic	**399 481**	**405 089**	**98 681**	**84 482**

Source: *© Statistics Canada, Uniform Crime Report Survey, Canadian Centre for Justice Statistics*
(1) Adults are defined as people age 18 and over, Youth between the ages of 12 and 17. (2) Data based on Homicide Survey.
(3) Includes impaired operation of a vehicle causing death, causing bodily harm, alcohol rate over 80 mg., failure/refusal to provide a breath/blood sample.

The National Anthem: O Canada

The music of *O Canada* was composed by Calixa Lavallée and the lyrics were written in French by Adolphe-Basile Routhier in Quebec City. Originally called *Chant National*, it was first performed at a banquet in Quebec City on June 24, 1880. The anthem grew in popularity in Quebec but was not heard in English until the early 1900s. There have been several English versions of the work, the most popular of which was written in 1908 by Robert Stanley Weir. In 1967 a Special Joint Committee of the Senate and the House of Commons was formed to recommend official versions of Canada's National and Royal Anthems. With a few minor changes, the official English version of *O Canada* is based on Weir's lyrics. On June 27, 1980, the House of Commons passed Bill C-36 designating both the music and lyrics of *O Canada* as Canada's national anthem. It was proclaimed July 1, 1980.

O Canada

O Canada! Terre de nos aïeux,

Ton front est ceint de fleurons glorieux!

Car ton bras sait porter l'épée,

Il sait porter la croix!

Ton histoire est une épopée

Des plus brillants exploits,

Et ta valeur, de foi trempée,

Protégera nos foyers et nos droits,

Protégera nos foyers et nos droits.

O Canada

O Canada! Our home and native land!

True patriot love in all thy sons command.

With glowing hearts we see thee rise,

The True North strong and free!

From far and wide, O Canada,

We stand on guard for thee.

God keep our land glorious and free!

O Canada, we stand on guard for thee.

O Canada, we stand on guard for thee!

The National Flag

The National Flag was adopted by Parliament December 15, 1964, and proclaimed by Queen Elizabeth II. It was inaugurated on February 15, 1965.

It is a red flag of the proportions two by length and one by width, containing in its centre a white square, the width of the flag, bearing a single, red, stylized maple leaf. The maple leaf has been looked upon as an emblem of Canada since the early 1700s. Red and white were declared Canada's official colours by King George V on November 21, 1921.

The National Flag is to be flown daily at all federal government buildings, airports and military bases and establishments within and outside Canada. When flown with other flags, it should be given a place of honour.

The National Coat of Arms

The creation of coats of arms dates back to the Middle Ages. Centuries ago few could read, nor did they have access to print material, pictures or the other means we now use to identify people. Heraldry was developed as a form of picture-writing, used to create visual emblems that identified individuals or members of a community or nation, particularly in battle.

Over time, such symbols became quite sophisticated; a coat of arms could identify not only the individual but tell if his father was still alive, his birth order, whether or not he was married and the prestige of his branch of the family. In war, the device was painted on a shield; in peace, it would be embroidered on a coat or banner. Because of its significance, heraldry came to be carefully regulated; colleges of arms controlled the grant and use of them.

At the time of Confederation, Canada did not have a coat of arms and used the Royal Arms of the United Kingdom to identify the offices of the Government of Canada. By 1868, however, a Great Seal was required and the government adopted a design that was also used as the Arms of Canada. The design showed the emblems of the original four provinces of the federation—Nova Scotia, New Brunswick, Quebec and Ontario—on a shield. When new provinces joined the federation, their emblems were added to the shield and the design became fragmented and confusing as the provinces multiplied. In 1919, the governor general convened a special committee to study the question of a Canadian coat of arms; a request for a grant of arms was later submitted to the sovereign.

Canada's Coat of Arms was granted by a royal proclamation of King George V on Nov. 21, 1921. Although simplified in 1957 and augmented in 1994, the coat of arms we have now is faithful to that original design.

The most important part of the design is the shield, which shows the emblems of the four founding peoples (English, Scottish, Irish and French) with an added sprig of distinctly Canadian maple leaves. The shield is supported on one side by the lion of England holding the Royal Union flag and the unicorn of Scotland holding a banner of royalist France on the other. A royal helmet and mantle sit above the shield, with a crest showing a royal lion holding a maple leaf on top of the helmet. (The crest is the symbol used on the governor general's standard.) The imperial crown above the crest represents the monarch as Canada's head of state.

Below the shield is Canada's motto, *A Mari usque ad Mare* (From sea to sea) which is based on a verse from Psalm 72 of the Bible: "He shall have dominion from sea to sea and from the river unto the ends of the earth." Around the shield is a ribbon with the motto of the Order of Canada: "Desiderantes Meliorem Patriam" (They desire a better country). The floral emblems of the four founding nations are found at the base of the design: the English rose, the Scottish thistle, the French fleur-de-lis and the shamrock of Ireland.

Canada's coat of arms represents national sovereignty and is used on federal government property such as buildings, official seals, money, passports, proclamations and publications as well as on badges of some members of the armed forces. This national symbol is protected from unauthorized commercial use by the Trade Marks Act.

CANADIAN HISTORY

■ Exploration and First Settlements

The first people who came to North America arrived during the last Ice Age, which began about 80,000 years ago and ended about 12,000 years ago. These Native People were hunters who crosssed from Asia via a land bridge that is now submerged beneath the Bering Sea. Although there is continuing debate among archeologists as to how early humans might have settled in what is now Canada, the earliest accepted occupation site is at the Bluefish Caves in the Yukon; artifacts at least 12,000 to 17,000 years old have been found there. As the glaciers of the Ice Age retreated, human settlements spread across Canada and gradually, these first Canadians developed lifestyles based on the environments in which they lived. They obtained their food by hunting, fishing, gathering, and in the case of Eastern Woodland tribes, by farming. By the time explorers from Europe reached Canada, the Native People had well developed trading patterns, arts and crafts, languages, writing, religious beliefs, laws and government.

There has been much conjecture as to who the first Europeans to come to Canada were. The claim that an Irish monk, St. Brendan, arrived about the year 550 has not been proven. However, the theory that Vikings settled in Newfoundland was confirmed by archeological excavations at L'Anse aux Meadows during the 1960s and 1970s.

A burst of European exploration didn't take place until the Age of Discovery in the 15th and 16th centuries. Explorers found what they called a New World while in search of a route to the Far East. In 1497, Giovanni Caboto (John Cabot), an Italian sailing for England, landed on the Canadian coast, likely in Cape Breton or Newfoundland, and claimed the land for Henry VII of England. Although Cabot probably died on a second expedition in 1498, his voyages helped open up the rich fishing grounds of the Grand Banks.

European navigators and fishermen continued to visit the shores of Canada, but the first serious exploration of the area was undertaken by Jacques Cartier, who discovered the Gulf of St. Lawrence while searching for a passage to Asia, in 1534. The next year he travelled up the St. Lawrence River as far as the native settlements of Stadacona (Quebec) and Hochelaga (Montreal). On this voyage, Cartier picked up the Iroquoian word for village, Kanata (thought to be the origin of "Canada"), and used it to apply to the whole region he had discovered. Cartier's discoveries gave France a claim to Canada and led to the first French settlements.

In 1541–42, Cartier and the Sieur de Roberval established a short-lived settlement at Charlesbourg-Royal just above Quebec. In 1605, the Sieur de Monts and Samuel de Champlain established the colony of Port Royal in what is now Nova Scotia. Champlain went on to establish a settlement at Quebec in 1608, to explore the interior and to draw maps of New France. Champlain also started a fur-trading network (mostly in beaver pelts) with the Algonquins and the Hurons who inhabited the St. Lawrence and Great Lakes regions. This trade relationship became a military alliance as Champlain supported these groups against the Iroquois. This enmity between the French and the Iroquois prevailed throughout most of the history of New France.

Circa 1000   Leif Ericsson and other **Vikings** visit Labrador and Newfoundland.

1497   John Cabot (Giovanni Caboto) claims Cape Breton Island (or possibly Newfoundland or Labrador) for Henry VII of England (June 24).

1498   Cabot makes his second voyage to North America.

1534   Jacques Cartier visits the Strait of Belle Isle (Newfoundland), and charts the Gulf of St Lawrence (landing in Gaspé July 14).

1535   Cartier sails up the St Lawrence River to **Quebec** and **Montreal**.

1541   Cartier and the Sieur de Roberval found Charlesbourg-Royal, the **first French settlement** in America.

1577   Martin Frobisher of England makes the first of his three attempts to find a northwest passage, sailing as far as Hudson Strait.

1600   King Henry IV of France grants a **fur-trading monopoly** in the Gulf of St Lawrence to a group of French merchants.

1605   Samuel de Champlain and the Sieur de Monts found Port Royal (Annapolis, NS).

1608   Champlain founds Quebec.

1609 Champlain supports the Algonquins against the Iroquois at Lake Champlain.

1610 **Étienne Brûlé** goes to live among the Huron and eventually becomes the first European to see Lakes Ontario, Huron and Superior. **Henry Hudson** explores Hudson Bay.

1617 Louis Hébert, the **first habitant (farmer),** arrives in Quebec.

1625 Jesuits arrive in Quebec to begin missionary work among the Indians.

1627 The **Company of One Hundred Associates** is founded (Apr. 29) to establish a French empire in North America.

■ The Growth of New France (1627–1660)

The economic foundation of New France was the fur trade. In fact, the French kings were content to let fur-trading companies run the colony. Although these companies expanded the territory's boundaries, they failed to encourage settlement. One of King Louis XIII's most able advisers, Cardinal Richelieu, tried to remedy this problem by granting a fur-trading monopoly to the Company of One Hundred Associates in 1627, on condition that it bring out several hundred settlers each year. However, war between England and France broke out and Quebec was captured in 1629. Even after peace was restored in 1633, the Company of One Hundred Associates failed to honour its commitment to bring out settlers.

Despite the lack of settlers, the colony was expanding in other ways. As governor, Champlain encouraged the expansion of the fur trade. The Jesuits had arrived in 1625 and were vigorously pursuing their missionary work among the Hurons.

Champlain died in 1635, just two years after the colony was restored to France. No leader possessing his vision or drive emerged to replace him. Next, despite their conviction, the French missionaries made few converts among the native people. Even Sainte-Marie among the Hurons, their central mission-post, was abandoned in 1649 in the face of invasion by the Iroquois, who dispersed the Hurons and disrupted the French fur-trading network. Finally, the security of the centre of the fur trade, Montreal (founded in 1642), and the rest of the colony was threatened by the wars against the Iroquois. When the wars were renewed in 1659–1660, after a brief peace,

there were still only about 3,000 French settlers in the colony. Clearly, the French king would have to act to secure France's foothold in North America.

1629 **David Kirke** captures Quebec for Britain (July 19).

1632 The **Treaty of Saint-Germain-en-Laye** returns Quebec to France.

1634–40 The **Huron nation** is reduced by half from European diseases (smallpox epidemic, 1639).

1637 **Kirke** is named first governor of Newfoundland.

1642 **Montreal** is founded (May 18) by the Sieur **de Maisonneuve.**

1649 The Jesuit Father **Jean de Brébeuf** is martyred by the **Iroquois** at St-Ignace (Mar. 16). The Iroquois disperse the Huron nation (1648–49).

1659 **François de Laval,** later to become Canada's first bishop, arrives in Quebec (June).

1660 **Adam Dollard des Ormeaux** makes his last stand against the Iroquois at Long Sault (May). The small party of French fights so well that the Iroquois decide not to attack Montreal.

■ Royal Government in New France (1663–1700)

In 1663 King Louis XIV made New France a crown colony. Regular troops were sent out and undertook a successful campaign against the Iroquois, which resulted in the signing of a peace treaty in 1667. Several hundred of these regulars stayed on as settlers, thereby adding to the security of the colony. A system of government headed by a governor, an intendant and a bishop was instituted. The governor, who was the king's representative, was charged with defence. The intendant was responsible for industry, trade and administrative affairs. The bishop looked after religious matters, which included education. In theory, this system provided for a clear separation of powers; but, in practice, there were frequent disputes among the three officials. Still, this system survived intact for the remainder of the colony's history, and it provided New France with some remarkably dynamic officials. Two of these arrived in the first years of the Royal Government.

The first intendant of New France, Jean Talon (1665–1672), introduced innovative measures, including awards for early marriage, to boost the population. As well, he tried to build a diversified economy on the St. Lawrence by promoting crafts, farming and local industry. Few subsequent officials in New France shared Talon's concern for settlement or economic diversity. Most were more interested in profits from the fur trade. Count Frontenac, governor for all but seven years between 1672 and 1698, threw his support behind the fur trade, not only raising profits but also encouraging exploration. Under his rule, French adventurers explored the Mississippi River from its upper reaches to the Gulf of Mexico, greatly expanding the fur-trading boundaries of New France. Frontenac gained more fame when he withstood the attack of an English army which besieged Quebec in 1690.

But Frontenac had not only exceeded his powers in promoting territorial expansion, he had also undermined the security of the colony. With its limited population, New France now found itself competing for the fur trade with the more populous English colonies around them. In the north, there was rivalry with the Hudson's Bay Company, founded in 1670. To the south, there was border warfare between French fur traders and their Indian allies, and the English with their Iroquois allies. New France fared well in the limited warfare of the 1680s and 1690s; but in the 18th century there was a series of major wars which resulted in disaster for the colony.

1663   Quebec becomes a **royal province**.

1665   The Carignan-Salières regiment is sent from France to Quebec to deal with the Iroquois. **Jean Talon** becomes Quebec's intendant.

1666   Canada's **first census** counts 3,215 non-native inhabitants in 668 families.

1670   The **Hudson's Bay Company** is formed and granted trade rights over all territory draining into Hudson Bay (May 2).

1672   Count **Frontenac** becomes Governor of Quebec.

1673   **Marquette** and **Jolliet** explore the Mississippi to its junction with the Arkansas.

1674   **Laval** becomes first Bishop of Quebec.

1678–79 Dulhut explores the headwaters of the Mississippi.

1682   **La Salle** explores the Mississippi to its mouth.

1686   **De Troyes** and **D'Iberville** capture the English posts of Moose Fort (June 20), Rupert House (July 3) and Fort Albany (July 26) on James Bay.

1689   The Iroquois kill many French settlers at Lachine.

1690   **Sir William Phips captures Port Royal** (May 11). Frontenac repels Phips's attack on Quebec (Oct.).

1697   The **Treaty of Ryswick** restores the status quo in the struggle between England and France. All captured territory is returned.

■ The Collapse of New France (1701–1763)

In the early years of the 18th century, New France stretched from Hudson Bay to the Gulf of Mexico, and from Newfoundland to the Great Lakes. Its population was thinly scattered in the north, south and west but its fur-trading posts in these regions gave legitimacy to its territorial claims. In the Atlantic region, there were several hundred colonists in Newfoundland and another 1,500 in Acadia. The heartland of New France was the settlement of about 20,000 colonists in Montreal, Quebec and in the small communities along the St. Lawrence. The prosperity of the French settlements was to be hurt by long periods of war.

The first of these was the War of the Spanish Succession fought between France and Austria (and their allies) between 1701–1714. Although the British failed to capture their main objective in the North American campaign, the fortress city of Quebec, they made other gains at the bargaining table. In the Treaty of Utrecht, which ended the conflict, France gave up claims to the Hudson Bay territory, all of Acadia except Cape Breton, and Newfoundland.

During a 30-year period of peace, New France enjoyed limited prosperity. The populaton grew, farm yields increased, some industry was established and furs were still exported. But military expenditure necessary to protect the colony was turning it into a financial burden for France. Much of that expenditure went into the huge fortress of

Louisbourg, built on Cape Breton Island to protect the offshore fisheries and guard the St. Lawrence.

Prussia, France, Spain, Naples, Bavaria and Saxony fought Austria and England when the War of Austrian Succession broke out in 1740 and Louisbourg was a natural target. The fortress fell to the British, although it was returned to France at the war's end in 1748. The British established their own military and naval base at Halifax in 1749.

The fragile peace was broken in 1754, when fighting broke out between the English and French colonists in the Ohio Valley. Within two years, Britain and France were officially at war again in what became known as the Seven Years' War. Despite some early victories, the French suffered the loss of Louisbourg in 1758. In the following year, General Wolfe defeated General Montcalm on the Plains of Abraham above the St. Lawrence at Quebec. Although Montreal did not fall until the next year, the loss of Quebec was an irreversible setback. The British army occupied New France, and in 1763 the treaty ending the Seven Years' War confirmed British sovereignty.

New France had fallen because of decisive military defeats at Louisbourg and Quebec, but more significant was the inability of France to supply its colony in the face of British naval supremacy. The British were now masters in North America.

1701 The **War of the Spanish Succession** begins in Europe; the conflict spreads to North America the following year.

1710 Francis Nicholson captures Port Royal for England.

1713 The **Treaty of Utrecht** confirms British possession of Hudson Bay, Newfoundland and Acadia (except Cape Breton Island). France starts building Fort **Louisbourg**.

1739 **La Vérendrye** expedition explores Lake Winnipeg.

1740 The **War of the Austrian Succession** pits Britain against France; the European conflict spreads to North America (**King George's War**) in 1744.

1745 Massachusetts Governor William Shirley takes the French fortress of **Louisbourg**.

1748 Louisbourg is returned to France by the **Treaty of Aix-la-Chapelle**.

1749 Britain founds **Halifax** to counter the French presence at Louisbourg.

1752 Canada's **first newspaper**, the Halifax *Gazette,* appears (Mar. 25).

1753 **George Washington**'s military expedition to the Monogahela is defeated by the French.

1754 Beginning of **French and Indian War** in America. Although war is not officially declared for another two years, this marks the final phase in the struggle between France and Britain in North America.

1755 Britain expels the **Acadians** from Nova Scotia, scattering them throughout her other North American colonies.

1756 Beginning of the **Seven Years' War** in Europe pits Britain against France. The Marquis **de Montcalm** assumes command of French troops in North America.

1758 The British under Generals Amherst and Wolfe take Louisbourg.

1759 **Wolfe takes Quebec**, defeating Montcalm on the Plains of Abraham (Sept. 13). Both generals are killed.

1760 General **James Murray** is appointed military governor of Quebec; he becomes civil governor in **1764**.

■ The First Years of British Rule (1763–1812)

The British had been active on the continent during their search for a northwest passage to the far east; however, their victory over the French encouraged a shift from exploration and fur trading to settlement and the strengthening of British customs in the new territory.

In 1763 a Royal Proclamation was imposed by the British government on the newly acquired territories of New France. The intent of this proclamation was clear. By encouraging the establishment of Protestant schools, by promoting the Church of England, and by stipulating that an assembly be elected, the proclamation aimed at Anglicization. The intent was most visible in the matter of the assembly. Although the French inhabitants were in the majority, under British law no Roman Catholic could hold office. If an assembly were elected, a few hundred British settlers would control about 65,000 Canadiens.

Fortunately for the French in Canada, James Murray, the governor of Quebec from 1760 to 1768, felt that the loyalty of the French colonists could more likely be gained by fair treatment. Murray refused to call elections for the assembly, and allowed French legal practices to continue. Murray's sympathies provoked a storm of protest from the British colonists in Quebec and he was recalled. But his successor, Guy Carleton, also realized that the Royal Proclamation of 1763 would only alienate the recently defeated colonists. Carleton saw that even if Anglicization were carried out, few colonists from the Thirteen Colonies in America or immigrants from Britain would be lured to the rugged colony of Quebec. Consequently, Carleton advised the government in London to replace the proclamation with more liberal legislation.

The result was the Quebec Act of 1774, which dropped the assembly in favour of an appointed council on which Catholics might serve. As well, the French system of civil law and the seigneurial system of land tenure were both guaranteed. Finally, the Quebec Act expanded the borders of the colony to include the rich lands of the Ohio Valley. The British had acted to win the support of the Canadiens. In doing so, however, the British government angered the citizens of the Thirteen Colonies, who resented the special treatment given to their former enemies. These English colonists were especially upset over the loss of the Ohio Valley, a region into which they expected to expand.

The Quebec Act was not the only cause for complaint in the Thirteen Colonies. Protests over British taxation policies and trade restriction led to talk of revolution. That talk led to action, and in 1775 an invading American army took Montreal. Quebec held out against the American siege until relieved by British forces. Although there was some sympathy for the American cause in both Quebec and Nova Scotia, it was not a strong enough sentiment to cause these two colonies to join the revolution.

During and immediately after the American Revolution, some American colonists who wished to retain their British ties fled from the newly created United States into the Maritimes and Quebec. The arrival of about 30,000 of these Loyalists in Nova Scotia resulted in the creation of a new colony, New Brunswick, in 1784. Similarly, the influx of 10,000 Loyalists into Quebec led to division of the colony, and in 1791, the western part of

the colony became Upper Canada. The remainder of the old colony was known as Lower Canada.

Despite these changes, fur trading remained an important economic activity in the interior of British North America. In fact, there was keen rivalry for furs between the Hudson's Bay Company and the newly formed (1784) North West Company based in Montreal which led to a flurry of western exploration. Alexander Mackenzie, a partner in the North West Company, explored a river (now known as the Mackenzie) to its mouth on the Beaufort Sea in 1789, and found a route to the Pacific via the Fraser and Bella Coola Rivers in 1793. Two other North West Company employees, Simon Fraser and David Thompson, also carried out voyages of discovery. Fraser followed the river named after him to the Pacific in 1808, and Thompson travelled down the Columbia River to the coast in 1811. These voyages, along with the earlier coastal explorations of James Cook in 1778 and George Vancouver in 1792–1795, helped establish Britain's claim to the northwest part of the continent.

1763 France cedes its North American possessions to Britain by the **Treaty of Paris.** A Royal Proclamation imposes British institutions on Quebec (Oct.). This proclamation also serves as the cornerstone for relations between Canadian aboriginal peoples and the Canadian government, preserving land for their use and giving the government exclusive right to negotiate treaties.

1768 **Guy Carleton** succeeds Murray as governor of Quebec.

1769 Frances Brooke publishes *The History of Emily Montague*, a novel with descriptions of geography, climate and social culture in the New World.

1774 The **Quebec Act** provides for British criminal law but restores French civil law and guarantees religious freedom for Roman Catholic colonists.

1775 Americans under Montgomery capture Montreal (Nov.) and attack Quebec (Dec. 31).

1776 Under Carleton, Quebec withstands American siege until the appearance of a British fleet (May 6).

1778 Captain **James Cook** anchors in Nootka Sound, Vancouver Island (Mar. 29–Apr. 26).

1783 The American Revolutionary War ends; the border between Canada and the US is accepted between the Atlantic Ocean and Lake of the Woods.

1784 United Empire Loyalists arrive in Canada. The province of **New Brunswick** is created. The **North West Company** is formed.

1789 Alexander Mackenzie journeys to the Beaufort Sea, following what would later be named the Mackenzie River.

1791 Constitutional Act divides Quebec into Upper and Lower Canada.

1792 George Vancouver begins his explorations of the Pacific coast.

1793 Alexander Mackenzie reaches the **Pacific.**

1794 Jay's Treaty (Nov. 19) between the US and Britain promises British evacuation of the Ohio Valley forts. The treaty's appointment of officials to settle boundary disputes marks the beginning of international arbitration through its provisions for boundary settlements.

1797 David Thompson joins the North West Company as a surveyor and mapmaker.

1806 *Le Canadien*, Quebec nationalist newspaper, is founded.

1808 Simon Fraser, a North West Company employee, travels the river named after him to the Pacific.

1811 David Thompson charts the Columbia River to the Pacific coast.

■ **The War of 1812**

Although the British and Americans signed a peace treaty in 1783 to end the American War of Independence, there was still friction between them. One source of conflict was the British fur-trading posts in the Ohio Valley which now belonged to the United States. Although Britain surrendered these posts in 1796 as stipulated by Jay's Treaty (1794), there were still American complaints that the British were arming the local native people. At the same time there was growing American resentment over British interference with shipping. The British, who were at war with France, claimed the right to search American ships for cargoes bound for the enemy. In the process, the British often forced American

sailors on these ships to join the British navy. Resentment grew among Americans until June 1812, when the United States declared war on Britain.

In the first year of the war, the Americans under General William Hull crossed the Detroit River to invade Upper Canada. Hull expected Canadian sympathizers to flock to his cause but he was disappointed. Without fighting a major battle, he retreated to Detroit. British General Isaac Brock and the Shawnees, under Chief Tecumseh, moved against Detroit, and General Hull surrendered. This British and Canadian victory was followed by a victory at Queenston Heights on the Niagara River. Brock was killed in this battle, which nevertheless gave confidence to the defenders of the British colonies.

In 1813, the Americans carried out a successful raid on York (now Toronto), and also gained a foothold in the Niagara district. But by the summer of that year the Americans had been pushed back across the Niagara River by British victories at Stoney Creek and Beaver Dam. Meanwhile, the Americans were building up a large fleet on the Great Lakes, and in September 1813 the Americans won control of Lake Erie at the Battle of Put-in-Bay. This victory prompted the British under General Proctor to abandon Fort Malden on the Detroit River. However, the American General Harrison caught the retreating forces at Moraviantown on the Thames River and defeated Proctor. Tecumseh was killed in this battle. In the east, a two-pronged attack on Montreal was repulsed. The American invaders were defeated on the Chateauguay River and at Crysler's Farm near Cornwall in the fall of 1813.

In 1814, the Americans again invaded the Niagara district but were halted at the Battle of Lundy's Lane. From Halifax, British forces attacked targets in Maine, and occupied most of that state. Another attack from Halifax was launched on the American capital, Washington. The British raiders burned the government buildings there in retaliation for the destruction of York the previous year. Despite these successes, a major British offensive against Plattsburgh on Lake Champlain failed. By now the war was in stalemate and both sides were tired. British and American negotiators signed the Treaty of Ghent in Dec. 1814, to end the war.

In the aftermath of the war, the two sides made an effort to settle outstanding differences. The Rush-Bagot Agreement of 1817 provided for naval disarmament on the Great Lakes. In the following year Britain and the United States agreed to accept the 49th parallel as the international boundary from the Lake of the Woods to the Rocky Mountains. In addition, they agreed to the joint occupation of the Oregon Territory for 10 years.

1812 The US declares war on Britain (June 18), beginning the **War of 1812**. Americans under General William Hull invade Canada from Detroit (July 11). The Red River settlement is begun in Canada's northwest (Aug.–Oct.). Battle of Queenston Heights (Oct. 13): Canadian victory. British **General Isaac Brock** is killed in this battle.

1813 Americans burn York (Apr. 27). Battle of Stoney Creek (June 5): Canadian victory. Battle of Beaver Dams (June 23): Canadian victory; **Laura Secord**, driving a cow, passes American sentries and walks 32 km through dense bush to warn of American attack. Battle of Put-in-Bay, Lake Erie (Sept. 10): American victory. Battle of Moraviantown (Oct. 5): American victory; the Indian Chief **Tecumseh** is killed. Battle of Chateauguay (Oct. 25): Canadian victory. Battle of Crysler's Farm (Nov. 11): Canadian victory.

1814 Battle of Chippewa (July 5): American victory. Battle of Lundy's Lane (July 25): Canadian victory. A British naval force takes Washington (Aug. 24). Battle of Lake Champlain (Sept. 6–11): American victory. The **Treaty of Ghent** ends the War of 1812 (Dec. 24).

■ Rebellion and Reform (1814–1839)

In the years after the War of 1812, there was considerable growth in British North America. The population increased as immigrants from both the United States and Britain arrived to take up land that was free or inexpensive. The economy became more diversified as lumbering, farming and ship-building developed in the Canadas and in the Maritimes. Finally, a sense of nationalism began to grow in parts of British North America. This feeling arose partly out of postwar patriotism and partly out of the shared experiences of a demanding colonial life.

As the colonies became more populous, political interest increased. In both the Canadas and the Maritimes friction between ruling elites and the ordinary colonists developed and was partially fuelled by the form of government in each colony. British governors or lieutenant-governors picked their own officials, including the members of legislative or executive councils. There were elected assemblies in each colony, but their powers were limited. Legislation might pass in the assembly but be turned down by the legislative council. The assemblies, the voice of the people, found themselves frustrated by the power of appointed officials.

By the mid-1830s, economic distress increased the discontent that had been building during the 1820s. In Lower Canada, where cultural prejudice against the Canadiens added to the tension, Louis Joseph Papineau emerged as leader of the radical Patriote Party. When the colonial authorities would not grant the reforms called for by Papineau and his followers, rebellion broke out in November 1837. But loyalist forces quickly defeated the badly organized and poorly led rebels. Papineau and other leaders fled to the United States.

In Upper Canada, the reform movement was able to gain a majority in the assembly in several elections. Still, the reformers could not turn their program into legislation because of Tory control of the Legislative Council. When an anti-reform lieutenant-governor, Sir Francis Bond Head, took over in 1836, some reformers became more radical. Their leader was William Lyon Mackenzie, a newspaper editor and member of the assembly. The Tories won the election of 1836, when Head directly intervened in the campaign. Mackenzie and his followers, spurred on by events in Lower Canada, took up arms in early December 1837. Mackenzie's disorganization, and lack of widespread support among the colonists, doomed the rebellion. After a skirmish north of Toronto the main body of rebels fled. An uprising in the western districts of Upper Canada was equally unsuccessful. Throughout the following year some rebels and American sympathizers mounted raids on Upper Canada from the United States, but these received no popular support.

In the aftermath of the rebellions came political change. The British government sent out Lord Durham to act as Governor General of British North America and investigate the rebellion. The Durham Report of 1839 contained two main recommendations: the first called for the union of Upper and Lower Canada as a first step in the eventual assimilation of the French Canadians; the second recommended the granting of responsible government (in which the executive is responsible to the assembly), a key demand of reformers.

1816 Agents of the North West Company kill Robert Semple, governor of the Hudson's Bay Company's Red River colony, and 21 others at White Oaks (June 19).

1817 The **Rush-Bagot** agreement limits the number of battleships on the Great Lakes.

1818 The **49th parallel** is accepted as **Canada's border** with the US from Lake of the Woods to the Rocky Mountains.

1821 The Hudson's Bay Company and the North West Company are amalgamated as the HBC.

1829 The **Lachine** and **Welland Canals** are completed.

1835 **William Lyon Mackenzie** becomes the first mayor of Toronto.

1836 Opening of Canada's **first railway line**, from St. Johns, Que., to La Prairie, Que.

1837 Unsuccessful **rebellions** in Upper and Lower Canada are led by Mackenzie and Louis-Joseph Papineau.

1839 **Lord Durham's Report** recommends union of Upper and Lower Canada and the establishment of responsible government.

■ The Road to Confederation (1840–1867)

The middle years of the 19th century were both satisfying and disturbing for British North Americans. Immigrants from Europe streamed into the colonies, more land was cleared and towns grew. Local industries were started while lumbering and ship-building activities increased. Montreal and Toronto became commercial centres and the ports of the Maritimes were prosperous, fuelled by shipbuilding and trade. Transportation improved as roads, canals and, by the 1850s, railways were built. Some British North Americans looked beyond their borders and began to think of a federation of British colonies that included not only Canada and the Maritimes, but the Red River settlement and the colonies in British Columbia.

Despite the prosperity, there were reasons to consider such an alliance. Until the mid-1840s, the colonies had enjoyed a preferential trading relationship whereby Britain reduced tariffs on colonial products. This advantage was lost in 1846 when Britain adopted free trade. At first, the colonies found some advantage in entering into a limited free trade arrangement with the United States. But the Americans allowed this Reciprocity Treaty of 1854 to lapse in 1866. British North Americans would have to look to themselves as trading partners.

There was also concern in British North America about the United States. That country seemed intent on fulfilling its "Manifest Destiny" to take over North America. The threat was especially clear during and after the American Civil War (1861–65). During the war, the Northern States were angered by British support for the South, and after the war, there was a fear that the large Northern army might march into British territory.

As well, there was a serious political problem in the colony of Canada. The union of Upper and Lower Canada in 1841 had resulted in the creation of a single legislature for the new colony, Canada. By the 1860s, however, this legislature was barely functioning. No single party could gain enough support from both Francophones and Anglophones to gain a majority. There had been 12 different governments in 15 years, and Canadian politicians were desperate for a solution.

Three powerful figures in Canada's legislature, John A. Macdonald, George Brown and George-Étienne Cartier formed a coalition and proposed a larger union of British North America as a way to end the political deadlock. In addition, this proposal would solve the problem of trade and provide security against the American threat. Meanwhile, on the East Coast there was interest in a union too, a union of the Maritimes. A conference had been called for Charlottetown in September 1864 to discuss that topic. When the leaders of the new Canadian coalition heard of this meeting, they asked for an invitation. At Charlottetown the British North American delegates decided on a federation of all the colonies. A second conference at Quebec in October 1864 resulted in a plan for federal union. A federal government would control defence, trade and other matters of national interest. Provincial governments would have power over local matters such as roads and education. The final details were hammered out at another conference in London, England, in 1866.

The British government, which supported this colonial initiative, passed the British North America Act in March 1867. On July 1, 1867, the provinces of Nova Scotia, New Brunswick, Ontario (formerly Canada West) and Quebec (formerly Canada East) became the Dominion of Canada.

1841 The **Act of Union** unites Upper and Lower Canada.

1842 The Ashburton-Webster Treaty settles the Maine–New Brunswick border dispute.

1843 **Fort Victoria** is built to bolster Britain's claim to Vancouver Island.

1846 Great Britain ends a preferential trading policy with the British North American colonies and enters into a **limited free trade agreement** with the United States.

1848 **Responsible government** is achieved in the Canadas and in the Maritimes, thanks to the work of **Robert Baldwin** and **Joseph Howe**.

1849 The boundary of the 49th parallel is extended to the Pacific Ocean. The province of Canada adopts both English and French as official languages. All bills of the United Canada Parliament, now Quebec and Ontario, are given assent in both English and French.

1851 Britain transfers control of the colonial postal system to Canada.

1854 The **Reciprocity Treaty** between Canada and the US is signed (June 6).

1857 **Ottawa** is named **Canada's capital** by Queen Victoria.

1860 Cornerstone of the **Parliament Buildings** is laid (Sept. 1).

1861 The **Grand Trunk Railway** through the length of the Province of Canada is completed.

1864 The **Charlottetown Conference** (Sept. 1–9) takes the first steps toward **Confederation**. The **Quebec Conference** (Oct. 10–27) sets out the basis for union.

1866 The **London Conference** (Dec. 4) passes resolutions which are redrafted to become the **British North America Act**. First raid into Canada by the **Fenians**, a radical Irish-American anti-British group, takes place (June 2). The American government allows the **Reciprocity Treaty of 1854** to lapse.

1867 **Confederation**. Britain's North American colonies are united by means of the **BNA Act** to become the **Dominion of Canada** (July 1). **Sir John A. Macdonald** is Canada's first prime minister. The BNA Act, now the **Constitution Act, 1867**, confirms the practice of **official bilingualism**, guaranteeing the use of French and English in the debates of the House of Commons and in the Senate, in federal courts and in publications of federal statutes. The provincial legislature, statutes and courts of Quebec are also made bilingual.

■ The Nation Expands (1867–1885)

Soon after the Confederation of Ontario, Quebec, New Brunswick and Nova Scotia in 1867, the new nation of Canada began to acquire more territory. In 1869, guided by the national vision of Prime Minister John A. Macdonald, the federal government bought Rupert's Land from the Hudson's Bay Company. This was a huge territory which included most of modern Manitoba, as well as parts of Saskatchewan, Alberta and the Northwest Territories. The few Ontario immigrants in the Red River Settlement there welcomed this move; but the far more numerous Métis (descendants of French fur traders and native people) were suspicious, especially because they had not been consulted beforehand. When newly appointed Lieutenant-Governor William McDougall tried to enter the settlement before the territory had officially been transferred to Canada, the Métis turned him back. In the absence of a legitimate government, the Métis, under their leader Louis Riel, seized Fort Garry on the Red River and proclaimed a provisional government. The Métis demanded the right to vote, land laws, the official use of both French and English, and the provision of both Roman Catholic and Protestant schools. The Métis list of rights became the terms for negotiating Manitoba's entry into Confederation in 1870.

In the same year, representatives from the colony of British Columbia arrived in Ottawa to discuss union. With the promise from Ottawa to build a transcontinental railway, British Columbia entered Confederation in 1871. Canada now stretched from sea to sea, but the work of nation building was still not complete.

In 1868, Nova Scotia elected an anti-Confederation provincial government and sent a delegation, led by veteran politician Joseph Howe, to London to seek a repeal of the union. But Britain was unsympathetic, and in 1869 Macdonald seized the opportunity to offer Nova Scotia better terms and Howe a cabinet position. With the Nova Scotia situation resolved, Macdonald turned his attention to Prince Edward Island. The Islanders were more attracted to the idea of union after an expensive railway project nearly bankrupted the colony. Macdonald agreed to assume the colony's debts, offered a cash subsidy and promised a steamer service to the mainland. In 1873, Prince Edward Island agreed to the terms and became Canada's seventh province.

In the 1870s and 1880s railways were built to link the provinces of the new nation. The Intercolonial Railway, joining central Canada to the Maritimes, was completed in 1876, but construction of a rail link to British Columbia ran into several delays. First, Macdonald's government was defeated in 1873 over charges of corruption associated with the railway project. The new prime minister, Alexander Mackenzie, refused to fund railway projects because the country was in the midst of a depression. However, after Macdonald's re-election in 1878, railway building began in earnest. In February 1881, the Canadian Pacific Railway Company (CPR) was incorporated, and in November 1885 the last spike was driven at Craigellachie in British Columbia to complete the link to the Pacific.

Even before it was fully completed, the CPR was used to carry troops to quell a rebellion in the spring of 1885. Trouble had started several years earlier when settlers in the North-West Territory (modern Alberta and Saskatchewan) complained to the government about land titles, shipping rates, and their lack of an elected government. Among those who complained were the Métis, some of whom had moved farther west after the Red River troubles of 1870. When the federal government was slow to respond, the Métis, again under Louis Riel, rose up in March 1885 against the territorial council appointed by Ottawa. By late April, 5,000 Canadian soldiers, who had travelled by the new railway, were on the march against Riel and his Métis and native followers. At the Battle of Batoche in May, the forces of General Middleton defeated the rebels. Riel was found guilty of treason by an English-speaking jury and executed.

1868 Confederationist **Thomas D'Arcy McGee** is **assassinated** by a Fenian in Canada's first political assassination.

1869 Canada purchases Rupert's Land from the Hudson's Bay Company for £300,000.

1870 **Louis Riel** leads the Métis in resisting Canadian authority in Canada's northwest. The Métis negotiate with the Canadian government over the right to vote, land laws, the official use of both French and English and the provision of Roman Catholic and Protestant schools. The Manitoba Act creates the province of **Manitoba**.

1871 **British Columbia** joins Confederation upon the promise from Ottawa to build a **transcontinental railway**.

1872 Macdonald's Conservatives win federal re-election.

1873 **Prince Edward Island** joins Confederation. A period of economic depression begins. The North-West Mounted Police are formed. **Alexander Mackenzie** becomes Canada's second prime minister after **Macdonald resigns** over the **Pacific Scandal**.

1874 **Liberals** win federal election.

1875 The **Supreme Court of Canada** is established.

1876 The **Intercolonial Railway** linking central Canada and the Maritimes is completed (July 1). The **Indian Act of 1876** defines special status for aboriginal people living on land reserves and sets out land regulations. Status Indians have no vote in Canadian elections and are exempted from taxation.

1878 Conservatives under Macdonald win federal election.

1879 Macdonald introduces **protective tariffs** as part of his **National Policy**.

1880 **Emily Stowe** receives her medical licence after practising medicine in Toronto since her graduation from a New York medical school in 1867.

1881 The **Canadian Pacific Railway** is incorporated.

1884 **Riel returns** to Canada.

1885 Métis and the NWMP clash at Duck Lake (Mar. 26). The Métis are defeated at Batoche (May 9–12). The **last spike of the transcontinental railway** is driven at Craigellachie in Eagle Pass, BC, by Donald

Smith (Nov. 7). **Louis Riel** is **hanged** in Regina (Nov. 16).

1887 Conservatives win federal election. Liberals choose **Wilfrid Laurier** as leader. The **first provincial premiers' conference** takes place in Quebec City.

1889 The **Dominion Women's Enfranchisement Association** is created to campaign for female voting rights in Canada.

1890 Manitoba Liberals under Thomas Greenway halt public funding of Catholic schools in Manitoba (Mar.).

1891 Conservatives win federal election. **Sir John A. Macdonald dies**. Sir John Abbott takes office as prime minister (June 16).

1892 Abbott resigns (Nov. 24). **Sir John Thompson** becomes prime minister (Dec. 5). He establishes the **Canadian Criminal Code**.

1894 Thompson dies (Dec. 12). **Sir Mackenzie Bowell** is asked by the governor general, the Earl of Aberdeen, to form the fourth Conservative government since 1891.

■ The Laurier Era (1896–1911)

Conservative Prime Minister John A. Macdonald died in 1891, soon after winning a federal election. The Conservatives could not find a suitable successor and by 1896 there had been four prime ministers—John Abbott, John Thompson, Mackenzie Bowell and Charles Tupper. During this period, the Conservatives had to deal with a crisis over school legislation introduced in Manitoba. The Manitoba legislature had replaced the dual school system (both Protestant and Catholic schools) which had been guaranteed in the terms of union, with a single Protestant system. Francophone Catholics across Canada were already bitter about Louis Riel's execution. Now the Manitoba schools legislation convinced them that English Protestant Canadians wanted to stamp out French Catholic rights. Extremists on both sides inflamed the issue, and the Conservatives' inability to settle the matter hurt them in the election of 1896. The Liberals, under Wilfrid Laurier, formed a government.

Laurier settled the Manitoba school question by adopting a compromise approach. Religious instruction would be allowed within the single system, and instruction in French could take place where numbers warranted. The issue died down, but Laurier remained sensitive to the tensions between Anglophone Protestants and Francophone Catholics. Many English Canadians were swept up in a great wave of pro-imperial sentiment associated with the Diamond Jubilee of Queen Victoria. In Britain the event was seen as an opportunity to strengthen ties within the British Empire. Laurier acknowledged Canada's support for the Empire, but resisted proposals for a closer relationship with Britain and the other colonies. The prime minister did not wish to yield Canadian autonomy, nor did he wish to lose support in French Canada. The issue of Canada's role in the Empire came to a head in 1899 during the Boer War when the South African Republic (Transvaal) and the Orange Free State fought against Britain. Once again steering a middle course, Laurier agreed to equip and transport Canadian volunteers to South Africa, but sent no official troops. Although this compromise did not satisfy all Canadians, it avoided a bitter dispute. For a time, imperial issues were forgotten, as Canadians enjoyed boom times after the turn of the century.

Laurier summed up the nation's mood when he declared that the "twentieth century is Canada's century." Impressive growth in both industrial and agricultural production provided support for his words. Canada's prospects appealed to immigrants who flocked to the industrial cities and to the farmland of the Prairies. Many of them were attracted by an extensive government advertising campaign and by the lure of free land in the West. As a result of this influx, two new provinces, Alberta and Saskatchewan, were created in 1905. The immigrant tide boosted Canada's population from 5,371,315 in 1901 to 7,206,643 in 1911. The mood of the country was so confident that two new transcontinental railway building projects got under way in the early years of the century.

The international scene, however, was not so bright. In 1903, the British sided with the Americans in the Alaska Boundary Dispute, a disagreement over the international boundary near the Klondike gold fields. Canadians were dismayed, but Britain was less concerned about the Canadian claim than for the need to maintain good relations with the United States. Tension in Europe was increasing and Britain found itself outside of the complicated system of alliances which had developed there. This same concern led both the British government and the Canadian pro-imperialists to pressure

Laurier into providing money to build British warships. Again, Laurier staked out a middle position by introducing a Naval Service Act which created a Canadian navy that could help Britain where the need arose.

Laurier's compromise on naval policy satisfied neither side. Some French Canadians supported the views of Quebec nationalist Henri Bourassa who claimed Laurier had betrayed his people. Anglophone pro-imperialists complained that Laurier's "tin pot navy" was not enough. Canada's naval policy became an issue in the 1911 election, as did the Liberal plan for free trade with the United States. Conservative leader Robert Borden was able to use both to characterize Laurier as not only disloyal to Britain but favouring annexation to the United States. The Conservatives won the election. Borden became prime minister and Laurier stayed on as leader of the Opposition, continuing to advocate conciliatory policies when the interests of French and English Canadians clashed.

1896 The economic depression ends. Bowell resigns, calling his cabinet a "nest of traitors" (Apr. 27). **Sir Charles Tupper** leads an interim government until the Liberals under Laurier win federal election on **Manitoba Schools Question** (June 23). Canada's minister of the interior, **Clifford Sifton,** develops an immigration plan that will bring farmers from Central and Eastern Europe to settle on the Prairies. Gold is discovered in the Klondike (Aug. 16).

1897 **Gold Rush** begins in the Klondike. **Clara Brett Martin** is the first woman admitted to the bar of Ontario.

1898 **Yukon** becomes a separate entity from the Northwest Territories. **Kit Coleman,** the first female Canadian war correspondent, covers the Spanish-American War for a Toronto newspaper.

1899 The first **Canadian troops** ever sent overseas are dispatched to the **Boer War** (Oct. 30).

1901 Marconi receives the **first transatlantic radio message** at St. John's, Newfoundland.

1903 Canada loses the **Alaska Boundary Dispute** when British tribunal representative Lord Alverstone sides with the US (Oct. 20). In northern Ontario, Fred LaRose throws hammer at what he thinks are fox's eyes and hits world's richest silver vein.

1904 Liberals win federal election.

1905 The provinces of **Alberta** and **Saskatchewan** are formed.

1907 The **National Council of Women** calls for "equal pay for equal work."

1908 Liberals win federal election.

1909 The Department of External Affairs is formed. John McCurdy's Silver Dart is first heavier-than-air machine to achieve powered flight in Canada at Baddeck, NS. University of Toronto wins **first Grey Cup** football match.

1910 Laurier creates a Canadian navy via the Naval Service Bill.

1911 **Robert Borden** and the Conservatives win federal election, defeating Laurier on the reciprocity issue.

■ Canada and the First World War (1914–1918)

In August 1914, Britain declared war on Germany and Austria–Hungary. The declaration automatically applied to Canada, as part of the British Empire. At first, there was an enthusiastic response, especially among recent British immigrants. When the minister of militia, Sam Hughes, called for 25,000 volunteers, nearly 33,000 appeared. In 1915, when the government asked the Canadian public to buy $50 million in war bonds, they bought $100 million. But enthusiasm for war began to fade as the casualties mounted and the realities of trench warfare became known.

Canadian troops sailed for Europe in October 1914 and, after training in Britain, went into action at Ypres, Belgium, in April 1915. There they gained a reputation for courage, holding their positions in the face of a poison-gas attack, a new weapon at the time. Canadians took part in the costly battles at St. Eloi and Mont Sorrel in 1916. By the Battle of the Somme, in late summer of 1916, Canada had four army divisions in France; in the spring of 1917, all four were deployed in the attack on Vimy Ridge, which resulted in the first real Canadian victory of the war. But by now it was clear that every battle would result in terrible losses. At Passchendaele in October 1917, the Canadians sustained more than 15,000 casualties.

Voluntary recruitment could not keep pace with the high casualty rates. Prime Minister Borden was forced to consider conscription to draft soldiers into the army and took the question to the electorate in 1917, unleashing one of the most bitterly fought campaigns in Canadian history. In Quebec, Henri Bourassa rallied anti-conscription supporters and argued that Canada had done enough. In Ontario, Borden's supporters condemned French-Canadian anti-conscriptionists as traitors. For his part, Borden introduced the Wartime Elections Act to help secure victory. This act removed the right to vote from enemy aliens, even though some were Canadian citizens. It also gave the right to vote to women relatives of soldiers. In the election, Borden won in every province except Quebec where he was soundly rejected. Conscription had created a deep division between Quebec and the rest of Canada and once in practice, it had little impact on the course of the war. When the first 400,000 conscripts were called up, 90 percent of them appealed for exemption, and by the war's end only about 24,000 conscripts had reached the front.

While the conscription crisis raged at home, Canadian soldiers played a major role in the events leading to an Allied victory. They took part in the successful battle at Amiens in August 1918 and helped to roll the Germans back to Mons by November. The Canadians were still fighting at Mons when the armistice was signed Nov. 11, 1918.

Canadians also served with distinction in other theatres of war. By 1918, Canadians made up almost 25 percent of the pilots in Britain's Royal Flying Corps. Other Canadians served in the Royal Navy or on coastal patrol in Canada's own small navy. Some served in forestry corps overseas and others operated the railways behind the British lines. Some, including women, served as ambulance drivers at the front. Many Canadian women also played key roles as nurses overseas and in the munitions factories in Canada.

Canada's war effort won the country a place in the Imperial War Cabinet during the war, and a seat in the League of Nations afterwards. There were other benefits, too. Women's contributions to the war effort helped them win the right to vote in federal elections and in provincial elections in seven of the provinces by 1919. Yet these advances came at a terrible cost. Overseas, 68,300 Canadians had died. At home, bitterness over the conscription issue had created a division between French and English Canadians that would be remembered for decades.

1914   CP ship *Empress of Ireland* sinks in the St Lawrence in 14 minutes after being rammed in fog, with the loss of 1,014 lives (May 29). **Canada is automatically at war** with Germany when Britain declares war (Aug. 4). The first Canadian troops leave for England (Oct. 3). Parliament passes the **War Measures Act**, allowing suspension of civil rights during periods of emergency. European immigration to Canada increases. Over one million settlers come between 1911 and 1913, bringing total immigration to three million since 1891.

1915   Canadians face German gas attack at **Ypres,** Belgium (Apr. 22). John McCrae writes "In Flanders Fields."

1916   Nellie McClung succeeds in persuading the Manitoba government to grant women the right to vote and to hold office (Jan.). The Parliament Buildings are destroyed by fire (Feb. 3). Canadian troops fight in the Battle of the **Somme** (July to Nov.); 24,713 Canadians and Newfoundlanders are killed. The unreliable, Canadian-made Ross rifle is withdrawn from war service (Aug.). **Emily Gowan Murphy** is the first woman magistrate appointed within the British Empire.

1917   Income tax is introduced as a "temporary wartime measure." Prime Minister Sir Robert Borden sits as a member of the Imperial War Cabinet (Feb. 23), giving Canada a voice in war policy. The Military Service Bill is introduced (June 11), leading to the **Conscription Crisis** between Quebec and English Canada. Unionist government under Borden wins federal election, in which **women vote** for the first time. **Louise McKinney** is elected to the Alberta legislature, the first woman in the British Commonwealth to hold such office. Canadians capture **Vimy Ridge,** France (Apr. 9–12). Canadians take **Passchendaele,** Belgium, (Nov. 7) in one of the war's worst battles; of the 20,000 Canadian troops sent into the two-week battle, 15,654 are killed or wounded. Explosion of a munitions ship in **Halifax harbour** wipes out two square miles (5.2 sq. km) of Halifax, killing almost 2,000 and injuring 9,000 (Dec. 6).

1918   Canadians break through German trenches at Amiens (Aug. 8), "the black day of the German army." The period from this date until the end of the war becomes known as "Canada's Hundred Days." Armistice ends war (Nov. 11).

■ Canada in the 1920s

As the soldiers returned home, many expected to find a Canada ready to reward them for their sacrifices. What they found was a nation in the midst of painful postwar readjustment. Industry had to convert to peacetime production, but interest rates were so high investment capital was scarce. Jobs were hard to find and wages were low, and tariffs on imported goods kept prices high. By 1921, 300,000 men and women—more than 15 percent of the work force—were unemployed. Farmers, especially on the Prairies, also suffered. During the war, the West had become the world's breadbasket: wheat prices had soared and many farmers had borrowed heavily to expand their production. But with the war's end, world markets collapsed; wheat prices fell by almost half within two years.

These conditions, along with resentment over wartime profiteering by big business, created unrest. The One Big Union movement, centred in western Canada, attempted to create a single union to represent all workers. The Winnipeg General Strike of 1919 grew out of the organizers' efforts and the general discontent. Although the Winnipeg workers were striking over such issues as the right to collective bargaining, better wages and improved working conditions, the opponents of the general strike characterized it as a Communist conspiracy by raising the spectre of a revolution similar to the one in Russia two years earlier. The federal government sided with the anti-strike forces. Immigration laws were amended to deport "alien" labour radicals, the strike leaders were arrested and the Royal North West Mounted Police fired into a rioting crowd on June 21, 1919—"Bloody Sunday"—killing one and wounding 30. The six-week strike was over and so was the growth of labour unions. In 1919 alone there were more than 400 strikes, but after the Winnipeg General Strike, the federal government and most governments at the provincial level opposed union activities. Throughout the 1920s there was a decline in union membership.

The reasons for unrest and discontent varied from region to region in the 1920s. The government takeover of five financially troubled railways had led to the creation of the Canadian National Railways in 1919, and railway rates in the Maritimes were raised 40 percent to bring them up to central Canadian levels. Angry over the rail rates and feeling that Ottawa was making decisions on the basis of central Canada's interests, many Maritimers protested by forming the Maritimes Rights movement, aimed at winning transportation concessions and federal subsidies. At the same time it promoted regional rights and pride.

Canadian farmers, resentful over low prices for farm products, high rail rates and high prices for manufactured goods, formed the United Farmers' movement. United Farmers' parties won provincial elections in Ontario in 1919, in Alberta in 1921, and in Manitoba in 1922. At the federal level, the Progressive Party embraced some of the program of the United Farmers' movement. The Progressives called for free trade, nationalization (especially in the case of railways) and more direct democracy (such as the use of a referendum to decide a controversial issue). Although they were a new party, the Progressives were to play an important role in politics in the 1920s.

The election of 1921 marked new directions in Canadian politics. Both major parties had new leaders: Arthur Meighen had replaced Borden as prime minister; William Lyon Mackenzie King had taken over as Liberal leader after Laurier's death. Of even greater significance was that for the first time, Canadians could vote for one of three parties at the federal level: the Liberals, the Conservatives or the Progressives. The Liberals won the 1921 election, but the Progressives finished second and formed the Opposition. Their position in the House of Commons was even more important after the 1925 election in which the Conservatives under Meighen won the most seats, but King remained in power by claiming the support of the Progressives. After 1925 the Progressives declined, and many of their supporters voted Liberal in King's 1926 election victory. But the influence of the Progressive movement was felt as King's government, anxious to keep their support, passed Canada's first Old Age Pension Act in 1927.

In foreign affairs, King made sure that Canada played a cautious role in the League of Nations, because he feared that Canada would be drawn into international disputes. In imperial matters, his insistence on autonomy contributed to a redefinition of the empire at the Imperial Conference of 1926. There it was acknowledged that Canada and the other British dominions were autonomous even in their external affairs. As a result, by 1929, Canada had diplomatic posts in Washington, Paris and Tokyo, and Britain had a high commissioner in Ottawa. The Governor General became a symbolic representative of the Crown rather than a representative of the British government.

At home, there were many signs that good times had finally come to Canada. World markets for Canadian manufactured goods had revived, and wheat prices were soaring to new levels. New mining and lumbering areas were developed. By 1928, more than a billion dollars' worth of products were being extracted from the newly developed primary industries of the Canadian Shield. Immigrants poured into Canada by the hundreds of thousands to provide labour in the growing industrial cities. Cars, radios, telephones, electrical appliances and other consumer goods were being bought, especially by middle-class Canadians, often using credit plans. Credit was also used to buy shares on the stock market, as the country became increasingly optimistic about its future. On both sides of the Canadian-American border, the Roaring Twenties were in full swing and there seemed no end in sight to the good times.

1919 Alcock and Brown take off from St. John's, Nfld, (June 14) on the first successful flight across the Atlantic to Cliften, Ireland. A **general strike paralyzes Winnipeg** (May–June), where an armed charge by the RCMP kills one person and injures 30 (June 21).

1920 **Canada joins** the **League of Nations** at its inception (Jan. 10). The flow of emigrants from the British Isles and Europe resumes, many going to urban centres. Federal legislation makes **women eligible** to sit in the **House of Commons**. The North West Mounted Police became the Royal Canadian Mounted Police (RCMP).

1921 Liberals under **Mackenzie King** defeat Conservatives under Arthur Meighen in federal election; the Progressive Party comes in second. **Agnes Macphail** becomes the first woman elected to Parliament. The world's fastest fishing schooner, the *Bluenose*, is launched at Lunenburg, NS. (Mar. 26). **Postwar economic depression** puts 300,000 men

and women out of work—more than 15 percent of the work force.

1922 Canada declines to rally to Britain's side during the Chanak Crisis. Sir Frederick **Banting**, Dr Charles **Best**, Dr J.J.R. MacLeod and J.B. Collip share Nobel Prize for the **discovery of insulin**.

1923 The Canadian Northern and Canadian Transcontinental are merged to form the **Canadian National Railways**. Canada signs the Halibut Treaty with the US without a corroborating British signature. Mackenzie King leads opposition to a common imperial policy ("one voice for the empire") at an Imperial Conference in London.

1924 The Saskatchewan Wheat Pool begins operations.

1925 Although Conservatives win more seats in federal election, Mackenzie King's Liberals remain in power with the support of the Progressives.

1926 King's Liberals win federal election. An Imperial Conference defines British dominions as autonomous (Balfour Report).

1927 Britain's Privy Council awards Labrador to Newfoundland instead of to Quebec (Mar. 1). The Diamond Jubilee of Confederation (July 1) is marked by Canada's first coast-to-coast radio network broadcast. King's government, with the support of the Progressive Party, passes Canada's first **Old Age Pension Act**.

1928 The Supreme Court of Canada rules that, according to the British North America Act, women are not "persons" who could hold public office. This decision is reversed by British Privy Council in 1929.

■ The Great Depression (1929–1939)

In 1929, Canadians looked with confidence toward the next decade and that confidence made the effects of the Great Depression of the 1930s even more bitter. The Depression was worldwide, but the effects were especially felt in Canada because about a third of the nation's gross national product was based on exports. The first signs of Canadian economic collapse appeared in October 1929 when wheat prices began to fall. In the same month the stock market collapsed, ruining thousands of shareholders, some of whom, on paper at least, had been millionaires. By 1930, the number of unemployed had doubled and the

Conservatives, under R.B. Bennett, won the 1930 federal election decisively as voters hoped a change in government would bring a change in fortune. However by 1933, one in five Canadians was unemployed.

Western Canada was hardest hit in "The Dirty Thirties" because of its reliance on wheat. The Prairie provinces also suffered from a drought which led to crop failure during these hard times. The combined results were devastating. In Saskatchewan, provincial income fell by 90 percent and two-thirds of the province's population had to go on welfare. In the 1930s, welfare, or "relief" as it was then known, became a burden for municipal and provincial governments across the country. By 1935, 10 percent of Canadians were on relief.

Bennett's government did not intervene to rebuild the economy. In the 1930s, politicians, economists and business leaders assumed that the Depression, like other downswings in the business cycle, would soon be followed by a recovery. Their experience, and most economic theory at the time, did not encourage them to consider major government spending as a way to stimulate a depressed economy.

One of the few federally financed programs created involved sending single unemployed men to camps where they did manual work in return for their keep and a small allowance. Working in isolated conditions, often at meaningless tasks, did nothing to satisfy the men, and those in the British Columbia camps took action. In 1935, about 1,500 camp inmates decided to present their complaints directly to Bennett in Ottawa. They began the "On to Ottawa" trek by taking over freight trains heading east. By the time they reached Regina, there were about 2,000 protesters and the railway refused to provide further transportation. Representatives of the Trekkers met with Prime Minister Bennett in Ottawa, but the talks were inconclusive. When the delegation returned to Regina, Bennett decided to arrest the protest leaders. On July 1, there was a bloody riot in Regina involving the Trekkers, local police and the RCMP, which left one policeman dead and several dozen rioters, constables and local citizens injured. The Trek was over and the protesters returned home over the next few days; but Bennett's handling of the affair hurt his image. In the election of 1935, the people turned to King again, in the hope that this time he could deal with the Depression.

After 1935, economic conditions began to improve slowly, yet federal politicians did little to speed this recovery. The failure of the Liberals and the Conservatives to deal with the Depression led to the rise of reform parties. A socialist party, the Co-operative Commonwealth Federation (CCF) won seven seats in the 1935 election and elected members to several provincial legislatures. Other new parties appeared at the provincial level. In Alberta, the Social Credit Party promised $25 prosperity certificates to each resident; but the plan fell flat because the province did not have the power to issue currency. In Quebec, Maurice Duplessis established the Union Nationale and promised economic reform. But the Union Nationale, like the other parties, could not end the Depression, the effects of which faded only with the outbreak of World War II in 1939.

1929   The **Great Depression** begins.

1930   **Cairine Wilson** is appointed Canada's first woman senator (Feb. 20). The Canadian Federation of Business and Professional Women's Clubs is organized. Conservatives under **R.B. Bennett** win federal election (Aug. 7).

1931   The **Statute of Westminster** (Dec. 11) grants Canada full legislative authority domestically and in external affairs. The Governor General becomes a representative of the Crown.

1932   Ottawa Agreements provide for preferential trade between Canada and other Commonwealth nations. The **Co-operative Commonwealth Federation (CCF)** is founded at Calgary.

1933   One in five Canadians is unemployed.

1934   The **Bank of Canada** is formed. The **Dionne quintuplets** are born in Callander, Ont.

1935   Ten percent of Canadians rely on welfare or "relief." The **On to Ottawa** trek by young men from government work camps ends in a riot at Regina (July 1). Liberals under Mackenzie King win federal election. The CCF win 7 seats. Social Credit claims 17. **William Aberhart** leads Social Credit into office in Alberta. The Canadian Wheat Board is created.

1936 Union Nationale under **Maurice Duplessis** wins its first election in Quebec.

1937 The **Rowell-Sirois Commission** is appointed to investigate the financial relationship between the federal government and the provinces. First regular flight of **Trans Canada Air Lines** (Sept. 1).

1938 Franklin D. Roosevelt becomes first US President in office to visit Canada, meeting Mackenzie King at Kingston.

■ Canada in World War II (1939–1945)

While most Canadians focused attention on the effects of the Depression at home, events in Europe during the 1930s were moving the world closer to another global conflict. After taking over Austria and Czechoslovakia (present-day Czech and Slovak republics), Germany invaded Poland in 1939; Britain and France responded by declaring war. Following Britain's action, King quickly summoned Parliament. On Sept. 10, one week after Britain had entered the conflict, the Canadian Parliament declared war on Germany and its allies.

Parliamentary support for the war declaration was based in part on King's known preference for a limited Canadian role and his assurance that there would be no conscription. Initially, only one Canadian division was sent to Britain. But by 1940, France had fallen and Britain faced invasion. King abandoned the concept of limited participation and decided to dispatch more troops. By late 1942, Canada had five divisions overseas. Canadian soldiers first saw action in December 1941 during the unsuccessful defence of Hong Kong. In August 1942, 5,000 Canadians took part in the disastrous raid on the French port of Dieppe, suffering casualties of 2,200 killed or captured. Despite these setbacks, the Canadian army played a major role in defeating enemy forces in Italy and took part in the Allied landings at Normandy in June 1944. After taking key targets in France, Canadian soldiers moved northward to liberate Holland in 1945.

Canadians contributed to the war effort in other important ways. The Royal Canadian Navy grew from six destroyers and less than 2,000 personnel in 1939 to 471 warships, 99,688 men and 6,500 women by the war's end in 1945. The navy helped win the Battle of the Atlantic against German submarines by providing protection to the convoys of merchant ships carrying essential supplies from North America to Britain. (Despite the protection, German U-boats sank 5,150 merchant ships.) Canadians also fought in the air as members of Britain's Royal Air Force, and, in increasing numbers throughout the war, in the Royal Canadian Air Force (RCAF). By 1945, there were 48 RCAF squadrons overseas. Other members of the RCAF were involved in the British Commonwealth Air Training Plan. Operating from Canadian airfields, this plan trained 131,000 aircrew from around the Commonwealth.

Canada also produced a wide variety of munitions, and provided important food supplies to the Allied war effort. Much of Canada's war production went directly to Britain, so did more than $3 billion in financial assistance.

While the contributions of Canadian men and women to the war effort were significant, the conflict raised disturbing issues at home. In reversing his earlier stand against conscription, Prime Minister King called for a national plebiscite on the issue in 1942. In all provinces except Quebec the electorate voted for conscription; relations between Quebec and the rest of Canada were strained, although not as severely as in World War I.

In a move that would later become controversial, Japanese-Canadians were interned and their property was confiscated in the name of national security after the Japanese attack on Pearl Harbor in 1941. The interned included Japanese-Canadians who had fought for Canada in World War I, and more than 40 years later, the Canadian government would officially apologize to the interned and their families.

By the war's end, more than a million Canadians had served in the armed forces and more than 42,000 had died. Canada's war effort enhanced its international image. At the same time, Canada had developed closer ties with the United States as the country's interests shifted away from Britain and Europe.

1939 **Canada declares war** on Germany (Sept. 10) after remaining neutral for a week following the British declaration. Quebec Premier Maurice Duplessis, who opposed Quebec participation in the war, is defeated by the provincial Liberals on that issue (Oct. 26).

1940 **Unemployment insurance** is introduced. Liberals win federal election (Mar. 26).

The Permanent Joint Board of Defence is formed between Canada and the US. **Thérèse Casgrain** wins women in Quebec the right to vote and to hold provincial office.

1941 Canadians are captured when Hong Kong falls to Japanese (Dec. 25); about 500 of the POWs subsequently die in Japanese camps. Immigration has changed Canadian demographic structure. Canadians of British ancestry now make up 49.7 percent of the population, of French descent 30.3 percent and of other ethnic backgrounds 20 percent.

1942 In the Canadian army's first European war action, many soldiers are captured or killed in the disastrous **Dieppe** raid (Aug. 19). Canadians of Japanese descent are moved inland from the coast of British Columbia as "security risks"; their property is confiscated. A national plebiscite releases Mackenzie King from his pledge of no conscription but reveals deep divisions between Quebec and the rest of Canada.

1943 Canadians participate in the invasion of Sicily (July 10). Canadians win the Battle of Ortona (Dec. 20–28). **Ernest C. Manning** wins first of nine successive elections for the Social Credit in Alberta.

1944 Canadian troops push farther inland than any other Allied unit on D-Day (June 6). Canadian forces fight as a separate army (July 23). Saskatchewan elects Tommy Douglas's CCF, the first socialist government in North America. Maurice Duplessis regains office for the Union Nationale in Quebec.

1945 War in Europe ends (May 8). One million Canadians fought in WW II; 42,042 were killed. Canadians killed while fighting for other Allied forces numbered 4,500. Liberals win federal election (June 11). First **family allowance payments** are **made** (June 20). Canada joins the **United Nations** (June 26). Igor Gouzenko defects from the Soviet embassy in Ottawa (Sept. 5) and reveals the existence in Canada of a Soviet spy network. Canada's first nuclear reactor begins operations at Chalk River, Ontario.

■ Postwar Canada: 1945–1968

In the years following World War II, Canadians enjoyed a standard of living that was in stark contrast to the Depression years. The economy had boomed during the war and the gross national product had doubled. The

war had prompted development in new industries which continued to expand in peacetime. Consumer spending had increased dramatically during the war, and continued to rise with the postwar baby boom. This boom, along with large numbers of European immigrants, resulted in a 40 percent population increase between the war's end and 1958. In Canada's quickly growing cities and suburbs, home ownership was made easier by the National Housing Act, designed to make mortgages easier to obtain. This example of government involvement in the economy was characteristic of the times. By 1945, unemployment insurance and family allowance legislation had been passed and other social welfare measures were being discussed.

Prime Minister King retired in 1948, and was followed as Liberal leader by Louis St. Laurent. One of St. Laurent's first achievements was the entry of Newfoundland into Confederation in 1949. In 1951, his government increased old age pensions and, in 1957, introduced a hospital insurance plan. St. Laurent negotiated with the United States to build the St. Lawrence Seaway, an impressive feat of engineering completed in 1959. In 1956, however, the government used closure (a limit on debate) to cut off the parliamentary debate concerning the building of the trans-Canada pipeline for oil and gas. In the election the following year, the Conservatives under John Diefenbaker won a minority victory. In 1958, Diefenbaker called another election to consolidate his position. This time the Conservatives swept the country, winning 208 of 265 seats.

Western agriculture found huge new markets when the government arranged wheat sales to China. In 1960, Diefenbaker's government introduced the Bill of Rights to protect the rights of all Canadians, and granted Native Canadians the right to vote in federal elections.

Despite continuing popular support for the British Commonwealth, the government of Canada signed the North American Air Defence Agreement (NORAD) with the United States to increase security during a time of international tension. But it could not deal with an economic recession that led to a devalued dollar and high unemployment. Also, the prime minister dealt Canada's fledgling aircraft industry a serious blow when he cancelled production of the Canadian-made Avro Arrow fighter jet, and his refusal to allow nuclear warheads on the American missiles based in Canada earned him the emnity of the US government. In the election of 1962, his government was returned to power, but in a minority situation that forced another election in 1963. The 1963 election also resulted in a minority government, but this time, the Liberals, under Lester B. Pearson, were in power.

As prime minister, Pearson, a career diplomat, concentrated on domestic matters. His government relied on the support of the New Democratic Party (formerly the CCF) to hold a majority in the House of Commons, and the partnership produced legislation that broadened social welfare by introducing Medicare, the Canada Pension Plan and the Canada Assistance Plan. Canadian nationalism was heightened with the adoption of the maple leaf flag in 1965, and in the same year another federal election produced a Liberal government one seat short of a clear majority. The opening of the world's fair, Expo in Montreal, in Canada's centennial year, 1967, marked a year of celebration across the country.

During the 1960s, Pearson was sensitive to growing nationalism in Quebec. His government established a Royal Commission on Bilingualism and Biculturalism in 1963, to demonstrate that Quebec's interests could be served by federalism, and he encouraged some of those closely associated with the Quiet Revolution to run for federal office. Quebec had been transformed from traditional to modern attitudes towards education, social reform and industrialization, a movement known as the Quiet Revolution, under Premier Jean Lesage. The Quebec government was implementing the ideas of the Quiet Revolution, and championed provincial rights with its slogan *maîtres chez nous* (masters in our own house). This sentiment took centre stage during Centennial celebrations. Visiting French President Charles de Gaulle ended a Montreal speech with the cry *"Vive le Québec libre!"* ("Long live free Quebec") which set off a storm of diplomatic protest and delighted local nationalists. Despite growing nationalist sentiment, many Quebeckers, including Pierre Trudeau, went to Ottawa. Trudeau was elected to the House of Commons in 1965, and was named minister of justice in 1967. In 1968, following Pearson's retirement, Trudeau became Liberal leader.

1947 Imperial Oil discovers the **Leduc oil field** (Feb. 13).

1948 **Louis St. Laurent** succeeds Mackenzie King as prime minister (Nov. 15).

1949 Under Premier **Joey Smallwood**, **Newfoundland** becomes Canada's tenth province (Mar. 31). Canada joins NATO. Canadian appeals to Britain's Judicial Committee of the Privy Council are abolished: Canada's Supreme Court becomes final court of appeal. Liberals under St Laurent defeat Conservatives under George Drew in federal election (June 3).

1950 The Korean War begins (June 25); Canadian troops participate in the conflict as part of a United Nations force.

1951 The midcentury census reports Canada's population as 14,009,429. **Postwar immigration** to Canada exceeds 100,000 annually during the 1950s, primarily moving from Central and Eastern Europe to hold manufacturing jobs in urban centres. The Massey Royal Commission reports that Canadian cultural life is dominated by American influences. Revisions to the **Indian Act**, beginning in 1951, limit its coverage of aboriginal people. Indian women married to non-Indian men are excluded from the act. This provision was removed in 1985 after much protest of discrimination. **Charlotte Whitton**, the first woman to be mayor of a major Canadian city, is elected in Ottawa.

1952 **Vincent Massey** becomes the first native-born Governor General of Canada. Canada's **first television** stations begin broadcasting in Montreal (Sept. 6) and Toronto (Sept. 8). **W.A.C. Bennett** begins **Social Credit**'s administration in British Columbia.

1953 Canada's National Library is established in Ottawa (Jan. 1). The Stratford Festival opens (July 13). The **Korean War** ends (July 27); total Canadian casualties are 314 killed and 1,211 wounded. Liberals under St Laurent defeat Conservatives under Drew in federal election (Aug. 10).

1954 An economic slump interrupts the postwar boom. Canada's **first subway** opens in Toronto (Mar. 30). Roger Bannister and John Landy run the "miracle mile" at the British Empire Games in Vancouver (Aug.), the first to run a mile in less than four minutes. Sixteen-year-old Marilyn Bell becomes the first person to swim Lake Ontario (Sept. 9).

Hurricane Hazel hits Toronto, killing 83 people (Oct. 15). The Geneva Conference on the Far East invites Canada to join India and Poland in **supervising peace in Indochina**. This peacekeeping commitment continues for nearly 20 years to 1973.

1955 The Canadian Labour Congress is formed. The suspension of Montreal Canadiens' hockey star Maurice (Rocket) Richard leads to rioting in Montreal (Mar. 17).

1956 The Liberals use closure to limit the **Pipeline Debate** (May 8–June 6), a manoeuvre that contributes to their electoral defeat the following year.

1957 Conservatives under **John Diefenbaker** win federal election (June 10) and form minority government. Ellen Fairclough becomes the first woman federal cabinet minister. The Canada Council is created to help foster Canadian cultural life. **Lester B. Pearson wins Nobel Prize** (Oct. 12) for his role in resolving the Suez Crisis. Canadian supply and services troops are sent to work with a multinational UN force around the **Gulf of Aqaba**. They stay until 1967 and return there in 1973.

1958 Conservatives under Diefenbaker win 208 seats in federal election (Mar. 31). Coal mine disaster at Springhill, NS, results in death of 74 miners.

1959 The **Avro Arrow** project is terminated, with a loss of almost 14,000 jobs (Feb. 20). The **St. Lawrence Seaway** is **opened** (June 26).

1960 Liberals under **Jean Lesage** win provincial election in Quebec (June 22), inaugurating the **Quiet Revolution**. A **Canadian Bill of Rights** is approved by Parliament. Native people get the right to vote in federal elections. During the 1960s French is recognized as a language of instruction in elementary and secondary schools in New Brunswick, Ontario and Manitoba. It is recognized subsequently in other provincial jurisdictions.

1961 The **New Democratic Party** replaces the CCF.

1962 Conservatives are reduced to minority status in federal election (June 18). Social Credit wins 30 seats and NDP take 19 to control the balance of power in the House of Commons. The Saskatchewan NDP introduces the first Canadian **Medicare** plan (July 1), and is opposed by a doctors' strike. **Trans-Canada Highway** officially opens (Sept. 3). Canadian-made satellite *Alouette* is launched (Sept. 29), making Canada the third nation in space. Canada's last execution, the double hanging of Ronald Turpin and Arthur Lucas, takes place (Dec. 11), at the Don Jail in Toronto.

1963 Liberals under Pearson win federal election (Apr. 8), and form a minority government. The Quebec separatist group **Front de libération du Québec (FLQ)** sets off a series of bombs in Montreal (Apr.–May). A Trans-Canada Airways flight crashes in Quebec, killing all 118 people aboard (Nov. 29). The **Royal Commission on Bilingualism and Biculturalism** begins its work.

1964 Canadians get social insurance cards (Apr.). Canada ends difficult peacekeeping duties in the Congo after four years of service with heavy casualties. Canadian troops join UN forces in Cyprus.

1965 Canada gets a new flag (Feb. 15). The **Autopact** between Canada and the US is signed. Canadian Roman Catholic Churches begin to celebrate mass in English (Mar. 7). Liberals win federal election (Nov. 8) to continue as a minority government. Failure of an Ontario Hydro relay device at Queenston plunges eastern North America into a power blackout (Nov. 9).

1966 The Munsinger Affair becomes Canada's first major parliamentary sex scandal (Mar. 4). The **Canada Pension Plan** is established. The CBC begins colour television broadcasting (Oct. 1).

1967 The Canadian army, navy and air forces are **unified** to become the Canadian **Armed Forces** (Apr. 25). Montreal hosts a world's fair, **Expo 67** (opened Apr. 27). Canada celebrates its **Centennial** (July 1). French President Charles **de Gaulle** delivers his "Vive le Québec Libre" speech in Montreal (July 24). The federal Department of Manpower and Immigration establishes the **"points system"** for immigrants. Patterns shift in the 1960s from European to Third World immigration as humanitarian objectives and family reunification policies increase multicultural immigration.

■ The Trudeau Years (1968–1984)

The Liberals won a majority victory in the election of 1968. Trudeau was a strong federalist, determined to show that Ottawa could promote the rights of French Canada. The Official Languages Act of 1969 recognized both English and French as official languages, and required federal institutions to provide services in both languages. Although the legislation was supported by all parties, it was not universally popular, even in Quebec.

In the October Crisis of 1970, separatist extremists belonging to the FLQ (Front de libération du Québec) kidnapped British trade commissioner James Cross, and killed Quebec Cabinet minister Pierre Laporte. Trudeau used the War Measures Act to apply emergency measures of arrest, detention and martial law. This move was generally accepted but was criticized by advocates of civil rights, especially since the FLQ had little real support and the Act was in effect across the country.

In his early years in power, Trudeau attempted to concentrate decision-making in Ottawa, and his newly created Prime Minister's Office led to western Canadian accusations of an eastern-dominated federal government. At the same time opposition parties charged that Trudeau was undermining both the power of the cabinet and of Parliament. The Liberals were almost defeated in the election of 1972, but retained office through a minority government that saw the New Democrats, under David Lewis, hold the balance of power. During this period the Foreign Investment Review Agency was set up (1973) to protect the Canadian economy against foreign domination; business critics claimed that it discouraged investment.

By 1974, the Liberals had regained a majority; their agenda was dominated by an economy battered by inflation. The government tried a variety of economic measures, including a three-year imposition of wage and price controls under the Anti-Inflation Act of 1975. Although the controls may have had some effect, world conditions, especially the international oil crisis, kept inflation high.

In 1976, the separatist Parti Québécois under René Lévesque defeated the provincial Liberals, led by Robert Bourassa in the Quebec election. This election fuelled public uncertainty over the future of Quebec (and

Canada), while continuing inflation and western alienation also undermined Liberal support. In the 1979 election, the Liberals lost, and Conservative leader Joe Clark took office as head of a minority government. Clark's government was short-lived as it suffered defeat in the House of Commons that same year.

The Liberals won the election of 1980, and Trudeau, lured out of planned retirement by the sudden election, embarked on an eventful term of office. He and members of his government actively campaigned on the victorious NO side in the 1980 Quebec referendum on sovereignty-association. The Liberals brought in the National Energy Program in the same year, again attempting to regulate ownership and control in part of the economy, and again succeeding in alienating foreign and local business interests. Resistance to the NEP, particularly in the West, was deep and persistent.

Then, after a long (18 months) and difficult campaign waged in Parliament, at federal-provincial meetings and in the media, Trudeau succeeded in getting an agreement on patriating the Canadian constitution amongst all provinces except Quebec. Patriation officially took place when Queen Elizabeth II proclaimed the new Constitution Act in Ottawa on April 17, 1982. The Canadian Charter of Rights and Freedoms was also proclaimed, entrenching bilingualism in the federal jurisdiction and providing for minority language education rights across Canada.

By 1984 the country was mired in a recession and in no mood for the international interest Trudeau was pursuing; he retired and John Turner became Liberal leader and prime minister for a brief period. The Liberal government was at the end of its mandate and Parliament was dissolved. After nearly 16 years of Liberal government, the voters were eager for a change.

1968 **Pierre Elliott Trudeau** succeeds Pearson as prime minister (Apr. 6), and leads Liberals to majority in federal election (June 25). A Royal Commission on the Status of Women is appointed. Canadian divorce law is reformed.

1969 Saturday postal deliveries end. Abortion law is liberalized (May). English and French become **official languages** of federal administration (July 9). New Brunswick declares official bilingualism. The Breathalyser comes into use as a test for alcohol-impaired drivers (Dec. 1).

1970 The FLQ kidnaps British trade commissioner James Cross (Oct. 5), precipitating the **October Crisis**. Quebec labour and immigration minister Pierre Laporte is kidnapped (Oct. 10), and found murdered (Oct. 17). The federal government invokes the **War Measures Act** (Oct. 16), leading to the arrest of 465 people.

1971 A policy of **multiculturalism** is adopted by the federal government. Canadian Gerhard Herzberg wins the Nobel Prize in chemistry for his studies of chemical reactions that help produce smog.

1972 Canada defeats the USSR in the first hockey series between the Soviets and Canadian professionals (Aug.–Sept.). Liberals win federal election with 109 seats to the Conservatives' 107, with the NDP holding the balance of power at 31 (Oct. 30).

1973 The separatist Parti Québécois becomes the Official Opposition in Quebec. Canadian troops are sent to the Middle East and serve with the United Nations Emergency Task Force there until 1979.

1974 Liberals under Trudeau win federal election and form majority government (July 8). **Pauline McGibbon** becomes the first female lieutenant-governor (Ontario) in the British Commonwealth.

1975 The **CN Tower**, the world's tallest free-standing structure at 553.339 metres, is completed in Toronto (Apr. 2). Federal government announces (July 18) its intention to screen foreign investment in Canada, via the Foreign Investment Review Agency (FIRA). Television cameras are allowed inside the House of Commons for the first time. Federal government imposes **wage and price controls** in an effort to fight inflation (Oct. 14). **Grace Hartman** is elected president of the Canadian Union of Public Employees.

1976 Canada announces 200-nautical-mile coastal fishing zone (June 4). **Death penalty** is **abolished** in a free vote (130–124) in Parliament (July 14). Montreal hosts **Olympic Games** (July 17–31). Team Canada wins the first **Canada Cup** hockey series

(Sept. 15). The **Parti Québécois** under René Lévesque wins provincial election in Quebec (Nov. 15).

1977 Quebec government passes Bill 101, restricting English-language schooling to children whose mother or father had attended English elementary school in Quebec (Aug. 26). Highway signs in most of Canada become metric (Sept. 6).

1978 **Soviet nuclear-powered satellite crashes** in Canadian north (Jan. 24). Sun Life Assurance Co. announces a head office move from Montreal to Toronto because of language laws and political instability in Quebec. **Hilda Watson**, first woman to lead a political party in Canada, wins leadership of Yukon Progressive Conservative party.

1979 Conservatives under **Joe Clark** win federal election (May 22). Canada's first gold bullion coin, the Maple Leaf, goes on sale (Sept. 5). Supreme Court of Canada declares Manitoba and Quebec legislation creating unilingual courts and legislatures unconstitutional (Dec. 13). Federal Conservatives lose non-confidence vote on budget (Dec. 13), forcing the government's resignation. **Antonine Maillet** wins the prestigious French literary prize, the Prix Goncourt, for her novel *Pélagie-la-Charette*.

1980 Canada's ambassador to Iran, Ken Taylor, arranges the successful **escape of six American embassy staff** from Tehran while their colleagues are held hostage (Jan. 28). Liberals win federal election (Feb. 18). Canada boycotts the Olympic Games in Moscow because of the Soviet invasion of Afghanistan. **Jeanne Sauvé** becomes the first female Speaker of the House of Commons (Apr. 14). **Quebec votes "no"** to "sovereignty-association" in a **referendum** (May 22). **"O Canada"** becomes Canada's national anthem (June 27). The Supreme Court awards Rosa Becker half the assets accumulated during a 19-year common-law relationship. **National Energy Program** is created to encourage oil self-sufficiency, increase Canadian ownership in the oil industry and obtain a larger share of Canadian energy revenues.

1981 Quebec bans public signs in English (Sept. 23). The federal government and every province except Quebec reach agreement on a method for patriating Canada's constitution (Nov. 5). The 1981 census indicates significant increases in the percentage of new Canadians from Asia, the Caribbean and Latin America.

1982 Bertha Wilson becomes Canada's first woman to be appointed a justice of the Supreme Court (Mar. 4). The Quebec Court of Appeal rejects the Quebec government's claim of veto power over constitutional change (Apr. 7). Canada gains a new **Constitution** and **Charter of Rights and Freedoms** (Apr. 17). Canada's GNP falls 4.8 percent in the worst recession since the Great Depression of the 1930s.

1983 Canadian pay-TV channels begin operation (Feb. 1). **Jeanne Sauvé** is Canada's first woman to be appointed Governor General (Dec. 23). Canada approves a US plan to test unarmed **cruise missiles** in western Canada beginning in 1984.

■ Mulroney in Power (1984–1993)

In the 1984 general election, the Conservatives, under Brian Mulroney, won a decisive victory, taking 211 of 282 seats in the House of Commons, including 58 seats in Quebec, a former Liberal stronghold. In contrast to the previous government, the Conservatives sought to strengthen ties with the United States and took steps to attract more foreign investment to Canada. The recession of the early 80s was over and business and government were both ready to expand.

One of the goals of the Mulroney government was to amend the Constitution Act of 1982 to obtain the support of Quebec. The prime minister and 10 provincial premiers reached an agreement, which became known as the Meech Lake Accord, on such an amendment in 1987; the agreement was to be taken to provincial legislatures and to Parliament for approval by June 23, 1990. Also in 1987, the government negotiated a Canada–US free trade agreement (FTA) which provided for the elimination of all cross-border tariffs over 10 years. But the deal was rejected by both opposition parties and Liberal leader John Turner announced that the Liberal-dominated Senate would not approve free trade unless the Conservatives obtained public support in a general election. Mulroney called an election for November 1988. The campaign that followed was fractious; emotions ran high and there were wide fluctuations in public opinion. Anti-FTA sentiment was split between the opposition parties, and the Conservatives won a second majority government. The FTA was approved in December and took effect Jan. 1, 1989.

As the deadline for ratification of the Meech Lake Accord approached, its confirmation became increasingly uncertain. Provincial governments had changed in the interim and both Manitoba and Newfoundland indicated that they had reservations about the agreement. Despite a last-minute first ministers' conference and a great deal of political pressure, the Manitoba legislature failed to ratify the accord and Newfoundland withdrew its consent; the deal lapsed on June 23, 1990. The following years were marked by numerous federal-provincial conferences, a variety of proposals and pressure from Quebec to include recognition of its distinct society. In August 1992, a new federal-provincial agreement was reached (the Charlottetown Accord) in time to be considered in a referendum Quebec Premier Robert Bourassa had pledged to hold on the future of Quebec. The other provinces also took part in a national referendum on the terms of the accord, which included not only recognition of Quebec as a distinct society, but also provisions to transfer mining, forestry, telecommunications and many other jurisdictions to the provinces. Canadians from all walks of life grappled with the issues raised by the terms of the Charlottetown Accord, and the question dominated national media, (aside from the sports pages, which were distracted by the prospect of a Canadian team, the Toronto Blue Jays, winning the 1992 World Series). The referendum was held on Oct. 26, 1992, and the deal was rejected by 54.8 percent of the voters.

The Conservatives' second term of office was also marked by the introduction of the Goods and Services Tax (GST), a tax designed to replace the manufacturers' tax and spread the tax burden more evenly across the economy. This tax was deeply unpopular and the Liberal-appointed members of the Senate vowed to block its passage in the upper chamber. Mulroney responded by temporarily increasing the number of senators to 112, with new appointees who would support the measure. The tax was the subject of heated debate and much protest across the country as Canadians transferred their frustration over the endless constitutional discussion, the now faltering economy and disappointment over the results of FTA to the government.

The GST took effect on Jan. 1, 1991, and the Conservative government continued to pursue wider trade agreements by joining the US and Mexico in negotiations for a North American Free Trade Agreement that would supersede the FTA. Amid much controversy, the deal was signed in December and the government's popularity continued to plumb the depths of the popularity polls. In February, Mulroney announced his decision to step aside as leader; Kim Campbell became the new leader of the Conservatives and the country's first female prime minister after a June leadership convention. As the Conservative mandate drew to a close, Campbell attempted to present herself as a brand-new prime minister at the head of a brand-new government. In the election in October 1993, Canadian voters made it clear they did not accept this stance: the Liberals under Jean Chrétien won a lopsided victory in an election that changed the political map of the country. The new government took office with a record number of rookie MPs, the Loyal Opposition was made up of members of the separatist Bloc Québécois, with the Reform Party from western Canada nearly matching the BQ's number of seats. The Conservatives elected only two members and the NDP also fared poorly at the hands of the electorate.

1984 **John Turner** succeeds Pierre Trudeau as prime minister (June 30). Conservatives under **Brian Mulroney** win federal election with 211 seats, the largest majority in Canada's history (Sept. 4). The **Pope visits Canada** (Sept. 9–20). **Marc Garneau** becomes the first Canadian in space, aboard US space shuttle *Challenger* (Oct. 5). Council for the Northwest Territories recognizes the use of **aboriginal languages** as well as English and French.

1985 The voyage through the Northwest Passage of US icebreaker *Polar Sea* challenges Canada's **Arctic sovereignty**. Prime Minister Mulroney and US President Reagan declare mutual support for **Star Wars research** and **free trade** between the two nations at "Shamrock Summit" (Mar. 18) in Quebec City. The Quebec provincial Liberals

under Robert Bourassa defeat the Parti Québécois (Dec. 2).

1986 The Canadian dollar hits a then all-time low of 70.20 cents US (Jan. 31). The **Expo 86** world's fair is held in Vancouver (May 2–Oct. 13). Canada joins other Commonwealth nations (Aug. 5) in adopting **economic sanctions against South Africa** because of its apartheid policy. Canada receives a United Nations award (Oct. 6) for providing a haven for world refugees. Canadian John Polanyi shares (with Dudley R. Herschbach and Yuan T. Lee) the Nobel Prize for chemistry.

1987 The Bank of Canada rate drops to a 13-year low of 7.49 percent (Jan. 28); 6-month residential mortgages are as low as 7.5 percent. Prime Minister Brian Mulroney and 10 provincial premiers agree on proposed constitutional amendments in the **Meech Lake Accord** (Apr. 30). Ontario passes the first **pay equity legislation** for the private sector enacted in North America (June). A free vote in Parliament on restoration of **capital punishment** defeats the proposal 148–127 (June). A **free trade** agreement between Canada and the United States is set out (Oct. 3). **Stock prices tumble** (Oct. 19) in Canada and throughout the world. The founding assembly of the **Reform Party of Canada** is held (November).

1988 Canada is left without an **abortion law** (Jan. 28) when the Supreme Court rules that existing legislation is unconstitutional. Canadian sprinter **Ben Johnson** sets a world record and wins a gold medal at the Summer Olympics in Seoul (Sept. 24) but is stripped of both (Sept. 26) after testing positive for steroids. Yukon Territory passes language legislation recognizing the use of aboriginal languages. Brian Mulroney's Progressive Conservatives win a second consecutive majority in the **federal election** (Nov. 21) after a bitter campaign fought over the free trade agreement with the US. Quebec's **French-only sign law** is struck down by the Supreme Court (Dec. 15) but is re-instated by Quebec (Dec. 21) using the "notwithstanding" clause in the Charter of Rights and Freedoms. Free trade legislation passes the House of Commons (Dec. 24) and the Senate (Dec. 30). The "Kamloops Amendment" to the Indian Act grants band councils jurisdiction over all reserve land, including the power to impose taxes.

1989 The Free Trade Agreement takes effect (Jan. 1). The federal government announces a new **goods and services tax** (GST) to take effect in January 1991. Audrey McLaughlin becomes Canada's **first female national party leader** as the NDP chooses a successor to Ed Broadbent (Dec. 2).

1990 Revisions to the Criminal Code provide choice of language in criminal hearings (January). Several Quebec Conservative MPs, led by cabinet minister Lucien Bouchard (May 21), leave the government to form the pro-independence **Bloc Québécois**. The **Meech Lake Accord dies** when both Newfoundland and Manitoba fail to ratify the constitutional agreement by the deadline (June 23). Manitoba MLA **Elijah Harper** refuses the unanimous consent required for debate and a vote on the Meech Lake Accord because the accord does not provide special status for aboriginal peoples as it does for Quebec. Jean Chrétien becomes leader of the federal Liberal party. A land dispute leads to a 78-day armed confrontation between Mohawk warriors and government forces at the Kanesatake reserve near **Oka**, Que. **Canada sends warships** to the Persian Gulf as part of the multinational force being assembled to force Iraq to withdraw from occupied Kuwait. Brian Mulroney's Conservative government stacks the Senate (Sept. 27) with new appointees to ensure passage of the federal **goods and services tax** (GST), which takes effect Jan. 1.

1991 Canadian military personnel participate with the Allied forces in the assault against Iraq beginning Jan. 16 (the **Gulf War**). Prime Minister Brian Mulroney and US President George Bush sign an **acid rain accord** with the goal of ending acid rain within 10 years. **Rita Johnston** succeeds BC Premier **William Vander Zalm** as premier, the first woman to enter the provincial premier's office in Canada. Mulroney's government announces a new **constitutional reform package** promising aboriginal self-government within 10 years and guaranteeing aboriginal representation in an elected Senate. **Gun control** is passed, imposing tougher controls and banning imported military assault weapons. **Yukon First Nations** sign an umbrella agreement on land claims and self-government; an agreement is reached on creation of Nunavut.

1992 A year-long crisis in the Atlantic **fisheries** results in a two-year shutdown of the cod fishery (July 2), a five-year ban on commercial salmon fishing in Newfoundland (Mar. 6) and international negotiations to protect the fish stocks. **Gwich'in Indians** sign a deal with Ottawa, giving them title to nearly 24,000 sq. km of land in the NWT and Yukon (Apr. 22). The details of the North American Free Trade Agreement (**NAFTA**) are announced Aug. 12. Prime Minister Mulroney signs the deal on Dec. 17. Negotiations on constitutional reform occur throughout the year, and the **Charlottetown Accord**, which wins Quebec's approval, is announced Aug. 19. Proposals include Senate reform, an enlarged House of Commons and self-government for native people. On Oct. 26, a national referendum is held on the accord; the rejectionists claim victory.

1993 The **Sahtu Tribe** of the Great Bear Lake region in the NWT settles a land claim to 41,437 sq. km; the **Cree** in northern Quebec win compensation from Hydro-Quebec for damage done around James Bay. On Jan. 19 Canadian troops begin the planned pull out from NATO bases. On Feb. 24 Prime Minister Mulroney announces his resignation, to take effect in June. Four members of the **Canadian Airborne Regiment**, in Somalia since January on a peacekeeping mission, are charged in the death of a Somali civilian. NAFTA legislation passes in the House of Commons on May 27. Yukon's 14 First Nations sign the **Umbrella Final Agreement** in Whitehorse on May 29; the settlement includes 41,400 sq. km of land and $280 million. Defence Minister **Kim Campbell** takes over the Conservative government after a second-ballot victory at the leadership convention on June 25. On Oct. 25, the Liberal Party wins a decisive victory in a federal election that sees the emergence of **two new parties**—the Bloc Québécois and the Reform party—and the near demise of the Progressive Conservatives. The cod moratorium of 1992 is extended to include the Gulf of St. Lawrence and is slated to last until the end of the decade.

1994 Most of the country west of the Rockies endures the coldest winter since the 1950s. **Cigarette taxes** are cut federally and provincially in an effort to curb a black market in cigarettes. The Liberals' first budget forecasts cuts in defence spending, UI benefits, tax deductions and foreign aid and freezes transfer payments and public sector salaries. The **Canada Pension Plan** posts a deficit for the first time in 28 years. Members of the **Saskatchewan Wheat Pool** vote to transform the organization, formed in 1924, into a public company. The prime minister and provincial premiers sign an agreement to end trade barriers among the provinces. The Inuit of Quebec sign a self-government deal with the Quebec government. **Canadian troops leave CFB Lahr**, officially ending 27 years of Canadian service for NATO in Europe. The **Algonquins** of Gold Lake, Ont., sign an agreement to begin negotiating an 8.5-million-acre land claim in southern Canada. Canadian sports fans are left hockey-less until the new year by a labour dispute and **NHL lock-out**.

1995 The Canadian Airborne Regiment is disbanded in January after a new scandal compounds damage done by the **Somalia Affair**. Federal fisheries officials seize the Spanish fishing vessel *Estai* in March in a battle over fishing rights on the Grand Banks. A settlement of the dispute in April gives the **North Atlantic Fishing Organization** greater powers; in the same month, Canada loses its triple-A bond rating courtesy of Moody's Investors Service of New York. BC's Fraser River salmon run is shut down in August because fish stocks are too low. In September, Newfoundland voters approve a proposal to shift control of education from the church to the province. In October, **Alexa McDonough** is elected leader of the federal NDP. On Oct. 30, after a bruising campaign that sees federal Opposition Leader Bouchard take over the YES side, the **proposal that Quebec separate from Canada** to form a sovereign state is narrowly defeated in a referendum—49.4 percent Yes, and 50.6 percent against.

1996 The Mint unveils the new $2 coin (Feb. 19). On May 29, Canada and the US sign a **softwood lumber agreement** after 15 years of controversy. On July 9, the **Innu** of Davis Inlet agree to relocate to Sango Bay. On July 20–21, **devastating floods** hit the Saguenay valley in Quebec. On Oct. 2, former Quebec premier **Robert Bourassa** dies. On Oct. 8, Gen. Jean Boyle resigns as head of Canada's armed forces after controversial evidence arises at the **Somalia inquiry**. On Nov. 18, Canada and Chile sign a free trade deal. In December, Canada signs a $4 billion contract with China for two **CANDU** reactors.

1997 The federal government announces an out-of-court settlement with Brian Mulroney in his libel suit over the **Airbus investigation** (Jan. 6). Voters in Alberta give Premier **Ralph Klein** another majority (Mar. 11). On Mar. 6, the federal government's **anti-smoking bill**, which limits tobacco-company funding of arts and sports activities, passes in the House of Commons. Census data taken in 1996 and released on Apr. 15 reveals that Quebec's share of Canada's population has fallen below 25 percent for the first time since 1867. Premier **Gary Filmon** declares an emergency in southern Manitoba as the **Red River** floods across the US border (Apr. 22). An independent auditor confirms that the gold in samples from the **Bre-X claim** in Indonesia are "negligible" (May 4). The **Confederation Bridge** officially opens to traffic between PEI and the mainland (May 31). The federal Liberals win re-election with a reduced majority; the Reform party becomes the Opposition (June 2). Casting ballots in a second referendum on creating secular schools, Newfoundland voters support the change (Sept. 2). A judge rules that the **Red Cross** is negligent in the tainted-blood scandal (Oct. 8). A bus crash in Quebec kills 43 in the worst road accident in Canadian history (Oct. 13). **Saskatchewan Conservatives** vote to mothball their party for at least two provincial elections (Nov. 9). The annual **APEC conference** is held in Vancouver (Nov. 21–25); the RCMP pepper-spray student demonstrators. Canada agrees to the **Kyoto Convention** on greenhouse gas emissions (Dec. 11).

1998 An **ice storm** cripples Quebec and eastern Ontario, leaving one million people without power and food (Jan. 6). Ottawa apologizes to Canada's aboriginals for past mistreatment (Jan. 7). On Feb. 17, **Ontario Hydro** reports a loss of $6.32 billion in 1997—the largest business loss in Canadian history. Canadian athletes at the **Nagano Winter Olympics** win a record 15 medals (Feb. 22). On Mar. 27, federal Conservative leader **Jean Charest** says he will run for leader of Quebec's Liberal party. On the same day, federal and provincial governments announce $1.1 billion in compensation for victims who contracted hepatitis C from tainted blood in 1986–90. Ottawa and Washington agree to save Pacific salmon. The **Nisga'a** people and the BC government sign a historic land claim treaty (July 15). The Supreme Court of Canada rules on **Quebec's proposed secession from Canada:** Canada–Quebec talks must begin after a majority in Quebec votes for independence in a referendum with an unambiguous question (Aug. 20). On Sept. 1, a new blood collection agency replaces the Canadian Red Cross. **Swissair Flight 111** crashes off the coast of Nova Scotia, killing all 229 passengers (Sept. 2). Ten thousand gun owners meet on Parliament Hill to protest firearm registration (Sept. 22). Canada wins a seat on the UN Security Council (Oct. 8). Canada's first diamond mine opens in NWT (Oct. 14). Statistics Canada reports that inflation has sunk to 1960s levels (Oct. 21). The *National Post* publishes its first edition (Oct. 27). Ontario passes the **Energy Competition Act** to end Ontario Hydro's monopoly on power provision in 2001 (Oct. 29). Former prime minister **Joe Clark** is elected leader of the federal Conservative party (Nov. 14). Canada pledges $100 million in hurricane relief to Central America over four years (Nov. 15). The Saskatchewan Court of Appeal rules that **Robert Latimer** must serve at least 10 years in prison for the 1993 killing of his disabled daughter (Nov. 23). **Environment Canada** declares 1998 the warmest year globally in 130–140 years (Nov. 30). On Dec. 1, federal justice minister **Anne McLellan** officially launches Canada's new gun control law. Statistics Canada reports that the national jobless rate fell to 8 percent in November—the lowest level this decade (Dec. 4). Finance Minister Paul Martin prohibits Canadian **bank mergers**, saying they would concentrate economic power in the hands of fewer bankers and reduce competition (Dec. 14).

1999 Toronto's task force on homelessness reports that the fastest-growing groups of **homeless people** are youths under age 18 and families with children (Jan. 14). The next day, snowfall in Toronto surpasses 120 cm for January and breaks an 1871 record for snowfall in one month. Statistics Canada says the number of self-employed and part-time workers steadily grew in the 1990s (Jan. 27). Prime Minister Chrétien gets nine premiers to agree to a **social union accord** after promising more health-care funding for the provinces but fails to secure Quebec's signature (Feb. 4). In his federal budget address, Finance Minister Paul Martin promises an $11.5 billion boost in **health-care transfers** to the provinces over the next five years (Feb. 16). The *Free Press* of Regina and Saskatoon declares bankruptcy

(Feb. 17). In Ottawa, **Kurds** hurl a gasoline bomb at a police line outside the Turkish embassy, setting one officer ablaze (Feb. 17); in Montreal, police and about 100 Kurds clash outside the Israeli consulate (Feb. 22). Ottawa and all provinces except Nova Scotia offer $1.5 billion in relief to 45,000 farm families facing financial hardship caused by falling international grain and hog markets (Feb. 24). Senator **Eric Berntson** becomes the fifteenth Conservative convicted in Saskatchewan's long-running expense-fraud scandal (Feb. 25). The Liberal government moves to bar federal Crown corporations from donating to political parties (Mar. 5). Canadian **CF-18 fighter-bombers** begin taking part in NATO air strikes against **Yugoslavia** (Mar. 24); in Toronto, Serbs throw rocks, paint and Molotov cocktails at the US consulate and police (Mar. 24–25). In Manitoba, an inquiry led by **Alfred Monnin** reports that senior Tories illegally recruited and backed supposedly independent aboriginal candidates in the 1995 provincial election to split popular support for the NDP (Mar. 29). For the first time in Canada, **Mohawks** on Quebec's Kahnawake reserve win the right to collect tax-like levies from non-natives on reserves (Mar. 30). MPs from all federal parties endorse Canadian participation in NATO's air war against **Yugoslavia** (Mar. 31). Nunavut becomes Canada's newest territory; **Paul Okalik** becomes its first premier (Apr. 1). Ontario sells **Highway 407** to a Quebec-led consortium for $3.1 billion in the biggest privatization in Canadian history to date (Apr. 13). Statistics Canada reports that the average household is no richer than it was 20 years ago (Apr. 14). **Wayne Gretzky** plays his last professional hockey game (Apr. 18). The Supreme Court of Canada says the courts put too many offenders behind bars, making Canada's incarceration rate one of the highest in the world (Apr. 23). Newfoundland's legislature unanimously votes to change the province's official name to Newfoundland and Labrador (Apr. 29). **David Milgaard**, who spent 22 years in prison for a murder he did not commit, gets a record $10 million in compensation from the Saskatchewan and federal governments (May 17). The Supreme Court of Canada rules that the **Ontario Family Law Act**'s definition of spouse—which applies only to heterosexual couples—is unconstitutional because it discriminates against gays; the court also opens band elections to off-reserve natives for the first time (May 20). Ottawa unanimously passes a law giving victims more voice in the criminal justice system (May 28). Ottawa agrees to liberalize trade with five Andean countries (May 31). The House of Commons passes a Reform party motion that says marriage is a union between man and woman (June 8). Defence Minister **Art Eggleton** announces the departure of another 500 peacekeepers to **Kosovo** (June 11), two days after Western generals and Yugoslavia sign a peace accord. The **Coast Guard** intercepts a cargo ship filled with 123 Chinese **illegal immigrants** off Vancouver Island (July 20). Statistics Canada reports that Canada's crime rate fell for the seventh year in a row and hit a 19-year low (July 21). Canadian goaltender **Steve Vézina** tests positive for banned stimulants at the **Pan American Games**; his roller hockey team is stripped of its gold medals (Aug. 1). In Winnipeg, the Pan American Games close after Canadian athletes win 196 medals, 64 of them gold (Aug. 8). Explosions rock an oil-recycling plant in Calgary (Aug. 9). A second cargo ship dumps 131 Chinese illegal immigrants in the Queen Charlotte Islands (Aug. 11). After 130 years, **Eaton's** files for bankruptcy protection and announces plans to close its stores (Aug. 20). BC Premier **Glen Clark** resigns following the revelation that he was under criminal investigation for awarding a casino license to a friend (Aug. 21). The NDP meets for a national convention in Ottawa; **Alexa McDonough** wins support for a policy of balanced budgets and moderate tax cuts (Aug. 27–29). The Canadian Forces, RCMP and Coast Guard rescue Chinese immigrants aboard a third ship near Vancouver Island (Aug. 31). A BC court sentences **Dave Stupich**, a provincial finance minister in the 1980s, to two years in prison for stealing hundreds of thousands of dollars from an NDP fundraising society in Nanaimo (Sept. 3). Prime Minister Chrétien says Canada will send up to 600 peacekeepers to **East Timor** (Sept. 12). Cape Breton's Phalen coal mine shuts down ahead of schedule; 400 workers lose their jobs (Sept. 13). **Donald Marshall** wins a victory in the Supreme Court of Canada defending historic Mi'kmaq fishing rights (Sept. 17). On Oct. 3, non-natives, angry that aboriginals have been allowed to fish off-season, destroy native lobster traps in **Miramichi Bay** off the coast of northeastern New Brunswick. (The Supreme Court of

Canada judgment on Sept. 17, 1999, ruled that terms of a 1760 Mi'kmaq treaty allowing East Coast natives to earn a moderate livelihood from hunting, fishing and gathering is valid.) On Oct. 10, Fisheries Minister **Herb Dhaliwal** announces future limits on native fishing. On Oct. 13, the **World Trade Organization** rules that the 1965 Canada–US auto pact violates rules that call for freer global trade. On Oct. 29, Ottawa agrees to pay **$3.6 billion in back pay** to thousands of mostly female workers to compensate for wage gaps between men and women. On Nov. 7, a labour dispute shuts down West Coast ports for everything but bulk grain shipments for a week, costing the **Port of Vancouver** alone $90 million a day. On Nov. 23, **Wayne Gretzky** is inducted into the Hockey Hall of Fame. On Nov. 23, Health Canada releases 1,200 pages of industry documents showing Canadian-based Imperial Tobacco Ltd. assessed smokers as young as nine and "fortified" products to increase their addictive qualities. On Dec. 3, the jobless rate is reported at 6.9 percent, the lowest in 18 years. **Air Canada** gains control of **Canadian Airlines** on Dec. 8 and reaches a release agreement with AMR Corp., Canadian's largest shareholder. **Merchant mariners** and the federal government reach a deal (Dec. 15) on compensation for civilian seamen who served aboard cargo ships during the Second World War.

2000   On Jan. 12, **Beverley McLachlin** is sworn in as chief justice of the Supreme Court of Canada—the first woman to hold the office. On Jan. 13, Ottawa announces it will pay $1 billion over the next two years to help farmers through the latest crisis in agricultural prices, but critics say the promised aid isn't enough. On Jan. 27, the Reform party opens the convention destined to create the **Canadian Alliance**. Human Resources Minister **Jane Stewart** spends much of January trying to play down reports that her department had misspent $1 billion on dubious projects. On Jan. 31, Ottawa approves the $8 billion takeover of **Canada Trust** by **Toronto Dominion Bank**. BC Attorney General **Ujjal Dosanjh**'s first ballot win (Feb. 20) at the NDP convention sets the stage for him to become Canada's first Indo-Canadian premier four days later. On Mar. 15, the House of Commons votes overwhelmingly for legislation to clarify the rules if Quebec, or any other province, holds a referendum on secession. On Apr. 11, the federal government's **same-sex bill** passes through the Commons as MPs vote overwhelmingly for the legislation. The bill gives same-sex pairs the same social and tax benefits as heterosexual couples. On Apr. 13, **Nisga'a leaders** smile and fight tears as a land-claim treaty started 113 years ago by their ancestors clears its last parliamentary hurdle. The BC First Nation receives self-government powers and $253 million in cash and economic funding. Ottawa promises $255 million toward the deal that will cost a total of $487 million. In late May, seven deaths in **Walkerton**, Ont., are blamed on the worst *E. coli* outbreak in Canadian history. The contamination by the deadly bacteria is traced to the town's water supply; local officials are accused of failing to alert townspeople to the danger. Alberta's controversial **Bill 11**, authorizing some private health-care services, receives royal assent on May 31; critics of the bill claim that its inclusion of provisions for private health care will make Canada's health-care system open to globalization. On June 4 in Windsor, Ont., **anti-globalization protesters** are blasted with pepper spray and arrested as police riot squads brace for the opening of the annual general assembly of the Organization of American States. On June 15, the Supreme Court upholds the five-year-old **Firearms Act** that requires every gun owner to get a licence and register every firearm by the end of 2000. Baton-wielding riot police dodge bricks, paint bombs and Molotov cocktails on June 15 as more than 1,000 **anti-poverty protesters** attempt to storm the Ontario legislature to protest the policies of the Harris government. Preston Manning places second to **Stockwell Day** on June 24 as the Canadian Alliance votes for its first leader. Manning loses two weeks later in a second ballot. On July 5, federal Agriculture Minister Lyle Vanclief declares that Canada's **agriculture ministers** signed a $5.5-billion deal to take some of the uncertainty out of the farming business. **Matthew Coon Come**, a Cree leader from northern Quebec, unseats Phil Fontaine as national chief of the Assembly of First Nations on July 12. Ninety **Chinese migrants** who arrived in BC by boat in 1999 return to China on July 27 to face jail and fines. On July 31, **CanWest Global Communications Corp.** announces a $3.5-billion takeover of all the major Canadian newspapers held by Conrad Black's **Hollinger Inc.**

On July 31, Ontario's highest court declares the law banning possession of **marijuana** unconstitutional and gives Ottawa one year to amend it. The Ontario Court of Appeal rules that Canada's marijuana law fails to recognize that people who suffer from chronic illnesses can use pot as medicine. On Aug. 3, armed Canadian soldiers drop from helicopters to take charge of the American cargo ship **GTS *Katie***, loaded with Canadian military equipment, which is refusing to complete its delivery because of a dispute over payment. Victims of Canada's tainted-blood tragedy agree to a $79-million compensation plan on Aug. 30. The people infected by **hepatitis C** and **HIV** were infected before 1986 or after 1990, making them ineligible for the $1.5 billion federal-provincial compensation package announced two years earlier. Premiers strike a **health-care deal** on Sept. 11 with Prime Minister Jean Chrétien that raises federal transfers to $18.3 billion next year. The provinces want federal transfer payments restored to 1994 levels of $18.7 billion, which they say will cost $4.2 billion annually. On Sept. 11, Canadian Alliance leader Stockwell Day and PC leader Joe Clark win seats in **federal by-elections**. On Sept. 13, Groupe Videotron Ltee. agrees to be taken over by **Quebecor Inc.** for $5.4 billion. Finance Minister **Paul Martin** announces Sept. 20 that the surplus for 1999–2000 is $12.3 billion, with a $11.4-billion surplus in the first four months of the latest fiscal year. On Sept. 28, former prime minister **Pierre Trudeau** dies at the age of 80; his body is brought to Ottawa to lie in state on Sept. 30 and his state funeral is held at Montreal's Notre-Dame Basilica on Oct. 3. On Oct. 27, RCMP arrest two men charged in connection with the 15-year-long investigation of the Air India Flight 182 bombing in 1985. **NASDAQ Canada**, the tech-oriented stock exchange, commences trading in Montreal on Nov. 21. On Nov. 27 the Liberals win the general election with a healthy majority of 173 seats; the CA takes 66 to become the Official Opposition. Canadian astronaut **Marc Garneau** lifts off on his third space mission on board the space shuttle *Endeavour* on Nov. 30. His mission is to take and install solar panels on the International Space Station. He returns to Earth on Dec. 11.

2001 Despite a last-minute rush to meet the Jan. 1 deadline, hundreds of thousands of

gun owners fail to register their guns. Two **gay couples**, one male and one female, are married on Jan. 14 in a Toronto church in a campaign to change Canada's ban on same-sex marriages. In a rare settlement, the **Correctional Service of Canada** agrees to pay $215,000 to a sexual-assault victim only hours before her civil suit against the prison system is due to begin. **Lorne Calvert** is elected leader of the NDP in Saskatchewan and the province's premier at a leadership convention in Saskatoon (Jan. 27). Ottawa bans the importation of **Brazilian beef** (Feb. 2) as a precaution against mad cow disease. Claiming there is no danger, Brazil says that the move is just part of a long-running trade battle. **Roger Grimes** becomes premier of Newfoundland and Labrador (Feb. 13). In February, the Supreme Court of Canada rules unanimously against extradition to countries that have **capital punishment**, unless there is assurance that detainees will not be executed if convicted of a crime carrying the death penalty. The ruling comes in the case of two Vancouver men, Glen Sebastian Burns and Atif Ahmad Rafay, wanted in Washington State for several murders. **Bernard Landry** is acclaimed premier of Quebec (Mar. 8). Alberta Premier **Ralph Klein** wins his third term in the Mar. 12 election. Hundreds of tractors and farm vehicles head for Ottawa in a Canada-wide protest to demand more financial support for **farmers**. The federal government had unveiled a $500-million aid package, but farmers—hurt by low commodity prices and poor harvests due to drought-like conditions—say it is not enough (Mar. 14). Canada's **softwood lumber** deal with the US expires on Mar. 31; US companies ask Washington to establish anti-dumping and countervailing duties against Canadian products. Health Minister **Allan Rock** appoints former Saskatchewan premier **Roy Romanow** to investigate Canadian health care and consider the role of private health care. A **VIA train** derails in Stewiacke, NS, injuring 24, after a switch lock is set incorrectly (Apr. 12). A teen is later charged with mischief. Astronaut **Chris Hadfield** becomes the first Canadian to walk in space as he deploys the new Canadarm2 during a mission to space station *Alpha* (Apr. 19). The **Summit of the Americas** is held in Quebec City (Apr. 20-22). More than 30,000 demonstrators march during the meeting of national leaders from North, Central and South America. Several hundred are arrested following battles with police and thousands are tear-gassed. Ontario Chief Justice Patrick LeSage approves a no-fault settlement in a class-action suit arising from the tainted-water tragedy in **Walkerton**, Ont. Under the settlement, all of the town's 5,000 residents plus visitors who got sick receive at least $2,000. American George Gillett buys 80 percent of the **Montreal Canadiens** from Molson Inc. for $275 million (May 7). (The NHL approves the deal in June, which becomes final in July.) On May 15, **eight Alliance MPs** leave their party and form a rebel faction due to leader Stockwell Day's poor performance. Ottawa announces that the last underground coal mine in **Cape Breton** will be shut down by the fall; 500 jobs will disappear along with a 280-year tradition (May 16). Liberal leader **Gordon Campbell** becomes premier of BC after his party defeats the NDP led by **Ujjal Dosanjh** (May 16). BC's NDP is reduced to two seats. Nova Scotia passes legislation giving **gay couples** registered with the Department of Vital Statistics some of the rights formerly reserved for married heterosexual couples. Members of Parliament vote to fast-track a new **pay package** for themselves, which includes a 20 percent raise but ends their tax-free expense allowance (June 5). Calgary-based **Gulf Canada Resources Ltd.** agrees to be taken over by Conoco Inc. of Houston for $9.8 billion. The Ontario government becomes the first provincial government to offer **tax credits** to families with children in private or independent religious schools (June 27). The credit is to be phased in over five years. The total of **Alliance defections** reaches 11 on June 27, putting the rebel group one member shy of official party status. Ontario Premier **Mike Harris** testifies before the Walkerton inquiry that he was never warned of risks to human health posed by funding cuts to the Environment Ministry (June 29). **Nortel Networks** announces the biggest quarterly loss in Canadian corporate history: US$19.4 billion in its second quarter (July 20). MPs from the Canadian Alliance and the Conservative party meet for two days in Halifax; on July 27, the group pledges to work together. Seven children, removed from their Aylmer, Ont., home by **Children's Aid** in a clash over spanking and medical care, are reunited with their Christian parents. On July 30, United Grain Growers and Agricore announce a merger to create **Agricore United**. The new company will control close to 40 percent of western Canadian grain. The **provincial premiers**, in a rare show of solidarity, demand $7 billion from Ottawa for their health-care systems to forestall cuts to service (Aug. 3). The US commerce department levies a 19.3 percent duty on Canadian **softwood lumber** from all provinces outside Atlantic Canada; the duty is made retroactive to mid-May and is projected to cost Canadian producers $4 billion a year (Aug. 10). **Conrad Black** announces the sale of his remaining half interest in the *National Post* to the Asper family's **CanWest Global Communications** (Aug. 24). By Aug. 28, 10 birds in Southern Ontario are found carrying the **West Nile virus**, which can be fatal in humans. On Sept. 11, three of the **Alliance dissidents** return to the party caucus and the remaining eight form a coalition with the Conservatives in the House of Commons. **Hundreds of flights** denied entry into US airspace are grounded in Canada after the terrorist attacks on New York City and Washington; thousands of travellers are put up in Canadian communities, from Gander to Vancouver, in hotels, school gyms and private homes. In the wake of the Sept. 11 attacks, **stricter surveillance** makes it tougher to cross the Canada–U.S. border and delays shipments, forcing thousands of layoffs in the Ontario auto industry. The ban on **air traffic** in Canada is lifted on the afternoon of Sept. 12; however, it takes days for air traffic to return to normal. On Sept. 14, 100,000 gather on Parliament Hill to pay respects to the victims of the terrorist attacks in the US. **Tropical storm Gabrielle** pounds the eastern coast of Newfoundland and Labrador with rain and winds of 111 km an hour (Sept. 19). The damage prompts the provincial government to apply for federal disaster relief. **General Motors** announces the closure of its assembly plant in Broisbriand, Que., for the fall of 2002, eliminating the province's auto industry (Sept. 25). On Sept. 26, Ottawa announces that it will freeze the assets of any group that the US government identifies as having terrorist links. On Oct. 2, Ottawa announces a **$160-million bailout** to help airlines cope with post-Sept. 11 financial losses. On Oct. 8, Defence Minister **Art Eggleton** outlines Canada's military aid to US-led operations in Afghanistan. Assistance includes six ships,

six aircraft and more than 2,000 personnel. An **anti-terrorism bill** in the House of Commons proposes to create new terrorist-related offences. The government considers giving new powers, such as the power to make preventive arrests and to monitor communications going outside Canada, to police and security forces (Oct. 15). A consortium of energy companies signs a deal with the **Mackenzie Valley Aboriginal Pipeline Corp.** and gives aboriginals a one-third stake in a proposed natural gas pipeline (Oct. 15). On Oct. 22, Health Minister **Allan Rock** approves the purchase of a generic version of the drug for treating exposure to **anthrax**; Bayer, holder of the patent for Cipro, threatens a lawsuit. The US Commerce Department places a second duty on Canadian **softwood lumber**, adding a 12.6 percent dumping duty to the existing 19.3 percent countervailing duty (Oct. 31). A Senate committee reviewing the **anti-terrorism bill** recommends placing a five-year limit on any new powers given to police. The committee also recommends that government ministers given new powers under the bill be strictly supervised to guarantee citizens' freedoms (Nov. 1). On Nov. 9, **Canada 3000**, the country's second-largest airline, leaves thousands of travellers stranded when it grounds its fleet and files for bankruptcy. Police and demonstrators clash when the **G-20 group of nations** meets in Ottawa (Nov. 17–18). On Nov. 29, released court documents show that **Samir Ait Mohamed**, an Algerian held in Vancouver and accused of plotting a terrorist attack in 1999 on the Los Angeles airport, had also planned attacks on Jews in Montreal. Alberta introduces regulations allowing some surgery in **private clinics** (Nov. 30). Thousands of Canadians, including Prime Minister Chrétien, take part in a "Canada Loves New York" rally in Manhattan to pay tribute to those who risked and lost their lives on Sept. 11, 2001 (Dec. 1). On Dec. 3, Canada and the US sign a **border security agreement** that includes more information sharing and border patrols by the US National Guard. Newfoundland's name officially changes to Newfoundland and Labrador (Dec. 6). On Dec. 12, the House of Commons releases a report on **reproductive technologies**, setting boundaries for researchers and users. The report calls for a ban on cloning humans and patenting human genes, but allows for experiments on human embryos left over from fertility treatments. **Stockwell Day** resigns as leader of the Canadian Alliance (Dec. 12). On Dec. 12, Ontario Premier Mike Harris announces plans to privatize **Hydro One** and open the province's electricity market to competition. Health Canada announces that **marijuana** grown in Flin Flon, Man., for medical use is available for shipment to eligible users (Dec. 21).

2002 A Montreal man, **Mokhtar Haouri**, is sentenced to 24 years in prison for his role in the plot to bomb the Los Angeles airport on the last day of 1999 (Jan. 16). The dollar hits a record low of US$0.62 (Jan. 17). On Jan 18, the first instalment of the report on **Walkerton** blames the Ontario Conservative government's emphasis on cost-cutting and deregulation for contributing to the May 2000 *E. coli* outbreak that killed seven people and made 2,300 ill. On Jan. 29, Defence Minister Eggleton confirms that **Canadian soldiers** have captured **al-Qaeda and Taliban fighters** and has handed them to US forces during the previous week. Former leader of the Reform party **Preston Manning** retires from politics (Jan. 31). On Feb. 4, 14,000 **Alberta teachers strike**. They are ordered back to work three weeks later. A $3.4-billion deal is signed by leaders of Quebec and the **Cree Nation**, opening Cree territory to future hydroelectric projects (Feb. 7). At the Olympics in Salt Lake City, the near-perfect performance of Canadian figure skaters **Jaime Salé** and **David Pelletier** on Feb. 11 wins them a silver medal. The gold goes to the Russian team, whose performance is flawed. A French judge later admits that she was pressured to favour the Russians. Salé and Pelletier get a new set of gold medals four days later. Federal Solicitor General **Lawrence MacAulay** gives in to provincial demands to create a national sex offender registry (Feb. 13). On Feb. 20, Ontario Premier **Mike Harris** files a $15-million lawsuit over a story in *The Globe and Mail* linking him to the 1995 police shooting of native protester **Dudley George**. An investigation into the **disappearance of 50 women** since 1983 leads police to a pig farm in Port Coquitlam, B.C. On Feb. 22, police charge the farm's owner, Robert William Pickton, with two counts of murder. About 45,000 **Ontario public servants** strike over wages and job security (Mar. 13). On Mar. 14, about 500 Canadian soldiers lead **Operation Harpoon**

against suspected terrorists in Afghanistan. The attack is the Canadian Forces' biggest ground offensive in more than 50 years. On Mar. 17, the **Arctic Winter Games** open in Iqaluit. The event is the largest held to date in Nunavut. **Stephen Harper** is elected leader of the Canadian Alliance (Mar. 20). On Apr. 3, **James Sabzali**, a Canadian living in the US, becomes the first foreign national convicted under the US law barring trade with Cuba. Prime Minister Chrétien begins a tour of six countries in Africa (Apr. 3). The report of an inquiry into **North Battleford's water** is released on Apr. 5, and the Saskatchewan government adopts all its recommendations. In March and April 2001, about 7,000 North Battleford residents became ill from a parasite contaminating the city's water. NDP MP **Svend Robinson** tries to visit **Yasser Arafat** in Ramallah on Apr. 6, but Robinson is removed by Israeli soldiers. Party leader **Alexa McDonough** distances the NDP from his visit and from the perception that the NDP favours either side in the Middle East conflict. **Ernie Eves** is sworn in as premier of Ontario (Apr. 15). In Afghanistan, **four Canadian soldiers die** and eight are wounded when a US F-16 fighter pilot bombs them during a live-fire training exercise at night. (Apr. 17) The pilot says later that he mistook the exercise for hostile fire and acted in self-defence. In Toronto, **Marcia and Tony Dooley** are convicted of murdering their seven-year-old son Randal in one of the worst cases of child abuse in Canadian history (Apr. 19). Two labour unions challenge the Ontario government's decision to sell **Hydro One** in court; on Apr. 19, the court rules that the province lacks the authority to sell. A military panel led by **Maurice Baril**, former chief of the defence staff, begins investigating the **deaths of four Canadian soldiers** killed in Afghanistan (Apr. 22). The federal government unveils a new anti-terrorism bill, the **Public Safety Act**, which replaces the bill tabled in the fall (Apr. 29). On May 1, the **Ontario electricity market** opens to competition. Prices are set by the market, not by a provincial regulator. Moody's Investor Service restores **Canada's Triple-A credit rating** on May 3; it had been downgraded in 1995. A jury finds **Hells Angels** leader Maurice (Mom) Boucher guilty of attempted murder and two counts of first degree murder in the 1997 shooting deaths of two prison guards (May 5). It is Boucher's second trial for the killings. On May 8,

Federal Auditor General **Sheila Fraser** recommends an RCMP investigation into $1.6 million worth of contracts awarded to a Montreal ad agency by **Alfonso Gagliano**, the former minister of public works. Fraser says the department "broke just about every rule in the book" in awarding the contracts, and the agency, Groupaction, may not have done the work. The informal inquiry into the contracts becomes a **criminal investigation** later in the month. On May 14, **1,700 people evacuate their homes** in Notre-Dame-du-Lac, Que., when fire destroys an abattoir and fear spreads that ammonia in the plant might be released. In Quebec City, a **bomb** blasts a hole in a door of the town's only **synagogue** (May 19). Ontario Public Safety Minister **Bob Runciman** announces that provincial police have shut down an **al-Qaeda "sleeper cell"** (May 22). On May 26, Prime Minister **Jean Chrétien** fires Defence Minister **Art Eggleton** for awarding a $36,500 military contract to an ex-girlfriend; Chrétien also takes the public works portfolio away from **Don Boudria**, who faces conflict of interest charges. On June 2, Prime Minister Chrétien dismisses Finance Minister **Paul Martin**. Inco Ltd. and the Newfoundland government sign a $2.9-billion deal to develop **Voisey Bay's** mineral deposit in Labrador in 2006 (June 11). On June 14, the federal government introduces a revised Indian Act: the **First Nations Governance Act**. Candidates for the new Action Démocratique du Québec party defeat their PQ rivals in **three Montreal by-elections** on June 17. On July 3, **B.C. holds a referendum** asking respondents to vote yes or no to eight principles proposed to guide B.C. in aboriginal treaty negotiations. Native groups call for a boycott, and critics say the questions are skewed to ensure agreement. Police reveal on July 10 that they have seized **$100 million worth of drugs** and have arrested 39 people in Halifax—one of the largest drug busts in Canadian history. The Alberta government announces a $324-million **drought relief package** (July 17). The province faces its third consecutive year of drought. Pope John Paul II and 200,000 young people from around the world come to Toronto for **World Youth Day** (July 23–28). Solicitor General **Lawrence MacAulay** bans al-Qaeda and six other extremist groups from Canada (July 23). On July 26, the World Trade Organization initially rules in favour of Canada in the **softwood lumber dispute**

between Canada and the US; the WTO denies US claims that Canada unfairly subsidizes producers. Mi'kmaq leaders in Burnt Church, N.B., and the federal government agree to end **the dispute over the lobster fishery** between native and non-native fishers (Aug. 1). Because the summer's drought left prairie farmers without feed for their herds, farmers in Ontario and Quebec launch the **"Hay West"** campaign in July. On Aug. 5, donated hay from Ontario starts arriving in Saskatchewan and Alberta. On Aug. 21, after months of public speculation, Prime Minister **Jean Chrétien** says that he will not run in the next election but will continue to lead Canada until February 2004. A B.C. court finds former premier **Glen Clark** not guilty of charges of breach of trust and accepting a benefit (Aug. 29). Prime Minister Chrétien announces at the World Summit on Sustainable Development that Canada will ratify the **Kyoto Accord** by year's end (Sept. 2). The first Canadian case of **West Nile virus** in a human is confirmed in an Ontario man (Sept. 6). Violence at **Montreal's Concordia University** forces visiting former Israeli prime minister **Benjamin Netanyahu** to cancel a planned speech (Sept. 9). The following day, he receives a standing ovation in Toronto. On Sept. 11, Canadians join in **remembrance ceremonies** for victims of the terrorist attacks in 2001 on the US. Prime Minister Chrétien visits Gander, Nfld, where thousands of air travellers had been stranded in 2001; he also visits New York later in the day. On Sept. 13, the US Air Force charges two pilots in the "friendly fire" incident that killed four Canadian soldiers and wounded eight in Afghanistan in April. Maj. **Harry Schmidt** is charged with involuntary manslaughter and assault; Maj. **William Umbach** is charged with aiding and abetting manslaughter and assault. On Sept. 18, Nova Scotia Premier **John Hamm** announces a $60-million clean-up of Halifax harbour. A **health-care workers strike** in Saskatchewan expands to 27 groups of health professionals—2,500 members of the Health Sciences Association of Saskatchewan—when bargaining breaks off in mid-September. At midnight on Sept. 30, Newfoundland and Labrador's **physicians strike** to gain wage parity with their counterparts in the rest of the Atlantic region. Only emergency room services remain available in the first such strike in the province's history. Deputy Prime

Minister **John Manley** says Canada no longer needs the monarchy as **Queen Elizabeth II** begins a 12-day tour of Canada (Oct. 4). American authorities deport **Maher Arar**, a Syrian-born Canadian citizen, to Syria for having alleged ties to terrorists (Oct. 8); in Syria, Arar is imprisoned and tortured for months. Auditor General **Sheila Fraser** declares that most provinces contravene the **Canada Health Act**, but Ottawa lacks the resources or will to crack down (Oct. 9). **Julian Fantino**, Toronto's police chief, announces an inquiry into the police department's treatment of black citizens (Oct. 25). Foreign Minister Bill Graham confirms that American officials have transferred **Omar Khadr**, a Canadian, from Afghanistan to Guantanamo Bay in Cuba where 600 suspected **al-Qaeda** combatants are imprisoned (Oct. 31). The Supreme Court of Canada grants **federal penitentiary inmates** the right to vote in federal elections (Nov. 1). In the House of Commons, Prime Minister **Jean Chrétien** loses the authority to single-handedly appoint the chairs of parliamentary committees (Nov. 6). **Lucille Poulin**, 78, a former Catholic nun, is sentenced to eight months in jail for assaulting children in a religious commune in PEI (Nov. 8). **Larry Campbell**, a former RCMP officer and coroner, becomes Vancouver's mayor and ends 16 years of conservative mayoral government (Nov. 18). The **Romanow report** on Canadian health care is released (Nov. 28); the report calls for a $15-billion infusion of federal funds by 2006 and rejects the need for increased private care. The House of Commons votes to ratify the **Kyoto Protocol** (Dec. 10). The **Innu**, one of Canada's most troubled native communities, begin moving from Davis Inlet to Natuashish in Labrador (Dec. 12). Ottawa declares that it will ban the political arm of **Hezbollah**, a Lebanese guerrilla organization (Dec. 13); Ottawa banned the Hezbollah's military arm in 2001. The Supreme Court of Canada rules that people in **common-law relationships** do not have an automatic right to a 50-50 division of assets after breaking up (Dec. 20).

2003 A court grants bankruptcy protection to the National Hockey League's **Ottawa Senators** (Jan. 9). Ottawa announces that it will invest $172.5 million over five years to upgrade security at Canada's **major seaports** (Jan. 22). A B.C. judge throws out the ban on publishing Atlantic Canada's vote before

Western polls close in federal elections (Jan. 29); Elections Canada appeals the decision. In early February, two severe **ice storms** hit south-central New Brunswick; they leave about 60,000 homes and businesses without power (Feb. 2). **Police in Regina** recover a missing computer hard drive containing personal and financial data on about 1 million Canadians (Feb. 4). Forty Edmontonians skate into the *Guinness Book of World Records* by playing the **world's longest outdoor hockey game** (80 hours) and raise more than $83,000 for cancer research (Feb. 17). The United States imposes a 3.94 percent tariff on **Canadian wheat** (Mar. 5). Edmonton passes a bylaw—the first in Canada—that allows police to ticket **schoolyard bullies** who repeatedly shove and name-call their peers (Mar. 11). A fire destroys much of Edmonton's **Old Strathcona**, the former staging ground for the Yukon gold rush (Mar. 13) Days after the World Health Organization (WHO) declares that **Severe Acute Respiratory Syndrome** (SARS) poses a worldwide threat to human life on Mar. 15, the virus affects people in the Toronto area. Ottawa pledges $250 million more in **aid to Afghanistan** (Mar. 17); the sum is double the amount given to Afghanistan since 1990 and is the largest Canadian aid commitment made to a single country. The military hearing on the "friendly fire" deaths of **four Canadian soldiers** in Afghanistan last year recommends that the American fighter pilots face administrative punishment instead of a court martial and criminal charges (Mar. 20). Ottawa pledges to establish 10 new **national parks** and protect marine areas over five years (Mar. 25). B.C. declares its intention to relax timber-cutting rules to revitalize the **softwood lumber industry** (Mar. 26). Newfoundland and Labrador becomes the first province to ban the use of **hand-held cellphones** while driving (Apr. 1). The federal government grants the **Yukon** full control of its natural resources (Apr. 1). In early April, heavy rain and melting snow flood homes and destroy roads and bridges in Nova Scotia, New Brunswick and parts of Newfoundland. **Alberta** announces its 10th straight budgetary surplus ($1.1 billion) alongside a spending increase of nearly 5 percent (Apr. 9). The federal government closes the **Atlantic cod fishery**, ending an 11-year moratorium on cod fishing and a centuries-old industry (Apr. 24); Ottawa offers about 1,000 commercial fishermen $44 million in compensation. B.C.'s Court of Appeal gives Ottawa and the provinces until July 2004 to change existing marriage laws to permit **same-sex marriage** (May 1). Ottawa declares Nazi sympathizer **Ernst Zundel** a national security risk (May 2). The federal government announces that Canada will assume command of the **international peacekeeping mission** in Kabul (May 5); the first 1,800 troops depart for Afghanistan in August 2003. The WHO removes Toronto from its list of **SARS-affected areas** (May 14); 12 days later, however, the WHO puts Toronto back on the list after the city discovers eight new probable and 26 suspected cases of SARS. A cow in Alberta is diagnosed with **"mad cow" disease** (May 20); the US, Australia, South Korea and Japan subsequently ban imports of Canadian beef, cattle and animal feed. Food inspectors single out nearly 1,000 cattle for slaughter and quarantine 17 farms in Alberta, B.C. and Saskatchewan (May 28). With the approval of Vancouver's Bishop **Michael Ingham**, an Anglican priest blesses a same-sex union (May 29). Prime Minister Chrétien's reform of **election financing** passes through Parliament (June 11); the law reduces corporate donations but requires taxpayers to pay $1.75 per vote per party based on the most recent election. Ottawa introduces legislation to make **same-sex marriages** legal while permitting churches and religious groups to "sanctify marriages as they see it" (June 17); the decision follows court rulings in favour of same-sex marriages in B.C., Quebec and Ontario. Photojournalist **Zahra Kazemi**, a dual citizen of Iran and Canada, is arrested in Iran while taking pictures of protestors outside a prison (June 23); she is subsequently beaten to death in custody. Privacy Commissioner **George Radwanski** resigns amid investigations by the auditor general and a parliamentary committee into his lavish food and travel spending (June 24). Canada becomes the first country to distribute **marijuana** to individuals with a medical right to use it (July 9). The eight-team **Canadian Baseball League** announces that it will shut down halfway through its first season (July 18). Ottawa recalls **Philip MacKinnon**, Canada's ambassador to Iran, after Iran ignores requests to return the body of **Zahra Kazemi** (July 25). In Montreal, during a meeting of the **World Trade Organization**, thousands of demonstrators protesting economic globalization clash with **riot police**; police arrest hundreds (July 27–29). In Toronto, almost 450,000 people attend Canada's largest rock concert—headlined by the **Rolling Stones**—to benefit SARS victims (July 30). B.C. declares an emergency when **forest fires** ravage the Okanagan and Kamloops regions (Aug. 2); firefighters and more than 2,200 soldiers use 27 aircraft and 115 helicopters to fight fires into September. In **Quebec**, heavy rain causes floods that destroy homes and uproot trees (Aug. 6). In **Halifax**, a blast in a grain elevator forces almost 400 people from their homes (Aug. 7). Ottawa unveils a $1.3-billion plan to cut greenhouse gas emissions in line with the **Kyoto Protocol** (Aug. 12); the measures include a $100-million subsidy for ethanol fuel and a $1,000 inducement to homeowners to make houses more energy efficient. Dr. **Nestor Yanga** becomes the 44th person to die of SARS in the Toronto area (Aug. 13). Ontario and Quebec lose electric power for two days during the continent's biggest **power blackout** (Aug. 14–15). Saskatchewan and North Battleford reach a $3.2-million settlement with 700 **North Battleford residents** who had become ill in 2001 after drinking water infected by a parasite (Aug. 21). In the Northwest Territories, **Dogrib natives** assume ownership of about 39,000 square km of land—including Canada's two biggest **diamond mines**—north of Great Slave Lake (Aug. 25). A North American Free Trade panel rules that the US has failed to prove that Canadian softwood exports threaten American lumber firms (Sept. 5). The House of Commons votes 137 to 132 to reject a motion by the **Canadian Alliance** that reaffirms marriage as a union between a man and a woman (Sept. 16). On Ellesmere Island, the **Ward Hunt ice shelf**, which jutted into the Arctic Ocean for more than 3,000 years, breaks up (Sept. 21); scientists say the region is warming. In Saskatchewan, the provincial death toll caused by **West Nile virus** rises to six people (Sept. 23); the province has the greatest number of cases— more than 400 confirmed and probable cases—of the virus in Canada. In Quebec, about 6,000 **day-care workers** hold walkouts, affecting more than 300 day-care centres (Sept. 26). In Nova Scotia, **Hurricane Juan** kills two people and causes extensive flooding and damage in Halifax (Sept. 29).

Aboriginal Languages

More than 975,000 people identified themselves as aboriginal in Canada's latest census in 2001. Aboriginal peoples include the First Nations (i.e., native Indians), Métis and Inuit.

Aboriginal people in Canada belong to 11 different language groups: the Algonkian, Athapaskan, Haidan, Inuktitut, Iroquoian, Kutenai (or Kootenay), Salishan, Siouan (or Dakotan), Tlingit, Tsimshian and Wakashan. Aboriginal people in Canada speak 50 different languages.

The three most common aboriginal languages in Canada are Cree, Inuktitut and Ojibway. Cree and Ojibway belong to the Algonkian language group. The least common languages include the Wakashan languages and Chipewyan. Chipewyan belongs to the Athapaskan language group.

Only one-quarter of aboriginal people in Canada, however, know enough of their ancestral languages to conduct conversations in them. A total of 235,075 people (24 percent) had this ability, according to the census of 2001.

The overall use of aboriginal languages in conversation in Canada is declining. In the

Population Reporting an Aboriginal Identity[1] by Mother Tongue[2] in Eastern Canada

	Canada	Nfld	PEI	NS	NB	Que.	Ont.
Aboriginal Population	976 305	18 775	1 345	17 010	16 990	79 400	188 310
Total Single Responses[4]	956 240	18 685	1 320	16 805	16 565	77 560	185 010
English	704 770	16 595	1 105	11 975	9 165	9 180	151 320
French	64 130	50	25	785	4 385	32 900	13 560
Non-Official Languages[3]	187 340	2 040	195	4 050	3 020	35 480	20 125
Aboriginal Languages	186 835	2 040	195	4 045	3 005	35 455	19 970
Cree	72 680	10	0	30	10	11 810	4 385
Inuktitut	29 005	545	10	10	20	8 620	160
Ojibway	20 890	0	0	10	10	20	9 670
Montagnais-Naskapi	9 655	1 470	0	0	0	8 180	0
Micmac	7 230	10	185	3 995	2 265	690	60
Dakota/Sioux	3 880	0	0	0	0	0	10
Blackfoot	2 740	0	0	0	0	10	25
Salish Languages	2 590	0	0	0	0	0	0
South Slave	1 380	0	0	0	0	0	0
Dogrib	1 860	0	0	0	0	0	10
Carrier	1 225	0	0	0	0	0	0
Wakashan Languages	1 275	0	0	0	0	0	0
Chipewyan	575	0	0	0	0	0	10
Other Aboriginal Languages	31 840	0	0	15	715	6 130	5 640
Non-Aboriginal Languages	505	0	0	0	15	30	155
Total Multiple Responses[5]	20 070	90	20	205	425	1 845	3 300
Multiple Aboriginal & Non-Aboriginal Responses	15 470	75	10	135	190	970	1 605
English and Aboriginal Language(s)	14 130	75	10	135	175	325	1 485
French and Aboriginal Language(s)	1 010	0	0	0	15	565	65
English, French and Aboriginal Language(s)	330	0	0	0	0	80	55
Other Multiple Responses	4 600	15	10	70	235	875	1 695

Source: *Statistics Canada, Census of Population (2001)*

(1) Refers to persons who identified with at least one aboriginal group (i.e, North American Indian, Métis or Inuit) and/or reported being Treaty Indians or Registered Indians as defined by the Indian Act of Canada and/or reported being members of an Indian band or First Nation. (2) Refers to the first language learned at home in childhood and still understood by the person in 2001. (3) Not English or French. (4) "Single responses" refers to respondents who reported only one language as mother tongue. (5) "Multiple responses" refers to respondents who reported more than one language as mother tongue.

census of 1996, Statistics Canada reported that 29 percent of the total of 799,010 aboriginal people could conduct a conversation in an aborginal language.

A closer look at aboriginal languages, however, shows that a few are increasing in use while others are declining. Eight of the 14 languages with at least 2,000 speakers in 2001 had increased since 1996 while six languages showed declines.

Between 1996 and 2001, the number of people who could conduct a conversation in Inuktitut, Dene, Montagnais-Naskapi and Attikamekw rose. Micmac, Dakota/Sioux and

Oji-Cree also posted small gains in speakers during the same period.

Between 1996 and 2001, Cree and Ojibway showed small declines in knowledge. The number of speakers of Blackfoot, which belongs to the Algonkian language group, fell from about 4,145 to 2,740 speakers in Canada.

According to Natural Resources Canada, about 10 once-flourishing aboriginal languages became extinct within the last 100 years in Canada. At least a dozen such languages are threatened with extinction now.

Population Reporting an Aboriginal Identity[1] by Mother Tongue[2] in Western and Northern Canada

	Man.	Sask.	Alta	BC	YT	NWT	Nun.
Aboriginal Population	150 040	130 190	156 220	170 025	6 545	18 725	22 720
Total Single Responses[4]	145 845	127 125	153 000	167 240	6 360	18 440	22 290
English	106 050	95 095	127 505	154 640	5 540	12 965	3 640
French	6 400	1 585	2 050	2 180	60	135	25
Non-Official Languages[3]	33 395	30 445	23 445	10 420	755	5 340	18 625
Aboriginal Languages	33 315	30 405	23 380	10 315	755	5 340	18 615
Cree	18 090	22 020	15 010	1 160	15	155	0
Inuktitut	70	50	100	50	20	760	18 605
Ojibway	8 840	1 370	625	275	10	65	0
Montagnais-Naskapi	0	0	0	0	0	0	0
Micmac	0	20	0	15	0	0	0
Dakota/Sioux	730	350	2 765	25	0	0	0
Blackfoot	25	15	2 630	35	10	0	0
Salish Languages	0	0	0	2 570	10	0	0
South Slave	0	0	250	100	20	1 005	0
Dogrib	0	10	10	20	0	1 830	0
Carrier	0	0	0	1 215	0	0	0
Wakashan Languages	0	0	0	1 270	0	0	0
Chipewyan	20	0	225	10	10	300	10
Other Aboriginal Languages	5 540	6 570	1 760	3 570	675	1 215	0
Non-Aboriginal Languages	75	45	70	105	0	0	10
Total Multiple Responses[5]	4 200	3 065	3 215	2 790	195	290	445
Multiple Aboriginal & Non-Aboriginal Responses	3 645	2 845	2 915	2 225	160	270	435
English and Aboriginal Language(s)	3 520	2 695	2 770	2 100	150	260	425
French and Aboriginal Language(s)	95	95	90	70	0	10	10
English, French and Aboriginal Language(s)	30	55	55	55	10	0	0
Other Multiple Responses	555	220	300	565	35	20	10

Source: *Statistics Canada, Census of Population (2001)*
(1) Refers to persons who identified with at least one aboriginal group (i.e., North American Indian, Métis or Inuit) and/or reported being Treaty Indians or Registered Indians as defined by the Indian Act of Canada and/or reported being members of an Indian band or First Nation. (2) Refers to the first language learned at home in childhood and still understood by the person in 2001. (3) Not English or French. (4) "Single responses" refers to respondents who reported only one language as mother tongue. (5) "Multiple responses" refers to respondents who reported more than one language as mother tongue.

Canadian Disasters

Aug. 29, 1583: Canada's first recorded marine disaster took 85 lives when the *Delight* was wrecked on Sable Island.

1710: Ships arriving in Quebec City from the West Indies brought a cargo that included yellow fever. The resulting epidemic killed a number of people, including six nurses, 12 priests and the ship's crew.

Aug. 23, 1711: As many as 950 drowned when ships attached to the British fleet preparing to attack Quebec were grounded and sank on the rocks of Ile-aux-Oeufs.

1746: Typhus broke out on a flotilla of French warships sailing for Port Royal in Acadia. Of the 3,150 soldiers aboard, 1,270 died at sea; another 1,130 died in the Bedford Basin while waiting for an army from Quebec. Typhus then spread to the Mi'kmaq population.

Oct. 5, 1825: A fire destroyed Newcastle and Douglastown, north of the Miramichi River, in New Brunswick. Between 200 and 500 people died.

1832–34: Cholera swept through Lower Canada when diseased Irish and English immigrants arrived in Quebec City. In Montreal, the disease killed at least 947 people between June 10–27, 1832.

Despite attempts by the authorities to quarantine infected immigrants on Grosse Île in the St Lawrence River, between 1833–34, the cholera killed about 3,800 people in Quebec City and 1,900 more in Montreal.

May 17, 1841: On this date, several large boulders from Cap Diamant tumbled down the precipitous cliffs above the Lower Town of Quebec City and demolished eight houses, killing 32 people.

1847: Ireland's potato famine prompted tens of thousands of Irish to sail for North America. Typhus killed about 5,000 immigrants at sea; at Grosse Île, medical inspectors buried at least 5,424 people throughout the year. From Grosse Île, some ships went to Pointe Saint-Charles, Montreal, where another 6,000 Irish immigrants died and were buried. The epidemic also spread to the population of Montreal and Quebec City.

1847–48: Under the command of Sir John Franklin, a British naval officer, 129 men perished of starvation and cold when their ships, HMS *Terror* and HMS *Erebus*, became trapped in pack ice west of King William Island in the Arctic archipelago. Franklin had been searching for the Northwest Passage.

Oct. 27, 1854: In one of the earliest Canadian train disasters, a gravel train running near Baptiste Creek, 24 km west of Chatham, Ont., was hit by an express train on the same line. In the collision, 52 persons were killed and 48 seriously injured.

June 29, 1864: Near St-Hilaire, Que., a passenger train was unable to stop for an open drawbridge at Beloeil on the Richelieu River. The train plunged through the opening onto passing barges, killing 99 and injuring 100 people.

Apr. 1, 1873: Sailing from Liverpool to New York, the steamer *Atlantic* struck Meager's Rock off the coast of Nova Scotia and sank with the loss of 535 people.

May 13, 1873: Sixty men died when a fire and subsequent explosion in a coal mine at Westville, Pictou County, NS, trapped firemen and workers. The mine was eventually sealed to starve the fire of oxygen and it was two years before all the bodies were recovered.

Aug. 25, 1873: The Great Nova Scotia Cyclone swept over Cape Breton Island. The hurricane destroyed 1,200 vessels and 900 buildings, demolished dikes, wharves and bridges and claimed 500 lives.

1885: A smallpox epidemic swept through Montreal killing 3,164 people—2,117 of whom were children. The catastrophe prompted city authorities to vaccinate the population, but some doctors said vaccination merely spread the disease. On Sept. 18, terrified rioters ransacked the home of the chief medical vaccinator, pharmacies, magistrates' homes and city hall.

May 3, 1887: In Nanaimo, BC, an explosion at the Number One mine, which was owned by the Vancouver Coal Mining and Land Company, killed 148 miners.

Jan. 24, 1888: Seventy-seven men lost their lives in a fire in the Number Five mine at Wellington, just outside of Nanaimo, BC.

Feb. 21, 1891: In the first of several major disasters in the coal mines of Springhill, NS, 125 men were killed in an explosion.

May 26, 1896: Fifty-five people were killed when a bridge at Point Ellice in Victoria, BC, collapsed while a streetcar was passing over it. The bridge was too weak to support the weight of a recently built tramline.

Sept. 19, 1899: A massive rockslide from the cliffs above Quebec City's Lower Town demolished most of Champlain St., killing 45 people.

Apr. 29, 1903: Parts of the town of Frank, Alta, were obliterated by a sudden landslide when over 90 million tonnes of limestone came crashing down Turtle Mountain, crossed the 4-km-wide valley floor and rolled up the other side of the valley. Approximately 75 people were killed. The landslide also sealed a mine entrance at the foot of the mountain and trapped 17 miners inside. The men were able to escape by digging a new tunnel to the surface.

Aug. 29, 1907: The Quebec Bridge, 11 km north of Quebec City, was the largest cantilevered bridge in the world at the time. As the bridge was nearing completion, the southern cantilever span collapsed, killing 75 workmen.

Aug. 2, 1908: A fire in BC's Kootenay Valley caused $5 million in damages and killed 70 people.

Mar. 5, 1910: Sixty-two train men and labourers died 2 km west of Rogers Pass, BC, when their engine was hit by an avalanche and hurtled 500 m into Bear Creek. Over 600 volunteers used pickaxes and shovels to dig through 10 m of snow in the search for survivors.

June 30, 1912: The worst tornado in Canadian history swept through Regina, Sask., killing 28 residents, injuring hundreds and causing $75 million damage (est. 1990 dollars).

Nov. 7–13, 1913: Thirty-four ships sank and 270 sailors drowned when a storm swept over Lake Erie and Lake Ontario. Winds reached speeds of 140 km/h. Days later, one ship was found afloat with its dead crew lashed to the mast.

Apr. 1, 1914: Seventy-seven sealers froze to death on the ice during a storm off the southeast coast of Labrador. At the storm's height, from Mar. 31 to Apr. 2, the temperature fell to –23°C and winds reached 64 km/h.

May 29, 1914: The Canadian Pacific liner *Empress of Ireland* collided with a Norwegian coal ship in the St. Lawrence River near Rimouski, Que., and sank in only 14 minutes with the loss of 1,014 lives. This was one of the worst naval disasters in history, with the eighth largest loss of life for a naval accident.

June 19, 1914: The worst coal mine disaster in Canadian history occurred at Hillcrest, Alta, when dust explosions killed 189 men.

July 29, 1916: A forest fire in northern Ontario, thought to have been started by lightning and locomotive sparks, engulfed the towns of Cochrane and Matheson, killing at least 233 persons.

Sept. 11, 1916: The Quebec Bridge was the scene of further tragedy when a new centre span being hoisted into position fell into the river below. Thirteen men were killed, bringing the loss of life during construction of the bridge to 88.

Dec. 6, 1917: Halifax was the scene of Canada's worst single disaster when a French munitions ship filled with explosives collided with a freighter in Halifax harbour. The French ship, the *Mont Blanc*, was split to the waterline; fuel oil spilled over its explosive cargo and started a fire in the hold. The crew abandoned ship without attempting to extinguish the fire.

In the explosion that followed, the *Mont Blanc* was tossed more than 1,000 m into the air. The explosion levelled homes and businesses in a large part of the city and set off explosives stockpiled on shore. The blast, heard as far away as Prince Edward Island, is thought to be the largest-ever accidental explosion, and the largest non-nuclear blast in history. More than 1,600 people were killed, 9,000 injured, and 6,000 left homeless. Property damage was estimated at $35 million.

Oct. 23, 1918: The Canadian Pacific steamship *Princess Sophia* ran onto Vanderbilt Reef while sailing from Alaska to Vancouver. The ship sank two days later on Oct. 25. All 343 aboard were drowned.

Jan. 9, 1927: A small fire that broke out in Montreal's Laurier Palace Theatre was quickly extinguished, but in the panic that ensued 12 people were crushed to death and 64 were asphyxiated, including many children.

Aug. 24–25, 1927: A hurricane struck Newfoundland, killing 56 people at sea. Throughout Atlantic Canada, the storm washed out roads, flooded houses and swamped boats.

Apr. 14, 1928: The 18-gun sloop *Acorn* sank near Halifax with 115 men on board.

Nov. 18, 1929: Newfoundland's Burin Peninsula was struck by a 4.5-m tidal wave. Property damage was extensive and 27 were killed.

June 26, 1930: A store of dynamite blew up when lightning struck the bow of the *John B. King*, a drillship on the St. Lawrence River. The explosion killed 30 people and injured 11 others.

1933–37: Throughout these years, the Prairies received only 60 percent of normal rainfall. The region turned into a dust bowl: Farmers lost thousands of animals to starvation and suffocation, crops withered, and 250,000 people left the Prairies to seek better lives elsewhere.

July 5–17, 1936: During an intense heat wave, 1,180 Canadians died in Manitoba and Ontario. Temperatures exceeding 44°C killed large numbers of infants and seniors; drowning killed about 400 people who went swimming to escape the heat.

Dec. 12, 1942: An arsonist set fire to the Knights of Columbus hostel in St John's. Because the hostel had no emergency lighting, the doors opened inwards and exits were restricted, 99 people died and another 100 were seriously injured.

May–June 1948: BC's worst flood of the century occurred when the Fraser River overflowed. The water destroyed 2,300 homes and forced 16,000 people to flee. Ten people drowned. For three weeks, Vancouver had no rail connection with the rest of Canada.

Sept. 17, 1949: Seven hundred people were aboard the Great Lakes excursion ship *Noronic* when it caught fire and burned at its pier in Toronto harbour. The ship's fire hydrants were dry and no alarm was sent to the city fire department until 15 minutes after the blaze was discovered. In the meantime, the single exit became blocked by fire and 118 lives were lost.

Spring 1950: The Red River flooded, forcing the evacuation of 100,000 people from southern Manitoba and damaging 5,000 homes. The provincial government responded by building the Winnipeg Floodway to forestall future floods.

Oct. 15, 1954: During the worst inland storm in Canadian history, Hurricane Hazel, over 10 cm of rain fell in Toronto in 12 hours. At that time, many houses in Toronto were built on low-lying flood plains. The storm and resulting floods caused 83 deaths and widespread property damage.

Nov. 1, 1956: A second major tragedy struck the coal mines at Springhill, NS, when an accident killed 39 men.

Dec. 9, 1956: A DC-4 North Star flown by Trans-Canada Airways (later Air Canada) crashed into the east face of Mount Slesse, BC, killing all 62 on board.

June 17, 1958: Design errors in Vancouver's Second Narrows Bridge caused one section to collapse. The accident killed 18 men, including the two engineers that an investigation later determined were responsible for the errors.

Oct. 23, 1958: A third mining accident in Springhill, NS, killed 75 when a tunnel collapsed.

June 20, 1959: More than 30 fishermen drowned and 22 salmon boats sank near Esuminac, NB, when a storm suddenly struck the Gulf of St. Lawrence.

Nov. 19, 1963: A Trans-Canada Airways DC-8F crashed after takeoff from Dorval in Montreal, killing 118.

July 5, 1970: At Toronto International Airport, an Air Canada DC-8 lost one starboard engine during a landing attempt. During the pilot's effort to take off and land again, the remaining starboard engine fell off. The aircraft crashed, killing all 109 persons aboard.

May 4, 1971: During a prolonged rainstorm in St-Jean-Vianney, Que., a giant sinkhole appeared in the ground. The hole swallowed 40 houses, several cars and a bus, and 31 people were killed.

Nov. 10, 1975: The 218-m ore carrier *Edmund Fitzgerald*, based in Sault Ste. Marie, broke apart during a storm on Lake Superior and sank in 156 m of water with all 29 members of the crew aboard. Two days later only two rubber rafts and some life preservers from the ship were found.

June 21, 1977: A fire that broke out in the cell block of the city police headquarters of St John, NB, was so hot that the locks on several cell doors were fused. Twenty prisoners were killed and 12 police officers who attempted to rescue the prisoners were injured.

Feb. 11, 1978: A Pacific Western Airlines aircraft crashed at Cranbrook, BC, killing 43 people.

Aug. 4, 1978: The brakes on a chartered bus failed near Eastman, Que. The bus plunged into a lake, and 41 passengers were killed.

Dec. 31, 1979: Forty-four persons were killed during New Year's Eve celebrations at a social club in Chapais, Que., in a fire caused by a man playing with a lighter who set decorations ablaze.

Feb. 15, 1982: The ocean drilling rig *Ocean Ranger* overturned and sank during a storm while operating 265 km east of Newfoundland, killing 84 men. Inadequate safety procedures and equipment were later blamed for the accident.

May 31, 1985: A midafternoon tornado struck Barrie, Ont., killing 12, including four children. Property damage was in the hundreds of millions of dollars.

Dec. 12, 1985: In the worst air crash in Canada, an Arrow Airlines DC-8, after refuelling in Gander en route to Hopkinsville, Ky., crashed seconds after takeoff, killing 256 passengers and crew.

Feb. 8, 1986: A 16-unit VIA Rail passenger train slammed head-on into a 118-unit CN freight train near Hinton, Alta. Twenty-six people were killed and dozens were seriously injured.

July 31, 1987: A tornado touched down in Edmonton, Alta, killing 26 people, injuring 250 others and causing an estimated $250 million damage.

Mar. 10, 1989: An Air Ontario jet crashed immediately after takeoff from Dryden, Ont., killing 24 people.

Feb. 12, 1990: One of the worst tire fires in North America broke out near Hagersville,

Ont., spewing oil and toxic smoke. The dump, which stored 14 million tires for recycling, burned for 16 days; the blaze was extinguished at a cost of $1.5 million.

May 9, 1992: Twenty-six miners died underground in the Westray coal mine near Plymouth, NS, after a methane gas explosion. Fifteen bodies were recovered but the bodies of the remaining victims could not be reached in the debris.

July 16, 1993: Nineteen people died when a truck towing tanks of diesel fuel collided with a van carrying senior citizens near Lac-Bouchette, Que.

July 19–20, 1996: Ten people died in the Lac-St-Jean Saguenay Region when flash floods from overflowing dams and reservoirs wiped out communities along the Saguenay River.

April–May 1997: Manitoba's Red River flooded 2,000 square km of valley land when water rose 12 m above winter levels—the highest for the river in the 20th century. Thousands of volunteers and soldiers fought the flood for days. Damage estimates reached half a billion dollars.

Oct. 13, 1997: Forty-four passengers were killed when the brakes failed on their sightseeing bus; the vehicle missed a turn at the bottom of a steep hill and crashed into a ravine in Les Eboulements, 110 km northeast of Quebec City.

Jan. 4–9, 1998: One of the most destructive ice storms in Canadian history struck Quebec and Eastern Ontario, causing hardship for 4 million people and costing $3 billion. Losses included 130 transmission towers, 120,000 km of power and phone lines, and millions of trees. Power outages lasted up to four weeks.

Sept. 2, 1998: All 229 passengers were killed when a Swissair MD-11 en route from New York to Geneva crashed in the Atlantic near Peggy's Cove, NS. The accident was the second worst in Canadian aviation history.

May 2000: At least seven people died and up to 2,300 people fell ill after drinking tap water infected by *E. coli* bacteria in Walkerton, Ont.

Prime Ministers of Canada

■ Sir John A. Macdonald

Canada's first prime minister, Sir John A. Macdonald, was born in Glasgow, Scotland, on Jan. 11, 1815. At age five he came to Canada with his parents who settled at Kingston, Upper Canada.

Called to the bar in 1836, Macdonald practised law in Kingston and then in Toronto. He established a reputation as a corporate lawyer, company director and businessman.

He was elected to the Legislative Assembly of the Province of Canada in 1844 and was re-elected in 1848, 1851, 1854, 1857, 1861 and 1863. In 1864, he joined a coalition with George Brown, leader of the Upper Canadian reformers, dedicated to bringing about Confederation. That same year, Macdonald was a delegate to the Charlottetown and Quebec conferences, and became the principal author of the Confederation resolutions agreed upon in Quebec. He was chairman of the London Conference (1866–67) and played a pivotal role in bringing about Confederation.

Macdonald became Canada's first prime minister when the Liberal-Conservative party won a majority of seats in Parliament following the first post-Confederation general election in 1867. Though he was re-elected in 1872, Macdonald's second administration was marred by the "Pacific Scandal" in 1873. The Liberal Opposition charged that his government had awarded the contract for the Canadian Pacific Railway to Sir Hugh Allan in return for political contributions. An investigation into these charges was held, and the government resigned on Nov. 5, 1873.

Macdonald's Liberal-Conservatives were re-elected Sept. 17, 1878, and Macdonald remained prime minister until his death in Ottawa on June 6, 1891.

During his first administration, the Dominion of Canada expanded to include the provinces of British Columbia, Prince Edward Island and the newly created Manitoba.

The building of the transcontinental railway is the most memorable feature of his second administration, but other accomplishments include the establishment of the "National Policy"—a system of tariff protection to aid the development of Canadian industries (1879)—and the increased settlement of the Western provinces that followed the construction of the railway.

■ Alexander Mackenzie

Alexander Mackenzie was born on Jan. 28, 1822 near Dunkeld, Perthshire, Scotland. He left school and became a stonemason at the age of 14.

He emigrated to Canada in 1842 and became a contractor at Lambton, Ontario, and then editor of the *Lambton Shield*. From 1866–74, he was a major in the 27th Lambton Battalion Volunteer Infantry.

In 1861, Mackenzie was elected to the Legislative Assembly of the Province of Canada, where he gave his support to the Confederation plan. When George Brown was defeated in the 1867 election, Mackenzie became *de facto* leader of the Opposition, though it was not until after the 1872 elections that he formally accepted this title.

It was Mackenzie who led the attack on the Macdonald administration over the "Pacific Scandal"; when Macdonald resigned on Nov. 5, 1873, Mackenzie became prime minister.

During his 5-year term of office, Mackenzie introduced changes to election laws that included the secret ballot and universal male suffrage. The Supreme Court of Canada was established under Mackenzie's rule, and Wilfrid Laurier was brought into Mackenzie's cabinet.

Severe economic depression plagued Canada during the Mackenzie years, and in 1878, his Liberal party was routed at the polls.

Mackenzie retained his own seat, however, and was still a member of Parliament when he died on Apr. 17, 1892, in Toronto.

■ Sir John Abbott

Sir John Joseph Caldwell Abbott was born on Mar. 12, 1821, at St. Andrews, Lower Canada —the first prime minister to be born on Canadian soil.

After taking his law degree from University of McGill College, he was admitted to the bar in 1847 and practised law in Montreal. From 1855–80 he was dean of the Faculty of Law, McGill University.

Abbott was elected to the Legislative Assembly of the Province of Canada in 1857, re-elected in 1861 and 1863, and sat until Confederation. He was then elected to the House of Commons in 1867, 1872 and 1874. He was last elected in 1882 and appointed to the Senate on May 12, 1887.

When Sir John A. Macdonald died in 1891, Abbott—though a senator—inherited the Conservative leadership. The three other leading Conservatives—Langevin, Tupper and Thompson—were unwilling or unable to assume the post. Abbott held the office of prime minister from June 16, 1891, until his resignation on Nov. 24, 1892. He died in Montreal on Oct. 30, 1893.

■ Sir John Thompson

Sir John Sparrow David Thompson was born in Halifax, NS, on Nov. 10, 1845.

Thompson was called to the Nova Scotia bar in 1865, and was instrumental in founding Dalhousie Law School in 1883, where he eventually became a lecturer.

In May 1882, Thompson became premier of Nova Scotia, but when his government was defeated two months later, he retired from politics and became a judge of the Supreme Court of Nova Scotia.

Prime Minister Macdonald coaxed Thompson back into politics, making him minister of justice in 1885. When Macdonald died in 1891, Thompson declined the leadership, fearing that his conversion to Roman Catholicism in 1870 would hinder his party's fortunes. However, the following year, Thompson changed his mind, and on Dec. 5, 1892, he became prime minister.

Though prime minister for just over 2 years, Thompson was largely responsible for the establishment of the Criminal Code and penetentiary reforms. He almost succeeded in bringing Newfoundland into Confederation in 1894, and successfully negotiated fisheries clauses in the Treaty of Washington.

He died while still in office on Dec. 12, 1894.

■ Sir Mackenzie Bowell

Mackenzie Bowell was born at Rickinghall, Suffolk, England, on Dec. 27, 1823, and came to Canada in 1832. In 1834, he became an

apprentice printer at Belleville, Upper Canada, and was later editor and proprietor of the Belleville *Intelligencer*. He served in the militia of the United Province of Canada during the American Civil War and the Fenian raids of 1866.

Bowell was elected to the House of Commons in 1867 for Hastings North, Ont., and was re-elected in 1872, 1874, 1878, 1887 and 1891.

As spokesman for the Orange Association of British America, Bowell was instrumental in having Louis Riel expelled from the Commons in 1874.

On Dec. 5, 1892, Bowell was appointed to the Senate and, after Thompson's death in 1894, was invited by the Governor General to form a government.

Perhaps the thorniest problem facing Prime Minister Bowell was the Manitoba Schools question. In 1890, Manitoba legislation had withdrawn school privileges from the Roman Catholic and primarily French minority in that province. By the time Bowell assumed office, attempts were being made to restore those lost school privileges by federal remedial legislation. Bowell was not equal to the political challenges facing him; he lost control of his cabinet ministers, several of whom eventually called for his resignation. Bowell denounced this cabinet rebellion as a "nest of traitors," but eventually he resigned on Apr. 27, 1896. He died in Belleville, Ont., on Dec. 10, 1917, at age 93.

■ Sir Charles Tupper

Charles Tupper was born at Amherst, NS, on July 2, 1821. He took a degree in medicine at Edinburgh University. At the age of 22, he began practising medicine in Amherst and became the first president of the Canadian Medical Association (1867–70).

The 1855 election that brought him to the Legislative Assembly of Nova Scotia was declared void on Feb. 24, 1857. He was subsequently re-elected in a by-election that same year and was elected again in 1859 and 1863.

Tupper was active in the Confederation movement and was a delegate to the Charlottetown, Quebec and London Conferences. He was elected to the House of Commons in 1867 and re-elected 1870, 1872, 1874, 1878 and 1882. He resigned in 1884 and served as High Commissioner for Canada in the United Kingdom from May 28 of that year to Jan. 26, 1887. In 1887, he was re-elected to the House of Commons, but resigned the following year and again served as High Commissioner from May 23, 1888, to Jan. 14, 1896.

In 1896, following the rebellion of Bowell's cabinet, Tupper became *de facto* leader of the administration until Bowell formally resigned on Apr. 27, 1896. At that time, the Governor General invited Tupper to form the government. Parliament was dissolved shortly thereafter and in the election that followed on June 23, Tupper's Conservatives were defeated. Tupper stayed on as leader of the Opposition until Feb. 5, 1901, then retired from public life. He died on Oct. 30, 1915 at Bexley Heath, Kent, England.

■ Sir Wilfrid Laurier

Wilfrid Laurier was born at St-Lin, Canada East, on Nov. 20, 1841. He first attended College de l'Assomption and then took his degree from McGill University.

He was called to the bar of Lower Canada in 1865. He practised law at Montreal and at Arthabaskaville, Que.

First elected to the Legislative Assembly of Quebec in 1871, Laurier resigned in January 1874 and later that year was elected to the House of Commons. He became leader of the Liberal Opposition in June 1887. Then, following the 1896 election that gave his party a 23-seat majority, Laurier became Canada's first French-speaking prime minister on July 11, 1896. The Liberals retained power in 1900 and won a landslide election victory in 1904.

Immigration increased during his time in office as Clifford Sifton, Laurier's minister of the interior from 1896–1905, mounted a powerful campaign to attract immigrants from Britain, the United States and Europe. In 1905, Laurier created the provinces of Alberta and Saskatchewan and established the boundaries of Manitoba. During Laurier's years in power the Canadian West became a major world wheat producer. In 1909, Laurier established the External Affairs Department.

His government's controversial support for the creation of a Canadian navy, and his unpopular attempt to enter into a reciprocal trade agreement with the United States (an agreement that would have reduced or eliminated duties on many imported goods) spelled trouble for Laurier in 1911. His party was defeated in the Sept. 21 election. He remained an Opposition MP until his death on Feb. 17, 1919, in Ottawa.

■ Sir Robert Borden

Robert Laird Borden was born at Grand Pré, NS, on June 26, 1854. At age 14 he gave up formal schooling to become an assistant master in classical studies. He taught classics and mathematics in New Jersey in 1873, before returning to Nova Scotia to study law. He was admitted to the Nova Scotia bar in 1878 and practised first in Halifax, then in Kentville, NS.

Borden was elected to the House of Commons in 1896 and 1900 and became leader of the Conservative party on Feb. 6, 1901. He served as Leader of the Opposition until 1911, when he led his party to victory in the Sept. 21 election.

Borden was prime minister throughout World War I, and during the war years his government was accused of scandal over British munitions contracts and its staunch support of the Ross Rifle—a weapon known to jam in battle. Borden's government introduced the first federal income tax, nationalized Canadian railways and introduced conscription in 1917.

In the election of Dec. 17, 1917, Borden led a re-organized Union Government made up of Conservatives and pro-conscription Liberals to victory. Borden headed the Canadian dele-

gation at the Paris Peace Conference in 1919, where the autonomy of Canada and other dominions within the British Commonwealth was successfully established. He resigned on July 10, 1920, and died in Ottawa on June 10, 1937.

■ Arthur Meighen

Arthur Meighen was born at Anderson, Ont., on June 16, 1874. Following his graduation from university in 1896, Meighen taught high school for a year, then moved to Winnipeg in 1898 to study law. He was called to the Manitoba bar in 1902, and practised at Portage La Prairie.

He was first elected to the House of Commons in 1908, re-elected in 1911, 1913 and 1917, defeated in 1921, and re-elected in 1922 and 1925.

Meighen first achieved national prominence in 1913 when he helped devise a closure rule which permitted the government to end debate on a bill which was to effect a $35-million contribution to the British navy. Prior to closure, the bill had been obstructed by a fierce and protracted Opposition party blockade.

Prime Minister Borden appointed Meighen his solicitor general on Oct. 2, 1915, and Meighen held this post for two years. A

strong supporter of conscription, Meighen essentially drafted Canada's 1917 conscription bill and put it into operation. He was also the chief draughtsman of the Wartime Elections Act.

When Borden resigned on July 10, 1920, Meighen succeeded him as prime minister. In the general election of Dec. 6, 1921, Meighen's party was defeated. Though his Conservatives won the most seats in the election of Oct. 29, 1925, the Liberals were able to stay in power with the support of Progressive and Labour members.

Following the resignation of William Lyon Mackenzie King's government on June 28, 1926, the Governor General invited Meighen to form a new ministry. This government was less than three months old, however, when it was defeated in the House of Commons (by only one vote) and Canadians again went to the polls.

Following a Liberal victory in the election of Sept. 14, 1926, Meighen resigned as Conservative leader in the House of Commons. He was appointed to the Senate on Feb. 3, 1932, during Richard Bennett's ministry and became government leader in the Senate. Then, following King's victory in 1935, he became Senate Opposition leader.

On Nov. 12, 1941, he once again became leader of the Conservative party, but failed in his bid to win a seat in the Commons in a federal by-election on Feb. 2, 1942. Following this defeat, he retired from politics and resumed his law practice in Toronto, where he died on Aug. 5, 1960.

■ Mackenzie King

William Lyon Mackenzie King, grandson of William Lyon Mackenzie, was born in Kitchener (then called Berlin), Ont., on Dec. 17, 1874.

He took his B.A. and law degrees from the University of Toronto and also studied at the University of Chicago and Harvard University.

He served as deputy minister of labour from 1900–08.

He was first elected to the House of Commons in 1908, and succeeded Laurier as leader of the Liberal party in 1919. King became prime minister when the Liberals won the general election of Dec. 6, 1921.

Though Meighen's Conservatives won a majority of seats in the general election of Oct. 29, 1925, King stayed in office with the help of Progressive and Labour members who supported his proposed tariff reductions and old-age pension legislation. King had lost his York North seat in the 1925 election but returned to the House of Commons as the member for Prince Albert, Sask., following a by-election on Feb. 15, 1926. King's government was shaken in 1926 by the revelation that the customs department was tainted with corruption and incompetence. In the furor that followed, King lost the support of many members of Parliament and, although never technically defeated in the House of Commons, decided that he could no longer hold his minority government. He appealed to Governor General Lord Byng to dissolve Parliament, even though the government had not been defeated. Byng refused. King subsequently resigned on June 28, 1926, and the Governor General invited Arthur Meighen to form a government which was subsequently defeated in the House of Commons.

In the general election of Sept. 14, 1926, King's Liberals regained power and held it until 1930. But the disastrous fall in the price of wheat and other Canadian exports in 1929 soured Canadians on their government, and King was defeated by Richard Bennett's Conservatives in the election of July 28, 1930.

Five years later, King was back in the prime minister's office, following the Liberal victory in the general election of Oct. 14, 1935. In the coming years, King, an ardent supporter of Canada's autonomy within the British Commonwealth, was faced with the issue of Canada's participation in an impending European war. To soothe French-Canadian concerns over Canadian support of Great Britain, King promised there would be no conscription; Canada declared war in September 1939. Later, however, heavy casualties in France and Italy in 1944 prompted King to break his promise and send conscripts overseas.

King's government began introducing postwar recovery legislation even before war was declared. These measures included reconstruction plans and social security schemes such as mother's allowances.

King resigned as prime minister on Nov. 15, 1948, supporting Louis St-Laurent as his successor. In poor health in his final years, King died on July 22, 1950, at Kingsmere, his estate in Wright County, Que.

■ Richard Bennett

Richard Bedford Bennett was born at Hopewell, NB, on July 3, 1870. Bennett studied law at Dalhousie University. He read and practised law in Chatham, NB, from 1893–97, before moving to Calgary where he entered a legal partnership with Senator James A. Lougheed.

Bennett was first elected to the House of Commons in 1911. He served as minister of justice in Arthur Meighen's 1921 cabinet, and minister of finance and minister of mines in Meighen's 1926 government.

Bennett was chosen to replace Meighen as Conservative leader at the party convention in

Winnipeg in 1927. He became prime minister following the Conservative victory in the election of July 28, 1930.

Bennett had the task of governing Canada during the worst years of the Depression. Virtually every measure his government

attempted ended in failure. High unemployment levels continued despite Bennett's efforts to reduce them. Negotiations for a reciprocity treaty with the United States did not succeed. A plan of preferential tariffs agreed to in 1930 at the Imperial Conference did little to ease Canada's economic woes.

Then, in 1935, near the end of his term, Bennett took an unexpected step to the political left. He proclaimed that "the old order is gone" and that it was time for a new economic system. That new system was to include a state-planned economy, new unemployment and health insurance legislation and old-age pension laws.

In the election of Oct. 14, 1935, Bennett's Conservatives suffered a devastating defeat, winning just 39 seats. Bennett remained in Opposition until 1937, when he retired to England. There he was given the title Viscount Bennett of Mickelham, Hopewell and Calgary.

Despite the overwhelming problems of the Great Depression, Bennett's term saw the creation of the Canadian Radio Broadcasting Corporation (the predecessor to the CBC) and the Bank of Canada. As well, it was during Bennett's tenure that the Statute of Westminster gave Canada increased autonomy in 1931.

Bennett died on June 27, 1947.

■ Louis St-Laurent

Louis Stephen St-Laurent was born at Compton, Que., on Feb. 1, 1882. Called to the Quebec bar in 1905, he practised law in Quebec City, and became professor of law at Université Laval. He was elected president of the Canadian Bar Association in 1930.

St-Laurent became justice minister in Mackenzie King's cabinet on Dec. 10, 1941. On Feb. 9, 1942, he was elected to the House of Commons in a by-election for Quebec East.

Originally planning to hold his cabinet post only during the war, St-Laurent was persuaded to stay on. On Dec. 10, 1946, he became secretary of state for external affairs. A firm believer in collective security, St-Laurent was one of the architects of the North

Atlantic Treaty Organization (NATO). On Aug. 7, 1948, he accepted his party's nomination to be King's successor, and on Nov. 15 he became prime minister.

While in power, St-Laurent ended the practice of appealing court cases to the Judicial Committee of the Privy Council in England, and made the Supreme Court of Canada the final Canadian court of appeal. He won the acceptance of a new apportionment of taxes in 1956 and, in negotiation with President Truman, laid the foundation for a US–Canada agreement to develop the St. Lawrence Seaway.

In 1958, he retired and returned to Quebec City to practise law. He died on July 25, 1973.

■ John Diefenbaker

John George Diefenbaker was born at Neustadt, Ont., on Sept. 18, 1895. He received his B.A. from the University of Saskatchewan in 1915 and his M.A. one year later.

After the outbreak of World War I, he joined the Canadian Officers' Training Corps, and served overseas as a lieutenant with the 105th "Saskatoon Fusiliers" Regiment from 1916 to 1917.

Returning to Saskatchewan, he took his law degree from the University of Saskatchewan in 1919 and established a law practice at Wakaw. He later moved to Prince Albert.

After several unsuccessful attempts to gain a seat, first in the federal, then in Saskatchewan's parliament, Diefenbaker was finally elected to the House of Commons in 1940. He was a candidate for leadership of the Progressive Conservative party at the 1942 and 1948 conventions, but did not win the nomination until Dec. 14, 1956.

The Progressive Conservatives won the election of June 10, 1957, by a slim margin, and on June 21, John Diefenbaker officially became prime minister. A year later, he called an election, hoping to turn his minority government into a clear majority. He was overwhelmingly successful, winning 208 of the 265 seats in the Mar. 31, 1958, election. He fared less well in the 1962 election, when only 116 Progressive Conservatives were elected, and in the general election of 1963, a Liberal victory relegated Diefenbaker to the role of Opposition leader. Diefenbaker remained Progressive Conservative leader until September 1967, when he was replaced by Robert Stanfield.

The Diefenbaker years (1957–63) saw the passage of the Canadian Bill of Rights, a "roads-to-resources" program to encourage the development of northern resources, support for agriculture, encouragement of technical training and improved health and welfare programs. Regional development was emphasized by significant public works such as construction of the South Saskatchewan Dam, and simultaneous translation was introduced in the House of Commons.

Diefenbaker died on Aug. 16, 1979, at his home in Rockliffe Park, Ottawa.

■ Lester Pearson

Lester Bowles Pearson was born at Newtonbrook, Ont., on Apr. 23, 1897. He took his B.A. at the University of Toronto and his M.A. at Oxford University.

After serving overseas in World War I, he became a history professor at the University of Toronto, where he taught from 1924–28. He joined Canada's foreign service in 1928, became Canada's ambassador to the United Nations in 1945, was appointed undersecretary of state for external affairs in 1946 and accepted the invitations of King and St-Laurent to become minister of external affairs in September 1948.

In 1956, following the Anglo-French-Israeli invasion of Egypt, Pearson helped establish a UN Emergency Force which kept peace on the Israeli–Egyptian border for the next decade. His settlement of the Suez crisis brought him the Nobel Peace Prize in 1957—the only time a Canadian has been so honoured.

Pearson was chosen leader of the Liberal party on Jan. 15, 1958. In the general election of Apr. 8, 1963, the Liberals won 129 seats in the House of Commons, and Pearson became the leader of a minority government.

In the 1965 election, the Liberals made slight gains, but were still short of a majority. Pearson announced his resignation in December 1967 and, in April 1968, was succeeded by Pierre Trudeau.

Under Pearson, the old age pension was extended and a national health plan created. He secured the adoption of a national flag and established the Royal Commission on Bilingualism and Biculturalism.

Though he retired in 1968, his international reputation prompted the World Bank to commission him to prepare a report on international aid programs.

He died in Ottawa on Dec. 27, 1972.

■ Pierre Trudeau

Pierre Elliott Trudeau was born in Montreal on Oct. 18, 1919. He attended the University of Montreal, Harvard University, Université de Paris and the London School of Economics. He was called to the Quebec bar in 1943. From 1949–51, he was a member of the Privy Council staff in Ottawa. In 1950, he co-founded the magazine *Cité Libre*. From 1952–62, he practised law and was a journalist and broadcaster in Montreal. From 1962–65, he was a law professor at the University of Montreal.

First elected to the House of Commons in 1965, Trudeau was named justice minister in Lester Pearson's cabinet in 1967. The following year, he won the Liberal leadership and became prime minister on Apr. 19, 1968. In the general election of the same year, the Liberals won a solid majority.

During his first four years in power, Trudeau faced the FLQ Crisis—the kidnapping of British diplomat James Cross and Quebec cabinet minister Pierre Laporte by the radical separatist organization Front de libération du Québec. (Laporte was later murdered.) In response Trudeau invoked the War Measures

Act, a statute giving the state broad powers of arrest and detention.

In the general election of 1972, Trudeau returned to power with a minority government. In 1974, he regained a majority.

In the general election of 1979, the Progressive Conservatives under Joe Clark won a narrow victory and were able to form a minority government. Trudeau announced his intention to retire, but when the Clark government fell later that year, Trudeau led the Liberals in the election and won a majority on Feb. 18, 1980.

Trudeau's final term in office was devoted to constitutional reform which, for the first time, allowed Canada's Parliament to amend the constitution without appeal to the British government. A constitutionally entrenched Charter of Rights and Freedoms was also introduced.

Trudeau's introduction of a National Energy Program led to bitter disputes between the federal government and the energy-producing provinces, particularly Alberta. The NEP was aimed at increasing Canadian control of the oil industry, promoting energy self-sufficiency and generating more federal revenues in the energy sector.

During his final year as prime minister Trudeau launched a world peace initiative, visiting more than 40 world leaders to appeal for peace and an end to the nuclear arms race.

In June of 1984, Trudeau resigned. He was succeeded by John Turner and left politics, eventually joining a Montreal law firm.

Trudeau died on Sept. 28, 2000, at his home in Montreal.

■ Joe Clark

Charles Joseph Clark was born at High River, Alta., on June 5, 1939. He was educated at the University of Alberta.

Clark was first elected to the House of Commons in 1972. In 1976 he became leader of the Progressive Conservative party and, in the general election of 1979, won enough seats to form a minority government. At 39, Clark was Canada's youngest prime minister. But his minority government fell in December 1979 on a vote of non-confidence on its proposed budget. In the February 1980 election, the Liberals returned to power.

At a national meeting of the Progressive Conservative party in January 1983, Clark received the support of only two-thirds of the delegates and called for a national party leadership convention. In June 1983, Clark lost the leadership to Brian Mulroney on the fourth ballot. He remained an MP and, when Mulroney became prime minister in 1984, Clark joined the cabinet as secretary of state for external affairs.

In 1991, he was appointed as minister responsible for constitutional affairs and given the task of succeeding where the Meech Lake Accord had failed. Late 1991 and the first half of 1992 were marked by weeks of cross-country constitutional negotiations under Clark's guidance. In August 1992, the Charlottetown Accord—an agreement to amend the Constitution Act of 1982—was agreed upon by all first ministers. The text of the agreement was presented to Canadians and a national referendum was held on Oct. 26, 1992, on the issue of whether or not to approve the deal. The agreement was rejected by the majority of voters across the country.

Clark left federal politics after the 1993 election. In 1998, he re-entered public life when Jean Charest left the leadership of the federal Progressive Conservatives to run in Quebec's provincial election. On Nov. 14, 1998, Clark was re-elected leader of the federal Progressive Conservative party.

Clark waited for more than a year before seeking a seat in the House of Commons. On Sept. 11, 2000, however, he won a by-election in Kings–Hants, NS, and on Nov. 27, 2000, he won a seat in Calgary Centre, Alta., during the general election.

In the House of Commons, Clark resisted attempts by the populist Reform party and its successor, the Canadian Alliance, to unite with the Progressive Conservatives. On Sept. 19, 2001, however, Clark became the leader of a coalition of Progressive Conservatives and ex-Canadian Alliance MPs. The coalition, known as the Progressive Conservative–Democratic Representative Caucus, collapsed on Apr. 9, 2002, when all but one of the DRC's members returned to the Canadian Alliance.

On May 30, 2003, during the Progressive Conservative leadership convention, Clark stepped down as party leader. He opposed the efforts of the party's new leader, Peter MacKay,

to merge the Progressive Conservative party and the Canadian Alliance; when members of both parties voted overwhelmingly to unite on Dec. 8, 2003, Clark refused to join the new Conservative Party of Canada.

On Feb. 2, 2004, Clark resumed sitting in the House of Commons. He refused to give up his designation as a Progressive Conservative. He did not seek re-election in June 2004.

■ John Turner

John Napier Turner was born at Richmond, Surrey, England, on June 7, 1929. He attended the University of British Columbia, Oxford

University and Université de Paris. He was called to the bar in England in 1953 and the bar in Quebec in 1954. He lectured for a time in the Faculty of Commerce at Sir George Williams University.

First elected to the House of Commons in 1962, Turner entered Lester Pearson's cabinet in 1965. He became minister of consumer and corporate affairs in 1967. In 1968, he was a candidate for the Liberal leadership, finishing third on the final ballot.

In 1968, Turner was appointed minister of justice in Pierre Trudeau's cabinet. In 1972, he became minister of finance, a post he held until his resignation in September 1975. In February 1976, he left politics and joined a Toronto law firm.

Turner remained in private practice until Trudeau's retirement in 1984, when he successfully ran for leader of the Liberal party and became prime minister on June 30, though he did not have a seat in the House of Commons. He dissolved Parliament on July 9, and in the ensuing general election the Liberals were overwhelmingly defeated by the Progressive Conservatives.

As leader of the Opposition, Turner used the Liberal majority in the Senate to block passage of the Progressive Conservatives' free trade legislation and force an election on the issue in 1988. The Progressive Conservatives won the election and formed another majority government.

Early in 1989, Turner announced plans to step down as leader; in June 1990, he was succeeded by Jean Chrétien.

■ Brian Mulroney

Martin Brian Mulroney was born at Baie Comeau, Que., on Mar. 20, 1939. He attended St. Francis Xavier University and Université Laval. Called to the bar of Quebec in 1965, Mulroney practised law in Montreal. In 1976, he joined the Iron Ore Company of Canada as executive vice-president and was elected company president the following year.

Mulroney made an unsuccessful bid for the Progressive Conservative party leadership in 1976. In 1983 he ran again, defeating the incumbent leader, Joe Clark, on the fourth ballot.

A by-election for the Maritime riding of Central Nova brought Mulroney into Parliament as leader of the Opposition. In the general election of 1984, he led the Progressive Conservatives to victory, winning the largest number of seats (211) in Canadian history.

Mulroney's major initiatives between 1984 and 1988 were the Meech Lake Accord—a package of constitutional changes designed to end Quebec's boycott of the 1982 constitutional reform—and the negotiation of a free trade agreement with the United States.

In 1988, with free trade the central election issue, Mulroney won a second majority government. The free trade agreement subsequently received final approval and took effect in 1989.

His term from 1988 to 1993 was marked by intense negotiations to bring about a new constitutional agreement to replace the Meech Lake Accord, which was not ratified by all provinces by the June 1990 deadline. Agreement was reached amongst federal and provincial officials in what became known as the Charlottetown Accord, but the proposals were rejected in a national referendum held on Oct. 26, 1992.

The Progressive Conservatives under Mulroney continued their free trade initiative and finalized a North American free trade deal (NAFTA) with the US and Mexico.

Mulroney announced his intention to retire in February 1993, and on June 25, 1993, he was replaced by Kim Campbell, newly elected leader of the Progressive Conservative party.

■ Kim Campbell

Avril Phaedra (Kim) Campbell was born on Mar. 10, 1947, in Port Alberni, BC. She attended the University of British Columbia, earning an honours degree in political science.

After an academic career in BC, she studied law at UBC. In September 1985, she joined BC Premier William Bennett's office as a policy advisor. In May 1986, Campbell ran in the provincial election and won a seat in the legislature, representing Vancouver–Point Grey. She served in the provincial legislature until October 1988 when she resigned her seat to contest the federal riding of Vancouver Centre. An ardent defender of free trade, Campbell joined Prime Minister Mulroney's cabinet with the Indian Affairs and Northern Development portfolio.

In 1990 Campbell became the first female minister of justice and attorney general. In January 1993, she became Canada's first female defence minister; she also became a candidate in the Progressive Conservative leadership contest. On June 13, 1993, she was elected leader on the second ballot; on June 25, she was sworn in as Canada's first female prime minister. In the election of Oct. 25, 1993, however, the Progressive Conservatives lost all but two seats in the House of Commons. Campbell's tenure as prime minister ended on Nov. 4; she stepped down as federal Progressive Conservative leader on Dec. 13, 1993.

■ Jean Chrétien

Jean Joseph Jacques Chrétien was born in Shawinigan, Que., on Jan. 11, 1934. He studied law at Laval University and was called to the bar of Quebec in 1958.

Chrétien was first elected to the House of Commons in 1963, and after re-election in 1965, served as parliamentary secretary to the prime minister (1965) and the finance minister (1966). He became minister of national revenue in 1968; after the June 1968 election, he became responsible for Indian affairs and northern development. In 1974, he was appointed president of the treasury board; in 1976, he served as minister of industry, trade and commerce. In 1977, he was named finance minister; in 1980 he became justice minister and attorney general and also served as minister of state for social development. Chrétien played an important role in patriating the Constitution. In 1982, he became minister of energy, mines and resources; in

1984, he became deputy prime minister and secretary of state for external affairs.

In 1984, Chrétien ran second to John Turner in the Liberal leadership race; in the 1984 election, Chrétien kept his seat in the House of Commons. In 1986, when the Liberals confirmed Turner's leadership at a party

convention, Chrétien resigned his seat to practice law.

In 1990, Turner resigned as Liberal leader after losing a second election to the Progressive Conservatives, and Chrétien won the Liberal leadership. He subsequently won a by-election in Beausejour and took his seat in the House of Commons as leader of the Opposition.

Chrétien inherited a party that was disorganized and almost bankrupt. His support for the Charlottetown Accord in 1992 cost him support among Quebec's nationalists. But in the election of Oct. 25, 1993, Chrétien led the Liberals to victory over the ruling Progressive Conservatives. He was re-elected in Saint-Maurice and sworn in as Canada's 20th prime minister.

The new government inherited a troubled economy. In 1993, Canada suffered from high unemployment, a large national debt and an alarming national deficit. Chrétien limited or cut federal spending, including subsidies to the provinces, to reduce the

national deficit. Chrétien also kept the Goods and Services Tax, despite an election pledge to abolish it.

In his first term, Chrétien struggled with Quebec's separatists. In 1993, the federal Liberals won only 20 seats in Quebec whereas the newly created Bloc Québécois won the remaining 54. On Oct. 30, 1995, in Quebec's second referendum on sovereignty, the federalists won by the slimmest of margins over the separatists. Chrétien's role in the federalist campaign was criticized.

In foreign policy, Chrétien stressed international trade. He led a series of well-publicized "Team Canada" missions around the globe and endorsed the North American Free Trade Agreement (NAFTA), which came into force on Jan. 1, 1994. Chrétien also established a cordial relationship with President Bill Clinton of the United States.

After leading the Liberals to another electoral victory on June 2, 1997, Chrétien continued the work of his first term. In 1998, the government delivered a balanced budget and eliminated the 25-year-old national deficit. In 1999, Chrétien committed Canadian troops to NATO's war against the Serbs in the Balkans. In 2000, the government passed the Clarity Act, spelling out the conditions under which Quebec could separate.

In the election of Nov. 27, 2000, Chrétien led the Liberals to a third majority. The improved economy initially allowed Chrétien to continue work on domestic issues, but terrorist attacks on the United States on Sept. 11, 2001, forced him to refocus on national security. Chrétien sent troops to Afghanistan to help the Americans fight terrorists there, but Canada's relationship with the United States deteriorated after Chrétien decided against sending troops to aid the Anglo-American invasion of Iraq in March 2003.

Chrétien also faced challenges from rivals within the Liberal party. Several cabinet ministers, including Finance Minister Paul Martin, sought to replace Chrétien as prime minister. In August 2002, Chrétien declared that he would not seek a fourth term. On Nov. 13, 2003, one day before a Liberal convention elected Paul Martin party leader, Chrétien relinquished the leadership of the Liberal party. Chrétien's last day in the prime minister's office was Dec. 11, 2003.

■ Paul Martin

Paul Edgar Philippe Martin was born in Windsor, Ont., on Aug. 28, 1938. His father was Paul Martin, Sr., who was a federal Liberal MP (1935–68), a federal cabinet minister (1945–57; 1963–69) and a Liberal senator (1968–74).

As a young man, Paul Martin, Jr., studied history, philosophy and law at St. Michael's College at the University of Toronto. He was called to the bar in Ontario in 1966.

Before entering politics, Martin worked in Montreal as an executive at Power Corporation of Canada. He later became chairman and chief executive officer of Canada Steamship Lines.

In 1988, Martin ran as a federal Liberal candidate and won the seat of LaSalle–Émard in Montreal. He was re-elected in 1993, 1997, 2000 and 2004 in the same riding.

In 1990, Martin ran for the leadership of the federal Liberal party. At the leadership convention, he finished in second place after Jean Chrétien.

Throughout 1991–93, when the Liberals occupied the Opposition benches in the House of Commons, Martin acted as associate finance critic and environment critic. In 1993, before the general election of that year, Martin co-authored *Creating Opportunity: The Liberal Plan for Canada* (the "Red Book").

On Oct. 25, 1993, the Liberal party won a majority of seats in the general election. On Nov. 4, 1993, Martin became finance minister in Prime Minister Chrétien's cabinet. Martin held the post until June 1, 2002.

During Chrétien's first term in office, Martin also became the minister responsible for the Federal Office of Regional Development in Quebec. He held the post from Nov. 4, 1993, to Jan. 24, 1996.

Throughout the Chrétien decade, Finance Minister Martin recorded five consecutive budget surpluses, eliminated a $42-billion deficit, paid down more than $36 billion in debt and effected some of the largest tax cuts in Canadian history. He also represented Canada at a series of international summit meetings.

In November 2003, the Liberal party held a leadership convention to determine Prime Minister Chrétien's successor. On Nov. 14, Martin defeated his only competitor, Minister of Canadian Heritage Sheila Copps, on the first ballot. On Dec. 12, 2003, after Chrétien resigned from office, Martin became Canada's 21st prime minister.

In December 2003, Martin named 38 ministers for his first cabinet. He named 22 new ministers, but he retained 16 ministers from Chrétien's last cabinet including Deputy Prime Minister Anne McLellan.

On June 28, 2004, the Liberals were re-elected in a general election, but they won only 135 of 308 seats in the House of Commons. The Liberals lost seats to the New Democratic Party, the Bloc Québécois and the newly formed Conservative Party of Canada. Martin subsequently formed the first federal minority government since 1979.

In August 2004, before the re-opening of Parliament, Martin named two female judges to the Supreme Court of Canada: Madam Justice Rosalie S. Abella and Madam Justice Louise V. Charron. The simultaneous appointment of these judges raised the number of females on the court to an unprecedented four out of nine. Martin also authorized an unprecedented parliamentary committee to review the two nominees before their official appointment to the court. The temporary committee consisted of Liberal MPs, Conservative MPs and legal experts.

Fathers of Confederation

In the 1860s, delegates from the British colonies in North America attended three constitutional conferences in Charlottetown, Quebec City and London. Their deliberations laid the foundation of the modern Canadian state in 1867.

Before Confederation, politicians had discussed the idea of uniting the colonies for years, but in the spring of 1864, the legislatures of New Brunswick, Nova Scotia and Prince Edward Island passed resolutions to hold a conference about Maritime union. In June, politicians in the Province of Canada (i.e., Ontario and Quebec) asked to attend the conference; they wanted to discuss the unification of all British North America. A conference was scheduled in PEI.

The Charlottetown Conference took place throughout Sept. 1–9, 1864. The delegates abandoned the idea of mere Maritime union and outlined a federal union for British North America. They also decided to continue their discussions in one month's time in Quebec City. The delegates acted quickly because they feared the northward march of American armies after the American Civil War. Some delegates also hoped that productive talks would end political deadlock in the Province of Canada between Protestant English and Roman Catholic French.

At the Quebec Conference, 33 delegates (including two from Newfoundland) drafted a more detailed plan for union throughout Oct. 10–27, 1864. The Province of Canada set the agenda, proposed resolutions and dominated the conference. The proposals for the future Parliament sparked the most controversy. PEI disliked the idea of electing members to a House of Commons according to representation by population. The delegates also fought battles over the distribution of seats in the Senate. John A. Macdonald and Oliver Mowat, however, made agreement over the division of federal and provincial powers easier. The conference adjourned with 72 resolutions.

The London Conference opened on Dec. 4, 1866, in Britain. Delegates from the Province of Canada, New Brunswick and Nova Scotia negotiated Confederation with the British government. The British were receptive to Confederation because they sought to divest themselves of some responsibilities in North America. Roman Catholic bishops won guarantees for separate religious schools in Ontario and Quebec. The final London Resolutions were redrafted as the British North America Act; this Act of Britain's Parliament became Canada's constitution and came into force on July 1, 1867.

In the table below, the names of the conference delegates are followed by the colonies they represented; "Canada" refers to the Province of Canada. C = Charlottetown; Q = Quebec; L = London.

Delegate (Colony)	Conference	Delegate (Colony)	Conference
Adams G. Archibald, NS	C,Q,L	Hector L. Langevin, Canada	C,Q,L
George Brown, Canada	C,Q	Jonathan McCully, NS	C,Q,L
Alexander Campbell, Canada	C,Q	A.A. Macdonald, PEI	C,Q
Frederick B.T. Carter, Nfld	Q	John A. Macdonald, Canada	C,Q,L
George-Étienne Cartier, Canada	C,Q,L	William McDougall, Canada	C,Q,L
Edward B. Chandler, NB	C,Q	Thomas D'Arcy McGee, Canada	C,Q
Jean-Charles Chapais, Canada	Q	Peter Mitchell, NB	Q,L
James Cockburn, Canada	Q	Oliver Mowat, Canada	Q
George H. Coles, PEI	C,Q	Edward Palmer, PEI	C,Q
Robert B. Dickey, NS	Q	William H. Pope, PEI	C,Q
Charles Fisher, NB	Q,L	John W. Ritchie, NS	L
Alexander T. Galt, Canada	C,Q,L	J. Ambrose Shea, Nfld	Q
John Hamilton Gray, NB	C,Q	William H. Steeves, NB	C,Q
John Hamilton Gray, PEI	C,Q	Sir Étienne-Paschal Taché, Canada	Q
Thomas Heath Haviland, PEI	Q	Samuel Leonard Tilley, NB	C,Q,L
William A. Henry, NS	C,Q,L	Charles Tupper, NS	C,Q,L
William P. Howland, Canada	L	Edward Whelan, PEI	Q
John M. Johnson, NB	C,Q,L	R.D. Wilmot, NB	L

GOVERNMENT OF CANADA

```
                    ┌─────────────┐
                    │  Sovereign  │
                    └─────────────┘
                           │
                    ┌─────────────┐
                    │  Governor   │
                    │   General   │
                    └─────────────┘
                           │
   ┌──────────────┐ ┌──────────────┐ ┌──────────────┐
   │  PARLIAMENT  │ │PRIME MINISTER│ │  JUDICIARY   │
   └──────────────┘ └──────────────┘ └──────────────┘
```

PARLIAMENT	PRIME MINISTER	JUDICIARY
House of Commons Senate		Supreme Court of Canada
		Federal Court of Canada
		Tax Court

Prime Minister's Office — Ministry — Privy Council Office

Federal Departments

Canada is an independent, self-governing democracy. Its form of government is constitutional monarchy. Government power is divided into three types: legislative, executive and judicial. In Canada the legislative and executive powers are joined, while the judiciary remains separate. The executive proposes legislation, presents budgets and implements laws; the legislature adopts laws and votes on recommendations for taxes or other revenue; the judiciary interprets the laws.

■ The Monarchy

The Queen (crowned Queen Elizabeth II on June 2, 1953) is Canada's official head of state. All government authority is derived from the Queen, and all laws are enacted in her name. The Queen's role is set out in the Constitution Act (formerly the British North America Act, 1867), which also gives the

monarch ultimate authority over Canada's armed forces.

In practice, however, the Queen has little or no part to play in Canadian government. She appoints the Governor General, but does so only on the prime minister's recommendation. Once appointed, it is the Governor General who performs the monarch's duties, and these duties have been mainly ceremonial for many years. Only during royal visits does the Queen carry out functions normally performed in her name by the Governor General such as the opening of Parliament.

■ The Governor General

The Governor General is selected by the prime minister and formally appointed by the Queen to act as her representative in Canada. The appointment is usually for five years but has sometimes been extended to seven.

Bills passed in the House of Commons and Senate do not become law until the Governor General has given them royal assent. The Governor General executes all orders-in-council and other state documents, appoints all superior court judges (on the advice of Cabinet) and summons, prorogues and dissolves Parliament (on the advice of the prime minister). Also, the Governor General invites the leader of the political party with the most support in the House of Commons to form a government. The leader of that party becomes prime minister.

The Imperial Conferences of 1926 and 1930 established that the Governor General was not the representative or agent of the British government and should act only on the advice of the Canadian prime minister and Cabinet. Therefore, the Governor General is obliged to respect the principle of responsible government and to follow the wishes of Canada's elected representatives. As a result, the role of the Governor General has become largely symbolic, with duties that are chiefly ceremonial.

Three members of the royal family have held the post: the Marquess of Lorne (1878–83), the Duke of Connaught (1911–16) and the Earl of Athlone (1940–46).

The first Canadian Governor General was Vincent Massey (1952–59).

The Legislature

Canada's legislature or Parliament consists of the Queen, an upper house (known as the Senate) and a lower house (known as the House of Commons). Senators are appointed by the Governor General on the advice of the prime minister.

The House of Commons is an elected assembly in which each member represents one of 308 electoral districts distributed according to population.

■ The Senate

The Senate is the upper house of the Canadian Parliament through which all legislation must pass before it becomes law. Its members, appointed by the Governor General on the recommendation of the prime minister, hold office until age 75. (Senators appointed before June 1965 held office for life.)

Originally, there were 72 senators, but through the years the Senate has increased as the number of provinces and the population have grown. In 1975 the Senate was increased to 104 members; in 1990 Prime Minister Brian Mulroney employed a never-before-used section of the Constitution Act to increase the number temporarily to 112.

After 1999, there were 105 Senate seats apportioned on a regional basis: 24 from the Maritime provinces (Nova Scotia, 10; New Brunswick, 10; Prince Edward Island, 4); 24 from Quebec; 24 from Ontario; 24 from the Western provinces (Manitoba, 6; Saskatchewan, 6; Alberta, 6; British Columbia, 6); 6 from Newfoundland; 1 each from the Yukon, Northwest Territories and Nunavut.

To be eligible for Senate appointment, a person must be a Canadian citizen, at least 30 years old, a resident of the province for which he or she is appointed, possess land in that province with an unencumbered value of $4,000 and have a net estate of $4,000. A senator for Quebec must either be resident in the division for which he or she is appointed, or have property qualification there.

A Speaker of the Senate, who is appointed by the Governor General on the prime minister's advice, presides over the proceedings. By custom, the appointment to the Speaker's chair alternates between anglophone and francophone members. The Speaker decides questions of privilege and points of order. The Speaker also represents the Senate when receiving parliamentary and foreign dignitaries.

Technically, the Senate's legislative powers are equal to those of the House of Commons with two restrictions: first, on certain constitutional amendments, the Senate may delay resolutions of the House of Commons for up to 180 days but cannot defeat them; second, the Senate cannot initiate money bills.

In practice, however, the Senate's chief role is to provide technical reviews of legislation proposed in the House of Commons rather than initiate political action. These reviews are done by Senate committees, which inspect each bill clause by clause and hear evidence from groups or individuals who may be affected by the proposed legislation.

Three types of Senate committee are worth noting. Standing committees, which are created at the start of a parliamentary session, study ongoing issues such as banking and foreign affairs. Standing committees may sit for up to five years. Special committees, which are created to deal with unusual or temporary issues, usually sit for six months before tabling their final reports in the Senate. Joint committees, which consist of representatives from the Senate and the House of Commons, work on issues that affect both chambers of Parliament.

Historically, the Senate rarely used its powers to impede legislation originating from the elected House of Commons. From 1984 to 1990, however, the Liberal-dominated Senate attempted several times to stall or block legislation approved by the Conservative majority in the House of Commons. In 1990, when the Senate blocked his government's goods and services tax, Prime Minister Mulroney temporarily increased the size of the Senate and added eight new Conservatives, ensuring that the measure would be made law.

In recent years, there have been repeated calls, especially from the West, for constitutional reform which would include an elected Senate with more representation from the Western provinces and Newfoundland and Labrador.

■ The House of Commons

The House of Commons is Canada's 308-member elected federal assembly. Its members are chosen in general elections held at least once every five years. By-elections are held if a member dies or resigns between general elections.

All bills governing matters within federal jurisdiction must be passed by a majority of members of Parliament to become law.

Members of Parliament usually belong to a political party and will normally vote with that party on any proposed legislation. Occasionally, members will break with their party on a vote and will leave the party they were affiliated with when elected to sit as independents or to join another political party within the House. Members of Parliament can also be elected as independent candidates who do not belong to a political party.

The prime minister is the leader of the political party able to command the support of a majority of the members of the House of Commons. The prime minister's command of a majority of members in the House also makes the prime minister the leader of the federal government. If no party holds a clear majority of seats, a "minority government" is formed, usually led by the party with the

most seats in Parliament, provided it has enough support from the other parties to enable it to pass legislation.

The Opposition consists of parties that win enough votes to elect members to the House but do not have enough seats in the House to form a majority government. These parties sit on benches across from the governing party in the House and debate the government's policies for the life of the legislature—a maximum of five years. The Opposition party with the largest number of seats is given the title of "Her Majesty's Loyal Opposition." The minimum requirement for "official party" status is 12 seats in the House.

When the House of Commons is in session it convenes at two o'clock daily and 11 o'clock on Fridays when the Speaker of the House takes the chair. After the mace is laid on the table in front of the Speaker and the daily prayer is read, business commences. Members of the government sit to the Speaker's right and the Opposition sits on the left. The leaders of other opposition parties sit on the left farther away from the Speaker's chair.

The Speaker of the House, who is elected from and by the members after a general election, presides over the legislature. This official decides all procedural questions and maintains order. The Speaker is impartial at all times, enforcing the House's rules without regard to party loyalty. The Speaker also chairs the Board of Internal Economy, which controls the House of Commons staff and its annual budget. Some Speakers resign their party membership and run as independents in subsequent elections to maintain their impartial standing in the House.

An important feature of Parliament is the daily question period when members question Cabinet ministers about their policies and actions. But most of Parliament's time is spent discussing proposed legislation introduced as "bills." Any member may introduce a bill, although this is usually done by a member of Cabinet. After an initial reading in the House, a bill is forwarded into committee for detailed examination.

The House of Commons features several types of committees. Standing committees, which are the most common, are created at the beginning of a parliamentary session. They investigate ongoing issues and may sit for up to five years. Special committees, which are sometimes called task forces, are created to deal with unusual issues (such as illegal drug use). Special committees usually sit for six months before tabling their final reports in the House. Legislative committees are created solely to examine a bill after its second reading in the House. These committees usually have no more than seven members and cease to exist after reporting to the House.

After a bill is examined by committee and read a third time in the House, members vote on the bill. If a majority of members vote for the bill, it is forwarded to the Senate for consideration.

The leader of the government in the House of Commons—who is a cabinet minister but not the prime minister—shepherds the government's bills through the legislature. The house leader of the government works with the leader of the government in the Senate to coordinate the smooth passage of bills there. The house leader of the government also keeps Opposition members informed about all legislative matters.

Before a vote on a bill occurs, the party whips—who are drawn from their respective caucuses—ensure that their party's members appear in the legislature or at committee meetings to vote. Party whips rely more on persuasion than coercion to ensure member attendance; occasionally whips offer minor rewards (e.g., trips and committee memberships) to party colleagues to ensure that they vote. In 2001, the Liberal government appointed the first woman—Marlene Catterall of Ontario West—to the post of chief government whip in the House of Commons.

When a major piece of legislation introduced by the government is defeated in the House of Commons, the government is obliged to resign. The Governor General may then call on the Leader of the Opposition to form a government but, in most cases, will call a general election so that the electorate can decide which party has the most public support for its policies.

The Executive

■ The Prime Minister

The prime minister is the pre-eminent figure in Canadian politics. The power and authority of the office come from the prime minister's leadership of the party (or group of parties) that has control of the most seats in the House of Commons. The prime minister is an elected member of Parliament as well as national party leader and has a mandate to govern via programs and policies and to speak on behalf of Canada.

The prime minister appoints and dismisses cabinet ministers, senior civil servants and parliamentary secretaries; the prime minister also appoints senators, judges, lieutenant-governors, privy councillors, provincial administrators and Speakers of the Senate. In addition, the prime minister recommends to the monarchy the appointment of the Governor General. The prime minister has the authority to dissolve Parliament and can therefore control the timing of an election. The prime minister also controls the organization of government, including the power to create or shut down Crown corporations; create, modify or merge cabinet portfolios and bureaucratic agencies; and appoint royal commissions.

■ The Cabinet

The Cabinet is a group of government ministers who, chosen and led by the prime minister, determine executive policies and are responsible for them to the House of Commons. Cabinet members are usually given responsibility for heading specific areas of the government such as finance or foreign policy and will introduce legislation pertaining to them in the House of Commons. They will also explain or defend government actions when questioned in the House.

Cabinet ministers are generally chosen from members of the government's party in the House of Commons, although senators are sometimes appointed to provide Cabinet representation from all parts of the country. When senators join the Cabinet they do not usually head a government department because a senator is constitutionally forbidden to introduce tax or "money bill" legislation.

There are five categories of cabinet ministers:

1. department ministers who assume responsibility for running one or more government departments

2. ministers with special parliamentary responsibilities

3. ministers without portfolios who do not have responsibility for running a department and are often appointed to

balance regional representation in the Cabinet

4. ministers of state for designated purposes who formulate and develop new policies outside normal departmental responsibilities

5. secretaries of state who may assist departmental ministers, though the departmental minister remains legally responsible for the duties and functions performed by the minister of state

■ The Privy Council Office

The Privy Council Office is directed by the senior member of the public service, the clerk of the Privy Council, who also serves as the secretary to the Cabinet. As part of the executive branch of government, the office staffs the Cabinet secretariat and provides services to ensure the smooth functioning of the Cabinet and Cabinet meetings. The Privy Council Office advises the prime minister on government appointments, relations with Parliament and the monarchy, the roles and responsibilities of ministers and the organization of government. The office assists in the co-ordination of policy, ensuring that new proposals are compatible both with existing policy and the government's objectives. During a transition period between governments, the Privy Council Office assists in the winding down of outgoing administrations and the startup of the newly elected government.

The Privy Council Office's primary responsibilities are to ensure the smooth functioning of the machinery of government and decision-making, provide support to the Cabinet, monitor developments throughout the government, and act as a broker to resolve governmental problems.

■ The Treasury Board

The Treasury Board is a committee of the Privy Council that reviews planned expenditures and programs proposed by government departments and assigns priorities to each. The board is responsible for preparing a long-range and comprehensive fiscal plan that projects government income and expenses for up to four years; it also prepares operational plans for departmental programs. The board's estimates of the costs of existing programs, major statutory payments (such as transfer payments) and public debt charges form the basis of the main estimates, which are tabled by the first of March each year for review by various House committees.

The Treasury Board is also responsible for administrative policy; organization of the public service; and financial, expenditure and personnel management. In 1988, the board was also given responsibility for the policies and programs of the Official Languages Act. The board's secretariat negotiates collective agreements with the federal public service, acting as employer on the government's behalf.

■ Departments

Legislation and government policies are administered through departments, departmental branches and corporations, corporations owned or controlled by the government, special boards and various commissions and advisory bodies. Departments and departmental corporations are accountable to a cabinet minister and ultimately to Parliament; they perform research, administrative, advisory, supervisory or regulatory roles. Crown corporations usually operate in a competitive or commercial environment and some are accountable to Parliament through a minister as well.

The Canadian Judiciary

■ The Supreme Court of Canada

The Supreme Court of Canada is Canada's highest court of law. It was created by federal statute in 1875. Originally, Supreme Court decisions could be appealed to a special tribunal in England, but such appeals were abolished for criminal cases in 1933 and for civil cases in 1949. Since then, the Supreme Court of Canada has been the court of last resort for every case—criminal or civil—commenced in a Canadian court.

The Supreme Court has jurisdiction to hear appeals from the courts of appeal of each province, as well as from the Federal Court of Canada. The Supreme Court is also empowered to consider questions referred to it by the federal Cabinet, and to rule on the legality of bills submitted by the government.

The Constitution Act, 1982, with its new Canadian Charter of Rights and Freedoms, has expanded the role of the courts in general and of the Supreme Court in particular. Though it has always been within the power of Canadian courts to declare laws or other government actions invalid, this power had narrow limits prior to 1982. Legislation could be struck down only if the government introducing it had exceeded its legislative authority as defined in the Constitution Act (formerly called the British North America Act, 1867). The federal government was not permitted to legislate on matters within provincial legislative authority, and the provincial governments were not permitted to legislate on matters within federal legislative authority. As long as the legislation satisfied that test, it was valid.

But after the Constitution Act was patriated from the United Kingdom in 1982, the courts have had the power to strike down legislation or invalidate other government actions if they infringe or deny any of the fundamental rights and freedoms recognized by the Canadian Charter of Rights and Freedoms. This new power has made Supreme Court judges the watchdogs of Parliament and, ultimately, the guardians of our constitutional rights. As the highest court in the land, the Supreme Court of Canada has the final word on whether laws violate the Constitution.

The Supreme Court consists of nine judges, including the chief justice. Three of the judges must be appointed from Quebec. By convention (although it is not legally required) three have been appointed from Ontario, two from the West and one from Atlantic Canada. All judges are appointed and paid by the federal government, and may hold office until age 75.

■ Federal Court of Canada

This court consists of a trial division and a court of appeal and has jurisdiction over a small range of specialized areas such as admiralty law, income tax, patents and customs. Once called the Exchequer Court, the Federal Court is administered by the federal government.

■ Appellate Courts

When a decision of the provincial superior courts is to be appealed, these courts hear the appeal and decide upon it. An appeal is not a new trial; there are rarely any witnesses called and the judges do not re-hear the whole case. Instead, they examine written transcripts of the trial and listen to legal arguments presented by the parties' lawyers. The appellate courts are provincial institutions and are called either the Court of Appeal or the Supreme Court Appeal Division; the judges are appointed by the federal government.

■ Superior Court of Original Jurisdiction

This is the highest court at the provincial level, with jurisdiction to hear all civil and criminal cases, unless a statute specifically says otherwise. The name of the superior court differs among provinces. It can be called the Court of Queen's Bench, the Superior Court, the Superior Court of Justice or the Supreme Court Trial Division. The judges of these courts are appointed and paid by the federal government.

■ District or County Courts

These trial courts hear all but the most serious criminal matters and civil matters up to a certain dollar value. The judges of these courts are also appointed by the federal government.

■ Provincial Courts

This is the lowest rung of the judicial ladder. The jurisdiction of the provincial courts is limited by statute to the less serious criminal matters and civil cases involving relatively small sums of money. These judges are appointed and paid by the province in which they serve.

■ Federal and Provincial Legislative Authority

Because Canada is a federal state, legislative powers are divided between two levels of government: federal and provincial. (Municipal governments only exercise powers delegated to them by the provincial government).

Each level of government has a distinct sphere of authority. With a few exceptions, neither level is permitted to encroach on the legislative authority of the other.

The Constitution Act lists the responsibilities over which the federal and provincial governments have exclusive authority. The federal government, in addition to a general power to make laws for the "peace, order and good government of Canada," has exclusive power in several areas including criminal law, unemployment insurance, postal service, regulation of trade, external relations, money and banking, transportation, citizenship, Indian affairs and defence. Matters exclusively within provincial legislative authority include property and civil rights, administration of justice, education, health and welfare, municipal institutions and matters of a merely local or private nature.

Many of the subject classes set out in the Constitution Act, 1867, are broadly worded, and considerable debate has arisen over which level of government has authority to pass certain laws. Confusion has also arisen over the proper distribution of powers to regulate matters that could not have been foreseen by the Fathers of Confederation, such as air travel, radio and television broadcasting, etc. These difficulties have led to long political debates and court challenges. The latter arise when a person adversely affected by a particular law claims that the law is invalid because it is *ultra vires*—beyond the powers of the level of government that enacted it. Before the passing of the Constitution Act, 1982, only statutes found to be *ultra vires* could be declared inoperative by the Supreme Court of Canada. Now, there is an additional restraint on the federal Parliament and the provincial legislatures to comply with constitutional provisions, including the Canadian Charter of Rights and Freedoms.

■ The Provincial Governments

Canada's 10 provinces have a system of government which parallels that of the federal government in several ways. A premier, like the prime minister, leads the government by virtue of being leader of the party with the most seats in the provincial legislature and forms a Cabinet from the elected members of the governing party. Members of a provincial legislature, like members of the federal Parliament, represent constituencies and approve legislation within their constitutional jurisdiction. A lieutenant-governor, like the Governor General, gives royal assent to the laws passed by the legislature.

The major difference between the provincial and federal systems is that the provinces have no equivalent body to Canada's Senate.

■ The Territorial Governments

The Yukon, Northwest Territories and Nunavut are governed by elected representatives. Although the administration of each territory is technically in the hands of a commissioner appointed by the federal government, in practice the role of the commissioner has become like a provincial lieutenant-governor's: a commissioner follows the wishes of the elected representatives when exercising their authority.

In the Northwest Territories, the legislature consists of elected members who run for office as independents rather than as members of political parties. This assembly selects the territory's political executives: a premier, who must win more than 50 percent of the vote, and other cabinet ministers.

In Nunavut, the legislature consists of elected members who also run for office as independents rather than as members of political parties. The territory's executive, which is drawn from this assembly, consists of a premier and other cabinet ministers.

Yukon also has a legislative assembly, which features political parties. The leader of the party supported by a majority of the assembly's elected representatives is named premier. Executive power is in the hands of an executive council, which functions like a provincial cabinet. Its members are appointed by Yukon's commissioner on the advice of the premier.

In the territories, the elected bodies have jurisdiction over such areas as education, housing, social services and renewable resources.

In 1990, the Northwest Territories established six aboriginal languages (Dogrib, Chipewyan, Gwich'in, Cree, Slavey and Inuktitut) as official languages, in addition to English and French.

■ Mechanics of Government

Formation of Government: General elections for the House of Commons occur at least every five years. But they may take place more often if the prime minister decides to call an early election or if the governing party loses the support of the majority of members of the House.

Following an election, the Governor General calls upon the leader of the party with the greatest House of Commons support to become prime minister. This is almost always the leader of the party with the most seats in the House but, under unusual circumstances, it could be the leader of another party which is able to gain majority support in Parliament.

The prime minister selects the Cabinet, usually from members of his party in the House of Commons. Formally, the prime minister and Cabinet act as advisors to the Governor General. In practice, however, they wield executive power and the Governor General's role is mainly ceremonial.

Passage of Legislation: To become law, proposed legislation (known as bills) must be passed by a majority of members in both the House of Commons and the Senate and then must be given royal assent by the Governor General. Most bills are introduced by members of the government in the House of Commons. Typically, a bill is given three "readings" in the House. The first reading is simply to introduce the bill. The second reading is accompanied by debate on the principle of the bill. The bill is then voted on and, if approved, is sent to a House committee composed of representatives of all parties to be considered clause by clause. The committee prepares a report and submits it to the House of Commons with any proposed amendments. These amendments, plus any others moved by any member of Parliament, are debated and usually voted on. A motion is then brought for the bill to be given third reading. If the vote is favorable, the bill is then introduced in the Senate where it undergoes a similar process. After a bill has been approved by both Houses, the Governor General gives it royal assent in a ceremony that takes place in the Senate chamber.

Defeat of a Government: Between elections, a government can be forced to resign if it is defeated in a vote on a major government bill. When this happens, the government is considered to have lost the support of the majority of Parliament's elected representatives. This typically occurs only when the party in power has formed a minority government—that is, if it holds more seats than any other single party but fewer seats than the combined Opposition parties. This last happened federally in 1979 when a minority Conservative government, elected earlier that year, introduced a budget which was defeated by the combined votes of the Liberal and New Democratic Party members in the House. Parliament was dissolved, an election was called and the Liberals regained power.

■ The Constitution of Canada

Canada's constitution consists of written documents and unwritten conventions. The written constitution is embodied in the Constitution Acts of 1867 and 1982. The 1867 legislation (originally titled the British North America Act) was a British statute that established a federal state with a Parliament modelled on the British system. The Act assembled the colonies of Nova Scotia, New Brunswick and Canada (Ontario and Quebec) into the "Dominion of Canada," created a federal government in Ottawa, and divided the powers of government between Ottawa and the provinces.

The BNA Act gave Ottawa broad jurisdiction over internal matters, including unlimited powers of taxation, while allowing the provinces only a narrow field of local control. In general, the Canadian constitution of the late 19th century was a centralist document.

Under the BNA Act, Britain still had the power to veto Canadian laws or to enact statutes affecting Canada. But the British had no desire to raise revenue in Canada, for example, or to tax Canadians directly. This approach extended to trade and tariffs. Gradually, the practice was established that where money was involved, even in trade treaties, Canada would determine its own policy.

The same was not true of political foreign policy. When Britain declared war on Germany in 1914, Canada, as part of the British Empire, was automatically at war. During this period, British courts also interpreted Canadian statutes, especially those involving the division of power between Ottawa and the provinces. Through this process, the constitution's strong centralist thrust was altered to give more authority to the provinces.

The constitution was also adjusted more directly, through amendments. But because the BNA Act was a British statute, Canada could make formal changes to it only with the consent of the British Parliament. Ottawa tended to seek such amendments only when they did not affect provincial powers or when the provinces agreed with the changes. This process worked at least some of the time: 29 times, in fact, between 1870 and 1975. In 1940, for example, unemployment insurance became a federal responsibility through an amendment to the BNA Act.

In 1931, Britain attempted to tidy up relations with Canada and other self-governing dominions within the Commonwealth by passing the Statute of Westminster. The Statute ceded full powers over foreign affairs and trade to Canada. But because the federal and provincial governments could not agree on a method for amending the BNA Act at home, the British Parliament retained ultimate power over Canada's constitution. Until 1949, British courts continued to review Canadian constitutional cases.

From 1927 until 1982, a succession of federal governments attempted to resolve the problem by getting the provinces to agree to an amending formula. These negotiations failed as the provinces used them as a means to gain concessions from Ottawa.

The catalyst in constitutional discussions during the late 20th century came from Quebec, where provincial governments since 1960 sought to expand the province's jurisdiction. To protect French culture, the Quebec government requested more powers over culture, the economy and social institutions.

Ottawa resisted the move under prime ministers Lester Pearson and Pierre Trudeau. Trudeau argued that without a strong central power a country as sprawling and diverse as Canada would be fatally weakened and might disintegrate.

In lengthy negotiations with the provinces, Trudeau failed to gain agreement on an amending formula, even when he offered increased powers in return. In 1976, the election of the separatist Parti Québécois in Quebec made constitutional compromise even more unlikely and the matter was set aside.

After Quebec's 1980 referendum on sovereignty-association was won by the federal-ists, constitutional renewal was back on the agenda. However, federal-provincial discussions became mired in disagreement through the summer of 1980. In September, Trudeau announced that the federal government, with the support of only Ontario and New Brunswick, would ask the British Parliament to amend the BNA Act to patriate the constitution and establish a Canadian Charter of Rights and Freedoms to protect individual liberties. The Charter would also protect minority rights in education and the mobility rights of Canadian citizens, and change the name of the constitution: the BNA Act became the Constitution Act, 1982.

It took 18 months to get the new amendments approved by the Canadian Parliament, resolve the concerns of eight provincial governments, and get the Act through the British Parliament. But, in April 1982, the Constitution Act was proclaimed—although the consent of the Quebec government was never given.

The Constitution Act, 1982, consolidated all the previous BNA Acts and added an amending formula and a Charter of Rights and Freedoms. The Charter, which provided for basic democratic rights, also contained a "notwithstanding" clause that allowed Parliament or any provincial legislature to over-ride its provisions.

The amending formula provided for two types of constitutional change. The division of powers between the federal and provincial governments could be modified with the consent of the federal Parliament and seven provincial legislatures in provinces totalling more than 50 percent of the Canadian population; matters such as the composition of the Supreme Court or the status of English or French, however, required unanimous consent. The formula also stipulated that no amendment could take longer than three years to be ratified by Ottawa and all 10 provinces.

Visiting Public Galleries in Parliament

W hen Parliament is in session, visitors may sit in public galleries to watch debates or question period. Visits to the Senate gallery do not require reservations, but visits to the House of Commons do. Individuals who want to watch the House in action should schedule their visit through their MP's office; groups of 10–50 people or more must schedule their visit through their MP's office or through Parliament's reservation office at (613) 996-0896.

Electoral Redistribution

Since 1867, Canada's elected representatives have wrestled with the problem of ensuring that each Canadian citizen receives fair representation in government while also ensuring that each region has a fair say in the nation's business. Representation in both the House of Commons and the Senate has always been based on geography, and Canada's vast and often sparsely populated territory has always made establishing fair representation a challenge.

THE QUEST FOR A FORMULA

The first formula for representation in the House of Commons used the population of Quebec as the benchmark for calculating what is known as the "electoral quotient." First, the population of Quebec was divided by 65 (the number of seats guaranteed by the first Constitution Act). The result was then divided into the populations of each of the other provinces to calculate the number of seats each province would have—giving each voter the same relative representation.

Recognizing the need for a process of future adjustment, Parliament legislated that the number of seats in the House of Commons would be re-examined and redistributed after each 10-year census, beginning in 1871. At the same time, because not all provinces' populations would grow equally, the formula was softened by what was known as the "one-twentieth rule": no province would lose seats unless its percentage of Canada's total population dropped by at least 5 percent between the last two censuses. Despite the rule, people soon realized that the formula was too harsh.

In 1915, a new rule was introduced, stating that no province would have fewer seats in the Commons than it had in the Senate. (Thus PEI was guaranteed four seats.) In 1946, the formula was again amended to calculate the electoral quotient by dividing Canada's total population by the number of seats (255) to ascertain the average population per electoral district. By 1951, emerging population trends (which continue today) threatened to erode the voting power of the smaller provinces too quickly. Nova Scotia, Manitoba and Saskatchewan all faced the loss of seats after the 1951 census. A new rule, known as the "15

percent clause" was adopted. It stated that no province, no matter what its population drop, could lose more than 15 percent of its seats in any one redistribution. The 1961 census showed more population loss in those provinces, as well as in Quebec, and the 15 percent clause again came into effect. The 1971 census added Newfoundland to the number of provinces losing seats as a result of population shifts. Concern over the continuing erosion of the position of some provinces prompted another overhaul of the rules for calculating the allocation of seats when the Representation Act, 1974, was enacted. It was based on the following assumption:

> The objective must be adequate and realistic representation of all Canadians bearing in mind the historical undertakings arising out of Confederation and its responsibilities. The allocation of seats (in the House of Commons) is at the very heart of the Confederation compromise.[1]

The Representation Act made radical changes to the rules for allocating seats:

1) The population of Quebec was again used to calculate the electoral quotient.
2) Quebec was guaranteed 75 seats instead of 65.
3) The number of seats assigned to Quebec was to grow by 4 at each readjustment in order to slow the growth in the average population per electoral district.
4) Categories of provinces were created to assist in balancing representation among large and small provinces. A small province was classed as having a population of less than 1.5 million; an intermediate province, between 1.5 million and 2.5 million; a large province, over 2.5 million.

The new formula was used in 1976 and the House increased to 282 seats. After the 1981

(1) The Standing Committee on Privileges and Elections, February 1974.

census, it was clear that the formula of 1974 would send the number of seats in the House soaring—possibly to 369 after 2001. The Representation Act, 1985, simplified the formula. It guides the redistribution triggered by the 2001 census. It provides for the following:

1) Subtract 1 seat for each of the territories (3) from the total number of seats in the House of Commons (282) to reach 279 seats.
2) Divide the total population of the provinces (29,914,315) by 279 seats to reach the national quotient: 107,220 people.
3) Divide a province's population in 2001 by 107,220 to reach the number of seats for the province.
4) Then apply the Special Clauses—the various senatorial and grandfather clauses—to arrive at the final allocation of seats shown in the table below.

Redistribution began on March 12, 2002, as soon as Elections Canada received the census data from the chief statistician. It is clear from the electoral quotient that while the goal is "one elector—one vote," not all votes carry equal weight. The Supreme Court of Canada was asked to address this issue in 1991 and, in its opinion, judged that the formula guaranteed the right of effective representation rather than equality of voting power.

BOUNDARY READJUSTMENT

Changing representation is a two-step process: once seats are allocated, boundaries for constituencies must be adjusted. This job rests with independent provincial commissions set up by Elections Canada. Chaired by a judge appointed by that province's chief justice, each commission includes two appointees named by the speaker of the House of Commons. Deliberations of the commissions are subject to public scrutiny. Maps of proposed changes are published and public hearings are held.

The most recent round of hearings ended in 2002, and all 10 provincial commissions filed their reports in the House of Commons by March 28, 2003. Throughout the summer of 2003, the commissions resolved objections to their proposed boundary changes from federal MPs. Then the number of electoral districts increased from 301 to 308. The Representation Order of 2003 that defined the 308 districts came into force upon the dissolution of Parliament on May 23, 2004.

For more information about Canada's electoral boundaries, visit Elections Canada, at www.elections.ca

Canada's Current Representation Formula, using 2001 Census Data

Province/ Territory	Minimum Number of Seats[2]	Calculations				Electoral Quotient[3]
		Population 2001	Divided by National Quotient[4] (rounded result)	Adjustments due to Special Clauses	Total Seats	
Newfoundland & Labrador	7	512 930	5	+2	7	73 276
Prince Edward Island	4	135 294	1	+3	4	33 824
Nova Scotia	11	908 007	8	+3	11	82 546
New Brunswick	10	729 498	7	+3	10	72 950
Quebec	75	7 237 479	68	+7	75	96 500
Ontario	95	11 410 046	106	0	106	107 642
Manitoba	14	1 119 583	10	+4	14	79 970
Saskatchewan	14	978 933	9	+5	14	69 924
Alberta	21	2 947 807	28	0	28	106 243
British Columbia	28	3 907 738	36	0	36	108 548
Nunavut	1	n.a.	n.a.	n.a.	1	n.a.
Northwest Territories	1	n.a.	n.a.	n.a.	1	n.a.
Yukon Territory	1	n.a.	n.a.	n.a.	1	n.a.
Total Seats	**282**				**308**	

(2) In accordance with the Constitution Act, 1867 and amendments. (3) Population divided by the actual number of seats. (4) Population of provinces divided by existing seats allocated to provinces: 29 914 315 / 279 = 107 220

Text of the Canadian Charter of Rights and Freedoms

Whereas Canada is founded upon principles that recognize the supremacy of God and the rule of law:

■ Guarantee of Rights and Freedoms

1 The Canadian Charter of Rights and Freedoms guarantees the rights and freedoms set out in it subject only to such reasonable limits prescribed by law as can be demonstrably justified in a free and democratic society.

■ Fundamental Freedoms

2 Everyone has the following fundamental freedoms: (a) freedom of conscience and religion; (b) freedom of thought, belief, opinion and expression, including freedom of the press and other media of communication; (c) freedom of peaceful assembly; and (d) freedom of association.

■ Democratic Rights

3 Every citizen of Canada has the right to vote in an election of members of the House of Commons or of a legislative assembly and to be qualified for membership therein.

4 (1) No House of Commons and no legislative assembly shall continue for longer than five years from the date fixed for the return of the writs at a general election of its members. (2) In time of real or apprehended war, invasion or insurrection, a House of Commons may be continued by Parliament and a legislative assembly may be continued by the legislature beyond five years if such continuation is not opposed by the votes of more than one-third of the members of the House of Commons or the legislative assembly, as the case may be.

5 There shall be a sitting of Parliament and of each legislature at least once every twelve months.

■ Mobility Rights

6 (1) Every citizen of Canada has the right to enter, remain in and leave Canada. (2) Every citizen of Canada and every person who has the status of a permanent resident of Canada has the right (a) to move to and take up residence in any province; and (b) to pursue the gaining of a livelihood in any province. (3) The rights specified in subsection (2) are subject to (a) any laws or practices of general application in force in a province other than those that discriminate among persons primarily on the basis of province of present or previous residence; and (b) any laws providing for reasonable residency requirements as a qualification for the receipt of publicly provided social services. (4) Subsections (2) and (3) do not preclude any law, program or activity that has as its object the amelioration in a province of conditions of individuals in that province who are socially or economically disadvantaged if the rate of employment in that province is below the rate of employment in Canada.

■ Legal Rights

7 Everyone has the right to life, liberty and security of the person and the right not to be deprived thereof except in accordance with the principles of fundamental justice.

8 Everyone has the right to be secure against unreasonable search or seizure.

9 Everyone has the right not to be arbitrarily detained or imprisoned.

10 Everyone has the right on arrest or detention (a) to be informed promptly of the reasons therefor; (b) to retain and instruct counsel without delay and to be informed of that right; and (c) to have the validity of the detention determined by way of *habeas corpus* and to be released if the detention is not lawful.

11 Any person charged with an offence has the right (a) to be informed without unreasonable delay of the specific offence; (b) to be tried within a reasonable time; (c) not to be compelled to be a witness in proceedings against that person in respect of the offence; (d) to be presumed innocent until proven guilty according to law in a fair and public hearing by an independent

and impartial tribunal; (e) not to be denied reasonable bail without just cause; (f) except in the case of an offence under military law tried before a military tribunal, to the benefit of trial by jury where the maximum punishment for the offence is imprisonment for five years or a more severe punishment; (g) not to be found guilty on account of any act or omission unless, at the time of the act or omission, it constituted an offence under Canadian or international law or was criminal according to the general principles of law recognized by the community of nations; (h) if finally acquitted of the offence, not to be tried for it again and, if finally found guilty and punished for the offence, not to be tried or punished for it again; and (i) if found guilty of the offence and if the punishment for the offence has been varied between the time of commission and the time of sentencing, to the benefit of the lesser punishment.

12 Everyone has the right not to be subjected to any cruel and unusual treatment or punishment.

13 A witness who testifies in any proceedings has the right not to have any incriminating evidence so given used to incriminate that witness in any other proceedings, except in a prosecution for perjury or for the giving of contradictory evidence.

14 A party or witness in any proceedings who does not understand or speak the language in which the proceedings are conducted or who is deaf has the right to the assistance of an interpreter.

■ Equality Rights

15 (1) Every individual is equal before and under the law and has the right to the equal protection and equal benefit of the law without discrimination and, in particular, without discrimination based on race, national or ethnic origin, colour, religion, sex, age or mental or physical disability. (2) Subsection (1) does not preclude any law, program or activity that has as its object the amelioration of conditions of disadvantaged individuals or groups including those that are disadvantaged because of race, national or ethnic origin,

colour, religion, sex, age or mental or physical disability.

■ Official Languages of Canada

16 (1) English and French are the official languages of Canada and have equality of status and equal rights and privileges as to their use in all institutions of the Parliament and government of Canada. (2) English and French are the official languages of New Brunswick and have equality of status and equal rights and privileges as to their use in all institutions of the legislature and government of New Brunswick. (3) Nothing in this Charter limits the authority of Parliament or a legislature to advance the equality of status or use of English and French.

17 (1) Everyone has the right to use English or French in any debates and other proceedings of Parliament. (2) Everyone has the right to use English or French in any debates and other proceedings of the legislature of New Brunswick.

18 (1) The statutes, records and journals of Parliament shall be printed and published in English and French and both language versions are equally authoritative. (2) The statutes, records and journals of the legislature of New Brunswick shall be printed and published in English and French and both language versions are equally authoritative.

19 (1) Either English or French may be used by any person in, or in any pleading in or process issuing from, any court established by Parliament. (2) Either English or French may be used by any person in, or in any pleading in or process issuing from, any court of New Brunswick.

20 (1) Any member of the public in Canada has the right to communicate with, and to receive available services from, any head or central office of an institution of the Parliament or government of Canada in English or French, and has the same right with respect to any other office of any such institution where (a) there is a significant demand for communications with and services from that office in such language; or (b) due to the nature of the office, it is reasonable that communications with and services from that office be available in both English and French. (2) Any member of the public in New

Brunswick has the right to communicate with, and to receive available services from, any office of an institution of the legislature or government of New Brunswick in English or French.

21 Nothing in sections 16 to 20 abrogates or derogates from any right, privilege or obligation with respect to the English and French languages, or either of them, that exists or is continued by virtue of any other provision of the Constitution of Canada.

22 Nothing in sections 16 to 20 abrogates or derogates from any legal or customary right or privilege acquired or enjoyed either before or after the coming into force of this Charter with respect to any language that is not English or French.

■ Minority Language Educational Rights

23 (1) Citizens of Canada (a) whose first language learned and still understood is that of the English or French linguistic minority population of the province in which they reside, or (b) who have received their primary school instruction in Canada in English or French and reside in a province where the language in which they received that instruction is the language of the English or French linguistic minority population of the province, have the right to have their children receive primary and secondary school instruction in that language in that province. (2) Citizens of Canada of whom any child has received or is receiving primary or secondary school instruction in English or French in Canada, have the right to have all their children receive primary and secondary school instruction in the same language. (3) The right of citizens of Canada under subsections (1) and (2) to have their children receive primary and secondary school instruction in the language of the English or French linguistic minority population of a province (a) applies wherever in the province the number of children of citizens who have such a right is sufficient to warrant the provision to them out of public funds of minority language instruction; and (b) includes, where the number of those children so warrants, the right to have them receive that instruction in minority language educational facilities provided out of public funds.

■ Enforcement

24. (1) Anyone whose rights or freedoms, as guaranteed by this Charter, have been infringed or denied may apply to a court of competent jurisdiction to obtain such remedy as the court considers appropriate and just in the circumstances. (2) Where, in proceedings under subsection (1), a court concludes that evidence was obtained in a manner that infringed or denied any rights or freedoms guaranteed by this Charter, the evidence shall be excluded if it is established that, having regard to all the circumstances, the admission of it in the proceedings would bring the administration of justice into disrepute.

■ General

25 The guarantee in this Charter of certain rights and freedoms shall not be construed so as to abrogate or derogate from any aboriginal, treaty or other rights or freedoms that pertain to the aboriginal peoples of Canada including (a) any rights or freedoms that have been recognized by the Royal Proclamation of October 7, 1763; and (b) any rights or freedoms that now exist by way of land claims agreements or may be so acquired.

26 The guarantee in this Charter of certain rights and freedoms shall not be construed as denying the existence of any other rights or freedoms that exist in Canada.

27 This Charter shall be interpreted in a manner consistent with the preservation and enhancement of the multicultural heritage of Canadians.

28 Notwithstanding anything in this Charter, the rights and freedoms referred to in it are guaranteed equally to male and female persons.

29 Nothing in this Charter abrogates or derogates from any rights or privileges guaranteed by or under the Constitution of Canada in respect of denominational, separate or dissentient schools.

30 A reference in this Charter to a province or to the legislative assembly or legislature or a province shall be deemed to include a reference to the Yukon Territory and the Northwest Territories, or to the appropriate legislative authority thereof, as the case may be.

31 Nothing in this Charter extends the legislative powers of any body or authority.

■ Application of Charter

32 (1) This Charter applies (a) to the Parliament and government of Canada in respect of all matters within the authority of Parliament including all matters relating to the Yukon Territory and Northwest Territories; and (b) to the legislature and government of each province in respect of all matters within the authority of the legislature of each province. (2) Notwithstanding subsection (1), section 15 shall not have effect until three years after this section comes into force.

33 (1) Parliament or the legislature of a province may expressly declare in an Act of Parliament or of the legislature, as the case may be, that the Act or a provision thereof shall operate notwithstanding a provision included in section 2 or sections 7 to 15 of this Charter. (2) An Act or a provision of an Act in respect of which a declaration made under this section is in effect shall have such operation as it would have but for the provision of this Charter referred to in the declaration. (3) A declaration made under subsection (1) shall cease to have effect five years after it comes into force or on such earlier date as may be specified in the declaration. (4) Parliament or the legislature of a province may re-enact a declaration made under subsection (1). (5) Subsection (3) applies in respect of a re-enactment made under subsection (4).

■ Citation

34 This Part may be cited as the Canadian Charter of Rights and Freedoms.

Canadian Orders and Decorations

For more information on Canada's orders and decorations, see the Web site of Governor General Adrienne Clarkson at http://www.gg.ca/honours and "Canadian Military Medals and Decorations" at the Web site of Veterans Affairs Canada at http://www.vac-acc.gc.ca/clients.

☐ National Orders

■ The Order of Canada

History Creation of the Order of Canada was announced by Prime Minister Lester B. Pearson in 1967. It was instituted on the centennial of Canadian Confederation, July 1, 1967.

Basis of Award To honour Canadians for outstanding achievement and service to their country or humanity. Appointments are announced twice annually, around July 1 and Jan. 1. Investitures occur three times a year, in February, April and October when the awards are given by the Governor General.

Eligibility Every living Canadian is eligible to become a member. Federal and provincial politicians and judges are ineligible while in office.

Membership There are three categories of membership. The first is Companion of the Order of Canada (C.C.). No more than 15 companions may be appointed in any one year, and no more than 165 living companions may hold the order at one time.

The second is Officer of the Order of Canada (O.C.). No more than 64 appoint-ments may be made annually.

The third is Member of the Order of Canada (C.M.)., which recognizes service in a locality or a field of activity. No more than 136 appointments may be made annually.

Badge A stylized snowflake bearing the crown with a ribbon in the same proportions of white and red which appear on the Canadian flag and the Latin motto *Desiderantes Meliorem Patriam*—"They Desire a Better Country." Worn at the neck by companions and officers and on the left breast by members.

■ The Order of Military Merit

History The Order of Military Merit was instituted on July 1, 1972.

Basis of Award To recognize exceptional service and conspicuous merit by regular and reserve members of Canada's Armed Forces.

Appointments are made by the Governor General on the recommendation of the chief of defence staff.

Eligibility Active members of the Canadian Armed Forces, regular and reserve. A formula limits the number of annual appointments per year to one-tenth of one percent of the average number of persons who were members of the Armed Forces during the previous year.

Membership There are three categories of membership. The first is Commander of the Order of Military Merit (C.M.M.). Six percent of annual appointments go to this category of membership.

The second is Officer of the Order of Military Merit (O.M.M.). Thirty percent of annual appointments go to this category of membership.

The third is Member of the Order of Military Merit (M.M.M.). The balance of annual appointments go to this category of membership.

Badge In the form of an enamelled blue cross having expanded arms, with a blue ribbon edged in gold. Bears the words "Merit Merite Canada." Worn at the neck by commanders and on the left breast by officers and members.

☐ Medals for Military Valour

The Military Valour Decorations, consisting of the Victoria Cross (Canadian), the Star of Military Valour and the Medal of Military Valour, enable Canada to recognize members of the Canadian Forces, or members of an allied armed force serving with the Canadian Forces, for deeds of military valour.

■ Victoria Cross (V.C.) (Canadian)

History Approved by Queen Elizabeth II on Feb. 2, 1993. The British Victoria Cross was created by Queen Victoria in 1856 and was awarded to Canadians in all wars until 1945. There have been 94 Canadian recipients of the British V.C. and none of the Canadian version.

Basis of Award In recognition of "the most conspicuous bravery, a daring or pre-eminent act of valour or self-sacrifice or extreme devotion to duty, in the presence of the enemy." The V.C. will be awarded by the Governor General on the advice of the Military Valour Advisory Committee. It is the highest in the order of precedence in Canadian honours.

Eligibility Members of the Canadian Forces or a member of an allied armed force that is serving with or in conjunction with the Canadian Forces on or after Jan. 1, 1993. The V.C. may be awarded posthumously.

Badge The Cross is a bronze straight armed cross, suspended from a crimson ribbon. The face has, in the middle of the cross, a lion guardant standing on the Royal Crown, with the Latin inscription *Pro Valore*—"For

Valour." The date of the act for which the decoration is bestowed is engraved in a raised circle on the reverse.

■ The Star of Military Valour (S.M.V.)

History Approved by Queen Elizabeth II on Feb. 2, 1993.

Basis of Award Awarded for distinguished and valiant service in the presence of the enemy.

Eligibility Members of the Canadian Forces or a member of an allied armed force that is serving with or in conjunction with the Canadian Forces on or after Jan. 1, 1993. The S.M.V. may be awarded posthumously.

Badge A gold star with four points with a maple leaf in each of the angles, on the face of which a gold maple leaf is superimposed in the centre of a sanguine field surrounded by a silver wreath of laurel and on the reverse of which the Royal Cypher and Crown and the Latin inscription *Pro Valore*—"For Valour" —appears. The Star shall be worn, suspended from a crimson ribbon with two white stripes, immediately after any order and before the Star of Courage.

■ The Medal of Military Valour (M.M.V.)

History Approved by Queen Elizabeth II on Feb. 2, 1993.

Basis of Award Awarded for an act of valour or devotion to duty in the presence of the enemy.

Eligibility Members of the Canadian Forces or a member of an allied armed force that is serving with or in conjunction with the Canadian Forces on or after Jan. 1, 1993. The M.M.V. may be awarded posthumously.

Badge A circular gold medal, on the face of which there is a maple leaf surrounded by a wreath of laurel and on the reverse of which the Royal Cypher and Crown and the Latin inscription *Pro Valore*—"For Valour"— appears. The medal shall be worn, from a crimson ribbon with three white stripes, immediately after the Meritorious Service Cross and before the Medal of Bravery.

☐ Decorations for Bravery

The Decorations for Bravery, consisting of the Cross of Valour, the Star of Courage and the Medal of Bravery honour those who have risked their lives to save or protect others. These three Canadian decorations replaced the following non-combatant Commonwealth medals: the George Cross, the George Medal and the Queen's Gallantry Medal, respectively.

■ The Cross of Valour (C.V.)

History   Created on May 1, 1972, the Cross of Valour takes precedence before all orders and other decorations except the Victoria Cross.

Basis of Award   Awarded for acts of the most conspicuous courage in circumstances of extreme peril.

Eligibility   May be awarded to civilians or members of the Canadian Forces. Only 19 have been awarded. May be awarded posthumously.

Badge   A gold cross bearing the words "Valour Vaillance."

■ The Star of Courage (S.C.)

History   Created on May 1, 1972.

Basis of Award   Awarded for acts of conspicuous courage in circumstances of great peril.

Eligibility   May be awarded to civilians or members of the Canadian Forces. May be awarded posthumously.

Badge   A four-pointed silver star with the word "Courage."

■ The Medal of Bravery (M.B.)

History   Created on May 1, 1972.

Basis of Award   Awarded for acts of bravery in hazardous circumstances.

Eligibility   May be awarded to civilians or members of the Canadian Forces. May be awarded posthumously.

Badge   A circular silver medal with the words "Bravery Bravoure."

■ The Meritorious Service Cross (M.S.C.) (military and civilian)

History   Military division created in 1984; civilian division created in 1991.

Basis of Award   *Military division*: awarded in recognition of a military deed or activity that has been performed in an outstandingly professional manner or according to a rare high standard that brings considerable benefit or great honour to the Canadian Forces. *Civilian division*: awarded in recognition of the performance of a deed or activity performed in an outstandingly professional manner or according to an uncommonly high standard that brings considerable benefit or great honour to Canada.

Eligibility   A member of the Canadian and allied forces, persons serving in conjunction with the Canadian Forces or other persons, Canadian or foreign.

Badge   A Greek cross of silver, ends splayed and convexed, ensigned with the Royal Crown. On the face appear a maple leaf within a circle and a laurel wreath between the arms. Recipients are entitled to use the letters "M.S.C." after their names.

■ The Meritorious Service Medal (M.S.M.) (military and civilian)

History   Created in 1991.

Basis of Award   *Military division*: awarded in recognition of a military deed or activity that has been performed in a highly professional manner or is of a very high standard that brings benefit or honour to the Canadian Forces. *Civilian division*: awarded in recognition of the performance of a deed or activity performed in a highly professional manner or of a very high standard that brings benefit or honour to Canada.

Eligibility   A member of the Canadian and allied forces, persons serving in conjunction with the Canadian Forces or other persons, Canadian or foreign.

Badge   A circular medal of silver ensigned with the Royal Crown. On the face appears the design of the cross. On the reverse appears the Royal Cypher and, within a double circle, the words "Meritorious Service Méritoire." Recipients are entitled to use the letters "M.S.M." after their names.

□ Other Notable Awards

The Governor General also bestows these awards.

■ The Academic Medal

Created in 1873. Awarded for academic excellence. Medals are distributed in March to colleges and universities and in April to high schools.

■ The Governor General's Caring Canadian Award

Created in 1996. Awarded to unpaid volunteers for their extraordinary contributions, performed behind the scenes and for several years, in support of family, community or humanitarian causes.

Governors General of Canada

Name	Date Appointed	Assumed Office	Term
Sir Charles Stanley, Viscount Monck	June 1, 1867	July 1, 1867	1867–69
Sir John Young, Baron Lisgar	Dec. 29, 1868	Feb. 2, 1869	1869–72
Frederick Temple Hamilton Blackwood, Earl of Dufferin	May 22, 1872	June 25, 1872	1872–78
John Douglas Sutherland Campbell, Marquess of Lorne	Oct. 5, 1878	Nov. 20, 1878	1878–83
Henry Charles Keith Petty-Fitzmaurice, Marquess of Lansdowne	Aug. 18, 1883	Oct. 23, 1883	1883–88
Frederick Arthur Stanley, Baron Stanley of Preston	May 1, 1888	June 11, 1888	1888–93
John Campbell Hamilton-Gordon, Earl of Aberdeen	May 22, 1893	Nov. 18, 1893	1893–98
Gilbert John Elliott Murray-Kynynmound, Earl of Minto	July 30, 1898	Nov. 12, 1898	1898–1904
Albert Henry George Grey, Earl Grey	Sept. 26, 1904	Dec. 10, 1904	1904–11
His Royal Highness The Prince Arthur, Field Marshal Duke of Connaught	Mar. 21, 1911	Oct. 13, 1911	1911–16
Victor Christian William Cavendish, Duke of Devonshire	Aug. 19, 1916	Nov. 11, 1916	1916–21
Julian Byng, General Baron Byng of Vimy and of Thorpe	Aug. 2, 1921	Aug. 11, 1921	1921–26
Sir Freeman Freeman-Thomas, Baron Willingdon of Ratton	Aug. 5, 1926	Nov. 2, 1926	1926–31
Vere Brabazon Ponsonby, Earl of Bessborough	Feb. 9, 1931	Apr. 4, 1931	1931–35
John Buchan, Baron Tweedsmuir	Aug. 10, 1935	Nov. 2, 935	1935–40
Alexander George Cambridge, Major General Earl of Athlone	Apr. 3, 1940	June 21, 1940	1940–46
Sir Harold George Alexander, Field Marshal Viscount Alexander of Tunis	Aug. 1, 1945	Apr. 18, 1946	1946–52
The Right Honourable Vincent Massey	Jan. 24, 1952	Feb. 22, 1952	1952–59
General the Right Honourable Georges P. Vanier	Aug. 1, 1959	Sept. 15, 1959	1959–67
The Right Honourable Daniel Roland Michener	Mar. 25, 1967	Apr. 15, 1967	1967–74
The Right Honourable Jules Léger	Oct. 5, 1973	Jan. 14, 1974	1974–79
The Right Honourable Edward Richard Schreyer	Dec. 7, 1978	Jan. 22, 1979	1979–83
The Right Honourable Jeanne Sauvé	Dec. 23, 1983	May 14, 1984	1984–90
The Right Honourable Ramon John Hnatyshyn	Oct. 6, 1989	Jan. 21, 1990	1990–95
The Right Honourable Roméo LeBlanc	Nov. 22, 1994	Feb. 8, 1995	1995–99
The Right Honourable Adrienne Clarkson	Sept. 8, 1999	Oct. 7, 1999	1999–

Prime Ministers of Canada

Prime Minister	Party	Term(s)	Born	P.M. at Age	Died
Sir John A. Macdonald	Conservative	July 1, 1867–Nov. 5, 1873 Oct. 9, 1878–June 6, 1891	Jan. 11, 1815	52	June 6, 1891
Alexander Mackenzie	Liberal	Nov. 5, 1873–Oct. 9, 1878	Jan. 28, 1822	51	Apr. 17, 1892
Sir John Abbott	Conservative	June 15, 1891–Nov. 24, 1892	Mar. 12, 1821	70	Oct. 30, 1893
Sir John Thompson	Conservative	Nov. 25, 1892–Dec. 12, 1894	Nov. 10, 1845	48	Dec. 12, 1894
Sir Mackenzie Bowell	Conservative	Dec. 13, 1894–Apr. 27, 1896	Dec. 27, 1823	70	Dec. 10, 1917
Sir Charles Tupper	Conservative	Apr. 27, 1896–July 8, 1896	July 2, 1821	74	Oct. 30, 1915
Sir Wilfrid Laurier	Liberal	July 11, 1896–Oct. 6, 1911	Nov. 20, 1841	54	Feb. 17, 1919
Sir Robert Borden	Conservative/ Unionist	Oct. 10, 1911–Oct. 12, 1917 Oct. 12, 1917–July 10, 1920	June 26, 1854	57	June 10, 1937
Arthur Meighen	Unionist/ Conservative	July 10, 1920–Dec. 29, 1921 June 29, 1926–Sept. 25, 1926	June 16, 1874	46	Aug. 5, 1960
Mackenzie King	Liberal	Dec. 29, 1921–June 28, 1926 Sept. 25, 1926–Aug. 6, 1930 Oct. 23, 1935–Nov. 15, 1948	Dec. 17, 1874	47	July 22, 1950
Richard B. Bennett	Conservative	Aug. 7, 1930–Oct. 23, 1935	July 3, 1870	60	June 27, 1947
Louis St. Laurent	Liberal	Nov. 15, 1948–June 21, 1957	Feb. 1, 1882	66	July 25, 1973
John Diefenbaker	Prog. Cons.	June 21, 1957–Apr. 22, 1963	Sept. 18, 1895	61	Aug. 16, 1979
Lester Pearson	Liberal	Apr. 22, 1963–Apr. 20, 1968	Apr. 23, 1897	65	Dec. 27, 1972
Pierre Trudeau	Liberal	Apr. 20, 1968–June 4, 1979 Mar. 3, 1980–June 30, 1984	Oct. 18, 1919	48	Sept. 28, 2000
Joe Clark	Prog. Cons.	June 4, 1979–Mar. 3, 1980	June 5, 1939	39	
John Turner	Liberal	June 30, 1984–Sept. 17, 1984	June 7, 1929	55	
Brian Mulroney	Prog. Cons.	Sept. 17, 1984–June 25, 1993	Mar. 20, 1939	45	
Kim Campbell	Prog. Cons.	June 25, 1993–Nov. 4, 1993	Mar. 10, 1947	46	
Jean Chrétien	Liberal	Nov. 4, 1993–Dec. 11, 2003	Jan. 11, 1934	59	
Paul Martin	Liberal	Dec. 12, 2003–	Aug. 28, 1938	65	

Canadian Cabinet Ministers and Ministers of State

(as of October 1, 2004)

Cabinet ministers are the most powerful elected officials in government. They are sworn to the Privy Council and are bound by collective responsibility. They work with their staffs to set policies for their ministries and present (or defend) those policies in the House of Commons. They shepherd their bills through various readings and committees before having their bills voted into law.

The prime minister appoints ministers of state to assist specific ministers. While they do not have independent portfolios, ministers of state—unlike the secretaries of state of the recent Chrétien era—are full members of the cabinet. Ministers of state are peers, not subordinates, of ministers. Ministers of state also participate in collective decision making and uphold the confidentiality of cabinet decisions.

■ The Cabinet

Prime Minister of Canada
The Right Hon. Paul Edgar Philippe Martin
(LaSalle–Émard, Quebec)
Telephone: (613) 992-4211
Fax: (613) 941-6900
E-mail: Martin.P@parl.gc.ca

Deputy Leader of the Government in the House of Commons; Minister responsible for Official Languages; Minister responsible for Democratic Reform; Associate Minister of National Defence
The Hon. Mauril Bélanger
(Ottawa–Vanier, Ontario)
Telephone: (613) 992-4766
Fax: (613) 992-6448
E-mail: Belanger.M@parl.gc.ca

Deputy Prime Minister of Canada; Minister of Public Safety and Emergency Preparedness
Responsible for emergency preparedness, crisis management, national security, corrections, policing, crime prevention and border control.
The Hon. A. Anne McLellan
(Edmonton Centre, Alberta)
Telephone: (613) 992-4524
Fax: (613) 943-0044
E-mail: McLellan.A@parl.gc.ca

Leader of the Government in the House of Commons
Responsible for planning the weekly business of the House of Commons.
The Hon. Tony Valeri
(Hamilton East–Stoney Creek, Ontario)
Telephone: (613) 992-6535
Fax: (613) 992-7764
E-mail: Valeri.T@parl.gc.ca

Leader of the Government in the Senate
Responsible for planning the weekly business in the Senate.
The Hon. Jacob (Jack) Austin
(Vancouver South, British Columbia)
Telephone: (613) 992-1437
Fax: (613) 995-7329
E-mail: Austin.J@sen.parl.gc.ca

Minister of Agriculture and Agri-Food
Responsible for producing, processing, marketing, inspecting and protecting crops and livestock. Responsible for soil protection.
The Hon. Andrew (Andy) Mitchell
(Parry Sound–Muskoka, Ontario)
Telephone: (613) 996-3434
Fax: (613) 991-2147
E-mail: Mitchell.A@parl.gc.ca

Minister of Atlantic Canada Opportunities Agency
Responsible for developing businesses and job opportunities in Atlantic Canada.
The Hon. Joseph Blair McGuire
(Egmont, Prince Edward Island)
Telephone: (613) 992-9223
Fax: (613) 992-1974
E-mail: McGuire.J@parl.gc.ca

Minister of Canadian Heritage; Minister of State (Status of Women)
Responsible for promoting Canadian culture, protecting Canada's heritage and encouraging active citizenship. Responsible for promoting gender equality.
The Hon. Liza Frulla
(Jeanne-Le Ber, Quebec)
Telephone: (613) 995-6403
Fax: (613) 995-6404
E-mail: Frulla.L@parl.gc.ca

▶

▶ **Minister of Citizenship and Immigration**
Responsible for admitting immigrants, visitors and temporary workers; resettling and protecting refugees; and helping newcomers become citizens.
The Hon. Judy Sgro
(York West, Ontario)
Telephone: (613) 992-7774
Fax: (613) 947-8319
E-mail: Sgro.J@parl.gc.ca

Minister of the Environment
Responsible for protecting and conserving Canada's air, water, land and wildlife. Monitors climate change.
The Hon. Stéphane Dion
(Saint-Laurent–Cartierville, Quebec)
Telephone: (613) 996-5789
Fax: (613) 996-6562
E-mail: Dion.S@parl.gc.ca

Minister of Finance
Responsible for preparing the budget, designing tax policies, regulating Canada's banks and transferring funds to the provinces and territories.
The Hon. Ralph Edward Goodale
(Wascana, Saskatchewan)
Telephone: (613) 996-4743
Fax: (613) 996-9790
E-mail: Goodale.R@parl.gc.ca

Minister of Fisheries and Oceans
Responsible for Canada's economic, ecological and scientific interests in oceans and inland waters.
The Hon. Geoff Regan
(Halifax West, Nova Scotia)
Telephone: (613) 996-3085
Fax: (613) 996-6988
E-mail: Regan.G@parl.gc.ca

Minister of Foreign Affairs
Rresponsible for supporting Canadians abroad, working toward a peaceful and secure world, and promoting Canadian culture and values internationally.
The Hon. Pierre S. Pettigrew
(Papineau, Quebec)
Telephone: (613) 995-8872
Fax: (613) 995-9926
E-mail: Pettigrew.P@parl.gc.ca

Minister of Health
Responsible for enforcing health regulations, promoting disease prevention and healthy living, and making provincial-type health services available to aboriginal people.
The Hon. Ujjal Dosanjh
(Vancouver South, British Columbia)
Telephone: (613) 957-0200
Fax: (613) 952-1154
E-mail: minister@www.hc-sc.gc.ca

Minister of Human Resources and Skills Development
Responsible for job training, employment insurance, old age pensions and social insurance cards.
The Hon. Joseph Volpe
(Eglinton–Lawrence, Ontario)
Telephone: (613) 992-6361
Fax: (613) 992-9791
E-mail: Volpe.J@parl.gc.ca

**Minister of Indian Affairs and Northern Development;
Federal Interlocutor for Métis and Non-Status Indians**
Responsible for negotiating aboriginal land claims and self-government agreements; providing education and housing to Status Indians on-reserve; and managing natural resources in the north.
The Hon. Andy Scott
(Fredericton, New Brunswick)
Telephone: (613) 992-1067
Fax: (613) 996-9955
E-mail: Scott.A@parl.gc.ca

Minister of Industry
Responsible for helping Canadians become more productive and competitive in the knowledge-based economy.
The Hon. David Emerson
(Vancouver Kingsway, British Columbia)
Telephone: (613) 995-9001
Fax: (613) 992-0302
E-mail: ministre.industrie@ic.gc.ca

Minister for International Cooperation
Responsible for administering economic and technical aid to developing countries.
The Hon. M. Aileen Carroll
(Barrie, Ontario)
Telephone: (613) 992-3394
Fax: (613) 996-7923
E-mail: Carroll.A@parl.gc.ca

Minister of International Trade
Responsible for aiding Canadian businesses expand internationally, attracting foreign investment, and negotiating and administering trade agreements.
The Hon. James Scott Peterson
(Willowdale, Ontario)
Telephone: (613) 992-4964
Fax: (613) 992-1158
E-mail: Peterson.J@parl.gc.ca

Minister of Justice and Attorney General of Canada
Responsible for assisting the government write and reform laws and for providing legal services to federal departments and agencies.
The Hon. Irwin Cotler
(Mount Royal, Quebec)
Telephone: (613) 995-0121
Fax: (613) 992-6762
E-mail: Cotler.I@parl.gc.ca

▶

▶ **Minister of Labour and Housing**
Responsible for enforcing the labour code (including health and safety provisions), mediating labour disputes and promoting affordable housing.
The Hon. Joseph Frank Fontana
(London North Centre, Ontario)
Telephone: (613) 992-0805
Fax: (613) 992-9613
E-mail: Fontana.J@parl.gc.ca

Minister of National Defence
Responsible for protecting Canada, defending North America with the United States and contributing to international peace and security.
The Hon. William (Bill) Graham
(Toronto Centre, Ontario)
Telephone: (613) 992-5234
Fax: (613) 996-9607
E-mail: Graham.B@parl.gc.ca

Minister of National Revenue
Responsible for administering the tax laws and for delivering socio-economic benefits through the tax system.
The Hon. John McCallum
(Markham–Unionville, Ontario)
Telephone: (613) 996-3374
Fax: (613) 992-3921
E-mail: McCallum.J@parl.gc.ca

Minister of Natural Resources
Responsible for the sustainable use of energy, minerals, metals and forests.
The Hon. R. John Efford
(Avalon, Newfoundland and Labrador)
Telephone: (613) 992-4133
Fax: (613) 992-7277
E-mail: Efford.J@parl.gc.ca

Minister of Public Works and Government Services
Responsible for building, leasing and managing federal government property.
The Hon. Scott Brison
(Kings–Hants, Nova Scotia)
Telephone: (613) 995-8231
Fax: (613) 996-9349
E-mail: Brison.S@parl.gc.ca

Minister of Social Development
Responsible for aiding families with children, seniors and people with disabilities.
The Hon. Ken Dryden
(York Centre, Ontario)
Telephone: (613) 994-2482
Fax: (613) 997-8504

Minister of Transport
Responsible for the safety and efficiency of rail, marine, road and air transportation.
The Hon. Jean-C. Lapierre

(Outremont, Quebec)
Telephone: (613) 991-0700
Fax: (613) 995-0327
E-mail: mintc@tc.gc.ca

Minister of Veterans Affairs
Responsible for aiding war veterans and commemorating their achievements.
The Hon. Albina Guarnieri
(Mississauga East–Cooksville, Ontario)
Telephone: (613) 996-0420
Fax: (613) 996-0279
E-mail: Guarnieri.A@parl.gc.ca

Minister of Western Economic Diversification; Minister of State (Sport)
Responsible for diversifying Western Canada's economy and supporting athletes and sporting events.
The Hon. Stephen Owen
(Vancouver Quadra, British Columbia)
Telephone: (613) 992-2430
Fax: (613) 995-0770
E-mail: Owen.S@parl.gc.ca

Minister responsible for the Economic Development Agency of Canada for the Regions of Quebec; Minister responsible for la Francophonie
Responsible for aiding small or medium-sized businesses in Quebec and for maintaining relations with francophones outside Canada.
The Hon. Jacques Saada
(Brossard—La Prairie, Quebec)
Telephone: (613) 996-3214
Fax: (613) 996-6412
E-mail: Saada.J@parl.gc.ca

President of the Queen's Privy Council for Canada; Minister of Intergovernmental Affairs
Responsible for managing federal-provincial relations and providing legal advice on constitutional issues.
The Hon. Lucienne Robillard
(Westmount–Ville-Marie, Quebec)
Telephone: (613) 996-7267
Fax: (613) 995-8632
E-mail: Robillard.L@parl.gc.ca

President of the Treasury Board; Minister responsible for the Canadian Wheat Board
Responsible for managing the government's finances, personnel and administration. He is also responsible for marketing farmers' wheat and barley.
The Hon. Reginald B. Alcock
(Winnipeg South, Manitoba)
Telephone: (613) 995-7517
Fax: (613) 943-1466
E-mail: Alcock.R@parl.gc.ca

▶

► ■ **Ministers of State**

Minister of State (Families and Caregivers)
The Hon. Tony Ianno
(Trinity–Spadina, Ontario)
Telephone: (613) 992-2352
Fax: (613) 992-6301
E-mail: Ianno.T@parl.gc.ca

Minister of State (Federal Economic Development Initiative for Northern Ontario)
The Hon. Joseph R. Comuzzi
(Thunder Bay–Superior North, Ontario)
Telephone: (613) 996-4792
Fax: (613) 996-9785
E-mail: Comuzzi.J@parl.gc.ca

Minister of State (Human Resources Development)
The Hon. Claudette Bradshaw
(Moncton–Riverview–Dieppe, New Brunswick)
Telephone: (613) 992-8072
Fax: (613) 992-8083
E-mail: Bradshaw.C@parl.gc.ca

Minister of State (Infrastructure and Communities)
The Hon. John Ferguson Godfrey
(Don Valley West, Ontario)
Telephone: (613) 992-2855
Fax: (613) 995-1635
E-mail: Godfrey.J@parl.gc.ca

Minister of State (Multiculturalism)
The Hon. Raymond Chan
(Richmond, British Columbia)
Telephone: (819) 997-9900
Fax: (819) 953-8055

Minister of State (Northern Development)
The Hon. Ethel Dorothy Blondin-Andrew
(Western Arctic, Northwest Territories)
Telephone: (613) 992-4587
Fax: (613) 992-7411
E-mail: Blondin-Andrew.E@parl.gc.ca

Minister of State (Public Health)
The Hon. Carolyn Bennett
(St. Paul's, Ontario)
Telephone: (613) 995-9666
Fax: (613) 947-4622
E-mail: Bennett.C@parl.gc.ca

Deputy Prime Ministers of Canada

(as of October 1, 2004)

The title of deputy prime minister is strictly honorary. It is conferred at the prime minister's discretion on a member of the cabinet. The title has no standing in law and carries no formal duties or tasks. Deputy prime ministers, however, often have other cabinet portfolios.

Prime Minister Pierre Trudeau named the first deputy prime minister during a press interview after the nomination of his cabinet on Sept. 16, 1977.

Since then only Prime Minister Joe Clark (1979–80) has not named a deputy prime minister.

In 1984, Prime Minister Brian Mulroney began the practice of appointing the deputy prime minister by "instrument of advice." An instrument of advice is a private letter written by the prime minister to the Crown. Since 1984, all deputy prime ministers have been appointed by this method.

Deputy Prime Minister	Date Appointed	Term Ended	Designated by Prime Minister
Allan J. MacEachen	Sept. 16, 1977	June 3, 1979	Pierre Trudeau
Allan J. MacEachen	Mar. 3, 1980	June 29, 1984	Pierre Trudeau
Jean Chrétien	June 30, 1984	Sept. 16, 1984	John Turner
Erik Nielsen	Sept. 17, 1984	June 29, 1986	Brian Mulroney
Donald Mazankowski	June 30, 1986	June 24, 1993	Brian Mulroney
Jean J. Charest	June 25, 1993	Nov. 3, 1993	Kim Campbell
Sheila M. Copps	Nov. 4, 1993	Apr. 30, 1996	Jean Chrétien
Sheila M. Copps	June 19, 1996	June 10, 1997	Jean Chrétien
Herbert E. Gray	June 11, 1997	Jan. 14, 2002	Jean Chrétien
John Paul Manley	Jan. 15, 2002	Dec. 11, 2003	Jean Chrétien
A. Anne McLellan	Dec. 12, 2003		Paul Martin

Source: *Library of Parliament, Information and Documentation Branch*

Public Accountability in Government

Several federal bodies monitor federal government activity to ensure that responsible actions are taken and the rights of citizens are respected. Independent of Cabinet and political parties, officials in these organizations report government shortcomings to the House of Commons and are often empowered to act on citizens' complaints.

THE AUDITOR GENERAL

The auditor general examines the handling of taxpayers' money. Authorized by the Auditor General Act and the Financial Administration Act, this official ensures that federal institutions keep accurate accounts and collect and spend their budgets as intended. The auditor general, employing a staff of accountants, lawyers, engineers, computer technicians, economists and management experts, looks for efficient spending and exposes fraud and carelessness. Appointed to a 10-year term in May 2001, the current auditor general is Sheila Fraser.

The Office of the Auditor General includes the commissioner of the environment and sustainable development. This commissioner ensures that government is improving the protection of the environment and fostering sustainable development—25 federal departments and agencies must prepare sustainable development strategies. The post was created in 1995 to give the public a way to pressure federal departments on environmental issues through a petition process. The current commissioner is Johanne Gélinas, appointed in August 2000.

Write to the Office of the Auditor General and the Commissioner of the Environment and Sustainable Development, 240 Sparks Street, Ottawa, Ontario KIA OG6 or phone (613) 995-3708. Regional offices exist in Vancouver, Edmonton, Montreal and Halifax/ Dartmouth. Visit http://www.oag-bvg.gc.ca.

PRIVACY COMMISSIONER

Authorized by the Privacy Act, the commissioner monitors the government's collection, use and disclosure of Canadians' personal information. The Act gives Canadians the right to examine any government-held information about them—110 federal organizations can hold personal information. The Act requires that the information be accurate, confidential and used only for its intended purpose. The commissioner investigates complaints about the misuse of government-held information and may act as an ombudsman. Although unable to impose penalties or force compliance, the commissioner may make recommendations to complainants and may take cases before the Federal Court. The commissioner can also launch privacy-related suits against the government in the public interest.

The commissioner serves for seven years. The current official, Jennifer Stoddart, was appointed in December 2003. Write to the Privacy Commissioner of Canada, 112 Kent Street, Place de Ville, Tower B, 3rd Floor, Ottawa, Ontario K1A 1H3 or phone 1 (800) 282-1376. Visit http://www.privcom.gc.ca.

INFORMATION COMMISSIONER

Authorized by the Access to Information Act, this commissioner ensures that Canadians obtain non-personal information collected by the government. As an ombudsman, the commissioner investigates complaints when the government denies access to public documents, mediates disputes and makes recommendations. The commissioner may also take cases to the Federal Court.

The commissioner serves for seven years. The current official, John Reid, was appointed in July 1998. Write to the Information Commissioner of Canada, 112 Kent Street, Place de Ville, Tower B, 22nd Floor, Ottawa, Ontario K1A IH3 or phone 1 (800) 267-0441. Visit http://www.infocom.gc.ca.

CANADIAN HUMAN RIGHTS COMMISSIONER

This commissioner is charged with ensuring that the Canadian Human Rights Act is upheld by resolving individual complaints, promoting understanding of human rights, upholding equality principles and assisting in reducing equality barriers in employment and access to services.

The chief commissioner serves for seven years. The current official, Mary Gusella, was appointed in August 2002. Write to the CHRC, 344 Slater Street, 8th Floor, Ottawa, Ontario K1A 1E1 or phone 1 (888) 214-1090. Visit http://www.chrc-ccdp.ca.

Members of Canada's Senate

(as of Oct. 1, 2004)

The Governor General appoints senators under the Great Seal of Canada on the prime minister's advice.

To be eligible for the Senate, a candidate must be a Canadian citizen and at least 30 years old. A candidate must also live in the region the appointment represents—either Ontario, Quebec, the West, the Maritimes or a territory. He or she must own land in that region with an unencumbered value of at least $4,000 and have a net estate worth at least $4,000. A senator from Quebec must either live in or have land in Quebec. A senator must retire at age 75.

Senator (Year of Birth)	Party	Date Nominated	Appointed by Prime Minister	Province (Senatorial Division)
Willie Adams (1934)	Lib.	Apr. 5, 1977	Trudeau (Lib.)	Nun.
Raynell Andreychuk (1944)	Con.	Mar. 11, 1993	Mulroney (PC)	Sask.
W. David Angus (1937)	Con.	June 10, 1993	Mulroney (PC)	Que. (Alma)
Norman Atkins (1934)	PC	June 30, 1986	Mulroney (PC)	Ont. (Markham)
Jack Austin (1932)	Lib.	Aug. 19, 1975	Trudeau (Lib.)	BC (Vancouver South)
Lise Bacon (1934)	Lib.	Sept. 15, 1994	Chrétien (Lib.)	Que. (De la Durantaye)
George Baker (1942)	Lib.	Mar. 26, 2002	Chrétien (Lib.)	Nfld. and Lab.
Tommy Banks (1936)	Lib.	Apr. 7, 2000	Chrétien (Lib.)	Alta. (Edmonton)
Michel Biron (1934)	Lib.	Oct. 4, 2001	Chrétien (Lib.)	Que. (Mille Isles)
John G. Bryden (1937)	Lib.	Nov. 23, 1994	Chrétien (Lib.)	NB
John Buchanan (1931)	Con.	Sept. 12, 1990	Mulroney (PC)	NS (Halifax)
Catherine Callbeck (1939)	Lib.	Sept. 23, 1997	Chrétien (Lib.)	PEI
Pat Carney (1935)	Con.	Aug. 30, 1990	Mulroney (PC)	BC
Sharon Carstairs (1942)	Lib.	Sept. 15, 1994	Chrétien (Lib.)	Man.
Maria Chaput (1942)	Lib.	Dec. 12, 2002	Chrétien (Lib.)	Man.
Ione Christensen (1933)	Lib.	Sept. 2, 1999	Chrétien (Lib.)	YT
Ethel Cochrane (1937)	Con.	Nov. 17, 1986	Mulroney (PC)	Nfld. and Lab.
Gerald Comeau (1946)	Con.	Aug. 30, 1990	Mulroney (PC)	NS
Joan Cook (1934)	Lib.	Mar. 6, 1998	Chrétien (Lib.)	Nfld. and Lab.
Anne Cools (1943)	Con.	Jan. 13, 1984	Trudeau (Lib.)	Ont. (Toronto-Center-York)
Eymard Corbin (1934)	Lib.	July 9, 1984	Turner (Lib.)	NB (Grand-Sault)
Jane Cordy (1950)	Lib.	June 9, 2000	Chrétien (Lib.)	NS
Joseph Day (1945)	Lib.	Oct. 4, 2001	Chrétien (Lib.)	NB (Saint John-Kennebecasis)
Pierre De Bané (1938)	Lib.	June 29, 1984	Trudeau (Lib.)	Que. (De la Vallière)
Consiglio Di Nino (1938)	Con.	Aug. 30, 1990	Mulroney (PC)	Ont.
C. William Doody (1931)	PC	Oct. 3, 1979	Clark (PC)	Nfld. and Lab. (Harbour Main–Bell Island)
Percy Downe (1954)	Lib.	June 26, 2003	Chrétien (Lib.)	PEI (Charlottetown)
John Trevor Eyton (1934)	Con.	Sept. 23, 1990	Mulroney (PC)	Ont.
Joyce Fairbairn (1939)	Lib.	June 29, 1984	Trudeau (Lib.)	Alta. (Lethbridge)
Marisa Ferretti Barth (1931)	Lib.	Sept. 22, 1997	Chrétien (Lib.)	Que. (Repentigny)
Isobel Finnerty (1930)	Lib.	Sept. 2, 1999	Chrétien (Lib.)	Ont.
D. Ross Fitzpatrick (1933)	Lib.	Mar. 6, 1998	Chrétien (Lib.)	BC (Okanagan–Similkameen)
John Michael Forrestall (1932)	Con.	Sept. 27, 1990	Mulroney (PC)	NS (Dartmouth/Eastern Shore)
Joan Fraser (1944)	Lib.	Sept. 17, 1998	Chrétien (Lib.)	Que. (De Lorimier)
George Furey (1948)	Lib.	Aug. 11, 1999	Chrétien (Lib.)	Nfld. and Lab.
Jean-Robert Gauthier (1929)	Lib.	Nov. 23, 1994	Chrétien (Lib.)	Ont. (Ottawa-Vanier)
Aurélien Gill (1933)	Lib.	Sept. 17, 1998	Chrétien (Lib.)	Que. (Wellington)
Jerahmiel Grafstein (1935)	Lib.	Jan. 13, 1984	Trudeau (Lib.)	Ont. (Metro Toronto)
Leonard Gustafson (1933)	Con.	May 26, 1993	Mulroney (PC)	Sask.
Mac Harb (1953)	Lib.	Sept. 9, 2003	Chrétien (Lib.)	Ont.
Daniel Hays (1939)	Lib.	June 29, 1984	Trudeau (Lib.)	Alta. (Calgary)

▶ Céline Hervieux-Payette (1941)	Lib.	Mar. 21, 1995	Chrétien (Lib.)	Que. (Bedford)
Elizabeth Hubley (1942)	Lib.	Mar. 8, 2001	Chrétien (Lib.)	PEI
Mobina Jaffer (1949)	Lib.	June 13, 2001	Chrétien (Lib.)	BC
Janis Johnson (1946)	Con.	Sept. 27, 1990	Mulroney (PC)	Man. (Winnipeg-Interlake)
Serge Joyal (1945)	Lib.	Nov. 26, 1997	Chrétien (Lib.)	Que. (Kennebec)
James Francis Kelleher (1930)	Con.	Sept. 23, 1990	Mulroney (PC)	Ont.
Colin Kenny (1943)	Lib.	June 29, 1984	Trudeau (Lib.)	Ont. (Rideau)
Wilbert Joseph Keon (1935)	Con.	Sept. 27, 1990	Mulroney (PC)	Ont. (Ottawa)
Noël Kinsella (1939)	Con.	Sept. 12, 1990	Mulroney (PC)	NB (Fredericton-York-Sunbury)
Michael Kirby (1941)	Lib.	Jan. 13, 1984	Trudeau (Lib.)	NS (South Shore)
Richard Kroft (1938)	Lib.	June 11, 1998	Chrétien (Lib.)	Man.
Laurier LaPierre (1929)	Lib.	June 13, 2001	Chrétien (Lib.)	Ont.
Jean Lapointe (1935)	Lib.	June 13, 2001	Chrétien (Lib.)	Que. (Saurel)
Raymond Lavigne (1945)	Lib.	Mar. 26, 2002	Chrétien (Lib.)	Que. (Montarville)
Marjory LeBreton (1940)	Con.	June 18, 1993	Mulroney (PC)	Ont.
Viola Léger (1930)	Lib.	June 13, 2001	Chrétien (Lib.)	NB (Acadie)
Rose-Marie Losier-Cool (1937)	Lib.	Mar. 21, 1995	Chrétien (Lib.)	NB (Tracadie)
John Lynch-Staunton (1930)	Con.	Sept. 23, 1990	Mulroney (PC)	Que. (Grandville)
Shirley Maheu (1931)	Lib.	Feb. 1, 1996	Chrétien (Lib.)	Que. (Rougemont)
Frank Mahovlich (1938)	Lib.	June 11, 1998	Chrétien (Lib.)	Ont.
Paul Massicotte (1951)	Lib.	June 26, 2003	Chrétien (Lib.)	Que. (De Lanaudière)
Michael Arthur Meighen (1939)	Con.	Sept. 27, 1990	Mulroney (PC)	Ont. (St. Marys)
Terry Mercer (1947)	Lib.	Nov. 7, 2003	Chrétien (Lib.)	NS (Northend Halifax)
Pana Merchant (1943)	Lib.	Dec. 12, 2002	Chrétien (Lib.)	Sask.
Lorna Milne (1934)	Lib.	Sept. 21, 1995	Chrétien (Lib.)	Ont. (Peel County)
Wilfred Moore (1942)	Lib.	Sept. 26, 1996	Chrétien (Lib.)	NS (Stanhope St./Bluenose)
Yves Morin (1929)	Lib.	Mar. 8, 2001	Chrétien (Lib.)	Que. (Lauzon)
Jim Munson (1946)	Lib.	Dec. 10, 2003	Chrétien (Lib.)	Ont. (Ottawa/Rideau Canal)
Lowell Murray (1936)	PC	Sept. 13, 1979	Clark (PC)	Ont. (Pakenham)
Pierre Claude Nolin (1950)	Con.	June 18, 1993	Mulroney (PC)	Que. (De Salaberry)
Donald Oliver (1938)	Con.	Sept. 7, 1990	Mulroney (PC)	NS
Landon Pearson (1930)	Lib.	Sept. 15, 1994	Chrétien (Lib.)	Ont.
Lucie Pépin (1936)	Lib.	Apr. 8, 1997	Chrétien (Lib.)	Que. (Shawinegan)
Gerard Phalen (1934)	Lib.	Oct. 4, 2001	Chrétien (Lib.)	NS
P. Michael Pitfield (1937)	Ind.	Dec. 22, 1982	Trudeau (Lib.)	Ont. (Ottawa-Vanier)
Madeleine Plamondon (1931)	Ind.	Sept. 9, 2003	Chrétien (Lib.)	Que. (The Laurentides)
Marie-Paule Poulin (1945)	Lib.	Sept. 21, 1995	Chrétien (Lib.)	Ont. (Northern Ontario)
Vivienne Poy (1941)	Lib.	Sept. 17, 1998	Chrétien (Lib.)	Ont. (Toronto)
Marcel Prud'homme (1934)	Ind.	May 26, 1993	Mulroney (PC)	Que. (La Salle)
Pierrette Ringuette (1955)	Lib.	Dec. 12, 2002	Chrétien (Lib.)	NB
Jean-Claude Rivest (1943)	Con.	Mar. 11, 1993	Mulroney (PC)	Que. (Stadacona)
Fernand Robichaud (1939)	Lib.	Sept. 22, 1997	Chrétien (Lib.)	NB (Saint-Louis-de-Kent)
William Rompkey (1936)	Lib.	Sept. 21, 1995	Chrétien (Lib.)	Nfld. and Lab. (North West River, Labrador)
Gerry St. Germain (1937)	Con.	June 23, 1993	Mulroney (PC)	BC (Langley-Pemberton-Whistler)
Nick Sibbeston (1943)	Lib.	Sept. 2, 1999	Chrétien (Lib.)	NWT
David Paul Smith (1941)	Lib.	June 25, 2002	Chrétien (Lib.)	Ont. (Cobourg)
Herbert Sparrow (1930)	Lib.	Feb. 9, 1968	Pearson (Lib.)	Sask.
Mira Spivak (1934)	Ind.	Nov. 17, 1986	Mulroney (PC)	Man.
Peter Stollery (1935)	Lib.	July 2, 1981	Trudeau (Lib.)	Ont. (Bloor and Yonge, Toronto)
Terence Stratton (1938)	Con.	Mar. 25, 1993	Mulroney (PC)	Man. (Red River)
David Tkachuk (1945)	Con.	June 8, 1993	Mulroney (PC)	Sask.
Marilyn Trenholme Counsell (1933)	Lib.	Sept. 9, 2003	Chrétien (Lib.)	NB
Charlie Watt (1944)	Lib.	Jan. 16, 1984	Trudeau (Lib.)	Que. (Inkerman)

Source: *Parliamentary Internet (Library of Parliament, Information and Documentation Branch)*
Con.—Conservative; Ind.—Independent; Lib.—Liberal; PC—Progressive Conservative.

Members of Parliament

(as of Oct. 1, 2004)

Correspondence to members of Parliament should be addressed individually and may be sent postage free to the following address: (Name of MP), House of Commons, Parliament Buildings, Ottawa, Ontario, K1A 0A6. For general information, call (613) 992-4793.

To contact a government department or minister's office via the Internet, go to http://canada.gc.ca (the Web site for the Government of Canada) and access "About Government."

■ Newfoundland and Labrador

Riding (population 2004)	Member (year of birth)	Party	Elected[1]
Avalon (79 548)	R. John Efford (1944)	Lib.	2002*
Bonavista—Exploits (89 743)	Scott Simms (n.a.)	Lib.	2004
Humber—St. Barbe—Baie Verte (76 467)	Gerry Byrne (1966)	Lib.	1996*
Labrador (27 864)	Lawrence O'Brien (1951)	Lib.	1996*
Random—Burin—St. George's (76 089)	Bill Matthews (1947)	Lib.	1997
St. John's North (81 007)	Norman Doyle (1945)	Con.	1997
St. John's South (82 212)	Loyola Hearn (1943)	Con.	2000*

■ Prince Edward Island

Riding (population 2004)	Member (year of birth)	Party	Elected[1]
Cardigan (34 777)	Lawrence MacAulay (1946)	Lib.	1988
Charlottetown (32 245)	Shawn Murphy (1951)	Lib.	2000
Egmont (35 208)	Joseph McGuire (1944)	Lib.	1988
Malpeque (33 064)	Wayne Easter (1949)	Lib.	1993

■ Nova Scotia

Riding (population 2004)	Member (year of birth)	Party	Elected[1]
Cape Breton—Canso (75 221)	Roger Cuzner (1955)	Lib.	2000
Central Nova (73 722)	Peter MacKay (1965)	Con.	1997
Dartmouth—Cole Harbour (88 507)	Michael Savage (1960)	Lib.	2004
Halifax (88 931)	Alexa McDonough (1945)	NDP	1997
Halifax West (79 933)	Geoff Regan (1959)	Lib.	2000
Kings—Hants (79 286)	Scott Brison (1967)	Con.	2000
North Nova (87 507)	William Casey (1945)	Con.	1997
Sackville—Eastern Shore (83 655)	Peter Stoffer (1956)	NDP	1997
South Shore—St. Margaret's (83 694)	Gerald Keddy (1953)	Con.	1997
Sydney—Victoria (79 294)	Mark Eyking (1960)	Lib.	2000
West Nova (88 257)	Robert Thibault (1959)	Lib.	2000

■ New Brunswick

Riding (population 2004)	Member (year of birth)	Party	Elected[1]
Acadie—Bathurst (76 392)	Yvon Godin (1955)	NDP	1997
Beauséjour (73 871)	Dominic LeBlanc (1967)	Lib.	2000
Fredericton (82 782)	Andy Scott (1955)	Lib.	1993
Fundy (67 675)	Rob Moore (1974)	Con.	2004
Madawaska—Restigouche (65 877)	Jean-Claude D'Amours (1972)	Lib.	2004
Miramichi (63 001)	Charles Hubbard (1940)	Lib.	1993
Moncton—Riverview—Dieppe (83 191)	Claudette Bradshaw (1949)	Lib.	1997
St. Croix—Belleisle (63 141)	Gregory Thompson (1947)	Con.	1997
Saint John (83 463)	Paul Zed (1956)	Lib.	1993
Tobique—Mactaquac (70 105)	Andy Savoy (1963)	Lib.	2000

▶

▶ ■ **Quebec**

Riding (population 2004)	Member (year of birth)	Party	Elected[1]
Abitibi—Témiscamingue (104 620)	Marc Lemay (n.a.)	BQ	2004
Ahuntsic (99 848)	Eleni Bakopanos (1954)	Lib.	1993
Alfred-Pellan (99 841)	Robert Carrier (n.a.)	BQ	2004
Argenteuil—Mirabel (98 467)	Mario Laframboise (1957)	BQ	2000
Beauce (102 072)	Claude Drouin (1956)	Lib.	1997
Beauharnois—Salaberry (103 808)	Alain Boire (n.a.)	BQ	2004
Beauport (98 990)	Christian Simard (1955.)	BQ	2004
Berthier—Maskinongé (103 516)	Guy André (n.a.)	BQ	2004
Bourassa (99 862)	Denis Coderre (1963)	Lib.	1997
Brome—Missisquoi (88 128)	Denis Paradis (1949)	Lib.	1995*
Brossard—La Prairie (100 489)	Jacques Saada (1947)	Lib.	1997
Chambly—Borduas (104 995)	Yves Lessard (n.a.)	BQ	2004
Charlesbourg (90 162)	Richard Marceau (1970)	BQ	1997
Charlevoix—Montmorency (89 257)	Michel Guimond (1953)	BQ	1993
Châteauguay—Saint Constant (102 709)	Denise Poirier-Rivard (n.a.)	BQ	2004
Chicoutimi—Le Fjord (98 739)	Robert Bouchard (n.a.)	BQ	2004
Compton—Stanstead (94 167)	France Bonsant (n.a.)	BQ	2004
Drummond (87 808)	Pauline Picard (1947)	BQ	1993
Gaspésie—Îles-de-la-Madeleine (84 202)	Raynald Blais (n.a.)	BQ	2004
Gatineau (102 898)	Françoise Boivin (1960)	Lib.	2004
Hochelaga (100 934)	Réal Ménard (1962)	BQ	1993
Honoré-Mercier (100 981)	Pablo Rodriguez (n.a.)	Lib.	2004
Hull—Aylmer (102 331)	Marcel Proulx (1946)	Lib.	1999*
Jeanne-Le Ber (103 092)	Liza Frulla (1949)	Lib.	2002*
Joliette (97 344)	Pierre Paquette (1955)	BQ	2000
Jonquière—Alma (98 167)	Sébastien Gagnon (1973)	BQ	2002*
Lac-Saint-Louis (101 919)	Francis Scarpaleggia (n.a.)	Lib.	2004
La Pointe-de-l'Île (98 878)	Francine Lalonde (1940)	BQ	1993
LaSalle—Émard (99 767)	Paul Martin (1938)	Lib.	1988
Laurentides—Labelle (96 133)	Johanne Deschamps (n.a.)	BQ	2004
Laurier (100 488)	Gilles Duceppe (1947)	BQ	1990*
Laval (98 831)	Nicole Demers (n.a.)	BQ	2004
Laval—Les Îles (100 137)	Raymonde Folco (1940)	Lib.	1997
Lévis—Bellechasse (102 310)	Réal Lapierre (n.a.)	BQ	2004
Longueuil (96 403)	Caroline St-Hilaire (1969)	BQ	1997
Lotbinière—Chutes-de-la-Chaudière (94 834)	Odina Desrochers (1951)	BQ	1997
Louis-Hébert (98 156)	Roger Clavet (n.a.)	BQ	2004
Louis-Saint-Laurent (94 294)	Bernard Cleary (n.a.)	BQ	2004
Manicouagan (84 872)	Gérard Asselin (1950)	BQ	1993
Marc-Aurèle-Fortin (99 044)	Serge Ménard (1941)	BQ	2004
Matapédia—Matane (74 475)	Jean-Yves Roy (1949)	BQ	2000
Mégantic—L'Érable (87 205)	Marc Boulianne (1941)	BQ	2004
Montcalm (105 678)	Roger Gaudet (1945)	BQ	2002*
Mount Royal (98 346)	Irwin Cotler (1940)	Lib.	1999*
Notre-Dame-de-Grâce—Lachine (101 698)	Marlene Jennings (1951)	Lib.	1997
Nunavik—Eeyou (80 052)	Yvon Lévesque (n.a.)	BQ	2004
Outremont (96 693)	Jean-C. Lapierre (1956)	Lib.	1979
Papineau (103 942)	Pierre Pettigrew (1951)	Lib.	1996*
Pierrefonds—Dollard (102 542)	Bernard Patry (1943)	Lib.	1993
Pontiac (89 950)	David Smith (1963)	Lib.	2004
Portneuf (87 141)	Guy Côté (1966)	BQ	2004
Québec (93 811)	Christiane Gagnon (1948)	BQ	1993
Repentigny (103 977)	Benoît Sauvageau (1963)	BQ	1997
Richelieu (92 650)	Louis Plamondon (1943)	BQ	1984
Richmond—Arthabaska (97 493)	André Bellevance (n.a.)	BQ	2004
Rimouski—Témiscouata (84 557)	Louise Thibault (n.a.)	BQ	2004
Rivière-des-Mille-Îles (92 929)	Gilles-A. Perron (1940)	BQ	1997
Rivière-du-Loup—Montmagny (87 126)	Paul Crête (1953)	BQ	1993
Rivière-du-Nord (90 419)	Monique Guay (1959)	BQ	1993

▶

▶ Roberval (81 373) .... Michel Gauthier (1950) .... BQ 1993
Rosemont—La Petite-Patrie (103 458) .... Bernard Bigras (1970) .... BQ 1997
Saint-Bruno—Saint-Hubert (99 755) .... Carole Lavallée (n.a.) .... BQ 2004
Saint-Hyacinthe—Bagot (94 084) .... Yvan Loubier (1959) .... BQ 1993
Saint-Jean (95 096) .... Claude Bachand (1951) .... BQ 1993
Saint-Lambert (92 946) .... Maka Kotto (1964) .... BQ 2004
Saint-Laurent—Cartierville (100 747) .... Stéphane Dion (1955) .... Lib. 1996*
Saint-Léonard—Saint-Michel (102 302) .... Massimo Pacetti (1962) .... Lib. 2002*
Saint-Maurice—Champlain (97 893) .... Marcel Gagnon (1936) .... BQ 2000
Shefford (94 939) .... Robert Vincent (n.a.) .... BQ 2004
Sherbrooke (97 882) .... Serge Cardin (1950) .... BQ 1998*
Terrebonne—Blainville (92 086) .... Diane Bourgeois (1949) .... BQ 2000
Trois-Rivières (92 206) .... Paule Brunelle (n.a.) .... BQ 2004
Vaudreuil-Soulanges (102 100) .... Meili Faille (n.a.) .... BQ 2004
Verchères—Les Patriotes (89 209) .... Stéphane Bergeron (1965) .... BQ 1993
Westmount—Ville-Marie (97 226) .... Lucienne Robillard (1945) .... Lib. 1995*

■ Ontario

Riding (population 2004)	Member (year of birth)	Party	Elected[1]
Ajax—Pickering (100 248)	Mark Holland (n.a.)	Lib.	2004
Algoma—Manitoulin—Kapuskasing (82 340)	Brent St. Denis (1950)	Lib.	1993
Ancaster—Dundas—Flamborough—Westdale (106 245)	Russ Powers (n.a.)	Lib.	2004
Barrie (103 710)	Aileen Carroll (1944)	Lib.	1997
Beaches—East York (108 913)	Maria Minna (1948)	Lib.	1993
Bramalea—Gore—Malton (119 886)	Gurbax Singh Malhi (1949)	Lib.	1993
Brampton—Springdale (116 775)	Ruby Dhalla (n.a.)	Lib.	2004
Brampton West (113 638)	Colleen Beaumier (1944)	Lib.	1993
Brant (118 580)	Lloyd St-Amand (n.a.)	Lib.	2004
Burlington (117 348)	Patricia (Paddy) Torsney (1962)	Lib.	1993
Cambridge (119 141)	Gary Goodyear (1958)	Con.	2004
Carleton—Lanark (111 149)	Gordon O'Connor (n.a.)	Con.	2004
Chatham-Kent—Essex (106 144)	Jerry Pickard (1940)	Lib.	1997
Clarington—Scugog—Uxbridge (107 435)	Bev Oda (n.a.)	Con.	2004
Davenport (111 705)	Mario Silva (1967)	Lib.	2004
Don Valley East (111 177)	Yasmin Ratansi (n.a.)	Lib.	2004
Don Valley West (115 539)	John Ferguson Godfrey (1942)	Lib.	1993
Dufferin—Caledon (101 608)	David Tilson (n.a.)	Con.	2004
Eglinton—Lawrence (106 879)	Joseph Volpe (1947)	Lib.	1988
Elgin—Middlesex—London (104 564)	Joe Preston (n.a.)	Con.	2004
Essex (114 330)	Jeff Watson (1971)	Con.	2004
Etobicoke Centre (111 792)	Borys Wrzesnewskyj (1961)	Lib.	2004
Etobicoke—Lakeshore (113 914)	Jean Augustine (1937)	Lib.	1993
Etobicoke North (112 411)	Roy Cullen (1944)	Lib.	1996*
Glengarry—Prescott—Russell (97 660)	Don Boudria (1949)	Lib.	1984
Grey—Bruce—Owen Sound (102 487)	Larry Miller (n.a.)	Con.	2004
Guelph (106 170)	Brenda Kay Chamberlain (1952)	Lib.	1993
Haldimand—Norfolk (104 575)	Diane Finley (1958)	Con.	2004
Haliburton—Kawartha Lakes—Brock (111 343)	Barry Devolin (n.a.)	Con.	2004
Halton (100 055)	Gary Carr (1955)	Lib.	2004
Hamilton Centre (118 186)	David Christopherson (1954)	NDP	2004
Hamilton East—Stoney Creek (115 709)	Tony Valeri (1957)	Lib.	1993
Hamilton Mountain (119 830)	Elizabeth Phinney (1938)	Lib.	1988
Huron—Bruce (104 063)	Paul Daniel Steckle (1942)	Lib.	1993
Kenora (60 572)	Roger Valley (n.a.)	Lib.	2004
Kingston and the Islands (115 833)	Peter Milliken (1946)	Lib.	1988
Kitchener Centre (108 840)	Karen Redman (1953)	Lib.	1997
Kitchener—Conestoga (96 708)	Lynn Myers (1951)	Lib.	1984
Kitchener—Waterloo (113 826)	Andrew Telegdi (1946)	Lib.	1993
Lanark—Frontenac—Lennox and Addington (113 077)	Scott Reid (1964)	Con.	2000
Leeds—Grenville (96 606)	Gord Brown (1960)	Con.	2004
London—Fanshawe (107 341)	Pat O'Brien (1948)	Lib.	1993

▶

▶ London North Centre (107 672)........................Joseph Frank Fontana (1950)......Lib.......1988
London West (110 988)..............................Susan Barnes (1952).............Lib......1993
Markham—Unionville (112 093)...................John McCallum (1950)...........Lib......2000
Middlesex—Kent—Lambton (105 291).............Rose-Marie Margaret Ur (1946)...Lib......1993
Mississauga—Brampton South (113 826).............Navdeep Bains (n.a.)...........Lib......2004
Mississauga East—Cooksville (122 566)............Albina Guarnieri (1953)...........Lib......1988
Mississauga—Erindale (120 354)....................Carolyn Parrish (1946)...........Lib......1993
Mississauga South (113 003)........................Paul Szabo (1948)................Lib......1993
Mississauga—Streetsville (118 305)..................Wajid Khan (n.a.)................Lib......2004
Nepean—Carleton (109 291).........................Pierre Poilievre (n.a.).............Con......2004
Newmarket—Aurora (105 955)........................Belinda Stronach (1966)..........Con......2004
Niagara Falls (120 797)..............................Robert Douglas Nicholson (1952)...Con......1984
Niagara West—Glanbrook (99 747)...................Dean Allison (n.a.)...............Con......2004
Nickel Belt (89 314).................................Raymond Bonin (1942)............Lib......1993
Nipissing—Timiskaming (89 961)....................Anthony Rota (n.a.)..............Lib......2004
Northumberland—Quinte West (118 906)..............Paul Harold Macklin (1944).......Lib......2000
Oak Ridges—Markham (111 276).....................Lui Temelkovski (n.a.)............Lib......2004
Oakville (109 642)..................................Bonnie Brown (1941).............Lib......1993
Oshawa (113 662)..................................Colin Carrie (n.a.)................Con......2004
Ottawa Centre (114 032)............................Edward Broadbent (1936).........NDP....1968
Ottawa—Orléans (103 435)..........................Marc Godbout (1948)............Lib......1993
Ottawa South (118 808).............................David McGuinty (1960)...........Lib......2004
Ottawa—Vanier (105 870)............................Mauril Bélanger (1955)...........Lib......1995*
Ottawa West—Nepean (112 509).....................Marlene Catterall (1939).........Lib......1988
Oxford (99 270).....................................Dave MacKenzie (1947)..........Con......2004
Parkdale—High Park (106 559)........................Sarmite (Sam) Bulte (1953).......Lib......1997
Parry Sound—Muskoka (84 789).....................Andrew Mitchell (1953)...........Lib......1993
Perth—Wellington (102 447)..........................Gary Schellenberger (1943).......Con......2003*
Peterborough (110 887)..............................Peter Adams (1936)..............Lib......1993
Pickering—Scarborough East (106 722)...............Dan McTeague (1962)............Lib......1993
Prince Edward—Hastings (109 407)...................Daryl Kramp (1947)..............Con......2004
Renfrew—Nipissing—Pembroke (96 421)..............Cheryl Gallant (1960)............Con......2000
Richmond Hill (109 394).............................Bryon Wilfert (1952).............Lib......1997
St. Catharines (111 452).............................Walt Lastewka (1940)............Lib......1993
St. Paul's (112 449).................................Carolyn Bennett (1950)...........Lib......1997
Sarnia—Lambton (104 556)...........................Roger John Gallaway (1948)......Lib......1993
Sault Ste. Marie (88 419).............................Tony Martin (1948)..............NDP....2004
Scarborough—Agincourt (110 669)....................Jim Karygiannis (1955)...........Lib......1988
Scarborough Centre (102 922).......................John Cannis (1951)..............Lib......1993
Scarborough—Guildwood (112 628)....................John McKay (1948)..............Lib......1997
Scarborough—Rouge River (115 437).................Derek Vincent Lee (1948).........Lib......1988
Scarborough Southwest (105 237)....................Tom Wappel (1950)..............Lib......1988
Simcoe—Grey (117 505)..............................Helena Guergis (n.a.)............Con......2004
Simcoe North (111 057)..............................Paul DeVillers (1946)............Lib......1993
Stormont—Dundas—South Glengarry (98 933).........Guy Lauzon (1948)...............Con......2004
Sudbury (89 443)...................................Diane Marleau (1943)............Lib......1988
Thornhill (116 840)..................................Susan Kadis (1953)..............Lib......2004
Thunder Bay—Rainy River (85 775)...................Ken Boshcoff (n.a.)..............Lib......2004
Thunder Bay—Superior North (83 657)................Joseph Comuzzi (1933)...........Lib......1988
Timmins—James Bay (84 001)........................Charlie Angus (1962).............NDP....2004
Toronto Centre (114 581)............................Bill Graham (1939)..............Lib......1993
Toronto—Danforth (109 713).........................Jack Layton (1950)..............NDP....2004
Trinity—Spadina (106 094)...........................Tony Ianno (1957)...............Lib......1993
Vaughan (112 049)..................................Maurizio Bevilacqua (1960).......Lib......1988
Welland (108 876)..................................John Maloney (1945)............Lib......1993
Wellington—Halton Hills (100 555)...................Mike Chong (n.a.)...............Con......2004
Whitby—Oshawa (112 802)...........................Judi Longfield (1947)...........Lib......1997
Willowdale (108 454)................................James Scott Peterson (1941)......Lib......1988
Windsor—Tecumseh (116 466).........................Joe Comartin (1947).............NDP....2000
Windsor West (117 041)..............................Brian Masse (1968)..............NDP....2002*
York Centre (113 420)...............................Ken Dryden (1947)..............Lib......2004
York—Simcoe (112 541)..............................Peter Van Loan (n.a.)............Con......2004 ▶

▶ York South—Weston (114 539) . . . . Alan Tonks (1943) . . . . Lib. 2000
York West (110 384) . . . . Judy Sgro (1944). . . . . Lib. 1999*

■ Manitoba

Riding (population 2004)	Member (year of birth)	Party	Elected[1]
Brandon—Souris (83 510)	Merv Tweed (n.a.)	Con.	2004
Charleswood—St. James (81 874)	Steven Fletcher (n.a.).	Con.	2004
Churchill (73 428)	Bev Desjarlais (1955).	NDP	1997
Dauphin—Swan River (77 586)	Inky Mark (1947).	Con.	1997
Elmwood—Transcona (77 997)	William (Bill) Blaikie (1951)	NDP	1979
Kildonan—St. Paul (77 131)	Joy Smith (1947)	Con.	2004
Portage—Lisgar (83 381)	Brian William Pallister (1954)	Con.	2000
Provencher (81 910)	Vic Toews (1952).	Con.	2000
Saint Boniface (81 239)	Raymond Simard (1958)	Lib.	2002*
Selkirk—Interlake (86 555)	James Bezan (1965)	Con.	2004
Winnipeg Centre (80 930)	Pat Martin (1955)	NDP	1997
Winnipeg North (79 332)	Judy Wasylycia-Leis (1951).	NDP	1997
Winnipeg South (76 871).	Reginald Alcock (1948)	Lib.	1993
Winnipeg South Centre (77 839)	Anita Neville (1942)	Lib.	2000

■ Saskatchewan

Riding (population 2004)	Member (year of birth)	Party	Elected[1]
Battlefords—Lloydminster (73 396)	Gerry Ritz (1951)	Con.	1997
Blackstrap (73 725)	Lynne Yelich (1953)	Con.	2000
Churchill River (64 416).	Jeremy Harrison (n.a.).	Con.	2004
Cypress Hills—Grasslands (65 216)	David Anderson (1957)	Con.	2000
Palliser (67 282).	Dave Batters (1969).	Con.	2004
Prince Albert (73 988)	Brian Fitzpatrick (1945)	Con.	2000
Regina—Lumsden—Lake Centre (66 374)	Tom Lukiwski (1952).	Con.	2004
Regina—Qu'Appelle (69 014)	Andrew Scheer (n.a.)	Con.	2004
Saskatoon—Humboldt (70 405)	Bradley Trost (1974)	Con.	2004
Saskatoon—Rosetown—Biggar (73 077)	Carol Skelton (1945)	Con.	2000
Saskatoon—Wanuskewin (72 429)	Maurice Vellacott (1955)	Con.	1997
Souris—Moose Mountain (66 223)	Ed Komarnicki (1950)	Con.	2004
Wascana (72 508)	Ralph Goodale (1949)	Lib.	1993
Yorkton—Melville (70 880)	Garry Breitkreuz (1945)	Con.	1993

■ Alberta

Riding (population 2004)	Member (year of birth)	Party	Elected[1]
Athabasca (88 882)	Brian Jean (n.a.)	Con.	2004
Calgary East (115 565).	Deepak Obhrai (1950)	Con.	1997
Calgary North Centre (117 252)	Jim Prentice (1957).	Con.	2004
Calgary Northeast (109 339)	Art Hanger (1943)	Con.	1993
Calgary—Nose Hill (100 026)	Diane Ablonczy (1949)	Con.	1993
Calgary South Centre (117 439).	Lee Richardson (1947)	Con.	1988
Calgary Southeast (107 432)	Jason Kenney (1968)	Con.	1997
Calgary Southwest (107 920).	Stephen Harper (1959)	Con.	1993
Calgary West (103 893)	Rob Anders (1972)	Con.	1997
Crowfoot (104 059)	Kevin Sorenson (1958)	Con.	2000
Edmonton—Beaumont (99 508)	David Kilgour (1941)	Lib.	1979
Edmonton Centre (115 900).	Anne McLellan (1950)	Lib.	1993
Edmonton East (119 160)	Peter Goldring (1944)	Con.	1997
Edmonton—Leduc (95 700)	James Rajotte (1970)	Con.	2000
Edmonton—St. Albert (113 146)	John Williams (1946)	Con.	1993
Edmonton—Sherwood Park (103 610)	Ken Epp (1939)	Con.	1993
Edmonton—Spruce Grove (111 622)	Rona Ambrose (1969)	Con.	2004
Edmonton—Strathcona (98 974).	Rahim Jaffer (1971).	Con.	1997
Lethbridge (106 132)	Rick Casson (1943)	Con.	1997
Macleod (97 578).	Ted Menzies (1952)	Con.	2004
Medicine Hat (105 009)	Monte Solberg (1958)	Con.	1993

▶

▶ Peace River (123 877) . . . . Charles Penson (1942) . . . . Con. 1993
Red Deer (105 070) . . . . Robert (Bob) Mills (1941) . . . . Con. 1993
Vegreville—Wainwright (107 771) . . . . Leon Earl Benoit (1950) . . . . Con. . . . 1993
Westlock—St. Paul (99 081) . . . . David Chatters (1946) . . . . Con. . . . 1993
Wetaskiwin (101 163) . . . . Dale Johnston (1941) . . . . Con. . . . 1993
Wild Rose (101 690) . . . . Myron Thompson (1936). . . . . Con. . . . 1993
Yellowhead (98 009) . . . . Rob Merrifield (1953) . . . . Con. . . . 2000

■ British Columbia

Riding (population 2004)	Member (year of birth)	Party	Elected[1]
Abbotsford (116 098)	Randy White (1948)	Con.	1993
Burnaby—Douglas (108 891)	Bill Siksay (n.a.)	NDP	2004
Burnaby—New Westminster (111 048)	Peter Julian (n.a.)	NDP	2004
Cariboo—Prince George (111 486)	Richard (Dick) Harris (1944)	Con.	1993
Chilliwack—Fraser Canyon (103 716)	Charles (Chuck) Strahl (1957)	Con.	1993
Delta—Richmond East (103 045)	John Cummins (1942)	Con.	1993
Dewdney—Alouette (110 577)	Randy Kamp (1953)	Con.	2004
Esquimalt—Juan de Fuca (110 909)	Keith Martin (1960)	Lib.	1993
Fleetwood—Port Kells (101 198)	Nina Grewal (n.a.)	Con.	2004
Kamloops—Thompson (111 721)	Betty Hinton (1950)	Con.	2000
Kelowna (111 206)	Werner Schmidt (1932)	Con.	1993
Kootenay—Columbia (88 637)	James Abbott (1942)	Con.	1993
Langley (111 046)	Mark Warawa (1950)	Con.	2004
Nanaimo—Alberni (112 972)	James Lunney (1951)	Con.	2000
Nanaimo—Cowichan (116 754)	Jean Crowder (n.a.)	NDP	2004
Newton—North Delta (111 050)	Gurmant Singh Grewal (1957)	Con.	1997
New Westminster—Coquitlam (109 301)	Paul Eugene Forseth (1946)	Con.	1993
North Okanagan—Shuswap (109 711)	Darrel Stinson (1945)	Con.	1993
North Vancouver (120 841)	Don Bell (n.a.)	Lib.	2004
Okanagan—Coquihalla (101 831)	Stockwell Day (1950)	Con.	2000
Port Moody—Westwood—Port Coquitlam (109 394)	James Moore (1976)	Con.	2000
Prince George—Peace River (104 257)	Jay Hill (1952)	Con.	1993
Richmond (106 621)	Raymond Chan (1951)	Lib.	1993
Saanich—Gulf Islands (110 284)	Gary Lunn (1957)	Con.	1997
Skeena—Bulkley Valley (99 474)	Nathan Cullen (n.a.)	NDP	2004
Southern Interior (96 144)	James William Gouk (1946)	Con.	1993
South Surrey—White Rock—Cloverdale (99 317)	Russ Hiebert (n.a.)	Con.	2004
Surrey North (106 904)	Chuck Cadman (1948)	Ind.	1997
Vancouver Centre (105 998)	Hedy Fry (1941)	Lib.	1993
Vancouver East (107 421)	Libby Davies (1953)	NDP	1997
Vancouver Island North (109 380)	John Morris Duncan (1948)	Con.	1993
Vancouver Kingsway (115 325)	David Emerson (1945)	Lib.	2004
Vancouver Quadra (112 985)	Stephen Owen (1948)	Lib.	2000
Vancouver South (113 063)	Ujjal Dosanjh (1947)	Lib.	2004
Victoria (104 561)	David Anderson (1937)	Lib.	1968
West Vancouver—Sunshine Coast (124 572)	John Douglas Reynolds (1942)	Con.	1997

■ Yukon

Riding (population 2004)	Member (year of birth)	Party	Elected[1]
Yukon (28 674)	Larry Bagnell (1949)	Lib.	2000

■ Northwest Territiories

Riding (population 2004)	Member (year of birth)	Party	Elected[1]
Western Arctic (37 360)	Ethel Blondin-Andrew (1951)	Lib.	1988

■ Nunavut

Riding (population 2004)	Member (year of birth)	Party	Elected[1]
Nunavut (26 745)	Nancy Karetak-Lindell (1957)	Lib.	1997

(1) The year shown is the year the MP was first elected. An asterisk indicates a by-election. BQ—Bloc Québécois; Con.—Conservative; Ind.—Independent; Lib.—Liberal; NDP—New Democratic Party; n.a.—not available.

Standing Committees of the Senate

(as of May 23, 2004)

Standing Committee on	Chair (Party)	Number of Subcommittees	Clerk's Telephone
Aboriginal Peoples	Nick Sibbeston (Lib.)	—	(613) 990-6160
Agriculture and Forestry	Donald Oliver (Con.)	—	(613) 993-8121
Banking, Trade and Commerce	Richard Kroft (Lib.)	—	(613) 993-4874
Energy, the Environment and Natural Resources	Tommy Banks (Lib.)	—	(613) 990-6080
Fisheries and Oceans	Gerald Comeau (Con.)	—	(613) 991-3620
Foreign Affairs	Peter Stollery (Lib.)	—	(613) 998-0424
Human Rights	Shirley Maheu (Lib.)	—	(613) 990-6081
Internal Economy, Budgets and Administration	Lise Bacon (Lib.)	—	(613) 992-2493
Legal and Constitutional Affairs	George Furey (Lib.)	—	(613) 943-7865
National Finance	Lowell Murray (PC)	—	(613) 990-6081
National Security and Defence	Colin Kenny (Lib.)	1	(613) 998-0371
Official Languages	Maria Chaput (Lib.)	—	(613) 990-6160
Rules, Procedures and the Rights of Parliament	Lorna Milne (Lib.)	—	(613) 991-9213
Selection	Rose-Marie Losier-Cool (Lib.)	—	(613) 990-5013
Social Affairs, Science and Technology	Michael Kirby (Lib.)	—	(613) 991-0719
Transport and Communications	Joan Fraser (Lib.)	—	(613) 991-3620

Con.—Conservative; Lib.—Liberal; PC—Progressive Conservative.

Standing Committees of the House of Commons

(as of May 23, 2004)

Standing Committee on	Chair (Party)	Number of Subcommittees	Clerk's Telephone
Aboriginal Affairs, Northern Development and Natural Resources	Guy St-Julien (Lib.)	1	(613) 992-3150
Agriculture and Agri-Food	Paul Steckle (Lib.)	1	(613) 992-3150
Canadian Heritage	Sarmite Bulte (Lib.)	—	(613) 992-3150
Citizenship and Immigration	Sarkis Assadourian (Lib.)	—	(613) 992-3150
Environment and Sustainable Development	Charles Caccia (Lib.)	1	(613) 992-3150
Finance	Roy Cullen (Lib.)	1	(613) 992-3150
Fisheries and Oceans	Tom Wappel (Lib.)	1	(613) 992-3150
Foreign Affairs and International Trade	Bernard Patry (Lib.)	3	(613) 992-3150
Government Operations and Estimates	Paul Szabo (Lib.)	1	(613) 992-3150
Health	Bonnie Brown (Lib.)	—	(613) 992-3150
Human Resources Development and the Status of Persons with Disabilities	Judi Longfield (Lib.)	—	(613) 992-3150
Industry, Science and Technology	Brent St. Denis (Lib.)	1	(613) 992-3150
Justice, Human Rights, Public Safety & Emergency Preparedness	Derek Lee (Lib.)	2	(613) 992-3150
Liaison	Judi Longfield (Lib.)	1	(613) 992-3150
National Defence and Veterans Affairs	Pat O'Brien (Lib.)	2	(613) 992-3150
Official Languages	Don Boudria (Lib.)	—	(613) 992-3150
Procedure and House Affairs	Peter Adams (Lib.)	3	(613) 992-3150
Public Accounts	John Williams (Con.)	2	(613) 992-3150
Transport	Raymond Bonin (Lib.)	—	(613) 992-3150

Con.—Conservative; Lib.—Liberal

Government of Canada Primary Internet Site

The Canada Site is the official Web site of the Canadian government. It provides access to information and services about Canada and Canadian governments. The starting point is http://canada.gc.ca, and the information appears in French and English. Across the top of the site, the following Web links appear in red:

WHAT'S NEW: This link connects you to an archive of government press releases and reports. The announcements are categorized by date and by government department and agency. You can find current data in Statistics Canada's *The Daily*, the Bank of Canada's *Weekly Financial Statistics* and the Canadian Forest Service's *National Forest Fire Situation Report.*

PUBLICATIONS AND REPORTS: This link connects you to Government of Canada Publications. You can find specialized books and CD-ROMs listed by topic, title or government agency. You can check for recent releases and order them online. (Some publications are free!) The "Canadian Library Gateway" allows you to browse through library Web sites and catalogues across Canada.

ABOUT GOVERNMENT: This link leads to sites that describe Canada's federal system of government. You can find an alphabetical list of government departments and agencies, information about the workings of Parliament, lists of Canadian municipalities and so on. This link also provides access to the texts of the throne speech, the federal budget, federal laws (e.g., the Official Languages Act) and the auditor general's report.

PROVINCES AND TERRITORIES: This link connects you to the official sites of Canada's provincial and territorial governments.

On the left of the Canada Site's home page, a vertical bar in black, red and gold provides more Web links:

PRIME MINISTER OF CANADA: This link takes you to the official Web site of the prime minister.

GOVERNMENT ANNOUNCEMENTS: This link takes you to a page of information that supplements government ads that have appeared on

television or in the newspapers. The site features information about tourism, climate change, safety on Canada's waterways, national security policy and recruitment of university graduates for the civil service.

ONLINE FORMS AND SERVICES: This link connects you to sites with printable government forms for air travel complaints, child tax benefits, GST/HST remittance etc. "Shop On-line" links you to sites that allow you to buy videos from the National Film Board or clothing from the RCMP's Musical Ride Boutique.

GOVERNMENT CONTACTS: Do you want to write or speak to a government official? This link connects you to directories of parliamentarians and federal public servants—including Canadian diplomats abroad. You can also find contact information for foreign embassies and consulates in Canada.

The centre of the Canada Site features four "gateway links":

CANADIANS AND RESIDENTS: This link connects you to a range of public services and information sites for consumers, job seekers, seniors, aboriginals, youth, rural dwellers, new immigrants and Canadians living abroad.

NON-CANADIANS: This links you to "Canada International," a site for tourists, immigrants and foreign investors. Several links connect you to pages that explain Canadian foreign policy and culture to non-Canadians.

CANADIAN BUSINESS: This links you to sites on business start-ups, taxation, financing, statistics analysis, and government tenders. Other links connect you to sites on employee management, exports and imports, technology, research and development.

ABOUT CANADA: This link connects you to Canadiana: maps, national symbols and landscape photos. Four sublinks lead you to facts about Canada's society, government, land and economy.

The Canada Site: a world of information at the click of a mouse!

If You're Not on the Internet...

*T*he Government of Canada provides a toll-free telephone inquiry service called 1 (800) O Canada. Operators at **1 (800) 622-6232** will direct callers to a service that will supply the needed information.

Salaries of Federal Political Figures

(as of October 2004)

The **GOVERNOR GENERAL OF CANADA** receives $110 000 per year.
Each provincial **LIEUTENANT-GOVERNOR** receives $105 800 per year.
Each **SENATOR** receives an annual sessional indemnity of $116 000 plus 64 travel points[1] per year.[2]

The following senators receive salaries on top of their annual sessional indemnities for performing specialized duties:

Leader of the Government in the Senate . . . . $67 680 plus $2 122 car allowance
Leader of the Opposition in the Senate $32 400
Speaker of the Senate . . . . $49 600 plus $3 000 residence allowance and $1 061 car allowance
Speaker pro tempore. $20 500
Deputy Leader of the Government in the Senate $32 400
Deputy Leader of the Opposition in the Senate $20 500
Government Whip $10 100
Opposition Whip $6 200
Chair of Standing Committee[3]. $10 100
Vice-Chair of Standing Committee[3] $5 300

Each **MEMBER OF PARLIAMENT** (MP) in the House of Commons receives an annual sessional indemnity of $141 000 plus 64 travel points[1] per year.[2]

The following MPs receive salaries on top of their annual sessional indemnities for performing specialized duties:

Prime Minister. . . . . $141 000 plus $2 122 car allowance
Cabinet Minister . . . . $67 600 plus $2 122 car allowance
Secretary of State $50 700
Speaker of the House . . . . $67 600 plus $1 061 car allowance and $3 000 rent allowance
Deputy Speaker of the House . . . . $35 200 plus $1 500 rent allowance
Leader of the Opposition in the House. . . . . $67 600 plus $2 122 car allowance
Leader: Other Party $48 200
Opposition House Leader $35 200
House Leader: Other Party $14 300
Chief Government Whip $25 600
Chief Opposition Whip $25 600
Deputy Government Whip $10 100
Deputy Opposition Whip $10 100
Whip: Other Party $10 100
Parliamentary Secretary $14 300
Deputy Chair, Committee of the Whole House. $14 300
Assistant Deputy Chair, Committee of the Whole House. $14 300
Chair of Standing or Standing Joint Committee[4] $10 100
Vice-Chair of Standing or Standing Joint Committee[4] $5 300

(1) One travel point is worth a business-class return air trip between Ottawa and a representative's riding. Travel points may be used by representatives, their spouses or dependents. Representatives may also take free trips on VIA Rail Canada for official business. (2) Representatives who travel at least 100 km from their principal residences in Canada on official business may claim as much as $20,000 in expenses for food, lodging etc. (3) Excludes the Standing Joint Committee on the Library of Parliament. (4) Excludes the Liaison Committee and the Standing Joint Committee on the Library of Parliament.

■ **SENATORS' OFFICE BUDGET**

Each senator is entitled to a budget of $130,700 per fiscal year for research and office expenses. The expenses must be incurred while the senator fulfills his or her parliamentary role.

■ **SENATORS' PENSION PLAN**

Senators must contribute 7 percent of their basic salaries (and may contribute up to 7 percent extra) to their pensions. Senators must serve at least six years to be eligible for a monthly pension for life. Senators who retire with fewer than six years' service get their pension contributions returned. Retirement benefits are indexed to the cost of living after age 60. No senator may collect pension benefits before age 55.

The maximum basic pension equals 75 percent of a senator's average best five years after 25 years of service (accrued at 3 percent annually). There is no maximum to extra salary pension, and the amount is accrued at 4 percent annually. After a senator dies, the surviving spouse is entitled to three-fifths of the senator's pension; up to three dependent children are entitled to a further one-tenth each of the deceased senator's pension.

■ MEMBERS' OFFICE BUDGET

Most members of the House of Commons have two offices: one in Ottawa and another in a home riding. These offices serve constituents who have problems when dealing with the federal government. The members' office budgets cover the costs of paying staff salaries, hiring contract labour, and renting, equipping and maintaining their offices. Office budgets also cover travel expenses, both within the riding and within the province.

The amount of money allocated to a member's office budget depends on whether the office is in a rural riding, an urban riding, an urban-rural riding, Nunavut or the Northwest Territories. The amounts allocated range between $234,600 and $251,400 per office. In general, urban offices cost less than rural offices to run. Territorial constituency offices are the most expensive to maintain.

Elector and Geographic Supplements: Members receive supplements for their main office budgets if they represent large constituencies. Offices in ridings that have at least 70,000 voters receive an extra $7,240, while offices in ridings that have at least 150,000 voters receive an extra $43,370. In addition, offices in ridings of at least 8,000 sq. km receive an extra $7,240 while offices in ridings of at least 500,001 sq. km receive an extra $43,550. These annual budgetary supplements cover the costs of hiring additional staff and some travel. Supplements often change after general elections when population sizes or riding boundaries change.

Other Services: To help meet the needs and requests of their constituents, members are also given access to printing, translation, mail and other support services that help them respond to the thousands of letters and requests they receive. (Canadians may write to members of Parliament free of charge from anywhere in Canada.) The services also allow members to keep the public up-to-date on the events in Ottawa through a parliamentary report known as a "householder." Finally, members are provided with desks, computers, photocopiers and other office supplies and equipment required to run an efficient office in Ottawa.

■ MEMBERS' PENSION PLAN

The Members of Parliament Retiring Allowances Act provides MPs with their pensions. Members must contribute 7 percent of their annual sessional allowance of $141,000 when in office. Members who receive extra salaries for being cabinet ministers, whips, parliamentary secretaries, etc., may contribute as much as 7 percent of their salaries as well. To collect, members must serve in the House of Commons for at least six years and be at least 55 years old when they retire, die or lose an election.

Pensions are payable at the rate of 3 percent per year of service (i.e., a minimum of 18 percent: 6 years × 3 percent) to a maximum of 75 percent (25 years of service) of the average of the best consecutive six years of earnings. Members who serve less than six years must withdraw their contributions.

The indexing of pensions begins only when members reach the age of 60, except for extraordinary situations such as disability. Survivors' benefits are payable to spouses and dependent children. If former members in receipt of pensions are re-elected to the House or appointed to the Senate, their pensions are suspended for their time in office. In 1995 the pension plan was amended to allow members to opt out, eliminate "double dipping" (drawing more than one pension after holding several positions), and provide that former members cannot receive pensions until they are at least 55 years old.

Sources: *Rideau Hall; Department of Canadian Heritage; Finance and Human Resources Directorate, House of Commons; Finance Directorate, Senate; Library of Parliament, Information and Documentation Branch.*

Supreme Court Justices of Canada

(as of October 2004)

Name	Date of Birth	Date Appointed	Appointed from
The Rt. Hon. Madam Justice Beverley McLachlin ...	Sept. 7, 1943	Mar. 30, 1989[1]	Supreme Court of BC
The Hon. Madam Justice Rosalie Abella	(n.a.)	Aug. 30, 2004	Ontario Court of Appeal
The Hon. Mr. Justice Michel Bastarache	June 10, 1947	Oct. 1, 1997	NB Court of Appeal
The Hon. Mr. Justice William Ian Corneil Binnie	Apr. 14, 1939	Jan. 8, 1998	Private law practice
The Hon. Madam Justice Louise Charron	(n.a.)	Aug. 30, 2004	Ontario Court of Appeal
The Hon. Madam Justice Marie Deschamps	Oct. 2, 1952	Aug. 7, 2002	Quebec Court of Appeal
The Hon. Mr. Justice Morris J. Fish.............	Nov. 16, 1938	July 31, 2003	Quebec Court of Appeal
The Hon. Mr. Justice Louis LeBel	Nov. 30, 1939	Jan. 7, 2000	Quebec Court of Appeal
The Hon. Mr. Justice John Charles Major	Feb. 20, 1931	Nov. 13, 1992	Alberta Court of Appeal

Source: *Supreme Court of Canada*   *n.a.—not available*   (1) Appointed Chief Justice Jan. 7, 2000

Chief Justices of the Supreme Court of Canada.

Name	Date of Birth	Date Appointed Chief Justice	Term Ended
The Hon. Sir William Buell Richards	May 2, 1815	Sept. 30, 1875	Jan. 10, 1879
The Hon. Sir William Johnston Ritchie...........	Oct. 28, 1813	Jan. 11, 1879	Sept. 25, 1892
The Rt. Hon. Sir Samuel Henry Strong...........	Aug. 13, 1825	Dec. 13, 1892	Nov. 18, 1902
The Rt. Hon. Sir Henri-Elzéar Taschereau	Oct. 7, 1836	Nov. 21, 1902	May 2, 1906
The Rt. Hon. Sir Charles Fitzpatrick	Dec. 19, 1853	June 4, 1906	Oct. 21, 1918
The Rt. Hon. Sir Louis Henry Davies	May 6, 1845	Oct. 23, 1918	May 1, 1924
The Rt. Hon. Francis Alexander Anglin...........	Apr. 2, 1865	Sept. 16, 1924	Feb. 28, 1933
The Rt. Hon. Sir Lyman Poore Duff	Jan. 7, 1865	Mar. 17, 1933	Jan. 7, 1944
The Rt. Hon. Thibaudeau Rinfret	June 22, 1879	Jan. 8, 1944	June 22, 1954
The Hon. Patrick Kerwin.......................	Oct. 25, 1889	July 1, 1954	Feb. 2, 1963
The Rt. Hon. Robert Taschereau	Sept. 10, 1896	Apr. 22, 1963	Sept. 1, 1967
The Rt. Hon. John Robert Cartwright............	Mar. 23, 1895	Sept. 1, 1967	Mar. 23, 1970
The Rt. Hon. Joseph Honoré Gérald Fauteux	Oct. 22, 1900	Mar. 23, 1970	Dec. 23, 1973
The Rt. Hon. Bora Laskin......................	Oct. 5, 1912	Dec. 27, 1973	Mar. 26, 1984
The Rt. Hon. Robert George Brian Dickson	May 25, 1916	Apr. 18, 1984	June 30, 1990
The Rt. Hon. Antonio Lamer...................	Jul. 8, 1933	July 1, 1990	Jan. 6, 2000
The Rt. Hon. Beverley McLachlin...............	Sept. 7, 1943	Jan. 7, 2000–	

Source: *Supreme Court of Canada and Canadian Parliamentary Guide*

Contacting the Supreme Court

*F*or information on the Supreme Court of Canada, turn to page 149. Visit the court's Web site at http://www.scc-csc.gc.ca for more information on judges, history, recent decisions, tours and news. You may also write to the Supreme Court of Canada, 301 Wellington Street, Ottawa, Ontario, K1A 0J1. Phone (613) 995-4330 or e-mail reception@scc-csc.gc.ca

Key Decisions of the Supreme Court of Canada

The Persons Case (1928): The court unanimously decided that women were not "persons" qualified for appointment to the Canadian Senate. In 1929, the British Privy Council overturned the decision on appeal, declaring the exclusion of women from public office "a relic of days more barbarous than ours."

Alberta Press Act Reference (1938): The court struck down an Alberta bill that would have required newspapers, when called upon by government officials, to publish the government's rebuttal of criticism that had appeared in the newspapers. The decision blocked one form of government interference with press freedom.

Saumur v City of Quebec (1953): The court narrowly upheld the province's right to authorize municipal bans on street pamphleteering. (The ban had been challenged by Jehovah's Witnesses who were distributing leaflets.) However, one majority judge declared that a Quebec law guaranteeing religious freedom prevented the authorities from banning the distribution of *religious* pamphlets. Thus the court attempted to protect this form of religious expression.

Switzman v Elbling (1957): The court struck down a Quebec law—the Act Respecting Communistic Propaganda of 1937—which criminalized the publication and distribution of Communist literature. The law, also known as the Padlock Act, empowered the attorney general to close buildings used by Communists for up to a year. The court ruled that the province lacked the constitutional power to pass criminal laws.

Roncarelli v Duplessis (1959): The court ruled that Maurice Duplessis, former premier and attorney general of Quebec, committed a civil wrong when he revoked the liquor licence of Roncarelli, a restaurateur, in 1946. Duplessis had revoked the licence, and had ruined Roncarelli's business, because Roncarelli had aided Jehovah's Witnesses who had been arrested for pamphleteering. The court ordered Duplessis to pay damages.

R. v Drybones (1970): The court used a clause declaring equality before the law in the Bill of Rights to strike down part of the Indian Act that made it an offence for a Native person to be drunk when off a reserve. The court decided that if a federal law cannot be applied without infringing on a citizen's rights, the law must be suspended until Parliament declares that the law still applies—regardless of the Bill of Rights. Then the court ruled that Drybones, an aboriginal man found drunk while away from his reserve, had been punished for his race under a law whose penalty differed for other Canadians.

R. v Kienapple (1975): The court abolished the practice of sentencing defendants twice for offences that amounted to being the same act.

CUPE Local 963 v New Brunswick Liquor Corp. (1979): The court affirmed the growing role of administrative tribunals and established when the courts can interfere with the tribunals' decisions.

Patriation Reference (1981): The court ruled that the federal government could patriate the constitution (then known as the British North America Act) without the consent of the provinces; however, the court also said that the federal government would violate a political tradition if it patriated the constitution without first securing "a substantial degree" of provincial consent.

The Bill 101 Case (1984): The court struck down two sections of Quebec's Bill 101 (The Charter of the French Language) that dealt with anglophone schooling. The sections attempted to make French the language of instruction in elementary schools for anglophones who had moved to Quebec from elsewhere in Canada. The court declared that this was incompatible with minority-language education guarantees in the Canadian Charter of Rights and Freedoms.

Hunter v Southam Inc. (1984): The court struck down two subsections of the Combines Investigation Act because they violated the guarantee in the Canadian Charter of Rights and Freedoms against unreasonable searches and seizures. Hunter, a government official investigating restrictive trade practices, had sent several officers without search warrants to enter Southam's corporate office in Edmonton to examine documents.

R. v Big M Drug Mart (1985): The court struck down the Lord's Day Act, a federal law passed in 1907 that banned business activities on Sundays. The court declared that, by forcing all members of society to observe the Christian Sabbath, the law infringed on the religious freedoms of non-Christian minorities; therefore, the Act was incompatible with the religious freedom guarantees in the Canadian Charter of Rights and Freedoms. Big M Drug Mart had been charged with selling merchandise on Sundays.

Singh et al. v Minister of Employment and Immigration (1985): The court ruled that foreign refugees in Canada may not be deported to countries where their lives or freedom are threatened. The guarantee of personal security in the Canadian Charter of Rights and Freedoms applied to everyone in Canada. The court also ruled that the Immigration Act's method for establishing refugee status failed to meet the Charter's requirements for fundamental justice. People seeking refugee status were entitled to a hearing.

R. v Oakes (1986): The court struck down a section of the Narcotic Control Act that conflicted with the presumption of innocence of accused persons—a presumption guaranteed in the Canadian Charter of Rights and Freedoms. The court also established a two-step test to see whether laws measure up to Charter guarantees. First, the government must prove the existence of a purpose important and urgent enough to justify the suppression of a right; second, the government's legislative methods must be reasonable, fair and proportionate to the goal.

Ford v Quebec (1988): The court struck down two more sections of Quebec's Bill 101. The provisions attempted to impose the exclusive use of French on public and commercial signs in Quebec. The court decided that these provisions violated the freedom of expression guarantees in the Canadian Charter of Rights and Freedoms, although the *predominant* use of French on such signs could be legally justified.

Daigle v Tremblay (1989): The court declared that fetuses have no constitutional rights; constitutional rights begin at the time of live birth. The court also decided that the father of a fetus may not use a court injunction to prevent the mother from exercising her right of choice to have an abortion. Tremblay had tried to stop his partner, Daigle, from aborting their unborn child.

R. v Stinchcombe (1990): The court unanimously affirmed that the Crown must reveal all its evidence against an accused to the defence so the defence can properly defend the accused. This responsibility of the Crown, which had existed in common law, became obligatory rather than merely voluntary. The ruling also required police and prosecutors to disclose all their evidence before the accused chose a mode of trial or entered a plea.

R. v Sparrow (1990): The court affirmed the rights of aboriginal peoples in the Constitution Act and declared that these rights must be interpreted broadly. The authorities had charged Sparrow, an aboriginal man, with breaking a federal fishing law. Sparrow successfully argued that the right to fish was protected by treaty and the constitution. The court also established criteria for interpreting aboriginal rights in the constitution.

Kindler v. Canada (1991): The court ruled that the extradition of a non-Canadian fugitive did not violate the guarantee in the Canadian Charter of Rights and Freedoms to life, liberty and security of person. Extradition also did not violate the Charter's ban on subjecting a person to cruel and unusual punishment. Kindler, an American who had been convicted of murder and kidnapping in Pennsylvania, had escaped from prison and fled to Canada where he was arrested. He faced a possible death sentence if returned to the US.

R. v Généreux (1992): The court found that judges in courts martial were vulnerable to financial and administrative pressures from senior officials in the Canadian Armed Forces. The decision paved the way for parliamentary reforms aimed at strengthening the independence and impartiality of military judges. Généreux, a corporal who had been court martialled for desertion and selling narcotics, had argued that he had not received an impartial trial.

R. v Tran (1994): The court ruled that an accused is entitled to full and contemporaneous translation in his or her native language during a trial. The court then ordered a new trial for Tran, a Vietnamese man who spoke no English or French and who had received inadequate translation service during his trial for sexual assault in Nova Scotia. This case was the first in which the Supreme Court of Canada dealt with an accused's right to an interpreter.

RJR-MacDonald Inc. v Canada (1995): The court declared that Parliament possessed the constitutional authority (in criminal law) to regulate the use of tobacco products. The court also said that Parliament had a valid interest in countering the harmful effects of tobacco on health. However, a 5–4 majority of justices struck down the Tobacco Products Control Act of 1988 because the law's broad ban on tobacco advertising violated the freedom of expression guarantees in the Canadian Charter of Rights and Freedoms.

Cooper v Canada (1996): The court ruled that the Canadian Human Rights Commission lacked the authority and expertise to rule on the constitutional validity of the mandatory age of retirement.

R. v Stillman (1997): The court decided that the common-law power to conduct a search incidental to an arrest excluded the right to seize body substances by force. The police had subjected a suspect, Stillman, to an intrusive body search without consent. The court ruled that such searches must meet three requirements to be legal: the arrest must be legal, the search must be incidental, and the search must be conducted in a reasonable way.

Delgamuukw v British Columbia (1997): The court defined the content and extent of aboriginal title to ancestral lands. The court required aboriginals seeking such title to prove that they occupied the territory before Canada's decla-

ration of sovereignty. The court also decided to consider admitting oral history as evidence.

Godbout v Longueuil (1997): The court unanimously declared that a municipal government may not dictate where its employees live. The City of Longueuil, Quebec, had demanded that its permanent employees live inside the town's limits.

R. v Caslake (1998): The court decided that a police search made for purposes of inventory, conforming to police policy but without a search warrant or permission, is an abusive search. Caslake had been arrested for possessing narcotics; an RCMP search of Caslake's van several hours after the arrest—which led to the seizure of more narcotics—prompted the dispute over "abusive searches" in court.

Quebec Secession Reference (1998): The court ruled unanimously that a unilateral declaration of independence by a province (i.e., Quebec) would be illegal according to the Canadian constitution and international law. However, a constitutional amendment would make secession possible. The court also said that if a clear majority of Quebeckers voted for secession in a referendum, the rest of Canada would be obliged to negotiate the terms of independence. The negotiations would have to respect democracy, federalism, the rule of law and the protection of minorities.

Vriend v Alberta (1998): The court unanimously declared that Alberta's failure to include sexual orientation as an illegal form of discrimination in its Individual Rights Protection Act violated the Canadian Charter of Rights and Freedoms. The court ruled that Vriend, a homosexual, had been wrongfully dismissed from his job at an Edmonton college after he acknowledged his sexual orientation to his employer.

Little Sister's Book and Art Emporium v Canada (2000): The court upheld the authority of customs officials to seize imported books, magazines and videos that may be sexually obscene. The justices also shifted the burden of proving illegal obscenity from importers to customs officials in open court. Little Sister's, a bookstore in Vancouver, had repeatedly complained about the seizure of homosexual erotica by customs agents.

The Conservative Party in Canada

The earliest conservatives in English Canada embraced British Toryism. Their supporters included United Empire Loyalists who fled from the United States after the American Revolution. The Loyalists were monarchists who favoured social hierarchy and law and order. In French Canada, the earliest conservatives were Roman Catholics. They also admired social hierarchy and sought to preserve their language and religion.

In 1854, John A. Macdonald entered a Liberal-Conservative coalition government in the Province of Canada. Macdonald subsequently shaped the Liberal-Conservative party and argued for the Confederation of British North America's colonies. In 1867, Macdonald became Canada's first prime minister.

Under Macdonald, the Liberal-Conservative party strengthened Canada through territorial expansion and national economic development. The party's very name expressed Macdonald's commitment to compromise and moderation. The Liberal-Conservatives attracted French Roman Catholics, English Tories and Orangemen, and businessmen from all founding provinces.

In 1873, the Pacific Scandal brought down Macdonald's government. In 1878, the Liberal-Conservatives returned to power with their new National Policy, which emphasized economic protectionism, western expansion and centralized government. The policy attracted manufacturers in Central Canada and opponents of American border tariffs. Macdonald included strong pro-British themes. The party was re-elected in 1882, 1887 and 1891.

Macdonald's gift for compromise failed during the North-West Rebellion of 1885. The execution of Louis Riel and weak leadership in Quebec led to a decline in the party's influence in Quebec after 1882. The party's emphasis on centralized government also provoked provincial demands for decentralization, which the Liberals exploited.

In 1891, Macdonald died. The shortlived governments of his successors—prime ministers Abbott, Thompson, Bowell and Tupper—were overwhelmed by religious and language crises such as the Manitoba Schools Question (1896). In 1894, the party simplified its name to Conservative. The party lost power in 1896 and stayed in Opposition for 15 years.

In 1901, Robert Borden became Conservative leader. A Nova Scotian, Borden advocated civil service reform and public ownership. He experimented with a Quebec lieutenant. The Conservatives lost the elections of 1904 and 1908 but won in 1911 by promoting the National Policy and British imperial ties.

The Conservative victory in 1911 depended in part on the support of anti-Laurier *nationalistes* in Quebec. The *nationalistes* were promised a referendum on naval aid to Britain, but they bitterly withdrew their support as World War I loomed and Borden sided with the pro-British imperialists in his caucus. The war extended Borden's mandate, but in 1917 the Conservatives faced a difficult election.

In 1917, Borden allied with pro-conscription Liberals to sustain wartime conscription. They formed a Union Government, but the victory created lasting enmity among French Canadians and (German) immigrants. When the Liberals left the coalition, Conservative popularity dropped. Railway nationalization prompted the defection of Montreal's business elite—the party's greatest source of funds.

In 1920, Arthur Meighen became party leader and replaced Borden as prime minister. Meighen's wartime support of conscription cost him votes in Quebec; his support of the National Policy cost him votes in the West. The Conservatives placed third in the election of 1921.

In 1925, the Conservatives increased their share of seats in the House of Commons but failed to win a majority. In 1926, after a scandal forced Liberal Prime Minister King to resign, Meighen became prime minister for three months. The Conservatives then lost a motion in the House and the election of 1926.

In 1927, Richard Bennett assumed the party's leadership. The onset of the Great Depression in 1929 during a Liberal administration assured a Conservative majority in the election of 1930. But Bennett's prescriptions for economic recovery—protecting industry, creating relief camps for the unemployed and seeking imperial preference for Canadian goods—failed. In 1935, continued economic depression ensured a crushing electoral defeat.

The party spent the next 22 years in Opposition. In English Canada, the Conservatives faced competition from new parties: ▶

▶ Social Credit and the CCF. In French Canada, the Conservatives made no headway even though in 1938 they selected Robert Manion— an anti-conscription Roman Catholic—as leader. When World War II began, Manion's conciliation of Quebec angered his caucus. Funds dried up; the party atrophied.

In 1942, the Conservatives shifted leftward to capitalize on popular reform sentiment. They chose Manitoba Premier John Bracken, a Progressive with no Conservative experience, as leader. They changed the party's name to Progressive Conservative. But the Liberals and the CCF moved leftward too and, in 1944, the PCs supported conscription again. In the election of 1945, the PCs could not find candidates to run in most of Quebec; the party placed fourth on the Prairies.

The PCs were becoming an Ontario party. In 1948, they selected Ontario Premier George Drew as leader. Canadian voters saw Drew as Ontario's man and the PCs suffered electoral defeats in 1949 and 1953.

In 1956, the PCs chose John Diefenbaker of Saskatchewan as leader. "Dief the Chief" was a populist and a fiery speaker. He excited Canadians who were tiring of 20 years of Liberal government. In the election of 1957, the PCs formed a minority government; in 1958, the PCs stunned Canada by winning 208 of 265 seats (including 50 in Quebec). For the first time since 1911, the party enjoyed support from coast to coast.

Diefenbaker passed the Bill of Rights and extended voting rights to aboriginal peoples. But Diefenbaker's populism cost him business support, and his failure to recognize Canada's biculturalism cost him votes in Quebec. In the election of 1962, the PCs formed a minority government; in the election of 1963, they lost to the Liberals. In 1967, Nova Scotia's Robert Stanfield replaced Diefenbaker as leader.

Diefenbaker had revived PC fortunes across Canada and won lasting support in Western Canada. But Diefenbaker's two successors failed to win majority governments in Ottawa. Stanfield failed to win in 1968, 1972 and 1974. In 1976, the PCs chose Alberta's Joe Clark as leader. In 1979, Clark exploited disaffection with Pierre Trudeau's Liberal regime to win a minority government. But the PCs soon lost a vote of confidence in the House and the election of 1980.

In 1983, the PCs selected Brian Mulroney, a bilingual Quebecer, as leader. Although Mulroney lacked parliamentary experience, he possessed executive skills and a shrewd knowledge of Quebec. He attracted *nationalistes* with promises of constitutional reform. In the election of 1984, the PCs won 211 of 282 seats—the biggest landslide in Canadian history.

Mulroney's first government promoted a pro-business agenda, privatized Crown corporations and negotiated the Free Trade Agreement (FTA) with the United States. Mulroney began talks to pass the Meech Lake Accord on constitutional reform. In 1988, voters excused several ministerial scandals and re-elected the PCs with a reduced majority.

Mulroney's second term was rocky. In the early 1990s, during an economic recession, the government passed the GST which increased daily living costs for all Canadians. In Ontario, people blamed the FTA for job losses. In 1990, the Meech Lake Accord collapsed; in 1992, voters rejected a second bundle of constitutional reforms—the Charlottetown Accord—in a referendum. Quebec's *nationalistes* withdrew their support. In the West, voters grew angry over delays in scrapping Trudeau's National Energy Program.

Facing angry voters in 1993, Mulroney resigned. The PCs chose Kim Campbell—a minister in Mulroney's cabinet—to lead them, but she couldn't distance herself from Mulroney's record. In 1993, the PCs suffered the worst federal electoral defeat in Canadian history. The party won two seats and lost official party status.

In 1993, Jean Charest became the PCs' first French-Canadian leader. In the election of 1997, the PCs won 20 seats and regained official party status. In 1998, Charest left the party for Quebec provincial politics; Clark returned to lead the federal PCs.

Charest and Clark faced a competitor for right-wing votes in the Reform party. Clark resisted efforts by Reform and its successor, the Canadian Alliance (CA), to unite with the PCs. However, Reform and the CA won more seats than the PCs in the elections of 1993, 1997 and 2000. In 2003, new PC leader Peter MacKay and CA leader Stephen Harper merged their parties. In 2004, the new Conservative party chose Harper as leader and won 99 seats in the election.

Lieutenant-Governors and Commissioners

(as of October 2004)

On the advice of the prime minister, the Governor General of Canada appoints 10 provincial lieutenant-governors and three territorial commissioners. Lieutenant-governors and commissioners represent the monarch and perform the same duties at the provincial and territorial levels that the Governor General performs at the federal level. They open, prorogue and dissolve legislatures and give royal assent to legislation and orders-in-council.

Lieutenant-governors and commissioners are paid by the federal government and usually serve terms of five years.

Province or Territory	Lieutenant-Governor/ Commissioner	Birthdate	Date Sworn in
Newfoundland and Labrador	Hon. Edward M. Roberts	Sept. 1, 1940	Nov. 1, 2002
Prince Edward Island	Hon. J. Léonce Bernard	May 23, 1943	May 28, 2001
Nova Scotia	Hon. Myra A. Freeman	May 17, 1949	May 17, 2000
New Brunswick	Hon. Herménégilde Chiasson	Apr. 7, 1946	Aug. 26, 2003
Quebec	Hon. Lise Thibault	Apr. 2, 1939	Jan. 30, 1997
Ontario	Hon. James K. Bartleman	Dec. 24, 1939	Mar. 7, 2002
Manitoba	Hon. John Harvard	June 4, 1938	June 30, 2004
Saskatchewan	Hon. Lynda M. Haverstock	Sept. 16, 1948	Feb. 21, 2000
Alberta	Hon. Lois Elsa Hole	1933	Feb. 10, 2000
British Columbia	Hon. Iona Campagnolo	Oct. 18, 1932	Sept. 25, 2001
Nunavut	Hon. Peter Irniq	1947	Apr. 1, 2000
Northwest Territories	Hon. Glenna F. Hansen	Aug. 10, 1956	Mar. 31, 2000
Yukon	Hon. Jack Cable	Aug. 17, 1934	Sept. 30, 2000

Provincial Premiers: An Historical Listing

(as of October 2004)

■ Newfoundland and Labrador

Premier	Term	Party	Elected or sworn in
Joseph R. Smallwood	1949–72	Liberal	Apr. 1, 1949
Frank D. Moores	1972–79	Conservative	Jan. 18, 1972
A. Brian Peckford	1979–89	Conservative	Mar. 26, 1979
Tom Rideout	1989	Conservative	Mar. 22, 1989
Clyde Wells	1989–96	Liberal	May 5, 1989
Brian Tobin	1996–2000	Liberal	Jan. 26, 1996
Beaton Tulk	2000–01	Liberal	Oct. 16, 2000
Roger Grimes	2001–03	Liberal	Feb. 13, 2001
Danny Williams	2003–	Conservative	Oct. 21, 2003

■ Prince Edward Island

Premier	Term	Party	Elected or sworn in
C. Pope	1873	Conservative	Apr., 1873
L. C. Owen	1873–76	Conservative	Sept., 1873
L. H. Davies	1876–79	Liberal (Coalition)	Aug.,1876
W. W. Sullivan	1879–89	Conservative	Apr. 25, 1879
N. McLeod	1889–91	Conservative	Nov., 1889
F. Peters	1891–97	Liberal	Apr. 27, 1891
A. B. Warburton	1897–98	Liberal	Oct., 1897
D. Farquharson	1898–1901	Liberal	Aug., 1898
A. Peters	1901–08	Liberal	Dec. 29, 1901
F. L. Haszard	1908–11	Liberal	Feb. 1, 1908
H. James Palmer	1911	Liberal	May 16, 1911
John A. Mathieson	1911–17	Conservative	Dec. 2, 1911
Aubin Arsenault	1917–19	Conservative	June, 21, 1917
J. H. Bell	1919–23	Liberal	Sept. 9, 1919
James D. Stewart	1923–27	Conservative	Sept. 5, 1923
Albert C. Saunders	1927–30	Liberal	Aug. 12, 1927
Walter M. Lea	1930–31	Liberal	May 20, 1930

▶

▶ James D. Stewart	1931–33	Conservative	Aug. 29, 1931
William J. P. MacMillan	1933–35	Conservative	Oct. 14, 1933
Walter M. Lea	1935–36	Liberal	Aug. 15, 1935
Thane A. Campbell	1936–43	Liberal	Jan. 14, 1936
J. Walter Jones	1943–53	Liberal	May 11, 1943
Alexander W. Matheson	1953–59	Liberal	May 25, 1953
Walter Shaw	1959–66	Prog. Conservative	Sept. 16, 1959
Alexander B. Campbell	1966–78	Liberal	July 28, 1966
William Bennett Campbell	1978–79	Liberal	Sept. 18, 1978
J. Angus MacLean	1979–81	Prog. Conservative	May 3, 1979
James M. Lee	1981–86	Prog. Conservative	Nov. 17, 1981
Joseph A. Ghiz	1986–93	Liberal	May 2, 1986
Catherine Callbeck	1993–96	Liberal	Jan. 25, 1993
Keith Milligan	1996	Liberal	Oct. 10, 1996
Patrick Binns	1996–	Prog. Conservative	Nov. 27, 1996

■ Nova Scotia

Premier	Term	Party	Elected or sworn in
H. Blanchard	1867	Conservative	July 4, 1867
William Annand	1867–75	Liberal	Nov. 7, 1867
P. C. Hill	1875–78	Liberal	May 11, 1875
S. H. Holmes	1878–82	Conservative	Oct. 22, 1878
John S. D. Thompson	1882	Conservative	May 25, 1882
W. T. Pipes	1882–84	Liberal	Aug. 3, 1882
W. S. Fielding	1884–96	Liberal	July 28, 1884
George H. Murray	1896–1923	Liberal	July 20, 1896
E. H. Armstrong	1923–25	Liberal	Jan. 24, 1923
E. N. Rhodes	1925–30	Conservative	July 16, 1925
Col. Gordon S. Harrington	1930–33	Conservative	Aug. 11, 1930
Angus L. Macdonald	1933–40	Liberal	Sept. 5, 1933
A. S. MacMillan	1940–45	Liberal	July 10, 1940
Angus L. Macdonald	1945–54	Liberal	Sept. 8, 1945
Harold Connolly	1954	Liberal	Apr. 13, 1954
Henry D. Hicks	1954–56	Liberal	Sept. 30, 1954
Robert L. Stanfield	1956–67	Prog. Conservative	Nov. 20, 1956
George Smith	1967–70	Prog. Conservative	Sept. 13, 1967
Gerald A. Regan	1970–78	Liberal	Oct. 28, 1970
John Buchanan	1978–90	Prog. Conservative	Oct. 5, 1978
Roger Bacon	1990–91	Prog. Conservative	Sept. 12, 1990
Donald Cameron	1991–93	Prog. Conservative	Feb. 9, 1991
John Savage	1993–97	Liberal	June 11, 1993
Russell MacLellan	1997–99	Liberal	July 18, 1997
John Hamm	1999–	Prog. Conservative	July 27, 1999

■ New Brunswick

Premier	Term	Party	Elected or sworn in
Andrew Wetmore	1867–70	Confederation Party	1867
G.E. King	1870–71	Conservative	1870
George Hatheway	1871–72	Conservative	1871
G.E. King	1872–78	Conservative	1872
James Fraser	1878–82	Conservative	1878
D. L. Hanington	1882–83	Conservative	1882
Andrew Blair	1883–96	Liberal	1883
James Mitchell	1896–97	Liberal	July, 1896
Henry Emmerson	1897–1900	Liberal	Oct. 29, 1897
L. J. Tweedie	1900–07	Liberal	Aug. 31, 1900
William Pugsley	1907	Liberal	Mar. 6, 1907
Clifford Robinson	1907–08	Liberal	May 31, 1907
John Douglas Hazen	1908–11	Conservative	Mar. 24, 1908
James K. Flemming	1911–14	Conservative	Oct. 16, 1911
George J. Clark	1914–17	Conservative	Dec. 17, 1914
James Murray	1917	Conservative	Feb. 1, 1917
Walter E. Foster	1917–23	Liberal	Apr. 4, 1917
Peter Veniot	1923–25	Liberal	Feb. 28, 1923
John B. M. Baxter	1925–31	Conservative	Sept. 14, 1925 ▶

▶ Charles D. Richards .... 1931–33 Conservative May 19, 1931
Leonard Tilley .... 1933–35 Conservative June 1, 1933
Allison Dysart .... 1935–40 Liberal July 16, 1935
John McNair .... 1940–52 Liberal Mar. 13, 1940
Hugh J. Flemming .... 1952–60 Prog. Conservative Oct. 8, 1952
Louis J. Robichaud .... 1960–70 Liberal July 12, 1960
Richard Hatfield .... 1970–87 Prog. Conservative Nov. 12, 1970
Frank McKenna .... 1987–97 Liberal Oct. 27, 1987
Ray Frenette (interim) .... 1997–98 Liberal Oct 14, 1997
Camille Thériault .... 1998–99 Liberal May 14, 1998
Bernard Lord .... 1999– Prog. Conservative June 21, 1999

■ Quebec

Premier	Term	Party	Elected or sworn in
Pierre-Joseph-Olivier Chauveau	1867–73	Conservative	July 15, 1867
Gédéon Ouimet	1873–74	Conservative	Feb. 26, 1873
Charles E. Boucher deBoucherville	1874–78	Conservative	Sept. 22, 1874
Henri Joly	1878–79	Liberal	Mar. 8, 1878
J. Adolphe Chapleau	1879–82	Conservative	Oct. 31, 1879
J. Alfred Mousseau	1882–84	Conservative	July 31, 1882
John J. Ross	1884–87	Conservative	Jan. 23, 1884
L. Olivier Taillon	1887	Conservative	Jan. 25, 1887
Honoré Mercier	1887–91	Liberal	Jan. 27, 1887
Charles E. Boucher deBoucherville	1891–92	Conservative	Dec. 21, 1891
L. Olivier Taillon	1892–96	Conservative	Dec. 16, 1892
Edmund J. Flynn	1896–97	Conservative	May 11, 1896
F. Gabriel Marchand	1897–1900	Liberal	May 24, 1897
S. Napoléon Parent	1900–05	Liberal	Oct. 3, 1900
Lomer Gouin	1905–20	Liberal	Mar. 23, 1905
L. Alexandre Taschereau	1920–36	Liberal	July 9, 1920
Adélard Godbout	1936	Liberal	June 11, 1936
Maurice Duplessis	1936–39	Union Nationale	Aug. 26, 1936
Adélard Godbout	1939–44	Liberal	Nov. 8, 1939
Maurice Duplessis	1944–59	Union Nationale	Aug. 30, 1944
Paul Sauvé	1959–60	Union Nationale	Sept. 11, 1959
Antonio Barrette	1960	Union Nationale	Jan. 8, 1960
Jean Lesage	1960–66	Liberal	July 5, 1960
Daniel Johnson	1966–68	Union Nationale	June 16, 1966
Jean-Jacques Bertrand	1968–70	Union Nationale	Oct. 2, 1968
Robert Bourassa	1970–76	Liberal	May 12, 1970
René Lévesque	1976–85	Parti Québécois	Nov. 25, 1976
Pierre-Marc Johnson	1985	Parti Québécois	Oct. 3, 1985
Robert Bourassa	1985–94	Liberal	Dec. 12, 1985
Daniel Johnson	1994–94	Liberal	Jan. 11, 1994
Jacques Parizeau	1994–96	Parti Québécois	Sept. 26, 1994
Lucien Bouchard	1996–2001	Parti Québécois	Jan. 29, 1996
Bernard Landry	2001–03	Parti Québécois	Mar. 8, 2001
Jean Charest	2003–	Liberal	Apr. 29, 2003

■ Ontario

Premier	Term	Party	Elected or sworn in
J.S. Macdonald	1867–71	Coalition	July 16, 1867
Edward Blake	1871–72	Liberal	Dec. 20, 1871
Oliver Mowat	1872–96	Liberal	Oct. 25, 1872
Arthur S. Hardy	1896–99	Liberal	July 25, 1896
George William Ross	1899–1905	Liberal	Oct. 21, 1899
Sir James P. Whitney	1905–14	Conservative	Feb. 8, 1905
Sir William Hearst	1914–19	Conservative	Oct. 2, 1914
Ernest C. Drury	1919–23	United Farmers of Ontario	Nov. 14, 1919
George Howard Ferguson	1923–30	Conservative	July 16, 1923
George Stewart Henry	1930–34	Conservative	Dec. 15, 1930
Mitchell F. Hepburn	1934–42	Liberal	July 10, 1934
Gordon Daniel Conant	1942–43	Liberal	Oct. 21, 1942
Harry C. Nixon	1943	Liberal	May 18, 1943
George Drew	1943–48	Prog. Conservative	Aug. 17, 1943
Thomas L. Kennedy	1948–49	Prog. Conservative	Oct. 19, 1948

▶

▶ Leslie M. Frost	1949–61	Prog. Conservative	May 4, 1949
John P. Robarts	1961–71	Prog. Conservative	Nov. 8, 1961
William G. Davis	1971–85	Prog. Conservative	Mar. 1, 1971
Frank Miller	1985	Prog. Conservative	Feb. 8, 1985
David Peterson	1985–90	Liberal	June 26, 1985
Bob Rae	1990–95	New Democratic	Oct. 1, 1990
Mike Harris	1995–2002	Prog. Conservative	June 28, 1995
Ernie Eves	2002–2003	Prog. Conservative	Apr. 15, 2002
Dalton McGuinty	2003–	Liberal	Oct. 2, 2003

■ Manitoba

Premier	Term	Party	Elected or sworn in
A. Boyd	1870–71	n.a.	Sept. 16, 1870
M. A. Girard	1871–72	Conservative	Dec. 14, 1871
H. H. Clarke	1872–74	n.a.	Mar. 14, 1872
M. A. Girard	1874	Conservative	July 8, 1874
R. A. Davis	1874–78	n.a.	Dec. 3, 1874
John Norquay	1878–87	Conservative	Oct. 16, 1878
D. H. Harrison	1887–88	Conservative	Dec. 26, 1887
T. Greenway	1888–1900	Liberal	Jan. 19, 1888
H. J. Macdonald	1900	Conservative	Jan. 8, 1900
Sir R. P. Roblin	1900–15	Conservative	Oct. 29, 1900
T. C. Norris	1915–22	Liberal	May 12, 1915
John Bracken	1922–43	Coalition[1]	Aug. 8, 1922
S. S. Garson	1943–48	Coalition	Jan. 8, 1943
D. L. Campbell	1948–58	Conservative	Nov. 11, 1948
Duff Roblin	1958–67	Prog. Conservative	June 16, 1958
Walter Weir	1967–69	Prog. Conservative	Nov. 25, 1967
Edward Schreyer	1969–77	New Democratic	July 15, 1969
Sterling Lyon	1977–81	Prog. Conservative	Nov. 24, 1977
Howard Pawley	1981–88	New Democratic	Nov. 30, 1981
Gary Filmon	1988–99	Prog. Conservative	Apr. 26, 1988
Gary Doer	1999–	New Democratic	Oct. 5, 1999

■ Saskatchewan

Premier	Term	Party	Elected or sworn in
Walter Scott	1905–16	Liberal	Sept. 5, 1905
W. M. Martin	1916–22	Liberal	Oct. 20, 1916
C. A. Dunning	1922–26	Liberal	Apr. 5, 1922
J. G. Gardiner	1926–29	Liberal	Feb. 26, 1926
J. T. M. Anderson	1929–34	Conservative	Sept. 9, 1929
J. G. Gardiner	1934–35	Liberal	July 19, 1934
W. J. Patterson	1935–44	Liberal	Nov. 1, 1935
Tommy Douglas	1944–61	C.C.F.[2]	July 10, 1944
W. S. Lloyd	1961–64	C.C.F.—N.D.P.	Nov. 7, 1961
W. Ross Thatcher	1964–71	Liberal	May 22, 1964
Allan E. Blakeney	1971–82	New Democratic	June 30, 1971
Grant Devine	1982–91	Prog. Conservative	May 8, 1982
Roy Romanow	1991–2001	New Democratic	Nov. 1, 1991
Lorne Calvert	2001–	New Democratic	Feb. 8, 2001

■ Alberta

Premier	Term	Party	Elected or sworn in
Alex Rutherford	1905–10	Liberal	Sept. 2, 1905
A. L. Sifton	1910–17	Liberal	May 26, 1910
Charles Stewart	1917–21	Liberal	Oct. 30, 1917
Herbert Greenfield	1921–25	United Farmers of Alberta	Aug. 13, 1921
John E. Brownlee	1925–34	United Farmers of Alberta	Nov. 23, 1925
Richard G. Reid	1934–35	United Farmers of Alberta	July 10, 1934
William Aberhart	1935–43	Social Credit	Sept. 3, 1935
E. C. Manning	1943–68	Social Credit	May 31, 1943
Harry Strom	1968–71	Social Credit	Dec. 12, 1968
Peter Lougheed	1971–85	Prog. Conservative	Sept. 10, 1971
Don Getty	1985–92	Prog. Conservative	Nov. 1, 1985
Ralph P. Klein	1992–	Prog. Conservative	Dec. 14, 1992

▶■ **British Columbia**

Premier	Term	Party	Elected or sworn in
J. F. McCreight	1871–72	n.a.	Nov. 13, 1871
Amor De Cosmos	1872–74	n.a.	Dec. 23, 1872
G. A. Walkem	1874–76	n.a.	Feb. 11, 1874
A. C. Elliott	1876–78	n.a.	Feb. 1, 1876
G. A. Walkem	1878–82	n.a.	June 25, 1878
Robert Beaven	1882–83	n.a.	June 13, 1882
William Smithe	1883–87	n.a.	Jan. 29, 1883
A. E. B. Davie	1887–89	n.a.	May 1, 1887
John Robson	1889–92	n.a.	Aug. 2, 1889
Theodore Davie	1892–95	n.a.	July 2, 1892
J. H. Turner	1895–98	n.a.	Mar. 4, 1895
C. A. Semlin	1898–1900	n.a.	Aug. 15, 1898
Joseph Martin	1900	n.a.	Feb. 28, 1900
James Dunsmuir	1900–02	n.a.	June 15, 1900
E. G. Prior	1902–03	n.a.	Nov. 21, 1902
Richard McBride	1903–15	Conservative	June 1, 1903
William J. Bowser	1915–16	Conservative	Dec. 15, 1915
Harlan C. Brewster	1916–18	Liberal	Nov. 23, 1916
John Oliver	1918–27	Liberal	Mar. 6, 1918
John D. MacLean	1927–28	Liberal	Aug. 20, 1927
Simon F. Tolmie	1928–33	Conservative	Aug. 21, 1928
T. D. Pattullo	1933–41	Liberal	Nov. 15, 1933
John Hart	1941–47	Liberal[3]	Dec. 9, 1941
Byron Johnson	1947–52	Liberal[3]	Dec. 29, 1947
W. A. C. Bennett	1952–72	Social Credit	Aug. 1, 1952
David Barrett	1972–75	New Democratic	Sept. 15, 1972
William R. Bennett	1975–86	Social Credit	Dec. 22, 1975
Bill Vander Zalm	1986–91	Social Credit	Aug. 6, 1986
Rita Johnston	1991–91	Social Credit	Apr. 2, 1991
Michael Harcourt	1991–96	New Democratic	Nov. 5, 1991
Glen Clark	1996–99	New Democratic	Feb. 22, 1996
Dan Miller	1999–2000	New Democratic	Aug. 25, 1999
Ujjal Dosanjh	2000–01	New Democratic	Feb. 24, 2000
Gordon Campbell	2001–	Liberal	June 5, 2001

■ **Nunavut**

Premier	Term	Party	Elected or sworn in
Paul Okalik	1999–	n.a.	Apr. 1, 1999

■ **Northwest Territories**

Premier	Term	Party	Elected or sworn in
George Braden	1980–83	n.a.	July 25, 1980
Richard Nerysoo	1984–85	n.a.	Jan. 12, 1984
Nick Sibbeston	1985–87	n.a.	Nov. 5, 1985
Dennis Patterson	1987–91	n.a.	Nov. 12, 1987
Nellie Cournoyea	1991–95	n.a.	Nov. 13, 1991
Don Morin	1995–98	n.a.	Nov. 20, 1995
James L. Antoine	1998–2000	n.a.	Dec. 10, 1998
Stephen Kakfwi	2000–03	n.a.	Jan. 19, 2000
Joseph Handley	2003–	n.a.	Dec. 10, 2003

■ **Yukon**

Premier	Term	Party	Elected or sworn in
Chris Pearson	1978–85	Prog. Conservative	
Willard Phelps	1985	Prog. Conservative	Mar. 20, 1985
Tony Penikett	1985–92[4]	New Democratic	May 29, 1985
John Ostashek	1992–96	Yukon Party	Nov. 7, 1992
Piers McDonald	1996–2000	New Democratic	Oct. 19, 1996
Pat Duncan	2000–02	Liberal	May 6, 2000
Dennis Fentie	2002–	Yukon Party	Nov. 30, 2002

Source: *Historical Statistics of Canada; Provincial Archives*

(1) United Farmer/Progressive, 1922–27; Coalition, 1927–37; Liberal—Progressive, 1937–43. (2) Co-operative Commonwealth Federation. (3) Coalition. (4) From 1989–92, Government Leader was designated Premier. (n.a.) not available.

Cabinets of the Provinces and Territories

(as of October 2004)

■ Newfoundland and Labrador

Ministry or Portfolio	Minister
Premier; Intergovernmental Affairs; Business	Danny Williams
Education	John Ottenheimer
Environment and Conservation	Tom Osborne
Finance; Treasury Board	Loyola Sullivan
Fisheries and Aquaculture; Labrador Affairs	Trevor Taylor
Government Services	Dianne Whalen
Health and Community Services; Strategic Social Plan	Elizabeth Marshall
Human Resources, Labour and Employment; Housing; Status of Women	Joan Burke
Innovation, Trade and Rural Development	Kathy Dunderdale
Justice and Attorney General	Tom Marshall
Municipal and Provincial Affairs	Jack Byrne
Natural Resources; House Leader	Ed Byrne
Tourism, Culture and Recreation	Paul Shelley
Transportation and Works; Aboriginal Affairs	Tom Rideout

■ New Brunswick

Ministry or Portfolio	Minister
Premier; Communications New Brunswick; Regional Development Corp.; Status of Disabled Persons; Youth	Bernard Lord
Deputy Premier; Supply and Services	Dale Graham
Agriculture, Fisheries and Aquaculture	David Alward
Business New Brunswick	Peter Mesheau
Education	Madeleine Dubé
Energy; New Brunswick Power Corp.	Bruce Fitch
Environment and Local Government	Brenda Fowlie
Family and Community Services; Social Union Framework Agreement	Tony J. Huntjens
Finance; Lotteries; NB Investment Management Corp.	Jeannot Volpé
Health and Wellness	Elvy Robichaud
Human Resources	Rose-May Poirier
Intergovernmental and International Relations; Culture and Sport; Francophonie; Service New Brunswick	Percy Mockler
Justice and Attorney General; Aboriginal Affairs	Bradley Green
Natural Resources	Keith Ashfield
Public Safety	Wayne Steeves
Tourism and Parks	Joan MacAlpine
Training and Employment Development; Status of Women	Margaret-Ann Blaney
Transportation; Acadian Peninsula Fisheries	Paul Robichaud

■ Nova Scotia

Ministry or Portfolio	Minister
Premier; Intergovernmental Affairs	John F. Hamm
Deputy Premier; Transportation and Public Works	Ronald S. Russell
Aboriginal Affairs; Attorney General and Justice; Treasury	Michael G. Baker
Acadian Affairs; Agriculture and Fisheries	Chris A. d'Entremont
African Nova Scotian Affairs; Service Nova Scotia and Municipal Relations	Barry Barnet
Community Services; Disabled Persons	David M. Morse
Economic Development; Communications Nova Scotia; Emergency Measures	Ernest L. Fage
Education; Youth	Jamie Muir
Energy	Cecil P. Clarke
Environment and Labour	Kerry Morash
Finance	Peter G. Christie
Health; Senior Citizens	Angus MacIsaac
Health Promotion; Tourism, Culture and Heritage	Rodney J. MacDonald

►

▶ Human Resources; Public Services; Status of Women .... Carolyn Bolivar-Getson
Natural Resources .... Richard Hurlburt

■ Prince Edward Island

Ministry or Portfolio	Minister
Premier; Intergovernmental Affairs	Patrick G. Binns
Agriculture, Fisheries, Aquaculture and Forestry	Kevin MacAdam
Attorney General; Environment and Energy	James W. Ballem
Community and Cultural Affairs	Elmer MacFadyen
Development and Technology	Michael Currie
Education	Mildred Dover
Health and Social Services	Chester Gillan
Provincial Treasury	P. Mitchell Murphy
Tourism	Philip Brown
Transportation and Public Works	Gail Shea

■ Quebec

Ministry or Portfolio	Minister
Premier	Jean Charest
Deputy Premier; International Relations	Monique Gagnon-Tremblay
Agriculture, Fisheries and Food	Françoise Gauthier
Canadian Intergovernmental Affairs and Native Affairs	Benoît Pelletier
Culture and Communications	Line Beauchamp
Education	Pierre Reid
Employment, Social Solidarity and Family Welfare	Claude Béchard
Environment	Thomas J. Mulcair
Family Welfare	Carole Théberge
Finance	Yves Séguin
Forests, Wildlife and Parks	Pierre Corbeil
Government Administration and Treasury	Monique Jérôme-Forget
Health and Social Services	Philippe Couillard
Health, Social Services and Status of Seniors	Vacant
Justice and Attorney General; Reform of Democratic Institutions	Jacques Dupuis
Labour	Michel Després
Municipal Affairs, Sports and Recreation	Jean-Marc Fournier
Natural Resources, Wildlife and Parks	Sam Hamad
Public Security	Jacques Chagnon
Regional and Economic Development and Research	Michel Audet
Regional Development and Tourism	Nathalie Normandeau
Relations with the Citizens and Immigration	Michelle Courchesne
Revenue	Lawrence S. Bergman
Transport	Yvon Marcoux
The Transports	Julie Boulet

■ Ontario

Ministry or Portfolio	Minister
Premier; Intergovernmental Affairs	Dalton McGuinty
Agriculture and Food	Steve Peters
Attorney General; Democratic Renewal; Native Affairs	Michael Bryant
Children and Youth Services; Citizenship and Immigration	Marie Bountrogianni
Community and Social Services; Women's Issues	Sandra Pupatello
Community Safety and Correctional Services	Monte Kwinter
Consumer and Business Services	Jim Watson
Culture; Francophone Affairs	Madeleine Meilleur
Economic Development and Trade	Joe Cordiano
Education	Gerard Kennedy
Energy; Chair of Cabinet; Government House Leader	Dwight Duncan
Environment	Leona Dombrowsky
Finance	Greg Sorbara
Health and Long-Term Care	George Smitherman
Labour	Chris Bentley
Management Board of Cabinet	Gerry Phillips
Municipal Affairs and Housing; Seniors	John Gerretsen
Natural Resources	David Ramsay
Northern Development and Mines	Rick Bartolucci

▶

▶ Public Infrastructure Renewal .... David Caplan
Tourism and Recreation .... Jim Bradley
Training, Colleges and Universities .... Mary Anne Chambers
Transportation .... Harinder Takhar

■ Manitoba

Ministry or Portfolio	Minister
Premier; Federal-Provincial Relations	Gary Albert Doer
Deputy Premier; Agriculture, Food and Rural Initiatives; Cooperative Development; Intergovernmental Affairs and Trade; International Relations Coordination	Rosann Wowchuk
Aboriginal and Northern Affairs	Oscar Lathlin
Advanced Education and Training	Diane McGifford
Conservation	Stan Struthers
Culture, Heritage and Tourism; Sport; Voluntary Sector	Eric Robinson
Education, Citizenship and Youth	Peter Bjornson
Energy, Science and Technology; Gaming; Hydro	Tim Sale
Family Services and Housing; People with Disabilities	Christine Melnick
Finance; French Language Services; Civil Service	Gregory F. Selinger
Health	David Walter Chomiak
Healthy Living; Seniors; Healthy Child Manitoba	Jim Rondeau
Industry, Economic Development and Mines; Emergency Measures; Liquor Control; Lotteries	Scott Smith
Justice and Attorney General; Constitutional Affairs; Government House Leader	Gord Mackintosh
Labour and Immigration; Multiculturalism; Status of Women; Workers Compensation	Nancy Allan
Transportation and Government Services	Ron Lemieux
Water Stewardship	Steve Ashton

■ Saskatchewan

Ministry or Portfolio	Minister
Premier	Lorne Calvert
Deputy Premier; Rural Revitalization	Clay Serby
Aboriginal Affairs; Highways and Transportation; Saskatchewan Government Insurance; Saskatchewan Telecommunications; Saskatchewan Transportation Company	Maynard Sonntag
Agriculture and Food	Mark Wartman
Community Resources and Employment; Disability Issues; Gaming	Joanne Crofford
Corrections and Public Safety; Saskatchewan Water Corp.	Peter Prebble
Crown Management Board; Immigration; Public Service	Pat Atkinson
Culture, Youth and Recreation	Joan Beatty
Environment; Energy Conservation	David Forbes
Finance; Government House Leader; SaskEnergy Inc.	Harry Van Mulligen
Government Relations	Len Taylor
Health; Seniors	John Nilson
Industry and Resources; Investment Saskatchewan Inc.	Eric Cline
Justice and Attorney General; Saskatchewan Power Corp.	Frank Quennell
Labour; Status of Women; Saskatchewan Property Management Corp.	Deb Higgins
Learning; Information Technology	Andrew Thomson
Northern Affairs	Buckley Belanger

■ Alberta

Ministry or Portfolio	Minister
Premier	Ralph Klein
Aboriginal Affairs and Northern Development	Pearl Calahasen
Agriculture, Food and Rural Development	Shirley McClellan
Children's Services	Iris Evans
Community Development	Gene Zwozdesky
Economic Development	Mark Norris
Energy	Murray Smith
Environment	Lorne Taylor
Finance	Patricia Nelson
Gaming	Ron Stevens
Government Services	David Coutts
Health and Wellness	Gary Mar
Human Resources and Employment	Clint Dunford
Infrastructure	Ty Lund
Innovation and Science	Victor Doerksen

▶

▶ International and Intergovernmental Relations .... Halvar Jonson
Justice and Attorney General; Government House Leader .... David Hancock
Learning .... Lyle Oberg
Municipal Affairs .... Guy Boutilier
Revenue .... Greg Melchin
Seniors .... Stan Woloshyn
Solicitor General .... Heather Forsyth
Sustainable Resource Development .... Mike Cardinal
Transportation .... Ed Stelmach

■ British Columbia

Ministry or Portfolio*	Minister
Premier	Gordon Campbell
Deputy Premier; Advanced Education	Shirley Bond
Agriculture, Food and Fisheries	John van Dongen
Attorney General; Treaty Negotiations	Geoff Plant
Children and Family Development	Stan Hagen
Community, Aboriginal and Women's Services	Murray Coell
Education	Tom Christensen
Energy and Mines	Richard Neufeld
Finance	Gary Collins
Forests	Michael de Jong
Health Services	Colin Hansen
Human Resources	Susan Brice
Management Services	Joyce Murray
Provincial Revenue	Rick Thorpe
Public Safety and Solicitor General	Rich Coleman
Skills Development and Labour	Graham Bruce
Small Business and Economic Development	John Les
Sustainable Resource Management	George Abbott
Transportation	Kevin Falcon
Water, Land and Air Protection	Bill Barisoff
Min. of State for Early Childhood Development	Linda Reid
Min. of State for Forestry Operations	Roger Harris
Min. of State for Immigration and Multicultural Services	Patrick Wong
Min. of State for Intergovernmental Relations	Sindi Hawkins
Min. of State for Mental Health and Addiction Services	Brenda Locke
Min. of State for Mining	Pat Bell
Min. of State for Resort Development	Sandy Santori
Min. of State for Women's and Seniors' Services	Ida Chong

■ Yukon Territory

Ministry or Portfolio	Minister
Premier; Finance; Economic Development; Women; Devolution, Land Claims & Youth	Dennis Fentie
Community Services; Highways and Public Works; Housing; Liquor	Glenn Hart
Education; Public Service	John Edzerza
Energy, Mines and Resources; Yukon Development Corp.; Yukon Energy Corp.	Archie Lang
Environment	Jim Kenyon
Health and Social Services; Yukon Workers' Compensation, Health and Safety	Peter Jenkins
Tourism and Culture; Justice	Elaine Taylor

■ Northwest Territories

Ministry or Portfolio	Minister
Premier; Aboriginal Affairs; Intergovernmental Affairs; NWT Power Corp.	Joseph (Joe) Handley
Deputy Premier; Finance; Public Works and Services	Floyd Roland
Education, Culture and Employment; Justice; Status of Women; Government House Leader	Charles Dent
Health and Social Services; Persons with Disabilities; Seniors	Michael Miltenberger
Municipal and Community Affairs; Transportation; Youth	Michael McLeod
NWT Housing Corp.; Workers' Compensation	David Krutko
Resources, Wildlife and Economic Development	Brendan Bell

■ Nunavut

Ministry or Portfolio	Minister
Premier; Executive and Intergovernmental Affairs; Justice	Paul Okalik
Deputy Premier; Health and Social Services; Status of Women	Levinia Brown
Community and Government Services; Nunavut Housing Corp.	Peter Kilabuk
Culture, Language, Elders and Youth; Human Resources	Louis Tapardjuk
Economic Development and Transportation; Energy; Qulliq Energy Corp.	David Simailak
Education; Homelessness and Immigration; Nunavut Arctic College	Ed Picco
Environment; Workers' Compensation	Olayak Akesuk
Finance; Government House Leader	Leona Aglukkaq

* In B.C. ministers of state are indicated; other officials are ministers.

POLITICS AND ELECTIONS

Registered Federal Political Parties

(as of October 2004)

Federal political parties can only be registered at election time, when they qualify for registration by fielding at least 50 candidates by the nomination deadline in a forthcoming election. In between elections, parties can be founded and organized, and can apply for registration to the chief electoral officer.

Bloc Québécois
Party Leader: Gilles Duceppe
National HQ: Ste 307, 3750 Crémazie Blvd E
Montreal, QC H2A 1B6
Tel.: (514) 526-3000
Fax: (514) 526-2868
Website: http://www.blocquebecois.org
Registered: Sept. 11, 1993

Canadian Action Party
Party Leader: Connie Fogal
National HQ: Ste 302, 99 Atlantic Ave
Toronto, ON M6K 3J8
Tel.: (416) 535-4144
Fax: (416) 535-6325
Website: http://www.canadianactionparty.ca
Registered: May 13, 1997

Christian Heritage Party
Party Leader: Ronald O. Gray
National HQ: PO Box 4958, Station E
Ottawa, ON K1S 5J1
Tel.: 1 (888) 868-3247
Fax: (819) 281-7174
Web site: http://www.chp.ca
Registered: May 28, 2004

Communist Party of Canada
Party Leader: Miguel Figueroa
National HQ: 290A Danforth Ave
Toronto, ON M4K 1N6
Tel.: (416) 469-2446
Fax: (416) 469-4063
Website: http://www.communist-party.ca
Registered: Nov. 8, 2000

Conservative Party of Canada
Party Leader: Stephen Harper
National HQ: Ste 1720, 130 Albert St
Ottawa, ON K1P 5G4
Tel.: (613) 755-2000
Fax: (613) 755-2001
Web site: http://www.conservative.ca
Registered: Dec. 7, 2003

The Green Party of Canada
Party Leader: Jim Harris
National HQ: Ste 300, 396 Cooper St
Ottawa, ON K2P 2H7
Tel.: 1 (866) 868-3447
Fax: (613) 482-4632
Web site: http://greenparty.ca
Registered: Aug. 8, 1984

Liberal Party of Canada
Party Leader: Paul Martin
National HQ: Ste 400, 81 Metcalfe St
Ottawa, ON K1P 6M8
Tel.: (613) 237-0740
Fax: (613) 235-7208
Website: http://www.liberal.ca
Registered: Apr. 4, 1972

Libertarian Party of Canada
Party Leader: Jean-Serge Brisson
National HQ: 2052 Ste. Marie
Embrun, ON K0A 1W0
Tel.: (613) 443-5423
Fax: (613) 443-5423
Registered: June 2, 2004

Marijuana Party
Party Leader: Marc-Boris St-Maurice
National HQ: Ste 100, 74 Rachel St E
Montreal, QC H2W 1C6
Tel.: (514) 842-4900
Fax: (514) 845-0263
Website: http://www.marijuanaparty.com
Registered: Nov. 6, 2000

Marxist-Leninist Party of Canada
Party Leader: Sandra L. Smith
National HQ: 1867 Amherst St
Montreal, QC H2L 3L7
Tel.: 1 (800) 749-9553
Fax: (514) 522-5872
Website: http://www.cpcml.ca
Registered: Sept. 28, 1993

New Democratic Party
Party Leader: Jack Layton
National HQ: Ste 300, 279 Laurier Ave W
Ottawa, ON K1P 5J9
Tel.: (613) 236-3613
Fax: (613) 230-9950
Website: http://www.ndp.ca
Registered: June 7, 1971

Progressive Canadian Party
Party Leader: Ernie Schreiber
National HQ: 118 Inverkip Ave
Ottawa, ON K1T 4B9
Tel.: (613) 247-1438
Fax: (613) 247-3387
Web site: http://www.pcparty.org
Registered: May 29, 2004

Source: *Elections Canada*

Federal Election Results, 1867–2004

🍁 1867–1904

	1867	1872	1874	1878	1882	1887	1891	1896	1900	1904
Canada										
Conservative	101	103	73	137	139	123	123	89	80	75
Liberal	80	97	133	69	71	92	92	117	133	139
Other	—	—	—	—	—	—	—	7	—	—
Prince Edward Island[1]										
Conservative	—	—	—	5	4	—	2	3	2	3
Liberal	—	—	6	1	2	6	4	2	3	1
Nova Scotia										
Conservative	3	11	4	14	15	14	16	10	5	—
Liberal	16	10	17	7	6	7	5	10	15	18
New Brunswick										
Conservative	7	7	5	5	10	10	13	9	5	6
Liberal	8	9	11	11	6	6	3	5	9	7
Quebec										
Conservative	45	38	32	45	48	33	30	16	7	11
Liberal	20	27	33	20	17	32	35	49	58	54
Other	—	—	—	—	—	—	—	5	—	—
Ontario										
Conservative	46	38	24	59	54	52	48	44	55	48
Liberal	36	50	64	29	37	40	44	43	37	38
Other	—	—	—	—	—	—	—	5	—	—
Manitoba[2]										
Conservative	—	3	2	3	2	4	4	4	4	3
Liberal	—	1	2	1	3	1	1	2	3	7
Other	—	—	—	—	—	—	—	1	—	—
British Columbia[3]										
Conservative	—	6	6	6	6	6	6	2	2	—
Liberal	—	—	—	—	—	—	—	4	4	7
Yukon[4]										
Conservative									—	1
Northwest Territories[2]										
Conservative	—	—	—	—	—	4	4	1	—	3
Liberal	—	—	—	—	—	—	—	2	4	7
Other	—	—	—	—	—	—	—	1	—	—

🍁 1908–1940

	1908	1911	1917[7]	1921	1925	1926	1930	1935	1940
Canada									
Conservative	85	133	153	50	116	91	137	39	39
Liberal	133	86	82	117	101	116	88	171	178
Progressive	—	—	—	64	25	—	2	—	—
CCF	—	—	—	—	—	—	—	7	8
Social Credit	—	—	—	—	—	—	—	17	10
Other	3	2	—	4	3	38	18	11	10
Prince Edward Island									
Conservative	1	2	2	—	2	1	3	—	—
Liberal	3	2	2	4	2	3	1	4	4
Nova Scotia									
Conservative	6	9	12	—	11	12	10	—	1
Liberal	12	9	4	16	3	2	4	12	10
CCF	—	—	—	—	—	—	—	—	1

▶

(1) Entered Confederation July 1, 1873. (2) Entered Confederation July 15, 1870. (3) Entered Confederation July 20, 1871. (4) Entered Confederation June 13, 1898. (5) Entered Confederation Mar. 31, 1949. (6) Entered Confederation Sept. 1, 1905. (7) For the 1917 election, Conservative refers to "Unionists," a coalition of Conservatives and pro-conscription Liberals; Liberals, for the 1917 election, are sometimes called "Laurier Liberals" because of their support for Laurier's anti-conscription stand. (8) The New Democratic Party (NDP) replaced the Co-operative Commonwealth Federation (CCF) in 1961. (9) In 1908–49, Yukon and NWT shared one representative. In 1953, the number was increased to two. (10) The Canadian Reform Conservative Alliance (or Canadian Alliance) replaced the Reform party in 2000. (11) Nunavut's first federal election occurred in 2000. (12) The Canadian Alliance and Progressive Conservative parties merged into the Conservative Party in 2003.

✦ 1908–1940	1908	1911	1917[7]	1921	1925	1926	1930	1935	1940
New Brunswick									
Conservative	2	5	7	5	10	7	10	1	5
Liberal	11	8	4	5	1	4	1	9	5
Other	—	—	—	1	—	—	—	—	—
Quebec									
Conservative	11	27	3	—	4	4	24	5	—
Liberal	53	37	62	65	60	60	40	55	61
Other	1	1	—	—	1	1	1	5	4
Ontario									
Conservative	48	72	74	37	68	53	59	25	25
Liberal	36	36	8	21	12	23	22	56	55
Progressive	—	—	—	24	2	4	—	—	—
Other	2	1	—	—	—	2	1	1	2
Manitoba									
Conservative	8	8	14	—	7	—	11	1	1
Liberal	2	2	1	2	1	4	1	12	14
CCF	—	—	—	—	—	—	—	2	1
Progressive	—	—	—	12	7	4	—	—	—
Other	—	—	—	1	2	9	5	2	1
Saskatchewan[6]									
Conservative	1	1	16	—	—	—	8	1	2
Liberal	9	9	—	1	15	16	11	16	12
CCF	—	—	—	—	—	—	—	2	5
Progressive	—	—	—	15	6	5	2	—	—
Social Credit	—	—	—	—	—	—	—	2	—
Other	—	—	—	—	—	—	—	—	2
Alberta[6]									
Conservative	3	1	11	—	3	1	4	1	—
Liberal	4	6	1	—	4	3	3	1	7
Progressive	—	—	—	10	9	—	—	—	—
Social Credit	—	—	—	—	—	—	—	15	10
United Farmers of Alta.	—	—	—	—	—	11	9	—	—
Other	—	—	—	2	—	1	—	—	—
British Columbia									
Conservative	5	7	13	7	10	12	7	5	4
Liberal	2	—	—	3	3	1	5	6	10
CCF	—	—	—	—	—	—	—	3	1
Progressive	—	—	—	2	1	—	—	—	—
Social Credit	—	—	—	—	—	—	—	—	—
Other	—	—	—	1	—	1	2	2	1
Yukon and Northwest Territories[9]									
Conservative	—	1	—	1	1	1	1	—	1
Liberal	1	—	—	—	—	—	—	—	—
Other	—	—	—	—	—	—	—	1	—

✦ 1945–1968	1945	1949	1953	1957	1958	1962	1963	1965	1968
Canada									
Conservative	67	41	51	112	208	116	95	97	72
Liberal	125	190	170	105	48	99	129	131	155
NDP (CCF)[8]	28	13	23	25	8	19	17	21	22
Social Credit	13	10	15	19	—	30	24	5	—
Other	12	8	6	4	1	1	—	11	15
Newfoundland[5]									
Conservative	—	2	—	2	2	1	—	—	6
Liberal	—	5	7	5	5	6	7	7	1
NDP (CCF)	—	—	—	—	—	—			
Prince Edward Island									
Conservative	1	1	1	4	4	4	2	4	4
Liberal	3	3	3	—	—	—	2	—	—

❀ 1945–1968

	1945	1949	1953	1957	1958	1962	1963	1965	1968
Nova Scotia									
Conservative	3	2	1	10	12	9	7	10	10
Liberal	8	10	10	2	—	2	5	2	1
NDP (CCF)	1	1	1	—	—	1			
New Brunswick									
Conservative	3	2	3	5	7	4	4	4	5
Liberal	7	7	7	5	3	6	6	6	5
Other	—	1	—	—	—	—	—	—	—
Quebec									
Conservative	1	2	4	9	50	14	8	8	4
Liberal	54	66	66	63	25	35	47	56	56
NDP (CCF)	—	—	—	—	—	—	—		
Social Credit	—	—	—	—	—	26	20		
Other	10	5	5	3	—	—	—	11	14
Ontario									
Conservative	48	25	33	61	67	35	27	25	17
Liberal	34	56	50	20	14	43	52	51	64
NDP (CCF)	—	—	—	3	3	6	6	9	6
Other	—	2	2	1	1	1	—	—	1
Manitoba									
Conservative	2	1	3	8	14	11	10	10	5
Liberal	10	12	8	1	—	1	2	1	5
NDP (CCF)	5	3	3	5	—	2	2	3	3
Saskatchewan									
Conservative	1	1	1	3	16	16	17	17	5
Liberal	2	14	5	4	—	1	—	—	2
NDP (CCF)	18	5	11	10	1	—	—	—	6
Alberta									
Conservative	2	2	2	3	17	15	14	15	15
Liberal	2	5	4	1	—	—	1	—	4
NDP (CCF)	—	—	—	—	—	—	—	—	—
Social Credit	13	10	11	13	—	2	2	2	—
British Columbia									
Conservative	5	3	3	7	18	6	4	3	—
Liberal	5	11	8	2	—	4	7	7	16
NDP (CCF)	4	3	7	7	4	10	9	9	7
Social Credit	—	—	4	6	—	2	2	3	
Other	2	1	—						
Yukon[9]									
Conservative	1	—	—	—	1	1	1	1	1
Liberal	—	1	2	1	—	—	—	—	—
NDP (CCF)	—	—	—	—	—	—	—	—	—
Northwest Territories[9]									
Conservative	n.a.	n.a.	n.a.	—	—	—	1	—	—
Liberal	n.a.	n.a.	n.a.	1	1	1	—	1	1
NDP (CCF)	n.a.	n.a.	n.a.	—	—	—	—	—	—

❀ 1972–2000

	1972	1974	1979	1980	1984	1988	1993	1997	2000
Canada									
Bloc Québécois	—	—	—	—	—	—	54	44	38
Conservative	107	95	136	103	211	169	2	20	12
Liberal	109	141	114	147	40	83	177	155	172
NDP	31	16	26	32	30	43	9	21	13
Reform/Canadian Alliance[10]	—	—	—	—	—	—	52	60	66
Social Credit	15	11	6	—	—	—	—	—	—
Other	2	1	—	—	1	—	1	1	—
Newfoundland									
Conservative	4	3	2	2	4	2	—	3	2
Liberal	3	4	4	5	3	5	7	4	5
NDP	—	—	1	—	—	—	—	—	—
Prince Edward Island									
Conservative	3	3	4	2	3	—	—	—	—
Liberal	1	1	—	2	1	4	4	4	4
NDP									—

▶ ❦ **1972–2000**	1972	1974	1979	1980	1984	1988	1993	1997	2000
Nova Scotia									
Conservative	10	8	8	6	9	5	—	5	4
Liberal	1	2	2	5	2	6	11	—	4
NDP	—	1	1	—	—	—	—	6	—
New Brunswick									
Conservative	5	3	4	3	9	5	1	5	3
Liberal	5	6	6	7	1	5	9	3	6
NDP	—	—	—	—	—	—	—	2	1
Other	—	1	—	—	—	—	—	—	—
Quebec									
Bloc Québécois	—	—	—	—	—	—	54	44	38
Conservative	2	3	2	1	58	63	1	5	1
Liberal	56	60	67	74	17	12	19	26	36
NDP	—	—	—	—	—	—	—	—	—
Social Credit	15	11	6	—	—	—	—	—	—
Other	1	—	—	—	—	—	1	—	—
Ontario									
Conservative	40	25	57	38	67	46	—	1	—
Liberal	36	55	32	52	14	43	98	101	100
NDP	11	8	6	5	13	10	—	—	1
Reform/Canadian Alliance[10]	—	—	—	—	—	—	1	—	2
Other	1	—	—	—	1	—	—	1	—
Manitoba									
Conservative	8	9	7	5	9	7	—	1	1
Liberal	2	2	2	2	1	5	12	6	5
NDP	3	2	5	7	4	2	1	4	4
Reform/Canadian Alliance[10]	—	—	—	—	—	—	1	3	4
Saskatchewan									
Conservative	7	8	10	7	9	4	—	—	—
Liberal	1	3	—	—	—	—	5	1	2
NDP	5	2	4	7	5	10	5	5	2
Reform/Canadian Alliance[10]	—	—	—	—	—	—	4	8	10
Alberta									
Conservative	19	19	21	21	21	25	—	—	1
Liberal	—	—	—	—	—	—	4	2	2
NDP	—	—	—	—	—	1	—	—	—
Reform/Canadian Alliance[10]	—	—	—	—	—	—	22	24	23
British Columbia									
Conservative	8	13	19	16	19	12	—	—	—
Liberal	4	8	1	—	1	1	6	6	5
NDP	11	2	8	12	8	19	2	3	2
Reform/Canadian Alliance[10]	—	—	—	—	—	—	24	25	27
Yukon									
Conservative	1	1	1	1	1	—	—	—	—
Liberal	—	—	—	—	—	—	—	—	1
NDP	—	—	—	—	—	1	1	1	—
Northwest Territories									
Conservative	—	—	1	1	2	—	—	—	—
Liberal	—	—	—	—	—	2	2	2	1
NDP	1	1	1	1	—	—	—	—°	—
Nunavut[11]									
Conservative									—
Liberal									1
NDP									

Historic Firsts of the Canadian Election of 2004

*S*everal "firsts" occurred during the election on June 28, 2004. In B.C., voters elected the first husband-and-wife team to the House of Commons: in Fleetwood–Port Kells, voters elected Nina Grewal, and in Newton–North Delta, voters re-elected her husband, Gurmant Singh Grewal. In Manitoba, voters elected the first quadriplegic man—Steven Fletcher—in Charleswood–St. James. In Ontario, voters elected the first Muslim woman—Yasmin Ratansi—in Don Valley East. Ontario voters also elected the first Sikh woman—Ruby Dhalla—in Brampton–Springdale. In Quebec, voters elected the first African immigrant—Maka Kotto—in Saint-Lambert.

🍁 2004–   2004

Canada
Bloc Québécois 54
Conservative[12] 99
Liberal 135
NDP 19
Other 1

Newfoundland and Labrador
Conservative[12] 2
Liberal 5
NDP . . . . —

Prince Edward Island
Conservative[12] . . . . —
Liberal 4
NDP . . . . —

Nova Scotia
Conservative[12] 3
Liberal 6
NDP 2

New Brunswick
Conservative[12] 2
Liberal 7
NDP 1

Quebec
Bloc Québécois 54
Conservative[12] . . . . —
Liberal 21
NDP . . . . —

Ontario
Conservative[12] 24
Liberal 75
NDP 7

Manitoba
Conservative[12] 7
Liberal 3
NDP 4

Saskatchewan
Conservative[12] 13
Liberal 1
NDP . . . . —

Alberta
Conservative[12] 26
Liberal 2
NDP . . . . —

British Columbia
Conservative[12] 22
Liberal 8
NDP 5
Other 1

Yukon
Conservative[12] . . . . —
Liberal 1
NDP . . . . —

Northwest Territories
Conservative[12] . . . . —
Liberal 1
NDP . . . . —

Nunavut
Conservative[12] . . . . —
Liberal 1
NDP . . . . —

Minority Governments in Canada

■ The Fourteenth Parliament — First Minority Government (Liberal)
Prime Minister William Lyon Mackenzie King

Election Date	Duration of Parliament[1]	Government Seats	Opposition Seats	Total Seats
Dec. 6, 1921	1 329 days	116	119	235

■ The Fifteenth Parliament — Second Minority Government (Liberal)
Prime Minister William Lyon Mackenzie King

Election Date	Duration of Parliament[1]	Government Seats	Opposition Seats	Total Seats
Oct. 29, 1925	207 days	99[2]	146	245

■ The Twenty-Third Parliament — Third Minority Government (Progressive Conservative)
Prime Minister John George Diefenbaker

Election Date	Duration of Parliament[1]	Government Seats	Opposition Seats	Total Seats
June 10, 1957	177 days	112	153	265

■ The Twenty-Fifth Parliament — Fourth Minority Government (Progressive Conservative)
Prime Minister John George Diefenbaker

Election Date	Duration of Parliament[1]	Government Seats	Opposition Seats	Total Seats
June 18, 1962	203 days	116	149	265

■ The Twenty-Sixth Parliament — Fifth Minority Government (Liberal)
Prime Minister Lester Bowles Pearson

Election Date	Duration of Parliament[1]	Government Seats	Opposition Seats	Total Seats
Apr. 8, 1963	854 days	129	136	265

■ The Twenty-Seventh Parliament — Sixth Minority Government (Liberal)
Prime Minister Lester Bowles Pearson

Election Date	Duration of Parliament[1]	Government Seats	Opposition Seats	Total Seats
Nov. 8, 1965	866 days	131	134	265

■ The Twenty-Ninth Parliament — Seventh Minority Government (Liberal)
Prime Minister Pierre Elliott Trudeau

Election Date	Duration of Parliament[1]	Government Seats	Opposition Seats	Total Seats
Oct. 30, 1972	535 days	109	155	264

■ The Thirty-First Parliament — Eighth Minority Government (Progressive Conservative)
Prime Minister Charles Joseph (Joe) Clark

Election Date	Duration of Parliament[1]	Government Seats	Opposition Seats	Total Seats
May 22, 1979	186 days	136	146	282

■ The Thirty-Eighth Parliament — Ninth Minority Government (Liberal)
Prime Minister Paul Edgar Philippe Martin

Election Date	Duration of Parliament[1]	Government Seats	Opposition Seats	Total Seats
June 28, 2004		135	173	308

(1) The number of days between the return of the writs after an election and the dissolution of Parliament. (2) This figure is 101 if two Independent Liberals are included.

Source: *Library of Parliament, Information and Documentation Branch*

Federal Election 2000: Total Votes by Province and Party

	Bloc Québécois	Canadian Alliance	Liberal	New Democrat	Progressive Conservative	Other[1]
Newfoundland	—	8 837	103 103	29 993	79 157	8 408
Prince Edward Island	—	3 719	35 021	6 714	28 610	400
Nova Scotia	—	41 752	158 870	104 277	126 557	3 813
New Brunswick	—	60 277	159 803	44 778	116 980	1 174
Quebec	1 377 727	212 874	1 529 642	63 611	192 153	80 891
Ontario	—	1 051 209	2 292 075	368 709	642 438	98 174
Manitoba	—	148 293	158 713	101 741	70 635	8 450
Saskatchewan	—	207 004	89 697	113 626	20 855	2 515
Alberta	—	739 514	263 008	68 363	169 093	16 021
British Columbia	—	797 518	446 624	182 993	117 614	69 972
Yukon	—	3 659	4 293	4 223	991	53
Northwest Territories	—	2 273	5 855	3 430	1 282	—
Nunavut	—	—	5 327	1 410	633	349
Total votes cast	**1 377 727**	**3 276 929**	**5 252 031**	**1 093 868**	**1 566 998**	**290 220**

Source: *Elections Canada. (1) Includes Canadian Action, Communist, Green, Marijuana, Marxist-Leninist, Natural Law, and Independent*

Federal Election 2000: % of Popular Vote by Province and Party

	Bloc Québécois	Canadian Alliance	Liberal	New Democrat	Progressive Conservative	Other[1]
Newfoundland	—	3.9	44.9	13.1	34.5	3.7
Prince Edward Island	—	5.0	47.0	9.0	38.4	0.5
Nova Scotia	—	9.6	36.5	24.0	29.1	0.9
New Brunswick	—	15.7	41.7	11.7	30.5	0.3
Quebec	39.9	6.2	44.2	1.8	5.6	2.3
Ontario	—	23.6	51.5	8.3	14.4	2.2
Manitoba	—	30.4	32.5	20.9	14.5	1.7
Saskatchewan	—	47.7	20.7	26.2	4.8	0.6
Alberta	—	58.9	20.9	5.4	13.5	1.3
British Columbia	—	49.4	27.7	11.3	7.3	4.3
Yukon	—	27.7	32.5	31.9	7.5	0.4
Northwest Territories	—	17.7	45.6	26.7	10.0	—
Nunavut	—	—	69.0	18.3	8.2	4.5
Canada	**10.7**	**25.5**	**40.8**	**8.5**	**12.2**	**2.3**
Total seats	**38**	**66**	**172**	**13**	**12**	**0**

Source: *Elections Canada. (1) Includes Canadian Action, Communist, Green, Marijuana, Marxist-Leninist, Natural Law, and Independent*

Voter Turnout at Canada's Federal Elections, 1867–2000

(percentage of eligible voters casting votes)

	Voter turnout[1]		Voter turnout[1]		Voter turnout[1]		Voter turnout[1]		Voter turnout[1]
1867	73%	1900	79%	1930	76%	1958	81%	1979	76%
1872	70	1904	84	1935	75	1962	80	1980	69
1874	75	1908	79	1940	71	1963	80	1984	75
1878	71	1911	72	1945	76	1965	76	1988	76
1882	72	1917	90	1949	75	1968	76	1993	70
1887	70	1921	71	1953	68	1972	77	1997	67
1891	65	1925	69	1957	75	1974	71	2000	61
1896	61	1926	70						

Source: *Elections Canada*

[1]Percentage of actual votes to eligible voters. In many early general elections, several electoral districts were won by acclamation; hence, no eligible voters nor actual votes were recorded. Furthermore, in some of the more remote districts, votes were cast but no voters' lists had been prepared.

Federal Political Party Leaders

■ Conservative Party

Leader	Term
Liberal Conservative	
Sir John Alexander Macdonald	July 1, 1867–June 6, 1891
Sir John Joseph Caldwell Abbott	June 16, 1891–Nov. 24, 1892
Sir John Sparrow David Thompson	Dec. 5, 1892–Dec. 12, 1894
Conservative	
Sir Mackenzie Bowell	Dec. 21, 1894–Apr. 27, 1896
Sir Charles Tupper	May 1, 1896–Feb. 5, 1901
Sir Robert Laird Borden	Feb. 6, 1901–July 9, 1920
Arthur Meighen	July 10, 1920–Sept. 24, 1926
Hugh Guthrie	Oct. 11, 1926–Oct. 11, 1927
Richard Bedford Bennett	Oct. 12, 1927–July 6, 1938
Robert James Manion	July 7, 1938–May 13, 1940
Richard Burpee Hanson[1]	May 14, 1940–Nov. 11, 1941
Arthur Meighen	Nov. 12, 1941–Dec. 9, 1942
Progressive Conservative	
John Bracken	Dec. 11, 1942–July 20, 1948
George Alexander Drew	Oct. 2, 1948–Nov. 29, 1956
John George Diefenbaker	Dec. 14, 1956–Sept. 8, 1967
Robert Lorne Stanfield	Sept. 9, 1967–Feb. 21, 1976
Charles Joseph (Joe) Clark	Feb. 22, 1976–Feb. 18, 1983
Charles Joseph (Joe) Clark[1]	Feb. 19, 1983–June 10, 1983
Martin Brian Mulroney	June 11, 1983–June 12, 1993
Avril Phaedra (Kim) Campbell	June 13, 1993–Dec. 13, 1993
Jean J. Charest	Dec. 14, 1993–Apr. 2, 1998
Elsie Eleanore Wayne[1]	Apr. 2, 1998–Nov. 13, 1998
Charles Joseph (Joe) Clark	Nov. 14, 1998–May 30, 2003
Peter Gordon MacKay	May 31, 2003–Feb. 1, 2004
Conservative[2]	
John Lynch-Staunton[1]	Dec. 8, 2003–Mar. 19, 2004
Stephen Joseph Harper	Mar. 20, 2004–

■ Reform/Canadian Alliance[3]

Leader	Term
Reform	
Ernest Preston Manning	Nov. 1, 1987–Mar. 26, 2000
Canadian Alliance	
Deborah C. Grey[1]	Mar. 27, 2000–July 7, 2000
Stockwell Burt Day	July 8, 2000–Dec. 11, 2001
Stephen Joseph Harper	Mar. 20, 2002–Jan. 21, 2004

■ Liberal Party

Leader	Term
Alexander Mackenzie	Mar. 6, 1873–Apr. 27, 1880
Edward Blake	May 4, 1880–June 2, 1887
Sir Wilfrid Laurier	June 23, 1887–Feb. 17, 1919
Daniel Duncan McKenzie[1]	Feb. 17, 1919–Aug. 7, 1919
William Lyon Mackenzie King	Aug. 7, 1919–Aug. 6, 1948
Louis Stephen St-Laurent	Aug. 7, 1948–Jan. 15, 1958
Lester Bowles Pearson	Jan. 16, 1958–Apr. 5, 1968
Pierre Elliott Trudeau	Apr. 6, 1968–June 15, 1984
John Napier Turner	June 16, 1984–June 22, 1990
Jean Joseph Jacques Chrétien	June 23, 1990–Nov. 13, 2003
Paul Edgar Philippe Martin	Nov. 14, 2003–

■ New Democratic Party[4]

Leader	Term
Co-operative Commonwealth Federation	
James Shaver Woodsworth[1]	Aug. 1, 1932–1933
James Shaver Woodsworth	1933–Mar. 21, 1942
Major James William Coldwell	July 1942–Aug. 10, 1960
Hazen Robert Argue	Aug. 11, 1960–Aug. 2, 1961
New Democrat	
Thomas Clement (Tommy) Douglas	Aug. 3, 1961–Apr. 23, 1971
David Lewis	Apr. 24, 1971–July 6, 1975
John Edward Broadbent	July 7, 1975–Dec. 4, 1989
Audrey Marlene McLaughlin	Dec. 4, 1989–Oct. 13, 1995
Alexa McDonough	Oct. 14, 1995–Jan. 24, 2003
Jack Layton	Jan. 25, 2003–

■ Bloc Québécois

Leader	Term
Lucien Bouchard	July 25, 1990–Jan. 15, 1996
Gilles Duceppe[1]	Jan. 15, 1996–Feb. 16, 1996
Michel Gauthier	Feb. 17, 1996–Mar. 14, 1997
Gilles Duceppe	Mar. 15, 1997–

(1) The individual is an acting or interim leader who fills a temporary vacancy in the post before a party leadership convention.
(2) The Progressive Conservative Party and the Canadian Alliance merged to form the Conservative Party in December 2003.
(3) The Canadian Alliance (formally the Canadian Reform Conservative Alliance) succeeded the Reform party in 2000.
(4) The NDP succeeded the Co-operative Commonwealth Federation in 1961.

Provincial Election Results

■ Newfoundland and Labrador

	1972	1975	1979	1982	1985	1989	1993	1996	1999	2003
Liberal	9	16	19	8	15	31	35	37	32	12
Progressive Conservative	33	30	33	44	36	21	16	9	14	34
New Democratic	—	—	—	—	1	—	1	1	2	2
Other	—	5	—	—	—	—	—	1	—	—
Size of legislature	42	51	52	52	52	52	52	48	48	48

■ Prince Edward Island

	1974	1978	1979	1982	1985	1989	1993	1996	2000	2003
Liberal	26	17	11	14	21	30	31	8	1	4
Progressive Conservative	6	15	21	18	11	2	1	18	26	23
New Democratic	—	—	—	—	—	—	—	1	—	—
Size of legislature	32	32	32	32	32	32	32	27	27	27

■ Nova Scotia

	1970	1974	1978	1981	1984	1988	1993	1998	1999	2003
Liberal	23	31	17	13	6	21	40	19	11	12
New Democratic[1]	2	3	4	1	3	2	3	19	11	15
Progressive Conservative[2]	21	12	31	37	42	28	9	14	30	25
Other	—	—	—	1	1	1	—	—	—	—
Size of legislature	46	46	52	52	52	52	52	52	52	52

■ New Brunswick

	1967	1970	1974	1978	1982	1987	1991	1995	1999	2003
Liberal	32	26	25	28	18	58	46	48	10	26
Progressive Conservative[3]	26	32	33	30	39	—	3	6	44	28
New Democratic	—	—	—	—	1	—	1	1	1	1
Confederation of Regions	—	—	—	—	—	—	8	—	—	—
Size of legislature	58	58	58	58	58	58	58	55	55	55

■ Quebec

	1966	1970	1973	1976	1981	1985	1989	1994	1998	2003
Crédit Social	—	12	2	1	—	—	—	—	—	—
Equality	—	—	—	—	—	—	4	—	—	—
Liberal	50	72	102	26	42	99	92	47	48	76
Parti Québécois[4]	—	7	6	71	80	23	29	77	76	45
Union Nationale	56	17	—	11	—	—	—	—	—	—
Other	2	—	—	1	—	—	—	1	1	4
Size of legislature	108	108	110	110	122	122	125	125	125	125

■ Ontario

	1971	1975	1977	1981	1985	1987	1990	1995	1999	2003
Liberal	20	36	34	34	48	95	36	30	35	72
New Democratic[5]	19	38	33	21	25	19	74	17	9	7
Progressive Conservative[3]	78	51	58	70	52	16	20	82	59	24
Independent	—	—	—	—	—	—	—	1	—	—
Size of legislature	117	125	125	125	125	130	130	130	103	103

■ Manitoba

	1969	1973	1977	1981	1986	1988	1990	1995	1999	2003
Liberal	4	5	1	—	1	20	7	3	1	2
New Democratic[5]	28	31	23	34	30	12	20	23	32	35
Progressive Conservative[6]	22	21	33	23	26	25	30	31	24	20
Other	3	—	—	—	—	—	—	—	—	—
Size of legislature	57	57	57	57	57	57	57	57	57	57

■ Saskatchewan

	1967	1971	1975	1978	1982	1986	1991	1995	1999	2003
Liberal	35	15	15	—	—	1	1	11	4	—
New Democratic[7]	24	45	39	44	8	25	55	42	29	30
Progressive Conservative[8]	—	—	7	17	56	38	10	5	—	—
Saskatchewan Party	—	—	—	—	—	—	—	—	25	28
Size of legislature	59	60	61	61	64	64	66	58	58	58

■ Alberta

	1967	1971	1975	1979	1982	1986	1989	1993	1997	2001
Liberal	3	—	—	—	—	4	8	32[9]	18	7
New Democratic[1]	—	1	1	1	2	16	16	—	22	2
Progressive Conservative[6]	6	49	69	74	75	61	59	51	63	74
Social Credit	55	24	4	4	—	—	—	—	—	—
Other	1	1	1	—	2	2	—	—	—	—
Size of legislature	65	75	75	79	79	83	83	83	83	83

■ British Columbia

	1966	1969	1972	1975	1979	1983	1986	1991	1996	2001
Liberal	6	5	5	1	—	—	—	17	33	77
New Democratic[5]	16	12	38	18	26	21	22	51	39	2
Progressive Conservative[6]	—	—	2	1	—	—	—	—	—	—
Social Credit	33	38	10	35	31	35	47	7	—	—
Other	—	—	—	—	—	1	—	—	3	—
Size of legislature	55	55	55	55	57	57	69	75	75	79

■ Yukon

	1978	1982	1985	1989	1992	1996	2000	2002
Liberal	2	—	2	—	1	3	10	1
New Democratic	1	6	8	9	6	11	6	5
Progressive Conservative	11	10	6	7	—	—	—	—
Yukon Party	—	—	—	—	7	3	1	12
Independent	2	—	—	—	3	—	—	—
Size of legislature	16	16	16	16	17	17	17	18

(1) Known as the Co-operative Commonwealth Federation until 1962. (2) Known as the Conservative Party until 1946. (3) Known as the Conservative Party until 1943. (4) Formed in 1968. (5) Known as the Co-operative Commonwealth Federation until 1961. (6) Known as the Conservative Party until 1944. (7) Known as the Co-operative Commonwealth Federation until 1967. (8) Known as the Conservative Party until 1945. (9) One Alberta Liberal became an independent.

Provincial Party Leaders[1]

(as of October 2004)

■ Newfoundland and Labrador

Progressive Conservative Party	Liberal Party	New Democratic Party
Tom Rideout 1989–91	Stephen Neary 1984–85	Peter Fenwick 1981–89
Len Simms 1991–95	Leo Barry 1985–87	Cle Newhook 1989–92
Lynn Verge............. 1995–96	Clyde Wells 1987–96	Jack Harris 1992–
Loyola Sullivan.......... 1996–98	Brian Tobin............. 1996–2000	
Ed Byrne................ 1998–2001	Beaton Tulk 2000–01	
Danny Williams 2001–	Roger Grimes........... 2001–	

■ Prince Edward Island

Progressive Conservative Party	Liberal Party	New Democratic Party
James M. Lee 1981–87	Catherine Callbeck 1993-96	David Burke 1982–83
Leone Bagnall 1987–88	Keith Milligan 1996–99	Jim Mayne 1983–89
Melbourne Gass 1988–90	Wayne Carew 1999–2000	Larry Duchesne 1991–95
Pat Mella 1990–96	Ron MacKinley........... 2000–03	Herb Dickieson 1995–2002
Patrick Binns 1996–	Robert Ghiz............. 2003–	Gary Robichaud 2002–

■ Nova Scotia

Progressive Conservative Party[2]	Liberal Party	New Democratic Party[3]
George I. Smith 1967–71	Vincent J. MacLean 1986–92	Jeremy Akerman 1968–80
John M. Buchanan 1971–90	John Savage 1992–97	Alexa McDonough 1980–94
Donald Cameron 1991–93	Russell MacLellan 1997–2000	John Holme............. 1994–96
Terence R.B. Donahoe 1993–95	Wayne Gaudet 2000–02	Robert Chisholm 1996–2000
Dr. John Hamm 1995–	Danny Graham 2002–04	Helen MacDonald 2000–01
	Wayne Gaudet.......... 2004	Darrell Dexter........... 2001–

■ New Brunswick

Progressive Conservative Party	Liberal Party	New Democratic Party
Richard B. Hatfield 1969–87	Doug Young 1982–83	Elizabeth Weir 1988–
Malcolm MacLeod 1987–89	Frank McKenna 1985–97	
Barbara Baird Filliter....... 1989–91	Ray Frenette 1997–98	
Dennis Cochrane 1991–95	Camille Theriault 1998–2001	
Bernard Valcourt.......... 1995–97	Bernard Richard 2001–02	
Bernard Lord 1997–	Shawn Graham 2002–	

■ Quebec

Parti Québécois	Parti Libéral	Action démocratique
René Lévesque 1968–85	Robert Bourassa 1970–77	Mario Dumont 1994–
Pierre-Marc Johnson 1985–88	Claude Ryan 1978–82	
Jacques Parizeau 1988–96	Robert Bourassa 1983–94	
Lucien Bouchard 1996–2001	Daniel Johnson 1994–98	
Bernard Landry........... 2001–	Jean Charest............. 1998–	

■ Ontario

Progressive Conservative Party	Liberal Party	New Democratic Party[4]
Larry Grossman 1985–87	Stuart Smith 1977–81	Stephen H. Lewis 1970–78
Andrew Brandt 1987–90	David Peterson 1982–90	Michael Cassidy 1978–82
Mike Harris 1990–2002	Lyn McLeod 1992–96	Bob Rae 1982–96
Ernie Eves 2002–04	Dalton McGuinty 1996–	Howard Hampton 1996–
John Tory 2004–		

■ Manitoba

Progressive Conservative Party	Liberal Party	New Democratic Party [4]
Sidney Spivak 1971–75	Paul Edwards 1993–96	A. Russell Paulley 1960–69
Sterling Lyon 1975–83	Ginny Hasselfield 1996–98	Edward R. Schreyer 1969–79
Gary Filmon 1983–2000	Neil Gaudry 1998	Howard R. Pawley 1979–88
Bonnie Mitchelson 2000	Jon Gerrard 1998–	Gary Doer 1988–
Stuart Murray 2000–		

■ Saskatchewan

Saskatchewan Party	Liberal Party	New Democratic Party [4]
Ken Karwetz 1997–98	Ron Osika 1996	Tommy Douglas 1944–61
Elwin Hermanson 1998–2004	Jim Melenchuk 1996–2001	Woodrow Lloyd 1961–70
Brad Wall 2004–	David Karwacki 2001–	Allan Blakeney 1970–78
		Roy Romanow 1987–2001
		Lorne Calvert 2001–

■ Alberta

Progressive Conservative Party	Liberal Party	New Democratic Party [4]
Milt Harradance 1962–64	Betty Hewes 1994	W. Grant Notley 1968–84
Peter Lougheed 1965–85	Grant Mitchell 1994–98	Ray Martin 1984–94
Donald R. Getty 1985–92	Nancy MacBeth 1998–2001	Ross Harvey 1994–96
Ralph P. Klein 1992–	Ken Nicol 2001–04	Pam Barrett 1996–2000
	Kevin Taft 2004–	Raj Pannu 2000–

■ British Columbia

Reform Party of British Columbia	New Democratic Party	Liberal
Ron Gamble 1993–95	Michael Harcourt 1987–96	Jevington Blair Tothill 1979–81
Jack Weisgerber 1995–97	Glen Clark 1996–99	Shirley McLoughlin 1981–83
Wilf Hanni 1997-98	Dan Miller 1999–2000	Arthur Lee 1984–87
Bill Vander Zalm 1998–2001	Ujjal Dosanjh 2000–01	Gordon Wilson 1987–93
	Joy MacPhail 2001–03	Gordon Campbell 1993–
	Carole James 2003–	

■ Yukon

Progressive Conservative Party	Liberal Party	New Democratic Party
Willard Phelps 1985–91	Ron Veale 1980–85	Fred Berger 1978–81
Chris Young 1991	Roger Coles 1985–92	Tony Penikett 1981–95
	Paul Theriault 1992–95	Piers McDonald 1995–2000
Yukon Party	Ken Taylor 1995–98	Trevor Harding 2000
John Ostashek 1991–2000	Pat Duncan 1998–	Eric Fairclough 2001–02
Peter Jenkins 2000–02		Todd Hardy 2002–
Dennis Fentie 2002–		

(1) Includes 10 provinces and 1 territory (Yukon); excludes the Northwest Territories and Nunavut because they lack party systems.
(2) Known as the Conservative Party until 1946.
(3) Known as the Co-operative Commonwealth Federation until 1962.
(4) Known as the Co-operative Commonwealth Federation until 1961.

DEFENCE

The Canadian Armed Forces are prepared for a wide range of tasks both at home and abroad. These tasks include active combat, peacekeeping, mine clearance and the protection of displaced persons. During emergencies, the duties of the Canadian Armed Forces include civil defence, seach and rescue, and disaster relief. Forces personnel also watch and control Canada's territory, airspace and sealanes.

In addition, the Canadian Armed Forces aid Canada's federal civilian authorities in thwarting terrorism, illegal immigration and narcotics trafficking. Forces personnel provide security for major international events such as the G8 summit and provide transportation for visiting dignitaries.

Canadian Regular Armed Forces Strength

Canada has an all-volunteer Armed Forces which, since 1968, has been a single body composed of what had been a separate army, navy and air force.

	Navy	Army	Air Force	Total Armed Forces			Navy	Army	Air Force	Total Armed Forces
1914	379	3 000	—	3 379		1951	11 082	34 986	22 359	68 427
1915	1 255	81 195	—	82 450		1952	13 505	49 278	32 611	95 394
1916	1 557	274 194	—	275 751		1953	15 546	48 458	40 423	104 427
1917	2 220	304 585	—	306 805		1955	19 207	49 409	49 461	118 077
1918	4 792	326 258	—	331 050		1960	20 675	47 185	51 737	119 597
1919	5 495	228 292	—	233 787		1965	19 756	46 264	48 144	114 164
1920	1 048	4 684	—	5 732		1970	—	—	—	93 353
1925	496	3 410	384	4 290		1975	—	—	—	79 817
1930	783	3 510	844	5 137		1980	—	—	—	80 166
1935	860	3 509	794	5 163		1985	—	—	—	83 740
1939	1 585	4 169	2 191	7 945		1990	—	—	—	87 976
1940	6 135	76 678	9 483	92 296		1995	—	—	—	72 079
1941	17 036	194 774	48 743	260 553		1996	—	—	—	61 336
1942	32 067	311 118	111 223	454 408		1997	—	—	—	60 320
1943	56 259	460 387	176 307	692 953		1998	—	—	—	60 942
1944	81 582	495 804	210 089	787 475		1999	—	—	—	58 567
1945	92 529	494 258	174 254	761 041		2000	—	—	—	56 706
1950	9 259	20 652	17 274	47 185		2001	—	—	—	58 419
						2002	—	—	—	60 391
						2003	—	—	—	61 753

Source: *Department of National Defence*

Senior Canadian Military Personnel

(as of Oct. 1, 2004)

Commander in Chief	Gov. Gen. Adrienne Clarkson
Chief of the Defence Staff	Gen. Ray R. Henault
Vice-Chief of the Defence Staff	Lt.-Gen. George Macdonald
Deputy Chief of the Defence Staff	Vice-Admiral Greg R. Maddison
Chief of the Land Staff	Lt.-Gen. Rick Hillier
Chief of the Maritime Staff	Vice-Admiral Ron D. Buck
Chief of the Air Staff	Lt.-Gen. Ken Pennie
Assistant Deputy Minister (Human Resources—Military)	Lt.-Gen. Christian Couture
Chief of Reserves and Cadets	Rear Admiral Raymond A. Zuliani
Judge Advocate General	Maj.-Gen. Jerry S.T. Pitzul

Source: *Department of National Defence*

Canadian Military Ranks

Army/Air Force

General Officers: General, Lieutenant-General, Major-General, Brigadier-General
Senior Officers: Colonel, Lieutenant-Colonel, Major
Junior Officers: Captain, Lieutenant, Second Lieutenant, Officer Cadet
Non-commissioned Members: Chief Warrant Officer, Master Warrant Officer, Warrant Officer, Sergeant, Master Corporal, Corporal, Private

Navy

Flag Officers: Admiral, Vice-Admiral, Rear Admiral, Commodore
Senior Officers: Captain (N), Commander, Lieutenant-Commander
Junior Officers: Lieutenant (N), Sub-Lieutenant, Acting Sub-Lieutenant, Naval Cadet
Non-commissioned Members: Chief Petty Officer 1st class, Chief Petty Officer 2nd class, Petty Officer 1st class, Petty Officer 2nd class, Master Seaman, Leading Seaman, Able Seaman, Ordinary Seaman

Source: *Department of National Defence*

Canadian Forces Units in Canada

National Defence Headquarters in Ottawa oversees a network of military installations across Canada. These installations for regular forces are classified differently.

Canadian Forces Bases (CFBs) support either land, air or naval units. Canadian Forces Stations (CFSs) are smaller than bases. Stations have fewer resources and personnel; they are organized for operations and lack support capability.

Area Support Units (ASUs) provide food, fuel, maintenance and transportation for nearby operational units. A Canadian Forces Support Unit (CFSU) is similar to an ASU. Forward Operating Locations (FOLs) are unmanned airstrips stocked with aviation fuel for use in emergencies. All FOLs are in the Arctic. The Western Area Training Centre (WATC) is a land force base.

Source: *Department of National Defence*

Air Force Bases:
CFB Bagotville (Que.)
CFB Cold Lake (Alta)
CFB Comox (BC)
CFB Gander (Nfld)
CFB Goose Bay (Nfld)
CFB Greenwood (NS)
CFB Moose Jaw (Sask.)
CFB North Bay (Ont.)
CFB Shearwater (NS)
CFB Trenton (Ont.)
CFB Winnipeg (Man.)

Training Base:
CFB Borden (Ont.)

Headquarters:
National HQ Ottawa (Ont.)
CFSU Ottawa (Ont.)
CFNA Yellowknife (NWT)

Land Force Bases:
CFB/ASU Edmonton (Alta)
CFB/ASU Gagetown (NB)
CFB/ASU Kingston (Ont.)
CFB/ASU Petawawa (Ont.)
CFB/ASU Valcartier (Que.)
CFB Suffield (Alta)
WATC Wainwright (Alta)

Naval Bases:
CFB Esquimalt (BC)
CFB Halifax (NS)

Other Units and Locations:
ASU Montreal (Que.)
ASU Shilo (Man.)
ASU Toronto (Ont.)
CFS Alert (Nun.)
CFS Leitrim (Ont.)
CFS St. John's (Nfld)
FOL Inuvik (NWT)
FOL Iqaluit (Nun.)
FOL Rankin Inlet (Nun.)
FOL Yellowknife (NWT)

Source: *Department of National Defence*   Note: as of October 2004

Humanitarian Missions

	Aid was brought to		Aid was brought to		Aid was brought to
1947	Japan	1979	St. Vincent	1996	Haiti
1948	British Columbia	1983	Grenada	1996	Quebec
1960	Congo, Chile	1988–91	Ethiopia	1997	Manitoba
1965	Zambia	1989	Montserrat	1998	Quebec, Ontario,
1967	India	1989–91	Northern Ontario		Nova Scotia, Italy,
1970	Peru	1991	Iraq		Central America
1971	Pakistan	1992	Bahamas, Florida	1999	Turkey
1973	West Africa, Newfoundland	1992–93	Somalia, CIS	2001	Manitoba, Nova Scotia, Newfoundland
1973–79	Nicaragua	1992–96	Sarajevo		
1974–89	Manitoba	1993–95	Somalia	2002	Afghanistan
1974	Saskatchewan	1994, 1996	Rwanda	2003	British Columbia

Source: *Department of National Defence*

Canadian Participation in UN Peacekeeping and Other Military Missions, 1947–2003

Location	Year	Mission (Canadian participation)
Korea	1947–48	Supervising elections (2)
India, Pakistan	1949–96	Supervising a ceasefire between India and Pakistan (39)
Korea	1950–53	Supervising the Armistice Agreement (6 146)
Korea	1953–2000	Supervising the armistice between North and South (1)
Cambodia, Laos, Vietnam	1954–74	Supervising the withdrawal of French forces (133)
Egypt (Sinai)	1956–67	Supervising the withdrawal of French, British and Israeli forces (1 007)
Lebanon	1958	Preventing infiltration across Lebanese borders (77)
Congo	1960–64	Keeping law and order (421)
West New Guinea (now West Irian)	1962–63	Maintaining peace and security (13)
Yemen	1963–64	Observing the withdrawal of Egyptian troops (36)
Dominican Republic	1965–66	Observing the withdrawal of OAS troops (1)
India, Pakistan	1965–66	Supervising a border ceasefire (112)
Nigeria	1968–70	Observing a ceasefire (2)
Egypt (Sinai)	1973–79	Supervising the redeployment of Israeli and Egyptian forces (1 145)
South Vietnam	1973	Supervising a truce (248)
Southern Lebanon	1978	Confirming the withdrawal of Israeli forces (117)
Afghanistan	1988–90	Confirming the withdrawal of Soviet troops (5)
Iran, Iraq	1988–91	Supervising a ceasefire and the withdrawal of forces (525)
Namibia	1989–90	Aiding the transition to independence (301)
Central America	1989–92	Verifying compliance with the Esquipulas Agreement (174)
Haiti	1990–91	Observing the 1990 elections (11)
Afghanistan, Pakistan	1990–92	Providing military advice (1)
Persian Gulf	1990–91	Securing the liberation of Kuwait
Iraq, Kuwait	1991	Participating in a UN-led mission to oversee the withdrawal of armed forces from a demilitarized zone and enforcing UN restrictions on Iraq's trade at sea (300)
Iraq, Kuwait	1991–2001	Enforcing UN restrictions on Iraq's trade at sea (236); monitoring the Iraqi-Kuwaiti border (2)
Western Sahara	1991–94	Monitoring a ceasefire; supervising a referendum (34)
Angola	1991–93	Monitoring a ceasefire (15)
Former Yugoslavia	1991–94	Monitoring a ceasefire (15); reporting on breaches of the and neighbouring states Geneva Convention (7)
El Salvador	1991–94	Investigating human rights abuses; monitoring the progress of military reform (55)
El Salvador	1992–95	Investigating human rights abuses; developing a process for military reform and elections (55)
Red Sea	1992	Participating in a naval embargo of Iraq after the Gulf War (250)
Cambodia	1992–93	Monitoring a ceasefire; establishing landmine awareness; monitoring disarmament (240)
Former Yugoslavia	1992–95	Helping to ensure the demilitarization of UN-protected areas in Croatia; monitoring ceasefires in Croatia and Bosnia-Herzegovina; protecting the airport at Sarajevo; delivering aid to civilians and monitoring no-fly zones in Bosnia-Herzegovina (2 400)
Somalia	1992–93	Providing headquarters staff (12)
Somalia, Kenya	1992–93	Distributing relief supplies (1 250)
Somalia	1993–95	Providing relief and political reconciliation (9)
Cambodia	1993–2000	Operating a school for landmine removal (60+)
Haiti	1993–94	Enforcing an embargo (250)
Mozambique	1993–95	Providing security, removing landmines; verifying a ceasefire (4)

▶

▶ Rwanda, Uganda..................	1993–94	Monitoring the border to enforce a military embargo (3)
Rwanda........................	1993–96	Providing security for refugees; distributing relief supplies (112)
Former Yugoslavia	1993–95	Enforcing a no-fly zone (13)
Dominican Republic	1994	Monitoring the DR-Haitian border; providing technical advice to the UN for enforcing a Haitian trade embargo (15)
Haiti	1994–97	Providing security and stability for the training of Haiti's military and police and for elections (650)
Guatemala.....................	1996	Verifying a ceasefire agreement (15)
Croatia	1996–2001	Monitoring the demilitarized zone in Prevlaka (1)
Guatemala.....................	1997–98	Monitoring the Comprehensive Agreement on Human Rights (15)
Arabian Gulf	1998	Supporting a multinational naval blockade of Iraq
Central African Republic	1998–99	Providing security, police training, advice and technical support (55); aiding voting during presidential elections (32)
Central Europe	1998–99	Taking part in OSCE military inspections in Macedonia and Slovakia and military evaluations in Estonia and Moldova
Kosovo	1998–2000	Supporting CF-18 fighter jets based in Italy; helping enforce NATO's no-fly zone; preparing for the 79-day NATO air war over Serbia in 1999 (300+)
Kosovo, Macedonia .... (Former Yugoslav Republic)	1999–2000	Supporting NATO land forces; aiding refugees; rebuilding schools and hospitals
Kosovo	1999–2002	Participating in UN interim administration (1)
Mozambique...................	1999	Clearing landmines (3)
East Timor	1999–2001	Securing peace and order; supporting a UN mission (650)
Eritrea, Ethiopia................	2000–01	Preserving a ceasefire (472)
Eritrea, Ethiopia................	2001–03	Monitoring a ceasefire between two countries (6)
Albania	2000–01	Helping to rebuild a civilian airport in Tirana (5)
Macedonia (Former Yugoslav Republic)	2001	Collecting weapons from armed insurgents (200)
Afghanistan, Arabian Gulf	2001–03	Fighting terrorism through maritime and air patrols; providing humanitarian aid; fighting with US-led coalition soldiers against the Taliban and al-Qaeda
Senegal.......................	2003–04	Resolving a border dispute between Nigeria and Cameroon (1)
Democratic Republic of Congo	2003	Supporting a multinational force to restore order at Bunia (50)
Haiti	2004	Participating in a UN-led force to restore social order and provide civilian relief (500)

Source: *Department of National Defence*

Current Canadian Participation in UN Peacekeeping and Other Military Missions

Location	Year	Mission (Canadian participation)
Middle East.....................	1954–	Supervising a 1949 armistice between Israel and Egypt, Lebanon, Jordan and Syria (7)
Cyprus	1964–	Maintaining a ceasefire since 1974 (1)
Israel, Syria...................	1974–	Supervising a ceasefire at Golan Heights (192)
Egypt (Sinai)...................	1986–	Supervising the 1979 Camp David Accord (29)
Bosnia-Herzegovina	1995–	Enforcing the Dayton Peace Accords (1 699)
Democratic Republic of Congo	1999–	Investigating ceasefire violations (8)
Sierra Leone	2000–	Monitoring the disarming and demobilizing of combatants (5); reorganizing the government's military (11)
Afghanistan.....................	2003–	Supporting NATO's International Security Assistance Force (2 152)

Source: *Department of National Defence*

FOCUS ON . . .

Canada–US Defence

Canada and the United States occupy most of the North American continent. They share similar democratic, social and cultural values; they enjoy peaceful and friendly relations; they profit from extensive bilateral trade. Because both countries share so many vital interests, Canada and the US are partners in continental defence as well.

Close military cooperation began during World War II. In 1940, Prime Minister Mackenzie King and President Franklin Roosevelt signed the Ogdensburg Agreement. The leaders acknowledged the indivisibility of North American security and pledged to aid each other in wartime. In 1941, the two leaders signed the Hyde Park Agreement which united the two North American economies for the war effort. Successful military cooperation in World War II paved the way for defence cooperation in later decades.

Today, the Canada–US defence partnership is close, entrenched and complex. The two governments uphold more than 80 treaty-level defence agreements, and their defence departments observe more than 250 memoranda of understanding. These arrangements cover joint planning and operations, combined exercises, defence production, logistics, communications, research and development, and intelligence sharing. Canadian and US officials also discuss common defence in about 145 bilateral venues.

Four bilateral institutions are worth noting.

The Permanent Joint Board on Defence, which was formed in 1940, is the highest defence forum. The board's members—senior diplomats and military officers—discuss issues affecting "the defence of the northern half of the Western Hemisphere." The Canadian and US co-chairs report respectively to the prime minister and the US president. In past decades, the board has examined the construction of Distant Early Warning radar stations in the Arctic, the joint operation of underwater acoustic surveillance, and military cooperation in space.

The Military Cooperation Committee, which was formed in 1945, creates detailed defence plans for North America during peace and wartime. The committee is a direct link between the military staffs of Canada and the US. The committee maintains the Canada–US Basic Security Plan (which coordinates land, sea and air forces in wartime) and the Combined Defence Plan. Subcommittees are responsible for mapping, meteorology, oceanography, communications, and logistics planning.

The North American Aerospace Defence Command (NORAD), which was established in 1958, is based in Colorado. NORAD warns of missile or air attacks against Canada and the US; the joint command also defends North America from air attacks. The US commander and the Canadian deputy commander both report to their respective civilian leaders through their respective commands. The North American Aerospace Defence Agreement is renewable in 2006.

The Canada–United States Planning Group is located at NORAD headquarters. The group coordinates maritime and aerospace intelligence to prevent terrorist attacks in North America. The group also devises contingency plans and exercises to ensure coordinated responses to emergencies. The group's formation was announced in 2002.

Several types of defence agreement are worth noting.

Canada and the US uphold **defence sharing arrangements**. The Defence Production Sharing Arrangement (DPSA) of 1956 promotes greater standardization in the production of military equipment for the Canadian and US armed forces. The DPSA also allows Canadian defence contractors to compete equally with their counterparts in the US market. The Defence Development Sharing Arrangement of 1963 promotes the joint funding of military research and development.

Canada and the US exchange **memoranda of understanding (MOUs)**. The Mutual Support and Integrated Lines of Communications MOUs, for example, permit cooperation in military training and operations. They permit the delivery of supplies and services during "non-routine situations." Canada may use US aircraft or ships to bring Canadian soldiers home from overseas.

The Canada–United States Test and Evaluation Program (CANUSTEP) of 1983 grants Canadian and US forces access to each other's ranges for testing military hardware. Equipment that has been tested in Canada under CANUSTEP includes electronic warfare technology, weapons effects simulators, light armoured vehicles, anti-armour munitions, sonobuoys, and unarmed air-launched cruise missiles. CANUSTEP is renegotiated every 10 years.

The United States is Canada's most important ally. In the uncertain world of the 21st century, Canada–US defence cooperation will continue.

Source: *Department of National Defence*

THE ECONOMY

Appreciation: the increase in the value of a currency relative to other currencies under free market conditions.

Balance of payments: a measure of all yearly business transactions between one country and the rest of the world, i.e., the difference between the value of exports and imports, plus the difference between investment money coming in and leaving.

Balanced budget: when a government's budget is balanced, revenues equal expenditures in a budget year. There is no surplus or deficit, but a national debt may still exist.

Bank of Canada: the sole money-issuing bank in Canada, acting as banker to all other financial institutions and the government. It is responsible for Canada's banking system, sets interest rates and regulates the money supply.

Bank rate: the interest rate at which the Bank of Canada lends money to the chartered banks.

Cartel: a group of companies in a specific industry that band together to restrict output and increase prices to get higher profits. In Canada, cartels are illegal.

Constant dollars: dollars expressed in relation to a specified base year in order to adjust for the effects of inflation (changes in purchasing power). Costs or income expressed in constant dollars compared over a range of time give a truer picture of price changes. Also called "real dollars."

Consumer price index: an indexed measure of the average prices of certain specified household goods to show inflationary trends; compiled monthly by Statistics Canada.

Cost of living: the cost of maintaining a particular standard of living measured in terms of purchased goods and services. The rise in the cost of living is the same as the rate of inflation.

Current dollars: cost of an asset or service expressed at the price in effect when it was acquired, i.e. prices are not adjusted for inflation.

Deficit spending: the practice whereby a government goes into debt to finance some expenditures.

Deflation: a decline in price levels, often caused by a reduction in the supply of money or credit.

Depreciation: the decrease in the value of a currency relative to other currencies under free market conditions. This differs from devaluation.

Depression: a long period of little business activity when prices are low, unemployment is high, and purchasing power decreases sharply.

Devaluation: the official lowering of the value of a nation's currency relative to foreign currencies.

Disposable income: income after taxes available to persons for spending and saving.

Equalization payments: transfers of tax revenues from the Canadian government to provinces with a high proportion of lower-income earners as compensation for their lower per capita tax revenues.

Exchange rate: the price of one country's currency relative to another country's currency.

Fiscal policy: the use of government budget measures (taxation and/or spending) to alleviate economic problems such as low GNP, high unemployment or inflation.

Free trade: the free movement of goods and services, investment money and workers between countries is neither restricted nor encouraged by governments.

Gross domestic product (GDP): the value of all goods and services produced in a country.

Gross national product (GNP): the value of all goods and services produced by citizens of a country both inside and outside the country.

Inflation: a steady rise in the average level of prices in an economy.

Less developed countries (LDCs): also known as Third World countries, these are countries considered economically underdeveloped relative to the western industrialized nations.

Monetary policy: the government's manipulation of interest rates and the money supply to achieve economic growth, employment and price stability.

Money supply: the amount of money in an economy, with money defined as all currency in circulation and in chequing accounts.

National debt: the debt of the central government; in Canada's case, the federal government.

Per capita GNP: also known as per capita income, a nation's gross national product divided by its population.

Prime interest rate: the rate charged by chartered banks on short-term loans to large commercial customers with the best credit ratings. ▶

▶ **Protectionism:** government policies to protect domestic industries by restricting imports. Policies include customs duties (tariffs) and restrictions on the quantity of imports (quotas).

Real GNP: GNP adjusted for inflation.

Recession: not as severe or long-lasting as a depression but with the same general characteristics: a decline in real GNP for two consecutive quarters, with unemployment and widespread softening in many sectors of the economy.

Stagflation: a high inflation rate combined with a high unemployment rate.

Supply-side economics: a belief that an economy can prosper through policies affecting costs of

production—i.e., production incentives to labour and greater financial rewards to investors.

Trade balance: the difference between the value of exports and imports.

Transfer payments: government payments to the provinces where no productive return is provided, such as pensions, EI and welfare.

Wage-price controls: wage, salary and price increases are set by government legislation to curb inflation.

Wage-price spiral: increased wages increase costs to the producers, who in turn increase prices. The increase in prices causes a demand for higher wages, resulting in spiralling inflation.

ECONOMIC INDICATORS

Canadian Gross Domestic Product

(millions of dollars)

Gross domestic product is the unduplicated value of production originating within Canada, regardless of the ownership of the factors of production.

There are three ways to measure the GDP. *Income Based Approach*: adding up all incomes earned in current production; *Expenditure Based Approach*: adding up all sales of current production to final users; or *Value Added Approach*: summing the difference between an industry's total revenue and the costs of materials and services purchased by that company.

In addition, there are two ways to express GDP: at Market Prices or at Factor Cost. At *Market Prices*: GDP is expressed in terms of the prices actually paid by the purchaser of the product or service—including indirect

taxes, but excluding subsidies. GDP at *Factor Cost* reflects the costs of the factors of production—expressed in terms of the expenses of the producer rather than the purchase price—again, including subsidies but not indirect taxes.

The costs themselves are then expressed either in Current Dollars—the prices in effect at the time that the data is for, or in Constant Dollars—also known as "real dollars." These are dollar figures adjusted for inflation growth in the economy. Constant Dollars allow us to compare data from different time periods (trends). The table below shows expenditure-based real GDP at market prices.

Expenditure-based GDP at Market Prices[1]

(millions of dollars)

Expenditure-based estimates	1993	1997	2001	2002	2003
Gross Domestic Product (GDP) at market prices...	772 498	882 734	1 036 017	1 071 815	1 096 437
Personal expenditure on consumer goods & services.	452 701	510 695	583 452	603 914	623 149
Government current expenditure on goods & services	178 686	171 756	193 660	199 071	206 722
Government gross fixed capital formation	20 355	20 104	27 208	29 486	32 064
Government investment in inventories	-3	5	13	-40	
Business gross fixed capital formation	115 277	154 737	184 900	187 581	196 956
Residential structures	41 278	43 519	50 666	57 926	62 283
Non-residential structures and equipment ..	74 150	111 218	134 234	129 655	134 673
Non-residential structures.............	33 436	43 872	48 607	44 575	45 032
Machinery and equipment.............	41 119	67 346	85 627	85 080	89 641
Business investment in inventories..........	-1 315	8 176	-7 240	-706	8 264
Business investment in non-farm inventories	-2 640	9 174	-5 652	837	5 493
Business investment in farm inventories....	1 413	-998	-1 588	-1 543	2 771
Exports of goods and services	244 260	348 604	443 409	447 847	440 209
Exports of goods......................	211 627	303 379	384 999	387 210	381 813
Exports of services	32 614	45 225	58 410	60 637	58 396
Deduct: imports of goods and services.......	236 738	331 271	388 696	394 477	410 320
Imports of goods	188 404	277 727	330 755	335 769	348 271
Imports of services	49 820	53 544	57 941	58 708	62 049
Statistical discrepancy.................	-2 015	-72	-689	-861	-621
Final domestic demand..................	767 177	857 292	989 220	1 020 052	1 058 891

Source: *Statistics Canada*

(1) Constant (1997) dollars.

Canadian Consumer Price Index by Year

(1992 = 100)

1915	7.3	1962	18.9	1977	40.0	1992	100.0
1920	13.5	1963	19.2	1978	43.6	1993	101.8
1925	10.9	1964	19.6	1979	47.6	1994	102.0
1930	10.9	1965	20.0	1980	52.4	1995	104.2
1935	8.6	1966	20.8	1981	58.9	1996	105.8
1940	9.5	1967	21.5	1982	65.3	1997	107.6
1945	10.8	1968	22.4	1983	69.1	1998	108.6
1950	14.9	1969	23.4	1984	72.1	1999	110.5
1955	16.8	1970	24.2	1985	75.0	2000	113.5
1956	17.1	1971	24.9	1986	78.1	2001	116.4
1957	17.6	1972	26.1	1987	81.5	2002	119.0
1958	18.0	1973	28.1	1988	84.8	2003	122.3
1959	18.2	1974	31.1	1989	89.0	2004[1]	123.5
1960	18.5	1975	34.5	1990	93.3		
1961	18.7	1976	37.1	1991	98.5		

Source: © *Statistics Canada*   (1) Year to date average as of July 2004.

Canadian Consumer Price Index by Item

(1992 = 100)

This table shows the relative costs, as far back as 1950, of categories of purchases made by Canadian consumers. To compare 2004 costs with those of another year, divide the 2004 index by the index for the year you wish to compare it with; then multiply that by your actual cost in the year for which you are making the comparison.

Example: you spent $65 per week on family food purchases in 1985. To calculate what that would be in today's dollars, divide the 2004 food index (124.2) by the 1985 food index (78.8). Now multiply the result by $65. The answer, $101.13, is what you now must spend to buy the same package of groceries that cost $65 in 1985.

	Food	Shelter	Household Oper. & Furn.	Clothing and Footwear	Gasoline	Health and Personal Care	Recreation and Education	Tobacco and Alcohol
1950	14.2	n.a.	n.a.	23.4	15.9	12.0	15.7	11.3
1955	15.5	n.a.	n.a.	25.3	16.2	14.9	18.9	11.8
1960	16.9	n.a.	n.a.	26.0	15.7	18.2	22.3	12.7
1965	18.8	n.a.	n.a.	28.5	16.5	20.6	23.8	13.4
1970	22.3	n.a.	n.a.	33.5	19.2	25.5	29.6	16.2
1975	36.4	n.a.	n.a.	42.5	28.2	34.6	39.3	20.6
1980	58.6	50.2	60.3	60.7	47.6	51.8	53.0	30.4
1985	78.8	74.7	82.3	75.2	93.6	73.1	72.9	52.9
1990	95.8	93.9	95.8	90.6	105.3	91.4	92.5	80.6
1995	104.5	102.9	103.1	101.7	101.9	103.5	109.5	84.9
2000	112.2	108.8	110.0	105.5	131.7	112.0	122.5	97.6
2001	117.2	112.8	112.2	106.0	128.3	114.2	124.3	105.1
2002	120.3	113.8	113.8	105.2	127.2	115.5	126.3	123.6
2003	122.4	117.5	114.6	103.3	135.4	117.0	127.3	136.0
2004[1]	124.2	119.6	115.2	103.0	148.5	118.6	127.4	142.4

Source: © *Statistics Canada*   (n.a.) Not available (1) Year to data average covering January to July 2004.

Canadian Inflation Rate by Year

This table shows annual inflation rates, as measured by the percentage change in the Consumer Price Index (CPI) from one year to the next. The CPI, determined monthly by Statistics Canada, is a "weighted" average of the cost of a package of goods and services — such as food, clothing, housing and health care — normally purchased by Canadian households. Weighted average means that some items are given more importance according to the proportion of household income spent on them.

Prices increase for several reasons: rising production costs, limited availability of the commodity, unfavourable exchange rates pushing up import prices, excessive consumer demand and too much currency in the economy.

Year	Rate	Year	Rate	Year	Rate	Year	Rate
1915	1.4	**1959**	1.7	**1975**	10.9	**1991**	5.6
1920	16.4	**1960**	1.1	**1976**	7.5	**1992**	1.5
1925	1.9	**1961**	1.1	**1977**	7.8	**1993**	1.8
1930	-0.9	**1962**	1.1	**1978**	9.0	**1994**	0.2
1935	1.2	**1963**	1.6	**1979**	9.2	**1995**	2.2
1940	3.3	**1964**	2.1	**1980**	10.1	**1996**	1.6
1945	0.9	**1965**	2.0	**1981**	12.4	**1997**	1.6
1950	2.8	**1966**	4.0	**1982**	10.9	**1998**	0.9
1951	10.1	**1967**	3.4	**1983**	5.8	**1999**	1.7
1952	3.0	**1968**	4.2	**1984**	4.3	**2000**	2.7
1953	-1.2	**1969**	4.5	**1985**	4.0	**2001**	2.6
1954	0.6	**1970**	3.4	**1986**	4.1	**2002**	2.2
1955	0.0	**1971**	2.9	**1987**	4.4	**2003**	2.8
1956	1.8	**1972**	4.8	**1988**	4.0	**2004**[1]	1.6
1957	2.9	**1973**	7.7	**1989**	5.0		
1958	2.3	**1974**	10.7	**1990**	4.8		

Source: © *Statistics Canada*   (1) Year to date average as of July 2004.

Canadian Unemployment Rates[1]

	1980	1985	1990	1995	2000	2001	2002	2003
Canada	**7.5**	**10.7**	**8.1**	**9.4**	**6.8**	**7.2**	**7.7**	**7.6**
Newfoundland and Labrador	13.1	20.8	16.9	18.1	16.7	16.1	16.9	16.7
Prince Edward Island	10.5	13.5	14.6	15.0	12.0	11.9	12.1	11.1
Nova Scotia	9.7	13.6	10.5	12.1	9.1	9.7	9.7	9.3
New Brunswick	11.1	15.3	12.1	11.2	10.0	11.2	10.4	10.6
Quebec	10.0	12.2	10.4	11.4	8.4	8.7	8.6	9.1
Ontario	6.8	8.1	6.2	8.7	5.7	6.3	7.1	7.0
Manitoba	5.5	8.4	7.3	7.2	4.9	5.0	5.2	5.0
Saskatchewan	4.2	8.3	7.0	6.6	5.2	5.8	5.7	5.6
Alberta	3.8	10.0	6.8	7.8	5.0	4.6	5.3	5.1
British Columbia	6.6	14.5	8.6	8.4	7.2	7.7	8.5	8.1

Source: © *Statistics Canada*   (1) number of unemployed persons expressed as a percentage of the labour force.

1992 = 100

*A*ll indexes measuring changes over time must have a specified time base. The time base is the reference point against which all levels are compared. Without a common time base, the indexes are meaningless. When quoting an index figure, the time base should always be included [e.g., all-items CPI in 1985 was 75.0 (1992 = 100)].

As of January 1998, the time base changed from 1986 to 1992. All constant dollar series were converted to 1992 dollars during the process, including historical tables for CPI.

New Vehicle Sales

	Total, new motor vehicles		Passenger cars		Total trucks[1]	
	Units	Dollars ($ 000)	Units	Dollars ($ 000)	Units	Dollars ($ 000)
1997	1 424 380	38 986 224	738 550	16 836 615	685 830	22 149 610
1998	1 428 932	40 255 777	740 809	17 054 244	688 123	23 201 534
1999	1 542 041	45 317 914	806 450	19 017 278	735 591	26 300 638
2000	1 587 561	46 930 514	849 171	20 790 660	738 390	26 139 852
2001	1 597 964	46 886 252	868 633	21 168 628	729 331	25 717 623
2002	1 733 318	52 227 499	934 704	23 191 483	798 614	29 036 014
2003	1 626 468	50 493 308	865 475	21 685 587	760 993	28 807 720

	Passenger cars made in North America		Passenger cars made overseas		Trucks[1] made in North America		Trucks[1] made overseas	
	Units	Dollars ($ 000)	Units	Dollars ($ 000)	Units	Dollars ($ 000)	Units	Dollars ($ 000)
1997	629 488	13 809 161	109 062	3 027 455	628 214	20 341 263	57 616	1 808 346
1998	590 667	13 101 703	150 142	3 952 541	627 256	21 165 239	60 867	2 036 296
1999	625 292	14 138 902	181 158	4 878 375	672 444	24 055 653	63 147	2 244 986
2000	640 856	15 089 665	208 315	5 700 994	669 492	23 745 933	68 898	2 393 922
2001	619 810	14 575 745	248 823	6 592 883	647 987	22 958 458	81 344	2 759 162
2002	651 305	15 521 295	283 399	7 670 192	698 870	25 633 136	99 744	3 402 877
2003	604 726	14 565 218	260 749	7 120 367	654 136	24 845 915	106 857	3 961 804

Source: *Statistics Canada*   (1) Trucks include minivans, sport-utility vehicles, light and heavy trucks, vans and buses.

Construction in Canada—Building Permits

(millions of dollars)

	Total	Annual % Change	Residential	Non-Residential Total	Industrial	Commercial	Institutional and Government
1960	2 025	-14.9	944	1 080	184	433	460
1965	3 810	16.6	1 757	2 053	430	783	840
1970	4 700	-4.0	2 312	2 389	498	807	1 084
1975	10 598	14.2	6 129	4 469	876	2 251	1 342
1980	15 452	9.2	7 468	7 984	1 911	4 322	1 751
1985	19 524	25.9	10 883	8 641	1 885	4 640	2 116
1990	32 131	-18.3	17 424	14 706	3 393	7 975	3 338
1991	28 468	-11.4	16 632	11 836	2 120	5 906	3 811
1992	26 995	-5.2	17 161	9 834	1 643	4 918	3 273
1993	25 586	-5.2	16 433	9 154	1 756	4 268	3 130
1994	27 637	8.0	17 590	10 047	2 250	4 993	2 803
1995	24 595	-11.0	13 242	11 353	2 823	5 441	3 089
1996	26 155	6.4	15 718	10 347	2 643	5 567	2 227
1997	30 838	17.9	18 317	12 521	3 455	6 520	2 546
1998	33 341	8.1	17 945	15 395	4 261	8 115	3 019
1999	35 736	7.2	19 957	15 779	3 630	8 463	3 686
2000	36 950	3.4	20 342	16 608	3 976	8 907	3 726
2001	40 856	10.3	22 619	18 237	3 665	9 307	5 265
2002	47 262	9.9	29 587	17 675	3 277	8 642	5 756
2003	50 772	7.1	31 971	18 801	3 618	9 323	5 859

Source: © *Statistics Canada*

Industrial Capacity Use Rates

An industry's "capacity use rate" is the ratio of actual production versus estimated potential production. Statistics Canada makes estimates of an industry's potential output from measures of that industry's physical resources and consults companies to produce survey-based industry measures. A company's measure of its level of operation, as a percentage of potential, takes into account changes in the obsolescence of facilities, capital-to-labour ratios and other characteristics of production techniques.

In 2003, Canada's industries were working at 82.2% capacity.

	Total Manufacturing	Food	Beverage	Tobacco	Textiles	Clothing	Leather & allied product	Wood product	Paper
1990	80.0	76.8	72.5	72.5	80.3	80.3	73.0	76.4	86.5
1991	74.0	79.7	63.6	63.6	73.8	75.5	62.7	70.1	83.1
1992	76.4	79.6	79.2	68.1	73.7	77.2	74.0	81.4	87.2
1993	79.8	79.4	82.9	75.0	79.3	79.3	70.2	90.1	88.3
1994	83.2	82.8	80.0	74.8	80.5	80.3	72.8	91.4	94.6
1995	83.8	81.5	83.2	78.4	82.9	82.0	72.6	87.2	93.0
1996	82.9	79.6	79.4	76.4	77.3	83.6	77.5	86.4	86.7
1997	83.1	78.0	81.9	86.3	81.7	80.5	79.9	86.0	92.5
1998	84.5	80.6	85.5	81.4	84.3	82.7	82.3	85.6	88.2
1999	85.2	79.9	84.1	78.6	83.3	87.6	73.8	83.3	90.2
2000	85.6	81.3	79.4	75.9	80.8	82.8	75.9	85.3	91.5
2001	82.9	81.8	82.8	76.9	77.4	84.5	73.7	82.4	89.7
2002	83.3	82.5	81.9	75.0	80.3	82.4	73.1	91.7	89.9
2003	82.2	77.6	79.6	66.2	77.7	76.5	69.1	94.9	91.8

	Printing	Petroleum and coal	Chemical	Plastics and rubber	Non-metallic mineral product	Primary metal	Fabricated metal	Machinery	Computers and electronics
1990	89.4	86.6	88.2	83.6	75.1	90.3	79.2	71.0	71.8
1991	74.7	83.4	80.7	76.6	63.8	80.5	70.1	62.9	69.8
1992	76.4	81.6	81.0	81.8	67.2	83.6	69.5	64.7	73.1
1993	74.8	87.1	83.8	82.5	71.4	90.0	71.9	73.8	69.8
1994	75.1	87.0	84.0	85.7	75.0	92.8	79.2	80.7	76.4
1995	77.6	87.3	84.8	80.7	75.8	90.2	77.9	87.1	87.7
1996	79.3	93.6	88.0	82.4	75.8	88.1	79.6	78.7	74.2
1997	79.6	91.1	78.2	83.4	83.7	86.6	80.0	81.9	75.0
1998	78.7	94.5	82.1	84.2	79.7	94.2	80.3	81.2	86.3
1999	82.2	97.1	79.5	86.3	81.4	89.5	85.3	78.4	91.0
2000	76.1	90.8	79.1	83.2	77.6	90.5	83.0	85.8	97.7
2001	74.8	94.0	81.8	84.4	81.8	90.0	79.3	80.1	76.1
2002	76.1	96.5	81.1	89.4	83.6	91.0	82.7	78.2	67.4
2003	72.7	98.5	84.8	86.8	89.1	91.5	80.4	78.0	68.1

	Electrical equipment, appliance and component	Transportation equipment	Furniture and related product	Misc.	Total industrial	Forestry and logging	Mining and oil and gas extraction	Electric power generation, transmission and distribution	Construction
1990	88.0	76.3	74.9	82.6	83.0	82.8	82.6	80.0	93.3
1991	73.6	72.9	66.2	79.8	78.0	74.8	83.4	84.9	82.8
1992	70.7	71.8	69.6	76.6	78.0	77.0	82.1	79.6	78.9
1993	76.0	77.3	73.8	77.8	79.9	87.6	85.2	78.7	76.1
1994	81.7	80.9	79.7	81.2	82.4	83.5	84.1	82.9	78.7
1995	77.4	83.9	79.3	74.5	81.7	83.3	81.9	80.7	75.1
1996	84.2	87.5	80.8	76.5	80.9	76.0	76.8	82.4	77.7
1997	85.7	88.0	80.8	84.8	81.9	82.3	76.8	81.8	82.5
1998	90.0	86.0	83.7	88.3	83.4	79.4	77.5	84.2	85.1
1999	93.2	88.0	85.9	87.0	83.5	78.4	74.5	82.8	86.3
2000	90.0	89.1	84.2	82.2	84.7	90.8	75.6	87.7	86.5
2001	78.6	88.2	82.1	79.3	83.3	82.4	75.3	89.2	89.2
2002	74.3	87.6	81.0	82.9	82.3	85.1	69.0	88.5	87.0
2003	70.9	84.0	77.6	75.4	81.2	90.1	68.5	85.2	85.9

Source: © *Statistics Canada*

(1) Each year represents data for the second quarter.

Annual Bankruptcies in Canada

	Personal	Business	Total		Personal	Business	Total
1970	2 732	2 927	5 659	1992	61 822	14 317	76 139
1975	8 335	2 958	11 293	1993	54 456	12 527	66 983
1980	21 025	6 595	27 620	1994	53 802	11 810	65 612
				1995	65 432	13 258	78 690
1985	19 752	8 663	28 415	1996	79 631	14 229	93 860
1986	21 765	8 502	30 267	1997	85 297	12 200	97 497
1987	24 384	7 659	32 043	1998	75 465	10 791	86 256
1988	25 817	8 031	33 848	1999	72 997	10 026	83 023
1989	29 202	8 664	37 866	2000	75 137	10 055	85 192
1990	42 782	11 642	54 424	2001	79 453	10 405	89 858
1991	62 277	13 496	75 773	2002	78 232	9 472	87 704
				2003	84 251	8 844	93 095

Source: © *Statistics Canada*

Commercial Bankruptcies by Industry

	1999	2000	2001	2002	2003
All Industries	10 026	10 055	10 405	9 472	8 844
Agriculture and related services	287	263	272	228	266
Fishing and trapping	22	18	12	10	17
Logging and forestry	151	143	203	150	163
Mining, quarrying and oil wells	66	66	32	61	64
Manufacturing	750	776	913	804	800
Construction	1 445	1 490	1 410	1 361	1 411
Transportation and storage	715	861	1 074	932	863
Communication and other utilities	116	118	126	135	145
Wholesale trade	479	552	519	480	541
Retail trade	1 964	1 821	1 814	1 451	1 418
Finance and insurance	89	87	120	117	153
Real estate operator and insurance agents	175	190	133	138	126
Business services	725	753	804	758	716
Government services	23	27	39	44	19
Educational services	26	36	62	31	28
Health and social services	128	133	141	123	134
Accommodation, food and beverage services	1 396	1 310	1 311	1 033	1 051
Other services	1 469	1 411	1 420	1 616	929

Source: *Statistics Canada*

Consumer Bankruptcies by Province, 2003

	Total Bankruptcies	Total Assets (thousands) $	Total Liabilities (thousands) $	Total Deficiency (thousands) $
Canada	84 251	2 048 368	4 817 515	2 769 146
Newfoundland and Labrador	2 153	57 820	102 533	44 713
Nova Scotia	3 503	30 484	172 277	141 793
Prince Edward Island	203	477	9 240	8 763
New Brunswick	2 254	13 905	114 200	100 295
Quebec	22 531	336 774	966 806	630 032
Ontario	30 223	686 843	1 951 603	1 264 760
Manitoba	2 609	78 138	133 189	55 051
Saskatchewan	2 191	99 361	124 232	24 871
Alberta	9 155	424 762	578 403	153 642
British Columbia	9 385	318 721	662 590	343 869
Northwest Territories	26	602	1 401	799
Yukon Territory	17	467	1 015	548
Nunavut	1	15	26	11

Source: © *Statistics Canada*

FEDERAL GOVERNMENT SPENDING

Federal Ministry Spending

(millions of dollars)

Department	1997–98	2000–01	2001–02	2002–03
Agriculture and Agri-Food	1 912	2 736	2 936	3 205
Canada Customs and Revenue Agency	2 442	4 561	3 936	3 825
Canadian Heritage (Communications)	2 620	3 124	3 409	3 610
Citizenship and Immigration	749	1 002	1 048	1 110
Consumer and Corporate Affairs	—1	—1	1	1
Energy, Mines & Resources	—2	—2	2	2
Environment	558	651	854	771
Finance	64 440	74 342	69 911	67 134
Fisheries and Oceans	1 152	1 528	1 512	1 522
Foreign Affairs and International Trade (External Affairs)	3 364	3 833	4 074	4 314
Governor General (and Lieutenant-Governors)	11	16	18	21
Health	1 884	2 717	3 210	3 347
Human Resources Development	24 944	27 022	27 873	28 146
Indian and Northern Affairs	4 556	5 107	5 145	5 370
Industry	4 523	4 077	4 908	4 725
Justice	828	1 258	1 373	1 384
Labour	—3	—3	3	3
Manpower/Employment and Immigration	—3	—3	3	3
National Defence	10 187	11 470	12 254	12 428
National Health and Welfare	—4	—4	4	4
Natural Resources	753	920	1 186	1 282
Parliament	297	345	394	419
Privy Council	339	469	334	311
Public Works and Government Services	3 757	4 313	4 442	2 605
Regional Economic (Industrial) Expansion	—1	—1	1	1
Science and Technology	—1	—1	1	1
Secretary of State	—5	—5	5	5
Solicitor General	2 738	3 135	3 583	3 815
Supply & Services	—6	—6	6	6
Transport	2 256	940	1 220	3 498
Treasury Board	1 151	4 179	1 554	1 471
Veterans Affairs	1 935	2 109	2 247	2 475
Total	**141 299**	**159 854**	**156 928**	**156 785**

Source: *Public Accounts of Canada*
(1) See Industry.
(2) See Natural Resources.
(3) Responsibilities moved to Human Resources Development.
(4) See Health.
(5) Split between Canadian Heritage and Human Resources Development.
(6) See Public Works.

Statement of Assets and Liabilities

(millions of dollars)

	2002	2003
Assets		
Cash and Accounts Receivable		
Cash	11 360	16 486
Tax receivables	45 605	43 597
Other accounts receivable	2 868	2 543
Foreign Exchange Accounts		
International reserves held in Exchange Fund Account	48 667	44 849
International Monetary Fund—Subscriptions	12 821	12 942
Less: International Monetary Fund—Notes payable	(9 442)	(8 841)
Loans, Investments and Advances		
Enterprise Crown corporations and other government business enterprises	13 688	14 555
National governments including developing countries & international organizations	7 342	6 597
Other loans, investments and advances	10 013	12 034
Less: allowance for valuation	(9 487)	(9 438)
Non-Financial Assets		
Tangible capital assets	45 724	47 034
Inventories	6 438	6 113
Prepaid expenses	1 200	1 093
Total Assets	**186 797**	**189 564**
Liabilities		
Accounts payable and accrued liabilities	35 286	37 731
Tax payables	34 284	33 549
Interest and matured debt	7 807	4 302
Allowance for guarantees	4 076	3 802
Interest-Bearing Debt		
Unmatured debt payable in Canadian currency		
Marketable bonds	293 843	288 245
Treasury bills	94 039	104 411
Canada savings and Canada premium bonds	23 966	22 584
Non-marketable bonds and notes	3 391	3 371
Unmatured debt payable in foreign currencies	27 032	21 141
Pension and other liabilities		
Public sector pensions	126 921	125 708
Other employee and veteran future benefits	38 280	38 844
Due to Canada Pension Plan	6 770	7 093
Other liabilities	8 647	9 359
Total Liabilities	**704 342**	**700 140**
Accumulated Deficit	517 545	510 576

Source: *Public Works and Government Services Canada (Receiver General)*

Interest on Public Debt

(millions of dollars)[1]

	Mun.	Prov.	Fed.	Total		Mun.	Prov.	Fed.	Total
1985	3 298	12 549	24 738	40 585	1994	4 219	25 221	40 157	69 597
1986	3 313	13 693	26 216	43 222	1995	4 316	26 957	46 254	77 527
1987	3 340	15 056	27 883	46 279	1996	4 176	26 756	45 352	76 284
1988	3 365	15 730	31 711	50 806	1997	3 949	26 679	43 407	74 035
1989	3 495	17 366	37 424	58 285	1998	3 588	27 978	43 910	75 476
1990	3 722	18 684	41 880	64 286	1999	3 412	27 986	43 632	75 030
1991	3 886	19 587	41 053	64 526	2000	3 175	28 017	45 299	76 491
1992	4 089	21 594	39 558	65 241	2001	3 192	28 033	41 830	73 055
1993	4 295	23 337	39 219	66 851	2002	3 042	26 895	36 907	66 844
					2003	2 975	26 659	35 090	64 724

Source: © *Statistics Canada*

(1) Expressed in constant dollars, 1992 = 100.

Statement of Revenue and Expenditure

for fiscal years ending March 31, annual (Dollars × 1,000,000)

	2001	2002	2003	2004
Total revenue	**193 825**	**192 304**	**191 418**	**199 801**
Income taxes	122 318	120 560	115 361	124 178
Personal income taxes	89 183	91 435	89 007	92 306
Corporation income taxes	28 823	24 976	21 977	27 705
Mining and logging taxes				
Consumption taxes	38 963	39 675	43 529	44 029
General sales tax	27 801	27 864	30 568	30 999
Alcoholic beverages and tobacco taxes	3 247	3 738	4 118	4425
Tobacco taxes	2 158	2 465	2 910	3 179
Amusement tax	15	14	15	14
Gasoline and motive fuel taxes	4 807	4 758	4 873	5 119
Custom duties	2 807	3 018	3 189	2 870
Other consumption taxes	285	284	765	603
Other taxes	585	518	496	503
Contributions to social security plans	19 116	18 496	18 753	17 893
Employment insurance contributions	19 029	18 414	18 661	17 800
Other social security plan contributions	87	82	92	92
Sales of goods and services	4 472	5 028	5 061	4 882
Investment income	7 057	6 833	7 231	6 740
Natural resource royalties	226	415	259	521
Other revenue from own sources	741	584	440	954
Total expenditures	**184 612**	**184 953**	**188 637**	**193 022**
General government services	8 905	7 396	7 855	7 355
Protection of persons and property	18 789	20 399	21 200	20 931
National defence	11 968	12 734	13 170	13 105
Transportation and communication	1 992	2 385	2 164	2 250
Health	3 630	3 286	3 498	6 044
Hospital care	1 070	76	65	1 533
Medical care	373	335	508	521
Preventive care	467	994	802	579
Social services	51 613	54 982	57 414	59 640
Education	5 104	4 970	4 982	4 771
Resource conservation & industrial development	6 791	7 154	7 894	7 630
Environment	1 554	1 627	1 719	1 750
Water purification and supply	644	609	656	613
Pollution control	315	416	424	612
Other environmental services	595	602	639	525
Recreation and culture	3 372	3 459	3 574	3 445
Labour, employment and immigration	2 409	2 471	2 796	2 650
Housing	1 885	1 910	1 979	2 065
Foreign affairs and international assistance	4 488	4 565	5 175	4 810
General purpose transfers to other gov't subsectors	26 015	27 147	28 889	31 758
Debt charges	45 650	40 139	36 464	34 632
Other expenditures	126	199	71	5
Surplus (deficit)	9 213	7 351	2 780	6 779

Source: © *Statistics Canada*

Federal Transfers to Provinces and Territories

The federal government transfers cash and tax revenues to the provinces and territories every year in order to support the delivery of programs and services in health care, post secondary education, social assistance, social services and early childhood development. The goal is to ensure that, as much as possible, all Canadians receive comparable levels of public services, regardless of where they live.

As of 2004–05; most federal government transfers will be administered through five major transfer programs:

1. **The Canada Health Transfer (CHT)** provides support for health care. In 2004–05, provinces and territories will receive $25.1 billion under the CHT, including an additional $2 billion for health announced in January 2004.

2. **The Canada Social Transfer (CST)** provides support for post-secondary education, social assistance and social services, including early childhood development and early learning and childcare. In 2004–05, provinces and territories will receive $14.9 billion under the CST.

3. **The Health Reform Transfer (HRT)** provides provinces and territories $16 billion over five years in support of health care reforms targeted to primary health care, home care and catastrophic drug coverage. Subject to a review by First Ministers of progress made in achieving the agreed-upon reforms by the end of 2007–08, funding provided through the HRT will be integrated into the CHT starting in 2008–09. In 2004–05, provinces and territories will receive $1.5 billion under the HRT.

4. **Equalization** ensures that less prosperous provinces have sufficient revenue to provide reasonably comparable levels of public services at reasonably comparable levels of taxation. Provinces can spend these payments according to their respective priorities.

5. **Territorial Formula Financing (TFF)** ensures that territorial governments can provide services to their residents, taking into account the higher costs in the North. In 2004–05, payments will total approximately $1.8 billion.

Total Major Federal Transfers to Provinces

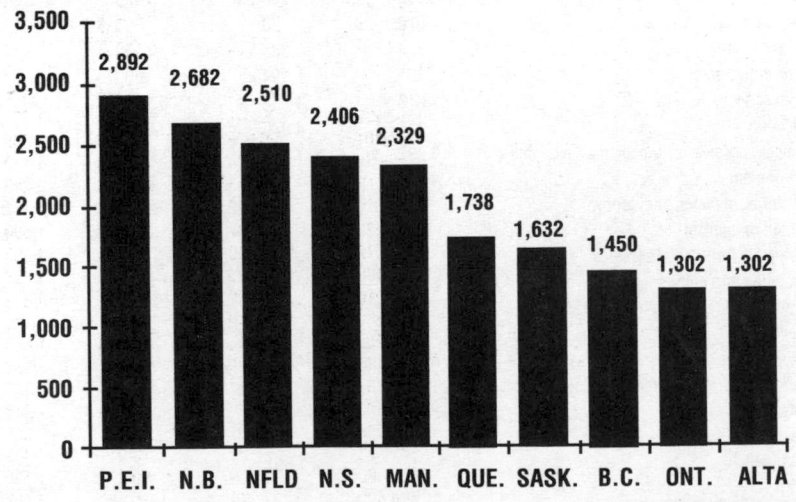

(CHT, CST, Health Reform Transfer and Equalization)
2004–05 ($ per capita)

Province	$ per capita
P.E.I.	2,892
N.B.	2,682
NFLD	2,510
N.S.	2,406
MAN.	2,329
QUE.	1,738
SASK.	1,632
B.C.	1,450
ONT.	1,302
ALTA	1,302

Federal Government Annual Surplus or Deficit

Fiscal Year Ending March 31 (millions of dollars)

	Surplus or Deficit[1]	% of GDP[2]		Surplus or Deficit[1]	% of GDP[2]		Surplus or Deficit[1]	% of GDP[2]
1960	-600	1.7	1974	-1 999	1.3	1989	-28 951	4.4
1961	-529	1.3	1975	-2 009	1.2	1990	-28 996	4.3
1962	-948	2.1	1976	-5 737	2.9	1991	-30 618	4.5
1963	-833	1.7	1977	-6 297	2.8	1992	-34 643	4.9
1964	-1 169	2.2	1978	-10 426	4.2	1993	-41 021	5.6
1965	-315	0.5	1979	-12 617	4.5	1994	-42 012	5.4
1966	-303	0.5	1980	-11 501	3.6	1995	-37 462	4.6
1967	-187	0.3	1981	-13 522	3.8	1996	-28 617	3.4
1968	-711	0.9	1982	-14 872	3.9	1997	-8 897	1.0
1969	-400	0.5	1983	-27 816	6.8	1998	3 478	0.4
1970	332	0.4	1984	-32 399	7.2	1999	2 884	0.3
1971	-780	0.8	1985	-38 324	7.9	2000	12 298	1.2
1972	-1 542	1.4	1986	-34 404	6.7	2001	17 148	1.7
1973	-1 675	1.3	1987	-30 733	5.5	2002	8 907	0.8
			1988	-28 201	4.6	2003	6 969	0.7

Source: *Public Accounts of Canada*

(1) A minus (-) sign indicates a deficit. (2) GDP (Gross Domestic Product) represents the value (in current dollars at market prices) of all goods and services produced in Canada.

Per Capita Accumulated Federal Debt[1]

	(millions of dollars)		(dollars)	
	Net Debt	Interest on Debt	Net Debt Per Capita	Interest Per Capita
1940	3 271	139	288	12
1945	11 298	409	936	34
1950	11 645	440	849	32
1955	11 263	478	718	30
1960	12 089	736	677	41
1965	15 504	1 012	789	52
1970	16 943	1 676	796	79
1975	19 276	3 164	849	139
1980	72 159	8 494	2 853	353
1985	199 092	22 445	7 911	892
1986	233 496	25 441	9 210	1 003
1987	264 101	26 658	10 306	1 040
1988	292 184	29 028	11 276	1 120
1989	320 918	33 183	12 240	1 266
1990	357 811	38 820	13 484	1 472
1991	388 429	42 537	14 424	1 590
1992	423 072	41 020	15 469	1 499
1993	466 198	38 825	16 301	1 356
1994	508 210	37 982	17 381	1 299
1995	545 672	42 046	18 435	1 420
1996	574 289	46 905	19 908	1 626
1997	583 186	44 973	19 247	1 484
1998	579 708	40 931	19 166	1 353
1999	576 824	41 394	18 918	1 358
2000	564 526	41 647	18 358	1 354
2001	547 378	42 094	18 242	1 403
2002	583 432	37 735	18 492	1 196
2003	526 492	37 270	16 480	1 167

Source: *Public Accounts of Canada*

(1) As of Mar. 31, on a public accounts basis.

FOREIGN TRADE

Canadian Imports – Top 50 Trading Partners

(millions of current dollars)

Country	1990	%	2002	%	2003	%
TOTAL (ALL COUNTRIES)[1]	$136 245	100	348 718	100.00	335 533	100.00
United States (U.S.).	87 875	53.83	218 332	62.61	203 550	60.66
China.	1 394	1.02	15 999	4.59	18 568	5.53
Japan.	9 525	6.99	15 421	4.42	13 815	4.12
Mexico.	1 748	1.28	12 734	3.65	12 184	3.63
United Kingdom (U.K.)	4 898	3.59	9 734	2.79	9 069	2.70
Germany	3 835	2.81	8 295	2.38	8 638	2.57
Korea, South	2 254	1.65	4 865	1.40	5 107	1.52
France (incl. Monaco, French Antilles).	2 448	1.79	5 855	1.68	5 067	1.51
Italy (includes Vatican City State)	1 954	1.43	4 439	1.27	4 619	1.38
Norway	1 683	1.24	3 933	1.13	4 314	1.29
Re-Imports (Canada).	—	—	5 369	1.54	4 112	1.23
Taiwan (Taipei)	2 108	1.55	4 243	1.22	3 761	1.12
Algeria.	62	0.05	1 724	0.49	2 400	0.72
Malaysia	380	0.28	2 019	0.58	2 278	0.68
Sweden	893	0.65	1 860	0.53	2 028	0.60
Brazil	798	0.59	1 905	0.55	1 993	0.59
Ireland.	257	0.19	1 736	0.50	1 902	0.57
Thailand.	406	0.30	1 777	0.51	1 865	0.56
Netherlands	719	0.53	1 466	0.42	1 685	0.50
Australia	764	0.56	1 721	0.49	1 633	0.49
India	226	0.17	1 326	0.38	1 423	0.42
Switzerland	646	0.47	1 514	0.43	1 416	0.42
Spain.	496	0.36	1 025	0.29	1 185	0.35
Belgium	539	0.40	1 392	0.40	1 162	0.35
Iraq	112	0.08	1 090	0.31	1 126	0.34
Denmark	248	0.18	1 025	0.29	1 076	0.32
Singapore	551	0.40	989	0.28	1 043	0.31
Austria.	406	0.30	1 008	0.29	1 037	0.31
Philippines.	202	0.15	1 113	0.32	975	0.29
Indonesia (includes East Timor)	202	0.15	964	0.28	927	0.28
Finland.	360	0.26	716	0.21	926	0.28
Saudi Arabia	708	0.52	749	0.21	919	0.27
Chile	180	0.13	670	0.19	886	0.26
Hong Kong	1 057	0.78	996	0.29	857	0.26
Russia	—	—	380	0.11	807	0.24
Venezuela	577	0.42	1 232	0.35	712	0.21
Israel	124	0.09	630	0.18	615	0.18
New Zealand	213	0.17	555	0.16	541	0.16
South Africa.	141	0.10	488	0.14	503	0.15
Turkey	84	0.06	401	0.11	467	0.14
Equatorial Guinea	—	—	294	0.08	460	0.14
Nigeria.	597	0.44	204	0.06	442	0.13
Argentina.	139	0.10	323	0.09	374	0.11
Colombia.	132	0.10	393	0.11	374	0.11
Poland	78	0.06	312	0.09	373	0.11
Cuba	130	0.10	325	0.09	371	0.11
Bangladesh	—	—	165	0.05	351	0.10
Vietnam	15	0.01	284	0.08	335	0.10
Costa Rica	—	—	247	0.07	297	0.09
Portugal.	171	0.13	251	0.07	278	0.08

Source: © *Statistics Canada*   (1) 219 Trading Partners

Canadian Exports – Top 50 Trading Partners

(millions of current dollars)

Country	1990	%	2002	%	2003	%
TOTAL (ALL COUNTRIES)[1]	**148 979**	**100**	**396 379**	**100.00**	**380 815**	**100.00**
United States (U.S.).	111 556	74.88	345 366	87.13	326 700	85.79
Japan.	8 230	5.52	8 366	2.11	8 144	2.14
United Kingdom (U.K.)	3 541	2.38	4 431	1.12	6 085	1.60
China.	1 706	1.15	4 130	1.04	4 766	1.25
Germany	2 323	1.56	2 955	0.75	2 882	0.76
Mexico.	88 302	59.27	2 419	0.61	2 210	0.58
France (incl. Monaco, French Antilles).	1 304	0.88	2 002	0.51	2 187	0.57
Korea, South	1 554	1.04	2 017	0.51	1 935	0.51
Belgium.	1 249	0.84	1 918	0.48	1 841	0.48
Italy (includes Vatican City State)	1 188	0.80	1 489	0.38	1 724	0.45
Netherlands.	1 649	1.11	1 774	0.45	1 621	0.43
Australia	902	0.61	1 170	0.30	1 471	0.39
Taiwan (Taipei)	798	0.54	1 127	0.28	1 232	0.32
Hong Kong	685	0.46	1 207	0.30	1 167	0.31
Norway	555	0.37	976	0.25	979	0.26
Brazil	502	0.34	766	0.19	895	0.23
Spain	387	0.26	949	0.24	857	0.23
India	321	0.22	674	0.17	765	0.20
Switzerland	1 054	0.71	518	0.13	490	0.13
Malaysia	256	0.17	491	0.12	481	0.13
Saudi Arabia	278	0.19	356	0.09	469	0.12
Thailand.	505	0.34	530	0.13	458	0.12
Indonesia (includes East Timor)	312	0.21	493	0.12	454	0.12
Ireland	139	0.09	366	0.09	452	0.12
Singapore	406	0.27	576	0.15	445	0.12
New Zealand	158	0.11	211	0.05	422	0.11
Philippines.	206	0.14	310	0.08	378	0.10
Finland.	146	0.10	277	0.07	351	0.09
Algeria	294	0.20	443	0.11	349	0.09
United Arab Emirates.	30	0.02	273	0.07	343	0.09
Russia	—	—	240	0.06	334	0.09
Chile	200	0.13	283	0.07	324	0.09
Sweden	327	0.22	287	0.07	317	0.08
South Africa.	180	0.12	254	0.06	317	0.08
Venezuela	287	0.19	546	0.14	309	0.08
Colombia	213	0.14	343	0.09	307	0.08
Pakistan.	—	—	86	0.02	288	0.08
Turkey	160	0.11	269	0.07	273	0.07
Denmark	138	0.09	402	0.10	273	0.07
Cuba	176	0.12	277	0.07	267	0.07
Austria.	158	0.11	244	0.06	250	0.07
Israel	145	0.10	388	0.10	246	0.06
Iran	360	0.24	168	0.04	237	0.06
Egypt	76	0.05	185	0.05	232	0.06
Luxembourg	—	—	86	0.02	231	0.06
Greece	97	0.07	146	0.04	186	0.05
Poland	—	—	134	0.03	183	0.05
Ecuador	—	—	134	0.03	149	0.04
Morocco	235	0.16	177	0.04	142	0.04
Peru.	8	0.04	169	0.04	134	0.04

Source: © Statistics Canada

(1) 219 Trading Partners

Canada's Top 50 Trading Partners by Balance of Trade

(millions of dollars)

Country	1999	2000	2001	2002	2003
TOTAL (ALL COUNTRIES)[1]	350 120	562 230	609 580	476 610	452 820
United States (U.S.)	925 020	1 296 290	1 334 560	1 270 350	1 231 500
Belgium	9 480	11 480	9 200	5 260	6 790
United Arab Emirates	1 520	790	1 370	2 440	3 130
Hong Kong	-1 610	-140	120	2 110	3 100
Iran	4 290	5 430	4 520	1 130	1 740
Luxembourg	190	300	100	30	1 720
Egypt	1 480	1 330	1 790	1 270	1 150
Greece	1 020	500	1 520	400	720
Tunisia	620	40	510	1 200	690
Sudan	300	210	660	610	590
Libya	510	210	200	470	580
Morocco	690	1 450	1 540	910	490
Bermuda	240	170	350	1 090	480
Panama	230	430	380	250	470
Oman (Muscat)	100	50	170	210	420
Barbados	300	260	250	310	400
Yemen	240	180	360	480	340
Kuwait	350	430	430	610	310
Korea, North	30	220	50	210	300
Qatar	50	130	120	280	290
Azerbaijan	10	30	40	30	280
Croatia	360	260	-20	-40	270
Angola	70	-350	-350	70	260
Tanzania	310	220	120	140	250
Jordan	190	190	300	280	250
Kazakhstan	-10	-40	90	270	230
Lebanon	310	260	240	240	210
St. Pierre-Miquelon	320	200	190	190	200
Ethiopia	70	50	10	0	180
Antigua and Barbuda	110	110	100	80	180
Mozambique	170	110	190	130	160
Iceland	-570	-610	-310	10	130
Senegal	200	180	450	100	130
Pakistan	-1 650	-1 900	-2 020	-2 030	130
Ghana	500	420	410	290	120
Latvia	-30	-220	-70	10	120
Cameroon	-100	-460	100	30	120
Congo (former Zaire)	60	50	50	120	110
Zambia (Zambi)	-90	60	40	70	110
Gibraltar	0	0	0	0	110
Togo	-200	100	220	130	90
French Polynesia	110	80	90	50	90
Saint Lucia	120	90	100	90	90
Afghanistan	0	0	0	20	80
Niger	-10	0	10	10	80
Dominica	40	30	20	20	80
Cayman Islands	70	80	380	50	80
Ecuador	-600	-210	-10	-260	70
Greenland	30	-60	20	30	70
Cyprus	190	110	10	190	60

Source: © *Statistics Canada*   (1) 219 trading partners; total represents the sum of trade surpluses and trade deficits

Trade Missions

Canada's small population means a small market for Canadian businesses. To create new jobs, these businesses must sell their goods and services elsewhere. According to the Department of Foreign Affairs and International Trade (DFAIT), exports accounted for more than 43 percent of all Canadian goods and services sold in 2002, and one in every three jobs in Canada was tied to exports. DFAIT estimates that every $1 billion in exports creates or supports 11,000 jobs in Canada.

As the tables on pages 215 and 216 show, Canada's biggest customer is the United States. The US is easily accessible, and it's compatible culturally and technologically too. But other foreign markets exist; e.g., in the Pacific Rim countries. DFAIT helps Canadian small or medium-sized firms export their products to these markets through high-profile Team Canada trade missions and regular trade missions.

Team Canada missions are led by the prime minister and include the federal minister for international trade, provincial premiers and territorial leaders. The missions often include academics and cultural ambassadors too. Business leaders—who must register beforehand and then be invited to participate—benefit through their association with high-profile Canadian figures in the destination countries.

Before a mission, DFAIT identifies the business sectors of greatest interest to the host countries. During a mission to Moscow in 2002, for example, officials focused on education, communications, metals, minerals, oil, gas, construction, agriculture and agri-food. In Munich in 2002, DFAIT added media, film and technology transfer to the mix but dropped oil, gas, metals and minerals. DFAIT works with foreign officials to create the understanding necessary for business development. The results include joint ventures and the creation of facilities in destination countries.

In recent years, Team Canada has also promoted exporters from distinct Canadian regions. Team Canada Atlantic aids businesses based in the four Atlantic provinces, and Team Canada West aids firms in Western Canada. Junior Team Canada sends university students abroad to work in their areas of interest with business mentors.

Team Canada alone has helped more than 2,800 Canadian business representatives and organizations gain access to senior government and private-sector leaders in international markets. It's estimated that the new business generated is worth $30.6 billion.

Other trade missions, led by the federal minister of international trade, focus on specific market sectors abroad. Delegates meet with potential clients and gain knowledge of how to do business in target countries. (See "Canadian Trade Missions" below.)

A publicly held company, the Canadian Commercial Corporation, also aids Canadian exporters and foreign buyers in Canada. Established in 1946, the corporation supplies pre-contract, contract advisory and post-contract services for a fee. The organization provides a government-backed guarantee of performance for Canadian exporters. Visit http://www.ccc.ca for more information.

Team Canada Missions

Year	Destinations	Year	Destinations	Year	Destinations
1994	China	1998	Argentina, Brazil, Chile,	2001	China
1996	India, Indonesia, Malaysia,		Mexico	2002	Germany, Russia
	Pakistan	1999	Japan	2002	USA (New York) [1]
1997	Korea, Philippines,	2000	USA (New England)[1]	2003	USA (Washington, DC)[1]
	Thailand	2001	USA (Atlanta)[1]	2004	Brazil
		2001	USA (Dallas, Los Angeles)[2]		

Regional missions: (1) Team Canada Atlantic; (2) Team Canada West

Canadian Trade Missions

Year	Destinations	Year	Destinations
1995	Argentina, Brazil, Chile	2000	Russia
1998	Italy	2000	Czech Republic, Hungary, Slovakia,
1999	Poland, Ukraine		Slovenia
1999	Israel, Palestine, Saudi Arabia, United	2000	Algeria, Morocco, Portugal, Spain
	Arab Emirates	2002	India
1999	USA (California)	2002	Mexico
1999	Ireland	2002	Nigeria, Senegal, South Africa
2000	Australia		

Source: *Department of Foreign Affairs and International Trade, www.tcm-mec.gc.ca*

Foreign Investment in Canada

(millions of dollars)

	Total	United States	United Kingdom	Other EU[1]	Japan	Other OECD[2]	All Other
1930	2 427	1 993	392	–	–	–	42
1935	2 284	1 870	373	–	–	–	41
1940	2 477	2 064	362	–	–	–	51
1945	2 831	2 422	348	–	–	–	61
1950	4 098	3 549	468	–	–	–	81
1955	8 010	6 778	905	–	–	–	327
1960	13 583	11 210	1 550	553	–	–	270
1965	17 864	14 408	2 107	968	10	240	131
1970	27 374	22 054	2 641	1 617	103	580	379
1975	38 728	30 506	3 830	2 520	257	987	628
1980	64 708	50 368	5 773	5 168	605	1 524	1 270
1985	90 358	67 874	8 643	6 774	2 250	2 562	2 255
1990	130 932	84 089	17 185	14 339	5 222	5 871	4 227
1991	135 234	86 396	16 224	14 908	5 596	6 803	5 308
1992	137 918	88 161	16 799	15 056	5 962	6 913	5 027
1993	141 493	90 600	15 872	15 732	6 249	7 312	5 727
1994	154 594	102 629	14 693	16 824	6 587	7 989	5 873
1995	168 167	112 948	14 097	21 778	6 987	5 827	6 529
1996	182 126	121 943	14 292	24 406	7 873	6 748	6 865
1997	194 277	128 978	15 748	25 508	7 990	8 860	7 193
1998	219 389	146 893	17 042	31 126	8 393	8 958	6 978
1999	252 563	176 045	15 279	36 341	8 270	10 115	6 514
2000	319 116	193 651	23 955	72 008	8 041	13 280	8 181
2001	341 011	220 211	26 476	65 966	7 893	10 893	9 572
2002	348 917	223 217	27 591	67 537	8 904	11 499	10 169
2003[3]	357 548	228 383	27 066	69 659	9 686	11 883	10 871

Source: © *Statistics Canada*

(1) Other European Union countries (EU) include Belgium, Denmark, Germany, France, Greece, Ireland, Italy, Luxembourg, Netherlands, Portugal, Spain; from January 1995, Austria, Finland and Sweden. (2) Other OECD countries include Australia, Iceland, New Zealand, Norway, Switzerland and Turkey; from July 1994, Mexico; from December 1995, Czech Republic; from May 1996, Hungary; from November 1996, Poland; and up to December 1994, Austria, Finland and Sweden. (3) Preliminary data.

Foreign Investment by Industry

(millions of dollars)

	Total	Wood & Paper	Energy & Metallic Minerals	Machinery & Transportation Equipment	Finance & Insurance	Services & Retailing	Other Industries
1991	**135 234**	7 902	31 706	18 212	25 939	10 363	41 112
1992	**137 918**	8 895	30 062	18 496	26 873	10 807	42 785
1993	**141 493**	9 109	30 846	20 641	26 685	11 010	43 203
1994	**154 594**	9 598	29 959	24 638	28 119	14 417	47 864
1995	**168 167**	10 010	29 061	25 305	29 086	16 885	57 820
1996	**182 126**	10 206	31 799	25 366	33 506	18 852	62 399
1997	**194 277**	12 595	33 923	28 043	35 781	19 460	64 476
1998	**219 389**	13 487	38 651	30 029	40 787	21 642	74 793
1999	**252 563**	15 345	42 884	30 563	52 755	23 462	87 555
2000	**319 116**	16 384	56 305	43 647	53 965	25 367	123 447
2001	**341 011**	14 477	74 934	46 619	68 611	25 728	110 641
2002	**348 917**	15 149	79 742	48 277	65 312	27 332	113 104
2003[1]	**357 548**	15 159	83 470	47 160	67 882	28 267	115 610

Source: © *Statistics Canada*   (1) Preliminary data.

Canadian Investment Abroad

(millions of dollars)

	Total	United States	United Kingdom	Other EU[1]	Japan	Other OECD[2]	All Other
1920	212	132	1	—	1	—	78
1925	246	144	1	—	1	—	100
1930	443	260	14	—	1	—	168
1935	485	266	46	—	—	—	173
1940	681	412	58	—	1	—	210
1945	720	455	54	—	2	—	209
1950	1 043	814	73	—	—	—	156
1955	1 835	1 362	145	—	6	—	322
1960	2 600	1 716	277	46	15	—	546
1965	3 655	2 178	510	125	28	44	769
1970	6 520	3 518	636	304	48	142	1 871
1975	11 091	5 975	1 105	633	74	699	2 605
1980	28 413	17 849	3 080	1 377	109	1 370	4 628
1985	60 292	41 851	4 865	2 868	276	2 293	8 139
1990	98 402	60 049	13 527	7 098	917	3 996	12 815
1991	109 068	63 379	15 262	8 505	2 182	3 548	16 192
1992	111 691	64 502	12 271	9 071	2 521	3 957	19 370
1993	122 427	67 677	12 907	11 478	2 845	4 355	23 165
1994	146 315	77 987	15 038	15 020	3 485	6 635	27 551
1995	161 237	84 562	16 412	18 106	2 739	7 166	32 251
1996	181 238	93 939	17 825	19 192	2 676	8 392	39 215
1997	218 607	110 707	22 722	22 416	2 985	9 284	50 493
1998	262 909	133 267	24 956	29 149	3 268	11 579	60 691
1999	290 730	151 775	25 686	28 384	3 853	12 381	68 651
2000	356 506	177 943	35 170	39 998	5 613	17 600	80 182
2001	398 855	190 528	39 786	42 124	7 013	25 170	94 233
2002	429 633	197 128	40 189	49 052	9 514	29 574	104 178
2003[3]	399 134	164 874	40 703	58 374	9 123	26 972	99 087

Source: © *Statistics Canada*
(1) Other European Union countries (EU) include Belgium, Denmark, Germany, France, Greece, Ireland, Italy, Luxembourg, Netherlands, Portugal, Spain; from January 1995, Austria, Finland and Sweden. (2) Other OECD countries include Australia, Iceland, New Zealand, Norway, Switzerland and Turkey; from July 1994, Mexico; from December 1995, Czech Republic; from May 1996, Hungary; from November 1996, Poland; and up to December 1994, Austria, Finland and Sweden. (3) Preliminary data.

Canadian Investment Abroad by Industry

(millions of dollars)

	Total	Wood & Paper	Energy & Metallic Minerals	Machinery & Transportation Equipment	Finance & Insurance	Services & Retailing	Other Industries
1991	109 068	3 473	22 051	2 794	32 443	10 043	38 264
1992	111 691	3 576	24 198	3 188	32 140	10 263	38 326
1993	122 427	3 727	27 008	4 030	37 353	10 423	39 887
1994	146 315	4 358	32 189	4 681	44 725	12 066	48 297
1995	161 237	5 340	37 219	5 207	48 932	17 892	46 646
1996	181 238	4 710	44 703	5 867	58 098	19 724	48 138
1997	218 607	6 154	53 079	7 715	73 714	21 760	56 184
1998	262 909	7 053	58 700	11 752	85 562	31 643	68 199
1999	290 730	7 636	60 444	10 036	104 111	30 130	78 373
2000	356 506	7 050	67 625	21 064	120 483	48 259	92 027
2001	398 855	8 839	75 933	25 363	151 635	55 887	81 198
2002	429 633	8 972	83 888	24 224	180 830	59 389	72 331
2003[1]	399 134	8 315	87 884	22 737	168 501	47 422	64 275

Source: © *Statistics Canada*

(1) Preliminary data.

BUSINESS

Agriculture in Canada

(millions of dollars)[1]

	1980	1990	2000	2002	2003[2]
Barley	553 596	545 232	477 987	504 880	353 811
Canola	673 559	789 573	1 560 025	1 783 099	1 755 119
Cattle	3 221 371	3 627 111	6 048 306	6 914 917	4 587 562
Corn	467 480	521 517	676 073	819 167	783 804
Dairy products	2 015 452	3 154 774	4 029 833	4 135 287	4 496 107
Eggs	407 034	482 308	511 052	574 980	566 033
Floriculture and nursery	276 246	913 634	1 588 698	1 831 293	1 928 639
Apples	90 618	131 895	192 361	152 243	148 442
Other tree fruits	46 721	56 749	67 919	74 453	85 390
Strawberries	28 862	46 982	53 553	52 398	53 475
Other berries and grapes	60 638	112 476	232 888	237 878	252 932
Fruits	226 839	348 102	546 721	516 972	540 239
Ginseng	2 800	30 472	46 716	68 155	67 307
Greenhouse vegetables	n.a.	n.a.	504 713	596 027	623 864
Hens and chickens	520 071	970 988	1 368 143	1 452 936	1 524 414
Hogs	1 404 169	2 021 243	3 355 238	3 284 628	3 390 189
Honey	44 791	45 046	69 489	132 561	143 148
Lentils	0	57 094	244 542	133 394	157 805
Maple products	34 087	70 750	180 680	150 075	153 216
Oats	53 471	80 952	196 413	307 737	243 509
Other vegetables	n.a.	n.a.	796 238	832 053	818 384
Potatoes	211 992	398 969	679 916	917 618	849 555
Sheep	2 887	2 310	5 214	3 568	4 402
Soybeans	183 283	256 602	677 947	587 746	714 605
Sugar beets	73 465	42 912	32 899	20 072	22 732
Tobacco	212 512	281 112	348 427	274 071	228 455
Turkeys	150 159	230 570	263 253	258 822	260 657
Vegetables	360 146	706 483	1 273 331	1 429 039	n.a.
Wheat	3 207 548	3 078 875	3 056 988	3 412 821	2 441 078

Source: © *Statistics Canada*   (1) Not adjusted for inflation. (2) Preliminary statistics. (n.a.) not available

FOCUS ON...

The Impact of BSE on the Farm Economy

The beef cattle sector is important to the Canadian agricultural industry and to the overall Canadian economy. Currently, one in three Canadian farm families operates a single unincorporated beef cattle farm that derives at least half of its agricultural sales from the sale of beef cattle and calves. In 2002, farm cash receipts from cattle and calves totalled nearly $8 billion, 21% of the total $36 billion farm cash receipts.

The growth in the Canadian beef cattle sector over the past decade has been fuelled by exports in both live animals and meat products, especially to the United States. The impact of the international trade ban on Canadian farm families operating beef cattle farms due to the discovery of bovine spongiform encephalopathy (BSE) in May 2003 has been significant. In 2003, Canadian farm cash receipts from cattle and calves were estimated at $5.2 billion, a sharp drop of $2.5 billion (33%) from 2002.

Families operating a single unincorporated beef cattle farm would have lost an average $20,000 due to the BSE situation. Average total income for families on beef cattle farms in 2000 would have declined by 33% from $60,000 to $40,000.

The farm families hardest hit from the BSE fallout will obviously be those operating large intensive cattle operations. The impact of the assumed scenario translates into a decline of $220,000 for the net farm operating income (before capital cost allowance) of families associated with unincorporated beef cattle farms with gross revenues of $500,000 or more. The calculated family income, assuming no other adjustments, would be negative $140,000. For families on large unincorporated beef cattle farms (revenues of $100,000 to $499,999), the average farm income loss from BSE is estimated at just over $36,000. Total family income for this group would have declined from $69,000 under the status quo to $33,000 under the BSE scenario.

Overall, 27% of families operating a single unincorporated beef cattle farm would have experienced total family income below $20,000 under the BSE scenario.

BSE impacts Canadian livestock sector

The announcement of bovine spongiform encephalopathy (BSE)—commonly called mad cow disease—in one cow in northern Alberta on May 20, 2003, led to a decision by more than 40 countries to immediately impose import restrictions on live ruminant animals (cattle, sheep, goats, bison, elk, deer), meat products and animal by-products from Canada.

The economic implications for the livestock sector, meat and animal feed manufacturers, and the vast array of service sectors, such as trucking, sales yards and brokers, which provide support to the livestock industry, are widespread. For the overall Canadian economy, it is estimated that for each $100 million in exports by the cattle sector, $80 million is added to the national gross domestic product (GDP) (at market prices), $228 million is generated in total output, $41 million is added to labour income, and 3,000 jobs are created.

Therefore, the potential negative impact on the Canadian economy from a $2.5 billion loss in cattle and calf exports due to BSE translates into a $2 billion loss in GDP, a $5.7 billion decline in total output in the Canadian economy, a $1 billion decline in labour income and a loss of 75,000 jobs.

According to a report prepared for the Canadian Animal Health Coalition, the direct economic cost to the Canadian livestock industry by early 2004 was estimated at nearly $3.3 billion. An additional loss in equity to the cow-calf sector was estimated at $3.0 billion, for a total economic impact from BSE of $6.3 billion.

The US government announced a partial lifting of the ban on August 8, 2003, which allowed boneless beef products from cattle less than 30 months of age, along with other selected ruminant-derived products to enter the American market under import permits beginning September 10. Exports of beef meat ▶

▶ ground to a halt from June through August 2003 under the full embargo. With the partial lifting of the ban, exports of meat products to the United States did recover. However, the January to November 2003 exports of beef meat of $1.3 billion are estimated to be 36% lower than during the same period of 2002. Canada is the first country with an indigenous case of BSE to regain access to the US market.

On August 11, 2003, Mexico followed with a similar decision as the United States on beef product imports. However, it was not until October 2, 2003, that Mexico actually lifted the ban on imports of fresh, refrigerated, frozen and processed beef from Canadian cattle less than 30 months of age.

On October 31, 2003, the United States Department of Agriculture (USDA) published a notice in the US Federal Register proposing that Canadian cattle less than 30 months of age be allowed to enter the US market.

However, before the 60-day public comment period ended, the first case of BSE in a single Holstein dairy cow in Washington State was announced on December 23, 2003. DNA testing confirmed that the cow was born on a farm in northern Alberta. On January 6, 2004, the USDA continued the live animal ban introduced the previous May. This export embargo contributed to a record 14.7 million head of cattle on Canadian farms as of January 1, 2004, 1.2 million head more than at the same time a year earlier.

Although science-based international standards exist for avoiding trade disruptions when BSE is discovered, inconsistent application has resulted in restrictive import policies. To improve the management of BSE within a North American context, Canada, the US, and Mexico committed in January 2004 to harmonize policies and regulations relating to BSE. In addition, Canada is reviewing its own import policy to take into account the potential new International Office of Epizootics (OIE) guidelines.

In early March 2004, the USDA reopened a 30-day comment period based on a rule, that if finalized, would allow live Canadian cattle under 30 months, other live animals and a broader range of animal products to enter the United States for the first time since May 20, 2003. This comment period ended on April 7, 2004 but no action had been taken as of the end of May.

In 2002, Canada's exports of beef (live animals and meat products) amounted to $4.1 billion, with about 90% destined to the US market. The corresponding farm value (excluding all other costs such as processing and transportation) amounted to $3.6 billion. This was nearly one-half of the total farm cash receipts for cattle in 2002.

Cattle on farms hit record high while receipts plunged

The number of cattle on Canadian farms on January 1, 2004 reached a record high 14.7 million head as the trade ban resulted in reduced marketings. Total Canadian cattle and calf receipts for 2003 were $5.2 billion, down 33% from $7.7 billion in 2002, as marketings and prices tumbled in the wake of the trade ban (Table A). This caused the largest percentage decline in total livestock receipts in more than a decade.

Receipts from international exports of live cattle and calves plunged 67% to $585 million, as almost all exports go to the United States and this market has collapsed.

Furthermore, receipts for slaughter cattle dropped 23% to $3.4 billion, as marketings and prices both fell because of reduced international demand for Canadian beef products following the ban. Receipts for slaughter calves declined 17% to $189 million due to lower prices.

The full impact of BSE on farm cash receipts can be best illustrated by considering the decline in cattle and calf receipts in the second half of 2003. Between July and December 2003, these receipts fell 48% compared with the same period in 2002.

Government program payments partially offset the economic hit in 2003. However, the estimated $582 million in government assistance to help offset the impact of the BSE-related ban in 2003 still resulted in a 25% decline in cattle and calf revenues compared to 2002.

Source: *Statistics Canada, catalogue no. 21-601-MIE*

Canadian Agriculture by Province, 2003

(millions of dollars)

	N&L	PEI	NS	NB	Que	Ont	Man	Sask	Alta	BC
Barley........	n.a	5 789	1 133	3 527	27 382	10 603	36 668	134 694	127 454	6 561
Canola	n.a	n.a	n.a.	n.a.	3 264	12 420	530 025	634 090	550 052	25 268
Cattle	858	16 865	16 604	17 169	198 688	797 453	288 597	550 476	2 539 369	161 483
Corn.........	n.a	n.a	4 025	n.a.	310 031	428 128	41 094	n.a.	526	n.a.
Dairy products .	28 241	55 023	97 726	76 250	1 691 406	1 470 486	174 422	124 747	384 704	393 102
Eggs.........	11 644	4 120	25 430	16 036	101 985	207 779	63 283	21 448	42 391	71 917
Floriculture & nursery	10 157	2 887	38 859	42 602	231 307	949 925	37 642	32 294	116 337	466 629
Fruit										
Apples	x	x	10 200	2 251	31 594	50 126	x	x	x	54 040
Other tree fruits	15	12	611	10	386	52 347	n.a.	11	0	31 998
Strawberries	375	1 080	4 700	1 850	17 770	17 925	1 175	300	900	7 400
Other berries & grapes ..	214	3 257	26 646	13 530	45 137	37 290	460	1 221	1 227	123 950
Ginseng	0	0	0	0	0	44 696	0	0	0	22 611
Greenhouse vegetables	239	421	6 153	710	54 192	320 083	444	722	25 718	215 182
Hens and chickens	x	x	53 285	43 518	421 428	496 942	63 345	50 454	123 488	245 962
Hogs	1 039	26 498	26 750	24 863	933 376	863 100	754 381	262 452	458 386	39 347
Honey	n.a.	217	1 786	629	5 076	20 484	26 058	30 042	51 566	7 290
Lentils	n.a	n.a.	n.a.	n.a.	n.a.	n.a.	710	155 408	1 688	n.a.
Maple products	n.a	0	1 383	6 820	134 546	10 467	n.a.	n.a.	n.a.	n.a.
Oats.........	n.a	701	219	699	16 716	7 102	112 992	77 494	22 855	4 731
Other vegetables	3 419	11 766	15 314	6 149	230 543	376 547	26 682	1 788	37 048	109 128
Potatoes......	2 065	186 462	9 204	96 464	90 328	86 226	138 130	58 095	132 085	50 500
Sheep........	0	0	43	9	682	2 889	127	81	253	318
Soybeans.....	0	1 125	0	0	117 703	560 322	35 455	0	0	0
Sugar beets ...	n.a	n.a	n.a.	n.a.	0	n.a.	0	n.a.	22 732	n.a.
Tobacco......	n.a	0	0	0	16 852	211 603	n.a.	n.a.	n.a.	n.a.
Turkeys	x	x	6 147	4 225	54 877	117 839	18 098	9 151	23 230	27 020
Vegetables										
Wheat	0	2 415	2 196	1 182	17 418	301 034	451 711	1 042 066	615 275	7 781

Source: © *Statistics Canada*   (n.a.) Not available (x) Confidential.

Mining in Canada

(millions of dollars)

	1960	1970	1980	1990	2000	2002	2003[1]
METALS							
Cadmium	3.3	15.3	7.6	11.6	.5	0.9	1.4
Cobalt	6.7	10.2	134.7	49.6	100.4	49.4	50.9
Copper	264.8	779.2	1 859.6	2 428.9	1 684.1	1 440.0	1 300.0
Gold	157.2	88.1	1 165.4	2 407.6	2 053.8	2 377	2 285.7
Iron Ore	175.1	588.6	1 700.9	1 258.8	1 424.5	1 278.1	1 444.9
Lead	43.9	123.1	273.7	279.3	96.6	71.9	53.2
Nickel	295.6	830.2	1 497.4	2 027.9	2 323.8	1 926.5	2 007.0
Platinum metals	28.9	43.6	159.1	189.4	478.5	502.4	269.9
Silver	30.2	81.9	828.8	249.7	279.0	315.7	275.2
Uranium	269.9	n.a.	702.0	887.9	473.2	613.2	504.4
Zinc	108.6	398.9	858.2	2 272.6	1 567.3	1 129.0	854.9
NON-METALS							
Asbestos	121.4	208.1	618.5	272.1	141.7	98.2	x
Diamonds					624.4	791.8	1 722.5
Gypsum	9.5	14.2	39.5	80.1	105.7	105.2	105.0
Potash	178.7	108.7	1 020.7	964.9	1 644.2	1 627.2	1 647.8
Salt	19.4	36.1	122.8	240.9	351.4	419.3	423.9
Sulphur (elemental)	4.3	28.4	444.1	368.9	92.4	77.3	246.4
STRUCTURAL MATERIALS							
Cement	93.3	155.7	581.4	991.4	1 258.7	1 437.4	1 495.9
Sand and gravel	111.2	133.6	508.4	817.3	971.2	1 053.7	1 047.0
Stone	60.6	87.9	341.2	663.4	881.3	1 003.8	979.5

Source: © *Statistics Canada*   (x) Confidential. (1) Preliminary figures.

Mining by Province, 2003[1]

(millions of dollars)

	N&L	PEI	NS	NB	Que	Ont	Man	Sask	Alta	BC	YT	NWT	NVT
METALS													
Copper				23.2	195.4	392.5	70.3	29.6		588.8			
Gold	17.6			4.1	457.2	1 253.0	64.5	33.7	83.1	354.5	25.8	44.7	29.9
Iron Ore	874.8				x					x			
Lead				49.2						4.1			
Nickel					321.7	1 192.4	493.0						
Zinc				318.9	290.8	84.8	96.7	6.2		57.5			
NON-METALS													
Diamonds												1 722.5	
STRUCTURAL MATERIALS													
Cement			x		326.7	613.8			x	264.9			
Sand & Gravel	9.2	x	x	12.0	88.3	410.4	35.2	38.9	234.9	177.5	10.6	3.5	
Stone	31.3		65.8	30.0	256.4	506.1	20.8		6.4	60.7		2.1	

Source: © *Statistics Canada*   (x) Confidential. (1) Preliminary figures.

Manufacturing in Canada

(millions of dollars)

	2001		2002		
	Manufacturing shipments[1]	Manufacturing value added	Manufacturing shipments[1]	Manufacturing value added	% Change of Goods Shipped 2001–02
All Industries	**543 782.5**	**214 573.8**	**550 244.4**	**217 257.5**	**1.2**
Food manufacturing	61 640.2	20 208.6	63 415.7	20 299.7	2.8
Beverage & tobacco product	11 684.9	7 253.5	11 923.9	7 466.0	2.0
Textile mills	4 223.8	1 917.3	4 130.6	1 949.0	-2.3
Textile product mills	2 659.2	1 334.8	2 765.0	1 271.5	3.8
Clothing manufacturing	7 838.6	4 204.4	7 571.8	3 893.5	-3.5
Leather & allied product	964.5	435.8	885.0	415.6	-9.0
Wood product manufacturing	30 074.9	11 671.6	32 174.4	12 675.2	6.5
Paper manufacturing	35 842.5	15 936.7	34 001.8	14 380.7	-5.4
Printing & related support activities	11 687.9	6 640.5	11 635.0	6 576.1	-0.5
Petroleum & coal products	33 407.5	5 243.6	33 660.2	4 841.3	0.8
Chemical manufacturing	38 406.8	15 033.2	40 546.3	16 466.3	5.3
Plastics and rubber products	22 950.4	10 877.8	24 720.9	11 737.5	7.2
Non-metallic mineral product	10 479.9	5 671.2	11 262.9	6 005.8	7.0
Primary metal	34 153.9	11 920.5	34 828.2	13 653.7	1.9
Fabricated metal product	30 164.8	15 002.5	31 101.9	15 643.3	3.0
Machinery manufacturing	26 445.2	13 776.0	26 815.7	13 623.2	1.4
Computer & electronic product	27 307.9	10 338.9	22 276.5	7 720.5	-22.6
Electrical equipment, appliance and component manufacturing	11 609.2	4 961.8	9 773.3	4 134.7	-18.8
Transportation equipment	122 360.6	41 676.8	125 738.2	43 257.5	2.7
Furniture & related product	13 062.0	6 717.4	13 273.4	6 946.4	1.6
Miscellaneous manufacturing	6 817.8	3 751.0	7 743.8	4 300.1	12.0

Source: © *Statistics Canada*   (1) = revenues from sales of manufactured goods, excludes other revenues

Operating Profits by Major Industry

(millions of dollars)

Year	Primary (including oil and gas)	Utilities	Manufact- uring	Construction	Transpor- tation	Trade	Finance, Insurance & Real Estate
1990	5 033	1 686	15 702	19 678	1 282	11 527	31 328
1995	5 539	2 051	39 193	2 894	4 259	7 429	38 437
1999	6 550	2 528	46 185	3 598	5 061	15 959	62 665
2000	23 844	2 234	52 379	3 406	4 789	16 482	76 778
2001	21 953	2 918	35 664	4 325	4 166	16 894	48 541
2002	16 006	3 131	39 523	4 722	6 825	20 758	33 890
2003	23 913	3 823	36 627	4 830	7 155	24 683	63 824

Year	Managerial & Related	Professional & Related	Information & Recreation	Accommodation & Food	Health & Social	Educational	Other Services
1990	22 107	675	4 604	126	705	86	526
1995	11 026	1 382	4 804	-88	742	-149	466
1999	14 975	1 168	6 496	1 840	1 486	108	1 057
2000	16 744	1 053	7 946	1 504	1 716	-9	1 111
2001	17 113	798	5 203	1 510	1 796	-133	623
2002	17 439	1 706	6 575	2 047	2 091	-97	1 079
2003	12 314	1 555	7 921	1 422	2 376	-102	1 622

Source: © *Statistics Canada*

Value of Manufacturing[1] by Province, 2003

(millions of dollars)

	Newfoundland and Labrador	Prince Edward Island	Nova Scotia	New Brunswick	Quebec	Ontario
All Industries	2 826.5	1 356.1	8 523.6	12 864.2	128 513.5	289 216.0
Food manufacturing	1 055.9	901.9	1 999.0	2 034.6	15 169.7	25 005.3
Beverage & tobacco product	144.1	x	x	225.4	3 965.3	5 315.6
Textile mills	x	x	x	x	2 045.9	1 027.5
Textile product mills	4.1	3.0	x	x	912.4	1 038.4
Clothing manufacturing	x	x	x	x	4 247.0	1 922.6
Leather and allied product	x	0.5	x	0.3	389.7	239.4
Paper manufacturing	x	x	874.9	2 083.5	10 620.2	10 825.5
Printing and related support activities	x	8.3	x	x	2 758.3	6 422.8
Petroleum & coal products	x	x	x	x	8 007.4	11 669.9
Chemical manufacturing	x	92.3	x	x	8 556.0	21 357.4
Plastics and rubber products	25.8	x	x	x	6 037.5	14 789.6
Wood product manufacturing	52.4	50.6	543.6	1 684.8	8 848.1	6 058.3
Non-metallic mineral product	x	x	x	x	2 678.9	5 559.8
Primary metal manufacturing	x	x	x	x	14 768.5	16 907.3
Fabricated metal product	153.3	26.9	x	x	6 596.7	17 460.2
Machinery manufacturing	10.7	21.3	176.6	202.5	4 919.6	13 687.6
Computer and electronic product	x	x	x	x	5 856.1	9 773.4
Electrical equipment, appliance and component	5.9	x	x	x	3 405.0	5 458.5
Transportation equipment	263.7	149.9	707.3	41.4	12 569.5	103 509.8
Furniture and related product	x	x	x	x	3 940.5	7 627.0
Miscellaneous manufacturing	x	7.4	x	x	2 221.3	3 560.0

	Manitoba	Saskatchewan	Alberta	British Columbia	Yukon	Northwest Territories	Nunavut
All Industries	11 412.6	7 913.4	45 837.7	37 222.9	12.3	63.4	2.9
Food manufacturing	2 456.8	1 947.0	7 975.8	4 889.7	–	–	–
Beverage and tobacco product	208.0	32.6	813.2	1 091.2	–	–	–
Textile mills	x	x	x	x	–	–	–
Textile product mills	x	x	x	x	–	–	–
Clothing manufacturing	263.6	28.3	139.4	x	–	–	–
Leather and allied product	x	2.6	x	22.9	–	–	–
Paper manufacturing	443.1	433.7	1 787.8	5 651.9	–	–	–
Printing & related support activities	509.7	146.6	661.5	758.5	–	–	–
Petroleum and coal products	32.9	x	8 199.7	x	–	–	–
Chemical manufacturing	814.4	798.8	8 285.3	1 083.9	–	–	–
Plastics and rubber products	568.4	107.0	835.8	1 155.9	–	–	–
Wood product manufacturing	697.3	468.1	2 931.5	9 913.0	–	–	–
Non-metallic mineral product	162.7	70.7	1 556.4	1 415.7	–	–	–
Primary metal manufacturing	x	x	1 812.1	1 995.2	–	–	–
Fabricated metal product	620.3	389.1	3 409.7	1 721.5	–	–	–
Machinery manufacturing	801.5	610.9	3 307.8	1 837.1	–	–	–
Computer and electronic product	x	x	1 520.2	1 101.2	–	–	–
Electrical equipment, appliance and component manufacturing	165.9	144.9	356.1	x	–	–	–
Transportation equipment	1 697.0	240.3	779.6	990.9	–	–	–
Furniture and related product	543.8	68.2	850.7	799.4	–	–	–
Miscellaneous manufacturing	175.4	54.7	534.1	651.5	x	2.9	x

Source: *Statistics Canada*   (1) Based on monthly data. (—) Not available. (x) Data suppressed to protect confidentiality.

Retail Merchandising in Canada

(millions of dollars)[1]

	1998	1999	2000	2001	2002	2003	2004[1]
Total, all trade groups	**255 626 913**	**270 629 442**	**286 911 433**	**299 487 384**	**318 531 997**	**330 502 942**	**163 826 718**
New car dealers	53 908 013	58 320 999	60 631 143	63 118 231	68 761 042	68 507 547	34 675 995
Used and recreational motor vehicle and parts dealers	11 037 505	11 392 689	12 872 207	14 009 336	14 303 021	14 393 896	7 469 118
Gasoline stations	19 606 841	21 535 226	26 676 245	26 986 111	28 138 391	29 847 864	15 710 060
Furniture stores	5 589 065	6 149 912	6 527 962	6 794 285	7 467 285	7 923 759	3 890 188
Home furnishings stores	2 563 471	2 732 784	2 974 593	3 222 267	3 701 197	3 971 591	1 973 767
Computer and software stores	1 838 480	2 032 249	2 209 619	1 988 867	1 967 688	1 941 061	907 800
Home electronics & appliance stores	5 799 598	6 221 251	7 002 164	7 543 210	8 361 114	9 028 704	3 927 347
Home centres and hardware stores	9 606 064	10 424 716	10 105 498	10 660 296	12 517 356	14 595 236	7 419 886
Specialized building materials and garden stores	3 473 879	3 398 933	3 484 514	3 841 627	4 234 114	4 368 090	2 183 851
Supermarkets	46 774 019	47 786 414	49 657 179	51 514 084	54 343 640	56 584 971	28 543 666
Convenience & specialty food stores	7 066 074	7 264 228	7 277 170	7 642 331	7 694 394	8 371 417	4 292 435
Beer, wine and liquor stores	9 306 803	10 055 661	10 580 137	11 332 001	12 103 235	12 673 555	5 963 697
Pharmacies & personal care stores	16 972 563	17 556 739	17 854 363	18 994 497	20 410 437	21 266 567	11 100 056
Clothing stores	12 211 150	12 673 181	13 461 188	13 976 141	14 219 966	14 567 138	6 557 697
Shoe, clothing accessories and jewellery stores	4 388 408	4 533 982	4 731 488	4 807 582	4 925 583	4 903 769	2 136 009
Department stores	16 367 272	17 372 306	17 716 719	18 992 130	20 112 546	20 800 829	9 375 187
Other general merchandise stores	15 246 170	16 424 337	17 488 458	17 599 916	18 306 983	19 210 190	9 306 984
Sporting goods, hobby, music and book stores	7 182 766	7 435 501	7 898 570	8 217 605	8 501 242	8 676 070	3 815 863
Miscellaneous store retailers	6 688 770	7 318 332	7 762 218	8 246 868	8 462 764	8 870 687	4 577 112
Total excluding new, used and recreational motor vehicle and parts dealers	190 681 393	200 915 753	213 408 083	222 359 818	235 467 934	247 601 497	121 681 605

Source: © *Statistics Canada*

(1) Data is for Jan-June 2004 only.

Retail Sales Reach New Heights in February 2004

*R*etail sales advanced at their fastest monthly rate in more than six years in February. Surging auto sales, combined with strong gains in the clothing, furniture, general merchandise and food sectors led total retail sales to new heights. Consumer spending in retail stores advanced 2.3% in February to $27.0 billion, after increasing 1.7% in January. February's gain was the strongest monthly increase since December 1997, when retail sales rose 3.6%.

Retailers enjoyed a resurgence in growth in the first two months of 2004, after experiencing poor sales in the second half of 2003. Previously, retail sales had generally been increasing since the fall of 2001.

Retail Merchandising by Province, 2003

(millions of dollars)

	N&L	PEI	NS	NB	Que.	Ont.	Man.	Sask.	Alta	BC	Terr.
Total retail, all stores. . . .	1 420.8	338.3	2 482.2	1 905.0	18 784.5	31 764.3	2 917.5	2 452.8	10 447.5	10 816.4	294.7
Supermarkets and grocery. . . .	373.9	87.7	560.8	459.7	3 959.6	5 410.0	645.7	560.8	2 144.7	2 426.9	61.3
Drugs & patent medicine.	84.4	24.1	172.3	128.8	820.8	1 844.4	118.1	123.5	483.0	665.9	x
Shoes	3.8	x	7.0	5.9	185.3	200.4	13.7	8.9	40.7	62.1	x
Men's clothing	4.3	x	6.5	9.1	77.2	199.5	14.0	8.5	60.5	49.0	x
Women's clothing	24.2	x	40.8	29.6	373.0	597.4	33.5	28.2	153.7	174.7	1.2
Other clothing	29.7	9.5	66.7	46.5	623.4	1 226.9	78.7	70.2	339.9	370.4	x
Household furniture & appliances	42.4	13.0	95.2	79.4	1 246.0	1 789.6	151.5	102.5	627.9	686.7	8.3
Other household furnishings. . . .	4.3	4.3	23.1	20.6	184.3	564.4	24.3	27.4	155.7	188.9	2.0
Motor & recreational vehicles .	268.5	49.4	468.4	354.9	4 260.2	6 672.8	713.8	561.3	2 334.6	2 070.8	x
Gasoline service stations.	122.3	35.5	208.6	156.2	1 359.7	2 093.9	215.5	202.8	722.5	718.3	x
Automotive parts, accessories and services	80.3	21.5	127.1	134.4	1 174.3	1 837.4	152.6	154.4	671.3	540.0	x
General merchandise.	256.0	43.6	376.6	275.8	2 227.0	4 478.2	447.1	362.5	1 378.6	1 394.7	88.3
Other semi-durable goods.	35.0	13.3	87.4	61.5	544.1	1 323.5	85.1	64.0	316.0	356.0	7.9
Other durable goods	28.3	7.3	74.4	43.1	551.0	1 062.0	67.8	66.4	307.7	358.6	6.4
Other retail stores, not classified	54.0	15.5	145.7	88.6	774.9	1 949.2	128.1	93.0	626.7	567.0	19.6

Source: © _Statistics Canada_

Knowledge Workers in Canada

Canada's science and communications technology industries place a high premium on knowledge workers, but these industries don't possess a monopoly on them, according to a new study.

Knowledge workers—highly skilled, highly educated people—are well represented across a diverse set of industries, not just in the high-tech sectors.

For the economy as a whole, only one out of every four workers is employed in a knowledge-based occupation. High-tech sectors that are associated with the growth of the new economy, such as information and communications technology (ICT) industries and science-based industries, are home to higher concentrations of knowledge workers.

In total, 63% of workers in ICT service industries are knowledge-based, as are about one-half of workers in ICT manufacturing.

One ICT service industry—computer and related services—sets the standard for knowledge workers. Workers in knowledge-based occupations make up 84% of employment in this industry. Architecture, engineering and scientific and technical services, a science-based service industry, follows close behind, with 78% of employees in knowledge-based occupations.

However, the study found that many industries with high concentrations of knowledge workers are located outside the ICT and research and development-intensive science sectors.

Certain industries that provide business or financial services have very high concentrations of knowledge workers. Knowledge-based occupations account for 69% of employment in management consulting and financial intermediaries, and 61% of workers in investment intermediaries.

Growth in high-knowledge financial services has been substantial. Long-run wage and employment growth in investment and financial intermediaries outpaced growth in ICT services. Financial industries have also become increasingly heavy consumers of technology-based products and services.

The study identifies other service industries that have a relatively large percentage of their workforce employed in knowledge-based occupations. These include accounting and bookkeeping services (55%) and lawyers and notaries (46%). In the goods-producing sector, 49% of employees in publishing industries are knowledge-based.

Knowledge workers are also well represented outside the business sector. About 71% of employment at universities and 73% of workers in medical and health laboratories are knowledge-based.

Source: _Statistics Canada, Canadian Economy in Transition series (no. 11-622-MIE2004005)_

Internet Web Site Presence and Purchasing

	% of Enterprises with a Web site		% of Enterprises using the Internet to make purchases		
	2002	2003	2001	2002	2003
All private sector	**31.5**	**34.0**	**22.4**	**31.7**	**37.2**
Agriculture, forestry, fishing and hunting	9.4	13.9	11.0	20.1	21.7
Mining and oil and gas extraction	35.5	24.8	14.5	26.4	31.3
Utilities	47.4	64.4	31.5	41.6	52.0
Construction	22.9	29.0	16.7	26.8	26.1
Manufacturing	54.7	56.5	29.1	40.5	47.8
Wholesale trade	40.7	43.9	26.4	36.3	45.1
Retail trade	30.7	36.4	16.9	29.1	34.8
Transportation and warehousing	15.8	16.9	11.6	19.2	26.9
Information and cultural industries	67.5	61.4	51.8	59.9	56.5
Finance and insurance	43.2	53.0	24.9	36.6	36.7
Real estate and rental and leasing	25.0	26.0	13.4	19.8	23.1
Professional, scientific and technical services	33.4	35.3	42.1	50.6	59.9
Management of companies and enterprises	23.2	20.2	8.4	21.1	24.1
Administrative and support, waste management and remediation services	35.1	34.5	30.9	28.5	36.6
Educational services	74.4	72.3	39.3	46.1	45.6
Health care and social assistance	18.2	21.8	20.0	29.5	32.1
Arts, entertainment and recreation	51.0	51.6	23.2	35.6	43.7
Accommodation and food services	21.7	26.0	9.4	18.2	22.4
Other services (except public administration)	30.4	33.3	14.8	23.4	27.6

Source: © *Statistics Canada* (n.a.) Not available.

Internet Sales

	% of Enterprises that use the Internet to make sales		Internet sales 2003		
	2002	2003	as % of Total Revenue	% to Consumers	% outside Canada
All private sector	**7.5**	**7.1**	**0.8**	**29.6**	**13.0**
Agriculture, forestry, fishing and hunting	5.0	0.0	n.a.	n.a.	n.a.
Mining and oil and gas extraction	3.2	0.5	x	x	x
Utilities	1.6	0.4	x	x	x
Construction	4.1	2.5	x	x	x
Manufacturing	12.1	11.5	0.4	20.9	30.2
Wholesale trade	12.6	13.8	1.2	7.0	2.2
Retail trade	11.4	11.3	0.6	81.6	25.5
Transportation and warehousing	3.6	2.4	3.7	13.3	1.2
Information and cultural industries	18.8	22.3	1.8	45.9	49.9
Finance and insurance	8.0	10.6	0.6	n.a.	0.3
Real estate and rental and leasing	4.1	3.5	0.4	68.5	n.a.
Professional, scientific and technical services	7.8	8.8	2.2	11.4	12.5
Management of companies and enterprises	5.9	5.0	0.8	68.0	n.a.
Administrative and support, waste management and remediation services	11.0	7.2	1.3	n.a.	8.9
Educational services	21.3	14.1	n.a.	n.a.	n.a.
Health care and social assistance	1.4	0.8	n.a.	n.a.	n.a.
Arts, entertainment and recreation	14.1	10.4	1.9	91.7	n.a.
Accommodation and food services	4.4	5.3	0.6	86.2	22.6
Other services (except public administration)	4.4	4.0	0.6	58.8	38.1

Source: © *Statistics Canada*
(n.a.) Not available. (x) Suppressed to protect confidentiality. (1) Stated as a percentage of total internet sales.

Establishments by Industry and Number of Employees, 2003

	Total	# of Employees not reported	Total reporting staff	1–4
Total	2 308 093	1 260 061	1 048 032	604 558
GOODS PRODUCING				
Agriculture, Forestry, Fishing and Hunting . . .	197 480	137 959	59 521	43 548
Mining and Oil and Gas Extraction.	16 108	7 957	8 151	4 737
Utilities	2 003	802	1 201	527
Construction	260 577	149 096	111 481	73 631
Manufacturing.	105 506	42 441	63 065	27 291
SERVICES				
Wholesale Trade	123 775	58 581	65 194	32 729
Retail Trade.	222 547	90 287	132 260	60 037
Transportation and Warehousing	111 237	65 061	46 176	31 317
Information and Cultural Industries.	32 094	18 254	13 840	7 444
Finance and Insurance.	108 860	74 231	34 629	17 740
Real Estate and Rental and Leasing.	171 957	131 839	40 118	25 182
Professional, Scientific and Technical Services	310 050	194 921	115 129	81 302
Management of Companies and Enterprises . .	86 650	69 654	16 996	10 282
Administrative and Support, Waste Management and Remediation Services	107 471	59 805	47 666	27 833
Educational Services	21 436	9 797	11 639	6 037
Health Care and Social Assistance.	95 885	13 073	82 812	47 718
Arts, Entertainment and Recreation.	42 416	24 333	18 083	10 313
Accommodation and Food Services	115 484	39 878	75 606	29 605
Other Services (except Public Administration)	168 570	72 035	96 535	64 985
Public Administration	7 987	57	7 930	2 300

	Number of Employees						
	5–9	10–19	20–49	50–99	100–199	200–499	500 +
Total	179 574	122 785	86 918	30 420	14 246	6 793	2 738
GOODS PRODUCING							
Agriculture, Forestry, Fishing and Hunting.	7 977	4 600	2 449	652	225	62	8
Mining and Oil and Gas Extraction.	1 089	899	740	328	183	125	50
Utilities.	207	145	140	59	42	42	39
Construction	16 689	10 318	7 277	2 323	875	305	63
Manufacturing	9 468	8 305	8 529	4 533	2 912	1 587	440
SERVICES							
Wholesale Trade	12 320	9 477	7 205	2 194	906	302	61
Retail Trade.	31 875	21 355	11 992	4 065	2 028	805	103
Transportation and Warehousing.	5 728	3 927	3 117	1 127	510	321	129
Information and Cultural Industries.	1 974	1 606	1 640	597	323	177	79
Finance and Insurance.	5 588	4 585	4 748	1 053	507	253	155
Real Estate and Rental and Leasing.	6 545	4 097	2 917	935	303	102	37
Professional, Scientific & Technical Services	15 005	9 433	6 232	1 922	766	360	109
Management of Companies and Enterprises	2 483	1 812	1 444	600	255	73	47
Administrative & Support, Waste Management and Remediation Services	7 962	5 346	3 941	1 407	669	379	129
Educational Services	1 881	1 417	1 020	393	250	216	425
Health Care and Social Assistance.	15 975	9 225	5 463	2 002	1 255	780	394
Arts, Entertainment and Recreation	3 148	2 155	1 506	535	258	127	41
Accommodation and Food Services.	14 922	14 260	11 211	4 049	1 175	314	70
Other Services (except Public Administration)	17 020	8 747	4 180	1 023	399	142	39
Public Administration	1 718	1 076	1 167	623	405	321	320

Source: © *Statistics Canada*

LABOUR

Provincial Employment by Industry

1993

	N&L	PEI	NS	NB	Que	Ont	Man	Sask	Alta	BC
Total, all industries	**241.1**	**66.0**	**429.5**	**344.6**	**3 505.2**	**5 581.1**	**558.6**	**490.9**	**1 431.9**	**1 855.6**
Goods-producing sector	59.2	19.9	101.0	90.1	915.2	1 436.4	138.2	152.1	395.4	431.6
Agriculture.	1.9	5.2	8.3	6.7	72.6	121.3	43.3	84.2	96.0	38.1
Forestry, fishing, mining, oil and gas	17.3	4.2	19.3	14.4	46.3	49.3	8.6	13.5	83.0	51.5
Utilities	2.9	.3	3.3	5.0	33.8	58.8	5.2	4.7	15.5	12.5
Construction	16.1	5.1	27.3	23.5	179.2	317.9	27.9	23.3	97.9	136.5
Manufacturing.	21.0	5.1	42.8	40.5	583.3	889.1	53.2	26.4	103.0	193.0
Services-producing sector	213.9	56.2	404.1	314.9	3 166.0	5 140.8	521.5	424.4	1 290.1	1 792.7
Trade.	39.6	9.1	69.1	57.2	530.3	834.6	88.1	71.5	212.9	296.7
Wholesale trade	5.7	1.5	11.3	10.7	113.3	156.2	19.4	16.8	44.5	69.3
Retail trade	33.9	7.5	57.8	46.5	417.0	678.5	68.7	54.7	168.5	227.3
Transportation and warehousing . .	10.8	2.9	19.2	16.7	155.0	238.6	34.7	21.3	65.2	106.7
Finance, insurance, real estate & leasing	7.9	2.4	21.7	14.5	198.9	383.3	29.7	25.0	78.3	117.6
Finance and insurance	5.5	1.4	14.9	10.2	147.5	257.3	20.1	17.7	48.5	70.1
Real estate and leasing	2.3	1.0	6.8	4.3	51.5	126.0	9.6	7.3	29.8	47.6
Professional, scientific & technical services	6.2	1.4	14.9	8.7	140.1	289.1	17.0	12.0	69.4	103.0
Business, building & other support services	4.4	1.3	10.3	9.0	84.9	177.3	13.8	9.4	41.8	53.5
Educational services	18.6	4.4	31.2	24.6	220.4	370.3	37.0	31.6	96.7	118.3
Health care and social assistance .	26.4	6.3	47.9	37.6	358.7	516.2	63.1	54.1	132.3	170.4
Information, culture and recreation	7.7	2.6	15.8	10.7	122.2	225.6	18.6	17.6	55.3	72.7
Accommodation and food services	11.8	5.1	25.7	19.4	210.4	314.2	36.7	30.9	93.3	135.1
Other services	12.9	3.7	23.0	18.1	175.5	242.2	26.7	22.8	69.8	99.1
Public administration	20.2	5.6	34.5	26.7	240.3	331.4	38.3	31.7	83.8	105.3

2003

	N&L	PEI	NS	NB	Que	Ont	Man	Sask	Alta	BC
Total, all industries	**261.4**	**77.5**	**480.1**	**385.8**	**4 016.5**	**6 694.1**	**598.6**	**515.8**	**1 814.9**	**2 202.1**
Goods-producing sector	59.8	21.3	111.4	96.3	1 019.9	1 740.4	147.2	128.9	502.2	457.9
Agriculture.	2.4	4.3	7.7	6.2	63.6	89.5	32.5	48.2	69.6	38.3
Forestry, fishing, mining, oil and gas	19.0	3.6	17.3	15.0	46.3	34.4	6.2	19.0	109.1	52.9
Utilities	2.3	.4	2.8	3.8	29.8	56.5	6.9	4.8	14.0	13.4
Construction	15.3	5.3	30.1	23.8	193.1	411.4	29.7	27.1	155.9	133.5
Manufacturing.	20.8	7.7	53.5	47.5	687.1	1 148.6	71.9	29.8	153.6	219.8
Services-producing sector	238.7	69.3	458.7	353.2	3 708.2	6 225.3	559.6	487.1	1 656.4	2 148.7
Trade.	40.0	11.1	78.4	57.2	637.6	983.7	87.0	80.3	274.7	336.5
Wholesale trade	5.4	1.6	14.9	11.5	143.9	234.9	20.5	17.3	69.6	78.2
Retail trade	34.7	9.6	63.5	45.7	493.6	748.8	66.5	63.0	205.1	258.3
Transportation and warehousing . .	14.9	3.1	21.3	19.8	170.5	293.6	35.1	24.5	98.8	119.1
Finance, insurance, real estate & leasing	7.7	2.5	21.4	15.2	194.9	444.8	28.6	27.8	89.0	130.1
Finance and insurance	4.6	1.5	13.6	9.6	142.4	326.1	21.3	20.5	57.3	84.0
Real estate and leasing	3.1	.9	7.8	5.6	52.5	118.7	7.3	7.4	31.7	46.1
Professional, scientific & technical services	8.4	2.9	20.0	16.1	222.5	461.4	24.2	18.4	122.9	147.7
Business, building & other support services	10.0	2.8	25.7	24.4	133.0	294.7	20.8	12.6	68.2	89.8
Educational services	17.6	5.1	34.8	23.8	263.5	399.2	43.9	41.7	112.2	150.6
Health care and social assistance .	34.7	8.1	55.6	46.0	443.2	618.1	74.7	60.6	163.9	218.0
Information, culture and recreation	9.0	3.1	18.6	13.5	168.5	311.0	24.1	21.8	75.2	115.4
Accommodation and food services	16.3	5.9	32.1	25.2	245.3	405.3	42.4	37.6	130.0	179.1
Other services	14.5	3.8	22.5	19.0	174.6	271.6	29.5	25.3	83.6	102.0
Public administration	17.8	7.3	28.5	20.6	222.2	313.4	33.7	28.3	74.2	93.8

Source: © Statistics Canada

Labour Force by Province, 2003

(thousands)

	Population 15 Years and Over	Labour Force[1]	Participation Rate (%)[2]	Employed	Employment Rate (%)	Un-employed	Unemploy-ment Rate (%)
Canada	25 403.9	17 187.4	67.7	15 920.7	62.7	1 266.8	7.4
Newfoundland and Labrador	439.4	262.8	59.8	215.6	49.1	47.2	18.0
Prince Edward Island . . .	113.7	78.1	68.7	70.2	61.7	7.9	10.1
Nova Scotia.	762.0	482.5	63.3	439.2	57.6	43.3	9.0
New Brunswick	610.6	384.2	62.9	346.1	56.7	38.1	9.9
Quebec	6 112.1	4 061.8	66.5	3 681.9	60.2	379.9	9.4
Ontario	9 857.3	6 736.2	68.3	6 285.8	63.8	450.4	6.7
Manitoba.	871.9	600.8	68.9	570.6	65.4	30.3	5.0
Saskatchewan	756.2	517.8	68.5	488.4	64.6	29.3	5.7
Alberta.	2 493.7	1 840.7	73.8	1 751.5	70.2	89.2	4.8
British Columbia	3 386.9	2 222.6	65.6	2 071.4	61.2	151.1	6.8

Source: © *Statistics Canada*
(1) The Labour Force consists of employed workers and those who are unemployed but actively seeking work.
(2) Participation rate is the percent of the population segment in the Labour Force.

Labour Force by Age, 2003

(thousands)

	Population	Labour Force[1]	Participation Rate (%)[2]	Employed	Employment Rate (%)	Un-employed	Unemploy-ment Rate (%)
Men							
15-19 years	1 050.3	569.6	54.2	455.8	43.4	113.7	20.0
20-24 years	1 074.9	875.9	81.5	764.2	71.1	111.7	12.8
25-29 years	1 061.5	966.6	91.1	886.5	83.5	80.1	8.3
30-34 years	1 109.7	1 035.6	93.3	964.4	86.9	71.2	6.9
35-39 years	1 199.9	1 115.1	92.9	1 038.7	86.6	76.4	6.9
40-44 years	1 373.7	1 272.9	92.7	1 195.7	87.0	77.2	6.1
45-49 years	1 219.1	1 114.4	91.4	1 049.1	86.1	65.3	5.9
50-54 years	1 091.2	960.0	88.0	903.9	82.8	56.1	5.8
55-59 years	899.8	681.6	75.8	635.6	70.6	46.0	6.7
60-64 years	671.8	353.6	52.6	328.9	49.0	24.8	7.0
65-69 years	534.7	112.1	21.0	107.0	20.0	5.1	4.5
70 years and over	1 122.8	78.5	7.0	77.0	6.9	1.5	1.9
Women							
15-19 years	999.0	548.6	54.9	459.7	46.0	88.9	16.2
20-24 years	1 041.0	797.9	76.6	727.1	69.8	70.7	8.9
25-29 years	1 044.2	847.2	81.1	788.3	75.5	58.9	7.0
30-34 years	1 101.8	891.2	80.9	829.4	75.3	61.8	6.9
35-39 years	1 212.5	995.4	82.1	927.9	76.5	67.5	6.8
40-44 years	1 357.7	1 116.7	82.2	1 042.1	76.8	74.6	6.7
45-49 years	1 258.5	1 030.1	81.9	974.1	77.4	56.0	5.4
50-54 years	1 076.1	822.4	76.4	775.7	72.1	46.7	5.7
55-59 years	922.9	551.1	59.7	519.7	56.3	31.3	5.7
60-64 years	704.4	224.4	31.9	212.1	30.1	12.3	5.5
65-69 years	582.4	57.3	9.8	54.8	9.4	2.5	4.4
70 years and over	1 540.9	28.7	1.9	28.3	1.8	.0	.0

Source: © *Statistics Canada*
(1) The labour force consists of the employed workers and those who are unemployed but actively seeking work.
(2) Participation rate is the percent of the population segment that is in the labour force.

Average Weekly Earnings

All employees (including overtime) (dollars)

	1999	2000	2001	2002	2003
Average weekly earnings	640.71	655.91	667.28	680.90	689.66
Goods producing industries	806.52	824.06	832.35	849.74	863.73
Forestry, logging and support	773.42	810.15	830.84	849.77	851.56
Mining and oil and gas extraction	1 101.04	1 137.37	1 153.12	1 167.98	1 182.29
Utilities	1 018.23	1 029.28	1 038.83	1 058.31	1 070.35
Construction	782.63	808.06	800.80	804.22	821.92
Manufacturing	782.43	796.89	808.10	830.14	842.33
Service producing industries	590.45	604.33	617.50	630.56	638.36
Trade	531.18	536.87	543.47	545.39	555.22
Wholesale trade	758.60	762.84	774.87	778.70	790.21
Retail trade	423.00	425.62	431.06	434.46	444.59
Transportation and warehousing	715.98	725.10	741.65	764.40	762.93
Information and cultural industries	766.73	780.32	798.88	821.09	819.85
Finance and insurance	824.82	845.54	852.32	852.78	868.03
Real estate and rental and leasing	577.63	590.93	611.35	609.79	598.02
Professional, scientific and technical services	831.34	870.38	886.09	899.14	914.06
Management of companies and enterprises .	855.85	829.82	839.66	846.25	859.07
Educational services	664.74	673.88	694.30	725.27	747.88
Health care and social assistance	544.79	562.39	581.34	605.12	612.92
Arts, entertainment and recreation	397.25	409.85	428.51	435.18	420.05
Other services (except public administration)	491.47	502.92	521.44	530.11	526.64
Public administration	761.05	781.15	791.95	833.52	858.43

Source: © Statistics Canada
(1) Unadjusted for seasonal variation and classified using the North American Industry Classification System (NAICS).

Labour Income

(millions of dollars)

	1999	2000	2001	2002	2003
Labour income	**502 726**	**545 204**	**570 008**	**592 692**	**613 718**
Wages and salaries	445 384	483 861	504 765	521 568	538 288
All good-producing industries	126 108	136 043	140 355	142 557	146 418
Agriculture, forestry, fishing and hunting . .	6 748	7 005	7 240	7 542	7 248
Mining and oil and gas extraction	8 531	9 991	11 203	10 837	11 592
Manufacturing	78 020	83 758	83 752	84 181	85 165
Construction	26 435	28 610	31 106	32 723	34 920
Utilities	6 374	6 680	7 054	7 274	7 492
All service-producing industries	319 275	347 818	364 410	379 011	391 871
Trade	61 475	65 664	68 960	71 318	74 367
Transportation and storage	24 823	26 070	27 103	27 655	27 900
Information and cultural industries	14 770	16 235	16 926	17 084	17 359
Finance, real estate and company management	41 103	45 830	48 397	49 207	50 616
Professional and personal services industries	74 209	83 032	87 743	91 722	93 592
Educational services	35 099	36 473	37 874	39 520	41 120
Health care and social assistance	35 958	38 898	41 292	43 810	46 000
Federal government public administration .	14 750	17 878	17 359	19 060	20 066
Military	3 383	3 508	3 833	3 949	4 242
Federal public administration excluding military	11 367	14 370	13 526	15 111	15 825
Provincial and territorial public administration	9 018	9 436	10 139	10 492	11 145
Local public administration	8 069	8 302	8 617	9 142	9 704
Supplementary labour income	57 343	61 342	65 243	71 124	75 430

Source: *© Statistics Canada*

Employment in Manufacturing

(thousands)

	Labour Force	Employment	Full-time Employment[1]	Part-time Employment[2]	Unemployed	Unemployment Rate (%)
1988	2 246.3	2 104.3	2 025.2	79.1	142.0	6.3
1989	2 272.6	2 129.7	2 044.4	85.3	142.9	6.3
1990	2 227.7	2 052.5	1 978.2	74.4	175.2	7.9
1991	2 101.7	1 891.8	1 814.9	76.9	209.9	10.0
1992	2 011.6	1 821.5	1 740.5	81.0	190.2	9.5
1993	1 957.3	1 786.4	1 707.6	78.8	170.9	8.7
1994	1 962.6	1 820.3	1 741.9	78.4	142.3	7.3
1995	2 037.1	1 905.5	1 821.8	83.7	131.6	6.5
1996	2 079.7	1 931.1	1 842.5	88.6	148.5	7.1
1997	2 143.6	2 022.4	1 937.9	84.5	121.2	5.7
1998	2 248.0	2 113.8	2 028.7	85.0	134.2	6.0
1999	2 344.8	2 217.4	2 135.3	82.1	127.4	5.4
2000	2 392.8	2 280.2	2 202.1	78.1	112.6	4.7
2001	2 422.5	2 274.5	2 190.4	84.1	148.0	6.1
2002	2 480.0	2 326.2	2 244.2	82.0	153.8	6.2
2003	2 440.2	2 294.0	2 207.2	86.8	146.2	6.0

Source: © *Statistics Canada*
(1) Full-time employment consists of persons who usually work 30 hours or more per week at their main or only job.
(2) Part-time employment consists of persons who usually work less than 30 hours per week at their main or only job.

Employment in Manufacturing by Sector

	Number of Manufacturing Establishments		Number of Production and Related Workers	
	2001	**2002**	**2001**	**2002**
Manufacturing	54 031	54 346	1 587 141	1 528 720
Food manufacturing	5 545	5 444	197 106	201 028
Beverage and tobacco product manufacturing	513	539	16 378	16 312
Textile mills	627	625	22 941	21 783
Textile product mills	912	897	16 928	16 092
Clothing manufacturing	2 842	2 788	94 260	78 851
Leather and allied product manufacturing	356	328	9 459	8 219
Wood product manufacturing	3 740	3 774	114 081	114 171
Paper manufacturing	850	845	76 261	74 670
Printing and related support activities	4 788	4 735	67 003	60 739
Petroleum and coal products manufacturing	251	234	7 163	7 321
Chemical manufacturing	2 067	2 145	55 046	56 610
Plastics and rubber products manufacturing	2 434	2 440	101 790	103 970
Non-metallic mineral product manufacturing	2 215	2 230	41 418	41 237
Primary metal manufacturing	673	678	70 885	69 532
Fabricated metal product manufacturing	7 924	8 020	158 980	151 830
Machinery manufacturing	5 000	5 063	113 551	106 564
Computer and electronic product manufacturing	2 043	2 037	62 785	52 306
Electrical equipment, appliance and component manufacturing	1 098	1 112	38 521	36 178
Transportation equipment manufacturing	2 250	2 338	187 966	178 775
Furniture and related product manufacturing	3 528	3 597	87 680	86 227
Miscellaneous manufacturing	4 375	4 477	46 939	46 305

Source: © *Statistics Canada*

Labour and Employment in Retail

(thousands)

	Labour Force		Employed		Full-time		Part-time		Unemployed		Unemployment Rate (%)	
	Men	Women	Men	Women	Men	Women	Men	Women	Men	Women	Men	Women
1988	832.6	900.7	783.2	841.5	626.9	485.8	156.3	355.7	49.4	59.2	5.9	6.6
1989	841.3	897.1	793.7	837.3	632.4	496.3	161.3	341.1	47.6	59.8	5.7	6.7
1990	843.2	922.5	790.6	858.4	627.8	501.3	162.8	357.1	52.6	64.1	6.2	6.9
1991	842.2	941.2	775.2	867.1	604.9	500.3	170.3	366.8	66.9	74.1	7.9	7.9
1992	855.2	915.8	787.8	844.6	614.0	492.9	173.8	351.7	67.5	71.2	7.9	7.8
1993	847.2	913.0	778.8	845.0	604.1	480.5	174.6	364.5	68.4	68.0	8.1	7.4
1994	847.8	923.5	786.1	863.8	606.5	494.7	179.6	369.0	61.7	59.7	7.3	6.5
1995	848.8	926.7	793.6	869.6	627.0	501.5	166.6	368.1	55.2	57.2	6.5	6.2
1996	851.6	919.1	795.0	866.3	623.8	488.5	171.3	377.8	56.6	52.8	6.6	5.7
1997	849.2	924.5	801.8	871.5	633.8	494.2	168.0	377.3	47.4	53.0	5.6	5.7
1998	836.9	953.0	794.1	901.3	622.2	523.6	172.0	377.7	42.7	51.6	5.1	5.4
1999	843.7	955.0	800.6	911.6	617.0	519.4	183.5	392.2	43.1	43.5	5.1	4.6
2000	854.8	999.3	816.1	953.8	631.9	566.5	184.2	387.3	38.7	45.5	4.5	4.6
2001	883.0	1033.3	841.5	988.0	645.8	580.1	195.7	407.8	41.6	45.3	4.7	4.4
2002	913.5	1064.2	865.2	1 011.1	662.6	583.5	202.5	427.7	48.3	53.1	5.3	5.0
2003	917.9	1 071.0	871.9	1 016.6	667.1	574.4	204.7	442.3	46.0	54.4	5.0	5.1

Source: © *Statistics Canada*

Retail Employment by Sector

	Total Number of Employees		Employees Paid by the Hour	
	2002	2003	2002	2003
Retail trade	1 550 141	1 597 035	1 091 068	1 088 523
Motor vehicle and parts dealers	162 230	169 616	71 425	79 273
Furniture and home furnishings stores	60 116	61 796	29 961	31 263
Electronics and appliance stores	57 963	58 023	26 458	26 786
Building material & garden equipment & supplies dealers .	76 652	77 797	46 821	47 617
Food and beverage stores	398 636	419 169	320 615	334 081
Health and personal care stores	124 646	132 116	n.a.	n.a.
Gasoline stations	86 017	85 381	66 642	63 150
Clothing and clothing accessories stores	179 249	183 903	n.a.	n.a.
Sporting goods, hobby, book and music stores	75 073	74 468	53 382	55 871
General merchandise stores	206 694	208 940	n.a.	n.a.
Miscellaneous store retailers	82 847	86 713	n.a.	n.a.
Non-store retailers	40 018	39 113	n.a.	n.a.
Electronic shopping and mail-order houses	10 424	10 828	6 738	7 091
Vending machine operators	6 062	5 580	3 929	3 768
Direct selling establishments	23 531	22 705	12 862	13 067
Information and cultural industries	334 139	343 540	127 001	122 988
Finance and insurance	568 837	574 683	116 387	116 963

Source: © *Statistics Canada*

(n.a.) Not available.

PERSONAL FINANCE

What's a Dollar Worth?[1]

This table shows how many current (2004) dollars it would take to equal the purchasing power of a single dollar in earlier years. For example, if you spent $30 a week on groceries in 1985 and want to know what that would be by today's standards, multiply $30 times the relative value of a 1985 dollar ($1.67) and you have your answer: $50.10. The relative value of a dollar for the years listed was calculated according to changes in the cost of living in Canada as measured by the Consumer Price Index (CPI).

Year	CPI	2004 Relative Value	Year	CPI	2004 Relative Value	Year	CPI	2004 Relative Value	Year	CPI	2004 Relative Value
1925	10.7	11.69	1963	19.1	6.55	1977	39.9	3.14	1991	98.9	1.26
1930	10.9	11.48	1964	19.5	6.42	1978	43.6	2.87	1992	100.0	1.25
1935	8.6	14.55	1965	20.1	6.22	1979	47.5	2.63	1993	101.6	1.23
1940	9.4	13.31	1966	20.8	6.01	1980	52.2	2.40	1994	101.6	1.23
1945	10.9	11.48	1967	21.5	5.82	1981	58.9	2.12	1995	104.4	1.20
1950	14.7	8.51	1968	22.3	5.61	1982	65.6	1.91	1996	105.9	1.18
1955	16.8	7.45	1969	23.5	5.32	1983	69.2	1.81	1997	107.7	1.16
1956	17.0	7.36	1970	24.2	5.17	1984	72.1	1.74	1998	108.8	1.15
1957	17.6	7.11	1971	24.8	5.04	1985	75.0	1.67	1999	110.5	1.13
1958	18.0	6.95	1972	25.8	4.85	1986	77.8	1.61	2000	113.7	1.10
1959	18.0	6.95	1973	27.9	4.48	1987	81.5	1.53	2001	117.5	1.06
1960	18.4	6.80	1974	31.1	4.02	1988	84.7	1.48	2002	119.0	1.05
1961	18.7	6.69	1975	34.3	3.65	1989	89.2	1.40	2003	122.1	1.02
1962	18.9	6.62	1976	37.0	3.38	1990	93.1	1.34	2004	125.1	1.00

Source: © *Statistics Canada*   (1) Based on Consumer Price Index as of June 2004. The current base period is 1992 = 100.

Personal Income and Savings

	Total Personal Income ($millions)	Annual Change in Personal Income (%)	Total Personal Disposable Income ($millions)	Total Personal Saving ($millions)	Personal Saving Rate (%)
1965	41 904	9.9	37 490	2 683	7.2
1970	67 932	8.4	56 042	4 284	7.6
1975	137 240	16.2	112 984	15 778	14.0
1980	248 761	13.9	206 266	32 065	15.5
1985	397 858	8.3	322 989	50 886	15.8
1986	425 757	7.0	340 403	45 761	13.4
1987	457 702	7.5	362 185	43 073	11.9
1988	502 542	9.8	395 217	48 691	12.3
1989	546 324	8.7	432 772	56 281	13.0
1990	586 566	7.4	457 400	59 286	13.0
1991	605 322	3.2	472 509	62 670	13.3
1992	620 653	2.5	483 370	62 879	13.0
1993	633 059	2.0	494 944	58 674	11.9
1994	646 348	2.1	501 678	47 427	9.5
1995	672 111	4.0	519 588	47 859	9.2
1996	687 203	2.2	527 783	37 041	7.0
1997	715 495	4.1	546 166	26 607	4.9
1998	748 321	4.6	568 766	27 610	4.9
1999	783 060	4.6	596 227	23 937	4.0
2000	840 382	7.3	639 567	29 919	4.7
2001	874 657	4.1	667 477	30 479	4.6
2002	897 901	2.7	692 691	22 044	3.2
2003	924 608	3.0	713 548	10 167	1.4
2004[1]	958 528	4.2	745 344	11 540	1.5

Source: © *Statistics Canada*   (1) Preliminary estimates.

Sources of Income by Family Type, 2002

(%)

Canadian taxfilers report income from a number of sources during any given tax year. The table below shows the percentage of taxfilers reporting a specific type of income, broken down by family type.

	Total Family Types	Couple Families	Lone-Parent Families	Non-Family Persons
Total families.....................	**13 299 610**	**7 249 010**	**1 404 260**	**4 646 340**
% REPORTING:				
Employment Income	75	86	79	58
Wages/salaries/commissions..............	71	82	76	53
Self-employment	16	22	9	8
Farm & fish self-employment.............	3	4	1	1
Other self-employment..................	14	19	8	7
Investment.............................	41	49	25	35
Government transfers......................	83	81	97	82
Employment Insurance...................	16	21	17	8
OAS/Net federal supp.	22	18	12	32
CPP/QPP	27	24	18	35
Canada Child Tax Benefit	24	33	63	n.a.
GST/HST credit.........................	56	42	83	70
Workers compensation	5	7	4	3
Social assistance	10	5	25	13
Provincial tax credits/Family Benefits........	47	37	74	54
Private pensions.........................	19	19	9	20
RRSP	3	3	1	3
Other income	25	31	24	17

Source: © *Statistics Canada*

Employment Income of Families with Children, 2002

	Total Families	Number of Children			
		0	1	2	3+
Total Couple Families	7 249 010	3 150 910	1 622 940	1 680 050	795 120
Median Employment Income of Husband in Single-Earner Family....................	$30 100	$18 500	$34 000	$42 900	$37 900
Median Employment Income of Wife in Single-Earner Family....................	$17 900	$16 700	$19 400	$21 000	$16 300
Median Employment Income of Couple in Dual-Earner Family......................	$66 000	$62 100	$65 200	$70 600	$65 900
Average Contribution of Wife in Dual-Earner Family......................	$28 500	$29 400	$28 200	$28 800	$26 000
LONE-PARENT FAMILIES					
Total Families with Employment Income	938 420	n.a.	527 230	295 740	115 450
Median Employment Income of Parent.........	$22 400	n.a.	$23 100	$23 200	$17 400

Source: © *Statistics Canada*

(n.a.) Not applicable.

Average Assets and Debts Held by Family Units, by Province, 1999

	Canada		Newfoundland & Labrador		Prince Edward Island	
Number of family units	12 215 629		198 630		54 205	
	% of Families[1]	$ Average	% of Families[1]	$ Average	% of Families[1]	$ Average
ASSETS	**100.0**	**237 163**	**100.0**	**114 687**	**100.0**	**194 919**
Financial assets............	93.0	74 774	80.8	37 801	92.0	54 450
Within registered plans	61.0	56 442	42.0	34 112	52.2	60 380
RRSPs & LIRAs[2]	54.9	51 189	39.1	32 658	45.4	57 255
Other registered plans[3]...	14.7	42 967	x	x	x	x
Outside registered plans....	90.0	39 047	79.5	20 424	88.5	21 016
Deposits in fin inst	87.9	14 970	78.1	7 657	84.6	8 060
Mutual & investmt funds......	30.0	53 928	19.4	15 407	30.4	28 732
Other financial assets[4]	8.9	64 948	x	x	x	x
Non-financial assets	100.0	138 593	100.0	77 755	100.0	102 550
Principal residence.........	60.4	149 661	73.2	66 440	67.2	92 108
Other real estate...........	16.5	116 999	17.0	42 225	x	x
Vehicles	77.2	13 329	77.1	10 616	84.0	11 913
Other non-financial assets[5] .	100.0	18 689	100.0	13 767	100.0	19 184
Equity in business...........	18.7	155 610	x	x	x	x
DEBTS	**68.0**	**55 155**	**75.3**	**29 332**	**74.5**	**31 853**
Mortgages.................	35.1	82 844	25.1	46 332	31.8	49 491
Principal residence.........	32.7	76 116	24.2	42 237	30.5	47 139
Other real estate...........	4.7	88 550	x	x	x	x
Line of credit.............	15.9	13 542	x	x	x	x
Cr card & installmt debt[6]......	38.5	3 033	52.6	2 614	48.2	2 628
Student loans	11.8	10 361	19.8	15 831	x	x
Vehicle loans..............	21.2	11 226	31.7	10 130	28.0	9 253
Other debt................	16.3	9 301	19.4	8 562	32.1	5 950
NET WORTH[7]	**99.9**	**199 789**	**100.0**	**92 612**	**100.0**	**171 189**

	Nova Scotia		New Brunswick		Quebec	
Number of family units	376 191		300 177		3 115 360	
	% of Families[1]	$ Average	% of Families[1]	$ Average	% of Families[1]	$ Average
ASSETS..............	**100.0**	**154 005**	**100.0**	**182 705**	**100.0**	**149 587**
Financial assets............	86.4	55 194	92.9	58 226	86.4	42 063
Within registered plans	54.0	43 020	57.2	49 632	48.0	41 585
RRSPs & LIRAs[2]	49.2	38 335	50.9	44 856	43.8	38 378
Other registered plans[3]......	13.6	32 174	12.1	45 716	11.9	26 146
Outside registered plans.....	81.3	30 045	90.5	28 423	83.7	19 595
Deposits in fin inst	78.1	10 598	89.4	11 491	81.2	10 670
Mutual & investmt funds......	30.4	31 983	21.8	49 374	23.3	27 992
Other financial assets[4]	9.9	65 025	6.3	74 464	x	x
Non-financial assets	100.0	94 340	100.0	101 815	100.0	91 874
Principal residence.........	64.4	87 382	55.4	109 481	70.2	78 715
Other real estate...........	19.4	50 615	16.8	101 942	19.7	52 090
Vehicles	76.9	12 122	72.8	11 740	82.2	12 779
Other non-financial assets[5] .	100.0	18 928	100.0	15 522	100.0	15 871
Equity in business...........	14.1	84 989	14.4	186 422	x	x
DEBTS..............	**74.5**	**34 523**	**65.1**	**42 297**	**72.8**	**30 796**
Mortgages.................	32.4	51 732	32.6	65 594	33.1	40 762
Principal residence.........	30.3	49 829	29.9	55 532	31.6	38 376
Other real estate...........	x	x	5.2	93 151	x	x
Line of credit.............	17.4	10 559	15.8	7 082	12.0	9 759
Cr card & installmt debt[6]......	45.6	2 626	33.8	2 081	49.0	2 373
Student loans	13.7	11 178	11.9	7 971	18.3	10 137
Vehicle loans..............	29.4	10 601	21.1	9 696	32.2	10 533
Other debt................	18.3	6 816	15.4	8 496	15.2	9 041
NET WORTH[7]	**99.8**	**128 502**	**100.0**	**155 261**	**100.0**	**127 155** ▶

Number of family units	Ontario 4 480 409		Manitoba 446 152		Saskatchewan 401 649	
	% of Families[1]	$ Average	% of Families[1]	$ Average	% of Families[1]	$ Average
ASSETS	100.0	264 348	100.0	190 268	100.0	224 291
Financial assets	94.6	87 690	92.2	70 312	94.5	72 337
Within registered plans	64.9	62 377	62.9	52 422	63.3	51 155
RRSPs & LIRAs[2]	58.5	55 119	55.3	47 802	56.2	47 644
Other registered plans[3]	17.0	48 485	17.1	38 271	16.8	33 345
Outside registered plans	87.7	46 451	87.7	36 342	91.2	39 416
Deposits in fin inst	89.6	17 893	84.1	16 227	88.6	19 311
Mutual & investmt funds	34.0	65 386	33.4	43 895	34.2	41 637
Other financial assets[4]	8.3	50 412	9.8	36 364	16.4	28 118
Non-financial assets	100.0	160 277	100.0	96 467	100.0	104 626
Principal residence	60.5	181 395	64.1	91 348	69.1	82 091
Other real estate	16.3	128 634	17.7	57 351	18.0	90 831
Vehicles	76.7	13 062	78.8	13 079	84.3	15 595
Other non-financial assets[5]	100.0	19 513	100.0	17 504	100.0	18 337
Equity in business	19.6	108 038	17.3	167 572	28.9	177 529
DEBTS	68.0	63 579	62.9	37 604	66.2	38 418
Mortgages	36.3	94 406	33.0	51 196	30.6	48 616
Principal residence	34.1	88 689	31.2	49 201	29.2	45 424
Other real estate	4.5	88 417	x	x	x	x
Line of credit	16.1	16 978	12.4	8 556	16.2	11 090
Cr card & installmt debt[6]	39.9	3 373	33.5	3 069	38.6	2 690
Student loans	12.2	11 680	x	x	11.4	11 309
Vehicle loans	19.4	11 529	21.5	11 201	26.9	12 839
Other debt	13.9	9 078	18.3	8 447	19.7	15 068
NET WORTH[7]	99.9	221 233	100.0	166 628	100.0	198 911

Number of family units	Alberta 1 157 207		British Columbia 1 685 649	
	% of Families[1]	$ Average	% of Families[1]	$ Average
ASSETS	100.0	278 016	100.0	302 934
Financial assets	93.2	79 624	92.8	82 775
Within registered plans	63.4	55 611	61.0	60 882
RRSPs & LIRAs[2]	58.7	53 703	54.7	56 644
Other registered plans[3]	14.2	26 533	14.1	43 822
Outside registered plans	89.4	43 553	90.4	43 882
Deposits in financial institutions	86.1	15 771	87.5	14 231
Mutual funds & investment funds stocks & bonds (saving & other)	33.2	42 022	33.3	53 280
Other financial assets[4]	12.9	88 595	11.2	84 493
Non-financial assets	100.0	146 583	100.0	189 208
Principal residence	66.4	135 917	57.7	225 202
Other real estate	16.2	126 108	14.3	183 179
Vehicles	84.3	15 870	78.6	15 087
Other non-financial assets[5]	100.0	22 513	100.0	21 140
Equity in business	25.1	228 367	20.9	176 758
DEBTS	71.9	58 441	69.1	74 860
Mortgages	41.0	78 108	36.4	115 849
Principal residence	38.1	72 687	33.4	107 152
Other real estate	5.7	76 536	5.8	108 932
Line of credit	17.2	14 543	16.4	18 547
Credit card & installment debt[6]	39.7	3 379	38.3	3 814
Student loans	11.0	9 242	9.7	10 433
Vehicle loans	23.1	13 032	18.2	12 278
Other debt	18.1	11 688	20.3	9 034
NET WORTH[7]	99.9	236 198	99.9	251 517

Source: © *Statistics Canada*

(x) Data unavailable, not applicable or confidential.
(1) Family units: economic families (a group of two or more persons who live in the same dwelling & are related to each other by blood, marriage, common law or adoption) & unattached individuals (a person living either alone or with others to whom he or she is unrelated). (2) Registered Retirement Savings Plans (RRSPs) & Locked-in Retirement Accounts (LIRAs). (3) Plans other than RRSPs or LIRAs e.g. Registered Retirement Income Funds (RRIFs), Deferred Profit Sharing Plans (DPSPs) & Registered Education Savings Plans (RESPs). (4) Includes treasury bills, mortgage-backed securities, money held in trust annuities, money owed to the respondent & other miscellaneous financial assets including shares of privately held companies not held within registered plans. (5) The value of the contents of the respondent's principal residence, valuables & collectibles, copyrights & patents, etc. (6) Includes major credit cards & retail store cards, gasoline station cards etc. Installment debt is the total amount owing on deferred payment or installment plans where the purchased item is to be paid for over a period of time. (7) Net worth = assets less debts.

Net Worth and Median Income by Family Type, 1998

	% of Family Units	% Economic Families	% Unattached Individuals	Median Net Worth	Median After-tax 1998 Income
All family units	100			$81 000	$33 400
Economic families of two or more. . .	68	100		$119 300	$43 000
Elderly families		14		$202 000	$32 000
Non-elderly families		86		$105 500	$48 400
Couples only		22		$125 800	$44 800
Couples with children under 18. . .		38		$100 500	$48 400
Lone-parent families		7		$14 600	$21 800
Other non-elderly families		18		$151 000	$52 300
Unattached individuals	32		100	$21 700	$16 700
Elderly men			7	$111 100	$17 700
Elderly women			20	$76 600	$15 300
Non-elderly men			42	$11 200	$19 800
Non-elderly women			32	$12 000	$15 600

Source: © *Statistics Canada*

Distribution of Net Worth, 1998

For the 1998 tax year, the median net worth of the close to 12.2 million family units in Canada was around $81,000. However, when family units were ranked from highest net worth to lowest, the median net worth of the top 10 percent (or top decile) was nearly $703,500, while the median net worth of the lowest decile was –$2,100. Further analysis showed that the wealthiest 10 percent of family units held 53 percent of all personal wealth. (By comparison, in the US, the top 10 percent of family units and unattached individuals held approximately two-thirds of total net worth.)

Family units ranked by net worth in deciles (units of 10%)	% of Total Net Worth	Median Net Worth
All family units	100	$81 000
Highest 10%	53	$703 500
Ninth 10%	17	$338 100
Eighth 10%	11	$220 800
Seventh 10%	8	$152 600
Sixth 10%	5	$101 500
Fifth 10%	3	$64 700
Fourth 10%	2	$35 500
Third 10%	1	$14 300
Second 10%	...	$3 100
Lowest 10%	...	–$2 100

Source: © *Statistics Canada*

Median Net Worth of Families by Income, 1998

After-tax Income in 1998	% of Family Units	Median Net Worth
All family units	100	$81 000
Less than $10 000	8	$1 700
$10 000 - $19 000	18	$14 600
$20 000 - $29 000	18	$52 000
$30 000 - $39 000	16	$82 800
$40 000 - $49 000	12	$109 200
$50 000 - $74 999	18	$153 500
$75 000 or more	10	$314 200

Source: © *Statistics Canada*

Median Net Worth by Province, 1998

"Median" refers to the point in a data grouping at which half of those in the group fall below the median number and half are above it—the middle value or mid-point in the series. "Net worth" includes financial assets such as investments, non-financial assets such as property, and equity in businesses.

	% of Total Family Units	% Owning Principal Residence	% with After-tax Family Income under $20 000	Median Net Worth
All provinces.	100	60	26	**$81 000**
Newfoundland and Labrador.	2	73	31	$53 000
Prince Edward Island	...	67	30	$76 100
Nova Scotia.	3	64	32	$68 100
New Brunswick.	2	70	31	$65 400
Quebec	26	55	31	$61 300
Ontario	37	60	21	$101 400
Manitoba.	4	64	28	$79 300
Saskatchewan.	3	69	30	$97 300
Alberta	9	66	24	$95 400
British Columbia	14	58	28	$94 800

Source: © *Statistics Canada*

Median Net Worth by Education, 1998

Highest Level of Education of Major Income Earner for Family	% of Family Units	Median Net Worth
Less than high school	27	$62 500
Graduated high school	23	$67 700
Non-university certificate	28	$78 700
University certificate:		
Bachelor's degree	15	$117 500
Master's or certificate above Bachelor's	5	$181 500
Doctorate.	1	$237 000
Degree in law, medicine, dentistry, veterinary medicine or optometry	1	$323 000

Source: © *Statistics Canada*

Median Net Worth by Occupation, 1998

Occupation of Major Income Earner for Family	% of Family Units	Median Net Worth	Median after-tax 1998 Income
All family units		**$81 000**	**$33 400**
Management.	8	$192 800	$56 100
Primary industry	2	$155 000	$35 800
Social science, education, government and religion . .	5	$112 200	$49 600
Health	4	$111 600	$46 000
Natural and applied sciences.	6	$90 500	$47 500
Trades, transportation and equipment operators	12	$79 000	$41 800
Business, finance and administration	10	$77 900	$39 700
No occupation.	32	$76 500	$20 700
Processing, manufacturing and utilities	6	$66 900	$41 700
Art, culture, recreation and sport	2	$65 000	$35 400
Sales and service	13	$40 000	$28 400

Source: © *Statistics Canada*

Canadian Income Tax

Income tax was introduced in 1917 as a temporary measure to finance Canada's participation in World War I. The law introducing the tax (the Income War Tax Act) was shorter and much simpler than our current legislation. It imposed tax at graduated rates, ranging from 4 percent on the first $1,500 to 25 percent for income over $100,000.

This "temporary" tax was not repealed when the war ended. But on Jan. 1, 1949, the federal government removed "war" from the title and gave the statute the name it has today—the Income Tax Act. This act has been amended many times—most notably in 1972 when a major overhaul of the tax system broadened the tax base and introduced a tax on capital gains. This is still the basis of our federal income tax laws today.

In 1988, all personal exemptions and many deductions were changed to non-refundable tax credits. Unlike deductions, which reduce taxable income, credits are used to reduce the amount of tax payable. The term "non-refundable" refers to the fact that, although you can use these credits to reduce or eliminate your federal tax payable, any unused portion is not refundable to you. In some cases, however, you may be able to transfer the unused portion of the credits to someone else.

Because the credits are calculated by multiplying eligible amounts by 15 percent—the same as the lowest personal tax rate—the change makes no difference to those whose income falls within the lowest tax bracket. But it increases taxes for most of those with higher incomes.

Source: *Revenue Canada*

For the 2003 income tax year, the federal income tax rates for the individual are: 16 percent on income up to $32,182; $5,149 plus 22 percent on the next $32,182 up to $64,367; $12,230 plus 26 percent on the next $40,319 up to $104,647; and $22,703 plus 29 percent on income in excess of $104,648. There is a maximum total tax for the first three brackets, but no maximum tax for the over $104,648 bracket.

Provincial Income Tax

In previous years, all provinces and territories except Quebec computed income tax as a percentage of basic federal tax ("tax-on-tax" system). In 2000, five provinces switched to the "tax-on-income" system, with the other provinces and three territories following suit for the 2001 tax year. All jurisdictions, except for Quebec, continue to use the federal definition of taxable income. However, under a tax-on-income system, provinces set their own rates, brackets and credits.

Filing Tax Returns

Though corporations must file tax returns each year, individuals need only file if they owe taxes or if they are eligible to claim tax credits such as the Child Tax Credit, or the Goods and Services Tax Credit. Persons owing money must file a return by April 30 of the year following the taxation year. Failure to do so makes the taxpayer liable to a late-filing penalty of 5 percent of unpaid tax plus an additional penalty of 1 percent per month on the amount outstanding, to a maximum of 12 months, plus interest on amounts owing.

Federal Income Tax Rates on Individual Income, 2004

The federal components of personal income tax rates apply to all taxpayers.

Federal Tax Brackets, Marginal Rates and Minimum Amounts of Tax

Basic Federal Tax Brackets	Other than Quebec		Quebec	
	Marginal Rate	Minimum Federal Tax Payable	Marginal Rate[2]	Minimum Federal Tax Payable
$8 012 to $35 000	16%	$0[1]	13.36%	$0[1]
$35 001 to $70 000	22%	$5 600	18.37%	$4 676
$70 001 to $113 804	26%	$13 300	21.71%	$11 106
over $113 804	29%	$24 689	24.22%	$20 615

Source: © *"Tax Facts and Figures," PricewaterhouseCoopers*

(1) The basic personal credit eliminates federal tax for taxable income below $8,012. (2) Marginal rates for the federal component of personal tax are adjusted by a factor of 83.5 percent in Quebec: 13.36 percent = 16 percent x 83.5 percent; 18.37 = 22 percent x 83.5 percent; 21.71 percent = 26 percent x 83.5 percent; 24.215 percent = 83.5 percent x 29 percent. The federal surtax is not affected. The 83.5 percent factor is what remains after the 16.5 percent abatement.

Individual Provincial Income Tax Rates, 2004

For 2003, all provinces and territories compute income tax as "tax-on-income" systems. All jurisdictions, except for Quebec, continued to use the federal definition of taxable income. However, under a tax-on-income system, provinces set their own rates, brackets and credits.

Five provinces have surtaxes, calculated as a percentage of provincial tax. Manitoba and Saskatchewan eliminated their flat taxes in 2002, while several provinces have eliminated their surtaxes.

	Basic Tax Credit Amount	Basic Brackets					Provincial Surtax[1] On Provincial Tax Above:	Reduction for Low Incomes
Nfld & Lab.	$7 410	$0 to $29 589 10.57%	$29 590 to $59 179 16.16%	over $59 180 18.02%			$7 032 9% of tax	No
PEI	$7 412	$0 to $30 753 9.8%	$30 754 to $61 508 13.8%	over $61 509 16.7%			$5 200 10% of tax	Yes
N. Scotia	$7 321	$0 to $29 590 8.79%	$25 590 to $59 180 24.5%	$59 180 to $93 000 17.5%	over $93 000 17.5%		$10 000 10% of tax	Yes
N. Brunswick	$7 756	$0 to $32 182	$32 183 to $64 368 9.68%	$64 369 to $104 647 14.82%	over $104 648 16.52%	17.84%	n.a.	Yes
Quebec[2]	$6 275	$0 to $27 635 16%	$27 635 to $55 280 20%	over $55 280 24%			n.a.	Yes
Ontario	$8 044	$0 to $33 375 6.05%	$33 375 to $66 752 9.15%	over $66 752 11.16%			$3 856 20% of tax; over $69 238 additional 36%	Yes
Manitoba	$7 634	$0 to $30 544 10.9%	$30 544 to $65 000 14%	over $65 000 17.4%			n.a.	Yes
Sask.	$8 264	$0 to $36 155 11%	$36 155 to $103 300 13%	over $103 300 15%			n.a.	Yes
Alberta	$14 337	on taxable income 10%					n.a.	No
B.C.	$8 523	$0 to $32 476 6.05%	$32 476 to $64 954 9.15%	$64 954 to $74 575 11.7%	$74 575 to $90 555 13.7%	over $90 555 14.7%	n.a.	No
Yukon	$8 012	$0 to $35 000 7.04%	$35 000 to $70 000 9.68%	$70 000 to $113 804 11.44%	over $113 804 12,76%	5%	$6 000 n.a.	Yes
Northwest Territories	$11 415	$0 to $33 245 7.2%	$33 245 to $66 492 9.9%	$66 492 to $108 101 11.95%	over $108 101 13.55%		n.a.	No
Nunavut	$10 495	$0 to $35 000 4%	$35 000 to $70 000 7%	$70 000 to $113 804 9%	over $113 804 11.5%		n.a.	No
Non-residents	$8 012	$0 to $35 000 7.68%	$35 000 to $70 000 10.56%	$70 000 to $113 804 12.48%	over $113 804 13.92%		n.a.	No

Source: © *"Tax Facts and Figures,"* PricewaterhouseCoopers (n.a.) Not applicable.
(1) Surtax rates are the percentage of provincial tax above the basic provincial tax thresholds.
(2) Quebec's basic amount is $9,200 under the simplified tax system.

Personal Tax Credits, 2004

(dollars)

	Federal Amount[13]	Federal Credit[14]
Basic	8 012	1 282
Spouse/Equivalent to Spouse[1]	6 803	1 088
Age 65[2]	3 912	626
Disability[3]	6 486	1 038
Infirm dependant[4]	3 784	605
Care giver[5]	3 784	605
Dependant[6]		
— 1st	—	—
— Children (Additional)	—	—
Single parent	—	—
Living alone	—	—
Pension income[7]	1 000	160
CPP/QPP[8]	1 832	293
Employment Insurance (EI)	772	124
Education (per month)[9]		
— Full-time	400	64
— Part-time	120	19
CREDITS AS PERCENTAGE OF ACTUAL PAYMENT		
Dividends[10]	—[13]	13.33%[14]
Charitable donations[11]		
First $200	—[13]	16%[14]
Over $2000	—[13]	29%[14]
Tuition[12]	—[13]	16%[14]

Source: © *"Tax Facts and Figures,"* *PricewaterhouseCoopers*

(1) The spousal and equivalent credits are reduced when the income of the spouse or qualifying dependent exceeds $659. Any net income of the spouse reduces the Quebec spouse credit. (2) The age credit is reduced if income exceeds $27,095. (3) Basic credit for individuals with severe and prolonged impairment. The under 18 supplement is reduced if childcare and attendant care expenses claimed for child exceed $2,145. (4) Reduced if dependent's income exceeds $5,115. Any income reduces the Quebec infirm dependant credit. (5) For providers of in-home care for an adult relative (reduced if relative's income exceeds $12,312). The caregiver credit for Quebec is refundable. (6) Quebec's childcare credit is refundable and depends on net family income, and ranges from 26% to 75% of the expense. To qualify for the additional credit for children, children must be full-time students or under 19 years of age at the end of the year. (7) Maximum pension credit is $160. (8) For employees, the maximum credit is $405, self-employed persons deduct half of CPP/QPP premiums paid for their own coverage and claim a credit for half of these premiums. (9) The education credit is $64/month for full-time students, $19/month for part-time students. Quebec's maximum education credit is $344 per term (maximum two terms per year) for a supporting Quebec parent, which is not transferable. (10) Credits for taxable Canadian dividends apply to the grossed-up amount (125 percent) of dividends. (11) Eligible donations are limited to 75% of net income. (12) Tuition credit is available only if at least $100 in fees is paid to an institution. (13) Provinces use their own amounts to determine credits. (14) Maximum dollar value of credits that are based on prescribed amounts. Provinces have their own maximum dollar value of credits.

Individual Tax Tables, 2004

This table shows the combined federal and provincial (or territorial) income taxes, including surtaxes and flat taxes, payable on the assumption that only the basic personal tax credit is available, and that all income is either interest or ordinary income (such as salary).

Amount of combined federal and provincial/territorial income tax

Taxable Income	Alberta	B.C.	Manitoba	N.B.	Nfld & Lab	Non-resident	N.W.T.
150 000	47 470	50 378	56 015	55 783	58 877	50 178	49 418
100 000	28 384	28 942	33 229	32 839	34 971	29 331	28 686
90 000	24 784	24 878	28 889	28 587	30 406	25 483	24 891
80 000	21 184	20 908	24 549	24 335	25 842	21 635	21 096
70 000	17 584	17 029	20 209	20 083	21 278	17 787	17 301
60 000	14 384	13 786	16 439	16 305	17 114	14 531	14 039
50 000	11 184	10 671	12 839	12 623	13 261	11 275	10 849
40 000	7 984	7 556	9 239	8 941	9 445	8 019	7 659
30 000	5 084	4 817	5 956	5 671	5 929	5 207	4 856

Taxable Income	N.S.	Nunavut	Ontario	P.E.I.	Quebec	Sask.	Yukon
150 000	57 106	45 439	53 030	56 825	59 738	52 706	49 268
100 000	33 395	25 948	30 239	33 554	35 976	31 186	28 674
90 000	28 898	22 448	25 898	29 117	31 405	27 286	24 873
80 000	24 478	18 948	21 557	24 680	26 834	23 386	21 072
70 000	20 211	15 448	17 216	20 243	22 263	19 486	17 306
60 000	16 344	12 548	13 809	16 254	18 026	15 986	14 138
50 000	12 635	9 648	10 672	12 562	14 001	12 486	10 970
40 000	8 940	6 748	7 557	8 982	10 164	8 986	7 802
30 000	5 545	4 298	4 846	5 732	6 577	5 909	5 066

Source: © *"Tax Facts and Figures,"* PricewaterhouseCoopers   (1) In some situations, the calculation of taxable income for federal and Quebec purposes may be different, and the amounts shown may require adjustments.

How much do average Canadians make?

*A*fter five consecutive years of growth, after-tax family income remained virtually unchanged between 2001 and 2002, as the three main components (market income, government transfers and personal income taxes) each remained more or less stable.

After-tax income for families of two people or more amounted to an estimated $60,500, virtually unchanged from $60,300 in 2001, after adjusting for inflation.

This lack of growth was in contrast to the increase of 3.2% in annual average after-tax income for these families between 1996 and 2001.

Family income is correlated with economic conditions. After reaching a peak at $53,900 in 1989, average family income declined through the recession of the early 1990s and stayed below $52,000 up to and including 1996. Since then, it has rebounded in step with the recovering economy.

The low-income rate among families of two people or more edged up slightly in 2002 after five consecutive years of declines. A small increase in the low-income rate was experienced by those aged 18 and over. However, the proportion of children younger than age 18 years old and living in a low-income family was marginally lower, continuing its long-term decline.

Unlike most other family types, average after-tax income declined in 2002 for single-parent families headed by women. However, their income gains were among the strongest between 1996 and 2002 because of the increase in labour force participation by single mothers.

For unattached individuals, after-tax income amounted to $25,900 in 2002, up 2.4% from 2001 and 17% from 1996. An estimated 1 million of these individuals lived in low income in 2002, about 25% of the total, down from 34% in 1996. **Source:** *The Daily*, May 20, 2004 © Statistics Canada

INVESTMENT

Investment: A Glossary of Terms

Annual report: A report issued by a company to its shareholders at the end of the fiscal year. It contains a report on company operations and formal financial statements.

Bankers' acceptance: A commercial draft backed by the guarantee of a bank. The bankers' acceptance promises repayment on a certain date, usually not more than 90 days ahead, and bears a rate of return competitive with other chartered bank securities.

Bear market: A market in which prices are falling.

Bid and ask: The bid price is the highest price anyone is willing to pay to buy a stock; the ask is the lowest price anyone will accept to sell a stock. Together, the bid and ask prices are a quote.

Blue chip stocks: Stocks with good investment qualities, usually common shares of well-established companies with good earnings records and long-time dividend payments.

Board lot: A unit of trading. Board lots on the Toronto Stock Exchange are: under 10 cents each—1000 shares; between 10 cents and 99 cents each—500 shares; at and above $1 each—100 shares.

Bond: A written promise or IOU by the issuer to repay a fixed amount of borrowed money on a specified date, and to pay a set annual rate of interest in the meantime, generally at semi-annual intervals. Bonds are usually considered a safe investment because the borrower (whether a company or the government) must make interest payments before its money is spent on anything else.

Bull market: A market in which prices are rising.

Call: An option to buy a fixed amount of a certain stock at a specified price within a specified time.

Canada Savings Bonds: These are issued each fall, and are popular with small investors because they come in denominations starting at $100. They are not traded. They have a term of several years and a minimum guaranteed rate of interest. However, the government sets an effective rate during the issuing period each year, and adjusts it when necessary to conform with interest rate trends. Interest can be awarded yearly or compounded, depending upon the type of bond.

Capital gain or loss: Profit or loss resulting from the sale of an asset, such as a security. The gain or loss is the difference between the buying and selling price of the security with commissions figured in.

Commercial paper: Short-term negotiable securities issued by corporations that call for the payment of a specific amount of money at a given time.

Common shares: Securities issued by the company that represent part-ownership in the company. Common shares sometimes carry a voting privilege and entitle the holder to a share in the company's profits, usually issued in the form of dividends.

Convertible bond: A corporate bond (see below) that may be converted into a stated number of shares of the corporation's common stock. Its price tends to fluctuate with the price of the stock, as well as with changes in interest rates.

Corporate bonds: Evidence of debt by a corporation. The bond bears interest much like a government bond, and matures at a certain date in the future. Considered safer than the common or preferred stock of the same company.

Day order: An order to buy or sell a security valid only for the day the order is given.

Dividend: A portion of a company's profit paid to the common and preferred shareholders. The amount is decided upon by the company's board of directors, and may be paid in cash or stock.

Equities: Common and preferred stocks that represent a share in the ownership of a company.

Ex-dividend: Without dividend. The buyer of shares quoted ex-dividend is not entitled to receive an already declared dividend. When shares are un-dividend, the purchaser will receive the declared dividend.

Floor trader: A brokerage-firm employee who works on the stock exchange trading floor, and is responsible for executing buy and sell orders on behalf of the firm and its clients.

Futures: Contracts to buy or sell specific quantities of a commodity or financial instrument with delivery delayed until some agreed-upon time in the future.

Government of Canada bonds: These bear a fixed rate of interest and a maturation date in the future, and are traded on the market, with the price rising and falling in response to interest rate trends. ▶

▶ Long-term government bonds are considered a safe investment. Provinces and municipalities may also issue long-term bonds.

Index: Statistical measure of the state of the stock market or economy, based on the performance of stocks or other components. Examples are the TSE 300 Composite Index and the Toronto 35 Index.

Limit order: An order to buy or sell securities in which the client has specified the price. The order can be executed only at the specified price or a better one.

Liquidity: The measure of how quickly an investor can turn securities into cash. A security is liquid if it can be bought and sold quickly with small price changes between transactions.

Long: A term signifying ownership of securities. "I am long 100 XYZ" means that the speaker owns 100 shares of XYZ.

Margin: The amount paid by clients when they use credit to buy a security, the balance being loaned by their brokers.

Market order: An order to buy a security immediately at the best possible price.

Money market: Part of the capital market established for short-term borrowing and lending of funds. Money market dealers conduct business over the telephone, and trade securities such as short-term (three years and less) government bonds, government treasury bills and commercial paper.

Mutual fund: A portfolio, or selection, of professionally bought and managed stocks in which the investor pools money with thousands of others. A share price is based on net asset value, or the value of all the investments owned by the fund, less any debt, divided by the total number of shares. The major advantage is less risk—an investment is spread out over many stocks, and if one or two do badly, the remainder may shield the investor from the losses. Bond funds are mutual funds that deal in the bond market exclusively. Money market mutual funds concentrate on debt instruments sold on the money market. Equity mutual funds place their investments in the common shares of companies.

Odd lot: A number of shares less than a board lot.

Open order: An order to buy or sell a security at a specified price, valid until executed or cancelled.

Over-the-counter: The over-the-counter (OTC) or unlisted market is the market maintained by securities dealers for issues not listed on a stock exchange.

Penny stock: Low-priced, often speculative issues selling at less than $1 a share.

Preferred shares: Shares that carry dividends at fixed rates that must be paid before any dividends are paid to common shareholders.

Price/earnings ratio: A common stock's current market price divided by the company's annual per share earnings.

Prospectus: A legal document describing securities being offered for sale to the public. It must be prepared in accordance with provincial securities commission regulations.

Put: An option to sell a fixed amount of a certain stock at a specified price within a specified time.

Registered representative: A salesperson or broker employed by an investment firm. Salespersons must be registered with the provincial securities commission.

Right: A temporary privilege granted to existing common shareholders to purchase additional shares directly from the company at a stated price.

Settlement date: The date on which a securities buyer must pay for a purchase or a seller must deliver the securities sold. In general, settlement must be made on or before the third business day following the transaction date.

Short sale: The sale of shares that the seller does not own. The seller is speculating that the stock price will fall, in the hope of later purchasing the same number of securities at a lower price, thereby making a profit. Sellers must advise their brokers when they are selling short.

Stock yield: The percentage of the dividend paid in relation to the price of the stock. For example, a stock selling at $40 a share with an annual dividend of $2 a share yields 5 percent.

Transfer agent: A trust company appointed by a company to keep a record of the names, addresses and numbers of shares held by its shareholders. Transfer agents are often responsible for distributing dividend cheques.

Underwriting: The purchase for resale of a new issue of securities by an investment dealer or group of dealers.

Warrant: A certificate giving the holder the right to purchase securities at a stipulated price within a specified period of time. They are often detachable and may be traded separately.

Canadian Investors by Province, 2002

	% of Taxfilers with Investment Income	Average Age of Investor	Median Total Income of Investor	Median Investment Income	% Investment Income from Dividends
CANADA................	13	54	$37,800	$1,000	62
Newfoundland and Labrador	6	52	36,700	400	61
Prince Edward Island.....	12	54	32,400	600	66
Nova Scotia............	12	55	35,100	800	75
New Brunswick.........	10	55	34,400	600	72
Quebec................	13	53	36,000	800	67
Ontario................	14	55	39,800	1,000	56
Manitoba..............	13	55	33,800	800	53
Saskatchewan...........	13	56	32,900	900	57
Alberta	15	53	41,200	1,000	67
British Columbia.........	13	56	36,500	1,300	62
Yukon.................	11	50	48,300	700	75
Northwest Territories	7	46	67,900	500	68
Nunavut...............	4	46	81,900	700	84

Source: © *Statistics Canada*

Canadian Investors by Age, 2002

	% Canadians with Investment Income					
	0–24	25–34	35–44	45–54	55–64	65 and over
CANADA	4	7	17	24	21	28
Newfoundland and Labrador ..	3	6	19	31	23	18
Prince Edward Island........	3	6	17	26	22	25
Nova Scotia	3	6	16	25	22	28
New Brunswick	3	6	16	25	22	28
Quebec	3	9	19	25	21	23
Ontario..................	4	7	16	22	21	31
Manitoba	4	7	15	23	21	30
Saskatchewan	4	6	15	24	20	31
Alberta..................	4	8	19	26	20	23
British Columbia	4	6	14	23	22	31
Yukon	3	8	20	33	23	13
Northwest Territories........	3	11	28	33	18	7
Nunavut.................	0	18	22	36	18	4

Source: © *Statistics Canada*

Canadian Investors by Gender, 2002

	% of Total Investment Income by Gender $ '000	Males	Females	Median Investment Income Total	Males	Females
Canada...................	21 781 629	58	42	$1,000	$900	$1,000
Newfoundland and Labrador ..	83 021	62	38	400	400	400
Prince Edward Island........	51 485	61	39	600	600	700
Nova Scotia	570 194	57	43	800	800	800
New Brunswick	317 015	60	40	600	600	700
Québec	4 576 640	66	34	800	900	800
Ontario..................	8 976 372	54	46	1000	900	1100
Manitoba	513 483	52	48	800	700	900
Saskatchewan	497 007	58	42	900	900	1000
Alberta..................	3 032 944	63	37	1000	900	1100
British Columbia	3 135 857	53	47	1300	1100	1600
Yukon	15 216	67	33	700	700	600
Northwest Territories........	8 567	66	34	500	500	500
Nunavut.................	3 827	75	25	700	700	800

Source: © *Statistics Canada*

Housing Affordability Table

The table below shows how expensive a home an individual or family could likely afford, using various income levels and mortgage interest rates—assuming a down-payment of 25 percent of the purchase price. As income rises, housing becomes more affordable, but it becomes less affordable as interest rates increase.

For example, most couples with a combined annual income of $60,000 would qualify for a mortgage on a home costing $192,170 at an 8 percent interest rate—provided they had a downpayment of $38,094 (25 percent of the purchase price). But at a 10 percent interest rate, the same couple earning the same income could only afford a $163,967 home.

The table assumes that mortgage payments, property taxes, heating costs and 50 percent of condominium fees should not exceed 32 percent of gross income (net income if self-employed). Most lending institutions use this percentage when calculating how large a mortgage you can afford. For this table, we have established annual costs of $2,400 for taxes and $2,400 for taxes and $2,400 for heating. Most lenders will also require that your total debt service ratio (mortgage payments, property taxes, heating cost, 50 percent of condo fees and any other liabilities such as car loans or other debts) does not·exceed 40 percent of gross income.

Mortgage Interest Rate (%)[1]	Annual Income							
	$30 000	$40 000	$50 000	$60 000	$70 000	$80 000	$90 000	$100 000
4.00	25 348	109 838	194 332	278 823	363 314	439 357	506 951	574 546
4.25	24 707	107 062	189 420	271 776	354 132	428 252	494 138	560 024
4.50	24 090	104 391	184 693	264 993	345 294	417 564	481 806	546 048
4.75	23 497	101 818	180 142	258 464	336 785	407 275	469 934	532 593
5.00	22 925	99 341	175 760	252 176	328 592	397 367	458 501	519 636
5.25	22 374	96 955	171 538	246 119	320 700	387 823	447 489	507 155
5.50	21 844	94 658	167 471	240 283	313 095	378 627	436 878	495 129
5.75	21 333	92 440	163 550	234 658	305 766	369 764	426 652	483 539
6.00	20 840	90 334	159 771	229 236	298 701	361 220	416 793	472 386
6.25	20 364	88 244	156 127	224 007	291 887	352 980	407 285	461 591
6.50	19 906	86 257	152 611	218 863	185 315	345 032	398 115	451 197
6.75	19 463	84 340	149 219	214 096	278 973	337 363	389 265	441 169
7.00	19 036	82 490	145 946	209 399	272 853	329 962	380 726	431 490
7.25	18 624	80 704	142 785	204 865	256 945	322 817	372 482	422 147
7.50	18 226	78 979	139 733	200 486	261 239	315 917	364 520	413 124
7.75	17 842	77 313	136 785	196 257	255 728	309 252	356 830	404 408
8.00	17 470	75 703	133 937	192 170	250 403	302 813	349 400	395 987
8.25	17 111	74 147	131 184	188 220	245 256	296 589	342 219	387 848
8.50	16 764	72 643	128 523	184 402	240 281	290 572	335 276	379 981
8.75	16 428	71 188	125 950	180 170	235 470	284 754	328 583	372 372
9.00	16 103	69 781	123 461	177 138	230 816	279 127	322 070	365 013
9.25	15 789	68 420	121 052	173 683	226 314	273 682	315 787	357 893
9.50	15 485	67 103	118 722	170 339	221 958	268 413	309 707	351 002
9.75	15 191	65 827	116 465	167 102	217 738	263 312	303 822	344 332
10.00	14 906	64 593	114 281	163 967	213 654	258 372	296 122	337 873
10.25	14 630	63 397	112 165	160 932	209 698	253 588	292 602	331 616
10.50	14 363	62 238	110 115	157 990	205 865	248 953	287 254	325 555
10.75	14 104	61 115	108 128	155 139	202 151	244 462	282 072	319 682
11.00	13 852	60 027	106 202	152 376	198 550	240 108	277 048	313 988
11.25	13 609	58 971	104 335	149 697	195 060	235 886	272 177	308 468
11.50	13 373	57 948	102 524	147 099	191 674	231 792	267 453	303 114
11.75	13 144	56 955	100 767	144 579	188 390	227 820	262 870	297 920
12.00	12 921	55 991	99 063	142 133	185 203	223 966	258 423	292 880
12.25	12 705	55 058	97 408	139 759	182 110	220 225	254 107	287 988
12.50	14 496	54 148	95 802	137 454	179 196	216 594	249 917	283 239
12.75	12 292	53 267	94 242	135 216	176 190	213 067	245 847	278 627
13.00	12 095	52 410	92 727	133 042	173 358	209 642	241 895	274 148

Source: *The Royal Bank of Canada*

(1) Compounded semi-annually. Mortgage payments based on a 25-year amortization.

The Effect of Interest Rate Changes on Mortgage Payments

The table below shows the monthly mortgage payment (principal and interest) for each $1,000 of mortgage debt. To calculate your payment at a given interest rate, choose the corresponding amount in the amortization column you select and multiply the amount by the number of thousands of dollars of debt. For example, if you want to know the cost per month to carry an $85,000 mortgage amortized over 25 years at 7.00 percent, multiply 7 by 85 and the result, $595, is your monthly payment. If the same mortgage was coming up for renewal at 8.00 percent, the new payment amount would be $648.66 (7.63 x 85) or $53.56 more each month.

Monthly Payments for Each $1 000 of Mortgage

Interest Rate (%)	Amortization Period							
	1 Year	2 Years	3 Years	5 Years	10 Years	15 Years	20 Years	25 Years
4.00	$85.13	$43.41	$29.51	$18.40	$10.11	$7.38	$6.04	$5.26
4.25	85.25	43.52	29.62	18.51	10.23	7.50	6.17	5.40
4.50	85.36	43.63	29.73	18.62	10.34	7.63	6.30	5.53
4.75	85.47	43.74	29.84	18.74	10.46	7.75	6.44	5.67
5.00	85.58	43.85	29.95	18.85	10.58	7.88	6.57	5.82
5.25	85.70	43.96	30.06	18.96	10.70	8.01	6.71	5.95
5.50	85.81	44.07	30.17	19.07	10.82	8.14	6.84	6.10
5.75	85.92	44.18	30.28	19.19	10.94	8.27	6.98	6.25
6.00	86.03	44.29	30.39	19.30	11.07	8.40	7.12	6.40
6.25	86.14	44.40	30.50	19.41	11.19	8.53	7.26	6.55
6.50	86.26	44.51	30.61	19.53	11.31	8.66	7.41	6.70
6.75	86.37	44.62	30.72	19.64	11.43	8.80	7.55	6.85
7.00	86.48	44.73	30.83	19.75	11.56	8.93	7.69	7.00
7.25	86.59	44.84	30.94	19.87	11.68	9.07	7.84	7.16
7.50	86.70	44.95	31.05	19.98	11.81	9.21	7.99	7.32
7.75	86.82	45.06	31.16	20.10	11.94	9.34	8.13	7.47
8.00	86.93	45.17	31.28	20.21	12.06	9.48	8.28	7.63
8.25	87.04	45.28	31.39	20.33	12.19	9.62	8.43	7.79
8.50	87.15	45.39	31.50	20.45	12.32	9.76	8.59	7.95
8.75	87.26	45.50	31.61	20.56	12.45	9.90	8.74	8.12
9.00	87.38	45.61	31.72	20.68	12.58	10.05	8.89	8.28
9.25	87.49	45.72	31.84	20.80	12.71	10.19	9.05	8.44
9.50	87.60	45.83	31.95	20.91	12.84	10.33	9.20	8.61
9.75	87.71	45.94	32.06	21.03	12.97	10.48	9.36	8.78
10.00	87.82	46.05	32.17	21.15	13.10	10.62	9.52	8.94
10.25	87.93	46.16	32.28	21.27	13.24	10.77	9.68	9.11
10.50	88.04	46.27	32.40	21.38	13.37	10.92	9.83	9.28
10.75	88.16	46.38	32.51	21.50	13.50	11.06	10.00	9.45
11.00	88.27	46.49	32.62	21.62	13.64	11.21	10.16	9.63
11.25	88.38	46.61	32.74	21.74	13.77	11.36	10.32	9.80
11.50	88.49	46.72	32.85	21.86	13.91	11.51	10.48	9.97
11.75	88.60	46.83	32.96	21.98	14.04	11.66	10.65	10.14
12.00	88.71	46.94	33.08	22.10	14.18	11.82	10.81	10.32
12.25	88.82	47.05	33.19	22.22	14.32	11.97	10.98	10.49
12.50	88.94	47.16	33.30	22.34	14.46	12.12	11.14	10.67
12.75	89.05	47.27	33.42	22.46	14.59	12.28	11.31	10.85
13.00	89.18	47.38	33.53	22.58	14.73	12.43	11.48	11.02

Source: *The Royal Bank of Canada*

New Home Building

The total value of investment in the housing sector in the first quarter of 2004 was $13.8 billion, up 15.4% from the first quarter of 2003, an exceptional year in residential construction. The growth was the result of higher expenditures in all three components of residential construction investment: new housing, renovations and acquisition costs.

The demand for new housing was buoyed by very attractive mortgage rates, the creation of 235,000 jobs since August 2003, and strong consumer confidence. An increase in the value of dwelling units also had a positive impact on the value of residential construction investment.

Investment in new housing totalled $7.1 billion in the first quarter of 2004, up 14.3% from the first quarter of 2003. The largest increase (in dollars) was in expenditures on new apartments/condominiums (+32.3% to $1.5 billion). The gain was the result of the continuing work on many apartment/condominium projects that began in late 2003, combined with a rise in the average value of dwelling units. Expenditures on new single-family dwellings also posted a sharp increase (+7.2% to $4.4 billion).

At the provincial level, Quebec had the largest dollar increase, as investment soared 30.3% from $2.4 billion to $3.2 billion in the province owing to heavy demand for new housing. There was also a very hefty gain in British Columbia (+32.7%) because of both new housing and renovations.

Note: Residential construction investment is divided into three main components. The first is new housing construction, which includes single dwellings, semi-detached dwellings, row housing and apartments, cottages, mobile homes and additional housing units created from non-residential buildings or other types of residential structures (conversions). The second component of residential construction investment, renovations, includes alterations and improvements in existing dwellings. The third component is acquisition costs, which refers to the value of services relating to the sale of new dwellings. These costs include sales tax, land development and service charges, as well as record-processing fees for mortgage insurance and the associated premiums.

Residential Construction Investment

Provinces/Territories	First quarter 2003	First quarter 2004	First quarter 2003 to first quarter 2004
	$ millions		% change
Canada	**11,930.4**	**13,765.1**	**15.4**
Newfoundland and Labrador	92.0	114.1	24.1
Prince Edward Island	38.1	34.6	-9.3
Nova Scotia	270.6	302.6	11.8
New Brunswick	155.6	185.8	19.4
Quebec	2,439.2	3,177.8	30.3
Ontario	4,914.4	5,247.6	6.8
Manitoba	249.9	299.0	19.6
Saskatchewan	206.5	262.3	27.0
Alberta	1,754.4	1,748.1	-0.4
British Columbia	1,768.5	2,347.4	32.7
Yukon	12.0	8.4	-30.3
Northwest Territories	21.2	30.6	44.2
Nunavut	8.0	6.8	-14.5

Source: *The Daily, June 1, 2004 © Statistics Canada*   Note: Data may not add to totals due to rounding.

Home Repairs and Renovations

Homeowners spent more than ever in 2002 on repairing and renovating their homes, according to data from the 2002 Homeowners Repair and Renovation Survey.

There are several possible reasons for this increase, including low interest rates, strong employment growth, higher disposable incomes and shortages in the rental and resale housing markets. These factors contributed to higher investment in new housing and in repairs and renovations of existing housing.

On average, homeowners spent $2,910 repairing or renovating their homes in 2002, about 9% more than they did in 2001 and approximately 58% higher than the average of $1,837 in 1998, which was a decade low. Figures from previous years used in comparisons have been adjusted using indexes that reflect price changes in the construction field.

Roughly two-thirds was devoted to work contracted out, and about one-third to materials purchased separately by the homeowner. This proportion remains unchanged from previous years.

In total, homeowners spent $23.4 billion on repairs and renovations in 2002, an increase of nearly 11% from 2001, and about 75% higher than the decade-low total of $13.4 billion in 1996.

One in four households that reported at least one repair or renovation expenditure spent less than $500, accounting for 1% of total repair and renovation spending. In contrast, 22% of reporting households spent $5,000 or more, accounting for 71% of repair and renovation spending.

The percentage of households reporting repairs and renovations was unchanged from 2001. About 76% of the nation's 8.1 million homeowner households indicated they had made at least one repair and renovation expenditure. The percentage of households reporting at least one such expenditure ranged from a high of 84% in Prince Edward Island, to a low of 67% in Alberta.

Painting remained the most common type of repair or renovation work reported, with 45% of owners undertaking some type of interior or exterior paint job. Also commonly reported were repairs to plumbing fixtures, to patios, fences or driveways, and to heating or air conditioning systems.

Total Homeowner Spending on Repairs and Renovations in Canada

(billions of dollars)

Year	Current dollars	Constant 2002 dollars[1]
1993	12.6	15.0
1994	12.8	14.7
1995	11.8	13.5
1996	11.8	13.4
1997	12.7	14.0
1998	12.6	13.8
1999	13.6	14.6
2000	...	...
2001	20.4	21.2
2002	23.4	23.4

Source: *The Daily, November 18, 2003 © Statistics Canada*

(1) To facilitate historical comparisons, data in this column have been adjusted using indices that reflect price and wage changes in the construction field. (...) Figures not available.

Average Resale Value of Canadian Homes[1]

In 2003 and 2004, the average resale value of Canadian homes continued to climb. The rate of housing sales remained strong across the country, despite an overall downward trend from the peak of January 2001. Particularly in the larger urban centres, a shortage of listings, combined with continued low interest levels, has been pushing prices up. Between March 2002 and March 2003, the national residential average price rose 8.6 percent to $201,662, setting a new record and breaking past the $200,000 level for the first time in history.

	1990	1995	2001	2002	2003	2004
Canada	139 922	150 321	171 897	184 855	208 525	219 754
Calgary	128 484	132 114	182 090	197 431	212 342	221 207
Edmonton	101 040	110 329	133 441	150 807	167 846	182 469
Halifax-Dartmouth	97 238	103 011	134 106	147 918	158 634	174 117
Montreal	111 956	109 929	128 851	144 280	173 813	186 337
Ottawa	141 562	143 127	175 972	203 283	225 381	233 478
Regina	71 054	76 629	96 943	98 512	99 318	113 839
Saint John	78 041	83 498	97 348	106 274	106 674	119 560
St. John's	88 939	89 655	105 237	113 860	124 468	133 302
Toronto[2]	254 890	203 028	251 508	282 765	297 175	304 159
Greater Vancouver	226 385	307 747	285 910	308 592	345 175	381 865
Victoria	160 743	210 669	259 138[3]	287 279	337 638	377 545

Source: *The Canadian Real Estate Association*
(1) Average price of all homes sold on the Multiple Listing Service in constant dollars.
(2) Includes Mississauga, Brampton, Durham, Orangeville and York Region figures.
(3) Figures from Victoria Real Estate Board; based on single family homes.

Mortgage Rates by Year[1]

	One-Year	Three-Year	Five-Year		One-Year	Three-Year	Five-Year
1980	13.98	n.a.	14.52	1991	10.08	10.90	11.13
1981	18.12	18.33	18.38	1992	7.87	8.95	9.51
1982	16.85	17.83	18.04	1993	6.91	8.10	8.78
1983	10.98	12.52	13.23	1994	7.83	8.99	9.53
1984	12.00	13.21	13.58	1995	8.38	8.82	9.16
1985	10.31	11.54	12.12	1996	6.19	7.37	7.93
1986	10.15	10.88	11.21	1997	5.54	6.56	7.07
1987	9.85	10.69	11.17	1998	6.50	6.77	6.93
1988	10.83	11.42	11.65	1999	6.80	7.37	7.56
1989	12.85	12.15	12.06	2000	7.85	8.17	8.35
1990	13.40	13.38	13.35	2001	6.14	6.88	7.40
				2002	5.17	6.28	7.02
				2003	4.84	5.82	6.39

Source: © *Statistics Canada* (n.a.) Not available.
(1) Annual averages of the most typical of those offered by the major chartered banks for conventional mortgages.

GLOBAL INFORMATION

GLOBAL SUPERLATIVES

Size of the earth's surface		510 000 000 sq. km
Largest continent	Asia	44 485 900 sq. km
Smallest continent	Australia	7 682 300 sq. km
Largest ocean	Pacific	166 241 000 sq. km
Smallest ocean	Arctic	9 485 000 sq. km
Deepest point of any ocean	Marianas Trench, Pacific Ocean	11 022 m
Largest sea	South China Sea	2 974 600 sq. km
Largest lake	Caspian Sea, Russian Fed., Kazakhstan, Turkmenistan, Iran, Azerbaijan	371 000 sq. km
Deepest lake	Lake Baykal, Russia	1 620 m
Largest freshwater lake	**Lake Superior, North America**	**82 100 sq. km**
Highest major lake	Lake Titicaca, Bolivia-Peru, South America	3 809 m
Lowest major lake	Caspian Sea, Russian Fed., Kazakhstan, Turkmenistan, Iran, Azerbaijan	-28 m
Largest island	Greenland, Denmark	2 175 600 sq. km
Longest reef	Great Barrier Reef, Australia-Papua New Guinea	2 027 km
Longest river	Nile, Africa	6 670 km
Largest nation	Russia	17 075 272 sq. km
Smallest nation	Vatican City	.44 sq. km
Most populous nation	People's Republic of China (July 2004 est.)	pop. 1 298 847 624
Oldest city	Damascus, Syria	continuously inhabited since c. 2500 B.C.
Highest point	Mount Everest, Nepal-Tibet	8 846 m
Lowest point	Dead Sea, Israel-Jordan	-400 m
Highest city	Cerro de Pasco, Peru	4 259 m
Coldest city	Norilsk, Russia	average temp. -10.9°C
Hottest city	Djibouti, Djibouti	average temp. 30°C
Coldest place	Plateau Station, Antarctica	-56.7°C
Hottest place	Dalol, Danakil Depression, Ethiopia	35°C avg.
Coldest recorded temperature	Vostok, Antarctica (Australian territory), July 21, 1983	-89.2°C
Hottest recorded temperature (shade)	Al-Aziziyah, Libya, Sept. 13, 1922	58°C
Wettest spot	Mount Waialeale, Kauai, Hawaii	avg. ann. rainfall of 16 800 mm
Driest spot	Atacama Desert, Chile	avg. ann. precipitation barely measurable
Greatest snowfall in 24 hrs	Silver Lake, Colorado, U.S., Apr. 14–15, 1921	193 cm
Greatest rainfall in 24 hrs	Cilaos, Reunion Island, Indian Ocean, Mar. 15–16, 1952	1 870 mm
Largest desert	Sahara, Africa	9 million sq. km
Largest waterfall (by volume)	Khone, Kampuchea-Laos	11 610 cu. m/sec.
Tallest waterfall	Angel Falls, Venezuela	807 m
Largest gorge	Grand Canyon, Colorado River, Arizona	349 km long; 6–20 km wide; 1.6 km deep
Deepest gorge	Colca River Canyon, Peru	3 223 m
Oldest tree	a bristlecone pine, Wheeler's Peak, Nevada	approx. age of 5 100 yrs.
Greatest tides	**Bay of Fundy, Nova Scotia**	**14.5 m**
Most devastating volcanic eruption	Tambora, Sumbawa, Indonesia, Apr. 5–7, 1815	92 000 deaths
Longest bridge	**Confederation, linking New Brunswick and Prince Edward Island**	**12.9 km** (main span 11 km); bridge between the tip of Florida and Key West is also 11 km
Largest man-made lake	Owen Falls, Uganda	2 700 000 cu. m
Tallest building	Sears Tower, Chicago, Illinois	110 storeys, 443 m

The Continents

Continent	Total Area (sq. km)	% of Earth's Land	Population	% of World Total
Asia	44 485 900	30.0	3 292 337 000	62.4
Africa	30 269 680	20.4	702 013 000	13.2
North and Central America	24 235 280	16.3	441 826 000	8.4
South America	17 820 770	12.0	309 634 000	5.9
Antarctica	13 209 000	8.9	uninhabited	
Europe	10 530 750	7.1	504 925 000	9.6
Oceania	7 830 682	5.3	27 752 000	.5

Source: *National Geographic Atlas of the World (1990), FAO Production Yearbook (1993)*

Highest and Lowest Points on Each Continent

Continent	Highest Point	(metres)	Lowest Point	(metres)
Asia	Everest	8 848	Dead Sea	-400
South America	Aconcagua	6 960	Valdés Peninsula	-40
North America	McKinley (Denali)	6 194	Death Valley	-86
Africa	Kilimanjaro	5 895	Lake Assal	-156
Europe	El'brus	5 642	Caspian Sea	-28
Antarctica	Vinson Massif	4 897	—	-2 538
Australia	Kosciusko	2 228	Lake Eyre	-16

Source: *National Geographic Atlas of the World (1990)*

World's Highest Cities

City	Altitude[1]	City	Altitude[1]
Cerro de Pasco, Peru	4 259 m	Quito, Ecuador	2 811 m
Shigatse, Tibet	3 800 m	Sucre, Bolivia	2 790 m
La Paz, Bolivia	3 636 m	Potosi, Bolivia	2 790 m
Lhasa, Tibet	3 606 m	Toluca de Lerdo, Mexico	2 680 m
Cuaco, Peru	3 400 m	Addis Ababa, Ethiopia	2 450 m

Source: *Global Atlas, Gage Educational Publishing Co., South American Handbook*
(1) Estimates vary, depending on source.

Oceans' Area and Depth

Ocean	Area (sq. km)	% of Earth's Water Area	Deepest Point	Depth (metres)
Pacific	166 241 000	46.0	Marianas Trench	11 022
Atlantic	86 557 000	23.9	Puerto Rico Trench	8 605
Indian	73 427 000	20.3	Java Trench	7 258
Arctic	9 485 000	2.6	Eurasia Basin	5 122

Source: *National Geographic Atlas of the World (1990)*

Major Seas of the World

Sea	Area (sq. km)	Average Depth (metres)	Sea	Area (sq. km)	Average Depth (metres)
South China	2 974 600	1 464	East Sea (Japan)	1 012 900	1 667
Caribbean	2 515 900	2 575	**Hudson Bay**	**730 100**	**93**
Mediterranean	2 510 000	1 501	East China	664 600	189
Bering	2 261 100	1 491	Andaman	564 900	1 118
Gulf of Mexico	1 507 600	1 615	Black	507 900	1 191
Sea of Okhotsk	1 392 100	973	Red	453 000	538

Source: *National Geographic Atlas of the World (1990)*

Largest Lakes of the World

Lake	Location	Area (sq. km)
Caspian (Sea)	Iran/Caspian Sea, Russian Fed., Kazakhstan, Turkmenistan, Iran, Azerbaijan	378 400
Superior	**Canada**/U.S.	**82 260**
Aral (Sea)	Kazakhstan-Uzbekistan	64 100
Victoria	Kenya/Tanzania/Uganda	62 940
Huron	**Canada**/U.S.	**59 580**
Michigan	U.S.	58 020
20 Tanganyika	Burundi/Tanzania/Zaire/Zambia	32 000
Baykal	Russia	31 500
Great Bear	**NWT, Canada**	**31 150**
Great Slave	**NWT, Canada**	**28 570**

Source: *World Facts and Figures, 1989; Victor Showers; John Wiley & Sons, Inc.*

Major Islands of the World

Island	Area (sq. km)	Island	Area (sq. km)
Greenland (Denmark)	2 175 600	Sumatra (Indonesia)	427 300
New Guinea (independent)	792 500	Honshu (Japan)	227 400
Borneo (Indonesia)	725 500	Great Britain (independent)	218 100
Madagascar (independent)	587 000	**Victoria (Canada)**	**217 300**
Baffin (Canada)	**507 500**	**Ellesmere (Canada)**	**196 200**

Source: *National Geographic Atlas of the World (1990)*

Highest Waterfalls in the World

Fall/Country	Height[1] (m)	Fall/Country	Height[1] (m)
Angel, Venezuela	807	Pilao, Brazil	524
Monge, Norway	774	Montoya, Venezuela	505
Itatinga, Brazil	628	Ribbon, United States	491
Ormeli, Norway	563	Great, Guyana	488
Tusse, Norway	533	Vestre Mardals, Norway	468

Source: *World Facts and Figures, 1989; Victor Showers; John Wiley & Sons Inc.*

(1) Height of the greatest individual leap.

Highest Mountains by Continent

Peak	Mountain Range or System	Location	Elevation[1] ft	m	First Ascent
■ Africa					
Kibo	n.a.	Tanganyika, Tanzania	19 340	5 890	1889
Mawensi	n.a.	Tanganyika, Tanzania	17 100	5 210	1912
Batian	n.a.	Kenya	17 050	5 200	1899
Nelion	n.a.	Kenya	17 020	5 190	1929
Margherita	Ruwenzori	Uganda/D. Rep. of Congo	16 760	5 110	1906
Alexandra	Ruwenzori	Uganda/D. Rep. of Congo	16 700	5 090	1906
Albert	Ruwenzori	Dem. Rep. of Congo	16 690	5 090	1932
Savoia	Ruwenzori	Uganda	16 330	4 980	1906
Elena	Ruwenzori	Uganda	16 300	4 970	1906
Elizabeth	Ruwenzori	Uganda	16 170	4 930	1953
■ Antarctica					
—	Sentinel	Antarctica	16 860	5140	1966
Tyree	Sentinel	Antarctica	16 290	4970	1967
Shinn	Sentinel	Antarctica	15 750	4800	1966
Gardner	Sentinel	Antarctica	15 370	4690	1966
Epperly	Sentinel	Antarctica	15 100	4600	n.a.
Kirkpatrick	Queen Alexandra	Antarctica	14 850	4530	n.a.
Llizabeth	Queen Alexandra	Antarctica	14 700	4480	n.a.
Markham	Queen Elizabeth	Antarctica	14 290	4360	n.a.
Bell	Queen Alexandra	Antarctica	14 120	4300	n.a.
Mackellar	Queen Alexandra	Antarctica	14 100	4300	n.a.
■ Asia					
Everest (alt Qomolangma, Chumulangma)	Nepal Himalaya	China/Nepal	29 030	8 850	1953
K2 (alt Chogori, Dapsang, Godwin Austen)	Karakoram	Pakistan-held Kashmir	28 250	8 610	1954
Kangchenjunga (alt Kanchenjunga): highest peak	Nepal Himalaya	India/Nepal	28 170	8 590	1955
Lhotse (alt E1, Luozi, Lotzu)	Nepal Himalaya	China/Nepal	27 890	8 500	1956
Kangchenjunga: S peak	Nepal Himalaya	India/Nepal	27 800	8 470	n.a.
Makalu I	Nepal Himalaya	China/Nepal	27 790	8 470	1955
Kangchenjunga: W peak	Nepal Himalaya	India/Nepal	27 620	8 420	1973
Lhotse Shar (alt Lhotse: E peak)	Nepal Himalaya	China/Nepal	27 500	8 380	1970
Dhaulagiri I (alt Daulagiri I)	Nepal Himalaya	Nepal	26 810	8 170	1960
Cho Oyu (alt Zhuoaoyu, Choaoyu): highest peak	Nepal Himalaya	China/Nepal	26 750	8 150	1954
■ Europe					
Elbrus (for Elborus): W peak	Caucasus (off Kavkaz)	Russia	18 480	5630	1874
Elbrus: E peak	Caucasus	Russia	18 360	5 590	1829
Shkhara: E peak	Caucasus	Georgia/Russia	17 060	5 200	1888
Dykh(-Tau): W peak	Caucasus	Russia	17 050	5 200	1888
Dykh(-Tau): E peak	Caucasus	Russia	16 900	5 150	1938
Koshtan(-Tau)	Caucasus	Russia	16 880	5 140	1888
Shkhara: W peak	Caucasus	Georgia/Russia	16 880	5 140	n.a.
Pushkina	Caucasus	Russia	16 730	5 100	1938
Dzhangi(-Tau): NW peak	Caucasus	Georgia	16 570	5 050	1903
Kazbek: E peak	Caucasus	Georgia	16 560	5 050	1868 ▶

► ■ **North America**

McKinley: S peak	Alaska	Alaska, U.S.	20 320	6 190	1913
Logan: central peak	**Saint Elias**	**Yukon, Canada**	**19 520**	**5 959**	**1925**
Logan: W peak	**Saint Elias**	**Yukon, Canada**	**19 470**	**5 930**	**1925**
McKinley: N peak	Alaska	Alaska, U.S.	19 470	5 930	1910
Logan: E peak	**Saint Elias**	**Yukon, Canada**	**19 420**	**5 920**	**1957**
Citlaltepetl (alt Orizaba)	Neovolcanica	Puebla-Veracruz, Mexico	18 410	5 610	1848
Logan: N peak	**Saint Elias**	**Yukon, Canada**	**18 270**	**5 570**	**1959**
Saint Elias	Saint Elias	Canada/U.S.	18 010	5 490	1897
Popocatepetl	Neovolcanica	Puebla, Mexico	17 930	5 460	1520
Foraker	Alaska	Alaska, U.S.	17 400	5 300	1934

■ **Oceania**

Jaya (for Carstensz, Djaja, Sukarno)	Sudirman (for Nassau)	Irian Jaya, Indonesia	16 500	5 030	1936
Daam	Jayawijaya (for Djajawidjaja, Orange)	Irian Jaya, Indonesia	16 150	4 920	n.a.
Pilimsit (for Idenburg)	Sudirman	Irian Jaya, Indonesia	15 750	4 800	1962
Trikora (for Wilhelmina)	Jayawijaya	Irian Jaya, Indonesia	15 580	4 750	1913
Mandala (for Juliana)	Jayawijaya	Irian Jaya, Indonesia	15 420	4 700	1959
Wilhelm	Bismarck	Papua New Guinea	15 400	4 690	n.a.
Wisnumurti (for Jan Pieterszoon Coen)	Jayawijaya	Irian Jaya, Indonesia	15 080	4 590	n.a.
Yamin (for Prins Hendrik)	Jayawijaya	Irian Jaya, Indonesia	14 860	4 530	n.a.
Kubor	Kubor	Papua New Guinea	14 300	4 360	n.a.
Herbert	Bismarck	Papua New Guinea	14 000	4 270	n.a.

■ **South America**

Aconcagua	Andes	Mendoza, Argentina	22 840	6 960	1897
Ojos del Salado: SE peak	Andes	Argentina/Chile	22 560	6 870	1937
Bonete	Andes	La Rioja, Argentina	22 550	6 870	1913
Pissis	Andes	Catamarca, La Rioja, Argentina	22 240	6 780	1937
Huascaran: S peak	Blanca (Andes)	Peru	22 210	6 770	1932
Mercedario	Andes	San Juan, Argentina	22 210	6 770	1934
Llullaillaco	Andes	Argentina/Chile	22 100[1]	6 730	bef 1550
Libertador (for Cachi: N peak)	Andes	Salta, Argentina	22 050	6 720	1950
Ojos del Salado: NW peak	Andes	Argentina/Chile	22 050	6 720	1937
Tupungato	Andes	Argentina/Chile	21 900	6 670	1897

Source: *World Facts and Figures, 1989; Victor Showers; John Wiley & Sons, Inc.*

(1) Rounded figures except for some Canadian peaks from Energy, Mines and Resources Canada. (n.a.) not available or not applicable.

Longest Rivers in the World

River	Outflow and Location	Length mi.	Length km
Nile-Kagera-Ruvuvu-Luvironza	Mediterranean Sea, Egypt	4 140	6 670
Amazon-Ucayali-Tambo-Ene-Apurimac	Atlantic Ocean, Amapa-Para, Brazil	4 080	6 570
Yangtze	East China Sea, Jiangsu, China	3 720	5 980
Mississippi-Missouri-Jefferson-Beaverhead-Red	Gulf of Mexico, Louisiana, U.S. Rock	3 710	5 970
Yenisey-Angara-Selenga-Ider	Yenisey Gulf of Kara Sea, Russia	3 650	5 870
Amur-Argun-Kerulen	Tatar Strait, Russia	3 590	5 780
Ob-Irtysh	Gulf of Ob of Kara Sea, Russia	3 360	5 410
Plata-Parana-Grande	Atlantic Ocean, Argentina-Uruguay	3 030	4 880
Huang	Gulf of Chihli of Yellow Sea, Shandong, China	3 010	4 840
Congo-Lualaba	Atlantic Ocean, Angola-Dem. Rep. of Congo	2 880	4 630

Source: *World Facts and Figures, 1989; Victor Showers; John Wiley & Sons, Inc.*

POPULATION

Global Population Trends

The Population Division of the United Nations carries out documentation and analytical work that is used by the UN General Assembly and the UN's Economic and Social Council, as well as by various conferences and member states. The information on population trends and other analysis that goes with the data gathering assists in the development of policy related to both population and social development at the national and international levels. The information below reflects projected population trends, based on population data as of July 1, 2002.

For more information about the United Nations Population Division, visit www.un.org/esa/population

Population Projections by Region

(000s)

Year	Africa	Asia	Europe	Latin America and the Caribbean[1]	Northern America[2]	Oceania[3]
2005	887 964	3 917 508	724 722	558 281	332 156	32 998
2010	984 225	4 148 948	719 714	594 436	348 139	34 821
2015	1 084 540	4 370 522	713 402	628 260	363 953	36 569
2020	1 187 584	4 570 131	705 410	659 248	379 589	38 275
2025	1 292 085	4 742 232	696 036	686 857	394 312	39 933
2030	1 398 004	4 886 647	685 440	711 058	407 532	41 468
2035	1 504 179	5 006 700	673 638	731 591	419 273	42 803
2040	1 608 329	5 103 021	660 645	747 953	429 706	43 938
2045	1 708 407	5 175 311	646 630	759 955	439 163	44 929

Source: *United Nations Population Division, World Populations Prospects Population Database*
(1) Includes South and Central America (2) Includes Bermuda, Canada, Greenland, Saint-Pierre-et-Miquelon, United States of America (3) Includes Australia, Melanesia, Micronesia, New Zealand, Polynesia

Projected Population Density by Region

(per square km)

Year	Africa	Asia	Europe	Latin America and the Caribbean	Northern America	Oceania
2005	29	123	32	27	15	4
2010	32	131	31	29	16	4
2015	36	138	31	31	17	4
2020	39	144	31	32	18	4
2025	43	149	30	33	18	5
2030	46	154	30	35	19	5
2035	50	158	29	36	19	5
2040	53	161	29	36	20	5
2045	56	163	28	37	20	5

Source: *United Nations Population Division, World Populations Prospects Population Database*

Projected Population Growth Rates by Region

(%)

Period	Africa	Asia	Europe	Latin America and the Caribbean	Northern America	Oceania
2005–2010	2.06	1.15	-0.14	1.26	0.94	1.08
2010–2015	1.94	1.04	-0.18	1.11	0.89	0.98
2015–2020	1.82	0.89	-0.23	0.96	0.84	0.91
2020–2025	1.69	0.74	-0.27	0.82	0.76	0.85
2025–2030	1.58	0.6	-0.31	0.69	0.66	0.76
2030–2035	1.46	0.49	-0.35	0.57	0.57	0.63
2035–2040	1.34	0.38	-0.39	0.44	0.49	0.52
2040–2045	1.21	0.28	-0.43	0.32	0.44	0.45
2045–2050	1.08	0.18	-0.46	0.2	0.4	0.39
2035–2040	1.55	0.51	-0.51	0.58	0.50	0.63
2040–2045	1.42	0.41	-0.55	0.49	0.46	0.55
2045–2050	1.26	0.32	-0.59	0.40	0.45	0.52

Source: *United Nations Population Division, World Populations Prospects Population Database*

Projected Net Migration Rate by Region

(per 1,000)

The net migration rate represents the number of immigrants minus the number of emigrants over the period shown, divided by the person-years lived by the population of the receiving country over that period.

Year	Africa	Asia	Europe	Latin America and the Caribbean	Northern America	Oceania
2005–2010	-0.2	-0.3	0.8	-1.0	3.9	2.5
2010–2015	-0.2	-0.3	0.8	-0.9	3.6	2.3
2015–2020	-0.2	-0.3	0.8	-0.8	3.4	2.0
2020–2025	-0.2	-0.3	0.8	-0.7	3.3	1.9
2025–2030	-0.2	-0.3	0.8	-0.7	3.2	1.9
2030–2035	-0.1	-0.2	0.8	-0.7	3.1	1.8
2035–2040	-0.1	-0.2	0.9	-0.6	3.0	1.8
2040–2045	-0.1	-0.2	0.9	-0.6	2.9	1.8
2045–2050	-0.1	-0.2	0.9	-0.6	2.9	1.7

Source: *United Nations Population Division, World Populations Prospects Population Database*

Median Age

The median age is the age at which there are as many persons with ages above the median as there are with ages below the median. In 2000, the median age in Canada was 36.9.

Year	Africa	Asia	Europe	Latin America and the Caribbean	Northern America	Oceania
2005	18.8	27.4	39.3	25.7	36.2	31.8
2010	19.3	28.6	40.8	27.4	36.7	32.8
2015	19.9	29.9	42.2	29.0	37.1	33.7
2020	20.6	31.4	43.6	30.7	37.6	34.7
2025	21.5	32.9	44.8	32.3	38.2	35.6
2030	22.5	34.3	46.1	34.0	38.8	36.7
2035	23.7	35.5	47.2	35.5	39.4	37.7
2040	24.8	36.7	47.9	37.1	39.7	38.6
2045	26.1	37.7	48.0	38.5	39.9	39.3
2050	27.5	38.7	47.7	39.8	40.2	39.9

Source: *United Nations Population Division, World Populations Prospects Population Database*

Sex Ratio

(number of males per 100 females)

Year	Africa	Asia	Europe	Latin America and the Caribbean	Northern America	Oceania
2005	99.2	104.0	93.1	97.8	96.8	100.7
2010	99.6	103.7	93.1	97.6	96.9	100.5
2015	100.1	103.3	93.1	97.4	97.0	100.4
2020	100.5	102.8	93.2	97.1	96.9	100.1
2025	100.8	102.2	93.2	96.9	96.8	99.9
2030	101.1	101.7	93.2	96.6	96.6	99.6
2035	101.3	101.2	93.2	96.3	96.5	99.4
2040	101.4	100.7	93.3	96.1	96.4	99.1
2045	101.5	100.2	93.4	95.8	96.5	99.0
2050	101.5	99.9	93.6	95.6	96.8	99.0

Source: *United Nations Population Division, World Populations Prospects Population Database*

Global Urbanization

% Urban Population, by Region

The continuing shift of Canada's population from rural to urban centres, as shown in the 2001 census data (see chapter entitled "The People"), is not happening in isolation—the urban dwelling trend is visible around the world. In March 2002, the United Nations Population Division (Department of Economic and Social Affairs) released population growth estimates based on 2001 population

statistics that emphasized the growing trend.

The report, entitled *World Urbanization Prospects: The 2001 Revision*, suggested that by 2007, half of the world's population would live in urban areas. In 2000, 2.9 billion—47% of global population—lived in urban centres, compared to just 30% in 1950. By 2030, the proportion is expected to rise to 60%.

Year	Africa	Asia	Europe	Latin America and the Caribbean	Northern America	Oceania
2005	40.0	40.2	74.2	77.4	78.5	75.1
2010	42.7	43.0	75.1	79.0	79.8	75.7
2015	45.3	45.9	76.3	80.5	81.1	76.1
2020	47.9	48.7	77.6	81.8	82.3	76.4
2025	50.4	51.4	79.1	83.0	83.5	76.8
2030	52.9	54.1	80.5	84.0	84.5	77.3

Source: *United Nations Population Division, World Populations Prospects Population Database*

Cities with 10 Million Inhabitants or More

In 1950, just one city—New York—had a population of over 10 million (12.3 million). By 1975, five cities claimed the honour: Tokyo (19.8); New York (15.9); Shanghai (11.4); Mexico City (10.7); and Sao Paulo (10.3). By 2001, there were 17 such cities and by 2015

the UN projects that 21 cities (or "urban agglomerates") will have more than 10 million inhabitants. In fact, by 2015, Tokyo, Dhaka, Mumbai, Sao Paulo, Delhi and Mexico City are all expected to have more than 20 million residents each.

2001 City	Population (millions)	2015 City	Population (millions)
1. Tokyo	26.5	1. Tokyo	27.2
2. Sao Paulo	18.3	2. Dhaka	22.8
3. Mexico City	18.3	3. Mumbai	22.6
4. New York	16.8	4. Sao Paulo	21.2
5. Mumbai	16.5	5. Delhi	20.9
6. Los Angeles	13.3	6. Mexico City	20.4
7. Calcutta	13.3	7. New York	17.9
8. Dhaka	13.2	8. Jakarta	17.3
9. Delhi	13.0	9. Calcutta	16.7
10. Shanghai	12.8	10. Karachi	16.2
11. Buenos Aires	12.1	11. Lagos	16.0
12. Jakarta	11.4	12. Los Angeles	14.5
13. Osaka	11.0	13. Shanghai	13.6
14. Beijing	10.8	14. Buenos Aires	13.2
15. Rio de Janeiro	10.8	15. Metro Manila	12.6
16. Karachi	10.4	16. Beijing	11.7
17. Metro Manila	10.1	17. Rio de Janeiro	11.5
		18. Cairo	11.5
		19. Istanbul	11.4
		20. Osaka	11.0
		21. Tianjin	10.3

Source: *United Nations Population Division, World Urbanization Prospects: The 2001 Revision*

United Nations (UN)

The first United Nations declaration was signed by 22 Allied governments on January 1, 1942, and was an alliance against Germany, Italy and Japan. This anti-Axis coalition was converted into an international body in 1945 when 51 nations signed a United Nations Charter to form an organization that would "save succeeding generations from the scourge of war." The Charter was drawn up at the Conference on International Organization held in San Francisco from April 25 to June 26, 1945, and took effect October 24, 1945. UN membership has since grown to 191.

The UN has six parts, with the General Assembly—the central organ—acting as the main deliberative body. General Assembly meetings have been held at UN Headquarters in New York since 1946. The International Court of Justice in The Hague, Netherlands, is the only major UN organ not based in New York. Specialized agencies are located throughout the world.

Mail requests for information to the Public Inquiries Unit, Dept. of Public Information, Room GA-053, United Nations, New York, NY 10017. Visit the UN Web site at www.un.org or send e-mail to inquiries@un.org. Write also to the United Nations Association in Canada, 309 Cooper St., Ste. 300 Ottawa, ON, K2P 0G5 or send e-mail to info@unac.org.

■ Structure of the United Nations

General Assembly The General Assembly is the UN's forum for discussing issues, reviewing UN activities and setting the agenda for initiatives. All member states are represented, and each is entitled to one vote. Resolutions require a majority vote before adoption. A president, 21 vice-presidents and six committee chairs head the Assembly, which sits from mid-September to mid-December or as required for the rest of the year. The six committees study (a) disarmament and international security issues; (b) economics and finance issues; (c) social, humanitarian and cultural issues; (d) special political and decolonization issues; (e) UN administration and budgets; and (f) legal matters. The committees report to a plenary session of the Assembly.

The General Assembly sets UN policies, admits new members on recommendation of the Security Council, approves the budget and receives reports from all other UN bodies.

Security Council The Security Council has the power to act for the maintenance of peace and security. It can enforce military action or economic sanctions, and it can send peace-keeping units (the Blue Berets) to troubled areas. The Security Council may also try to negotiate a cease fire in the case of conflicts.

The Council has 15 members, five permanent and 10 elected by the General Assembly for two-year terms. Decisions require nine affirmative votes, but all permanent members have the right to veto. The permanent members are: China, France, the United Kingdom, the United States and the Russian Federation. Canada served its sixth term as a non-permanent member of the Council (from Jan. 1, 1999, to Dec. 31, 2000). The Security Council is permanently in session and representatives are on call 24 hours a day.

Economic and Social Council The Economic and Social Council co-ordinates the economic and social work of the UN and its related agencies. The Council's 54 members hold two month-long sessions each year: one in New York, the other in Geneva. Each member, including Canada until 2006, is elected by the General Assembly for a three-year term.

Trusteeship Council The council, created to oversee the independence of trust territories, is now in abeyance.

International Court of Justice (World Court) The Security Council elects 15 judges to the Court for nine-year terms. No two members may be from the same nation. The Court, located in The Hague, only sits in judgment on disputes between states. Both member and non-member states may submit grievances (border disputes, resource access, breach of treaty, etc.).

Countries can opt out of any proceeding, unless required to participate by treaty provisions. But after agreeing to become a party in a case, a nation must comply with the Court's decision, enforced by the Security Council.

Secretariat The Secretariat administers the programs and policies laid out by other UN bodies. The Secretary General is the Chief Administrative Officer of the Secretariat, which administers the work of the UN as directed by the General Assembly, Security Council and other organs.

Glossary of United Nations Acronyms

FAO: Food and Agriculture Organization
IAEA: International Atomic Energy Agency
IBRD: International Bank for Reconstruction and Development
ICAO: International Civil Aviation Organization
IDA: International Development Association
IFAD: International Fund for Agricultural Development
IFC: International Finance Corporation
ILO: International Labour Organization
IMF: International Monetary Fund
INSTRAW: International Research and Training Institute for the Advancement of Women
ITU: International Telecommunications Union
MINUGUA: United Nations Mission for the Verification of Human Rights in Guatemala
MINURSO: United Nations Mission for the Referendum in Western Sahara
MINUSTAH: United Nations Stabilization Mission in Haiti
MONUC: United Nations Mission in the Democratic Republic of the Congo
ONUB: United Nations Operation in Burundi
UNAMA: United Nations Assistance Mission in Afghanistan
UNAMI: United Nations Assistance Mission in Iraq
UNAMSIL: United Nations Mission in Sierra Leone
UNCTAD: United Nations Conference on Trade and Development
UNDOF: United Nations Disengagement Observer Force
UNDP: United Nations Development Programme
UNEP: United Nations Environment Programme
UNESCO: United Nations Educational, Scientific and Cultural Organization
UNFICYP: United Nations Peacekeeping Force in Cyprus
UNFPA: United Nations Population Fund
UN-Habitat: United Nations Human Settlements Programme
UNHCR: Office of the United Nations High Commissioner for Refugees
UNICEF: United Nations Children's Fund
UNIDIR: United Nations Institute for Disarmament Research
UNIDO: United Nations Industrial Development Organization
UNIFIL: United Nations Interim Force in Lebanon

UNITAR: United Nations Institute for Training and Research
UNMEE: United Nations Mission in Ethiopia and Eritrea
UNMIK: United Nations Interim Administration Mission in Kosovo
UNMIL: United Nations Mission in Liberia
UNMISET: United Nations Mission of Support in East Timor
UNMOGIP: United Nations Military Observer Group in India and Pakistan
UNOCHA: United Nations Office for the Coordination of Humanitarian Affairs
UNOCI: United Nations Operation in Côte d'Ivoire
UNOMIG: United Nations Mission of Observers in Georgia
UNRWA: United Nations Relief and Works Agency for Palestine Refugees in the Near East
UNTSO: United Nations Truce Supervision Organization
UNU: United Nations University
UNV: United Nations Volunteers
UPU: Universal Postal Union
WFP: World Food Programme
WHO: World Health Organization
WIPO: World Intellectual Property Organization
WMO: World Meteorological Organization
WTO: World Tourism Organization
WTO: World Trade Organization (formerly General Agreement on Tariffs and Trade)

■ Functional Commissions

Commission for Social Development
Commission of Sustainable Development
Commission on Human Rights
Commission on Narcotic Drugs
Commission on the Status of Women
Population Commission
Statistical Commission

■ Regional Commissions

ECA: Economic Commission for Africa
ECE: Economic Commission for Europe
ECLAC: Economic Commission for Latin America and the Caribbean
ESCAP: Economic and Social Commission for Asia and the Pacific
ESCWA: Economic and Social Commission for Western Asia

The United Nations System

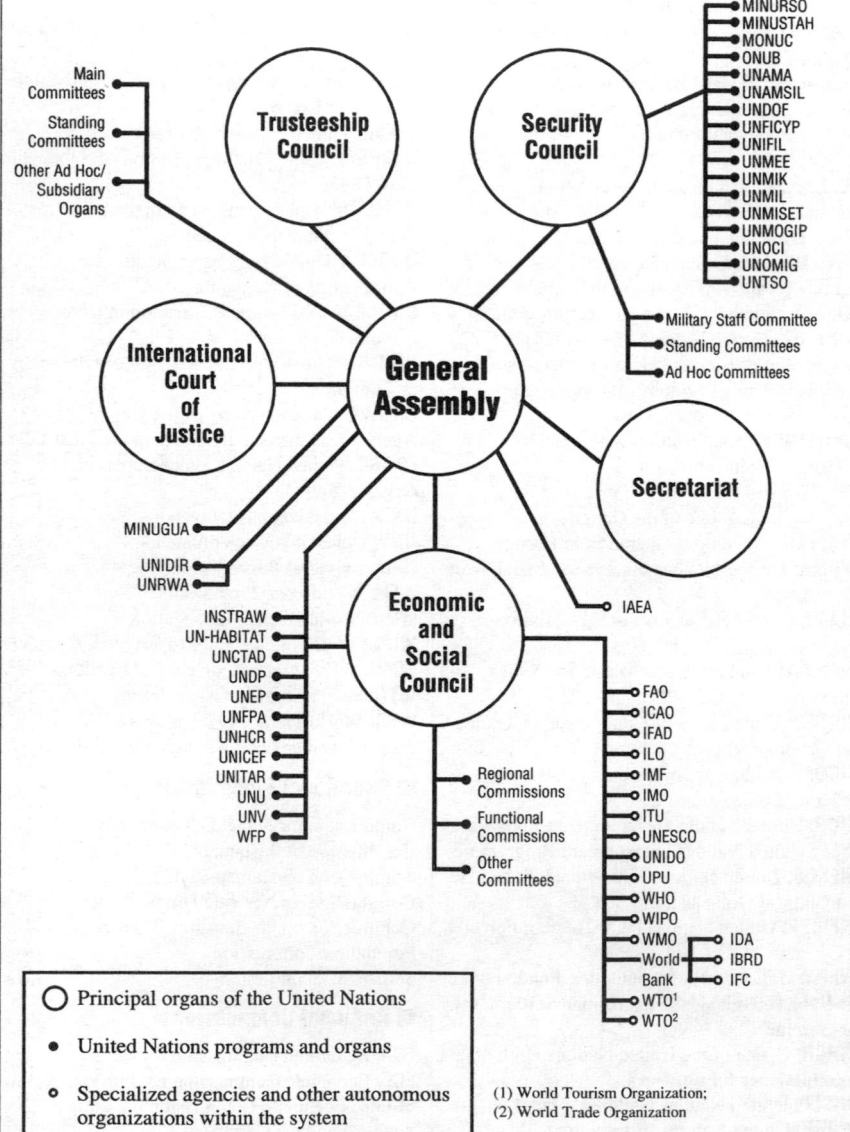

Main Committees
Standing Committees
Other Ad Hoc/ Subsidiary Organs

Trusteeship Council

Security Council

MINURSO
MINUSTAH
MONUC
ONUB
UNAMA
UNAMSIL
UNDOF
UNFICYP
UNIFIL
UNMEE
UNMIK
UNMIL
UNMISET
UNMOGIP
UNOCI
UNOMIG
UNTSO

International Court of Justice

General Assembly

Military Staff Committee
Standing Committees
Ad Hoc Committees

Secretariat

MINUGUA
UNIDIR
UNRWA

IAEA

INSTRAW
UN-HABITAT
UNCTAD
UNDP
UNEP
UNFPA
UNHCR
UNICEF
UNITAR
UNU
UNV
WFP

Economic and Social Council

Regional Commissions
Functional Commissions
Other Committees

FAO
ICAO
IFAD
ILO
IMF
IMO
ITU
UNESCO
UNIDO
UPU
WHO
WIPO
WMO
World Bank — IDA / IBRD / IFC
WTO[1]
WTO[2]

○ Principal organs of the United Nations

• United Nations programs and organs

○ Specialized agencies and other autonomous organizations within the system

(1) World Tourism Organization;
(2) World Trade Organization

N.B. The International Criminal Court came into effect on July 1, 2002, but it is independent and not shown on this chart.

United Nations Association in Canada – August 2004

Roster of the United Nations

(as of October 2004)

The 191 members of the United Nations, with the years in which they became members.

Member	Year	Member	Year	Member	Year
Afghanistan	1946	Ethiopia	1945	Micronesia	1991
Albania	1955	Fiji	1970	Moldova	1992
Algeria	1962	Finland	1955	Monaco	1993
Andorra	1993	France	1945	Mongolia	1961
Angola	1976	Gabon	1960	Morocco	1956
Antigua and Barbuda	1981	Gambia	1965	Mozambique	1975
Argentina	1945	Georgia	1992	Myanmar (formerly Burma)	1948
Armenia	1992	Germany	1973	Namibia	1990
Australia	1945	Ghana	1957	Nauru	1999
Austria	1955	Greece	1945	Nepal	1955
Azerbaijan	1992	Grenada	1974	Netherlands	1945
Bahamas	1973	Guatemala	1945	New Zealand	1945
Bahrain	1971	Guinea	1958	Nicaragua	1945
Bangladesh	1974	Guinea-Bissau	1974	Niger	1960
Barbados	1966	Guyana	1966	Nigeria	1960
Belarus	1945	Haiti	1945	Norway	1945
Belgium	1945	Honduras	1945	Oman	1971
Belize	1981	Hungary	1955	Pakistan	1947
Benin	1960	Iceland	1946	Palau	1995
Bhutan	1971	India	1945	Panama	1945
Bolivia	1945	Indonesia	1950	Papua New Guinea	1975
Bosnia and Herzegovina	1992	Iran	1945	Paraguay	1945
Botswana	1966	Iraq	1945	Peru	1945
Brazil	1945	Ireland	1955	Philippines	1945
Brunei Darussalam	1984	Israel	1949	Poland	1945
Bulgaria	1955	Italy	1955	Portugal	1955
Burkina Faso	1960	Jamaica	1962	Qatar	1971
Burundi	1962	Japan	1956	Romania	1955
Cambodia	1955	Jordan	1955	Russian Federation	1945
Cameroon	1960	Kazakhstan	1992	Rwanda	1962
Canada	1945	Kenya	1963	Saint Kitts and Nevis	1983
Cape Verde	1975	Kiribati	1999	Saint Lucia	1979
Central African Republic	1960	Korea, North	1991	Saint Vincent and the	
Chad	1960	Korea, South	1991	Grenadines	1980
Chile	1945	Kuwait	1963	Samoa	1976
China	1945	Kyrgyzstan	1992	San Marino	1992
Colombia	1945	Laos	1955	São Tomé and Príncipe	1975
Comoros	1975	Latvia	1991	Saudi Arabia	1945
Congo	1960	Lebanon	1945	Senegal	1960
Costa Rica	1945	Lesotho	1966	Seychelles	1976
Côte d'Ivoire	1960	Liberia	1945	Sierra Leone	1961
Croatia	1992	Libya	1955	Singapore	1965
Cuba	1945	Liechtenstein	1990	Slovak Republic	1993
Cyprus	1960	Lithuania	1991	Slovenia	1992
Czech Republic	1993	Luxembourg	1945	Solomon Islands	1978
Democratic Republic of the		Macedonia, Former Yugoslav		Somalia	1960
Congo (formerly Zaire)	1960	Republic of	1993	South Africa	1945
Denmark	1945	Madagascar	1960	Spain	1955
Djibouti	1977	Malawi	1964	Sri Lanka	1955
Dominica	1978	Malaysia	1957	Sudan	1956
Dominican Republic	1945	Maldives	1965	Suriname	1975
Ecuador	1945	Mali	1960	Swaziland	1968
Egypt	1945	Malta	1964	Sweden	1946
El Salvador	1945	Marshall Islands	1991	Switzerland	2002
Equatorial Guinea	1968	Mauritania	1961	Syria	1945
Eritrea	1993	Mauritius	1968	Tajikistan	1992
Estonia	1991	Mexico	1945	Tanzania	1961

Member	Year	Member	Year	Member	Year
Thailand	1946	Tuvalu	2000	Vanuatu	1981
Timor-Leste	2002	Uganda	1962	Vietnam	1977
Togo	1960	Ukraine	1945	Venezuela	1945
Tonga	1999	United Arab Emirates	1971	Yemen	1947
Trinidad and Tobago	1962	United Kingdom	1945	Yugoslavia, Federal Republic of	
Tunisia	1956	United States of America	1945	(Serbia and Montenegro)	1945
Turkey	1945	Uruguay	1945	Zambia	1964
Turkmenistan	1992	Uzbekistan	1992	Zimbabwe	1980

Source: *United Nations Association www.un.org*

United Nations Secretaries-General

The Secretary-General, heading the Secretariat, is responsible for the UN's administration and for alerting the Security Council to any threats to international peace and security, and acts as spokesperson for the UN. The Secretary-General is elected by the General Assembly on the recommendation of the Security Council and cannot be from one of the five permanent members of the Security Council.

Secretary, Nation	Date Installed	Secretary, Nation	Date Installed
Trygve Lie, Norway	Feb. 1946	Javier Pérez de Cuéllar, Peru	Dec. 1981
Dag Hammarskjöld, Sweden	Apr. 1953	Boutros Boutros-Ghali, Egypt	Jan. 1992
U Thant, Burma	Nov. 1961	Kofi Annan, Ghana	Jan. 1997
Kurt Waldheim, Austria	Dec. 1971		(to Dec. 31, 2006)

Source: *United Nations Association*

Canadian Ambassadors to the United Nations

Ambassador	Date Appointed	Ambassador	Date Appointed
Andrew McNaughton	Jan. 1948	Saul Forbes Rae	June 1972
John Holmes	Jan. 1950	William Barton	May 1976
Gerald Riddell	June 1950	Michel Dupuy	Mar. 1980
David Johnson	Oct. 1951	Gérard Pelletier	Aug. 1981
Robert MacKay	June 1955	Stephen H. Lewis	Oct. 1984
Charles Ritchie	Nov. 1957	Yves Fortier	July 1988
Paul Tremblay	May 1962	Louise Fréchette	Jan. 1992
George Ignatieff	Mar. 1966	Robert K. Fowler	Jan. 1995
Yvon Beaulne	Jan. 1969	Paul Heinbecker	June 2000
		Allan Rock	Jan. 2004

Source: *Dept. of Foreign Affairs*

Canada's New Ambassador to the United Nations

*O*n January 5, 2004, Allan Rock became Canada's newest ambassador and permanent representative to the United Nations in New York. Prime Minister Paul Martin announced the appointment in December 2003.

Rock is a career politician. In 1993, he was elected to Canada's House of Commons as the Liberal member for Etobicoke Centre in Toronto. He was re-elected in the same riding in 1997 and 2000.

Rock served in several cabinet posts in the government of Prime Minister Jean Chrétien. In 1993, Rock was appointed minister of justice and attorney general; in 1997, he was appointed minister of health; and in 2002, he was appointed minister of industry.

Before entering public life, Rock worked as a lawyer. He graduated from the University of Ottawa with a bachelor of arts and a bachelor of laws. He was born in 1947.

Rock replaced Paul Heinbecker as Canada's ambassador to the United Nations. Heinbecker has served Canada as a career diplomat since 1965.

World Health Organization (WHO)

The World Health Organization (WHO) is a specialized agency of the United Nations. The WHO declares in its constitution that every person has a right to good health and seeks to achieve the best possible health for all people in the world. The organization was established on April 7, 1948; its headquarters is in Geneva, Switzerland.

The WHO works with 192 governments to prevent and control the spread of disease. The agency promotes better sanitation and quarantine standards, cleaner water, proper food supply and nutrition, and better maternal and child care. The WHO sponsors medical research, encourages the investigation of new diseases, promotes immunization, and delivers medicine and medical equipment to needy countries. The agency can send teams to a site within 24 hours to control epidemics.

The WHO also promotes co-operation among non-governmental scientific and health organizations. These include UN agencies, bilateral agencies and "collaborating centres." The latter are national institutions (e.g., medical departments, research labs or training schools) that support the WHO's mandate and programs. Some publish medical information or devise new technologies; others provide advice on scientific, technical or policy issues.

The supreme decision-making body in the WHO is the World Health Assembly (WHA). This assembly consists of representatives from the WHO's 192 member states. The WHA decides major policy questions and approves the WHO's program and budget for the next two years. The assembly elects an executive board and appoints a director general. The WHA meets annually in Geneva in May.

The executive board consists of 32 health professionals who hold office for three-year terms. The board advises the WHA and implements the WHA's decisions. In January, the board prepares the agenda, reports and resolutions for the assembly's consideration in May. Another board meeting occurs in May after the assembly meets.

The WHO includes a secretariat of 3,500 health professionals and staff. These people work in Geneva, in the WHO's six regional offices and elsewhere. A director general leads the secretariat for five years. The director general is nominated by the executive board and approved by the assembly in May. The current director general is Dr. Lee Jong-wook of South Korea; he took office on July 21, 2003.

On May 19–28, 2003, the 56th session of the WHA occurred in Geneva. More than 2,000 people attended, including many ministers of health. The participants focused on the fight against tobacco use and a deadly new disease called severe acute respiratory syndrome (SARS).

On May 21, after four years of international negotiations, the WHA unanimously adopted the Framework Convention on Tobacco Control. This agreement—the world's first public health treaty— aims to protect people from the harmful effects of tobacco. The convention seeks to restrict tobacco advertising, increase tobacco taxes and eliminate the illegal cigarette trade. At least 40 governments must ratify the treaty before it enters into force. By June 29, 2004, however, only 23 governments (excluding Canada's) had ratified the convention.

The assembly also passed two resolutions about SARS. One declared that SARS was "the first severe infectious disease to emerge in the 21st century" and earmarked US$100 million in public and private funds to fight SARS. The other resolution confirmed the WHO's authority to verify outbreaks of disease by checking all official and unofficial sources and called for changes to international health law by 2005 to authorize the WHO to help control disease through on-site investigations.

The WHO will also continue its campaign against the epidemic of human immunodeficiency virus (HIV) and acquired immune deficiency syndrome (AIDS). The agency plans to reach its "three-by-five target" by providing anti-retroviral medicines to 3 million people in developing countries by the end of 2005.

WHO Regional Office Locations

Brazzaville, Congo (Africa)

Cairo, Egypt (Eastern Mediterranean)

Copenhagen, Denmark (Europe)

Manila, Philippines (Western Pacific)

New Delhi, India (Southeast Asia)

Washington, DC, USA (The Americas)

Source: *World Health Organization www.who.int*

World Trade Organization (WTO)

The World Trade Organization presides over the rules of international trade for more than 140 countries. The organization seeks to make international trade predictable, open and smooth. The WTO also provides a forum for trade talks, promotes freer trade and resolves trade disputes. The organization's binding rules, which are called the WTO Agreements, are negotiated and signed by the WTO's member governments.

The WTO appeared on January 1, 1995, after trade representatives from 125 countries negotiated for eight years (1986–94) to reform the rules of international trade. The talks, which were known as the "Uruguay Round," aimed at overhauling the older General Agreement on Tariffs and Trade (GATT) and concluded with the signing of a 22,000-page agreement in Marrakesh, Morocco, on April 5, 1994.

The WTO's creation marked the biggest reform of international trade since the establishment of the GATT in 1948. The WTO took over the administration of the amended GATT, which covered trade in goods alone, and got the authority to preside over newer agreements covering trade in services and intellectual property (e.g., designs and inventions) as well. The reformed trading system also attracted more prospective member governments.

The GATT, however, remains at the centre of the WTO Agreements. Since 1995, the WTO has incorporated the GATT's basic principles—which are reflected in rules barring discrimination among trading partners and favouring lower tariffs—in the more recent General Agreement on Trade in Services (GATS) and the Agreement on Trade-Related Aspects of Intellectual Property Rights (TRIPS).

The WTO has 147 members. The majority are sovereign countries, but a few are customs territories that have control over their trade policies. (An example is the Separate Customs Territory of Taiwan, Penghu, Kinmen and Matsu.) The membership also includes most of the world's industrial powers—such as Canada, which signed the GATT in 1948—although more than three-quarters of the WTO's members are "developing" or "least developed" countries.

Thirty "observer governments" are negotiating to join the WTO. They must begin talks to join the WTO within five years of acquiring observer status. Current observers include significant states such as Russia and Saudi Arabia. The Vatican is also an observer, although it is exempt from the need to begin negotiations for membership within five years.

■ The Structure of the WTO

The WTO's highest executive authority is the Ministerial Conference. It consists of government ministers from all WTO members and meets at least once every two years. The Ministerial Conference rules on matters under the WTO Agreements. The most recent Ministerial Conference met in Cancun, Mexico, in 2003.

In between Ministerial Conferences, the General Council directs the WTO's daily business. The General Council consists of all WTO members, acts on behalf of the Ministerial Conference and reports to the Ministerial Conference. The General Council also convenes as the Trade Policy Review Body (to examine members' trade policies) and as the Dispute Settlement Body (to resolve conflicts between members and uphold the WTO Agreements).

Three more councils, each responsible for different areas of trade, report to the General Council: the Council for Trade in Goods, the Council for Trade in Services and the Council for Trade-Related Aspects of Intellectual Property. These councils also consist of all WTO members and have numerous subsidiary committees as well.

The WTO's Secretariat is located in Geneva, Switzerland. The Secretariat's roles include organizing the Ministerial Conference, providing technical help to the WTO's councils and committees, analyzing trends in world trade and providing information to the public. The Secretariat's director-general is Dr. Supachai Panitchpakdi of Thailand; he assumed his post on September 1, 2002, for a term of three years.

WTO Ministerial Conferences (date of occurrence)

Singapore (Dec. 9–13, 1996)

Geneva, Switzerland (May 18 and 20, 1998)

Seattle, USA (Nov. 30–Dec. 3,1999)

Doha, Qatar (Nov. 9–14, 2001)

Cancun, Mexico (Sept. 10–14, 2003)

Source: *World Trade Organization, www.wto.org*

North Atlantic Treaty Organisation (NATO)

The North Atlantic Treaty Organisation (NATO) is a political and military alliance. It was created in Washington on April 4, 1949, when 12 states in Europe and North America signed the North Atlantic Treaty. NATO defends the peace and freedom of its members through collective security without sacrificing members' sovereignty. Headquarters is in Brussels, Belgium.

NATO was created to defend Western and Southern Europe from the threat of invasion by the Soviet Union following World War II. Western leaders began negotiating in 1948, after a Soviet attempt to deny Western access to West Berlin.

Today, 26 countries belong to NATO. The original 12 are Belgium, Canada, Denmark, France, Iceland, Italy, Luxembourg, the Netherlands, Norway, Portugal, the United Kingdom and the United States. The 14 newer members are Greece and Turkey (1952); West Germany (1955); Spain (1982); the Czech Republic, Hungary and Poland (1999); Bulgaria, Estonia, Latvia, Lithuania, Romania, Slovakia and Slovenia (2004). United Germany became a NATO ally after the reunification of West and East Germany in 1990.

The highest authority within NATO is the North Atlantic Council (NAC). It consists of permanent representatives, who act as ambassadors for their respective countries, and is directed by a secretary general. Meetings are weekly; the NAC also convenes less frequent meetings of foreign or defence ministers or heads of state. Discussions cover political, economic, military and scientific issues. The NAC reaches decisions only after all member states have been consulted. It cannot impose decisions on any of its members, although members can block the wishes of others by withholding consent.

The NAC can create subordinate committees and planning groups. The most important are the Defence Planning Committee and the Nuclear Planning Group. The Defence Planning Committee, which consists of permanent representatives and defence ministers, deals with collective defence planning. The Nuclear Planning Group, which consists of defence ministers, deals with nuclear weapons issues. Both are chaired by the NAC's secretary general. This post is currently held by Jaap de Hoop Scheffer of the Netherlands, who took office on January 5, 2004.

At the Rome Summit in 1991, NATO outlined a new strategy for Europe after the collapse of the Soviet-led Warsaw Pact: reduced dependence on nuclear weapons, reductions in the size and readiness of military forces, improvements in military flexibility, greater use of multinational military units and a new focus on peacekeeping.

Also concurrent with the disintegration of the Soviet Union, NATO created mechanisms for consultation and co-operation with former Warsaw Pact states, including the North Atlantic Cooperation Council (NACC) (1991), the Partnership for Peace program (1994) and the Euro-Atlantic Partnership Council (1997). In 1997, NATO and Russia signed the NATO–Russia Founding Act, which obliged the signatories to co-operate as equal partners. In 2002, NATO and Russia strengthened their partnership by creating the NATO–Russia Council. The goal of these organizations was peaceful progress toward a new security environment in Europe.

In 1995, NATO first sent land troops outside NATO territory when 60,000 personnel went into Bosnia and Herzegovina under United Nations' authority to enforce the Dayton Peace Accord, negotiated to end armed conflict in the former Yugoslavia. NATO forces and troops from 19 non-NATO countries, including Russia, worked together during the mission, first as part of the Implementation Force (IFOR) and then as the Stabilisation Force (SFOR).

On March 23, 1999, the NAC authorized air strikes by NATO forces against targets in the Federal Republic of Yugoslavia to end that country's campaign against ethnic Albanians in Kosovo. The air strike campaign continued until June 10 when the withdrawal of Yugoslav forces from the Kosovo region began. As of June 12, 1999, NATO forces joined a UN-mandated peacekeeping force (Kosovo Force or KFOR), to enforce the withdrawal agreement.

On September 12, 2001, less than 24 hours after terrorist attacks on the United States, NATO declared that the attacks were against all 19 NATO countries and began to aid the United States in its campaign against terrorism. Today, NATO supports US-led military operations against terrorists in Afghanistan and provide most of the troops in the UN-mandated International Security Assistance Force (ISAF) to stabilize Afghanistan.

REGIONAL ORGANIZATIONS

European Union (EU)

The European Union (EU) represents a unique relationship among democratic nations, with the aim of constructing a united Europe. The EU is more than an international organization but not a full-blown federation. It is the world's largest trading entity, accounting for well over 20 percent of world trade. Its population totals about 450 million people.

The European Union originated as the European Coal and Steel Community (ECSC). Formed in 1951 by France, West Germany, Italy, the Netherlands, Belgium and Luxembourg, it became operational in 1952.

The success of the ECSC spurred the same six countries to apply the same approach to the entire economy. In 1957, the Six formed the European Economic Community (EEC), creating a common market for all sectors of the economy. The EEC committed the Six to dismantle trade barriers and to allow the free movement of goods, services, capital and people. At the same time, the Six formed the European Atomic Energy Community (Euratom) to further the use of nuclear energy for peaceful purposes.

In 1967, the institutions of the ECSC, Euratom and the EEC were merged. In 1973, Denmark, Ireland and the United Kingdom became members, as did Greece in 1981, Spain and Portugal in 1986 and Austria, Finland and Sweden in 1995. Cyprus, the Czech Republic, Estonia, Hungary, Latvia, Lithuania, Malta, Poland, the Slovak Republic and Slovenia joined in 2004, creating an EU of 25 nations. Negotiations continue with Romania and Bulgaria. Turkey and Croatia have also been recognized as candidates. The basic principle of the accession negotiations is that all applicants must accept existing EU law.

From its inception, the EU has been dedicated to ensuring economic and social progress and strengthening the unity of the economies of its member states. To help promote their harmonious development the EU uses the European Regional Development Fund, the European Social Fund, the European Agricultural Guidance and Guarantee Fund and the Cohesion Fund.

Part of the Single European Act, which came into force in 1987, was the Europe 1992 project. This aimed at completing the common market and creating a single internal market by dismantling the remaining physical, technical and fiscal barriers among the member states.

The Maastricht Treaty on European Union, which came into effect in 1993, created a European Union of three pillars. The first pillar is the European Community with its joint supranational institutions. The two new pillars are intergovernmental co-operation in foreign and security policy and in justice and home affairs.

The Maastricht Treaty committed the member states to create an economic and monetary union, including the establishment of a European Central Bank in Frankfurt. In January 1999, the EURO (€) was introduced as a single EU currency. In January 2002, EURO coins and banknotes began circulating in 12 member states, replacing their national currencies. The treaty also committed the member states to develop a common foreign and security policy.

The treaty gave the regions a part to play by setting up a Committee of the Regions. It also introduced the principle of "subsidiarity," by which the EU deals only with matters it is better equipped to deal with than the member states.

In 1997, the member states agreed to revise the founding treaties. Coming into force in May 1999, the Treaty of Amsterdam contained four major objectives. They were to

• ensure citizens' rights;
• ensure the free movement of citizens;
• strengthen the union's foreign policy; and
• make the union's decision-making process more effective.

The treaty also introduced the new position of high representative for the common foreign and security policy.

The Treaty of Nice, which came into force in 2003, again amended the founding treaties to prepare the EU for the accession of more countries. The treaty allowed further qualified-majority voting for decisions that previously required unanimity. It also changed the weighting of votes in the council and reallocated the number of seats among the member states in the European Parliament.

In 2001, the European Council convened a convention to prepare for the Intergovernmental Conference a draft treaty establishing a constitution for Europe. In June 2004, the 25 EU leaders agreed on a new constitutional treaty for Europe. Innovations include the creation of the posts of president of the

European Council and of minister for foreign affairs and the introduction of a new double majority voting system in the council which requires decisions to be taken by 55 percent of the member states representing at least 65 percent of the EU's population. But this treaty must be ratified first in the various countries according to national procedures (e.g., referendum or parliamentary ratification).

■ INSTITUTIONS OF THE EU

The European Union creates its own laws and policies through the following institutions:

The European Commission proposes legislation, implements policy and enforces the treaties. It has investigative powers and can take legal action. It also represents the EU in trade negotiations. The Commission is headed by 25 commissioners. The commissioners are appointed for five years.

The European Parliament is directly elected by the citizens of the union. Its 732 members debate issues and question the commission and council. On a wide range of issues it shares legislative decision-making power with the council of the EU. It can dismiss the commission and has final approval over the EU budget. MPs sit according to political affiliation and not nationality. Elections take place every five years. The number of MPs from each country are: Germany 99, France 78, Italy 78, the United Kingdom 78, Poland 54, Spain 54, Netherlands 27, Belgium 24, Czech Republic 24, Greece 24, Hungary 24, Portugal 24, Sweden 19, Austria 18, Denmark 14, Finland 14, Slovakia 14, Ireland 13, Lithuania 13, Latvia 9, Slovenia 7, Estonia 6, Cyprus 6, Luxembourg 6 and Malta 5.

The Council of the European Union is composed of ministers from each of the member countries. The council acts on commission proposals and is, with the European Parliament, the EU's legislative decision-making body. Participation changes according to the agenda. Agricultural ministers, for instance, decide on agricultural matters and economic and finance ministers on economic and monetary matters. Ministers represent and defend the interests of their countries while seeking agreements that promote the union's goals. The presidency of the council rotates among the member states every six months. The Single European Act and subsequent treaties have gradually extended majority voting in the council in areas that previously required unanimity.

The European Council consists of the heads of state or government of the EU member states and the commission president. It meets in principle four times a year to define major internal and foreign policy orientations. The European Council does not legislate, but its written conclusions provide guidance.

The Court of Justice is the EU's supreme court. It interprets EU law and its rulings are binding—including on member states. The court has one judge from each member state, assisted by advocates-general. Both groups are appointed for six years by mutual consent of the member states.

The Court of Auditors audits the accounts of the EU and EU bodies.

The Committee of the Regions and the **Economic and Social Committee** must be consulted in certain areas by the commission and the council on policies and proposals for legislation.

The European Central Bank governs monetary policy.

Members of the European Union

(as of October 2004)

Member/Yr. Joined	Member/Yr. Joined	Member/Yr. Joined	Member/Yr. Joined	Member/Yr. Joined
Austria (1995)	Estonia (2004)	Hungary (2004)	Luxembourg (1952)	Slovakia (2004)
Belgium (1952)	Finland (1995)	Ireland (1973)	Malta (2004)	Slovenia (2004)
Cyprus (2004)	France (1952)	Italy (1952)	Netherlands (1952)	Spain (1986)
Czech Republic (2004)	Germany (1952)	Latvia (2004)	Poland (2004)	Sweden (1995)
Denmark (1973)	Greece (1981)	Lithuania (2004)	Portugal (1986)	United Kingdom (1973)

Source: *Commission of the European Communities*

For Internet information, visit: europa.eu.int and www.delcan.cec.eu.int

Asia-Pacific Economic Co-operation (APEC)

APEC is an association of 21 Pacific Rim countries seeking greater prosperity through freer trade. APEC's members include large, industrialized nations such as the United States and small, developing nations such as Papua New Guinea. The total population of APEC countries is 2.6 billion. About 47 percent of global trade moved through APEC countries; the combined gross domestic product of APEC's members was more than US$18 trillion.

APEC was established in 1989 at a conference of trade and foreign ministers in Canberra, Australia. The 12 founding countries (including Canada) agreed to meet annually in different member countries for informal ministerial talks. They also agreed to hold alternate ministerial meetings in APEC countries belonging to the Association of Southeast Asian Nations (ASEAN).

Subsequent meetings of trade and foreign ministers in the early 1990s produced several key decisions. In 1991, for example, APEC's members committed themselves to free enterprise and "open regionalism." In the same year, APEC admitted three Chinese states— China, Taiwan and Hong Kong—as members. In 1992, APEC decided to create a permanent Secretariat in Singapore and a central fund to cover its administration.

In 1993, APEC's international profile rose when, after a ministerial meeting in Seattle, all the political leaders of APEC countries met for a separate meeting on nearby Blake Island. They released an Economic Vision Statement that recognized the interdependence of all Pacific Rim economies. In subsequent years, APEC's political leaders have met for separate talks after each annual meeting of trade and foreign ministers.

In 1994, APEC's political leaders released the Bogor Declaration of Common Resolve in Indonesia. The statement pledged APEC's industrialized members to achieve total free trade and investment by 2010 and APEC's developing members to achieve the same goal by 2020. In 1998, during a serious financial crisis in Asia, APEC welcomed its three latest members: Russia, Vietnam and Peru.

APEC operates by consensus. Each year, a different country chairs and hosts the annual meetings of trade and foreign ministers and of political leaders. In 2004, Chile is chairing and hosting these meetings.

At the annual ministerial meeting, APEC sets tasks for its four committees, 11 working groups and other forums. The Committee on Trade and Investment pursues the liberalization of international trade; the Economic Committee analyzes economic trends; the Budget and Management Committee evaluates APEC's administration; and the Senior Officials' Meeting (SOM) Committee on Economic and Technical Cooperation helps APEC's senior officials coordinate their economic and technical agendas.

APEC's working groups—most of which were established in 1990 and 1991—focus on specific issues: small and medium-sized enterprises; energy; fisheries; human resources development; industrial science and technology; marine resource conservation; tourism; telecommunications and information; trade promotion; transportation; and agricultural technical co-operation. Other forums study issues such as the role of women in APEC and sustainable economic development.

Two other institutions provide advice. APEC's Secretariat provides research and technical support to APEC's member economies and committees. The Secretariat also promotes APEC to the world. The APEC Business Advisory Council (ABAC), which was created in Japan in 1995 and consists of business executives drawn from APEC countries, advises on the execution of APEC's plans.

A 10-year moratorium on new member economies is in effect. In 2007, APEC will accept applications for new members.

Member Economies (date of membership)

Australia (1989)	Papua New Guinea (1993)
Brunei Darussalam (1989)	Peru (1998)
Canada (1989)	Philippines (1989)
Chile (1994)	Russia (1998)
China (1991)	Singapore (1989)
Hong Kong (1991)	South Korea (1989)
Indonesia (1989)	Taiwan (1991)
Japan (1989)	Thailand (1989)
Malaysia (1989)	United States (1989)
Mexico (1993)	Vietnam (1998)
New Zealand (1989)	

Source: *Asia-Pacific Economic Co-operation.* Visit www.apec.org

Other Organizations in International News

African Union
(formerly the Organization of African Unity)
Headquarters: Addis Ababa, Ethiopia
Established: July 9, 2002, in Durban, Republic of South Africa
Aim: to promote solidarity, defend territorial integrity and accelerate socio-economic integration among African states
Members: 53 governments including Western Sahara, a territory occupied by Morocco
Note: The Organization of African Unity was established on May 25, 1963.
Web site: http://www.africa-union.org

Amnesty International
Secretariat: London, United Kingdom
Established: July 1961 in London, England
Aim: to prevent and end grave abuses to human rights worldwide
Members: more than 1.8 million members, supporters and subscribers in over 150 countries
Web site: http://www.amnesty.org

Andean Community
(formerly the Andean Pact)
General Secretariat: Lima, Peru
Established: Aug. 1, 1997
Aim: to promote balanced economic growth in the region, create an Andean common market and raise living standards for inhabitants
Members: (5) Bolivia, Colombia, Ecuador, Peru and Venezuela
Note: The Cartagena Agreement created the Andean Pact on May 24, 1969
Web site: http://www.comunidadandina.org

Arctic Council
Secretariat: Reykjavik, Iceland
Established: Sept. 19, 1996, in Ottawa, Canada
Aim: to promote sustainable development and environmental protection throughout the circumpolar region
Members: (8) Canada, Denmark (including Greenland and the Faroe Islands), Finland, Iceland, Norway, Russia, Sweden and the USA; plus six international aboriginal organizations with permanent participant status
Web site: http://www.arctic-council.org

Association of Southeast Asian Nations
Secretariat: Jakarta, Indonesia
Established: Aug. 8, 1967, in Bangkok, Thailand
Aim: to promote regional economic, social and cultural progress as well as peace and stability
Members: (10) Brunei Darussalam, Cambodia, Indonesia, Laos, Malaysia, Myanmar, the Philippines, Singapore, Thailand and Vietnam
Web site: http://www.aseansec.org

Caribbean Community and Common Market (CARICOM)
Secretariat: Georgetown, Guyana
Established: Aug. 1, 1973, by the Treaty of Chaguaramas, Trinidad and Tobago
Aim: to encourage economic growth, full employment and improved living standards
Members: (15) Antigua and Barbuda, Bahamas, Barbados, Belize, Dominica, Grenada, Guyana, Haiti, Jamaica, Montserrat, St. Lucia, St. Kitts and Nevis, St. Vincent and the Grenadines, Suriname, and Trinidad and Tobago; plus five associate members
Note: Bahamas belongs to the community but not the common market.
Web site: http://www.caricom.org

Christian Democrat International
Headquarters: Brussels, Belgium
Established: Nov. 21, 1961
Aim: to promote cooperation among Christian democrat and people's parties worldwide; to protect human rights, families, the poor and nature within free-market societies
Members: 79 member parties worldwide and 14 observer parties in 2003
Web site: http://www.idc-cdi.org

The Commonwealth
Secretariat: London, United Kingdom
Established: Dec. 11, 1931, in London, England
Aim: to promote democracy and cooperation among former member countries of the British Empire
Members: 53 countries including Canada
Web site: http://www.thecommonwealth.org

Economic Community of West African States (ECOWAS)
Secretariat: Abuja, Nigeria
Founding Treaty Signed: May 28, 1975, in Lagos, Nigeria
Aim: to promote full regional economic integration and closer political ties
Members: (15) Benin, Burkina Faso, Cape Verde, Côte d'Ivoire, Gambia, Ghana, Guinea, Guinea Bissau, Liberia, Mali, Niger, Nigeria, Senegal, Sierra Leone and Togo
Web site: http://www.ecowas.int

Group of Eight (G8)
Headquarters: No permanent headquarters or secretariat
Established: November 1975 in Rambouillet, France
Aim: to manage macroeconomic issues, international trade, relations with developing countries, energy and regional security
Members: (8) Canada, France, Germany, Italy, Japan, Russia, the UK and the USA; plus the European Union
Web site (unofficial): http://www.G8.utoronto.ca

International Civil Aviation Organization
Headquarters: Montreal, Canada
Established: Dec. 7, 1944, in Chicago, USA (a UN agency)
Aim: to promote international cooperation in civil aviation
Members: 188 contracting states including Canada
Web site: http://www.icao.int

International Criminal Court
Location: The Hague, The Netherlands
Founding Treaty Signed: July 17, 1998 in Rome, Italy
Aim: to prosecute persons responsible for war crimes, crimes against humanity and genocide
Members: 94 states parties (i.e., countries) including Canada
Web site: http://www.icc-cpi.int

International Criminal Police Organization (Interpol)
General Secretariat: Lyon, France
Established: Sept. 3–7, 1923, in Vienna, Austria, as the International Criminal Police Commission
Aim: to promote cooperation among national police forces in fighting international crime
Members: 181 countries including Canada
Web site: http://www.interpol.int

International Federation of Journalists
Headquarters: Brussels, Belgium
Established: 1926
Aim: to promote international action to defend press freedom and social justice through strong, free and independent trade unions of journalists
Members: 159 trade unions, including three Canadian unions, in 113 countries
Web site: http://www.ifj.org

International Federation of Red Cross and Red Crescent Societies (formerly Red Cross)
Secretariat: Geneva, Switzerland
Established: 1919 in Paris, France
Aim: to promote humanitarianism, prepare for disaster relief, provide relief after disasters and promote health in communities
Members: 178 national societies worldwide including Canada
Web site: http://www.ifrc.org

International Labour Organization
Headquarters: Geneva, Switzerland
Established: April 1919 in Paris, France (now a UN agency)
Aim: to promote social justice and internationally recognized human and labour rights
Members: 177 countries including Canada
Web site: http://www.ilo.org

International Monetary Fund
Headquarters: Washington DC, USA
Founding Conference: July 22, 1944, in Bretton Woods, USA (a UN agency)
Aim: to promote international monetary cooperation, exchange stability and orderly exchange arrangements; to foster economic growth and high levels of employment; to provide temporary financial help to countries to ease balance of payments adjustment
Members: 184 countries including Canada
Web site: http://www.imf.org

International Olympic Committee
Headquarters: Lausanne, Switzerland
Established: June 23, 1894, in France
Aim: to promote Olympic ideals and administer the Olympic games
Members: 202 National Olympic Committees including Canada worldwide
Note: The 2006 Winter Olympics will be in Turin, Italy; the 2008 Summer Olympics will be in Beijing, China.
Web site: http://www.olympic.org

International Organization for Standardization
Central Secretariat: Geneva, Switzerland
Established: Feb. 23, 1947, in Geneva, Switzerland
Aim: to promote the development of international standards; to aid the international exchange of goods and services
Members: 99 (national) member bodies including Canada; 35 (national) correspondent members
Web site: http://www.iso.org

Inter-Parliamentary Union
Headquarters: Geneva, Switzerland
Established: June 30, 1889, in Paris, France
Aim: to promote dialogue and cooperation among parliamentarians worldwide
Members: 140 national parliaments including Canada's; plus five associate international parliaments
Web site: http://www.ipu.org

League of Arab States (also known as the Arab League)
Headquarters: Cairo, Egypt
Established: Mar. 22, 1945, in Cairo, Egypt
Aim: to promote economic, social, political and military cooperation among member states
Members: (22) Algeria, Bahrain, Comoros, Djibouti, Egypt, Iraq, Jordan, Kuwait, Lebanon, Libya, Mauritania, Morocco, Oman, Palestine, Qatar, Saudi Arabia, Somalia, Sudan, Syria, Tunisia, United Arab Emirates, Yemen
Web site: http://www.arableagueonline.org

Liberal International
Headquarters: London, United Kingdom
Established: Apr. 10–14, 1947, in Oxford, England
Aim: to strengthen ties among liberal political parties and governments worldwide
Members: 61 full member parties including Canada's; plus 18 observer parties; plus nine cooperating organizations
Web site: http://www.liberal-international.org

Mercosur
Headquarters: Montevideo, Uruguay
Founding Treaty Signed: Mar. 26, 1991, in Asunción, Paraguay
Aim: to create a regional common market
Members: (4) Argentina, Brazil, Paraguay and Uruguay; plus associate members Bolivia and Chile
Web site: http://www.mercosur.org

Organisation for Economic Co-operation and Development (formerly the Organisation for European Economic Co-operation)
Secretariat: Paris, France

Founding Conference: Dec. 14, 1960, in Paris, France

Aim: supports democracy and the market economy; researches economic and social issues to influence government policy throughout the industrialized world

Members: 30 countries including Canada

Note: The Organisation for European Economic Co-operation was established on Apr. 16, 1948.

Web site: http://www.oecd.org

Organisation Internationale de la Francophonie

Secretariat: Paris, France

Founding Conference: Dec. 2–4, 1998, in Bucharest, Romania

Aim: to promote peace, democracy and French culture throughout the French-speaking world

Members: 51 governments including Canada, New Brunswick, Quebec and French-speaking Belgium; plus five observer states

Web site: http://www.francophonie.org

Organization for Security and Co-operation in Europe
(formerly the Conference on Security and Co-operation in Europe)

Headquarters: Vienna, Austria

Established: Dec. 5–6, 1994, in Budapest, Hungary

Aim: to promote security through arms control, conflict prevention, democratization, human rights, election-monitoring and other measures

Members: 55 states in Europe, Central Asia and North America including Canada

Note: The Conference on Security and Co-operation in Europe was established under the Helsinki Final Act of Aug. 1, 1975.

Web site: http://www.osce.org

Organization of American States

Headquarters: Washington DC, USA

Established: Apr. 30, 1948, in Bogota, Colombia

Aim: to strengthen democracy, advance human rights, promote peace and security, expand trade and reduce poverty, narcotics and corruption

Members: 35 states including Canada

Note: Cuba, although a member of the OAS, has been barred from participating by a resolution passed in 1962.

Web site: http://www.oas.org

Organization of the Petroleum Exporting Countries

Secretariat: Vienna, Austria

Established: Sept. 10–14, 1960, in Baghdad, Iraq

Aim: to coordinate and stabilize oil and gas policies to benefit member states

Members: (11) Algeria, Indonesia, Iran, Iraq, Kuwait, Libya, Nigeria, Qatar, Saudi Arabia, United Arab Emirates and Venezuela

Web site: http://www.opec.org

Organization of the Islamic Conference

General Secretariat: Jeddah, Saudi Arabia

Established: Sept. 25, 1969, in Rabat, Morocco

Aim: to strengthen Islamic solidarity and cooperation among member states; to protect the dignity, independence and national rights of Muslims

Members: 57 member states; plus three observer states

Web site: http://www.oic-un.org

Non-Aligned Movement

Headquarters: No permanent headquarters or secretariat

Established: Sept. 1–6, 1961, in Belgrade, Yugoslavia

Aim: to promote Third World perspectives on colonialism, disarmament, minority rights, apartheid and poverty

Members: 106 national governments including Yugoslavia, which was suspended in 1992; 17 observer national governments; seven observer organizations

Web site: http://www.nam.gov.za

Socialist International

Secretariat: London, United Kingdom

Established (in its present form): June 30–July 3, 1951, in Frankfurt, West Germany

Aim: to strengthen ties among social democratic, socialist and labour parties worldwide

Members: 107 full member parties including Canada's NDP; plus 31 consultative parties; plus 16 observer parties; plus fraternal and associated organizations

Web site: http://www.socialistinternational.org

World Council of Churches

Ecumenical Centre: Geneva, Switzerland

Established: Aug. 23, 1948, in Amsterdam, The Netherlands

Aim: to promote the visible unity of Christianity

Members: 342 Christian churches in more than 120 countries

Web site: http://www.wcc-coe.org

World Economic Forum

Headquarters: No permanent headquarters or secretariat

Established: January 1971 in Davos, Switzerland

Aim: to provide collaborative opportunities for world leaders to address global issues and promote entrepreneurship in the global public interest

Members: executives primarily drawn from the world's 1,000 leading global companies

Web site: http://www.weforum.org

WWF International
(formerly the World Wildlife Fund)

Secretariat: Gland, Switzerland

Established: Sept. 11, 1961, in Switzerland

Aim: to stop the degradation of the planet's natural environment and help humans live in harmony with nature

Members: five million supporters worldwide

Web site: http://www.panda.org

WORLD HISTORY

■ Ancient History: 5000 BC to AD 476

5000–3501 BC: During the Neolithic Age, people in western Europe devise polished stone weapons and tools and live in agriculturally based settlements. The earliest known cities emerge in Mesopotamia—in southwestern Asia between the Tigris and Euphrates rivers on a plain rendered fertile by canals. In southern Mesopotamia, Sumerians write on clay tablets; they use as many as 2,000 different pictographs. Sumerians and Egyptians smelt gold and silver. In Egypt, people use a calendar regulated by the sun and moon; musicians play harps and flutes. Painted pottery appears along the Mediterranean coast; Cretan ships sail on the Mediterranean Sea. Coloured ceramic ware from Russia reaches China.

3500–2001 BC: The Middle East's Bronze Age begins around 3500. Sumerian civilization, located in the region of the Euphrates River, reaches its zenith. Sumerians devise a cuneiform script, use numerals and write poetry. They irrigate farmland. They use pottery wheels, wheeled vehicles, oil-burning lamps and metal coins as legal tender. They make linen, barley, bread and beer. The Sumerians also build brick temples and create medicines. China's earliest recorded dynasty, the Yao, appears (2500–2300). The Chinese calculate equinoxes and solstices. In Egypt, pharoahs rule as god-kings (2200–525). The Egyptians build the Great Sphinx of Giza, wear colourful glass beads and wrestle for sport. The Egyptians mummify their dead and build the first library. They also introduce the bow and arrow to warfare. In India, the Indus civilization begins.

2000–1501 BC: Ancient Egyptian civilization reaches its zenith during the Eighteenth Dynasty. Egyptians irrigate their land, build great stone monuments and use an alphabet of 24 signs. They devise bathrooms with water and use contraceptives. Egyptians also write narratives such as *The Story of Sinuhe*. The Persian Empire emerges (1750–1550). The king of Babylonia, Hammurabi, drafts one of the earliest known legal codes. Babylonians use geometry for astronomical measurements and describe the signs of the Zodiac. Cretans perform religious dances. The first of

seven periods of Chinese literature begins. Stonehenge is built on Salisbury Plain in England. Abraham, patriarch of the Jewish religion, lives (c. 1800).

1500–1001 BC: The Israelites, led by Moses, escape bondage in Egypt; they eventually settle in Canaan in 1250. At Mt. Sinai, Moses reveals the Ten Commandments to his people. The decline of Egyptian power begins (1200–1090). Greeks destroy the city of Troy after years of war (1193–83). The Iron Age begins in the Mediterranean basin (1000). The Egyptians use obelisks as sundials. Phoenicia becomes the dominant trading power in the Mediterranean. The first Chinese dictionary is written; the Chinese also make silk fabrics. Pre-Columbian Americans build the Pyramid of the Sun at Teotihuacán in Mexico.

1000–901 BC: Phoenicians forge trade links between Asiatic and Greek civilizations. King David rules a united Judah and Israel (1000–960); Jerusalem is his capital. David's son, King Solomon, extends his kingdom's borders and builds magnificent palaces (960–25). The Hebrews develop an alphabet and literature. In Greece, pagan classicism flourishes. In India, pantheistic beliefs and belief in reincarnation prevail; the caste system takes hold. In China, the Chou Dynasty promotes rational philosophy; the Chinese paint with brush and ink. In northern Europe, people make gold vessels and jewellery. The Germanic peoples begin mass migrations. Pinto Indians build huts in southwestern North America.

900–601 BC: In North Africa, Carthage is founded (813). The *Iliad* and *Odyssey* are written and credited to the poet Homer (c. 800). The first recorded Olympic Games occur in Greece (776); subsequent games take place once every four years. Rome is founded, according to legend, by the twins Romulus and Remus (753). A hymn carved on a Sumerian tablet becomes the earliest known record of music. Pharoah Nechos orders the building of a canal between the Nile River and the Red Sea. The Assyrians destroy Babylon and divert the Euphrates River to flood the city. The Babylonians and their allies later destroy their Assyrian enemies and divide the Assyrian Empire. In Tuscany, Etruscan art flourishes. The Athenians build the Acropolis, a fortified temple on a hill. Greeks use limestone and marble to build other temples. Greeks play flutes and lyres to accompany songs; Greek choral and lyric poetry feature the strophe and antistrophe. In Persia, the prophet Zoroaster teaches religion (c. 628–551).

600–451 BC: Preclassical Mayan civilization flourishes in Mexico. In Babylon, Nebuchadnezzer orders the refortification of his city and the building of terraced, hanging gardens (600). The Babylonians destroy the Jewish Temple of Jerusalem and enslave the Jews. During their captivity, Jews write the early books of the Bible. In Nepal, the Indian prince Siddhartha Gautama is born (563). In midlife, he renounces his kingdom, practises asceticism and searches for religious enlightenment. As the Buddha, he teaches monks to spread his ideas. In China, Confucius is born (551). His moral philosophy, expressed in the *Analects*, spreads throughout China and influences Chinese rulers. Cyrus II the Great of Persia conquers Babylon and transforms Persia into a vast empire (c. 540). He frees the Jews in 536 and aids their return to Israel. Darius I divides the Persian Empire into 20 provinces and introduces a common currency, regular taxes and a standing army. Solon's laws are adopted in Athens. Athlete Milo of Crotona is crowned six times at the Olympic Games (536). Chinese feudalism weakens during the Chou Dynasty (c. 500–451). Greek cities fend off Persian domination when the Greeks in Cyprus win the Persian Wars (490–49). The Greeks build a marble temple for Apollo at Delphi in 478 and the statue of Zeus—the centrepiece of the temple at Olympia—in 460. Aeschylus writes *Prometheus Bound* (460). A former Phrygian slave writes the *Fables of Aesop*.

450–301 BC: During Greece's Periclean Age, Socrates and Plato discuss philosophy, Sophocles and Euripides write dramas, and Thucydides and Herodotus write histories. In India, an empire based in Magadha (the "cradle of Buddhism") emerges. The Torah becomes the moral code of the Jewish people. Celtic settlements appear in the British Isles. In Greece, the Spartans use chemicals (charcoal, sulphur and pitch) in warfare; the Athenians

build the Parthenon (447–32). Greece's population rises to 2 million citizens and 1 million slaves. The Peloponnesian Wars (431–04) end when the Spartan navy destroys the Athenian fleet at Aegospotami; Athenian power declines. Mesopotamians use the first horoscopes (c. 410). Athens condemns Socrates to death; he commits suicide (399). Brennus the Gaul sacks Rome (390). The Romans rebuild their city (387) and add city walls (377). Plato founds the Academy, one of the most influential schools in the world (c. 387). Armies begin using catapults in war. Aristotle, the Greek philosopher, is born (384). Alexander the Great is born in Macedon (356). Alexander's father, Philip II, is assassinated (336). After conquering Jerusalem, Tyre and Persia, Alexander leads his army east to the Indus River in India where his generals force him to turn back. Alexander dies in Babylon (323). Alexander's generals divide his empire and begin fighting civil wars (321). Greece's Hellenistic Age begins (330–20); Greek culture spreads into Asia Minor. Greek philosophies such as stoicism, epicureanism and cynicism flourish. Euclid writes *Elements*, a standard work on geometry (323). Alexandria becomes the centre of Greek learning.

300–151 BC: In Mexico, the sun temple Atetello is built at Teotihuacán (300). Chinese astronomers compile accurate star maps (c. 300). In Rome, plebeians achieve full equality in law with patricians (287). Archimedes, the Greek mathematician, is born (287). The establishment of the city of Seleucia heralds the end of Babylonian history (275). Manetho, a high priest of Egypt, writes a history of Egypt in Greek (275). The Colossus at Rhodes is completed (275). The Lighthouse of Pharos is completed at Alexandria (275). A dispute over the Sicilian cities of Messana and Syracuse sparks the First Punic War between the Carthaginians and the Romans (264–41). The Romans win naval battles at Mylae (260) and Cape Ecnomus (256) but lose in Africa (255). A Roman victory in the Aegadian Isles (241) leads to peace and wins Sicily for Rome, but the Romans break the peace and invade Sardinia and Corsica. The Egyptians introduce leap year into their calendar (239). The Greeks and Romans play ball games, dice and board games. The death of Sun-tsi ends the era of Chinese classical philosophy. The Chinese build the Great Wall of China (2,400 km long) to keep out invaders (221–10). The Second Punic War (218–01) opens when Hannibal of Carthage conquers the city of Saguntum, a Roman ally, in Spain; Rome declares war. Hannibal invades Italy from the north (217) and allies with Philip V of Macedon (216), but the Romans defeat Hannibal at Zama in Africa (202). Carthage surrenders its war fleet and Spanish province to Rome. The Second Macedonian War (200–197) ends when the Romans under Flamius defeat Philip V of Macedon. The use of gears leads to the invention of the ox-driven water wheel for irrigation (200). The Rosetta Stone, which features demotic, Greek and hieroglyphic scripts, is engraved (c. 200). Antiochus IV of Syria persecutes the Jews in Israel and desecrates the Temple of Jerusalem (168). The Jews revolt under Judas Maccabeus and repel the Syrians; the Jews rededicate the Temple of Jerusalem and begin the observance of Hanukkah (165). Hipparchus of Nicaea, the inventor of trigonometry, is born (160).

150–1 BC: During the Third Punic War (149–46), the Romans destroy Corinth and massacre the inhabitants of Carthage. Alexandros of Antioch sculpts the *Venus de Milo* (c. 140). The Roman orator Cicero is born (106). The first Chinese ships reach the east coast of India (100). The Roman poet Virgil is born (70); he pens the epic *Aeneid*. Horace, the lyric poet, is born (65). Julius Caesar, Roman military commander, organizes the First Triumvirate (60) with Pompey, commander-in-chief of the army, and Marcus Crassus. Caesar conquers the northern Gauls (55) and the Britons. Caesar and Pompey battle for control of Rome after Caesar crosses the Rubicon River and provokes a civil war. Caesar emerges victorious (48). Rome adopts the Julian calendar and leap year (46). Cleopatra, the last queen of Egypt, orders the death of Pompey. Caesar, now dictator of Rome, is murdered by a group headed by Marcus Brutus and Cassius Longinus (44). Mark Antony, Octavian and Lepidus form the Second Triumvirate; they defeat Brutus and Cassius at Phillipi (42). Mark Antony returns to Egypt (38) where he and Cleopatra commit suicide after being defeated by Octavian at Actium (31). Octavian, titled Augustus by the Roman Senate, becomes de facto emperor of Rome (30–AD 14). The Romans appoint Herod king of Judea (c. 40). The probable date of the birth of Jesus in Bethlehem is AD 4.

AD 1–150: In Galilee, Jesus preaches his religious philosophy for about three years; he wins disciples but also makes enemies (c. 30). In Jerusalem, Jesus is crucified by the Romans at the behest of local political and religious leaders. Gaius Caesar (nicknamed Caligula) becomes emperor of Rome (37). After a reign marked by ruthlessness and insanity, Gaius is assassinated by Rome's Praetorian Guard (42). Gaius' successor, Claudius I, consolidates and reinvigorates the empire. Paul begins his missionary travels to spread Christianity (45). Claudius dies (54). Nero, emperor of Rome, becomes the first to persecute the Christians for purportedly burning half of Rome (64). The Christian Gospels are written. The Jews revolt against Rome; the Romans destroy the second Temple of Jerusalem and enslave many local inhabitants (70). A thousand Jewish Zealots hold off 15,000 Roman legionnaires for three years on the mountaintop fortress of Masada; the Zealots eventually commit suicide to escape capture (73). The Roman Empire pushes out to its farthest boundaries under Emperor Trajan, who conquers Dacia and much of Parthia (98–116). The Chinese make paper but not for writing (c. 100). The Romans build Hadrian's Wall in England (122–26). The Greek physician and writer Galen (c. 130–200) demonstrates—through experiment and animal dissection—that arteries carry blood (not air), the brain controls speech and the spinal cord influences muscle movement. In India, the earliest known Sanskrit inscriptions are written (150).

151–300: Ptolemy, a Greco-Egyptian thinker, compiles *Almagest*, a 13-volume work on ancient astronomy (which features an earth-centred universe), mathematics, geography and science. In central America, the oldest known Mayan monuments are built (c. 164). In Greece, the philosophy of neoplatonism emerges (c. 200). Koreans export silkworms to China and Japan (c. 200). Roman authorities grant citizenship to every freeborn subject in the Roman Empire (212). The Huns invade Afghanistan (200). The Goths invade Asia Minor and the Balkan Peninsula (220). In China, the end of the Han Dynasty precedes four centuries of division (220). The southern part of India breaks into several kingdoms. Roman persecution of Christians increases and martyrs are revered as saints (c. 250). The first book of algebra is written by Diophantus of Alexandria (c. 250). The Goths attack settlements around the Black Sea (257); they also attack Athens, Sparta and Corinth (268). Pappus of Alexandria documents the use of the cogwheel, lever, pulley, screw and wedge (c. 285). Rome is partitioned into western and eastern empires. In western Europe, five distinct German dukedoms of Saxons, Franks, Alemanni, Thuringians and Goths emerge (c. 300).

301–400: Constantine the Great reunites the Western and Eastern Roman empires and becomes sole emperor (310–37). Constantine orders the toleration of Christianity with the Edict of Milan (313). The seat of the Roman Empire moves to Constantinople (c. 331). In Rome, the Basilican Church of St. Peter is erected (330). Emperor Constantine receives Christian baptism on his deathbed (337). The Huns invade Europe (360) and Russia (376). Books begin to replace scrolls (360). Lo-Tsun, a Chinese monk, founds the Caves of the Thousand Buddhas in Kansu (360). Theodosius the Great becomes the last emperor of a united Roman Empire (392). Alaric, king of the Visigoths, invades Greece (396), plundering Athens and the Balkans (398). The first surviving records of Japanese history appear (400), although legend claims Japan was founded in 660 BC.

401–76: The Visigoths invade Italy (401). Alaric sacks Rome (410). Roman legions withdraw from England to defend Italy from the Visigoths (410). Barbarians settle in Roman provinces (425). Attila becomes ruler of the Huns (433). St. Augustine, Christian theologian, writes *The City of God* (411). Alchemists begin a fruitless search for the philosopher's stone and the elixir of life. Pre-Incan culture develops in Peru. Venice is founded by refugees from Attila's Huns (452). The Vandals sack Rome (455) and destroy the Roman fleet at Cartegena (460). The Huns leave Europe (470). Mayan civilization flourishes in southern Mexico (c. 470). The Japanese build the first Shinto religious shrines to foster nature and ancestor worship (478). The German barbarian Odoacer conquers Ravenna and deposes Emperor Romulus Augustulus, ending the Western Roman Empire (476). Aryabhata, a Hindu astronomer and mathematician born in 476, studies the powers and roots of numbers.

■ Dark and Middle Ages: 477–1450

477–529: In western Europe, Clovis becomes king of the Franks (481) and converts to Christianity (496). The first schism between the Western and Eastern Christian churches occurs when Pope Felix III excommunicates Patriarch Acacius of Constantinople (484–519). The Armenian Church separates from Byzantium and Rome (491). In Peru, the Moshica culture of the Chimic Indians develops agriculture, pottery and textiles. In Rome, the Vatican Palace is planned (500). Tamo, a Buddhist monk born in India, carries tea from India to China (c. 500). Clovis kills Alaric II and annexes the Visigoths' kingdom of Toulouse (507); Clovis's realm is divided among his four sons upon his death (511). Emperor Wu-Ti converts to Buddhism and encourages the new religion in central China (517). Justinian I becomes Byzantine emperor (527); he introduces heavy taxes, promotes public works and codifies Roman law. In England, the Saxon kingdoms of Essex and Middlesex emerge. Chosroes I reigns in Persia (531–79) and encourages culture and art.

530–99: Arthur, the semi-legendary king of the Britons, is first mentioned at the Battle of Mt. Badon (c. 540). The earliest Chinese roll paintings (of landscapes) appear in Tunhuang. War breaks out between Persia and the Byzantine Empire (539–62). St. Gildas writes the first major source of early British history, *De excido et conquestu Brittaniae* (542). Earthquakes occur around the world (543). The plague of Constantinople, imported by rats from Egypt and Syria, spreads throughout Europe and reaches England (547). The golden era of Byzantine art begins (550). Poles settle in western Galicia; Ukrainians settle in eastern Galicia (550). Chess appears in India (c. 550). Emperor Shotoko Taishi (c. 552–621) introduces Buddhism to Japan, and the first Buddhist monastery is founded in Japan (587). Japan's Asuka Period begins (592). Justinian sends missionaries to China and Ceylon to smuggle out silkworms; the European silk industry becomes a Byzantine state monopoly (553). Mohammed, the founder of Islam, is born (570). Persia and the Byzantine Empire renew their war (572–91); Chosroes II rules in Persia (590–628) and renews the war yet again. The plague ends in Europe after killing half the population (542–94). The first account of decimal number use is verified in India (595). The first known English school is established at Canterbury (598). Jews compile the Talmud Babli, a compilation of Jewish oral law with rabbinical interpretations.

600–749: The Chinese print books (600). The Czechs move into Bohemia and Moravia (c. 600). Smallpox spreads from India through China and Asia Minor to southern Europe. The oldest surviving wooden building in the world, the Horyu-ji temple and hospital, is completed in Japan (607). Mohammed experiences a religious vision on Mt. Hira (610). The Japanese use petroleum, called "burning water" (615). The Chinese form orchestras (619) and produce porcelain (620). In Arabia, Mohammed flees to Yathrib (later renamed Medina) from hostile Mecca (622); Muslims refer to this flight as the Hegira, and 622 becomes the first year in the Muslim calendar. Isidore of Seville writes an encyclopedia of arts and sciences (622). In Japan, Tori builds the Shaka Trinity, a noted altarpiece of the Kondo, or Golden Hall (623). Mohammed begins to dictate the Koran in Arabic (625). The Byzantines decisively defeat the Persians at Nineveh (627). Mohammed captures Mecca and writes to world leaders to explain the Muslim faith (628). Cotton is introduced to Arab countries (630). Buddhism becomes the state religion in Tibet (632). Medina becomes the seat of the first caliph, Abu Bakr (Mohammed's father-in-law). The Arabs attack Persia (633). Damascus becomes the new capital of the caliphs (635–70). The Arabs capture Jerusalem (637) and Alexandria (641). Under Omar, the Arabs destroy the Persian Empire: caliphs rule the area until 1258 and Islam prevails over the religion of Zoroaster. The Arab conquest of Egypt, Mesopotamia and Syria also weakens the Eastern Roman Empire (642). Work begins on the Dome of the Rock, a mosque, in Jerusalem (643). A Muslim fleet destroys the Byzantine fleet at Lycia (655). Croats and Serbs settle in Bosnia (650). Chinese artists invent lampblack ink and woodblock printing (c. 650). Caliphs organize the first news service (650). The Korean-born priest Gyogi (c. 668–749)

reconciles the tenets of Japanese Buddhism and Shintoism. The Byzantines use "Greek fire"—a highly flammable liquid made of sulphur, salt, resin and petroleum—as a weapon against the Arabs at the siege of Constantinople (671–78). Glass windows appear in English churches (674). The first Arab coins are introduced (695). The Arabs destroy Carthage (697). Greek, instead of Latin, becomes the official language of the Eastern Roman Empire (700). The Arabs conquer Algiers (700) and almost eliminate Christianity in northern Africa. In China, the population grows rapidly (700) and the first large cities appear. The Great Mosque of Damascus is built (705). Buddhist monasteries in Japan become centres of civilization (710). The first history of Japan, *Kojiki*, is compiled (712). The power of the Lombard kingdom in northern Italy reaches its zenith (c. 600–c. 799). The Muslim world extends from the Pyrenees in Spain to China; Damascus is its capital (715). The earliest Islamic paintings appear (715). Caliph Omar II grants tax exemption to all Muslim believers' (717). The Chinese capital Ch'ang-an is the largest city in the world and Constantinople is the second largest (725). North American Indians build Casa Grande, a fort and large irrigation works, in Arizona (725). Charles Martel, mayor of the Frankish court, defeats the Arabs in the battle of Tours and halts their advance into western Europe (732). The first printed newspaper is published in Yenching, China (748).

750–849: Pueblos (Indian villages) appear in southwestern North America (750–900). Under Arab influence, Spain becomes a centre of progress for mathematics, optics and chemistry (c. 750). Kiev becomes a major trading centre (750). The Turkish Empire is founded by a Tartar tribe in Armenia (760). Charlemagne becomes ruler of the Franks after the deaths of his father, Pepin the Short, in 768 and brother Carloman (771). Arabic learning flourishes during the reigns of Caliph Harun al-Rashid (790) and Caliph Mamun (813–33). The Byzantine Empress Irene usurps the throne of her son Constantine VI (797). Charlemagne is crowned Holy Roman Emperor in Rome (800). The earliest records of Persian poetry and literature appear (800). Vikings dominate Ireland (802). Under Indian influence, Arabs devise their own numerals (814). The Arabs conquer Crete and move toward the Greek Isles (826); the Arabs begin their conquest of Italy and Sardinia (827). Prince Mimir founds the Great Moravian Empire (830), a confederation of Slavs in Bohemia, Moravia, Slovakia, Hungary and Transylvania. The Treaty of Verdun divides the Frankish Empire into France, Germany and Italy (843). In China, the use of paper currency causes inflation and state bankruptcy (845). Abu Tamman writes *Hamasa*, a collection of Arabian legends, proverbs and heroic stories (845). The Arabs sack Rome (846), damage the Vatican and destroy the Venetian fleet.

850–99: In Italy, Salerno University is founded (850). The discovery of coffee is credited to Arabia (850). Jews settling in Germany develop the Yiddish language (c. 850). Kudara Kuwanari, a significant Japanese painter, dies (853). Entering the Mediterranean Sea, Norse pirates sack the coast as far away as Asia Minor (859). The Norse discover Iceland (861). Russians sack parts of France (861) and attack Constantinople (865). Emperor Basil I of Byzantium compiles the Basilican Code, reforming finance and law and restoring the prestige of the military. He also founds the Macedonian Dynasty (867). In England, King Alfred the Great recaptures London from the Danes (878). Emperor Charles III becomes king of France and reunites the empire of Charlemagne (884); Charles is deposed (887) and the territories of Germany and France permanently separate. In England, King Alfred establishes a regular militia and navy, extends the power of the king's courts and founds fairs and markets (890).

900–99: The Norse discover Greenland (900). In the Americas, the Mayans abandon their settlements in the lowlands of Mexico and move to the Yucatan Peninsula (900). The English divide their country into shires with county courts to safeguard their rights (900). The writing of Arabian tales in *A Thousand and One Nights* begins (900). In Europe, castles become seats of the nobility (900). In Spain, Cordoba is the centre of Arab learning, science, commerce and industry (930). In China, Yenching—which is later renamed Peking—becomes the new capital city (938). In Japan, revolts against imperial rule instigate civil war (939–1185). The Arab Empire creates advanced postal and news services

(942). The earliest record of a London bridge appears (963). Work on a Chinese encyclopedia of 1,000 volumes begins (978–84). The rule of nobles in Rome ends (980). Venice and Genoa carry out a flourishing trade between Asia and western Europe (983). Systematic musical notation develops (990). The canonization of Christian saints begins.

1000–99: The epic heroic poem *Beowulf* is written in Old English by an unknown author (1000). Leif Ericsson, son of Eric the Red, sails to North America (1000). The Chinese invent gunpowder (1000). On the Yucatan Peninsula, Mayan civilization reaches its zenith (1000). Sridhara, an Indian mathematician, describes the importance of zero (1000). Muslims sack the Holy Sepulchre in Jerusalem (1009). Danes under King Canute control England (1016); Canute conquers Norway (1028). Prince Jaroslav the Wise reigns in Kicv (1020–54); he codifies Russian law and builds cities, schools and churches. Byzantine power begins to decline (1025). Canute dies (1035); Canute's three sons divide the kingdom of England, Norway and Denmark. After murdering King Duncan, Macbeth becomes king of Scotland (1040). Malcolm murders Macbeth (1057). Musical composers give time values to musical notes (1050). The separation of the Roman and Eastern churches becomes permanent (1054). In England, Westminster Abbey is consecrated (1065). William of Normandy successfully invades England and is crowned William the Conqueror (1066). A comet, later known as Halley's Comet, passes earth and is seen (1066). Emperor She-tsung of China nationalizes agricultural production and distribution (1068). Constantine the African brings Greek medicine to the western world (1071). The English build the original Tower of London (1078). William the Conqueror orders a comprehensive tax assessment of England; the Domesday Book records the results (1086). Pope Urban II proclaims the First Crusade to recapture the Holy Land from the Muslims (1096). Crusaders take Jerusalem (1099).

1100–99: Middle English replaces Old English (c. 1100). Islamic science begins to decline. Secular music first appears. Robert of Normandy recognizes Henry I as king of England with the Treaty of Alton (1101). The colonization of eastern Germany begins (1105). The earliest known miracle play is found in Dunstable, England (1110): based on Christian scriptures and the lives of saints, the plays are performed until the 16th century. Bologna University is founded (1119). Alexander Neckham records the earliest account of a mariner's compass (1125). The Second Crusade begins (1146) and fails one year later. Paris University is founded (1150). Bologna's medical school is founded (1150). The first recorded fire and plague insurance appears in Iceland (1151). The Japanese clans Taira and Minamoto fight each other (1156). Eric of Sweden conquers Finland (1157). Thomas à Becket is elected Archbishop of Canterbury (1162) to curb church power, but he later quarrels with King Henry II over growing royal power. Becket is murdered by Norman knights (1170) and buried at Canterbury. Jails are ordered erected in all English counties and boroughs (1166). Oxford University is founded (1167). Rules for the canonization of saints are established by Pope Alexander III (1170). The first authenticated influenza epidemics occur (1173). The Campanile ("Leaning Tower") of Pisa is built (1174). Walter Map organizes the Arthurian legends in their present form (1176). All Jews are banished from France (1182). The Third Crusade (1189–93) fails to recapture Jerusalem from the Muslims. Moses Maimonides, a Jewish philosopher, attempts to reconcile Aristotelian and Jewish philosophy in *Guide to the Perplexed* (1190); he is also credited with organizing all Jewish law for lay and religious educators.

1200–49: Cambridge University is founded (1200). Islam takes root in India. The Fourth Crusade begins with crusaders from Venice fighting Constantinople and establishing a Latin Kingdom of Jerusalem (1204). St. Francis of Assisi issues the first rules of his brotherhood of educators and missionaries, the Franciscans (1209). In the Children's Crusade (1212), thousands of children from Europe leave for the Holy Land, but most are either sold as slaves or die of hunger or disease. Genghis Khan becomes chief prince of the Mongols (1206) and conquers most of the Chinese Empire in northern China (1213–15); he also conquers Turkistan, Afghanistan and Transoxania (1218–24) and raids Persia and eastern Europe. Genghis

Khan's empire is divided among his descendants upon his death (1227). The Council of St. Albans is the precursor to the British Parliament (1213). Under compulsion by his barons, King John puts his seal on England's Magna Carta at Runnymede (1215): it defines the limitations of royal power and sets out basic civil rights. The Fifth Crusade fails in Egypt (1217–21). The oldest national flag in the world, Danneborg, is adopted by Denmark (1218). The sonnet develops in Italian poetry (1221). St. Thomas Aquinas (1225–74) theorizes philosophical proofs for the existence of God and reconciles Greek ideas with Christian theology. Emperor Frederick II leads the Sixth Crusade (1228). Crusaders bring leprosy to Europe (1230); they secure a temporary truce with the Muslims. Three later crusades against Muslims in the 13th century fail. Coal is mined for the first time in Newcastle, England (1233). The Inquisition begins as the pope makes Dominicans responsible for ending heresy (1233). Alexander Nevski is made Grand Duke of Novgorod (1236).

1250–99: Kublai Khan becomes governor of China (1251) and ruler of the Mongol peoples (1259–94). He fails to conquer Japan (1274), southeast Asia and Indonesia, but he defeats the Sung Dynasty of China (1279). Instruments of torture are first used in the Inquisition (1252). The Sorbonne is founded by Robert de Sorbon as the Paris School of Theology (1254). The House of Commons is established in England (1258). Mongols take control of Baghdad and end the caliphate (1258). Roger Bacon writes *De computo naturali* (1264). The glass mirror is invented (1278). Marco Polo, the Venetian explorer, journeys to China (1271–95) and enters the diplomatic service of Kublai Khan (1275–92). Florence, Italy, is the leading European city in commerce and finance (c. 1282). The Teutonic Order, a German military and religious order, conquers Prussia (1283) after killing the native "heathens" and replacing them with Germans. Spectacles (eyeglasses) are invented (1290). The crusades end and the Knights of St. John of Jerusalem settle in Cyprus (1291).

1300–99: Trade fairs occur at Bruges, Antwerp, Lyons and Geneva (c. 1300). Edward I of England standardizes the yard and the acre (1305). Dante composes his

Divina Commedia (1307–21). Mechanical clocks are driven by weights in Europe. Salic Law, excluding women from succession to the throne, is adopted in France (1317). Nō plays originate in Japan (1325). The Aztecs establish Mexico City (1327). The sawmill is invented (1328). Weaving at York is first documented (1331). The Hundred Years War between France and England begins (1337) over lands held by the English crown in France; the English and French later fight over the French crown itself. The first scientific weather forecasts are attempted by William Merlee of Oxford (1337). The Black Death (bubonic plague) devastates Europe, killing about 75 million people, more than one third of the population (1347–51). Boccaccio writes the *Decameron* (1348–53), which is intended to be a diversion from the horrors of the plague. Timur the Lame (Tamerlane) begins his conquest of Asia (1363). The Aztecs of Mexico build their capital, Tenochtitlan (1364). The Mongol Yüan Dynasty in China is overthrown by the national Ming Dynasty (1368–1644). The building of the Bastille begins in Paris (1369). "Robin Hood," the legendary hero who robbed the rich to help the poor, appears in English ballads and literature. The Great Schism (1378–1417) in the Catholic Church begins when, after the death of Pope Gregory XI, two popes are elected in Rome and Avignon. Venice wins its Hundred Years War against Genoa (1256–1381). Briton John Wyclif calls for the reform of church practices (1379). He is condemned as a heretic (1380; 1382) and inspires the first English translation of the Latin Bible, the Wyclif Bible. Chaucer writes *The Canterbury Tales*. The rival southern and northern courts of Japan's divided imperial family reunite after 50 years of strife. Denmark, Sweden and Norway unite under Queen Margaret of Denmark in the Union of Kalmar (1397).

1400–39: Russia's greatest icon painter, Andrei Rublev, creates *Trinity* (1411). England and France sign a perpetual peace treaty upon the marriage of Henry V and Catherine of Valois (1420). Joan of Arc and her French followers defeat the English at Orleans (1429) and march triumphantly to Paris: she is then taken prisoner by the Burgundians (1430) and condemned and executed (1431) in a political inquisition and trial. Complete suits of metal plate armour replace chain mail in Europe (1430). China shuts out the western world and bans voyages there (1433) because Confucian doctrine sees little merit in trade. The Portuguese find the way around Cape Bojador (on the west coast of Africa) under Henry the Navigator (1434). The Greek (Eastern or Byzantine) Church unites with the Roman Church (1439) to save itself from the Turkish threat. Montezuma becomes ruler of the Aztecs in Mexico (1440) and begins to conquer surrounding tribes.

■ European Renaissance: 1440–1650

1440–69: The rise of the Italian city-states heralds the Renaissance (1440–50), and the richest families (such as the Medici) vie with each other as patrons of art and learning (mainly in Florence). The first oil painter, Jan van Eyck, dies in Flanders (1441). France defeats England at Castillion, ending the Hundred Years War (1453); the English give up everything in France except Calais. Zimbabwe, the great African kingdom, declines after 200 years of expansion (1450) because of food shortages. Constantinople, the old capital of the Byzantine Empire, falls to the Muslim Ottomans (1453); they rename the city Istanbul. A treaty unites rival Italian city-states (1454), requiring them to protect each other from outside aggression. Ming porcelain pottery appears in Europe (1460). The Bible is printed mechanically with metal typefaces and oil-based ink by Johann Gutenberg (1455). The Wars of the Roses begin in England (1455) as a struggle for the throne between the houses of York and Lancaster; the wars end when Henry VII of the house of Lancaster prevails over Richard III (1485). Plato's writings are translated into Latin at the Platonic Academy in Florence (1469).

1470–99: Music sheets, maps and posters are mechanically printed (1470s). Vlad the Impaler dies in Transylvania (1477); the mass murderer becomes the source for Dracula legends. Inca rule, based in Peru, expands to include the entire Andean region (3,200 sq. km) under Pachacuti and his son Topa Inca (1470). Inca civilization features terracing, irrigation, pantheistic religion with human sacrifice, advanced metalwork, tapestry making and construction. Spain's Christian Inquisition begins (1478). King Ferdinand V of Aragón and Queen Isabella I of Castile unite their crowns in Spain to ward off Alfonso V of Portugal (1479). Ivan the Great declares Russian independence (1480) from the Mongols when he refuses to continue paying them tribute. The first European manual of navigation and nautical almanac is prepared in Portugal by mathematical experts who calculate the latitude of the sun, based on the work of the Jewish astronomer Abraham Zacuto (1484). Pope Innocent VIII attacks the spread of witchcraft and heresy in Germany (1484), and he authorizes Dominican inquisitors to torture and burn witches. The publication of an encyclopedia of witchcraft, *Malleus Maleficarum* (1486), adds to the hysteria. The Genoese seaman Christopher Columbus secures the sponsorship of Queen Isabella of Spain (1486) for his expedition to discover a western route to Asia. (He sets sail with his three ships: *Santa María, Pinta* and *Niña* in 1492). The Aztecs of Mexico inaugurate the Great Temple of Tenochtitlan (1487) when they ritually tear the hearts from 20,000 living people. The Portuguese explorer Bartholomew Dias rounds the Cape of Good Hope off South Africa (1488). Leonardo da Vinci is in his prime in Italy as an artist, scientist, inventor and philosopher (1488). He designs inventions centuries ahead of their time such as flying machines and an apparatus that enables humans to breathe under water. The Great Wall of China is rebuilt by Ming emperors as a defence against attacks by northern barbarians (1488). The first terrestrial globe is made by Martin Behaim, a German (1492). Jews are ordered by Spain's Christian rulers to choose between expulsion or forced conversion (1492); later the rulers change the options to conversion or death (1498). Spain conquers Granada (1492), the last Muslim kingdom in Spain. Spain and Portugal sign a treaty dividing lands discovered in the new world, but Spain benefits the most from the treaty (1494). French armies in Italy bring a virus later identified as syphilis to Naples and an epidemic spreads through Europe (1495). Columbus brings tobacco back from the Americas (1496). The Chinese invent a toothbrush (1498). Vasco da Gama discovers a sea route to India around the Cape of Good Hope in southern Africa (1498). The Italian navigator Amerigo Vespucci explores the northeast coast of South America (1499) and reports the existence of cannibals (1502).

Portugal's Pedro Cabral discovers the east coast of Brazil and observes natives using stone to cut wood (1499).

1500–25: The discovery of plays and poems by Hroswitha of Gandersheim, a 10th-century Saxon, makes her the first European playwright since the Classical Age (1500). King Ferdinand of Spain levies tribute payments on Indians in the Americas and uses Indians as forced labour (1501). Shiite Islam becomes the state religion in Persia (1502) and Sunni Muslim dissenters are executed there. A hand-held timepiece, made possible by the invention of the coiled mainspring, is constructed by German locksmith Peter Henlein (1502). *David*, a 4-metre statue, is completed by Michelangelo Buonarrotti (1504) in Florence, Italy. Leonardo da Vinci paints the *Mona Lisa* (1505). Venice dominates Mediterranean trade (c. 1507). A European map calls the New World "America" after Amerigo Vespucci (1507) and shows it as a distinct continent. The German artist Albrecht Dürer—a painter and engraver—paints *Adam and Eve* in oil (1507). Nicholas Copernicus writes *Commentariolus*, stating his theory that the earth revolves around the sun (1507–15). Michelangelo paints the ceiling of the Sistine Chapel (1508–12). Sebastian Cabot sails around Cuba and proves it is an island (1508); he later reaches Hudson Bay in search of a northwest passage. The first African slaves are brought to the Americas; they land in Cuba (1510). Erasmus, the Dutch humanist, writes the satirical *In Praise of Folly* (1511). Juan Ponce de León claims Florida for Spain (1513) while searching for the fountain of youth. Niccolo Machiavelli writes *The Prince* (1513) which discusses the uses and abuses of power. Vasco Núñez de Balboa discovers the "South Sea," or Pacific Ocean, for Spain (1513). Spain orders natives in the Americas to convert to Christianity under threat of enslavement or death (1514). Henry VIII of England puts forth measures to protect peasants from enclosure—the dividing and closing off of common land (1515). Sir Thomas More writes *Utopia* which depicts an ideal state (1516). Martin Luther, a German Augustinian monk, attacks the Church's sale of indulgences granting the forgiveness of sins in his *Ninety-Five Theses* (1517) and nails the document to the door of Wittenberg's church. English sailors complain to

King Henry VIII about the growing number of French cod fishermen in Newfoundland (1517). The rule of Suleiman I the Magnificent sees the Ottoman Turks reach the zenith of their empire with the conquest of Egypt, Syria and Hungary (1520). Ferdinand Magellan begins a three-year voyage to circumnavigate the globe (1519). Hernán Cortés lands at Vera Cruz in Mexico to wage war against the Aztecs (1519); the Aztecs, led first by emperors Montezuma II and then by Cuauhtémoc, surrender (1521). Chocolate is introduced to Europe from Mexico (1520). Martin Luther translates the Bible into German (1522).

1526–49: Lutheran German troops sack and burn Rome (1527). Hippocrates' ancient idea of the four humours governing bodily health is first disputed (1528). Henry VIII separates from the Church of Rome and becomes head of the English Church (1534) after he is refused an annulment of his first marriage. The Jesuit order of missionaries is founded by Ignatius Loyola (1534). Jacques Cartier searches for riches in North America along the St. Lawrence River (1535). John Calvin, the French leader of the Protestant Reformation in Geneva, emphasizes predestination and God's omniscience in his theology (1536). The first mechanical artificial limbs appear for crippled war veterans (1539). The founder of the Sikh religion, Guru Nanak, dies in India (1539). Henry VIII becomes king of Ireland and head of the Irish Church (1541). John Knox leads the Calvinist Reformation in Scotland (1541). Oil is discovered in North America by the Spaniards (1543). Portuguese traders are the first to sell guns in Japan (1543). Nostradamus, the French astrologer, begins making predictions (1547). Ivan IV (nicknamed Dread or Terrible) is crowned the first czar of Russia (1547): he calls the first national assembly (1549).

1550–99: Jesuit missionaries try to protect natives in the Americas from slavery (1551). Ivan the Terrible defeats the Mongols (1552) and conquers land as far away as the Caspian Sea (1556). Queen Mary Tudor has Lady Jane Grey executed for treason in England (1554). Mary restores papal authority in England and Wales (1554); she becomes known as "Bloody Mary" for persecuting the Protestants (1555). Charles V relinquishes the Holy Roman Empire and Spain to enter a monastery (1556). An influenza epidemic hits Europe (1557). Elizabeth I becomes queen of England (1558) and rejects papal power in England (1559). The Edict of Orleans suspends persecution of Huguenots (French Calvinists) in France (1561). The Peace of Amboise ends the first War of Religion in France and the Huguenots are granted limited toleration (1563). Andreas Vesalius, the Flemish founder of modern anatomy, dies (1564). Nobunaga deposes the Japanese shogunate and centralizes the government (1567). The Iroquois Confederacy of five North American nations (Mohawk, Oneida, Onondaga, Cayuga and Seneca) is founded (c. 1570). The Huguenots are massacred on St. Bartholomew's Day in Paris (1572). The Dutch War of Independence begins (1572). The Union of Utrecht founds the Dutch Republic (1579). William of Orange accepts the sovereignty of the northern Netherlands and is assassinated (1584). The first English colony in Newfoundland is founded (1582). Elizabeth I of England orders Mary Queen of Scots beheaded for treason (1587). Christopher Marlowe completes *Dr. Faustus* (1588). The first Spanish Armada leaves for England and is defeated by the English under Charles Howard (1588). Sir Francis Drake, with 18,000 men, fails to take Lisbon for England (1589). William Shakespeare completes the play *Romeo and Juliet* (1594). The Second Spanish Armada leaves for England but is scattered by storms (1597). An English Act of Parliament calls for convicted criminals to serve their terms in the colonies (1597).

1600–49: France boasts the largest population in central Europe, with 16 million persons (1600). William Shakespeare completes *Hamlet* (1600). Dutch opticians invent the telescope (1600). The Dutch East India Company—first modern public company—is founded (1602). Guy Fawkes is arrested for trying to blow up King James I and the House of Lords during the opening of Parliament (1605); Fawkes is sentenced to death (1606). The first English settlement on the American mainland is founded at Jamestown, Virginia (1607). Shakespeare writes his *Sonnets* (1609). The first cheques appear in the Netherlands as "cash letters" (1608). The *King James Bible* is published (1611). Peter Paul Rubens paints *Descent from the Cross* (1611). The North American Indian princess Pocahontas marries English colonist John

Rolfe (1614). Galileo Galilei, an Italian astronomer, faces the Inquisition for the first time for abandoning the Ptolemaic system of an earth-centred universe and endorsing the Copernican sun-centred system (1615). The Thirty Years War begins in Prague as Protestants rebel against Roman Catholic oppression (1618). Slavery in North America begins when the first Africans are brought to Virginia (1619). The triangular slave trade in the Atlantic begins: the British trade their goods in west Africa for slaves; the slaves are traded for agricultural products in the Americas; agricultural products are exported from the Americas to Britain. Pilgrims arriving on the *Mayflower* found Plymouth Colony, Massachusetts (1620). Patent law is created in England to protect inventors (1623). Construction begins on the Taj Mahal, a royal mausoleum, in northern India (1628). Charles I Stuart dissolves the English Parliament for 11 years (1629). Cardinal Richelieu, chief minister of King Louis XIII of France, governs France (1630–42). The Inquisition forces Galileo to cease promulgating Copernican astronomical theories (1633). Japan forbids foreign books, Christianity and European contacts (1637). René Descartes, called the father of modern philosophy, writes *Discourse on Method* (1637). In China, the Manchu Dynasty (1644–1912) supersedes the Ming Dynasty. Charles I of England and Parliament wage the English Civil War 1642–48; Oliver Cromwell, the victorious parliamentarian, has Charles executed for treason (1649).

1650–99: Bishop James Ussher dates the creation of the world at Oct. 23, 4004 BC (1650). The massacre of North American Indians by European settlers begins (1650). Thomas Hobbes writes *Leviathan*, a defence of absolute monarchy in England (1651). Oliver Cromwell becomes Lord Protector in England, dissolves Parliament, divides England into 11 districts, prohibits Anglican services (1653) and readmits Jews to England after 365 years (1655). Blaise Pascal develops the basic laws of probability (1654). The Portuguese drive the Dutch out of Brazil (1654). The first London opera house opens (1656). Dutch peasants (Boers) first settle in South Africa (1660). The Royal Society is founded in London to promote scientific discussion among great thinkers (1660). The

earliest condemnation of industrial pollution, *The Inconvenience of the Air and Smoke of London Dissipated*, is written by John Evelyn (1661). Louis XIV, the Sun King, begins to build the palace at Versailles (1662). Jean Baptiste Colbert forms the North American colony of New France with Quebec as its capital (1663). The British annex New Netherlands from the Dutch and rename the main city New York (1664). Isaac Newton begins to experiment with gravity and develops calculus (1664–66). The cell is named and described by Briton Robert Hooke (1665). The French army uses the first hand grenades (1667). Portugal gains independence from Spain through the Treaty of Lisbon (1668). Dutch scientist Anton van Leeuwenhoek discovers microorganisms (1669) and bacteria (1683). A British royal charter incorporates the Hudson's Bay Company and authorizes the firm to trade in North American lands where rivers drain into Hudson Bay (1670). Dutch philosopher Baruch Spinoza writes *Ethics* (1675). The poems of Bashu—a pseudonym—popularize Japanese haiku poetry (1675). The *Declaration of the People of Virginia* by Nathaniel Bacon supports a rebellion against authorities in the colonies (1676). Roman Catholics are excluded from Parliament in England (1678). The Habeas Corpus Amendment Act in England protects citizens from unjust imprisonment (1679). The French colonial empire of North America, stretching from Quebec to the mouth of the Mississippi River, is organized (1680). The large dodo bird with small, flightless wings becomes extinct (1680). Sir Isaac Newton writes *Principles of Natural Philosophy* (1687), which discusses universal gravitation. The Glorious Revolution establishes the constitutional monarchy in England (1688–89); King William of Orange III and Queen Mary II ascend the throne. Peter the Great becomes czar of Russia (1689). John Locke writes *Essay Concerning Human Understanding* and *Two Treatises on Civil Government* (1690).

1700–49: The childlessness of Charles II, Hapsburg king of Spain, prompts the War of the Spanish Succession (1701–14) between French Bourbons and Austrian Hapsburgs. Czar Peter's westernization of Russia sparks a rebellion in Astrakhan (1705). England and Scotland form Great Britain (1707). The

Peace of Utrecht is signed between Spain and England: Spain cedes Gibraltar and Minorca to England (1713) and Philip of France retains the Spanish crown. D.G. Fahrenheit constructs a mercury thermometer with a temperature scale (1714). George F. Handel writes *Water Music* for King George I (1717). Daniel Defoe writes *The Life and Strange Surprising Adventures of Robinson Crusoe* (1719). The German composer and virtuoso organist J.S. Bach composes *The Brandenburg Concertos* (1721). Johnathan Swift writes *Gulliver's Travels* (1726). Benjamin Franklin—an American statesman, scientist and printer—writes *Poor Richard's Almanack* (1732). John Kay patents the fly shuttle loom which revolutionizes weaving (1733). Alexander Pope, English poet and verse satirist, writes *Essay on Man* (1733). A Swede, Carolus Linnaeus, introduces the modern classification of plants and animals (1735). Alaska is discovered by Victor Behring (1740). In Prussia, King Frederick the Great introduces freedom of the press and freedom of worship (1740). Rodriguez Pereire creates a sign language for the deaf (1749).

■ Industrial Revolution: 1750–1850

1750–99: Benjamin Franklin experiments with static electricity and invents the lightning conductor (1752). In the Seven Years War (1756–63), Britain declares war on France and, in the North American colonies, the French drive the British from the Great Lakes region (1756). The French lose Quebec to the British (1759) during the battle on the Plains of Abraham. Voltaire writes the philosophical novel *Candide* (1759). Catherine II (the Great) becomes czarina of Russia (1762). Swiss-French philosopher Jean-Jacques Rousseau describes his theory of "natural man" in the *Social Contract* (1762). The Peace of Paris (1763) ends the war between England and France and gives Canada to England. Eight-year-old Wolfgang Amadeus Mozart writes his first symphony (1764). In Britain, James Hargreaves invents the spinning jenny, which spins up to 120 threads at once (1764). The British Parliament passes the Stamp Act to tax American colonists; in Virginia and New York, people challenge the right of Britain to tax them without granting elected representation (1766). English surveyors draw the Mason-Dixon Line between Pennsylvania and Mary-

land (1767); the boundary later divides "slave" and "free" states. Daniel Rutherford and Joseph Priestley independently discover nitrogen (1772). The Bolshoi Ballet is founded in Russia (1773). During the Boston Tea Party, American colonists protesting British taxes dress as Indians and dump the cargo of three tea ships in Boston harbour (1773). James Watt, Scottish inventor, perfects the steam engine (1775). The American Revolution begins (1775). The Second Continental Congress assembles at Philadelphia and appoints George Washington commander-in-chief of the American forces. The Americans proclaim the *Declaration of Independence* (July 4, 1776). Edward Gibbon begins *Decline and Fall of the Roman Empire* (1776). Adam Smith completes *Wealth of Nations* (1776). After the American victory in the Saratoga campaign (1777), France allies with the Americans (1778). General Washington's army suffers at Valley Forge (1778). James Cook discovers Hawaii (1778). Franz Mesmer practises hypnotism (1778). Spain joins the American War of Independence against Britain (1779). The Dutch support the American side (1780). Sir William Herschel discovers Uranus (1781). British General Cornwallis surrenders to the Americans (October 1781) at the end of the Yorktown campaign, and the Treaty of Paris recognizes American independence (1783). John Wesley writes the *Deed of Declaration*, the charter of Wesleyan Methodism (1784). The British colony of Australia is founded (1788). The French Revolution begins (1789). A Parisian mob opposing the monarchy storms the Bastille jail. French royalists begin to emigrate. The French revolutionaries proclaim the *Decrees of August 4* and the *Declaration of the Rights of Man and of the Citizen*. The revolutionary government limits the monarchy's power, abolishes the remnants of French feudalism, extends religious tolerance to Jews and Protestants, and reorganizes the Roman Catholic Church. A.L. Lavoisier completes the *Table of Thirty-One Chemical Elements* (1790). The Constitutional Act divides Britain's Canadian colony into English-speaking Upper Canada and French-speaking Lower Canada (1791). Thomas Paine writes *The Rights of Man* in defence of the French Revolution (1791). French King Louis XVI and Queen Marie Antoinette are beheaded for treason (January 1793). The

Jacobin Reign of Terror, which features the guillotine execution of prisoners, ends with the execution of Jacobin leader Maximilien Robespierre. Robert Burns' *Auld Lang Syne* is published (1794). Edward Jenner discovers a smallpox vaccine (1796).

1800–09: Ottawa is founded (1800). Eli Whitney makes muskets with interchangeable parts (1800). Thomas Jefferson establishes the Library of Congress in Washington, DC (1800). Alessandro Volto produces the first battery from zinc and copper plates (1800). William Herschel discovers infrared solar rays (1800). American civil engineer Robert Fulton makes the first submarine *Nautilus* (1801). John Dalton proposes an atomic theory of chemistry (1802). The United States buys land from France in the Louisiana Purchase (1803). Henry Shrapnel invents the shell for use in warfare (1803). Napoleon crowns himself emperor of the French (1804) and king of Italy (1805). In Egypt, Mehemet Ali becomes pasha and establishes a more modern state (1805). F.W.A. Satürner isolates morphine (1805). Napoleon wins his greatest victory at Austerlitz over the Austrians and Russians (1805). British naval officers looking for deserters almost cause a war when they stop and board the American frigate *Chesapeake* (1807). Ludwig van Beethoven, the German composer who united classical and romantic styles, performs his *Fifth Symphony* (written for Napoleon) and *Sixth Symphony* (1808). The first part of J.W. von Goethe's *Faust* is published (1808). Washington Irving writes *Rip van Winkle* (1809).

1810–19: Simón Bolívar becomes a leading figure in South American politics (1810). Philippe Girard invents a machine for spinning flax (1812). German folklorist Jakob Grimm completes *Grimm's Fairy Tales* (1812–15). Napoleon Bonaparte's first military setback occurs in the Peninsular War in Spain (1808–14), and he later retreats from an unsuccessful invasion of Russia. A battle at Tippecanoe (1811) presages the War of 1812 between Britain and the United States (1812–14). Jane Austen writes *Pride and Prejudice* (1813), depicting English country life and mores. Austria, Russia and Prussia form an alliance against Napoleon and defeat him at Leipzig (1813) and recapture Paris (1814). Napoleon abdicates and is exiled to

Elba Island. The War of 1812 continues in North America as the British capture Washington, DC (1814), but the Americans win battles at Fort McHenry, Thames (killing Tecumseh, an Indian ally of the British) and Plattsburgh (1814). The British initiate peace in the Treaty of Ghent (1814), but this news travels too slowly to stop the Battle of New Orleans (1815), won by the Americans. Napoleon escapes from exile and returns to march on Paris. He is defeated at Waterloo (1815), abdicates again and is banished to St. Helena Island. The German Confederation, dominated by Austria and Prussia, is created to replace the Holy Roman Empire (1815). Argentina declares independence from Spain (1816). The classical economist David Ricardo writes about the determination of wages and value in *The Principles of Political Economy and Taxation* (1817). Georg Hegel writes his all-embracing *Encyclopedia of the Philosophical Sciences* (1817). Mary Shelley writes *Frankenstein* (1818). Lord Byron begins *Don Juan* (1818–23). Chile proclaims its independence from Spain (1818). The Danish physicist Hans C. Oersted discovers electromagnetism (1819). Simón Bolívar liberates Greater Colombia (Panama, Venezuela, Ecuador and Colombia) from Spanish rule (1819).

1820–29: The Frenchman Andre Ampere writes *Laws of Electrodynamic Action* (1820). The Washington Colonization Society founds Liberia in western Africa to repatriate black slaves (1820). Sir Walter Scott writes *Ivanhoe* (1820). John Keats writes *Ode to a Nightingale* (1820). Sir Charles Wheatstone invents an electric recording device for sound reproduction (1821). Peru and Guatemala declare their independence from Spain (1821). The Greek War of Independence from Ottoman Turkish rule begins (1821). Franz Liszt, the Hungarian pianist who revolutionizes romantic music and invents the symphonic poem, makes his debut at age 11 in Vienna (1822). Brazil declares independence from Portugal (1822). The Monroe Doctrine closes the American continent to colonial settlement by European powers (1823). Simón Bolívar defeats the Spanish in Peru; Peruvian independence is recognized (1824). Bolívar creates his namesake, Bolivia (1825). The first steam-powered railroads carrying freight and passengers, operated by the Stockton and

Darlington Railway, run in England (1825). The Erie Canal opens, linking the Hudson River and the Great Lakes (1825). The first major American author, James Fenimore Cooper, writes *The Last of the Mohicans* (1826). Felix Mendelssohn composes the overture to *A Midsummer Night's Dream* (1826). The great cholera epidemic begins in India (1826) and spreads from Russia into central Europe. J.J. Audubon writes *Birds of North America* (1827). Noah Webster writes the *American Dictionary of the English Language* (1828). Uruguay declares independence from Brazil (1828). The Peace of Adrianople ends the Russo-Turkish war and Turkey acknowledges the independence of Greece (1829). Frederic Chopin, the Polish pianist, debuts in Vienna (1829). Venezuela withdraws from Greater Colombia and becomes independent (1829).

1830–39: Charles Lyell of Scotland divides the geological system into three eras: Eocene, Miocene and Pliocene (1830). Ecuador declares independence (1830). Mass demonstrations in Swiss cities lead to liberal reforms (1831). Charles Darwin sails on the HMS *Beagle* as a naturalist, surveying South America, New Zealand and Australia (1831–36). The leading antislavery leader in the United States, W.L. Garrison, begins publishing *The Liberator* in Boston (1831). In Britain, the Industrial Revolution creates a wealthy middle class which is enfranchised, doubling the number of voters (1832). The New England Anti-Slavery Society is founded in Boston (1832). Slavery is abolished in the British Empire (1833). The Spanish Inquisition, begun during the 13th century, is finally abolished (1834). France's leading writer, Victor Hugo, writes *The Hunchback of Notre Dame* (1834). The Poor Law Amendment Act decrees that no able-bodied person (such as those displaced by the Industrial Revolution) in Britain shall receive assistance unless he or she enters a workhouse (1834). Hans Christian Andersen writes his first stories for children (1835). The American writer Ralph Waldo Emerson writes *Nature* (1836). The People's Charter initiates Britain's first national working-class movement; it calls for universal male suffrage and voting by ballot (1836). The Dutch (Afrikaner) farmers begin "The Great Trek" of emigration across the Orange and Vaal rivers in South Africa

(1836). The American Asa Gray writes the first botanical textbook, *The Elements of Botany* (1836). Victoria becomes Queen of Great Britain (1837). Citizens stage unsuccessful rebellions in Lower and Upper Canada (1837). Louis Braille invents his reading system for the blind (1837). Charles Dickens's *Oliver Twist*, a critique of British industrial society, is a bestseller (1838). Kirkpatrick Macmillan, a Scot, invents the first bicycle (1839). Theodor Schwann proposes his cell-growth theory (1839). Christian Schönbein, a German-Swiss chemist, discovers ozone (1839). American Charles Goodyear develops vulcanization, making the commercial use of rubber possible (1839). Louis Daguerre and Nicephore Niepce invent the daguerreotype, a photograph produced on a silver-coated copperplate treated with iodine vapour (1839). The First Opium War between Britain and China begins (1839).

1840–49: New Zealand becomes a British colony (1840). Philosopher Thomas Carlyle writes *On Heroes, Hero-Worship and the Heroic in History* in support of strong government (1841). Thomas Cook, the British father of the guided tour, arranges his first trip (1841). Showman P.T. Barnum gains fame after opening his American museum of "freak" exhibitions (1841). The Webster-Ashburton Treaty between Britain and the United States settles American border disputes with Canada (1842). The Treaty of Nanking ends the Opium War between Britain and China and confirms the cession of Hong Kong to Britain (1842). Riots and strikes erupt in northern England's industrial areas (1842). German composer Richard Wagner finishes the opera *The Flying Dutchman* (1843). English physicist James P. Joule determines the amount of work required to produce a unit of heat, the joule (1843). American social reformer Dorothea Dix reports shocking conditions in prisons and asylums and influences the establishment of state hospitals for the insane in Europe and North America (1843). Samuel Morse's telegraph is used for the first time between Baltimore and Washington (1844). In Ireland, a potato famine kills 1 million people and prompts massive emigration (1845–50). After American troops defeat the Mexicans at Palo Alto (1846), the United States Congress formally declares war on Mexico, and American forces take Santa Fe and annex New Mexico. The Smithsonian Institution, a research and educational centre, is founded in Washington, DC (1846). Dentist W.T. Morton first uses ether as an anaesthetic (1846). Sisters Charlotte and Emily Brontë publish *Jane Eyre* and *Wuthering Heights* respectively (1847). American troops capture Mexico City (1847). The Treaty of Guadalupe Hidalgo ends the war between Mexico and the United States (1848); the United States acquires Texas and much of the surrounding territory in return for $15 million. Gold discoveries in California lead to the first gold rush (1848). A revolt in Paris causes King Louis Philippe to abdicate (1848). A revolution in Vienna causes Prince Klemens von Metternich's resignation (1848). Revolution spreads to Venice, Berlin, Milan, Rome and Parma (1848). The first Public Health Act is introduced in Britain (1848). The first women's rights convention, organized by Elizabeth Stanton and Lucretia Mott, is held in Seneca Falls, New York (1848). The Germans Karl Marx and Friedrich Engels publish *The Communist Manifesto* (1848), championing the working class and promoting radical socialist theory.

1850–59: Harriet Beecher Stowe writes her antislavery novel *Uncle Tom's Cabin* (1852). The Transvaal is granted self-government (1852). The Crimean War (1853–56) begins when Russia occupies Moldavia and Walachia, and Turkey declares war. The Russians destroy the Turkish fleet off Sinope; England, France and Sardinia join Turkey's fight. After a long siege, the Russian base at Sebastopol falls to the allied forces (1855); after the allied victory at Balaklava, Russia recognizes the integrity of Turkey (1856). English nurse Florence Nightingale founds modern nursing while tending soldiers during the Crimean War (1853–56). Alexander Wood uses the first hypodermic syringe (1853). Samuel Colt revolutionizes the manufacture of small arms (1853). Commander Matthew Perry negotiates the first treaty between the United States and Japan, permitting American ships to use two Japanese ports (1854). The Elgin Reciprocity Treaty between Britain and the United States introduces free trade between Canada and the United States (1854). Henry Bessemer introduces a converter into his process for making steel and makes steel production inexpensive (1855). Pure cocaine is extracted from coca leaves (1856). Gustave Flaubert, the French master of realistic novels, writes *Madame Bovary* (1856). Louis Pasteur discovers that fermentation is caused by microorganisms (1857); he later invents pasteurization and discovers a vaccine for rabies. The first Neanderthal skeleton is found in a cave in the Neander Valley near Düsseldorf, Germany. The Indian Mutiny against British rule (1857) causes the British siege and capture of Delhi. The British Royal Navy destroys the Chinese fleet, and Britain and France take Canton (1857). Giuseppe Garibaldi forms the Italian National Association for the unification of Italy (1857). The Treaty of Tientsin ends the Anglo-Chinese war (1858). Charles Darwin writes *On the Origin of Species* explaining his theory of evolution (1859). The German National Association is formed to unite Germany under Prussia (1859). In Britain, John Stuart Mill writes his essay *On Liberty* (1859).

■ Modern Era

1860–64: Garibaldi and his redshirts sail from Genoa to take Palermo and Naples. King Victor Emmanuel II of Sardinia invades the Papal States and defeats the papal troops; Garibaldi proclaims Emmanuel II king of Italy (1860). Anglo-French troops defeat the Chinese at Pa-li-Chau (1860) and sign the Treaty of Peking. The first Food and Drugs Act is enacted in Britain (1860). Lenoir constructs the first internal-combustion engine (1860). An American, Christopher L. Sholes, creates a primitive form of typewriter (1860). Russian troops fire at anti-Russian demonstrators in Poland during the Warsaw Massacre (1861). T.S. Mort builds the first machine-chilled cold storage unit (1861). Krupp begins arms production in Essen, Germany (1861). The archaeopteryx, the skeleton linking reptiles and birds, is discovered at Solnhofen, Germany (1861). The American Civil War (1861–65) begins after Abraham Lincoln is elected president. Eleven southern states, led by South Carolina, secede from the union to form the Confederacy; they defend states' rights and oppose the abolition of slavery. Lincoln issues the Emancipation Proclamation (1862), calling for the freedom of black slaves in Confederate territory. Jean Henri Dunant, a Swiss humanist, proposes the creation of the Red Cross to provide relief for the sick and wounded (1862). An American, Richard Gatling, invents the first form of the machine gun (1862). Otto von Bismarck becomes the prime minister of Prussia (1862); he begins building the system of poltical and military alliances that result in German pre-eminence in Europe. Victor Hugo writes *Les Miserables* (1862). Leo Tolstoy writes *War and Peace* (1864). The Geneva Convention establishes the neutrality of battlefield medical facilities (1864). Pope Pius IX condemns liberalism, socialism and rationalism in *Syllabus Errorum* (1864). Cheyenne and Arapahoe Indians are massacred at Sand Creek, Colorado (1864). Karl Marx founds the First International Workingmen's Association in London and New York (1864). Confederate troops surrender at Appomattox in Virginia (1865), marking the end of the American Civil War and victory for the Union. The Thirteenth Amendment abolishes slavery in the United States. The actor John Wilkes Booth assassinates President Lincoln at Ford's Theater in Washington, DC (1865).

1865–69: In Britain, Lewis Carroll writes *Alice's Adventures in Wonderland* (1865). Joseph Lister initiates antiseptic surgery by using carbolic acid on a compound wound (1865). The German mathematician Julius Plücker invents line geometry (1865). Gregor Mendel, an Austrian monk, describes his *Law of Heredity* (1865). Bismarck, the Prussian foreign minister, provokes the brief Austro-Prussian War by invading the duchies of Schleswig-Holstein and overrunning the German states allied with Austria. After seven weeks, a peace settlement gives Schleswig-Holstein, Hanover, Hesse, Nassau and Frankfurt to Prussia and excludes Austria from influence in German affairs (1866). Fyodor Dostoevsky publishes *Crime and Punishment* (1866). Alfred Nobel invents dynamite (1866). Johann Strauss popularizes the Viennese waltz with *Blue Danube* (1866). Robert Whitehead, an English engineer, invents the underwater torpedo (1866). Ernst Haeckel publishes the fundamental law of biogenetics in *General Morphology* (1866). Claude Monet, a French founder of impressionism, paints *Camille* (1866). Russia sells Alaska to the United States for $7.2 million (1867). Karl Marx writes the first volume of *Das Kapital* (1867). The British North Amer-

ica Act establishes the Dominion of Canada and John A. Macdonald becomes prime minister (1867). Louisa May Alcott describes Victorian life in America in *Little Women* (1868). A skeleton of Cro-Magnon man from the Upper Paleolithic age—the first *Homo sapiens* in Europe, successor to the Neanderthal man—is found in France by Louis Lartet (1868). The first regular Trades Union Congress is held in Manchester, England (1868). Dmitri Mendeleyev formulates his periodic law for the classification of the elements (1869). John Stuart Mill writes *On the Subjection of Women* (1869). Francis Galton publishes a major early treatise on eugenics, *Hereditary Genius* (1869). J.W. Hyatt invents celluloid (1869). The First Nihilist Congress is held in Basel, Switzerland (1869). The Suez Canal opens in Egypt (1869). Pope Pius IX establishes the doctrine of papal infallibility during Vatican Council I (1869–79).

1870–79: American industrialist John D. Rockefeller founds the Standard Oil Company (1870). T.H. Huxley, English biologist and educator, writes the *Theory of Biogenesis* (1870). The Franco-Prussian War begins (1870) and France under Emperor Napoleon III capitulates. Wilhelm I, king of Prussia, is proclaimed the German emperor at Versailles; at the Peace of Frankfurt France cedes Alsace-Lorraine to Germany (1871). The Italian Law of Guarantees allows the pope possession of the Vatican (1871). Labour unions become legal in Britain (1871). Charles Darwin writes *The Descent of Man* (1871). The Great Fire ravages Chicago (1871). Explorer Sir Henry M. Stanley is sent to find David Livingstone in Africa (1871). The first modern luxury liner, SS *Oceanic*, is launched (1871). Civil war in Spain ends with the Carlists' defeat (1872). In Berlin, the Three Emperors League allies Germany, Russia and Austria-Hungary (1872). Colour photographs are first developed (1873). James C. Maxwell writes *Electricity and Magnetism* (1873). Wilhelm Wundt, known for the experimental method, writes *Principles of Physiological Psychology* (1873). Under Prime Minister Benjamin Disraeli, Britain expands its imperial power by annexing the Fiji islands (1874). Johannes Brahms composes the *Hungarian Dances* (1874). Johann Strauss II performs the operetta *Die Fledermaus* in Vienna

(1874). Bosnia and Herzegovina rebel against Turkish rule (1875); the Turkish sultan promises reforms (1875). Mary Baker Eddy writes *Science and Health* (1875) and she founds the Christian Science movement (1879). Georges Bizet performs *Carmen* in Paris (1875). Britain's Queen Victoria is crowned empress of India (1876). Britain annexes the Transvaal (1877). American Lt.-Col. George Custer is killed with his cavalry by Cheyenne and Sioux Indians in the Battle of Little Bighorn (1876). Alexander Graham Bell constructs a telephone (1876). The first national lawn tennis championship is played at Wimbledon (1877). German historian Heinrich Treitschke begins an anti-Semitic movement (1878). Gilbert and Sullivan write *HMS Pinafore* (1878). Zulus massacre British troops in Isandhlwana, Africa (1879). The British occupy the Khyber Pass near Afghanistan and are massacred in Kabul (1879). Norwegian playwright Henrik Ibsen completes *A Doll's House* (1879). Chile invades Bolivia and Peru after Bolivia cancels a Chilean company's contract to exploit Bolivia's nitrate deposits (1879).

1880–84: Auguste Rodin sculpts *The Thinker* (1880). France annexes Tahiti (1880). The Transvaal declares its independence from Britain, and the Boers establish a republic after a brief war with Britain (1880–81). Working independently, Thomas Edison and J.W. Swan make the first practical electrical lights (1880). Charles Laveran discovers the malaria parasite (1880). American steel baron Andrew Carnegie develops the first large steel furnace (1880). The Vatican opens its archives to scholars (1881). The first Japanese political parties are founded (1881). Russians condone pogroms against Russian Jews (1881–1917), causing large-scale Jewish emigration to western Europe and North America. The Federation of Organized Trades and Labor Unions of the United States and Canada is formed (1881). Germany, Austria-Hungary and Italy form an alliance (1882). The three-mile limit for territorial waters is agreed upon at the Hague Convention (1882). Peter I. Tchaikovsky composes the *1812 Overture* (1882). Joseph Breuer, an Austrian, uses hypnosis to treat hysteria (1882). Thomas Edison designs the first hydroelectric plant in Wisconsin (1882). The Orient Express train between Paris and Istanbul makes its first run

(1883). British scientist William Thomson—later Lord Kelvin—publishes *On the Size of Atoms* (1883). Peace is restored between Peru and Chile (1883). The German philosopher Friedrich Nietzsche begins *Thus Spake Zarathustra* (1884–91). The discovery of gold in the Transvaal (1884) helps the growth of Johannesburg. A truce is signed between Bolivia and Chile; Bolivia cedes its only coastal territory to Chile (1884). The *Oxford English Dictionary* begins publication (1884–1928). Fourteen European countries meet at the Berlin Conference to discuss African affairs (1884).

1885–89: Karl Benz builds the single-cylinder engine for motor cars (1885). Sir Francis Galton proves the individuality of finger-prints (1885). The first Indian National Congress meets (1886). France presents the Statue of Liberty to the United States (1886). Ernst von Bergmann first uses steam to steril-ize surgical instruments (1886). Irish politi-cian Charles Parnell, the Fenians and British Prime Minister William Gladstone try unsuc-cessfully to pass the first Irish Home Rule Bill to give Ireland control over domestic affairs (1886). Sir Arthur Conan Doyle writes the first Sherlock Holmes story, *A Study in Scarlet* (1887). Wilhelm II becomes emperor (or kaiser) of Germany (1888). Vincent Van Gogh paints his series of sunflowers (1888) and later, *Starry Night*. The electric motor is first constructed by Nikola A. Tesla and manufactured by George Westinghouse (1888). Working independently, Heinrich Hertz and Oliver Lodge discover that radio waves belong to the same family as light waves (1888). George Eastman produces the Kodak box camera (1888). "Jack the Ripper" murders seven women in London (1888). Alexander G. Eiffel designs the Eiffel Tower for the Paris World Exhibition (1889).

1890–94: The first Japanese general election is held (1890). German Emperor Wilhelm II dismisses Chancellor Bismarck from office (1890). The first moving picture shows appear in New York (1890). Oscar Wilde writes *The Picture of Dorian Gray* (1890). Emil von Behring discovers antitoxins (1890). Engineers in Chicago build the first entirely steel-framed building (1890). The Triple Alliance between Austria-Hungary, Germany and Italy is renewed for 12 years (1891). In Britain, Thomas Hardy writes *Tess* *of the d'Urbervilles* (1891). Henri Toulouse-Lautrec produces his first music hall posters (1891). Samuel P. Langley publishes *Experiments in Aero-Dynamics* (1891). The All-Deutschland Verband (Pan-Germany League) is founded (1891). Russia experiences widespread famine (1891). An earthquake in Japan kills 10,000 people (1891). Dutch anthropologist Eugène Dubois discovers Java Man (*Pithecanthropus homo erectus*) in Indonesia (1891). French painter Paul Gauguin creates *By the Sea* in Tahiti (1892). German designer Rudolph Diesel patents his internal-combustion engine (1892). Tchaikovsky performs the music for *The Nutcracker* ballet in St. Petersburg (1892). Karl Benz constructs his four-wheel car (1893). Alfred Dreyfus, a Jewish officer in the French army, is wrongly convicted of spying for Germany (1894). Rudyard Kipling writes *The Jungle Book* (1894). After sending troops to Seoul in Korea, Japan declares war on China and defeats the Chinese at Port Arthur (1894). Emil Berliner develops a horizontal gramophone disc, replacing the record cylinder for sound reproduction (1894).

1895–99: The Sino-Japanese War ends in Japanese victory: China cedes Taiwan and Port Arthur to Japan, but Japan later returns the territories to China for payment (1895). H.G. Wells writes *The Time Machine* (1895). William B. Yeats writes *Poems* (1895). William Röntgen discovers X-rays (1895). G. Marchese Marconi invents radio telegraphy (1895). Konstantin Tsiolkovsky develops the principle of rocket reaction propulsion (1895). Athens hosts the first modern Olympic Games (1896). The Russian Anton Chekhov writes *The Sea Gull* (1896). Alfred Nobel establishes five annual Nobel prizes for persons who have contributed the most to the fields of physics, physiology and medicine, chemistry, literature and peace (1896). Wilfrid Laurier becomes the first French-Canadian prime minister of Canada (1896–1911). The Klondike gold rush in Bonanza Creek, Canada, begins (1896). Edmond Rostand writes *Cyrano de Bergerac* (1897). Queen Victoria celebrates her Diamond Jubilee (1897). French writer Emile Zola writes an open letter, *J'accuse*, condemning the Dreyfus espionage trial, and he is imprisoned (1898). Colonel Henry admits forging documents in the Dreyfus case (1898), and

Captain Dreyfus is pardoned after a retrial (1899). The Dreyfus case polarizes French politics for decades. The United States declares war on Spain over Cuba and destroys the Spanish fleet at Manila (1898). Spain cedes Cuba, Puerto Rico, Guam and the Philippines to the United States for $20 million at the Treaty of Paris. Chinese Boxers form to expel Western influences from their country (1898). The Boer War begins as the South African Republic (Transvaal) and the Orange Free State unite against the British (1898). Marie and Pierre Curie discover radium and polonium (1898). German Count Ferdinand von Zeppelin builds his airship (1898). Photographs using artificial light are first taken (1898). G. Marchese Marconi invents the radio (1899).

1900: The Boer War continues, and Canadian troops set sail for South Africa to fight for Britain in their first foreign war. China's Boxer Rebellion, which is supported by the Dowager Empress Tzu-hsi, continues against Christian missionaries and Western foreigners. The Austrian psychoanalyst Sigmund Freud completes *The Interpretation of Dreams*. Wilhelm Wundt writes *Comparative Psychology*. The Japanese reinstate Shintoism to counter Buddhist influences. The Commonwealth of Australia is created. Max Planck formulates the quantum theory. Canadian-born scientist R.A. Fessenden first transmits human speech by radio waves. Holland's Senate creates an international arbitration court at The Hague. Millions are reported starving in India. Botanist Hugo de Vries rediscovers Gregor Mendel's laws of heredity after 30 years. Ten thousand Ashanti attack a British force of 400 at Cape Coast, Ghana, and are defeated. Henri Matisse leads the Fauves, artists who paint with very bright colours.

1901: Queen Victoria dies; her son becomes King Edward VII. The Dutch Boers begin organized guerrilla warfare against the British. The Cuba Convention makes Cuba a protectorate of the United States. President William McKinley is assassinated in Buffalo, New York; Vice President Theodore Roosevelt becomes president. A treaty is signed to build the Panama Canal under American supervision. The hormone adrenaline is first isolated. Walter Nernst postulates the "third law of thermodynamics." John Pierpont Morgan organizes the United States Steel Corp., the first billion-dollar corporation. The Peace of Peking ends the Boxer uprising; China pays an indemnity of $333 million to the Allies to amend commercial treaties in favour of foreign nationals and allows the posting of foreign troops in Peking. French physicist Henri Becquerel determines that atoms have an internal structure. Race riots occur in New Orleans when American black leader Booker T. Washington is invited to the White House. The Trans-Siberian railroad reaches Port Arthur on the east coast of Russia. Oil drilling begins in Persia (Iran).

1902: An Anglo-Japanese treaty recognizes the independence of China and Korea. The Treaty of Vereeniging ends the Boer War, and the Orange Free State becomes a British colony. The Triple Alliance between Germany, Austria-Hungary and Italy is renewed for another six years. The United States acquires perpetual control over the Panama Canal. The Colonial Conference meets in London. The Committee of Imperial Defence meets in London for the first time. Jean Sibelius, Finnish composer and conductor, completes *Symphony No. 2*. Singer Enrico Caruso makes his first gramophone record. Egypt's Aswan Dam opens.

1903: France and Britain establish the "Entente Cordiale" to counter German imperialism. The Russian Social Democratic Party splits into a Menshevik faction (led by Georgi Plekhanov) and a Bolshevik faction (led by Vladimir Lenin and Leon Trotsky). Joseph John Thomson publishes *The Conduction of Electricity through Gases*. George Bernard Shaw writes *Man and Superman*. Orville and Wilbur Wright successfully fly a powered airplane near Kitty Hawk, North Carolina. Wilhelm Einthoven invents the electrocardiograph, which records heart action. In Britain, Emmeline Pankhurst founds the National Women's Social and Political Union and campaigns for women's right to vote. Prince Albert I of Monaco founds the International Peace Institute. Henry Ford founds the Ford Motor Company. The Boston Red Sox win the first World Series. W.E.B. Du Bois publishes *The Souls of Black Folk*.

1904: The Russo-Japanese War breaks out over Korea and Manchuria. The Japanese besiege Port Arthur and occupy Seoul. The Russian fleet is partially destroyed off Port Arthur. The Russians are defeated at Mukden and Tsushima Straits. Max Weber writes *The Protestant Ethic and the Spirit of Capitalism*. The first performance of Giacomo Puccini's opera *Madame Butterfly* takes place in Milan. The first radio transmission of music occurs at Graz, Austria. Ernest Rutherford and Frederick Soddy postulate the theory of radioactivity. W.C. Gorgas eradicates yellow fever in the Panama Canal Zone. F.S. Kipping discovers silicones. New York City's subway opens.

1905: Albert Einstein publishes four papers on the theory of relativity, the relationship between mass and energy, the Brownian theory of motion and the photon theory of light. The Russian city of Port Arthur surrenders to the Japanese. In Russia, troops fire at peaceful protest marchers heading for the czar's Winter Palace in St. Petersburg; the event becomes known as "Bloody Sunday." Emperor Wilhelm II of Germany and Czar Nicholas II of Russia sign the Treaty of Bjorko for mutual help in Europe. The Treaty of Portsmouth ends the Russo-Japanese War. A general strike in Russia, prompted by Bloody Sunday, includes a sailors' mutiny on the battleship *Potemkin* and the creation of the first workers' council, or *soviet*, in St. Petersburg. Czar Nicholas establishes a constitutional government (the Imperial Duma). The Norwegian parliament decides to separate from Sweden. The Anglo-Japanese alliance is renewed for 10 years. The Sinn Fein nationalist party forms in Ireland. George Santayana writes his philosophical work *The Life of Reason*.

1906: In Russia, the czar dissolves the duma to end social and democratic reforms. Aga Khan founds the All-India Muslim League. Clemens von Pirquet introduces the term "allergy." Norwegian explorer Roald Amundsen determines the position of the magnetic North Pole. Many countries forbid night-shift work for women. The San Francisco earthquake kills 700 people and causes $400 million in property losses. The Transvaal and Orange River colonies win self-government.

1907: The second Russian duma meets in March. Its radical proposals lead to its dissolution five months later. The United States prohibits Japanese immigration. Lenin leaves Russia and founds the newspaper *The Prole-*

tarian. Grigori Rasputin, a Russian mystic, gains influence with the royal family when he treats the hemophiliac son of Czar Nicholas II. New Zealand becomes a dominion within the British Empire. Robert Baden-Powell forms the Boy Scouts. Korea becomes a Japanese protectorate. Russian artist Marc Chagall paints *Peasant Women.* The Austrian composer Gustav Mahler writes *Symphony No. 8.* In Russia, Ivan Pavlov studies conditioned reflexes in dogs. The SS *Lusitania* beats the SS *Mauritania* in a race from Ireland to New York. Pablo Picasso paints *Les Desmoiselles d'Avignon* in the cubist style.

1908: Austria-Hungary occupies Bosnia and Herzegovina. Bulgaria declares independence from Turkey. Isadora Duncan emerges as a popular modern dancer. A zeppelin airship crashes near Echterdingen. General Motors Corp. is formed in the United States. Henry Ford designs the inexpensive, standardized Model T automobile while pioneering assembly line techniques for autos. An earthquake in Sicily and Calabria kills 150,000 people. Gertrude Stein writes *Three Lives.* The French writer Anatole France completes the political satire *Penguin Island.* Canadian Lucy Maud Montgomery writes *Anne of Green Gables.*

1909: Turkey and Serbia acknowledge Austro-Hungarian control of Bosnia and Herzegovina. The sultan of Turkey is deposed and replaced by his brother. Ezra Pound writes *Exultations.* The first newsreels appear. Film director D.W. Griffith features Canadian-born Mary Pickford, who becomes the first film star. Sergei Diaghilev presents his *Ballets Russes*, revolutionizing dance, in Paris. Hector Blériot flies from Calais to Dover in 37 minutes, and Henri Farman makes the first 100-mile flight. W.E.B. Du Bois cofounds the National Negro Committee which becomes the National Association for the Advancement of Colored People in 1910. The Girl Guides are organized in Britain. Thomas Hunt Morgan begins research in genetics. American explorer Robert E. Peary reaches the North Pole.

1910: The Union of South Africa becomes a dominion within the British Empire with Louis Botha as premier. China abolishes slavery. Japan takes over Korea. Montenegro becomes an independent kingdom. Portugal becomes a republic after a revolution ends the monarchy. Albania rebels against Turkish rule. Roger Fry arranges an exhibition of post-impressionist art in London with works by Cezanne, van Gogh and Matisse. Igor Stravinsky performs his ballet score *The Firebird* in Paris. A dance craze for the South American tango sweeps Europe and North America. Murray and Hjort launch the first deep-sea research expedition. The five-day work week is instituted in the United States, making the "weekend" possible.

1911: American-Japanese and Anglo-Japanese commercial treaties are signed. Porfirio Diaz, president of Mexico since 1877, surrenders power but revolutions continue. The Kaiser's Hamburg speech promises Germany's "Place in the Sun." War erupts between Turkey and Italy, and aircraft are first used for military offensives. A revolution in central China presages the fall of the Manchu Dynasty (in power since 1644) and the proclamation of a Chinese Republic. Sun Yat-sen is elected president; he appoints Chiang Kai-shek as his military adviser. The Russian premier, Peter Stolypin, is assassinated. Roald Amundsen reaches the South Pole. Marie Curie is the first person to win a second Nobel Prize, in chemistry. Ernest Rutherford formulates his theory of atomic structure. Richard Strauss composes *Der Rosenkavalier.*

1912: British dock workers, coal miners and transport workers strike. The German-Austrian-Italian alliance is renewed. Lenin becomes editor of *Pravda.* Sun Yat-sen founds the Kuomintang (Chinese Nationalist Party). Montenegro declares war against Turkey and Bulgaria; Greece and Serbia mobilize. Carl Jung writes *The Theory of Psychoanalysis.* A Polish chemist, Kasimir Funk, coins the term "vitamin." Vilhjalmur Stefansson and Anderson explore Arctic Canada. Wilson's cloud chamber (particle detector) photographs lead to the detection of protons and electrons. Britain establishes the Royal Flying Corps (later the Royal Air Force). The SS *Titanic* sinks on its first voyage after colliding with an iceberg: 1,513 people drown.

1913: The London Peace Treaty ending the First Balkan War is signed; Turkey loses all possessions in Europe except eastern Thrace. The Second Balkan War breaks out as

Bulgaria attacks Serbia and Greece. Russia declares war on Bulgaria. Bulgaria and Turkey settle a peace treaty and Turkey regains Thrace. Serbia invades Albania. Greece and Turkey make peace. Police crack down on suffragist demonstrations led by Emmeline Pankhurst in London. Maxim Gorky, the father of Soviet literature, writes *My Childhood*. Charlie Chaplin first stars in movies. Niels Bohr formulates his theory of atomic structure. Albert Schweitzer, medical missionary, opens his famous hospital in Lambaréné, French Congo. Henry Ford creates the first moving assembly line.

1914: A Serbian nationalist murders Archduke Franz Ferdinand, heir to the Austro-Hungarian throne, in Sarajevo—capital of the Austro-Hungarian province of Bosnia (June 28). Austria-Hungary declares war on Serbia (July 28). Russia and France support Serbia and mobilize their troops. In response, Austria-Hungary's German ally declares war on Russia and France. The members of the Triple Entente (Britain, France and Russia) declare war on Ottoman Turkey after the Turks attack Russia. Germany, Austria-Hungary and Turkey form the Central Powers; Britain, members of the British Empire, France, Russia, Belgium, Japan and Serbia form the Allied Powers. In the west, Germany invades Belgium and attacks France; in the east, Germany fights the Russians at Tannenberg and the Masurian Lakes. In the west, the Germans are stopped after battles at the Marne River in France (Sept. 6). The First Battle of Ypres, in Belgium, is waged to prevent the Germans from cutting British supply lines to France. Austria-Hungary fails in three attacks on Serbia and, after the Russians capture the province of Galicia, Austro-Hungarian troops retreat to their own territory. The Western Front, which stretches 720 km across Belgium and northeast France to the Swiss border, stabilizes (Nov. 14). The Panama Canal opens. American President Woodrow Wilson intervenes in Mexico's civil war and orders the marines to Vera Cruz. Irish writer James Joyce writes *Dubliners*. John B. Watson writes *Behavior: An Introduction to Comparative Psychology*. The first successful heart surgery is performed on a dog by Dr. Alexis Carrel. Millions of immigrants leave southern and eastern Europe between 1905 and 1914.

1915: The Allied campaign at Gallipoli to neutralize Turkey fails; Australian and New Zealand troops suffer heavy losses. The first German submarine (U-boat) attack occurs at Le Havre. The German blockade of Britain begins. At the Second Battle of Ypres, Canadian forces stall the German advance despite the Germans' use of artillery, chlorine gas and flame throwers. Italy joins the Allied Powers, declares war on Austria-Hungary (May 23) and opens the Italian front. A German submarine sinks the *Lusitania* (May 7). The first zeppelin attack takes place on London. Ottoman-controlled Mesopotamia surrenders to Britain. Turkish troops begin a massacre of Armenians. Italians fight Austria-Hungary in continuous battles at Isonzo (1915–17). Germans invade Warsaw and Brest-Litovsk. Allied troops land at Salonika. Hugo Junkers builds the first fighter airplane. Henry Ford develops a farm tractor. James Kendall, a British chemist, isolates the dysentery bacillus. American feminist Margaret Sanger writes the first book advocating birth control; she is sent to jail for publishing obscenity. Filmmaker D.W. Griffith makes *Birth of a Nation*.

1916: Germany stages a zeppelin raid on Paris and declares war on Portugal. Portugal and Romania later join the Allied Powers. In the Middle East, T.E. Lawrence leads an Arab revolt against Turkey. Heavy casualties occur at Verdun (Feb. 21). British and German fleets clash at the Battle of Jutland (May 31–June 1). A Newfoundland regiment is annihilated along with 624,000 Allied troops during the July offensive on the Somme. The HMS *Hampshire* is sunk. Italy declares war on Germany. The Germans first use gas masks and steel helmets. Peace notes are exchanged between Germany and the Allies. Lloyd George becomes British prime minister. British troops put down the Easter Uprising in Ireland. In Mexico, American troops under General "Black Jack" Pershing search in vain for rebel leader Pancho Villa. Blood for transfusion is first refrigerated. F.W. Mott describes shell shock. Paul Langevin builds an underwater ultrasonic source for submarine detection. Britain initiates daylight-saving time. The United States purchases the Virgin Islands for $25 million.

1917: The Russian Black Sea fleet mutinies at Sebastopol. Revolution breaks out in

Russia in February and the czar abdicates (Mar. 16). Alexander Kerensky becomes Russian premier and continues the war. The United States enters World War I on the Allied side (Apr. 6). The Germans withdraw on the Western Front. Canadian forces seize Vimy Ridge in northern France. Germany stages air attacks on Britain. Greece joins the Allies (July). China declares war on Germany and Austria-Hungary. The British-led offensive at the Third Battle of Ypres (Passchendaele) fails (July 31). Austria-Hungary defeats the Italian army at Caporetto. The Bolsheviks overthrow Kerensky's government in Petrograd (formerly St. Petersburg) in October. Lenin is appointed chief commissar. Trotsky becomes commissar for foreign affairs, and Russia seeks peace with Germany. The first tank battle occurs in the west at Cambrai. Starvation sweeps Germany. Finland declares independence from Russia. The Allies execute dancer Mata Hari as a spy. Lord Arthur Balfour, the British foreign secretary, issues the Balfour Declaration which declares British support for a Jewish national homeland in Palestine. Women are arrested for demanding suffrage in the United States.

1918: Russia, Ukraine and the Central Powers conclude the Treaties of Brest-Litovsk. The first treaty establishes the (temporary) independence of Ukraine; the second strips Russia of its Baltic and Polish possessions. The Turks surrender to the British at Jerusalem. President Woodrow Wilson puts forth his Fourteen Points for world peace, which include a proposal for a League of Nations (Jan. 18). Romania signs a peace treaty with the Central Powers. Germany launches three final offensives on the Western Front (Mar. 21). The Germans bomb Paris. The Allies win the Second Battle of the Marne (July 15–Aug. 6). The Allies win victories on all fronts in the fall. The Japanese push into Siberia. Germany and Austria-Hungary agree to retreat to their own territory before an armistice is signed. The Hungarian premier is assassinated. The Turkish and Austro-Hungarian empires and Bulgaria surrender to the Allies (Nov. 3). The German fleet mutinies at Kiel and the emperor flees for the Netherlands. An armistice between the Allies and Germany is signed (Nov. 11). Germany agrees to the provisions of the Treaty of Versailles after the Allies threaten

to invade. Emperor Charles of Austria-Hungary loses his throne. The Austro-Hungarian Empire breaks apart: sovereign states appear in Hungary, Czechoslovakia and Yugoslavia (the Kingdom of the Serbs, Croats and Slovenes). Austria becomes a republic and Poland breaks away from Russia. Iceland becomes an independent state. Throughout the Russian Empire, Bolshevik Reds and anti-Bolshevik Whites wage civil war. British, French and American troops intervene against the Reds. The British government abandons Home Rule for Ireland. Former Czar Nicholas II and his family are executed by Russian revolutionaries in Ekaterinburg. Hsu-Shih-Chang becomes president of the Chinese Republic. Women over 30 get the vote in Britain. Psychologists debate the divergent theories of Sigmund Freud and Carl Gustav Jung. The true dimensions of the Milky Way are discovered by Harlow Shapley, an American astronomer.

1919: President Woodrow Wilson heads the first League of Nations meeting in Paris. The peace conference opens at Versailles. Benito Mussolini founds the *Fasci di Combattimento* in Italy. Radical socialist governments appear briefly in Austria and Budapest. The Treaty of Versailles is signed with Germany (June 28). The final treaty exacts heavy financial penalties on Germany, restricts the size of the German army and navy, blames Germany for provoking the war and establishes the League of Nations. The United States Senate refuses to ratify the treaty, and the United States is excluded from League membership. The Allied peace treaty with Austria is signed at St. Germain (Sept. 10). The Treaty of Neuilly with Bulgaria is signed (Nov. 27). The International Labor Congress in Washington endorses the eight-hour workday. The Bolshevik forces win successive battles in the Russian civil war. J.W. Alcock and A. Whitten Brown make the first nonstop flight across the Atlantic from Newfoundland to Ireland. Lady Astor is elected to Britain's Parliament, becoming the first female MP.

1920: The League of Nations establishes its headquarters in Geneva. Britain gains control of Palestine from the Turks. The Hague becomes the International Court of Justice. The "Little Entente" is formed between Czechoslovakia, Romania and the Kingdom of the Serbs, Croats and Slovenes. The

Treaty of Trianon is signed with Hungary (June 4). The Treaty of Sevres is signed with the Ottoman Empire. The 19th Amendment gives American women the right to vote. Two hundred thousand Chinese die in an earthquake in Kansu province. The world population rises to 1.8 billion. Britain establishes separate parliaments for northern and southern Ireland. Adolf Hitler founds the Nazi party in Munich and announces a 25-point program. Hitler and other German nationalists blame Germany's military defeat on Jews and communists. Mohandas (Mahatma) Gandhi becomes India's leader in its struggle for independence from Britain. Prohibition of the manufacture, sale and consumption of liquor goes into effect in the United States. A worldwide influenza epidemic, which began in 1918, leaves 22 million dead. American author Sinclair Lewis publishes *Main Street.* British author Agatha Christie publishes her first mystery novel.

1921: The first Indian parliament meets. In Paris, the Allies fix German reparation payments at 132 thousand million gold marks. Hitler's storm troopers (SA) begin to terrorize their opponents. Mackenzie King is elected prime minister of Canada. The British Broadcasting Company (later Corporation) is founded. The Spanish prime minister and Japanese premier are assassinated. The founder of the Portuguese republic is murdered. Ex-emperor Charles stages two failed coup attempts to regain the Hungarian throne. Russia's civil war ends in Bolshevik victory. Britain and the Bolshevik government sign a trade treaty (Mar. 16). The Bolshevik government and newly independent Poland sign the Treaty of Riga (Mar. 18). Britain and Ireland sign a peace treaty. The German mark falls and rapid inflation plagues the economy. The Four Power Treaty, which checks Japanese expansion in the Pacific, is signed in Washington, DC (Dec. 13). Friedrich Bergius successfully hydrogenates coal into oil. Albert Calmette and Camille Guerin develop the tuberculosis vaccine. American biologist Thomas Morgan proposes the chromosome theory of heredity. Albert Einstein wins the Nobel Prize for physics. Ku Klux Klan members terrorize blacks and black sympathizers in the southern United States. One of the founders of modern aeronautics, Hermann

J. Oberth, writes *The Rocket into Interplanetary Space.*

1922: The Naval Treaty and the Nine Power Treaty are signed in Washington, DC (Feb. 6). Gandhi is sentenced to six years' imprisonment for civil disobedience. Britain recognizes the independence of Egypt (Feb. 28). German reconstruction minister Walter Rathenau is assassinated by radical nationalists. The Arab Congress at Nablus rejects British control of Palestine. Austria denounces "Anschluss" (union with Germany). Mussolini stages the March on Rome and forms the first fascist government. The Irish Free State is proclaimed. Kemal Ataturk overthrows the last sultan in Turkey. British archaeologists Lord Carnarvon and Howard Carter find the tomb of Egyptian pharoah Tutankhamen. John Harwood invents the self-winding wristwatch (which is patented in 1924). A stock market "boom" begins in the United States. Russian Bolsheviks form the Union of Soviet Socialist Republics (USSR). Germany and Soviet Russia sign the Treaty of Rapallo (Apr. 16). Diabetic patients first receive insulin, prepared by Canadian physicians Frederick Banting, Charles Best and John Macleod. James Joyce publishes *Ulysses.*

1923: French and Belgian troops occupy Germany's Ruhr (Jan. 11). An earthquake kills 120,000 people in Tokyo and Yokohama. Adolf Hitler fails to overthrow the German government in the "Beer Hall Putsch." The Greek army overthrows the monarch. The Allies sign the Treaty of Lausanne with Turkey (July 24). Jewish philosopher Martin Buber writes the theological work *I and Thou.* J.N. Brönsted postulates the theory of acids and bases. Lee de Forest demonstrates the process for making motion pictures with sound. The first commercial airline, Aeroflot, is founded in the USSR. Blues singer Bessie Smith makes her first record; George Gershwin composes *Rhapsody in Blue.*

1924: Ramsay MacDonald forms the first labour government in Britain. Britain recognizes the Soviet Union (Feb. 1). Adolf Hitler writes *Mein Kampf* during an eight-month jail term. R.C. Andrews discovers the skeletons of Mesozoic dinosaurs in the Gobi desert. Winston Churchill is named chancellor of the exchequer in Britain. In the Soviet Union, Lenin dies; Stalin, Zinoviev and

Kamenev ally against Trotsky. Britain's Foreign Office publishes the "Zinoviev letter" which purports to call for a communist revolution in Britain. The Dawes Agreements are signed in London (Aug. 30). The Teapot Dome scandal—the fraudulent leases of naval oil reserves—rocks President Warren Harding's government in the United States. Greece becomes a republic. Elections are held in Italy, and Mussolini wins the support of 65 percent of the electorate. Fascists murder Giacomo Matteoti, the leader of the Italian socialists. The Albanian Republic is founded. The League of Nations adopts the Geneva Protocol (Oct. 2). Sigmund Freud begins his *Collected Writings* (12 vols. 1924–39). In India, Gandhi fasts for 21 days to protest feuds between Hindus and Muslims. British astronomer Arthur Eddington discovers that the luminosity of a star is approximately related to its mass. Insecticides are used for the first time. V.K. Zworkin, a Russian-American inventor, files a patent application for the iconoscope (an early version of television). Danish polar explorer Knud Rasmussen completes the longest dog-sled journey ever made across the North American Arctic. British Imperial Airways begins commercial air flights.

1925: Britain rejects the Geneva Protocol (Mar. 10). Nellie Taylor Ross of Wyoming becomes the first woman governor in the United States. In Tennessee, John Scopes is convicted for teaching Darwinian evolutionary theory in a public school; the sentence is set aside. The Locarno Treaty between Germany, France, Belgium, Poland, Britain, Italy and Czechoslovakia creates a demilitarized zone in the Rhineland and fixes the borders between Belgium, France and Germany (Dec. 1). A Scottish inventor, John Logie Baird, transmits recognizable human features on a television. Walter P. Chrysler founds the Chrysler Corp. The (Franz) Fischer and (Hans) Tropsch synthesis leads to the industrial development of synthetic oil. Heisenberg, Bohr and Jordan develop quantum mechanics for atoms. Robert Andrews Millikan, an American physicist, detects cosmic rays in the upper atmosphere. The "flapper" era begins. An international convention condemns the illegal narcotics trade.

1926: The League of Nations admits German membership (Sept. 10). Fascist youth organi-

zations appear: the *Balilla* in Italy and *Hitlerjugend* in Germany. Josef Pilsudski successfully stages a coup d'état in Poland and begins a military dictatorship. A general strike hurts commerce in Britain. Hirohito succeeds his father Taisho as emperor of Japan. The United States sends the marines to Nicaragua during a revolt; they stay until 1933. Robert H. Goddard fires the first liquid fuel rocket. B. Jansen and W. Donath isolate vitamin B. Kodak produces the first 16-mm movie film. British Imperial Chemical Industries (ICI) begins operations. H.L. Mencken writes *Notes on Democracy*. Turkish reforms include the abolition of polygamy, the modernization of female attire and the adoption of the Latin alphabet (1926–28). American author Ernest Hemingway publishes *The Sun Also Rises*.

1927: Chinese nationalists establish their government at Hankow (Jan. 1). The Allied military control of Germany ends. Fifty-two countries attend an economic conference in Geneva. An Austrian court acquits Nazis of political murder; socialists riot in Vienna to protest. In the USSR, the communist party expels Leon Trotsky (Dec. 18). Al Jolson stars in the first film with sound, a "talkie" called *The Jazz Singer*. Lev Theremin invents the earliest electronic musical instrument. Charles Lindbergh flies the monoplane *Spirit of St. Louis* in the first solo transatlantic flight, nonstop from New York to Paris, in 33.5 hours. Airplanes first spray Canadian forests with insecticides. Georges Lemaître speculates on the origin of the universe with the "Big Bang" theory. The first vehicular tunnel, the Holland Tunnel, links New York and New Jersey.

1928: Sixty-five states sign the Pact of Paris (the Kellogg-Briand Pact) outlawing war (Aug. 27). Josef Stalin emerges as leader of Soviet Union. The first economic five-year plan begins in the USSR. Chiang Kai-shek is elected president of China. Overproduction of coffee leads to the collapse of Brazil's economy. Alexander Fleming, a Scot, discovers penicillin. American anthropologist Margaret Mead writes *Coming of Age in Samoa*. George Eastman exhibits the first colour motion pictures in Rochester, New York. J.L. Baird presents colour television. Mickey Mouse makes his Walt Disney debut.

1929: The Hague Conference approves the Young Plan (Aug. 31). The US stock exchange collapses (Oct. 28); the Great Depression, a world economic crisis, begins. It is primarily caused by easy credit and stock market overspeculation, the overproduction of goods, and tariff and war-debt policies. Six Chicago-area gangsters are machine-gunned to death in the St. Valentine's Day Massacre. In the Kingdom of the Serbs, Croats and Slovenes, the monarch establishes a dictatorship and changes the country's name to Yugoslavia. Trotsky is exiled from USSR. Talks on Indian sovereignty begin between Indian leaders and the British viceroy. The Lateran Treaty establishes the independence of Vatican City. American astronomer Edwin Hubble proposes the theory of an expanding universe. W.A. Morrison makes precise timekeeping possible with quartz-crystal clocks. The airship *Graf Zeppelin* flies around the world in 21 days.

1930: Austria and Italy sign a friendship treaty. Britain, the United States, Japan, France and Italy sign a naval treaty in London (Apr. 22). A right-wing coalition comes to power in Germany; the Nazis later capture 107 more seats in an election. Allied troops evacuate the Rhineland (June 30). A right-wing government is formed in Poland. Roman Catholic-Fascist units are established in Austria. Revolution in Argentina brings a military dictatorship to power. At Lowell Observatory, C.W. Tombaugh discovers the planet Pluto. South African microbiologist Max Theiler develops a vaccine for yellow fever. The photoflash bulb is introduced. The word "technocracy," meaning the domination of technology, comes into use. Ernest Lawrence, an American physicist, devises the cyclotron.

1931: The collapse of Austria's Credit-Anstalt causes a financial crisis in central Europe. All German banks close following the bankruptcy of the German Danatbank. Germany and Austria agree on a customs union (Mar. 21). A small fascist party forms in Britain. The Statute of Westminster establishes the British Commonwealth as a free association of nations sharing a common allegiance to the British crown; the statute also declares that Britain's Parliament can no longer legislate for any member state unless requested to do so. In the United States, President Herbert Hoover proposes a one-year moratorium on the payment of reparations and war debts. American scientist Harold Urey discovers heavy hydrogen. An American court convicts gangster Al Capone for tax evasion. The Scottsboro trial begins in Alabama, exposing the depth of southern racism. Japan begins military operations in Chinese Manchuria (Sept. 19). Britain abandons the gold standard (Sept. 21). The Spanish overthrow their king and declare a republic. The first trans-African railroad is completed, Benguella-Katanga. Franz and Toni Schmid climb the northern face of the Matterhorn for the first time.

1932: The Indian National Congress, a party dedicated to home rule, is declared illegal and its leader, Mahatma Gandhi, is arrested. The United States criticizes Japanese aggression in Manchuria. The Nazis sweep the German Reichstag elections; Marshall Paul von Hindenburg, a hero of the First World War, wins the presidential election. Hitler refuses Hindenburg's offer to become vice chancellor, and the Austrian-born Hitler receives German citizenship. The Reparation Agreement is signed in Lausanne (July 9). Britain and its dominions sign trade agreements in Ottawa (Aug. 20). The British mandate over Iraq ends (Oct. 20). War veterans march on Washington, DC; they are forcibly dispelled. Franklin D. Roosevelt wins the presidential election in the United States. Famine sweeps the USSR. Zuider Zee, a huge dam and drainage project in Holland, is completed. Amelia Earheart is the first woman to fly solo across the Atlantic. Japan conquers world markets by undercutting prices. About 30 million people are unemployed worldwide. James Chadwick discovers the neutron. Vitamin D is discovered.

1933: The Reichstag is burned in Berlin, and Hitler uses the event to justify banning opposition parties and labour unions. Hitler is appointed German chancellor (Jan. 30) and granted dictatorial powers with the Enabling Law. Nazi Hermann Goering becomes Prussian prime minister. Joseph Goebbels becomes Hitler's minister of propaganda. Parliamentary government is suspended in Austria. Starvation spreads in the USSR. The League of Nations passes a resolution on Manchuria (Feb. 24); Japan withdraws from the League. The World Economic Conference opens (June 12). The Nazis build their first concentration camps in Germany to hold Jews and other opponents. The Nazis burn books by non-Nazi and Jewish authors. Germans begin to boycott and restrict Jewish services. Germany announces its withdrawal from the disarmanent conference and the League of Nations (Oct. 14). In Munich, Cardinal von Faulhaber publishes an anti-Nazi treatise called *Judaism-Christendom-Germanism.* Assyrian Christians are massacred in Iraq. President Franklin Roosevelt launches the New Deal, and the United States goes off the gold standard. The United States creates the Tennessee Valley Authority to construct dams and generate electricity. The United States repeals the ban on making, selling and drinking alcohol.

1934: A revolution in Austria overthrows the Social Democrats; Nazis assassinate the Austrian chancellor. A general strike takes place in France. Winston Churchill warns the British Parliament of the German air menace. Hitler orders a blood purge of his associates and opponents. A national vote makes Hitler führer (leader). Stalin's purge of the Soviet communist party begins; he oversees the murder of millions of people. The League of Nations admits the USSR (Sept. 18). King Alexander of Yugoslavia is assassinated in Marseilles (Oct. 9). Albert Einstein, a German Jewish scientist, flees Germany for the United States. Japan renounces the Washington treaties of 1922 and 1930. Mao Tse-tung, leader of the Chinese communists, leads 100,000 guerillas into northern China on the Long March.

1935: Italy and France sign an agreement (Jan. 7). The Nazis repudiate the military clauses of the Treaty of Versailles (Mar. 16); Germany reintroduces compulsory military service. The Franco-Soviet Pact is signed (May 2). The autonomous territory of Saarland votes for reunion with Germany. An Anglo-German Naval Agreement is concluded. The Nazis implement the Nuremberg Laws against Jews, stripping them of civic rights and forbidding intermarriage with non-Jews. Mussolini invades Abyssinia (Oct. 2); the League of Nations retaliates by imposing sanctions (Nov. 18). Louisiana Governor Huey Long is murdered. The Chaco War, a three-year conflict between Paraguay and Bolivia over barren but oil-rich territory, ends after 100,000 lives are lost. (The peace

treaty isn't concluded until 1938.) Robert Watson Watt builds radar equipment to detect aircraft. Oil pipelines between Iraq, Haifa and Tripoli open. Persia changes its name to Iran.

1936: King George V of England dies; King Edward VIII succeeds him. German troops occupy the demilitarized zone in the Rhineland (Mar. 7). Hitler wins the German elections with 99 percent of the vote. Italy, Austria and Hungary sign the Rome Pact. Italy annexes Abyssinia (May 9). Britain, France and the United States sign the London Naval Convention. An Austro-German convention acknowledges Austrian independence. The Spanish Civil War begins (July 18); General Francisco Franco leads nationalist insurgents and fascists in their revolt against the legal republican government. The nationalists lay siege to Madrid, take Malaga, destroy Guernica and Gijon, and begin a naval blockade (1937). In Germany, Heinrich Himmler is appointed head of the Gestapo; he becomes responsible for operating the Nazis' concentration camps (1936–45). King Edward VIII abdicates to marry American divorcee Wallis Simpson. Mussolini and Hitler proclaim the Rome-Berlin Axis. Germany and Japan sign the Anti-Comintern Pact. Chiang Kai-shek declares war on Japan. Dr. Alexis Carrel develops an artificial heart. The airship *Hindenburg* explodes at Lakehurst, New Jersey, after a transatlantic flight. Black American athlete Jesse Owens upsets the Nazis when he wins four gold medals at the Olympic Games in Berlin.

1937: Poland refuses to return Danzig to Germany. The first worldwide radio broadcast occurs when George VI is crowned king of Britain. President Roosevelt signs the Neutrality Act to keep the United States out of a possible European war. Trotsky, exiled from the Soviet Union in 1929, is forced to leave Norway and settles in Mexico. In Japan, the newly appointed premier, Prince Konoye, launches a more ambitious war policy. Japan begins an undeclared war in China (July 8), seizing Chinese cities (Peking, Tianjin, Shanghai, Nanjing and Hangzhou) and forcing Chinese nationalists and communists to unite. The Chinese government makes Chungking its capital. The Royal Commission on Palestine recommends the establishment of Arab and Jewish states. Stalin purges the Soviet Union's military command amid show trials of old Bolshevik leaders. Britain signs naval agreements with Germany and the USSR. Germany guarantees Belgian sovereignty. Italy joins the Anti-Comintern Pact and withdraws from the League of Nations. Japanese planes sink an American gunboat in Chinese waters. Amelia Earheart disappears during a Pacific flight. Pablo Picasso paints *Guernica*.

1938: Germany annexes Austria during the "Anschluss" (Mar. 12). France calls up reservists. At Munich, Great Britain, France and Italy agree to let Germany absorb the Sudetenland in Czechoslovakia in a policy of appeasement (Sept. 29); Germany promises to cease aggressive expansion. British foreign minister Anthony Eden resigns in protest against appeasement, and Winston Churchill also voices opposition. General Franco begins an offensive against the Spanish loyalists in Catalonia. Italy enacts anti-Jewish legislation. During Kristallnacht, or "Night of Broken Glass," the Nazis orchestrate a national pogrom against German Jews. The United States and Germany recall their respective ambassadors. Japan withdraws from the League of Nations and sets up a puppet Chinese government in Nanking. Howard Hughes flies around the world in less than four days. Orson Welles broadcasts *War of the Worlds*, a play based on H.G. Wells' novel, on American radio stations.

1939: President Roosevelt demands assurances from Hitler and Mussolini that they have no plans to attack other countries. Germany breaks the Munich Pact and occupies Bohemia and Moravia (Mar. 15). Slovakia is placed under German "protection." The Spanish Civil War ends with Franco's nationalists victorious (Apr. 1). Italy invades Albania (Apr. 7). Britain introduces conscription (May 26). Germany renounces the nonaggression pact with Poland and the naval agreement with England, and concludes a 10-year alliance with Italy. Germany signs a nonaggression pact with the USSR (Aug. 23); Germany and the USSR secretly plan to divide Poland between them. World War II begins when Germany launches a lightning invasion (blitzkrieg) of Poland and annexes Danzig (Sept. 1). Britain and France declare war on Germany (Sept. 3). Britain and France lead the Allied Powers; Germany leads the

Axis Powers. Canada declares war on Germany (Sept. 10). President Roosevelt announces American neutrality. The Soviets invade Poland from the east (Sept. 17). The Germans quickly overrun western Poland, taking Brest-Litovsk and Warsaw. France masses troops along the Maginot Line on the eastern frontier of France; Germany sends troops to its parallel Siegfried Line. The British Expeditionary Force is sent to France. The USSR invades Finland and is expelled from the League of Nations. Japan occupies Hainan and blockades the British at Tientsin. The United States renounces the Japanese trade agreement of 1911. Spain joins the Anti-Comintern Pact and leaves the League of Nations. Britain and Poland sign a treaty of mutual assistance. Women and children are first evacuated from London. A Russian-American, Igor Sikorsky, builds the first helicopter. The American economy booms from arms sales to Europe.

1940: Food rationing begins in Britain. Finland surrenders (March) and signs a peace treaty with the USSR. Germany invades Norway and Denmark (Apr. 9). Winston Churchill becomes British prime minister (May 10). Norway falls (June). Germany invades Belgium, Luxembourg and the Netherlands (May 10). Holland and Belgium surrender to Germany; 400,000 Allied forces are trapped in Belgium, but 338,000 are evacuated from Dunkirk, a seaport on the English channel (May 29–June 3). Italy declares war on France and Britain. Germans attack France from the north and enter Paris (June 14). France concludes an armistice with Germany. Southern France remains unoccupied until 1942 and is ruled by the Vichy government. The USSR seizes Estonia, Latvia and Lithuania in the summer. The Royal Navy sinks the French fleet in Oran. The Royal Air Force begins night bombing of Germany. The Battle of Britain in August is the first battle fought completely in the air. Hitler begins night bombing of Britain in the fall and winter. Japan, Germany and Italy sign a military and economic pact. The United States trades 50 destroyers for leases on British bases in the Western Hemisphere; the United States introduces the Selective Service Act. President Franklin Roosevelt wins an unprecedented third term in office. Germany intensifies U-boat warfare in the

Atlantic. Italian forces attempt to take Egypt and Libya to cut off British access to Middle East oil and the Suez Canal. The British Eighth Army opens an offensive in North Africa and defeats the Italian forces. A Stalinist agent murders Trotsky in Mexico. Fulgencio Batista becomes president of Cuba. Wall paintings dating to about 20,000 BC are discovered in the Lascaux caves in France. A giant cyclotron is built at the University of California for producing mesotrons from atomic nuclei. NBC airs the first official television broadcast.

1941: The British invade Ethiopia and defeat the Italians (May). Germany opens a counteroffensive in North Africa to aid Italy. German General Irwin Rommel regains Libya and Egypt. The Germans launch an airborne invasion of Crete, securing an important base in the Mediterranean by the end of May. Britain sinks the German battleship *Bismarck* to protect vital American shipments to Great Britain. The Allies develop radar and sonar to track U-boats. German air raids over London continue. The United States freezes German and Italian assets; President Roosevelt signs the Lend Lease Act. The Germans invade the Soviet Union during Operation Barbarossa (June 22). Churchill and Roosevelt sign the Atlantic Charter (Aug. 14). German troops surround Leningrad and Moscow (November), but an early, harsh winter stalls the German advance. Marshal Timoshenko launches the Soviet counteroffensive. The United States ambassador to Japan warns President Roosevelt of a possible Japanese attack. The Japanese bomb Pearl Harbor (Dec. 7); the United States and Britain declare war on Japan (Dec. 8). China declares war on the Axis (Dec. 9). Japan invades the Philippines. Germany and Italy declare war on the United States; the United States declares war on Germany and Italy. British Hong Kong surrenders to the Japanese. As an official war artist, Henry Moore draws refugees in London air raid shelters. Dmitri Shostakovich writes *Symphony No. 7* during the German siege of Leningrad. The German dramatist Bertolt Brecht writes *Mother Courage and Her Children* while in exile from the Nazis.

1942: Hitler's Final Solution, the systematic murder of 6 million Jews in Nazi gas chambers at death camps such as Auschwitz-Birkenau, begins. The 26 Allied nations agree not to make separate treaties with the Axis powers. Rommel breaks through British lines and reaches El Alamein (320 km from the Suez Canal). Field Marshall Montgomery of the British Eighth Army decisively defeats Rommel at El Alamein. The Germans reach Stalingrad in the Soviet Union. Four hundred thousand American troops land in French North Africa. Rommel, in full retreat, loses Tobruk and Benghazi. Japan invades Burma, the Dutch East Indies and Singapore. The British bomb Cologne and Lübeck. The United States and Canada intern citizens of Japanese heritage. In the Philippines, the Japanese capture many American and Philippino soldiers who die during the Bataan Death March. The Americans bomb Tokyo. The Americans begin their successful island-hopping strategy against Japan and win the battles of the Coral Sea and Midway. The French navy loses in Toulon. British and Indian troops advance in Burma. In the United States, Enrico Fermi achieves the first controlled nuclear chain reaction when he splits the atom; intensive atomic research begins with the Manhattan Project. The first "electronic brain" or automatic computer is developed in the United States. German engineers invent plastic magnetic recording tape. Gandhi demands independence from Britain and is arrested.

1943: German troops surrender at Stalingrad (Feb. 2) and begin to withdraw from the Caucasus. The Russians destroy a German army southwest of Stalingrad. The Russians recapture Rostov and Kharkov. Churchill and Roosevelt meet in Casablanca. American troops drive the Japanese from Guadalcanal. The British Eighth Army reaches Tripoli. British and American armies in Africa link up and Rommel retreats. The last Axis troops in North Africa surrender in Tunisia (May 13). The Royal Air Force raids Berlin. American planes sink the 22-ship Japanese convoy in the Battle of the Bismarck Sea. An armed Jewish uprising begins in the Warsaw ghetto, but it is crushed by German troops (1943–44). The RAF bombs Ruhr dams. American forces land in New Guinea. The Americans recapture the Aleutian Islands from the Japanese. The Allies land in Sicily (July 10). Churchill, Roosevelt and Mackenzie King meet in Quebec. American troops bomb Ploesti's oil fields in Romania and enter Messina in Sicily. The Allies land in Salerno Bay and invade Italy, which unconditionally surrenders (Sept. 8). The Russians retake Kiev. Chinese General and Madame Chiang Kai-shek meet with Roosevelt and Churchill in Cairo and pledge to liberate Korea after Japan is defeated. Churchill, Stalin and Roosevelt hold the Tehran Conference. Allied round-the-clock bombing of Germany begins. The British use the first fully electronic computer to crack German military codes. Penicillin is used to treat chronic diseases. Bengal is swept by famine. Rationing of selected foods begins in the United States. Race riots occur in some American cities.

1944: Germany continues air raids on London. Russian offensives continue in the Ukraine and Crimea. The Allies bomb Berlin. The Allies liberate Rome. The Allies invade Normandy, France, with over 700 ships and 4,000 landing craft on D-Day (June 6); Canadian troops lead the trek inland from the beaches. The Germans launch their first flying bomb (V-1) on London. The United States bombs southern Japan. American troops take Saipan. The Russians capture 100,000 Germans at Minsk. German officers fail to assassinate Hitler. The Russians reach Brest-Litovsk. The Americans capture Guam from the Japanese. The British Eighth Army takes Florence. At the Bretton Woods Conference, Allied officials propose the creation of the International Monetary Fund and the World Bank; at Dumbarton Oaks in Washington, officials discuss the creation of a United Nations. Charles De Gaulle leads the Free French into Paris (Aug. 25). The Allies liberate Belgium. The first V-2 rockets land in Britain. Churchill and Roosevelt meet in Quebec. The Americans cross the German frontier near Trier. British airborne forces land at Eindhoven and Arnheim but withdraw. American troops land in the Philippines. The Russians and Yugoslavs enter Belgrade. The Russian army occupies Hungary. The Japanese suffer heavy losses in Battle of Leyte Gulf. The Battle of the Bulge in the Ardennes Forest results in an Allied victory. France regains Lorraine. Rommel commits suicide. Vietnam, under Ho Chi Minh, declares independence from France. Quinine is synthesized. American playwright Tennessee Williams completes *The Glass Menagerie*. Richard Strauss completes the opera *Die Liebe der Danae* in Austria, but its performance is cancelled when the Nazis shut down the theatres. French playwright Jean-Paul Sartre writes *Being and Nothingness*. Swedish sociologist Gunnar Myrdal describes race relations in *An American Dilemma*.

1945: Britain begins an offensive in Burma. The Russians take Warsaw, capture Krakow and reach the Oder River. Churchill, Roosevelt and Stalin meet at Yalta. The Americans enter Manila. The Russians take Budapest. British troops reach the Rhine. The United States Air Force raids Tokyo, Cologne and Danzig. The Americans capture Okinawa. The British Second Army crosses the Rhine. The last German V-2 rocket falls on Britain. President Franklin Roosevelt dies; Vice President Harry S Truman succeeds him. The Russians reach Berlin. Bologna is captured. American and Soviet troops meet at Torgau; both liberate Nazi death camps, finding gas chambers and crematoriums. A new United Nations charter is drawn up at a conference in San Francisco (April–June). The Allies capture Bremen, Genoa, Verona and Venice. The Allies cross the Elbe. Italian partisans execute Mussolini. Hitler commits suicide (Apr. 30). The German army on the Italian front surrenders. Berlin surrenders to the Russians (May 2) and Germany capitulates to the Allies (May 7). V-E Day (Victory in Europe) ends the war in Europe (May 8). Germany is divided into four zones by the Allies and the occupation of Berlin begins. Churchill, Truman and Stalin meet at Potsdam. Labour leader Clement Attlee replaces Churchill as prime minister of Britain in an electoral landslide. America's atomic scientists (J. Robert Oppenheimer, Enrico Fermi and others) devise the first atomic bomb; it is detonated near Alamogordo, New Mexico (July 16). The Soviet Union declares war on Japan and occupied Manchuria. The United States drops atomic bombs on Hiroshima (Aug. 6) and Nagasaki (Aug. 9). Japan surrenders and World War II ends. The war dead are estimated at 35 million plus the victims of Nazi concentration camps. The Nuremberg trials of Nazi war criminals begin. The League of Nations holds its final meeting in Geneva and turns over its assets to the United Nations (October). Charles De

Gaulle is elected president of the French provisional government. Marshall Josip Broz Tito becomes chief of state of the new Federal People's Republic of Yugoslavia. Chinese nationalists and communists resume their civil war. The Arab League is founded to oppose the creation of a Jewish state. Japan abolishes shintoism. Vitamin A is synthesized. Black markets for food, clothing and cigarettes develop in Europe. The United Nations World Bank (International Bank for Reconstruction and Development) is founded with authorized share capital of $27 billion. ENIAC, the first electronic computer, is built.

1946: Albania, Bulgaria, Hungary and Transjordan become sovereign states. The United Nations General Assembly holds its first session in London (Jan. 7), electing Trygve Lie of Norway as its first secretary general; its permanent headquarters is established in New York. Winston Churchill warns that an "Iron Curtain" is descending in Soviet-occupied Europe. Juan Perón is elected president of Argentina. A peace conference of 21 nations is held in Paris. Twelve leading Nazis are executed following the Nuremberg trials, and others get life imprisonment. Power in Japan is transferred from the emperor to an elected assembly. The United Nations Atomic Energy Commission is formed to monitor member nations. After a referendum in Italy, the king abdicates. Italy becomes a republic and de Gasperi becomes head of state. Chester Carlson invents xerography (photocopying). Dr. Benjamin Spock writes *Baby and Child Care*, the "baby boom" reference book.

1947: Britain nationalizes its coal industry. In Paris, Italy, Romania, Bulgaria, Hungary and Finland sign peace treaties. The Dead Sea Scrolls, dating from about 22 BC to AD 100, are discovered in Qumran, Palestine. President Truman declares the Truman Doctrine to aid Greece and Turkey in their efforts to resist Soviet expansion. The United States proposes the Marshall Plan to aid Western European economic recovery. Black baseball player Jackie Robinson joins the Brooklyn Dodgers. American Chuck Yeager flies the first airplane at supersonic speeds. Scientists at Bell Telephone Laboratory invent the transistor. The United Nations divides Palestine, which is under a British mandate, into a Jewish and an Arab state (November); the

British withdraw six months later. India gains independence from Britain; the territory is partitioned into India, and East and West Pakistan. *The Diary of Anne Frank* is published by Anne's father, the only member of the German-Jewish family to survive the Holocaust.

1948: A Hindu murders Mahatma Gandhi (Jan. 30). Burma and Ceylon win independence (Jan 4; Feb. 4). A communist coup takes place in Czechoslovakia (Feb. 23–25). The United States Congress approves the Marshall Plan, providing $17 billion in aid for Europe. Winston Churchill chairs the Hague Congress for European unity. Israel is proclaimed with Chaim Weizmann as president and David Ben-Gurion as premier (May 14). Neighbouring Arab states declare war (1948–49) on Israel, but Israel succeeds in increasing its territory. The Western powers begin airlifting supplies into Berlin (June 26) after the USSR imposes a land and water blockade on the city (June 24). The first international schism in the communist world occurs when Yugoslavia and the Soviet Union break relations. The republic of South Korea is proclaimed. Bread rationing ends in Britain. The World Council of Churches is organized in Amsterdam. American biologist Alfred C. Kinsey writes *Sexual Behavior in the Human Male*. The first World Health Assembly meets in Geneva. The first port radar system is installed in Liverpool, Britain. In Japan, war-crimes trials end in the imprisonment of 18 leaders and the execution of seven others—including former premier Hideki Tojo. Indonesia wins independence from the Netherlands.

1949: Tianjin, China, falls to the communists. Chiang Kai-shek resigns as president of China and removes his forces to Taiwan. The communist People's Republic of China is proclaimed under Mao Tse-tung with Chou En-lai as premier. In Washington, Western powers (Belgium, Canada, Denmark, France, Iceland, Italy, Luxembourg, the Netherlands, Norway, Portugal, Britain and the United States) sign the North Atlantic Treaty and create NATO. The Soviet blockade of Berlin lifts. The German Federal Republic (West Germany) comes into being with Bonn as its capital and Konrad Adenauer as chancellor. The republic of Eire is proclaimed with its capital in Dublin. Transjordan is renamed the

Hashemite Kingdom of Jordan. The state of Vietnam, under Ho Chi Minh, is established at Saigon. Civil war looms in Korea. South Africa institutes racial apartheid. The Democratic Republic is established in East Germany with Pieck as president. India becomes a federal republic with Pandit Nehru as prime minister. The USSR tests its first atomic bomb. The United States launches a guided missile to a height of 400 km, the highest altitude yet. George Orwell publishes *Nineteen Eighty-Four*.

1950: Communist China and the Soviet Union sign a treaty of friendship and mutual assistance; Britain also recognizes communist China. United States Senator Joseph McCarthy claims the Department of State is infiltrated with communists. Robert Schuman proposes the Schuman Plan to foster greater cooperation in Europe's coal and steel industries. Protesters are killed in anti-apartheid riots in South Africa. Vietnam, Laos and Cambodia gain independence from France. North Korea invades South Korea, capturing Seoul and forcing President Syngman Rhee to flee. The United States Atomic Energy Commission begins work on a hydrogen bomb. Troops under General Douglas MacArthur's command land in South Korea and push north of the 38th parallel; China enters the Korean War. The United States recognizes Vietnam and sends military supplies and instructors; the United States also signs a military assistance pact with Vietnam, Laos, Cambodia and France. Puerto Rican nationalists fail to assassinate President Truman.

1951: North Korean forces reach the 38th parallel and capture Seoul: attempts to negotiate peace fail. President Truman sacks General MacArthur as commander in Korea for threatening massive retaliation against China. Winston Churchill forms the government in Britain. Six countries form the European Coal and Steel Community; it becomes effective in 1952. Remington Rand produces UNIVAC, the first large-scale, general-purpose computer. Atomic energy produces electricity in the United States. J. Andre-Thomas devises a heart-lung machine. Penicillin and streptomycin become available in the United States. In San Francisco, 49 countries sign the Japanese peace treaty (Sept. 8). Libya gains independence (Dec. 24).

1952: Dwight D. Eisenhower is elected American president. Britain produces an atomic bomb. Queen Elizabeth II ascends the throne in Britain. Egypt is rocked by anti-British riots: the premier resigns and the army seizes power. The Mau-Maus rebel in Kenya; the British colonial government declares an emergency. The United States explodes the first hydrogen bomb at Eniwetok Atoll in the Pacific. British Overseas Airways introduces the world's first jet passenger service from London to Rome. Sony markets the first pocket-sized transistor radio in Japan. Ralph Ellison publishes *The Invisible Man*.

1953: Soviet leader Joseph Stalin dies (Mar. 5); Georgi Malenkov replaces him. Sweden's Dag Hammarskjöld begins his term as United Nations secretary general (Apr. 10). Yugoslavia proclaims a new constitution and Marshall Tito becomes president. Francis Crick and James Watson publish their discovery of the molecular model of DNA (April–May). Edmund Hillary and Tenzing Norgay become the first to scale Mt. Everest (May 29). East Berliners revolt against Soviet rule; Soviet tanks crush the revolt (June). Egyptian generals establish a dictatorship and proclaim a republic (June 18). A nationalist government in Iran is overthrown with CIA help. Rebels from Vietnam attack Laos. Fidel Castro begins his campaign to overthrow Cuban dictator Fulgencio Batista. American authorities execute Ethel and Julius Rosenberg for passing atomic bomb designs to the Soviet Union (June 19). An armistice signed at Panmunjom ends the Korean War (July 27). The Soviet Union explodes a hydrogen bomb (Aug. 20). The first successful open heart surgery is performed in the United States. Researchers associate lung cancer with cigarette smoking.

1954: The Soviet Union grants sovereignty to East Germany (Mar. 23). Vietnamese communists defeat the French at Dien Bien Phu (May 7). The United States Supreme Court bans racial segregation in public schools (May 17). Gamal Abdel Nasser becomes leader in Egypt. The United States Senate censures Senator Joseph McCarthy for launching a witchhunt of real and alleged communists. Canada and the United States plan a joint radar defence system in the north: the Distant Early Warning Line. The USS

Nautilus becomes the first nuclear-powered submarine. The government of Guatemala is overthrown with CIA help. The Southeast Asian Treaty, forming SEATO, is signed in Manila (Sept. 8). Dr. Jonas Salk begins inoculating children against polio. Algerian nationalists launch their war for independence (November). The oral contraceptive pill is introduced in the United States. The first successful kidney transplant is performed in the United States. Roger Bannister becomes the first to run a mile in less than four minutes.

1955: Bulganin succeeds Malenkov as Soviet premier (Feb. 8). Churchill resigns in Britain; Anthony Eden succeeds him (Apr. 6). West Germany becomes a sovereign state (May 5). Eight East European communist countries adopt the Warsaw Pact mutual defence treaty (May 14). West Germany joins NATO. Border clashes between Israel and Jordan increase. Juan Perón is ousted by a military coup in Argentina (Sept. 19). The first optical fibres are produced in Britain. Rosa Parks, a black American woman, refuses to sit at the back of a bus; Dr. Martin Luther King, Jr., begins a boycott of the bus company in Alabama (Dec. 1). Two large American labour unions—the AFL and the CIO—unite (Dec. 5).

1956: Soviet leader Nikita Khrushchev denounces Stalin's "cult of the individual" and Stalinism's excesses (Feb. 24). The United States tests the first aerial hydrogen bomb at Bikini Atoll (May 21). Nasser is elected Egyptian president. Egypt seizes control of the Suez Canal. The Soviets quell an uprising in Poznan, Poland (June 28–30). Soviet troops crush an anti-communist rebellion in Hungary (Oct. 23–Nov. 4). Israeli troops invade Egypt and push towards the Suez Canal (Oct. 29). British and French forces invade Egypt (Nov. 5). A United Nations force arrives in Egypt, prompting a ceasefire. Jordan and Israel accept United Nations truce proposals for the dispute. Sudan becomes a democratic republic. Pakistan becomes an Islamic republic. Morocco gains independence. Dr. Martin Luther King, Jr., leads the campaign against racial segregation in the American south. Transatlantic telephone service begins. Scientists devise the first computer programming language (FORTRAN) in the United States. Swedish

filmmaker Ingmar Bergman makes *The Seventh Seal*. American beatnik poet Allen Ginsberg composes *Howl*.

1957: Israeli troops withdraw from Egypt, and the Gaza Strip comes under United Nations jurisdiction. The United Nations reopens the Suez Canal. President Eisenhower warns that the United States will oppose communist takeovers in the Middle East (Jan. 5). The attempt to racially integrate a high school in Arkansas prompts President Eisenhower to send troops to quell mob violence (Sept. 24). The space race begins as the USSR launches the first earth-orbiting satellite, *Sputnik* (Oct. 4). Belgium, France, Italy, Luxembourg, the Netherlands and West Germany sign the Rome Treaty to extend the common market established for the steel industry to all sectors of the economy. Harold Macmillan leads the new conservative government in Britain.

1958: The European Economic Community (or Common Market) becomes effective (Jan. 1). Pope Pius XII dies; he is succeeded by Pope John XXIII. The United States launches its first space satellite, *Explorer I* (Jan. 31). Scientists in the USSR send two dogs into space and return them safely to earth. Egypt and Syria form the United Arab Republic (Feb. 1). Nikita Khrushchev becomes Soviet premier (Mar. 27). Charles de Gaulle becomes premier of France (June 1). President Eisenhower sends the marines to Lebanon (July 15). France gains a new constitution, which inaugurates the Fifth Republic (Sept. 28). Iraq's King Faisal is assassinated in a military coup. Alaska becomes the 49th American state. Charles de Gaulle is elected president of France (Dec. 21).

1959: Fidel Castro overthrows Fulgencio Batista in Cuba (Jan. 1); the new government subsequently expropriates sugar mills owned by American firms. Soviet premier Khrushchev visits the United States. American Vice President Richard Nixon visits the Soviet Union and has the "kitchen debate" with Khrushchev. The USSR sends a space probe to the moon and photographs its hidden side. The first commercial photocopier is introduced. The Dalai Lama flees Tibet for India (Mar. 31). The St. Lawrence Seaway opens (Apr. 25); ocean ships begin sailing to the Midwest.

Hawaii becomes the 50th state to join the United States.

1960: An American U-2 spy plane is shot down over the USSR (May 1); Soviet premier Nikita Khrushchev cancels a Soviet-American summit meeting (May 16). Fifty black South African protesters are massacred at Sharpeville. The Congo gains independence from Belgium, sparking civil war and United Nations intervention. Senegal, Ghana, Nigeria and Madagascar gain independence from European rule. Cyprus becomes independent; Archbishop Makarios wins the first presidential election. Israeli agents capture former Nazi official Adolf Eichmann in Argentina (May 23); they smuggle him to Israel for trial. Germany bans neo-Nazi political groups. The two communist giants, China and the USSR, openly feud. John F. Kennedy is elected president in the United States. Nine hundred American military advisors work in South Vietnam. Americans launch the first weather and communications satellites. The first heart pacemaker is developed.

1961: The United States breaks off diplomatic ties with Cuba (Jan. 3). Soviet Major Yuri Gagarin becomes the first man in space (Apr. 12). Aided by the United States, Cuban exiles attempt an invasion of Cuba at the Bay of Pigs but fail to topple Fidel Castro (Apr. 17). Astronaut Alan Shepard becomes the first American to make a suborbital flight in space (May 5). An American astronaut flies over the Atlantic Ocean (July 21). Soviet cosmonaut Gherman Titov orbits the earth in *Vostok II* (Aug. 6). East Germany builds the Berlin Wall to stop its citizens from moving to the West (Aug. 13). The Soviet Union tests a 50-megaton hydrogen bomb, the biggest manmade explosion to date (Oct. 29). Kuwait gains independence from Britain; Britain sends troops to counter Iraqi annexation threats. United Nations Secretary General Dag Hammarskjöld dies in a plane crash over Northern Rhodesia. The number of American military advisors in South Vietnam rises to 2,000. Britain applies for membership in the Common Market. Texas Instruments patents the silicon chip.

1962: Fearing nuclear war, many North Americans build fallout shelters. John Glenn becomes the first American astronaut to orbit the earth (Feb. 20). The United States establishes a military council in South Vietnam. France cedes sovereignty to Algeria after ending their war (July 3). The discovery of Soviet missiles in Cuba leads to an American naval blockade; the Cuban missile crisis ends when Soviet leader Khrushchev agrees to dismantle the bases (August–November). United Nations troops quell rebellion in the Congo's Katanga province. Escorted by federal police, black American James Meredith registers at the all-white University of Mississippi (Oct. 1). The United Nations votes in favour of economic sanctions against South Africa. Pope John XXIII opens the Second Vatican Council to modernize the Roman Catholic Church (Oct. 11). Burundi, Western Samoa, Uganda, Jamaica and Trinidad and Tobago gain independence. Americans launch the TV satellite *Telstar*. Cuba releases more than 1,100 prisoners captured during the Bay of Pigs invasion (Dec. 24). Rachel Carson warns of the dangers posed by manmade toxins in *Silent Spring*.

1963: France and West Germany sign a cooperation treaty (Jan. 27). The United States, Soviet Union and Britain ban nuclear tests in the atmosphere. South Vietnamese leader Ngo Dinh Diem is assassinated in a military coup. The United States sends financial aid to South Vietnam; the number of American military advisers in South Vietnam rises to 15,000. Zanzibar and Kenya gain independence. The British application to join the Common Market is rejected after French opposition. The British government is rocked by the Profumo affair; the scandal forces the resignation of a senior minister (June). Pope John XXIII dies (June 3); Pope Paul VI succeeds him (June 21). The United States Supreme Court rules that no one may require the recitation of Bible verses or the Lord's Prayer in public schools (June 17). Archaeologists find the remains of a thousand-year-old Viking settlement in Newfoundland. Dr. Martin Luther King leads 200,000 people in the March on Washington seeking equality for American blacks (Aug. 28). The White House and the Kremlin establish the "hot line" emergency communications link (Aug. 30) to avert accidental war. The first liver and lung transplants are performed. Soviet cosmonaut Valentina Tereshkova becomes the first female in space. Lee Harvey Oswald assassinates President Kennedy in Dallas, Texas; Lyndon Johnson succeeds Kennedy as president (Nov. 22). Jack Ruby, a nightclub owner, shoots and kills Oswald (Nov. 24). Betty Friedan publishes *The Feminine Mystique*.

1964: Harold Wilson becomes prime minister in Britain. Communist China announces it has developed an atomic bomb. The United States escalates its military role in Vietnam following a reported North Vietnamese attack on American destroyers in the Gulf of Tonkin. In Mississippi, the Ku Klux Klan murders three civil rights workers (June). The President's Commission on the Assassination of President Kennedy—the Warren Commission—concludes that Oswald acted alone. A South African court sentences black leader Nelson Mandela to life imprisonment (June 11). The Palestine Liberation Organization (PLO) is formed. Zambia, Malta and Malawi become independent. The sultan of Zanzibar is banished and the country is declared a republic. Zanzibar unites with Tanganyika to form Tanzania. Northern Rhodesia declares independence and adopts the name Zambia. Leonid Brezhnev and Alexei Kosygin become Soviet leaders after Khrushchev is deposed. International Business Machines (IBM) devises the first word processor. In the United States, the Beatles appear on *The Ed Sullivan Show* and "Beatlemania" sweeps North America.

1965: Police in Alabama arrest Dr. Martin Luther King and 2,600 blacks in Selma during demonstrations against voter registration rules (Feb. 1). American black leader Malcolm X is slain in New York City (Feb. 21). The United States marines land in the Dominican Republic (Apr. 28). A race riot erupts in Watts, Los Angeles, (Aug. 11–16). Ferdinand Marcos is elected president of the Philippines. Gambia and Rhodesia declare independence from Britain. Rhodesia's declaration is met by an oil embargo. A massive power failure blacks out most of the northeastern United States and eastern Canada (Nov. 9). Pope Paul VI reaffirms the Roman Catholic Church's opposition to birth control. A Soviet cosmonaut is the first to leave a spacecraft and "float" in space. Two American *Gemini* capsules rendezvous in space. Ralph Nader critiques the American auto industry in *Unsafe at Any Speed*.

1966: Chairman Mao launches the Great Proletarian Cultural Revolution in China; Red Guards demonstrate against Western influences. Indira Gandhi becomes India's prime minister. Floods destroy art treasures in Florence, Italy. In Houston, Dr. Michael DeBakey implants the first artificial heart in a human (Apr. 21). De Gaulle asks that NATO forces leave France. South African President Hendrik Verwoerd is stabbed to death in parliament. Lesotho and Guyana become independent. Civilian protests against the Vietnam War escalate in the United States. The government in Ghana is overthrown by a military coup. The Soviet Union lands an unmanned spacecraft on the moon.

1967: American manned space flights are suspended after astronauts Grissom, White and Chaffee die in an *Apollo* capsule fire (Jan. 27). Biafra attempts to secede from Nigeria (May 30). Egypt, Syria and Jordan attack Israel in the Six Day War; the war ends with Israel in command of the Sinai Peninsula, the Golan Heights, the Gaza Strip and the east bank of the Suez Canal (June 5). China announces the explosion of its first hydrogen bomb (June 17). Expo 67 opens in Montreal. A Soviet cosmonaut becomes the first reported casualty of the space race. Race riots erupt in American cities during the "long hot summer." Canada celebrates its centennial (July 1). Dr. Christiaan Barnard of South Africa performs the world's first successful human heart transplant (Dec. 3); the patient survives for 18 days.

1968: North Korea captures the American spy ship *Pueblo* (Jan. 23). Vietnamese communists launch the Tet offensive (January–February). American troops in South Vietnam massacre hundreds of civilians at My Lai (Mar. 16). Lyndon Johnson refuses to seek another term as America's president (Mar. 31). Dr. Martin Luther King, Jr., is assassinated in Memphis, Tennessee (Apr. 4). Presidential candidate Robert Kennedy is assassinated in Los Angeles (June 5–6). Soviet troops crush liberalizing reforms in Czechoslovakia (Aug. 20). Sixty-two countries sign a treaty limiting the military use of outer space. University students protest worldwide. Richard Nixon is elected American president. Peace talks between the United States and North Vietnam begin in Paris. The British colony of Mauritius becomes independent. Pope Paul VI issues an encyclical banning artificial birth control. Three American astronauts circle the moon and return to Earth. The unmanned ship *Surveyor 7* lands on the moon.

1969: Yasser Arafat becomes PLO chairman. North Vietnamese leader Ho Chi Minh dies at age 79. The International Red Cross estimates that 1.5 million Biafrans died, mostly by starvation, in the civil war in Nigeria. The United States begins withdrawing troops from Vietnam. The Stonewall riot in New York City marks the beginning of the modern gay rights movement (June 28). American astronauts Neil Armstrong and Edwin Aldrin become the first men to walk on the moon as *Apollo 11* lands on the lunar surface (July 20). More than 400,000 people congregate at Woodstock's music festival in New York (Aug. 15–17). Golda Meir becomes Israeli prime minister. The Concorde supersonic airliner makes its first flight. The *Mariner* space probes transmit pictures of Mars back to earth. *Sesame Street* debuts on American television. The Internet—originally known as (ARPAnet) goes online.

1970: Scientists at the University of Wisconsin announce the first complete synthesis of a gene. Arab commandos hijack three jets bound for New York from Europe. The civil wars in Nigeria end when Biafra capitulates (Jan. 15). Severing its final ties with Britain, Rhodesia declares itself a racially segregated republic (Mar. 1). American troops in Vietnam invade Cambodia (May 1). National Guardsmen kill four students at Kent State University in Ohio during antiwar protests at the campus (May 4); two students are killed at Jackson State following similar demonstrations. The United States Senate repeals the Gulf of Tonkin Resolution (June 24). In Canada, the Front de Libération du Québec (FLQ) kidnaps British trade commissioner James Cross, and kidnaps and murders Quebec cabinet minister Pierre Laporte; the Canadian government responds to this "October Crisis" by invoking the War Measures Act (October–December). Israel and the United Arab Republic declare a 99-day truce in their latest conflict. Gambia becomes a republic. A cyclone and tidal wave hit offshore islands in the Ganges Delta of East Pakistan, leaving at least 168,000 people dead and about 1 million homeless. A coup

attempt in Chile fails to unseat Marxist President Salvador Allende.

1971: American planes bomb Cambodia, attacking Vietcong supply routes. Fighting in Indochina spreads to Laos. The United States conducts large bombing raids against North Vietnam. Antiwar demonstrators disrupt government business in Washington, DC; police arrest as many as 12,000 people (May 3). Communist China replaces Taiwan in the United Nations (Oct. 25). Women win the right to vote in Switzerland. Violence in Northern Ireland escalates after Britain introduces internment without trial. India fights with Bengali rebels against Pakistan. The United States and USSR sign a treaty banning nuclear weapons on the ocean floor. Algeria seizes majority control of all French oil and gas interests within its borders but promises restitution. Idi Amin Dada takes control of Uganda. Mao Tse-tung's heir-apparent, Lin Piao, dies in a mysterious air crash. The USSR soft-lands a space capsule on Mars. A Los Angeles earthquake kills 60 people and causes $1 billion in damage. Dr. Choh Hao Li at the University of California synthesizes the hormone that controls human growth. *The New York Times* publishes the *Pentagon Papers*, revealing American government deception in the conduct of the Vietnam war.

1972: The world's largest diamond (969.8 carats) is unearthed in Sierra Leone. President Richard Nixon meets Mao Tse-tung in China (Feb 21–27). Britain imposes direct rule on Northern Ireland (Mar. 24); violence between Roman Catholics and Protestants kills 467 people. Governor George Wallace of Alabama survives an assassination attempt (May 15). Ceylon becomes a republic and changes its name to Sri Lanka. Philippine President Ferdinand Marcos assumes near-dictatorial powers. A Soviet spacecraft soft-lands on Venus. More than 70 nations sign a treaty prohibiting the stockpiling of biological weapons. The United States conducts its heaviest B-52 bombing raids of the war against North Vietnam but continues to withdraw troops, despite lack of progress at the Paris peace talks. Arab terrorists massacre 11 Israeli athletes in a stand-off with West German police at the summer Olympic Games in Munich (Sept. 5). Richard Leakey and Glynn Isaac discover a 2.5-million-year-old human skull in northern Kenya. A United States federal grand jury indicts seven persons, including two former White House aids, on conspiracy charges for breaking into the Democratic National Headquarters in the Watergate building in Washington, DC. Richard Nixon is re-elected American president.

1973: Britain, Ireland and Denmark formally join the Common Market (Jan. 1). The United States Supreme Court rules on Roe v. Wade, an abortion rights case (Jan. 22). A ceasefire agreement, intended to end the Vietnam war, is signed in Paris (Jan. 27). The United States Senate begins televised hearings on the Watergate scandal; it is revealed that President Nixon secretly taped all conversations in his White House office. Vice President Spiro Agnew resigns when caught evading payment of income taxes. Greece's military junta abolishes the monarchy and declares a republic (June 1). American combat in Indochina officially ends as American planes halt their bombing of Cambodia (Aug. 15). Typhoon Nora leaves 800,000 Filipinos homeless on the island of Luzon. The Bahamas win independence from Britain after three centuries of colonial rule. Chilean President Allende commits suicide during a CIA-backed coup (Sept. 11); a military junta led by General Augusto Pinochet takes power. The Yom Kippur War between Israeli and Arab forces begins (Oct. 6). Arab oil-producing states cut petroleum exports to the United States, Western Europe and Japan because of their support for Israel. Egypt and Israel sign an American-sponsored peace accord (Nov. 11). The Shah of Iran nationalizes foreign-owned oil companies.

1974: Oil-producing nations boost their prices; worldwide inflation accelerates as economic growth slows to near zero in most industrialized nations. China launches a new "Cultural Revolution" aimed at condemning both the Chinese philosopher Confucius and former Defence Minister Lin Piao. West German Chancellor Willy Brandt resigns after a scandal involving an East German spy. The IRA bombs the Tower of London and the British Parliament. Soviet Nobel Prize-winning author Aleksandr Solzhenitsyn is stripped of his citizenship and exiled. The Portuguese dictatorship is ended by a military coup and democratic reforms are initiated.

Rebels supported by Greece overthrow the government in Cyprus: Turkish forces take over much of the island. India explodes a nuclear device. Syria and Israel agree to the boundaries of a demilitarized zone in the Golan Heights, and they begin withdrawing troops from the region. President Richard Nixon resigns to avoid impeachment by Congress for his coverup of the Watergate scandal (Aug. 8). Gerald Ford replaces Nixon as American president (Aug. 9). The United States and the Soviet Union reach a tentative agreement to limit the numbers of their strategic offensive nuclear weapons and delivery vehicles. Severe drought threatens millions in Africa. Scientists warn of the effects of chloroflourocarbons (CFCs) on the ozone layer.

1975: Portugal's new constitution grants most power to the military. Angola, Cape Verde, São Tomé and Principe, and Mozambique gain independence from Portugal. Turkish Cypriots establish a separate state in the northern half of the island. The United States evacuates Vietnam as North Vietnamese forces seizes Saigon. Led by Pol Pot, the Khmer Rouge take over Cambodia (April). Cambodian forces seize the American merchant ship *Mayaguez*; American forces retake the vessel but lose 38 men (May 15). *Soyuz* and *Apollo* spacecraft take off for a US-Soviet link-up in space (July 15). President Ford escapes two assassination attempts (Sept. 5; Sept 22). Egypt reopens the Suez Canal, closed since the 1967 Arab-Israeli war. A United Nations Security Council resolution calling for an arms embargo against South Africa is vetoed by the United States, Britain and France. Generalissimo Franco, Spain's chief of state, dies; King Juan Carlos I replaces him as head of state. A military coup ousts Peru's president; a general assumes power. A democratic republic is proclaimed in Laos. Papua New Guinea and Surinam become independent. Civil war breaks out in Beirut between Christians and Muslims. Rebels in Eritrea provoke battles with the Ethiopian government.

1976: Communist Chinese leaders Chou En-lai and Mao Tse-tung die within months of each other. Riots against apartheid erupt in the all-black township of Soweto outside of Johannesburg and spread to Cape Town. Reports surface that Libyan leader Colonel

Muammar al-Qadhafi is financing, training and arming a terrorist network. Overturning an earlier ruling, the United States Supreme Court declares that the death penalty is constitutionally acceptable (July 3). The United States celebrates its bicentennial (July 4). In Uganda, Israeli airborne commandos free 103 hostages taken by pro-Palestinian hijackers (July 4). Jimmy Carter is elected American president (Nov. 2). The Gang of Four (Mao Tse-tung's widow and three others) attempt a coup in China. Venezuela nationalizes its petroleum industry. The president of Argentina is overthrown by a military junta. Spanish Sahara is released from Spain's jurisdiction and divided between Morocco and Mauritania. North and South Vietnam reunite under a communist government. A military coup in Thailand succeeds. Nine thousand refugees flee Angola's new civil war. Worldwide earthquakes kill an estimated 780,000 people.

1977: American scientists identify the bacterial cause of Legionnaire's Disease (Jan. 21). President Carter pardons draft evaders (Jan. 21). American scientists report using bacteria in labs to create insulin (May 23). Cambodian refugees report mass death following the communists' capture of Phnom Penh. Egypt severs diplomatic relations with Syria, Iraq, Libya, Algeria and South Yemen for disrupting its peace overtures to Israel. More than 570 die in the world's worst aviation disaster when two Boeing 747s collide on the runway on the Canary Island of Tenerife. Black South African leader Steven Biko dies in police custody (Sept. 12). Fifteen countries, including the United States and the USSR, sign a treaty designed to halt the spread of nuclear weapons to other states (Sept. 21). The French territories of Afars and Issa unite to form the Republic of Djibouti. The government of Pakistan is overthrown and martial law is imposed. Leonid Brezhnev becomes the USSR's president and communist party chief. Somalian-backed Eritrean guerrillas are stopped by the Ethiopian army. Thailand's government is seized by a military junta. Rhodesia's white government begins negotiations with the country's black majority. A cyclone in India leaves 20,000 dead and 2 million homeless. Unmanned American spacecraft *Voyager I* and *II* begin journeys to the outer solar system. The neutron bomb, which causes great loss of life but little property damage, is developed in the United States.

1978: In Rhodesia, Prime Minister Ian Smith and three black leaders agree to move toward black-majority rule (Feb. 15). The United States Senate votes to transfer control of the Panama Canal to Panama by 2000 (Apr. 18). A Soviet-supported military junta takes power in Afghanistan. In Italy, Red Brigades kidnap Italy's former premier Aldo Moro (Mar. 16); Moro is found dead (May 6). Christian and Muslim militias and Palestinian guerrillas plague Lebanon; the Arab League intervenes to try to restore peace. Israeli forces withdraw. Syria declares a unilateral ceasefire in and around Beirut, Lebanon. Egyptian President Anwar Sadat and Israeli Premier Menachem Begin sign peace accords, mediated by President Jimmy Carter (Sept. 17). Shah Mohammed Reza Pahlevi of Iran imposes martial law to suppress antigovernment demonstrations. Sandinista guerrillas attempt to overthrow the government of Nicaraguan President Anastasio Somoza. The United States establishes full diplomatic relations with communist China. The first peaceful transfer of power takes place in Dominican Republic. Zaïre (formerly the Congo) is invaded by secessionist rebels: African nations, France and Belgium send defence aid after the massacre of Europeans. A military junta seizes power in Honduras. The army seizes power in Bolivia. John Paul II (Karol Wojtyla) of Poland becomes the first non-Italian Pope in four centuries (Oct. 16). The first "test-tube baby"—a human baby conceived outside the womb—is born in Britain. The followers of Reverend Jim Jones commit mass suicide in Jonestown, Guyana (Nov. 18).

1979: The Vietnamese army invades Cambodia, takes Phnom Penh and overthrows Pol Pot (Jan. 7). Oil spills pollute the Atlantic and Gulf of Mexico (Jan. 1; June 8; July 21). The Shah of Iran flees his country (Jan. 16); Islamic revolutionaries under the leadership of Ayatollah Khomeini take control of Iran (Feb. 1). A malfunction in the cooling system of a nuclear reactor at Three Mile Island in Pennsylvania closes down the reactor and radiation escapes into the air (Mar. 28). Conservative Margaret Thatcher becomes Britain's first female prime minister (May 3).

A black government is installed in Rhodesia; the country's name changes to Zimbabwe. China and the United States establish formal commercial relations for the first time since 1949. St. Vincent and the Grenadines and St. Lucia become independent. A coup in Grenada occurs. President Idi Amin Dada of Uganda is overthrown. Egypt is expelled from the Arab League after signing the Camp David peace treaty. The first elections for the European Parliament are held. The US-USSR SALT (Strategic Arms Limitation Treaty) Agreement is signed in Vienna (June 14). In Nicaragua, President Anastasio Somoza Debayle resigns and flees to Miami (July 17); the Sandinistas form a revolutionary government (July 19). A bomb blast kills Earl Mountbatten—a World War II hero—and three others on a boat off the Irish coast (Aug. 27). Iranian students demanding the Shah's return to stand trial seize hostages at the American embassy (Nov. 4). Iran nationalizes its remaining privately owned industries without providing compensation. Sharp oil price increases contribute to high inflation worldwide. South Korean President Park Chung Hee and his chief body guard are assassinated by a government official. Emperor Bokassa of the Central African Empire is overthrown. The president of El Salvador is ousted by a military coup. The Soviet Union invades Afghanistan to prop up the native communist government (Dec. 27); the Soviet occupation stirs protest worldwide.

1980: Six American embassy aides escape from Iran with Canadian help (Jan. 29). The United States breaks diplomatic relations with Iran (Apr. 7). An American attempt to rescue the remaining hostages in Tehran fails; eight American troops die and five are injured when a helicopter and cargo plane crash in the Iranian desert (Apr. 15). The United States Supreme Court upholds limits on federal aid for abortions (June 30). The Shah of Iran dies in exile (July 27). Soviet dissident Andrei Sakharov, a Nobel Prize-winning physicist, is arrested in Moscow. Human interferon, a promising natural disease-fighting substance, is made by gene splicing. Mt. St. Helens erupts in Washington State; the blast sends debris 20 km up into the atmosphere. In a political comeback, Indira Gandhi wins a landslide victory in India's parliamentary elections. In response

to the Soviet war in Afghanistan, the United States bans the sale of grain and high technology to the Soviet Union, and 50 nations boycott the Moscow Olympics. Roman Catholic Archbishop Oscar Arnulfo Romero, an El Salvadoran reformer, is assassinated while saying mass. Some 10,800 Cubans seek asylum in Peru's Cuban embassy, and more than 125,000 Cubans escape by boat to the United States. Former Nicaraguan dictator Anastasio Somoza Debayle is assassinated in Paraguay (Sept. 17). Liberian President William Tolbert, Jr., is killed in a coup. A military coup occurs in Turkey. Zimbabwe gains independence from Britain. About 350 Bengalis are massacred by tribal people in India. Black guerrillas successfully bomb two South African petroleum plants and a refinery. Large labour strikes in Poland force the government to allow independent trade unions, including Solidarity, led by Lech Walesa. Twenty bomb attacks take place in France. The Iran-Iraq war begins when Iraqi fighter-bombers attack Iranian airfields and lay siege to Iran's southwestern cities (Sept. 19). Ronald Reagan is elected American president (Nov. 4). Three American nuns and a lay worker are found murdered in El Salvador (Dec. 4). Earthquakes in southern Italy kill 3,000 people. Twenty thousand people die in two earthquakes in Algeria. *Voyager I* sends back the first pictures of Saturn. The wreck of the *Titanic* is found in the North Atlantic. John Lennon of the Beatles is shot dead in New York City (Dec. 8). Smallpox is vanquished.

1981: Iran releases 52 American hostages on the day that President Ronald Reagan is sworn into office (Jan. 20). A gunman wounds President Reagan and aides (Mar. 30). Aquired Immune Deficiency Syndrome (AIDS) is discovered in the United States. In El Salvador, heavy fighting occurs between the government and leftist insurgents. The world's first reusable spacecraft, the space shuttle *Columbia*, flies into space. Sandra Day O'Connor becomes the first woman nominated to sit on the United States Supreme Court (July 7). Clashes between Syrian troops and Christian militiamen in Lebanon prompt Israeli bombing in support of Christian forces. Artificial bone and skin are developed in the United States. Pope John Paul II is shot and wounded outside the Vatican by a Turkish terrorist (May 14). Israel is condemned worldwide after Israeli warplanes destroy an Iraqi atomic reactor near Baghdad. Irish prisoners in Belfast stage hunger strikes to force the British government to grant political-prisoner status to Irish nationalist inmates, and some die. South African troops invade Angola in pursuit of guerrillas. Belize, formerly British Honduras, becomes independent. Muslim extremists murder President Anwar el-Sadat of Egypt during a military parade. Israel formally annexes the Golan Heights. Ecuador and Peru fight a five-day war. Greece joins the European Community. The Italian government is rocked by revelations that nearly 1,000 key government, army and business leaders support a secret outlawed Masonic lodge. The president of Bangladesh is assassinated. The Iranian president, prime minister and 29 others die in a bomb attack. Five thousand people die when an Indonesian ferry sinks in the Java Sea. The Polish regime declares martial law in the face of continued labour unrest. IBM introduces the personal computer in the United States.

1982: Argentina invades the Falkland Islands (Malvinas); Britain defeats Argentina in the subsequent war (Apr. 2–June 15). Canada's constitution is patriated from Britain. The Israelis turn the Sinai over to Egypt, fulfilling their 1979 peace treaty. Israel invades Lebanon to attack the PLO (June 4); PLO leaders leave Lebanon under United Nations protection. A series of IRA bombs explode in London, killing nine and wounding 51. In the United States, proponents of the Equal Rights Amendment fail to win ratification (June 30). Western nations debate a proposed Soviet oil pipeline to western Europe. Lech Walesa, former leader of Solidarity, the outlawed Polish labour union, is freed after 11 months in prison. Military coups occur in Bangladesh and Guatemala. Princess Grace of Monaco dies in a car accident (Sept. 14). In West Beirut, Lebanese Christian Phalangists massacre Palestinians in refugee camps (Sept. 15); Israel is accused of indirectly aiding the attack. Iran invades Iraq. Soviet leader Leonid Brezhnev dies (Nov. 10); Yuri Andropov succeeds him (Nov. 15). In Cambodia, support for the Khmer Rouge grows as Prince Sihanouk joins a coalition against the Vietnamese-backed government.

As many as 1,200 Afghanistani civilians and Soviet soldiers die in a tunnel explosion caused by the collision of two trucks. The first permanent artificial heart is transplanted into Dr. Barney B. Clark, 61, in Utah (Dec. 2). The Mexican volcano, El Chichón, erupts, blasting debris into the stratosphere.

1983: The second American space shuttle, *Challenger*, makes a successful maiden voyage (Apr. 4). Bolivia deports Klaus Barbie, former chief of the German Gestapo in Lyons, France, during World War II, to France to face charges of crimes against humanity. France, Spain, the United States and Britain expel Soviet citizens and diplomats accused of espionage. The United States government illegally aids Nicaraguan Contra rebels. Anti-government protests increase in Chile. Ethiopia appeals for aid for 4 million victims of drought and famine. Sally Ride, 32, becomes the first American woman to fly into space (June 18). The United States government admits to shielding Klaus Barbie after World War II (Aug. 15). Sri Lankan Sinhalese and Tamil forces clash, killing hundreds and destroying the homes of thousands of others. About 1,200 people die in an earthquake in Turkey. The Polish regime lifts martial law. The Organization of Petroleum Exporting Countries (OPEC) agrees to cut crude oil prices for the first time in its 23-year history. Benigno Aquino, an opponent of Philippine President Ferdinand Marcos, returns to Manila and is assassinated (Aug. 21). The Soviet Union shoots down a South Korean airliner, claiming that the plane had been spying when it strayed into Soviet airspace; all 269 passengers die (Aug. 30). Suicide terrorists kill 241 American marines and sailors and 40 French paratroopers—all members of a multinational peacekeeping force in Lebanon (Oct. 23). The United States and France support Chad's government against Libyan-supported guerrillas. The Israeli withdrawal from Lebanon is followed by fighting between Lebanese ethnic and religious groups. American-led forces invade Grenada (Oct. 25). American cruise missiles are deployed in Britain despite Soviet and civilian opposition. White South Africans approve a new constitution granting limited political participation for persons of mixed race and Asians, but not for blacks, in a new tricameral legislature.

Yasser Arafat and PLO guerrillas are evacuated under United Nations sponsorship from Lebanon to Tunis. Riots in Assam, India, claim 5,000 lives; 300,000 refugees flee. The compact disc is introduced. After an 11-year journey in space, *Pioneer 10* leaves the solar system.

1984: France receives the first delivery of Soviet natural gas (Jan. 1). The United States and the Vatican exchange diplomats after a 116-year interlude (Jan. 10). After finishing a 10-year study, American researchers link cholesterol to heart disease. The Apple Macintosh with clickable mouse enters the personal computer market. Konstantin Chernenko becomes Soviet leader (Feb. 9) following the death of Yuri Andropov. American astronauts fly free of the space shuttle *Challenger*, the first humans to do so without a tether. Italy and the Vatican agree to end Roman Catholicism as Italy's state religion (Feb. 18). American and United Nations forces withdraw from Lebanon. President Reagan ends the American role in Beirut by withdrawing the Sixth Fleet from the international peacekeeping force (Mar. 30). French and American researchers, working separately, say they have identified viruses that appear to cause AIDS. Iran and Iraq attack Saudi, Greek and Swiss tankers in the Persian Gulf; Saudi Arabia shoots down two Iranian jets. The United States Congress rebukes President Reagan for using federal funds to mine Nicaraguan harbours (Apr. 10). Daniel Ortega, the Sandinista leader, wins in Nicaraguan elections. The Soviet Union withdraws from the Olympic Games in Los Angeles (May 7); other Soviet allies follow suit. José Napoleón Duarte becomes president of El Salvador (May 11). Hundreds die in a battle for the Golden Temple in Amritsar between Sikh militants and police in India (June 6). In New Delhi, Indian Prime Minister Indira Gandhi is slain by her two Sikh bodyguards; anti-Sikh riots kill 1,000 people and Rajiv Gandhi becomes prime minister (Oct. 31). Several countries send aid to starving Ethiopians. President Reagan is re-elected (Nov. 6). In a secret operation, Israel airlifts 25,000 Ethiopian Jews (Falashas) out of the Sudan. Britain and China finalize an agreement which guarantees Hong Kong's capitalist system for 50 years after the colony's return to China in 1997. A Union

Carbide chemical plant leaks poison gas and kills 2,500 in Bhopal, India (Dec. 3). The European Space Agency launches the largest telecommunications satellite in the world.

1985: South African police kill 18 blacks commemorating the Sharpville massacre in 1960; 19 more are killed in a funeral procession. Later the South African government declares an emergency. Daniel Ortega becomes president of Nicaragua. President Reagan urges military aid to Nicaraguan opposition forces, but Congress approves only humanitarian aid. Soviet leader Konstantin Chernenko dies (Mar. 11). Iraq turns back an Iranian military offensive. Shiite Muslim hijackers release hostages after 17 days of captivity in Beirut, having demanded the release of hundreds of Shiites detained by Israeli forces. Argentina's president imposes drastic measures to cut an inflation rate of 1,010 percent. Top French officials are linked to the bombing of the *Rainbow Warrior*, a ship owned by Greenpeace, in New Zealand. Two leading Soviet KGB officials defect to Britain and the United States, where both name Soviet spies in the two countries. A cyclone and tidal waves hit Bangladesh, killing 10,000. A Mexican earthquake kills more than 7,000 and leaves thousands homeless. A border dispute between Mali and Burkina Faso leads to war but is eventually referred to the International Court of Justice. Nicaragua suspends civil rights. Four Palestinians seize the Italian cruise ship *Achille Lauro* near Egypt and murder an American (Oct. 7–8). President Reagan and new Soviet leader Mikhail Gorbachev meet at "the fireside summit," the first superpower summit in six years (Nov. 19). Ninety-five Colombians die when 60 rebels seize the Palace of Justice in Bogotá and take more than 300 hostages. In Malta, 60 passengers die when Egyptian forces storm a hijacked Egyptian jetliner (Nov. 23–24). A volcanic eruption in Colombia kills 20,000 people. Guatemala elects its first civilian president following three decades of military rule. Uruguay's military government is replaced by a civilian government. The Sudanese and Ugandan presidents are ousted by military coups. Terrorists kill 20 people at airports in Rome and Vienna, both at the ticket counters of El Al, Israel's national airline. The Live Aid rock concert in

London and Philadelphia raises more than $60 million for African famine relief.

1986: Portugal and Spain join the European Economic Community (Jan. 1). The *Voyager II* spacecraft passes Uranus (Jan. 26). The American space shuttle *Challenger* explodes one minute after liftoff; all seven crew members die (Jan. 28). Jean-Claude Duvalier, Haiti's "president for life," flees to France in the face of nationwide protest (Feb. 7). Philippine President Ferdinand Marcos flees to the United States after allegations of electoral fraud; his newly elected opponent, Corazon Aquino, becomes president (Feb. 26). Portugal elects its first civilian president in 60 years. Mikhail Gorbachev calls for "radical reform" of the Soviet economy and reshapes the leadership of the communist party. Swedish Prime Minister Olof Palme is assassinated (Feb. 28). Former United Nations secretary general Kurt Waldheim is elected president of Austria. Waldheim's service as a German officer in Yugoslavia during World War II is revealed (Mar. 3). The United States bombs Libya, citing retaliation after missile attacks (Apr. 14). In South Africa, Desmond Tutu is elected archbishop (Apr. 14). An accident occurs at the Chernobyl nuclear plant in the USSR (Apr. 26); escaped radiation spreads across Europe. The United States Supreme Court reaffirms abortion rights (June 11). The World Court declares that the United States broke international law by mining Nicaragua's harbours (June 27). South African forces attack African National Congress (ANC) bases in neighbouring Botswana, Zambia and Zimbabwe. *The New York Times* first links Panama's General Manuel Noriega with drug and arms trafficking. President Reagan publicly acknowledges his government's role in the "Iran-Contra Affair": the illegal sale of weapons to Iran in exchange for cash used to fund Contra rebels in Nicaragua (November). In Rome, Israeli agents kidnap Mordechai Vanunu, the Israeli technician who alerted the world to Israel's nuclear weapons plant in Dimona, and return him to Israel to stand trial.

1987: Soviet leader Mikhail Gorbachev begins a campaign for openness (glasnost) and reconstruction (perestroika). Tamil separatists kill hundreds of Sri Lankans, mostly Sinhalese, and clash with government forces.

German pilot Mathias Rust, 19, embarrasses the Soviets when he lands his single-engine Cessna in Red Square, Moscow. Moscow's communist party chief, Boris Yeltsin, is dismissed after criticizing Mikhail Gorbachev. South Africa withdraws its troops from Angola. An Iraqi warplane's missile kills 37 American sailors aboard the USS *Stark* in the Persian Gulf (May 17); the United States escorts Kuwaiti oil tankers despite the danger posed by the Iran-Iraq war. Four hundred Iranian pilgrims in Mecca die in battles with Saudi police. Prime Minister Margaret Thatcher wins a rare third term in Britain (June 11). A French court sentences Klaus Barbie to life imprisonment for war crimes (July 4). The United States Congress holds an inquiry into the Iran-Contra affair (July–August). Twenty-four nations sign a treaty to protect the ozone layer. Portugal and China agree that the Portuguese colony of Macao will return to China in 1999. Stock market prices plunge worldwide. The Palestinian intifada (uprising) begins against Israeli authorities in the Gaza Strip and West Bank; thousands of protesters are imprisoned. An Israeli court convicts Mordechai Vanunu of treason and sentences him to 18 years in prison. Syrian troops enter Beirut, attempting to impose a ceasefire. The Lebanese prime minister dies in a bomb attack. A military coup ousts a coalition government in Chad. Two thousand people die in the Philippines when a ferry sinks.

1988: Nicaraguan Contras and the Sandinista government reach a ceasefire agreement. The United States and Soviet Union sign a treaty on intermediate-range nuclear forces (INF). Soviet troops begin to pull out of Afghanistan after a nine-year occupation. Nationalist groups in Soviet-controlled Azerbaijan and Armenia clash. Colombian drug cartels defy government attempts to bring them to justice and fight among themselves. An American warship accidentally shoots down a commercial Iranian airliner over the Persian Gulf, killing all 290 persons aboard (July 3). The Soviet communist party backs Mikhail Gorbachev's plan for perestroika. Iran and Iraq agree on a ceasefire to end their eight-year war. Iraq uses poison gas on its Kurdish minority and razes Kurdish villages. Libya and Chad formally end their war. Thailand and Laos fight a brief border war. Ethiopia and Somalia end 11 years of border disputes with a peace treaty. Solidarity supporters stage widespread strikes in Poland. A military coup occurs in Burma; thousands die in antigovernment riots. Yugoslavia's inflation rate tops 250 percent; ethnic Albanians in Kosovo demand freedom from Serbian rule. An explosion on board a plane kills Pakistani President Zia ul-Haq (Aug. 17). George Bush, Sr., is elected president of the United States (Nov. 8). Benazir Bhutto, daughter of a former Pakistani president, becomes the first female prime minister of Pakistan (Dec. 1). Two hundred and fifty-nine people die when a bomb blows up a Pan Am jetliner over Lockerbie, Scotland (Dec. 21). Twenty-five thousand Armenians die during an earthquake.

1989: The Canada-United States Free Trade Agreement takes effect (Jan. 1). Japanese Prime Minister Noboru Takeshita is toppled by financial scandal. Japan's Emperor Hirohito dies (Jan. 7). Iran's Ayatollah Khomeini calls for the execution of British author Salman Rushdie for blaspheming the prophet Mohammed in *The Satanic Verses* (Feb. 14). The oiltanker *Exxon Valdez* runs aground in Alaska and creates a massive oil spill; the environmental disaster is one of the worst in American history (Mar. 24). The Soviet Union holds historic multicandidate parliamentary elections and Boris Yeltsin emerges as Russian leader. Chinese students lead more than one million in demonstrations for democratic reforms in Beijing's Tiananmen Square, but the government ends the protest by sending tanks and killing thousands (Apr. 19–June 4). A United States jury convicts Lieutenant-Colonel Oliver North for his role in the Iran-Contra affair (May 4). Hungary opens its border with Austria and moves toward political and economic reform. Anti-communist forces continue to battle the government in Afghanistan. Mikhail Gorbachev becomes Soviet president (May 25). P.W. Botha quits as South Africa's president (Aug. 14). Fighting between Christians and Muslims in Beirut intensifies. Ninety people die in ethnic violence in Soviet Uzbekistan. Poles participate in their first open election in 40 years, and Solidarity wins a solid victory. The three Baltic states—Estonia, Latvia and Lithuania—protest Soviet domination. A Colombian presidential candidate is slain, prompting a renewed crackdown on illegal drug traffickers. Thousands of East Germans flee to West Germany; the East German government proposes political reforms. Vietnamese forces withdraw from Cambodia. The Burmese dictatorship imposes martial law, arrests thousands (including democratic activist Aung San Suu Kyi) and renames the country Myanmar. The spaceship *Atlantis* is launched on a journey to Jupiter. Panama's General Manuel Noriega annuls presidential elections after an opposition party victory. Eighty nations agree to limit the production of chlorofluorocarbons (CFCs) to protect the ozone layer. Paraguay's president is toppled by a military coup. The *Voyager II* spacecraft reaches Neptune (Aug. 29). East Germany opens the Berlin Wall after 28 years and lifts visa and emigration restrictions (Nov. 11). Tens of thousands demonstrate in Czechoslovakia and force the communist government to resign; dissident playwright Vaclav Havel is elected president. East German communist leader Erich Honecker is removed from power, and is later charged with corruption. Romanian President Nicolae Ceausescu is overthrown and hastily executed with his wife for genocide, abuse of power and theft (Dec. 15–25). The United States invades Panama (Dec. 20); Noriega goes into hiding.

1990: Panama's Manuel Noriega surrenders to American authorities (Jan. 3). Violence erupts in Soviet Azerbaijan as Azerbaijanis attack Armenians. Yugoslavia's communists end their 45-year monopoly on power (Jan. 22). Communists in the Soviet Union relinquish their monopoly on power (Feb. 7). Violeta Chamorro defeats Sandinista leader Daniel Ortega to become the Nicaraguan president. The South African government lifts restrictions on opposition organizations and declares an amnesty for political prisoners. Black leader Nelson Mandela is freed after 27 years in prison (Feb. 11). The United States, France, Britain and the Soviet Union reach agreement on a reunited Germany. Lithuania proclaims its sovereignty and Soviet troops move in. Namibia gains independence from South Africa. Newly released Soviet documents prove Soviet secret police killed 15,000 Polish military officers in the Katyn forest massacre of 1940. The $1.5-billion Hubble Space Telescope is sent into space (Apr. 25); its flawed light-gathering mirrors distort transmissions. Iran's worst earthquake kills 40,000. More than 1,400 Muslim pilgrims to Mecca suffocate in a stampede in an overcrowded tunnel. An American court overturns Oliver North's conviction in the Iran-Contra scandal (July 20). Ukraine declares its sovereignty within the Soviet Union. Czechoslovakia and Romania hold their first free elections in the postwar era. Iraq invades Kuwait over disagreements regarding oil production (Aug. 2); Iraq appears ready to invade Saudi Arabia. The United Nations passes sweeping trade and financial sanctions against Iraq, and aid and troops pour into Saudi Arabia. Civil war in black South African townships kills hundreds. The first human gene therapy for disease is done by blood transfusion. South Africa bans racial discrimination in public places. Mozambique adopts a constitution allowing for a multiparty democracy. Civil war in Chad ends with the overthrow of the president. A military coup in Bangladesh unseats the president. Soviet President Mikhail Gorbachev proposes the Union Treaty to restructure the Soviet Union. The two Germanys reunite, merging their economic, legal and political systems (Oct. 3). Helmut Kohl is elected chancellor of unified Germany. Mikhail Gorbachev assumes emergency powers (Nov. 17). British Prime Minister Margaret Thatcher resigns (Nov. 22). Lech Walesa is elected president of Poland (Dec. 9). The African National Congress (ANC) holds its first conference in South Africa in 31 years. Reverend Jean-Bertrand Aristide is elected president of Haiti (Dec. 17). Eduard Shevardnadze resigns as Soviet foreign minister. Slovenia and Croatia initiate their secession from Yugoslavia.

1991: Iraq ignores the deadline for withdrawal from Kuwait (Jan. 15); Allied forces (including the United States, Canada, Britain, France, Italy, Japan, Pakistan and members of the Arab League) launch a six-week air attack (Jan. 15). The United States and Italy begin the rescue of foreigners trapped in Somalia's civil war. Limited integration of schools begins in South Africa; sweeping legal reforms of apartheid are proposed. The Allies launch a ground assault on Iraqi forces; an informal ceasefire ends the war (Apr. 3). A deadly earthquake rocks Pakistan and Afghanistan. Lithuanians vote to secede from the Soviet Union; Estonia and Latvia

follow suit. The Soviets suppress independence movements in the Baltic republics. Violent antigovernment protests occur in Belgrade. Europeans end their sanctions against South Africa (Apr. 15). The communist regime in Albania resigns (June 4). Jiang Qing, Mao Tse-tung's widow and a leader of the Gang of Four, commits suicide (June 4). The Kuwaiti government resigns after failing to establish postwar order. A United Nations ceasefire formally ends the Gulf War in April and Kurds flee from Iraq. South Africa's parliament repeals apartheid laws (June 5). The Warsaw Pact dissolves (July 1). President Bush and Mikhail Gorbachev negotiate an arms limitation treaty (July 31). The Soviet republic of Georgia votes for independence. China accepts the nuclear nonproliferation treaty (Aug. 10). Rajiv Gandhi is assassinated during India's election campaign. Boris Yeltsin is elected president of Russia. Fighting between the Yugoslav military and Slovenian nationalists escalates. Soviet hardliners attempt a coup against Mikhail Gorbachev: its failure accelerates the dissolution of the communist party and Soviet state. Rebels oust Haitian President Jean-Bertrand Aristide. Serbia and Croatia reach a political settlement but civil war continues. Israel and the Soviet Union resume relations after 24 years (Oct. 18). Lebanese terrorists free Anglican envoy Terry Waite and professor Thomas Sutherland (Nov. 14). A peace accord is signed in El Salvador, paving the way to end an 11-year civil war. Warring factions in Cambodia sign a peace accord. Rebels fighting in Somalia claim to take over Mogadishu and depose the president. Gorbachev resigns as the USSR formally dissolves; the Commonwealth of Independent States (CIS) succeeds the USSR (Dec. 25). Germany recognizes Slovenia and Croatia as independent states. The Islamic Salvation Front leads in Algerian elections. Sierra Leone's civil war begins. The World Wide Web debuts on the Internet. Throughout the year, a cholera epidemic kills 3,500 in Latin America and 12,500 in Africa.

1992: Algeria's national assembly is dissolved to prevent Islamists from taking power after democratic elections (Jan. 4); the move provokes a seven-year terrorist war that kills about 150,000 Algerians. Russia begins experimenting with free markets (January);

the "shock therapy" triggers soaring inflation and consumer shortages. Yugoslavia breaks up (Jan. 15). Presidents Bush and Yeltsin formally proclaim the end of the Cold War (Feb. 1). The United States lifts trade sanctions against China (Feb. 21). Bosnia-Herzegovina declares independence from Yugoslavia (Mar. 3); civil war worsens in the territory throughout the year. White South Africans vote in a referendum to end apartheid and create a multiracial government (Mar. 18). In Peru, President Alberto Fujimori illegally dissolves congress and suspends constitutional rights; he cites the need to crush Shining Path guerrillas and drug barons (Apr. 5). The United Nations sends forces to Somalia to aid 4.5 million people threatened by starvation and civil war (April); the year-long mission fails to end the fighting. A race riot breaks out in Los Angeles after a court acquits four white policemen of beating motorist Rodney King, a black man (Apr. 29). In Brazil, Rio de Janeiro hosts the United Nation's "Earth Summit"; 108 world leaders and 30,000 participants discuss worldwide environmental protection (June 3–14). In Lebanon, terrorists free their last Western hostages (June 29). An American court sentences General Noriega, Panama's former dictator, to 40 years in prison for narcotics offences (July 10). An American court overturns the conviction of Joseph Hazelwood, former captain of the oiltanker *Exxon Valdez*, for negligence (July 10). Hurricane Andrew devastates Florida (August). The United Nations expels Yugoslavia, which now consists of Serbia and Montenegro, from the General Assembly (Sept. 22). The United States Senate ratifies the second Strategic Arms Limitation Treaty (Oct. 1). The *Pioneer* spacecraft plunges into the scorching atmosphere of Venus, ending a 14-year mission (Oct. 12). Americans elect Democrats Bill Clinton as president and Al Gore as vice president (Nov. 3). The Russian parliament approves the START Treaty (Nov. 4). American forces leave the Philippines, ending a military presence that lasted almost a century (Nov. 24). In Britain, Prince Charles and Princess Diana agree to separate (Dec. 9). President Bush pardons officials in President Reagan's administration who were involved in the Iran-Contra affair (Dec. 24).

1993: Czechoslovakia peacefully divides into the Czech and Slovak Republics (Jan. 1). President Clinton agrees to compromise on the American military's ban on homosexuals (Jan. 29). In New York, six die and more than 1,000 are injured when Muslim fundamentalists explode a car bomb inside the World Trade Center (Feb. 26). The United States begins airlifting supplies to besieged Bosnian towns (Feb. 28). In Waco, Texas, federal agents besiege a compound of Branch Davidians after six are killed in a raid; the siege ends in a paramilitary assault on the compound and the death of 72 Branch Davidians (Mar. 1–Apr. 19). One of the longest civil wars in Africa ends when Eritreans vote for independence from Ethiopia in a United Nations-supervised referendum (Apr. 23–25). More than 300,000 people march on Washington, DC, to demand equal rights for homosexuals (Apr. 25). The president of Sri Lanka is murdered (May 1). The United Nations declares "safe areas" in Bosnia to protect civilians from civil war (May 6). Twenty-two troops belonging to the United Nations are killed in Somalia (June 5). Iraq accepts United Nations weapons monitoring (July 19). Vincent Foster, Jr., a legal advisor to President Clinton, commits suicide (July 22). In Washington, DC, Palestinian leader Yasser Arafat and Israeli Prime Minister Yitzak Rabin endorse a peace agreement negotiated in Norway; it grants Palestinian autonomy and recognizes Israel's right to exist (Sept. 13). In Russia, President Yeltsin dissolves parliament and declares new elections; his parliamentary opponents name Vice President Rutskoi acting head of state and barricade themselves in the parliament; Yeltsin's forces besiege parliament and crush a communist riot; the parliamentarians surrender (Sept. 21–Oct. 4). In Burundi, the murder of President Melchior Ndadaye and six ministers during a failed military coup provokes ethnic violence and sends thousands of refugees into Rwanda (October). In Somalia, American troops battle militiamen loyal to warlord Mohammed Farah Aidid in Mogadishu (Oct. 3). China breaks a moratorium on nuclear tests (Oct. 5). Europe's Maastricht Treaty takes effect, creating the European Union (Nov. 1). The North American Free Trade Agreement (NAFTA) is approved by the United States House of Representatives (Nov. 17) and Senate (Nov.

21). A new Russian constitution grants sweeping powers to the president (December). Pablo Escobar, Colombia's wealthiest narcotics baron, is killed while escaping police (Dec. 2). South Africa's parliament ratifies a new constitution that requires majority rule (Dec. 22).

1994: In Mexico, armed Zapatista rebels in Chiapas demand land reforms and recognition of native Indian rights (Jan. 1). An earthquake jolts California (Jan. 17). A Bosnian Serb mortar attack on a marketplace in besieged Sarajevo kills 66 and injures 200 (Feb. 5). President Clinton ends the American trade embargo on Vietnam (Feb. 9). A militant Jewish settler massacres 29 Palestinians praying in a mosque in Hebron (Feb. 25). Luis Colosio, the leading presidential candidate in Mexico's election, is shot dead (Mar. 23). In Rwanda, President Habyarimana dies when his plane is shot down; Hutu radicals begin killing 800,000 Tutsis and moderate Hutus in about 100 days (Apr. 6). Nelson Mandela is elected president in South Africa's first multiracial national election (Apr. 29). Palestinian leader Arafat and Israeli Prime Minister Rabin sign the accord that begins Palestinian self-rule in the Gaza Strip and Jericho (May 4). The United States Supreme Court approves limits on protests against abortion (June 30). Kim Il Sung, North Korea's communist dictator, dies (July 8); his son, Kim Jong Il, succeeds him. A string of comet fragments known as Shoemaker-Levy 9 crash into Jupiter, causing massive explosions in the planet's atmosphere—the first such collisions in the solar system ever witnessed by humans (July 16–22). In Sudan, French agents capture international terrorist Ilich Ramirez Sanchez— "Carlos the Jackal" (Aug. 14). The IRA declares a ceasefire in Northern Ireland (Aug. 31). An American-led force lands in Haiti (Sept. 19). Exiled Haitian President Jean-Bertrand Aristide returns home to a joyous welcome (Oct. 4). Earthquakes rock Japan (Oct. 4). The United States sends forces to the Persian Gulf (Oct. 7). Ulster Protestants declare a ceasefire (Oct. 13). Israel and Jordan normalize relations (Nov. 6). President Clinton orders an end to the Bosnian arms embargo (Nov. 10). The Russian military attack on secessionist Chechnya begins (Dec. 11). Bosnian Serb militiamen kidnap

United Nations peacekeepers and use them as human shields to halt NATO air strikes (December). Throughout 1994, German officials seize shipments of plutonium apparently smuggled out of Russia.

1995: In Japan, Kobe is struck by a deadly earthquake (Jan. 17). The United States rescues Mexico from a financial crisis with a US$20 billion loan but imposes austerity measures and requires the reform of Mexico's electoral process (Feb. 21). In Singapore, at the 232-year-old Barings Bank, a rogue trader's speculation on the currency market costs the bank US$1.4 billion; Barings collapses (Feb. 26). In Japan, the Aum Shinrikyo ("Supreme Truth") cult releases nerve gas in a Tokyo subway during rush hour, leaving at least eight dead and 5,500 injured (Mar. 20); two more incidents occur in April in Yokohama before police find and arrest Shoko Asahara, the cult's leader. The United Nation's Security Council votes for easier sanctions against Iraq (Apr. 14). In Oklahoma City, Timothy McVeigh— a Persian Gulf War veteran sympathetic to radical American militiamen—detonates a car bomb outside a federal government building, killing 168 people and injuring more than 400 (Apr. 19). Fighting escalates in Bosnia and Croatia (May 1). The military regime in Myanmar (formerly Burma) frees democratic activist Aung San Suu Kyi from house arrest (July 10). Croatian troops regain territory in Krajina that had been lost to Croatian Serbs in 1991 (August). An American space shuttle docks with the Russian space station (Aug. 11). France explodes a nuclear device in the South Pacific despite international protests (Sept. 5). China hosts the United Nation's Fourth World Conference on Women; women from 185 countries meet in Beijing (September). Israelis and Palestinians agree to transfer the West Bank to the Arabs (Sept. 24). In Los Angeles, a jury finds ex-football player O.J. Simpson not guilty of murder (Oct. 3). Pope John Paul II visits the United States (Oct. 4–8). Louis Farrakhan of the Nation of Islam draws hundreds of thousands of black men to Washington, DC, in the "Million Man March" (Oct. 16). In Israel, a Jewish law student kills Prime Minister Rabin (Nov. 4). Nigeria's military regime executes Ken Saro-Wiwa, an Ogoni activist, and eight others

(Nov. 10). In Poland, ex-communist Alexander Kwasniewski defeats President Lech Walesa in elections (Nov. 19). The Irish vote to end the constitutional ban on divorce (Nov. 24). The Dayton Accord, negotiated in November at an air force base in Ohio, ends Bosnia's civil war (Dec. 14). The *Galileo* spacecraft arrives at Jupiter after travelling 3.7 billion km over six years; *Galileo* drops a probe into Jupiter's atmosphere (Dec. 15).

1996: Francois Mitterand, former president of France, dies (Jan. 8). France conducts a nuclear test (Jan. 27); President Jacques Chirac declares an end to further tests (Jan. 29). The IRA ends a 17-month ceasefire by bombing the Docklands in London (Feb. 10). Cuban fighter planes shoot down two civilian American aircraft for violating Cuban air space (Feb. 24). Suicide bombers kill 59 in Israel (Mar. 4). A gunman kills 16 kindergarten children, their teacher and himself in Dunblane, Scotland (Mar. 13). In Britain, officials declare that a probable link exists between Bovine Spongiform Encephalopathy—"mad cow disease"—and a new variant of Creutzfeld-Jacob's Disease, a fatal brain disease found in humans (Mar. 20); the announcement provokes a panic, bans on exports of British beef and the eventual destruction of thousands of cattle to contain the disease. The Bank of Tokyo and Mitsubishi Bank merge to create the world's largest bank (Apr. 1). Ron Brown, American secretary of commerce, dies in a plane crash (Apr. 3). The Liberian capital of Monrovia is torn by factional fighting (Apr. 6). President Clinton blocks a ban on late-term abortions (Apr. 10). The PLO revokes its charter clauses that call for the destruction of Israel (Apr. 24). Bulgaria's currency collapses (May); hyperinflation paralyzes the economy. South Africa's main political parties agree on a new constitution (May 8). Russia and Chechnya end their war; Chechnya wins limited autonomy (May 27). Balkan leaders sign an accord on arms limits (June 14). Jazz singer Ella Fitzgerald dies (June 15). A truck bomb kills 19 at an American base in Saudi Arabia (June 25). In Russia, President Yeltsin is re-elected in a run-off election (July 3). In Britain, Prince Charles and Princess Diana agree to divorce (July 12). A bomb explodes at the Olympic Games in Atlanta, Georgia (July 25). China tests an underground nuclear device and then declares a moratorium on nuclear tests (July 29). The United States Congress passes welfare reform (Aug. 2). Iraqis attack a Kurdish enclave (Aug. 31); the United States attacks Iraq's southern air defences (Sept. 2–3). Iraq halts attacks on American planes and enforces flight exclusion zones in the north and south (Sept. 13). A North Korean submarine runs aground in South Korea; most crew members die on South Korean soil (September). In Jerusalem, the opening of an archaeological tunnel bordering the Al Aqsa Mosque provokes violent protest (Sept. 24). In Afghanistan, the Taliban capture Kabul (Sept. 27). Ethnic violence breaks out in Zaire's refugee camps (Oct. 13); thousands of refugees from Rwanda and Burundi abandon the camps (Oct. 21). President Clinton and Vice President Gore win re-election in the United States (Nov. 5). Pakistan's president dismisses Prime Mininster Benazir Bhutto's government and calls for elections in the wake of corruption allegations (November). Hundreds of thousands of refugees return to Rwanda (Nov. 15–18). Thousands march in Belgrade (Dec. 26) to protest President Slobodan Milosevic's annulment of election results in November. The marches continue into February 1997.

1997: Israel agrees to give up a large part of Hebron in the West Bank (Jan. 16). In Pakistan, the Muslim League wins in national elections (Feb. 3). Deng Xiaoping, Chinese communist leader, dies (Feb. 19). In Scotland, embryologist Ian Wilmut and four colleagues at Roslin Institute reveal a cloned sheep named Dolly (Feb. 22–23); Dolly—the first mammal to be successfully cloned—was born on July 5, 1996. The Israeli government approves a Jewish settlement in East Jerusalem (Feb. 26). In Thailand, an economic crisis forces the government to halt trading of all bank and financial stocks (March). The Hale-Bopp Comet flies closest to earth before 4397 (Mar. 22). Members of Heaven's Gate, a cult in California, commit suicide (Mar. 27). Tiger Woods breaks multiple records in the Masters golf tournament (Apr. 13). In Zaire, President Mobutu Sese Seko relinquishes power and flees as a rebel army advances on Kinshasa (May 16); the war in Zaire, renamed Democratic Republic of the Congo, soon affects six neighbouring countries. China reclaims the British colony of Hong Kong, ending a 99-year lease (July 1). *Pathfinder*, an American spacecraft, begins transmitting pictures from Mars to earth for 250 days (July 4). The Thai government devalues the baht (July); Asian neighbours offer loans to help maintain foreign currency reserves; the Philippines, Malaysia and Indonesia devalue their currencies; the IMF offers aid in exchange for economic reforms. The worst flood to hit central Europe in a century occurs (July). Fashion designer Gianni Versace is murdered (July 15). In Paris, Princess Diana and two others die in a car crash (Aug. 31). Mother Teresa dies (Sept. 5). The space shuttle *Atlantis* docks with the *Mir* space station (Oct. 6). In Nevada, British pilot Andy Green breaks the sound barrier by driving a jet-propelled automobile at 1,229.775 kph (Oct. 13). The United States launches the space probe *Cassini* for Saturn (Oct. 15). In late October, the value of Hong Kong's stock market drops more than 10 percent in four days; global markets follow suit. Iraq expels all American weapons inspectors (Oct. 29). In Egypt, Muslim terrorists kill 68 people—mostly tourists—at Luxor (Nov. 17). In Japan, Yamichi Securities—one of Japan's largest brokerages—shuts down amid the collapse of stock prices and a payoff scandal (Nov. 24); the closure leaves US$24 billion in debts. In Kyoto, representatives from 150 countries meet to devise controls on greenhouse gases to slow ozone damage and global warming (Dec. 1–10). British Prime Minister Tony Blair and Gerry Adams, leader of Northern Ireland's Sinn Fein, meet at Downing Street in London to discuss peace in Northern Ireland—the first such meeting since the 1920s (Dec. 11). An American firm launches the first commercial spy satellite (Dec. 24). A court in Paris convicts "Carlos the Jackal" of murder (Dec. 24).

1998: An American court sentences Ramzi Ahmed Yousef, a Muslim cleric, to life in prison for the bombing of New York's World Trade Center in 1993 (Jan. 9). In Cuba, Pope John Paul II visits Roman Catholics and Fidel Castro (Jan. 21–25). The United States launches its last shuttle to aid Russia's aging *Mir* space station (Jan. 22). American tobacco executives admit that smoking endangers health and agree to a US$368.5-billion settlement in exchange for immunity from further lawsuits (Jan. 29). In Kosovo, violence erupts between Serbs and ethnic Albanians (Mar. 5). In Sri Lanka, suicide bombers using boats packed with explosives ram a naval convoy transporting troops to Jaffna; two vessels sink and at least 40 soldiers die (March). The United States Food and Drug Administration approves Viagra, a male impotence drug (Mar. 27). The British government and warring factions in Northern Ireland reach the Good Friday Accord, agreeing to a referendum on the creation of a self-governing assembly in Northern Ireland (Apr. 10). In Cambodia, Pol Pot, the Khmer Rouge leader responsible for the deaths of 2 million Cambodians in the 1970s, dies (Apr. 15). The war in Kosovo spills into Albania (May). While exchanging artillery fire over the disputed Kashmiri border, India tests five underground nuclear devices (May 11, 13) and Pakistan announces five underground nuclear tests (May 28). After students occupy Indonesia's parliament, President Suharto resigns (May 21). Nigeria's dictator, General Sani Abacha, dies (June 8). In Bangladesh, monsoons strand 8 million people near the capital (July). In Russia, the remains of Czar Nicholas and his family are interred in St. Petersburg (July 17). The Dow Jones stock exchange loses 10 percent of its value (late July—Aug. 7); other stock markets around the world follow suit. In Kenya, a car bomb explodes outside the American embassy; in Tanzania, a second car bomb explodes outside the American embassy (Aug. 7). China suffers its worst flood season in 50 years (August). In Northern Ireland, IRA dissidents explode a car bomb in Omagh (Aug. 15). In retaliation for the terrorist attacks in Kenya and Tanzania, the United States fires missiles into suspected terrorist camps of Osama bin Laden in Sudan and Afghanistan (Aug. 20). Massive flooding in northern and eastern India strands some 1.5 million people (Aug. 27). In Russia, after President Yeltsin fires prime ministers Chernomyrdin and Kiriyenko and their cabinets, and then fails to reappoint Chernomyrdin, Yeltsin and the parliament agree to appoint Prime Minister Yevgeny Primakov (Sept. 10–14). Iran lifts the death threat against British author Salman Rushdie (Sept. 24). General Augusto Pinochet, Chile's former dictator, is arrested in London, England (Oct.

16). Hurricane Mitch, the fourth strongest Atlantic hurricane on record, devastates Central America (Oct. 24–Nov. 1). The United States and European Union agree to send food aid to Russia after a poor harvest (Nov. 6). United States Senator John Glenn, 77, the oldest person to enter space, returns to earth in the shuttle *Discovery* after nine days in orbit (Nov. 7). President Clinton agrees to pay US$850,000 to Paula Jones to settle her sexual harassment suit (Nov. 13). After receiving the report of South Africa's Truth and Reconciliation Commission on Oct. 29, President Mandela declares that some amnesties are possible for crimes committed during the apartheid era (Dec. 6). The United States and Britain launch air strikes against Iraq's military forces; the attacks are prompted by President Saddam Hussein's refusal to co-operate with United Nations weapons inspectors but lack the United Nations Security Council's support (Dec. 16–20). The United States House of Representatives impeaches President Clinton for perjury and obstruction of justice in the Monica Lewinsky sex scandal (Dec. 18).

1999: The European Union introduces the EURO in 11 countries (Jan. 1). An American rocket carrying the *Polar Lander* takes off for Mars (Jan. 3). In Switzerland, the International Olympic Committee, facing corruption allegations, suspends six members (Jan. 23–24); four more IOC members resign later in January. In Australia, Queensland suffers its worst flood in a century (February). King Hussein of Jordan dies (Feb. 7). The United States Senate acquits President Clinton of perjury and obstruction charges (Feb. 12). In Israel, 200,000 ultra-Orthodox Jews pray near the supreme court in Jerusalem to protest the court's alleged religious persecution of them (Feb. 14). Bertrand Piccard and Brian Jones become the first to fly nonstop around the world in a balloon (Mar. 1–20). Baseball star Joe DiMaggio dies (Mar. 8). During his visit to Italy, President Mohammad Khatami becomes the first Iranian leader to visit the West since the revolution of 1979 (Mar. 9–11). NATO admits former Warsaw Pact states as members: Poland, Hungary and the Czech Republic (Mar. 12). The 20-member European Commission resigns when found guilty of fraud, nepotism and mismanagement (Mar. 16). NATO begins air strikes

against Yugoslavia to stop Serbian attacks on Albanians in Kosovo (Mar. 24). In the United States, a court convicts Dr. Jack Kevorkian of murder in an assisted-suicide case (Mar. 26). Bill Clinton becomes the first sitting American president to be found in contempt of court when a judge declares that Clinton lied in his 1998 deposition in the Paula Jones case (Apr. 12). A Pakistani court convicts former prime minister Benazir Bhutto in absentia of corruption (Apr. 15). American astronomers announce the first discovery of another solar system, which orbits the star Upsilon Andromeda (Apr. 15). Two student gunmen kill 13 people and themselves in a high school in Littleton, Colorado (Apr. 20). NATO mistakenly bombs the Chinese embassy in Belgrade (May 7). North Korean officials admit "thousands" of their people have died from famine since 1995 (May 8). President Yeltsin names Sergei Stepashin prime minister (May 12). Indian fighter jets attack Muslim guerrillas in Jammu and Kashmir for the first time since 1971 (May 26); Pakistan shoots down three Indian aircraft during border fighting (May 27–28). Pope John Paul II speaks to 700,000 people near Gdansk, Poland (June 5). Indonesia conducts its first democratic elections in 44 years (June 7). Yugoslavia agrees to withdraw troops from Kosovo after 11 weeks of NATO air attacks (June 9). North and South Korean navies battle in the Yellow Sea (June 15). Britain's Prince Edward and Sophie Rhys-Jones wed at Windsor (June 19). A Turkish court sentences Abdullah Ocalan to death for leading the Kurdish rebellion (June 29). The Chinese government bans the Falun Gong and arrests 30,000 of the sect's members (July 21–22). Berlin replaces Bonn as the capital of Germany (Aug. 9). Russian President Yeltsin sacks Prime Minister Stepashin and his cabinet, and appoints Vladimir Putin prime minister (Aug. 9). In Belgrade, almost 150,000 demonstrators demand the resignation of President Milosevic (Aug. 19). In East Timor, after enduring 25 years of state-sponsored violence, people vote for independence from Indonesia (Aug. 30). Dozens of people are exposed to radiation in Japan's worst nuclear accident (Sept. 30). Russia sends troops back into Chechnya to end border clashes with Muslim militants (Oct. 1). The world's human population rises to 6 billion (Oct. 11). In Pakistan, General Pervez

Musharraf seizes power in a bloodless coup (Oct. 12). A supercyclone strikes the Bay of Bengal, killing 10,000 and leaving 15 million people homeless (Oct. 29). China launches its first spacecraft (Nov. 21). In Florida, Elián González, a Cuban child refugee, gets caught in a politically charged custody battle (Nov. 25). In Seattle, Washington, "anti-globalization" activists and riot police clash during a meeting of the World Trade Organization (Nov. 30). Northern Ireland begins self-rule for the first time in 25 years (Dec. 2). The *Polar Lander* crashes on Mars (Dec. 3). In Sri Lanka, President Kumaratunga is injured in one of two bomb blasts that kill at least 18 people and injure 150 others at election rallies (Dec. 18). China reclaims Macau, ending 442 years of Portuguese rule (Dec. 20). Panama takes control of the Panama Canal from the United States (Dec. 31). Russian President Yeltsin declares his resignation and hands presidential powers to Prime Minister Vladimir Putin (Dec. 31).

2000: A revolution overthrows President Jamil Mahuad in Ecuador (Jan. 21). One million Spaniards gather in Madrid to protest bombings by Basque terrorists (Jan. 22). Britain ends self-rule in Northern Ireland when the IRA misses a disarmament deadline (Feb. 11). The Near Earth Asteroid Rendezvous (NEAR) spacecraft becomes the first to orbit an asteroid (Feb. 14). Technology stocks crash on the New York stock market: the NASDAQ index records a drop in value from US$6.71 trillion to US$5.61 trillion (Mar. 10–Apr. 4). Pope John Paul II asks for God's forgiveness for the sins of Roman Catholics inflicted on Jews, women and minorities throughout the ages (Mar. 12). In Uganda, more than 900 members of a religious cult—the Movement for the Restoration of the Ten Commandments—are found dead (March). Zimbabwe's government legalizes the confiscation and redistribution of white-owned farmland to landless blacks (Apr. 6). In Japan, 16,000 people are evacuated from villages on Hokkaido as Mt. Usu sends ash and rocks into the air and mud slides down its slopes (April). Israel withdraws troops from southern Lebanon after 22 years of occupation (May 24). Britain restores parliamentary powers to Northern Ireland when Sinn Fein agrees to disarm (June 4). The presidents of North and South Korea sign a

peace accord, easing 50 years of enmity (June 15). Scientists in the United States and Britain produce a "rough draft" of the 3 billion letters of genetic code in a single human being (June 26). Elián González returns to Cuba with his father (June 28). Mexicans elect Vicente Fox president, ending 71 years of rule by the Institutional Revolutionary Party (July 2). More than 13,000 Japanese suffer from food poisoning caused by contaminated milk products (July). One hundred families from South and North Korea reunite in Seoul and Pyongyang 50 years after Korea's division into two antagonistic states (August). Chile's supreme court strips General Augusto Pinochet of immunity from prosecution for crimes committed during his presidency (Aug. 8). More than 2,000 Somalis meet in Djibouti to form a central Somali government and end a decade of anarchy (Aug. 13). The Russian nuclear submarine *Kursk* explodes and sinks in the Barents Sea (Aug. 14). Myanmar's regime places democratic activist Aung San Suu Kyi under house arrest (September 2000). The Dutch parliament votes to give same-sex couples the right to marry, adopt children and divorce (Sept. 12). In New York, Chase Manhattan Corp. agrees to buy J.P. Morgan & Co. for US$36 billion (Sept. 13). The six-year federal search for fraud in the Clintons' Whitewater real estate transactions before they entered the White House ends without indictments (Sept. 20). Palestinians launch the Al Aqsa intifada—waves of suicide attacks against Israeli civilians and soldiers (Sept. 28). The United States Senate approves RU-486, the "abortion pill" (Sept. 28). Britain incorporates the European Convention on Human Rights into its judicial system (Oct. 2). Yugoslavs overthrow President Slobodan Milosevic (Oct. 5); Vojislav Kostunica is sworn in as president (Oct. 7). In Yemen, a terrorist's bomb explodes on the USS *Cole* (Oct. 12). Eva Morris, the world's oldest woman, dies at age 114 (Nov. 2). In Ethiopia, the 25-year-old remains of Emperor Haile Selassie are laid to rest in Addis Ababa (Nov. 5). In Cambodia, the worst floods in 70 years displace 3.4 million people (November). The American presidential contest between Republican candidate George W. Bush, Jr., and Democratic candidate Al Gore ends in stalemate; a recount of votes to decide the winner begins in Florida (Nov. 7). In the

Philippines, the House of Representatives impeaches President Joseph Estrada for corruption and bribery (Nov. 13). George W. Bush, Jr., is certified the winner of the presidential election (Nov. 26). Dutch parliamentarians vote to allow euthanasia and physician-assisted suicide in special cases (Nov. 28). Ukrainian engineers shut down the last nuclear reactor in Chernobyl (Dec. 15).

2001: Two earthquakes strike El Salvador (Jan. 13; Feb. 16). Congolese president Laurent Kabila is shot dead by his bodyguard (Jan. 16). In Beijing, five supporters of the Falun Gong set themselves ablaze in Tiananmen Square to protest the government's imprisonment of sect members (Jan. 23). In India, an earthquake hits Gujarat, killing 15,000, injuring 60,000 and leaving 600,000 homeless (Jan. 26). In the Netherlands, a court convicts a Libyan agent for blowing up a plane over Lockerbie, Scotland, in 1988 (Jan. 30). Nine people die when the USS *Greenville*, a nuclear submarine, surfaces underneath a Japanese fishing boat near Hawaii (Feb. 9). American and British jets bomb nearly 20 radar sites near Baghdad (Feb. 16). In Brazil, more than 20,000 inmates coordinate deadly riots in prisons in Sao Paulo state (Feb. 18). An 11-month epidemic of foot-and-mouth disease in Britain's livestock begins (Feb. 19); 4 million cattle and sheep are subsequently destroyed. In Afghanistan, the Taliban destroy two huge fifth-century Buddhas on a mountainside at Bamiyan (Mar. 10). France confirms the first case of foot-and-mouth disease in its livestock (Mar. 12); Argentina, Saudi Arabia and the United Arab Emirates subsequently report cases. In Macedonia, ethnic Albanians begin a six-month revolt (Mar. 15). In Medina, Saudi Arabian commandos free more than 100 passengers aboard a Russian airliner hijacked by Chechens (Mar. 16). In the South Atlantic, three explosions rock the Petrobras rig—the world's biggest offshore oil platform—killing 10 workers (Mar. 16), but over 160 people are saved before the rig sinks north of Rio de Janeiro (Mar. 20). Russia's space station *Mir* burns up in the air over the South Pacific (Mar. 23). President Bush abandons the Kyoto Protocol (Mar. 29). In China, an American spy plane and a Chinese fighter plane collide (Apr. 1). An American court convicts Ahmed Ressam, an

Algerian, of conspiracy to commit terrorism by importing explosives into the United States from Canada to disrupt the year 2000 celebrations (Apr. 6). A race riot breaks out in Cincinnati (Apr. 7). Dennis Tito becomes the world's first space tourist when he visits the international space station *Alpha* (Apr. 28). Race riots erupt in at least five towns in northern England (May–July). Nepal's Crown Prince Dipendra kills his parents, nine other family members and himself (June 1). Timothy McVeigh, the Oklahoma City bomber, is executed (June 11). Yugoslavia sends Slobodan Milosevic to the Netherlands to stand before the United Nation's war crimes tribunal and face charges of crimes against humanity (June 28). Doctors in Kentucky implant the first self-contained artificial heart in a human (July 2). In Nablus, Palestine, Israeli military helicopters destroy the headquarters of Hamas, a militant Palestinian organization (July 31). President Bush approves federal funds for medical studies on stem cells extracted from human embryos (Aug. 9). The United Nation's World Conference Against Racism in Durban, South Africa, sees rancorous debates over slavery and Zionism (Aug. 31–Sept. 8). Surgeons in New York successfully perform a gallbladder operation on a patient in Strasbourg, France, by sending high-speed signals to robots (Sept. 7). The United States suffers the worst terrorist attack in its history when Islamist hijackers fly two American passenger planes into both towers of New York's World Trade Center and a third American passenger plane into the Pentagon. A fourth hijacked plane crashes outside Shanksville, Pennsylvania. Casualties total more 3,000 people (Sept. 11). The United States begins building a global alliance to combat terrorism. The United States, Britain, Germany and Canada detain suspected terrorist supporters. The United States and its allies focus attention on Osama bin Laden, a Saudi Arabian terrorist in Afghanistan. Many countries mourn for America's dead (Sept. 14). The American stock market loses a trillion dollars in value (October). In Ukraine, a stray missile hits a Russian airliner over the Black Sea, killing all 78 people on board (Oct. 4). American and British air forces begin bombing Osama bin Laden's camps and Taliban sites in Afghanistan (Oct. 7). Four men get life sentences for the American embassy bombings in Tanzania and Kenya in 1998 (Oct. 18). Russia legalizes the private sale of urban land for the first time since 1917 (Oct. 26). Antigovernment rebels in Sri Lanka sink a government oil tanker (Oct. 29). The Taliban flee Kabul (November). In Morocco, representatives from 178 governments (except the United States) agree on the final details of the Kyoto Protocol (Nov. 11). Cuba agrees to buy food from American companies to replace damaged crops, marking the first commercial export of food from the United States to Cuba since 1959 (Nov. 21). An Israeli military helicopter kills Mahmoud Abu Hanoud, a Hamas leader, with a missile in Nablus (Nov. 23). American ground troops begin fighting in Afghanistan (Nov. 25). American energy giant Enron Corp. files for bankruptcy protection (Dec. 2). At a United Nations-led conference in Germany, Hamid Karzai emerges as president of Afghanistan's new interim government (Dec. 5). Indian and Pakistani troops exchange fire over Kashmir (Dec. 28).

2002: President Eduardo Duhalde defaults on Argentina's debt (Jan. 3); runs on banks, riots and economic hardship follow. American forces begin moving captured enemy fighters from Afghanistan to a prison in Guantanamo Bay, Cuba (Jan. 10). Zimbabwe places new legal restrictions on free expression and foreign election monitors (Jan. 10). An American court convicts John Geoghan, an ex-priest protected for years by Boston's Roman Catholic Church, of child molestation (Jan. 18). In Sierra Leone, President Ahmed Tejan Kabbah commemorates the end of his country's 10-year civil war (Jan. 18). TV-6—Russia's last independent national TV station—complies with a court order and stops broadcasting (Jan. 21). Colm Murphy is convicted for the IRA bombing in Omagh in 1998 (Jan. 25). President Bush describes Iran, Iraq and North Korea as an "axis of evil" (Jan. 29). Zimbabwe places legal restrictions on foreign news media (Jan. 31). In Gujarat, India, sectarian violence kills hundreds of Hindus and Muslims (February –March). President Bush unveils "Green Skies"—an alternative to the Kyoto Protocol—to reduce greenhouse gas emissions and pollution from power plants (Feb. 14). In Colombia, President Andres Pastrana orders the military to seize the FARC enclave, a

legally sanctioned refuge the size of Switzerland for the country's biggest insurgent army (Feb. 20); FARC steps up kidnappings and murders of legislators and other citizens. Jonas Savimbi, leader of UNITA's forces in Angola, dies in battle (Feb. 22). Rising temperatures in Antarctica cause the Larsen B Shelf—a mass of ice 3,250 sq. km wide and 200 metres thick—to fall into the ocean (March). Israeli forces attack Palestinian President Yasser Arafat's headquarters in Gaza City (Mar. 10) and Ramallah (Mar. 29; June 6). The leaders of Serbia, Montenegro and the Federal Republic of Yugoslavia agree to maintain a joint state named Serbia and Montenegro (Mar. 14). Zimbabwe's President Robert Mugabe claims a re-election victory (Mar. 14). The British Commonwealth suspends Zimbabwe's membership for one year (Mar. 19). Pope John Paul II condemns child sexual abuse by priests as "grievously evil" (Mar. 22). Angola's government and UNITA agree to end their 27-year-old civil war (Apr. 4). Dutch Prime Minister Wim Kok and his ministers resign (Apr. 16) upon learning that Dutch peace-keeping troops under the United Nations flag failed to prevent the Serbian massacre of about 8,000 Muslim males in Srebrenica during Bosnia's civil war in 1995. Colombia suffers its worst civilian massacre in four decades of civil war when FARC mortars a church in Bojaya and kills 117 people (May 2). The United States government rejects the authority of the International Criminal Court over American citizens (May 6). Dutch electoral candidate Pim Fortuyn is shot dead (May 6). In Myanmar, the military regime frees Aung San Suu Kyi from house arrest (May 6). East Timor achieves full independence (May 20). In Moscow, Russian and American leaders sign the Strategic Offensive Reductions Treaty (SORT) to reduce nuclear arsenals (May 24). The European Union recognizes Russia as a market economy (May 30). The United States withdraws from the Antiballistic Missile Treaty (June 13). Israel begins construction of a 640-km barrier to cordon off the West Bank (June 18). The Russian parliament legalizes the private sale of farmland (June 26). North and South Korea fight a deadly naval battle— their first in three years—over a disputed sea boundary (June 30). The International Criminal Court is established at The Hague to prosecute persons responsible for war crimes, genocide and crimes against humanity (July 1). WorldCom, the second-largest long-distance telecommunications firm in the United States, files for bankruptcy protection (July 21). President Bush calls for regime change in Iraq (July 8). Israeli forces kill two Hamas leaders: Salah Shehada in Gaza City (July 23); Nasir Jarrar in the West Bank (Aug. 14). In Colombia, FARC bombs kill 20 people at President Alvaro Uribe's inauguration (Aug. 6); the blast is the second FARC bomb attack on Uribe in four months. Terrorist Abu Nidal is found dead in Baghdad (Aug. 20). Brazil's government announces the creation of Tumucumaque National Park, the world's largest rain forest reserve, in the northern Amazon (Aug. 23). The presidents of the Democratic Republic of Congo (DRC) and Uganda sign a peace accord; Ugandan troops agree to leave the eastern Congo (Sept. 6). In India, shortly before a state election in Kashmir, a government minister is assassinated and more than 600 people die in sectarian violence (September). The two Koreas agree to clear land mines in their demilitarized border zone (Sept. 14). Iraq agrees to allow United Nations weapons inspections (Sept. 16). In Côte d'Ivoire, a military revolt provokes civil disorder (Sept. 19–Oct. 17). Two snipers terrorize Washington, DC (Oct. 2–24). North Korea admits to having a covert nuclear weapons program (Oct. 4). Terrorists' bombs kill 202 people— mostly Western tourists—at a nightclub in Bali, Indonesia (Oct. 12). Chechen terrorists take 763 hostages in a Moscow theatre; Russian forces gas the building to end the stalemate but kill 116 people (Oct. 23–26). The United Nations Security Council calls on Iraq to disarm or face "serious consequences" (Nov. 8); Iraqi President Saddam Hussein denies having weapons of mass destruction. In Venezuela, President Hugo Chavez sends troops into Caracas to wrest control of the capital's police from the mayor, his staunch opponent; demonstrations and clashes with police result (Nov. 17). United Nations arms inspectors arrive in Iraq to search for weapons of mass destruction (Nov. 18). The United States Senate votes to create the Department of Homeland Security (Nov. 19). A large oil tanker, the *Prestige*, breaks in half off the Spanish coast (Nov. 19). A United Nations report declares that 42 million people are infected with HIV worldwide (Nov. 26). In South Africa, the Congo (DRC), rebel factions and opposition parties agree to end their four-year war (Dec. 17); neighbouring countries withdraw their troops from the DRC and leave 3 million dead from fighting, disease and malnutrition. Chechen suicide bombers blow up the pro-Russian government in Grozny, killing 46 and wounding others (Dec. 27).

2003: North Korea decides to withdraw from the Treaty on the Nonproliferation of Nuclear Weapons (Jan. 9). George Ryan, governor of Illinois, commutes all 167 death sentences for inmates in the state's prisons (Jan. 11). United Nations weapons inspectors in Iraq say the Iraqis are uncooperative but also find no evidence of a revived nuclear weapons program (Jan. 27). President Bush addresses Congress to argue for war with Iraq (Jan. 28). The space shuttle *Columbia* explodes upon re-entering the earth's atmosphere (Jan. 29). A general strike in Venezuela ends after nine weeks and fails to unseat President Hugo Chavez (Feb. 2). Yugoslavia's parliament votes to rename the country Serbia and Montenegro (Feb. 4). In the United Nation's Security Council, American Secretary of State Colin Powell declares that Iraq threatens world security, deceives United Nations weapons inspectors and cooperates with al-Qaeda (Feb. 5). Large demonstrations against the impending war in Iraq occur in New York, London, Paris, Melbourne and other cities (Feb. 15). In Germany, a court in Hamburg convicts Mounir El-Motassadeq of aiding the terrorists who flew passenger planes into New York's World Trade Center and the Pentagon in 2001 (Feb. 19). The former president of Bosnia, Biljana Plavsic, is sentenced to 11 years in prison for persecuting Muslims and Croats in Bosnia during the war in 1992–95 (Feb. 27). Turkey rejects an American proposal to base 62,000 troops in Turkey to open a northern front in Iraq (Mar. 1). President Bush declares that Iraq threatens the United States and that the United States will attack Iraq unilaterally if necessary (Mar. 6). Zoran Djindjic, the prime minister of Serbia, is murdered (Mar. 12). The World Health Organization (WHO) declares that a new virus called Severe Acute Respiratory Syndrome (SARS) is a worldwide threat to human life (Mar. 15). The

United States and Britain launch the war against Iraq with air strikes on Baghdad (Mar. 19). Ground troops in Nasiriya and Basra encounter heavy fighting (Mar. 23). American troops take Baghdad (Apr. 4–9). Basra falls to British troops (Apr. 7). In Baghdad, American troops topple a statue of Saddam Hussein before an Iraqi crowd and TV cameras (Apr. 10). The Kurds seize Kirkuk (Apr. 11). American troops seize Tikrit, Saddam Hussein's home town (Apr. 14). In Sierra Leone, a postwar Truth and Reconciliation Commission begins public hearings (Apr. 14). South Africa agrees to pay US$85 million in reparations to the families of more than 19,000 victims of apartheid (Apr. 15). Palestine's first prime minister, PLO member Mahmoud Abbas, is sworn into office (Apr. 29). On board the USS *Lincoln*, President Bush declares the end of the war in Iraq—but armed Iraqi resistance to the American and British occupation of their country continues (May 1). A sex scandal prompts Australia's governor general, Peter Hollingsworth, to resign (May 11). American diplomat Paul Bremer becomes civil administrator in occupied Iraq (May 12). In Casablanca, Morocco, 12 suicide bombers coordinate attacks (May 17). In Indonesia, President Megawati Sukarnoputri declares martial law in Aceh and sends troops to quell a long-simmering revolt (May 18–19).The WHO adopts the Framework Convention on Tobacco Control, the world's first public health treaty (May 21). The United Nation's Security Council votes to end 13 years of economic sanctions against Iraq (May 22). Scientists announce the first cloning of a mule, named Idaho Gem (May 29). In Myanmar, the authorities place Aung San Suu Kyi under house arrest again (May 30). British Prime Minister Tony Blair and American Secretary of State Colin Powell deny distorting information used to justify the war in Iraq (May 30). A coup attempt in Mauritania fails (June 8). Britain rejects the use of EURO currency (June 9). ASEAN condemns Myanmar for suppressing democratic dissent (June 16). The International Atomic Energy Agency discovers Iran's secret nuclear program (June 18). In Italy, Prime Minister Silvio Berlusconi—on trial for corruption—and four other lawmakers win immunity from prosecution while in office (June 18). The United States Supreme Court upholds the right of affirma-

tive action in higher education (June 23). In Hong Kong, 500,000 people protest against a proposed "anti-subversion" law (July 1). The WHO declares that SARS has been contained (July 5). The inauguration of Iraq's interim governing council occurs (July 13). American troops kill Saddam Hussein's sons in a firefight in Mosul (July 22). The first Australian-led peacekeepers land in the Solomon Islands to restore civil order (July 24). American and Nigerian troops arrive in Liberia to restore order (July 25; Aug. 4). A military coup fails in the Philippines (July 27). In Britain, Lord Hutton opens an inquiry into the suicide of David Kelly, a defence scientist; Kelly had been quoted by a BBC reporter as saying that the British government had "sexed up" information about Iraq's weapons of mass destruction to justify the war (Aug. 11). Liberian President Charles Taylor surrenders his office and flees to Nigeria (Aug. 11). In its first mission outside Europe, NATO assumes control of peacekeeping forces in Afghanistan (Aug. 11). In North America, eight American states, Ontario and Quebec lose electric power for two days during the continent's biggest power blackout (Aug. 14–15). Libya accepts blame for the destruction of a passenger plane over Lockerbie, Scotland, in 1988 and agrees to pay compensation to the victims' families (Aug. 15). Idi Amin Dada, Uganda's former dictator, dies in exile in Saudi Arabia (Aug. 16). In Iraq, a suicide bomber attacks the United Nations headquarters in Baghdad, killing United Nations envoy Sergio Vieira de Mello and others (Aug. 19). In Venezuela, tens of thousands demonstrate against President Hugo Chavez (Aug. 20). In Iraq, American troops capture Ali Hassan al-Majid —"Chemical Ali"—who is responsible for the poison gas attack on Kurdish civilians in 1988 (Aug. 21). British Prime Minister Tony Blair testifies before the Hutton Inquiry (Aug. 28). Russia reports the loss of another nuclear-powered submarine in the Barents Sea (Aug. 30). South Korea's worst typhoon in a century strikes the southeast coast (September). Prime Minister Abbas of Palestine resigns after losing a vote of confidence (Sept. 6). Sweden's foreign minister is murdered (Sept. 10). Italy suffers a power blackout (Sept. 28). Californians elect actor Arnold Schwarzenegger as governor (Oct. 7). President Bush signs a bill that outlaws partial-birth abortions (Nov. 5). In Alabama, a judicial court removes Judge Roy Moore from office for refusing to remove a stone monument of the Ten Commandments from a courthouse (Nov. 13). A high court in Massachusetts rules in favour of homosexual marriages (Nov. 18). Georgian President Eduard Shevardnadze resigns after weeks of protests (Nov. 23). An American court sentences John Muhammad to death for sniper attacks in Washington, DC (Nov. 24). American troops capture Iraq's deposed president, Saddam Hussein (Dec. 13).

2004: Two American rover spacecraft land on Mars and begin to transmit photos to earth (Jan. 3; 25). Mikhail Saakashvili is elected president of Georgia (Jan. 4). Afghanistan's *loya jirga*, or grand council, approves a new constitution and renames the nation the Islamic Republic of Afghanistan (Jan. 4). The United States begins fingerprinting and photographing some foreign visitors (Jan. 5). Former Iraqi dictator Saddam Hussein wins prisoner-of-war status (Jan. 9). Iran's Guardian Council disqualifies more than 3,600 people from running in parliamentary elections (Jan. 11); President Khatami says his entire administration will resign unless reformers are allowed to run (Jan. 14); the council reinstates more than 1,160 candidates (Jan. 30). President Bush allows Canadian firms to bid on reconstruction contracts in Iraq (Jan. 13). Andrew Fastow, former CFO of Enron Corp., pleads guilty to defrauding the firm and agrees to pay US$23 million in fines (Jan. 13). About 100,000 Iraqis march to support Grand Ayatollah Ali al-Sistani, who calls for direct elections (Jan. 19). The Salvation Army announces the receipt of a gift of US$1.5 billion from the estate of Joan Kroc (Jan. 20). David Kay, the CIA's chief weapons inspector, resigns; he says his 1,400-member team failed to find weapons of mass destruction in Iraq (Jan. 23). In Pakistan, President Pervez Musharraf says Pakistani scientists probably sold nuclear-weapons designs to other countries for personal profit (Jan. 23). President Hamid Karzai signs Afghanistan's new constitution into law (Jan. 26). In Britain, Lord Hutton exonerates Prime Minister Tony Blair of distorting information used to justify the war in Iraq (Jan. 28). One third of Iran's parliament resigns to protest the Guardian Coun-

cil's disqualification of more than 2,000 candidates in elections (Feb. 1). In Saudi Arabia, more than 250 Muslim pilgrims die during the *hajj* (Feb. 1). In northern Iraq, a suicide bomber kills about 100 people, including Kurdish political leaders, and injures hundreds of others (Feb. 1). Massachusetts' supreme court rules in favour of homosexual marriages (Feb. 4). Abdul Qadeer Khan, the "father" of Pakistan's nuclear weapons program, admits he illegally passed nuclear weapons designs and technologies to countries such as North Korea, Iran and Libya (Feb. 4). President Musharraf pardons Khan (Feb. 5). A team of Russian and American scientists creates two new chemical elements, provisionally named Ununtrium and Ununpentium (Feb. 12). Homosexual couples legally marry in San Francisco (Feb. 18). An accidental explosion kills more than 300 Iranian passengers on a train (Feb. 18). In Iran, religious conservatives win a majority in parliamentary elections (Feb. 20). Russian President Vladimir Putin sacks Prime Minister Mikhail Kasyanov and his cabinet two weeks before elections (Feb. 24). Clare Short, a former member of the British cabinet, declares that Britain bugged United Nations Secretary General Kofi Annan's office in the weeks before the Iraqi war (Feb. 26). In the United States, a study by the John Jay College of Criminal Justice concludes that 4,392 priests molested 10,667 children between 1950–2002 (Feb. 26). In Haiti, after weeks of civil disorder, President Jean-Bertrand Aristide resigns and flees to the Central African Republic (Feb. 29); President Bush sends troops to Haiti. President Putin appoints Mikhail Fradkin as premier (Mar. 1). NASA suggests water once covered part of Mars (Mar. 2). Iraq's governing council signs an interim constitution (Mar. 8). Boniface Alexandre is sworn in as Haiti's interim president (Mar. 8). An American court sentences John Muhammad, the Washington, DC, sniper of 2002, to death (Mar. 9); the court sentences Muhammad's accomplice, Lee Malvo, to life imprisonment (Mar. 10). Gérard Latortue is sworn in as Haiti's interim prime minister (Mar. 10). At least 10 bombs explode on trains in Madrid, killing 191 people and injuring more than a thousand, in Spain's worst terrorist attack; (Mar. 11); al-Qaeda takes responsibility. South Korea's parliament votes to impeach

President Roh Moo-hyun for violating election laws (Mar. 12). Vladimir Putin wins re-election as Russia's president (Mar. 14). NASA reports the discovery of a planetoid, named Sedna, three times farther from the sun than Pluto (Mar. 15). Pakistani troops begin an attack against foreign Muslim militants (including al-Qaeda) in South Waziristan (Mar. 16). NATO deploys extra soldiers to Kosovo to pacify an outburst of Serbo-Albanian violence (Mar. 18). The United States declares that Pakistan's diplomatic status will rise to "major non-NATO ally"; the United States promises to grant Pakistan access to its military and counterterrorism technology (Mar. 18). In Taiwan, an assassination attempt on President Chen Shui-bian and Vice President Annette Lu fails during an election campaign (Mar. 19). In Gaza City, Israelis assassinate Sheik Ahmed Yassin, a founder of Hamas, and others in a rocket attack for ordering suicide bombers to Israel (Mar. 22). In Libya, British Prime Minister Tony Blair and Colonel Qadhafi meet, ending nearly three decades of Libyan diplomatic isolation (Mar. 25). NATO admits seven ex-communist states—Bulgaria, Estonia, Lithuania, Latvia, Romania, Slovakia and Slovenia—in the largest expansion in NATO's history (Mar. 29). In Washington, DC, high officials of the Clinton and Bush administrations testify before a commission ("the 9/11 commission") investigating the terrorist attacks on the United States on Sept. 11, 2001 (Mar. 23–30). The Bush administration admits to withholding documents from the 9/11 commission (Apr. 1). American troops face an Iraqi uprising, ordered by Muslim cleric Muqtada al-Sadr, in Fallujah and other cities (April–May). The Bush administration releases a secret document, dated Aug. 6, 2001, entitled "Bin Laden Determined to Attack Inside United States" (Apr. 10). In South Africa, the ANC wins national elections (Apr. 15). In Gaza, Israelis assassinate Abdel Aziz Rantisi, the leader of Hamas, in a rocket attack (Apr. 17). Spain's newly elected premier, José Luis Rodriguez Zapatero, recalls Spanish troops from Iraq (Apr. 18). In North Korea, a deadly explosion derails a train in Ryongchon (Apr. 22). President Bush ends trade sanctions against Libya (Apr. 23). The reunification of Cyprus is rejected by a majority of Greeks but approved by a majority of Turks in a referendum (Apr. 24). In Washington, DC, hundreds of thousands demonstrate for abortion rights in the largest pro-choice march in 12 years (Apr. 25). President Bush and Vice President Richard Cheney testify before the 9/11 commission behind closed doors (Apr. 29). President Bush condemns photos of American soldiers abusing Iraqi prisoners in Abu Ghraib prison in Iraq (Apr. 30). Ten countries join the European Union, including eight ex-communist states (May 1). Pablo Picasso's *Boy with a Pipe* (1905) sells for US$104.1 million at a Sotheby's auction—the most money ever paid for a painting (May 5). In Grozny, Chechnya, a bomb kills President Akhmad Kadyrov and others during a parade (May 9). President Bush places trade sanctions on Syria for failing to prevent terrorists from entering Iraq (May 11). In India, Prime Minister Atal Bihari Vajpayee resigns after the Indian National Congress party wins in parliamentary elections (May 13). South Korea's constitutional court reinstates Roh Moo-hyun, the nation's recently impeached leader, as president (May 14). A suicide bomber kills the president of Iraq's governing council, Ezzidin Salim, in Baghdad (May 17). Sonia Gandhi, the Italian-born leader of the Indian National Congress party, refuses the premiership (May 18); Manmohan Singh accepts the post. Nigeria declares an emergency in Plateau where Christian and Muslim militias are fighting (May 18). American and Iraqi troops raid the office of Ahmad Chalabi, an American ally and member of the Iraqi governing council (May 20). Sudan's Islamic government and Sudanese rebels reach a peace accord to end two decades of civil war (May 26); however, fighting in western Darfur between Arab militias and black Africans continues. Floods kill 1,950 people in Haiti and the Dominican Republic (May 26). An American court convicts Terry Nichols, a confederate in the Oklahoma City bombing of 1995, of mass murder (May 26). America's Surgeon General declares that cigarette smoking can cause cancer of the cervix, kidney, pancreas and stomach (May 27). Iyad Alawi is chosen as Iraq's interim premier (May 28). Two hundred thousand people—including 100,000 veterans—attend the dedication of the United States World War II memorial in Washington, DC (May 29). (See also "News Events of 2003–04" on pages 341–67.)

October 1, 2003, to September 30, 2004

(See also Obituaries pages 870–881.)

OCTOBER 2003

WORLD

Azerbaijan: As widely expected, Ilham Aliyev succeeded his father by winning the presidential election on October 15. Azerbaijan had been ruled by Aliyev's father for 34 years. **Bolivia:** President Gonzalo Sanchez de Lozada called in the military on October 12 to stem the rising tide of anti-government protests in the capital, La Paz. The demonstrators, opposed to government plans for exporting natural gas, called for the president's resignation. Lozada resigned five days later. **Brazil:** On October 7, Brazil announced that it would begin enriching uranium in 2004. The uranium, which Brazil has large reserves of, would initially be used to fuel its two nuclear power plants, but would eventually be exported. **China:** Lieutenant-Colonel Yang Liwei became the first Chinese astronaut, after successfully orbiting Earth 14 times in 21 hours on October 14. China became the third country to send a man into space, after the U.S. and Russia. **Indonesia:** At a summit meeting in Bali on October 8, the Association of Southeast Asian Nations signed an accord to establish an EU-style free-trade zone by 2020. The agreement also pledged to move towards greater security cooperation. **Israel and the Palestinian Territories:** On October 1, the Israeli government approved the expansion of its controversial security barrier into parts of the Palestinian-controlled West Bank to protect Jewish settlements. A day later, Israel announced plans to build more than 600 homes in three West Bank settlements. On the eve of Yom Kippur, a female suicide bomber attacked a Haifa restaurant, killing 19 people and wounding about 50 others (October 4). In response to escalating violence, on October 5 Yasser Arafat declared a state of emergency and named a new cabinet, with Ahmed Qurei as the new prime minister. **Iran:** Lawyer Shirin Ebadi, a vocal campaigner for women's rights in Iran, won the Nobel Peace Prize on October 10, the first Muslim woman to do so. **Iraq:** A number of countries, as well as the World Bank and the International Monetary Fund, collectively pledged $13 billion over five years for the reconstruction of Iraq at a donor conference in Madrid, Spain on October 24. The U.S. was seeking $30 billion. Bombs continued to rock high-profile American and Iraqi Governing Council targets in Baghdad throughout the month, ahead of the October 26 start of Ramadan, the holy month of fasting observed by Muslims. **Italy:** In the Vatican, the Pope celebrated 25 years as leader of the Roman Catholic Church on October 17. Two days later, the Pope beatified Mother Teresa. **Nepal:** On October 12, Maoist rebels stormed a police training centre and killed 12 policemen in western Nepal as part of an escalating rebel campaign following the breakdown of a seven-month peace process in August 2003. **North Korea:** U.S. President George Bush outlined on October 20 a security guarantee for North Korea if it dismantles its nuclear weapons program. **Pakistan:** On October 14, Pakistan conducted its third nuclear-capable missile test in less than two weeks, launching a medium-range missile capable of hitting many targets inside India. **Russia:** Mikhail Khodorkovsky, the head of Russia's largest oil company, Yukos, was arrested on October 25 on charges of fraud and tax evasion. Prosecutors later froze more than 40 percent of Yukos' shares, unnerving foreign investors and triggering a slump on the Russian stock market. Many observers claimed the arrest of Khodorkovsky, who has been publicly critical of President Vladimir Putin, was politically motivated. **South Korea:** President Roh Moo-hyun called a referendum on his leadership on October 13. His approval rating had dropped considerably since assuming the presidency in December 2002. **Sudan:** On October 22, the Sudanese government committed to signing a peace deal with rebels from the country's non-Muslim south, to end a civil war that has been fought for nearly 50 years and has left more than 1.5 million people dead. **Switzerland:** In an October 19 election, the right-wing People's Party won the highest share of the vote, making it the biggest party in a four-way coalition. **Syria:** Reflecting a shift in tactics, on October 5 Israel bombed what it called a Palestinian terrorist training camp outside of Damascus, Syria. The Israeli strike was the first inside Syria in 30 years. **Turkey:** On October 8, Parliament voted in favour of deploying troops to Iraq in support of American forces, although they would not be deployed to the Kurdish areas of the country. The Iraqi Governing Council voiced their strong opposition to the decision. **United Kingdom:** On October 21, the Irish Republican Army announced that it had been destroying its arms and would continue to do so. Following the announcement, British Prime Minister Tony Blair set dates for elections for the Northern Ireland Assembly. The *Concorde* jet touched down for the last time at London's Heathrow Airport on October 24, marking an end to the world's only commercial supersonic flights. **United Nations:** On October 16, the Security Council unanimously approved a resolution supporting an international force in Iraq under U.S. authority. The resolution also called on the Iraqi Governing Council to set a timetable for drafting a constitution and holding elections. The October 22 report into the bombing of the UN headquarters in Baghdad on August 19, 2003, placed most of the blame on the UN's own security system, which it called "dysfunc-

tional." **United States:** Davis Kay, the lead weapons inspector in Iraq, told Congress that his team had found equipment and evidence of weapons-related activities violating UN resolutions, but no weapons of mass destruction (October 2). California governor Gray Davis was ousted in an October 7 recall vote. Austrian-born actor Arnold Schwarzenegger was elected to replace Mr. Davis, receiving nearly 49 percent of the vote. The Senate voted 64-34 in support of a federal ban on partial-birth abortion procedures, the most significant restriction on abortion procedures since the *Roe v. Wade* ruling of 1973 (October 21). President Bush declared the California wildfires a national disaster on October 27, paving the way for federal assistance. The wildfire, one of the largest in the state's history, destroyed hundreds of thousands of acres and more than 3,500 homes. It was believed to have been set by arsonists. On October 31, the House of Representatives voted to give the Bush administration billions for the military and reconstruction in Iraq and Afghanistan. Three-quarters of the $87.5 billion will be spent on military operations.

CANADA

The first of three reports on the 2002–03 SARS epidemic was released on October 1, urging that a federal centre for disease control be established and that $700 million in new funding be made available for the next public health emergency. Statistics Canada reported on October 2 that gun-related murders had fallen to an all-time low in Canada: more people were killed with knives than guns in 2003. On October 2, the family of Dudley George, a Native man killed by Ontario Provincial Police during a protest eight years ago, dropped its lawsuit against the Ontario government and accepted a $100,000 settlement from the OPP. A British Columbia jury convicted Jay Handel of first-degree murder for killing his six children on October 2, rejecting the notion he was mentally incompetent at the time. While the jury was out, Handel attempted suicide by slashing his wrists. After 374 days in a Syrian jail, Maher Arar was released to his family in Ottawa on October 5. The 33-year-old Canadian citizen was changing planes in New York in October 2002 when American officials detained and deported him to Syria on suspicion of being an al-Qaeda terrorist. On October 6, the Supreme Court announced that it would reserve judgment on a request by religious and family groups to appeal the Ontario Court ruling allowing gay marriage. At least 1,000 gay and lesbian couples had married in Ontario and British Columbia since lower courts in those provinces ruled in June 2003 that existing marriage laws were discriminatory. The trial of Mohammed Reza Aghadam Ahmadi, accused of beating Canadian photojournalist Zahra Kazemi to death in a Tehran prison in July 2003, began in Iran on October 7. Ahmadi, an intelligence officer, was charged with "quasi-intentional murder." Nine-year-old Cecilia Zhang was abducted from her suburban Toronto home in the middle of the night on October 20, sparking a city-wide manhunt. Newfoundlanders and Labradorians went to the polls on October 21, electing Progressive Conservative millionaire Danny Williams with nearly 60 percent of the popular vote. After five referendums in 30 years, the Mennonite town of Steinbach, Manitoba, voted to allow alcohol to be served in local restaurants on October 22.

NOVEMBER 2003

WORLD

Afghanistan: A draft constitution was unveiled on November 3, calling for the creation of an Islamic republic with a strong presidential system and equal rights for all citizens. The draft did not, however, mention *sharia*, or Islamic law. **China:** On November 19, China warned Taiwan president Chen Shui-bian that he "risks war" if he launches an independence bid.

China has long threatened military action against Taiwan, which it sees as a renegade province. On November 24, the government suspended nearly 700 state-run newspapers as part of broad press reforms aimed at bringing the industry in line with a free-market economy and reducing government spending. **Dominican Republic:** Six people were killed in clashes with troops during a student protest on November 12 against high prices and regular power cuts. **France:** Three former executives of the state-owned oil company Elf received long prison sentences on November 12 for corruption and embezzling public funds. **Georgia:** After three weeks of demonstrations, President Eduard Shevardnadze resigned on November 23. The protests began after the preliminary results of the November 2 parliamentary elections suggested that the results were rigged. **India:** The first formal ceasefire between India and Pakistan in the disputed state of Kashmir began on November 26. **Indonesia:** Flooding caused by torrential rain on the island of Sumatra left over 100 people dead on November 3. **Israel and the Palestinian Territories:** On November 27, Israel said it would continue building a security barrier deep into the West Bank, despite a U.S. announcement that it would withhold a $290-million loan guarantee in protest. **Iraq:** Insurgents shot down an American helicopter on November 2, killing 16 U.S. soldiers and injuring 21 others. Another helicopter crash five days later in Tikrit claimed the lives of six U.S. soldiers. On November 12, a fuel truck exploded outside an Italian police compound in Nasiriya, killing at least 27 and injuring 100. On November 14, the U.S. agreed to transfer power to an interim Iraqi government in early 2004. Two U.S. helicopters collided on November 15, killing at least 17 soldiers. U.S. President George Bush made a secret trip to Baghdad to celebrate Thanksgiving with troops on November 27. Iraqi guerrillas fired rocket-propelled grenades at a car carrying eight Spanish intelligence officers, killing seven of them on November 28. Also that day, two Japanese diplomats were killed following an ambush by insurgents. In a shootout north of Baghdad on November 30, U.S. troops killed at least 46 Iraqi insurgents. **Japan:** Prime Minister Junichiro Koizumi's governing Liberal Democratic Party and its coalition partners held on to power in parliamentary elections on November 9. The opposition Democratic Party, however, made big gains. **Myanmar:** On November 24, the government released five senior opposition politicians from house arrest. The politicians are members of democracy advocate Aung San Suu Kyi's National League for Democracy. Aung San Suu Kyi herself was not freed. **Saudi Arabia:** A bomb blast at a housing complex in the capital, Riyadh, killed at least 18 people and wounded dozens on November 9. Al-Qaeda was blamed for the attack. **Sri Lanka:** Claiming that Prime Minister Ranil Wickremesinghe was making too many concessions in negotiations with the rebel Tamil Tigers, President Chandrika Kumaratunga suspended Parliament and fired several of Wickremesinghe's ministers on November 4. A day later, Kumaratunga declared a state of emergency. The Prime Minister maintained his hold on power. **South Africa:** On November 19, the government approved a plan to give free anti-AIDS drugs to those who need them. Under the plan, the government will establish a network of centres to distribute the anti-retroviral drugs to fight the disease. Over five million South Africans have AIDS. **Turkey:** Twenty-five people were killed and 300 wounded following simultaneous blasts at synagogues in Istanbul on November 15. On November 20, truck explosions outside the British consulate and the British Bank HSBC in Istanbul killed 26 people and wounded 400. Al-Qaeda was suspected in the bombings. **United Nations:** While stopping short of recommending sanctions, on November 26 the International Atomic Energy Agency passed a resolution censuring Iran over its nuclear program. **United States:** On November 1, Reverend V. Gene Robinson became the first openly gay bishop of the U.S. Episcopalian Church. The World Trade Organization ruled against American steel tariffs on November 10, saying that the Bush administration violated trade laws by imposing steep tariffs on steel imports to the U.S. Also on November 10, the Supreme Court announced that it would hear its first appeals related to the Bush administration's anti-terrorism policies, and decide whether detainees held at the Guantanamo Bay Naval Base in Cuba can challenge their imprisonment in the U.S. court system. John A. Muhammad, accused of killing 10 people in the October 2002 Washington, D.C.-area sniper shootings, was found guilty on November 17. A week later, the jury recommended the death sentence. The Massachusetts Supreme Court ruled on November 18 that barring gays and lesbians from marrying violates the state constitution. Also on November 18, federal prosecutors arrested 47 participants in the foreign-exchange markets for defrauding big banks and small investors. On November 19, a warrant was issued for the arrest of pop star Michael Jackson on multiple charges of child-sex abuse. Following an all-night session on November 22, the House of Representatives voted 220-215 to overhaul the Medicare system. The Senate approved the $400-billion bill three days later. The passage of the Medicare Bill represented the biggest change to the government program since 1965. Most Democrats voted against the legislation.

CANADA

Finance Minister John Manley announced on November 3 that the federal surplus would be much smaller in 2003 as compared to previous years. Of the estimated $3.5-billion surplus, over $2 billion was targeted to go to the provinces for health care. Former Ontario premier Mike Harris took himself out of the running for the leadership of a united federal Conservative Party on November 3. His decision set off fears among old-line Progressive Conservatives that the party was being taken over by the Canadian Alliance. Saskatchewan went to the polls on November 5, re-electing Premier Lorne Calvert and his New Democratic Party with 30 seats, compared to 28 for the conservative Saskatchewan Party of Elwin Hermanson. The major issue in the race was Calvert's allegation that Hermanson would sell Saskatchewan's Crown corporations. On November 6, Quebec police raided four Hells Angels drug cells and arrested 31 people. Those arrested included prominent Montreal lawyer Benoit Cliche, who was charged with running the criminal operations of one of his clients. Also on November 6, a new bell tower was lifted atop the rebuilt St. John's Anglican Church in Lunenburg, Nova Scotia, two years after a fire destroyed the 250-year-old structure. On November 13, Prime Minister Jean Chrétien announced that he would hasten his planned retirement, and hand power to Paul Martin on December 12. A November 19 Canada-U.S. report laid blame for the massive August 2003 power blackout that swept through Ontario and eight U.S. states on short-circuited power lines and a faulty alarm system at an Ohio utility. On November 19, Solicitor General Wayne Easter acknowledged that Canada and other countries provided information to U.S. authorities on Maher Arar, the Ottawa man who was sent to Syria after being detained during a stopover in New York. Easter also suggested that Canada might be more reluctant to share intelligence with the U.S. if the rights of Canadian citizens are not respected. Breaking an election promise, Ontario's new Liberal government announced in its Throne speech on November 20 that it will lift an electricity price freeze introduced by the Conservative government. On November 24, six Vancouver police officers pleaded guilty to common assault for dragging three suspected drug dealers to a remote area of Stanley Park, and striking them. Quebec ordered the demolition of the heavily fortified Hells Angels bunker near Quebec City on November 25. The building, which Justice Minister Marc Bellemare called a "symbol of gangsterism," was seized under federal anti-gang laws. Alliance Leader Stephen Harper stripped Regina member of parliament Larry Spencer of his job as critic for family issues after Spencer told a newspaper that he believes homosexuality should be illegal (November 27).

DECEMBER 2003

WORLD

Afghanistan: American air strikes in southeastern Afghanistan on December 6 missed their Taliban targets and killed 15 civilians, mostly children. About 500 delegates gathered in Kabul on December 14 for a grand council, or *loya jirga*, to debate and approve a constitution. **China:** The government announced its first new case of Severe Acute Respiratory Syndrome, or SARS, on December 27. **Cyprus:** Elections in northern (Turkish) Cyprus ended with the pro-European opposition parties, who also support UN plans for reunification, narrowly winning the vote (December 15). **European Union:** Summit-level talks on a European Union constitution broke down with no agreement on December 14. The biggest stumbling-block was a dispute over countries' voting weights that pitted smaller EU countries such as Spain against larger ones such as France and Germany. **France:** President Jacques Chirac announced plans for a ban on the Muslim headscarf and other "ostentatious" religious symbols in schools and other public buildings, as recommended by an independent government commission on secularism (December 17). **Greece:** Fifteen members of the terrorist organization November 17 were convicted on December 8 for a series of attacks that killed 23 people between 1975 and 2000.

Guatemala: Óscar Berger, a conservative businessman and former mayor of Guatemala city, was elected president on December 29 with 54 percent of the vote. **Guinea:** Dozens of soldiers were arrested during the run-up to the December 21 presidential election, amid rumours that a coup was being plotted against the gravely ill President Lansana Conté. **Haiti:** On December 11, opponents of President Jean-Bertrand Aristide staged a general strike and demonstrations aimed at forcing his resignation. **Iran:** A massive earthquake, measuring 6.6 on the Richter scale, destroyed most of the ancient city of Bam, located in Iran's southeast (December 26). As many has 30,000 of the town's 80,000 people died. **Iraq:** American troops captured Saddam Hussein under a hut belonging to his former cook, near his hometown of Tikrit on December 13. Hussein was found in dishevelled condition in an eight-foot-deep pit and surrendered without a fight. On December 14, the Governing Council announced that it would establish a war-crimes tribunal without UN or international involvement, raising fears that the alleged perpetrators of atrocities under Saddam Hussein's rule might not receive fair trials. **Israel and the Palestinian Territories:** Israeli Prime Minister Ariel Sharon ordered the dismantling of four unauthorized Jewish settlement outposts in the West Bank on December 29. **Italy:** Parliament passed a media law on December 3, which critics said would benefit Prime Minister Silvio Berlusconi, who has direct influence over most of Italy's media outlets. **Japan:** On December 9, the government agreed to send up to 1,000 troops to Iraq within a year, the largest deployment of Japanese troops since the Second World War. Since the Japanese constitution bans the country from going to war, the contingent would be limited to a humanitarian role only. **Libya:** U.S. President Bush and British Prime Minister Tony Blair announced on December 19 that Libyan leader Muammar Qaddafi had agreed to give up his country's

nuclear, biological and chemical weapons programs. **Nicaragua:** Former president Arnoldo Alemén was convicted of fraud, money laundering and misuse of public funds and sentenced to 20 years in jail on December 8. **North Korea:** On December 9, the government announced that it would freeze its nuclear program in exchange for concessions from the United States, including fuel aid and its removal from the list of sponsors of state terrorism. The United States countered with a plan demanding the dismantling of North Korea's entire nuclear-weapons program. **Pakistan:** President Pervez Musharraf narrowly survived an assassination attempt on December 14 after a half-ton remote control bomb exploded seconds after his motorcade passed it. Musharraf's motorcade was attacked a second time, on December 25, by two suicide bombers. Musharraf escaped unharmed, but 14 were killed. **Russia:** Nearly 50 people were killed and about 150 wounded when suicide bombers struck a commuter train travelling near the republic of Chechnya on December 5. The December 8 general election gave President Vladimir Putin's United Russia party and its allies a two-thirds majority in the Duma, enough to push through a number of economic reforms supported by the president. **Rwanda:** On December 3, the International Criminal Tribunal for Rwanda found three high-profile Rwandan media figures guilty of genocide in the slaughter of the Tutsi minority in 1994. **Serbia and Montenegro:** Extreme nationalists saw big gains in the Serbian elections on December 28. The Radical Party, led by indicted and jailed war-crimes suspect Vojislav Seselj, won 27 percent of the vote. The party of former dictator Slobodan Milosevic (also indicted and in jail) fared well too. **South Korea:** On December 17, the government announced that it would send 3,000 troops to Iraq. **Switzerland:** On December 20, the Swiss parliament elected Christoph Blocher of the far-right Swiss People's Party to the country's seven-man cabinet.

Taiwan: President Chen Shui-bian said that he would press on with plans for a referendum calling for China to cease its military threats against Taiwan (December 8). China later vowed to "crush" Taiwanese attempts at independence.

United States: On December 4, President Bush reversed a previous decision by eliminating tariffs on imported steel. The decision came weeks after the World Trade Organization ruled the tariffs illegal and authorized European Union countries to impose retaliatory tariffs. A Pentagon directive on December 9 barred Canada, France, Germany and Russia from bidding on lucrative contracts for rebuilding Iraq. Only the U.S. and its coalition partners were deemed eligible to bid. On December 23, a Virginia jury sentenced Lee Malvo, the second sniper involved in the Washington, D.C. area sniper killings in October 2002, to life in prison.

Zimbabwe: On December 7, Zimbabwe pulled itself out of the 54-nation Commonwealth of Nations, a voluntary group of countries tied together by their former association with Great Britain. Zimbabwe had been suspended from the Commonwealth for nearly two years due to President Robert Mugabe's alleged election fraud and human rights abuses.

CANADA

In a warning report on the supply of fresh water, Statistics Canada stated on December 3 that the St. Lawrence River was at one of its lowest ebbs in a century and that Canada's glaciers were the smallest they have been in nearly 10,000 years. Minister of Natural Resources Herb Dhaliwal, who had clashed with Paul Martin during the Liberal leadership race, announced his retirement from politics on December 3. On December 6, members of the Progressive Conservative Party approved a proposal to merge with its larger, more socially conservative rival, the Canadian Alliance. The new party, the Conservative Party of Canada, was formed as part of efforts to "unite the right" and

dent the Liberals' hold on power. A construction accident caused the wall of Toronto's historic Uptown Theatre to collapse onto a neighbouring language school on December 8. A Costa Rican man was killed protecting a 10-year-old Korean boy. On December 8, Ottawa banned commercial fishing and oil and gas exploration in most of the Sable Gully, a unique two-kilometre-deep collection of underwater canyons off the coast of Nova Scotia. The ban was seen as a next-to-last step toward declaring the rare ecosystem a marine protected area. In its final cabinet meeting, the Chrétien government approved a proclamation that acknowledged the historic wrongs done by the British Crown between 1755 and 1763, when 11,000 Acadians were expelled from the Maritimes (December 10). Quebec police arrested 25 minors, aged 13 to 17, for buying and selling marijuana at two high schools in small communities south of Montreal (December 11). Former finance minister Paul Martin formally replaced Jean Chrétien as leader of the Liberal Party and prime minister of Canada on December 12. His 38-member ministry included only 16 ministers who served on Jean Chrétien's team. A fierce winter storm in Atlantic Canada over the Christmas holiday closed roads, snapped power lines, and killed five people in New Brunswick. On December 28, the Royal Canadian Mounted Police stormed the legislative offices of two British Columbia cabinet ministers and seized files as part of a 20-month probe into marijuana smuggling and money laundering. No arrests were made. The raids were focused on two high-ranking ministerial aides, who were heavily involved in Prime Minister Paul Martin's leadership campaign.

JANUARY 2004

WORLD

Afghanistan: At their *loya jirga* on January 4, 502 Afghan leaders agreed to a constitution that established a strong presidency and a two-chamber parliament, an independent judiciary, and gave equal rights to women. The constitution became law on January 26. A Canadian peacekeeper and an Afghan civilian were killed in a suicide attack in Kabul on January 27. **Algeria:** At least 23 people were killed and 74 injured in an explosion at Algeria's largest gas refinery on January 20. Foul play was not suspected. **Dominican Republic:** Workers held a two-day general strike in protest of President Hipólito Mejía's decision to adopt the policies of the International Monetary Fund to help mend the shattered economy (January 29-30). Five people died in clashes with police. **Egypt:** An Egyptian charter flight crashed into the Red Sea on January 3, killing all 148 on board, most of them French tourists. Foul play was not suspected. **Georgia:** Mikhail Saakashvili was elected president in a landslide victory on January 4. Only two months earlier, the 36-year-old American-educated lawyer was leading weeks of peaceful protest that forced former president Eduard Shevardnadze to resign in November 2003. **India:** At their first meeting in more than two years, Prime Minister Atal Bihari Vajpayee and Pakistani Prime Minister Pervez Musharaff agreed to restart peace talks between their two countries (January 5). **Internet:** In a massive attack, a computer worm called MyDoom or Novarg spread through Internet servers worldwide on January 26, infecting about one in every 12 e-mail messages. **Iraq:** A U.S. Black Hawk helicopter was downed by a missile near Fallujah on January 8, killing nine soldiers. On January 9, Saddam Hussein was designated a prisoner of war, giving him access to the services of the Red Cross. On January 15, Iraq's most influential Shia Muslim cleric, Ayatollah Ali Sistani, called for direct elections to an interim parliament that is supposed to choose a full-fledged Iraqi government by July. The U.S. wants the Parliament to be chosen by caucuses of notable Iraqis. A suicide bomber attacked the Coalition Provisional Authority headquarters in Baghdad on January 18, killing at least 25 people, most of them Iraqis. **Israel and the Palestinian Territories:** On January 14, a mother of two children killed herself and four Israeli security officers in the Gaza Strip. The attack marked the first time that Hamas used a woman as a suicide bomber. Israel agreed to free 436 mostly Palestinian prisoners in exchange for the release of a kidnapped Israeli businessman and the bodies of three soldiers (January 24). **Italy:** The constitutional court ruled on January 14 that a law passed in June 2003 giving Prime Minister Silvio Berlusconi and four other top officials immunity from prosecution was unconstitutional. A suspended trial of Mr. Berlusconi on judge-bribing charges was expected to resume. **Pakistan:** On January 5, the United States said that it believes Pakistani scientists supplied Libya, and possibly Iran and North Korea, with nuclear weapons designs and technology. President Pervez Musharaff admitted to the claim on January 23. **Russia:** U.S. Secretary of State Colin Powell visited Moscow on January 26 to meet with President Vladimir Putin and other officials. In a newspaper article, Powell sharply criticized Russia for its lack of democracy, suppression of free media and the war in Chechnya. **Sudan:** The government and the Sudan People's Liberation Army agreed on a formula for sharing the country's oil wealth on January 6. The deal represents a major step towards a formal peace agreement to a civil war that has raged for decades. A separate civil war, however, continued in the western region of Darfur. **Thailand:** The government announced on January 22 that it is investigating three possible cases of the avian flu virus, which had recently infected over ten people and forced a cull of millions of chickens in nearby Vietnam. The virus was later found to have spread to China, Japan, South Korea, Cambodia, Taiwan, Indonesia, Pakistan and Laos. **United Kingdom:**

Heeding warnings from the United States about possible terrorist attacks, the British government grounded a number of flights to the United States on January 1 and 2. In releasing his report on intelligence on Iraq's weapons programs, Lord Hutton said that Prime Minister Tony Blair did not intentionally exaggerate intelligence to justify the war. Hutton's report accused the British Broadcasting Corporation of sloppy reporting and editorial judgment, prompting the resignation of its chairman (January 28). **United States:** A new security system began operation on January 5, requiring many international travellers to the U.S. to be fingerprinted and photographed. On January 14, President Bush announced that the U.S. intends to launch another manned mission to the moon by 2020. Massachusetts senator John Kerry staged a surprise win during the Iowa Democratic caucuses on January 19, with North Carolina senator John Edwards placing a strong second. Howard Dean, the former frontrunner for the Democratic nomination, took third place. In his State of the Union address on January 20, President Bush suggested he would introduce a constitutional amendment to ban gay marriage. The Salvation Army announced on January 20 that it had received a gift of $1.5 billion, possibly the largest that any charity has ever received. The Central Intelligence Agency's chief weapons inspector, David Kay, resigned on January 23, saying that his 1,400 member Iraqi Survey Group failed to find any evidence of chemical, biological and nuclear weapons in Iraq. Five days later, Kay called for an independent investigation into the intelligence gathered before the U.S.-led war in Iraq. Senator John Kerry placed first in the New Hampshire Democratic primary on January 27.

CANADA

Labour leaders in Newfoundland vowed on January 6 to take the new Conservative government, led by premier Danny Williams, to task for freezing public sector wages. The wage freeze came after a review of the province's fiscal position projected deficits of more than $1 billion annually. In a blow to Canada's beef industry, officials from both Canada and the U.S. announced on January 6 that DNA tests confirmed a cow that tested positive for "mad cow disease" in Washington state came from Alberta. Five active and one retired Toronto police officers, members of a disgraced and disbanded drug squad, were charged with 40 counts of corruption, extortion, theft and obstruction of justice as part of a two-year investigation by the Royal Canadian Mounted Police (January 7). On January 12, angry Mohawk warriors burned down the house of Kanesetake reserve Chief James Gabriel and held 55 constables hostage. The Quebec government negotiated the release of the constables. The violence was in response to Chief Gabriel's attempt to evict alleged drug runners from the reserve. In his meeting with U.S. President George Bush at a summit in Mexico on January 13, Prime Minister Martin won agreement for Canadian companies to bid on a second round of contracts to rebuild Iraq. Bush also promised not to deport Canadian citizens to other countries without first consulting Ottawa, as had happened with Maher Arar. Ottawa announced on January 14 that the federal government would fund most of a $325,000 study to examine the possibility of building a causeway or tunnel between Labrador and Newfoundland. On January 21, the British Columbia government instructed its approximately 300 marriage commissioners to perform same-sex weddings, and that they would be asked to resign if they did not comply. Pakistan confirmed to the Canadian government on January 24 that Egyptian-born Canadian Ahmed Said Khadr, an aid worker accused of ties to al-Qaeda, was killed in a gun battle in 2003 with security forces. Canadian peacekeeper Corporal James Murphy and an Afghan civilian were killed and three other Canadian soldiers were injured by a suicide bomber in Kabul on January 27. On January 28, investigators found the remains of 10 more women at the Port Coquitlam pig farm owned by accused murder Robert Pickton, bringing to 31 the number of missing women found at the farm. After months denying the need for one, on January 28 Public Safety Minister Anne McLellan called a public inquiry into the case of Maher Arar, who was deported to Syria by U.S. officials in September 2002 and allegedly tortured while in detention. The head of the inquiry, Justice Dennis O'Connor, was given the power to see classified documents. On January 30, the Supreme Court upheld a century-old law that allowed parents and, in some cases, teachers and caregivers to spank children, so long as "reasonable" force was used and guidelines were set.

FEBRUARY 2004

WORLD

Australia: The death of an aboriginal teenager following a police chase sparked riots in Sydney on February 16. Rioters set fire to a railway station and 40 police officers were injured. **Austria:** On February 11, the Organization of Petroleum Exporting Countries (OPEC) made a surprise decision to cut output by 10 percent by lowering quotas, even though the price of oil was considerably more expensive than the organization's target of $22-28 a barrel. **China:** Six-party talks over North Korea's nuclear program began in Beijing on February 25. North Korea expressed its desire for aid and security guarantees before freezing its program. **France:** Supported by both government and opposition parties, and despite mass protests by French Muslims, on February 11 the National Assembly overwhelmingly approved a ban on the wearing of Muslim headscarves and other supposedly ostentatious religious symbols. **Germany:** Chancellor Gerhard Schroeder unexpectedly resigned as chairman of the centre-left

Social Democratic Party on February 6. The decision came after mounting criticism in the party of his economic reform agenda. Schroeder stayed on as Chancellor. **Haiti:** Violent protests against President Jean-Bertrand Aristide's government on February 5 overwhelmed the Haitian military and police. Opposition stemmed from concerns over high unemployment, extreme poverty, and the legitimacy of Aristide's presidency. The same day, armed rebels took control of Gonaïves in Haiti's northeast. In the week following, the violence had spread to a dozen other towns, killing over 40 people. After rebels attacked a police station in central Haiti and killed the police chief on February 17, President Aristide appealed to the international community for help. On February 22, rebels took control of Cap Haitien, Haiti's second largest city. Under pressure from the U.S., President Aristide resigned on February 29, fleeing to the Central African Republic. Haiti's Chief Justice, Boniface Alexandre, was sworn in to replace Aristide. **Iran:** About one-third of Iran's parliamentarians resigned on February 1 in protest of a move by the hard-line Guardian Council to bar more than 3,600 reformist candidates from running in parliamentary elections. About 300 people were killed when a train carrying fertilizer, fuel and sulphur derailed and exploded in Iran's northeast on February 18. With thousands of reformist candidates not allowed to run, religious conservatives cruised to electoral victory and took a clear majority in parliament on February 20. **Iraq:** Suicide bombings outside a police station in Iskandariyah on February 10 killed at least 53 people, mostly civilians lining up to apply for jobs. Another suicide bombing on February 11 in Baghdad killed 47 people seeking jobs with Iraq's new army. **Israel and the Palestinian Territories:** Israeli Prime Minister Ariel Sharon shocked many Israelis by announcing on February 2 that he was planning to order the evacuation of all Jewish settlements in the Gaza Strip as part of his plan to "disengage" from the territories occupied by Israel since the war of 1967. About 7,500 Jews live alongside 1.2 million Palestinians in Gaza. **Morocco:** An earthquake in northern Morocco on February 24 killed at least 564 people and left 20,000 without homes. **Pakistan:** Abdul Qadeer Khan, considered the "father" of Pakistan's nuclear weapons program, confessed to selling nuclear weapon designs and technology to North Korea, Iran and Libya (February 4). He denied that the government had sanctioned the deals. **Russia:** On February 24, President Vladimir Putin unexpectedly fired his entire cabinet as well as Prime Minister Mikhail M. Kasyanov two weeks before nationwide elections. **Saudi Arabia:** During the annual *hajj*, or pilgrimage, to Mecca on February 1, 251 pilgrims were crushed to death in a stampede during a "devil-stoning" ceremony. **Sri Lanka:** In the latest move in the power struggle between the president and prime minister, on February 8 President Chandrika Kumaratunga dissolved parliament and called for elections on April 2. Kumaratunga later fired 39 government ministers. **South Korea:** On February 12, scientists announced that they had created 30 human embryos by cloning for the purposes of embryonic stem cell research. **Sudan:** The government announced on February 9 that it had crushed rebel forces fighting against it in the western region of Darfur. The rebels denied the claim. Over 800,000 people fled the region during the conflict. **Turkmenistan:** On February 25, autocratic President Saparmurat Niyazov passed a decree forbidding young men to wear long hair or beards, and banned car radios, smoking in the street, and opera and ballet performances. **Uganda:** The Lord's Resistance Army rebel group killed at least 200 unarmed civilians in northern Uganda on February 22. The group has been trying to overthrow the government for 18 years. **United Nations:** Former British cabinet minister Clare Short claimed on February 26 that British intelligence employed electronic surveillance to spy on UN Secretary-General Kofi Annan and Security Council members in the weeks preceding the war in Iraq. **United States:** Under growing political pressure and the failure of U.S. weapons inspectors to find evidence of chemical, biological and nuclear weapons in Iraq, on February 2 President George Bush called for an independent commission to study the country's intelligence-gathering operations. Three Senate buildings were closed when the toxin ricin was found in the office of Senate majority leader Bill Frist on February 3. Massachusetts senator John Kerry won five more states on February 3, solidifying his position as frontrunner in the Democratic presidential nomination race. Senator Joe Lieberman, former Vice-President Al Gore's running mate in 2000, dropped out of the race. On February 4, the Massachusetts Supreme Court ruled in support of gay marriage. A distant third behind Senators John Kerry and John Edwards, early frontrunner Howard Dean dropped out of the Democratic Presidential race on February 18. Consumer advocate Ralph Nader announced on February 22 that he would once again run for president as an independent candidate. Democrats, who fear that Nader's candidacy would split votes from their party, expressed outrage. **Venezuela:** President Hugo Chávez devalued Venezuela's currency, the bolívar, by 16.7 percent to boost the local currency value of the government's oil income.

CANADA

Quebec police suspected arson behind the February 2 fire at the Auberge Grand-Mère, the Shawinigan hotel at the centre of a controversy surrounding former prime minister Jean Chrétien in 2000. Owner Yvon Duhaime was later charged with arson and insurance fraud. In the February 4 Speech from the Throne, Governor-General Adrienne Clarkson set out the government's legislative program, pledged budgetary discipline, and offered extra money for cities and health care. The opposition blasted the speech as election-eering. On February 10, Auditor-General Sheila Fraser released a report criticizing the government under former Prime Minister Jean Chrétien for the "blatant misuse" of public money during a C$250-million publicity campaign to promote federalism in Quebec between 1997 and 2003. The "sponsorship scandal" sent public support falling to 12-year lows and sparked speculation that Prime Minister Paul Martin would put on hold plans to call an early election. On February 10 the Quebec Court of Appeal upheld the firing of two Montreal paramedics who refused to help a dying man because they were on break. Federal Finance Minister Ralph Goodale announced on February 10 that Ottawa's budgetary surplus could reach $7 billion in 2004, much higher than originally anticipated. On February 15, a British Broadcasting Corporation investigation showed that Canadian photojournalist Zahra Kazemi, beaten to death last June while in the custody of Iranian security officials, was taken to hospital for her injuries but prevented from receiving medical treatment. New Brunswick's auditor general accused Premier Bernard Lord of misleading the public by claiming a $1-million surplus when the province actually had a $109-million deficit. Premier Lord dismissed the charge as a dispute over accounting semantics (February 18). A mild strain of the avian flu virus that was ravaging poultry farms in southeast Asia turned up at a chicken farm in British Columbia on February 20. Japan and the European Union later banned Canadian poultry imports from British Columbia. At the February 25 inaugural meeting of the Council of the Federation, which had replaced the annual premiers' conference, the country's premiers warned that without more federal funding and reforms Canada's health-care system could not survive. Alberta premier Ralph Klein suggested that his province might opt out of the system.

MARCH 2004

WORLD

Afghanistan: On March 31, about 50 nations pledged more than $4.4 billion in grants and loans to Afghanistan. More than half came from the United States. **Greece:** The conservative New Democracy Party convincingly won the Greek election on March 8, sweeping out the Socialist Party after a decade in power. New Democracy Party leader Costas Karamanlis became Greece's youngest-ever prime minister at 47. **Haiti:** An international force composed of troops from the U.S., France, Canada and Chile began to arrive in Haiti on March 1 with a UN mandate to provide security. While in exile, former president Jean-Bertrand Aristide claimed that he had been toppled and abducted by U.S. forces. American officials retorted that he had left voluntarily. On March 4, South Africa joined calls by Caribbean leaders for an inquiry into the circumstances surrounding Aristide's departure. On March 10, lawyer Gérard Latortue was appointed as interim prime minister. **Iraq:** About 170 Shiite Muslims marking the religious festival of *ashoura* at mosques in Baghdad and Karbala were killed by suicide bombers on March 2. Twenty-five members of the Governing Council signed an interim constitution on March 8. The document, which would take effect in July 2004 when the U.S.-led coalition was to transfer power to Iraq, calls for a federal government to oversee the entire country, and makes Islam "a," not "the," source of Iraqi legislation. On March 31, an Iraqi mob shot, mutilated and dragged the bodies of four American civilian contract workers through the streets of Fallujah. Two of the bodies were later hung from a bridge. **Ireland:** On March 29, the Irish government became the first in Europe to implement a smoking ban in all workplaces, including pubs and restaurants. **Israel and the Palestinian Territories:** On March 22, Sheik Ahmed Yassin, the leader and founder of the military group Hamas, was killed in a missile attack by Israeli forces as he was leaving a mosque in Gaza City. The next day, Hamas appointed Dr. Abdel Aziz Rantisi as its leader. **Libya:** British Prime Minister Tony Blair ended nearly 30 years of diplomatic isolation of Libya with a visit to Tripoli on March 25. Blair and Libyan leader Mu'ammar Qadhafi promised to fight terrorism. **NATO:** In the largest expansion in the Alliance's 55-year history, the North Atlantic Treaty Organization formally admitted seven east European countries, bringing its membership to 26. The new members are Bulgaria, Estonia, Lithuania, Latvia, Romania, Slovakia and Slovenia (March 29). **Pakistan:** Amid rumours that Ayman al-Zawahiri, al-Qaeda's deputy leader, was hiding in South Waziristan, Pakistani troops launched an assault on hundreds of foreign militants in the area on March 16. **Russia:** President Vladimir Putin named Russia's ambassador to the European Union, Mikhail Fradkov, as prime minister on March 1. On March 14, Putin was overwhelmingly re-elected to a second term. **Rwanda:** The French newspaper *Le Monde* reported on March 10 that a French police investigation blamed current Rwandan president Paul Kagame for shooting down a predecessor's plane in 1994—an assassination that was used as a pretext for the genocide that followed. Kagame, the rebel leader who ended the genocide, has always denied the charge. **Serbia and Montenegro:** Dozens of people died in violence between Serbs and ethnic Albanians in Kosovo on March 17. In previous weeks, Albanians had burned Serb homes and churches, and Serbs had burned down Albanian mosques. On March 18, NATO deployed 1,000 peacekeepers to boost the 18,000-strong force already there. **South Korea:** On March 12, the National Assembly voted 193-2 to impeach President Roh Moo-Hyun for allegedly violating election laws. Prime Minister Koh Gun took over as head of state. **Spain:** In the worst terrorist attack in Spanish history, at least 10 bombs exploded on four commuter trains during rush hour in Madrid, killing 191 people and wounding more than a thousand (March 11). While the Basque separatist group ETA was initially blamed for the attack, on March 14 officials found a videotape on which al-Qaeda took responsibility. Also on March 14, the governing Popular Party, led by Prime Minister José María Aznar, was upset by José Luis Rodríguez Zapatero and the opposition Socialists in a general election. Many blamed the election loss on Aznar's handling of the tragedy and his support for the U.S. war in Iraq. Zapatero swiftly promised to pull Spanish troops out of Iraq. **Taiwan:** On the eve of the general election, President Chen Shui-bian and Vice President Annette Lu were shot while campaigning in Tainan (March 19). Neither sustained life-threatening injuries. The next day, Chen was re-elected by a slim margin, beating Nationalist Party candidate Lien Chen 50.1 percent to 49.9 percent. **United States:** On March 2, NASA announced that its Mars robot explorer *Opportunity* had detected sedimentary rocks that appear to have been formed under flowing saltwater. Winning nine of ten states in the "Super Tuesday" Democratic primaries and caucuses on March 2, Massachusetts Senator John Kerry informally secured his nomination as the Democratic candidate for the presidential election. Senator John Edwards dropped out of the race the next day. Martha Stewart was found guilty of four counts of obstruction of justice on March 5, stemming from her December 2001 sale of shares of the biotech stock ImClone. On March 11, the California Supreme Court ordered the city of San Francisco to stop issuing marriage licenses to same-sex couples. The Bush administration's former counter-terrorism chief, Richard Clarke, said that Bush's inner circle failed to heed his warnings in 2001 of an imminent attack by al-Qaeda, and were focused instead on Iraq (March 21). On March 23, Secretary of State Colin Powell and Secretary of Defense Donald Rumsfeld appeared before the 9/11 Commission investigating the September 11, 2001, terrorist attacks. Former President Bill Clinton's Defense Secretary William Cohen and Secretary of State Madeleine Albright also testified. **Uzbekistan:** Several terrorist bombings and shootings on March 28 killed more than 40 people in the capital Tashkent and the city of Bukhara. President Islam Karimov blamed Islamic militants. Two days later, three police officers were killed when 20 suicide bombers blew themselves up. **Venezuela:** Five days of opposition protests across the country started on March 2 after the country's electoral council invalidated 1.8 million of 3.4 million signatures on a petition calling for a recall vote on unpopular President Hugo Chávez.

CANADA

On March 5, about 500 Canadian Forces troops and six helicopters were deployed to Haiti as part of international efforts to stabilize the security situation in the country and facilitate the delivery of humanitarian aid. On March 5, the Quebec Court of Appeal overturned a lower court judgment and rejected a Sikh student's right to wear the _kirpan_, a ceremonial dagger, to school. The Court ruled that security concerns trumped religious demands. Former Liberal cabinet minister Sheila Copps lost a hotly contested nomination fight in her Hamilton riding to Minister of Transport Tony Valeri on March 6. Citing alleged voting irregularities, Copps asked the party to overturn the result, and later asked the RCMP to investigate. On March 10, the Department of National Defence reported a C$160-million accounting fraud involving computer company Hewlett-Packard. HP denied it had anything to do with the

decade-long scam. On March 11, British Columbia health officials warned that pork from the Port Coquitlam pig farm of accused mass murderer Robert Pickton may be contaminated with human remains. Bombardier announced on March 17 that it would shut seven rail plants in Europe and cut 6,600 jobs worldwide. The restructuring came in response to a loss of C$448 million in the latest quarter. On March 19, former New Brunswick premier Frank McKenna turned down Prime Minister Paul Martin's invitation to be a "star candidate" in the Liberal government. In an effort to stem the spread of the avian flu virus, Health Canada ordered the culling of 275,000 chickens and turkeys on ten large farms within a high-risk region of British Columbia on March 24. Once completed, the cull killed a total of 365,000 birds, or about 10 percent of the province's poultry population. Quebec radio personality Robert Gillet was convicted of sex with an underage prostitute on March 26. Gillet, who said he thought the girl was of legal age, was the star witness in the case of an alleged teen prostitution ring that resulted in charges against 43 men. A hiker found Cecilia Zhang's remains in a ravine in Mississauga, Ontario, on March 27, nearly six months after her disappearance from her Toronto home. Auditor-General Sheila Fraser reported that, despite a plan to spend nearly $8 billion to improve national security, Canada's security agencies were failing to cooperate effectively to combat terrorism. Fraser also cited vulnerabilities at airports and border crossings (March 30).

APRIL 2004

WORLD

Afghanistan: The governor of Faryab Province stepped down on April 8, as forces loyal to warlord General Abdul Rashid Dostrum took control of several districts. **Argentina:** An international arrest warrant was issued for former president Carlos Menem on April 20.

Menem is accused of fraudulently using public funds. **Cyprus:** About 75 percent of Greek Cypriots rejected the United Nations plan to reunify the divided island. However, 65 percent of Turkish Cypriots approved the plan (April 24). **India:** The first phase of India's general elections—which involves four stages over three weeks and 670 million voters—began on April 20. **Iraq:** On April 4, eight U.S. soldiers in several southern Iraq cities died in coordinated attacks ordered by radical Shia cleric Muqtada al-Sadr, after his newspaper had been closed down by the Americans for inciting violence. Shiites loyal to al-Sadr continued their assault on U.S. and allied forces throughout the month. On April 7, U.S. officials reported evidence that Shiite and Sunni leaders were uniting against the U.S.-led occupation. Three Japanese civilians were taken hostage on April 8 by Iraqi militants, who threatened to kill them unless Japan withdrew its troops from the country. A day later, an American contract worker was taken hostage. On April 15, the U.S. agreed to a plan to replace the Iraqi Governing Council with a caretaker government when sovereignty is to transfer to Iraq on June 30. Five coordinated suicide bombings targetting police buildings on April 21 in Basra killed 68 people, including 23 children. United Nations envoy to Iraq Lakhdar Brahimi announced on April 27 that he would select a transitional government to run Iraq until elections are held in 2005. **Israel and the Palestinian Territories:** On the eve of an April 13 visit to the U.S., Prime Minister Ariel Sharon announced that as part of his proposal to unilaterally separate from Palestinians, he would leave five West Bank settlements under Israeli control. U.S. President George Bush endorsed Sharon's separation plan, eliciting outrage among Arab leaders. Israeli missiles killed Hamas leader Dr. Abdel Aziz Rantisi in the Gaza Strip on April 17. Dr. Rantisi replaced Sheik Ahmed Yassin after Yassin's assassination in March. **Italy:**

Despite efforts to the contrary, the media bill pushed through by Silvio Berlusconi's government became law on April 30. The president of Italy's state-run television network resigned in protest. **Jordan:** The government announced on April 17 that it had foiled a terrorist attack involving chemical weapons against the headquarters of its intelligence service. Al-Qaeda was accused of planning the attack. **Lithuania:** President Rolandas Paksas was ousted after a close impeachment vote in parliament on April 6. An earlier parliamentary report called Paksas a threat to national security, and charged that his office was under the influence of criminals and shady political lobbyists. **North Korea:** A massive explosion occurred when a train car carrying explosives touched a live power cable in Ryongchon on April 22, killing at least 160 people. The normally insular North Korean government asked the United Nations for assistance. **Pakistan:** Scientist Abdul Qadeer Khan, who confessed to selling nuclear technology to North Korea in February, reported on April 13 that North Korea possesses nuclear weapons, and that he had personally seen three such devices in a North Korean nuclear plant five years ago. **Peru:** On April 27, a mob protesting corruption lynched the mayor of the town of Ilave, and attacked the police station with gasoline bombs. **Saudi Arabia:** A suicide bomber blew up the headquarters of the security service in the capital Riyadh on April 21, killing at least four people. A radical Islamist militant group claimed responsibility. **Slovakia:** Populist politician Ivan Gasparovic became Slovakia's new president, beating frontrunner Vladimir Meciar in a run-off election on April 18. **South Africa:** Led by President Thabo Mbeki, the African National Congress won the general election on April 15, with 70 percent of the vote. **Spain:** Tunisian Sarhane Ben Abdelmajid Fakhet, who allegedly led and coordinated the March train bombings in Madrid, killed himself and three others in a blast at an apartment building in the capital. The explosion occurred as police were raiding the building (April 3). The day after being sworn in as prime minister, José Luis Rodríguez Zapatero ordered Spain's soldiers back from Iraq (April 18). **Taiwan:** During a visit to China on April 14, U.S. Vice-President Dick Cheney confirmed that the United States did not support Taiwan's independence, nor any reunification between China and Taiwan brought about by force. **Thailand:** On April 28, gang members armed with machetes attacked police and security stations in the Muslim-dominated south, killing more than 110 people. Government officials blamed Muslim separatists for the violence. **United Kingdom:** In a reversal of position, on April 19 Prime Minister Tony Blair declared that there would be a referendum on the EU constitution. Most polls had shown strong opposition among Britons to the proposed constitution. **United States:** National Security Advisor Condoleezza Rice testified before the 9/11 Commission on April 8, telling members that President George Bush was warned of suspicious activity by terrorists before the attacks occurred, but that there was no information that said an attack was imminent. In its preliminary report on April 14, the commission harshly criticized the U.S. intelligence community for failing to follow up on important leads and not making counter-terrorism a priority. On April 15, the Environmental Protection Agency told 31 governors that the air pollution in their states did not meet federal health standards. In the largest abortion rights rally in 12 years, hundreds of thousands of people gathered in Washington, D.C. to protest the Bush administration's policy on reproductive rights (April 25). In a closed-door meeting on April 29, President Bush and Vice-President Dick Cheney were interviewed by members of the 9/11 Commission. Abuses of prisoners at Abu Ghraib prison by U.S. soldiers were reported on April 30, along with images of American soldiers smiling as they stood over groups of Iraqis in sexually abusive situations.

CANADA

Twenty thousand Newfoundland civil servants walked off the job on April 1, in opposition to the Conservative government's decision to freeze public sector wage increases. The province responded with plans to lay off as many as 4,000 to address its $840-million deficit. On April 2, Prime Minister Paul Martin appointed former British Columbia New Democratic Party premier Ujjal Dosanjh as a "star candidate" for the Liberals in the next election. Despite the protests of environmentalists worldwide, an estimated 5,000 sealers began the largest cull of seals in Canada in 40 years off the coast of Newfoundland and Labrador on April 12. The government explained that the exploding seal population was responsible for a decline in fish stocks, and that the seal cull was conducted as humanely as possible. Making a rare prime ministerial visit to a military base, on April 15 Paul Martin announced that Canada would acquire three new support ships for the navy at a total cost of $2.1 billion. New Democratic Party MP Svend Robinson stunned supporters on April 15 by admitting that, while attending a public jewellery sale, he stole an expensive ring. Robinson said that he had been battling severe stress for a few months and that "something just snapped." The family of Maher Arar announced on April 22 that it was suing the federal government, the Royal Canadian Mounted Police, the Canadian Security Intelligence Service and several Canadian consular officers for $400 million. The suit claimed authorities breached Arar's Charter rights and were guilty of racism when they pursued an investigation into his alleged extremism links in 2002. Huguette Tremblay, the career civil servant who handled the paperwork in the controversial sponsorship program, directly contradicted former minister Alfonso Gagliano's testimony that he only met those in charge of the program a couple of times annually (April 26). Tremblay told a parliamentary committee that the program directors were in weekly contact with Gagliano and other senior Liberals, and that civil servants were told to "blindly follow" directives from above. On April 27, the federal government unveiled a new $690-million national security policy, aimed at tightening port security, funding cyber-security initiatives, improving the national fingerprinting system, and enhancing Canada's intelligence capabilities. Quebec's justice minister, Marc Bellemare, resigned on April 28, stating that he was disappointed with Premier Jean Charest's Liberal government and the slow pace of reforms.

MAY 2004

WORLD

Burundi: The country's main rebel group walked out of a power-sharing government on May 3, raising fears of a return to civil war. On May 21, the United Nations Security Council voted to send a 5,500-strong peacekeeping force to Burundi to take over from African Union operations there. **European Union:** Ten countries, eight of them former Communist states, joined the European Union on May 1, bringing total membership to 25. **Greece:** Fears grew over security at the summer Olympic Games when three small bombs went off outside a central Athens police station on May 5, injuring one policeman. A Greek extremist group called "Revolutionary Struggle" claimed responsibility for the attack. **Haiti:** Adding to the ills of the violence-ravaged country, flooding caused by several days of heavy rains in late May killed nearly 2,000 people in Haiti and neighbouring Dominican Republic. **Honduras:** A fire in a severely overcrowded prison in Honduras on May 17 killed 103 inmates. All of the victims were members of youth gangs. **India:** Prime Minister Atal Bihari Vajpayee

resigned on May 13 following a surprising electoral loss to the Indian National Congress Party. The Congress Party named their leader, Italian-born Sonia Gandhi, as Prime Minister. On May 18, Sonia Gandhi announced that she would not become prime minister due to controversy over her birthplace. Former finance minister Manmohan Singh was named to the post. **Indonesia:** A month after voting was completed, Indonesia's election results were announced on May 5. Golkar, the party of former president Suharto, came out on top with 22 percent of the vote. President Megawati Sukarnoputri's party finished second. **Iraq:** On May 4, about 150 influential Shia leaders met in Baghdad and urged rebel Shia cleric Muqtada al-Sadr to hand over weapons and remove his militia from Najaf and Karbala. The meeting came as U.S. troops began an assault on a militia loyal to al-Sadr in Karbala and Diwaniya in southern Iraq. A videotape broadcast on an Islamist Web site on May 8 showed the murder and decapitation of Nicholas Berg, a 26-year-old American businessman seeking work in Iraq. The Web site stated that Abu Musab al-Zarqawi, who claimed to be an al-Qaeda leader, cut off Berg's head. On May 10, U.S. soldiers destroyed al-Sadr's headquarters in Baghdad. Ezzidin Salim, the president of the Iraqi Governing Council, was killed by a suicide bomber on May 17. Ghazi Mashal Ajil al-Yawer was chosen to succeed him. In a May 27 agreement, al-Sadr agreed to pull his militia from the streets after the U.S. agreed to withdraw from Najaf and suspend the arrest warrant for al-Sadr. On May 28, former exile and member of the Iraqi Governing Council Iyad Alawi was chosen to serve as interim premier after the U.S. plans to transfer sovereignty on June 30. **Israel and the Palestinian Territories:** Israeli Prime Minister Ariel Sharon suffered a setback when his Likud Party voted against his proposal to withdraw settlers and soldiers from the Gaza Strip (May 3). Six Israeli soldiers were killed and their body parts confiscated by Palestinian militants on May 11. In an Egyptian-brokered deal, the Palestinians returned the remains in exchange for Israeli withdrawal of troops from Gaza City on May 13. In pursuit of Palestinian militants, Israeli troops and bulldozers raided a Palestinian neighbourhood in the Gaza Strip on May 18, killing at least 39 people, demolishing more than 100 houses, and leaving some 1,000 homeless. The UN Security Council condemned the act. More than three dozen people were killed when an Israeli helicopter gunship opened fire on a protest march in the Gaza Strip on May 20. **Nigeria:** On May 12, 10 people were killed in two days of rioting by Muslims in the northern city of Kano. The rioters were demanding the government take action after a massacre of Muslims in the previous week by a Christian militia. **Panama:** Martín Torrijos won the presidential election in Panama on May 3. Torrijos is the son of the Panamanian military dictator who repatriated the Panama Canal from the United States. **Russia:** Akhmad Kadyrov, a former rebel leader who was elected as Chechen president in 2003, died when a bomb exploded during a parade at a stadium in Grozny (May 9). **Saudi Arabia:** On May 29, gunmen opened fire on a complex that housed foreigners and took several hostages. The next day, Saudi commandos stormed the complex, freeing most of the hostages and capturing several militants. Twenty-two people were killed in the fighting. **South Korea:** The Constitutional Court reinstated Roh Moo-Hyun as president on May 14, after dismissing his March impeachment by Parliament for alleged violation of electoral laws. **Sudan:** The government reached an accord with the People's Liberation Army on May 26, formally ending their decades' long civil war. Meanwhile, violence continued in a separate conflict in the western region of Darfur. **Syria:** U.S. President George Bush imposed sanctions (excluding food and medicine) on Syria on May 11, citing its alleged support of terrorism and for trying to undermine American policy in Iraq. **United Kingdom:** At an art auction at London's Sotheby's on May 5, Pablo Piacasso's work *Boy with a Pipe* (1905) sold for $104.1 million, smashing the previous record held by Vincent Van Gogh's *Portrait of Dr. Gachet,* which sold for $82.5 million in 1990. **United States:** On May 4, the Pentagon revised its plan to reduce the number of troops in Iraq, stating that 135,000 soldiers would remain in Iraq through 2005. In a May 5 interview on the prisoner abuse scandal, President George Bush called the acts "abhorrent," but drew criticism for not apologizing for the incidents. Bush formally apologized the next day at a White House meeting with King Abdullah II of Jordan. On May 6, the Food and Drug Administration ignored the opinion of its expert advisory panel and banned over-the-counter sales of the "morning-after pill." At hearings before the Senate and House Armed Service committees on May 7, Secretary of Defense Donald Rumsfeld apologized to Iraqis for the prisoner abuses, but rejected calls for his resignation. On May 16, President Bush changed his AIDS drugs policy to allow countries in Africa and the Caribbean to buy American drugs cheaper and administer them more efficiently. May 19, in the first court-martial of the Iraqi prisoner abuse scandal, specialist Jeremy Sivits was sentenced to one year in prison for mistreating detainees.

CANADA

Toronto's beleaguered police force, already facing allegations of corruption, came under more pressure when it was revealed on May 3 that the Royal Canadian Mounted Police had been investigating the force. Four policemen were later charged with 26 offences related to organized crime and gambling. The British Columbia government attempted to order 43,000 striking health care workers back to their jobs on May 3. The government's order also included a 15 percent wage cut and an increase in weekly working hours. Supported by other unions, the workers refused. Union leaders, however, eventually accepted the government's demands, sending angry employees back to work. Canadian authorities boarded five foreign fishing vessels just outside the 200-mile Economic Exclusion Zone on May 6, and issued two citations to one Portuguese ship for illegal overfishing. Ottawa and the Nova Scotia government announced a 10-year $400 million plan to clean up the infamous Sydney tar ponds (May 12). Rock singer Bono appeared in Ottawa on May 12 to praise Prime Minister Paul Martin's recently announced commitment to fighting HIV/AIDS, including giving $100 million to the World Health Organization to bring anti-retroviral drugs to AIDS patients in developing countries. The federal government announced on May 13 that Canada's new National Microbiology Laboratory, created in response to the 2002–03 SARS crisis, would be based in Winnipeg. On May 23, Prime Minister Paul Martin dropped the writ for a general election for June 28. Polls were suggesting, however, that the Liberal Party may be reduced to a minority government. The Liberal Party released its health care platform on May 25, promising billions of dollars over five years to launch a national homecare program, shorten waiting times and add more family doctors. At an evening event on May 26, New Democratic Party leader Jack Layton accused Paul Martin of causing the deaths of homeless people by clawing back funding for housing projects when he was finance minister during the 1990s. Citing the Prairie drought and the mad cow crisis, Statistics Canada reported on May 27 that farm incomes fell to their lowest level in 25 years in 2003. As many as 10 million Canadians were unable to fully access their accounts and paycheques after internal computer problems at the Royal Bank starting on May 31 made it impossible to process direct deposits for almost a week.

JUNE 2004

WORLD

Afghanistan: In the face of growing violence, President Hamid Karzai called on NATO to send more troops to Afghanistan ahead of the October elections (June 29). **Argentina:** On June 9, a Chilean judge refused a second request by an Argentine court to extradite former president Carlos Menem, for questioning over corruption allegations. **Columbia:** The National Liberation Army, Colombia's second-largest leftist guerrilla group, agreed to start peace talks with the government on June 11. On June 16, 34 coca pickers were massacred in a small town close to the border with Venezuela. Police blamed the left-wing rebel group FARC, who battle right-wing paramilitaries for control of the country's drug trade. **European Union:** Most voters stayed away from the June 13 European elections. Those who did vote tended to punish their governments or support parties sceptical about further EU integration. The result was regarded as a blow to ongoing efforts to draft an EU constitution. The EU summit ended on June 18 with an agreement on a new constitution that included fewer vetoes by single countries and greater centralization. **Haiti:** A Brazilian-led and mostly Latin American United Nations force arrived in Haiti on June 1, taking over from the U.S.-led multinational force. The 8,000 UN soldiers will maintain the fragile peace and help survivors of the recent flooding. **Iran:** On June 21, the Iranian Revolutionary Guards captured three vessels and eight British servicemen, accusing them of straying into the Shatt al-Arab waterway between Iran and Iraq. They were released three days later. **Iraq:** On June 1, as the Iraqi Governing Council disbanded, a new government formed with a cabinet of 36 Iraqis, including Sunnis, Shiites, Kurds and Christians. Sheik Ghazi Ajil al-Yawer was named as president and Iyad Allawi as prime minister. The Mahdi Army, loyal to Muqtada al-Sadr, withdrew from Najaf and Karbala on June 5. On June 11, Muqtada al-Sadr endorsed the new government and urged his leaders to observe the existing ceasefire. The next day, he announced his intentions to form a political party and participate in the 2005 elections. Deputy Foreign Minister Bassam Salih Kubba was fatally shot in Baghdad on June 12; two other ministry officials were killed in the following week. As violence intensified in the lead-up to the June 30 transfer of power, a car bomb exploded near the Iraqi army's recruiting station on June 17, killing at least 40 people and wounding well over 100. Terrorists linked to Abu Musab al-Zaraqawi beheaded South Korean interpreter Kim Sun Il on June 22, after the South Korean government refused to pull its troops from Iraq. In an attempt to thwart attacks by insurgents, the U.S. handed power over to Iraqis on June 28, two days earlier than planned. **Israel and the Palestinian Territories:** On June 4, Israeli Prime Minister Ariel Sharon fired two cabinet members who opposed his plan to withdraw settlers and troops from the Gaza Strip. Two days later, Sharon's coalition government approved his plan. On June 30, the Israeli Supreme Court ordered Israel to dismantle a 20.5 mile portion of the security wall in the West Bank because it separates Palestinian landowners from their land. The ruling stated, however, that Israel has a legal right to build the fence. **North Korea:** The two Koreas agreed on June 5 to open transport links through the militarized zone that divides the two countries. The two countries also agreed on other measures that would reduce military tensions. During negotiations on North Korea's nuclear weapons program on June 23, the U.S. offered delivery of fuel oil and a "provisional security guarantee" if North Korea disclosed details of its program, allowed inspections, and dismantled it. The next day, North Korea threatened to test one of its nuclear weapons. **Philippines:** The vote count of presidential elections was finally completed on June 20, six weeks after the election. The count confirmed that Filipinos had re-elected Gloria Arroyo as president. The opposition claimed the poll was marred by irregularities. **Saudi Arabia:** Paul Johnson, an American engineer, was kidnapped by an al-Qaeda cell demanding that the Saudi government release militants from prison (June 12). On June 18, the kidnappers decapitated Johnson. **Turkey:** At a June 16 meeting in Istanbul, the 57-member Organization of the Islamic Conference endorsed Iraq's new interim government, and the organization's secretary-general urged Muslim countries to try harder to be democratic. **United Nations:** On June 8, the Security Council voted 15-0 in favour of an American and British resolution to transfer power to an interim Iraqi government on June 30. The resolution also called for elections by January 31, 2005. The World Health Organization reported on June 22 that the polio virus had made a resurgence across Africa, reaching ten previously polio-free countries. **United States:** On June 1, a federal judge in San Francisco ruled that the ban on "partial birth" abortions, signed into law last year, was unconstitutional and compromised a woman's right to choose. The Justice Department said it would challenge the judgment and uphold the will of Congress. Central Intelligence Agency Director George Tenet unexpectedly resigned on June 3, after serving for seven years. He cited personal reasons, but many speculated his resignation was related to criticism of the CIA's intelligence failures regarding the September 11, 2001, terrorist attacks and weapons of mass destruction in Iraq. Former President Ronald Reagan, the 40th president of the United States, died at age 93 on June 3. Reagan had long suffered from Alzheimer's disease. The U.S. announced on June 7 that it planned to withdraw 12,500 of its 37,000 troops stationed in South Korea in 2006. The 9/11 Commission investigating the terrorist attacks against the United States reported on June 16 that it had found no link between al-Qaeda and Iraq. For the first time in four years, the Federal Reserve raised its key interest rate, from 1 percent to 1.25 percent (June 30). **Venezuela:** The country's electoral authority ruled on June 9 that opponents of Hugo Chávez had collected enough signatures to force the president to submit to a recall referendum. The referendum was set for August 15.

CANADA

Conservative Party health critic Rob Merrifield sparked an uproar on June 1 when he suggested that women wanting abortions should be required to go through third-party counselling. This was the first in a series of hot-button social issues that forced Conservative Party leader Stephen Harper to rein in a number of his candidates. In an unexpected move, on June 3 the United States proposed lowering duties on Canadian softwood lumber, from 27.2 percent to an average of 13.2 percent. The move raised optimism that the long-standing bilateral dispute over softwood lumber duties would soon end. Stephen Harper unveiled his party's platform on June 5, promising deep tax cuts and heavy spending to improve Canada's health care system and the military. On June 11, Edmonton police and the Royal Canadian Mounted Police discovered the body of another prostitute in a field outside the city, bringing to nine the number of murdered sex workers found in the city and its outskirts. Police established a special task force and stated that they may be looking for a serial killer. Reflecting the perception that the Liberals and Conservatives were in a dead heat, the French- and English-language televised debates on June 14 and 15, respectively, were heavy in attacks on Prime Minister Paul Martin and Conservative leader Stephen Harper. None of the leaders stumbled badly in the debates, which focused mostly on the sponsorship scandal, minority rights, health care and child care,

but Martin spent most of the time on the defensive. Alberta Premier Ralph Klein announced on June 17 that he planned to introduce changes to his province's health care system just two days after the federal election to allow for more private health care options. Prime Minister Martin seized upon the statement as proof that Canada's health care system would be in danger under a Conservative government. Klein later reversed his decision. The federal commission examining the case of Maher Arar got underway in Ottawa on June 21. The first witness was Ward Elcock, the former head of the Canadian Security Intelligence Service, who testified about the basic workings of the Service. New Brunswick Premier Bernard Lord caused a fury on June 23 after announcing the closure of 298 hospital beds and six hospitals across the province. On June 28, after one of the closest campaigns in recent Canadian history, the Liberal Party received a fourth consecutive mandate from voters—albeit as a minority government—by capturing 37 percent of the vote. The Liberals took 135 seats, most in seat-rich Ontario. The Conservative Party of Canada, only one point behind the Liberals at the final poll, received about 30 percent of the vote. The New Democratic Party came in at 16 percent and the Bloc Québécois, which captured two-thirds of Quebec seats, received 12 percent.

JULY 2004

WORLD

Afghanistan: Afghanistan's Election Commission announced on July 9 that the country's presidential election would take place on October 9, although Afghans will have to wait until April 2005 to elect local and national assemblies. Médecins Sans Frontières, a Nobel prize-winning international humanitarian group, announced on July 28 that it planned to leave Afghanistan because the government had failed to prosecute the suspect in the murder of five of its aid workers. **Austria:** President Thomas Klestil died after suffering heart failure on July 6, on the eve of his departure to make way for Heinz Fischer. **China:** The head of China's space agency announced on July 7 that his country plans to send an unmanned mission to the moon in 2007. **France:** President Jacques Chirac announced on July 14 that France would join other countries in holding a referendum on the European Union constitution. **India:** More than 80 children died when an elementary school caught fire in southern India on July 16. **Iraq:** Former Iraqi president Saddam Hussein, now in Iraqi hands, appeared in court on July 1 with 11 co-defendants, on charges of crimes against humanity stemming from the 1988 gassing of Iraqi Kurds, the 1990 invasion of Kuwait, and the persecution of political opponents. The Iraqi government arrested more than 500 people on July 13, to show its resolve in checking violent crime. Iraqi insurgents led by Abu Musab al-Zarqawi beheaded another hostage, a Bulgarian truck driver, on July 14. Also that day, the governor of the northern province of Nineveh was killed in an ambush. A surge of kidnappings—of Kuwaitis, Egyptians and Jordanians—occurred in late July, following Philippine President Gloria Arroyo's accession to kidnappers' demands that Filipino troops be withdrawn from Iraq. At least 70 people died on July 28 when a suicide bomb exploded outside a police station in Baquba. **Israel and the Palestinian Territories:** In a July 9 ruling, the International Court of Justice said that the portion of Israel's security barrier cutting into occupied Palestinian land in the West Bank is illegal. The non-binding ruling advised Israel to remove the barrier. Israel ignored the verdict. Palestinian Prime Minister Ahmed Qurei submitted his resignation to leader Yasser Arafat on July 17 following days of unrest in the Gaza Strip. Arafat refused to accept the resignation. Qurei withdrew it ten days later, after Arafat agreed to hand over

some control of security agencies. On July 20, the United Nations General Assembly passed a resolution demanding that Israel comply with the International Court of Justice ruling on its security barrier. **Japan:** For the first time since 1989, Japan's opposition won partial elections for the upper house on July 11. The ruling Liberal Democratic Party, collecting only 49 of the 121 seats, contested. The LDP's coalition, however, retained its majority in both houses. **Mexico:** On July 23, a special prosecutor accused former president Luis Echeverría of genocide for ordering the 1971 massacre of 25 student protestors. A federal judge dismissed the case the next day. **The Netherlands:** The opening of the defence case by Slobodan Milosevic at the war-crimes tribunal in The Hague was postponed on July 16 due to the former Yugoslav president's ill health. **Portugal:** Enormous underdog Greece took the Euro 2004 soccer championship in Lisbon on July 5. **Sudan:** U.S. Secretary of State Colin Powell and Secretary-General of the United Nations Kofi Annan visited Sudan on July 1 and urged the government to rein in the Arab militias attacking the black population of Darfur. Calls for the UN to impose sanctions on Sudan grew stronger throughout July, as government-backed Arab militias continued to commit atrocities in Darfur. France urged the African Union to deal with the problem without western intervention, while the Sudanese government said it was prepared to use force if foreign troops entered the country. **Thailand:** Officials gathered in Bangkok on July 11 for the 15th International AIDS Conference, to discuss the state of the worldwide epidemic. The World Health Organization said that the world has "failed miserably" to combat the spread of the disease. **United Kingdom:** On July 14, the Butler Report on intelligence in the run-up to the war in Iraq faulted the British government for relying on "seriously flawed" intelligence to make the case for war. The report, however, did not find evidence that Prime Minister Tony Blair misled the public or intentionally exaggerated the threat posed by Saddam Hussein. **United Nations:** A July 15 report by the UN Development Program found that life expectancy in seven African countries dropped to below 40 years, largely because of the spread of AIDS. Ashraf Qazi, Pakistan's ambassador to the United States, was appointed as the UN's new special representative for Iraq. He replaced Sergio Vieira de Mello, who was killed in a bombing last August. **United States:** The cornerstone of the Freedom Tower, which will be constructed on the site of the World Trade Center, was laid during a ceremony on July 4. Presumptive Democratic presidential nominee John Kerry announced on July 6 that he would select Senator John Edwards as his vice-presidential running mate. The Department of Defense established the Combat Status Review Tribunal on July 7, allowing nearly 600 prisoners in Guantánamo Bay to challenge their status as enemy combatants. The Senate Intelligence Committee unanimously reported on July 9 that information on Iraq's weapons programs was flawed and exaggerated. The assessment was particularly critical of the CIA. On July 9, a federal appeals court ruled against the Energy Department's plan for burying nuclear waste at Nevada's Yucca Mountain. On July 14, the Senate voted 50–48 against a proposed constitutional amendment to ban gay marriage. The director of the Los Alamos nuclear weapons laboratory shut down operations on July 16, after a series of security and safety lapses, including the disappearance of classified information. Domestic diva Martha Stewart was sentenced to five months in prison and fined $30,000 on July 16 after being found guilty of four counts of obstruction of justice and lying to federal investigators. On July 29, Senator John Kerry officially accepted the nomination as the Democratic candidate for president at the Democratic National Convention in Boston. On July 30, the White House predicted a $445-billion deficit for the current fiscal year, the largest in history.

CANADA

Nine people were detained on July 6 after more than 500 kilograms of cocaine with a street value of C$16 million was discovered in a sailboat off the coast of Nova Scotia. On July 6, Regina police began a sweeping search for a five-year-old Native girl, Tamra Jewel Keepness, who disappeared from her home in the city the night before. Police and volunteers combed the city and surrounding area, but ended their search a week after she was last seen. Alberta Premier Ralph Klein announced on July 12 that the province would pay off its outstanding public debt and become Canada's only debt-free province. Two Ontario men were convicted of the largest Goods and Services Tax fraud in Canadian history on July 12, and given four years in jail. The pair defrauded Ottawa of $24 million in a complex, multi-year scam involving fictitious cars. The Canadian Radio-television and Telecommunications Commission sparked controversy on July 13 after pulling the license of "shock-jock" radio station CHOI-FM in Quebec City. The CRTC said that the station had ignored repeated warnings to curb offensive on-air content that violated the Broadcasting Act. Ottawa recalled its ambassador to Iran on July 18 in protest after Tehran broke a promise to allow Canadian observers to attend the trial of the intelligence agent charged with killing photojournalist Zahra Kazemi. The agent was acquitted the following week; Minister of Foreign Affairs Pierre Pettigrew expressed Canada's dissatisfaction with the acquittal. Prime Minister Paul Martin's new cabinet was announced and sworn in on July 20. The ministry reflected a blend of experienced ministers and a host of newcomers, including former NHL hockey player Ken Dryden and British Columbia forestry executive David Emerson. Opposition parties called the new cabinet tired and familiar. On July 22, police in

Brampton, Ontario, arrested 21-year-old Min Chen, a visa student from China, for the murder of Cecilia Zhang, who was abducted from her Toronto home in October 2003, sparking a city-wide manhunt. After a decade of political limbo, Ottawa announced on July 23 that it would buy 28 navy helicopters for $3.2 billion from U.S.-based Sikorsky Aircraft Corporation to replace the Canadian Forces' fleet of ageing *Sea King* helicopters. Ignoring a proposal from a legislative committee, on July 28 New Brunswick Premier Bernard Lord forced insurance companies in the province to offer inexpensive, no-frills options and tighten regulations in an attempt to bring down rates.

AUGUST 2004

WORLD

Australia: On August 29, Prime Minister John Howard called a general election for October 9. Howard is seeking a fourth term as prime minister, but is expected to face stiff competition from Labour Party leader Mark Latham. **Burundi:** About 160 people, mostly Congolese Tutsi women and children, were massacred by members of the National Liberation Forces rebel group at a United Nations refugee camp on August 13. **Greece:** Amid heightened security and sluggish ticket sales, the Games of the XXVIII Olympiad opened in Athens on August 13, the first time the Games had returned to Greece since the birth of the modern Olympics in 1896. After two incident-free weeks, the U.S., Russia and China placed first, second and third, respectively. **Indonesia:** The convictions of four soldiers and policemen accused of human rights abuses during East Timor's independence referendum in 1999 were overturned by an appeal court on August 6. Indonesia has dismissed or overturned all charges against its officials for their actions in the former province. **Iraq:** Four Christian churches were attacked

in coordinated car bombings in Baghdad and Mosul on August 1. Shia cleric Muqtada al-Sadr, after moving his army into a base at the Imam Ali mosque in Najaf, ordered an uprising against American and allied troops on August 5. The subsequent violence killed hundreds of Iraqis and broke a fresh ceasefire. As negotiations between the Iraqi government and al-Sadr broke down on August 14, Iraqi and U.S. troops prepared to attack the insurgents. Facing imminent attack, al-Sadr announced on August 18 that he would leave the mosque and transform his army into a political group. On August 31, a dozen Nepalese labourers were executed by the Army of Ansar al-Sunna, an Iraqi militant organization. **Israel and the Palestinian Territories:** Prime Minister Ariel Sharon suffered a political setback on August 18 when his Likud Party voted against his plan to form a coalition with the opposition Labour Party. Sharon required the Labour Party's support to follow through with his plan to unilaterally withdraw Jewish settlements from the Gaza Strip. **North Korea:** A defence newsmagazine reported on August 3 that North Korea may be developing a sea-based missile system that could bring the U.S. within range of a nuclear strike by the Stalinist state. **Norway:** In a daring midday robbery at Oslo's crowded Munch Museum, thieves made away with two of Edvard Munch's most famous paintings, *The Scream* and *Madonna* on August 22. **Paraguay:** Almost 500 people died when a fire swept through a supermarket complex on August 1 near the capital, Asunción. Two days later, prosecutors charged six people with murder after survivors claimed that security guards trapped customers inside by locking the doors to prevent looting. **Russia:** On August 25, two passenger planes crashed within minutes of each other, killing all 89 people aboard. Finding traces of explosives on both planes, Russian officials declared the incidents as acts of Chechen terrorism.

In the Chechen presidential elections on August 30, the Kremlin's choice for president, Alu Alkhanov, won in a landslide. International observers questioned the fairness of the process. The following day, a woman suicide bomber detonated a bomb outside a Moscow subway station, killing nine others and wounding more than 50. **South Korea:** On August 11, an area in the centre of the country was selected as the site for a new capital. The new city is intended to reduce Seoul's overcrowding and economic dominance, and is scheduled for completion by 2030. **United Kingdom:** On August 4, Defence Secretary Geoff Hoon upset the Spanish government by visiting Gibraltar to mark the 300th anniversary of the colony's acquisition by Britain. **United States:** A devastating hurricane season began for Floridians as Hurricane Bonnie pounded the Florida Panhandle on August 12, forcing the evacuation of about 1.9 million people. Hurricane Charley struck Florida's west coast the next day, forcing two million people to evacuate, killing at least 20, and leaving tens of thousands homeless. President Bush announced on August 16 that the U.S. will withdraw about a third of its stationed forces overseas—up to 70,000 troops—from Europe and Asia over the next decade. On August 24, a report of the independent panel investigating the prisoner abuse scandal at Iraq's Abu Ghraib prison criticized senior commanders and top administration officials for oversight failures. Amid hundreds of thousands of protesters marching in midtown Manhattan, the Republican Party gathered in New York during the week of August 30 to hold their national convention and confirm George Bush as the party's nominee for President. **Venezuela:** On August 15, President Hugo Chávez survived a recall referendum by a 59 percent to 41 percent margin. Opposition parties protested the results, claiming the vote was rigged.

CANADA

On August 3, Alberta's auditor general reported that the province's three largest meat packers nearly tripled their profits when the U.S. shut its doors to Canadian beef due to a single case of BSE (bovine spongiform encephalopathy, also known as Mad Cow disease). Despite plunging prices for cattle, consumer prices for beef changed little. The Canadian branch of the United Food and Commercial Workers became the first to gain a presence in a North American Wal-Mart store, after becoming certified to represent 180 workers in Jonquiere, Quebec, on August 3. The union vowed to organize other Canadian stores owned by the U.S. retailer. Ottawa announced on August 4 that it was investigating whether the Israeli spy agency Mossad was using altered Canadian passports to move around the world after promising in 1997 never to do so again. New research published in the Canadian Medical Association Journal on August 4 showed that a deadly bacterium called Clostridium difficile was infecting patients at a hospital in Sherbrooke, Quebec. The "superbug" had already been blamed for at least 80 deaths in Montreal and Calgary. Defence Minister Bill Graham announced on August 5 that Canada had signed an amendment to the North American Aerospace Defence Command (NORAD) Agreement that would allow NORAD to share its missile-warning information with the organization responsible for the U.S. ballistic missile defence program. Reports on August 13 suggested that U.S.-based discount chain Target Corporation was considering buying the Hudson's Bay Company, which opened Canada's Northwest over three hundred years ago. Manitoba pedophile Robert Arthurson, currently serving a life sentence for abducting and killing a 13-year-old girl in The Pas in 1994, surprised his parole board by admitting to sexually abusing 15 or 16 other young girls (August 18). By the close of the Olympic Games in Athens, Greece, on August 29, Canadian athletes had won a total of 12 medals, including three gold. The medal count was lower than in the previous Games in Australia, sparking calls for increased funding for amateur Canadian sport.

SEPTEMBER 2004

WORLD

Caribbean: Dozens were killed as Hurricane Ivan smashed through the Caribbean in mid-September. Grenada was worst hit with 37 dead and more than 90 percent of its homes damaged or destroyed, but Barbados, Cuba, the Dominican Republic, Haiti, Jamaica, and the southern United States also suffered significant damage. **Haiti:** Already devastated after a year of civil violence and flooding, Haiti suffered another blow when Hurricane Jeanne swept through the country on September 22, causing severe flooding and more than 2,000 deaths. About 300,000 people were left homeless. **Indonesia:** A car bomb exploded outside the Australian Embassy in Jakarta on September 7, killing eight people and wounding nearly 200. **Iraq:** The U.S. death toll in Iraq reached 1,000 on September 7 following violence between rebel cleric Muqtada al-Sadr's Mahdi Army and U.S. and Iraqi troops. On September 12, suicide bombings and attacks by insurgents across the country killed nearly 60 people. Two days later, a suicide bomber killed nearly 50 young men lining up to apply for jobs at the Baghdad police headquarters. Hours after a massive car bomb killed nearly 47 people outside a police station in Baghdad on September 14, Iraqi officials suggested that the spiralling violence may force a delay to the country's proposed January 2005 elections. A series of bomb blasts on September 30 ripped through a street celebration at the opening of a refurbished

sewage plant, killing at least 41 people, including 34 children. **Israel and the Palestinian Territories:** Israeli Prime Minister Ariel Sharon agreed on September 6 to change the path of the security barrier that cuts through the Palestinian West Bank. The new route would be closer to the line that divided the territories after the war of 1967, while still looping around large Jewish settlements in the West Bank. **North Korea:** A massive blast in a province close to the Chinese border occurred on September 9 as North Korea celebrated its National Day, causing speculation that it was a nuclear explosion. Reports in the days following the blast suggested it was not nuclear. **Russia:** About 30 armed guerillas, most of them Chechen separatists, took about 1,200 schoolchildren, parents and teachers hostage in a school in the southern Russian town of Beslan on September 1. The three-day standoff ended in tragedy on September 3 after explosives inside the school were detonated and armed Russian commandos stormed the building. Russian authorities reported that at least 330 people, mostly children, died. The hostage-takers were demanding Russian withdrawal from Chechnya. On September 28, Beslan residents accounting for the missing reported 150 more victims than the government acknowledged. **South Korea:** The government told the International Atomic Energy Agency on September 2 that a group of "rogue scientists" had produced a small amount of weapons-grade uranium, in violation of several international treaties. **Sudan:** U.S. Secretary of State Colin Powell testified on September 9 that the rapes, mass killings and destruction of property in Darfur qualify that conflict as genocide and urged the United Nations to take action. Use of the term genocide does not legally oblige countries to act to stop violence, but does increase the moral and political pressure to address the situation. **United Kingdom:** Thousands of members of England's rural aristocracy took to London on September 15 to protest a vote to ban the centuries-old tradition of foxhunting. Five protestors broke into the House of Commons, raising concerns about security. At his Liberal Party convention on September 28, Prime Minister Tony Blair delivered an address that amounted to an apology for having asserted that Iraq possessed chemical and biological weapons. **United Nations:** Secretary-General Kofi Annan reported on September 1 that the Sudanese government had failed to disarm Arab militias or stop attacks on civilians in Darfur, despite the Security Council's directive to do so or face sanctions. Despite the report, Russia, a veto-wielding permanent member of the Security Council, refused to agree to impose sanctions. **United States:** Hurricanes continued to pound Florida, which was hit by enormous and slow-moving Hurricane Frances on September 4, causing nearly $40 billion in damage and killing about 20. President Bush's military records were released on September 7, indicating that Bush logged 336 hours as a pilot before failing to appear for a medical exam. Other memos suggested that Bush received preferential treatment in joining the National Guard. On September 8, a space capsule containing samples of the sun crashed when its parachutes failed to open. Scientists were optimistic, however, that some of the valuable data inside the probe could be recovered. Up to 25 people were reported dead after Hurricane Ivan made landfall in Louisiana, Alabama and the Florida Panhandle on September 16. The fourth major hurricane to hit Florida, Hurricane Jeanne, pounded the state on September 26. The price of crude oil hit $50 per barrel for the first time in history on September 28, amid fears of disruptions to shipments around the world.

CANADA

The inquiry into the "Sponsorship Scandal" headed by Justice John Gomery got underway in Ottawa on September 7. Auditor-General Sheila Fraser and other senior bureaucrats appeared before the inquiry during its first week. The following week, the Commission learned that in 1997 the Clerk of the Privy Council sent a memo to Prime Minister Jean Chrétien telling him that he was directly responsible for the sponsorship program. More than 25,000 Revenue Canada workers and members of the Public Service Alliance of Canada began rotating strikes on September 8 in a dispute over wages and working conditions. It was widely expected that the strike would spread to more than 100,000 other public servants in early October. National Hockey League team owners announced on September 15 that they were locking out the players until a new contract could be negotiated, putting the entire 2004-05 season in jeopardy. After three days of complicated negotiations, Prime Minister Paul Martin and the country's provincial premiers and territorial leaders signed a 10-year, $41-billion health care deal on September 16. The agreement saw both sides compromise on their initial demands, with the federal government providing $18 billion over six years instead of $12 billion, and the provinces agreeing to national standards for waiting times. In an important gesture, Quebec was given the right to design its waiting-list plan according to its own standards and objectives. Major League Baseball announced on September 29 that the Montreal Expos, Canada's first major league baseball team, would be relocated to Washington, D.C., in 2005. Paul Martin announced on September 30 that he had asked Governor-General Adrienne Clarkson to extend her term by one year to September 2005; he cited her potential role in a minority Parliament as his reason for doing so.

THE STATISTICS SHOWN ARE INTENDED TO PRESENT an informative and comparative picture of the various nations of the world and their dependent territories. All data, including the geographic, population and government data, are taken from the latest available sources. The economic and finance/trade data indicate the size of the national economies and the amount of economic activity in the respective countries; the population, health and education data, and communications and transportation data give some evidence of the quality of life and the state of the infrastructure in each nation.

All dollar amounts are in US dollars. International dollar price weights have been used instead of an official currency exchange rate in an attempt to make more equitable comparisons.

The "Total Fertility Rate" figure represents the number of children born per woman, and indicates the potential for population growth. A high total fertility rate will have an impact on a nation's workforce—women's participation may be limited; it may also have an impact on the amount of education available and the level of education achieved in the general population.

The information contained in this section reflects data available up to and including October 1, 2004. Sources used for information include:
CIA World Fact Book 2003 • *"Compendium of Statistics: Illiteracy" (UNESCO)* • *Demographic Yearbook (UN)* • *Encyclopedia Britannica* • *Direction of Trade Statistics (International Monetary Fund)* • *Foreign Affairs Canada* • *Government Finance Statistics Monthly (International Monetary Fund)* • *"Human Development Report" (UN Development Programme)* • *International Financial Statistics Yearbook (International Monetary Fund)* • *International Financial Statistics (monthly IMF update)* • *Monthly Bulletin of Statistics (UN Statistical Division)* • *"Population and Vital Statistics Report" (UN Dept. of International Economic and Social Affairs)* • *World Bank Atlas (World Bank)* • *World Book Encyclopedia* • *World Culture Report (UNESCO)* • *World Debt Tables* • *"World Development Report" (World Bank)* • *"World Motor Vehicle Data" (Motor Vehicle Manufacturers Assoc. of the US Inc.)* • *"World Population" (UNESCO)* • *World Resources (World Resources Institute)* • *"World Tables" (Johns Hopkins UP)* • *Year Book of Labour Statistics (International Labour Office, Geneva).*

Afghanistan

Long-Form Name: Islamic State of Afghanistan
Capital: Kabul

■ GEOGRAPHY

Area: 647,500 sq. km
Coastline: none: landlocked
Climate: arid to semi-arid; cold winters and hot summers, considerable snowfall
Environment: damaging earthquakes occur in Hindu Kush mountains; poor soil, flooding, desertification, overgrazing, deforestation (largely due to logging for building materials and fuel), pollution, soil degradation. Drought and land mines remaining from the war make it impossible in many areas to grow even the most essential food supplies
Terrain: mostly rugged mountains; plains in north and southwest

Land Use: arable land: 12.13%, permanent crops: 0.22%, other: 87.65%, includes about 23,860 sq. km of irrigated farmland
Location: SW Asia (Middle East)

■ PEOPLE

Population: 28,717,213 (July 2003 est.)
Nationality: Afghan
Age Structure: 0–14 yrs: 41.8%; 15–64: 55.4%; 65+: 2.8% (2003 est.)
Population Growth Rate: 3.38% (2003 est.)
Net Migration: 10.32 migrants/1,000 population (2003 est.)
Ethnic Groups: 38% Pathan, 25% Tajik, 6% Uzbek, 19% Hazara; minor ethnic groups include Charar Aimaks, Turkoman, Baloch and others
Languages: 35% Pushtu (official), 50% Afghan Persian (Dari), 11% Turkic languages (primarily Uzbek and Turmen), 4% thirty minor languages (primarily Balochi and Pahai); much bilingualism
Religions: Islam (84% Sunni Muslim, 15% Shi'a Muslim), 1% other
Birth Rate: 40.63/1,000 population (2003 est.)

Death Rate: 17.15/1,000 population (2003 est.)
Infant Mortality: 142.48 deaths/1,000 live births (2003 est.)
Life Expectancy at Birth: 47.67 years male, 46.23 years female (2003 est.)
Total Fertility Rate: 5.64 children born/woman (2003 est.)
Literacy: 36.09% (2002 est.)

■ GOVERNMENT

Leader(s): President Hamid Karzai
Government Type: transitional
Administrative Divisions: 30 provinces (velayat, sing. & pl.)
Nationhood: Aug. 19, 1919 (from UK)
National Holiday: Victory of the Muslim Nation, Apr. 28; Remembrance Day for Martyrs and Disabled, May 4; Independence Day, August 19

■ ECONOMY

Overview: a poor country, largely dependent on farming (wheat) and livestock (sheep and goats); the economy is adversely affected by political and military disruptions; much of the population continues to suffer from insufficient food, clothing, housing and medical care; inflation remains a serious problem; government efforts to encourage foreign investment have failed
GDP: US$19 billion; per capita US$700; real growth rate n.a.
Inflation: n.a.
Industries: accounts for 20% of GDP; small-scale production of textiles, soap, furniture, shoes, fertilizer and cement; handwoven carpets; natural gas, oil, coal, copper
Labour Force: 11.7 million (2002); 80% agriculture and animal husbandry, 10% industry, 10% services and other
Unemployment: n.a.
Agriculture: largely subsistence farming and nomadic animal husbandry; cash products— opium poppies, wheat, fruit, nuts, karakul pelts, wool, mutton, barley, corn; production is limited due to the shortage of modern machinery, high-grade seed and fertilizer. Accounts for 60% of GDP.
Natural Resources: natural gas, crude oil, copper, coal, salt, talc, barites, sulphur, lead, zinc, iron ore, slate, precious and semi-precious stones, especially lapis lazuli, amethysts, rubies

■ FINANCE/TRADE

Currency: afghani (Af) = 100 puls
International Reserves Excluding Gold: n.a.
Gold Reserves: n.a.

Budget: revenues US$200 million; expenditures US$550 million, including capital expenditures of US$n.a. (2003 plan est.)
Defence Expenditures: 7.7% of GDP (2002)
Education Expenditures: n.a.
External Debt: n.a.
Exports: US$98 million (2002 est.); commodities: natural gas 55%, fruit and nuts 24%, handwoven carpets, wool, cotton, hides, gemstones; partners: Pakistan, Germany, India, Belgium, Russia, United Arab Emirates
Imports: US$1.007 billion (2002 est.); commodities: capital goods, food and petroleum products, most consumer goods; partners: Pakistan, Kenya, Japan, India, South Korea, Turkmenistan

■ COMMUNICATIONS

Daily Newspapers: 5/1,000 inhabitants (2000)
Televisions: 14/1,000 inhabitants (2002)
Radios: 114/1,000 inhabitants (2001)
Telephones: 1 line/1,000 inhabitants (2002)
Internet: users: 1,000 (2002)

■ TRANSPORTATION

Motor Vehicles: 67,000; 35,000 passenger cars
Roads: 21,000 km; 2,793 km paved
Railway: 9.6 km from Kushka (Turkmenistan) to Towraghondi, and 15.0 km from Termez (Uzbekistan) to Kheyrabad
Air Traffic: 150,000 passengers carried (2002)
Airports: 47; 10 have paved runways (2003 est.)

Canadian Embassy: c/o The Canadian Embassy, House 256, Street 15, Wazir-Akbar-Khan, Kabul, Afghanistan. Tel: (011-93-70) 294-281. Fax: none. e-mail: homcanadakabul@yahoo.com
Embassy in Canada: Embassy of Afghanistan, 246 Queen St., Suite 400, Ottawa, K1P 4E3 Tel: (613) 563-4223. Fax: (613) 563-4962 e-mail: afghanembott@hotmail.com

Albania

Long-Form Name: Republic of Albania
Capital: Tirana

■ GEOGRAPHY

Area: 28,748 sq. km
Coastline: 362 km
Climate: mild temperate; cool, cloudy, wet winters; hot, clear, dry summers; interior is cooler and wetter, with severe winters
Environment: subject to destructive earthquakes; soil erosion; water pollution; tsunami occur along southwestern coast; deforestation and water pollution are still current issues

Terrain: mostly mountains and hills; small plains along coast
Land Use: arable land: 21.09%, permanent crops: 4.45%, other: 74.46%; includes 3,400 sq. km irrigated
Location: SE Europe, bordering on Adriatic Sea

■ PEOPLE

Population: 3,582,205 (July 2003 est.)
Nationality: Albanian
Age Structure: 0–14 yrs: 28.1%; 15–64: 64.6%; 65+: 7.3% (2003 est.)
Population Growth Rate: 1.03% (2003 est.)
Net Migration: -1.39 migrants/1,000 population (2003 est.)
Ethnic Groups: 95% Albanian, 3% Greek, 2% others (Vlachs, Gypsies, Serbs and Bulgarians)
Languages: Albanian (Tosk is official dialect, also Gheg dialect), Greek
Religions: 70% Muslim, 20% Albanian Orthodox, 10% Roman Catholic
Birth Rate: 18.20/1,000 population (2003 est.)
Death Rate: 6.48/1,000 population (2003 est.)
Infant Mortality: 37.28 deaths/1,000 live births (2003 est.)
Life Expectancy at Birth: 69.53 years male, 75.42 years female (2003 est.)
Total Fertility Rate: 2.22 children born/woman (2003 est.)
Literacy: 86.5% (2003 est.)

■ GOVERNMENT

Leader(s): President Alfred Moisiu, Prime Minister Fatos Nano
Government Type: in transition to democracy
Administrative Divisions: 36 districts (rrethe, sing. —rreth) and 1 municipality (bashki)
Nationhood: Nov. 28, 1912 (from Ottoman Empire); People's Socialist Republic of Albania declared Jan. 11, 1946
National Holiday: Independence Day, Nov. 28

■ ECONOMY

Overview: the poorest country in Europe, it is a Stalinist-type economy (central planning and state ownership of the means of production); though largely self-sufficient in food until 1990, the recent break-up of co-operative farms and the general economic decline has forced Albania to rely increasingly on foreign aid; the government has taken strong measures to restore public order and to revive economic activity and trade
GDP: US$15.69 billion, per capita US$4,400; real growth rate 7.3% (2002)
Inflation: 6.0% (2002)
Industries: accounts for 27% of GDP (2002); food processing, textiles and clothing, lumber,

oil, cement, chemicals, basic metals, hydroelectricity; most industries produce at only fraction of past levels
Labour Force: 1.6 million (2002); 50% agriculture, 50% industry and services
Unemployment: 22.7% (2002)
Agriculture: accounts for 49% of GDP (2002); arable land per capita among lowest in Europe; one-half of workforce engaged in farming; produces wide range of temperate-zone crops and livestock; claims self-sufficiency in grain output; 80% of all arable land is now in private ownership. Products include wheat, corn, potatoes, fruits, meat, dairy products.
Natural Resources: crude oil, natural gas, coal, chromium, copper, timber, nickel, petroleum

■ FINANCE/TRADE

Currency: lek (L) = 100 quintars
International Reserves Excluding Gold: US$1.005 billion (Jan. 2004)
Gold Reserves: 0.069 million fine troy ounces (Jan. 2004)
Budget: revenues US$1.65 billion; expenditures US$2.0 billion, including capital expenditures of US$406 million. (2004 est.)
Defence Expenditures: 3.7% of central government expenditures (2002)
Education Expenditures: n.a.
External Debt: US$1.312 billion (2002)
Exports: US$446 million (2003); commodities: textiles, footwear, asphalt, bitumen, petroleum products, metals and metallic ores, electricity, oil, vegetables, fruit, tobacco; partners: Italy, Yugoslavia, Germany, Greece
Imports: US$1.835 billion (2003); commodities: machinery, machine tools, iron and steel products, foodstuffs, textiles, chemicals, pharmaceuticals; partners: Italy, Greece, Turkey, Germany, Bulgaria

■ COMMUNICATIONS

Daily Newspapers: 35/1,000 inhabitants (2000)
Televisions: 318/1,000 inhabitants (2002)
Radios: 260/1,000 inhabitants (2001)
Telephones: 71 lines/1000 persons (2002)
Internet: hosts: 172 (2002); users: 17,000 (2003)

■ TRANSPORTATION

Motor Vehicles: 233,900; 152,000 passenger cars
Roads: 18,000 km; 5,400 km paved
Railway: 447 km
Air Traffic: 138,000 passengers carried (2002)
Airports: 12; 4 have paved runways (2003 est.)

Canadian Embassy: Consulate of Canada, Rr: Bulevardi Shan d'Ark, Kulla Teknoprojekt Nr.

2, Ap.1, Tirana, Albania. Tel: (011 355 4) 257 274 / 257 275. Fax: (011 355 4) 257 073 e-mail: canadaalb@canada.gov.al
Embassy in Canada: Embassy of the Republic of Albania, 130 Albert St, Ste 302, Ottawa ON K1P 5G4. Tel: (613) 236-4114. Fax: (613) 236-0804. e-mail: embassyrepublicofalbania@on.aivn.com

Algeria

Long-Form Name: Democratic and Popular Republic of Algeria
Capital: Algiers

■ GEOGRAPHY

Area: 2,381,740 sq. km
Coastline: 998 km
Climate: arid to semi-arid; mild, wet winters with hot, dry summers along coast; drier with cold winters and hot summers on high plateau; sirocco is a hot, dust/sand-laden wind especially common in summer
Environment: mountainous areas subject to severe earthquakes; desertification; industrial and domestic pollution and soil erosion contribute to environmental problems
Terrain: mostly high plateau and desert; some mountains; narrow, discontinuous coastal plain
Land Use: arable land: 3.21%, permanent crops: 0.21%, other: 96.58%; includes 5,600 sq. km irrigated
Location: N Africa, bordering on Mediterranean Sea

■ PEOPLE

Population: 32,818,500 (July 2003 est.)
Nationality: Algerian
Age Structure: 0–14 yrs: 32.8%; 15–64: 63.0%; 65+: 4.2% (2003 est.)
Population Growth Rate: 1.65% (2003 est.)
Net Migration: -0.40 migrants/1,000 population (2003 est.)
Ethnic Groups: 99% Arab-Berber, less than 1% European
Languages: Arabic (official), French, Berber dialects
Religions: 99% Sunni Muslim (state religion); 1% Christian and Jewish
Birth Rate: 21.94/1,000 population (2003 est.)
Death Rate: 5.09/1,000 population (2003 est.)
Infant Mortality: 37.74 deaths/1,000 live births (2003 est.)
Life Expectancy at Birth: 69.14 years male, 72.01 years female (2003 est.)
Total Fertility Rate: 2.55 children born/woman (2003 est.)
Literacy: 68.9% (2002)

■ GOVERNMENT

Leader(s): President Abdelaziz Bouteflika, Prime Minister Ahmed Ouyahia
Government Type: republic
Administrative Divisions: 48 provinces (wilayas, sing. —wilaya)
Nationhood: July 5, 1962 (from France)
National Holiday: Anniversary of the Revolution, Nov. 1

■ ECONOMY

Overview: the economy is largely based on the exploitation of oil and natural gas products; dropping oil and gas prices have contributed to Algeria's most serious social and economic crisis since independence; recently, reforms have been implemented to combat social and economic problems
GDP: US$173.8 billion, per capita US$5,400; real growth rate 3.3% (2002 est.)
Inflation: 3.09% (2002 est)
Industries: petroleum, light industries, natural gas, mining, electrical, petrochemical, food processing. Accounts for 60% of GDP
Labour Force: 11.0 million (2002); 11% industry, 25% agriculture, 29% government, 15% construction and public works, 20% other
Unemployment: 29.8% (2002)
Agriculture: accounts for 8% of GDP and employs 25% of labour force; products include wheat, barley, grapes, oats, olives, fruit, livestock; must import more than one-third of its food
Natural Resources: crude oil, natural gas, iron. ore, phosphates, uranium, lead, zinc

■ FINANCE/TRADE

Currency: dinar (DA) = 100 centimes
International Reserves Excluding Gold: US$33.268 billion (Jan. 2004)
Gold Reserves: 5.583 million fine troy ounces (Jan. 2004)
Budget: revenues US$18.5 billion; expenditures US$22.7 billion, including capital expenditures US$5.8 billion (2003 est.)
Defence Expenditures: 12.0% of central government expenditure (2001)
Education Expenditures: n.a.
External Debt: US$22.80 billion (2002)
Exports: US$24.96 billion (2003 est.); commodities: petroleum and natural gas 97%; partners: Italy, France, US, Spain, Brazil
Imports: US$12.42 billion (2003 est.); commodities: capital goods, consumer goods, food and beverages; partners: France, Italy, Germany, US, Spain

■ COMMUNICATIONS

Daily Newspapers: 27/1,000 inhabitants (2000)
Televisions: 114/1,000 inhabitants (2002)
Radios: 244/1,000 inhabitants (2001)
Telephones: 61 lines/1,000 inhabitants (2002)
Internet: hosts: 821 (2002); users: 500,000 (2002)

■ TRANSPORTATION

Motor Vehicles: 930,000; 500,000 passenger cars
Roads: 104,000 km; 71,656 km paved
Railway: 3,973 km
Air Traffic: 3,027,000 passengers carried (2002)
Airports: 136; 54 have paved runways (2003 est.)

Canadian Embassy: The Canadian Embassy, 18 Mustapha Khalef St, Ben Aknoun, Algiers, Algeria; mailing address: P.O. Box 48, Alger-Gare, 16035 Alger, Algeria. Tel: (011-213-21) 914951. Fax: (011-213-21) 914973. e-mail: alger@dfait-maeci.gc.ca
Embassy in Canada: Embassy of the People's Democratic Republic of Algeria, 500 Wilbrod St. Ottawa, ON, K1N 6N2 Tel: (613) 789-8505 Fax: (613) 789-1406. e-mail: ambalgcan@rogers.com

American Samoa

Long-Form Name: Territory of American Samoa
Capital: Pago Pago (on Tutuila Island)

■ GEOGRAPHY

Area: 199 sq. km
Climate: tropical maritime, plentiful rainfall, temperatures consistent throughout the year
Land Use: arable land: 5%, permanent crops: 10%, other: 85%; n.a. km irrigated
Location: S Pacific Ocean, E of Australia and New Zealand

■ PEOPLE

Population: 70,260 (July 2003 est.)
Nationality: American Samoan; nationals of the United States
Ethnic Groups: Samoan (Polynesian) 89%, Caucasian 2%, Tongan 4%, other 5%
Languages: Samoan (a Polynesian dialect), English

■ GOVERNMENT

Colony/Territory of: Dependent Territory of the United States
Leader(s): President George W. Bush Jr.; Governor Togiola Tulafono
Government Type: US dependency with democratically elected governor: unorganized unincorporated territory

National Holiday: Territorial Flag Day, Apr. 17

■ ECONOMY

Overview: agriculture: taro, bread-fruit, yams, bananas, coconuts; livestock includes pigs, goats, poultry; industries: fish (tuna) canning; economic activity is closely tied to US; tourism is slowly developing

■ FINANCE/TRADE

Currency: American dollar (US$) = 100 cents

Canadian Embassy: c/o The Canadian Embassy, 501 Pennsylvania Ave. NW, Washington DC. 20001 USA Tel: (202) 682-1740 Fax: (202) 682-7726 e-mail: wshdc@dfait-maeci.gc.ca
Representative to Canada: c/o Embassy of the United States of America, 490 Sussex Drive, PO Box 866, Station "B," Ottawa, ON, K1P 5T1. Tel: (613) 238-5335. Fax: (613) 688-3080. e-mail inquiries are not accepted.

Andorra

Long-Form Name: Principality of Andorra
Capital: Andorra-la-Vella

■ GEOGRAPHY

Area: 468 sq. km
Coastline: none: landlocked
Climate: temperate; snowy, cold winters and warm, dry summers
Environment: deforestation, overgrazing, soil erosion; avalanches are a natural hazard
Terrain: rugged mountains separated by narrow valleys
Land Use: arable land: 2.22%, permanent crops: 0%, other: 97.78%; n.a. km irrigated
Location: SW Europe

■ PEOPLE

Population: 69,150 (July 2003 est.)
Nationality: Andorran
Age Structure: 0–14 yrs: 15.1%; 15–64: 71.7%; 65+: 13.2% (2003 est.)
Population Growth Rate: 1.06% (2003 est.)
Net Migration: 6.67 migrants/1,000 population (2003 est.)
Ethnic Groups: Catalan stock; 43% Spanish, 33% Andorran, 11% Portuguese, 7% French, 6% other
Languages: Catalan (official); many also speak some French and Spanish
Religions: predominantly Roman Catholic
Birth Rate: 9.65/1,000 population (2003 est.)
Death Rate: 5.74/1,000 population (2003 est.)

Infant Mortality: 4.06 deaths/1,000 live births (2003 est.)
Life Expectancy at Birth: 80.58 years male, 86.58 years female (2003 est.)
Total Fertility Rate: 1.27 children born/woman (2003 est.)
Literacy: 100% (2002)

■ GOVERNMENT

Leader(s): Co-Heads of State: President Jacques Chirac (France) and Bishop Joan Enric Vives Sicilia (Spain), Premier Marc Forné Molné
Government Type: parliamentary democracy; retains as its heads of state a co-principality of president of France and Spanish bishop of Seo de Urgel, who are represented locally by officials called veguers
Administrative Divisions: 7 parishes (parroquies, sing.—parroquia)
Nationhood: 1278 (from France and Spain)
National Holiday: Mare de Deu de Meritxell, Sept. 8

■ ECONOMY

Overview: tourism is the backbone of the economy, due to its duty-free status and year-round resorts; most food is imported due to a scarcity of arable land
GDP: US$1.3 billion, per capita US$19,000; real growth rate 3.8% (2000 est.)
Inflation: 4.3% (2001 est.)
Industries: tourism (particularly skiing), sheep, timber, tobacco, banking
Labour Force: exact figures n.a.; 1% agriculture, 21% industry, 78% services
Unemployment: 0%
Agriculture: sheep raising, small quantities of tobacco, rye, wheat, barley, buckwheat, maize, oats and some vegetables, especially potatoes
Natural Resources: hydroelectricity, mineral water, timber, iron ore, lead

■ FINANCE/TRADE

Currency: French Franc = 100 centimes, Spanish peseta (F Ptas) = 100 centimos, Euro (€).
International Reserves Excluding Gold: n.a.
Gold Reserves: n.a.
Budget: n.a.
Defence Expenditures: defence is the responsibility of Spain and France
Education Expenditures: n.a.
External Debt: n.a.
Exports: exact figures unavailable; commodities: electricity, tobacco products, furniture; partners: France, Spain

Imports: exact figures unavailable; commodities: consumer goods, food; partners: France, Spain, US

■ COMMUNICATIONS

Daily Newspapers: 3 in total
Televisions: n.a.
Radios: n.a.
Telephones: 512 lines/1,000 inhabitants (2001)
Internet: hosts: 3,200 (2001); users: 24,500 (2001)

■ TRANSPORTATION

Motor Vehicles: 36,000; 35,500 passenger cars
Roads: 269 km; 198 km paved
Railway: none
Air Traffic: n.a.
Airports: none

Canadian Embassy: The Canadian Embassy to Andorra, c/o The Canadian Embassy, Calle Nunez de Balboa, 35, Madrid, 28001, Spain; postal address: Apartado 587, 28080, Madrid, Spain. Tel: (011-34) 91-423-3250. Fax: (011-34) 91-423-3251. e mail: mdrid@dfait-maeci.gc.ca
Embassy in Canada: c/o Embassy of the Principality of Andorra, 2 United Nations Plaza, 25th Fl, New York NY 10017, USA. Tel: (212) 750-8064. Fax: (212) 750-6630. e-mail: n.a.

Angola

Long-Form Name: Republic of Angola
Capital: Luanda

■ GEOGRAPHY

Area: 1,246,700 sq. km
Coastline: 1,600 km
Climate: semi-arid in south and along coast to Luanda; north has cool, dry season (May to October) and hot, rainy season (Nov. to Apr.)
Environment: locally heavy rainfall causes periodic flooding on plateau; desertification, especially on coastal plain, soil erosion and water pollution; deforestation
Terrain: narrow coastal plain rises abruptly to vast interior plain
Land Use: arable land: 2.41%, permanent crops: 0.4%, other: 97.19%; includes 750 sq. km irrigated
Location: SW Africa

■ PEOPLE

Population: 10,766,471 (July 2003 est.)
Nationality: Angolan
Age Structure: 0–14 yrs: 43.5%; 15–64: 53.7%; 65+: 2.8% (2003 est.)
Population Growth Rate: 1.97% (2003 est.)

Net Migration: 0 migrants/1,000 population (2003 est.)
Ethnic Groups: 37% Ovimbundu, 25% Kimbundu, 13% Bakongo, 2% Mestiço, 1% European, 22% other
Languages: Portuguese (official); Bantu dialects spoken include Ovimbundu, Kimbundu, Bakongo and Chokwe
Religions: 38% Roman Catholic, 15% Protestant, 47% Animist (indigenous beliefs)
Birth Rate: 45.57/1,000 population (2003 est.)
Death Rate: 25.83/1,000 population (2003 est.)
Infant Mortality: 193.82 deaths/1,000 live births (2003 est.)
Life Expectancy at Birth: 36.13 years male, 37.83 years female (2003 est.)
Total Fertility Rate: 6.38 children born/woman (2003 est.)
Literacy: 42% (2002)

■ GOVERNMENT

Leader(s): President José Eduardo dos Santos; Prime Minister Fernando da Piedade Dias dos Santos
Government Type: transitional government, nominally a democracy with strong presidential system
Administrative Divisions: 18 provinces (provincias, sing. —provincia)
Nationhood: Nov. 11, 1975 (from Portugal)
National Holiday: Independence Day, Nov. 11

■ ECONOMY

Overview: subsistence agriculture is the main livelihood of the population, but oil production is the most lucrative activity; recent internal war has weakened the economy, and food must be imported
GDP: US$18.36 billion, per capita US$1,700; real growth rate 9.4% (2002 est.)
Inflation: 106% (2002)
Industries: accounts for 67% of GDP (2001); petroleum, mining (phosphate rock, uranium, gold, iron ore, bauxite, feldspar, diamonds), fish processing, brewing, tobacco, sugar, textiles, cement, food processing, building construction
Labour Force: 6.1 million (2002); 85% agriculture, 15% industry and services
Unemployment: extensive unemployment and underemployment affects more than half the population (2000 est.)
Agriculture: accounts for 8% of GDP (2001); cash crops—coffee, sisal, corn, cotton, sugar, manioc, tobacco; food crops—cassava, corn, vegetables, plantains, bananas and other local foodstuffs, fish

Natural Resources: petroleum, diamonds, iron ore, phosphates, copper, feldspar, gold, bauxite, uranium

■ FINANCE/TRADE

Currency: new kwanza (Kz) = 100 lwei
International Reserves Excluding Gold: US$469 million (Jan. 2004)
Gold Reserves: n.a.
Budget: n.a.
Defence Expenditures: 5.4% of GDP (2002)
Education Expenditures: n.a.
External Debt: US$10.134 billion (2002)
Exports: US$6.380 billion (2001); commodities: oil, coffee, diamonds, sisal, fish and fish products, timber, cotton; partners: US, China, South Korea, countries of the European Union
Imports: US$3.179 billion (2001); commodities: machinery and electrical equipment, food, vehicles and spare parts, textiles and clothing, medicines, substantial military deliveries; partners: EU, Brazil, South Korea, South Africa

■ COMMUNICATIONS

Daily Newspapers: 11/1,000 inhabitants (2000)
Televisions: 52/1,000 inhabitants (2002)
Radios: 74/1,000 inhabitants (2001)
Telephones: 6 lines/1,000 inhabitants (2002)
Internet: hosts: 7 (2002); users: 41,000 (2002)

■ TRANSPORTATION

Motor Vehicles: 225,000; 200,000 passenger cars
Roads: 51,429 km; 5,349 km paved
Railway: 2,761 km
Air Traffic: 190,000 passengers carried (2002)
Airports: 243; 32 have paved runways (2003 est.)

Canadian Embassy: Consulate of Canada, Rua Rei Katyavala 113, Luanda, Angola; mailing address C.P. 3360, Luanda, Angola. Tel: (011-244-2) 448-371. Fax: (011-244-2) 44-94-94.
Embassy in Canada: Embassy of the Republic of Angola, 189 Laurier Ave. E., Ottawa, ON K1N 6P1. Tel: (613) 234-1152. Fax: (613) 234-1179. e-mail: info@embangola-can.org

Anguilla

Long-Form Name: Anguilla
Capital: The Valley

■ GEOGRAPHY

Area: 91 sq. km
Climate: dry and sunny, tropical with moderating northeast trade winds
Land Use: arable land: 0%, permanent crops: 0%, other: 100%, (mostly rock with sparse

scrub oak, few trees, some commercial salt
ponds)
Location: West Indies, E of Puerto Rico

■ PEOPLE

Population: 12,738 (July 2003 est.)
Nationality: Anguillan
Ethnic Groups: of English ancestry, black/mixed-black African
Languages: English (official)

■ GOVERNMENT

Colony/Territory of: Dependent Territory of the United Kingdom
Leader(s): Head of State: Queen Elizabeth II, Governor Peter Johnstone
Government Type: dependent overseas territory of the U.K.
National Holiday: Anguilla Day, May 30

■ ECONOMY

Overview: agriculture: pigeon peas, corn, sweet potatoes; fishing; livestock includes sheep, goats, cattle, poultry; main trading partner: U.K.; there are few natural resources and the economy depends heavily on tourism

■ FINANCE/TRADE

Currency: Eastern Caribbean dollar (EU$) = 100 cents

Canadian Embassy: c/o The Canadian High Commission, Macdonald House 1, Grosvenor Square, London W1K 4AB, England, UK. Tel: (011-44-20) 7258-6600. Fax: (011-44-20) 7258-6333. e-mail: ldn@dfait-maeci.gc.ca
Representative to Canada: c/o British High Commission, 80 Elgin St, Ottawa ON K1P 5K7. Tel: (613) 237-1530. Fax: (613) 237-7980. e-mail should be sent using the appropriate form at the British High Commission's Website at http://www.britain-in-canada.org

Antigua and Barbuda

Long-Form Name: Antigua and Barbuda
Capital: Saint John's (on Antigua)

■ GEOGRAPHY

Area: 442 sq. km; includes Redonda (1.3 sq. km)
Coastline: 153 km
Climate: tropical marine; little seasonal temperature variation
Environment: subject to hurricanes and tropical storms (July to Oct.); insufficient freshwater resources are decreased further by clear-cutting of trees, which promotes rain run-off; occasional

long periods of drought; deeply indented coastline provides many natural harbours
Terrain: mostly low-lying limestone and coral islands with some higher volcanic areas
Land Use: arable land: 18.18%, permanent crops: 0%, other: 81.82%; n.a. km irrigated
Location: Caribbean islands, SE of Puerto Rico

■ PEOPLE

Population: 67,897 (July 2003 est.)
Nationality: Antiguan, Barbudan
Age Structure: 0–14 yrs: 28.1%; 15–64: 67.4%; 65+: 4.5% (2003 est.)
Population Growth Rate: 0.64% (2003 est.)
Net Migration: -6.19 migrants/1,000 population (2003 est.)
Ethnic Groups: almost entirely of black African origin; some of British, Portuguese, Lebanese and Syrian origin
Languages: English (official), local dialects
Religions: Anglican (predominant), other Protestant sects, some Roman Catholic
Birth Rate: 18.23/1,000 population (2003 est.)
Death Rate: 5.64/1,000 population (2003 est.)
Infant Mortality: 20.90 deaths/1,000 live births (2003 est.)
Life Expectancy at Birth: 68.99 years male, 73.75 years female (2003 est.)
Total Fertility Rate: 2.28 children born/woman (2003 est.)
Literacy: 85.8% (2002)

■ GOVERNMENT

Leader(s): Head of State: Queen Elizabeth II, Governor General James B. Carlisle, Prime Minister Spencer Baldwin
Government Type: constitutional parliamentary democracy
Administrative Divisions: 6 parishes, 2 dependencies
Nationhood: Nov. 1, 1981 (from UK)
National Holiday: Independence Day, Nov. 1

■ ECONOMY

Overview: Tourism is the backbone of this service-oriented economy, therefore economic downturns, particularly in the US, can have adverse effects. A labour shortage is plaguing some sectors of the economy; agriculture is a minor but growing sector of the economy
GDP: US$750 million, per capita US$11,000; real growth rate 3.0% (2002 est.)
Inflation: 0.4% (2000)
Industries: accounts for 19% of GDP; tourism, construction, light manufacturing (clothing, alcohol, household appliances)
Labour Force: 30,000; 82% commerce and services, 11% agriculture, 7% industry

Unemployment: 8% (2001 est.)

Agriculture: accounts for 4% of GDP; expanding output of cotton, fruit, vegetables and livestock; other crops—bananas, coconuts, sugar cane, cucumbers, mangoes; not self-sufficient in food

Natural Resources: negligible; pleasant climate and beautiful beaches foster tourism

■ FINANCE/TRADE

Currency: East Caribbean dollar ($EU) = 100 cents

International Reserves Excluding Gold: US$98 million (Jan. 2004)

Gold Reserves: n.a.

Budget: revenues US$123.7 million; expenditures US$145.9 million, including capital expenditures US$ n.a. (2000 est.)

Defence Expenditures: n.a.

Education Expenditures: n.a.

External Debt: n.a.

Exports: US$689 million (2002 est.); commodities: petroleum products 48%, manufactures 23%, food and live animals 4%, machinery and transport equipment 17%; partners: Trinidad and Tobago, Barbados, US

Imports: US$692 million (2002 est.); commodities: food and live animals, machinery and transport equipment, manufactures, chemicals, oil; partners: US, UK, OECS, Canada

■ COMMUNICATIONS

Daily Newspapers: 1 in total

Televisions: n.a.

Radios: n.a.

Telephones: 563 lines/1,000 inhabitants (2002)

Internet: hosts: 622 (2002); users: 10,000 (2002)

■ TRANSPORTATION

Motor Vehicles: 14,800; 13,400 passenger cars

Roads: 250 km paved

Railway: 77 km

Air Traffic: 1,510,000 passengers carried (2001 est.)

Airports: 3; 2 have paved runways (2002 est.)

Canadian Embassy: c/o The Canadian High Commission, Bishop's Court Hill, Bridgetown, Barbados; mailing address: P.O. Box 404, Bridgetown, Barbados. Tel: 1-246-429-3550. Fax: 1-246-429-3780. e-mail: bdgtn@dfait-maeci.gc.ca

Embassy in Canada: c/o High Commission for the countries of the Organization of Eastern Caribbean States, 130 Albert St, Ste 700, Ottawa ON K1P 5G4. Tel: (613) 236-8952. Fax: (613) 236-3042. e-mail: echcc@travel-net.com

Argentina

Long-Form Name: Argentine Republic

Capital: Buenos Aires

■ GEOGRAPHY

Area: 2,766,890 sq. km

Coastline: 4,989 km

Climate: mostly temperate; arid in southeast; subantarctic in southwest

Environment: Tucamán and Mendoza areas in Andes subject to earthquakes; pamperos are violent windstorms that can strike the Pampas and northeast; irrigated soil degradation; desertification; air and water pollution in Buenos Aires; erosion is a current problem

Terrain: rich plains of the Pampas in northern half, flat to rolling plateau of Patagonia in south, rugged Andes along western border

Land Use: arable land: 9.14%, permanent crops: 0.8%, other: 90.06%; includes 15,610 sq. km irrigated

Location: SE South America

■ PEOPLE

Population: 38,740,807 (July 2003 est.)

Nationality: Argentine or Argentinian

Age Structure: 0–14 yrs: 26.2%; 15–64: 63.4%; 65+: 10.4% (2003 est.)

Population Growth Rate: 1.05% (2003 est.)

Net Migration: 0.62 migrants/1,000 population (2003 est.)

Ethnic Groups: 97% white (mostly Spanish and Italian), 3% mestizo, Indian, or other non-white groups

Languages: Spanish (official), English, Italian, German, French

Religions: 90% nominally Roman Catholic (less than 20% practising), 2% Protestant, 2% Jewish, 6% other

Birth Rate: 17.47/1,000 population (2003 est.)

Death Rate: 7.58/1,000 population (2003 est.)

Infant Mortality: 16.16 deaths/1,000 live births (2003 est.)

Life Expectancy at Birth: 71.72 years male, 79.44 years female (2003 est.)

Total Fertility Rate: 2.28 children born/woman (2002 est.)

Literacy: 97.0% (2002)

■ GOVERNMENT

Leader(s): President Nestor Kirchner, Vice President Daniel Scioli

Government Type: republic

Administrative Divisions: 23 provinces (provincias, sing. — provincia) and 1 federal district (distrito federal)

Nationhood: July 9, 1816 (from Spain)
National Holiday: Revolution Day, May 25

■ ECONOMY

Overview: though the country possesses abundant natural resources and a diversified industrial base, burgeoning debt is weakening the economy; high unemployment rates have been a persistent problem, largely because of rigid labour laws
GDP: US$403.8 billion, per capita US$10,500; real growth rate -10.9% (2003 est.)
Inflation: 3.7% (2003)
Industries: accounts for 28% of GDP (2001); food processing (especially meat packing), motor vehicles, consumer durables, textiles, chemicals and petrochemicals, printing, metallurgy, steel
Labour Force: 15.7 million (2002); 13% agriculture, 34% industry, 53% services
Unemployment: 17.8% (2002)
Agriculture: accounts for 5% of GNP (including fishing) (2001); produces abundant food for both domestic consumption and exports; among world's top five exporters of grain and beef; principal crops—wheat, corn, sorghum, soybeans, sugar beets, peanuts, grapes, tea, lemons, tobacco
Natural Resources: fertile plains of the Pampas, lead, zinc, tin, copper, iron ore, manganese, crude oil, uranium

■ FINANCE/TRADE

Currency: nuevo peso argentino = 100 centavos
International Reserves Excluding Gold: US$14.697 billion (Jan. 2004)
Gold Reserves: 0.570 million fine troy ounces (Jan. 2004)
Budget: revenues US$44 billion; expenditures US$48 billion, including capital expenditures of US$ n.a. (2000 est.)
Defence Expenditures: 8.1% of central government expenditure (2002)
Education Expenditures: 13.7% of total government expenditure (2002)
External Debt: US$132.314 billion (2002)
Exports: US$29.350 billion (2003); commodities: meat, cereal grains, corn, oilseed, hides, wool; partners: US , Chile, Spain, Brazil
Imports: US$13.813 billion (2003); commodities: machinery and equipment, metals, chemicals, motor vehicles, plastics, agricultural products; partners: US, Brazil, Germany, China

■ COMMUNICATIONS

Daily Newspapers: 37/1,000 inhabitants (2000)
Televisions: 326/1,000 inhabitants (2002)
Radios: 681/1,000 inhabitants (2001)
Telephones: 219 lines/1,000 inhabitants (2002)
Internet: hosts: 495,920 (2002); users: 4.1 million (2002)

■ TRANSPORTATION

Motor Vehicles: 6,840,000; 5,294,000 passenger cars
Roads: 215,471 km; 63,348 km paved
Railway: 34,463 km
Air Traffic: 5,257,000 passengers carried (2002)
Airports: 1,342; 145 have paved runways (2003 est.)

Canadian Embassy: The Canadian Embassy, 2828 Tagle, 1425 Buenos Aires; mailing address: Casilla de Correo 1598 C1000WAP, Buenos Aires, Argentina. Tel: (011-54-11) 4808-1000. Fax: (011-54-11) 4808-1111.
Embassy in Canada: Embassy of the Argentine Republic, Royal Bank Centre, 90 Sparks St, Ste 910, Ottawa ON K1P 5B4. Tel: (613) 236-2351. Fax: (613) 235-2659.

Armenia

Long-Form Name: Republic of Armenia
Capital: Yerevan

■ GEOGRAPHY

Area: 29,800 sq. km
Coastline: none: landlocked
Climate: severe winters; hot summers; dry year-round
Environment: prone to earthquakes; little land suitable for cultivation; air and water pollution; deforestation and drought; soil pollution is a current problem
Terrain: rugged highlands; 70% is mountains; little forest land; fast-flowing rivers; Aras River Valley has good soil
Land Use: arable land: 17.52%, permanent crops: 2.3%, other: 80.18%; includes 2,870 sq. km irrigated; most farmland lies in the Aras Valley; animal herding predominant in the highlands
Location: SW Asia

■ PEOPLE

Population: 3,326,448 (July 2003 est.)
Nationality: Armenian
Age Structure: 0–14 yrs: 21.1%; 15–64: 68.3%; 65+: 10.6% (2003 est.)
Population Growth Rate: -0.07% (2003 est.)
Net Migration: -3.15 migrants/1,000 population (2003 est.)
Ethnic Groups: 93% Armenians, 2% Russians, 3% Azerbaijanis, 2% other, predominantly Kurds

Languages: Armenian (official), Azerbaijan, Russian
Religions: predominantly Armenian Orthodox
Birth Rate: 12.57/1,000 population (2003 est.)
Death Rate: 10.16/1,000 population (2003 est.)
Infant Mortality: 40.86 deaths/1,000 live births (2003 est.)
Life Expectancy at Birth: 62.41 years male, 71.17 years female (2003 est.)
Total Fertility Rate: 1.56 children born/woman (2003 est.)
Literacy: 99.4% (2002)

■ GOVERNMENT

Leader(s): President Robert Kocharian, Prime Minister Andranik Markaryan
Government Type: republic
Administrative Divisions: 10 provinces (marzer, sing. —marz) and 1 city (k'aghak'ner, sing. — k'aghak')
Nationhood: Sept. 21, 1991 (from Soviet Union)
National Holiday: Independence Day, Sept. 21

■ ECONOMY

Overview: predominantly manufacturing and agriculture; much of Armenia's population remains heavily dependent on remittances from relatives abroad
GDP: US$12.13 billion, per capita US$3,600; real growth rate 12.9% (2002 est.)
Inflation: 1.1% (2002)
Industries: accounts for 26% of GDP; electrical equipment and machinery, chemicals, machine tools, vehicles, textiles
Labour Force: 1.6 million (2002); 25% industry, 45% agriculture and forestry, 30% services
Unemployment: 9.3% (2001)
Agriculture: accounts for approximately 30% of GDP; fruit, grapes, vegetables, tobacco, grains, beetroot, potatoes, geranium oil, cattle and sheep herding
Natural Resources: marble, precious metals, iron, tufa, small deposits of gold, copper, molybdenum, zinc, alumina

■ FINANCE/TRADE

Currency: dram = 100 luma
International Reserves Excluding Gold: US$508 million (Jan. 2004)
Gold Reserves: none (Jan. 2004)
Budget: revenues US$402 million; expenditures US$482 million, including capital expenditures of US$ n.a (2003 est.)
Defence Expenditures: 6.5% of GDP (2001)
Education Expenditures: n.a.
External Debt: US$1.149 billion (2002)

Exports: US$678 million (2003); commodities include cotton, diamonds, brandy, copper ore, fruit, olives, pomegranates, machine tools, instruments, shoes. Partners: Belgium, Iran, Russia, US.
Imports: US$1.269 billion (2003); commodities include machinery, energy, consumer goods, diamonds. Partners: Russia, US, Belgium, Iran

■ COMMUNICATIONS

Daily Newspapers: 5/1,000 inhabitants (2000)
Televisions: 229/1,000 inhabitants (2002)
Radios: 225/1,000 inhabitants (2001)
Telephones: 143 lines/1,000 persons (2002)
Internet: hosts: 2,850 (2002); users: 60,000 (2002)

■ TRANSPORTATION

Motor Vehicles: n.a.
Roads: 15,918 km; 15,329 km paved
Railway: 852 km
Air Traffic: 408,000 passengers carried (2002)
Airports: 15; 8 have paved runways (2003)

Canadian Embassy: c/o The Canadian Embassy 23 Starokonyushenny Pereulok, Moscow, 119002 Russia (No tel., fax or e-mail info provided.)
Embassy in Canada: Embassy of the Republic of Armenia, 7 Delaware Ave, Ottawa ON K2P 0Z2. Tel: (613) 234-3710. Fax: (613) 234-3444. e-mail: erac@ican.net

Aruba

Long-Form Name: Aruba
Capital: Oranjestad

■ GEOGRAPHY

Area: 193 sq. km
Climate: tropical marine; little seasonal temperature variation
Land Use: arable land: 10.53%, (including aloe 0.01%) permanent crops: 0%, other: 89.47%; 0.01 sq. km irrigated
Location: Caribbean island, off N coast of South America

■ PEOPLE

Population: 70,844 (July 2003 est.)
Nationality: Aruban
Ethnic Groups: 80% mixed European/Caribbean Indian
Languages: Dutch (official), Papiamento (a Spanish, Portuguese, Dutch, English dialect), English (widely spoken), Spanish

■ GOVERNMENT

Colony/Territory of: Dependent Territory of the Netherlands

Leader(s): Head of State: Queen Beatrix (Netherlands), Governor Fredis Refenjol, Prime Minister Nelson Oduber

Government Type: part of the Dutch realm; parliamentary democracy; autonomy in internal affairs obtained in 1986. Dutch government retains responsibility for defense and foreign affairs.

National Holiday: Flag Day, Mar. 18

■ ECONOMY

Overview: Tourism is the mainstay; banking and oil refinery are also important

■ FINANCE/TRADE

Currency: Aruban florin (Af) or guilder = 100 cents

Canadian Embassy: c/o The Canadian Embassy, Sophialaan 7, 2514JP, The Hague, Netherlands. Tel.: (011-31-70) 311-1600. Fax: (011-31-70) 311-1620. e-mail: hague@dfait-maeci.gc.ca

Representative to Canada: c/o Embassy of the Kingdom of the Netherlands, 350 Albert St, Ste 2020, Ottawa ON K1R 1A4. Tel: (613) 237-5030. Fax: (613) 237-6471. e-mail: nlgovott@netcom.ca

---

Australia

Long-Form Name: Commonwealth of Australia
Capital: Canberra

■ GEOGRAPHY

Area: 7,686,850 sq. km; includes Macquarie Island

Coastline: 25,760 km

Climate: generally arid to semi-arid; temperate in south and east; tropical in north

Environment: subject to severe droughts and floods; cyclones along coast; limited fresh water availability; soil degradation; regular, tropical, invigorating, sea breeze known as "the Doctor" occurs along west coast in summer; desertification. Shipping activities and tourism are threatening the Great Barrier Reef

Terrain: mostly low plateau with deserts; fertile plain in southeast

Land Use: arable land: 6.88%, permanent crops: 0.03%, other: 93.09%; includes 24,000 sq. km irrigated

Location: continent of the eastern hemisphere, SE of Asia and S. of the equator; divides Indian and Pacific Oceans

■ PEOPLE

Population: 19,731,984 (July 2003 est.)

Nationality: Australian

Age Structure: 0–14 yrs: 20.2%; 15–64: 67.1%; 65+: 12.7% (2003 est.)

Population Growth Rate: 0.93% (2003 est.)

Net Migration: 4.05 migrants/1,000 population (2003 est.)

Ethnic Groups: 92% Caucasian, 7% Asian, 1% Aboriginal and other

Languages: English, native languages

Religions: 26.1% Anglican, 26% Roman Catholic, 24.3% other Christian; most of the rest do not profess a religion

Birth Rate: 12.55/1,000 population (2003 est.)

Death Rate: 7.31/1,000 population (2003 est.)

Infant Mortality: 4.83 deaths/1,000 live births (2003 est.)

Life Expectancy at Birth: 77.27 years male, 83.13 years female (2003 est.)

Total Fertility Rate: 1.76 children born/woman (2003 est.)

Literacy: 100% (2002)

■ GOVERNMENT

Leader(s): Head of State: Queen Elizabeth II, Governor General Michael Jeffrey, Prime Minister John Howard

Government Type: federal parliamentary state

Administrative Divisions: 6 states, 2 territories; dependent areas includes Ashmore and Cartier Islands (uninhabited), Australian Antarctic Territory (uninhabited except for scientific staff), Cocos (Keeling) Islands, Coral Sea Islands Territory (uninhabited), Christmas Island, Heard and McDonald Islands (uninhabited), Norfolk Island

Nationhood: Jan. 1, 1901 (federation of UK colonies)

National Holiday: Australia Day, Jan. 26

■ ECONOMY

Overview: successful Western-style capitalist economy and a major exporter of natural resources and agricultural products; is looking to increase exports of manufactured goods

GDP: US$525.5 billion, per capita US$26,900; real growth rate 3.6% (2002)

Inflation: 2.8% (2002)

Industries: accounts for 26% of GDP (2001); mining, industrial and transportation equipment, food processing, chemicals, steel, motor vehicles

Labour Force: 10.0 million (2002); 73% services, 22% industry, 5% agriculture

Unemployment: 5.9% (Mar. 2004)

Agriculture: accounts for 3% of GDP and 30% of export revenues; world's largest exporter of beef and wool, second largest for mutton, and among top wheat exporters; major crops—wheat, barley, sugar cane, fruit; livestock—cattle, sheep, poultry

Natural Resources: bauxite, coal, iron ore, copper, tin, silver, uranium, nickel, tungsten, mineral sands, lead, zinc, diamonds, natural gas, crude oil

■ FINANCE/TRADE

Currency: dollar ($A) = 100 cents
International Reserves Excluding Gold: US$29.294 billion (Jan. 2004)
Gold Reserves: 2.563 million fine troy ounces (Jan. 2004)
Budget: revenues US$86.8 billion; expenditures US$84.1 billion, including capital expenditures US$ n.a. (FY2000/01 est.)
Defence Expenditures: 7.5% of central government expenditure (2002)
Education Expenditures: 13.8% of government expenditure (2002)
External Debt: US$176.8 billion (2002 est.)
Exports: US$69.873 billion (2003 est.); commodities: wheat, barley, beef, lamb, dairy products, wool, gold, coal, iron ore; partners: developing countries, Japan, US, New Zealand, S Korea, Singapore, countries of the European Union
Imports: US$87.094 billion (2003 est.); commodities: manufactured raw materials, capital equipment, consumer goods; partners: developing countries, EU, US, Japan

■ COMMUNICATIONS

Daily Newspapers: 293/1,000 inhabitants (2000)
Televisions: 731/1,000 inhabitants (2002)
Radios: 1,999/1,000 inhabitants (2001)
Telephones: 539 lines/1,000 inhabitants (2002)
Internet: hosts: 2,564,339 (2002); users: 9.472 million (2002)

■ TRANSPORTATION

Motor Vehicles: 10,900,000; 9,000,000 passenger cars
Roads: 811,603 km; 314,090 km paved
Railway: 41,588 km
Air Traffic: 32,483,000 passengers carried (2002)
Airports: 444; 294 have paved runways (2003 est.)

Canadian Embassy: The Canadian High Commission, Commonwealth Ave, Canberra A.C.T. 2600, Australia. Tel: (011-61-2) 6270-4000. Fax: (011-61-2) 6273-3285. e-mail: cnbra@dfait-maeci.gc.ca
Embassy in Canada: Australian High Commission, 50 O'Connor St, Ste 710, Ottawa ON K1P 6L2.

Tel: (613) 236-0841. Fax: (613) 236-4376. e-mail: n.a.

Austria

Long-Form Name: Republic of Austria
Capital: Vienna

■ GEOGRAPHY

Area: 83,858 sq. km
Coastline: none: landlocked
Climate: temperate; continental, cloudy; cold winter with frequent rain in lowlands and snow in mountains; cool summers with occasional showers
Environment: because of steep slopes, poor soils and cold temperatures, population is concentrated on eastern lowlands; air and soil pollution is due to emissions by coal, and oil-fired power stations and industrial plants
Terrain: mostly mountains with Alps in west and south; flat, with gentle slopes along eastern and northern margins
Land Use: arable land: 16.89%, permanent crops: 0.99%, other: 82.12%; includes 457 sq. km irrigated
Location: C Europe

■ PEOPLE

Population: 8,188,207 (July 2003 est.)
Nationality: Austrian
Age Structure: 0–14 yrs: 16.2%; 15–64: 68.3%; 65+: 15.5% (2003 est.)
Population Growth Rate: 0.22% (2003 est.)
Net Migration: 2.44 migrants/1,000 population (2003 est.)
Ethnic Groups: 98% German, 2% Croatian, Slovene and others
Languages: German (official); Slovene, Hungarian, and a Croatian dialect also spoken
Religions: 85% Roman Catholic, 6% Protestant, 9% other
Birth Rate: 9.43/1,000 population (2003 est.)
Death Rate: 9.69/1,000 population (2003 est.)
Infant Mortality: 4.33 deaths/1,000 live births (2003 est.)
Life Expectancy at Birth: 75.02 years male, 81.48 years female (2003 est.)
Total Fertility Rate: 1.41 children born/woman (2003 est.)
Literacy: 100% (2002)

■ GOVERNMENT

Leader(s): Chancellor Wolfgang Schuessel, President Heinz Fischer
Government Type: federal republic

Administrative Divisions: 9 states (bundeslaender, sing. — bundesland)
Nationhood: Nov. 12, 1918 (from Austro-Hungarian Empire)
National Holiday: National Day, Oct. 26

■ ECONOMY

Overview: prosperous, Western capitalist economy, as well as substantial welfare benefits and extensive nationalized industry; unemployment is a continuing problem
GDP: US$227.7 billion, per capita US$27,900; real growth rate 1.1% (2002)
Inflation: 1.8% (2002)
Industries: accounts for 33% of GDP (2002); foods, iron and steel, machines, textiles, chemicals, electrical, paper and pulp, tourism, mining
Labour Force: 3.8 million (2002); 67% services, 29% industry and crafts, 4% agriculture and forestry; an estimated 200,000 Austrians are employed in other European countries; foreign labourers in Austria number 177,840, about 6% of labour force
Unemployment: 9.1% (Jan. 2004)
Agriculture: accounts for 2% of GDP (including forestry) (2002); principal crops and animals—grains, fruit, potatoes, sugar beets, sawn wood, cattle, pigs, poultry; 80–90% self-sufficient in food
Natural Resources: iron ore, crude oil, timber, magnesite, lead, coal, lignite, copper, hydro-electricity

■ FINANCE/TRADE

Currency: schilling (S) = 100 groschen; Euro (€); on January 1, 2002 the Euro became the sole currency for everyday transactions.
International Reserves Excluding Gold: US$8.607 billion (Jan. 2004)
Gold Reserves: 10.208 million fine troy ounces (Jan. 2004)
Budget: revenues US$67 billion; expenditures US$70 billion, capital expenditures US$ n.a. (2004 est.)
Defence Expenditures: 2.0% of total government expenditure (2002)
Education Expenditures: 15.1% of total government expenditure (2002)
External Debt: US$12.1 billion (2001 est.)
Exports: US$87.559 billion (2003 est.); commodities: machinery and equipment, iron and steel, lumber, textiles, paper products, chemicals; partners: countries of the European Union, Switzerland, US, Hungary
Imports: US$88.235 billion (2003 est.); commodities: petroleum, foodstuffs, machinery and equipment, vehicles, chemicals, textiles and

clothing, pharmaceuticals; partners: Germany, Italy, France, Switzerland, US, Hungary

■ COMMUNICATIONS

Daily Newspapers: 296/1,000 inhabitants (2000)
Televisions: 637/1,000 inhabitants (2001)
Radios: 753/1,000 inhabitants (2001)
Telephones: 489 lines/1,000 inhabitants (2002)
Internet: hosts: 367,933 (2002); users: 3.34 million (2002)

■ TRANSPORTATION

Motor Vehicles: 4,380,000; 4,044,000 passenger cars
Roads: 200,00 km, all paved
Railway: 6,024 km
Air Traffic: 7,070,000 passengers carried (2002)
Airports: 55; 24 have paved runways (2003 est.)

Canadian Embassy: The Canadian Embassy, Laurenzerberg 2 A-1010 Vienna, Austria. Tel: (011-43-1) 531-38-3000. Fax: (011-43-1) 531-38-3321. e-mail: vienn@dfait-maeci.gc.ca
Embassy in Canada: Embassy of the Republic of Austria, 445 Wilbrod St, Ottawa ON K1N 6M7. Tel: (613) 789-1444. Fax: (613) 789-3431. e-mail: ottawa-ob@bmaa.gv.at

Azerbaijan

Long-Form Name: Azerbaijani Republic
Capital: Baku (or Baki)

■ GEOGRAPHY

Area: 86,600 sq. km
Coastline: none; landlocked. Inland coastline (Caspian Sea) approximately 800 km
Climate: Alpine to subtropical; dry, semi-arid steppe subject to drought
Environment: severe air and water pollution render Aspheron Peninsula, including Baku and Sumgait, the "most ecologically devastated area in the world," according to local scientists
Terrain: fertile central lowlands; large flat Kura-Aras Lowland; Caucasus Mountains in north; western uplands
Land Use: arable land: 19.31%, permanent crops: 3.04%, other: 77.65% (includes 14,550 sq. km irrigated); grazing land in the Caucasus Mountains; farming in lowlands
Location: SW Asia, bordering on Caspian Sea

■ PEOPLE

Population: 7,830,764 (July 2003 est.)
Nationality: Azerbaijani
Age Structure: 0–14 yrs: 27.7%; 15–64: 64.7%; 65+: 7.6% (2003 est.)

Population Growth Rate: 0.32% (2003 est.)
Net Migration: -5.16 migrants/1,000 population (2003 est.)
Ethnic Groups: 90% Azerbaijani, 2.5% Russians, 2% Armenians, 3.2% Daghestanis, 2.3% other
Languages: Azerbaijani (official), Armenian, Russian, 6% other
Religions: Muslim 93.4%, Russian Orthodox 2.3%, Armenian Orthodox 2.3%, other 1.8%
Birth Rate: 19.28/1,000 population (2003 est.)
Death Rate: 9.68/1,000 population (2003 est.)
Infant Mortality: 82.41 deaths/1,000 live births (2003 est.)
Life Expectancy at Birth: 58.95 years male, 67.58 years female (2003 est.)
Total Fertility Rate: 2.34 children born/woman (2002 est.)
Literacy: 97% (2002)

■ GOVERNMENT

Leader(s): President Ilham Aliyev, Prime Minister Artur Rasizade
Government Type: republic
Administrative Divisions: 59 (rayonlar, sing. — rayon), 11 cities (saharlar, sing. — sahar), 1 autonomous republic (muxtar respublika, rayons)
Nationhood: Aug. 30, 1991 (from Soviet Union)
National Holiday: Independence Day (Founding of the Democratic Republic of Azerbaijan), May 28

■ ECONOMY

Overview: cotton and refining industries are most prominent; Azerbaijan is least industrially developed of the Transcaucasian States
GDP: US$28.61 billion, per capita US$3,700; real growth rate 10.6% (2002)
Inflation: 2.6% (2002)
Industries: accounts for 33% of GDP (2001); oil extraction and refining, steel, cement, textiles, chemicals, petrochemicals
Labour Force: 3.7 million (2002); 41% agriculture and forestry, 7% industry, 52% services
Unemployment: 1.3% (2002)
Agriculture: accounts for 20% of GDP; cotton, grain, rice, grapes, tea, citrus fruit, vegetables, sheep and horse breeding, pigs and goats
Natural Resources: oil reserves, minerals, iron, aluminum

■ FINANCE/TRADE

Currency: manat = 100 gopik
International Reserves Excluding Gold: US$760 million (Jan. 2004)
Gold Reserves: none

Budget: Revenues US$786 million, expenditures US$807 million, including capital expenditures of US $n.a. (2001)
Defence Expenditures: 10.2% of central government expenditure (2002)
Education Expenditures: 23.1% of central government expenditure (2002 est.)
External Debt: US$1.398 billion (2002)
Exports: US$2.605 billion (2003 est.); oil and gas and related equipment, textiles, cotton. Partners: Italy, Turkey, Russia, Georgia, Israel
Imports: US$2.498 billion (2003 est.); machinery and parts, foodstuffs, textiles, consumer durables. Partners: US, Russia, Turkey, Kazakhstan, Germany

■ COMMUNICATIONS

Daily Newspapers: 27/1,000 inhabitants (2000)
Televisions: 332/1,000 inhabitants (2002)
Radios: 27/1,000 inhabitants (2001)
Telephones: 113 lines/1,000 persons (2002)
Internet: hosts: 1,139 (2002); users: 300,000 (2002)

■ TRANSPORTATION

Motor Vehicles: 405,000; 328,000 passenger cars
Roads: 24,981 km; 23,057 km hard-surfaced
Railway: 2,125 km (does not include industrial lines)
Air Traffic: 575,000 passengers carried (2002)
Airports: 71; 27 have paved runways (2003 est.)

Canadian Embassy: c/o The Canadian Embassy, Nenehatun Caddesi No. 75, Gaziosmanpasa 06700, Ankara, Turkey. Tel: (011-90-312) 459-9200. Fax: (011-90-312) 459-9361. e-mail: ankra@dfait-maeci.gc.ca
Embassy in Canada: Embassy of the Republic of Azerbaijan, 275 Slater Street, Suite 904-C, Ottawa, ON, K1P 5H9. Tel: (613) 288-0497. Fax: (613) 230-8089. e-mail: n.a.

Bahamas

Long-Form Name: Commonwealth of The Bahamas
Capital: Nassau

■ GEOGRAPHY

Area: 13,940 sq. km
Coastline: 3,542 km
Climate: tropical marine; moderated by warm waters of Gulf Stream
Environment: subject to hurricanes and other tropical storms that cause extensive flood and wind damage; coral reef decay is a current issue

Terrain: long, flat coral islands with some low, rounded hills
Land Use: arable land: 0.6%, permanent crops: 0.4%, other: 99%; n.a. km irrigated
Location: Caribbean islands, E of Florida

■ PEOPLE

Population: 297,477 (July 2003 est.)
Nationality: Bahamian
Age Structure: 0–14 yrs: 28.8%; 15–64: 65.4%; 65+: 5.8% (2003 est.)
Population Growth Rate: 0.77% (2003 est.)
Net Migration: -2.21 migrants/1,000 population (2003 est.)
Ethnic Groups: 85% black, 12% white, 3% Asian and Hispanic
Languages: English; some Creole among Haitian immigrants
Religions: 32% Baptist, 20% Anglican, 19% Roman Catholic, smaller groups of other Protestants, Greek Orthodox and Jews
Birth Rate: 18.57/1,000 population (2003 est.)
Death Rate: 8.68/1,000 population (2003 est.)
Infant Mortality: 26.21 deaths/1,000 live births (2003 est.)
Life Expectancy at Birth: 62.30 years male, 69.18 years female (2003 est.)
Total Fertility Rate: 2.25 children born/woman (2003 est.)
Literacy: 95.5% (2002)

■ GOVERNMENT

Leader(s): Head of State: Queen Elizabeth II, Governor General Ivy Dumont, Prime Minister Perry Christie
Government Type: constitutional parliamentary democracy
Administrative Divisions: 21 districts
Nationhood: July 10, 1973 (from UK)
National Holiday: Independence Day, July 10

■ ECONOMY

Overview: tourism and offshore banking are features of this stable, middle-income developing nation
GDP: US$4.59 billion, per capita US$15,300; real growth rate 0.1% (2002 est.)
Inflation: 2.0% (2001)
Industries: accounts for 7% of GDP; banking, tourism, cement, oil refining and transshipment, salt production, rum, aragonite, pharmaceuticals, spiral welded steel pipe
Labour Force: approx. 156,000; 40% hotels and restaurants, 50% other services, 5% industry, 5% agriculture
Unemployment: n.a.

Agriculture: accounts for 3% of GDP; dominated by small-scale producers; principal products— citrus fruit, vegetables, poultry; large net importer of food
Natural Resources: salt, aragonite, timber

■ FINANCE/TRADE

Currency: Bahamian dollar ($B) = 100 cents
International Reserves Excluding Gold: US$503 million (Jan. 2004)
Gold Reserves: none
Budget: revenues US$918.5 million; expenditures US$956.5 million, including capital expenditures US$106.7 million (FY1999/2000)
Defence Expenditures: 2.91% of central government expenditure (2001)
Education Expenditures: 19.8% of central government expenditure (2000)
External Debt: US$371.6 million (2001 est.)
Exports: US$617 million (2002); commodities: pharmaceuticals, cement, rum, crawfish; partners: US, UK, France, Germany
Imports: US$1.614 billion (2002); commodities: foodstuffs, manufactured goods, mineral fuels; partners: US, South Korea, Italy, Japan

■ COMMUNICATIONS

Daily Newspapers: 3 in total
Televisions: n.a.
Radios: n.a.
Telephones: 421 lines/1,000 inhabitants (2002)
Internet: hosts: 32 (2002); users: 60,000 (2002)

■ TRANSPORTATION

Motor Vehicles: 59,000; 47,000 passenger cars
Roads: 2,693 km; 1,546 km paved
Railway: none
Air Traffic: 850,000 passengers carried (2001 est.)
Airports: 64; 30 have paved runways (2003 est.)

Canadian Embassy: Consulate of Canada, Shirley Street Plaza, Nassau; mailing address: Consulate of Canada, P.O. Box SS-6371, Nassau, Bahamas. Tel: (1-242) 393-2123. Fax: (1-242) 393-1305. e-mail: cdncon@bahamas.net.bs
Embassy in Canada: High Commission for the Commonwealth of the Bahamas, 50 O'Connor St, Ste 1313, Ottawa ON K1P 6L2. Tel: (613) 232-1724. Fax: (613) 232-0097. e-mail: ottawa-mission@bahighco.com

Bahrain

Long-Form Name: Kingdom of Bahrain
Capital: Manama

■ GEOGRAPHY

Area: 620 sq. km
Coastline: 161 km
Climate: arid; mild, pleasant winters; very hot, humid summers
Environment: there are no natural fresh water resources; ground water and sea water are the sole sources for all water needs; dust storms; desertification; drought; coastal degradation resulting from oil industry
Terrain: mostly low desert plain rising gently to low central escarpment
Land Use: arable land: 4.35%, permanent crops: 4.35%, other: 91.3%; includes 50 sq. km irrigated
Location: Persian Gulf, E of Saudi Arabia

■ PEOPLE

Population: 667,238 (July 2003 est.)
Nationality: Bahraini
Age Structure: 0–14 yrs: 28.8%; 15–64: 68.0%; 65+: 3.2% (2003 est.)
Population Growth Rate: 1.61% (2003 est.)
Net Migration: 1.07 migrants/1,000 population (2003 est.)
Ethnic Groups: 63% Bahraini, 19% Asian, 10% other Arab, 8% Iranian
Languages: Arabic (official); English also widely spoken; Farsi, Urdu
Religions: Muslim (70% Shi'a, 30% Sunni)
Birth Rate: 19.02/1,000 population (2003 est.)
Death Rate: 3.99/1,000 population (2003 est.)
Infant Mortality: 18.59 deaths/1,000 live births (2003 est.)
Life Expectancy at Birth: 71.28 years male, 76.24 years female (2003 est.)
Total Fertility Rate: 2.71 children born/woman (2003 est.)
Literacy: 88.5% (2002)

■ GOVERNMENT

Leader(s): King Hamad bin Isa al-Khalifa Prime Minister Khalifa bin Salman Al Khalifa
Government Type: constitutional hereditary monarchy
Administrative Divisions: 12 municipalities (manatiq, sing. —mintaqah)
Nationhood: Aug. 15, 1971 (from UK)
National Holiday: National Day, Dec. 16

■ ECONOMY

Overview: petroleum production and processing are the backbone of the economy and any change in the world oil market affects the economy
GDP: US$9.91 billion, per capita US$15,100; real growth rate 2.9% (2002 est.)
Inflation: 0.5% (2002 est.)

Industries: accounts for 35% of GDP (2001); petroleum processing and refining, aluminum smelting, offshore banking, ship repairing
Labour Force: exact figures n.a.; 42% of labour force is Bahraini; 79% industry, commerce and services, 20% government, 1% agriculture
Unemployment: n.a.
Agriculture: including fishing, accounts for 1% of GDP (2001); not self-sufficient in food production; heavily subsidized sector produces fruit, vegetables, poultry, dairy products, shrimp and fish
Natural Resources: oil, associated and non-associated natural gas, fish

■ FINANCE/TRADE

Currency: Bahraini dinar (BD) = 1,000 fils
International Reserves Excluding Gold: US$1.776 billion (Jan. 2004)
Gold Reserves: 0.15 million fine troy ounces (Jan. 2004)
Budget: revenues US$1.8 billion; expenditures US$2.2 billion, capital expenditures US$700 million (2002 est.)
Defence Expenditures: 15.23% of total government expenditures (2001)
Education Expenditures: 12.84% of central government expenditure (2000)
External Debt: US$3.7 billion (2002)
Exports: US$6.364 billion (2003 est.); commodities: petroleum 80%, aluminum 7%, other 13%; partners: US, Japan, Saudi Arabia, India, South Korea
Imports: US$5.116 billion (2003 est.); commodities: non-oil 59%, crude oil 41%; partners: UK, Saudi Arabia, US, France, Japan

■ COMMUNICATIONS

Daily Newspapers: 4 in total
Televisions: n.a.
Radios: n.a.
Telephones: 267 lines/1,000 inhabitants (2002)
Internet: hosts: 1,339 (2002); users: 165,000 (2002)

■ TRANSPORTATION

Motor Vehicles: 178,000; 143,000 passenger cars
Roads: 3,261 km; 2,531 km paved
Railway: none
Air Traffic: 1,410,000 passengers carried (2001 est.)
Airports: 4; 3 have paved runways (2003 est.)

Canadian Embassy: The Canadian Embassy to Bahrain, c/o The Canadian Embassy, P.O. Box 94321, Riyadh 11693, Saudi Arabia. Tel: (011-966-1) 488-2288. Fax: (011-966-1) 488-1997. e-mail: ryadh@dfait-maeci.gc.ca

Embassy in Canada: c/o The Embassy of the Kingdom of Bahrain, 3502 International Dr NW, Washington DC 20008, USA. Tel: (202) 342-0741. Fax: (202) 362-2192. e-mail: n.a.

Bangladesh

Long-Form Name: People's Republic of Bangladesh
Capital: Dhaka

■ GEOGRAPHY

Area: 144,000 sq. km
Coastline: 580 km
Climate: tropical; cool, dry winter (Oct. to Mar.); hot, humid summer (Mar. to June)
Environment: vulnerable to droughts; much of country routinely flooded during summer monsoon season (June to Oct.); overpopulation; deforestation; cyclones
Terrain: mostly flat alluvial plain; hilly in southeast
Land Use: arable land: 60.7%, permanent crops: 2.61%, other: 36.69%; includes 38,440 sq. km irrigated
Location: S Asia, bordering on Bay of Bengal

■ PEOPLE

Population: 138,448,210 (July 2003 est.)
Nationality: Bangladeshi
Age Structure: 0–14 yrs: 34.1%; 15–64: 62.5%; 65+: 3.4% (2003 est.)
Population Growth Rate: 2.06% (2003 est.)
Net Migration: -0.72 migrants/1,000 population (2003 est.)
Ethnic Groups: 98% Bengali, 250,000 Biharis, less than 1 million tribals
Languages: Bangla (official), English widely used, 5% tribal dialects
Religions: 83% Muslim, 16% Hindu, less than 1% Buddhist, Christian and other
Birth Rate: 29.90/1,000 population (2003 est.)
Death Rate: 8.63/1,000 population (2003 est.)
Infant Mortality: 66.08 deaths/1,000 live births (2003 est.)
Life Expectancy at Birth: 61.46 years male, 61.20 years female (2003 est.)
Total Fertility Rate: 3.17 children born/woman (2003 est.)
Literacy: 41.1% (2002)

■ GOVERNMENT

Leader(s): President Iajuddin Ahmed, Prime Minister Khaleda Zia
Government Type: parliamentary democracy
Administrative Divisions: 5 divisions

Nationhood: Dec. 16, 1971 (from Pakistan; Bangladesh formerly known as East Pakistan)
National Holiday: Independence Day, Mar. 26 (date of independence from West Pakistan); Victory Day, Dec. 16 (commemorates the official creation of the state of Bangladesh.

■ ECONOMY

Overview: one of the poorest nations in the world; the economy is based on a small number of agricultural exports, which are vulnerable to natural disasters; few natural resources; frequent cyclones and floods, a rapidly growing labour force that cannot be absorbed by agriculture, a low level of industrialization, government interference with the economy, failure to exploit energy reserves, and inadequate power supplies all contribute to stifling economic growth
GDP: US$238.2 billion, per capita US$1,800; real growth rate 4.8% (2002 est.)
Inflation: 3.1% (2002)
Industries: accounts for 19% of GDP (2001), jute manufacturing, food processing, cotton textiles, petroleum, urea fertilizer
Labour Force: 72.4 million (2002); 63% agriculture, 26% services, 11% industry; extensive export of labour to Saudi Arabia, United Arab Emirates, Oman and Kuwait
Unemployment: 3.3% (2002)
Agriculture: accounts for about 35% of GDP (2001), 65% of employment and 20% of exports; imports 10% of foodgrain requirements; world's largest exporter of jute; commercial products—jute, rice, wheat, tea, sugar cane, potatoes, tobacco, spices, beef, milk, poultry
Natural Resources: natural gas, arable land, timber

■ FINANCE/TRADE

Currency: taka (Tk) = 100 poisha
International Reserves Excluding Gold: US$2.549 billion (Jan. 2004)
Gold Reserves: 0.112 million fine troy ounces (Jan. 2004)
Budget: revenues US$4.9 billion; expenditures US$6.8 billion, including capital expenditures of US$ n.a. (2000 est.)
Defence Expenditures: 11.2% of central government expenditure (2002)
Education Expenditures: 15.8% of total government expenditure (2002)
External Debt: US$17.037 billion (2002)
Exports: US$4.566 billion (2002); commodities: jute, tea, garments, leather, shrimp, manufacturing; partners: US, Germany, UK, France, Netherlands, Italy 4%

Imports: US$7.913 billion (2002); commodities: food, petroleum and other energy, non-food consumer goods, semi-processed goods and capital equipment; partners: India, EU, Japan, Singapore, China

■ COMMUNICATIONS

Daily Newspapers: 53/1,000 inhabitants (2000)
Televisions: 59/1,000 inhabitants (2002)
Radios: 49/1,000 inhabitants (2001)
Telephones: 5 lines/1,000 inhabitants (2002)
Internet: hosts: 2 (2002); users: 204,000 (2002)

■ TRANSPORTATION

Motor Vehicles: 225,000; 152,000 passenger cars
Roads: 207,486 km; 19,773 km paved
Railway: 2,706 km
Air Traffic: 1,544,000 passengers carried (2002)
Airports: 18; 15 have paved runways (2003 est.)

Canadian Embassy: The Canadian High Commission, House CWN 16/A, Rd. 48, Gulshan; mailing address: G.P.O. Box 569, Dhaka, Bangladesh. Tel: (011-880-2) 988-7091. Fax: (011-880-2) 882-30-43. e-mail: dhakada@dfait-maeci.gc.ca.
Embassy in Canada: High Commission for the People's Republic of Bangladesh, 275 Bank St, Ste 302, Ottawa ON K2P 2L6. Tel: (613) 236-0138. Fax: (613) 567-3213. e-mail: bang@bellnet.ca

---

Barbados

Long-Form Name: Barbados
Capital: Bridgetown

■ GEOGRAPHY

Area: 430 sq. km
Coastline: 97 km
Climate: tropical; rainy season (June to Oct.)
Environment: subject to hurricanes, especially June to Oct.; water pollution and soil erosion; landslides
Terrain: relatively flat; rises gently to a central highland region
Land Use: arable land: 37.21%, permanent crops: 2.33%, other: 60.46%; includes 10 sq. km irrigated
Location: Caribbean islands, N of Venezuela

■ PEOPLE

Population: 277,264 (July 2003 est.)
Nationality: Barbadian, or Bajan (colloquial)
Age Structure: 0–14 yrs: 21.2%; 15–64: 70.0%; 65+: 8.8% (2003 est.)
Population Growth Rate: 0.38% (2003 est.)

Net Migration: -0.31 migrants/1,000 population (2003 est.)
Ethnic Groups: 80% African, 16% mixed, 4% European
Languages: English
Religions: 67% Protestant, 9% Methodist, 4% Roman Catholic, 9% other, including Moravian
Birth Rate: 13.15/1,000 population (2003 est.)
Death Rate: 9.02/1,000 population (2003 est.)
Infant Mortality: 12.72 deaths/1,000 live births (2003 est.)
Life Expectancy at Birth: 69.56 years male, 74.14 years female (2003 est.)
Total Fertility Rate: 1.65 children born/woman (2003 est.)
Literacy: 99.7% (2002)

■ GOVERNMENT

Leader(s): Head of State: Queen Elizabeth II, Governor General Sir Clifford Husbands. Prime Minister Owen Seymour Arthur
Government Type: parliamentary democracy
Administrative Divisions: 11 parishes
Nationhood: Nov. 30, 1966 (from UK)
National Holiday: Independence Day, Nov. 30

■ ECONOMY

Overview: has one of the highest standards of living of islands in the region; the tourist industry and traditional sugar cane cultivation are main parts of the economy; manufacturing and tourism have become increasingly important in recent years
GDP: US$4.153 billion, per capita US$15,000; real growth rate -2.8% (2002 est.)
Inflation: -0.6% (2002 est.)
Industries: accounts for 16% of GDP; tourism, sugar, light manufacturing, component assembly for export
Labour Force: 128,500 (2001 est.); 75% community, social and business services, 15% industry, 10% agriculture
Unemployment: 10% (Nov. 2001)
Agriculture: accounts for 6% of GDP; major cash crop is sugar cane; other crops—vegetables and cotton; not self-sufficient in food
Natural Resources: crude oil, fishing, natural gas

■ FINANCE/TRADE

Currency: Barbadian dollar ($BDS) = 100 cents
International Reserves Excluding Gold: US$747 million (Jan. 2004)
Gold Reserves: none
Budget: revenues US$847 million; expenditures US$886 million, including capital expenditures of US$ n.a. (2000 est.)
Defence Expenditures: n.a.
Education Expenditures: n.a.

External Debt: US$692 million (2002)
Exports: US$210 million (2003); commodities: sugar and molasses, electrical components, clothing, rum, machinery and transport equipment; partners: Caribbean community, US, UK
Imports: US$1.133 billion (2003); commodities: foodstuffs, consumer durables, raw materials, crude oil; partners: US, CARICOM, Japan, UK, Canada

■ COMMUNICATIONS

Daily Newspapers: 2 in total
Televisions: n.a.
Radios: n.a.
Telephones: 481 lines/1,000 inhabitants (2002)
Internet: hosts: 160 (2002); users: 30,000 (2002)

■ TRANSPORTATION

Motor Vehicles: 48,500; 45,000 passenger cars
Roads: 1,793 km; 1,719 km paved
Railway: none
Air Traffic: n.a.
Airports: 1, with a paved runway (2003 est.)

Canadian Embassy: c/o The Canadian High Commission, Bishop's Court Hill, Bridgetown, Barbados; mailing address: P.O. Box 404, Bridgetown, Barbados. Tel: 1-246-429-3550. Fax: 1-246-429-3780. e-mail: bdgtn@dfait-maeci.gc.ca
Embassy in Canada: High Commission for Barbados, 130 Albert St, Ste 1204, Ottawa ON K1P 5G4. Tel: (613) 236-9517. Fax: (613) 230-4362. e-mail: ottawa@foreign.gov.bb

Belarus

Long-Form Name: Republic of Belarus
Capital: Minsk

■ GEOGRAPHY

Area: 207,600 sq. km
Coastline: none; landlocked
Climate: mild and moist, transitional between continental and maritime
Environment: southern region is badly contaminated with nuclear fallout from 1986 Chernobyl reactor accident; pesticide use results in extensive soil pollution
Terrain: land of forests, lakes, rivers, and marshes; soil poor, sandy, marshy
Land Use: arable land: 29.76%, permanent crops: 0.69%, other: 69.55%; includes 1,150 sq. km irrigated
Location: W Asia, bordering on Poland

■ PEOPLE

Population: 10,322,151 (July 2003 est.)
Nationality: Belarusian
Age Structure: 0–14 yrs: 16.8%; 15–64: 68.9%; 65+: 14.3% (2003 est.)
Population Growth Rate: -0.12% (2003 est.)
Net Migration: 2.66 migrants/1,000 population (2003 est.)
Ethnic Groups: 77.9% Byelorussian, 13.2% Russian, 4.1% Polish, 2.9% Ukrainian, 1.9% other
Languages: Byelorussian, Russian
Religions: predominantly Roman Catholic and Eastern Orthodox
Birth Rate: 10.18/1,000 population (2003 est.)
Death Rate: 14.05/1,000 population (2003 est.)
Infant Mortality: 13.87 deaths/1,000 live births (2003 est.)
Life Expectancy at Birth: 62.54 years male, 74.60 years female (2003 est.)
Total Fertility Rate: 1.34 children born/woman (2003 est.)
Literacy: 99.7% (2002)

■ GOVERNMENT

Leader(s): President Aleksandr Lukashenko, Prime Minister Sergei Sidorsky
Government Type: republic
Administrative Divisions: 6 regions (voblastsi, sing. — voblasts), 1 municipality (harady, sing. — horad)
Nationhood: Aug. 25, 1991 (from former Soviet Union)
National Holiday: Independence Day, July 3

■ ECONOMY

Overview: strong emphasis on mining and agriculture, with growing manufacturing (heavy machinery, chemicals, fertilizer) and services sector; Belarus is an important transport link for the former Soviet states
GDP: US$90.19 billion, per capita US$8,700; real growth rate 4.7% (2002 est.)
Inflation: 42.8% (2002 est.)
Industries: accounts for 40% of GDP (2002); machinery, tools, refineries, fertilizer production; about 50% of labour force is employed in industry
Labour Force: 5.3 million (2002); 27.4% manufacturing, 22.4% community, social and business services, 21.9% agriculture
Unemployment: 2.3%, but large numbers of underemployed (2002)
Agriculture: accounts for 15% of GDP (2002); potatoes, flax, rye, oats, barley, wheat, cattle breeding, milk, vegetables, pigs, potatoes, peat, forest resources

Natural Resources: oil and natural gas, potassium, forest land, peat deposits

■ **FINANCE/TRADE**

Currency: Belarusian ruble
International Reserves Excluding Gold: US$595 million (Dec. 2003)
Gold Reserves: n.a.
Budget: n.a.
Defence Expenditures: 4.5% of total government expenditures (2002)
Education Expenditures: 3.87% of total government expenditures (2000)
External Debt: US$908 million (2002)
Exports: US$9.964 billion (2003 est.); agricultural and transport machinery, chemicals, metals, textiles; partners: Russia, Ukraine, Poland, Germany
Imports: US$11.505 billion (2003 est.); commodities: fuels, raw materials, textiles, sugar; partners: Russia, Germany, Poland

■ **COMMUNICATIONS**

Daily Newspapers: 152/1,000 inhabitants (2000)
Televisions: 362/1,000 inhabitants (2002)
Radios: 199/1,000 inhabitants (2001)
Telephones: 299 lines/1,000 inhabitants (2002)
Internet: hosts: 4,025 (2002); users: 808,700 (2002)

■ **TRANSPORTATION**

Motor Vehicles: 1,400,000; 1,350,000 passenger cars
Roads: 74,385 km; 66,203 km hard-surfaced
Railway: 5,563 km (does not include industrial lines) (2000)
Air Traffic: 205,000 passengers carried (2002)
Airports: 124; 28 have paved runways (2003 est.)

Canadian Embassy: The Canadian Embassy to Belarus, c/o The Canadian Embassy, ul. Jana Matejki 1/5, 00-481 Warsaw, Poland. Tel: (011-48-22) 584-3100. Fax: (011-48-22) 584-3190 e-mail: wsaw@dfait-maeci.gc.ca
Embassy in Canada: Embassy of the Republic of Belarus, 130 Albert St, Ste 600, Ottawa ON K1P 5G4. Tel: (613) 233-9994. Fax: (613) 233-8500. e-mail: belamb@igs.net

---

Belgium

Long-Form Name: Kingdom of Belgium
Capital: Brussels

■ **GEOGRAPHY**

Area: 30,510 sq. km
Coastline: 66 km

Climate: temperate; mild winters, cool summers; rainy, humid, cloudy
Environment: air and water pollution; acid rain
Terrain: flat coastal plains in northwest central rolling hills, rugged mountains of Ardennes Forest in southeast
Land Use: arable land: 27.4%, permanent crops: 0%, other: 72.6%, note: includes Luxembourg; includes 40 sq. km irrigated
Location: NW Europe, bordering on North Sea

■ **PEOPLE**

Population: 10,289,088 (July 2003 est.)
Nationality: Belgian
Age Structure: 0–14 yrs: 17.2%; 15–64: 65.6%; 65+: 17.2% (2003 est.)
Population Growth Rate: 0.14% (2003 est.)
Net Migration: 0.97 migrants/1,000 population (2003 est.)
Ethnic Groups: 58% Flemish, 31% Walloon, 11% mixed or other
Languages: Dutch or Flemish spoken in north (Flanders), French in south (Wallonia), both languages official; small English-speaking minority in east, German 1%
Religions: 75% Roman Catholic, remainder Protestant or other
Birth Rate: 10.45/1,000 population (2003 est.)
Death Rate: 10.07/1,000 population (2003 est.)
Infant Mortality: 4.57 deaths/1,000 live births (2003 est.)
Life Expectancy at Birth: 74.97 years male, 81.78 years female (2003 est.)
Total Fertility Rate: 1.62 children born/woman (2003 est.)
Literacy: 100% (2002)

■ **GOVERNMENT**

Leader(s): Head of State: King Albert II, Prime Minister Guy Verhofstadt
Government Type: federal parliamentary democracy under a constitutional monarch
Administrative Divisions: 10 provinces and 1 region
Nationhood: Oct. 4, 1830 (from the Netherlands)
National Holiday: Independence Day, July 21

■ **ECONOMY**

Overview: a small, private enterprise-based economy possessing few natural resources, it is therefore highly vulnerable to the state of world markets; burgeoning public debt offsets economic growth
GDP: US$299.7 billion, per capita US$29,200; real growth rate 0.7% (2002)
Inflation: 1.7% (2002)

Industries: accounts for 24% of GDP (2001); engineering and metal products, processed food and beverages, chemicals, basic metals, textiles, glass, petroleum, coal
Labour Force: 4.3 million (2002); 73% community, social and business services, 25% industry, 2% agriculture
Unemployment: 12.8% (Feb. 2004)
Agriculture: accounts for 1% of GDP (2001); emphasis on livestock production—beef, veal, pork, milk; major crops are sugar beets, fresh vegetables, fruit, grain and tobacco; net importer of farm products
Natural Resources: coal, natural gas

■ FINANCE/TRADE

Currency: Belgian franc (BF) = 100 centimes; Euro (€); on January 1, 2002 the Euro became the sole currency for everyday transactions.
International Reserves Excluding Gold: US$10.901 billion (Jan. 2004)
Gold Reserves: 8.291 million fine troy ounces (Jan. 2004)
Budget: revenues US$113.4 billion, expenditures US$106 billion, including capital expenditures of US$7.17 billion (2000)
Defence Expenditures: 3.2% of central government expenditure (2002)
Education Expenditures: 11.6% of total government expenditures (2002)
External Debt: n.a.
Exports: US$255.404 billion (2003 est.) Belgium-Luxembourg Economic Union; commodities: iron and steel, transportation equipment, tractors, diamonds, petroleum products; partners: European Community, US
Imports: US$235.466 billion (2003 est.) Belgium-Luxembourg Economic Union; commodities: fuels, grains, chemicals, foodstuffs; partners: Netherlands, Germany, France, UK, US

■ COMMUNICATIONS

Daily Newspapers: 160/1,000 inhabitants (2000)
Televisions: 541/1,000 inhabitants (2002)
Radios: 793/1,000 inhabitants (2001)
Telephones: 494 lines/1,000 inhabitants (2002)
Internet: hosts: 336,604 (2002); users: 3.4 million (2002)

■ TRANSPORTATION

Motor Vehicles: 5,290,000; 4,750,000 passenger cars
Roads: 148,216 km, 116,687 km paved
Railway: 3,471 km
Air Traffic: n.a. (2002)
Airports: 42; 25 have paved runways (2003 est.)

Canadian Embassy: The Canadian Embassy, 2, Avenue de Tervuren, 1040 Brussels, Belgium. Tel: (011-32-2) 741-0611. Fax: (011-32-2) 741-0643. e-mail: bru@dfait-maeci.gc.ca
Embassy in Canada: Embassy of the Kingdom of Belgium, 360 Albert Street, 8th Floor, Suite 820, Ottawa, ON, K1R 7X7. Tel: (613) 236-7267. Fax: (613) 236-7882. e-mail: ottawa@diplobel.org

Belize

Long-Form Name: Belize
Capital: Belmopan

■ GEOGRAPHY

Area: 22,960 sq. km
Coastline: 386 km
Climate: tropical; very hot and humid; rainy season (May to Feb.)
Environment: frequent devastating hurricanes (Sept. to Dec.) and coastal flooding, especially in south; deforestation; industrial and agricultural water pollution
Terrain: flat, swampy coastal plain; low mountains in south
Land Use: arable land: 2.81%, permanent crops: 1.1%, other: 96.09%; includes 30 sq. km irrigated
Location: Central (Latin) America, just S of Mexico bordering on Caribbean Sea

■ PEOPLE

Population: 266,440 (July 2003 est.)
Nationality: Belizean
Age Structure: 0–14 yrs: 41.1%; 15–64: 55.3%; 65+: 3.5% (2003 est.)
Population Growth Rate: 2.44% (2003 est.)
Net Migration: 0 migrants/1,000 population (2003 est.)
Ethnic Groups: 31% Creole, 44.1% Mestizo, 9.2% Maya, 6.2% Garifuna, 9.5% other
Languages: English (official), Spanish, Maya, Garifuna (Carib)
Religions: 62% Roman Catholic, 30% Protestant sects, 2% none, 6% other
Birth Rate: 30.46/1,000 population (2003 est.)
Death Rate: 6.05/1,000 population (2003 est.)
Infant Mortality: 27.07 deaths/1,000 live births (2003 est.)
Life Expectancy at Birth: 65.19 years male, 69.63 years female (2003 est.)
Total Fertility Rate: 3.86 children born/woman (2003 est.)
Literacy: 76.9% (2002)

■ GOVERNMENT

Leader(s): Head of State: Queen Elizabeth II, Governor General Colville Young. Prime Minister Said Musa
Government Type: parliamentary democracy
Administrative Divisions: 6 districts
Nationhood: Sept. 21, 1981 (from UK; Belize formerly known as British Honduras)
National Holiday: Independence Day, Sept. 21

■ ECONOMY

Overview: economy primarily based on agriculture and merchandising; sugar is the main crop; tourism and construction are becoming increasingly important
GDP: US$1.28 billion, per capita US$4,900; real growth rate 3.7% (2002 est.)
Inflation: 1.9% (2002 est.)
Industries: accounts for 24% of GDP (2001); sugar refining, clothing, timber and forest products, furniture, rum, soap, beverages, cigarettes, tourism, garment production, citrus concentrates
Labour Force: 90,000; 27% agriculture, 55% services, 18% industry (2001 est.)
Unemployment: n.a.
Agriculture: accounts for 18% of GDP (including fish and forestry) and 75% of export earnings (2001); commercial crops include sugar cane, bananas, coca, citrus fruit; expanding output of lumber and cultured shrimp; net importer of basic foods
Natural Resources: arable land potential, timber, fish, hydroelectric power

■ FINANCE/TRADE

Currency: Belizean dollar ($BZ) = 100 cents
International Reserves Excluding Gold: US$105 million (Jan. 2004)
Gold Reserves: n.a.
Budget: revenues US$224 million; expenditures US$209 million, including capital expenditures of US$70 million (2002 est.)
Defence Expenditures: 1.87% of GDP (2001)
Education Expenditures: n.a.
External Debt: US$835 million (2002)
Exports: US$205 million (2003 est.); commodities: sugar, clothing, seafood, molasses, bananas, citrus, wood and wood products; partners: EU, US, UK, CARICOM, Canada
Imports: US$552 million (2003 est.); commodities: machinery and transportation equipment, food, beverages, tobacco, manufactured goods, fuels, chemicals, pharmaceuticals; partners: US, Mexico, Central America, UK

■ COMMUNICATIONS

Daily Newspapers: none
Televisions: n.a.
Radios: n.a.
Telephones: 119 lines/1,000 inhabitants (2002)
Internet: hosts: 1,498 (2002); users: 30,000 (2002)

■ TRANSPORTATION

Motor Vehicles: 5,600; 2,400 passenger cars
Roads: 2,872 km; 488 km paved
Railway: none
Air Traffic: n.a.
Airports: 42; 4 have paved runways (2003 est.)

Canadian Embassy: Consulate of Canada, 80 Princess Margaret Drive, Belize City, Belize. Mailing address: P.O. Box 610, Belize City, Belize. Tel: (011-501) 2-31-060. Fax: (011-501) 2-30060. e-mail: cdcon.bze@btl.net
Embassy in Canada: High Commission for Belize, 350 Albert Street, Suite 2120, Ottawa, ON, K1R 1A4. Tel: (613) 232-2826. Fax: (613) 232-4279. e-mail: hcbelize@bellnet.ca

Benin

Long-Form Name: Republic of Benin
Capital: Porto Novo (official); Cotonou (de facto)

■ GEOGRAPHY

Area: 112,620 sq. km
Coastline: 121 km
Climate: tropical; hot, humid in south; semi-arid in north
Environment: hot, dry, dusty harmattan wind may affect north in winter; deforestation; desertification; recent droughts have severely affected marginal agriculture in north; insufficient safe drinking water
Terrain: mostly flat to undulating plain; some hills and low mountains
Land Use: arable land: 15.28%, permanent crops: 1.36%, other: 83.36%; includes 120 sq. km irrigated
Location: WC Africa, bordering on South Atlantic Ocean

■ PEOPLE

Population: 7,041,490 (July 2003 est.)
Nationality: Beninese (sing. & pl.)
Age Structure: 0–14 yrs: 47.0%; 15–64: 50.7%; 65+: 2.3% (2003 est.)
Population Growth Rate: 2.95% (2003 est.)
Net Migration: 0 migrants/1,000 population (2003 est.)

Ethnic Groups: 99% African (42 ethnic groups, most important being Fon, Adja, Yoruba, Bariba); 5,500 Europeans
Languages: French (official); also Fon, Yoruba, Fulami, Bariba
Religions: majority Animist, 15% Islam, 15% Christian
Birth Rate: 43.15/1,000 population (2003 est.)
Death Rate: 13.65/1,000 population (2003 est.)
Infant Mortality: 86.76 deaths/1,000 live births (2003 est.)
Life Expectancy at Birth: 50.35 years male, 51.84 years female (2003 est.)
Total Fertility Rate: 6.04 children born/woman (2003 est.)
Literacy: 39.8% (2002)

■ GOVERNMENT

Leader(s): President Mathieu Kerekou
Government Type: republic under multiparty democratic rule
Administrative Divisions: 6 provinces
Nationhood: Aug. 1, 1960 (from France; Benin formerly known as Dahomey)
National Holiday: National Day, Aug. 1

■ ECONOMY

Overview: one of the least developed countries in the world; limited natural resources and an underdeveloped infrastructure characterize the economy; agricultural products are a major export
GDP: US$7.38 billion, per capita US$1,100; real growth rate 6.0% (2002 est.)
Inflation: 3.3% (2002 est.)
Industries: accounts for 15% of GDP; palm oil and palm kernel oil processing, textiles, beverages, petroleum, cigarettes, construction materials, foodstuffs
Labour Force: 3.0 million (2002); 70.2% agriculture, 23.1% services, 6.6% industry
Unemployment: n.a.
Agriculture: accounts for 38% of GDP (2002); small farms produce 90% of agricultural output; production is dominated by food crops—corn, sorghum, cassava, yams, beans and rice; cash crops include cotton, palm oil and peanuts; poultry and livestock output has not kept up with consumption
Natural Resources: small offshore oil deposits, limestone, marble, timber

■ FINANCE/TRADE

Currency: Communauté financière africaine franc (CFAF) = 100 centimes
International Reserves Excluding Gold: US$480 million (Nov. 2003)

Gold Reserves: n.a.
Budget: revenues US$377.4 million; expenditures US$561.8 million, including capital expenditures of US$ n.a. (2001)
Defence Expenditures: 2.7% of GDP (2002)
Education Expenditures: n.a
External Debt: US$1.843 billion (2002)
Exports: US$378 million (2002); commodities: cotton, crude oil, cocoa, palm products; partners: Brazil, France, Indonesia, Thailand, Morocco, Portugal, Côte d'Ivoire
Imports: US$664 million (2002); commodities: foodstuffs, tobacco, petroleum products, capital goods; partners: France, US, China, Côte d'Ivoire, Netherlands, Japan

■ COMMUNICATIONS

Daily Newspapers: 5/1,000 inhabitants (2000)
Televisions: 32/1,000 inhabitants (2002)
Radios: 441/1,000 inhabitants (2001)
Telephones: 9 lines/1,000 inhabitants (2002)
Internet: hosts: 574 (2002); users: 50,000 (2002)

■ TRANSPORTATION

Motor Vehicles: 60,000; 38,000 passenger cars
Roads: 6,787 km; 1,357 km paved
Railway: 578 km
Air Traffic: 46,000 passengers carried (2002)
Airports: 5; 1 has a paved runway (2003 est.)

Canadian Embassy: The Canadian Embassy, c/o The Canadian Embassy, P.O. Box 4104, Abidjan 01, Côte d'Ivoire. Tel: (011-225) 21-20-09. Fax: none. e-mail: abdjn@dfait-maeci.gc.ca
Embassy in Canada: Embassy of the Republic of Benin, 58 Glebe Ave, Ottawa ON K1S 2C3. Tel: (613) 233-4429. Fax: (613) 233-8952. e-mail: ambaben2@on.aira.com

---

Bermuda

Long-Form Name: Commonwealth of Bermuda
Capital: Hamilton

■ GEOGRAPHY

Area: 58.8 sq. km
Climate: subtropical; mild, humid; gales, strong winds common in winter
Land Use: arable land: 6%, permanent crops: 0%, other: 94%, (55%, developed, 45%, rural/open space); includes n.a. sq. km irrigated
Location: North Atlantic Ocean, E of United States

■ PEOPLE

Population: 64,482 (July 2003 est.)
Nationality: Bermudian

Age structure: 0–14 years: 19.2%;15–64 years: 69.3%; 65 years and over: 11.5% (2003 est.)
Population Growth Rate: 0.72% (2003 est.)
Net Migration: 2.56 migrant(s)/1,000 population (2003 est.)
Ethnic Groups: 58% black, 36% white, 6% other
Languages: English (official), Portuguese
Religions: 39% non-Anglican Protestant, 27% Anglican, 15% Roman Catholic, 19% other
Birth Rate: 12.13 births/1,000 population (2003 est.)
Death Rate: 7.46 deaths/1,000 population (2003 est.)
Infant Mortality: 9.05 deaths/1,000 live births (2003 est.)
Life Expectancy at Birth: 75.38 years male, 79.49 years female (2003 est.)
Total Fertility Rate: 1.90 children born/woman (2003 est.)
Literacy: 98% (2000)

■ GOVERNMENT

Colony/Territory of: Dependent Territory of the United Kingdom
Leader(s): Head of State: Queen Elizabeth II, Governor John Vereker, Premier Alex Scott
Government Type: dependent territory of the UK, with internal self-government
National Holiday: Bermuda Day, May 24

■ ECONOMY

Overview: a successful tourist industry accounts for its high per capita income; the industrial sector is small, and agriculture is limited by the lack of suitable land; 80% of food must be imported

■ FINANCE/TRADE

Currency: Bermudian dollar ($Ber) = 100 cents

Canadian Embassy: Consulate of Canada, P.O. Box HM140, Hamilton, HMFX, Bermuda. Street Address: Consulate of Canada, Reid House, 31 Church Street, Hamilton, HMFX, Bermuda. Tel: (1 441) 294 3611. Fax: (1 441) 294 42929. e-mail: none
Representative to Canada: c/o British High Commission, 80 Elgin St, Ottawa ON K1P 5K7. Tel: (613) 237-1530. Fax: (613) 237-7980. e-mail should be sent using the appropriate form at the British High Commission's Website at http://www.britain-in-canada.org

Bhutan

Long-Form Name: Kingdom of Bhutan
Capital: Thimphu

■ GEOGRAPHY

Area: 47,000 sq. km
Coastline: none: landlocked
Climate: varies; tropical in southern plains; cool winters and hot summers in central valleys; severe winters and cool summers in Himalayas
Environment: violent storms coming from the Himalayas were the source of the country's name, which means Land of the Thunder Dragon; soil erosion and limited access to water are ongoing problems
Terrain: mostly mountainous with some fertile valleys and savanna
Land Use: arable land: 2.98%, permanent crops: 0.43%, other: 96.59%; includes 400 sq. km irrigated
Location: S Asia

■ PEOPLE

Population: 2,139,549 (July 2003 est.)
Nationality: Bhutanese (sing. & pl.)
Age Structure: 0–14 yrs: 39.6%; 15–64: 56.4%; 65+: 4.0% (2003 est.)
Population Growth Rate: 2.14% (2003 est.)
Net Migration: 0 migrants/1,000 population (2003 est.)
Ethnic Groups: 50% Bhote, 35% ethnic Nepalese, 15% indigenous or migrant tribes
Languages: Bhotes speak various Tibetan dialects—the most widely spoken dialect is Dzongkha (official); Nepalese speak various Nepalese dialects
Religions: 75% Mahayana Buddhism (state religion), Hinduism (25%, mainly ethnic Nepalese)
Birth Rate: 34.82/1,000 population (2003 est.)
Death Rate: 13.47/1,000 population (2003 est.)
Infant Mortality: 104.68 deaths/1,000 live births (2003 est.)
Life Expectancy at Birth: 53.90 years male, 53.25 years female (2003 est.)
Total Fertility Rate: 4.94 children born/woman (2003 est.)
Literacy: 47.0% (2002 est.)

■ GOVERNMENT

Leader(s): King Jigme Singye Wangchuk, Prime Minister Yeshey Zimba
Government Type: monarchy; special treaty relationship with India
Administrative Divisions: 18 districts (dzongkhag, sing. & pl.)
Nationhood: Aug. 8, 1949 (from India)
National Holiday: National Day, Dec. 17

■ ECONOMY

Overview: agriculture and forestry are the bedrock of the economy; it is poorly developed due to omnipresent rugged topography
GDP: US$2.7 billion, per capita US$1,300; real growth rate 7.7% (2002 est.)
Inflation: 3.0% (2002)
Industries: accounts for 10% of GDP (2002 est.); cement, chemical products, mining, distilling, food processing, handicrafts, wood products, calcium carbide. Industries are small and technologically underdeveloped
Labour Force: exact figures not available; there is a massive lack of skilled labour. 93% of the population is employed in agriculture, 5% in service, 2% in industry and commerce.
Unemployment: n.a.
Agriculture: accounts for 45% of GDP (2002), provides a living for 90% of the population; based on subsistence farming and animal husbandry; self-sufficient in food except for foodgrains; other production—rice, corn, root crops, citrus fruit, dairy and eggs
Natural Resources: timber, hydroelectricity, gypsum, calcium carbide, tourism potential

■ FINANCE/TRADE

Currency: ngultrum (Nu) = 100 chetrum; Indian currency is also legal tender
International Reserves Excluding Gold: US$328 million (Sept. 2003)
Gold Reserves: n.a.
Budget: exact figures n.a.; the government of India finances almost 60% of Bhutan's expenditures
Defence Expenditures: 1.9% of GDP (2002)
Education Expenditures: 15.14% of central government expenditure (2001)
External Debt: US$120 million (2002)
Exports: US$108 million (2002); commodities: cardamom, gypsum, timber, handicrafts, cement, fruit, electricity, precious stones, spices; partners: India, Bangladesh
Imports: US$165 million (2002); commodities: fuel and lubricants, grain, machinery and parts, vehicles, fabrics, rice; partners: India, Japan, UK, Germany, US

■ COMMUNICATIONS

Daily Newspapers: none
Televisions: n.a.
Radios: n.a.
Telephones: 10 lines/1,000 inhabitants (2002)
Internet: hosts: 1,242 (2002); users: 10,000 (2002)

■ TRANSPORTATION

Motor Vehicles: n.a.
Roads: 3,690 km; 2,240 km surfaced
Railway: none
Air Traffic: 44,000 passengers carried (2001 est.)
Airports: 2; 1 has paved runway (2003)

Canadian Embassy: Canadian Co-operation Office, P.O. Office 201,Thimpu (Bhutan), India. Tel: (900 975) 2332 109. Fax: none. e-mail: canada@drunknet.bet
Embassy in Canada: Consular Representation of Bhutan, 255 Consumers Road, Ste 401, Toronto ON M2J 5B6. Tel: (416) 498-3150. Fax: (416) 498-7296. e-mail: ecsondra@web.ca

Bolivia

Long-Form Name: Republic of Bolivia
Capital: La Paz (seat of government); Sucre (legal capital and seat of judiciary)

■ GEOGRAPHY

Area: 1,098,580 sq. km
Coastline: none: landlocked
Climate: varies with altitude; humid and tropical to cold and semi-arid
Environment: cold, thin air of high plateau is obstacle to efficient fuel combustion; over-grazing, soil erosion, desertification; deforestation, pollution of drinking water
Terrain: Andes Mountains, high plateau, hills, lowland plains in Amazon basin
Land Use: arable land: 1.73%, permanent crops: 0.21%, other: 98.06%; includes 1,280 sq. km irrigated
Location: C South America

■ PEOPLE

Population: 8,586,443 (July 2003 est.)
Nationality: Bolivian
Age Structure: 0–14 yrs: 37.1%; 15–64: 58.4%; 65+: 4.5% (2003 est.)
Population Growth Rate: 1.63% (2003 est.)
Net Migration: -1.37 migrants/1,000 population (2003 est.)
Ethnic Groups: 30% Quechua, 25% Aymara, 30% mixed,15% European
Languages: Spanish, Quechua and Aymara (all official)
Religions: 95% Roman Catholic; 5% Protestant, especially Methodist
Birth Rate: 25.53/1,000 population (2003 est.)
Death Rate: 7.91/1,000 population (2003 est.)
Infant Mortality: 56.05 deaths/1,000 live births (2003 est.)

Life Expectancy at Birth: 62.20 years male, 67.48 years female (2003 est.)
Total Fertility Rate: 3.23 children born/woman (2003 est.)
Literacy: 86.7% (2002)

■ GOVERNMENT

Leader(s): President Carlos Diego Mesa Gisbert
Government Type: republic
Administrative Divisions: 9 departments (departmentos, sing. —departmento)
Nationhood: Aug. 6, 1825 (from Spain)
National Holiday: Independence Day, Aug. 6

■ ECONOMY

Overview: a poor economy vulnerable to price fluctuations for its small number of exports; market-oriented economic reforms and tighter fiscal discipline are leading to generally improving economic conditions
GDP: US$21.15 billion, per capita US$2,500; real growth rate 2.8% (2002 est.)
Inflation: 1.6% (2001)
Industries: accounts for 20% of GDP (2002); mining, smelting, petroleum, food and beverage, tobacco, handicrafts, clothing; illicit drug industry reportedly produces the largest revenues
Labour Force: 3.6 million (2002); 29.1% trade and tourism, 26.2% community, social and business services, 19.4% manufacturing
Unemployment: 5.2% (2002)
Agriculture: accounts for about 20% of GDP (including forestry and fisheries) (2002); principal commodities—soybeans, coffee, coca, cotton, corn, sugar cane, rice, potatoes, timber; self-sufficient in food
Natural Resources: tin, natural gas, crude oil, zinc, tungsten, antimony, silver, iron ore, lead, gold, timber, hydroelectric power

■ FINANCE/TRADE

Currency: Boliviano ($b) = 100 centavos
International Reserves Excluding Gold: US$644 million (Jan. 2004)
Gold Reserves: 0.911 million fine troy ounces (Jan. 2004)
Budget: revenues US$4 billion; expenditures US$4 billion, including capital expenditures of US$ n.a. (2002 est.)
Defence Expenditures: 6.1% of central government expenditure (2002)
Education Expenditures: 18.4% of government expenditure (2002)
External Debt: US$4.867 billion (2002)
Exports: US$1.573 billion (2003); commodities: metals 45%, natural gas 32%, coffee, soybeans,

sugar, cotton, gold, timber; partners: US, Peru, Colombia, UK, Brazil
Imports: US$1.613 billion (2003); commodities: food, petroleum, consumer goods, capital goods; partners: US, Brazil, Argentina, Chile, Peru

■ COMMUNICATIONS

Daily Newspapers: 55/1,000 inhabitants (2000)
Televisions: 121/1,000 inhabitants (2002)
Radios: 676/1,000 inhabitants (2001)
Telephones: 68 lines/1,000 inhabitants (2002)
Internet: hosts: 1,413 (2002); users: 270,000 (2002)

■ TRANSPORTATION

Motor Vehicles: 433,000; 200,000 passenger cars
Roads: 53,790 km; 3,496 km paved
Railway: 3,519 km
Air Traffic: 1,509,000 passengers carried (2002)
Airports: 1,081 airfields; 12 have paved runways (2003 est.)

Canadian Embassy: The Consulate of Canada Calle Victor Sanjinez No. 2678 Edificio Barcelona, 2nd Floor, Plaza Espana, Sopacachi, La Paz; mailing address: Casilla Postal 13032, La Paz, Bolivia. Tel: (011-591-2) 241-5021. Fax: (011-591-2) 241-4453. e-mail: lapaz@dfait-maeci.gc.ca
Embassy in Canada: Embassy of the Republic of Bolivia, 130 Albert St, Ste 416, Ottawa ON K1P 5G4. Tel: (613) 236-5730. Fax: (613) 236-8237. e-mail: info@boliviaembassy.ca

Bosnia and Herzegovina

Long-Form Name: Republic of Bosnia and Herzegovina
Capital: Sarajevo

■ GEOGRAPHY

Area: 51,129 sq. km
Coastline: 20 km
Climate: hot summers and cold winters; regions with high elevation have short, cool summers and long, severe winters; mild, rainy winters along the coast
Environment: air pollution; scarce water; waste disposal sites limited; subject to frequent destructive earthquakes
Terrain: mountains and valleys
Land Use: arable land: 9.8%, permanent crops: 2.94%, other: 87.26%; includes 20 sq. km irrigated
Location: SE Europe

■ PEOPLE

Population: 3,989,018 (July 2003 est.)
Nationality: Bosnian, Herzegovinian
Age Structure: 0–14 yrs: 19.4%; 15–64: 70.5%; 65+: 10.1% (2003 est.)
Population Growth Rate: 0.48% (2003 est.)
Net Migration: 0.32 migrants/1,000 population (2003 est.)
Ethnic Groups: 31% Serb, Bosniak 44%, Croat 17%, Yugoslav 5.5%, other 2.5%; Note: Bosniak has replaced Muslim as an ethnic term, partly to avoid confusion with the religious term Muslim, an adherent of Islam.
Languages: Croatian, Serbian, Bosnian
Religions: 40% Muslim, 31% Orthodox, 15% Catholic, 4% Protestant, 10% other
Birth Rate: 12.65/1,000 population (2003 est.)
Death Rate: 8.21/1,000 population (2003 est.)
Infant Mortality: 22.70 deaths/1,000 live births (2003 est.)
Life Expectancy at Birth: 69.56 years male, 75.22 years female (2003 est.)
Total Fertility Rate: 1.71 children born/woman (2003 est.)
Literacy: 94.6% (2002)

■ GOVERNMENT

Leader(s): Presidential Chairman Sulejman Tihic. Note: the central government is headed by a tripartite presidency with one representative of each of the three major ethnic constituencies
Government Type: emerging federal democratic republic
Administrative Divisions: 2 first-order administrative divisions
Nationhood: Mar. 1, 1992 (from Yugoslavia)
National Holiday: Bilt National Day, Nov. 25

■ ECONOMY

Overview: though farms are almost entirely privately owned, they are small and inefficient, and food must be imported; inter-ethnic warfare has caused sharp decreases in industrial output and soaring unemployment
GDP: US$7.3 billion, per capita US$1,900; real growth rate 2.3% (2002 est.)
Inflation: 3.5% (2002 est.)
Industries: accounts for 41% of GDP; steel production, mining (esp. coal, iron ore, lead, zinc), manufacturing (esp. vehicle assembly, textiles, tobacco products, wood furniture), oil refining
Labour Force: 1.9 million (2002); 2% agriculture, 45% industry and mining

Unemployment: n.a.
Agriculture: accounts for 13% of GDP; regularly produces less than half the region's food needs; foothills of northern Bosnia support orchards, vineyards, livestock and some wheat and corn; long winters and heavy precipitation reduce agricultural output in mountains; farms are generally not very productive
Natural Resources: coal, iron, bauxite, manganese, timber, copper, lead, zinc, chromium, hydroelectric power

■ FINANCE/TRADE

Currency: convertible marka = 100 convertible pfenniga
International Reserves Excluding Gold: n.a.
Gold Reserves: n.a.
Budget: expenditures US$1.6 billion; revenues and capital expenditures n.a. (2000 est.)
Defence Expenditures: 4.5% of GDP (2002)
Education Expenditures: n.a.
External Debt: US$2.515 billion (2002)
Exports: $1.020 billion (2002); partners include: Croatia, Switzerland, Italy, Germany
Imports: $4.066 billion (2002); commodities: foodstuffs, machinery and transport equipment, textiles, petroleum products. partners include: Croatia, Slovenia, Germany, Italy

■ COMMUNICATIONS

Daily Newspapers: 152/1,000 inhabitants (2000)
Televisions: 116/1,000 inhabitants (2002)
Radios: 243/1,000 inhabitants (2001)
Telephones: 237 lines/1,000 inhabitants (2002)
Internet: hosts: 5,702 (2002); users: 100,000 (2002)

■ TRANSPORTATION

Motor Vehicles: n.a.
Roads: 21,846 km; 11,424 km paved
Railway: 1,021 km
Air Traffic: 66,000 passengers carried (2002)
Airports: 32; 14 have paved runways (2003 est.)

Canadian Embassy: The Canadian Embassy, 4 Grbavicka, 71000 Sarajevo, Bosnia and Herzegovina. Tel: (011-387-33) 222-033. Fax: (011-387-33) 222-038. e-mail: sjevo@dfait-maeci.gc.ca
Embassy in Canada: Embassy of Bosnia and Herzogovina, 130 Albert St., Ste 805, Ottawa ON K1P 5G4. Tel: (613) 236-0028. Fax: (613) 236-1139. e-mail: embassyofbih@magma.ca

Botswana

Long-Form Name: Republic of Botswana
Capital: Gaborone

■ GEOGRAPHY

Area: 600,370 sq. km
Coastline: none: landlocked
Climate: subtropical to semi-arid; warm winters and hot summers
Environment: overgrazing; desertification; limited resources of fresh water, periodic droughts, sand and dust storms
Terrain: predominantly flat to gently rolling tableland; Kalahari Desert in southwest
Land Use: arable land: 0.61%, permanent crops: 0.01%, other: 99.38%; includes 10 sq. km irrigated
Location: S Africa

■ PEOPLE

Population: 1,573,267 (July 2003 est.)
Nationality: Motswana (sing.), Batswana (pl.)
Age Structure: 0–14 yrs: 39.5%; 15–64: 56.0%; 65+: 4.5% (2003 est.)
Population Growth Rate: -0.55% (2003 est.)
Net Migration: 0 migrants/1,000 population (2003 est.)
Ethnic Groups: 95% Batswana; about 4% Kalanga, Basarwa and Kgalagadi; about 1% white
Languages: English (official), Setswana
Religions: 50% indigenous beliefs, 50% Christian
Birth Rate: 25.50/1,000 population (2003 est.)
Death Rate: 31.00/1,000 population (2003 est.)
Infant Mortality: 67.34 deaths/1,000 live births (2003 est.)
Life Expectancy at Birth: 32.20 years male, 32.32 years female (2003 est.)
Total Fertility Rate: 3.27 children born/woman (2003 est.)
Literacy: 78.9% (2002)

■ GOVERNMENT

Leader(s): President Festus Gontebanye Mogae, Vice President Seretse Ian Khama
Government Type: parliamentary republic
Administrative Divisions: 10 districts and 4 town councils
Nationhood: Sept. 30, 1966 (from UK; Botswana formerly known as Bechuanaland)
National Holiday: Independence Day, Sept. 30

■ ECONOMY

Overview: economy based on mining (diamonds) and traditionally, cattle raising and crops; exhibits high unemployment

GDP: US$13.48 billion, per capita US$8,500; real growth rate 4.2% (2002 est.)
Inflation: 8.1% (2002)
Industries: accounts for 44% of GDP (2000); livestock processing; mining of diamonds, copper, nickel, coal, salt, soda ash, potash; tourism
Labour Force: 800,000 (2002); 36.6% community, social and business services; 18% trade and tourism, 11.2% manufacturing; 19,000 are employed in various mines in South Africa
Unemployment: 15.8% (2002 est.)
Agriculture: plagued by erratic rainfall and poor soil; accounts for only 4% of GDP; subsistence farming predominates; cattle raising supports 50% of the population; must import large share of food needs. Products include sorghum, millet, corn, peanuts, beans, livestock.
Natural Resources: diamonds, copper, nickel, salt, soda ash, potash, coal, iron ore, silver, natural gas

■ FINANCE/TRADE

Currency: pula (P) = 100 thebe
International Reserves Excluding Gold: US$5.189 billion (Nov. 2003)
Gold Reserves: n.a.
Budget: revenues US$2.3 billion; expenditures US$2.4 billion, including capital expenditures of US$ n.a. (FY2001/02)
Defence Expenditures: 3.5% of GDP (2002)
Education Expenditures: n.a.
External Debt: US$480 million (2002)
Exports: US$2.256 billion (2002); commodities: diamonds 72%, copper and nickel 5%, meat 4%, cattle, animal products; partners: Switzerland, US, UK, other European Community-associated members of Southern African Customs Union
Imports: US$1.672 billion (2002 est.); commodities: foodstuffs, vehicles, textiles, petroleum products; partners: Southern African Customs Union, EFTA, Zimbabwe

■ COMMUNICATIONS

Daily Newspapers: 27/1,000 inhabitants (2000)
Televisions: 44/1,000 inhabitants (2002)
Radios: 150/1,000 inhabitants (2001)
Telephones: 87 lines/1,000 inhabitants (2002)
Internet: hosts: 1,617 (2002); users: 50,000 (2002)

■ TRANSPORTATION

Motor Vehicles: 110,000; 49,000 passenger cars
Roads: 10,217 km; 5,620 km paved
Railway: 888 km
Air Traffic: 175,000 passengers carried (2002)
Airports: 86; 10 have paved runways (2003 est.)

Canadian Embassy: The Consulate of Canada, Vision Hire Building, Plot 182, Queen's Road,

Gaborone, Botswana; mailing address: P.O. Box 882, Gaborone, Botswana. Tel: & Fax: (011-267) 3904-411. e-mail: n.a.
Embassy in Canada: c/o High Commission for the Republic of Botswana, 1531-1533 New Hampshire Ave. NW, Washington DC 20036, USA. Tel: (202) 244-4990. Fax: (202) 244-4164. e-mail: n.a.

Brazil

Long-Form Name: Federative Republic of Brazil
Capital: Brasilia

■ GEOGRAPHY

Area: 8,511,965 sq. km; includes Arquipélago de Fernando de Noronha, Atol das Rocas, Ilha da Trindade, Ilhas Martin Vaz and Penedos de São Pedro e São Paulo
Coastline: 7,491 km
Climate: mostly tropical, but temperate in south
Environment: recurrent droughts in northeast; floods and frost in south; deforestation in Amazon basin; air and water pollution in Rio de Janeiro and São Paulo and several other large cities
Terrain: mostly flat to rolling lowlands in north; some plains, hills, mountains and narrow coastal belt
Land Use: arable land: 6.3%, permanent crops: 1.42%, other: 92.28%; includes 26,560 sq. km irrigated
Location: E South America

■ PEOPLE

Population: 182,032,604 (July 2003 est.)
Nationality: Brazilian
Age Structure: 0–14 yrs: 27.1%; 15–64: 67.2%; 65+: 5.7% (2003 est.)
Population Growth Rate: 1.15% (2003 est.)
Net Migration: -0.03 migrants/1,000 population (2003 est.)
Ethnic Groups: Portuguese, Italian, German, Japanese, black, Amerindian; 55% white, 38% mixed, 6% black, 1% other
Languages: Portuguese (official), Spanish, English, French
Religions: 70% Roman Catholic (nominal)
Birth Rate: 17.67/1,000 population (2003 est.)
Death Rate: 6.13/1,000 population (2003 est.)
Infant Mortality: 31.74 deaths/1,000 live births (2003 est.)
Life Expectancy at Birth: 67.16 years male, 75.30 years female (2003 est.)
Total Fertility Rate: 2.01 children born/woman (2003 est.)
Literacy: 86.4% (2002)

■ GOVERNMENT

Leader(s): President Luiz Inacio Lula da Silva, Vice President Jose Alencar
Government Type: federative republic
Administrative Divisions: 26 states (estados, sing. — estado) and 1 federal district (distrito federal)
Nationhood: Sept. 7, 1822 (from Portugal)
National Holiday: Independence Day, Sept. 7

■ ECONOMY

Overview: inflation has dropped sharply and sweeping reforms have boosted the economy, but the domestic debt remains burdensome. Brazil's natural resources remain a major, long-term economic strength
GDP: US$1.376 trillion, per capita US$7,600; real growth rate 1.5% (2002 est.)
Inflation: 8.3% (2002)
Industries: accounts for 32% of GDP (2000); textiles and other consumer goods, shoes, chemicals, cement, lumber, iron ore, steel, motor vehicles and auto parts, metalworking, capital goods, tin
Labour Force: 81.7 million (2002); 53% community, social and business services, 23% agriculture, 24% industry
Unemployment: 9.4% (2002)
Agriculture: accounts for 9% of GDP (2000); world's largest producer and exporter of coffee and orange juice concentrate and second-largest exporter of soybeans; self-sufficient in food, except for wheat. Products also include rice, corn, cocoa
Natural Resources: iron ore, manganese, bauxite, nickel, uranium, phosphates, tin, hydro-electricity, gold, platinum, crude oil, timber

■ FINANCE/TRADE

Currency: real (CR$) = 100 centavos
International Reserves Excluding Gold: US$53.084 billion (Jan. 2004)
Gold Reserves: 0.446 million fine troy ounces (Jan. 2004)
Budget: revenues US$100.6 billion; expenditures US$91.6 billion, including capital expenditures of US$ n.a. (2000)
Defence Expenditures: 5.2% of total government expenditure (2002)
Education Expenditures: 10.4% of central government expenditure (2002)
External Debt: US$227.932 billion (2002)
Exports: US$73.084 billion (2003 est.); commodities: coffee, soybeans, footwear, metallurgical products, foodstuffs, iron ore, automobiles and parts; partners: US, Argentina, Germany, Japan, Italy, Netherlands

Imports: US$50.665 billion (2003 est.); commodities: crude oil, capital goods, chemical products, foodstuffs, coal; partners: US, Argentina, Germany, Japan, Italy

COMMUNICATIONS

Daily Newspapers: 43/1,000 inhabitants (2000)
Televisions: 349/1,000 inhabitants (2002)
Radios: 433/1,000 inhabitants (2001)
Telephones: 223 lines/1,000 inhabitants (2002)
Internet: hosts: 2,237,527 (2002); users: 14.3 million (2002)

TRANSPORTATION

Motor Vehicles: 16,700,000; 13,100,000 passenger cars
Roads: 1.725 million km; 94,871 km paved
Railway: 31,543 km
Air Traffic: 35,890,000 passengers carried (2002)
Airports: 3,590 airfields; 665 have paved runways (2003 est.)

Canadian Embassy: Avenida das Nacoes, Quadra 803, Lote 16, Brasilia DF, 70410-900; mailing address: Caixa Postal 341, 70359-900 Brasilia DF, Brazil. Tel: (011-55-61) 424-5400. Fax: (011-55-61) 424-5490. e-mail: brsla@dfait-maeci.gc.ca
Embassy in Canada: Embassy of the Federative Republic of Brazil, 450 Wilbrod St, Ottawa ON K1N 6M8. Tel: (613) 237-1090. Fax: (613) 237-6144. e-mail: mailbox@brasembottawa.org

British Indian Ocean Territory

Long-Form Name: British Indian Ocean Territory
Capital: None; Victoria (Seychelles) is administrative headquarters

GEOGRAPHY

Area: 60 sq. km
Climate: tropical maritime, hot and humid, moderated by trade winds
Land Use: arable land: NEGL permanent crops: 0%, other: 100%
Location: Indian Ocean, the Chagos Archipelago island group E of Madagascar, S of India

PEOPLE

Population: no indigenous inhabitants; US and UK military personnel
Nationality: n.a.
Ethnic Groups: n.a. — no indigenous population
Languages: n.a. — no indigenous population

GOVERNMENT

Colony/Territory of: Dependent Territory of the United Kingdom
Leader(s): Head of State: Queen Elizabeth II, Commissioner to the BIOT Alan Huckle, Administrator Charles Hamilton
Government Type: dependent overseas territory of Great Britain
National Holiday: n.a.

ECONOMY

Overview: fishing, coconuts, guano fertilizer; all economic activity takes place on the largest island, Diego Garcia, where joint US–UK defence facilities are located; there are no industrial or agricultural activities on the islands

FINANCE/TRADE

Currency: pound sterling (£ or £ stg)

Canadian Embassy: c/o of the Canadian High Commission, Macdonald House, 1 Grosvenor Square, London W1K 4AB, England, UK. Tel: (011-44-20) 7258-6600. Fax: (011-44-20) 7258-6333. e-mail: ldn@dfait-maeci.gc.ca
Representative to Canada: c/o British High Commission, 80 Elgin St, Ottawa ON K1P 5K7. Tel: (613) 237-1530. Fax: (613) 237-7980. e-mail should be sent using the appropriate form at the British High Commission's Website at http://www.britain-in-canada.org

British Virgin Islands

Long-Form Name: British Virgin Islands
Capital: Road Town

GEOGRAPHY

Area: 150 sq. km; includes the island of Anegada
Climate: subtropical and humid; moderated by trade winds; hurricanes, and tropical storms occur from July to Oct.
Land Use: arable land: 20%, permanent crops: 6.67%, other: 73.33%
Location: Caribbean islands, E of Puerto Rico

PEOPLE

Population: 21,730 (July 2003 est.)
Nationality: British Virgin Islander
Ethnic Groups: 90% black, 10% white, Asian, and other
Languages: English (official)

GOVERNMENT

Colony/Territory of: Dependent territory of the UK

Leader(s): Head of State: Queen Elizabeth II, Governor Thomas T. Macan, Chief Minister Orlando Smith
Government Type: overseas territory of Great Britain
National Holiday: Territory Day, July 1

ECONOMY

Overview: one of the most prosperous economies in the Caribbean; highly dependent on tourism

FINANCE/TRADE

Currency: US dollar ($) = 100 cents

Canadian Embassy: c/o The Canadian High Commission, Macdonald House, 1 Grosvenor Square, London, W1K 4AB, England, UK. Tel: (011-44-20) 7258-6600. Fax: (011-44-20) 7258-6333. e-mail: ldn@dfait-maeci.gc.ca
Representative to Canada: c/o British High Commission, 80 Elgin St, Ottawa ON K1P 5K7. Tel: (613) 237-1530. Fax: (613) 237-7980. e-mail should be sent using the appropriate form at the British High Commission's Website at http://www.britain-in-canada.org

---

Brunei Darussalam

Long-Form Name: Negara Brunei Darussalam
Capital: Bandar Seri Begawan

GEOGRAPHY

Area: 5,770 sq. km
Coastline: 161 km
Climate: tropical; hot, humid, rainy
Environment: typhoons, earthquakes and severe floods occasionally occur
Terrain: flat coastal plain rises to mountainous east; hilly lowland in west
Land Use: arable land: 0.57%, permanent crops: 0.76%, other: 98.67%; includes 10 sq. km irrigated
Location: Indonesia (island of Borneo), bordering on South China Sea and Malaysia

PEOPLE

Population: 358,098 (July 2003 est.)
Nationality: Bruneian
Age Structure: 0–14 yrs: 29.6%; 15–64: 67.6%; 65+: 2.8% (2003 est.)
Population Growth Rate: 2.0% (2003 est.)
Net Migration: 3.75 migrants/1,000 population (2003 est.)
Ethnic Groups: 62% Malay, 15% Chinese, 6% indigenous, 17% other
Languages: Malay (official), English and Chinese

Religions: Islam (official, mainly Sunni Muslims); majority of Chinese are Buddhist, Confucian or Taoist
Birth Rate: 19.68/1,000 population (2003 est.)
Death Rate: 3.39/1,000 population (2003 est.)
Infant Mortality: 13.50 deaths/1,000 live births (2003 est.)
Life Expectancy at Birth: 71.90 years male, 76.82 years female (2003 est.)
Total Fertility Rate: 2.37 children born/woman (2003 est.)
Literacy: 93.9% (2002)

GOVERNMENT

Leader(s): Sultan, Prime Minister and Minister of Defence Sir Hassanal Bolkiah
Government Type: constitutional sultanate
Administrative Divisions: 4 districts (daerahdaerah, sing. —daerah)
Nationhood: Jan. 1, 1984 (from UK)
National Holiday: National Day, Feb. 23

ECONOMY

Overview: economy is based on crude oil and natural gas exports and the per capita GDP is one of the highest for underdeveloped nations; almost totally supported by exports of crude oil and natural gas
GDP: US$6.5 billion, per capita US$18,600; real growth rate 3.0% (2002 est.)
Inflation: -2.0% (2002 est.)
Industries: accounts for 45% of GDP (2001 est.); petroleum, liquefied natural gas, construction
Labour Force: approx. 150,000; 42% production of oil, natural gas and construction; 48% government, 10% agriculture, forestry and fishing
Unemployment: n.a.
Agriculture: accounts for 5% of GDP; imports about 80% of its food needs; principal crops and livestock include rice, cassava, bananas, buffalo and pigs
Natural Resources: crude oil, natural gas, timber

FINANCE/TRADE

Currency: Bruneian dollar ($B) = 100 cents
International Reserves Excluding Gold: n.a.
Gold Reserves: n.a.
Budget: n.a.
Defence Expenditures: 5.0% of GDP (2002)
Education Expenditures: n.a.
External Debt: none
Exports: US$4.320 billion (2003 est.); commodities: crude oil, liquefied natural gas, petroleum products; partners: Japan, US, South Korea, Thailand
Imports: US$1.312 billion (2003 est.); commodities: machinery and transport equipment, manu-

factured goods, food, beverages, tobacco, consumer goods; partners: Singapore, UK, Malaysia, US

■ COMMUNICATIONS

Daily Newspapers: 1 in total
Televisions: n.a.
Radios: n.a.
Telephones: 256 lines/1,000 inhabitants (2002)
Internet: hosts: 8,668 (2002); users: 35,000 (2002)

■ TRANSPORTATION

Motor Vehicles: 166,000; 148,000 passenger cars
Roads: 2,525 km; all paved
Railway: 13 km private line
Air Traffic: 1,050,000 passengers carried (2001 est.)
Airports: 2; 1 has paved runway (2002 est.)

Canadian Embassy: The High Commission of Canada, 5th Floor, Jalan McArthur Bldg., Bandar Seri Begawan; mailing address: P.O. Box 2808, Bandar Seri, Begawan B58675, Brunei Darussalam. Tel: (011-673-2) 22-00-43. Fax (011-673-2) 22-00-40. e-mail: bsbgn@dfait-maeci.gc.ca
Embassy in Canada: High Commission for Brunei, 395 Laurier Ave E, Ottawa ON K1N 6R4. Tel: (613) 234-5656. Fax: (613) 234-4397. e-mail: bhco@bellnet.ca

Bulgaria

Long-Form Name: Republic of Bulgaria
Capital: Sofia

■ GEOGRAPHY

Area: 110,910 sq. km
Coastline: 354 km
Climate: temperate; cold, damp winters; hot, dry summers
Environment: subject to earthquakes, landslides, deforestation, air and water pollution
Terrain: mostly mountains with lowlands in north and south
Land Use: arable land: 39%, permanent crops: 1.8%, other: 59.2%; includes 8,000 sq. km irrigated
Location: SE Europe, bordering on Black Sea

■ PEOPLE

Population: 7,537,929 (July 2003 est.)
Nationality: Bulgarian
Age Structure: 0–14 yrs: 14.2%; 15–64: 68.8%; 65+: 17.0% (2003 est.)
Population Growth Rate: -1.09% (2003 est.)

Net Migration: -4.58 migrants/1,000 population (2003 est.)
Ethnic Groups: 83% Bulgarian, 8.5% Turk, 2.6% Gypsy, 2.5% Macedonian, 3.4% Armenian, Russian, Tatar and other
Languages: Bulgarian (official), Turkish; secondary languages closely correspond to ethnic breakdown
Religions: 85% Bulgarian Orthodox, 13% Muslim (practised by Turkish and Pomak minorities), 0.8% Jewish, 0.7% Roman Catholic, 0.5% Protestant, Gregorian-Armenian and other
Birth Rate: 8.02/1,000 population (2003 est.)
Death Rate: 14.34/1,000 population (2003 est.)
Infant Mortality: 13.70 deaths/1,000 live births (2003 est.)
Life Expectancy at Birth: 68.26 years male, 75.56 years female (2003 est.)
Total Fertility Rate: 1.13 children born/woman (2003 est.)
Literacy: 98.6% (2002)

■ GOVERNMENT

Leader(s): President Georgi Purvanov, Prime Minister Simeon Saxe-Coburg Gotha
Government Type: parliamentary democracy
Administrative Divisions: 28 provinces (oblasti, sing. —oblast)
Nationhood: March 3, 1878 (from Ottoman Empire)
National Holiday: Liberation Day, Mar. 3

■ ECONOMY

Overview: heavily in debt with low growth, the economy is also hindered by antiquated industrial plants; continues to adjust to a market economy; the government's structural reform program includes privatization and, where appropriate, liquidation of state-owned enterprises; agricultural policies have been liberalized
GDP: US$49.23 billion, per capita US$6,500; real growth rate 4.8% (2002)
Inflation: 5.9% (2002)
Industries: accounts for 29% of GDP (2001); food processing, machine building and metal working, electronics, chemicals
Labour Force: 4.1 million (2002); 31% industry, 26% agriculture, 43% community, social and business services
Unemployment: 19.4% (2002)
Agriculture: accounts for 14% of GNP (2001); climate and soil conditions support livestock raising and the growing of various grain crops, oilseeds, vegetables, fruit and tobacco; more than one-third of the arable land devoted to grain; world's fourth largest tobacco exporter; surplus food producer

Natural Resources: bauxite, copper, lead, zinc, coal, timber, arable land

■ FINANCE/TRADE

Currency: lev (pl. leva) (Lv) = 100 stotinki
International Reserves Excluding Gold: US$5.826 billion (Jan. 2004)
Gold Reserves: 1.281 million fine troy ounces (Jan. 2004)
Budget: revenues US$6.68 billion; expenditures US$6.69 billion, capital expenditures US$ n.a. (2002 est.)
Defence Expenditures: 7.9% of total government expenditure (2002)
Education Expenditures: 4.34% of central government expenditure (2000)
External Debt: US$10.462 billion (2002)
Exports: US$7.428 billion (2003 est.); commodities: machinery and equipment 60.5%, agricultural products 14.7%, manufactured consumer goods 10.6%, fuels, minerals, raw materials and metals 8.5%, other 5.7%; partners: Italy, Turkey, Germany, Greece, Serbia and Montenegro
Imports: US$10.717 billion (2003 est.); commodities: fuels, minerals, raw materials 45.2%, machinery and equipment 39.8%, manufactured consumer goods 4.6%, agricultural products 3.8%, other 6.6%; partners: Russia, Germany, Italy, France

■ COMMUNICATIONS

Daily Newspapers: 116/1,000 inhabitants (2000)
Televisions: 453/1,000 inhabitants (2002)
Radios: 543/1,000 inhabitants (2001)
Telephones: 368 lines/1,000 inhabitants (2002)
Internet: hosts: 32,986 (2002); users: 630,000 (2002)

■ TRANSPORTATION

Motor Vehicles: 2,080,000; 1,830,000 passenger cars
Roads: 37,286 km; 35,049 km paved
Railway: 4,294 km
Air Traffic: 163,000 passengers carried (2002)
Airports: 216; 128 have paved runways (2003 est.)

Canadian Embassy: Consulate of Canada, 11, Assen Slatarov St., 1st Floor, Sofia 1504, Bulgaria. Tel: (011 359 2) 943 3704. Fax: (011 359 2) 946 1913. e-mail: canada@mail.techno-link.com
Embassy in Canada: Embassy of the Republic of Bulgaria, 325 Stewart St, Ottawa ON K1N 6K5. Tel: (613) 789-3215. Fax: (613) 789-3524. e-mail: mailmn@storm.ca

Burkina Faso

Long-Form Name: Burkina Faso
Capital: Ouagadougou

■ GEOGRAPHY

Area: 274,200 sq. km
Coastline: none: landlocked
Climate: tropical; warm, dry winters; hot, wet summers
Environment: recent droughts and desertification severely affecting marginal agricultural activities, population distribution, economy; overgrazing;
Terrain: mostly flat to dissected, undulating plains; hills in west and southeast
Land Use: arable land: 12.43%, permanent crops: 0.18%, other: 87.39%; includes 250 sq. km irrigated
Location: WC Africa

■ PEOPLE

Population: 13,228,460 (July 2003 est.)
Nationality: Burkinabe (sing. & pl.)
Age Structure: 0–14 yrs: 46.1%; 15–64: 51.0%; 65+: 2.9% (2003 est.)
Population Growth Rate: 2.6% (2003 est.)
Net Migration: 0.0 migrants/1,000 population (2003 est.)
Ethnic Groups: more than 50 tribes; principal tribe is Mossi (over 40% of pop.); other important groups are Gurunsi, Senufo, Lobi, Bobo, Mande and Fulani
Languages: French (official); tribal languages belong to Sudanic family, spoken by 90% of population
Religions: 40% indigenous beliefs, about 50% Muslim, 10% Christian (mainly Roman Catholic)
Birth Rate: 44.78/1,000 population (2003 est.)
Death Rate: 18.76/1,000 population (2003 est.)
Infant Mortality: 99.78 deaths/1,000 live births (2003 est.)
Life Expectancy at Birth: 43.02 years male, 45.94 years female (2003 est.)
Total Fertility Rate: 6.34 children born/woman (2003 est.)
Literacy: 12.8% (2002)

■ GOVERNMENT

Leader(s): Head of State: Captain Blaise Compaoré, Prime Minister Paramango Ernest Yonli
Government Type: parliamentary democracy
Administrative Divisions: 45 provinces
Nationhood: Aug. 5, 1960 (from France; Burkina Faso formerly known as Upper Volta)
National Holiday: Republic Day — December 11

■ ECONOMY

Overview: a poor economy with high population density and few natural resources, it relies heavily on subsistence agriculture; economic development is hindered by a poor communications network; agriculture provides approximately one-third of national income
GDP: US$14.51 billion, per capita US$1,100; real growth rate 4.6% (2002 est.)
Inflation: 4.9% (2001)
Industries: accounts for 28% of GDP (2000); agricultural processing plants; brewery, cement and brick plants; soap, cigarettes, textiles, gold mining and extraction; a few other small consumer goods enterprises
Labour Force: 5.8 million (2002); 90% agriculture, 4.3% industry, 5% services; 20% of male labour force migrates annually to neighbouring countries for seasonal employment
Unemployment: n.a.
Agriculture: accounts for 31% of GDP (2000); cash crops—peanuts, shea nuts, sesame, cotton; food crops—sorghum, millet, corn, rice; livestock; not self-sufficient in foodgrains
Natural Resources: manganese, limestone, marble; small deposits of gold, antimony, copper, nickel, bauxite, lead, phosphates, zinc, silver

■ FINANCE/TRADE

Currency: Communauté financière africaine franc (CFAF) = 100 centimes
International Reserves Excluding Gold: US$399 million (Jan. 2004)
Gold Reserves: 0.231 million fine troy ounces (Oct. 2003)
Budget: revenues US$316 million; expenditures US$ n.a., including capital expenditures of US$ n.a. (2001)
Defence Expenditures: 1.4% of GDP (2002)
Education Expenditures: n.a.
External Debt: US$1.580 billion (2002)
Exports: US$272 million (2003 est.); commodities: oilseeds, cotton, live animals, gold; partners: Italy, France, Venezuela, Benelux
Imports: US$622 million (2003 est.); commodities: grain, dairy products, petroleum, machinery; partners: Côte d'Ivoire, Venezuela, France

■ COMMUNICATIONS

Daily Newspapers: 1/1,000 inhabitants (2000)
Televisions: 79/1,000 inhabitants (2002)
Radios: 433/1,000 inhabitants (2001)
Telephones: 5 lines/1,000 inhabitants (2002)
Internet: hosts: 409 (2002); users: 25,000 (2002)

■ TRANSPORTATION

Motor Vehicles: 55,000; 35,600 passenger cars

Roads: 12,506 km; 2,001 km paved
Railway: 622 km
Air Traffic: 53,000 passengers carried (2002)
Airports: 33; 2 have paved runways (2003 est.)

Canadian Embassy: The Canadian Embassy, rue Agostino Neto, Ouagadougou; mailing address: Office of the Canadian Embassy, P.O. Box 548, Ouagadougou 01, Province du Kadiogo, Burkina Faso. Tel: (011-226) 50-31-18-94. Fax (011-226) 50-31-19-00. e-mail: ouaga@dfait-maeci.gc.ca
Embassy in Canada: Embassy of Burkina Faso, 48 Range Rd, Ottawa ON K1N 8J4. Tel: (613) 238-4796. Fax: (613) 238-3812. e-mail: burkina.faso@sympatico.ca

Burma

see Myanmar

Burundi

Long-Form Name: Republic of Burundi
Capital: Bujumbura

■ GEOGRAPHY

Area: 27,830 sq. km
Coastline: none: landlocked
Climate: temperate; warm; occasional frost in uplands
Environment: soil exhaustion; soil erosion; deforestation; flooding and landslides are natural hazards
Terrain: mostly rolling to hilly highland; some plains
Land Use: arable land: 29.98%, permanent crops: 12.85%, other: 57.17%; includes 740 sq. km irrigated
Location: EC Africa

■ PEOPLE

Population: 6,096,156 (July 2003 est.)
Nationality: Burundian
Age Structure: 0–14 yrs: 46.7%; 15–64: 50.6%; 65+: 2.7% (2003 est.)
Population Growth Rate: 2.18% (2003 est.)
Net Migration: -0.12 migrants/1,000 population (2003 est.)
Ethnic Groups: Africans: 85% Hutu (Bantu), 14% Tutsi (Hamitic), 1% Twa (Pygmy); non-Africans: 3,000 Europeans, 2,000 South Asians
Languages: Kirundi and French (official); Swahili used commercially
Religions: about 67% Christian (62% Roman Catholic, 5% Protestant), 32% indigenous beliefs, 1% Muslim

Birth Rate: 39.72/1,000 population (2003 est.)
Death Rate: 17.80/1,000 population (2003 est.)
Infant Mortality: 71.54 deaths/1,000 live births (2003 est.)
Life Expectancy at Birth: 42.54 years male, 43.88 years female (2003 est.)
Total Fertility Rate: 5.99 children born/woman (2003 est.)
Literacy: 50.4% (2002)

■ GOVERNMENT

Leader(s): President Domitien Ndayizeye; Vice President Alphonse Kadege
Government Type: republic
Administrative Divisions: 16 provinces
Nationhood: July 1, 1962 (from UN trusteeship under Belgian administration)
National Holiday: Independence Day, July 1

■ ECONOMY

Overview: economy is heavily dependent on the coffee crop and therefore vulnerable to market conditions; there are only a few basic industries; massive ethnic-based violence has also interfered with economic activity
GDP: US$3.146 billion, per capita US$500; real growth rate 4.5% (2002 est.)
Inflation: 12.0% (2002)
Industries: accounts for 19% of GDP (2002 est.); light consumer goods such as blankets, shoes, soap; assembly of imports; public works construction; food processing
Labour Force: 3.9 million (2002); 39.6% community, social and business services, 14.8% manufacturing
Unemployment: n.a.
Agriculture: accounts for 50% of GDP (2002 est.); 90% of population dependent on subsistence farming; marginally self-sufficient in food production; cash crops—coffee, cotton, tea; food crops—corn, sorghum, sweet potatoes, bananas, manioc; livestock—meat, milk, hides and skins
Natural Resources: nickel, uranium, rare earth oxide, peat, cobalt, copper, platinum (not yet exploited), vanadium, hydroelectric power

■ FINANCE/TRADE

Currency: Burundi franc (FBu) = 100 centimes
International Reserves Excluding Gold: US$70 million (Jan. 2004)
Gold Reserves: 0.001 million fine troy ounces (Jan. 2004)
Budget: revenues US$125 million, expenditures US$176 million, including capital expenditures of US$ n.a. (2000 est.)

Defence Expenditures: 27.1% of central government expenditure (2002)
Education Expenditures: 21.8% of central government expenditure (2002)
External Debt: US$1.204 billion (2002)
Exports: US$38 million (2003); commodities: coffee 88%, tea, sugar, cotton, hides and skins; partners: US, India, China, Japan, Singapore
Imports: US$156 million (2003); commodities: capital goods 31%, petroleum products 15%, foodstuffs, consumer goods; partners: EU, Tanzania, Zambia, India, China

■ COMMUNICATIONS

Daily Newspapers: 2/1,000 inhabitants (2000)
Televisions: 31/1,000 inhabitants (2002)
Radios: 220/1,000 inhabitants (2001)
Telephones: 3 lines/1,000 inhabitants (2002)
Internet: hosts: 3 (2002); users: 8,400 (2002)

■ TRANSPORTATION

Motor Vehicles: 20,000; 8,200 passenger cars
Roads: 14,480 km; 1,028 km paved
Railway: none
Air Traffic: 12,600 passengers carried (2001 est.)
Airports: 7; 1 has paved runways (2003 est.)

Canadian Embassy: c/o The Canadian High Commission, Limuru Road, Gigiri, Nairobi, Kenya. Postal Address: The Canadian High Commission, P.O. Box 1013, 00621 Nairobi, Kenya. Tel: (011 254 20) 366 3000. Fax: (011 254 20) 366 3900. e-mail: nrobi@dfait-maeci.gc.ca
Embassy in Canada: Embassy of the Republic of Burundi, 325 Dalhousie St., Suite 815, Ottawa ON K1N 7G2. Tel (613) 789-0414. Fax (613) 789-9537. e-mail: ambabucanada@infonet.ca

Cambodia

Long-Form Name: Kingdom of Cambodia
Capital: Phnom Penh

■ GEOGRAPHY

Area: 181,040 sq. km
Coastline: 443 km
Climate: tropical; rainy, monsoon season (May to Oct.); dry season (Dec. to Mar.); little seasonal temperature variation
Environment: a land of paddies and forests dominated by Mekong River and Tonle Sap; deforestation, monsoons; logging and strip mining are resulting in environmental degradation
Terrain: mostly low, flat plains; mountains in southwest and north

Land Use: arable land: 20.96%, permanent crops: 0.61%, other: 78.43%; includes 2,700 sq. km irrigated

Location: SE Asia, bordering on the Gulf of Siam

■ PEOPLE

Population: 13,124,764 (July 2003 est.)
Nationality: Cambodian
Age Structure: 0–14 yrs: 39.3%; 15–64: 57.6%; 65+: 3.1% (2003 est.)
Population Growth Rate: 1.8% (2003 est.)
Net Migration: 0 migrants/1,000 population (2003 est.)
Ethnic Groups: 90% Khmer (Cambodian), 5% Vietnamese, 1% Chinese, 4% other minorities
Languages: Khmer (official), French
Religions: 95% Theravada Buddhism, 5% Christianity
Birth Rate: 27.28/1,000 population (2003 est.)
Death Rate: 9.26/1,000 population (2003 est.)
Infant Mortality: 75.94 deaths/1,000 live births (2003 est.)
Life Expectancy at Birth: 55.49 years male, 60.47 years female (2003 est.)
Total Fertility Rate: 3.58 children born/woman (2003 est.)
Literacy: 69.4% (2002)

■ GOVERNMENT

Leader(s): King Norodom Sihanouk, Prime Minister Hun Sen
Government Type: liberal democracy under constitutional monarchy
Administrative Divisions: 20 provinces (khett, sing. & pl.) and 4 municipalities (krong, sing. & pl.)
Nationhood: Nov. 9, 1953 (from France)
National Holiday: Independence Day, Nov. 9

■ ECONOMY

Overview: a desperately poor country; the economy has suffered badly due to internal war; the country has not been able to feed its people; economy remains essentially rural, with 90% of the population dependent mainly on subsistence agriculture
GDP: US$20.42 billion, per capita US$1,600; real growth rate 4.5% (2002 est.)
Inflation: 3.3% (2002 est.)
Industries: accounts for 15% of GDP (2000); rice milling, fishing, wood and wood products, rubber, cement, gem mining
Labour Force: 6.6 million (2002); 80% agriculture, 5% industry, 15% services
Unemployment: 1.8% (2002 est.)
Agriculture: accounts for 50% of GDP (2000), mainly subsistence farming except for rubber plantations; main crops—rice, rubber, corn; food shortages—rice, meat, vegetables, dairy products, sugar, flour
Natural Resources: timber, gemstones, some iron ore, manganese, phosphates, hydroelectricity potential

■ FINANCE/TRADE

Currency: new riel (KR) = 100 sen
International Reserves Excluding Gold: US$816 million (Jan. 2004)
Gold Reserves: 0.400 million fine troy ounces (Dec. 2003)
Budget: revenues US$438 million, expenditures US$630 million, including capital expenditures of US$291 (2002 est.)
Defence Expenditures: 3.0% of GDP (2001 est.)
Education Expenditures: 10.1% of total government expenditures (2002)
External Debt: US$2.907 billion total (2002)
Exports: US$1.616 billion (2003 est.); commodities: timber, garments, rubber, rice, fish; partners: Singapore, US, Vietnam, Germany, UK
Imports: US$2.124 billion (2003 est.); commodities: cigarettes, gold, construction materials, petroleum products, machinery, motor vehicles; partners: Singapore, Vietnam, Hong Kong, China, Thailand

■ COMMUNICATIONS

Daily Newspapers: 2/1,000 inhabitants (2000)
Televisions: 8/1,000 inhabitants (2002)
Radios: 119/1,000 inhabitants (2001)
Telephones: 3 lines/1,000 inhabitants (2002)
Internet: hosts: 1,391 (2002); users: 30,000 (2002)

■ TRANSPORTATION

Motor Vehicles: 75,000; 62,000 passenger cars (2000)
Roads: 12,323 km; 1,966 km paved
Railway: 603 km, much inoperational since 1973
Air Traffic: 125,000 passengers carried (2002)
Airports: 21; 5 have paved runways (2003 est.)

Canadian Embassy: The Canadian Embassy, Villa 9, RV Senei Vinnavaut Oum, Chaktamouk, Daun Penh District, Phnom Penh. Tel: (011-855-23) 213-470. Fax: (011-855-23) 211-389. e-mail: pnmpn@dfait-maeci.gc.ca
Embassy in Canada: c/o Embassy of the Kingdom of Cambodia, 866 UN Plaza, Ste. 420, New York, NY 10017, USA. Tel (212) 223-0676. Fax (212) 223-0425. e-mail: cambodia@un.int

Cameroon

Long-Form Name: Republic of Cameroon
Capital: Yaoundé

■ GEOGRAPHY

Area: 475,440 sq. km
Coastline: 402 km
Climate: varies with terrain from tropical along coast to semi-arid and hot in north
Environment: recent volcanic activity with release of poisonous gases; deforestation; overgrazing; desertification; diseases transmitted through the water supply are common
Terrain: coastal plain in southwest, dissected plateau in centre, mountains in west, plains in north
Land Use: arable land: 12.81%, permanent crops: 2.58%, other: 84.61%; includes 330 sq. km irrigated
Location: WC Africa, bordering on South Atlantic Ocean

■ PEOPLE

Population: 15,746,179 (July 2003 est.)
Nationality: Cameroonian
Age Structure: 0–14 yrs: 42.3%; 15–64: 54.5%; 65+: 3.2% (2003 est.)
Population Growth Rate: 2.02% (2003 est.)
Net Migration: 0 migrants/1,000 population (2003 est.)
Ethnic Groups: over 200 tribes of widely differing background; 31% Cameroon Highlanders, 19% Equatorial Bantu, 11% Kirdi, 10% Fulani, 8% Northwestern Bantu, 7% Eastern Nigritic, 13% other African, less than 1% non-African
Languages: English and French (official), 24 major African language groups, including Fang, Bamileke, Duala
Religions: 51% indigenous beliefs, 33% Christian, 16% Muslim
Birth Rate: 35.49/1,000 population (2003 est.)
Death Rate: 15.30/1,000 population (2003 est.)
Infant Mortality: 70.12 deaths/1,000 live births (2003 est.)
Life Expectancy at Birth: 47.15 years male, 48.97 years female (2003 est.)
Total Fertility Rate: 4.63 children born/woman (2003 est.)
Literacy: 67.9% (2002)

■ GOVERNMENT

Leader(s): President Paul Biya, Prime Minister Peter Mafany Musonge
Government Type: unitary republic; multiparty presidential regime

Administrative Divisions: 10 provinces
Nationhood: Jan. 1, 1960 (from UN trusteeship under French administration; Cameroon formerly known as French Cameroon)
National Holiday: Republic Day, May 20

■ ECONOMY

Overview: an offshore oil industry has boosted the economy but the government is now emphasizing diversification, particularly in agriculture
GDP: US$26.84 billion, per capita US$1,700; real growth rate 4.0% (2002 est.)
Inflation: 4.5% (2002)
Industries: accounts for 20% of GDP (2000); crude oil products, small aluminum plant, food processing, light consumer goods industries, textiles, sawmills
Labour Force: 6.5 million (2002); 70% agriculture, 13% industry, 17% services
Unemployment: n.a.
Agriculture: the agriculture and forestry sectors provide employment for the majority of the population, contributing 44% to GNP (2000) and providing a high degree of self-sufficiency in staple foods
Natural Resources: crude oil, bauxite, iron ore, timber, hydroelectricity potential

■ FINANCE/TRADE

Currency: Communauté financière africaine franc (CFAF) = 100 centimes
International Reserves Excluding Gold: US$640 million (Dec. 2003)
Gold Reserves: 0.03 million fine troy ounces (Dec. 2003)
Budget: revenues US$2.2 billion; expenditures US$2.1 billion, including capital expenditures of US$ n.a. (FY2000/01 est.)
Defence Expenditures: 10.4% of total government expenditure (2002)
Education Expenditures: 12.5% of central government expenditure (2002)
External Debt: US$8.502 billion (2002)
Exports: US$2.282 billion (2002); commodities: petroleum products 56%, coffee, cocoa, cotton, aluminum, timber, manufacturing; partners: Italy, France, Netherlands
Imports: US$2.852 million (2002); commodities: machines and electrical equipment, transport equipment, chemical products, consumer goods; partners: France, Japan, US, Germany

■ COMMUNICATIONS

Daily Newspapers: 7/1,000 inhabitants (2000)
Televisions: 75/1,000 inhabitants (2002)
Radios: 163/1,000 inhabitants (2001)

Telephones: 7 lines/1,000 inhabitants (2002)
Internet: hosts: 439 (2002); users: 60,000 (2002)

■ TRANSPORTATION

Motor Vehicles: 153,000; 92,000 passenger cars
Roads: 34,300 km; 4,288 km paved
Railway: 1,008 km
Air Traffic: 243,000 passengers carried (2002)
Airports: 49; 11 have paved runways (2003 est.)

Canadian Embassy: The Canadian High Commission, Immeuble Stamiatades, Place de l'Hotel de Ville, Yaoundé, Cameroon; mailing address: P.O. Box 572, Yaounde, Cameroon. Tel: (011-237) 223-2311. Fax: (011-237) 222-1090. e-mail: yunde@dfait-maeci.gc.ca
Embassy in Canada: High Commission for the Republic of Cameroon, 170 Clemow Ave, Ottawa ON K1S 2B4. Tel: (613) 236-1522. Fax: (613) 236-3885. e-mail: cameroon@comnet.ca

Canada

Long-Form Name: Canada
Capital: Ottawa

■ GEOGRAPHY

Area: 9,976,140 sq. km
Coastline: 202,080 km
Climate: varies from temperate in south to subarctic and arctic in north
Environment: 80% of population concentrated within 160 km of US border; permafrost in north a serious obstacle to development; acid rain and ocean-water pollution resulting from industrial and agricultural activities are an increasing problem
Terrain: mostly plains with mountains in west and lowlands in southeast
Land Use: arable land: 4.94%, permanent crops: 0.02%, other: 95.04%; includes 7,200 sq. km irrigated
Location: N North America, bordering on North Atlantic Ocean, Arctic Ocean, North Pacific Ocean and United States

■ PEOPLE

Population: 32,207,113 (July 2003 est.)
Nationality: Canadian
Age Structure: 0–14 yrs: 18.5%; 15–64: 68.6%; 65+: 12.9% (2003 est.)
Population Growth Rate: 0.94% (2003 est.)
Net Migration: 6.01 migrants/1,000 population (2003 est.)
Ethnic Groups: 28% British, 23% French, 15% other European, 2% Amerindian, 6% Arab, 26% mixed background

Languages: English and French (both official)
Religions: 45% Roman Catholic, 12% United Church, 8% Anglican, 35% other
Birth Rate: 10.99/1,000 population (2003 est.)
Death Rate: 7.61/1,000 population (2003 est.)
Infant Mortality: 4.88 deaths/1,000 live births (2003 est.)
Life Expectancy at Birth: 76.44 years male, 83.38 years female (2003 est.)
Total Fertility Rate: 1.61 children born/woman (2003 est.)
Literacy: approaching 100% (2002)

■ GOVERNMENT

Leader(s): Head of State: Queen Elizabeth II, Governor General Adrienne Clarkson, Prime Minister Paul Martin
Government Type: confederation with parliamentary democracy
Administrative Divisions: 10 provinces, 3 territories
Nationhood: July 1, 1867 (from UK)
National Holiday: Canada Day, July 1

■ ECONOMY

Overview: abundant natural resources, skilled labour force, and high-tech industrialization characterize a market-oriented economy; Canada can anticipate solid economic prospects in the future
GDP: US$934.1 billion, per capita US$29,300; real growth rate 3.3% (2002)
Inflation: 2.2% (2002)
Industries: accounts for 27% of GDP (2001); processed and unprocessed minerals, food products, wood and paper products, transportation equipment, chemicals, fish products, petroleum, natural gas
Labour Force: 16.8 million (2002); 74% services, 15% manufacturing, 5% construction, 3% agriculture, 3% other
Unemployment: 7.9% (Feb. 2004)
Agriculture: accounts for 2% of GDP (2001); one of the world's major producers and exporters of grain (wheat and barley); key source of US agricultural imports; large forest resources cover 35% of total land area. Products also include fruits, vegetables, tobacco, fish and dairy products
Natural Resources: nickel, zinc, copper, gold, lead, molybdenum, potash, silver, fish, timber, wildlife, coal, crude oil, natural gas

■ FINANCE/TRADE

Currency: dollar ($ or $Can) = 100 cents

International Reserves Excluding Gold: US$36.323 billion (Jan. 2004)
Gold Reserves: 0.109 million fine troy ounces (Jan. 2004)
Budget: revenues US$178.6 billion; expenditures US$161.4 billion, capital expenditures US$ n.a. (FY2000/01)
Defence Expenditures: 6.2% of central government expenditure (2002)
Education Expenditures: 3.2% of central government expenditure (2001)
External Debt: US $1.9 billion (2000)
Exports: US$269.446 billion (2003); commodities: newsprint, wood pulp, timber, grain, crude petroleum, natural gas, electricity, ferrous and non-ferrous ores, motor vehicles; partners: US, Japan, UK, Germany, other European Community
Imports: US$236.214 billion (2003 est.); commodities: processed foods, beverages, crude petroleum, chemicals, industrial machinery, motor vehicles, durable consumer goods, electronic computers; partners: US, Japan, UK, countries of the European Community

■ **COMMUNICATIONS**

Daily Newspapers: 159/1,000 inhabitants (2000)
Televisions: 691/1,000 inhabitants (2002)
Radios: 1,047/1,000 inhabitants (2001)
Telephones: 635 lincs/1,000 inhabitants (2002)
Internet: hosts: 2,993,982 (2002); users: 16.11 million (2002)

■ **TRANSPORTATION**

Motor Vehicles: 18,680,000; 14,750,000 passenger cars
Roads: 1.408 million km; 497,306 km paved
Railway: 49,422 km; 36,114 km operational
Air Traffic: 23,323,000 passengers carried (2002)
Airports: 1,389; 507 have paved runways (2003 est.)

Canadian Embassy: n.a.
Embassy in Canada: n.a.

Cape Verde

Long-Form Name: Republic of Cape Verde
Capital: Praia

■ **GEOGRAPHY**

Area: 4,033 sq. km
Coastline: 965 km
Climate: temperate; warm, dry, very erratic summer precipitation
Environment: subject to prolonged droughts; harmattan wind can obscure visibility; volcanically and seismically active; deforestation; desertification; overgrazing and overfishing

Terrain: steep, rugged, rocky, volcanic
Land Use: arable land: 9.68%, permanent crops: 0.5%, other: 89.82%; includes 30 sq. km irrigated
Location: Atlantic Ocean W of Africa

■ **PEOPLE**

Population: 412,137 (July 2003 est.)
Nationality: Cape Verdean
Age Structure: 0–14 yrs: 41.0%; 15–64: 52.3%; 65+: 6.7% (2003 est.)
Population Growth Rate: 0.79% (2003 est.)
Net Migration: -12.16 migrants/1,000 population (2003 est.)
Ethnic Groups: approx. 71% Creole (mulatto), 28% African, 1% European
Languages: Portuguese and Crioulo, a blend of Portuguese and West African tongues
Religions: Roman Catholicism fused with indigenous beliefs
Birth Rate: 26.95/1,000 population (2003 est.)
Death Rate: 6.86/1,000 population (2003 est.)
Infant Mortality: 50.50 deaths/1,000 live births (2003 est.)
Life Expectancy at Birth: 66.53 years male, 73.23 years female (2003 est.)
Total Fertility Rate: 3.77 children born/woman (2003 est.)
Literacy: 75.7% (2002)

■ **GOVERNMENT**

Leader(s): President Pedro Pires, Prime Minister Jose Maria Pereira Neves
Government Type: republic
Administrative Divisions: 14 districts (concelhos, sing. —concelho)
Nationhood: July 5, 1975 (from Portugal)
National Holiday: Independence Day, July 5

■ **ECONOMY**

Overview: a service-oriented economy, which suffers from a poor natural resource base, a high birth rate and a long-term drought
GDP: US$600 million, per capita US$1,400; real growth rate 4.0% (2002 est.)
Inflation: 3.0% (2002)
Industries: accounts for 17% of GDP (2001), fish processing, salt mining, clothing factories, ship repair, construction materials, food and beverage production
Labour Force: n.a.; 52% agriculture (mostly subsistence), 25% services, 23% industry
Unemployment: n.a.
Agriculture: accounts for 11% of GDP (2001); largely subsistence farming; bananas are the only export crop; growth potential limited by

poor soils and limited rainfall. Approximately 90% of food needs must be imported
Natural Resources: salt, basalt rock, pozzolana, limestone, kaolin, fish

■ FINANCE/TRADE

Currency: Cape Verdean escudo (C.V. Esc.) = 100 centavos
International Reserves Excluding Gold: US$94 million (Jan. 2004)
Gold Reserves: n.a.
Budget: revenues US$112 million; expenditures US$198 million, capital expenditures US$ n.a. (2000)
Defence Expenditures: 1.6% of GDP (2002)
Education Expenditures: n.a.
External Debt: US$414 million (2002)
Exports: US$12 million (2002 est.); commodities: fuel, shoes, garments, fish, bananas, salt; partners: Portugal, UK, Germany, Guinea-Bissau
Imports: US$268 million (2002 est.); commodities: petroleum, foodstuffs, consumer goods, industrial products; partners: Portugal, Germany, France, UK

■ COMMUNICATIONS

Daily Newspapers: none
Televisions: n.a.
Radios: n.a.
Telephones: 172 lines/1,000 inhabitants (2002)
Internet: hosts: 48 (2002); users: 16,000 (2002)

■ TRANSPORTATION

Motor Vehicles: 18,000; 11,000 passenger cars
Roads: 1,100 km; 858 km paved
Railway: none
Air Traffic: 286,000 passengers carried (2001 est.)
Airports: 9; 6 have paved runways (2003 est.)

Canadian Embassy: c/o The Canadian Embassy, P.O. Box 3373, Dakar, Senegal. Tel: (011-221) 889-4700. Fax: (011-221) 889-4720. e-mail: dakar@dfait-maeci.gc.ca
Embassy in Canada: c/o Embassy of the Republic of Cape Verde, 3415 Massachusetts Ave NW, Washington DC 20007, USA. Tel: (202) 965-6820. Fax: (202) 965-1207. e-mail: n.a.

Cayman Islands

Long-Form Name: Cayman Islands
Capital: George Town (on Grand Cayman Island)

■ GEOGRAPHY

Area: 259 sq. km (three islands: Grand Cayman, Little Cayman, Cayman Brac)

Climate: tropical maritime; warm, rainy summers (May to Oct.); cool season: Nov. to March, hurricane-prone July to Nov.
Land Use: arable land: 0%, permanent crops: 0%, other: 100%
Location: Caribbean Sea, S of Cuba

■ PEOPLE

Population: 41,934 (July 2003 est.)
Nationality: Caymanian
Ethnic Groups: 40% mixed, 20% white, 20% black, 20% expatriates of various ethnic groups, various Hispanic strains, descendants of European settlers
Languages: English (official)

■ GOVERNMENT

Colony/Territory of: Overseas territory of the United Kingdom
Leader(s): Head of State: Queen Elizabeth II, Governor Bruce H. Dinwiddy
Government Type: British crown colony
National Holiday: Constitution Day (first Monday in July)

■ ECONOMY

Overview: chiefly tourism (75% of GDP and 75% of export earnings) and financial services; main export turtle products; imports: foodstuffs (about 90% of food and consumer goods must be imported), manufactured items, textiles, building materials, cars, petroleum products

■ FINANCE/TRADE

Currency: Caymanian dollar (CI$) = 100 cents

Canadian Embassy: c/o The Canadian High Commission, Macdonald House, 1 Grosvenor Square, London W1K 4AB, England, UK. Tel: (011-44-20) 7258-6600. Fax: (011-44-20) 7258-6333. e-mail: ldn@dfait-maeci.gc.ca
Representative to Canada: British High Commission, 80 Elgin St, Ottawa ON K1P 5K7. Tel: (613) 237-1530. Fax: (613) 237-7980. e-mail should be sent using the appropriate form at the British High Commission's Website at http://www.britain-in-canada.org

Central African Republic

Long-Form Name: Central African Republic
Capital: Bangui

■ GEOGRAPHY

Area: 622,984 sq. km
Coastline: none: landlocked

Climate: tropical; hot, dry winters; mild to hot, wet summers

Environment: hot, dry, dusty harmattan winds affect northern areas; poaching has diminished reputation as one of last great wildlife refuges; desertification and flooding; tap water is not safe to drink

Terrain: vast, flat to rolling, monotonous plateau; scattered hills in northeast and southwest

Land Use: arable land: 3.1%, permanent crops: 0.14%, other: 96.76%

Location: C Africa

■ PEOPLE

Population: 3,683,538 (July 2003 est.)

Nationality: Central African

Age Structure: 0–14 yrs: 43.1%; 15–64: 53.5%; 65+: 3.4% (2003 est.)

Population Growth Rate: 1.62% (2003 est.)

Net Migration: 0 migrants/1,000 population (2003 est.)

Ethnic Groups: about 80 ethnic groups, the majority of which have related ethnic and linguistic characteristics; 34% Baya, 27% Banda, 10% Sara, 21% Mandjia, 4% Mboum, 4% m'Baka; 6,500 Europeans, of whom 3,600 are French

Languages: French (official); Sangho (lingua franca and national language); Arabic, Hunsa, Swahili

Religions: 25% indigenous beliefs, 25% Protestant, 25% Roman Catholic, 15% Muslim, 10% other; animistic beliefs and practices strongly influence the Christian majority

Birth Rate: 35.93/1,000 population (2003 est.)

Death Rate: 19.73/1,000 population (2003 est.)

Infant Mortality: 93.30 deaths/1,000 live births (2003 est.)

Life Expectancy at Birth: 40.18 years male, 43.29 years female (2003 est.)

Total Fertility Rate: 4.68 children born/woman (2003 est.)

Literacy: 48.6% (2002)

■ GOVERNMENT

Leader(s): President Francois Bozize, Prime Minister Abel Goumba

Government Type: republic

Administrative Divisions: 14 prefectures, 2 economic prefectures, 1 capital commune

Nationhood: Aug. 13, 1960 (from France; formerly known as Central African Empire)

National Holiday: Republic Day (proclamation of the republic), Dec. 1

■ ECONOMY

Overview: subsistence agriculture and forestry are the backbone of the economy. It suffers from a poor transportation infrastructure and a weak human resource base; diamond industry accounts for 54% of export earnings

GDP: US$4.296 billion, per capita US$1,200; real growth rate 1.5% (2002 est.)

Inflation: 3.6% (2001)

Industries: accounts for 20% of GDP (2001 est.); sawmills, breweries, diamond mining, textiles, footwear, assembly of bicycles and motorcycles

Labour Force: 1.8 million (2002); 32.6% construction industries, 30.5% manufacturing, 17.6% agriculture

Unemployment: n.a.

Agriculture: accounts for 55% of GDP (2001 est.); self-sufficient in food production except for grain; commercial crops—cotton, coffee, tobacco, timber; food crops—manioc, yams, millet, corn, bananas

Natural Resources: diamonds, uranium, timber, gold, oil, hydroelectric potential

■ FINANCE/TRADE

Currency: Communauté financière africaine franc (CFAF) = 100 centimes

International Reserves Excluding Gold: US$132 million (Dec. 2003)

Gold Reserves: 0.011 million fine troy ounces (Dec. 2003)

Budget: n.a.

Defence Expenditures: 1.1% of GDP (2002)

Education Expenditures: n.a.

External Debt: US$1.066 billion (2002)

Exports: US$146 million (2002); commodities: diamonds, cotton, coffee, timber, tobacco; partners: France, Benelux, Italy, Côte d'Ivoire, Spain, China

Imports: US$120 million (2002); commodities: food, textiles, petroleum products, machinery, electrical equipment, motor vehicles, chemicals, pharmaceuticals, consumer goods, industrial products; partners: France, Germany, Japan, Cameroon, Benelux, Côte d'Ivoire

■ COMMUNICATIONS

Daily Newspapers: 2/1,000 inhabitants (2000)

Televisions: 6/1,000 inhabitants (2002)

Radios: 80/1,000 inhabitants (2001)

Telephones: 2 lines/1,000 inhabitants (2002)

Internet: hosts: 6 (2002); users: 5,000 (2002)

■ TRANSPORTATION

Motor Vehicles: 20,000; 11,000 passenger cars

Roads: 23,810 km; 643 km paved

Railway: none

Air Traffic: 46,000 passengers carried (2002)
Airports: 50; 3 have paved runways (2003 est.)

Canadian Embassy: The Canadian High Commission, Immeuble Stamiatades, Place de l'Hotel de Ville, Yaoundé, Cameroon; mailing address: P.O. Box 572, Yaounde, Cameroon. Tel: (011-237) 22-32-311. Fax: (011-237) 22-21-090. e-mail: yunde@dfait-maeci.gc.ca
Embassy in Canada: c/o Embassy of the Central African Republic, 1618-22nd St NW, Washington DC 20008, USA. Tel: (202) 483-7800. Fax: (202) 332-9893. e-mail: n.a.

Chad

Long-Form Name: Republic of Chad
Capital: N'Djamena

■ GEOGRAPHY

Area: 1,284,000 sq. km
Coastline: none: landlocked
Climate: tropical in south, desert in north
Environment: hot, dry, dusty harmattan winds occur in north; drought and desertification adversely affecting south; subject to plagues of locusts; unsafe water supply
Terrain: broad, arid plains in centre, desert in north, mountains in northwest, lowlands in south
Land Use: 2.78%, permanent crops: 0.02%, other: 97.2%, includes 200 sq. km irrigated
Location: NC Africa

■ PEOPLE

Population: 9,253,493 (July 2003 est.)
Nationality: Chadian
Age Structure: 0–14 yrs: 47.9%; 15–64: 49.3%; 65+: 2.8% (2003 est.)
Population Growth Rate: 3.07% (2003 est.)
Net Migration: 0 migrants/1,000 population (2003 est.)
Ethnic Groups: some 200 distinct ethnic groups, most of whom are Muslims in the north and centre, and non-Muslims in the south; some 150,000 non-indigenous, of whom 1,000 are French
Languages: French and Arabic (official); Sara and Sango in south; more than 100 different languages and dialects are spoken
Religions: 50% Muslim, 25% Christian, 25% animism
Birth Rate: 47.06/1,000 population (2003 est.)
Death Rate: 16.38/1,000 population (2003 est.)
Infant Mortality: 95.74 deaths/1,000 live births (2003 est.)
Life Expectancy at Birth: 46.97 years male, 50.10 years female (2003 est.)

Total Fertility Rate: 6.44 children born/woman (2003 est.)
Literacy: 45.8% (2002)

■ GOVERNMENT

Leader(s): President Idriss Deby, Prime Minister Moussa Faki Mahamat
Government Type: republic
Administrative Divisions: 14 prefectures
Nationhood: Aug. 11, 1960 (from France)
National Holiday: Independence Day, Aug. 11

■ ECONOMY

Overview: one of the world's most under-developed countries; civil war, drought and food shortages have adversely affected the economy, which is based on subsistence farming and fishing
GDP: US$9.297 billion, per capita US$1,000; real growth rate 7.4% (2002 est.)
Inflation: 6.0% (2002 est.)
Industries: accounts for 13% of GDP (2001 est.), cotton textile mills, slaughterhouses, soap, cigarettes, brewery, natron (sodium carbonate), construction materials
Labour Force: 4.0 million (2002); more than 80% of the labour force is engaged in agriculture.
Unemployment: n.a.
Agriculture: accounts for 38% of GDP (2001 est.); largely subsistence farming, herding, fishing; cotton most important cash crop; food crops include sorghum, millet, peanuts, rice, potatoes, manioc; livestock—cattle, sheep, goats, camels; self-sufficient in food in years of adequate rainfall
Natural Resources: small quantities of crude oil (unexploited but exploration beginning), uranium, natron, kaolin, fish (Lake Chad)

■ FINANCE/TRADE

Currency: Communauté financière africaine franc (CFAF) = 100 centimes
International Reserves Excluding Gold: US$187 million (Dec. 2003)
Gold Reserves: 0.011 million fine troy ounces (Dec. 2003)
Budget: n.a.
Defence Expenditures: 1.9% of GDP (2002)
Education Expenditures: n.a.
External Debt: US$1.281 billion (2002)
Exports: US$190 million (2002); commodities: cotton 43%, cattle 35%, textiles 5%, fish; partners: Costa Rica, Nigeria, Portugal, Germany, Thailand, France
Imports: US$1.0 billion (2002); commodities: machinery and transportation equipment 39%, industrial goods 20%, petroleum products 13%,

foodstuffs 9%; partners: France, Cameroon, Nigeria, India

■ COMMUNICATIONS

Daily Newspapers: less than 1/1,000 inhabitants (2000)
Televisions: 2/1,000 inhabitants (2002)
Radios: 236/1,000 inhabitants (2001)
Telephones: 2 lines/1,000 inhabitants (2002)
Internet: hosts: 11 (2002); users: 15,000 (2002)

■ TRANSPORTATION

Motor Vehicles: 24,600; 10,000 passenger cars
Roads: 33,400 km; 267 km paved
Railway: none
Air Traffic: 46,000 passengers carried (2002)
Airports: 50; 7 have paved runways (2003 est.)

Canadian Embassy: The Canadian High Commission, Immeuble Stamiatades, Place de l'Hotel de Ville, Yaoundé, Cameroon; mailing address: P.O. Box 572, Yaounde, Cameroon. Tel: (011-237) 22-32-311. Fax: (011-237) 22-21-090. e-mail: yunde@dfait-macci.gc.ca
Embassy in Canada: c/o Embassy of the Republic of Chad, 2002 R St NW, Washington DC 20009, USA. Tel: (202) 462-4009. Fax: (202) 265-1937. e-mail: info@chadembassy.org

Channel Islands

Long-Form Name: Channel Islands; Guernsey: Bailiwick of Guernsey; Jersey: Bailiwick of Jersey
Capital: St. Helier (Jersey), St. Peter Port (Guernsey)

■ GEOGRAPHY

Area: Jersey: 116 sq. km; Guernsey: 194 sq. km
Climate: temperate, with mild winters and cool summers
Land Use: Jersey: 66% arable; remainder n.a.; Guernsey: n.a.
Location: English Channel, off the coast of France

■ PEOPLE

Population: Jersey: 90,156; Guernsey: 64,818 (July 2003 est.)
Nationality: Channel Islander
Ethnic Groups: English, French
Languages: English (official), French (official only on Jersey), Norman-French dialect

■ GOVERNMENT

Colony/Territory of: Dependent Territory of the United Kingdom

Leader(s): Head of State: Queen Elizabeth II; Jersey: Lieutenant Governor John Cheshire, Guernsey: Lieutenant Governor John Foley
Government Type: largely self-governing British Crown dependency
National Holiday: Liberation Day, May 9

■ ECONOMY

Overview: Jersey: economy is based chiefly on financial services, agriculture and tourism, vegetable and flower exports, Jersey cattle; Guernsey: tourism, financial services, Guernsey cattle, and tomato and flower exports make up backbone of the economy

■ FINANCE/TRADE

Currency: Jersey pound, Guernsey pound, both = 100 pence; both are at par with the British £

Canadian Embassy: c/o The Canadian High Commission, Macdonald House, 1 Grosvenor Square, London W1K 4AB, England, UK. Tel: (011-44-20) 7258-6600. Fax: (011-44-20) 7258-6333. e-mail: ldn@dfait-maeci.gc.ca
Representative to Canada: c/o British High Commission, 80 Elgin St, Ottawa ON K1P 5K7. Tel: (613) 237-1530. Fax: (613) 237-7980. e-mail should be sent using the appropriate form at the British High Commission's Website at http://www.britain-in-canada.org

Chile

Long-Form Name: Republic of Chile
Capital: Santiago

■ GEOGRAPHY

Area: 756,950 sq. km
Coastline: 6,435 km
Climate: temperate; desert in north; cool and damp in south
Environment: subject to severe earthquakes, active volcanism, tsunami; Atacama Desert one of world's driest regions; desertification; deforestation; air and water pollution
Terrain: low coastal mountains; fertile central valley; rugged Andes in east
Land Use: arable land: 2.65%, permanent crops: 0.42%; other: 96.93%; includes 18,000 sq. km irrigated
Location: SW South America

■ PEOPLE

Population: 15,665,216 (July 2003 est.)
Nationality: Chilean
Age Structure: 0–14 yrs: 26.4%; 15–64: 66.0%; 65+: 7.7% (2003 est.)

Population Growth Rate: 1.05% (2003 est.)
Net Migration: 0 migrants/1,000 population (2003 est.)
Ethnic Groups: 95% European and European-Amerindian, 3% Amerindian, 2% other
Languages: Spanish
Religions: 89% Roman Catholic, 11% Protestant and small Jewish population
Birth Rate: 16.10/1,000 population (2003 est.)
Death Rate: 5.63/1,000 population (2003 est.)
Infant Mortality: 8.88 deaths/1,000 live births (2003 est.)
Life Expectancy at Birth: 73.04 years male, 79.82 years female (2003 est.)
Total Fertility Rate: 2.09 children born/woman (2003 est.)
Literacy: 95.7% (2002)

■ GOVERNMENT

Leader(s): President Ricardo Lagos
Government Type: republic
Administrative Divisions: 13 regions (regiones, sing. —region)
Nationhood: Sept. 18, 1810 (from Spain)
National Holiday: Independence Day, Sept. 18

■ ECONOMY

Overview: economy remains largely dependent on a few sectors, particularly copper mining (copper is the single largest export product), fishing and forestry
GDP: US$156.1 billion, per capita US$10,100; real growth rate 2.1% (2002 est.)
Inflation: 2.5% (2002)
Industries: accounts for 38% of GDP (2000); copper (Chile is the world's largest producer and exporter of copper), other minerals, foodstuffs, fish processing, iron and steel, wood and wood products, transport equipment, textiles, cement
Labour Force: 6.5 million (2002); 59% services, 27% industry, 14% agriculture
Unemployment: 7.4% (Nov. 2003)
Agriculture: accounts for about 8% of GDP (including fishing and forestry) (2000); major exporter of fruit, fish and timber products; major crops—wheat, corn, grapes, beans, sugar beets, potatoes, fruit; beef, poultry, fish; net agricultural importer
Natural Resources: copper, timber, iron ore, nitrates, precious metals, molybdenum

■ FINANCE/TRADE

Currency: peso ($CH) = 100 centavos
International Reserves Excluding Gold: US$16.017 billion (Jan. 2004)

Gold Reserves: 0.008 million fine troy ounces (Jan. 2004)
Budget: revenues US$14.7 billion; expenditures US$15.6 billion, including capital expenditures US$ n.a. (2003 est.)
Defence Expenditures: 12.4% of total government expenditure (2002)
Education Expenditures: 17.5% of central government expenditure (2002)
External Debt: US$41.945 billion (2002)
Exports: US$21.046 billion (2003 est.); commodities: copper 48%, industrial products 33%, molybdenum, iron ore, wood pulp, fishmeal, fruit; partners: US, Japan, UK, Brazil, China
Imports: US$19.413 billion (2003 est.); commodities: petroleum, wheat, capital goods, spare parts, raw materials; partners: US, Argentina, Brazil, China, Japan

■ COMMUNICATIONS

Daily Newspapers: 98/1,000 inhabitants (2000)
Televisions: 323/1,000 inhabitants (2002)
Radios: 759/1,000 inhabitants (2001)
Telephones: 230 lines/1,000 inhabitants (2002)
Internet: hosts: 135,155 (2002); users: 3.575 million (2002)

■ TRANSPORTATION

Motor Vehicles: 2,080,000; 1,360,000 passenger cars
Roads: 79,814 km; 15,484 km paved
Railway: 6,585 km
Air Traffic: 4,987,000 passengers carried (2002)
Airports: 363; 71 have paved runways (2003 est.)

Canadian Embassy: The Canadian Embassy, Edificio World Trade Centre, 12th Fl., Nueva Tajamar 481, Santiago, Chile; mailing address: Casilla 139-10, Santiago, Chile. Tel: (011-56-2) 362-9660. Fax: (011-56-2) 362-9663. e-mail: stago@dfait-maeci.gc.ca
Embassy in Canada: Embassy of the Republic of Chile, 50 O'Connor St, Ste 1413, Ottawa ON K1P 6L2. Tel: (613) 235-9940. Fax: (613) 235-1176. e-mail: echileca@chile.ca

China

Long-Form Name: People's Republic of China
Capital: Beijing

■ GEOGRAPHY

Area: 9,596,960 sq. km
Coastline: 14,500 km
Climate: extremely diverse; tropical in south to subarctic in north

Environment: frequent typhoons (about five times per year along southern and eastern coasts), damaging floods, tsunamis, earthquakes; deforestation; soil erosion; industrial pollution; water and air pollution; desertification; lack of safe drinking water

Terrain: mostly mountains, high plateaus, deserts in west; plains, deltas and hills in east

Land Use: arable land: 13.31%, permanent crops: 1.2%, other: 85.49%; includes 525,800 sq. km irrigated

Location: SE Asia, bordering on South China Sea, Yellow Sea

■ PEOPLE

Population: 1,286,975,468 (July 2003 est.)

Nationality: Chinese

Age Structure: 0–14 yrs: 23.1%; 15–64: 69.5%; 65+: 7.4% (2003 est.)

Population Growth Rate: 0.6% (2003 est.)

Net Migration: -0.23 migrants/1,000 population (2003 est.)

Ethnic Groups: 91.9% Han Chinese; 8.1% Zhuang, Uigur, Hui, Yi, Tibetan, Miao, Manchu, Mongol, Buyi, Korean and other nationalities

Languages: Standard Chinese (Putonghua) or Mandarin (based on the Beijing dialect), Yue (Cantonese), Wu (Shanghainese), Minbei (Fuzhou), Minnan. The Tibetans, Uigurs, Mongols and others have their own languages

Religions: officially atheist, but traditionally pragmatic and eclectic; Confucianism, Taoism and Buddhism; approx. 2–3% Muslim, 1% Christian

Birth Rate: 12.96/1,000 population (2003 est.)

Death Rate: 6.74/1,000 population (2003 est.)

Infant Mortality: 25.26 deaths/1,000 live births (2003 est.)

Life Expectancy at Birth: 70.33 years male, 74.28 years female (2003 est.)

Total Fertility Rate: 1.70 children born/woman (2003 est.)

Literacy: 90.9% (2002)

■ GOVERNMENT

Leader(s): President Hu Jintao, Premier Wen Jiabao

Government Type: Communist Party-led state

Administrative Divisions: 23 provinces (sheng, sing. & pl.), 5 autonomous regions (zizhigu, sing. & pl.), 4 government-controlled municipalities (shi, sing. & pl.)

Nationhood: People's Republic established Oct. 1, 1949

National Holiday: National Day, Oct. 1 (Founding of the People's Republic of China

■ ECONOMY

Overview: the Soviet-style, centrally planned economy has been recently altered to include increased local authority, which has led to greater production; population control is vital, but has been weakened by popular resistance and loss of authority by rural cadres. Decentralization of the economic system is slowly progressing

GDP: US$5.989 trillion, per capita US$4,700; real growth rate 8.0% (2002)

Inflation: -0.8% (2002)

Industries: accounts for 49% of GDP (2001 est.); iron, steel, coal, machine building, armaments, textiles, petroleum, chemical fertilizer, cement, consumer durables, food processing

Labour Force: 769.3 million (2002); 50% agriculture, 22% industry, 28% services

Unemployment: 3.1% (2002)

Agriculture: accounts for 18% of GDP (2001 est.); among the world's largest producers of rice, potatoes, sorghum, peanuts, tea, millet, barley and pork; commercial crops include cotton, other fibres and oilseeds; produces variety of livestock products; self-sufficient in food

Natural Resources: coal, iron ore, crude oil, mercury, tin, tungsten, antimony, manganese, molybdenum, vanadium, magnetite, aluminum, lead, zinc, uranium, world's greatest hydroelectricity potential

■ FINANCE/TRADE

Currency: yuan (¥), pl. yen; = 10 jiao

International Reserves Excluding Gold: US$420.608 billion (Jan. 2004)

Gold Reserves: 19.290 million fine troy ounces (Nov. 2003)

Budget: revenues US$228.4 billion; expenditures US$267.1 billion, capital expenditures US$ n.a. (2002 est.)

Defence Expenditures: 19.2% of total government expenditure (2002)

Education Expenditures: 1.71% of central government expenditure (2001)

External Debt: US$168.255 billion (2002)

Exports: US$437.899 billion (2003 est.); commodities: machinery and equipment, manufactured goods, agricultural products, oilseeds, grain (rice and corn), oil, minerals; partners: US, Hong Kong, Japan, South Korea, Germany, Netherlands, UK

Imports: US$413.062 billion (2003 est.); commodities: grain (mostly wheat), chemical fertilizer, steel, industrial raw materials, machinery, equipment; partners: Japan, Taiwan, US, South Korea, Germany, Hong Kong, Russia, Malaysia

■ COMMUNICATIONS

Daily Newspapers: 39 in total
Televisions: 350/1,000 inhabitants (2002)
Radios: 339/1,000 inhabitants (2001)
Telephones: 167 lines/1,000 inhabitants (2002)
Internet: hosts: 156,531 (2002); users: 59.1 million (2002)

■ TRANSPORTATION

Motor Vehicles: 15,400,000; 5,900,000 passenger cars
Roads: 1,402,698 km; 314,204 km paved
Railway: 71,600 km
Air Traffic: 83,672,000 passengers carried (2002)
Airports: 500; 351 have paved runways (2003 est.)

Canadian Embassy: The Canadian Embassy, 19 Dong Zhi Men Wai St, Chao Yang District, Beijing 100600, People's Republic of China. Tel: (011-86-10) 6532-3536. Fax (011-86-10) 6532-4311. e-mail: bejing@dfait-maeci.gc.ca
Embassy in Canada: Embassy of the People's Republic of China, 515 St. Patrick St, Ottawa ON K1N 5H3. Tel: (613) 789-3434. Fax: (613) 789-1911. e-mail: n.a.

Christmas Island

Long-Form Name: Territory of Christmas Island
Capital: The Settlement

■ GEOGRAPHY

Area: 135 sq. km (land area); includes one of the largest coral islands in the Pacific
Climate: tropical, with little seasonal variation; heat and humidity moderated by trade winds
Land Use: arable land: 0%, permanent crops: 0%, other: 100%, note: mainly tropical rainforest; 63% of the island is a national park
Location: SE Asia, between Australia and Indonesia

■ PEOPLE

Population: 433 (July 2003 est.)
Nationality: Christmas Islander
Ethnic Groups: 61% Chinese, 25% Malay, 11% European, 3% other. There is no indigenous population
Languages: English, Chinese, Oriental and European-speaking minorities

■ GOVERNMENT

Colony/Territory of: Dependent Territory of Australia
Leader(s): Head of State: Queen Elizabeth II, Administrator Evan Williams (appointed by Governor General of Australia)

Government Type: dependency of Australia
National Holiday: n.a.

■ ECONOMY

Overview: extraction and export of rock phosphate dust was the only significant economic activity until 1987, when the mine was closed; it was reopened in 1990

■ FINANCE/TRADE

Currency: Australian dollar = 100 cents

Canadian Embassy: c/o The Canadian High Commission, Commonwealth Ave, Canberra A.C.T. 2600, Australia. Tel: (011-61-2) 6270-4000. Fax: (011-61-2) 6273-3285. e-mail: cnbra@dfait-maeci.gc.ca
Representative to Canada: c/o Australian High Commission, 50 O'Connor St, Ste 710, Ottawa ON K1P 6L2. Tel: (613) 236-0841. Fax: (613) 236-4376. e-mail: n.a.

Cocos (Keeling) Islands

Long-Form Name: Territory of Cocos (Keeling) Islands
Capital: West Island

■ GEOGRAPHY

Area: 14 sq. km
Climate: tropical maritime modified by southeast trade wind for 9 months of the year; moderate rainfall
Land Use: arable land: 0%, permanent crops: 0%, other: 100%
Location: Indian Ocean, SW of Sumatra

■ PEOPLE

Population: 630 (July 2003 est.)
Nationality: Cocos Islander
Ethnic Groups: West Island: Europeans; Home Island: Cocos Malays
Languages: English, Malay

■ GOVERNMENT

Colony/Territory of: Dependent Territory of Australia
Leader(s): Head of State: Queen Elizabeth II, Administrator Evan Williams (appointed by Governor General of Australia)
Government Type: territory of Australia; dependency placed under Australian government. authority by Cocos (Keeling) Islands Act of 1955
National Holiday: n.a.

■ ECONOMY

Overview: little industrial activity; agriculture limited to copra and coconut cultivation

■ FINANCE/TRADE

Currency: Australian dollar = 100 cents

Canadian Embassy: c/o The Canadian High Commission, Commonwealth Ave, Canberra A.C.T. 2600, Australia. Tel: (011-61-2) 6270-4000. Fax: (011-61-2) 6273-3285. e-mail: cnbra@dfait-maeci.gc.ca

Representative to Canada: c/o Australian High Commission, 50 O'Connor St, Ste 710, Ottawa ON K1P 6L2. Tel: (613) 236-0841. Fax: (613) 236-4376. e-mail: n.a.

Colombia

Long-Form Name: Republic of Colombia
Capital: Bogotá

■ GEOGRAPHY

Area: 1,138,910 sq. km; includes Isla de Malpelo, Roncador Cay, Serrana Bank, and Serranilla Bank
Coastline: 3,208 km
Climate: tropical along coast and eastern plains; cooler in highlands
Environment: highlands subject to volcanic eruptions; deforestation; soil damage from overuse of pesticides; periodic droughts; air pollution
Terrain: mixture of flat coastal lowlands, plains in east, central highlands, some high mountains (Andes)
Land Use: arable land: 1.9%, permanent crops: 1.96%, other: 96.14%; includes 8,500 sq. km irrigated
Location: NW South America, bordering on Caribbean Sea, Pacific Ocean

■ PEOPLE

Population: 41,662,073 (July 2003 est.)
Nationality: Colombian
Age Structure: 0–14 yrs: 31.3%; 15–64: 63.7%; 65+: 4.9% (2003 est.)
Population Growth Rate: 1.56% (2003 est.)
Net Migration: -0.32 migrants/1,000 population (2003 est.)
Ethnic Groups: 58% mestizo, 20% white, 14% mulatto, 4% black, 3% mixed black-Amerindian, 1% Amerindian
Languages: Spanish
Religions: 95% Roman Catholic
Birth Rate: 21.59/1,000 population (2003 est.)
Death Rate: 5.63/1,000 population (2003 est.)

Infant Mortality: 22.47 deaths/1,000 live births (2003 est.)
Life Expectancy at Birth: 67.29 years male, 75.12 years female (2003 est.)
Total Fertility Rate: 2.61 children born/woman (2003 est.)
Literacy: 92.1% (2002)

■ GOVERNMENT

Leader(s): President Alvaro Uribe Velez; Vice President Francisco Santos
Government Type: republic; executive branch dominates government structure
Administrative Divisions: 32 departments (departmentos, sing. —departmento), 1 capital district (distrito capital)
Nationhood: July 20, 1810 (from Spain)
National Holiday: Independence Day, July 20

■ ECONOMY

Overview: traditionally coffee has been the main export, though other industries such as oil and coal are developing; drug-related violence is an increasing threat to economic growth
GDP: US$251.6 billion, per capita US$6,100; real growth rate 1.5% (2002 est.)
Inflation: 6.2% (2002 est.)
Industries: accounts for 26% of GDP (2001 est.); textiles, food processing, oil, clothing and footwear, beverages, chemicals, metal products, cement; mining—gold, coal, emeralds, iron, nickel, silver, salt
Labour Force: 19.4 million (2002); 46% community, social and business services, 24% industry, 30% agriculture
Unemployment: 17.9% (2002)
Agriculture: accounts for 19% of GDP (2001 est.); crops make up two-thirds and livestock one-third of agricultural output; climate and soils permit a wide variety of crops, such as coffee, bananas, rice, tobacco, corn, sugar cane, cocoa beans, oilseeds, vegetables; forest products and shrimp farming are increasing in importance
Natural Resources: crude oil, natural gas, coal, iron ore, nickel, gold, copper, emeralds

■ FINANCE/TRADE

Currency: peso ($Col) = 100 centavos
International Reserves Excluding Gold: US$11.112 billion (Jan. 2004)
Gold Reserves: 0.327 million fine troy ounces (Jan. 2004)
Budget: revenues US$24 billion; expenditures US$25.6 billion, including capital expenditures US$ n.a. (2002 est.)
Defence Expenditures: 18.8% of total government expenditure (2002)

Education Expenditures: 18.0% of central government expenditure (2002)
External Debt: US$33.853 billion (2002)
Exports: US$12.671 billion (2003 est.); commodities: coffee 30%, petroleum 24%, coal, bananas, fresh-cut flowers; partners: US, European Community, Andean Community of Nations
Imports: US$13.892 billion (2003 est.); commodities: industrial equipment, transportation equipment, foodstuffs, chemicals, paper products; partners: US, European Community, Andean Community of Nations, Japan

■ COMMUNICATIONS

Daily Newspapers: 46/1,000 inhabitants (2000)
Televisions: 303/1,000 inhabitants (2002)
Radios: 549/1,000 inhabitants (2001)
Telephones: 179 lines/1,000 inhabitants (2002)
Internet: hosts: 55,626 (2002); users: 2 million (2002)

■ TRANSPORTATION

Motor Vehicles: 2,090,000; 1,760,000 passenger cars
Roads: 110,000 km; 26,000 km paved
Railway: 3,304 km
Air Traffic: 9,395,000 passengers carried (2002)
Airports: 1,050; 96 have paved runways (2003 est.)

Canadian Embassy: The Canadian Embassy, Carrera 7, No. 115-33, Piso 14, Bogotá, Colombia; mailing address: Apartado Aereo 110067, Bogotá 2, Colombia. Tel: (011-57-1) 657-9800. Fax (011-57-1) 657-9912. e-mail: bgota@dfait-maeci.gc.ca
Embassy in Canada: Embassy of the Republic of Colombia, 360 Albert St, Ste 1002, Ottawa ON K1R 7X7. Tel: (613) 230-3760. Fax: (613) 230-4416. e-mail: embajada@embajadacolombia.ca

---

Comoros

Long-Form Name: Union of the Comoros
Capital: Moroni

■ GEOGRAPHY

Area: 2,170 sq. km
Coastline: 340 km
Climate: tropical marine; rainy season (Nov. to May)
Environment: soil degradation and erosion, resulting from crop cultivation on slopes without proper terracing; deforestation; cyclones possible during rainy season

Terrain: volcanic islands, interiors vary from steep mountains to low hills
Land Use: arable land: 34.98%, permanent crops: 17.94%, other: 47.08%
Location: E of Africa, Indian Ocean/ Mozambique Channel

■ PEOPLE

Population: 632,948 (July 2003 est.)
Nationality: Comoran
Age Structure: 0–14 yrs: 42.9%; 15–64: 54.2%; 65+: 2.9% (2003 est.)
Population Growth Rate: 2.96% (2003 est.)
Net Migration: 0 migrants/1,000 population (2003 est.)
Ethnic Groups: Antalote, Cafre, Makoa, Oimatsaha, Sakalava
Languages: French and Arabic (both official), Shaafi Islam (a Swahili dialect), Malagasy; majority speaks Comoran
Religions: 86% Sunni Muslim, 14% Roman Catholic
Birth Rate: 38.50/1,000 population (2003 est.)
Death Rate: 8.86/1,000 population (2003 est.)
Infant Mortality: 79.51 deaths/1,000 live births (2003 est.)
Life Expectancy at Birth: 58.92 years male, 63.50 years female (2003 est.)
Total Fertility Rate: 5.21 children born/woman (2003 est.)
Literacy: 56.2% (2002)

■ GOVERNMENT

Leader(s): President of the Union: Colonel Assoumani Azali
Government Type: republic
Administrative Divisions: 3 islands and 4 municipalities
Nationhood: July 6, 1975 (from France)
National Holiday: Independence Day, July 6

■ ECONOMY

Overview: agriculture is the main sector of the economy, though it does not feed citizens adequately; lack of natural resources makes Comoros one of the world's poorest countries
GDP: US$441 million, per capita US$700; real growth rate 2.0% (2002 est.)
Inflation: 3.5% (2001)
Industries: accounts for 4% of GDP (2001 est.); perfume distillation, textiles, furniture, jewellery, soft drinks, construction materials
Labour Force: approx. 150,000; 80% agriculture, 6% industry, 14% services
Unemployment: n.a.
Agriculture: accounts for 40% of GDP (2001 est.); most of population works in subsistence

agriculture and fishing; plantations produce cash crops for export—vanilla, cloves, perfume essences and copra; principal food crops—coconuts, bananas, cassava; large net food importer
Natural Resources: negligible

■ FINANCE/TRADE

Currency: Comoran franc (CFAF) = 100 centimes
International Reserves Excluding Gold: US$94 million (Dec. 2003)
Gold Reserves: n.a.
Budget: revenues US$27.6 million; expenditures US$ n.a., including capital expenditures US$ n.a. (2001 est.)
Defence Expenditures: 3.0% of GDP (2002)
Education Expenditures: n.a.
External Debt: US$270 million (2002)
Exports: US$28 million (2002); commodities: vanilla, cloves, perfume oil, copra; partners: France, US, Singapore, Germany
Imports: US$88 million (2002 est.); commodities: rice and other foodstuffs, cement, petroleum products, consumer goods, paper products, fuels, electricity; partners: France, South Africa, Kenya, Pakistan

■ COMMUNICATIONS

Daily Newspapers: none
Televisions: n.a.
Radios: n.a.
Telephones: 17 lines/1,000 inhabitants (2002)
Internet: hosts: 12 (2002); users: 3,200 (2002)

■ TRANSPORTATION

Motor Vehicles: n.a.
Roads: 880 km; 673 km paved
Railway: none
Air Traffic: 32,000 passengers carried (2001 est.)
Airports: 4; all have paved runways (2003 est.)

Canadian Embassy: Canadian Embassy to the Comoros, c/o The Canadian High Commission, P.O. Box 1022, Dar-es-Salaam, Tanzania. Tel: (011-255-22) 211-2831. Fax: (011-255-22) 211-6897. e-mail: dslam@dfait-maeci.gc.ca
Embassy in Canada: Embassy of the Comoros, c/o Permanent Mission of the Comoros to the UN, 420 East 50th Street, New York, NY 10022, USA. Tel: (212) 972-8010. Fax: (212) 983-4712. e-mail: comun@undp.org

Congo

Long-Form Name: Republic of the Congo
Capital: Brazzaville

■ GEOGRAPHY

Area: 342,000 sq. km
Coastline: 169 km
Climate: tropical; rainy season (Mar. to June); dry season (June to Oct.); constant high temperatures and humidity; particularly enervating climate astride the equator
Environment: Deforestation; air and water pollution; unsafe water supply; about 70% of the population lives in Brazzaville, Pointe Noire or along the railroad between them
Terrain: coastal plain, southern basin, central plateau, northern basin
Land Use: arable land: 0.5%, permanent crops: 0.13%, other: 99.37%; includes 10 sq km irrigated
Location: WC Africa, bordering on South Atlantic Ocean

■ PEOPLE

Population: 2,954,258 (July 2003 est.)
Nationality: Congolese (sing. & pl.)
Age Structure: 0–14 yrs: 38.4%; 15–64: 58%; 65+: 3.6% (2003 cst.)
Population Growth Rate: 1.53% (2003 est.)
Net Migration: 0 migrants/1,000 population (2003 est.)
Ethnic Groups: about 15 ethnic groups divided into some 75 tribes, almost all Bantu; most important ethnic groups are Kongo (48%) in south, Sangha (20%) and M'Bochi (12%) in the north, Teke (17%) in the centre; about 8,500 Europeans, mostly French
Languages: French (official); many African languages with Lingala and Kikongo most widely used
Religions: 50% Christian, 48% animist, 2% Muslim
Birth Rate: 29.46/1,000 population (2003 est.)
Death Rate: 14.2/1,000 population (2003 est.)
Infant Mortality: 94.34 deaths/1,000 live births (2003 est.)
Life Expectancy at Birth: 49.04 years male, 51.02 years female (2003 est.)
Total Fertility Rate: 3.65 children born/woman (2003 est.)
Literacy: 83.8% (2003 est.)

■ GOVERNMENT

Leader(s): President Denis Sassou-Nguesso
Government Type: republic
Administrative Divisions: 9 regions, 1 commune
Nationhood: Aug. 15, 1960 (from France)
National Holiday: Congolese National Day, (Independence Day), Aug. 15

■ ECONOMY

Overview: oil revenues are responsible for one of the highest growth rates in Africa, though the country faces increasing foreign debt and is vulnerable to the oil market. Recent efforts at economic reform are beginning to show results
GDP: US$2.5 billion, per capita US$900; real growth rate 3.0% (2002 est.)
Inflation: 4.0% (2002)
Industries: accounts for 48% of GDP (2001 est.); petroleum, lumbering, cement, sawmills, brewery, sugar mills, palm oil, soap, cigarettes
Labour Force: 1.5 million (2002); 62.4% agriculture, 25.6% services, 11.9% industry
Unemployment: n.a.
Agriculture: accounts for 10% of GDP (including fishing and forestry); cassava accounts for 90% of food output; other crops—rice, corn, peanuts, vegetables; cash crops include coffee and cocoa; forest products important export earner; imports over 90% of food needs
Natural Resources: petroleum, timber, potash, lead, zinc, uranium, copper, phosphate, natural gas, hydroelectric potential

■ FINANCE/TRADE

Currency: Communauté financière africaine franc (CFAF) = 100 centimes
International Reserves Excluding Gold: US$35 million (Dec. 2003)
Gold Reserves: 0.011 million fine troy ounces (Dec. 2003)
Budget: n.a.
Defence Expenditures: 2.8% of GDP (2001)
Education Expenditures: 12.6% of total government expenditures (2002)
External Debt: US$5.152 billion (2002)
Exports: US$2.293 billion (2003 est.); commodities: crude petroleum 50%, lumber, plywood, coffee, cocoa, sugar, diamonds; partners: US, South Korea, China, Germany
Imports: US$666.9 billion (2003 est.); commodities: foodstuffs, consumer goods, intermediate manufactures, construction materials, capital equipment; partners: France, US, Italy, Belgium

■ COMMUNICATIONS

Daily Newspapers: 8/1,000 inhabitants (2000)
Televisions: 13/1,000 inhabitants (2002)
Radios: 123/1,000 inhabitants (2001)
Telephones: 7 lines/1,000 inhabitants (2002)
Internet: hosts: 36 (2002); users: 5,000 (2002)

■ TRANSPORTATION

Motor Vehicles: 47,000; 30,000 passenger cars
Roads: 12,800 km; 1,242 km paved

Railway: 894 km
Air Traffic: 128,000 passengers carried (2002)
Airports: 31; 4 have paved runways (2003 est.)

Canadian Embassy: The Canadian Embassy to the Republic of the Congo, P.O. Box 4037, Libreville, Gabon. Tel: (011-241) 73-73-54. Fax: (011-241) 73-73-88. e-mail: lbrve@dfaitmaeci.gc.ca
Embassy in Canada: c/o Embassy of the Republic of the Congo, 4891 Colorado Ave NW, Washington DC 20011, USA. Tel: (202) 726-5500. Fax: (202) 726-1860. e-mail: n.a.

Congo (Democratic Republic)

Long-Form Name: Democratic Republic of the Congo (formerly known as Belgian Congo and also Zaire)
Capital: Kinshasa

■ GEOGRAPHY

Area: 2,345,410 sq. km
Coastline: 37 km
Climate: tropical; hot and humid in equatorial river basin; cooler and drier in southern highlands; cooler and wetter in eastern highlands
Environment: dense tropical rainforest in central river basin and eastern highlands; periodic droughts in south; water pollution, deforestation; poaching negatively affects wildlife populations
Terrain: vast central basin is a low-lying plateau; mountains in east
Land Use: arable land: 2.96%, permanent crops: 0.52%, other: 96.52%; includes 110 sq. km irrigated
Location: C Africa, just barely bordering on South Atlantic Ocean

■ PEOPLE

Population: 56,625,039 (July 2003 est.)
Nationality: Congolese (sing. & pl.)
Age Structure: 0–14 yrs: 48.3%; 15–64: 49.2%; 65+: 2.5% (2003 est.)
Population Growth Rate: 2.9% (2003 est.)
Net Migration: -1.26 migrants/1,000 population (2003 est.)
Ethnic Groups: over 200 African ethnic groups, the majority are Bantu; four largest tribes—Mongo, Luba, Kongo (all Bantu) and the Mangbetu-Azande (Hamitic)—make up 45% of the population
Languages: French (official), Lingala, Swahili, Kinggwana, Kikongo, Tshiluba
Religions: 50% Roman Catholic, 20% Protestant, 10% Kimbanguist, 10% Muslim, 10% other syncretic sects and traditional beliefs

Birth Rate: 45.12/1,000 population (2003 est.)
Death Rate: 14.87/1,000 population (2003 est.)
Infant Mortality: 96.56 deaths/1,000 live births (2003 est.)
Life Expectancy at Birth: 46.83 years male, 51.09 years female (2003 est.)
Total Fertility Rate: 6.69 children born/woman (2003 est.)
Literacy: 65.5% (2003 est.)

■ GOVERNMENT

Leader(s): President Joseph Kabila
Government Type: dictatorship; ostensibly undergoing a transition to representative government
Administrative Divisions: 10 provinces and 1 city
Nationhood: June 30, 1960 (from Belgium)
National Holiday: Independence Day, June 30

■ ECONOMY

Overview: despite its vast potential wealth, the Democratic Republic of the Congo continues to suffer from a decline in the national economy; tight fiscal policies have curbed inflation and currency depreciation; a barter economy flourishes in all but the largest cities
GDP: US$34 billion, per capita US$900; real growth rate 0% (2002 est.)
Inflation: 16% (2002 est.)
Industries: accounts for 58% of GDP; mining, mineral processing, consumer products (including textiles, footwear and cigarettes), processed foods and beverages, cement, diamonds
Labour Force: 21.4 million (2002); 65% agriculture, 16% industry, 19% services
Unemployment: n.a.
Agriculture: accounts for 54% of GDP; cash crops: coffee, sugar, palm oil, rubber, quinine; food crops: cassava, bananas, root crops, corn, rice, peanuts, cocoa
Natural Resources: cobalt, copper, cadmium, crude oil, industrial and gem diamonds, gold, silver, zinc, manganese, tin, germanium, uranium, radium, bauxite, iron ore, coal, hydroelectric potential

■ FINANCE/TRADE

Currency: Congolese franc
International Reserves Excluding Gold: n.a.
Gold Reserves: n.a.
Budget: n.a.
Defence Expenditures: n.a.
Education Expenditures: n.a.
External Debt: US$8.726 billion (2002)
Exports: US$1.417 billion (2002 est.); commodities: copper 37%, coffee 24%, diamonds 12%, cobalt, crude oil; partners: US, Benelux, South Africa, Finland, Italy

Imports: US$933 million (2002 est.); commodities: consumer goods, foodstuffs, mining and other machinery, transport equipment, fuels; partners: South Africa, Benelux, Nigeria, Kenya, China

■ COMMUNICATIONS

Daily Newspapers: 3/1,000 inhabitants (2000)
Televisions: 2/1,000 inhabitants (2002)
Radios: 386/1,000 inhabitants (2001)
Telephones: less than 1 line/1,000 inhabitants (2002)
Internet: hosts: 134 (2002); users: 50,000 (2002)

■ TRANSPORTATION

Motor Vehicles: 530,000; 330,000 passenger cars
Roads: 157,000 km; n.a. km paved
Railway: 4,772 km
Air Traffic: 47,000 passengers carried (2002)
Airports: 229; 24 have paved runways (2003 est.)

Canadian Embassy: The Canadian Embassy to the Democratic Republic of Congo, 17 avenue Pumbu, Commune de Gombe, Democratic Republic of Congo; mailing address: P.O. Box 8341, Kinshasa 1, Democratic Republic of Congo. Tel: (011-243) 895-0310. Fax: (011-243) 884-1277. e-mail: knsha@dfait-maeci.gc.ca
Embassy in Canada: Embassy of the Democratic Republic of Congo, 18 Range Rd, Ottawa ON K1N 8J3. Tel: (613) 230-6391. Fax: (613) 230-1945. e-mail: n.a.

Cook Islands

Long-Form Name: Cook Islands
Capital: Avarua (on Rarotonga Island)

■ GEOGRAPHY

Area: 240 sq. km
Climate: mild year-round, moderated by trade winds
Land Use: arable land: 17.39%, permanent crops: 13.04%, other: 69.57%
Location: S Pacific Ocean, NE of New Zealand

■ PEOPLE

Population: 21,008 (July 2003 est.)
Nationality: Cook Islander
Ethnic Groups: Polynesian 81.3%, Polynesian-European mixture 7.7%, Polynesian-other mixture 7.7%, European 2.4%, other 0.9%
Languages: English (official), Cook Islands Maori

■ GOVERNMENT

Colony/Territory of: Self-governing territory in free association with New Zealand
Leader(s): Head of State: Queen Elizabeth II, Prime Minister Robert Woonton
Government Type: self-governing territory in free association with New Zealand; Cook Island is fully responsible for internal affairs; New Zealand retains responsibility for external affairs, in consultation with the Cook Islands
National Holiday: Constitution Day, first Monday in August

■ ECONOMY

Overview: agriculture provides the backbone of the economy: copra, fruits, tomatoes; livestock: pigs, goats; fishing; manufacturing is limited

■ FINANCE/TRADE

Currency: New Zealand dollar (NZ$) = 100 cents

Canadian Embassy: c/o The Canadian High Commission, 3rd Fl, 61 Molesworth St, Thorndon, Wellington, New Zealand; postal address: c/o Box 12-049, Thorndon, Wellington, New Zealand. Tel: (011-64-4) 473-9577. Fax: (011-64-4)471-2082. e-mail: wlgtn@dfait-maeci.gc.ca
Representative to Canada: c/o New Zealand High Commission, Clarica Centre, 99 Bank St, Ste 727, Ottawa ON K1P 6G3. Tel: (613) 238-5991. Fax: (613) 238-5707. e-mail: info@nzhcottawa.org

---

Costa Rica

Long-Form Name: Republic of Costa Rica
Capital: San José

■ GEOGRAPHY

Area: 51,100 sq. km; includes Isla del Coco
Coastline: 1,290 km
Climate: tropical; dry season (Dec. to Apr.); rainy season (May to Nov.)
Environment: subject to occasional earthquakes, hurricanes along Atlantic coast; frequent flooding of lowlands at onset of rainy season; active volcanoes; deforestation; soil erosion
Terrain: coastal plains separated by rugged mountains
Land Use: arable land: 4.41%, permanent crops: 5.48%, other: 90.11%; includes 1,260 sq. km irrigated
Location: Central (Latin) America, bordering on Caribbean Sea, Pacific Ocean

■ PEOPLE

Population: 3,896,092 (July 2003 est.)
Nationality: Costa Rican
Age Structure: 0–14 yrs: 30.1%; 15–64: 64.4%; 65+: 5.4% (2003 est.)
Population Growth Rate: 1.56% (2003 est.)
Net Migration: 0.51 migrants/1,000 population (2003 est.)
Ethnic Groups: 94% white (including mestizo), 3% black, 1% Indian, 1% Chinese, 1% other
Languages: Spanish (official), English is spoken around Puerto Limon
Religions: 95% Roman Catholic
Birth Rate: 19.40/1,000 population (2003 est.)
Death Rate: 4.31/1,000 population (2003 est.)
Infant Mortality: 10.56 deaths/1,000 live births (2003 est.)
Life Expectancy at Birth: 73.87 years male, 79.11 years female (2003 est.)
Total Fertility Rate: 2.38 children born/woman (2003 est.)
Literacy: 95.8% (2002)

■ GOVERNMENT

Leader(s): President Abel Pacheco
Government Type: democratic republic
Administrative Divisions: 7 provinces (provincias, sing. —provincia)
Nationhood: Sept. 15, 1821 (from Spain)
National Holiday: Independence Day, Sept. 15

■ ECONOMY

Overview: inflation and external debt are high, many people are underemployed; coffee and banana crops are vital
GDP: US$32.0 billion, per capita US$8,300; real growth rate 2.8% (2002 est.)
Inflation: 9.1% (2002 est.)
Industries: accounts for 37% of GDP (2000); food processing, textiles and clothing, plastics products, construction materials, fertilizer, tourism
Labour Force: 1.6 million (2002); 58% community, social and business services, 20% agriculture, 22% industry
Unemployment: 6.4% (2002), but there is much underemployment
Agriculture: accounts for 11% of GDP (2000) and 70% of exports; cash commodities—coffee, pineapples, beef, bananas, sugar; normally self-sufficient in food except for grain; depletion of forest resources resulting in lower timber output
Natural Resources: hydroelectricity potential

■ FINANCE/TRADE

Currency: colón (pl. colones) (C/) = 100 centimes
International Reserves Excluding Gold: US$1.676 billion (Jan. 2004)
Gold Reserves: 0.002 million fine troy ounces (Jan. 2004)
Budget: revenues US$2.17 billion, expenditures US$2.84 billion, including capital expenditures of US$ n.a. (2002 est.)
Defence Expenditures: n.a.
Education Expenditures: 21.1% of central government expenditure (2002)
External Debt: US$4.834 billion (2002)
Exports: US$6.101 billion (2003); commodities: coffee, bananas, textiles, sugar, electronics, medical equipment; partners: US, EU, Central America, Puerto Rico, Mexico
Imports: US$7.643 billion (2003); commodities: petroleum, machinery, consumer durables, chemicals, fertilizer, foodstuffs; partners: US, EU, Mexico, Venezuela, Central America

■ COMMUNICATIONS

Daily Newspapers: 91/1,000 inhabitants (2000)
Televisions: 231/1,000 inhabitants (2002)
Radios: 816/1,000 inhabitants (2001)
Telephones: 251 lines/1,000 inhabitants (2002)
Internet: hosts: 7,725 (2002); users: 800,000 (2002)

■ TRANSPORTATION

Motor Vehicles: 500,000; 300,000 passenger cars (2000)
Roads: 35,892 km; 7,896 km paved
Railway: 950 km
Air Traffic: 620,000 passengers carried (2002)
Airports: 151; 30 have paved runways (2003 est.)

Canadian Embassy: The Canadian Embassy, Oficentro Ejecutivo La Sabana-detrás de la Contraloría, Sabana Sur, San José; mailing address: Canadian Embassy, P.O. Box 351-1007, Centro Colon, San José, Costa Rica. Tel: (011-506) 242-4400. Fax: (011-506) 242-4410. e-mail: sjcra@dfait-maeci.gc.ca
Embassy in Canada: Embassy of the Republic of Costa Rica, 325 Dalhousie St., Suite 407, Ottawa ON K1N 7G2. Tel: (613) 562-2855. Fax: (613) 562-2582. e-mail: n.a.

Côte d'Ivoire (Ivory Coast)

Long-Form Name: Republic of Côte d'Ivoire
Capital: Yamoussoukro; Abidjan remains the administrative centre.

■ GEOGRAPHY

Area: 322,460 sq. km
Coastline: 515 km
Climate: tropical along coast, semi-arid in far north; three seasons: warm and dry (Nov. to Mar.), hot and dry (Mar. to May), hot and wet (June to Oct.)
Environment: coast has heavy surf and no natural harbours; severe deforestation; water pollution; heavy flooding is possible during rainy season
Terrain: mostly flat to undulating plains; mountains in northwest
Land Use: arable land: 9.28%, permanent crops: 13.84%, other: 76.88%; includes 730 sq. km irrigated
Location: WC Africa, bordering on South Atlantic Ocean

■ PEOPLE

Population: 16,962,491 (July 2003 est.)
Nationality: Ivorian
Age Structure: 0–14 yrs: 45.4%; 15–64: 52.4%; 65+: 2.2% (2003 est.)
Population Growth Rate: 2.15% (2003 est.)
Net Migration: -0.08 migrants/1,000 population (2003 est.)
Ethnic Groups: over 60 ethnic groups; most important are the Baoule 23%, Bete 18%, Senoufou 15%, Malinke 11% and Agni; about 2 million foreign Africans mostly Burkinabe; about 130,000 to 330,000 non-Africans (30,000 French and 100,000–300,000 Lebanese)
Languages: French (official), 60 native dialects, of which Dioula is the most widely spoken
Religions: 28% indigenous, 60% Muslim, 12% Christian
Birth Rate: 40.01/1,000 population (2003 est.)
Death Rate: 18.41/1,000 population (2003 est.)
Infant Mortality: 98.33 deaths/1,000 live births (2003 est.)
Life Expectancy at Birth: 40.34 years male, 45.04 years female (2003 est.)
Total Fertility Rate: 5.51 children born/woman (2003 est.)
Literacy: 49.7% (2002)

■ GOVERNMENT

Leader(s): President Laurent Gbagbo, Prime Minister Seydou Diarra
Government Type: republic; multiparty presidential regime
Administrative Divisions: 58 departments (departements, sing. —departement)
Nationhood: Aug. 7, 1960 (from France)
National Holiday: Independence Day, Aug. 7

■ ECONOMY

Overview: despite attempts to diversify, the economy is largely dependent on agriculture and related industries; highly sensitive to fluctuations in world prices for coffee and cocoa and to weather conditions
GDP: US$24.03 billion, per capita US$1,400; real growth rate -1.6% (2002 est.)
Inflation: 3.2% (2002 est.)
Industries: accounts for 29% of GDP (2000); foodstuffs, wood processing, oil refinery, automobile assembly, textiles, fertilizer, beverages
Labour Force: 6.7 million (2002); 45.4% community, social and business services, 15.6% industry, 13.8% agriculture
Unemployment: n.a.
Agriculture: contributes 28% to GDP and 80% to exports (2000); cash crops include coffee, cocoa beans, rice, timber, bananas, palm kernels, rubber; food crops; not self-sufficient in bread grain and dairy products
Natural Resources: crude oil, diamonds, manganese, iron ore, cobalt, bauxite, copper

■ FINANCE/TRADE

Currency: Communauté financière africaine franc (CFAF) = 100 centimes
International Reserves Excluding Gold: US$2.002 billion (Nov. 2003)
Gold Reserves: 0.045 million fine troy ounces (Jun. 2000)
Budget: revenues US$1.72 billion; expenditures US$2.4 billion, including capital expenditures of US$420 million (2001 est.)
Defence Expenditures: 3.7% of central government expenditure (2002)
Education Expenditures: 21.5% of total government expenditures (2002)
External Debt: US$11.816 billion (2002)
Exports: US$5.157 million (2002) commodities: cocoa 33%, coffee 20%, tropical woods 11%, cotton, bananas, pineapples, palm oil, petroleum; partners: France, Germany, Netherlands, US, Italy
Imports: US$3.799 million (2002) commodities: manufactured goods and semi-finished products 50%, consumer goods 40%, raw materials and fuels 10%; partners: France, Nigeria, China, Italy, Germany

■ COMMUNICATIONS

Daily Newspapers: 16/1,000 inhabitants (2000)
Televisions: 61/1,000 inhabitants (2002)
Radios: 183/1,000 inhabitants (2001)
Telephones: 20 lines/1,000 inhabitants (2002)

Internet: hosts: 4,397 (2002); users: 90,000 (2002)

■ TRANSPORTATION

Motor Vehicles: 255,000; 160,000 passenger cars
Roads: 50,400 km; 4,889 km paved
Railway: 660 km
Air Traffic: 46,000 passengers carried (2002)
Airports: 36; 7 have paved runways (2003 est.)

Canadian Embassy: The Canadian Embassy, Immeuble Trade-Center, 23 rue Nogues, Le Plateau, Abidjan; mailing address: BP 4104, Abidjan 01, Côte d'Ivoire. Tel: (011-225) 20-30-07-00. Fax: (011-225) 20-30-07-20. e-mail: abdjn@dfait-maeci.gc.ca
Embassy in Canada: Embassy of the Republic of Côte d'Ivoire, 9 Marlborough Ave, Ottawa ON K1N 8E6. Tel: (613) 236-9919. Fax: (613) 563-8287. e-mail: embaci@ican.net

Croatia

Long-Form Name: Republic of Croatia
Capital: Zagreb

■ GEOGRAPHY

Area: 56,542 sq. km
Coastline: 5,835 km
Climate: hot summers and cold winters; along coast, mild winters and dry summers
Environment: air pollution (including acid rain), damaged forests, coastal pollution; subject to frequent and destructive earthquakes
Terrain: flat plains along Hungarian border, low mountains and highlands along Adriatic coast, coastline and islands
Land Use: arable land: 23.55%, permanent crops: 2.24%, other: 74.21%; includes 30 sq. km irrigated
Location: S Europe, bordering on Adriatic Sea

■ PEOPLE

Population: 4,422,248 (July 2003 est.)
Nationality: Croat
Age Structure: 0–14 yrs: 18.3%; 15–64: 66.1%; 65+: 15.6% (2003 est.)
Population Growth Rate: 0.31% (2003 est.)
Net Migration: 1.61 migrants/1,000 population (2003 est.)
Ethnic Groups: 78.1% Croat, 12.2% Serb, 0.9% Muslim, 0.5% Hungarian, 0.5% Slovenian, 0.4% Czech, 0.3% Albanian, 0.3% Montenegrin, 0.2% Roma, 6.6% other
Languages: Croatian 96%, other 4% (including Italian, Hungarian, Czech, Slovak and German)

Religions: 76.5% Catholic, 11.1% Orthodox, 1.2% Slavic Muslim, 0.4% Protestant, 10.8% others and unknown
Birth Rate: 12.76/1,000 population (2003 est.)
Death Rate: 11.25/1,000 population (2003 est.)
Infant Mortality: 6.92 deaths/1,000 live births (2003 est.)
Life Expectancy at Birth: 70.76 years male, 78.20 years female (2003 est.)
Total Fertility Rate: 1.93 children born/woman (2003 est.)
Literacy: 98.1% (2002)

■ GOVERNMENT

Leader(s): President Stjepan Mesic, Prime Minister Ivo Sanader
Government Type: parliamentary democracy
Administrative Divisions: 20 counties (zvpanije, sing. —zvpanija), 1 city
Nationhood: June 25, 1991, secession from federal Yugoslavia
National Holiday: Statehood Day, May 30

■ ECONOMY

Overview: tourism, manufacturing including chemicals, food products, petroleum, ships and textiles; war and internal strife have severely disrupted economy
GDP: US$43.12 billion, per capita US$9,800; real growth rate 5.2% (2002)
Inflation: 2.2% (2002 est.)
Industries: accounts for 33% of GDP (2002 est.); mining, fertilizers, plastics, chemicals, fabricated metal, pig iron and rolled steel products, paper, wood products, shipbuilding, food processing, beverages, sugar, cotton fabrics, machinery
Labour Force: 2.1 million (2002); 13.2% agriculture, 25.4% industry, 46.4% services
Unemployment: 14.1% (Feb. 2003)
Agriculture: accounts for 9% of GDP (2002 est.); Croatia normally produces a food surplus, but much land has been put out of production by fighting; products include wheat, maize, sugar, beets, olives, potatoes, plums, fish, livestock, esp. cattle, sheep, pigs, poultry, cereal grains, citrus fruit, vegetables
Natural Resources: oil, salt, coal, bauxite, brown coal and lignite, iron ore, china clay, silver, hydroelectric power, calcium, natural asphalt

■ FINANCE/TRADE

Currency: Croatian kuna = 100 lipas
International Reserves Excluding Gold: US$8.242 billion (Jan. 2004)
Gold Reserves: none (Dec. 2002)

Budget: revenues US$8.6 billion, expenditures US$9 billion, including capital expenditures of US$ n.a. (2001 est.)
Defence Expenditures: 5.9% of total government expenditure (2002)
Education Expenditures: 7.33% of central government expenditure (2001)
External Debt: US$15.347 billion (2002)
Exports: US$6.162 billion (2003 est.); machinery and transportation equipment, fuels, chemicals, textiles, and other manufactured goods; partners: Italy, Germany, Bosnia and Herzegovina, Slovenia, Austria, France
Imports: US$14.136 billion (2003 est.); machinery and transportation equipment, chemicals, raw materials. Partners: Germany, Italy, Russia, Slovenia, Austria, France

■ COMMUNICATIONS

Daily Newspapers: 114/1,000 inhabitants (2000)
Televisions: 293/1,000 inhabitants (2002)
Radios: 340/1,000 inhabitants (2001)
Telephones: 417 lines/1,000 inhabitants (2002)
Internet: hosts: 29,644 (2002); users: 789,000 (2002)

■ TRANSPORTATION

Motor Vehicles: 1,200,000; 1,080,000 passenger cars
Roads: 28,123 km; 23,792 km paved
Railway: 2,296 km
Air Traffic: 1,127,000 passengers carried (2002)
Airports: 59; 16 have paved runways (2003 est.)

Canadian Embassy: The Canadian Embassy, Prilaz Gjure Dezelica #4, 10000 Zagreb. Tel: (011-385-1) 488-1200. Fax: (011-385-1) 488-1230. e-mail: zagrb@dfait-maeci.gc.ca
Embassy in Canada: Embassy of the Republic of Croatia, 229 Chapel St., Ottawa ON K1N 7Y6. Tel: (613) 562-7820. Fax: (613) 562-7821. e-mail: n.a,

Cuba

Long-Form Name: Republic of Cuba
Capital: Havana

■ GEOGRAPHY

Area: 110,860 sq. km
Coastline: 3,735 km
Climate: tropical; moderated by trade winds; dry season (Nov. to Apr.); rainy season (May to Oct.)
Environment: averages one hurricane every two years; water pollution and deforestation
Terrain: mostly flat to rolling plains with rugged hills and mountains in the southeast

Land Use: arable land: 33.04%, permanent crops: 7.61%, other: 59.35%; including 870 sq. km irrigated
Location: West Indies, bordering on Caribbean Sea, Atlantic Ocean

■ PEOPLE

Population: 11,263,429 (July 2003 est.)
Nationality: Cuban
Age Structure: 0–14 yrs: 20.1%; 15–64: 69.6%; 65+: 10.2% (2003 est.)
Population Growth Rate: 0.34% (2003 est.)
Net Migration: -1.05 migrants/1,000 population (2003 est.)
Ethnic Groups: 51% mulatto, 37% white, 11% black, 1% Chinese
Languages: Spanish
Religions: Christianity (majority Roman Catholic)
Birth Rate: 11.87/1,000 population (2003 est.)
Death Rate: 7.38/1,000 population (2003 est.)
Infant Mortality: 7.15 deaths/1,000 live births (2003 est.)
Life Expectancy at Birth: 74.38 years male, 79.36 years female (2003 est.)
Total Fertility Rate: 1.61 children born/woman (2003 est.)
Literacy: 96.9% (2002)

■ GOVERNMENT

Leader(s): President of the Council of State: Fidel Castro Ruz
Government Type: communist state
Administrative Divisions: 14 provinces (provincias, sing. —provincia) and 1 special municipality (municipio especial)
Nationhood: May 20, 1902 (from Spain Dec. 10, 1898; administered by the US from 1898 to 1902)
National Holiday: Independence Day, Dec. 10

■ ECONOMY

Overview: state plays the primary role in the economy and controls practically all foreign trade; recent government reforms aim at alleviating serious shortages of food, consumer goods and services; tourism plays a key role in foreign currency earnings
GDP: US$30.69 billion, per capita US$2,700; real growth rate 1.1% (2002)
Inflation: 7.1% (2002 est.)
Industries: accounts for 35% of GDP; sugar milling, petroleum refining, food and tobacco processing, textiles, chemicals, paper and wood products, metals (particularly nickel), cement, fertilizers, consumer goods, agricultural machinery

Labour Force: 5.6 million (2002); 51% services, 25% industry, 24% agriculture
Unemployment: 3.3% (2002 est.)
Agriculture: accounts for 8% of GDP (including fishing and forestry); key commercial crops—sugar cane, tobacco and citrus fruit; other products—coffee, rice, potatoes, meat, beans; world's largest sugar exporter; not self-sufficient in food
Natural Resources: cobalt, nickel, iron ore, copper, manganese, salt, timber, silica, petroleum

■ FINANCE/TRADE

Currency: peso ($) = 100 centavos
International Reserves Excluding Gold: n.a.
Gold Reserves: n.a.
Budget: revenues US$14.9 billion, expenditures US$15.6 billion, includes capital expenditures of US$ n.a. (2001 est.)
Defence Expenditures: n.a.
Education Expenditures: 16.8% of total government expenditures (2002)
External Debt: US$12.3 billion; another $15–20 billion is owed to Russia (2002 est.).
Exports: US$1.467 billion (2003 est.); commodities: sugar, nickel, shellfish, citrus, tobacco, coffee; partners: Netherlands, Russia, Canada, Spain, China
Imports: US$4.531 billion (2003 est.); commodities: capital goods, industrial raw materials, machinery and transport equipment, food, petroleum; partners: Spain, France, Canada, China, Italy

■ COMMUNICATIONS

Daily Newspapers: 118/1,000 inhabitants (2000)
Televisions: 251/1,000 inhabitants (2002)
Radios: 185/1,000 inhabitants (2001)
Telephones: 51 lines/1,000 inhabitants (2002)
Internet: hosts: 1,133 (2002); users: 120,000 (2002)

■ TRANSPORTATION

Motor Vehicles: 360,000; 180,000 passenger cars
Roads: 60,858 km; 29,820 km paved
Railway: 3,442 km
Air Traffic: 589,000 passengers carried (2002)
Airports: 161; 70 have paved runways (2003 est.)

Canadian Embassy: The Canadian Embassy, Calle 30, No. 518 Esquina 7a, Avenida Miramar, Havana, Cuba. Tel: (011-53-7) 204-25-16. Fax: (011-53-7) 204-97-72. e-mail: havan@dfait-maeci.gc.ca
Embassy in Canada: Embassy of the Republic of Cuba, 388 Main St, Ottawa ON K1S 1E3. Tel:

(613) 563-0141. Fax: (613) 563-0068. e-mail: cuba@iosphere.net

Cyprus

Long-Form Name: Republic of Cyprus
Capital: Nicosia

■ GEOGRAPHY

Area: 9,250 sq. km
Coastline: 648 km
Climate: temperate, Mediterranean with hot, dry summers and cool, wet winters
Environment: moderate earthquake activity; water resource problems (no natural reservoir catchments, seasonal disparity in rainfall and most potable resources concentrated in the Turkish-Cypriot area)
Terrain: central plain with mountains to north and south, plain along south coast
Land Use: arable land: 14.4%, permanent crops: 4.5%, other: 81.1%, (2001 est.); including 400 sq. km irrigated
Location: Middle East, in the Mediterranean Sea

■ PEOPLE

Population: 771,657 (July 2003 est.)
Nationality: Cypriot
Age Structure: 0–14 yrs: 21.9%; 15–64: 67.0%; 65+: 11.1% (2003 est.)
Population Growth Rate: 0.56% (2003 est.)
Net Migration: 0.43 migrants/1,000 population (2003 est.)
Ethnic Groups: 78% Greek; 18% Turkish; 4% other
Languages: 80% Greek, Turkish, English
Religions: 78% Greek Orthodox; 18% Muslim; 4% Maronite, Armenian, Apostolic and other
Birth Rate: 12.77/1,000 population (2003 est.)
Death Rate: 7.63/1,000 population (2003 est.)
Infant Mortality: 7.54 deaths/1,000 live births (2003 est.)
Life Expectancy at Birth: 74.94 years male, 79.71 years female (2003 est.)
Total Fertility Rate: 1.88 children born/woman (2003 est.)
Literacy: 96.8% (2002)

■ GOVERNMENT

Leader(s): President Tassos Papadopoulos
Government Type: republic; Greek Cypriots control the only internationally recognized government, however the country is divided by a UN-patrolled buffer zone. The northern portion of the island (approx. 40%) is a Turkish-Cypriot administered area. (In 1983 this area was declared the Turkish Republic of Northern Cyprus, but Turkey is the only nation to recognize this jurisdiction)
Administrative Divisions: 6 districts
Nationhood: Aug. 16, 1960 (from UK)
National Holiday: Independence Day, Oct. 1 (Nov. 15 is celebrated as Independence Day in the Turkish area)

■ ECONOMY

Overview: remains heavily dependent on agriculture and government service, which together employ about 50% of the workforce
GDP: Greek Cypriot area: revenues US$9.4 billion, per capita US$15,000; real growth rate 1.7%; Turkish Cypriot area: revenues US$787 million, per capita US$6,000; real growth rate 2.6% (2001)
Inflation: Greek Cypriot area: 2.8%; Turkish Cypriot area: 24.5% (2002 est.)
Industries: accounts for 20–21% of GDP; mining (iron pyrites, gypsum, asbestos); manufactured products—beverages, footwear, clothing and cement—are principally for local consumption, tourism
Labour Force: 377,300 (2000); Greek Cypriot area: 73% services, 22% industry, 5% agriculture; Turkish Cypriot area: 56% services, 23% industry, 21% agriculture
Unemployment: n.a.
Agriculture: accounts for 5–8% of GDP; major crops—potatoes, vegetables, barley, grapes, olives and citrus fruit; vegetables and fruit provide 25% of export revenues
Natural Resources: copper, pyrites, asbestos, gypsum, timber, salt, marble, clay earth pigment

■ FINANCE/TRADE

Currency: Cypriot pound (£ or £C) = 100 cents and Turkish lira (TL) = 100 kurus
International Reserves Excluding Gold: US$3.152 billion (Jan. 2004)
Gold Reserves: 0.465 million fine troy ounces (Jan. 2004)
Budget: Greek area: revenues US$4.4 billion; expenditures US$3.7 billion, including capital expenditures of US$539 million; Turkish area: revenues US$231.3 million; expenditures US$432.8 million, including capital expenditures of US$ n.a. million (2003 est.)
Defence Expenditures: 3.8% of GDP (2002)
Education Expenditures: n.a.
External Debt: Greek Cypriot area: US $8 billion Turkish Cypriot area: n.a. (2002)
Exports: US$908 million (2003 est.); commodities: citrus, potatoes, grapes, wine, cement, clothing

and shoes; partners: EU, Russia, Syria, Lebanon, Turkey, UK
Imports: US$4.420 billion (2003 est.); commodities: consumer goods 23%, petroleum and lubricants 12%, food and feed grains, machinery; partners: EU, US

■ COMMUNICATIONS

Daily Newspapers: 9 in total
Televisions: n.a.
Radios: n.a.
Telephones: n.a.
Internet: hosts: 2,692 (2002); users: 210,000 (2002)

■ TRANSPORTATION

Motor Vehicles: 340,000; 230,000 passenger cars
Roads: 13,491 km; 7,798 km paved
Railway: none
Air Traffic: 1,530,000 passengers carried (2001 est.)
Airports: 16; 13 have paved runways (2003 est.)

Canadian Embassy: Consulate of Canada, P.O. Box 22125, 1095, Nicosia 1517, Cyprus. Tel: (011-357-2) 775-508, Fax: (011-357-2) 779-905. e-mail: n.a.
Embassy in Canada: c/o Embassy of the Republic of Cyprus, 2211 R St NW, Washington DC 20008, USA. Tel: (202) 462-5772. Fax: (202) 483-6710. e-mail: n.a.

Czech Republic

Long-Form Name: Czech Republic
Capital: Prague

■ GEOGRAPHY

Area: 78,866 sq. km
Coastline: none: landlocked
Climate: temperate; cool summers; cold, cloudy, humid winters
Environment: air and water pollution and acid rain, which also damages the forests; recently there has been severe flooding
Terrain: Bohemia in the west consists of rolling plains, hills and plateaus surrounded by low mountains; Moravia in east consists of very hilly country
Land Use: arable land: 40%, permanent crops: 3.04%, other: 56.96%; includes 240 sq. km irrigated
Location: C Europe

■ PEOPLE

Population: 10,249,216 (July 2003 est.)
Nationality: Czech

Age Structure: 0–14 yrs: 15.4%; 15–64: 70.6%; 65+: 14.0% (2003 est.)
Population Growth Rate: -0.08% (2003 est.)
Net Migration: 0.97 migrants/1,000 population (2003 est.)
Ethnic Groups: 81.2% Czech, 3.1% Slovak, 0.2% Hungarian, 0.5% German, 0.6% Polish, 13.2% Moravian, 0.4% Silesian, 0.3% Gypsy, 0.5% other
Languages: Czech and Slovak
Religions: 39.8% atheist, 39.2% Roman Catholic, 4.6% Protestant, 3% Orthodox, 13.4% other
Birth Rate: 9.01/1,000 population (2003 est.)
Death Rate: 10.74/1,000 population (2003 est.)
Infant Mortality: 5.37 deaths/1,000 live births (2003 est.)
Life Expectancy at Birth: 71.69 years male, 78.87 years female (2003 est.)
Total Fertility Rate: 1.18 children born/woman (2003 est.)
Literacy: approaching 100% (2002)

■ GOVERNMENT

Leader(s): President Vaclav Klaus, Prime Minister Stanislav Gross
Government Type: parliamentary democracy
Administrative Divisions: 13 regions (Kraje, sing, —Kraj), 1 capital city
Nationhood: Jan. 1, 1993 (from Czechoslovakia)
National Holiday: National Liberation Day, May 8; Founding of the Republic, Oct. 28

■ ECONOMY

Overview: economy is beginning the transition from a command to a market economy; economic growth is less important at this point than economic restructuring
GDP: US$157.1 billion, per capita US$15,300; real growth rate 2.0% (2003 est.)
Inflation: 0.6% (2002 est.)
Industries: accounts for 41% of GDP (2001); fuels, ferrous metallurgy, machinery and equipment, coal, motor vehicles, glass, armaments
Labour Force: 5.7 million (2002); 35% industry, 5% agriculture, 60% services
Unemployment: 10.1% (Sept. 2003)
Agriculture: accounts for 4% of GDP (2001); largely self-sufficient in food production; diversified crop and livestock production, including grains, sugar beets, potatoes, hops, fruit, hogs, cattle and poultry
Natural Resources: hard and soft coal, kaolin, clay, graphite

■ FINANCE/TRADE

Currency: koruna (pl. koruny) (Kcs) = 100 haleru
International Reserves Excluding Gold: US$26.463 billion (Jan. 2004)
Gold Reserves: 0.442 million fine troy ounces (Jan. 2004)
Budget: revenues US$16.7 billion; expenditures US$18 billion, including capital expenditures US$ n.a. (2001 est.)
Defence Expenditures: 5.4% of total government expenditure (2002)
Education Expenditures: 9.7% of central government expenditure (2002)
External Debt: US$26.419 billion (2002)
Exports: US$47.987 billion (2003); commodities: machinery and equipment 58.5%, industrial consumer goods 15.2%, fuels, chemicals, minerals and metals 10.6%, agricultural and forestry products 6.1%, other products 15.2%; partners: former USSR countries, Germany, Slovakia, UK, Austria, Poland
Imports: US$50.418 billion (2002); commodities: machinery and equipment 41.6%, fuels, minerals, metals 32.2%, agricultural and forestry products 11.5%, industrial consumer goods 6.7%, other products 8%; partners: Germany, Slovakia, Russia, Italy, Austria

■ COMMUNICATIONS

Daily Newspapers: 254/1,000 inhabitants (2000)
Televisions: 538/1,000 inhabitants (2002)
Radios: 803/1,000 inhabitants (2001)
Telephones: 362 lines/1,000 inhabitants (2002)
Internet: hosts: 226,429 (2002); users: 2.6 million (2002)

■ TRANSPORTATION

Motor Vehicles: 3,700,000; 3,400,000 passenger cars
Roads: 55,408 km; all paved
Railway: 9,462 km
Air Traffic: 2,801,000 passengers carried (2002)
Airports: 144; 44 have paved runways (2003 est.)

Canadian Embassy: The Canadian Embassy, Mickiewiczova 6, 16000 Prague 6, Czech Republic. Tel: (011-420-2) 7210-1800. Fax: (011-420-2) 7210-1890. e-mail: prgue@dfait-maeci.gc.ca
Embassy in Canada: Embassy of the Czech Republic, 251 Cooper St. Ottawa ON, K2P 0G2. Tel: (613) 562-3875. Fax: (613) 562-3878. e-mail: ottawa@embassy.mzv.cz

Denmark

Long-Form Name: Kingdom of Denmark
Capital: Copenhagen

■ GEOGRAPHY

Area: 43,094 sq. km; includes the island of Bornholm in the Baltic Sea and the rest of metropolitan Denmark, but excludes the Faroe Islands and Greenland
Coastline: 7,314 km (includes fjords)
Climate: temperate; humid and overcast; mild, windy winters and cool summers
Environment: air and water pollution; pollution of drinking water
Terrain: low and flat to gently rolling plains
Land Use: arable land: 55.74%, permanent crops: 0.19%, other: 44.07%; includes 4,760 sq. km irrigated
Location: N Europe, bordering on North Sea, Baltic Sea

■ PEOPLE

Population: 5,384,384 (July 2003 est.)
Nationality: Dane
Age Structure: 0–14 yrs: 18.7%; 15–64: 66.3%; 65+: 15.0% (2003 est.)
Population Growth Rate: 0.29% (2003 est.)
Net Migration: 2.01 migrants/1,000 population (2003 est.)
Ethnic Groups: Scandinavian, Inuit, Faroese, German
Languages: Danish, Faroese, Greenlandic (an Inuit dialect); small German-speaking minority
Religions: 91% Evangelical Lutheran, 2% other Protestant and Roman Catholic, 7% other
Birth Rate: 11.52/1,000 population (2003 est.)
Death Rate: 10.72/1,000 population (2003 est.)
Infant Mortality: 4.90 deaths/1,000 live births (2003 est.)
Life Expectancy at Birth: 74.48 years male, 79.87 years female (2003 est.)
Total Fertility Rate: 1.73 children born/woman (2003 est.)
Literacy: approaching 100% (2002)

■ GOVERNMENT

Leader(s): Head of State: Queen Margrethe II, Prime Minister Anders Fogh Rasmussen
Government Type: constitutional monarchy
Administrative Divisions: 14 counties (amter, sing. —amt) and 2 kommunes; dependent areas includes Faroe Islands, Greenland (see Greenland entry for details)
Nationhood: became a constitutional monarchy in 1849

National Holiday: none designated. Constitution Day, June 5, is generally viewed as the National Day.

■ ECONOMY

Overview: advanced agriculture and industry; extensive government welfare measures; highly dependent on foreign trade
GDP: US$155.3 billion, per capita US$28,900; real growth rate 1.6% (2002)
Inflation: 2.3% (2002 est.)
Industries: accounts for 26% of GDP (2002 est.); food processing, machinery and equipment, textiles and clothing, chemical products, electronics, construction, furniture and other wood products
Labour Force: 2.9 million (2002); 79% community, social and business services, 17% industry, 4% agriculture
Unemployment: 5.6% (Aug. 2003)
Agriculture: accounts for 3% of GNP (2002 est.) and employs 5.6% of labour force (includes fishing); farm products account for nearly 15% of export revenues; principal products—meat, dairy, grain, potatoes, rape, sugar beets, fish; self-sufficient in food production
Natural Resources: crude oil, natural gas, fish, salt, limestone, sand and gravel

■ FINANCE/TRADE

Currency: krone (pl. kroner) (DKr) = 100 oere
International Reserves Excluding Gold: US$34.891 billion (Jan. 2004)
Gold Reserves: 2.140 million fine troy ounces (Jan. 2004)
Budget: revenues US$52.9 billion; expenditures US$51.3 billion, including capital expenditures US$500 million (2001 est.)
Defence Expenditures: 4.3% of total government expenditure (2002)
Education Expenditures: 15.3% of central government expenditure (2002)
External Debt: US$21.7 billion (2000)
Exports: US$65.397 billion (2003 est.); commodities: meat and meat products, dairy products, transport equipment, fish, chemicals, furniture, industrial machinery; partners: EU, US, Norway
Imports: US$55.857 billion (2003 est.); commodities: petroleum, machinery and equipment, chemicals, grain and foodstuffs, textiles, paper; partners: US, Germany, Netherlands, Sweden, UK, France, Italy

■ COMMUNICATIONS

Daily Newspapers: 283/1,000 inhabitants (2000)

Televisions: 859/1,000 inhabitants (2002)
Radios: 1,400/1,000 inhabitants (2001)
Telephones: 689 lines/1,000 inhabitants (2002)
Internet: hosts: 836,631 (2002); users: 2.756 million (2002)

■ TRANSPORTATION

Motor Vehicles: 2,250,000; 1,930,000 passenger cars
Roads: 71,591 km; all paved
Railway: 3,164 km; 2,859 km operational
Air Traffic: 6,322,000 passengers carried (2002)
Airports: 104; 28 have paved runways (2003 est.)

Canadian Embassy: The Canadian Embassy, Kr. Bernikowsgade 1, 1105 Copenhagen K, Denmark. Tel: (011-45) 33-48-32-00. Fax: (011-45) 33-48-32-20. e-mail: copen@dfait-maeci.gc.ca
Embassy in Canada: Embassy of the Kingdom of Denmark, 47 Clarence St, Ste 450, Ottawa ON K1N 9K1. Tel: (613) 562-1811. Fax: (613) 562-1812. e-mail: danemb@cyberus.ca

Djibouti

Long-Form Name: Republic of Djibouti
Capital: Djibouti

■ GEOGRAPHY

Area: 22,000 sq. km
Coastline: 314 km
Climate: desert; torrid, dry
Environment: vast wasteland; desertification; droughts and earthquakes; occasional cyclones; inadequate safe drinking water
Terrain: coastal plain and plateau separated by central mountains
Land Use: arable land: 0%, permanent crops: 0%, other: 100%; includes 10 sq. km irrigated
Location: E Africa, bordering on Gulf of Aden

■ PEOPLE

Population: 457,130 (July 2003 est.)
Nationality: Djiboutian
Age Structure: 0–14 yrs: 43.1%; 15–64: 53.9%; 65+: 3.0% (2003 est.)
Population Growth Rate: 2.13% (2003 est.)
Net Migration: 0 migrants/1,000 population (2003 est.)
Ethnic Groups: 60% Somali (Issa), 35% Afar, 5% French, Arab, Ethiopian and Italian
Languages: French and Arabic (both official); Somali and Afar widely used
Religions: 94% Muslim, 6% Christian
Birth Rate: 40.78/1,000 population (2003 est.)

Death Rate: 19.45/1,000 population (2003 est.)
Infant Mortality: 106.96 deaths/1,000 live births (2003 est.)
Life Expectancy at Birth: 41.82 years male, 44.48 years female (2003 est.)
Total Fertility Rate: 5.56 children born/woman (2003 est.)
Literacy: 65.5% (2002)

■ GOVERNMENT

Leader(s): President Ismail Omar Guelleh, Prime Minister Mohamed Dileita
Government Type: republic
Administrative Divisions: 5 districts (cercles, sing. —cercle)
Nationhood: June 27, 1977 (from France; formerly known as French Territory of the Afars and Issao)
National Holiday: Independence Day, June 27

■ ECONOMY

Overview: based on service activities related to country's strategic location and status as a free trade zone; Djibouti is heavily dependent on foreign aid
GDP: US$619 million, per capita US$1,300; real growth rate 3.5% (2002 est.)
Inflation: 2.0% (2002 est.)
Industries: accounts for 10% of GDP (2001 est.); limited to a few small-scale enterprises, such as dairy products and mineral-water bottling
Labour Force: approx. 282,000; 79% agriculture, 17% industry, 4% services
Unemployment: 50% (2000 est.)
Agriculture: accounts for only 3% of GDP (2001 est.); scanty rainfall limits crop production to mostly fruit and vegetables; half of population pastoral nomads herding goats, sheep and camels; imports bulk of food needs
Natural Resources: geothermal areas

■ FINANCE/TRADE

Currency: Djiboutian franc (DF) = 100 centimes
International Reserves Excluding Gold: US$100 million (Dec. 2003)
Gold Reserves: n.a.
Budget: n.a.
Defence Expenditures: 4.4% of GDP (2002)
Education Expenditures: n.a.
External Debt: US$335 million (2002)
Exports: US$155 million (2002 est.); commodities: hides and skins, coffee (in transit); partners: Somalia, Yemen, Ethiopia
Imports: US$665 million (2002 est.); commodities: foods, beverages, transport equipment,

chemicals, petroleum products; partners: France, Ethiopia, Italy, Saudi Arabia, UK

■ COMMUNICATIONS

Daily Newspapers: none
Televisions: n.a.
Radios: n.a.
Telephones: 21 lines/1,000 inhabitants (2002)
Internet: hosts: 498 (2002); users: 4,500 (2002)

■ TRANSPORTATION

Motor Vehicles: 16,500; 13,500 passenger cars
Roads: 2,890 km; 364 km paved
Railway: 100 km
Air Traffic: n.a.
Airports: 13; 2 have paved runways (2003 est.)

Canadian Embassy: The Canadian Embassy to Djibouti, c/o The Canadian Embassy, P.O. Box 1130, Addis Ababa, Ethiopia. Tel: (011-251-1) 71-30-22. Fax: (011-251-1) 71-30-33. e-mail: addis@dfait-maeci.gc.ca
Embassy in Canada: c/o Embassy of the Republic of Djibouti, 1156 15th St. NW, Ste 515, Washington DC 20005, USA. Tel: (202) 331-0270. Fax: (202) 331 0302. e-mail: n.a.

Dominica

Long-Form Name: Commonwealth of Dominica
Capital: Roseau

■ GEOGRAPHY

Area: 754 sq. km
Coastline: 148 km
Climate: tropical; moderated by northeast trade winds; heavy rainfall
Environment: flash floods a constant hazard; occasional hurricanes
Terrain: rugged mountains of volcanic origin
Land Use: arable land: 4%, permanent crops: 16%, other: 80%; includes n.a. sq. km irrigated
Location: Caribbean islands, northern end of the Windward Islands

■ PEOPLE

Population: 69,655 (July 2002 est.)
Nationality: Dominican
Age Structure: 0–14 yrs: 27.8%; 15–64: 64.3%; 65+: 7.9% (2003 est.)
Population Growth Rate: -0.63% (2003 est.)
Net Migration: -16.11 migrants/1,000 population (2003 est.)
Ethnic Groups: mostly black; some Carib Indians
Languages: English (official); French patois widely spoken

Religions: 77% Roman Catholic; 15% Protestant, 2% none, 1% unknown, 5% other
Birth Rate: 16.78/1,000 population (2003 est.)
Death Rate: 6.99/1,000 population (2003 est.)
Infant Mortality: 15.34 deaths/1,000 live births (2003 est.)
Life Expectancy at Birth: 71.23 years male, 77.15 years female (2003 est.)
Total Fertility Rate: 1.99 children born/woman (2003 est.)
Literacy: 76.4% (2002)

■ GOVERNMENT

Leader(s): President Nicholas J.O. Liverpool, Prime Minister Roosevelt Skerrit
Government Type: parliamentary democracy
Administrative Divisions: 10 parishes
Nationhood: Nov. 3, 1978 (from UK)
National Holiday: Independence Day, Nov. 3

■ ECONOMY

Overview: dependent on agriculture and vulnerable to climatic conditions; tourist potential (undeveloped)
GDP: US$380 million, per capita US$5,400; real growth rate 1.2% (2002 est.)
Inflation: 1.0% (2001 est.)
Industries: agricultural processing, tourism, soap and other coconut-based products, cigars, pumice mining, cement blocks, shoes. Industries account for 24% of GDP (2002 est.)
Labour Force: approx. 25,000; agriculture 40%, industry and commerce 32%, services 28%
Unemployment: n.a.
Agriculture: accounts for 18% of GDP (2001 est.); principal crops—bananas, citrus fruit, mangoes, coconuts, root crops; bananas provide the bulk of export earnings; forestry and fisheries potential not exploited
Natural Resources: timber, hydroelectric power, arable land

■ FINANCE/TRADE

Currency: East Caribbean dollar ($EC) = 100 cents
International Reserves Excluding Gold: US$57 million (Jan. 2004)
Gold Reserves: n.a.
Budget: revenues US$73.9 million, expenditures US$84.4 million, including capital expenditures of US$ n.a. (2001)
Defence Expenditures: n.a.
Education Expenditures: n.a.
External Debt: US$207 million (2002)
Exports: US$39 million (2003 est.); commodities: bananas, coconuts, grapefruit, oranges, soap, galvanized sheets; partners: CARICOM countries, UK, US
Imports: US$126 million (2003 est.); commodities: food, oils and fats, chemicals, fuels and lubricants, manufactured goods, machinery and equipment; partners: US, CARICOM, UK, Netherlands, Canada

■ COMMUNICATIONS

Daily Newspapers: none
Televisions: n.a.
Radios: n.a.
Telephones: 338 lines/1,000 inhabitants (2002)
Internet: hosts: 464 (2002); users: 12,500 (2002)

■ TRANSPORTATION

Motor Vehicles: 5,700; 2,800 passenger cars
Roads: 780 km; 393 km paved
Railway: none
Air Traffic: n.a.
Airports: 2; both have paved runways (2003 est.)

Canadian Embassy: c/o The Canadian High Commission, Bishop's Court Hill, St. Michael, Barbados; mailing address: P.O. Box 404, Bridgetown, Barbados. Tel: (246) 429-3550. Fax: (246) 429-3780. e-mail: bdgtn@dfait-maeci.gc.ca
Embassy in Canada: c/o High Commission for the Countries of the Organization of Eastern Caribbean States, 130 Albert St, Ste 700, Ottawa ON K1P 5G4. Tel: (613) 236-8952. Fax: (613) 236-3042. e-mail: echcc@travel-net.com

Dominican Republic

Long-Form Name: Dominican Republic
Capital: Santo Domingo

■ GEOGRAPHY

Area: 48,730 sq. km
Coastline: 1,288 km
Climate: tropical maritime; little seasonal temperature variation
Environment: subject to occasional hurricanes (July to Oct.); deforestation; erosion and water shortage
Terrain: rugged highlands and mountains interspersed with fertile valleys
Land Use: arable land: 21.08%, permanent crops: 9.92%, other: 69%; includes 2,590 sq. km irrigated
Location: West Indies, bordering on Haiti, Caribbean Sea, Atlantic Ocean

■ PEOPLE

Population: 8,715,602 (July 2003 est.)
Nationality: Dominican
Age Structure: 0–14 yrs: 33.6%; 15–64: 61.2%;
65+: 5.2% (2003 est.)
Population Growth Rate: 1.36% (2003 est.)
Net Migration: -3.43 migrants/1,000 population
(2003 est.)
Ethnic Groups: 73% mixed, 16% white, 11% black
Languages: Spanish
Religions: 95% Roman Catholic
Birth Rate: 23.94/1,000 population (2003 est.)
Death Rate: 6.88/1,000 population (2003 est.)
Infant Mortality: 34.19 deaths/1,000 live births
(2003 est.)
Life Expectancy at Birth: 66.41 years male, 69.58
years female (2003 est.)
Total Fertility Rate: 2.92 children born/woman
(2003 est.)
Literacy: 84.4% (2002)

■ GOVERNMENT

Leader(s): President Leonel Fernandez Reyna,
Vice President Rafael Alburquerque de Castro
Government Type: representative democracy
Administrative Divisions: 29 provinces (provin-
cias, sing. —provincia) and 1 district (distrito)
Nationhood: Feb. 27, 1844 (from Haiti)
National Holiday: Independence Day, Feb. 27

■ ECONOMY

Overview: agriculture is the backbone of the
economy (sugar cane); tourism and a free trade
zone help; hurricane damage has adversely
affected agriculture and infrastructure; the
government is attempting to increase electric
generating capacity, but there have been
numerous delays
GDP: US$53.78 billion, per capita US$6,300;
real growth rate 4.1% (2002 est.)
Inflation: 5.3% (2002 est.)
Industries: accounts for 34% of GDP (2000);
tourism, sugar processing, nickel and gold
mining, textiles, cement, tobacco
Labour Force: 3.9 million (2002); 17% agriculture, 59% services and government, 24%
industry
Unemployment: 15.6% (2002)
Agriculture: accounts for 11% of GDP (2000)
and employs almost half of labour force; sugar
cane most important commercial crop, followed
by coffee, cotton and cocoa; food crops include
rice, beans, potatoes, corn; animal output; not
self-sufficient in food
Natural Resources: nickel, bauxite, gold, silver

■ FINANCE/TRADE

Currency: Dominican peso ($RD) = 100 centavos
International Reserves Excluding Gold: US$254
million (Jan. 2004)
Gold Reserves: 0.018 million fine troy ounces
(Jan. 2004)
Budget: revenues US$2.9 billion; expenditures
US$3.2 billion, including capital expenditures
of US$1.1 billion (2001 est.)
Defence Expenditures: 5.57% of total govern-
ment expenditure (2002)
Education Expenditures: 13.2% of central govern-
ment expenditure (2002)
External Debt: US$6.256 billion (2002)
Exports: US$834 million (2002); commodities:
sugar, coffee, cocoa, tobacco, gold, nickel;
partners: US, Netherlands, Canada, France
Imports: US$6.037 billion (2002); commodities:
foodstuffs, petroleum, cotton and fabrics,
chemicals and pharmaceuticals; partners: US,
Mexico, Japan, Venezuela

■ COMMUNICATIONS

Daily Newspapers: 27/1,000 inhabitants (2000)
Televisions: 97/1,000 inhabitants (2000)
Radios: 181/1,000 inhabitants (2001)
Telephones: 110 lines/1,000 inhabitants (2002)
Internet: hosts: 45,508 (2002); users: 300,000
(2002)

■ TRANSPORTATION

Motor Vehicles: 209,000; 114,200 passenger cars
Roads: 12,600 km; 6,224 km paved
Railway: 757 km
Air Traffic: 11,000 passengers carried (2001 est.)
Airports: 30; 13 have paved runways (2003 est.)

Canadian Embassy: The Canadian Embassy,
Capitan Eugenio de Marchena, No. 39, La
Esperilla, Santo Domingo; mailing address:
Apartado 2054, Santo Domingo 1, Dominican
Republic. Tel: (809) 685-1136. Fax: (809) 682-
2691. e-mail: sdmgo@dfait-maeci.gc.ca
Embassy in Canada: Embassy of the Dominican
Republic, 130 Albert St., Suite 418, Ottawa ON,
K1P 5G4. Tel: (613) 569-9893. Fax: (613) 569-
8673. e-mail: n.a.

East Timor

Long-Form Name: Democratic Republic of
Timor-Leste
Capital: Dili

■ GEOGRAPHY

Area: 14,609 sq. km

Coastline: 706 km
Climate: tropical with little seasonal temperature variation and high annual rainfall.
Environment: lack of safe drinking water; water is mainly underground and often far from villages
Terrain: extremely mountainous, volcanic island, much of it covered in forest; flat and arable in the south
Land Use: n.a.%, permanent crops: n.a.%, other: n.a.%; 1,065 sq. km irrigated
Location: eastern half of the island of Timor, which lies between Indonesia and Australia at the eastern end of Malay Archipelago.

■ PEOPLE

Population: 997,853 (July 2003 est.)
Nationality: East Timorese
Age Structure: 0–14 yrs: 49%; 15–64 yrs: 49%; 65 yrs +: 2%; (2001)
Population Growth Rate: 2.13% (2003 est.)
Net Migration: 0 migrants/1,000 population (2003 est.)
Ethnic Groups: Malay and Papuan, including 33% Tetum, 12% Mambai, 8% Kemak, 10% Makasai, 8% Galoli and 8% Tokodede
Languages: 9 Austronesian language groups: Tetum (spoken by about 60% of the population), Mambai, Tokodede, Kemak, Galoli, Idate, Waima'a, Naueti and 3 Papuan langauge groups (Bunak, Makasae, Fataluku). Under Indonesian rule the official language was Bahasa. Some Timorese still speak Portuguese
Religions: Roman Catholic 91.4%; Other (Muslim, Protestant, Hindu, Buddhist)
Birth Rate: 27.75/1,000 population (2003 est.)
Death Rate: 6.41/1,000 population (2003 est.)
Infant Mortality: 50.47 deaths/1,000 live births (2003 est.)
Life Expectancy at Birth: 62.97 years male; 67.55 years female (2003 est.)
Total Fertility Rate: 3.79 children born/woman (2003 est.)
Literacy: 58.6% (2002 est.)

■ GOVERNMENT

Leader(s): President Jose Alexandre ("Xanana") Gusmao, Prime Minister Mari Bin Amude Alkatiri
Government Type: republic
Administrative Divisions: 13 districts

Nationhood: May 20, 2002 is the official date of international recognition of East Timor's independence from Indonesia
National Holiday: Independence Day, August 30; National Day, November 28

■ ECONOMY

Overview: fierce fighting in struggle for independence has damaged or destroyed most of East Timor's infrastructure; East Timor hopes to revive its economy by export profits from its high-quality, organically grown coffee crop
GDP: US$440 million, per capita US$500; real growth rate 18.1% (2001)
Inflation: 3.0% (2001), down from 76.7% in 1999
Industries: oil and natural gas, and the processing of agricultural products including coffee, fish, spices, coconuts and cacao. Industrial production accounts for 17% of DGP (2001)
Labour Force: 230,400 (2001 est.)
Unemployment: 6% (2001 est.)
Agriculture: cornerstone of East Timorese economy. It employs over 80% of the population and is the major source of foreign exchange revenue. While paddy and rain-fed rice is the leading cash crop, other principal crops include food crops 51%, plantations 25.8%, livestock 20.5%, forestry 1% and fisheries 1%. High-quality arabica coffee is also being produced. Agricultural production accounts for 25% of GDP (2001)
Natural Resources: extremely rich in oil, natural gas and manganese

■ FINANCE/TRADE

Currency: US dollar (US$) = 100 cents
International Reserves Excluding Gold: n.a.
Gold Reserves: n.a.
Budget: revenues US$36 million expenditures, US$97 million, including capital expenditures of US$ n.a. (2003 est.)
Defence Expenditures: n.a.
Education Expenditures: n.a.
External Debt: n.a.
Exports: US$4 million (2001); commodities: coffee, copra, palm oil, rice, wax and hides; partners: Australia, Portugal
Imports: US$237 million (2001); partners: Australia, Portugal

■ COMMUNICATIONS

Daily Newspapers: n.a.
Televisions: n.a.
Radios: n.a.
Telephones: n.a.
Internet: n.a.

■ TRANSPORTATION

Motor Vehicles: n.a.
Roads: 3,800 km; 428 km paved
Railway: none
Air Traffic: n.a.
Airports: 8; 3 have paved runways (2003 est.)

Canadian Embassy: c/o The Canadian Embassy, World Trade Centre, 6th Floor, Jl. Jend. Sudirman, Kav. 29, Jakarta 12920, Indonesia. Postal Address: The Canadian Embassy, P.O. Box 8324/JKS.MP, Jakarta 12083, Indonesia. Tel: (011 62 21) 2550-7800. Fax: (011 62 21) 2550-7811. e-mail: jkrta@dfait-maeci.gc.ca
Embassy in Canada: c/o Embassy of the Republic of Indonesia, 55 Parkdale Avenue, Ottawa, ON, K1Y 1E5. Tel: (613) 724-1100. Fax: (613) 724-1105. e-mail: info@prica.org

Ecuador

Long-Form Name: Republic of Ecuador
Capital: Quito

■ GEOGRAPHY

Area: 283,560 sq. km
Coastline: 2,237 km
Climate: tropical along coast becoming cooler inland
Environment: subject to frequent earthquakes, landslides, volcanic activity; deforestation; desertification; soil erosion; periodic droughts
Terrain: coastal plain, inter-Andean central highlands and flat to rolling eastern jungle
Land Use: arable land: 5.69%, permanent crops: 5.15%, other: 89.16%; includes 8,650 sq. km irrigated
Location: NW South America, bordering on Pacific Ocean

■ PEOPLE

Population: 13,710,234 (July 2003 est.)
Nationality: Ecuadorian
Age Structure: 0–14 yrs: 34.9%; 15–64: 60.6%; 65+: 4.5% (2003 est.)
Population Growth Rate: 1.91% (2003 est.)

Net Migration: -0.52 migrants/1,000 population (2003 est.)
Ethnic Groups: 65% mestizo (mixed Indian and Spanish), 25% Indian, 7% Spanish, 3% black
Languages: Spanish (official), Indian languages, especially Quechua
Religions: 95% Roman Catholic
Birth Rate: 24.94/1,000 population (2003 est.)
Death Rate: 5.29/1,000 population (2003 est.)
Infant Mortality: 31.97 deaths/1,000 live births (2003 est.)
Life Expectancy at Birth: 69.06 years male, 74.86 years female (2003 est.)
Total Fertility Rate: 2.99 children born/woman (2003 est.)
Literacy: 91.0% (2002)

■ GOVERNMENT

Leader(s): President Lucio Gutierrez Borbua, Vice President Alfredo Palacio
Government Type: republic
Administrative Divisions: 22 provinces (provincias, sing. —provincia)
Nationhood: May 24, 1822 (from Spain; Battle of Pichincha)
National Holiday: Independence Day, Aug. 10

■ ECONOMY

Overview: vulnerable to international oil prices; the banana crop, second in importance only to oil, has been hurt by EU import quotas and banana blight; strict austerity program has resulted in economic stabilization
GDP: US$42.65 billion, per capita US$3,200; real growth rate 3.4% (2002 est.)
Inflation: 12.5% (2002 est.)
Industries: accounts for 25% of GDP (2000); food processing, textiles, metal works, paper products, chemicals, fishing, timber, petroleum
Labour Force: 5.1 million (2002); 30% agriculture, 45% services, 25% industry
Unemployment: 11.0% (2002)
Agriculture: accounts for 11% of GDP (2000) and 35% of labour force (including fishing and forestry); leading producer and exporter of bananas and balsawood; crop and livestock sector; coffee, cocoa, rice, potatoes, net importer of foodgrain, dairy products and sugar
Natural Resources: petroleum, fish, timber, hydroelectric power

■ FINANCE/TRADE

Currency: US dollar ($) = 100 cents
International Reserves Excluding Gold: US$903 million (Jan. 2004)

Gold Reserves: 0.845 million fine troy ounces (Jan. 2004)
Budget: revenues US$6.3 billion; expenditures US$5.3 billion, including capital expenditures of US$1.6 billion (2002 est.)
Defence Expenditures: n.a.
Education Expenditures: 8.0% of total government expenditures (2002)
External Debt: US$16.452 billion (2002)
Exports: US$6.039 billion (2003 est.); commodities: petroleum 47%, coffee, bananas, cocoa products, shrimp, fish products; partners: US, Chile, Peru, Colombia, Italy
Imports: US$6.535 billion (2003 est.); commodities: transport equipment, vehicles, machinery, chemicals, petroleum; partners: US, Colombia, Japan, Venezuela, Brazil

■ **COMMUNICATIONS**

Daily Newspapers: 96/1,000 inhabitants (2000)
Televisions: 237/1,000 inhabitants (2002)
Radios: 413/1,000 inhabitants (2001)
Telephones: 110 lines/1,000 inhabitants (2002)
Internet: hosts: 2,648 (2002); users: 537,900 (2002)

■ **TRANSPORTATION**

Motor Vehicles: 640,000; 580,000 passenger cars
Roads: 43,197 km; 8,165 km paved
Railway: 966 km
Air Traffic: 1,292,000 passengers carried (2002)
Airports: 205; 61 have paved runways (2003 est.)

Canadian Embassy: The Canadian Embassy, Avenida 6 de Diciembre, 2816 y Paul Rivet, Edificio Josueth Gonzalez, 4th Fl., Quito, Ecuador; mailing address: P.O. Box 17-11-6512, Quito, Ecuador. Tel: (011-593-2) 223-2114. Fax: (011-593-2) 2503-108. e-mail: quito@dfait-maeci.gc.ca
Embassy in Canada: Embassy of the Republic of Ecuador, 50 O'Connor St, Ste 316, Ottawa ON K1P 6L2. Tel: (613) 563-8206. Fax: (613) 235-5776. e-mail: mecuacan@rogers.com

---

Egypt

Long-Form Name: Arab Republic of Egypt
Capital: Cairo

■ **GEOGRAPHY**

Area: 1,001,450 sq. km
Coastline: 2,450 km
Climate: desert; hot, dry summers with moderate winters
Environment: Nile is only perennial water source; increasing soil salinization below Aswan High Dam; hot, driving windstorm called khamsin occurs in spring; water pollution; desertification; urbanization and erosion are decreasing the arable land available
Terrain: vast desert plateau interrupted by Nile valley and delta
Land Use: arable land: 2.85%, permanent crops: 0.47%, other: 96.68%; includes 33,000 sq. km irrigated
Location: NE Africa, bordering on Mediterranean Sea, Red Sea

■ **PEOPLE**

Population: 74,718,797 (July 2003 est.)
Nationality: Egyptian
Age Structure: 0–14 yrs: 33.9%; 15–64: 61.9%; 65+: 4.2% (2003 est.)
Population Growth Rate: 1.88% (2003 est.)
Net Migration: -0.23 migrants/1,000 population (2003 est.)
Ethnic Groups: 99% Eastern Hamitic stock; 1% Greek, Italian, Syro-Lebanese, Armenian
Languages: Arabic (official); English and French
Religions: 94% Muslim (mostly Sunni), 6% Coptic Christian and other
Birth Rate: 24.36/1,000 population (2003 est.)
Death Rate: 5.35/1,000 population (2003 est.)
Infant Mortality: 35.26 deaths/1,000 live births (2003 est.)
Life Expectancy at Birth: 67.94 years male, 73.00 years female (2003 est.)
Total Fertility Rate: 3.02 children born/woman (2003 est.)
Literacy: 55.6% (2002)

■ **GOVERNMENT**

Leader(s): President Mohammed Hosni Mubarak, Prime Minister Ahmed Mohamed Nazif
Government Type: republic
Administrative Divisions: 26 governorates (muhafazat, sing. —muhafazah)
Nationhood: Feb. 28, 1922 (from UK; formerly known as United Arab Republic)
National Holiday: Anniversary of the Revolution, July 23

■ **ECONOMY**

Overview: urban population growth puts pressure on the agricultural sector; having difficulty with its debt servicing; vulnerable to oil prices; unemployment has become a growing problem
GDP: US$289.8 billion, per capita US$4,000; real growth rate 3.2% (2002 est.)
Inflation: 4.3% (2002 est.)
Industries: accounts for 30% of GDP (2001), textiles, food processing, tourism, chemicals, petroleum, construction, cement, metals

Labour Force: 25.9 million (2002); 29% agriculture, 49% community, social and business services, 22% industry
Unemployment: 9.0% (2002)
Agriculture: accounts for 14% of GDP (2001), employs more than one-third of labour force; dependent on irrigation water from the Nile; world's fifth largest cotton exporter; other crops include rice, corn, wheat, beans, fruit, vegetables; livestock production; not self-sufficient in food
Natural Resources: crude oil, natural gas, iron ore, phosphates, manganese, limestone, gypsum, talc, asbestos, lead, zinc

■ FINANCE/TRADE

Currency: Egyptian pound (LE) = 100 piasters
International Reserves Excluding Gold: US$13.589 billion (Jan. 2004)
Gold Reserves: 2.432 million fine troy ounces (Jan. 2004)
Budget: revenues US$14 billion; expenditures US$18.1 billion, including capital expenditures of US$2.7 billion (2003 est.)
Defence Expenditures: 10.2% of central government expenditure (2002)
Education Expenditures: n.a.
External Debt: US$30.750 billion (2002)
Exports: US$4.708 billion (2002); commodities: raw cotton, crude and refined petroleum, cotton yarn, textiles; partners: US, EU, Middle East, Asian countries
Imports: US$12.552 billion (2002); commodities: foods, machinery and equipment, fertilizers, wood products, durable consumer goods, capital goods; partners: Germany, Italy, France, US, Asian countries, Middle East

■ COMMUNICATIONS

Daily Newspapers: 31/1,000 inhabitants (2000)
Televisions: 229/1,000 inhabitants (2002)
Radios: 339/1,000 inhabitants (2001)
Telephones: 110 lines/1,000 inhabitants (2002)
Internet: hosts: 3,061 (2002); users: 1.9 million (2002)

■ TRANSPORTATION

Motor Vehicles: 1,711,000; 1,300,000 passenger cars
Roads: 64,000 km; 49,984 km paved
Railway: 5,105 km
Air Traffic: 4,478,000 passengers carried (2002)
Airports: 89; 71 have paved runways (2003 est.)

Canadian Embassy: The Canadian Embassy, #26 Kamel El Shenawy St., Garden City, Cairo, Egypt; mailing address: P.O. Box 1667, Cairo, Egypt. Tel: (011-20-2) 794-3110. Fax: (011-20-2) 796-3548. e-mail: cairo@dfait-maeci.gc.ca

Embassy in Canada: Embassy of the Arab Republic of Egypt, 454 Laurier Ave E, Ottawa ON K1N 6R3. Tel: (613) 234-4931. Fax: (613) 234-4398. e-mail: egyptemb@sympatico.ca

El Salvador

Long-Form Name: Republic of El Salvador
Capital: San Salvador

■ GEOGRAPHY

Area: 21,040 sq. km
Coastline: 307 km
Climate: tropical; rainy season (May to Oct.), dry season (Nov. to Apr.)
Environment: the Land of Volcanoes; subject to frequent and sometimes very destructive earthquakes; deforestation; soil erosion and pollution; water pollution
Terrain: mostly mountains with narrow coastal belt and central plateau
Land Use: arable land: 27.27%, permanent crops: 12.11%, other: 60.62%; includes 360 sq. km irrigated
Location: Central (Latin) America, bordering on Pacific Ocean

■ PEOPLE

Population: 6,470,379 (July 2003 est.)
Nationality: Salvadoran
Age Structure: 0–14 yrs: 37.1%; 15–64: 57.9%; 65+: 5.1% (2003 est.)
Population Growth Rate: 1.81% (2003 est.)
Net Migration: -3.81 migrants/1,000 population (2003 est.)
Ethnic Groups: 90% mestizo, 1% Amerindian, 9% white
Languages: Spanish, Nahua spoken among some Indians
Religions: approx. 75% Roman Catholic, with activity by Protestant groups throughout the country
Birth Rate: 27.90/1,000 population (2003 est.)
Death Rate: 6.01/1,000 population (2003 est.)
Infant Mortality: 26.75 deaths/1,000 live births (2003 est.)
Life Expectancy at Birth: 67.02 years male, 74.40 years female (2003 est.)
Total Fertility Rate: 3.25 children born/woman (2003 est.)
Literacy: 79.7% (2002)

■ GOVERNMENT

Leader(s): President Elias Antonio Saca, Vice President Ana Vilma de Escobar
Government Type: republic
Administrative Divisions: 14 departments (departmentos, sing. —departmento)

Nationhood: Sept. 15, 1821 (from Spain)
National Holiday: Independence Day, Sept. 15

■ ECONOMY

Overview: in recent years inflation has fallen to unprecedented levels and exports have grown considerably; even so, sizeable fiscal deficits persist; the trade deficit has been offset by remittances from the many Salvadorans living abroad
GDP: US$29.41 billion, per capita US$4,600; real growth rate 2.1% (2002 est.)
Inflation: 3.8% (2001)
Industries: accounts for 30% of GDP (2000); food processing, textiles, non-metallic products, tobacco, beverages, clothing, petroleum products, cement
Labour Force: 2.8 million (2002); 30% agriculture, 55% community, social and business services, 15% industry
Unemployment: 6.2% (2002)
Agriculture: accounts for 10% of GDP (2000) and 40% of labour force (including fishing and forestry); coffee most important commercial crop; other products—sugar cane, corn, rice, beans, oilseeds, beef, dairy products, shrimp; not self-sufficient in food
Natural Resources: hydroelectricity and geothermal power, crude oil

■ FINANCE/TRADE

Currency: colón (pl. colones) (C/) = 100 centavos; also US dollar ($) =100 cents
International Reserves Excluding Gold: US$1.935 billion (Jan. 2004)
Gold Reserves: 0.469 million fine troy ounces (Jan. 2004))
Budget: revenues US$2.1 billion, expenditures US$2.5 billion, including capital expenditures of US$ n.a. (2001 est.)
Defence Expenditures: 31.2% of total government expenditure (2002)
Education Expenditures: 19.4% of central government expenditure (2002)
External Debt: US$5.828 billion (2002)
Exports: US$1.255 billion (2003); commodities: coffee 60%, sugar, cotton, shrimp, electricity; partners: US, Guatemala, Honduras, EU
Imports: US$4.382 billion (2003); commodities: petroleum products, electricity, consumer goods, foodstuffs, machinery, construction materials, fertilizer; partners: US, Guatemala, EU, Mexico

■ COMMUNICATIONS

Daily Newspapers: 28/1,000 inhabitants (2000)
Televisions: 233/1,000 inhabitants (2002)

Radios: 478/1,000 inhabitants (2001)
Telephones: 103 lines/1,000 inhabitants (2002)
Internet: hosts: 269 (2002); users: 300,000 (2002)

■ TRANSPORTATION

Motor Vehicles: 390,000; 190,000 passenger cars
Roads: 10,029 km; 1,986 km paved
Railway: 562 km; 283 km operational
Air Traffic: 1,804,000 passengers carried (2002)
Airports: 82; 4 have paved runways (2003 est.)

Canadian Embassy: Office of the Canadian Embassy, Centro Financiero Gigante, Alameda Roosevelt y 63 Avenida Sur, Torre A, Lobby 2, Colonia Escalon, San Salvador, El Salvador. Tel: (011-503) 279-4655. Fax: (011-503) 279-0765. e-mail: ssal@dfait-maeci.gc.ca
Embassy in Canada: Embassy of the Republic of El Salvador, 209 Kent St, Ottawa ON K2P 1Z8. Tel: (613) 238-2939. Fax: (613) 238-6940. e-mail: embajada@elsalvador.ca.org

Equatorial Guinea

Long-Form Name: Republic of Equatorial Guinea
Capital: Malabo

■ GEOGRAPHY

Area: 28,051 sq. km
Coastline: 296 km
Climate: tropical; always hot, humid
Environment: subject to violent windstorms; desertification; unsafe drinking water
Terrain: coastal plains rise to interior hills; islands are volcanic
Land Use: arable land: 4.63%, permanent crops: 3.57%, other: 91.8%; includes n.a. sq. km irrigated
Location: WC Africa, bordering on South Atlantic Ocean

■ PEOPLE

Population: 510,473 (July 2003 est.)
Nationality: Equatorial Guinean or Equatoguinean
Age Structure: 0–14 yrs: 42.2%; 15–64: 54.0%; 65+: 3.8% (2003 est.)
Population Growth Rate: 2.44% (2003 est.)
Net Migration: 0 migrants/1,000 population (2003 est.)
Ethnic Groups: indigenous population of Bioko, primarily Bubi, some Fernandinos; Rio Muni, primarily Fang; less than 1,000 Europeans, mostly Spanish

Languages: Spanish (official), pidgin English, Fang, Bubi, Ndowe, Bujeba, Anobones and Corisqueño
Religions: natives all nominally Christian and predominantly Roman Catholic; some pagan practices retained (5%)
Birth Rate: 36.94/1,000 population (2003 est.)
Death Rate: 12.54/1,000 population (2003 est.)
Infant Mortality: 89.02 deaths/1,000 live births (2003 est.)
Life Expectancy at Birth: 52.63 years male, 56.93 years female (2003 est.)
Total Fertility Rate: 4.75 children born/woman (2003 est.)
Literacy: 84.2% (2002)

■ GOVERNMENT

Leader(s): President Teodoro Obiang Nguema Mbasogo, Prime Minister Miguel Abia Biteo Borico
Government Type: republic
Administrative Divisions: 7 provinces (provincias, sing. —provincia)
Nationhood: Oct. 12, 1968 (from Spain; formerly Spanish Guinea)
National Holiday: Independence Day, Oct. 12

■ ECONOMY

Overview: the economy is recovering from destruction by a past regime; subsistence agriculture, forestry and fishing predominate; little industry; many undeveloped natural resources, but increased exploitation of recently discovered natural gas resources is boosting the economy
GDP: US$1.27 billion, per capita US$2,700; real growth rate 20.0% (2002 est.)
Inflation: 6% (2002 est.)
Industries: accounts for 60% of GDP; petroleum, fishing, sawmilling
Labour Force: n.a.; 66% agriculture, 23% services, 11% industry
Unemployment: n.a.
Agriculture: accounts for 20% of GDP; cash crops—timber and coffee from Rio Muni, cocoa from Bioko; food crops—rice, yams, cassava, bananas, tobacco, oil, palm nuts, manioc, livestock, timber production
Natural Resources: timber, crude oil, small unexploited deposits of gold, manganese, uranium

■ FINANCE/TRADE

Currency: Communauté financière africaine franc (CFAF) = 100 centimes

International Reserves Excluding Gold: US$238 million (Dec. 2003)
Gold Reserves: n.a.
Budget: revenues US$200 million; expenditures US$158 million, capital expenditures US$ n.a. (2001 est.)
Defence Expenditures: 2.5% of GDP (2002)
Education Expenditures: n.a.
External Debt: US$260 million (2002)
Exports: US$2.1 billion (2003 est.); commodities: petroleum, coffee, timber, cocoa beans; partners: China, Japan, US, South Korea
Imports: US$1.371 billion (2003 est.); commodities: petroleum, food, beverages, clothing, machinery; partners: US, France, Spain, Italy

■ COMMUNICATIONS

Daily Newspapers: 1 in total
Televisions: n.a.
Radios: n.a.
Telephones: 17 lines/1,000 persons (2002)
Internet: hosts: 3 (2002); users: 1,800 (2002)

■ TRANSPORTATION

Motor Vehicles: 10,500; 6,500 passenger cars
Roads: 2,880 km, none paved
Railway: none
Air Traffic: 25,000 passengers carried (2001 est.)
Airports: 3; 2 have paved runways (2003 est.)

Canadian Embassy: The Canadian Embassy to Equatorial Guinea, c/o P.O. Box 4037, Libreville, Gabon. Tel: (011-241) 73-73-54. Fax (011-241) 73-73-88. e-mail: lbrve@dfait-maeci.gc.ca
Embassy in Canada: c/o Embassy of Equatorial Guinea, 2020 16th St, NW, Washington DC 20009, USA. Tel: (202) 518-5700. Fax: (202) 518-5252. e-mail: n.a.

Eritrea

Long-Form Name: State of Eritrea
Capital: Asmara (formerly Asmera)

■ GEOGRAPHY

Area: 121,320 sq. km
Coastline: 1,151 km mainland coast; 2,234 km including island coastlines
Climate: hot, dry desert along Red Sea coast, cooler and wetter in central highlands, semi-arid in west
Environment: frequent droughts, famine, deforestation, soil erosion, overgrazing

Terrain: highlands descending to coastal desert in east, hilly in northwest, flat to rolling plains in southwest
Land Use: arable land: 3.87%, permanent crops: 0.02%, other: 96.11%; includes 220 sq. km irrigated
Location: E Africa

■ PEOPLE

Population: 4,362,254 (July 2003 est.)
Nationality: Eritrean
Age Structure: 0–14 yrs: 44.7%; 15–64: 52.0%; 65+: 3.3% (2003 est.)
Population Growth Rate: 1.28% (2003 est.)
Net Migration: -13.38 migrants/1,000 population (2003 est.)
Ethnic Groups: 50% ethnic Tigrinya, 40% Tigre and Kunama, 4% Afar, 3% Saho (Red Sea coast-dwellers), 3% other
Languages: Afar, Amharic, Tigre and Kunama, Cushitic dialects, Tigrinya, Nora Bana, Arabic
Religions: Muslim, Coptic Christian, Roman Catholic, Protestant
Birth Rate: 39.44/1,000 population (2003 est.)
Death Rate: 13.23/1,000 population (2003 est.)
Infant Mortality: 76.32 deaths/1,000 live births (2003 est.)
Life Expectancy at Birth: 51.48 years male, 54.92 years female (2003 est.)
Total Fertility Rate: 5.74 children born/woman (2003 est.)
Literacy: 56.7% (2002)

■ GOVERNMENT

Leader(s): President Isaias Afworki
Government Type: transitional govt.
Administrative Divisions: 8 provinces (awraja)
Nationhood: May 24, 1993 (from Ethiopia)
National Holiday: National Day (independence from Ethiopia), May 24

■ ECONOMY

Overview: with independence from Ethiopia, Eritrea faces the bitter economic problems of a small and desperately poor nation; subsistence farming will continue to be the people's economic mainstay; production is augmented by remittances from abroad, and there are long-term prospects for revenue from offshore oil development, offshore fishing, and tourism; Ethiopia is largely dependent on Eritrean ports for foreign trade
GDP: US$3.3 billion, per capita US$700; real growth rate 2.0% (2002 est.)
Inflation: 15.0% (2001 est.)

Industries: accounts for 29% of GDP (2001 est.); food processing, beverages, textiles, clothing manufacture
Labour Force: 2.2 million (2002); 80% agriculture, 20% industry and commerce
Unemployment: n.a.
Agriculture: accounts for 17% of GDP (2001 est.); livestock, fish, vegetables, sorghum, lentils, vegetables, corn, cotton, coffee and tobacco
Natural Resources: gold, potash, copper, zinc, salt, fish

■ FINANCE/TRADE

Currency: nafka = 100 cents
International Reserves Excluding Gold: n.a.
Gold Reserves: none (Jan. 2004)
Budget: revenues US$206.4 million; expenditures US$615.7 million, capital expenditures US$ n.a. (2000 est.)
Defence Expenditures: 12% of GDP (2002)
Education Expenditures: n.a.
External Debt: US$528 million (2002)
Exports: US$56 million (2003 est.); commodities: livestock, sorghum, textiles, food, small manufactures; partners: Ethiopia, Sudan, Japan, UAE, Italy
Imports: US$600 million (2003 est.); commodities: processed goods, machinery, petroleum products; partners: Italy, United Arab Emirates, Germany, UK, Korea

■ COMMUNICATIONS

Daily Newspapers: none
Televisions: 50/1,000 inhabitants (2002)
Radios: 464/1,000 inhabitants (2001)
Telephones: 9 lines/1,000 inhabitants (2002)
Internet: hosts: 859 (2002); users: 9,000 (2002)

■ TRANSPORTATION

Motor Vehicles: n.a.
Roads: 4,010 km, 874 km paved
Railway: 317 km; not operational
Air Traffic: n.a.
Airports: 18; 4 have paved runways (2003 est.)

Canadian Embassy: c/o The Canadian High Commission, Limuru Road, Gigiri, Nairobi, Kenya. Postal Address: The Canadian High Commission, P.O. Box 1013, 00621 Nairobi, Kenya. Tel: (011 254 20) 366 3000. Fax: (011 254 20) 366 3900. e-mail: nrobi@dfait-maeci.gc.ca
Embassy in Canada: Embassy of the State of Eritrea, 75 Albert St., Suite 610, Ottawa, ON K1P 5E7. Tel: (613) 234-3989. Fax: (613) 234-6213. e-mail: n.a.

Estonia

Long-Form Name: Republic of Estonia
Capital: Tallinn

■ GEOGRAPHY

Area: 45,226 sq. km
Coastline: 3,794 km
Climate: wet, moderate winter; long windy autumn; warm sunny summer; late and short spring
Environment: severe air pollution, soil and ground water contamination (chemicals and petroleum products), radioactive waste; frequent spring floods are a natural hazard
Terrain: marshy lowlands, sloping coastal plain; islands account for 10% of the region
Land Use: arable land: 26.5%, permanent crops: 0.35%, other: 73.15%; includes 40 sq. km irrigated
Location: NE Europe, bordering on Baltic Sea

■ PEOPLE

Population: 1,408,556 (July 2003 est.)
Nationality: Estonian
Age Structure: 0–14 yrs: 15.8%; 15–64: 68.8%; 65+: 15.4% (2003 est.)
Population Growth Rate: -0.49% (2003 est.)
Net Migration: -0.71 migrants/1,000 population (2003 est.)
Ethnic Groups: 65.1% Estonian, 28.1% Russian, 2.5% Ukrainian, 1.5% Byelorussian, 1% Finn, 1.8% other
Languages: Estonian (official), Russian, Latvian, Lithuanian, English and German also spoken
Religions: Lutheran, Orthodox Christian
Birth Rate: 9.24/1,000 population (2003 est.)
Death Rate: 13.42/1,000 population (2003 est.)
Infant Mortality: 12.03 deaths/1,000 live births (2003 est.)
Life Expectancy at Birth: 64.36 years male, 76.57 years female (2003 est.)
Total Fertility Rate: 1.27 children born/woman (2003 est.)
Literacy: 99.8% (2002)

■ GOVERNMENT

Leader(s): President Arnold Ruutel, Prime Minister Juhan Parts
Government Type: parliamentary democracy
Administrative Divisions: 15 counties (maakonnad, sing. —maakond)
Nationhood: Sept. 6, 1991 (from Soviet Union)
National Holiday: Independence Day, Feb. 24 (1918 from Soviet Russia); Sept. 6 (1991, from the Soviet Union)

■ ECONOMY

Overview: market reforms and stabilizing measures are rapidly transforming the economy; living standards and incomes are rising, but so are unemployment and inflation
GDP: US$15.52 billion, per capita US$11,000; real growth rate 6.0% (2002)
Inflation: 3.7% (2002)
Industries: accounts for 29% of GDP (2001); electronics, electrical engineering, textiles, clothing, footwear, shipbuilding
Labour Force: 800,000 (2002); 20% industry, 69% community, social and business services, 11% agriculture
Unemployment: 5.8% (Mar. 2003); large numbers of underemployed
Agriculture: contributes 6% to GDP (2001), and employs 11% of labour force; dairy products, pork, poultry, eggs, fruit, vegetables; net exports of meat, fish, dairy products, potatoes
Natural Resources: fish, shale, phosphorites, amber, limestone, peat, dolomite, arable land

■ FINANCE/TRADE

Currency: kroon (pl. kroons) = 100 sents
International Reserves Excluding Gold: US$1.194 billion (Jan. 2004)
Gold Reserves: 0.008 million fine troy ounces (Jan. 2004)
Budget: revenues US$3.13 billion; expenditures US$3.0 billion, capital expenditures US$ n.a. (2003 est.)
Defence Expenditures: 5.6% of government expenditure (2002)
Education Expenditures: 10.24% of central government expenditure (2000)
External Debt: US$4.741 billion (2002)
Exports: US$4.459 billion (2003); dairy products, fish, furniture, electrical power, meat; partners: Latvia, Finland, Sweden, Germany, UK
Imports: US$6.400 billion (2003); machinery 45%, oil 13%, chemicals 12%, foodstuffs, textiles; partners: Finland, Russia, Sweden, Germany, Japan

■ COMMUNICATIONS

Daily Newspapers: 176/1,000 inhabitants (2000)
Televisions: 502/1,000 inhabitants (2002)
Radios: 1,136/1,000 inhabitants (2001)
Telephones: 351 lines/1,000 inhabitants (2002)
Internet: hosts: 63,364 (2002); users: 444,000 (2002)

■ TRANSPORTATION

Motor Vehicles: 570,000; 480,000 passenger cars

Roads: 51,411 km; 10,334 km paved
Railway: 968 km
Air Traffic: 254,000 passengers carried (2002)
Airports: 38; 14 have paved runways (2003 est.)

Canadian Embassy: Office of the Canadian Embassy, Toom Kooli 13, 2nd Fl, 10130 Tallinn, Estonia. Tel: (011-372) 627-3311. Fax: (011-372) 627-3312. e-mail: tallinn@canada.ee
Embassy in Canada: c/o Embassy of the Republic of Estonia, 260 Dalhousie St, Ste 210, Ottawa ON K1N 7E4. Tel: (613) 789-4222. Fax: (613) 789-9555. e-mail: estonianembassy@rogers.com

---

Ethiopia

Long-Form Name: Federal Democratic Republic of Ethiopia
Capital: Addis Ababa

■ GEOGRAPHY

Area: 1,127,127 sq. km
Coastline: none; landlocked
Climate: tropical with wide topographic-induced variation; prone to extended droughts
Environment: geologically active Great Rift Valley susceptible to earthquakes, volcanic eruptions; deforestation; overgrazing; soil erosion; desertification; frequent droughts; famine
Terrain: high plateau with central mountain range divided by Great Rift Valley
Land Use: arable land: 9.9%, permanent crops: 0.65%, other: 89.45%; includes 1,900 sq. km irrigated
Location: E Africa, between Somalia and Sudan

■ PEOPLE

Population: 66,557,553 (July 2003 est.)
Nationality: Ethiopian
Age Structure: 0–14 yrs: 44.8%; 15–64: 52.4%; 65+: 2.8% (2003 est.)
Population Growth Rate: 1.96% (2003 est.)
Net Migration: 0.0 migrants/1,000 population (2003 est.)
Ethnic Groups: 40% Oromo, 32% Amhara and Tigrean, 9% Sidamo, 6% Shankella, 6% Somali, 4% Afar, 2% Gurage, 1% other
Languages: Amharic (official), Tigrinya, Orominga, Guaraginga, Somali, Arabic, English (major foreign language taught in schools)
Religions: 45–50% Muslim, 35–40% Ethiopian Orthodox, 12% animist, 5% other
Birth Rate: 39.81/1,000 population (2003 est.)
Death Rate: 20.17/1,000 population (2003 est.)
Infant Mortality: 103.22 deaths/1,000 live births (2003 est.)

Life Expectancy at Birth: 40.39 years male, 42.11 years female (2003 est.)
Total Fertility Rate: 5.55 children born/woman (2003 est.)
Literacy: 41.5% (2002)

■ GOVERNMENT

Leader(s): President Girma Woldegiorgis, Premier Meles Zenawi
Government Type: federal republic
Administrative Divisions: 9 states and 2 self-governing administrations
Nationhood: oldest (at least 2,000 years) independent country in Africa and one of the oldest in the world
National Holiday: National Day, May 28

■ ECONOMY

Overview: remains one of the poorest and least developed countries in the world; its economy is based on agriculture and suffers from recent periods of drought, poor cultivation practices and the deterioration of internal security conditions
GDP: US$48.53 billion, per capita US$700; real growth rate 3.0% (2002 est.)
Inflation: 4.0% (2003 est.)
Industries: accounts for 11% of GDP (2000), cement, textiles, food processing, beverages, chemicals, metals processing, oil refinery
Labour Force: 28.9 million (2002); 80% agriculture, 12% services, 8% industry
Unemployment: n.a.
Agriculture: accounts for 52% of GDP (2000) even though frequent droughts, poor cultivation practices and state economic policies keep farm output low; famines not uncommon; estimated 50% of agricultural production at subsistence level. Products include cereals, coffee, oilseed
Natural Resources: small reserves of gold, platinum, copper, potash, natural gas

■ FINANCE/TRADE

Currency: birr (Br) = 100 cents
International Reserves Excluding Gold: US$956 million (Dec. 2003)
Gold Reserves: none (Jan. 2004)
Budget: revenues US$1.4 billion; expenditures US$2.4 billion, capital expenditures US$788 million (2003 est.)
Defence Expenditures: 43.0% of central government expenditure (2002)
Education Expenditures: 13.8% of total government expenditures (2002)
External Debt: US$6.522 billion (2002)

Exports: US$478 million (2002); commodities: coffee 60%, gold, oilseed, hides; partners: Germany, Djibouti, Japan, Saudi Arabia
Imports: US$1.659 billion (2002); commodities: food, fuels, machinery and motor vehicles, capital goods; partners: Italy, US, Saudi Arabia, Russia

■ COMMUNICATIONS

Daily Newspapers: less than 1/1,000 inhabitants (2000)
Televisions: 6/1,000 inhabitants (2002)
Radios: 189/1,000 inhabitants (2001)
Telephones: 5 lines/1,000 inhabitants (2002)
Internet: hosts: 41 (2002); users: 50,000 (2002)

■ TRANSPORTATION

Motor Vehicles: 69,000; 46,400 passenger cars
Roads: 31,571 km; 3,789 km paved
Railway: 681 km
Air Traffic: 1,103,000 passengers carried (2002)
Airports: 83; 14 have paved runways (2003 est.)

Canadian Embassy: The Canadian Embassy, Old Airport Area, Higher 23, Kebele 12, House Number 122, Addis Ababa; mailing address: P.O. Box 1130, Addis Ababa, Ethiopia. Tel: (011-251-1) 71-30-22. Fax: (011-251-1) 71-30-33. e-mail: addis@dfait-maeci.gc.ca
Embassy in Canada: Embassy of the Federal Democratic Republic of Ethiopia, 151 Slater St, Ste 210, Ottawa ON K1P 5H3. Tel: (613) 235-6637. Fax: (613) 235-4638. e-mail: infoethi@magi.com

Faeroe Islands

Long-Form Name: Faeroe Islands
Capital: Tórshavn (island of Stremoy)

■ GEOGRAPHY

Area: 1,399 sq. km (total of 18 islands and some reefs)
Climate: cold and windy; mild winters, cool summers; foggy
Land Use: arable land: 2.14%, permanent crops: 0%, other: 97.86%
Location: Norwegian Sea (N Atlantic Ocean), N of Scotland

■ PEOPLE

Population: 46,345 (July 2003 est.)
Nationality: Faeroese (sing. & pl.)
Ethnic Groups: Scandinavian
Languages: Faeroese (derived from Old Norse), Danish

■ GOVERNMENT

Colony/Territory of: Dependent Territory of Denmark
Leader(s): Queen Margrethe II of Denmark, High Commissioner Birgit Kleis, Prime Minister Joannes Eidesgaard
Government Type: dependency with some degree of self-rule
National Holiday: Olaifest, July 29

■ ECONOMY

Overview: fishing main industry, now in decline, which poses great danger to the economy; steep coastline and treacherous currents make trading by sea difficult; exports: fish and fish products; partners: Denmark, Norway, Sweden, Germany, United States

■ FINANCE/TRADE

Currency: Danish krone (kr) = 100 oere

Canadian Embassy: c/o The Canadian Embassy, Kr. Bernikowsgade 1, 1105 Copenhagen K, Denmark. Tel: (011-45) 33-48-32-00. Fax: (011-45) 33-48-32-20. e-mail: copen@dfait-maeci.gc.ca
Representative to Canada: c/o Embassy of the Kingdom of Denmark, 47 Clarence St, Ste 450, Ottawa ON K1N 9K1. Tel: (613) 562-1811. Fax: (613) 562-1812. e-mail: danemb@cyberus.ca

Falkland Islands

Long-Form Name: Colony of the Falkland Islands
Capital: Stanley (on East Falkland)

■ GEOGRAPHY

Area: numerous islands covering 12,173 sq. km
Climate: damp, cool, temperate; strong winds, esp. in spring; occasional snow all year
Land Use: arable land: 0%, permanent crops: 0%, other: 100%, (99%, permanent pastures, 1%, other)
Location: S South America, in the South Atlantic Ocean

■ PEOPLE

Population: 2,967 (July 2003 est.)
Nationality: Falkland Islander
Ethnic Groups: almost 100% British descent
Languages: English

■ GOVERNMENT

Colony/Territory of: Dependent Territory of the United Kingdom

Leader(s): Head of State: Queen Elizabeth II, Governor Howard J.S. Pearce, Chief Executive Chris Simpkins
Government Type: overseas territory of the UK, although in 1990 Argentina declared the Falklands and other British-held South Atlantic Islands part of new Argentine province Tierra del Fuego
National Holiday: Liberation Day, June 14

■ ECONOMY

Overview: heavily agricultural, esp. sheep farming, with wool main product; fishing: illex squid; exports tend to outweigh imports in value; chief trading partner: United Kingdom

■ FINANCE/TRADE

Currency: Falkland Islands pound (FKP) = 100 pence, at parity with the British pound sterling

Canadian Embassy: c/o The Canadian High Commission, Macdonald House, 1 Grosvenor Square, London W1K 4AB, England, UK. Tel: (011-44-20) 7258-6600. Fax: (011-44-20) 7445-3302. e-mail: ldn@dfait-maeci.gc.ca
Representative to Canada: c/o British High Commission, 80 Elgin St, Ottawa ON K1P 5K7l. Tel: (613) 237-1530. Fax: (613) 237-7980. e-mail should be sent using the appropriate form at the British High Commission's Website at http://www.britain-in-canada.org

Fiji

Long-Form Name: Republic of the Fiji Islands
Capital: Suva

■ GEOGRAPHY

Area: 18,270 sq. km; includes 332 islands of which approx. 110 are inhabited
Coastline: 1,129 km
Climate: tropical marine; only slight seasonal temperature variation
Environment: subject to hurricanes from Nov. to Jan.; deforestation and soil erosion
Terrain: mostly mountains of volcanic origin
Land Use: arable land: 10.95%, permanent crops: 4.65%, other: 84.4%; includes 30 sq. km irrigated
Location: Pacific Ocean, N of New Zealand

■ PEOPLE

Population: 868,531 (July 2003 est.)
Nationality: Fijian
Age Structure: 0–14 yrs: 32.0%; 15–64: 64.1%; 65+: 3.8% (2003 est.)
Population Growth Rate: 1.41% (2003 est.)

Net Migration: -3.24 migrants/1,000 population (2003 est.)
Ethnic Groups: 44% Indian, 51% Fijian, 5% European, other Pacific Islanders, overseas Chinese and others
Languages: English (official); Fijian; Hindi
Religions: Christianity 52%, Hinduism 38%, Muslim 8%, other 2%
Birth Rate: 23.06/1,000 population (2003 est.)
Death Rate: 5.70/1,000 population (2003 est.)
Infant Mortality: 13.35 deaths/1,000 live births (2003 est.)
Life Expectancy at Birth: 66.43 years male, 71.44 years female (2003 est.)
Total Fertility Rate: 2.81 children born/woman (2003 est.)
Literacy: 92.9% (2002)

■ GOVERNMENT

Leader(s): President Ratu Josefa Iloilo, Prime Minister Laisenia Qarase
Government Type: republic. The government was destabilized by a coup and hostage taking that began May 19, 2000; it ended with the release of final hostages of deposed elected government on July 13, 2000. A new president was elected by the Great Council of Chiefs on July 13
Administrative Divisions: 4 divisions and 1 dependency
Nationhood: Oct. 10, 1970 (from UK)
National Holiday: Independence Day, second Monday in October

■ ECONOMY

Overview: the economy, based on agriculture, has recovered from military coups, droughts and a drop in tourism; sugar exports are a major source of income
GDP: US$4.822 billion, per capita US$5,600; real growth rate 4.6% (2002 est.)
Inflation: 2.0% (2002 est.)
Industries: accounts for 25% of GDP (2000); sugar, copra, tourism, gold, silver, fishing, clothing, lumber, small cottage industries
Labour Force: approx. 235,000; 70% of the population is engaged in agriculture and subsistence farming
Unemployment: n.a.
Agriculture: accounts for 17% of GDP (2000); principal cash crop is sugar cane; coconuts, cassava, rice, sweet potatoes and bananas; small livestock sector includes cattle, pigs, horses and goats; annual fish catch is significant
Natural Resources: timber, fish, gold, copper, offshore oil potential

■ FINANCE/TRADE

Currency: Fijian dollar ($F) = 100 cents
International Reserves Excluding Gold: US$424 million (Dec. 2003)
Gold Reserves: 0.001 million fine troy ounces (Jan. 2004)
Budget: revenues US$427 million; expenditures US$531.4 million, including capital expenditures US$ n.a. (2000 est.)
Defence Expenditures: 2.2% of GDP (2002)
Education Expenditures: 12.2% of total government expenditures (2002)
External Debt: US$210 million (2002)
Exports: US$550 million (2002); commodities: sugar 49%, garments, gold, copra, processed fish, lumber; partners: Australia, US, UK, Japan, other Pacific island countries, New Zealand
Imports: US$898 million (2002); commodities: food 15%, petroleum products, machinery, consumer goods; partners: New Zealand, Australia, Singapore, Japan, Hong Kong, US, Taiwan

■ COMMUNICATIONS

Daily Newspapers: 1 in total
Televisions: n.a.
Radios: n.a.
Telephones: 114 lines/1,000 inhabitants (2002)
Internet: hosts: 785 (2002); users: 50,000 (2002)

■ TRANSPORTATION

Motor Vehicles: 59,000; 30,000 passenger cars
Roads: 3,440 km; 1,692 km paved
Railway: 597 km
Air Traffic: 620,000 passengers carried (2001 est.)
Airports: 27; 3 have paved runways (2002 est.)

Canadian Embassy: Consulate of Canada, P.O. Box 10690, Nadi Airport, Suva, Fiji. Tel: (011 679) 72 24 00. Fax (011 679) 72 19 36. e-mail: none
Embassy in Canada: c/o Embassy of the Republic of Fiji, 630 Third Ave, 7th Fl, New York NY 10017, USA. Tel: (212) 687-4130. Fax: (212) 687-3963. e-mail: n.a.

Finland

Long-Form Name: Republic of Finland
Capital: Helsinki

■ GEOGRAPHY

Area: 337,030 sq. km
Coastline: 1,126 km excluding islands and coastal indentations
Climate: cold temperate; potentially subarctic, but comparatively mild because of moderating influence of the North Atlantic Current, Baltic Sea and more than 60,000 lakes
Environment: permanently wet ground covers approx. 30% of land; air and water pollution
Terrain: mostly low, flat to rolling plains interspersed with lakes and low hills
Land Use: arable land: 6.98%, permanent crops: 0.01%, other: 93.01%; includes 640 sq. km irrigated
Location: N Europe, bordering on Baltic Sea

■ PEOPLE

Population: 5,190,785 (July 2003 est.)
Nationality: Finn
Age Structure: 0–14 yrs: 17.7%; 15–64: 66.9%; 65+: 15.4% (2003 est.)
Population Growth Rate: 0.14% (2003 est.)
Net Migration: 0.63 migrants/1,000 population (2003 est.)
Ethnic Groups: 93% Finn, 6% Swede, 0.11% Lapp, 0.12% Gypsy, 0.02% Tatar
Languages: 93.5% Finnish, 6.3% Swedish (both official); small Lapp- and Russian-speaking minorities; business language is English
Religions: 89% Evangelical Lutheran, 9% atheist, 1% Eastern Orthodox, 1% other
Birth Rate: 10.54/1,000 population (2003 est.)
Death Rate: 9.82/1,000 population (2003 est.)
Infant Mortality: 3.73 deaths/1,000 live births (2003 est.)
Life Expectancy at Birth: 74.28 years male, 81.68 years female (2003 est.)
Total Fertility Rate: 1.70 children born/woman (2003 est.)
Literacy: approaching 100% (2002)

■ GOVERNMENT

Leader(s): President Tarja Halonen, Prime Minister Matti Taneli Vanhanen
Government Type: republic
Administrative Divisions: 6 provinces (laanit, sing. -laani)
Nationhood: Dec. 6, 1917 (from Soviet Union)
National Holiday: Independence Day, Dec. 6

■ ECONOMY

Overview: the manufacturing sector and trade are vital to this highly industrialized, largely free market economy; because of the climate, agricultural development is limited to maintaining self-sufficiency in basic products. Unemployment is a continuing problem.
GDP: US$133.8 billion, per capita US$25,800; real growth rate 1.6% (2002)
Inflation: 1.9% (2002 est.)
Industries: accounts for 34% of GDP (2002 est.); metal manufacturing and shipbuilding, forestry

and wood processing (pulp, paper), copper refining, foodstuffs, textiles, clothing
Labour Force: 2.6 million (2002); 32% com-. munity, social and business services, 22% industry, 14% commerce, 32% other
Unemployment: 11.7% (Feb. 2004)
Agriculture: accounts for 4% of GDP (2002 est.) (including forestry); livestock production, especially dairy cattle, predominates; forestry is an important export earner; main crops—cereals, sugar beets, potatoes; 85% self-sufficient, but short of food and fodder grains
Natural Resources: timber, copper, zinc, iron ore, silver

■ FINANCE/TRADE

Currency: markkaa, or Finmark = 100 pennia; Euro (€); on January 1, 2002 the Euro became the sole currency for everyday transactions.
International Reserves Excluding Gold: US$10.764 billion (Jan. 2004)
Gold Reserves: 1.577 million fine troy ounces (Jan. 2004)
Budget: revenues US$36.1 billion; expenditures US$31 billion, including capital expenditures of US$ n.a. (2000 est.)
Defence Expenditures: 4.4% of central government expenditure (2002)
Education Expenditures: 12.4% of total government expenditures (2002)
External Debt: n.a.
Exports: US$52.340 billion (2003 est.); commodities: timber, paper and pulp, ships, machinery, clothing and footwear; partners: Germany, US, UK, Sweden, Russia, France
Imports: US$41.133 billion (2003 est.); commodities: foodstuffs, petroleum and petroleum products, chemicals, transport equipment, iron and steel, machinery, textile yarn and fabrics, fodder grains; partners: Germany, Sweden, Russia, US, UK, France

■ COMMUNICATIONS

Daily Newspapers: 445/1,000 inhabitants (2000)
Televisions: 670/1,000 inhabitants (2002)
Radios: 1,624/1,000 inhabitants (2001)
Telephones: 523 lines/1,000 inhabitants (2002)
Internet: hosts: 1,220,062 (2002); users: 2.65 million (2002)

■ TRANSPORTATION

Motor Vehicles: 2,400,000; 2,100,000 passenger cars
Roads: 77,943 km; 50,305 km paved
Railway: 5,850 km
Air Traffic: 6,414,000 passengers carried (2002)

Airports: 150; 74 have paved runways (2003 est.)

Canadian Embassy: The Canadian Embassy, Pohjois Esplanadi 25B, 00100 Helsinki; mailing address: Box 779, 00101 Helsinki, Finland. Tel: (011-358-9) 22-85-30. Fax (011-358-9) 60-10-60. e-mail: hsnki@dfait-maeci.gc.ca
Embassy in Canada: Embassy of Finland, 55 Metcalfe St, Ste 850, Ottawa ON K1P 6L5. Tel: (613) 288-2233 Fax: (613) 288-2244. e-mail: embassy@finland.ca

---

France

Long-Form Name: French Republic
Capital: Paris

■ GEOGRAPHY

Area: 547,030 sq. km; includes Corsica and the rest of metropolitan France, but excludes the overseas administrative divisions
Coastline: 3,427 km (includes Corsica, 644 km)
Climate: generally cool winters and mild summers, but mild winters and hot summers along the Mediterranean
Environment: most of large urban areas and industrial centres in Rhône, Garonne, Seine or Loire River basins; occasional warm, tropical winds known as mistrals are in central south; air and water pollution; acid rain
Terrain: mostly flat plains or gently rolling hills in north and west; remainder is mountainous, especially Pyrenees in south and Alps in east
Land Use: arable land: 33.3%, permanent crops: 2.11%, other: 64.59%; includes 20,000 sq. km irrigated
Location: W Europe, bordering on Atlantic Ocean, Mediterranean Sea

■ PEOPLE

Population: 60,180,529 (July 2003 est.)
Nationality: Frenchman, Frenchwoman
Age Structure: 0–14 yrs: 18.6%; 15–64: 65.1%; 65+: 16.3% (2003 est.)
Population Growth Rate: 0.42% (2003 est.)
Net Migration: 0.66 migrants/1,000 population (2003 est.)
Ethnic Groups: Celtic and Latin with Teutonic, Slavic, North African, Indochinese and Basque minorities
Languages: French (100% of population); rapidly declining regional dialects (Provençal, Breton, Alsatian, Corsican, Catalan, Basque, Flemish)
Religions: 90% Roman Catholic, 2% Protestant, 1% Jewish, 1% Muslim (North African workers), 6% unaffiliated

Birth Rate: 12.54/1,000 population (2003 est.)
Death Rate: 9.05/1,000 population (2003 est.)
Infant Mortality: 4.37 deaths/1,000 live births (2003 est.)
Life Expectancy at Birth: 75.63 years male, 83.11 years female (2003 est.)
Total Fertility Rate: 1.85 children born/woman (2003 est.)
Literacy: approaching 100% (2002)

■ GOVERNMENT

Leader(s): President Jacques Chirac, Prime Minister Jean-Pierre Raffarin
Government Type: republic
Administrative Divisions: 22 regions; dependent areas includes Bassas da India, Clipperton Island, Europa Island, Glorioso Islands, Juan de Nova Island, Tromelin Island, French Polynesia, Guadeloupe, Guiana (French Guiana), Martinique, Mayotte, New Caledonia, Réunion, St. Pierre and Miquelon, Southern and Antarctic Territories, Wallis and Futuna Islands
Nationhood: unified by Clovis in 486, First Republic proclaimed in 1792
National Holiday: Taking of the Bastille, July 14

■ ECONOMY

Overview: one of the world's most developed economies; largely self-sufficient in agricultural products; the leading agricultural producer in Western Europe; highly diversified industrial sector; economic integration into the European Community has unknown consequences; unemployment is rising rapidly
GDP: US$1.558 trillion, per capita US$26,000 real growth rate 1.2% (2002)
Inflation: 1.8% (2002 est.)
Industries: accounts for 26% of GDP (2002 est.); steel, machinery, chemicals, automobiles, metallurgy, aircraft, electronics, mining, textiles, food processing, tourism
Labour Force: 27.0 million (2002); 71% community, social and business services, 25% industry, 4% agriculture
Unemployment: 8.9% (2002)
Agriculture: accounts for 3% of GNP (2002 est.) (including fishing and forestry); one of the world's top five wheat producers; self-sufficient for most temperate-zone foods; shortages include fats and oils and tropical produce, but overall net exporter of farm products
Natural Resources: coal, iron ore, bauxite, fish, timber, zinc, potash

■ FINANCE/TRADE

Currency: franc (F or FF) = 100 centimes; Euro (€); on January 1, 2002, the Euro became the sole currency for everyday transactions
International Reserves Excluding Gold: US$34.731 billion (Jan. 2004)
Gold Reserves: 97.245 million fine troy ounces (Jan. 2004)
Budget: revenues US$217 billion; expenditures US$274 billion, including capital expenditures of US$23 billion (2003 est.)
Defence Expenditures: 6.4% of central government expenditure (2002)
Education Expenditures: 11.5% of total government expenditures (2002)
External Debt: n.a.
Exports: US$365.359 billion (2003 est.); commodities: machinery and transportation equipment, chemicals, foodstuffs, agricultural products, iron and steel products, textiles and clothing; partners: Germany, UK, Spain, Italy, US
Imports: US$370.351 billion (2003 est.); commodities: crude oil, machinery and equipment, agricultural products, chemicals, iron and steel products; partners: Germany, Benelux, Italy, UK, US

■ COMMUNICATIONS

Daily Newspapers: 201/1,000 inhabitants (2000)
Televisions: 632/1,000 inhabitants (2002)
Radios: 950/1,000 inhabitants (2001)
Telephones: 569/1,000 inhabitants (2002)
Internet: hosts: 1,388,681 (2002); users: 18.716 million (2002)

■ TRANSPORTATION

Motor Vehicles: 34,300,000; 28,500,000 passenger cars
Roads: 894,000 km; all paved
Railway: 32,682 km
Air Traffic: 49,096,000 passengers carried (2002)
Airports: 477; 273 have paved runways (2003 est.)

Canadian Embassy: The Canadian Embassy, 35-37 avenue Montaigne, 75008, Paris, France. Tel: (011-33-1) 44-43-29-00. Fax: (011-33-1) 44-43-29-99. e-mail: paris@dfait-maeci.gc.ca
Embassy in Canada: Embassy of France, 42 Sussex Dr, Ottawa ON K1M 2C9. Tel: (613) 789-1795. Fax: (613) 562-3735. e-mail: politique@ambafrance-ca.org

French Guiana

Long-Form Name: Department of Guiana
Capital: Cayenne

■ GEOGRAPHY

Area: 91,000 sq. km
Coastline: 378 km
Climate: tropical, warm and humid, little seasonal temperature variation
Terrain: low-lying coastal plains rising to hills and small mountains
Land Use: arable land: 0.11%, NEGL permanent crops: 0.03%, other: 99.86%, (90%, forest, 10%, other); 20 sq. km are irrigated
Location: N South America, bordering on Atlantic Ocean

■ PEOPLE

Population: 186,917 (July 2003 est.)
Nationality: French Guianese
Ethnic Groups: 66% black or mulatto, 12% Caucasian, 12% East Indian, Chinese, Amerindian, 10% other
Languages: French (official), Creole patois

■ GOVERNMENT

Colony/Territory of: Overseas Department of France
Leader(s): Head of State: President Jacques Chirac (France); Prefect Ange Mancini, President of General Council Antoine Karam
Government Type: overseas department of France
National Holiday: Taking of the Bastille, July 14

■ ECONOMY

Overview: economy is closely tied to that of France through subsidies and imports; agriculture: rice, manioc, sugar cane, livestock; forestry, fisheries, food processing industry; chief trading partners: France, EU countries, Japan, US; unemployment is particularly serious among younger workers

■ FINANCE/TRADE

Currency: French franc = 100 centimes, Euro (€)

Canadian Embassy: c/o The Canadian Embassy, 35-57 avenue Montaigne, Paris 75008, France. Tel: (011-33-1) 44-43-29-00. Fax: (011-3-1) 44-43-29-99. e-mail: paris@dfait-maeci.gc.ca
Representative to Canada: c/o Embassy of France, 42 Sussex Dr, Ottawa ON K1M 2C9. Tel: (613) 789-1795. Fax: (613) 562-3735. e-mail: politique@ambafrance-ca.org

French Polynesia

Long-Form Name: Territory of French Polynesia
Capital: Papeete (Windward Islands)

■ GEOGRAPHY

Area: 4,167 sq. km, consisting of five island archipelagoes scattered widely over Eastern Pacific; uninhabited Clipperton Territory is a dependency of French Polynesia but does not form part of the territory
Climate: warm and humid; tropical but moderate
Environment:
Land Use: arable land: 1.64%, permanent crops: 6.01%, other: 92.35%
Location: south Pacific Ocean, NE of New Zealand

■ PEOPLE

Population: 262,125 (July 2003 est.)
Nationality: French Polynesian
Ethnic Groups: 78% Polynesian, 12% Chinese, 6% local French, 4% metropolitan French
Languages: French and Tahitian (both official)

■ GOVERNMENT

Colony/Territory of: Overseas Territory of France
Leader(s): President Jacques Chirac (France), represented by High Commissioner to French Polynesia Michel Mathieu
Government Type: French overseas territory
National Holiday: Taking of the Bastille, July 14

■ ECONOMY

Overview: agriculture: copra, tropical fruits grown for local consumption; tourism accounts for approximately 20% of GDP and is primary source of revenue; trading partners: France, UK, US

■ FINANCE/TRADE

Currency: CFP franc = 100 centimes

Canadian Embassy: c/o The Canadian Embassy, 35-37 avenue Montaigne, Paris 75008, France. Tel: (011-33-1) 44-43-29-00. Fax: (011-33-1) 44-43-29-99. e-mail: paris@dfait-maeci.gc.ca
Representative to Canada: c/o Embassy of France, 42 Sussex Dr, Ottawa ON K1M 2C9. Tel: (613) 789-1795. Fax: (613) 562-3735. e-mail: politique@ambafrance-ca.org

Gabon

Long-Form Name: Gabonese Republic
Capital: Libreville

■ GEOGRAPHY

Area: 267,667 sq. km
Coastline: 885 km
Climate: tropical; always hot, humid
Environment: deforestation and poaching

Terrain: narrow coastal plain; hilly interior; savanna in east and south
Land Use: arable land: 1.26%, permanent crops: 0.66%, other: 98.08%; includes 150 sq. km irrigated
Location: WC Africa, bordering on South Atlantic Ocean

■ PEOPLE

Population: 1,321,560 (July 2003 est.)
Nationality: Gabonese (sing. & pl.)
Age Structure: 0–14 yrs: 42.3%; 15–64: 53.5%; 65+: 4.2% (2003 est.)
Population Growth Rate: 0.97% (2003 est.)
Net Migration: 0 migrants/1,000 population (2003 est.)
Ethnic Groups: about 40 Bantu tribes, including four major tribal groupings (Fang, Eshira, Bapounou, Bateke); approx. 154,000 other Africans and Europeans, including 6,000 French and 11,000 persons of mixed background
Languages: French (official), Fang, Myene, Bateke, Bapounou/Eschira, Bandjabi
Religions: 55–75% Roman Catholic, 1% Muslim, remainder animist
Birth Rate: 36.54/1,000 population (2003 est.)
Death Rate: 11.17/1,000 population (2003 est.)
Infant Mortality: 55.05 deaths/1,000 live births (2003 est.)
Life Expectancy at Birth: 55.45 years male, 58.84 years female (2003 est.)
Total Fertility Rate: 4.83 children born/woman (2003 est.)
Literacy: 71.0% (2002)

■ GOVERNMENT

Leader(s): President El Hadj Omar Bongo, Premier Jean-François Ntoutoume-Emane
Government Type: republic; multiparty presidential regime
Administrative Divisions: 9 provinces
Nationhood: Aug. 17, 1960 (from France)
National Holiday: Founding of the Gabonese Democratic Party, March 12

■ ECONOMY

Overview: economy is dependent on oil, which has contributed to an increase in per capita income; agricultural and industrial sectors are relatively underdeveloped
GDP: US$8.354 billion, per capita US$6,500; real growth rate 0.2% (2002 est.)
Inflation: 2.3% (2002 est.)
Industries: accounts for 60% of GDP; sawmills, cement, petroleum, food and beverages; mining of increasing importance (especially manganese and uranium)

Labour Force: 600,000 (2002); 60% agriculture, 15% industry, 25% services
Unemployment: n.a.
Agriculture: accounts for 10% of GDP (including fishing and forestry); cash crops—cocoa, coffee, palm oil; livestock not developed; importer of food; okoume (a tropical softwood) is the most important timber product; rubber; fish
Natural Resources: crude oil, manganese, uranium, gold, timber, iron ore

■ FINANCE/TRADE

Currency: Communauté financière africaine franc (CFAF) = 100 centimes
International Reserves Excluding Gold: US$197 million (Dec. 2003)
Gold Reserves: 0.013 million fine troy ounces (Dec. 2003)
Budget: revenues US$1.8 billion; expenditures US$1.8 billion, capital expenditures US$310 million (2002 est.)
Defence Expenditures: 2.0% of GDP (2002)
Education Expenditures: n.a.
External Debt: US$3.533 billion (2002)
Exports: US$2.646 billion (2001); commodities: crude oil 70%, manganese 11%, wood 12%, uranium 6%; partners: France, US, China, Netherlands Antilles
Imports: US$858 million (2001); commodities: foodstuffs, chemical products, petroleum products, construction materials, manufacturers, machinery; partners: France, US, Belgium, Côte d'Ivoire

■ COMMUNICATIONS

Daily Newspapers: 30/1,000 inhabitants (2000)
Televisions: 308/1,000 inhabitants (2002)
Radios: 501/1,000 inhabitants (2001)
Telephones: 25 lines/1,000 inhabitants (2002)
Internet: hosts: 79 (2002); users: 25,000 (2002)

■ TRANSPORTATION

Motor Vehicles: 39,500; 23,800 passenger cars
Roads: 8,454 km; 838 km paved
Railway: 814 km
Air Traffic: 366,000 passengers carried (2002)
Airports: 57; 10 have paved runways (2003 est.)

Canadian Embassy: The Canadian Embassy, P.O. Box 4037 Libreville, Gabon. Tel: (011-241) 73-73-54. Fax: (011-241) 73-73-88. e-mail: lbrve@dfait-maeci.gc.ca
Embassy in Canada: Embassy of the Gabonese Republic, 4 Range Rd, Ottawa ON K1N 8J5. Tel: (613) 232-5301. Fax: (613) 232-6916. e-mail: ambgabon@sprint.ca

Gambia

Long-Form Name: Republic of the Gambia
Capital: Banjul

■ GEOGRAPHY

Area: 11,300 sq. km
Coastline: 80 km
Climate: tropical; hot, rainy season (June to Nov.); cooler, dry season (Nov. to May)
Environment: deforestation and desertification; diseases spread through the water supply are common
Terrain: flood plain of the Gambia River flanked by some low hills
Land Use: arable land: 19.5%, permanent crops: 0.5%, other: 80%; includes 20 sq. km irrigated
Location: W Africa, bordering on Atlantic Ocean

■ PEOPLE

Population: 1,501,050 (July 2003 est.)
Nationality: Gambian
Age Structure: 0–14 yrs: 44.9%; 15–64: 52.4%; 65+: 2.7% (2003 est.)
Population Growth Rate: 3.03% (2003 est.)
Net Migration: 1.89 migrants/1,000 population (2003 est.)
Ethnic Groups: 99% African (42% Mandinka, 18% Fula, 16% Wolof, 10% Jola, 9% Serahuli, 4% other); 1% non-Gambian
Languages: English (official); Mandinka, Wolof, Fula, other indigenous vernaculars
Religions: 90% Muslim, 9% Christian, 1% indigenous beliefs
Birth Rate: 40.77/1,000 population (2003 est.)
Death Rate: 12.35/1,000 population (2003 est.)
Infant Mortality: 74.93 deaths/1,000 live births (2003 est.)
Life Expectancy at Birth: 52.39 years male, 56.44 years female (2003 est.)
Total Fertility Rate: 5.53 children born/woman (2003 est.)
Literacy: 37.8% (2002)

■ GOVERNMENT

Leader(s): Head of State Yahya Jammeh, Vice President Isatou Njie-Saidy
Government Type: republic
Administrative Divisions: 5 divisions and 1 city (Banjul)
Nationhood: Feb. 18, 1965 (from UK)
National Holiday: Independence Day, Feb. 18

■ ECONOMY

Overview: a poor country, lacking in natural resources and possessing a limited agricultural base of peanut products; the recent rebound in tourism has helped the economy
GDP: US$2.582 billion, per capita US$1,800; real growth rate 5.7% (2002 est.)
Inflation: 5.5% (2002 est.)
Industries: accounts for 12% of GDP; peanut processing, tourism, beverages, agricultural machinery assembly, woodworking, metal-working, clothing
Labour Force: 700,000 (2002); 75% agriculture, 19% industry, commerce and services, 6% government
Unemployment: 13.8% (2001)
Agriculture: accounts for 21% of GDP; imports one-third of food requirements; major export crop is peanuts; also millet, sorghum, rice, corn; forestry and fishing resources not fully exploited
Natural Resources: fish

■ FINANCE/TRADE

Currency: dalasi (D) = 100 butut
International Reserves Excluding Gold: US$102 million (June 2003)
Gold Reserves: n.a.
Budget: revenues US$90.5 million; expenditures US$80.9 million, including capital expenditures US$4.1 million (2001 est.)
Defence Expenditures: 0.3% of GDP (2002)
Education Expenditures: 14.2% of total government expenditures (200)
External Debt: US$573 million (2002)
Exports: US$2.0 million (2002); commodities: peanuts and peanut products, fish, cotton lint, palm kernels; partners: Benelux, Japan, UK, Brazil
Imports: US$148 million (2002); commodities: foodstuffs, manufacturers, raw materials, fuel, machinery and transport equipment; partners: China, UK, Netherlands, France, Brazil

■ COMMUNICATIONS

Daily Newspapers: 2/1,000 inhabitants (2000)
Televisions: 15/1,000 inhabitants (2002)
Radios: 396/1,000 inhabitants (2001)
Telephones: 28 lines/1,000 inhabitants (2002)
Internet: hosts: 568 (2002); users: 25,000 (2002)

■ TRANSPORTATION

Motor Vehicles: 9,000; 8,000 passenger cars
Roads: 2,700 km; 956 km paved
Railway: none
Air Traffic: n.a.

Airports: 1, with paved runway (2003 est.)

Canadian Embassy: The Canadian High Commission to the Gambia, c/o The Canadian Embassy, P.O. Box 3373, Dakar, Senegal. Tel: (011-221) 889-4700. Fax: (011-221) 889-4720. e-mail: dakar@dfait-maeci.gc.ca
Embassy in Canada: c/o High Commission for the Republic of the Gambia, 1155 15th St NW, Ste 905, Washington DC 20005 USA. Tel: (202) 785-1399. Fax: (202) 785-1430. e-mail: n.a.

Gaza Strip

Long-Form Name: none
Capital: none

■ GEOGRAPHY

Area: 360 sq. km
Climate: temperate, mild winters, dry and warm to hot summers
Land Use: arable land: 26.32%, permanent crops: 39.47%, other: 34.21%; includes 120 sq. km irrigated
Location: Middle East, bordering on Mediterranean Sea, Egypt and Israel.

■ PEOPLE

Population: 1,274,868, plus more than 5,000 Israeli settlers (July 2002)
Nationality: n.a.
Ethnic Groups: Palestinian Arab and other 99.4%, Jewish 0.6%
Languages: Arabic, Hebrew (spoken by Israeli settlers and many Palestinians), English (widely understood)

■ GOVERNMENT

Colony/Territory of: claimed and occupied by Israel
Leader(s): local Palestinian authority is headed by Yasser Arafat, subject to Israeli authority
Government Type: Palestinian Legislative Council (Jan. 1996) has limited powers under interim self-governing agreements with Israel. Originally designated as a five-year interim arrangement in 1993, permanent status still under negotiation
National Holiday: n.a.

■ ECONOMY

Overview: economic conditions in the Gaza Strip, under the responsibility of the Palestinian Authority since the Cairo Agreement of May 1994, have deteriorated since the early 1990s; the most serious negative social effect has been the emergence of chronic unemployment, which has risen to over 20%

■ FINANCE/TRADE

Currency: 1 new Israeli shekel = 100 new agorot

Canadian Embassy: n.a.
Representative to Canada: n.a.

Georgia

Long-Form Name: Republic of Georgia
Capital: T'bilisi

■ GEOGRAPHY

Area: 69,700 sq. km
Coastline: 310 km
Climate: Alpine to subtropical with warm, humid coastlands
Environment: soil, air and water pollution from toxic chemicals
Terrain: largely mountainous in north and south; lowlands open to Black Sea in west; Kura River Basin in east; good soils in river valley, flood plains and lowlands
Land Use: arable land: 11.21%, permanent crops: 4.09%, other: 84.7%; includes 4,700 sq. km irrigated
Location: SW Asia, bordering on Black Sea

■ PEOPLE

Population: 4,934,413 (July 2003 est.)
Nationality: Georgian
Age Structure: 0–14 yrs: 18.6%; 15–64: 68.4%; 65+: 13.0% (2003 est.)
Population Growth Rate: -0.52% (2003 est.)
Net Migration: -2.30 migrants/1,000 population (2003 est.)
Ethnic Groups: 70.1% Georgian, 8.1% Armenian, 6.3% Russian, 5.7% Azerbaijani, 3% Ossetian, 1.9% Greek, 1.8% Abkhazian, 1% Ukrainian, 2.1% other
Languages: Armenian 7%, Azeri 6%, Georgian 71% (official), Russian 9%, other 7%
Religions: Christian Orthodox 75%, Muslim 11%, Armenian Apostolic 8%, unknown 6%
Birth Rate: 11.79/1,000 population (2003 est.)
Death Rate: 14.71/1,000 population (2003 est.)
Infant Mortality: 51.24 deaths/1,000 live births (2003 est.)
Life Expectancy at Birth: 61.33 years male, 68.36 years female (2003 est.)
Total Fertility Rate: 1.51 children born/woman (2003 est.)
Literacy: approaching 100% (2002)

■ GOVERNMENT

Leader(s): President Mikheil Saakashvili, Prime Minister Zurab Zhvania
Government Type: republic
Administrative Divisions: 53 rayons (raionebi, sing. —raioni), 9 cities (k'alak'ebi, sing. — k'alak'i) and 2 autonomous regions (avtomnoy respubliki, sing. —avtom respublika)
Nationhood: April 9, 1991 (from Soviet Union)
National Holiday: Independence Day, May 26

■ ECONOMY

Overview: Steel processing and light industry predominate; agriculture hindered by extensive wooded areas; international transportation services through key ports are Georgia's main hope for the future
GDP: US$16.05 billion, per capita US$3,200; real growth rate 5.4% (2002)
Inflation: 5.2% (2002 est.)
Industries: accounts for 25% of GDP (2002 est.); coal and non-ferrous metals refining, machinery and instruments, electrical engineering, chemical production, food processing, cloth, hosiery, shoes, vehicles, mining, esp. manganese, coal, baryta
Labour Force: 2.6 million (2002); 20% industry and construction, 40% agriculture and forestry, 40% services
Unemployment: 11.0% (2002 est.)
Agriculture: accounts for 20% of GDP (2002 est.); grapes, tobacco, bay leaves, tea, citrus fruit, sugar, vegetables, grains, tobacco, tung, silk, orchard fruit, potatoes, livestock
Natural Resources: manganese deposits; sulphur and other medicinal springs, forest resources, hydro power, coal and oil

■ FINANCE/TRADE

Currency: lari (GEL) = 100 tetri
International Reserves Excluding Gold: n.a.
Gold Reserves: none (Jan. 2002)
Budget: revenues US$499 million; expenditures US$554 million, including capital expenditures of US$ n.a. (2001 est.)
Defence Expenditures: 4.9% of total government expenditure (2002)
Education Expenditures: 13.1% of central government expenditure (2002)
External Debt: US$1.838 billion (2002)
Exports: US$349 million (2002); grain, fruit, vegetables, tea, electric mine cars, seamless pipes; partners: Russia, Turkey, Azerbaijan, US, Germany
Imports: US$733 million (2002); fuel, foodstuffs, machinery, equipment; partners: Russia, Turkey, Azerbaijan, Germany, US

■ COMMUNICATIONS

Daily Newspapers: 5/1,000 inhabitants (2000)
Televisions: 357/1,000 inhabitants (2002)
Radios: 556/1,000 inhabitants (2001)
Telephones: 131 lines/1,000 inhabitants (2002)
Internet: hosts: 3,032 (2002); users: 73,500 (2002)

■ TRANSPORTATION

Motor Vehicles: 345,000; 270,000 passenger cars
Roads: 20,362 km; 19,038 km hard-surfaced
Railway: 1,612 km
Air Traffic: 112,000 passengers carried (2002)
Airports: 40; 22 have paved runways (2003 est.)

Canadian Embassy: The Canadian Embassy to Georgia, c/o The Canadian Embassy, Nenehatun Caddesi No. 75, Gaziosmanpasa 06700, Ankara, Turkey. Tel: (011-90-312) 459-9200. Fax: (011-90-312) 459-9362. e-mail: ankra@dfait-maeci.gc.ca
Embassy in Canada: c/o Embassy of the Republic of Georgia, 1615 New Hampshire Ave. NW, Suite 300, Washington DC 20009, USA. Tel: (202) 387-2390. Fax: (202) 393-4537. e-mail: n.a.

Germany

Long-Form Name: Federal Republic of Germany
Capital: Berlin

■ GEOGRAPHY

Area: 357,021 sq. km
Coastline: 2,389 km
Climate: temperate; cool, wet summers; cool to cold, cloudy winters with frequent rain and snow; occasional warm, tropical föhn wind; high relative humidity
Environment: air and water pollution; significant deforestation in mountain regions due to environmental pollution
Terrain: flat plains; lowlands in north; central uplands; Bavarian Alps in southwest
Land Use: arable land: 33.88%, permanent crops: 0.65%, other: 65.47%; includes 4,850 sq. km irrigated
Location: NC Europe, bordering on North Sea, Baltic Sea

■ PEOPLE

Population: 82,398,326 (July 2003 est.)
Nationality: German
Age Structure: 0–14 yrs: 14.9%; 15–64: 67.3%; 65+: 17.8% (2003 est.)
Population Growth Rate: 0.04% (2003 est.)
Net Migration: 2.18 migrants/1,000 population (2003 est.)

Ethnic Groups: German 91.5%, Turkish 2.4%, Italian 0.7%, Greek 0.4%. Polish 0.4%, other 4.6%
Languages: German (official)
Religions: 45% Protestant, 37% Roman Catholic, 18% unaffiliated
Birth Rate: 8.60/1,000 population (2003 est.)
Death Rate: 10.34/1,000 population (2003 est.)
Infant Mortality: 4.23 deaths/1,000 live births (2003 est.)
Life Expectancy at Birth: 75.46 years male, 81.55 years female (2003 est.)
Total Fertility Rate: 1.37 children born/woman (2003 est.)
Literacy: approaching 100% (2002)

■ GOVERNMENT

Leader(s): President Horst Koehler, Chancellor Gerhard Schroeder
Government Type: federal republic
Administrative Divisions: 16 states (Laender, sing. —Land)
Nationhood: January 18, 1871 (unification of German Empire); West Germany and East Germany were unified on Oct. 3, 1990
National Holiday: German Unity Day, Oct. 3

■ ECONOMY

Overview: possesses the world's third most technologically powerful economy, after the US and Japan, but its capitalistic economy has begun to struggle under the burden of generous social benefits; unemployment is a long-term, not just cyclical, problem; the integration and upgrading of the Eastern German economy remains a costly long-term problem
GDP: US$2.16 trillion, per capita US$26,200; real growth rate 0.2% (2002)
Inflation: 1.3% (2002 est.)
Industries: accounts for 31% of GDP (2002 est.); iron, steel, coal, chemicals, vehicles, ships, machinery, food and beverages, electronics, brown coal, shipbuilding, textiles, petroleum refining
Labour Force: 41.1 million (2002); 33% industry, 64% community, social and business services, 3% agriculture
Unemployment: 12.3% (Feb. 2004)
Agriculture: agriculture, including fishing and forestry, accounts for about 1% of GDP (2000); diversified crop and livestock farming, including wheat, potatoes, barley, sugar beets, fruit, cabbages, livestock products; net importer of food
Natural Resources: iron ore, coal, potash, natural gas, copper, salt, nickel, timber

■ FINANCE/TRADE

Currency: Deutsche Mark (DM) = 100 Pfennige; Euro (€); on January 1, 2002, the Euro became the sole currency for everyday transactions
International Reserves Excluding Gold: US$50.971 billion (Jan. 2004)
Gold Reserves: 110.584 million fine troy ounces (Jan. 2004)
Budget: revenues US$802 billion; expenditures US$825 billion, including capital expenditures US$ n.a. (2001 est.)
Defence Expenditures: 4.7% of central government expenditure (2002)
Education Expenditures: 9.9% of total government expenditures (2002)
External Debt: n.a.
Exports: US$478.609 billion (2003); manufactured goods 88%, agricultural products 5%, raw materials 2.3%, other 4.7%; partners: France, US, UK, Netherlands, Austria, Belgium, Spain, Switzerland
Imports: US$601.828 billion (2003); manufactured goods 74%, agricultural products 10%, fuels 6.4%, raw materials 6%, other 3.6%; partners: France, Netherlands, US, UK, Italy, Belgium, Japan, Austria

■ COMMUNICATIONS

Daily Newspapers: 305/1,000 inhabitants (2000)
Televisions: 661/1,000 inhabitants (2002)
Radios: 570/1,000 inhabitants (2001)
Telephones: 651 lines/1,000 inhabitants (2002)
Internet: hosts: 2,594,323 (2002); users: 34 million (2002)

■ TRANSPORTATION

Motor Vehicles: 50,000,000; 43,000,000 passenger cars
Roads: 656,140 km; 650,891 km paved
Railway: 45,514 km
Air Traffic: 61,043,000 passengers carried (2002)
Airports: 551; 328 have paved runways (2003 est.)

Canadian Embassy: The Canadian Embassy, Friedrichstrasse 95, 10117, Berlin, Germany. Tel: (011-49-30) 20-312-0. Fax: (011-49-30) 20-312-590. e-mail: brlin@dfait-maeci.gc.ca
Embassy in Canada: Embassy of the Federal Republic of Germany, 1 Waverley St, Ottawa ON K2P 0T8. Tel: (613) 232-1101. Fax: (613) 594-9330. e-mail: GermanEmbassyOttawa@ on.aibn.com

Ghana

Long-Form Name: Republic of Ghana
Capital: Accra

■ GEOGRAPHY

Area: 238,540 sq. km
Coastline: 539 km
Climate: tropical; warm and comparatively dry along southeast coast; hot and humid in southwest; hot and dry in north
Environment: recent drought in north severely affecting marginal agricultural activities; deforestation; overgrazing; soil erosion; dry, northeasterly harmattan wind (Jan. to Mar.); water pollution and insufficient safe drinking water
Terrain: mostly low plains with dissected plateau in south-central area
Land Use: arable land: 15.82%, permanent crops: 7.47%, other: 76.71%; includes 110 sq. km irrigated
Location: WC Africa, bordering on South Atlantic Ocean

■ PEOPLE

Population: 20,467,747 (July 2003 est.)
Nationality: Ghanaian
Age Structure: 0–14 yrs: 38.9%; 15–64: 57.5%; 65+: 3.6% (2003 est.)
Population Growth Rate: 1.45% (2003 est.)
Net Migration: -0.83 migrants/1,000 population (2003 est.)
Ethnic Groups: 99.8% black African (major tribes—44% Akan, 16% Moshi-Dagomba, 13% Ewe, 8% Ga, 18.8% other), 0.2% European and other
Languages: English (official); African languages include Akan, Moshi-Dagomba, Ewe and Ga
Religions: 38% indigenous beliefs, 30% Muslim, 24% Christian, 8% other
Birth Rate: 25.84/1,000 population (2003 est.)
Death Rate: 10.53/1,000 population (2003 est.)
Infant Mortality: 53.02 deaths/1,000 live births (2003 est.)
Life Expectancy at Birth: 55.66 years male, 57.43 years female (2003 est.)
Total Fertility Rate: 3.32 children born/woman (2003 est.)
Literacy: 73.8% (2002)

■ GOVERNMENT

Leader(s): President John Agyekum Kufuor, Vice President Aliu Mahama
Government Type: constitutional democracy
Administrative Divisions: 10 regions
Nationhood: Mar. 6, 1957 (from UK, formerly known as Gold Coast)
National Holiday: Independence Day, Mar. 6

■ ECONOMY

Overview: heavily dependent on cocoa, gold and timber exports; international assistance boosts this economy, which depends on good harvests; population growth is a burden
GDP: US$41.25 billion, per capita US$2,000; real growth rate 4.5% (2002 est.)
Inflation: 14.5% (2002 est.)
Industries: accounts for 25% of GDP (2000); mining, lumbering, light manufacturing, fishing, aluminum, food processing
Labour Force: 9.7 million (2002); 60% agriculture, 15% industry, 25% services
Unemployment: n.a.
Agriculture: accounts for 36% of GDP (2000); major cash crop is cocoa; other crops: rice, coffee, cassava, peanuts, corn, bananas, timber; normally self-sufficient in food
Natural Resources: gold, timber, industrial diamonds, bauxite, manganese, fish, rubber

■ FINANCE/TRADE

Currency: cedi (C/) = 100 pesewas
International Reserves Excluding Gold: US$1.353 billion (Dec. 2003)
Gold Reserves: 0.281 million fine troy ounces (Dec. 2003)
Budget: revenues US$1.603 billion; expenditures US$1.975 billion, capital expenditures US$ n.a. (2001 est.)
Defence Expenditures: 0.6% of GDP (2002)
Education Expenditures: n.a.
External Debt: US$7.338 billion (2002)
Exports: US$2.642 billion (2003 est.); commodities: cocoa 60%, timber, gold, tuna, bauxite, and aluminum; partners: Togo, UK, Italy, Netherlands, Germany, US, France
Imports: US$3.24 billion (2003 est.); commodities: petroleum 16%, consumer goods, foods, intermediate goods, capital equipment; partners: US, UK, Nigeria, Germany, Italy, Spain

■ COMMUNICATIONS

Daily Newspapers: 14/1,000 inhabitants (2000)
Televisions: 53/1,000 inhabitants (2002)
Radios: 710/1,000 inhabitants (2001)
Telephones: 13 lines/1,000 inhabitants (2002)
Internet: hosts: 313 (2002); users: 170,000 (2002)

■ TRANSPORTATION

Motor Vehicles: 135,000; 90,000 passenger cars
Roads: 39,409 km; 11,665 km hard-surfaced
Railway: 953 km
Air Traffic: 256,000 passengers carried (2002)
Airports: 12; 7 have paved runways (2003 est.)

Canadian Embassy: Canadian High Commission, 42 Independence Ave, Accra, Ghana; P.O. Box 1639, Accra, Ghana. Tel: (011-233-21) 22-85-55. Fax: (011-233-21) 77-37-92. e-mail: accra@dfait-maeci.gc.ca
Embassy in Canada: High Commission for the Republic of Ghana, 1 Clemow Ave, Ottawa ON K1S 2A9. Tel: (613) 236-0871. Fax: (613) 236-0874. e-mail: n.a.

Gibraltar

Long-Form Name: Gibraltar
Capital: Gibraltar

■ GEOGRAPHY

Area: 6.5 sq. km
Climate: warm, temperate, low precipitation, mild winters, warm summers
Land Use: arable land: 0%, permanent crops: 0%, other: 100%
Location: Iberian Peninsula of S Spain, bordering on Mediterranean Sea

■ PEOPLE

Population: 27,776 (July 2003 est.)
Nationality: Gibraltarian
Ethnic Groups: Portuguese, Maltese, Spanish, Italian, English
Languages: English (used in schools and for official purposes), Spanish, Italian, Portuguese, Russian

■ GOVERNMENT

Colony/Territory of: Dependent Territory of United Kingdom
Leader(s): Head of State: Queen Elizabeth II, Governor Francis Richards, Chief Minister Peter Caruana
Government Type: dependent overseas territory of the UK
National Holiday: Commonwealth Day (second Monday in March), National Day, Sept. 10

■ ECONOMY

Overview: tourism most important; industries: construction materials, beverage bottling; re-exports: tobacco, petroleum, wine; exports of local products negligible; must import all food; more than 70% of the economy is in the public sector

■ FINANCE/TRADE

Currency: Gibraltar pound = 100 pence

Canadian Embassy: c/o The Canadian High Commission, Macdonald House, 1 Grosvenor Square, London W1K 4AB, England, UK. Tel:

(011-44-20) 7258-6600. Fax: (011-44-20) 7258-6333. e-mail: ldn@dfait-maeci.gc.ca
Representative to Canada: c/o British High Commission, 80 Elgin St, Ottawa ON K1P 5K7. Tel: (613) 237-1530. Fax: (613) 237-7980. e-mail should be sent using the appropriate form at the British High Commission's Website at http://www.britain-in-canada.org

Greece

Long-Form Name: Hellenic Republic
Capital: Athens

■ GEOGRAPHY

Area: 131,940 sq. km
Coastline: 13,676 km
Climate: temperate; mild, wet winter; hot, dry summer
Environment: subject to severe earthquakes; air pollution; archipelago of 2,000 islands; water pollution
Terrain: mostly mountainous with ranges extending into sea as peninsulas or chains of islands
Land Use: arable land: 22%, permanent crops: 8%, other: 70% (2004 est.); includes 14,220 sq. km irrigated
Location: S Europe, bordering on Adriatic Sea

■ PEOPLE

Population: 10,665,989 (July 2003 est.)
Nationality: Greek
Age Structure: 0–14 yrs: 14.7%; 15–64: 67.0%; 65+: 18.3% (2003 est.)
Population Growth Rate: 0.19% (2003 est.)
Net Migration: 1.96 migrants/1,000 population (2003 est.)
Ethnic Groups: 98% Greek, 2% others
Languages: Greek (official); English, German and French widely understood
Religions: 98% Greek Orthodox, 1.3% Muslim, 0.7% other
Birth Rate: 9.79/1,000 population (2003 est.)
Death Rate: 9.86/1,000 population (2003 est.)
Infant Mortality: 6.12 deaths/1,000 live births (2003 est.)
Life Expectancy at Birth: 76.32 years male, 81.65 years female (2003 est.)
Total Fertility Rate: 1.35 children born/woman (2003 est.)
Literacy: 97.3% (2002)

■ GOVERNMENT

Leader(s): President Konstandinos "Kostis" Stefanopoulos, Prime Minister Konstandinos Karamanlis

Government Type: presidential parliamentary government
Administrative Divisions: 51 prefectures (nomoi, sing. —omós) and 1 autonomous region
Nationhood: 1829 (from the Ottoman Empire)
National Holiday: Independence Day (proclamation of the war of independence), Mar. 25

■ ECONOMY

Overview: a large commodity trade deficit is offset by the successful tourism industry; economy is characterized by low GDP growth and high national debt
GDP: US$203.3 billion, per capita US$19,100; real growth rate 4.0% (2002)
Inflation: 3.6% (2002 est.)
Industries: accounts for 22% of GDP (2002); food and tobacco processing, textiles, chemicals, metal products, tourism, mining, petroleum
Labour Force: 4.6 million (2002); 20% agriculture, 59% community, social and business services, 21% industry
Unemployment: 9.6% (2002)
Agriculture: accounts for 8% of GDP (2002) (including fishing and forestry); self-sufficient in food; principal products—wheat, corn, barley, sugar beets, olives, tomatoes, wine, tobacco, potatoes, beef, mutton, pork, dairy products
Natural Resources: bauxite, lignite, magnesite, crude oil, marble, hydro power

■ FINANCE/TRADE

Currency: drachma (Dr) = 100 lepta; Euro (€); on January 1, 2002 the Euro became the sole currency for everyday transactions.
International Reserves Excluding Gold: US$3.593 billion (Jan. 2004)
Gold Reserves: 3.451 million fine troy ounces (Jan. 2004)
Budget: n.a.
Defence Expenditures: 15.6% of central government expenditure (2002)
Education Expenditures: 7.0% of total government expenditures (2002)
External Debt: US$63.4 billion (2002 est.)
Exports: US$10.315 billion (2002); commodities: manufactured goods, food and live animals, fuels and lubricants, raw materials; partners: Germany, Italy, UK, US
Imports: US$31.164 billion (2002); commodities: machinery and transport equipment, light manufactures, fuels and lubricants, foodstuffs, chemicals; partners: Italy, Germany, France, Netherlands

■ COMMUNICATIONS

Daily Newspapers: 23/1,000 inhabitants (2000)
Televisions: 519/1,000 inhabitants (2002)
Radios: 478/1,000 inhabitants (2001)
Telephones: 491 lines/1,000 inhabitants (2002)
Internet: hosts: 160,829 (2002); users: 1,704,900 (2002)

■ TRANSPORTATION

Motor Vehicles: 3,700,000; 2,700,000 passenger cars
Roads: 117,000 km; 107,406 km paved
Railway: 2,571 km
Air Traffic: 7,579,000 passengers carried (2002)
Airports: 79; 66 have paved runways (2003 est.)

Canadian Embassy: The Canadian Embassy, 4 Ioannou Gennadiou St, Athens 115 21, Greece. Tel: (011-30-210) 727-3400. Fax: (011-30-210) 727-3460. e-mail: athns@dfait-maeci.gc.ca
Embassy in Canada: Embassy of the Hellenic Republic, 80 MacLaren St, Ottawa ON K2P 0K6. Tel: (613) 238-6271. Fax: (613) 238-5676. e-mail: embassy@greekembassy.ca

Greenland

Long-Form Name: Grønland
Capital: Nuuk (Godthab)

■ GEOGRAPHY

Area: 2,175,600 sq. km
Climate: arctic to subarctic; cool summers, cold winters
Land Use: arable land: 0%, permanent crops: 0%, other: 100%
Location: N North America, bordering on Atlantic Ocean, Greenland Sea, Arctic Ocean, Baffin Bay

■ PEOPLE

Population: 56,385 (July 2003 est.)
Nationality: Greenlander
Ethnic Groups: 87% Greenlander (Inuit and Greenland-born Caucasians), 13% Danish and others
Languages: Inuit dialects, Danish

■ GOVERNMENT

Colony/Territory of: Dependent Territory of Denmark
Leader(s): Queen Margrethe II of Denmark, represented by High Commissioner Peter Lauritzen, Premier Hans Enoksen
Government Type: part of the Danish realm; self-governing overseas administrative division

National Holiday: June 21 (longest day of the year)

■ ECONOMY

Overview: dependent on annual subsidy from the Danish government; unemployment is on the increase; fishing is the most important industry; mineral resource exploitation is limited to lead and zinc

■ FINANCE/TRADE

Currency: Danish krone (DKr) = 100 oere

Canadian Embassy: c/o The Canadian Embassy, Kr. Bernikowsgade 1, 1105 Copenhagen K, Denmark. Tel. (011-45) 33-48-32-00. Fax: (011-45) 33-48-32-20. e-mail: copen@dfait-maeci.gc.ca
Representative to Canada: c/o Royal Danish Embassy, 47 Clarence St Ste 450, Ottawa ON K1N 9K1. Tel: (613) 562-1811. Fax: (613) 562-1812. e-mail: danemb@cyberus.ca

Grenada

Long-Form Name: Grenada
Capital: Saint George's

■ GEOGRAPHY

Area: 340 sq. km
Coastline: 121 km
Climate: tropical; tempered by northeast trade winds
Environment: lies on edge of hurricane belt; hurricane season lasts from June to Nov.
Terrain: volcanic in origin with central mountains
Land Use: arable land: 5.88%, permanent crops: 26.47%, other: 67.65%
Location: Caribbean islands, just north of Venezuela

■ PEOPLE

Population: 89,258 (July 2003 est.)
Nationality: Grenadian
Age Structure: 0–14 yrs: 35.1%; 15–64: 61.3%; 65+: 3.6% (2003 est.)
Population Growth Rate: 0.08% (2003 est.)
Net Migration: -14.56 migrants/1,000 population (2003 est.)
Ethnic Groups: 82% black, some East Indians, Europeans, a few Arawak
Languages: English (official); some French patois
Religions: largely Roman Catholic; Anglican; other Protestant sects

Birth Rate: 22.87/1,000 population (2003 est.)
Death Rate: 7.46/1,000 population (2003 est.)
Infant Mortality: 14.63 deaths/1,000 live births (2003 est.)
Life Expectancy at Birth: 62.74 years male, 66.31 years female (2003 est.)
Total Fertility Rate: 2.45 children born/woman (2003 est.)
Literacy: 94.4 (2002)%

■ GOVERNMENT

Leader(s): Head of State: Queen Elizabeth II, Governor General Daniel Williams, Prime Minister Keith Mitchell
Government Type: constitutional democracy
Administrative Divisions: 6 parishes and 1 dependency
Nationhood: Feb. 7, 1974 (from UK)
National Holiday: Independence Day, Feb. 7

■ ECONOMY

Overview: economy is based on agriculture (spices, tropical plants) and tourism; unemployment is high
GDP: US$440 million, per capita US$5,000; real growth rate 2.5% (2002 est.)
Inflation: 2.8% (2001 est.)
Industries: accounts for 24% of GDP (2000); food and beverage, textiles, light assembly operations, tourism, construction
Labour Force: approx. 45,000; services 62%, agriculture 24%, construction 8%, manufacturing 5%, other 1%
Unemployment: n.a.
Agriculture: accounts for 8% of GDP (2000), 80% of exports and employs 24% of the labour force; bananas, cocoa, nutmeg and mace are major crops; citrus, root crops, avocados; small-scale farms predominate
Natural Resources: timber, tropical fruit, deep-water harbours

■ FINANCE/TRADE

Currency: East Caribbean dollar ($EC) = 100 cents
International Reserves Excluding Gold: US$83 million (Jan. 2004)
Gold Reserves: n.a.
Budget: n.a.
Defence Expenditures: n.a.
Education Expenditures: n.a.
External Debt: US$339 million (2002)
Exports: US$46 million (2002 est.); commodities: nutmeg 35%, cocoa beans 15%, bananas 13%, mace 7%, textiles; partners: CARICOM countries, UK, US, Netherlands

Imports: US$208 million (2002 est.); commodities: machinery 24%, food 22%, manufactured goods 19%, petroleum 8%; partners: US, CARICOM, UK, Japan

■ COMMUNICATIONS

Daily Newspapers: n.a.
Televisions: n.a.
Radios: n.a.
Telephones: 375 lines/1,000 inhabitants (2002)
Internet: hosts: 14 (2002); users: 15,000 (2002)

■ TRANSPORTATION

Motor Vehicles: n.a.
Roads: 1,040 km; 638 km paved
Railway: none
Air Traffic: n.a.
Airports: 3; all have paved runways (2003 est.)

Canadian Embassy: The Canadian High Commission to Grenada, c/o The Canadian High Commission, Bishop's Court Hill, Bridgetown, Barbados; mailing address: P.O. Box 404, Bridgetown, Barbados. Tel: 1-246-429-3550. Fax: 1-246-429-3780. e-mail: bdgtn@dfait-maeci.gc.ca
Embassy in Canada: c/o High Commission for the Countries of the Organization of Eastern Caribbean States, 130 Albert St, Ste 700, Ottawa ON K1P 5G4. Tel: (613) 236-8952. Fax: (613) 236-3042. e-mail: echcc@travel-net.com

Guadeloupe

Long-Form Name: Department of Guadeloupe
Capital: Basse-Terre (seat of government); each of the 7 inhabited islands has its own chief town

■ GEOGRAPHY

Area: 1,780 sq. km (2 main islands, 5 small islands, one small island group called Iles des Saintes)
Climate: subtropical tempered by trade winds; hot and humid May–Dec., cool and dry Dec.–April
Land Use: arable land: 10.65%, permanent crops: 4.14%, other: 85.21%; includes 20 sq. km irrigated
Location: Caribbean, halfway along the Lesser Antilles arch between Puerto Rico and S America

■ PEOPLE

Population: 440,189 (July 2003 est.)
Nationality: Guadeloupian
Ethnic Groups: 90% black or mulatto, 5% white, less than 5% East Indian, Lebanese, Chinese

Languages: French, Creole dialect

■ GOVERNMENT

Colony/Territory of: Overseas Department of France
Leader(s): Head of State: President Jacques Chirac (France), Prefect Paul Girot de Langlade, President of the General Council Jacques Gillot
Government Type: overseas department of France
National Holiday: Taking of the Bastille, July 14

■ ECONOMY

Overview: economy depends on agriculture, tourism, light industry and services; unemployment is especially high among youth; agriculture: includes bananas, sugar cane, rum, flowers, livestock; vegetables and tobacco grown for local consumption; forestry, fisheries, tourism, food processing; partners: France, Martinique

■ FINANCE/TRADE

Currency: French franc = 100 centimes; Euro as of March 1, 2002

Canadian Embassy: c/o The Canadian Embassy, 35-37 avenue Montaigne, Paris, 75008, France. Tel: (011-331) 44-43-29-00. Fax: (011-331) 44-43-29-99. e-mail: paris@dfait-maeci.gc.ca
Representative to Canada: c/o Embassy of France, 42 Sussex Dr, Ottawa ON K1M 2C9. Tel: (613) 789-1795. Fax: (613) 562-3735. e-mail: politique@ambafrance-ca.org

Guam

Long-Form Name: Territory of Guam
Capital: Hagatna (Agana)

■ GEOGRAPHY

Area: 549 sq. km
Climate: tropical maritime, with little seasonal variation, but typhoon-prone and suffers from earthquakes; wet all year
Land Use: arable land: 10.91%, permanent crops: 10.91%, other: 78.18%; interior is mountainous and volcanic hills dominate the south, but many forests in northern Guam have been cleared for farming and the construction of airfields; coconut trees grow throughout the island
Location: N Pacific Ocean, E of the Philippines

■ PEOPLE

Population: 163,941 (July 2003 est.)
Nationality: Guamanian

Ethnic Groups: 47% Chamorro, 25% Filipino, 10% Caucasian, 18% Chinese, Japanese, Korean and other
Languages: English (official), Chamorro, Japanese

■ GOVERNMENT

Colony/Territory of: Unincorporated Outlying Territory of the United States
Leader(s): Head of State: President George W. Bush, Jr. (US), Governor Felix P. P. Camacho
Government Type: unincorporated outlying territory of the US; executive powers of the legislature similar to those of an American state legislature
National Holiday: Guam Discovery Day (first Monday in March); also Liberation Day, July 21

■ ECONOMY

Overview: economy depends mainly on US military spending and on tourism; agriculture: corn, coconuts, sweet potatoes, cucumbers, watermelons, beans, livestock, esp. cattle and pigs, fruit, vegetables, fish; industry: textile manufacture, cement, petroleum, printing, plastics, ship repair; tourism of growing importance

■ FINANCE/TRADE

Currency: American dollar = 100 cents

Canadian Embassy: c/o The Canadian Embassy, 501 Pennsylvania Avenue NW, Washington DC 20001, USA. Tel: (202) 682-1740. Fax: (202) 682-7726. e-mail: wshdc@dfait-maeci.gc.ca
Representative to Canada: c/o Embassy of the United States of America, 490 Sussex Drive, PO Box 866, Station "B," Ottawa, ON, K1P 5T1. Tel: (613) 238-5335. Fax: (613) 688-3080. e-mail inquiries are not accepted.

Guatemala

Long-Form Name: Republic of Guatemala
Capital: Guatemala

■ GEOGRAPHY

Area: 108,890 sq. km
Coastline: 400 km
Climate: tropical; hot, humid in lowlands; cooler in highlands
Environment: numerous volcanoes in mountains, with frequent violent earthquakes; Caribbean coast subject to hurricanes and other tropical storms; deforestation; soil erosion; water pollution

Terrain: mostly mountainous with narrow coastal plains and rolling limestone plateau (Petén)
Land Use: arable land: 12.54%, permanent crops: 5.03%, other: 82.43%; includes 1,250 sq, km irrigated
Location: northernmost Central (Latin) America, bordering on Caribbean Sea, Pacific Ocean

■ PEOPLE

Population: 13,909,384 (July 2003 est.)
Nationality: Guatemalan
Age Structure: 0–14 yrs: 42.9%; 15–64: 53.8%; 65+: 3.3% (2003 est.)
Population Growth Rate: 2.66% (2003 est.)
Net Migration: -1.71 migrants/1,000 population (2003 est.)
Ethnic Groups: 56% Ladino (mestizo-mixed Indian and European ancestry), 44% Indian
Languages: 60% Spanish, but 40% of the population speaks an Indian language as a primary tongue (23 Indian dialects, including Quiche, Cakchiquel, Kekchi)
Religions: predominantly Roman Catholic; also Protestant, traditional Mayan
Birth Rate: 35.05/1,000 population (2003 est.)
Death Rate: 6.78/1,000 population (2003 est.)
Infant Mortality: 37.92 deaths/1,000 live births (2003 est.)
Life Expectancy at Birth: 64.31 years male, 66.21 years female (2003 est.)
Total Fertility Rate: 4.67 children born/woman (2003 est.)
Literacy: 69.9% (2002)

■ GOVERNMENT

Leader(s): President Oscar Berger, Vice President Eduardo Stein
Government Type: constitutional democratic republic
Administrative Divisions: 22 departments (departamento, pl. departamentos)
Nationhood: Sept. 15, 1821 (from Spain)
National Holiday: Independence Day, Sept. 15

■ ECONOMY

Overview: the inflation rate has dropped significantly as a result of government economic reforms, but political uncertainty casts a shadow over the agriculturally based economy
GDP: US$53.2 billion, per capita US$3,900; real growth rate 2.2% (2002 est.)
Inflation: 8.1% (2002 est.)
Industries: accounts for 20% of GDP (2000); sugar, textiles and clothing, furniture, chemicals, petroleum, metals, rubber, tourism

Labour Force: 4.5 million (2002); 35% community, social and business services, 50% agriculture, 15% industry
Unemployment: 3.1% (2002 est.)
Agriculture: accounts for 23% of GDP (2000) and employs 60% of the labour force; principal crops—sugar cane, corn, bananas, coffee, beans, cardamom; livestock—cattle, sheep, pigs, chickens; food importer
Natural Resources: crude oil, nickel, rare woods, fish, chicle, hydro power

■ FINANCE/TRADE

Currency: quetzal (pl. quetzalas) (Q) = 100 centavos, also US ($) = 100 cents
International Reserves Excluding Gold: US$2.808 billion (Jan. 2004)
Gold Reserves: 0.220 million fine troy ounces (Jan. 2004)
Budget: revenue US$2.3 billion, expenditures US$2.7 billion, including capital expenditures of US$750 million (2002 est.)
Defence Expenditures: n.a.
Education Expenditures: 11.4% of total government expenditures (2002)
External Debt: US$4.676 billion (2002)
Exports: US$2.494 billion (2003 est.); commodities: coffee 38%, bananas 7%, sugar 7%, cardamom 4%; partners: US, El Salvador, Costa Rica, Nicaragua, Germany
Imports: US$6.058 billion (2003 est.); commodities: fuel and petroleum products, machinery, grain, fertilizers, motor vehicles; partners: US, Mexico, South Korea, El Salvador, Venezuela

■ COMMUNICATIONS

Daily Newspapers: 33/1,000 inhabitants (2000)
Televisions: 95/1,000 inhabitants (2002)
Radios: 79/1,000 inhabitants (2001)
Telephones: 71 lines/1,000 inhabitants (2002)
Internet: hosts: 9,789 (2002); users: 400,000 (2002)

■ TRANSPORTATION

Motor Vehicles: 199,000; 102,000 passenger cars
Roads: 14,118 km; 4,871 km paved
Railway: 886 km
Air Traffic: 506,000 passengers carried (2001 est.)
Airports: 466; 11 have paved runways (2003 est.)

Canadian Embassy: The Canadian Embassy, 13 Calle 8-44, Zone 10, Guatemala City; mailing address: P.O. Box 400, Guatemala City, Guatemala, C.A. Tel: (011-502) 363-4348. Fax: (011-502) 365-1211. e-mail: gtmla@dfait-maeci.gc.ca

Embassy in Canada: Embassy of the Republic of Guatemala, 130 Albert St, Ste 1010, Ottawa ON K1P 5G4. Tel: (613) 233-7237. Fax: (613) 233-0135. e-mail: embguate@webruler.com

Guinea

Long-Form Name: Republic of Guinea
Capital: Conakry

■ GEOGRAPHY

Area: 245,857 sq. km
Coastline: 320 km
Climate: generally hot and humid; monsoonal-type rainy season (June to Nov.) with south-westerly winds; dry season (Dec. to May) with northeasterly harmattan winds
Environment: hot, dry, dusty harmattan haze may reduce visibility during dry season; deforestation; insufficient safe drinking water
Terrain: generally flat coastal plain, hilly to mountainous interior
Land Use: arable land: 3.6%, permanent crops: 2.44%, other: 93.96%; includes 950 sq. km irrigated
Location: W Africa, bordering on Atlantic Ocean

■ PEOPLE

Population: 9,030,220 (July 2003 est.)
Nationality: Guinean
Age Structure: 0–14 yrs: 44.4%; 15–64: 52.4%; 65+: 3.2% (2003 est.)
Population Growth Rate: 2.37% (2003 est.)
Net Migration: -3.14 migrants/1,000 population (2003 est.)
Ethnic Groups: 40% Peuhl, 30% Malinke, 20% Sousou, 10% smaller tribes
Languages: French (official); each tribe has its own language; 8 official languages are taught in schools, including Fulani, Malinke, Soussou
Religions: 85% Muslim, 7% indigenous beliefs, 8% Christian
Birth Rate: 42.50/1,000 population (2003 est.)
Death Rate: 15.70/1,000 population (2003 est.)
Infant Mortality: 93.30 deaths/1,000 live births (2003 est.)
Life Expectancy at Birth: 48.28 years male, 50.83 years female (2003 est.)
Total Fertility Rate: 5.90 children born/woman (2003 est.)
Literacy: 41.0% (2002)

■ GOVERNMENT

Leader(s): President General Lansana Conté, Premier Lamine Sidime
Government Type: republic

Administrative Divisions: 33 prefectures and 1 special zone (zone speciale)
Nationhood: Oct. 2, 1958 (from France; formerly known as French Guinea)
National Holiday: Anniversary of the Second Republic, Apr. 3. Independence Day, Oct. 2

■ ECONOMY

Overview: although possessing numerous natural resources and potential for agricultural development, it is one of the poorest countries in the world; mining accounts for the bulk of Guinea's exports, and apart from the bauxite industry, foreign investment remains low
GDP: US$18.69 billion, per capita US$2,100; real growth rate 3.7% (2002 est.)
Inflation: 6% (2002 est.)
Industries: accounts for 38% of GDP (2000); bauxite mining, alumina, diamond mining, light manufacturing and agricultural processing industries
Labour Force: 3.7 million (2002); 80% agriculture, 20% industry and services
Unemployment: n.a.
Agriculture: accounts for 24% of GDP (2000) and employs 80% of the workforce (including fishing and forestry); mostly subsistence farming; principal products—rice, coffee, pineapples, palm kernels, cassava, sweet potatoes, timber; livestock—cattle, sheep and goats
Natural Resources: bauxite, iron ore, diamonds, gold, uranium, hydroelectricity, fish

■ FINANCE/TRADE

Currency: Guinean franc = 100 centimes
International Reserves Excluding Gold: US$194 million (June 2002)
Gold Reserves: n.a.
Budget: revenues US$ n.a., expenditures US$417.7 million, including capital expenditures US$ n.a. (2000 est.)
Defence Expenditures: 8.5% of central government expenditure (2002)
Education Expenditures: 25.6% of total government expenditures (2002)
External Debt: US$3.401 billion (2002)
Exports: US$726 million (2003 est.) commodities: alumina, bauxite, gold, diamonds, coffee, pineapples, bananas, palm kernels; partners: Belgium, US, Ireland, Russia
Imports: US$646 million (2003 est.) commodities: petroleum products, metals, machinery, transport equipment, foodstuffs, textiles and grain; partners: US, France, Belgium, Côte d'Ivoire

■ COMMUNICATIONS

Daily Newspapers: none
Televisions: 47/1,000 inhabitants (2002)
Radios: 52/1,000 inhabitants (2001)
Telephones: 3 lines/1,000 inhabitants (2002)
Internet: hosts: 251 (2002); users: 35,000 (2002)

■ TRANSPORTATION

Motor Vehicles: 33,000; 13,700 passenger cars
Roads: 30,500 km; 5,033 km paved
Railway: 1,115 km
Air Traffic: 64,000 passengers carried (2001 est.)
Airports: 15; 5 have paved runways (2003 est.)

Canadian Embassy: The Canadian Embassy, P.O. Box 99, Conakry, Guinea. Tel: (011-224) 46-23-95. Fax: (011-224) 46-42-35. e-mail: cnaky@dfait-maeci.gc.ca
Embassy in Canada: Embassy of the Republic of Guinea, 483 Wilbrod St, Ottawa ON K1N 6N1. Tel: (613) 789-8444. Fax: (613) 789-7560. e-mail: ambaguineaott@sympatico.ca

Guinea-Bissau

Long-Form Name: Republic of Guinea-Bissau
Capital: Bissau

■ GEOGRAPHY

Area: 36,120 sq. km
Coastline: 350 km
Climate: tropical; generally hot and humid; monsoon-type rainy season (June to Nov.) with southwesterly winds; dry season (Dec. to May) with northeasterly harmattan winds
Environment: hot, dry, dusty harmattan haze may reduce visibility during dry season; deforestation, soil erosion
Terrain: mostly low coastal plain rising to savanna in east
Land Use: arable land: 10.67%, permanent crops: 1.78%, other: 87.55%; includes 170 sq. km irrigated
Location: W Africa, bordering on Atlantic Ocean

■ PEOPLE

Population: 1,360,827 (July 2003 est.)
Nationality: Guinean
Age Structure: 0–14 yrs: 41.9%; 15–64: 55.2%; 65+: 2.9% (2003 est.)
Population Growth Rate: 2.02% (2003 est.)
Net Migration: -1.60 migrants/1,000 population (2003 est.)
Ethnic Groups: approx. 99% African (including 30% Balanta, 20% Fula, 14% Manjaca, 13% Mandinga, 7% Papel); less than 1% European and mulatto

Languages: Portuguese (official); Crioulo (a Portuguese-based Creole), Balante and numerous African languages
Religions: 65% indigenous beliefs, 30% Muslim, 5% Christian
Birth Rate: 38.41/1,000 population (2003 est.)
Death Rate: 16.62/1,000 population (2003 est.)
Infant Mortality: 110.29 deaths/1,000 live births (2003 est.)
Life Expectancy at Birth: 45.09 years male, 48.91 years female (2003 est.)
Total Fertility Rate: 5.07 children born/woman (2003 est.)
Literacy: 39.6% (2002)

■ GOVERNMENT

Leader(s): President Henrique Rosa, Prime Minister Carlos Gomes Jr.
Government Type: republic
Administrative Divisions: 9 regions (regiões, singular–região)
Nationhood: Sept. 10, 1974 (from Portugal; formerly known as Portuguese Guinea)
National Holiday: Independence Day, Sept. 24

■ ECONOMY

Overview: this poor country is focusing on agricultural development; exploitation of mineral deposits is hampered by a weak infrastructure and high costs. The heavy foreign debt is a burden
GDP: US$901.4 million, per capita US$700; real growth rate -4.3% (2002 est.)
Inflation: 4% (2002 est.)
Industries: accounts for 15% of GDP; agricultural processing, beer, soft drinks
Labour Force: 700,000 (2002); 82% agriculture, 18% other
Unemployment: n.a.
Agriculture: accounts for 54% of GDP; nearly 100% of exports and 80% of employment; rice is the staple; not self-sufficient in food; fishing and forestry not fully exploited; crops include corn, beans, cassava, cashew nuts, peanuts, palm kernels, cotton, timber and fish
Natural Resources: unexploited deposits of petroleum, bauxite, phosphates; fish, timber

■ FINANCE/TRADE

Currency: Communauté financière africaine (CFAF) franc = 100 centimes
International Reserves Excluding Gold: US$151 million (Nov. 2003)
Gold Reserves: none (Dec. 2002)
Budget: n.a.
Defence Expenditures: 2.8% of GDP (2002)

Education Expenditures: 4.8% of total government expenditures (2002)
External Debt: US$699 million (2002)
Exports: US$54 million (2002); commodities: cashews, fish, peanuts, palm kernels; partners: India, Italy, South Korea, Belgium
Imports: US$104 million (2002); commodities: capital equipment, consumer goods, semi-processed goods, foods, petroleum; partners: Portugal, Senegal, Thailand, China

■ COMMUNICATIONS

Daily Newspapers: 5/1,000 inhabitants (2000)
Televisions: 36/1,000 inhabitants (2002)
Radios: 204/1,000 inhabitants (2001)
Telephones: 9 lines/1,000 inhabitants (2002)
Internet: hosts: 20 (2002); users: 5,000 (2002)

■ TRANSPORTATION

Motor Vehicles: 6,900; 4,000 passenger cars
Roads: 4,400 km; 453 km paved
Railway: none
Air Traffic: 20,000 passengers carried (2001 est.)
Airports: 28; 3 have paved runways (2003 est.)

Canadian Embassy: The Canadian Embassy to Guinea-Bissau, c/o The Canadian Embassy, P.O. Box 3373, Dakar, Senegal. Tel: (011-221) 889-4700. Fax: (011-221) 889-4720. e-mail: dakar@dfait-maeci.gc.ca
Embassy in Canada: c/o Embassy of the Republic of Guinea-Bissau, 15929 Yukon Lane (Rockville, Maryland), Washington DC 20855, USA. Tel: (301) 947-3958. Fax: (301) 947-3958. e-mail: n.a.

Guyana

Long-Form Name: Co-operative Republic of Guyana
Capital: Georgetown

■ GEOGRAPHY

Area: 214,970 sq. km
Coastline: 459 km
Climate: tropical; hot, humid, moderated by northeast trade winds; two rainy seasons (May to mid-Aug., mid-Nov. to mid-Jan.)
Environment: flash floods a constant threat during rainy seasons; water pollution; deforestation
Terrain: mostly rolling highlands; low coastal plain; savanna in south
Land Use: arable land: 2.44%, permanent crops: 0.08%, other: 97.48%; includes 1,500 sq. km irrigated
Location: N South America, bordering on Atlantic Ocean

■ PEOPLE

Population: 702,100 (July 2003 est.)
Nationality: Guyanese
Age Structure: 0–14 yrs: 27.0%; 15–64: 67.9%; 65+: 5.1% (2003 est.)
Population Growth Rate: 0.44% (2003 est.)
Net Migration: -4.16 migrants/1,000 population (2003 est.)
Ethnic Groups: 51% East Indian, 44% black and mixed, 4% Amerindian, 1% European and Chinese
Languages: English, Hindi, Urdu, Amerindian dialects
Religions: 60% Christian, 30% Hindu, 9% Muslim, 1% other
Birth Rate: 17.87/1,000 population (2003 est.)
Death Rate: 9.27/1,000 population (2003 est.)
Infant Mortality: 37.55 deaths/1,000 live births (2003 est.)
Life Expectancy at Birth: 60.51 years male, 65.79 years female (2003 est.)
Total Fertility Rate: 2.07 children born/woman (2003 est.)
Literacy: 96.5% (2002)

■ GOVERNMENT

Leader(s): President Bharrat Jagdeo, Prime Minister Samuel Hinds
Government Type: republic
Administrative Divisions: 10 regions
Nationhood: May 26, 1966 (from UK; formerly known as British Guyana)
National Holiday: Republic Day, Feb. 23

■ ECONOMY

Overview: one of the world's poorest countries, with a per capita income less than one-fifth the South American average; electricity has been in short supply and constitutes a major barrier to production
GDP: US$2.628 billion, per capita US$3,800; real growth rate 1.1% (2002 est.)
Inflation: 4.7% (2002 est.)
Industries: accounts for 21% of GDP (2002); bauxite mining, sugar, rice milling, timber, fishing (shrimp), textiles, gold mining
Labour Force: 418,000 (2001 est.) 26% industry, 27% agriculture, 47% services
Unemployment: n.a.
Agriculture: most important sector, accounting for 35% of GDP (2002); sugar and rice are main crops; livestock include beef, pork, poultry; not self-sufficient in food; development potential exists for fishing and forestry, wheat, vegetable oils
Natural Resources: bauxite, gold, diamonds, hardwood timber, shrimp, fish

■ FINANCE/TRADE

Currency: Guyanese dollar ($G) = 100 cents
International Reserves Excluding Gold: US$274 million (Jan. 2004)
Gold Reserves: n.a.
Budget: revenues US$227 million; expenditures US$235.2 million, including capital expenditures of US$93.4 million (2000)
Defence Expenditures: n.a.
Education Expenditures: n.a.
External Debt: US$1.459 billion (2002)
Exports: US$637 million (2003 est.); commodities: bauxite, sugar, rice, shrimp, gold, molasses, timber, rum; partners: Canada, US, UK, Netherlands Antilles
Imports: US$1.161 billion (2003 est.); commodities: manufactures, machinery, food, petroleum; partners: US, Trinidad and Tobago, Netherlands Antilles, UK

■ COMMUNICATIONS

Daily Newspapers: 2 in total
Televisions: n.a.
Radios: n.a.
Telephones: 115 lines/1,000 inhabitants (2002)
Internet: hosts: 63 (2002); users: 125,000 (2002)

■ TRANSPORTATION

Motor Vehicles: 33,000; 24,000 passenger cars
Roads: 7,970 km; 590 km paved
Railway: 187 km; no public railroads
Air Traffic: 150,000 passengers carried (2001 est.)
Airports: 51; 8 have paved runways (2003 est.)

Canadian Embassy: Canadian High Commission, High and Young Streets, Georgetown; mailing address: P.O. Box 10880, Georgetown, Guyana. Tel: (011-592) 227-2081. Fax: (011-592) 225-8380. e-mail: grgtn@dfait-maeci.gc.ca
Embassy in Canada: High Commission for the Co-operative Republic of Guyana, Burnside Bldg, 151 Slater St, Ste 309, Ottawa ON K1P 5H3. Tel: (613) 235-7249. Fax: (613) 235-1447. e-mail: n.a.

Haiti

Long-Form Name: Republic of Haiti
Capital: Port-au-Prince

■ GEOGRAPHY

Area: 27,750 sq. km
Coastline: 1,771 km
Climate: tropical; semi-arid where mountains in east cut off trade winds
Environment: lies in the middle of the hurricane belt and subject to severe storms from June to

Oct.; occasional flooding and earthquakes; deforestation; soil erosion, insufficient safe drinking water
Terrain: mostly rough and mountainous
Land Use: arable land: 20.3%, permanent crops: 12.7%, other: 67%; includes 750 sq. km irrigated
Location: West Indies, bordering on Caribbean Sea, Atlantic Ocean

■ PEOPLE

Population: 7,527,817 (July 2003 est.)
Nationality: Haitian
Age Structure: 0–14 yrs: 42.7%; 15–64: 53.6%; 65+: 3.7% (2003 est.)
Population Growth Rate: 1.67% (2003 est.)
Net Migration: -4.03 migrants/1,000 population (2003 est.)
Ethnic Groups: 95% black, 5% mulatto and European
Languages: French (official) spoken by only 10% of population; all speak Creole
Religions: 80% Roman Catholic (of which an overwhelming majority also practice Voodoo), 16% Protestant, 4% other
Birth Rate: 34.06/1,000 population (2003 est.)
Death Rate: 13.36/1,000 population (2003 est.)
Infant Mortality: 76.01 deaths/1,000 live births (2003 est.)
Life Expectancy at Birth: 50.36 years male, 52.92 years female (2003 est.)
Total Fertility Rate: 4.86 children born/woman (2003 est.)
Literacy: 51.9% (2002)

■ GOVERNMENT

Leader(s): President Boniface Alexandre, Prime Minister Gerard Latortue
Government Type: elected government
Administrative Divisions: 9 départments (départements, sing. —département)
Nationhood: Jan. 1, 1804 (from France)
National Holiday: Independence Day, Jan. 1

■ ECONOMY

Overview: about 75% of the population live in absolute poverty, and do not have access to safe drinking water, medical care or sufficient food; agriculture based on small-scale subsistence farming; trade sanctions have further damaged the economy
GDP: US$10.6 billion, per capita US$1,400; real growth rate -0.9% (2002 est.)
Inflation: 14.2% (2001)
Industries: accounts for 20% of GDP (2001 est.); sugar refining, textiles, flour milling, cement

manufacturing, bauxite mining, tourism, light assembly industries based on imported parts
Labour Force: 3.6 million (2002); 66% agriculture, 25% services, 9% industry
Unemployment: 70%; widespread underemployment
Agriculture: accounts for 30% of GDP (2001 est.) and employs 70% of workforce; mostly small-size subsistence farms; commercial crops include coffee, mangoes, and sugar cane; staple crops include rice, corn, sorghum and mangoes
Natural Resources: bauxite, copper, gold, calcium carbonate

■ FINANCE/TRADE

Currency: gourde (G) = 100 centimes
International Reserves Excluding Gold: US$66 million (Nov. 2003)
Gold Reserves: 0.001 million fine troy ounces (Jan. 2004)
Budget: revenues US$273 million; expenditures US$361 million, including capital expenditures US$ n.a. (FY2000/01 est.)
Defence Expenditures: 1.3% of GDP (2000)
Education Expenditures: n.a.
External Debt: US$1.248 billion (2002)
Exports: US$332 million (2003 est.); commodities: light manufactures 65%, coffee 17%, other agriculture 8%, other products 10%; partners: US, EU
Imports: US$1.140 billion (2003 est.); commodities: machines and manufactures 36%, food and beverages 21%, petroleum products 11%, fats and oils 12%, chemicals 12%; partners: US, EU, Dominican Republic

■ COMMUNICATIONS

Daily Newspapers: 3/1,000 inhabitants (2000)
Televisions: 6/1,000 inhabitants (2002)
Radios: 18/1,000 inhabitants (2001)
Telephones: 16 lines/1,000 inhabitants (2002)
Internet: hosts: NA users: 80,000 (2002)

■ TRANSPORTATION

Motor Vehicles: 53,000; 32,000 passenger cars
Roads: 4,160 km; 1,011 km paved
Railway: 40 km
Air Traffic: n.a.
Airports: 12; 2 have paved runways (2003 est.)

Canadian Embassy: The Canadian Embassy, Édifice Banque de Nova Scotia, route de Delmas, 18 Port-au-Prince, Haiti; mailing address: C.P. 826, Port-au-Prince, Haiti. Tel: (011-509) 298-3050. Fax: (011-509) 298-3801. e-mail: prnce@dfait-maeci.gc.ca

Embassy in Canada: Embassy of the Republic of Haiti, 130 Albert St, Ste 1409, Ottawa ON K1P 5G4. Tel: (613) 238-1628. Fax (613) 238-2986. e-mail: bohio@sympatico.ca

Honduras

Long-Form Name: Republic of Honduras
Capital: Tegucigalpa

■ GEOGRAPHY

Area: 112,090 sq. km
Coastline: 820 km
Climate: subtropical in lowlands, temperate in mountains
Environment: subject to frequent, but generally mild, earthquakes; damaging hurricanes along Caribbean coast; deforestation; soil erosion; mining pollution of freshwater resources
Terrain: mostly mountainous in interior, narrow coastal plains
Land Use: arable land: 15.15%, permanent crops: 3.13%, other: 81.72%; includes 760 sq. km irrigated
Location: Central (Latin) America, bordering on Caribbean Sea, Pacific Ocean

■ PEOPLE

Population: 6,669,789 (July 2003 est.)
Nationality: Honduran
Age Structure: 0–14 yrs: 41.6%; 15–64: 54.8%; 65+: 3.6% (2003 est.)
Population Growth Rate: 2.32% (2003 est.)
Net Migration: -2.04 migrants/1,000 population (2003 est.)
Ethnic Groups: 90% mestizo (mixed Indian and European), 7% Indian, 2% black, 1% white
Languages: Spanish, Indian dialects
Religions: about 97% Roman Catholic; small Protestant minority
Birth Rate: 31.67/1,000 population (2003 est.)
Death Rate: 6.44/1,000 population (2003 est.)
Infant Mortality: 29.96 deaths/1,000 live births (2003 est.)
Life Expectancy at Birth: 65.31 years male, 68.06 years female (2003 est.)
Total Fertility Rate: 4.07 children born/woman (2003 est.)
Literacy: 80.0% (2002)

■ GOVERNMENT

Leader(s): President Ricardo Maduro
Government Type: democratic constitutional republic

Administrative Divisions: 18 departments (departamentos, sing. —departamento, plus 1 probable central district)
Nationhood: Sept. 15, 1821 (from Spain)
National Holiday: Independence Day, Sept. 15

■ ECONOMY

Overview: one of the poorest countries in the western hemisphere, with a high population growth rate, a high unemployment rate, a lack of basic services and an export sector vulnerable to world prices (coffee, bananas)
GDP: US$16.29 billion, per capita US$2,500; real growth rate 2.5% (2002 est.)
Inflation: 7.7% (2002 est.)
Industries: accounts for 32% of GDP (2002); agricultural processing (sugar and coffee), textiles, clothing, wood products
Labour Force: 2.6 million (2002); 34% agriculture, 45% community, social and business services, 21% industry
Unemployment: 3.8% (2002)
Agriculture: accounts for 14% of GDP (2002), over 60% of the labour force and 20% of exports; main products include bananas, coffee, timber, beef, citrus fruit, shrimp; importer of wheat
Natural Resources: timber, gold, silver, copper, lead, zinc, iron ore, antimony, coal, fish

■ FINANCE/TRADE

Currency: lempira (L) = 100 centavos
International Reserves Excluding Gold: US$1.373 billion (Jan. 2004)
Gold Reserves: 0.021 million fine troy ounces (Jan. 2004)
Budget: n.a.
Defence Expenditures: n.a.
Education Expenditures: n.a.
External Debt: US$5.395 billion (2002)
Exports: US$1.360 billion (2003 est.); commodities: bananas, coffee, shrimp, lobster, minerals, lumber; partners: US, El Salvador, Germany, Belgium, Guatemala
Imports: US$3.161 billion (2003 est.); commodities: machinery and transport equipment, chemical products, manufactured goods, fuel and oil, foodstuffs; partners: US, Guatemala, El Salvador, Mexico, Japan

■ COMMUNICATIONS

Daily Newspapers: 55/1,000 inhabitants (2000)
Televisions: 119/1,000 inhabitants (2002)
Radios: 413/1,000 inhabitants (2001)
Telephones: 48 lines/1,000 inhabitants (2002)

Internet: hosts: 160 (2002); users: 168,600 (2002)

■ TRANSPORTATION

Motor Vehicles: 400,000; 335,000 passenger cars
Roads: 13,603 km; 2,775 km paved
Railway: 699 km
Air Traffic: 570,000 passengers carried (2001 est.)
Airports: 115; 12 have paved runways (2003 est.)

Canadian Embassy: The Office of the Canadian Embassy, Centro Financiero BANEXPO, 3rd Floor, Bulevar San Juan Bosco, Colonia Payaqui, Tegucigalpa, Honduras, Postal Address: The Office of the Canadian Embassy, P.O. Box 3552, Tegucigalpa, Honduras. Tel: (011 504) 232-4551. Fax: (011 504) 239-7767. e-mail: tglpa@dfait-maeci.gc.ca
Embassy in Canada: Embassy of the Republic of Honduras, 151 Slater St, Ste 805, Ottawa ON K1P 5H3. Tel: (613) 233-8900. Fax: (613) 232-0193. e-mail: embhonca@magma.ca

Hong Kong

Long-Form Name: Hong Kong Special Administrative Region
Capital: none

■ GEOGRAPHY

Area: 1,092 sq. km
Climate: tropical monsoon; cool and humid in winter, hot and rainy from spring through summer, warm and sunny in fall
Land Use: arable land: 5.05%, permanent crops: 1.01%, other: 93.94%; includes 20 sq. km irrigated
Location: SE Asia, bordering on South China Sea

■ PEOPLE

Population: 7,394,170 (July 2003 est.)
Nationality: Chinese
Ethnic Groups: 95% Chinese, 5% other
Languages: Chinese (Cantonese), English

■ GOVERNMENT

Colony/Territory of: Special Administrative Region (SAR) of the People's Republic of China
Leader(s): President Hu Jintao (China), Chief Executive Tung Chee-hwa
Government Type: reverted to China July 1, 1997
National Holiday: National Day, Oct. 1; July 1 is celebrated as Hong Kong Special Administrative Region Establishment Day

■ ECONOMY

Overview: manufacturing and services (finance, business and professional) are the basis of the economy; natural resources are limited and food and raw materials must be imported

■ FINANCE/TRADE

Currency: Hong Kong dollar (HK$) = 100 cents

Canadian Embassy: c/o The Canadian Embassy, 19 Dong Zhi Men Wai, Chao Yang District 100600, Beijing, PDR China. Tel: (011-86-10) 6532-3536. Fax: (011-86-10) 6532-4311. e-mail: bejing@dfait-maeci.gc.ca
Representative to Canada: c/o Embassy of the People's Republic of China, 515 St. Patrick St, Ottawa ON K1N 5H3. Tel: (613) 789-3434. Fax: (613) 789-1911. e-mail: n.a.

Hungary

Long-Form Name: Republic of Hungary
Capital: Budapest

■ GEOGRAPHY

Area: 93,030 sq. km
Coastline: none: landlocked
Climate: temperate; cold, cloudy, humid winter; warm summer
Environment: levees are common along many streams, but flooding occurs almost every year; pollution of air, soil and underground water resources
Terrain: mostly flat to rolling plains
Land Use: arable land: 52.2%, permanent crops: 2.46%, other: 45.34%; includes 2,100 sq. km irrigated
Location: C Europe

■ PEOPLE

Population: 10,045,407 (July 2003 est.)
Nationality: Hungarian
Age Structure: 0–14 yrs: 16.1%; 15–64: 69.0%; 65+: 14.9% (2003 est.)
Population Growth Rate: -0.29% (2003 est.)
Net Migration: 0.78 migrants/1,000 population (2003 est.)
Ethnic Groups: 89.9% Hungarian, 4% Gypsy, 2% Serb, 2.6% German, 0.8% Slovak, 0.7% Romanian
Languages: Hungarian (Magyar, official), 1.8% other
Religions: 67.5% Roman Catholic, 20% Calvinist, 5% Lutheran, 7.5% atheist and other
Birth Rate: 9.32/1,000 population (2003 est.)
Death Rate: 13.00/1,000 population (2003 est.)
Infant Mortality: 8.58 deaths/1,000 live births (2003 est.)

Life Expectancy at Birth: 67.84 years male, 76.81 years female (2003 est.)
Total Fertility Rate: 1.25 children born/woman (2003 est.)
Literacy: 99.3% (2002)

■ GOVERNMENT

Leader(s): President Ferenc Madl, Prime Minister Peter Medgyessy
Government Type: parliamentary democracy
Administrative Divisions: 19 counties (megyek, sing. —megye), 20 urban counties and 1 capital city (fovaros)
Nationhood: 1001 (unification by King Stephen I)
National Holiday: St. Stephen's Day, Aug. 20 (National Day)

■ ECONOMY

Overview: consolidated its stabilization program and undergone enough restructuring to become an established market economy; it appears to have entered a period of sustainable growth, gradually falling inflation, and stable external balances; the government's main economic priorities are to complete structural reforms, particularly in pension, taxation, and health-care reforms
GDP: US$134.0 billion, per capita US$13,300; real growth rate 3.3% (2002)
Inflation: 5.3% (2002 est.)
Industries: accounts for 34% of GDP (2000); mining, metallurgy, engineering industries, processed foods, textiles, chemicals (especially pharmaceuticals)
Labour Force: 4.9 million (2002); 27% industry, 65% community, social and business services, 8% agriculture
Unemployment: 5.5% (Nov. 2003)
Agriculture: accounts for 4% of GDP (2000) (including forestry) and 16% of employment; highly diversified crop-livestock farming; main crops—wheat, corn, sunflowers, potatoes, sugar beets; livestock—hogs, cattle, poultry and dairy products; self-sufficient in food
Natural Resources: bauxite, coal, natural gas, fertile soils, arable land

■ FINANCE/TRADE

Currency: forint (Ft) = 100 filler
International Reserves Excluding Gold: US$13.137 billion (Jan. 2004)
Gold Reserves: 0.101 million fine troy ounces (Jan. 2004)
Budget: revenues US$13 billion; expenditures US$14.4 billion, including capital expenditures of US$ n.a. (2000 est.)
Defence Expenditures: 4.4% of central government expenditure (2002)

Education Expenditures: 14.1% of total government expenditure (2002)
External Debt: US$34.958 billion (2002)
Exports: US$41.910 billion (2003 est.); commodities: capital goods 36%, foods 24%, consumer goods 18%, fuels and minerals 11%, other 11%; partners: Germany, Austria, Italy, US
Imports: US$46.897 billion (2003 est.); commodities: machinery and transport 28%, fuels 20%, chemical products 14%, manufactured consumer goods 16%, agriculture 6%, other 16%; partners: former USSR countries 43%, Germany, Italy, Austria, Russia

■ COMMUNICATIONS

Daily Newspapers: 456/1,000 inhabitants (2000)
Televisions: 475/1,000 inhabitants (2002)
Radios: 690/1,000 inhabitants (2001)
Telephones: 361 lines/1,000 inhabitants (2002)
Internet: hosts: 194,503 (2002); users: 1.6 million (2002)

■ TRANSPORTATION

Motor Vehicles: 2,750,000; 2,400,000 passenger cars
Roads: 188,203 km; 81,680 km paved
Railway: 7,875 km
Air Traffic: 2,134,000 passengers carried (2002)
Airports: 49; 17 have paved runways (2003 est.)

Canadian Embassy: The Canadian Embassy, Zugligeti ut. 51-53, 1121 Budapest, Hungary. Tel.: (011-36-1) 392-3360. Fax: (011-36-1) 392-3390. e-mail: bpest@dfait-maeci.gc.ca
Embassy in Canada: Embassy of the Republic of Hungary, 299 Waverley St, Ottawa ON K2P 0V9. Tel: (613) 230-2717. Fax: (613) 230-7560. e-mail: sysadmin@huembott.org

---

Iceland

Long-Form Name: Republic of Iceland
Capital: Reykjavik

■ GEOGRAPHY

Area: 103,000 sq. km
Coastline: 4,988 km
Climate: temperate; moderated by North Atlantic Current; mild, windy winters; damp, cool summers
Environment: subject to earthquakes and volcanic activity; water pollution
Terrain: mostly plateau interspersed with mountain peaks, ice fields; coast deeply indented by bays and fjords
Land Use: arable land: 1%, permanent crops: 0%, permanent pastures: 28%, forest and woodlands: 1%, other: 70%

Location: NW Europe, island in Norwegian Sea, Atlantic Ocean

■ PEOPLE

Population: 280,798 (July 2003 est.)
Nationality: Icelander
Age Structure: 0–14 yrs: 22.7%; 15–64: 65.4%; 65+: 11.9% (2003 est.)
Population Growth Rate: 0.49% (2003 est.)
Net Migration: -2.26 migrants/1,000 population (2003 est.)
Ethnic Groups: homogeneous mixture of descendants of Norwegians and Celts
Languages: Icelandic
Religions: Christianity (predominantly Protestant)
Birth Rate: 14.13/1,000 population (2003 est.)
Death Rate: 6.95/1,000 population (2003 est.)
Infant Mortality: 3.50 deaths/1,000 live births (2003 est.)
Life Expectancy at Birth: 77.54 years male, 82.22 years female (2003 est.)
Total Fertility Rate: 1.98 children born/woman (2003 est.)
Literacy: approaching 100% (2002)

■ GOVERNMENT

Leader(s): President Olafur Ragnar Grimsson, Prime Minister David Oddsson
Government Type: constitutional republic
Administrative Divisions: 23 counties (syslar, sing. —sysla) and 14 independent towns (kaupstadhir, sing. —kaupstadhur)
Nationhood: June 17, 1944 (from Denmark)
National Holiday: Anniversary of the Establishment of the Republic, June 17

■ ECONOMY

Overview: basically capitalistic, but it has an extensive welfare system, low unemployment, and an unusually even distribution of income; depends heavily on the fishing industry and is vulnerable to changing world fish prices
GDP: US$8.444 billion, per capita US$30,200; real growth rate -0.6% (2002)
Inflation: 5.2% (2002 est.)
Industries: accounts for 21% of GDP (2001 est.); fish processing, aluminum smelting, ferro-silicon production, hydroelectricity
Labour Force: 159,000 (2000); 55% commerce, finance and services, 13% other manufacturing, 5.1% agriculture, 12% fish processing, 15% other
Unemployment: 3.1% (Nov. 2003)
Agriculture: accounts for about 15% of GDP (includes fishing) (2001 est.); fishing is the most important economic activity, contributing nearly 75% to export earnings; principal crops include potatoes and turnips; livestock—cattle, sheep; self-sufficient in crops
Natural Resources: fish, hydroelectric and geothermal power, diatomite

■ FINANCE/TRADE

Currency: króna (pl. krónur) (ISK) = 100 aurar
International Reserves Excluding Gold: US$787 million (Jan. 2004)
Gold Reserves: 0.063 million fine troy ounces (Jan. 2004)
Budget: n.a.
Defence Expenditures: none
Education Expenditures: n.a.
External Debt: n.a.
Exports: US$2.358 billion (2003 est.); commodities: fish and fish products, animal products, aluminum, diatomite; partners: UK, Germany, Netherlands, US, Portugal, Spain, Norway
Imports: US$2.755 billion (2003 est.); commodities: machinery and transportation equipment, petroleum, foodstuffs, textiles; partners: Germany, US, Denmark, Norway, UK, Netherlands

■ COMMUNICATIONS

Daily Newspapers: 5 in total
Televisions: n.a.
Radios: n.a.
Telephones: 673 lines/1,000 inhabitants (2002)
Internet: hosts: 68,261 (2002); users: 186,600 (2002)

■ TRANSPORTATION

Motor Vehicles: 144,000; 125,300 passenger cars
Roads: 12,955 km; 3,863 km paved
Railway: none
Air Traffic: 1,600,000 passengers carried (2001 est.)
Airports: 86; 13 have paved runways (2003 est.)

Canadian Embassy: The Consulate General of Canada, Tungata 14, 101 Reykjavik, Iceland, Postal Address: The Consulate General of Canada, P.O. Box 1510, 121 Reykjavik, Iceland. Tel: (011 354) 575-6500. Fax: (011-354) 575-6501. e-mail: rkjvk@dfait-maeci.gc.ca
Embassy in Canada: Embassy of the Republic of Iceland, 360 Albert St, 7th Fl Ste 710, Ottawa ON K1R 7X7. Tel: (613) 482-1944. Fax: (613) 482-1945. e-mail: n.a.

India

Long-Form Name: Republic of India
Capital: New Delhi

■ GEOGRAPHY

Area: 3,287,590 sq. km
Coastline: 7,000 km
Climate: varies from tropical monsoon in south to temperate in north
Environment: deforestation; soil erosion; overgrazing; air and water pollution; desertification, droughts, flash floods, severe thunderstorms common; earthquakes are a hazard
Terrain: upland plain (Deccan Plateau) in south, flat to rolling plain along the Ganges, deserts in west, Himalayas in north
Land Use: arable land: 54.35%, permanent crops: 2.66%, other: 42.99%; includes 590,000 sq. km irrigated
Location: S Asia, bordering on Arabian Sea, Indian Ocean, Bay of Bengal

■ PEOPLE

Population: 1,049,700,118 (July 2003 est.)
Nationality: Indian
Age Structure: 0–14 yrs: 32.2%; 15–64: 63.0%; 65+: 4.8% (2003 est.)
Population Growth Rate: 1.47% (2003 est.)
Net Migration: -0.07 migrants/1,000 population (2003 est.)
Ethnic Groups: 72% Indo-Aryan, 25% Dravidian, 3% Mongoloid and other
Languages: Hindi (official, spoken by 30%); English; 19 regional languages, including Bengali, Tlegu, Marathi, Tamil, Urdu, Gujarati, Malayalam, Kannada, Oriya, Punjabi, Assamese, Kashmiri, Sindhi and Sanskrit; 24 languages spoken by a million or more persons each; numerous other languages
Religions: 80% Hindu, 14% Muslim, 2.4% Christian, 2% Sikh, 0.7% Buddhist, 0.5% Jains, 0.4% other
Birth Rate: 23.28/1,000 population (2003 est.)
Death Rate: 8.49/1,000 population (2003 est.)
Infant Mortality: 59.59 deaths/1,000 live births (2003 est.)
Life Expectancy at Birth: 62.92 years male, 64.37 years female (2003 est.)
Total Fertility Rate: 2.91 children born/woman (2003 est.)
Literacy: 61.31% (2002)

■ GOVERNMENT

Leader(s): President A.P.J. Abdul Kalam, Prime Minister Manmohan Singh
Government Type: federal republic
Administrative Divisions: 28 states and 7 union territories
Nationhood: Aug. 15, 1947 (from UK)
National Holiday: Anniversary of the Proclamation of the Republic, Jan. 26

■ ECONOMY

Overview: a mixture of traditional village farming and handicrafts, modern agriculture, old and new branches of industry and a multitude of support services; millions still live in poverty, hoping to benefit from modern farming techniques
GDP: US$2.664 trillion, per capita US$2,600; real growth rate 4.3% (2002)
Inflation: 5.4% (2002 est.)
Industries: accounts for 25% of GDP (2002 est.), textiles, food processing, steel, machinery, transportation equipment, cement, jute manufactures, mining, petroleum, power, chemicals, pharmaceuticals, electronics
Labour Force: 470.2 million (2002); 60% agriculture, 17% industry, 23% services
Unemployment: n.a.
Agriculture: accounts for 25% of GDP (2002 est.) and employs two-thirds of labour force; self-sufficient in foodgrains; main crops—rice, wheat, oilseeds, cotton, jute, tea, sugar cane, potatoes; livestock—cattle, buffalo, sheep, goats and poultry; in top 10 of fishing nations
Natural Resources: coal, iron ore, manganese, mica, bauxite, titanium ore, chromite, petroleum, natural gas, diamonds, crude oil, limestone

■ FINANCE/TRADE

Currency: rupee (Rs) = 100 paise
International Reserves Excluding Gold: US$102.097 billion (Jan. 2004)
Gold Reserves: 11.502 million fine troy ounces (Jan. 2004)
Budget: revenues US$48.3 billion; expenditures US$78.2 billion, including capital expenditures of US$13.5 billion (FY2001/02 est.)
Defence Expenditures: 2.3% of GDP (2002)
Education Expenditures: 12.7% of central government expenditure (2002)
External Debt: US$104.429 billion (2002)
Exports: US$55.828 billion (2003 est.); commodities: tea, coffee, iron ore, fish products, manufactures; partners: US, UK, Germany, Japan, Benelux
Imports: US$70.485 billion (2003 est.); commodities: petroleum, edible oils, textiles, clothing, capital goods; partners: UK, US, Belgium, Japan, Germany

■ COMMUNICATIONS

Daily Newspapers: 60/1,000 inhabitants (2000)
Televisions: 83/1,000 inhabitants (2002)
Radios: 120/1,000 inhabitants (2001)
Telephones: 40 lines/1,000 inhabitants (2002)
Internet: hosts: 78,595 (2002); users: 16.58 million (2002)

■ TRANSPORTATION

Motor Vehicles: 10,400,000; 6,200,000 passenger cars
Roads: 3,319,644 km; 1,517,077 km hard-surfaced
Railway: 63,518 km
Air Traffic: 18,225,000 passengers carried (2002)
Airports: 334; 232 have paved runways (2003 est.)

Canadian Embassy: The Canadian High Commission, 7/8 Shantipath, Chanakyapuri, New Delhi 110021; mailing address: The Canadian High Commission, P.O. Box 5207, Chanakyapuri, New Delhi 110021, India. Tel: (011-91-11) 5178-2000. Fax: (011-91-11) 5178-2020. e-mail: delhi@dfait-maeci.gc.ca
Embassy in Canada: High Commission for the Republic of India, 10 Springfield Rd, Ottawa ON K1M 1C9. Tel: (613) 744-3751. Fax: (613) 744-0913. e-mail: hicomind@hciottawa.ca

Indonesia

Long-Form Name: Republic of Indonesia
Capital: Jakarta

■ GEOGRAPHY

Area: 1,919,440 sq. km (13,677 islands)
Coastline: 54,716 km
Climate: tropical; hot, humid; more moderate in highlands
Environment: archipelago of more than 13,500 islands (6,000 inhabited); occasional floods, severe droughts and tsunamis; deforestation; environmental pollution
Terrain: mostly coastal lowlands; larger islands have interior mountains
Land Use: arable land: 9.9%, permanent crops: 7.2%, other: 82.9%; includes 48,150 sq. km irrigated
Location: SE Asia, bordering on Indian Ocean

■ PEOPLE

Population: 234,893,453 (July 2003 est.)
Nationality: Indonesian
Age Structure: 0–14 yrs: 29.7%; 15–64: 65.4%; 65+: 4.9% (2003 est.)
Population Growth Rate: 1.52% (2003 est.)
Net Migration: 0.0 migrants/1,000 population (2003 est.)
Ethnic Groups: majority of Malay stock comprising 45% Javanese, 14% Sundanese, 7.5% Madurese, 7.5% coastal Malays, 26% other
Languages: Bahasa Indonesia (modified form of Malay; official); English and Dutch leading foreign languages; 25 local dialects, the most widely spoken of which is Javanese
Religions: 87% Muslim, 6% Protestant, 3% Roman Catholic, 2% Hindu, 1% Buddhist, 1% other
Birth Rate: 21.49/1,000 population (2003 est.)
Death Rate: 6.26/1,000 population (2003 est.)
Infant Mortality: 38.09 deaths/1,000 live births (2003 est.)
Life Expectancy at Birth: 66.54 years male, 71.47 years female (2003 est.)
Total Fertility Rate: 2.50 children born/woman (2003 est.)
Literacy: 87.9% (2002)

■ GOVERNMENT

Leader(s): President Susilo Bambang Yudhoyono, Vice President Hamzah Haz
Government Type: republic
Administrative Divisions: 27 provinces (propinsi-propinsi, sing. —propinsi), 2 special regions (daerah-daerah istimewa, sing. —daerah istimewa) and 1 special capital city district (daerah khusus ibukota)
Nationhood: Aug. 17, 1945 (Indonesia became legally independent from the Netherlands on Dec. 27, 1949; formerly known as Netherlands or Dutch East Indies)
National Holiday: Independence Day, Aug. 17

■ ECONOMY

Overview: a mixed economy with many socialist institutions and central planning but with a recent emphasis on deregulation and private enterprise; hampered by large population growth; possesses abundant natural wealth
GDP: US$714.2 billion, per capita US$3,100; real growth rate 3.7% (2002 est.)
Inflation: 11.9% (2002 est.)
Industries: accounts for 41% of GDP (2001 est.); petroleum, textiles, mining, cement, chemical fertilizer production, timber, food, rubber
Labour Force: 104.2 million (2002); 45% agriculture, 16% industry, 39% services
Unemployment: 6.1%; 50% underemployment (2002)
Agriculture: accounts for 17% of GDP (2001 est.); subsistence food production; small-holder and plantation production for export; rice, cassava, peanuts, rubber, cocoa, coffee, copra, other tropical products; poultry, beef, pork, eggs; the staple crop is rice; once the world's largest rice importer, Indonesia is now nearly self-sufficient

Natural Resources: crude oil, tin, natural gas, nickel, timber, bauxite, copper, fertile soils, coal, gold, silver

■ FINANCE/TRADE

Currency: rupiah (Rp) = 100 sen
International Reserves Excluding Gold: US$34.672 billion (Jan. 2004)
Gold Reserves: 3.101 million fine troy ounces (Jan. 2004)
Budget: revenues US$39 billion; expenditures US$43 billion, including capital expenditures of US$ n.a. (2003 est.)
Defence Expenditures: 4.6% of central government expenditure (2002)
Education Expenditures: 9.6% of central government expenditure (2002)
External Debt: US$132.208 billion (2002)
Exports: US$62.631 billion (2003); commodities: petroleum and liquefied natural gas 40%, timber 15%, textiles 7%, rubber 5%, coffee 3%; partners: Japan, US, Singapore, South Korea, China, Malaysia
Imports: US$41.682 billion (2003); commodities: machinery 39%, chemical products 19%, manufactured goods 16%; partners: Japan, Singapore, US, South Korea, China, Australia

■ COMMUNICATIONS

Daily Newspapers: 23/1,000 inhabitants (2000)
Televisions: 153/1,000 inhabitants (2002)
Radios: 159/1,000 inhabitants (2001)
Telephones: 37 lines/1,000 inhabitants (2002)
Internet: hosts: 61,279 (2002); users: 8 million (2002)

■ TRANSPORTATION

Motor Vehicles: 5,700,000; 3,200,000 passenger cars
Roads: 342,700 km; 158,670 km paved
Railway: 6,458 km
Air Traffic: 12,114,000 passengers carried (2002)
Airports: 631; 153 have paved runways (2003 est.)

Canadian Embassy: The Canadian Embassy, Jalan Jendral Sudirman, Jakarta 12920; mailing address: P.O. Box 8324/JKS.MP, Jakarta 12083, Indonesia. Tel: (011-62-21) 2550-7800. Fax: (011-62-21) 2550-7811. e-mail: jkrta@dfait-maeci.gc.ca
Embassy in Canada: Embassy of the Republic of Indonesia, 55 Parkdale Ave, Ottawa ON K1Y 1E5. Tel: (613) 724-1100. Fax: (613) 724-1105. e-mail: info@prica.org

Iran

Long-Form Name: Islamic Republic of Iran
Capital: Tehran

■ GEOGRAPHY

Area: 1,648,000 sq. km
Coastline: 2,440 km
Climate: mostly arid or semi-arid, subtropical along Caspian coast
Environment: deforestation; overgrazing; desertification; air and water pollution; periodic droughts and floods
Terrain: rugged mountainous rim; high, central basin with deserts, mountains; small, discontinuous plains along both coasts
Land Use: arable land: 10.17%, permanent crops: 1.16%, other: 88.67%; includes 75,620 sq. km irrigated
Location: SW Asia (Middle East), bordering on Persian Gulf

■ PEOPLE

Population: 68,278,826 (July 2003 est.)
Nationality: Iranian
Age Structure: 0–14 yrs: 29.3%; 15–64: 65.9%; 65+: 4.8% (2003 est.)
Population Growth Rate: 1.08% (2003 est.)
Net Migration: -0.86 migrants/1,000 population (2003 est.)
Ethnic Groups: 51% Persian, 24% Azerbaijani, 7% Kurd, 8% Gilaki and Mazandarani, 2% Lur, 2% Baloch, 3% Arab, 2% Turkmen, 1% other
Languages: Farsi (Persian) (official) 58%, Turkic and Turkic dialects 26%, Kurdish 9%, Luri 2%, Balochi 1%, Turkish 1%, Arabic 1%, 2% other
Religions: 99% Muslim (89% Shia, 10% Sunni); Christianity, Judaism, Zoroastrianism 1%
Birth Rate: 17.23/1,000 population (2003 est.)
Death Rate: 5.54/1,000 population (2003 est.)
Infant Mortality: 34.17 deaths/1,000 live births (2003 est.)
Life Expectancy at Birth: 68.04 years male, 70.73 years female (2003 est.)
Total Fertility Rate: 1.99 children born/woman (2003 est.)
Literacy: 77.1% (2002)

■ GOVERNMENT

Leader(s): President Mohammed Khatami, Supreme Religious Leader Ayatollah Mohammed Ali Hoseini Khamenei
Government Type: theocratic republic

Administrative Divisions: 28 provinces (ostanha, sing. —ostan)
Nationhood: Apr. 1, 1979, Islamic Republic of Iran proclaimed
National Holiday: Islamic Republic Day, Apr. 1

■ ECONOMY

Overview: economy is a mixture of central planning, state ownership of oil and other large enterprises, village agriculture, and small-scale private trading and service ventures; soaring external debt and high unemployment impede progress towards recovery from the economic devastation of the war with Iraq
GDP: US$458.3 billion, per capita US$6,800; real growth rate 7.6% (2002)
Inflation: 15.3% (2002)
Industries: accounts for 26% of GDP (2002 est.); petroleum, petrochemicals, textiles, cement and other building materials, food processing (particularly sugar refining and vegetable oil production), metal fabricating (steel and copper)
Labour Force: 21.1 million (2002); 30% agriculture, 25% industry, 45% services
Unemployment: 14% (2000 est.)
Agriculture: accounts for 19% of GDP (2002 est.); principal products—rice, other grains, sugar beets, fruits, nuts, cotton, wheat, dairy products, wool, caviar; not self-sufficient in food
Natural Resources: petroleum, natural gas, coal, chromium, copper, iron ore, lead, manganese, zinc, sulphur

■ FINANCE/TRADE

Currency: 10 rials (RIs) = 1 toman
International Reserves Excluding Gold: n.a.
Gold Reserves: n.a.
Budget: revenues US$41.2 billion; expenditures US$43.4 billion, including capital expenditures of US$ 7.6 billion (2003 est.)
Defence Expenditures: 17.2% of central government expenditure (2002)
Education Expenditures: 21.7% of central government expenditure (2002)
External Debt: US$9.154 billion (2002)
Exports: US$33.837 billion (2003 est.); commodities: petroleum 90%, carpets, fruit, nuts, hides; partners: Japan, Italy, UAE, France, China
Imports: US$24.088 billion (2003 est.); commodities: machinery, military supplies, metal works, foodstuffs, pharmaceuticals, technical services, refined oil products; partners: Germany, Italy, China, Japan, UAE

■ COMMUNICATIONS

Daily Newspapers: 28/1,000 inhabitants (2000)
Televisions: 173/1,000 inhabitants (2002)

Radios: 281/1,000 inhabitants (2001)
Telephones: 187 lines/1,000 inhabitants (2002)
Internet: hosts: 3,491 (2002); users: 3.168 million (2002)

■ TRANSPORTATION

Motor Vehicles: 2,239,000; 1,630,000 passenger cars
Roads: 167,157 km; 94,104 km paved or hard surfaced
Railway: 7,201 km
Air Traffic: 10,085,000 passengers carried (2002)
Airports: 309; 122 have paved runways (2003 est.)

Canadian Embassy: The Canadian Embassy to the Islamic Republic of Iran, 57 Shahid Javad-e-Sarafraz, Ostad-Motahari Ave, 15868 Tehran; mailing address: P.O. Box 11365-4647, Tehran, Iran. Tel: (011-98-21) 873-2623. Fax: (011-98-21) 873-3202. e-mail: teran@dfait-maeci.gc.ca
Embassy in Canada: Embassy of the Islamic Republic of Iran, 245 Metcalfe St, Ottawa ON K2P 2K2. Tel: (613) 235-4726. Fax: (613) 238-5712. e-mail: iranemb@salamiran.org

Iraq

Long-Form Name: Republic of Iraq
Capital: Baghdad

■ GEOGRAPHY

Area: 437,072 sq. km
Coastline: 58 km
Climate: desert; mild to cool winters with dry, hot, cloudless summers; northern mountainous regions experience cold winters with occasionally heavy snows
Environment: development of Tigris-Euphrates river systems contingent upon agreements with upstream riparians (Syria and Turkey); air and water pollution; soil degradation (salinization) and erosion; desertification
Terrain: mostly broad plains; reedy marshes in southeast; mountains along borders with Iran and Turkey
Land Use: arable land: 11.89%, permanent crops: 0.78%, other: 87.33%; includes 35,250 sq. km irrigated
Location: SW Asia (Middle East), bordering on Persian Gulf

■ PEOPLE

Population: 24,683,313 (July 2003 est.)
Nationality: Iraqi
Age Structure: 0–14 yrs: 40.7%; 15–64: 56.3%; 65+: 3.0% (2003 est.)

Population Growth Rate: 2.78% (2003 est.)
Net Migration: 0 migrants/1,000 population (2003 est.)
Ethnic Groups: 75–80% Arab, 15–20% Kurdish, 5% Turkoman and other
Languages: Arabic (official), Kurdish (official in Kurdish region), Assyrian, Armenian
Religions: 97% Muslim (60–65% Shi'a, 32–37% Sunni), 3% Christian or other
Birth Rate: 33.66/1,000 population (2003 est.)
Death Rate: 5.84/1,000 population (2003 est.)
Infant Mortality: 55.16 deaths/1,000 live births (2003 est.)
Life Expectancy at Birth: 66.70 years male, 68.99 years female (2003 est.)
Total Fertility Rate: 4.52 children born/woman (2003 est.)
Literacy: 40.4% (2003 est.)

■ **GOVERNMENT**

Leader(s): President Ghazi al-Ujayl al-Yawr, Prime Minister Ayad Allawi
Government Type: republic (in transition following April 2003 defeat of Saddam Hussein regime by US-led coalition)
Administrative Divisions: 18 provinces (muhafazat, sing. —muhafazah)
Nationhood: Oct. 3, 1932 (from League of Nations mandate under British administration)
National Holiday: Anniversary of the Revolution, July 17

■ **ECONOMY**

Overview: Iraq's economy is dominated by the oil sector, which has traditionally provided about 95% of foreign exchange earnings. Political instability (the eight-year war with Iran during the 1990s; the invasion of Kuwait and the hostilities and sanctions that followed) has been at the root of Iraq's substantial debt-load. The drop in GDP in 2001–02 was largely the result of the global economic slowdown and lower oil prices. Most recently, the military victory of the US-led coalition in March/April 2003 resulted in the shutdown of much of the country's central economic administrative structure.
GDP: US$58 billion, per capita US$2,400; real growth rate -3% (2002 est.)
Inflation: 70% (2002 est.)
Industries: accounts for 13% of GDP; petroleum, chemicals, textiles, construction materials, food processing
Labour Force: 6.8 million (2002)
Unemployment: n.a.
Agriculture: principal products: wheat, barley, rice, vegetables, dates, other fruit, cotton, wool;

livestock: cattle, sheep; not self-sufficient in food output
Natural Resources: petroleum, natural gas, phosphates, sulphur

■ **FINANCE/TRADE**

Currency: dinar = 1,000 fils
International Reserves Excluding Gold: n.a.
Gold Reserves: n.a.
Budget: revenues US$12.8 billion; expenditures US$13.4 billion, including capital expenditures of US$ n.a. (2004 plan)
Defence Expenditures: n.a.
Education Expenditures: n.a.
External Debt: US$120 billion (2002 est.)
Exports: US$7.542 billion (2003 est.); commodities: crude oil and refined products, machinery, chemicals, dates; partners: US, Italy, France, Netherlands
Imports: US$6.521 billion (2003 est.); commodities: manufactures, medicines, food; partners: France, Australia, Italy, Germany

■ **COMMUNICATIONS**

Daily Newspapers: 19/1,000 inhabitants (2000)
Televisions: 83/1,000 inhabitants (2002)
Radios: 222/1,000 inhabitants (2001)
Telephones: 28 lines/1,000 inhabitants (2002)
Internet: users: 25,000 (2002)

■ **TRANSPORTATION**

Motor Vehicles: 1,040,000; 672,000 passenger cars
Roads: 45,550 km; 38,400 km paved
Railway: 1,963 km
Air Traffic: n.a.
Airports: 150; 77 have paved runways (2003 est.)

Canadian Embassy: The Canadian Embassy to Iraq, c/o The Canadian Embassy, P.O. Box 815403, Amman, Jordan, 11180. Tel: (011-962-6) 566-61-24. Fax: (011-962-6) 568-92-27. e-mail: amman@dfait-maeci.gc.ca
Embassy in Canada: Embassy of the Republic of Iraq, 215 McLeod St, Ottawa ON K2P 0Z8. Tel: (613) 236-9177. Fax: (613) 567-1101. e-mail: n.a.

Ireland

Long-Form Name: Ireland
Capital: Dublin

■ **GEOGRAPHY**

Area: 70,280 sq. km
Coastline: 1,448 km

Climate: temperate maritime; modified by North Atlantic Current; mild winters, cool summers; consistently humid; overcast about half the time

Environment: deforestation and water pollution, especially of lakes, from agricultural runoff

Terrain: mostly level to rolling interior plains surrounded by rugged hills and low mountains; sea cliffs on west coast

Land Use: arable land: 19.49%, permanent crops: 0.04%, other: 80.47%; includes n.a. sq. km irrigated

Location: NW Europe, (British Isles), bordering on Atlantic Ocean and Irish Sea

■ PEOPLE

Population: 3,924,140 (July 2003 est.)

Nationality: Irish

Age Structure: 0–14 yrs: 21.2%; 15–64: 67.4%; 65+: 11.4% (2003 est.)

Population Growth Rate: 1.03% (2003 est.)

Net Migration: 3.57 migrants/1,000 population (2003 est.)

Ethnic Groups: Celtic, with English minority

Languages: Irish (official first language, but use is limited) and English; English is the language generally used, with Gaelic spoken in a few areas, mostly along the western seaboard

Religions: 93% Roman Catholic, 3% Anglican, 1% atheist, 3% other

Birth Rate: 14.63/1,000 population (2003 est.)

Death Rate: 7.94/1,000 population (2003 est.)

Infant Mortality: 5.34 deaths/1,000 live births (2003 est.)

Life Expectancy at Birth: 74.58 years male, 80.31 years female (2003 est.)

Total Fertility Rate: 1.89 children born/woman (2003 est.)

Literacy: approaching 100% (2002)

■ GOVERNMENT

Leader(s): President Mary McAleese, Prime Minister Bertie Ahern

Government Type: republic

Administrative Divisions: 26 counties

Nationhood: Dec. 6, 1921 (from UK)

National Holiday: St. Patrick's Day, Mar. 17

■ ECONOMY

Overview: a small, open economy that is trade dependent; unemployment is high but inflation has been considerably lowered and the deficit burden relieved

GDP: US$113.7 billion, per capita US$29,300; real growth rate 6.9% (2002)

Inflation: 4.6% (2002 est.)

Industries: account for 46% of GDP (2002), 80% of exports and employs almost 30% of the workforce; food products, brewing, textiles, clothing, chemicals, pharmaceuticals, machinery, transportation equipment, glass and crystal

Labour Force: 1.7 million (2002); 64% community, social and business services, 28% industry, 8% agriculture

Unemployment: 4.5% (Nov. 2003)

Agriculture: accounts for 5% of GDP (2002) and 8% of the labour force; principal crops include turnips, barley, potatoes, sugar, beets, wheat; livestock—meat and dairy products; 85% self-sufficient in food; food shortages include bread grain, fruits, vegetables

Natural Resources: zinc, lead, natural gas, barite, copper, gypsum, limestone, dolomite, peat, silver

■ FINANCE/TRADE

Currency: Irish pound (£ or £Ir) = 100 pence; Euro (€); on January 1, 2002 the Euro became the sole currency for everyday transactions.

International Reserves Excluding Gold: US$4.055 billion (Jan. 2004)

Gold Reserves: 0.176 million fine troy ounces (Jan. 2004)

Budget: revenues US$30.7 billion; expenditures US$30.5 billion, including capital expenditures of US$55.5 billion (2002)

Defence Expenditures: 2.8% of central government expenditure (2002)

Education Expenditures: 10.7% of total government expeditures (2002)

External Debt: n.a.

Exports: US$92.431 billion (2003 est.); commodities: live animals, animal products, chemicals, data processing equipment, industrial machinery; partners: European Community, US

Imports: US$53.315 billion (2003 est.); commodities: food, animal feed, chemicals, petroleum and petroleum products, machinery, textiles, clothing; partners: UK, Germany, France, Netherlands, US, Japan

■ COMMUNICATIONS

Daily Newspapers: 150/1,000 inhabitants (2000)

Televisions: 694/1,000 inhabitants (2002)

Radios: 695/1,000 inhabitants (2001)

Telephones: 502 lines/1,000 inhabitants (2002)

Internet: hosts: 136,487 (2002); users: 1.065 million (2002)

■ TRANSPORTATION

Motor Vehicles: 1,570,000; 1,350,000 passenger cars

Roads: 92,500 km; 87,042 km paved

Railway: 3,314 km

Air Traffic: 19,729,000 passengers carried (2002)
Airports: 36; 16 have paved runways (2003 est.)

Canadian Embassy: The Canadian Embassy, 65 St Stephen's Green, Dublin 2, Ireland. Tel: (011-353-1) 417-4100. Fax: (011-353-1) 417-4101. e-mail: dubln@dfait-maeci.gc.ca
Embassy in Canada: Embassy of Ireland, 130 Albert St, Ste 1105, Ottawa ON K1P 5G4. Tel: (613) 233-6281. Fax: (613) 233-5835. e-mail: embassyofireland@rogers.com

Isle of Man

Long-Form Name: Isle of Man
Capital: Douglas

■ GEOGRAPHY

Area: 572 sq. km
Climate: temperate maritime, cool summers and mild winters, humid, overcast about half the time
Land Use: 9% arable; 0% permanent crops; 46% permanent pastures; 6% forests and woodland; 39% other;
Location: Irish Sea, between Great Britain and Northern Ireland

■ PEOPLE

Population: 74,261 (July 2003 est.)
Nationality: Manxman, Manxwoman
Ethnic Groups: Manx (Norse-Celtic descent), Briton
Languages: English, Manx, Gaelic

■ GOVERNMENT

Colony/Territory of: Dependency of United Kingdom
Leader(s): Head of State: Queen Elizabeth II, Lieutenant Governor Ian David Macfadyen, Chief Minister Richard Corkill
Government Type: parliamentary democracy
National Holiday: Tynwald Day, July 5

■ ECONOMY

Overview: offshore banking, manufacturing, and tourism are key sectors of the economy; the government's policy of offering incentives to high-technology companies and financial institutions to locate on the island has paid off in expanding employment opportunities in high-income industries

■ FINANCE/TRADE

Currency: Manx pound = 100 pence; on a par with British pound sterling

Canadian Embassy: c/o The Canadian High Commission, Macdonald House, 1 Grosvenor Square, London W1K 4AB, England, UK. Tel: (011-44-20) 7258-6600. Fax: (011-44-20) 7258-6333. e-mail: Ldn@dfait-maeci.gc.ca
Representative to Canada: c/o British High Commission, 80 Elgin St, Ottawa ON K1P 5K7. Tel: (613) 237-1530. Fax: (613) 237-7980. e-mail should be sent using the appropriate form at the British High Commission's Website at http://www.britain-in-canada.org

Israel

Long-Form Name: State of Israel
Capital: Jerusalem

■ GEOGRAPHY

Area: 20,770 sq. km
Coastline: 273 km
Climate: temperate; hot and dry in desert areas
Environment: sandstorms may occur during spring and summer; limited arable land and natural water resources pose serious constraints; deforestation
Terrain: Negev Desert in the south; low coastal plain; central mountains; Jordan Rift Valley
Land Use: arable land: 17.02%, permanent crops: 4.17%, other: 78.81%; includes 1,990 sq. km irrigated
Location: SW Asia (Middle East), bordering on Mediterranean Sea

■ PEOPLE

Population: 6,116,533; includes about 187,000 Israeli settlers in the West Bank, about 20,000 in the Israeli-occupied Golan Heights, more than 5,000 in the Gaza Strip, and fewer than 177,000 in East Jerusalem (Feb. 2003 est.)
Nationality: Israeli
Age Structure: 0–14 yrs: 26.9%; 15–64: 63.2%; 65+: 9.9% (2003 est.)
Population Growth Rate: 1.39% (2003 est.)
Net Migration: 1.39 migrants/1,000 population (2003 est.)
Ethnic Groups: 80.1% Jewish, 19.9% non-Jewish (mostly Arab)
Languages: Hebrew (official); Arabic used officially for Arab minority; European languages (mostly English)
Religions: 82% Judaism, 14% Islam (mostly Sunni Muslim), 2% Christian and Druze, 2% other
Birth Rate: 18.67/1,000 population (2003 est.)
Death Rate: 6.20/1,000 population (2003 est.)

Infant Mortality: 7.37 deaths/1,000 live births (2003 est.)
Life Expectancy at Birth: 76.95 years male, 81.19 years female (2003 est.)
Total Fertility Rate: 2.58 children born/woman (2003 est.)
Literacy: 95.3% (2002)

■ GOVERNMENT

Leader(s): Prime Minister Ariel Sharon, President Moshe Katzav
Government Type: parliamentary democracy
Administrative Divisions: 6 districts (mehozot, sing. —mehoz)
Nationhood: May 14, 1948 (from League of Nations mandate under British administration)
National Holiday: Independence Day, May 14; the Jewish calendar is lunar and the holiday may occur in Apr. or May

■ ECONOMY

Overview: a market economy with government participation; despite limited natural resources, this country has strong agriculture and industry sectors; transfer payments and foreign loans offset the deficit; the Palestinian uprising and Russian immigration stifle growth; high Jewish immigration from the former Soviet states has created massive housing problems
GDP: US$117.4 billion, per capita US$19,500; real growth rate -0.8% (2002)
Inflation: 5.7% (2002 est.)
Industries: accounts for 37% of GDP (2001 est.); food processing, diamond cutting and polishing, textiles, clothing, chemicals, metal products, military equipment, transport equipment, electrical equipment, miscellaneous machinery, potash mining, high-technology electronics, tourism
Labour Force: 2.9 million (2002); 77% services, 20% industry, 3% agriculture
Unemployment: 11.0% (Nov. 2003)
Agriculture: accounts for 3% of GDP (2001 est.); largely self-sufficient in food production, except for bread grains; principal products—citrus and other fruit, vegetables, cotton; livestock products —beef, dairy and poultry
Natural Resources: copper, phosphates, bromide, potash, clay, sand, sulphur, asphalt, manganese, small amounts of natural gas and crude oil

■ FINANCE/TRADE

Currency: new Israeli shekel (NIS) = 100 new agorot
International Reserves Excluding Gold: US$26.030 billion (Jan. 2004)

Gold Reserves: none (Jan. 2004)
Budget: revenues US$38.5 billion; expenditures US$45.1 billion, capital expenditures US$ n.a. (2002 est.)
Defence Expenditures: 16.6% of central government expenditure (2001)
Education Expenditures: 13.54% of central government expenditure (2000)
External Debt: US$42.8 billion (2001 est.)
Exports: US$31.577 billion (2003); commodities: polished diamonds, citrus and other fruit, textiles and clothing, processed foods, fertilizer and chemical products, military hardware, electronics; partners: US, Benelux, Hong Kong, Germany, UK, Japan
Imports: US$34.769 billion (2003 est.); commodities: military equipment, rough diamonds, oil, chemicals, machinery, iron and steel, cereals, textiles, vehicles, ships, aircraft; partners: US, Benelux, Germany, UK, Switzerland, Italy

■ COMMUNICATIONS

Daily Newspapers: 290/1,000 inhabitants (2000)
Televisions: 330/1,000 inhabitants (2002)
Radios: 526/1,000 inhabitants (2001)
Telephones: 467 lines/1,000 inhabitants (2002)
Internet: hosts: 146,791 (2002); users: 2 million (2002)

■ TRANSPORTATION

Motor Vehicles: 1,650,000; 1,400,000 passenger cars
Roads: 16,281 km, all paved
Railway: 640 km
Air Traffic: 3,731,000 passengers carried (2002)
Airports: 52; 28 have paved runways (2003 est.)

Canadian Embassy: The Canadian Embassy, 3 Nirim St., 4th Fl, Tel Aviv, 67060; mailing address: P.O. Box 9442, Tel Aviv, Israel. Tel: (011-972-3) 636-3300. Fax: (011-972-3) 636-3380. e-mail: taviv@dfait-maeci.gc.ca
Embassy in Canada: Embassy of Israel, 50 O'Connor St, Ste 1005, Ottawa ON K1P 6L2. Tel: (613) 567-6450. Fax: (613) 237-8865. e-mail: info@ottawa.mfa.gov.il

Italy

Long-Form Name: Italian Republic
Capital: Rome

■ GEOGRAPHY

Area: 301,230 sq. km; includes Sardinia and Sicily

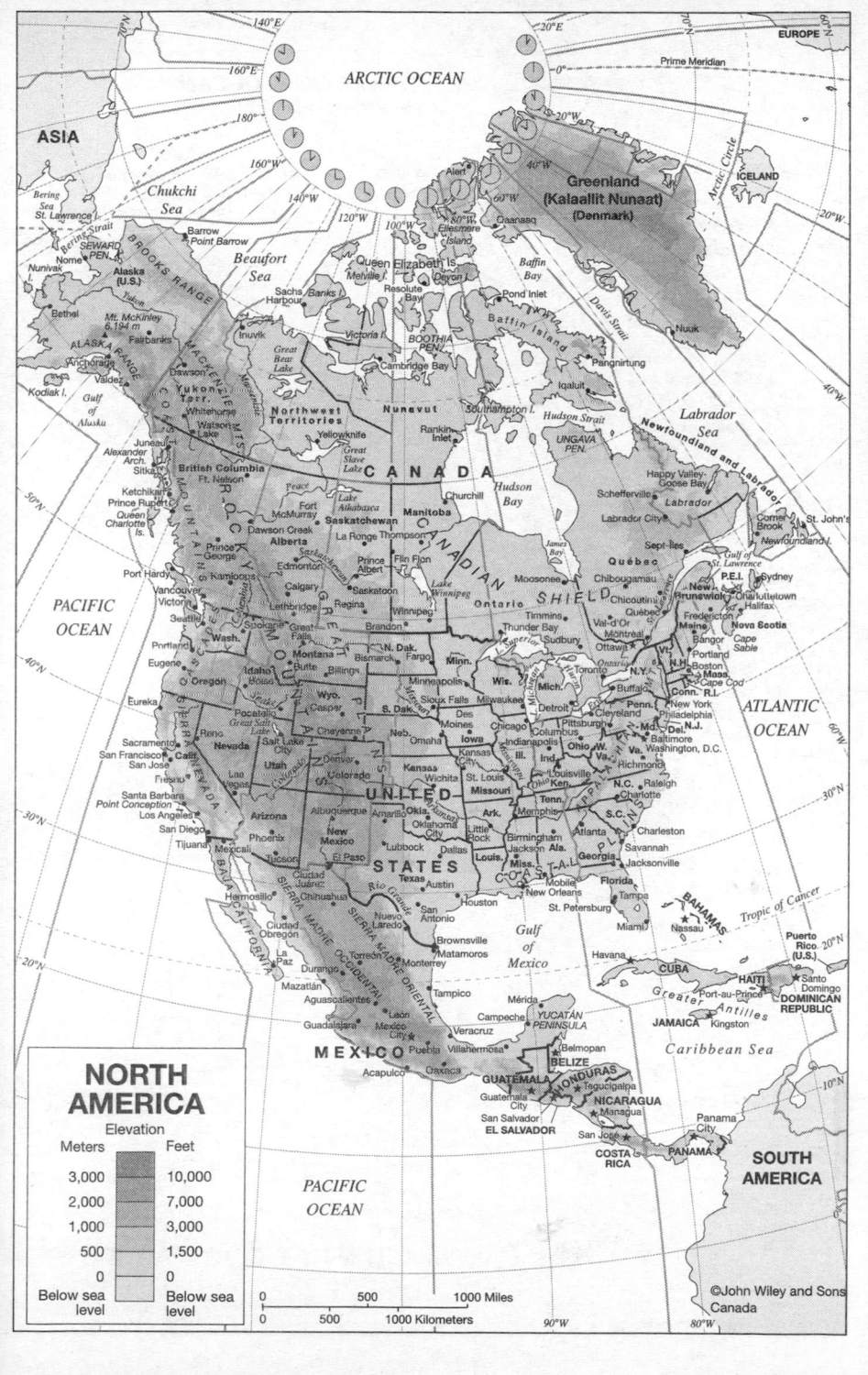

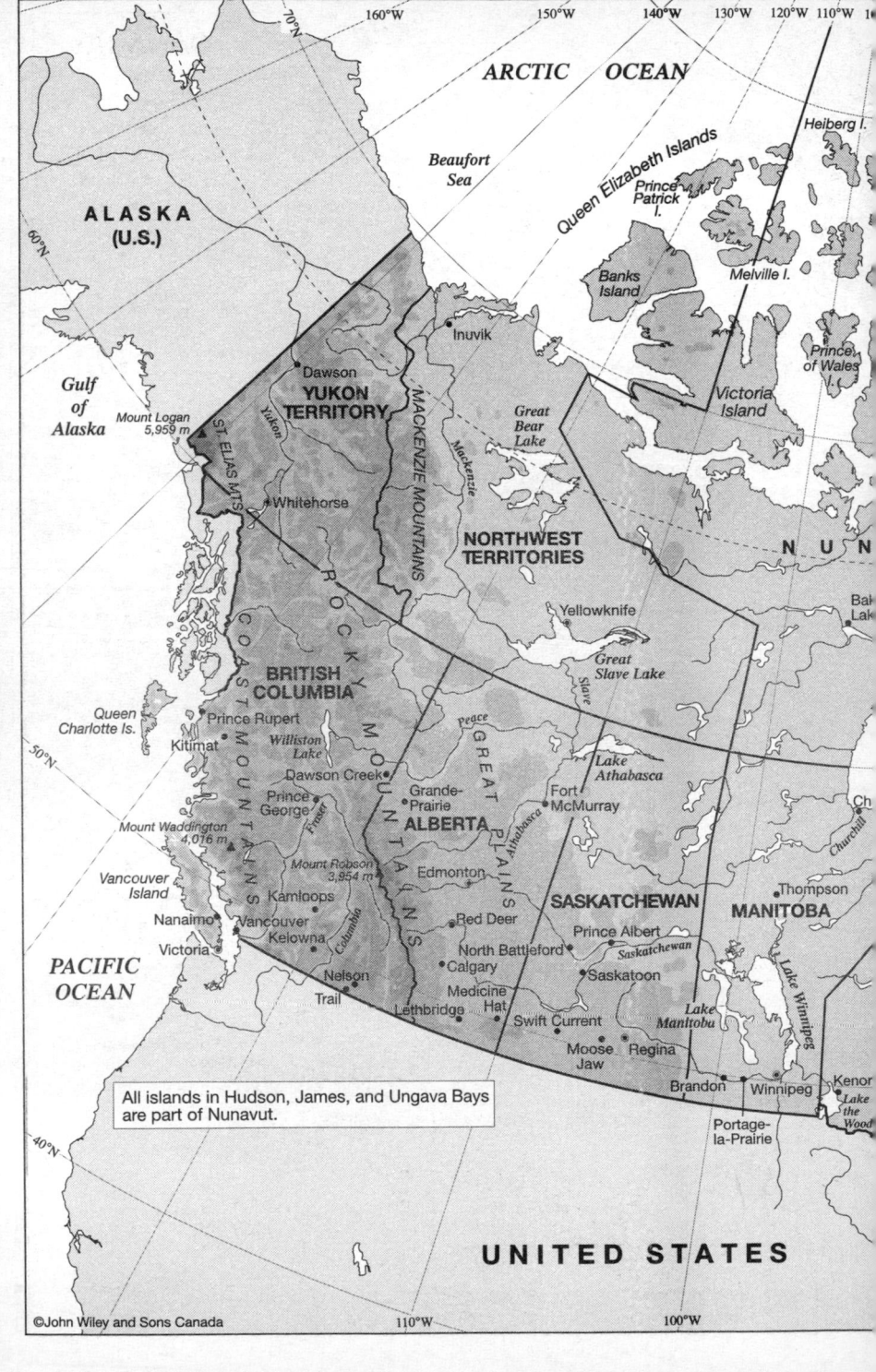

All islands in Hudson, James, and Ungava Bays are part of Nunavut.

©John Wiley and Sons Canada

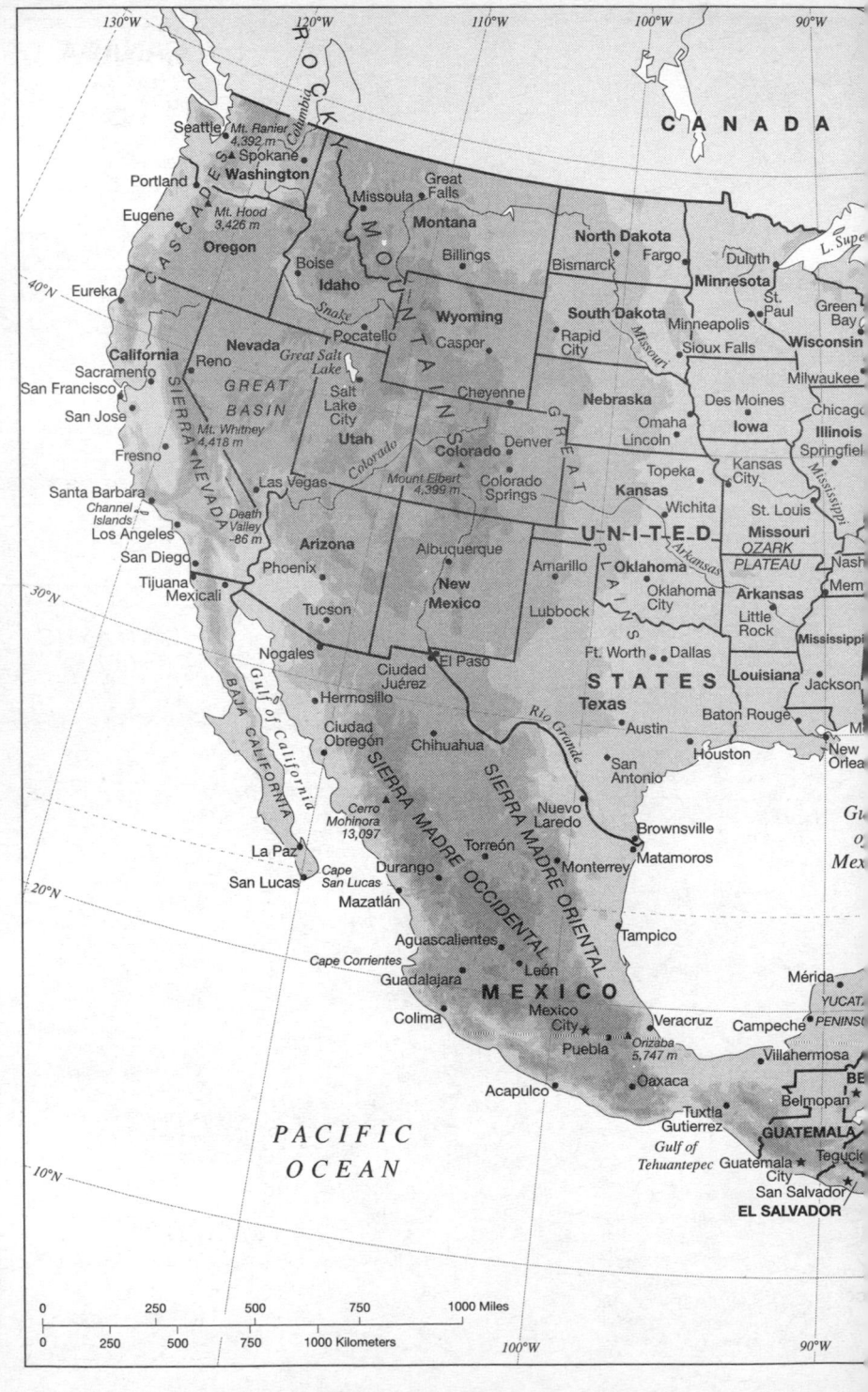

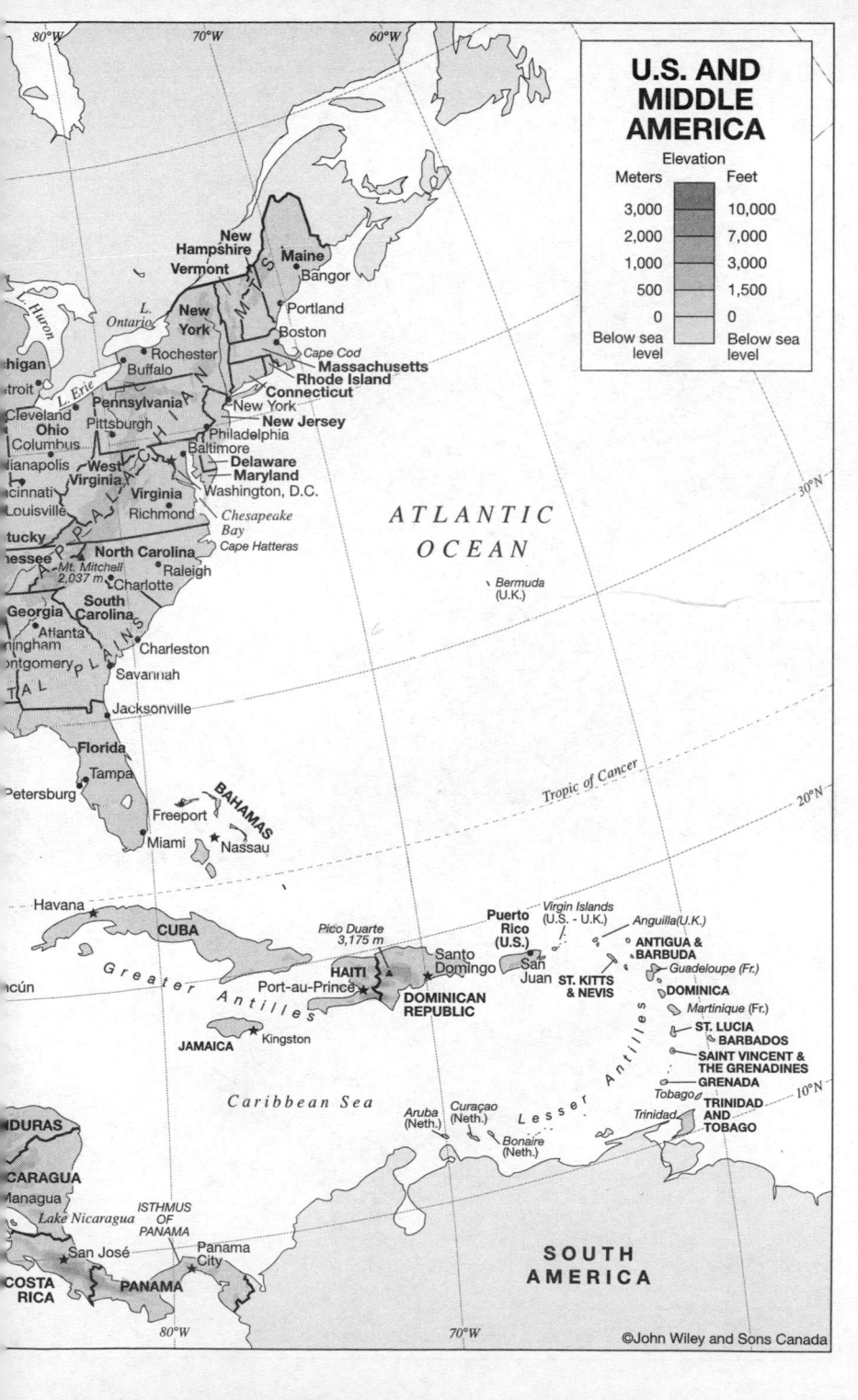

U.S. AND MIDDLE AMERICA

Elevation

Meters		Feet
3,000		10,000
2,000		7,000
1,000		3,000
500		1,500
0		0
Below sea level		Below sea level

New Hampshire
Vermont
Maine
Bangor
L. Ontario
New York
Portland
Boston
Rochester
Buffalo
Cape Cod
Massachusetts
Rhode Island
Connecticut
higan
troit
Cleveland
Pennsylvania
New York
New Jersey
Ohio
Pittsburgh
Philadelphia
Columbus
Baltimore
ianapolis
West
Delaware
Virginia
Maryland
cinnati
Virginia
Washington, D.C.
Louisville
Richmond
Chesapeake Bay
kucky
essee
North Carolina
Cape Hatteras
Mt. Mitchell
2,037 m
Raleigh
Charlotte
Georgia
South Carolina
Atlanta
ningham
Charleston
ntgomery
Savannah
AL
Jacksonville

ATLANTIC
OCEAN

Bermuda
(U.K.)

Florida
Tampa
Petersburg

Tropic of Cancer

BAHAMAS
Freeport
Miami
Nassau

Havana
CUBA
Pico Duarte
3,175 m
Virgin Islands
(U.S. - U.K.)
Puerto Rico
(U.S.)
Anguilla(U.K.)
Santo Domingo
San Juan
ANTIGUA & BARBUDA
Guadeloupe (Fr.)
cún
HAITI
Port-au-Prince
DOMINICAN REPUBLIC
ST. KITTS & NEVIS
DOMINICA
Martinique (Fr.)
JAMAICA
Kingston
ST. LUCIA
BARBADOS
SAINT VINCENT & THE GRENADINES
GRENADA
Caribbean Sea
Aruba (Neth.)
Curaçao (Neth.)
Tobago
TRINIDAD AND TOBAGO
Trinidad
Bonaire (Neth.)

Greater Antilles

Lesser Antilles

NDURAS
CARAGUA
Managua
Lake Nicaragua
ISTHMUS OF PANAMA
San José
Panama City
SOUTH AMERICA
COSTA RICA
PANAMA

©John Wiley and Sons Canada

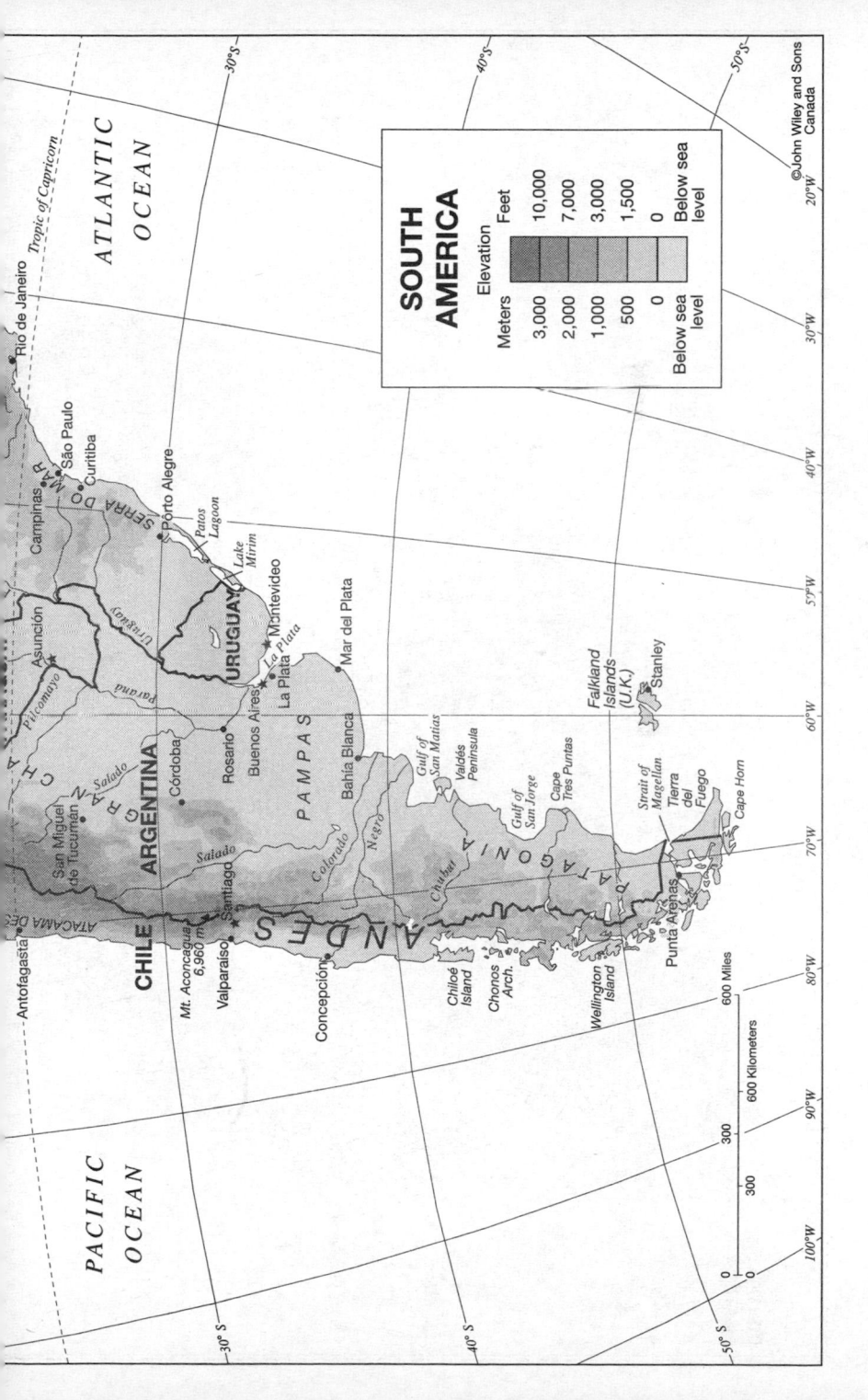

Barents
Sea

Murmansk

KOLA
PENINSULA

White
Sea

Arkhangelsk

N. Dvina

WESTERN
SIBERIAN
LOWLAND

Ob

Ob

Irtysh

Pechora

U R A L   M O U N T A I N S

Tyumen

Kurgan

N

ILAND

Lake
Onega

Lake
Ladoga

KAMA
UPLAND

Perm

Yekaterinburg

Chelyabinsk

Izhevsk

Ufa

50°N

lsinki

St. Petersburg

RUSSIA

Tallinn

Velikiy
Novgorod

Lake
Peipus

TONIA

LATVIA

Riga

Yaroslavl

Volga

Kazan

Nizhny
Novgorod

Tver

Samara

Orenburg

Moscow

Oka

Ural

JANIA

Smolensk

Ryazan

nius

Vitsyebsk

Minsk

CENTRAL
RUSSIAN
UPLAND

Saratov

Volga

BELARUS

Voronezh

Hornyel

CASPIAN
DEPRESSION

Brest

Belgorod

ASIA

Kiev

Kharkiv

Volgograd

UKRAINE

Luhansk

Caspian
Sea

Lviv

Vinnytsya

Dnipropetrovsk

Donetsk

Don

Zaporizhya

PEAN PLAIN

EUROPEAN PLAIN

RPATHIAN MTS.

MOLDOVA

Mariupol

Rostov-na-Donu

uj-
apoca

Chisinau

Odesa

Dnieper

Sea of
Azov

Krasnodar

Makhachkala

40°N

ROMANIA

CRIMEA

CAUCASUS MOUNTAINS

Craiova

Bucharest

Sevastopol

Mt. Elbrus
5,642 m

GEORGIA

Baku

Danube

Constanta

Black   Sea

Batumi

T'bilisi

AZERBAIJAN

BULGARIA

Varna

ARMENIA

Sofia

Plovdiv

Burgas

Yerevan

opje

Istanbul

AZER.

A

TURKEY

essaloniki

EECE

Aegean Sea

thens

Rhodes

Crete

EUROPE

Elevation

Meters		Feet
4,000		14,000
2,000		7,000
1,000		3,000
500		1,500
0		0
Below sea level		Below sea level

30°E   ©John Wiley and Sons Canada

30°E   40°E   50°E   60°E   70°E

ASIA

Elevation

Meters	Feet
4,000	13,000
2,000	7,000
1,000	3,000
500	1,500
0	0
Below sea level	Below sea level

OCEAN

East Siberian Sea

New Siberian Is.

North Land

Laptev Sea

Taimyr Peninsula

CENTRAL

SIBERIAN

USSIA

PLATEAU

Stony Tunguska

Angara

Lena

Vilyuy

KOLYMA RANGE

Kolyma

CHERSKY MTS.

VERKHOYANSK RANGE

CENTRAL RANGE

Kamchatka Peninsula

Bering Sea

Sea of Okhotsk

Sakhalin

Kuril Islands

Hokkaido

Sapporo

Vladivostok

Sea of Japan

Honshu

JAPAN

Tokyo

Lena

Aldan

Amur

SIKHOTE-ALIN RANGE

Tatar Strait

Lake Baikal

Irkutsk

SAYAN MTS.

Selenga

Ulaanbaatar

MONGOLIAN PLATEAU

MONGOLIA

GOBI DESERT

Argun

Amur

Sungari

Harbin

DA HINGGAN LING

MANCHURIAN PLAIN

Shenyang

Yalu

NORTH KOREA

P'yongyang

Seoul

SOUTH KOREA

Osaka

Hiroshima

Fukuoka

Kyushu

Shikoku

Korea Str.

Beijing

Tianjin

NORTH CHINA PLAIN

Yellow Sea

Huang (Yellow)

Huang (Yellow)

Lanzhou

Wei

Xi'an

QIN LING

Nanjing

Shanghai

East China Sea

Ryukyu Is.

Tropic of Cancer

CHINA

TAINS

Mekong

TIBET

Chang (Yangzi)

Salween

Chang

Chongqing

Wuhan

Changsha

Taipei

TAIWAN

PACIFIC OCEAN

BHUTAN

Hongshi

Guangzhou

Xi

Hong Kong

Macau

Red

Hainan

Luzon

South China Sea

Manila

PHILIPPINES

MYANMAR (BURMA)

Hanoi

LAOS

Vientiane

Mekong

THAILAND

VIETNAM

Yangon (Rangoon)

Bangkok

CAMBODIA

Ho Chi Minh City

Andaman Is. (India)

Phnom Penh

Mekong Delta

Gulf of Thailand

Bandar Seri Begawan

BRUNEI

Sulu Sea

Mindanao

Davao

Celebes Sea

Equator

MALAY PEN.

MALAYSIA

Kuala Lumpur

SINGAPORE

Borneo

Nicobar Is.

©John Wiley and Sons Canada

100°E   110°E   120°E   130°E

70°N   60°N   50°N   40°N   30°N   20°N   10°N   0°   10°S

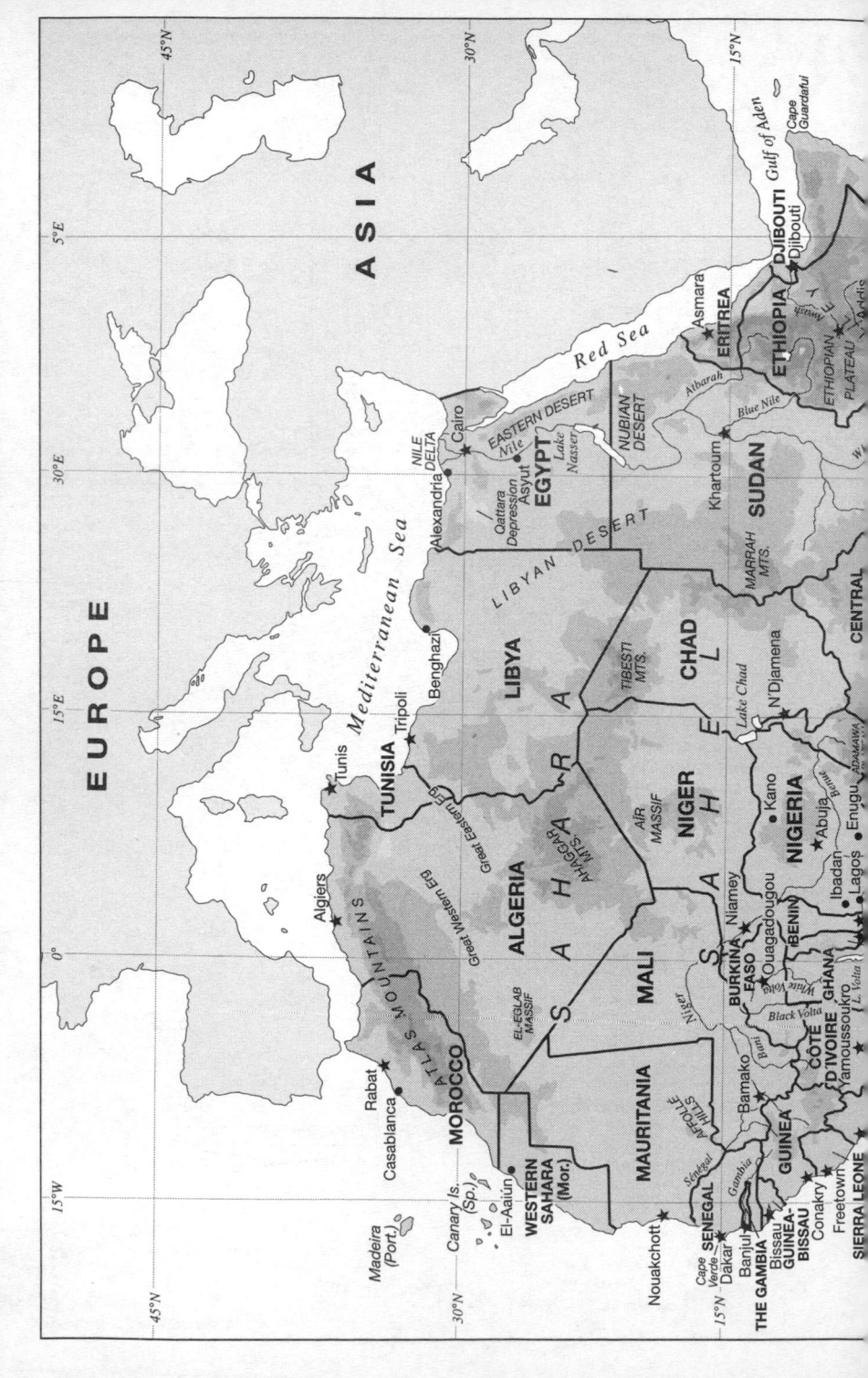

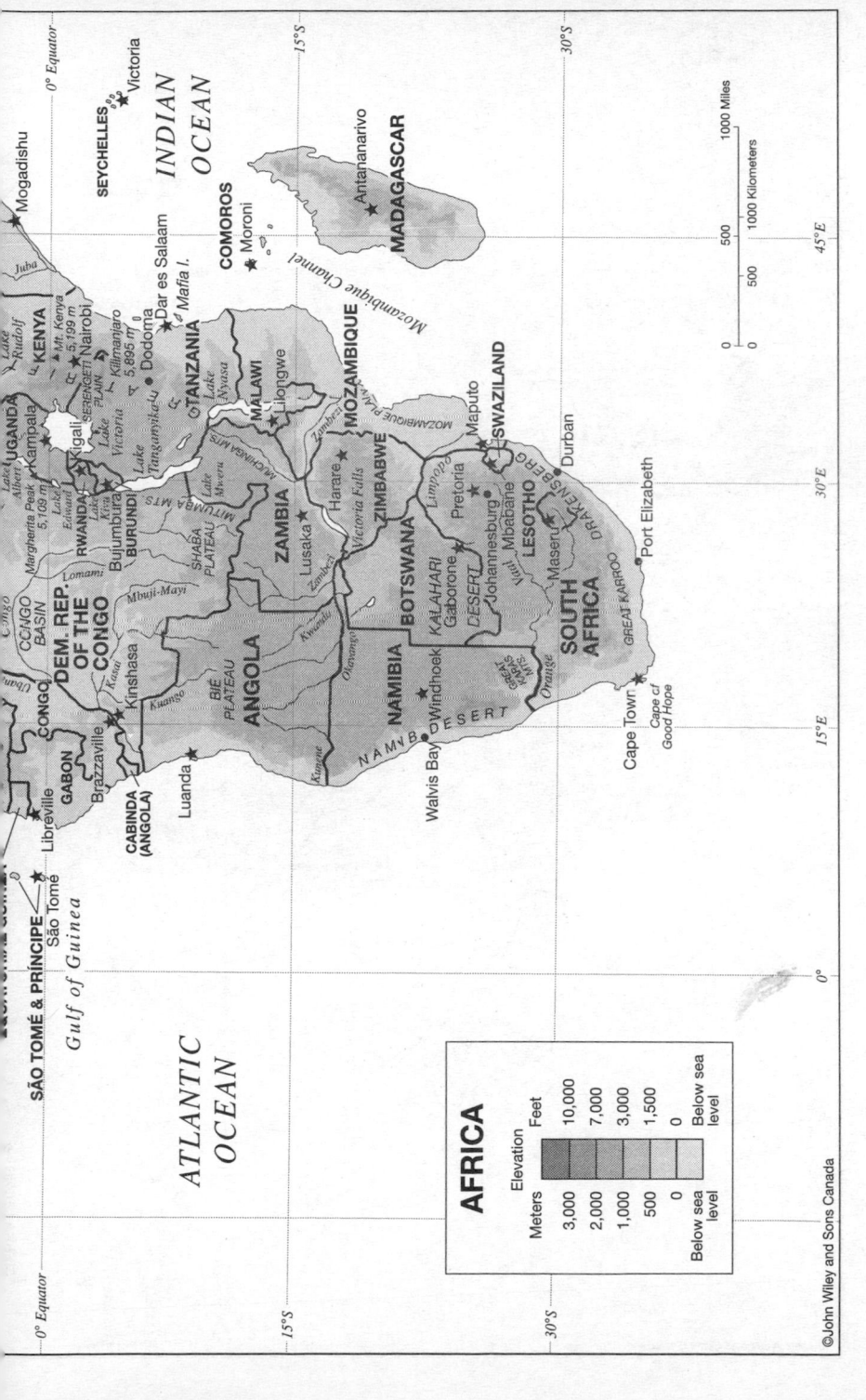

©John Wiley and Sons Canada

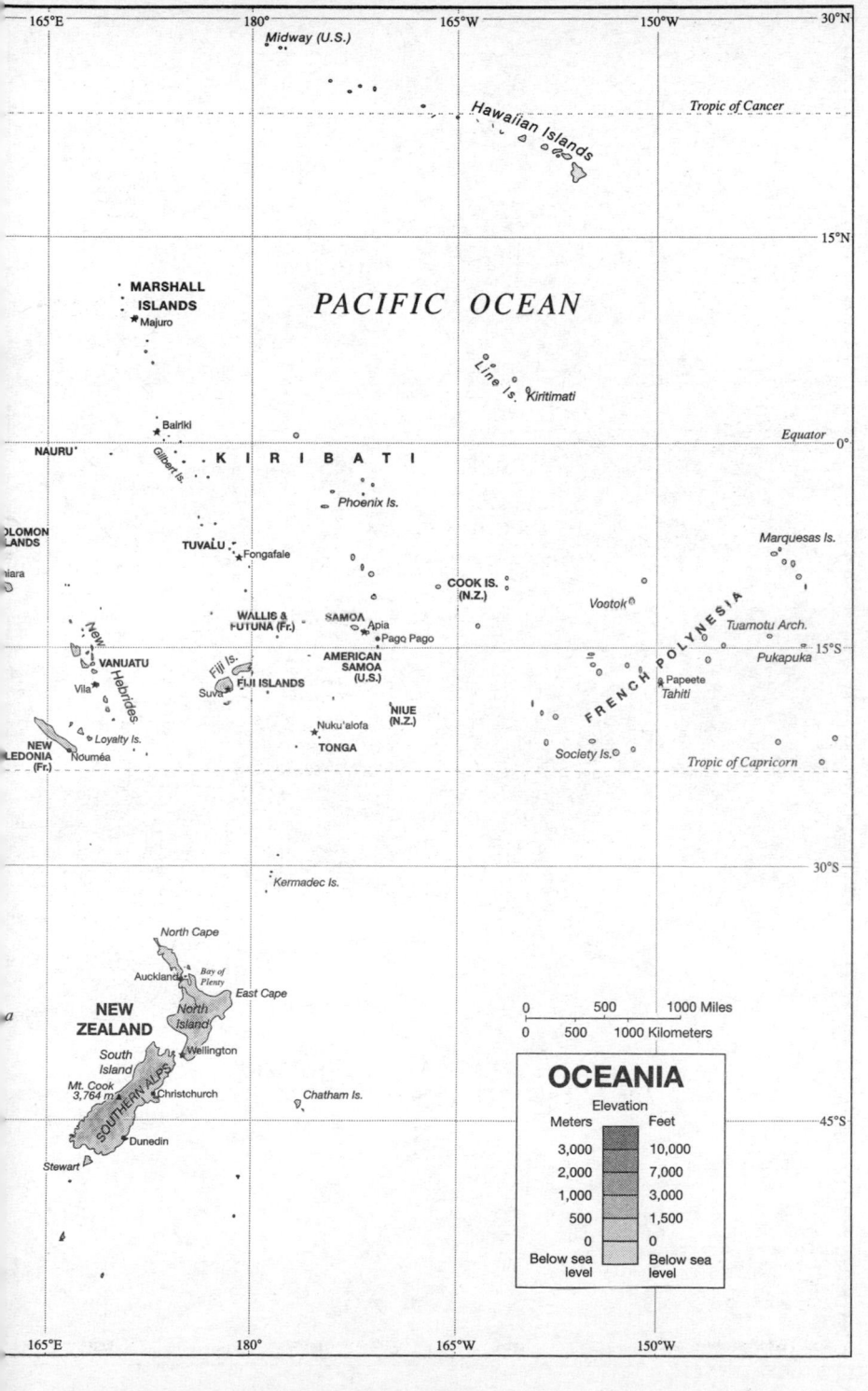

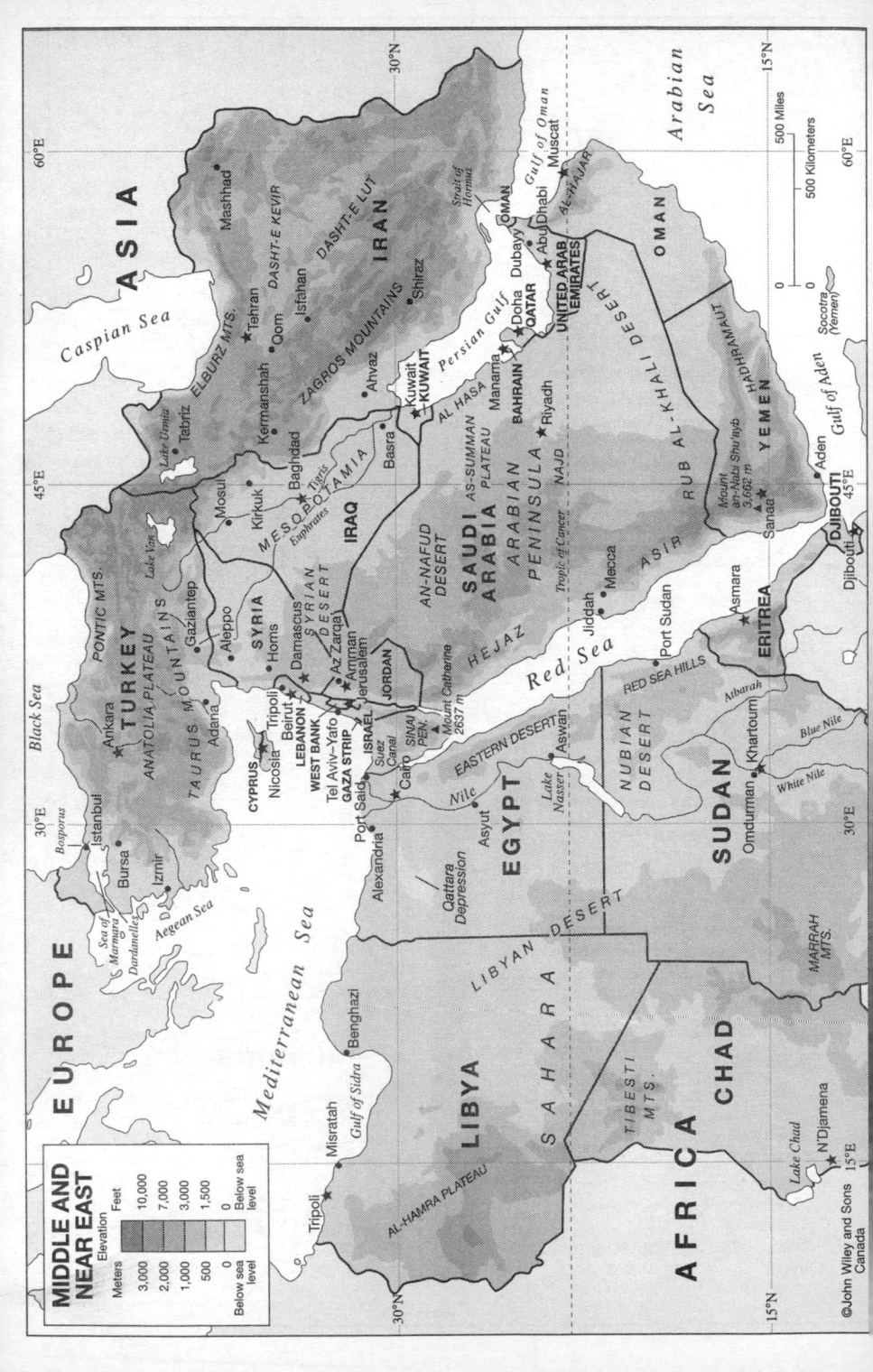

Coastline: 7,600 km
Climate: predominantly Mediterranean; Alpine in far north; hot, dry in south
Environment: regional risks include landslides, mudflows, snowslides, earthquakes, volcanic eruptions, flooding; land sinkage in Venice; serious air and water pollution
Terrain: mostly rugged and mountainous; some plains, coastal lowlands
Land Use: arable land: 28.07%, permanent crops: 9.25%, other: 62.68%; includes 26,980 sq. km irrigated
Location: S Europe, bordering on Adriatic Sea, Mediterranean Sea

■ PEOPLE

Population: 57,998,353 (July 2002 est.)
Nationality: Italian
Age Structure: 0–14 yrs: 14.0%; 15–64: 67.2%; 65+: 18.8% (2003 est.)
Population Growth Rate: 0.11% (2003 est.)
Net Migration: 2.07 migrants/1,000 population (2003 est.)
Ethnic Groups: primarily Italian but population includes small clusters of German-, French- and Slovene-Italians in the north and Albanian-Italians in the south; Sicilians; Sardinians
Languages: Italian; parts of Trentino-Alto Adige region are predominantly German-speaking; significant French-speaking minority in Valle d'Aosta region; Slovene-speaking minority in the Trieste-Gorizia area
Religions: almost 100% nominally Roman Catholic
Birth Rate: 9.18/1,000 population (2003 est.)
Death Rate: 10.12/1,000 population (2003 est.)
Infant Mortality: 6.19 deaths/1,000 live births (2003 est.)
Life Expectancy at Birth: 76.47 years male, 82.52 years female (2003 est.)
Total Fertility Rate: 1.26 children born/woman (2003 est.)
Literacy: 98.5% (2002)

■ GOVERNMENT

Leader(s): President Carlo Azeglio Ciampi, Prime Minister Silvio Berlusconi
Government Type: republic
Administrative Divisions: 20 regions (regioni, sing. —regione)
Nationhood: Mar. 17, 1861, Kingdom of Italy proclaimed
National Holiday: Anniversary of the Republic, June 2

■ ECONOMY

Overview: country is divided into a developed industrial north and an undeveloped agricultural south; an inadequate communications system, high pollution and economic integration into the European Union pose continuing challenges
GDP: US$1.455 trillion, per capita US$25,100; real growth rate 0.4% (2002)
Inflation: 2.4% (2002 est.)
Industries: accounts for 30% of GDP (2001 est.); machinery and transportation equipment, iron and steel, chemicals, food processing, textiles, motor vehicles
Labour Force: 25.7 million (2002); 32% industry, 5% agriculture, 63% community, social and business services
Unemployment: 9.0% (2002)
Agriculture: accounts for 2% of GDP (2001 est.) and 10% of the workforce; self-sufficient in foods other than meat and dairy products; principal crops—fruit, vegetables, grapes, potatoes, sugar beets, soybeans, grain, olives
Natural Resources: mercury, potash, marble, sulphur, dwindling natural gas and crude oil reserves, fish, coal

■ FINANCE/TRADE

Currency: lira (Lit) = 100 centesimi; Euro (€); on January 1, 2002 the Euro became the sole currency for everyday transactions.
International Reserves Excluding Gold: US$30.649 billion (Jan. 2004)
Gold Reserves: 78.829 million fine troy ounces (Jan. 2004)
Budget: revenues US$504 billion; expenditures US$517 billion, including capital expenditures US$ n.a. (2001 est.)
Defence Expenditures: 4.8% of central government expenditure (2002)
Education Expenditures: 9.5% of total government expenditures (2002)
External Debt: n.a.
Exports: US$285.883 billion (2003 est.); commodities: textiles, wearing apparel, metals, transportation equipment, chemicals; partners: EU, US
Imports: US$286.445 billion (2003 est.); commodities: petroleum, industrial machinery, chemicals, metals, foods, agricultural products; partners: Germany, France, Netherlands, UK, US

■ COMMUNICATIONS

Daily Newspapers: 104/1,000 inhabitants (2000)
Televisions: 494/1,000 inhabitants (2002)
Radios: 878/1,000 inhabitants (2001)

Telephones: 481 lines/1,000 inhabitants (2002)
Internet: hosts: 672,638 (2002); users: 19.9 million (2002)

■ TRANSPORTATION

Motor Vehicles: 35,000,000; 31,200,000 passenger cars
Roads: 479,688 km; all paved
Railway: 19,493 km
Air Traffic: 28,245,000 passengers carried (2002)
Airports: 134; 96 have paved runways (2003 est.)

Canadian Embassy: The Canadian Embassy, Via G.B. de Rossi 27, 00161 Rome, Italy. Tel: (011-39-06) 445981. Fax: (011-39-06) 445 98750. e-mail: rome@dfait-maeci.gc.ca
Embassy in Canada: Embassy of the Italian Republic, 275 Slater St, 21st Fl, Ottawa ON K1P 5H9. Tel: (613) 232-2401. Fax: (613) 233-1484. e-mail: ambital@italyincanada.org

Jamaica

Long-Form Name: Jamaica
Capital: Kingston

■ GEOGRAPHY

Area: 10,990 sq. km
Coastline: 1,022 km
Climate: tropical; hot, humid; temperate interior
Environment: subject to hurricanes (especially July to Nov.); deforestation; water pollution
Terrain: mostly mountainous with narrow, discontinuous coastal plain
Land Use: arable land: 16.07%, permanent crops: 9.23%, other: 74.7%; includes 250 sq. km irrigated
Location: West Indies, island in Caribbean Sea, just south of Cuba

■ PEOPLE

Population: 2,695,867 (July 2003 est.)
Nationality: Jamaican
Age Structure: 0–14 yrs: 28.6%; 15–64: 64.5%; 65+: 6.8% (2003 est.)
Population Growth Rate: 0.61% (2003 est.)
Net Migration: -5.78 migrants/1,000 population (2003 est.)
Ethnic Groups: 90.9% African, 7.3% mixed, 1.3% East Indian and Afro-East Indian, 0.2% white, 0.2% Chinese and Afro-Chinese, 0.1% other
Languages: English (official), Creole
Religions: 60% Protestant, 5% Roman Catholic, 35% other
Birth Rate: 17.35/1,000 population (2003 est.)
Death Rate: 5.42/1,000 population (2003 est.)

Infant Mortality: 13.26 deaths/1,000 live births (2003 est.)
Life Expectancy at Birth: 73.84 years male, 77.97 years female (2003 est.)
Total Fertility Rate: 2.01 children born/woman (2003 est.)
Literacy: 87.6% (2002)

■ GOVERNMENT

Leader(s): Head of State: Queen Elizabeth II, Governor General Howard Cooke, Prime Minister Percival James Patterson
Government Type: parliamentary democracy
Administrative Divisions: 14 parishes
Nationhood: Aug. 6, 1962 (from UK)
National Holiday: Independence Day, first Monday in Aug.

■ ECONOMY

Overview: key sectors in this island economy are bauxite and tourism; continued tight fiscal policies have helped slow inflation and stabilize the exchange rate, but have resulted in the slowdown of economic growth
GDP: US$10.08 billion, per capita US$3,800; real growth rate 1.0% (2002 est.)
Inflation: 7.0% (2002 est.)
Industries: accounts for 31% of GDP (2002); tourism, bauxite mining, textiles, food processing, light manufactures
Labour Force: 1.4 million (2002); 21% agriculture, 60% community, social and business services, 19% industry
Unemployment: 15.7% (2001)
Agriculture: accounts for about 6% of GDP (2002), 22% of workforce and 17% of exports; principal crops—sugar cane, bananas, coffee, citrus, potatoes and vegetables; not self-sufficient in grain, meat and dairy products
Natural Resources: bauxite, gypsum, limestone

■ FINANCE/TRADE

Currency: Jamaican dollar ($J) = 100 cents
International Reserves Excluding Gold: US$1.195 billion (Dec. 2003)
Gold Reserves: n.a.
Budget: revenues US$2.23 billion; expenditures US$2.56 billion, including capital expenditures of US$232.5 million (2000 est.)
Defence Expenditures: 1.63% of central government expenditure (2001)
Education Expenditures: 12.3% of central government expenditure (2002)
External Debt: US$5.477 billion (2002)
Exports: US$1.114 billion (2002); commodities: bauxite, alumina, sugar, bananas; partners: US, EU, UK, Canada

Imports: US$3.533 billion (2002); commodities: petroleum, machinery, food, consumer goods, construction goods; partners: US, CARICOM countries, Latin America, EU

■ COMMUNICATIONS

Daily Newspapers: 62/1,000 inhabitants (2000)
Televisions: 274/1,000 inhabitants (2002)
Radios: 796/1,000 inhabitants (2001)
Telephones: 170 lines/1,000 inhabitants (2002)
Internet: hosts: 1,276 (2002); users: 600,000 (2002)

■ TRANSPORTATION

Motor Vehicles: 58,900; 43,500 passenger cars
Roads: 18,700 km; 13,109 km paved
Railway: 272 km
Air Traffic: 2,016,000 passengers carried (2002)
Airports: 35; 11 have paved runways (2003 est.)

Canadian Embassy: The Canadian High Commission, 3 West Kings House Road, Kingston 10, Jamaica; mailing address: The Canadian High Commission, P.O. Box 1500, Kingston 10, Jamaica. Tel: (876) 926-1500. Fax: (876) 511-3494. e-mail: kngtn@dfait-maeci.gc.ca
Embassy in Canada: Jamaican High Commission, 275 Slater St, Ste 800, Ottawa ON K1P 5H9. Tel: (613) 233-9311. Fax: (613) 233-0611. e-mail: hc@jhcottawa.ca

Japan

Long-Form Name: Japan
Capital: Tokyo

■ GEOGRAPHY

Area: 377,835 sq. km; includes Bonin Islands (Ogasawara-gunto), Daito-shoto, Minamijima, Okinotori-shima, Ryukyu Islands (Nansei-shoto) and Volcano Islands (Kazan-retto)
Coastline: 29,751 km
Climate: varies from tropical in south to cool temperate in north
Environment: many dormant and some active volcanoes; about 1,500 seismic occurrences (mostly tremors) every year; subject to tsunamis; acid rain caused by industrial emissions
Terrain: mostly rugged and mountainous
Land Use: arable land: 12.13%, permanent crops: 1.01%, other: 86.86%; includes 26,790 sq. km irrigated
Location: E Asia, bordering on Sea of Japan, North Pacific Ocean

■ PEOPLE

Population: 127,214,499 (July 2003 est.)

Nationality: Japanese
Age Structure: 0–14 yrs: 14.4%; 15–64: 67.0%; 65+: 18.6% (2003 est.)
Population Growth Rate: 0.11% (2003 est.)
Net Migration: 0 migrants/1,000 population (2003 est.)
Ethnic Groups: 99.4% Japanese, 0.6% other (mostly Korean)
Languages: Japanese
Religions: most Japanese observe both Shinto and Buddhist rites; about 16% belong to other faiths, including 0.8% Christian
Birth Rate: 9.61/1,000 population (2003 est.)
Death Rate: 8.55/1,000 population (2003 est.)
Infant Mortality: 3.30 deaths/1,000 live births (2003 est.)
Life Expectancy at Birth: 77.63 years male, 84.41 years female (2003 est.)
Total Fertility Rate: 1.38 children born/woman (2003 est.)
Literacy: approaching 100% (2002)

■ GOVERNMENT

Leader(s): Emperor Tsegu no Miya Akihito, Prime Minister Junichiro Koizumi
Government Type: constitutional monarchy with a parliamentary government
Administrative Divisions: 47 prefectures
Nationhood: 660 BC, traditional founding by Emperor Jimmu; May 3, 1947 constitutional monarchy established
National Holiday: Birthday of the Emperor, Dec. 23

■ ECONOMY

Overview: impressive economic growth and status as the second largest industrial economy in the world is due to government-industry co-operation and a strong work ethic; known for high-tech industry; the crowding of habitable land and the ageing population are two major long-term problems
GDP: US$3.651 trillion, per capita US$28,700; real growth rate 0.2% (2002)
Inflation: -0.9% (2002 est.)
Industries: accounts for 31% of GDP (2001 est.), metallurgy, engineering, electrical and electronics, textiles, chemicals, automobiles, fishing
Labour Force: 68.0 million (2002); 70% community, social and business services, 25% industry; 5% agriculture
Unemployment: 5% (Feb. 2004)
Agriculture: accounts for 1% of GDP (2001 est.); highly subsidized and protected sector, with crop yields among highest in the world; main crops—rice, sugar beets, vegetables, fruit; animal products include fish, pork, poultry,

dairy and eggs; about 50% self-sufficient in food

Natural Resources: negligible mineral resources, fish

■ FINANCE/TRADE

Currency: yen (pl. yen) (¥)
International Reserves Excluding Gold: US$731.411 billion (Jan. 2004)
Gold Reserves: 24.602 million fine troy ounces (Jan. 2004)
Budget: revenues US$380 billion; expenditures US$746 billion, including capital expenditures of US$71 billion (2003–2004 est.)
Defence Expenditures: 1.0% of GDP (2002)
Education Expenditures: 10.5% of total government expenditures (2002)
External Debt: n.a.
Exports: US$462.305 billion (2003 est.); commodities: manufactures 97% (including machinery 38%, motor vehicles 17%, consumer electronics 10%); partners: US, China, South Korea, Taiwan, Hong Kong
Imports: US$375.494 billion (2003 est.); commodities: manufactures 42%, fossil fuels 30%, foodstuffs 15%, non-fuel raw materials 13%; partners: US, China, South Korea, Taiwan, Indonesia

■ COMMUNICATIONS

Daily Newspapers: 578/1,000 inhabitants (2000)
Televisions: 785/1,000 inhabitants (2002)
Radios: 956/1,000 inhabitants (2001)
Telephones: 558 lines/1,000 inhabitants (2002)
Internet: hosts: 9,260,117 (2002); users: 57.2 million (2002)

■ TRANSPORTATION

Motor Vehicles: 72,600,000; 52,000,000 passenger cars
Roads: 1,161,894 km; 534,471 km paved
Railway: 23,168 km
Air Traffic: 109,247,000 passengers carried (2002)
Airports: 172; 141 have paved runways (2003 est.)

Canadian Embassy: The Canadian Embassy, 3-38 Akasaka 7-chome, Minato-ku, Tokyo 107-8503, Japan. Tel: (011-81-3) 5412-6200. Fax: (011-81-3) 5412-6303. e-mail: tokyo@dfait-maeci.gc.ca
Embassy in Canada: Embassy of Japan, 255 Sussex Dr, Ottawa ON K1N 9E6. Tel: (613) 241-8541. Fax: (613) 241-2232. e-mail: n.a.

Jordan

Long-Form Name: Hashemite Kingdom of Jordan
Capital: Amman

■ GEOGRAPHY

Area: 92,300 sq. km
Coastline: 26 km
Climate: mostly arid desert; rainy season in west (Nov. to Apr.)
Environment: lack of natural water resources; deforestation; overgrazing; soil erosion; desertification
Terrain: mostly desert plateau in east, highland area in west; Great Rift Valley separates East and West Banks of the Jordan River
Land Use: arable land: 2.87%, permanent crops: 1.52%, other: 95.61%; includes 750 sq. km irrigated
Location: SW Asia (Middle East), on Arabian Peninsula

■ PEOPLE

Population: 5,460,265(July 2003 est.)
Nationality: Jordanian
Age Structure: 0–14 yrs: 35.9%; 15–64: 60.5%; 65+: 3.6% (2003 est.)
Population Growth Rate: 2.78% (2003 est.)
Net Migration: 6.78 migrants/1,000 population (2003 est.)
Ethnic Groups: 98% Arab, 1% Circassian, 1% Armenian
Languages: Arabic (official); English widely understood among upper and middle classes
Religions: Islam (92% Sunni Muslim, Shia minority), 8% Christianity
Birth Rate: 23.68/1,000 population (2003 est.)
Death Rate: 2.62/1,000 population (2003 est.)
Infant Mortality: 18.86 deaths/1,000 live births (2003 est.)
Life Expectancy at Birth: 75.42 years male, 80.50 years female (2003 est.)
Total Fertility Rate: 3.00 children born/woman (2003 est.)
Literacy: 90.9% (2002)

■ GOVERNMENT

Leader(s): King Abdullah II, Prime Minister Faisal al-Fayez
Government Type: constitutional monarchy
Administrative Divisions: 12 governorates (muhafazat, sing. —muhafazah)
Nationhood: May 25, 1946 (from League of Nations mandate under British administration; formerly known as Trans-Jordan)

National Holiday: Independence Day, May 25

■ ECONOMY

Overview: imports are outweighing exports and foreign aid makes up the difference; droughts are a potential threat; debt, poverty and unemployment remain problems; economic recovery is unlikely without substantial foreign aid, debt relief and economic reform
GDP: US$22.63 billion, per capita US$4,300; real growth rate 4.9% (2002)
Inflation: 3.3% (2002 est.)
Industries: accounts for 26% of GDP (2001 est.); phosphate mining, petroleum refining, cement, potash, light manufacturing
Labour Force: 1.6 million (2002); 83% services, 13% industry, 5% agriculture
Unemployment: 13.2% (2002)
Agriculture: accounts for 4% of GDP (2001 est.); principal products are wheat, barley, citrus fruit, tomatoes, melons, olives; livestock—sheep, goats, poultry; large net importer of food
Natural Resources: phosphates, potash, shale oil

■ FINANCE/TRADE

Currency: Jordanian dinar (JD) = 1,000 fils
International Reserves Excluding Gold: US$5.201 billion (Jan. 2004)
Gold Reserves: 0.411 million fine troy ounces (Jan. 2004)
Budget: revenues US$3.3 billion; expenditures US$3.7 billion, including capital expenditures of US$582 million (2003 est.)
Defence Expenditures: 26.5% of central government expenditure (2002)
Education Expenditures: 20.6% of central government expenditure (2002)
External Debt: US$8.094 billion (2002)
Exports: US$2.889 billion (2003 est.); commodities: fruit and vegetables, phosphates, fertilizers; partners: India, US, Saudi Arabia, Israel
Imports: US$5.429 billion (2003 est.); commodities: crude oil, textiles, capital goods, motor vehicles, foodstuffs; partners: Germany, US, Italy, France

■ COMMUNICATIONS

Daily Newspapers: 75/1,000 inhabitants (2000)
Televisions: 177/1,000 inhabitants (2002)
Radios: 372/1,000 inhabitants (2001)
Telephones: 127 lines/1,000 inhabitants (2002)
Internet: hosts: 4,116 (2002); users: 307,500 (2002)

■ TRANSPORTATION

Motor Vehicles: 265,000; 175,000 passenger cars

Roads: 7,245 km, all paved
Railway: 505 km
Air Traffic: 1,300,000 passengers carried (2002)
Airports: 17; 15 have paved runways (2003 est.)

Canadian Embassy: The Canadian Embassy, Pearl of Shmeisani Bldg, Shmeisani, Amman, Jordan; mailing address: P.O. Box 815403, Amman, Jordan 11180. Tel: (011-962-6) 566-61-24. Fax: (011-962-6) 568-92-27. e-mail: amman@dfait-maeci.gc.ca
Embassy in Canada: Embassy of the Hashemite Kingdom of Jordan, 100 Bronson Ave, Ste 701, Ottawa ON K1R 6G8. Tel: (613) 238-8090. Fax: (613) 232-3341. e-mail: n.a.

Kazakhstan

Long-Form Name: Republic of Kazakhstan
Capital: Astana; in December 1998 the government was moved from Almaty to Astana

■ GEOGRAPHY

Area: 2,717,300 sq. km
Coastline: none; landlocked; Kazakhstan borders the Aral Sea (1,070 km) and the Caspian Sea (1,894 km)
Climate: dry desert climate; arid and semi-arid; hot summers and cold winters
Environment: drought and desertification; lack of fresh water; drying up of Aral Sea is causing increased concentrations of chemical pesticides and natural salts; industrial pollution, including radioactive or toxic chemical sites
Terrain: desert and steppe; plains in western Siberia to oasis and desert in Central Asia
Land Use: arable land: 11.23%, permanent crops: 0.05%, other: 88.72%; includes 23,320 sq. km irrigated
Location: C Asia, bordering on Caspian Sea

■ PEOPLE

Population: 16,763,795 (July 2003 est.)
Nationality: Kazakhstani
Age Structure: 0–14 yrs: 25.4%; 15–64: 66.8%; 65+: 7.9% (2003 est.)
Population Growth Rate: 0.17% (2003 est.)
Net Migration: -5.89 migrants/1,000 population (2003 est.)
Ethnic Groups: 46% Kazakh, 34.7% Russian, 4.9% Ukrainian, 3.1% German, 2.3% Uzbek, 1.9% Tatar, 7.1% other
Languages: Kazakh (official, spoken by over 40% of population), Russian (official, spoken by two-thirds of population), German, Ukrainian

Religions: primarily Sunni Muslim (47%) and Eastern Orthodox (44%), Protestant (2%), other 7%
Birth Rate: 18.36/1,000 population (2003 est.)
Death Rate: 10.78/1,000 population (2003 est.)
Infant Mortality: 58.73 deaths/1,000 live births (2003 est.)
Life Expectancy at Birth: 58.16 years male, 69.06 years female (2003 est.)
Total Fertility Rate: 2.16 children born/woman (2003 est.)
Literacy: 99.4% (2002)

■ GOVERNMENT

Leader(s): President Nursultan A. Nazarbayev, Prime Minister Daniyal Akhmetov
Government Type: republic
Administrative Divisions: 14 oblasts (oblystar, sing. —oblysy) and 3 cities (gala, sing. —galasy)
Nationhood: Dec. 16, 1991 (from Soviet Union)
National Holiday: Day of the Republic, Oct. 25

■ ECONOMY

Overview: predominantly mining and manufacturing; agriculture possible only with irrigation; serious pollution problems, lack of modern technology and little experience in foreign markets hamper economic progress
GDP: US$120 billion, per capita US$7,200; real growth rate 9.5% (2002 est.)
Inflation: 6.0% (2002 est.)
Industries: accounts for 40% of GDP (2002); coal refining, oil and natural gas extraction, mining, agricultural machinery, electric motors, construction materials
Labour Force: 7.4 million (2002); 50% community, social and business services, 20% agriculture, 30% industry
Unemployment: 13.7%; large numbers of underemployed (2001)
Agriculture: accounts for 9% of GDP (2002), and employs one-fifth of labour force; wheat, cotton, rice, vineyard and orchard crops, sheep, cattle
Natural Resources: fish, oil, natural gas, zinc, coal, lead, iron ore, rare metals, tungsten, copper, zinc, manganese, bauxite, gold

■ FINANCE/TRADE

Currency: tenge = 100 tiyn
International Reserves Excluding Gold: US$4.738 billion (Jan. 2004)
Gold Reserves: 1.747 million fine troy ounces (Jan. 2004)
Budget: revenues US$4.2 billion; expenditures US$5.1 billion, including capital expenditures of US$ n.a. (2001 est.)

Defence Expenditures: 6.8% of central government expenditure (2002)
Education Expenditures: 3.64% of central government expenditure (2000)
External Debt: US$17.538 billion (2002)
Exports: US$12.900 billion (2003 est.): fuels, karakul fleece, wool, industrial products; partners: Russia, China, Germany
Imports: US$8.327 billion (2003 est.): fuel, industrial products; partners: Russia, Germany, US

■ COMMUNICATIONS

Daily Newspapers: 3 in total
Televisions: 338/1,000 inhabitants (2002)
Radios: 411/1,000 inhabitants (2001)
Telephones: 130 lines/1,000 inhabitants (2002)
Internet: hosts: 16,562 (2002); users: 250,000 (2002)

■ TRANSPORTATION

Motor Vehicles: 1,440,000; 1,100,000 passenger cars
Roads: n.a.
Railway: 13,601 km
Air Traffic: 593,000 passengers carried (2002)
Airports: 488 airfields; 60 have paved runways (2003 est.)

Canadian Embassy: The Canadian Embassy, 34 Karasai Batir St, Almaty 480100, Kazakhstan. Tel: (011-7-3272) 50-11-51. Fax: (011-7-3272) 582-493. e-mail: almat@dfait-maeci.gc.ca
Embassy in Canada: c/o The Embassy of the Republic of Kazakhstan, 1401 16th Street NW, Washington, DC 20036, USA. Tel: (202) 232-5488. Fax: (202) 232-5845. e-mail: kazak@intr.net

Kenya

Long-Form Name: Republic of Kenya
Capital: Nairobi

■ GEOGRAPHY

Area: 582,650 sq. km
Coastline: 536 km
Climate: varies from tropical along coast to arid in interior
Environment: unique physiography supports abundant and varied wildlife of scientific and economic value, but poaching is a continuing problem; deforestation; soil erosion; desertification; glaciers on Mt Kenya; deteriorating water quality
Terrain: low plains rise to central highlands bisected by Great Rift Valley; fertile plateau in west

Land Use: arable land: 7.03%, permanent crops: 0.91%, other: 92.06%; includes 670 sq. km irrigated
Location: E Africa, bordering on Indian Ocean

■ PEOPLE

Population: 31,639,091 (July 2003 est.)
Nationality: Kenyan
Age Structure: 0–14 yrs: 41.3%; 15–64: 55.8%; 65+: 2.9% (2003 est.)
Population Growth Rate: 1.27% (2003 est.)
Net Migration: -0.15 migrants/1,000 population (2003 est.)
Ethnic Groups: 22% Kikuyu, 14% Luhya, 13% Luo, 12% Kalenjin, 11% Kamba, 6% Kisii, 6% Meru, 1% Asian, European and Arab, 15% other
Languages: English and Swahili (official); Kikuyu and Luo are widely spoken; numerous indigenous languages
Religions: 28% Roman Catholic, 26% indigenous beliefs, 38% Protestant, 8% other
Birth Rate: 28.81/1,000 population (2003 est.)
Death Rate: 16.01/1,000 population (2003 est.)
Infant Mortality: 63.36 deaths/1,000 live births (2003 est.)
Life Expectancy at Birth: 45.02 years male, 45.43 years female (2003 est.)
Total Fertility Rate: 3.47 children born/woman (2003 est.)
Literacy: 84.3% (2002)

■ GOVERNMENT

Leader(s): President Mwai Kibaki, Vice President Moody Awori
Government Type: republic
Administrative Divisions: 7 provinces and 1 area
Nationhood: Dec. 12, 1963 (from UK; formerly known as British East Africa)
National Holiday: Independence Day, Dec. 12

■ ECONOMY

Overview: a large annual population growth, a deteriorating infrastructure and a shortage of arable land threaten economic growth; vulnerable to weather conditions
GDP: US$32.89 billion, per capita US$1,100; real growth rate 1.1% (2002 est.)
Inflation: 1.9% (2002 est.)
Industries: accounts for 16% of GDP (2000); small-scale consumer goods (plastic, furniture, batteries, textiles, soap, cigarettes, flour), agricultural processing, oil refining, cement, tourism
Labour Force: 16.3 million (2002); 75–80% of the population is engaged in agriculture
Unemployment: n.a.

Agriculture: accounts for 23% of GDP (2000) and 65% of exports; cash crops include coffee, tea, sisal, pineapple; food products—corn, wheat, sugar cane, fruit, vegetables, dairy products, poultry, eggs; food output not sufficient for existing population
Natural Resources: gold, limestone, diatomite, salt barytes, magnesite, feldspar, sapphires, fluorspar, garnets, wildlife, hydro power

■ FINANCE/TRADE

Currency: Kenyan shilling (KSh) = 100 cents
International Reserves Excluding Gold: US$1.456 billion (Jan. 2004)
Gold Reserves: 0.001 million fine troy ounces (Jan. 2004)
Budget: revenues US$2.91 billion; expenditures US$2.97 billion, including capital expenditures of US$ n.a. (2000 est.)
Defence Expenditures: 5.8% of central government expenditure (2002)
Education Expenditures: 22.5% of central government expenditure (2002)
External Debt: US$6.031 billion (2002)
Exports: US$2.424 billion (2003 est.); commodities: coffee 20%, tea 18%, manufactures 15%, petroleum products 10%; partners: US, Tanzania, Uganda, Germany
Imports: US$3.704 billion (2003 est.); commodities: machinery and transportation equipment 36%, raw materials 33%, fuels and lubricants 20%, food and consumer goods 11%; partners: UK, UAE, Japan, India

■ COMMUNICATIONS

Daily Newspapers: 10/1,000 inhabitants (2000)
Televisions: 26/1,000 inhabitants (2002)
Radios: 221/1,000 inhabitants (2001)
Telephones: 10 lines/1,000 inhabitants (2002)
Internet: hosts: 2,963 (2002); users: 400,000 (2002)

■ TRANSPORTATION

Motor Vehicles: 364,900; 271,000 passenger cars
Roads: 63,942 km; 7,737 km paved
Railway: 2,778 km
Air Traffic: 1,600,000 passengers carried (2002)
Airports: 230; 19 have paved runways (2003 est.)

Canadian Embassy: The Canadian High Commission, Limuru Road, Gigiri, Nairobi, Kenya. Postal Address: The Canadian High Commission, P.O. Box 1013, 00621 Nairobi, Kenya. Tel: (011 254 20) 366 3000. Fax: (011 254 20) 366 3900. e-mail: nrobi@dfait-maeci.gc.ca
Embassy in Canada: High Commission for the Republic of Kenya, 415 Laurier Ave E, Ottawa

ON K1N 6R4. Tel: (613) 563-1773. Fax: (613) 233-6599. e-mail: kenrep@on.aibn.com

Kiribati

Long-Form Name: Republic of Kiribati
Capital: Tarawa

■ GEOGRAPHY

Area: 717 sq. km
Coastline: 1,143 km
Climate: tropical; marine, hot and humid, moderated by trade winds
Environment: typhoons can occur anytime, but usually Nov. to Mar.
Terrain: mostly low-lying coral atolls surrounded by extensive reefs
Land Use: arable land: 0%, permanent crops: 50.68%, other: 49.32%; includes n.a. sq. km irrigated
Location: SW Pacific Ocean, NE of Australia

■ PEOPLE

Population: 98,549 (July 2003 est.); only 20 of Kiribati's 33 islands are inhabited
Nationality: I-Kiribati (sing. & pl.)
Age Structure: 0–14 yrs: 39.7%; 15–64: 57.0%; 65+: 3.3% (2003 est.)
Population Growth Rate: 2.26% (2003 est.)
Net Migration: 0 migrants/1,000 population (2003 est.)
Ethnic Groups: Micronesian
Languages: English (official), Gilbertese
Religions: 52.6% Roman Catholic, 40.9% Protestant (Congregatioñal), some Seventh-Day Adventist and Baha'i
Birth Rate: 31.24/1,000 population (2003 est.)
Death Rate: 8.63/1,000 population (2003 est.)
Infant Mortality: 51.26 deaths/1,000 live births (2003 est.)
Life Expectancy at Birth: 57.97 years male, 64.03 years female (2003 est.)
Total Fertility Rate: 4.28 children born/woman (2003 est.)
Literacy: n.a.

■ GOVERNMENT

Leader(s): President Atone Tong, Vice President Teima Onorio
Government Type: republic
Administrative Divisions: 3 units
Nationhood: July 12, 1979 (from UK; formerly known as Gilbert Islands)
National Holiday: Independence Day, July 12

■ ECONOMY

Overview: economy has fluctuated widely in recent years and copra production and a good fish catch have provided a boost; at present there is a moderate but steady growth trend
GDP: US$79 million, per capita US$800; real growth rate 1.5% (2001). Kiribati's revenues are supplemented by a nearly equal amount from external sources
Inflation: 2.5% (2001 est.)
Industries: accounts for 7% of GDP; fishing, handicrafts
Labour Force: 7,870 (2001 est.)
Unemployment: n.a., but massive underemployment
Agriculture: accounts for 30% of GDP (including fishing); copra and fish contribute 65% to exports; subsistence farming predominates; food crops—taro, breadfruit, sweet potatoes, vegetables, fish; not self-sufficient in food
Natural Resources: tuna fishing

■ FINANCE/TRADE

Currency: Australian dollar.($A) = 100 cents
International Reserves Excluding Gold: n.a.
Gold Reserves: n.a.
Budget: revenues US$28.4 million; expenditures US$37.2 million, capital expenditures US$ n.a. (2000 est.)
Defence Expenditures: n.a.
Education Expenditures: n.a.
External Debt: n.a.
Exports: US$35 million (2002); commodities: fish 55%, copra 42%; partners: Japan, Bangladesh, US, Australia, Brazil, Poland
Imports: US$83 million (2002); commodities: foodstuffs, fuel, transportation equipment; partners: Australia, Japan, Fiji, Poland, US

■ COMMUNICATIONS

Daily Newspapers: none
Televisions: n.a.
Radios: n.a.
Telephones: 46 lines/1,000 inhabitants (2002)
Internet: users: 2,000 (2002)

■ TRANSPORTATION

Motor Vehicles: n.a.
Roads: 670 km; n.a. km paved
Railway: none
Air Traffic: 33,500 passengers carried (2001 est.)
Airports: 20; 4 have paved runways (2003 est.)

Canadian Embassy: The Canadian High Commission to Kiribati, c/o The Canadian High Commission, P.O. Box 12-049, Thorndon, Wellington, New Zealand. Tel: (011-64-4) 473-

9577. Fax: (011-64-4) 471-2082. e-mail:
wlgtn@dfait-maeci.gc.ca
Embassy in Canada: c/o New Zealand High
Commission, Clarica Centre, 99 Bank St,
Ste 727, Ottawa, ON K1P 6G3. Tel: (613)
238-5991. Fax: (613) 238-5707. e-mail:
info@nzhcottawa.org

Korea (North)

Long-Form Name: Democratic People's Republic
of Korea
Capital: P'yongyang

■ GEOGRAPHY

Area: 120,540 sq. km
Coastline: 2,495 km
Climate: temperate with rainfall concentrated in
summer
Environment: isolated mountainous interior,
nearly inaccessible and sparsely populated; late-
spring droughts often followed by severe
flooding
Terrain: mostly hills and mountains separated by
deep, narrow valleys; coastal plains wide in
west, discontinuous in east
Land Use: arable land: 14.12%, permanent crops:
2.49%, other: 83.39%; includes 14,600 sq. km
irrigated
Location: E Asia, bordering on Yellow Sea, Sea
of Japan

■ PEOPLE

Population: 22,466,481 (July 2003 est.)
Nationality: Korean
Age Structure: 0–14 yrs: 25.0%; 15–64: 67.8%;
65+: 7.2% (2003 est.)
Population Growth Rate: 1.07% (2003 est.)
Net Migration: 0 migrants/1,000 population
(2003 est.)
Ethnic Groups: Korean (racially homogeneous)
Languages: Korean
Religions: Buddhism and Confucianism; Taoism,
Shamanism, Chonodogyu; autonomous religious
activities are now almost nonexistent; government-
sponsored religious groups exist to provide an
illusion of religious freedom
Birth Rate: 17.61/1,000 population (2003 est.)
Death Rate: 6.93/1,000 population (2003 est.)
Infant Mortality: 25.66 deaths/1,000 live births
(2003 est.)
Life Expectancy at Birth: 68.10 years male, 73.61
years female (2003 est.)
Total Fertility Rate: 2.25 children born/woman
(2003 est.)
Literacy: 99% (2002)

■ GOVERNMENT

Leader(s): Chairman National Defense Commis-
sion Kim Jong-il, Chairman of Supreme
People's Assembly Presidium Kim Yong-nam
Government Type: authoritarian socialist state;
one-person dictatorship
Administrative Divisions: 9 provinces (do, sing.
& pl.) and 3 special cities (si, sing. & pl.)
Nationhood: Sept. 9, 1948
National Holiday: Independence Day (DPRK
Foundation Day), Sept. 9

■ ECONOMY

Overview: a command economy that is almost
completely socialized, with state-owned industry
and collectivization of agriculture; state control
over economic affairs is unusually tight even for
a socialist country
GDP: US$22.26 billion, per capita US$1,000;
real growth rate 1.0% (2002)
Inflation: n.a.
Industries: accounts for 32% of GDP (2000);
machine building, military products, electric
power, chemicals, mining, metallurgy, textiles,
food processing
Labour Force: 11.8 million (2002); 36% agricultural, 64% services and industry
Unemployment: n.a.
Agriculture: accounts for about 30% of GNP
(2000) and 36% of workforce; principal crops—
rice, corn, potatoes, soybeans, pulses; fish;
livestock and livestock products—cattle, hogs,
pork, eggs; not self-sufficient in grain
Natural Resources: coal, lead, tungsten, zinc,
graphite, magnesite, iron ore, copper, gold,
pyrites, salt, fluorspar, hydroelectricity

■ FINANCE/TRADE

Currency: North Korean won (Wn) = 100 chon
International Reserves Excluding Gold: n.a.
Gold Reserves: n.a.
Budget: n.a.
Defence Expenditures: 33.9% of GDP (2002)
Education Expenditures: n.a.
External Debt: n.a.
Exports: US$1.044 billion (2002 est.); commodi-
ties: minerals, metallurgical products, agri-
cultural products, manufactures; partners:
former USSR countries, China, Japan, South
Korea
Imports: US$2.042 billion (2002 est.); commodi-
ties: petroleum, machinery and equipment,
coking coal, grain; partners: China, South
Korea, Japan

■ COMMUNICATIONS

Daily Newspapers: 208/1,000 inhabitants (2000)

Televisions: 162/1,000 inhabitants (2002)
Radios: 154/1,000 inhabitants (2001)
Telephones: 21 lines/1,000 inhabitants (2002)
Internet: users: n.a.

■ TRANSPORTATION

Motor Vehicles: n.a.
Roads: 31,200 km; 1,997 km paved
Railway: 5,214 km
Air Traffic: 84,000 passengers carried (2002)
Airports: 72; 34 have paved runways (2003 est.)

Canadian Embassy: The Canadian Embassy to the Democratic People's Republic of Korea, c/o The Canadian Embassy, 19 Dong Zhi Men Wai St., Chao Yang District, Beijing 100600, People's Republic of China. Tel: (011-86-10) 6532-3536. Fax: (011-86-10) 6532-4311. e-mail: bejing@dfait-maeci.gc.ca
Embassy in Canada: c/o Permanent Mission of the Democratic People's Republic of Korea to the United Nations, 820 Second Ave., 13th Floor, New York 10017, USA. Tel: (212) 972-3105. Fax: (212) 972-3154. e-mail: n.a.

Korea (South)

Long-Form Name: Republic of Korea
Capital: Seoul

■ GEOGRAPHY

Area: 99,392 sq. km
Coastline: 2,413 km
Climate: temperate, with rainfall heavier in summer than winter
Environment: occasional typhoons bring high winds and floods; earthquakes in southwest; air and water pollution in large cities
Terrain: mostly hilly and mountainous; wide coastal plains in west and south
Land Use: arable land: 17.44%, permanent crops: 2.05%, other: 80.51%; includes 11,590 sq. km irrigated
Location: E Asia, bordering on Yellow Sea, East Sea

■ PEOPLE

Population: 47,900,037 (July 2003 est.)
Nationality: Korean
Age Structure: 0–14 yrs: 20.6%; 15–64: 71.5%; 65+: 7.9% (2003 est.)
Population Growth Rate: 0.98% (2004 est.)
Net Migration: 0 migrants/1,000 population (2003 est.)
Ethnic Groups: homogeneous; small Chinese minority (about 20,000)

Languages: Korean; English widely taught in high school
Religions: 48.6% Christianity, 47.4% Buddhism, 3% Confucianism, 1% other
Birth Rate: 12.60/1,000 population (2003 est.)
Death Rate: 6.03/1,000 population (2003 est.)
Infant Mortality: 7.31 deaths/1,000 live births (2003 est.)
Life Expectancy at Birth: 71.73 years male, 79.32 years female (2003 est.)
Total Fertility Rate: 1.56 children born/woman (2003 est.)
Literacy: 98.1% (2003 est.)

■ GOVERNMENT

Leader(s): President Roh Moo-hyun, Prime Minister Lee Hae-chan
Government Type: republic
Administrative Divisions: 9 provinces (do, sing. & pl.) and 7 special cities (gwangyoksi, sing. & pl.)
Nationhood: Aug. 15, 1948
National Holiday: Liberation Day, Aug. 15

■ ECONOMY

Overview: dynamic growth is attributed to the planned development of an export-oriented economy in a strongly entrepreneurial society; labour unrest has hurt its record of non-inflationary growth; economic growth has recovered in recent years
GDP: US$941.5 billion, per capita US$19,600; real growth rate 6.3% (2002)
Inflation: 3.5% (2003 est.)
Industries: accounts for 42% of GDP (2002 est.); textiles, clothing, footwear, food processing, chemicals, steel, electronics, automobile production, shipbuilding
Labour Force: 23 million (2003); 69% services, 21% industry, 10% agriculture
Unemployment: 3.2% (June 2004)
Agriculture: accounts for 4% of GDP (2002 est.) and 21% of workforce (including fishing and forestry); main crops—rice, root crops, barley, vegetables, fruit; livestock and livestock products—cattle, hogs, chickens, milk, eggs; self-sufficient in food, except for wheat; fish catch is seventh largest in the world
Natural Resources: coal, tungsten, graphite, molybdenum, lead, hydroelectricity

■ FINANCE/TRADE

Currency: South Korean won (W)
International Reserves Excluding Gold: US$157.375 billion (Jan. 2004)
Gold Reserves: 0.452 million fine troy ounces (Jan. 2004)

Budget: revenues US$127 billion; expenditures US$108 billion, including capital expenditures of US$23.5 billion (2002)
Defence Expenditures: 2.8% of GDP (2002)
Education Expenditures: 17.4% of total government expenditures (2002)
External Debt: US$159.8 billion (2003)
Exports: US$208.4 billion (2004); commodities: textiles, clothing, electronic and electrical equipment, footwear, machinery, steel, automobiles, ships, fish; partners: US, China, Japan, Hong Kong, Taiwan
Imports: US$178.5 billion (2004); commodities: machinery, electronics and electronic equipment, oil, steel, transport equipment, textiles, organic chemicals, grains; partners: Japan, US, China, Saudi Arabia, Australia

■ COMMUNICATIONS

Daily Newspapers: 393/1,000 inhabitants (2000)
Televisions: 363/1,000 inhabitants (2002)
Radios: 1,034/1,000 inhabitants (2001)
Telephones: 489/1,000 inhabitants (2002)
Internet: hosts: 407,318 (2002); users: 26.27 million (2002)

■ TRANSPORTATION

Motor Vehicles: 12,300,000; 8,250,000 passenger cars
Roads: 86,990 km; 64,808 km paved
Railway: 3,125 km
Air Traffic: 34,512,000 passengers carried (2002)
Airports: 102; 69 have paved runways (2003 est.)

Canadian Embassy: The Canadian Embassy, Kolon Building, 45 Mugyo-Dong, Jung-Ku, Seoul 100-170, Korea; mailing address: P.O. Box 6299, Seoul 100-662 Korea. Tel: (011-82-2) 3455-6000. Fax: (011-82-2) 755-0686. e-mail: seoul@dfait-maeci.gc.ca
Embassy in Canada: Embassy of the Republic of Korea, 150 Boteler St, Ottawa ON K1N 5A6. Tel: (613) 244-5010. Fax: (613) 244-5043. e-mail: cultural@emb-korea.ottawa.on.ca

Kuwait

Long-Form Name: State of Kuwait
Capital: Kuwait

■ GEOGRAPHY

Area: 17,820 sq. km
Coastline: 499 km
Climate: dry desert; intensely hot summers; short, cool winters
Environment: large and sophisticated desalination plants are required for adequate drinking water supply; air and water pollution; desertification
Terrain: flat to slightly undulating desert plain
Land Use: arable land: 0.34%, permanent crops: 0.06%, other: 99.6%; includes 60 sq. km irrigated
Location: SW Asia (Middle East), on Arabian Peninsula, bordering on Persian Gulf

■ PEOPLE

Population: 2,183,161; includes 1,291,354 non-nationals (July 2003 est.)
Nationality: Kuwaiti
Age Structure: 0–14 yrs: 27.9%; 15–64: 69.5%; 65+: 2.6% (2003 est.)
Population Growth Rate: 3.34% (2003 est.)
Net Migration: 14.04 migrants/1,000 population (2003 est.)
Ethnic Groups: 45% Kuwaiti, 35% other Arab, 9% South Asian, 4% Iranian, 7% other
Languages: Arabic (official); Kurdish, Farsi, English (commercial) widely spoken
Religions: 85% Muslim (30% Shi'a, 45% Sunni, 10% other), 15% Christian, Hindu, Parsi and other
Birth Rate: 21.83/1,000 population (2003 est.)
Death Rate: 2.45/1,000 population (2003 est.)
Infant Mortality: 10.57 deaths/1,000 live births (2003 est.)
Life Expectancy at Birth: 75.72 years male, 77.62 years female (2003 est.)
Total Fertility Rate: 3.08 children born/woman (2003 est.)
Literacy: 82.9% (2002)

■ GOVERNMENT

Leader(s): Prime Minister Sabah al-Ahmad al-Jabir al-Sabah, Emir Shaikh Jabir al-Ahmad al-Jabir al-Sabah
Government Type: nominal constitutional monarchy
Administrative Divisions: 5 governorates (muhafazat, sing. -muhafazah)
Nationhood: June 19, 1961 (from UK)
National Holiday: National Day, Feb. 25

■ ECONOMY

Overview: a small and relatively open economy with crude oil reserves of about 10% of world reserves; lacks water and has practically no arable land, thus preventing development of agriculture; with the exception of fish, it depends almost wholly on food imports
GDP: US$36.85 billion, per capita US$17,500; real growth rate -2.0% (2002 est.)
Inflation: 2.0% (2002 est.)

Industries: petroleum (accounts for 60% of GDP and 90% of export revenues), petrochemicals, desalination, food processing, salt, construction
Labour Force: 1.0 million (2002); 45% services, 20% construction, 12% trade, 9% manufacturing, 3% finance and real estate, 2% agriculture, 2% power and water, 1% mining and quarrying
Unemployment: 0.8% (2002)
Agriculture: virtually none; dependent on imports for food; about 75% of potable water (adversely affected by the Gulf War) must be distilled or imported
Natural Resources: petroleum, fish, shrimp, natural gas

■ **FINANCE/TRADE**

Currency: dinar (KD) = 1,000 fils
International Reserves Excluding Gold: US$7.540 billion (Jan. 2004)
Gold Reserves: 2.539 million fine troy ounces (Jan. 2004)
Budget: revenues US$11.0 billion; expenditures US$19.5 billion, including capital expenditures US$ n.a. (FY2003–04)
Defence Expenditures: 18.8% of central government expenditure (2002)
Education Expenditures: n.a.
External Debt: US$10.4 billion (2000)
Exports: US$15.369 billion (2002); commodities: oil 90%; fertilizers; partners: Japan, US, South Korea, Singapore, Netherlands, Pakistan, Indonesia, UK
Imports: US$9.007 billion (2002); commodities: food, construction material, vehicles and parts, clothing; partners: Japan, US, Germany, UK, France, Australia, Netherlands

■ **COMMUNICATIONS**

Daily Newspapers: 374/1,000 inhabitants (2000)
Televisions: 418/1,000 inhabitants (2002)
Radios: 624/1,000 inhabitants (2001)
Telephones: 204 lines/1,000 inhabitants (2002)
Internet: hosts: 3,261 (2002); users: 250,000 (2002)

■ **TRANSPORTATION**

Motor Vehicles: 693,000; 538,000 passenger cars
Roads: 4,450 km; 3,587 km paved
Railway: none
Air Traffic: 2,299,000 passengers carried (2002)
Airports: 6; 3 have paved runways (2003 est.)

Canadian Embassy: The Canadian Embassy, Villa 24, Area 4, 24 Mutawakel St, Da Aiyah, Kuwait; mailing address: P.O. Box 25281, 13113, Safat, Kuwait City, Kuwait. Tel: (011-965) 256-3025. Fax: (011-965) 256-0173. e-mail: kwait@dfait-maeci.gc.ca
Embassy in Canada: Embassy of the State of Kuwait, 333 Sussex Drive, Ottawa, ON, K1N 1J9. Tel: (613) 780-9999. Fax: (613) 780-9905. e-mail: info@embassyofkuwait.com

Kyrgyzstan

Long-Form Name: Kyrgyz Republic
Capital: Bishkek

■ **GEOGRAPHY**

Area: 198,500 sq. km
Coastline: none: landlocked
Climate: dry continental to polar in high Tien Shan; subtropical in south; glacial Alpine; moderate in valley regions
Environment: frequent severe earthquakes; water pollution and water-borne diseases are widespread
Terrain: mountainous; 75% of land covered by snow and glaciers; peaks of Tien Shan rise to 7,000 meters, and associated valleys and basins encompass the entire nation
Land Use: 7.04%, permanent crops: 0.39%, other: 92.57%, note: Kyrgyzstan has the world's largest natural growth walnut forest; includes 10,740 sq. km irrigated
Location: C Asia, bordering on China

■ **PEOPLE**

Population: 4,892,808 (July 2003 est.)
Nationality: Kyrgyzstani
Age Structure: 0–14 yrs: 33.8%; 15–64: 59.9%; 65+: 6.3% (2003 est.)
Population Growth Rate: 1.46% (2003 est.)
Net Migration: -2.37 migrants/1,000 population (2003 est.)
Ethnic Groups: 52.4% Kirghiz, 18% Russian, 12.9% Uzbeks, 2.5% Ukrainian, 2.4% German, 1.6% Tatars, 10.2% other
Languages: Kirghiz and Russian (both official) and Dungan
Religions: 75% Muslim, 20% Eastern Orthodox, 5% other
Birth Rate: 26.06/1,000 population (2003 est.)
Death Rate: 9.10/1,000 population (2003 est.)
Infant Mortality: 75.34 deaths/1,000 live births (2003 est.)
Life Expectancy at Birth: 59.49 years male, 68.03 years female (2003 est.)
Total Fertility Rate: 3.12 children born/woman (2003 est.)
Literacy: 97.0% (2002)

■ GOVERNMENT

Leader(s): President Askar Akayev, Prime Minister Nikolai Tanayev
Government Type: republic
Administrative Divisions: 7 provinces (oblastar, pl., sing. —oblasty) and 1 city
Nationhood: August 31, 1991 (from Soviet Union)
National Holiday: National Day, Dec. 2; also Independence Day, Aug. 31

■ ECONOMY

Overview: a small, poor, mountainous country with a predominantly agricultural economy; has been one of the most progressive countries of the former Soviet Union in carrying out market reforms; foreign assistance played a substantial role in the country's recent economic turn-around
GDP: US$13.88 billion, per capita US$2,900; real growth rate 5.3% (2002 est.)
Inflation: 2.1% (2002 est.)
Industries: accounts for 25% of GDP (2002); small machinery, cement, shoes, furniture and appliances, electronics, electrical engineering, silk making, rare earth metals
Labour Force: 2.2 million (2002); 55% agriculture and forestry, 15% industry and construction, 30% other services
Unemployment: 8.6% (2002)
Agriculture: accounts for 35% of GDP (2002); irrigation required; wheat, barley, beets, cotton, fruit, vegetables, potatoes, cotton, grain, tobacco, livestock: sheep, goats, cattle
Natural Resources: mercury, antimony, zinc, tungsten deposits, coal, natural gas, oil, nepheline, bismuth, mercury, lead, zinc

■ FINANCE/TRADE

Currency: Kyrgyzstani som = 100 tyiyn
International Reserves Excluding Gold: US$394 million (Jan. 2004)
Gold Reserves: 0.083 million fine troy ounces (Jan. 2004)
Budget: n.a.
Defence Expenditures: 9.7% of central government expenditure (2002)
Education Expenditures: 18.6% of central government expenditure (2002)
External Debt: US$1.797 billion (2002)
Exports: US$488 million (2002); agricultural products, antimony, silk, carpets, non-ferrous metals, electrical equipment, cotton, wool, meat, tobacco, gold, mercury, hydro power, machinery, consumer goods; partners: Germany, Russia, Kazakhstan, Uzbekistan, China

Imports: US$592 million (2002); grain, lumber, industrial products, metals, fuel, machinery, consumer goods; partners: Russia, Kazakhstan, Uzbekistan, US, Turkey

■ COMMUNICATIONS

Daily Newspapers: 27/1,000 inhabitants (2000)
Televisions: 49/1,000 inhabitants (2002)
Radios: 110/1,000 inhabitants (2001)
Telephones: 77 lines/1,000 inhabitants (2002)
Internet: hosts: 5,930 (2002); users: 152,000 (2002)

■ TRANSPORTATION

Motor Vehicles: 187,000; 183,000 passenger cars
Roads: 18,500 km; 16,854 km paved or graveled
Railway: 420 km
Air Traffic: 177,000 passengers carried (2002)
Airports: 68; 18 have paved runways (2003 est.)

Canadian Embassy: c/o The Canadian Embassy, 34 Karasai Batir St, Almaty 480100, Kazakhstan. Tel: (011-7-3272) 50-11-51. Fax: (011-7-3272) 582-493. e-mail: almat@dfait-maeci.gc.ca
Embassy In Canada: c/o Embassy of the Kyrgyz Republic, 1732 Wisconsin Ave NW, Washington DC 20007, USA. Tel: (202) 338-5141. Fax: (202) 338-5139. e-mail: n.a.

Laos

Long-Form Name: Lao People's Democratic Republic
Capital: Vientiane

■ GEOGRAPHY

Area: 236,800 sq. km
Coastline: none: landlocked
Climate: tropical monsoon; rainy season (May to Nov.); dry season (Dec. to Apr.)
Environment: deforestation; soil erosion; subject to floods; limited safe drinking water
Terrain: mostly rugged mountains; some plains and plateaus
Land Use: arable land: 3.47%, permanent crops: 0.23%, other: 96.3%; includes between 750 and 1,640 sq. km irrigated
Location: SE Asia

■ PEOPLE

Population: 5,921,545 (July 2003 est.)
Nationality: Laotian or Lao
Age Structure: 0–14 yrs: 42.2%; 15–64: 54.6%; 65+: 3.2% (2003 est.)
Population Growth Rate: 2.45% (2003 est.)
Net Migration: 0 migrants/1,000 population (2003 est.)

Ethnic Groups: mostly Laotian; Vietnamese, Kha, Thai, Meo, Hmong, Yao, Chinese, European, Indian and Pakistani minorities
Languages: Lao (official), French, English, tribal languages
Religions: 60% Buddhist, 40% animist and other
Birth Rate: 36.93/1,000 population (2003 est.)
Death Rate: 12.39/1,000 population (2003 est.)
Infant Mortality: 88.94 deaths/1,000 live births (2003 est.)
Life Expectancy at Birth: 52.34 years male, 56.33 years female (2003 est.)
Total Fertility Rate: 4.94 children born/woman (2003 est.)
Literacy: 52.8% (2003 est.)

■ GOVERNMENT

Leader(s): President Khamtai Siphandon, Prime Minister Boungnang Volachit
Government Type: communist state
Administrative Divisions: 16 provinces (khoueng, sing. & pl.) and 1 municipality (kampheng nakhon, sing. & pl.) and 1 special zone (khetphiset, sing. & pl.)
Nationhood: July 19, 1949 (from France)
National Holiday: National Day (proclamation of the Lao People's Democratic Republic), Dec. 2

■ ECONOMY

Overview: one of the world's poorest nations, landlocked with a primitive infrastructure; while traditionally a communist centrally planned economy with government ownership and control of productive enterprises, the government is now decentralizing control and encouraging some private enterprise; heavily dependent on foreign aid
GDP: US$10.4 billion, per capita US$1,800; real growth rate 5.7% (2002 est.)
Inflation: 10.0% (2002 est.)
Industries: accounts for 22% of GDP (2000); tin mining, timber, electric power, agricultural processing
Labour Force: 2.6 million (2002); 80% agriculture, 5% industry, 15% services
Unemployment: n.a.
Agriculture: accounts for 53% of GDP (2000) and employs most of the labour force; subsistence farming predominates; normally self-sufficient; principal crops—rice (80% of cultivated land), potatoes, vegetables, coffee, tea, sugar cane, cotton
Natural Resources: timber, hydroelectricity, gypsum, tin, gold, gemstones

■ FINANCE/TRADE

Currency: new kip (NK) = 100 at

International Reserves Excluding Gold: US$209 million (Dec. 2003)
Gold Reserves: 0.117 million fine troy ounces (Dec. 2003)
Budget: n.a.
Defence Expenditures: n.a.
Education Expenditures: 10.6% of total government expenditures (2002)
External Debt: US$2.665 billion (2002)
Exports: US$378 million (2003); wood products, electricity, tin, consumer goods; partners: Thailand, Germany, France, UK, Belgium
Imports: US$524 million (2003); machinery and equipment, fuel, vehicles; partners: Thailand, Japan, China, Singapore, Hong Kong

■ COMMUNICATIONS

Daily Newspapers: 4/1,000 inhabitants (2000)
Televisions: 52/1,000 inhabitants (2002)
Radios: 148/1,000 inhabitants (2001)
Telephones: 11 lines/1,000 inhabitants (2002)
Internet: hosts: 281 (2002); users: 15,000 (2002)

■ TRANSPORTATION

Motor Vehicles: 21,000; 10,000 passenger cars
Roads: 21,716 km; 9,664 km paved
Railway: none
Air Traffic: 220,000 passengers carried (2002)
Airports: 51; 9 have paved runways (2003 est.)

Canadian Embassy: The Canadian Embassy to Laos, c/o P.O. Box 2090, Bangkok 10501 Thailand. Tel: (011-66-2) 636-0540. Fax: (011-66-2) 636-0565. e-mail: bngkk@dfait-maeci.gc.ca
Embassy in Canada: c/o Embassy of the Lao People's Democratic Republic, 2222 S St NW, Washington DC 20001, USA. Tel: (202) 332-6416. Fax: (202) 332-4923. e-mail: n.a.

Latvia

Long-Form Name: Republic of Latvia
Capital: Riga

■ GEOGRAPHY

Area: 64,589 sq. km
Coastline: 531 km
Climate: maritime, wet, moderate winters
Environment: air and water pollution, soil and groundwater contaminated with chemicals and petroleum products at military bases
Terrain: hilly, forested land with many lakes and shallow valleys
Land Use: arable land: 29.01%, permanent crops: 0.48%, other: 70.51%; includes 200 sq. km irrigated
Location: NE Europe, bordering on Baltic Sea

■ PEOPLE

Population: 2,348,784 (July 2003 est.)
Nationality: Latvian
Age Structure: 0–14 yrs: 15.1%; 15–64: 68.9%; 65+: 16.0% (2003 est.)
Population Growth Rate: -0.73% (2003 est.)
Net Migration: -1.19 migrants/1,000 population (2003 est.)
Ethnic Groups: 56.5% Latvian, 30.4% Russian, 4.3% Belorussian, 2.8% Ukrainian, 2.6% Polish, 3.4% other
Languages: Lettish (official), Lithuanian, Russian, some others
Religions: Lutheran, Catholic, Russian Orthodox
Birth Rate: 8.55/1,000 population (2003 est.)
Death Rate: 14.70/1,000 population (2003 est.)
Infant Mortality: 14.59 deaths/1,000 live births (2003 est.)
Life Expectancy at Birth: 63.46 years male, 75.45 years female (2003 est.)
Total Fertility Rate: 1.20 children born/woman (2003 est.)
Literacy: 99.7% (2002)

■ GOVERNMENT

Leader(s): President Vaira Vike-Freiberga, Prime Minister Indulis Emsis
Government Type: parliamentary democracy
Administrative Divisions: 26 counties (sing. — rajons) and 7 municipalities
Nationhood: Aug. 21, 1991 (from Soviet Union)
National Holiday: Independence Day, Nov. 18

■ ECONOMY

Overview: lacks natural resources, aside from its arable land and small forests; its most valuable economic asset is its workforce, which is better educated and disciplined than in most of the former Soviet republics; rapidly moving towards a dynamic market economy.
GDP: US$20.99 billion, per capita US$8,900; real growth rate 6.1% (2002)
Inflation: 2.0% (2002 est.)
Industries: accounts for 26% of GDP (2001) and 31% of labour force; manufacturing of railroad cars, paper, woollen goods, electronics and engineering, food processing
Labour Force: 1.3 million (2002); 25% industry, 15% forestry and agriculture, 60% services
Unemployment: 8.9% (March 2003)
Agriculture: accounts for 5% of GDP (2001), employs 9% of labour force and has become largely privatized; poor soil hinders agriculture products including grain, beets, potatoes, cattle and dairy farming, poultry, eggs, fishing
Natural Resources: forests, peat deposits, amber, dolomite, hydroelectric power, arable land

■ FINANCE/TRADE

Currency: lat = 100 santims
International Reserves Excluding Gold: US$1.425 billion (Jan. 2004)
Gold Reserves: 0.249 milllion fine troy ounces (Jan. 2004)
Budget: revenues US$2.4 billion, expenditures US$2.6 billion, including capital expenditures of US$ n.a. (2002 est.)
Defence Expenditures: 3.9% of central government expenditure (2002)
Education Expenditures: 5.62% of central government expenditure (2000)
External Debt: US$6.690 billion (2002)
Exports: US$2.865 billion (2003); vehicles, household appliances, electric power, textiles; partners: Germany, UK, Sweden, Lithuania, Russia
Imports: US$5.190 billion (2003): fuels, cars, chemicals and metal products; partners: Russia, Germany, Lithuania, Finland, Sweden

■ COMMUNICATIONS

Daily Newspapers: 135/1,000 inhabitants (2000)
Televisions: 850/1,000 inhabitants (2002)
Radios: 700/1,000 inhabitants (2001)
Telephones: 301 lines/1,000 inhabitants (2002)
Internet: hosts: 35,492 (2002); users: 312,000 (2002)

■ TRANSPORTATION

Motor Vehicles: 665,000; 556,000 passenger cars
Roads: 73,202 km; 28,256 km paved
Railway: 2,347 km
Air Traffic: 265,000 passengers carried (2002)
Airports: 38; 22 have paved runways (2003 est.)

Canadian Embassy: The Canadian Embassy, 20/22 Baznicas Street, 6th Floor, Riga, LV-1010, Latvia. Tel: (011 371) 781 3945. Fax (011 371) 781 3960. e-mail: riga@dfait-maeci.gc.ca
Embassy in Canada: Embassy of the Republic of Latvia, 280 Albert St Ste 300, Ottawa, ON, K1P 5G8. Tel: (613) 238-6014. Fax: (613) 238-7044. e-mail: embassy.canada@mfa.gov.lv

Lebanon

Long-Form Name: Lebanese Republic
Capital: Beirut

■ GEOGRAPHY

Area: 10,400 sq. km
Coastline: 225 km
Climate: Mediterranean; mild to cool, wet winters with hot, dry summers; heavy snowfall in winter in Lebanon Mountains

Environment: deforestation; soil erosion; air and water pollution; desertification
Terrain: narrow coastal plain; al Biqa' separates Lebanon and Anti-Lebanon Mountains; rugged terrain historically helped isolate, protect and develop numerous factional groups based on religion, clan and ethnicity.
Land Use: arable land: 17.6%, permanent crops: 12.51%, other: 69.89%; includes 1,200 sq. km irrigated
Location: SW Asia (Middle East), bordering on Mediterranean Sea

■ PEOPLE

Population: 3,727,703 (July 2003 est.)
Nationality: Lebanese (sing. & pl.)
Age Structure: 0–14 yrs: 27.1%; 15–64: 66.1%; 65+: 6.8% (2003 est.)
Population Growth Rate: 1.34% (2003 est.)
Net Migration: 0 migrants/1,000 population (2003 est.)
Ethnic Groups: 95% Arab, 4% Armenian, 1% other
Languages: Arabic and French (both official); Armenian, English, Kurdish
Religions: Muslim 70% (Sunni, Shia and Druse), Christian 30% (mainly Maronite; also, Armenian, Greek and Syrian sects and Protestants)
Birth Rate: 16.68/1,000 population (2003 est.)
Death Rate: 6.32/1,000 population (2003 est.)
Infant Mortality: 26.43 deaths/1,000 live births (2003 est.)
Life Expectancy at Birth: 69.64 years male, 74.61 years female (2003 est.)
Total Fertility Rate: 1.98 children born/woman (2003 est.)
Literacy: 86.5% (2002)

■ GOVERNMENT

Leader(s): President Emile Jamil Lahud, Prime Minister Rafiq Hariri
Government Type: republic
Administrative Divisions: 5 governorates (muhafazat, sing. —muhafazah)
Nationhood: Nov. 22, 1943 (from League of Nations mandate under French administration)
National Holiday: Independence Day, Nov. 22

■ ECONOMY

Overview: Factional infighting has led to deterioration of the infrastructure and disrupted normal economic activity in what used to be the centre for Middle Eastern banking; high unemployment; growing shortages; international aid is vital
GDP: US$17.61 billion, per capita US$4,800; real growth rate 2.0% (2002 est.)
Inflation: 3.5% (2002 est.)

Industries: accounts for 21% of GDP (2000); banking, food processing, textiles, cement, oil refining, chemicals, jewellery, some metal fabricating
Labour Force: 1.6 million (2002); 27.4% industry, 58.4% services, 14.3% agriculture
Unemployment: n.a.
Agriculture: accounts for about 12% of GDP (2000); principal products—citrus fruit, grapes, tomatoes, apples, vegetables, potatoes, olives, tobacco, hemp (hashish), sheep and goats; not self-sufficient in grain
Natural Resources: limestone, iron ore, salt; water-surplus state in a water-deficit region

■ FINANCE/TRADE

Currency: Lebanese pound (£L) = 100 piasters
International Reserves Excluding Gold: US$12.579 billion (Jan. 2004)
Gold Reserves: 9.222 million fine troy ounces (Jan. 2004)
Budget: revenues US$4.5 billion; expenditures US$7.1 billion, including capital expenditures of US$ n.a. (2003 est.)
Defence Expenditures: 14% of central government expenditure (2002)
Education Expenditures: 11.1% of central government expenditure (2002)
External Debt: US$17.077 billion (2002)
Exports: US$1.524 billion (2003); commodities: agricultural products, chemicals, tobacco, textiles, metals and jewellery; partners: 21% Saudi Arabia, UAE, Switzerland, US, France, Iraq, Jordan, Kuwait, Syria
Imports: US$7.171 billion (2003); commodities: consumer goods, machinery and transport equipment, metals, petroleum products; partners: Italy, France, Germany, US, Switzerland, Japan, China, Syria, UK

■ COMMUNICATIONS

Daily Newspapers: 107/1,000 inhabitants (2000)
Televisions: 357/1,000 inhabitants (2002)
Radios: 182/1,000 inhabitants (2001)
Telephones: 199 lines/1,000 inhabitants (2002)
Internet: hosts: 7,199 (2002); users: 400,000 (2002)

■ TRANSPORTATION

Motor Vehicles: 1,200,000; 1,135,000 passenger cars (2000)
Roads: 7,300 km; 6,200 km paved
Railway: 399 km; railroad system in disrepair, considered inoperable
Air Traffic: 874,000 passengers carried (2002)
Airports: 8; 5 have paved runways (2003 est.)

Canadian Embassy: The Canadian Embassy, 43 Jal-el-Dib Highway, 1st floor, Jal-ed-Dib, Lebanon; mailing address: P.O. Box 60163, Jal-el-Dib, Beirut, Lebanon. Tel: (011-961-4) 713-900. Fax: (011-961-4) 710-595. e-mail: berut@dfait-maeci.gc.ca
Embassy in Canada: Embassy of the Lebanese Republic, 640 Lyon St, Ottawa ON K1S 3Z5. Tel: (613) 236-5825. Fax: (613) 232-1609. e-mail: info@lebanonembassy.ca

Lesotho

Long-Form Name: Kingdom of Lesotho
Capital: Maseru

■ GEOGRAPHY

Area: 30,355 sq. km
Coastline: none: landlocked
Climate: temperate; cool to cold, dry winters; hot, wet summers
Environment: population pressure forcing settlement in marginal agricultural areas results in overgrazing, severe soil erosion, soil exhaustion; desertification
Terrain: mostly highland with some plateaus, hills and mountains
Land Use: arable land: 10.71%, permanent crops: 0%, other: 89.29%; includes 10 sq. km irrigated
Location: S Africa

■ PEOPLE

Population: 1,861,959 (July 2003 est.)
Nationality: Mosotho (sing.), Basotho (pl.)
Age Structure: 0–14 yrs: 37.7%; 15–64: 56.8%; 65+: 5.5% (2003 est.)
Population Growth Rate: 0.19% (2003 est.)
Net Migration: -0.74 migrants/1,000 population (2003 est.)
Ethnic Groups: 99.7% Sotho; 0.3% Europeans, Asians and other
Languages: Sesotho (southern Sotho) and English (official); also Zulu and Xhosa
Religions: 80% Christian, indigenous beliefs
Birth Rate: 27.26/1,000 population (2003 est.)
Death Rate: 24.58/1,000 population (2003 est.)
Infant Mortality: 86.21 deaths/1,000 live births (2003 est.)
Life Expectancy at Birth: 36.76 years male, 37.13 years female (2003 est.)
Total Fertility Rate: 3.52 children born/woman (2003 est.)
Literacy: 81.4% (2002)

■ GOVERNMENT

Leader(s): King Letsie III, Prime Minister Bethuel Pakalitha Mosisili

Government Type: parliamentary constitutional monarchy
Administrative Divisions: 10 districts
Nationhood: Oct. 4, 1966 (from UK: formerly known as Basutoland)
National Holiday: Independence Day, Oct. 4

■ ECONOMY

Overview: the economy is hampered by the geography of the country (small, landlocked and mountainous) and the lack of natural resources other than water; subsistence farming is the main occupation; labourers in South Africa make remittances; industry is growing in importance
GDP: US$5.106 billion, per capita US$2,700; real growth rate 4.0% (2002 est.)
Inflation: 10.0% (2002 est.)
Industries: accounts for 38% of GDP (2001); light manufacturing, milling, canning, leather, jute production, textiles, clothing, light engineering, food, beverages, handicrafts, tourism
Labour Force: 700,000 (2002); 86% agriculture
Unemployment: 45% (2000 est.)
Agriculture: accounts for 18% of GDP (2001); very primitive, mostly subsistence farming and livestock; principal crops are corn, wheat, pulses, sorghum and barley
Natural Resources: some diamonds and other minerals, water, agricultural and grazing land

■ FINANCE/TRADE

Currency: loti, maloti (pl.) = 100 lisente; also the South African rand
International Reserves Excluding Gold: US$477 million (Jan. 2004)
Gold Reserves: n.a.
Budget: revenues US$76 million, expenditures US$80 million, including capital expenditures of $US n.a. (2000 est.)
Defence Expenditures: 6.4% of central government expenditure (2002)
Education Expenditures: 18.4% of total government expenditures (2002)
External Debt: US$637 million (2002)
Exports: US$469 million (2003); commodities: wool, mohair, wheat, cattle, peas, beans, corn, hides, skins, baskets; partners: South African Customs Union, North American countries
Imports: US$998 million (2003); commodities: corn, building materials, clothing, vehicles, machinery, medicines, petroleum, oil and lubricants; partners: South African Customs Union, Asian countries

■ COMMUNICATIONS

Daily Newspapers: 8/1,000 inhabitants (2000)
Televisions: 35/1,000 inhabitants (2002)
Radios: 53/1,000 inhabitants (2001)
Telephones: 13 lines/1,000 inhabitants (2002)
Internet: hosts: 45 (2002); users: 21,000 (2002)

■ TRANSPORTATION

Motor Vehicles: n.a.
Roads: 5,940 km; 1,087 km paved
Railway: 2.6 km, owned, operated by and included in the statistics for South Africa
Air Traffic: n.a.
Airports: 28; 4 have paved runways (2003)

Canadian Embassy: The Canadian High Commission to Lesotho, 1103 Arcadia St., Hatfield, Pretoria 0028. Mailing address: c/o Canadian Embassy, Private Bag X13, Hatfield 0028, Pretoria, South Africa. Tel: (011-27-12) 422-3000. Fax: (011-27-12) 422-3052. e-mail: pret@dfait-maeci.gc.ca
Embassy in Canada: c/o High Commission for the Kingdom of Lesotho, 2511 Massachusetts Ave NW, Washington DC 20008, USA. Tel: (202) 797-5533. Fax: (202) 234-6815. e-mail: n.a.

Liberia

Long-Form Name: Republic of Liberia
Capital: Monrovia

■ GEOGRAPHY

Area: 111,370 sq. km
Coastline: 579 km
Climate: tropical; hot, humid; dry winters with hot days and cool to cold nights; wet, cloudy summers with frequent heavy showers
Environment: West Africa's largest tropical rainforest, subject to deforestation; soil erosion is increasingly a problem; river pollution
Terrain: mostly flat to rolling coastal plains rising to rolling plateau and low mountains in northeast
Land Use: arable land: 1.97%, permanent crops: 2.08%, other: 95.95%; includes 30 sq. km irrigated
Location: W Africa, bordering on South Atlantic Ocean

■ PEOPLE

Population: 3,317,176 (July 2003 est.)
Nationality: Liberian
Age Structure: 0–14 yrs: 43.4%; 15–64: 53.0%; 65+: 3.6% (2003 est.)

Population Growth Rate: 1.67% (2003 est.)
Net Migration: -10.70 migrants/1,000 population (2003 est.)
Ethnic Groups: 95% indigenous African tribes, including Kpelle, Bassa, Gio, Kru, Grego, Mano, Krahn, Gola, Gbandi, Lom, Kissi, Vai and Bella; 2.5% descendants of repatriated slaves known as Americo-Liberians, and 2.5% Congo People (descendants of immigrants from the Caribbean who had been slaves)
Languages: English (official); 20 local languages of the Niger-Congo language group; English used by approx. 20%
Religions: 70% traditional, 20% Muslim, 10% Christian
Birth Rate: 45.28/1,000 population (2003 est.)
Death Rate: 17.84/1,000 population (2003 est.)
Infant Mortality: 132.18 deaths/1,000 live births (2003 est.)
Life Expectancy at Birth: 47.03 years male, 49.30 years female (2003 est.)
Total Fertility Rate: 6.23 children born/woman (2003 est.)
Literacy: 57.5% (2003 est.)

■ GOVERNMENT

Leader(s): Chairman Gyude Bryant, Vice Chairman Wesley Johnson
Government Type: republic
Administrative Divisions: 13 counties
Nationhood: July 26, 1847
National Holiday: Independence Day, July 26

■ ECONOMY

Overview: civil war since 1990 has destroyed much of Liberia's economy, especially the infrastructure in and around Monrovia; many businesspeople have fled the country, taking capital and expertise with them; the government must encourage foreign investment to restore the infrastructure and to raise incomes
GDP: US$3.116 billion, per capita US$1,000; real growth rate 2.0% (2002 est.)
Inflation: 15.0% (2002 est.)
Industries: accounts for 10% of GDP; rubber processing, food processing, construction materials, furniture, palm oil processing, mining (iron ore, diamonds)
Labour Force: 1.3 million (2002); 70% agriculture, 22% services, 8% industry
Unemployment: 70%
Agriculture: including fishing and forestry, accounts for 60% of GDP (2001 est.); principal products—rubber, timber, coffee, cocoa, rice, cassava, palm oil, sugar cane, bananas, sheep

and goats; not self-sufficient in food, imports 25% of rice consumption
Natural Resources: iron ore, timber, diamonds, gold, hydro power

■ FINANCE/TRADE

Currency: Liberian dollar ($L) = 100 cents
International Reserves Excluding Gold: none (Sept. 2003)
Gold Reserves: n.a.
Budget: revenues US$85.4 million; expenditures US$90.5 million, capital expenditures US$ n.a. (2000 est.)
Defence Expenditures: 1.3% of GDP (2002)
Education Expenditures: n.a.
External Debt: US$2.324 billion (2002)
Exports: US$1.079 billion (2002 est.); commodities: diamonds, iron ore, rubber, timber, coffee, cocoa; partners: Belgium, Germany, Italy, US
Imports: US$5.051 billion (2002 est.); commodities: mineral fuels, chemicals, machinery, foodstuffs; partners: France, South Korea, Japan, Singapore

■ COMMUNICATIONS

Daily Newspapers: 12/1,000 inhabitants (2000)
Televisions: 25/1,000 inhabitants (2002)
Radios: 274/1,000 inhabitants (2001)
Telephones: 2 lines/1,000 inhabitants (2002)
Internet: users: 1,000 (2002)

■ TRANSPORTATION

Motor Vehicles: 28,700; 17,800 passenger cars
Roads: 10,600 km; 657 km paved
Railway: 490 km
Air Traffic: n.a.
Airports: 47; 2 have paved runways (2003 est.)

Canadian Embassy: The Canadian Embassy, Immeuble Trade-Center, 23 rue Nogues, Le Plateau, Abidjan; mailing address: BP 4104, Abidjan 01, Côte d'Ivoire. Tel: (011-225) 20-30-07-00. Fax: (011-225) 20-30-07-20. e-mail: abdjn@dfait-maeci.gc.ca
Embassy in Canada: c/o Consulate of Liberia, 1441 Ontario St., Burlington, ON, L7S 1G5. Tel: (905) 333-4000. Fax: (905)632-4000. e-mail: n.a.

Libya

Long-Form Name: Socialist People's Libyan Arab Jamahiriya
Capital: Tripoli

■ GEOGRAPHY

Area: 1,759,540 sq. km
Coastline: 1,770 km
Climate: Mediterranean along coast; dry, extreme desert interior
Environment: hot, dry, dust-laden ghibli (a southern wind lasting one to four days in spring and fall); desertification; dust storms; sparse natural surface-water resources
Terrain: mostly barren, flat to undulating plains, plateaus, depressions
Land Use: arable land: 1.03%, permanent crops: 0.17%, other: 98.8%; includes 4,700 sq. km irrigated
Location: N Africa, bordering on Mediterranean Sea

■ PEOPLE

Population: 5,499,074; includes 166,510 non-nationals (July 2003 est.)
Nationality: Libyan
Age Structure: 0–14 yrs: 34.5%; 15–64: 61.4%; 65+: 4.1% (2003 est.)
Population Growth Rate: 2.39% (2003 est.)
Net Migration: 0 migrants/1,000 population (2003 est.)
Ethnic Groups: 97% Berber and Arab; some Greeks, Maltese, Italians, Egyptians, Pakistanis, Turks, Indians and Tunisians
Languages: Arabic (official); Italian and English widely understood in major cities, Berber
Religions: 97% Sunni Muslim, 3% Christian and other
Birth Rate: 27.43/1,000 population (2003 est.)
Death Rate: 3.49/1,000 population (2003 est.)
Infant Mortality: 26.80 deaths/1,000 live births (2003 est.)
Life Expectancy at Birth: 73.91 years male, 78.34 years female (2003 est.)
Total Fertility Rate: 3.49 children born/woman (2003 est.)
Literacy: 81.7% (2002)

■ GOVERNMENT

Leader(s): Colonel Mu'ammar Abu Minyar al-Qadhafi, Secretary General of People's Congress Muhammad al-Zanati
Government Type: Jamahiriya (a state of the masses); in theory, governed by the populace through local councils; in fact, a military dictatorship
Administrative Divisions: 25 municipalities (baladiyat, sing. —baladiyah)
Nationhood: Dec. 24, 1951 (from Italy)
National Holiday: Revolution Day, Sept. 1

■ ECONOMY

Overview: a socialist-oriented economy that depends largely on revenues from the oil sector; cutbacks on imports due to declining oil revenues have led to shortages of foodstuffs and basic goods; must import 75% of its food needs, as poor soil and climate limit agricultural production
GDP: US$33.36 billion, per capita US$6,200; real growth rate 1.2% (2002 est.)
Inflation: 1.0% (2002 est.)
Industries: accounts for 47% of GDP; petroleum, food processing, textiles, handicrafts, cement
Labour Force: 1.6 million (2002); 29% industry, 54% services, 17% agriculture
Unemployment: 30% (2000 est.)
Agriculture: accounts for 7% of GDP; cash crops—wheat, barley, olives, dates, citrus fruit, peanuts, soybeans; 75% of food is imported
Natural Resources: crude oil, natural gas, gypsum

■ FINANCE/TRADE

Currency: Libyan dinar (LD) = 1,000 dirhams
International Reserves Excluding Gold: US$19.752 billion (Jan. 2004)
Gold Reserves: n.a.
Budget: revenues US$10.2 billion; expenditures US$7.8 billion, including capital expenditures of US$ n.a. (2003 est.)
Defence Expenditures: 3.9% of GDP (2000)
Education Expenditures: n.a.
External Debt: US$4.4 billion (2001 est.)
Exports: US$8.020 billion (2002); commodities: petroleum, peanuts, hides; partners: Italy, Germany, Spain, Turkey, France, Tunisia
Imports: US$4.402 billion (2002); commodities: machinery, transport equipment, food, manufactured goods; partners: Italy, Germany, UK, Tunisia, France, South Korea.

■ COMMUNICATIONS

Daily Newspapers: 15/1,000 inhabitants (2000)
Televisions: 137/1,000 inhabitants (2002)
Radios: 273/1,000 inhabitants (2001)
Telephones: 118 lines/1,000 inhabitants (2002)
Internet: hosts: 83 (2002); users: 125,000 (2002)

■ TRANSPORTATION

Motor Vehicles: 904,000; 592,000 passenger cars
Roads: 83,200 km; 47,590 km paved
Railway: none
Air Traffic: 559,000 passengers carried (2002)
Airports: 136; 58 have paved runways (2003 est.)

Canadian Embassy: The Canadian Embassy, Al-Fateh Tower, 7th Fl, P.O. Box 93392, Al-Fateh Tower Post Office, Tripoli, Libya. Tel: (011-218-21) 335-1633. Fax: (011-218-21) 335-1630. e-mail: trpli@dfait-maeci.gc.ca
Embassy in Canada: Embassy of the Socialist People's Libyan Arab Jamahiriya, 81 Metcalfe St Ste 1000, Ottawa ON K1P 6K7. Tel: (613) 230-0919. Fax: (613) 230-0683. e-mail: n.a.

Liechtenstein

Long-Form Name: Principality of Liechtenstein
Capital: Vaduz

■ GEOGRAPHY

Area: 160 sq. km
Coastline: none: landlocked
Climate: continental; cold, cloudy winters with frequent snow or rain; cool to moderately warm, cloudy, humid summers
Environment: variety of microclimatic variations based on elevation
Terrain: mostly mountainous (Alps) with Rhine Valley in western third
Land Use: arable land: 25%, permanent crops: 0%, other: 75%; includes n.a. sq. km irrigated
Location: C Europe, bordering on Switzerland and Austria

■ PEOPLE

Population: 33,145 (July 2003 est.)
Nationality: Liechtensteiner
Age Structure: 0–14 yrs: 18.1%; 15–64: 70.6%; 65+: 11.3% (2003 est.)
Population Growth Rate: 0.90% (2003 est.)
Net Migration: 4.89 migrants/1,000 population (2003 est.)
Ethnic Groups: 87.5% Alemannic, 12.5% Italian, Turkish and other
Languages: German (official), also Alemannic dialect
Religions: 87.3% Roman Catholic, 8.3% Protestant, 2.8% other; 1.6% unknown
Birth Rate: 10.92/1,000 population (2003 est.)
Death Rate: 6.85/1,000 population (2003 est.)
Infant Mortality: 4.85 deaths/1,000 live births (2003 est.)
Life Expectancy at Birth: 75.63 years male, 82.87 years female (2003 est.)
Total Fertility Rate: 1.5 children born/woman (2003 est.)
Literacy: approaching 100% (2003 est.)

■ GOVERNMENT

Leader(s): Head of State: Prince Hans Adam II von und zu Liechtenstein, Prime Minister Otmar Hasler
Government Type: hereditary constitutional monarchy
Administrative Divisions: 11 communes (gemeinden, sing. —gemeinde)
Nationhood: Jan. 23, 1719, Imperial Principality of Liechtenstein established
National Holiday: Assumption Day, Aug. 15

■ ECONOMY

Overview: a prosperous economy based mainly on small-scale light industry and some farming; economy closely tied to that of Switzerland in a customs union; known for low business taxes and easy incorporation rules
GDP: n.a.
Inflation: 1.0% (2001)
Industries: electronics, metal manufacturing, textiles, ceramics, pharmaceuticals, food products, precision instruments, tourism
Labour Force: approx. 29,000 (2001), of which approx. 15,000 are foreigners; 48% industry, trade and building, 51% services, 1% agriculture, fishing, forestry and horticulture
Unemployment: n.a.
Agriculture: livestock, vegetables, corn, barley, wheat, potatoes, grapes
Natural Resources: hydroelectric potential, arable land

■ FINANCE/TRADE

Currency: Swiss franc, franken, or franco (SwF) = 100 centimes, rappen, or centesimi
International Reserves Excluding Gold: n.a.
Gold Reserves: n.a.
Budget: n.a.
Defence Expenditures: defence is the responsibility of Switzerland
Education Expenditures: n.a.
External Debt: none
Exports: exact figures not available; small speciality machinery, dental products, stamps, hardware, pottery; partners: EU, US, Switzerland
Imports: exact figures not available; commodities: machinery, metal goods, textiles, foodstuffs, motor vehicles; partners: EU countries, Switzerland

■ COMMUNICATIONS

Daily Newspapers: 2 in total
Televisions: n.a.

Radios: n.a.
Telephones: 607 lines/1,000 inhabitants (2002)
Internet: users: 20,000 (2002)

■ TRANSPORTATION

Motor Vehicles: n.a.
Roads: 250 km; all paved
Railway: 18.5 km, owned, operated and included in statistics for Austria
Air Traffic: n.a.
Airports: none

Canadian Embassy: The Canadian Embassy, Kirchenfeldstrasse 88, Bern, 3005, Switzerland. Mailing address: The Canadian Embassy to Liechtenstein, c/o the Canadian Embassy, P.O. Box 3000, Berne 6, Switzerland. Tel: (011-41-31) 357-32-00. Fax: (011-41-31) 357-32-10. e-mail: bern@dfait-maeci.gc.ca
Embassy in Canada: Embassy of Liechtenstein, c/o Embassy of Switzerland, 5 Marlborough Ave, Ottawa ON K1N 8E6. Tel: (613) 235-1837. Fax: (613) 563-1394. e-mail: vertretung@ott.rep.admin.ch

Lithuania

Long-Form Name: Republic of Lithuania
Capital: Vilnius

■ GEOGRAPHY

Area: 65,200 sq. km
Coastline: 99 km
Climate: transitional, between maritime and continental; mild, with moderate precipitation
Environment: risk of accidents from the two Chernobyl-type reactors; at military bases, contamination of soil and groundwater with chemicals and petroleum products
Terrain: undulating glacial terrain; rivers, lakes and swamps predominate
Land Use: arable land: 45.46%, permanent crops: 0.93%, other: 53.61%; includes 90 sq. km irrigated
Location: NE Europe, bordering on Baltic Sea

■ PEOPLE

Population: 3,592,561 (July 2003 est.)
Nationality: Lithuanian
Age Structure: 0–14 yrs: 17.6%; 15–64: 68.4%; 65+: 14.0% (2003 est.)
Population Growth Rate: -0.23% (2003 est.)
Net Migration: 0.14 migrants/1,000 population (2003 est.)
Ethnic Groups: 80.6% Lithuanian, 8.7% Russian, 7% Polish, 1.6% Byelorussian, 2.1% other
Languages: Lithuanian (official), Russian, Polish

Religions: predominantly Protestant, Roman Catholic, Russian Orthodox
Birth Rate: 10.48/1,000 population (2003 est.)
Death Rate: 12.89/1,000 population (2003 est.)
Infant Mortality: 14.17 deaths/1,000 live births (2003 est.)
Life Expectancy at Birth: 63.78 years male, 75.70 years female (2003 est.)
Total Fertility Rate: 1.43 children born/woman (2003 est.)
Literacy: 99.6% (2002)

■ GOVERNMENT

Leader(s): Acting President Arturas Paulauskas, Prime Minister Algirdas Mikolas Brazauskas
Government Type: parliamentary democracy
Administrative Divisions: 10 counties (apskritys, sing. —apskritis)
Nationhood: Sept. 6, 1991 (from Soviet Union)
National Holiday: Independence Day, Feb. 16

■ ECONOMY

Overview: arable land and strategic location are Lithuania's only important natural resources; Lithuania remains highly dependent on Russia for energy, raw materials, grains and markets for its products
GDP: US$30.08 billion, per capita US$8,400; real growth rate 6.7% (2002)
Inflation: 0.8% (2002 est.)
Industries: accounts for 31% of GDP (2001 est.) and employs 42% of labour force; heavy engineering, shipbuilding, production of building materials, nuclear and electric power production; electric motors, television sets, appliances, refining, fertilizer
Labour Force: 1.8 million (2002); 30% industry, 50% community, social and business services, 20% agriculture
Unemployment: 9.7% (Nov. 2003)
Agriculture: accounts for 8% of GDP (2001 est.) and employs approximately 18% of labour force; beef and dairy cattle and related products, pigs, poultry, grains, flax, potatoes and other vegetables, eggs, fish, dairy products; net exporter of meat, milk, eggs and fish
Natural Resources: amber, peat

■ FINANCE/TRADE

Currency: litas (pl. litai) = 100 centas
International Reserves Excluding Gold: US$3.318 billion (Jan. 2004)
Gold Reserves: 0.186 million fine troy ounces (Jan. 2004)
Budget: revenues US$1.59 billion; expenditures US$1.77 billion, capital expenditures US$ n.a. (2001 est.)

Defence Expenditures: 6.8% of central government expenditure (2002)
Education Expenditures: 5.82% of central government expenditure (2000)
External Debt: US$6.199 billion (2002)
Exports: US$7.124 billion (2003); 18% electronics, 5% petroleum products, 10% food, 6% chemicals; partners: UK, Latvia, Germany, Russia, Poland
Imports: US$9.682 billion (2003); 24% oil, 14% machinery, 8% chemicals, grain, textiles and clothing; partners: Russia, Germany, Poland, Italy, France

■ COMMUNICATIONS

Daily Newspapers: 29/1,000 inhabitants (2000)
Televisions: 487/1,000 inhabitants (2002)
Radios: 524/1,000 inhabitants (2001)
Telephones: 270 lines/1,000 inhabitants (2002)
Internet: hosts: 54,605 (2002); users: 500,000 (2002)

■ TRANSPORTATION

Motor Vehicles: 1,240,000; 1,140,000 passenger cars
Roads: 75,243 km; 68,697 km paved
Railway: 1,998 km
Air Traffic: 304,000 passengers carried (2002)
Airports: 87; 22 have paved runways (2003 est.)

Canadian Embassy: Office of the Canadian Embassy, Gedimino pr. 64, 2001 Vilnius, Lithuania. Tel: (011-370) 5-249-0950. Fax: (011-370) 5-249-7865. e-mail: vilnius@canada.lt
Embassy in Canada: Embassy of the Republic of Lithuania, 130 Albert St, Ste 204, Ottawa, ON K1P 5G4. Tel: (613) 567-5458. Fax: (613) 567-5315. e-mail: litemb@storm.ca

---

Luxembourg

Long-Form Name: Grand Duchy of Luxembourg
Capital: Luxembourg

■ GEOGRAPHY

Area: 2,586 sq. km
Coastline: none: landlocked
Climate: modified continental with mild winters, cool summers
Environment: deforestation; air and water pollution in urban areas
Terrain: mostly gently rolling uplands with broad, shallow valleys; uplands to slightly mountainous in the north; steep slope down to Moselle floodplain in the southeast

Land Use: arable land: 25%, permanent crops: 0%, other: 75% (includes Belgium); including 40 sq. km irrigated shared with Belgium
Location: NC Europe, bordering on Belgium, France and Germany

■ PEOPLE

Population: 454,157 (July 2003 est.)
Nationality: Luxembourger
Age Structure: 0–14 yrs: 18.9%; 15–64: 66.9%; 65+: 14.2% (2002 est.)
Population Growth Rate: 1.23% (2003 est.)
Net Migration: 9.14 migrants/1,000 population (2003 est.)
Ethnic Groups: Celtic base, with French and German blend; also guest and worker residents
Languages: Luxembourgisch (official), German (written language of commerce and press), French (administrative), English
Religions: 97% Roman Catholic, 3% Protestant and Jewish
Birth Rate: 11.92/1,000 population (2003 est.)
Death Rate: 8.78/1,000 population (2003 est.)
Infant Mortality: 4.65 deaths/1,000 live births (2003 est.)
Life Expectancy at Birth: 74.38 years male, 81.15 years female (2003 est.)
Total Fertility Rate: 1.70 children born/woman (2003 est.)
Literacy: approaching 100% (2002)

■ GOVERNMENT

Leader(s): Head of State: Henri, Grand Duke of Luxembourg, Prime Minister Jean-Claude Juncker
Government Type: constitutional monarchy
Administrative Divisions: 3 districts
Nationhood: 1839 (Grand Duchy)
National Holiday: National Day (public celebration of the Grand Duke's birthday), June 23

■ ECONOMY

Overview: a stable economy featuring moderate growth, low inflation and negligible unemployment; is in an economic union with Belgium for trade and most financial matters, and is also closely connected economically with the Netherlands; financial sector is strong; industrial sector is becoming increasingly diversified
GDP: US$21.94 billion, per capita US$48,900; real growth rate 0.4% (2002)
Inflation: 1.6% (2002 est.)
Industries: accounts for 30% of GDP; banking, iron and steel, food processing, chemicals, metal products, engineering, tires, glass, aluminum

Labour Force: 248,000 (2000); 90% community, social and business services, 8% industries, 2% agriculture
Unemployment: 4.5% (Jan. 2004)
Agriculture: accounts for only 1% of GDP (including forestry); principal products—barley, oats, potatoes, wheat, fruits, wine grapes; cattle-raising widespread
Natural Resources: iron ore (no longer exploited), arable land

■ FINANCE/TRADE

Currency: Luxembourg franc (LuxF) = 100 centimes; Euro (€); on January 1, 2002 the Euro became the sole currency for everyday transactions.
International Reserves Excluding Gold: US$266 million (Jan. 2004)
Gold Reserves: 0.075 million fine troy ounces (Jan. 2004)
Budget: revenues US$5.5 billion; expenditures US$5.5 billion, including capital expenditures US$760 million (2002 est.)
Defence Expenditures: 0.8% of GDP (2002)
Education Expenditures: n.a
External Debt: n.a.
Exports: US$10.194 billion (2003 est.); commodities: finished steel products, chemicals, rubber products, glass, aluminum, other industrial products; partners: Germany, France, Belgium, US
Imports: US$13.571 billion (2003 est.); commodities: minerals, metals, foodstuffs, quality consumer goods; partners: Germany, Belgium, France, US

■ COMMUNICATIONS

Daily Newspapers: 5 in total
Televisions: n.a.
Radios: n.a.
Telephones: 792 lines/1,000 inhabitants (2002)
Internet: hosts: 17,260 (2002); users: 165,000 (2002)

■ TRANSPORTATION

Motor Vehicles: 251,000; 233,000 passenger cars
Roads: 5,189 km; all paved
Railway: 274 km
Air Traffic: 665,000 passengers carried (2001 est.)
Airports: 2; 1 has paved runways (2003 est.)

Canadian Embassy: The Canadian Embassy to Luxembourg, c/o 2, Avenue de Tervuren, 1040 Brussels, Belgium. Tel: (011-32-2) 741-0611. Fax: (011-32-2) 741-0643. e-mail: bru@dfait-maeci.gc.ca
Embassy in Canada: c/o Embassy of the Grand Duchy of Luxembourg, 2200 Massachusetts

Ave NW, Washington DC 20008, USA. Tel: (202) 265-4171. Fax: (202) 328-8270. e-mail: info@luxembourg-usa.org

Macau

Long-Form Name: Macau Special Administrative Region
Capital: none

■ GEOGRAPHY

Area: 21 sq. km (a peninsula and three small islands)
Climate: subtropical maritime; marine with cool winters, warm summers
Land Use: arable land: 0%, permanent crops: 0%, other: 100%, note: "green areas" represent 22.4%
Location: SE coast of China, bordering on South China Sea

■ PEOPLE

Population: 469,903 (July 2003 est.)
Nationality: Chinese
Ethnic Groups: Chinese 95%, Portuguese 3%, other 2%
Languages: Portuguese (official), Cantonese, English widely spoken

■ GOVERNMENT

Colony/Territory of: Special Administrative Region of China
Leader(s): President Hu Jintao (China), Chief Executive Edmund Ho Hau-wah
Government Type: reverted to China Dec. 20, 1999
National Holiday: National Day, Oct. 1; Dec. 20 is celebrated as Macau Special Administrative Region Establishment Day

■ ECONOMY

Overview: gambling and tourism; industry confined to textiles, fireworks, toy-making, plastics; imports almost all energy, food and water from China

■ FINANCE/TRADE

Currency: pataca (pl. patacas) = 100 avos

Canadian Embassy: c/o The Canadian Embassy, 19 Dong Zhi Men Wai Street, Chao Yang District, Beijing 100600, China. Tel: (011 86 10) 6532 3536. Fax: (011 86 10) 6532 4311. e-mail: bejing@dfait-maeci.gc.ca
Representative to Canada: c/o Embassy of the People's Republic of China, 515 St. Patrick Street, Ottawa, ON, K1N 5H3. Tel: (613) 789-3434. Fax: (613) 789-1911. e-mail: n.a.

Macedonia

Long-Form Name: The Former Yugoslav Republic of Macedonia
Capital: Skopje

■ GEOGRAPHY

Area: 25,333 sq. km
Coastline: none: landlocked
Climate: hot, dry summers and autumns; winters relatively cold with heavy snowfall
Environment: high earthquake hazard; air pollution from metallurgical plants
Terrain: mountainous, with deep valleys and basins; three large lakes
Land Use: arable land: 23.59%, permanent crops: 1.85%, other: 74.56%; includes 550 sq. km irrigated
Location: SE Europe

■ PEOPLE

Population: 2,063,122 (July 2003 est.)
Nationality: Macedonian
Age Structure: 0–14 yrs: 21.9%; 15–64: 67.5%; 65+: 10.6% (2003 est.)
Population Growth Rate: 0.40% (2003 est.)
Net Migration: -1.46 migrants/1,000 population (2003 est.)
Ethnic Groups: 66.6% Macedonian, 22.7% Albanian, 4% Turkish, 2.1% Serb, 2.2% Gypsies, 2.4% other
Languages: 70% Macedonian, 21% Albanian, 3% Turkish, 3% Serbo-Croatian, 3% other
Religions: 67% Eastern Orthodox, 30% Muslim, 3% other
Birth Rate: 13.20/1,000 population (2003 est.)
Death Rate: 7.78/1,000 population (2003 est.)
Infant Mortality: 12.14 deaths/1,000 live births (2003 est.)
Life Expectancy at Birth: 72.23 years male, 76.94 years female (2003 est.)
Total Fertility Rate: 1.75 children born/woman (2003 est.)
Literacy: 96.0% (2002)

■ GOVERNMENT

Leader(s): President Branko Crvenkovski, Prime Minister Hari Kostov
Government Type: parliamentary democracy
Administrative Divisions: 123 municpalities (opstini, sing. —opstina)
Nationhood: Sept. 17, 1991 (from Yugoslavia)
National Holiday: Independence Day, Sept. 8; Uprising Day, Aug. 2

■ ECONOMY

Overview: although it is the poorest of the six republics of the dissolved Yugoslav federation,

Macedonia can meet its basic food requirements; new economic ties are necessary,
however, to keep living standards from falling
to a bare subsistence level; all oil, gas, modern
machinery and parts must be imported;
continued political upheaval prevents return to
settled economic conditions; an important
supplement to GDP is the remittances from
thousands of Macedonians working in Germany
and other West European countries; continued
recovery depends on Macedonia's ability to
attract investment, to redevelop trade ties with
Greece and Serbia and Montenegro, and to
maintain its commitment to economic liberalization
GDP: US$10.57 billion, per capita US$5,100;
real growth rate 0.7% (2002)
Inflation: 1.1% (2002 est.)
Industries: accounts for 31% of GDP (2001 est.);
level of technology is generally low; basic
liquid fuels, coal, metallic chromium, lead, zinc;
Macedonia is one of the seven legal cultivators
of the opium poppy for the world pharmaceutical industry
Labour Force: 1 million (2002); 35.2% industry,
20.2% community, social and business services,
11.6% trade and tourism
Unemployment: 31.9% (2002)
Agriculture: highly labour-intensive; accounts for
11% of GDP (2001 est.). Rice, tobacco, corn,
sesame, citrus, millet and wheat are the chief
crops; livestock production includes beef, pork
and poultry
Natural Resources: chromium, lead, zinc,
manganese, tungsten, nickel, iron ore, asbestos,
timber

■ **FINANCE/TRADE**

Currency: denar = 100 deni
International Reserves Excluding Gold: US$864
million (Jan. 2004)
Gold Reserves: 0.089 million fine troy ounces
(Jan. 2004)
Budget: revenues US$1.03 billion; expenditures
US$1.05 billion, capital expenditures US$80
million (2003 est.)
Defence Expenditures: 6% of GDP (2002)
Education Expenditures: n.a.
External Debt: US$1.619 billion (2002)
Exports: US$1.112 billion (2002); manufactured
goods, machinery and transportation equipment,
raw materials, food and livestock, tobacco and
beverages, chemicals; partners: Serbia and
Montenegro, Germany, Greece, Italy, US
Imports: US$1.928 billion (2002); fuel and
lubricants, machinery and transport equipment,
food and livestock, chemicals, raw materials,

manufactures; partners: Germany, Greece,
Serbia and Montenegro, Russia, Slovenia

■ **COMMUNICATIONS**

Daily Newspapers: 21/1,000 inhabitants (2000)
Televisions: 282/1,000 inhabitants (2002)
Radios: 205/1,000 inhabitants (2001)
Telephones: 271 lines/1,000 inhabitants (2002)
Internet: hosts: 3,167 (2002); users: 100,000
(2002)

■ **TRANSPORTATION**

Motor Vehicles: n.a.
Roads: 8,684 km; 5,540 km paved
Railway: 699 km
Air Traffic: 166,000 passengers carried (2002)
Airports: 18; 10 have paved runways (2003 est.)

Canadian Embassy: Canadian Embassy, 12-ta
Udarna Brigada 2-a, Skopje 91000, Macedonia.
Tel: (389 91) 125 228. Fax: (389 91) 122 681. e-
mail: dfaitmk@unet.com.mk
Embassy in Canada: Embassy of the Former
Yugoslav Republic of Macedonia, 130 Albert St
Ste 1006, Ottawa, ON, K1P 5G4. Tel: (613)
234-3882. Fax: (613) 233-1852. e-mail:
emb.macedonia.ottawa@sympatico.ca

Madagascar

Long-Form Name: Republic of Madagascar
Capital: Antananarivo

■ **GEOGRAPHY**

Area: 587,040 sq. km
Coastline: 4,828 km
Climate: tropical along coast, temperate inland,
arid in south
Environment: subject to periodic cyclones;
deforestation; overgrazing; soil erosion;
desertification; water pollution
Terrain: narrow coastal plain; high plateau and
mountains in centre
Land Use: arable land: 4.99%, permanent crops:
1.03%, other: 93.98%, (2000 est.); includes
10,900 sq. km irrigated
Location: island in the Indian Ocean, E of Africa

■ **PEOPLE**

Population: 16,979,744 (July 2003 est.)
Nationality: Malagasy
Age Structure: 0–14 yrs: 45.0%; 15–64: 51.9%;
65+: 3.1% (2003 est.)
Population Growth Rate: 3.03% (2003 est.)
Net Migration: 0 migrants/1,000 population
(2003 est.)
Ethnic Groups: basic split between highlanders of
predominantly Malayo-Indonesian origin

(Merina and Betsileo) and coastal tribes, collectively termed the Côtiers, with mixed African, Malayo-Indonesian and Arab ancestry (Betsimisaraka, Tsimihety, Antaiska, Sakalava)
Languages: French and Malagasy (both official)
Religions: 52% indigenous beliefs; approx. 41% Christian, 7% Muslim
Birth Rate: 42.16/1,000 population (2003 est.)
Death Rate: 11.88/1,000 population (2003 est.)
Infant Mortality: 80.21 deaths/1,000 live births (2003 est.)
Life Expectancy at Birth: 53.82 years male, 58.53 years female (2003 est.)
Total Fertility Rate: 5.73 children born/woman (2003 est.)
Literacy: 67.3% (2002)

■ GOVERNMENT

Leader(s): President Marc Ravalomanana, Prime Minister Jacques Sylla
Government Type: republic
Administrative Divisions: 6 provinces (faritany)
Nationhood: June 26, 1960 (from France; formerly known as Malagasy Republic)
National Holiday: Independence Day, June 26

■ ECONOMY

Overview: a poor country, hampered by high population growth and a GDP growth rate that is not keeping pace; agriculture is the basis of the economy; industrial development is hurt by government policies restricting imports of equipment and spare parts
GDP: US$12.59 billion, per capita US$800; real growth rate -11.9% (2002 est.)
Inflation: 6.9% (2001)
Industries: accounts for 14% of GDP (2000); agricultural processing (meat canneries, soap factories, breweries, tanneries, sugar refining), light consumer goods industries (textiles, glassware), cement, automobile assembly plant, paper, petroleum
Labour Force: 7.8 million (2002); 59.2% community, social and business services, 26.7% agriculture
Unemployment: n.a.
Agriculture: accounts for 30% of GDP (2000); cash crops—coffee, vanilla, sugar cane, cloves, cocoa; food crops—rice, cassava, beans, bananas, peanuts; almost self-sufficient in rice
Natural Resources: graphite, chromite, coal, bauxite, salt, quartz, tar sands, semi-precious stones, mica, fish

■ FINANCE/TRADE

Currency: Malagasy franc (FMG) = 100 centimes

International Reserves Excluding Gold: US$430 million (Jan. 2004)
Gold Reserves: n.a.
Budget: revenues US$459.8 million, expenditures US$798.9 million, including captial expenditures of US$331 million (2001)
Defence Expenditures: 7.1% of central government expenditure (2002)
Education Expenditures: n.a.
External Debt: US$4.518 billion (2002)
Exports: US$505 million (2002); commodities: coffee 45%, vanilla 15%, cloves 11%, shellfish, sugar, petroleum products; partners: France, Japan, Italy, Germany, US, UK
Imports: US$507 million (2002); commodities: intermediate manufactures 30%, capital goods 28%, petroleum 15%, consumer goods 14%, food 13%; partners: France, Hong Kong, China, Singapore, Japan

■ COMMUNICATIONS

Daily Newspapers: 5/1,000 inhabitants (2000)
Televisions: 25/1,000 inhabitants (2002)
Radios: 216/1,000 inhabitants (2001)
Telephones: 4 lines/1,000 inhabitants (2002)
Internet: hosts: 509 (2002); users: 55,000 (2002)

■ TRANSPORTATION

Motor Vehicles: 74,700; 58,900 passenger cars
Roads: 49,837 km; 5,781 km paved
Railway: 732 km
Air Traffic: 549,000 passengers carried (2002)
Airports: 121; 29 have paved runways (2003 est.)

Canadian Embassy: The Canadian Embassy to Madagascar, P.O. Box 1022, Dar-es-Salaam, Tanzania. Tel: (011-255-22) 211-2831. Fax: (011-255-22) 211-6897. e-mail: dslam@dfait-aeci.gc.ca
Embassy in Canada: Embassy of the Republic of Madagascar, 200 Catherine Street, Suite 510 Ottawa, ON, K2P 2K9. Tel: (613) 567-0505. Fax: (613) 567-2882. e-mail: n.a.

Malawi

Long-Form Name: Republic of Malawi
Capital: Lilongwe

■ GEOGRAPHY

Area: 118,480 sq. km
Coastline: none: landlocked
Climate: tropical; rainy season (Nov. to May); dry season (May to Nov.)
Environment: deforestation; water pollution; soil degradation

Terrain: narrow elongated plateau with rolling plains, rounded hills, some mountains
Land Use: arable land: 19.93%, permanent crops: 1.33%, other: 78.74%; includes 280 sq. km irrigated
Location: SE Africa

■ PEOPLE

Population: 11,651,239 (July 2003 est.)
Nationality: Malawian
Age Structure: 0–14 yrs: 46.8%; 15–64: 50.5%; 65+: 2.7% (2003 est.)
Population Growth Rate: 2.21% (2003 est.)
Net Migration: 0 migrants/1,000 population (2003 est.)
Ethnic Groups: Chewa, Nyanja, Tumbuko, Yao, Lomwe, Sena, Tonga, Ngoni, Ngonde, Asian, European
Languages: English and Chichewa (both official); other languages important regionally
Religions: 55% Protestant, 20% Roman Catholic, 25% Muslim, traditional indigenous beliefs
Birth Rate: 44.70/1,000 population (2003 est.)
Death Rate: 22.64/1,000 population (2003 est.)
Infant Mortality: 105.15 deaths/1,000 live births (2003 est.)
Life Expectancy at Birth: 37.57 years male, 38.39 years female (2003 est.)
Total Fertility Rate: 6.10 children born/woman (2003 est.)
Literacy: 61.8% (2002)

■ GOVERNMENT

Leader(s): President Bingu wa Mutharika, Vice President Cassim Chilumpha
Government Type: multiparty democracy
Administrative Divisions: 24 districts
Nationhood: July 6, 1964 (from UK; formerly known as Nyasaland)
National Holiday: Independence Day, July 6; Republic Day, July 6

■ ECONOMY

Overview: one of the world's least developed countries; the economy is predominantly agricultural, with about 90% of the population living in rural areas; economy depends heavily on foreign aid
GDP: US$6.811 billion, per capita US$600; real growth rate 1.7% (2002 est.)
Inflation: 27.4% (2001 est.)
Industries: accounts for 19% of GDP (2000); agricultural processing (tea, tobacco, sugar), sawmilling, cement, consumer goods
Labour Force: 5.2 million (2002); 86% agriculture, 14% industry and services

Unemployment: n.a.
Agriculture: accounts for 40% of GDP (2000); crops: tobacco, sugar cane, cotton, tea, corn, potatoes, cassava; subsistence crops: cattle and goats
Natural Resources: limestone; unexploited deposits of uranium, coal and bauxite

■ FINANCE/TRADE

Currency: kwacha (K) = 100 tambala
International Reserves Excluding Gold: US$115 million (Oct. 2003)
Gold Reserves: 0.013 million fine troy ounces (Oct. 2003)
Budget: revenues US$490 million, expenditures US$523 million, including capital expenditures of US$ n.a. (2000 est.)
Defence Expenditures: 0.7% of GDP (2002)
Education Expenditures: n.a.
External Debt: US$2.912 billion (2002)
Exports: US$407 million (2002); commodities: tobacco, tea, sugar, coffee, peanuts; partners: US, UK, South Africa, Germany, Japan, Netherlands
Imports: US$696 million (2002); commodities: food, petroleum, semi-manufactures, consumer goods, transportation equipment; partners: South Africa, Japan, US, UK, Zimbabwe, Germany, Zambia

■ COMMUNICATIONS

Daily Newspapers: 3/1,000 inhabitants (2000)
Televisions: 4/1,000 inhabitants (2002)
Radios: 499/1,000 inhabitants (2001)
Telephones: 7 lines/1,000 inhabitants (2002)
Internet: hosts: 17 (2002); users: 27,000 (2002)

■ TRANSPORTATION

Motor Vehicles: 54,300; 25,400 passenger cars
Roads: 28,400 km; 5,254 km paved
Railway: 797 km
Air Traffic: 105,000 passengers carried (2002)
Airports: 43; 6 have paved runways (2003 est.)

Canadian Embassy: The Canadian High Commission to Malawi, c/o The Canadian High Commission, 5199 United Nations Ave, Lusaka; mailing address: P.O. Box 31313 Lusaka, Zambia. Tel: (011-260-1) 25-08-33. Fax: (011-260-1) 25-41-76. e-mail: lsaka@dfait-maeci.gc.ca
Embassy in Canada: High Commission for the Republic of Malawi, 7 Clemow Ave, Ottawa ON K1S 2A9. Tel: (613) 236-8931. Fax: (613) 236-1054. e-mail: malawi.highcommission@bellnet.ca

Malaysia

Long-Form Name: Malaysia
Capital: Kuala Lumpur

■ GEOGRAPHY

Area: 329,750 sq. km; includes Sabah and Sarawak
Coastline: 4,675 km total (2,068 km Peninsular Malaysia, 2,607 km East Malaysia)
Climate: tropical; annual southwest (Apr. to Oct.) and northeast (Oct. to Feb.) monsoons
Environment: subject to flooding; air and water pollution; deforestation
Terrain: coastal plains rising to hills and mountains
Land Use: arable land: 5.54%, permanent crops: 17.61%, other: 76.85%; includes 3,650 sq. km irrigated
Location: SE Asia, bordering on South China Sea

■ PEOPLE

Population: 23,092,940 (July 2003 est.)
Nationality: Malaysian
Age Structure: 0–14 yrs: 33.7%; 15–64: 61.9%; 65+: 4.4% (2003 est.)
Population Growth Rate: 1.86% (2003 est.)
Net Migration: 0 migrants/1,000 population (2003 est.)
Ethnic Groups: 58% Malay and other indigenous, 26% Chinese, 7% Indian, 9% other
Languages: Peninsular Malaysia: Malay (official), English, Chinese dialects, Tamil; State of Sabah: English, Malay, numerous tribal dialects; Chinese State of Sarawak: English, Malay, Mandarin, numerous tribal languages
Religions: Peninsular Malaysia: Muslim (Malays), Buddhist (Chinese), Hindu (Indians); State of Sabah: 38% Muslim, 17% Christian, 45% other; Chinese State of Sarawak: 35% tribal religions, 24% Buddhist and Confucianist, 20% Muslim, 16% Christian, 5% other
Birth Rate: 23.70/1,000 population (2003 est.)
Death Rate: 5.12/1,000 population (2003 est.)
Infant Mortality: 19.00 deaths/1,000 live births (2003 est.)
Life Expectancy at Birth: 69.01 years male, 74.51 years female (2003 est.)
Total Fertility Rate: 3.13 children born/woman (2003 est.)
Literacy: 88.7% (2002)

■ GOVERNMENT

Leader(s): Paramount Ruler: Tuanku Syed Sirajuddin ibni Almarhum Tuanku Syed Putra Jamalullail, Prime Minister Abdullah bin Ahmad Badawi
Government Type: constitutional monarchy nominally headed by the paramount ruler (king) and a bicameral parliament
Administrative Divisions: 13 states (negeri-negeri, sing. —negeri) and 2 federal territories (wilaya-wilaya persekutuan, sing. —wilayah perseku-tuan)
Nationhood: Aug. 31, 1957 (from UK)
National Holiday: Independence/Malaysia Day, Aug. 31

■ ECONOMY

Overview: vulnerable to recession or a fall in world commodity prices because of its high export dependence; the world's largest producer of semiconductor devices; the majority of the rural population subsists at the poverty level but recent increases in economic output have improved living standards and real income; foreign investment has increased significantly in recent years
GDP: US$198.4 billion, per capita US$8,800; real growth rate 4.1% (2002 est.)
Inflation: 1.9% (2002 est.)
Industries: accounts for 40% of GDP (2001); rubber and oil palm processing and manufacturing, light manufacturing industries, electronics, tin mining and smelting, logging and processing timber, petroleum production, agriculture processing
Labour Force: 10.3 million (2002); 16% agriculture, 27% industry, 10% services, trade and tourism 28%, other 19%
Unemployment: 3.91% (2002)
Agriculture: accounts for 12% of GDP (2001); Peninsular Malaysia—natural rubber, palm oil, cocoa, rice; Sabah—mainly subsistence; main crops—rubber, timber, coconut, rice; Sarawak—main crops—rubber, timber, pepper; there is a deficit of rice in all areas
Natural Resources: tin, crude oil, timber, copper, iron ore, natural gas, bauxite

■ FINANCE/TRADE

Currency: ringgit ($M) = 100 sen
International Reserves Excluding Gold: US$47.338 billion (Jan. 2004)
Gold Reserves: 1.170 million fine troy ounces (Jan. 2004)

Budget: revenues US$25.2 billion; expenditures US$28.9 billion, including capital expenditures of US$9.4 billion (2004 est.)
Defence Expenditures: 10.6% of central government expenditure (2002)
Education Expenditures: 25.2% of total government expenditures (2002)
External Debt: US$48.557 billion (2002)
Exports: US$99.370 billion (2003 est.); commodities: natural rubber, palm oil, tin, timber, petroleum, electronics, light manufactures; partners: US, Singapore, Japan, Hong, Kong, Netherlands, China, Thailand
Imports: US$81.949 billion (2003 est.); commodities: food, crude oil, consumer goods, intermediate goods, capital equipment, chemicals; partners: Japan, US, Singapore, Taiwan, China, Germany, Thailand

■ COMMUNICATIONS

Daily Newspapers: 158/1,000 inhabitants (2000)
Televisions: 210/1,000 inhabitants (2002)
Radios: 420/1,000 inhabitants (2001)
Telephones: 190 lines/1,000 inhabitants (2002)
Internet: hosts: 86,285 (2002); users: 7.841 million (2002)

■ TRANSPORTATION

Motor Vehicles: 4,400,000; 3,700,000 passenger cars (2000)
Roads: 65,877 km; 49,935 km paved
Railway: Peninsular Malaysia: 1,672 km; Sabah: 134 km; Sarawak: none
Air Traffic: 16,208,000 passengers carried (2002)
Airports: 114; 35 have paved runways (2003 est.)

Canadian Embassy: The Canadian High Commission, Menara Tan + Tan, 17th floor, 207 Jalan Tun Razak, 50400 Kuala Lumpur, Malaysia; mailing address: P.O. Box 10990, 50732 Kuala Lumpur, Malaysia. Tel: (011-60-3) 2718-3333. Fax: (011-60-3) 2718-3399. e-mail: klmpr@dfait-maeci.gc.ca
Embassy in Canada: High Commission for Malaysia, 60 Boteler St, Ottawa ON K1N 8Y7. Tel: (613) 241-5182. Fax: (613) 241-5214. e-mail: mwottawa@istar.ca

Maldives

Long-Form Name: Republic of Maldives
Capital: Malé

■ GEOGRAPHY

Area: 300 sq. km; 1,190 coral islands grouped in 26 atolls

Coastline: 644 km
Climate: tropical; hot, humid; dry, northeast monsoon (Nov. to Mar.); rainy, southwest monsoon (June to Aug.)
Environment: future rise in ocean level could obliterate large parts of the country; freshwater supplies are limited
Terrain: flat with elevations of only 2.5 metres
Land Use: arable land: 3.33%, permanent crops: 6.67%, other: 90%; includes n.a. sq. km irrigated
Location: islands in the Indian Ocean, S of India

■ PEOPLE

Population: 329,684 (July 2003 est.)
Nationality: Maldivian
Age Structure: 0–14 yrs: 44.9%; 15–64: 52.1%; 65+: 3.0% (2003 est.)
Population Growth Rate: 2.91% (2003 est.)
Net Migration: 0 migrants/1,000 population (2003 est.)
Ethnic Groups: mixtures of Sinhalese, Dravidian, Arab and African
Languages: Dhivehi (Maldivian dialect of Sinhara; script derived from Arabic); English spoken by most government officials
Religions: Sunni Muslim
Birth Rate: 36.71/1,000 population (2003 est.)
Death Rate: 7.65/1,000 population (2003 est.)
Infant Mortality: 60.13 deaths/1,000 live births (2003 est.)
Life Expectancy at Birth: 62.07 years male, 64.60 years female (2003 est.)
Total Fertility Rate: 5.26 children born/woman (2003 est.)
Literacy: 97.2% (2002)

■ GOVERNMENT

Leader(s): President Maumoun Abdul Gayoom
Government Type: republic
Administrative Divisions: 19 atolls (atolhu, sing. & pl.) and 1 other first-order administrative division
Nationhood: July 26, 1965 (from UK)
National Holiday: Independence Day, July 26

■ ECONOMY

Overview: Based on fishing, tourism and shipping; fishing is the largest industry; tourism has become one of the largest and most important sources of revenue
GDP: US$1.25 billion, per capita US$3,900; real growth rate 2.3% (2002 est.)
Inflation: 1.0% (2002 est.)
Industries: accounts for 18% of GDP (2000); fishing and fish processing, tourism, shipping,

boat building, some coconut processing, garments, woven mats, coir (rope), handicrafts
Labour Force: approx. 88,000; 22% agriculture, 18% industry, 60% services
Unemployment: negligible
Agriculture: accounts for almost 20% of GDP (including fishing); fishing more important than farming; limited production of coconuts, corn, sweet potatoes; most staple foods must be imported
Natural Resources: fish

■ FINANCE/TRADE

Currency: rufiyaa (Rf) = 100 laari
International Reserves Excluding Gold: US$163 million (Jan. 2004)
Gold Reserves: 0.002 million fine troy ounces (Jan. 2004)
Budget: revenues US$224 million, expenditures US$282 million, including capital expenditures US$80 million (2002 est.)
Defence Expenditures: 8.6% of GDP (2002)
Education Expenditures: 17.79% of central government expenditure (2000)
External Debt: US$270 million (2002)
Exports: US$113 million (2003 est.); commodities: fish 57%, clothing 39%; partners: Japan, UK, Sri Lanka, US.
Imports: US$471 million (2003 est.); commodities: intermediate and capital goods 47%, consumer goods 42%, petroleum products 11%; partners: Singapore, India, Sri Lanka, Japan, Canada

■ COMMUNICATIONS

Daily Newspapers: 2 in total
Televisions: n.a.
Radios: n.a.
Telephones: 90 lines/1,000 inhabitants (2002)
Internet: hosts: n.a.; users: 15,000 (2002)

■ TRANSPORTATION

Motor Vehicles: n.a.
Roads: Malé has 9.6 km of coral highways within the city
Railway: none
Air Traffic: n.a.
Airports: 5; 2 have paved runways (2003 est.)

Canadian Embassy: The Canadian High Commission to Maldives, c/o The Canadian High Commission, P.O. Box 1006, Colombo 7, Sri Lanka. Tel: (011 94 11) 269 5841. Fax: (011 94 11) 268-7049. e-mail: clmbo@dfait-maeci.gc.ca

Embassy in Canada: Embassy of the Maldives, c/o High Commission for the Democratic Socialist Republic of Sri Lanka, 333 Laurier Ave W, Ste 1204, Ottawa ON K1P 1C1. Tel: (613) 233-8449. Fax: (613) 238-8448. e-mail: lankacom@magi.com

Mali

Long-Form Name: Republic of Mali
Capital: Bamako

■ GEOGRAPHY

Area: 1,240,000 sq. km
Coastline: none: landlocked
Climate: subtropical to arid; hot and dry Feb. to June; rainy, humid and mild June to Nov.; cool and dry Nov. to Feb.
Environment: hot, dust-laden harmattan haze common during dry seasons; soil erosion; desertification; deforestation
Terrain: mostly flat to rolling northern plains covered with sand; savanna in south, rugged hills in northeast
Land Use: arable land: 3.77%, permanent crops: 0.04%, other: 96.19%; includes 1,380 sq. km irrigated
Location: NW Africa

■ PEOPLE

Population: 11,626,219 (July 2003 est.)
Nationality: Malian
Age Structure: 0–14 yrs: 47.2%; 15–64: 49.8%; 65+: 3.0% (2003 est.)
Population Growth Rate: 2.82% (2003 est.)
Net Migration: -0.34 migrants/1,000 population (2003 est.)
Ethnic Groups: 50% Mande (Bambara, Malinke, Sarakole), 17% Peul, 12% Voltaic, 6% Songhai, 10% Tuareg and Moor, 5% other
Languages: French (official); Bambara spoken by about 80% of the population; numerous African languages
Religions: 90% Muslim, 9% indigenous beliefs, 1% Christian
Birth Rate: 47.79/1,000 population (2003 est.)
Death Rate: 19.21/1,000 population (2003 est.)
Infant Mortality: 119.20 deaths/1,000 live births (2003 est.)
Life Expectancy at Birth: 44.70 years male, 46.19 years female (2003 est.)
Total Fertility Rate: 6.66 children born/woman (2003 est.)
Literacy: 19.0% (2002)

■ GOVERNMENT

Leader(s): President Amadou Toumani Toure, Prime Minister Ousmane Issoufi Maiga
Government Type: republic
Administrative Divisions: 8 regions
Nationhood: Sept. 22, 1960 (from France; formerly French Sudan)
National Holiday: Anniversary of the Proclamation of the Republic, Sept. 22

■ ECONOMY

Overview: among the poorest countries in the world, with 65% of its land area desert or semi-desert; economic activity is largely confined to the area irrigated by the Niger; industrial activity is concentrated on processing farm commodities
GDP: US$9.775 billion, per capita US$900; real growth rate 4.5% (2002 est.)
Inflation: 4.5% (2002 est.)
Industries: accounts for 17% of GDP (2001 est.); small local consumer goods and processing, construction, phosphate, gold, fishing
Labour Force: 5.6 million (2002); 80% agriculture and fishing
Unemployment: n.a.
Agriculture: accounts for 45% of GDP (2001 est.); most production based on small subsistence farms; cotton and livestock products account for over 70% of exports; other crops—millet, rice, corn, vegetables, peanuts; livestock—cattle, sheep and goats
Natural Resources: gold, phosphates, kaolin, salt, limestone, uranium; bauxite, iron ore, manganese, tin and copper deposits are known but not exploited

■ FINANCE/TRADE

Currency: Communauté financière africaine franc (CFAF) = 100 centimes
International Reserves Excluding Gold: US$831 million (Nov. 2003)
Gold Reserves: 0.19 million fine troy ounces (Aug. 2000)
Budget: revenues US$764 million; expenditures US$828 million, capital expenditures US$ n.a. (2002 est.)
Defence Expenditures: 15.0% of GDP (2002)
Education Expenditures: n.a.
External Debt: US$2.803 billion (2002)
Exports: US$885 million (2002); commodities: livestock, peanuts, dried fish, cotton, skins; partners: Brazil, South Korea, Italy, Canada
Imports: US$876 million (2002); commodities: textiles, vehicles, petroleum products, machinery,

sugar, cereals; partners: Côte d'Ivoire, France, Senegal, Germany, Benelux

■ COMMUNICATIONS

Daily Newspapers: 1/1,000 inhabitants (2000)
Televisions: 33/1,000 inhabitants (2002)
Radios: 180/1,000 inhabitants (2001)
Telephones: 5 lines/1,000 inhabitants (2002)
Internet: hosts: 158 (2002); users: 25,000 (2002)

■ TRANSPORTATION

Motor Vehicles: 41,800; 24,700 passenger cars
Roads: 15,100 km; 1,827 km paved
Railway: 729 km
Air Traffic: 46,000 passengers carried (2002)
Airports: 26; 7 have paved runways (2003 est.)

Canadian Embassy: The Canadian Embassy, P.O. Box 198, Bamako, Mali. Tel: (011-223) 221-22-36. Fax: (011-223) 221-4362. e-mail: bmako@ dfait-maeci.gc.ca
Embassy in Canada: Embassy of the Republic of Mali, 50 Goulburn Ave, Ottawa ON K1N 8C8. Tel: (613) 232-1501. Fax: (613) 232-7429. e-mail: ambassadedumali@rogers.com

Malta

Long-Form Name: Republic of Malta
Capital: Valletta

■ GEOGRAPHY

Area: 316 sq. km
Coastline: 196.8 km
Climate: Mediterranean with mild, rainy winters and hot, dry summers
Environment: numerous bays provide good harbours; fresh water very scarce, increasing reliance on desalination
Terrain: mostly low, rocky, flat to dissected plains; many coastal cliffs
Land Use: arable land: 31.25%, permanent crops: 3.13%, other: 65.62%; includes 20 sq. km irrigated
Location: Mediterranean Sea, S of Sicily

■ PEOPLE

Population: 400,420 (July 2003 est.)
Nationality: Maltese (sing. & pl.)
Age Structure: 0–14 yrs: 19.5%; 15–64: 67.5%; 65+: 13.0% (2003 est.)
Population Growth Rate: 0.73% (2003 est.)
Net Migration: 2.34 migrants/1,000 population (2003 est.)
Ethnic Groups: mixture of Arab, Sicilian, Norman, Spanish, Italian, English

Languages: Maltese and English (both official), Italian widely spoken
Religions: 98% Roman Catholic
Birth Rate: 12.75/1,000 population (2003 est.)
Death Rate: 7.80/1,000 population (2003 est.)
Infant Mortality: 5.62 deaths/1,000 live births (2003 est.)
Life Expectancy at Birth: 75.94 years male, 81.14 years female (2003 est.)
Total Fertility Rate: 1.91 children born/woman (2003 est.)
Literacy: 92.8% (2003 est.)

■ GOVERNMENT

Leader(s): President Edward Fenech Adami, Prime Minister Lawrence Gonzi
Government Type: republic
Administrative Divisions: none
Nationhood: Sept. 21, 1964 (from UK)
National Holiday: Independence Day, Sept. 21

■ ECONOMY

Overview: manufacturing and tourism are important; economy is dependent on foreign trade and services (food, water and energy); Malta produces only 20% of its food needs, has a limited supply of fresh water and lacks domestic energy sources
GDP: US$6.818 billion, per capita US$17,200; real growth rate 1.2% (2002)
Inflation: 2.4% (2002 est.)
Industries: accounts for 26% of GDP; tourism, ship repair, clothing, construction, food manufacturing, textiles, footwear, beverages, tobacco
Labour Force: 160,000 (2002 est.); 24% industry, 71% services, 5% agriculture
Unemployment: 5.1% (Aug. 2003)
Agriculture: accounts for 3% of GDP; 20% self-sufficient overall; main products—potatoes, cauliflower, grapes, wheat, barley, tomatoes, citrus, cut flowers, green peppers, hogs, poultry, eggs; adequate supplies of vegetables, milk, pork products; seasonal or periodic shortages
Natural Resources: limestone, salt

■ FINANCE/TRADE

Currency: Maltese lira (LM) = 100 cents
International Reserves Excluding Gold: US$2.573 million (Sept. 2003)
Gold Reserves: 0.004 million fine troy ounces (Sept. 2003)
Budget: revenues US$1.5 billion; expenditures US$1.6 billion, including capital expenditures of US$ n.a. (2000)
Defence Expenditures: 1.7% of GDP (2000)
Education Expenditures: n.a.

External Debt: US$1.531 billion (2001)
Exports: US$2.223 billion (2002); commodities: clothing, textiles, footwear, ships; partners: US, Germany, France, UK, Italy
Imports: US$2.840 billion (2002); commodities: food, beverages, tobacco, petroleum, non-food raw materials; partners: Italy, France, US, UK, Germany

■ COMMUNICATIONS

Daily Newspapers: 2 in total
Televisions: n.a.
Radios: n.a.
Telephones: 521 lines/1,000 inhabitants (2002)
Internet: hosts: 7,355 (2002); users: 82,900 (2002)

■ TRANSPORTATION

Motor Vehicles: 141,200; 122,100 passenger cars
Roads: 2,254 km; 1,972 km paved
Railway: none
Air Traffic: 1,250,000 passengers carried (2001 est.)
Airports: 1, with a paved runway (2003 est.)

Canadian Embassy: The Canadian High Commission to Malta, c/o The Canadian Embassy, Via G.B. de Rossi 27, 00161 Rome, Italy. Tel: (011-39-06) 445981. Fax: (011-39-06) 445 98750. e-mail: rome@dfait-maeci.gc.ca
Embassy in Canada: c/o High Commission for Malta, 2017 Connecticut Ave NW, Washington DC 20008, USA. Tel: (202) 462-3611. Fax: (202) 387-5470. e-mail: n.a.

Marshall Islands

Long-Form Name: Republic of the Marshall Islands
Capital: Majuro

■ GEOGRAPHY

Area: 181.3 sq. km; 2 island chains of 30 atolls and 1,152 islands
Coastline: 370.4 km
Climate: islands border typhoon belt; wet season, May to Nov.; hot and humid
Environment: occasional typhoons; insufficient fresh water
Terrain: low coral limestone and sand islands
Land Use: arable land: 16.67%, permanent crops: 0%, other: 83.33%; includes no irrigated land
Location: Oceania, in North Pacific Ocean, SW of Hawaii

■ PEOPLE

Population: 56,429 (July 2003 est.)
Nationality: Marshallese (sing. & pl.)

Age Structure: 0–14 yrs: 39.1%; 15–64: 58.2%; 65+: 2.7% (2003 est.)
Population Growth Rate: 2.30% (2003 est.)
Net Migration: -6.18 migrants/1,000 population (2003 est.)
Ethnic Groups: Micronesian
Languages: English (official), two major Marshallese dialects, Japanese
Religions: Christian (predominantly Protestant)
Birth Rate: 34.18/1,000 population (2003 est.)
Death Rate: 5.03/1,000 population (2003 est.)
Infant Mortality: 31.58 deaths/1,000 live births (2003 est.)
Life Expectancy at Birth: 67.49 years male, 71.40 years female (2003 est.)
Total Fertility Rate: 4.12 children born/woman (2003 est.)
Literacy: 93%

■ GOVERNMENT

Leader(s): President Kessai Note
Government Type: constitutional government in free association with the US
Administrative Divisions: 33 municipalities
Nationhood: Oct. 21, 1986 (from US-administered UN trusteeship)
National Holiday: Constitution Day, May 1

■ ECONOMY

Overview: agriculture and tourism are the backbone of the economy; industry is on a small scale, limited to handicrafts, copra and fish processing; imports far exceed exports; foreign aid is vital
GDP: US$115 million, per capita US$1,600; real growth rate 1.0% (2001 est.)
Inflation: 2.0% (2001 est.)
Industries: accounts for 16% of GDP (2000); copra, fish, tourism, crafts; offshore banking is in its infancy
Labour Force: n.a.; 21% agriculture, 21% industry, 58% services
Unemployment: n.a.
Agriculture: accounts for 14% of GDP (2000); coconuts, taro, cacao, breadfruit, fruits, poultry, tomatoes, melons, cattle, pigs
Natural Resources: phosphate, marine products, minerals

■ FINANCE/TRADE

Currency: US$ = 100 cents
International Reserves Excluding Gold: n.a.
Gold Reserves: n.a.
Budget: n.a.
Defence Expenditures: defence is the responsibility of the US
Education Expenditures: n.a.

External Debt: US$86.5 million (2000 est.)
Exports: US$9 million (2000); fish, coconut oil, trochus shells; partners: US, Japan, Australia
Imports: US$54 million (2000); foodstuffs, machinery, equipment, fuels, beverages, tobacco; partners: US, Japan, Australia, New Zealand, Singapore, Fiji, China, Philippines

■ COMMUNICATIONS

Daily Newspapers: n.a.
Televisions: n.a.
Radios: n.a.
Telephones: 60 lines/ 1,000 inhabitants (2002)
Internet: hosts: 5 (2002); users: 1,300 (2002)

■ TRANSPORTATION

Motor Vehicles: n.a.
Roads: paved roads on major islands only
Railway: none
Air Traffic: 35,600 passengers carried (2001 est.)
Airports: 15; 4 have paved runways (2003 est.)

Canadian Embassy: The Canadian Embassy to the Marshall Islands, c/o The Canadian High Commission, Commonwealth Ave., Canberra A.C.T., Australia. Tel: (011-61-2) 6270-4000. Fax: (011-61-2) 6273-3285. e-mail: cnbra@dfait-maeci.gc.ca
Embassy in Canada: c/o Embassy of the Republic of the Marshall Islands, 2433 Massachusetts Ave NW, Washington DC 20008, USA. Tel: (202) 234-5414. Fax: (202) 232-3236. e-mail: n.a.

Martinique

Long-Form Name: Department of Martinique
Capital: Fort-de-France

■ GEOGRAPHY

Area: 1,100 sq. km
Climate: tropical, moderated by trade winds; rainy season (June to Oct.)
Land Use: arable land: 9.43%, permanent crops: 11.32%, other: 79.25%; includes 30 sq. km irrigated
Location: Caribbean Islands, halfway along the Lesser Antilles arch between Puerto Rico and Venezuela

■ PEOPLE

Population: 425,966 (July 2003 est.)
Nationality: Martiniquais
Ethnic Groups: 90% black, remainder a mix of black African and Latin ancestry, Caucasian 5%
Languages: French (official), majority speak Creole

■ GOVERNMENT

Colony/Territory of: Overseas Department of France
Leader(s): President Jacques Chirac (France), Prefect Yves Dassonville
Government Type: overseas department of France
National Holiday: Taking of the Bastille, National Day, July 14

■ ECONOMY

Overview: most of the meat, vegetable and grain requirements must be imported; industry: food processing, oil refining, chemical engineering; agriculture: pineapples, tobacco, cotton, bananas, sugar, rum, livestock; forest products; fishing; chief trading partners: France, UK, Guadeloupe

■ FINANCE/TRADE

Currency: French franc (F) = 100 centimes, Euro (€)

Canadian Embassy: c/o The Canadian Embassy 35-37 avenue Montaigne, 75008 Paris, France. Tel: (011-33-1) 44-43-29-00. Fax: (011-33-1) 44-43-29-99. e-mail: paris@dfait-maeci.gc.ca
Representative to Canada: c/o Embassy of France, 42 Sussex Dr, Ottawa ON K1M 2C9. Tel: (613) 789-1795. Fax: (613) 562-3735. e-mail: politique@ambafrance-ca.org

---

Mauritania

Long-Form Name: Islamic Republic of Mauritania
Capital: Nouakchott

■ GEOGRAPHY

Area: 1,030,700 sq. km
Coastline: 754 km
Climate: desert; constantly hot, dry, dusty
Environment: hot, dry, dust/sand-laden sirocco wind blows primarily in Mar. and Apr.; desertification; only perennial river is the Senegal; overgrazing and insufficient fresh water
Terrain: mostly barren, flat plains of the Sahara; some central hills
Land Use: arable land: 0.48%, permanent crops: 0.01%, other: 99.51%; includes 490 sq. km irrigated
Location: NW Africa, bordering on Atlantic Ocean

■ PEOPLE

Population: 2,912,584 (July 2003 est.)
Nationality: Mauritanian

Age Structure: 0–14 yrs: 46.0%; 15–64: 51.8%; 65+: 2.2% (2003 est.)
Population Growth Rate: 2.91% (2003 est.)
Net Migration: 0 migrants/1,000 population (2003 est.)
Ethnic Groups: 30% Maur, 40% mixed Maur-black, 30% black
Languages: Hasaniya Arabic and Wolof (both official), Pular, Soninke
Religions: nearly 100% Muslim
Birth Rate: 42.16/1,000 population (2003 est.)
Death Rate: 13.04/1,000 population (2003 est.)
Infant Mortality: 73.80 deaths/1,000 live births (2003 est.)
Life Expectancy at Birth: 49.78 years male, 54.13 years female (2003 est.)
Total Fertility Rate: 6.08 children born/woman (2003 est.)
Literacy: 41.2% (2002)

■ GOVERNMENT

Leader(s): President Maaouya Ould Sid Ahmed Taya, Prime Minister Sghair Ould Mbareck
Government Type: republic
Administrative Divisions: 12 regions and 1 capital district
Nationhood: Nov. 28, 1960 (from France)
National Holiday: Independence Day, Nov. 28

■ ECONOMY

Overview: most of the population is engaged in agricultural and livestock production; substantial iron ores; threatened by foreign overexploitation of fishing areas; in recent years, droughts, conflicts with Senegal, rising energy costs and economic mismanagement have resulted in a substantial build-up of foreign debt
GDP: US$4.891 billion, per capita US$1,700; real growth rate 3.3% (2002 est.)
Inflation: 3.0% (2002 est.)
Industries: accounts for 29% of GDP (2001 est.); fishing, fish processing, mining of iron ore and gypsum
Labour Force: 1.3 million (2002); 50% agriculture, 40% services, 10% industry
Unemployment: n.a.
Agriculture: accounts for 25% of GDP (including fishing) (2001 est.); largely subsistence farming, nomadic cattle and sheep herding except in Senegal river valley; crops—dates, millet, sorghum, root crops, rice, corn; fish products number-one export; large food deficit in years of drought
Natural Resources: iron ore, gypsum, fish, copper, phosphate

■ FINANCE/TRADE

Currency: ouguiya (UM) = 5 Khoums
International Reserves Excluding Gold: US$415 million (Dec. 2003)
Gold Reserves: 0.012 million fine troy ounces (Dec. 2003)
Budget: revenues US$421 million; expenditures US$378 million, including capital expenditures of US$154 million (2002 est.)
Defence Expenditures: 3.7% of GDP (2002)
Education Expenditures: n.a.
External Debt: US$2.309 billion (2002)
Exports: US$541 million (2002); commodities: iron ore, processed fish, small amounts of gum arabic and gypsum, unrecorded but numerically significant cattle exports to Senegal; partners: France, Japan, Italy, Spain
Imports: US$860 million (2002); commodities: foodstuffs, consumer goods, petroleum products, capital goods; partners: France, US, Spain, Algeria, Germany, Benelux, Senegal

■ COMMUNICATIONS

Daily Newspapers: less than 1/1,000 inhabitants (2000)
Televisions: 99/1,000 inhabitants (2002)
Radios: 149/1,000 inhabitants (2001)
Telephones: 12 lines/1,000 inhabitants (2002)
Internet: hosts: 79 (2002); users: 10,000 (2002)

■ TRANSPORTATION

Motor Vehicles: 27,000; 17,800 passenger cars
Roads: 7,720 km; 830 km paved
Railway: 717 km
Air Traffic: 106,000 passengers carried (2002)
Airports: 26; 10 have paved runways (2003 est.)

Canadian Embassy: The Canadian Embassy to Mauritania, c/o The Canadian Embassy, P.O. Box 3373, Dakar, Senegal. Tel: (011-221) 889-4700. Fax: (011-221) 889-4720. e-mail: dakar@dfait-maeci.gc.ca
Embassy in Canada: Embassy of the Islamic Republic of Mauritania, 121 Sherwood Dr, Ottawa ON K1Y 3V1. Tel: (613) 237-3283. Fax: (613) 237-3287. e-mail: info@mauritania-canada.ca

Mauritius

Long-Form Name: Republic of Mauritius
Capital: Port Louis

■ GEOGRAPHY

Area: 1,860 sq. km; includes Agalega Islands, Cargados Carajos Shoals (St. Brandon) and Rodriques
Coastline: 177 km
Climate: tropical modified by southeast trade winds; warm, dry winter (May to Nov.); hot, wet, humid summer (Nov. to May)
Environment: subject to cyclones (Nov. to Apr.); almost completely surrounded by reefs; water pollution is a growing problem
Terrain: small coastal plain rising to discontinuous mountains encircling central plateau
Land Use: arable land: 49.26%, permanent crops: 2.96%, other: 47.78%, (2000 est.); includes 200 sq. km irrigated
Location: Indian Ocean, E of Africa (E of Madagascar)

■ PEOPLE

Population: 1,210,447 (July 2003 est.)
Nationality: Mauritian
Age Structure: 0–14 yrs: 25.1%; 15–64: 68.5%; 65+: 6.4% (2003 est.)
Population Growth Rate: 0.84% (2003 est.)
Net Migration: -0.91 migrants/1,000 population (2003 est.)
Ethnic Groups: 68% Indo-Mauritian, 27% Creole, 3% Sino-Mauritian, 2% Franco-Mauritian
Languages: English (official), Creole, French, Hindi, Urdu, Hakka, Bojpoori
Religions: 52% Hindu, 28% Christian (mostly Roman Catholic with a few Anglicans), 17% Muslim, 3% other
Birth Rate: 16.10/1,000 population (2003 est.)
Death Rate: 6.81/1,000 population (2003 est.)
Infant Mortality: 16.11 deaths/1,000 live births (2003 est.)
Life Expectancy at Birth: 67.82 years male, 75.85 years female (2003 est.)
Total Fertility Rate: 1.98 children born/woman (2003 est.)
Literacy: 84.3% (2002)

■ GOVERNMENT

Leader(s): President Anerood Jugnauth, Prime Minister Paul Raymond Berenger
Government Type: parliamentary democracy
Administrative Divisions: 9 administrative districts and 3 dependencies
Nationhood: Mar. 12, 1968 (from UK)
National Holiday: Independence Day, Mar. 12

■ ECONOMY

Overview: based on sugar, manufacturing (textiles) and tourism; industrialization programs stress increasing exports
GDP: US$12.15 billion, per capita US$10,100; real growth rate 2.3% (2002 est.)
Inflation: 6.4% (2002 est.)
Industries: accounts for 33% of GDP; food processing (largely sugar milling), textiles, wearing apparel, chemical and chemical products, metal products, transport equipment, non-electrical machinery, tourism
Labour Force: 500,000 (2002); 14% agriculture, 36% industry, 24% community, social and business services, 26% other
Unemployment: 8.0% (2002 est.)
Agriculture: accounts for 6% of GDP; about 90% of cultivated land in sugar cane (which accounts for 40% of export earnings); other products—tea, corn, potatoes, bananas, pulses, cattle, goats, fish; net food importer, especially rice and fish
Natural Resources: arable land, fish

■ FINANCE/TRADE

Currency: rupee (Mau Rs) = 100 cents
International Reserves Excluding Gold: US$1.590 billion (Jan. 2004)
Gold Reserves: 0.062 million fine troy ounces (Jan. 2004)
Budget: n.a.
Defence Expenditures: 0.8% of total government expenditure (2002)
Education Expenditures: 13.3% of central government expenditure (2002)
External Debt: US$1.803 billion (2002)
Exports: US$1.916 billion (2003 est.); commodities: textiles 44%, sugar 40%, light manufactures 10%; partners: UK, France, US, South Africa, Germany, Italy
Imports: US$2.353 billion (2003 est.); commodities: manufactured goods 50%, capital equipment 17%, foodstuffs 13%, petroleum products 8%, chemicals 7%; partners: South Africa, France, India, Hong Kong, UK

■ COMMUNICATIONS

Daily Newspapers: 119/1,000 inhabitants (2000)
Televisions: 299/1,000 inhabitants (2002)
Radios: 379/1,000 inhabitants (2001)
Telephones: 270 lines/1,000 inhabitants (2002)
Internet: hosts: 3,462 (2002); users: 120,000 (2002)

■ TRANSPORTATION

Motor Vehicles: 125,000; 93,000 passenger cars
Roads: 1,926 km; 1,868 km paved

Railway: none
Air Traffic: 1,025,000 passengers carried (2002)
Airports: 5; 2 have paved runways (2003 est.)

Canadian Embassy: The Canadian High Commission to Mauritius, c/o 1103 Arcadia St., Hatfield, Pretoria 0028. Mailing address: c/o Canadian Embassy, Private Bag X13, Hatfield 0028, Pretoria, South Africa. Tel: (011-27-12) 422-3000. Fax: (011-27-12) 422-3052. e-mail: pret@dfait-maeci.gc.ca
Embassy in Canada: c/o Embassy of Mauritius, 4301 Connecticut Avenue NW, Ste 441, Washington DC 20008, USA. Tel: (202) 244-1491. Fax: (202) 966-0983. e-mail: mauritius.embassy@prodigy.net

Mayotte

Long-Form Name: Territorial Collectivity of Mayotte
Capital: Mamoutzou

■ GEOGRAPHY

Area: 374 sq. km
Climate: tropical maritime; hot, humid rainy season during northeastern monsoon (Nov. to May), dry season is cooler (May to Nov.)
Land Use: arable land: n.a.%, permanent crops: n.a.%, other: n.a.%
Location: Mozambique Channel, off E coast of Africa

■ PEOPLE

Population: 178,437 (July 2003 est.)
Nationality: Mahorais (sing. & pl.)
Ethnic Groups: Antalote, Cafre, Makoa, Oimatsaha, Sakalava
Languages: French (official), Mahorian (a Swahili dialect)

■ GOVERNMENT

Colony/Territory of: Territorial Collectivity of France
Leader(s): President Jacques Chirac (France), Prefect Jean-Jacques Brot
Government Type: French territorial collectivity
National Holiday: Taking of the Bastille, July 14

■ ECONOMY

Overview: industry: lobster, shrimp; agriculture: pineapples, bananas, mangoes, breadfruit, cassava, ylang-ylang, vanilla, coffee, spices; must import a large portion of its food requirements, mainly from France; chief trading partners: France, UK, South Africa, Bahrain, Thailand, Réunion

■ FINANCE/TRADE

Currency: French franc (F) = 100 centimes; also Euro (€) as of March 1, 2002

Canadian Embassy: c/o The Canadian Embassy, 35-37 avenue Montaigne, 75008 Paris, France. Tel: (011-33-1) 44-43-29-00. Fax: (011-33-1) 44-43-29-99. e-mail: paris@dfait-maeci.gc.ca
Representative to Canada: c/o Embassy of France, 42 Sussex Dr., Ottawa ON K1M 2C9. Tel: (613) 789-1795. Fax: (613)562-3735. e-mail: politique@ambafrance-ca.org

Mexico

Long-Form Name: United Mexican States
Capital: Mexico City

■ GEOGRAPHY

Area: 1,972,550 sq. km
Coastline: 9,330 km
Climate: varies from tropical to desert
Environment: subject to tsunamis along the Pacific coast and destructive earthquakes in the centre and south; natural water resources scarce and polluted; deforestation; erosion widespread; desertification; serious air pollution
Terrain: high, rugged mountains, low coastal plains, high plateaus and desert
Land Use: arable land: 13.2%, permanent crops: 1.1%, other: 85.7%; includes 65,000 sq. km irrigated
Location: Central (Latin) America, bordering on United States, Gulf of Mexico, Pacific Ocean

■ PEOPLE

Population: 104,907,991 (July 2003 est.)
Nationality: Mexican
Age Structure: 0–14 yrs: 32.3%; 15–64: 63.1%; 65+: 4.6% (2003 est.)
Population Growth Rate: 1.43% (2003 est.)
Net Migration: -2.65 migrants/1,000 population (2003 est.)
Ethnic Groups: 60% mestizo (Indian-Spanish), 30% Amerindian or predominantly Amerindian, 9% white or predominantly white, 1% other
Languages: Spanish, also indigenous (Mayan) languages
Religions: 89% Roman Catholic, 6% Protestant, 5% other
Birth Rate: 21.92/1,000 population (2003 est.)
Death Rate: 4.97/1,000 population (2003 est.)
Infant Mortality: 23.68 deaths/1,000 live births (2003 est.)
Life Expectancy at Birth: 69.26 years male, 75.49 years female (2003 est.)

Total Fertility Rate: 2.53 children born/woman (2003 est.)
Literacy: 90.5% (2002)

■ GOVERNMENT

Leader(s): President Vicente Fox Quesada
Government Type: federal republic operating under a centralized government
Administrative Divisions: 31 states (estados, sing. —estado) and 1 federal district (distrito federal)
Nationhood: Sept. 16, 1810 (from Spain)
National Holiday: Independence Day, Sept. 16

■ ECONOMY

Overview: outlook remains positive, but this country still needs to overcome many structural problems as it strives to modernize its economy and raise living standards; income distribution is very unequal, with the top 20% of income earners accounting for 55% of income; trade with the US and Canada has nearly doubled since NAFTA was implemented in 1994
GDP: US$924.4 billion, per capita US$8,900; real growth rate 0.7% (2002 est.)
Inflation: 6.4% (2002 est.)
Industries: accounts for 26% of GDP (2001 est.); food and beverages, tobacco, chemicals, iron and steel, petroleum, mining, textiles, clothing, transportation equipment, tourism
Labour Force: 42.3 million (2002); 56% services, 20% agriculture, 24% industry
Unemployment: 2.4% (2002); plus considerable underemployment
Agriculture: accounts for 5% of GDP (2001 est.) and 20% of labour force; large number of small farms at subsistence level; major food crops— corn, wheat, rice, beans, soybeans; cash crops— cotton, coffee, fruit, tomatoes, beef, poultry, dairy products
Natural Resources: crude oil, silver, copper, gold, lead, zinc, natural gas, timber

■ FINANCE/TRADE

Currency: peso ($Mex) = 100 centavos
International Reserves Excluding Gold: US$62.953 billion (Jan. 2004)
Gold Reserves: 0.166 million fine troy ounces (Jan. 2004)
Budget: revenues US$174 billion; expenditures US$176 billion, capital expenditures US$ n.a. (2004 est.)
Defence Expenditures: 3.2% of central government expenditure (2002)
Education Expenditures: 22.6% of central government expenditure (2002)
External Debt: US$141.264 billion (2002)

Exports: US$165.396 billion (2003 est.); commodities: crude oil, oil products, silver, fruits, vegetables, coffee, shrimp, engines, cotton; partners: US, Canada, Germany, Spain, Netherlands Antilles, Japan, UK, Venezuela
Imports: US$170.490 billion (2003 est.); commodities: grain, metal manufactures, agricultural machinery, electrical equipment, motor vehicle and aircraft parts; partners: US, Japan, Germany, Canada, China, South Korea, Taiwan, Italy, Brazil

■ COMMUNICATIONS

Daily Newspapers: 94/1,000 inhabitants (2000)
Televisions: 282/1,000 inhabitants (2002)
Radios: 330/1,000 inhabitants (2001)
Telephones: 147 lines/1,000 inhabitants (2002)
Internet: hosts: 1,107,795 (2002); users: 10.033 million (2002)

■ TRANSPORTATION

Motor Vehicles: 16,400,000; 11,050,000 passenger cars
Roads: 329,532 km; 108,087 km paved
Railway: 19,510 km
Air Traffic: 19,282,000 passengers carried (2002)
Airports: 1,823; 231 have paved runways (2003 est.)

Canadian Embassy: The Canadian Embassy, Calle Schiller no. 529, Rincon del Bosque, Colonia Polanco, 11580 Mexico; mailing address: Apartado Postal 105-05, 11580 Mexico, Mexico. Tel: (011-52) 55-57-24-79-00. Fax: (011-52) 55-57-24-79-80. e-mail: mxico@dfait-maeci.gc.ca
Embassy in Canada: Embassy of the United Mexican States, 45 O'Connor St, Ste 1500, Ottawa ON K1P 1A4. Tel: (613) 233-8988. Fax: (613) 235-9123. e-mail: info@embamexcan.com

Micronesia

Long-Form Name: Federated States of Micronesia
Capital: Palikir

■ GEOGRAPHY

Area: 702 sq. km.; 4 major island groups totalling 607 islands
Coastline: 6,112 km
Climate: tropical; heavy rainfall all year long, particularly in the eastern islands
Environment: occasional severe typhoons mostly from June to Dec.
Terrain: varies from high, mountainous islands to low coral atolls; volcanic outcroppings
Land Use: arable land: 5.71%, permanent crops: 45.71%, other: 48.58%

Location: Oceania, in the N Pacific Ocean, NE of Australia

■ PEOPLE

Population: 108,143 (July 2003 est.)
Nationality: Micronesian
Age Structure: 0–14 yrs: 38.4%; 15–64: 58.5%; 65+: 3.2% (2003 est.)
Population Growth Rate: 0.04% (2003 est.)
Net Migration: -20.98 migrants/1,000 population (2003 est.)
Ethnic Groups: 9 Micronesian and Polynesian groups
Languages: English (official and common), local languages including Pohnpeian, Yapese, Trukese and Kosrean
Religions: Roman Catholic 50%, Protestant 47%, other or none 3%
Birth Rate: 26.47/1,000 population (2003 est.)
Death Rate: 5.10/1,000 population (2003 est.)
Infant Mortality: 32.39 deaths/1,000 live births (2003 est.)
Life Expectancy at Birth: 67.39 years male, 70.95 years female (2003 est.)
Total Fertility Rate: 3.50 children born/woman (2003 est.)
Literacy: 89%

■ GOVERNMENT

Leader(s): President Joseph J. "Joe" Urusemal, Vice President Redley Killion
Government Type: constitutional government in free association with the United States
Administrative Divisions: 4 states
Nationhood: Nov. 3, 1986 (from US-administered UN Trusteeship)
National Holiday: Proclamation of the Federated States of Micronesia, May 10

■ ECONOMY

Overview: mostly subsistence farming and fishing; few economically viable mineral deposits; region's remote location and lack of adequate facilities hinders development of tourism potential; considerably dependent on financial assistance from the US
GDP: US$277 million, per capita US$2,000; real growth rate 1.0% (2002 est.)
Inflation: 1.0% (2002 est.)
Industries: accounts for 4% of GDP; fish processing, crafts, tourism, construction
Labour Force: n.a.; two-thirds are government employees
Unemployment: n.a.
Agriculture: accounts for 50% of GDP (2000); pepper, tropical fruits and vegetables, coconuts, sweet potatoes, pigs, chickens

Natural Resources: forests, marine products, deep-sea minerals

■ FINANCE/TRADE

Currency: US dollar ($) = 100 cents
International Reserves Excluding Gold: US$82 million (Jan. 2004)
Gold Reserves: n.a.
Budget: n.a.
Defence Expenditures: n.a.
Education Expenditures: n.a.
External Debt: US$53.1 million (2003 est.)
Exports: exact figures not available; commodities: fish, garments, bananas, pepper; partners: Japan, US, Guam
Imports: exact figures not available; commodities: food, manufactures, machinery and equipment, beverages; partners: US, Japan, Australia

■ COMMUNICATIONS

Daily Newspapers: n.a.
Televisions: n.a.
Radios: n.a.
Telephones: 74 lines/1,000 inhabitants (2002)
Internet: users: 6,000 (2002)

■ TRANSPORTATION

Motor Vehicles: n.a.
Roads: 240 km; 42 km paved
Railway: none
Air Traffic: n.a.
Airports: 7; 6 have paved runways (2003 est.)

Canadian Embassy: Canadian Embassy to the Federated States of Micronesia, c/o The Canadian High Commission, Commonwealth Avenue, Canberra ACT 2600, Australia, Tel: (011 61 2) 6270-4000. Fax: (011 61 2) 6273-3285. e-mail: cnbra@dfait-maeci.gc.ca
Embassy in Canada: c/o The Embassy of the Republic of the Philippines, 130 Albert St Ste 606, Ottawa, ON K1P 5G4. Tel: (613) 233-1121. Fax: (613) 233-4165. e-mail: embassyofphilippines@rogers.com

Moldova

Long-Form Name: Republic of Moldova
Capital: Chisinau

■ GEOGRAPHY

Area: 33,843 sq. km
Coastline: none: landlocked
Climate: mild sunny winters; warm rainy summers; long dry autumns

Environment: heavy use of agricultural chemicals, including banned pesticides such as DDT, has contaminated groundwater and soil; erosion severe due to poor farming methods
Terrain: hilly plains in north; southern steppe
Land Use: arable land: 54.08%, permanent crops: 12.1%, other: 33.82%; includes 3,070 sq. km irrigated
Location: E Europe, bordering on Ukraine and Romania

■ PEOPLE

Population: 4,439,502 (July 2003 est.)
Nationality: Moldovan
Age Structure: 0–14 yrs: 21.1%; 15–64: 68.7%; 65+: 10.2% (2003 est.)
Population Growth Rate: 0.13% (2003 est.)
Net Migration: -0.27 migrants/1,000 population (2003 est.)
Ethnic Groups: 64.5% Moldavian, 13.8% Ukrainian, 13% Russian, 3.5% Gagauz, 1.5% Jews, 3.7% other
Languages: Moldavan (official), Russian, Ukrainian, Gagauz (a Turkish dialect)
Religions: 98.5% Eastern Orthodox, 1.5% Jewish, minority Baptists (note that almost all churchgoers are ethnic Moldovan; the Slavic population are not churchgoers)
Birth Rate: 14.31/1,000 population (2003 est.)
Death Rate: 12.70/1,000 population (2003 est.)
Infant Mortality: 41.58 deaths/1,000 live births (2003 est.)
Life Expectancy at Birth: 60.63 years male, 69.35 years female (2003 est.)
Total Fertility Rate: 1.74 children born/woman (2003 est.)
Literacy: 99.0% (2002)

■ GOVERNMENT

Leader(s): President Vladimir Voronin, Prime Minister Vasile Tarlev
Government Type: republic
Administrative Divisions: 10 juletule (sing. juletul), 1 autonomous territorial unit and 1 municipality
Nationhood: Aug. 27, 1991 (from Soviet Union)
National Holiday: Independence Day, Aug. 27

■ ECONOMY

Overview: predominantly agricultural, with important manufacturing sector; Moldova has a climate favourable to agriculture, and this is where the bulk of economic development has taken place
GDP: US$11.51 billion, per capita US$2,600; real growth rate 6.5% (2002 est.)
Inflation: 5.5% (2002 est.)

Industries: accounts for 23% of GDP (2000); machinery and appliances, hosiery, refined sugar, vegetable oil, canned food, shoes, textiles
Labour Force: 2.2 million (2002); 40% agriculture, 46% other; 14% industry
Unemployment: 7.3%; also large numbers of underemployed (2002)
Agriculture: accounts for 28% of GDP (2000); grapes and other fruits, vegetables, sugar, wheat and cereal grains, tobacco, oil, essential oil crops, beets, wine; beef, milk.
Natural Resources: lignite, phosphorites, gypsum, arable land

■ FINANCE/TRADE

Currency: leu (pl. lei)
International Reserves Excluding Gold: US$311 million (Jan. 2004)
Gold Reserves: n.a.
Budget: n.a.
Defence Expenditures: 1.2% of central government expenditure (2002)
Education Expenditures: 15.0% of total government expenditure (2002)
External Debt: US$1.349 billion (2002)
Exports: US$570 million (2001); wine, grapes, other agricultural products, machinery, pumps; partners: Russia, Ukraine, Italy, Germany, Romania
Imports: US$897 million (2001); fuels, metals and metal products, consumer products, foodstuffs; partners: Russia, Romania, Ukraine, Germany, Italy

■ COMMUNICATIONS

Daily Newspapers: 13/1,000 inhabitants (2000)
Televisions: 296/1,000 inhabitants (2002)
Radios: 758/1,000 inhabitants (2001)
Telephones: 161 lines/1,000 inhabitants (2002)
Internet: hosts: 2,189 (2002); users: 150,000 (2002)

■ TRANSPORTATION

Motor Vehicles: 360,000; 280,000 passenger cars
Roads: 12,657 km; 11,012 km hard-surfaced
Railway: 1,328 km, which does not include industrial lines
Air Traffic: 129,000 passengers carried (2002)
Airports: 36; 8 have paved runways (2003 est.)

Canadian Embassy: The Canadian Embassy to Moldova, 36 Nicolae Iorga St., 71118 Bucharest, Romania. Mailing address: c/o The Canadian Embassy, P.O. Box 117, Post Office No. 22, 71118 Bucharest, Romania. Tel: (011-40-21) 307-5000. Fax: (011-40-21) 307-5010. e-mail: bucst@dfait-maeci.gc.ca

Embassy in Canada: Embassy of the Republic of Moldova, 2101 S. St NW, Washington DC 20008, USA. Tel: (202) 667-1130. Fax: (202) 667-1204. e-mail: moldova@dgsys.com

Monaco

Long-Form Name: Principality of Monaco
Capital: Monaco

■ GEOGRAPHY

Area: 1.95 sq. km
Coastline: 4.1 km
Climate: Mediterranean with mild, wet winters and hot, dry summers
Environment: almost entirely urban
Terrain: hilly, rugged, rocky
Land Use: arable land: 0%, permanent crops: 0%, other: 100%, (urban area)
Location: W Europe, bordering on France and Mediterranean Sea

■ PEOPLE

Population: 32,130 (July 2003 est.)
Nationality: Monegasque or Monacan
Age Structure: 0–14 yrs: 15.5%; 15–64: 62.1%; 65+: 22.4% (2003 est.)
Population Growth Rate: 0.44% (2003 est.)
Net Migration: 7.78 migrants/1,000 population (2003 est.)
Ethnic Groups: 47% French, 16% Monegasque, 16% Italian, 21% other
Languages: French (official), English, Italian, Monegasque
Religions: 95% Roman Catholic
Birth Rate: 9.46/1,000 population (2003 est.)
Death Rate: 12.82/1,000 population (2003 est.)
Infant Mortality: 5.63 deaths/1,000 live births (2003 est.)
Life Expectancy at Birth: 75.37 years male, 83.37 years female (2003 est.)
Total Fertility Rate: 1.76 children born/woman (2002 est.)
Literacy: 99%

■ GOVERNMENT

Leader(s): Prince Rainier III, Minister of State Patrick Leclercq
Government Type: constitutional monarchy
Administrative Divisions: 4 districts (quartiers, sing. —quartier)
Nationhood: 1419, rule by the House of Grimaldi
National Holiday: National Day, Nov. 19

■ ECONOMY

Overview: a popular resort, attracting tourists to its casinos and pleasant climate; no income tax

and low business taxes make it a tax haven; no data is published on the economy
GDP: n.a.
Inflation: n.a.
Industries: pharmaceuticals, food processing, precision instruments, glassmaking, printing, tourism
Labour Force: n.a.
Unemployment: n.a.
Agriculture: none
Natural Resources: none

■ FINANCE/TRADE

Currency: French franc (F) = 100 centimes; also Euro (€)as of March 1, 2002
International Reserves Excluding Gold: n.a.
Gold Reserves: n.a.
Budget: n.a.
Defence Expenditures: defence is the responsibility of France
Education Expenditures: n.a.
External Debt: n.a.
Exports: n.a.; full customs integration with France, which collects and rebates Monegasque trade duties
Imports: n.a.; full customs integration with France, which collects and rebates Monegasque trade duties

■ COMMUNICATIONS

Daily Newspapers: 1 in total
Televisions: n.a.
Radios: n.a.
Telephones: n.a.
Internet: users: 16,000 (2002)

■ TRANSPORTATION

Motor Vehicles: 21,000; 17,000 passenger cars
Roads: 50 km paved city streets only
Railway: 1.7 km
Air Traffic: 50,000 passengers carried (2001 est.)
Airports: none; Monaco is linked to the airport in Nice, France, by helicopter service

Canadian Embassy: The Canadian Consulate General, c/o The Canadian Embassy, 35 av Montaigne, 75008 Paris, France. Tel: (011-33-1) 44-43-22-51. Fax: (011-33-1) 44-43-29-99. e-mail: paris@dfait-maeci.gc.ca
Embassy in Canada: Consulate of Monaco, 20 Queen St. W., Suite 3300, Toronto, ON, M5H 3R3. Tel: (416) 971-4848, Fax: (416) 971-4849. e-mail: blette@lette.com

---

Mongolia

Long-Form Name: Mongolia

Capital: Ulan Bator, or Ulaanbaatar

■ GEOGRAPHY

Area: 1,565,000 sq. km
Coastline: none: landlocked
Climate: desert; continental (large daily and seasonal temperature ranges)
Environment: harsh and rugged; water resources are severely limited; deforestation is a problem; spring dust storms are a natural hazard
Terrain: vast semi-desert and desert plains; mountains in west and southwest; Gobi Desert in southeast
Land Use: arable land: 0.84%, permanent crops: 0%, other: 99.16%; includes 840 sq. km irrigated
Location: EC Asia, bordering China and Russia

■ PEOPLE

Population: 2,712,315 (July 2003 est.)
Nationality: Mongolian
Age Structure: 0–14 yrs: 30.7%; 15–64: 65.7%; 65+: 3.6% (2003 est.)
Population Growth Rate: 1.42% (2003 est.)
Net Migration: 0 migrants/1,000 population (2003 est.)
Ethnic Groups: 90% Mongol, 4% Kazakh, 2% Chinese, 2% Russian, 2% other
Languages: Kazakh and Khalkha Mongol is spoken by over 90% of population; minor languages include Turkic, Russian, Chinese and English
Religions: no state religion; predominantly Buddhist Lamaism and Shamanism, Islam 4%
Birth Rate: 21.39/1,000 population (2003 est.)
Death Rate: 7.18/1,000 population (2003 est.)
Infant Mortality: 57.16 deaths/1,000 live births (2003 est.)
Life Expectancy at Birth: 61.63 years male, 66.09 years female (2003 est.)
Total Fertility Rate: 2.28 children born/woman (2003 est.)
Literacy: 97.8% (2002)

■ GOVERNMENT

Leader(s): President Natsagiin Bagabandi, Prime Minister Tsakhiagiyn Elbedorj
Government Type: republic
Administrative Divisions: 18 provinces (aymguud, sing. —aymag) and 3 municipalities (hotuud, sing. —hot)
Nationhood: July 11, 1921 (from China; formerly known as Outer Mongolia)
National Holiday: Independence/Revolution Day, July 11

■ ECONOMY

Overview: severe climate, widely dispersed population and largely unproductive land have hindered economic development; one-quarter of the population lives below the poverty line; economy is traditionally based on agriculture and the breeding of livestock (has highest number of livestock per person in the world); recently extensive mineral resources have been developed
GDP: US$5.06 billion, per capita US$1,900; average real growth rate 3.9% (2002 est.)
Inflation: 3.0% (2002 est.)
Industries: accounts for 30% of GDP (2000); processing of animal products, building materials, food and beverage, mining (particularly coal), copper
Labour Force: 1.2 million (2002); primarily engaged in herding and agriculture
Unemployment: 5.7% (2001)
Agriculture: accounts for 32% of GDP (2000) and 90% of exports, and provides livelihood for about 50% of the population; livestock raising predominates (sheep, goats, cattle, camels, horses); crops—wheat, barley, potatoes, forage
Natural Resources: oil, coal, copper, molybdenum, tungsten, phosphates, tin, nickel, zinc, wolfram, fluorspar, gold

■ FINANCE/TRADE

Currency: tughrik (Tug) = 100 mongos
International Reserves Excluding Gold: US$171 million (Jan. 2004)
Gold Reserves: 0.032 million fine troy ounces (Jan. 2004)
Budget: revenues US$387 million, expenditures of US$428 million, including capital expenditures of US$ n.a. (2001 est.)
Defence Expenditures: 7.5% of central government expenditure (2002)
Education Expenditures: 8.68% of central government expenditure (2000)
External Debt: US$1.037 billion (2002)
Exports: US$448 million (2001); commodities: livestock, animal products, wool, hides, cashmere, copper, fluorspar, non-ferrous metals, minerals; partners: China, US, Russia, Japan
Imports: US$630 million (2001); commodities: machinery and equipment, fuels, food products, industrial consumer goods, chemicals, building materials, sugar, tea; partners: Russia, China, Japan, South Korea, US

■ COMMUNICATIONS

Daily Newspapers: 30/1,000 inhabitants (2000)
Televisions: 79/1,000 inhabitants (2002)
Radios: 50/1,000 inhabitants (2001)

Telephones: 53 lines/1,000 inhabitants (2002)
Internet: hosts: 127 (2002); users: 50,000 (2002)

■ TRANSPORTATION

Motor Vehicles: 83,000; 48,000 passenger cars
Roads: 49,250 km; 1,724 km paved
Railway: 1,815 km
Air Traffic: 270,000 passengers carried (2002)
Airports: 50; 10 have paved runways (2003 est.)

Canadian Embassy: The Canadian Embassy to Mongolia, c/o The Canadian Embassy, 19 Dong Zhi Men Wai St, Chao Yang District, Beijing 100600, China. Tel: (011-86-10) 6532-3536. Fax: (011-86-10) 6532-4311. e-mail: bejing@dfait-maeci.gc.ca
Embassy in Canada: Embassy of Mongolia, 151 Slater St. Suite 503, Ottawa, ON, K1P 5H3. Tel: (613)569-3830 Fax: (613)569-3916. e-mail: mail@mongolembassy.org

Montserrat

Long-Form Name: Montserrat
Capital: Plymouth (abandoned in 1997 due to volcanic activity); interim government buildings are located in Brades

■ GEOGRAPHY

Area: 100 sq. km
Climate: tropical, no well-defined rainy season; June to Nov. hottest; prone to hurricanes
Land Use: arable land: 20%, permanent crops: 0%, other: 80%; includes n.a. sq. km irrigated
Location: Caribbean island, SE of Puerto Rico

■ PEOPLE

Population: 8,995 (July 2003 est.)
Nationality: Montserratian
Ethnic Groups: descendants of British, French, Irish settlers; also black
Languages: English (official)

■ GOVERNMENT

Colony/Territory of: Crown Colony of the United Kingdom
Leader(s): Head of State: Queen Elizabeth II, Acting Governor Howard Fergus, Chief Minister John Osborne
Government Type: dependent territory of the UK
National Holiday: Celebration of the Birthday of the Queen, second Saturday in June

■ ECONOMY

Overview: manufacturing accounts for 85% of exports: leather goods, cotton clothing, electronics, plastic bags, herbal teas, ornamental plants, tropical fruit; the economy is heavily dependent on imports, making it vulnerable to fluctuations in world prices; ongoing major volcanic activity is hindering economic activity

■ FINANCE/TRADE

Currency: Eastern-Caribbean dollar = 100 cents

Canadian Embassy: c/o Macdonald House, 1 Grosvenor Square, London WIK 4AB, England, UK. Tel: (011-44-20) 7258-6600. Fax: (011-44-20) 7258-6333. e-mail: ldn@dfait-maeci.gc.ca
Representative to Canada: c/o High Commission for the Countries of the Organization of Eastern Caribbean States, 130 Albert St, Ste 700, Ottawa ON K1P 5G4. Tel: (613) 236-8952. Fax: (613) 236-3042. e-mail: echcc@travel-net.com

Morocco

Long-Form Name: Kingdom of Morocco
Capital: Rabat

■ GEOGRAPHY

Area: 446,550 sq. km
Coastline: 1,835 km
Climate: Mediterranean, becoming more extreme in the interior
Environment: northern mountains geologically unstable and subject to earthquakes; desertification; unsafe water supply; land degradation
Terrain: mostly mountains with rich coastal plains
Land Use: arable land: 20.12%, permanent crops: 2.05%, other: 77.83%; includes 12,910 sq. km irrigated
Location: NW Africa, bordering on Atlantic Ocean

■ PEOPLE

Population: 31,689,265 (July 2003 est.)
Nationality: Moroccan
Age Structure: 0–14 yrs: 33.2%; 15–64: 62.0%; 65+: 4.8% (2003 est.)
Population Growth Rate: 1.64% (2003 est.)
Net Migration: -1.03 migrants/1,000 population (2003 est.)
Ethnic Groups: 99.1% Arab-Berber, 0.7% non-Morrocan, 0.2% Jewish
Languages: Arabic (official); several Berber dialects; French is language of business, government, diplomacy and post-primary education
Religions: 98.7% Sunni Muslim, 1.1% Christian, 0.2% Jewish
Birth Rate: 23.26/1,000 population (2003 est.)
Death Rate: 5.78/1,000 population (2003 est.)

Infant Mortality: 44.87 deaths/1,000 live births (2003 est.)
Life Expectancy at Birth: 67.77 years male, 72.41 years female (2003 est.)
Total Fertility Rate: 2.89 children born/woman (2003 est.)
Literacy: 50.7% (2002)

■ GOVERNMENT

Leader(s): King Sidi Mohammed VI, Prime Minister Driss Jettou
Government Type: constitutional monarchy
Administrative Divisions: 37 provinces and 2 municipalities (wilayas)
Nationhood: Mar. 2, 1956 (from France)
National Holiday: Throne Day or Sete de Throne, July 30 (anniversary of King Mohammed VI's accession to the throne)

■ ECONOMY

Overview: faces the problems typical of developing countries: restraining government spending, reducing constraints on private activity and foreign trade, and keeping inflation manageable
GDP: US$121.8 billion, per capita US$3,900; real growth rate 4.6% (2002 est.)
Inflation: 3.6% (2002 est.)
Industries: accounts for 33% of GDP (2000), phosphate rock mining and processing, food processing, leather goods, textiles, construction, tourism
Labour Force: 12.1 million (2002); 50% agriculture, 35% services, 15% industry
Unemployment: 22.0% (2001)
Agriculture: accounts for 15% of GDP (2000); 50% of employment and 30% of export value; not self-sufficient in food; cereal farming and livestock raising predominate; barley, wheat, citrus fruit, wine, vegetables, olives
Natural Resources: phosphates, iron ore, manganese, lead, zinc, fish, salt

■ FINANCE/TRADE

Currency: dirham (DH) = 100 centimes
International Reserves Excluding Gold: US$13.654 billion (Jan. 2004)
Gold Reserves: 0.708 million fine troy ounces (Jan. 2004)
Budget: revenues US$13.8 billion; expenditures of US$14.0 billion, including capital expenditures of US$2.1 billion (2004 est.)
Defence Expenditures: 12.4% of central government expenditure (2002)
Education Expenditures: n.a.
External Debt: US$17.7 billion (2002)

Exports: US$7.484 billion (2002); commodities: food and beverages 30%, semi-processed goods 23%, consumer goods 21%, phosphates 17%; partners: France, Spain, UK, Italy, Germany, India, US

Imports: US$11.868 billion (2002); commodities: capital goods 24%, semi-processed goods 22%, raw materials 16%, fuel and lubricants 16%, food and beverages 13%, consumer goods 10%; partners: France, Spain, Germany, Italy, UK, US

■ COMMUNICATIONS

Daily Newspapers: 28/1,000 inhabitants (2000)
Televisions: 167/1,000 inhabitants (2002)
Radios: 243/1,000 inhabitants (2001)
Telephones: 38 lines/1,000 inhabitants (2002)
Internet: hosts: 2,680 (2002); users: 700,000 (2002)

■ TRANSPORTATION

Motor Vehicles: 1,600,000; 1,270,000 passenger cars
Roads: 57,707 km; 32,547 km paved
Railway: 1,907 km
Air Traffic: 3,146,000 passengers carried (2002)
Airports: 63; 26 have paved runways (2003 est.)

Canadian Embassy: The Canadian Embassy, 13 bis, rue Jaafar As-Sadik; Rabat-Agdal; mailing address: CP 709, Rabat-Agdal, Morocco. Tel: (011-212-37) 68-74-00. Fax: (011-212-37) 68-74-30. e-mail: rabat@dfait-maeci.gc.ca.
Embassy in Canada: Embassy of the Kingdom of Morocco, 38 Range Rd, Ottawa ON K1N 8J4. Tel: (613) 236-7391. Fax: (613) 236-6164. e-mail: sifamaot@bellnet.ca

Mozambique

Long-Form Name: Republic of Mozambique
Capital: Maputo

■ GEOGRAPHY

Area: 801,590 sq. km
Coastline: 2,470 km
Climate: tropical to subtropical
Environment: severe drought and floods occur in south; desertification; water pollution; danger of cyclones
Terrain: mostly coastal lowlands, uplands in centre, high plateaus in northwest, mountains in west
Land Use: arable land: 3.98%, permanent crops: 0.29%, other: 95.73%; includes 1,070 sq. km irrigated
Location: SE Africa, bordering on Mozambique Channel

■ PEOPLE

Population: 17,479,266 (July 2003 est.)
Nationality: Mozambican
Age Structure: 0–14 yrs: 42.1%; 15–64: 55.3%; 65+: 2.6% (2003 est.)
Population Growth Rate: 0.82% (2003 est.)
Net Migration: 0 migrants/1,000 population (2003 est.)
Ethnic Groups: 99.66% indigenous tribal groups; about 0.06% Europeans, 0.2% Euro-Africans, 0.08% Indians
Languages: Portuguese (official); English; many indigenous dialects
Religions: 50% indigenous beliefs, 30% Christian, 20% Muslim
Birth Rate: 38.20/1,000 population (2003 est.)
Death Rate: 30.04/1,000 population (2003 est.)
Infant Mortality: 199.00 deaths/1,000 live births (2003 est.)
Life Expectancy at Birth: 30.98 years male, 31.63 years female (2003 est.)
Total Fertility Rate: 4.87 children born/woman (2003 est.)
Literacy: 46.5% (2002)

■ GOVERNMENT

Leader(s): President Joaquím Alberto Chissano, Prime Minister Luisa Diogo
Government Type: republic
Administrative Divisions: 10 provinces (provincias, sing. —provincia)
Nationhood: June 25, 1975 (from Portugal)
National Holiday: Independence Day, June 25

■ ECONOMY

Overview: internal disorder, lack of government administrative control and a growing foreign debt have contributed to the country's failure to exploit the economic potential of its agricultural, hydro power and transportation resources; depends on much foreign aid; industry operates at only 20–40% of capacity
GDP: US$19.52 billion, per capita US$1,100; real growth rate 7.7% (2002 est.)
Inflation: 15.2% (2002 est.)
Industries: accounts for 25% of GDP (2000); food, beverages, chemicals (fertilizer, soap, paints), petroleum products, textiles, non-metallic mineral products (cement, glass, asbestos), tobacco
Labour Force: 9.6 million (2002); 81% agriculture, 6% industry, 13% services
Unemployment: n.a.
Agriculture: accounts for 33% of GDP (2000), over 90% of labour force and about 90% of exports; cash crops—cotton, cashew nuts, sugar cane, tea, shrimp; other crops—cassava, corn, rice, tropical fruit; beef, poultry, not self-sufficient in food

Natural Resources: coal, titanium, natural gas, hydro power

■ FINANCE/TRADE

Currency: metical (pl. meticais) (Mt) = 100 centavos
International Reserves Excluding Gold: US$987 million (Jan. 2004)
Gold Reserves: n.a.
Budget: revenues US$393.1 million; expenditures US$1.025 billion, including capital expenditures US$479.4 million (2001 est.)
Defence Expenditures: 1.0% of GDP (2000)
Education Expenditures: n.a.
External Debt: US$4.609 billion (2002)
Exports: US$795 million (2003 est.); commodities: shrimp 48%, cashews 21%, sugar 10%, copra 3%, citrus 3%, cotton, electricity; partners: South Africa, Zimbabwe, Spain, Portugal
Imports: US$1.142 billion (2003 est.); commodities: food, clothing, farm equipment, petroleum, chemicals, metals; partners: South Africa, Portugal, US, Australia

■ COMMUNICATIONS

Daily Newspapers: 2/1,000 inhabitants (2000)
Televisions: 14/1,000 inhabitants (2002)
Radios: 44/1,000 inhabitants (2001)
Telephones: 5 lines/1,000 inhabitants (2002)
Internet: hosts: 1,925 (2002); users: 30,000 (2002)

■ TRANSPORTATION

Motor Vehicles: 88,800; 67,600 passenger cars
Roads: 30,400 km; 5,685 km paved
Railway: 3,123 km
Air Traffic: 282,000 passengers carried (2002)
Airports: 165; 22 have paved runways (2003 est.)

Canadian Embassy: The Canadian Embassy, avenida Julius Nyerere, No. 1128, Maputo; mailing address: P.O. Box 1578, Maputo, Mozambique. Tel: (011-258-1) 492-623. Fax: (011-258-1) 492-667. e-mail: canembas@ecanada.uem.mz
Embassy in Canada: c/o High Commission for the Republic of Mozambique, 1990 M St NW, Ste 570, Washington DC 20036, USA. Tel: (202) 293-7146. Fax: (202) 835-0245. e-mail: n.a.

Myanmar

Long-Form Name: Union of Myanmar (formerly Burma)
Capital: Rangoon (Yangon)

■ GEOGRAPHY

Area: 678,500 sq. km

Coastline: 1,930 km
Climate: tropical monsoon; cloudy, rainy, hot, humid summers (southwest monsoon, June to Sept.); less cloudy, scant rainfall, mild temperatures, lower humidity during winter (northeast monsoon, Dec. to Apr.)
Environment: subject to destructive earthquakes and cyclones; flooding and landslides common during rainy season (June to Sept.); deforestation
Terrain: central lowlands ringed by steep, rugged highlands
Land Use: arable land: 14.53%, permanent crops: 0.9%, other: 84.57%; includes 15,920 sq. km irrigated
Location: SE Asia, bordering on Bay of Bengal

■ PEOPLE

Population: 42,510,537 (July 2003 est.)
Nationality: Burmese
Age Structure: 0–14 yrs: 28.1%; 15–64: 67.0%; 65+: 4.9% (2003 est.)
Population Growth Rate: 0.52% (2003 est.)
Net Migration: -1.81 migrants/1,000 population (2003 est.)
Ethnic Groups: 68% Burmese, 9% Shan, 7% Karen, 4% Rakhine, 3% Chinese, 2% Mon, 2% Indian, 5% other
Languages: Myanmar (Burmese); minority ethnic groups have their own languages
Religions: 89% Buddhist, 11% animist beliefs, Muslim, Christian or other
Birth Rate: 19.15/1,000 population (2003 est.)
Death Rate: 12.17/1,000 population (2003 est.)
Infant Mortality: 70.35 deaths/1,000 live births (2003 est.)
Life Expectancy at Birth: 54.12 years male, 57.56 years female (2003 est.)
Total Fertility Rate: 2.15 children born/woman (2003 est.)
Literacy: 85.3% (2002)

■ GOVERNMENT

Leader(s): Chairman of the State Peace and Development Council Senior General Than Shwe, Prime Minister General Khin Nyunt
Government Type: military regime
Administrative Divisions: 7 divisions (yin-mya, sing. —yin), 7 states (pyine-mya, sing. —pyine)
Nationhood: Jan. 4, 1948 (from UK)
National Holiday: Independence Day, Jan. 4

■ ECONOMY

Overview: dependent on agriculture and vulnerable to world market conditions (especially for rice); has been unable to achieve much improvement in export earnings due to falling prices for many of its export commodities
GDP: US$73.69 billion, per capita US$1,700; real growth rate 5.3% (2002 est.)
Inflation: 53.7% (2002 est.)

Industries: accounts for 9% of GDP (2000); agricultural processing; textiles and footwear; wood and wood products; petroleum refining; mining of copper, tin, tungsten, iron; construction materials; pharmaceuticals; fertilizer
Labour Force: 26.1 million (2002); 65% agriculture, 25% services, 10% industry
Unemployment: n.a.
Agriculture: accounts for 60% of GDP (2000); self-sufficient in food; principal crops: rice, corn, oilseed, sugar cane, pulses; world's largest stand of hardwood trees; rice and teak account for 55% of exports; world's largest producer of opium poppies
Natural Resources: crude oil, timber, tin, antimony, zinc, copper, tungsten, lead, coal, some marble, limestone, precious stones, natural gas

■ **FINANCE/TRADE**

Currency: kyat (K) = 100 pyas
International Reserves Excluding Gold: US$520 million (Oct. 2003)
Gold Reserves: 0.231 million fine troy ounces (Oct. 2003)
Budget: n.a.
Defence Expenditures: 26.6% of central government expenditure (2002)
Education Expenditures: 18.1% of central government expenditure (2002)
External Debt: US$6.556 billion (2002)
Exports: US$3.046 billion (2002); commodities: teak, rice, oilseed, metals, rubber, gems; partners: US, India, China, Japan, Singapore
Imports: US$2.348 billion (2002); commodities: machinery, transport equipment, chemicals, food products; partners: China, Singapore, South Korea, Japan, Taiwan

■ **COMMUNICATIONS**

Daily Newspapers: 9/1,000 inhabitants (2000)
Televisions: 8/1,000 inhabitants (2002)
Radios: 65/1,000 inhabitants (2001)
Telephones: 7 lines/1,000 inhabitants (2002)
Internet: hosts: 2; users 25,000 (2002)

■ **TRANSPORTATION**

Motor Vehicles: 69,000; 35,000 passenger cars
Roads: 28,200 km; 3,440 km paved
Railway: 3,955 km
Air Traffic: 1,186,000 passengers carried (2002)
Airports: 80; 8 have paved runways (2003 est.)

Canadian Embassy: The Canadian Embassy to Myanmar, c/o The Canadian Embassy, 990 Rama IV, Abdulrahim Place, 15th Fl, Bangrak, Bangkok 10500, Thailand; mailing address: P.O. Box 2090, Bangkok 10501, Thailand. Tel:

(011-66-2) 636-0540. Fax: (011-66-2) 636-0566. e-mail: bngkk@dfait-maeci.gc.ca
Embassy in Canada: c/o Embassy of the Union of Myanmar, 85 Range Rd, Ste 902/903, Ottawa ON K1N 8J6. Tel: (613) 232-6434. Fax: (613) 232-6435. e-mail: meott@magma.ca

---

Namibia

Long-Form Name: Republic of Namibia
Capital: Windhoek

■ **GEOGRAPHY**

Area: 825,418 sq. km
Coastline: 1,572 km
Climate: desert; hot, dry; rainfall sparse and erratic
Environment: inhospitable with very limited natural water resources; drought and desertification
Terrain: mostly high plateau; Namib Desert along coast; Kalahari Desert in east
Land Use: arable land: 0.99%, permanent crops: 0%, other: 99.01%; includes 70 sq. km irrigated
Location: SW Africa, bordering on South Atlantic Ocean

■ **PEOPLE**

Population: 1,927,447 (July 2003 est.)
Nationality: Namibian
Age Structure: 0–14 yrs: 42.5%; 15–64: 54.0%; 65+: 3.5% (2003 est.)
Population Growth Rate: 1.49% (2003 est.)
Net Migration: 0 migrants/1,000 population (2003 est.)
Ethnic Groups: 87.5% black, 6% white, 6.5% mixed; about 50% of the population belong to the Ovambo tribe and 9% to the Kavangos tribe
Languages: white population: 60% Afrikaans, 33% German, 7% English (all official); several indigenous languages
Religions: 90% Christian, 10% traditional religions
Birth Rate: 34.10/1,000 population (2003 est.)
Death Rate: 19.17/1,000 population (2003 est.)
Infant Mortality: 68.44 deaths/1,000 live births (2003 est.)
Life Expectancy at Birth: 44.27 years male, 41.22 years female (2003 est.)
Total Fertility Rate: 4.71 children born/woman (2003 est.)
Literacy: 83.3% (2002)

■ **GOVERNMENT**

Leader(s): President Sam Nujoma, Prime Minister Theo-Ben Gurirab
Government Type: republic
Administrative Divisions: 13 regions
Nationhood: Mar. 21, 1990 (from South Africa)
National Holiday: Independence Day, Mar. 21

■ ECONOMY

Overview: very dependent on the mining industry to extract and process minerals for export; world's fifth largest producer of uranium; rich diamond deposits; more than 50% of the population depends on subsistence agriculture
GDP: US$13.15 billion, per capita US$6,900; real growth rate 2.3% (2002 est.)
Inflation: 9.5% (2001)
Industries: meat packing, fish processing, dairy products; mining accounts for 28% of GDP (2000) (copper, lead, zinc, diamonds, uranium)
Labour Force: 800,000 (2002); 47% agriculture, 20% industry, 33% services
Unemployment: 33.8% (2002)
Agriculture: accounts for 11% of GDP (2000) (including fishing); mostly subsistence farming; livestock raising major source of cash income; crops: millet, sorghum, peanuts; large unfulfilled fish catch potential; needs to import food
Natural Resources: diamonds, copper, uranium, gold, lead, tin, zinc, salt, vanadium, natural gas, fish, hydroelectric potential; suspected deposits of coal and iron ore

■ FINANCE/TRADE

Currency: Namibian dollar = 100 cents, also the South African Rand
International Reserves Excluding Gold: US$394 million (Jan. 2004)
Gold Reserves: none (Jan. 2002)
Budget: n.a.
Defence Expenditures: 9.1% of central government expenditure (2002)
Education Expenditures: 21.0% of total government expenditures (2002)
External Debt: US$517 million (2002 est.)
Exports: US$1.182 billion (2001); commodities: diamonds, uranium, zinc, copper, meat, processed fish, karakul skins; partners: South Africa, UK, Spain, Japan
Imports: US$1.546 billion (2001 est.); commodities: foodstuffs, manufactured consumer goods, machinery and equipment, chemicals; partners: South Africa, Germany, US

■ COMMUNICATIONS

Daily Newspapers: 19/1,000 inhabitants (2000)
Televisions: 69/1,000 inhabitants (2002)
Radios: 141/1,000 inhabitants (2001)
Telephones: 65 lines/1,000 inhabitants (2002)
Internet: hosts: 3,709 (2002); users: 50,000 (2002)

■ TRANSPORTATION

Motor Vehicles: 145,000; 69,000 passenger cars
Roads: 66,467 km; 9,172 km paved

Railway: 2,382 km
Air Traffic: 222,000 passengers carried (2002)
Airports: 135; 21 have paved runways (2003 est.)

Canadian Embassy: The Canadian High Commission to Namibia, c/o The Canadian High Commission, 1103 Arcadia St, Hatfield 0028, Pretoria; mailing address: Private Bag X13, Hatfield 0028, Pretoria, South Africa. Tel.: (011-27-12) 422-3000. Fax: (011-27-12) 422-3052. e-mail: pret@dfait-maeci.gc.ca
Embassy in Canada: High Commission for the Republic of Namibia, 1605 New Hampshire Ave NW, Washington DC 20009, USA. Tel: (202) 986-0540. Fax: (202) 986-0443. e-mail: n.a.

Nauru

Long-Form Name: Republic of Nauru
Capital: no capital city as such; government offices in Yaren

■ GEOGRAPHY

Area: 21 sq. km
Coastline: 30 km
Climate: tropical; monsoonal; rainy season (Nov. to Feb.)
Environment: only 53 km south of equator; periodic droughts; water supply limited and unreliable
Terrain: sandy beach rises to fertile ring around raised coral reefs with phosphate plateau in centre
Land Use: arable land: 0%, permanent crops: 0%, other: 100%
Location: island in the Pacific Ocean, NE of Australia

■ PEOPLE

Population: 12,570 (July 2003 est.)
Nationality: Nauruan
Age Structure: 0–14 yrs: 38.9%; 15–64: 59.3%; 65+: 1.8% (2003 est.)
Population Growth Rate: 1.90% (2003 est.)
Net Migration: 0 migrants/1,000 population (2003 est.)
Ethnic Groups: 58% Nauruan, 26% other Pacific Islander, 8% Chinese, 8% European
Languages: Nauruan, a distinct Pacific Island language (official); English widely understood, spoken and used for most government and commercial purposes
Religions: Christian (two-thirds Nauruan Protestant, one-third Roman Catholic)
Birth Rate: 26.09/1,000 population (2003 est.)
Death Rate: 7.08/1,000 population (2003 est.)
Infant Mortality: 10.33 deaths/1,000 live births (2003 est.)
Life Expectancy at Birth: 58.41 years male, 65.66 years female (2003 est.)

Total Fertility Rate: 3.40 children born/woman (2003 est.)
Literacy: n.a.

■ GOVERNMENT

Leader(s): President Ludwig Scotty
Government Type: republic
Administrative Divisions: 14 districts
Nationhood: Jan. 31, 1968 (from UN trusteeship under Australia, New Zealand and UK; formerly known as Pleasant Island)
National Holiday: Independence Day, Jan. 31

■ ECONOMY

Overview: most resources are imported; has one of the highest per capita incomes in the Third World; the rehabilitation of mined land and the replacement of income from phosphates are serious long-term considerations
GDP: US$60 million; per capita US$5,000; real growth rate n.a. (2001 est.)
Inflation: n.a.
Industries: phosphate mining, financial services, coconuts
Labour Force: n.a.
Unemployment: 0%
Agriculture: coconuts; other agricultural activities are negligible; almost completely dependent on imports for food and water
Natural Resources: phosphates

■ FINANCE/TRADE

Currency: Australian dollar ($A) = 100 cents
International Reserves Excluding Gold: n.a.
Gold Reserves: n.a.
Budget: n.a.
Defence Expenditures: no formal defence structure
Education Expenditures: n.a.
External Debt: US$33.3 million (2002)
Exports: US$18 million (2002); commodities: phosphates; partners: Australia, New Zealand, South Korea, US
Imports: US$31 million (2002); commodities: food, fuel, manufacturers, building materials, machinery; partners: Australia, US, UK, Indonesia, India

■ COMMUNICATIONS

Daily Newspapers: none
Televisions: n.a.
Radios: n.a.
Telephones: n.a.
Internet: users: 300 (2002)

■ TRANSPORTATION

Motor Vehicles: n.a.
Roads: 30 km; 24 km paved
Railway: 5 km
Air Traffic: n.a.

Airports: 1, with a paved runway (2003 est.)

Canadian Embassy: c/o The Canadian High Commission, Commonwealth Ave, Canberra A.C.T. 2600, Australia. Tel: (011-61-2) 6270-4000. Fax: (011-61-2) 6273-3285. e-mail: cnbra@dfait-maeci.gc.ca
Embassy in Canada: c/o Australian High Commission, 50 O'Connor St, Ste 710, Ottawa ON K1P 6L2. Tel: (613) 236-0841. Fax: (613) 236-4376. e-mail: n.a.

Nepal

Long-Form Name: Kingdom of Nepal
Capital: Kathmandu

■ GEOGRAPHY

Area: 140,800 sq. km
Coastline: none: landlocked
Climate: varies from cool summers and severe winters in north to subtropical summers and mild winters in south
Environment: contains eight of the world's 10 highest peaks; flooding, drought, landslides; deforestation; soil erosion; water pollution
Terrain: flat river plain of the Ganges in south, central hilly region, rugged Himalayas in north
Land Use: arable land: 20.27%, permanent crops: 0.49%, other: 79.24%; includes 11,350 sq. km irrigated
Location: SC Asia, bordering on India and Tibet

■ PEOPLE

Population: 26,469,569 (July 2003 est.)
Nationality: Nepalese
Age Structure: 0–14 yrs: 39.7%; 15–64: 56.7%; 65+: 3.6% (2003 est.)
Population Growth Rate: 2.26% (2003 est.)
Net Migration: 0 migrants/1,000 population (2003 est.)
Ethnic Groups: Newars, Indians, Tibetans, Gurungs, Magars, Tamangs, Bhotias, Rais, Limbus, Sherpas, as well as many smaller groups
Languages: Nepali (official); 20 languages divided into numerous dialects
Religions: 90% Hindu, 5% Buddhist, 3% Muslim, 2% other; only official Hindu state in the world, although no sharp distinction between many Hindu and Buddhist groups; small groups of Muslims and Christians
Birth Rate: 32.46/1,000 population (2003 est.)
Death Rate: 9.84/1,000 population (2003 est.)
Infant Mortality: 70.57 deaths/1,000 live births (2003 est.)
Life Expectancy at Birth: 59.36 years male, 58.63 years female (2003 est.)
Total Fertility Rate: 4.39 children born/woman (2003 est.)

Literacy: 44.0% (2002)

■ GOVERNMENT

Leader(s): King Gyanendra Bir Bikram Shah Dev, Prime Minister Sher Bahadur Deuba
Government Type: parliamentary democracy
Administrative Divisions: 14 zones (anchal, sing. & pl.)
Nationhood: 1768, unified by Prithvi Narayan Shah
National Holiday: Birthday of His Majesty the King, July 7

■ ECONOMY

Overview: one of the poorest and most underdeveloped countries in the world; agriculture provides the backbone of the economy, employing more than 80% of the population; there have been attempts to expand into other economic sectors
GDP: US$37.32 billion, per capita US$1,400; real growth rate -0.6% (2002 est.)
Inflation: 2.8% (2001)
Industries: accounts for 22% of GDP; small rice, jute, sugar and oilseed mills, cigarettes, textiles, cement, brick; tourism, carpet production
Labour Force: 11.3 million (2002); 81% agriculture, 16% services, 3% industry
Unemployment: 1.1% (2001)
Agriculture: accounts for 41% of GDP and 80% of workforce; farm products—rice, corn, wheat, sugar cane, root crops, milk, buffalo meat; not self-sufficient in food, particularly in drought years
Natural Resources: quartz, water, timber, hydroelectric potential, scenic beauty; small deposits of lignite, copper, cobalt, iron ore

■ FINANCE/TRADE

Currency: rupee (NRs) = 100 paisa
International Reserves Excluding Gold: US$1.375 billion (Jan. 2004)
Gold Reserves: 0.153 million fine troy ounces (Jan. 2004)
Budget: revenues US$665 million; expenditures US$1.1 billion, capital expenditures US$ n.a. (2000 est.)
Defence Expenditures: 8.6% of central government expenditure (2002)
Education Expenditures: 13.9% of central government expenditure (2002)
External Debt: US$2.953 billion (2002)
Exports: US$660 million (2003); commodities: clothing, carpets, leather goods, grain; partners: India, US, Germany
Imports: US$1.748 billion (2003); commodities: petroleum products 20%, fertilizer 11%, machinery and equipment 10%; partners: India, Singapore, China, Hong Kong

■ COMMUNICATIONS

Daily Newspapers: 12/1,000 inhabitants (2000)
Televisions: 8/1,000 inhabitants (2002)
Radios: 39/1,000 inhabitants (2001)
Telephones: 14 lines/1,000 inhabitants (2002)
Internet: hosts: 1,206 (2002); users: 80,000 (2002)

■ TRANSPORTATION

Motor Vehicles: n.a.
Roads: 13,223 km; 4,073 km paved
Railway: 59 km
Air Traffic: 681,000 passengers carried (2002)
Airports: 45; 9 have paved runways (2003 est.)

Canadian Embassy: The Canadian Embassy to Nepal, c/o The Canadian Cooperation Office, Lazimpat, Kathmandu, Nepal; mailing address: P.O. Box 4574, Kathmandu, Nepal. Tel: (011-9771) 415-193. Fax: (011-9771) 410-422. e-mail: cco@cco.org.np
Embassy in Canada: Embassy of the Kingdom of Nepal, 2131 Leroy Place NW, Washington DC 20008, USA. Tel: (202) 667 4550. Fax: (202) 667-5534. e-mail: nepali@erols.com

---

Netherlands

Long-Form Name: Kingdom of the Netherlands
Capital: Amsterdam; seat of government: The Hague

■ GEOGRAPHY

Area: 41,526 sq. km
Coastline: 451 km
Climate: temperate; marine; cool summers and mild winters
Environment: nearly half of the land area is below sea level and protected from the North Sea by dikes; water and air pollution
Terrain: mostly coastal lowland and reclaimed land (polders); some hills in southeast
Land Use: arable land: 26.53%, permanent crops: 1.03%, other: 72.44%; includes 5,650 sq. km irrigated
Location: NW Europe, bordering on North Sea

■ PEOPLE

Population: 16,150,511 (July 2003 est.)
Nationality: Dutchman, Dutchwoman
Age Structure: 0–14 yrs: 18.2%; 15–64: 67.9%; 65+: 13.9% (2003 est.)
Population Growth Rate: 0.50% (2003 est.)
Net Migration: 2.35 migrants/1,000 population (2003 est.)
Ethnic Groups: 91% Dutch, 9% Moroccans, Turks and others
Languages: Dutch, Frisian

Religions: 62% Christianity, of which 34% is Roman Catholic and 25% is Protestant; most of the rest do not profess a religion
Birth Rate: 11.31/1,000 population (2003 est.)
Death Rate: 8.66/1,000 population (2003 est.)
Infant Mortality: 4.26 deaths/1,000 live births (2003 est.)
Life Expectancy at Birth: 75.85 years male, 81.76 years female (2003 est.)
Total Fertility Rate: 1.65 children born/woman (2003 est.)
Literacy: approaching 100% (2002)

■ GOVERNMENT

Leader(s): Head of State: Queen Beatrix, Premier Jan Peter Balkenende
Government Type: constitutional monarchy
Administrative Divisions: 12 provinces (provincien, sing. provincie); dependent areas: Aruba, Netherlands Antilles
Nationhood: 1579 (from Spain)
National Holiday: Queen's Day, Apr. 30

■ ECONOMY

Overview: a highly developed and affluent economy based on private enterprise; numerous government-backed welfare programs; trade and financial sectors are the strongest part of the economy
GDP: US$437.8 billion, per capita US$27,200; real growth rate 0.2% (2002)
Inflation: 3.4% (2002 est.)
Industries: contributes 26% to the GDP (2001 est.); agro-industries, metal and engineering products, electrical machinery and equipment, chemicals, petroleum, fishing, construction, micro-electronics
Labour Force: 7.5 million (2002); 73% community, social and business services, 23% industry, 4% agriculture
Unemployment: 4.2% (Jan. 2004)
Agriculture: accounts for 3% of GDP (2001 est.) and 4% of labour force; animal production predominates; crops—grains, potatoes, sugar beets, fruits, vegetables; shortages of grain, fats and oils
Natural Resources: natural gas, crude oil, fertile soil

■ FINANCE/TRADE

Currency: guilder, gulden or florin (f.) = 100 cents; Euro (€); on January 1, 2002 the Euro became the sole currency for everyday transactions.
International Reserves Excluding Gold: US$11.130 billion (Jan. 2004)
Gold Reserves: 24.996 million fine troy ounces (Jan. 2004)

Budget: revenues US$134 billion; expenditures US$134 billion, including capital expenditures of US$ n.a. (2001 est.)
Defence Expenditures: 4.0% of central government expenditures (2002)
Education Expenditures: 10.4% of total government expenditures (2002)
External Debt: none
Exports: US$222.406 billion (2002); commodities; agricultural products, processed foods and tobacco, natural gas, chemicals, metal products, textiles, clothing; partners: EU (Germany, Benelux, UK, France, Italy)
Imports: US$193.784 billion (2002); commodities: raw materials and semi-finished products, consumer goods, transportation equipment, crude oil, food products; partners: Germany, Benelux, UK, France, US

■ COMMUNICATIONS

Daily Newspapers: 306/1,000 inhabitants (2000)
Televisions: 648/1,000 inhabitants (2002)
Radios: 980/1,000 inhabitants (2001)
Telephones: 618 lines/1,000 inhabitants (2002)
Internet: hosts: 3,137,203 (2002); users: 8.2 million (2002)

■ TRANSPORTATION

Motor Vehicles: 6,870,000; 6,170,000 passenger cars
Roads: 116,500 km; 104,850 km paved
Railway: 2,808 km
Air Traffic: 22,931,000 passengers carried (2002)
Airports: 28; 21 have paved runways (2003 est.)

Canadian Embassy: The Canadian Embassy, Sophialaan 7, 2514JP, The Hague, Netherlands. Tel: (011-31-70) 311-1600. Fax: (011-31-70) 311-1620. e-mail: hague@dfait-maeci.gc.ca
Embassy in Canada: Embassy of the Kingdom of the Netherlands, 350 Albert St, Ste 2020, Ottawa ON K1R 1A4. Tel: (613) 237-5030. Fax: (613) 237-6471. e-mail: nlgovott@netcom.ca

Netherlands Antilles

Long-Form Name: Netherlands Antilles
Capital: Willemstad

■ GEOGRAPHY

Area: 960 sq. km, 2 island groups
Climate: tropical maritime, moderated by northeasterly trade winds, short rainy season
Land Use: arable land: 10%, permanent crops: 0%, other: 90%; includes n.a. sq. km irrigated
Location: West Indies, just north of Venezuela

■ PEOPLE

Population: 216,226 (July 2003 est.)

Nationality: Netherlands Antillean, or Dutch Antillean
Ethnic Groups: mixed African 85%, Carib Indian, European, Latin, Oriental
Languages: Dutch (official), Papiamento (derived from Dutch, Spanish, Portuguese), English

■ **GOVERNMENT**

Colony/Territory of: Dependent Territory of the Netherlands
Leader(s): Chief of State: Queen Beatrix, Governor Frits Goedgedrag, Prime Minister Etienne Ys
Government Type: dependency with internal self-government; the Dutch government retains responsibility for defense and foreign affairs.
National Holiday: Queen's Day, Apr. 30

■ **ECONOMY**

Overview: unlike many Latin American countries, the Netherlands Antilles has avoided crushing external debt; Curaçao has one of the largest ship-repair dry docks in the western hemisphere; almost all consumer goods must be imported; chief trading partner: UK

■ **FINANCE/TRADE**

Currency: Netherlands Antilles guilder, gulden or florin = 100 cents; also the Euro

Canadian Embassy: c/o The Canadian Embassy, 7, 2514JP The Hague, Netherlands. Tel: (011-31-70) 311-1600. Fax: (011-31-70) 311-1620. e-mail: hague@dfait-maeci.gc.ca
Representative to Canada: c/o Embassy of the Kingdom of the Netherlands, 350 Albert St, Ste 2020, Ottawa ON K1R 1A4. Tel: (613) 237-5030. Fax: (613) 237-6471. e-mail: nlgovott@netcom.ca

New Caledonia

Long-Form Name: Territory of New Caledonia and Dependencies
Capital: Nouméa

■ **GEOGRAPHY**

Area: 19,060 sq. km (a peninsula and three small islands)
Climate: humid, subtropical maritime, modified by southeast trade winds
Land Use: arable land: 0.38%, permanent crops: 0.33%, other: 99.29%; includes 160 sq. km irrigated
Location: SW Pacific Ocean (Melanesia), E of Australia

■ **PEOPLE**

Population: 210,798 (July 2003 est.)
Nationality: New Caledonian

Ethnic Groups: 42.5% Melanesian, 37.1% European, 8.4% Wallisian, 3.8% Polynesian, 3.6% Indonesian, 1.6% Vietnamese, 3% other
Languages: French (official), 28 Melanesian and Polynesian languages

■ **GOVERNMENT**

Colony/Territory of: Overseas Territory of France
Leader(s): President Jacques Chirac (France), High Commissioner Daniel Constantin
Government Type: overseas territory of France since 1956
National Holiday: Taking of the Bastille, July 14

■ **ECONOMY**

Overview: only a negligible portion of the land is arable; and most food must be imported; the backbone of the economy is nickel export

■ **FINANCE/TRADE**

Currency: CFP franc = 100 centimes

Canadian Embassy: c/o The Canadian Embassy, 35-37 avenue Montaigne 75008 Paris, France. Tel: (011-33-1) 44-43-29-00. Fax: (011-33-1) 44-43-29-99. e-mail: paris@dfait-maeci.gc.ca
Representative to Canada: c/o Embassy of France, 42 Sussex Dr, Ottawa ON K1M 2C9. Tel: (613) 789-1795. Fax: (613) 562-3735. e-mail: politique@ambafrance-ca.org

New Zealand

Long-Form Name: New Zealand
Capital: Wellington

■ **GEOGRAPHY**

Area: 268,680 sq. km
Coastline: 15,134 km
Climate: temperate with sharp regional contrasts
Environment: earthquakes are common though usually not severe; deforestation and soil degradation are increasing; occasional volcanic activity
Terrain: predominantly mountainous with some large coastal plains
Land Use: arable land: 5.8%, permanent crops: 6.44%, other: 87.76%; includes 2,850 sq. km irrigated
Location: SE of Australia, bordering on Tasman Sea, Pacific Ocean

■ **PEOPLE**

Population: 3,951,307 (July 2003 est.)
Nationality: New Zealander
Age Structure: 0–14 yrs: 21.9%; 15–64: 66.5%; 65+: 11.6% (2003 est.)
Population Growth Rate: 1.09% (2003 est.)
Net Migration: 4.26 migrants/1,000 population (2003 est.)

Ethnic Groups: 79.1% European, 9.7% Maori, 3.8% Pacific Islander, 7.4% other
Languages: English (official), Maori
Religions: 75% Christian, 18% unspecified, 7% Hindu, Confucian, other
Birth Rate: 14.14/1,000 population (2003 est.)
Death Rate: 7.54/1,000 population (2003 est.)
Infant Mortality: 6.07 deaths/1,000 live births (2003 est.)
Life Expectancy at Birth: 75.34 years male, 81.44 years female (2003 est.)
Total Fertility Rate: 1.79 children born/woman (2003 est.)
Literacy: approaching 100% (2002)

■ GOVERNMENT

Leader(s): Head of State: Queen Elizabeth II, Governor General Silvia Cartwright, Prime Minister Helen Clark
Government Type: parliamentary democracy
Administrative Divisions: 93 counties, 9 districts, 3 town districts; dependent areas includes the Cook Islands, the Kermadec Islands, Niue, the Ross Dependency (uninhabited except for scientific personnel), Tokelau
Nationhood: Sept. 26, 1907 (from UK)
National Holiday: Waitangi Day, Feb. 6

■ ECONOMY

Overview: government has been reorienting from an agrarian to an open, free-market economy that can compete in the global community; inflation and unemployment have been reduced
GDP: US$78.4 billion, per capita US$20,100; real growth rate 3.3% (2002 est.)
Inflation: 2.7% (2002)
Industries: accounts for 23% of GDP; food processing, wool production, wood and paper products, textiles, machinery, transportation equipment, banking and insurance, tourism, mining
Labour Force: 2.0 million (2002); 6.5% community, social and business services, 25% industry, 10% agriculture
Unemployment: 4.5% (Nov. 2003)
Agriculture: accounts for 8% of GDP and 10% of workforce; livestock predominates: wool, meat, dairy products; crops: wheat, barley, potatoes, pulses, fruit and vegetables; fish; surplus producer of farm products
Natural Resources: natural gas, iron ore, sand, coal, timber, hydroelectricity, gold, limestone

■ FINANCE/TRADE

Currency: New Zealand dollar (NZ$) = 100 cents
International Reserves Excluding Gold: US$4.645 billion (Jan. 2004)
Gold Reserves: none (Jan. 2002)

Budget: revenues US$29.2 billion; expenditures US$31.2 billion, including capital expenditures US$ n.a. (2002 est.)
Defence Expenditures: 4.0% of central government expenditure (2002)
Education Expenditures: 16.29% of central government expenditure (2000)
External Debt: US$33.0 billion (2002 est.)
Exports: US$16.209 billion (2003 est.); commodities: wool, lamb, mutton, beef, fruit, fish, cheese, manufactures, chemicals, forestry products; partners: Japan, Australia, US, UK, South Korea, China
Imports: US$18.207 billion (2003); commodities: petroleum, consumer goods, motor vehicles, industrial equipment; partners: Australia, US, Japan, UK, China, Germany

■ COMMUNICATIONS

Daily Newspapers: 362/1,000 inhabitants (2000)
Televisions: 557/1,000 inhabitants (2002)
Radios: 997/1,000 inhabitants (2001)
Telephones: 448 lines/1,000 inhabitants (2002)
Internet: hosts: 432,957 (2002); users: 1.908 million (2002)

■ TRANSPORTATION

Motor Vehicles: 2,650,000; 2,200,000 passenger cars
Roads: 92,053 km; 57,809 km paved
Railway: 3,898 km
Air Traffic: 12,240,000 passengers carried (2002)
Airports: 113; 46 have paved runways (2003 est.)

Canadian Embassy: The Canadian High Commission, 61 Molesworth St, 3rd Floor, Thorndon, Wellington; mailing address: P.O. Box 12049, Thorndon, Wellington, New Zealand. Tel: (011-64-4) 473-9577. Fax: (011-64-4) 471-2082. e-mail: wlgtn@dfait-maeci.gc.ca
Embassy in Canada: c/o New Zealand High Commission, Clarica Centre, 99 Bank St, Ste 727, Ottawa ON K1P 6G3. Tel: (613) 238-5991. Fax: (613) 238-5707. e-mail: info@nzhcottawa.org

---

Nicaragua

Long-Form Name: Republic of Nicaragua
Capital: Managua

■ GEOGRAPHY

Area: 129,494 sq. km
Coastline: 910 km
Climate: tropical in lowlands, cooler in highlands
Environment: subject to destructive earthquakes, volcanoes, landslides and occasional severe hurricanes; deforestation; soil erosion; water pollution

Terrain: extensive Atlantic coastal plains rising to central interior mountains; narrow Pacific coastal plain interrupted by volcanoes
Land Use: arable land: 20.24%, permanent crops: 2.38%, other: 77.38%; includes 880 sq. km irrigated
Location: Central (Latin) America, bordering on Caribbean Sea, Pacific Ocean

■ PEOPLE

Population: 5,128,517 (July 2003 est.)
Nationality: Nicaraguan
Age Structure: 0–14 yrs: 37.7%; 15–64: 59.2%; 65+: 3.0% (2003 est.)
Population Growth Rate: 2.03% (2003 est.)
Net Migration: -1.27 migrants/1,000 population (2003 est.)
Ethnic Groups: 69% mestizo, 17% white, 9% black, 5% Indian
Languages: Spanish (official); English- and Indian-speaking minorities on Atlantic coast
Religions: 95% Roman Catholic, 5% Protestant
Birth Rate: 26.29/1,000 population (2003 est.)
Death Rate: 4.69/1,000 population (2003 est.)
Infant Mortality: 31.39 deaths/1,000 live births (2003 est.)
Life Expectancy at Birth: 67.68 years male, 71.79 years female (2003 est.)
Total Fertility Rate: 3.00 children born/woman (2003 est.)
Literacy: 76.7% (2002)

■ GOVERNMENT

Leader(s): President Enrique Bolanos, Vice President Jose Rizo
Government Type: republic
Administrative Divisions: 15 departments (departamentos, sing. —departamento) and 2 autonomous regions (regiones autonomistas, sing. —region autonomista)
Nationhood: Sept. 15, 1821 (from Spain)
National Holiday: Independence Day, Sept. 15

■ ECONOMY

Overview: based on the export of coffee and cotton; government control is extensive, including the financial system, wholesale purchasing, production, sales, foreign trade and distribution of goods; many shortages; high inflation
GDP: US$11.16 billion, per capita US$2,200; real growth rate 1.1% (2002 est.)
Inflation: 3.7% (2002 est.)
Industries: accounts for 26% of GDP (2002); food processing, chemicals, metal products, textiles, clothing, petroleum refining and distribution, beverages, footwear
Labour Force: 2.2 million (2002); 43% services, 42% agriculture, 15% industry

Unemployment: 11.2%; underemployment approximately 36% (2002 est.)
Agriculture: accounts for 30% of GDP (2002); cash crops—coffee, bananas, sugar cane, cotton, tobacco; food crops—rice, corn, cassava, citrus fruit, beans; variety of animal products—beef, veal, pork, poultry, dairy; war has lowered self-sufficiency in food
Natural Resources: gold, silver, copper, tungsten, lead, zinc, timber, fish

■ FINANCE/TRADE

Currency: gold córdoba ($C) = 100 centavos
International Reserves Excluding Gold: US$539 million (Jan. 2004)
Gold Reserves: n.a.
Budget: revenues US$726 million; expenditures US$908 million, including capital expenditures US$ n.a. (2000 est.)
Defence Expenditures: 2.6% of central government expenditure (2002)
Education Expenditures: 13.0% of total government expenditures (2002)
External Debt: US$6.485 billion (2002)
Exports: US$596 million (2002); commodities: coffee, cotton, sugar, bananas, seafood, meat, chemicals; partners: US, Germany, Canada, Costa Rica, Honduras
Imports: US$1.795 billion (2002); commodities: petroleum, food, chemicals, machinery, clothing; partners: US, Costa Rica, Venezuela, Guatemala, Mexico

■ COMMUNICATIONS

Daily Newspapers: 30/1,000 inhabitants (2000)
Televisions: 123/1,000 inhabitants (2002)
Radios: 270/1,000 inhabitants (2001)
Telephones: 32 lines/1,000 inhabitants (2002)
Internet: hosts: 3,370 (2002); users: 90,000 (2002)

■ TRANSPORTATION

Motor Vehicles: 150,000; 65,000 passenger cars
Roads: 19,032 km; 2,094 km paved
Railway: 6 km
Air Traffic: 61,000 passengers carried (2002)
Airports: 176; 11 have paved runways (2003 est.)

Canadian Embassy: The Office of the Canadian Embassy, Costado Oriental de la Casa Nazareth, Una Quadra Arriba, Calle Noval, Managua. Mailing address: The Office of the Canadian Embassy, Apartado Postal 25, Managua, Nicaragua. Tel: (011-505) 268-0433. Fax: (011-505) 268-0437. e-mail: mngua@dfait-maeci.gc.ca
Embassy in Canada: c/o Embassy of the Republic of Nicaragua, 1627 New Hampshire Ave NW, Washington DC 20009, USA. Tel: (202) 939-6570. Fax: (202) 939-6545. e-mail: n.a.

Niger

Long-Form Name: Republic of Niger
Capital: Niamey

■ GEOGRAPHY

Area: 1,267,000 sq. km
Coastline: none: landlocked
Climate: mostly hot, dry, dusty; tropical in extreme south
Environment: recurrent drought and desertification severely affecting marginal agricultural activities; overgrazing; soil erosion
Terrain: desert and sand dunes; hills in north
Land Use: arable land: 3.94%, permanent crops: 0%, other: 96.06%; includes 660 sq. km irrigated
Location: WC Africa

■ PEOPLE

Population: 11,058,590 (July 2003 est.)
Nationality: Nigerien
Age Structure: 0–14 yrs: 47.6%; 15–64: 50.2%; 65+: 2.2% (2002 est.)
Population Growth Rate: 2.71% (2003 est.)
Net Migration: -0.69 migrants/1,000 population (2003 est.)
Ethnic Groups: 56% Hausa; 22% Djerma; 8.5% Fula; 8% Tuareg; 4.3% Beri Beri (Kanouri); 1.2% Arab, Toubou and Gourmantche; about 1,200 French expatriates
Languages: French (official); Hausa (50%), Djerma, also Tuareg, Fulani
Religions: 80% Muslim, remainder indigenous beliefs and Christians
Birth Rate: 49.54/1,000 population (2003 est.)
Death Rate: 21.71/1,000 population (2003 est.)
Infant Mortality: 123.64 deaths/1,000 live births (2003 est.)
Life Expectancy at Birth: 42.29 years male, 49.12 years female (2003 est.)
Total Fertility Rate: 6.91 children born/woman (2003 est.)
Literacy: 17.1% (2002)

■ GOVERNMENT

Leader(s): President Mamadou Tandja, Prime Minister Hama Amadou
Government Type: republic
Administrative Divisions: 7 departments (departements, sing. —departement); 1 capital district (capitale district)
Nationhood: Aug. 3, 1960 (from France)
National Holiday: Republic Day, Dec. 18

■ ECONOMY

Overview: about 90% of the population is engaged in livestock rearing and farming; depends heavily on exploitation of uranium deposits, thus vulnerable to demand for uranium; increasing external debt is a problem; GDP growth cannot keep pace with the rapid population growth
GDP: US$8.713 billion, per capita US$800; real growth rate 2.9% (2002 est.)
Inflation: 3.0% (2002)
Industries: accounts for 17% of GDP (2000); cement, brick, rice mills, small cotton gins, textiles, chemicals, oilseed presses, slaughterhouses and a few other small light industries; uranium production began in 1971
Labour Force: 5.4 million (2002); 90% agriculture, 6% industry, 4% government
Unemployment: n.a.
Agriculture: accounts for 41% of GDP (2000) and 90% of labour force; cash crops—cowpeas, cotton, peanuts; food crops—millet, sorghum, cassava, rice; livestock—cattle, sheep, goats, camels, poultry; self-sufficient in food except in drought years
Natural Resources: uranium, coal, iron ore, tin, phosphates, gold, petroleum

■ FINANCE/TRADE

Currency: Communauté financière africaine franc (CFAF) = 100 centimes
International Reserves Excluding Gold: US$40 million (Nov. 2003)
Gold Reserves: 0.011 million fine troy ounces (Aug. 2000)
Budget: revenues US$320 million; expenditures US$320 million, including capital expenditures of US$178 million (2002 est.)
Defence Expenditures: 1.1% of GDP (2002)
Education Expenditures: n.a.
External Debt: US$1.797 billion (2002)
Exports: US$282 million (2002); commodities: uranium 76%, livestock, cowpeas, onions, hides, skins; partners: France, Nigeria, Spain, US
Imports: US$400 million (2002); commodities: petroleum products, primary materials, machinery, vehicles and parts, electronic equipment, pharmaceuticals, chemical products, cereals, foodstuffs; partners: France, Côte d'Ivoire, Nigeria, US

■ COMMUNICATIONS

Daily Newspapers: less than 1/1,000 inhabitants (2000)
Televisions: 27/1,000 inhabitants (2002)
Radios: 121/1,000 inhabitants (2001)
Telephones: 2 lines/1,000 inhabitants (2002)
Internet: hosts: 119 (2002); users: 15,000 (2002)

■ TRANSPORTATION

Motor Vehicles: 51,600; 37,500 passenger cars

Roads: 10,100 km; 798 km paved
Railway: none
Air Traffic: 46,000 passengers carried (2002)
Airports: 27; 9 have paved runways (2003 est.)

Canadian Embassy: Office of the Canadian Embassy, Boulevard Mali Béro, Niamey, Niger; mailing address: Box 362, Niamey, Niger. Tel: (011-227) 75-36-86. Fax: (011-227) 75-31-07. e-mail: niamy@dfait-maeci.gc.ca
Embassy in Canada: Embassy of the Republic of Niger, 38 Blackburn Ave, Ottawa ON K1N 8A3. Tel: (613) 232-4291. Fax: (613) 230-9808. e-mail: n.a.

Nigeria

Long-Form Name: Federal Republic of Nigeria
Capital: Abuja

■ GEOGRAPHY

Area: 923,768 sq. km
Coastline: 853 km
Climate: varies; equatorial in south, tropical in centre, arid in north
Environment: recent droughts in north severely affecting marginal agricultural activities; desertification; soil degradation, rapid deforestation
Terrain: southern lowlands merge into central hills and plateaus; mountains in southeast, plains in north
Land Use: arable land: 30.96%, permanent crops: 2.79%, other: 66.25%; includes 2,330 sq. km irrigated
Location: WC Africa, bordering on South Atlantic Ocean

■ PEOPLE

Population: 133,881,703 (July 2003 est.)
Nationality: Nigerian
Age Structure: 0–14 yrs: 43.6%; 15–64: 53.6%; 65+: 2.8% (2003 est.)
Population Growth Rate: 2.53% (2003 est.)
Net Migration: 0.26 migrants/1,000 population (2003 est.)
Ethnic Groups: more than 250 tribal groups; Hausa and Fulani of the north, Yoruba of the southwest and Ibos of the southeast make up 65% of the population; about 27,000 non-Africans
Languages: English (official); Hausa, Yoruba, Ibo, Fulani and several other languages also widely used
Religions: 50% Muslim, 40% Christian, 10% indigenous beliefs
Birth Rate: 38.75/1,000 population (2003 est.)
Death Rate: 13.76/1,000 population (2003 est.)

Infant Mortality: 71.35 deaths/1,000 live births (2003 est.)
Life Expectancy at Birth: 50.89 years male, 51.14 years female (2003 est.)
Total Fertility Rate: 5.40 children born/woman (2003 est.)
Literacy: 66.8% (2002)

■ GOVERNMENT

Leader(s): President Olusegun Obasanjo, Vice President Atiku Abubakar
Government Type: republic in transition from military to civilian rule.
Administrative Divisions: 36 states and 1 territory
Nationhood: Oct. 1, 1960 (from UK)
National Holiday: Independence Day, Oct. 1

■ ECONOMY

Overview: dependent on oil and vulnerable to oil prices; agricultural production cannot keep pace with rapid population growth and Nigeria, once a large exporter of food, must now import foodstuffs; high inflationary pressures are a concern; government efforts to reduce Nigeria's dependence on oil exports and to sustain non-inflationary economic growth have been hampered by inadequate new investment and endemic corruption
GDP: US$112.5 billion, per capita US$900; real growth rate 3.2% (2002 est.)
Inflation: 14.2% (2002 est.)
Industries: accounts for 20% of GDP (2002); crude oil, natural gas, coal, tin, columbite; palm oil, peanut, cotton, rubber, petroleum, wood, hides and skins; textiles, cement, building materials, food products, footwear, chemicals, printing, ceramics, steel
Labour Force: 52.9 million (2002); 70% agriculture, 20% services, 10% industry
Unemployment: n.a.
Agriculture: accounts for 45% of GDP (2002) and half of labour force; inefficient small-scale farming dominates; once a large net exporter of food and now an importer; cash crops—cocoa, peanuts, palm oil, rubber; food crops—corn, rice, sorghum, millet, cassava, yams, fishing and forestry, livestock
Natural Resources: crude oil, tin, columbite, iron ore, coal, limestone, lead, zinc, natural gas

■ FINANCE/TRADE

Currency: naira (N) = 100 kobo
International Reserves Excluding Gold: US$7.949 billion (Jan. 2004)
Gold Reserves: 0.687 million fine troy ounces (Jan. 2004)

Budget: revenues US$3.4 billion; expenditures US$3.6 billion, including capital expenditures of US$ n.a. (2000 est.)
Defence Expenditures: 1.0% of GDP (2002)
Education Expenditures: n.a.
External Debt: US$30.476 billion (2002)
Exports: US$19.243 billion (2003 est.); commodities: oil 95%, cocoa, palm kernels, rubber; partners: US, Spain, India, France, Brazil
Imports: US$11.027 billion (2003 est.); commodities: consumer goods, capital equipment, chemicals, raw materials; partners: UK, US, France, Germany, China

■ COMMUNICATIONS

Daily Newspapers: 24/1,000 inhabitants (2000)
Televisions: 103/1,000 inhabitants (2002)
Radios: 200/1,000 inhabitants (2001)
Telephones: 6 lines/1,000 inhabitants (2002)
Internet: hosts: 1,030 (2002); users: 420,000 (2002)

■ TRANSPORTATION

Motor Vehicles: 970,000; 590,200 passenger cars
Roads: 194,394 km; 60,068 km paved, but much of the road system is barely usable.
Railway: 3,557 km
Air Traffic: 512,000 passengers carried (2002)
Airports: 70; 36 have paved runways (2003 est.)

Canadian Embassy: The Canadian High Commission, 3A Bobo St, Maitama, Abuja FCT, Nigeria. Tel: (011-234-9) 413-9910. Fax: (011-234-9) 413-9911. e-mail: abuja@dfait-maeci.gc.ca
Embassy in Canada: High Commission for the Federal Republic of Nigeria, 295 Metcalfe St, Ottawa, ON K2P 1R9. Tel: (613) 236-0522. Fax: (613) 236-0529. e-mail: hc@nigeriahighcommottawa.com

---

Niue

Long-Form Name: Niue
Capital: Alofi

■ GEOGRAPHY

Area: 260 sq. km, world's largest uplifted coral island
Climate: tropical maritime, modified by southeasterly trade winds
Land Use: arable land: 19.23%, permanent crops: 7.69%, other: 73.08%; includes n.a. sq. km irrigated
Location: Pacific Ocean, NE of New Zealand

■ PEOPLE

Population: 2,145 (July 2003 est.)
Nationality: Niuean

Ethnic Groups: Polynesian
Languages: English, Polynesian closely related to Tongan and Samoan

■ GOVERNMENT

Colony/Territory of: Self-governing territory in free association with New Zealand
Leader(s): Head of State: Queen Elizabeth II, New Zealand High Commissioner Sandra Lee-Vercoe, Premier Young Vivian
Government Type: self-governing parliamentary democracy in free association with New Zealand
National Holiday: Waitangi Day, Feb. 6

■ ECONOMY

Overview: heavily dependent on aid from New Zealand; government expenditures regularly exceed revenues; agriculture includes coconuts, honey, limes, root crops, livestock; chief trading partner: New Zealand

■ FINANCE/TRADE

Currency: New Zealand dollar = 100 cents

Canadian Embassy: c/o The Canadian High Commission, 3rd Fl, 61 Molesworth St, Thorndon, Wellington, New Zealand; Mailing address: c/o P.O. Box 12-049, Thorndon, Wellington, New Zealand. Tel: (011-64-4) 473-9577. Fax: (011-64-4) 471-2082. e-mail: wlgtn@dfait-maeci.gc.ca
Representative to Canada: c/o New Zealand High Commission, Clarica Centre, 99 Bank St, Ste 727, Ottawa ON K1P 6G3. Tel: (613) 238-5991. Fax: (613) 238-5707. e-mail: nzhcott@istar.ca

---

Norfolk Island

Long-Form Name: Territory of Norfolk Island
Capital: Kingston (administrative centre), Burnt Pine (commercial centre)

■ GEOGRAPHY

Area: 34.6 sq. km
Climate: subtropical, mild, little seasonal variation
Land Use: arable land: 0%, permanent crops: 0%, other: 100%; includes no irrigated land
Location: S Pacific Ocean, E of Australia

■ PEOPLE

Population: 1,853 (July 2003 est.)
Nationality: Norfolk Islander
Ethnic Groups: majority descendants of Polynesians and British (the latter crew members of the British naval ship *Bounty*)
Languages: English (official), Norfolk (a mixture of 18th-century English and ancient Tahitian)

■ GOVERNMENT

Colony/Territory of: Dependent Territory of Australia
Leader(s): Queen Elizabeth II, represented by Administrator Grant Tambling
Government Type: a largely self-governing dependency, territory of Australia
National Holiday: Pitcairners' Arrival Day Anniversary, June 8

■ ECONOMY

Overview: tourism is backbone of economy; revenues from tourism have helped the agricultural sector become self-sufficient in beef, poultry and eggs; export of indigenous fruit and vegetables

■ FINANCE/TRADE

Currency: Australian dollar = 100 cents

Canadian Embassy: c/o The Canadian High Commission, Commonwealth Ave, Canberra, A.C.T. 2600, Australia. Tel: (011-61-2) 6270-4000. Fax: (011-61-2) 6273-3285. e-mail: cnbra@dfait-maeci.gc.ca
Representative to Canada: c/o Australian High Commission, 50 O'Connor St, Ste 710, Ottawa ON K1P 6L2. Tel: (613) 236-0841. Fax: (613) 236-4376. e-mail: n.a.

Northern Marianas

Long-Form Name: The Commonwealth of the Northern Mariana Islands
Capital: Saipan

■ GEOGRAPHY

Area: 477 sq. km (combined land area of 14 islands)
Coastline: 1,482 km
Climate: tropical maritime, moderated by northeasterly trade winds; little seasonal temperature variation
Terrain: southern islands are limestone with level terraces and fringing coral reefs; northern islands are volcanic
Land Use: arable land: 15.22%, permanent crops: 6.52%, other: 78.26%; no irrigated land
Location: Pacific Ocean, E of the Philippines

■ PEOPLE

Population: 80,006 (July 2003 est.)
Nationality: no descriptive term; American citizenship
Ethnic Groups: Chamorro, Carolinians and other Micronesians, Caucasian, Japanese, Chinese, Korean
Languages: English (official), Chamorro, Carolinian, Japanese; 86% of the population speaks a language other than English at home

■ GOVERNMENT

Colony/Territory of: Commonwealth in political union with the United States
Leader(s): Head of State: President George W. Bush Jr. (US), Governor Juan N. Babauta
Government Type: commonwealth in political union with the US; self-governing with locally elected governing body
National Holiday: Commonwealth Day, Jan. 8

■ ECONOMY

Overview: economy benefits from US financial assistance, but the rate of funding has declined as local revenues have increased; tourism is growing in importance and now employs approximately 50% of the workforce; agriculture: cattle, coconuts, breadfruit, vegetables

■ FINANCE/TRADE

Currency: American dollar = 100 cents

Canadian Embassy: c/o The Canadian Embassy, 501 Pennsylvania Ave. NW, Washington DC 20001, USA. Tel: (202) 682-1740. Fax: (202) 456-7726. e-mail: wshdc-outpack@dfait-maeci.gc.ca
Representative to Canada: c/o Embassy of the United States of America, 490 Sussex Drive, PO Box 866, Station "B," Ottawa, ON, K1P 5T1. Tel: (613) 238-5335. Fax: (613) 688-3080. e-mail inquiries are not accepted.

Norway

Long-Form Name: Kingdom of Norway
Capital: Oslo

■ GEOGRAPHY

Area: 324,220 sq. km
Coastline: 21,925 km (3,491 km mainland; 2,413 km large islands; 16,093 km long fjords; numerous small islands and minor indentations); one of the longest and most rugged coastlines in the world
Climate: temperate along coast, modified by North Atlantic Current; colder interior; rainy year-round on west coast
Environment: air and water pollution; acid rain damages forests and adversely affects lakes and threatens fish stocks
Terrain: glaciated; mostly high plateaus and rugged mountains broken by fertile valleys; small, scattered plains; coastline deeply indented by fjords; arctic tundra in north
Land Use: arable land: 2.94%, permanent crops: 0%, other: 97.06%; includes 1,270 sq. km irrigated
Location: N Europe, bordering on Norwegian Sea, North Sea

■ PEOPLE

Population: 4,546,123 (July 2003 est.)
Nationality: Norwegian
Age Structure: 0–14 yrs: 19.9%; 15–64: 65.2%; 65+: 14.9% (2003 est.)
Population Growth Rate: 0.46% (2003 est.)
Net Migration: 2.09 migrants/1,000 population (2003 est.)
Ethnic Groups: Germanic (Nordic, Alpine, Baltic) and racial-cultural minority of 20,000 Lapps
Languages: Norwegian (official); small Lapp- and Finnish-speaking minorities
Religions: Lutheran (88%, state church), other Protestant and Roman Catholic 4%, none 3.2%, other 4.8%
Birth Rate: 12.17/1,000 population (2003 est.)
Death Rate: 9.72/1,000 population (2003 est.)
Infant Mortality: 3.87 deaths/1,000 live births (2003 est.)
Life Expectancy at Birth: 76.15 years male, 82.22 years female (2003 est.)
Total Fertility Rate: 1.80 children born/woman (2003 est.)
Literacy: approaching 100% (2002)

■ GOVERNMENT

Leader(s): King Harald V, Prime Minister Kjell Magne Bondevik
Government Type: constitutional monarchy
Administrative Divisions: 19 provinces (fylker, sing. —fylke); dependent areas include Bouvet Island (uninhabited), Jan Mayen (uninhabited), Peter I Island (uninhabited), Queen Maud Land (uninhabited), Svalbard
Nationhood: Oct. 26, 1905 (from Sweden)
National Holiday: Constitution Day, May 17

■ ECONOMY

Overview: a small country with high dependence on international trade; a prosperous capitalist nation that has extensive welfare measures; concerns are the ageing population, increased economic integration with Europe and the balance between private and public influence in economic decisions
GDP: US$149.1 billion, per capita US$33,000; real growth rate 1.0% (2002)
Inflation: 3.0% (2001)
Industries: accounts for 31% of GDP (2000); petroleum and gas, food processing, ship-building, pulp and paper products, metal, chemicals, timber, mining, textiles, fishing
Labour Force: 2.4 million (2002); 74% community, social and business services, 22% industry, 4% agriculture, forestry and fishing
Unemployment: 4.3% (Aug. 2003)
Agriculture: accounts for 2% of GDP (2000); among world's top 10 fishing nations; livestock output exceeds value of crops; over half of food needs imported. Domestic products include barley, other grains, potatoes, beef, milk and fish.
Natural Resources: rich in natural resources: crude oil, copper, natural gas, pyrites, nickel, iron ore, zinc, lead, fish, timber, hydro power

■ FINANCE/TRADE

Currency: krone (pl. kroner) (NKr) = 100 oere
International Reserves Excluding Gold: US$25.181 billion (Jan. 2004)
Gold Reserves: 1.184 million fine troy ounces (Jan. 2004)
Budget: revenues US$71.7 billion, expenditures US$57.6 billion, including capital expenditures US$ n.a. (2000)
Defence Expenditures: 5.9% of central government expenditure (2002)
Education Expenditures: 16.2% of total government expenditures (2002)
External Debt: none
Exports: US$66.293 billion (2003 est.); commodities: petroleum and petroleum products 25%, natural gas 11%, fish 7%, aluminum 6%, ships 3.5%, pulp and paper; partners: UK, France, Germany, Netherlands, Sweden, US
Imports: US$38.821 billion (2003 est.); commodities: machinery, fuels and lubricants, transportation equipment, chemicals, foodstuffs, clothing, ships; partners: Sweden, Germany, UK, Denmark, France, US

■ COMMUNICATIONS

Daily Newspapers: 569/1,000 inhabitants (2000)
Televisions: 884/1,000 inhabitants (2002)
Radios: 3,324/1,000 inhabitants (2001)
Telephones: 734 lines/1,000 inhabitants (2002)
Internet: hosts: 255,742 (2002); users: 2.288 million (2002)

■ TRANSPORTATION

Motor Vehicles: 2,300,000; 1,860,000 passenger cars
Roads: 91,454 km; 69,505 km paved
Railway: 4,178 km
Air Traffic: 13,706,000 passengers carried (2002)
Airports: 102; 66 have paved runways (2003 est.)

Canadian Embassy: The Canadian Embassy, Wergelandsveien #7, 0244 Oslo, Norway. Tel: (011-47) 22-99-53-00. Fax: (011-47) 22-99-53-01. e-mail: oslo@dfait-maeci.gc.ca
Embassy in Canada: Embassy of the Kingdom of Norway, Royal Bank Centre, 90 Sparks St, Ste 532, Ottawa ON K1P 5B4. Tel: (613) 238-6571. Fax: (613) 238-2765. e-mail: emb.ottawa@mfa.no

Oman

Long-Form Name: Sultanate of Oman
Capital: Masqat or Muscat

■ GEOGRAPHY

Area: 212,460 sq. km
Coastline: 2,092 km
Climate: dry desert; hot, humid along coast; hot, dry interior; strong southwest summer monsoon (May to Sept.) in far south
Environment: summer winds often raise large sandstorms and dust storms in interior; sparse natural freshwater resources are threatened by increasing soil salinity
Terrain: vast central desert plain, rugged mountains in north and south
Land Use: arable land: 0.08%, permanent crops: 0.22%, other: 99.7%; includes 620 sq. km irrigated
Location: SW Asia (Middle East), bordering on Arabian Sea

■ PEOPLE

Population: 2,807,125; includes 577,293 non-nationals (July 2003 est.)
Nationality: Omani
Age Structure: 0–14 yrs: 42.2%; 15–64: 55.4%; 65+: 2.4% (2003 est.)
Population Growth Rate: 3.38% (2003 est.)
Net Migration: 0.29 migrants/1,000 population (2003 est.)
Ethnic Groups: almost entirely Arab, with small Balochi, Zanzibari, Pakistani and Indian groups
Languages: Arabic (official); English, Balochi, Urdu, Indian dialects
Religions: 75% Ibadhi Muslim; remainder Sunni Muslim, Shi'a Muslim, Hindu minority
Birth Rate: 37.47/1,000 population (2003 est.)
Death Rate: 3.97/1,000 population (2003 est.)
Infant Mortality: 21.01 deaths/1,000 live births (2003 est.)
Life Expectancy at Birth: 70.40 years male, 74.86 years female (2003 est.)
Total Fertility Rate: 5.94 children born/woman (2003 est.)
Literacy: 74.4 (2002)

■ GOVERNMENT

Leader(s): Sultan and Prime Minister Qaboos Bin Sa'id
Government Type: absolute monarchy; independent, with residual UK influence
Administrative Divisions: 6 regions (mintaqat, sing. —mintaqah) and 2 governorates (muhafazat, sing. —muhafazah)
Nationhood: 1650, expulsion of the Portuguese
National Holiday: National Day (Birthday of Sultan Qaboos), Nov. 18

■ ECONOMY

Overview: depends on the success of its oil industry, which has 15 years' supply at the current rate of extraction; subsistence agriculture is the major employment, and the general populace relies on imported food
GDP: US$22.4 billion, per capita US$8,300; real growth rate 2.2% (2002 est.)
Inflation: -0.5% (2002 est.)
Industries: accounts for 40% of GDP; crude oil production and refining, natural gas production, construction, cement, copper
Labour Force: 700,000 (2002); 50% agriculture, 21.8% industry, 28.6% services; 58% of labour force are non-Omani
Unemployment: n.a.
Agriculture: accounts for 3% of GDP and 50% of labour force (including fishing); less than 2% of land cultivated; largely subsistence farming (dates, limes, bananas, alfalfa, vegetables, camels, cattle); not self-sufficient in food
Natural Resources: crude oil, copper, asbestos, some marble, limestone, chromium, gypsum, natural gas

■ FINANCE/TRADE

Currency: Omani rial (RO) = 1,000 baiza
International Reserves Excluding Gold: US$3.689 billion (Jan. 2004)
Gold Reserves: 0.001 million fine troy ounces (Jan. 2004)
Budget: revenues US$9.2 billion; expenditures US$6.9 billion, including capital expenditures of US$ n.a. (2000 est.)
Defence Expenditures: 40.70% of central government expenditure (2002)
Education Expenditures: 15.17% of central government expenditure (2000)
External Debt: US$4.639 billion (2002)
Exports: US$11.172 billion (2002); commodities: petroleum, re-exports, processed copper, dates, nuts, fish; partners: Japan, South Korea, Thailand, China, United Arab Emirates, US
Imports: US$6.005 billion (2002); commodities: machinery, transportation equipment, manufactured goods, food, livestock, lubricants; partners: Japan, United Arab Emirates, UK, Germany, US, Italy.

■ COMMUNICATIONS

Daily Newspapers: 29/1,000 inhabitants (2000)
Televisions: 533/1,000 inhabitants (2002)
Radios: 621/1,000 inhabitants (2001)
Telephones: 84 lines/1,000 inhabitants (2002)
Internet: hosts: 676 (2002); users: 180,000 (2002)

■ TRANSPORTATION

Motor Vehicles: 300,000; 209,000 passenger cars
Roads: 34.965 km; 9,673 km paved
Railway: none
Air Traffic: 2,104,000 passengers carried (2002)
Airports: 139; 6 have paved runways (2003 est.)

Canadian Embassy: The Canadian Embassy to Oman, c/o The Canadian Embassy, P.O. Box 94321, Riyadh 11693, Saudi Arabia. Tel: (011-966-1) 488-2288. Fax: (011-966-1) 488-1997. e-mail: ryadh@dfait-maeci.gc.ca
Embassy in Canada: c/o Embassy of the Sultanate of Oman, 2535 Belmont Rd. NW, Washington DC 20008, USA. Tel: (202) 387-1980. Fax: (202) 745-4933. e-mail: n.a.

Pakistan

Long-Form Name: Islamic Republic of Pakistan
Capital: Islamabad

■ GEOGRAPHY

Area: 803,940 sq. km
Coastline: 1,046 km along Gulf of Oman and Arabian Sea
Climate: mostly hot, dry desert; temperate in northwest; arctic in north
Environment: frequent earthquakes, occasionally severe especially in north and west; flooding along the Indus after heavy rains (July and Aug.); deforestation; soil erosion; desertification; water pollution from raw sewage
Terrain: flat Indus plain in east; mountains in north and northwest; Balochistan plateau in west
Land Use: arable land: 27.81%, permanent crops: 0.79%, other: 71.4%; includes 180,000 sq. km irrigated
Location: SW Asia (Middle East), bordering on Arabian Sea

■ PEOPLE

Population: 150,694,740 (July 2003 est.)
Nationality: Pakistani
Age Structure: 0–14 yrs: 39.3%; 15–64: 56.5%; 65+: 4.2% (2003 est.)
Population Growth Rate: 2.01% (2003 est.)
Net Migration: -0.79 migrants/1,000 population (2003 est.)
Ethnic Groups: Punjabi, Sindhi, Pashtun (Pathan), Baloch, Muhajir (immigrants from India and their descendants)
Languages: Urdu (official), Punjab (spoken by majority), Sindhi, Pushto, English
Religions: 97% Muslim (77% Sunni, 20% Shi'a), 3% Christian, Hindu and other
Birth Rate: 29.59/1,000 population (2003 est.)
Death Rate: 8.79/1,000 population (2003 est.)

Infant Mortality: 76.53 deaths/1,000 live births (2003 est.)
Life Expectancy at Birth: 61.30 years male, 63.14 years female (2003 est.)
Total Fertility Rate: 4.10 children born/woman (2003 est.)
Literacy: 41.5% (2002)

■ GOVERNMENT

Leader(s): President Pervez Musharraf, Prime Minister Chaudhry Shujaat Hussain
Government Type: federal republic
Administrative Divisions: 4 provinces, 1 territory and 1 capital territory
Nationhood: Aug. 14, 1947 (from UK; formerly West Pakistan)
National Holiday: Republic Day (proclamation of the republic), Mar. 23

■ ECONOMY

Overview: long-standing economic weaknesses such as indebtedness, a small tax base, large population and dependence on cotton exports hamper the economy
GDP: US$295.3 billion, per capita US$2,000; real growth rate 4.4% (2002 est.)
Inflation: 3.9% (2002 est.)
Industries: accounts for 25% of GDP (2002 est.); textiles, food processing, beverages, petroleum products, construction materials, clothing, paper products, international finance, shrimp
Labour Force: 55.3 million (2002); 44% agriculture, 17% industry, 39% community, social and business services
Unemployment: 7.8% (2002)
Agriculture: 24% of GDP (2002), over 50% of labour force; world's largest continuous irrigation system; cotton, wheat, rice, sugar cane, fruits, vegetables, livestock (milk, beef, mutton, eggs); self-sufficient in foodgrain
Natural Resources: land, extensive natural gas reserves, limited crude oil, poor quality coal, iron ore, copper, salt, limestone

■ FINANCE/TRADE

Currency: Pakistani rupee (PRs) = 100 paisa
International Reserves Excluding Gold: US$10.882 billion (Jan. 2004)
Gold Reserves: 2.096 million fine troy ounces (Jan. 2004)
Budget: revenues US$12.2 billion; expenditures US$12.3 billion, including capital expenditures US$ n.a. (FY2002/03 est.)
Defence Expenditures: 21.6% of central government expenditure (2002)
Education Expenditures: 7.8% of total government expenditure (2002)
External Debt: US$33.672 billion (2002)

Exports: US$11.910 billion (2003 est.); commodities: rice, cotton, textiles, clothing; partners: US, UK, UAE, Hong Kong, Germany
Imports: US$13.014 billion (2003 est.); commodities: petroleum, petroleum products, machinery, transportation, equipment, vegetable oils, animal fats, chemicals; partners: Kuwait, UAE, Saudi Arabia, US, Japan

■ COMMUNICATIONS

Daily Newspapers: 40/1,000 inhabitants (2000)
Televisions: 150/1,000 inhabitants (2002)
Radios: 105/1,000 inhabitants (2001)
Telephones: 25 lines/1.000 inhabitants (2002)
Internet: hosts: 12,707 (2002); users: 1.5 million (2002)

■ TRANSPORTATION

Motor Vehicles: 1,300,000; 735,000 passenger cars
Roads: 254,410 km; 109,396 km paved
Railway: 8,163 km
Air Traffic: 4,141,000 passengers carried (2002)
Airports: 124; 87 have paved runways (2003 est.)

Canadian Embassy: The Canadian High Commission, Diplomatic Enclave, Sector G-5, Islamabad; mailing address: The Canadian High Commission, G.P.O. Box 1042, Islamabad, Pakistan. Tel: (011-92-51) 227-91-00. Fax: (011-92-51) 227-91-88. e-mail: isbad@dfait-maeci.gc.ca
Embassy in Canada: High Commission for the Islamic Republic of Pakistan, 10 Range Road, Ottawa ON K1N 8J3. Tel: (613) 238-7881. Fax: (613) 238-7296. e-mail: parepottawa@sprint.ca

---

Palau

Long-Form Name: Republic of Palau
Capital: Koror (on Koror Island); a new capital is being built 20 km northeast

■ GEOGRAPHY

Area: 458 sq. km (26 islands and 300+ islets)
Coastline: 1,519 km
Climate: tropical, warm year-round; wet season, May to Dec.; dry season, Jan. to April; typhoon-prone with violent winds and heavy rain, esp. in July
Environment: inadequate facilities for waste management; typhoons
Terrain: about 200 islands; topography varies from high and mountainous to low coral reef islands; northern islands of volcanic origin, fertile and extensively cultivated; southern islands too rugged for habitation

Land Use: arable land: 21.74%, permanent crops: 0%, other: 78.26%
Location: W Pacific Ocean (Micronesia), E of the Philippines

■ PEOPLE

Population: 19,717 (July 2003 est.)
Nationality: Palauan
Age Structure: 0–14 yrs: 26.7%; 15–64: 68.7%; 65+: 4.6% (2003 est.)
Population Growth Rate: 1.54% (2003 est.)
Net Migration: 3.40 migrants/1,000 population (2003 est.)
Ethnic Groups: Polynesian, Malayan, Melanesian, mixtures
Languages: English (official in all states), Sonsorolese, Angaur, Japanese, Tobi, Palauan
Religions: Christian, Modekngei, a religion indigenous to Palau
Birth Rate: 19.02/1,000 population (2003 est.)
Death Rate: 7.00/1,000 population (2003 est.)
Infant Mortality: 15.76 deaths/1,000 live births (2003 est.)
Life Expectancy at Birth: 66.37 years male, 72.82 years female (2003 est.)
Total Fertility Rate: 2.47 children born/woman (2003 est.)
Literacy: 92%

■ GOVERNMENT

Leader(s): President Tommy Remengesau, Vice President Sandra Pierantozzi
Government Type: constitutional government in free association with the US
Administrative Divisions: 18 states
Nationhood: Oct. 1, 1994 (from US-administered UN trusteeship)
National Holiday: Constitution Day, July 9

■ ECONOMY

Overview: subsistence agriculture and fishing; some tourism; government is main employer; phosphate deposits on northern islands; largely dependent on imports from the US
GDP: US$174 million, per capita US$9,000; real growth rate 1.0% (2001 est.)
Inflation: 3.4% (2000 est.)
Industries: some fishing and agriculture, tourism, crafts, garment making
Labour Force: 9,860 (2001 est.); 20% agriculture
Unemployment: 2.3% (2000 est.)
Agriculture: subsistence-level cultivation of coconuts, copra, yams, cassava
Natural Resources: marine resources, minerals (especially gold), forests

■ FINANCE/TRADE

Currency: American dollar (US$) = 100 cents

International Reserves Excluding Gold: n.a.
Gold Reserves: n.a.
Budget: n.a.
Defence Expenditures: defence is the responsibility of the US
Education Expenditures: n.a.
External Debt: none
Exports: US$18 million (2001 est.); fish, copra, handicrafts; partners: US, Japan, Singapore
Imports: US$99 million (2001 est.); machinery, equipment, fuels; partners: US

■ COMMUNICATIONS

Daily Newspapers: n.a.
Televisions: n.a.
Radios: n.a.
Telephones: n.a.

■ TRANSPORTATION

Motor Vehicles: n.a.
Roads: 61 km; 36 km paved
Railway: none
Air Traffic: n.a.
Airports: 3; 1 has a paved runway (2003 est.)

Canadian Embassy: c/o The Canadian Embassy, 501 Pennsylvania Ave NW, Washington DC 20001, USA. Tel: (202) 682-1740. Fax: (202) 456-7726. e-mail: washdc-outpack@dfait-maeci.gc.ca
Embassy in Canada: c/o Embassy of the United States of America, 490 Sussex Drive, PO Box 866, Station "B," Ottawa, ON, K1P 5T1. Tel: (613) 238-5335. Fax: (613) 688-3080. e-mail inquiries are not accepted.

Panama

Long-Form Name: Republic of Panama
Capital: Panama

■ GEOGRAPHY

Area: 78,200 sq. km
Coastline: 2,490 km
Climate: tropical; hot, humid, cloudy; prolonged rainy season (May to Jan.), short dry season (Jan. to May)
Environment: dense tropical forest in east and northwest is threatened by deforestation; water pollution and soil degradation
Terrain: interior mostly steep, rugged mountains and dissected, upland plains; coastal areas largely plains and rolling hills
Land Use: arable land: 6.72%, permanent crops: 2.08%, other: 91.2%; includes 320 sq. km irrigated
Location: Central (Latin) America, bordering on S America, Caribbean Sea, Pacific Ocean

■ PEOPLE

Population: 2,960,784 (July 2003 est.)

Nationality: Panamanian
Age Structure: 0–14 yrs: 30.6%; 15–64: 63.3%; 65+: 6.1% (2003 est.)
Population Growth Rate: 1.36% (2003 est.)
Net Migration: -0.97 migrants/1,000 population (2003 est.)
Ethnic Groups: 70% mestizo (mixed Indian and European ancestry), 14% West Indian, 10% white, 6% Indian
Languages: Spanish (official), 14% English; many Panamanians are bilingual
Religions: 85% Roman Catholic, 15% Protestant
Birth Rate: 20.78/1,000 population (2003 est.)
Death Rate: 6.25/1,000 population (2003 est.)
Infant Mortality: 21.44 deaths/1,000 live births (2003 est.)
Life Expectancy at Birth: 69.97 years male, 74.79 years female (2003 est.)
Total Fertility Rate: 2.53 children born/woman (2003 est.)
Literacy: 92.3% (2002)

■ GOVERNMENT

Leader(s): President Mireya Elisa Moscoso de Gruber, First Vice President Arturo Ulises Vallarino
Government Type: constitutional republic
Administrative Divisions: 9 provinces (provincias, sing. provincia) and 1 territory (comarca)
Nationhood: Nov. 3, 1903 (from Colombia; became independent from Spain Nov. 28, 1821)
National Holiday: Independence Day, Nov. 3

■ ECONOMY

Overview: political instability, lack of credit and the erosion of business confidence have drastically hurt the economy resulting in a recent overall economic slump; exports are stagnant; unemployment and economic reform are two of the greatest challenges the government must face
GDP: US$18.06 billion, per capita US$6,200; real growth rate 0.7% (2001 est.)
Inflation: 0.3% (2001)
Industries: accounts for 17% of GDP (2000); manufacturing and construction activities, petroleum refining, brewing, cement and other construction materials, sugar mills
Labour Force: 1.3 million (2002); 61% community, social and business services; 21% agriculture, 18% industry
Unemployment: 13.2% (2002)
Agriculture: accounts for 7% of GDP (2000) and almost one-third of labour force; bananas, rice, corn, coffee, sugar cane, livestock, fishing, importer of foodgrain, vegetables, milk products
Natural Resources: copper, mahogany forests, shrimp, hydroelectric potential

■ FINANCE/TRADE

Currency: balboa (B) = 100 centesimos, also the US dollar ($) = 100 cents.
International Reserves Excluding Gold: US$1.224 million (Jan. 2004)
Gold Reserves: n.a.
Budget: revenues US$2.8 billion; expenditures US$2.9 billion, including capital expenditures of US$471 million (2000 est.)
Defence Expenditures: 4.2% of central government expenditure (2002)
Education Expenditures: 7.3% of central government expenditure (2002)
External Debt: US$8.298 billion (2002)
Exports: US$804 million (2003 est.); commodities: bananas 40%, shrimp 27%, coffee 4%, sugar, petroleum products; partners: US, Sweden, Benelux, Costa Rica
Imports: US$2.963 billion (2003 est.); commodities: foodstuffs 16%, capital goods 9%, crude oil 16%, consumer goods, chemicals; partners: US, Ecuador, Venezuela, Japan

■ COMMUNICATIONS

Daily Newspapers: 62/1,000 inhabitants (2000)
Televisions: 191/1,000 inhabitants (2002)
Radios: 300/1,000 inhabitants (2001)
Telephones: 122 lines/1,000 inhabitants (2002)
Internet: hosts: 7,393 (2002); users: 120,000 (2002)

■ TRANSPORTATION

Motor Vehicles: 320,000; 230,000 passenger cars
Roads: 11,400 km; 3,944 km paved
Railway: 355 km
Air Traffic: 1,048,000 passengers carried (2002)
Airports: 103; 41 have paved runways (2003 est.)

Canadian Embassy: The Canadian Embassy, World Trade Center, 1st Floor, Calle 53 Este Marbella y Calle 5 B Sur, Urbanización Marbella, Panama City, Panama; Postal Address: The Canadian Embassy, Apartado Postal 0832-2446, Estafeta World Trade Center, Panama City, Panama. Tel: (011-507) 264-9731. Fax: (011-507) 263-8083. e-mail: panam@dfaitmaeci.gc.ca
Embassy in Canada: Embassy of the Republic of Panama, 130 Albert St, Ste 300, Ottawa ON K1P 5G4. Tel: (613) 236-7177. Fax: (613) 236-5775. e-mail: pancanem@rapidweb.ca

---

Papua New Guinea

Long-Form Name: Independent State of Papua New Guinea
Capital: Port Moresby

■ GEOGRAPHY

Area: 462,840 sq. km

Coastline: 5,152 km
Climate: tropical; northwest monsoon (Dec. to Mar.), southeast monsoon (May to Oct.); slight seasonal temperature variation
Environment: one of the world's largest swamps along southwest coast; some active volcanoes; frequent earthquakes and mudslides; pollution and deforestation
Terrain: mostly mountains with coastal lowlands and rolling foothills
Land Use: arable land: 0.13%, permanent crops: 1.35%, other: 98.52%; includes n.a. sq. km irrigated
Location: Pacific Ocean, Coral Sea N of Australia

■ PEOPLE

Population: 5,295,816 (July 2003 est.)
Nationality: Papua New Guinean
Age Structure: 0–14 yrs: 38.4%; 15–64: 57.8%; 65+: 3.8% (2003 est.)
Population Growth Rate: 2.34% (2003 est.)
Net Migration: 0 migrants/1,000 population (2003 est.)
Ethnic Groups: predominantly Melanesian and Papuan; some Negrito, Micronesian and Polynesian
Languages: pidgin, English, Motu (all official); also 715 local languages
Religions: 22% Roman Catholic, 16% Lutheran, 8% Presbyterian/Methodist/London Missionary Society, 5% Anglican, 4% Evangelical Alliance, 1% Seventh-Day Adventists, 10% other Protestant sects, 34% indigenous beliefs
Birth Rate: 31.07/1,000 population (2003 est.)
Death Rate: 7.63/1,000 population (2003 est.)
Infant Mortality: 54.84 deaths/1,000 live births (2003 est.)
Life Expectancy at Birth: 62.07 years male, 66.42 years female (2003 est.)
Total Fertility Rate: 4.13 children born/woman (2003 est.)
Literacy: 64.6% (2002)

■ GOVERNMENT

Leader(s): Head of State: Queen Elizabeth II, Governor General Paulius Matane, Prime Minister Michael Somare
Government Type: parliamentary democracy
Administrative Divisions: 20 provinces
Nationhood: Sept. 16, 1975 (from UN trusteeship under Australian administration)
National Holiday: Independence Day, Sept. 16

■ ECONOMY

Overview: country has abundant natural resources but exploitation has been hampered by the rugged terrain and the high cost of developing an infrastructure; subsistence agriculture is the livelihood for 85% of the

population; mining accounts for about 60% of export earnings
GDP: US$10.86 billion, per capita US$2,100; real growth rate -3.1% (2002 est.)
Inflation: 9.8% (2002 est.)
Industries: accounts for 44% of GDP (2000); copra crushing, palm oil processing, plywood processing, wood chip production, gold, silver, copper, construction, tourism
Labour Force: 2.7 million (2002); 85% agriculture, 10% industry, 5% other
Unemployment: n.a.
Agriculture: accounts for 26% of GDP (2000); fertile soils and favourable climate permit cultivating a wide variety of crops; cash crops: coffee, cocoa, coconuts, palm kernels; other products: tea, rubber, sweet potatoes, fruit, vegetables, poultry, pork; net importer of food for urban centres
Natural Resources: gold, copper, silver, natural gas, timber, oil potential, fisheries

■ FINANCE/TRADE

Currency: kina (K) = 100 toea
International Reserves Excluding Gold: US$484 million (Jan. 2004)
Gold Reserves: 0.063 million fine troy ounces (Jan. 2004)
Budget: revenues US$894 million; expenditures US$1.1 billion, including capital expenditures of US$344 million (2000 est.)
Defence Expenditures: 3.3% of central government expenditures (2002)
Education Expenditures: n.a.
External Debt: US$2.485 billion (2002)
Exports: US$2.162 billion (2003); commodities: gold, copper ore, coffee, copra, palm oil, timber, lobster; partners: Germany, Japan, Australia, China, South Korea, UK, Philippines, US
Imports: US$1.290 billion (2003); commodities: machinery and transport equipment, fuels, food, chemicals, consumer goods; partners: Australia, Singapore, Japan, New Zealand, Indonesia, Malaysia, US

■ COMMUNICATIONS

Daily Newspapers: 14/1,000 inhabitants (2000)
Televisions: 21/1,000 inhabitants (2002)
Radios: 86/1,000 inhabitants (2001)
Telephones: 12 lines/1,000 inhabitants (2002)
Internet: hosts: 517 (2002); users: 75,000 (2002)

■ TRANSPORTATION

Motor Vehicles: 99,300; 21,600 passenger cars
Roads: 19,600 km; 686 km paved
Railway: none
Air Traffic: 1,235,000 passengers carried (2002)
Airports: 491; 21 have paved runways (2003 est.)

Canadian Embassy: The Canadian High Commission to Papua New Guinea, c/o The Canadian High Commission, Commonwealth Ave, Canberra A.C.T. 2600, Australia. Tel: (011-61-2) 6270-4000. Fax: (011-61-2) 6273-3285. e-mail: cnbra@dfait-maeci.gc.ca
Embassy in Canada: c/o High Commission for Papua New Guinea, 1779 Massachusetts Ave NW, Ste 805, Washington DC 20036, USA. Tel: (202) 745-3680. Fax: (202) 745-3679. e-mail: n.a.

Paraguay

Long-Form Name: Republic of Paraguay
Capital: Asunción

■ GEOGRAPHY

Area: 406,750 sq. km
Coastline: none: landlocked
Climate: subtropical; varies from temperate in east to semi-arid in far west
Environment: local flooding in southeast (early Sept. to June); poorly drained plains may become boggy (early Oct. to June); deforestation and water pollution are increasing
Terrain: grassy plains and wooded hills east of Río Paraguay; Gran Chaco region west of Río Paraguay mostly low, marshy plain near the river and dry forest and thorny scrub elsewhere
Land Use: arable land: 5.54%, permanent crops: 0.21%, other: 94.25%; includes 670 sq. km irrigated
Location: C South America

■ PEOPLE

Population: 6,036,900 (July 2003 est.)
Nationality: Paraguayan
Age Structure: 0–14 yrs: 38.4%; 15–64: 56.8%; 65+: 4.7% (2003 est.)
Population Growth Rate: 2.54% (2003 est.)
Net Migration: -0.08 migrants/1,000 population (2003 est.)
Ethnic Groups: 95% mestizo (Spanish and Indian), 5% white and Indian
Languages: Spanish (official), Guarani
Religions: 90% Roman Catholic; 10% Mennonite and other Protestant denominations
Birth Rate: 30.14/1,000 population (2003 est.)
Death Rate: 4.64/1,000 population (2003 est.)
Infant Mortality: 27.71 deaths/1,000 live births (2003 est.)
Life Expectancy at Birth: 71.89 years male, 77.03 years female (2003 est.)
Total Fertility Rate: 4.02 children born/woman (2003 est.)
Literacy: 91.6% (2002)

■ GOVERNMENT

Leader(s): President Nicanor Duarte Frutos, Vice President Luis Castiglioni
Government Type: constitutional republic
Administrative Divisions: 17 departments (departamentos, sing. —departamento) and 1 capital city
Nationhood: May 14, 1811 (from Spain)
National Holiday: Independence Days, May 14–15

■ ECONOMY

Overview: in the absence of significant mineral or petroleum resources, the economy is based on agriculture; has a large hydroelectric power potential; is vulnerable to climatic conditions and international commodity prices for agricultural exports; non-traditional exports are growing rapidly
GDP: US$25.19 billion, per capita US$4,300; real growth rate -2.7% (2002 est.)
Inflation: 10.5% (2002 est.)
Industries: accounts for 26% of GDP (2000); meat packing, oilseed crushing, milling, brewing, textiles, other light consumer goods, cement, construction
Labour Force: 2.1 million (2002); 45% agriculture
Unemployment: 16% (2000 est.)
Agriculture: accounts for 29% GDP (2000) and 45% of labour force; cash crops: cotton, sugar cane; other crops: corn, wheat, tobacco, soybeans, cassava, fruit and vegetables; animal products: beef, pork, eggs, milk; surplus producer of timber; self-sufficient in most foods
Natural Resources: iron ore, manganese, limestone, hydro power, timber

■ FINANCE/TRADE

Currency: guaraní (pl. guaraníes) (G/) = 100 centimos
International Reserves Excluding Gold: US$934 million (Jan. 2004)
Gold Reserves: 0.035 million fine troy ounces (Jan. 2004)
Budget: n.a.
Defence Expenditures: 5.0% of central government expenditure (2002)
Education Expenditures: 9.7% of total government expenditures (2002)
External Debt: US$2.967 billion (2002)
Exports: US$990 million (2001); commodities: cotton, soybeans, timber, vegetable oils, coffee, tung oil, meat products, electricity; partners: Brazil, Uruguay, Argentina
Imports: US$1.989 billion (2001); commodities: capital goods 35%, consumer goods 20%, fuels and lubricants 19%, raw materials 16%, foodstuffs, beverages and tobacco 10%; partners: Argentina, Brazil, Uruguay

■ COMMUNICATIONS

Daily Newspapers: 43/1,000 inhabitants (2000)
Televisions: 218/1,000 inhabitants (2002)
Radios: 182/1,000 inhabitants (2001)
Telephones: 47 lines/1,000 inhabitants (2002)
Internet: hosts: 4,351 (2002); users: 100,000 (2002)

■ TRANSPORTATION

Motor Vehicles: 121,000; 71,000 passenger cars
Roads: 29,500 km; 14,986 km hard-surfaced
Railway: 971 km
Air Traffic: 269,000 passengers carried (2002)
Airports: 879; 11 have paved runways (2003 est.)

Canadian Embassy: The Canadian Embassy to Paraguay, The Canadian Embassy, 2828 Tagle, 1425 Buenos Aires; mailing address: Casilla de Correo 1598 C1000WAP, Buenos Aires, Argentina. Tel: (011-54-11) 4808-1000. Fax: (011-54-11) 4808-1111. e-mail: n.a.
Embassy in Canada: Embassy of the Republic of Paraguay, 151 Slater St, Ste 501, Ottawa, ON K1P 5H3. Tel: (613) 567-1283. Fax: (613) 567-1679. e-mail: embapar@magmacom.com

---

Peru

Long-Form Name: Republic of Peru
Capital: Lima

■ GEOGRAPHY

Area: 1,285,220 sq. km
Coastline: 2,414 km
Climate: varies from tropical in east to dry desert in west
Environment: subject to earthquakes, tsunamis, landslides, mild volcanic activity; deforestation; overgrazing; soil erosion; desertification; air pollution in Lima; shares control of Lago Titicaca, world's highest navigable lake, with Bolivia
Terrain: western coastal plain (costa), high and rugged Andes in centre (sierra), eastern lowland jungle of Amazon Basin (selva)
Land Use: arable land: 2.85%, permanent crops: 0.38%, other: 96.77%; includes 11,950 sq. km irrigated
Location: W South America, bordering on Pacific Ocean

■ PEOPLE

Population: 28,409,897 (July 2003 est.)
Nationality: Peruvian
Age Structure: 0–14 yrs: 33.5%; 15–64: 61.5%; 65+: 5.0% (2003 est.)

Population Growth Rate: 1.61% (2003 est.)
Net Migration: -1.03 migrants/1,000 population (2003 est.)
Ethnic Groups: 45% Indian; 37% mestizo (mixed Indian and European ancestry); 15% white; 3% black, Japanese, Chinese and other
Languages: Spanish and Quechua (official), Aymara
Religions: predominantly Roman Catholic
Birth Rate: 22.81/1,000 population (2003 est.)
Death Rate: 5.69/1,000 population (2003 est.)
Infant Mortality: 36.97 deaths/1,000 live births (2003 est.)
Life Expectancy at Birth: 68.45 years male, 73.43 years female (2003 est.)
Total Fertility Rate: 2.81 children born/woman (2003 est.)
Literacy: 85.0% (2002)

■ GOVERNMENT

Leader(s): President Alejandro Toledo, Prime Minister Carlos Ferrero Costa
Government Type: constitutional republic
Administrative Divisions: 24 departments (departamentos, sing. —departamento) and 1 constitutional province (provincia constitucional)
Nationhood: July 28, 1821 (from Spain)
National Holiday: Independence Day, July 28

■ ECONOMY

Overview: revival of growth in GDP continues to be restricted by the large amount of public and private resources being devoted to strengthening internal security; deficit spending and poor relations with international lenders are problems; labour unrest has cut production; food shortages; world's largest producer of coca (for cocaine)
GDP: US$138.8 billion, per capita US$5,000; real growth rate 5.3% (2002 est.)
Inflation: 0.2% (2002 est.)
Industries: accounts for 35% of GDP (2001 est.), mining of metals, petroleum, fishing, textiles, clothing, food processing, cement, auto assembly, steel, shipbuilding, metal fabrication
Labour Force: 10.4 million (2002); 34.1% trade and tourism, 28.6% community, social and business services, 6% finance
Unemployment: 8.7%, plus extensive underemployment (2002)
Agriculture: accounts for 10% of GDP (2001 est.) and 35% of labour force; commercial crops: coffee, cotton, sugar cane; other crops: rice, wheat, potatoes, plantains, coca; animal products: poultry, meats, dairy, wool; not self-sufficient in grain or vegetable oil; fish catch of 6.9 million metric tons

Natural Resources: copper, silver, gold, petroleum, timber, fish, iron ore, coal, phosphate, potash

■ FINANCE/TRADE

Currency: nuevo sol (pl. soles) (S/.) = 100 centimos
International Reserves Excluding Gold: US$10.134 billion (Jan. 2004)
Gold Reserves: 1.115 million fine troy ounces (Jan. 2004)
Budget: revenues US$10.4 billion, expenditures US$10.4 billion, including capital expenditures of US$ n.a. (2002 est.)
Defence Expenditures: 9.2% of central government expenditure (2002)
Education Expenditures: 21.1% of total government expenditures (2002)
External Debt: US$28.167 billion (2002)
Exports: US$8.954 billion (2003 est.); commodities: fishmeal, cotton, sugar, coffee, copper, iron ore, refined silver, lead, zinc, crude petroleum and by-products; partners: US, UK, Switzerland, China, Japan, Chile, Brazil
Imports: US$8.244 billion (2003); commodities: foodstuffs, machinery, transport equipment, iron and steel semi-manufactures, chemicals, pharmaceuticals; partners: US, Chile, Spain, Venezuela, Colombia, Brazil, Japan

■ COMMUNICATIONS

Daily Newspapers: 74 in total
Televisions: 172/1,000 inhabitants (2002)
Radios: 269/1,000 inhabitants (2001)
Telephones: 66 lines/1,000 inhabitants (2002)
Internet: hosts: 19,447 (2002); users: 2.5 million (2002)

■ TRANSPORTATION

Motor Vehicles: 1,200,000; 750,000 passenger cars
Roads: 72,900 km; 9,331 km paved
Railway: 1,829 km
Air Traffic: 1,879,000 passengers carried (2002)
Airports: 233; 49 have paved runways (2003 est.)

Canadian Embassy: The Canadian Embassy, Calle Libertad 130, Miraflores, Lima 18, Peru; mailing address: Casilla 18-1126, Correo Miraflores, Lima, Peru. Tel: (011-51-1) 444-4015. Fax: (011-51-1) 242-4050. e-mail: lima@dfait-maeci.gc.ca
Embassy in Canada: Embassy of the Republic of Peru, 130 Albert St, Ste 1901, Ottawa ON K1P 5G4. Tel: (613) 238-1777. Fax: (613) 232-3062. e-mail: embperuca@bellnet.ca

Philippines

Long-Form Name: Republic of the Philippines

Capital: Manila

■ GEOGRAPHY

Area: 300,000 sq. km
Coastline: 36,289 km
Climate: tropical marine; northeast monsoon (Nov. to Apr.); southwest monsoon (May to Oct.)
Environment: astride typhoon belt, usually affected by 15 and struck by five to six cyclonic storms per year; subject to landslides, active volcanoes, destructive earthquakes, tsunami; deforestation; soil erosion; water pollution
Terrain: mostly mountains with narrow to extensive coastal lowlands
Land Use: arable land: 18.45%, permanent crops: 14.76%, other: 66.79%; includes 15,500 sq. km irrigated
Location: SE of China, bordering on South China Sea, Pacific Ocean

■ PEOPLE

Population: 84,619,974 (July 2003 est.)
Nationality: Filipino
Age Structure: 0–14 yrs: 36.2%; 15–64: 59.9%; 65+: 3.9% (2003 est.)
Population Growth Rate: 1.92% (2003 est.)
Net Migration: -1.50 migrants/1,000 population (2003 est.)
Ethnic Groups: 91.5% Christian Malay, 4% Muslim Malay, 1.5% Chinese, 3% other
Languages: Pilipino (native national language based on Tagalog) and English (both official); Spanish also spoken, also 76 indigenous languages including Cebuano, Tagalog, Iloco, Ifugao
Religions: 83% Roman Catholic, 9% Protestant, 5% Muslim, 3% Buddhist and other
Birth Rate: 26.30/1,000 population (2003 est.)
Death Rate: 5.60/1,000 population (2003 est.)
Infant Mortality: 24.98 deaths/1,000 live births (2003 est.)
Life Expectancy at Birth: 66.44 years male, 72.28 years female (2003 est.)
Total Fertility Rate: 3.29 children born/woman (2003 est.)
Literacy: 92.6% (2002)

■ GOVERNMENT

Leader(s): President Gloria Macapagal-Arroyo, Vice President Noli de Castro
Government Type: republic
Administrative Divisions: 14 regions, divided into 73 provinces and 61 chartered cities
Nationhood: July 4, 1946 (from US)
National Holiday: Independence Day (from Spain), June 12

■ ECONOMY

Overview: drought and power supply problems have hampered production; world's largest exporter of coconuts and coconut products
GDP: US$379.7 billion, per capita US$4,600; real growth rate 4.4% (2002 est.)
Inflation: 3.1% (2002 est.)
Industries: accounts for 30% of GDP (2000); textiles, pharmaceuticals, chemicals, wood products, food processing, electronics assembly, petroleum refining, fishing
Labour Force: 34.2 million (2002); 45% agriculture, 40% services, 15% industry
Unemployment: 10.6% (Jan. 2003)
Agriculture: accounts for 17% of GDP (2000) and 45% of labour force; major crops: rice, coconuts, corn, sugar cane, bananas, pineapples, mangoes; animal products: pork, eggs, beef: net exporter of farm products: fish catch of 2 million metric tons annually
Natural Resources: timber, crude oil, nickel, cobalt, silver, gold, salt, copper

■ FINANCE/TRADE

Currency: peso (P) = 100 centavos
International Reserves Excluding Gold: US$12.848 billion (Jan. 2004)
Gold Reserves: 8.076 million fine troy ounces (Jan. 2004)
Budget: revenues US$10.9 billion; expenditures US$15.1 billion, including capital expenditures US$2.4 million (2002 est.)
Defence Expenditures: 5.1% of central government expenditure (2002)
Education Expenditures: 18.72% of central government expenditure (2000)
External Debt: US$59.342 billion (2002)
Exports: US$35.829 billion (2003 est.); commodities: electrical equipment 19%, textiles 16%, minerals and ores 11%, farm products 10%, coconut 10%, chemicals 5%, fish 5%, forest products 4%; partners: US, Japan, Netherlands, Singapore, Taiwan, Hong Kong
Imports: US$39.630 billion (2003 est.); commodities: raw materials 53%, capital goods 17%, petroleum products 17%; partners: Japan, US, EU, South Korea, Singapore, Taiwan

■ COMMUNICATIONS

Daily Newspapers: 82/1,000 inhabitants (2000)
Televisions: 182/1,000 inhabitants (2002)
Radios: 161/1,000 inhabitants (2001)
Telephones: 42 lines/1,000 inhabitants (2002)
Internet: hosts: 38,440 (2002); users: 3.5 million (2002)

■ TRANSPORTATION

Motor Vehicles: 2,700,000; 845,000 passenger cars
Roads: 201,994 km; 42,419 km paved
Railway: 897 km
Air Traffic: 5,660,000 passengers carried (2002)
Airports: 275; 82 have paved runways (2003 est.)

Canadian Embassy: The Canadian Embassy, Level 6 to 8, Tower 2, RCBC Plaza, 6819 Ayala Avenue, Makati City, Manila, Philippines. Postal Address: The Canadian Embassy, P.O. Box 2168, Makati Central Post Office, Manila,1261, Philippines. Tel: (011 63 2) 857 9000. Fax: (011 63 2) 843 1082. e-mail manil@dfait-maeci.gc.ca
Embassy in Canada: Embassy of the Republic of the Philippines, 130 Albert St, Ste 606, Ottawa ON K1P 5G4. Tel: (613) 233-1121. Fax: (613) 233-4165. e-mail: embassyofphilippines@rogers.com

Pitcairn Islands

Long-Form Name: Pitcairn, Henderson, Ducie and Oeno Islands
Capital: Adamstown

■ GEOGRAPHY

Area: 47 sq. km (Pitcairn and 3 small uninhabited islands)
Climate: tropical, hot, humid, modified by southeasterly trade winds; rainy season from Nov. to March
Land Use: arable land: n.a.%, permanent crops: n.a.%, other: n.a.%
Location: S Pacific Ocean, E of French Polynesia

■ PEOPLE

Population: 47 (July 2003 est.)
Nationality: Pitcairn Islander
Ethnic Groups: descendants of Polynesians and British (the latter crew members of the British naval ship *Bounty*)
Languages: English (official), Tahitian-English dialect

■ GOVERNMENT

Colony/Territory of: Dependent Territory of the United Kingdom
Leader(s): Queen Elizabeth II (UK), Governor Richard Fell
Government Type: dependency of the UK
National Holiday: Celebration of the birthday of the Queen, second Saturday in June

■ ECONOMY

Overview: inhabitants subsist on fishing and farming; fertile soil of the valleys produces wide variety of fruit and vegetables; bartering is an important part of the economy; imports: fuel oil, machinery, building materials; no exports other than small tourist trade with passing ships

■ FINANCE/TRADE

Currency: New Zealand dollar = 100 cents

Canadian Embassy: c/o The Canadian High Commission, Macdonald House, 1 Grosvenor Square, London, W1K 4AB. Tel: (011-44-20) 7258-6600. Fax: (011-44-20) 7258-6333. e-mail: ldn@dfait-maeci.gc.ca
Representative to Canada: c/o British High Commission, 80 Elgin St, Ottawa ON K1P 5K7. Tel: (613) 237-1530. Fax: (613) 237-7980. e-mail should be sent using the appropriate form at the British High Commission's Website at http://www.britain-in-canada.org

Poland

Long-Form Name: Republic of Poland
Capital: Warsaw

■ GEOGRAPHY

Area: 312,683 sq. km
Coastline: 491 km along Baltic Sea
Climate: temperate with cold, cloudy, moderately severe winters with frequent precipitation; mild summers with frequent showers and thundershowers
Environment: plain crossed by a few meandering streams; severe air and water pollution in south; flat terrain; lack of natural barriers; recently there has been severe flooding
Terrain: mostly flat plain, mountains along southern border
Land Use: arable land: 45.81%, permanent crops: 1.23%, other: 52.96%; includes 1,000 sq. km irrigated
Location: NE Europe, bordering on Baltic Sea

■ PEOPLE

Population: 38,622,660 (July 2003 est.)
Nationality: Polish, Pole
Age Structure: 0–14 yrs: 17.5%; 15–64: 69.8%; 65+: 12.7% (2003 est.)
Population Growth Rate: 0.0% (2003 est.)
Net Migration: -0.49 migrants/1,000 population (2003 est.)
Ethnic Groups: 97.6% Polish, 1.3% German, 0.6% Ukrainian, 0.5% Byelorussian
Languages: Polish
Religions: 95% Roman Catholic (about 75% practising), 5% Russian Orthodox, Protestant and other
Birth Rate: 10.47/1,000 population (2003 est.)
Death Rate: 9.96/1,000 population (2003 est.)
Infant Mortality: 8.95 deaths/1,000 live births (2003 est.)

Life Expectancy at Birth: 69.77 years male, 78.28 years female (2003 est.)
Total Fertility Rate: 1.37 children born/woman (2003 est.)
Literacy: 99.7% (2002)

■ GOVERNMENT

Leader(s): President Aleksander Kwasniewski, Acting Prime Minister Marek Belka
Government Type: republic
Administrative Divisions: 16 provinces (wojewodztwa, sing. —wojewodztwo)
Nationhood: Nov. 11, 1918, independent republic proclaimed
National Holiday: Constitution Day, May 3; Independence Day, Nov. 11

■ ECONOMY

Overview: continues to make good progress in the difficult transition to a free-market economy; in contrast to the vibrant expansion of private non-farm activity, the large agricultural component remains handicapped by structural problems, surplus labour, inefficient small farms, and lack of investment
GDP: US$373.2 billion, per capita US$9,700; real growth rate 1.4% (2002)
Inflation: 1.9% (2002 est.)
Industries: accounts for 32% of GDP (2000), machine building, iron and steel, extractive industries, chemicals, shipbuilding, food processing, glass, beverages, textiles
Labour Force: 19.9 million (2002); 28% agriculture, 22.1% industry, 50% community, social and business services
Unemployment: 20.6% (Jan. 2004)
Agriculture: accounts for 3% GDP (2000) and 27% of labour force; 75% of output from private farms, 25% from state farms; low productivity; leading European producer of rye, rapeseed and potatoes; wide variety of other crops and livestock; major exporter of pork products
Natural Resources: coal, sulphur, copper, natural gas, silver, lead, salt

■ FINANCE/TRADE

Currency: zloty (pl. zlotych) (Zl) = 100 groszy
International Reserves Excluding Gold: US$35.408 billion (Jan. 2004)
Gold Reserves: 3.308 million fine troy ounces (Jan. 2004)
Budget: n.a.
Defence Expenditures: 5.3% of central government expenditure (2002)
Education Expenditures: 12.2% of total government expenditure (2000)
External Debt: US$69.521 billion (2002)
Exports: US$41.032 billion (2002); commodities: machinery and equipment 63%, fuels,

minerals and metals 14%, manufactured consumer goods 14%, agricultural and forestry products 5%; partners: Germany, Italy, France, UK
Imports: US$55.141 billion (2002); commodities: machinery and equipment 36%, fuels, minerals and metals 35%, manufactured consumer goods 9%, agricultural and forestry products 12%; partners: Germany, Russia, Italy, France

■ COMMUNICATIONS

Daily Newspapers: 102/1,000 inhabitants (2000)
Televisions: 422/1,000 inhabitants (2002)
Radios: 523/1,000 inhabitants (2001)
Telephones: 295 lines/1,000 inhabitants (2002)
Internet: hosts: 657,495 (2002); users: 8.88 million (2002)

■ TRANSPORTATION

Motor Vehicles: 11,800,000; 10,000,000 passenger cars
Roads: 364,656 km; 249,060 km paved
Railway: 23,420 km
Air Traffic: 2,846,000 passengers carried (2002)
Airports: 150; 88 have paved runways (2003 est.)

Canadian Embassy: The Canadian Embassy, ul. Jana Matejki 1/5, 00-481, Warsaw, Poland. Tel: (011-48-22) 584-3100. Fax: (011-48-22) 584-3190. e-mail: wsaw@dfait-maeci.gc.ca
Embassy in Canada: Embassy of the Republic of Poland, 443 Daly Ave, Ottawa ON K1N 6H3. Tel: (613) 789-0468. Fax: (613) 789-1218. e-mail: n.a.

Portugal

Long-Form Name: Portuguese Republic
Capital: Lisbon

■ GEOGRAPHY

Area: 92,391 sq. km; includes Azores and Madeira Islands
Coastline: 1,793 km
Climate: maritime temperature; cool and rainy in north, warmer and drier in south
Environment: air pollution and soil degradation are accelerating; coastal water pollution; Azores subject to severe earthquakes
Terrain: mountainous north, rolling plains in south
Land Use: arable land: 20.57%, permanent crops: 7.74%, other: 71.69%; includes 6,320 sq, km irrigated
Location: SW Europe, bordering on North Atlantic Ocean

■ PEOPLE

Population: 10,102,022 (July 2003 est.)
Nationality: Portuguese

Age Structure: 0–14 yrs: 16.8%; 15–64: 67.2%; 65+: 16.0% (2003 est.)
Population Growth Rate: 0.17% (2003 est.)
Net Migration: 0.49 migrants/1,000 population (2003 est.)
Ethnic Groups: homogeneous Mediterranean stock in mainland, Azores and Madeira Islands; citizens of black African descent who immigrated to mainland during decolonization number less than 100,000
Languages: Portuguese (official), English, French
Religions: 97% Roman Catholic, 1% Protestant, 2% other
Birth Rate: 11.45/1,000 population (2003 est.)
Death Rate: 10.21/1,000 population (2003 est.)
Infant Mortality: 5.73 deaths/1,000 live births (2003 est.)
Life Expectancy at Birth: 72.86 years male, 80.07 years female (2003 est.)
Total Fertility Rate: 1.49 children born/woman (2003 est.)
Literacy: 92.5% (2002)

■ GOVERNMENT

Leader(s): President Jorge Sampaio, Premier Pedro Santana Lopes
Government Type: parliamentary democracy
Administrative Divisions: 18 districts (distritos, sing. —distrito) and 2 autonomous regions (regioes autonomas, sing. —regiao autonoma)
Nationhood: 1143; independent republic proclaimed Oct. 5, 1910
National Holiday: Day of Portugal, June 10

■ ECONOMY

Overview: the economy has grown recently due to strong domestic consumption and investment spending; government is promoting privatization measures; the global slowdown and tight financial policies to combat inflation have caused economic growth to slow
GDP: US$195.2 billion, per capita US$19,400; real growth rate 0.4% (2002 est.)
Inflation: 3.7% (2002 est.)
Industries: accounts for 29% of GDP (2001); textiles and footwear; wood pulp, paper and cork; metalworking; oil refining; chemicals; fish canning; wine; tourism
Labour Force: 5.2 million (2002); 60% community, social and business services, 30% industry, 10% agriculture
Unemployment: 5.1% (Oct. 2002)
Agriculture: accounts for 4% of GDP (2001) and 20% of labour force; small inefficient farms; imports more than half of food needs; major crops: grain, potatoes, olives, grapes; livestock sector: sheep, cattle, goats, poultry, meat, dairy products

Natural Resources: fish, forests (cork), tungsten, iron ore, uranium ore, marble

■ FINANCE/TRADE

Currency: escudo (Esc) = 100 centavos; Euro (€); on January 1, 2002 the Euro became the sole currency for everyday transactions.
International Reserves Excluding Gold: US$5.602 billion (Jan. 2004)
Gold Reserves: 16.627 million fine troy ounces (Jan. 2004)
Budget: revenues US$45 billion, expenditures US$48 billion, including capital expenditures of US$ n.a. (2001 est.)
Defence Expenditures: 5.4% of central government expenditures (2002)
Education Expenditures: 12.8% of total government expenditures (2002)
External Debt: n.a.
Exports: US$30.714 billion (2003); commodities: cotton textiles, cork and cork products, canned fish, wine, timber and timber products, resin, machinery, appliances; partners: EU, US
Imports: US$40.843 billion (2003); commodities: petroleum, cotton, foodgrains, industrial machinery, iron and steel, chemicals; partners: Spain, Germany, France, Italy, UK, US, Japan

■ COMMUNICATIONS

Daily Newspapers: 32/1,000 inhabitants (2000)
Televisions: 413/1,000 inhabitants (2002)
Radios: 304/1,000 inhabitants (2001)
Telephones: 421 lines/1,000 inhabitants (2002)
Internet: hosts: 164,711 (2002); users: 3.6 million (2002)

■ TRANSPORTATION

Motor Vehicles: 3,500,000; 3,230,000 passenger cars
Roads: 68,732 km; 59,110 km surfaced
Railway: 2,850 km
Air Traffic: 6,894,000 passengers carried (2002)
Airports: 66; 40 have paved runways (2003 est.)

Canadian Embassy: The Canadian Embassy, Avenida da Liberdade, 196-200, 3rd Floor, 1269-121 Lisbon, Portugal. Tel: (011-351) 21-316-46-00. Fax: (011-351) 21-316-46-91. e-mail: lsbon@dfait-maeci.gc.ca
Embassy in Canada: Embassy of Portugal, 645 Island Park Dr, Ottawa ON K1Y 0B8. Tel: (613) 729-0883. Fax: (613) 729-4236. e-mail: embportugal@embportugal-ottawa.org

Puerto Rico

Long-Form Name: Commonwealth of Puerto Rico

Capital: San Juan

■ GEOGRAPHY

Area: 9,104 sq. km
Climate: tropical marine, mild, little seasonal temperature variation
Land Use: arable land: 3.7%, permanent crops: 5.1%, other: 91.2%; includes 400 sq. km irrigated
Location: West Indies, bordering on Caribbean Sea, Atlantic Ocean

■ PEOPLE

Population: 3,885,877 (July 2003 est.)
Nationality: Puerto Rican (US citizens)
Ethnic Groups: almost entirely Hispanic
Languages: Spanish (official); English is widely understood

■ GOVERNMENT

Colony/Territory of: Commonwealth associated with the US
Leader(s): President George W. Bush Jr., Governor Sila Maria Calderon
Government Type: Commonwealth associated with the US
National Holiday: US Independence Day, July 4

■ ECONOMY

Overview: economy (one of the most dynamic in the Caribbean region) has benefited from heavy US investment; new industries include pharmaceuticals and electronics; tourism is important; sugar production has lost out to dairy production and other livestock products as the main facet of the agricultural sector

■ FINANCE/TRADE

Currency: American dollar ($US) = 100 cents

Canadian Embassy: c/o The Canadian Embassy, 501 Pennsylvania Ave NW, Washington DC 20001, USA. Tel: (202) 682-1740. Fax: (202) 456-7726. e-mail: wshdc@dfait-maeci.gc.ca
Representative to Canada: c/o Embassy of the United States of America, 490 Sussex Drive, PO Box 866, Station "B," Ottawa, ON, K1P 5T1. Tel: (613) 238-5335. Fax: (613) 688-3080. e-mail inquiries are not accepted.

Qatar

Long-Form Name: State of Qatar
Capital: Doha

■ GEOGRAPHY

Area: 11,437 sq. km
Coastline: 563 km
Climate: desert; hot, dry; humid and sultry in summer
Environment: haze, dust storms, sandstorms common; limited freshwater resources mean increasing dependence on large-scale desalination facilities
Terrain: mostly flat and barren desert covered with loose sand and gravel
Land Use: arable land: 1.27%, permanent crops: 0.27%, other: 98.46%; includes 130 sq. km irrigated
Location: SW Asia (Middle East, Arabian Peninsula), bordering on Persian Gulf

■ PEOPLE

Population: 817,052 (July 2002 est.)
Nationality: Qatari
Age Structure: 0–14 yrs: 24.7%; 15–64: 72.4%; 65+: 2.9% (2003 est.)
Population Growth Rate: 2.87% (2003 est.)
Net Migration: 17.48 migrants/1,000 population (2003 est.)
Ethnic Groups: 40% Arab, 18% Pakistani, 18% Indian, 10% Iranian, 14% other
Languages: Arabic (official); English is commonly used as second language
Religions: Islam (native Qataris—less than one-third of the population—principally adhere to orthodox Wahhabi sect of Sunni Muslims)
Birth Rate: 15.68/1,000 population (2003 est.)
Death Rate: 4.43/1,000 population (2003 est.)
Infant Mortality: 20.03 deaths/1,000 live births (2003 est.)
Life Expectancy at Birth: 70.65 years male, 75.76 years female (2003 est.)
Total Fertility Rate: 3.02 children born/woman (2003 est.)
Literacy: 84.2% (2002)

■ GOVERNMENT

Leader(s): Amir Shaykh Hamad bin Khalifa Al Thani, Prime Minister Shaykh Abdallah bin Khalifa Al Thani
Government Type: traditional monarchy
Administrative Divisions: 9 municipalities (baladiyah, sing. —baladiyah)
Nationhood: Sept. 3, 1971 (from UK)
National Holiday: Independence Day, Sept. 3

■ ECONOMY

Overview: has one of the highest per capita GDPs in the world, due to oil revenues; reserves should not be completely depleted for about 20 years; production and export of natural gas is becoming increasingly important; oil has given Qatar a per capita GDP comparable to the leading West European industrial countries
GDP: US$15.91 billion, per capita US$20,100; real growth rate 4.6% (2002 est.)
Inflation: 1.9% (2002)

Industries: accounts for 49% of GDP; crude oil production and refining, fertilizers, petrochemicals, steel, cement
Labour Force: n.a.; 3% agriculture, 28% industry, 69% services; 83% of labour force in private sector is non-Qatari
Unemployment: n.a.
Agriculture: farming and grazing on small scale, less than 1% of GDP; commercial fishing increasing in importance; most food imported. Domestic products include fruits, vegetables, poultry, dairy products.
Natural Resources: crude oil, natural gas, fish

■ FINANCE/TRADE

Currency: Qatari riyal (QR) = 100 dirhams
International Reserves Excluding Gold: US$2.970 billion (Jan. 2004)
Gold Reserves: 0.019 million fine troy ounces (Jan. 2004)
Budget: revenues US$5 billion; expenditures US$5.5 billion, including capital expenditures of US$2.2 billion (FY2002/03 est.)
Defence Expenditures: 10.0% of GDP (2000)
Education Expenditures: n.a.
External Debt: US$15.4 billion (2002 est.)
Exports: US$12.36 billion (2003 est.); commodities: petroleum products 90%, steel, fertilizers; partners: Japan, Singapore, South Korea, US, UAE
Imports: US$4.052 billion (2002); commodities: foodstuffs, beverages, animal and vegetable oils, chemicals, machinery and equipment; partners: UK, Japan, Germany, US, Italy

■ COMMUNICATIONS

Daily Newspapers: 5 in total
Televisions: n.a.
Radios: n.a.
Telephones: 223 lines/1,000 inhabitants (2002)
Internet: hosts: 171 (2002); users: 70,000 (2002)

■ TRANSPORTATION

Motor Vehicles: 184,000; 97,000 passenger cars
Roads: 1,230 km; 1,107 km paved
Railway: none
Air Traffic: n.a.
Airports: 4; 2 have paved runways (2003 est.)

Canadian Embassy: The Canadian Embassy to Qatar, c/o The Canadian Embassy, Villa 24, Area 4, Plot 121, 24 Al-Mutawakel St, Da Aiyah, Kuwait City, Kuwait; mailing address: P.O. Box 25281, 13113, Safat, Kuwait City, Kuwait. Tel: (011-965) 256-3025. Fax: (011-965) 256-0173. e-mail: kwait@dfait-maeci.gc.ca
Embassy in Canada: Embassy of the State of Qatar, c/o Permanent Mission of the State of Qatar to the United Nations, 809 UN Plaza, First

Ave 4th Fl, New York NY 10017, USA. Tel: (212) 486-9335. Fax: (212) 758-4952. e-mail: n.a.

Réunion

Long-Form Name: Department of Réunion
Capital: Saint-Denis

■ GEOGRAPHY

Area: 2,512 sq. km; uninhabited islands of Juan de Nova, Europa, Bassas da India, Iles Glorieuses, Tromelin administered by Réunion but do not form part of the territory; Mauritius and the Seychelles claim Tromelin, Madagascar claims all 5 islands
Climate: tropical, but more moderate at higher elevations; May to Nov.: cool and dry; Nov. to April: hot and rainy
Land Use: arable land: 13.2%, permanent crops: 2%, other: 84.8%; includes 120 sq. km irrigated
Location: Indian Ocean, E of Africa (E of Madagascar)

■ PEOPLE

Population: 755,171 (July 2003 est.)
Nationality: Réunionese
Ethnic Groups: French Creoles, African, Malagasy, Pakistani, Indian and Chinese minorities
Languages: French (official), Creole vernacular

■ GOVERNMENT

Colony/Territory of: Overseas Department of France
Leader(s): President Jacques Chirac (France), Prefect Dominique Vian
Government Type: overseas department of France
National Holiday: Taking of the Bastille, July 14

■ ECONOMY

Overview: agriculture-based economy, of which sugar cane is the backbone; government is promoting the development of the tourist industry; socio-economic tensions between classes with widely disparate living standards; economy heavily depends on financial assistance from France

■ FINANCE/TRADE

Currency: French franc = 100 centimes

Canadian Embassy: c/o The Canadian Embassy, 35-37 avenue Montaigne, 75008, Paris, France. Tel: (011-33-1) 44-43-29-00. Fax: (011-33-1) 44043-29-99. e-mail: paris@dfait-maeci.gc.ca
Representative to Canada: c/o Embassy of France, 42 Sussex Dr, Ottawa ON K1M 2C9. Tel: (613) 789-1795. Fax: (613) 562-3735. e-mail: politique@ambafrance-ca.org

Romania

Long-Form Name: Romania
Capital: Bucharest

■ GEOGRAPHY

Area: 237,500 sq. km
Coastline: 225 km
Climate: temperate; cold, cloudy winters with frequent snow and fog; sunny summers with frequent showers and thunderstorms
Environment: frequent earthquakes most severe in south and southwest; geologic structure and climate promote landslides; water pollution; air pollution in south; soil degradation
Terrain: central Transylvanian Basin is separated from the plain of Moldavia on the east by the Carpathian Mountains and separated from the Walachian Plain on the south by the Transylvanian Alps
Land Use: arable land: 40.57%, permanent crops: 2.4%, other: 57.03%; includes 28,800 sq. km irrigated
Location: SE Europe, bordering on Black Sea

■ PEOPLE

Population: 22,271,839 (July 2003 est.)
Nationality: Romanian
Age Structure: 0–14 yrs: 16.9%; 15–64: 69.0%; 65+: 14.0% (2003 est.)
Population Growth Rate: -0.21% (2003 est.)
Net Migration: -0.6 migrants/1,000 population (2003 est.)
Ethnic Groups: 89.5% Romanian; 7.1% Hungarian; 0.5% German; 2.9% Ukrainian, Serb, Croat, Russian, Turk and Gypsy
Languages: Romanian (official), Hungarian, German; French and English also spoken
Religions: 70% Romanian Orthodox; 6% Roman Catholic; 24% Calvinist, Lutheran, Jewish, Baptist, unaffiliated
Birth Rate: 10.79/1,000 population (2003 est.)
Death Rate: 12.25/1,000 population (2003 est.)
Infant Mortality: 18.40 deaths/1,000 live births (2003 est.)
Life Expectancy at Birth: 66.88 years male, 74.59 years female (2003 est.)
Total Fertility Rate: 1.36 children born/woman (2003 est.)
Literacy: 97.3% (2002)

■ GOVERNMENT

Leader(s): President Ion Iliescu, Prime Minister Adrian Nastase
Government Type: republic
Administrative Divisions: 40 counties (judete, sing. —judet) and 1 municipality (municipiu)
Nationhood: 1881 (from Turkey); republic proclaimed Dec. 30, 1947

National Holiday: National Day/Unification Day, Dec. 1

■ ECONOMY

Overview: industry suffers from an ageing capital plant and shortages of energy; agriculture sector has suffered from drought and mismanagement; private enterprise is increasing in importance; growing budget deficit, inflation, unemployment and a deteriorating infrastructure hamper economic progress
GDP: US$169.3 billion, per capita US$7,600; real growth rate 4.9% (2002 est.)
Inflation: 22.5% (2002 est.)
Industries: accounts for 30% of GDP (2000); mining, timber, construction materials, metallurgy, chemicals, machine building, food processing, petroleum
Labour Force: 10.7 million (2002); 25% industry, 40% agriculture, 35% community, social and business services
Unemployment: 7.6% (Jan. 2004)
Agriculture: accounts for 15% of GDP (2000) and 28% of labour force; major wheat and corn producer, sugar beets, sunflower seeds, grapes, potatoes, milk, eggs, meat
Natural Resources: crude oil (reserves being exhausted), timber, natural gas, coal, iron ore, salt, arable land, hydro power

■ FINANCE/TRADE

Currency: leu (pl. lei) = 100 bani
International Reserves Excluding Gold: US$9.042 billion (Jan. 2004)
Gold Reserves: 3.378 million fine troy ounces (Jan. 2004)
Budget: revenues US$8.2 billion; expenditures US$9.6 billion, including capital expenditures of US$ n.a. (2002 est.)
Defence Expenditures: 8.1% of central government expenditure (2002)
Education Expenditures: n.a.
External Debt: US$14.683 billion (2002)
Exports: US$17.619 billion (2003); commodities: machinery and equipment 34.7%, fuels, minerals and metals 24.7%, manufactured consumer goods 16.9%, agricultural materials and forestry products 11.9%, other 11.6%; partners: Italy, Germany, France, Turkey, US
Imports: US$24.003 billion (2003); commodities: fuels, minerals and metals 51%, machinery and equipment 26.7%, agricultural and forestry products 11%, manufactured consumer goods 4.2%; partners: Italy, Germany, France, Russia

■ COMMUNICATIONS

Daily Newspapers: 300/1,000 inhabitants (2000)
Televisions: 497/1,000 inhabitants (2002)
Radios: 358/1,000 inhabitants (2001)

Telephones: 194 lines/1,000 inhabitants (2002)
Internet: hosts: 40,971 (2002); users: 1.8 million (2002)

■ TRANSPORTATION

Motor Vehicles: 3,570,000; 3,100,000 passenger cars
Roads: 198,603 km; 98,308 km paved
Railway: 11,385 km
Air Traffic: 961,000 passengers carried (2002)
Airports: 65; 26 have paved runways (2003 est.)

Canadian Embassy: The Canadian Embassy, 36, Nicolae Iorga, 71118 Bucharest, Romania; Postal Address: P.O. Box 117, Post Office No. 22, Bucharest, Romania. Tel: (011-40-1) 307-5000. Fax: (011-40-1) 307-5010. e-mail: bucst@dfait-maeci.gc.ca
Embassy in Canada: Embassy of Romania, 655 Rideau St, Ottawa ON K1N 6A3. Tel: (613) 789-3709. Fax: (613) 789-4365. e-mail: romania@cyberus.ca

Russia

Long-Form Name: Russian Federation
Capital: Moscow

■ GEOGRAPHY

Area: 17,075,200 sq. km
Coastline: 37,653 km
Climate: ranges from steppes in south through humid continental, subarctic in Siberia to tundra in polar north; winters vary—cool along Black Sea, frigid in Siberia; summers—warm in the steppes to cool along Arctic coast
Environment: cold desert in north; volcanic activity; only small percentage of land is arable—much is too far north; permafrost over much of Siberia; severe land, air and water pollution; deforestation and soil erosion
Terrain: rolling western plains, north-south ridge of Ural Mountains, central plateau, rugged eastern uplands
Land Use: arable land: 7.46%, permanent crops: 0.11%, other: 92.43%; includes 46,630 sq. km irrigated
Location: E Europe and N Asia, bordering on Barents Sea, Baltic Sea, Black Sea, Caspian Sea

■ PEOPLE

Population: 144,526,278 (July 2003 est.)
Nationality: Russian
Age Structure: 0–14 yrs: 16.0%; 15–64: 70.4%; 65+: 13.6% (2003 est.)
Population Growth Rate: -0.30% (2003 est.)
Net Migration: 0.91 migrants/1,000 population (2003 est.)

Ethnic Groups: 81.5% Russians; 3.8% Tatars, 1.2% Chuvash, 0.9% Bashkir, 0.8% Belorussian, 3% Ukrainian, remainder includes Chechens, Germans, Udmurts, Mari, Kazakhs, Avars, Jews, Moldavians and Armenians
Languages: Russian (official), Tartar, Ukrainian
Religions: Christianity (Russian Orthodox) with substantial Muslim populations and other religious minorities
Birth Rate: 10.09/1,000 population (2003 est.)
Death Rate: 13.99/1,000 population (2003 est.)
Infant Mortality: 19.51 deaths/1,000 live births (2003 est.)
Life Expectancy at Birth: 62.46 years male, 73.11 years female (2003 est.)
Total Fertility Rate: 1.33 children born/woman (2003 est.)
Literacy: 99.6% (2002)

■ GOVERNMENT

Leader(s): President Vladimir V. Putin, Premier Mikhail Yefimovich Fradkov
Government Type: federation
Administrative Divisions: 49 oblasts (oblastey, sing. —oblast), 21 autonomous republics (avtonomnyk respublik, sing. —avtonomnaya respublika), 10 autonomous okrugs (avtonomnykh okrugov, sing. —avtonomnyy okrug), 6 krays (krayer, sing. — kray), 2 federal cities (gorod) and 1 autonomous oblast (avtonomnaya oblast)
Nationhood: Aug. 24, 1991 (from Soviet Union)
National Holiday: Independence Day, June 12

■ ECONOMY

Overview: a vast country with a great many natural resources, a well-educated population, and a diverse but declining industrial base; 25% of the population live below the poverty line and the country continues to experience formidable difficulties in moving from its old centrally planned economy to a modern market economy; the severity of Russia's economic problems is dramatized by the large annual decline in population, caused by environmental hazards, poor health care, and other factors
GDP: US$1.409 trillion, per capita US$9,700; real growth rate 4.3% (2002)
Inflation: 15.0% (2002 est.)
Industries: accounts for 35% of GDP (2002); natural gas refining, steel and coal production and processing, all forms of machine building, shipbuilding, transportation equipment, consumer durables, communications and agricultural equipment, medical and scientific instruments
Labour Force: 77.6 million (2002); 22.7% industry, 65% community, social and business services, 12.3% agriculture
Unemployment: 8.9% (2002)

Agriculture: accounts for 6% of GDP (2002); grain, sugar beets, sunflower seeds, meat, milk, vegetables, fruit

Natural Resources: iron ore, coal, oil, gold, platinum, copper, zinc, lead, tin, rare metals; climate, terrain and distance hinder exploitation

■ FINANCE/TRADE

Currency: ruble (rbl.) = 100 kopeks
International Reserves Excluding Gold: US$80.227 billion (Jan. 2004)
Gold Reserves: 12.545 million fine troy ounces (Jan. 2004)
Budget: revenues US$70 billion; expenditures US$62 billion, including capital expenditures US$ n.a. (2002 est.)
Defence Expenditures: 15.4% of central government expenditure (2002)
Education Expenditures: 10.6% of total government expenditure (2002)
External Debt: US$147.541 billion (2002)
Exports: US$133.520 billion (2003 est.); commodities: fuels, wood products, metals, chemicals, wide range of manufactured products; partners: Germany, US, Italy, China, Belarus, Ukraine
Imports: US$57.309 billion (2003 est.); commodities: machinery, medicine, foodstuffs, consumer products; partners: Germany, Belarus, Ukraine, US, Kazakhstan, Italy

■ COMMUNICATIONS

Daily Newspapers: 105/1,000 inhabitants (2000)
Televisions: 538/1,000 inhabitants (2002)
Radios: 418/1,000 inhabitants (2001)
Telephones: 242 lines/1,000 inhabitants (2002)
Internet: hosts: 409,229 (2002); users: 6 million (2002)

■ TRANSPORTATION

Motor Vehicles: 25,500,000; 19,100,000 passenger cars
Roads: 532,393 km; 358,833 km hard-surfaced
Railway: 87,157 km
Air Traffic: 20,892,000 passengers carried (2002)
Airports: 2,743; 471 have paved runways (2003 est.)

Canadian Embassy: The Canadian Embassy, Starokonyushenny Per 23, Moscow 119002, Russia. Tel: (011-7-095) 105-6000. Fax: (011-7-095) 105-6025. e-mail: mosco@dfait-maeci.gc.ca
Embassy in Canada: Embassy of the Russian Federation, 285 Charlotte St, Ottawa ON K1N 8L5. Tel: (613) 235-4341. Fax: (613) 236-6342. e-mail: rusemb@intranet.ca

Rwanda

Long-Form Name: Rwandese Republic
Capital: Kigali

■ GEOGRAPHY

Area: 26,338 sq. km
Coastline: none: landlocked
Climate: temperate; two rainy seasons (Feb. to Apr., Nov. to Jan.); mild in mountains with frost and snow possible
Environment: deforestation; overgrazing; soil exhaustion; soil erosion; periodic droughts
Terrain: mostly grassy uplands and hills; mountains in west
Land Use: arable land: 32.43%, permanent crops: 10.13%, other: 57.44%; includes 40 sq. km irrigated
Location: EC Africa

■ PEOPLE

Population: 7,810,056 (July 2003 est.)
Nationality: Rwandan
Age Structure: 0–14 yrs: 42.5%; 15–64: 54.8%; 65+: 2.7% (2003 est.)
Population Growth Rate: 1.84% (2003 est.)
Net Migration: 0.0 migrants/1,000 population (2003 est.)
Ethnic Groups: 84% Hutu, 15% Tutsi, 1% Twa (Pygmoid)
Languages: Kinyarwanda, French, English (all official); Kiswahili used in commercial centres
Religions: 65% Christian (mostly Roman Catholic), 9% Protestant, 1% Muslim, 25% indigenous beliefs and other
Birth Rate: 40.10/1,000 population (2003 est.)
Death Rate: 21.72/1,000 population (2003 est.)
Infant Mortality: 102.61 deaths/1,000 live births (2003 est.)
Life Expectancy at Birth: 38.51 years male, 40.18 years female (2003 est.)
Total Fertility Rate: 5.10 children born/woman (2003 est.)
Literacy: 69.2% (2002)

■ GOVERNMENT

Leader(s): President Paul Kagame, Prime Minister Bernard Makuza
Government Type: republic; presidential system in which military leaders hold key offices
Administrative Divisions: 12 prefectures
Nationhood: July 1, 1962 (from UN trusteeship under Belgian administration)
National Holiday: Independence Day, July 1

■ ECONOMY

Overview: a poor nation whose economy is severely hampered by civil war, which has damaged infrastructure and economic prospects; agricultural sector dominates, with coffee and tea making up 80–90% of total exports; manufacturing is largely restricted to the processing of agricultural products

GDP: US$8.92 billion, per capita US$1,200; real growth rate 9.7% (2002 est.)

Inflation: 5.5% (2002 est.)

Industries: accounts for 20% of GDP (2002); mining of cassiterite (tin ore) and wolframite (tungsten ore), tin, cement, agricultural processing, small-scale beverage production, soap, furniture, shoes, plastic goods, textiles, cigarettes

Labour Force: 4.4 million (2002); 90% agriulture

Unemployment: n.a.

Agriculture: accounts for 45% of GDP (2002) and about 90% of labour force; cash crops: coffee, tea, pyrethrum (insecticide made from chrysanthemums); main food crops: bananas, beans, sorghum, potatoes; stock raising; self-sufficiency declining; country imports foodstuffs as farm production fails to keep up with population growth; coffee and tea constitute 80–90% of total exports

Natural Resources: gold, cassiterite (tin ore), wolframite (tungsten ore), natural gas, hydro power

■ FINANCE/TRADE

Currency: Rwandan franc (RF) = 100 centimes

International Reserves Excluding Gold: US$231 million (Jan. 2004)

Gold Reserves: none (Dec. 2002)

Budget: revenues US$199.3 million; expenditures US$443 million, including capital expenditures of US$ n.a. (2001 est.)

Defence Expenditures: 3.0% of GDP (2002)

Education Expenditures: n.a.

External Debt: US$1.435 billion (2002)

Exports: US$61 million (2003 est.); commodities: coffee 85%, tea, tin, cassiterite, wolframite, pyrethrum; partners: EU, Pakistan, US, China, Malaysia

Imports: US$233 million (2003 est.); commodities: textiles, foodstuffs, machines and equipment, capital goods, steel, petroleum products, cement and construction material; partners: Kenya, EU, US, India, Tanzania

■ COMMUNICATIONS

Daily Newspapers: less than 1/1,000 inhabitants (2000)

Televisions: 0/1,000 inhabitants (2000)

Radios: 76/1,000 inhabitants (2001)

Telephones: 3 lines/1,000 inhabitants (2002)

Internet: hosts: 1,233 (2002); users: 25,000 (2002)

■ TRANSPORTATION

Motor Vehicles: 27,800; 11,900 passenger cars

Roads: 12,000 km; 996 km paved

Railway: none

Air Traffic: n.a.

Airports: 9; 4 have paved runways (2003 est.)

Canadian Embassy: Office of the Canadian Embassy, rue Akagera, P.O. Box 1177, Kigali, Rwanda. Tel: (011-250) 573210. Fax: (011-250) 572719. e-mail: kgali@dfait-maeci.gc.ca

Embassy in Canada: c/o Embassy of the Republic of Rwanda, 1714 New Hampshire NW, Washington DC 20009, USA. Tel: (202) 232-2882. Fax: (202) 232-4544. e-mail: n.a.

Saint Helena

Long-Form Name: Saint Helena

Capital: Jamestown

■ GEOGRAPHY

Area: 410 sq. km

Climate: tropical marine; little seasonal variation

Land Use: arable land: 12.9%, permanent crops: 0%, other: 87.1%; includes n.a. sq. km irrigated

Location: S Atlantic Ocean, SW of Africa

■ PEOPLE

Population: 7,367 (July 2003 est.)

Nationality: Saint Helenian

Ethnic Groups: Europeans, East Indians, Africans

Languages: English (official)

■ GOVERNMENT

Colony/Territory of: Dependent Territory of the United Kingdom

Leader(s): Head of State: Queen Elizabeth II, Governor Michael Clancy

Government Type: dependent territory of the UK

National Holiday: Celebration of the Birthday of the Queen, second Saturday in June

■ ECONOMY

Overview: depends primarily on financial assistance from UK; fishing, livestock raising and sale of handicrafts provide income for local population; due to the lack of jobs, many inhabitants have emigrated

■ FINANCE/TRADE

Currency: Saint Helenian pound = 100 pence (at par with British pound)

Canadian Embassy: c/o The Canadian High Commission, Macdonald House, 1 Grosvenor Square, London W1K 4AB, England, UK. Tel: (011-44-20) 7258-6600. Fax: (011-44-20) 7258-6333. e-mail: ldn@dfait-maeci.gc.ca

Representative to Canada: c/o British High Commission, 80 Elgin St, Ottawa ON K1P 5K7. Tel: (613) 237-1530. Fax: (613) 237-7980. e-mail should be sent using the appropriate form at the British High Commission's Website at http://www.britain-in-canada.org

Saint Kitts and Nevis

Long-Form Name: Federation of Saint Kitts and Nevis
Capital: Basseterre

■ GEOGRAPHY

Area: 261 sq. km
Coastline: 135 km
Climate: subtropical tempered by constant sea breezes; little seasonal temperature variation; rainy season (May to Nov.)
Environment: subject to hurricanes (July to Oct.)
Terrain: volcanic with mountainous interiors
Land Use: arable land: 16.67%, permanent crops: 2.78%, other: 80.55%; includes n.a. sq. km irrigated
Location: Caribbean islands E of Puerto Rico

■ PEOPLE

Population: 38,763 (July 2003 est.)
Nationality: Kittsian or Kittitian, Nevisian
Age Structure: 0–14 yrs: 29.0%; 15–64: 62.4%; 65+: 8.5% (2003 est.)
Population Growth Rate: 0.13% (2003 est.)
Net Migration: -8.31 migrants/1,000 population (2003 est.)
Ethnic Groups: mainly of black African descent
Languages: English
Religions: Anglican, other Protestant sects, Roman Catholic
Birth Rate: 18.45/1,000 population (2003 est.)
Death Rate: 8.85/1,000 population (2003 est.)
Infant Mortality: 15.39 deaths/1,000 live births (2003 est.)
Life Expectancy at Birth: 68.76 years male, 74.56 years female (2003 est.)
Total Fertility Rate: 2.37 children born/woman (2003 est.)
Literacy: n.a.

■ GOVERNMENT

Leader(s): Head of State: Queen Elizabeth II, Governor General Cuthbert Montraville Sebastian, Prime Minister Denzil Douglas
Government Type: constitutional monarchy
Administrative Divisions: 14 parishes
Nationhood: Sept. 19, 1983 (from UK)
National Holiday: Independence Day, Sept. 19

■ ECONOMY

Overview: traditionally dependent on the growing and processing of sugar cane and on remittances from overseas workers; tourism and export-oriented manufacturing are increasing
GDP: US$339 million, per capita US$8,800; real growth rate -1.9% (2002 est.)
Inflation: 1.7% (2001 est.)
Industries: accounts for 26% of GDP (2001); sugar processing, tourism, cotton, salt, copra, clothing, footwear, beverages
Labour Force: n.a.
Unemployment: n.a.
Agriculture: accounts for 4% of GDP (2001); cash crop: sugar cane; subsistence crops: rice, yams, vegetables, bananas; fishing potential but not fully exploited; most food imported
Natural Resources: negligible

■ FINANCE/TRADE

Currency: East Caribbean dollar ($EC) = 100 cents
International Reserves Excluding Gold: US$63 million (Jan. 2004)
Gold Reserves: n.a.
Budget: revenues US$89.7 million, expenditures US$128.2 million, including capital expenditures of US$19.5 million (2003 est.)
Defence Expenditures: n.a.
Education Expenditures: n.a.
External Debt: US$255 million (2002)
Exports: US$70 million (2002 est.); commodities: sugar, manufactures, electronics, tobacco, postage stamps; partners: US, UK, CARICOM countries
Imports: US$195 million (2002 est.); commodities: foodstuffs, intermediate manufactures, machinery, fuels; partners: US, CARICOM countries, UK

■ COMMUNICATIONS

Daily Newspapers: none
Televisions: n.a.
Radios: n.a.
Telephones: 607 lines/1,000 inhabitants (2002)
Internet: hosts: 2 (2002); users: 10,000 (2002)

■ TRANSPORTATION

Motor Vehicles: n.a.
Roads: 320 km; 136 km paved
Railway: 50 km
Air Traffic: n.a.
Airports: 2, both with paved runways (2003 est.)

Canadian Embassy: The Canadian High Commission to Saint Kitts and Nevis, c/o The Canadian High Commission, Bishop's Court Hill, St. Michael, Barbados; mailing address: P.O. Box 404, Bridgetown, Barbados. Tel: (246) 429-3550. Fax: (246) 429-3780. e-mail: bdgtn@dfait-maeci.gc.ca

Embassy in Canada: c/o High Commission for the Countries of the Organization of Eastern Caribbean States, 130 Albert St Ste 700, Ottawa ON K1P 5G4. Tel: (613) 236-8952. Fax: (613) 236-3042. e-mail: echcc@travel-net.com

Saint Lucia

Long-Form Name: Saint Lucia
Capital: Castries

■ GEOGRAPHY

Area: 620 sq. km
Coastline: 158 km
Climate: tropical, moderated by northeast trade winds; dry season from Jan. to Apr., rainy season from May to Aug.
Environment: subject to hurricanes and volcanic activity; deforestation; soil erosion
Terrain: volcanic and mountainous with some broad, fertile valleys
Land Use: arable land: 4.9%, permanent crops: 23%, other: 72.1%; includes 30 sq. km irrigated
Location: Caribbean islands, N of Venezuela

■ PEOPLE

Population: 162,157 (July 2003 est.)
Nationality: Saint Lucian
Age Structure: 0–14 yrs: 31.1%; 15–64: 63.7%; 65+: 5.2% (2003 est.)
Population Growth Rate: 1.25% (2003 est.)
Net Migration: -3.15 migrants/1,000 population (2003 est.)
Ethnic Groups: 90% African descent, 6% mixed, 3% East Indian, 1% Caucasian
Languages: English (official), French patois
Religions: 90% Roman Catholic, 7% Protestant, 3% Anglican
Birth Rate: 20.93/1,000 population (2003 est.)
Death Rate: 5.24/1,000 population (2003 est.)
Infant Mortality: 14.37 deaths/1,000 live births (2003 est.)
Life Expectancy at Birth: 69.52 years male, 76.90 years female (2003 est.)
Total Fertility Rate: 2.29 children born/woman (2003 est.)
Literacy: n.a.

■ GOVERNMENT

Leader(s): Head of State: Queen Elizabeth II, Governor General Calliopa Pearlette Louisy, Prime Minister Kenny Anthony
Government Type: parliamentary democracy
Administrative Divisions: 11 quarters
Nationhood: Feb. 22, 1979 (from UK)
National Holiday: Independence Day, Feb. 22

■ ECONOMY

Overview: depends on strong agricultural (bananas) and tourist industry sectors; expanding industrial base supported by foreign investment in manufacturing and activities such as data processing; vulnerable to droughts and tropical storms
GDP: US$866 million, per capita US$5,400; real growth rate 3.3% (2002 est.)
Inflation: 3.0% (2001 est.)
Industries: accounts for 20% of GDP (2002); clothing, electronic component assembly, beverages, tourism, lime and coconut processing
Labour Force: 43,800 (2001); 43% agriculture, 39% services, 18% industry and commerce
Unemployment: n.a.
Agriculture: accounts for 7% of GDP (2002) and 43% of labour force; crops: bananas, coconuts, vegetables, citrus fruit, root crops, cocoa; imports food for the tourist industry
Natural Resources: forests, sandy beaches, minerals (pumice), mineral springs, geothermal potential

■ FINANCE/TRADE

Currency: East Caribbean dollar (EC$) = 100 cents
International Reserves Excluding Gold: US$121 million (Jan. 2004)
Gold Reserves: n.a.
Budget: revenues US$141.2 million; expenditures US$146.7 million, including capital expenditures of US$25.1 million (2002 est.)
Defence Expenditures: n.a.
Education Expenditures: n.a.
External Debt: US$415 million (2002)
Exports: US$38 million (2002 est.); commodities: bananas 67%, cocoa, vegetables, fruit, coconut oil, clothing; partners: UK, US, CARICOM countries
Imports: US$254 million (2002 est.); commodities: manufactured goods 22%, machinery and transportation equipment 21%, food and live animals 20%, mineral fuels, foodstuffs, machinery and equipment, fertilizers, petroleum products; partners: US, CARICOM countries, Japan, Canada

■ COMMUNICATIONS

Daily Newspapers: none
Televisions: n.a.
Radios: n.a.
Telephones: 322 lines/1,000 inhabitants (2002)
Internet: hosts: 29 (2002); users: 13,000 (2002)

■ TRANSPORTATION

Motor Vehicles: 12,300; 11,400 passenger cars
Roads: 1,210 km; 63 km paved

Railway: none
Air Traffic: n.a.
Airports: 2, both with paved runways (2003 est.)

Canadian Embassy: The Canadian High Commission to Saint Lucia, c/o The Canadian High Commission, Bishop's Court Hill, St. Michael, Barbados; mailing address: P.O. Box 404, Bridgetown, Barbados. Tel: (246) 429-3550. Fax: (246) 429-3780. e-mail: bdgtn@dfait-maeci.gc.ca
Embassy in Canada: c/o High Commission for the Countries of the Organization of Eastern Caribbean States, 130 Albert St Ste 700, Ottawa ON K1P 5G4. Tel: (613) 236-8952. Fax: (613) 236-3042. e-mail: echcc@travel-net.com

Saint Pierre and Miquelon

Long-Form Name: Territorial Collectivity of Saint Pierre and Miquelon
Capital: Saint-Pierre

■ GEOGRAPHY

Area: 242 sq. km, 8 small islands
Climate: cold and wet, misty and foggy, windy spring and autumn, moist, temperate summers, cold and snowy winters
Land Use: arable land: 13.04%, permanent crops: 0%, other: 86.96%; includes n.a. km irrigated
Location: N Atlantic Ocean, S of Newfoundland

■ PEOPLE

Population: 6,976 (July 2003 est.)
Nationality: Frenchman, Frenchwoman
Ethnic Groups: descendants of French settlers, Basques and Bretons (French fishermen)
Languages: French, English

■ GOVERNMENT

Colony/Territory of: Territorial Collectivity of France
Leader(s): President Jacques Chirac (France), Prefect Claude Valleix
Government Type: territorial collectivity with internal self-government
National Holiday: Taking of the Bastille, July 14

■ ECONOMY

Overview: fishing, and the servicing of fishing fleets operating off the coast of Newfoundland, have long been an important part of the economy; agriculture: some vegetables and livestock for local consumption; partners: UK, Canada, EU

■ FINANCE/TRADE

Currency: French franc = 100 centimes; also the Euro (€)

Canadian Embassy: c/o The Canadian Embassy, 35-37 avenue Montaigne, 75008 Paris, France. Tel: (011-33-1) 44-43-29-00. Fax: (011-33-1) 44-43-29-99. e-mail: paris@dfait-maeci.gc.ca
Representative to Canada: c/o Embassy of France, 42 Sussex Dr, Ottawa ON K1M 2C9. Tel: (613) 789-1795. Fax: (613) 562-3735. e-mail: politique@ambafrance-ca.org

Saint Vincent and the Grenadines

Long-Form Name: Saint Vincent and the Grenadines
Capital: Kingstown

■ GEOGRAPHY

Area: 389 sq. km
Coastline: 84 km
Climate: tropical; little seasonal temperature variation; rainy season (May to Nov.)
Environment: subject to hurricanes; Soufrière volcano is a constant threat; water pollution along coasts
Terrain: volcanic, mountainous; Soufrière volcano on the island of Saint Vincent
Land Use: arable land: 10.3%, permanent crops: 17.9%, other: 71.8%; includes 10 sq. km irrigated
Location: Caribbean islands, N of Venezuela

■ PEOPLE

Population: 116,812 (July 2003 est.)
Nationality: Saint Vincentian or Vincentian
Age Structure: 0–14 yrs: 28.2%; 15–64: 65.5%; 65+: 6.4% (2003 est.)
Population Growth Rate: 0.34% (2003 est.)
Net Migration: -7.66 migrants/1,000 population (2003 est.)
Ethnic Groups: 66% black African descent; remainder mixed, with some white, East Indian, Carib Indian
Languages: English (official), some French patois
Religions: Anglican, Methodist, Roman Catholic, Seventh-Day Adventist
Birth Rate: 17.16/1,000 population (2003 est.)
Death Rate: 6.08/1,000 population (2003 est.)
Infant Mortality: 15.70 deaths/1,000 live births (2003 est.)
Life Expectancy at Birth: 71.30 years male, 74.92 years female (2003 est.)
Total Fertility Rate: 1.95 children born/woman (2003 est.)
Literacy: 83.1% (2002)

■ GOVERNMENT

Leader(s): Head of State: Queen Elizabeth II, Governor General Frederick Nathaniel Ballantyne, Prime Minister Ralph Gonsalves
Government Type: parliamentary democracy
Administrative Divisions: 6 parishes

Nationhood: Oct. 27, 1979 (from UK)
National Holiday: Independence Day, Oct. 27

■ ECONOMY

Overview: overdependence on the weather-plagued banana crop as a major export earner has caused high unemployment; has been unsuccessful in diversifying into new industries
GDP: US$339 million, per capita US$2,900; real growth rate -0.5% (2002 est.)
Inflation: 0.8% (2001)
Industries: accounts for 26% of GDP (2001 est.); food processing (sugar, flour), cement, furniture, rum, starch, sheet metal, beverage
Labour Force: n.a.
Unemployment: n.a.
Agriculture: accounts for 10% of GDP (2001 est.) and 60% of labour force; provides bulk of exports; products: bananas, arrowroot (world's largest producer), coconuts, sweet potatoes, spices; small numbers of cattle, sheep, hogs, goats; small fish catch used locally
Natural Resources: negligible

■ FINANCE/TRADE

Currency: East Caribbean dollar ($EC) = 100 cents
International Reserves Excluding Gold: US$72 million (Jan. 2004)
Gold Reserves: n.a.
Budget: revenues US$94.6 million; expenditures US$85.8 million, including capital expenditures US$ n.a. (2002 est.)
Defence Expenditures: negligible
Education Expenditures: 16.45% of total government expenditure (2000)
External Debt: US$206 million (2002)
Exports: US$38 million (2003 est.); commodities: bananas, eddoes and dasheen (taro), arrowroot starch, copra; partners: CARICOM, UK, US
Imports: US$200 million (2003 est.); commodities: foodstuffs, machinery and equipment, chemicals and fertilizers, minerals and fuels; partners: US, CARICOM countries, UK

■ COMMUNICATIONS

Daily Newspapers: none
Televisions: n.a.
Radios: n.a.
Telephones: 234 lines/1,000 inhabitants (2002)
Internet: hosts: n.a. users: 7,000 (2002)

■ TRANSPORTATION

Motor Vehicles: 8,200; 5,000 passenger cars
Roads: 1,040 km; 320 km paved
Railway: none

Air Traffic: n.a.
Airports: 6, 5 with paved runways (2003 est.)

Canadian Embassy: The Canadian High Commission to Saint Vincent and the Grenadines, c/o The Canadian High Commission, Bishop's Court Hill, St. Michael, Barbados; mailing address: P.O. Box 404, Bridgetown, Barbados. Tel: (246) 429-3550. Fax: (246) 429-3780. e-mail: bdgtn@dfait-maeci.gc.ca
Embassy in Canada: c/o High Commission for the Countries of the Organization of Eastern Caribbean States, 130 Albert St Ste 700, Ottawa ON K1P 5G4. Tel: (613) 236-8952. Fax: (613) 236-3042. e-mail: echcc@travel-net.com

Samoa

Long-Form Name: Independent State of Samoa
Capital: Apia

■ GEOGRAPHY

Area: 2,860 sq. km
Coastline: 403 km
Climate: tropical; rainy season lasts from Oct. to March, dry season from May to Oct.
Environment: volcanism and typhoons are natural hazards; soil erosion
Terrain: interior is rocky, with volcanic mountains; narrow coastal plain
Land Use: arable land: 19.43%, permanent crops: 23.67%, other: 56.9%; includes n.a. sq. km irrigated
Location: South Pacific Ocean, E of Australia and NE of New Zealand

■ PEOPLE

Population: 178,173 (July 2003 est.)
Nationality: Samoan
Age Structure: 0–14 yrs: 29.4%; 15–64: 64.6%; 65+: 6.1% (2003 est.)
Population Growth Rate: -0.27% (2003 est.)
Net Migration: -11.67 migrants/1,000 population (2003 est.)
Ethnic Groups: 92.6% Samoan, 7% European-Polynesian; 0.4% Europeans
Languages: Samoan (Polynesian), also English
Religions: almost 100% Christianity
Birth Rate: 15.41/1,000 population (2003 est.)
Death Rate: 6.41/1,000 population (2003 est.)
Infant Mortality: 29.73 deaths/1,000 live births (2003 est.)
Life Expectancy at Birth: 67.35 years male, 73.00 years female (2003 est.)
Total Fertility Rate: 3.21 children born/women (2003 est.)
Literacy: 88.7% (2002)

■ GOVERNMENT

Leader(s): Head of State: Tanumafili II Malietoa, Prime Minister Sailele Malielegaoi Tuialepa
Government Type: constitutional monarchy under a native chief
Administrative Divisions: 11 districts
Nationhood: Jan. 1, 1962
National Holiday: Independence Day, June 1

■ ECONOMY

Overview: Recent economic growth has been impressive, but overall the economy remains heavily agriculture-oriented, and disease and pests have done much damage in recent years; tourism has become the most important growth industry; the flexibility of the labour market is a basic strength for future economic gains
GDP: US$1 billion; per capita US$5,600, real growth rate 5.0% (2002 est.)
Inflation: 4.0% (2001)
Industries: accounts for 18% of GDP (2000); fishing, timber, food processing, tourism
Labour Force: 90,000 (2000 est.); 65% agriculture, 30% services, 5% industry
Unemployment: n.a.
Agriculture: makes up 16% of GDP (2000); mostly coconuts and fruit
Natural Resources: fish, forest resources, hydroelectric potential

■ FINANCE/TRADE

Currency: tala ($WS) = 100 sene
International Reserves Excluding Gold: US$86 million (Jan. 2004)
Gold Reserves: n.a.
Budget: revenues US$105 million; expenditures US$119 million, including capital expenditures US$ n.a. (FY2001/02)
Defence Expenditures: n.a.
Education Expenditures: n.a.
External Debt: US$234 million (2002)
Exports: US$15 million (2003 est.); commodities: coconut oil and cream, copra, fish, beer; partners: New Zealand, American Samoa, Australia, Indonesia, US
Imports: US$135 million (2003 est.); commodities: intermediate goods, food, capital goods; partners: New Zealand, Australia, Fiji, US, Japan

■ COMMUNICATIONS

Daily Newspapers: none
Televisions: n.a.
Radios: n.a.
Telephones: 58 lines/1,000 inhabitants (2002)
Internet: hosts: 5,705 (2002); users: 4,000 (2002)

■ TRANSPORTATION

Motor Vehicles: 2,600; 1,200 passenger cars
Roads: 790 km; 332 km paved
Railway: none
Air Traffic: 88,500 passengers carried (2001 est.)
Airports: 4; 3 have paved runways (2003 est.)

Canadian Embassy: The Canadian High Commission to Western Samoa, c/o The Canadian High Commission, P.O. Box 12049, Thorndon, Wellington, New Zealand. Tel: (011-64-4) 473-9577. Fax: (011-64-4) 471-2082. e-mail: wlgtn@dfait-maeci.gc.ca
Embassy in Canada: c/o Samoa High Commission, 800 Second Ave, Ste 400J, New York NY 10017, USA. Tel: (212) 599-6196. Fax: (212) 599-0797. e-mail: samoa@un.int

San Marino

Long-Form Name: Republic of San Marino
Capital: San Marino

■ GEOGRAPHY

Area: 60.5 sq. km
Coastline: none; landlocked
Climate: Mediterranean; mild to cool winters; warm, sunny summers
Environment: dominated by the Apennines
Terrain: rugged mountains
Land Use: arable land: 16.67%, permanent crops: 0%, other: 83.33%; includes n.a. sq. km irrigated
Location: S Europe (E Italy)

■ PEOPLE

Population: 28,119 (July 2003 est.)
Nationality: Sammarinese
Age Structure: 0–14 yrs: 16.3%; 15–64: 67.1%; 65+: 16.6% (2003 est.)
Population Growth Rate: 1.38% (2003 est.)
Net Migration: 11.13 migrants/1,000 population (2003 est.)
Ethnic Groups: Sammarinese, Italian
Languages: Italian
Religions: Roman Catholic
Birth Rate: 10.49/1,000 population (2003 est.)
Death Rate: 7.86/1,000 population (2003 est.)
Infant Mortality: 5.97 deaths/1,000 live births (2003 est.)
Life Expectancy at Birth: 77.90 years male, 85.26 years female (2003 est.)
Total Fertility Rate: 1.31 children born/woman (2003 est.)
Literacy: 96%

■ GOVERNMENT

Leader(s): Captains-Regent: Paulo Bollini and Marino Riccardi

Government Type: republic
Administrative Divisions: 9 municipalities (castelli, sing. —castello)
Nationhood: 301 (by tradition)
National Holiday: Anniversary of the Foundation of the Republic, Sept. 3

■ ECONOMY

Overview: tourism and the sale of postage stamps are vital to the economy; tourism itself contributes more than 50% to the GDP; key industries are clothing, electronics, ceramics, agricultural products, wine and cheese
GDP: US$940 million, per capita $34,600; real growth rate 7.5% (2001 est.)
Inflation: 3.3% (2001)
Industries: wine, olive oil, cement, leather, textiles, tourism
Labour Force: n.a.; 57% services, 42% industry, 1% agriculture
Unemployment: 2.8% (Dec. 2000)
Agriculture: employs 2% of labour force; products: wheat, grapes, corn, olives, meat, cheese, hides; small numbers of cattle, pigs, horses; depends on Italy for food imports
Natural Resources: building stone

■ FINANCE/TRADE

Currency: Italian lire (Lit) = 100 centesimi; also the Euro. San Marino also mints its own coins
International Reserves Excluding Gold: n.a.
Gold Reserves: n.a.
Budget: revenues US$400 million, expenditures US$400 million, including capital expenditures of US$ n.a. (2000 est.)
Defence Expenditures: n.a.
Education Expenditures: n.a.
External Debt: n.a.
Exports: n.a.; trade data are included in the statistics for Italy. Products include building stone, lime, wood, chestnuts, wheat, wine, baked goods, hides, ceramics
Imports: n.a.; trade data are included in the statistics for Italy. Products include a wide variety of consumer manufactures and food-stuffs

■ COMMUNICATIONS

Daily Newspapers: 3 in total
Televisions: n.a.
Radios: n.a.
Telephones: 744 lines/1,000 inhabitants (2002)
Internet: users: 14,300 (2002)

■ TRANSPORTATION

Motor Vehicles: 30,000; 25,000 passenger cars
Roads: 220 km; all km paved
Railway: none
Air Traffic: n.a.
Airports: none

Canadian Embassy: The Canadian Consulate to San Marino, c/o The Canadian Embassy, Via G.B. de Rossi, 27, 00161 Rome, Italy. Tel: (011-39-06) 445981. Fax: (011-39-06) 445 98750. e-mail: rome@dfait-maeci.gc.ca
Embassy in Canada: none at present.

São Tomé and Príncipe

Long-Form Name: Democratic Republic of São Tomé and Príncipe
Capital: São Tomé

■ GEOGRAPHY

Area: 1,001 sq. km
Coastline: 209 km
Climate: tropical; hot, humid; one rainy season (Oct. to May)
Environment: deforestation; soil degradation
Terrain: volcanic, mountainous
Land Use: arable land: 2%, permanent crops: 41%, other: 57%; includes 100 sq. km irrigated
Location: S Atlantic Ocean, off W African Coast

■ PEOPLE

Population: 175,883 (July 2003 est.)
Nationality: São Toméan
Age Structure: 0–14 yrs: 47.7%; 15–64: 48.3%; 65+: 4.0% (2003 est.)
Population Growth Rate: 3.18% (2003 est.)
Net Migration: -2.93 migrants/1,000 population (2003 est.)
Ethnic Groups: mestiço, angolares (descendants of Angolan slaves), forros (descendants of freed slaves), servicais (contract labourers from Angola, Mozambique and Cape Verde), tongas (children of servicais born on the islands) and European (primarily Portuguese)
Languages: Portuguese (official), Crioulo
Religions: Roman Catholic, Evangelical Protestant, Seventh-Day Adventist
Birth Rate: 41.87/1,000 population (2003 est.)
Death Rate: 7.11/1,000 population (2003 est.)
Infant Mortality: 46.04 deaths/1,000 live births (2003 est.)
Life Expectancy at Birth: 64.79 years male, 67.82 years female (2003 est.)
Total Fertility Rate: 5.88 children born/woman (2003 est.)
Literacy: 83.1% (2002)

■ GOVERNMENT

Leader(s): President Fradique de Menezes, Prime Minister Maria das Neves
Government Type: republic
Administrative Divisions: 2 provinces
Nationhood: July 12, 1975 (from Portugal)
National Holiday: Independence Day, July 12

■ ECONOMY

Overview: the economy is hampered by over-dependence on cocoa production, which has substantially declined in recent years because of drought and mismanagement; imports 90% of food needs as well as all fuels and most manufactured goods; government is attempting to restructure economy and reduce debt burden

GDP: US$200 million, per capita US$1,200; real growth rate 4.0% (2002 est.)

Inflation: 9.0% (2002 est.)

Industries: accounts for 19% of GDP; light construction, shirts, soap, beer, fisheries, shrimp processing

Labour Force: n.a.; most of population engaged in subsistence agriculture and fishing. There are shortages of skilled workers

Unemployment: n.a.

Agriculture: 23% of GDP; primary source of exports; cash crops: cocoa (85%), coconuts, palm kernels, coffee, copra, cinnamon, pepper; food products: bananas, papayas, beans, poultry, fish; not self-sufficient in foodgrain and meat

Natural Resources: fish, hydro power

■ FINANCE/TRADE

Currency: dobra (Db) = 100 centimos

International Reserves Excluding Gold: n.a.

Gold Reserves: n.a.

Budget: n.a.

Defence Expenditures: 0.8% of GP (2001)

Education Expenditures: n.a.

External Debt: US$333 million (2002)

Exports: US$6.479 million (2003 est.); commodities: cocoa 85%, copra, coffee, palm oil; partners: Spain, Netherlands, Portugal

Imports: US$30.03 million (2003 est.); commodities: machinery and electrical equipment 54%, food products 23%, other 23%; partners: Portugal, France, UK

■ COMMUNICATIONS

Daily Newspapers: none

Televisions: n.a.

Radios: n.a.

Telephones: 36 lines/1,000 inhabitants (2002)

Internet: hosts: 1,069 (2002); users: 11,000 (2002)

■ TRANSPORTATION

Motor Vehicles: n.a.

Roads: 320 km; 218 km paved

Railway: none

Air Traffic: 27,800 passengers carried (2001 est.)

Airports: 2, both with paved runways (2003 est.)

Canadian Embassy: The Canadian Embassy to São Tomé and Príncipe, c/o The Canadian Embassy, P.O. Box 4037 Libreville, Gabon.

Tel: (011-241) 73-73-54. Fax: (011-241) 73-73-88. e-mail: lbrve@dfait-maeci.gc.ca

Embassy in Canada: c/o Embassy of São Tomé and Príncipe, 400 Park Ave, 7th Fl, New York, NY 10022. Tel: (212) 317-0533. Fax: (212) 317-0580. e-mail: n.a.

Saudi Arabia

Long-Form Name: Kingdom of Saudi Arabia

Capital: Riyadh (royal); Jeddah (administrative)

■ GEOGRAPHY

Area: 1,960,582 sq. km

Coastline: 2,640 km

Climate: harsh, dry desert with great extremes of temperature

Environment: no perennial rivers or permanent water bodies; developing extensive coastal seawater desalination facilities; desertification; coastal pollution; frequent dust and sandstorms

Terrain: mostly uninhabited, sandy desert

Land Use: arable land: 1.72%, permanent crops: 0.06%, other: 98.22%; includes 16,200 sq. km irrigated

Location: SW Asia (Middle East), bordering on Persian Gulf, Arabian Sea, Red Sea

■ PEOPLE

Population: 24,293,844; includes 5,576,076 non-nationals (July 2003 est.)

Nationality: Saudi

Age Structure: 0–14 yrs: 42.3%; 15–64: 54.8%; 65+: 2.9% (2003 est.)

Population Growth Rate: 3.27% (2003 est.)

Net Migration: 1.23 migrants/1,000 population (2003 est.)

Ethnic Groups: 90% Arab, 10% Afro-Asian

Languages: Arabic (official); English (business language)

Religions: Muslim (85% Sunni, 15% Shia)

Birth Rate: 37.20/1,000 population (2003 est.)

Death Rate: 5.79/1,000 population (2003 est.)

Infant Mortality: 47.94 deaths/1,000 live births (2003 est.)

Life Expectancy at Birth: 66.99 years male, 70.55 years female (2003 est.)

Total Fertility Rate: 6.15 children born/woman (2003 est.)

Literacy: 77.9% (2002)

■ GOVERNMENT

Leader(s): King and Prime Minister Fahd bin Abdul Aziz al Saud

Government Type: monarchy

Administrative Divisions: 13 provinces (mintaqat, sing. —mintaqah)

Nationhood: Sept. 23, 1932 (unification)

National Holiday: Unification of the Kingdom, Sept. 23

■ ECONOMY

Overview: has the largest reserves of petroleum in the world and is the largest exporter of petroleum; the government is working toward the privatization of the economy
GDP: US$268.9 billion, per capita US$11,400; real growth rate 1.0% (2002 est.)
Inflation: 1.0% (2002 est.)
Industries: accounts for 48% of GDP (2000); crude oil production, petroleum refining, basic petrochemicals, cement, small steel-rolling mill, construction, fertilizer, plastic
Labour Force: 7.2 million (4 million foreign workers) (2001); 25% industry, 63% services, 12% agriculture
Unemployment: n.a.
Agriculture: accounts for 7% of GDP (2000); fastest growing economic sector; subsidized by government; products: wheat, barley, tomatoes, melons, dates, citrus fruit, mutton, chickens, eggs, milk; approaching self-sufficiency in food
Natural Resources: crude oil, natural gas, iron ore, gold, copper

■ FINANCE/TRADE

Currency: riyal (SR) = 100 halalah
International Reserves Excluding Gold: US$23.865 billion (Jan. 2004)
Gold Reserves: 4.596 million fine troy ounces (Jan. 2004)
Budget: revenues US$78.7 billion; expenditures US$66.7 billion, including capital expenditures US$ n.a. (2003 est.)
Defence Expenditures: 13.0% of GDP (2000)
Education Expenditures: n.a.
External Debt: US$25.9 billion (2003 est.)
Exports: US$72.550 billion (2002); commodities: petroleum and petroleum products 89%; partners: Japan, US, South Korea, Singapore, India
Imports: US$32.312 billion (2002); commodities: manufactured goods, transportation equipment, construction materials, processed food products; partners: US, Japan, Germany, UK

■ COMMUNICATIONS

Daily Newspapers: 326/1,000 inhabitants (2000)
Televisions: 265/1,000 inhabitants (2002)
Radios: 326/1,000 inhabitants (2001)
Telephones: 144 lines/1,000 inhabitants (2002)
Internet: hosts: 14,788 (2002); users: 1,418,900 (2002)

■ TRANSPORTATION

Motor Vehicles: 3,000,000; 1,710,000 passenger cars
Roads: 151,470 km; 45,592 km paved
Railway: 1,392 km
Air Traffic: 13,564,000 passengers carried (2002)

Airports: 209; 70 have paved runways (2003 est.)

Canadian Embassy: The Canadian Embassy, Diplomatic Quarter, Riyadh; mailing address: P.O. Box 94321, Riyadh 11693, Saudi Arabia. Tel: (011-966-1) 488-2288. Fax: (011-966-1) 488-1997. e-mail: ryadh@dfait-maeci.gc.ca
Embassy in Canada: Royal Embassy of Saudi Arabia, 99 Bank St, Ste 901, Ottawa ON K1P 6B9. Tel: (613) 237-4100. Fax: (613) 237-0567. e-mail: n.a.

Senegal

Long-Form Name: Republic of Senegal
Capital: Dakar

■ GEOGRAPHY

Area: 196,190 sq. km
Coastline: 531 km
Climate: tropical; hot, humid; rainy season (Dec. to Apr.) has strong southeast winds; dry season (May to Nov.) dominated by hot, dry harmattan wind
Environment: lowlands seasonally flooded; deforestation; overgrazing; soil degradation; wildlife populations are endangered by poaching
Terrain: generally low, rolling, plains rising to foothills in southeast
Land Use: arable land: 11.58%, permanent crops: 0.19%, other: 88.23%; includes 710 sq. km irrigated
Location: W Africa, bordering on Atlantic Ocean

■ PEOPLE

Population: 10,580,307 (July 2003 est.)
Nationality: Senegalese (sing. & pl.)
Age Structure: 0–14 yrs: 43.7%; 15–64: 53.3%; 65+: 3.0% (2003 est.)
Population Growth Rate: 2.56% (2003 est.)
Net Migration: 0.21 migrants/1,000 population (2003 est.)
Ethnic Groups: 43.3% Wolof, 23.8% Fulani, 14.7% Serer, 3.7% Diola, 3% Mandingo, 1% European and Lebanese, 10.5% other
Languages: French (official); Wolof, Pulaar, Diola, Mandingo
Religions: 92% Muslim, 6% indigenous beliefs, 2% Christian (mostly Roman Catholic)
Birth Rate: 36.23/1,000 population (2003 est.)
Death Rate: 10.88/1,000 population (2003 est.)
Infant Mortality: 57.57 deaths/1,000 live births (2003 est.)
Life Expectancy at Birth: 54.83 years male, 57.95 years female (2003 est.)
Total Fertility Rate: 4.93 children born/woman (2003 est.)
Literacy: 39.3% (2002)

■ GOVERNMENT

Leader(s): President Abdoulaye Wade, Prime Minister Idrissa Seck
Government Type: republic under multiparty democratic rule
Administrative Divisions: 10 regions
Nationhood: April 4, 1960 (from France)
National Holiday: Independence Day, Apr. 4

■ ECONOMY

Overview: tourism has emerged as a great boon to the economy; fishing is the main economic resource; mining (phosphate) has been hurt by reduced worldwide demand for fertilizers in recent years; limited resource base, environmental degradation and very high population growth continue to delay improvements
GDP: US$15.64 billion, per capita US$1,500; real growth rate 2.4% (2002 est.)
Inflation: 3.0% (2002 est.)
Industries: accounts for 26% of GDP (2000); fishing, agricultural processing, phosphate mining, petroleum refining, building materials
Labour Force: 4.4 million (2002); 70% agriculture
Unemployment: n.a.; urban youth 40%
Agriculture: including fishing, accounts for 18% of GDP (2000); major products: peanuts (cash crop), millet, corn, sorghum, rice, cotton, tomatoes, green vegetables; estimated two-thirds self-sufficient in food, cattle, poultry, pigs; fish catch of 354,000 metric tons
Natural Resources: fish, phosphates, iron ore

■ FINANCE/TRADE

Currency: Communauté financière africaine franc (CFAF) = 100 centimes
International Reserves Excluding Gold: US$788 million (Nov. 2003)
Gold Reserves: none (Dec. 2002)
Budget: revenues US$1.373 billion, expenditures US$1.373 billion, including capital expenditures of US$357 million (2002 est.)
Defence Expenditures: 6.8% of central government expenditure (2002)
Education Expenditures: n.a.
External Debt: US$3.918 billion (2002)
Exports: US$1.23 billion (2003 est.); commodities: manufactures 30%, fish products 27%, peanuts 11%, petroleum products 11%, phosphates 10%; partners: France, Italy, Spain, Côte d'Ivoire
Imports: US$1.753 billion (2003 est.); commodities: semi-manufactures 30%, food 27%, durable consumer goods 17%, petroleum 12%, capital goods 14%; partners: France, Nigeria, Germany, US, Italy

■ COMMUNICATIONS

Daily Newspapers: 5/1,000 inhabitants (2000)
Televisions: 78/1,000 inhabitants (2002)
Radios: 126/1,000 inhabitants (2001)
Telephones: 22 lines/1,000 inhabitants (2002)
Internet: hosts: 761 (2002); users: 105,000 (2002)

■ TRANSPORTATION

Motor Vehicles: 150,000; 115,000 passenger cars
Roads: 14,576 km; 4,271 km paved
Railway: 906 km
Air Traffic: 245,000 passengers carried (2002)
Airports: 20; 9 have paved runways (2003 est.)

Canadian Embassy: The Canadian Embassy, 45 av. de la République, P.O. Box 3373, Dakar, Senegal. Tel: (011-221) 889-4700. Fax: (011-221) 889-4720. e-mail: dakar@dfait-maeci.gc.ca
Embassy in Canada: Embassy of the Republic of Senegal, 57 Marlborough Ave, Ottawa ON K1N 8E8. Tel: (613) 238-6392. Fax: (613) 238-2695. e-mail: ambassn@sympatico.ca

Serbia and Montenegro

Long-Form Name: Serbia and Montenegro
Capital: Belgrade (Serbia), Podgorica (Montenegro)

■ GEOGRAPHY

Area: 102,350 sq. km (Serbia 88,412 sq. km, Montenegro 13,938 sq. km)
Coastline: 199 km (Montenegro 199 km, Serbia 0 km)
Climate: continental in north; continental and Mediterranean in central region; south—Adriatic climate along coast, hot and dry summers, relatively cold winters, with heavy snowfall inland
Environment: coastal water pollution from sewage outlets, esp. in tourist-related areas; air and water pollution; subject to earthquakes
Terrain: varied: rich fertile plain in north, limestone ranges and basins in east, mountains and hills in southeast, high shoreline with no islands in southwest
Land Use: arable land: 36.34%, permanent crops: 3.44%, other: 60.22%; includes 570 sq. km irrigated
Location: S Europe, bordering Adriatic Sea

■ PEOPLE

Population: 10,655,774 (July 2003 est.)
Nationality: Serb, Montenegrin
Age Structure: 0–14 yrs: 19.3%; 15–64: 65.4%; 65+: 15.3% (2003 est.)
Population Growth Rate: 0.07% (2003 est.)

Net Migration: -1.38 migrants/1000 population (2003 est.)
Ethnic Groups: 62.6% Serb, 16.5% Albanian, 5% Montenegrin, 3.4% Yugoslav, 3.3% Hungarian, 9.2% other
Languages: 95% Serbian, 5% Albanian
Religions: 65% Orthodox, 19% Muslim, 4% Roman Catholic, 1% Protestant, 11% other
Birth Rate: 12.74/1000 population (2003 est.)
Death Rate: 10.62/1,000 population (2003 est.)
Infant Mortality: 16.90 deaths/1,000 live births (2003 est.)
Life Expectancy at Birth: 71.03 years male, 77.16 years female (2003 est.)
Total Fertility Rate: 1.77 children born/woman (2003 est.)
Literacy: n.a.

■ GOVERNMENT

Leader(s): President and Chairman of the Council of Ministers Svetozar Marovic
Government Type: republic
Administrative Divisions: 2 republics (republike, sing. —republika) and 2 nominally autonomous provinces (autonomna pokrajine, sing. — autonomna pokrajina)
Nationhood: April 11, 1992 (from Yugoslavia)
National Holiday: St. Vitus Day, June 28

■ ECONOMY

Overview: ethnic warfare has caused destabilization of republic boundaries and the break-up of important inter-republic trade connections; the economic boom anticipated by the government after the suspension of UN sanctions has failed to take place, largely due to government mismanagement of the economy. International sanctions have now been lifted, and Serbia and Montenegro is in the initial stages of economic reform
GDP: US$23.15 billion, per capita US$2,200; real growth rate 4.0% (2002)
Inflation: 19.0% (2002 est.)
Industries: accounts for 36% of GDP (2001 est.); machine building, metallurgy, mining, consumer goods, electronics, petroleum products, chemicals, pharmaceuticals
Labour Force: 3.9 million (2002); 41% industry, 35% services, 12% trade and tourism, 7% transportation and communication, 5% agriculture
Unemployment: 22.3% (2002 est.)
Agriculture: accounts for 26% of GDP (2001 est.); cereals, cotton, oilseed plants, chicory, fodder crops, fruit, vegetables, tobacco, olives, citrus, rice, livestock (sheep, goats)
Natural Resources: oil, gas, coal, antimony, copper, lead, gold, chrome, pyrite, hydro power

■ FINANCE/TRADE

Currency: Yugoslav New Dinar (YD) = 100 paras. Also the Euro: in Montenegro the Euro is legal tender, in Kosovo both the Euro and the Dinar are legal tender.
International Reserves Excluding Gold: n.a.
Gold Reserves: n.a.
Budget: revenues US$3.9 billion, expenditures US$4.3 billion, including capital expenditures of US$ n.a. (2001 est.)
Defence Expenditures: n.a.
Education Expenditures: n.a.
External Debt: US$12.688 billion (2002)
Exports: US$2.667 billion (2003 est.); manufactured goods, food, live animals, raw materials; partners: Italy, Bosnia and Herzegovina, Macedonia, Germany
Imports: US$7.144 billion (2003 est.); machinery, transport equipment, fuels and lubricants, manufactured goods, chemicals, food, live animals, raw materials; partners: Germany, Italy, Russia, Greece

■ COMMUNICATIONS

Daily Newspapers: 107/1,000 inhabitants (2000)
Televisions: 282/1,000 inhabitants (2002)
Radios: 297/1,000 inhabitants (2001)
Telephones: 233 lines/1,000 inhabitants (2001)
Internet: hosts: 16,972 (2002); users: 640,000 (2002)

■ TRANSPORTATION

Motor Vehicles: 2,000,000; 1,800,000 passenger cars
Roads: 49,805 km; 31,029 km paved
Railway: 4,059 km
Air Traffic: 1,186,000 passengers carried (2002)
Airports: 45; 19 have paved runways (2003 est.)

Canadian Embassy: The Canadian Embassy, 75 Kneza Milosa, 11000 Belgrade, Serbia and Montenegro. Tel: (011-381-11) 306-3000. Fax: (011-381-11) 306-3042. e-mail: bgrad@dfait-maeci.gc.ca
Embassy in Canada: Embassy of Serbia and Montenegro, 17 Blackburn Ave, Ottawa ON K1N 8A2. Tel: (613) 233-6289. Fax: (613) 233-7850. e-mail: diplomat@yuemb.ca

Seychelles

Long-Form Name: Republic of Seychelles
Capital: Victoria

■ GEOGRAPHY

Area: 455 sq. km
Coastline: 491 km

Climate: tropical marine; humid; cooler season during southeast monsoon (late May to Sept.); warmer season during northwest monsoon (Mar. to May)

Environment: lies outside the cyclone belt, so severe storms are rare; short droughts possible; no fresh water, catchments collect rain

Terrain: 40 granitic and about 50 coralline islands; Mahé Group is granitic, narrow coastal strip, rocky, hilly; others are coral, flat, elevated reefs

Land Use: arable land: 2.22%, permanent crops: 13.33%, other: 84.45%; includes n.a. sq. km irrigated

Location: Indian Ocean, NE of Madagascar

■ PEOPLE

Population: 80,469 (July 2003 est.)
Nationality: Seychellois (sing. & pl.)
Age Structure: 0–14 yrs: 27.3%; 15–64: 66.5%; 65+: 6.2% (2003 est.)
Population Growth Rate: 0.46% (2003 est.)
Net Migration: -5.84 migrants/1,000 population (2003 est.)
Ethnic Groups: Seychellois (mixture of Asians, Africans, Europeans)
Languages: English, French (both official), Creole
Religions: 90% Roman Catholic, 8% Anglican, 2% other
Birth Rate: 16.88/1,000 population (2003 est.)
Death Rate: 6.49/1,000 population (2003 est.)
Infant Mortality: 16.41 deaths/1,000 live births (2003 est.)
Life Expectancy at Birth: 65.78 years male, 76.88 years female (2003 est.)
Total Fertility Rate: 1.79 children born/woman (2003 est.)
Literacy: n.a.

■ GOVERNMENT

Leader(s): President James Alix Michel, Vice President Joseph Belmont
Government Type: republic
Administrative Divisions: 23 administrative districts
Nationhood: June 29, 1976 (from UK)
National Holiday: Constitution Day, June 18 (1993 adoption of a new constitution)

■ ECONOMY

Overview: the government is moving to reduce the high dependence on tourism by promoting the development of farming, fishing and small-scale manufacturing, yet it is also encouraging foreign investment in order to upgrade hotels and other services
GDP: US$626 million, per capita US$7,800; real growth rate 1.5% (2002 est.)
Inflation: 0.5% (2002 est.)

Industries: accounts for 26.3% of GDP; tourism employs 30% of labour force; mostly subsistence farming; cash crops: coconuts, cinnamon, vanilla; other products: sweet potatoes, cassava, bananas; broiler chickens; large share of food needs imported; expansion of tuna fishing under way
Labour Force: n.a.; 19% industry, 71% services, 10% agriculture
Unemployment: n.a.
Agriculture: accounts for 4% of GDP, mostly subsistence farming; cash crops: coconuts, cinnamon, vanilla, yams, bananas; large share of food needs to be imported; tuna fishing is increasing in importance
Natural Resources: fish, copra, cinnamon trees

■ FINANCE/TRADE

Currency: Seychelles rupee (SRe) = 100 cents
International Reserves Excluding Gold: US$66 million (Jan. 2004)
Gold Reserves: n.a.
Budget: n.a.
Defence Expenditures: 1.8% of GDP (2002)
Education Expenditures: 7.10% of government expenditure (2000)
External Debt: US$253 million (2002)
Exports: US$228 million (2002); commodities: fish, copra, cinnamon bark, petroleum products (re-exports); partners: France, Italy, UK, Netherlands
Imports: US$420 million (2002); commodities: manufactured goods, food, tobacco, beverages, machinery and transportation equipment, petroleum products; partners: Italy, South Africa, France, UK, Singapore

■ COMMUNICATIONS

Daily Newspapers: 1 in total
Televisions: n.a.
Radios: n.a.
Telephones: 271 lines/1,000 inhabitants (2002)
Internet: hosts: 266 (2002); users: 11,700 (2002)

■ TRANSPORTATION

Motor Vehicles: 8,500; 6,800 passenger cars
Roads: 373 km; 315 km paved
Railway: none
Air Traffic: n.a.
Airports: 14; 7 have paved runways (2003 est.)

Canadian Embassy: The Canadian High Commission to Seychelles, c/o The Canadian High Commission, 38 Mirambo St, Dar-es-Salaam; mailing address: P.O. Box 1022, Dar-es-Salaam, Tanzania. Tel: (011-255-22) 211-2831. Fax: (011-255-22) 211-6897. e-mail: dslam@dfait-maeci.gc.ca
Embassy in Canada: c/o High Commission for the Republic of Seychelles, 800 Second Ave,

Ste 400C, New York NY 10017, USA. Tel: (212) 972-1785. Fax: (212) 972-1786. e-mail: seychelles@un.int

Sierra Leone

Long-Form Name: Republic of Sierra Leone
Capital: Freetown

■ GEOGRAPHY

Area: 71,740 sq. km
Coastline: 402 km
Climate: tropical; hot, humid; summer rainy season (May to Dec.); winter dry season (Dec. to Apr.)
Environment: extensive mangrove swamps hinder access to sea; sand and dust storms; deforestation; soil degradation; population pressure negatively affects land
Terrain: coastal belt of mangrove swamps, wooded hill country, upland plateau, mountains in east
Land Use: arable land: 6.76%, permanent crops: 0.78%, other: 92.46%; includes 290 sq. km irrigated
Location: W Africa, bordering on North Atlantic Ocean

■ PEOPLE

Population: 5,732,681 (July 2003 est.)
Nationality: Sierra Leonean
Age Structure: 0–14 yrs: 44.8%; 15–64: 52.0%; 65+: 3.2% (2003 est.)
Population Growth Rate: 2.94% (2003 est.)
Net Migration: 6.19 migrants/1,000 population (2003 est.)
Ethnic Groups: 90% native African (30% Temne, 39% Mende, 30% other); 10% Creole, European, Lebanese and Asian
Languages: English (official); regular use limited to literate minority; principal vernaculars are Mende in south and Temne in north; Krio is the language of the resettled ex-slave population of the Freetown area and is lingua franca
Religions: 60% Muslim, 10% Christian, 30% traditional beliefs
Birth Rate: 43.89/1,000 population (2003 est.)
Death Rate: 20.66/1,000 population (2003 est.)
Infant Mortality: 146.86 deaths/1,000 live births (2003 est.)
Life Expectancy at Birth: 40.33 years male, 45.42 years female (2003 est.)
Total Fertility Rate: 5.86 children born/woman (2003 est.)
Literacy: 36.0% (2002)

■ GOVERNMENT

Leader(s): President Ahmad Tejan Kabbah, Vice President Solomon Berewa

Government Type: constitutional democracy
Administrative Divisions: 3 provinces and 1 area
Nationhood: Apr. 27, 1961 (from UK)
National Holiday: Independence Day, Apr. 27

■ ECONOMY

Overview: the economic and social infrastructure is underdeveloped; subsistence agriculture is the backbone of the economy; problems include unemployment, large trade deficits; diamond mining is an important source of national income
GDP: US$2.826 billion, per capita US$500; real growth rate 6.6% (2002 est.)
Inflation: 1.0% (2002 est.)
Industries: accounts for 27% of GDP (2000); mining (diamonds, bauxite, rutile), small-scale manufacturing (beverages, textiles, cigarettes, footwear), petroleum refinery
Labour Force: 2.0 million (2002); 69.6% agriculture, 14.1% industry, 16.4% services
Unemployment: n.a.
Agriculture: accounts for 43% of GDP (2000) and two-thirds of the labour force, largely subsistence farming; cash crops: coffee, cocoa, palm kernels; harvest of food staple rice meets 80% of domestic needs; annual fish catch averages 53,000 metric tons
Natural Resources: diamonds, titanium ore, bauxite, iron ore, gold, chromite

■ FINANCE/TRADE

Currency: leone (Le) = 100 cents
International Reserves Excluding Gold: US$57 million (Jan. 2004)
Gold Reserves: n.a.
Budget: revenues US$96 million, expenditures US$351 million, including capital expenditures of US$ n.a. (2000 est.)
Defence Expenditures: 1.5% of GDP (2001)
Education Expenditures: n.a.
External Debt: US$1.448 billion (2002)
Exports: US$95 million (2003); commodities: rutile 50%, bauxite 17%, cocoa 11%, diamonds 3%, coffee 3%; partners: New Zealand, US, Belgium, France
Imports: US$311 million (2003); commodities: capital goods 40%, food 32%, petroleum 12%, consumer goods 7%, light industrial goods; partners: Czech Republic, US, UK, Netherlands

■ COMMUNICATIONS

Daily Newspapers: 4/1,000 inhabitants (2000)
Televisions: 13/1,000 inhabitants (2002)
Radios: 259/1,000 inhabitants (2001)
Telephones: 5 lines/1,000 inhabitants (2002)
Internet: hosts: 277 (2002); users: 8,000 (2002)

■ TRANSPORTATION

Motor Vehicles: 42,500; 21,000 passenger cars
Roads: 11,330 km; 895 km paved
Railway: 84 km
Air Traffic: 14,000 passengers carried (2002)
Airports: 10; 1 has paved runway (2003 est.)

Canadian Embassy: The Canadian High Commission to Sierra Leone, c/o The Canadian Embassy, PO Box 99, Conakry, Guinea. Tel: (011-224) 46-23-95. Fax: (011-224) 46-42-35. e-mail: cnaky@dfait-maeci.gc.ca
Embassy in Canada: c/o High Commission for the Republic of Sierra Leone, 1701-19th St NW, Washington DC 20009, USA. Tel: (202) 939-9261. Fax: (202) 483-1793. e-mail: slehoc@starpower.net

Singapore

Long-Form Name: Republic of Singapore
Capital: Singapore

■ GEOGRAPHY

Area: 647.5 sq. km
Coastline: 193 km
Climate: tropical; hot, humid, rainy; no pronounced rainy or dry seasons; thunderstorms occur on 40% of all days (67% of days in Apr.)
Environment: mostly urban and industrialized; water supply is limited
Terrain: lowland; gently undulating central plateau contains water catchment area and nature preserve
Land Use: arable land: 1.64%, permanent crops: 0%, other: 98.36%; includes n.a. sq. km irrigated
Location: SE Asia (southern tip of Malaysia), bordering on South China Sea

■ PEOPLE

Population: 4,608,595 (July 2003 est.)
Nationality: Singaporean
Age Structure: 0–14 yrs: 17.3%; 15–64: 75.5%; 65+: 7.2% (2003 est.)
Population Growth Rate: 3.42% (2003 est.)
Net Migration: 25.76 migrants/1,000 population (2003 est.)
Ethnic Groups: 77% Chinese, 14% Malay, 7.6% Indian, 1.4% other
Languages: Chinese (Mandarin), Malay, Tamil and English (all official); Malay (national)
Religions: majority of Chinese are Buddhists or atheists; Malays nearly all Muslim (minorities are Christians, Hindus, Sikhs, Taoists, Confucianists)
Birth Rate: 12.75/1,000 population (2003 est.)
Death Rate: 4.31/1,000 population (2003 est.)
Infant Mortality: 3.57 deaths/1,000 live births (2003 est.)
Life Expectancy at Birth: 77.46 years male, 83.60 years female (2003 est.)
Total Fertility Rate: 1.24 children born/woman (2003 est.)
Literacy: 92.5% (2002)

■ GOVERNMENT

Leader(s): President Sellapan Rama Nathan, Prime Minister Lee Hsien Loong
Government Type: parliamentary republic within Commonwealth
Administrative Divisions: none
Nationhood: Aug. 9, 1965 (from Malaysia)
National Holiday: Independence Day, Aug. 9

■ ECONOMY

Overview: has an open entrepreneurial economy with strong service and manufacturing sectors and good international trading links; growth has traditionally run at high rates; per capita GDP is among the highest in Asia; rising labour costs continue to adversely affect Singapore's competitiveness
GDP: US$112.4 billion, per capita US$25,200; real growth rate -2.2% (2002 est.)
Inflation: -0.4% (2002 est.)
Industries: accounts for 33% of GDP (2001 est.); petroleum refining, electronics, oil drilling equipment, rubber processing and rubber products, processed food and beverages, ship repair, entrepôt trade, financial services, biotechnology
Labour Force: 2 million (2002); 27% industry, 22.8% trade and tourism, 21.6% community, social and business services
Unemployment: 3.4% (Dec. 2002)
Agriculture: minor importance in the economy; self-sufficient in poultry and eggs; must import most other food; major crops: rubber, copra, fruit, vegetables, fish
Natural Resources: fish, deepwater ports

■ FINANCE/TRADE

Currency: Singapore dollar ($S) = 100 cents
International Reserves Excluding Gold: US$97.680 billion (Jan. 2004)
Gold Reserves: n.a.
Budget: revenues US$17.4 billion; expenditures US$17.6 billion, including capital expenditures US$5.6 billion (FY2003–2004 est.)
Defence Expenditures: 22.8% of central government expenditure (2002)
Education Expenditures: 21.03% of central government expenditure (2000)
External Debt: US$8.2 billion (2002)
Exports: US$144.740 billion (2003 est.); commodities (includes transshipments to Malaysia): petroleum products, rubber electronics, manufactured goods; partners: US, Malaysia, Hong Kong, Japan, Taiwan, Thailand, China, South Korea

Imports: US$127.381 billion (2003 est.); commodities (includes transshipments from Malaysia): capital equipment, petroleum, chemicals, manufactured goods, foodstuffs; partners: Japan, Malaysia, US, China, Taiwan, Thailand, South Korea, Saudi Arabia

■ COMMUNICATIONS

Daily Newspapers: 298/1,000 inhabitants (2000)
Televisions: 303/1,000 inhabitants (2002)
Radios: 672/1,000 inhabitants (2001)
Telephones: 463 lines/1,000 inhabitants (2002)
Internet: hosts: 338,349 (2002); users: 2.31 million (2002)

■ TRANSPORTATION

Motor Vehicles: 740,000; 540,000 passenger cars
Roads: 3,066 km; all paved
Railway: 38.6 km
Air Traffic: 17,257,000 passengers carried (2002)
Airports: 9; all have paved runways (2003 est.)

Canadian Embassy: Canadian High Commission, IBM Towers, 14th & 15th Fls, 80 Anson Rd, Singapore 079907; mailing address: Robinson Rd, P.O. Box 845, Singapore 901645. Tel: (011-65) 6325-3200. Fax: (011-65) 6325-3297. e-mail: spore@dfait-maeci.gc.ca
Embassy in Canada: c/o High Commission for the Republic of Singapore, 231 East 51st St, New York NY 10022, USA. Tel: (212) 826-0840. Fax: (212) 826-2964. e-mail: n.a.

Slovakia

Long-Form Name: Slovak Republic
Capital: Bratislava

■ GEOGRAPHY

Area: 48,845 sq. km
Coastline: none: landlocked
Climate: temperate: cool summers, cold, cloudy, humid winters
Environment: severe damage to forests from acid rain; industrial air pollution from metallurgical plants poses risks to human health
Terrain: rugged mountains in central region and north, lowlands in south
Land Use: arable land: 30.74%, permanent crops: 2.64%, other: 66.62%; includes 1,740 sq. km irrigated
Location: C Europe

■ PEOPLE

Population: 5,430,033 (July 2003 est.)
Nationality: Slovak
Age Structure: 0–14 yrs: 17.8%; 15–64: 70.5%; 65+: 11.7% (2003 est.)
Population Growth Rate: 0.14% (2003 est.)

Net Migration: 0.53 migrants/1,000 population (2003 est.)
Ethnic Groups: 85.7% Slovak, 10.6% Hungarian, 1.6% Gypsy, 1.0% Czech, 0.3% Ruthenian, 0.3% Ukrainian, 0.1% German, 0.1% Polish, 0.3% other
Languages: Slovak (official), Hungarian
Religions: 60.3% Roman Catholic, 9.7% atheist, 8.4% Protestant, 4.1% Orthodox, 17.5% other
Birth Rate: 10.10/1,000 population (2003 est.)
Death Rate: 9.22/1,000 population (2003 est.)
Infant Mortality: 8.55 deaths/1,000 live births (2003 est.)
Life Expectancy at Birth: 70.44 years male, 78.64 years female (2003 est.)
Total Fertility Rate: 1.25 children born/woman (2003 est.)
Literacy: 99.7% (2002)

■ GOVERNMENT

Leader(s): President Ivan Gasparovic, Prime Minister Mikulas Dzurinda
Government Type: parliamentary democracy
Administrative Divisions: 8 regions (kraje, sing. —kraj)
Nationhood: Jan. 1, 1993 (from Czechoslovakia)
National Holiday: Slovak Constitution Day, Sept. 1; Anniversary of Slovak National Uprising, Aug. 29

■ ECONOMY

Overview: continues the difficult transition from a centrally controlled economy to a modern market-oriented economy; private activity now makes up more than two-thirds of GDP. Slovakia continues to experience difficulty in attracting foreign investment
GDP: US$67.34 billion, per capita US$12,400; real growth rate 4.4% (2002)
Inflation: 3.3% (2002)
Industries: accounts for 32% of GDP (2000); mining, chemicals, metalworking, consumer appliances, plastics, armaments
Labour Force: 3.0 million (2002); 29.3% industry, 26.4% community, social and business services, 12.4% agriculture
Unemployment: 17.1% (Feb. 2003)
Agriculture: accounts for 4% of GDP (2000); very diversified crop and livestock production including grains, livestock, poultry; mostly self-sufficient in food
Natural Resources: brown coal and lignite, iron ore, copper, manganese, salt, gas

■ FINANCE/TRADE

Currency: koruna (pl. koruny) (Kc) = 100 halierov
International Reserves Excluding Gold: US$11.789 billion (Jan. 2004)

Gold Reserves: 1.129 million fine troy ounces (Jan. 2004)
Budget: n.a.
Defence Expenditures: 4.9% of central government expenditure (2002)
Education Expenditures: 13.8% of central government expenditure (2002)
External Debt: US$13.013 billion (2002)
Exports: US$21.549 billion (2003); machinery and transport equipment, chemicals, fuels, minerals, agricultural products; partners: Germany, Italy, Austria, Czech Republic
Imports: US$23.281 billion (2003); machinery and transport equipment, fuels, lubricants, manufactured goods, chemicals, agricultural products; partners: Germany, Italy, Czech Republic, Russia

■ COMMUNICATIONS

Daily Newspapers: 131/1,000 inhabitants (2000)
Televisions: 409/1,000 inhabitants (2002)
Radios: 695/1,000 inhabitants (2001)
Telephones: 268 lines/1,000 inhabitants (2002)
Internet: hosts: 85,998 (2002); users: 862,800 (2002)

■ TRANSPORTATION

Motor Vehicles: 1,440,000; 1,280,000 passenger cars
Roads: 42,717 km; 37,036 km paved
Railway: 3,668 km
Air Traffic: 39,000 passengers carried (2002)
Airports: 37; 20 have paved runways (2003 est.)

Canadian Embassy: The Office of the Canadian Embassy, Carlton Courtyard & Savoy Buildings, Mostova 2, 811 02, Bratislava, Slovakia. Tel: (011 421 2) 59 20 40 31. Fax: (011 421 2) 54 43 42 27. e-mail: office@canemb.sk
Embassy in Canada: Embassy of the Slovak Republic, 50 Rideau Terrace, Ottawa ON K1M 2A1. Tel: (613) 749-4442. Fax: (613) 749-4989. e-mail: slovakemb@sprint.ca

Slovenia

Long-Form Name: Republic of Slovenia
Capital: Ljubljana

■ GEOGRAPHY

Area: 20,253 sq. km
Coastline: 46.6 km
Climate: Mediterranean climate on the coast, continental climate with mild to hot summers and cold winters in the plateaus and eastern valleys
Environment: pollution of Sava River; heavy metals and toxic chemicals along coast; forest damage from air pollution; subject to flooding and earthquakes
Terrain: short coastal strip, alpine mountain region, mixed mountains and valleys and numerous rivers in east
Land Use: arable land: 11.48%, permanent crops: 2.68%, other: 85.84%; includes 20 sq. km irrigated
Location: southern Europe, bordering on Adriatic Sea

■ PEOPLE

Population: 1,935,677 (July 2003 est.)
Nationality: Slovene
Age Structure: 0–14 yrs: 15.3%; 15–64: 70.0%; 65+: 14.7% (2003 est.)
Population Growth Rate: 0.14% (2003 est.)
Net Migration: 2.34 migrants/1,000 population (2003 est.)
Ethnic Groups: 88% Slovene, 3% Croat, 2% Serb, 1% Bosniak, 0.6% Yugoslav, 0.4% Hungarian, 5% other
Languages: 91% Slovenian, 6% Serbo-Croatian, 3% other
Religions: 71% Roman Catholic, 1% Lutheran, 1% Muslim, 4.3% athiest, 23% other
Birth Rate: 9.23/1,000 population (2003 est.)
Death Rate: 10.15/1,000 population (2003 est.)
Infant Mortality: 4.42 deaths/1,000 live births (2003 est.)
Life Expectancy at Birth: 71.65 years male, 79.58 years female (2003 est.)
Total Fertility Rate: 1.27 children born/woman (2003 est.)
Literacy: 99.7% (2003 est.)

■ GOVERNMENT

Leader(s): President Janez Drnovsek, Prime Minister Anton Rop
Government Type: parliamentary democratic republic
Administrative Divisions: 136 municipalities (obcine, sing. —obcina) and 11 urban municipalities (obcine mestne, sing. —obcina mestna)
Nationhood: June 25, 1991 (from Yugoslavia)
National Holiday: National Statehood Day, June 25

■ ECONOMY

Overview: tourism has suffered due to internal strife; destruction of trade channels and the influx of tens of thousands of refugees have interfered with economic recovery after secession from Yugoslavia; there are efforts toward the privatization of major industrial firms; inflation and unemployment rates are gradually beginning to drop
GDP: US$37.06 billion, per capita US$19,200; real growth rate 3.2% (2002)
Inflation: 7.4% (2002 est.)

Industries: accounts for 36% of GDP (2001 est.); metallurgy, furniture, sports equipment, steel, cars, sugar, cement, textiles, machine tools
Labour Force: 1.0 million (2002); 39.3% industry, 23.1% community, social and business services, 11.1% trade and tourism
Unemployment: 11.3% (Jan. 2004)
Agriculture: accounts for 3% of GDP (2001 est.); products include wheat, maize, grapes, sugar beets, potatoes, cabbages, livestock (esp. cattle, sheep, pigs, poultry); fishing, forestry; many other agricultural products must be imported
Natural Resources: brown coal and lignite deposits, lead, zinc, mercury, uranium, silver, hydro power

■ FINANCE/TRADE

Currency: Slovenian tolar = 100 stotins (at parity with Yugoslav dinar)
International Reserves Excluding Gold: US$8.491 billion (Jan. 2004)
Gold Reserves: 0.243 million fine troy ounces (Jan. 2004)
Budget: revenues US$9.9 billion; expenditures US$10.5 billion, including capital expenditures US$n.a. (2003 est.)
Defence Expenditures: 3.5% of central government expenditure (2002)
Education Expenditures: n.a.
External Debt: US$7.9 billion (2001)
Exports: US$13.013 billion (2003 est.); machinery, semi-finished goods, raw materials, electric motors, transportation equipment, clothing, foodstuffs; partners: Germany, Italy, Croatia, Austria, France
Imports: US$12.434 billion (2003 est.); raw materials, semi-finished goods, machinery, foodstuffs; partners: Germany, Italy, France, Austria, Croatia

■ COMMUNICATIONS

Daily Newspapers: 169/1,000 inhabitants (2000)
Televisions: 366/1,000 inhabitants (2002)
Radios: 405/1,000 inhabitants (2001)
Telephones: 506 lines/1,000 inhabitants (2002)
Internet: hosts: 35,791 (2002); users: 750,000 (2002)

■ TRANSPORTATION

Motor Vehicles: 900,000; 820,000 passenger cars
Roads: 20,177 km; 20,157 km paved
Railway: 1,201 km
Air Traffic: 721,000 passengers carried (2002)
Airports: 16; 6 have paved runways (2003 est.)

Canadian Embassy: The Canadian Embassy to Slovenia, c/o The Canadian Embassy Zugligeti ut. 51-53, 1121 Budapest, Hungary. Tel.: (011-36-1) 392-3360. Fax: (011-36-1) 392-3390. e-mail: bpest@dfait-maeci.gc.ca
Embassy in Canada: Embassy of the Republic of Slovenia, 150 Metcalfe St, Ste 2101, Ottawa, ON K2P 1P1. Tel: (613) 565-5781. Fax: (613) 565-5783. e-mail: vot@mzz-dkp.sigov.si

Solomon Islands

Long-Form Name: Solomon Islands
Capital: Honiara (on island of Guadalcanal)

■ GEOGRAPHY

Area: 28,450 sq km
Coastline: 5,313 km
Climate: tropical monsoon; few extremes of temperature and weather
Environment: subject to typhoons, which are rarely destructive; geologically active region with frequent earth tremors; soil degradation and deforestation; deterioration of coral reefs
Terrain: mostly rugged mountains with some low coral atolls
Land Use: arable land: 1.5%, permanent crops: 0.64%, other: 97.86%; includes n.a. sq. km irrigated
Location: Melanesia, Pacific Ocean, E of New Guinea

■ PEOPLE

Population: 509,190 (July 2003 est.)
Nationality: Solomon Islander
Age Structure: 0–14 yrs: 42.9%; 15–64: 54.0%; 65+: 3.1% (2003 est.)
Population Growth Rate: 2.83% (2003 est.)
Net Migration: 0 migrants/1,000 population (2003 est.)
Ethnic Groups: 93% Melanesian, 4% Polynesian, 1.5% Micronesian, 0.8% European, 0.3% Chinese, 0.4% other
Languages: English (official), Pidgin, 120 local languages
Religions: 34% Anglican, 19% Roman Catholic, 17% South Seas Evangelical, 25% other Protestant, 5% other
Birth Rate: 32.45/1,000 population (2003 est.)
Death Rate: 4.12/1,000 population (2003 est.)
Infant Mortality: 22.88 deaths/1,000 live births (2003 est.)
Life Expectancy at Birth: 69.64 years male, 74.68 years female (2003 est.)
Total Fertility Rate: 4.34 children born/woman (2003 est.)
Literacy: 76.6% (2002)

■ GOVERNMENT

Leader(s): Head of State: Queen Elizabeth II, Governor General Nathaniel Waena, Prime Minister Sir Allan Kemakeza
Government Type: parliamentary democracy

Administrative Divisions: 7 provinces and 1 town
Nationhood: July 7, 1978 (from UK; formerly known as British Solomon Islands)
National Holiday: Independence Day, July 7

■ ECONOMY

Overview: about 90% of the population depend on subsistence agriculture, fishing and forestry for at least part of their livelihood; possesses an abundance of undeveloped mineral resources; little manufacturing activity—most manufactured goods must be imported; uncontrolled government spending is leading to national financial ruin despite a rich natural resource base
GDP: US$800 million, per capita US$1,700; real growth rate -10.0% (2001 est.)
Inflation: 1.8% (2001 est.)
Industries: account for 11% of GDP; copra, fish (tuna)
Labour Force: approx. 27,000; 20% community, social and business services, 75% agriculture, 5% industry
Unemployment: n.a.
Agriculture: including fishing and forestry, accounts for approx. 42% of GDP; mostly subsistence farming; cash crops: cocoa, beans, coconuts, palm kernels, timber; other products: rice, potatoes, vegetables, fruit, cattle, pigs; not self-sufficient in foodgrains; 90% of fish catch is exported
Natural Resources: fish, forests, gold, bauxite, phosphates, lead, zinc, nickel

■ FINANCE/TRADE

Currency: Solomon Islands dollar ($SI) = 100 cents
International Reserves Excluding Gold: US$37 million (Dec. 2003)
Gold Reserves: n.a.
Budget: revenues US$38 million, expenditures US$ n.a., including capital expenditures of US$ n.a. (2001)
Defence Expenditures: negligible
Education Expenditures: n.a.
External Debt: US$180 million (2002)
Exports: US$90 million (2002 est.); commodities: fish 46%, timber 31%, copra 5%, palm oil 5%; partners: Japan, China, Philippines, South Korea, UK, Thailand
Imports: US$100 million (2002 est.); commodities: equipment and machinery 30%, fuel 19%, food 16%; partners: Australia, Singapore, New Zealand, Japan, US

■ COMMUNICATIONS

Daily Newspapers: none
Televisions: n.a.
Radios: n.a.
Telephones: 13 lines/1,000 inhabitants (2002)

Internet: hosts: 470 (2002); users: 2,200 (2002)

■ TRANSPORTATION

Motor Vehicles: n.a.
Roads: 1,360 km; 34 km paved
Railway: none
Air Traffic: n.a.
Airports: 32; 2 have paved runways (2003 est.)

Canadian Embassy: The Canadian High Commission to Solomon Islands, c/o The Canadian High Commission, Commonwealth Ave, Canberra A.C.T. 2600, Australia. Tel: (011-61-2) 6270-4000. Fax: (011-61-2) 6273-3285. e-mail: cnbra@dfait-maeci.gc.ca
Embassy in Canada: c/o High Commission for the Solomon Islands, 800-2nd Ave, Ste 400L, New York NY 10017, USA. Tel: (212) 599-6192. Fax: (212) 661-8925. e-mail: simny@solomons.com

Somalia

Long-Form Name: Somalia
Capital: Mogadishu

■ GEOGRAPHY

Area: 637,657 sq. km
Coastline: 3,025 km
Climate: desert; northeast monsoon (Dec. to Feb.), cooler southwest monsoon (May to Oct.); irregular rainfall; hot, humid periods (tangambili) between monsoons
Environment: recurring droughts; frequent dust storms over eastern plains in summer; deforestation; overgrazing; soil erosion; desertification
Terrain: mostly flat to undulating plateau rising to hills in north
Land Use: arable land: 1.66%, permanent crops: 0.04%, other: 98.3%; includes 2,000 sq. km irrigated
Location: E Africa, bordering on Gulf of Aden, Indian Ocean

■ PEOPLE

Population: 8,025,190 (July 2003 est.)
Nationality: Somali
Age Structure: 0–14 yrs: 44.8%; 15–64: 52.5%; 65+: 2.7% (2003 est.)
Population Growth Rate: 3.43% (2003 est.)
Net Migration: 5.56 migrants/1,000 population (2003 est.)
Ethnic Groups: 85% Somali, rest mainly Bantu; 30,000 Arabs, 3,000 Europeans, 800 Asians
Languages: Somali (official); Arabic, Italian, English
Religions: almost entirely Sunni Muslim, small Christian community
Birth Rate: 46.42/1,000 population (2003 est.)
Death Rate: 17.64/1,000 population (2003 est.)

Infant Mortality: 120.34 deaths/1,000 live births (2003 est.)
Life Expectancy at Birth: 45.67 years male, 49.05 years female (2003 est.)
Total Fertility Rate: 6.98 children born/woman (2003 est.)
Literacy: 37.8% (2001)

■ GOVERNMENT

Leader(s): President Abdikassim Salad Hassan, Prime Minister Hassan Abshir Farah
Government Type: parliamentary
Administrative Divisions: 18 regions (plural n.a., sing. —gobolka)
Nationhood: July 1, 1960 (from a merger of British Somaliland, which became independent from the UK on June 26, 1960, and Italian Somaliland, which became independent from the Italian-administered UN trusteeship on July 1, 1960, to form the Somali Republic)
National Holiday: Anniversary of the Revolution, Oct. 21, Foundation of the Somali Republic, July 1

■ ECONOMY

Overview: nomads or semi-nomads who are dependent upon livestock for their livelihoods make up about 50% of the population; one of the world's least developed countries, possessing few resources; problems include high external debt, triple-digit inflation and bitter civil war, which has devastated much of the economy
GDP: US$4.27 billion, per capita US$600; real growth rate 3.5% (2002)
Inflation: over 100%; businesses print their own money (2002 est.)
Industries: accounts for 10% of GDP (2000); based on processing of agricultural products; sugar refining, textiles, petroleum refining
Labour Force: 4.0 million (2002); 71% agriculture, 29% industry and services
Unemployment: n.a.
Agriculture: livestock accounts for 65% of GDP (2000) and 65% of export revenue: cattle, sheep, goats; fishing potential largely unexploited; crops: bananas, sorghum, corn, mangoes, sugar cane, beans, fish; not self-sufficient in food
Natural Resources: uranium and largely unexploited reserves of iron ore, tin, gypsum, bauxite, copper, salt

■ FINANCE/TRADE

Currency: Somali shilling (So.Sh.) = 100 cents
International Reserves Excluding Gold: n.a.
Gold Reserves: n.a.
Budget: n.a.
Defence Expenditures: 0.9% of GDP (2002)
Education Expenditures: n.a.
External Debt: US$2.688 billion (2002)

Exports: US$79 million (2002 est.); commodities: livestock, hides, skins, bananas, fish; partners: Saudi Arabia, UAE, Yemen
Imports: US$344 million (2002 est.); commodities: textiles, petroleum products, foodstuffs, construction materials; partners: Djibouti, Kenya, India

■ COMMUNICATIONS

Daily Newspapers: 1/1,000 inhabitants (2000)
Televisions: 14/1,000 inhabitants (2002)
Radios: 60/1,000 inhabitants (2001)
Telephones: 10 lines/1,000 inhabitants (2002)
Internet: users: 89,000 (2002)

■ TRANSPORTATION

Motor Vehicles: 20,000; 10,000 passenger cars
Roads: 22,100 km; 2,608 km paved
Railway: none
Air Traffic: n.a.
Airports: 60; 6 have paved runways (2003 est.)

Canadian Embassy: c/o The Canadian High Commission, Limuru Road, Gigiri, Nairobi, Kenya. Postal Address: The Canadian High Commission, P.O. Box 1013, 00621 Nairobi, Kenya. Tel: (011 254 20) 366 3000. Fax: (011 254 20) 366 3900. e-mail: nrobi@dfait-maeci.gc.ca
Embassy in Canada: c/o The High Commission for the Republic of Kenya, 415 Laurier Ave E, Ottawa ON K1N 6R4. Tel: (613) 563-1773. Fax: (613) 233-6599. e-mail: kenrep@on.aibn.com

South Africa

Long-Form Name: Republic of South Africa
Capital: Pretoria (administrative), Cape Town (legislative), Bloemfontein (judicial)

■ GEOGRAPHY

Area: 1,219,912 sq. km; includes Walvis Bay, Marion Island and Prince Edward Island
Coastline: 2,798 km
Climate: mostly semi-arid; subtropical along coast; sunny days, cool nights
Environment: lack of important arterial rivers or lakes requires extensive water conservation and control measures; prolonged droughts and increasing water pollution exacerbate the problem
Terrain: vast interior plateau rimmed by rugged hills and narrow coastal plain
Land Use: arable land: 12.13%, permanent crops: 0.77%, other: 87.1%; includes 13,500 sq. km irrigated
Location: S Africa, bordering on Indian Ocean, South Atlantic Ocean

■ PEOPLE

Population: 42,768,678 (July 2003 est.)

Nationality: South African
Age Structure: 0–14 yrs: 30.0%; 15–64: 65.0%; 65+: 5.0% (2003 est.)
Population Growth Rate: 0.01% (2003 est.)
Net Migration: -0.35 migrants/1,000 population (2003 est.)
Ethnic Groups: 75.2% black, 13.6% white, 8.6% coloured, 2.6% Indian
Languages: 11 official languages: Afrikaans, English, Ndebele, Pedi, Sotho, Swazi, Tsonga, Tswana, Venda, Xhosa, Zulu
Religions: most of whites, coloureds and approx. 60% of blacks are Christian; approx. 60% of Indians are Hindu, 20% Muslim
Birth Rate: 18.87/1,000 population (2003 est.)
Death Rate: 18.42/1,000 population (2003 est.)
Infant Mortality: 60.84 deaths/1,000 live births (2003 est.)
Life Expectancy at Birth: 46.57 years male, 46.54 years female (2002 est.)
Total Fertility Rate: 2.24 children born/woman (2002 est.)
Literacy: 86.0% (2002)

■ GOVERNMENT

Leader(s): President Thabo Mvuyelwa Mbeki
Government Type: republic
Administrative Divisions: 9 provinces; after the election bringing Mandela to power, all 10 black homelands and 4 provinces existing earlier were dissolved
Nationhood: May 31, 1910 (from UK)
National Holiday: Freedom Day, April 27

■ ECONOMY

Overview: there is great disparity in living standards between the white minority (favoured) and the black majority; international embargoes against the country (because of its policy of apartheid) hurt the economy; other problems include crime, corruption and HIV/AIDS; burgeoning unemployment; has rich mineral resources (diamonds)
GDP: US$427.7 billion, per capita US$10,000; real growth rate 3.0% (2002 est.)
Inflation: 9.9% (2002 est.)
Industries: accounts for 31% of GDP (2000); mining (world's largest producer of platinum, gold, chrome), automobile assembly, metalworking, machinery, textile, iron and steel, chemical, fertilizer, foodstuffs
Labour Force: 18.1 million (2002); 25% industry, 45% community, social and business services, 30% agriculture
Unemployment: 29.5% (2002)
Agriculture: accounts for 3% of GDP (2000) and 30% of labour force; diversified agriculture, with emphasis on livestock; products: cattle, poultry, sheep, wool, milk, beef, corn, wheat;

sugar cane, fruit, vegetables; self-sufficient in food
Natural Resources: gold, chromium, antimony, coal, iron ore, manganese, nickel, phosphates, tin, uranium, gem diamonds, platinum, copper, vanadium, salt, natural gas

■ FINANCE/TRADE

Currency: rand (R) = 100 cents
International Reserves Excluding Gold: US$6.516 billion (Jan. 2004)
Gold Reserves: 3.975 million fine troy ounces (Jan. 2004)
Budget: revenues US$22.6 billion, expenditures US$24.7 billion, including capital expenditures of US$ n.a. (FY2002/03)
Defence Expenditures: 5.4% of central government expenditure (2002)
Education Expenditures: 18.1% of total government expenditures (2002)
External Debt: US$25.041 billion (2002)
Exports: US$34.148 billion (2003); commodities: gold 40%, minerals and metals 23%, food 6%, chemicals 3%; partners: EU, US, Japan, Mozambique
Imports: US$38.587 billion (2003); commodities: machinery 27%, chemicals 11%, vehicles and aircraft 11%, textiles, scientific instruments, base metals; partners: EU, US, Saudi Arabia, Japan

■ COMMUNICATIONS

Daily Newspapers: 32/1,000 inhabitants (2000)
Televisions: 177/1,000 inhabitants (2002)
Radios: 338/1,000 inhabitants (2001)
Telephones: 107 lines/1,000 inhabitants (2002)
Internet: hosts: 198,853 (2002); users: 3.1 million (2002)

■ TRANSPORTATION

Motor Vehicles: 6,230,000; 4,100,000 passenger cars (2000)
Roads: 362,099 km; 73,506 km paved
Railway: 22,298 km
Air Traffic: 8,167,000 passengers carried (2002)
Airports: 727; 143 have paved runways (2003 est.)

Canadian Embassy: The Canadian High Commission, 1103 Arcadia, Hatfield 0028, Pretoria; mailing address: Private Bag X13, Hatfield 0028, South Africa. Tel: (011-27-12) 422-3000. Fax: (011-27-12) 422-3052. e-mail: pret@dfait-maeci.gc.ca
Embassy in Canada: Embassy of the Republic of South Africa, 15 Sussex Dr, Ottawa ON K1M 1M8. Tel: (613) 744-0330. Fax: (613) 741-1639. e-mail: rsafrica@sympatico.ca

Spain

Long-Form Name: Kingdom of Spain
Capital: Madrid

■ GEOGRAPHY

Area: 504,782 sq. km; includes Balaeric Islands, Canary Islands, Ceuta, Melilla, Islas Chafarinas, Peñón de Vélez de la Gomera
Coastline: 4,964 km
Climate: temperate; clear, hot summers in interior, more moderate and cloudy along coast; cloudy, cold winters in interior, partly cloudy and cool along coast
Environment: deforestation; air and water pollution; soil degradation; desertification; periodic droughts
Terrain: large, flat to dissected, rugged hills; Pyrenees in north
Land Use: arable land: 28.6%, permanent crops: 9.56%, other: 61.84%; includes 36,400 sq. km irrigated
Location: SW Europe, bordering on Mediterranean Sea and N Atlantic Ocean

■ PEOPLE

Population: 40,217,413 (July 2003 est.)
Nationality: Spanish or Spaniard
Age Structure: 0–14 yrs: 14.4%; 15–64: 68.0%; 65+: 17.6% (2003 est.)
Population Growth Rate: 0.16% (2003 est.)
Net Migration: 0.99 migrants/1,000 population (2003 est.)
Ethnic Groups: composite of Mediterranean and Nordic types
Languages: Castilian Spanish; second languages include 17% Catalan (northeast), 7% Galician (northwest), 2% Basque (north)
Religions: 99% Roman Catholic, 1% other sects
Birth Rate: 10.08/1,000 population (2003 est.)
Death Rate: 9.48/1,000 population (2003 est.)
Infant Mortality: 4.54 deaths/1,000 live births (2003 est.)
Life Expectancy at Birth: 75.87 years male, 82.80 years female (2003 est.)
Total Fertility Rate: 1.26 children born/woman (2003 est.)
Literacy: 97.7% (2002)

■ GOVERNMENT

Leader(s): King Juan Carlos I, President Jose Luis Rodriguez Zapatero
Government Type: parliamentary monarchy
Administrative Divisions: 17 autonomous communities (comunidades autonomas, sing. — comunidad autonoma)
Nationhood: 1492 (expulsion of the Moors and unification)
National Holiday: National Day, Oct. 12

■ ECONOMY

Overview: advocates liberalization, privatization, and deregulation of the economy, and has introduced some tax reforms to that end; adjustment to the monetary and other economic policies of an integrated Europe will pose difficult challenges in the next few years
GDP: US$850.7 billion, per capita US$21,200; real growth rate 2.0% (2002)
Inflation: 3.0% (2002 est.)
Industries: accounts for 28% of GDP (2000); textiles and apparel (including footwear), food and beverages, metals and metal manufacturing, chemicals, shipbuilding, automobiles, machine tools
Labour Force: 18.1 million (2002); 64% services, 29% manufacturing and mining, 7% agriculture
Unemployment: 11.2% (Nov. 2003)
Agriculture: accounts for 4% of GDP (2000) and 14% of labour force; major products: grain, vegetables, olives, wine grapes, sugar beets, citrus fruit, beef, pork, poultry, dairy; largely self-sufficient in food; fish catch of 1.4 million metric tons
Natural Resources: coal, lignite, iron ore, uranium, mercury, pyrites, fluorspar, gypsum, zinc, lead, tungsten, copper, kaolin, potash, hydro power

■ FINANCE/TRADE

Currency: peseta (Pta) = 100 centimos; Euro (€) on January 1, 2002 the Euro became the sole currency for everyday transactions
International Reserves Excluding Gold: US$17.429 billion (Jan. 2004)
Gold Reserves: 16.827 million fine troy ounces (Jan. 2004)
Budget: revenues US$105 billion, expenditures US$109 billion, including capital expenditures US$12.8 billion (2000 est.)
Defence Expenditures: 4.2% of central government expenditure (2002)
Education Expenditures: 11.3% of total government expenditures (2002)
External Debt: n.a.
Exports: US$123.563 billion (2002); commodities: foodstuffs, live animals, wood, footwear, machinery, chemicals; partners: EU, Latin America, US
Imports: US$163.575 billion (2002); commodities: petroleum, footwear, machinery, chemicals, grain, soybeans, coffee, tobacco, iron and steel, timber, cotton, transport equipment; partners: France, Germany, Italy, Benelux, UK, OPEC countries, US, Japan, Latin America

■ COMMUNICATIONS

Daily Newspapers: 100/1,000 inhabitants (2000)
Televisions: 564/1,000 inhabitants (2002)
Radios: 330/1,000 inhabitants (2001)
Telephones: 506 lines/1,000 inhabitants (2002)
Internet: hosts: 589,979 (2002); users: 7.388 million (2001)

■ TRANSPORTATION

Motor Vehicles: 18,700,000; 16,300,000 passenger cars
Roads: 663,795 km; 657,157 km paved
Railway: 14,189 km
Air Traffic: 40,585,000 passengers carried (2002)
Airports: 152; 93 have paved runways (2003 est.)

Canadian Embassy: The Canadian Embassy, Calle Nunez de Balboa, 35, 28001 Madrid; mailing address: Apartado 587, 28080 Madrid, Spain. Tel: (011-34) 91-423-3252. Fax: (011-34) 91-423-3251. e-mail: mdrid@dfait-maeci.gc.ca
Embassy in Canada: Embassy of the Kingdom of Spain, 74 Stanley Ave, Ottawa ON, K1M IP4. Tel: (613) 747-2252. Fax: (613) 744-1224. e-mail: embespca@mail.mae.es

Sri Lanka

Long-Form Name: Democratic Socialist Republic of Sri Lanka
Capital: Colombo (administrative); Sri Jayewardenepura Kotte (legislative)

■ GEOGRAPHY

Area: 65,610 sq. km
Coastline: 1,340 km
Climate: tropical; monsoonal; northeast monsoon (Dec. to Mar.); southwest monsoon (June to Oct.)
Environment: occasional cyclones, tornadoes; deforestation; soil erosion; pollution of fresh water resources
Terrain: mostly low, flat to rolling plain; mountains in south-central interior
Land Use: arable land: 13.43%, permanent crops: 15.78%, other: 70.79%; includes 6,510 sq. km irrigated
Location: Indian Ocean, S of India

■ PEOPLE

Population: 19,742,439 (July 2003 est.)
Nationality: Sri Lankan
Age Structure: 0–14 yrs: 25.2%; 15–64: 67.9%; 65+: 6.9% (2003 est.)
Population Growth Rate: 0.83% (2003 est.)
Net Migration: -1.35 migrants/1,000 population (2003 est.)

Ethnic Groups: 74% Sinhalese; 18% Tamil; 7% Moor; 1% Burgher, Malay and Veddha
Languages: Sinhala (official); Sinhala and Tamil are the national languages; Sinhala spoken by about 74% of population, Tamil spoken by about 18%; English commonly used in government and spoken by about 10% of the population
Religions: 69% Buddhist, 15% Hindu (Tamil speakers), 8% Christian, 8% Muslim
Birth Rate: 16.12/1,000 population (2003 est.)
Death Rate: 6.46/1,000 population (2003 est.)
Infant Mortality: 15.22 deaths/1,000 live births (2003 est.)
Life Expectancy at Birth: 70.09 years male, 75.29 years female (2003 est.)
Total Fertility Rate: 1.90 children born/woman (2003 est.)
Literacy: 92.1% (2002)

■ GOVERNMENT

Leader(s): President Chandrika Bandaranaike Kumaratunga, Prime Minister Mahinda Rajapaksa
Government Type: republic
Administrative Divisions: 8 provinces
Nationhood: Feb. 4, 1948 (from UK; formerly known as Ceylon)
National Holiday: Independence and National Day, Feb. 4

■ ECONOMY

Overview: sustained economic growth, coupled with low population growth, has pushed Sri Lanka from the ranks of the poorest countries, however civil war between Sinhalese and Tamils continues to disrupt economic progress
GDP: US$73.7 billion, per capita US$3,700; real growth rate 3.2% (2002 est.)
Inflation: 9.6% (2002 est.)
Industries: accounts for 27% of GDP (2000); processing of rubber, tea, coconuts and other agricultural commodities; cement, petroleum refining, textiles, tobacco. The apparel industry has surpassed all other kinds of manufacturing
Labour Force: 8.4 million (2002); 38% agriculture, 45% community, social and business services, 17% industry
Unemployment: 8.2% (2002)
Agriculture: accounts for 21% of GDP (2000) and almost 45% of labour force; most important staple crop is paddy rice; other field crops: sugar cane, grains, pulses, oilseeds, roots; spices; cash crops: tea, rubber, coconuts; animal products: milk, eggs, hides, meat; not self-sufficient in rice production
Natural Resources: limestone, graphite, mineral sands, gems, phosphates, clay, hydro power

■ FINANCE/TRADE

Currency: rupee (SL Re) = 100 cents
International Reserves Excluding Gold: US$1.889 billion (July 2003)
Gold Reserves: 0.063 million fine troy ounces (June 2003)
Budget: revenues US$2.8 billion; expenditures US$4.1 billion, including capital expenditures of US$ n.a. (2001 est.)
Defence Expenditures: 14.7% of central government expenditure (2002)
Education Expenditures: 9.60% of government expenditure (2000)
External Debt: US$9.611 billion (2002)
Exports: US$4.699 billion (2002); commodities: tea, textiles and garments, petroleum products, coconut, rubber, agricultural products, gems and jewellery, marine products; partners: US, UK, Middle East, Germany, Japan
Imports: US$6.105 billion (2002); commodities: petroleum, machinery and equipment, textiles and textile materials, wheat, transportation equipment, electrical machinery, sugar, rice; partners: Japan, India, Hong Kong, Singapore, South Korea

■ COMMUNICATIONS

Daily Newspapers: 29/1,000 inhabitants (2000)
Televisions: 117/1,000 inhabitants (2002)
Radios: 215/1,000 inhabitants (2001)
Telephones: 47 lines/1,000 inhabitants (2002)
Internet: hosts: 2,335 (2002); users: 200,000 (2002)

■ TRANSPORTATION

Motor Vehicles: 720,000; 235,000 passenger cars
Roads: 11,285 km; 10,721 km paved
Railway: 1,508 km
Air Traffic: 1,741,000 passengers carried (2002)
Airports: 15, 14 have paved runways (2003 est.)

Canadian Embassy: The Canadian High Commission, 6 Gregory's Rd, Cinnamon Gardens, Colombo 7, Sri Lanka; mailing address: P.O. Box 1006, Colombo 7, Sri Lanka. Tel: (011 94 11) 269 5841. Fax: (011 94 11) 268-7049. e-mail: clmbo@dfait-maeci.gc.ca
Embassy in Canada: High Commission for the Democratic Socialist Republic of Sri Lanka, 333 Laurier Ave W, Ste 1204, Ottawa ON K1P 1C1. Tel: (613) 233-8449. Fax: (613) 238-8448. e-mail: lankacom@magi.com

Sudan

Long-Form Name: Republic of the Sudan
Capital: Khartoum

■ GEOGRAPHY

Area: 2,505,810 sq. km
Coastline: 853 km
Climate: tropical in south; arid desert in north; rainy season (Apr. to Oct.)
Environment: dominated by the Nile and its tributaries; dust storms; desertification; unsafe drinking water resources; overhunting threatens wildlife population
Terrain: generally flat, featureless plain; mountains in east and west
Land Use: arable land: 7.03%, permanent crops: 0.08%, other: 92.89%; includes 19,500 sq. km irrigated
Location: NE Africa, bordering on Red Sea

■ PEOPLE

Population: 38,114,160 (July 2003 est.)
Nationality: Sudanese
Age Structure: 0–14 yrs: 44.0%; 15–64: 53.8%; 65+: 2.2% (2003 est.)
Population Growth Rate: 2.71% (2003 est.)
Net Migration: 0.24 migrants/1,000 population (2003 est.)
Ethnic Groups: 52% black, 39% Arab, 6% Beja, 2% foreigners, 1% other
Languages: Arabic (official), Nubian, Ta Bedawie, diverse dialects of Nilotic, Nilo-Hamatic and Sudanic languages, English; program of Arabization in process
Religions: 70% Sunni Muslim (in north), 25% indigenous beliefs, 5% Christian (mostly in south and Khartoum)
Birth Rate: 36.48/1,000 population (2003 est.)
Death Rate: 9.59/1,000 population (2003 est.)
Infant Mortality: 65.59 deaths/1,000 live births (2003 est.)
Life Expectancy at Birth: 56.59 years male, 58.93 years female (2003 est.)
Total Fertility Rate: 5.10 children born/woman (2003 est.)
Literacy: 59.9% (2002)

■ GOVERNMENT

Leader(s): President Omar Hassan Ahmed al-Bashir
Government Type: authoritarian regime
Administrative Divisions: 26 states (wilayat, sing. —wilayah)
Nationhood: Jan. 1, 1956 (from Egypt and UK; formerly known as Anglo-Egyptian Sudan)
National Holiday: Independence Day, Jan. 1

■ ECONOMY

Overview: a very poor country, hurt by civil war, chronic political instability, adverse weather and counterproductive governmental economic policies; agriculture is the economic base. It employs 80% of the labour force and focuses chiefly on processing agricultural produce; international aid is helping the country manage a high foreign debt, but creditors want economic reform

GDP: US$52.9 billion, per capita US$1,400; real growth rate 5.1% (2002 est.)

Inflation: 9.2% (2002 est.)

Industries: accounts for 17% of GDP; cotton ginning, textiles, cement, edible oils, sugar, soap distilling, shoes, petroleum refining

Labour Force: 13.2 million (2002); 80% agriculture, 10% industry, 6% services, 4% other

Unemployment: n.a.

Agriculture: accounts for 39% of GDP and 80% of labour force; untapped potential for higher farm production; water shortages; two-thirds of land area suitable for crops and livestock; major products: cotton, oilseeds, sorghum, millet, wheat, gum arabic, papaya, bananas, sheep; marginally self-sufficient in most foods

Natural Resources: modest reserves of crude oil, iron ore, copper, chromium ore, zinc, tungsten, mica, silver

■ FINANCE/TRADE

Currency: Sudanese dinar (LSd) = 100 piastres; Sudanese pound was discontinued in July 1999

International Reserves Excluding Gold: US$848 million (Dec. 2003)

Gold Reserves: n.a.

Budget: revenues US$1.6 billion; expenditures US$1.9 billion, including capital expenditures of US$ n.a. (2001 est.)

Defence Expenditures: 27.4% of central government expenditure (2002)

Education Expenditures: n.a.

External Debt: US$16.389 billion (2002)

Exports: US$2.45 billion (2003 est.); commodities: cotton 43%, sesame, gum arabic, peanuts, livestock, sugar; partners: Japan, China, Saudi Arabia, Germany

Imports: US$2.383 billion (2003 est.); commodities: petroleum products, manufactured goods, machinery and equipment, medicines and chemicals; partners: China, Saudi Arabia, UK, Germany

■ COMMUNICATIONS

Daily Newspapers: 26/1,000 inhabitants (2000)

Televisions: 386/1,000 inhabitants (2002)

Radios: 466/1,000 inhabitants (2001)

Telephones: 21 lines/1,000 inhabitants (2002)

Internet: hosts: n.a.; users: 84,000 (2002)

■ TRANSPORTATION

Motor Vehicles: 75,000; 35,000 passenger cars

Roads: 11,900 km; 4,320 km paved

Railway: 5,978 km

Air Traffic: 409,000 passengers carried (2002)

Airports: 63; 12 have paved runways (2003 est.)

Canadian Embassy: Office of the Canadian Embassy, 29 Africa Road, Block 56, Khartoum 1, Sudan. Tel: (011 249 11) 79 03 20/22. Fax (011 249 11) 79 03 21. e-mail: david.hutchings @dfait-maeci.gc.ca

Embassy in Canada: Embassy of the Republic of the Sudan, 354 Stewart St, Ottawa ON K1N 6K8. Tel: (613) 235-4000. Fax: (613) 235-6880. e-mail: sudanembassy-canada@rogers.com

Suriname

Long-Form Name: Republic of Suriname

Capital: Paramaribo

■ GEOGRAPHY

Area: 163,270 sq. km

Coastline: 386 km

Climate: tropical; moderated by trade winds

Environment: mostly tropical rainforest; deforestation resulting from logging for export; mining causes pollution of inland waterways

Terrain: mostly rolling hills; narrow coastal plain with swamps

Land Use: arable land: 0.37%, permanent crops: 0.06%, other: 99.57%; includes 490 sq. km irrigated

Location: N South America, bordering on Atlantic Ocean

■ PEOPLE

Population: 435,449 (July 2003 est.)

Nationality: Surinamer

Age Structure: 0–14 yrs: 30.7%; 15–64: 63.3%; 65+: 6.0% (2003 est.)

Population Growth Rate: 0.37% (2003 est.)

Net Migration: -8.84 migrants/1,000 population (2003 est.)

Ethnic Groups: 37% Hindustani (East Indian), 31% Creole (black and mixed), 15% Javanese, 10% Maroons, 2% Amerindian, 2% Chinese, 1% European, 2% other

Languages: Dutch (official), Hindustani 32%, Javanese 15%; the majority can speak the native language Sranang Tongo (Taki-Taki); English is also widely spoken

Religions: 27.4% Hindu, 19.6% Muslim, 22.8% Roman Catholic, 25.2% Protestant (predominantly Moravian), about 5% indigenous beliefs

Birth Rate: 19.40/1,000 population (2003 est.)

Death Rate: 6.83/1,000 population (2003 est.)

Infant Mortality: 24.74 deaths/1,000 live births (2003 est.)

Life Expectancy at Birth: 66.79 years male, 71.78 years female (2003 est.)
Total Fertility Rate: 2.40 children born/woman (2003 est.)
Literacy: 94.0% (2002)

■ GOVERNMENT

Leader(s): President Ronald Venetiaan, Vice President Jules Rattankoemar Ajodhia
Government Type: constitutional democracy
Administrative Divisions: 10 districts (distrikten, sing. distrikt)
Nationhood: Nov. 25, 1975 (from Netherlands; formerly known as Netherlands Guiana or Dutch Guiana)
National Holiday: Independence Day, Nov. 25

■ ECONOMY

Overview: the economy is vulnerable to world prices for its bauxite, which provides more than 15% of the GDP and 65+% of export earnings. Guerrilla activity has targeted the economic infrastructure; high inflation, high unemployment, widespread black-market activity and hard currency shortfalls continue to characterize the economy
GDP: US$1.469 billion, per capita US$3,400; real growth rate 1.2% (2002 est.)
Inflation: 17.0% (2002 est.)
Industries: accounts for 22% of GDP; bauxite mining, alumina and aluminum production, lumbering, food processing, fishing
Labour Force: approx. 100,000; 20% agriculture, 8.9% industry, 49.4% services, 15.2% trade and tourism
Unemployment: n.a.
Agriculture: accounts for 13% of GDP and 25% of export earnings; paddy rice planted on 85% of arable land and represents 60% of total farm output; other products: bananas, palm kernels, coconuts, plantains, peanuts, beef, chicken; shrimp and forestry products of increasing importance
Natural Resources: timber, hydro power potential, fish, shrimp, bauxite, iron ore and modest amounts of nickel, copper, platinum, gold

■ FINANCE/TRADE

Currency: Surinamese guilder, gulden or florin (Sf) = 100 cents
International Reserves Excluding Gold: US$114 million (Jan. 2004)
Gold Reserves: 0.021 million fine troy ounces (Jan. 2004)
Budget: n.a.
Defence Expenditures: n.a.
Education Expenditures: n.a.
External Debt: US$512 million (2002 est.)

Exports: US$495 million (2002); commodities: alumina, bauxite, aluminum, rice, wood and wood products, shrimp and fish, bananas; partners: Netherlands, US, Norway, France, Japan, UK
Imports: US$604 million (2002); commodities: capital equipment, petroleum, foodstuffs, cotton, consumer goods; partners: US, Netherlands, Trinidad and Tobago, Brazil, UK, Japan

■ COMMUNICATIONS

Daily Newspapers: 2 in total
Televisions: n.a.
Radios: n.a.
Telephones: 180 lines/1,000 inhabitants (2002)
Internet: hosts: 24 (2002); users: 20,000 (2002)

■ TRANSPORTATION

Motor Vehicles: 66,000; 46,900 passenger cars
Roads: 4,492 km; 1,168 km paved
Railway: 166 km
Air Traffic: 330,000 passengers carried (2001 est.)
Airports: 46; 5 have paved runways (2003 est.)

Canadian Embassy: The Canadian Embassy to Suriname, c/o Canadian High Commission, High and Young Streets, Georgetown; mailing address: P.O. Box 10880, Georgetown, Guyana. Tel: (011-592) 227-2081. Fax: (011-592) 225-8380. e-mail: grgtn@dfait-maeci.gc.ca
Embassy in Canada: c/o Embassy of the Republic of Suriname, Van Ness Center, 4301 Connecticut Ave NW, Ste 460, Washington DC 20008, USA. Tel: (202) 244-7488. Fax: (202) 244-5878. e-mail: embsur@erols.com

Svalbard

Long-Form Name: Svalbard
Capital: Longyearbyen

■ GEOGRAPHY

Area: 62,049 sq. km, 5 large islands, many smaller ones
Climate: arctic, tempered by mild Atlantic winds, cool summers, cold winters
Land Use: arable land: 0%, permanent crops: 0%, other: 100%, (no trees, and the only bushes are crowberry and cloudberry)
Location: Arctic Ocean, midway between Norway and the North Pole

■ PEOPLE

Population: 2,811 (July 2003 est.)
Nationality: Norwegian
Ethnic Groups: 62% Russian and Ukrainian; 38% Norwegian
Languages: Norwegian, Russian

■ GOVERNMENT

Colony/Territory of: Dependent Territory of Norway
Leader(s): Head of State: King Harald V (Norway), District Governor Odd Olsen Ingerø
Government Type: Territory of Norway
National Holiday: n.a.

■ ECONOMY

Overview: tourism most important; coal mining only industry (the Norwegian state-owned company employs almost 60% of the population); some trapping of seal, polar bear, fox and walrus

■ FINANCE/TRADE

Currency: Norwegian krone = 100 oere

Canadian Embassy: c/o The Canadian Embassy, Wergelandsveien 7, 0244 Oslo, Norway. Tel: (011-47) 22-99-53-00. Fax: (011-47) 22-99-53-01. e-mail: oslo@dfait-maeci.gc.ca
Representative to Canada: c/o Embassy of the Kingdom of Norway, Royal Bank Centre, 90 Sparks St, Ste 532, Ottawa ON K1P 5B4. Tel: (613) 238-6571. Fax: (613) 238-2765. e-mail: emb.ottawa@mfa.no

Swaziland

Long-Form Name: Kingdom of Swaziland
Capital: Mbabane (administrative); Lobamba (legislative)

■ GEOGRAPHY

Area: 17,363 sq. km
Coastline: none: landlocked
Climate: varies from tropical to near temperate
Environment: overhunting and overgrazing; soil degradation; soil erosion; limited safe drinking water
Terrain: mostly mountains and hills; some moderately sloping plains
Land Use: arable land: 9.77%, permanent crops: 0.7%, other: 89.53%; includes 690 sq. km irrigated
Location: S Africa

■ PEOPLE

Population: 1,161,219 (July 2003 est.)
Nationality: Swazi
Age Structure: 0–14 yrs: 41.4%; 15–64: 55.1%; 65+: 3.5% (2003 est.)
Population Growth Rate: 0.83% (2003 est.)
Net Migration: 0 migrants/1,000 population (2003 est.)
Ethnic Groups: 97% African, 3% European
Languages: English and siSwati (official); government business conducted in English

Religions: 60% Christian, 40% indigenous beliefs
Birth Rate: 29.37/1,000 population (2003 est.)
Death Rate: 21.08/1,000 population (2003 est.)
Infant Mortality: 67.44 deaths/1,000 live births (2003 est.)
Life Expectancy at Birth: 41.02 years male, 37.87 years female (2003 est.)
Total Fertility Rate: 4.92 children born/woman (2003 est.)
Literacy: 80.9% (2002)

■ GOVERNMENT

Leader(s): King Mswati III, Prime Minister Absalom Themba Dlamini
Government Type: monarchy; independent member of Commonwealth
Administrative Divisions: 4 districts
Nationhood: Sept. 6, 1968 (from UK)
National Holiday: Somhlolo (Independence) Day, Sept. 6

■ ECONOMY

Overview: is based on subsistence agriculture and is closely tied to that of its neighbour, South Africa, from which it receives 90% of its imports and to which it sends about half of its exports; manufacturing focuses on the processing of agricultural products; mining is becoming less important; overgrazing, soil deterioration and recurrent droughts are persistent problems
GDP: US$5.542 billion, per capita US$4,800; real growth rate 1.6% (2002 est.)
Inflation: 11.8% (2002 est.)
Industries: accounts for 46% of GDP; mining (coal and asbestos), wood pulp, sugar; asbestos is declining in importance
Labour Force: 400,000 (2002); 74% agriculture, 17% services, 9% industry; 24,000–29,000 employed in South Africa
Unemployment: n.a.
Agriculture: accounts for 10% of GDP and over two-thirds of labour force; mostly subsistence agriculture; cash crops: sugar cane, citrus fruit, cotton, tobacco, pineapple; other crops and livestock: corn, sorghum, peanuts, cattle, goats, sheep; not self-sufficient in grain
Natural Resources: asbestos, coal, clay, tin, hydroelectric power, quarry stone, talc, forests and small gold and diamond deposits

■ FINANCE/TRADE

Currency: lilangeni (pl. emalangeni) (E) = 100 cents
International Reserves Excluding Gold: US$305 million (Jan. 2004)
Gold Reserves: n.a.

Budget: revenues US$448 million, expenditures US$506.9 million, including capital expenditures of US$147 million (FY2001/02)
Defence Expenditures: 5.2% of central government expenditure (2002)
Education Expenditures: 19.84% of central government expenditure (2000)
External Debt: US$342 million (2002)
Exports: US$937 million (2002); commodities: sugar, asbestos, wood pulp, citrus, canned fruit, soft drink concentrates; partners: South Africa, US, Mozambique, EU, UK
Imports: US$983 million (2002); commodities: motor vehicles, machinery, transport equipment, chemicals, petroleum products, foodstuffs; partners: South Africa, EU, Japan, Singapore

■ COMMUNICATIONS

Daily Newspapers: 26/1,000 inhabitants (2000)
Televisions: 84/1,000 inhabitants (2002)
Radios: 162/1,000 inhabitants (2001)
Telephones: 34 lines/1,000 inhabitants (2002)
Internet: hosts: 1,329 (2002); users: 20,000 (2002)

■ TRANSPORTATION

Motor Vehicles: 79,000; 39,000 passenger cars
Roads: 3,000 km; 1,064 km paved
Railway: 301 km
Air Traffic: 90,000 passengers carried (2002)
Airports: 18; 1 has a paved runway (2003 est.)

Canadian Embassy: The Canadian High Commission to Swaziland, c/o The Canadian Embassy, 1103 Arcadia St, Hatfield 0028, Pretoria; mailing address: Private Bag X13, Hatfield 0028, Pretoria, South Africa. Tel: (011-27-12) 422-3000. Fax (011-27-12) 422-3052. e-mail: pret@dfait-maeci.gc.ca
Embassy in Canada: c/o High Commission for the Kingdom of Swaziland, 1712 New Hampshire Ave. NW, Washington DC, 20009, Tel: (202) 234-5002, Fax: (202) 234-8254. e-mail: swaziland@compuserve.com

Sweden

Long-Form Name: Kingdom of Sweden
Capital: Stockholm

■ GEOGRAPHY

Area: 449,964 sq. km
Coastline: 3,218 km
Climate: temperate in south with cold, cloudy winters and cool, partly cloudy summers, subarctic in north
Environment: water pollution; acid rain; ice floes in coastal waters hinder navigation

Terrain: mostly flat or gently rolling lowlands; mountains in west
Land Use: arable land: 6.8%, permanent crops: 0%, other: 93.2%; includes 1,150 sq. km irrigated
Location: N Europe, bordering on Baltic Sea

■ PEOPLE

Population: 8,878,085 (July 2003 est.)
Nationality: Swedish, Swede
Age Structure: 0–14 yrs: 17.7%; 15–64: 65.0%; 65+: 17.3% (2003 est.)
Population Growth Rate: 0.01% (2003 est.)
Net Migration: 1.00 migrants/1,000 population (2003 est.)
Ethnic Groups: homogeneous white population; small Lappish minority; about 12% foreign born or first-generation immigrants (Finns, Yugoslavs, Danes, Norwegians, Greeks, Turks)
Languages: Swedish (official), small Lapp- and Finnish-speaking minorities; immigrants speak native languages
Religions: 94% Evangelical Lutheran, 1.5% Roman Catholic, 4.5% other
Birth Rate: 9.71/1,000 population (2003 est.)
Death Rate: 10.58/1,000 population (2003 est.)
Infant Mortality: 3.42 deaths/1,000 live births (2003 est.)
Life Expectancy at Birth: 77.31 years male, 82.78 years female (2003 est.)
Total Fertility Rate: 1.54 children born/woman (2003 est.)
Literacy: approaching 100% (2002)

■ GOVERNMENT

Leader(s): King Carl XVI Gustaf, Prime Minister Goran Persson
Government Type: constitutional monarchy
Administrative Divisions: 21 counties (lan, sing. & pl.)
Nationhood: June 6, 1523, constitutional monarchy established
National Holiday: Day of the Swedish Flag, June 6

■ ECONOMY

Overview: a mixed system of high-tech capitalism and extensive welfare benefits; has benefited from neutrality in world wars; economy is heavily oriented toward foreign trade; has excellent communications systems
GDP: US$230.7 billion, per capita US$26,000; real growth rate 1.9% (2002)
Inflation: 2.2% (2002 est.)
Industries: accounts for 28% of GDP (2001); iron and steel, precision equipment (bearings, radio and telephone parts, armaments), wood pulp and paper products, processed foods, motor vehicles

Labour Force: 4.8 million (2002); 74% community, social and business services, 24% industry, 2% agriculture
Unemployment: 5.3% (Jan. 2004)
Agriculture: accounts for 2% of GDP (2001); animal husbandry predominates, with milk and dairy products accounting for 37% of farm income; main crops: grains, sugar beets, potatoes; 100% self-sufficient in grains and potatoes, 85% self-sufficient in sugar beets
Natural Resources: zinc, iron ore, lead, copper, silver, timber, uranium, hydro power potential

■ FINANCE/TRADE

Currency: krona (pl. kronor) (Skr) = 100 oere
International Reserves Excluding Gold: US$20.111 billion (Jan. 2004)
Gold Reserves: 5.961 million fine troy ounces (Jan. 2004)
Budget: revenues US$119 billion, expenditures US$110 billion, including capital expenditures of US$ n.a. (2001 est.)
Defence Expenditures: 5.4% of government expenditure (2002)
Education Expenditures: 13.6% of total government expenditure (2002)
External Debt: n.a.
Exports: US$99.356 billion (2003 est.); commodities: machinery, motor vehicles, paper products, pulp and wood, iron and steel products, chemicals, petroleum and petroleum products; partners: Germany, UK, Denmark, Finland, US, Norway
Imports: US$81.167 billion (2003 est.); commodities: machinery, petroleum and petroleum products, chemicals, motor vehicles, foodstuffs, iron and steel, clothing; partners: Germany, UK, Denmark, Netherlands, US, France, Norway

■ COMMUNICATIONS

Daily Newspapers: 410/1,000 inhabitants (2000)
Televisions: 965/1,000 inhabitants (2002)
Radios: 2,811/1,000 inhabitants (2001)
Telephones: 736 lines/1,000 inhabitants (2002)
Internet: hosts: 849,174 (2002); users: 5.125 million (2002)

■ TRANSPORTATION

Motor Vehicles: 4,380,000; 4,000,000 passenger cars
Roads: 212,402 km; 166,523 km paved
Railway: 11,481 km
Air Traffic: 12,696,000 passengers carried (2002)
Airports: 245; 145 have paved runways (2003 est.)

Canadian Embassy: The Canadian Embassy, Tegelbacken 4 (Flr 7), Stockholm, Sweden; mailing address: P.O. Box 16129; S-10323 Stockholm, Sweden. Tel: (011-46-8) 453-3000. Fax: (011-46-8) 453-3016. e-mail: stkhm@dfait-maeci.gc.ca
Embassy in Canada: Embassy of Sweden, Mercury Court, 377 Dalhousie St, Ottawa ON K1N 9N8. Tel: (613) 241-8553. Fax: (613) 241-2277. e-mail: sweden@cyberus.ca

Switzerland

Long-Form Name: Swiss Confederation
Capital: Bern

■ GEOGRAPHY

Area: 41,290 sq. km
Coastline: none: landlocked
Climate: temperate, but varies with altitude; cold, cloudy, rainy/snowy winters; cool to warm, cloudy, humid summers with occasional showers
Environment: dominated by Alps; air and water pollution; avalanches, flash floods and landslides are natural hazards
Terrain: mostly mountains (Alps in south, Jura in northwest) with a central plateau of rolling hills, plains and large lakes
Land Use: arable land: 10.57%, permanent crops: 0.61%, other: 88.82%; includes 250 sq. km irrigated
Location: C Europe

■ PEOPLE

Population: 7,318,638 (July 2003 est.)
Nationality: Swiss (sing. & pl.)
Age Structure: 0–14 yrs: 16.6%; 15–64: 67.8%; 65+: 15.6% (2003 est.)
Population Growth Rate: 0.21% (2003 est.)
Net Migration: 1.37 migrants/1,000 population (2003 est.)
Ethnic Groups: total population: 65% German, 18% French, 10% Italian, 1% Romansch, 6% other
Languages: 65% German, 18% French, 12% Italian, 1% Raeto-Romansch (all official), 4% other
Religions: 47.6% Roman Catholic, 44.3% Protestant, 8.1% other
Birth Rate: 9.59/1,000 population (2003 est.)
Death Rate: 8.82/1,000 population (2003 est.)
Infant Mortality: 4.36 deaths/1,000 live births (2003 est.)
Life Expectancy at Birth: 77.11 years male, 83.02 years female (2003 est.)
Total Fertility Rate: 1.48 children born/woman (2003 est.)
Literacy: approaching 100% (2002)

■ GOVERNMENT

Leader(s): President Joseph Deiss, Vice President Samuel Schmid

Government Type: federal republic
Administrative Divisions: 26 cantons
Nationhood: Aug. 1, 1291
National Holiday: Anniversary of the Founding of the Swiss Confederation, Aug. 1

■ ECONOMY

Overview: country has the highest per capita output, general living standards, education and science, health-care and diet standards in Europe; important banking and tourist sectors; low inflation and negligible unemployment are due partly to government policies; has rejected membership in the European Economic Community
GDP: US$233.4 billion, per capita US$32,000; real growth rate 0.1% (2002)
Inflation: 0.5% (2002 est.)
Industries: accounts for 34% of GDP (2002 est.); machinery, chemicals, watches, textiles, precision instruments
Labour Force: 3.9 million (2002); 26% industry, 69% community, social and business services, 5% agriculture
Unemployment: 4.2% (Feb. 2004)
Agriculture: accounts for 2% of GDP (2002 est.); dairy farming predominates; less than 50% self-sufficient; food shortages: fish, refined sugar, fats and oils (other than butter), grains, eggs, fruit, vegetables, meat
Natural Resources: hydro power potential, timber, salt; scenic beauty

■ FINANCE/TRADE

Currency: Swiss franc, franken, or franco (SwF) = 100 centimes, rappen, or centesimi
International Reserves Excluding Gold: US$49.921 billion (Jan. 2004)
Gold Reserves: 51.708 million fine troy ounces (Jan. 2004)
Budget: revenues US$30 billion; expenditures US$30 billion, including capital expenditures of US$ n.a. (2001 est.)
Defence Expenditures: 4.2% of central government expenditure (2002)
Education Expenditures: 15.2% of total government expenditure (2002)
External Debt: n.a.
Exports: US$95.908 billion (2003); commodities: machinery and equipment, precision instruments, metal products, foodstuffs, textiles and clothing; partners: Germany, France, Italy, UK, US, Japan
Imports: US$90.827 billion (2003); commodities: agricultural products, machinery and transportation equipment, chemicals, textiles, construction materials; partners: Germany, France, Italy, Netherlands, UK, US

■ COMMUNICATIONS

Daily Newspapers: 373/1,000 inhabitants (2000)
Televisions: 552/1,000 inhabitants (2002)
Radios: 1,002/1,000 inhabitants (2001)
Telephones: 744 lines/1,000 inhabitants (2002)
Internet: hosts: 560,902 (2002); users: 2.556 million (2002)

■ TRANSPORTATION

Motor Vehicles: 3,900,000; 3,600,000 passenger cars
Roads: 71,011 km; all paved
Railway: 4,511 km
Air Traffic: 13,292,000 passengers carried (2002)
Airports: 66; 41 have paved runways (2003 est.)

Canadian Embassy: The Canadian Embassy, Kirchenfeldstrasse 88, Bern, 3005, Switzerland. Mailing address: P.O. Box 3000, Berne 6, Switzerland. Tel: (011-41-31) 357-32-00. Fax: (011-41-31) 357-32-10. e-mail: bern@dfait-maeci.gc.ca
Embassy in Canada: Embassy of Switzerland, 5 Marlborough Ave, Ottawa ON K1N 8E6. Tel: (613) 235-1837. Fax: (613) 563-1394. e-mail: vertretung@ott.rep.admin.ch

Syria

Long-Form Name: Syrian Arab Republic
Capital: Damascus

■ GEOGRAPHY

Area: 185,180 sq. km; including 1,295 sq. km of Israeli-occupied territory
Coastline: 193 km
Climate: mostly desert; hot, dry, sunny summers (June to Aug.) and mild, rainy winters (Dec. to Feb.) along coast
Environment: deforestation; overgrazing; soil erosion; desertification; unsafe drinking water
Terrain: primarily semi-arid and desert plateau; narrow coastal plain; mountains in west
Land Use: arable land: 25.96%, permanent crops: 4.08%, other: 69.96%; includes 12,130 sq. km irrigated
Location: SW Asia (Middle East), bordering on Mediterranean Sea

■ PEOPLE

Population: 17,585,540 (July 2003 est.)
Nationality: Syrian
Age Structure: 0–14 yrs: 38.6%; 15–64: 58.2%; 65+: 3.2% (2003 est.)
Population Growth Rate: 2.45% (2003 est.)
Net Migration: 0 migrants/1,000 population (2003 est.)
Ethnic Groups: 90.3% Arab; 9.7% Kurds, Armenians and other

Languages: Arabic (official), Kurdish, Armenian, Aramaic, Circassian; English and French widely understood
Religions: 74% Sunni, 16% Alawite, Druze and other Muslim sects, 10% Christian
Birth Rate: 29.54/1,000 population (2003 est.)
Death Rate: 5.04/1,000 population (2003 est.)
Infant Mortality: 31.67 deaths/1,000 live births (2003 est.)
Life Expectancy at Birth: 68.18 years male, 70.67 years female (2003 est.)
Total Fertility Rate: 3.72 children born/woman (2003 est.)
Literacy: 82.9% (2002)

■ GOVERNMENT

Leader(s): President Bashar al-Asad, Vice President Abd al-Halim ibn Said Khaddam
Government Type: republic under left-wing military regime
Administrative Divisions: 14 provinces (muhafazat, sing. —muhafazah)
Nationhood: Apr. 17, 1946 (from League of Nations mandate under French administration; formerly known as United Arab Republic)
National Holiday: Independence Day, Apr. 17

■ ECONOMY

Overview: economic difficulties are due, in part, to severe drought in several recent years, costly but unsuccessful attempts to match Israel's military strength, a fall-off in Arab aid and insufficient foreign exchange earnings to buy needed imports; agricultural output is poor; a major long-term concern is the additional drain of upstream Euphrates water by Turkey once its vast dam and irrigation projects are completed
GDP: US$63.48 billion, per capita US$3,700; real growth rate 3.6% (2002 est.)
Inflation: 0.9% (2002 est.)
Industries: accounts for 23% of GDP (2000), textiles, food processing, beverages, tobacco, phosphate rock mining, petroleum
Labour Force: 5.6 million (2002); 40% services, 40% agriculture, 20% industry
Unemployment: 11.2% (2002 est.)
Agriculture: accounts for 27% of GDP (2000); all major crops (wheat, barley, cotton, lentils, chickpeas) grown on rain-fed land causing wide swings in yields; animal products: beef, lamb, eggs, poultry, milk; not self-sufficient in grain or livestock products
Natural Resources: crude oil, phosphates, chrome and manganese ores, asphalt, iron ore, rock salt, marble, gypsum

■ FINANCE/TRADE

Currency: Syrian pound (£S) = 100 piastres
International Reserves Excluding Gold: n.a.

Gold Reserves: 0.833 million fine troy ounces (Sept. 2003)
Budget: revenues US$4.3 billion; expenditures US$8.6 billion, including capital expenditures of US$3.6 billion (2004 est.)
Defence Expenditures: 24.2% of central government expenditure (2002)
Education Expenditures: n.a.
External Debt: US$21.504 billion (2002)
Exports: US$6.831 billion (2002); commodities: petroleum, textiles, fruit and vegetables, phosphates; partners: Italy, Germany, France, Turkey, Saudi Arabia
Imports: US$5.097 billion (2002); commodities: petroleum, machinery, base metals, foodstuffs and beverages, textiles and chemicals; partners: France, Italy, Lebanon, China, Germany, South Korea, Turkey, US

■ COMMUNICATIONS

Daily Newspapers: 20/1,000 inhabitants (2000)
Televisions: 82/1,000 inhabitants (2002)
Radios: 276/1,000 inhabitants (2001)
Telephones: 123 lines/1,000 inhabitants (2002)
Internet: hosts: 11 (2002); users: 220,000 (2002)

■ TRANSPORTATION

Motor Vehicles: 500,000; 154,000 passenger cars
Roads: 43,381 km; 10,021 km hard-surfaced
Railway: 2,743 km
Air Traffic: 824,000 passengers carried (2002)
Airports: 92; 24 have paved runways (2003 est.)

Canadian Embassy: The Canadian Embassy, Lot 12, Mezzeh Autostrade, Damascus, Syria; mailing address: P.O. Box 3394, Damascus, Syria. Tel: (011-963-11) 611-6692. Fax: (011-963-11) 611-4000. e-mail: dmcus@dfait-maeci.gc.ca
Embassy in Canada: Embassy of the Syrian Arab Republic, 151 Slater St., Suite 1000, Ottawa, ON, K1P 5H3, Tel: (613) 569-5556, Fax: (613) 569-3800. e-mail: syrianembassy@on.aibn.com

Taiwan

Long-Form Name: Taiwan
Capital: Taipei

■ GEOGRAPHY

Area: 35,980 sq. km; includes the Pescadores, Matsu and Quemoy
Coastline: 1,566.3 km
Climate: tropical; marine; rainy season during southwest monsoon (June to Aug.)
Environment: subject to earthquakes and typhoons; water and air pollution
Terrain: eastern two-thirds mostly rugged mountains; flat to gently rolling plains in west

Land Use: arable land: 24%, permanent crops: 1%, other: 75%; includes n.a. sq. km irrigated
Location: island, SE of China, bordering on South and East China Seas, Pacific Ocean

■ PEOPLE

Population: 22,603,001 (July 2003 est.)
Nationality: Taiwanese
Age Structure: 0–14 yrs: 20.1%; 15–64: 70.6%; 65+: 9.3% (2003 est.)
Population Growth Rate: 0.65% (2003 est.)
Net Migration: 0.00 migrants/1,000 population (2003 est.)
Ethnic Groups: 84% Taiwanese, 14% mainland Chinese, 2% aborigine
Languages: Mandarin Chinese (official); Taiwanese and Hakka dialects also used
Religions: 93% mixture of Buddhist, Islam, Confucian and Taoist, 5% Christian, 2% other
Birth Rate: 12.74/1,000 population (2003 est.)
Death Rate: 6.20/1,000 population (2003 est.)
Infant Mortality: 6.65 deaths/1,000 live births (2003 est.)
Life Expectancy at Birth: 74.12 years male, 79.88 years female (2003 est.)
Total Fertility Rate: 1.57 children born/woman (2003 est.)
Literacy: 94%

■ GOVERNMENT

Leader(s): President Chen Shui-bian, Vice President Annette Lu, Premier Yu Shyi-Kun
Government Type: multiparty democratic regime
Administrative Divisions: 16 counties (hsien, sing. & pl.), 5 municipalities (shih, sing. & pl.), 2 special municipalities (chuan-shih, sing. & pl.)
Nationhood: Taiwanese
National Holiday: National Day (Anniversary of the Revolution), Oct. 10

■ ECONOMY

Overview: dynamic capitalist economy with gradually decreasing guidance of investment and foreign trade by government authorities and partial government ownership of some large banks and industrial firms
GDP: US$406 billion, per capita US$18,000; real growth rate 3.5% (2002 est.)
Inflation: -0.2% (2002 est.)
Industries: accounts for 31% of GDP (2002), textiles, clothing, chemicals, electronics, food processing, plywood, sugar milling, cement, shipbuilding, petroleum
Labour Force: 10.0 million (2003 est.); 56% services, 36% industry, 8% agriculture
Unemployment: 3% (2000 est.)
Agriculture: accounts for 2% of GDP (2002); heavily subsidized sector; major crops: rice, sugar cane, sweet potatoes, fruit, vegetables, tea;

livestock: hogs, poultry, beef, milk, cattle; not self-sufficient in wheat, soybeans, corn; fish catch expanding, 1.4 million metric tons
Natural Resources: small deposits of coal, natural gas, limestone, marble and asbestos

■ FINANCE/TRADE

Currency: New Taiwan dollar (NT$) = 100 cents
International Reserves Excluding Gold: n.a.
Gold Reserves: n.a.
Budget: revenues US$52.5 billion; expenditures US$63.0 billion, including capital expenditures of US$14.4 billion (2002)
Defence Expenditures: 2.7% of GDP (2002)
Education Expenditures: n.a.
External Debt: US$24.7 billion (2002)
Exports: US$143 billion (2003 est.); commodities: textiles 16%, electrical machinery 19%, general machinery and equipment 14%, telecommunications equipment 9%, basic metals and metal products 5%, foodstuffs 0.9%, plywood and wood products 1.3%; partners: US Hong Kong, Europe, Japan
Imports: US$119.6 billion (2003 est.); commodities: machinery and equipment 15.9%, crude oil 5%, chemical and chemical products 11.1%, basic metals 7.4%, foodstuffs 2%, minerals, precision equipment; partners: Japan, US, European countries, South Korea

■ COMMUNICATIONS

Daily Newspapers: n.a.
Televisions: n.a.
Radios: n.a.
Telephones: n.a.
Internet: hosts: 2,170,233 (2002); users: 8.59 million (2002)

■ TRANSPORTATION

Motor Vehicles: 5,225,000; 4,300,000 passenger cars
Roads: 35,931 km; 31,583 km paved
Railway: 1,108 km
Air Traffic: n.a.
Airports: 39; 37 have paved runways (2003 est.)

Canadian Embassy: Canadian Trade Office, 13th floor, 365 Fu Hsing Nord Road, Taipei 10483, Taiwan. Tel: (011 886 2) 2544 3000. Fax: (011 886 2) 2544 3592. e-mail: tapei@dfait-maeci.gc.ca
Embassy in Canada: none

Tajikistan

Long-Form Name: Republic of Tajikistan
Capital: Dushanbe

■ GEOGRAPHY

Area: 143,100 sq. km
Coastline: none; landlocked
Climate: continental; severe winters in east; extremely hot summers; wet spring; semi-arid to polar in Pamir mountains
Environment: lack of fresh water; little land suitable for cultivation; industrial pollution
Terrain: mountains and glaciers constitute 93% of land area, predominantly herding and non-agricultural
Land Use: arable land: 5.4%, permanent crops: 0.9%, other: 93.7%; includes 7,200 sq. km irrigated
Location: C Asia, bordering on China and Afghanistan

■ PEOPLE

Population: 6,863,752 (July 2003 est.)
Nationality: Tajik, Tajikistani
Age Structure: 0–14 yrs: 39.8%; 15–64: 55.5%; 65+: 4.7% (2003 est.)
Population Growth Rate: 2.13% (2003 est.)
Net Migration: -3.06 migrants/1,000 population (2003 est.)
Ethnic Groups: 64.9% Tajik, 25% Uzbek, 3.5% Russian (declining due to emigration), 6.6% other
Languages: Tajik (official), Uzbek, Russian
Religions: 80% Sunni Muslim, 5% Shia Muslim, 15% other
Birth Rate: 32.78/1,000 population (2003 est.)
Death Rate: 8.46/1,000 population (2003 est.)
Infant Mortality: 113.43 deaths/1,000 live births (2003 est.)
Life Expectancy at Birth: 61.39 years male, 67.50 years female (2002 est.)
Total Fertility Rate: 4.17 children born/woman (2002 est.)
Literacy: 99.5% (2002)

■ GOVERNMENT

Leader(s): President Emomali Rahmonov, Prime Minister Oqil Oqilov
Government Type: republic
Administrative Divisions: 2 oblasts (viloyatho, sing. —viloyat) and 1 autonomous oblast (viloyati mukhtori)
Nationhood: Sept. 9, 1991 (from Soviet Union)
National Holiday: Independence Day, Sept. 9

■ ECONOMY

Overview: mostly mining and manufacturing with strong agricultural sector; industry and agriculture have been producing at reduced capacity due to civil unrest; currency incompatibility with neighbouring countries is straining trade relations; depends on aid from Russia and Uzbekistan and on international aid for much of its basic subsistence needs
GDP: US$8.476 billion, per capita US$1,300; real growth rate 9.1% (2002 est.)
Inflation: 12.0% (2001 est.)
Industries: accounts for 26% of GDP (2002); aluminum and electrochemical plants, textile machinery, silk and carpet mills; zinc, lead, chemicals and fertilizers, cement, vegetable oil, refrigerators and freezers
Labour Force: 2.5 million (2002); 67% agriculture and forestry, 8% industry, 25% services
Unemployment: n.a.
Agriculture: accounts for 19% of GDP (2002); cotton, grapes, fruit, grains, silkworm farming, cattle breeding, sheep, goats, pigs
Natural Resources: coal, oil, rare metals, rock crystal, mica, gold, hydro power potential, uranium, mercury, zinc, lead

■ FINANCE/TRADE

Currency: Tajik somoni
International Reserves Excluding Gold: n.a.
Gold Reserves: 0.015 million fine troy ounces (Jan. 2004)
Budget: revenues US$502 million, expenditures US$520 million, including capital expenditures of US$86 million (2002 est.)
Defence Expenditures: 10.1% of central government expenditure (2002)
Education Expenditures: 3.15% of total government expenditure (2000)
External Debt: US$1.153 billion (2002)
Exports: US$737 million (2002); commodities: fruit, plant products, aluminum, electricity; partners: European countries, Uzbekistan, Russia
Imports: US$721 million (2002); commodities: fuel, machinery, foodstuffs; partners: European nations, Uzbekistan, Russia

■ COMMUNICATIONS

Daily Newspapers: 20/1,000 inhabitants (2000)
Televisions: 357/1,000 inhabitants (2002)
Radios: 141/1,000 inhabitants (2001)
Telephones: 37 lines/1,000 inhabitants (2002)
Internet: hosts: 302 (2002); users: 3,500 (2002)

■ TRANSPORTATION

Motor Vehicles: n.a.
Roads: 29,900 km; 21,400 km hard-surfaced
Railway: 482 km, not including industrial lines
Air Traffic: 397,000 passengers carried (2002)
Airports: 66; 13 have paved runways (2003 est.)

Canadian Embassy: The Canadian Embassy to Tajikistan, c/o The Canadian Embassy, 34 Kasarai Batir St, Almaty 480100, Kazakhstan.

Tel: (011-7-3272) 50-11-51. Fax: (011-7-3272) 582-493. e-mail: almat@dfait-maeci.gc.ca
Embassy in Canada: c/o Embassy of the Republic of Kazakhstan, 1401 16th Street, N.W., Washington, 20036, USA. Tel: (202) 232-5488. Fax: (202) 232-5845. e-mail: kazak@intr.net

Tanzania

Long-Form Name: United Republic of Tanzania
Capital: Dar es Salaam

■ GEOGRAPHY

Area: 945,087 sq. km (includes the islands of Mafia, Pemba and Zanzibar)
Coastline: 1,424 km
Climate: varies from tropical along coast to temperate in highlands
Environment: deforestation; lack of water limits agriculture; recent droughts affected marginal agriculture
Terrain: plains along coast; central plateau; highlands in north, south; Kilimanjaro is highest point in Africa
Land Use: arable land: 4.24%, permanent crops: 1.02%, other: 94.74%; includes 1,550 sq. km irrigated
Location: E Africa, bordering on Indian Ocean

■ PEOPLE

Population: 35,922,454 (July 2003 est.)
Nationality: Tanzanian
Age Structure: 0–14 yrs: 44.3%; 15–64: 53.1%; 65+: 2.6% (2003 est.)
Population Growth Rate: 1.72% (2003 est.)
Net Migration: -4.91 migrants/1,000 population (2003 est.)
Ethnic Groups: 99% native African consisting of well over 100 tribes; 1% Asian, European and Arab
Languages: Swahili and English (official); English primarily language of commerce, administration and higher education; Swahili widely understood and generally used for communication between ethnic groups
Religions: mainland: 30% Christian, 35% Muslim, 35% indigenous beliefs; Zanzibar: almost all Muslim
Birth Rate: 39.50/1,000 population (2003 est.)
Death Rate: 17.38/1,000 population (2003 est.)
Infant Mortality: 103.68 deaths/1,000 live births (2003 est.)
Life Expectancy at Birth: 43.33 years male, 45.83 years female (2003 est.)
Total Fertility Rate: 5.24 children born/woman (2003 est.)
Literacy: 77.1% (2002)

■ GOVERNMENT

Leader(s): President Benjamin William Mkapa, Premier Frederick Sumaye
Government Type: republic
Administrative Divisions: 25 regions
Nationhood: April 26, 1964; Tanganyika became independent on Dec. 9, 1961 (from UN trusteeship under British administration); Zanzibar became independent Dec. 19, 1963 (from UK); Tanganyika united with Zanzibar Apr. 26, 1964 to form the political unit that was renamed Tanzania on Oct. 29, 1964
National Holiday: Union Day, Apr. 26

■ ECONOMY

Overview: world aid is increasing the availability of imports and providing funds to rehabilitate this country's deteriorated economic infrastructure; this poor economy is heavily dependent on agriculture; industry is largely confined to processing agricultural products; mining is increasing in importance; recent banking reforms have helped increase private sector growth and investment
GDP: US$20.42 billion, per capita US$600; real growth rate 6.1% (2002 est.)
Inflation: 4.8% (2002 est.)
Industries: accounts for 15% of GDP (2000); primarily agricultural processing (sugar, beer, cigarettes, sisal twine); diamond mines, oil refineries, shoes, cement, textiles, wood products, fertilizer
Labour Force: 18.1 million (2002); 80% agriculture, 20% industry and commerce
Unemployment: n.a.
Agriculture: accounts for 45% of GDP (2000), 85% of exports and employs 90% of workforce; topography and climatic conditions limit cultivated crops to only 5% of land area; cash crops: coffee, sisal, tea, cotton, pyrethrum (insecticide made from chrysanthemums), cashews, tobacco, cloves (Zanzibar); corn, wheat, beans, fruit and vegetables grown for local consumption
Natural Resources: hydro power potential, tin, phosphates, iron ore, coal, diamonds, gemstones, gold, natural gas, nickel

■ FINANCE/TRADE

Currency: Tanzania shilling (TSh) = 100 cents
International Reserves Excluding Gold: US$1.987 billion (Jan. 2004)
Gold Reserves: n.a.
Budget: revenues US$1.2 billion; expenditures US$2.0 billion, including capital expenditures of US$ n.a. (FY2002/03 est.)
Defence Expenditures: 0.2% of GDP (2002)
Education Expenditures: n.a.
External Debt: US$7.244 billion (2002)

Exports: US$656 million (2003 est.); commodities: gold, coffee, cashew nuts, manufactures, cotton; partners: Germany, Japan, India, Belgium

Imports: US$1.449 billion (2003 est.); commodities: manufactured goods, machinery and transportation equipment, cotton piece goods, crude oil, foodstuffs; partners: Australia, Japan, UK, South Africa

■ COMMUNICATIONS

Daily Newspapers: 4/1,000 inhabitants (2000)
Televisions: 45/1,000 inhabitants (2002)
Radios: 406/1,000 inhabitants (2001)
Telephones: 5 lines/1,000 inhabitants (2002)
Internet: hosts: 1,731 (2002); users: 80,000 (2002)

■ TRANSPORTATION

Motor Vehicles: 133,800; 55,000 passenger cars
Roads: 88,200 km; 3,704 paved
Railway: 3,690 km
Air Traffic: 138,000 passengers carried (2002)
Airports: 123; 11 have paved runways (2003 est.)

Canadian Embassy: The Canadian High Commission, 38 Mirambo St, Dar-es-Salaam; mailing address: P.O. Box 1022, Dar-es-Salaam, Tanzania. Tel: (011-255-22) 211-2831. Fax: (011-255-22) 211-6897. e-mail: dslam@dfait-maeci.gc.ca

Embassy in Canada: High Commission for the United Republic of Tanzania, 50 Range Rd, Ottawa ON, K1N 8J4. Tel: (613) 232-1500. Fax: (613) 232-5184. e-mail: tzottawa@synapse.net

Thailand

Long-Form Name: Kingdom of Thailand
Capital: Bangkok

■ GEOGRAPHY

Area: 514,000 sq. km
Coastline: 3,219 km
Climate: tropical; rainy, warm, cloudy southwest monsoon (mid-May to Sept.); dry, cool, northeast monsoon (Nov. to mid-Mar.); southern isthmus always hot and humid
Environment: air and water pollution; land subsidence in Bangkok area; deforestation; soil erosion; illegal hunting threatens wildlife populations
Terrain: central plain; eastern plateau (Khorat); mountains elsewhere
Land Use: arable land: 32.88%, permanent crops: 7%, other: 60.12%; includes 47,490 sq. km irrigated
Location: SE Asia, bordering on Gulf of Siam and Andaman Sea

■ PEOPLE

Population: 64,265,276 (July 2003 est.)
Nationality: Thai (sing. & pl.)
Age Structure: 0–14 yrs: 24.2%; 15–64: 68.8%; 65+: 7.0% (2003 est.)
Population Growth Rate: 0.95% (2003 est.)
Net Migration: 0 migrants/1,000 population (2003 est.)
Ethnic Groups: 75% Thai, 14% Chinese, 11% other
Languages: Thai; English is the secondary language of the elite; small minorities speak Chinese, Malay, indigenous languages
Religions: 95% Buddhist (Theravada), 3.8% Muslim, 0.5% Christianity, 0.1% Hinduism, 0.6% other
Birth Rate: 16.37/1,000 population (2003 est.)
Death Rate: 6.86/1,000 population (2003 est.)
Infant Mortality: 21.83 deaths/1,000 live births (2003 est.)
Life Expectancy at Birth: 69.07 years male, 73.53 years female (2003 est.)
Total Fertility Rate: 1.91 children born/woman (2003 est.)
Literacy: 92.6% (2002)

■ GOVERNMENT

Leader(s): King Phumiphon Adunyadet (Rama IX), Premier Thaksin Chinnawat
Government Type: constitutional monarchy
Administrative Divisions: 76 provinces (changwat, sing. & pl.)
Nationhood: 1238 (traditional founding date); never colonized
National Holiday: Birthday of His Majesty the King, Dec. 5

■ ECONOMY

Overview: with the currency depreciation and the collapse of domestic demands, imports have fallen by more than a third recently; foreign investment for new projects, the long-time catalyst of Thailand's economic growth, has also slowed
GDP: US$445.8 billion, per capita US$7,000; real growth rate 5.3% (2002 est.)
Inflation: 0.6% (2002 est.)
Industries: accounts for 40% of GDP (2000), tourism is the largest source of foreign exchange; textiles and garments, agricultural processing, beverages, tobacco, cement, other light manufacturing, such as jewellery; electric appliances and components, integrated circuits, furniture, plastics
Labour Force: 37.5 million (2002); 54% agriculture, 31% services, 15% industry
Unemployment: 1.8% (Nov. 2003)
Agriculture: accounts for 11% of GDP (2001) and 57% of labour force; leading producer and exporter of rice and cassava; other crops:

rubber, corn, sugar cane, coconuts, soybeans; self-sufficient in food except for wheat
Natural Resources: tin, rubber, natural gas, tungsten, tantalum, timber, lead, fish, gypsum, lignite, fluorite

■ FINANCE/TRADE

Currency: baht (pl. baht) (B) = 100 satang
International Reserves Excluding Gold: US$41.166 billion (Jan. 2004)
Gold Reserves: 2.600 million fine troy ounces (Jan. 2004)
Budget: revenues US$21 billion; expenditures US$22 billion, including capital expenditures of US$5 billion (2000)
Defence Expenditures: 7.1% of central government expenditure (2002)
Education Expenditures: 28.3% of government expenditure (2002)
External Debt: US$59.211 billion (2002)
Exports: US$79.697 billion (2003); commodities: textiles 12%, fishery products 12%, rice 8%, tapioca 8%, jewellery 6%, manufactured gas, corn, tin; partners: US, Japan, Singapore, Malaysia, Hong Kong, China
Imports: US$75.002 billion (2003); commodities: machinery and parts 23%, petroleum products 13%, chemicals 11%, iron and steel, electrical appliances; partners: Japan, US, Singapore, Malaysia, China, Taiwan

■ COMMUNICATIONS

Daily Newspapers: 64/1,000 inhabitants (2000)
Televisions: 300/1,000 inhabitants (2002)
Radios: 235/1,000 inhabitants (2001)
Telephones: 105 lines/1,000 inhabitants (2002)
Internet: hosts: 100,132 (2002); users: 4.8 million (2002)

■ TRANSPORTATION

Motor Vehicles: 5,700,000; 1,550,000 passenger cars
Roads: 64,600 km; 62,985 km paved
Railway: 4,071 km
Air Traffic: 18,112,000 passengers carried (2002)
Airports: 111; 62 have paved runways (2003 est.)

Canadian Embassy: The Canadian Embassy, 990 Rama IV, Abdulrahim Place, 15th Fl, Bangkok 10500, Thailand; mailing address: P.O. Box 2090, Bangkok 10501, Thailand. Tel: (011-66-2) 636-0540. Fax: (011-66-2) 636-0566. e-mail: bngkk@dfait-maeci.gc.ca
Embassy in Canada: The Royal Thai Embassy, 180 Island Park Dr, Ottawa ON K1Y 0A2. Tel: (613) 722-4444. Fax: (613) 722-6624. e-mail: thaiott@magma.ca

Togo

Long-Form Name: Togolese Republic
Capital: Lomé

■ GEOGRAPHY

Area: 56,785 sq. km
Coastline: 56 km
Climate: tropical; hot, humid in south; semi-arid in north
Environment: hot, dry harmattan wind; recent droughts affecting agriculture; deforestation
Terrain: gently rolling savanna in north; low coastal plain with extensive lagoons and marshes
Land Use: arable land: 41.37%, permanent crops: 1.84%, other: 56.79%; includes 70 sq. km irrigated
Location: WC Africa, bordering on South Atlantic Ocean

■ PEOPLE

Population: 5,429,299 (July 2003 est.)
Nationality: Togolese (sing. & pl.)
Age Structure: 0–14 yrs: 44.5%; 15–64: 53.0%; 65+: 2.5% (2003 est.)
Population Growth Rate: 2.37% (2003 est.)
Net Migration: 0 migrants/1,000 population (2003 est.)
Ethnic Groups: 37 tribes; largest and most important are Ewe, Mina and Kabyè; under 1% European and Syrian-Lebanese
Languages: French, both official and language of commerce; major African languages are Ewe and Mina in the south and Dagomba and Kabyè in the north
Religions: about 70% indigenous beliefs, 20% Christian, 10% Muslim
Birth Rate: 35.23/1,000 population (2003 est.)
Death Rate: 11.51/1,000 population (2003 est.)
Infant Mortality: 68.73 deaths/1,000 live births (2003 est.)
Life Expectancy at Birth: 51.47 years male, 55.45 years female (2003 est.)
Total Fertility Rate: 4.97 children born/woman (2003 est.)
Literacy: 59.6% (2002)

■ GOVERNMENT

Leader(s): President General Gnassingbé Eyadéma, Prime Minister Koffi Sama
Government Type: republic; one-party presidential regime under transition to multiparty democratic rule
Administrative Divisions: 5 regions
Nationhood: Apr. 27, 1960 (from UN trusteeship under French administration; formerly known as French Togo)
National Holiday: Independence Day, Apr. 27

■ ECONOMY

Overview: an underdeveloped country that is heavily dependent on subsistence agriculture and phosphate mining; self-sufficient in basic foodstuffs when harvests are normal; political unrest and widespread strikes have interfered with economic activity
GDP: US$7.594 billion, per capita US$1,400; real growth rate 2.9% (2002 est.)
Inflation: 4.0% (2002 est.)
Industries: accounts for 21% of GDP (2001 est.); phosphate mining, agricultural processing, cement, handicrafts, textiles, beverages
Labour Force: 2.0 million (2002); 65% agriculture, 5% industry, 30% services
Unemployment: n.a.
Agriculture: accounts for 42% of GDP (2001 est.) and 64% of labour force; cash crops: coffee, cocoa, cotton; food crops: yams, cassava, corn, beans, rice, millet, sorghum, fish, livestock
Natural Resources: phosphates, limestone, marble, arable land

■ FINANCE/TRADE

Currency: Communauté financière africaine franc (CFAF) = 100 centimes
International Reserves Excluding Gold: US$184 million (Nov. 2003)
Gold Reserves: none (Dec. 2002)
Budget: n.a.
Defence Expenditures: 1.8% of GDP (2002)
Education Expenditures: 23.2% of total government expenditures (2002)
External Debt: US$1.581 billion (2002)
Exports: US$434 million (2003); commodities: phosphates, cocoa, coffee, cotton, manufactures, palm kernels; partners: Benin, Nigeria, Belgium, Ghana
Imports: US$561 million (2003); commodities: food, fuels, durable consumer goods, other intermediate goods, capital goods; partners: Ghana, China, France, Côte d'Ivoire

■ COMMUNICATIONS

Daily Newspapers: 2/1,000 inhabitants (2000)
Televisions: 37/1,000 inhabitants (2002)
Radios: 265/1,000 inhabitants (2001)
Telephones: 10 lines/1,000 inhabitants (2002)
Internet: hosts: 80 (2002); users: 200,000 (2002)

■ TRANSPORTATION

Motor Vehicles: 110,000; 75,000 passenger cars
Roads: 7,520 km; 2,376 km paved
Railway: 525 km
Air Traffic: 46,000 passengers carried (2002)
Airports: 9; 2 have paved runways (2003 est.)

Canadian Embassy: The Canadian Embassy to Togo, c/o Canadian High Commission, 42 Independence Ave, Accra, Ghana; P.O. Box 1639, Accra, Ghana. Tel: (011-233-21) 22-85-55. Fax: (011-233-21) 77-37-92. e-mail: accra@dfait-maeci.gc.ca
Embassy in Canada: Embassy of the Republic of Togo, 12 Range Rd, Ottawa ON K1N 8J3. Tel: (613) 238-5916. Fax: (613) 235-6425. e-mail: n.a.

Tokelau

Long-Form Name: Tokelau
Capital: none; each atoll has its own administrative centre

■ GEOGRAPHY

Area: 10 sq. km, 3 atolls
Climate: tropical maritime, moderated by trade winds (April–Nov.)
Land Use: arable land: 0%, (soil is thin and infertile) permanent crops: 0%, other: 100%; includes no irrigated land
Location: S Pacific Ocean, NE of Australia

■ PEOPLE

Population: 1,418 (July 2003 est.)
Nationality: Tokelauan
Ethnic Groups: Polynesian
Languages: Tokelauan, English

■ GOVERNMENT

Colony/Territory of: Overseas Territory of New Zealand
Leader(s): Head of State: Queen Elizabeth II, Administrator Neil Walter
Government Type: territory of New Zealand
National Holiday: Waitangi Day, Feb. 6

■ ECONOMY

Overview: Tokelau's small size, great distance from markets and lack of resources greatly hinder economic development; copra is only agricultural product of significance; the people rely on aid from New Zealand, supplemented by revenue from postage stamps, souvenir coins, and handicrafts

■ FINANCE/TRADE

Currency: New Zealand dollar = 100 cents

Canadian Embassy: c/o The Canadian High Commission, 3rd Fl, 61 Molesworth St. Thorndon, Wellington, New Zealand; mailing address: P.O. Box 12049, Thorndon, Wellington, New Zealand. Tel: (011-64-4) 6270-4000. Fax: (011-64-4) 471-2082. e-mail: wlgtn@dfait-maeci.gc.ca

Representative to Canada: c/o New Zealand High Commission, Clarica Centre, 99 Bank St, Ste 727, Ottawa ON K1P 6G3. Tel: (613) 238-5991. Fax: (613) 238-5707. e-mail: info@nzhcottawa.org

Tonga

Long-Form Name: Kingdom of Tonga
Capital: Nuku'alofa

■ GEOGRAPHY

Area: 748 sq. km; archipelago of 170 islands, of which 36 are inhabited
Coastline: 419 km
Climate: tropical; modified by trade winds; warm season (Dec. to May), cool season (May to Dec.)
Environment: subject to cyclones (Oct. to Apr.); deforestation and overhunting of native animals
Terrain: most islands have limestone base formed from uplifted coral formation; others have limestone overlying volcanic base
Land Use: arable land: 23.61%, permanent crops: 43.06%, other: 33.33%; includes n.a. sq. km irrigated
Location: Pacific Ocean, NW of New Zealand

■ PEOPLE

Population: 108,141 (July 2003 est.)
Nationality: Tongan
Age Structure: 0–14 yrs: 38.2%; 15–64: 57.6%; 65+: 4.1% (2003 est.)
Population Growth Rate: 1.90% (2003 est.)
Net Migration: 0 migrants/1,000 population (2003 est.)
Ethnic Groups: Polynesian; about 300 Europeans
Languages: Tongan, English
Religions: Christian; Free Wesleyan Church claims over 30,000 adherents
Birth Rate: 24.51/1,000 population (2003 est.)
Death Rate: 5.54/1,000 population (2003 est.)
Infant Mortality: 13.35 deaths/1,000 live births (2003 est.)
Life Expectancy at Birth: 66.43 years male, 71.44 years female (2003 est.)
Total Fertility Rate: 3.0 children born/woman (2003 est.)
Literacy: n.a.

■ GOVERNMENT

Leader(s): King Taufa'ahau Tupou IV, Prime Minister Prince Lavaka ata Ulukalala
Government Type: hereditary constitutional monarchy
Administrative Divisions: three island groups
Nationhood: June 4, 1970 (from UK; formerly known as Friendly Islands)
National Holiday: Independence Day, June 4

■ ECONOMY

Overview: the economy's base is agriculture though the country must import a high proportion of its food, for the most part from New Zealand; tourism is the main source of hard currency; the country also remains dependent on sizeable external aid and remittances to offset its trade deficit
GDP: US$236 million, per capita US$2,200; real growth rate 3.0% (2001 est.)
Inflation: 8.3% (2001)
Industries: accounts for 10% of GDP (2001 est.); tourism, fishing
Labour Force: n.a.; 65% agriculture, 35% mining
Unemployment: n.a.
Agriculture: accounts for 30% of GDP and 70% of labour force; dominated by coconut, copra and banana production; squash, vanilla beans, cocoa, coffee, ginger, black pepper, fish
Natural Resources: fish, fertile soil

■ FINANCE/TRADE

Currency: pa'anga ($T) = 100 seniti
International Reserves Excluding Gold: US$30 million (Oct. 2003)
Gold Reserves: n.a.
Budget: revenues US$39.9 million, expenditures US$54.2 million, including capital expenditures of US$1.9 million (2000 est.)
Defence Expenditures: n.a.
Education Expenditures: n.a.
External Debt: US$74 million (2002)
Exports: US$7 million (2001); commodities: coconut oil, desiccated coconut, copra, bananas, taro, vanilla beans, fruit, vegetables, fish; partners: New Zealand, Australia, US, Fiji, Japan
Imports: US$73 million (2001); commodities: food products, beverages, tobacco, fuels, machinery, transport equipment, chemicals, building materials; partners: New Zealand, Australia, Japan, US, Fiji

■ COMMUNICATIONS

Daily Newspapers: 1 in total
Televisions: n.a.
Radios: n.a.
Telephones: 106 lines/1,000 inhabitants (2002)
Internet: hosts: n.a.; users: 2,900 (2002)

■ TRANSPORTATION

Motor Vehicles: n.a.
Roads: 680 km; 184 km paved
Railway: none
Air Traffic: 57,000 passengers carried (2001 est.)
Airports: 6; 1 has a paved runways (2003 est.)

Canadian Embassy: The Canadian High Commission to Tonga, c/o The Canadian High Commission, 61 Molesworth St, 3rd Floor, Thorndon, Wellington; mailing address: P.O. Box 12-049, Thorndon, Wellington, New Zealand. Tel: (011-64-4) 473-9577. Fax: (011-64-4) 471-2082. e-mail: wlgtn@dfait-maeci.gc.ca
Embassy in Canada: c/o Embassy of the Kingdom of Tonga, 250 East 51st St, New York NY 10022, USA. Tel: (917) 369-1025. Fax: (917) 369-1024. e-mail: n.a.

Trinidad and Tobago

Long-Form Name: Republic of Trinidad and Tobago
Capital: Port of Spain

■ GEOGRAPHY

Area: 5,128 sq. km
Coastline: 362 km
Climate: tropical; rainy season (June to Dec.)
Environment: outside usual path of hurricanes and other tropical storms; water pollution and soil deterioration; oil pollution of beaches
Terrain: mostly plains with some hills and low mountains
Land Use: arable land: 14.6%, permanent crops: 9.2%, other: 76.2%; includes 30 sq. km irrigated
Location: West Indies, off N coast of South America

■ PEOPLE

Population: 1,104,209 (July 2003 est.)
Nationality: Trinidadian, Tobagonian
Age Structure: 0–14 yrs: 22.1%; 15–64: 70.0%; 65+: 7.9% (2003 est.)
Population Growth Rate: -0.68% (2003 est.)
Net Migration: -10.79 migrants/1,000 population (2003 est.)
Ethnic Groups: 40% black, 40% East Indian, 14% mixed, 1% white, 1% Chinese, 4% other
Languages: English (official), Hindi, French, Spanish, Chinese
Religions: Christianity 61%, Hinduism 24%, Islam 6%, 9% other
Birth Rate: 12.74/1,000 population (2003 est.)
Death Rate: 8.71/1,000 population (2003 est.)
Infant Mortality: 24.97 deaths/1,000 live births (2003 est.)
Life Expectancy at Birth: 67.07 years male, 72.23 years female (2003 est.)
Total Fertility Rate: 1.78 children born/woman (2003 est.)
Literacy: 98.5% (2002)

■ GOVERNMENT

Leader(s): President George Maxwell Richards, Prime Minister Patrick Manning
Government Type: parliamentary democracy

Administrative Divisions: 8 counties, 3 municipalities and 1 ward
Nationhood: Aug. 31, 1962 (from UK)
National Holiday: Independence Day, Aug. 31

■ ECONOMY

Overview: the economy has suffered in recent years because of the sharp decline in the price of oil; the unemployment rate has risen due to the government's austerity programs; the government is seeking to diversify the country's export base
GDP: US$11.07 billion, per capita US$10,000; real growth rate 3.2% (2002 est.)
Inflation: 4.3% (2002 est.)
Industries: accounts for 43% of GDP (2000); petroleum, chemicals, tourism, food processing, cement, beverage, cotton textiles
Labour Force: 600,000 (2002); 64% community, social and business services, 10% agriculture, 12% construction
Unemployment: 13.1% (2001)
Agriculture: accounts for approx. 2% of GDP (2000); highly subsidized sector; major crops: cocoa and sugar cane; sugar cane acreage is being shifted into rice, citrus, coffee, vegetables; must import large share of food needs
Natural Resources: crude oil, natural gas, asphalt

■ FINANCE/TRADE

Currency: Trinidad and Tobago dollar ($TT) = 100 cents
International Reserves Excluding Gold: US$2.451 billion (Dec. 2003)
Gold Reserves: 0.061 million fine troy ounces (Dec. 2003)
Budget: n.a.
Defence Expenditures: n.a.
Education Expenditures: 13.4% of total government expenditures (2002)
External Debt: US$2.672 billion (2002)
Exports: US$3.881 billion (2002); commodities (including re-exports): petroleum and petroleum products 70%, fertilizer, chemicals 15%, steel products, sugar, cocoa, coffee, citrus; partners: US, CARICOM countries, Latin America, EU
Imports: US$3.643 billion (2002); commodities: raw materials 41%, capital goods 30%, consumer goods 29%; partners: US, Venezuela, EU, CARICOM countries

■ COMMUNICATIONS

Daily Newspapers: 123/1,000 inhabitants (2000)
Televisions: 345/1,000 inhabitants (2002)
Radios: 532/1,000 inhabitants (2001)
Telephones: 250 lines/1,000 inhabitants (2002)
Internet: hosts: 7,209 (2002); users: 138,000 (2002)

■ TRANSPORTATION

Motor Vehicles: 155,000; 128,000 passenger cars
Roads: 8,320 km; 4,252 km paved
Railway: minimal agricultural railway system near San Fernando
Air Traffic: 1,269,000 passengers carried (2002)
Airports: 6; 3 have paved runways (2003 est.)

Canadian Embassy: The Canadian High Commission, Maple House, 3-3A Sweet Briar Road, St. Clair, Port-of-Spain, Trinidad and Tobago; mailing address: P.O. Box 1246, Port-of-Spain, Trinidad and Tobago. Tel: (868) 622-6232. Fax: (868) 628-1830. e-mail: pspan@dfait-maeci.gc.ca
Embassy in Canada: High Commission for the Republic of Trinidad and Tobago, 200 First Ave, 3rd Level, Ottawa ON K1S 2G6. Tel: (613) 232-2418. Fax: (613) 232-4349. e-mail: ottawa@ttmissions.com

---

Tunisia

Long-Form Name: Republic of Tunisia
Capital: Tunis

■ GEOGRAPHY

Area: 163,610 sq. km
Coastline: 1,148 km
Climate: temperate in north with mild, rainy winters and hot, dry summers; desert in south
Environment: deforestation; overgrazing; soil erosion; desertification; ineffective disposal of toxic and hazardous wastes
Terrain: mountains in north; hot, dry central plain; semi-arid south merges into the Sahara
Land Use: arable land: 18.67%, permanent crops: 12.87%, other: 68.46%; includes 3,800 sq. km irrigated
Location: N Africa, bordering on Mediterranean Sea

■ PEOPLE

Population: 9,924,742 (July 2003 est.)
Nationality: Tunisian
Age Structure: 0–14 yrs: 27.0%; 15–64: 66.6%; 65+: 6.4% (2003 est.)
Population Growth Rate: 1.09% (2003 est.)
Net Migration: -0.60 migrants/1,000 population (2003 est.)
Ethnic Groups: 98% Arab-Berber, 1% European, less than 1% Jewish
Languages: Arabic (official); Arabic and French (commerce)
Religions: 98% Muslim, 1% Christian, less than 1% Jewish
Birth Rate: 16.53/1,000 population (2003 est.)
Death Rate: 5.02/1,000 population (2003 est.)
Infant Mortality: 26.91 deaths/1,000 live births (2003 est.)

Life Expectancy at Birth: 72.77 years male, 76.51 years female (2003 est.)
Total Fertility Rate: 1.90 children born/woman (2003 est.)
Literacy: 73.2% (2002)

■ GOVERNMENT

Leader(s): President General Zine El Abidine Ben Ali, Prime Minister Mohamed Ghannouchi
Government Type: republic
Administrative Divisions: 23 governorates
Nationhood: Mar. 20, 1956 (from France)
National Holiday: Independence Day, Mar. 20

■ ECONOMY

Overview: diverse economy, with important agriculture, mining, energy, tourism, and manufacturing sectors; governmental control of economic affairs has gradually lessened over the past decade with increasing privatization of trade and commerce, simplification of the tax structure, and a prudent approach to debt
GDP: US$67.13 billion, per capita US$6,800; real growth rate 4.8% (2002 est.)
Inflation: 2.5% (2002 est.)
Industries: accounts for 32% of GDP (2003); petroleum, mining (particularly phosphate and iron ore), textiles, footwear, food, beverages, tourism
Labour Force: 4.0 million (2002); 22% agriculture, 23% industry, 55% services
Unemployment: 15.6% (2000 est.)
Agriculture: accounts for 12% of GDP (2003); output subject to severe fluctuations because of frequent droughts; export crops: olives, dates, oranges, almonds; other products: grain, sugar beets, wine grapes, poultry, beef, dairy; not self-sufficient in food
Natural Resources: crude oil, phosphates, iron ore, lead, zinc, salt, arable land

■ FINANCE/TRADE

Currency: Tunisian dinar (D) = 1,000 millimes
International Reserves Excluding Gold: US$2.945 billion (Dec. 2003)
Gold Reserves: 0.218 million fine troy ounces (Dec. 2003)
Budget: revenues US$5.2 billion; expenditures US$5.7 billion, including capital expenditures of US$1.6 billion (2002 est.)
Defence Expenditures: 5.2% of central government expenditure (2002)
Education Expenditures: 17.4% of total government expenditure (2002)
External Debt: US$12.625 billion (2002)
Exports: US$7.967 billion (2003); commodities: hydrocarbons, agricultural products, phosphates and chemicals; partners: France, Italy, Germany, Belgium, Libya

Imports: US$10.818 billion (2003); commodities: industrial goods and equipment 57%, hydrocarbons 13%, food 12%, consumer goods; partners: France, Germany, Italy, Spain, Belgium

■ COMMUNICATIONS

Daily Newspapers: 19/1,000 inhabitants (2000)
Televisions: 207/1,000 inhabitants (2002)
Radios: 158/1,000 inhabitants (2001)
Telephones: 117 lines/1,000 inhabitants (2002)
Internet: hosts: 341 (2002); users: 505,500 (2002)

■ TRANSPORTATION

Motor Vehicles: 700,000; 420,000 passenger cars
Roads: 18,997 km; 12,310 km paved
Railway: 2,152 km
Air Traffic: 1,789,000 passengers carried (2002)
Airports: 30; 14 have paved runways (2003 est.)

Canadian Embassy: Canadian Embassy, 3, rue du Sénégal, Place d'Afrique, 1002 Tunis-Belvedere, Tunisia; mailing address: CP 31, Le Belvédère, 1002, Tunis-Belvedere, Tunisia. Tel: (011-216-71) 104-000. Fax: (011-216-71) 104-191. e-mail: tunis@dfait-maeci.gc.ca
Embassy in Canada: Embassy of the Republic of Tunisia, 515 O'Connor St, Ottawa ON, K1S 3P8. Tel: (613) 237-0330. Fax: (613) 237-7939. e-mail: n.a.

Turkey

Long-Form Name: Republic of Turkey
Capital: Ankara

■ GEOGRAPHY

Area: 780,580 sq. km
Coastline: 7,200 km
Climate: temperate; hot, dry summers with mild, wet winters; harsher in interior
Environment: subject to severe earthquakes, especially along major river valleys in west; water and air pollution; desertification
Terrain: mostly mountains; narrow coastal plain; high central plateau (Anatolia)
Land Use: arable land: 34.53%, permanent crops: 3.36%, other: 62.11%; includes 42,000 sq. km irrigated
Location: SW Asia (Near East), bordering on Mediterranean Sea, Black Sea, Aegean Sea

■ PEOPLE

Population: 68,109,469 (July 2003 est.)
Nationality: Turk
Age Structure: 0–14 yrs: 27.2%; 15–64: 66.4%; 65+: 6.4% (2003 est.)
Population Growth Rate: 1.16% (2003 est.)

Net Migration: 0 migrants/1,000 population (2003 est.)
Ethnic Groups: 80% Turkish, 20% Kurd
Languages: Turkish (official), Kurdish 7%, Arabic; English (business language)
Religions: 99.8% Muslim (mostly Sunni), 0.2% other (mostly Christian and Jewish)
Birth Rate: 17.59/1,000 population (2003 est.)
Death Rate: 5.95/1,000 population (2003 est.)
Infant Mortality: 44.20 deaths/1,000 live births (2003 est.)
Life Expectancy at Birth: 69.41 years male, 74.30 years female (2003 est.)
Total Fertility Rate: 2.03 children born/woman (2003 est.)
Literacy: 86.5% (2002)

■ GOVERNMENT

Leader(s): President Ahmet Necdet Sezer, Prime Minister Recep Tayyip Erdogan
Government Type: republican parliamentary democracy
Administrative Divisions: 80 provinces (iller, sing. —il)
Nationhood: Oct. 29, 1923 (successor state to the Ottoman Empire)
National Holiday: Anniversary of the Declaration of the Republic, Oct. 29

■ ECONOMY

Overview: has a strong and rapidly growing private sector, yet the state still plays a major role in basic industry, banking, transport and communications; its most important industry and largest export is textiles and clothing, which are almost entirely in private hands. Note: Major economic disruption in August 1999 due to a massive earthquake
GDP: US$489.7 billion, per capita US$7,300; real growth rate 7.8% (2002)
Inflation: 45.2% (2002 est.)
Industries: accounts for 30% of GDP (2001); textiles, food processing, mining (coal, chromite, copper, boron minerals), steel, petroleum, construction, lumber, paper
Labour Force: 33.7 million (2002); 40% agriculture, 22% industry, 38% community, social and business services; about 1,000,000 Turks work abroad
Unemployment: 9.4% (Aug. 2003)
Agriculture: accounts for 13% of GDP (2001) and 46% the labour force; products: tobacco, cotton, grain, olives, sugar beets, pulses, citrus fruit, variety of animal products; self-sufficient in food most years
Natural Resources: antimony, coal, chromium, mercury, copper, borate, sulphur, iron ore

■ FINANCE/TRADE

Currency: Turkish lira (TL) = 100 kurus

International Reserves Excluding Gold: US$33.719 billion (Jan. 2004)
Gold Reserves: 3.733 million fine troy ounces (Jan. 2004)
Budget: revenues US$42.4 billion; expenditures US$69.1 billion, including capital expenditures of US$ n.a. (2001)
Defence Expenditures: 10% of central government expenditure (2002)
Education Expenditures: 9.63% of total government expenditure (2000)
External Debt: US$131.556 billion (2002)
Exports: US$46.576 billion (2003 est.); commodities: industrial products 70%, crops and livestock products 25%; partners: Germany, US, Italy, UK, France, Russia
Imports: US$65.637 billion (2003 est.); commodities: crude oil, machinery, transport equipment, metals, pharmaceuticals, dyes, plastics, rubber, mineral fuels, fertilizers, chemicals; partners: Germany, Italy, Russia, US, France, UK

■ COMMUNICATIONS

Daily Newspapers: 511/1,000 inhabitants (2000)
Televisions: 423/1,000 inhabitants (2002)
Radios: 487/1,000 inhabitants (2001)
Telephones: 281 lines/1,000 inhabitants (2002)
Internet: hosts: 154,585 (2002); users: 4.9 million (2002)

■ TRANSPORTATION

Motor Vehicles: 5,700,000; 4,240,000 passenger cars
Roads: 385,960 km; 113,226 km paved
Railway: 8,607 km operational
Air Traffic: 10,640,000 passengers carried (2002)
Airports: 120; 86 have paved runways (2003 est.)

Canadian Embassy: The Canadian Embassy, Nenehatun Caddesi 75, Gaziosmanpasa, 06700 Ankara, Turkey. Tel: (011-90-312) 459-9200. Fax: (011-90-312) 459-9361. e-mail: ankra@dfait-maeci.gc.ca
Embassy in Canada: Embassy of the Republic of Turkey, 197 Wurtemburg St, Ottawa ON K1N 8L9. Tel: (613) 789-4044. Fax: (613) 789-3442. e-mail: turkishottawa@mfa.gov.tr

---

Turkmenistan

Long-Form Name: Turkmenistan
Capital: Ashkhabad

■ GEOGRAPHY

Area: 488,100 sq. km
Coastline: landlocked; 1,768 km inland coastline along Caspian Sea

Climate: subtropical desert; long, extremely hot summers; short and cold winters; rainfall occurs only in the mountains
Environment: soil and groundwater contaminated with chemicals and pesticides; salinization and waterlogging of soil due to poor irrigation methods; desertification in some areas; prone to earthquakes
Terrain: flat to rolling sandy desert; Caspian Sea in west
Land Use: arable land: 3.6%, permanent crops: 0.1%, other: 96.3% (2003 est.); includes 17,500 sq. km irrigated
Location: WC Asia, bordering on Caspian Sea

■ PEOPLE

Population: 4,775,544 (July 2003 est.)
Nationality: Turkmen
Age Structure: 0–14 yrs: 36.8%; 15–64: 59.2%; 65+: 4.1% (2003 est.)
Population Growth Rate: 1.82% (2003 est.)
Net Migration: -0.92 migrants/1,000 population (2003 est.)
Ethnic Groups: 77% Turkmen, 6.7% Russian, 9.2% Uzbek, 2% Kazakh, 5.1% other
Languages: 72% Turkmen (official), 12% Russian, 9% Uzbek, 7% other
Religions: 89% Muslim, 9% Eastern Orthodox, 2% unknown
Birth Rate: 28.02/1,000 population (2003 est.)
Death Rate: 8.87/1,000 population (2003 est.)
Infant Mortality: 73.17 deaths/1,000 live births (2003 est.)
Life Expectancy at Birth: 57.72 years male, 64.84 years female (2003 est.)
Total Fertility Rate: 3.50 children born/woman (2003 est.)
Literacy: 98.8% (2002)

■ GOVERNMENT

Leader(s): President Saparmurad Niyazov
Government Type: republic
Administrative Divisions: 5 regions (welayatlar, sing. —welayat)
Nationhood: Oct. 27, 1991 (from Soviet Union)
National Holiday: Independence Day, Oct. 27

■ ECONOMY

Overview: mining produces the greatest part of Turkmenistan's economic production value, but agriculture is the chief occupation; industry leans heavily toward the energy sector (gas, oil), but the lack of pipeline access to hard currency markets limits expansion; efforts at gas and oil export expansion will take many more years to pay off. Privatization goals remain limited.
GDP: US$31.34 billion, per capita US$6,700; real growth rate 21.1% (2002 est.)
Inflation: 5.0% (2002 est.)

Industries: accounts for 45% of GDP (2000); oil production and refining, natural gas extraction, chemicals, electrical engineering, fertilizer, carpets, textiles and clothing, food processing
Labour Force: 2.1 million (2002); 48% agriculture and forestry, 15% industry and construction, 37% services
Unemployment: n.a.
Agriculture: accounts for 27% of GDP (2000); irrigation is mandatory for agriculture; products include cotton, grains, livestock, fish
Natural Resources: extensive mineral deposits, including the world's largest sulfur deposits; oil, natural gas, coal, potassium, salts, sulphur

■ FINANCE/TRADE

Currency: manat = 100 tenesi
International Reserves Excluding Gold: n.a.
Gold Reserves: n.a.
Budget: n.a.
Defence Expenditures: n.a.
Education Expenditures: n.a.
External Debt: US$2.5 billion (2000 est.)
Exports: US$3.355 billion (2003 est.); oil, natural gas, electric power, clothing and textiles, petroleum products, carpets; partners: Turkey, Ukraine, Iran, Italy, Switzerland
Imports: US$2.472 billion (2003 est.); machinery, foodstuffs, consumer products, plastics and rubber, textiles; partners: Ukraine, Russia, Turkey, UAE, France

■ COMMUNICATIONS

Daily Newspapers: 7/1,000 inhabitants (2000)
Televisions: 182/1,000 inhabitants (2002)
Radios: 256/1,000 inhabitants (2001)
Telephones: 77 lines/1,000 inhabitants (2002)
Internet: hosts: 2,020 (2002); users: 8,000 (2002)

■ TRANSPORTATION

Motor Vehicles: n.a.
Roads: 24,000 km; 19,488 km paved
Railway: 2,440 km
Air Traffic: 1,464,000 passengers carried (2002)
Airports: 76; 13 have paved runways (2003 est.)

Canadian Embassy: c/o The Canadian Embassy, Nenehatun Caddesi 75, Gaziosmanpasa 06700, Ankara, Turkey. Tel: (011-90-312) 459-9200. Fax: (011-90-312) 459-9361. e-mail: ankra@dfait-maeci.gc.ca
Embassy in Canada: c/o Embassy of the Republic of Turkmenistan, 2207 Massachusetts Ave NW, Washington DC 20008, USA. Tel: (202) 588-1500. Fax: (202) 588-0697. e-mail: n.a.

Turks and Caicos

Long-Form Name: The Turks and Caicos Islands

Capital: Cockburn Town (on Grand Turk Island)

■ GEOGRAPHY

Area: 430 sq. km; 30+ small cays, of which only 8 are inhabited
Climate: sunny, relatively dry, equable climate with moderating winds; occasional hurricanes
Land Use: arable land: 2.3%, permanent crops: 0%, other: 97.7%; includes n.a. sq. km irrigated
Location: West Indies (S Atlantic Ocean), N of Dominican Republic

■ PEOPLE

Population: 19,350 (July 2003 est.)
Nationality: none (British citizens)
Ethnic Groups: black majority
Languages: English (official)

■ GOVERNMENT

Colony/Territory of: Colony of the United Kingdom
Leader(s): Head of State: Queen Elizabeth II, Governor Jim Poston, Head of government: Chief Minister Michael Eugene Misick
Government Type: dependent territory of the United Kingdom
National Holiday: Constitution Day, Aug. 30

■ ECONOMY

Overview: fishing is the most important activity; exports include lobster, conch, other fish products; imports include food and drink, tobacco, maufactured goods; tourism; offshore banking; chief trading partner: US

■ FINANCE/TRADE

Currency: US dollar (US$) = 100 cents

Canadian Embassy: c/o The Canadian High Commission, Macdonald House, 1 Grosvenor Square, London W1K 4AB, England, UK. Tel: (011-44-20) 7258-6600. Fax: (011-44-20) 7258-6333. e-mail: ldn@dfait-maeci.gc.ca
Representative to Canada: c/o British High Commission, 80 Elgin St, Ottawa ON K1P 5K7. Tel: (613) 237-1530. Fax: (613) 237-7980. e-mail should be sent using the appropriate form at the British High Commission's Website at http://www.britain-in-canada.org

---

Tuvalu

Long-Form Name: Tuvalu
Capital: Funafuti

■ GEOGRAPHY

Area: 26 sq. km
Coastline: 24 km

Climate: tropical; moderated by easterly trade winds (Mar. to Nov.); westerly gales and heavy rain (Nov. to Mar.)
Environment: severe tropical storms are rare; no natural safe drinking water resources
Terrain: very low-lying and narrow coral atolls
Land Use: arable land: 0%, permanent crops: 0%, other: 100%
Location: S Pacific Ocean, NE of Australia

■ PEOPLE

Population: 11,305 (July 2003 est.)
Nationality: Tuvaluan
Age Structure: 0–14 yrs: 31.9%; 15–64: 63.0%; 65+: 5.1% (2003 est.)
Population Growth Rate: 1.42% (2003 est.)
Net Migration: 0 migrants/1,000 population (2003 est.)
Ethnic Groups: 96% Polynesian
Languages: Tuvaluan, English
Religions: 97% Congregationalist (Church of Tuvalu), 1.4% Seventh Day Adventists, 1% Baha'i, 0.6% other
Birth Rate: 21.58/1,000 population (2003 est.)
Death Rate: 7.34/1,000 population (2003 est.)
Infant Mortality: 21.34 deaths/1,000 live births (2003 est.)
Life Expectancy at Birth: 65.15 years male, 69.59 years female (2003 est.)
Total Fertility Rate: 3.05 children born/woman (2003 est.)
Literacy: n.a.

■ GOVERNMENT

Leader(s): Head of State: Queen Elizabeth II, Governor General Sir Tomasi Puapua, Prime Minister Koloa Talake
Government Type: constitutional monarchy with a parliamentary democracy
Administrative Divisions: none
Nationhood: Oct. 1, 1978 from UK (formerly known as Ellice Islands)
National Holiday: Independence Day, Oct. 1

■ ECONOMY

Overview: scattered group of 9 coral atolls with poor soil; a small economy, no known mineral resources and few exports; receives money from the sale of stamps and coins and worker remittances as well as an international trust fund; subsistence farming and fishing are the primary economic activities
GDP: US$12.2 million; per capita US$1,100; real growth rate 3.0% (2000 est.)
Inflation: 5.0% (2000 est.)
Industries: fishing, tourism, copra, fish
Labour Force: 7,000 (2001 est.); people make a living primarily through exploitation of sea resources
Unemployment: n.a.

Agriculture: coconuts, copra, fish
Natural Resources: fish

■ FINANCE/TRADE

Currency: Australian dollar ($A) or Tuvaluan dollar ($T) = 100 cents
International Reserves Excluding Gold: n.a.
Gold Reserves: n.a.
Budget: revenues US$22.5 million, expenditures US$11.2 million, including capital expenditures of US$4.2 million (2000 est.)
Defence Expenditures: n.a.
Education Expenditures: n.a.
External Debt: n.a.
Exports: US$1 million (2002); commodities: copra; partners: Fiji, Germany, Iceland, Sweden
Imports: US$79 million (2002); commodities: food, animals, fuels, machinery, manufactures; partners: Fiji, Australia, Portugal, New Zealand

■ COMMUNICATIONS

Daily Newspapers: none
Televisions: n.a.
Radios: n.a.
Telephones: n.a.
Internet: users: 1,300 (2002)

■ TRANSPORTATION

Motor Vehicles: n.a.
Roads: 8 km gravel roads
Railway: none
Air Traffic: n.a.
Airports: 1; no paved runway (2003 est.)

Canadian Embassy: The Canadian High Commission to Tuvalu, c/o The Canadian High Commission, 61 Molesworth St, 3rd Fl, Thorndon, Wellington; mailing address: P.O. Box 12-049, Thorndon, Wellington, New Zealand. Tel: (011-64-4) 473-9577. Fax: (011-64-4) 471-2082. e-mail: wlgtn@dfait-maeci.gc.ca
Embassy in Canada: c/o New Zealand High Commission, Clarica Centre, 99 Bank St, Ste 727, Ottawa, ON K1P 6G3. Tel: (613) 238-5991. Fax: (613) 238-5707. e-mail: info@nzhcottawa.org

U.S. Virgin Islands

Long-Form Name: Virgin Islands of the United States
Capital: Charlotte Amalie

■ GEOGRAPHY

Area: 352 sq. km
Climate: subtropical, tempered by easterly trade winds, relatively low humidity, little seasonal temperature variation; rainy season May to Nov.
Land Use: arable land: 15%, permanent crops: 6%, other: 79%; includes n.a. sq. km irrigated

Location: Caribbean islands, just E of Puerto Rico

■ PEOPLE

Population: 124,778 (July 2003 est.)
Nationality: Virgin Islander
Ethnic Groups: 74% West Indian (45% born in the Virgin Islands and 29% born elsewhere in the West Indies), 13% US mainland, 5% Puerto Rican, 8% other (80% black, 15% white, 5% other); 14% of Hispanic origin
Languages: English (official), but Spanish and Creole are widely spoken

■ GOVERNMENT

Colony/Territory of: Dependent Territory of the United States
Leader(s): Head of State: President George W. Bush Jr., Governor Charles Wesley Turnbull
Government Type: organized, unincorporated territory of the US
National Holiday: Transfer Day, Mar. 27 (1917, from Denmark to the US)

■ ECONOMY

Overview: tourism is the primary economic activity accounting for more than 70% of GDP and 70% of employment; some manufacturing; small agricultural sector (most food is imported); international business and financial services are a small but growing sector

■ FINANCE/TRADE

Currency: US dollar ($) = 100 cents

Canadian Embassy: c/o The Canadian Embassy, 501 Pennsylvania Ave NW, Washington DC 20001, USA. Tel: (202) 682-1740. Fax: (202) 456-7726. e-mail: wshdc@dfait-maeci.gc.ca
Representative to Canada: c/o Embassy of the United States of America, 490 Sussex Drive, PO Box 866, Station "B," Ottawa, ON, K1P 5T1. Tel: (613) 238-5335. Fax: (613) 688-3080. e-mail inquiries are not accepted.

Uganda

Long-Form Name: Republic of Uganda
Capital: Kampala

■ GEOGRAPHY

Area: 236,040 sq. km
Coastline: none: landlocked
Climate: tropical; generally rainy with two dry seasons (Dec. to Feb., June to Aug.); semi-arid in northeast
Environment: straddles equator; deforestation; overgrazing; soil erosion; widespread poaching
Terrain: mostly plateau with rim of mountains

Land Use: arable land: 25.34%, permanent crops: 8.77%, other: 65.89%; includes 90 sq. km irrigated
Location: EC Africa

■ PEOPLE

Population: 25,632,794 (July 2003 est.)
Nationality: Ugandan
Age Structure: 0–14 yrs: 50.8%; 15–64: 46.8%; 65+: 2.4% (2003 est.)
Population Growth Rate: 2.96% (2003 est.)
Net Migration: 0.0 migrants/1,000 population (2003 est.)
Ethnic Groups: 17% Baganda, 12% Karamojong, 8% Basogo, 8% Iteso, 6% Langi, 6% Rwanda, 5% Bagisu, 4% Acholi, 4% Lugbara, 3% Bunyro, 27% other
Languages: English (official); Luganda and Swahili widely used; other Bantu and Nilotic languages
Religions: 33% Roman Catholic, 33% Protestant, 16% Muslim, rest indigenous beliefs
Birth Rate: 46.57/1,000 population (2003 est.)
Death Rate: 16.95/1,000 population (2003 est.)
Infant Mortality: 87.90 deaths/1,000 live births (2003 est.)
Life Expectancy at Birth: 43.42 years male, 46.38 years female (2003 est.)
Total Fertility Rate: 6.72 children born/woman (2003 est.)
Literacy: 68.9% (2002)

■ GOVERNMENT

Leader(s): President Yoweri Kaguta Museveni, Prime Minister Apollo Nsibambi
Government Type: republic
Administrative Divisions: 45 districts
Nationhood: Oct. 9, 1962 (from UK)
National Holiday: Independence Day, Oct. 9

■ ECONOMY

Overview: despite substantial natural resources, the economy has been ruined by years of political instability, mismanagement and civil war; the government has started a reform program that is partly aimed at lowering high inflation and increasing export earnings; agriculture is the most important economic sector
GDP: US$30.49 billion, per capita US$1,200; real growth rate 5.5% (2002 est.)
Inflation: 0.1% (2002 est.)
Industries: accounts for 18% of GDP (2000); sugar, brewing, tobacco, cotton textiles, cement
Labour Force: 12.1 million (2002); 82% agriculture, 5% industry, 13% services
Unemployment: n.a.
Agriculture: accounts for 44% (2000) of GDP; coffee, tea and tobacco are the main export

crops. Domestic products also include cotton, corn, millet and livestock
Natural Resources: copper, cobalt, limestone, salt, hydro power, arable land

■ FINANCE/TRADE

Currency: Ugandan shilling (USh) = 100 cents
International Reserves Excluding Gold: US$1.335 billion (Jan. 2004)
Gold Reserves: n.a.
Budget: n.a.
Defence Expenditures: 10.1% of central government expenditure (2002)
Education Expenditures: n.a.
External Debt: US$4.100 billion (2002)
Exports: US$561 million (2003 est.); commodities: coffee 97%, fish and fish products, cotton, tea; partners: Germany, Netherlands, US, Spain, Belgium
Imports: US$1.246 billion (2003 est.); commodities: petroleum products, machinery, cotton piece goods, metals, transportation equipment, food; partners: Kenya, US, India, South Africa, Japan

■ COMMUNICATIONS

Daily Newspapers: 2/1,000 inhabitants (2000)
Televisions: 18/1,000 inhabitants (2002)
Radios: 127/1,000 inhabitants (2001)
Telephones: 2 lines/1,000 inhabitants (2002)
Internet: hosts: 2,242 (2002); users: 100,000 (2002)

■ TRANSPORTATION

Motor Vehicles: 120,000; 48,400 passenger cars
Roads: 27,000 km; 1,809 km paved
Railway: 1,241 km
Air Traffic: 41,000 passengers carried (2002)
Airports: 27; 4 have paved runways (2003 est.)

Canadian Embassy: c/o The Canadian High Commission, Limuru Road, Gigiri, Nairobi, Kenya. Postal Address: The Canadian High Commission, P.O. Box 1013, 00621 Nairobi, Kenya. Tel: (011 254 20) 366 3000. Fax: (011 254 20) 366 3900. e-mail: nrobi@dfait-maeci.gc.ca
Embassy in Canada: High Commission for the Republic of Uganda, 231 Cobourg St, Ottawa ON K1N 8J2. Tel: (613) 789-7797. Fax: (613) 789-8909. e-mail: ugacom@comnet.ca

---

Ukraine

Long-Form Name: Ukraine
Capital: Kiev

■ GEOGRAPHY

Area: 603,700 sq. km
Coastline: 2,782 km

Climate: temperate continental; subtropical on southern Crimean coast; moderate rainfall in north; drier in southern regions
Environment: air and water pollution, unsafe drinking water, deforestation, radiation contamination around Chernobyl nuclear power plant
Terrain: Carpathian mountains in west, marshy in north, remainder flat fertile plains (steppes) and plateaux
Land Use: arable land: 57.1%, permanent crops: 1.73%, other: 41.17%; includes 24,540 sq. km irrigated
Location: E Europe, bordering on Black Sea

■ PEOPLE

Population: 48,055,439 (July 2003 est.)
Nationality: Ukrainian
Age Structure: 0–14 yrs: 16.3%; 15–64: 68.7%; 65+: 15.0% (2003 est.)
Population Growth Rate: -0.69% (2003 est.)
Net Migration: -0.41 migrants/1,000 population (2003 est.)
Ethnic Groups: 73% Ukrainian, 22% Russian, 1% Jewish, 4% other
Languages: Ukrainian, Russian, Romanian, Polish
Religions: predominantly Eastern Orthodox and Roman Catholic; Uniate Church re-legalized in 1991; also, Autocephalous Orthodox Church, Greek rite Catholic
Birth Rate: 9.89/1,000 population (2003 est.)
Death Rate: 16.39/1,000 population (2003 est.)
Infant Mortality: 20.87 deaths/1,000 live births (2003 est.)
Life Expectancy at Birth: 61.10 years male, 72.17 years female (2003 est.)
Total Fertility Rate: 1.34 children born/woman (2003 est.)
Literacy: 99.6% (2002)

■ GOVERNMENT

Leader(s): President Leonid Kuchma, Prime Minister Viktor Yanukovych
Government Type: republic
Administrative Divisions: 24 oblasts (oblasti, sing. —oblast), 1 autonomous republic (avtomnaya respublika), 2 municipalities (mista, sing. —misto) with oblast status
Nationhood: Aug. 24, 1991 (from Soviet Union)
National Holiday: Independence Day, Aug. 24

■ ECONOMY

Overview: mining and heavy industry, with very strong agricultural sector; food surplus area of former USSR
GDP: US$218 billion, per capita US$4,500; real growth rate 4.8% (2002 est.)
Inflation: -1.2% (2002 est.)
Industries: accounts for 40% of GDP (2000) and 33% of labour force; industries include: mining,

manufacturing of machinery, food processing, chemicals, electric and electronic equipment, coal, electric power, food processing (esp. sugar)
Labour Force: 24.9 million (2002); 32% industry and construction, 24% agriculture and forestry, 17% health and cultural services, 27% other
Unemployment: 11.1% (2002)
Agriculture: accounts for about 13% of GDP (2000); corn, wheat, sugar beets, sunflower seeds, barley, tobacco; livestock includes cattle, pigs, goats, sheep, vegetables, milk
Natural Resources: coal, manganese, oil, gypsum, iron, lead, zinc, titanium, natural gas, oil, salt, sulphur, graphite, mercury, timber, arable land

■ FINANCE/TRADE

Currency: hryvnia (pl. hryvni) = 100 kopiykas
International Reserves Excluding Gold: US$6.864 billion (Jan. 2004)
Gold Reserves: 0.497 million fine troy ounces (Jan. 2004)
Budget: revenues US$10.2 billion; expenditures US$11.1 billion, including capital expenditures US$ n.a. (2002 est.)
Defence Expenditures: 9.8% of central government expenditure (2002)
Education Expenditures: 15.0% of total government expenditure (2002)
External Debt: US$13.555 billion (2002)
Exports: US$23.080 billion (2003): minerals, agricultural products, heavy machinery, vehicles, airplanes; partners: Russia, Turkey, Italy, Germany
Imports: US$23.021 billion (2003): machinery and equipment, chemicals, textiles, energy; partners: Russia, Turkmenistan, Germany, US

■ COMMUNICATIONS

Daily Newspapers: 175/1,000 inhabitants (2000)
Televisions: 456/1,000 inhabitants (2002)
Radios: 889/1,000 inhabitants (2001)
Telephones: 216 lines/1,000 inhabitants (2002)
Internet: hosts: 71,691 (2002); users: 900,000 (2002)

■ TRANSPORTATION

Motor Vehicles: 5,000,000 passenger cars
Roads: 169,491 km; 163,898 km paved
Railway: 22,473 km
Air Traffic: 1,512,000 passengers carried (2002)
Airports: 790; 182 have paved runways (2003 est.)

Canadian Embassy: The Canadian Embassy, 31 Yaroslaviv Val St, Kiev 01901, Ukraine. Tel: (011-380-44) 464-1144. Fax: (011-380-44) 464-0598. e-mail: kiev@dfait-maeci.gc.ca

Embassy in Canada: Embassy of Ukraine, 310 Somerset St W, Ottawa ON K2P 0J9. Tel: (613) 230-2961. Fax: (613) 230-2400. e-mail: emb_ca@ukremb.ca

United Arab Emirates

Long-Form Name: United Arab Emirates
Capital: Abu Dhabi

■ GEOGRAPHY

Area: 82,880 sq. km
Coastline: 1,318 km
Climate: desert; cooler in eastern mountains
Environment: frequent dust- and sandstorms; lack of natural freshwater resources being overcome by desalination plants; desertification
Terrain: flat, barren coastal plain; desert wasteland; mountains in east
Land Use: arable land: 0.48%, permanent crops: 0.49%, other: 99.03%; includes 720 sq. km irrigated
Location: SW Asia (Middle East), Arabian Peninsula bordering on Persian Gulf

■ PEOPLE

Population: 2,484,818 (July 2003 est.)
Nationality: Emirati
Age Structure: 0–14 yrs: 26.7%; 15–64: 70.4%; 65+: 2.9% (2003 est.)
Population Growth Rate: 1.57% (2003 est.)
Net Migration: 1.22 migrants/1,000 population (2003 est.)
Ethnic Groups: 19% Emiri, 23% other Arab, 50% South Asian (fluctuating), 8% other expatriates (includes Westerners and East Asians); less than 20% of the population are United Arab Emirates citizens
Languages: Arabic (official); Farsi and English widely spoken in major cities; Hindi, Urdu
Religions: 96% Muslim (16% Shi'a); 4% Christian, Hindu and other
Birth Rate: 18.48/1,000 population (2003 est.)
Death Rate: 4.02/1,000 population (2003 est.)
Infant Mortality: 15.58 deaths/1,000 live births (2003 est.)
Life Expectancy at Birth: 72.28 years male, 77.35 years female (2003 est.)
Total Fertility Rate: 3.09 children born/woman (2003 est.)
Literacy: 77.3% (2002)

■ GOVERNMENT

Leader(s): President Zayid bin Sultan Al Nuhayyan, Vice President and Prime Minister Maktoum bin Rashid al-Maktoum
Government Type: federation with specified powers delegated to the United Arab Emirates central government and other powers reserved to member emirates

Administrative Divisions: 7 emirates (imarat, sing. -imarah)
Nationhood: Dec. 2, 1971 (from UK; formerly known as Trucial States)
National Holiday: Independence Day, Dec. 2

■ ECONOMY

Overview: an open economy tied to the world prices for oil and gas; currently has a high standard of living; crude oil reserves should last for over 100 years at present levels of production; the government is encouraging privatization measures
GDP: US$53.97 billion, per capita US$22,100; real growth rate 1.8% (2002 est.)
Inflation: 2.8% (2002 est.)
Industries: accounts for 46% of GDP (2000); petroleum, fishing, petrochemicals, construction materials, some boat building, handicrafts, pearling
Labour Force: 1.6 million (2002): 15% industry, 7% agriculture, 78% services
Unemployment: 2.3% (2002)
Agriculture: accounts for 3% of GDP (2000) and 8% of labour force; cash crop: dates; food products: vegetables, watermelons, poultry, eggs, dairy, fish; only 25% self-sufficient in food
Natural Resources: crude oil and natural gas

■ FINANCE/TRADE

Currency: Emirian dirham (Dh) = 100 fils
International Reserves Excluding Gold: US$14.811 billion (Sept. 2003)
Gold Reserves: 0.198 million fine troy ounces (Sept. 2003)
Budget: revenues US$15.6 billion; expenditures US$23.5 billion, including capital expenditures US$3.4 billion (2003 est.)
Defence Expenditures: 30.1% of central government expenditure (2002)
Education Expenditures: n.a.
External Debt: US$18.5 billion (2002 est.)
Exports: US$56.73 billion (2003 est.); commodities: crude oil 75%, natural gas, re-exports, dried fish, dates; partners: US, European Community, Japan, Singapore, Korea, India, Oman, Iran
Imports: US$37.16 billion (2003 est.); commodities: food, consumer and capital goods; partners: Japan, US, UK, Italy, Germany, South Korea

■ COMMUNICATIONS

Daily Newspapers: 156/1,000 inhabitants (2000)
Televisions: 252/1,000 inhabitants (2002)
Radios: 318/1,000 inhabitants (2001)
Telephones: 314 lines/1,000 inhabitants (2002)
Internet: hosts: 52,332 (2002); users: 1,175,600 (2002)

■ TRANSPORTATION

Motor Vehicles: 400,000; 320,000 passenger cars

Roads: 4,835 km, 1,088 km paved
Railway: none
Air Traffic: 9,667,000 passengers carried (2002)
Airports: 41; 22 have paved runways (2003 est.)

Canadian Embassy: The Canadian Embassy, Villa No. 440, 26th St, Rowdah District, Abu Dhabi, UAE; mailing address: P.O. Box 6970, Abu Dhabi, UAE. Tel: (011-971-2) 407-1300. Fax: (011-971-2) 407-1399. e-mail: abdbi@dfait-maeci.gc.ca
Embassy in Canada: c/o Embassy of the United Arab Emirates, 45 O'Connor St, Ste 1800 World Exchange Plaza, Ottawa, ON, K1P 1A4, Tel: (613) 565-7272, Fax: (613) 565-8007. e-mail: safara@uae-embassy.com

---

United Kingdom

Long-Form Name: United Kingdom of Great Britain and Northern Ireland
Capital: London

■ GEOGRAPHY

Area: 244,820 sq. km
Coastline: 12,429 km
Climate: temperate; moderated by prevailing southwest winds over the North Atlantic Current; more than half of the days are overcast
Environment: pollution control measures improving air, water quality; because of heavily indented coastline, no location is more than 125 km from tidal waters
Terrain: mostly rugged hills and low mountains; level to rolling plains in east and southeast
Land Use: arable land: 26.41%, permanent crops: 0.18%, other: 73.41%; includes 1,080 sq. km irrigated
Location: NW Europe, bordering on North Sea, Atlantic Ocean

■ PEOPLE

Population: 60,094,648 (July 2003 est.)
Nationality: British or Briton
Age Structure: 0–14 yrs: 18.3%; 15–64: 66.1%; 65+: 15.6% (2003 est.)
Population Growth Rate: 0.30% (2003 est.)
Net Migration: 2.20 migrants/1,000 population (2003 est.)
Ethnic Groups: 81.5% English, 9.6% Scottish, 2.4% Irish, 1.9% Welsh, 1.8% Ulster, 2.8% West Indian, Indian, Pakistani and other
Languages: English, Welsh (about 26% of population of Wales), Scottish form of Gaelic (about 60,000 in Scotland)
Religions: 73% Anglican, 23% Roman Catholic, 3% Muslim, 0.1% Sikh, 0.2% Presbyterian, 0.5% Methodist, 0.2% Jewish
Birth Rate: 10.99/1,000 population (2003 est.)
Death Rate: 10.21/1,000 population (2003 est.)

Infant Mortality: 5.28 deaths/1,000 live births (2003 est.)
Life Expectancy at Birth: 75.74 years male, 80.70 years female (2003 est.)
Total Fertility Rate: 1.66 children born/woman (2003 est.)
Literacy: approaching 100% (2002)

■ GOVERNMENT

Leader(s): Head of State: Queen Elizabeth II, Prime Minister Tony Blair
Government Type: constitutional monarchy
Administrative Divisions: England: 47 boroughs, 36 counties, 29 London boroughs, 12 cities and boroughs, 10 counties, 12 cities, 3 royal boroughs, Northern Ireland: 24 districts, 2 cities; Scotland: 32 council areas; Wales: 11 county boroughs, 9 counties, 2 cities and counties. Dependent areas include: Anguilla, Bermuda, British Antarctic Territory (uninhabited except for variable population of research stations — about 300 persons), British Indian Ocean Territory, British Virgin Islands, Cayman Islands, Channel Islands, Falkland Islands, Gibraltar, Guernsey, Isle of Man, Jersey, Montserrat, Pitcairn, Saint Helena, South Georgia (uninhabited except for scientific station and 500 persons in a whaling/sealing settlement), South Sandwich Islands (uninhabited), Turks and Caicos Islands
Nationhood: Jan. 1, 1801, United Kingdom established
National Holiday: Celebration of the Birthday of the Queen, second Saturday in June

■ ECONOMY

Overview: essentially capitalist economy; intensive agricultural practices produce 60% of domestic food needs with only 1% of the labour force; strong service sector; industry is declining in importance
GDP: US$1.528 trillion, per capita US$25,500; real growth rate 1.8% (2002)
Inflation: 2.1% (2002 est.)
Industries: accounts for 25% of GDP (2000) and 25% of labour force; machinery and transportation equipment, metals, food processing, paper and paper products, textiles, chemicals, clothing, other consumer goods, motor vehicles, aircraft, shipbuilding, petroleum, coal
Labour Force: 29.6 million (2002); 74% services, 25% industry, 1% agriculture
Unemployment: 3.1% (Jan. 2004)
Agriculture: accounts for only 1% of GDP (2000); highly mechanized and efficient farms; wide variety of crops and livestock products produced; about 60% self-sufficient in food and feed needs

Natural Resources: coal, crude oil, natural gas, tin, limestone, iron ore, salt, clay, chalk, gypsum, lead, silica

■ FINANCE/TRADE

Currency: pound sterling (£ or £ stg) = 100 pence
International Reserves Excluding Gold: US$42.066 billion (Jan. 2004)
Gold Reserves: 10.070 million fine troy ounces (Jan. 2004)
Budget: revenues US$565 billion; expenditures US$540 billion, including capital expenditures US$ n.a. (2001)
Defence Expenditures: 7.0% of central government expenditure (2002)
Education Expenditures: 11.4% of total government expenditure (2002)
External Debt: n.a.
Exports: US$299.768 billion (2003 est.); commodities: manufactured goods, machinery, fuels, chemicals, semi-finished goods, transport equipment; partners: Germany, France, Netherlands, Ireland, US
Imports: US$375.170 billion (2003 est.); commodities: manufactured goods, machinery, semi-finished goods, foodstuffs, consumer goods; partners: Germany, France, Netherlands, Benelux, US

■ COMMUNICATIONS

Daily Newspapers: 329/1,000 inhabitants (2000)
Televisions: 950/1,000 inhabitants (2002)
Radios: 1,446/1,000 inhabitants (2001)
Telephones: 591 lines/1,000 inhabitants (2002)
Internet: hosts: 2,865,930 (2002); users: 25 million (2002)

■ TRANSPORTATION

Motor Vehicles: 23,400,000; 22,900,000 passenger cars
Roads: 371,913 km, all paved
Railway: 16,893 km
Air Traffic: 71,892,000 passengers carried (2002)
Airports: 470; 334 have paved runways (2003 est.)

Canadian Embassy: The Canadian High Commission, Macdonald House, 1 Grosvenor Square, London W1K 4AB, England, UK. Tel: (011-44-20) 7258-6600. Fax: (011-44-20) 7258-6333. e-mail: ldn@dfait-maeci.gc.ca
Embassy in Canada: British High Commission, 80 Elgin St, Ottawa ON K1P 5K7. Tel: (613) 237-1530. Fax: (613) 237-7980. e-mail should be sent using the appropriate form at the British High Commission's Website at http://www.britain-in-canada.org

United States

Long-Form Name: United States of America
Capital: Washington, D.C.

■ GEOGRAPHY

Area: 9,629,091 sq. km; includes only the 50 states and District of Columbia
Coastline: 19,924 km
Climate: mostly temperate, but varies from tropical (Hawaii) to arctic (Alaska); arid to semi-arid in west with occasional warm, dry chinook wind
Environment: pollution control measures improving air and water quality; acid rain; agricultural fertilizer and pesticide pollution; management of sparse natural water resources in west; desertification; tsunamis, volcanoes and earthquake activity around Pacific; permafrost in Alaska
Terrain: vast central plain, mountains in west, hills and low mountains in east; rugged mountains and broad river valleys in Alaska; rugged, volcanic topography in Hawaii
Land Use: arable land: 19.3%, permanent crops: 0.2%, other: 80.5%; includes 214,000 sq. km irrigated
Location: North America, bordering on Canada, Mexico, Pacific Ocean, Atlantic Ocean

■ PEOPLE

Population: 290,342,554 (July 2003 est.)
Nationality: American
Age Structure: 0–14 yrs: 20.9%; 15–64: 66.7%; 65+: 12.4% (2003 est.)
Population Growth Rate: 0.92% (2003 est.)
Net Migration: 3.52 migrants/1,000 population (2003 est.)
Ethnic Groups: 83.5% white, 12.4% black, 3.3% Asian, 0.8% other
Languages: predominantly English; sizable Spanish-speaking minority
Religions: 56% Protestant (including 21% Baptist, 12% Methodist, 8% Lutheran, 4% Presbyterian, 3% Episcopalian), 28% Roman Catholic, 2% Jewish, 4% other; 10% none
Birth Rate: 14.14/1,000 population (2003 est.)
Death Rate: 8.44/1,000 population (2003 est.)
Infant Mortality: 6.75 deaths/1,000 live births (2003 est.)
Life Expectancy at Birth: 74.37 years male, 80.05 years female (2003 est.)
Total Fertility Rate: 2.07 children born/woman (2003 est.)
Literacy: approaching 100% (2002)

■ GOVERNMENT

Leader(s): President George W. Bush Jr., Vice President Richard B. Cheney
Government Type: federal republic
Administrative Divisions: 50 states and 1 district; dependent areas include: American Samoa, Baker Island, Federated States of Micronesia, Guam, Howland Island, Jarvis Island, Johnston Atoll, Kingman Reef, Marshall Islands, Midway Islands (inhabited by U.S. military personnel), Northern Marianas, Palau, Palmyra Atoll, Puerto Rico (for details see Puerto Rico entry), Virgin Islands (for details see Virgin Islands entry), Wake Island (military base), Navassa Island
Nationhood: July 4, 1776 (from England)
National Holiday: Independence Day, July 4

■ ECONOMY

Overview: market-oriented economy with a very large private sector; a powerful and diversified economy, with high per capita GNP; problems include the significant budget and trade deficits, large medical costs for the ageing population and inadequate investment in industry and infrastructure
GDP: US$10.45 trillion, per capita US$36,300; real growth rate 2.4% (2002)
Inflation: 1.6% (2002)
Industries: accounts for 18% of GDP and 25.3% of labour force (2002); highly diversified industry; petroleum, steel, motor vehicles, aerospace, telecommunications, chemicals, electronics, food processing, consumer goods, fishing, lumber, mining
Labour Force: 148.31 million (2002); 30.2% managerial and professional, 29.2% technical, sales and administrative support, 13.5% services, 24.6% manufacturing, mining, transportation and crafts, 2.5% farming, forestry and fishing.
Unemployment: 6.0% (Feb. 2004)
Agriculture: accounts for 2% of GDP (2002) and 2.5% of labour force; favourable climate and soils support a wide variety of crops and livestock production; world's second largest producer and top exporter of grain; surplus food producer; fish catch of 4.4 million metric tons
Natural Resources: coal, copper, lead, phosphates, uranium, bauxite, gold, iron, mercury, nickel, potash, silver, tungsten, zinc, crude oil, natural gas, timber

■ FINANCE/TRADE

Currency: $US = 100 cents
International Reserves Excluding Gold: US$74.212 billion (Jan. 2004)
Gold Reserves: 261.536 million fine troy ounces (Jan. 2004)
Budget: revenues US$1.946 trillion; expenditures US$2.052 trillion, including capital expenditures US$ n.a. (2002 est.)
Defence Expenditures: 16.0% of central government expenditure (2002)
Education Expenditures: 15.5% of government expenditure (2002)
External Debt: n.a.
Exports: US$723.805 billion (2003 est.); commodities: capital goods, automobiles, industrial

supplies and raw materials, consumer goods, agricultural products; partners: Canada, Mexico, Japan, UK, Germany, France, Netherlands
Imports: US$1.305 trillion (2003 est.); commodities: crude and partly refined petroleum, machinery, automobiles, consumer goods, industrial raw materials, food and beverages; partners: Japan, Canada, China, Mexico, Germany, UK, Taiwan

■ COMMUNICATIONS

Daily Newspapers: 213/1,000 inhabitants (2000)
Televisions: 938/1,000 inhabitants (2000)
Radios: 2,117/1,000 inhabitants (2001)
Telephones: 646 lines/1,000 inhabitants (2002)
Internet: hosts: 115,311,958 (2002); users: 159 million (2002)

■ TRANSPORTATION

Motor Vehicles: 218,000,000; 135,000,000 passenger cars
Roads: 6,334,859 km; 3,737,567 km paved
Railway: 212,433 km; 194,731 km operational
Air Traffic: 593,246,000 passengers carried (2002)
Airports: 14,801; 5,131 have paved runways (2003 est.)

Canadian Embassy: The Canadian Embassy, 501 Pennsylvania Ave, NW, Washington DC 20001, USA. Tel: (202) 682-1740. Fax: (202) 682-7726. e-mail: wshdc-outpack@dfait-maeci.gc.ca
Embassy in Canada: Embassy of the United States of America, 490 Sussex Drive, PO Box 866, Station "B," Ottawa, ON, K1P 5T1. Tel: (613) 238-5335. Fax: (613) 688-3080. e-mail inquiries are not accepted.

Uruguay

Long-Form Name: Oriental Republic of Uruguay
Capital: Montevideo

■ GEOGRAPHY

Area: 176,220 sq. km
Coastline: 660 km
Climate: warm temperate; freezing temperatures almost unknown
Environment: subject to seasonally high winds, droughts, floods; industrial pollution from Brazil
Terrain: mostly rolling plains and low hills; fertile coastal lowland
Land Use: arable land: 7.21%, permanent crops: 0.27%, other: 92.52%; includes 1,800 sq. km irrigated
Location: SE South America, bordering on Atlantic Ocean

■ PEOPLE

Population: 3,413,329 (July 2003 est.)
Nationality: Uruguayan

Age Structure: 0–14 yrs: 24.3%; 15–64: 62.6%; 65+: 13.1% (2003 est.)
Population Growth Rate: 0.79% (2003 est.)
Net Migration: -0.35 migrants/1,000 population (2003 est.)
Ethnic Groups: 88% white, 8% mestizo, 4% black
Languages: Spanish, Brazilero
Religions: 66% nominally Roman Catholic, 2% Protestant, 2% Jewish, 30% other
Birth Rate: 17.19/1,000 population (2003 est.)
Death Rate: 8.97/1,000 population (2003 est.)
Infant Mortality: 13.80 deaths/1,000 live births (2003 est.)
Life Expectancy at Birth: 72.54 years male, 79.38 years female (2003 est.)
Total Fertility Rate: 2.35 children born/woman (2003 est.)
Literacy: 97.7% (2002)

■ GOVERNMENT

Leader(s): President Jorge Batlle Ibanez, Vice President Luis Hierro
Government Type: constitutional republic
Administrative Divisions: 19 departments (departamentos, sing. —departamento)
Nationhood: Aug. 25, 1828 (from Brazil)
National Holiday: Independence Day, Aug. 25

■ ECONOMY

Overview: a small economy with favourable climate, good soils and considerable hydro power potential; problems include high inflation rates, a large and growing domestic debt and frequent strikes; growth in the agriculture and fishing sectors has spurred recovery; unemployment is on the rise and hobbles economic progress
GDP: US$26.82 billion, per capita US$7,900; real growth rate -10.8% (2002 est.)
Inflation: 14.1% (2002 est.)
Industries: accounts for 29% of GDP (2001) and 19% of labour force; meat packing, oil refining, manufacturing, foodstuffs, engineering, transport equipment, sugar, textiles, leather apparel, tires
Labour Force: 1.6 million (2002); 70% community, social and business services, 16% industry, 14% agriculture
Unemployment: 17.2% (2002)
Agriculture: accounts for 6% of GDP (2000) and 11% of labour force; meat processing, wool and hides, sugar, textiles, footwear, leather apparel, tires, cement, fishing, petroleum refining, wine, wheat, rice, corn, sorghum; livestock and fish; self-sufficient in most basic foods
Natural Resources: arable land, hydro power potential, minor minerals

■ FINANCE/TRADE

Currency: new peso (N$Ur) = 100 centesimos

International Reserves Excluding Gold: US$2.130 billion (Jan. 2004)
Gold Reserves: 0.008 million fine troy ounces (Jan. 2004)
Budget: revenues US$2.74 billion; expenditures US$3.4 billion, including capital expenditures of US$193 million (2002)
Defence Expenditures: 4.2% of central government expenditure (2002)
Education Expenditures: 10.0% of total government expenditure (2002)
External Debt: US$10.736 billion (2002)
Exports: US$2.164 billion (2003 est.); commodities: hides and leather goods 17%, beef 10%, wool 9%, fish 7%, rice 4%; partners: EU, US
Imports: US$1.989 billion (2003 est.); commodities: fuels and lubricants 15%, metals, machinery, transportation equipment, industrial chemicals; partners: MERCOSUR partners, EU, US

■ **COMMUNICATIONS**

Daily Newspapers: 293/1,000 inhabitants (2000)
Televisions: 530/1,000 inhabitants (2002)
Radios: 603/1,000 inhabitants (2001)
Telephones: 280 lines/1,000 inhabitants (2002)
Internet: hosts: 78,660 (2002); users: 400,000 (2002)

■ **TRANSPORTATION**

Motor Vehicles: 585,000; 530,000 passenger cars
Roads: 8,983 km; 8,081 km paved
Railway: 2,073 km
Air Traffic: 525,000 passengers carried (2002)
Airports: 64; 15 have paved runways (2003 est.)

Canadian Embassy: The Canadian Embassy, Plaza Independencia 749, off. 102, 11100 Montevideo, Uruguay. Tel: (011-598-2) 902-20-30. Fax: (011-598-2) 902-20-29. e-mail: mvdeo@dfait-maeci.gc.ca
Embassy in Canada: Embassy of the Oriental Republic of Uruguay, 130 Albert St, Ste 1905, Ottawa ON K1P 5G4. Tel: (613) 234-2727. Fax: (613) 233-4670. e-mail: uruott@iosphere.net

---

Uzbekistan

Long-Form Name: Republic of Uzbekistan
Capital: Tashkent

■ **GEOGRAPHY**

Area: 447,400 sq. km
Coastline: landlocked; 420 km inland coastline along Aral Sea
Climate: dry continental; warm to hot summers; cool to cold winters; semi-arid grassland in east
Environment: drying up of the Aral Sea is resulting in increasing concentrations of chemical pesticides and natural salts; water and soil pollution
Terrain: flat to rolling deserts and semi-deserts, mountains, shrinking Aral Sea in west

Land Use: arable land: 10.8%, permanent crops: 0.91%, other: 88.29%; includes 42,810 sq. km irrigated
Location: C Asia

■ **PEOPLE**

Population: 25,981,647 (July 2003 est.)
Nationality: Uzbekistani
Age Structure: 0–14 yrs: 34.7%; 15–64: 60.5%; 65+: 4.7% (2003 est.)
Population Growth Rate: 1.63% (2003 est.)
Net Migration: -1.83 migrants/1,000 population (2003 est.)
Ethnic Groups: 80% Uzbek, 5.5% Russian, 1.5% Tartars, 5% Tajiks, 3% Kazakhs, 2.5% Kara-Kalpaks, 2.5% other
Languages: 74.3% Uzbek (official), 14.2% Russian, 4.4% Tajik, 7.1% other
Religions: predominantly Sunni Muslim and Eastern Orthodox
Birth Rate: 26.09/1,000 population (2003 est.)
Death Rate: 7.97/1,000 population (2003 est.)
Infant Mortality: 71.51 deaths/1,000 live births (2003 est.)
Life Expectancy at Birth: 60.53 years male, 67.64 years female (2003 est.)
Total Fertility Rate: 3.00 children born/woman (2003 est.)
Literacy: 99.3% (2002)

■ **GOVERNMENT**

Leader(s): President Islam A. Karimov, Prime Minister Shavkat Mirziyayev
Government Type: republic
Administrative Divisions: 12 (wiloyatlar, sing. — wiloyat), 1 autonomous republic (respublikasi), 1 city (shahri)
Nationhood: Aug. 31, 1991 (from Soviet Union)
National Holiday: Independence Day, Sept. 1

■ **ECONOMY**

Overview: despite the need for irrigation, agriculture is the predominant economic sector; small industrial sector, mining; inflation is skyrocketing and economic problems are numerous; more than 60% of the population is living in overcrowded rural villages
GDP: US$66.06 billion, per capita US$2,600; real growth rate 4.2% (2002 est.)
Inflation: 26% (2002 est.)
Industries: accounts for 24% of GDP (2000); chemicals and gas, machine building, metalmaking, textile manufacture, clothing, butter, preserves, vegetable oil, textiles
Labour Force: 11.0 million (2002); 44% agriculture and forestry, 20% industry and construction, 36% services
Unemployment: n.a.; also large numbers of underemployed
Agriculture: accounts for 33% of GDP (2000), vegetables, cotton, grains, almonds, fruit, livestock; 97% of all crops are grown on irrigated land

Natural Resources: gold, non-ferrous metals, coal, natural gas, petroleum, uranium, silver, copper

■ FINANCE/TRADE

Currency: Uzbekistani sum
International Reserves Excluding Gold: n.a.
Gold Reserves: n.a.
Budget: revenues US$2.42 billion, expenditures US$2.45 billion, including capital expenditures of US$ n.a. (2003 est.)
Defence Expenditures: n.a.
Education Expenditures: n.a.
External Debt: US$4.568 billion (2002)
Exports: US$2.988 billion (2002): cotton, agricultural products, machinery, gold, natural gas; partners: Russia, Switzerland, UK, Ukraine, South Korea, Kazakhstan
Imports: US$2.712 billion (2002): foodstuffs, machinery, consumer products; partners: Russia, South Korea, Germany, US, Ukraine, Kazakhstan

■ COMMUNICATIONS

Daily Newspapers: 3/1,000 inhabitants (2000)
Televisions: 280/1,000 inhabitants (2002)
Radios: 456/1,000 inhabitants (2001)
Telephones: 66 lines/1,000 inhabitants (2002)
Internet: hosts: 281 (2002); users: 275,000 (2002)

■ TRANSPORTATION

Motor Vehicles: n.a.
Roads: 81,600 km; 71,237 km hard-surfaced
Railway: 3,950 km
Air Traffic: 1,451,000 passengers carried (2002)
Airports: 273 airfields; 27 have paved runways (2003 est.)

Canadian Embassy: c/o The Canadian Embassy, 23 Starokonyushenny Pereulok, Moscow 121002, Russia. Tel: (011-7-095) 105-6000. Fax: (011-7-095) 105-6025. e-mail: mosco@ dfait-maeci.gc.ca
Embassy in Canada: c/o The Embassy of the Republic of Uzbekistan, 1746 Massachusetts Ave. NW, Washington, DC 20036. Tel: (202) 887-5300. Fax: (202) 293-6804. e-mail: n.a.

Vanuatu

Long-Form Name: Republic of Vanuatu
Capital: Port Vila

■ GEOGRAPHY

Area: 12,200 sq. km
Coastline: 2,528 km
Climate: tropical; moderated by southeast trade winds
Environment: subject to tropical cyclones or typhoons (Jan. to Apr.); volcanism causes minor earthquakes; lack of safe drinking water
Terrain: mostly mountains of volcanic origin; narrow coastal plains

Land Use: arable land: 2.46%, permanent crops: 7.38%, other: 90.16%; includes n.a. sq. km irrigated
Location: South Pacific Ocean, NE of Australia

■ PEOPLE

Population: 199,414 (July 2003 est.)
Nationality: Ni-Vanuatu (sing. & pl.)
Age Structure: 0–14 yrs: 34.8%; 15–64: 61.8%; 65+: 3.4% (2003 est.)
Population Growth Rate: 1.61% (2003 est.)
Net Migration: 0 migrants/1,000 population (2003 est.)
Ethnic Groups: 94% indigenous Melanesian, 4% French, remainder Vietnamese, Chinese and various Pacific Islanders
Languages: English and French (both official); pidgin (known as Bislama or Bichelama)
Religions: 36.7% Presbyterian, 15% Anglican, 15% Catholic, 7.6% indigenous beliefs, 6.2% Seventh-Day Adventist, 3.8% Church of Christ, 15.7% other
Birth Rate: 24.26/1,000 population (2003 est.)
Death Rate: 8.13/1,000 population (2003 est.)
Infant Mortality: 58.11 deaths/1,000 live births (2003 est.)
Life Expectancy at Birth: 60.28 years male, 63.21 years female (2003 est.)
Total Fertility Rate: 2.98 children born/woman (2003 est.)
Literacy: 34.0% (2002)

■ GOVERNMENT

Leader(s): President Kalkot Mataskelekele, Prime Minister Serge Vohor
Government Type: republic
Administrative Divisions: 6 provinces
Nationhood: July 30, 1980 (from France and UK; formerly known as New Hebrides)
National Holiday: Independence Day, July 30

■ ECONOMY

Overview: economy is based on subsistence farming, fishing and tourism; few mineral deposits; a small light industry sector sees to local needs; tax revenues come largely from import duties
GDP: US$563 million, per capita US$2,900; real growth rate -0.3% (2002 est.)
Inflation: 3.7% (2001)
Industries: accounts for 12% of GDP (2000); food and fish freezing, meat canning, wood processing
Labour Force: n.a.; 65% agriculture, 30% services, 5% industry
Unemployment: n.a.
Agriculture: accounts for 26% of GDP (2000) and 65% of labour force; export crops: cocoa, coffee and fish; subsistence crops: copra, taro, yams, coconuts, fruit and vegetables
Natural Resources: manganese, hardwood forests, fish

■ FINANCE/TRADE

Currency: vatu (VT) = 100 centimes
International Reserves Excluding Gold: US$45 million (Jan. 2004)
Gold Reserves: n.a.
Budget: n.a.
Defence Expenditures: negligible
Education Expenditures: n.a.
External Debt: US$84 million (2002)
Exports: US$15 million (2002 est.); commodities: copra 37%, cocoa 11%, meat 9%, fish 8%, timber 4%; partners: Japan, Belgium, US, Germany
Imports: US$89 million (2002 est.); commodities: machines and vehicles 25%, food and beverages 23%, basic manufactures 18%, raw materials and fuels 11%, chemicals 6%; partners: Australia, Singapore, New Zealand, Japan, US

■ COMMUNICATIONS

Daily Newspapers: none
Televisions: n.a.
Radios: n.a.
Telephones: 34 lines/1,000 inhabitants (2002)
Internet: hosts: 551 (2002); users: 7,000 (2002)

■ TRANSPORTATION

Motor Vehicles: 6,300; 4,000 passenger cars
Roads: 1,070 km; 256 km paved
Railway: none
Air Traffic: 89,000 passengers carried (2001 est.)
Airports: 30; 3 have paved runways (2002)

Canadian Embassy: The Canadian High Commission to Vanuatu, c/o The Canadian High Commission, Commonwealth Ave, Canberra A.C.T. 2600, Australia. Tel: (011-61-2) 6270-4000. Fax: (011-61-2) 6273-3285. e-mail: cnbra@dfait-maeci.gc.ca
Embassy in Canada: n.a.

Vatican City

Long-Form Name: State of the Vatican City, or the Holy See
Capital: Vatican City

■ GEOGRAPHY

Area: 0.44 sq. km
Coastline: none: landlocked
Climate: temperate; mild, rainy winters (Sept. to mid-May) with hot, dry summers (May to Sept.)
Environment: urban
Terrain: low hill
Land Use: arable land: 0%, permanent crops: 0%, other: 100%, (urban area)
Location: S Europe (W Italy)

■ PEOPLE

Population: 911 (July 2003 est.)
Nationality: n.a.
Age Structure: n.a.
Population Growth Rate: 0.01% (2003 est.)
Net Migration: n.a.
Ethnic Groups: primarily Italians and Swiss but also many other nationalities
Languages: Italian, Latin and various other languages
Religions: Roman Catholic
Birth Rate: n.a.
Death Rate: n.a.
Infant Mortality: n.a.
Life Expectancy at Birth: n.a.
Total Fertility Rate: n.a.
Literacy: 100%

■ GOVERNMENT

Leader(s): Head, Roman Catholic Church, Pope John Paul II (Karol Wojtyla)
Government Type: monarchical-sacerdotal state
Administrative Divisions: none
Nationhood: Feb. 11, 1929 (from Italy)
National Holiday: Installation Day of the Pope (John Paul II), Oct. 22; also Christmas, Easter, Feast of Saints Peter and Paul (June 29), and other holy days of obligation

■ ECONOMY

Overview: economy is supported financially by contributions (known as Peter's Pence) from Roman Catholics throughout the world, the sale of postage stamps, tourist mementos, fees for admission to museums and the sale of publications
GDP: n.a.
Inflation: n.a.
Industries: printing and production of a small amount of mosaics and staff uniforms; worldwide banking and financial activities
Labour Force: approximately 1,500 Vatican City employees divided into three categories: executives, office workers, salaried employees
Unemployment: n.a.
Agriculture: none
Natural Resources: none

■ FINANCE/TRADE

Currency: Vatican Lira (Lit) = 100 centesimi (at par with Italian lira)
International Reserves Excluding Gold: n.a.
Gold Reserves: n.a.
Budget: n.a.
Defence Expenditures: defence is the responsibility of Italy
Education Expenditures: n.a.
External Debt: n.a.
Exports: n.a.
Imports: n.a.

■ COMMUNICATIONS

Daily Newspapers: 1 in total
Televisions: n.a.
Radios: n.a.
Telephones: n.a.
Internet: n.a.

■ TRANSPORTATION

Motor Vehicles: n.a.
Roads: no highways, all city streets
Railway: 862 m
Air Traffic: none
Airports: none

Canadian Embassy: The Canadian Embassy, Via della Conciliazione 4/D, 00193 Rome, Italy. Tel: (011-39-06) 6830-7316. Fax: (011-39-06) 6880-6283. e-mail: vatcn@dfait-maeci.gc.ca
Embassy in Canada: Apostolic Nunciature, 724 Manor Ave, Rockcliffe Park, Ottawa ON K1M 0E3. Tel: (613) 746-4914. Fax: (613) 746-4786. c-mail: nuncioap@istar.ca

Venezuela

Long-Form Name: The Bolivarian Republic of Venezuela
Capital: Caracas

■ GEOGRAPHY

Area: 912,050 sq. km
Coastline: 2,800 km
Climate: tropical; hot, humid; more moderate in highlands
Environment: subject to floods, rockslides, mud slides; periodic droughts; increasing industrial pollution in Caracas and Maracaibo
Terrain: Andes Mountains and Maracaibo lowlands in northwest; central plains (llanos); Guyana highlands in southwest
Land Use: arable land: 2.99%, permanent crops: 0.96%, other: 96.05%; includes 540 sq. km irrigated
Location: N South America, bordering on Caribbean Sea

■ PEOPLE

Population: 24,654,694 (July 2003 est.)
Nationality: Venezuelan
Age Structure: 0–14 yrs: 31.0%; 15–64: 64.1%; 65+: 4.9% (2003 est.)
Population Growth Rate: 1.48% (2003 est.)
Net Migration: -0.07 migrants/1,000 population (2003 est.)
Ethnic Groups: 67% mestizo, 21% white, 10% black, 2% Indian
Languages: Spanish (official); Indian dialects spoken by approximately 200,000 Amerindians in the remote interior
Religions: 96% nominally Roman Catholic, 2% Protestant, 2% other
Birth Rate: 19.78/1,000 population (2003 est.)
Death Rate: 4.90/1,000 population (2003 est.)
Infant Mortality: 23.79 deaths/1,000 live births (2003 est.)
Life Expectancy at Birth: 70.78 years male, 77.07 years female (2003 est.)
Total Fertility Rate: 2.36 children born/woman (2003 est.)
Literacy: 93.1% (2002)

■ GOVERNMENT

Leader(s): President Hugo Chavez Frias, Vice President Jose Vicente Rangel
Government Type: republic
Administrative Divisions: 23 states (estados, sing. —estado), 1 federal district (distrito federal) and 1 federal dependency (dependencia federal)
Nationhood: July 5, 1811 (from Spain)
National Holiday: Independence Day, July 5

■ ECONOMY

Overview: petroleum is the backbone of the economy, accounting for 27% of GDP, 78% of total exports and more than half of government revenue; it is likely to become even more important as the state petroleum company plans to double its production over the next 10 years
GDP: US$131.7 billion, per capita US$5,400; real growth rate -8.9% (2002 est.)
Inflation: 31.2% (2002 est.)
Industries: accounts for 40% of GDP (2001 est.); petroleum, iron-ore mining, construction materials, food processing, textiles, steel, aluminum, motor vehicle assembly
Labour Force: 10.5 million (2002); 64% community, social and business services, 23% industry, 13% agriculture
Unemployment: 12.8% (2002)
Agriculture: accounts for 5% GDP (2001 est.); products: corn, sorghum, sugar cane, rice, bananas, vegetables, coffee, beef, pork, milk, eggs, fish; not self-sufficient in food other than meat
Natural Resources: crude oil, natural gas, iron ore, gold, bauxite, other minerals, hydro power, diamonds

■ FINANCE/TRADE

Currency: bolívar (Bs) = 100 centimos
International Reserves Excluding Gold: US$16.85 billion (Jan. 2004)
Gold Reserves: 11.460 million fine troy ounces (Jan. 2004)
Budget: revenues US$20.1 billion; expenditures US$23.3 billion, including capital expenditures of US$2.6 billion (2002 est.)
Defence Expenditures: 6.1% of central government expenditure (2002)
Education Expenditures: 22.13% of central government expenditure (2000)
External Debt: US$32.563 billion (2002)
Exports: US$25.861 billion (2003 est.); commodities: petroleum 81%, bauxite and aluminum, iron ore, agricultural products, basic manufactures; partners: US, Brazil, Colombia, Italy, Spain
Imports: US$10.71 billion (2003 est.); commodities: foodstuffs, chemicals, manufactures, machinery and transport equipment; partners: US, Colombia, Brazil, Germany, Italy

■ COMMUNICATIONS

Daily Newspapers: 206/1,000 inhabitants (2000)

Televisions: 186/1,000 inhabitants (2002)
Radios: 294/1,000 inhabitants (2001)
Telephones: 113 lines/1,000 inhabitants (2002)
Internet: hosts: 24,138 (2002); users: 1,274,400 (2002)

■ **TRANSPORTATION**

Motor Vehicles: 2,025,000; 1,500,000 passenger cars
Roads: 96,155 km; 32,308 km paved
Railway: 682 km
Air Traffic: 6,370,000 passengers carried (2002)
Airports: 373; 127 have paved runways (2003 est.)

Canadian Embassy: The Canadian Embassy, Avenida Francisco de Miranda con Avenida Sur de Altamira, Altamira, Caracas, Venezuela. mailing address: Apartado 62302, Caracas 1060A, Venezuela. Tel: (011-58-212) 600-3000. Fax: (011-58-212) 261-8741. e-mail: crcas@dfait-maeci.gc.ca
Embassy in Canada: Embassy of the Republic of Venezuela, 32 Range Rd, Ottawa ON K1N 8J4. Tel: (613) 235-5151. Fax: (613) 235-3205. e-mail: info.canada@misionvenezuela.org

Vietnam

Long-Form Name: Socialist Republic of Vietnam
Capital: Hanoi

■ **GEOGRAPHY**

Area: 329,560 sq. km
Coastline: 3,444 km (excluding islands)
Climate: tropical in south; monsoonal in north with hot, rainy season (mid-May to mid-Sept.) and warm, dry season (mid-Oct. to mid-Mar.)
Environment: occasional typhoons (May to Jan.) with extensive flooding; soil deterioration; inadequate supply of safe drinking water
Terrain: low, flat delta in south and north; central highlands; hilly, mountainous far north and northwest
Land Use: arable land: 17.41%, permanent crops: 4.71%, other: 77.88%; includes 30,000 sq. km irrigated
Location: SE Asia, bordering on South China Sea

■ **PEOPLE**

Population: 81,624,716 (July 2003 est.)
Nationality: Vietnamese (sing. & pl.)
Age Structure: 0–14 yrs: 30.2%; 15–64: 64.2%; 65+: 5.6% (2003 est.)
Population Growth Rate: 1.29% (2003 est.)
Net Migration: -0.46 migrants/1,000 population (2003 est.)
Ethnic Groups: 85–90% predominantly Vietnamese; 3% Chinese; more than 60 ethnic minorities including Muong, Thai, Meo, Khmer, Man, Cham; other mountain tribes

Languages: Vietnamese (official), French, Chinese, English, Khmer, tribal languages (Mon-Khmer and Malayo-Polynesian)
Religions: Buddhist, Confucian, Taoist, Roman Catholic, indigenous beliefs, Islamic, Protestant
Birth Rate: 19.58/1,000 population (2003 est.)
Death Rate: 6.19/1,000 population (2003 est.)
Infant Mortality: 30.83 deaths/1,000 live births (2003 est.)
Life Expectancy at Birth: 67.58 years male, 72.70 years female (2003 est.)
Total Fertility Rate: 2.24 children born/woman (2003 est.)
Literacy: 90.3% (2002)

■ **GOVERNMENT**

Leader(s): President Tran Duc Luong, Prime Minister Phan Van Khai
Government Type: communist state
Administrative Divisions: 58 provinces (tinh, sing. & pl.), 3 municipalities (thu do, sing. & pl.)
Nationhood: Sept. 2, 1945 (from France)
National Holiday: Independence Day, Sept. 2

■ **ECONOMY**

Overview: centrally planned, developing economy with extensive government ownership and control of production facilities; dependent on foreign aid; high rate of population growth and high unemployment combine to form the economy's most serious problem
GDP: US$183.8 billion, per capita US$2,300; real growth rate 7.0% (2002 est.)
Inflation: 3.9% (2002 est.)
Industries: accounts for 34% of GDP (2000); food processing, textiles, machine building, mining, cement, chemical fertilizer, glass, tires, oil, fishing
Labour Force: 41.8 million (2002); 67% agriculture, 33% industry and services
Unemployment: n.a.
Agriculture: accounts for 25% of GDP (2000); rice, corn, potatoes make up 50% of farm output; commercial crops (rubber, soybeans, coffee, tea, bananas) and animal products other 50%; not self-sufficient in rice
Natural Resources: phosphates, coal, manganese, bauxite, chromate, offshore oil deposits, forests

■ **FINANCE/TRADE**

Currency: dong (pl. dong) (D) = 100 xu
International Reserves Excluding Gold: US$6.083 billion (Sept. 2003)
Gold Reserves: n.a.
Budget: n.a.
Defence Expenditures: n.a.
Education Expenditures: 13.93% of total government expenditure (2000)
External Debt: US$13.349 billion (2002)
Exports: US$16.530 billion (2002); commodities: agricultural and handicraft products, coal, minerals, ores, coffee, rubber, tea; partners: Israel, Jordan, Gaza Strip

Imports: US$19.000 billion (2002); commodities: petroleum, steel products, railroad equipment, chemicals, medicines, raw cotton, fertilizer, grain; partners: Japan, Singapore, South Korea, Taiwan, China, Thailand, Hong Kong

■ COMMUNICATIONS

Daily Newspapers: 4/1,000 inhabitants (2000)
Televisions: 197/1,000 inhabitants (2002)
Radios: 109/1,000 inhabitants (2001)
Telephones: 48 lines/1,000 inhabitants (2002)
Internet: hosts: 529 (2002); users: 1.5 million (2002)

■ TRANSPORTATION

Motor Vehicles: 178,000; 80,000 passenger cars
Roads: 93,300 km; 23,418 km paved
Railway: 3,142 km
Air Traffic: 4,082,000 passengers carried (2002)
Airports: 47; 24 have paved runways (2003 est.)

Canadian Embassy: The Canadian Embassy, 31 Hung Vuong Street, Hanoi, Vietnam, Tel: (011 84 4) 734-5000, Fax: (011 84 4) 734-5049. e-mail: hanoi@dfait-maeci.gc.ca
Embassy in Canada: Embassy of the Socialist Republic of Vietnam, 470 Wilbrod St, Ottawa, ON KIN 6M8. Tel: (613) 236-0772. Fax: (613) 236-2704. e-mail: vietem@istar.ca

Wallis and Futuna

Long-Form Name: Territory of the Wallis and Futuna Islands
Capital: Mata-Utu

■ GEOGRAPHY

Area: 274 sq. km
Climate: tropical maritime, rainy season (Nov. to April); cool, dry season (May to Oct.)
Land Use: arable land: 5%, permanent crops: 20%, other: 75%; includes n.a. sq. km irrigated
Location: SW Pacific Ocean, E of Australia

■ PEOPLE

Population: 15,734 (July 2003 est.)
Nationality: Wallisian, Futunan, or Wallis and Futuna Islanders
Ethnic Groups: Polynesians, and descendants of French settlers
Languages: Wallisian, Futunian (Polynesian languages), French

■ GOVERNMENT

Colony/Territory of: Overseas Territory of France
Leader(s): Head of State: President Jacques Chirac (France), High Administrator Christian Job
Government Type: overseas territory of France
National Holiday: Bastille Day, July 14

■ ECONOMY

Overview: agriculture includes copra, cassava, yams, taro roots, bananas; livestock includes pigs and goats; considerable imports, negligible exports

■ FINANCE/TRADE

Currency: CFP franc = 100 centimes

Canadian Embassy: c/o The Canadian Embassy, 35-37 avenue Montaigne, 75008, Paris, France. Tel: (011-33-1) 44-43-29-00. Fax: (011-33-1) 44-43-29-99. e-mail: paris@dfait-maeci.gc.ca
Representative to Canada: c/o Embassy of France, 42 Sussex Dr, Ottawa ON K1M 2C9. Tel: (613) 789-1795. Fax: (613) 562-3735. e-mail: politique@ambafrance-ca.org

West Bank

Long-Form Name: none
Capital: none

■ GEOGRAPHY

Area: 5,860 sq. km
Climate: temperate, temperature and precipitation vary with altitude, warm to hot summers, cool to mild winters
Land Use: arable land: 0%, permanent crops: 0%, other: 100%; includes n.a. sq. km irrigated
Location: Middle East, between Israel and Jordan

■ PEOPLE

Population: 2,237,194 (July. 2002 est.)
Nationality: n.a.
Ethnic Groups: Palestinian Arab and other 83%, Jewish 17%
Languages: Arabic, Hebrew (spoken by Israeli settlers and many Palestinians), English (widely understood)

■ GOVERNMENT

Colony/Territory of: claimed and occupied by Israel
Leader(s): local Palestinian authority is headed by Yasser Arafat, subject to Israeli authority
Government Type: Palestinian Legislative Council (Jan. 1996) has limited powers under interim self-governing agreements with Israel. Originally designated as a five-year interim arrangement in 1993, permanent status still under negotiation.
National Holiday: n.a.

■ ECONOMY

Overview: as for Gaza Strip

■ FINANCE/TRADE

Currency: 1 new Israeli shekel= 100 new agorot; 1 Jordanian dinar = 1,000 fils.

Canadian Embassy: n.a.
Representative to Canada: n.a.

Western Sahara

Long-Form Name: Western Sahara
Capital: none

■ GEOGRAPHY

Area: 266,000 sq. km
Coastline: 1,110 km
Climate: Mediterranean to arid; hot, dry desert; rain is rare; cold offshore air currents produce fog and heavy dew
Environment: desertification, sparse water and arable land; hot and dry and dust/sand-laden sirocco wind; harmattan haze
Terrain: mostly barren rocky desert; small mountains in south and northeast
Land Use: arable land: 0%, permanent crops: 0%, other: 100%; includes n.a. sq. km irrigated
Location: NW Africa, bordering on Atlantic Ocean

■ PEOPLE

Population: 261,794 (July 2003 est.)
Nationality: Sahrawi, Sahraoui
Age Structure: n.a.
Population Growth Rate: 2.29% (2000 est.)
Net Migration: -6.05 migrants/1,000 population (2000 est.)
Ethnic Groups: Arabs, Berbers
Languages: Hassaniya Arabic, Moroccan Arabic
Religions: Islam (almost 100% Sunni Muslim)
Birth Rate: 45.07/1,000 population (2000 est.)
Death Rate: 16.11/1,000 population (2000 est.)
Infant Mortality: 133.59 deaths/1,000 live births (2000 est.)
Life Expectancy at Birth: 48.65 years male, 51.33 years female (2000 est.)
Total Fertility Rate: 6.64 children born/woman (2000 est.)
Literacy: n.a.

■ GOVERNMENT

Leader(s): under de facto control of Morocco
Government Type: under Moroccan occupation; legal status and matters of sovereignty remain unresolved
Administrative Divisions: none (under de facto control of Morocco)
Nationhood: n.a.
National Holiday: n.a.

■ ECONOMY

Overview: economy severely disrupted by Moroccan occupation and ongoing guerrilla warfare; poor in natural resources and with inadequate rainfall, most food must be imported; all aspects of the economy are controlled by the Moroccan government
GDP: n.a.
Inflation: n.a.

Industries: phosphate mining, fishing, handicrafts
Labour Force: approx. 12,000; 50% of the people are engaged in subsistence farming and animal husbandry
Unemployment: n.a.
Agriculture: limited to subsistence agriculture; some grain production, livestock (esp. sheep, goats, camels); cash economy exists largely for the garrison forces
Natural Resources: rich phosphate deposits, iron ore

■ FINANCE/TRADE

Currency: Moroccan dirham (DH) = 100 centimes
International Reserves Excluding Gold: n.a.
Gold Reserves: n.a.
Budget: n.a.
Defence Expenditures: n.a.
Education Expenditures: n.a.
External Debt: n.a.
Exports: exact figures n.a.; phosphates main export product; Morocco claims and administers Western Sahara, so trade partners are included in overall Moroccan accounts
Imports: exact figures n.a.; fuel for fishing fleet; most of the country's food supply must be imported; partners, see exports

■ COMMUNICATIONS

Daily Newspapers: n.a.
Televisions: n.a.
Radios: n.a.
Telephones: n.a.
Internet: n.a.

■ TRANSPORTATION

Motor Vehicles: n.a.
Roads: 6,200 km; 1,350 km surfaced
Railway: none
Air Traffic: n.a.
Airports: 11; 3 have paved runways (2003)

Canadian Embassy: none
Embassy in Canada: none

Yemen

Long-Form Name: Republic of Yemen
Capital: Sana'a (political capital); Aden (commercial capital)

■ GEOGRAPHY

Area: 527,970 sq. km
Coastline: 1,906 km
Climate: hot, dry desert in the south to temperate in central region and north; harsh desert in the east
Environment: desertification, overgrazing, lack of natural fresh water, soil erosion, summer dust and sandstorms
Terrain: narrow coastal plain; western mountains, northern desert interior

Land Use: arable land: 2.75%, permanent crops: 0.21%, other: 97.04%; includes 4,900 sq. km irrigated
Location: SW Asia (Middle East), bordering on Red Sea

■ PEOPLE

Population: 19,349,881 (July 2003 est.)
Nationality: Yemeni
Age Structure: 0–14 yrs: 46.8%; 15–64: 50.4%; 65+: 2.8% (2003 est.)
Population Growth Rate: 3.42% (2003 est.)
Net Migration: 0 migrants/1,000 population (2003 est.)
Ethnic Groups: predominantly Arab; Afro-Arab, Indian, Somali and European minorities
Languages: Arabic
Religions: predominantly Muslim; Christian and Hindu minorities in the south
Birth Rate: 43.23/1,000 population (2003 est.)
Death Rate: 9.04/1,000 population (2003 est.)
Infant Mortality: 65.02 deaths/1,000 live births (2003 est.)
Life Expectancy at Birth: 59.16 years male, 62.87 years female (2003 est.)
Total Fertility Rate: 6.82 children born/woman (2003 est.)
Literacy: 49.0% (2002)

■ GOVERNMENT

Leader(s): President Ali Abdallah Salih, Prime Minister Abd al-Qadir Ba Jamal
Government Type: republic
Administrative Divisions: 17 governorates (muhafazat, sing. —muhafazah)
Nationhood: May 22, 1990
National Holiday: Unification Day, May 22

■ ECONOMY

Overview: future economic level depends heavily on Western assistance; North: low level of domestic industry once self-sufficient in food but now dependent on imports; South: economic growth among the slowest of all Arab countries
GDP: US$15.07 billion, per capita US$800; real growth rate 4.1% (2002 est.)
Inflation: 12.2% (2002 est.)
Industries: accounts for 40% of GDP (2000); petroleum, cotton, textiles, leather goods, food processing, handicrafts, cement, small aluminum products factory
Labour Force: 5.9 million (2002); most people are employed in agriculture
Unemployment: n.a.
Agriculture: in the north, agriculture accounts for 20% GDP; main crops include fruit (grapes) and cotton; in the south, agriculture accounts for 17% GDP and 45% of the labour force; the main agricultural product is livestock (cattle, camels, sheep, goats, poultry)
Natural Resources: salt deposits, petroleum, fish, marble, coal, gold, lead, nickel, copper

■ FINANCE/TRADE

Currency: Yemeni rial (YR) = 100 fils
International Reserves Excluding Gold: US$5.043 billion (Jan. 2004)
Gold Reserves: 0.050 million fine troy ounces (Jan. 2004)
Budget: revenues US$3.78 billion; expenditures US$4.13 billion, including capital expenditures of US$ n.a. (2004 est.)
Defence Expenditures: 18.8% of central government expenditure (2002)
Education Expenditures: 32.8% of government expenditure (2002)
External Debt: US$5.290 billion (2002)
Exports: US$3.92 billion (2003 est.); crude oil, cotton, coffee, vegetables, cotton, animal hides, fish; partners: Saudi Arabia, Japan, Singapore, Thailand, China, South Korea
Imports: US$3.042 billion (2003 est.); textiles and other manufactured consumer goods, petroleum products, sugar, grain, flour, other foodstuffs, cement, consumer goods, crude oil, machinery, chemicals; partners: Saudi Arabia, UAE, US, France, Italy

■ COMMUNICATIONS

Daily Newspapers: 15/1,000 inhabitants (2000)
Televisions: 308/1,000 inhabitants (2002)
Radios: 65/1,000 inhabitants (2001)
Telephones: 28 lines/1,000 inhabitants (2002)
Internet: hosts: 113 (2002); users: 100,000 (2002)

■ TRANSPORTATION

Motor Vehicles: 516,000; 230,000 passenger cars
Roads: 67,000 km; 7,705 km paved
Railway: none
Air Traffic: 869,000 passengers carried (2002)
Airports: 44; 16 have paved runways (2003 est.)

Canadian Embassy: The Canadian Embassy to Yemen, c/o Canadian Embassy, Diplomatic Quarter, P.O. Box 94321, Riyadh 11693, Saudi Arabia. Tel: (011-966-1) 488-2288. Fax: (011-966-1) 488-1997. e-mail: ryadh@dfait-maeci.gc.ca
Embassy in Canada: Embassy of the Republic of Yemen, 788 Island Park Drive, Ottawa ON K1Y OC2. Tel: (613) 729-6627. Fax: (613) 729-8915. e-mail: info@yemenincanada.ca

Yugoslavia

see Serbia and Montenegro

Zambia

Long-Form Name: Republic of Zambia
Capital: Lusaka

■ GEOGRAPHY

Area: 752,614 sq. km
Coastline: none: landlocked

Climate: tropical; modified by altitude; rainy season (Oct. to Apr.)

Environment: deforestation; soil erosion; desertification; air pollution and resultant acid rain; tropical storms are a natural hazard from Nov. to Apr.

Terrain: mostly high plateau with some hills and mountains

Land Use: arable land: 7.08%, permanent crops: 0.03%, other: 92.89%; includes 460 sq. km irrigated

Location: SC Africa

■ PEOPLE

Population: 10,307,333 (July 2003 est.)

Nationality: Zambian

Age Structure: 0–14 yrs: 46.3%; 15–64: 50.9%; 65+: 2.8% (2003 est.)

Population Growth Rate: 1.52% (2003 est.)

Net Migration: 0.0 migrants/1,000 population (2003 est.)

Ethnic Groups: 98.7% African, 1.1% European, 0.2% other

Languages: English (official); about 70 indigenous languages

Religions: 50–75% Christian, 24–49% Muslim and Hindu, remainder indigenous beliefs

Birth Rate: 39.53/1,000 population (2003 est.)

Death Rate: 24.30/1,000 population (2003 est.)

Infant Mortality: 99.29 deaths/1,000 live births (2003 est.)

Life Expectancy at Birth: 35.25 years male, 35.25 years female (2003 est.)

Total Fertility Rate: 5.25 children born/woman (2003 est.)

Literacy: 79.9% (2002)

■ GOVERNMENT

Leader(s): President Levy Mwanawasa, Vice President Nevers Mumba

Government Type: republic

Administrative Divisions: 9 provinces

Nationhood: Oct. 24, 1964 (from UK; formerly known as Northern Rhodesia)

National Holiday: Independence Day, Oct. 24

■ ECONOMY

Overview: economy continues to decline due to a sustained drop in copper production and ineffective economic policies; problems include a high inflation rate, high population growth and severe drought

GDP: US$8.24 billion, per capita US$800; real growth rate 2.3% (2002 est.)

Inflation: 21.0% (2002 est.)

Industries: accounts for 25% of GDP (2000); copper mining and processing, transport, construction, foodstuffs, beverages, chemicals, textiles and fertilizer

Labour Force: 4.4 million (2002); 85% agriculture, 6% industry, 9% services

Unemployment: 50% (2000 est.)

Agriculture: accounts for 24% of GDP (2000) and 85% of labour force; food production is insufficient for country's needs; crops: corn (food staple), sorghum, rice, peanuts, sunflower, tobacco, cotton, sugar cane, cassava; cattle, goats, beef, eggs produced; marginally self-sufficient in corn

Natural Resources: copper, cobalt, zinc, lead, coal, emeralds, gold, silver, uranium, hydro power potential

■ FINANCE/TRADE

Currency: kwacha (K) = 100 ngwee

International Reserves Excluding Gold: US$245 million (Jan. 2004)

Gold Reserves: n.a.

Budget: revenues US$1.2 billion; expenditures US$1.25 billion, including capital expenditures of US$ n.a. (2001 est.)

Defence Expenditures: 0.9% of GDP (2002)

Education Expenditures: n.a.

External Debt: US$5.969 billion (2002)

Exports: US$1.039 billion (2003 est.); commodities: copper, zinc, cobalt, lead, tobacco, electricity; partners: UK, South Africa, Switzerland, Malawi

Imports: US$1.128 billion (2003 est.); commodities: machinery, transportation equipment, foodstuffs, fuels, manufactures; partners: South Africa, UK, Zimbabwe, US

■ COMMUNICATIONS

Daily Newspapers: 12/1,000 inhabitants (2000)

Televisions: 51/1,000 inhabitants (2002)

Radios: 169/1,000 inhabitants (2001)

Telephones: 8 lines/1,000 inhabitants (2002)

Internet: hosts: 1,621 (2002); users: 52,400 (2002)

■ TRANSPORTATION

Motor Vehicles: 215,500; 142,000 passenger cars

Roads: 66,781 km; n.a. km paved

Railway: 2,173 km

Air Traffic: 47,000 passengers carried (2002)

Airports: 109; 11 have paved runways (2003 est.)

Canadian Embassy: The Canadian High Commission, 5199 United Nations Ave, Lusaka; mailing address: P.O. Box 31313, 10101 Lusaka, Zambia. Tel: (011-260-1) 25-08-33. Fax: (011-260-1) 25-41-76. e-mail: lsaka@dfait-maeci.gc.ca

Embassy in Canada: c/o High Commision for the Republic of Zambia, 2419 Massachusetts Ave NW, Washington DC 20008, USA. Tel: (202) 265-9717. Fax: (202) 332-0826. e-mail: embzamb@aol.com

---

Zimbabwe

Long-Form Name: Republic of Zimbabwe

Capital: Harare

■ GEOGRAPHY

Area: 390,580 sq. km

Coastline: none: landlocked

Climate: tropical; moderated by altitude; rainy season (Nov. to Mar.)

Environment: recurring droughts; floods and severe storms are rare; deforestation; soil erosion; air and water pollution; desertification; poaching has significantly reduced the black rhinoceros population, which was once the largest concentration of the species anywhere in the world

Terrain: mostly high plateau with higher central plateau (high veld); mountains in east

Land Use: arable land: 8.4%, permanent crops: 0.34%, other: 91.26%; includes 1,170 sq. km irrigated

Location: S Africa

■ PEOPLE

Population: 12,576,742 (July 2003 est.)
Nationality: Zimbabwean
Age Structure: 0–14 yrs: 39.2%; 15–64: 57.4%; 65+: 3.4% (2003 est.)
Population Growth Rate: 0.83% (2003 est.)
Net Migration: neg. 1 migrants/1,000 population (2003 est.)
Ethnic Groups: 98% African (71% Shona, 16% Ndebele, 11% other), 1% white, 1% mixed and Asian
Languages: English (official); Shona and Sindebele, numerous minor tribal dialects
Religions: 50% syncretic (part Christian, part indigenous beliefs), 25% Christian, 24% indigenous beliefs, a few Muslim
Birth Rate: 30.34/1,000 population (2003 est.)
Death Rate: 22.02/1,000 population (2003 est.)
Infant Mortality: 66.47 deaths/1,000 live births (2003 est.)
Life Expectancy at Birth: 40.09 years male, 37.89 years female (2003 est.)
Total Fertility Rate: 3.66 children born/woman (2003 est.)
Literacy: 90.0% (2002)

■ GOVERNMENT

Leader(s): President Robert Mugabe, Vice President Joseph Msika
Government Type: parliamentary democracy
Administrative Divisions: 8 provinces and 2 cities with provincial status
Nationhood: Apr. 18, 1980 (from UK; formerly known as Southern Rhodesia)
National Holiday: Independence Day, Apr. 18

■ ECONOMY

Overview: severe droughts have adversely affected this agriculture-based economy in recent years; the government is working to consolidate earlier progress in developing a market-oriented economy
GDP: US$26.07 billion, per capita US$2,100; real growth rate -13.0% (2002 est.)
Inflation: 134.5% (2002 est.)
Industries: accounts for 14% of GDP (2000); mining (minerals and metals account for 40% of exports), steel, clothing and footwear, chemicals,

foodstuffs, fertilizer, beverages, transportation equipment, wood products
Labour Force: 6.1 million (2002); 24% community, social and business services, 66% agriculture, 10% industry
Unemployment: 6.0% (2001)
Agriculture: accounts for 11% of GDP (2000); 40% of land area divided into 4,500 large commercial farms and 42% in communal lands; crops: corn (food staple), cotton, tobacco, wheat, coffee, sugar cane, peanuts; livestock: cattle, sheep, goats, pigs; self-sufficient in food
Natural Resources: coal, chromium ore, asbestos, gold, nickel, copper, iron ore, vanadium, lithium, tin

■ FINANCE/TRADE

Currency: Zimbabwean dollar ($Z) = 100 cents
International Reserves Excluding Gold: US$82 million (Aug. 2002)
Gold Reserves: 0.139 million fine troy ounces (Aug. 2002)
Budget: revenues US$1.4 billion; expenditures US$2.0 billion, including capital expenditures US$ n.a. (2003)
Defence Expenditures: 9.4% of central government expenditure (2002)
Education Expenditures: n.a.
External Debt: US$4.066 billion (2002)
Exports: US$1.261 billion (2003 est.); commodities: agriculture 34% (tobacco 21%, other 13%), manufactures 19%, gold 11%, ferrochrome 15%, cotton 6%; partners: South Africa, UK, Japan, Germany, China
Imports: US$1.691 billion (2003); commodities: machinery and transportation equipment 37%, other manufactures 22%, chemicals 16%, fuels 15%; partners: South Africa, UK, Germany, US, Japan

■ COMMUNICATIONS

Daily Newspapers: 18/1,000 inhabitants (2002)
Televisions: 56/1,000 inhabitants (2002)
Radios: 362/1,000 inhabitants (2001)
Telephones: 25 lines/1,000 inhabitants (2002)
Internet: hosts: 2,382 (2002); users: 500,000 (2002)

■ TRANSPORTATION

Motor Vehicles: 358,000; 250,000 passenger cars
Roads: 18,338 km; 8,692 km paved
Railway: 3,077 km
Air Traffic: 251,000 passengers carried (2002)
Airports: 430; 17 have paved runways (2003 est.)

Canadian Embassy: The Canadian High Commission, 45 Baines Ave, Harare, Zimbabwe; mailing address: P.O. Box 1430, Harare, Zimbabwe. Tel: (011-263-4) 252-181. Fax: (011-263-4) 252-186. e-mail: hrare@dfait-maeci.gc.ca
Embassy in Canada: High Commission for the Republic of Zimbabwe, 332 Somerset St W, Ottawa ON K2P 0J9. Tel: (613) 237-4388. Fax: (613) 563-8269. e-mail: zim.highcomm@sympatico.ca

SCIENCE AND NATURE

Science in the News, 2003–04

■ July 2003

An international team of astronomers has detected the most ancient planet yet known orbiting a binary system thousands of light-years away, in the globular cluster M4. The new discovery indicates that planet formation in the Milky Way may have started sooner and been more widespread than previously believed. Because globular clusters have low concentrations of heavy elements—necessary building blocks for planets—scientists had thought they were unlikely to be the home of many planets. "This is tremendously encouraging that planets are probably abundant in globular star clusters," said astronomer Harvey Richer of the University of British Columbia, co-author of the report in the journal *Science*.

■ August 2003

The electric power grid in northeastern North America suffered a huge breakdown on the afternoon of Aug. 14 when lights winked out from Ohio and Ontario to New York. The outage, which affected more than 50 million people, was blamed on a local system failure in Ohio.

The blackout began a few minutes after 4 p.m. (EDT), and power was not restored for four days in some parts of the United States, while parts of Ontario suffered rolling blackouts for more than a week. The economic impact was dramatic: in Canada, gross domestic product was down 0.7 percent in August, there was a net loss of 18.9 million work hours, and manufacturing shipments in Ontario were down $2.3 billion. The blackout was estimated to cost the U.S. up to $10 billion (U.S.)

■ September 2003

Scientists in the Netherlands have developed a new version of electronic paper that can switch quickly from one colour to another, giving it the ability to display moving images—and someday, perhaps, full-scale video. The researchers made an electronic-paper prototype, in which each pixel is a tiny chamber that has a water-repelling base over a white background. These containers are filled with coloured oil and topped off with water. Left alone, the oil forms a flat film between the bottom and the water. But when electricity is applied to the base, the oil contracts and moves aside, allowing light to reflect from the white background and changing the appearance of the pixel. Full-colour displays can be made by combining cells of yellow, cyan and magenta.

■ October 2003

China became the third nation to put a human in space on October 14. Lt. Col. Yang Liwei orbited Earth 14 times in 21 hours before his entry capsule parachuted to the ground in Inner Mongolia. Yang stayed in space much longer than the other two "first men in space"—Russian cosmonaut Yuri Gagarin and American astronaut Alan Shepard. As well, the spacecraft left behind an orbital module that may be carrying a high-resolution military camera.

Belgian scientists discovered a bright purple, bloated frog in southern India that may merit the establishment of not only a new species but also a new family. Franky Bossuyt and S.D. Biju of the Free University of Brussels reported in the journal *Nature* that the creature—dubbed *Nasikabatrachus sahyadrensis*—diverged from its closest relatives about 130 million years ago. One commentator said the classification of the frog as a new family would make it "a once-in-a-century find."

■ November 2003

The World Conservation Union's so-called Red List—published yearly—now includes a total of 12,259 species that are characterized as critically endangered, endangered or vulnerable. The number of threatened species is increasing partly because the number of known species is also on the rise. For example, a botanical survey of Ecuador found 1,164 new plant species, more than 800 of which are in danger. But human activities, such as farming and forestry, also play a major role in the endangerment of species.

■ December 2003

The blood and guts of an autopsy may soon be replaced by a virtual autopsy procedure that requires neither scalpel nor a strong stomach. The procedure, described at the annual meeting of the Radiological Society of America, uses two types of imaging—computed tomography (CT) and magnetic resonance (MR)—to generate a 3-D computer model of the body. Other techniques provide information on such things as wounds and time of death. However, the process is expensive compared with the old-fashioned exam.

■ January 2004

Two new Mars rovers—*Spirit* and *Opportunity*—began exploring the red planet's surface, touching down on Mars three weeks apart after seven months in space. *Spirit* landed in Gusev Crater, a wide basin that may once have held a lake. *Opportunity* landed in Meridiani Planum, an area about halfway around Mars from Gusev that has a broad outcropping of a mineral—grey hematite—that usually forms in the presence of liquid water. The rovers were expected to be functional only until April, but by August 2004 they were still producing what NASA called "bonus science," although they were operating under some mechanical and software restrictions. The goal of the exploration was to see if Mars might once have had water. Both rovers struck paydirt, finding strong evidence that rocks near their landing sites were chemically altered by water. ▶

▶ ■ **March 2004**

On March 30, NASA flew an experimental hypersonic jet—dubbed the X-43—that shattered a four-decades' old record and showed that an air-breathing engine can operate at more than five times the speed of sound. The unpiloted 12-foot-long aircraft actually flew at seven times the speed of sound—nearly 7,680 km/h—for about 11 seconds, then splashed down in the Pacific Ocean. The X-43 engine—a "scramjet," or supersonic combustion ramjet—relies on the shape of the aircraft itself, moving at hypersonic speeds, to compress the air so fuel combustion can take place. The technology allows aircraft to fly where oxygen is sparse.

For the last half of March, five of Earth's planetary neighbours lined up across the sky. Next-door neighbour Venus, looming in the west, shone more brightly than anything except the full moon. Mercury was a bit below Venus and somewhat to the right, Mars was at the upper left of Venus, while farther to the upper left was Saturn. Finally, Jupiter was visible as a big, bright star high in the eastern sky.

Astronomers at the California Institute of Technology reported a new object in our solar system that is much, much farther away than anything ever seen before. Nicknamed Sedna, for the goddess whom the Inuit believe to have created all sea life, it is nearly three times farther from the sun than Pluto. Sedna is the first object found within a distant zone called the Oort Cloud, which theory suggests is home to trillions of comets. However, Sedna is too large—somewhere between 1,200 and 1,800 kilometres across—to be a comet.

■ **May 2004**

About 1 in 13 patients in Canadian hospitals will experience "an adverse event," according to a study by researchers from seven Canadian universities. The rate is about twice as high as in the United States. The study, in the journal of the Canadian Medical Association, found 185,000 of some 2.5 million medical and surgical hospital admissions in Canada in 2000 were associated with an adverse event—defined as "an unintended injury or complication … caused by healthcare management." Co-author Ross Baker of the University of Toronto said 37 percent of the adverse events could have been prevented, but added not all such events are preventable.

■ **June 2004**

Two research teams demonstrated "teleportation"—but not the kind seen in the television show *Star Trek*. Instead, properties of an atom, called its quantum states—such as its energy level, motion or magnetic field—were transferred from one point to another without benefit of physical forces. This teleportation of information could someday lead to ultra-fast quantum computers, although experts caution that such machines are decades from realization.

■ **July 2004**

The *Cassini* spacecraft entered orbit around Saturn, beginning a four-year mission to explore the giant ringed planet and its 31 known moons, after travelling nearly 3.5 billion kilometres since its 1997 launch. The spacecraft began by sending back images of unprecedented detail of the planet's clouds, taken from only about 20,000 km. *Cassini* also captured images of the rings from nearly point-blank range, revealing incredible detail, and even plunged through the rings, entering a zone called the Cassini Gap, which scientists had predicted was devoid of ring material. In the coming years, the bus-sized spacecraft is scheduled to fly close to Saturn 76 times and to visit Titan, its largest moon, 45 times. It also will execute 52 close fly-bys of seven of the other moons. At the end of this year, the Huygens probe, which has piggy-backed aboard *Cassini*, will attempt the closest view of Titan, the most distant object from Earth yet contacted by a probe.

AIDS activists fear the ambitious goal of getting 3 million of the sickest victims treated with state-of-the-art drugs by the end of the year is out of reach, due to by shortfalls in funding and delays in putting together the foundations to make the project work. The International AIDS Conference in Bangkok noted that the pandemic is continuing to rage and efforts to contain it are still falling short. U.N. Secretary-General Kofi Anan admitted: "We are not doing nearly well enough." At the end of 2003, nearly 40 million people around the world were infected with human immuno-deficiency virus (HIV), which causes AIDS.

■ **MILESTONES**

Sept. 9, 2003–Edward Teller, 95, an inventor of the hydrogen bomb whose zeal for nuclear-weapons development made him a model for filmmaker Stanley Kubrick's *Dr. Strangelove*, died of a stroke.

Sept. 21, 2003–The 13-year-old *Galileo* spacecraft obliterated itself by crashing into the planet Jupiter, as directed by NASA engineers. Launched in 1989, *Galileo* stayed in orbit an extra six years and amassed a long list of firsts: the first asteroid fly-by; the first sighting of a moon orbiting an asteroid; the first detailed analysis of Jupiter's atmosphere.

Dec. 17, 2003–The 100th anniversary of the first powered flight. On Dec. 17, 1903, Orville Wright flew for 12 seconds and 120 feet, then bumped down into the sand.

April 15, 2004–Tim Berners-Lee, inventor of the World Wide Web, wins the inaugural Millennium Technology Prize. The $1 million Euro prize is bestowed by the Finnish Technology Award Foundation.

July 28, 2004–Francis Crick, co-discover of DNA molecular structure and considered to be a founder of molecular biology, died of colon cancer. Crick, James Watson and Maurice Wilkens won the 1962 Nobel Prize in Medicine for their discovery.

ASTRONOMY AND SPACE

Astronomy has taught us that the universe is more complex than the ancients thought. Though less dependent on the "patterns" in the sky, we continue the exploration. The skies act not simply as a guide, but also as a frontier to be explored.

Our Solar System

Our solar system consists of our sun, at least nine planets and smaller bodies such as asteroids, comets and moons. The dominant member of this family is the sun, our nearest star. The sun is an enormous ball of hot, glowing gas, mostly hydrogen and helium. Its powerful pull of gravity holds the planets, asteroids and comets in orbit around it.

The planets have been known since people first turned their gaze skyward. The ancient Greeks called them "wanderers" because they moved through the sky relative to the fixed stars. Five planets can be seen without a telescope: Mercury, Venus, Mars, Jupiter and Saturn. They are visible because they reflect the light of the sun.

In order of distance from the sun, the planets are Mercury, Venus, Earth, Mars, Jupiter, Saturn, Uranus, Neptune and Pluto.

All the planets revolve (orbit) around the sun in the same counter-clockwise direction. The closer to the sun, the greater their speed. Except for Pluto, all the orbits lie in nearly the same plane in space, like marbles rolling on a table top.

Our Place in the Universe Although the solar system seems enormous, it is quite small compared to the whole universe. Our sun is only one star among the hundreds of billions that make up our spiral-shaped galaxy, the **Milky Way**. It takes our sun, with planets in tow, about 250 million years to orbit around the Milky Way just once. All the stars that we see at night are in a small, nearby portion of our galaxy. There may be billions of galaxies in the universe, each containing billions of stars of its own.

The Birth of Our Solar System Approximately 4.6 billion years ago (billions of years after the galaxies were formed) astronomers believe that a vast cloud of gas and dust collapsed and formed a spinning disk. Gravitation compacted so much material in the centre that extremely high pressures and temperatures lit a nuclear fire—our sun began to shine. Meanwhile, any remaining lumps of hot solids and gases slowly collected to become the planets, moons, asteroids and comets.

Our Solar System The planets of the solar system can be divided into two groups. The inner planets, Mercury, Venus, Earth and Mars, are the **terrestrial**, or Earth-like, planets. These are small rocky worlds with metal cores and thin atmospheres, except for airless Mercury. Jupiter, Saturn, Uranus and Neptune make up the realm of the **gas giants**. These planets do not have a solid surface, but are made up of layers of gases and clouds, possibly with rocky cores the size of Earth. The gas giants are huge: a thousand Earths could easily fit inside Jupiter. Saturn's rings may be the most famous feature of the solar system but rings are also found around Jupiter, Uranus and Neptune.

Pluto is unique and does not fit into either of these two groups. It is a tiny world of rock and ice, smaller than the Earth's moon, and with an extremely thin atmosphere.

Separating the terrestrial planets from the gas giants is the **asteroid belt**, a region of space between Mars and Jupiter where as many as 50,000 rocky objects may orbit the sun. Asteroids, often called minor planets, range from gravel-size, or smaller, to the 1,000-km-wide Ceres. They may be the remains of a small, shattered planet.

More than 130 moons, or satellites, are found in the solar system. All the planets, except for Mercury and Venus, have at least one moon orbiting them. Some of these moons are fascinating worlds in their own right: **Phobos** and **Deimos**, the moons of Mars, may be captured asteroids; **Io**, one of Jupiter's moons, has many active volcanoes; **Europa**, another one of Jupiter's moons, appears to have a frozen ocean; **Titan**, a moon of Saturn, has an atmosphere thicker than Earth's. Jupiter with its 63 known moons, Saturn with its 31 and Uranus with its 27 are like miniature solar systems.

▶

Exploring the Solar System Most of the planets have been visited by space probes from Earth: Mercury was visited in 1974 by *Mariner 10*, Soviet *Venera* spacecraft landed on Venus several times in the 1970s while *Viking 1* and *2* landed on Mars in 1976. The best spacecraft views of Jupiter and Saturn were obtained by *Voyager 1* and *2* in 1979 and 1980–81 respectively. *Voyager 2* went on to Uranus in 1986 and Neptune in August 1989. These spacecraft made discoveries not possible from the Earth: craters on Mercury, volcanoes and great valleys on Mars, Jupiter's ring and 10 new moons of Uranus were only a few.

Recent missions include the *Ulysses* mission, launched in 1990, which finished its second orbit of the sun in 1997–98. The spacecraft performed a south polar pass of the sun from September 2000 to January 2001. The combined NASA/ESA (European Space Agency) *Cassini* mission to Saturn was launched in October 1997. *Cassini* entered orbit around Saturn in July 2004, and began sending back unprecedented amounts of information about the planets and its rings and satellites. (See Science in the News, page 610.)

Mars has been the target of several missions, beginning with the *Mariner* and *Viking* spacecraft in the early and mid-1970s. *Mars Global Surveyor* became the first successful mission to the red planet in two decades when it launched in November 1996 and entered Mars' orbit less than a year later. Its launch was followed quickly by *Pathfinder*, which landed on Mars on July 4, 1997. In 2002, the *Mars Observer* detected underground ice, and the 2003 *Mars Express* is continuing the search for water. Two flights in 2003 landed exploration robots—dubbed *Spirit* and *Opportuinity*—on Mars early in 2004. The *Mars Reconnaissance Orbiter* is to be launched in 2005, carrying the most powerful camera that has ever been used to photograph the planet's surface.

The *Messenger* spacecraft, launched Aug. 3, 2004, will be the first to orbit Mercury. It is expected to enter orbit around the solar system's innermost planet in 2011.

Our Solar System at a Glance

	Distance from Sun (million km)	Equatorial Diameter (km)	Gravity (Earth=1)	Mass (Earth=1)	Period of Orbit about the Sun	Period of Rotation on Axis (days)	Number of Known Moons
Sun	—	1 392 000	27.90	332 830	—	25.38	—
Mercury	57.9	4 878	0.38	0.06	88.0 days	58.60	0
Venus	108.2	12 104	0.91	0.8	224.7 days	243.00	0
Earth	149.6	12 756	1.00	1.0	365.3 days	0.99	1
Mars	227.9	6 787	0.38	0.1	1.88 years	1.02	2
Jupiter	778.4	142 800	2.14	317.8	11.86 years	0.41	63
Saturn	1 426.7	120 000	0.74	95.2	29.4 years	0.44	31
Uranus	2 870.9	51 200	0.86	14.4	83.97 years	0.71	27
Neptune	4 498.2	49 528	1.10	17.2	164.80 years	0.67	13
Pluto	5 906.3	2 390	0.08	0.002	247.92 years	6.38	1

Source: *solarsystem.nasa.gov*

Canadians Enter Private Space Race

*T*he *$10-million Ansari X PRIZE, created in 1996, is aimed at stimulating private enterprise to create passenger-carrying spacecraft. Two Canadians teams—the Toronto-based Da Vinci Project and the London-based Canadian Arrow—are among the 26 contenders for the prize. To win, a team's craft must reach an altitude of 100 kilometres, carrying at least three people, and return safely. It then must repeat the performance within two weeks. The Da Vinci Project's spacecraft, dubbed Wild Fire, was to make its first competition flight Oct. 2, 2004, from a site in Saskatchewan. The Canadian Arrow was beginning test flights in August.*

International Space Station (ISS)

Sixteen countries have been contributing to the International Space Station (ISS), a project that first got serious attention (and funding) in 1993. That project is now a reality that orbits 400 km above the Earth, at an inclination of 51.6° to the equator.

The assembly of the ISS began in 1998, when the first stage—the Functional Cargo Block—was launched from Kazakhstan. That first launch put the propulsion, command and control systems in place with the Zarya module. A six-man crew went up in December 1998 to do some assembly of the space station in orbit—they added the Unity module. In June 1999, tools and a crane were added to assist in construction. On May 19, 2000, a seven-member crew began to ready the space station for residents. On July 25, 2000, the third big component of the station, Zvezda, docked with the ISS. A NASA mission in mid-September took supplies up after a Russian supply ship with oxygen generators, toilet components and other gear had made Zvezda habitable. The September NASA mission installed equipment such as power and data cables as well as bringing supplies.

Canada's Marc Garneau visited the station as part of a mission (Nov. 30–Dec. 11, 2000) to install the station's first solar panels, which will generate 110 kilowatts of power. Col. Chris Hadfield became the first Canadian to walk in space (Apr. 19–May 1, 2001), when he installed CANADARM2.

Canada's contribution to the ISS is the Mobile Servicing System (MSS); the sophisticated CANADARM2 is part of this system, as is a robotic hand (known formally as a Special Purpose Dexterous Manipulator or SPDM). These pieces and the CANADARM2 will be used for assembly and maintenance tasks on the space station. The arm, together with the hand, can manipulate delicate objects; the CANADARM2 can work with large objects. The Canadian Space Agency is developing a Canadian Space Vision System to assist those using the equipment. Ground support for the devices will be at CSA headquarters in St. Hubert, Quebec.

The station is expected to be finished in 2006.

Other contributions to the project include a pressurized lab and logistics transport vehicles (European Space Agency); a lab with "attached exposed facility" and logistics transport vehicles (Japan); and research modules, a service module with its own life support and habitation system, a science power platform to supply electrical power, more logistics transport vehicles and a Soyuz spacecraft for emergency crew return and transfer (Russia).

The completed station would weigh more than 180,000 kg, were it on Earth. The station currently has a habitable volume of 425 cubic metres. It is 44.5 metres long (and 52 metres when a *Progress* spacecraft is docked) and 27.5 metres high. It is 73 metres wide, measuring across the solar panels that supply much of the station's power. Its orbit was chosen because it can be reached by launch vehicles from each of the international partners; the orbit also allows observation of 85 percent of the globe and 95 percent of the world's population.

The ISS was originally planned to establish a permanent laboratory where gravity, temperature and air pressure could be manipulated to create conditions that would be impossible to achieve in Earth-bound labs. The participants in the ISS program are the United States; Canada; European Space Agency partners Belgium, Denmark, France, Germany, Italy, the Netherlands, Norway, Spain, Sweden, Switzerland, and the United Kingdom; plus Japan, Russia and Brazil. Each partner will contribute astronauts to crew the finished station, and have access to its labs for research and experiments.

For more news and information, visit space-flight.nasa.gov/station or www.space.gc.ca

Some Astronomical Terms

Asteroid: Any of the thousands of small, rocky objects that orbit the Sun. Some pass closer to the Sun than Earth does and others have orbits that take them well beyond Jupiter. The largest asteroid is one called Ceres.

Big Bang: The primeval explosion that most astronomers think gave rise to the universe as we see it today, in which clusters of galaxies are moving apart from one another. Astronomers calculate the Big Bang happened about 15 to 20 billion years ago.

Black Hole: An object whose gravitational pull is so strong that—within a certain distance of it—nothing can escape, not even light. Black holes are thought to result from the collapse of certain very massive stars, but other kinds have been postulated as well: **mini black holes**, for example, which might have been formed in the turbulence shortly after the Big Bang. **Supermassive black holes**—with masses millions of times the Sun's—may exist in the cores of large galaxies.

Comet: A small chunk of ice, dust and rocky material (a few kilometres across) which, when it comes close enough to the Sun, can develop a tenuous "tail." The tail of a comet is made of gas and dust that have been driven off the comet's surface by the Sun's energy. The tail always points away from the Sun (no matter in what direction the comet is moving).

Eclipse: The blocking of all or part of the light from one object by another.

Galaxy: A large assemblage of stars (and sometimes interstellar gas and dust), typically containing millions to hundreds of billions of member stars. A galaxy is held together by the gravitational attraction of its member stars (and other material) to one another.

Light-Year: The distance light travels in one year in a vacuum. Since light travels at a speed of about 300,000 km per second, a light-year is roughly 9.5 trillion km long.

Magnitude: A way of expressing the brightness of astronomical objects, inherited from the Greeks. In the magnitude system, a lower number indicates a brighter object (for example, a 1st-magnitude star is brighter than a 3rd-magnitude star). Each step in magnitude corresponds to a brightness difference of about 2.5. Stars of the 6th magnitude are the faintest the unaided human eye can see.

Meteor: A bit of solid debris from space, burning up in the Earth's atmosphere because of friction with the air. Before entering Earth's atmosphere, the body is called a meteoroid. If any of the object survives its fiery passage through the air, the parts that hit the ground are called **meteorites.**

Milky Way Galaxy: A spiral galaxy, with a disk approximately 100,000 light-years across, containing roughly 400 billion stars. Our Sun is in the disk about two-thirds of the way from the centre. It takes about 200 million years to orbit the centre of the Milky Way once.

Neutron Star: A crushed remnant left over when a very massive star explodes. Some neutron stars are known to spin very rapidly, at least at the beginning, and can be detected as **pulsars**: rapidly flashing sources of radio radiation or visible light. The pulses are produced by the spinning of a neutron star, much as a lighthouse beacon appears to flash off, on and off.

Nova: A star that abruptly and temporarily increases its brightness by a factor of hundreds of thousands.

Orbit: The path of one body around another (such as the Moon around the Earth) or around the centre of gravity of a number of objects (such as the Sun's 200-million-year path around the centre of our galaxy).

Planet: A major object that orbits around a star.

Quasar: One of a class of very distant (typically billions of light years away), extremely bright, and very small objects. Quasar means "quasi-star"—that is, something that looks like a star but can't actually be a star.

Red Giant: A very large, distended, and relatively cool star in the final stages of its life.

Solar System: The Sun and all things orbiting it, including the nine major planets, their satellites, and all the asteroids and comets.

Supernova: An explosion that marks the end of a very massive star's life. When it occurs, the star can outshine all the other stars in a galaxy in total for several days, and may leave behind a crushed core (perhaps a neutron star or a black hole).

White Dwarf: The collapsed remnant of a relatively low-mass star (roughly one and a half times the Sun's mass and less), which has exhausted the fuel for its nuclear reactions and shines only by radiating its stored-up heat.

Source: *The Astronomical Society of the Pacific, San Francisco, CA*

2005 Phases of the Moon

(Eastern Standard Time)

New Moon	First Quarter	Full Moon	Last Quarter
			Jan 3 12:46 PM
Jan 10 7:03 AM	Jan 17 1:57 AM	Jan 25 5:32 AM	Feb 2 2:27 AM
Feb 8 5:28 PM	Feb 16 7:16 PM	Feb 24 11:54 PM	Mar 3 12:36 PM
Mar 10 4:10 AM	Mar 17 2:19 PM	Mar 25 3:58 PM	Apr 2 7: 50 PM
Apr 8 3:32 PM	Apr 16 9:37 AM	Apr 24 5:06 AM	May 1 1:24 AM
May 8 8 45	May 16 8 56	May 23 20 18	May 30 11 47
Jun 6 4:55 PM	Jun 15 8:22 PM	Jun 22 11:14 PM	Jun 28 1:23 PM
Jul 6 7:02 AM	Jul 14 10:20 AM	Jul 21 6:00 AM	Jul 28 10:19 PM
Aug 5 10:05 PM	Aug 13 9:38 PM	Aug 19 12:53 PM	Aug 26 10:18 AM
Sep 3 1:45 PM	Sep 11 6:37 AM	Sep 18 9:01 PM	Sep 25 1:41 AM
Oct 3 5:28 AM	Oct 10 2:01 PM	Oct 17 7:14 AM	Oct 25 8:17 AM
Nov 2 8:24 PM	Nov 9 8:57 PM	Nov 16 7:57 PM	Nov 23 5:11 PM
Dec 1 10:01 AM	Dec 8 4:36 AM	Dec 15 11:15 AM	Dec 23 2:36 PM
Dec 31 10:12 PM			

Daylight Saving Time (Summer Time) is kept in most places across Canada. It starts at 2 a.m. on the first Sunday in April, when clocks go forward one hour. Clocks return to Standard Time at 2 a.m. on the last Sunday in October, when clocks go back one hour. To get wristwatch time in the Eastern Time Zone during daylight saving *add* one hour to the times listed.

Across Canada, there are six Standard Time Zones. To adjust to wristwatch time in another time zone, add or subtract the following to the times listed in the table: Newfoundland (+1hr 30m), Atlantic (+1hr), Central (-1hr), Mountain (-2hr), Pacific (-3hr).

Organizations

Canadian Astronomical Society

An organization of professional astronomers. Contact: Hugh Couchman, CASCA Secretary Department of Physics & Astronomy, McMaster University, Hamilton, ON L8S 4M1
Business office: R. Hanes
Dept. of Physics, Queen's University, Kingston, ON K7L 3N6
Tel: (613) 533-6439; Fax: (613) 533-6463
Web site: www.casca.ca

Royal Astronomical Society of Canada (RASC)

The Society is an organization of amateur and professional astronomers that is open to anyone interested in astronomy. The Society publishes the annual *Observer's Handbook* as well as other publications. It has more than 4,900 members in 27 centres across Canada. National Headquarters: 136 Dupont Street, Toronto, ON M5R 1V2
Tel: (888) 924-RASC
Web site: www.rasc.ca

Scientists Watch "Movie" of Neutron Star Explosion in Real-Time

*S*cientists at the Canadian Institute for Theoretical Astrophysics (CITA) and NASA have taken an unprecedented second-by-second "movie" of an explosion on the surface of a neutron star—dubbed 4U 1820-30—that is 25,000 light-years from Earth. (A light-year is the distance light, moving at approximately 300,000 km/s, travels in a year.) Dr. David Ballantyne of CITA at the University of Toronto and colleagues at NASA used a satellite called the Rossi X-ray Timing Explorer to capture details of the explosion, which poured out more energy in three hours than our sun does in 100 years. Such explosions can serve as a laboratory to study the flow of hot gas swirling around neutron stars and black holes attracted by the strong gravity of those regions. The neutron star 4U 1820-30 contains about the same mass as our sun, packed into a sphere no larger than Toronto.

Source: *University of Toronto*

Events in the 2005 Sky

January

3   Quadrantids meteor shower. The Quadrantids shower is named for the constellation Quadrans Muralis. The moon is in the last quarter, so the viewing should be good.

13   Saturn is at opposition. Opposition occurs when a planet farther from the sun than Earth appears opposite the sun in the sky. It is the best time to observe a planet.

March

20   The vernal equinox occurs at 7:33 a.m. EST. There will be equal amounts of daylight and darkness. This is also the first day of spring in the northern hemisphere.

April

3   Jupiter is at opposition. This is the best time to view and photograph the giant planet and its moons. The moon is in its last quarter, which may improve viewing.

8   A rare annular/total eclipse of the sun. (See Eclipses, page 618.) The eclipse will only be visible in a thin corridor beginning southeast of New Zealand and stretching across the Pacific to Panama, Columbia and Venezuela.

21   Lyrids meteor shower. The moon will be brightening toward full, which may hamper viewing.

24   Penumbral eclipse of the moon. (See Eclipses, page 618.) The moon will set before the eclipse ends for observers in eastern North America, but those further west will be able to witness the entire event.

May

4   Eta Aquarids meteor shower. The moon will have just entered the last quarter, so viewing should be good.

June

3   Pluto is at opposition. The outermost planet is only visible with high-powered telescopes.

21   The summer solstice occurs at 2:46 a.m. EDT. This is the first day of summer in the northern hemisphere. It is the longest period of daylight in the year.

July

17   Mars is at perihelion, the point in its orbit when it is nearest to the sun.

27   Delta Aquarids meteor shower. The moon is entering its last quarter, which may help make the Aquarids a good show.

August

8   Neptune is at opposition. Like Pluto, Neptune is hard to see with home-based telescopes, even though opposition is the best time to view.

11   Perseids meteor shower. The Perseids shower is created by the dust trail of Comet 109P/Swift-Tuttle. There could be a good show this year, since the moon is still in its new phase.

31   Uranus is at opposition.

September

22   The autumnal equinox occurs at 6:23 p.m. EDT. The daytime and night-time are equal in length. This is also the first day of autumn in the northern hemisphere.

October

3   An annular eclipse of the sun will be seen in the eastern hemisphere. (See Eclipses, page 618.)

8   Draconids meteor shower. The shower is created by the dust trail of Comet 21P/Giacobini-Zinner.

17   Partial eclipse of the moon. (See Eclipses, page 618.)

20   Orionids meteor shower. The moon is still full.

November

2   Taurids meteor shower. The moon is new, so the viewing could be good.

16   Leonids meteor shower. The full moon may make it hard to see the show.

December

9   Venus is at its greatest brilliancy, with a magnitude of −4.7.

12   Geminids meteor shower. Unfortunately, the moon will be entering its full phase, so after moonrise, its light may wash out the meteor show.

22   The winter solstice takes place at 1:35 p.m. EST. This is the shortest day of the year and the first day of winter in the northern hemisphere.

Source: www.astronomy.com

Eclipses in 2005

The year 2005 features two solar eclipses, including a rare hybrid eclipse, and two lunar eclipses. However, only the lunar eclipses will be visible from North America.

April 8

The first solar eclipse of 2005 is a rare type known either as annular-total or hybrid. In other words, some observers will see the sun completely obscured by the moon, while others will see a ring of sunlight around the moon. In this case, the eclipse will begin annular, change to total for the middle portion, and revert to annular near the end. The eclipse will be visible in a thin corridor beginning southeast of New Zealand and stretching across the Pacific to Panama, Columbia and Venezuela. However, observers in New Zealand, much of the South Pacific, South America, and the southern U.S. will be able to see a partial eclipse.

April 24

The year's first lunar eclipse will be visible from most of the western hemisphere; for observers in eastern North America, the moon will set before the eclipse ends, but those further west will be able to witness the entire event. However, this event is a penumbral eclipse, meaning the moon does not enter the deepest part of the Earth's shadow, and so will be difficult to observe. Still, a distinct shading should be visible across the northern half of the moon at the height of the eclipse.

October 3

The second solar eclipse—this one of the more common annular variety—will only be visible from the eastern hemisphere. The central track of the eclipse crosses the Iberian Peninsula—including Madrid and Valencia in Spain, but just missing Porto, Portugal—and stretches across the African continent. The rest of Europe, Western Asia, the Middle East, India and most of Africa will see partial eclipses.

October 17

The last event of 2005 is a partial eclipse of the moon, visible over North America. The eclipse begins at 4:51 a.m. EST but most observers won't be able to see the shadow until about 5:30. If you're watching from east of the Great Lakes, you'll see the start of the event, but the moon will set before it's over; observers farther west will be able to see the whole thing.

> **WARNING: SPECIAL PRECAUTIONS MUST BE TAKEN TO OBSERVE THE SUN AT ALL TIMES. AT NO TIME DURING A PARTIAL SOLAR ECLIPSE CAN THE SUN BE OBSERVED SAFELY WITH THE UNPROTECTED HUMAN EYE.**

Source: *sunearth.gsfc.nasa.gov/eclipse*

Space Information on the World Wide Web

*N*ASA Home Page: *www.nasa.gov*
NASA provides links to the massive amount of information the agency has placed on the Web, as well as links to other space-related sites in the United States and other countries.

Space Telescope Science Institute: *www.stsci.edu*
This is the site for the Hubble Telescope.

Cassini Mission to Saturn: *saturn.jpl.nasa.gov Images, mission status, student activities.*

Getting down on Mars: *A one-stop shopping site for people interested in all aspects of the Red Planet is mars.jpl.nasa.gov/. Learn about the evidence for water, the search for traces of former life, and the spacecraft that are studying Mars' surface. If you dream of walking on the ochre dunes of Mars, try spaceflight.nasa.gov/mars/, where you'll learn about plans for human exploration of the solar system.*

Canadian Space Agency: *The agency has a home page dedicated to its activities in space. You'll find details of past work and plans for the future, as well as information about space science, a huge gallery of images of current and past Canadian astronauts, and details about all of the agency's programs. (See p. 619.) Visit www.space.gc.ca*

The Canadian Space Agency (CSA)

With the launch of *Alouette I* on September 9, 1962, Canada became the third country—after the USSR and the U.S.—to have a satellite orbiting the Earth. *Alouette I* was the first satellite to return useful information; its goal was to study the ionosphere (the layer of the atmosphere that affects long-distance radio and television transmissions). The Canadian Space Agency, created by Parliament on December 14, 1990, carries on a long tradition of activity in space for Canadians—a tradition that continues to this day.

Alouette paved the way for further scientific satellites, and, in 1972, Canada broke new ground with the launch of *Anik A-1*, making us the first country to have a commercial communications satellite. It made nation-wide, real-time television possible, and—for the first time—brought reliable telephone service to the far North. A successor satellite, *Anik E-2*, still provides services to television networks and facilitates activities such as the transmission of newspaper copy to printing plants around the country. (A new satellite in the same tradition, *Anik F-2*, was launched on July 17, 2004.)

Joint ventures with other countries are the norm for Canadian space activities; starting with *Alouette*, our satellites have been launched using boosters provided by other nations. In 1976, the U.S. and Canada launched Hermes, a joint venture communications satellite that became the prototype for direct broadcast satellites. And in 1981, the Canadian-designed and built Remote Manipulator System was installed on the U.S. space shuttle *Columbia*. The RMS—soon to be better known as the Canadarm—was operated by two hand controls from inside the *Columbia*'s cabin, allowing astronauts to take satellites from the cargo bay and place them in space. The Canadarm is also designed to snare satellites from orbit and put them in the cargo bay for repair or a return to Earth.

The Canadian Astronaut Program has been in operation since 1983. (See the next page for the role Canada's astronauts and science have played in building the International Space Station.)

But much of Canada's space activity was undertaken by different departments; the creation of the CSA was intended to coordinate Canada's space programs and manage our space-related activities. Its formal mission is to "promote the peaceful use and development of space for the social and economic benefit of Canadians."

Working with scientists and the private sector, the CSA has been involved in a series of important commercial and scientific satellites.

RadarSat, launched in 1995, is the country's first Earth Observation satellite. This remote sensing satellite is in a near-polar orbit 800 km above the Earth. *RadarSat* produces images of the Earth's surface using a microwave Synthetic Aperture Radar (SAR) system. (Similar devices use optical sensors; unlike them, *RadarSat* can function night or day, and through clouds, fog or smoke.)

Among projects for the future is the second *RadarSat*, intended to be launched in 2005.

But one of the most exciting new projects is Canada's first space telescope, the Microvariability and Oscillations of STars or MOST. No bigger than a suitcase, and costing less than $10 million, MOST was launched the day before Canada Day, 2003, using a Russian Stiletto rocket, and was immediately seen to be working perfectly.

The 54-kg MOST has already made a major scientific discovery. In early 2004, it monitored the star Procyon, which scientists had thought varied in its emissions, as our sun does. But the satellite found no changes ▶

▶ at all, which is sending theorists who study the evolution of stars back to the drawing board.

MOST will also be used to help determine the age of the universe by training its modest telescope on the same distant star for as long as seven weeks—something that previously would have needed a huge satellite to get the necessary accuracy.

But a Toronto space technology company, Dynacon Enterprises Ltd., came up with a tiny device to accurately control what's called the satellite's orientation, which determines where the telescope points.

Another small satellite, the 150-kilogram SCISAT-1, was launched in early August 2003. The $42-million spacecraft houses pioneering instruments to decipher chemical reactions in the atmosphere.

Depending on how much money is available, the CSA wants to launch either a microsat (like MOST, under 100 kilograms) or a smallsat (like SCISAT, under 500 kilograms) every year.

Also depending on money is Canada's participation in the biggest space mission of the decade: a science laboratory destined to land on Mars in 2009. NASA has invited the CSA to take part, but that may require Parliament to open its purse strings—something the agency is seeking.

Canada's Astronauts

The Canadian Astronaut Program began in 1983 when Canada was invited to send an astronaut on the U.S. space shuttle. A permanent corps of Canadian astronauts who could co-ordinate and conduct Canadian experiments in space was created as a result.

Dr. Marc Garneau was the first Canadian astronaut to fly in space. He conducted a set of experiments in space science, space technology, and life sciences during Mission 41-G, from October 5 to 13, 1984, aboard the space shuttle *Challenger*.

Dr. Roberta Bondar flew aboard *Discovery* from January 22 to 30, 1992, as the prime Canadian Payload Specialist for the first International Microgravity Laboratory mission; she conducted more than 43 experiments on behalf of 13 countries.

Dr. Steve MacLean flew aboard the shuttle *Columbia* from October 22 to November 1, 1992, and conducted a second set of these experiments.

Col. Chris Hadfield, in November 1995, was the first Canadian to serve as a full crew member and the first Canadian on board the Russian Space Station *Mir* when he flew aboard *Atlantis* from November 12 to 20, 1995.

Dr. Marc Garneau made his second space flight in May 1996, as a Mission Specialist aboard Space Shuttle *Endeavor*.

Dr. Robert Thirsk flew as a Payload Specialist on June 20, 1996, aboard *Columbia*.

Bjarni Tryggvason was Payload Specialist on August 7, 1997, for *Discovery*.

Dr. Dave Williams flew on board *Columbia* from April 17 to May 3, 1998.

Julie Payette flew aboard *Discovery* in August 1996, as part of a 10-day logistics and resupply mission to the International Space Station (ISS).

Dr. Marc Garneau flew his third space mission November 30, 2000, when he installed the first of four sets of solar panels on the ISS.

Col. Chris Hadfield became the first Canadian to walk in space in April 2001, when he installed and tested CANADARM2 (part of Canada's contribution to the multi-billion-dollar-project) on the ISS.

Dr. Steve MacLean was scheduled to fly on *Endeavor* in late May 2003, but all flights were grounded in the wake of the February 1, 2003, mishap that destroyed the shuttle *Columbia*.

Source: *Canadian Space Agency www.space.gc.ca*

Constellations

Astronomers have divided the sky into 88 well-defined areas called constellations. They are named after people, animals or objects. The pattern of bright stars in some constellations (such as Orion or Scorpius) resembles the person, animal, or object they are named after, but in most constellations it is difficult to see a pattern among the stars. The largest constellation is Hydrus, followed by Virgo and Ursa Major. The smallest is Crux.

Constellation	Meaning
Andromeda	Daughter of Cassiopeia
Antlia	The Air Pump
Apus	Bird of Paradise
Aquarius	The Water-bearer
Aquila	The Eagle
Ara	The Altar
Aries	The Ram
Auriga	The Charioteer
Bootes	The Herdsman
Caelum	The Chisel
Camelopardalis	The Giraffe
Cancer	The Crab
Canes Venatici	The Hunting Dogs
Canis Major	The Big Dog
Canis Minor	The Little Dog
Capricornus	The Horned Goat
Carina	The Keel
Cassiopeia	The Queen
Centaurus	The Centaur
Cepheus	The King
Cetus	The Whale
Chamaeleon	The Chameleon
Circinus	The Compasses
Columba	The Dove
Coma Berenices	Berenice's Hair
Corona Australis	The Southern Crown
Corona Borealis	The Northern Crown
Corvus	The Crow
Crater	The Cup
Crux	The Cross
Cygnus	The Swan
Delphinus	The Dolphin
Dorado	The Goldfish
Draco	The Dragon
Equuleus	The Little Horse
Eridanus	A River
Fornax	The Furnace
Gemini	The Twins
Grus	The Crane (bird)
Hercules	The Son of Zeus
Horologium	The Clock
Hydra	The Water Snake (f)
Hydrus	The Water Snake (m)
Indus	The Indian

Constellation	Meaning
Lacerta	The Lizard
Leo	The Lion
Leo Minor	The Little Lion
Lepus	The Hare
Libra	The Balance
Lupus	The Wolf
Lynx	The Lynx
Lyra	The Lyre
Mensa	Table Mountain
Microscopium	The Microscope
Monoceros	The Unicorn
Musca	The Fly
Norma	The Square
Octans	The Octant
Ophiuchus	The Serpent-bearer
Orion	The Hunter
Pavo	The Peacock
Pegasus	The Winged Horse
Perseus	Rescuer of Andromeda
Phoenix	The Phoenix
Pictor	The Painter
Pisces	The Fishes
Piscis Austrinus	The Southern Fish
Puppis	The Stern
Pyxis	The Compass
Reticulum	The Reticule
Sagitta	The Arrow
Sagittarius	The Archer
Scorpius	The Scorpion
Sculptor	The Sculptor
Scutum	The Shield
Serpens	The Serpent
Sextans	The Sextant
Taurus	The Bull
Telescopium	The Telescope
Triangulum	The Triangle
Triangulum Australe	The Southern Triangle
Tucana	The Toucan
Ursa Major	The Great Bear[1]
Ursa Minor	The Little Bear[2]
Vela	The Sails
Virgo	The Maiden
Volans	The Flying Fish
Vulpecula	The Fox

(1) Commonly known as the Big Dipper. (2) Commonly known as the Little Dipper.

Observatories in Canada

Maritime Region

☐ Burke-Gaffney Observatory

Department of Astronomy and Physics, Saint Mary's University, Halifax, NS B3H 3C3. From November to March, open at 7 pm; from April to June at 9 pm, every 1st and 3rd Saturday; from June to September, open every Saturday. Tel: (902) 496-8257.
Web site: apwww.stmarys.ca/bgo

Central Canada

☐ David Dunlap Observatory

Richmond Hill, Ont. Tours are held Saturday evenings from May to October, and Friday and Saturdays in July and August. Tickets are sold on a first-come, first-served basis. Tel: (905) 884-2112. Web site: www.astro.utoronto.ca/ddo

☐ Helen Sawyer Hogg Observatory

Canada Science and Technology Museum. 1867 St. Laurent Blvd, Ottawa, ON K1G 5A3. Tel: (613) 991-3044. ▶

▶ ☐ **Hume Cronyn Memorial Observatory**
University of Western Ontario, London, ON N6A 3K7.
Open late October to early April by reservation, and
from June to August on Saturday evenings at 8:30 pm.
Tel: (519) 661-2111. Web site: www.astro.uwo.ca/
~dfgray/cronyn.html

Western Canada

☐ **Climenhaga Observatory**
Dept. of Physics and Astronomy, University of Victoria,
PO Box 3055, Stn Csc, Victoria, BC V8W 3P6.
Tel: (250) 721-7700. Web site: astrowww.phys.uvic.ca/
climenhaga/obs/telescope.html

☐ **Rothney Astrophysical Observatory**
Physics and Astronomy Dept., University of Calgary,
Calgary, AB T2N 1N4. Tel: (403) 220-5385. Web site:
phas.ucalgary.ca/rao/

☐ **Dominion Astrophysical Observatory**
Little Saanich Mountain, 5071 West Saanich Road,
Victoria, BC, Canada V9E 2E7. Star parties and other
special events. Tel: (250) 363-8262. Web site: www.hia-
iha.nrc.gc.ca

☐ **Dominion Radio Astrophysical Observatory**
PO Box 248, Penticton, BC V2A 6K3. Guide available
on weekends, 10 am to 5 pm, at the visitors' centre.
Open weekdays during normal business hours, but no
guides available. Tel: (250) 493-2277.

☐ **H.R. MacMillan Planetarium and Gordon
Southam Observatory** 1100 Chestnut St., Vancouver,
BC V6J 3J9. Tel: (604) 738-7827. Web site:
www.hrmcmillanspacecentre.com

☐ **Devon Observatory** Dept. of Physics, University
of Alberta, Edmonton, AB T6G 2J1. Web site:
www.phys.ualberta.ca/research/astrophyscis/devon.html

☐ **University of Saskatchewan Observatory**
Wiggins Avenue off College Drive, 116 Science Place,
Saskatoon, SK S7N 5E2. Open to the public every
Saturday evening. Tel: (306) 966-6429. Web site:
128.233.95.140//observatory

☐ **University of British Columbia Observatory**
2219 Main Mall, Vancouver, BC V6T 1W5. Free public
observing on clear Saturday evenings. Tel: (604) 224-6186.
Web site: www.astro.ubc.ca/telescope/telescope.html

Planetariums

Maritime Region

☐ **The Halifax Planetarium**
The education section of the Nova Scotia Museum of
Natural History is located in the Sir James Dunn Building
at Dalhousie University. (902) 424-7353. Web site:
Halifax.rasc.ca/hp/

Central Canada

☐ **Doran Planetarium**
Laurentian University, Ramsey Lake Rd, Sudbury, ON
P3E 2C6. Tel: (705) 675-1151, ext. 2227. Web site:
laurentian.ca/physics/PLANETARIUM/Planetarium.html/

☐ **Planetarium de Montréal** 1000 St. Jacques St.
W., Montreal, QC H3C 1G7. Tel: (514) 872-4530.
Live shows in French and English. Web site:
www.planetarium.montreal.qc.ca/

☐ **Roberta Bondar Planetarium**
Seneca College, Newnham Campus, on Finch Ave. E.
between Highway 404 and Don Mills Road.
Tel: (416) 491-5050, ext. 2227. Planned reopening
delayed by construction.

☐ **William J. McCallion Planetarium**
Department of Physics and Astronomy, McMaster
University, 1280 Main Street, Hamilton, ON L8S 4M1.
Tel: (905) 525-9140, ext. 27777. Web site:
www.physics.mcmaster.ca/planetarium

Western Canada

☐ **Calgary Science Centre**
15 701–11 St. S.W., Calgary, AB Tel: (403) 268-8300
Open daily. Web site: www.calgaryscience.ca

☐ **Edmonton Odyssium**
1121-142 St., Edmonton, AB T5M 4A1.
Tel: (780) 452-9100. Features planetarium Star Theatre,
IMAX film theatre, exhibit galleries, telescope shop and
bookstore. Open daily. Web site: www.odyssium.com

☐ **Manitoba Planetarium**
190 Rupert Ave., Winnipeg, MB R3B 0N2.
Tel: (204) 956-2830 (switchboard). Shows daily except
some Mondays. Museum gift shop has scientific books
and equipment. Web site: wwwmanitobamusem.ca

EARTH SCIENCES

The earth sciences include **geology** (the study of earth's origin and composition), **oceanography** (the study of ocean water, currents, life-forms and the ocean floor), **paleontology** (the study of fossils and ancient life-forms), and **meteorology** (the study of earth's atmosphere, including weather and climate).

The Geological Survey of Canada

The Geological Survey of Canada (GSC) is Canada's first scientific agency, and one of the first of its kind in the world. The agency was created to survey and map mineral deposits in Canada's nearly 1 million square kilometres of land and freshwater lakes, and more than 6 million square kilometres of coastal boundaries.

The Survey began life in Montreal in 1842. Under the first director, William Edmond Logan, a Canadian businessman turned geologist, its initial task was a search for coal, the main industrial fuel at the time. The search, throughout Upper and Lower Canada, was unsuccessful, but Logan did find mineable deposits of copper and other metallic minerals.

Soon Survey geologists were undertaking expeditions westward. In the 1880s another director, George Mercer Dawson, became a noted ethnologist in Western Canada, as well as a pioneer geologist. His reports included observations of the Haida people of British Columbia. During his expeditions he took many photographs of settlements and totem poles, capturing a glimpse of a vanishing landscape.

In 1992 the Geological Survey marked its 150th anniversary. While the task of mapping Canada's geology remains its central focus, the computerized Survey of the 1990s is very different from the one started by Sir William Logan. The Survey now undertakes an ever-expanding range of research—from exploring questions related to global change to those concerning natural hazards such as earthquakes, landslides, volcanoes, floods and ground instability.

For more information on the Geological Survey and its programs, contact: Communications Office, Geological Survey of Canada, 601 Booth Street, Ottawa, Ontario K1A OE8.

When the Seabed Burps

Giant, gassy sea-floor burps could be causing underwater slides that threaten submarine pipelines, cables and even shoreline structures such as lighthouses and shipping terminals, says University of Calgary engineer Jocelyn Grozic. "We see all these re-occurring submarine slides on the continental shelf [and] no one knows for certain exactly what triggers them," Grozic says. But gas in the soil—generated by seabed micro-organisms—is a possible culprit. One clue is that the slides usually happen at low tide, when the pressure keeping the gas in soil is lower. "It's like twisting the lid off a bottle of pop … you get a lot of gas coming out of the solution," she says. That's still a hypothesis, but what is known is that the submarine slides are extremely powerful—they can easily snap cables or pipelines, so planners need to take them into account when building underwater structures.

Source: *NSERC*

Common Geological Terms

Continental shelf: Submerged edge of continent, extending to depths of less than 200 metres, and largely made up of sedimentary rock.

Earthquake: A sudden motion or trembling in the earth caused by the release of slowly accumulated strain along a fault line or through volcanic activity.

Echo Sounding: A determination of water depth by measuring the time required for a sonic or ultrasonic signal to travel to the bottom of a body of water and back to the ship emitting the signal.

Epicentre: Point on the earth's surface directly above the focus of an earthquake, usually the location of the most severe damage.

Erosion: Breakdown and wearing away of rocks on the earth's surface by the action of water, waves, glaciers, wind and underground water. ▶

▶ **Fault:** A fracture in the earth's crust along which there has been displacement of the rock on either side, relative to one another.

Geothermal Energy: Energy that can be extracted from the earth's internal heat, usually in the form of emissions of hot water, steam, and gas.

Glacier: A large ice mass formed on land by recrystallization of compacted snow.

Ice Field: An extensive area of interconnected glaciers. An ice field is known as pack ice when floating on the sea.

Igneous Rock: Rock formed when a mass of molten magma cools and solidifies on or below earth's surface. One of three main classes of rock.

Magma: Molten rocky material (mostly silica) beneath the earth's surface. Reaching the surface red hot through volcanic activity, it cools and becomes lava.

Metamorphic Rock: Rock formed when pre-existing rocks are altered by marked changes in temperature, pressure, or shearing stress. One of three major rock groups.

Sedimentary Rock: Rock formed from the accumulation of loose material deposited by water, wind and ice, and solidified by compaction.

Seismograph: A device that records the seismic vibrations of an earthquake. The wave disturbances caused by earthquakes have different speeds and require different lengths of time to reach the surface.

Tectonic Plates: Rigid outer layer of the earth's crust consists of about ten large plates, which "float" horizontally across the denser inner crust. The boundaries of these plates are zones of intense activity, and give rise to mountain building, volcanoes, changes in the ocean floor, and earthquakes.

Tsunami: Particular form of ocean wave produced by an earthquake in the ocean floor, noted for its destructive force.

Volcano: A vent in the earth's crust through which magma, rock fragments, dust, gases and ash are ejected from below earth's surface.

Composition of the Earth

Core: The earth's core lies about 2,900 km below the surface, and consists of two layers: a solid inner core and an outer liquid layer. The inner core is a solid mass, 3,200 km in diameter, probably composed of compressed iron with small amounts of other metals such as nickel. The outer core (the only liquid layer) is about 3,470 km in radius and gives rise to Earth's magnetic fields.

Mantle: Accounting for about 82 percent of Earth's volume, the mantle is denser than the crust, and probably increases in density close to the core. The mantle extends from the core to about 90 km below the higher mountains, and to about 5 km beneath parts of the ocean crust.

Crust: The outside crust of planet Earth ranges in thickness from 5 to 50 km. The relatively light, granite-like rock forming the continents overlies a thinner magnesium-iron layer that makes up the ocean floor. The continental blocks "float" on the denser layer forming the ocean bed.

Hydrosphere: A layer of water covering over 70 percent of the earth's crust, including all water on or near the surface of the planet.

Atmosphere: The lightest part of Earth is the atmosphere, a gaseous envelope surrounding the planet. The atmosphere consists of nitrogen, oxygen, water vapour and argon. Less than 0.1 percent is composed of other gases. Gases have weight, so the atmosphere is densest near Earth's surface, and thins towards the vacuum of space.

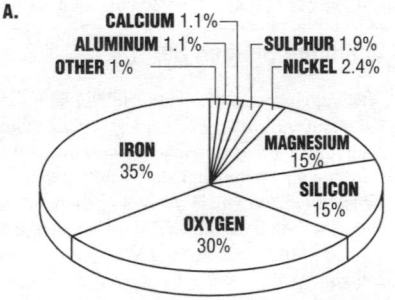

A.

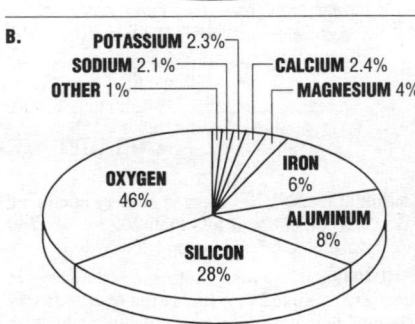

B.

▲

Relative abundance of elements by weight of elements in the whole earth (A) and in the earth's crust (B).

Earthquakes

Although the earth's surface seems completely stable, it is constantly moving and changing. Layers of rock in the earth's crust, called plates, push and pull each other until they bend or stretch.

Vibrations or "seismic waves" emanate from the source of the breakage out through the earth, causing the planet to quiver or ring like a tuning fork. The waves can be so minor that the quake will not be felt by humans, or so severe it will change the physical landscape of the area.

Earthquakes can happen all over the world, but they tend to recur along weaknesses in the crust, called faults. By studying the patterns of earthquakes, scientists determine the areas at greatest risk and compile the information in seismic zoning maps. In this way, building regulations can be applied to earthquake zones to minimize possible damage.

The most common method of measuring an earthquake's magnitude is the Richter Scale. It estimates the force from recordings of seismic waves taken by an instrument called a seismometer. The scale is logarithmic, so that each numeric reading is ten times greater in recorded amplitude.

The intensity of an earthquake can also be measured through the Modified Mercali Scale. In addition to mechanical recordings, it uses witness accounts to describe the effects of an earthquake.

Measuring Earthquakes

Richter		Modified Mercali	
2.5	Generally felt, but not recorded.	I	Not felt except by a very few.
		II	Felt only by a few persons at rest, especially on upper floors of buildings.
3.5	Felt by many people.	III	Felt noticeably indoors. Standing cars may rock slightly. Most people do not recognize.
		IV	During daytime felt by many indoors, outdoors by a few. Dishes, windows and doors disturbed; walls creak. At night, some awaken. Sensation like a heavy truck passing.
		V	Felt by nearly everyone; many awakened. Some dishes and windows broken; some objects over-turned. Trees, poles and other tall objects disturbed.
4.5	Some local damage may occur.	VI	Felt by all, many run outdoors. Heavy furniture moves; occasionally plaster falls and chimneys damaged. Overall damage slight.
		VII	Everyone runs outdoors. Well-built structures suffer negligible damage; slight to moderate damage in well-built homes; poorly constructed buildings suffer considerable damage. Noticed by people in moving cars.
6.0	A destructive earthquake	VIII	Damage slight in specially designed structures; considerable in ordinary substantial buildings, with partial collapse; great in poorly built structures. Chimneys fall. Heavy furniture overturned. Disturbs people driving cars. Sand and mud ejected in small amounts.
		IX	Damage to specially designed structures considerable. Buildings shifted off foundations. Conspicuous ground cracks. Underground pipes broken.

►

▶ Richter		Modified Mercali	
7.0	A major earthquake, about 10 occur each year	X	Some well-built wooden structures destroyed; most masonry and frame structures destroyed. Ground badly cracked. Rails bent. Landslides considerable.
8.0	Great earthquake, occurs once every five to 10 years	XI	Few masonry structures remain standing. Bridges destroyed. Broad fissures in ground. Underground pipelines out of service. Earth slumps, and land slips in soft ground.
		XII	Damage total. Waves seen on ground surface. Lines of sight and levels distorted. Objects thrown upward into air.

World's Major Earthquakes

Date		Location	Deaths	Magnitude
1902	Dec. 16	Turkestan	4 500	—
1905	Apr. 4	India, Kangra	19 000	8.6
1905	Sep. 8	Italy, Calabria	2 500	7.9
1906	Aug. 17	Chile, Santiago	20 000	8.6
1907	Oct. 21	Central Asia	12 000	8.1
1908	Dec. 28	Italy, Messina	83 000	7.5
1915	Jan. 13	Italy, Avezzano	29 980	7.5
1920	Dec. 16	China, Gansu	200 000	8.6
1923	Sep. 1	Japan, Kwanto-Tokyo-Yokohama	143 000	8.3
1925	Mar. 16	China, Yunnan	5 000	7.1
1927	Mar. 7	Japan, Tango	3 020	7.9
1927	May 22	China, near Xining	200 000	8.3
1929	May 1	Iran	3 300	7.4
1932	Dec. 25	China, Gansu	70 000	7.6
1933	Mar. 2	Japan, Sanriku	2 990	8.9
1934	Jan. 15	India, Behar-Nepal	10 700	8.4
1935	Apr. 20	Formosa	3 280	7.1
1935	May 30	Pakistan, Quetta	30 000	7.6
1939	Jan. 25	Chile, Chillan	28 000	8.3
1939	Dec. 26	Turkey, Erzincan	30 000	7.6
1948	June 28	Japan, Fukui	5 390	7.3
1949	Aug. 5	Ecuador, Ambato	6 000	6.8
1960	Feb. 29	Morocco, Agadir	15 000	5.9
1960	May 22	Chile	5 000	7.3
1966	Aug. 19	Turkey, Varto	2 520	7.1
1968	Aug. 31	Iran	20 000	7.3
1970	May 31	Peru	66 000	7.8
1972	Apr. 10	Southern Iran	5 054	7.1
1972	Dec. 23	Nicaragua, Managua	5 000	6.2
1974	Dec. 28	Pakistan	5 300	6.2
1976	Feb. 4	Guatemala	23 000	7.5
1976	June 30	Indonesia, Westirian	5 000	7.1
1976	July 27	China, Tangshan	255 000	8.0
1976	Aug. 16	Philippines, Mindanao	8 000	7.9
1976	Nov. 24	Turkey	4 000	7.3
1978	Sep. 16	Iran	25 000	7.8
1980	Oct. 10	Algeria	4 500	7.7
1980	Nov. 23	Southern Italy	4 800	7.2
1981	June 11	Southern Iran	3 000	6.9
1985	Sep. 19	Mexico, Michoacan	15 000	8.1
1988	Dec. 7	USSR, Turkey	25 000	7.0
1990	June 20	Western Iran	50 000	7.7
1993	Sept. 30	India	9 500	6.4
1995	Jan. 17	Kobe, Japan	6 000	7.2
1998	Feb. 1	Afghanistan	5 000	6.9
1999	Aug. 17	Turkey	12 000	7.4
2001	Jan, 26	India, Gujarat	20 085	7.7
2003	May 21	Algeria	2 666	6.8

Source: *U.S. Geological Survey*

Earthquakes in Canada

Scientists estimate that more than 1,000 earthquakes are recorded in Canada each year. Most measure less than 3 on the Richter scale. The southwest corner of British Columbia is the most active earthquake region (more than 200 every year). Other active regions include coastal BC, the southern Yukon, the Mackenzie Valley in the Northwest Territories, the Arctic Islands, and parts of Ontario and Quebec (especially the Ottawa and St. Lawrence valleys).

Date		Location	Magnitude
1918	Dec. 6	Vancouver Island	7.0
1925	Mar. 1	Charlevoix-Kamouraska region, Québec	6.7
1929	May 6	Off Queen Charlotte Islands	7.0
1929	Nov. 18	Atlantic Ocean, south of Newfoundland	7.2
1933	Nov. 20........	Baffin Bay	7.3
1935	Nov. 1	Québec–Ontario border	6.2
1946	June 23	Vancouver Island	7.3
1949	Aug. 22	Off Queen Charlotte Islands	8.1
1958	July 10	Alaska–BC border	7.9
1970	June 24	South of Queen Charlotte Islands	7.4
1976	Dec. 20	West of Vancouver Island	6.8
1979	Feb. 28	Yukon–Alaska border	7.5
1980	Dec. 17	West of Vancouver Island	6.8
1985	Dec. 23	Mackenzie region, NWT	6.9
1988	Nov. 25	Saguenay region, Quebec	6.0
1989	Dec. 25	Northern Quebec	6.1
1992	Apr. 6	West of Vancouver Island	6.8
2001	Sept. 14	West of Vancouver Island	6.0
2003	July 12	277 km west of Prince Rupert, B.C.	6.1

Source: *Geological Survey of Canada*

For more information, contact the National Earthquake Hazards Program of the Geological Survey of Canada (www.seismo.nrcan.gc.ca):

East
7 Observatory Cres.
Ottawa, ON
K1A 0Y3
(613) 995-5548

West
P.O. Box 6000
9860 West Saanich
Sidney, BC V8L 4B2
(250) 363-6500

Geological Time Periods

The story of planet earth is one of continuous change. Fossils, rock records and radioactive dating show three marked changes in the patterns of plant and animal life. These times of change in the most recent 570 million years of the earth's history are divided by geologists into three eras: Paleozoic (ancient life); Mesozoic (age of reptiles); and Cenozoic (age of mammals). The more than 4 billion years before the start of the Paleozoic era are referred to as Precambrian time. Each geological unit is divided further: the eras into periods, the periods into epochs.

The names of the time periods are taken either from the geographic locality where the fossil information was best displayed or first studied, or from some characteristic of the geological formations. For example, the Jurassic period is named from the Jura Mountains of France and Switzerland, and the Carboniferous is named from the coal-bearing sedimentary rocks. ▶

Era	Period	Epoch	Years Ago	Changes and Characteristics
▶ Precambrian Time			4.5 bil.?	Cooling and melting of the earth's crust. Evidence of bacteria, the first known living things, about 3.5 billion years ago.
Paleozoic	Cambrian		575 mil.	Seas spread across North America. First fish appear. Greatest development of invertebrates.
	Ordovician		480 mil.	Floods sometimes cover two-thirds of North America. Jawless fish appear. Algae become plentiful.
	Silurian		435 mil.	Coral reefs are formed. First amphibians and forests of fernlike trees appear.
	Devonian		405 mil.	Gas and oil are formed. Many kinds of fish in seas and fresh water. First insects appear.
	Carboniferous —Mississippian		350 mil.	Warm, moist climate produces great forests that later become coal beds. Fish and amphibians plentiful.
	—Pennsylvanian		310 mil.	Appalachian Mountains are formed. Large amounts of coal are formed. First reptiles appear.
	Permian		270 mil.	Ural Mountains are formed. Glaciers in southern hemisphere melt. Gas, oil and salt are formed. Reptiles developing.
Mesozoic	Triassic		225 mil.	Reptiles dominate the earth. First mammals appear.
	Jurassic		180 mil.	Shallow seas invade continents. Dinosaurs reach their largest size. First birds appear.
	Cretaceous		130 mil.	Seas spread over the land. Flowering plants appear. Dinosaurs die out. Most chalk deposits are made.
Cenozoic	Tertiary	Paleocene	65 mil.	Mountains become higher. Climates less uniform. Mammals, flowering plants become common.
		Eocene	50 mil.	Climate mild. Seas flood shores of continents. Primitive apes, early horses and elephants appear.
		Oligocene	38 mil.	Climate mild. Alps and Himalayas begin to rise. Many volcanoes. Oil and natural gas are formed.
		Miocene	27 mil.	Climate mild. Rocky Mountains and Sierra Nevadas forming. Flowering plants and trees resemble modern kinds.
		Pliocene	10 mil.	Climate cooling. Mountains rising in western Canada. Many volcanoes. Birds and mammals spread around the world. Humans appear near end of epoch.
	Quaternary	Pleistocene	1.5 mil.	Great ice sheets cover northern hemisphere. Climate cool. Mountains continue to rise in North America. Early humans reach Europe and North America.
		Recent, or Holocene	10 000	Glaciers melt and Great Lakes are formed. Climate warm. Humans live in most parts of the earth, develop agriculture, use metals, domesticate animals.

Source: *Gage Canadian Dictionary by Walter S. Avis, et al. Copyright © 1983 Gage Publishing Limited. Reproduced by permission.*

Minerals

Minerals are all around us—everything from ice on the sidewalk in winter to the salt you sprinkle on French fries. Each mineral species has a definite chemical composition and a crystal structure.Therefore, ice is mineral because it is solid, but water is not because it is liquid. Sea shells are not minerals because, although they are solid, they are organic—formed by living creatures.

The physical properties of minerals—their form and hardness—are easy to recognize. Specimens may be composed of large showy crystals or millions of tiny crystals fused together. The external shape (or habit) is determined by the internal arrangement of atoms. The atoms are joined together in a framework to form minute building blocks. Called the crystal structure, the arrangement of atoms is unique for each mineral. The habit is also partly the result of the environment in which a mineral grows. If there is enough space during growth, the mineral develops smooth external crystals. However, conditions are seldom ideal and more often than not, minerals grow together as masses of fibres, grains, plates or spheres. The hardness of a mineral—its resistance to scratching—is measured by the Mohs scale.

The optical properties of minerals—lustre, colour and transparency—are easily observed by the unaided eye; other optical properties are determined with microscopes. Lustre is the quality of light reflected from the surface of a mineral. For instance, the highly reflective surfaces of pyrite produce the metallic lustre characteristics of most sulphide minerals. Many silicates, carbonates and other minerals have a softer, but still bright, glassy or vitreous lustre. Minerals with surfaces that reflect light more diffusely, such as serpentine asbestos or cyanotrichite, are said to have silky or earthly lustres. Lustre is a reliable means of distinguishing minerals.

Colour can also be very distinctive, but is not always reliable in identifying most minerals because even minerals of the same species can occur in many colours. Quartz, which is quite common, can be as clear as water or the deepest purple because of flaws in the mineral's crystal structure. Colour can also be affected by the presence of major elements in the mineral: copper in azurite produces an intense azure blue; arsenic makes realgar appear red; and curite is coloured orange by uranium. Colour can also be produced by physical structure. When light strikes very thin layers within the structure of labradorite, the mineral glows with iridescent colours, an effect much like that of sunlight striking a film of gasoline on a puddle, causing a rainbow of colour.

Determining the chemical composition and crystal structure of minerals requires laboratory techniques and tools such as the electron microbe, a reliable tool for analysing chemical composition. Crystal structure is determined using an X-ray diffractometer. Other mineral properties such as magnetism, fluorescence and radioactivity are more easily detected: magnetite and pyrrhotite are noticeably magnetic; some minerals, such as scheelite, fluoresce strongly in ultra-violet light; and all uranium and thorium-bearing minerals are radioactive. The radiation can easily be detected with a Geiger counter or scintillometer.

Mohs Scale of Hardness

Mohs scale indicates the relative hardness of minerals. Each mineral listed is hard enough to scratch a smooth surface of those below it. On this scale, a polymer-like polyethylene would have a hardness of about 1, a finger nail 2.5, a penny 5, window glass 5.5, and the blade of a pocket knife 6.5. Tool steel has a hardness of about 7, and easily cuts glass.

10	Diamond	**5**	Apatite
9	Corundum	**4**	Fluorite
8	Topaz	**3**	Calcite
7	Quartz	**2**	Gypsum
6	Orthoclase	**1**	Talc

Source: *Geological Survey of Canada*

Earth Sciences Museums

Maritime Region:

☐ **St. Lawrence Miner's Museum**
PO Box 128, St. Lawrence, NL A0E 2V0. Tel: (709)
873-2222. No charge. Open in summer.

☐ **Fundy Geological Museum**
Two Island Road, PO Box 640, Parrsboro, NS
B0M 1S0. Tel: 902-254-3814. Open daily from 9:30
am to 5:30 pm, June 1 to October 15; open Tuesday
to Saturday from 9 am to 5 pm, Sundays from 1 to
5 pm, from October 16 to May 31. Web site:
museum.gov.ns.ca/fgm/

☐ **Inverness Miner's Museum**
Lower Railway St., Inverness NS B0E 1N0. Tel:
(902) 258-2097. Donations. Open from June to
September, 9 am to 5 pm weekdays, and noon to
5 pm on weekends. Web site: members.tripod.com/
~Dongael/museum.htm

☐ **Springhill Miner's Museum**
Black River Road, Springhill, NS B0M 1X0. Tel:
(902) 597-3449. Open spring, summer and fall.
Web site: town.springhill.ns.ca/Miners_Museum.htm

Central Canada:

☐ **Canadian Museum of Nature,**
Viola Macmillan Mineral Gallery
240 McLeod St., Ottawa, ON K1P 6P4. Tel: (613)
566-4700. Open daily. Web site: www.nature.ca

☐ **Logan Hall**
Geological Survey of Canada, 601 Booth St., Ottawa,
ON K1A 0E8. Tel: (613) 996-3919. Open 8 am to
4 pm weekdays. Web site: gsc.nrcan.gc.ca/logan/

☐ **Musée de Géologie**
Laval University, Pavillon Pouliot, 4th floor, Sainte
Foy, QC G1K 7P4. Tel: (418) 656-2131. Open all year.

☐ **Musée mineralogique et minier de Thetford**
Mines 711 Frontenac Blvd. W., Thetford Mines, QC
G6G 5T3. Tel: (418) 335-2123. Open all year. Web
site: www.mmmtm.qc.ca/

☐ **Musée régional mines de Malartic**
650 rue da la Paix, Malartic, QC J0Y 1Z0. Tel: (819)
757-4677. Open daily in summer; weekdays in
winter. Web site: www.museemalartic.qc.ca/

☐ **Earth Sciences Museum**
University of Waterloo, Waterloo, ON N2L 3G1.
Tel: (519) 888-4567, ext. 2469. Web site:
www.science.uwaterloo.ca/earth/museum/
museum.html

☐ **Miller Museum of Geology**
Queen's University, Miller Hall, Kingston, ON K7L
3N6. Tel: (613) 533-6767. Open weekdays. Web
site: geol.queensu.ca/museum/museum/html

☐ **The Petrolia Discovery Foundation**
4381 Discovery Line, Petrolia, ON N0N 1R0.
Tel: (519) 882-0897. Open in summer and fall.
Web site: www.petroliadiscovery.com

☐ **Royal Ontario Museum,**
INCO Gallery of Earth Sciences
1100 Queen's Park, Toronto, ON M5S 2C6.
Tel: (416) 586-5549. Closed Christmas, New Year's
Day. Web site: www.rom.on.ca

☐ **Timmins Museum**
70 Legion Drive, South Porcupine, ON P4N 1B3.
Tel: (705) 235-5066. Open all year. Web site:
www.city.timmins.on.ca/Timmins-Museum.htm

Western Canada:

☐ **Royal Saskatchewan Museum**
2445 Albert Street, Regina, SK S4P 3V7.
Tel: (306) 787-2815. Open all year.
Web site: www.royalsaskmuseum.ca/

☐ **Frank Slide Interpretive Centre**
PO Box 959, Blairmore, AB T0K 0E0. Located 1 km
north of Frank, AB Tel: (403) 562-7388. Open all
year. Web site: www.frankslide.com

☐ **Royal Tyrrell Museum of Palaeontology**
Hwy. 838, Midland Provincial Park, Drumheller,
AB T0J 0Y0. Tel: (403) 823-7707. Open all year.
Web site: www.tyrrellmuseum.com

☐ **Dinosaur Provincial Park**
Patricia, AB T0J 2K0. Tel: (403) 378-4342. Open all
year. Web site: www.cd.gov.ab.ca/parks/dinosaur

☐ **British Columbia Museum of Mining**
PO Box 188, Britannia Beach, BC V0N 1J0.
Tel: 1-800-896-4044. Open all year. Web site:
www.bcmuseumofmining.org

☐ **Pacific Mineral Museum**
848 West Hastings St., Vancouver, BC V6C 1C8.
Tel: (604) 689-8700. Open all year. Web site:
www.pacificmineralmuseum.org

☐ **Princeton and District Museums**
167 Vermilion St., Princeton, BC V0X 1W0.
Tel: (250) 295-7588. Open April through October.
Web site: town.princeton.bc.ca/museum/museum/htm

PHYSICAL SCIENCES

Physics and chemistry constitute the physical sciences. **Chemistry** concerns itself with the composition, properties and reactions of substances. Organic chemistry, one of the two main branches of chemistry, specializes in the composition, properties and reactions of hydrocarbon compounds. The other branch, inorganic chemistry, deals primarily with the elements and compounds that do not include hydrocarbons. **Physics** concerns itself with universal aspects of nature—forces, energy, structure of matter, and their interactions. Some of its particular fields are: plasma physics, optics and quantum optics, particle physics, geophysics, biophysics and acoustics. As basic sciences, physics and chemistry permeate all sciences and technologies.

Common Chemistry Terms

Acid: A substance that in liquid form will turn blue litmus paper red, react with alkalis (bases) to form salts, and dissolve metals to form salts.

Alkali: Any compound that has chemical qualities of a base, such as reacting with acid to form salts.

Atomic Weight (Mass): The relative mass of an atom, based on a scale in which a specific carbon atom is assigned a mass value of 12.

Base: An alkaline substance, either molecular or ionic in form, that will accept or receive a proton from another chemical unit.

Catalyst: A substance that accelerates a chemical reaction without becoming a part of the end product of the reaction.

Compound: A substance formed by the combination of two or more chemical elements that cannot be separated from the combination by physical means. The constituent atoms, however, can usually be separated by means of chemical reactions.

Electron: A negatively charged particle that moves in orbit about the nucleus of an atom.

Element: A substance composed of atoms with the same atomic number or the same number of protons in their nuclei.

Isotope: One of two or more atoms having the same atomic number, but a different mass number.

Mass Number: The atomic weight of an isotope, calculated from the number of protons and neutrons in the nucleus.

Matter: Anything that has weight or fills space, such as a solid, liquid or gas.

Polymer: A huge molecule composed of repeating units of the same molecule.

Valence: A number that represents the combining power of an element, ion or radical.

Common Physics Terms

Acceleration: The rate of change of velocity with respect to time.

Anode: The positive terminal of an electric current flow. In a vacuum tube, electrons flow from the cathode to the anode.

Cathode: The negative terminal of an electric current system. In vacuum tube, the filament serves as the source electrons.

Conduction: The transfer of heat by molecular motion from a source of high temperature to a region of lower temperature, tending towards a result of equalized temperatures.

Convection: The mechanical transfer of heated molecules of a gas or liquid from a source to another area, as when a room is warmed by the movement of air molecules heated by a radiator.

Electromotive Force: The force that causes the movement of electrons through an electrical circuit.

Energy: The ability to perform work. Energy may be changed from one form to another, as from heat to light, but normally it cannot be created or destroyed.

Force: The influence on a body that causes it to accelerate.

Heat: A form of energy that results from the disordered motion of molecules. As the motion becomes more rapid and disordered, the amount of heat is increased.

Mass: A measure of the amount of matter. Near the surface of the Earth, it is roughly equivalent to weight.

Momentum: The mathematical product of the mass of a moving object and its velocity.

Velocity: The speed with which an object travels over a specified distance during a measured amount of time.

Weight: The force on a body produced by the downward pull of gravity on it.

Basic Laws of Physics

■ Newton's Laws of Motion

Newton's laws apply to objects in a vacuum, and are difficult to observe in the "real" world where forces such as friction affect all objects.

First Law: Any object at rest tends to stay at rest, and a body in motion will continue that motion with a constant velocity unless acted upon by some external unbalanced force.

Second Law: The acceleration of an object is directly proportional to the force acting upon it, and is inversely proportional to the mass of the object.

Third Law: Every action generates an equal and opposite reaction.

■ Gravity

When an object is dropped near the surface of the Earth, it increases in speed as it falls. By rolling balls down inclined planes Galileo discovered that acceleration due to gravity is the same for all objects, independent of their weight (mass). For example, if you drop this book and a brick simultaneously, they will reach to floor at the same time. You can try the same experiment with a heavy book and a single sheet of paper. The paper is affected by the resistance of the air. Then crumple the paper, and try again.

Gravity is the force that tends to attract objects to the centre of a celestial body, such as the Earth, the moon or Mars. The weight of an object at the Earth's surface is mainly due to the force of gravity between the Earth and the object. The force exerted by the Earth varies with the object's distance from the centre of the Earth. Therefore the weight of an object is not the same at the Earth's surface as it is on the moon or in space.

■ Laws of Thermodynamics

Sadi Carnot (1796–1832) stated in his work *Reflections on the Motive Power of Fire* that mechanical energy could be produced by the simple transfer of heat.

First Law: In a closed system, energy appears to be conserved in all but nuclear reactions and other extreme conditions.

Second Law: In a closed system, heat never travels from a low to a higher temperature in a self sustaining process. In a closed system, entropy (disorder) always increases.

■ Two Basic Laws of Quantum Physics

Heisenberg's Uncertainty Principle: It is impossible to specify completely the position and momentum of a particle, such as an electron.

Pauli's Exclusion Principle: No two electrons of the same atom can have identical values for all four quantum numbers: at least one quantum number must be different.

Loudness of Sounds

Sound is measured in decibels. A decibel is a unit for measuring the relative intensity of a sound, equal to one-tenth of a bel. A bel indicates the amount of energy in the form of sound transmitted to one square centimetre of the ear. The bel was named after Alexander Graham Bell.

The decibel scale advances geometrically instead of arithmetically. Twenty decibels represents not twice as much noise as ten, but 10 times as much. The 80-decibel level of a pneumatic drill is 100 times as noisy as the 60-decibel level of a quiet motor.

Source: *Dictionary of Science, Barnhardt, American Heritage Series*

Intensity (decibels)	Loudness	Intensity (decibels)	Loudness
0	Threshold of hearing	70	Loud conversation
10 (1 bel)	Virtual silence	80	Door slamming
20	Quiet room	90	Busy typing room
30	Watch ticking at 1 m	100	Near loud motor horn
40	Quiet street	110	Pneumatic drill
50	Quiet conversation	120	Near airplane engine
60	Quiet motor at 1 m	130	Threshold of pain

The Elements

An element is a substance composed of atoms that are chemically alike—each atom has an identical number of protons in its nucleus. Furthermore, there is no known process to break these elements down into more fundamental substances.

Name	Symbol	Number	Name	Symbol	Number	Name	Symbol	Number
actinium	Ac	89	gold	Au	79	potassium	K	19
aluminum	Al	13	hafnium	Hf	72	praseodymium . .	Pr	59
americium	Am	95	hassium	Hs	108	promethium.	Pm	61
antimony	Sb	51	helium	He	2	protactinium	Pa	91
argon.	Ar	18	holmium	Ho	67	radium	Ra	88
arsenic.	As	33	hydrogen	H	1	radon.	Rn	86
astatine	At	85	indium	In	49	rhenium.	Re	75
barium	Ba	56	iodine	I	53	rhodium.	Rh	45
berkelium	Bk	97	iridium	Ir	77	roentgenium	Rg	111
beryllium	Be	4	iron	Fe	26	rubidium	Rb	37
bismuth	Bi	83	krypton	Kr	36	ruthenium	Ru	44
bohrium.	Bh	107	lanthanum	La	57	rutherfordium . . .	Rf	104
boron.	B	5	lawrencium	Lr	103	samarium	Sm	62
bromine.	Br	35	lead	Pb	82	scandium.	Sc	21
cadmium	Cd	48	lithium	Li	3	seaborgium	Sg	106
calcium	Ca	20	lutetium	Lu	71	selenium	Se	34
californium	Cf	98	magnesium	Mg	12	silicon	Si	14
carbon	C	6	manganese	Mn	25	silver	Ag	47
cerium	Ce	58	meitnerium	Mt	109	sodium	Na	11
cesium.	Cs	55	mendelevium	Md	101	strontium.	Sr	38
chlorine	Cl	17	mercury	Hg	80	sulfur.	S	16
chromium	Cr	24	molybdenum	Mo	42	tantalum	Ta	73
cobalt	Co	27	neodymium	Nd	60	technetium	Tc	43
copper	Cu	29	neon	Ne	10	tellurium	Te	52
curium	Cm	96	neptunium	Np	93	terbium	Tb	65
darnstadtium	Ds	110	nickel	Ni	28	thallium	Tl	81
dubnium	Db	105	niobium	Nb	41	thorium	Th	90
dysprosium	Dy	66	nitrogen	N	7	thulium	Tm	69
einsteinium	Es	99	nobelium	No	102	tin	Sn	50
erbium	Er	68	osmium	Os	76	titanium	Ti	22
europium	Eu	63	oxygen	O	8	tungsten	W	74
fermium	Fm	100	palladium	Pd	46	ununbium*	Uub	112
fluorine	F	9	phosphorus	P	15	ununquadium* . .	Uuq	114
francium	Fr	87	platinum	Pt	78	ununhexium*	Uuh	116
gadolinium	Gd	64	plutonium	Pu	94	ununoctium*	Uuo	118
gallium	Ga	31	polonium	Po	84	uranium	U	92
germanium	Ge	32				vanadium.	V	23
						xenon	Xe	54
						ytterbium.	Yb	70
						yttrium.	Y	39
						zinc	Zn	30
						zirconium	Zr	40

*temporary name

What is the Periodic Table?

*T*he *Periodic Table of Elements (shown on the next page) has its roots in the 19th century when chemists calculated how much one atom of an element weighed in comparison to another. The resulting weight was known as the atomic mass and measured in atomic mass units (amu). (An amu is a mass equal to ¹⁄₁₂ of the mass of the most common form of carbon atom.) As the list of elements was compiled and ranked in order of mass, chemists noted that every seven or eight elements had similar properties.*

By 1869 Dimitri Mendeleyev was confident enough to rearrange the list of elements to group those with similar properties and leave blanks for the missing ones. Mendeleyev only had 63 elements; the table now has 110 named elements (some artificially created) and at least five others have been found but not named.

Early in the 20th century, the table was further refined when atoms were found to be made up of protons and electrons. The number of protons and electrons is equal in one atom and this number was designated the element's atomic number. The table now shows the elements in order according to their atomic number and their atomic mass.

Periodic Table of Elements

transition metals

non-metals

other metals

gases

rare earth elements

1 H 1.00																	2 He 4.00
3 Li 6.94	4 Be 9.01											5 B 10.81	6 C 12.01	7 N 14.01	8 O 15.99	9 F 18.99	10 Ne 20.18
11 Na 22.98	12 Mg 24.30											13 Al 26.98	14 Si 28.08	15 P 30.97	16 S 32.06	17 Cl 35.45	18 Ar 39.95
19 K 39.09	20 Ca 40.08	21 Sc 44.95	22 Ti 47.88	23 V 50.94	24 Cr 51.99	25 Mn 54.94	26 Fe 55.84	27 Co 58.93	28 Ni 58.69	29 Cu 63.54	30 Zn 65.39	31 Ga 69.72	32 Ge 72.61	33 As 74.92	34 Se 78.96	35 Br 79.90	36 Kr 83.80
37 Rb 85.46	38 Sr 87.62	39 Y 88.90	40 Zr 91.22	41 Nb 92.91	42 Mo 95.94	43 Tc (98)	44 Ru 101.07	45 Rh 102.91	46 Pd 106.42	47 Ag 107.87	48 Cd 112.41	49 In 114.82	50 Sn 118.71	51 Sb 121.76	52 Te 127.60	53 I 126.90	54 Xe 131.29
55 Cs 132.90	56 Ba 137.33	71 Lu 174.97	72 Hf 178.49	73 Ta 180.95	74 W 183.84	75 Re 186.21	76 Os 190.2	77 Ir 192.22	78 Pt 195.08	79 Au 196.90	80 Hg 200.59	81 Tl 204.38	82 Pb 207.2	83 Bi 208.98	84 Po (209)	85 At (210)	86 Rn (222)
87 Fr (223)	88 Ra 226.02	103 Lr (262)	104 Rf (263)	105 Db (262)	106 Sg (266)	107 Bh (264)	108 Hs (269)	109 Mt (268)	110 Ds (271)	111 Rg (272)	112 Uub (277)	114 Uuq (289)			116 Uuh (289)		118 Uuo (293)

lanthanoids

57 La 138.91	58 Ce 140.12	59 Pr 140.91	60 Nd 144.24	61 Pm (145)	62 Sm 150.36	63 Eu 151.96	64 Gd 157.25	65 Tb 158.93	66 Dy 162.50	67 Ho 164.93	68 Er 167.26	69 Tm 168.93	70 Yb 173.04

actinoids

89 Ac 227.03	90 Th 232.04	91 Pa 231.04	92 U 238.03	93 Np 237.05	94 Pu (244)	95 Am (243)	96 Cm (247)	97 Bk (247)	98 Cf (251)	99 Es (252)	100 Fm (257)	101 Md (258)	102 No (259)

This is a table which shows the properties of the elements, in the order of their atomic mass or number, and arranged in horizontal rows (periods) and vertical columns (groups) to illustrate the occurence of similarities in the structure of their atoms. When the elements are arranged in this order, their chemical and physical properties show repeatable trends. This pattern in properties occurs periodically; that is, the pattern is repeated in an orderly manner over time.

The order of the elements is that of their atomic numbers, the integers which are equal to the positive electrical charges of the atomic nuclei expressed in electronic units. Elements that are listed with their atomic weights in brackets are radioactive and have variable weights. Since the various isotopes weigh differently at different times due to decay (that is, an isotope will be heavier at its creation than later on), the atomic mass of the most stable isotope is listed.

Canadian Light Source

In one corner of the University of Saskatchewan's campus is Canada's biggest science project in decades—the Canadian Light Source (CLS). With a price-tag of $174 million, the CLS is giving Canadian scientists a cutting-edge tool for research ranging from archaeology to zoology.

The CLS is a synchrotron—a device for creating intense beams of light that can be used to probe deep inside almost anything, showing details hidden to other methods of investigation. It has been described as a "Swiss army knife" for scientific research because of its enormous versatility.

Information obtained by scientists using the synchrotron can be employed to help design new drugs, examine the structure of surfaces in order to develop more effective motor oils, build more powerful computer chips, develop new materials for safer medical implants, and help with clean-up of mining wastes, to name just a few applications.

■ Research Tool

Indeed, Canadian scientists already use synchrotrons in other countries—even Brazil, Korea and Taiwan have their own—because they have become indispensable in many areas of research. For example:

• Mineralogist Jenne Percival of Natural Resources Canada wants to use the CLS to study how uranium binds to clay. This will have important implications for the way uranium mining is done.

• Biochemist Michele Loewen of the National Research Council is using offshore synchrotrons to study the behaviour of proteins. She's looking forward to doing the work in Canada.

• Geochemist Alan Anderson of St. Francis Xavier University wants to use the CLS to study how ore deposits are formed by hot fluids, which may shed light on where to develop new mines.

The synchrotron is based on some fundamental facts of physics. First, a moving electron (or any subatomic particle) that is forced to change direction will lose energy. Second, that energy comes in packets called photons, the particles of light.

■ Brighter Than Sunlight

The CLS speeds billions of electrons up to nearly the speed of light, using microwave energy. Then the (now highly energetic) electrons are sent into a large ring, 171.5 metres in circumference, where they are propelled in a multi-sided near-circle by 24 guide magnets, as well as by 108 smaller focussing magnets. Every time the electrons pass one of the guide magnets, they change direction, forcing them to emit photons, in a beam millions of times as bright as sunlight.

A similar phenomenon happens every winter, when charged particles from the sun approach the earth in a straight line. But when they hit the earth's magnetic field, they are forced into a spiral motion and begin shedding the photons that we see as the northern lights.

The difference is that the CLS lets researchers capture, tune, and use different parts of the light spectrum, from infrared to x-rays, in what are called "beamlines." In principle, the CLS could have a beamline for every guide magnet and still more to use light created when the focussing magnets herd the electrons back into line.

Initially, however, only seven are being built, with more being added later as money is available and demand grows. The first seven are:

• High Resolution Far-Infrared Spectroscopy
• Mid-Infrared Microscopy
• Plane Grating Monochromator
• Spherical Grating Monochromator
• Soft X-ray Spectromicroscopy
• Macromolecular Protein Crystallography
• X-ray Absorption Spectroscopy with Microprobe Capabilities.

▶

▶ The first seven beamlines are either working or under construction; another five have been approved and money allocated. Because of the beamlines, publicity for the CLS often calls it "Canada's Field of Beams."

More than 2,000 academic and industrial researchers a year from across Canada and from other countries are expected to use the facility once the full complement of beamlines is developed.

■ Wide Range of Support

The University of Saskatchewan is the home of the CLS, but dozens of other Canadian universities are supporting it, as well as industrial partners, such as the pharmaceutical giant GlaxoSmithKline, and research organizations, such as the Canadian Institute for Health Research.

The CLS began as an idea floated by the Natural Sciences and Engineering Council, Canada's largest scientific granting council, in 1994. Two years later, an international committee recommended the bid put together by the University of Saskatchewan. And in 1999, the Canada Foundation for Innovation gave the green light, when it announced a $56.4-million contribution toward building costs.

That was slightly more than a third of the $141 million needed to construct the machine and the building to house it (an existing building and equipment accounted for the other $33 million of the $174 million price-tag).

So the CLS consortium had to raise the rest; it came from various sources, including $2.4 million from the city of Saskatoon, $500,000 for the drug company Boehringer Ingelheim, $25 million from the Saskatchewan government, and so on.

■ "Third-Generation" Synchrotron

The CLS is one of only 17 "third-generation" synchrotrons either in existence or planned. Third-generation synchrotrons have devices inserted to produce even more light from the electron stream. This makes it possible to do such things as medical imaging faster and cheaper and to "see" much smaller entities than has been possible before.

This first-in-Canada 2.9 GeV (giga-electron volt) synchrotron light source will be fully competitive with the best available internationally and is expected to attract industrial and academic researchers from coast to coast.

■ Reverse "Brain Drain"

Indeed, a reverse brain drain began happening even before the CLS was ready to start work. Physicist Dean Chapman of the Illinois Institute of Technology, world-renowned for his use of synchrotron light in medical and biological applications, agreed to relocate to Saskatoon. CLS Director Bill Tomlinson, with more than 25 years of experience in developing synchrotrons, came from the European Synchrotron Radiation Facility. All told, more than 25 researchers have moved to the University of Saskatchewan to take advantage of the CLS, and still others have taken up posts at nearby universities.

As well, an independent consulting firm estimated in 1996 that the CLS, once it's running, will attract $35 million a year to Canada in commercial research and development spending, add $12 million a year to Canada's gross domestic product and create 200 permanent jobs.

Building the CLS was an engineering challenge. Because it must be absolutely rock-steady, the main hall that houses the machine is anchored by 632 concrete piles driven between 10 and 20 metres into the Prairie soil. The main hall itself has an area of 6,806 square metres or about 1.7 acres—that's roughly the same size as four double tennis courts or 50 sheets of curling ice. But that's still only about half the area of the whole facility, including office space and other areas.

Building the structure took 7,000 cubic metres of concrete—enough for 160 new 1,200-square-foot homes. That's equivalent to 1,200 truckloads of concrete, weighing about 16,800 tonnes. Also needed was 1,300 tonnes of steel to frame the building and 5,280 square metres of wall sheathing.

The CLS Web site is at www.lightsource.ca

The International System of Units (SI)

The Systeme Internationale (SI) or metric system was developed in France in 1799. By 1880 many European countries and much of South America had adopted the system as a common language of measurements.

The pressures of global trade have persuaded many of the English-speaking countries to adopt a uniform international standard of measure. Canada adopted the metric system in 1970.

Name	Symbol	Quantity
■ SI Base Units		
metre	m	length
kilogram	kg	mass
second	s	time
ampere	A	electric current
kelvin	K	thermodynamic temperature
mole.............	mol	amount of substance
candela..........	cd	luminous intensity
■ SI Supplementary Units		
radian	rad	plane angle
steradian	sr	solid angle
■ Common SI Derived Units With Special Names		
hertz	Hz	frequency
pascal	Pa	pressure, stress
wall	W	power, radiant flux
volt	V	electric potential, electromotive force
newton	N	force
joule	J	energy, work
coulomb	C	electric charge
ohm	Ω	electric resistance
farad	F	electric capacitance
■ Common Units Used With the SI		
litre.............	L	volume or capacity ($= 1$ dm^3)
degree Celsius	°C	temperature ($= 1$ K; 0°C $= 273.2$ K)

	Symbol	Quantity
hectare	ha	area ($= 10\ 000$ m^2)
tonne	t	mass ($= 1000$ kg)
electronvolt........	eV	energy ($= 0.160$ aJ)
nautical mile.......	M	distance (navigation) ($= 1852$ m)
knot	kn	speed (navigation) ($= 1$ M/h)
standard atmosphere	atm	atmospheric pressure ($= 101.3$ kPa)

■ SI Prefixes

Name	Symbol	Multiplying Factor*
exa-	E	10^{18}
peta-.............	P	10^{15}
tera-	T	10^{12}
giga-.............	G	10^{9}
mega-.............	M	10^{6}
kilo-.............	k	10^{3}
hecto-............	h	10^{2}
deca-	da	10
deci-.............	d	10^{-1}
centi-.............	c	10^{-2}
milli-	m	10^{-3}
micro-	μ	10^{-6}
nano-	n	10^{-9}
pico-.............	p	10^{-12}
femto-.............	f	10^{-15}
atto-	a	10^{-18}

*$10^2 = 100$; $10^3 = 1\ 000$; $10^{-1} = 0.1$; $10^{-2} = 0.01$; Thus, 2 km = $2 \times 1\ 000 = 2\ 000$ m ; 3 cm = $3 \times 0.01 = 0.03$ m

Source: *Gage Canadian Dictionary*

Large Numbers

1 thousand	1 000
1 million..	1 000 000 or 10^6
1 milliard: used in Europe, USSR, former French possessions	1 000 000 000 or 10^9
1 billion:	1 000 000 000 000 or 10^{12}
—Canada, the United States and France	1 000 000 000 or 10^9
1 trillion:	1 000 000 000 000 000 000 or 10^{18}
—Canada and the United States......................................	1 000 000 000 000 or 10^{12}

Source: *World Weights and Measures*

Science Centres and Museums

Maritime Region:

☐ **Discovery Centre**
1593 Barrington St., Halifax, NS. Open daily.
Tel: (902) 492-4422.
Web site: www.discoverycentre.ns.ca

☐ **Newfoundland Science Centre**
5 Beck's Cove, St. John's. A1C 5N5
Tel: (709) 754-0823. Open all year.
Web site: www.nlsciencecentre.com

☐ **Nova Scotia Museum of Natural History**
1747 Summer St., Halifax, NS B3H 3A6
Tel: (902) 424-7353. Closed Monday in winter.
Web site: www.museum.gov.ns.ca/mnh

☐ **Science East**
668 Brunswick St., Fredericton, NB.E3B 1H6
Tel: (506) 457-2340. Open all year.
Web site: www.scienceeast.nb.ca

Central Canada:

☐ **Montreal Science Centre**
333 Commune St. W. Montreal H2Y 2E2
Tel: (514) 496-1960. Open all year.
Web site: www.centredessciencesdemontreal.com

☐ **Museum of Visual Science and Optometry**
200 University Ave. W., Waterloo, ON N2L 3G1.
Open weekdays. Web site:
www.optometry.uwaterloo.ca/~museum

☐ **National Museum of Science and Technology**
1867 St. Laurent Blvd, Ottawa, ON K1G 5A3.
Tel: (613) 991-3044. Open all year.
Web site: www.science-tech.technomuses.ca

☐ **Ontario Science Centre**
7770 Don Mills Rd, Toronto, ON M3C 1T3.
Tel : (416) 429-4100. Open all year.
Web site: www.ontariosciencecentre.ca/

☐ **Science North**
100 Ramsey Lake Rd, Sudbury, ON P3E 5S9.
Tel: (705) 522-3701. Open all year.
Web site: www.sciencenorth.ca

Western Canada:

☐ **Calgary Science Centre**
701-11 Street S.W., Calgary, AB T2P 2M5.
Tel: (403) 268-8300. Open all year.
Web site: www.calgaryscience.ca

☐ **Manitoba Children's Museum**
45 Forks Market Rd., Winnipeg MB R3C 4T6
Tel: (204) 924-4000. Open all year.
Web site: www.childrensmuseum.com

☐ **The Manitoba Museum**
190 Rupert Ave., Winnipeg MB R3B 0N2
Tel: (204) 956-2830. Open all year.
Web site: www.manitobamuseum.mb.ca

☐ **Odyssium**
11211-142 St., Edmonton, AB T5M 4A1.
Tel: (403) 452-9100. Open all year.
Web site: www.odyssium.com

☐ **Oil Sands Discovery Centre**
515 MacKenzie Blvd. Fort McMurray, AB T9H 4X3
Tel: (780) 743-7167. Closed Mondays in winter.
Web site: www.oilsandsdiscovery.com

☐ **Okanagan Science Centre**
2704 Highway 6, Vernon, BC V1T 5G5.
Tel : (250) 545-3644. Closed Mondays.
Web site: www.okscience.ca

☐ **Saskatchewan Science Centre**
2903 Powerhouse Dr., Regina, SK S4N 0A1.
Tel: 1-800-667-6300. Open all year.
Web site: www.sasksciencecentre.com

☐ **Science World**
1455 Quebec St., Vancouver, BC V6A 3Z7.
Tel: (604) 443-7440. Open all year. Web site:
www.scienceworld.bc.ca

Shocking Research Points to Ways to Protect Technology

*T*oronto's 553-metre-high CN Tower is acting as a lightning laboratory, teaching scientists how to protect delicate electronic equipment against high-voltage surges. Lightning strikes the tower an average of 75 times a year and is directed into the ground by metallic conductors, linked to 42 grounding rods buried deep in the nearby soil. But the unusual shape of the tower's observation decks obstructs the downward flow of electricity and causes the current to peak in certain areas, University of Toronto researcher Wasyl Janischewskyj and his colleagues found. The ability to identify such patterns will be critical to designing protective measures for sensitive electronic equipment, he said, both on tall buildings and in mountainous regions. "More and more electronic equipment has very sensitive components," Janischewskyj said. "Even a small over-voltage can cause equipment to malfunction." The research at the CN Tower, he said, "gives us a better understanding of … a lightning strike to a tall structure [and] can help designers incorporate the appropriate precautions."

Source: *University of Toronto*

SCIENCE AT WORK

Individual Canadians have been awarded recognition in the ranks of the world's pre-eminent scientists and researchers, as our lists of Nobel Prize winners and the Canadian Engineering and Science Hall of Fame both show.

Canadian Nobel Laureates in Science and Medicine

1923	Drs. Banting, Macleod and Collip	Medicine and Physiology	For the discovery of insulin
1971	Dr. Gerhard Herzberg	Chemistry	For his contributions to the knowledge of electronic structure, particularly free radicals
1986	Dr. John Polanyi	Chemistry	For contributions concerning the dynamics of elementary chemical reactions
1993	Dr. Michael Smith	Chemistry	Co-winner for work on genetic codes
1994	Bertram Brockhouse	Physics	Co-winner for study on atoms

2003 Nobel Prize Winners

Each October, the Swedish academies for physics, chemistry and medicine announce the winners of the Nobel prizes in science. The awards are named after Alfred Nobel, the Swedish-born chemist and businessman who invented dynamite and smokeless gunpowder. The science prizes, as well as one for literature and one for peace, are financed by an endowment from Nobel's estate. The prize for economics is financed by the Swedish national bank.

In 2003, the prize for literature went to South African writer J.M. Coetzee. The peace prize was awarded to Iranian lawyer, judge, lecturer, writer and activist Shirin Ebadi for her efforts on behalf of democracy and human rights. The economics prize went to two American economists, Robert F. Engle and Clive W.J. Granger, for their work analyzing economic trends over time.

For their contributions to the theory of superconductors and superfluids, the 2003 Nobel Prize in physics went to Alexei A. Abrikosov, of the Argonne National Laboratory in Illinois; Vitaly L. Ginzburg of the P.N. Lebedev Physical Institute, Moscow; and Anthony J. Leggett, of the University of Illinois at Urbana, Illinois. The Nobel in chemistry went to Peter Agre, of Johns Hopkins University School of Medicine, Baltimore, and Roderick MacKinnon of the Rockefeller University, New York, "for discoveries concerning channels in cell membranes." And the 2003 Nobel prize in physiology or medicine went to Paul C. Lauterbur, also of the University of Illinois at Urbana, and Peter Mansfield of the University of Nottingham, Nottingham, U.K. for their work on magnetic resonance imaging.

For more information, see www.nobel.se.

Nobel Prize in Physics

2003 Alexei A. Abrikosov, Vitaly L. Ginzburg, Anthony J. Leggett
2002 Raymond Davis Jr., Masatoshi Koshiba, Riccardo Giacconi
2001 Eric A. Cornell, Wolfgang Ketterle, Carl E. Wieman
2000 Zhores I. Alferov, Herbert Kroemer, Jack S. Kilby
1999 Gerardus 't Hooft, Martinus J.G. Veltman
1998 Robert B. Laughlin, Horst L. Störmer, Daniel C. Tsui
1997 Steven Chu, Claude Cohen-Tannoudji, William D. Phillips
1996 David M. Lee, Douglas D. Osheroff, Robert C. Richardson
1995 Martin L. Perl, Frederick Reines
1994 Bertram N. Brockhouse, Clifford G. Shull
1993 Russell A. Hulse, Joseph H. Taylor Jr.
1992 Georges Charpak

▶

▶ 1991 Pierre-Gilles de Gennes
1990 Jerome I. Friedman, Henry W. Kendall, Richard E. Taylor
1989 Norman F. Ramsey, Hans G. Dehmelt, Wolfgang Paul
1988 Leon M. Lederman, Melvin Schwartz, Jack Steinberger
1987 J. Georg Bednorz, K. Alex Müller
1986 Ernst Ruska, Gerd Binnig, Heinrich Rohrer
1985 Klaus von Klitzing
1984 Carlo Rubbia, Simon van der Meer
1983 Subramanyan Chandrasekhar, William A. Fowler
1982 Kenneth G. Wilson
1981 Nicolaas Bloembergen, Arthur L. Schawlow, Kai M. Siegbahn
1980 James Cronin, Val Fitch
1979 Sheldon Glashow, Abdus Salam, Steven Weinberg
1978 Pyotr Kapitsa, Arno Penzias, Robert Woodrow Wilson
1977 Philip W. Anderson, Sir Nevill F. Mott, John H. van Vleck
1976 Burton Richter, Samuel C.C. Ting
1975 Aage N. Bohr, Ben R. Mottelson, James Rainwater
1974 Martin Ryle, Antony Hewish
1973 Leo Esaki, Ivar Giaever, Brian D. Josephson
1972 John Bardeen, Leon N. Cooper, Robert Schrieffer
1971 Dennis Gabor
1970 Hannes Alfvén, Louis Néel
1969 Murray Gell-Mann
1968 Luis Alvarez
1967 Hans Bethe
1966 Alfred Kastler
1965 Sin-Itiro Tomonaga, Julian Schwinger, Richard P. Feynman
1964 Charles H. Townes, Nicolay G. Basov, Aleksandr M. Prokhorov
1963 Eugene Wigner, Maria Goeppert-Mayer, J. Hans D. Jensen
1962 Lev Landau
1961 Robert Hofstadter, Rudolf Mössbauer
1960 Donald A. Glaser
1959 Emilio Segrè, Owen Chamberlain
1958 Pavel A. Cherenkov, Il´ja M. Frank, Igor Y. Tamm
1957 Chen Ning Yang, Tsung-Dao Lee
1956 William B. Shockley, John Bardeen, Walter H. Brattain
1955 Willis E. Lamb, Polykarp Kusch
1954 Max Born, Walther Bothe
1953 Frits Zernike
1952 Felix Bloch, E. M. Purcell
1951 John Cockcroft, Ernest T.S. Walton
1950 Cecil Powell
1949 Hideki Yukawa

1948 Patrick M.S. Blackett
1947 Edward V. Appleton
1946 Percy W. Bridgman
1945 Wolfgang Pauli
1944 Isidor Isaac Rabi
1943 Otto Stern
1942 The prize money was ⅓ allocated to the Main Fund and ⅔ to the special Fund of this prize section
1941 The prize money was ⅓ allocated to the Main Fund and ⅔ to the special Fund of this prize section
1940 The prize money was ⅓ allocated to the Main Fund and ⅔ to the special Fund of this prize section
1939 Ernest Lawrence
1938 Enrico Fermi
1937 Clinton Davisson, George Paget Thomson
1936 Victor F. Hess, Carl D. Anderson
1935 James Chadwick
1934 The prize money was ⅓ allocated to the Main Fund and ⅔ to the special Fund of this prize section
1933 Erwin Schrödinger, Paul A.M. Dirac
1932 Werner Heisenberg
1931 The prize money was allocated to the Special Fund of this prize section
1930 Venkata Raman
1929 Louis de Broglie
1928 Owen Willans Richardson
1927 Arthur H. Compton, C.T.R. Wilson
1926 Jean Baptiste Perrin
1925 James Franck, Gustav Hertz
1924 Manne Siegbahn
1923 Robert A. Millikan
1922 Niels Bohr
1921 Albert Einstein
1920 Charles Edouard Guillaume
1919 Johannes Stark
1918 Max Planck
1917 Charles Glover Barkla
1916 The prize money was allocated to the Special Fund of this prize section
1915 William Bragg, Lawrence Bragg
1914 Max von Laue
1913 Heike Kamerlingh Onnes
1912 Gustaf Dalén
1911 Wilhelm Wien
1910 Johannes Diderik van der Waals
1909 Guglielmo Marconi, Ferdinand Braun
1908 Gabriel Lippmann
1907 Albert A. Michelson
1906 J.J. Thomson
1905 Philipp Lenard
1904 Lord Rayleigh

1903 Henri Becquerel, Pierre Curie, Marie Curie
1902 Hendrik A. Lorentz, Pieter Zeeman
1901 Wilhelm Conrad Röntgen

Nobel Prize in Chemistry

2003 Peter Agre, Roderick MacKinnon
2002 John B. Fenn, Koichi Tanaka, Kurt Wüthrich
2001 William S. Knowles, Ryoji Noyori, K. Barry Sharpless
2000 Alan Heeger, Alan G. MacDiarmid, Hideki Shirakawa
1999 Ahmed Zewail
1998 Walter Kohn, John Pople
1997 Paul D. Boyer, John E. Walker, Jens C. Skou
1996 Robert F. Curl Jr., Sir Harold Kroto, Richard E. Smalley
1995 Paul J. Crutzen, Mario J. Molina, F. Sherwood Rowland
1994 George A. Olah
1993 Kary B. Mullis, Michael Smith
1992 Rudolph A. Marcus
1991 Richard R. Ernst
1990 Elias James Corey
1989 Sidney Altman, Thomas R. Cech
1988 Johann Deisenhofer, Robert Huber, Hartmut Michel
1987 Donald J. Cram, Jean-Marie Lehn, Charles J. Pedersen
1986 Dudley R. Herschbach, Yuan T. Lee, John C. Polanyi
1985 Herbert A. Hauptman, Jerome Karle
1984 Bruce Merrifield
1983 Henry Taube
1982 Aaron Klug
1981 Kenichi Fukui, Roald Hoffmann
1980 Paul Berg, Walter Gilbert, Frederick Sanger
1979 Herbert C. Brown, Georg Wittig
1978 Peter Mitchell
1977 Ilya Prigogine
1976 William Lipscomb
1975 John Cornforth, Vladimir Prelog
1974 Paul J. Flory
1973 Ernst Otto Fischer, Geoffrey Wilkinson
1972 Christian Anfinsen, Stanford Moore, William H. Stein
1971 Gerhard Herzberg
1970 Luis Leloir
1969 Derek Barton, Odd Hassel
1968 Lars Onsager
1967 Manfred Eigen, Ronald G.W. Norrish, George Porter

1966 Robert S. Mulliken
1965 Robert B. Woodward
1964 Dorothy Crowfoot Hodgkin
1963 Karl Ziegler, Giulio Natta
1962 Max F. Perutz, John C. Kendrew
1961 Melvin Calvin
1960 Willard F. Libby
1959 Jaroslav Heyrovsky
1958 Frederick Sanger
1957 Lord Todd
1956 Sir Cyril Hinshelwood, Nikolay Semenov
1955 Vincent du Vigneaud
1954 Linus Pauling
1953 Hermann Staudinger
1952 Archer J.P. Martin, Richard L.M. Synge
1951 Edwin M. McMillan, Glenn T. Seaborg
1950 Otto Diels, Kurt Alder
1949 William F. Giauque
1948 Arne Tiselius
1947 Sir Robert Robinson
1946 James B. Sumner, John H. Northrop, Wendell M. Stanley
1945 Artturi Virtanen
1944 Otto Hahn
1943 George de Hevesy
1942 The prize money was $\frac{1}{3}$ allocated to the Main Fund and $\frac{2}{3}$ to the special Fund of this prize section
1941 The prize money was $\frac{1}{3}$ allocated to the Main Fund and $\frac{2}{3}$ to the special Fund of this prize section
1940 The prize money was $\frac{1}{3}$ allocated to the Main Fund and $\frac{2}{3}$ to the special Fund of this prize section
1939 Adolf Butenandt, Leopold Ruzicka
1938 Richard Kuhn
1937 Norman Haworth, Paul Karrer
1936 Peter Debye
1935 Frédéric Joliot, Irène Joliot-Curie
1934 Harold C. Urey
1933 The prize money was $\frac{1}{3}$ allocated to the Main Fund and $\frac{2}{3}$ to the Special Fund of this prize section
1932 Irving Langmuir
1931 Carl Bosch, Friedrich Bergius
1930 Hans Fischer
1929 Arthur Harden, Hans von Euler-Chelpin
1928 Adolf Windaus
1927 Heinrich Wieland
1926 The Svedberg
1925 Richard Zsigmondy
1924 The prize money was allocated to the Special Fund of this prize section
1923 Fritz Pregl

1922 Francis W. Aston
1921 Frederick Soddy
1920 Walther Nernst
1919 The prize money was allocated to the Special Fund of this prize section
1918 Fritz Haber
1917 The prize money was allocated to the Special Fund of this prize section
1916 The prize money was allocated to the Special Fund of this prize section
1915 Richard Willstätter
1914 Theodore W. Richards
1913 Alfred Werner
1912 Victor Grignard, Paul Sabatier
1911 Marie Curie
1910 Otto Wallach
1909 Wilhelm Ostwald
1908 Ernest Rutherford
1907 Eduard Buchner
1906 Henri Moissan
1905 Adolf von Baeyer
1904 Sir William Ramsay
1903 Svante Arrhenius
1902 Emil Fischer
1901 Jacobus H. van 't Hoff

Nobel Prize in Physiology or Medicine

2003 Paul C. Lauterbur, Sir Peter Mansfield
2002 Sydney Brenner, H. Robert Horvitz, John E. Sulston
2001 Leland H. Hartwell, Tim Hunt, Sir Paul Nurse
2000 Arvid Carlsson, Paul Greengard, Eric R. Kandel
1999 Günter Blobel
1998 Robert F. Furchgott, Louis J. Ignarro, Ferid Murad
1997 Stanley B. Prusiner
1996 Peter C. Doherty, Rolf M. Zinkernagel
1995 Edward B. Lewis, Christiane Nüsslein-Volhard, Eric F. Wieschaus
1994 Alfred G. Gilman, Martin Rodbell
1993 Richard J. Roberts, Phillip A. Sharp
1992 Edmond H. Fischer, Edwin G. Krebs
1991 Erwin Neher, Bert Sakmann
1990 Joseph E. Murray, E. Donnall Thomas
1989 J. Michael Bishop, Harold E. Varmus
1988 Sir James W. Black, Gertrude B. Elion, George H. Hitchings
1987 Susumu Tonegawa
1986 Stanley Cohen, Rita Levi-Montalcini
1985 Michael S. Brown, Joseph L. Goldstein
1984 Niels K. Jerne, Georges J.F. Köhler, César Milstein
1983 Barbara McClintock

1982 Sune K. Bergström, Bengt I. Samuelsson, John R. Vane
1981 Roger W. Sperry, David H. Hubel, Torsten N. Wiesel
1980 Baruj Benacerraf, Jean Dausset, George D. Snell
1979 Allan M. Cormack, Godfrey N. Hounsfield
1978 Werner Arber, Daniel Nathans, Hamilton O. Smith
1977 Roger Guillemin, Andrew V. Schally, Rosalyn Yalow
1976 Baruch S. Blumberg, D. Carleton Gajdusek
1975 David Baltimore, Renato Dulbecco, Howard M. Temin
1974 Albert Claude, Christian de Duve, George E. Palade
1973 Karl von Frisch, Konrad Lorenz, Nikolaas Tinbergen
1972 Gerald M. Edelman, Rodney R. Porter
1971 Earl W. Sutherland, Jr.
1970 Sir Bernard Katz, Ulf von Euler, Julius Axelrod
1969 Max Delbrück, Alfred D. Hershey, Salvador E. Luria
1968 Robert W. Holley, H. Gobind Khorana, Marshall W. Nirenberg
1967 Ragnar Granit, Haldan K. Hartline, George Wald
1966 Peyton Rous, Charles B. Huggins
1965 François Jacob, André Lwoff, Jacques Monod
1964 Konrad Bloch, Feodor Lynen
1963 Sir John Eccles, Alan L. Hodgkin, Andrew F. Huxley
1962 Francis Crick, James Watson, Maurice Wilkins
1961 Georg von Békésy
1960 Sir Frank Macfarlane Burnet, Peter Medawar
1959 Severo Ochoa, Arthur Kornberg
1958 George Beadle, Edward Tatum, Joshua Lederberg
1957 Daniel Bovet
1956 André F. Cournand, Werner Forssmann, Dickinson W. Richards
1955 Hugo Theorell
1954 John F. Enders, Thomas H. Weller, Frederick C. Robbins
1953 Hans Krebs, Fritz Lipmann
1952 Selman A. Waksman
1951 Max Theiler
1950 Edward C. Kendall, Tadeus Reichstein, Philip S. Hench
1949 Walter Hess, Egas Moniz
1948 Paul Müller
1947 Carl Cori, Gerty Cori, Bernardo Houssay
1946 Hermann J. Muller
1945 Sir Alexander Fleming, Ernst B. Chain, Sir Howard Florey
1944 Joseph Erlanger, Herbert S. Gasser
1943 Henrik Dam, Edward A. Doisy
1942 The prize money was ⅓ allocated to the Main Fund and ⅔ to the special Fund of this prize section

1941	The prize money was ⅓ allocated to the Main Fund and ⅔ to the special Fund of this prize section	**1921**	The prize money was allocated to the Special Fund of this prize section
1940	The prize money was ⅓ allocated to the Main Fund and ⅔ to the special Fund of this prize section	**1920**	August Krogh
		1919	Jules Bordet
1939	Gerhard Domagk	**1918**	The prize money was allocated to the Special Fund of this prize section
1938	Corneille Heymans	**1917**	The prize money was allocated to the Special Fund of this prize section
1937	Albert Szent-Györgyi		
1936	Sir Henry Dale, Otto Loewi	**1916**	The prize money was allocated to the Special Fund of this prize section
1935	Hans Spemann		
1934	George H. Whipple, George R. Minot, William P. Murphy	**1915**	The prize money was allocated to the Special Fund of this prize section
1933	Thomas H. Morgan	**1914**	Robert Bárány
1932	Sir Charles Sherrington, Edgar Adrian	**1913**	Charles Richet
1931	Otto Warburg	**1912**	Alexis Carrel
1930	Karl Landsteiner	**1911**	Allvar Gullstrand
1929	Christiaan Eijkman, Sir Frederick Hopkins	**1910**	Albrecht Kossel
1928	Charles Nicolle	**1909**	Theodor Kocher
1927	Julius Wagner-Jauregg	**1908**	Ilya Mechnikov, Paul Ehrlich
1926	Johannes Fibiger	**1907**	Alphonse Laveran
1925	The prize money was allocated to the Special Fund of this prize section	**1906**	Camillo Golgi, Santiago Ramón y Cajal
		1905	Robert Koch
1924	Willem Einthoven	**1904**	Ivan Pavlov
1923	Frederick G. Banting, John Macleod	**1903**	Niels Ryberg Finsen
1922	Archibald V. Hill, Otto Meyerhof	**1902**	Ronald Ross
		1901	Emil von Behring

2004 Gairdner Award Winners

The Gairdner Foundation was created in 1957, by Toronto businessman James Arthur Gairdner, to recognize and reward the achievements of medical researchers whose work contributes significantly to improving the quality of human life. Throughout his life, Gairdner had a practical interest in clinical medicine and medical research, which led to his conviction that the achievements of medical scientists should be recognized in a tangible way. Since the first awards were made in 1959, the Gairdner Award has come to be a recognition of merit second only to the Nobel Prize. Indeed, of the 268 winners of the award, 61 have gone on to win a Nobel Prize in either medicine and physiology or chemistry.

The 2004 International Gairdner Awards went to Seymour Benzer, to George Sachs, and jointly to Reginald John Ellis, Franz Ulrich Hartl and Arthur Horwich.

Seymour Benzer is professor of biology at the California Institute of Technology, and a pioneer in understanding the link between genetics and behaviour. This has implications for understanding behavioural and neurological disorders as well as ageing. His work has led to the discovery and cloning of specific genes that participate in various behavioral phenomena, including the biological clock, learning, sexual courtship, vision, neurodegeneration and nociception.

George Sachs is professor of medicine and physiology at the University of California in Los Angeles, who was cited for his "monumental contributions to improving the care of patients with peptic ulcer disease, gastroesophageal reflux disease, esophageal cancer, and gastric cancer." Therapy based on his experimental work has dramatically reduced the morbidity and mortality associated with these conditions.

The joint award went to Reginald John Ellis of the University of Warwick, Coventry, United Kingdom, Franz Ulrich Hartl, of the Max Planck-Institut für Biochemie, Martinsried, Germany, and Arthur Horwich, professor of genetics at Yale University School of Medicine. They were cited for their "seminal contributions in establishing the principles and discovering the key mechanisms and pathways in cellular protein folding." The discoveries have a direct relevance to many diseases, such as cystic fibrosis, Alzheimer disease, and even some cancers, which are thought to arise from protein misfolding.

Source: *www.gairdner.org*

2003 Manning Award Winners

The Manning Awards recognize and encourage innovation in Canada by honouring individuals who have created and promoted a new concept, process or product that is beneficial to society. Administered by the Calgary-based Ernest C. Manning Foundation, the awards are presented annually. For the 2004 winners, visit www.manningawards.ca

PRINCIPAL AWARD: Nancy Mathis, of Fredericton, New Brunswick, transformed her breakthrough doctoral research into a unique, non-invasive thermal effusivity sensor that determines the heat-transferring characteristics of a wide range of materials. Mathis Instruments Ltd.'s patented sensors are used by major companies around the world for unprecedented quality control of materials in the laboratory, during production and for the testing of finished goods.

AWARD OF DISTINCTION: Chris Griffiths, of St. John's, Newfoundland, invented the patented Griffiths Active Bracing System, a one-piece glass fibre unit that forms the structural frame of all Garrison Guitars. The system produces the most affordable, high-quality, solid wood acoustic guitar in the world, an instrument with superior sound and playability that makes beautiful music for professional recording artists and beginning players alike.

INNOVATION AWARD: Tim Edmonds, of inNOVAcorp. in Dartmouth, Nova Scotia, developed the Air Chamber Crab Processor, a "sea change" in crab-processing technology that provides a cost-effective, safe and health method of removing meat from hard-shell segments of crab.

Kirk Swinimer, of Chester, Nova Scotia, invented the only code-evaluated, engineered footing form for construction tubes that enables the integral pouring of the footing and the column. F&S Manufacturing Inc.'s patented Bigfoot Systems, a cone-shaped, high-density plastic footing form that saves time and reduces labour costs, is used by builders throughout Canada and exported worldwide.

YOUNG CANADIAN INNOVATION AWARDS: Adrian Maler, of Crysler, Ontario ("We Got Rhythm," a project that simulates the brain's 'timekeeper' (circadian clock) using mathematical equations); Ildiko Beres, of Windsor, Ontario ("Go Green," a bacterial bio-reporting system that can be used to detect heavy metal ion contamination); Kara Barfett, of London, Ontario (a biotechnology solution that uses artificial cells as a fish feed additive for pollution control in aquaculture); Spencer Hughes, of Timmins, Ontario (a method to turn flooded mines into useful thermo-ionic bioreactors).

Source: *The Manning Awards*

Patents

If you have an idea for a new gadget, you'd probably like to patent it. After all, you'll need a patent to protect your intellectual property as you try to market your device. Indeed, without patent protection, many people might not invest the time and money involved in devising and perfecting new products.

To be eligible for a patent, an invention must be the first of its kind, it must be useful and must work, and it must be clearly ingenious to people familiar with the field. A patent gives you the right to prevent others from making, selling or using your gadget for up to 20 years from the date of filing for a patent.

Patent rights are a national affair: a Canadian patent only applies in Canada and a U.S. patent in the U.S. In Canada, patents are issued by the Canadian Intellectual Property Office, which has an on-line guide to applying for a patent. The CIPO Web site is cipo.gc.ca.

Here are several other sites of interest to inventors:

The Canadian Innovation Centre (www.innovationcentre.ca)

The Canada Foundation for Innovation (www.innovation.ca)

The U.S. Patent and Trademark Office (www.uspto.gov)

Canadian Science and Engineering Hall of Fame

The inductees into the Canadian Science and Engineering Hall of Fame are outstanding researchers, inventors and innovators who have won worldwide recognition for their accomplishments. The Hall of Fame Web site can be accessed at www.sciencetech.technomuses.ca/english/about/hallfame/u_main_e.cfm

The Inductees

Maude Abbott (1869–1940) . . . . Pathologist and specialist in congenital heart disease

Sir Frederick Banting (1891–1941) . . . . Co-discoverer of insulin; Nobel laureate

Alexander Graham Bell (1847–1922) . . . . . . Inventor of the telephone

J. Armand Bombardier (1907–1964) . . . . Inventor of the snowmobile

Bertram Brockhouse (1918–) . . . . Physicist who pioneered use of neutron scattering in study of atoms; Nobel laureate

Douglas Harold Copp (1915–1998) . . . . Discoverer of calcitonin, used to treat osteoporosis

Pierre Dansereau (1911–) . . . . Pioneered a new approach to the study of ecology

John William Dawson (1820-1899) . . . . Pioneering paleobotanist

Reginald Fessenden (1866–1932) . . . . Pioneer in the development of the radio

Sir Sanford Fleming (1827–1915) . . . . Architect of the transcontinental railway; inventor of time zones

Gerald Heffernan (1919–) . . . . Developer of the environment-friendly "mini-mill"

Gerhard Herzberg (1904–99) . . . . Astrophysicist; Nobel laureate

Helen Sawyer Hogg (1905-1993) . . . . Among the first women to be a professional astronomer

Harold Elford Johns (1915–1998) . . . . Developer of the cobalt-60 cancer therapy unit in 1951.

George J. Klein (1904–92) . . . . Design engineer, the most productive inventor in 20th century Canada

Hugh Le Caine (1914–77) . . . . Physicist; designed the first musical synthesizer

Raymond Urgel Lemieux (1920-2000) . . . . . Chemist who first synthesized sugar

Sir William Logan (1798–1875) . . . . First director of the Geological Survey of Canada

Elizabeth "Elsie" MacGill (1905–80) . . . . . . Oversaw WWII production of Hawker Hurricane aircraft

Frances G. McGill (1877–1959) . . . . Pioneer in forensic pathology

Frère Marie-Victorin (1885–1944) . . . . Botanist, author and teacher

Andrew G.L. MacNaughton (1887–1966) . . . Inventor of cathode-ray detection finder and military leader

Margaret Newton (1887–1971) . . . . Plant pathologist who developed techniques to combat wheat rust

Joseph-Alphonse Ouimet (1908–88) . . . . . . Inventor, engineer and CBC president

Wilder Penfield (1891–1976) . . . . Neurosurgeon who developed surgical treatments for epilepsy

John Polanyi (1929–) . . . . Contributed to the development of laser chemistry; Nobel laureate

Charles E. Saunders (1867–1937) . . . . Developed fast-ripening Marquis wheat

Charles Scriver (1930–) . . . . Innovator in medical genetics

Michael Smith (1932–2000) . . . . Chemistry researcher, genetic codes and DNA; Nobel laureate

Edgar William Richard Steacie (1900–62) . . Researcher (free radical chemistry), educator

Wallace Turnbull (1870–1954) . . . . Inventor of the variable pitch propellor

John Tuzo Wilson (1908–1993) . . . . Contributed to development of plate tectonics

Source: *National Research Council*

The National Research Council

Canada's National Research Council was established in 1916, with the country at war and millions of men and women serving overseas. The NRC's goal was to develop Canadian science—a goal that is still its focus. Some highlights from the NRC's history:

1916–27: Magnesite, a mineral used in the coating of high-temperature industrial furnaces, was imported for years because domestic ores weren't pure enough. NRC-financed researchers found a simple way of eliminating the impurities, so Canada could cut its dependence on imports.

1928–32: From 1924 to 1938, Canadian medical researchers worked with the NRC to find a vaccine against tuberculosis. Their work helped make the BCG vaccine the main weapon against the disease.

George Klein (1904–92), a Canadian inventor and a longtime NRC employee, produced an almost endless list of inventions: aircraft skis, an electric wheelchair for quadriplegics, a microsurgery staple gun and a retractable antenna that is still standard equipment on satellites

1933–45: The NRC helped develop radar (for "radio distance and ranging") during World War II. Today, radar is essential to make travel safer by air, land and sea.

Before World War II began, the NRC enlisted **Sir Frederick Banting**, the discoverer of insulin, to lead research on combat-related medicine. Banting's team worked on wound infections, shock, penicillin, a typhus vaccine, blood substitutes and plastic surgery.

If you've ever played a **synthesizer**, you owe the experience to an NRC scientist. Hugh Le Caine invented the world's first in 1945.

1946–52: **Canola oil,** which can sometimes take the place of butter on popcorn, is used to make margarine, cooking oils, lubricants and inks. In the 1940s, the NRC helped to develop a hybrid canola plant, and today canola is one of Canada's leading cash crops.

If you or someone you know wears a **pacemaker**, the technology that made it possible was developed by the NRC in the late 1940s by Jack Hopps.

1953–63: The NRC's Harry Stevinson developed a reliable emergency locator beacon for downed aircraft. In 1957, the Crash Position Indicator was introduced for military use, and by 1960 was available for commercial aircraft.

In 1958, the NRC built one of the world's earliest cesium beam atomic clocks—accurate to a few millionths of a second per year. By the 1970s, NRC time was being used to set official time scales and clocks around the world.

1964–71: In 1971, Dr. Gerhard Herzberg of the NRC won a Nobel Prize in chemistry for his work in identifying molecules in space.

1972–80: In 1973, the NRC opened a centre to retrieve and analyse data from flight recorders (more commonly known as black boxes).

Also in 1973, the **Canada–France–Hawaii Telescope** opened, high on the frigid, barren top of the Hawaiian volcano Mauna Kea. It can produce images almost as sharp as those from the Hubble Space Telescope—and it's much easier to repair.

1981–89: The NRC developed an optical security patch that changes colour in different lights. The patch is used on paper money and drivers' licences to prevent counterfeiting.

Saran Narang made a major medical breakthrough when he produced **synthetic insulin** for use by diabetics.

1990–2001: In May 1996, Canadian astronaut Marc Garneau retrieved a satellite in flight using the CANADARM—with the help of the Space Vision System, a technology developed by the NRC.

Early 1990s: NRC experts introduced various fingerprint detection methods that are still used by the RCMP and other police forces.

Sudbury Inside Out

*A*bout 1.8 billion years ago, a huge meteorite crashed into what is now Sudbury, Ontario— so violently that it flipped parts of the earth's crust inside out, spewing melted rock and precious metals from deep inside the ground around the top of the impact site, according to University of Toronto professor Dr. James Mungall. The ancient crater was filled both by melted rock from up to 40 km below the earth's crust and by the valuable metals such as nickel for which Sudbury is known. There are also hints that the meteorite vaporized in a great burst of heat rather than being deposited deep in the ground, Mungall reported in the journal Nature.
Source: *NSERC*

ATMOSPHERIC SCIENCE

A Glossary of Weather Terms

Air mass: An extensive body of air with a fairly uniform distribution of moisture and temperature throughout.

Alberta clipper: Named after the clipper sailing ships, which at one time were the fastest vessels on the seas. These storms zip along at 64 km/h, preceded by about 5 cm of light, powdery snow and followed by violent winds capable of reaching 100 km/h. This often results in severe blowing and drifting with blizzard conditions that can leave many roads impassable.

Atmosphere: The envelope of air surrounding the earth. Most weather events are confined to the lower 10 km of the atmosphere.

Atmospheric pressure: The force exerted on the earth by the weight of the atmosphere.

Blizzard: Severe winter weather condition characterized by low temperatures, strong winds above 40 km/h, and visibility of less than 1 km due to blowing snow; condition lasts three hours or more.

Blowing snow: Snow lifted from the earth's surface by the wind to a height of two metres or more. Blowing snow is higher than drifting snow.

Bright sunshine: Sunshine intense enough to burn a mark on recording paper mounted in the Campbell-Stokes sunshine recorder. The daily period of bright sunshine is less than that of visible sunshine because the sun's rays are not intense enough to burn the paper just after sunrise, near sunset and under cloudy conditions.

Chinook (also snow-eater): A dry, warm, strong wind that blows down the eastern slopes of the Rocky Mountains in North America. The warmth and dryness are due principally to heating by compression as the air descends the mountain slope.

Cold wave: An occurrence of dangerous cold conditions, when temperatures often dip below -18°C, that usually lasts longer than a few days.

Crepuscular rays: Clouds to excite any sky photographer, crepuscular rays are caused by streaks or beams of sunlight shining through openings in large cumulonimbus clouds on the horizon. The beams reach down and outward from behind the clouds. If they focus upward, toward a point in the sky opposite the sun, they are called anticrepuscular rays. Sometimes they are called sun beams crossing the sky or Jacob's ladder. Sailors refer to them as "the sun drawing water." The dark bands you see crossing the sky are the shadows from clouds.

Cyclone: A generic term that describes all classes of storms from local thunderstorms and tiny dust devils to monstrous hurricanes and typhoons. It comes from the Greek word *kyklon*, meaning cycle, circle or coil of a snake and refers to all circular wind systems.

Deep low: Used to describe the central barometric pressure of a low (usually when it is about 975 millibars [97.50 kPa or less]). Often has winds of gale to storm force around the low.

Developing low: A low in which the central pressure is decreasing with time. Winds normally increase as the low deepens.

Dew point temperature: The temperature at which air becomes saturated, allowing condensation of water vapour as frost, fog, dew, mist or precipitation.

Drizzle: Precipitation consisting of numerous minute water droplets which appear to float; the droplets are much smaller than in rain.

El Niño: Near the end of most years, the normally cold Peru Current that sweeps northward along the South American coast from southern Chile to the equator is replaced by a warm southward flowing coastal current. Centuries ago the local fishermen named this the "Christ child current," because it appeared around the Christmas season. Every few years it was unusually intense and over time the term El Niño became more closely associated with occasional intense warmings.

Filling low: A low in which the central pressure is increasing with time., i.e., the low is gradually weakening.

Flash floods: A very rapid rise of water with little or no advance warning, most often when an intense thunderstorm drops a huge rainfall on a fairly small area in a very short space of time.

Fog: A cloud based at the earth's surface consisting of tiny water droplets or, under very cold conditions, ice crystals or ice fog; generally found in calm or low wind conditions. Under foggy conditions, visibility is reduced to less than one kilometre.

▶

▶ **Frazil ice:** [French Canadian] During the freeze-up period ice forms on the river surface and ice crystals or frazil develop within the river, especially in open, turbulent water slightly below 0°C. Frazil ice is very common in rapids.

Freezing precipitation: Supercooled water drops of drizzle, or rain which freeze on impact to form a coating of ice upon the ground or any objects they strike.

Front: The boundary between two different air masses which have originated from widely separated regions. A cold front is the leading edge of an advancing cold air mass, while a warm front is the trailing edge of a retreating cold air mass.

Frost: The deposit of ice crystals that occurs when the air temperature is at or below the freezing point of water. The term frost is also used to describe the icy deposits of water vapor that may form on the ground or on other surfaces like car windshields, which are colder than the surrounding air and which have a temperature below freezing.

Gale: A strong wind. A gale warning is issued for expected winds of 65 to 100 km/h (34 to 47 knots).

Gust: A sudden, brief increase in wind speed, for generally less than 20 seconds.

Heat wave: A period with more than three consecutive days of maximum temperatures at or above 32°C.

High pressure: A term for an area of high (maximum) pressure with a closed, clockwise (in the Northern Hemisphere) circulation of air.

Humidex: A measure of what hot weather "feels like." Air of a given temperature and moisture content is equated in comfort to air with a higher temperature and that of negligible moisture content. At a humidex of 30°C some people begin to experience discomfort. (See chart on p. 603.)

Hurricanes: Tropical systems are classed into several categories depending on maximum strength, usually measured by maximum sustained wind speed. A *tropical disturbance* is simply a moving area of thunderstorms in the tropics that maintains its identity for 24 hours or more. A *tropical depression* is a cyclonic system originating over the tropics with a highest sustained wind speed of up to 61 km/h. A *tropical storm* has a highest sustained wind speed of between 62 and 117 km/h. A *hurricane* has wind speeds of 118 km/h or more.

Ice pellets: Precipitation consisting of fragments of ice, 5 mm or less in diameter, that bounce when hitting a hard surface, making a sound upon impact.

Inversion: The term refers to a temperature increase with height, where the usual pattern is a decrease in temperature within increasing height.

Isobar: A line on a weather map or chart connecting points of equal pressure. The large concentric lines on television or newspaper weather maps are isobars.

Killing frost: A frost severe enough to end the growing season, usually when the air temperature falls below –2°C.

Land breeze: A small-scale wind set off when the air temperature over water is warmer than that over adjacent land. The land breeze develops at night and blows from the land out to the sea or onto the lake. Its counterpart is the sea or lake breeze.

Low pressure: An area of low (minimum) atmospheric pressure that has a closed counterclockwise circulation in the Northern Hemisphere.

Peak wind (gust): The highest instantaneous wind speed recorded for a specific time period.

Plough winds: These belong to a family of strong, straight-line downburst winds found in thunderstorms. These winds rush to the ground with great force, maybe 100 to 150 km/h and occasionally even higher. Damage usually covers an area less than 3 km across. Plough winds are capable of toppling trees, lifting roofs, and ripping apart houses and other structures.

Precipitation: Any and all forms of water, whether liquid or solid, that fall from the atmosphere and reach the earth's surface. A day with measurable precipitation is a day when the water equivalent of the precipitation is equal to or greater than 0.2 mm.

Probability of precipitation (POP): Subjective numerical estimates of your chances of encountering measurable precipitation at some time during the forecast period. For example, a 40% probability of rain means there are four chances in 10 of getting wet. They cannot be used to predict when, where or how much precipitation will occur.

Relative humidity: The ratio of water vapour in the air at a given temperature to the maximum which could exist at that temperature. It is usually expressed as a percentage.

Ridge: An elongated area of high pressure extending from the centre of a high pressure region; the opposite of a trough. ▶

▶ **Sea breeze:** A small-scale wind set off when the air temperature over land is greater than that over the adjacent sea. The sea breeze develops during the day and blows from the sea to the land. Its counterpart is the land breeze.

Sleet: This is not what you think. In the United States, sleet is frozen raindrops that bounce when they hit the surface. It is not as treacherous to drive on as is freezing rain. What Americans call sleet a Canadian would call ice pellets or frozen raindrops. They are spherical or irregular shapes with a diameter of 5 mm or less. Pellets do not stick to trees or wires. On the other hand, sleet to a British weather watcher is a mix of rain and partly melted snowflakes.

Small craft warning: Issued when winds over the coastal marine areas are expected to reach and maintain speeds of 20 to 33 knots.

Snow: Precipitation consisting of white or translucent ice crystals and often agglomerated into snowflakes. A day with measurable snow is a day when the total snowfall is at least 0.2 cm.

Squall: A strong, sudden wind which generally lasts a few minutes then quickly decreases in speed. Squalls are generally associated with severe thunderstorms.

Storm track: The path taken by a low-pressure centre.

Storm warning: The wind warning that is issued to mariners when winds are expected to be from 48 to 63 knots.

Thunderstorm: A local storm, usually produced by a cumulonimbus cloud, and always accompanied by thunder and lightning. A thunderstorm day is a day when thunder is heard or when lightning is seen (rain and snow need not have fallen).

Tornado (also twister): A violently rotating column of air that is usually visible as a funnel cloud hanging from dark thunderstorm clouds. It is one of the least extensive of all storms, but in violence, it is the most destructive.

Trough: An elongated area of low pressure extending from the centre of a low pressure region; the opposite of a ridge.

Tsunami: Also known (incorrectly) as a tidal wave. "Tsunami" is a Japanese word that means "harbour wave." It is a wave set in motion by an undersea movement such as an earthquake or a landslide. These waves can travel up to 1,000 km/h over long distances, hitting the shore with tremendous force.

Typhoon: A severe tropical cyclone in the Western Pacific Ocean, counterpart of the Atlantic hurricane.

Virga: Streaks of falling rain that evaporate before reaching the ground.

Watches and warnings: Environment Canada alerts Canadians to severe storms by issuing weather watches and warnings. Usually the first message is the severe thunderstorm watch. If a watch is issued in your area, maintain your routine, but keep an eye skyward for threatening weather, and listen to radio and television for further weather information. When severe local storms are building, or have actually been sighted or detected by radar, then warnings are issued and updated. These may be either severe thunderstorm warnings or tornado warnings. Warnings mean you should be on the alert.

Waterspout: A waterspout is not really a waterspout. Often called a tornado over water, the actual water spray involved does not extend from the surface to the cloud, but 3 to 10 metres above the water surface. Like the tornado, the waterspout is very brief. Sailors believed one way of breaking up a waterspout was to fire a cannon through it.

Weatheradio: This is the name of Environment Canada's weather information broadcast network. The network has transmitters in every region and listeners need a receiver, which can be purchased from electronic equipment dealers, to pick up the broadcasts. Weatheradio signals warnings of severe weather automatically to receivers equipped with special alarm devices for that purpose.

Westerlies (west-wind belt): The pronounced west-to-east motion of the atmosphere centred over middle latitudes from about 35° to 65° latitude.

Willy-willies: Refers to small, circular winds such as dust devils or whirlwinds in Australia, not very hazardous. Before 1950, willy-willies referred to much larger, more destructive typhoons or hurricanes.

Wind chill: A measure of the effect we feel when strong winds are combined with freezing temperatures. The index is in temperature-like units, explaining the way skin feels in a comparable temperature on a calm day, i.e., if it's −10°C and the wind chill is −20, it means your skin feels as cold as it would on a calm day at −20°C.

Wind direction: The direction from which the wind is blowing.

Source: *Environment Canada*

Humidex

DRY BULB TEMPERATURE (DEGREES CELSIUS) vs **RELATIVE HUMIDITY (%)**

Temp \ RH	100	95	90	85	80	75	70	65	60	55	50	45	40	35	30	25	20
43													56	54	51	49	47
42												56	54	52	50	48	46
41											56	54	52	50	48	46	44
40										57	54	52	51	49	47	44	43
39									56	54	53	51	49	47	45	43	41
38							57	56	54	52	51	49	47	46	43	42	40
37					58	57	55	53	51	50	49	47	45	43	42	40	
36			58	57	56	54	53	51	50	48	47	45	43	42	40	38	
35		58	57	56	54	52	51	49	48	47	45	43	42	41	38	37	
34	58	57	55	53	52	51	49	48	47	45	43	42	41	39	37	36	
33	55	54	52	51	50	48	47	46	44	43	42	40	38	37	36	34	
32	52	51	50	49	47	46	45	43	42	41	39	38	37	36	34	33	
31	50	49	48	46	45	44	43	41	40	39	38	36	35	34	33	31	
30	48	47	46	44	43	42	41	40	38	37	36	35	34	33	31	31	
29	46	45	44	43	42	41	39	38	37	36	34	33	32	31	30		
28	43	42	41	41	39	38	37	36	35	34	33	32	31	29	28		
27	41	40	39	38	37	36	35	34	33	32	31	30	29	28	28		
26	39	38	37	36	35	35	33	32	31	31	29	28	28	27			
25	37	36	35	34	33	33	32	31	30	29	28	27	27	26			
24	35	34	33	33	32	31	30	29	28	28	27	26	26	25			
23	33	32	32	31	30	29	28	27	27	26	25	24	23				
22	31	29	29	28	28	27	26	26	24	24	23	23					
21	29	29	28	27	27	26	26	24	24	23	23	22					

Humidex (°C)	Degree of Comfort
20–29	Comfortable
30–39	Varying degrees of discomfort
40–45	Almost everyone uncomfortable
46 and over	Many types of labour must be restricted

■ In hot weather, our bodies regulate core temperature by using our sweat glands to shed water. Sweating doesn't cool the body, but the evaporation of sweat on your skin removes heat because it takes energy (heat) to change the liquid on your skin to vapour in the air. However, when it's humid, the air itself is already full of moisture and it can't absorb the moisture we are trying to shed, making us sticky and uncomfortable.

Ultra-Violet Index

Ultra-violet radiation is short-wavelength radiation that is part of the spectrum, just beyond visible violet light. These waves can harm both plant and animal life—the shorter of the UV wavelengths, known as UV-B, can cause sunburn, skin cancer and cataracts in humans and animals, and can also reduce agricultural productivity.

These rays are usually blocked by the protective ozone layer in the stratosphere, found between 10 and 50 km above the earth. Ozone is a form of oxygen that has three atoms instead of two and is created when ordinary oxygen interacts with ultraviolet radiation from the sun. Ozone can be destroyed by chemicals released into the air—most notably by the breakdown of chlorofluorocarbons (CFCs). CFCs have been used in air-conditioning, refrigeration and in some plastics manufacturing and CFC molecules are stable enough to last 100 years in the atmosphere—long enough to drift into the stratosphere where UV-B rays can break them down to produce free chlorine atoms. It is the chlorine atoms that destroy ozone.

In the 1970s, scientists had a theory that the chemicals drifting in the atmosphere could destroy the ozone layer. In the winter of 1985 NASA discovered a hole in the ozone layer over Antarctica. In recent years the continuing depletion of the ozone layer has resulted in its general thinning, and in holes of varying sizes at the poles from time to time. Various attempts have been made to phase out the use of ozone-depleting chemicals all over the world, particularly at the Earth Summit in Rio de Janeiro in June 1992. While progress has been made, it is important to realize that more UV-B rays are getting through the atmosphere and there is a higher risk of UV-B generated health problems.

In May 1992, Canada's weather service launched a daily ultraviolet index as part of the forecast, the first country in the world to do so. The purpose of the index is to warn people about the dangers of over-exposure to the sun. Several other countries, including Australia, New Zealand, the Netherlands, Germany, Great Britain and the United States, have now started their own programs closely modelled on the Canadian UV index.

The amount of UV-B is measured on a scale of 0 to 10, with 10 being a typical amount you would receive on a summer day in the tropics. The higher the number, the faster you'll sunburn. (Sunburn times are for light, untanned skin; times would be somewhat longer for those with darker skin.)

UV Index	Category	Sunburn Time
over 9	extreme	less than 15 minutes
7–9	high	about 20 minutes
4–7	moderate	about 30 minutes
0–4	low	more than one hour

Source: *Environment Canada*

Icebound and Loving It

*T**he Canadian research icebreaker CCGS* AMUNDSEN, *refitted by the Canada Foundation for Innovation at a cost of $30 million, is providing a new platform for polar research. The variety of research on the* AMUNDSEN *is virtually endless—ranging from investigating the link between global warming and the reduction in sea ice to studying how organisms survive in the polar environment. That latter study is part of a NASA-funded project that is part of the larger goal to look for life on Europa and Mars. Even when the ice around the* AMUNDSEN *is a metre thick, researchers have access to sea water through an access door dubbed the "moon pool." But, says University of Manitoba polar researcher David Barber, that also means aquatic life has direct access to the* AMUNDSEN. *"We've had visits from ring seals and one of them has been trying to take up residence in the ship," Dr. Barber said. The seal liked hanging out next to the ship's heaters inside the moon pool and had to be shooed away—a challenge, since the local wildlife has no fear of humans.*

Source: *NSERC*

Weather Records

	Canada	United States	World
Highest maximum air temperature	45.0° Midale and Yellowgrass, Sask. July 5, 1937	56.7° Death Valley, CA July 10, 1913	58.0° Al'azizyah, Libya Sept. 13, 1922
Lowest minimum air temperature	-63.0° Snag, YT Feb. 3, 1947	-62.1° Prospect Creek Camp, AK Jan. 23, 1971	-89.6° Vostok, Antarctica July 21, 1983
Coldest month	-47.9° Eureka, NWT Feb. 1979		
Highest sea-level pressure	107.95 kPa Dawson, YT Feb. 2, 1989	107.86 kPa Northway, AK Jan. 31, 1989	108.38 kPa Agata, Siberia USSR Dec. 31, 1968
Lowest sea-level pressure	94.02 kPa St. Anthony, Nfld Jan. 20, 1977	89.23 kPa Matecumbe Key, FL Sept. 2, 1935	87 kPa in eye of Typhoon Tip (Pacific Ocean) Oct. 12, 1979
Greatest precipitation in 24 hrs	489.2 mm Ucluelet Brynnor Mines, BC Oct. 6, 1967	1 090 mm Alvin, TX July 28, 1979	1 869.9 mm Cilaos, La Réunion Is. March 15, 1952
Greatest precipitation in one month	2 235.5 mm Swanson Bay, BC Nov. 1917	2 717.8 mm Kukui, HI March 1942	9 300 mm Cherrapunji, India July 1861
Greatest precipitation in one year	9 341.1 mm Henderson Lake, BC 1998	17 902.7 mm Kukui, HI 1982	26 461.2 mm Cherrapunji, India Aug. 1860-July 1861
Greatest average annual precipitation	6655 mm Henderson Lake, BC	11 684 mm Mt. Waialeaie, Kauai, HI	11 684 mm Mt. Waialeaie, Kauai, HI
Least annual precipitation	12.7 mm Arctic Bay, NWT 1949	0.0 mm Bagdad, CA Oct. 3, 1912 to Nov. 8, 1914	0.0 mm Arica, Chile—no rain for 14 years
Greatest average annual snowfall	1 433 cm Glacier Mt. Fidelity, BC	1 461 cm Rainer Paradise Ranger Station, WA	
Greatest snowfall in one season	2 446.9 cm Revelstoke/Mt. Copeland, BC 1971–72	2 850 cm Rainer Paradise Ranger Station, WA 1971–72	
Greatest snowfall in one month	535.9 cm Haines Apps. No 2, BC Dec. 1959	990.6 cm Tamarack, CA Jan. 1911	
Greatest snowfall in one day	118 cm Lakelse Lake, BC Jan. 17,1974	193 cm Silver Lake, CO April 14–15, 1921	
Highest average annual number of thunderstorm days	34 days London, Ont.	96 days Fort Meyers, FL	322 days Bogor, Indonesia
Heaviest hailstone	290 g Cedoux, Sask. Aug. 27, 1973	758 g Coffeyville, KS Sept. 3, 1970	15 000 g Guangdong province of China April 19, 1995
Highest average annual wind speed	36 km/h Cape Warwick, Resolution Island, NWT	56.3 km/h Mt. Washington, NH	
Highest wind speed for 1 hr	201.1 km/h Cape Hopes Advance (Quaqtaq), Que. Nov. 18, 1931	362.0 km/h Mt. Washington, NH April 12, 1934	
Highest average hours of fog	1 890 hrs Argentia, Nfld	2 552 hrs Cape Disappointment, WA	

Source: *Environment Canada*

Wind Chill Hazards

Check the wind chill before you go outdoors in the winter, and make sure you are well prepared for the weather. Even moderate wind chills can be dangerous if you are outside for long periods.

In parts of the country with a milder climate (Southern Ontario, Southern British Columbia and the Atlantic provinces except Labrador), a wind chill warning is issued at –35°C. Further north, people have grown more accustomed to the cold, and have adapted to the more severe conditions. Because of this, Environment Canada issues warnings at progressively colder wind chill values as you move north. Most of Canada hears a warning at –45°C. The residents of the Arctic and Northern Manitoba, Northern Ontario and Northern Quebec are warned at –53°C, and –63°C in the high Arctic.

Wind Chill (°C)	Description	Health Concern	What to do
0 to –9	Low	• Slight increase in discomfort.	• Dress warmly, with the outside temperature in mind.
–9 to –24	Moderate	• Uncomfortable. • Exposed skin feels cold. • Risk of hypothermia if outside for long periods without adequate protection.	• Dress in layers of warm clothing, with an outer layer that is wind resistant. • Wear a hat, mittens and scarf. • Keep active.
–25 to –44	Cold	• Risk of skin freezing (frostbite). Check extremities (fingers, toes, ears and face) for numbness or whiteness. Risk of hypothermia if outside for long periods without adequate protection.	• Dress in layers of warm clothing, with an outer layer that is wind resistant. • Cover all exposed skin, particularly your face and hands. Wear a hat, mittens and a scarf, neck tube or face mask. • Keep active.
–45 to –62	Very cold WARNING LEVEL	• Exposed skin may freeze in minutes. Check extremities frequently for numbness or whiteness (frostbite). Serious risk of hypothermia if outside for long periods.	• Be careful. Dress very warmly in layers of clothing, with an outer layer that is wind resistant. Cover all exposed skin, particularly your face and hands. Wear a hat, mittens and a scarf, neck tube or face mask. Limit outdoor activities to short periods. Be ready to cut short or cancel outdoor activities. Keep active.
–63 and colder	Extreme DANGER!	• Outdoor conditions are hazardous. Exposed skin may freeze in seconds.	• Stay indoors.

Source: *Environment Canada*

Why Wind Chill Matters

O n a calm winter day, our bodies insulate us from cold temperatures by warming a thin layer of air close to our skin (the boundary layer). When the wind blows, it takes away this protective layer, exposing our skin to cold, moving air. Our bodies expend more energy warming up a new layer, and if each one keeps getting blown away, our skin temperature will drop, and we will feel colder.

How much heat you keep or lose depends not just on the wind. Good-quality clothing with high insulating properties traps air, for a thicker boundary layer around the body to keep in the heat. Wet clothing or footwear loses this property; the water creates body-heat loss that nearly equals the condition of exposed skin.

Your body type also determines how quickly you lose or increase heat—people with a tall, slim build become cold much faster than those who are shorter and heavier. Physical activity (walking or skiing) increases metabolism and generates body heat; those with less muscle mass (children or the elderly) find it harder to get warm.

The Beaufort Wind Scale

Beaufort forces range from 0 in calm conditions, to 12 in a hurricane. Rear-Admiral Sir Francis Beaufort of the British Royal Navy devised the scale in 1805. It originally referred to the amount of sail a full-rigged ship could carry in specific wind conditions. In light air, just one sail would be taken in; in a moderate gale, seven would come down; and in a heavy storm the number would be eleven, therefore Beaufort force 11. The Beaufort scale has been modified and modernized several times. Basically, however, the idea is to estimate wind speed by watching the effects of wind on such things as flags, trees, smoke, water surface and even people. The scale is still widely used today.

Beaufort Wind Force	Wind Speed (km/h)	Wind Type	Descriptive Effects
0	0–1	calm	smoke rises vertically
1	2–5	light air	smoke drifts slowly
2	6–11	light breeze	leaves rustle; wind vanes move
3	12–19	gentle breeze	leaves and twigs in constant motion
4	20–29	moderate breeze	small branches move; raises dust and loose paper moves along
5	30–38	fresh breeze	small trees sway
6	39–50	strong breeze	large branches in continuous motion; telephone wires whistle
7	51–61	near gale	whole trees in motion; wind affects walking
8	62–74	gale	twigs and small branches break off trees
9	75–87	strong gale	branches break; shingles blow from roofs
10	88–101	storm	trees snap and uproot; some damage to buildings
11	102–117	violent storm	property damage widespread
12	118–	hurricane	severe and extensive damage

Source: *Environment Canada*

Tornado Intensity Scale

Tornadoes are classified by the destruction they leave behind. They are rated from F0 to F5, F standing for Fujita, one of the world's leading experts on tornadoes.

F-Scale	Winds (km/h)	Length (km)	Width	Damage
0 (very weak)	under 116	< 1.5	under 15m	Light damage; minor roof, tree, chimney, antenna and sign damage
1 (weak)	117–180	1.6–5	16–50m	Moderate damage; barns torn apart; mobile homes pushed off foundations; trees snapped; cars pushed off roads; sheet metal buildings destroyed
2 (strong)	181–252	5.1–15.9	51–160m	Considerable damage; roofs torn off schools, homes and businesses; debris from barns scattered; trailers disintegrated; large trees uprooted; concrete block buildings destroyed
3 (severe)	253–332	16–50	161–500m	Severe damage; roofs and walls of schools, homes and buildings blown away; large trees uprooted; weaker homes completely disappear
4 (devastating)	333–419	51–159	0.5–1.4km	Interior and exterior walls of all homes blown apart; cars thrown more than 300m in the air
5 (incredible)	420–512	160–507	1.5–16km	Strongly built homes completely blown away; bizarre phenomena such as straw driven through fence posts

Source: *Environment Canada*

The Saffir-Simpson Hurricane Intensity Scale

Category	Maximum Sustained Wind Speed (km/h)	Minimum Surface Pressure (kPa)	Storm Surge (m)	Remarks
1 (minimal)	119–153	>=98.0	1.0–1.7	Damage to trees and signs. Low-lying flooding. Small craft torn from mooring.
2 (moderate)	154–177	97.9–96.5	1.8–2.6	Trees blown down; damage to mobile homes and roofs. Marinas flooded; evacuation of shores.
3 (extensive)	178–209	96.4–94.5	2.7–3.8	Some structural damage to small buildings; serious coastal flooding; mobile homes destroyed.
4 (extreme)	210–249	94.4–92.0	3.9–5.6	Extensive damage: doors, roofs, windows; major damage to lower floors of buildings near shore. Major beach erosion. Massive evacuation from shore possible.
5 (catastrophic)	>250	<92.0	>5.6	Small buildings blown away; complete destruction of mobile homes; massive evacuation within 10 to 20 km of shore possible.

Source: *H.S. Saffir, P.E. and Dr. R. Simpson*

Hurricane Names in 2005

*T*he names chosen for tropical storms in the Atlantic Ocean, Gulf of Mexico and the Caribbean Sea for 2005 are: Arlene, Bret, Cindy, Dennis, Emily, Franklin, Gert, Harvey, Irene, Jose, Katrina, Lee, Maria, Nate, Ophelia, Philippe, Rita, Stan, Tammy, Vince, and Wilma. The names for eastern Pacific tropical storms (those west of 140° W) are: Adrian, Beatriz, Calvin, Dora, Eugene, Fernanda, Greg, Hilary, Irwin, Jova, Kenneth, Lidia, Max, Norma, Otis, Pilar, Ramon, Selma, Todd, Veronica, Wiley, Xina, York, and Zelda. Other regions of the world have their own naming systems: see http://www.nhc.noaa.gov/aboutnames.shtml

Since 1953, Atlantic tropical storms have been named from lists originated by the National Hurricane Centre and now maintained and updated by an international committee of the World Meteorological Organization (WMO). The lists featured only women's names until 1979, when men's and women's names were alternated. Six lists are used in rotation. Thus, the 2005 list will be used again in 2011.

Hurricanes that have a severe impact on lives or the economy are remembered for generations, and some go into weather history. If a hurricane has had a major impact, any country affected by the storm can request that the name of the hurricane be "retired" by agreement of the WMO. Retiring a name actually means that it cannot be reused for at least 10 years, to facilitate historic references, legal actions, insurance claim activities, etc. and avoid public confusion with another storm of the same name.

Air Quality

Poor quality air—or air pollution—affects the health of all of us, especially children, the elderly and people with lung conditions (bronchitis or asthma) or heart problems. Effects can range from irritation to eyes, nose and throat to decreased lung capacity, or an intensifying of the impact of existing respiratory diseases. Even healthy, active Canadians can feel the effects of pollution. They may notice they're breathing less efficiently when they are active during times of high pollution levels.

When we think of air pollution, we usually think of smog. Smog is composed mostly of ground-level ozone and fine particles.

Ozone (O_3), is a colourless, odourless gas. It's the result of a chain of chemical reactions between nitrogen oxides and volatile organic compounds warmed by sunlight. High levels typically occur from May to September, between noon and early evening, when the warm temperatures (over 25°C) accelerate the process. (Areas in Canada that have been experiencing warmer summers have also experienced an increase in air quality problems or smog alerts during the last few years for this reason.)

Nitrogen oxides are emitted by burning fossil fuels (coal and oil); volatile organic compounds are found in the unburned gasoline emitted in car exhaust; they are also emitted by solvents, oil-based paints or similar materials.

Exposure to high levels of O_3 results in chest tightness, coughing and wheezing. People with respiratory and heart problems are at a higher risk for these problems. Ozone also causes noticeable damage in many crops, garden plants and trees—reducing crop yields and stunting growth.

Fine suspended particles in the atmosphere consist of either solid particles or fine liquid droplets. They include aerosols, smoke, fumes, dust, fly ash (fine ash from the fuel burned in power stations or at brick works) and pollen.

Particles in the atmosphere have been characterized according to size, mainly because of the different health effects from particles of different diameters. Particles with diameters less than 100 microns (millionths of a metre) are classified as total suspended particles (TSP). Most particle emissions from human activity fall into the TSP size range. Particles less than 10 microns and 2.5 microns in diameter are defined as inhalable particles (PM_{10}) and respirable particles ($PM_{2.5}$), respectively. The smaller the particle, the further it will penetrate into the lungs—respirable particles penetrate the furthest and aggravate bronchitis, asthma and other respiratory diseases the most. ▶

Levels of Inhalable Airborne Particles in Canadian Cities (PM_{10} and $PM_{2.5}$)

Year	PM$_{10}$ (mg/m3) mean	PM$_{10}$ (mg/m3) mean peak	PM$_{2.5}$ (mg/m3) mean	PM$_{2.5}$ (mg/m3) mean peak
1991	23.1	48.4	11.9	30.6
1992	27.5	67.6	13.9	30.9
1993	22.9	53.3	11.9	33.0
1994	21.2	53.9	11.1	28.3
1995	18.0	44.5	9.0	24.5
1996	17.0	36.1	8.6	19.9
1997	18.1	36.9	9.3	20.8
1998	20.7	49.2	10.1	26.7
1999	19.7	46.9	9.4	23.6
2000	18.0	39.2	8.9	22.3
2001	18.1	41.3	9.0	24.4
2002	18.1	48.6	10.2	27.4

Source: *Environmental Technology Centre, Environment Canada, Ottawa, Ontario*   Last update: 2003

► Particles come from both natural and man-made sources. Natural sources include wind-blown soil and mineral particles, volcanic ash, sea salt spray and biological materials such as pollen, spores, bacteria and smoke from forest fires. Man-made sources include wind-blown dust from agricultural soil, roads and construction sites and particles from combustion of fossil fuels.

Aside from smog, the air can also include the following:

Nitrogen dioxide (NO_2), a reddish-brown gas with a pungent and irritating odour, transforms in the air to make gaseous nitric acid and toxic organic nitrates. NO_2, of course, plays a major role in the production of ground-level ozone, and is also a precursor to nitrates, which contribute to increased respirable particle levels.

All combustion in air produces oxides of nitrogen, of which NO_2 is the major one. Much of it comes from the transportation sector—cars and trucks. Most of the remainder comes from power generation, metal production and incineration. There are also a few natural sources of NO_2.

NO_2 irritates the lungs and can lower resistance to respiratory infection. People with asthma and bronchitis are especially sensitive.

Sulphur dioxide (SO_2), a colourless gas, smells like burnt matches. It can be oxidized to sulphur trioxide, which in the presence of water is transformed to sulphuric acid mist or rain. SO_2 can be oxidized to form acid aerosols. It is also a precursor to sulphates, one of the main components of particles in the atmosphere that can penetrate deep into the lungs. SO_2 comes mainly from smelters and utilities, iron and steel mills, petroleum refineries and pulp and paper mills. Small sources include residential, commercial and industrial space heating.

Exposure to high levels of SO_2 can cause breathing problems, respiratory illness, a weakening of the lung's defences and a worsening of respiratory and cardiovascular disease. People with asthma or chronic lung or heart disease are the most sensitive to SO_2. It also damages trees and crops.

Carbon monoxide (CO), a colourless, odourless and tasteless but poisonous gas, is produced primarily by incomplete burning of fossil fuels. Most of it comes from cars and trucks, but a significant amount is produced by metal production.

CO enters the bloodstream and reduces oxygen delivery to the organs and tissues. People with heart disease are particularly sensitive. Exposure to high levels is linked to impairment of vision, work capacity, learning ability and performance of difficult tasks, as well as premature death.

Total reduced sulphur compounds (TRS) produce offensive odours similar to those of rotten eggs or cabbage. Industrial sources of TRS include the steel industry, pulp and paper mills, refineries and sewage treatment facilities. Natural sources include swamps, bogs and marshes.

TRS compounds are not normally considered a health hazard. They are, however, a primary cause of odours.

How Is Air Quality Measured?

The federal government, the provinces and many municipalities have created a measure known as an Air Quality Index (AQI). This uses real-time data from measuring stations to calculate the amount of the above common pollutants in the air. The list of measured pollutants varies from place to place, but Ontario's Air Quality Index serves as an example.

In Ontario, a network of 33 monitoring stations continuously measures the six common pollutants: ozone, suspended particles, nitrogen dioxide, sulphur dioxide, carbon monoxide and total reduced sulphur compounds. The quantity of each is measured on an appropriate scale and the AQI for a locality is based on whichever is highest on a particular day. (See Ontario's air quality Web site: www.airqualityontario.com)

If the AQI falls below 32, the air is considered good or very good. An AQI reading between 32 and 49 indicates moderate air quality, and an AQI reading from 50 to 99 indicates poor air quality. A reading over 100 indicates very poor air quality.

Sources: *Government of Ontario, Environment Canada*

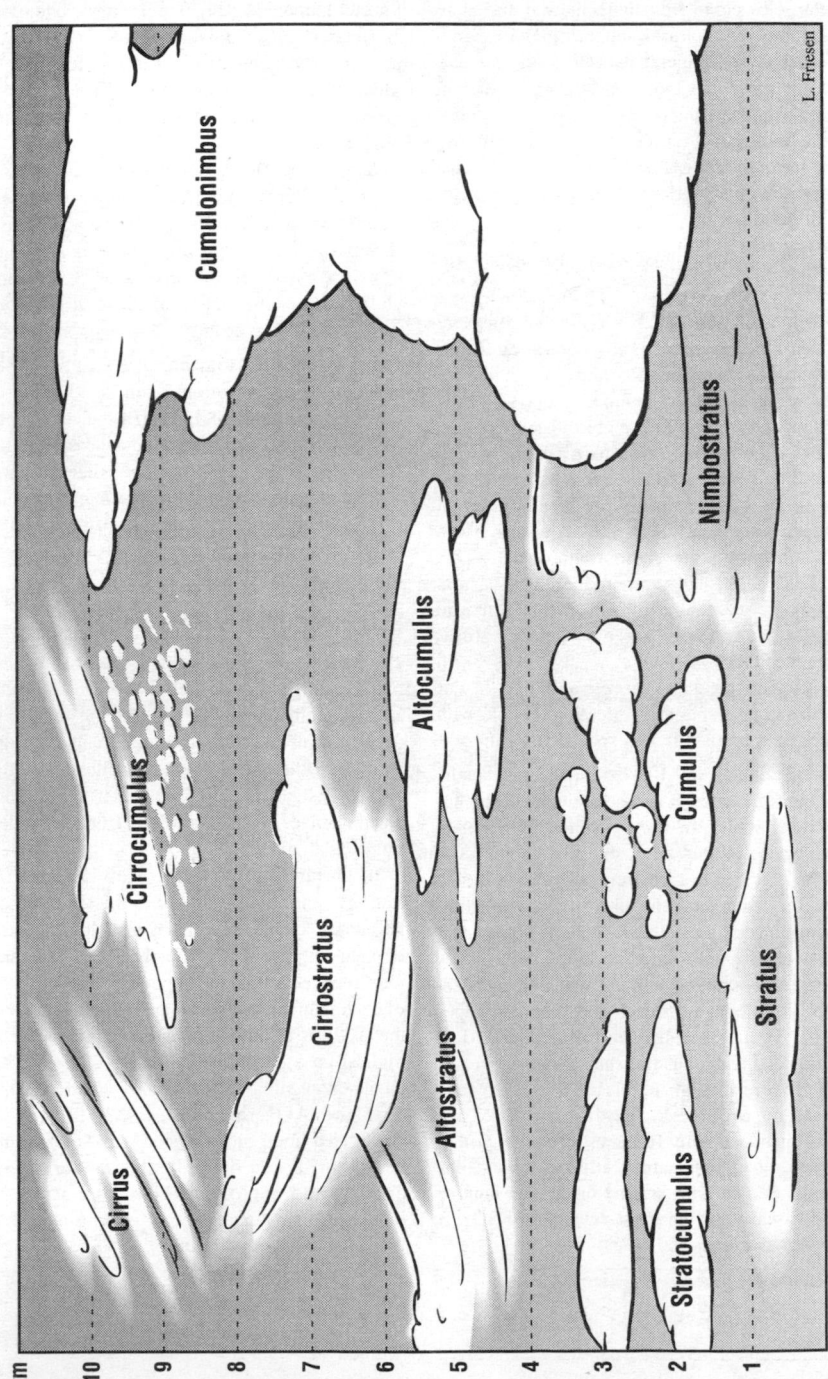

Ten Basic Cloud Types

1. Cirrus
Thin wispy small white clouds that often occur as feathery filaments or long streamers stretching across the sky. Often their ends are swept by strong winds giving it the look of a mare's tail.

2. Cirrostratus
White uniform veil of thin transparent cloud. Sky still appears bright with a halo around the sun. Cloud sheets are small or extensive.

3. Cirrocumulus
Thin bands of either continuous or patchy small clouds, white or pale grey in colour. Cloud base occurs above 6,000 m.; ripple or rib pattern gives it a look of fish-scales, often referred to as a "mackerel sky."

4. Altocumulus
Either patchy or continuous middle cumulus cloud with a dappled or rippled appearance. Thicker and lower version of cirrocumulus that is associated with changeable weather and perhaps rain.

5. Altostratus
Grey pale uniform layer of cloud in which the sun may appear weakly. Too thick and low for halos to be seen; however, through the overcast, the sun can be seen weakly. A sign of precipitation within a few hours.

6. Stratocumulus
Low layers of grey or whitish clouds with occasional dark patches that have a well-defined rounded or undulating appearance. May

have a few breaks, but usually total cloud cover extends for hundreds of kilometres.

7. Stratus
A grey uniform low blanket of cloud that may be continuous or patchy, often producing light drizzle. The base is between the surface and 300 m, often obscuring hill tops and tall buildings. Looks like high drifting fog or making for a dull, grey day.

8. Nimbostratus
A thick low-level (600 m) deck of cloud providing continuous rain or snow. Usually covers the entire sky and completely hides the sun.

9. Cumulus
White puffy clouds that often form by day and disappear by night. Well-defined base begins at 600 to 1,200 m; upper parts are cauliflower-like. Associated with fair weather, blue sky and no precipitation.

10. Cumulonimbus
Giant impressive cumulus clouds with dark base and a smooth anvil-shaped top. Called the kings of the sky, they are the biggest of all clouds, often towering in excess of 10 km. Often associated with severe thunderstorms and sometimes hail or tornadoes. In heavy rain, cumulonimbus clouds have a dark ominous base and a curtain of rain.

Source: *Environment Canada*

Weather Symbols

Meteorologists all around the world use a standard set of symbols in constructing detailed weather maps. Here are some samples of these universal weather symbols:

Dust or Sandstorm	Cumulonimbus clouds
Smoke	Cirrus clouds
Haze	Dust devil
Drizzle	Funnel cloud
Thunderstorms (with hail)	50 knot wind
Freezing Rain (moderate or heavy)	Sky obscured
Fog	Snow
Hail	Drifting Snow

Source: *Environment Canada*

Revisiting the Kyoto Protocol

■ Signing on to Kyoto

The fate of the international Kyoto climate accord—the focus of much controversy both in Canada and around the world—is coming down to a decision by a single country: Russia.

The accord comes into effect when enough countries have agreed to it. But the actual number needed reflects a compromise between environmentalism and economic development. There are two key numbers. The accord comes into effect when 55 nations have ratified it—provided those 55 include enough developed nations to account for 55 percent of the world's 1990 carbon dioxide emissions. By August 2004, 124 countries had signed on—including Canada—but not enough of the developed nations. Of the remaining developed countries that could sign, only Russia and the United States are large enough to bring the treaty into force. However, the U.S.—one of the largest emitters of carbon dioxide—has pulled out, arguing that the science behind the accord is unsound and that implementing it would harm the U.S. economy. Debate on the issue within Russia remains intense but President Vladimir Putin has hinted strongly he will ratify the accord.

■ The Rationale for Kyoto

Climate change is a global problem that affects all countries; a central cause of climate change is greenhouse gases (GHGs), such as methane and carbon dioxide. Many GHGs form naturally, but without human activity, it's unlikely there would be a crisis. Heating and cooling buildings, using energy at home and work, driving vehicles to move people and goods, powering industrial processes—all contribute extra GHGs. Greenhouse gases are so called because they act like the glass in a greenhouse, trapping the warmth of the sun. This is a good thing for hothouse tomatoes, but a bad thing for the earth: scientists believe that the warming trend they see will damage the polar ice caps, cause sea levels to rise, increase the number of extremely violent weather events, and cause agricultural patterns to change. The Intergovernmental Panel on Climate Control (IPCC), set up by the World Meteorological Organization and United Nations Environment Program, estimates that world temperatures will rise on average by between 1.4 and 5.8 degrees this century. In Canada, climate change will affect fishing, farming, forestry, lakes, rivers, coastal communities and the North. To deal with the issue, more than 160 countries from around the world gathered in Kyoto, Japan, in December 1997, and agreed to reduce GHG emissions. The agreement that set out those targets, and the options available to countries to achieve them, became known as the Kyoto Protocol. Canada ratified the agreement Dec. 17, 2002, after a fractious debate. Our target is to reduce GHG emissions to 6 percent below 1990 levels by the period between 2008 and 2012.

■ What Is the Cost?

Economists are divided on the costs of climate control. Clearly, there will be losses in the traditional industries related to the production and export of fossil fuels. However, another view says that changing our economies and lifestyles to slow global climate change is likely to add jobs and growth—although not in the conventional energy sector. Alternative technologies, such as solar and wind power, as well as the production of alternative fuels, would be the new growth areas. There is also, of course, a cost for doing nothing. One of the prime costs, according to the World Wealth Organization, is the impact on public health care. WHO has estimated that the penalty for failing to reduce the levels of air pollution could be as high as 8 million additional deaths around the world between 2000 and 2020.

Former prime minister Jean Chrétien said Canada wants to meet most of its Kyoto obligations through "domestic action" and the government has produced a climate change plan; in the 2004 election, Prime Minister Paul Martin campaigned partly on a promise to implement the plan. Canada is already set to reduce emissions by 65 megatons —one-third of the Kyoto target—and will be looking for ways to achieve the rest in the next few years.

For various views, see these Web sites: unfccc.int/index.html; www.davidsuzuki.org; www3.gov.ab.ca/env/; climatechange.gc.ca

LIFE SCIENCES

The life sciences consist of diverse disciplines that share a knowledge base centred on the same fundamental question, "What is life?" Beginning with biology (the study of living organisms), the life sciences soon included: zoology (the study of animals), botany (the study of plants), and taxonomy (the study of the classification of living things).

Over the last century, an ever-increasing variety of subdisciplines and approaches to studying life have arisen: microbiology (the study of microorganisms), genetics (the study of heredity), biochemistry (the study of chemical compounds and reactions in living organisms), ecology (the study of the relationships between living things and their environment), and ethology (the study of animal behaviour). Most recently these disciplines have been joined by biotechnology (the study and use of organisms or their components for the manufacture or production of commercial substances, aided by techniques of genetic manipulation).

Common Life Sciences Terms

Aerobic: Life processes that depend on the presence of oxygen.

Algae: Simple rootless plants that grow in bodies of water in relative proportion to the amount of nutrients available.

Allergen: Any of various sorts of material that, as a result of coming into contact with appropriate tissues, induce a state of sensitivity and/or resistance to infection or toxic substances.

Anaerobic: Life processes that occur in the absence of oxygen.

Animal: A vertebrate (having a bony skeleton or one made of cartilage) or invertebrate (lacking a spine or skeleton) species including, but not limited to, humans and other mammals, birds, fish, and shellfish.

Bacteria: Single cell microorganisms that possess cell walls. Some cause disease and some are beneficial.

Baleen: Horny plates with fringed inner edges attached to the upper jaw of Mysticeti type whales, such as right and blue whales. The baleen are used to filter plankton and other food from water.

Biodiversity: The total diversity within an ecosystem, including genetic variation among species, diversity of life forms, and ecosystem diversity.

Biomass: The amount of living matter in a given unit of the environment.

Biosphere: The portion of earth (upwards at least to a height of 10,000 m and downward to the ocean floor and 100 km below the planet's surface) and the atmosphere surrounding it that supports life.

Bloom: A seasonal, dense growth of small marine plants, i.e., phytoplankton.

Coniferous: Refers to a softwood, cone-bearing tree.

Deciduous: Refers to a hardwood, leaf-dropping tree.

Effluent Waste: Material discharged into the environment, treated or untreated.

Flood Tide: Interim period of tide between low and high water; a rising tide.

Lagoon: Shallow pond where sunlight, bacterial action and oxygen work to purify waste water.

Marsh: Wet, soft, low-lying land that provides a natural habitat for many plants and animals.

Molt: The periodic casting off or shedding of the outer body covering (feathers, hair, skin or cuticle) by birds, mammals, arachnids and reptiles.

Nutrients: Elements or compounds essential to growth and development of living things: carbon, oxygen, nitrogen, potassium and phosphorus.

Osmosis: Tendency of a fluid to pass through a permeable membrane, such as the wall of a living cell, into a less concentrated solution, so as to equalize concentrations on both sides of the membrane.

Photosynthesis: A process of biochemical change in which plant cells, using light as an energy source, manufacture simple sugars from oxygen and carbon dioxide.

Regeneration (forests): The renewal of a forest by natural processes (self-sown seed or root suckers), as well as by sowing or planting new tree stock.

Synthesis: Production of a substance by the union of elements or simpler chemical compounds. ▶

► **Tailings:** Residue of raw materials or waste separated out during the processing of wood or minerals products.

Tidal Marsh: Low, flat marshlands crossed by interlaced channels and tidal sloughs, and subject to tidal inundation from the ocean, normally, the only vegetation present is salt-tolerant rushes and grasses.

Tide: Alternate rising and falling of water levels twice each lunar day, due to gravitational attraction of the moon and the sun in conjunction with the earth's rotational force.

Major Groups of Living Organisms

All life forms are classified in a hierarchical series of groups. Taxonomy, the science of such classification, was introduced by Swedish scientist Carolus Linneaus (1707–78).

The purpose of classification is to provide each plant or animal on the planet with a unique name by which it is known; to describe it so it may be recognized by anyone; and to place it within a system that shows its relationship to other plants and animals.

The system is flexible, allowing updating as more is learned about individual species and their history.

Naming

The scientific naming of species involves two Latin names. The first word in the species name denotes the Genus the species belongs to. For example, the first word in the scientific name of the Monarch butterfly is *Danaus*. The Monarch belongs to the Genus Danaus.

The second word in the scientific name is particular to a species and can be quite arbitrary. Sometimes species names refer to a person, a country, a particular feature of the animal or plant, or a food source. The second word in the scientific name for the Monarch is *plexippus*. Thus, the scientific name of the Monarch is *Danaus plexippus.*

A species usually also has a common or more familiar name. For example, people seldom refer to the Monarch butterfly as Danaus plexippus.

Species

The basic level in the system is species. The interpretation of differences and similarities between species is often subjective, so the number and name of a species may change. New species are still being found and identified.

Genus

Species with a number of common features are grouped together in Genera. The number of different species in a genus can vary from one to several hundred. Again identification is subjective and the number of genera is not fixed.

Family

Genera are further grouped into Families. Butterfly genera are broadly divided into four major families: 1) Papilionidae (swallowtails); 2) Pierodae (whites and sulphurs); 3) Nymphalidae (brush-footed); and 4) Lycaenidae (hairstreaks, coppers and blues).

Order

Families that share major characteristics are grouped into Orders. For example, butterflies, along with moths, belong to the Order Lepidoptera or insects with scales. The word comes from the Greek words *lepis* (scale) and *pteron* (wing). Classification at this level can be a very complex structure of orders, sub-orders, and sub-sub-orders.

Class

Further up the hierarchy, all Orders belong to a Class. Members of each class show characteristics indicating a common evolutionary descent.

Phylum

At the next level, butterflies, for example, are members of the Phylum Arthropoda, along with millipedes, spiders, and crustaceans, among others. The word Phylum comes from the Greek *phulon* or race.

Kingdom

At the highest level of the hierarchy, butterflies, along with other living creatures, including humans, are members of the Animal Kingdom.

Extinct and Endangered Species in Canada, 2004

The following list has been prepared by the Committee on the Status of Endangered Wildlife in Canada.

The "Extinct" category refers to any species that is indigenous to Canada that no longer exists anywhere in the world. The "Extirpated" category refers to any species that no longer exists in the wild but does occur elsewhere. The "Endangered" category refers to any species threatened with imminent extinction or extirpation throughout all or most of its Canadian range.

For more information, visit the web site www.speciesatrisk.gc.ca.

Species	Habitat	Year Documented
EXTINCT CATEGORY		
Mammals		
Caribou, Woodland	(Queen Charlotte Islands population) BC	1920s, 1984
Mink, Sea	Atlantic coastal waters	1894
Birds		
Auk, Great	QC, NB, NS, NF	1844
Duck, Labrador	QC, NB, NS, NF	1875
Pigeon, Passenger	SK, MB, ON, QC, NB, NS, PE	1914
Fish		
Cisco, Deepwater	ON	1952
Dace, Banff Longnose	AB	1986
Stickleback, Benthic (Hadley Lake)	BC	1999
Stickleback, Limnetic (Hadley Lake)	BC	1999
Walleye, Blue	ON	1965
Molluscs		
Limpet, Eelgrass	QC, NS, NF	1929
Mosses		
Moss, Macoun's Shining	ON	not observed since 1864
EXTIRPATED CATEGORY		
Mammals		
Bear, Grizzly	(Prairie population) AB, SK, MB	1880s
Ferret, Black-footed	AB, SK, MB	1974
Walrus, Atlantic	Atlantic coastal waters	1850
Whale, Grey	Atlantic population	prior 1800
Birds		
Grouse, Sage	(British Columbia population) BC	not observed since 1960's
Prairie-Chicken, Greater	AB, SK, MB, ON	last reported 1987 (SK)
Reptiles		
Lizard, Pygmy Short-Horned	(British Columbia population) BC	last reported 1898, near Osoyoos, BC
Rattlesnake, Timber	ON	1941
Snake, Pacific Gopher	BC	Not seen since 1957
Turtle, Pacific Pond	BC	Not seen since 1959
Fish		
Chub, Gravel	ON	last reported 1958, Thames River drainage
Paddlefish	ON	1917
Amphibians		
Salamander, Tiger	ON	Not observed since 1915
Molluscs		
Wedgemussel, Dwarf	NB	1968
Snail, Puget Oregonian	BC	not observed since 1905
Lepidopterans[1]		
Blue, Karner	ON	1991
Elfin, Frosted	ON	1988
Marble, Island	BC	prior 1910
Plants		
Blue-eyed Mary	ON	not observed since 1954
Tick-trefoil, Illinois	ON	not observed since 1888

▶

Species	Habitat	Year Documented
Mosses		
▶ Moss, Incurved Grizzled	ON	2002

ENDANGERED CATEGORY

Mammals

Species	Habitat	Year Documented
Badger, American	BC, ON	2000
Caribou, Peary	(Banks Island population) (High Arctic population) NT, NU	1991
Caribou, Woodland	(Atlantic - Gaspésie population) QC	2000
Fox, Swift	AB, SK	1998
Marmot, Vancouver Island	BC	1997
Marten, American	(Newfoundland population) NF	1996
Mole, Townsend's	BC	2003
Whale, Beluga	eastern Hudson Bay population NU, QC	2004
Whale, Beluga	Ungava Bay population QC	2004
Whale, Blue	Atlantic and Pacific populations	2002
Whale, Bowhead	Eastern Arctic population	1980
	Western Arctic population	1986
Whale, Killer	Northeast Pacific southern resident population	2001
Whale, North Atlantic Right	Atlantic Ocean	2003
Whale, North Pacific Right	Pacific Ocean	1990
Whale, Northern Bottlenose	(Scotian Shelf population) Atlantic Ocean	2002
Whale, Sei	(Pacific population) Pacific Ocean	2003
Wolverine	(Eastern population) QC, NF	2003

Birds

Species	Habitat	Year Documented
Bobwhite, Northern	ON	1994
Chat, Western Yellow-breasted	BC	2000
Crane, Whooping	NT, NU	1978
Crossbill, Red	NF	2004
Curlew, Eskimo	All provinces and territories except BC	2000
Flycatcher, Acadian	ON	1994
Grouse, Sage	(Prairie population) AB, SK	1998
Lark, Horned	BC	2003
Owl, Barn	(Eastern population) ON, QC	1999
Owl, Burrowing	BC, AB, MB, SK	1995
Owl, Northern Spotted	BC	1999
Plover, Mountain	AB, SK	1987
Plover, Piping	AB, SK, MB, ON, QC, NB, NS, PE, NF	1985
Rail, King	ON	1994
Screech-owl, Western	BC	2002
Shrike, Loggerhead	(Eastern population) MB, ON, QC	1991
Sparrow, Henslow's	ON	1993
Tern, Roseate	QC, NB, NS	1999
Thrasher, Sage	BC, AB, SK	1992
Warbler, Kirtland's	ON	1999
Warbler, Prothonotary	ON	1996
Woodpecker, White-headed	BC	2000

Amphibians

Species	Habitat	Year Documented
Frog, Northern Cricket	ON	1990
Frog, Northern Leopard	(Southern Mountain population) BC	1998
Frog, Oregon Spotted	BC	1999
Frog, Rocky Mountain Tailed	BC	2000
Salamander, Small-mouthed	ON	2004
Salamander, Tiger	BC	2001

Reptiles

Species	Habitat	Year Documented
Racer, Blue	ON	1991
Skink, Prairie	MB	2004
Snake, Lake Erie Water	ON	1991
Snake, Night	BC	2001
Snake, Sharp-tailed	BC	1999
Turtle, Leatherback	Atlantic & Pacific Oceans	1981
Turtle, Spotted	ON, QC	2004 ▶

Species	Habitat	Year Documented
Fish		
Cod, Atlantic	(Newfoundland and Labrador population) Atlantic Ocean	2003
Dace, Nooksack	BC	1996
Dace, Speckled	BC	2002
Lamprey,	Morrison Creek BC	1999
Madtom, Northern	ON	2002
Salmon, Atlantic	(Inner Bay of Fundy populations) NB, NS	2001
Salmon, Coho	(Interior Fraser population) BC	2002
Salmon, Sockeye	(Cultus population) BC	2003
Salmon, Sockeye	(Sakinaw population) BC	2003
Shark, Porbeagle	Atlantic Ocean	2004
Shiner, Pugnose	ON	2002
Stickleback, Benthic	Paxton Lake (Texada Island)BC	1999
Stickleback, Benthic	Enos Lake, BC	2002
Stickleback, Benthic	Vananda Creek BC	1999
Stickleback, Limnetic	Paxton Lake (Texada Island)BC	1999
Stickleback, Limnetic	Vananda Creek BC	1999
Sturgeon, White	BC	2003
Sucker, Salish	BC	1986
Trout, Aurora	ON	2000
Whitefish, Atlantic (Acadian)	NS	1984
Molluscs		
Bean, Rayed	ON	1999
Hickorynut, Round	ON	2003
Forestsnail, Oregon	BC	2002
Kidneyshell	ON	2003
Lampmussel, Wavy-rayed	ON	1999
Mussel, Mudpuppy	ON	2001
Physa, Hotwater	BC	1998
Pigtoe, Round	ON	2004
Riffleshell, Northern	ON	1999
Snail, Banff Springs	AB	1997
Snail, Lake Winnipeg Physa	MB	2002
Snuffbox	ON	2001
Lepidopterans[1]		
Blue, Island	BC	2000
Checkerspot, Taylor's	BC	2000
Metalmark, Mormon	(Southern Mountain population) BC	2003
Moth, Sand-verbena	BC	2003
Moth, Yucca	AB	2002
Ringlet, Maritime	QC, NB	1997
Plants		
Agalinis, Gattinger's	ON	1999
Agalinis, Skinner's	ON	1999
Ammannia, Scarlet	BC, ON	1999
Avens, Eastern Mountain	NS	1999
Balsamroot, Deltoid	BC	1996
Bluehearts	ON	1998
Braya, Long's	NF	1997
Bugbane, Tall	BC	2001
Bulrush, Bashful (Few-flowered Club-rush)	ON	2000
Bush-clover, Slender	ON	1999
Buttercup, Water-plantain	BC	1996
Cactus, Eastern Prickly Pear	ON	1998
Catchfly, Coastal Scouler's	BC	2003
Coreopsis, Pink	NS	1999
Cryptanthe, Tiny	AB, SK	1998
Fern, Southern Maidenhair	BC	1998
Gentian, White Prairie	ON	1991
Ginseng, American	ON, QC	1999
Goat's-rue, Virginia	ON	1996

Species	Habitat	Year Documented
▶ Goldenrod, Showy	ON	1999
Grass, Forked Three-awned	ON, QC	2002
Lady's-slipper, Small White	MB, ON	1999
Lipocarpha, Small-flowered	BC, ON	2002
Lotus, Seaside Birds-foot	BC	1996
Lousewort, Furbish's	NB	1998
Lupine, Prairie	BC	1996
Lupine, Streambank	BC	2002
Milkwort, Pink	ON	1998
Mountain-mint, Hoary	ON	1998
Mulberry, Red	ON	1999
Orchid, Eastern Prairie Fringed	ON	2003
Orchid, Western Prairie Fringed	MB	2000
Owl-clover, Bearded	BC	1998
Owl-clover, Rosy	BC	2004
Paintbrush, Golden	BC	1995
Plantain, Heart-leaved	ON	1998
Pogonia, Large Whorled	ON	1998
Pogonia, Nodding	ON	1999
Pogonia, Small Whorled	ON	1998
Pussytoes, Stoloniferous	BC	2004
Quillwort, Engelmann's	ON	1992
Rush, Kellogg's	BC	2003
Sand-verbena, Pink	BC	2004
Sand-verbena, Small-flowered	AB, SK	2002
Sandwort, Dwarf	BC	2004
Sanicle, Bear's-foot	BC	2001
Sedge, False Hop	ON, QC	1997
Sedge, Juniper	ON	1999
Spike-rush, Horsetail	ON	2000
Sundew, Thread-leaved	NS	1991
Thistle, Pitcher's	ON	1999
Tonella, Small-flowered	BC	2003
Toothcup	BC, ON	1999
Tree, Cucumber	ON	1999
Trefoil, Bog Bird's-foot	BC	2004
Trillium, Drooping	ON	1996
Triteleia, Howell's	BC	2003
Twayblade, Purple	ON	1999
Violet, Bird's-foot	ON	2002
Willow, Barrens	NF	2001
Wintergreen, Spotted	YT, NT, BC, AB	2000
Wood-poppy	ON	1993
Woodsia, Blunt-lobed	ON, QC	1994
Woolly-heads, Dwarf	BC	2003
Woolly-heads, Tall	(Pacific population) BC	2001
Lichens		
Lichen, Boreal Felt	NB, NS	2002
Seaside Centipede	BC	1996
Mosses		
Moss, Apple	BC	1997
Moss, Margined Streamside	BC	2002
Moss, Poor Pocket	BC	2001
Moss, Silver Hair	BC	2002
Moss, Spoon-leaved	ON	2003

Source: *Committee on Status of Endangered Wildlife in Canada*
(1) Lepidopteran: Order of insects with four wings covered by fine scales; butterflies and moths.

FOCUS ON...

Emerging Diseases

It sounds almost amusing: "Mad Cow Disease." But bovine spongiform encephalopathy, or BSE, is no laughing matter. It is devastating to the animals that get it—and it's one of a number of animal diseases that can make the leap to humans. For that reason, even the hint of BSE in a nation's cattle herds is enough to cause other countries to shut their borders to cows and beef products from the affected region.

The Canadian beef industry is only now starting to recover from the effects of such a ban, which occurred after a BSE-infected cow was discovered and removed from a slaughterhouse in Alberta in May 2003. No meat from the cow was ever processed, but the damage was done: the U.S., Japan, and several other countries banned Canadian beef, costing the industry hundreds of millions of dollars.

The disease is caused by misfolded proteins, called prions, and versions of it arise spontaneously in many animals including humans. The prions cause holes to develop in the brain, eventually making it look like a sponge. The spontaneous human version, called Creutzfeldt-Jakob Disease, or CJD, will strike about one in a million people, eventually causing dementia and death. But eating beef from a cow with BSE can lead to a transmitted version of the disease, called variant CJD. Only one case of vCJD has ever been found in Canada, in a man who had lived in Britain and eaten beef during the mad-cow crisis there.

Animal infections that make the jump to humans are called zoonoses, and more than 150 known diseases fall into this category. The flu, for instance, is actually a bird virus that has made the jump to humans. And experts think it's extremely likely that more zoonoses are in our future. Indeed, no one has ever been more wrong than former U.S. Surgeon-General William Stewart, who in 1967 declared that "the war on infectious diseases has been won."

Unfortunately, Stewart didn't reckon on economic and social changes that have meant a constant parade of new diseases. Nor did he take into account the resilience of some of the older diseases that are now bouncing back. Increased travel, global trade, changes in land use, alterations in weather, climate or ecosystems, poverty, war, and inequality are some of the factors contributing to the rise of new diseases.

Severe Acute Respiratory Syndrome (SARS) is thought to have its roots in a virus found in civet cats. It originated in China and spread worldwide in 2003, causing an estimated 800 deaths. The West Nile virus is carried by birds and spread by mosquitoes. Until a few years ago, it was found only in Europe and Africa. Then somehow the virus made it to North America. Once here, mosquitoes picked up the virus and transmitted it first to other birds, and then to mammals, including humans.

The most devastating zoonosis is HIV, the Human Immunodeficiency Virus, which researchers think jumped from chimpanzees or other primates. HIV causes Acquired Immune Deficiency Syndrome, or AIDS, which has caused millions of deaths around the world.

Canada was hard hit by SARS in 2003; there were 44 deaths and Toronto was the subject of a travel advisory, telling people not to visit the city. Hospitals were under severe restrictions to prevent the spread of the disease and several were shut down entirely. But although new cases of SARS have been reported in China in 2004, Canada has not seen any.

The world response to SARS was swift and effective and may be the model for the response to new diseases. In Canada, the government's National Microbiology Laboratory in Winnipeg will play a key role in dealing with any new outbreaks. As well, across North America, officials are putting together early-warning systems to detect outbreaks.

The greatest fear is that the next outbreak of SARS or something like it will not take place in North America, Europe, or even relatively developed regions like Hong Kong and China. Instead, experts fear the effects on places like Africa, where medical infrastructure is limited and where millions of people have weakened immune systems owing to HIV.

For more information, try these Web sites: www.bt.cdc.gov/; www.fas.org/promed; and www.nml.ca

Zoos and Aquariums*

Maritime Region:

☐ **Aquarium and Marine Centre**
100 Aquarium St., Shippigan, NB E0B 2P0.
Tel: (506) 336-3013. Open May to September.
Web site: www.gnb.ca/0181/index-e.asp

☐ **Cherry Brook Zoo**
901 Foster Thurston Dr., Saint John, NB E2K 5H9.
Tel: (506) 634-1440. Open all year.

☐ **Magnetic Hill Zoo**
100 Worthington Ave., Moncton, NB E1C 9Z3.
Tel: (506) 384-0303. Open May to October, with
limited openings on winter weekends. Web site:
http://new-brunswick.net/new-brunswick/moncton/
zoo.html

Central Canada:

☐ **Aquarium du Québec**
1675, ave. des Hotels, Ste-Foy, QC G1W 4S3
Tel: (418) 659-5264. Open daily. Web site:
www.spsnq.qc.ca/

☐ **The Biodome de Montréal**
4777, ave. Pierre-de Coubenin, Montréal, QC
H1V 1B3. Tel: (514) 868-3000. Open all year.
Web site: www.ville.montreal.qc.ca/biodome/ebdm.htm

☐ **African Lion Safari and Game Farm**
RR #1, Cambridge, ON N1R 5S2. Tel: (800) 461-WILD.
Open spring through fall. Web site: www.lionsafari.com/

☐ **Parc safari Africain**
850 Route 202, Hemmingford, QC J0L 1H0.
Tel: (514) 247-2727. Open mid-May to Labour Day.
Web site: www.parcsafari.com

☐ **Bowmanville Zoo**
340 King St. E., Bowmanville, ON L1C 3K5.
Tel: (905) 623-5655. Open daily in summer.
Web site: www.bowmanvillezoo.com

☐ **Centre for Conservation of Boreal Diversity**
2230 boul. du Jardin, Saint-Félicien, QC G8K 2P8.
Tel: 1-800-667-5687. Open mid-May to mid-October.
Web site: www.borealie.org

☐ **Zoo de Granby**
525, rue Saint-Hubert, Granby, QC J2G 5P3.
Tel: 1-877-472-6299. Open May to September.
Web site: www.zoogranby.qc.ca

☐ **Indian River Reptile Zoo**
Indian River, ON K0L 2B0.
Tel: (705) 639-1443. Open daily.
Web site: www.reptilezoo.com

☐ **Jungle Cat World**
3667 Concession 6, Orono, ON L0B 1M0.
Tel: (905) 983-5016. Open daily.
Web site: www.junglecatworld.com

☐ **Marineland**
7657 Portage Road, Niagara Falls, ON.
Tel: (905) 356-9565. Open daily in summer.
Web site: www.marinelandcanada.com

☐ **Toronto Zoo**
361A Old Finch Ave., Scarborough, ON M1B 5K7.
Tel: (416) 392-5900. Open all year.
Web site: www.torontozoo.com

Western Canada:

☐ **Assiniboine Park Zoo**
54 Zoo Dr., Winnipeg, MB R3P 0R5.
Tel: (204) 982-0660. Open all year.
Web site: www.zoosociety.com

☐ **Saskatoon Zoo**
1903 Forest Dr., Saskatoon, SK S7S 1G9.
Tel: (306) 975-3382. Open all year.

☐ **Calgary Zoo**
1300 Zoo Road N.E., Calgary, AB T2M 4R8.
Tel: (403) 232-9300. Open all year.
Web site: www.calgaryzoo.ab.ca

☐ **Dolphin Lagoon**
West Edmonton Mall, #2472, 8770-170 St.,
Edmonton, AB T5T 4M2. Tel: 1-800-661-8890.
Web site: www.westedmall.com/parks/dolphin.htm

☐ **Valley Zoo**
PO Box 2359, 13315 Buena Vista Rd, Edmonton, AB
T5J 2R7. Tel: (780) 496-8787. Open all year.
Web site: www.gov.edmonton.ab.ca/valleyzoo/

☐ **Crystal Garden**
613 Pandora Ave., Victoria, BC V8W 1N8.
Tel: (250) 953-8800. Open all year.
Web site: www.bcpcc.com/crystal

☐ **Greater Vancouver Zoological Centre**
5048-264 St., Aldergrove, BC V4W 1N7.
Tel: (604) 856-6825. Open daily.
Web site: www.greatervancouverzoo.com

☐ **Kamloops Wildlife Park**
PO Box 698, East Trans Canada Highway, Kamloops,
BC V2C 5L7. Tel: (250) 573-3242. Open all year.
Web site: www.kamloopswildlife.org

☐ **Mountain View Farms Breeding and
Conservation Centre** 23898 Rowlinson Cres.,
Langley, BC V3A 4P9. Tel: (604) 882-9313. Open
daily. Web site: www.mtnviewfarms.com

☐ **Vancouver Aquarium Marine Science Centre**
PO Box 3232, Stanley Park, Vancouver, BC
V6B 3X8. Tel: (604) 659-3474. Open all year.
Web site: www.vanaqua.org

*Accredited by the Canadian Association of Zoos and
Aquariums.

ARTS AND MEDIA

Canada may well have been one of the best kept secrets on the world's arts and entertainment scene, but the secret is getting harder and harder to keep as artists like Atom Egoyan, Alanis Morissette, Robert LePage, and Yann Martel make their mark. Historically, the small size and scattered nature of the Canadian market made dissemination of Canadian works of art and entertainment products difficult. But the years following World War II saw an explosion of activity in every sector, fuelled by public institutions such as the CBC, the Canada Council for the Arts, and the National Film Board and similar provincial and local agencies. Canadian content requirements for broadcasters and tax and investment measures favouring Canadian publishers have also helped foster successful, if fragile, publishing and recording industries. In 2001–2002 all levels of government devoted $6.1 billion to culture (this includes federal support for the CBC and provincial and local support for public libraries). Restraints on public spending over the past two decades have caused emphasis to be placed on private investment and on production for foreign markets. During the 1990s, film and TV production saw a 200 percent increase in foreign investment and a 33 percent increase in private sector Canadian investment. At the same time Canadian authors, agents and publishers found the sale of foreign rights to be a lucrative stream of revenue in a world hungry to read the work of writers such as Carol Shields, Michael Ondaatje, Anne Michaels and Ann-Marie MacDonald.

MAJOR ARTS COUNCILS

The Canada Council: 350 Albert St, Box 1047, Ottawa, ON K1P 5V8, tel: (613) 566-4414 (toll-free: 1-800-263-5588); fax: (613) 566-4390; e-mail: [employee name]@canadacouncil.ca (see personnel directory at Web site); Web site: www.canadacouncil.ca

Alberta Foundation for the Arts: Alberta Community Development, 901 Standard Life Centre, 10405 Jasper Ave, Edmonton, AB T5J 4R7; tel: (780) 427-9968; fax: (780) 422-9132; e-mail: afa@mcd.gov.ab.ca; Web site: www.affta.ab.ca

British Columbia Arts Council: Box 9819, Stn Prov. Govt, Victoria, BC V8W 9W3; tel: (250) 356-1718; fax: (250) 387-4099; e-mail: BCArtsCouncil @gems2.gov.bc.ca; Web site: www.bcartscouncil.ca

Manitoba Arts Council: 525-93 Lombard Ave, Winnipeg, MB R3B 3B1; tel: (204) 945-2237; fax: (204) 945-5925; e-mail: info@artscouncil.mb.ca; Web site: www.artscouncil.mb.ca

New Brunswick Arts Board: 634 Queen St, Ste 300, Fredericton, NB E3B 1C2; tel: 1-866-460-ARTS; e-mail: [employee name]@artsnb.ca (see personnel directory at Web site); Web site: www.artsnb.ca

Newfoundland and Labrador Arts Council: Box 98, St. John's, NF A1C 5H5; tel: 1-866-726-2212; fax: (709)726-0619; e-mail: nlacmail@nfld.net; web site: www.nlac.nf.ca

Northwest Territories Arts Council: Department of Education, Culture and Employment, Government of the Northwest Territories, Box 1320, Yellowknife, NT X1A 2L9; tel: (867) 920-3103; fax: (867) 873-0205

Nova Scotia Arts and Culture Partnership Council: World Trade and Convention Centre, 1800 Argyle St, Ste 402, PO Box 456, Halifax, NS B3J 2R5; tel: (902) 424-6471; fax (902) 424-0170; e-mail: turnerpm@gov.ns.ca

Ontario Arts Council: 151 Bloor St W, 5th floor Toronto, ON M5S 1T6; tel: (416) 961-1660 (toll-free in Ontario: 1-800-387-0058); fax: (416) 961-7796; e-mail: info@arts.on.ca; Web site: www.arts.on.ca

P.E.I. Council of the Arts: 115 Richmond St, Charlottetown, PE C1E 1H7; tel: (902) 368-6176; fax: (902) 368-4418; e-mail: peiarts@peiartscouncil.com; Web site: www.peiartscouncil.com

Conseil des arts et des lettres du Quebec: Quebec bureau: 79, boul René-Lévesque Est, 3e étage, Quebec, QC G1R 5N5; tel: (418) 643-1707 (toll-free: 1-800-897-1707); fax: (418) 643-4558; Montreal bureau: 500, Place d'Armes, 15e étage, Montréal, QC H2Y 2W2; tel: (514) 864-3350 (toll-free1-800-608-3350); fax: (514) 864-4160; e-mail: affaires.publiques@calq.gouv.qc.ca; Web site: www.calq.gouv.qc.ca

Saskatchewan Arts Board: 2135 Broad St, Regina, SK S4P 3V7; tel: (306) 787-4056 (toll-free in Saskatchewan: 1-800-667-7526); fax: (306) 787-4199; e-mail: sab@artsboard.sk.ca; Web site: www.artsboard.sk.ca

Yukon Tourism, Arts Branch: PO Box 2703, Whitehorse, YT Y1A 2C6; tel: (867) 667-5386 (toll-free in Yukon: 1-800-661-0408); fax: (867) 667-8023; e-mail: arts@gov.yk.ca; Web site: www.btc.gov.yk.ca/cultural/MAJOR ARTS

TELEVISION

Television first reached Canada in the 1940s from border stations in the United States. The Canadian Broadcasting Corporation's TV services were launched in 1952. The launch in English Canada was less than auspicious; the first image to appear on the screen was the CBC logo presented upside down. The CBC recovered its poise and the network grew rapidly, opening stations across the country and broadcasting its programs on affiliated private stations.

CBC TV was joined by the private Canadian Television Network in 1961. The CanWest/Global system began in the 1970s and has become Canada's third major television network. Through the 1980s and 1990s the CRTC has licensed dozens of specialty cable services to ensure that Canadian services offer viewers a full range of choices.

While the most-watched television programs in Canada continue to be American dramas and situation comedies, Canadian broadcasters have scored considerable success with programs such as *Traders* and *DaVinci's Inquest*, *Street Legal*, and *Due South*. Canadian producers have been particularly successful with children's programs such as *Mr. Dressup* and with sketch comedy programs including *SCTV*, *Codco*, and *This Hour Has 22 Minutes*.

Today the television market accounts for 70 percent of the 14,000 film projects undertaken in Canada each year. Much of that production is destined for air in the United States and other countries as international coproduction becomes an increasingly popular way of funding television programs around the world.

Canada's Television Classification System

In the fall of 1997, a television classification system was formally launched on Canadian airwaves to help Canadians identify programming suitable to various age groups. There are seven classification levels. Although violence is the most important content consideration, each classification also includes information on coarse language, nudity and sex. The classifications are designed for use with V-chip technology which enables parents to block reception of undesirable programs. In 2001, Canada implemented a V-chip system using the following classifications:

 Children: Might contain occasional comedic, unrealistic depictions of violence. No offensive language. No sex or nudity.

 Children Over 8 Years: Might include mild physical violence, comedic violence, comic horror, special effects; fantasy, supernatural, or animated violence. No profanity. No sex or nudity.

 General: Violence is minimal and infrequent. Contains no frightening special effects not required by the storyline. May contain inoffensive slang. No profanity. No sex or nudity.

 Parental Guidance: Moderate violence which must be justified within the context of the storyline. Might contain mild profanity, suggestive language, some nudity.

 Over 14 Years: Might contain intense scenes of violence. Could include frequent profanity. Might include scenes of nudity and/or sexual activity.

 Adults: Depictions of violence are intended for adult viewing, and thus are not suitable for audiences under 18 years of age. Might contain graphic language and explicit portrayals of sex and/or nudity.

Exempt: News, sports, documentaries, and other information programming, talk shows, music videos, and variety programming.

Source: *Media Awareness Network, www.media-awareness.ca*

The CRTC: Canada's Communications Watchdog

The Canadian Radio-television and Tele-communications Commission (CRTC) regulates all aspects of the Canadian broadcasting system. It grants licences to radio and television broadcasters, enforces the conditions of those licences and reviews broadcaster performance at regularly scheduled hearings. Created under the Broadcasting Act of 1968, the Commission inherited a long tradition of government supervision of broadcasting in Canada. Radio broadcasting was regulated in its early days under the Radiotelegraph Act. In the 1930s responsibility for radio was shifted to the newly created Canadian Broadcasting Corporation. Private broadcasters were unhappy with a system that gave their public sector competitor the right to supervise their businesses and so an independent regulator, the Board of Broadcast Governors (BBG) was formed in 1958. The Broadcasting Act of 1968 replaced the BBG with the CRTC. The commission scored a success with the establishment of Canadian content regulations in 1971 for radio. Through the 1980s and 1990s it insisted on higher levels of quality Canadian programming from private television broadcasters and oversaw the introduction of dozens of new specialty services on cable and satellite television. While the CRTC also supervises telecommunications it announced in 1999 that it would not attempt to regulate the Internet.
Web site: www.crtc.gc.ca

The Gemini Awards, 1988–2002

The Gemini Awards were established in 1986 to honor outstanding contributions to the Canadian television industry. Given out annually by the Academy of Canadian Cinema and Television, the Geminis grew out of the former ACTRA Awards, last presented in 1985. The 18th annual Geminis were held Oct. 18–20, 2003, in Toronto.

1986
Dramatic Series . . . . *Night Heat*
Comedy Series . . . . *Seeing Things*
TV Movie . . . . *Love & Larceny*
Actor (Dramatic Series) . . . . Robert Clothier, *The Beachcombers*
Actress (Dramatic Series) . . . . Marnie McPhail, *The Edison Twins*

1987
Dramatic Series . . . . *Night Heat*
Comedy Series . . . . *Seeing Things*
TV Movie . . . . *The Marriage Bed*
Actor (Dramatic Series) . . . . . . Winston Rekert, *Adderly*, Eric Peterson, *Street Legal*
Actress (Dramatic Series) . . . . Dixie Seatle, *Adderly*

1988
Dramatic Series . . . . *Degrassi Jr. High*
TV Movie . . . . *Skate*
Actor (Dramatic Series) Pat Mastroianni, *Degrassi Jr. High*
Actress (Dramatic Series) . . . Sonja Smits, *Street Legal*

1989
Dramatic Series . . . . *Degrassi Jr. High*
Comedy Series . . . . *Codco*
TV Movie . . . . *The Squamish Five*
Actor (Dramatic Series) . . . . Eric Peterson, *Street Legal*
Actress (Dramatic Series) . . . . Stacy Mistysyn, *Degrassi Jr. High*

1990
Dramatic Series . . . . *E.N.G.*
Comedy Series . . . . *Material World*
TV Movie . . . . *Where The Spirit Lives*
Actor (Dramatic Series) . . . . Art Hindle, *E.N.G.*
Actress (Dramatic Series) . . . . Jackie Burroughs, *Road to Avonlea*

1991
Awards not presented

1992
Dramatic Series . . . . *E.N.G.*
Comedy Series . . . . *Codco*
TV Movie . . . . *Journey Into Darkness: The Bruce Curtis Story*
Actor (Dramatic Series) . . . . Eric Peterson, *Street Legal*
Actress (Dramatic Series) . . . . Jackie Burroughs, *Road to Avonlea*

1993
Dramatic Series . . . . *E.N.G.*
Comedy Series . . . . *The Kids in the Hall*
TV Movie . . . . *Scales of Justice*
Actor (Dramatic Series) . Cedric Smith, *Road to Avonlea*
Actress (Dramatic Series) . . . . . . Sarah Botsford, *E.N.G.*

1994
Dramatic Series . . . . *E.N.G.*
Comedy Series . . . . *The Kids in the Hall*
TV Movie . . . . *The Diviners*
Actor (Dramatic Series) . . James Purcell, *Counterstrike*
Actress (Dramatic Series) . . . . Jackie Burroughs, *Road to Avonlea* ▶

▶ **1995**
Dramatic Series . . . . *Due South*
Comedy Series . . . . *This Hour Has 22 Minutes*
TV Movie . . . . *Due South*
Actor (Dramatic Series) . . . . Paul Gross, *Due South*
Actress (Dramatic Series)Lally Cadeau, *Road to Avonlea*

1996
Dramatic Series . . . . *Due South*
Comedy Series . . . . *This Hour Has 22 Minutes*
TV Movie . . . . *Butterbox Babies*
Actor (Dramatic Series) . . . . Paul Gross, *Due South*
Actress (Dramatic Series) . . . . . . Joely Collins, *Madison*

1997
Dramatic Series . . . . *Due South*
Comedy Series . . . . *This Hour Has 22 Minutes*
TV Movie . . . . *Net Worth*
Actor (Dramatic Series) . . . . David Cubitt, *Traders*
Actress (Dramatic Series) . . . . Tina Keeper, *North of 60*

1998 (12th annual)
Dramatic Series . . . . *Traders*
Comedy Series . . . . *This Hour Has 22 Minutes*
TV Movie . . . . *Hiroshima*
Actor (Dramatic Series) . . . . Bruce Gray, *Traders*
Actress (Dramatic Series) Patti Harras, *Jake and the Kid*

1998 (13th annual)
Dramatic Series . . . . *Traders*
Comedy Series . . . . *This Hour Has 22 Minutes*
TV Movie . . . . *The Sleep Room*
Actor (Dramatic Series) . . . . . Patrick McKenna, *Traders*
Actress (Dramatic Series) . . . . Sheila McCarthy,
Emily of New Moon

1999
Dramatic Series . . . . *Da Vinci's Inquest*
Comedy Series . . . . *Made In Canada*
TV Movie . . . . *Milgaard*
Actor (Dramatic Series) . . . . . Michael Riley, *Powerplay*
Actress (Dramatic Series) . . . . Arsinée Khanjian,
Foolish Heart
Newscast . . . . *The National*, Swissair Disaster

2000
Dramatic Series . . . . *Da Vinci's Inquest*
Comedy Series . . . . *This Hour Has 22 Minutes*
TV Movie . . . . *Dr Lucille: The Lucille Teasdale Story*
Actor (Dramatic Series) . . . . . Michael Riley, *Powerplay*
Actress (Dramatic Series) . . . . Torri Higginson, *The City*
Newscast . . . . *The National*, May 5, 1999

2001
Dramatic Series . . . . *Da Vinci's Inquest*
Comedy Series . . . . *Made In Canada*
TV Movie . . . . *Scorn*
Actor (Dramatic Series) . . . . Nicholas Campbell,
Da Vinci's Inquest
Actress (Dramatic Series) . . . . Babz Chula,
These Arms of Mine
Newscast . . . . *The National*, Oct. 2

2002
Dramatic Series . . . . *Da Vinci's Inquest*
Comedy Series . . . . *An American In Canada*
TV Movie . . . . *Torso*
Actor (Dramatic Series) . . . . Donnelly Rhodes,
Da Vinci's Inquest
Actress (Dramatic Series) . . . Julie Stewart, *Cold Squad*
Newscast . . . . *The National*

The Gemini Awards, 2003

Dramatic series . . . . *The Eleventh Hour*
Comedy series . . . . *This Hour Has 22 Minutes*
TV movie . . . . *100 Days in the Jungle*
Actor (dramatic series) . . . . Jeff Seymour, *The Eleventh Hour*
Actor (dramatic program) . . . . Michael Riley, *The Interrogation of Michael Crowe*
Supporting actor (dramatic program or mini-series) . . . . Ted Whittall, *Agent of Influence*
Supporting actor (dramatic series) . . . . Peter MacNeil, *The Eleventh Hour*
Actress (dramatic series) . . . . Marina Orsini, *The Last Chapter II: The War Continues*
Actress (dramatic program) . . . . Wendy Crewson, *The Many Trials of One Jane Doe*
Supporting actress (dramatic program or mini-series) . . . . Janet Wright, *Betrayed*
Supporting actress (dramatic series) . . . . Jennie Raymond, *Blue Murder*
Performance (performing arts program or series) . . . . . Peter James, Antoine Carabinier-Lepine, Jean (Jano) Chiasson, Marie-Michelle Faber, Geneviève Gauthier, Thanh Dinh Huynh, Van Anh Le Tran, Andréane Leclerc, Geneviève Lemay, Manuel Roque, Édith Sauvé-Letellier, Samuel Tétreault, Lucie Vigneault, Shira Wohlberg, Koichi Yano, *Cirque Orchestra*
Ensemble Performance (comedy program or series) . . . . Cathy Jones, Colin Mochrie, Greg Thomey, Mary Walsh, *This Hour Has 22 Minutes—Season X*, "Episode 14"
Performance or Host (variety program or series) . . . . Sean Cullen, *17th Annual Gemini Awards*
Animated program or series . . . . *Doodlez*, p. Gretha Rose
Children's or youth fiction program or series . . . . . . *Degrassi: The Next Generation*, p. Linda Schuyler, Stephen Stohn
Children's or youth non-fiction program or series . . . . *Street Cents*, p. Barbara Kennedy, Wendy Purves
Documentary series . . . . *Rough Cuts*, p. Andrew Johnson
Lifestyle/general information series . . . . *Taking It Off*, p. Margaret Mardirossian
Best Talk Series . . . . *Studio 2*, p. Doug Grant, Jane Jankovic
Sports program or series . . . . *The Hockey Nomad*, p. Nick de Pencier, Mike Downie News
Information series . . . . *CBC News: Disclosure*
Newscast . . . . *CBC News: The National*
Performing arts program or series . . . . *Stormy Weather: The Music of Harold Arlen*, p. Larry Weinstein
Short dramatic program . . . . *When I Was Seven*, p. Andrea Bastin
Science, technology, nature, environment or adventure documentary program . . . . *The Nature of Things*, "The Investigation of Swiss Air 111," p. Howard Green, Michael Allder, Kurt Schaad

Source: *Academy of Canadian Cinema and Television*

The Most-Watched Television Programs in Canada[1]

Top 10 Programs[2]

1. Academy Awards (CTV)
2. Golden Globe Awards (CTV)
3. Academy Awards Pre-show (CTV)
4. *World Idol* (Results) (CTV)
5. *Harry Potter and the Philosopher's Stone* (CBC)
6. *World Idol* (CTV)
7. CBC News: *Canada Votes 2* (CBC)
8. *Barbara Walters* (CTV)
9. Golden Globe Awards Pre-show(CTV)
10. People's Choice Awards (CTV)

Top 10 Regularly Scheduled Programs

1. *American Idol 3* (Performances) (CTV)
2. *American Idol 3* (Results) (CTV)
3. *C.S.I.* (CTV)
4. *C.S.I. Miami* (CTV)
5. *Canadian Idol 2* (Performances) (CTV)
6. *E.R.* (CTV)
7. *Canadian Idol* (Auditions) (CTV)
8. *Amazing Race 5* (CTV)
9. *American Idol 3* (Specials) (CBC)
10. *Canadian Idol 2* (Results) (CTV))

Source: *Nielsen Media Research*
(1) Persons 2+ for the period Sept. 1, 2003–Aug. 29, 2004 (2) Specials, not including sports.

The Primetime Emmy Awards, 2003–2004

The Emmy Awards are presented annually on behalf of the U.S. Academy of Television Arts and Sciences. The 56th annual Primetime Emmy Awards were presented September 19, 2004 at the Shrine auditorium in Los Angeles, California.

OUTSTANDING DRAMA SERIES . . . . *The Sopranos*
Actor (drama series) . . . . James Spader, *The Practice*
Actress (drama series) . . . . Allison Janney, *The West Wing*
Supporting actor (drama series) . . . . : . . . . Michael Imperioli, *The Sopranos*
Supporting actress (drama series) . . . . Drea de Matteo, *The Sopranos*
Directing (drama series) . . . . Walter Hill, *Dreadwood* (Pilot)
Writing (drama series) . . . . Terence Winter, "Long Term Parking," *The Sopranos*

OUTSTANDING COMEDY SERIES . . . . *Arrested Development*
Actor (comedy series) . . . . Kelsey Grammer, *Frasier*
Actress (comedy series) . . . . Sarah Jessica Parker, *Sex And The City*
Supporting actor (comedy series) . . . . David Hyde Pierce, *Frasier*
Supporting actress (comedy series) . . . . Cynthia Nixon, *Sex And The City*
Directing (comedy series) . . . . Joe Russo, Anthony Russo, *Arrested Development* (Pilot)
Writing (comedy series) . . . . Michael Hurwitz, *Arrested Development* (Pilot)

OUTSTANDING MINISERIES . . . . *Angels In America*
Actor (comedy series) . . . . Al Pacino, *Angels In America*
Actress (miniseries) . . . . Meryl Streep, *Angels In America*
Supporting actor (miniseries) . . . . Jeffrey Wright, *Angels In America*
Supporting actress (miniseries) . . . . Mary-Louise Parker, *Angels In America*
Directing (miniseries) . . . . Mike Nichols, *Angels In America*
Writing (miniseries) . . . . Tony Kushner, *Angels In America*

OUTSTANDING VARIETY, MUSIC OR COMEDY SERIES . . . . *The Daily Show With Jon Stewart*
Directing (variety or music) . . . . Louis J. Horvitz, The 76th Annual Academy Awards
Writing (variety or music) . . . . David Javerbaum *et al*, *The Daily Show With Jon Stewart*
Performance (variety or music) . . . . Elaine Stritch, *Elaine Stritch: At Liberty*
Outstanding TV movie . . . . *Something the Lord Made*

OUTSTANDING REALITY/COMPETITION PROGRAM . . . . *The Amazing Race*

All-Time Highest Rated TV Programs in Canada

Rank	Year[1]	Network	Program	Audience (000)[2]
1.	1983	CBC	M*A*S*H (Final episode)	9 030
2.	2002	CBC	Olympic Hockey (Gold Medal Game)	8 960
3.	1992	CTV	World Series Game 6	6 717
4.	1998	CTV	Academy Awards	6 605
5.	1992	CTV	World Series Game 2	6 280
6.	1984	CBC	Stanley Cup Final Game 5	6 192
7.	1992	CTV	World Series Game 3	6 103
8.	1986	CBC	Anne of Green Gables Pt.2	5 837
9.	1974	CBC	Canada/USSR Hockey....................	5 774
10.	1993	CTV	World Series Game 6	5 721
11.	1987	CBC	Anne of Green Gables Sequel Pt.1	5 666
12.	1992	CTV	World Series Game 4	5 611
13.	1984	CBC	NHL Playoffs Game 4	5 319
14.	2001	CTV	Academy Awards	5 100
15.	1993	CTV	World Series Game 5	5 016
16.	1988	CBC	Ben Johnson 100 metres, Seoul Olympics	5 015
17.	1997	CTV	Academy Awards	5 008
18.	1996	CTV	Academy Awards	4 984
19.	1987	CBC	Anne of Green Gables Sequel Pt.2	4 974
20.	1994	CBC	NHL Playoff Game 7	4 957
21.	1984	CBC	NHL Semi-final Game 7.....................	4 936
22.	1986	CBC	Anne of Green Gables Pt.1	4 908
23.	1989	CBC	NHL Playoff Game 5	4 788
24.	1992	CTV	World Series Game 2	4 771
25.	1994	CBC	NHL Playoff Game 3	4 762
26.	2002	CBC	Olympic Hockey (Gold Medal Game)	4 536

Source: *CBC Research (Nielsen)*
(1) After Sept. 1989, average minute audience measured with people meter data. Before Sept. 1989, average quarter-hour audience based on diary measurement. (2) All demographics, aged 2+. Only CBC and CTV audiences reported.

Average TV Viewing Hours In Canada[1]

Sex	Age group	Hrs. Weekly
M&F	2 to 11 years	14.6
M&F	12 to 17 years	13.7
Males	18 years and over..................	21.0
Males	18 to 24 years	12.6
Males	25 to 34 years	16.6
Males	35 to 49 years	18.9
Males	50 to 59 years	22.7
Males	60 years and over..................	31.9
Females.............	18 years and over..................	25.8
Females.............	18 to 24 years	16.3
Females.............	25 to 34 years	21.7
Females.............	35 to 49 years	22.7
Females.............	50 to 59 years	27.5
Females.............	60 years and over..................	35.9

Source: *Statistics Canada*   (1) Data collected over 4-week period, November 2002.

Television Networks and Cable Services

Arts & Entertainment Network (A&E):
235 E 45th St, New York, NY 10017
(212) 210-1400 www.aetv.com

Atlantic Television System & Atlantic Satellite Network: 2885 Robie St, Halifax, NS B3K 5Z4
(902) 453-4000 www.atv.ca

Bravo!: 299 Queen St W, Toronto, ON
M5V 2Z5 (416) 591-5757 www.bravo.ca

Canadian Broadcasting Corporation (CBC):
Box 500, Stn A, Toronto, ON M5W 1E6
(416) 205-3311 www.cbc.ca

Canal Famille: 2100 Sainte-Catherine ouest,
Bureau 800, Montreal, QC H3H 2T3
(514) 939-3150

CanWest/Global Communications Corp.:
201 Portage Ave, 31st Flr, TD Centre,
Winnipeg, MB R3B 3L7 (204) 956-2025

CTV Television Network Ltd: Box 9, Stn O,
9 Channel Nine Ct, Scarborough, ON M1S 4B5
(416) 332-5000 www.ctv.ca

Discovery Channel: 9 Channel Nine Ct,
Scarborough, ON M1S 4B5 (416) 332-5000
www.discovery.ca

The Family Channel Inc.: BCE Place,
181 Bay St, Box 787, Toronto, ON M5J 2T3
(416) 956-2030 www.family.ca

Global Television Network: 81 Barber Greene
Rd, Don Mills, ON M3C 2A2 (416) 446-5311
www.canada.com

Life Network: 121 Bloor St E, Ste 200, Toronto, ON
M4W 3M5 (416) 967-0022 www.lifenetwork.ca

The Movie Network/Viewers Choice: BCE Place,
181 Bay St, Box 787, Toronto, ON M5J 2T3

(416) 956-2010, www.themovienetwork.ca,
www.viewerschoice.ca

MuchMusic, MuchMoreMusic: 299 Queen St W,
Toronto, ON M5V 2Z5 (416) 591-5757
www.muchmusic.com, www.muchmore
music.com

MusiquePlus: 355 Sainte-Catherine est,
Montreal, QC H3B 1A5 (514) 284-7587
www.musiqueplus.com

Showcase Television Inc.: 121 Bloor St E,
#200, Toronto, ON M4W 1B9 (416) 967-3253
www.showcase.ca

Télé-Québec: 1000, rue Fullum, Montreal,
QC H2K 3L7 1-800-361-4301 www.telequebec.
qc.ca

The Sports Network (TSN): 9 Channel Nine Ct,
Scarborough, ON M1S 4B5 (416) 332-5000
www.tsn.ca

Telelatino Network Inc.: 5125 Steeles Ave W,
Weston, ON M9L 1R5 (416) 744-8200
www.tlntv.com

TVOntario (TVO): Box 200, Stn Q, Toronto, ON
M4T 2T1 (416) 484-2600 www.tvo.org

Vision TV: 80 Bond St, Toronto, ON M5B 1X2
(416) 368-3194 www.visiontv.ca

W Network: W Network, 64 Jefferson Ave,
Unit 18, Toronto, ON M6K 3H4 (416) 534-1191
ext. 5155 www.wnetwork.com

YTV Canada Inc.: 64 Jefferson Ave, Unit 18,
Toronto, ON M6K 3H4. (416) 534-1191
www.ytv.com

MUSIC

The watershed year in the Canadian music industry was 1971, when the federal government imposed Canadian content regulations on the country's radio stations. These regulations helped build a domestic recording industry that has produced several generations of world-class pop stars including Bryan Adams, Céline Dion, Sarah MacLachlan and Shania Twain.

Montreal, Toronto and Vancouver have consistently served as centres for the Canadian popular music industry. But other cities have served as hotbeds at various periods. Winnipeg in the 1960s was dubbed the Liverpool of Canada for a scene that launched the careers of Neil Young and The Guess Who. The Ottawa

Valley has long been a place of musical ferment owing to the interaction of Irish, Scottish and French settlers. Bruce Cockburn and Alanis Morrissette are two of the National Capital Region's best-known alumni.

Nova Scotia and Newfoundland have historically been home to vibrant Celtic folk traditions and the 1990s saw the rise of Atlantic Canada as a major centre for music production in Canada. Those traditions have been parlayed into commercial success for artists such as Great Big Sea, The Rankins, singer Rita MacNeil, and folk/rock fiddlers Ashley MacIsaac and Natalie MacMaster.

The Juno Awards, 1995–2004

The Juno Awards were established in 1975 to honour achievement in the Canadian recording industry. The name was chosen to honour Pierre Juneau, former head of the Canadian Radio-television and Telecommunications Commission (CRTC) which instituted "Canadian content" requirements in the nation's broadcast industry.

Nominations for most major Juno categories are determined by record sales, although the actual winners are selected by a vote of members of the Canadian Academy of Recording Arts & Sciences.

Nominees must be Canadian citizens or landed immigrants and must have resided in Canada during the year prior to their nomination. Eligible recordings don't require national distribution, but must be available for retail sale in Canada.

The latest awards were announced April 4, 2004. The awards ceremony was broadcast live from Edmonton.

Canadian Entertainer of the Year
1995 . . . . The Tragically Hip
1996 . . . . Shania Twain

Juno Fan Choice Award
2003 . . . . Shania Twain
2004 . . . . Nickelback

Best Selling Album (Foreign or Domestic)
2000 . . . . *Millennium*, Backstreet Boys
2001 . . . . *The Marshall Mathers LP*, Eminem
2002 . . . . *Hotshot*, Shaggy

International Album of the Year
2003 . . . . *The Eminem Show*, Eminem
2004 . . . . *Get Rich Or Die Tryin'*, 50 Cent

Best Album
1995 . . . . *Colour of My Love*, Céline Dion
1996 . . . . *Jagged Little Pill*, Alanis Morissette
1997 . . . . . . *Trouble at the Henhouse*, The Tragically Hip
1998 . . . . *Clumsy*, Our Lady Peace
1999 . . . . *Let's Talk About Love*, Céline Dion
2000 . . . . *Supposed Former Infatuation Junkie*,
 Alanis Morissette
2001 . . . . *Maroon*, The Barenaked Ladies
2002 . . . . *The Look of Love*, Diana Krall
2003 . . . . *Let Go*, Avril Lavigne
2004 . . . . *We Were Born In a Flame*, Sam Roberts

Best Single
1995 . . . . "Could I Be Your Girl," Jann Arden
1996 . . . . "You Oughta Know," Alanis Morissette
1997 . . . . "Ironic," Alanis Morissette
1998 . . . . "Building a Mystery," Sarah McLachlan
1999 . . . . "One Week," The Barenaked Ladies
2000 . . . . "Bobcaygeon," The Tragically Hip
2001 . . . . "I'm Like A Bird," Nelly Furtado
2002 . . . . "How You Remind Me," Nickelback
2003 . . . . "Complicated," Avril Lavigne
2004 . "Powerless (Say What You Want)," Nelly Furtado

Best Artist
2002 . . . . Diana Krall
2003 . . . . Shania Twain
2004 . . . . Sam Roberts

Best Female Artist
1995 . . . . Jann Arden
1996 . . . . Alanis Morissette
1997 . . . . Céline Dion
1998 . . . . Sarah McLachlan
1999 . . . . Céline Dion
2000 . . . . Chantal Kreviazuk
2001 . . . . Jann Arden

Best Male Artist
1995 . . . . Neil Young
1996 . . . . Colin James
1997 . . . . Bryan Adams
1998 . . . . Paul Brandt
1999 . . . . Jim Cuddy
2000 . . . . Bryan Adams
2001 . . . . Neil Young

Best Group
1995 . . . . The Tragically Hip
1996 . . . . Blue Rodeo
1997 . . . . The Tragically Hip
1998 . . . . Our Lady Peace
1999 . . . . The Barenaked Ladies
2000 . . . . Matthew Good Band
2001 . . . . The Barenaked Ladies
2002 . . . . Nickelback
2003 . . . . Sum 41
2004 . . . . Nickelback

Best Songwriter
1995 . . . . Jann Arden
1996 . . . . Alanis Morissette, Glen Ballard
1997 . . . . Alanis Morissette, Glen Ballard
1998 . . . . Sarah McLachlan, Pierre Marchand
1999 . Bryan Adams, Phil Thornalley "On A Day Like Today";
 Bryan Adams, Eliott Kennedy, "When You're Gone" ▶

▶ 2000 . . . . Shania Twain, Robert John "Mutt" Lange, "Man! I Feel Like A Woman," "You've Got A Way," "That Don't Impress Me Much"

2001 . . . . Nelly Furtado, "Turn Off The Light," "I'm Like A Bird," "...on the radio (remember the days)"

2002 . . . . . . Jann Arden, Russell Brown, "Never Mind,"

2003 . . . . Chad Kroeger/Nickelback, "Hero"; Nickelback, "Too Bad," "How You Remind Me"

2004 . . . . Sarah McLachlan-Pierre Marchand, "World On Fire," "Fallen," "Stupid"

Best New Solo Artist

1995	Susan Aglukark
1996	Ashley MacIsaac
1997	Terri Clark
1998	Holly McNarland
1999	Melanie Doane
2000	Tal Bachman
2001	Nelly Furtado
2002	Hawksley Workman
2003	Avril Lavigne
2004	Michael Bublé

Best New Group

1995	Moist
1996	The Philosopher Kings
1997	The Killjoys
1998	Leahy
1999	Johnny Favourite Swing Orchestra
2000	Sky
2001	Nickelback
2002	Default
2003	Theory of a Deadman
2004	Billy Talent

Best Francophone Album

1995	*Coup de tête*
1996	*D'eux*
1997	*Live À Paris*
1998	*Marie Michèle Desrosiers Chante Les Classiques de Noël*
1999	*S'il Suffisait D'Aimer*, Céline Dion
2000	*En Catimini*, La Chicane
2001	*Un grand noël d'amour*, Ginette Reno
2002	*Les Vents ont changé*, Kevin Parent
2003	*Rêver Mieux*, Daniel Bélanger
2004	*Wilfred Le Bouthillier*, Wilfred Le Bouthillier

Best Country Recording

2003	"I'm Gonna' Getcha' Good," Shania Twain
2004	"Up!" Shania Twain

Best Country Artist

2002	Carolyn Dawn Johnson
2003	Shania Twain

Best Country Female Artist

1995	Michelle Wright
1996	Shania Twain
1997	Shania Twain
1998	Shania Twain
1999	Shania Twain
2000	Shania Twain
2001	Terri Clark

Best Country Male Artist

1995	Charlie Major
1996	Charlie Major
1997	Paul Brandt
1998	Paul Brandt
1999	Paul Brandt
2000	Paul Brandt
2001	Paul Brandt

Best New Country Artist/Group

2002	Ennis Sisters

Best Country Group or Duo

1995	Prairie Oyster
1996	Prairie Oyster
1997	The Rankin Family
1998	Farmer's Daughter
1999	Leahy
2000	The Rankins
2001	The Wilkinsons

Best Pop/Adult Album

2000	*Colour Moving And Still*, Chantal Kreviazuk
2001	*Maroon*, The Barenaked Ladies
2002	*Morning Orbit*, David Usher
2003	*Let Go*, Avril Lavigne
2004	*Afterglow*, Sarah McLachlan

Best Rock Album

1995	*Suffersystem*, Monster Voodoo Machine
1996	*Jagged Little Pill*, Alanis Morissette
2000	*Beautiful Midnight*, Matthew Good Band
2001	*Music @ Work*, The Tragically Hip
2002	*Silver Side Up*, Nickelback
2003	*Gravity*, Our Lady Peace
2004	*We Were Born In a Flame*, Sam Roberts

Best Alternative Album

1998	*Glee*, Bran Van 3000
1999	*Rufus Wainwright*, Rufus Wainwright
2000	*Julie Doiron and the Wooden Stars*, Julie Doiron and the Wooden Stars
2001	*Mass Romantic*, The New Pornographers
2002	*Poses*, Rufus Wainwright
2003	*You Forgot It In People*, Broken Social Scenes
2004	*Talkin' Honky Blues*, Buck 65

Best Rap Recording

1995	"Certified," Ghetto Concept
1996	"E-Z On Tha Motion," Ghetto Concept ▶

1997	"What It Takes," Choclair
1998	"Cash Crop," Rascalz
1999	"Northern Touch," Rascalz featuring Choclair, Kardinal Offishall, Thrust and Checkmate
2000	"Ice Cold," Choclair
2001	"Balance," Swollen Members
2002	"Bad Dreams," Swollen Members
2003	"Monsters in the Closet," Swollen Members
2004	"Flagrant," Choclair

Best Dance Recording

1995	"Higher Love (Club Mix)," Capital Sound
1996	"A Deeper Shade of Love (Extended Mix)," Camille
1997	"Astroplane" (City of Love Mix)," BKS
1998	"Euphoria" (Rabbit in the Moon Mix)," Delerium
1999	"Broken Bones," Love Inc.
2000	"Silence," Delerium
2001	"Into the Night," Love Inc.
2002	"Spaced Invaders," Hatiras
2003	"The Sound Bluntz," Billie Jean
2004	"Something About You," The Sound Bluntz

Best Contemporary Jazz Album

1995	*The Merlin Factor*, Jim Hillman & The Merlin Factor
1996	*NOJO*, Neufeld-Occhipinti Jazz Orchestra
1997	*Africville Suite*, Joe Sealy
1998	*Metalwood*, Metalwood
1999	*Metalwood 2*, Metalwood
2000	*...so far*, D.D. Jackson
2001	*Compassion*, François Carrier Trio
2002	*Live*, François Bourassa Trio + André LeRoux
2003	*tales from the blue lounge*, Richard Underhill
2004	*bLOW tHE hOUSE dOWN*, Great Uncles of the Revolution

Best Vocal Jazz Album

2000	*When I Look In Your Eyes*, Diana Krall
2001	*Both Sides Now*, Joni Mitchell
2002	*The Look of Love*, Diana Krall
2003	*Live In Paris*, Diana Krall
2004	*Shade*, Holly Cole

Best Mainstream/Traditional Jazz Album

1995	*Free Trade*, Free Trade
1996	*Vernal Fields*, Ingrid Jensen
1997	*Ancestors*, Renee Rosnes
1998	*In the Mean Time*, The Hugh Fraser Quintet
1999	*The Atlantic Sessions*, Kirk MacDonald
2000	*Deep In A Dream*, Pat LaBarbera
2001	*Rob McConnell Tentet*, Rob McConnell Tentet
2002	*Murley, Bickert & Wallace: Live at the Senator*
2003	*Life On Earth*, Renee Rosnes, Mike Murley
2004	*Lost In The Stars*, Guido Basso

Best R&B/Soul Recording

1995	"First Impressions for the Bottom Jigglers," Bass is Base
1996	"Deborah Cox," Deborah Cox
1997	"Feelin' Alright," Carlos Morgan

1998	"Things Just Ain't the Same," Deborah Cox
1999	"One Wish," Deborah Cox
2000	"Thinkin' About You," 2Rude featuring Latoya & Miranda
2001	"Sleepless," jacksoul
2002	"Don't You Forget It," Glenn Lewis
2003	"The Way I Feel," Remy Shand
2004	"The Master Plan," In Essence

Best Blues/Gospel Album

1995	*Joy to the World Jubilation V*, Montreal Jubilation Gospel Choir
1996	*That River*, Jim Byrnes
1997	*Right To Sing The Blues*, Long John Baldry

Best Blues Album

1998	*National Steel*, Colin James
1999	*Blues Weather*, Fathead
2000	*Gust Of Wind*, Ray Bonneville
2001	*Love Comin' Down*, Sue Foley
2002	*Big Mouth*, Colin Linden
2003	*6-String Lover*, Jack de Keyzer
2004	*Painkiller*, Morgan Davis

Best Gospel Album

1998	*Romantics and Mystics*, Steve Bell
1999	*Life Is*, Sharon Riley & Faith Chorale
2000	*Legacy Of Hope*, Deborah Klassen
2001	*Simple Songs*, Steve Bell
2002	*Downhere*, Downhere
2003	*Instrument of Praise*, Toronto Mass Choir
2004	*Jill Paquette*, Jill Paquette

Best Reggae/Calypso Recording

1995	*Class and Credential*, Carla Marshall
1996	*Now and Forever*, Sattalites
1997	*Nana Maclean*, Nana Maclean
1998	*Catch de Vibe*, Messenjah
1999	*Vision*, Frankie Wilmot
2000	*Heart & Soul*, Lazo
2001	*Lenn Hammond*, Lenn Hammond
2002	*Love (African Woman)*, Blessed
2003	*You Won't See Me Any More*, Sonia Collymore
2004	*Rent a Tile*, Leroy Brown

Best Global/ World Music Album

1995	*Africa+*, Eval Manigat
1996	*Music From Africa*, Takadja
1997	*Africa Do Brasil*, Paulo Ramos Group
1998	*La Llorona*, Lhasa
1999	*La Llorona*, Lhasa
2000	*Omnisource*, Madagascar Slim
2001	*Ritmo + Soul*, Jane Bunnett and the Spirits of Havana
2002	*The Journey*, Alpha Yaya Diallo
2003	*Balagane*, Jeszcze Raz
2004	*Beyond Boundaries*, Kiran Ahluwalia ▶

Best Roots and Traditional Album

1995 . . . . *The Mask and Mirror,* Loreena McKennitt
1996 . *Hi: How Are You Today?,* Ashley MacIsaac (solo);
Gypsies & Lovers, The Irish Descendants (group)
1997 . . . . *drive-in movie,* Fred Eaglesmith (solo);
Matapedia, Kate & Anna McGarrigle (group)
1998 . . . . *Other Songs,* Ron Sexsmith (solo)
Molinos, The Paperboys (group)
1999 . . . . *Heartstrings,* Willie P Bennett (solo)
The McGarrigle Hour, Kate & Anna McGarrigle (group)
2000 . . . *Breakfast In New Orleans, Dinner In Timbuktu,*
Bruce Cockburn (solo)
Kings Of Love, Blackie & The Rodeo Kings (group)
2001 . . . . *Jenny Whiteley,* Jenny Whiteley (solo)
Tri-Continental, Tri-Continental, Bill Bourne,
Lester Quitzau, Madagascar Slim (group)
2002 . . . . *Cordial,* La Bottine Souriante
2003 . . . .*Unravel,* Lynn Miles (solo),
Chicken Scratch, Zubot & Dawson (group)
2004 . . . . *Skating Rink,* David Francey (solo)
Maudite Moisson, Le Vent du Nord (group)

Instrumental Artist(s) of the Year

1995 . . . . André Gagnon
1996 . . . . Liona Boyd
1997 . . . . Ashley MacIsaac
1998 . . . . Leahy

Best Instrumental Album

1999 . . . . . . *My Roots Are Showing,* Natalie MacMaster
2000 . . . . *In My Hands,* Natalie MacMaster
2001 . . . . *Free Fall,* Jesse Cook
2002 . . . . *Armando's Fire,* Oscar Lopez
2004 . . . . *Italian Love Songs,* I Sorenti

Best Classical Album (solo or chamber ensemble)

1995 . . . . . *Erica Goodman Plays Canadian Harp Music,*
Erica Goodman
1996 . . . . *Aikan: Grande Sonate/Sonatine,*
Marc-André Hamelin
1997 . . . . *Scriabin: The Complete Piano Sonatas,*
Marc-André Hamelin
1998 . . . . *Marc-André Hamelin plays Franz Liszt,*
Marc-André Hamelin
1999 . . . . *Bach: Well-Tempered Clavier – Book 1,*
Angela Hewitt
2000 . . . . *Schumann: String Quartets,*
St. Lawrence String Quartet
2001 . . *Bach: The Six Sonatas & Partitas For Solo Violin*
James Ehnes
2002 . . . . *Bach Arrangements,* Angela Hewitt
2003 . . . . *Allegro,* Robert Michaels
2004 . . . . *Murphy, Chan, Hatzis, Kulescha:*
Canadian Premieres, Gryphon Trio

Best Classical Album (large ensemble)

1995 . *Bach: Brandenburg Concertos Nos 1-6,* Tafelmusik
1996 . . . . . *Shostakovich: Symphonies 5 & 9, Orchestra*
Symphonique de Montréal
1997 . . . . *Ginastera/Villa-Lobos/Evangelista,*
I Musici de Montreal

1998 . . . . *Mozart Horn Concertos,* James Sommerville,
CBC Vancouver Orchestra, Mario Bernardi
1999 . . . . *Handel: Music For The Royal Fireworks,*
Tafelmusik, Jeanne Lamon (Musical Director)
2000 . . . . . *Respighi: La Boutique Fantasque,* Orchestre
Symphonique de Montréal
2001 . . . . . *Sibelius: Lemminkäinen Suite — Night Ride*
And Sunrise, Toronto Symphony Orchestra
2002 . . . . . . *Max Bruch, Concertos 1 & 3,* James Ehnes,
violin—Orchestre Symphonique de Montréal
2003 . . . . *Bruch Concertos: Vol II,* James Ehnes/
Mario Bernardi/Orchestre symphonique de Montréal
2004 . . . . . *CONCERTOS: Music of Jacques Hétu,* André
Laplante, piano/Christopher Millard, bassoon/Robert
Cram, flute/Joaquin Valdepenas, clarinet/CBC Radio
Orchestra/Mario Bernardi, conductor

Best Classical Album (vocal or choral performance)

1995 . . . . *Berlioz: Les Troyens,* Vocal Soloists,
Choeur et Orchestre symphonique de Montréal
1995 *Ben Heppner Sings Richard Strauss,* Ben Heppner,
Toronto Symphony Orchestra, Andrew Davis, conductor
1997 *Berlioz: La Damnation de Faust,* Choeur et Orchestre
symphonique de Montreal, Charles Dutoit, Conductor
1998 . . *Soirée Francaise,* Michel Schade, Russel Braun,
Canadian Opera Company Orchestra, Richard Bradshaw
1999 . . . . *Songs Of Travel,*
Gerald Finley (baritone), Stephen Ralls (piano)
2000 . . . . *German Romantic Opera,* Ben Heppner
2001 . . . . *G.F Handel: Apollo e Dafne Silete Venti,*
Karina Gauvin; Russell Braun; Les violons du Roy
2002 . . . . *Air Français,* Ben Heppner
2003 . . . . *Mozart Requiem,* Les Violons du roi
2004 . . . . . . *Azul?o,* Isabel Bayrakdarian, James Parker,
Cello Ensemble

Best Classical Composition

1995 . . . . *Sketches From Natal,* Malcolm Forsyth
1996 *Concerto For Violin and Orchestra,* Andrew P MacDonald
1997 . . . . *Picasso Suite,* Harry Somers
1998 . . . . *Electra Rising,* Malcolm Forsyth
1999 . . . . *Concerto for Wind Orchestra,* Colin McPhee
2000 . . . *Shattered Night, Shivering Stars,* Alexina Louie
2001 . . .*From The Diary of Anne Frank,* Oskar Morawetz
2002 . . . . *Par-çi, par la,* Chan Ka Nin
2003 . . . . .*Requiem for a Charred Skull,* Bramwell Tovey
2004 . . . . *String Quartet No. 8,* R. Murray Schaeffer,
Quatuor Morinari

Best Children's Album

1995 . . . . *Bananaphone,* Raffi
1996 . . . . *Celery Stalks at Midnight,* Al Simmons
1997 . . . . . *Songs From the Treehouse,* Martha Johnson
1998 . . . . *Livin' in a Shoe,* Judy & David
1999 . . . . *Mozart's Magnificent Voyage,*
Susan Hammond's Classical Kids
2000 . . . . *Skinnamarink TV,* Sharon, Lois and Bram
2001 . . . . *Sing & Dance,* Jack Grunsky
2002 . . . *A Classical Kids Christmas,* Susan Hammond
2003 . . . . *Sing with Fred,* Fred Penner
2004 . . . . *A Duck In New York City,* Connie Kaldor ▶

Producer of the Year

1995	Robbie Robertson
1996	Michael-Phillip Wojewoda
1997	Garth Richardson
1998	Pierre Marchand
1999	Colin James (co-producer, Joe Hardy)
2000	Tal Bachman and Bob Rock
2001	Gerald Eaton, Brian West and Nelly Furtado
2002	Daniel Lanois (co-producer Brian Eno), "Beautiful Day," "Elevation," U2
2003	Alannis Morrissette, "Hands Clean," "So Unsexy"
2004	Gavin Brown

Best Video

1995	*Tunnel of Trees* (Gogh Van Go), Lyne Charlebois
1996	*Good Mother* (Jann Arden), Jeth Weinrich
1997	*Burned Out Car* (Junkhouse), Jeth Weinrich
1998	*Gasoline* (Moist), Javier Aguilera

Source: *Canadian Academy of Recording Arts & Sciences*

1999	*Forestfire (David Usher)*, Javier Aguilera
2000	*So Pure*, Alanis Morissette
2001	*Alive* (Edwin), Rob Heydon
2002	*Jealous of Your Cigarette* (Hawksley Workman), Sean Michael Turrell
2003	*Weapon*, Ante Kovac, Matthew Good
2004	*Fighter*, Floria Sigismundi, Christina Aguilera

Best Music of Aboriginal Canada Recording

1995	Susan Aglukark
1996	Jerry Alfred & The Medicine Beat
1997	Buffy Ste. Marie
2000	*Falling Down*, Chester Knight & The Wind
2001	*Nipaiamianan*, Florent Voliant
2002	*On and On*, Eagle & Hawk
2003	*Lovesick Blues*, Derek Miller
2004	*Big Feeling*, Susan Aglukark

Canadian Music Hall of Fame

The Canadian Academy of Recording Arts and Sciences instituted a Hall of Fame Award in 1978 to honour Canadians who have contributed to the greater international recognition of Canadian artists and music.

■ Winners

Year	Winner	Year	Winner	Year	Winner
1978	Guy Lombardo	1987	The Guess Who		Zal Yanovsky
	Oscar Peterson	1989	The Band	1997	Lenny Breau
1979	Hank Snow	1990	Maureen Forrester		Gil Evans
1980	Paul Anka	1991	Leonard Cohen		Maynard Ferguson
1981	Joni Mitchell	1992	Ian & Sylvia		Moe Kauffman
1982	Neil Young	1993	Anne Murray		Rob McConnell
1983	Glenn Gould	1994	Rush	1998	David Foster
1984	The Crewcuts	1995	Buffy Sainte-Marie	1999	Luc Plamondon
	The Diamonds	1996	David Clayton-Thomas	2000	Bruce Fairbairn
	The Four Lads		Denny Doherty	2001	Bruce Cockburn
1985	Wilf Carter		Domenic Troiano	2002	Daniel Lanois
1986	Gordon Lightfoot		John Kay	2003	Tom Cochrane

2004 INDUCTEE
■ Bob Ezrin

This Canadian-born producer extraordinaire is one of the most commercially successful and sonically creative masters of the recording studio in rock history. In the mid-1970s, he teamed with Jack Richardson and Dave Greene to build Soundstage Studios in Toronto. It became one of the most in-demand studios in North America, and many of rock's superstars travelled to the city to work there. Ezrin and Alice Cooper struck multi-platinum together on such early 1970s albums as *Killer, School's Out* and *Billion Dollar Babies* and continued making hits together for over 10 years. KISS had a smash with the Ezrin-produced *Destroyer* in 1976. Bob was also at the helm for Peter Gabriel's self-titled debut, also in 1976. Bob worked on records by an amazingly diverse range of artists in the 1970s and 1980s. These included Lou Reed (the critically hailed masterpiece, *Berlin*), Poco, Flo & Eddie, Rhinoceros, Mitch Ryder, Roberta Flack (*Blue Lights in the Basement*), Hanoi Rocks, Air Supply, Rod Stewart, and Julian Lennon.

A milestone credit came in 1979 with his production of Pink Floyd's *The Wall*, now viewed as one of the most important rock albums of all time.

Source: *Canadian Academy of Recording Arts and Sciences* www.juno-awards.ca/caras/

The East Coast Music Awards, 2004

The East Coast Music Awards were established in 1989 to honour outstanding contributions to the Canadian music industry by artists performing, recording, or rooted in Atlantic Canada, and to celebrate that region's distinct musical heritage in English and in French. The ECMAs were presented February 12–15, 2004, in St. John's, Nfld.

Male Artist of the Year. . . . . Jimmy Rankin
Female Artist of the Year. . . . . Damhnait Doyle
Group of the Year . . . . Crush
Bluegrass Recording of the Year . . *The Shores of Nova Scotia*, Birchmountain Bluegrass Band
Songwriter of the Year . Corie Tetford, Gordie Sampson, "King for a Day"
Single of the Year . . . . "King for a Day," Crush
Video of the Year . . . . Sloan, "The Rest of My Life"
Album of the Year . . . . . . *Get Back Change*, Ron Hymes
New Artist of the Year . . . . Matt Mays
Entertainer of the Year . . . . Crush
Country Recording of the Year . . . . . . *Get Back Change*, Ron Hymes
Pop Recording of the Year . . . . *Davnet*, Damhnait Doyle
Rock Recording of the Year . . *Face in the Crowd*, Crush
Instrumental Recording of the Year. . . . . *Infectious*, Richard Wood

Alternative Recording of the Year . *Talkin' Honky Blues* Buck 65
Jazz Recording of the Year . . . . *HavanaFax* Live, Jeff Goodspeed & Jorge Chicoy
Blues Recording of the Year. . . . . *Live At Last*, Matt Minglewood
Gospel Recording of the Year *A Burke Family Christmas*, The Burkes
Urban Recording of the Year *I Took the Long Way Home*, Dutch Robinson
Classical Recording of the Year. . . . . *Stravinsky: Works for Violin & Piano*, Jasper Wood
Roots/Traditional Solo Recording of the Year *Handmade*, Jimmy Rankin
Roots/Traditional Group Recording of the Year *Can't Be The Same*, Ennis Sisters
Francophone Recording of the Year *Blou Blanc Rouge*, Blou

The Grammy Awards, 1999–2003

Grammy winners are selected annually by the 6,000 voting members of The Recording Academy, based on artistic and/or technical excellence.

The titles for song of the year are followed by the names of the songwriters. The 2003 Grammy winners were announced Feb. 8, 2004.

Best Record
1999 . . . . . "Smooth," Santana featuring Rob Thomas
2000 . . . . "Beautiful Day," U2
2001 . . . . "Walk On," U2
2002 . . . . "Don't Know Why," Norah Jones
2003 . . . . "Clocks," Coldplay

Best Album
1999 . . . . *Supernatural*, Santana
2000 . . . . *Two Against Nature*, Steely Dan
2001 . . . . *O Brother, Where Art Thou?* (soundtrack), Various Artists
2002 . . . . *Come Away With Me*, Norah Jones
2003. . . . . *Speakerboxxx/The Love Below*, OutKast

Best Song
1999 . "Smooth," Itaal Shur & Rob Thomas, songwriters
2000 . . . . "Beautiful Day," U2
2001 . . . . "Fallin,'" Alicia Keys
2002 . . . . "Don't Know Why," Jesse Harris
2003 . . . . "Dance With My Father," Richard Marx & Luther Vandross

Best Male Pop Vocal
1999 . . . . "Brand New Day," Sting
2000 . . . . "Again," Lenny Kravitz
2001 . . "Don't Let Me Be Lonely Tonight," James Taylor
2002 . . . . "Your Body Is a Wonderland," John Mayer
2003 . . . . "Cry Me A River," Justin Timberlake

Best Female Pop Vocal
1999 . . . . . **"I Will Remember You," Sarah McLachlan**
2000 . . . . "There Goes the Neighborhood," Sheryl Crow
2001 . . . . **"I'm Like a Bird," Nelly Furtado**
2002 . . . . "Don't Know Why," Norah Jones
2003 . . . . "Beautiful," Christina Aguilera

Best Rap Album
1999 . . . . *The Slim Shady LP*, Eminem
2000 . . . . *The Marshall Mathers LP*, Eminem
2001 . . . . *Stankonia*, Outkast
2002 . . . . *The Eminem Show*, Eminem

Best Male Country Vocal Performance
1999 . . . . "Choice," George Jones
2000 . . . . "Solitary Man," Johnny Cash
2001 . . . . "O Death," Ralph Stanley
2002 . . . . "Give My Love to Rose," Johnny Cash
2003 . . . . "Next Big Thing," Vince Gill

Best Female Country Vocal Performance
1999 . . . . **"Man! I Feel Like A Woman!" Shania Twain**
2000 . . . . "Breathe," Faith Hill
2001 . . . . "Shine," Dolly Parton
2002 . . . . "Cry," Faith Hill
2003 . . . "Keep On The Sunny Side," June Carter Cash

Best Jazz Vocal Album
2003 . . . . *A Little Moonlight*, Dianne Reeves ▶

▶

Best Jazz Vocal Performance
1999 ..... "When I Look In Your Eyes," Diana Krall
2000 "In the Moment—Live in Concert," Dianne Reeves
2001 .... "The Calling," Dianne Reeves

Best Instrumental Soloist(s) Performance (with Orchestra)
1999 "Prokofiev: Piano Concertos. Nos. 1 & 3; Bartók: Piano Con. No. 3," Martha Argerich & the Montreal Symphony Orchestra
2000 .... "Maw: Violin Concerto," Joshua Bell & the London Philharmonic Orchestra

2001 .... Strauss Wind Concertos (Horn Concerto; Oboe Concerto, Etc.)," Daniel Barenboim
2002 "Brahms/Stravinsky Violin Concertos," Hilary Hahn
2003 .... "Britten: Violin Concerto/Walton: Viola Concerto," Mstislav Rostropovich, conductor; Maxim Vengerov, violin & viola.

Best New Artist
1999 .... Christina Aguilera
2000 .... Shelby Lynne
2001 .... Alicia Keys
2002 .... Norah Jones
2003........................... Evanescence

Source: *National Academy of Recording Arts & Sciences*

The ADISQ ("Félix") Awards, 2003

The Felix Awards have been presented annually since 1978 by ADISQ, the umbrella group representing the Québec music, video, and performance industry, to acknowledge achievement in Canada's French language music and performance scene. The 25th awards were held at ADISQ's annual gala, October 20, 2003.

Popular Song of the Year......... "Et c'est pas fini," Various Artists
Group of the Year .... Les Cowboys Fringuants
Best Female Vocalist............... Isabelle Boulay
Best Male Vocalist............... Sylvain Cossette
Album of the Year (alternative) .... Attache ta tuquel, Les Cowboys Fringuants
Album of the Year (popular) .... Star Académie, Various Artists
Album of the Year (pop-rock) .... Aquanaute, Ariane Moffatt
Album of the Year (rock) .... La vallée des réputations, Jean Leloup
Album of the Year (contemporary folk) Je marche á toi, Chloé Sainte-Marie
Album of the Year (hip-hop) ... J'rêvolutionne, Muzion
Album of the Year (jazz) .... Then & Now, Oliver Jones and Skip Bey
Bestselling Album ..... Star Académie, Various Artists
Album of the Year (electronic/techno) .. Train to Reofa, Les Jardiniers
Best Quebec Artist in a Language Other than French .... Bob Walsh

Best Artist from "la francophonie," .... Indochine
Album of the Year (traditional). . Wô, Les Charbonniers de l'enfer
Album of the Year (world music)...... Intakto, Intakto
Writer/Composer of the Year .... Jérôme Minière
Album of the Year (country) ... Chansons consignées, Les Ours
Album of the Year (classical, large ensemble) ......
Max Bruch—Concerto no. 2 / Scottish Fantasy, James Ehnes, Orchestre symphonique de Montréal
Album of the Year (classical, soloist/small ensemble)
Handel—Love Duets, Suzie LeBlanc, Daniel Taylor and Arion
Video of the Year ... Dans un spoutnik, Daniel Bélanger
Album of the Year (children's)...... Annie Brocoli d l'espace, Annie Brocoli
Album of the Year (instrumental) ..... Piano Solitude, André Gagnon
Album of the Year (humour)....... L'album Pirate de François Pérusse, François Pérusse
Album of the Year (original soundtrack) ... Un homme et son péché, Michel Cusson

www.musiccentre.ca: The Canadian Music Centre On-line

*W*ith offices in Toronto, Montreal, Vancouver, Calgary and Sackville, the Canadian Music Centre promotes the works of its Associate Composers, and encourages the performance and appreciation of Canadian music, making it available to the public through its sales operations and through lending libraries at each of its locations. These services have now been enhanced by on-line services available on the CMC web site. An on-line catalogue search gives visitors access to the centre's database of nearly 600 composers' works, including score samples and audio clips. Scores may be borrowed free of charge. A selection of published and unpublished music is available for purchase. The site's "Buy a Recording" area offers access to the most complete commercial CD catalogue in the world of recorded music by Canadian composers.

The Canadian Academy of Recording Arts and Sciences (CARAS)

*T*his organization was originally created to administer and promote the Juno Awards. It has since expanded its mandate to link members of the Canadian music community and members of the public interested in the Canadian music and recording industry. The Junos themselves remain the centrepiece, to recognize (and reward) outstanding achievement in recorded music. The broadcast of the Junos brings singers, musicians, songwriters, producers and other creative talent together and to the attention of both a national audience and foreign markets.

Beginning with jazz and big band legends Oscar Peterson and Guy Lombardo in 1978, CARAS has inducted a figure from the Canadian music scene into the Canadian Music Hall of Fame each year. A database of these inductees is maintained on the Juno awards web site, www. juno-awards.ca. Just click the Juno History button on the Junos' home page. CARAS is in the process of expanding this database to provide complete biographical information on each inductee. The Junos' web site offers complete contact information on CARAS and information on the Junos nomination process.

Top 50 Albums in Canada, 2003

Artist, Title	Artist, Title
1. Norah Jones, *Come Away With Me*	26. Eminem, *Eminem Show*
2. **Shania Twain, *Up!***	27. Various Artists, *Don Juan*
3. 50 Cent, *Get Rich or Die Tryin'*	28. **Michael Bublé, *Michael Bublé***
4. **Various, *Star Académie***	29. Various Artists, *Big Shiny Tunes 8*
5. Evanescence, *Fallen*	30. Clay Aiken, *Measure of a Man*
6. **Avril Lavigne, *Let Go***	31. ***Wilfred Le Bouthillier, Wilfred Le Bouthillier***
7. **Sarah McLachlan, *Afterglow***	32. Black Eyed Peas, *Elephunk*
8. Sean Paul, *Dutty Rock*	33. *Chicago*, Soundtrack
9. Linkin Park, *Meteora*	34. Josh Groban, *Josh Groban*
10. **Celine Dion, *One Heart***	35. Various Artists, *Now! 8*
11. **Nickelback, *Long Road***	36. Rod Stewart, *Great America Song Book*
12. Coldplay, *Rush of Blood to the Head*	37. Britney Spears, *In The Zone*
13. Hilary Duff, *Metamorphosis*	38. Blink 182, *Blink 182*
14. Metallica, *St. Anger*	39. *8 Mile*, Soundtrack
15. Sheryl Crow, *Very Best of Sheryl Crow*	40. Kelly Clarkson, *Thankful*
16. Various Artists, MuchDance 2004	41. Radiohead, *Hail to the Thief*
17. Christina Aguilera, *Stripped*	42. Various, *Grammy Nominees 2003*
18. Rod Stewart, *Vol. II-Great American Songs*	43. **Bruno Pelletier, *Concert de Noël***
19. Josh Groban, *Closer*	44. **Celine Dion, *Une fille et 4 types***
20. Dixie Chicks, *Home*	45. *Bad Boys II*, Soundtrack
21. Dido, *Life For Rent*	46. Outkast, *Speakerboxx-Love*
22. White Stripes, *Elephant*	47. Various Artists, *MuchDance 2003/DansePlus*
23. *Lizzie McGuire Movie*, Soundtrack	48. Justin Timberlake, *Justified*
24. Beyoncé, *Dangerously In Love*	49. Elton John, *Greatest Hits 1970-2002*
25. Good Charlotte, *Young & the Hopeless*	50. G-Unit, *Beg For Mercy*

Source: *Chart Information Supplied By Soundscan. Copyright (C) 2003 By Soundscan, Inc. All Rights Reserved.*
Note: Canadian artists set in bold type.

Nielsen
SoundScan

Canadian Country Music Awards, 2004

Fans' Choice Award . . . . Terri Clark
Female Artist of the Year . . . . Terri Clark
Male Artist of the Year . . . . Jason McCoy
Single of the Year . . . . "Simple Life," Carolyn Dawn Johnson
Album of the Year . . . . *Dress Rehearsal*, Carolyn Dawn Johnson
Duo or Group of the Year . . . . Doc Walker
Music Video of the Year . . . . *Simple Life*, Carolyn Dawn Johnson
Song of the Year . . . . "Die of a Broken Heart," Carolyn Dawn Johnson & Shaye Smith
Roots Artist or Group of the Year . . . . The Corb Lund Band
Rising Star . . . . George Canyon
CCMA Hall of Fame Inductee . . . . The Good Brothers

Source: *Canadian Country Music Awards*

Top 50 Singles in Canada, 2004

Artist, Title	Artist, Title
1. Clay Aiken, "Bridge Over Troubled Water"	26. Christina Aguilera, "Beautiful"
2. **Ryan Malcolm, "Something More"**	27. Dixie Chicks, "Landslide"
3. Ruben Studdard, "Flying Without Words"	28. Radiohead, "Go To Sleep-CD2"
4. 50 Cent, "In Da Club"	29. Beyoncé, "Baby Boy"
5. **Celine Dion, "I Drove All Night"**	30. Linkin Park, "Somewhere I Belong"
6. Evanescence, "Bring Me to Life"	31. Sean Paul, "Like Glue"
7. Beyoncé, "Crazy In Love"	32. Outkast, "Hey Ya!"
8. **Nickelback, "Someday"**	33. Madonna, "Die Another Day"
9. Hilary Duff, "So Yesterday"	34. Christina Aguilera, "Dirrty"
10. Madonna, "American Life"	35. Kelly Clarkson, "Low"
11. Kid Rock feat. Moorer, "Allis Picture"	36. Shaggy, "Hey Sexy Lady"
12. Las Ketchup, "Ketchup Song (Hey Hay)"	37. **Shawn Desman, "Shook"**
13. Radiohead, "There There"	38. Santana, "Game of Love"
14. Simply Red, "Sunrise"	39. Nelly, "Dilemma"
15. **Shania Twain, "Up!-I'm Gonna' Getcha' Good"**	40. **Shania Twain, "I'm Gonna' Getcha' Good"**
16. Eminem, "Sing for the Moment," (Ltd. Ed)	41. Norah Jones, "Come Away With Me"
17. T.A.T.U., "All The Things She Said"	42. P!nk, "Trouble"
18. **Shania Twain, "Forever and For Always"**	43. Jay Z, "Bonnie & Clyde"
19. Christina Aguilera, "Fighter"	44. **Keshia Chante, "Unpredictable"**
20. 50 Cent, "21 Questions"	45. Sigur Ros, "Untitled Track No. 1"
21. Elvis Pesley, "Rubberneckin'"	46. Eagles, "Hole In The World"
22. Daniel Bedingfield, "If You're Not The One"	47. **Au de Montigny, "Même les anges"**
23. Eminem, "Lose Yourself"	48. Busta Rhymes, "I Know What You Want"
24. VA-American Juniors, "One Step Closer"	49. Robbie Williams, "Feel"
25. Jennifer Lopez, "Jenny From The Block"	50. American Idol Finalists, "What The World Needs Now"

Source: *Chart Information Supplied By Soundscan. Copyright (C) 2003 By Soundscan, Inc. All Rights Reserved.*
Note: Canadian artists set in bold type.

Nielsen
SoundScan

MTV Video Music Awards, 2004

Best Video Of The Year	"Hey Ya!,"Outkast
Best Rock Video	"Are You Gonna Be My Girl," Jet,
Best Hip Hop Video	"Hey Ya!,"Outkast
Best R&B Video	"If I Ain't Got You, " Alicia Keys
Viewer's Choice	"Breaking The Habit," Linkin Park
Best Rap Video	"99 Problems," Jay-Z
Best Female Video	"Naughty Girl," Beyoncé,
Best Pop Video	"It's My Life," No Doubt,
Best Videogame Soundtrack	Tony Hawke's Underground
Best New Artist	"This Love," Maroon5
Best Group Video	"It's My Life," No Doubt,
Best Male Video	"Yeah!," Usher Featuring Lil Jon & Ludacris
Best Dance Video	"Yeah!," Usher Featuring Lil Jon & Ludacris
Best Breakthrough Video	"Take Me Out," Franz Ferdinand
Best Art Direction	"Hey Ya!,"Outkast
Special Effects	"Hey Ya!,"Outkast
Best Editing	"99 Problems," Jay-Z
Best Choreography	"Hey Mama," Black Eyed Peas
Best Cinematography	"99 Problems," Jay-Z
Mtv2 Award	"Ocean Avenue," Yellowcard

Source: *MTV: Music Television*

MuchMusic Video Awards, 2004

Favourite Canadian Artist	Avril Lavigne, "Don't Tell Me"
Trail Blazer Award	Beastie Boys
Best Video	Finger Eleven, "One Thing"
Best Pop Video	Nelly Furtado, "Powerless"
MuchLOUD Best Rock Video	Billy Talent, "Try Honesty"
Best French Video	Corneille, "parce qu'on vient de loin"
MuchVIBE Best Rap Video	Jelleestone f. Elephant Man, "Who Dat"
Best R&B Video	In Essence, "Friend Of Mine"
Best Director	Sam Roberts, "Hard Road"
Best Post-Production	Sam Roberts, "Hard Road"
Best Cinematography	Sam Roberts, "Hard Road"
Best Independent Video	Pilate, "Into Your Hideout"
MuchMoreMusic Award	Sarah McLachlan, "Fallen"
Best International Video Artist	Beyoncé (f/Jay-Z), "Crazy In Love"
Best International Video Group	Outkast, "Hey Ya"
VideoFACT Award	Alexisonfire, "Counterparts And Number Them"

Source: *MuchMusic Network*

Music Festivals in Canada

Classical music festivals and competitions across Canada have played an essential role in the development of the country's musical talent since the first local music festival was organized in Edmonton in 1908. By 1953, every province had at least one festival in operation. The Federation of Canadian Music Festivals was founded in 1949 to coordinate their activities and, in Canada's centennial year (1967), the first all-Canadian music competition was held in Saint John, N.B.

Today, the Federation reports a total of 230 festivals occurring in Canada each year. These festivals attract some 140,000 entries involving the participation of as many as half a million people. Attendance at local festivals averages 450,000, while provincial festivals average audiences of 6,000 people. The festivals are important to young musicians as much for the prestige they bestow on participants as for the prizes and scholarships offered to help with their studies. The Federation is made up of provincial associations that are responsible for supporting local festivals and organizing festivals to determine the provincial champions at various levels. These champions represent their home province at the National Music Festival. In 1973, the national competition was instituted on an annual basis. Since 1981, the national festival has been held in a different province each year.

Major Classical and New Music Festivals

In addition to the network of amateur music festivals sponsored by the Federation of Canadian Music Festivals, a number of other amateur music festivals and professional festivals take place across Canada each year.

Vancouver Early Music Festival, mid-July–mid-August, 2005, VancouverOne of North America's leading early music festivals, featuring acclaimed performers and ensembles from the international scene, often in consort with Vancouver's finest musicians. This eclectic festival offers a unique series of concerts devoted to vocal and instrumental music from the Mediæval, Renaissance, Baroque and Classical eras, with occasional forays into 'early music' from other cultures as well as contemporary music. www.earlymusic.bc.ca

The Winnipeg Symphony Orchestra New Music Festival, Winnipeg, Manitoba, January 29–Feb.4, 2005: First presented in January 1992, the Festival has drawn international participation, earned critical acclaim, and enjoyed a growing audience. It is now considered one of Canada's most important forums for new work. Tel. (204) 949-3999.

The Ottawa International Chamber Music Festival, Ottawa, Ont., July–August: The Ottawa Chamber Music Society produces a two-week summer programme of chamber music featuring the highest calibre of local, national and international artists. Concerts take place in downtown Ottawa, mostly in churches. Tel. (613) 234-8008. www.chamberfest.com.

Festival of the Sound, Parry Sound, Ont. July–August: Talks by renowned scholars, open rehearsals and concerts reflecting a wide variety of classical genres make this a noted Ontario festival on the shores of Georgian Bay. Tel. (705) 746-2410. www.festivalofthesound.on.ca.

The Saskatoon Symphony Festival of New Music, Saskatoon, Saskatchewan, April: Events include small chamber groups, a jazz brunch, concerts by the Saskatchewan Chamber Orchestra, and an after hours club. Also includes world premieres of new works such as *Batoche* a chamber opera based on the life of Louis Riel, by composer Bill Pura. The Festival of New Music puts the prairies on the cutting edge of creative music making. Tel. (306) 665-6414.

Festival international de Lanaudière, Joliette, Québec, July 8–Aug. 7, 2005: This six-week event is one of largest and longest classical music festivals in Canada. Some 30 concerts are presented by as many as 1,300 musicians for up to 48,000 visitors. Most concerts for soloists and smaller ensembles are held in the many churches of the Joliette area. Larger groups such as the Montréal Symphony Orchestra perform at the Lanaudière Amphitheatre. The festival is renowned for its emphasis on new work and young artists. Tel. 1-800-245-7636. www.lanaudiere.org

MusicFest Canada, Richmond, B.C., May 17–21, 2005: This six day annual national event brings together more than 11,000 of Canada's finest young musicians who perform for recognition as the country's foremost musical ensembles. Participants range in age from 12–24 years and are drawn from the elementary, high school, college and university levels. Tel. (403) 717-1766. www.musicfest.ca

Recording Industry Sales, 2003–2004[1]

These two charts examine the amount—and dollar value—of music purchased in a variety of forms between June 30–May 31, for 2002 and 2003. Sales information is supplied by members of the Canadian Recording Industry Association. Units and dollar amounts are expressed in the thousands.

'000s Units Shipped	2004	2003	% change
VHS	152	240	-37%
DVDs	1546	1076	44%
Singles	222	421	-47%
CDs	18 874	18 449	2%
GRAND TOTAL	**20 794**	20 186	3%

Net Value of Sales ($000s)	2004	2003	% change
VHS	854	1776	-52%
DVDs	22 759	18 183	25%
Singles	1054	1373	-53%
CDs	203 335	211 927	-4%
GRAND TOTAL	**228 002**	**233 259**	**-2%**

Note: The categories of DCC/Mini Disc and Cassette Single have been eliminated from the report due to negligible sales.

Source: *Canadian Recording Industry Association*   (1) For the period ending June 30.

The Rock and Roll Hall of Fame

The Rock and Roll Hall of Fame was established in 1984. The Rock and Roll Hall of Fame and Museum opened in September 1995 in Cleveland, Ohio.

■ ARTISTS (Year Elected)

Aerosmith (2001)

The Allman Brothers Band (1995)

The Animals (1994)

LaVern Baker (1991)

Hank Ballard (1990)

The Band (1994)

The Beach Boys (1988)

The Beatles (1988)

The Bee Gees (1997)

Chuck Berry (1986)

Bobby "Blue" Bland (1992)

Booker T. & The MG's (1992)

David Bowie (1996)

James Brown (1986)

Ruth Brown (1993)

Jackson Browne (2004)

Buffalo Springfield (1997)

Solomon Burke (2001)

The Byrds (1991)

David Byrne (2002)

Johnny Cash (1992)

Ray Charles (1986)

Eric Clapton (2000)

The Clash (2003)

The Coasters (1987)

Eddie Cochran (1987)

Sam Cooke (1986)

Elvis Costello and the Attractions (2003)

Cream (1993)

Creedence Clearwater Revival (1993)

Crosby, Stills and Nash (1997)

Bobby Darin (1990)

The Dells (2004)

Bo Diddley (1987)

Dion (1989)

Fats Domino (1986)

The Doors (1993)

The Drifters (1988)

Bob Dylan (1988)

The Eagles (1998)

Earth, Wind and Fire (2000)

Duane Eddy (1994)

The Everly Brothers (1986)

The Flamingos (2001)

Fleetwood Mac (1998)

The Four Seasons (1990)

The Four Tops (1990)

Aretha Franklin (1987)

Marvin Gaye (1987)

The Grateful Dead (1994)

Al Green (1995)

Bill Haley (1987)

George Harrison (2004)

Isaac Hayes (2002)

Buddy Holly (1986)

The Jimi Hendrix Experience (1992)

John Lee Hooker (1991)

The Impressions (1991)

The Isley Brothers (1992)

Michael Jackson (2001)

Etta James (1993)

Jefferson Airplane (1996)

Billy Joel (1999)

Elton John (1994)

Janis Joplin (1995)

B.B. King (1987)

The Jackson Five (1997)

The Kinks (1990)

Gladys Knight and the Pips (1996)

Led Zeppelin (1995)

Lloyd Price (1998)

Brenda Lee (2002)

John Lennon (1994)

Jerry Lee Lewis (1986)

▶

Little Richard (1986)
Little Willie John (1996)
The Lovin' Spoonful (2000)
Frankie Lyman and the Teenagers (1993)
The Mamas and the Papas (1998)
Bob Marley (1994)
Martha and the Vandellas (1995)
Curtis Mayfield (1999)
Paul McCartney (1999)
Joni Mitchell (1997)
Clyde McPhatter (1987)
The Moonglows (2000)
Van Morrison (1993)
Ricky Nelson (1987)
Roy Orbison (1987)
Parliament Funkadelic (1997)
Carl Perkins (1987)
Tom Petty (2002)
Wilson Pickett (1991)
Pink Floyd (1996)
Gene Pitney (2002)
The Platters (1990)
Elvis Presley (1986)
Prince (2004)
Queen (2001)
Bonnie Raitt (2000)
Dee Dee Ramone (2002)
Otis Redding (1989)
Jimmy Reed (1991)
The Righteous Brothers (2003)
Smokey Robinson (1987)
The Rolling Stones (1989)
Sam & Dave (1992)
Santana (1998)
Bob Seger (2004)
Del Shannon (1999)
The Shirelles (1996)
Paul Simon (2001)
Simon and Garfunkel (1990)
Sly and the Family Stone (1993)
Dusty Springfield (1999)

Bruce Springsteen (1999)
Steely Dan (2001)
Rod Stewart (1994)
The Supremes (1988)
The Staple Singers (1999)
James Taylor (2000)
The Temptations (1989)
Traffic (2004)
Ike and Tina Turner (1991)
Big Joe Turner (1987)
Ritchie Valens (2001)
Gene Vincent (1998)
The Velvet Underground (1996)
Muddy Waters (1987)
The Who (1990)
Jackie Wilson (1987)
Stevie Wonder (1989)
The Yardbirds (1992)
The Young Rascals (1997)
Neil Young (1995)
Frank Zappa (1995)
ZZ Top (2004)

■ **NON-PERFORMERS**

Paul Ackerman (1995)
Dave Bartholomew (1991)
Ralph Bass (1991)
Chris Blackwell (2001)
Leonard Chess (1987)
Dick Clark (1993)
Clive Davis (2000)
Tom Donahue (1996)
Lamont Dozier, Brian Holland & Eddie Holland (1990)
Ahmet Ertegun (1987)
Leo Fender (1992)
Alan Freed (1986)
Milt Gabler (1993)
Gerry Goffin & Carole King (1990)
Berry Gordy, Jr. (1988)
Bill Graham (1992)
Jerry Leiber & Mike Stoller (1987)
George Martin (1999)

Syd Nathan (1997)
Johnny Otis (1994)
Sam Phillips (1986)
Doc Pomus (1992)
Phil Spector (1989)
Allen Toussaint (1998)
Jann S. Wenner (2004)
Jerry Wexler (1987)

■ **LIFETIME ACHIEVEMENT AWARDS**
Willie Dixon (1994)
Nesuhl Ertegun (1991)
John Hammond (1986)

■ **EARLY INFLUENCES**
Louis Armstrong (1990)
Charles Brown (1999)
Charlie Christian (1990)
Nat "King" Cole (2000)
Willie Dixon (1994)
Woody Guthrie (1988)
Billie Holiday (2000)
Howlin' Wolf (1991)
The Ink Spots (1989)
Mahalia Jackson (1997)
Elmore James (1992)
Robert Johnson (1986)
Louis Jordan (1987)
Lead Belly (1988)
Bill Monroe (1997)
Jelly Roll Morton (1998)
The Orioles (1995)
Les Paul (1988)
Professor Longhair (1992)
Ma Rainey (1990)
Jimmie Rodgers (1986)
Pete Seeger (1996)
Bessie Smith (1989)
The Soul Stirrers (1989)
T-Bone Walker (1987)
Dinah Washington (1993)
Hank Williams (1987)
Bob Wills & His Texas Playboys (1999)
Jimmy Yancey (1986)

Source: *Rock and Roll Hall of Fame Foundation* Note: Canadian artists set in bold type.

FOCUS ON ...

Downloading: Entertainment's Hottest Issue

The war over illegal downloading of music and other intellectual property on the Internet continued to heat up in 2004. On February 11, the Canadian Recording Industry Association (CRIA), demanded in court that five of Canada's major Internet Service Providers (Bell/Sympatico, Rogers Communications, Shaw Communications, TELUS and Videotron Ltd.) be required to divulge the identities of what it called "flagrant downloaders." While the court rejected the request on March 31, the war of words escalated as CRIA immediately appealed the decision.

There's no question that illegal downloading is having a dramatic impact on the recording industry worldwide. In early April, the international recording association IFPI reported a 7.6 percent drop in sales of recorded music in 2003 as compared to 2002. CRIA claimed that the Canadian industry was one of the world's hardest hit markets on a per capita basis, with sales down $425 million since 1999 and layoffs reaching the 20 percent mark at Canadian recording companies.

In the U.S. a Harris Interactive poll in April showed that while 88 percent of respondents aged 8 to 18 knew that material on free file-sharing networks was protected by copyright, 56 percent downloaded anyway. A March report from the Pew Internet and American Life Project reported that there were 23 million regular downloaders in the United States. That number was up from 18 million reported in late 2003 but still lower than the peak of 35 million downloaders reported in the spring of 2003, when CRIA'sister organization, the Recording Industry Association of America, began threatening Internet pirates with legal action. RIAA, which says that music sales in the U.S. have dropped from $13.2 billion to $11.2 billion (U.S.), has sued more than 1,000 downloaders, some of them as young as 12. In April 2004, the U.S. Justice Department began a crackdown targeting networks suspected of stealing as much as $50 million in software, music and movie downloads. A bill was also being sponsored in the U.S. Congress that, if passed, would impose a three-year prison sentence for those convicted of downloading 1,000 or more songs.

In the wake of the Canadian court decision, CRIA reported half a million downloading attempts on "Vaccination Scar," the new single by rock band The Tragically Hip. "To me it's an ethical question," said Hip lead singer Gord Downie. "If you hear something you like, go out and support the artist." Singers Jann Arden, Kathleen Edwards and Ed Robertson of The Barenaked Ladies also added their voices to the campaign against illegal downloading.

"Downloading music from the Internet is ironically the hope, and alarmingly the impending decay and destruction, of the music industry," said Arden. "Unless these downloads are monitored and artists are compensated for their work, there will be NO work to download. None of us, as writers and performers, can afford to keep making the music that has always, and will always, make the world a little easier to swallow in troubled times."

CRIA is encouraging downloaders to patronize legal sites like www.puretracks.com and www.archambaultzik.ca which quote prices in Canadian dollars that average 99 cents per track.

Some companies have emerged with an innovative approach to file sharing and copyright rules. One such is Magnatune of Berkeley, California, which offers music from techno to classical and allows downloaders to pay what they can in a range from $5 to $18 (U.S.) for whole albums. Magnatune's underlying philosophy is that there's more profit to be made if their artists' music becomes more available. The artists take 50 percent of sales and are free to sign with other labels. The approach sits well with lesser-known and emerging artists, and with more established artists who have seen their revenues and conventionally distributed work disappear in a morass of legal and business wrangling. But the pay-what-you-can approach does not sit well with the recording establishment. Negotiations between the American industry and file-sharing companies such as Blubster and Piolet have so far foundered over the industry's right to set prices.

MOVIES

Canada has been a world leader in documentary filmmaking, producing renowned artists such as Donald Brittain and Harry Rasky primarily through the National Film Board of Canada. The film board has also helped bring Canada to prominence as a producer of animation, and short subjects. Canadians have made an enormous contribution to the Hollywood feature film industry, from film mogul Louis B. Mayer to acclaimed director Norman Jewison to stars including Mary Pickford, Dan Aykroyd, Michael J. Fox, John Candy and Keanu Reeves. The Department of Canadian Heritage estimates that 20 percent of those employed in the Hollywood film industry are Canadian and that about 60 percent of the software used in U.S. film productions was developed by Canadians. Made-in-Canada features by filmmakers such as Denys Arcand, David Cronenberg, Atom Egoyan and Patricia Rozema have enjoyed considerable critical and "art house" success around the world. In the 1990s, Canadian features twice won the Special Grand Jury Prize at the Cannes Film Festival. However, with US distribution houses controlling 85 percent of the theatrical market, only one in twenty features gaining commercial release in Canada is produced in Canada.

Toronto International Film Festival, 2004

The 29th annual festival was held Sept. 9–18, 2004, showing 328 films from 60 countries. This is widely regarded as North America's major film festival.

People's Choice Award . . . . *Hotle Rwanda*, Terry George, UK/South Africa/ Italy
Discovery Award . . . . *Omagh*, Pete Travis, Ireland/ UK
Fipresci Award . . . . *In My Father's Den*, Brad McGann, New Zealand/UK
Best Canadian First Feature . . . . **La Peau Blanche**, Daniel Roby
Best Canadian Feature Film . . . . *It's All Gone Pete Tongr*, Michael Dowse
Short Cuts Canada Award . . . . *Man Feel Pain*, Dylan Akio Smith

Source: *Toronto International Film Festival*

Montreal World Film Festival, 2004

The 28th annual Festival des Films du Monde was held from Aug. 26th to Sept 6th, 2004.

Grand Prix of the Americas . . . . *The Syrian Bride*, Eran Riklis, (Israel/France/Germany)
Jury Award . . . (tie) *The Parking Lot Attendant In July*, An Zhaniun (China); *Around The Bend*, Jordan Roberts (USA)
Best Director. . . . . Carolos Saura, *The Seventh Day* (Spain/France)
Best Artistic Contribution . . . . **The Five of Us, Ghyslaine Coté (Canada)**
Best Actress . . . . Karin Viard, *The Role of Her Life* (France)
Best Actor. . . . (tie) Fan Wei, *The Parking Lot Attendant In July* (China); Christopher Walken, *Around The Bend* (USA)
Best Screenplay François Favrat, Jule Lopes-Cuvral, Jérôme Beauséjour, Roger Bohbot, *The Role of Her Life* (France)
Best Short Film . . . . *The Little Terrorist*, Ashvin Kumar (India)
Jury Award (Short Film) . . . . **Mabel's Saga**, Jo Dee Samuelson (Canada)
People's Choice Award . . . . *The Syrian Bride* (Israel/France/Germany)
Fipresci Prize. . . . . *The Syrian Bride* (Israel/France/Germany)
Most Popular Canadian Film . . . . **The Five of Us, Ghyslaine Coté**
Best Canadian Short Film . . . . **Mabel's Saga, Jo Dee Samuelson**

Source: *Montreal World Film Festival*

Genie Awards, 1980–2003

The Genie Awards have been presented since 1980 by the Academy of Canadian Cinema and Television to honour achievement in the Canadian film industry. Awards apply to films released in the previous year. Voting is conducted in a two-step process whereby the winners are chosen by all academy members from among the five nominees selected in each category by their respective craft branches. The 2003 awards were presented May 1, 2004.

1980
Picture............................ *The Changeling*
Actor........ Christopher Plummer, *Murder By Decree*
Actress........................... Kate Lynch, *Meatballs*
Sup. Actor............. Gordon Pinsent, *Jack London's Klondike Fever*
Sup Actress...... Geneviève Bujold, *Murder By Decree*
Director................ Bob Clark, *Murder By Decree*

1981
Picture............................ *Les Bons débarras*
Actor ... Thomas Peacocke, *The Hounds of Notre Dame*
Actress................. Marie Tifo, *Les Bons débarras*
Sup. Actor........ Germain Houde, *Les Bons débarras*
Sup Actress............ Kate Reid, *Atlantic City, U.S.A.*
Director....... Francis Mankiewicz, *Les Bons débarras*

1982
Picture................................. *Les Plouffes*
Actor................. Nick Mancuso, *Ticket To Heaven*
Actress.............. Margot Kidder, *Heartaches*
Sup. Actor............ Saul Rubinek, *Ticket To Heaven*
Sup Actress........... Denise Filiatrault, *Les Plouffes*
Director.................... Gilles Carle, *Les Plouffes*

1983
Picture................................ *The Grey Fox*
Actor.................. Donald Sutherland, *Threshold*
Actress.............. Rae Dawn Chong, *Quest For Fire*
Sup. Actor .. R.H. Thomson, *If You Could See What I Hear*
Sup Actress.......... Jackie Burroughs, *The Grey Fox*
Director.............. Phillip Borsos, *The Grey Fox*

1984
Picture.......................... *The Terry Fox Story*
Actor.................. Eric Fryer, *The Terry Fox Story*
Actress...................... Martha Henry, *The Wars*
Sup. Actor...... Michael Zelniker, *The Terry Fox Story*
Sup Actress............. Jackie Burroughs, *The Wars*
Director................ Bob Clark, *A Christmas Story*, David Cronenberg, *Videodrome*

1985
Picture................................. *The Bay Boy*
Actor........ Gabriel Arcand, *Le Crime d'Ovide Plouffe*
Actress........... Louise Marleay, *La Femme de l'hôtel*
Sup. Actor............... Alan Scarfe, *The Bay Boy*
Sup Actress .... Linda Sorensen, *Draw!*
Director................. Micheline Lanctôt, *Sonatine*

1986
Picture........................ *My American Cousin*

Actor............. John Wildman, *My American Cousin*
Actress....... Margaret Langrick, *My American Cousin*
Sup. Actor.......... Alan Arkin, *Joshua Then and Now*
Sup Actress.... Linda Sorensen, *Joshua Then and Now*
Director.......... Sandy Wilson, *My American Cousin*

1987
Picture............ *The Decline of the American Empire*
Actor............ Gordon Pinsent, *John and the Missus*
Actress............ Martha Henry, *Dancing in the Dark*
Sup. Actor............................ Gabriel Arcand, *The Decline of the American Empire*
Sup Actress............................ Louise Portal, *The Decline of the American Empire*
Director................................ Denys Arcand, *The Decline of the American Empire*

1988
Picture................................. *Un Zoo la nuit*
Actor .... Roger Le Bel, *Un Zoo la nuit*
Actress............... Sheila McCarthy, *I've Heard the Mermaids Singing*
Sup. Actor........... Germaine Houde, *Un Zoo la nuit*
Sup. Actress.......... Paule Baillargeon, *I've Heard the Mermaids Singing*
Director.......... Jean-Claude Lauzon, *Un Zoo la nuit*

1989
Picture.................................. *Dead Ringers*
Actor..................... Jeremy Irons, *Dead Ringers*
Actress............... Jackie Burroughs, *A Winter Tan*
Sup. Actor........ Rémy Girard, *Les Portes tournantes*
Sup. Actress............. Colleen Dewhurst, *Obsessed*
Director............. David Cronenberg, *Dead Ringers*

1990
Picture............................ *Jésus de Montréal*
Actor .... Lothaire Bluteau, *Jésus de Montréal*
Actress.............. Rebecca Jenkins, *Bye Bye Blues*
Sup. Actor............ Remy Girard, *Jésus de Montréal*
Sup. Actress............ Robyn Stevan, *Bye Bye Blues*
Director............ Denys Arcand, *Jésus de Montréal*

1991
Picture.................................... *Black Robe*
Actor..................... Remy Girard, *Amoureux fou*
Actress .... Pascare Montpetit, *H*
Sup. Actor.......... August Schellenberg, *Black Robe*
Sup. Actress.......... Danielle Proulx, *Amoureux fou*
Director................. Bruce Beresford, *Black Robe*

1992

Picture . . . . *Naked Lunch*
Actor . . . . Tony Nardi, *La Sarrasine*
Actress . . . . Janet Wright, *Bordertown Café*
Sup. Actor . . . . Michael Hogan, *Solitaire*
Sup. Actress . . . . Monique Mercure, *Naked Lunch*
Director . . . . David Cronenberg, *Naked Lunch*

1993

Picture . . . . *Thirty-Two Short Films about Glenn Gould*
Actor . . . . Tom McCamus, *I Love A Man in Uniform*
Actress . . . . Sheila McCarthy, *The Lotus Eaters*
Sup. Actor . . . . Kevin Tighe, *I Love A Man in Uniform*
Sup. Actress . . . . Nicola Cavendish, *The Grocer's Wife*
Director . . . . François Girard, *Thirty-Two Short Films
about Glenn Gould*

1994

Picture . . . . *Exotica*
Actor . . . . Maury Chaykin, *Whale Music*
Actress . . . . Sandra Oh, *Double Happiness*
Sup. Actor . . . . Don McKellar, *Exotica*
Sup. Actress . . . . Martha Henry, *Mustard Bath*
Director . . . . Atom Egoyan, *Exotica*

1995

Picture . . . . *Le Confessionnal*
Actor . . . . David La Haye, *L'Enfant D'Eau*
Actress . . . . . . Helena Bonham Carter, *Margaret's Museum*
Sup. Actor . . . . Kenneth Welsh, *Margaret's Museum*
Sup. Actress . . . . Kate Nelligan, *Margaret's Museum*
Director . . . . Robert Lepage, *Le Confessionnal*

1996

Picture . . . . *Lilies*
Actor . . . . . . William Hutt, *Long Day's Journey Into Night*
Actress . . . Martha Henry, *Long Day's Journey Into Night*
Sup. Actor . . . Peter Donaldson, *Long Day's Journey Into Night*
Sup. Actress . . . . Martha Burns, *Long Day's Journey Into Night*
Director . . . . David Cronenberg, *Crash*

1997

Picture . . . . *The Sweet Hereafter*
Actor . . . . Ian Holm, *The Sweet Hereafter*
Actress . . . . Molly Parker, *Kissed*
Sup. Actor . . . . Peter MacNeill, *The Hanging Garden*
Sup. Actress . . . . . Seana McKenna, *The Hanging Garden*
Director . . . . Atom Egoyan, *The Sweet Hereafter*

1998

Picture . . . . *The Red Violin*
Actor . . . . Roshan Seth, *Such a Long Journey*
Actress . . . . Sandra Oh, *Last Night*
Sup. Actor . . . . Callum Keith Rennie, *Last Night*
Sup. Actress . . . . Monique Mercure, *Conquest*
Director . . . . François Girard, *The Red Violin*

1999

Picture . . . . *Sunshine*
Actor . . . . Bob Hoskins, *Felicia's Journey*

Actress . . . . Sylvie Moreau, *Post Mortem*
Sup. Actor . . . . Mark McKinney, *Dog Park*
Sup. Actress . . . . . Catherine O'Hara, *The Life Before This*
Director . . . . Jeremy Podeswa, *The Five Senses*

2000

Picture . . . . *Maelström*
Actor . . . . Tony Nardi, *My Father's Angel*
Actress . . . . Marie-Josée Croze, *Maelström*
Sup. Actor . . . . Martin Cummins, *Love Come Down*
Sup. Actress . . . . Helen Shaver, *We All Fall Down*
Director . . . . Denis Villeneuve, *Maelström*

2001

Picture . . . . *Atanarjuat (The Fast Runner)*
Actor . . . . Brendan Fletcher, *The Law of Enclosures*
Actress . . . . Élise Guilbault, *La femme qui boit
(The Woman Who Drinks)*
Sup. Actor . . . . Vincent Gale, *Last Wedding*
Sup. Actress . . . . Molly Parker, *Last Wedding*
Director . Zacharias Kunuk, *Atanarjuat (The Fast Runner)*

2002

Picture . . . . *Ararat*
Actor . . . . Luc Picard, *Savage Messiah*
Actress . . . . Arsinée Khanjian, *Ararat*
Sup. Actor . . . . Elias Koteas, *Ararat*
Sup. Actress . . . . Pascale Montpetit, *Savage Messiah*
Director . . . . David Cronenberg, *Spider*

2003

Picture . . . . *Les Invasions barbares*
Actor . . . . Rémy Girard, *Les Invasions barbares*
Actress . . . . Sarah Polly, *My Life Without Me*
Sup. Actor . . Stéphane Rousseau, *Les Invasions barbares*
Sup. Actress . Marie-Josée Croze, *Les Invasions barbares*
Director . . . . Denys Arcand, *Les Invasions barbares*
Original Screenplay . . . . Denys Arcand,
Les Invasions barbares
Cinematography . . . . . Allen Smith, *La Grande séduction*
Film Editing . . . . David Wharnsby,
The Saddest Music in the World
Art Direction . Rob Gray, Christina Kuhnigk, *Falling Angels*
Costume Design . . . . Meg McMillan,
The Saddest Music in the World
Overall Sound . . . . . . D. Bruce Carwardine, Todd Beckett,
Michael O'Farrell, Don White, *The Statement*
Sound Editing . . . . Michael O'Farrell, Mark Gingras,
Paul Intson, Goro Koyama, John Laing, Andy Malcolm,
Jill Purdy, John Douglas Smith, *The Statement*
Music Score . . . . Christopher Dedrick,
The Saddest Music in the World
Best Documentary . . . . Betsy Carson, Nettie Wild,
Fix: The Story of an Addicted City
Best Animated Short . . . . . Marcy Page, Munro Ferguson,
Falling In Love Again
Best Live Action Short Drama . . . . Christiane Ciupka,
Jean-François Rivard, *No.I Blank*

Motion Picture Academy Awards (Oscars™), 1927–2003

1927–28
Picture . . . . *Wings*, Paramount
Actor . . . . Emil Jannings, *The Way of All Flesh*
Actress . . . . Janet Gaynor, *7th Heaven*
Director . . Frank Borzage, *7th Heaven;* Lewis Milestone,
Two Arabian Knights

1928–29
Picture . . . . *The Broadway Melody*, MGM
Actor . . . . Warner Baxter, *In Old Arizona*
Actress . . . . Mary Pickford, *Coquette*
Director . . . . Frank Lloyd, *The Divine Lady*

1929–30
Picture . . . . . . *All Quiet on the Western Front*, Universal
Actor . . . . George Arliss, *Disraeli*
Actress . . . . Norma Shearer, *The Divorcee*
Director Lewis Milestone, *All Quiet on the Western Front*

1930–31
Picture . . . . *Cimarron*, RKO
Actor . . . . Lionel Barrymore, *A Free Soul*
Actress . . . . Marie Dressler, *Min and Bill*
Director . . . . Norman Taurog, *Skippy*

1931–32
Picture . . . . *Grand Hotel*, MGM
Actor . . . . Fredric March, *Dr. Jekyll and Mr. Hyde*
Wallace Beery, *The Champ* (tie)
Actress . . . . Helen Hayes, *Sin of Madelon Claudet*
Director . . . . Frank Borzage, *Bad Girl*
Special . . . . Walt Disney, *Mickey Mouse*

1932–33
Picture . . . . *Cavalcade*, Fox
Actor . . Charles Laughten, *The Private Life of Henry VIII*
Actress . . . . Katharine Hepburn, *Morning Glory*
Director . . . . Frank Lloyd, *Cavalcade*

1934
Picture . . . . *It Happened One Night*, Columbia
Actor . . . . Clark Gable, *It Happened One Night*
Actress . . . . . Claudette Colbert, *It Happened One Night*
Director . . . . Frank Capra, *It Happened One Night*

1935
Picture . . . . *Mutiny on the Bounty*, MGM
Actor . . . . Victor McLaglen, *The Informer*
Actress . . . . Bette Davis, *Dangerous*
Director . . . . John Ford, *The Informer*

1936
Picture . . . . *The Great Ziegfeld*, MGM
Actor . . . . Paul Muni, *The Story of Louis Pasteur*
Actress . . . . Luise Rainer, *The Great Ziegfeld*
Sup. Actor . . . . Walter Brennan, *Come and Get It*
Sup. Actress . . . . . Gale Sondergaard, *Anthony Adverse*
Director . . . . Frank Capra, *Mr. Deeds Goes to Town*

1937
Picture . . . . *Life of Emile Zola*, Warner Bros.
Actor . . . . Spencer Tracy, *Captains Courageous*
Actress . . . . Luise Rainer, *The Good Earth*
Sup. Actor . . . . . . Joseph Schildkraut, *Life of Emile Zola*
Sup. Actress . . . . Alice Brady, *In Old Chicago*
Director . . . . Leo McCarey, *The Awful Truth*

1938
Picture . . . . *You Can't Take It With You*, Columbia
Actor . . . . Spencer Tracy, *Boys Town*
Actress . . . . Bette Davis, *Jezebel*
Sup. Actor . . . . Walter Brennan, *Kentucky*
Sup. Actress . . . . Fay Bainter, *Jezebel*
Director . . . . . . Frank Capra, *You Can't Take It With You*

1939
Picture . . . . . *Gone With the Wind*, Selznick International
Actor . . . . Robert Dowel, *Goodbye, Mr. Chips*
Actress . . . . Vivien Leigh, *Gone With the Wind*
Sup. Actor . . . . Thomas Mitchell, *StageCoach*
Sup. Actress . . . . Hattie McDaniel, *Gone With the Wind*
Director . . . . Victor Fleming, *Gone With the Wind*

1940
Picture . . . . *Rebecca*, Selznick International
Actor . . . . James Stewart, *The Philadelphia Story*
Actress . . . . Ginger Rogers, *Kitty Foyle*
Sup. Actor . . . . Walter Brennan, *The Westerner*
Sup. Actress . . . . . . Jane Darwell, *The Grapes of Wrath*
Director . . . . John Ford, *The Grapes of Wrath*

1941
Picture . . . *How Green Was My Valley*, 20th Century-Fox
Actor . . . . Gary Cooper, *Sergeant York*
Actress . . . . Joan Fontaine, *Suspicion*
Sup. Actor . . . Donald Crisp, *How Green Was My Valley*
Sup. Actress . . . . Mary Astor, *The Great Lie*
Director . . . . John Ford, *How Green Was My Valley*

1942
Picture . . . . *Mrs. Miniver*, MGM
Actor . . . . James Cagney, *Yankee Doodle Dandy*
Actress . . . . Greer Garson, *Mrs. Miniver*
Sup. Actor . . . . Van Heflin, *Johnny Eager*
Sup. Actress . . . . Teresa Wright, *Mrs. Miniver*
Director . . . . William Wyler, *Mrs. Miniver*

1943
Picture . . . . *Casablanca*, Warner Bros.
Actor . . . . Paul Lukas, *Watch On the Rhine*
Actress . . . . . . Jennifer Jones, *The Song of Bernadette*
Sup. Actor . . . . . Charles Coburn, *The More the Merrier*
Sup. Actress . . Katina Paxinou, *For Whom the Bell Tolls*
Director . . . . Michael Curtiz, *Casablanca*

1944
Picture . . . . *Going My Way*, Paramount
Actor . . . . Bing Crosby, *Going My Way*

Actress . . . . Ingrid Bergman, *Gaslight*
Sup. Actor . . . . Barry Fitzgerald, *Going My Way*
Sup. Actress . Ethel Barrymore, *None But the Lonely Heart*
Director. . . . . Leo McCarey, *Going My Way*

1945
Picture . . . . *The Lost Weekend*, Paramount
Actor . . . . Ray Milland, *The Lost Weekend*
Actress . . . . Joan Crawford, *Mildred Pierce*
Sup. Actor . . . . James Dunn, *A Tree Grows in Brooklyn*
Sup. Actress . . . . Anne Revere, *National Velvet*
Director . . . . Billy Wilder, *The Lost Weekend*

1946
Picture . . . . *The Best Years of Our Lives,* Goldwyn, RKO
Actor . . . . . Fredric March, *The Best Years of Our Lives*
Actress . . . . Olivia de Havilland, *To Each His Own*
Sup. Actor . Harold Russell, *The Best Years of Our Lives*
Sup. Actress. . . . . Anne Baxter, *The Razor's Edge*
Director . . . . William Wyler, *The Best Years of Our Lives*

1947
Picture . . . . . *Gentleman's Agreement*, 20th Century-Fox
Actor . . . . Ronald Colman, *A Double Life*
Actress. . . . . . . Loretta Young, *The Farmer's Daughter*
Sup. Actor . . . . Edmund Gwenn, *Miracle on 34th Street*
Sup. Actress . . . Celeste Holm, *Gentleman's Agreement*
Director . . . . Elia Kahn, *Gentleman's Agreement*

1948
Picture . *Hamlet*, Two Cities Film, Universal International
Actor . . . . Laurence Olivier, *Hamlet*
Actress . . . . Jane Wyman, *Johnny Belinda*
Sup. Actor. . . . . Walter Huston,
 The Treasure of the Sierra Madre
Sup. Actress . . . . Claire Trevor, *Key Largo*
Director John Huston, *The Treasure of the Sierra Madre*

1949
Picture. . . . . *All the King's Men*, Columbia
Actor . . . . Broderick Crawford, *All the King's Men*
Actress . . . . Olivia de Havilland, *The Heiress*
Sup. Actor. . . . . Dean Jagger, *Twelve O'Clock High*
Sup. Actress . Mercedes McCambridge, *All the King's Men*
Director . . Joseph L. Mankiewicz, *A Letter to Three Wives*

1950
Picture . . . . *All About Eve*, 20th Century-Fox
Actor . . . . Jose Ferrer, *Cyrano de Bergerac*
Actress . . . . Judy Holliday, *Born Yesterday*
Sup. Actor . . . . George Sanders, *All About Eve*
Sup. Actress . . . . Josephine Hull, *Harvey*
Director. . . . . Joseph L. Mankiewicz, *All About Eve*

1951
Picture . . . . *An American in Paris*, MGM
Actor . . . . Humphrey Bogart, *The African Queen*
Actress . . . . Vivien Leigh, *A Streetcar Named Desire*
Sup. Actor. . . . . Karl Malden, *A Streetcar Named Desire*
Sup. Actress. . . . Kim Hunter, *A Streetcar Named Desire*
Director. . . . . George Stevens, *A Place in the Sun*

1952
Picture. . . . . *The Greatest Show on Earth*,
 C.B. DeMille, Paramount
Actor . . . . Gary Cooper, *High Noon*
Actress . . . . Shirley Booth, *Come Back, Little Sheba*
Sup. Actor. . . . . Anthony Quinn, *Viva Zapata!*
Sup. Actress Gloria Grahame, *The Bad and the Beautiful*
Director . . . . John Ford, *The Quiet Man*

1953
Picture . . . . *From Here to Eternity*, Columbia
Actor . . . . William Holden, *Stalag 17*
Actress . . . . Audrey Hepburn, *Roman Holiday*
Sup. Actor . . . . Frank Sinatra, *From Here to Eternity*
Sup. Actress . . . . . Donna Reed, *From Here to Eternity*
Director. . . . . . . Fred Zinnemann, *From Here to Eternity*

1954
Picture *On the Waterfront,* Horizon-American, Columbia
Actor . . . . Marlon Brando, *On the Waterfront*
Actress . . . . Grace Kelly, *The Country Girl*
Sup. Actor. . . . Edmond O'Brien, *The Barefoot Contessa*
Sup. Actress . . . . . . Eva Marie Saint, *On the Waterfront*
Director . . . . Elia Kazan, *On the Waterfront*

1955
Picture *Marty*, Hecht and Lancaster's Steven Prods, U.A.
Actor . . . . Ernest Borgnine, *Marty*
Actress. . . . . Anna Magi, *The Rose Tattoo*
Sup. Actor. . . . . Jack Lemmon, *Mister Roberts*
Sup. Actress . . . . Jo Van Fleet, *East of Eden*
Director . . . . Delbert Mann, *Marty*

1956
Picture . . . . *Around the World in 80 Days*,
 Michael Todd, U.A.
Actor . . . . Yul Brynner, *The King and I*
Actress . . . . Ingrid Bergman, *Anastasia*
Sup. Actor . . . . Anthony Quinn, *Lust for Life*
Sup. Actress . . . . Dorothy Malone, *Written on the Wind*
Director . . . . George Stevens, *Giant*

1957
Picture . . . . . . *The Bridge on the River Kwai*, Columbia
Actor . . . . Alec Guinness, *The Bridge on the River Kwai*
Actress . . . Joanne Woodward, *The Three Faces of Eve*
Sup. Actor . . . . Red Buttons, *Sayonara*
Sup. Actress. . . . . Miyoshi Umeki, *Sayonara*
Director. . . . . David Lean, *The Bridge on the River Kwai*

1958
Picture. . . . . *Gigi*, Arthur Freed Production, MGM
Actor. . . . . David Niven, *Separate Tables*
Actress. . . . . Susan Hayward, *I Want to Live*
Sup. Actor. . . . . Burl Ives, *The Big Country*
Sup. Actress. . . . . Wendy Hiller, *Separate Tables*
Director. . . . . Vincente Minnelli, *Gigi*

1959
Picture . . . . *Ben-Hur*, MGM
Actor . . . . Charlton Heston, *Ben-Hur*
Actress. . . . . Simone Signoret, *Room at the Top*

Sup. Actor .... Hugh Griffith, *Ben-Hur*
Sup. Actress . Shelley Winters, *The Diary of Anne Frank*
Director .... William Wyler, *Ben-Hur*

1960
Picture .... *The Apartment*, Mirisch Co., U.A.
Actor .... Burt Lancaster, *Elmer Gantry*
Actress .... Elizabeth Taylor, *Butterfield 8*
Sup. Actor .... Peter Ustenov, *Spartacus*
Sup. Actress............ Shirley Jones, *Elmer Gantry*
Director............... Billy Wilder, *The Apartment*

1961
Picture........ *West Side Story*, Mirisch Pictures, U.A.
Actor ..... Maximilian Schell, *Judgment at Nuremberg*
Actress .... Sophia Loren, *Two Women*
Sup. Actor .... George Chakiris, *West Side Story*
Sup. Actress .... Rita Moreno, *West Side Story*
Director Jerome Robbins, Robert Wise, *West Side Story*

1962
Picture .... *Lawrence of Arabia*, Columbia
Actor .... Gregory Peck, *To Kill a Mockingbird*
Actress .... Anne Bancroft, *The Miracle Worker*
Sup. Actor .... Ed Begley, *Sweet Bird of Youth*
Sup. Actress........ Patty Duke, *The Miracle Worker*
Director .... David Lean, *Lawrence of Arabia*

1963
Picture *Tom Jones*, Woodfall Prod., U.A.-Lopert Pictures
Actor .... Sidney Poitier, *Lilies of the Field*
Actress...................... Patricia Neal, *Hud*
Sup. Actor .... Melvyn Douglas, *Hud*
Sup. Actress........ Margaret Rutherford, *The V.I.P.s*
Director............... Tony Richardson, *Tom Jones*

1964
Picture .... *My Fair Lady*, Warner Bros.
Actor .... Rex Harrison, *My Fair Lady*
Actress .... Julie Andrews, *Mary Poppins*
Sup. Actor .... Peter Ustinov, *Topkapi*
Sup. Actress .... Lila Kedrova, *Zorba the Greek*
Director .... George Cukor, *My Fair Lady*

1965
Picture .... *The Sound of Music*, 20th Century-Fox
Actor................... Lee Marvin, *Cat Ballou*
Actress .... Julie Christie, *Darling*
Sup. Actor .... Marlin Balsam, *A Thousand Clowns*
Sup. Actress .... Shelley Winters, *A Patch of Blue*
Director.......... Robert Wise, *The Sound of Music*

1966
Picture .... *A Man for All Seasons*, Columbia
Actor.......... Paul Scofield, *A Man for All Seasons*
Actress . Elizabeth Taylor, *Who's Afraid of Virginia Woolf?*
Sup. Actor .... Walter Matthau, *The Fortune Cookie*
Sup. Actress Sandy Dennis, *Who's Afraid of Virginia Woolf?*
Director ...... Fred Zinnemann, *A Man for All Seasons*

1967
Picture .... *In the Heat of the Night*, Mirisch Corp., U.A

Actor .... Rod Steiger, *In the Heat of the Night*
Actress...................... Katharine Hepburn,
Guess Who's Coming to Dinner
Sup. Actor .... George Kennedy, *Cool Hand Luke*
Sup. Actress .... Estelle Parsons, *Bonnie and Clyde*
Director............... Mike Nichols, *The Graduate*

1968
Picture........................ *Oliver!*, Columbia
Actor .... Cliff Robertson, *Charly*
Actress ...... Katharine Hepburn, *The Lion in Winter*,
Barbra Streisand, *Funny Girl* (tie)
Sup. Actor .... Jack Albertson, *The Subject Was Roses*
Sup. Actress......... Ruth Gordon, *Rosemary's Baby*
Director.................... Sir Carol Reed, *Oliver!*

1969
Picture .... *Midnight Cowboy*, United Artists
Actor .... John Wayne, *True Grit*
Actress.. Maggie Smith, *The Prime of Miss Jean Brodie*
Sup. Actor. Gig Young, *They Shoot Horses. Don't They?*
Sup. Actress........... Goldie Hawn, *Cactus Flower*
Director .... John Schlesinger, *Midnight Cowboy*

1970
Picture .... *Patton*, 20th Century-Fox
Actor .... George C. Scott, *Patton* (refused)
Actress .... Glenda Jackson, *Women in Love*
Sup. Actor .... John Mills, *Ryan's Daughter*
Sup. Actress .... Helen Hayes, *Airport*
Director .... Franklin J. Schaffner, *Patton*

1971
Picture ..... *The French Connection*, 20th Century-Fox
Actor .... Gene Hackman, *The French Connection*
Actress....................... Jane Fonda, *Ionic*
Sup. Actor ...... Ben Johnson, *The Last Picture Show*
Sup. Actress . Cloris Leachman, *The Last Picture Show*
Director...... William Friedkin, *The French Connection*

1972
Picture................... *The Godfather*, Paramount
Actor .... Marlon Brando, *The Godfather* (refused)
Actress..................... Liza Minnelli, *Cabaret*
Sup. Actor .... Joel Grey, *Cabaret*
Sup. Actress ...... Eileen Heckart, *Butterflies Are Free*
Director .... Bob Fosse, *Cabaret*

1973
Picture .... *The Sting*, Universal
Actor .... Jack Lemmon, *Save the Tiger*
Actress .... Glenda Jackson, *A Touch of Class*
Sup. Actor ...... John Houseman, *The Paper Chase*
Sup. Actress............. Tatum O'Neal, *Paper Moon*
Director .... George Roy Hill, *The Sting*

1974
Picture .... *The Godfather Part II*, Paramount
Actor................... Art Carney, *Harry and Tonto*
Actress. Ellen Burstyn, *Alice Doesn't Live Here Anymore*
Sup. Actor ...... Robert De Niro, *The Godfather Part II*

Sup. Actress . . . . Ingrid Bergman,
Murder on the Orient Express
Director . . . Francis Ford Coppola, *The Godfather Part II*

1975
Picture. *One Flew Over the Cuckoo's Nest*, United Artists
Actor Jack Nicholson, *One Flew Over the Cuckoo's Nest*
Actress. . . . . Louise Fletcher,
One Flew Over the Cuckoo's Nest
Sup. Actor . . . . George Burns, *The Sunshine Boys*
Sup. Actress . . . . Lee Grant, *Shampoo*
DirectorMilos Forman, *One Flew Over the Cuckoo's Nest*

1976
Picture. . . . . *Rocky*, United Artists
Actor . . . . Peter Finch, *Network*
Actress . . . . Faye Dunaway, *Network*
Sup. Actor . . . . Jason Robards, *All the President's Men*
Sup. Actress . . . . Beatrice Straight, *Network*
Director . . . . John G. Avildsen, *Rocky*

1977
Picture. . . . . *Annie Hall*, United Artists
Actor . . . . Richard Dreyfuss, *The Goodbye Girl*
Actress . . . . Diane Keaton, *Annie Hall*
Sup. Actor. . . . . .Jason Robards, *Julia*
Sup. Actress . . . . Vanessa Redgrave, *Julia*
Director . . . . Woody Allen, *Annie Hall*

1978
Picture . . . . *The Deer Hunter*, Universal
Actor. . . . . Jon Voight, *Coming Home*
Actress. . . . . Jane Fonda, *Coming Home*
Sup. Actor . . . . . Christopher Walken, *The Deer Hunter*
Sup. Actress . . . . Maggie Smith, *California Suite*
Director . . . . Michael Cimino, *The Deer Hunter*

1979
Picture . . . . *Kramer vs. Kramer*, Columbia
Actor . . . . Dustin Hoffman, *Kramer vs. Kramer*
Actress . . . . Sally Field, *Norma Rae*
Sup. Actor . . . . Melvyn Douglas, *Being There*
Sup. Actress. . . . . . . Meryl Streep, *Kramer vs. Kramer*
Director . . . . Robert Benton, *Kramer vs. Kramer*

1980
Picture . . . . *Ordinary People*, Paramount
Actor . . . . Robert De Niro, *Raging Bull*
Actress . . . . Sissy Spacek, *Coal Miner's Daughter*
Sup. Actor . . . . Timothy Hutton, *Ordinary People*
Sup. Actress. . . Mary Steenburgen, *Melvin and Howard*
Director. . . . . Robert Redford, *Ordinary People*

1981
Picture. . . . . *Chariots of Fire*, Warner Bros.
Actor . . . . Henry Fonda, *On Golden Pond*
Actress . . . . Katharine Hepburn, *On Golden Pond*
Sup. Actor. . . . . John Gielgud, *Arthur*
Sup. Actress . . . . Maureen Stapleton, *Reds*
Director . . . . Warren Beatty, *Reds*

1982
Picture . . . . *Gandhi*, Columbia
Actor. Ben Kingsley, *Gandhi*
Ac tress. . . . . Meryl Streep, *Sophie's Choice*
Sup. Actor . . . . Louis Gossett, Jr.,
An Officer and a Gentleman
Sup. Actress . . . . Jessica Lange, *Tootsie*
Director . . . . Richard Attenborough, *Gandhi*

1983
Picture. . . . . *Terms of Endearment*, Paramount
Actor. . . . . Robert Duvall, *Tender Mercies*
Actress . . . . Shirley Maclaine, *Terms of Endearment*
Sup. Actor . . . . . Jack Nicholson, *Terms of Endearment*
Sup. Actress . Linda Hunt, *The Year of Living Dangerously*
Director . . . . . . James L. Brooks, *Terms of Endearment*

1984
Picture. . . . . *Amadeus*, Orion
Actor . . . . F. Murray Abraham, *Amadeus*
Actress . . . . Sally Field, *Places in the Heart*
Sup. Actor . . . . Haing S. Ngor, *The Killing Fields*
Sup. Actress . . . . . . Peggy Ashcroft, *A Passage to India*
Director . . . . Milos Forman, *Amadeus*

1985
Picture . . . . *Out of Africa*, Universal
Actor . . . . William Hurt, *Kiss of the Spider Woman*
Actress . . . . Geraldine Page, *The Trip to Bountiful*
Sup. Actor . . . . Don Ameche, *Cocoon*
Sup. Actress . . . . Anjelica Huston, *Prizzi's Honor*
Director . . . . Sydney Pollack, *Out of Africa*

1986
Picture . . . . *Platoon*, Orion
Actor . . . . Paul Newman, *The Color of Money*
Actress . . . . . . Marlee Matlin, *Children of a Lesser God*
Sup. Actor . . . . . Michael Caine, *Hannah and Her Sisters*
Sup. Actress . . . . Dianne Wiest, *Hannah and Her Sisters*
Director. . . . . Oliver Stone, *Platoon*

1987
Picture . . . . *The Last Emperor*, Columbia
Actor. . . . . Michael Douglas, *Wall Street*
Actress. . . . . Cher, *Moonstruck*
Sup. Actor . . . . Sean Connery, *The Untouchables*
Sup. Actress . . . . Olympia Dukakis, *Moonstruck*
Director. . . . . . . Bernardo Bertolucci, *The Last Emperor*

1988
Picture . . . . *Rain Man*, United Artists
Actor . . . . Dustin Hoffman, *Rain Man*
Actress . . . . Jodie Foster, *The Accused*
Sup. Actor. . . . . Kevin Kline, *A Fish Called Wanda*
Sup. Actress . . . . . Geena Davis, *The Accidental Tourist*
Director . . . . Barry Levinson, *Rain Man*

1989
Picture . . . . *Driving Miss Daisy*, Warner Bros.
Actor . . . . Daniel Day Lewis, *My Left Foot*
Actress . . . . Jessica Tandy, *Driving Miss Daisy*
Sup. Actor. . . . . Denzel Washington, *Glory*

Sup. Actress . . . . Brenda Fricker, *My Left Foot*
Director . . . . . . Oliver Stone, *Born on the Fourth of July*

1990

Picture. . . . . *Dances With Wolves*, Orion
Actor. . . . . Jeremy Irons, *Reversal of Fortune*
Actress . . . . Kathy Bates, *Misery*
Sup. Actor. . . . . Joe Pesci, *Good Fellas*
Sup. Actress . . . . Whoopi Goldberg, *Ghost*
Director . . . . Kevin Costner, *Dances With Wolves*

1991

Picture . . . . The Silence of the Lambs, Orion
Actor . . . . . Anthony Hopkins, *The Silence of the Lambs*
Actress . . . . Jodie Foster, *The Silence of the Lambs*
Sup. Actor . . . . Jack Palance, *City Slickers*
Sup. Actress. . . . . . . Mercedes Ruehl, *The Fisher King*
Director . . Jonathan Demme, *The Silence of the Lambs*

1992

Picture. . . . . *Unforgiven*, p. Clint Eastwood
Actor . . . . Al Pacino, *Scent of A Woman*
Actress . . . . Emma Thompson, *Howards End*
Sup. Actor. . . . . Gene Hackman, *Unforgiven*
Sup. Actress. . . . . Marisa Tomei, *My Cousin Vinny*
Director. . . . . Clint Eastwood, *Unforgiven*

1993

Picture . . . . *Schindler's List*, p. Steven Spielberg,
Gerald R. Molen, Branko Lustig
Actor . . . . Tom Hanks, *Philadelphia*
Actress . . . . Holly Hunter, *The Piano*
Sup. Actor. . . . . Tommy Lee Jones, *The Fugitive*
Sup. Actress . . . . Anna Paquin, *The Piano*
Director . . . . Steven Spielberg, *Schindler's List*

1994

Picture. *Forrest Gump*, p. Steve Tisch, Wendy Finerman,
Steve Sharkey
Actor. . . . . Tom Hanks, *Forrest Gump*
Actress. . . . . Jessica Lange, *Blue Sky*
Sup. Actor. . . . . Martin Landau, *Ed Wood*
Sup. Actress . . . . Dianne Wiest, *Bullets Over Broadway*
Director . . . . Robert Zemeckis, *Forrest Gump*

1995

Picture . . . . *Braveheart*, p. Mel Gibson,
Alan Ladd, Jr., and Bruce Davey
Actor. . . . . Nicolas Cage, *Leaving Las Vegas*
Actress . . . . Susan Sarandon, *Dead Man Walking*
Sup. Actor . . . . Kevin Spacey, *The Usual Suspects*
Sup. Actress. . . . . Mira Sorvino, *Mighty Aphrodite*
Director. . . . . Mel Gibson, *Braveheart*

1996

Picture . . . . *The English Patient*, p. Saul Zaentz
Actor. . . . . Geoffrey Rush, *Shine*
Actress . . . . Frances McDormand, *Fargo*
Sup. Actor . . . . Cuba Gooding. Jr., *Jerry Maguire*

Sup. Actress . . . . Juliette Binoche, *The English Patient*
Director . . . . . . Anthony Minghella, *The English Patient*

1997

Picture *Titanic*, James Cameron, Jon Landau, producers
Actor . . . . Mart Damon, *Good Will Hunting*
Actress . . . . Helen Hunt, *As Good as It Gets*
Sup. Actor. . . . . Robin Williams, *Good Will Hunting*
Sup. Actress . . . . Kim Basinger, *LA Confidential*
Director . . . . James Cameron, *Titanic*

1998

Picture . . *Shakespeare in Love*, p. Donna Gigliotti, Mar
Norman, David Parfitt, Harvey Weinstein, Edward Zwick
Actor . . . . Roberto Benigni, *Life Is Beautiful*
Actress . . . . Gwyneth Paltrow, *Shakespeare in Love*
Sup. Actor. . . . . James Coburn, *Affliction*
Sup. Actress. . . . . Judi Dench, *Shakespeare in Love*
Director . . . . . . Steven Spielberg, *Saving Private Ryan*

1999

Picture *American Beauty*, p. Bruce Cohen and Dan Jinks
Actor. . . . . Kevin Spacey, *American Beauty*
Actress. . . . . Hilary Swank, *Boys Don't Cry*
Sup. Actor . . . . . Michael Caine, *The Cider House Rules*
Sup. Actress . . . . Angelina Jolie, *Girl Interrupted*
Director. . . . . Sam Mendes, *American Beauty*

2000

Picture. . . . . *Gladiator*, p. Douglas Wick,
David Franzoni, Branko Lustig
Actor . . . . Russell Crowe, *Gladiator*
Actress . . . . Julia Roberts, *Erin Brockovich*
Sup. Actor. . . . . Benicio Del Toro, *Traffic*
Sup. Actress . . . . Marcia Gay Harden, *Pollock*
Director . . . . Steven Soderbergh, *Traffic*

2001

Picture. *A Beautiful Mind*, p. Douglas Wick, Brian Grazer
and Ron Howard
Actor . . . . Denzel Washington, *Training Day*
Actress . . . . Halle Berry, *Monster's Ball*
Sup. Actor. . . . . Jim Broadbent, *Iris*
Sup. Actress . . . . . . Jennifer Connelly, *A Beautiful Mind*
Director . . . . Ron Howard, *A Beautiful Mind*

2002

Picture . . . . *Chicago*, p. Martin Richards
Actor . . . . Adrien Brody, *The Pianist*
Actress . . . . Nicole Kidman, *The Hours*
Sup. Actor. . . . . Chris Cooper, *Adaptation*
Sup. Actress. . . . . Catherine Zeta-Jones, *Chicago*
Director. . . . . Roman Polanski, *The Pianist*

2003

Picture. . . . *The Lord of the Rings: The Return of the King*,
New Line

Source: © *Academy of Motion Picture Arts and Sciences* Oscars® for the 75th Annual Academy Awards were presented on March 22, 2003, by the Academy of Motion Picture Arts and Sciences.

Actor . . . . Sean Penn, *Mystic River*
Actress . . . . Charlize Theron, *Monster*
Sup. Actor . . . . Tim Robbins, *Mystic River*
Sup. Actress . . . . Renée Zellweger, *Cold Mountain*
Director. . . . . Peter Jackson, The Lord of the Rings:
The Return of the King
Foreign-Language Film. . . . . Les Invasions barbares
(The Barbarian Invasions), Canada
Original Screenplay . . Sofia Coppola, *Lost In Translation*
Screenplay Adaptation . . Fran Walsh, Philippa Boyens &
Peter Jackson, *The Lord of the Rings:*
The Return of the King
Cinematography . . . . Russell Boyd,
Master and Commander: The Far Side of the World
Editing . . . . Jamie Selkirk, *The Lord of the Rings:*
The Return of the King
Original Score (Dramatic) . . . . Howard Shore,
The Lord of the Rings: The Return of the King
Original Song. . . . . Fran Walsh, Howard Shore,
Annie Lennox, "Into The West,"
The Lord of the Rings: The Return of the King

Art Direction. . . . . . Grant Major, Don Hennah, Alan Lee,
The Lord of the Rings: The Return of the King
Costume Design . . . . Ngila Dickson, Richard Taylor,
The Lord of the Rings: The Return of the King
Sound Mixing. . . Christopher Boyes, Michael Semanick,
Michael Hedges and Hammond Peek,
The Lord of the Rings: The Return of the King
Sound Editing . . Richard King, *Master and Commander:*
The Far Side of the World
Makeup. . . . . Richard Taylor, Peter King,
The Lord of the Rings: The Return of the King
Visual Effects . . . . Jim Rygiel, Joe Letteri,
Randall William Cook, Alex Funke,
The Lord of the Rings: The Return of the King
Documentary Feature. . . Errol Morris, Michael Williams,
The Fog of War
Documentary Short Subject . . . . Maryann DeLeo,
Chernobyl Heart

2003 Oscar™ Nominations

Picture: *Lord of the Rings: The Return of the King*, *Lost In Translation*, *Master and Commander*, *Mystic River*, *Seabiscuit*

Actor: Johnny Depp, *Pirates of the Caribbean: The Curse of the Black Pearl*; Ben Kingsley, *House of Sand and Fog*; Jude Law, *Cold Mountain*; Bill Murray, *Lost In Translation*; Sean Penn, *Mystic River*

Actress: Keisha Castle-Hughes, *Whale Rider*; Diane Keaton, *Something's Gotta Give*; Samantha Morton, *In America*; Charlize Theron, *Monster*; Naomi Watts, *21 Grams*

Sup. Actor: Alec Baldwin, *The Cooler*; Benicio Del Toro, *21 Grams*; Djimon Hounsou, *In America*; Tim Robbins, *Mystic River*; Ken Watanabe, *The Last Samurai*

Sup. Actress: Shohreh Aghdashloo, *House of Sand and Fog*; Patricia Clarkson, *Pieces of April*; Marcia Gay Harden, *Mystic River*; Holly Hunter, *Thirteen*; Renée Zellweger, *Cold Mountain*

Director: Fernando Meirelles, *City of God*; Peter Jackson, *The Lord of the Rings: The Return of the King*; Peter Weir, *Master and Commander: The Far Side of the World*; Clint Eastwood, *Mystic River*

Foreign Language Film: *The Barbarian Invasions*,

Canada; *Evil*, Sweden; *The Twilight Samurai*, Japan; *Twin Sisters*, The Netherlands; *Zelary*, Czech Republic

Original Screenplay: Denys Arcand, *The Barbarian Invasions*; Steven Knight, *Dirty Pretty Things*; Andrew Stanton, Bob Peterson, David Reynolds, *Finding Nemo*; Jim Sheridan, Naomi Sheridan, Kirsten Sheridan, *In America*; Sofia Coppola, *Lost In Translation*

Adapted Screenplay: Robert Pulcini, Shari Springer Berman, *American Splendor*; Braulio Mantovani, *City of God*; Fran Walsh, Philippa Boyens, Peter Jackson, *The Lord of the Rings: The Return of the King*; Gary Ross, *Seabiscuit*

Cinematography: Cesar Charlone, *City of God*; John Seale, *Cold Mountain*; Eduardo Serra, *Girl with a Pearl Earring*; Russell Boyd, *Master and Commander: The Far Side of the World*; John Schwartzman, *Seabiscuit*

Original Song: Fran Walsh, **Howard Shore**, Annie Lennox, "Into the West," *The Lord of the Rings: The Return of the King*; Michael McKean, Annette O'Toole, "A Kiss at the End of the Rainbow," *A Mighty Wind*; T Bone Burnett, Elvis Costello, "Scarlet Tide," *Cold Mountain*; Benoit Charest, Sylvain Chomet, "Belleville Rendez-vous," *The Triplets of Belleville*; Sting, "You Will Be My One True Love," *Cold Mountain*

Source: © *Academy of Motion Picture Arts and Sciences*

The Berlin Film Festival Awards

The awards of the 54th annual Berlin Film Festival (also known as the "Berlinale") were announced February 14, 2004.

Golden Berlin Bear . . . . *Head On*, dir. Faith Akin
Silver Berlin Bear . . *Lost Embrace*, dir. Daniel Burman
Best Actress . . . Catalina Sandina Moreno, *Maria Full of Grace*; Charlize Theron, *Monster*
Best Actor . . . . Daniel Hendler, *Lost Embrace*

Best Director . . . . Kim Ki-Duk, *Samaritan Girl*
Alfred Bauer Prize (for first feature film) . . . . *Maria Full of Grace*, dir. Joshua Marston
Best European Film . . . . . . *Daybreak*, dir. Björn Runge

Source: *Berlin Film Festival*

The Sundance Film Festival Awards

The Sundance Film Festival was held January 15–25, 2004, in Park City, Utah.

Documentary Grand Jury Prize . *Dig!*, dir. Ondi Timoner
Dramatic Grand Jury Prize . . *Primer*, dir. Shane Carruth
Documentary Audience Award . . . . *Born Into Brothels*, dirs. Ross Kauffman, Zana Briski
Dramatic Audience Award . . . . *Maria Full of Grace*, dir. Joshua Marston
World Cinema Dramatic Audience Award *Seducing Dr. Lewis*, dir. Jean-François Pouliot
World Cinema Documentary Audience Award . . . . *The Corporation*, dirs. Mark Achbar, Jennifer Abbott
Documentary Directing Award . . . . . Morgan Spurlock, *Supersize Me*
Dramatic Directing Award . . . . Debra Granick, *Down to the Bone*

The Freedom of Expression Award . . . . . . *Repatriation*, dir. Kim Dong-won
Waldo Salt Screenwriting Award . . . . Larry Gross, *We Don't Live Here Any More*
Dramatic Special Jury Prize . . . . . . *Brother to Brother* dir. Rodney Evans; Vera Farmiga (performance) *Down to the Bone*
Documentary Special Jury Prize . . . . *Farmingville*, dirs. Catherine Tambini, Carlos Sandoval
Jury Prize in Short . . . . . *The Trespasser*, dir. Beto Brant
Jury Prize in Short Filmmaking *When The Storm Came*, dir. Shilpi Gupta; *Gowanus Brooklyn*, dir. Ryan Fleck
Jury Prize in International Short Filmmaking . . . *Tomo*, dir. Paul Catling

Source: *Sundance Film Festival*

The Cannes Film Festival Awards, 1998–2004

1998

Grand Jury Prize . . . . *La Vita e Bella* (Italy)
Special Jury Prize . . . . *La Classe de Neige* (France); *Festen* (Denmark)
Best Director . . . . John Boorman, *The General* (UK)
Best Actor. . . . . Peter Mullan, *My Name Is Joe* (UK)
Best Actress. . . . . Elodie Bouchez and Natacha Regnier, *La Vie Revee des Anges* (France)
Palme d'Or. *Eternity and a Day*, Theo Angelopoulos (Greece)

1999

Grand Jury Prize . . . . *L'humanité* (France)
Jury Prize . . . . *A Carta* (Portugal)
Best Director. . . . . Pedro Almodovar, *Todo Sobre Mi Madre* (Spain)
Best Actor . . . . Emmanuel Schotté, *L'humanité* (France)
Best Actress (tie) Séverine Cancele, *L'humanité* (France) and Emilie Dequenne, *Rosetta* (Belgium)
Palme d'Or. . . . . *Rosetta*, Luc and Jean-Pierre Dardenne (Belgium)

2000

Grand Prize . . . . *Guizi Lai Le*, Jiang Wen (China)
Jury Prize. . . . . *Sånger Från Andra Våningen* (Sweden), *Takhté Siah* (Iran)
Best Director. . . . . Edward Yang, *Yi Yi* (Taiwan)
Best Actor . . . . Tony Leung Chiu-Wai, *In the Mood for Love* (China)
Best Actress . . . . . Björk, *Dancer in the Dark* (Denmark)
Palme d'Or . . . . *Dancer in the Dark*, Lars von Trier (Denmark)

2001

Grand Prize. . . . . *The Piano Teacher*, Michael Haneke (Austria/France)
Caméra d'Or . . . . ***Atanarjuat (The Fast Runner)***, **Zacharias Kunuk (Canada)**

Best Director . . . . (tie) Joel Coen, *The Man Who Wasn't There* (USA); David Lynch, *Mulholland Drive* (USA)
Best Actor. Benoit Magimel, *The Piano Teacher* (France)
Best Actress . . . . Isabelle Huppert, *The Piano Teacher* (France)
Palme d'Or . . . . . *The Son's Room*, Nanni Moretti (Italy)

2002

Grand Prize . . . . *The Man Without a Past*, Aki Kaurismäki dir. (Iceland)
Caméra d'Or . *Bord de mer*, Julie Lopes-Curval (France)
Best Director . . . . (tie) Im Kwon-Taek, *Chihwaseon (South Korea);* Paul Thomas Anderson, *Punch-Drunk Love (USA)*
Best Actor . . . . Olivier Gourmet, *Les Fils*
Best Actress Kati Outinen, *The Man Without a Past* (Iceland)
Palme d'Or . . *The Pianist*, Roman Polanski dir. (France)

2003

Grand Prize . . . . . . *Uzak*, Nuri Bilge Cevlan, dir. (Turkey)
Caméra d'Or*Reconstruction*, Christopher Boe (Denmark)
Best Director . . . . Gus Van Sant, *Elephant* (USA)
Best Actor . . . . (tie) Muzaffer Ozdemir, Mehmen Ermin Toprak, *Uzak*
Best Actress . . . . **Marie Josée Croze,** ***Barbarian Invasions* (Canada)**
Palme d'Or. . . . . *Elephant*, Gus Van Sant, dir. (USA)

2004

Grand Prize . . . *Old Boy*, Chan-Wook Park dir. (S.Korea)
Caméra d'Or . . . . *Or*, Keren Yedaya (Israel)
Best Director. . . . . Tony Gatlif, *Exils* (France)
Best Actor . . . . . . Yuuya Yagira, *Nobody Knows* (Japan)
Best Actress . . . . Maggie Cheung, *Clean* (China)
Palme d'Or. . *Fahrenheit 9/11*, Michael Moore dir. (USA)

Source: *The Cannes Film Festival*

CANADIAN ARTS AWARDS

Governor General's Performing Arts Awards

The Governor General's Performing Arts Awards were inaugurated in 1992 to pay tribute to the lifetime achievements of outstanding artists in a variety of creative fields. The motto of the awards, "The Arts Engage and Inspire Us," reflects the cultural contribution made by recipients chosen from theatre, dance, classical music/opera, popular music, film and broadcasting. The awards are presented annually in November by the Governor General and are administered by the Governor General's Performing Arts Awards Foundation.

■ Winners 1999–2003

1999

Mario Bernardi
David Cronenberg
Denise Filiatrault
Mavor Moore
Louis Quilico
Ginette Reno
Sam Sniderman
Michel Tremblay

2000

Janette Bertrand
Walter Carsen
Tom C. ("Stompin' Tom") Connors

Fernand Nault
Christopher Newton
Teresa Stratas
Donald Sutherland

2001

Mario Bernardi
Diane Dufresne
Max Ferguson, O.C.
Evelyn Hart, C.C.
Christopher Plummer, C.C.
Anne-Claire Poirier
Thea Borlase
Édouard Lock

2002

André Brassard

Joy Coghill
The Guess Who
Karen Kain
Phil Nimmons
Jean-Pierre Perreault
Father Fernand Lindsay
Angela Hewitt

2003

Pierrette Allaire
Dave Broadfoot
Douglas Campbell
Marie Chouinard
Norman Jewison
Micheline Lanctôt
Jim and Sandra Pitblado
Ian Tyson

2004 Winners

■ Kate and Anna McGarrigle

As singers, songwriters, performers and recording artists, Kate and Anna McGarrigle express a particular Canadian ideal of the fundamental bonds of music and family. Born in Montréal of mixed English and French-Canadian origin, they were taught music by the nuns of the Laurentian village of St-Sauveur and developed their passion for music through regular sessions around the family piano. In the 1960s, they were inspired by a Pete Seeger concert in Montreal to form their own trio and subsequently appeared in coffeehouses. They began to write their own songs and achieved a breakthrough at the 1970 Philadelphia Folk Festival, where they opened

for Jerry Jeff Walker, who was struck with the power and imagination of their song *Heart Like a Wheel*, which became a major hit for Linda Ronstadt. In 1975, they recorded their first album, *Kate and Anna McGarrigle*. Their subsequent albums include *Dancer with Bruised Knees*, *Pronto Monto*, *Love Over and Over*, *Matapedia*, *The McGarrigle Hour*, and most recently *La Vache Qui Pleure*. They have created hit songs for Emmylou Harris, Nana Mouskouri, Judy Collins and Maria Muldaur, and have sung with Joan Baez, Lou Reed, Gilles Vigneault, Robert Charlebois, and The Chieftains.

Rick Mercer

Rick Mercer's skill in satire without malice has endeared him to his 'victims' as much as the audience at large. Born in Middle Cove, Newfoundland, in 1969, Rick gained his earliest stage experience in a troupe formed from his high-school theatre class known as "Cory and Wade's Playhouse." He burst onto the national scene in 1990 with his outstanding one-man stage show *Show Me the Button, I'll Push It*. His outstanding contribution to TV comedy with a political punch has been rec-

ognized with over 20 Gemini Awards for both writing and performing on the top-rated series *This Hour Has 22 Minutes*. In 2002, Mercer won two more Geminis for his hit satire of the Canadian television production industry, *Made In Canada*. His newest series, *Monday Report*, was an instant hit in the fall of 2003 and will be returning in the fall of 2004 for a second season. *Rick Mercer's Talking to Americans* was the highest rated comedy special in the history of Canadian television. In 1998, his first book, *Streeters*, based on his signature straight-to-the-camera monologues, was published and quickly rose to the top of the bestseller list.

Constance V. Pathy

Mrs. Pathy studied law at Leiden University in her native Netherlands, before coming to Canada in 1960. In Montreal, she earned two performance degrees from McGill University in cello and viola da gamba which led to her playing in chamber groups such as the Quatuor Morency and Le Consort Royall. A committee member of Montreal's oldest chamber music society, the Ladies' Morning Musical Club since 1968, she first served as

president in 1975 and has held that office since 1990. Mrs. Pathy has also served on the board of the Canadian Guild of Crafts for more than 25 years, 17 of them as chair. She founded Brome Beaux Arts, an organization providing chamber music concerts free of charge in the Eastern Townships, and has also been deeply involved with the Canadian Arts Summit since its inception in 1998.

Gordon Pinsent

Gordon Pinsent has contributed to Canada's entertainment heritage as an actor, director, writer, and producer. Born in Grand Falls, Nfld, in 1930, he served with the Royal Canadian Regiment and worked as a dance instructor and illustrator before he talked himself into his first job as an actor at the Winnipeg Repertory Theatre. While in Winnipeg, he was also involved in many of the first radio dramas and the first live network television programs to be broadcast from that city. His roles range from establish-

ment figures such as a Member of Parliament *(Quentin Durgens M.P.),* President of the United States *(The Forbin Project),* Sergeant Scott of the *Forest Rangers,* and Constable Fraser Sr. on *Due South* to iconoclasts such as Will Cole *(The Rowdyman)* and John in *John and the Missus,* both of which films he wrote. He has three Genie Awards for his film work, five Gemini Awards for his work in television and has won the Dora Mavor Moore Award for his stage work. He is also the recipient of ACTRA's Lifetime Achievement Award and the Banff Television Festival Award for Lifetime Achievement. His most recent work includes the acclaimed film *The Shipping News* and the CBC Radio drama *Test Drive.*

■ Joseph Rouleau

Internationally renowned bass Joseph Rouleau has sung on the world's most prestigious stages. He was born in Matane, Quebec, in 1929. After following classical studies at Collège Jean de Brébeuf, he enrolled in political science at Université de Montréal. In 1947, he studied voice with Édouard Wooley and Albert Cornellier. In 1949, he won the Prix Archambault and became the first singing student to be admitted to the Conservatoire de musique du Québec in Montreal. In 1952, he pursued voice studies in Milan with Mario Basiola and Antonio Narducci. In 1955, he made his debut in the United States in the role of Colline *(La Bohème* by Puccini). In 1956, he joined the Royal Opera House at Covent Garden (London) where, over 30

years, he took part in 850 performances in over 48 operas. His impressive discography includes *Semiramide* (Rossini), *Boris Godounov* (Mussorgsky), *Romeo and Juliet, Don Carlos*

(Verdi), and the songs of Félix Leclerc. He has performed on television and radio, and recorded several video performances including *L'Africaine* (Meyerbeer), *Don Carlos* (Verdi), and *Who's Afraid of Opera?*

■ Jean-Louis Roux

For more than 60 years, Jean-Louis Roux has made his mark on the Canadian cultural landscape as a director, playwright, translator, author, and cultural organizer. Born in Montreal on May 18, 1923, he completed his classical studies at Collège Sainte-Marie before pursuing medical studies at Université de Montréal from 1942 to 1946. After the war, he went to Paris and Europe to absorb the latest trends, then returned to Montreal in 1949 to co-found the Théâtre d'essai. In 1951, he co-founded

the Théâtre du Nouveau Monde and held the positions of secretary general (1953–63) and artistic director (1966–82). He has performed over 150 theatrical roles in more than 70 productions. In addition to writing two of his own plays, *Rose Latulippe* and *Bois Brûlés*, he has translated and adapted over 20 works by the likes of Shakespeare, Tennessee Williams, and Peter Shaeffer. He has written screenplays for television and radio, and he has portrayed some 50 roles in TV series such as *La Famille Plouffe* and *Septième Nord*. In film, he has appeared in *Cordélia* by Jean Beaudin and *L'empereur du Pérou* by Fernando Arrabal. He has been president of the Société des auteurs (1953–62) and of the Centre canadien du théâtre (1959–68), director general of the National Theatre School of Canada (1981–86), and president of the Canada Council for the Arts (1998–2003).

■ Veronica Tennant

Born in London, England, Veronica began dancing at the age of four. After arriving in Canada, she studied with Betty Oliphant and at 18 was cast by Celia Franca as Juliet for her debut with the National Ballet of Canada as principal dancer. For 25 years, she danced on the international stage with the greatest male

dancers of our time, including Erik Bruhn, Rudolf Nureyev, and Mikhail Baryshnikov, earning acclaim in every major classical role as well as having ballets choreographed for her unique talents. She moved swiftly to the forefront of another career: the challenging world of arts television. Her first three CBC TV specials—*Salute to Dancers For Life, Margie Gillis: Wild Hearts in Strange Times* and *Karen Kain: Dancing In The Moment*,

each won awards and critical acclaim, with the latter receiving an International Emmy Award in 1999. Since forming Veronica Tennant Productions in 1997, she has conceived, produced and directed a significant body of work as an independent filmmaker, including *The Dancers' Story: The National Ballet of Canada, Trio* and *Northern Light*.

■ Eric Till

As a director of film and television, Eric Till is recognized as a brilliant and passionate artist whose early productions for the *Festival* series became the first CBC productions to contend for international Emmy awards. Born and educated in England, Eric began his professional career at a British radio station in Hamburg. Arriving in Canada in 1954, he was

hired as Company Manager for the National Ballet, where he became a lasting friend of Glenn Gould, with whom he produced and directed three of Gould's television specials. Till wrote and directed the multiple award-winning *Glenn Gould—A Portrait*, following the pianist's death. He has directed/produced ballet programs on television for the Royal Ballet, the Bolshoi Ballet, the National Ballet of Canada, the Royal Winnipeg Ballet and such acclaimed miniseries as *The National Dream, Glory Enough for All*, and *Talking to a Stranger*. His best-known Canadian films include *Small Gifts, Getting Married in Buffalo Jump* and *A Nest of Singing Birds*. His international film credits include *Bethune* with Donald Sutherland, *A Fan's Notes* with Jerry Orbach, *A Walking Stick* with David Hemmings, and *Hot Millions*, a classic comedy starring Maggie Smith.

The National Aboriginal Achievement Awards, 2004

The National Aboriginal Achievements Foundation established these awards in conjunction with the United Nations' International Decade of the World's Indigenous peoples. The awards recognize career achievements by Aboriginal professionals in diverse occupations. The foundation presents awards to outstanding First Nations citizens in the fields of arts and culture, medicine, business, law, heritage and sports, education, the environment, public service and community development. The 12th annual National Aboriginal Achievement Awards were held April 4, 2004, in Calgary. The following biographies are of those who received awards in the arts.

■ Winners, Arts and Culture, 1997–2003[1]

1997
Kiawak Ashoona
Gil Cardinal
Graham Greene

1998
Tantoo Cardinal
Daphne Odjig
Buffy Sainte-Marie

2000
Tsa-qwa-supp (Art Thompson)
Leetia Ineak

2001
Tomson Highway
Zacharias Kunuk

2002
Ohito Ashoona
Freda Diesing
Gail Guthrie Valaskakis

2003
John Arcand
Tom King
Robbie Robertson

(1) In 1999, there were no recipients in the area of arts and culture.

2004 Winners

■ Osuitok Ipeelee, sculptor: Osuitok Ipeelee is an internationally known carver and printmaker who was instrumental in the development of both of these important art forms. Born in a camp near Cape Dorset, Osuitok learned his art by watching his father. By the age of 13, Osuitok was making his own toys. Soon after, he began selling soapstone and ivory sculptures to the Hudson's Bay Company and to local missionaries. By 1951, he had become one of the best carvers on the south Baffin coast. Since then his work has been included in countless

museum and gallery exhibitions around the world and forms part of the permanent collections of the Metropolitan Museum of Art in New York, the Canadian Museum of Civilization, the Beaverbrook Art Gallery, the Art Gallery of Ontario, the Glenbow Museum and the McMichael Canadian Collection.

■ Tina Keeper, actor: Tina Keeper is best known to television audiences in her role as RCMP constable Michelle Kenidi in the highly successful CBC series *North of 60*. She was born in northern Manitoba and moved to Winnipeg with her family when she was four. She completed the acting program at the University of Manitoba. In 1982

she began work in theatre, first as a wardrobe assistant, then as a stage manager and finally as an actor, dancer, mime artist and improv performer. With only two film roles under her belt, she landed the role in *North of 60*, which won her a Gemini Award for Best Actress in 1997. Keeper has also appeared in several TV movies including *Dreamstorm* and *In The Blue Ground*, for which she won Best Actress at the Native American Film Festival.

■ Basil Johnston, heritage and spirituality:

Basil Johnston is a respected author, storyteller and preserver of the Anishnaabe language. A member of the Cape Croker

First Nation in Ontario, he has written 15 books in English and five in Ojibway, as well as numerous articles that have been published in newspapers, anthologies and periodicals. He is a strong proponent of the idea that the key to understanding culture is language. In service of that idea he has developed audio language programs on cassette and CD and continues to teach Anishnaabe language classes to adults and to youth. From 1970 to 1994 he worked in the ethnology department of the Royal Ontario Museum. He has taught and lectured at both the secondary and post-secondary levels. His best known book, *Indian School Days*, is a humorous and poignant account of his experience in the residential school system.

■ Susan Point, artist:

Born in 1952, Susan Point is from the Musqueam First Nation on the edge of Vancouver. While raising the profile of Coast Salish art on local, national and international levels, she has developed her own personal style, produc-

ing her fine art in precious metals, serigraphs, wood block prints and acrylic paintings. A self-taught artist, she began exploring and creating large-scale public art in various media using stained glass, steel, bronze, concrete, wood, terra cotta and forton casting. Her large works welcome visitors to Vancouver International Airport and appear in many public buildings and corporate developments. Governor General Adrienne Clarkson recently invited her on a state visit to South America as a cultural ambassador. She was awarded an honorary doctorate in Fine Arts from the University of Victoria.

■ Suzanne Rochon-Burnett, broadcaster:

Suzanne Rochon-Burnett began her career at age 18 with a radio station in St. Jerome, Quebec. Over the next 20 years, she worked as a journalist and broadcaster in Montreal, Paris

and New York. In 1974, she moved to the Niagara Peninsula in southwestern Ontario. There she developed a program called *Chanson à la Français* which was distributed to 22 Ontairo radio stations. Today she is president and CEO of R.B. Communications Ltd. which owns radio station Spirit FM 91.7. She also owns Kakekalanicks Inc., a company that focuses on Aboriginal art and issues.

Source: *The National Aboriginal Achievement Foundation*

THEATRE

Toronto is now considered the third-largest production centre of live theatre in the English-speaking world (following New York, and London, England). The English Canadian theatre scene has undergone exponential growth since the birth of the Stratford Shakespearean Festival at Stratford, Ont., in 1953. The alternative theatre movement that swept English Canada in the 1970s established producers of Canadian drama in every large centre. Diminishing government support in the 1980s and 1990s led to more emphasis on commercial Canadian productions of British, French and American "megamusicals" while development of new and experimental work has passed increasingly to independent artists often appearing at a cross-Canada network of "fringe" festivals.

Theatrical activity in French Canada burgeoned in the 1950s and 1960s as playwrights such as Marcel Dubé (*Un Simple Soldat*) and Gratien Gélinas (*'Tit Coq*) explored the social and moral issues confronting Québecers in their own dialect. This movement reached its apex in the work of Michel Tremblay in the early 1970s. More recently, Quebec theatre has also excelled in less verbal forms of theatre such as the spectacles produced by Cirque du Soleil, while the "total theatre" productions of Quebec City writer/performer/director Robert Lepage have garnered critical acclaim around the world.

Dora Mavor Moore Awards, 2004

The 2004 Dora Mavor Moore Awards, honouring the best of the Toronto community's performing arts, were held June 28, 2004, at the Princess of Wales Theatre.

General Theatre
Outstanding New Play . . . . *Confederation*, Michael Hollingsworth
Outstanding New Musical . . . . *Tequila Vampire Matinee*, Kevin Quain
Outstanding Production of a Play . . . . Tie: *Remnants*, Tarragon Theatre; *The Syringa Tree*, CanStage
Outstanding Production of a Musical . . . . *The Producers*, David & Ed Mirvish
Outstanding Direction of a Play . . . . Richard Rose, *Remnants*
Outstanding Direction of a Musical . . . . Susan Stroman, *The Producers*
Outstanding Performance by a Male in a Principle Role-Play . . . . William Hutt, *No Man's Land*
Outstanding Performance by a Female in a Principal Role-Play . . . . Caroline Cave, *The Syringa Tree*
Outstanding Performance by a Male in a Principal Role-Musical . . . . Michael Therriault, *The Producers*
Outstanding Performance by a Female in a Principal Role-Musical . . . . . . Jackie Richardson, *Cookin' At The Cookery*
Outstanding Performance in a Featured Role-Play or Musical . . . . Juan Chioran, *The Producers*
Outstanding Production for Young Audiences . . . . *Bluffer's Moon*, Cliffhanger Productions
Outstanding Set Design . . . . Charlotte Dean, *Rune Arlidge*, Tarragon Theatre
Outstanding Costume Design . . . . Astrid Janson & Julie Renton, *Confederation*, VideoCabaret
Outstanding Lighting Design . . . . Graeme Thomson

Independent Theatre
Outstanding New Play or Musical . . . . *Stories from the Rains of Love and Death*, Abas Na'lbandian,
Trans. by Soheil Parsa & Peter Farbridge,
Outstanding Production . . . . *something about a river*, bluemouth inc.
Outstanding Direction . . . . Soheil Parsa, *Stories from the Rains of Love and Death*
Outstanding Performance by a Female . . . . Michelle Polak, *For Sale*
Outstanding Performance by a Male . . . . Ashwatthama JD, *Ek Qatra Khoon-A Drop of Blood*
Outstanding Set Design . . . . Trevor Schwellnus, *For Sale*
Outstanding Costume Design . . . . Rhoma Spencer & Albert Otoo, *Anowa*
Outstanding Lighting Design . . . . Andrea Lundy, *Stories from the Rains of Love and Death*

Dance
Outstanding New Choreography . . . . Daniel Léveillé, *Amour, acide et noix*, DanceWorks
Outstanding Performance . . . . Tom Casey, *Thok*, CanAsian Dance Festival

Opera
Outstanding Production . . . . *Die Walküre*, Canadian Opera Company
Outstanding Performance . . . . Adrianne Pieczonka, *Die Walküre*, Canadian Opera Company

Source: *Toronto Theatre Alliance*

Jessie Awards, 2004

Named for professional theatre pioneer Jessie Richardson, these awards honour excellence in and raise awareness of professional theatre in Vancouver. Winners of the 22nd Jessies were announced June 14, 2004, in the Commodore Ballroom.

Small Theatre

Outstanding Production . . . . *Practicing Democracy*, Headlines Theatre
Outstanding Direction . . . . Sarah Rodgers, *Cat and Mouse (Sheep)*, Sea Theatre
Outstanding Performance by an Actress in a Lead Role . . . Christiane Raymond, *Émilie ne sera plus jamais cuellie par l'anémone*, Théâtre la Seizième
Outstanding Performance by an Actor in a Lead Role . . . . Jonathon Young, *The Palace Grand*, Electric Company
Outstanding Performance by an Actress in a Supporting Role . . . . . . Colleen Wheeler, *The Underpants*, Quickchange Productions
Outstanding Performance by an Actor in a Supporting Role . . . . James Long, *Hunted*, Urban Ink Productions
Outstanding Costume Design . . . . Marina Szijarto, *Asylum of the Universe*, NeWorld Theatre
Outstanding Set Design of a Play . . . . Jonathon Young, John Webber, *The Palace Grand*, Electric Company
Outstanding Lighting Design . . . . John Webber, *The Palace Grand*, Electric Company
Outstanding Sound Design or Original Composition . . . . Joelysa Pankanea, .*Maharaja's Daughter*, Urban Crawl
Significant Artistic Achievement (Demonstrating the power of theatre in the community) . . David Diamond, *Practicing Democracy*, Headlines Theatre

Large Theatre

Outstanding Production . . . . *Equus*, The Vancouver Playhouse
Outstanding Direction . . . . Glynis Leyshon, *Equus*, The Vancouver Playhouse
Outstanding Performance by an Actress in a Lead Role . . . . Susinn McFarlen, *Hello, Dolly!*, The Vancouver Playhouse
Outstanding Performance by an Actor in a Lead Role . . . . Bill Dow, *Equus*, The Vancouver Playhouse
Outstanding Performance by an Actress in a Supporting Role Laara Sadiq, *The Matka King*, Arts Club Theatre Company
Outstanding Performance by an Actor in a Supporting Role . . . . . Christopher Gaze, *Equus*, The Vancouver Playhouse
Outstanding Costume Design . . . . Nancy Bryant, *Hello, Dolly!*, The Vancouver Playhouse
Outstanding Set Design of a Play . . . . Pam Johnson, *Equus*, The Vancouver Playhouse
Outstanding Lighting Design . . . . John Webber, *Soulless*, Rumble Productions
Outstanding Sound Design or Original Composition . . . . Noah Drew, *Pericles, Prince of Tyre*, Bard on the Beach
Significant Artistic Achievement (Choreography/Ensemble and Movement) . . . . Wendy Gorling & the Horses: Christopher Frary, Bob Frazer, Andrew McNee, Stuart Pierre, Chris Van Hyfte, *Equus*, The Vancouver Playhouse

Source: *Jessie Richardson Society*

Theatre Highlights for 2005

Arts Club Theatre, Vancouver

Stanley Theatre Series: *Enchanted April* by Matthew Barber, Feb. 4–Mar. 6—The tale of four characters who come together to rent an Italian villa and find an escape from their unfulfilling London routines; *Unless* by Carol Shields & Sara Cassidy, Apr. 1–May 1—A successful writer's placid existence is cracked wide open when her daughter drops out of life; *Miss Saigon* by Claude-Michel Schönberg and Alain Boubil, May 19–Jun. 19—An American soldier has a brief and passionate affair with an innocent Vietnamese girl, only to be tragically separated in the turmoil of the U.S. exodus. Granville Island Series: *The Dishwashers* by Morris Panych, Feb. 2—A new and absurd comedy. *Shear Madness* by Marilyn Abrams & Bruce Jordan, Jun. 3–Jul. 2—With the audience's participation, two undercover cops and an outrageous cast of characters put on a different mystery every night.

Vancouver Playhouse

Humble Boy by Charlotte Jones, Jan. 29–Feb. 19—Astrophysicist Felix Humble leaves the safety of his Cambridge studies to return home for the funeral of his father. *Copenhagen* by Michael Frayn, Feb. 26–Mar. 19—Speculates on what actually happened when German physicist Werner Heisenberg travelled to Nazi-occupied Denmark to meet with his Jewish former mentor, Niels Bohr, in 1941. *Trying* by Joanna McClelland Glass, Apr. 9–30—Francis Biddle, former Attorney General under President Franklin D. Roosevelt and now in the final year of his life, has hired Sarah, a young woman from Saskatchewan, to be his personal secretary.

Theatre Calgary

Macbeth by William Shakespeare, Feb.1–26—The immortal tragedy of a Scottish nobleman whose ambition leads to murder and to his undoing. *West Side Story* Mar. 8–Apr. 3—The musical adaptation of Shakespeare's *Romeo and Juliet*. *Humble Boy* by Charlotte Jones, Apr. 12–May 1 (see Vancouver Playhouse).

Globe Theatre, Regina

Strawberries In January by Evelyne de la Chenelière, Jan. 26–Feb. 12—Two couples-to-be share views on the search for true love. *Wingfield On Ice* by Dan Needles, Feb. 23–Mar. 12—Stockbroker-turned-farmer Walt Wingfield is overwhelmed when an ice storm hits the region. *Twelfth Night* by William Shakespeare, Apr. 20–May 7—Shipwrecked on the island of Illyria, Sebastian and his twin sister Viola are separated in a comic tale of mistaken identity. Sandbox Series: *Out of My Skin* by Shannan Calcutt and Sue Morrison, Jan. 11–21—Calcutt's stage character Izzy struggles with the consequences after Calcutt's car is broken into and Izzy's sets, makeup and costumes are stolen; *Fusion* by Joey Tremblay, Feb. 16–19—A group of theatre artists are given a starting point and create new works; *The Shape of Things* by Neil LaBute, April 5–9—A modern re-telling of the Pygmalion myth.

Manitoba Theatre Centre, Winnipeg

Much Ado About Nothing by William Shakespeare, Jan. 6–29—Beatrice and Benedick outwardly ridicule and argue with each other until they are thrown together to defend the honour of friend and family. *Trying* by Joanna McClelland Glass, Feb. 10–Mar. 5 (see Vancouver Playhouse). *The Dresser* by Ronald Harwood, Mar. 17–Apr. 9—In wartime England, a travelling theatre company prepares to perform *King Lear* while "Sir," the actor in the title role, spirals into madness. *Mama Mia!* by Benny Andersson and Björn Ulvaeus, Aug. 16–28—A mother confronts her past as her 20-year-old daughter is about to be married, set to the music of ABBA. Warehouse series: *Hosanna* by Michel Tremblay, Jan. 20–Feb. 5—A misfit farm boy becomes Hosanna, the drag queen with the biggest mouth in Montreal; *Provenance* by Ronnie Burkett, Feb. 17–Mar. 5—Burkett's acclaimed adult puppetry features in a play that is tender, exotic and erotic. *The Last Five Years* by Jason Robert Brown, Mar. 31–Apr. 16—A contemporary musical chronicles a young couple's romance.

Mirvish Productions, Toronto

Da Kink In My Hair, Jan. 8–Feb. 27, Wintergarden Theatre—Six women in a West Indian hair salon in Toronto tell their moving and often hilarious stories. *Wicked*, Mar. 7–May 1—Two friends meet in the Land of Oz pre-Dorothy and end up becoming the Wicked Witch of the West and the Good Witch of the North. *We Will Rock You*, May–June—Earth is now run by a corporate entity that demands conformity. Set to the music of Queen.

Canadian Stage, Toronto

Berkeley St. Theatre: *The Glass Menagerie* by Tennessee Williams, Jan 10–Feb. 19—An overbearing mother suffocates the adult children she seeks to protect; *My Mother's Feet* by Gina Wilkinson, Mar. 2–Apr. 7—An unrelenting tale of betrayal, forgiveness and a pair of prosthetic feet; *Trying* by Joanna McClelland Glass, May 2–Jun. 11 (see Vancouver Playhouse). Bluma Appel Theatre: *Take Me Out*, by Richard Greenberg, Jan. 17–Feb. 12—Centre-fielder Darren has three lucky strikes: handsome, rich, famous. And he's out. *Unless* by Carol Shields & Sara Cassidy, Feb 21–Mar. 19 (see Arts Club Theatre, Vancouver); *Ain't Misbehavin'* April 7–30—Jackie Richardson returns in Fats Waller's upbeat 1930s musical revue.

National Arts Centre, Ottawa

Main Stage Series: *Love's Labours Lost*, by William Shakespeare, Jan. 13–29—The King of Navarre and his three loyal companions take an oath to forswear the company of women in the pursuit of learning; *Humble Boy* by Charlotte Jones, Mar. 2–19 (see Vancouver Playhouse); *Vanya* by Tom Wood, Apr. 20–May 7—Chekhov's *Uncle Vanya* transposed to a Northern Alberta farm in 1928. Studio Series: *Portrait of an Unidentified Man* by Pierre Brault, Feb. 8–19—Elmyr de Hory becomes one of the greatest art forgers of the 20th century; *A Woman In Waiting* by Thembi Mtshali, Apr. 12–23—A compelling one-woman show about the voyages made out of apartheid by the women of South Africa.

Centaur Theatre, Montreal

The Goat, or Who Is Sylvia? by Edward Albee, Feb. 1–Mar. 13—Albee chronicles a perfect American family in which someone falls in love with a goat. *Tales From Ovid*, by Ted Hughes, Mar. 8–Apr. 3—Developed in association with the National Theatre School. *Wade In The Water* by George Boyd, Apr. 5–May 15—A man in search of his roots, journeys from Civil War-era Georgia to Sierra Leone. *Long Day's Journey Into Night* by Eugene O'Neill, May 10–June 5—An Irish-American family faces its ruination.

Theatre New Brunswick, Fredericton

Mary's Wedding by Stephen Massicotte, Jan. 27–Feb. 13—A love story set against the tumultuous events of WWI. *Oh, Coward!*, Mar. 17–Apr. 3—Songs, biographical anecdotes and sketches celebrate the life and work of British legend Sir Noel Coward. *Lucien Snowbird* by Marshall Button, Apr. 18–May 16—Canada's favourite blue-collar philosopher realizes his dream of becoming a tourist in Florida.

Neptune Theatre, Halifax

Over the River and Through the Woods by Joe DiPietro, Mar. 1–27—A young man's decision about his future sparks an eruption of meddling from his four Italian-American grandparents. *Friends* and *Traces*, Feb. 22–Mar. 13—*Friends*, written by Micheál Mac Liammóir, is a celebration of Ireland's tumultuous history seen through the eyes of a select few of the country's dramatists, poets, wits and revolutionaries; *Traces*, by Robbie O'Neill with Leo Kennedy, reacquaints us with a beloved Nova Scotian from Canso—Leo Kennedy. *Cat On a Hot Tin Roof* by Tennessee Williams, Jan. 25–Feb. 20—Big Daddy is dying; his oldest son schemes to secure his inheritance; and his favourite son, Brick, climbs inside a whisky bottle for solace. *The Goat or Who Is Sylvia?*, by Edward Albee Mar. 22–Apr. 10 (see Centaur Theatre).

Major Theatre Companies in Canada

ATLANTIC CANADA

Charlottetown Festival: Charlottetown, P.E.I.
www.confederationcentre.com
Mermaid Theatre of Nova Scotia: Windsor, N.S.
www.mermaidtheatre.ns.ca
Neptune Theatre Foundation: Halifax, N.S.
www.neptunetheatre.com
Theatre New Brunswick: Fredericton, N.B.
www.tnb.nb.ca
Stephenville Festival: Stephenville, Nfld www.stf.nf.ca

CENTRAL CANADA

Blyth Festival: Blyth, Ont. www.blythfestival.com
Buddies in Bad Times: Toronto, Ont.
www.buddiesinbadtimestheatre.com
Canadian Stage Company: Toronto, Ont.
www.canstage.com
Centaur Theatre Company: Montreal, Que.
www.centaurtheatre.com
Factory Theatre: Toronto, Ont. www.factorytheatre.ca
Grand Theatre Company (Theatre London):
London, Ont. www.grandtheatre.com
Great Canadian Theatre Company: Ottawa, Ont.
www.gctc.ca
Gryphon Theatre: Barrie, Ont. www.gryphontheatre.com
Huron Country Playhouse: Grand Bend, Ont.
www.huroncountryplayhouse.com
Kawartha Summer Theatre P.O. Box 161, 2 Lindsay St. S.
Lindsay, ON K9V 4S1
Magnus Theatre Company: Thunder Bay, Ont.
www.magnustheatre.on.ca
National Arts Centre: Ottawa, Ont. www.nac-cna.ca
Native Earth Performing Arts: Toronto, Ont.
www.nativeearth.ca
The Piggery: North Hatley, Que. www.piggery.com
Mirvish Productions: Toronto, Ont. www.mirvish.com
Saidye Bronfman Centre for the Arts: Montreal, Que.
www.saidyebronfman.org
Shaw Festival Theatre: Niagara-on-the-Lake, Ont.
www.shawfest.com
Soulpepper Theatre Company: Toronto, Ont.
www.soulpepper.ca

Stratford Shakespearean Festival: Stratford, Ont.
www.stratfordfestival.ca
Sudbury Theatre Centre: Sudbury, Ont.
www.sudburytheatre.on.ca
Tarragon Theatre: Toronto, Ont.
www.tarragontheatre.com
Theatre Aquarius: Hamilton, Ont.
www.theatreaquarius.org
Théâtre de la Bordée: Quebec City, Que.
www.bordee.qc.ca
Théâtre du Nouveau Monde: Montreal, Que.
www.tnm.qc.ca
Théâtre du Rideau Vert: Montreal, Que.
www.rideauvert.qc.ca
Theatre Passe Muraille: Toronto, Ont.
www.passemuraille.on.ca

WESTERN CANADA

Alberta Theatre Projects: Calgary, Alta
www.atplive.com
Arts Club Theatre: Vancouver, B.C. www.artsclub.com
Belfry Theatre: Victoria, B.C. www.belfry.bc.ca
Citadel Theatre: Edmonton, Alta
www.citadeltheatre.com
Globe Theatre: Regina, Sask. www.globetheatrelive.com
Manitoba Theatre Centre: Winnipeg, Man.
www.mtc.mb.ca
Persephone Theatre: Saskatoon, Sask.
www.persephonetheatre.org
Prairie Theatre Exchange: Winnipeg, Man.
www.pte.mb.ca
Theatre Calgary: Calgary, Alta www.theatrecalgary.com
25th Street Theatre: Saskatoon, Sask.
www.25thstreettheatre.com
Vancouver Playhouse: Vancouver, B.C.
www.vancouverplayhouse.com
Western Canada Theatre Company: Kamloops, B.C.
www.westerncanadatheatre.ca

Sources Include: *The Professional Association of Canadian Theatres*

DANCE

Canada is home to strong traditions in both classical and contemporary dance. Founded in 1938, The Royal Winnipeg Ballet is the second oldest company in North America and was the first in the Commonwealth to receive a Royal charter. Since 1951, the Toronto-based National Ballet of Canada has provided a home to major talents including prima ballerinas Karen Kain and Veronica Tennant. It has also been a favoured stopping place for international greats such as the late Rudolph Nureyev. The National Ballet was instrumental in facilitating the 1979 defection of Russia's Mikhail Baryshnikov in Toronto. Baryshnikov danced his first performances as a free man with the National Ballet, an event whose anniversary was marked in 1999 with the presentation of an honorary doctorate to Baryshnikov at the University of Toronto.

Major Ballet Companies

Alberta Ballet: 141-18th Avenue SW, Calgary, AB T2S 0B8

Ballet British Columbia: #102, 1101 West Broadway, Vancouver, BC V6H 1G2

Ballet Jorgen: 213B Glebeholme Blvd, Toronto, ON M4J 1S8

Ballet North: 12245-131 St, Edmonton, AB T5L 1M8

Les Grands Ballets Canadiens: 4816 rue Rivard, Montreal, QC H2J 2N6

Royal Winnipeg Ballet: 380 Graham Ave, Winnipeg, MB R3C 4K2

The National Ballet of Canada: The Walter Carson Centre, 470 Queen's Quay W, Toronto, ON M5V 3K4

Major Contemporary and Jazz Dance Companies

Les Ballets Jazz de Montréal: 3450 rue St-Urbain, Montreal, QC H2X 2N5

Contemporary Dancers Canada: 109 Pulford St, Winnipeg, MB R3L 1X8

Dancemakers: 927 Dupont St, Toronto, ON M6H 1Z1

Decidedly Jazz Danceworks: 1514-4th St SW, Calgary, AB T2R 0Y4

Desrosiers Dance Theatre: 103-219 Broadview Ave, Toronto, ON M4M 2G3

Fortier Danse Création: PO Box 605, Stn C, Montreal, QC H2L 4L5

Margie Gillis Dance Foundation: 502-3575 boul St Laurent, #502, Montreal, QC H2X 2T7

Danny Grossman Dance Company: 511 Bloor St W, Toronto, ON M5S 1Y4

LaLaLa Human Steps: #206, 5655 ave du Parc, Montreal, QC H2V 4H2

Le Groupe de la Place Royale: 2 Daly Ave, Ste 2, Ottawa, ON K1N 6E2

Karen Jamieson Dance Company: 221 E 16th Ave, Vancouver, BC V5T 2T5

Kompany!: #810, 10136-100th St, Edmonton, AB T5J 0P1

Mascall Dance: 1130 Jervis St, Vancouver, BC V6E 2C7

O Vertigo Danse: 4455 rue de Rouen, Montreal, QC H1V 1H1

La Fondation Jean-Pierre Perreault: 2022 rue Sherbrooke est, Montreal, QC H2K 1B9

Gina Lori Riley Dance Enterprises: 3277 Sandwich St, Windsor, ON N9C 1A9

Toronto Dance Theatre: 80 Winchester St, Toronto, ON M4X 1B2

Canadian Children's Dance Theatre: 509 Parliament St, Toronto, ON M4X 1P3

Compagnie Marie Chouinard: #615-3981 boul St-Laurent, Montreal, QC H2W 1Y5

Dance Arts Vancouver: #402-873 Beatty St, Vancouver, BC V6B 2M6

Source: *Dance Umbrella of Ontario*

BOOKS, MAGAZINES, NEWSPAPERS

According to the Association of Canadian Book Publishers, book publishing is a $1.7-billion enterprise in Canada. Eleven million English-speaking Canadians regularly read books, twice as many as in 1978, and Canadian-owned publishing firms publish over 80 percent of Canadian-authored titles. The association also reports that export of Canadian books has tripled since 1989. Canadian authors regularly win international acclaim and in recent years Canadians have won the Pulitzer Prize, the Booker Prize, and the Orange Prize for Fiction. In 2002, the Canadian publishing industry experienced a major crisis with the collapse of Stoddart Publishing. Most critical was the failure of Stoddart's distribution arm, which handled the books of several important small publishers.

Magazine publishing in Canada is an $866-million business in which domestic magazines take a 30 percent share of the market. The industry was dealt a serious blow in 2000 when the federal government was forced by the World Trade Organization to abandon tax measures aimed at protecting the advertising market from nominally Canadian "split run" editions of U.S. magazines. In 2001 the federal government responded with the creation of the $150,000,000 Canada Magazine Fund designed to offset revenue losses due to increased foreign competition.

Recent years have seen major shifts in newspaper ownership. Montreal-based Québecor Inc. took control of the Sun newspaper chain. Canada's oldest newspaper dynasty, that of the Thomson family, divested itself of most of its newspaper holdings, while in 2000 the newspaper empire of Conrad Black's Hollinger Inc. sold its interests in Southam Newspapers to Winnipeg television magnate Izzy Asper's Canwest/Global Corporation.

The Governor General's Literary Awards, 1994–2003

The Governor General's Literary Awards, Canada's foremost literary prizes, are presented annually to recognize and reward Canadian writers. The awards were initiated in 1937 by the Canadian Authors' Association with the agreement of Governor General Baron Tweedsmuir (novelist John Buchan), and were administered by the Association until 1958.

The Awards are now administered by the Canada Council, which appoints juries composed of literary specialists who select the best English- and French-language works in each of six categories: drama, fiction, poetry, non-fiction, and, beginning in 1987, children's literature (text and illustration) and translation. The juries review all books by Canadian authors, illustrators and translators published in Canada or abroad during the previous year (Oct. 1–Sept. 30). In the case of translation, the original work must also be a Canadian-authored title. Winners receive a medal from the Governor General, $10,000 and a specially bound copy of their award-winning book. The 2003 winners were announced November 12, 2003, in Ottawa.

English

—1994—

Fiction . . . . *A Discovery of Strangers*, Rudy Wiebe
Non-fiction . . . . *Rogue Primate: An Exploration of Human Domestication*, John A. Livingston
Poetry . . . . *Cantos from a Small Room*, Robert Hilles
Drama . . . . *The Ends of the Earth*, Morris Panych

—1995—

Fiction . . . . *The Roaring Girl*, Greg Hollingshead
Non-fiction . . . . *Shadow Maker: The Life of Gwendolyn MacEwen*, Rosemary Sullivan
Poetry . . . . *Voice*, Anne Szumigalski
Drama . . . . *Three in the Back, Two in the Head*, Jason Sherman

—1996—

Fiction . . . . *The Englishman's Boy*, Guy Vanderhaeghe
Non-fiction . . . . *The Unconscious Civilization*, John Ralston Saul
Poetry. . . . . *Apostrophes: Woman at a Piano*, E.D. Blodgett
Drama . . . . *The Monument*, Colleen Wagner

—1997—

Fiction . . . . *The Underpainter*, Jane Urquhart
Non-fiction . . . . *Drumblair—Memories of a Jamaican Childhood*, Rachel Manley
Poetry . . . . *Land to Light On*, Dionne Brand
Drama . . . . *fareWel*, Ian Ross

—1998—

Fiction. . . . . *Forms of Devotion*, Diane Schoemperlen
Non-fiction . . . . *Lines on the Water—A Fisherman's Life on the Miramichi*,
David Adams Richards
Poetry. . . . . *White Stone: The Alice Poems*, Stephanie Bolster
Drama . . . . *Harlem Duet*, Djanet Sears

—1999—

Fiction. . . . . *Elizabeth and After*, Matt Cohen
Non-fiction . . . . *Water*, Marq de Villiers
Poetry . . . . *Songs for Relinquishing the Earth*, Jan Zwicky
Drama . . . . *The Drawer Boy*, Michael Healey

—2000—

Fiction . . . . *Anil's Ghost*, Michael Ondaatje
Non-fiction . . . . *Notes from the Hyena's Belly*, Nega Mezlekia
Poetry. . . . . *Another Gravity*, Don McKay
Drama . . . . *Elizabeth Rex*, Timothy Findley

—2001—

Fiction . . . . *Clara Callan*, Richard B. Wright
Non-fiction. . . . . *The Ingenuity Gap*, Thomas Homer-Dixon
Poetry. . . . . *Execution Poems*, George Elliott Clarke
Drama . . . . *The Harps of God*, Kent Stetson

—2002—

Fiction . . . . *A Song for Nettie Johnson*, Gloria Sawai
Non-fiction. . . . . *Saboteurs: Wiebo Ludwig's War Against Big Oil*, Andrew Nikiforuk
Poetry. . . . . *Surrender*, Roy Miki
Drama . . . . *Unity (1918)*, Kevin Kerr

—2003—

Fiction . . . . *Elle*, Douglas Glover
Non-fiction . . . . *Paris 1919*, Margaret MacMillan
Poetry . . . . *Kill-site*, Tim Lilburn
Drama . . . . *Einstein's Gift*, Vern Thiessen
Translation . . . . *Memoirs of a Less Traveled Road: A Historian's Life*, Jane Brierley
Children's Literature (Illustration) . . . . *The Song Within My Heart*, Allen Sapp
Children's Literature (Text) . . . . *Stitches*, Glen Huser

French

—1994—

Fiction	*Le Petit Aigle à tête blanche*, Robert Lalonde
Non-fiction	*Du sida*, Chantal Saint-Jarre
Poetry	*Aknos*, Fulvio Caccia
Drama	*French Town*, Michel Ouellette

—1995—

Fiction	*Les Oiseaux de Saint-John Perse*, Nicole Houde
Non-fiction	*Louis-Antoine Dessaulles*, Yvan Lamonde
Poetry	*Pour orchestre et poète seul*, Émile Martel
Drama	*Les Quatre Morts de Marie*, Carole Fréchette

—1996—

Fiction	*Soifs*, Marie-Claire Blais
Non-fiction	*Le Naufrage de l'université*, Michel Freitag
Poetry	*Le Quatuor de l'errance*, Serge Patrice Thibodeau
Drama	*Le Passage de l'Indiana*, Normand Chaurette

—1997—

Fiction	*Cet imperceptible mouvement*, Aude
Non-fiction	*Enfants du néant et mangeurs d'âmes—Guerre, culture et société en Iroquoisie ancienne*, Roland Viau
Poetry	*Romans-fleuves*, Pierre Nepveu
Drama	*Dits et Inédits*, Yvan Bienvenue

—1998—

Fiction	*La Terre ferme*, Christiane Frenette
Non-fiction	*Intérieurs du Nouveau Monde*, Pierre Nepveu
Poetry	*Le Part de feu/Le Deuil de la rancune*, Suzanne Jacob
Drama	*15 secondes*, François Archambault

—1999—

Fiction	*La Danse juive*, Lise Tremblay
Non-fiction	*Le Mal du Nord*, Pierre Perrault
Poetry	*Conversations*, Herménégilde Chiasson
Drama	*Il n'y a que l'amour*, Jean Marc Dalpé

—2000—

Fiction	*Un vent se lève qui éparpille*, Jean Marc Dalpé
Non-fiction	*Genèse des nations et cultures du Nouveau Monde*, Gérard Bouchard
Poetry	*La Marche de l'aveugle sans son chien*, Normand de Bellefeuille
Drama	*Littoral*, Wajdi Mouawad

—2001—

Fiction	*Le ravissement*, Andrée A. Michaud
Non-fiction	*Quel Canada pour les Autochtones? La fin de l'exclusion*, Renée Dupuis
Poetry	*Des ombres portées*, Paul Chanel Malenfant
Drama	*Le Petit Köchel*, Normand Chaurette

—2002—

Fiction	*La Gloire de Cassiodore*, Monique LaRue
Non-fiction	*Mark Twain et la parole noire*, Judith Lavoie
Poetry	*Humains paysages en temps de paix relative*, Robert Dickson
Drama	*Le Langue-à-Langue des chiens de roche*, Daniel Danis

—2003—

Fiction	*La maison étrangère*, Élise Turcotte
Non-fiction	*Raconter et mouri: aux sources narratives de l'imaginaire occidental*, Thierry Hentsch
Poetry	*Lignes aériennes*, Pierre Nepveu
Drama	*Deux pas vers les étoiles*, Jean-Rock Gaudreault
Translation	*Un amour de Salomé*, Agnès Guitard
Children's Literature (Illustration)	*Recette d'éléphant à la sauce vieux pneu*, Virginie Egger
Children's Literature (Text)	*J'ai vendu ma soeur*, Danielle Simard

Source: *The Canada Council*

The Giller Prize, 1994–2003

The Giller Prize awards $25,000 annually to the author of the best Canadian novel or short story collection published in English. The award was founded in 1994 by Toronto businessman Jack Rabinovitch in honour of his late wife, literary journalist Doris Giller.

The 2002 Giller Prize was presented November 4, 2003.

Year	Author	Title
1994	M.G. Vassanji	*The Book of Secrets*
1995	Rohinton Mistry	*A Fine Balance*
1996	Margaret Atwood	*Alias Grace*
1997	Mordecai Richler	*Barney's Version*
1998	Alice Munro	*The Love of a Good Woman*
1999	Bonnie Burnard	*A Good House*
2000 (joint winners)	Michael Ondaatje	*Anil's Ghost*
	David Adams Richards	*Mercy Among the Children*
2001	Richard B. Wright	*Clara Callan*
2002	Austin Clarke	*The Polished Hoe*
2003	M.G. Vassanji	*The In-Between World of Vikram Lall*

The Man-Booker Prize, 1994–2003

The Man-Booker Prize recognizes the best work of English fiction published in the Commonwealth, South Africa and Ireland. Since April 2002 it has been sponsored by Man Group plc, a global provider of alternative investment funds, and administered by the Booker Prize Book Foundation, a British educational charity. Since 1984, the value of the Booker Prize has been £15,000.

Year	Author	Title
1994	James Kelman	*How Late It Was, How Late*
1995	Pat Barker	*The Ghost Road*
1996	Graham Swift	*Last Orders*
1997	Arundhati Roy	*The God of Small Things*
1998	Ian McEwan	*Amsterdam*
1999	J.M. Coetzee	*Disgrace*
2000	**Margaret Atwood**	***The Blind Assassin***
2001	Peter Carey	*The True Story of the Kelly Gang*
2002	**Yann Martel**	***Life of Pi***
2003	DBC Pierre	*Vernon God Little*

Pulitzer Prizes, 2004

The winners of these annual American literary awards were announced on May 24, 2004.

Fiction — Edward P. Jones, *The Known World*

Non-fiction — Diane McWhorter, *Carry Me Home: Birmingham, Alabama, and the Climactic Battle of the Civil Rights Revolution*

Poetry — Franz Wright, *Walking to Martha's Vineyard*

Drama — Doug White, *I Am My Own Wife*

Biography — William Taubman, *Krushchev: The Man and His Era*

History — Steven Hahn, *A Nation Under Our Feet*

News Reporting — Staff, *The Los Angeles Times*

Investigative Reporting — Michael D. Sallah, Mitch Weiss and Joe Mahr, *The Blade*, Toledo, Ohio

The Griffin Poetry Prize, 2002–2004

Consisting of two $40,000 awards presented annually, the Griffin Poetry Prize is one of the world's largest awards for poets. The Griffin Trust for Excellence in Poetry gives one prize to a Canadian poet and one to an international poet. The competition is judged by a panel of Canadian and international literary figures. The 2004 Griffin Prize was announced June 3 in Toronto.

■ **Canada**

Year	Author	Title
2002	Christian Bök	*Eunoia*
2003	Margaret Avison	*Concrete and Wild Carrot*
2004	Anne Simpson	*Loop*

■ **International**

Year	Author	Title
2002	Alice Notley (USA)	*Disobedience*
2003	Paul Muldoon (UK)	*Moy Sand and Gravel*
2004	August Kleinzahler (USA)	*The Strange Hours Travellers Keep*

The Stephen Leacock Medal for Humour, 1999–2004

Stephen Butler Leacock was born in England in 1869. He was educated at Upper Canada College, University of Toronto (B.A.), and the University of Chicago (Ph.D.). He taught at UCC, and later lectured in political science at McGill. His literary output included works in history, economics and political science, although by far the most popular were his humour books. By the time of his death in 1944, he was the best-known humourist in the English-speaking world.

Canada's highest award for humour is given annually at a ceremony in Leacock's hometown of Orillia, Ontario.

Year	Author	Title
1999	Stuart McLean	*Home from the Vinyl Café*
2000	Arthur Black	*Black Tie and Tales*
2001	Stuart McLean	*Vinyl Café Unplugged*
2002	Will Ferguson	*Generica*
2003	Dan Needles	*With Axe and Flask—A History of Persephone Township from Pre-Cambrian Times to the Present*
2004	Ian Ferguson	*In the Village of Small Houses*

Source: www.leacock.com

www.archives.ca: The National Archives On-line

*I*n May 2001, the National Archives of Canada launched its official web site designed as an introduction to its collections and services. Digitization of the archives' materials is ongoing, but for the moment the site gives visitors an opportunity to get a glimpse of the fascinating items in the archival vaults. The "Living Memory" segment of the site was inspired by the **Treasured Memories** exhibition held in 1999 to mark the archives' 125th anniversary. Among the documents and artefacts displayed are the Canadian Bill of Rights, illustrations from the Log book of the HMS **Pegasus** as it carried out the first visit by a member of the Royal family to Canada in 1820 and the Torah of the Shearith Israel Congregation of 18th-century Montreal. The database is searchable by Theme, Period and Media Type. It contains maps, documentary art, photographs and government records. A short description of each item is provided with selections from the item in question: for example, a page of former Governor General Georges Vanier's report on his 1945 visit to the recently liberated concentration camp at Buchenwald in his capacity as Canada's Ambassador to France.

The research section of the web site offers an introduction to Research Services at the National Archives. The ArchiviaNet on-line research and consultation tool gives access to information about items stored in the archives' general inventory.

Bestselling Books in Canada, 2003

Fiction

1. ***Oryx and Crake*, Margaret Atwood**
2. *The Lovely Bones*, Alice Sebold
3. *Harry Potter and the Order of the Phoenix*, J.K. Rowling
4. *The Da Vinci Code*, Dan Brown
5. ***The Way the Crow Flies*, Anne-Marie MacDonald**
6. *Crossroads of Twilight*, Robert Jordan
7. *The Curious Incident of the Dog in the Night-Time*, Mark Haddon
8. *Shopaholic Ties the Knot*, Sophie Kinsella
9. *The King of Torts*, John Grisham
10. *Confessions of a Shopaholic*, Sophie Kinsella

Source: *The Globe and Mail*   Canadian books set in bold type.

Non-fiction

1. *Stupid White Men*, Michael Moore
2. ***Paris 1919*, Margaret MacMillan**
3. ***Dropped Threads 2*, Carol Shields, Marjorie Anderson, eds.**
4. ***How To Be A Canadian*, Will and Ian Ferguson**
5. *A Short History of Nearly Everything*, Bill Bryson
6. *Living History*, Hillary Rodham Clinton
7. *Leap of Faith*, Queen Noor
8. *Krakatoa*, Simon Winchester
9. *Dude, Where's My Country?*, Michael Moore
10. ***Dropped Threads*, Carol Shields, Marjorie Anderson, eds.**

National Magazine Awards, 2004

These annual awards were presented June 11, 2004, by the National Magazine Awards Foundation. In 2004 there were gold and silver awards in 33 categories, including writing, design, illustration, and photography and art direction. Gold award winners are listed below.

Humour . . . . Anne Marie Lecomte, "Suis-je encore sexy?" *Châtelaine*
Business . . . . Paul Webster, "Send Lawyers, Guns and Money," *Report On Business Magazine*
Science & Technology Health and Medicine . . . Paul Webster, " Is the West Rearming Russia?," *The Walrus Magazine*
. . . . Marci McDonald, "Smog Sleuth," *Canadian Geographic*
Still-Life Photography . . . . Karin Bubas, "Shoe Story," *Toro*
Fashion . . . . Christopher Griffith, Cameron Williamson, Alicia Kowalewski, Alon Freeman, "Take That!," *Toro*
Politics . . . . Jay Teitel, "Is Jean Chrétien Canada's Greatest Politician Ever?" *Saturday Night*
Investigative Reporting . . . . Marci McDonald, "Blind Trust," *The Walrus Magazine*
Fiction . . . . Jay Teitel, "Luck," *Toronto Life*
Arts and Entertainment . . . . Debra Kirshner, "The Genius of Django," *The Walrus Magazine*
Sports and Recreation . . . . Adam Killick, "So This Is What It's Like to Sail Through a Hurricane," *explore*
Photojournalism . . . . Gregory Crow, "Ring Dogs," *Vancouver*
Personal journalism . . . . Sophie Lees, "Conundrum of Kites," *Alberta Views*
Portrait Photography . . . . Mark Gilbert, "The Trauma Guy," *Toro*
Columns . . . . Pierre Fortin, *L'actualité*
Service: Health & Family . . . . John Hoffman, Wendy Haaf, Sarah Cassidy,
Steve Brearton, "Safe Streets, Safe Kids," *Today's Parent*
Service: Personal Finance & Business . . . . Moshe Milevsky, Felix Vikhman, Camilla Cornell, Bruce Gillespie,
Julie McCann, David Dias, John Guise, Wayne Lilley, Charles Davies, Mary Theresa Bitti, Norah Murphy,
Mark Anderson, "A Survival Guide to Family Finances," *National Post Business*
Service: Leisure Pursuits Travel . . . . Kevin Arnold, "Best Gear '03," *explore*
Philip Preville, "Living On Lobster Time," *Saturday Night*
Spot Illustration . . . . Todd Julie, "Canada's Prime Ministers: Secrets to Their Success," *Maisonneuve*
How-To . . . . Louise Gendron, Philippe Daoust, Isabelle Grégoire, "Comment choisir une école?," *L'actualité*
Essays . . . . Janice Kulyk Keefer, "War Gaze," *Border Crossings*
Profiles . . . . Daniel Wood, "George Bowering's Home Run," *Elm Street*
Poetry . . . . Steven Heighton, "2001," "An Elegy," "Blackjack," "Ravines," *The New Quarterly*
Art Direction for a Single Article . . . . Diti Katona, John Pylypczak, "Between Life and Death," *Azure*
Editorial Package . . . . Staff, "Le mélodie du Québec en 10 chansons," *L'actualité*
Words and Pictures . . . . Sarah Fulford, Tobi Asmoucha, Sandra Latini, "Arrivals," *Toronto Life*
Magazine Covers . . . . Maarten Sluyter, "Free Spirited Decorating," *Canadian House & Home*
President's Medal . . . . *Border Crossings*
Magazine of the Year . . . . *Canadian Geographic*
Alexander Ross Award for Best New Magazine Writer . . . . Chantal Shrivastava
Foundation Award for Outstanding Achievement . . . . Stephen Osbourne

Source: *National Magazine Awards Foundation*

Top Canadian Paid-Circulation Magazines, 2004

Magazine	Circulation[1]
Reader's Digest (Canadian English edition)	955,145
Chatelaine (English-language edition)	680,020
Canadian Living	534,005
Homemaker's	509,722
TV Guide	370,536
Maclean's	452,950
Sélection du Reader's Digest (Canadian French edition)	231,867
Time (Canadian edition)	230,158
Canadian Geographic	212,003
Coup de Pouce	228,071
Châtelaine (French language edition)	189,581
L'Actualité	187,151
Flare	160,844
TV Hebdo	153,998
Fashion	124,927
Today's Parent	117,591
7 Jours	108,835
Elle (Canadian edition)	100,390

Source: *CARD: Media Information Network* (1) Average total paid circulation for most recently reported 6-month period as of June 2004.

Canada's Newspapers On-Line

Southam Newspapers—www.canada.com: *Operated by CanWest Interactive, this site links to sites for Southam newspapers in major Canadian cities including* **The Vancouver Sun,** *the* **Vancouver Province,** *the* **Calgary Herald,** *the* **Edmonton Journal,** *the* **Ottawa Citizen** *and the* **Montreal Gazette***. The sites each offer a home page containing the day's lead story plus "sections" such as a "front" section, news section, sports, entertainment, etc., each containing a selection of stories from that day's edition. The newspapers' archives can be accessed on a pay basis at www.infomart.ca.*

The Toronto Star—www.thestar.com: *The official site of Canada's largest circulation daily offers a selection of articles from sections including the Greater Toronto, Sports, Business and Entertainment sections of each day's edition, plus access to stories from weekly sections. A 14-day archive may be searched free of charge. Paid archive searches for articles dating as far back as January 1985 may be conducted for a nominal fee payable by credit card.*

The Globe and Mail—www.globeandmail.com: *"Canada's National Newspaper" includes a selection of approximately 10 stories per section of its daily print edition. Weekly features such as columns by the paper's 31 columnists are also available.*

National Post—www.nationalpost.com: *As well as a selection of stories from each day's edition, the National Post site offers a 14-day searchable database of its stories. Weekly features such as Saturday Post, Post Movies and Driver's Edge are available, as are specials such as* **Inside Entertainment** *and* **National Post Business Magazine***.*

The Winnipeg Free Press—www.winnipegfreepress.com: *The* **Free Press** *offers full on-line access only to subscribers of its print edition inside Manitoba. Readers outside Manitoba may subscribe to the paper on-line for a charge of $5.00 per month. Available free on the web site are auto listings, classifieds, obituaries, careers and special sections.*

The Chronicle Herald, Mail Star and **Sunday Herald,** Halifax—**www.herald.ns.ca:** *Subscribers to the print edition can register for free access to the full edition on-line. On-line subscriptions to the papers are $13 per month.*

Top Canadian Daily Newspapers, 2004

| | Circulation[1] | | |
Newspaper	Daily[2]	Saturday	Sunday
Toronto Star............................	463,840	662,784	434,916
Globe and Mail.........................	317,411	389,062	
Le Journal de Montréal	262,161	314,893	264,820
National Post	246,632	275,944	
Toronto Sun............................	201,612	166,513	342,367
La Presse	201,499	283,670	213,777
Vancouver Sun..........................	183,004 (M.-Th.)	239,269	
	210,995 (F.)		
Vancouver Province......................	160, 482	198,954	
Montreal Gazette	140,503	163,606	134,075
Ottawa Citizen	130,431	165,989	123,857
Edmonton Journal	127,799 (M-Th.-Sat.)	128,243	
	146,431 (F.)		
Winnipeg Free Press	115,896	167,894	115,855
Calgary Herald	109,857 (M.-Th.)	122,840	112,861
	137,618 (F.)		
Hamilton Spectator	105,893	120,148	
Halifax Chronicle Herald...................	93,116 (M.-Sat. A.M.)		64,799
	13,847 (M.-Sat. P.M.)		
London Free Press......................	92,536	111,503	
Le Journal de Québec.....................	91,178	120,498	98,726
Le Soleil..............................	78,364	113,207	84,797
Windsor Star		73,030	83,436
Edmonton Sun..........................	69,274 (M.-Sat.)		98,853
Victoria Times-Columnist	68,019 (M.-Th.)	77,348 (F.-Sat.)	71,250

Sources: *CARD: Media Information Network, Canadian Newspaper Association*
(1) Average total paid circulation for most recently reported 6-month period as of August 2004. Ranked by weekday circulation.
(2) Monday to Friday unless otherwise indicated.

National Newspaper Awards, 2004

These annual awards were announced in Vancouver on June 5, 2004.

Editorial Writing..	Jonathan Kay, *National Post*
News Photography	Stephen MacGillivray, *Fredericton Daily Gleaner*
Feature Photography.......................................	Greg Southam, *Edmonton Journal*
Breaking News Reporting......................................	Kevin Donovan, Theresa Boyle, *Toronto Star*
International Reporting	Stephanie Nolen, *Globe and Mail*
Sports Writing	Morgan Campbell, *Toronto Star*
Long Feature Writing	Mark MacKinnon, *Globe and Mail*
Short Feature Writing..	Oakland Ross, *Toronto Star*
Columns	Denis Gratton, *Le Droit*
Sports Photography...	Hans Deryk, *Toronto Star*
Investigations...	Dan Lett, *Winnipeg Free Press*
Explanatory Work	Ian Brown, *Globe and Mail*
Presentation	Jocelyne Potelle, *La Presse*
Editorial Cartooning...	Serge Chapleau, *La Presse*
Business Reporting...	Tony Van Alphen, *Toronto Star*
Special Project	"Poison," *Hamilton Spectator*
Local Reporting...	Jennifer Pritchett, *The Kingston Whig Standard*

Source: *Canadian Newspaper Association*

THE INTERNET

What's It All About?

The Internet is a complex international web composed of hundreds of thousands computer-based networks. Originally linked by conventional telephone lines, today's users increasingly rely on high-speed media including cable modem and DSL. The Internet was created by the U.S. Defence Department in the late 1960s as a means of linking U.S. government agencies and as an alternative means of emergency communication. Consumer applications were developed in the 1980s with the emergence of service providers such as CompuServe and America Online. The 1990s saw an explosion of activity, making the new medium an essential service in every aspect of day-to-day living.

Estimates of the number of people connected to the Internet worldwide have risen from three million in 1993 to 600 million a decade later.

With a highly advanced telecommunications sector already in place, Canada was well positioned to take advantage of the new medium. Today Canadians are among the heaviest Internet users per capita in the world. Recent studies report that Canadians conduct 575 million searches in a given month with an average of 40 searches per user. That average is higher than in the U.S. where searchers conduct an average of 35 conducted searches per month.

As the Internet has grown in its pervasiveness, concern has also mounted regarding its potential invasiveness. In 1999 the Canadian Radio-Television and Telecommunications Commission ruled that it would not regulate content on the Internet. But as hackers place increasing numbers of viruses on the Net, and entrepreneurs engage in the delivery of unsolicited SPAM e-mails and download invasive Spyware and Adware onto home and business computers, pressure is mounting for governments to take action.

Internet Use in Canada

(Percentage of households)*

Date	Location of use	Home	Work	School	Public library	Other locations	Any location
	Type of household						
1997	All households	16.0	19.9	9.3	3.7	2.8	29.0
	Single family with unmarried children under age 18						
	....	21.7	26.0	16.5	5.6	4.1	37.9
	Single family without unmarried children under age 18						
	....	15.5	18.8	6.4	2.9	2.0	27.2
	One-person household	7.1	11.6	2.3	1.5	2.0	16.4
	Multi-family household	24.7	27.8	15.8	6.4	4.6	42.9
2002	All households	51.4	34.2	22.9	8.2	10.4	61.6
	Single family with unmarried children under age 18						
	....	69.7	45.2	47.5	13.0	14.3	81.2
	Single family without unmarried children under age 18						
	....	51.1	32.0	13.3	5.9	8.2	58.9
	One-person household	26.2	21.9	3.9	4.3	7.3	37.5
	Multi-family household	61.8	41.3	28.6	12.3	17.2	75.3

*"Household: Any person or group of persons living in a dwelling. A household may consist of any combination of one: one person living alone, one or more family, a group of people who are not related but who share the same dwelling."

Source: *Statistics Canada*

Total Internet Users Worldwide, 2004*

Canada 17,458   United States 156,313   Worldwide 531,378

Source: © comScore Networks   *Reporting period: May 2004

Top 20 News & Information Websites in Canada, 2004*

		Total Visitors (000)	% Reach			Total Visitors (000)	% Reach
	Total Audience	17,458	100	11.	Globe Web Centre	1,805	10.3
	Total News/Info Audience	13,996	80.2	12.	CBS.COM	1,458	8.4
1.	Weather Network/Meteomedia	4,179	23.9	13.	BBC Sites	1,383	7.9
2.	Canada.com Network	3,121	17.9	14.	CYBERPRESSE.CA	1,225	7.0
3.	ABOUT.COM	2,958	16.9	15.	CTV	1,211	6.9
4.	CBC Sites	2,864	16.4	16.	NEWGROUNDS.COM	1,138	6.5
5.	MSNBC	2,819	16.1	17.	The Weather Channel	1,023	5.9
6.	CANOE.CA	2,657	15.2	18.	BRANCHEZ-VOU.COM	923	5.3
7.	CANOE.QC.CA	2,494	14.3	19.	Canoe LCN	884	5.1
8.	CNN	2,065	11.8	20.	Toronto Star	765	4.4
9.	Yahoo! News	1,999	11.5				
10.	Radio Canada Sites	1,874	10.7				

Source: © comScore Networks   *Reporting period: May 2004

Top 50 Internet Properties In Canada, 2004*

		Total Visitors (000)	% Reach			Total Visitors (000)	% Reach
	Total Audience	17,458	100	26.	MARIGNY.COM	2,674	15.3
1.	MSN-Microsoft Sites	16,720	95.8	27.	Tickle.Inc.	2,623	15
2.	Yahoo! Sites	13,358	76.5	28.	Wanadoo Sites	2,576	14.8
3.	Google Sites	12,608	72.2	29.	Sony Online	2,547	14.6
4.	Time Warner Network	9,824	56.3	30.	Walt Disney Internet Group	2,512	14.4
5.	eBay	8,999	51.5	31.	Expedia Travel	2,511	14.4
6.	Canoe Network	6,365	36.5	32.	Vivendi-Universal Sites	2,507	14.4
7.	Bell Sympatico	6,323	36.2	33.	Lycos Europe Sites	2,502	14.3
8.	Terra Lycos	6,241	35.7	34.	DESJARDINS.COM	2,497	14.3
9.	Excite Network	5,692	32.6	35.	iVillage.com	2,424	13.9
10.	About/Primedia	5,440	31.2	36.	Apple Computer, Inc.	2,360	13.5
11.	Amazon Sites	4,888	28	37.	Verizon Communications	2,314	13.3
12.	Bell Globemedia	4,569	26.2	38.	Sears Sites	2,258	12.9
13.	Symantec	4,290	24.6	39.	eUniverse Network	2,231	12.8
14.	CNET Networks	4,210	24.1	40.	LAVALIFE.COM	2,217	12.7
15.	Weather Network/Meteomedia	4,179	23.9	41.	Transcontinental Women's	2,153	12.3
16.	RBC Financial Group	4,170	23.9	42.	MINICLIP.COM	2,085	11.9
17.	Viacom Online	4,032	23.1	43.	Tiscali Sites	2,021	11.6
18.	Telus Sites	3,881	22.2	44.	Monster	2,004	11.5
19.	Real.com Network	3,862	22.1	45.	EA Online	2,004	11.5
20.	Yellow Pages Group	3,727	21.3	46.	GOUV.QC.CA	1,988	11.4
21.	Gorilla Nation Media	3,442	19.7	47.	Classmates.com Sites	1,981	11.3
22.	Canwest Interactive Sites	3,296	18.9	48.	Macromedia	1,937	11.1
23.	CBC Sites	2,864	16.4	49.	Bank of Commerce	1,937	11.1
24.	Iliad/Free.fr Sites	2,861	16.4	50.	HRDC-DRHC.GC.CA	1,906	10.9
25.	TD Financial Group	2,840	16.3				

Source: *© comScore Networks*   *Reporting period: May 2004

GALLERIES AND MUSEUMS

Canadian art is a time-honoured tradition with the oldest surviving work of prehistoric First Nations carving dating back to 5,000 B.C. European traditions were slow to take hold in the colonial regime. Bishop Laval established the country's first school of art near Quebec in 1675 and religious art dominated the Canadian scene until the 19th century when Paul Kane and Cornelius Krieghoff became the country's first genre painters, rendering scenes of native and settler life respectively. After the establishment of major art institutions such as the Royal Canadian Academy of Art (1880) and the Ontario College of Art (1875), landscape became the dominant form of Canadian painting, a trend that peaked with the formation of the Group of Seven in 1920 (see article below). Abstract art reached Canada in the 1940s and gained its first domestic expression in the work of Montreal's automatiste painters, lead by Jean Paul Riopelle and Paul-Émile Borduas, working under the influence of cubism and the French surrealists. Art in English Canada remained under the sway of the Group of Seven and that of British representational trends in portraiture and urban landscape until the formation in 1954 and subsequent international success of Painters Eleven in Toronto. This group, which featured Jack Bush, Kazuo Nakamura, Jock MacDonald, William Ronald, and Harold Town, drew heavily on the abstract expressionist movement in the United States for inspiration and its members scored success in New York critical circles of the period. Leadership reverted to Montreal in the 1960s with the emergence of painters devoted to the op art school focussing on experiments in visual effects and surface dynamics. While hyperrealist painters such as Nova Scotia's Alex Colville, and Newfoundland's Christopher Pratt and Manitoba-born naïve painter William Kurelek kept representational painting popular through the 1970s, a new generation of artists such as Michael Snow, Greg Curnoe, General Idea, and Iain Baxter followed the international trend away from painting into conceptual art exploring new media such as film, photography, performance and installation art. The 1980s saw a rebirth in interest in representational painting with the emergence of neo-expressionist–influenced work from groups such as Vancouver's New Romantics and Toronto's ChromaZone Collective. Today the Canadian art scene features artists working in every conceivable medium and genre. Their work is shown in artist-run collectives, commercial galleries and larger public galleries in every major centre.

The Group of Seven

The Group of Seven held its first exhibition at the Art Gallery of Toronto in May 1920. The original members included J.E.H. MacDonald, Lawren Harris, A.Y. Jackson, Arthur Lismer, F.H. Varley, Frank Johnston and Franklin Carmichael.

In 1924, Johnston resigned from the Group and, in 1926, A.J. Casson was invited to join. In the later years of the Group, two new members, Edwin Holgate and Lionel Lemoine FitzGerald, were added. The Group held its final exhibition in Dec. 1931 and disbanded in 1932.

Tom Thomson, who drowned in 1917, was never a member of the Group of Seven, though his boldly coloured works depicting the rugged landscape of northern Ontario became associated with its style of painting.

By breaking with the traditional, European, painting style popular in Canada in the 1920s, the Group of Seven made a huge impact on Canadian art. Although originally reviled by critics, the Group had gained wide acceptance and popularity by the 1930s. Today, the Group's paintings are exhibited in every major gallery in Canada.

J.E.H. **MacDonald** (1873–1932)
Lawren **Harris** (1885–1970)
Alexander Young (A.Y.) **Jackson** (1882–1974)
Arthur **Lismer** (1885–1969)
Frederick Horsman (F.H.) **Varley** (1881–1969)
Frank Hans **Johnston** (1888–1949)
Frank **Carmichael** (1890–1945)
Alfred Joseph (A.J.) **Casson** (1898–1992)
Edwin **Holgate** (1892–1977)
Lionel Lemoine **FitzGerald** (1890–1956)
Tom **Thomson** (1877–1917)

Source: *Looking at Landscape*, Dwight Siegner, The McMichael Canadian Art Collection

Gallery and Museum Highlights, 2005

Glenbow Museum, Calgary

In celebration of Alberta's 100th anniversary in 2005, Glenbow Museum is planning a series of special exhibitions, and the development of a new permanent gallery that traces Alberta's legendary tales, maverick personalities, and romanticized livelihoods of the West. In winter 2005, visitors will take a journey down Alberta's lifeline in *The Bow: Living With A River*. This special exhibition will examine geological, floral and faunal, cultural, historical, and artistic aspects of the Bow River. The Bow River has been a source of spiritual inspiration for many artists and cultures, yet it is also one of the most heavily engineered rivers in Canada that supports one-third of Alberta's total population base. As one of the most innovative and interdisciplinary exhibitions ever produced by Glenbow Museum, *The Bow* will share the story of how this precious resource has helped shape and define this region.

Winnipeg Art Gallery

The Power of Dreams (to June 5): This exhibition explores the role of dreams in Inuit culture and the imaginative visual forms used by artists to express them. In over 50 prints, drawings, and sculptures, dreams take the form of future events, directions to be followed, and communication with the spirit world. *Steve Gouthro: Through the Mill* (to Mar. 6) Based on photographs taken in the Gerdau MRM steel mill in Selkirk, this series reflects Winnipeg artist Steve Gouthro's fascination with the process of decay and growth as embodied in heavy industry and its products in our modern world. *Beauty In a Common Thing: Drawings and Prints by L.L. Fitzgerald* (to Mar. 13): This exhibition by Winnipeg artist Lionel LeMoine FitzGerald (1890–1956) examines the inspiration he found in everyday things, presenting a thematic survey of his preferred subjects through 60 works in graphite, watercolour, coloured pencil, drypoints, and woodcuts. *Between Earth and Sky: Geoffrey Hendricks*, (Jan.–Apr. 10): The paintings, installations, and multi-media works in this exhibition explore the sky as an integral part of Hendricks' experience with the landscape, in particular that of Cape Breton, his

home since 1965. *Peter Pitseolak: Inuit Photographer & Inuit Sculpture from the Collection* (Jan. 22–Apr. 24): A camp leader, storyteller, and self-taught photographer, Pitseolak was among the first to record Inuit life as it really was. *Rita Letendre Aux Couleurs du Jour* (Apr. 9–June 26): A retrospective of the work of one of Canada's most important abstract artists. *Ivan Eyre* (Apr. 30–Aug.): This exhibition will draw upon 60 to 100 key works in this Manitoba artist's oeuvre, featuring his insistent and unique vision through the media of painting, drawing and sculpture. *Peggy Nicol Macleod: A Life In Art* (May 21–July 31): This exhibition paints a vivid picture of a Canadian artist who was both a product of and a contributor to the artistic and intellectual world of Canada during the critical and developmental decades between the First and Second World Wars. *Manitoba Modernism: 1942–1972* (Aug. 24–Jan. 2, 2006): Drawings, plans, building models, photographs, period furnishings, clothing, advertising, and other lifestyle products combine in this survey of an important period of Manitoba architectural history.

The Royal Ontario Museum, Toronto

Pearls: A Natural History (to Jan. 9): The natural and cultural history of pearls illustrated through more than 500 objects, including some of the world's oldest, largest and most valuable pearls and the jewellery and fashions that have adorned royalty and celebrities. *Feathered Dinosaurs and the Origin of Flight* (Mar.–Aug. 28): A showcase of rare dinosaur and bird fossils and life-size feathered sculptural restorations of raptors and gigantic flightless birds examines the origins of flying reptiles and birds. *Lalique in Canada* (opens Dec. 15): Drawn from the ROM's collection, close to 100 original René Lalique Art Deco glass pieces and other glass objects influenced by this French artist demonstrate the popularity of Lalique glass in Canada in the 1920s and 30s. *Canada Collects* (opens Dec. 15): Illustrating the depth and diversity of collecting in Canada, 40 different public museums and private collectors from across Canada display some of their stellar pieces of art and natural science specimens at the ROM. This exhibit celebrates the opening of the ROM's new addition, the Michael A. Lee-Chin Crystal, designed by Daniel Libeskind.

The National Gallery of Canada, Ottawa

The Sixties in Canada (Feb. 4–Apr. 24): The exhibition will address the abundance of artistic expressions of the time as they occurred throughout Canada: Neo-dadaist and Pop art, minimalism, mass media–influenced experiments with art and technology, high modernist paintings, early conceptual and photo-based art works and, finally, the first use of video technology and experimental films. *British Drawings from the National Gallery of Canada* (May–Sept.): The show covers three centuries of British draughtsmanship, from the 18th century to the 20th, and will feature major works by William Hogarth, Benjamin West, Paul Sandby, Thomas Gainsborough, J.M.W. Turner, John Constable, Samuel Palmer, Dante Gabriel Rossetti, Charles Rennie Mackintosh and Henry Moore. *Leonardo, Michelangelo and the Renaissance in Florence* (May 27–Sept. 5): Michelangelo, Leonardo da Vinci, Andrea del Sarto, Domenico Puligo, Bronzino, Puligo, Soligliani and Piero di Cosimo, are just some of the artists whose extraordinary creativity will be represented in this exhibition of some 120 paintings, sculptures, drawings and prints never before seen together. *Christopher Pratt: Celebrating Art and Life* (Sept. 30–Jan. 8, 2006): This retrospective of Newfoundland artist Christopher Pratt's work highlights iconic pieces produced since the 1960s, along with 50 large-scale paintings made in the last 20 years, especially his famous boats and interiors spaces.

Canadian Museum of Civilization, Hull

The Rocket, Maurice Richard (closes Mar. 13) traces the story of hockey immortal Maurice "The Rocket" Richard, illustrated by treasures from his own memorabilia collection, plus fan scrapbooks, newspaper clippings, music, photographs, video and rare artifacts. With *Living in New France* (closes March 28), the Canadian Museum of Civilization celebrates the 400th anniversary of French settlement in North America. Through rich artifacts from over 40 collections, the exhibition provides a look at life in New France in the 17th and 18th

centuries. *Beads of Life: Eastern and Southern African Adornments from Canadian Collections* (Apr. 15–Feb. 26, 2006): The history of personal adornment in eastern and southern Africa is examined through a range of objects drawn from Canadian collections. *Made In Canada: Craft and Design in the Sixties* (Feb. 25–Nov. 27): Examines two concurrent influences on the design of everyday objects. During the 1960s, the federal government sought to re-design the country through the adoption of legislation to create a vital, new nation. Simultaneously, popular culture was influencing the choices of young, independent and streetwise consumers. Together, these two factors provided for an exciting creative environment for designers and craftspeople.

Montreal Museum of Fine Art

A Dealer For "Living Art": Selected Works From the Max and Iris Stern Donation to Montreal (to Jan. 23): Considered one of the most important art dealers in Canadian history, Max Stern (1904–87) played a leading role in promoting this country's modern artists. The exhibition will include 50 works by Canadian artists including Paul-Émile Borduas, Emily Carr, Stanley Cosgrove, Jean Dallaire, John Lyman, J.E.H. MacDonald, Alfred Pellan and Jean-Paul Riopelle. *Eternal Egypt: Masterworks of Ancient Art from the British Museum* (Jan. 27–May 22): The first exhibition tour in North America to be drawn solely from the British Museum's outstanding collection of Egyptian antiquities. Taking an art historical view of this great culture, the exhibition will feature nearly 150 objects spanning the full range of 3000 years of pharaonic history. *Edwin Holgate: Master of the Human Figure* (May 19–Oct. 23): This major retrospective devoted to Edwin Holgate (1892–1977), a central figure in Montreal's art community and in the history of Canadian art, will feature 120 works, a selection of paintings, drawings, watercolours, prints, book illustrations and archival photographs. *Sam Borenstein* (June 16–Aug. 21): This retrospective—which includes some 70 works coming for the first time from public and private collections—will show not only the urban and country landscapes that made Borenstein famous, but portraits and still-lives. *Right Under the Sun: Painting in Provence from Classicism to*

Modernism (Sept. 22–Jan. 8, 2006): The exhibition will showcase more than 180 works, including masterpieces by such renowned names as Vernet, Loubon, Monet, Gauguin, Van Gogh, Cézanne and Braque. The presentation will focus primarily on landscape and light as depicted in Romanticism, Naturalism, Impressionism, Post-Impressionism, Fauvism and Cubism.

The Art Gallery of Nova Scotia

The Acadian Heritage in Prints (to Jan. 16): This survey of Acadia marks the 400th anniversary of the arrival of Pierre Du Gua de Monts and Samuel de Champlain at La Héve on the shores of Nova Scotia on May 8, 1604. Champlain's six small views constitute the only direct images of the Acadian presence. A selection of maps records the presence of Acadia at the focus of the belligerent relationship between France and England during this period, and another selection of prints documents the French presence at Louisbourg after 1720. *Rodin: A Magnificent Obsession*, (Feb. 26–May 22): A complete retrospective of the artist's career, including more than 60 bronzes from small studies as well as monumental works. Seventy-three cast bronze sculptures organized and circulated by the Iris & B. Gerald Cantor Foundation.

Museums Online

*M*ost major museums have Web sites that offer the public access to their collections, research documents, and education resources and activities. Here's a description of what you'll find at sites for some major Canadian and international museums:

The British Museum, London, England (www.thebritishmuseum.ac.uk) *The "Compass" section of this site gives the visitor access to a database containing images and descriptions of 5,000 objects from the museum collections. Virtual tours are available on a variety of subjects. A "Children's Compass" is available for young visitors.*

The Canadian Museum of Civilization, Hull, Quebec (www.civilization.ca) *This site's "Collections Storage Space" offers images and descriptions of furnishings, tools, personal items and other artifacts in the fields of archaeology, ethnology, folk culture and history. A virtual tour of the museum's Canada Hall is available, as well as an extensive selection of articles and images concerning the collections and recent exhibitions.*

The Kunsthistorisches Museum, Vienna, Austria (www.khm.at) *Visitors may survey collections from a dozen departments. Notable are collections of 15th- to 18th-century art and items from the treasuries of the Hapsburg-Lorraine household and the Holy Roman Empire.*

Musée du Louvre, Paris, France (www.louvre.fr) *The site offers a selection of works from each of nine departments. A virtual tour offers 70 images drawn from 50 rooms in the museum.*

The Royal British Columbia Museum, Victoria, B.C. (rbcm1.rbcm.gov.bc.ca) *This site reflects the RBCM's mandate to explore and preserve B.C.'s cultural and natural heritage. Its "Object Database" provides an opportunity to survey a collection rich in artifacts from Northwest First Nations peoples, as well as from pioneer and modern periods.*

The Royal Ontario Museum, Toronto, Ont. (www.rom.on.ca) *An "Interactive" section offers quizzes, contests, electronic postcards from the collection, and activities such as how to make a dinosaur out of chicken bones.*

The Smithsonian Institution, Washington, D.C., U.S.A. (www.si.edu) *An extensive "Explore and Learn" online resource section includes floor-by-floor virtual tours, audio presentations by famous performing artists, "Closer Look" brochures on museum installations, photo exhibits, and games and activities for children.*

Major Public Art Galleries in Canada

Art Gallery of Greater Victoria: 1040 Moss St, Victoria, BC V8V 4P1 (604) 384-4101

Art Gallery of Nova Scotia: PO Box 2262, Halifax, NS B3J 3C8 (902) 424-7542

Art Gallery of Ontario: 317 Dundas St W, Toronto, ON M5T 1G4 (416) 979-6648

Art Gallery of Windsor: 3100 Howard Ave, Windsor, ON N8X 3Y8 (519) 258-7111

Beaverbrook Art Gallery: PO Box 605, Fredericton, NB E3B 5A6 (506) 458-8545

Confederation Centre Art Gallery and Museum: 145 Richmond St, Charlottetown, PE C1A 1J1 (902) 628-6111

Dunlop Art Gallery: PO Box 2311, Regina, SK S4P 3Z5 (306) 777-6040

Edmonton Art Gallery: 2 Sir Winston Churchill Sq, Edmonton, AB T5J 2C1 (403) 422-6223

McMichael Canadian Art Collection: 10365 Islington Ave, Kleinburg, ON L0J 1C0 (905) 893-1121

Montreal Museum of Fine Arts: 1379-1380 Sherbrooke St W, PO Box 3000, Stn H, Montreal, QC H3G 2T9 (514) 285-1600

Musee d'Art Contemporain de Montreal: 185, rue Ste Catherine ouest, Montreal, QC H2X 1Z8 (514) 847-6212

Musée du Québec: Parc des Champs de Bataille, 1, rue Wolfe/Montcalm, Quebec, QC G1R 5H3 (418) 643-2150

National Gallery of Canada: 380 Sussex Dr, Ottawa, ON K1N 9N4 (613) 990-1985

Thunder Bay Art Gallery: PO Box 1193, Stn F, Thunder Bay, ON P7C 4X9 (807) 577-6427

Vancouver Art Gallery: 750 Hornby St, Vancouver, BC V6Z 2H7 (604) 662-4700

Winnipeg Art Gallery: 300 Memorial Blvd, Winnipeg, MB R3C 1V1 (204) 786-6641

Major Public Museums in Canada

Canadian Centre for Architecture: 1920 rue Baile, Montreal, QC H3A 1E9 (514) 939-7000

Canadian Museum of Civilization: 100 Laurier St, Box 3100, Stn B, Hull, QC J8X 4H2 (819) 776-7000

Canadian Museum of Contemporary Photography: 1 Rideau Canal, PO Box 465, Stn A, Ottawa, ON K1N 9N6 (613) 990-8257

Canadian Museum of Nature: PO Box 3443, Stn D, Ottawa, ON K1P 6P4 (613) 566-4700

Canadian War Museum: 330 Sussex Dr, Ottawa, ON K1A 0M8 (613) 996-1420

Glenbow-Alberta Institute: 130-9th Ave. SE, Calgary, AB T2G 0P3 (403) 268-4100

Manitoba Museum of Man and Nature: 190 Rupert Ave, Winnipeg, MB R3B 0N2 (204) 956-2830

Maritime Museum of the Atlantic: 1675 Lower Water St, Halifax, NS B3J 1S3 (902) 429-7490

McCord Museum of Canadian History: 690, rue Sherbrooke ouest, Montreal, QC H3A 1E9 (514) 398-7100

Musée de la Civilisation: 85, rue Dalhousie, CP 155, Succursale B, Quebec, QC G1K 7A6 (418) 643-2158

New Brunswick Museum: 277 Douglas Ave, Saint John, NB E2K 1E5 (506) 643-2300

Newfoundland Museum: 285 Duckworth St, PO Box 8700, St. John's, NF A1B 4J6 (709) 729-2329

Nova Scotia Museum: 1747 Summer St, Halifax, NS B3H 3A6 (902) 424-6471

Prince of Wales Northern Heritage Centre: PO Box 1320, Yellowknife, NT X1A 2L9 (867) 873-7551

Provincial Museum of Alberta: 12845-102nd Ave, Edmonton, AB T5N 0M6 (403) 453-9100

Royal British Columbia Museum: PO Box 9815, Stn Prov. Govt, Victoria, BC V8W 9W2 (250) 387-3701

Royal Ontario Museum: 100 Queen's Park, Toronto, ON M5S 2C6 (416) 586-8000

Royal Saskatchewan Museum: Wascana Park, College and Albert, Regina, SK S4P 3V7 (306) 787-2815

Vancouver Museum: 1100 Chestnut St, Vancouver, BC V6J 3J9 (604) 736-4431

Prince Edward Island Museum and Heritage Foundation: 2 Kent St, Charlottetown, PE C1A 1M6 (902) 368-6600

Governor General's Awards in Visual and Media Arts

These annual awards, funded and administered by the Canada Council for the Arts, were created in June 1999. Six prizes are awarded for distinguished career achievement in the visual and media arts, and one prize for distinguished contributions to the visual and media arts through voluntarism, philanthropy, board governance or community outreach activities. The fifth annual Governor General's awards were announced March 3, 2004.

2004 Winners

■ **Iain Baxter:** Iain Baxter studied zoology and education at the University of Idaho before earning an MFA from Washington State University. His pioneering conceptual art and experiments in photography, light boxes, painting, video, earth works, information systems and multimedia installations, have built his reputation as a provocateur, devil's advocate, activist and social critic. He is currently Professor Emeritus in the School of Visual Arts at the University of Windsor, where he has taught since 1988.

■ **Eric Cameron:** In a career that stretches over 40 years, Eric Cameron has demonstrated a fierce dedication to the practice of art, as well as to his work as art historian and teacher. He studied painting at King's College, University of Durham, in Newcastle-Upon-Tyne, and art history at the Courtauld Institute in London. He has taught at the University of Leeds, England, the University of Guelph, Ontario, the Nova Scotia College of Art and Design and is currently teaching at the University of Calgary.

■ **Istvan Kantor:** Istvan Kantor (also known previously as Monty Cantsin) is a media artist/producer active in performance art, robotics, installation, sound, music, video and new media. Kantor's interactive robotic performance work has been featured at Ars Electronica 2000. He has received the Telefilm Canada Award for Best Canadian Video (1998) and the Transmediale 2001 video award in Berlin. His avant-garde work has been described by the media as rebellious and anti-authoritarian, as well as technically innovative and highly experimental.

■ **Garry Neill Kennedy:** Conceptual painter and educator Garry Neill Kennedy studied at the Ontario College of Art, the University of Buffalo and the University of Ohio. In 1967, at the age of 32, he was appointed president of the Nova Scotia College of Art and Design, the youngest ever to serve in that position. He headed the college for 23 years. He has exhibited extensively, including a major show at the National Gallery of Canada in 2000. He was awarded the Portia White Prize by the Arts Council of Nova Scotia in 2000.

■ **John Oswald:** A media/sound artist, composer, performance and dance artist, John Oswald defies categorization: everything is material for his art. He coined the term "plunderphonics" in the late 80s to describe his plundering, or appropriating, well-known music and images and manipulating them in original ways. Oswald has an international reputation as a leading contemporary composer. He explores his electroacoustic creativity as Director of Research at Toronto's Mystery Lab.

■ **Ian Wallace:** Considered the "grandfather" of conceptual art in Vancouver, Ian Wallace broke new ground in his approach to photography and painting. He taught at both UBC (1970-87) and at the Emily Carr Institute of Art and Design (1972–98). He was an innovator, marrying art history with contemporary art and media. He has lectured and exhibited extensively in Europe (notably in France, Belgium, Italy and England), the U.S. and Canada. Through his lectures and writings he has influenced several generations of students at Emily Carr, UBC and beyond.

■ **Tom Hill:** As a curator, writer, art historian, volunteer and artist, Tom Hill has played an influential role in the development of Aboriginal visual arts. A Konadaha Seneca, Hill studied at the Ontario College of Art; he also has a certificate in museum studies from the Ontario Museums Association. From his involvement in the Indians of Canada Pavilion at Expo '67, he went on to become the first Aboriginal art curator in Canada. He has been museum director at the Woodland Cultural Centre near Brantford for over 20 years. Tom Hill lives in Ohsweken, Ontario.

FASHION AND DESIGN

The Substance of Style

The garment industry has been a major presence in Canadian business since the early 20th century. Today Quebec remains the country's top fashion centre, with apparel manufacturers employing 48,000 workers, 55 percent of the national total. Ontario follows with 25,000 workers and 28 percent of the industry workforce centred at the King-Spadina Fashion District. Manitoba is considered the centre of the country's outerwear industry. Clothing design in Canada ranges from the celebrated Tilley Endurables outdoor wear pioneered by Alex Tilley, to the black satin hotpants developed by Marilyn Brooks. First Nations motifs have had a strong influence on the work of designers such as Linda Lundstrom, while Dorothy Grant and D'arcy Moses draw from their respective Haida and Cree heritages.

Canada has emerged as an important centre in the fields of modern and postmodern architecture. Architects such as Frank Gehry, Arthur Erickson, Moshe Safdie and Raymond Moriyama have carved out international reputations. The Royal Architectural Institute of Canada estimates that 35,000 people work in this industry. Architectural firms generate an estimated $1.2 billion in revenues annually.

The industrial, interior, graphic, landscape and other design sectors employee 44,000 designers working in 5,700 firms across Canada. One of the country's most famous designs was the electric kettle developed by designer Fred Moffatt. Today, Karim Rashid is one of the country's most sought-after designers of items ranging from tableware to furniture to garbage cans.

National Post Design Exchange Awards 2003

The 2003 *National Post* Design Exchange Awards were presented in Toronto on November 30, 2003.

Products
Gold . . . . OHM Industrial Designers Inc., Fox 40 Marine
Silver . BW Technologies Product & Development Team, Gas Alert Micro—Compact 4-Gas Detector
Bronze . . . . Mark Müller, Vox Office™
Merit . . . . David Tonizzo, Zoom Zone
Merit . . . . DW Product Development Inc.& Camalor Manufacturing Inc., Black & Decker Workmate WM375

New Media
Gold . . . . CBC Radio 3, CBC Radio 3 Web Design
Gold . . . . IN_situ, IN_situ
Bronze . . . . Frost, DNA Condos Web design

Fashion
Gold . . . . . . Charlotte McKeough, The Brave Brown Bag
Silver . . . . Carla Romagnoli Inc., Pleatonics
Bronze . . . . . Joanna Notkin, LoooLo Sustainable Textiles
Merit . . . . JACQ's, Accordion Knit Accessories
Merit . . . . Nikki Kavakonis Designs, Ode to the Right Angle

Visual Communications
Gold . . . . Claire Dawson Design, Prefix Photo Magazine (Re-Design)
Silver . . . . Hahn Smith Design, Cuisipro Corporate & Brand Identity
Bronze . . . . Signals Design Group Inc., Canstruction Vancouver Marketing Materials

Interiors
Gold . . . . Gauthier, Daoust Lestage Inc., CDP Capital Centre
Silver . . . . MacLennan Jaunkains Miller Architects, Polar Capital Headquarters

Silver . . . . . . HCA Architecture Incorporated Architects, Stillwater Spa, Park Hyatt Toronto
Merit . . . . Burdifilek, Teknion Exhibit 2001
Merit . . . . . . Fiorino Design Inc., Liquor Control Board of Ontario, Summerhill store, Toronto

Environments
Gold . . . . Janet Rosenberg & Associates Landscape Architects, Jackson-Triggs Niagara Estate Winery
Gold . . . . Kuwabara Payne McKenna Blumberg Architects, Jackson-Triggs Niagara Estate Winery
Silver . . . . Group 90—0 (Atelier In Situ / Vlan Paysages), International Garden Festival, Les Jardins de Métis / Reford Gardens
Bronze . . . . Diamond and Schmitt Architects Inc., Bahen Centre for Information Technology, University of Toronto
Merit . . . . Brown & Storey Architects, Yonge-Dundas Square, Toronto
Merit . . . . Hariri Pontarini Architects, MacLaren Art Centre
Merit . . . . Watt IDG, La Maison Simons

Sustainable Design
Gold . . . . Robert Burgers Architects, Freybe Gourmet Foods
Silver . . . . . Prairie Architects Inc., Mountain Equipment Co-op Winnipeg Retail Outlet
Bronze . . . . Martin Liefhebber Architects Inc., Natural Life Network, Wilson House
Merit . . . . Robert Burgers Architects, Freybe Gourmet Foods
Merit . . . . Sustainable EDGE, EcoCité Habitat I

2003 Special Award-CEO with the Best Design Strategy
Paul Reichmann, Reichmann International

The Lycra British Style Awards 2003

The 2003 Lycra British Style Awards were presented September 25, 2003, in London, England.

British Designer of the Year: ..... Alexander McQueen
New Generation Designer: .... Sophia Kokosalaki
Accessory Designer: .... Manolo Blahnik
Glamour Designer of the Year: ..... Julien Macdonald
Contemporary Designer: .... Paul Smith
High Street Fashion Retailer: .... Reiss
Menswear Designer: .... Paul Smith
Most Stylish Photographer: .... Mario Testino
Most Stylish Model: .... Erin O'Connor

Stylist: .... Katie Grand
Most Stylish Female TV Personality: ..... Kim Cattrall
Most Stylish Male TV Personality: .... Ant & Dec
Most Stylish Movie Actress: .... Minnie Driver
Most Stylish Movie Actor: .... Ewan McGregor
Most Stylish Male Music Artist: ..... Robbie Williams
Most Stylish Female Music Artist: .. Victoria Beckham
Most Stylish Sports Personality: ..... David Beckham

THE CFDA Fashion Awards 2004

The CFDA Fashion Awards were presented by the Council of Fashion Designers of America in New York on June 8, 2004.

Womenswear Designer of the Year .. Carolina Herrera
Menswear Designer of the Year ..... Sean Combs for Sean John
Accessory Designer of the Year .... Reed Krakoff for Coach
Swarovski Perry Ellis Award for Emerging Talent (Ready-to-Wear).................... Zac Posen

Swarovski Perry Ellis Award for Emerging Talent (Accessory Design)................. Eugenia Kim
Eugenia Sheppard Award Teri Agins, *Wall Street Journal*
Eleanor Lambert Award .... Irving Penn
International Award .... Miuccia Prada
Lifetime Achievement............... Donna Karan
Special Tribute...................... Tom Ford
Fashion Icon................ Sarah Jessica Parker

Governor General's Medals in Architecture 2004

The Governor General's Medals in Architecture were presented in Ottawa on May 11, 2004, by the Royal Architectural Institute of Canada (RAIC) and the Canada Council for the Arts. The following projects were honoured:

Brentwood Skytrain Station – Busby + Associates Architects (Vancouver), Peter Busby, FRAIC

Nicola Valley Institute of Technology – Busby + Associates Architects (Vancouver), Peter Busby, FRAIC

Lore Krill Housing Co-op and City of Vancouver Parkade – Henriquez Partners Architects (Vancouver), Gregory Henriquez, MRAIC

Agosta House – Patkau Architects Inc. (Vancouver), John Patkau, FRAIC

Shaw House – Patkau Architects Inc. (Vancouver), John Patkau, FRAIC

James Stewart Centre for Mathematics, McMaster University – Kuwabara Payne McKenna Blumberg Architects (Toronto), Bruce Kuwabara, FRAIC

House in Erin – Ian MacDonald Architect Inc. (Toronto), Ian MacDonald

Muskoka Boathouse – Shim Sutcliffe Architects (Toronto), Brigitte Shim, MRAIC & Howard Sutcliffe, MRAIC

Weathering Steel House – Shim Sutcliffe Architects (Toronto), Brigitte Shim, MRAIC & Howard Sutcliffe, MRAIC

FESTIVALS AND EVENTS, 2005

In addition to festivals in the various branches of the performing arts, communities across Canada celebrate local, national and international culture with a wide variety of events. Here is a sample of the fairs and festivals available to visitors across Canada. Note that dates are subject to change and interested visitors should contact the numbers given, or the tourist bureaus of the respective provinces and territories.

■ Newfoundland and Labrador

Gander's Annual Festival of Flight, Gander, Aug.: Described as "Newfoundland's Biggest Kitchen Party," the festival includes live music, seafood, fireworks and demolition derbies. (709) 651-5927

Trinity-Conception Fall Fair, Harbour Grace, late Sept.: The annual fair will include the Miss Newfoundland & Labrador Pageant, a talent search contest, farm days, arts & crafts contest, agricultural contests, amusement park, parade, and nightly entertainment. (709) 596-6201

Grand Falls-Windsor Red Maple Festival, Grand Falls-Windsor, Oct. 28–Nov. 5: This community fall festival features swimming, hockey, tournament, ball hockey tournament, teen dances, adult dances and community skating. It concludes with a huge bonfire and mini-fireworks at Centennial Field. (709) 489-0450

■ Prince Edward Island

Lucy Maud Montgomery Festival, Cavendish and Area, Aug.: Two days of wholesome family fun and an opportunity to learn more about Montgomery and her time. Experience old-fashioned community events and hear readings from Montgomery's work. Improve your writing skills at writers' workshops. Enjoy traditional and children's entertainment. (902) 963-7874

Festival of Lights, Charlottetown Waterfront, July: The Festival of Lights has become the premier celebration of the Canada Day weekend in Atlantic Canada. Festivities include nightly concerts, international buskers, carnival midway and the July 1st fireworks over Charlottetown Harbour. Toll-free: 1-800-955-1864

Summerside Highland Gathering, College of Piping, Summerside, late June: Competitions for pipe bands, solo pipers and drummers, Highland and step dancers, and heavy-weight athletes. Celtic entertainment with concerts, ceilidhs, fiddling, clans, and children's activities. Daily and weekend passes available. (902) 436-5377, toll-free: 1-877-BAGPIPE

Festival Rendez-vous Rustico, Rustico, late July: An Acadian festival of traditional music, dance, culture, food and games, featuring ECMA award winner Lenny Gallant. Horse and wagon rides, games, races, carnival blow-ups, face painting are among the family activities. (902) 963-3252

The Indian River Festival Midsummer Magic Weekend, Indian River, late July: Four nights of fabulous music performed by internationally acclaimed musicians, recorded for broadcast by CBC Radio. Music you can hear with your heart in an acoustic and architectural treasure. (902) 836-4933, toll-free: 1-800-565-3688

■ Nova Scotia

Yarmouth Seafest, Yarmouth, mid-July: This community event celebrates Yarmouth's connection to a seafaring heritage. Key elements include a giant street parade, antique car show, bagpiper's walk and tea with the Mayor. It also features the largest fireworks display in Southwest Nova Scotia and the fabulous Fish Feast. (902) 742-5355

Festival Acadien de Clare, Clare, July: Canada's largest and oldest Acadian festival. Theatre, hikes, races, parades, a deep-sea fishing tournament and other competitions are all part of the event. (902) 769-3655

Nova Scotia International Tattoo, Halifax, beginning of June–July: The world's largest annual indoor show presents acts performed by over 2,000 military and civilian performers from Canada and around the world. The program offers a unique combination of music, dance, drama, gymnastics, comedy and military displays. (902) 420-1114

Antigonish Highland Games, Antigonish, July: A traditional Scottish Highland Games including clan gatherings, Scottish heritage workshops and concerts. Concentrated in the last three days are piping, dancing, drumming and heavy event competitions, along with one of Canada's finest outdoor tattoos and the "Concert Under the Stars." (902) 863-4275

Congrès mondial acadien, provincewide, Aug. 4th: In 2004, the 3rd Congrès mondial acadien will celebrate a homecoming to the birthplace of L'Acadie. Over 250,000 participants will walk the land where their ancestors once lived. Music, song, dance, pageantry and joyful reunions will abound. (902) 424-7104

Celtic Colours, Cape Breton, Oct. : Voted one of the "Top 100 Events in North America" for 2003 by the American Bus Association. Autumn is the time when the sounds of fiddles, pipes and voices in song echo over the island with Celtic Colours International Festival. An event to remember with over 250 musicians, dancers, singers, and storytellers at venues across the Island with Celtic Colours International Festival. The festival's goal is to increase international awareness of Cape Breton's own world-class Celtic talent and to help preserve Cape Breton's "living" Celtic culture. (902) 539-8800

■ **New Brunswick**

Shediac Lobster Festival, Shediac, second week of July: The Shediac Lobster Festival is an annual event held in the first week of July. Visitors are invited to discover the region's lobster and Acadian culture. Parades, races, entertainment and fireworks are all part of the festivities. (506) 532-1122

New Brunswick Highland Games and Scottish Festival, Fredericton, late July: This event features pipeband competitions, individual piping and drumming competitions, highland dancing competitions, heavy events contests, clan heritage genealogy workshop, Celtic music, ceilidh and concerts under the stars. It also includes fiddling, whisky tasting, Celtic guitar and step dancing. (506) 452-9244, toll-free: 1-888-368-4444

La Foire Brayonne, Edmundston, August: Internationally renowned, this popular festival offers three main activities: concerts, cultural activities and sports events. It celebrates the heritage of local Francophones and it is one of the biggest Francophone festivals outside Québec. (506) 739-6608

■ **Quebec**

The Québec Winter Carnival, Quebec City, Feb.: This is a unique and exciting event that enlivens the world's snow capital. It draws nearly 1,000,000 visitors every year. For 17 consecutive days, the Carnival offers sporting, artistic, and cultural activities that provide grown-ups and children alike an opportunity to rediscover the wonders of winter. The main Carnival attractions are located in the heart of Old Québec. These include dogsled races, canoe races, parades, ice fishing, flapjack breakfasts and. toboggan runs. Toll-free: 1-877-BONJOUR

Journées de la culture, Abitibi-Témiscamingue, Bas-Saint-Laurent, Centre-du-Québec, Charlevoix, Chaudière-Appalaches, Duplessis, Gaspésie, Greater Québec City Area, Îles-de-la-Madeleine, Lanaudière, Laurentians, Laval, Manicouagan, Mauricie, Montérégie, Montréal, Northern Québec, Outaouais, Saguenay-Lac-Saint-Jean, Eastern Townships. Late Sept: Each year, artists, craftspeople and cultural workers hold their own original activities to reveal the secrets of their art or throw a spotlight on the hidden treasures of their community. With 2000 activities all over Québec, they extend a hand to the people not normally reached and open the art and culture for all. Toll-free: 1-877-BONJOUR

Quebec Summer Festival, Quebec City, July: This is the biggest French-language stage and street performance event in North America. Over 1,000 artists from up to 20 countries perform in as many as 500 shows. Toll-free: 1-877-BONJOUR

■ **Ontario**

The Toronto International Carnival, Toronto, Aug.: Formerly known as Caribana, this is the largest festival rooted in Caribbean culture in North America. The two-week festival attracts over a million participants annually. (416) 465-4884

Winterlude, Ottawa, weekends in Feb.: The world's largest skating rink (the Rideau Canal) is the centrepiece of this annual winter carnival. But the bed races, polar bear golf, buskers on ice, hot air balloon fiesta, ice sculptures and figure skating that contribute to the festivities take place throughout the National Capital Region. Toll-free: 1-800-363-4465

Great Rendezvous Festival, Thunder Bay, second week of July: This 10-day festival commemorates the historic arrival of the voyageur brigades and features rustic camps, authentic canoes, unique crafts, historic games, music and spirited fun. (807) 625-2149

■ Manitoba

Northern Manitoba Trapper's Festival, The Pas, Feb. 9–13: This winter festival, originating in 1916, celebrates the cultural heritage of the northern pioneer with skill displays and entertainments. Events include the World Championship Dog Race and King Trapper events, including canoe packing, trap setting, moose calling, bannock baking and more. An arts and crafts show, beard-growing contest and children's games are also part of the fun. (204) 623-2912; www.trappersfestival.com

Festival du Voyageur, Winnipeg, Feb. 11–20: This is western Canada's largest winter festival: a celebration of Canada's fur-trading era combines the joie de vivre of the voyageurs with more than 400 music performances, magnificent snow sculptures, historical interpretation of early 19th-century life at Fort Gibraltar, live entertainment, traditional dishes, arets and crafts, the voyageur International Sled Dog Classic and governor's ball. (204) 237-7692; www.festivalvoyageur.mb.ca

Royal Manitoba Winter Fair, Keystone Centre, Brandon, Mar. 28–Apr. 2: A week of continuous excitement with world-class equestrian events, children's shows, agricultural shows and auctions. (204) 726-3590; www.brandon.com/provinciale

Red River Exhibition, Winnipeg, June 23–July 2: Family entertainment starts with a parade and continues with a giant midway, nightly entertainment and attractions, innovative displays and creative exhibits. (204) 888-6990; www.redriverex.com

Flin Flon Trout Festival, Flin Flon, June 28–July 1: Starting at sunrise at the beginning of June, the official cast opens the month-long catch-and-release lake trout fishing derby. The July 1st long weekend is a celebrated festival event with pancake breakfast, parade, ceremonies, Main Street extravaganzas, amusements, sporting events and a regional showcase. Take part in a day of canoeing in the Canadian Open Gold Rush Canoe Derby. (204) 687-3469

A Taste of Manitoba, Winnipeg, July 6–10: Twenty-eight of Manitoba's great restaurants dish out over 80 different menu items along with a main stage, children's entertainment, buskers and attractions. (204) 783-9955; www.dinemanitoba.com

Canada's National Ukrainian Festival, Dauphin, July 29–31: Special celebration of Ukraine's independence is an opportunity to experience the flavour of the old traditions and culture through song, dance, costume and delectably satisfying Ukrainian cuisine. (204) 622-4600; www.cnuf.ca

Winnipeg International Children's Festival, Winnipeg, June 9–12: The Winnipeg International Children's Festival provides world-standard performing arts and participatory activities that are educational, entertaining and accessible to young people from all social, economic and ethnic backgrounds. Activities include Authors' Reading Tent, Circus and Magic Partnership Tent, hands-on activities, puppet-making and more. (204) 958-4730; www.kidsfest.ca

■ Saskatchewan

The Prince Albert Winter Festival, Prince Albert, Feb.: The 26th annual Prince Albert Winter Festival includes children's carnival, talent shows, arts & crafts, international food and entertainment, guest artists, sled dog races and snow sculptures. (306) 764-7595

Vesna Festival, Saskatoon, May: A celebration of Ukrainian culture including artisans, fine arts, cultural displays and, of course, lots of dancing. (306) 934-1803

Taste of Saskatchewan, Saskatoon, July: More than 24 Saskatoon restaurants serve three of their favourite house dishes in an outdoor setting in Friendship Park. Available for sampling are Chinese, Greek, Italian, Indian, Native and Cajun foods. Live entertainment includes some of Saskatchewan's finest performers. (306) 975-3175

■ Alberta

Stampede 2004, Calgary, July: The Calgary Stampede is Canada's premiere celebration of western heritage and culture and one of the top such events in all of North America. Organizers promise visitors more to see and do over 10 days than they will ever be able to manage— from midway rides to pancakes, horses to light shows, rodeos to stage shows, chuckwagons to displays of Alberta Agriculture and top name entertainers. Western duds are a must! General information: 1-800-661-1260; tickets: 1-800-661-1767; www.calgarystampede.com

Klondike Days, Edmonton, July 18–27: More than 750,000 fair visitors attend this exposition which starts with a colourful parade and continues with 10 days of midway rides and attractions, excellent live entertainment, chuckwagon racing, the Feature Country Showcase, great shopping and the mini-donuts that have become the fair's trademark. Each afternoon, there is live entertainment with bathtub racing and the Taste of Edmonton restaurant showcase downtown. Each night a show of fireworks completes the day's excitement. Toll-free: 1-888-800-7275; www.klondikedays.com

Cold Lake-Maple Flag Event, Cold Lake, mid-May to mid-June: Airforce flying demonstrations take place at the Cold Lake airbase for six weeks every summer. Fighter pilots are training for the Canadian Forces and Top Gun crews from all over the world. Toll-free: 1-800-840-6140; www.airforce.forces.ca/4wing/index_e.cfm

■ **British Columbia**

Kamloops Cowboy Festival, Kamloops, Mar.: The B.C. Cowboy Heritage Society presents this festival, which includes a western trade show, art, music and cowboy poetry. It supports the preservation of cowboy heritage in B.C. and institutions such as the B.C. Cowboy Hall of Fame, which holds its induction ceremony at the festival. Toll-free: 1-888-763-2224; www.bcchs.com /festival.htm

Victoria Harbour Festival, Victoria, May: This 10-day celebration bridges two holiday long weekends, Canada's Victoria Day and U.S. Memorial Day. Featured under the festival umbrella are events ranging from a literary festival to a rodeo, with many family-oriented entertainment, cultural and sporting events in between. The Victoria Day Parade and internationally renowned Swiftsure International Yacht Race are part of the festivities. Swiftsure: (250) 592-9098

Nanaimo Marine Festival, Nanaimo, fourth weekend of July: The main event of this four-day sea festival on Vancouver Island is a bathtub race featuring a variety of unusual home-made watercraft. (250) 753-7223; www.bathtub. island.net/

HSBC Celebration of Light, Vancouver, July–Aug.: Three countries put on fabulous fireworks displays in this dazzling competition in the skies over Vancouver. The four-night competition attracts 1.2 million viewers, including residents from all over the lower mainland, tourists and cruise ship passengers. Jugglers, face painters, magicians and musicians entertain visitors on their way from parking lots to the fireworks festival viewing areas at English Bay, Kitsilano, Vanier Park, Jericho Beach and West Vancouver. (604) 641-1193; www.celebration-of-light.com

Okanagan Wine Festivals, Okanagan Valley, throughout the year: The Okanagan Ice Wine Festival in mid-January incorporates winter recreation with wine education and cuisine. The Okanagan Spring Wine Festival in May focusses on the culinary arts and features a vine cycling event. The Okanagan Summer Wine Festival in earlu August is a relaxing and tasty event. And the Okanagan Fall Wine Festival in September and October celebrates the harvest. (250) 861-6654; www.thewinefestivals.com

■ **Yukon**

Yukon Sourdough Rendezvous Festival, Whitehorse, Feb.: This winter festival has sports, arts, as well as traditional games. The entertainment ranges from dog races to cancan dancers, from snowshoe shufflers to the International Winter Air Show. (867) 667-2148

■ **Northwest Territories**

Caribou Carnival, Yellowknife, March: The Caribou Carnival is Yellowknifers' favourite spring event. The Queen and Princess contests are featured, as well as snowmobile races. Also included in the carnival is the NMI Mobility Canadian Championship Dog Derby. The biggest purse in the Northwest Territories is offered for this three-day, 240-km (142-mile) race on Great Slave Lake. The annual race will feature mushers from across North America and around the world. (867) 873-4262

■ **Nunavut**

Nunavut Day, throughout Nunavut, July 9: Residents of Nunavut celebrate both the coming of summer and the founding of Nunavut on this day. Events take place across the new territory. Among the activities in Baker Lake are foot and bicycle races, a tea-boiling contest and traditional Inuit games. Toll-free: 1-800-491-7910

Sports Year in Review

Because this publication goes to press in October of each year, our year in review presents more of a "fiscal" timeline of the year in sports—from October to September—reserving the standard calendar year-in-review retrospectives for the daily newspapers of the world.

OCTOBER 2003: Jordin Tootoo plays in the Nashville Predators' opening game, becoming the first Inuit hockey player to play in the NHL. • The Florida Marlins win their second world championship in eight years. • Los Angeles Laker Kobe Bryant participates in team training camp while jetting back and forth to Colorado for court activity of another kind related to his alleged rape of an Eagle, Colorado, hotel employee.

NOVEMBER 2003: Paul Tracy, a native of Scarborough, Ontario, becomes the second Canadian driver to win the Champ Car drivers championship and helps Canada to its first-ever Nations Cup win on the CART circuit. • The Edmonton Eskimos defeat the Montreal Alouettes to win the 91st Grey Cup Championship, marking the Eskimos' 12th Grey Cup win in franchise history. • Canadian Mike Weir's 3-2-0 record helps lead the International squad to a halved decision at the 2003 Presidents Cup golf match play competition.

DECEMBER 2003: Oakville, Ontario, native and Indianapolis Colts placekicker Mike Vanderjagt sets an NFL record for consecutive field goals when he kicks a 43-yarder for his 41st consecutive field goal.

JANUARY 2004: With the publication of his new book, *My Prison Without Bars*, baseball's all-time hits leader Pete Rose publicly admits for the first time that he bet on the outcomes of baseball games, allegations for which he was thrown out of baseball in 1989. • At the Sony Open in Hawaii, 14-year-old golf phenom Michelle Wie missed the cut of this men's professional golf tournament by a single stroke.

FEBRUARY 2004: The New England Patriots defeat the Carolina Panthers, 32-29, to win Super Bowl XXXVIII. Jamaal Magloire of the New Orleans Hornets becomes the second Canadian to play in an NBA all-star game.

MARCH 2004: Winger Todd Bertuzzi of the Vancouver Canucks lands a vicious blind-side punch on a prone Colorado Avalanche centre Steve Moore. Moore receives fractured vertebrae and an uncertain NHL future from the blow. Bertuzzi receives suspension, assault charges, and an uncertain NHL future for the blow.

APRIL 2004: The University of Connecticut connects on a rare double-double, winning both the men's and women's U.S. national college basketball championships.

MAY 2004: Smarty Jones is this year's triple-crown near-miss. The three-year-old demolished the fields at the Kentucky Derby and the Preakness Stakes before faltering at horse racing's coveted third leg, the Belmont Stakes.

JUNE 2004: Behind the stellar goaltending of Miikka Kiprusoff and offensive skills of Jarome Iginla, the Calgary Flames make a surprising run to the Stanley Cup finals before losing in the seventh game to the Tampa Bay Lightning. • The Detroit Pistons surprise the heavily favoured Los Angeles Lakers to take the NBA Finals crown. • Canadian cross-country skier Beckie Scott received her gold medal as 2002 Olympic champion of the women's pursuit event. Scott finished third in the actual race, but the top two finishers were subsequently stripped of their medals because of positive drug tests.

JULY 2004: With a 1-0 win over Portugal, Greece pulled off a shocking upset to win the Euro 2004 European soccer championship. • Just seven months after receiving his Canadian citizenship, golfer Stephen Ames of Calgary posted a 10-under-par score of 274 to win his first PGA Tour title, the Cialis Western Open tournament played just outside Chicago. • American cyclist Lance Armstrong finishes first in the Tour de France an unprecedented sixth consecutive time.

AUGUST 2004: Nearly 11,000 athletes compete in the 2004 Summer Olympic Games in Athens. The United States dominates the medal podium, winning 103 medals. Canadian Olympians take home 12 medals, including 3 golds.

SEPTEMBER 2004: Canadian Mike Weir falls just short of becoming the first Canadian golfer to win the Bell Canadian Open in 50 years when he loses to Vijay Singh, in a three-hole playoff. • Roger Federer of Switzerland completes an impressive performance in tennis's major championships by winning the U.S. Open to go along with earlier wins at the Australian Open and Wimbledon. • NHL owners lock out NHL players, threatening the 2004–05 season—and possibly beyond. • Major League Baseball finally pulls out of Montreal with the announcement that the Expos will relocate to Washington, D.C., in time for the 2005 season.

American League Final Standings, 2004

Eastern Division

TEAM	W	L	PCT	GB
Y-New York	101	61	.623	-
X-Boston	98	64	.605	3.0
Baltimore	78	84	.481	23.0
Tampa Bay	70	91	.435	30.5
Toronto	67	94	.416	33.5

Central Division

TEAM	W	L	PCT	GB
Y-Minnesota	92	70	.568	-
Chicago	83	79	.512	9.0
Cleveland	80	82	.494	12.0
Detroit	72	90	.444	20.0
Kansas City	58	104	.358	34.0

Western Division

TEAM	W	L	PCT	GB
Y-Anaheim	92	70	.568	-
Oakland	91	71	.562	1.0
Texas	89	73	.549	3.0
Seattle	63	99	.389	29.0

Source: *Major League Baseball*

X — Wild Card Y — Division Title.

American League Leaders, 2004

Batting

Batting Average

I. Suzuki, Sea	.372
M. Mora, Bal	.340
V. Guerrero, Ana	.337
I. Rodriguez, Det	.334
E. Durazo, Oak	.321
C. Guillon, Det	.318
J. Lopez, Bal.	.316
M. Kotsay, Oak.	.314
M. Young, Tex	.313
T. Hafner, Cle.	.311
M. Tejada, Bal	.311

On-Base Percentage

M. Mora, Bal	.419
I. Suzuki, Sea.	.414
T. Hafner, Cle.	.410
J. Posada, NYY	.400
E. Chavez, Oak.	.397
M. Ramirez, Bos.	.397
E. Durazo, Oak.	.396
G. Sheffield, NYY	.393
V. Guerrero, Ana	.391
H. Matsui, NYY.	.390
J. Varitek, Bos	.390

Runs

V. Guerrero, Ana	124
J. Damon, Bos	123
G. Sheffield, NYY	117
M. Young, Tex	114
A. Rodriguez, NYY	112
D. Jeter, NYY	111
M. Mora, Bal	111
M. Lawton, Cle.	109
H. Matsui, NYY.	109
M. Ramirez, Bos.	108

Hits

I. Suzuki, Sea.	262
M. Young, Tex	216
V. Guerrero, Ana	206
M. Tejada, Bal	203
M. Kotsay, Oak.	190
J. Damon, Bos	189
D. Jeter, NYY	188
M. Mora, Bal	187
C. Crawford, TB	185
J. Lopez, Bal.	183

Runs Batted In

M. Tejada, Bal	150
D. Ortiz, Bos.	139
M. Ramirez, Bos.	130
V. Guerrero, Ana	126
G. Sheffield, NYY	121
P. Konerko, CWS	117
M. Teixeira, Tex	112
H. Blalock, Tex.	110
T. Hafner, Cle.	109
V. Martinez, Cle	108
H. Matsui, NYY.	108

Doubles

B. Roberts, Bal.	50
R. Belliard, Cle	48
D. Ortiz, Bos.	47
D. Jeter, NYY	44
M. Ramirez, Bos.	44
T. Hafner, Cle.	41
J. Lugo, TB.	41
M. Mora, Bal	41
M. Tejada, Bal	40
E. Byrnes, Oak	39
V. Guerrero, Ana	39

Triples

C. Crawford, TB	19
C. Figgins, Ana.	17
C. Guillen, Det	10
O. Infante, Det	9
M. Young, Tex	9
J. Cruz, TB	8
O. Hudson, Tor	7
B. Inge, Det	7
K. Lofton, NYY	7
D. Newhan, Bal.	7
A. Rios, Tor	7

Home Runs

M. Ramirez, Bos.	43
P. Konerko, CWS	41
D. Ortiz, Bos.	41
V. Guerrero, Ana	39
M. Teixeira, Tex	38
A. Rodriguez, NYY	36
G. Sheffield, NYY	36
M. Tejada, Bal	34
H. Blalock, Tex.	32
C. Delgado, Tor.	32

Slugging Percentage

M. Ramirez, Bos.	.613
D. Ortiz, Bos.	.603
V. Guerrero, Ana	.598
T. Hafner, Cle.	.583
M. Mora, Bal	.562
M. Teixeira, Tex	.560
A. Rowand, CWS	.544
C. Guillen, Det	.542
C. Delgado, Tor.	.535
P. Konerko, CWS	.535

Stolen Bases

C. Crawford, TB	59
I. Suzuki, Sea.	36
C. Figgins, Ana.	34
B. Roberts, Bal.	29
A. Rodriguez, NYY	28
D. Jeter, NYY	23
M. Lawton, Cle.	23
T. Hunter, Min	21
J. Lugo, TB.	21
R. Winn, Sea	21

Walks

E. Chavez, Oak.	95
G. Sheffield, NYY	92
M. Bellhorn, Bos	88
H. Matsui, NYY.	88
J. Posada, NYY	88
R. Palmeiro, Bal.	86
B. Williams, NYY	85
M. Ramirez, Bos.	82
A. Rodriguez, NYY	80
J. Cruz, TB	76
J. Damon, Bos	76

Total Bases

V. Guerrero, Ana	366
D. Ortiz, Bos.	351
M. Tejada, Bal	349
M. Ramirez, Bos.	348
M. Young, Tex	333
I. Suzuki, Sea.	320
H. Blalock, Tex.	312
C. Lee, CWS.	310
M. Mora, Bal	309
A. Rodriguez, NYY	308

▶

Pitching

Wins – Losses

C. Schilling, Bos.	21–6
J. Santana, Min	20–6
K. Rogers, Tex	18–9
B. Colon, Ana	18–12
M. Mulder, Oak	17–8
P. Martinez, Bos.	16–9
M. Buehrle, CWS	16–10
C. Lee, Cle	14–8
J. Lieber, NYY	14–8
C. Silva, Min.	14–8
6 others with 14 wins	

Winning Percentage

C. Schilling, Bos.	.778
J. Santana, Min	.769
M. Mulder, Oak	.680
T. Hudson, Oak	.667
K. Rogers, Tex	.667
J. Rincon, Min	.647
P. Martinez, Bos.	.640
C. Lee, Cle	.636
J. Lieber, NYY	.636
C. Silva, MIN	.636

Earned Run Average

J. Santana, Min	2.61
C. Schilling, Bos.	3.26
J. Westbrook, Cle.	3.38
B. Radke, Min.	3.48
T. Hudson, Oak	3.53
R. Lopez, Bal	3.59
F. Garcia, CWS	3.81
M. Buehrle, CWS	3.89
P. Martinez, Bos.	3.90
K. Escobar, Ana	3.93

Strikeouts

J. Santana, Min	265
P. Martinez, Bos.	227
C. Schilling, Bos.	203
K. Escobar, Ana	191
F. Garcia, CWS	184
J. Bonderman, Det.	168
T. Lilly, Tor	168
R. Harden, Oak.	167
M. Buehrle, CWS	165
B. Zito, Oak	163

Saves

M. Rivera, NYY.	53
F. Cordero, Tex.	49
J. Nathan, Min	44
T. Percival, Ana	33
K. Foulke, Bos	32
D. Baez, TB.	30
O. Dotel, Oak	22
J. Julio, Bal	22
U. Urbina, Det	21
S. Takatsu, CWS	19

Shutouts

J. Bonderman, Det	2
T. Hudson, Oak	2
S. Ponson, Bal	2
Many more tied with 1	

Innings Pitched

M. Buehrle, CWS	245.1
J. Santana, Min	228.0
C. Schilling, Bos.	226.2
M. Mulder, Oak	225.2
B. Radke, Min.	219.2
J. Garland, CWS.	217.0
M. Maroth, Det.	217.0
P. Martinez, Bos.	217.0
S. Ponson, Bal	215.2
J. Westbrook, Cle.	215.2

Pitched Games

P. Quantrill, NYY	86
T. Gordon, NYY	80
J. Rincon, Min	77
B. Ryan, Bal	76
M. Timlin, Bos	76
M. Myers, Bos	75
D. Marte, CWS	74
M. Rivera, NYY.	74
J. Romero, Min	74
J. Grimsley, Bal	73
J. Nathan, Min	73

Complete Games

M. Mulder, Oak	5
S. Ponson, Bal	5
J. Westbrook, Cle.	5
M. Buehrle, CWS	4
T. Hudson, Oak	3
D. May, KC.	3
C. Schilling, Bos.	3
12 players tied with	2

Source: *Major League Baseball*

National League Final Standings, 2004

Eastern Division

TEAM	W	L	PCT	GB
Y-Atlanta	96	66	.593	-
Philadelphia	86	76	.531	10.0
Florida	83	79	.512	13.0
New York	71	91	.438	25.0
Montreal	67	95	.414	29.0

Central Division

TEAM	W	L	PCT	GB
Y-St. Louis	105	57	.648	-
X-Houston	92	70	.568	13.0
Chicago	89	73	.549	16.0
Cincinnati	76	86	.469	29.0
Pittsburgh	72	89	.447	32.5
Milwaukee	67	94	.416	37.5

Western Division

TEAM	W	L	PCT	GB
Y-Los Angeles	93	69	.574	-
San Francisco	91	71	.562	2.0
San Diego	87	75	.537	6.0
Colorado	68	94	.420	25.0
Arizona	51	111	.315	42.0

Source: *Major League Baseball*   X — Wild Card Y — Division Title.

National League Leaders, 2004

Batting

Batting Average

B. Bonds, SF	.362
T. Helton, Col	.347
M. Loretta, SD	.335
A. Beltre, LA.	.334
A. Pujols, StL	.331
J. Pierre, Fla.	.326
S. Casey, Cin	.324
J. Kendall, Pit.	.319
A. Ramirez, CHC.	.318
L. Berkman, Hou	.316

On-Base Percentage

B. Bonds, SF	.609
T. Helton, Col.	.469
L. Berkman, Hou	.450
J. Drew, Atl	.436
B. Abreu, Phi	.428
J. Edmonds, StL.	.418
A. Pujols, StL.	.415
S. Rolen, StL	.409
J. Kendall, Pit.	.399
J. Thome, Phi.	.396

Runs

A. Pujols, StL.	133
B. Bonds, SF	129
J. Rollins, Phi.	119
B. Abreu, Phi	118
J. Drew, Atl	118
T. Helton, Col	115
B. Wilkerson, Mon	112
S. Rolen, StL	109
M. Loretta, SD	108
M. Alou, CHC	106

Hits

J. Pierre, Fla.	221
M. Loretta, SD	208
J. Wilson, Pit	201
A. Beltre, LA	200
A. Pujols, StL	196
C. Izturis, LA	193
T. Helton, Col	190
J. Rollins, Phi.	190
S. Casey, Cin	185
J. Kendall, Pit.	183

Runs Batted In

V. Castilla, Col	131
S. Rolen, StL	124
A. Pujols, StL	123
A. Beltre, LA.	121
M. Cabrera, Fla.	112
J. Edmonds, StL.	111
T. Batista, Mon.	110
J. Burnitz, Col.	110
J. Kent, Hou.	107
M. Alou, CHC.	106
L. Berkman, Hou	106

Doubles

L. Overbay, Mil.	53
A. Pujols, StL.	51
T. Helton, Col	49
B. Abreu, Phi.	47
C. Biggio, Hou	47
M. Loretta, SD	47
S. Casey, Cin	44
M. Lowell, Fla.	44
V. Castilla, Col	43
J. Rollins, Phi.	43

Triples

J. Pierre, Fla.	12
J. Rollins, Phi.	12
J. Wilson, Pit	12
C. Izturis, LA	9
J. Drew, Atl	8
R. Durham, SF	8
R. Freel, Cin	8
J. Kent, Hou	8
6 players tied with	7

Home Runs

A. Beltre, LA.	48
A. Dunn, Cin.	46
A. Pujols, StL.	46
B. Bonds, SF	45
J. Edmonds, StL.	42
J. Thome, Phi.	42
M. Alou, CHC	39
J. Burnitz, Col.	37
S. Finley, LA.	36
A. Ramirez, CHC.	36

Slugging Percentage

B. Bonds, SF	.812
A. Pujols, StL	.657
J. Edmonds, StL.	.643
A. Beltre, LA.	.629
T. Helton, Col	.620
S. Rolen, StL	.598
J. Thome, Phi.	.581
A. Ramirez, CHC.	.578
J. Drew, Atl	.569
A. Dunn, Cin.	.569

Stolen Bases

JS. Podsednik, Mil	70
J. Pierre, Fla.	45
B. Abreu, Phi	40
R Freel, Cin	37
D. Roberts, LA	33
E. Chavez, Mon	32
C. Patterson, CHC	32
J. Rollins, Phi.	30
R. Furcal, Atl	29
C. Beltran, Hou.	28

Walks

B. Bonds, SF	232
B. Abreu, Phi	127
L. Berkman, Hou	127
T. Helton, Col	127
J. Drew, Atl	118
A. Dunn, Cin	108
B. Wilkerson, Mon	106
J. Thome, Phi.	104
J. Edmonds, StL.	101
J. Bagwell, Hou	96

Total Bases

A. Pujols, StL.	389
A. Beltre, LA.	376
T. Helton, Col.	339
M. Alou, CHC.	335
A. Dunn, Cin.	323
J. Edmonds, StL.	320
A. Ramirez, CHC.	316
B. Abreu, Phi.	312
V. Castilla, Col	312
M. Cabrera, Fla.	309

Pitching

Wins – Losses

RR. Oswalt, Hou.	20–10
R. Clemens, Hou	18–4
J. Schmidt, SF	18–7
C. Pavano, Fla	18–8
C. Zambrano, CHC	16–8
J. Suppan, StL	16–9
G. Maddux, CHC.	16–11
R. Johnson, Ari	16–14
C. Carpenter, StL	15–5
J. Peavy, SD.	15–6
6 others with 15 wins	

Winning Percentage

R. Clemens, Hou	.818
C. Carpenter, StL	.750
J. Lima, LA.	.722
J. Schmidt, SF	.720
J. Peavy, SD.	.714
E. Milton, Phi	.700
C. Pavano, Fla	.692
T. Jones, Phi	.688
J. Marquis, StL.	.682
R. Oswalt, Hou.	.667
C. Zambrano, CHC	.667

Earned Run Average

J. Peavy, SD.	2.27
R. Johnson, Ari	2.60
B. Sheets, Mil.	2.70
C. Zambrano, CHC	2.75
R. Clemens, Hou	2.98
O. Perez, Pit	2.98
C. Pavano, Fla	3.00
J. Schmidt, SF	3.20
A. Leiter, NYM	3.21
O. Perez, LA.	3.25

Strikeouts

R. Johnson, Ari	290
B. Sheets, Mil.	264
J. Schmidt, SF	251
O. Perez, Pit	239
R. Clemens, Hou	218
R. Oswalt, Hou.	206
M. Clement, CHC	190
C. Zambrano, CHC	188
L. Hernandez, Mon	186
J. Peavy, SD.	173

Saves

A. Benitez, Fla.	47
J. Isringhausen, StL.	47
E. Gagne, LA	45
J. Smoltz, Atl	44
J. Mesa, Pit	43
D. Graves, Cin	41
T. Hoffman, SD	41
D. Kolb, Mil	39
S. Chacon, Col	35
B. Lidge, Hou.	29
B. Looper, NYM	29

Shutouts

C. Lidle, Phi	3
J. Schmidt, SF	3
L. Hernandez, Mon	2
K. Ishii, LA	2
R. Johnson, Ari	2
M. Morris, StL	2
R. Oswalt, Hou.	2
C. Pavano, Fla	2
Many more tied with 1	

Innings Pitched

L. Hernandez, Mon	255.0
R. Johnson, Ari	245.2
R. Oswalt, Hou.	237.0
B. Sheets, Mil.	237.0
J. Schmidt, SF	225.0
C. Pavano, Fla	222.1
J. Weaver, LA.	220.0
R. Clemens, Hou	214.1
G. Maddux, CHC.	212.2
T. Glavine, NYM	212.1

Pitched Games

J. Brower, SF	89
R. King, StL	86
R. Cormier, Phi	84
C. Reitsma, Atl	84
S. Torres, Pit	84
S. Eyre, SF	83
M. Stanton, NYM	83
L. Ayala, Mon	81
B. Lidge, Hou.	80
A. Alfonseca, Atl.	79

Complete Games

L. Hernandez, Mon	9
C. Lidle, Phi	5
B. Sheets, Mil.	5
R. Johnson, Ari	4
J. Schmidt, SF	4
M. Morris, StL	3
10 players tied with 2	

Source: *Major League Baseball*

Major League Pennant Winners, 1961–2003

National League					American League			
Year	Winner	Won	Lost	%	Year	Winner	Won	Lost	%
1961	Cincinnati	93	61	.604	1961	New York	109	53	.673
1962	San Francisco	103	62	.624	1962	New York	96	66	.593
1963	Los Angeles	99	63	.611	1963	New York	104	57	.646
1964	St. Louis	93	69	.574	1964	New York	99	63	.611
1965	Los Angeles	97	65	.599	1965	Minnesota	102	60	.630
1966	Los Angeles	95	67	.586	1966	Baltimore	97	63	.606
1967	St. Louis	101	60	.627	1967	Boston	92	70	.568
1968	St. Louis	97	65	.599	1968	Detroit	103	59	.636
1969	New York	100	62	.617	1969	Baltimore	109	53	.673
1970	Cincinnati	102	60	.630	1970	Baltimore	108	54	.667
1971	Pittsburgh	97	65	.599	1971	Baltimore	101	57	.639
1972	Cincinnati	95	59	.617	1972	Oakland	93	62	.600
1973	New York	82	79	.509	1973	Oakland	94	68	.580
1974	Los Angeles	102	60	.630	1974	Oakland	90	72	.556
1975	Cincinnati	108	54	.667	1975	Boston	95	65	.594
1976	Cincinnati	102	60	.630	1976	New York	97	62	.610
1977	Los Angeles	98	64	.605	1977	New York	100	62	.617
1978	Los Angeles	95	67	.586	1978	New York	100	63	.613
1979	Pittsburgh	98	64	.605	1979	Baltimore	102	57	.642
1980	Philadelphia	91	71	.562	1980	Kansas City	97	65	.599
1981	Los Angeles	63	47	.573	1981	New York	59	48	.551
1982	St. Louis	92	70	.568	1982	Milwaukee	95	67	.586
1983	Philadelphia	90	72	.556	1983	Baltimore	98	64	.605
1984	San Diego	92	70	.568	1984	Detroit	104	58	.642
1985	St. Louis	101	61	.623	1985	Kansas City	91	71	.562
1986	New York	108	54	.667	1986	Boston	95	66	.590
1987	St. Louis	95	67	.586	1987	Minnesota	85	77	.525
1988	Los Angeles	94	67	.584	1988	Oakland	104	58	.642
1989	San Francisco	92	70	.568	1989	Oakland	99	63	.611
1990	Cincinnati	91	71	.562	1990	Oakland	103	59	.636
1991	Atlanta	94	68	.580	1991	Minnesota	95	67	.586
1992	Atlanta	98	64	.605	1992	**Toronto**	**96**	**66**	**.593**
1993	Philadelphia	97	65	.599	1993	**Toronto**	**95**	**67**	**.586**
1994[1]	no winner				1994[1]	no winner			
1995	Atlanta	90	54	.625	1995	Cleveland	100	44	.694
1996	Atlanta	96	66	.593	1996	New York	92	70	.569
1997	Florida	92	70	.568	1997	Cleveland	86	75	.534
1998	San Diego	98	64	.605	1998	New York	114	48	.704
1999	Atlanta	103	59	.639	1999	New York	98	64	.605
2000	New York	94	68	.580	2000	New York	87	74	.540
2001	Arizona	92	70	.568	2001	New York	95	65	.594
2002	San Francisco	95	66	.590	2002	Anaheim	99	63	.611
2003	Florida	91	71	.562	2003	New York	101	61	.623

Source: *Canadian Press*   (1) Players strike Aug. 12, 1994; owners suspended season, Sept. 14, 1994.

World Series Results, 1903–2003

Year	Champion	Opponent	Series Result	MVP
1903	Boston Red Sox	Pittsburgh Pirates	5-3	
1905	New York Giants	Philadelphia A's	4-1	
1906	Chicago White Sox	Chicago Cubs	4-2	
1907	Chicago Cubs	Detroit Tigers	4-0	
1908	Chicago Cubs	Detroit Tigers	4-1	
1909	Pittsburgh Pirates	Detroit Tigers	4-3	
1910	Philadelphia A's	Chicago Cubs	4-1	
1911	Philadelphia A's	New York Giants	4-2	
1912	Boston Red Sox	New York Giants	4-3	
1913	Philadelphia A's	New York Giants	4-1	
1914	Boston Braves	Philadelphia A's	4-0	
1915	Boston Red Sox	Philadelphia Phillies	4-1	
1916	Boston Red Sox	Brooklyn Dodgers	4-1	
1917	Chicago White Sox	New York Giants	4-2	
1918	Boston Red Sox	Chicago Cubs	4-2	
1919	Cincinnati Reds	Chicago White Sox	5-3	
1920	Cleveland Indians	Brooklyn Dodgers	5-2	
1921	New York Giants	New York Yankees	5-3	
1922	New York Giants	New York Yankees	4-0	
1923	New York Yankees	New York Giants	4-2	
1924	Washington Senators	New York Giants	4-3	
1925	Pittsburgh Pirates	Washington Senators	4-3	
1926	St. Louis Cardinals	New York Yankees	4-3	
1927	New York Yankees	Pittsburgh Pirates	4-0	
1928	New York Yankees	St. Louis Cardinals	4-0	
1929	Philadelphia A's	Chicago Cubs	4-1	
1930	Philadelphia A's	St. Louis Cardinals	4-2	
1931	St. Louis Cardinals	Philadelphia A's	4-3	
1932	New York Yankees	Chicago Cubs	4-0	
1933	New York Giants	Washington Senators	4-1	
1934	St. Louis Cardinals	Detroit Tigers	4-3	
1935	Detroit Tigers	Chicago Cubs	4-2	
1936	New York Yankees	New York Giants	4-2	
1937	New York Yankees	New York Giants	4-1	
1938	New York Yankees	Chicago Cubs	4-0	
1939	New York Yankees	Cincinnati Reds	4-0	
1940	Cincinnati Reds	Detroit Tigers	4-3	
1941	New York Yankees	Brooklyn Dodgers	4-1	
1942	St. Louis Cardinals	New York Yankees	4-1	
1943	New York Yankees	St. Louis Cardinals	4-1	
1944	St. Louis Cardinals	St. Louis Browns	4-2	
1945	Detroit Tigers	Chicago Cubs	4-3	
1946	St. Louis Cardinals	Boston Red Sox	4-3	
1947	New York Yankees	Brooklyn Dodgers	4-3	
1948	Cleveland Indians	Boston Braves	4-2	
1949	New York Yankees	Brooklyn Dodgers	4-1	
1950	New York Yankees	Philadelphia Phillies	4-0	
1951	New York Yankees	New York Giants	4-2	

▶

Year	Champion	Opponent	Series Result	MVP
▶ 1952	New York Yankees	Brooklyn Dodgers	4-3	
1953	New York Yankees	Brooklyn Dodgers	4-2	
1954	New York Giants	Cleveland Indians	4-0	a
1955	Brooklyn Dodgers	New York Yankees	4-3	Johnny Podres, Bkl
1956	New York Yankees	Brooklyn Dodgers	4-3	Don Larsen, NYY
1957	Milwaukee Braves	New York Yankees	4-3	Lew Burdette, Mil
1958	New York Yankees	Milwaukee Braves	4-3	Bob Turley, NYY
1959	Los Angeles Dodgers	Chicago White Sox	4-2	Larry Sherry, LA
1960	Pittsburgh Pirates	New York Yankees	4-3	Bobby Richardson, NYY
1961	New York Yankees	Cincinnati Reds	4-1	Whitey Ford, NYY
1962	New York Yankees	San Francisco Giants	4-3	Ralph Terry, NYY
1963	Los Angeles Dodgers	New York Yankees	4-0	Sandy Koufax, LA
1964	St. Louis Cardinals	New York Yankees	4-3	Bob Gibson, StL
1965	Los Angeles Dodgers	Minnesota Twins	4-3	Sandy Koufax, LA
1966	Baltimore Orioles	Los Angeles Dodgers	4-0	Frank Robinson, Bal
1967	St. Louis Cardinals	Boston Red Sox	4-3	Bob Gibson, StL
1968	Detroit Tigers	St. Louis Cardinals	4-3	Mickey Lolich, Det
1969	New York Mets	Baltimore Orioles	4-1	Donn Clendenon, NYM
1970	Baltimore Orioles	Cincinnati Reds	4-1	Brooks Robinson, Bal
1971	Pittsburgh Pirates	Baltimore Orioles	4-3	Roberto Clemente, Pit
1972	Oakland A's	Cincinnati Reds	4-3	Gene Tenace, Oak
1973	Oakland A's	New York Mets	4-3	Reggie Jackson, Oak
1974	Oakland A's	Los Angeles Dodgers	4-1	Rollie Fingers, Oak
1975	Cincinnati Reds	Boston Red Sox	4-3	Pete Rose, Cin
1976	Cincinnati Reds	New York Yankees	4-0	Johnny Bench, Cin
1977	New York Yankees	Los Angeles Dodgers	4-2	Reggie Jackson, NYY
1978	New York Yankees	Los Angeles Dodgers	4-2	Bucky Dent, NYY
1979	Pittsburgh Pirates	Baltimore Orioles	4-3	Willie Stargell, Pit
1980	Philadelphia Phillies	Kansas City Royals	4-2	Mike Schmidt, Phi
1981	Los Angeles Dodgers	New York Yankees	4-2	Guerrero/Cey/Yeager, LA
1982	St. Louis Cardinals	Milwaukee Brewers	4-3	Darrell Porter, StL
1983	Baltimore Orioles	Philadelphia Phillies	4-1	Rick Dempsey, Bal
1984	Detroit Tigers	San Diego Padres	4-1	Alan Trammell, Det
1985	Kansas City Royals	St. Louis Cardinals	4-3	Bret Saberhagen, KC
1986	New York Mets	Boston Red Sox	4-3	Ray Knight, NYM
1987	Minnesota Twins	St. Louis Cardinals	4-3	Frank Viola, Min
1988	Los Angeles Dodgers	Oakland A's	4-1	Orel Hershiser, LA
1989	Oakland A's	San Francisco Giants	4-0	Dave Stewart, Oak
1990	Cincinnati Reds	Oakland A's	4-0	Jose Rijo, Cin
1991	Minnesota Twins	Atlanta Braves	4-3	Jack Morris, Min
1992	Toronto Blue Jays	Atlanta Braves	4-2	Pat Borders, Tor
1993	Toronto Blue Jays	Philadelphia Phillies	4-2	Paul Molitor, Tor
1994	No World Series held; season cancelled Sept. 15, 1994			
1995	Atlanta Braves	Cleveland Indians	4-2	Tom Glavine, Atl
1996	New York Yankees	Atlanta Braves	4-2	John Wetteland, NYY
1997	Florida Marlins	Cleveland Indians	4-3	Livan Hernandez, Fla
1998	New York Yankees	San Diego Padres	4-0	Scott Brosius, NYY
1999	New York Yankees	Atlanta Braves	4-0	Mariano Rivera, NYY
2000	New York Yankees	New York Mets	4-1	Derek Jeter, NYY
2001	Arizona Diamondbacks	New York Yankees	4-3	Schilling/Johnson, Ari
2002	Anaheim Angels	San Francisco Giants	4-3	Troy Glaus, Ana
2003	Florida Marlins	New York Yankees	4-2	Josh Beckett, Fla

Source: *Canadian Press*

a No World Series MVP award existed before 1955.

Cy Young Award Winners, 1964–2003

Player, Club		Player, Club	
1964[1]	Dean Chance, California Angels	**1985** (NL)	Dwight Gooden, New York Mets
1965[1]	Sandy Koufax, Los Angeles Dodgers	(AL)	Bret Saberhagen, Kansas City Royals
1966[1]	Sandy Koufax, Los Angeles Dodgers	**1986** (NL)	Mike Scott, Houston Astros
1967 (NL)	Mike McCormick, San Francisco Giants	(AL)	Roger Clemens, Boston Red Sox
(AL)	Jim Lonborg, Boston Red Sox	**1987** (NL)	Steve Bedrosian, Philadelphia Phillies
1968 (NL)	Bob Gibson, St. Louis Cardinals	(AL)	Roger Clemens, Boston Red Sox
(AL)	Dennis McLain, Detroit Tigers	**1988** (NL)	Orel Hershiser, Los Angeles Dodgers
1969 (NL)	Tom Seaver, New York Mets	(AL)	Frank Viola, Minnesota Twins
(AL)	Dennis McLain, Detroit Tigers	**1989** (NL)	Mark Davis, San Diego Padres
(AL)	Mike Cuellar, Baltimore Orioles	(AL)	Bret Saberhagen, Kansas City Royals
1970 (NL)	Bob Gibson, St. Louis Cardinals	**1990** (NL)	Doug Drabek, Pittsburgh Pirates
(AL)	Jim Perry, Minnesota Twins	(AL)	Bob Welch, Oakland A's
1971 (NL)	Ferguson Jenkins, Chicago Cubs	**1991** (NL)	Tom Glavine, Atlanta Braves
(AL)	Vida Blue, Oakland A's	(AL)	Roger Clemens, Boston Red Sox
1972 (NL)	Steve Carlton, Philadelphia Phillies	**1992** (NL)	Greg Maddux, Chicago Cubs
(AL)	Gaylord Perry, Cleveland Indians	(AL)	Dennis Eckersley, Oakland A's
1973 (NL)	Tom Seaver, New York Mets	**1993** (NL)	Greg Maddux, Atlanta Braves
(AL)	Jim Palmer, Baltimore Orioles	(AL)	Jack McDowell, Chicago White Sox
1974 (NL)	Mike Marshall, Los Angeles Dodgers	**1994** (NL)	Greg Maddux, Atlanta Braves
(AL)	Jim (Catfish) Hunter, Oakland A's	(AL)	David Cone, Kansas City Royals
1975 (NL)	Tom Seaver, New York Mets	**1995** (NL)	Greg Maddux, Atlanta Braves
(AL)	Jim Palmer, Baltimore Orioles	(AL)	Randy Johnson, Seattle Mariner
1976 (NL)	Randy Jones, San Diego Padres	**1996** (NL)	John Smoltz, Atlanta Braves
(AL)	Jim Palmer, Baltimore Orioles	**(AL)**	**Pat Hentgen, Toronto Blue Jays**
1977 (NL)	Steve Carlton, Philadelphia Phillies	**1997 (NL)**	**Pedro Martinez, Montreal Expos**
(AL)	Sparky Lyle, New York Yankees	**(AL)**	**Roger Clemens, Toronto Blue Jays**
1978 (NL)	Gaylord Perry, San Diego Padres	**1998** (NL)	Tom Glavine, Atlanta Braves
(AL)	Ron Guidry, New York Yankees	**(AL)**	**Roger Clemens, Toronto Blue Jays**
1979 (NL)	Bruce Sutter, Chicago Cubs	**1999** (NL)	Randy Johnson, Arizona Diamondbacks
(AL)	Mike Flanagan, Baltimore Orioles	(AL)	Pedro Martinez, Boston Red Sox
1980 (NL)	Steve Carlton, Philadelphia Phillies	**2000** (NL)	Randy Johnson, Arizona Diamondbacks
(AL)	Steve Stone, Baltimore Orioles	(AL)	Pedro Martinez, Boston Red Sox
1981 (NL)	Fernando Valenzuela, Los Angeles Dodgers	**2001** (NL)	Randy Johnson, Arizona Diamondbacks
(AL)	Rollie Fingers, Milwaukee Brewers	(AL)	Roger Clemens, New York Yankees
1982 (NL)	Steve Carlton, Philadelphia Phillies	**2002** (NL)	Randy Johnson, Arizona Diamondbacks
(AL)	Pete Vuckovich, Milwaukee Brewers	(AL)	Barry Zito, Oakland A's
1983 (NL)	John Denny, Philadelphia Phillies	**2003** (NL)	Eric Gagne, Los Angeles Dodgers
(AL)	LaMarr Hoyt, Chicago White Sox	(AL)	Roy Halladay, Toronto Blue Jays
1984 (NL)	Rick Sutcliffe, Chicago Cubs		
(AL)	Willie Hernandez, Detroit Tigers		

Source: *Canadian Press*   (1) One award, 1962–66.

Most Valuable Player, 1963–2003

	National League	American League
1963	Sandy Koufax, Los Angeles Dodgers	Elston Howard, New York Yankees
1964	Ken Boyer, St. Louis Cardinals	Brooks Robinson, Baltimore Orioles
1965	Willie Mays, San Francisco Giants	Zoilo Versalles, Minnesota Twins
1966	Roberto Clemente, Pittsburgh Pirates	Frank Robinson, Baltimore Orioles
1967	Orlando Cepeda, St. Louis Cardinals	Carl Yastrzemski, Boston Red Sox
1968	Bob Gibson, St. Louis Cardinals	Denny McLain, Detroit Tigers
1969	Willie McCovey, San Francisco Giants	Harmon Killebrew, Minnesota Twins
1971	Joe Torre, St. Louis Cardinals	Vida Blue, Oakland Athletics
1972	Johnny Bench, Cincinnati Reds	Dick Allen, Chicago White Sox
1975	Joe Morgan, Cincinnati Reds	Fred Lynn, Boston Red Sox
1976	Joe Morgan, Cincinnati Reds	Thurman Munson, New York Yankees
1979	Keith Hernandez, St. Louis Cardinals; Willie Stargell, Pittsburgh Pirates	Don Baylor, California Angels
1980	Mike Schmidt, Philadelphia Phillies	George Brett, Kansas City Royals
1981	Mike Schmidt, Philadelphia Phillies	Rollie Fingers, Milwaukee Brewers
1982	Dale Murphy, Atlanta Braves	Robin Yount, Milwaukee Brewers
1983	Dale Murphy, Atlanta Braves	Cal Ripken, Jr., Baltimore Orioles
1984	Ryne Sandberg, Chicago Cubs	Willie Hernandez, Detroit Tigers
1985	Willie McGee, St. Louis Cardinals	Don Mattingly, New York Yankees
1986	Mike Schmidt, Philadelphia Phillies	Roger Clemens, Boston Red Sox
1987	André Dawson, Chicago Cubs	**George Bell, Toronto Blue Jays**
1988	Kirk Gibson, Los Angeles Dodgers	Jose Canseco, Oakland Athletics
1989	Kevin Mitchell, San Francisco Giants	Robin Yount, Milwaukee Brewers
1990	Barry Bonds, Pittsburgh Pirates	Rickey Henderson, Oakland Athletics
1991	Terry Pendleton, Atlanta Braves	Cal Ripken, Jr., Baltimore Orioles
1992	Barry Bonds, Pittsburgh Pirates	Dennis Eckersley, Oakland A's
1993	Barry Bonds, San Francisco Giants	Frank Thomas, Chicago White Sox
1994	Jeff Bagwell, Houston Astros	Frank Thomas, Chicago White Sox
1995	Barry Larkin, Cincinnati Reds	Mo Vaughn, Boston Red Sox
1996	Ken Caminiti, San Diego Padres	Juan Gonzalez, Texas Rangers
1997	Larry Walker, Colorado Rockies	Ken Griffey Jr., Seattle Mariners
1998	Sammy Sosa, Chicago Cubs	Juan Gonzalez, Texas Rangers
1999	Chipper Jones, Atlanta Braves	Ivan Rodriguez, Texas Rangers
2000	Jeff Kent, San Francisco Giants	Jason Giambi, Oakland A's
2001	Barry Bonds, San Francisco Giants	Ichiro Suzuki, Seattle Mariners
2002	Barry Bonds, San Francisco Giants	Miguel Tejada, Oakland A's
2003	Barry Bonds, San Francisco Giants	Alex Rodriguez, Texas Rangers

Source: *Baseball Almanac*

A Banner Cy Young Year for Canada

*T*he Cy Young award is given to the most outstanding pitcher in each league. In 2003, the Cy Young award had a distinct Canadian flavour in both the National and American Leagues. Montreal native Eric Gagne earned the National League Cy Young award with 28 of 32 first-place votes following a record-breaking year as the Los Angeles Dodgers' closer. Gagne tied the National League record with 55 saves during the season, midway through converting a record-shattering 84 consecutive save changes over three seasons. Gagne is the ninth relief pitcher to win the award. Toronto Blue Jays ace Roy Halladay also dominated Cy Young voting in the American League, taking 26 of 28 first-place votes on the way to earning the American League Cy Young award. Halladay led all American League pitchers in wins, innings pitched, shutouts, and complete games, and rung up 204 strikeouts on the way to a 22–7 record. Halladay is the third Blue Jays pitcher to win the award; Roger Clemens was a two-time winner while with the Blue Jays, and Pat Hentgen won it once. **Source:** *Major League Baseball*

Batting Champions, 1964–2004

	National League				American League	
	Player, Club	**%**			**Player, Club**	**%**
1964	Roberto Clemente, Pittsburgh	.339		**1964**	Tony Oliva, Minnesota	.323
1965	Roberto Clemente, Pittsburgh	.329		**1965**	Tony Oliva, Minnesota	.321
1966	Matty Alou, Pittsburgh	.342		**1966**	Frank Robinson, Baltimore	.316
1967	Roberto Clemente, Pittsburgh	.357		**1967**	Carl Yastrzemski, Boston	.326
1968	Pete Rose, Cincinnati	.335		**1968**	Carl Yastrzemski, Boston	.301
1969	Pete Rose, Cincinnati	.348		**1969**	Rod Carew, Minnesota	.332
1970	Rico Carty, Atlanta	.366		**1970**	Alex Johnson, California	.329
1971	Joe Torre, St. Louis	.363		**1971**	Tony Oliva, Minnesota	.337
1972	Billy Williams, Chicago	.333		**1972**	Rod Carew, Minnesota	.318
1973	Pete Rose, Cincinnati	.338		**1973**	Rod Carew, Minnesota	.350
1974	Ralph Garr, Atlanta	.353		**1974**	Rod Carew, Minnesota	.364
1975	Bill Madlock, Chicago	.354		**1975**	Rod Carew, Minnesota	.359
1976	Bill Madlock, Chicago	.339		**1976**	George Brett, Kansas City	.333
1977	Dave Parker, Pittsburgh	.338		**1977**	Rod Carew, Minnesota	.388
1978	Dave Parker, Pittsburgh	.334		**1978**	Rod Carew, Minnesota	.333
1979	Keith Hernandez, St. Louis	.344		**1979**	Fred Lynn, Boston	.333
1980	Bill Buckner, Chicago	.324		**1980**	George Brett, Kansas City	.390
1981	Bill Madlock, Pittsburgh[1]	.341		**1981**	Carney Lansford, Boston	.336
1982	**Al Oliver, Montreal**	**.331**		**1982**	Willie Wilson, Kansas City	.332
1983	Bill Madlock, Pittsburgh	.323		**1983**	Wade Boggs, Boston	.361
1984	Tony Gwynn, San Diego	.351		**1984**	Don Mattingly, New York	.343
1985	Willie McGee, St. Louis	.353		**1985**	Wade Boggs, Boston	.368
1986	**Tim Raines, Montreal**	**.334**		**1986**	Wade Boggs, Boston	.357
1987	Tony Gwynn, San Diego	.370		**1987**	Wade Boggs, Boston	.363
1988	Tony Gwynn, San Diego	.313		**1988**	Wade Boggs, Boston	.366
1989	Tony Gwynn, San Diego	.336		**1989**	Kirby Puckett, Minnesota	.339
1990	Willie McGee, St. Louis	.335		**1990**	George Brett, Kansas City	.329
1991	Terry Pendleton, Atlanta	.319		**1991**	Julio Franco, Texas	.341
1992	Gary Sheffield, San Diego	.330		**1992**	Edgar Martinez, Seattle	.343
1993	Andres Galarraga, Colorado	.370		**1993**	**John Olerud, Toronto**	**.363**
1994	Tony Gwynn, San Diego[1]	.394		**1994**	Paul O'Neill, New York[1]	.359
1995	Tony Gwynn, San Diego	.368		**1995**	Edgar Martinez, Seattle	.356
1996	Tony Gwynn, San Diego	.353		**1996**	Alex Rodriguez, Seattle	.358
1997	Tony Gwynn, San Diego	.372		**1997**	Frank Thomas, Chicago	.347
1998	Larry Walker, Colorado	.363		**1998**	Bernie Williams, New York	.339
1999	Larry Walker, Colorado	.379		**1999**	Nomar Garciaparra, Boston	**.357**
2000	Todd Helton, Colorado	.372		**2000**	Nomar Garciaparra, Boston	.372
2001	Larry Walker, Colorado	.350		**2001**	Ichiro Suzuki, Seattle	.350
2002	Barry Bonds, San Francisco	.370		**2002**	Manny Ramirez, Boston	.349
2003	Albert Pujols, St. Louis	.359		**2003**	Bill Mueller, Boston	.326
2004	Barry Bonds, San Francisco	.362		**2004**	Ichiro Suzuki, Seattle	.372

Source: *Canadian Press*

(1) Strike abbreviated season.

Home Run Seasons

HR	Player, Team	Year	HR	Player, Team	Year	HR	Player, Team	Year
73	Barry Bonds, SF	2001	57	Alex Rodriguez,	2002	52	Mark McGwire, Oak	1996
70	Mark McGwire, StL	1998	57	Luis Gonzalez, Ari	2001	52	Alex Rodriguez, Tex	2001
66	Sammy Sosa, Chi Cubs	1998	56	Hack Wilson, Chi Cubs	1930	51	Ralph Kiner, Pit	1947
65	Mark McGwire, StL	1999	56	Ken Griffey Jr., Sea	1998	51	Johnny Mize,	
64	Sammy Sosa, Chi Cubs	2001	56	Ken Griffey Jr., Sea	1997		NY Giants	1947
63	Sammy Sosa, Chi Cubs	1999	54	Babe Ruth, NYY	1920	51	Willie Mays, NY Giants	1955
61	Roger Maris, NYY	1961	54	Babe Ruth, NYY	1928	51	Cecil Fielder, Det	1990
60	Babe Ruth, NYY	1927	54	Ralph Kiner, Pit	1949	50	Jimmie Foxx, Bos	1938
59	Babe Ruth, NYY	1921	54	Mickey Mantle, NYY	1961	50	Albert Belle, Cle	1995
58	Jimmie Foxx, Phi Athletics	1932	52	Mickey Mantle, NYY	1956	50	Brady Anderson, Bal	1996
58	Hank Greenberg, Det	1938	52	Willie Mays, SF	1965	50	Greg Vaughn, SD	1998
58	Mark McGwire, Oak/ StL	1997	52	George Foster, Cin	1977			

Source: *Canadian Press*

Individual Earned Run Average Leaders, 1963–2004

National League			American League		
Player, Team		ERA	Player, Team		ERA
1963	Sandy Koufax, LA	1.88	1963	Gary Peters, Chi	2.33
1964	Sandy Koufax, LA	1.74	1964	Dean Chance, LA	1.65
1965	Sandy Koufax, LA	2.04	1965	Sam McDowell, Cle	2.18
1966	Sandy Koufax, LA	1.73	1966	Gary Peters, Chi	1.98
1967	Phil Niekro, Atl	1.87	1967	Joel Horlen, Chi	2.06
1968	Bob Gibson, StL	1.12	1968	Luis Tiant, Cle	1.60
1969	Juan Marichal, SF	2.10	1969	Dick Bosman, Wash	2.19
1970	Tom Seaver, NY	2.81	1970	Diego Segui, Oak	2.56
1971	Tom Seaver, NY	1.76	1971	Vida Blue, Oak	1.82
1972	Steve Carlton, Pha	1.97	1972	Luis Tiant, Bos	1.91
1973	Tom Seaver, NY	2.08	1973	Jim Palmer, Bal	2.40
1974	Buzz Capra, Atl	2.28	1974	Catfish Hunter, Oak	2.49
1975	Randy Jones, SD	2.24	1975	Jim Palmer, Bal	2.09
1976	John Denny, StL	2.52	1976	Mark Fidrych, Det	2.34
1977	John Candelaria, Pgh	2.34	1977	Frank Tanana, Cal	2.54
1978	Craig Swan, NY	2.43	1978	Ron Guidry, NY	1.74
1979	J.R. Richard, Hou	2.71	1979	Ron Guidry, NY	2.78
1980	Don Sutton, LA	2.21	1980	Rudy May, NY	2.47
1981	Nolan Ryan, Hou	1.69[1]	1981	Steve McCatty, Oak	2.32[1]
1982	Steve Rogers, Mtl	2.40	1982	Rick Sutcliffe, Cle	2.96
1983	Atlee Hammaker, SF	2.25	1983	Rick Honeycutt, Tex	2.42
1984	Alejandro Pena, LA	2.48	1984	Mike Boddicker, Bal	2.79
1985	Dwight Gooden, NY	1.53	1985	Dave Stieb, Tor	2.48
1986	Mike Scott, Hou	2.22	1986	Roger Clemens, Bos	2.48
1987	Nolan Ryan, Hou	2.76	1987	Jimmy Key, Tor	2.76
1988	Joe Magrane, StL	2.18	1988	Allan Anderson, Min	2.45
1989	Scott Garrelts, SF	2.28	1989	Bret Saberhagen, KC	2.16
1990	Danny Darwin, Hou	2.21	1990	Roger Clemens, Bos	1.93
1991	Dennis Martinez, Mtl	2.39	1991	Roger Clemens, Bos	2.62
1992	Bill Swift, SF	2.08	1992	Roger Clemens, Bos	2.41
1993	Greg Maddux, Atl	2.36	1993	Kevin Appier, KC	2.56
1994	Greg Maddux, Atl	1.56[1]	1994	Steve Ontiveras, Oak	2.65[1]
1995	Greg Maddux, Atl	1.63	1995	Randy Johnson, Sea	2.48
1996	Kevin Brown, Fla	1.89	1996	Juan Guzman, Tor	2.93
1997	Pedro Martinez, Mtl	1.90	1997	Roger Clemens, Tor	2.05
1998	Greg Maddux, Atl	2.22	1998	Roger Clemens, Tor	2.65
1999	Randy Johnson, Ari	2.48	1999	Pedro Martinez, Bos	2.07
2000	Kevin Brown, LA	2.58	2000	Pedro Martinez, Bos	1.74
2001	Randy Johnson, Ari	2.49	2001	Freddy Garcia, Sea	3.05
2002	Randy Johnson, Ari	2.32	2002	Pedro Martinez, Bos	2.26
2003	Jason Schmidt, SF	2.34	2003	Pedro Martinez, Bos	2.22
2004	Jake Peavy, SD	2.27	2004	Johan Santana, Min	2.61

(1) Strike abbreviated season.

Directory of Selected Baseball Organizations in Canada

Canadian Federation of Amateur Baseball	*Major League Baseball*	*Montreal Expos Baseball Club*	*Toronto Blue Jays*
2212 Gladwin Crescent, Suite A7 Ottawa, ON K1B 5N1 Tel: (613) 748-5606 Fax: (613) 748-5767 www.baseball.ca	350 Park Ave. New York, NY 10022 Tel: (212) 339-7800 www.mlb.com	P.O. Box 500, Station M Montreal, QC H1V 3P2 Tel: (514) 253-3434 Fax: (514) 253-8282 www.montrealexpos.com	The Skydome 300 The Esplanade West, Suite 3200 Toronto, ON M5V 3B3 Tel: (416) 341-1000 www.bluejays.ca

Canadian Players in Major League Baseball, 2004

Player	TEAM	POS	G	AB	R	H	2B	3B	HR	RBI	TB	BB	SO	SB	CS	OBP	SLG	AVG
Larry Walker	StL/COL	OF	82	258	51	77	16	4	17	47	152	49	57	6	0	.424	.589	.298
Jason Bay	PIT	OF	120	411	61	116	24	4	26	82	226	41	129	4	6	.358	.550	.282
Justin Morneau	MIN	1B	74	280	39	76	17	0	19	58	150	28	54	0	0	.340	.536	.271
Matt Stairs	KC	OF	126	439	48	117	21	3	18	66	198	49	92	1	0	.345	.451	.267
Corey Koskie	MIN	3B	118	422	68	106	24	2	25	71	209	49	103	9	3	.342	.495	.251
Cody McKay	StL	C	35	74	7	17	2	0	0	6	19	2	14	0	0	.269	.257	.230
Simon Pond	TOR	OF	16	49	4	8	2	0	1	6	13	5	12	0	0	.250	.265	.163
Aaron Guiel	KC	OF	42	135	15	21	4	0	5	13	40	17	42	1	1	.263	.296	.156

POS = position; G = games played; AB = at bats; R = runs; H = hits; 2B = doubles; 3B = triples; HR = home runs; RBI = runs batted in; TB = total bases; BB = walks; SO = strikeouts; SB = stolen bases; CS = caught stealing; OBP = on-base percentage; SLG = slugging percentage; AVG = batting average

Pitcher	TEAM	W	L	ERA	G	GS	CG	SHO	SV	SVO	IP	H	R	ER	HR	BB	SO
Jesse Crain	MIN	3	0	2.00	22	0	0	0	0	1	27.0	17	6	6	2	12	14
Eric Gagne	LA	7	3	2.19	70	0	0	0	45	47	82.1	53	24	20	5	22	114
Rheal Cormier	PHI	4	5	3.56	84	0	0	0	0	7	81.0	70	32	32	7	26	46
Ryan Dempster	CHC	1	1	3.92	23	0	0	0	2	2	20.2	16	9	9	1	13	18
Rich Harden	OAK	11	7	3.99	31	31	0	0	0	0	189.2	171	90	84	16	81	167
Chris Reitsma	ATL	6	4	4.07	84	0	0	0	2	9	79.2	89	38	36	9	20	60
Erik Bedard	BAL	6	10	4.59	27	26	0	0	0	0	137.1	149	83	70	13	71	121
Paul Quantrill	NYY	7	3	4.72	86	0	0	0	1	5	95.1	124	54	50	5	20	37
Jeff Francis	COL	3	2	5.15	7	7	0	0	0	0	36.2	42	22	21	8	13	32
Aaron Myette	CIN	0	0	8.31	5	0	0	0	0	0	4.1	3	4	4	0	8	6
Shawn Hill	MON	1	2	16.00	3	3	0	0	0	0	9.0	17	16	16	1	7	10

W = wins; L = losses; ERA = earned run average; G = games played; GS = games started; CG = complete games; SHO = shutouts; SV = saves; SVO = save opportunities; IP = innings pitched; H = hits; R = runs; ER = earned runs; HR = home runs allowed; BB = walks; SO = strikeouts

Source: *Major League Baseball; SLAM! Sports*

Career Records of Some Canadian Major League Players of the Past

Player	Years	G	AB	R	H	HR	RBI	AVG	OBP	SLG	BB	SO	SB	CS
Tip O'Neill	1922-23	1054	4255	880	1386	52	757	.326	.392	.458	421	146	161	—
Pop Smith	1880-91	1110	4230	642	939	24	358	.300	.287	.313	325	345	169	—
Doc Mille	1910-14	557	1717	184	507	12	235	.295	.343	.390	121	149	64	—
Jeff Heath	1936-49	1383	4937	777	1447	194	887	.293	.370	.509	593	670	56	47
Goody Rosen	1937-46	551	1916	310	557	22	197	.291	.364	.398	218	166	12	—
George Selkirk	1934-42	846	2790	503	810	108	576	.290	.400	.483	486	319	49	32
Terry Puhl	1977-91	1531	4855	676	1361	62	435	.280	.349	.388	505	507	217	99
Bill Phillips	1879-88	1038	4255	562	1130	17	534	.266	.299	.374	178	215	39	—

Pitcher	Years	W	L	IP	ERA	G	GS	CG	SV	H	ER	BB	SO
Fergie Jenkins	1965-83	284	226	4500.2	3.34	664	594	267	7	4142	1669	997	3192
Kirk McCaskill	1985-96	106	108	1729.0	4.12	380	242	30	7	1748	791	665	1003
Reggie Cleveland	1969-81	105	106	1809.0	4.02	428	203	57	25	1843	807	543	930
John Hiller	1965-80	87	76	1242.0	2.83	545	43	13	125	1040	391	535	1036
Phil Marchildon[1]	1940-50	68	75	1214.1	3.93	185	162	82	2	1084	530	684	481
Dick Fowler	1941-52	66	79	1303.0	4.11	221	170	75	4	1367	595	578	382
Claude Raymond	1959-71	46	53	721.0	3.66	449	7	2	83	711	293	225	497
Ron Taylor	1962-72	45	43	800.0	3.93	491	17	3	72	794	349	209	464

G=games played; AB=at bats; R=runs; H=hits; HR=home runs; RBI=runs batted in; AVG=batting average; OBP=on-base percentage; SLG=slugging percentage; BB=walks; SO=strikeouts; SB=stolen bases; CS=caught stealing

W=wins; L=losses; IP=innings pitched; ERA=earned run average; G=games pitched; GS=games started; CG=complete games; SV=saves; H=hits; ER=earned runs; BB=walks; SO=strikeouts

Source: *Sportspic.com*

Montreal Expos Year-By-Year Record, 1969–2004

	Won	Lost	%	Pos.	Home Attendance	Manager		Won	Lost	%	Pos.	Home Attendance	Manager
1969...	52	110	.321	6th	1 212 608	Gene Mauch	**1987**...	91	71	.562	3rd	1 850 324	Buck Rodgers
1970...	73	89	.451	6th	1 424 683	Gene Mauch	**1988**...	81	81	.500	3rd	1 478 659	Buck Rodgers
1971...	71	90	.441	5th	1 290 963	Gene Mauch	**1989**...	81	81	.500	4th	1 783 533	Buck Rodgers
1972...	70	86	.449	5th	1 142 145	Gene Mauch	**1990**...	85	77	.525	3rd	1 421 388	Buck Rodgers
1973...	79	83	.488	4th	1 246 863	Gene Mauch	**1991**...	70	91	.441	6th	978 045	B. Rodgers/
1974...	79	82	.491	4th	1 019 134	Gene Mauch							T. Runnells
1975...	75	87	.463	5th	908 292	Gene Mauch	**1992**...	87	75	.537	2nd	1 731 566	T. Runnells/
1976...	55	107	.340	6th	646 704	K. Kuehl/C. Fox							F. Alou
1977...	75	87	.463	5th	1 433 757	Dick Williams	**1993**...	94	68	.580	2nd	1 641 437	Felipe Alou
1978...	76	86	.469	4th	1 427 007	Dick Williams	**1994**...	74	40	.649	1st(a)	1 276 250	Felipe Alou
1979...	95	65	.594	2nd	2 102 173	Dick Williams	**1995**...	66	78	.458	5th	1 309 618	Felipe Alou
1980...	90	72	.556	2nd	2 208 175	Dick Williams	**1996**...	88	74	.543	2nd	1 618 573	Felipe Alou
1981...	60	48	.556	—	1 534 564	D. Williams/	**1997**...	78	84	.481	4th	1 175 000	Felipe Alou
						J.Fanning	**1998**...	65	97	.401	4th	914 909	Felipe Alou
1982...	86	76	.531	3rd	2 318 292	Jim Fanning	**1999**...	68	94	.420	4th	773 277	Felipe Alou
1983...	82	80	.506	3rd	2 320 651	Bill Virdon	**2000**...	67	95	.414	4th	926 427	Felipe Alou
1984...	78	83	.484	5th	1 606 531	B. Virdon/	**2001**...	68	94	.420	5th	642 745	F. Alou/J. Torborg
						J. Fanning	**2002**...	83	79	.512	2nd	749 104	Frank Robinson
1985...	84	77	.522	3rd	1 502 494	Buck Rodgers	**2003**...	83	79	.512	4th	1 025 640	Frank Robinson
1986...	78	83	.484	4th	1 128 981	Buck Rodgers	**2004**...	67	95	.414	5th	749 550	Frank Robinson

Source: *Canadian Press*   (a) Eastern Division: first year with three divisions.

Montreal Expos Individual Statistics, 2004

Batting

Player	POS	G	AB	R	H	2B	3B	HR	RBI	TB	BB	SO	SB	CS	OBP	SLG	AVG
J Rivera.........	OF	134	391	48	120	24	1	12	49	182	34	45	6	2	.364	.465	.307
J Vidro..........	2B	110	412	51	121	24	0	14	60	187	49	43	3	1	.367	.454	.294
J Carroll	2B	102	218	36	63	14	2	0	16	81	32	21	5	1	.378	.372	.289
E Chavez........	OF	132	502	65	139	20	6	5	34	186	30	40	32	7	.318	.371	.277
H Mateo	2B	40	44	3	12	2	0	0	0	14	1	9	2	3	.289	.318	.273
T Sledge	OF	133	398	45	107	20	6	15	62	184	40	66	3	3	.336	.462	.269
B Schneider	C	135	436	40	112	20	3	12	49	174	42	63	0	1	.325	.399	.257
B Wilkerson	1B	160	572	112	146	39	2	32	67	285	106	152	13	6	.374	.498	.255
C Everett........	OF	39	127	8	32	10	0	2	14	48	8	19	0	0	.319	.378	.252
N Johnson	1B	73	251	35	63	16	0	7	33	100	40	58	6	3	.359	.398	.251
L Hernandez......	P	34	81	2	20	7	0	1	10	30	1	8	0	0	.256	.370	.247
O Cabrera	SS	103	390	41	96	19	2	4	31	131	28	31	12	3	.298	.336	.246
T Batista	3B	157	606	76	146	30	2	32	110	276	26	78	14	6	.272	.455	.241
E Diaz............	C	55	139	9	31	6	1	1	11	42	11	10	2	0	.293	.302	.223
M Cepicky........	OF	32	60	4	13	4	0	1	3	20	1	18	1	0	.230	.333	.217
P Bergeron	OF	11	42	2	9	0	0	0	1	9	2	16	0	1	.250	.214	.214
S Kim	P	41	28	1	6	2	0	0	5	8	0	9	1	0	.214	.286	.214
M Izturis........	SS	32	107	10	22	5	2	1	4	34	10	20	4	0	.286	.318	.206
V Pascucci	OF	32	62	6	11	1	0	2	6	18	10	22	1	0	.297	.290	.177
R Church.......	OF	30	63	6	11	1	0	1	6	15	7	16	0	0	.257	.238	.175
B Harris..........	2B	23	59	4	10	3	0	1	3	16	3	12	0	0	.222	.271	.169
R Calloway	OF	46	84	4	14	2	0	1	10	19	5	22	2	0	.211	.226	.167
L Lopez..........	1B	11	26	0	4	0	0	0	0	4	0	9	0	0	.185	.154	.154
A Fox	SS	34	43	2	4	0	0	1	1	7	0	16	0	0	.093	.163	.093

POS = position; G = games played; AB = at bats; R = runs; H = hits; 2B = doubles; 3B = triples; HR = home runs; RBI = runs batted in; TB = total bases; BB = walks; SO = strikeouts; SB = stolen bases; CS = caught stealing; OBP = on-base percentage; SLG = slugging percentage; AVG = batting average

Source: *Major League Baseball*

Pitching

Player	W	L	ERA	G	GS	CG	SHO	SV	SVO	IP	H	R	ER	HR	HBP	BB	SO
J Rauch	3	0	1.54	9	2	0	0	0	0	23.1	14	4	4	1	0	7	18
L Ayala	6	12	2.69	81	0	0	0	2	7	90.1	92	30	27	6	5	15	63
C Cordero	7	3	2.94	69	0	0	0	14	18	82.2	68	28	27	8	1	43	83
J Horgan	4	1	3.15	47	0	0	0	2	3	40.0	35	18	14	5	3	22	30
T Ohka	3	7	3.40	15	15	0	0	0	0	84.2	98	40	32	11	1	20	38
L Hernandez	11	15	3.60	35	35	9	2	0	0	255.0	234	105	102	26	10	83	186
T Tucker	4	2	3.72	54	1	0	0	0	2	67.2	73	28	28	5	4	17	44
G Majewski	0	1	3.86	16	0	0	0	1	2	21.0	28	15	9	2	2	5	12
Z Day	5	10	3.93	19	19	1	1	0	0	116.2	117	53	51	13	4	45	61
J Eischen	0	1	3.93	21	0	0	0	0	1	18.1	16	10	8	2	1	8	17
S Kim	4	6	4.58	43	17	0	0	0	0	135.2	145	80	69	17	13	55	87
T Armas	2	4	4.88	16	16	0	0	0	0	72.0	66	41	39	13	4	45	54
J Patterson	4	7	5.03	19	19	0	0	0	0	98.1	100	58	55	18	8	46	99
S Downs	3	6	5.14	12	12	1	1	0	0	63.0	79	47	36	9	3	23	38
C Vargas	5	5	5.25	45	14	0	0	0	0	118.1	120	75	69	26	7	64	89
J Fikac	1	2	5.40	19	0	0	0	0	0	25.0	26	16	15	5	0	13	22
F Beltran	2	2	5.47	45	0	0	0	1	1	49.1	47	31	30	11	2	27	48
C Bentz	0	3	5.86	36	0	0	0	0	0	27.2	23	19	18	5	2	23	18
R Corcoran	0	0	6.75	5	0	0	0	0	0	5.1	7	4	4	0	0	5	4
R Biddle	4	8	6.92	47	9	0	0	11	15	78.0	98	69	60	15	8	31	51
R Beltran	0	0	13.50	2	0	0	0	0	0	0.2	1	1	1	0	0	0	0
S Hill	1	2	16.00	3	3	0	0	0	0	9.0	17	16	16	1	1	7	10

W = wins; L = losses; ERA = earned run average; G = games played; GS = games started; CG = complete games; SHO = shutouts; SV = saves; SVO = save opportunities; IP = innings pitched; H = hits; R = runs; ER = earned runs; HR = home runs allowed; HBP = hit by pitch; BB = walks; SO = strikeouts

Source: *Major League Baseball*

Montreal Expos Team Records, through 2004 Season

Batting

Single Season

Batting Average: Vladimir Guerrero, 2000, .345
At Bats: Warren Cromartie, 1979, 659
Games: Rusty Staub, 1971, 162; Ken Singleton, 1973, 162; Warren Cromartie, 1980, 162; Orlando Cabrera, 2001, 2003, 162
Hits: Vladimir Guerrero, 2002, 206
Runs: Tim Raines, 1983, 133
Singles: Tim Raines, 1986, 140
Doubles: Mark Grudzielanek, 1997, 54
Triples: Rodney Scott, 1980, 13; Tim Raines, 1985, 13; Mitch Webster, 1986, 13
Home Runs: Vladimir Guerrero, 2000, 44
Runs Batted In: Vladimir Guerrero, 1999, 131
Total Bases: Vladimir Guerrero, 2000, 379
Slugging Percentage: Vladimir Guerrero, 2000, .664
On-Base Percentage: Tim Raines, 1987, .431
Stolen Bases: Ron LeFlore, 1980, 97
Strikeouts: Andres Galarraga, 1990, 169
Walks: Ken Singleton, 1973, 123

Career Leaders

Batting average: .323, Vladimir Guerrero
At Bats: Tim Wallach, 6 529
Games: Tim Wallach, 1 767
Hits: Tim Wallach, 1 694
Runs: Tim Raines, 947
Singles: Tim Raines, 1,148
Doubles: Tim Wallach, 360
Triples: Tim Raines, 82
Home Runs: Vladimir Guerrero, 234
Runs Batted In: Tim Wallach, 905
Total Bases: Tim Wallach, 2,728
Slugging Percentage: V. Guerrero, .588
On-Base Percentage: Rusty Staub, .402
Stolen Bases: Tim Raines, 635
Strikeouts: Tim Wallach, 1,009
Walks: Tim Raines, 793

Pitching

Single Season

Games: Mike Marshall, 1973, 92
Games Started: Steve Rogers, 1977, 40
Complete Games: Bill Stoneman, 1971, 20
Innings Pitched: Steve Rogers, 1977, 302
Wins: Ross Grimsley, 1978, 20
Losses: Steve Rogers, 1974, 22
Saves: John Wetteland, 1993, 43
Earned Run Average: Ugueth Urbina, 1998, 1.30
Strikeouts: Pedro Martinez, 1997, 305

Career Leaders

Games: Tim Burke, 425
Games Started: Steve Rogers, 393
Complete Games: Steve Rogers, 129
Innings Pitched: Steve Rogers, 2 838
Wins: Steve Rogers, 158
Losses: Steve Rogers, 152
Saves: Jeff Reardon, 152
Earned Run Average: Tim Burke, 2.61
Strikeouts: Steve Rogers, 1,621

Source: *Major League Baseball*

Montreal Expos Player of the Year, 1969–2003

1969	Rusty Staub	1978	Ross Grimsley	1986	Tim Raines	1995	David Segui
1970	Carl Morton	1979	Larry Parrish	1987	Tim Wallach	1996	Hank Rodriguez
1971	Ron Hunt	1980	Gary Carter	1988	Andres Galarraga	1997	Pedro Martinez
1972	Mike Marshall	1981	Andre Dawson	1989	Tim Wallach	1998	Vladimir Guerrero
1973	Mike Marshall	1982	Al Oliver	1990	Tim Wallach	1999	Vladimir Guerrero
1974	Willie Davis	1983	Andre Dawson;	1991	Dennis Martinez	2000	Vladimir Guerrero
1975	Gary Carter		Tim Raines (tie)	1992	Larry Walker	2001	Orlando Cabrera
1976	Woodie Fryman	1984	Gary Carter	1993	Marquis Grissom	2002	Vladimir Guerrero
1977	Gary Carter	1985	Tim Raines	1994	Moises Alou	2003	Orlando Cabrera

Expo Uncertain Future Finally (Seems to Be) Certain

*M*ajor League Baseball (MLB) Commissioner Bud Selig announced on September 29, 2004, the move of the Montreal Expos to Washington, D.C. After years of threats, MLB finally made it official that the Expos franchise would no longer be based in Montreal where it had played since entering the league in 1969. The team will begin play in the U.S. capital city in 2005. During its 35-year history, the Expos very early captured the hearts of baseball fans in Quebec and throughout Canada, and the team started to challenge for postseason play first in 1973 and then more regularly by the end of the 1970s. However, the team's only playoff experience came in 1981, when the Los Angeles Dodgers defeated the Expos in the National League Championship Series to advance to the World Series. Ironically, the Expos' best season record came in 1994, the season that was interrupted by a player strike. The Expos had the best overall record in the major leagues, but the strike forced the cancellation of the season and the playoffs that year. Franchise uncertainty began after original Expos owner Charles Bronfman sold control of the team in 1991. Two more owners held control of the franchise until MLB assumed control in 2002, setting the final stage for the team's departure.

Key Dates in Montreal Expos History

May 27, 1968: Major League Baseball (MLB) awards an expansion franchise to a group headed by Charles Bronfman. The team will begin play as the Montreal Expos in 1969.

April 8, 1969: The Expos win the franchise's first major league game over the New York Mets, 11-10, at Shea Stadium in New York.

April 14, 1969: The Expos play their first home game, at Jarry Park, and defeat the St. Louis Cardinals, 8-7.

April 17, 1969: Right-hander Bill Stoneman tosses the franchise's first-ever no-hitter, against the Philadelphia Phillies. It would be the first of four no-hitters in franchise history.

April 15, 1977: The Expos play their first home game at Olympic Stadium, losing to the Phillies, 7-2.

September 30, 1979: The Expos complete their first winning season, with a record of 95 wins and 65 losses, good for second place behind the Pittsburgh Pirates in the NL East.

October 3, 1981: In the strike-shortened 1981 season, the Expos win the second-half NL East title by defeating the Mets, 5-4, at Shea Stadium. The Expos advance to the National League Division Series against NL East first-half winner Philadelphia.

October 11, 1981: The Expos defeat the Phillies, 3 games to 2, to advance to the National League Championship Series against the Los Angeles Dodgers.

October 19, 1981: The Expos fall to the Dodgers in the fifth and deciding game of the National League Championship Series. The Dodgers advance to the World Series.

July 13, 1982: The All-Star Game is played at Olympic Stadium, with four Expos in the National League's starting lineup.

June 14, 1991: A group of businessmen led by Expos team president Claude Brochu purchase the franchise from original owner Charles Bronfman.

July 28, 1991: Dennis Martinez pitches the franchise's only perfect game against the Dodgers in Los Angeles.

May 22, 1992: Felipe Alou begins a nine-year tenure as manager of the Expos. When he leaves the team in 2001, Alou is the winningest manager in team history.

August 12, 1994: MLB players go on strike. When the season and subsequent playoffs are later cancelled, the Expos are left with a valueless record of 74 wins and 40 losses, the best record in baseball that year.

December 9, 1999: Jeffery Loria becomes the Expos' new owner.

February 12, 2002: Major League Baseball assumes control of the team.

April 11, 2003: The Expos play the first of 44 home games to be played in San Juan, Puerto Rico, during the 2003 and 2004 seasons.

July 27, 2003: Former Expos catcher Gary Carter becomes the first player to be inducted into the Baseball Hall of Fame with an Expos cap on the player's plaque.

September 30, 2004: MLB Commissioner Bud Selig announces the Expos will relocate to Washington, D.C., beginning with the 2005 season. On this same day, over 31,000 fans witness the Expos final home game in Montreal at Olympic Stadium, and the team loses to the Florida Marlins, 9-1.

October 3, 2004: The franchise plays its final game as the Montreal Expos, losing to the Mets, 8-1, in the same place where it all began 35 years before, New York's Shea Stadium.

Source: *Major League Baseball*

Toronto Blue Jays Year-By-Year Record, 1977–2004

	Won	Lost	%	Pos.	Home Attendance	Manager		Won	Lost	%	Pos.	Home Attendance	Manager
1977	54	107	.335	7th	1 701 052	Roy Hartsfield	**1989**	89	73	.549	1st	3 375 573	Williams/Gaston
1978	59	102	.366	7th	1 562 585	Roy Hartsfield	**1990**	86	76	.531	2nd	3 885 284	Cito Gaston
1979	53	109	.327	7th	1 431 651	Roy Hartsfield	**1991**	91	71	.562	1st	4 001 526	Cito Gaston
1980	67	95	.414	7th	1 400 327	Bob Mattick	**1992**	96	66	.593	1st	4 028 318	Cito Gaston
1981	37	69	.349	—	755 083	Bob Mattick	**1993**	95	67	.586	1st	4 057 947	Cito Gaston
1st half ..	16	42	.276	7th	—		**1994**	55	60	.476	3rd[2]	2 907 933	Cito Gaston
2nd half	21	27	.438	7th	—		**1995**	56	88	.389	5th	2 826 483	Cito Gaston
1982	78	84	.481	6th[1]	1 275 978	Bobby Cox	**1996**	74	88	.457	4th	2 559 563	Cito Gaston
1983	89	73	.549	4th	1 930 415	Bobby Cox	**1997**	76	86	.469	5th	2 589 297	Cito Gaston[3]
1984	89	73	.549	2nd	2 110 009	Bobby Cox	**1998**	88	74	.543	3rd	2 454 303	Tim Johnson
1985	99	62	.615	1st	2 468 925	Bobby Cox	**1999**	84	78	.518	3rd	2 163 473	Jim Fregosi
1986	86	76	.531	4th	2 455 477	Jimy Williams	**2000**	83	78	.516	3rd	1 819 886	Jim Fregosi
1987	96	66	.593	2nd	2 778 459	Jimy Williams	**2001**	80	82	.494	3rd	1 915 438	Buck Martinez
1988	87	75	.537	3rd	2 595 175	Jimy Williams	**2002**	78	84	.481	3rd	1 637 900	Martinez/Tosca
							2003	86	76	.531	3rd	1 799 458	Carlos Tosca
							2004	67	94	.416	5th	1 900 041	Tosca/Gibbons

(1) Tied. (2) Eastern Division: first year with three divisions (3) Gaston was fired with five games remaining in the 1997 season.

Source: *Canadian Press*

Toronto Blue Jays Individual Statistics, 2004

Batting

Player	POS	G	AB	R	H	2B	3B	HR	RBI	TB	BB	SO	SB	CS	OBP	SLG	AVG
R Adams	SS	22	72	10	22	2	1	4	10	38	5	5	1	0	.359	.528	.306
F Catalanotto ...	OF	75	249	27	73	19	1	1	26	97	17	33	1	0	.344	.390	.293
A Rios	OF	111	426	55	122	24	7	1	28	163	31	84	15	3	.338	.383	.286
C Gomez	SS	109	341	41	96	11	1	3	37	118	28	41	3	2	.337	.346	.282
F Menechino ...	2B	84	269	40	74	13	4	9	26	122	37	52	0	2	.371	.454	.275
V Wells	OF	134	536	82	146	34	2	23	67	253	51	83	9	2	.337	.472	.272
O Hudson	2B	135	489	73	132	32	7	12	58	214	51	98	7	3	.341	.438	.270
R Johnson	OF	141	537	68	145	25	2	10	61	204	28	98	6	3	.320	.380	.270
C Delgado	1B	128	458	74	123	26	0	32	99	245	69	115	0	1	.372	.535	.269
G Zaun	C	107	338	46	91	24	0	6	36	133	47	61	0	2	.367	.393	.269
D Berg	OF	58	154	13	39	4	0	3	23	52	4	27	0	1	.278	.338	.253
E Hinske	3B	155	570	66	140	23	3	15	69	214	54	109	12	8	.312	.375	.246
C Woodward ...	SS	69	213	21	50	13	4	1	24	74	14	46	1	2	.283	.347	.235
B Estalella	C	5	13	1	3	0	0	0	0	3	3	5	0	0	.412	.231	.231
G Myers	C	8	18	0	4	2	0	0	1	6	2	4	0	0	.300	.333	.222
H Clark	OF	40	115	17	25	9	0	3	12	40	13	15	0	0	.292	.348	.217
G Quiroz	C	17	52	2	11	2	0	0	6	13	2	8	1	0	.263	.250	.212
G Gross	OF	44	129	18	27	4	0	3	16	40	19	31	2	2	.311	.310	.209
K Cash	C	60	181	18	35	9	0	4	21	56	10	59	0	0	.249	.309	.193
S Pond	OF	16	49	4	8	2	0	1	6	13	5	12	0	0	.250	.265	.163
E Crozier	DH	14	33	5	5	2	0	2	4	13	6	19	0	0	.282	.394	.152

POS = position; G = games played; AB = at bats; R = runs; H = hits; 2B = doubles; 3B = triples; HR = home runs; RBI = runs batted in; TB = total bases; BB = walks; SO = strikeouts; SB = stolen bases; CS = caught stealing; OBP = on-base percentage; SLG = slugging percentage; AVG = batting average ▶

Pitchers

Player	W	L	ERA	G	GS	CG	SHO	SV	SVO	IP	H	R	ER	HR	HBP	BB	SO
B League	1	0	0.00	3	0	0	0	0	0	4.2	3	0	0	0	0	1	2
F Menechino	0	0	0.00	1	0	0	0	0	0	0.1	2	0	0	0	0	0	0
G Chacin	1	1	2.57	2	2	0	0	0	0	14.0	8	4	4	0	1	3	6
D Bush	5	4	3.69	16	16	1	1	0	0	97.2	95	47	40	11	6	25	64
J Speier	3	8	3.91	62	0	0	0	7	11	69.0	61	32	30	8	5	25	52
R Glynn	1	0	4.05	6	2	0	0	0	0	20.0	19	9	9	4	3	8	14
T Lilly	12	10	4.06	32	32	2	1	0	0	197.1	171	92	89	26	6	89	168
J Frasor	4	6	4.08	63	0	0	0	17	19	68.1	64	31	31	4	2	36	54
R Halladay	8	8	4.20	21	21	1	1	0	0	133.0	140	66	62	13	1	39	95
V Chulk	1	3	4.66	47	0	0	0	2	5	56.0	59	30	29	6	1	27	44
M Batista	10	13	4.80	38	31	2	1	5	5	198.2	206	115	106	22	3	96	104
B File	1	0	4.81	24	0	0	0	0	0	33.2	45	19	18	4	2	12	15
J Towers	9	9	5.11	21	21	0	0	0	0	116.1	148	70	66	16	9	26	51
A Lopez	1	1	6.00	18	0	0	0	0	0	21.0	21	15	14	5	2	13	13
J Kershner	0	1	6.04	24	2	0	0	0	0	22.1	30	16	15	3	0	8	15
J Miller	3	4	6.06	19	15	0	0	0	0	81.2	101	58	55	14	5	42	47
V De Los Santos	0	0	6.17	17	0	0	0	0	1	11.2	11	8	8	0	0	10	10
S Douglass	0	2	6.28	14	3	0	0	0	0	38.2	37	27	27	6	2	28	36
K Ligtenberg	1	6	6.38	57	0	0	0	3	5	55.0	73	40	39	6	2	25	49
K Frederick	0	2	6.59	22	0	0	0	0	1	28.2	32	21	21	4	1	16	22
P Hentgen	2	9	6.95	18	16	0	0	0	0	80.1	90	67	62	16	4	42	33
M Nakamura	0	3	7.36	19	0	0	0	0	0	25.2	27	23	21	7	2	7	24
A Peterson	0	0	16.87	3	0	0	0	0	0	2.2	7	5	5	1	0	3	2
D Maurer	0	0	54.00	3	0	0	0	0	0	1.1	6	8	8	1	0	5	1

W = wins; L = losses; ERA = earned run average; G = games played; GS = games started; CG = complete games; SHO = shutouts; SV = saves; SVO = save opportunities; IP = innings pitched; H = hits; R = runs; ER = earned runs; HR = home runs allowed; HBP = hit by pitch; BB = walks; SO = strikeouts

Source: *Major League Baseball*

Toronto Blue Jays Team Records, through 2004 Season

Batting

Single Season

Batting Average: John Olerud, 1993, .363

At Bats: Tony Fernandez, 1986, 687

Games: Tony Fernandez, 1986, 163

Hits: Vernon Wells, 2003, 215

Runs: Shawn Green, 1999, 134

Singles: Tony Fernandez, 1986, 161

Doubles: Carlos Delgado, 2000, 57

Triples: Tony Fernandez, 1990, 17

Home Runs: George Bell, 1987, 47

Runs Batted In: Carlos Delgado, 2003, 145

Total Bases: Carlos Delgado, 2000, 378

Slugging Percentage: Carlos Delgado, 2000, .664

On-Base Percentage: John Olerud, 1993, .473

Stolen Bases: Dave Collins, 1984, 60

Strikeouts: José Canseco, 1998, 159

Walks: Carlos Delgado, 2000, 123

Career Leaders

Batting Average: Roberto Alomar, .307

At Bats: Tony Fernandez, 5,335

Games: Tony Fernandez, 1,450

Hits: Tony Fernandez, 1,583

Runs: Carlos Delgado, 889

Singles: Tony Fernandez, 1,035

Doubles: Carlos Delgado, 343

Triples: Tony Fernandez, 72

Home Runs: Carlos Delgado, 336

Runs Batted In: Carlos Delgado, 1,058

Total Bases: Carlos Delgado, 2,786

Slugging Percentage: Carlos Delgado, .556

On-Base Percentage: John Olerud, .395

Stolen Bases: Lloyd Moseby, 255

Strikeouts: Carlos Delgado, 1,242

Walks: Carlos Delgado, 827

Pitching

Single Season	Career Leaders
Games: Mark Eichhorn, 1987, 89	**Games:** Duane Ward, 452
Games Started: Jim Clancy, 1982, 40	**Games Started:** Dave Stieb, 408
Complete Games: Dave Stieb, 1982, 19	**Complete Games:** Dave Stieb, 103
Innings Pitched: Dave Stieb, 1982, 288	**Innings Pitched:** Dave Stieb, 2,873
Wins: Roy Halladay, 2003, 22	**Wins:** Dave Stieb, 175
Losses: Jerry Garvin, 1977, 18; Phil Huffman, 1979, 18	**Losses:** Jim Clancy, 140
Saves: Duane Ward, 1993, 45	**Saves:** Tom Henke, 217
Earned Run Average: Mark Eichhorn, 1986, 1.72	**Earned Run Average:** Tom Henke, 2.48
Strikeouts: Roger Clemens, 1997, 292	**Strikeouts:** Dave Stieb, 1 658

Source: *Major League Baseball*

Toronto Blue Jays Player of the Year, 1977–2003

1977	Bob Bailor	1986	Jesse Barfield	1995	Roberto Alomar
1978	Bob Bailor	1987	George Bell	1996	Ed Sprague
1979	Alfredo Griffin	1988	Fred McGriff	1997	Carlos Delgado
1980	John Mayberry	1989	George Bell	1998	Carlos Delgado
1981	Dave Stieb	1990	Kelly Gruber	1999	Shawn Green
1982	Damaso Garcia	1991	Roberto Alomar	2000	Carlos Delgado
1983	Lloyd Moseby	1992	Roberto Alomar	2001	Jose Cruz Jr.
1984	Dave Collins	1993	Paul Molitor	2002	Vernon Wells
1985	Jesse Barfield	1994	Joe Carter	2003	Roy Halladay

2004 Major League Baseball Milestones

■ Hitting

October 3: Ichiro Suzuki of the Seattle Mariners singles for hit number 262, an all-time single-season hit record, breaking the 84-year-old mark of 257 hits set by George Sisler in 1920.

October 2: Sammy Sosa of the Chicago Cubs hits career home run number 574 to pass Harmon Killebrew for seventh place on the all-time home run list.

September 23: Barry Bonds of the San Francisco Giants scores career run number 2,063 to pass Willie Mays for sixth place on the all-time run list.

September 22: Rafael Palmeiro of the Baltimore Orioles hits career home run number 549 to pass Mike Schmidt for tenth place on the all-time home run list.

September 17: Barry Bonds of the San Francisco Giants hits career home run number 700, only the third player in MLB history to achieve that milestone.

July 4: Barry Bonds of the San Francisco Giants earns career walk number 2,191 to pass Rickey Henderson for first place on the all-time base-on-balls list.

June 20: Ken Griffey, Jr. of the Cincinnati Reds hits career home run number 500, becoming the 20th player in MLB history to achieve that milestone.

April 13: Barry Bonds of the San Francisco Giants hits career home run number 661 to pass Willie Mays for third place on the all-time home run list.

■ Pitching

September 18: Trevor Hoffman of the San Diego Padres earns career save number 391 to pass Dennis Eckersley for third place on the all-time save list.

September 15: Randy Johnson of the Arizona Diamondbacks records career strikeout number 4,137 to pass Steve Carlton for third place on the all-time strikeout list.

September 14: Roger Clemens of the Houston Astros wins career victory number 327 to pass Eddie Plank for eleventh place on the all-time win list.

September 12: Mariano Rivera of the New York Yankees earns career save number 331 to pass John Wetteland for eighth place on the all-time save list.

August 7: Greg Maddux of the Chicago Cubs wins career victory 300, only the 22nd player in MLB history to achieve that milestone.

July 3: Eric Gagne of the Los Angeles Dodgers earns consecutive save number 84, the all-time record for consecutive saves.

May 5: Roger Clemens of the Houston Astros records career strikeout number 4,137 to pass Steve Carlton for second place on the all-time strikeout list.

Source: Major League Baseball

BASKETBALL

National Basketball Association, 2003–04

Final Regular Season Standings

Eastern Conference

■ Atlantic Division

	W	L	PCT	GB
New Jersey (2)[a]	47	35	.566	—
Miami (4)	42	40	.512	5
New York (7)	39	43	.476	8
Boston (8)	36	46	.439	11
Philadelphia	33	49	.402	14
Washington	25	57	.305	22
Orlando	21	61	.256	26

■ Central Division

	W	L	PCT	GB
Indiana (1)[b]	61	21	.744	—
Detroit (3)	54	28	.659	7
New Orleans (5)	41	41	.500	20
Milwaukee (6)	41	41	.500	20
Cleveland	35	47	.427	26
Toronto	33	49	.402	28
Atlanta	28	54	.349	33
Chicago	23	59	.280	38

Western Conference

■ Midwest Division

	W	L	PCT	GB
Minnesota (1)[c]	58	24	.707	—
San Antonio (3)	57	25	.695	1
Dallas (5)	52	30	.634	6
Memphis (6)	50	32	.610	8
Houston (7)	45	37	.549	13
Denver (8)	43	39	.524	15
Utah	42	40	.512	16

■ Pacific Division

	W	L	PCT	GB
L.A. Lakers (2)	56	26	.683	—
Sacramento (4)	55	27	.671	1
Portland	41	41	.500	15
Golden State	37	45	.451	19
Seattle	37	45	.451	19
Phoenix	29	53	.354	27
L.A. Clippers	28	54	.341	28

a Number in brackets indicates seeding in conference playoffs   b Top seed in Eastern Conference playoffs   c Top seed in Western Conference playoffs

Source: *NBA*

NBA Playoff Results, 2003–04

Eastern Conference

First Round (best-of-7 series)
Indiana defeated Boston, 4–0
New Jersey defeated New York, 4–0
Detroit defeated Milwaukee 4–1
Miami defeated New Orleans 4–3

Semifinals (best-of-7 series)
Indiana defeated Miami 4–2
Detroit defeated New Jersey 4–3

Finals (best-of-7 series)
Detroit defeated Indiana 4–2

Western Conference

First Round (best-of-7 series)
Minnesota defeated Denver 4–1
L.A. Lakers defeated Houston 4–1
San Antonio defeated Memphis 4–0
Sacramento defeated Dallas 4–1

Semifinals (best-of-7 series)
Minnesota defeated Sacramento 4–3
L.A. Lakers defeated San Antonio 4–2

Finals (best-of-7 series)
L.A. Lakers defeated Dallas 4–2

NBA FINALS

Detroit Pistons defeated Los Angeles Lakers 4–1
Game 1:
Detroit 87 – L.A. Lakers 75
Game 2:
Detroit 91 – **L.A. Lakers 99**
Game 3:
Detroit 88 – L.A. Lakers 68
Game 4:
Detroit 88 – L.A. Lakers 80
Game 5:
Detroit 100 – L.A. Lakers 87

Source: *NBA*

Pistons' Coach Brown Champion at Two (Almost Three) Levels

*I*n coaching the Detroit Pistons to the 2003–04 NBA championship, veteran head coach Larry Brown became the first head coach to win an NBA title and an NCAA college basketball national championship (with the University of Kansas in 1988). Brown had coached 22 years with 7 NBA franchises before realizing competitive basketball's pinnacle achievement in his first year with the Pistons. Brown nearly captured an unprecedented coaching hat trick later in the summer of 2004 when he coached the United States' men's basketball squad to a bronze medal at the Olympic Summer Games in Athens. Alas, Brown can console himself with the gold medal he earned as a player on the U.S. Olympic men's basketball team in 1964 in Melbourne.

NBA Champions and Most Valuable Players

Year	Champion	Runner-up	G	MVP
1946-47	Philadelphia Warriors	Chicago Stags	4-1	
1947-48	Baltimore Bullets	Philadelphia Warriors	4-2	
1948-49	Minneapolis Lakers	Washington Capitols	4-2	
1949-50	Minneapolis Lakers	Syracuse Nationals	4-2	
1950-51	Rochester Royals	New York Knicks	4-3	
1951-52	Minneapolis Lakers	New York Knicks	4-3	
1952-53	Minneapolis Lakers	New York Knicks	4-1	
1953-54	Minneapolis Lakers	Syracuse Nationals	4-3	
1954-55	Syracuse Nationals	Fort Wayne Pistons	4-3	
1955-56	Philadelphia Warriors	Fort Wayne Pistons	4-1	
1956-57	Boston Celtics	St. Louis Hawks	4-3	
1957-58	St. Louis Hawks	Boston Celtics	4-2	
1958-59	Boston Celtics	Minneapolis Lakers	4-0	
1959-60	Boston Celtics	St. Louis Hawks	4-3	
1960-61	Boston Celtics	St. Louis Hawks	4-1	
1961-62	Boston Celtics	Los Angeles Lakers	4-3	
1962-63	Boston Celtics	Los Angeles Lakers	4-2	
1963-64	Boston Celtics	San Francisco Warriors	4-1	
1964-65	Boston Celtics	Los Angeles Lakers	4-1	
1965-66	Boston Celtics	Los Angeles Lakers	4-3	
1966-67	Philadelphia 76ers	San Francisco Warriors	4-2	
1967-68	Boston Celtics	Los Angeles Lakers	4-2	[a]
1968-69	Boston Celtics	Los Angeles Lakers	4-3	Jerry West, L.A.
1969-70	New York Knicks	Los Angeles Lakers	4-3	Willis Reed, N.Y.
1970-71	Milwaukee Bucks	Baltimore Bullets	4-0	Kareem Abdul-Jabbar, Mil.
1971-72	Los Angeles Lakers	New York Knicks	4-1	Wilt Chamberlain, L.A.
1972-73	New York Knicks	Los Angeles Lakers	4-1	Willis Reed, N.Y.
1973-74	Boston Celtics	Milwaukee Bucks	4-3	John Havlicek, Bos.
1974-75	Golden State Warriors	Washington Bullets	4-0	Rick Barry, G.S.
1975-76	Boston Celtics	Phoenix Suns	4-2	Jo Jo White, Bos.
1976-77	Portland Trail Blazers	Philadelphia 76ers	4-2	Bill Walton, Por.
1977-78	Washington Bullets	Seattle SuperSonics	4-3	Wes Unseld, Was.
1978-79	Seattle SuperSonics	Washington Bullets	4-1	Dennis Johnson, Sea.
1979-80	Los Angeles Lakers	Philadelphia 76ers	4-2	Magic Johnson, L.A.
1980-81	Boston Celtics	Houston Rockets	4-2	Cedric Maxwell, Bos.
1981-82	Los Angeles Lakers	Philadelphia 76ers	4-2	Magic Johnson, L.A.
1982-83	Philadelphia 76ers	Los Angeles Lakers	4-0	Moses Malone, Phi.
1983-84	Boston Celtics	Los Angeles Lakers	4-3	Larry Bird, Bos.
1984-85	Los Angeles Lakers	Boston Celtics	4-2	Kareem Abdul-Jabbar, L.A.
1985-86	Boston Celtics	Houston Rockets	4-2	Larry Bird, Bos.
1986-87	Los Angeles Lakers	Boston Celtics	4-2	Magic Johnson, L.A.
1987-88	Los Angeles Lakers	Detroit Pistons	4-3	James Worthy, L.A.
1988-89	Detroit Pistons	Los Angeles Lakers	4-0	Joe Dumars, Det.
1989-90	Detroit Pistons	Portland Trail Blazers	4-1	Isiah Thomas, Det.
1990-91	Chicago Bulls	Los Angeles Lakers	4-1	Michael Jordan, Chi.
1991-92	Chicago Bulls	Portland Trail Blazers	4-2	Michael Jordan, Chi.
1992-93	Chicago Bulls	Phoenix Suns	4-2	Michael Jordan, Chi.
1993-94	Houston Rockets	New York Knicks	4-3	Hakeem Olajuwon, Hou.
1994-95	Houston Rockets	Orlando Magic	4-0	Hakeem Olajuwon, Hou.
1995-96	Chicago Bulls	Seattle SuperSonics	4-2	Michael Jordan, Chi.
1996-97	Chicago Bulls	Utah Jazz	4-2	Michael Jordan, Chi.
1997-98	Chicago Bulls	Utah Jazz	4-2	Michael Jordan, Chi.
1998-99	San Antonio Spurs	New York Knicks	4-1	Tim Duncan, S.A.
1999-00	Los Angeles Lakers	Indiana Pacers	4-2	Shaquille O'Neal, L.A..
2000-01	Los Angeles Lakers	Philadelphia 76ers	4-1	Shaquille O'Neal, L.A..
2001-02	Los Angeles Lakers	New Jersey Nets	4-0	Shaquille O'Neal, L.A..
2002-03	San Antonio Spurs	New Jersey Nets	4-2	Tim Duncan, S.A.
2003-04	Detroit Pistons	Los Angeles Lakers	4-3	Chauncey Billups, Det.

(a) No finals most valuable player award existed before 1969.

Individual Statistical Leaders, Regular Season, 2003–04

■ **Points Per Game**

Player	G	FG	FT	P	PG
1. Tracy McGrady (Orlando Magic) 67		653	398	1,878	28.0
2. Predrag Stojakovic (Sacramento Kings) 81		665	394	1,964	24.3
3. Kevin Garnett (Minnesota Timberwolves) 82		804	368	1,987	24.2
4. Kobe Bryant (Los Angeles Lakers) 65		516	454	1,557	24.0
5. Paul Pierce (Boston Celtics) 80		602	517	1,836	23.0
6. Baron Davis (New Orleans Hornets) 67		554	237	1,532	22.9
7. **Vince Carter (Toronto Raptors)** 73		608	336	1,645	22.5
8. Tim Duncan (San Antonio Spurs) 69		592	352	1,538	22.3
9. Dirk Nowitzki (Dallas Mavericks) 77		605	371	1,680	21.8
10. Michael Redd (Milwaukee Bucks) 82		633	383	1,776	21.7

■ **Rebounds Per Game**

Player	G	OFF	DEF	REB	RPG
1. Kevin Garnett (Minnesota Timberwolves) 82		3.0	10.9	1,139	13.9
2. Tim Duncan (San Antonio Spurs) 69		3.3	9.2	859	12.4
3. Ben Wallace (Detroit Pistons) 81		4.0	8.4	1,006	12.4
4. Erick Dampier (Golden State Warriors) 74		4.6	7.3	887	12.0
5. Carlos Boozer (Cleveland Cavaliers) 75		3.1	8.4	857	11.4
6. Zach Randolph (Portland Trail Blazers) 81		3.0	7.5	851	10.5
7. **Jamaal Magloire** (New Orleans Hornets) 82		3.3	7.1	847	10.3
8. Brad Miller (Sacramento Kings) 72		2.7	7.7	743	10.3
9. Kenny Thomas (Philadelphia 76ers) 74		3.5	6.6	750	10.1
10. Marcus Camby (Denver Nuggets) 72		2.9	7.2	727	10.1

■ **Field Goal Percentage**

Player	FGM	FGA	%
1. Shaquille O'Neal (Los Angeles Lakers)	554	948	.584
2. Mark Blount (Boston Celtics)	342	604	.566
3. Erick Dampier (Golden State Warriors)	348	650	.535
4. Antawn Jamison (Dallas Mavericks)	488	913	.535
5. Nene Hilario (Denver Nuggets)	334	630	.530
6. Carlos Boozer (Cleveland Cavaliers)	471	900	.523
7. Yao Ming (Houston Rockets)	535	1,025	.522
8. Brad Miller (Sacramento Kings) . . .	373	731	.510
9. Corliss Williamson (Detroit Pistons)	304	602	.505
10. Tim Duncan (San Antonio Spurs) . .	592	1,181	.501

■ **Assists Per Game**

Player	GP	AST	AVG
1. Jason Kidd (New Jersey Nets)	67	618	9.2
2. Stephon Marbury (New York/Phoenix) .	81	719	8.9
3. **Steve Nash** (Dallas Mavericks)	78	687	8.8
4. Baron Davis (New Orleans Hornets)	67	501	7.5
5. Sam Cassell (Minnesota Timberwolves)	81	592	7.3
6. Eric Snow (Philadelphia 76ers)	82	563	6.9
7. Jason Williams (Memphis Grizzlies)	72	492	6.8
8. Kirk Hinrich (Chicago Bulls)	76	517	6.8
9. Steve Francis (Houston Rockets) . .	79	493	6.2
10. Jeff McInnis (Cleveland/Portland) . .	70	430	6.1

■ **Free Throw Percentage**

Player	FTM	FTA	%
1. Peja Stojakovic (Sacramento Kings) .	394	425	.927
2. **Steve Nash** (Dallas Mavericks) . . .	230	251	.916
3. Allan Houston (New York Knicks) .	157	172	.913
4. Ray Allen (Seattle SuperSonics) . .	245	271	.904
5. Reggie Miller (Indiana Pacers) . . .	146	165	.885
6. Chauncey Billups (Detroit Pistons)	404	460	.878
7. Brian Cardinal (Golden State Warriors)	238	271	.878
8. Dirk Nowitzki (Dallas Mavericks) . .	371	423	.877
9. Earl Boykins (Denver Nuggets) . . .	142	162	.877
10. Damon Stoudamire (Portland Trail Blazers)	127	145	.876

■ **Three-Point Field Goals Percentage**

Player	3FG	3FGA	%
1. Anthony Peeler (Sacramento Kings)	68	141	.482
2. Brent Barry (Seattle SuperSonics) .	114	252	.452
3. Brian Cardinal (Golden State Warriors)	55	124	.444
4. Fred Hoiberg (Minnesota Timberwolves) .	76	172	.442
5. Aaron McKie (Philadelphia 76ers) . .	75	172	.436
6. Peja Stojakovic (Sacramento Kings) .	240	554	.433
7. Allan Houston (New York Knicks) . .	87	202	.431
8. Hedo Turkoglu (San Antonio Spurs)	101	241	.419
9. Casey Jacobsen (Phoenix Suns) . .	75	180	.417
10. Charlie Ward (New York/San Antonio) .	84	206	.408

■ Steals Per Game

Player	GP	STL	SPG
1. Baron Davis (New Orleans Hornets)	67	158	2.36
2. Shawn Marion (Phoenix Suns)	79	167	2.11
3. Ron Artest (Indiana Pacers)	73	152	2.08
4. Andrei Kirilenko (Utah Jazz)	78	150	1.92
5. Doug Christie (Sacramento Kings)	82	151	1.84
6. Stephen Jackson (Atlanta Hawks)	80	142	1.78
7. Manu Ginobili (San Antonio Spurs)	77	136	1.77
8. Ben Wallace (Detroit Pistons)	81	143	1.77
9. Steve Francis (Houston Rockets)	79	139	1.76
10. Andre Miller (Denver Nuggets)	82	142	1.73

■ Blocked Shots Per Game

Player	GP	BLK	AVG
1. Theo Ratliff (Atlanta/Portland)	85	307	3.61
2. Ben Wallace (Detroit Pistons)	81	246	3.04
3. Andrei Kirilenko (Utah Jazz)	78	215	2.76
4. Tim Duncan (San Antonio Spurs)	69	185	2.68
5. Marcus Camby (Denver Nuggets)	72	187	2.60
6. Jermaine O'Neal (Indiana Pacers)	78	199	2.55
7. Zydrunas Ilgauskas (Cleveland Cavaliers)	81	201	2.48
8. Shaquille O'Neal (Los Angeles Lakers)	67	166	2.48
9. Samuel Dalembert (Philadelphia 76ers)	82	189	2.30
10. Elton Brand (Los Angeles Clippers)	69	154	2.23

Source: *ESPN.com*   **Bold** indicates player is from Canada or plays on a Canada-based team.

All-Time NBA Statistical Leaders

(as of the end of the 2003–04 season)

■ Total points, career

Player	GP	FG	FT	PPG	PTS
1. Kareem Abdul-Jabbar	1,560	15,837	6,712	24.6	38,387
2. Karl Malone*	1,476	13,528	9,787	25.0	36,928
3. Michael Jordan	1,072	12,192	7,327	30.1	32,292
4. Wilt Chamberlain	1,045	12,681	6,057	30.1	31,419
5. Moses Malone	1,329	9,435	8,531	20.6	27,409
6. Elvin Hayes	1,303	10,976	5,356	21.0	27,313
7. Hakeem Olajuwon	1,238	10,749	5,423	21.8	26,946
8. Oscar Robertson	1,040	9,508	7,694	25.7	26,710
9. Dominique Wilkins	1,074	9,963	6,031	24.8	26,668
10. John Havlicek	1,270	10,513	5,369	20.8	26,395

■ Total rebounds, career

Player	GP	OFF	DEF	RPG	REB
1. Wilt Chamberlain	1,045	0[a]	0	22.9	23,924
2. Bill Russell	963	0	0	22.5	21,620
3. Kareem Abdul-Jabbar	1,560	2,975	9,394	11.2	17,440
4. Elvin Hayes	1,303	2,778	6,973	12.5	16,279
5. Moses Malone	1,329	6,731	9,481	12.2	16,212
6. Karl Malone*	1,476	3,562	11,406	10.1	14,968
7. Robert Parish	1,611	4,598	10,117	9.1	14,715
8. Nate Thurmond	964	744	1,827	15.0	14,464
9. Walt Bellamy	1,043	264	481	13.7	14,241
10. Wes Unseld	984	2,085	4,974	14.0	13,769

[a] Offensive and defensive rebounds were not recorded prior to 1973–74 season.

■ Total assists, career

Player	GP	APG	AST
1. John Stockton	1,504	10.5	15,806
2. Mark Jackson*	1,296	8.0	10,334
3. Magic Johnson	906	11.2	10,141
4. Oscar Robertson	1,040	9.5	9,887
5. Isiah Thomas	979	9.3	9,061
6. Gary Payton*	1,109	7.2	8,039
7. Rod Strickland*	1,078	7.4	7,948
8. Maurice Cheeks	1,101	6.7	7,392
9. Lenny Wilkens	1,077	6.7	7,211
10. Terry Porter	1,274	5.6	7,160

■ Total blocked shots, career

Player	GP	AVG	BLK
1. Hakeem Olajuwon	1,238	3.09	3,830
2. Kareem Abdul-Jabbar	1,560	2.57	3,189
3. Mark Eaton	875	3.50	3,064
4. Dikembe Mutombo*	929	3.22	2,996
5. David Robinson	987	2.99	2,954
6. Patrick Ewing	1,183	2.45	2,894
7. Tree Rollins	1,156	2.20	2,542
8. Robert Parish	1,611	1.47	2,361
9. Shaquille O'Neal*	809	2.60	2,102
10. Manute Bol	624	3.34	2,086

Source: *NBA*   * Active player during 2003–04 season   [a] Blocked shots were not recorded prior to the 1973–74 season.

Toronto Raptors Individual Statistics, 2003–04

Player	G	MIN	FGM-A	FG%	3PM-A	3P%	FTM-A	FT%	PTS	PPG
Vince Carter	73	2,785	608-1,457	.417	93-243	.383	336-417	.806	1,645	22.5
Donyell Marshall[a]	66	2,580	413-884	.467	120-298	.403	120-162	.741	1,066	16.2
Jalen Rose[b]	50	1,968	308-752	.410	46-148	.311	148-180	.822	810	16.2
Chris Bosh	75	2,510	327-712	.459	5-14	.357	202-288	.701	861	11.5
Alvin Williams	56	1,730	201-496	.405	26-89	.292	66-85	.776	494	8.8
Morris Peterson	82	2,148	238-587	.405	126-340	.371	76-94	.809	678	8.3
Lamond Murray	33	518	76-215	.353	21-60	.350	24-35	.686	197	6.0
Rod Strickland[c]	15	282	28-84	.333	0-3	.000	15-22	.682	71	4.7
Dion Glover[d]	14	178	25-65	.385	4-14	.286	10-14	.714	64	4.6
Milt Palacio	59	1,211	104-298	.349	4-26	.154	45-68	.662	257	4.4
Roger Mason Jr.[e]	23	285	31-87	.356	12-33	.364	19-22	.864	93	4.0
Michael Curry	70	1,229	76-196	.388	3-15	.200	49-58	.845	204	2.9
Jerome Moiso	35	417	40-84	.476	0-1	.000	22-38	.579	102	2.9
Corie Blount[f]	16	294	18-47	.383	0-0	.000	2-3	.667	38	2.4
Robert Archibald[g]	30	246	8-30	.267	0-0	.000	13-27	.481	29	1.0

Player	REB	OFF	DEF	RPG	AST	APG	STL	BLK	TO	PF
Vince Carter	349	95	254	4.8	348	4.8	88	65	223	212
Donyell Marshall	709	182	527	10.7	94	1.4	80	104	95	200
Jalen Rose	202	27	175	4.0	273	5.5	39	18	171	139
Chris Bosh	557	191	366	7.4	78	1.0	59	106	107	215
Alvin Williams	150	18	132	2.7	224	4.0	55	10	78	114
Morris Peterson	261	35	226	3.2	113	1.4	88	14	69	206
Lamond Murray	90	14	76	2.7	28	0.8	15	7	38	47
Rod Strickland	37	10	27	2.5	59	3.9	8	4	18	17
Dion Glover	29	4	25	2.1	15	1.1	10	2	19	17
Milt Palacio	102	15	87	1.7	184	3.1	41	11	87	90
Roger Mason Jr.	28	1	27	1.2	23	1.0	10	6	18	31
Michael Curry	87	22	65	1.2	53	0.8	23	5	48	153
Jerome Moiso	113	41	72	3.2	8	0.2	17	12	25	42
Corie Blount	69	22	47	4.3	10	0.6	11	5	8	49
Robert Archibald	50	21	29	1.7	12	0.4	13	3	9	49

Source: *NBA*

[a] Marshall's statistics do not reflect an additional 16 games with the Chicago Bulls.
[b] Rose's statistics do not reflect an additional 16 games with the Chicago Bulls.
[c] Strickland's statistics do not reflect an additional 46 games with the Orlando Magic.
[d] Glover's statistics do not reflect an additional 55 games with the Atlanta Hawks.
[e] Mason's statistics do not reflect an additional 3 games with the Chicago Bulls.
[f] Blount's statistics do not reflect an additional 46 games with the Chicago Bulls.
[g] Archibald's statistics do not reflect an additional 2 games with the Phoenix Sun and the Orlando Magic.

G= games played; MIN = total minutes (season); FGM-A = field goals made-attempts; FG% = field goal percentage; 3PM-A = three-point field goals made-attempts; 3P% = three-point field goal percentage; FTM-A = free throws made-attempts; FT% = free throw percentage; PTS = total points (season); PPG = points per game; REB = total rebounds (season); OFF = total offensive rebounds (season); DEF = total defensive rebounds (season); RPG = rebounds per game; AST = total assists (season); APG = assists per game; STL = total steals (season); BLK = total blocked shots (season); TO = total turnovers (season); PF = total personal fouls (season)

Toronto's Jamaal Magloire Named NBA All-Star

*T*oronto's Jamaal Magloire became the second Canadian NBA player to be named to an NBA all-star team. The annual game features 24 of the league's best players, 10 of whom are voted to the team by NBA fans. Magloire was one of seven players named to the Eastern Conference squad by NBA coaches. In his fourth season for the New Orleans Hornets franchise, Magloire had shown steady improvement from year to year, but the 2003–04 season proved to be a breakout year. At the time of his selection, Magloire was averaging over 9 rebounds and 11 points per game, which he upped to nearly 14 points per game and 10.3 rebounds per game, the latter good enough for 7th in the league. Victoria native Steve Nash was the first Canadian named to an NBA all-star team. Nash has earned the honour twice (in 2002 and 2003), but was not selected for the most recent game. **Source:** *NBA; Canadian Press*

Toronto Raptors Year-By-Year Record, 1995–2004

Year	Won	Lost	%	Conference Standing	Avg. Home Attendance	Coach
1995–96 21	61	.256	14th	23,179	Brendan Malone
1996–97 30	52	.366	12th	18,267	Darrell Walker
1997–98 16	66	.195	15th	16,470	Walker/Butch Carter
1998–99[a] 23	27	.460	10th	17,568	Butch Carter
1999–00 45	37	.549	6th[b]	18,451	Butch Carter
2000–01 47	35	.573	5th[c]	19,348	Lenny Wilkens
2001–02 42	40	.512	7th[d]	19,760	Lenny Wilkens
2002–03 24	58	.293	14th	18,964	Lenny Wilkens
2003–04 33	49	.402	10th	18,308	Kevin O'Neill

Source: *NBA; Canadian Press*
[a]Season shortened by player lockout
[b]Made playoffs; eliminated in first round
[c]Made playoffs; eliminated in conference semi-finals
[d]Made playoffs; eliminated in first round

Toronto Raptors Draft Picks, through 2003–04

1995
Damon Stoudamire, University of Arizona (1st round, 7th pick overall)
Jimmy King, University of Michigan (2nd round, 35th pick overall)

1996
Marcus Camby, University of Massachusetts (1st round, 2nd pick overall)

1997
Tracy McGrady, Mt. Zion Christian Academy (1st round, 9th pick overall)

1998
Antawn Jamison, University of North Carolina (1st round, 4th pick overall)[a]
Tyson Wheeler, University of Rhode Island (2nd round, 47th pick overall)

1999
Jonathan Bender, Picayune (Mississippi) High School (1st round, 5th pick overall)[b]
Aleksandar Radojevic, Barton County (Kansas) Community College (1st round, 12th pick overall)

2000
Morris Peterson, Michigan State University (1st round, 21st pick overall)
DeeAndre Hulett, Las Vegas, IBL (2nd round, 46th pick overall)

2001
Michael Bradley, Villanova University (1st round, 17th pick overall)

2002
Kareem Rush, University of Missouri (1st round, 20th pick overall)[c]

2003
Chris Bosh, Georgia Tech University (1st round, 4th pick overall)
Matt Bonner, University of Florida (2nd round, 45th pick overall)
Remon Van de Hare, F.C. Barcelona (2nd round, 52nd pick overall)

2004
Rafael Araujo, Brigham Young University (1st round, 8th pick overall)
Albert Miralles, Spain (2nd round, 39th pick overall)

Source: *NBA*
[a]Traded to Golden State Warriors for the draft rights to Vince Carter (5th pick overall) and cash
[b]Traded to Indiana Pacers for Antonio Davis
[c]Traded with Tracy Murray to Los Angeles Lakers for the draft rights to Chris Jefferies (27th pick overall) and Lindsey Hunter

FOOTBALL

Canadian Football League

(2003 Regular Season Standings)

Team	GP	W	L	T	F	A	PTS
East Division							
Montreal	18	13	5	0	562	409	26
Toronto	18	9	9	0	473	433	18
Ottawa..........	18	7	11	0	467	581	14
Hamilton	18	1	17	0	293	583	2

Team	GP	W	L	T	F	A	PTS
West Division							
Edmonton	18	13	5	0	569	414	26
Winnipeg........	18	11	7	0	514	487	22
Saskatchewan	18	11	7	0	535	430	22
B.C.............	18	11	7	0	531	430	22
Calgary	18	5	13	0	323	502	10

Playoffs

Sunday, November 2, 2003
East Division Semi-Final —
British Columbia 7 at Toronto 28
Attendance: 21,029
West Division Semi-Final —
Saskatchewan 37 at Winnipeg 21
Attendance: 22,110

Sunday, November 9, 2003
East Division Final —
Toronto 26 at Montreal 30
Attendance: 60,007
West Division Final —
Saskatchewan 23 at Edmonton 30
Attendance: 40,081

Sunday, November 16, 2003 — **Edmonton 34 vs Montreal 22**
Grey Cup Championship at Taylor Field, Regina—Attendance: 50,909

Source: *Canadian Football League*

CFL All-Stars, 2003

(voted by Football Reporters of Canada)

Offence

Quarterback: Anthony Calvillo, Montreal
Running Back: Mike Pringle, Edmonton
Running Back: Charles Roberts, Winnipeg
Slotback: Jeremaine Copeland, Montreal
Slotback: Geroy Simon, British Columbia
Wide Receiver: Ed Hervey, Edmonton
Wide Receiver: Tony Miles, Toronto
Centre: Bryan Chiu, Montreal
Tackle: Bruce Beaton, Edmonton
Tackle: Uzooma Okeke, Montreal
Guard: Andrew Greene, Saskatchewan
Guard: Scott Flory, Montreal

Defence

Defensive Tackle: Joe Fleming, Calgary
Defensive Tackle: Eric England, Toronto
Defensive End: Daved Benefield, Winnipeg
Defensive End: Ray Jacobs, British Columbia
Middle Linebacker: Barrin Simpson, British Columbia
Outside Linebacker: Reggie Hunt, Saskatchewan
Outside Linebacker: Jackie Mitchell, Saskatchewan
Cornerback: Adrion Smith, Toronto
Cornerback: Omarr Morgan, Saskatchewan
Defensive Back: Donny Brady, Edmonton
Defensive Back: Clifford Ivory, Toronto
Safety: Orlondo Steinauer, Toronto

Special Teams

Punter:
Noel Prefontaine, Toronto

Placekicker:
Lawrence Tynes, Ottawa

Special Team:
Bashir Levingston, Toronto

Source: *Canadian Football League*

A CFL Turnaround in Southern Ontario

*O*ne year ago, the future of the CFL's two southern Ontario franchises— the Toronto Argonauts and the Hamilton Tiger-Cats— was uncertain. The league had taken control of the management of both teams until new ownership stepped forward for each franchise. Money problems had led to the league's action— Toronto's management stopped paying its bills; Hamilton's leadership failed to meet its players' payroll. What a difference a year makes. Toronto-area entrepreneurs Howard Sokolowski and David Cynamon took over control of the Argonauts; Hamilton native Bob Young assumed ownership of the Tiger-Cats. The rejuvenated franchise typified the league's strong attendance numbers in 2004.

The Grey Cup, 1909–2003

The Grey Cup was donated in 1909 by Governor General Earl Grey for the "Rugby Football Championship of Canada." Since 1954, only teams in the Canadian Football League have challenged for the trophy, with the winners of the East and West divisions meeting in the championship game.

1909	U. of Toronto 26, Parkdale 6
1910	U. of Toronto 16, Ham. Tigers 7
1911	U. of Toronto 14, Toronto 7
1912	Ham. Alerts 11, Toronto 4
1913	Ham. Tigers 44, Parkdale 2
1914	Toronto 14, U. of Toronto 2
1915	Ham. Tigers 13, Tor. R.A.A. 7
1916–19	No games held.
1920	U. of Toronto 16, Toronto 3
1921	Toronto 23, Edmonton 0
1922	Queen's U. 13, Edmonton 1
1923	Queen's U. 54, Regina 0
1924	Queen's U. 11, Balmy Beach 3
1925	Ott. Senators 24, Winnipeg 1
1926	Ott. Senators 10, U. of Toronto 7
1927	Balmy Beach 9, Ham. Tigers 6
1928	Ham. Tigers 30, Regina 0
1929	Ham. Tigers 14, Regina 3
1930	Balmy Beach 11, Regina 6
1931	Mtl. A.A.A. 22, Regina 0
1932	Ham. Tigers 25, Regina 6
1933	Toronto 4, Sarnia 3
1934	Sarnia 20, Regina 12
1935	Winnipeg 18, Ham. Tigers 12
1936	Sarnia 26, Ott. R.R. 20
1937	Toronto 4, Winnipeg 3
1938	Toronto 30, Winnipeg 7
1939	Winnipeg 8, Ottawa 7
1940[1]	Ottawa 12, Balmy Beach 5
	Ottawa 8, Balmy Beach 2
1941	Winnipeg 18, Ottawa 16
1942	Tor. R.C.A.F. 8, Win. R.C.A.F. 5
1943	Ham. F. Wild 23, Win. R.C.A.F. 14
1944	Mtl. St. H.D. Navy 7, Ham. F. Wild 6
1945	Toronto 35, Winnipeg 0
1946	Toronto 28, Winnipeg 6
1947	Toronto 10, Winnipeg 9
1948	Calgary 12, Ottawa 7
1949	Mtl. Als. 28, Calgary 15
1950	Toronto 13, Winnipeg 0
1951	Ottawa 21, Saskatchewan 14
1952	Toronto 21, Edmonton 11
1953	Hamilton 12, Winnipeg 6
1954	Edmonton 26, Montreal 25
1955	Edmonton 34, Montreal 19
1956	Edmonton 50, Montreal 27
1957	Hamilton 32, Winnipeg 7
1958	Winnipeg 35, Hamilton 28
1959	Winnipeg 21, Hamilton 7
1960	Ottawa 16, Edmonton 6
1961	Winnipeg 21, Hamilton 14
1962	Winnipeg 28, Hamilton 27
1963	Hamilton 21, BC 10
1964	BC 34, Hamilton 24
1965	Hamilton 22, Winnipeg 16
1966	Saskatchewan 29, Ottawa 14
1967	Hamilton 24, Saskatchewan 1
1968	Ottawa 24, Calgary 21
1969	Ottawa 29, Saskatchewan 11
1970	Montreal 23, Calgary 10
1971	Calgary 14, Toronto 11
1972	Hamilton 13, Saskatchewan 10
1973	Ottawa 22, Edmonton 18
1974	Montreal 20, Edmonton 7
1975	Edmonton 9, Montreal 8
1976	Ottawa 23, Saskatchewan 20
1977	Montreal 41, Edmonton 6
1978	Edmonton 20, Montreal 13
1979	Edmonton 17, Montreal 9
1980	Edmonton 48, Hamilton 10
1981	Edmonton 26, Ottawa 23
1982	Edmonton 32, Toronto 16
1983	Toronto 18, BC 17
1984	Winnipeg 47, Hamilton 17
1985	BC 37, Hamilton 24
1986	Hamilton 39, Edmonton 15
1987	Edmonton 38, Toronto 36
1988	Winnipeg 22, BC 21
1989	Saskatchewan 43, Hamilton 40
1990	Winnipeg 50, Edmonton 11
1991	Toronto 36, Calgary 21
1992	Calgary 24, Winnipeg 10
1993	Edmonton 33, Winnipeg 23
1994	BC 26, Baltimore 23
1995	Baltimore 37, Calgary 20
1996	Toronto 43, Edmonton 37
1997	Toronto 47, Saskatchewan 23
1998	Calgary 26, Hamilton 24
1999	Hamilton 32, Calgary 21
2000	BC 28, Montreal 26
2001	Calgary 27, Winnipeg 19
2002	Montreal 25, Edmonton 16
2003	Edmonton 34, Montreal 22

Source: *Canadian Press*

(1) A 2-game total point series.

All-Time Leading CFL Players

(up to the end of the 2003 season)

Playing Records

Games Played, Career

408 . . . . . . Lui Passaglia (B.C.) 1976–2000
394 . . . . . . Bob Cameron (Winnipeg) 1980–2002
321 . . . . . . Miles Gorrell (five teams) 1978–1996
315 . . . . . . Damon Allen (five teams) 1985–2003
304 . . . . . . Paul Osbaldiston (three teams) 1986–2003

Consecutive Games Played

353 . . . . . . Bob Cameron (Winnipeg) 1980–2000
268 . . . . . . Paul Osbaldiston (three teams) 1988–2002
262 . . . . . . Mark McLoughlin (Calgary) 1988–2002
253 . . . . . . Dave Cutler (Edmonton) 1969–1984
252 . . . . . . Leo Groenewegen (three teams) 1987–2000

Seasons Played, Career

25 . . . . Lui Passaglia (B.C.) 1976–2000
23 . . . . Bob Cameron (Winnipeg) 1980–2002
22 . . . . Eddie Emerson (Ottawa) 1911–1937
20 . . . . Hank Ilesic (three teams) 1977–1993, 1995, 1998, 2001
19 . . . . Ron Lancaster (two teams) 1960–1978
19 . . . . Miles Gorrell (five teams) 1978–1996

Consecutive Seasons Played

25 . . . . Lui Passaglia (B.C.) 1976–2000
21 . . . . Bob Cameron (Winnipeg) 1980–2002
19 . . . . Miles Gorrell (Five teams) 1978–1997
19 . . . . Ron Lancaster (Two Teams) 1960–1978
19 . . . . Damon Allen (five teams) 1985–2003

Scoring Records

Points, Career

3991 . . . . . Lui Passaglia (B.C.) 1976–2000
2953 . . . . . Mark McLoughlin (Calgary) 1988–2003
2939 . . . . . Paul Osbaldiston (three teams) 1986–2003
2374 . . . . . Dave Ridgway (Saskatchewan) 1982–1994
2237 . . . . . Dave Cutler (Edmonton) 1969–1984

Most Points, One Season

236 . . . . . . Lance Chomyc (Toronto) 1991
235 . . . . . . Roman Anderson (San Antonio) 1995
233 . . . . . . Paul Osbaldiston (Hamilton) 1989
233 . . . . . . Dave Ridgway (Saskatchewan) 1990
228 . . . . . . Carlos Huerta (Baltimore) 1995

Most Points, One Game

36 . . . . Bob McNamara (Winnipeg) Oct 13, 1956
30 . . . . Ernie Pitts (Winnipeg) Aug 29, 1959
30 . . . . Fred Burket (Saskatchewan) Oct 26, 1959
30 . . . . Earl Lunsford (Calgary) Sept 2, 1962
30 . . . . Martin Patton (Shreveport) Aug 5, 1995
30 . . . . Eric Blount (Edmonton) Sept 15, 1995

Most Touchdowns, One Season

23 . . . . Milt Stegall (Winnipeg) 2002
22 . . . . Cory Philpot (B.C.) 1995
21 . . . . Allen Pitts (Calgary) 1994
20 . . . . Pat Abbruzzi (Montreal) 1956
20 . . . . Darrell K. Smith (Toronto) 1990
20 . . . . Blake Marshall (Edmonton) 1991
20 . . . . Jon Volpe (B.C.) 1991

Touchdowns, Career

137 . . . . . . George Reed (Saskatchewan) 1963–1975
128 . . . . . . Mike Pringle (four teams) 1992–2003
117 . . . . . . Allen Pitts (Calgary) 1990–2000
97 . . . . Brian Kelly (Edmonton) 1979–1987
91 . . . . Dick Shatto (Toronto) 1954–1965
91 . . . . Tom Scott (three teams) 1974–1984

Most Touchdowns, One Game

6 . . . . Eddie James (Winnipeg) Sept 28, 1932
6 . . . . Bob McNamara (Winnipeg) Oct 13, 1956
5 . . . . Ernie Pitts (Winnipeg) Aug 29, 1959
5 . . . . Fred Burket (Saskatchewan) Oct 26, 1959
5 . . . . Earl Lunsford (Calgary) Sept 2, 1962
5 . . . . Martin Patton (Shreveport) Aug 5, 1995
5 . . . . Eric Blount (Edmonton) Sept 15, 1995

Source: *Canadian Football League*

CFL Outstanding Player Awards (1983–2003)[1]

Outstanding Player

1983	Warren Moon, Edm	1990	Mike Clemons, Tor	1997	Doug Flutie, Tor
1984	Willard Reaves, Wpg	1991	Doug Flutie, BC	1998	Mike Pringle, Mtl
1985	Mervyn Fernandez, BC	1992	Doug Flutie, Cal	1999	Danny McManus, Ham
1986	James Murphy, Wpg	1993	Doug Flutie, Cal	2000	Dave Dickenson, Cal
1987	Tom Clements, Wpg	1994	Doug Flutie, Cal	2001	Khari Jones, Wpg
1988	David Williams, BC	1995	Mike Pringle, Bal	2002	Milt Stegall, Wpg
1989	Tracy Ham, Edm	1996	Doug Flutie, Tor	2003	Anthony Calvillo, Mtl

Outstanding Canadian

1983	Paul Bennett, Wpg	1990	Ray Elgaard, Sask	1997	Sean Millington, BC
1984	Nick Arakgi, Mtl	1991	Blake Marshall, Edm	1998	Mike Morreale, Ham
1985	Paul Bennett, Ham	1992	Ray Elgaard, Sask	1999	Mike O'Shea, Tor
1986	Joe Poplawski, Wpg	1993	Dave Sapunjis, Cal	2000	Sean Millington, BC
1987	Scott Flagel, Wpg	1994	Gerald Wilcox, Wpg	2001	Doug Brown, Wpg
1988	Ray Elgaard, Sask	1995	Dave Sapunjis, Cal	2002	Ben Cahoon, Mtl
1989	Rocky DiPietro, Ham	1996	Leroy Blugh, Edm	2003	Ben Cahoon, Mtl

Outstanding Defensive Player

1983	Greg Marshall, Ott	1990	Greg Battle, Wpg	1997	Willie Pless, Edm
1984	James Parker, BC	1991	Greg Battle, Wpg	1998	Joe Montford, Ham
1985	Tyrone Jones, Wpg	1992	Willie Pless, Edm	1999	Calvin Tiggle, Ham
1986	James Parker, BC	1993	Jearld Baylis, Sask	2000	Joe Montford, Ham
1987	Gregg Stumon, BC	1994	Willie Pless, Edm	2001	Joe Montford, Ham
1988	Grover Covington, Ham	1995	Willie Pless, Edm	2002	Elfrid Payton, Edm
1989	Danny Bass, Edm	1996	Willie Pless, Edm	2003	Joe Fleming, Cal

Outstanding Offensive Lineman

1983	Rudy Phillips, Ott	1990	Jim Mills, BC	1997	Mike Kiselak, Tor
1984	John Bonk, Wpg	1991	Jim Mills, BC	1998	Fred Childress, Cal
1985	Nick Bastaja, Wpg	1992	Rob Smith, Ott	1999	Uzooma Okeke, Mtl
1986	Roger Aldag, Sask	1993	Chris Walby, Wpg	2000	Pierre Vercheval, Mtl
1987	Chris Walby, Wpg	1994	Shar Pourdanesh, Bal	2001	Dave Mudge, Wpg
1988	Roger Aldag, Sask	1995	Mike Withycombe, Bal	2002	Brian Chiu, Mtl
1989	Rod Connop, Edm	1996	Mike Kiselak, Tor	2003	Andrew Greene, Sask

Outstanding Rookie

1983	Johnny Shepherd, Ham	1990	Reggie Barnes, Ott	1997	Derrell Mitchell, Tor
1984	Dwaine Wilson, Mtl	1991	Jon Volpe, BC	1998	Steve Muhammad, BC
1985	Michael Gray, BC	1992	Mike Richardson, Wpg	1999	Pat LaCoste, BC
1986	Harold Hallman, Cal	1993	Michael O'Shea, Ham	2000	Albert Johnson III, Wpg
1987	Gill Fenerty, Tor	1994	Matt Goodwin, Bal	2001	Barrin Simpson, BC
1988	Orville Lee, Ott	1995	Shalon Baker, Edm	2002	Jason Clermont, BC
1989	Stephen Jordan, Ham	1996	Kelvin Anderson, Cal	2003	Frank Cutolo, BC

Source: *Canadian Football League*

(1) Winners are chosen by a vote of the Football Reporters of Canada; prior to 1989 they were known as the Schenley Awards.

Canadian Football Hall of Fame

(players only)

Player, Year Elected, Team(s)

Ah You, Junior (1997) Mtl
Aldag, Roger, (2002) Sask
Atchison, Ron, (1978) Sask
Bailey, Byron (1975) BC
Baker, Bitt (1994) Sask/BC
Barrow, John (1976) Ham
Bass, Danny (2000) Tor/Cgy/Edm
Batstone, Harry (1963) Tor/Queen's
Beach, Ormond (1963) Sarnia
Benecick, Al (1996) Sask
Bennett, Paul (2002) Tor/Wpg/Ham
Box, Ab (1965) Balmy Beach/Tor
Breen, Joseph (1963) U of Toronto/Tor
Bright, Johnny (1970) Edm/Cal
Brock, Ralph Dieter (1995) Wpg/Ham
Brown, Tom (1984) BC
Browne, Less (2002) Ham/Wpg/Ott/BC
Burden, Willie (2001) Cal
Campbell, Jerry "Soupy" (1996) Cal/Ott
Casey, Tom (1964) Wpg
Charlton, Ken (1992) Ott/Sask
Clements, Tom (1994) Ott/Sask/Ham/Wpg
Clark, Bill (1996) Sask
Coffey, Tommy Joe (1977) Edm/Cal
Conacher, Lionel (1963) Tor
Copeland, Royal (1988) Tor
Corrigal, Jim (1990) Tor
Covington, Grover (2000) Ham
Cox, Ernest (1963) Ham
Craig, Ross (1964) Ham
Cronin, Carl (1967) Wpg
Cutler, Dave (1998) Edm
Cutler, Wes (1968) Tor
Dalla Riva, Peter (1993) Mtl
Dipietro, Rocky (1997) Ham
Dixon, George (1974) Mtl
Elgaard, Ray (2002) Sask
Eliowitz, Abe (1969) Ott/Mtl
Emerson, Eddie (1963) Ott
Estay, Ron (2003) BC/Edm
Etcheverry, Sam (1969) Mtl
Evanshen, Terry (1984) Mtl/Cal/Ham/Tor
Faloney, Bernie (1974) Edm/Ham
Fear, Cap (1967) Tor/Mtl/Ham
Fennell, Dave (1990) Edm
Ferraro, John (1966) Ham/Mtl
Fieldgate, Norm (1979) BC
Fleming, Willie (1982) BC
Frank, Bill (2001) BC/Tor/Wpg

Player, Year Elected, Team(s)

Gabriel, Tony (1984) Ham/Ott
Gaines, Geve (1994) Mtl/Ott
Gall, Hugh (1963) U of Toronto
Golab, Tony (1964) Ott
Grant, Tom (1995) Ham/Wpg
Gray, Herb (1983) Wpg
Griffing, Dean (1965) Sask/Cal
Hanson, Fritz (1963) Wpg
Harris, Dickie (1998) Mtl
Harris, Wayne (1976) Cal
Harrison, Herman (1993) Cal
Helton, John (1985) Cal/Wpg
Henley, Garney (1979) Ham
Highbaugh, Larry (2004) BC/Edm
Hinton, Tom (1991) BC
Holloway, Condredge (1998) O/Tor/BC
Huffman, Dick (1987) Wpg/Cal
Isbister, Bob (1965) Ham
Jackson, Russ (1973) Ott
Jacobs, Jack (1963) Wpg
James, Eddie (1963) Wpg/Reg
James, Gerry (1981) Wpg
Kabat, Greg (1966) Wpg
Kapp, Joe (1984) Cal/BC
Keeling, Jerry (1989) Cal/Ott/Ham
Kelly, Brian (1991) Edm
Kelly, Ellison (1992) Edm/Ham
Kepley, Dan (1996) Edm
Krol, Joe (1963) Tor/Ham
Kwong, Normie (1969) Cal/Edm
Lawson, Smirle (1963) U. of Toronto
Leadlay, Frank (1963) Queen's/Ham
Lear, Les (1974) Wpg/Cal
Lewis, Leo (1973) Wpg
Lunsford, Earl (1983) Cal
Luster, Marv (1990) Mtl/Tor
Luzzi, Don (1985) Cal
McCance, Chester (1976) Wpg/Mtl
McGill, Frank (1965) Mtl
McGowan, George (2003) Edm
McQuarters, Ed (1988) Sask
Miles, Rollie (1980) Edm
Moon, Warren (2001) Edm
Morris, Frank (1983) Tor/Edm
Morris, Ted (1964) Tor
Mosca, Angelo (1987) Ham
Murphy, James (2000) Wpg
Nelson, Roger (1985) Edm
Neumann, Peter (1979) Ham
O'Quinn, Red (1981) Mtl

Player, Year Elected, Team(s)

Pajaczkowski, Tony (1988) Cal/Mtl
Parker, Jackie (1971) Edm/Tor/BC
Parker, James (2001) Edm/BC/Tor
Passaglia, Lui (2004) BC
Patterson, Hal (1971) Mtl/Ham
Perry, Gordon (1970) Mtl
Perry, Norman (1963) Sarnia
Ploen, Ken (1975) Wpg
Poplawski, Joe (1998) Wpg
Quilty, Silver (1966) U. of Ottawa
Raimy, Dave (2000) Wpg/Tor
Rebholz, Russ (1963) Wpg
Reed, George (1979) Sask
Reeve, Ted (1963) Tor
Ridgway, Dave (2003) Sask
Rigney, Frank (1984) Wpg
Robinson, Larry (1998) Cal
Rodden, Michael (1964) Queen's/Tor
Rowe, Paul (1964) Cal
Ruby, Martin (1974) Sask
Russel, Jeff (1963) Ott
Scott, Tom (1998) Wpg/Edm
Scott, Vince (1982) Ham
Shatto, Dick (1975) Tor
Simpson, Benjamin (1963) Ham
Simpson, Bob (1976) Ott
Sprague, David (1963) Ham/Ott
Stevenson, Art (1969) Wpg
Stewart, Ron (1977) Ott
Stirling, Bummer (1966) Sarnia
Sutherin, Don (1992) Ham/Ott
Symons, Bill (1997) BC/Tor
Thelen, Dave (1989) Ott/Tor
Timmis, Brian (1963) Ham/Ott
Tinsley, Buddy (1982) Wpg
Tommy, Andrew (1989) Ott/Tor
Trawick, Herb (1975) Mtl
Tubman, Joe (1968) Ott
Tucker, Whit (1993) Ott
Urness, Ted (1989) Sask
Vaughn, Kaye (1978) Ott
Wagner, Virgil (1980) Mtl
Walby, Chris (2003) Mtl/Wpg
Welch, Huck (1964) Ham/Mtl
Wilkinson, Tom (1987) Edm
Wilson, Al (1997) BC
Wylie, Harvey (1980) Cal
Yochum, Dan (2004) Mtl/Edm
Young, Jim (1991) BC
Zambiasi, Ben (2004) Ham/Tor
Zock, William (1984) Tor/Edm

Source: *Canadian Football League*

2004 CFL Hall of Fame Inductees

Five new inductees entered the Canadian Football Hall of Fame during ceremonies in Hamilton, Ontario, September 30 to October 2, 2004. Of the inductees, four are entering as players and one is in the builder category.

■ Larry Highbaugh (Player)

During a 14-year career — mostly with the Edmonton Eskimos — defensive back Larry Highbaugh was named CFL All-Star three times and Western Division All-Star four times. Eskimo teams that he played on went to the Grey Cup nine times, winning six of those.

■ Cal Murphy (Builder)

At various times, Cal Murphy was a coach, head coach, and general manager with five CFL teams, including 14 years with the Winnipeg Blue Bombers. During his leadership in Winnipeg, the Blue Bombers played in five Grey Cups and won three, including the 1984 Grey Cup that was Winnipeg's first championship in 22 years. Murphy also coached with the B.C., Montreal, Edmonton, and Saskatchewan franchises.

■ Lui Passaglia (Player)

Lui Passaglia holds many CFL individual records, including most regular seasons played (25), most regular season games played (408), and most career regular-season points (3,991). He was the first player to score 200 points in a season, accumulating 214 points in 1987.

Passaglia spent his entire career as a kicker and wide receiver with the B.C. Lions, and was named Western Division All-Star nine times and a CFL All-Star four times.

■ Dan Yochum (Player)

A four-time CFL All-Star, offensive tackle Dan Yochum spent most of his nine-year career with the Montreal Alouettes. Yochum was also named an Eastern Division All-Star seven times, and was named the league's Most Outstanding Offensive Lineman in 1976. Yochum finished his CFL career in 1980 as an Edmonton Eskimo.

■ Ben Zambiasi (Player)

Linebacker Ben Zambiasi's career with the Hamilton Tiger-Cats started with a bang and continued strong throughout his 11 years in the league, finishing with Toronto in 1988. Zambiasi was named the Eastern Division's Most Outstanding Rookie in the Eastern Division in 1978. That year, he also earned Eastern Division All-Star and CFL All-Star honours, the first of eight times and six times, respectively. Zambiasi won the league's Most Outstanding Defensive Player Award in 1979.

Source: *Canadian Football League*

Canadian Football Hall of Fame

*I*nterested in Canadian Football? Visit the Canadian Football Hall of Fame. In the Hands-On zone you can kick a virtual field goal and view videos showing production of football equipment and in the Heritage zone you can view photos of Gridiron Greats. The Hall also offers student education programs that help kids build language skills as they discover the star players and explore exhibits. The CFL Hall of Fame itself is located at 58 Jackson Street West, Hamilton, Ontario and is open year round Tuesday to Saturday, 9:30 a.m. till 4:30 p.m. It's closed Statutory holidays and long weekends. For information call (905) 528-7566 or click on www.footballhof.com.

NFL Final Standings, 2003–04

American Football Conference

■ AFC East	W	L	T	PCT	PF	PA
New England (*YZ)	14	2	0	.875	348	238
Miami	10	6	0	.625	311	261
Buffalo	6	10	0	.375	243	279
N.Y. Jets	6	10	0	.375	283	299

■ AFC North	W	L	T	PCT	PF	PA
Baltimore (Y)	10	6	0	.625	391	281
Cincinnati	8	8	0	.500	346	384
Pittsburgh	6	10	0	.375	300	327
Cleveland	5	11	0	.312	254	322

■ AFC South	W	L	T	PCT	PF	PA
Indianapolis (Y)	12	4	0	.750	447	336
Tennessee (X)	12	4	0	.750	435	324
Jacksonville	5	11	0	.312	276	331
Houston	5	11	0	.312	255	380

■ AFC West	W	L	T	PCT	PF	PA
Kansas City (YZ)	13	3	0	.812	484	332
Denver (X)	10	6	0	.625	381	301
Oakland	4	12	0	.250	270	379
San Diego	4	12	0	.250	313	441

National Football Conference

■ NFC East	W	L	T	PCT	PF	PA
Philadelphia (*YZ)	12	4	0	.750	374	287
Dallas (X)	10	6	0	.625	289	260
Washington	5	11	0	.312	287	372
N.Y. Giants	4	12	0	.250	243	387

■ NFC North	W	L	T	PCT	PF	PA
Green Bay (Y)	10	6	0	.625	442	307
Minnesota	9	7	0	.562	416	353
Chicago	7	9	0	.438	283	346
Detroit	5	11	0	.312	270	379

■ NFC South	W	L	T	PCT	PF	PA
Carolina (Y)	11	5	0	.688	325	304
New Orleans	8	8	0	.500	340	326
Tampa Bay	7	9	0	.438	301	264
Atlanta	5	11	0	.312	299	422

■ NFC West	W	L	T	PCT	PF	PA
St. Louis (YZ)	12	4	0	.750	447	328
Seattle (X)	10	6	0	.625	404	327
San Francisco	7	9	0	.438	384	337
Arizona	5	11	0	.312	262	417

Source: *National Football League*

(x) Clinched playoff berth; (y) clinched division title; (z) clinched first round bye; (*) clinched home field advantage in playoffs

Playoffs

■ Wild Cards

Saturday, Jan. 3, 2004

Tennessee Titans 20

At Baltimore Ravens 17

Saturday, Jan. 3, 2004

At Carolina Panthers 29

Dallas Cowboys 10

Sunday, Jan. 4, 2004

At Green Bay Packers 33

Seattle Seahawks 27

Sunday, Jan. 4, 2004

At Indianapolis Colts 41

Denver Broncos 10

■ Divisional Playoffs

Saturday, Jan. 10, 2004

Carolina Panthers 29

At St. Louis Rams 23

Saturday, Jan. 10, 2004

At New England Patriots 17

Tennessee Titans 14

Sunday, Jan. 11, 2004

Indianapolis Colts 38

At Kansas City Chiefs 31

Sunday, Jan. 11, 2004

At Philadelphia Eagles 20

Green Bay Packers 17

■ Conference Championship

Sunday, Jan. 18, 2004

At New England Patriots 24

Indianapolis Colts 14

Sunday, Jan. 18, 2004

Carolina Panthers 14

At Philadelphia Eagles 3

■ Super Bowl XXXVIII at Reliant Stadium Houston, Texas

Sunday, Feb. 1, 2004

New England Patriots 32

Carolina Panthers 29

Source: *National Football League*

Super Bowl Champions and Most Valuable Players

Game	Date	Result	MVP
I	Jan. 15, 1967	Green Bay Packers 35, Kansas City Chiefs 10	Bart Starr, GB
II	Jan. 14, 1968	Green Bay Packers 33, Oakland Raiders 14	Bart Starr, GB
III	Jan. 12, 1969	New York Jets 16, Baltimore Colts 7	Joe Namath, NY
IV	Jan. 11, 1970	Kansas City Chiefs 23, Minnesota Vikings 7	Len Dawson, KC
V	Jan. 17, 1971	Baltimore Colts 16, Dallas Cowboys 13	Chuck Howley, DAL
VI	Jan. 16, 1972	Dallas Cowboys 24, Miami Dolphins 3	Roger Staubach, DAL
VII	Jan. 14, 1973	Miami Dolphins 14, Washington Redskins 7	Jake Scott, MIA
VIII	Jan. 13, 1974	Miami Dolphins 24, Minnesota Vikings 7	Larry Csonka, MIA
IX	Jan. 12, 1975	Pittsburgh Steelers 16, Minnesota Vikings 6	Franco Harris, PIT
X	Jan. 18, 1976	Pittsburgh Steelers 21, Dallas Cowboys 17	Lynn Swann, PIT
XI	Jan. 9, 1977	Oakland Raiders 32, Minnesota Vikings 14	Fred Biletnikoff, OAK
XII	Jan. 15, 1978	Dallas Cowboys 27, Denver Broncos 10	Randy White, Harvey Martin, DAL
XIII	Jan. 21, 1979	Pittsburgh Steelers 35, Dallas Cowboys 31	Terry Bradshaw, PIT
XIV	Jan. 20, 1980	Pittsburgh Steelers 31, Los Angeles Rams 19	Terry Bradshaw, PIT
XV	Jan. 25, 1981	Oakland Raiders 27, Philadelphia Eagles 10	Jim Plunkett, OAK
XVI	Jan. 24, 1982	San Francisco 49ers 26, Cincinnati Bengals 21	Joe Montana, SF
XVII	Jan. 30, 1983	Washington Redskins 27, Miami Dolphins 17	John Riggins, WAS
XVIII	Jan. 22, 1984	Los Angeles Raiders 38, Washington Redskins 9	Marcus Allen, LA
XIX	Jan. 20, 1985	San Francisco 49ers 38, Miami Dolphins 16	Joe Montana, SF
XX	Jan. 26, 1986	Chicago Bears 46, New England Patriots 10	Richard Dent, CHI
XXI	Jan. 25, 1987	New York Giants 39, Denver Broncos 20	Phil Simms, NY
XXII	Jan. 31, 1988	Washington Redskins 42, Denver Broncos 10	Doug Williams, WAS
XXIII	Jan. 22, 1989	San Francisco 49ers 20, Cincinnati Bengals 16	Jerry Rice, SF
XXIV	Jan. 28, 1990	San Francisco 49ers 55, Denver Broncos 10	Joe Montana, SF
XXV	Jan. 27, 1991	New York Giants 20, Buffalo Bills 19	Ottis Anderson, NY
XXVI	Jan. 26, 1992	Washington Redskins 37, Buffalo Bills 24	Mark Rypien, WAS
XXVII	Jan. 31, 1993	Dallas Cowboys 52, Buffalo Bills 17	Troy Aikman, DAL
XXVIII	Jan. 30, 1994	Dallas Cowboys 30, Buffalo Bills 13	Emmitt Smith, DAL
XXIX	Jan. 29, 1995	San Francisco 49ers 49, San Diego Chargers 26	Steve Young, SF
XXX	Jan. 28, 1996	Dallas Cowboys 27, Pittsburgh Steelers 17	Larry Brown, DAL
XXXI	Jan. 26, 1997	Green Bay Packers 35, New England Patriots 21	Desmond Howard, GB
XXXII	Jan. 25, 1998	Denver Broncos 31, Green Bay Packers 24	Terrell Davis, DEN
XXXIII	Jan. 31, 1999	Denver Broncos 34, Atlanta Falcons 19	John Elway, DEN
XXXIV	Jan. 30, 2000	St. Louis Rams 23, Tennessee Titans 16	Kurt Warner, STL
XXXV	Jan. 28, 2001	Baltimore Ravens 34, New York Giants 7	Ray Lewis, BAL
XXXVI	Feb. 3, 2002	New England Patriots 20, St. Louis Rams 17	Tom Brady, NE
XXXVII	Jan. 26, 2003	Tampa Bay Buccaneers 48, Oakland Raiders 21	Dexter Jackson, TB
XXXVIII	Feb. 1, 2004	New England Patriots 32, Carolina Panthers 29	Tom Brady, NE

National Football League Individual Leaders, 2003

■ PASSING

PLAYER	TEAM	YDS	ATT	CMP	TDS	INTS	LONG	RATING
Peyton Manning........	IND	4267	566	379	29	10	79	99.0
Trent Green	KC	4039	523	330	24	12	67	92.6
Marc Bulger...........	STL	3845	532	336	22	22	48	81.4
Matt Hasselbeck........	SEA	3841	513	313	26	15	80	88.8
Brad Johnson..........	TB	3811	570	354	26	21	76	81.5
Tom Brady	NE	3620	527	317	23	12	82	85.9
Jon Kitna	CIN	3591	520	324	26	15	82	87.4
Aaron Brooks..........	NO	3546	518	306	24	8	76	88.8
Daunte Culpepper	MIN	3479	454	295	25	11	59	96.4
Tommy Maddox........	PIT	3414	519	298	18	17	53	75.3

■ RECEIVING

PLAYER	TEAM	REC	YDS	AVG	TDS	LONG
Torry Holt............	STL	117	1696	14.5	12	48
Randy Moss...........	MIN	111	1632	14.7	17	72
Anquan Boldin	ARI	101	1377	13.6	8	71
LaDainian Tomlinson	SD	100	725	7.3	4	73
Hines Ward	PIT	95	1163	12.2	10	50
Derrick Mason	TEN	95	1303	13.7	8	50
Marvin Harrison........	IND	94	1272	13.5	10	79
Chad Johnson	CIN	90	1355	15.1	10	82
Steve Smith	CAR	88	1110	12.6	7	67
Keenan McCardell	TB	84	1174	14.0	8	76

■ RUSHING

PLAYER	TEAM	YDS	ATT	AVG	TDS	LONG
Jamal Lewis...........	BAL	2066	387	5.3	14	82
Ahman Green..........	GB	1883	355	5.3	15	98
LaDainian Tomlinson	SD	1645	313	5.3	13	73
Deuce McAllister	NO	1641	351	4.7	8	76
Clinton Portis..........	DEN	1591	290	5.5	14	65
Fred Taylor...........	JAC	1572	345	4.6	6	62
Stephen Davis	CAR	1444	318	4.5	8	40
Shaun Alexander	SEA	1435	326	4.4	14	55
Priest Holmes	KC	1420	320	4.4	27	31
Ricky Williams	MIA	1372	392	3.5	9	45

■ SACKS

PLAYER	TEAM	SACKS	TAC
Michael Strahan	NYG	18.5	76
Adewale Ogunleye	MIA	15	62
Simeon Rice.........	TB	15	50
Jason Taylor.........	MIA	13	57
Shaun Ellis..........	NYJ	12.5	69
Leonard Little........	STL	12.5	47
Terrell Suggs	BAL	12	27
Mike Rucker.........	CAR	12	58
Aaron Schobel	BUF	11.5	60
Bert Berry...........	DEN	11.5	36

■ SCORING

PLAYER	TEAM	POINTS	TDS	XPT	FG
Jeff Wilkins .... STL		163	0	46	39
Priest Holmes........ KC		162	27	0	0
Mike Vanderjagt ..... IND		157	0	46	37
Matt Stover .... BAL		134	0	35	33
John Kasay.......... CAR		125	0	29	32
Gary Anderson .... TEN		123	0	42	27
Jason Elam.......... DEN		120	0	39	27
Ahman Green........ GB		120	20	0	0
Ryan Longwell ...... GB		120	0	51	23
Josh Brown .... SEA		114	0	48	22
David Akers .... PHI		114	0	42	24

Source: *NFL*

2004 PGA Scoring Leaders

(as of October 4, 2004)

Rank	Player (Country)	Average Strokes per Round	Rank	Player (Country)	Average Strokes per Round
1	Vijay Singh (Fiji)	68.92	14	Jerry Kelly (USA)	70.09
2	Phil Mickelson (USA)	68.94	14	Loren Roberts (USA)	70.09
3	Ernie Els (South Africa)	68.96	16	Bo Van Pelt (USA)	70.10
4	Tiger Woods (USA)	69.10	17	Jay Haas (USA)	70.13
5	Retief Goosen (South Africa)	69.49	17	Nick Price (Zimbabwe)	70.13
6	Stewart Cink (USA)	69.73	19	Shigeki Maruyama (Japan)	70.17
7	Sergio Garcia (Spain)	69.79	19	Jesper Parnevik (Sweden)	70.17
8	**Stephen Ames (Canada)**	**69.88**	**21**	**Mike Weir (Canada)**	**70.19**
9	Scott Verplank (USA)	69.94	22	Kenny Perry (USA)	70.22
10	Davis Love III (USA)	69.99	23	Chris DiMarco (USA)	70.23
11	Adam Scott (Australia)	70.02	24	David Toms (USA)	70.26
12	Luke Donald (England)	70.04	25	Tom Lehman (USA)	70.28
13	Zach Johnson (USA)	70.08	**186**	**David Morland IV (Canada)**	**72.31**

Source: *Professional Golf Association*

2004 PGA Tour Money Leaders

(as of October 4, 2004 — in US dollars)

Rank	Player (Country)	Events	Earnings ($)	Rank	Player (Country)	Events	Earnings($)
1	Vijay Singh (Fiji)	26	9 455 566	15	Rory Sabbatini (South Africa)	25	2 342 197
2	Phil Mickelson (USA)	19	5 672 323	16	Steve Flesch (USA)	28	2 341 886
3	Ernie Els (South Africa)	15	5 629 025	17	Mark Hensby (Australia)	26	2 334 791
4	Tiger Woods (USA)	18	4 717 472	18	Chad Campbell (USA)	25	2 244 977
5	Stewart Cink (USA)	26	4 344 670	19	John Daly (USA)	19	2 242 507
6	Adam Scott (Australia)	15	3 619 384	20	Zach Johnson (USA)	27	2 237 405
7	Sergio Garcia (Spain)	17	3 115 415	21	Shigeki Maruyama (Japan)	24	2 133 440
8	Davis Love III (USA)	21	3 075 092	22	Scott Verplank (USA)	21	2 052 477
9	**Stephen Ames (Canada)**	**24**	**3 014 679**	23	K.J. Choi (South Korea)	22	1 982 975
10	Todd Hamilton (USA)	26	2 970 178	24	Fred Funk (USA)	25	1 943 943
11	Chris DiMarco (USA)	25	2 816 427	25	Jerry Kelly (USA)	25	1 914 232
12	Stuart Appleby (Australia)	21	2 784 943	**194**	**David Morland IV (Canada)**	**25**	**164 435**
13	Retief Goosen (South Africa)	14	2 747 323	**213**	**Glen Hnatiuk (Canada)**	**9**	**103 500**
14	**Mike Weir (Canada)**	**20**	**2 513 536**				

Source: *Professional Golf Association*

Canadian PGA Tour Tournament Champions

Stephen Ames	2004 Cialis Western Open		1968 Tucson Open
Al Balding	1955 Mayfair Open		1972 Robinson Open
	1957 Miami Beach Open	Ian Leggatt	2002 Tucson Open
	1957 West Palm Beach Open	Stan Leonard	1957 Greater Greensboro Open
	1957 Havana Invitational		1958 Tournament of Champions
Dave Barr	1981 Quad Cities Open		1960 Western Open
	1987 Georgia-Pacific Atlanta Golf Classic	Mike Weir	1999 Air Canada Championship
	2003 Royal Caribbean Golf Classic (Champions Tour)		2000 WGC-American Express Championship
Kenneth Black (amateur)	1936 Vancouver Golden Jubilee		2001 The Tour Championship
Dan Halldorson	1980 Pensacola Open		2003 Bob Hope Chrysler Classic
	1986 Deposit Guaranty Golf Classic		2003 Nissan Open
George Knudson	1961 Coral Gables Open		2003 Masters
	1963 Portland Open		2004 Nissan Open
	1964 Fresno Open	Richard Zokol	1992 Greater Milwaukee Open
	1967 New Orleans Open		
	1968 Phoenix Open		

Official World Golf Ranking

(as of October 4, 2004)

Rank	Player (Country)	Pts. Avg.	Rank	Player (Country)	Pts. Avg.	Rank	Player (Country)	Pts. Avg.
1	Vijay Singh (Fiji)	14.14	35	Robert Allenby (Australia)	2.97	69	Loren Roberts (USA)	1.93
2	Ernie Els (South Africa)	12.48	36	Jonathan Kaye (USA)	2.89	70	Carlos Franco (Paraguay)	1.92
3	Tiger Woods (USA)	11.54	37	Nick Price (Zimbabwe)	2.88	71	Jonathan Byrd (USA)	1.91
4	Phil Mickelson (USA)	8.55	38	John Daly (USA)	2.79	72	Ben Curtis (USA)	1.91
5	Retief Goosen (South Africa)	7.26	39	Jerry Kelly (USA)	2.75	73	Geoff Ogilvy (Australia)	1.86
6	Davis Love-III (USA)	7.04	39	Chris Riley (USA)	2.75	74	Arron Oberholser (USA)	1.81
7	**Mike Weir (Canada)**	**6.77**	41	Zach Johnson (USA)	2.73	75	Tim Clark (South Africa)	1.80
8	Padraig Harrington (Ireland)	5.98	42	Thomas Levet (France)	2.69	76	Craig Parry (Australia)	1.79
9	Stewart Cink (USA)	5.33	43	Charles Howell III (USA)	2.64	77	Bernhard Langer (Germany)	1.79
10	Sergio Garcia (Spain)	4.96	44	Alex Cejka (Germany)	2.62	78	Brian Davis (England)	1.78
11	Adam Scott (Australia)	4.95	45	Lee Westwood (England)	2.62	79	Phillip Price (Wales)	1.76
12	Jim Furyk (USA)	4.69	46	Fred Funk (USA)	2.52	80	S.K. Ho (South Korea)	1.75
13	Darren Clarke (N. Ireland)	4.64	47	Joakim Haeggman (Sweden)	2.51	81	John Huston (USA)	1.74
14	Chris DiMarco (USA)	4.48	48	Brad Faxon (USA)	2.48	82	Bob Estes (USA)	1.72
15	Stuart Appleby (Australia)	4.48	49	Trevor Immelman (South Africa)	2.44	83	Raphael Jacquelin (France)	1.66
16	Chad Campbell (USA)	4.38	50	Stephen Leaney (Australia)	2.41	84	Eduardo Romero (Argentina)	1.66
17	Kenny Perry (USA)	4.27	51	David Howell (England)	2.39	85	Tim Petrovic (USA)	1.65
18	Todd Hamilton (USA)	4.24	52	Nick O'Hern (Australia)	2.36	86	Briny Baird (USA)	1.65
19	Miguel A Jimenez (Spain)	3.95	53	Bob Tway (USA)	2.36	87	Mark O'Meara (USA)	1.62
20	**Stephen Ames (Canada)**	**3.85**	54	Mark Hensby (Australia)	2.34	88	Skip Kendall (USA)	1.60
21	David Toms (USA)	3.74	55	Jeff Maggert (USA)	2.30	89	Ricardo Gonzalez (Argentina)	1.59
22	Scott Verplank (USA)	3.74	56	Tim Herron (USA)	2.29	90	Jeff Sluman (USA)	1.59
23	Jay Haas (USA)	3.51	57	Rodney Pampling (Australia)	2.28	91	Graeme McDowell (N. Ireland)	1.58
24	K.J. Choi (South Korea)	3.45	58	Kirk Triplett (USA)	2.28	92	Woody Austin (USA)	1.57
25	Paul Casey (England)	3.37	59	Duffy Waldorf (USA)	2.24	93	Steve Lowery (USA)	1.57
26	Shigeki Maruyama (Japan)	3.37	60	Shaun Micheel (USA)	2.17	94	Brendan Jones (Australia)	1.56
27	Fred Couples (USA)	3.35	61	Peter Lonard (Australia)	2.17	95	Tom Lehman (USA)	1.56
28	Thomas Bjorn (Denmark)	3.26	62	Ian Poulter (England)	2.10	96	Joey Sindelar (USA)	1.54
29	Justin Leonard (USA)	3.12	63	Justin Rose (England)	2.04	97	David Lynn (England)	1.52
30	Luke Donald (England)	3.11	64	Shingo Katayama (Japan)	2.03	98	Bo Van Pelt (USA)	1.51
31	Rory Sabbatini (South Africa)	3.10	65	Paul McGinley (Ireland)	2.01	99	Thongchai Jaidee (Thailand)	1.50
32	Angel Cabrera (Argentina)	3.08	66	Colin Montgomerie (Scotland)	1.98	100	John Rollins (USA)	1.49
33	Steve Flesch (USA)	3.06	67	Scott Hoch (USA)	1.95	278	**David Hearn (Canada)**	**0.51**
34	Fredrik Jacobson (Sweden)	3.05	68	Michael Campbell (New Zealand)	1.94	315	**Glen Hnatiuk (Canada)**	**0.43**

Source: *The Official World Golf Ranking*

2003–04 PGA Tour Tournament Champions

(October 8, 2003–October 4, 2004)

Date	Tournament	Location	Champion
Oct. 8–12, 2003	Las Vegas Invitational	Las Vegas, NV	Stuart Appleby
Oct. 16–19, 2003	Chrysler Classic of Greensboro	Greensboro, NC	Shigeki Maruyama
Oct. 23–26, 2003	Funai Classic at the Walt Disney World Resort	Palm Lake Buena Vista, FL	Vijay Singh
Oct. 30–Nov. 2, 2003	Chrysler Championship	Palm Harbor, FL	Retief Goosen
Nov. 3–9, 2003	The Tour Championship	Houston, TX	Chad Campbell
Jan. 5–11, 2004	Mercedes Championships	Kapalua, HI	Stuart Appleby
Jan. 12–18, 2004	Sony Open in Hawaii	Honolulu, HI	Ernie Els
Jan. 19–25, 2004	Bob Hope Chrysler Classic	La Quinta, CA	Phil Mickelson
Jan. 26–Feb. 1, 2004	FBR Open	Scottsdale, AZ	Jonathan Kaye
Feb. 2–8, 2004	AT&T Pebble Beach National Pro-Am	Pebble Beach, CA	Vijay Singh
Feb. 9–15, 2004	Buick Invitational	San Diego, CA	John Daly
Feb. 16–22, 2004	Nissan Open	Pacific Palisades, CA	**Mike Weir**
Feb. 23–29, 2004	WGC-Accenture Match Play Championship	Carlsbad, CA	Tiger Woods
Feb. 23–29, 2004	Chrysler Classic of Tucson	Tucson, AZ	Heath Slocum
March 1–7, 2004	Ford Championship at Doral	Miami, FL	Craig Parry
March 8–14, 2004	The Honda Classic	Palm Beach Gardens, FL	Todd Hamilton
March 15–21, 2004	Bay Hill Invitational	Orlando, FL	Chad Campbell
March 22–28, 2004	The Players Championship	Ponte Vedra Beach, FL	Adam Scott
March 29–April 4, 2004	BellSouth Classic	Duluth, GA	Zach Johnson
April 5–11, 2004	The Masters #	Augusta, GA	Phil Mickelson
April 12–18, 2004	MCI Heritage	Hilton Head Island, SC	Stewart Cink
April 19–25, 2004	Shell Houston Open	Houston, TX	Vijay Singh
April 26–May 2, 2004	HP Classic of New Orleans	New Orleans, LA	Vijay Singh
May 3–9, 2004	Wachovia Championship	Charlotte, NC	Joey Sindelar
May 10–16, 2004	EDS Byron Nelson Championship	Irving, TX	Sergio Garcia
May 17–23, 2004	Bank of America Colonial	Ft. Worth, TX	Steve Flesch
May 24–30, 2004	FedEx St. Jude Classic	Memphis, TN	David Toms
May 31–June 6, 2004	The Memorial Tournament	Dublin, OH	Ernie Els
June 7–13, 2004	Buick Classic	Harrison, NY	Sergio Garcia
June 14–20, 2004	U.S. Open #	Southampton, NY	Retief Goosen
June 21–27, 2004	Booz Allen Classic	Potomac, MD	Adam Scott
June 28–July 4, 2004	Cialis Western Open	Lemont, IL	**Stephen Ames**
July 5–11, 2004	John Deere Classic	Silvis, IL	Mark Hensby
July 12–18, 2004	British Open #	Ayrshire, Scotland	Todd Hamilton
July 12–18, 2004	B. C. Open	Endicott, NY	Jonathan Byrd
July 19–25, 2004	U.S. Bank Championship	Milwaukee, WI	Carlos Franco
July 26–Aug. 1, 2004	Buick Open	Grand Blanc, MI	Vijay Singh
Aug. 2–8, 2004	The International	Castle Rock, CO	Rod Pampling
Aug. 9–15, 2004	PGA Championship #	Kohler, WI	Vijay Singh
Aug. 16–22, 2004	WGC-NEC Invitational	Akron, OH	Stewart Cink
Aug. 16–22, 2004	Reno-Tahoe Open	Reno, NV	Vaughn Taylor
Aug. 23–29, 2004	Buick Championship	Cromwell, CN	Woody Austin
Aug. 30–Sept. 6, 2004	Deutsche Bank Championship	Norton, MA	Vijay Singh
Sept. 6–12, 2004	Bell Canadian Open	Oakville, Ontario, Canada	Vijay Singh
Sept. 13–19, 2004	Valero Texas Open	San Antonio, TX	Bart Bryant
Sept. 20–26, 2004	84 Lumber Classic	Farmington, PA	Vijay Singh
Sept. 27–Oct. 3, 2004	WGC-American Express Championship	Kilkenny, Ireland	Ernie Els
Sept. 27–Oct. 3, 2004	Southern Farm Bureau Classic	Madison, MS	Fred Funk

Source: *Professional Golf Association*

\# Major Championships

2004 LPGA Scoring Leaders

(as of October 4, 2004)

Rank	Player (Country)	Average Strokes per Round	Rank	Player (Country)	Average Strokes per Round
1	Annika Sorenstam (Sweden)	69.04	15	Christina Kim (USA)	71.01
2	Lorena Ochoa (Mexico)	69.88	16	Shi Hyun Ahn (Korea)	71.09
3	Grace Park (Korea)	70.19	17	Laura Davies (England)	71.13
4	Mi-Hyun Kim (Korea)	70.45	17	Se Ri Pak (Korea)	71.13
5	Lindsey Wright (England)	70.50	17	Rosie Jones (USA)	71.13
6	Cristie Kerr (USA)	70.52	20	Catriona Matthew (Scotland)	71.15
7	Karrie Webb (Australia)	70.61	21	Jennifer Rosales (Philippines)	71.16
8	Karen Stupples (England)	70.76	22	Leta Lindley (USA)	71.18
9	Meg Mallon (USA)	70.80	23	Carin Koch (Sweden)	71.26
10	Hee-Won Han (Korea)	70.86	24	Patricia Meunier-Lebouc (France)	71.28
11	Pat Hurst (USA)	70.90	25	Candie Kung (Taiwan)	71.32
11	Juli Inkster (USA)	70.90	**26**	**Lorie Kane (Canada)**	**71.36**
13	Jeong Jang (Korea)	70.91	**63**	**Dawn Coe-Jones (Canada)**	**72.34**
14	Michele Redman (USA)	70.93	**81**	**A.J. Eathorne (Canada)**	**72.67**

Source: *Ladies Professional Golf Association*

2004 LPGA Tour Money Leaders

(as of October 4, 2004 — in US dollars)

Rank	Player (Country)	Earnings ($)	Rank	Player (Country)	Earnings ($)
1	Annika Sorenstam (Sweden)	1 864 608	15	Catriona Matthew (Scotland)	565 932
2	Meg Mallon (USA)	1 313 623	16	Jeong Jang (Korea)	529 729
3	Lorena Ochoa (Mexico)	1 263 043	17	Shi Hyun Ahn (Korea)	519 643
4	Grace Park (Korea)	1 003 845	18	Rachel Teske (Australia)	514 847
5	Cristie Kerr (USA)	986 936	19	Candie Kung (Taiwan)	497 358
6	Mi-Hyun Kim (Korea)	886 608	20	Pat Hurst (USA)	479 727
7	Karen Stupples (England)	845 200	**21**	**Lorie Kane (Canada)**	**467 692**
8	Hee-Won Han (Korea)	746 870	22	Michele Redman (USA)	462 047
9	Se Ri Pak (Korea)	648 860	23	Rosie Jones (USA)	439 648
10	Jennifer Rosales (Philippines)	619 394	24	Kim Saiki (USA)	437 328
11	Karrie Webb (Australia)	608 642	25	Gloria Park (Korea)	421 157
12	Christina Kim (USA)	588 530	**53**	**Dawn Coe-Jones (Canada)**	**189 573**
13	Juli Inkster (USA)	588 378	**76**	**Isabelle Beisiegel (Canada)**	**120 586**
14	Wendy Doolan (Australia)	575 983	**81**	**A.J. Eathorne (Canada)**	**111 698**

Canadian LPGA Tour Tournament Champions

Jocelyne Bourassa	1973 La Canadienne	Sandra Post	1968 LPGA Championship
Dawn Coe-Jones	1994 HEALTHSOUTH Palm Beach Classic		1978 Colgate Dinah Shore Winners Circle
	1991 Women's Kemper Open		1979 Colgate Dinah Shore Winner's Circle
Gail Graham	1997 Alpine Australian Ladies Masters		1978 Lady Stroh's Open
	1995 Fieldcrest Cannon Classic		1979 Lady Michelob
Lorie Kane	2001 LPGA Takefuji Classic		1979 ERA Real Estate Classic
	2000 Mizuno Classic		1980 West Virginia Classic
	2000 New Albany Golf Classic		1981 McDonald's Kids Classic
	2000 Michelob Light Classic		

The Presidents Cup

The Presidents Cup is a biennial match-play competition between a team from the United States and an international team made up of players from outside the United States and Europe. The four-day event features foursomes (teams of two golfers alternate shots), four-ball (teams of two golfers each playing their own shot), and singles (one-on-one) matches. The United States holds the overall lead in matches with three wins against one loss and one half.

The fifth Presidents Cup competition was held in South Africa, November 20–23, 2003. The competition was halved at 17 points each.

Day One—Foursomes

Nick Price/**Mike Weir** (Int.) def. David Toms/Phil Mickelson, 1-up

Retief Goosen/Vijay Singh (Int.) def. Chris DiMarco/Jerry Kelly, 3 and 2

Davis Love III/Kenny Perry (U.S.) def. Peter Lonard/Tim Clark, 4 and 2

Ernie Els/Adam Scott (Int.) def. Justin Leonard/Jim Furyk, 1-up

Jay Haas/Fred Funk (U.S.) halved with Robert Allenby/Stephen Leaney

Tiger Woods/Charles Howell III (U.S.) def. Stuart Appleby/K.J. Choi, 4 and 3

Day Two—Four-ball

Allenby/**Weir** (Int.) def. Mickelson/Toms, 3 and 1

Perry/Love III (U.S.) def. Goosen/Choi, 2 and 1

Furyk/Haas (U.S.) def. Appleby/Scott, 6 and 5

DiMarco/Leonard (U.S.) def. Singh/Price, 1 up

Els/Clark (Int.) def. Woods/Howell III, 5 and 3

Day Two—Foursomes

Perry/Kelly (U.S.) def. Choi/Lonard, 2 and 1

Funk/Toms (U.S.) def. Allenby/Leaney, 4 and 3

Woods/Howell III (U.S.) def. Clark/Goosen, 1 up

Els/Scott (Int.) def. DiMarco/Mickelson, 1 up

Furyk/Leonard (U.S.) def. Singh/**Weir**, 5 and 4

Day Three—Four-ball

Lonard/Leaney (Int.) def. Funk/Mickelson, 2 and 1

Els/Clark (Int.) def. Furyk/Haas, 3 and 2

Scott/Choi (Int.) def. Perry/Kelly, 5 and 4

Singh/Goosen (Int.) def. Woods/Howell, 2 and 1

Weir/Allenby (Int.) def. DiMarco/Leonard, 1 up

Price/Appleby (Int.) def Love/Toms, 2 and 1

Day Four—Singles

Furyk (U.S.) def. **Weir**, 3 and 1

Kelly (U.S.) def. Clark, 1 up

Perry (U.S.) def. Price, 1 up

Choi (Int.) def. Leonard, 4 and 2

Howell (U.S.) def. Scott, 5 and 4

Haas (U.S.) def. Leaney, 4 and 3

Goosen (Int.) def. Mickelson, 2 and 1

Lonard (Int.) def. Funk, 4 and 3

DiMarco (U.S.) def. Appleby, 1 up

Singh (Int.) def. Toms, 4 and 3

Woods (U.S.) def. Els, 4 and 3

Love (U.S.) halved with Allenby

Canadians in Presidents Cup Competion

Player	Year	Wins	Losses	Halves
Mike Weir	2003	3	2	0
Mike Weir	2000	3	2	0

Bell Canadian Open Champions

The Bell Canadian Open is the world's third oldest national open championship, behind the Open Championship in Great Britain and the United States Open Championship. Seven Canadians have won the national championship, but none since Pat Fletcher of Saskatoon did so in 1954. The following list of past championship winners includes the winning scores (in parentheses) and host courses.

1980 Bob Gilder (274) Royal Montreal	1989 Steve Jones (271) Glen Abbey	1998 Billy Andrade (275) Glen Abbey
1981 Peter Oosterhuis (280) Glen Abbey	1990 Wayne Levi (278) Glen Abbey	1999 Hal Sutton (275) Glen Abbey
1982 Bruce Lietzke (277) Glen Abbey	1991 Nick Price (273) Glen Abbey	2000 Tiger Woods (266) Glen Abbey
1983 John Cook (277) Glen Abbey	1992 Greg Norman (280) Glen Abbey	2001 Scott Verplank (266) Royal
1984 Greg Norman (278) Glen Abbey	1993 David Frost (279) Glen Abbey	Montreal
1985 Curtis Strange (279) Glen Abbey	1994 Nick Price (275) Glen Abbey	2002 John Rollins (272) Angus Glen
1986 Bob Murphy (280) Glen Abbey	1995 Mark O'Meara (274) Glen Abbey	2003 Bob Tway (272) Hamilton Golf
1987 Curtis Strange (276) Glen Abbey	1996 Dudley Hart (202) Glen Abbey	Club
1988 Ken Green (275) Glen Abbey	1997 Steve Jones (275) Royal Montreal	2004 Vijay Singh (275) Glen Abbey

The Ryder Cup

The Ryder Cup is a biennial match-play competition between a team from the United States and a team from Europe. The three-day event features foursomes (teams of two golfers alternate shots), four-ball (teams of two golfers each playing their own shot), and singles (one-on-one) matches. The United States holds the overall lead in matches with 24 wins against 9 losses and 2 halves.

The 35th Ryder Cup competition was held in Michigan, September 17–19, 2004. Team Europe defeated the United States, 18.5 to 9.5.

Day One—Four-ball

Colin Montgomerie/Padraig Harrington (Eur.) def. Phil Mickelson/Tiger Woods, 2 and 1

Darren Clarke/Miguel Angel Jiménez (Eur.) def. Davis Love III/Chad Campbell, 5 and 4

Paul McGinley/Luke Donald (Eur.) halved with Chris Riley/Stewart Cink

Sergio Garcia/Lee Westwood (Eur.) def. David Toms/Jim Furyk, 5 and 3

Day One—Foursomes

Chris DiMarco/Jay Haas (U.S.) def. Jiménez/Thomas Levet, 3 and 2

Montgomerie/Harrington (Eur.) def. Love/Fred Funk, 4 and 2

Clarke/Westwood (Eur.) def. Mickelson/Woods, 1 up

Garcia/Donald (Eur.) def. Kenny Perry/Cink, 2 and 1

Day Two—Four-ball

Garcia/Westwood (Eur.) halved with Haas/DiMarco

Woods/Riley (U.S.) def. Clarke/Ian Poulter, 4 and 3

Paul Casey/David Howell (Eur.) def. Furyk/Campbell, 1 up

Cink /Love (U.S.) def. Montgomerie/Harrington, 3 and 2

Day Two—Foursomes

Clarke/Westwood (Eur.) def. Haas/DiMarco, 5 and 4

Mickelson/Toms (U.S.) def. Jiménez/Levet, 4 and 3

Garcia/Donald (Eur.) def. Furyk/Funk, 1 up

Harrington/McGinley (Eur.) def. Love/Woods, 4 and 3

Day Three—Singles

Woods (U.S.) def. Casey, 3 and 2

Garcia (Eur.) def. Mickelson, 3 and 2

Clarke (Eur.) halved with Love

Furyk (U.S.) def. Howell, 6 and 4

Westwood (Eur.) def. Perry, 1 up

Montgomerie (Eur.) def. Toms, 1 up

Campbell (U.S.) def. Donald, 5 and 3

DiMarco (U.S.) def. Jiménez, 1 up

Levet (Eur.) def. Funk, 1 up

Poulter (Eur.) def. Riley, 3 and 2

Harrington (Eur.) def. Haas, 1 up

McGinley (Eur.) def. Cink, 3 and 2

NATIONAL HOCKEY LEAGUE, 2003–04

Conference Standings

Conference standings reflect the order in which teams qualify for the playoffs. Teams with the best record in the conference (marked with a *z*) and division leaders (marked with a *y*) are automatically seeded first through third. The Detroit Red Wings earned the Presidents' Trophy with the league's best record. Other playoff participants are marked with an *x*.

Eastern Conference

Rank	Team	GP	W	L	T	OTL	GF	GA	PTS
1	z - Tampa Bay	82	46	22	8	6	245	192	106
2	y - Boston	82	41	19	15	7	209	188	104
3	y - Philadelphia	82	40	21	15	6	229	186	101
4	x - Toronto	82	45	24	10	3	242	204	103
5	x - Ottawa	82	43	23	10	6	262	189	102
6	x - New Jersey	82	43	25	12	2	213	164	100
7	x - Montreal	82	41	30	7	4	208	192	93
8	x - NY Islanders	82	38	29	11	4	237	210	91
9	Buffalo	82	37	34	7	4	220	221	85
10	Atlanta	82	33	37	8	4	214	243	78
11	Carolina	82	28	34	14	6	172	209	76
12	Florida	82	28	35	15	4	188	221	75
13	NY Rangers	82	27	40	7	8	206	250	69
14	Washington	82	23	46	10	3	186	253	59
15	Pittsburgh	82	23	47	8	4	190	303	58

Western Conference

Rank	Team	GP	W	L	T	OTL	GF	GA	PTS
1	z - Detroit	82	48	21	11	2	255	189	109
2	y - San Jose	82	43	21	12	6	219	183	104
3	y - Vancouver	82	43	24	10	5	235	194	101
4	x - Colorado	82	40	22	13	7	236	198	100
5	x - Dallas	82	41	26	13	2	194	175	97
6	x - Calgary	82	42	30	7	3	200	176	94
7	x - St Louis	82	39	30	11	2	191	198	91
8	x - Nashville	82	38	29	11	4	216	217	91
9	Edmonton	82	36	29	12	5	221	208	89
10	Minnesota	82	30	29	20	3	188	183	83
11	Los Angeles	82	28	29	16	9	205	217	81
12	Anaheim	82	29	35	10	8	184	213	76
13	Phoenix	82	22	36	18	6	188	245	68
14	Columbus	82	25	45	8	4	177	238	62
15	Chicago	82	20	43	11	8	188	259	59

Source: *National Hockey League*

GP - Games Played; W – Wins; L – Losses; T – Ties; GF - Goals; GA - Goals Against; OTL - Overtime Losses (worth one point); PTS - Points

Division Standings

Eastern Conference

■ ATLANTIC	GP	W	L	T	OTL	PTS	GF	GA	HOME	AWAY
y - Philadelphia . .	82	40	21	15	6	101	229	186	24-11-3-3	16-10-12-3
x - New Jersey . . .	82	43	25	12	2	100	213	164	22-13-5-1	21-12-7-1
x - NY Islanders . .	82	38	29	11	4	91	237	210	25-11-4-1	13-18-7-3
NY Rangers	82	27	40	7	8	69	206	250	13-21-3-4	14-19-4-4
Pittsburgh	82	23	47	8	4	58	190	303	13-22-6-0	10-25-2-4

■ NORTHEAST	GP	W	L	T	OTL	PTS	GF	GA	HOME	AWAY
y - Boston	82	41	19	15	7	104	209	188	18-12-9-2	23-7-6-5
x - Toronto	82	45	24	10	3	103	242	204	22-14-3-2	23-10-7-1
x - Ottawa	82	43	23	10	6	102	262	189	23-8-5-5	20-15-5-1
x - Montreal	82	41	30	7	4	93	208	192	23-13-4-1	18-17-3-3
Buffalo	82	37	34	7	4	85	220	221	21-13-4-3	16-21-3-1

■ SOUTHEAST	GP	W	L	T	OTL	PTS	GF	GA	HOME	AWAY
z - Tampa Bay . . .	82	46	22	8	6	106	245	192	24-10-4-3	22-12-4-3
Atlanta	82	33	37	8	4	78	214	243	18-17-4-2	15-20-4-2
Carolina	82	28	34	14	6	76	172	209	13-18-8-2	15-16-6-4
Florida	82	28	35	15	4	75	188	221	16-15-7-3	12-20-8-1
Washington	82	23	46	10	3	59	186	253	13-20-6-2	10-26-4-1

Western Conference

■ CENTRAL	GP	W	L	T	OTL	PTS	GF	GA	HOME	AWAY
p - Detroit	82	48	21	11	2	109	255	189	30-7-4-0	18-14-7-2
x - St Louis	82	39	30	11	2	91	191	198	23-11-7-0	16-19-4-2
x - Nashville	82	38	29	11	4	91	216	217	22-10-7-2	16-19-4-2
Columbus	82	25	45	8	4	62	177	238	17-18-4-2	8-27-4-2
Chicago	82	20	43	11	8	59	188	259	13-17-6-5	7-26-5-3

■ NORTHWEST	GP	W	L	T	OTL	PTS	GF	GA	HOME	AWAY
y - Vancouver	82	43	24	10	5	101	235	194	21-13-7-0	22-11-3-5
x - Colorado	82	40	22	13	7	100	236	198	19-14-6-2	21-8-7-5
x - Calgary	82	42	30	7	3	94	200	176	21-14-5-1	21-16-2-2
Edmonton	82	36	29	12	5	89	221	208	22-12-4-3	14-17-8-2
Minnesota	82	30	29	20	3	83	188	183	19-13-7-2	11-16-13-1

■ PACIFIC	GP	W	L	T	OTL	PTS	GF	GA	HOME	AWAY
y - San Jose	82	43	21	12	6	104	219	183	24-8-7-2	19-13-5-4
x - Dallas	82	41	26	13	2	97	194	175	26-7-8-0	15-19-5-2
Los Angeles	82	28	29	16	9	81	205	217	15-16-9-1	13-13-7-8
Anaheim	82	29	35	10	8	76	184	213	19-11-7-4	10-24-3-4
Phoenix	82	22	36	18	6	68	188	245	11-19-7-4	11-17-11-2

Source: *ESPN.com*

x- clinched playoff spot

y- clinched division title

z- clinched best record in conference

*- clinched Presidents' Trophy (best regular-season record)

NHL Playoff Results 2003–04

■ CONFERENCE QUARTER-FINALS

Eastern Conference – 1

Matchup	Result

Tampa Bay vs. NY Islanders
Game 1: At Tampa Bay 3, NY Islanders 0
Game 2: NY Islanders 3, at Tampa Bay 0
Game 3: Tampa Bay 3, at NY Islanders 0
Game 4: Tampa Bay 3, at NY Islanders 0
Game 5: At Tampa Bay 3, NY Islanders 2 (OT)
Tampa Bay wins series 4-1

Eastern Conference – 2

Matchup	Result

Boston vs. Montreal
Game 1: At Boston 3, Montreal 0
Game 2: At Boston 2, Montreal 1 (OT)
Game 3: At Montreal 3, Boston 2
Game 4: Boston 4, Montreal 3 (2OT)
Game 5: Montreal 5, at Boston 1
Game 6: At Montreal 5, Boston 2
Game 7: Montreal 2, at Boston 0
Montreal wins series 4-3

Eastern Conference – 3

Matchup	Result

Philadelphia vs. New Jersey
Game 1: At Philadelphia 3, New Jersey 2
Game 2: At Philadelphia 3, New Jersey 2
Game 3: At New Jersey 4, Philadelphia 2
Game 4: Philadelphia 3, at New Jersey 0
Game 5: At Philadelphia 3, New Jersey 1
Philadelphia wins series 4-1

Eastern Conference – 4

Matchup	Result

Toronto vs. Ottawa
Game 1: Ottawa 4, at Toronto 2
Game 2: At Toronto 2, Ottawa 0
Game 3: Toronto 2, at Ottawa 0
Game 4: At Ottawa 4, Toronto 1
Game 5: At Toronto 2, Ottawa 0
Game 6: At Ottawa 2, Toronto 1 (2OT)
Game 7: At Toronto 4, Ottawa 1
Toronto wins series 4-1

Western Conference – 1

Matchup	Result

Detroit vs. Nashville
Game 1: At Detroit 3, Nashville 1
Game 2: At Detroit 2, Nashville 1
Game 3: At Nashville 3, Detroit 1
Game 4: At Nashville 3, Detroit 0
Game 5: At Detroit 4, Nashville 1
Game 6: Detroit 2, at Nashville 0
Detroit wins series 4-2

Western Conference – 2

Matchup	Result

San Jose vs. St. Louis
Game 1: At San Jose 1, St. Louis 0 (OT)
Game 2: At San Jose 3, St. Louis 1
Game 3: At St. Louis 4, San Jose 1
Game 4: San Jose 4, at St. Louis 3
Game 5: At San Jose 3, St. Louis 1
San Jose wins series 4-1

Western Conference – 3

Matchup	Result

Vancouver vs. Calgary
Game 1: At Vancouver 5, Calgary 3
Game 2: Calgary 2, at Vancouver 1
Game 3: Vancouver 2, at Calgary 1
Game 4: At Calgary 4, Vancouver 0
Game 5: Calgary 2, at Vancouver 1
Game 6: Vancouver 5, at Calgary 4 (3OT)
Game 7: Calgary 3, at Vancouver 2 (OT)
Calgary wins series 4-3

Western Conference – 4

Matchup	Result

Colorado vs. Dallas
Game 1: At Colorado 3, Dallas 1
Game 2: At Colorado 5, Dallas 2
Game 3: At Dallas 4, Colorado 3 (OT)
Game 4: Colorado 3, at Dallas 2 (2OT)
Game 5: At Colorado 5, Dallas 1
Colorado wins series 4-1

▶

▶ ■ CONFERENCE SEMI-FINALS

Eastern Conference – 1
Matchup Result

Tampa Bay vs. Montreal
Game 1: At Tampa Bay 4, Montreal 0
Game 2: At Tampa Bay 3, Montreal 1
Game 3: Tampa Bay 4, at Montreal 3 (OT)
Game 4: Tampa Bay 3, at Montreal 1
Tampa Bay wins series 4–0

Western Conference – 1
Matchup   Result

Detroit vs. Calgary
Game 1: Calgary 2, at Detroit 1 (OT)
Game 2: At Detroit 5, Calgary 2
Game 3: At Calgary 3, Detroit 2
Game 4: Detroit 4, at Calgary 2
Game 5: Calgary 1, at Detroit 0
Game 6: At Calgary 1, Detroit 0 (OT)
Calgary wins series 4–2

Eastern Conference – 2
Matchup Result

Philadelphia vs. Toronto
Game 1: At Philadelphia 3, Toronto 1
Game 2: At Philadelphia 2, Toronto 1
Game 3: At Toronto 4, Philadelphia 1
Game 4: At Toronto 3, Philadelphia 1
Game 5: At Philadelphia 7, Toronto 2
Game 6: Philadelphia 3, at Toronto 2 (OT)
Philadelphia wins series 4–2

Western Conference – 2
Matchup   Result

San Jose vs. Colorado
Game 1: At San Jose 5, Colorado 2
Game 2: At San Jose 4, Colorado 1
Game 3: San Jose 1, at Colorado 0
Game 4: At Colorado 1, San Jose 0 (OT)
Game 5: Colorado 2, at San Jose 1 (OT)
Game 6: San Jose 3, at Colorado 1
San Jose wins series 4–2

■ CONFERENCE FINALS

EASTERN CONFERENCE FINAL
Matchup   Result

Tampa Bay vs. Philadelphia
Game 1: At Tampa Bay 3, Philadelphia 1
Game 2: Philadelphia 6, at Tampa Bay 2
Game 3: Tampa Bay 4, at Philadelphia 1
Game 4: At Philadelphia 3, Tampa Bay 2
Game 5: At Tampa Bay 4, Philadelphia 2
Game 6: At Philadelphia 5, Tampa Bay 4 (OT)
Game 7: At Tampa Bay 2, at Philadelphia 1
Tampa Bay wins series 4–3

WESTERN CONFERENCE FINAL
Matchup   Result

San Jose vs. Calgary
Game 1: Calgary 4, at San Jose 3 (OT)
Game 2: Calgary 4, at San Jose 1
Game 3: San Jose 3, at Calgary 0
Game 4: San Jose 4, at Calgary 2
Game 5: Calgary 3, at San Jose 0
Game 6: At Calgary 3, San Jose 1
Calgary wins series 4-2

STANLEY CUP FINALS
Tampa Bay vs. Calgary
Game 1: Calgary 4, at Tampa Bay 1
Game 2: At Tampa Bay 4, Calgary 1
Game 3: At Calgary 3, Tampa Bay 0
Game 4: Tampa Bay 1, at Calgary 0
Game 5: Calgary 3, at Tampa Bay 2 (OT)
Game 6: Tampa Bay 3, at Calgary 2 (2OT)
Game 7: At Tampa Bay 2, Calgary 1
Tampa Bay wins Stanley Cup 4–3

Source: *The Hockey Nut*

Stanley Cup Champions, 1926–2004

The Stanley Cup, the oldest trophy competed for by professional athletes in North America, was donated by Frederick Arthur, Lord Stanley of Preston, in 1893. Originally presented to the amateur hockey champions of Canada, it has been awarded to the top professional team since 1910 and, since 1926, has been competed for only by NHL teams.

Year	Champion	Final Opponent	Series Result	Winning Coach	Winning General Manager
1926	Montreal Maroons	Victoria	3-1	Eddie Gerard	Eddie Gerard
1927	Ottawa Senators	Boston	2-0	Dave Gill	Dave Gill
1928	New York Rangers	Montreal	3-2	Lester Patrick	Lester Patrick
1929	Boston Bruins	New York	2-0	Cy Denneny	Art Ross
1930	Montreal Canadiens	Boston	2-0	Cecil Hart	Cecil Hart
1931	Montreal Canadiens	Chicago	3-2	Cecil Hart	Cecil Hart
1932	Toronto Maple Leafs	New York	3-0	Dick Irvin	Conn Smythe
1933	New York Rangers	Toronto	3-1	Lester Patrick	Lester Patrick
1934	Chicago Black Hawks	Detroit	3-1	Tommy Gorman	Tommy Gorman
1935	Montreal Maroons	Toronto	3-0	Tommy Gorman	Tommy Gorman
1936	Detroit Red Wings	Toronto	4-0	Jack Adams	Jack Adams
1937	Detroit Red Wings	New York	3-2	Jack Adams	Jack Adams
1938	Chicago Black Hawks	Toronto	4-1	Bill Stewart	Bill Stewart
1939	Boston Bruins	Toronto	4-1	Art Ross	Art Ross
1940	New York Rangers	Toronto	4-2	Frank Boucher	Lester Patrick
1941	Boston Bruins	Detroit	4-0	Cooney Weiland	Art Ross
1942	Toronto Maple Leafs	Detroit	4-3	Hap Day	Conn Smythe
1943	Detroit Red Wings	Boston	4-0	Jack Adams	Jack Adams
1944	Montreal Canadiens	Chicago	4-0	Dick Irvin	Tommy Gorman
1945	Toronto Maple Leafs	Detroit	4-3	Hap Day	Conn Smythe
1946	Montreal Canadiens	Boston	4-1	Dick Irvin	Tommy Gorman
1947	Toronto Maple Leafs	Montreal	4-2	Hap Day	Conn Smythe
1948	Toronto Maple Leafs	Detroit	4-0	Hap Day	Conn Smythe
1949	Toronto Maple Leafs	Detroit	4-0	Hap Day	Conn Smythe
1950	Detroit Red Wings	New York	4-3	Tommy Ivan	Jack Adams
1951	Toronto Maple Leafs	Montreal	4-1	Joe Primeau	Conn Smythe
1952	Detroit Red Wings	Montreal	4-0	Tommy Ivan	Jack Adams
1953	Montreal Canadiens	Boston	4-1	Dick Irvin	Frank Selke
1954	Detroit Red Wings	Montreal	4-3	Tommy Ivan	Jack Adams
1955	Detroit Red Wings	Montreal	4-3	Jimmy Skinner	Jack Adams
1956	Montreal Canadiens	Detroit	4-1	Toe Blake	Frank Selke
1957	Montreal Canadiens	Boston	4-1	Toe Blake	Frank Selke
1958	Montreal Canadiens	Boston	4-2	Toe Blake	Frank Selke
1959	Montreal Canadiens	Toronto	4-1	Toe Blake	Frank Selke
1960	Montreal Canadiens	Toronto	4-0	Toe Blake	Frank Selke
1961	Chicago Black Hawks	Detroit	4-2	Rudy Pilous	Tommy Ivan
1962	Toronto Maple Leafs	Chicago	4-2	Punch Imlach	Punch Imlach
1963	Toronto Maple Leafs	Detroit	4-1	Punch Imlach	Punch Imlach
1964	Toronto Maple Leafs	Detroit	4-3	Punch Imlach	Punch Imlach
1965	Montreal Canadiens	Chicago	4-3	Toe Blake	Sam Pollock
1966	Montreal Canadiens	Detroit	4-2	Toe Blake	Sam Pollock
1967	Toronto Maple Leafs	Montreal	4-2	Punch Imlach	Punch Imlach
1968	Montreal Canadiens	St. Louis	4-0	Toe Blake	Sam Pollock
1969	Montreal Canadiens	St. Louis	4-0	Claude Ruel	Sam Pollock
1970	Boston Bruins	St. Louis	4-0	Harry Sinden	Milt Schmidt
1971	Montreal Canadiens	Chicago	4-3	Al MacNeil	Sam Pollock
1972	Boston Bruins	New York	4-2	Tom Johnson	Milt Schmidt
1973	Montreal Canadiens	Chicago	4-2	Scotty Bowman	Sam Pollock
1974	Philadelphia Flyers	Boston	4-2	Fred Shero	Keith Allen
1975	Philadelphia Flyers	Buffalo	4-2	Fred Shero	Keith Allen
1976	Montreal Canadiens	Philadelphia	4-0	Scotty Bowman	Sam Pollock
1977	Montreal Canadiens	Boston	4-0	Scotty Bowman	Sam Pollock
1978	Montreal Canadiens	Boston	4-2	Scotty Bowman	Sam Pollock

▶

Year	Champion	Final Opponent	Series Result	Winning Coach	Winning General Manager
▶ 1979	Montreal Canadiens	New York	4-1	Scotty Bowman	Irving Grundman
1980	N.Y. Islanders	Philadelphia	4-2	Al Arbour	Bill Torrey
1981	N.Y. Islanders	Minnesota	4-1	Al Arbour	Bill Torrey
1982	N.Y. Islanders	Vancouver	4-0	Al Arbour	Bill Torrey
1983	N.Y. Islanders	Edmonton	4-0	Al Arbour	Bill Torrey
1984	Edmonton Oilers	New York	4-1	Glen Sather	Glen Sather
1985	Edmonton Oilers	Philadelphia	4-1	Glen Sather	Glen Sather
1986	Montreal Canadiens	Calgary	4-1	Jean Perron	Serge Savard
1987	Edmonton Oilers	Philadelphia	4-3	Glen Sather	Glen Sather
1988	Edmonton Oilers	Boston	4-0	Glen Sather	Glen Sather
1989	Calgary Flames	Montreal	4-2	Terry Crisp	Cliff Fletcher
1990	Edmonton Oilers	Boston	4-1	John Muckler	Glen Sather
1991	Pittsburgh Penguins	Minnesota	4-2	Bob Johnson	Craig Patrick
1992	Pittsburgh Penguins	Chicago	4-0	Scotty Bowman	Craig Patrick
1993	Montreal Canadiens	Los Angeles	4-1	Jacques Demers	Serge Savard
1994	New York Rangers	Vancouver	4-3	Mike Keenan	Neil Smith
1995	New Jersey Devils	Detroit	4-0	Jacques Lemaire	Lou Lamoriello
1996	Colorado Avalanche	Florida	4-0	Marc Crawford	Pierre Lacroix
1997	Detroit Red Wings	Philadelphia	4-0	Scotty Bowman	Scotty Bowman
1998	Detroit Red Wings	Washington	4-0	Scotty Bowman	Ken Holland
1999	Dallas Stars	Buffalo	4-2	Ken Hitchcock	Bob Gainey
2000	New Jersey Devils	Dallas	4-2	Larry Robinson	Lou Lamoriello
2001	Colorado Avalanche	New Jersey	4-3	Bob Harley	Pierre Lacroix
2002	Detroit Red Wings	Carolina	4-1	Scotty Bowman	Ken Holland
2003	New Jersey Devils	Anaheim	4-3	Pat Burns	Lou Lamoriello
2004	Tampa Bay Lightning	Calgary	4-3	John Tortorella	Jay Feaster

Source: *National Hockey League*

Selected Hockey Organizations

Hockey Hall of Fame
BCE Place
30 Yonge St.
Toronto, Ont.
M5E 1X8
Tel: (416) 360-7735
Fax: (416) 360-1501
www.hhof.com

National Hockey League
1251 Avenue of the Americas
New York, NY
10020
Tel: (212) 789-2000
www.nhl.com

National Hockey League
Players' Association
777 Bay St., Suite 2400
Toronto, Ont.
M5G 2C8
Tel: (416) 313-2300
Fax: (416) 313-2301
www.nhlpa.com

Hockey Information web sites

Canadian Hockey League
www.chl.ca
Info on Canadian junior
hockey with links to various
leagues

The Hockey News
www.thn.com
News and stats

Ontario Hockey League
www.ontariohockeyleague.com
Scores, standings, game
recaps and news

Hockey Future: The Hockey
Propects Resource
www.hockeysfuture.com
Learn about the stars of
tomorrow today

American Hockey League
www.theahl.com
Stats, rosters and team info

The Hockey Nut
www.hockeynut.com
An ice hockey webzine with
up-to-date news, scores and
statistics.

NHL Scoring Leaders, 2003–04

Regular Season

Player	Team	GP	G	A	Pts	+/-	PIM
Martin St. Louis	TAM	82	38	56	94	35	24
Ilya Kovalchuk	ATL	81	41	46	87	-10	63
Joe Sakic	COL	81	33	54	87	11	42
Markus Naslund	VAN	78	35	49	84	24	58
Marian Hossa	OTT	81	36	46	82	4	46
Patrik Elias	NJD	82	38	43	81	26	44
Daniel Alfredsson	OTT	77	32	48	80	12	24
Cory Stillman	TAM	81	25	55	80	18	36
Robert Lang	DET	69	30	49	79	4	24
Brad Richards	TAM	82	26	53	79	14	12
Alex Tanguay	COL	69	25	54	79	30	42
Milan Hejduk	COL	82	35	40	75	19	20
Mats Sundin	TOR	81	31	44	75	11	52
Mark Recchi	PHI	82	26	49	75	18	47
Jaromir Jagr	NYR	77	31	43	74	-5	38
Jarome Iginla	CGY	81	41	32	73	21	84
Steve Sullivan	NAS	80	24	49	73	1	48
Joe Thornton	BOS	77	23	50	73	18	98
Keith Tkachuk	STL	75	33	38	71	8	83
Scott Gomez	NJD	80	14	56	70	18	70
Bill Guerin	DAL	82	34	35	69	14	109
Martin Havlat	OTT	68	31	37	68	12	46
Pavel Datsyuk	DET	75	30	38	68	2	35
Shane Doan	PHO	79	27	41	68	-11	47
Brett Hull	DET	81	25	43	68	-4	12

Playoffs

Player	Team	GP	G	A	Pts	+/-	PIM
Brad Richards	TAM	23	12	13	25	5	4
Martin St. Louis	TAM	23	9	15	24	6	14
Jarome Iginla	CGY	26	13	9	22	13	45
Fredrik Modin	TAM	23	8	11	19	7	12
Craig Conroy	CGY	26	6	11	17	12	12
Vincent Lecavalier	TAM	23	9	7	16	-2	25
Keith Primeau	PHI	18	9	7	16	11	22
Martin Gelinas	CGY	26	8	6	14	10	32
Vincent Damphousse	SAN	17	7	7	14	0	20
Alexei Zhamnov	PHI	18	4	10	14	-1	8
Dave Andreychuk	TAM	23	1	13	14	-2	14
Ruslan Fedotenko	TAM	22	12	1	13	0	14
Jeremy Roenick	PHI	18	4	9	13	4	8
Patrick Marleau	SAN	17	8	4	12	0	6
Joe Sakic	COL	11	7	5	12	0	8
Marcus Nilson	CGY	26	4	7	11	0	12
Peter Forsberg	COL	11	4	7	11	6	12
Saku Koivu	MON	11	3	8	11	1	10
Alexei Kovalev	MON	11	6	4	10	2	8
Shean Donovan	CGY	24	5	5	10	0	23
Michal Handzus	PHI	18	5	5	10	7	10
Jonathan Cheechoo	SAN	17	4	6	10	4	10
Sami Kapanen	PHI	18	3	7	10	5	6
Robyn Regehr	CGY	26	2	8	10	7	20
Dan Boyle	TAM	23	2	8	10	7	16

Source: *The Hockey Nut*

GP – games played; G – goals; A – assists; Pts – total points; plus/minus (when player is on ice, the number of goals scored/the number of goals allowed per 60 minutes of play); PIM – penalty minutes

NHL Goalie Statistics, 2003–04 Season

Regular Season

■ WINS

Goaltender	Team	GPI	W	L	T
Martin Brodeur........	NJD	75	38	26	11
Marty Turco	DAL	73	37	21	13
Ed Belfour	TOR	59	34	19	6
Tomas Vokoun	NAS	73	34	29	10
Dan Cloutier..........	VAN	60	33	21	6
Jose Theodore	MON	67	33	28	5
David Aebischer.......	COL	62	32	19	9
Evgeni Nabokov	SAN	59	31	19	8
Chris Osgood.........	STL	67	31	25	8
Andrew Raycroft	BOS	57	29	18	9
Nikolai Khabibulin	TAM	55	28	19	7
Martin Biron..........	BUF	52	26	18	5

■ GOALS-AGAINST AVERAGE (minimum 27 games)

Goaltender	Team	GPI	GA	AVG
Miikka Kiprusoff...	CGY	38	65	1.69
Dwayne Roloson ..	MIN	48	89	1.88
Marty Turco	DAL	73	144	1.98
Martin Brodeur ...	NJD	75	154	2.03
Robert Esche	PHI	40	79	2.04
Andrew Raycroft ..	BOS	57	117	2.05
Vesa Toskala	SAN	28	53	2.06
John Grahame	TAM	29	58	2.06
David Aebischer ..	COL	62	129	2.09
Martin Prusek	OTT	29	54	2.12
Manny Legace	DET	41	82	2.12
Ed Belfour	TOR	59	122	2.13

■ SHUTOUTS

Goaltender	Team	GPI	SO
Martin Brodeur........	NJD	75	11
Ed Belfour	TOR	59	10
Evgeni Nabokov	SAN	59	9
Marty Turco	DAL	73	9
Roberto Luongo.......	FLA	72	7
Kevin Weekes.........	CAR	66	6
Jose Theodore	MON	67	6
Brian Boucher	PHO	40	5
Dwayne Roloson	MIN	48	5
Roman Cechmanek	LOS	49	5
Rick DiPietro	NYI	50	5
Patrick Lalime	OTT	57	5
Dan Cloutier..........	VAN	60	5
Marc Denis...........	CLB	66	5

■ SAVE PERCENTAGE (minimum 27 GPI)

Goaltender	Team	GPI	GA	SA	SPCT
Dwayne Roloson .	MIN	48	89	1323	.933
Miikka Kiprusoff..	CGY	38	65	966	.933
Roberto Luongo.	FLA	72	172	2475	.931
Vesa Toskala	SAN	28	53	760	.930
Andrew Raycroft .	BOS	57	117	1586	.926
David Aebischer..	COL	62	129	1703	.924
Evgeni Nabokov ..	SAN	59	127	1610	.921
Manny Legace ...	DET	41	82	1019	.920
Jose Theodore ..	MON	67	150	1860	.919
Ed Belfour	TOR	59	122	1483	.918
Marc Denis......	CLB	66	162	1970	.918
Martin Gerber....	ANA	32	64	785	.918
Martin Prusek ...	OTT	29	54	651	.917

Playoffs

■ WINS

Goaltender	Team	GPI	W	L
Nikolai Khabibulin	TAM	23	16	7
Miikka Kiprusoff..	CGY	26	15	11
Robert Esche	PHI	18	11	7
Evgeni Nabokov ..	SAN	17	10	7
David Aebischer..	COL	11	6	5
Ed Belfour	TOR	13	6	7
Curtis Joseph....	DET	9	4	4
Jose Theodore ...	MON	11	4	7
Patrick Lalime ...	OTT	7	3	4
Andrew Raycroft .	BOS	7	3	4

■ SHUTOUTS

Goaltender	Team	GPI	SO
Nikolai Khabibulin	TAM	23	5
Miikka Kiprusoff.......	CGY	26	5
Ed Belfour	TOR	13	3
Evgeni Nabokov	SAN	17	3
Rick DiPietro	NYI	5	1
Tomas Vokoun	NAS	6	1
Andrew Raycroft	BOS	7	1
Curtis Joseph.........	DET	9	1
David Aebischer.......	COL	11	1
Jose Theodore	MON	11	1

■ GOALS-AGAINST AVERAGE

Goaltender	Team	GPI	GA	AVG
Curtis Joseph....	DET	9	12	1.39
Evgeni Nabokov ..	SAN	17	30	1.71
Nikolai Khabibulin	TAM	23	40	1.71
Miikka Kiprusoff..	CGY	26	51	1.85
Patrick Lalime ...	OTT	7	13	1.96
Tomas Vokoun ...	NAS	6	12	2.02
David Aebischer..	COL	11	23	2.08
Ed Belfour	TOR	13	27	2.09
Andrew Raycroft .	BOS	7	16	2.15
Dan Cloutier	VAN	3	5	2.17

■ SAVE PERCENTAGE

Goaltender	Team	GPI	GA	SA	SPCT
Roman Turek	CGY	1	0	3	1.000
Tommy Salo.....	COL	1	0	7	1.000
Reinhard Divis ...	STL	1	0	8	1.000
Mathieu Garon ...	MON	1	0	6	1.000
Curtis Joseph...	DET	9	12	197	.939
Tomas Vokoun ...	NAS	6	12	197	.939
Evgeni Nabokov ..	SAN	17	30	461	.935
Nikolai Khabibulin	TAM	23	40	598	.933
Martin Prusek ...	OTT	1	1	15	.933
Ed Belfour	TOR	13	27	379	.929

Source: *The Hockey Nut*

AVG = Average; GPI = Games Played; GA = Goals Against; L = Losses; SA = Saves; SO = Shut outs; SPCT = Save percentage; T = Ties; W = Wins.

Regular Season NHL Scoring Champions, 1961–2004

Season	Player, Team	GP	G	A	PTS	Season	Player, Team	GP	G	A	PTS
1960–61	Bernie Geoffrion, Mtl	64	50	45	95	1982–83	Wayne Gretzky, Edm.	80	71	125	196
1961–62	Bobby Hull, Chi	70	50	34	84	1983–84	Wayne Gretzky, Edm.	74	87	118	205
1962–63	Gordie Howe, Det	70	38	48	86	1984–85	Wayne Gretzky, Edm.	80	73	135	208
1963–64	Stan Mikita, Chi	70	39	50	89	1985–86	Wayne Gretzky, Edm.	80	52	163	215
1964–65	Stan Mikita, Chi	70	28	59	87	1986–87	Wayne Gretzky, Edm.	79	62	121	183
1965–66	Bobby Hull, Chi.	65	54	43	97	1987–88	Mario Lemieux, Pitt	77	70	98	168
1966–67	Stan Mikita, Chi	70	35	62	97	1988–89	Mario Lemieux, Pitt	76	85	114	199
1967–68	Stan Mikita, Chi	72	40	47	87	1989–90	Wayne Gretzky, L.A.	73	40	102	142
1968–69	Phil Esposito, Bos.	74	49	77	126	1990–91	Wayne Gretzky, L.A.	78	41	122	163
1969–70	Bobby Orr, Bos	76	33	87	120	1991–92	Mario Lemieux, Pitt	64	44	87	131
1970–71	Phil Esposito, Bos.	78	76	76	152	1992–93	Mario Lemieux, Pitt	60	69	91	160
1971–72	Phil Esposito, Bos.	76	66	67	133	1993–94	Wayne Gretzky, L.A.	81	38	92	130
1972–73	Phil Esposito, Bos.	78	55	75	130	1994–95	Jaromir Jagr[1], Pitt	48[2]	32	38	70
1973–74	Phil Esposito, Bos.	78	68	77	145	1995–96	Mario Lemieux, Pitt	70	69	92	161
1974–75	Bobby Orr, Bos	80	46	89	135	1996–97	Mario Lemieux, Pitt	76	50	72	122
1975–76	Guy Lafleur, Mtl	80	56	69	125	1997–98	Jaromir Jagr, Pitt	77	35	67	102
1976–77	Guy Lafleur, Mtl	80	56	80	136	1998–99	Jaromir Jagr, Pitt	81	44	83	127
1977–78	Guy Lafleur, Mtl	78	60	72	132	1999–00	Jaromir Jagr, Pitt	63	42	54	96
1978–79	Bryan Trottier, NYI	76	47	87	134	2000–01	Jaromir Jagr, Pitt	81	52	69	121
1979–80	Marcel Dionne, L.A.	80	53	84	137	2001–02	Jarome Iginla, Cal.	82	52	44	96
1980–81	Wayne Gretzky, Edm.	80	55	109	164	2002–03	Peter Forsberg, Col.	75	29	77	106
1981–82	Wayne Gretzky, Edm.	80	92	120	212	2003–04	Martin St. Louis, T.B.	82	38	56	94

Source: *The Hockey Nut*
(1) Jagr tied with Lindros (Phi); awarded title based on most goals scored. (2) Season shortened to 48 games due to owner/player dispute.

NHL Player Lockout Threatens 2004–05 Season

*S*eptember 15 may turn out to be the beginning of the end of the 2004–05 NHL season. On that date, NHL owners locked out NHL players, effectively shutting down the opportunity for fans to see professional hockey played at its highest level for the foreseeable future. The issues surrounding the labour dispute are varied and complex, with the high-profile issues of player salary cap and franchise ticket prices garnering most of the headlines. Nevertheless, the global issues require agreement on a new collective bargaining agreement (CBA) between owners and players, one that will replace the CBA that expired on September 15. At press time, little progress had been made in reaching an agreement; indeed, little progress had been made in actually getting the two sides to a negotiating table, save for separate national town hall sessions on CBC's The National with NHL Commissioner Gary Bettman and NHL Players Association Executive Director Bob Goodenow.

By the end of September, the gradual cancellation of the season's scheduled games began, with NHL franchises given the green light to cancel home games as far as 30 days in advance so that arenas could be freed up for other events. October games were quickly wiped out, and it was left to pundits to speculate how many more months of hockey dates would be gone before the league decided to cancel the entire season.

2004 NHL Draft — First Round Selections

PICK	TEAM	PLAYER	POSITION	PREVIOUS TEAM	PREVIOUS LEAGUE
1	Washington	Alexander Ovechkin	LW	Dynamo	RUS
2	Pittsburgh	Evgeni Malkin	C/W	Magnitogorsk	RUS
3	Chicago	Cameron Barker	D	Medicine Hat	WHL
4	Carolina (from Columbus)	Andrew Ladd	LW	Calgary	WHL
5	Phoenix	Blake Wheeler	RW	Breck	USHSW
6	New York Rangers	Al Montoya	G	U. of Michigan	CCHA
7	Florida	Rostislav Olesz	C	Vitkovice	CZE
8	Columbus (from Carolina)	Alexandre Picard	LW	Lewiston	QMJHL
9	Anaheim	Ladislav Smid	D	Liberec	CZE
10	Atlanta	Boris Valabik	D	Kitchener	OHL
11	Los Angeles	Lauri Tukonen	RW	Blues	FIN
12	Minnesota	A.J. Thelen	D	Michigan State	CCHA
13	Buffalo	Drew Stafford	RW	U. of North Dakota	WCHA
14	Edmonton	Devan Dubnyk	G	Kamloops	WHL
15	Nashville	Alexander Radulov	RW	Tver	RUS
16	New York Islanders	Petteri Nokelainen	C/W	Saipa	FIN
17	St. Louis	Marek Schwarz	G	Sparta	CZE
18	Montreal	Kyle Chipchura	C	Prince Albert	WHL
19	New York Rangers (from Calgary)	Lauri Korpikoski	C/W	Tps Jr.	FIN JR.
20	New Jersey (from Dallas)	Travis Zajac	C	Salmon Arm	BCHL
21	Colorado	Wojtek Wolski	LW	Brampton	OHL
22	San Jose (from New Jersey)	Lukas Kaspar	RW	Litvinov	CZE
23	Ottawa	Andrej Meszaros	D	Trencin	SVK
24	Calgary (from Toronto)	Kris Chucko	LW	Salmon Arm	BCHL
25	Edmonton (from Philadelphia)	Rob Schremp	C	London	OHL
26	Vancouver	Cory Schneider	G	Phillips-Andover	USHSE
27	Washington (from Boston)	Jeff Schultz	D	Calgary	WHL
28	Dallas (from San Jose)	Mark Fistric	D	Vancouver	WHL
29	Washington (from Detroit)	Mike Green	D	Saskatoon	WHL
30	Tampa Bay	Andy Rogers	D	Calgary	WHL

Source: *National Hockey League*

NHL All-Stars, 1999–2004

First Team	Second Team	First Team	Second Team
1999		**2002**	
Dominik Hasek, Buf, G	Bryon Dafoe, Bos, G	Patrick Roy, Col, G	Jose Theodore, Mtl, G
Al MacInnis, StL, D	Raymond Bourque, Bos, D	Nicklas Lidstrom, Det, D	Rob Blake, Col, D
Nicklas Lidstrom, Det, D	Eric Desjardins, Pha, D	Chris Chelios, Det, D	Sergei Gonchar, Was, D
Peter Forsberg, Col, C	Alexei Yashin, Ott, C	Markus Naslund, Van, LW	Brendan Shanahan, Det, LW
Jaromir Jagr, Pitt, RW	Teemu Selanne, Ana, RW	Joe Sakic, Col, C	Mats Sundin, Tor, C
Paul Kariya, Ana, LW	John LeClair, Phil, LW	Jarome Iginla, Cal, RW	Bill Guerin, Bos, RW
2000		**2003**	
Olaf Kolzig, Was, G	Roman Turek, StL, G	Martin Brodeur, NJ, G	Marty Turco, Dal, G
Chris Pronger, StL, D	Rob Blake, LA, D	Marcus Naslund, Van, LW	Paul Kariya, Ana, LW
Nicklas Lidstrom, Det, D	Eric Desjardins, Phil, D	Todd Bertuzzi, Van, RW	Milan Hejduk, Col, RW
Steve Yzerman, Det, C	Mike Modano, Dal, C	Peter Forsberg, Col, C	Joe Thornton, Bos, C
Jaromir Jagr, Pitt, RW	Pavel Bure, Fla, RW	Al MacInnis, StL, D	Sergei Gonchar, Was, D
Brendan Shanahan, Det, LW	Paul Kariya, Ana, LW	Nicklas Lidstrom, Det, D	Derian Hatcher, Dal, D
2001		**2004**	
Dominik Hasek, Det, G	Roman Cechmanek, Phil, G	Martin Brodeur, NJ, G	Joe Sakic, Col, C
Ray Bourque, Col, D	Rob Blake, Col, D	Roberto Luongo, Fla, G	Mats Sundin, Tor, C
Nicklas Lidstrom, Det, D	Scott Stevens, NJD, D	Markus Naslund, Van, LW	Zdeno Chara, Ott, D
Joe Sakic, Col, C	Mario Lemieux, Pitt. C	Ilya Kovalchuk, Atl, LW	Chris Pronger, StL, D
Jaromir Jagr, Wash, RW	Pavel Bure, Fla, RW	Martin St. Louis, TB, RW	Scott Niedermayer, NJ, D
Patrik Elias, NJD, LW	Luc Robitaille, Det, LW	Jarome Iginla, Cal, RW	Bryan McCabe, Tor, D

Source: *National Hockey League*   As selected by members of the Professional Hockey Writers' Association.

NHL Individual Award Winners, 1984–2004

Hart Trophy (Most Valuable Player)[1]

1984 Wayne Gretzky, Edm	**1991** Brett Hull, StL	**1998** Dominik Hasek, Buf
1985 Wayne Gretzky, Edm	**1992** Mark Messier, NYR	**1999** Jaromir Jagr, Pitt
1986 Wayne Gretzky, Edm	**1993** Mario Lemieux, Pitt	**2000** Chris Pranger, StL
1987 Wayne Gretzky, Edm	**1994** Sergei Fedorov, Det	**2001** Joe Sakic, Col
1988 Mario Lemieux, Pitt	**1995** Eric Lindros, Phil	**2002** Jose Theodore, Mtl
1989 Wayne Gretzky, LA	**1996** Mario Lemieux, Pitt	**2003** Peter Forsberg, Col
1990 Mark Messier, Edm	**1997** Dominik Hasek, Buf	**2004** Martin St. Louis, TB

Calder Trophy (Outstanding Rookie)[1]

1984 Tom Barrasso, Buf	**1991** Ed Belfour, Chl	**1998** Sergei Samsonov, Bos
1985 Mario Lemieux, Pitt	**1992** Pavel Bure, Vcr	**1999** Chris Drury, Col
1986 Gary Suter, Cal	**1993** Teemu Selanne, Wpg	**2000** Scott Gomez, NJ
1987 Luc Robitaille, LA	**1994** Martin Brodeur, NJ	**2001** Evgeni Nabokov, SJ
1988 Joe Nieuwendyk, Cal	**1995** Peter Forsberg, Que	**2002** Dany Heatley, Atl
1989 Brian Leetch, NYR	**1996** Daniel Alfredsson, Ott	**2003** Barret Jackman, StL
1990 Sergei Makarov, Cal	**1997** Bryan Berard, NYI	**2004** Andrew Raycroft, Bos

James Norris Trophy (Outstanding Defenceman)[1]

1984 Rod Langway, Wash	**1991** Raymond Bourque, Bos	**1998** Rob Blake, LA
1985 Paul Coffey, Edm	**1992** Brian Leetch, NYR	**1999** Al MacInnis, StL
1986 Paul Coffey, Edm	**1993** Chris Chelios, Chi	**2000** Chris Pranger, StL
1987 Raymond Bourque, Bos	**1994** Raymond Bourque, Bos	**2001** Nicklas Lidstrom, Det
1988 Raymond Bourque, Bos	**1995** Paul Coffey, Det	**2002** Nicklas Lidstrom, Det
1989 Chris Chelios, Mtl	**1996** Chris Chelios, Chi	**2003** Nicklas Lidstrom, Det
1990 Raymond Bourque, Bos	**1997** Brian Leetch, NYR	**2004** Scott Niedermayer, NJ

Veniza Trophy (Outstanding Goalkeeper)[2]

1984 Tom Barrasso, Buf	**1991** Ed Belfour, Chi	**1998** Dominik Hasek, Buf
1985 Pelle Lindbergh, Phil	**1992** Patrick Roy, Mtl	**1999** Dominik Hasek, Buf
1986 John Vanbiesbrouck, NYR	**1993** Ed Belfour, Chi	**2000** Olaf Kolzig, Wash
1987 Ron Hextall, Phil	**1994** Dominik Hasek, Buf	**2001** Dominik Hasek, Buf
1988 Grant Fuhr, Edm	**1995** Dominik Hasek, Buf	**2002** Jose Theodore, Mtl
1989 Patrick Roy, Mtl	**1996** Jim Carey, Wash	**2003** Martin Brodeur, NJ
1990 Patrick Roy, Mtl	**1997** Dominik Hasek, Buf	**2004** Martin Brodeur, NJ

Lady Byng Trophy (Sportsmanship)[1]

1984 Mike Bossy, NYI	**1991** Wayne Gretzky, LA	**1998** Ron Francis, Pitt
1985 Jari Kurri, Edm	**1992** Wayne Gretzky, LA	**1999** Wayne Gretzky, NYR
1986 Mike Bossy, NYI	**1993** Pierre Turgeon, NYI	**2000** Pavol Demitra, StL
1987 Joe Mullen, Cal	**1994** Wayne Gretzky, LA	**2001** Joe Sakic, Col
1988 Mats Naslund, Mtl	**1995** Ron Francis, Pitt	**2002** Ron Francis, Car
1989 Joe Mullen, Cal	**1996** Paul Kariya, Ana	**2003** Alexander Mogilny, Tor
1990 Brett Hull, StL	**1997** Paul Kariya, Ana	**2004** Brad Richards, TB

▶

(1) As selected at the end of the regular season by members of the Professional Hockey Writers' Association in the NHL cities. (2) Since the 1981–82 season, Vezina Trophy winners have been selected by general managers of the NHL clubs. In earlier seasons the trophy was awarded to the goalkeeper(s) of the team allowing the fewest goals during the regular season.

Conn Smythe Trophy (Most Valuable in Playoffs)[3]

1984 Mark Messier, Edm	**1991** Mario Lemieux, Pitt	**1998** Steve Yzerman, Det
1985 Wayne Gretzky, Edm	**1992** Mario Lemieux, Pitt	**1999** Joe Nieuwendyk, Dal
1986 Patrick Roy, Mtl	**1993** Patrick Roy, Mtl	**2000** Scott Stevens, NJ
1987 Ron Hextall, Phil	**1994** Brian Leetch, NYR	**2001** Patrick Roy, Col
1988 Wayne Gretzky, Edm	**1995** Claude Lemieux, NJ	**2002** Nicklas Lidstrom, Det
1989 Al MacInnis, Cal	**1996** Joe Sakic, Col	**2003** Jean-Sebastien Giguere, Ana
1990 Bill Ranford, Edm	**1997** Mike Vernon, Det	**2004** Brad Richards, TB

Frank J. Selke Trophy (Outstanding Defensive Forward)[1]

1984 Doug Jarvis, Wash	**1991** Dirk Graham, Chi	**1998** Jere Lehtinen, Dal
1985 Craig Ramsay, Buf	**1992** Guy Carbonneau, Mtl	**1999** Jere Lehtinen, Dal
1986 Troy Murray, Chi	**1993** Doug Gilmour, Tor	**2000** Steve Yzerman, Det
1987 Dave Poulin, Phil	**1994** Sergei Fedorov, Det	**2001** John Madden, NJ
1988 Guy Carbonneau, Mtl	**1995** Ron Francis, Det	**2002** Mike Peca, NYI
1989 Guy Carbonneau, Mtl	**1996** Sergei Fedorov, Det	**2003** Jere Lehtinen, Dal
1990 Rick Meagher, StL	**1997** Mike Peca, Buf	**2004** Kris Draper, Det

Jack Adams Trophy (Coach of the Year)

1984 Bryan Murray, Wash	**1991** Brian Sutter, StL	**1998** Pat Burns, Bos
1985 Mike Keenan, Phil	**1992** Pat Quinn, Van	**1999** Jacques Martin, Ott
1986 Glen Sather, Edm	**1993** Pat Burns, Tor	**2000** Joel Quenneville, StL
1987 Jacques Demers, Det	**1994** Jacques Lemaire, NJ	**2001** Bill Barber, Phil
1988 Jacques Demers, Det	**1995** Marc Crawford, Que	**2002** Bob Francis, Phnx
1989 Pat Burns, Det	**1996** Scotty Bowman, Det	**2003** Jacques Lemaire, Min
1990 Bob Murdoch, Wpg	**1997** Ted Nolan, Buf	**2004** John Tortorella, TB

Source: *The Hockey Nut*

(3) As selected by members of the Professional Hockey Writers' Association at the end of the last game of the Stanley Cup finals.

Top NHL Draft Picks Since 1980

Player, Team Selected by, Position, Junior Team	Player, Team Selected by, Position, Junior Team
1980 Doug Wickenheiser, Montreal, C, Regina (WHL)	**1993** Alexandre Daigle, Ottawa, C, Victoriaville (QMJHL)
1981 Dale Hawerchuk, Winnipeg, C, Cornwall (QMJHL)	**1994** Ed Jovanovski, Florida, D, Windsor (OHL)
1982 Gord Kluzak, Boston, D, Billings (WHL)	**1995** Bryan Berard, Ottawa, D, Detroit (OHL)
1983 Brian Lawton, Minnesota, C, Mount St. Charles HS	**1996** Chris Phillips, Ottawa, D, Prince Albert (WHL)
1984 Mario Lemieux, Pittsburgh, C, Laval (QMJHL)	**1997** Joe Thornton, Boston, C, Sault Ste. Marie (OHL)
1985 Wendel Clark, Toronto, LW-D, Saskatoon (WHL)	**1998** Vincent Lecavalier, Tampa Bay, C, Rimouski (QMJHL)
1986 Joe Murphy, Detroit, C, Michigan State	**1999** Patrik Stefan, Atlanta, C, Long Beach (IHL)
1987 Pierre Turgeon, Buffalo, C, Granby (QMJHL)	**2000** Rick DiPietro, N.Y. Islanders, G, Boston University
1988 Mike Modano, Minnesota, C, Prince Albert (WHL)	**2001** Ilya Kovalchuk, Atlanta, C, Spartak (Russia, Div. 1)
1989 Mats Sundin, Quebec, RW, Nacka (Sweden)	**2002** Rick Nash, Columbus, LW, London (OHL)
1990 Owen Nolan, Quebec, RW, Cornwall (OHL)	**2003** Marc-Andre Fleury, Pittsburgh, G, Cape Breton (QMJHL)
1991 Eric Lindros, Quebec, C, Oshawa (OHL)	**2004** Alexander Ovechkin, Washington, LW, Dynamo (RUS)
1992 Roman Hamrlik, Tampa Bay, D, ZPS Zin (Czech)	

Source: *National Hockey League*

2004 World Cup of Hockey

Held at various sites in North America and Europe, August 30–September 14

Canada Captures World Cup Crown

The second World Cup of Hockey tournament (a reincarnation of the Summit Series and Canada Cup tournaments that took place in the 1970s and 1980s) featured eight teams from North America and Europe in a competitive tournament that was very likely to be the last NHL-style hockey to be played for many months. (Two days after the World Cup's completion, the NHL announced a player lockout while negotiations for a new collective bargaining agreement continued at a standstill.)

Team Canada continued its stellar international play, sailing through the tournament undefeated to claim its fourth international tournament gold medal in as many tries. Led by tournament MVP Vincent Lecavalier and standout goaltender Martin Brodeur (defenceman Adam Foote was a third Canadian named to the all-tournament team), Canada defeated a plucky Finland team 3-2 to capture the cup.

ROUND ROBIN STANDINGS (all teams advance to quarterfinal round)

■ European Pool

Team	W	L	T	GF	GA	PTS
Finland	2	0	1	11	4	5
Sweden	2	0	1	13	9	5
Czech Republic	1	2	0	10	10	2
Germany	0	3	0	4	15	0

Quarterfinal Round

Finland 2, Germany 1 (0-0, 1-0, 1-1)

Czech Republic 6, Sweden 1 (2-0, 1-0, 3-1)

USA 5, Russia 3 (1-0, 1-1, 3-2)

Canada 5, Slovakia 0 (0-0, 4-0, 1-0)

■ North American Pool

Team	W	L	T	GF	GA	PTS
Canada	3	0	0	10	3	6
Russia	2	1	0	9	6	4
USA	1	2	0	5	6	2
Slovakia	0	3	0	4	13	0

Semifinal Round

Canada 4, Czech Republic 3 (0-0, 2-1, 1-2, 0-1)

Finland 2, USA 1 (0-0, 0-1, 2-0)

Final
Canada 3, Finland 2 (1-1, 1-1, 1-0)

Source: *Hockey Canada, The Hockey Nut*

2004 World Cup of Hockey Scoring Leaders

Player	Team	GP	G	A	P	PIM	+/-	Player	Team	GP	G	A	P	PIM	+/-
Fredrik Modin	SWE	4	4	4	8	2	1	Mats Sundin	SWE	4	1	4	5	0	1
Vincent Lecavalier	**CAN**	**6**	**2**	**5**	**7**	**8**	**1**	Saku Koivu	FIN	6	3	1	4	2	2
Keith Tkachuk	USA	5	5	1	6	23	5	**Ryan Smyth**	**CAN**	**6**	**3**	**1**	**4**	**2**	**0**
Joe Sakic	**CAN**	**6**	**4**	**2**	**6**	**2**	**4**	Marek Zidlicky	CZE	5	3	1	4	2	3
Martin Havlat	CZE	5	3	3	6	2	6	**Kris Draper**	**CAN**	**5**	**2**	**2**	**4**	**2**	**5**
Kimmo Timonen	FIN	6	1	5	6	2	3	Bill Guerin	USA	5	2	2	4	8	6
Joe Thornton	**CAN**	**6**	**1**	**5**	**6**	**0**	**4**	**Martin St. Louis**	**CAN**	**6**	**2**	**2**	**4**	**0**	**1**
Michael Modano	USA	5	0	6	6	0	4	Teemu Selanne	FIN	6	1	3	4	4	1
Daniel Alfredsson	SWE	4	0	6	6	2	1	Jere Lehtinen	FIN	6	1	3	4	2	1
Patrik Elias	CZE	5	3	2	5	10	3	Vaclav Prospal	CZE	4	1	3	4	0	1
Milan Hejduk	CZE	4	3	2	5	2	1	Kim Johnsson	SWE	4	1	3	4	0	-1
Tomas Holmstrom	SWE	4	3	2	5	8	-3	**Eric Brewer**	**CAN**	**6**	**1**	**3**	**4**	**4**	**6**
Mario Lemieux	**CAN**	**6**	**1**	**4**	**5**	**2**	**4**								

Source: *International Ice Hockey Federation*

GP – games played; G – goals; A – assists; Pts – total points; plus/minus (when player is on ice, the number of goals scored/the number of goals allowed per 60 minutes of play); PIM – penalty minutes

2004 World Cup of Hockey Team Canada Statistics

Player	Birthplace	Position	GP	G	A	Pts	PIM	+/-
Vincent Lecavalier	Ile Bizard, QC	C	6	2	5	7	8	1
Joe Sakic	Burnaby, BC	C	6	4	2	6	2	4
Joe Thornton	London, ON	C	6	1	5	6	0	4
Mario Lemieux	Montreal, QC	C	6	1	4	5	2	4
Eric Brewer	Vernon, BC	D	6	1	3	4	4	6
Kris Draper	Toronto, ON	C	5	2	2	4	2	5
Brad Richards	Murray Harbour, PEI	C	6	1	3	4	0	2
Martin St. Louis	Laval, QC	R	6	2	2	4	0	1
Ryan Smyth	Banff, AB	L	6	3	1	4	2	0
Adam Foote	Toronto, ON	D	6	0	3	3	0	7
Jarome Iginla	Edmonton, AB	R	6	2	1	3	2	5
Shane Doan	Halkirk, AB	R	6	1	1	2	2	4
Simon Gagné	Ste-Foy, QC	L	6	1	1	2	0	2
Scott Niedermayer	Cranbrook, BC	D	6	1	1	2	9	1
Dany Heatley	Freiburg, Germany	R	6	0	2	2	2	0
Scott Hannan	Richmond, BC	D	5	0	1	1	4	3
Wade Redden	Lloydminster, SK	D	2	0	1	1	0	0
Jay Bouwmeester	Edmonton, AB	D	4	0	0	0	0	3
Robyn Regehr	Recife, Brazil	D	6	0	0	0	6	2
Ed Jovanovski	Windsor, ON	D	1	0	0	0	0	0
Brenden Morrow	Carlyle, SK	L	1	0	0	0	4	0
Kirk Maltby	Guelph, ON	F	0	0	0	0	0	0
Patrick Marleau	Aneroid, SK	F	0	0	0	0	0	0

Player	Birthplace	Position	GPI	GA	GAA	SA	SPCT	SO
Martin Brodeur	Montreal, QC	GK	5	5	1.00	124	.961	1
Roberto Luongo	Montreal, QC	GK	1	3	2.82	37	.925	0
José Théodore	Laval, QC	GK	0	0	0.00	0	.000	0

Head coach: Pat Quinn, Hamilton, ON (Toronto Maple Leafs, NHL)

Source: *International Ice Hockey Federation; Hockey Canada*

GP – games played; G – goals; A – assists; Pts – total points; plus/minus (when player is on ice, the number of goals scored/the number of goals allowed per 60 minutes of play); PIM – penalty minutes; GPI – games played; GAA – average goals against per game; SO – shutouts; SA – saves; GA – goals against; SPCT – percentage of saves made on attempted shots

---

Hockey Hall of Fame

*I**nterested in learning about ice hockey? Visit the Hockey Hall of Fame inside Toronto's BCE Place. Tours last about three hours and educational programs exist for junior, intermediate and senior students. Outreach programs such as* Shut Out, Shutdown, *and the* Legends of Hockey Mobile Exhibit *are also available.*

Among the permanent exhibits here are the original Stanley Cup trophy, memorabilia from the arenas of the "Original Six" NHL franchises, two theaters offering historic NHL highlights and Stanley Cup retrospectives, and some lucky Canadian loonies, including the coin that was buried below center ice at the Salt Lake City Winter Olympics before the games in which Canada's men's and women's hockey squads each won the 2002 gold medal and the coin that rested in the goal webbing during the 2003 Senior Men's World Championship final, also won by Canada. The loonies are part of the RBC Olympic Excellence display that showcases the history of Olympic hockey. Kids and parents alike will enjoy the interactive exhibits, including a chance to take on goalie Eddie Belfour — or at least a simulated likeness of him — or to call your own NHL game.

The Hockey Hall of Fame is in BCE Place at 30 Yonge Street, Toronto. It's open every day except Christmas, New Year's Day and Induction Day. See their web site at www.hhof.com or call (416) 360-7735 for more information.

Men's World Hockey Championships, 2004

Held in the Czech Republic, April 24–May 9

Canada Wins Second Consecutive World Championship

For the first time in over 40 years, Team Canada won consecutive World Championships, capturing the 2004 International Ice Hockey Federation Men's World Hockey Championship with a 5–3 victory over Sweden in the gold medal game. The win gave Canada its 17th gold medal in World Championship play. Canada's Dany Heatley was named the tournament's Most Valuable Player.

PRELIMINARY ROUND STANDINGS: (Top three in each group advance to qualification round)

■ Group A

Team	W	L	T	GF	GA	GDF	PTS
Czech Republic	3	0	0	15	2	13	6
Latvia	1	1	1	5	5	0	3
Germany	1	1	1	6	8	-2	3
Kazakhstan	0	0	3	3	14	-11	0

■ Group B

Team	W	L	T	GF	GA	GDF	PTS
Slovakia	2	1	0	10	5	5	5
Finland	2	0	1	11	8	3	4
USA	1	1	1	12	8	4	3
Ukraine	0	0	3	2	14	-12	0

■ Group C

Team	W	L	T	GF	GA	GDF	PTS
Sweden	3	0	0	13	4	9	6
Russia	2	0	1	14	6	8	4
Denmark	1	0	2	7	14	-7	2
Japan	0	0	3	5	15	-10	0

■ Group D

Team	W	L	T	GF	GA	GDF	PTS
Canada	2	1	0	8	3	5	5
Austria	1	2	0	12	6	6	4
Switzerland	1	1	1	11	7	4	3
France	0	0	3	0	15	-15	0

QUALIFICATION ROUND STANDINGS: (Top four in each group advance to quarterfinals)

■ Group E

Team	W	L	T	GF	GA	GDF	PTS
Czech Republic	5	0	0	19	5	14	10
Canada	3	1	1	15	10	5	7
Latvia	1	2	2	8	9	-1	4
Switzerland	1	2	2	8	11	-3	4
Germany	1	1	3	6	14	-8	3
Austria	0	2	3	9	16	-7	2

■ Group F

Team	W	L	T	GF	GA	GDF	PTS
Slovakia	3	2	0	18	5	13	8
Sweden	3	2	0	12	5	7	8
Finland	3	1	1	17	8	9	7
USA	2	1	2	17	15	2	5
Russia	1	0	4	10	14	-4	2
Denmark	0	0	5	6	33	-27	0

Quarterfinal

Sweden 4, Latvia 1 (3-0, 0-0, 1-1)
USA 3, Czech Republic 2 (0-0, 1-2, 1-0, 1-0)
Canada 5, Finland 4 (0-2, 3-1, 1-1, 1-0)
Slovakia 3, Switzerland 1 (0-1, 2-0, 1-0)

Semifinal

Canada 2, Slovakia 1 (0-0, 1-1, 1-0)
Sweden 3, USA 2 (2-0, 1-1, 0-1)

Bronze Medal Game

USA 1, Slovakia 0 (0-0, 0-0, 0-0, 1-0)

Gold Medal Game

Canada 5, Sweden 3 (1-2, 2-1, 2-0)

Source: *International Ice Hockey Federation*
W – wins; L – losses; T – ties; GF – goals scored; GA – goals allowed; GDF – goal differential; PTS – points

2004 World Championship Scoring Leaders

Scoring leaders

Player	Team	GP	G	A	P	PIM	+/-
Dany Heatley	**CAN**	**9**	**8**	**3**	**11**	**4**	**3**
Ville Peltonen	FIN	7	4	6	10	2	6
Jaromir Jagr	CZE	7	5	4	9	6	2
Martin Rucinsky	CZE	7	5	4	9	6	5
Olli Jokinen	FIN	7	5	3	8	6	6
Richard Park	USA	9	5	3	8	0	5
Pavol Demitra	SVK	9	4	4	8	4	5
Miroslav Satan	SVK	9	4	4	8	4	4
Danny Briere	**CAN**	**9**	**2**	**6**	**8**	**6**	**2**
Shawn Horcoff	**CAN**	**9**	**3**	**4**	**7**	**8**	**4**
Vaclav Prospal	CZE	7	3	4	7	2	5
Marian Hossa	SVK	9	2	5	7	2	5
Tomi Kallio	FIN	7	2	5	7	0	8
Thomas Vanek	AUT	6	2	5	7	0	2
Brendan Morrison	**CAN**	**9**	**1**	**6**	**7**	**6**	**-1**
Radek Dvorak	CZE	7	0	7	7	16	5
Jonas Hoglund	SWE	9	5	1	6	2	-2
Daniel Alfredsson	SWE	8	4	2	6	8	5
Marian Gaborik	SVK	9	4	2	6	4	5
Dick Tarnstrom	SWE	9	4	2	6	6	7
Chris Drury	USA	9	3	3	6	27	3
Jukka Hentunen	FIN	7	3	3	6	2	4
Matt Cullen	USA	9	2	4	6	4	2
Rob Niedermayer	**CAN**	**9**	**2**	**4**	**6**	**22**	**3**
Michael Nylander	SWE	7	2	4	6	8	-1

Source: *International Ice Hockey Federation*

GP – games played; G – goals; A – assists; Pts – total points; plus/minus (when player is on ice, the number of goals scored/the number of goals allowed per 60 minutes of play); PIM – penalty minutes

2004 World Championship Team Canada Statistics

Player	Birthplace	Position	GP	G	A	Pts	PIM	+/-
Dany Heatley	Freiburg, Germany	F	9	8	3	11	4	3
Danny Brière	Gatineau, QC	F	9	2	6	8	6	2
Shawn Horcoff	Trail, BC	F	9	3	4	7	8	4
Brendan Morrison	Pitt Meadows, BC	F	9	1	6	7	6	-1
Rob Niedermayer	Cranbrook, BC	F	9	2	4	6	22	3
Scott Niedermayer	Cranbrook, BC	D	9	3	2	5	12	4
Derek Morris	Edmonton, AB	D	9	0	5	5	35	-2
Matt Cooke	Belleville, ON	F	9	2	2	4	8	5
Glen Murray	Halifax, NS	F	9	2	2	4	4	0
Ryan Smyth	Banff, AB	F	9	2	2	4	2	-1
Jay Bouwmeester	Edmonton, AB	D	9	2	1	3	0	5
Brenden Morrow	Carlyle, SK	F	9	0	3	3	12	2
Eric Brewer	Vernon, BC	D	9	1	1	2	6	4
Steve Staios	Hamilton, ON	D	9	1	1	2	6	1
Jean-Pierre Dumont	Montreal, QC	F	9	0	1	1	0	0
Nick Schultz	Strasbourg, SK	D	9	0	1	1	0	0
Patrice Bergeron	Ancienne-Lorette, QC	F	9	1	0	1	4	-1
Jeff Friesen	Meadow Lake, SK	F	9	0	1	1	4	-1
Justin Williams	Cobourg, ON	F	9	0	0	0	4	-1
Willie Mitchell	Port McNeill, BC	D	9	0	0	0	0	-2
Jamie Heward	Regina, SK	D	0	0	0	0	0	0
Jeff Shantz	Duchess, AB	F	0	0	0	0	0	0

Player	Birthplace	Position	GPI	GA	GAA	SA	SPCT	SO
Roberto Luongo	Montreal, QC	GK	7	17	2.32	194	.919	1
Jean-Sebastien Giguere	Montreal, QC	GK	2	1	0.50	39	.975	1
Marc Denis	Montreal, QC	GK	0	0	0.00	0	.000	0

Head coach: Mike Babcock, Saskatoon, SK (Anaheim Mighty Ducks, NHL)

Source: *International Ice Hockey Federation; Hockey Canada*

GP – games played; G – goals; A – assists; Pts – total points; plus/minus (when player is on ice, the number of goals scored/the number of goals allowed per 60 minutes of play); PIM – penalty minutes; GPI – games played; GAA – average goals against per game; SO – shutouts; SA – saves; GA – goals against; SPCT – percentage of saves made on attempted shots

World Hockey Championships, 1981–2004
Team Canada's Leading Scorers

		GP	G	A	PTS			GP	G	A	PTS
1981	Dennis Maruk	8	5	3	8	1993	Eric Lindros	8	11	6	17
1982	Wayne Gretzky	10	6	8	14	1994	Paul Kariya	8	5	7	12
1983	Michel Goulet	10	1	8	9	1995	Andrew McKim	8	6	7	13
1984	Marcel Dionne	10	6	3	9	1996	Yanic Perrault	8	6	3	9
1985	Mario Lemieux	9	4	6	10	1997	Travis Green	11	3	5	8
1986	Brent Sutter	8	4	7	11	1998	Ray Whitney	6	4	2	6
1987	Tony Tanti	10	6	2	8	1999	Corey Stillman	10	4	4	8
1989[1]	Brian Bellows	10	8	7	15	2000	Todd Bertuzzi	9	5	4	9
1990	Steve Yzerman	10	9	10	19	2001	Brad Richards	7	3	3	6
1991	Joe Sakic	10	6	5	11	2002	Andy McDonald	7	4	1	5
1992	Steve Thomas	6	2	2	4	2003	Dan Heatley	9	7	3	10
						2004	Dan Heatley	9	8	3	11

Source: *International Ice Hockey Federation*   (1) No championship held in 1988.

World Junior Hockey Medal Winners, 1981–2004

1981	Sweden, Finland, Soviet Union	1993	**Canada**, Sweden, Czech-Slovak
1982	**Canada**, Czechoslovakia, Finland	1994	**Canada**, Sweden, Russia
1983	Soviet Union, Czechoslovakia, **Canada**	1995	**Canada**, Russia, Sweden
1984	Soviet Union, Finland, Czechoslovakia	1996	**Canada**, Sweden, Russia
1985	**Canada**, Czechoslovakia, Soviet Union	1997	**Canada**, United States, Russia
1986	Soviet Union, **Canada**, United States	1998	Finland, Russia, Switzerland
1987	Finland, Czechoslovakia, Sweden	1999	Russia, **Canada**, Slovakia
1988	**Canada**, Soviet Union, Finland	2000	Czech Republic, Russia, **Canada**
1989	Soviet Union, Sweden, Czechoslovakia	2001	Czech Republic, Finland, **Canada**
1990	**Canada**, Soviet Union, Czechoslovakia	2002	Russia, **Canada**, Finland
1991	**Canada**, Soviet Union, Czechoslovakia	2003	Russia, **Canada**, Finland
1992	C.I.S., Sweden, United States	2004	USA, **Canada**, Finland

Source: *Hockey Canada*

2005 IIHF World Championships

Tournament	Location	Dates
Men's World Hockey Championship	Vienna and Innsbruck, Austria	April 30–May 15, 2005
World Junior Hockey Championship	Grand Forks, ND, and Thief River Falls, MN, USA	December 25, 2004–January 4, 2005
World Women's Hockey Championship	Linköping and Norrköping, Sweden	April 2–9, 2005

2004 World Junior Hockey Championship

Held in Finland, December 26, 2003–January 5, 2004

■ **Preliminary Round Standings:** (Top three in each group advance)

Group A	W	L	T	GF	GA	Pts	Group B	W	L	T	GF	GA	Pts
USA	4	0	0	21	04	8	Canada	4	0	0	25	04	8
Slovakia	2	1	1	09	07	5	Finland	3	0	1	19	06	6
Russia	2	1	1	11	10	5	Czech Republic	2	0	2	14	09	4
Sweden	1	0	3	13	10	2	Switzerland	1	0	3	14	11	2
Austria	0	0	4	01	24	0	Ukraine	0	0	4	01	43	0

■ **Quarterfinal**

USA advances with a bye
Canada advances with a bye
Czech Republic 4, Slovakia 2 (1-1, 3-1, 0-1)
Finland 4, Russia 3 (1-1, 1-1, 2-1)

■ **Semifinal**

Canada 7, Czech Republic 2 (2-1, 1-0, 4-0)
USA 2, Finland 1 (1-0, 0-0, 1-1)

■ **Bronze Medal Game**

Finland 2, Czech Republic 1 (0-0, 0-1, 2-0)

■ **Gold Medal Game**

USA 4, **Canada** 3 (1-1, 0-2, 3-0)

Source: *International Ice Hockey Federation*

■ A Third Consecutive Silver Medal for Canada

Team Canada earned the silver medal in the 2004 International Ice Hockey Federation World Junior Hockey Championship, losing to the United States in the gold medal game. Finland defeated the Czech Republic to capture the bronze medal.

2004 World Junior Hockey Championship Team Canada Statistics

Player	Hometown	Position	GP	G	A	Pts	PIM	+/-
Anthony Stewart	Scarborough, ON	F	6	5	6	11	2	11
Nigel Dawes	Winnipeg, MB	F	6	6	5	11	0	10
Jeff Carter	London, ON	F	6	5	2	7	2	5
Ryan Getzlaf	Regina, SK	F	6	3	3	6	4	3
Brent Burns	Ajax, ON	F	6	0	6	6	20	3
Mike Richards	Kenora, ON	F	6	2	3	5	2	11
Jeff Tambellini	Port Moody, BC	F	6	2	3	5	0	4
Sidney Crosby	Cole Harbour, NS	F	6	2	3	5	4	4
Dion Phaneuf	Edmonton, AB	D	6	2	2	4	29	6
Daniel Paillé	Welland, ON	F	6	4	0	4	2	4
Josh Gorges	Kelowna, BC	D	6	0	3	3	4	8
Braydon Coburn	Shaunavon, SK	D	6	2	1	3	2	5
Brent Seabrook	Tsawwassen, BC	D	6	1	2	3	2	3
Maxime Talbot	St-Bruno, QC	F	6	0	3	3	2	2
Tim Brent	Cambridge, ON	F	6	1	2	3	4	1
Shawn Belle	Edmonton, AB	D	6	0	1	1	0	8
Derek Meech	Winnipeg, MB	D	6	0	1	1	2	5
Stephen Dixon	Halifax, NS	F	6	0	1	1	0	0
Kevin Klein	Kitchener, ON	D	6	0	0	0	0	3
Jeremy Colliton	Blackie, AB	F	6	0	0	0	2	2

Player	Hometown	Position	GPI	GA	GAA	SA	SPCT	SO
Marc Andre Fleury	Sorel, QC	GK	5	9	1.81	103	.920	1
Josh Harding	Regina, SK	GK	1	0	0.00	11	1.000	1

Head coach: Mario Durocher, Sherbrooke, QC (Lewiston, QMJHL)

Source: *International Ice Hockey Federation; Hockey Canada*

GP – games played; G – goals; A – assists; Pts – total points; plus/minus (when player is on ice, the number of goals scored/the number of goals allowed per 60 minutes of play); PIM – penalty minutes; GPI – games played; GAA – average goals against per game; SO – shutouts; SA – saves; GA – goals against; SPCT – percentage of saves made on attempted shots

2004 World Women's Hockey Championship

Held in Nova Scotia, March 30–April 6

Another Gold for Canadian Women

Team Canada captured its eighth gold medal in eight tries at the International Ice Hockey Federation World Women's Hockey Championship, defeating the United States 2–0 in the gold medal game to remain the only nation to win this tournament. Finland defeated Sweden to capture the bronze medal.

PRELIMINARY ROUND STANDINGS: (Top three in each group advance to qualification round)

■ **Group A**

Team	W	L	T	GF	GA	PTS
Canada	2	0	0	24	0	4
Germany	1	0	1	4	15	2
China	0	0	2	2	15	0

■ **Group B**

Team	W	L	T	GF	GA	PTS
USA	2	0	0	17	1	4
Russia	1	0	1	2	9	2
Switzerland	0	0	2	2	11	0

■ **Group C**

Team	W	L	T	GF	GA	PTS
Sweden	1	1	0	10	4	3
Finland	1	1	0	3	3	2
Japan	0	0	2	2	9	0

(Teams are reseeded for qualifying round: Top finishers from each preliminary round group are in Group D, second-place finishers are in Group E, and third-place finishers are in Group F.)

QUALIFYING ROUND STANDINGS: (Top four in each group advance to quarterfinals)

■ **Group D**

Team	W	L	T	GF	GA	PTS
USA	2	0	0	12	3	4
Canada	1	0	1	8	4	2
Sweden	0	0	2	3	16	0

■ **Group E**

Team	W	L	T	GF	GA	PTS
Finland	2	0	0	6	1	4
Russia	1	0	1	5	4	2
Germany	0	0	2	2	8	0

■ **Group F**

Team	W	L	T	GF	GA	PTS
China	2	0	0	11	5	4
Switzerland	1	0	1	7	6	2
Japan	0	0	2	2	9	0

(The third-place finisher from Group D and the top finisher from Group E face off in the bronze medal game. The first and second place finishers from Group D play in the gold medal game.)

Bronze Medal Game

Finland 3, Sweden 2 (1-0, 1-2, 1-0)

Gold Medal Game

Canada 2, USA 0 (0-0, 1-0, 1-0)

Source: *International Ice Hockey Federation*
W – wins; L – losses; T – ties; GF – goals scored; GA – goals allowed; GDF – goal differential; PTS – points

2004 World Women's Hockey Championship Team Canada Statistics

Player	Hometown	Position	GP	G	A	Pts	PIM	+/-
Jennifer Botterill	Winnipeg, MB	F	5	3	8	11	0	8
Jayna Hefford	Kingston, ON	F	5	7	3	10	2	6
Caroline Ouellette	Montreal, QC	F	5	3	6	9	0	10
Cherie Piper	Scarborough, ON	F	5	1	6	7	4	7
Danielle Goyette	St-Nazaire, QC	F	5	2	5	7	6	7
Dana Antal	Esterhazy, SK	F	5	2	3	5	0	7
Hayley Wickenheiser	Shaunavon, SK	F	5	3	2	5	2	6
Cassie Campbell	Brampton, ON	F	5	1	4	5	0	6
Delaney Collins	Pilot Mound, MB	D	5	3	1	4	4	10
Gillian Apps	Unionville, ON	F	5	4	0	4	10	6
Therese Brisson	Dollard-des-Ormeaux, QC	D	5	0	3	3	6	10
Cheryl Pounder	Mississauga, ON	D	5	0	3	3	2	8
Gillian Ferrari	Thornhill, ON	D	5	0	2	2	6	9
Colleen Sostorics	Kennedy, SK	D	5	1	1	2	2	8
Gina Kingsbury	Rouyn-Noranda, QC	F	5	1	1	2	4	4
Vicky Sunohara	Scarborough, ON	F	5	2	0	2	0	0
Kelly Béchard	Sedley, SK	F	5	1	0	1	0	3
Becky Kellar	Hagersville, ON	D	4	0	0	0	0	4
Sarah Vaillancourt	Sherbrooke, QC	F	0	0	0	0	0	0

Player	Hometown	Position	GPI	GA	GAA	SA	SPCT	SO
Kim St-Pierre	Châteauguay, QC	GK	4	3	1.00	59	.952	3
Sami Jo Small	Winnipeg, MB	GK	2	1	0.50	21	.955	1
Charline Labonté	Boisbriand, QC	GK	0	0	0.00	0	.000	0

Head coach: Karen Hughes, Agincourt, ON (University of Toronto, CIS)

Source: *International Ice Hockey Federation; Hockey Canada*
GP – games played; G – goals; A – assists; Pts – total points; plus/minus (when player is on ice, the number of goals scored/the number of goals allowed per 60 minutes of play); PIM – penalty minutes; GPI – games played; GAA – average goals against per game; SO – shutouts; SA – saves; GA – goals against; SPCT – percentage of saves made on attempted shots

International Hockey Competitions

■ WORLD MEN'S CHAMPIONSHIP

	GOLD	SILVER	BRONZE
1920...	Canada	United States	Czechoslovakia
1924...	Canada	United States	Britain
1928...	Canada	Sweden	Switzerland
1930...	Canada	Germany	Switzerland
1931...	Canada	United States	Austria
1932...	Canada	United States	Germany
1933...	United States	Canada	Czechoslovakia
1934...	Canada	United States	Germany
1935...	Canada	Switzerland	Britain
1936...	Britain	Canada	United States
1937...	Canada	Britain	Switzerland
1938...	Canada	Britain	Czechoslovakia
1939...	Canada	United States	Switzerland

1940-46 WORLD WAR II — NO EVENT HELD

	GOLD	SILVER	BRONZE
1947...	Czechoslovakia	Sweden	Austria
1948...	Canada	Czechoslovakia	Switzerland
1949...	Czechoslovakia	Canada	United States
1950...	Canada	United States	Switzerland
1951...	Canada	Sweden	Switzerland
1952...	Canada	United States	Sweden
1953...	Sweden	Germany	Switzerland
1954...	Soviet Union	Canada	Sweden
1955...	Canada	Soviet Union	Czechoslovakia
1956...	Soviet Union	United States	Canada
1957...	Sweden	Soviet Union	Czechoslovakia
1958...	Canada	Soviet Union	Sweden
1959...	Canada	Soviet Union	Czechoslovakia
1960...	United States	Canada	Soviet Union
1961...	Canada	Czechoslovakia	Soviet Union
1962...	Sweden	Canada	United States
1963...	Soviet Union	Sweden	Czechoslovakia
1964...	Soviet Union	Sweden	Czechoslovakia
1965...	Soviet Union	Czechoslovakia	Sweden
1966...	Soviet Union	Czechoslovakia	Canada
1967...	Soviet Union	Sweden	Canada
1968...	Soviet Union	Czechoslovakia	Canada
1969...	Soviet Union	Sweden	Czechoslovakia
1970...	Soviet Union	Sweden	Czechoslovakia
1971...	Soviet Union	Czechoslovakia	Sweden
1972...	Czechoslovakia	Soviet Union	Sweden
1973...	Soviet Union	Sweden	Czechoslovakia
1974...	Soviet Union	Czechoslovakia	Sweden
1975...	Soviet Union	Czechoslovakia	Sweden
1976...	Czechoslovakia	Soviet Union	Sweden
1977...	Czechoslovakia	Sweden	Soviet Union
1978...	Soviet Union	Czechoslovakia	Canada
1979...	Soviet Union	Czechoslovakia	Sweden
1981...	Soviet Union	Sweden	Czechoslovakia
1982...	Soviet Union	Czechoslovakia	Canada
1983...	Soviet Union	Czechoslovakia	Canada
1985...	Czechoslovakia	Canada	Soviet Union
1986...	Soviet Union	Sweden	Canada
1987...	Sweden	Soviet Union	Czechoslovakia
1989...	Soviet Union	Canada	Czechoslovakia
1990...	Soviet Union	Sweden	Czechoslovakia
1991...	Sweden	Canada	Soviet Union
1992...	Sweden	Finland	Czechoslovakia
1993...	Russia	Sweden	Czechoslovakia
1994...	Canada	Finland	Sweden
1995...	Finland	Sweden	Canada
1996...	Czech Republic	Canada	United States
1997...	Canada	Sweden	Czech Republic
1998...	Sweden	Finland	Czech Republic
1999...	Czech Republic	Finland	Sweden
2000...	Czech Republic	Slovakia	Finland
2001...	Czech Republic	Finland	Sweden
2002...	Slovakia	Russia	Sweden
2003...	Canada	Sweden	Slovakia
2004...	Canada	Sweden	USA

■ OLYMPIC GAMES

	GOLD	SILVER	BRONZE
1924...	Canada	United States	Britain
1928...	Canada	Sweden	Switzerland
1932...	Canada	United States	Germany
1936...	Britain	Canada	United States
1948...	Canada	Czechoslovakia	Switzerland
1952...	Canada	United States	Sweden
1956...	Soviet Union	United States	Canada
1960...	United States	Canada	Soviet Union
1964...	Soviet Union	Sweden	Czechoslovakia
1968...	Soviet Union	Czechoslovakia	Canada
1972...	Soviet Union	United States	Czechoslovakia
1976...	Soviet Union	Czechoslovakia	Germany
1980...	United States	Soviet Union	Sweden
1984...	Soviet Union	Czechoslovakia	Sweden
1988...	Soviet Union	Finland	Sweden
1992...	Unified Team	Canada	Czechoslovakia
1994...	Sweden	Canada	Finland
1998...	Czech Republic	Russia	Finland
2002...	Canada	United States	Russia

■ WORLD CUP OF HOCKEY

	WINNER	RUNNER-UP
1996...	United States	Canada
2004...	Canada	Finland

■ CANADA CUP

	WINNER	RUNNER-UP
1976...	Canada	Czechoslovakia
1981...	Soviet Union	Canada
1984...	Canada	Sweden

▶

► 1987... Canada ...... Soviet Union
1991... Canada ...... United States

■ **WORLD JUNIOR CHAMPIONSHIP**

	GOLD	SILVER	BRONZE
1977...	Soviet Union ..	Canada	Czechoslovakia
1978...	Soviet Union ..	Sweden......	Canada
1979...	Soviet Union ..	Czechoslovakia	Sweden
1980...	Soviet Union ..	Finland	Sweden
1981...	Sweden	Finland	Soviet Union
1982...	Canada	Czechoslovakia	Finland
1983...	Soviet Union ..	Czechoslovakia	Canada
1984...	Soviet Union ..	Finland	Czechoslovakia
1985..	Canada	Czechoslovakia	Soviet Union
1986...	Soviet Union ..	Canada	United States
1987...	Finland.......	Czechoslovakia	Sweden
1988...	Canada	Soviet Union ..	Finland
1989...	Soviet Union ..	Sweden......	Czechoslovakia
1990...	Canada	Soviet Union ..	Czechoslovakia
1991...	Canada	Soviet Union ..	Czechoslovakia
1992...	Soviet Union ..	Sweden......	United States
1993...	Canada	Sweden	Czechoslovakia

1994...	Canada	Sweden......	Russia
1995...	Canada	Russia.......	Sweden
1996...	Canada	Sweden......	Russia
1997...	Canada	United States..	Russia
1998...	Finland.......	Russia.......	Switzerland
1999...	Russia.......	Canada	Slovakia
2000...	Czech Republic	Russia.......	Canada
2001...	Czech Republic	Finland	Canada
2002...	Russia.......	Canada	Finland
2003...	Russia.......	Canada	Finland
2004...	United States..	Canada	Finland

■ **WORLD WOMEN'S CHAMPIONSHIP**

	GOLD	SILVER	BRONZE
1990...	Canada	United States..	Finland
1992...	Canada	United States..	Finland
1994...	Canada	United States..	Finland
1997...	Canada	United States..	Finland
1999...	Canada	United States..	Finland
2000...	Canada	United States..	Finland
2001...	Canada	United States..	Russia
2004...	Canada	United States..	Finland

Memorial Cup Winners, 1962–2004

(Canadian Junior Hockey Champions)

1962	Hamilton Red Wings	**1984**	Ottawa 67's
1963	Edmonton Oil Kings	**1985**	Prince Albert Raiders
1964	Toronto Marlboros	**1986**	Guelph Platers
1965	Niagara Falls Flyers	**1987**	Medicine Hat Tigers
1966	Edmonton Oil Kings	**1988**	Medicine Hat Tigers
1967	Toronto Marlboros	**1989**	Swift Current Broncos
1968	Niagara Falls Flyers	**1990**	Oshawa Generals
1969	Montreal Jr. Canadiens	**1991**	Spokane Chiefs
1970	Montreal Jr. Canadiens	**1992**	Kamloops Blazers
1971	Quebec Ramparts	**1993**	Sault Ste. Marie Greyhounds
1972	Cornwall Royals	**1994**	Kamloops Blazers
1973	Toronto Marlboros	**1995**	Kamloops Blazers
1974	Regina Pats	**1996**	Granby Predateurs
1975	Toronto Marlboros	**1997**	Hull Olympiques
1976	Hamilton Fincups	**1998**	Portland Winter Hawks
1977	New Westminster Bruins	**1999**	Ottawa 67s
1978	New Westminster Bruins	**2000**	Rimouski Oceanic
1979	Peterborough Petes	**2001**	Red Deer Rebels
1980	Cornwall Royals	**2002**	Kooteny Ice
1981	Cornwall Royals	**2003**	Kitchener Rangers
1982	Kitchener Rangers	**2004**	Kelowna Rockets
1983	Portland Winter Hawks		

Source: *Canoe Limited Partnership*

OLYMPICS

Summer Olympics

Location	Date of Competition	Competitors		Nations Repre-sented	Unofficial Winners
		Men	Women		
1896 Athens, Greece	Apr. 6–15	311	0	13	United States
1900 Paris, France	May 20–Oct. 28	1 319	11	22	United States
1904 St. Louis, United States	July 1–Nov. 23	681	6	12	United States
1906[1] Athens, Greece	Apr. 22–May 2	877	7	20	United States
1908 London, England	Apr. 27–Oct. 31	1 999	36	23	United States
1912 Stockholm, Sweden	May 5–July 22	2 490	57	28	United States
1916 Cancelled because of World War I					
1920 Antwerp, Belgium	Apr. 20–Sept. 12	2 543	64	29	United States
1924 Paris, France	May 4–July 27	2 956	136	44	United States
1928 Amsterdam, Netherlands	May 17–Aug. 12	2 724	290	46	United States
1932 Los Angeles, United States	July 30–Aug. 14	1 281	127	37	United States
1936 Berlin, Germany	Aug. 1–16	3 738	328	49	Germany
1940 Cancelled because of World War II					
1944 Cancelled because of World War II					
1948 London, England	July 29–Aug. 14	3 714	385	59	United States
1952 Helsinki, Finland	July 19–Aug. 3	4 407	518	69	United States
1956 Melbourne, Australia[2]	Nov. 22–Dec. 8	2 958	384	67	USSR
1960 Rome, Italy	Aug. 25–Sept. 11	4 738	610	83	USSR
1964 Tokyo, Japan	Oct. 10–24	4 457	683	93	United States
1968 Mexico City, Mexico	Oct. 12–27	4 750	781	112	United States
1972 Munich, West Germany	Aug. 26–Sept. 10	5 848	1 299	122	USSR
1976 Montreal, Canada	July 17–Aug. 1	4 834	1 251	92[3]	USSR
1980 Moscow, USSR	July 19–Aug. 3	4 265	1 088	81	USSR
1984 Los Angeles, United States	July 28–Aug. 12	5 458	1 620	141	United States
1988 Seoul, South Korea	Sept. 17–Oct. 2	7 105	2 476	160	USSR
1992 Barcelona, Spain	July 25–Aug. 9	7 555	3 008	172	Unified Team
1996 Atlanta, United States	July 19–Aug. 4	7 000	3 800	197	United States
2000 Sydney, Australia	Sept. 16–Oct. 1	6 582	4 069	199	United States
2004 Athens, Greece	Aug. 13–29	6 452	4 412	202	United States
2008 Beijing, China	Aug. 8–24				

Source: *Canadian Olympic Association, International Olympic Committee*

(1) 1906 Games were not recognized by the International Olympic Committee.

(2) The equestrian events were held in Stockholm, Sweden, June 10–17, 1956.

(3) Most sources list this figure as 88. Cameroon, Egypt, Morocco and Tunisia all boycotted the 1976 Olympics; however, their athletes had already competed before the boycott was officially announced.

Winter Olympics

Year	Location	Date of Competition	Competitors		Nations Repre- sented	Unofficial Winners
			Men	Women		
1924	Chamonix, France	Jan. 25–Feb. 4	281	13	16	Norway
1928	St. Moritz, Switzerland	Feb. 11–19	468	27	25	Norway
1932	Lake Placid, United States	Feb. 4–15	274	32	17	United States
1936	Garmisch-Partenkirchen, Germany	Feb. 6–16	675	80	28	Norway
1940	Cancelled because of World War II					
1944	Cancelled because of World War II					
1948	St. Moritz, Switzerland	Jan. 30–Feb. 8	636	77	28	Sweden
1952	Oslo, Norway	Feb. 14–25	623	109	30	Norway
1956	Cortina d'Ampezzo, Italy	Jan. 26–Feb. 5	686	132	32	U.S.S.R.
1960	Squaw Valley, United States	Feb. 18–28	521	144	30	U.S.S.R.
1964	Innsbruck, Austria	Jan. 29–Feb. 9	986	200	36	U.S.S.R.
1968	Grenoble, France	Feb. 6–18	1 081	212	37	Norway
1972	Sapporo, Japan	Feb. 3–13	1 015	217	35	U.S.S.R.
1976	Innsbruck, Austria	Feb. 4–15	900	228	37	U.S.S.R.
1980	Lake Placid, United States	Feb. 14–23	833	234	37	East Germany
1984	Sarajevo, Yugoslavia	Feb. 7–19	1 180	409	49	U.S.S.R.
1988	Calgary, Canada	Feb. 13–28	1 128	317	57	U.S.S.R.
1992	Albertville, France	Feb. 8–23	1 545	602	64	Germany
1994	Lillehammer, Norway	Feb. 12–27	1 216	521	67	Norway
1998	Nagano, Japan	Feb. 7–22	1 488	814	72	Germany
2002	Salt Lake City, United States	Feb. 8–24	1 513	886	77	Germany
2006	Turin, Italy	Feb. 10–26				
2010	Vancouver/Whistler, Canada	Feb. 12–26				

Source: *International Olympic Committee, Canadian Olympic Association*

Vancouver's 2010 Winter Olympics Planning on Target

*T*he organizing committee for the 2010 Winter Olympic Games in Vancouver reported to the International Olympic Committee (IOC) that plans for the upcoming games in Canada are "on track." While still very early in the organization's post-Olympic-bid existence (over 2,000 days from opening ceremonies at the time of the organizing committee's report), enough progress has been made to satisfy the IOC, including a draft schedule for the Games and updates on proposed event venues and support facilities. Vancouver was selected over Pyeongchang, South Korea, and Salzburg, Austria, to become the third Canadian city to host an Olympic Games and the second to host the Winter Games. The Games will take place over a 17-day period in February 2010 at a variety of existing and yet-to-be-constructed facilities in Vancouver and Whistler.

Source: *Vancouver Organizing Committee for the 2010 Olympic and Paralympic Winter Games (VANOC)*

Canada's Olympic Medalists, 1900–2004

Summer Olympic Games

1900

Bronze: Men's athletics, 400m hurdles George Orton (Although a Canadian citizen, he represented the University of Pennsylvania; Canada did not officially appear at the Olympics until 1904.)

1904

Gold: Men's athletics, 56lb weight throw Étienne Desmarteau
Gold: Men's golf George Lyon
Gold: Men's team football (soccer)
Gold: Men's team lacrosse
Silver: Men's rowing, eight with coxswain

1908

Gold: Men's athletics, 200m Robert Kerr
Gold: Men's team lacrosse
Gold: Men's trapshooting Walter Ewing
Silver: Men's team shooting, clay pigeons
Silver: Men's trapshooting George Beattie
Silver: Men's athletics, triple jump J. Garfield MacDonald
Bronze: Men's athletics, 100m Robert Kerr
Bronze: Men's freestyle wrestling, bantamweight Aubert Cote
Bronze: Men's athletics, hammer throw Cornelius Walsh
Bronze: Men's athletics, long jump Calvin Bricker
Bronze: Men's athletics, pole vault Edward Archibald
Bronze: Men's rowing, coxless pair Norman Jackes Fred Toms
Bronze: Men's rowing, eight with coxswain
Bronze: Men's team cycling (1 980-yard pursuit) William Anderson Walter Andrews Frederick McCarthy William Morton
Bronze: Men's team shooting (rifle)

1912

Gold: Men's athletics, 10 000m walk George Goulding
Gold: Men's swimming, 1 500m freestyle George Hodgson
Gold: Men's swimming, 400m freestyle George Hodgson
Silver: Men's athletics, hammer throw Duncan Gillis
Silver: Men's athletics, long jump Calvin Bricker
Bronze: Men's athletics, pentathlon Frank Lukeman
Bronze: Men's athletics, pole vault William Happenny
Bronze: Men's rowing, single sculls Everard Butler

1920

Gold: Men's athletics, 110m hurdles Earl Thomson
Gold: Men's boxing, welterweight Julius Schneider
Silver: Men's boxing, bantamweight Clifford Graham
Silver: Men's boxing, middleweight George Prud'homme
Silver: Men's swimming, 1 500m freestyle George Vernot
Bronze: Men's boxing, lightweight Clarence Newton
Bronze: Men's boxing, middleweight Montgomery Herscovitch
Bronze: Men's swimming, 400m freestyle George Vernot

1924

Silver: Men's rowing, eight with coxswain
Silver: Men's rowing, four without coxswain Archibald Black, George MacKay, A. Mariacher, William Wood
Silver: Men's team shooting, clay pigeons
Bronze: Men's boxing, welterweight Douglas Lewis

1928

Gold: Men's athletics, 100m Percy Williams
Gold: Men's athletics, 200m Percy Williams
Gold: Women's athletics, 4x100m relay Myrtle Cook, Fanny Rosenfeld, Ethel Smith, Jean Thompson
Gold: Women's athletics, high jump Ethel Catherwood
Silver: Men's athletics, 400m James Ball
Silver: Men's freestyle wrestling, middleweight Donald Stockton
Silver: Men's rowing, double sculls John Guest, Joseph Wright Jr.
Silver: Women's athletics, 100m Fanny Rosenfeld
Bronze: Men's athletics, 4x400m relay James Ball, Philip Edwards, Stanley Glover, Alexander Wilson
Bronze: Men's boxing, welterweight Raymond Smillie
Bronze: Men's freestyle wrestling, bantamweight James Trifunov
Bronze: Men's freestyle wrestling, welterweight Maurice Letchford
Bronze: Men's rowing, eight with coxswain
Bronze: Men's swimming, 4x200m freestyle relay Garnet Ault, Frederick Bourne, Walter Spence, James Thompson
Bronze: Women's athletics, 100m Ethel Smith

1932

Gold: Men's athletics, high jump Duncan McNaughton
Gold: Men's boxing, bantamweight Horace Gwynne ▶

▶ Silver: **Men's athletics, 800m** Alexander Wilson
Silver: **Men's freestyle wrestling, welterweight** Daniel MacDonald
Silver: **Sailing, 8m mixed**
Silver: **Women's athletics, 100m** Hilda Strike-Sisson
Silver: **Women's athletics, 4x100m relay** Mary Frizzell, Mildred Frizzell, Lillian Palmer-Alderson, Hilda Strike-Sisson
Bronze: **Men's athletics, 1 500m** Philip Edwards
Bronze: **Men's athletics, 400m** Alexander Wilson
Bronze: **Men's athletics, 4x400m relay** James Ball, Philip Edwards, Raymond Lewis, Alexander Wilson
Bronze: **Men's athletics, 800m** Philip Edwards
Bronze: **Men's rowing, double sculls** Noel De Mille, Charles Pratt
Bronze: **Men's rowing, eight with coxswain**
Bronze: **Sailing, 6m mixed** Gardner Boultbee, Kenneth Glass, Philip Rogers, Gerald Wilson
Bronze: **Women's athletics, high jump** Eva Dawes-Spinks

1936

Gold: **Men's 1 000m canoe single** Frank Amyot
Silver: **Men's 10 000m canoe double** Harvey Charters, Frank Saker
Silver: **Men's athletics, 400m hurdles** John Loaring
Silver: **Men's team basketball**
Bronze: **Men's 1 000m canoe double** Harvey Charters, Frank Saker
Bronze: **Men's athletics, 800m** Philip Edwards
Bronze: **Men's freestyle wrestling, welterweight** Joseph Schleimer
Bronze: **Women's athletics, 4x100m relay** Dorothy Brookshaw, Hilda Cameron, Mildred Dolson-Cavill, Aileen Meagher
Bronze: **Women's athletics, 80m hurdles** Elizabeth Taylor-Campbell

1948

Silver: **Men's 1 000m canoe single** Douglas Bennett
Bronze: **Men's 10 000m canoe single** Norman Lane
Bronze: **Women's athletics, 4x100m relay** Dianne Foster, Patricia Jones, Nancy MacKay-Murrall, Violet Meyers

1952

Gold: **Men's trapshooting** George Genereux
Silver: **Men's 10 000m canoe double** Donald Hawgood, Kenneth Lane
Silver: **Men's weightlifting, middleweight** Gerald Gratton

1956

Gold: **Men's shooting, 50m rifle prone** Gerald Ouellette
Gold: **Men's rowing, four without coxswain** Donald Arnold, Ignace D'Hondt, Lorne Loomer, Archibald MacKinnon
Silver: **Men's rowing, eight with coxswain**
Bronze: **Men's shooting, 50m rifle prone** Gilmore Boa
Bronze: **Mixed team equestrian**
Bronze: **Women's diving, 3m springboard** Irene MacDonald

1960

Silver: **Men's rowing, eight with coxswain**

1964

Gold: **Men's rowing, coxless pair** George Hungerford, Roger Jackson
Silver: **Men's athletics, 800m** William Crothers
Silver: **Men's judo, heavyweight** Alfred Rogers
Bronze: **Men's athletics, 100m** Harry Jerome

1968

Gold: **Mixed team equestrian**
Silver: **Men's swimming, 400m freestyle** Ralph Hutton
Silver: **Women's swimming, 100m backstroke** Elaine Tanner
Silver: **Women's swimming, 200m backstroke** Elaine Tanner
Bronze: **Women's swimming, 4x100m freestyle relay** Marilyn Corson-Whitney, Angela Coughlaw, Marion Lay, Elaine Tanner

1972

Silver: **Men's swimming, 100m butterfly** Bruce Robertson
Silver: **Women's swimming, 400m individual medley** Leslie Cliff
Bronze: **Mixed sailing, fleet/match race keelboat open** Paul Cote, John Ekels, David Miller
Bronze: **Men's swimming, 4x100m medley relay** Erik Fish, Robert Kasting, William Mahony, Bruce Robertson

1976

Silver: **Men's 1 500m canoe single** John Wood
Silver: **Men's athletics, high jump** Gregory Joy
Silver: **Men's swimming, 4x100 medley relay** Clayton Evans, Gary MacDonald, Stephen Pickell, Graham Smith
Silver: **Mixed individual equestrian** Michel Vaillancourt ▶

▶ Silver: **Women's swimming, 400m individual medley** Cheryl Gibson

Bronze: **Women's swimming, 100m backstroke** Nancy Garapick

Bronze: **Women's swimming, 200m backstroke** Nancy Garapick

Bronze: **Women's swimming, 400m freestyle** Shannon Smith

Bronze: **Women's swimming, 400m individual medley** Rebecca Smith

Bronze: **Women's swimming, 4x100 medley relay** Wendy Cook-Hogg, Robin Corsiglia, Anne Jardin, Susan Smith-Sloan

Bronze: **Women's swimming, 4x100m freestyle relay** Gail Amundrud, Barbara Clark, Anne Jardin, Rebecca Smith

1984

Gold: **Men's 1 000m kayak double** Lawrence Cain, Hugh Fisher

Gold: **Men's 1 000m kayak double** Hugh Fisher, Alwyn Morris

Gold: **Men's rowing, eight with coxswain**

Gold: **Men's swimming, 200m breaststroke** Victor Davis

Gold: **Men's swimming, 200m individual medley** Alexander Baumann

Gold: **Men's swimming, 400m individual medley** Alexander Baumann

Gold: **Women's diving, 3m springboard** Sylvie Bernier

Gold: **Women's shooting, 25m pistol** Linda Thom

Gold: **Women's swimming, 200m breaststroke** Anne Ottenbrite

Silver: **Men's 1 000m canoe single** Lawrence Cain

Silver: **Men's boxing, heavyweight** Willie Dewit

Silver: **Men's boxing, light-middleweight** Shawn O'Sullivan

Silver: **Men's cycling, 1km time trial** Curtis Harnett

Silver: **Men's cycling, individual road race** Stephen Bauer

Silver: **Men's freestyle wrestling, super heavyweight** Robert Molle

Silver: **Men's swimming, 100m breaststroke** Victor Davis

Silver: **Men's swimming, 4x100m medley relay** Victor Davis, Donald Goss, Thomas Ponting, Michael West

Silver: **Men's weightlifting, middleweight** Jacques Demers

Silver: **Mixed sailing, flying Dutchman** Terence McLaughlin, Evert Bastet

Silver: **Women's 500m kayak double** Alexandra Barre, Susan Holloway

Silver: **Women's athletics, 4x100m relay** Angela Bailey, France Gareau, Marita Payne-Wiggins, Angella Taylor-Issajenko

Silver: **Women's athletics, 4x400m relay** Charmaine Crooks, Molly Killingbeck, Marita Payne-Wiggins, Jillian Richardson-Briscoe

Silver: **Women's rowing, four-oared shell with coxswain** Barbara Armbrust, Marilyn Brain, Angela Schneider, Lesley Thompson, Jane Tregunno

Silver: **Women's rowing, pair without coxswain** Elizabeth Craig, Patricia Smith

Silver: **Women's swimming, 100m breaststroke** Anne Ottenbrite

Silver: **Women's synchronized swimming, duet** Sharon Hambrook, Kelly Kryczka

Silver: **Women's synchronized swimming, solo** Carolyn Waldo

Bronze: **Men's 500m kayak double** Hugh Fisher, Alwyn Morris

Bronze: **Men's athletics, 100m** Ben Johnson

Bronze: **Men's athletics, 4x100m relay** Sterling Hinds, Ben Johnson, Anthony Sharpe, Desai Williams

Bronze: **Men's boxing, bantamweight** Dale Walters

Bronze: **Men's freestyle wrestling, middleweight** Christopher Rinke

Bronze: **Men's judo, heavyweight** Marc Berger

Bronze: **Men's rowing, quadruple sculls without coxswain** Bruce Ford, Douglas Hamilton, Michael Hughes, Philip Monckton

Bronze: **Men's rowing, single sculls** Robert Mills

Bronze: **Men's sailing, single-handed dinghy** Terence Neilson

Bronze: **Men's swimming, 100m backstroke** Michael West

Bronze: **Men's swimming, 200m backstroke** Cameron Henning

Bronze: **Mixed sailing, fleet/match race keelboat open** Stephen Calder, Hans Fogh, John Kerr

Bronze: **Women's 500m kayak four** Alexandra Barre, Lucie Guay, Susan Holloway, Barbara Olmstead

Bronze: **Women's athletics, 3 000m** Lynn Williams

Bronze: **Women's rowing, double sculls** Daniele Laumann, Silken Laumann

Bronze: **Women's swimming, 4x100m medley relay** Reema Abdo, Michelle MacPherson, Anne Ottenbrite, Pamela Rai

1988

Gold: **Men's boxing, super heavyweight** Lennox Lewis

Gold: **Women's synchronized swimming, duet** Michelle Cameron, Carolyn Waldo

Gold: **Women's synchronized swimming, solo** Carolyn Waldo

▶

▶ Silver: Men's boxing, middleweight Egerton Marcus
Silver: Men's swimming, 4x100m medley relay Victor Davis, Donald Goss, Thomas Ponting, Mark Tewksbury
Bronze: Men's athletics, decathlon David Steen
Bronze: Men's boxing, light-middleweight Raymond Downey
Bronze: Mixed sailing, flying Dutchman Frank McLaughlin, John Millen
Bronze: Mixed team equestrian
Bronze: Women's swimming, 4x100m medley relay Allison Higson, Jane Kerr, Lori Melien, Andrea Nugent

1992

Gold: Men's athletics, 110m hurdles Mark McKoy
Gold: Men's rowing, eight with coxswain
Gold: Men's swimming, 100m backstroke Mark Tewksbury
Gold: Women's rowing, coxless four Jennifer Barnes, Jessica Monroe, Brenda Taylor, Kay Worthington
Gold: Women's rowing, eight with coxswain
Gold: Women's rowing, pair without coxswain Kathleen Heddle, Marnie McBean
Gold: Women's synchronized swimming, solo Sylvie Frechette
Silver: Men's athletics, 20km race walk Guillaume Leblanc
Silver: Men's boxing, light-welterweight Mark Leduc
Silver: Men's freestyle wrestling, super heavyweight Jeffrey Thue
Silver: Women's synchronized swimming, duet Penny Vilagos, Vicky Vilagos
Bronze: Men's boxing, middleweight Christopher Johnson
Bronze: Men's cycling, sprint Curtis Harnett
Bronze: Men's judo, middleweight Nicolas Gill
Bronze: Men's swimming, 4x100m medley relay Stephen Clarke, Jonathan Cleveland, Marcel Gery, Mark Tewksbury
Bronze: Mixed sailing, two-person keelboat open Eric Jespersen, Ross MacDonald
Bronze: Women's athletics, 3 000m Angela Chalmers
Bronze: Women's rowing, single sculls Silken Laumann

1996

Gold: Men's athletics, 100m Donovan Bailey
Gold: Men's athletics, 4x100m relay Donovan Bailey, Robert Esmie, Glenroy Gilbert, Bruny Surin
Gold: Women's rowing, double sculls Kathleen Heddle, Marnie McBean
Silver: Men's boxing, heavyweight David Defiagbon
Silver: Men's cycling, points race Brian Walton

Silver: Men's freestyle wrestling, bantamweight Giuvi Sissaouri
Silver: Men's rowing, lightweight coxless four Dave Boyes, Gavin Hassett, Jeffrey Lay, Brian Peaker
Silver: Men's rowing, single sculls Derek Porter
Silver: Women's 500m kayak single Caroline Brunet
Silver: Women's mountain bike, cross-country Alison Sydor
Silver: Women's rowing, eight with coxswain
Silver: Women's rowing, single sculls Silken Laumann
Silver: Women's swimming, 200m individual medley Marianne Limpert
Silver: Women's team synchronized swimming
Bronze: Men's beach volleyball John Child, Mark Heese
Bronze: Men's cycling, sprint Curtis Harnett
Bronze: Men's swimming, 200m individual medley Curtis Myden
Bronze: Men's swimming, 400m individual medley Curtis Myden
Bronze: Women's cycling, individual road race Clara Hughes
Bronze: Women's cycling, individual time trial Clara Hughes
Bronze: Women's diving, 3m springboard Annie Pelletier
Bronze: Women's rowing, quadruple sculls without coxswain Laryssa Biesenthal, Kathleen Heddle, Marnie McBean, Diane O'Grady

2000

Gold: Men's freestyle wrestling, 63–69kg Daniel Igali
Gold: Men's tennis, doubles Sebastien Lareau, Daniel Nestor
Gold: Men's triathlon, individual Simon Whitfield
Silver: Men's judo, half-heavyweight Nicolas Gill
Silver: Women's 500m kayak single Caroline Brunet
Silver: Women's synchronized diving, 10m platform Emilie Heymans, Anne Montminy
Bronze: Men's 1 000m canoe single Stephen Giles
Bronze: Men's swimming, 400m individual medley Curtis Myden
Bronze: Men's trampoline, individual Mathieu Turgeon
Bronze: Women's diving, 10m platform Anne Montminy
Bronze: Women's rowing, eight with coxswain
Bronze: Women's team synchronized swimming
Bronze: Women's trampoline, individual Karen Cockburn

2004

Gold: Men's 500m K-1 kayak single Adam van Koeverden
Gold: Men's artistic gymnastics, floor exercise Kyle Shewfelt
Gold: Women's sprint cycling Lori-Ann Muenzer ▶

Silver: **Men's 3m springboard diving** Alexandre Despatie
Silver: **Men's rowing, coxless four**
Silver: **Men's yachting, Star class** Ross Macdonald, Mike Wolfs
Silver: **Women's freestyle wrestling, 55kg** Tonya Verbeek
Silver: **Women's mountain bike, cross-country** Marié-Hélène Prémont

Silver: **Women's synchronized diving, 10m platform** Emilie Heymans, Blythe Hartley
Silver: **Women's trampoline, individual** Karen Cockburn
Bronze: **Men's 1 000m K-1 kayak single** Adam van Koeverden
Bronze: **Women's 500m K-1 kayak single** Caroline Brunet

Source: *International Olympic Committee*

Winter Olympic Games

1920

Gold: **Men's ice hockey** (Although the Winter Games did not begin until 1924, ice hockey was an official event at the 1920 Summer Games.)

1924

Gold: **Men's ice hockey**

1928

Gold: **Men's ice hockey**

1932

Gold: **Men's ice hockey**
Silver: **Men's speed skating, 1 500m** Alexander Hurd
Bronze: **Men's figure skating** Montgomery Wilson
Bronze: **Men's speed skating, 1 500m** William Logan
Bronze: **Men's speed skating, 10 000m** Frank Stack
Bronze: **Men's speed skating, 5 000m** William Logan
Bronze: **Men's speed skating, 500m** Alexander Hurd

1936

Silver: **Men's ice hockey**

1948

Gold: **Men's ice hockey**
Gold: **Women's figure skating** Barbara Ann Scott
Bronze: **Pairs figure skating** Wallace Diestelmeyer, Suzanne Morrow

1952

Gold: **Men's ice hockey**
Bronze: **Men's speed skating, 500m** Gordon Audley

1956

Silver: **Pairs figure skating** Norris Bowden, Frances Dafoe
Bronze: **Men's ice hockey**
Bronze: **Women's alpine skiing, downhill** Lucile Wheeler

1960

Gold: **Pairs figure skating** Robert Paul, Barbara Wagner
Gold: **Women's alpine skiing, slalom** Anne Heggtveit
Silver: **Men's ice hockey**
Bronze: **Men's figure skating** Donald Jackson

1964

Gold: **Men's bobsleigh, four-man** Douglas Anakin, John Emery, Victor Emery, Peter Kirby
Bronze: **Pairs figure skating** Debbi Wilkes, Guy Revell
Bronze: **Women's figure skating** Petra Burka

1968

Gold: **Women's alpine skiing, giant slalom** Nancy Greene
Bronze: **Men's ice hockey**
Bronze: **Women's alpine skiing, slalom** Nancy Greene

1972

Silver: **Women's figure skating** Karen Magnussen

1976

Gold: **Women's alpine skiing, giant slalom** Kathy Kreiner
Silver: **Women's speed skating, 500m** Cathy Priestner
Bronze: **Men's figure skating** Toller Cranston

1980

Silver: **Men's speed skating, 1 000m** Gaetan Boucher
Bronze: **Men's alpine skiing, downhill** Steve Podborski

1984

Gold: **Men's speed skating, 1 000m** Gaetan Boucher
Gold: **Men's speed skating, 1 500m** Gaetan Boucher
Silver: **Men's figure skating** Brian Orser
Bronze: **Men's speed skating, 500m** Gaetan Boucher ▶

▶ 1988

Silver: Men's figure skating Brian Orser
Silver: Women's figure skating Elizabeth Manley
Bronze: Pairs ice dancing Robert McCall, Tracy Wilson
Bronze: Women's alpine skiing, downhill Karen Percy
Bronze: Women's alpine skiing, super-G Karen Percy

1992

Gold: Women's alpine skiing, downhill Kerrin Lee-Gartner
Gold: Women's short track speed skating, 3 000m relay Angela Cutrone, Sylvie Daigle, Nathalie Lambert, Annie Perreault
Silver: Men's ice hockey
Silver: Men's short track speed skating, 1 000m Frédéric Blackburn
Silver: Men's short track speed skating, 5 000m relay Frédéric Blackburn, Laurent Daignault, Michel Daignault, Sylvain Gagnon, Mark Lackie
Bronze: Pairs figure skating Isabelle Brasseur, Lloyd Eisler
Bronze: Women's biathlon, 15km Myriam Bedard

1994

Gold: Men's freestyle skiing, moguls Jean-Luc Brassard
Gold: Women's biathlon, 15km Myriam Bedard
Gold: Women's biathlon, 7.5km Myriam Bedard
Silver: Men's figure skating Elvis Stojko
Silver: Men's freestyle skiing, aerials Philippe Laroche
Silver: Men's ice hockey
Silver: Women's short track speed skating, 1 000m Nathalie Lambert
Silver: Women's short track speed skating, 3 000m relay Christine Boudrias, Isabelle Charest, Angela Cutrone, Sylvie Daigle, Nathalie Lambert
Silver: Women's speed skating, 500m Susan Auch
Bronze: Men's alpine skiing, downhill Ed Podivinsky
Bronze: Men's freestyle skiing, aerials Lloyd Langlois
Bronze: Men's short track speed skating, 1 000m Marc Gagnon
Bronze: Pairs figure skating Isabelle Brasseur, Lloyd Eisler

1998

Gold: Men's bobsleigh, two-man Pierre Lueders, David MacEachern
Gold: Men's short track speed skating, 5 000m relay Eric Bedard, Derrick Campbell, François Drolet, Marc Gagnon
Gold: Men's snowboard, giant-slalom Ross Rebagliati
Gold: Women's curling Jan Betker, Atina Ford, Marcia Gudereit, Joan McCusker, Sandra Schmirler

Gold: Women's short track speed skating, 500m Annie Perreault
Gold: Women's speed skating, 500m Catriona LeMay Doan
Silver: Men's curling Mike Harris, Richard Hart, George Karrys, Collin Mitchell, Paul Savage
Silver: Men's figure skating Elvis Stojko
Silver: Men's speed skating, 500m Jeremy Wotherspoon
Silver: Women's ice hockey
Silver: Women's speed skating, 500m Susan Auch
Bronze: Men's short track speed skating, 1 000m Eric Bedard
Bronze: Men's speed skating, 500m Kevin Overland
Bronze: Women's short track speed skating, 3 000m relay Christine Boudrias, Isabelle Charest, Annie Perreault, Tania Vicent
Bronze: Women's speed skating, 1 000m Catriona LeMay Doan

2002

Gold: Men's ice hockey
Gold: Men's short track speed skating, 5 000m relay Eric Bedard, Marc Gagnon, Jonathan Guilmette, François-Louis Tremblay, Mathieu Turcotte
Gold: Men's short track speed skating, 500m Marc Gagnon
Gold: Pairs figure skating David Pelletier, Jamie Sale
Gold: Women's ice hockey
Gold: Women's speed skating, 500m Catriona LeMay Doan
Silver: Men's curling Don Bartlett, Kevin Martin, Carter Rycroft, Ken Tralnberg, Don Walchuk
Silver: Men's short track speed skating, 500m Jonathan Guilmette
Silver: Women's cross-country skiing, 5km pursuit Beckie Scott
Silver: Women's freestyle skiing, aerials Veronica Brenner
Bronze: Men's short track speed skating, 1 000m Mathieu Turcotte
Bronze: Men's short track speed skating, 1 500m Marc Gagnon
Bronze: Women's curling Kelley Law, Diane Nelson, Cheryl Noble, Julie Skinner, Georgina Wheatcroft
Bronze: Women's freestyle skiing, aerials Deidra Dionne
Bronze: Women's short track speed skating, 3 000m relay Isabelle Charest, Marie-Eve Drolet, Amelie Goulet-Nadon, Alanna Kraus, Tania Vicent
Bronze: Women's speed skating, 3 000m Cindy Klassen
Bronze: Women's speed skating, 5 000m Clara Hughes

Source: *International Olympic Committee*

Games of the XXVIII Olympiad

Summer Olympic Games
Athens, Greece, August 13–29, 2004
Final Medal Standings

Country	Gold	Silver	Bronze	Total	Country	Gold	Silver	Bronze	Total
United States 35	39	29	103		Jamaica 2	1	2	5
Russia 27	27	38	92		Uzbekistan 2	1	2	5
China 32	17	14	63		Croatia 1	2	2	5
Australia. 17	16	16	49		Egypt 1	1	3	5
Germany. 14	16	18	48		Switzerland. 1	1	3	5
Japan 16	9	12	37		Azerbaijan. 1	0	4	5
France 11	9	13	33		DPR Korea 0	4	1	5
Italy 10	11	11	32		Georgia. 2	2	0	4
Korea 9	12	9	30		Indonesia 1	1	2	4
Great Britain. 9	9	12	30		Latvia 0	4	0	4
Cuba. 9	7	11	27		Mexico 0	3	1	4
Ukraine. 9	5	9	23		Slovenia 0	1	3	4
Netherlands 4	9	9	22		Morocco. 2	1	0	3
Romania. 8	5	6	19		Chile. 2	0	1	3
Spain 3	11	5	19		Lithuania 1	2	0	3
Hungary. 8	6	3	17		Zimbabwe. 1	1	1	3
Greece 6	6	4	16		Belgium 1	0	2	3
Belarus. 2	6	7	15		Portugal 0	2	1	3
Canada. **3**	**6**	**3**	**12**		Estonia. 0	1	2	3
Bulgaria 2	1	9	12		Bahamas 1	0	1	2
Brazil 4	3	3	10		Israel 1	0	1	2
Turkey 3	3	4	10		Finland 0	2	0	2
Poland 3	2	5	10		Serbia/Montenegro. . . . 0	2	0	2
Thailand 3	1	4	8		Nigeria 0	0	2	2
Denmark. 2	0	6	8		Venezuela. 0	0	2	2
Kazakhstan. 1	4	3	8		Cameroon. 1	0	0	1
Czech Republic. 1	3	4	8		Dominican Republic. . . 1	0	0	1
Sweden 4	1	2	7		Ireland 1	0	0	1
Austria 2	4	1	7		United Arab Emirates . . 1	0	0	1
Ethiopia 2	3	2	7		Hong Kong. 0	1	0	1
Kenya. 1	4	2	7		India. 0	1	0	1
Norway. 5	0	1	6		Paraguay 0	1	0	1
Iran. 2	2	2	6		Colombia 0	0	1	1
Slovakia 2	2	2	6		Eritrea. 0	0	1	1
Argentina 2	0	4	6		Mongolia 0	0	1	1
South Africa 1	3	2	6		Syrian Arab Republic . . 0	0	1	1
New Zealand. 3	2	0	5		Trinidad/Tobago 0	0	1	1
Chinese Taipei 2	2	1	5						

Source: *International Olympic Committee*

FOCUS ON . . .

Performance Enhancing Drugs

During a sports year that witnessed the emotional drama of Perdita Felicien's unsuccessful quest for Olympic gold in Athens, the beauty of the lowly single as the Seattle Mariners' Ichiro Suzuki pursued an 84-year-old single-season hits record (he hit 225 of them in his record-setting 2004 campaign), and the joyful relief on golfer Phil Mickelson's face after he birdied the 18th hole of The Masters to capture his first major championship in 48 tries, it's hard to imagine that same sports year could be so consumed with scandal. And yet, the spectre of doping and performance enhancing drugs hung over the sporting world throughout 2004.

The news on the cheating front wasn't just limited to the Olympic Games either, as performance enhancing drugs stole the attention of baseball and football fans as well. Most of the activity revolves around the steroid tetrahydrogestrinone (THG), a so-called "undetectable steroid," and the company that distributes the drug, Balco Laboratories. It remains unclear when THG started to appear on the sporting scene, but the United States Anti-Doping Agency (USADA) first became aware of it in mid-2003 when a track coach anonymously sent the agency a syringe with a THG sample. Investigations ensued, leading to U.S. grand jury testimony from some of the biggest names in sports, including baseball's Barry Bonds and Jason Giambi, track's Marion Jones and Tim Montgomery, Olympic gold-medal swimmer Amy Van Dyken, and several members of football's Oakland Raiders franchise. The world's anti-doping agencies also were able to use the submitted sample to create a test to make the undetectable detectable, and athletes participating at the Summer Olympic Games in Athens were tested for the steroid.

In February 2004, indictments having to do with conspiracy, money laundering, and steroid distribution were handed down to four individuals connected with Balco, including two of Balco's executives, a track coach, and a personal trainer to slugger Bonds. As of press time, no athletes have been suspended or banned because of the relatively young steroid. However, several U.S. track athletes have been notified by the USADA of a possible ban, with hearings pending.

News about possible THG use and testing for that steroid was nearly as prolific during the Athens Summer Olympic Games as the results of the medal events themselves. And the murky circumstances under which Greek sprinters Costas Kenteris and Ekaterini Thanou were able to evade drug testing at the Athens games before subsequently pulling out of the competition didn't help matter either.

What the investigations have presented, however, is suspicion in the eyes of sports fans and observers alike about the impact of THG and other performance enhancing drugs on the results of games people watch year in and year out. Even mere allegations of use facing such superstar athletes as Barry Bonds and Marion Jones are enough to raise doubt about the worthiness of their achievements.

Hearings for the track stars that are facing participation bans from the USADA were scheduled to begin in November. Regardless of the outcome of those hearings, the furor surrounding THG—and the athletes most feeling the heat of that furor—will not soon dissipate.

OTHER SPORTS

Canadian Curling Champions

Men

Skip, Province	Skip, Province	Skip, Province
1928 Gordon Hudson, Man.	1956 Billy Walsh, Man.	1981 Kerry Burtnyk, Man.
1929 Gordon Hudson, Man.	1957 Matt Baldwin, Alta	1982 Al Hackner, N. Ont.
1930 Howard Wood, Man.	1958 Matt Baldwin, Alta	1983 Ed Werenich, Ont.
1931 Bob Gourley, Man.	1959 Ernie Richardson, Sask.	1984 Mike Riley, Man.
1932 Jim Congalton, Man.	1960 Ernie Richardson, Sask.	1985 Al Hackner, N. Ont.
1933 Cliff Manahan, Alta	1961 Hec Gervais, Alta	1986 Ed Lukowich, Alta
1934 Leo Johnson, Man.	1962 Ernie Richardson, Sask.	1987 Russ Howard, Ont.
1935 Gordon Campbell, Ont.	1963 Ernie Richardson, Sask.	1988 Pat Ryan, Alta
1936 Ken Watson, Man.	1964 Lyall Dagg, BC	1989 Pat Ryan, Alta
1937 Cliff Manahan, Alta	1965 Terry Braunstein, Man.	1990 Ed Werenich, Ont.
1938 Ab Gowanlock, Man.	1966 Ron Northcott, Alta	1991 Kevin Martin, Alta
1939 Bert Hall, Ont.	1967 Alf Phillips, Jr., Ont.	1992 Vic Peters, Man.
1940 Howard Wood, Man.	1968 Ron Northcott, Alta	1993 Russ Howard, Ont.
1941 Howard Palmer, Alta	1969 Ron Northcott, Alta	1994 Rick Folk, BC
1942 Ken Watson, Man.	1970 Don Duguid, Man.	1995 Kerry Burtnyk, Man
1946 Billy Rose, Alta	1971 Don Duguid, Man.	1996 Jeff Stoughton, Man
1947 Jimmy Welsh, Man.	1972 Orest Meleschuk, Man.	1997 Kevin Martin, Alta
1948 Frenchy D'Amour, BC	1973 Harvey Mazinke, Sask.	1998 Wayne Middaugh, Ont.
1949 Ken Watson, Man.	1974 Hector Gervais, Alta	1999 Jeff Stoughton, Man.
1950 Tom Ramsay, N. Ont.	1975 Bill Tetley, N. Ont.	2000 Greg McAuley, BC
1951 Don Oyler, NS	1976 Jack MacDuff, Nfld.	2001 Randy Ferbey, Alta
1952 Billy Walsh, Man.	1977 Jim Ursel, Que.	2002 Randy Ferbey, Alta
1953 Ab Gowanlock, Man.	1978 Ed Lukowich, Alta	2003 Randy Ferbey, Alta
1954 Matt Baldwin, Alta	1979 Barry Fry, Man.	2004 Mark Dacey, NS
1955 Garnet Campbell, Sask.	1980 Rick Folk, Sask.	

Women

Skip, Province	Skip, Province	Skip, Province
1961 Joyce McKee, Sask.	1976 Lindsay Davie, BC	1991 Julie Sutton, BC
1962 Ina Hansen, BC	1977 Myrna McQuarrie, Alta.	1992 Connie Laliberte, Man.
1963 Mabel DeWare, NB	1978 Cathy Pidzarko, Man.	1993 Sandra Peterson, Sask.
1964 Ina Hansen, BC	1979 Lindsay Sparkes, BC	1994 Sandra Peterson, Sask
1965 Peggy Casselman, Man.	1980 Marj Mitchell, Sask.	1995 Connie Laliberte, Man.
1966 Gail Lee, Alta.	1981 Susan Seitz, Alta.	1996 Marilyn Bodogh, Ont.
1967 Betty Duguid, Man.	1982 Colleen Jones, NS	1997 Sandra Schmirler, Sask.
1968 Hazel Jamieson, Alta.	1983 Penny LaRocque, NS	1998 Cathy Borst, Alta.
1969 Joyce McKee, Sask.	1984 Connie Laliberte, Man.	1999 Colleen Jones, NS
1970 Dorenda Schoenhais, Sask.	1985 Linda Moore, BC	2000 Kelly Law, BC
1971 Vera Pezer, Sask.	1986 Marilyn Darte, Ont.	2001 Colleen Jones, NS
1972 Vera Pezer, Sask.	1987 Pat Sanders, BC	2002 Colleen Jones, NS
1973 Vera Pezer, Sask.	1988 Heather Houston, Ont.	2003 Colleen Jones, NS
1974 Emily Farnham, Sask.	1989 Heather Houston, Ont.	2003 Colleen Jones, NS
1975 Lee Tobin, Que.	1990 Alison Goring, Ont.	

Source: *Canadian Curling Association*

All rankings below are current as of October 3, 2004. The top ranking for the year in men's tennis will be determined following the season-ending Tennis Masters Cup, to be held November 13–21, 2004, in Houston, Texas. The top ranking for the year in women's tennis will be determined following the season-ending WTA Tour Championships, to be held November 10–15, 2004, in Los Angeles, California.

Association of Tennis Professionals' Ranking

Rank	Player (Country)	Rank	Player (Country)
1	Roger Federer (Switzerland)	11	David Nalbandian (Argentina)
2	Andy Roddick (USA)	12	Tommy Robredo (Spain)
3	Lleyton Hewitt (Australia)	13	Dominik Hrbaty (Slovakia)
4	Carlos Moya (Spain)	14	Joachim Johansson (Sweden)
5	Guillermo Coria (Argentina)	15	Nicolas Kiefer (Germany)
6	Tim Henman (Great Britain)	16	Fernando Gonzalez (Chile)
7	Gaston Gaudio (Argentina)	17	Nicolas Massu (Chile)
8	Marat Safin (Russia)	18	Guillermo Canas (Argentina)
9	Andre Agassi (USA)	18	Juan Ignacio Chela (Argentina)
10	Sebastien Grosjean (France)	20	Vincent Spadea (USA)

Source: *Association of Tennis Professionals*

Association of Tennis Professionals' Top Money Earners

Ranking	Player (Country)	Earnings (in US$)	Ranking	Player (Country)	Earnings (in US$)
1	Roger Federer (Switzerland)	4 837 547	6	Carlos Moya (Spain)	1 238 209
2	Andy Roddick (USA)	2 126 440	7	Tim Henman (Great Britain)	1 212 577
3	Lleyton Hewitt (Australia)	1 977 421	8	Andre Agassi (USA)	1 011 154
4	Guillermo Coria (Argentina)	1 607 155	9	Marat Safin (Russia)	988 333
5	Gaston Gaudio (Argentina)	1 514 589	10	Tommy Robredo (Spain)	763 207

Source: *Association of Tennis Professionals*

Women's Tennis Association Rankings

Rank	Player (Country)	Rank	Player (Country)
1	Amelie Mauresmo (France)	11	Vera Zvonareva (Russia)
2	Lindsay Davenport (USA)	12	Venus Williams (USA)
3	Justine Henin-Hardenne (Belgium)	13	Nadia Petrova (Russia)
4	Anastasia Myskina (Russia)	14	Ai Sugiyama (Japan)
5	Svetlana Kuznetsova (Russia)	15	Patty Schnyder (Switzerland)
6	Elena Dementieva (Russia)	16	Paola Suarez (Argentina)
7	Kim Clijsters (Belgium)	17	Elena Bovina (Russia)
8	Jennifer Capriati (USA)	18	Karolina Sprem (Croatia)
9	Serena Williams (USA)	19	Magdalena Maleeva (Bulgaria)
10	Maria Sharapova (Russia)	20	Alicia Molik (Australia)

Source: *Women's Tennis Association*

Women's Tennis Association Top Money Earners

Ranking	Player (Country)	Earnings (in US$)	Ranking	Player (Country)	Earnings (in US$)
1	Svetlana Kuznetsova (Russia)	1 828 878	6	Maria Sharapova (Russia)	1 319 380
2	Lindsay Davenport (USA)	1 697 011	7	Serena Williams (USA)	1 317 198
3	Anastasia Myskina (Russia)	1 481 863	8	Amelie Mauresmo (France)	1 299 236
4	Justine Henin-Hardenne (Belgium)	1 425 406	9	Paola Suarez (Argentina)	1 157 526
5	Elena Dementieva (Russia)	1 418 420	10	Jennifer Capriati (USA)	809 961

Source: *Women's Tennis Association*

The Davis Cup

The Davis Cup international tennis competition began in 1900, and with 142 nations competing for a spot in the World Group, it is the largest annual international team competition in world sport. Only 16 countries each year can qualify for a spot in the World Group first playoff round to compete for the Davis Cup. During each round, nations face off in five-match—or *rubber*—competitions—called *ties*—over a three-day period. In each tie, the first day features two singles matches, followed the doubles match on day two, with two final singles matches to wrap up the tie on day three. In the Davis Cup's 103-year history, the United States and Australia have dominated the competition, winning 32 and 28 Davis Cups, respectively.

Canada participated in the 2004 World Group for the first time since 1992. However, losses to The Netherlands and Romania prevented Team Canada from advancing to the 2005 World Group.

■ World Group, First Round Ties 2004 — *February 6–8, 2004*

(Winning nations advance to 2004 World Group quarter-final round and qualify for 2005 World Group;
losing nations compete in play-off round to complete 2005 World Group field.)

Sweden 4, Australia 1
USA 5, Austria 0
Belarus 3, Russia 2
Argentina 5, Morocco 0
Switzerland 3, Romania 2
France 4, Croatia 1
Netherlands 4, **Canada 1**

R1: Sjeng Schalken (Netherlands) def.
Frank Dancevic (Canada)
6-3, 5-7, 6-2, 6-1
R2: Martin Verkerk (Netherlands) def.
Simon Larose (Canada)
6-4, 7-6(9), 4-6, 6-3
R3: **Daniel Nestor / Frederic Niemeyer (Canada)** def. Paul Haarhuis / Martin Verkerk (Netherlands) 7-6(10), 1-0 retired

R4: Martin Verkerk (Netherlands) def.
Frank Dancevic (Canada)
6-7(5), 6-2, 7-5, 6-3
R5: Sjeng Schalken (Netherlands) def.
Simon Larose (Canada)
6-2, 7-5
Spain 3, Czech Republic 2

■ World Group, Quarter-final Ties 2004

April 9–11, 2004
USA 4, Sweden 1
Belarus 5, Argentina 0
France 3, Switzerland 2
Spain 4, Netherlands 1

■ World Group, Semi-final Ties 2004

September 24–26, 2004
USA 4, Belarus 0
Spain 4, France 1

■ World Group, Final Tie 2004

December 3–5, 2004
USA vs. Spain (to be held in Spain)

■ World Group, Play-off Ties 2004 — *September 24–26, 2004*

(Winning nations advance to 2005 World Group; losing nations compete in 2005 Zonal Group.)

Australia 4, Morocco 1
Chile 5, Japan 0
Croatia 3, Belgium 2
Czech Republic 5, Paraguay 0
Slovak Republic 3, Germany 2
Austria 3, Great Britain 2
Romania 4, **Canada 1**

R1: Andrei Pavel (Romania) def.
Simon Larose (Canada)
7-5, 6-3, 6-2
R2: Victor Hanescu (Romania) def.
Frank Dancevic (Canada)
5-7, 6-3, 3-6, 6-3, 6-4
R3: **Daniel Nestor / Frederic Niemeyer (Canada)** def. Victor Ionita / Florin Mergea (Romania) 6-4, 6-4, 2-6, 6-2

R4: Andrei Pavel (Romania) def. **Frank Dancevic (Canada)** 6-2, 6-4, 6-2
R5: Victor Ionita (Romania) def.
Simon Larose (Canada) 4-2
retired
Russia 5, Thailand 0

■ Draw for World Group 2005 — *Dates:* First Round: March 4–6, 2005 ■ Quarterfinals: July 15–17, 2005

Semifinals: September 23–25, 2005 ■ Final: December 2–4, 2005

First Round Ties *(host nation in italics)*

Spain vs. *Slovak Republic*
Switzerland vs. Netherlands
Australia vs. Austria
Argentina vs. Czech Republic

Chile vs. *Russia*
Sweden vs. *France*
Romania vs. Belarus
Croatia vs. *United States*

(Note: Canada to compete as top seed in Americas Group 1 in Zonal Group competition in 2005 and will face the winner of the Venezuela–Peru tie April 29–May 1, 2005.)

National Lacrosse League (NLL), 2004

■ 2003–04 FINAL STANDINGS

Eastern Division	GP	W	L	PCT	GB	FOR	AG
y-**Toronto Rock** 16	10	6	.625	—	202	176
x-Rochester Knighthawks 16	8	8	.500	2	173	186
x-Buffalo Bandits 16	8	8	.500	2	205	198
Philadelphia Wings 16	7	9	.438	3	192	198

Central Division	GP	W	L	PCT	GB	FOR	AG
y-Colorado Mammoth . . . 16	13	3	.813	—	223	173
x-San Jose Stealth 16	11	5	.688	2	204	201
x-**Calgary Roughnecks** . . 16	10	6	.667	3	214	187
Arizona Sting 16	7	9	.438	6	200	208
Vancouver Ravens 16	5	11	.313	8	183	213
Anaheim Storm 16	1	15	.063	12	171	227

y-Clinched division title   x-Clinched playoff berth

■ PLAYOFFS

Wild Card Round
April 16–18
Buffalo Bandits 13 Rochester Knighthawks 9
Calgary Roughnecks 15 San Jose Stealth 14

Semi-Finals
April 23–25
Calgary Roughnecks 13 Colorado Mammoth 11
Buffalo Bandits 19 **Toronto Rock** 10

Championship Game
May 7, 2004
Calgary Roughnecks 14 Buffalo Bandits 11
Game MVP: Curtis Palidwor (Calgary)

Source: *National Lacrosse League*

NLL Scoring Leaders, 2004

Player, Team	GP	G	A	PTS	AVG/G
Gary Gait, COL 16	55	38	93	5.81
John Tavares, BUF 16	49	44	93	5.81
Gavin Prout, COL 16	34	57	91	5.69
Blaine Manning, TOR 16	36	54	90	5.62
Josh Sanderson, SJS 16	28	61	89	5.56
Colin Doyle, TOR 16	33	55	88	5.50
Pat Maddalena, ARZ 16	42	41	83	5.19
Shawn Williams, ROC 16	45	36	81	5.06
Derek Malawsky, ROC 16	24	54	78	4.88
Dan Dawson, ARZ 16	26	48	74	4.62

Source: *National Lacrosse League*

Lacrosse—The Mann Cup, 1910–2004

The Mann Cup was presented by the late Sir Donald Mann, builder of the Canadian Northern Railway, for the Senior Amateur Championship of Canada and was originally a challenge cup.

1910	Young Torontos, Toronto, Ont.
1911	Vancouver Athletic Club, Vancouver, BC
1912	Vancouver Athletic Club, Vancouver, BC
1913	Vancouver Athletic Club, Vancouver, BC
1914	Vancouver Athletic Club, Vancouver, BC
1915	Salmonbellies, New Westminster, BC
1916	Salmonbellies, New Westminster, BC
1917	Salmonbellies, New Westminster, BC
1918	Coughlans, Vancouver, BC
1919	Foundation Club, Vancouver, BC
1920–25	Salmonbellies, New Westminster, BC
1926	Westonmen, Weston, Ont.
1927	Salmonbellies, New Westminster, BC
1928	Emmets, Ottawa, Ont.
1929	Generals, Oshawa, Ont.
1930	Excelsiors, Brampton, Ont.
1931	Excelsiors, Brampton, Ont.
1932	Mountaineers, Mimico, Ont.
1933	Tigers, Hamilton, Ont.
1934	Terriers, Orillia, Ont.
1935	Terriers, Orillia, Ont.
1936	Terriers, Orillia, Ont.
1937	Salmonbellies, New Westminster, BC
1938	Athletics, St. Catharines, Ont.
1939	Adanacs, New Westminster, BC
1940	Athletics, St. Catharines, Ont.
1941	Athletics, St. Catharines, Ont.
1942	Combines, Mimico/Brampton, Ont.
1943	Salmonbellies, New Westminster, BC
1944	Athletics, St. Catharines, Ont.
1945	Burrards, Vancouver, BC
1946	Athletics, St. Catharines, Ont.
1947	Adanacs, New Westminster, BC
1948	Tigers, Hamilton, Ont.
1949	Burrards, Vancouver, BC
1950	Crescents, Owen Sound, Ont.
1951	Timbermen, Peterborough, Ont.
1952	Timbermen, Peterborough, Ont.
1953	Timbermen, Peterborough, Ont.
1954	Timbermen, Peterborough, Ont.
1955	Shamrocks, Victoria, BC
1956	Timbermen, Nanaimo, BC
1957	Shamrocks, Victoria, BC
1958	Salmonberries, New Westminster, BC
1959	O'Keefes, New Westminster, BC
1960	Sailors, Port Credit, Ont.
1961	Burrards, Vancouver, BC
1962	O'Keefes, New Westminster, BC
1963	Carlings, Vancouver, BC
1964	Carlings, Vancouver, BC
1965	Salmonbellies, New Westminster, BC
1966	Lakers, Peterborough, Ont.
1967	Carlings, Vancouver, BC
1968	Redmen, Brooklin, Ont.
1969	Redmen, Brooklin, Ont.
1970	Salmonbellies, New Westminster, BC
1971	Warriors, Brantford, Ont.
1972	Salmonbellies, New Westminster, BC
1973	Lakers, Peterborough, Ont.
1974	Salmonbellies, New Westminster, BC
1975	Burrards, Vancouver, BC
1976	Salmonbellies, New Westminster, BC
1977	Burrards, Vancouver, BC
1978	Red Oaks, Peterborough, Ont.
1979	Shamrocks, Victoria, BC
1980	Excelsiors, Brampton, Ont.
1981	Salmonbellies, New Westminster, BC
1982	Lakers, Peterborough, Ont.
1983	Payless, Victoria, BC
1984	Lakers, Peterborough, Ont.
1985	Redmen, Brooklin, Ont.
1986	Salmonbellies, New Westminster, BC
1987	Redmen, Brooklin, Ont.
1988	Redmen, Brooklin, Ont.
1989	Salmonbellies, New Westminster, BC
1990	Redmen, Brooklin, Ont.
1991	Salmonbellies, New Westminster, BC
1992	Excelsiors, Brampton, Ont.
1993	Excelsiors, Brampton, Ont.
1994	Chiefs, Six Nations, Ont.
1995	Chiefs, Six Nations, Ont.
1996	Chiefs, Six Nations, Ont.
1997	Shamrocks, Victoria, BC
1998	Excelsiors ,Brampton, Ont.
1999	Shamrocks, Victoria, BC
2000	Redmen, Brooklin, Ont.
2001	Adanacs, Coquitlam, BC
2002	Excelsiors, Brampton, Ont.
2003	Shamrocks, Victoria, BC
2004	Lakers, Peterborough, Ont.

Source: *Canadian Lacrosse Association*

Figure Skating Champions, 1958–2004

	Canadian Champions		**World Champions**	
	Men	**Women**	**Men**	**Women**
1958	Charles Snelling	Margaret Crosland	Dave Jenkins, US	Carol Heiss, US
1959	Donald Jackson	Margaret Crosland	Dave Jenkins, US	Carol Heiss, US
1960	Donald Jackson	Wendy Griner	Alain Giletti, France	Carol Heiss, US
1961	Donald Jackson	Wendy Griner	—1	—1
1962	Donald Jackson	Wendy Griner	Don Jackson, Canada	Sjoukje Dijkstra, Neth.
1963	Donald McPherson	Wendy Griner	Don McPherson, Canada	Sjoukje Dijkstra, Neth.
1964	Charles Snelling	Petra Burka	Manfred Schnelldorfer, W. Germany	Sjoukje Dijkstra, Neth.
1965	Donald Knight	Petra Burka	Alain Calmat, France	Petra Burka, Canada
1966	Donald Knight	Petra Burka	Emmerich Danzer, Austria	Peggy Fleming, US
1967	Donald Knight	Valerie Jones	Emmerich Danzer, Austria	Peggy Fleming, US
1968	Jay Humphry	Karen Magnussen	Emmerich Danzer, Austria	Peggy Fleming, US
1969	Jay Humphry	Linda Carbonetto	Tim Wood, US	Gabriele Seyfert, E. Germany
1970	David McGillivray	Karen Magnussen	Tim Wood, US	Gabriele Seyfert, E. Germany
1971	Toller Cranston	Karen Magnussen	Ondrej Nepela, Czech.	Beatrix Schuba, Austria
1972	Toller Cranston	Karen Magnussen	Ondrej Nepela, Czech.	Beatrix Schuba, Austria
1973	Toller Cranston	Karen Magnussen	Ondrej Nepela, Czech.	Karen Magnussen, Canada
1974	Toller Cranston	Lynn Nightingale	Jan Hoffman, E. Germany	Christine Errath, E. Germany
1975	Toller Cranston	Lynn Nightingale	Sergei Volkov, USSR	Dianne de Leeuw, Neth.-US
1976	Toller Cranston	Lynn Nightingale	John Curry, Gr. Brit.	Dorothy Hamill, US
1977	Ron Shaver	Lynn Nightingale	Vladimir Kovalev, USSR	Linda Fratianne, US
1978	Brian Pockar	Heather Kemkaran	Charles Tickner, US	Anett Poetzsch, E. Germany
1979	Brian Pockar	Janet Morrisey	Vladimir Kovalev, USSR	Linda Fratianne, US
1980	Brian Pockar	Heather Kemkaran	Jan Hoffmann, E. Germany	Anett Poetzsch, E. Germany
1981	Brian Orser	Tracey Wainman	Scott Hamilton, US	Denise Biellmann, Switzerland
1982	Brian Orser	Kay Thomson	Scott Hamilton, US	Elaine Zayak, US
1983	Brian Orser	Kay Thomson	Scott Hamilton, US	Rosalyn Sumners, US
1984	Brian Orser	Kay Thomson	Scott Hamilton, US	Katarina Witt, E. Germany
1985	Brian Orser	Elizabeth Manley	Alexandre Fadeev, USSR	Katarina Witt, E. Germany
1986	Brian Orser	Tracey Wainman	Brian Boitano, US	Debi Thomas, US
1987	Brian Orser	Elizabeth Manley	Brian Orser, Canada	Katarina Witt, E. Germany
1988	Brian Orser	Elizabeth Manley	Brian Boitano, US	Katarina Witt, E. Germany
1989	Kurt Browning	Karen Preston	Kurt Browning, Canada	Midori Ito, Japan
1990	Kurt Browning	Lisa Sargeant	Kurt Browning, Canada	Jill Trenary, US
1991	Kurt Browning	Josée Chouinard	Kurt Browning, Canada	Kristi Yamaguchi, US
1992	Michael Slipchuk	Karen Preston	Victor Petrenko, Russia	Kristi Yamaguchi, US
1993	Kurt Browning	Josée Chouinard	Kurt Browning, Canada	Oksana Baiul, Ukraine
1994	Elvis Stojko	Josée Chouinard	Elvis Stojko, Canada	Yuka Sato, Japan
1995	Sebastien Britten	Netty Kim	Elvis Stojko, Canada	Lu Chen, China
1996	Elvis Stojko	Jennifer Robinson	Todd Eldredge, US	Michelle Kwan, US
1997	Elvis Stojko	Susan Humphreys	Elvis Stojko, Canada	Tara Lapinski, US
1998	Elvis Stojko	Angela Derochie	Alexei Yagudin, Russia	Michelle Kwan, US
1999	Elvis Stojko	Jennifer Robinson	Alexei Yagudin, Russia	Maria Butyrskaya, Russia
2000	Elvis Stojko	Jennifer Robinson	Alexei Yagudin, Russia	Michelle Kwan, US
2001	Emmanuel Sandhu	Jennifer Robinson	Evgeny Plushenko, Russia	Michelle Kwan, US
2002	Elvis Stojko	Jennifer Robinson	Alexei Yagudin, Russia	Irina Slutskaya, Russia
2003	Emmanuel Sandhu	Jennifer Robinson	Evgeny Plushenko, Russia	Michelle Kwan, US
2004	Emmanuel Sandhu	Cynthia Phaneuf	Evgeny Plushenko, Russia	Shizuka Arakawa, Japan

Source: *Canadian Figure Skating Association*

(1) The 1961 world championships were cancelled after an air crash killed the entire US team travelling to the competition.

The Queen's Plate, 1970–2004

The Queen's Plate, first run in 1860, is North America's oldest annual sports event. The race for 3-year-olds foaled in Canada is run at Toronto's Woodbine Race Track in late June or July.

	Winner	Jockey	Time		Winner	Jockey	Time
1970	Almoner	Sandy Hawley	2:04.4	1987	Market Control	Ken Skinner	2:03.2
1971	Kennedy Road	Sandy Hawley	2:03	1988	Regal Intention	Jack Lauzon	2:06.1
1972	Victoria Song	Robin Platts	2:03.1	1989	With Approval	Don Seymour	2:03
1973	Royal Chocolate	Ted Colangelo	2:08	1990	Izvestia	Don Seymour	2:01.4
1974	Amber Herod	Robin Platts	2:09.1	1991	Dance Smartly	Pal Day	2:03.2
1975	L'Enjoleur	Sandy Hawley	2:02.3	1992	Alydeed	Craig Perret	2:04.6
1976	Norcliffe	Jeffrey Fell	2:05	1993	Peteski	Craig Perret	2:04.2
1977	Sound Reason	Robin Platts	2:06.3	1994	Basqueian	Jack Laron	2:03.4
1978	Regal Embrace	Sandy Hawley	2:02	1995	Regal Discovery	Todd Kabel	2:03.4
1979	Steady Growth	Brian Swatuk	2:06.3	1996	Victor Cooley	Emke Ramsammy	2:03.8
1980	Driving Home	Bill Parsons	2:04.1	1997	Awesome Again	A.E. Smith	2:04
1981	Fiddle Dancer Boy	David Clark	2:04.4	1998	Archer's Bay	Kent Desormeaux	2:02.1
1982	Son of Briartic	John-Paul Souter	2:04.3	1999	Woodcarver	Mickey Walls	2:03
1983	Bompago	Larry Attard	2:04.1	2000	Scatter the Gold	Todd Kabel	1:56.0
1984	Key to the Moon	Robin Platts	2:03.4	2001	Dancethruthedawn	Gary Boulanger	2:03.8
1985	La Lorgnette	David Clark	2:04.3	2002	TJ's Lucky Moon	Steven Bahen	2:06.8
1986	Golden Choice	Vince Bracciale	2:07.1	2003	Wando	Patrick Husbands	2:02.4
				2004	Niigon	Robert Landry	2:04.7

Source: *Woodbine Entertainment Group*

Thoroughbred Racing

Thoroughbred racing's coveted Triple Crown has only been won 11 times: Sir Barton (1919); Gallant Fax (1930); Omaha (1935); War Admiral (1937); Whirlaway (1941); Count Fleet (1943); Assault (1946); Citation (1948); Secretariat (1973); Seattle Slew (1977) and Affirmed (1978). The challenge will be taken up anew in 2005: The Kentucky Derby will be held at Churchill Downs on May 7, 2005; the Preakness Stakes will be held at Pimlico on May 21, 2005; and the Belmont Stakes will be held on June 11, 2005.

Triple Crown	Date	Winner
Kentucky Derby	May 1, 2004	Smarty Jones
Preakness Stakes	May 15, 2004	Smarty Jones
Belmont Stakes	June 7, 2004	Birdstone

Source: *ESPN Network*

Harness Racing

Event	Date	Winner	Driver	Time
North America Cup	June 19, 2004	Mantacular	Cat Manzi	1:51.2
The Canadian Pacing Derby	September 4, 2004	Casimir Camotion	Pat Lachance	1:48.3
The Metro Pace	September 4, 2004	Dawn Ofa New Day	John Campbell	1:52.3
Maple Leaf Trot	September 18, 2004	Mr Muscleman	Ron Pierce	1:53.2
Canadian Trotting Classic	September 25, 2004	Cincinnati Kid	Trevor Ritchie	1:54.4

Source: *Woodbine Entertainment Group*

Prince of Wales Stakes, 1962–2004

	Winner	Jockey	Time[1]		Winner	Jockey	Time[1]
1962	King Gorm	Hugo Dittfach	2:21.1	1983	Archdeacon	Vince Bracciale	2:32.0
1963	Canebora	Hugo Dittfach	2:30.3	1984	Val Dansant	John LeBlanc	2:48.3
1964	Canadillis	Avelino Gomez	2:35.0	1985	Imperial Choice	Irwin Driedger	2:34.3
1965	Good Old Mort	S. McComb	2:22.4	1986	Golden Choice	Vince Bracciale	2:44.2
1966	He's A Smoothie	Hugo Dittfach	2:19.0	1987	Coryphee	Brian Swatuk	2:39.3
1967	Battling	Hugo Dittfach	2:21.0	1988	Regal Classic	Sandy Hawley	2:00.1
1968	Rouletabille	Richard Grubb	2:18.3	1989	With Approval	Don Seymour	1:56.4
1969	Sharp-Eyed Quillo	H. Gustines	2:16.3	1990	Izvestia	Don Seymour	1:56.2
1970	Almoner	Sandy Hawley	2:19.4	1991	Dance Smartly	Pal Day	1:56.3
1971	New Pro	Jim Kelly	2:15.1	1992	Benburb	Larry Attard	1:57.2
1972	Presidial	John LeBlanc	2:16.3	1993	Peteski	Dave Penna	1:34.4
1973	Tara Road	Sandy Hawley	2:16.4	1994	Bruce's Mill	Craig Perret	1:53.4
1974	Rushton's Corsair	Jim Kelly	2:23.2	1995	Kiridashi	Larry Attard	1:55.0
1975	L'Enjoleur	Sandy Hawley	2:32.2	1996	Stephanotis	Mickey Walls	1:55.2
1976	Norcliffe	Jeff Fell	2:30.1	1997	Cryptocloser	W. Martinez	1:560
1977	Dance in Time	Gary Stahlbaum	2:31.4	1998[2]	Archer's Bay	Robert Landry	1:55.1
1978	Overskate	Robin Platts	2:34.2	1999	Gandria	Constant Montpellier	1:56.4
1979	Mass Rally	George Ho Sang	2:33.2	2000	Scatter the Gold	Todd Kabel	1:56.0
1980	Allan Blue	Joe Belowus	2:34.4	2001	Fantastic Light	Frankie Dettori	2:04.4
1981	Cadet Corps	Robin Platts	2:34.4	2002	Le Cinquieme Essai	Brian Bochinski	1:56.5
1982	Runaway Groom	Robin Platts	2:38.2	2003	Wando	Patrick Husbands	1:55.8
				2004	A Bit O'Gold	Jono Jones	1:57.3

Source: *Woodbine Entertainment Group*   (1) Fractions of a second are in fifths. (2) Held July 25, 1999.

Breeders Stakes, 1962–2004

	Winner	Jockey	Time[1]		Winner	Jockey	Time[1]
1962	Crafty Lace	Ron Turcotte	2:52	1984	Bounding Away	David Clark	2:32.3
1963	Canebora	Manuel Ycaza	2:32.1	1985	Crowning Honors	Brian Swatuk	2:50
1964	Artic Hills	R. Armstrong	2:33.3	1986	Carotene	Richard Dos Ramos	2:32.3
1965	Good Old Mort	P. Kallai	2:43	1987	Hangin On a Star	Dave Penna	2:30
1966	Titled Hero	Avelino Gomez	2:31.2	1988	King's Deputy	Sandy Hawley	2:30.3
1967	Pine Point	Avelino Gomez	2:32.1	1989	With Approval	Don Seymour	2:29
1968	No Parando	John LeBlanc	2:30	1990	Izvestia	Don Seymour	2:33.2
1969	Grey Whiz	John LeBlanc	2:29	1991	Dance Smartly	Pal Day	2:31.2
1970	Mary of Scotland	Richard Grubb	2:38.2	1992	Blitzer	Don Seymour	2:35.3
1971	Belle Geste	Noel Turcotte	2:28	1993	Peteski	Craig Perret	2:30.4
1972	Nice Dancer	Sandy Hawley	2:35.4	1994	Basqueian	Jack Lauzon	2:47.4
1973	Come In Dad	Wayne Green	2:33.3	1995	Charlie's Dewan	Craig Perret	2:26.4
1974	Haymaker's Jig	Robin Platts	2:30.4	1996	Chief Bearheart	Mickey Walls	2:28.3
1975	Momigi	Gary Melanson	2:38.1	1997	John The Magician	Steven Bahen	2:35
1976	Tiny Tinker	Sandy Hawley	2:31.1	1998[2]	Pinafore Park	Robert Landry	2:30.1
1977	Dance in Time	Gary Stahlbaum	3:01.3	1999	Free Vacation	Laurie Gulas	2:28.4
1978	Overskate	Robin Platts	2:29.2	2000	Lodge Hill	Todd Pletcher	2:28
1979	Bridle Path	Sandy Hawley	2:29.3	2001	Sweetest Thing	James McAleney	2:29.9
1980	Ben Fab	Gary Stahlbaum	2:31.3	2002	Portcullis	Slade Callaghan	2:29.8
1981	Social Wizard	George Ho Sang	2:48.4	2003	Wando	Patrick Husbands	2:28.7
1982	Runaway Groom	Robin Platts	2:32.1	2004	A Bit O'Gold	Jono Jones	2:27.1
1983	Kingsbridge	Robin Platts	2:32.2				

Source: *Woodbine Entertainment Group*   (1) Fractions of a second are in fifths. (2) August 15, 1999.

Championship Auto Racing Teams (CART), 2004

(as of October 4, 2004)

Race	Date	Winner
Toyota Grand Prix of Long Beach	April 18	Paul Tracy
Tecate Telmex Monterrey Grand Prix	May 23	Sebastien Bourdais
Milwaukee Mile	June 5	Ryan Hunter-Reay
Champ Car Grand Prix of Portland	June 20	Sebastien Bourdais
Champ Car Grand Prix of Cleveland	July 3	Sebastien Bourdais
Molson Indy Toronto	July 11	Sebastien Bourdais
Molson Indy Vancouver	July 25	Paul Tracy
Grand Prix of Road America (Elkhart Lake)	August 8	Alex Tagliani
Centrix Financial Grand Prix of Denver	August 15	Sebastien Bourdais
Molson Indy Montreal	August 29	Bruno Junqueira
Grand Prix of Monterey	September 12	Patrick Carpentier
Las Vegas Bridgestone 400	September 26	Sebastien Bourdais

CART races for the balance of the 2004 season:

Lexmark Indy 300 (Australia)	October 24, 2004	
Gran Premio Telmex (Mexico City)	November 7, 2004	

Source: *CART Inc.*

CART Champions

Paul Tracy, a native of Scarborough, Ontario, became the second Canadian driver to win the points race on the CART circuit (Jacques Villeneuve of St-Jean-Sur-Richelieu, Quebec, won in 1995). His 226 points also helped Canada win its first Nations Cup, the third nation to do so (Brazil and the United States are four-time winners). Other Canadian drivers on the 2003 tour were Patrick Carpentier and Alex Tagliani.

Year	Winner	Team	Points
1979	Rick Mears	Penske Racing	4 060
1980	Johnny Rutherford	Chaparral Racing	4 723
1981	Rick Mears	Penske Racing	304
1982	Rick Mears	Penske Racing	294
1983	Al Unser	Penske Racing	151
1984	Mario Andretti	Newman/Haas Racing	176
1985	Al Unser	Penske Racing	151
1986	Bobby Rahal	Truesports	179
1987	Bobby Rahal	Truesports	188
1988	Danny Sullivan	Penske Racing	182
1989	Emerson Fittipaldi	Patrick Racing	196
1990	Al Unser, Jr	Galles-Kraco Racing	210
1991	Michael Andretti	Newman/Haas Racing	234
1992	Bobby Rahal	Rahal-Hogan Racing	196
1993	Nigel Mansell	Newman/Haas	191
1994	Al Unser, Jr	Malboro Team Penske	225
1995	Jacques Villeneuve	Team Green	172
1996	Jimmy Vasser	Target Chip Ganassi	154
1997	Alex Zanardi	Target Chip Ganassi	195
1998	Alex Zanardi	Target Chip Ganassi	285
1999	Juan Montoya	Target Chip Ganassi	212
2000	Gil de Ferran	Marlboro Team Penske	168
2001	Gil de Ferran	Marlboro Team Penske	199
2002	Cristiano da Matta	Newman/Haas Racing	237
2003	Paul Tracy	Forsythe Championship Racing	226

Source: *CART Inc.*

Tour de France: Winners, 1983–2004

American cyclist Lance Armstrong rode to a sixth consecutive Tour de France in 2004, marking the first time a rider has won the prestigious event six times—much less six times in a row. (Four previous Tour winners had won the event five times.)

The story is well told of how Armstrong battled and overcame testicular cancer—cancer so strong that it had spread to his lungs and brain—and then won his first Tour just two years later. What is often overlooked, however, is how overwhelming his Tour wins have been. Throw out his 2003 victory (by a close margin of just over one minute), and Armstrong's average margin of victory has been 6 minutes, 48 seconds, a time bested by only one Tour winner in the 10 years before Armstrong won his first. In the 40 years before Armstrong started his amazing win streak, only 12 winners had a larger margin of victory than the 6:48 average.

Armstrong has not yet committed to racing for an unprecedented seventh consecutive Tour de France victory in 2005. No matter his decision, he will remain one of cycling's—indeed, one of sport's—most inspirational and exceptional champions.

1983	Laurent Fignon, France		1994	Miguel Indurain, Spain
1984	Laurent Fignon, France		1995	Miguel Indurain, Spain
1985	Bernard Hinault, France		1996	Bjarne Riis, Denmark
1986	Greg LeMond, United States		1997	Jan Ullrich, Germany
1987	Stephen Roche, Ireland		1998	Marco Pantani, Italy
1988	Pedro Delgado, Spain		1999	Lance Armstrong, United States
1989	Greg LeMond, United States		2000	Lance Armstrong, United States
1990	Greg LeMond, United States		2001	Lance Armstrong, United States
1991	Miguel Indurain, Spain		2002	Lance Armstrong, United States
1992	Miguel Indurain, Spain		2003	Lance Armstrong, United States
1993	Miguel Indurain, Spain		2004	Lance Armstrong, United States

Source: *ESPN.com*

Mountain Bike World Championships

■ Cross Country Elite Men

Place	Name	Time
1.	Absalon, Julien (Fra)	2:20:37
2.	Ravanel, Cedric (Fra)	2:21:34
3.	Frischknecht, Thomas (Sui)	2:22:21
4.	Paulissen, Roel (Bel)	2:22:25
5.	Galinski, Marek (Pol)	2:23:34
15.	**Kabush, Geoff (Can)**	**2:30:19**
16.	**Sheppard, Chris (Can)**	**2:30:29**
26.	**Federau, Ricky (Can)**	**2:35:31**
51.	**Toulouse, Mathieu (Can)**	**-1 lap**
58.	**Wedge, Peter (Can)**	**-1 lap**
65.	**Lega, Roddi (Can)**	**-1 lap**

■ Cross Country Elite Women

Place	Name	Time
1.	Dahle, Gunn-Rita (Nor)	2:02:12
2.	Wloszczowska, Maja (Pol)	2:03:18
3.	**Sydor, Alison (Can)**	**2:03:57**
4.	**Premont, Marie-Helene (Can)**	**2:06:33**
5.	Spitz, Sabine (Ger)	2:06:45
14.	**Bisaro, Kiara (Can)**	**2:12:51**
25.	**Redden, Chrissy (Can)**	**2:20:21**
42.	**Sinclair, Trish (Can)-1 lap**	
46.	**Pendrel, Catherine -1 lap (Can)**	
56.	**De Wolfe, Karen (Can)-1 lap**	

■ The Espoir (under 23)

Place	Name	Time
1.	Fumic, Manuel (Ger)	1:56:10
2.	Killeen, Liam (GBr)	1:56:14
3.	Vogel, Florian (Sui)	1:58:24
3.	Lejarreta Errasti, Inaki (Esp)	1:59:57
5.	Ruzafa Cueto, Ruben (Esp)	2:01:24
24.	**Plaxton, Max (Can)**	**2:08:01**
31.	**Sneddon, Kris (Can)**	**2:09:33**
49.	**Zandstra, Derek (Can)**	**2:14:16**
62.	**Lazarski, Martin (Can)-1 lap**	
71.	**Hadley, Matthew (Can)-2 laps**	
76.	**Watson, Andrew (Can)-2 laps**	

Source: *Union Cycliste Internationale*

UEFA Euro 2004

Held in Portugal — June 12 to July 4, 2004

Greece won its first European football championship at the 12th quadrennial Euro 2004, defeating the host country, Portugal, 1-0. Germany leads all nations with three championships.

GROUP STANDINGS

(top 2 teams in each group advance to quarterfinals)

■ Group A

Team	MP	W	D	L	GF	GA	Pts
Portugal	3	2	0	1	4	2	6
Greece	3	1	1	1	4	4	4
Spain	3	1	1	1	2	2	4
Russia	3	1	0	2	2	4	3

■ Group B

Team	MP	W	D	L	GF	GA	Pts
France	3	2	1	0	7	4	7
England	3	2	0	1	8	4	6
Croatia	3	0	2	1	4	6	2
Switzerland	3	0	1	2	1	6	1

■ Group C

Team	MP	W	D	L	GF	GA	Pts
Sweden	3	1	2	0	8	3	5
Denmark	3	1	2	0	4	2	5
Italy	3	1	2	0	3	2	5
Bulgaria	3	0	0	3	1	9	0

■ Group D

Team	MP	W	D	L	GF	GA	Pts
Czech Republic	3	3	0	0	7	4	9
Netherlands	3	1	1	1	6	4	4
Germany	3	0	2	1	2	3	2
Latvia	3	0	1	2	1	5	1

■ Group A Scores
Greece 2, Portugal 1
Spain 1, Russia 0
Greece 1, Spain 1
Portugal 2, Russia 0
Portugal 1, Spain 0
Russia 2, Greece 1

■ Group B Scores
Switzerland 0, Croatia 0
France 2, England 1
England 3, Switzerland 0
Croatia 2, France 2
England 4, Croatia 2
France 3, Switzerland 1

■ Group C Scores
Denmark 0, Italy 0
Sweden 5, Bulgaria 0
Denmark 2, Bulgaria 0
Italy 1, Sweden 1
Italy 2, Bulgaria 1
Denmark 2, Sweden 2

■ Group D Scores
Germany 1, Netherlands 1
Czech Republic 2, Latvia 1
Latvia 0, Germany 0
Czech Republic 3,
Netherlands 2
Netherlands 3, Latvia 0
Czech Republic 2, Germany 1

■ Quarterfinals
Portugal 2 (6-5), England 2
Greece 1, France 0
Netherlands 0 (5-4), Sweden 0
Czech Republic 3, Denmark 0

■ Semifinals
Portugal 2, Netherlands 1
Greece 1, Czech Republic 0

FINAL
Greece 1, Portugal 0

MP: Matches played; W: Won; D: Drawn; L: Lost; GF: Goals for; GA: Goals against; Pts: Points

FIFA World Cup 2006 Update

To be held in Germany — June 9 to July 9, 2006

The long road to qualifying as one of 32 nations to participate in the 2006 World Cup began in September 2003 and continued through the summer of 2004. Qualifying matches will continue through 2005. Team Canada made it through the first stage of qualifying in its zone (North/Central America and Caribbean Zone), with two 4-0 victories over Belize. The second stage of qualifying has not been as successful for Canada, which at press time sat in last place in its group with three matches to play.

North/Central America and Caribbean Zone Standings

Group 1 Standings

Team	MP	W	D	L	F	A	Pts
USA	3	1	2	0	4	2	5
Jamaica	3	1	1	1	5	3	4
Panama	3	1	1	1	4	4	4
El Salvador	3	1	0	2	2	6	3

Group 2 Standings

Team	MP	W	D	L	F	A	Pts
Guatemala	3	2	1	0	6	3	7
Honduras	3	1	2	0	8	5	5
Costa Rica	3	1	0	2	4	7	3
Canada	3	0	1	2	1	4	1

Group 3 Standings

Team	MP	W	D	L	F	A	Pts
Trinidad & Tobago	3	2	0	1	5	4	6
Mexico	1	1	0	0	3	1	3
St. Vincent/ Grenadines	2	1	0	1	1	2	3
St. Kitts & Nevis	2	0	0	2	1	3	0

MP: Matches played; W: Won; D: Drawn; L: Lost; GF: Goals for; GA: Goals against; Pts: Points

Rugby World Cup 2003

Australia, October 10–November 22, 2003

Canada's national rugby team qualified for the 2003 Rugby World Cup by winning the Americas Rugby World Cup qualifying group in August 2002. Team Canada finished fourth in its pool and did not qualify for quarter-final play.

QUALIFYING POOL STANDINGS

(top 2 teams in each pool qualify for quarter-finals)

■ Pool A

Team	PL	W	D	L	PF	PA	PD	TP
Australia	4	4	0	0	273	32	241	18
Ireland	4	3	0	1	141	56	85	15
Argentina	4	2	0	2	140	57	83	11
Romania	4	1	0	3	65	192	-127	5
Namibia	4	0	0	4	28	310	-282	0

■ Pool B

Team	PL	W	D	L	PF	PA	PD	TP
France	4	4	0	0	204	70	134	20
Scotland	4	3	0	1	102	97	5	14
Fiji	4	2	0	2	98	114	-16	10
USA	4	1	0	3	86	125	-39	6
Japan	4	0	0	4	79	163	-84	0

■ Pool C

Team	PL	W	D	L	PF	PA	PD	TP
England	4	4	0	0	255	47	208	19
South Africa	4	3	0	1	184	60	124	15
Samoa	4	2	0	2	138	117	21	10
Uruguay	4	1	0	3	56	255	-199	4
Georgia	4	0	0	4	46	200	-154	0

■ Pool D

Team	PL	W	D	L	PF	PA	PD	TP
New Zealand	4	4	0	0	282	57	225	20
Wales	4	3	0	1	132	98	34	14
Italy	4	2	0	2	77	123	-46	8
Canada	4	1	0	3	54	135	-81	5
Tonga	4	0	0	4	46	178	-132	1

PL: played; W: won; D: drawn; L: lost; PF: points for; PA: points against; PD: points difference; TP: total points, including bonus points

QUARTER-FINAL MATCHES
New Zealand 29, South Africa 9

Australia 33, Scotland 16

France 43, Ireland 21

England 28, Wales 17

SEMI-FINAL MATCHES
Australia 22, New Zealand 10

England 24, France 7

THIRD-PLACE MATCH
New Zealand 40, France 13

FINAL MATCH
England 20, Australia 17

Source: *Rugby Canada*

Want to Surf for Sports Info?

Basketball

Basketball Canada
www.basketball.ca
Official site of Canadian basketball, providing information on national teams and all national basketball associations.

FIBA (Federation Internationale Basketall Association)
www.fiba.com
Official site of the international governing body of basketball, featuring tournament information, press releases and rules.

Cycling
Canadian Cycling Association
www.canadian-cycling.com
Governing body of cycling in Canada with information on national teams, championships, coaching and rules.

Lacrosse
National Lacrosse League
www.nll.com
Official site of the National Lacrosse league with schedules, team rosters, standings and statistics.

Football
Canadian Football League
www.cfl.ca
All you need to know about the CFL

National Football League
www.nfl.com
All the information you want on the NFL

Canadian Junior Football League
www.cjfl.ca
Scores, standings and stats

Rugby

Rugby Canada
www.rugbycanada.ca
Official site of Canadian rugby with information on Canadian national teams, super league, national championships, refereeing and coaching.

Soccer

Canadian Soccer Association
www.canadasoccer.com
Governing body for both men's and women's soccer in Canada with constantly updated information on competitions, national teams and players.

Canada's Sports Hall of Fame

(living members as of October 1, 2004)

Anakin, Douglas, bobsled
Arnold, Don, rowing
Athans, George, Jr., water skiing
Aubut, Marcel, hockey builder
Bailey, Donovan, track sprint*
Balding, Al, golf
Baldwin, Matt, curling
Bassett-Seguso, Carling, tennis
Baumann, Alex, swimming
Bédard, Myriam, biathlon
Bedard, Robert, tennis
Béliveau, Jean, hockey
Bell, Marilyn, marathon swimming
Bernier, Sylvie, diving
Betger, Jan, curling
Boldt, Arnie, field high jump
Boucher, Gaetan, speed skating
Bower, Johnny, hockey
Bowman, Scotty, hockey*
Box, Ab, football
Boys, Bev, diving
Brasseur, Isabelle, figure skating
Brooks, Lela, speed skating
Browning, Kurt, figure skating
Burka, Ellen, figure skating builder
Burka, Petra, figure skating
Burka, Sylvia, speed skating
Cain, Larry, canoeing
Cameron, Michelle, synchro swimming
Carnegie, Herb, hockey
Chuvalo, George, boxing
Cliff, Leslie, swimming
Clifford, Betsy, skiing
Cowan, Gary, golf
Cranston, Toller, figure skating
Crothers, Bill, track mid-distance
D'hondt, Walter, rowing
Dafoe, Frances, figure skating
Day, James, equestrian
Dexter, Glen, yachting
Dionne, Marcel, hockey
Dojack, Paul, football builder
Drake, Clare, hockey builder
Drayton, Jerome, marathon running
Dryden, Ken, hockey
Duguid, Don, curling
Dunnell, Milt, sports broadcaster
Durelle, Yvon, boxing
Eisler, Lloyd, figure skating

Elder, James, equestrian
Emery, Dr. John, bobsled
Emery, Victor, bobsled
Esaw, Johnny, all-around builder
Esposito, Phil, hockey
Filion, Hervé, harness racing
Fisher, Hugh, canoeing
Fogh, Hans, yachting
Fortier, Sylvie, synchro swimming
Frechette, Sylvie, synchro swimming
Fung, Lori, rhythmic gymnastics*
Gabriel, Tony, football
Gainey, Bob, hockey
Galbraith, Sheldon, figure skating builder
Gate, George, swimming builder
Gaudaur, Jake, Jr., football builder
Gayford, Tom, equestrian
Geoffrion, Bernard "Boom Boom," hockey
Golab, Tony, football
Gowan, Geoff, builder
Graham, Laurie, skiing
Greene, Nancy, skiing
Grenier, Jean, speed skating builder
Gretzky, Wayne, hockey
Gudereit, Marcia, curling
Hall, Glenn, hockey
Hartman, Barney, skeet shooting
Hawley, Sandy, horse racing
Heddle, Kathleen, rowing
Heggtveit, Anne, skiing
Henderson, Paul, hockey
Hepburn, Doug, weightlifting
Hildebrand, Ike, lacrosse
Hiller, John, baseball
Hoffman, Abby, track mid-distance*
Howe, Gordie, hockey
Hull, Bobby, hockey
Hungerford, George W., rowing
Hunter, Bill, builder
Huot, Jules, golf
Hutton, Ralph, swimming
Jackson, Donald, figure skating
Jackson, Dr. Roger, rowing
Jackson, Russ, football
Jelinek, Maria, figure skating
Jelinek, Otto, figure skating
Jenkins, Ferguson, baseball
Josenhans, Andreas, yachting
Kelly, Leonard (Red), hockey

▶

▶ **Kidd,** Bruce, track mid-distance
Kirby, Peter, bobsled
Kreiner, Kathy, skiing
Krol, Joe, football
Kwong, Norm, football
Lafleur, Guy, hockey
Lambert, Nathalie, speed skating
Lancaster, Ron, football
Laumann, Silken, rowing
Lee-Gartner, Kerrin, skiing
Lemieux, Mario, hockey
Leonard, Stan, golf
Lessard, Lucille, archery
Lidstone, Dorothy, archery
Lindsay, Robert B.T. (Ted), hockey
Longden, Johnny, horse racing
Loomer, Lorne, rowing
Lovell, Jocelyn, cycling
Luftspring, Sammy, boxing
MacDonald, Irene, diving
MacDonald, Noel, basketball
MacMillan, Sandy, yachting
Magnussen, Karen, figure skating
Mahovlich, Frank, hockey
Mara, George, multi-sport builder
Martini, Paul, figure skating
McBean, Marnie, rowing
McCusker, Joan, curling
McLarnin, Jimmy, boxing
McPherson, Donald, figure skating
Miles, John C., marathon swimming
Millar, Ian, equestrian
Mitchell, Ray, bowling
Morris, Alwyn, canoeing
Muir, Debbie, synchro swim builder
Nattrass, Susan, trap shooting
Nicholas, Cindy, marathon swimming
Northcott, Ron, curling
O'Donnell, Bill, harness racing
Orr, Robert (Bobby), hockey
Orser, Brian, figure skating
Ottenbrite, Anne, swimming
Parker, Jackie, football
Pashby, Dr. Tom, multi-sport builder
Paul, Robert, figure skating
Peden, Doug, multi-sport
Percy, Karen, skiing
Perry, Gordon, football
Podborski, Steve, skiing

Pollock, Sam, hockey builder
Post, Sandra, golf
Potvin, Denis, hockey
Presley, Gerald, bobsled
Primrose, John, trap shooting
Ramage, Pat, skiing builder
Read, Ken, skiing
Reed, George, football
Richard, Henri, hockey
Richardson, Arnold, curling
Richardson, Ernie, curling
Richardson, Garnet, curling
Richardson, Wes, curling
Robertson, Bruce, swimming
Robinson, Larry, hockey*
Rogers, Doug, judo
Saunders, Claude, rowing builder
Schmidt, Milt, hockey
Scott, Barbara Ann, figure skating
Shedd, Marjory, badminton
Smith, Graham, swimming
Sorensen, Gerry, skiing
Steen, Dave, decathlon
Stewart, Marlene, golf
Stewart, Ron, football
Storey, R.A. (Red), all-around
Stukus, Annis, football builder
Tanner, Elaine, swimming
Taylor, Ron, baseball
Tewksbury, Mark, swimming
Thom, Linda, pistol shooting
Thompson, James, speedboating builder
Thorburn, Cliff, snooker
Townsend, Cathy, bowling
Turcotte, Ron, horse racing
Underhill, Barbara, figure skating
Van Vliet, Maury, builder
Vanderburg, Helen, synchro swimming
Wagner, Barbara, figure skating
Waldo, Carolyn, synchro swimming
Waples, Keith, harness racing
Weslock, Nick, golf
Wheeler, Lucille, skiing
Whitaker, Brig. Gen. Denis, equestrian builder
Wilson, Bruce, soccer
Worrall, Jim, builder
Young, Jim, football
Young, Michael, bobsled

Source: *Canada's Sports Hall of Fame*

CANADIAN HALL OF FAME

The following list is not meant to be exhaustive, but rather a general listing of prominent Canadians, and those whose reputation is inextricably linked to Canada.

A

ABBOTT, Sir John Joseph Caldwell, politics. St. Andrews, Lower Canada, 1821–93. Canada's third prime minister.

ABBOTT, Maude Elizabeth Seymour, medicine. St Andrews, Que., 1869–1940. Specialist in congenital heart disease. *History of Medicine in the Province of Quebec.*

ABBOTT, Roger, performing arts. Eng., 1946. Actor and co-producer of CBC's *Royal Canadian Air Farce.*

ABEL, Sidney Gerald (Sid), sports. Melville, Sask., 1918–2000. Hockey player; 1949–52 considered best offensive unit when centred with Gordie Howe and Ted Lindsay (Detroit Red Wings); four-time all-star.

ABERDEEN, Lady Ishbel Maria Marjoribanks Gordon, public service. Eng., 1857–1939. Helped create National Council of Women, Victorian Order of Nurses.

ABERHART, William "Bible Bill," politics. Hibbard Twp, Ont., 1878–1943. Founded Social Credit party; Alberta premier 1935–43.

ACORN, Milton, literary arts. Charlottetown, P.E.I., 1923–86. Radical poet. "The Island Means Minago."

ADAIR, Jean, performing arts. Toronto, Ont., 1873–1953. Character actress best known in her role as Aunt Martha Brewster in the movie *Arsenic and Old Lace. Something in the Wind; Living in a Big Way.*

ADAMS, Bryan, performing arts. Kingston, Ont., 1959. Singer/songwriter; rock star; photographer. *Reckless.*

ADAMS, Ian, literary arts. Tanzania, 1937. Novelist, non-fiction writer. *S, Portrait of a Spy; The Trudeau Papers.*

ADAMS, Lawrence, performing arts. St. Boniface, Man., 1937–2003. Dancer with the National Ballet of Canada 1954–69; after his retirement he and his wife, Miriam Weinstein, created Dance Collection Danse, Canada's largest dance archive and publisher. *Encyclopedia of Theatre Dance in Canada.*

ADAMS, Thomas, city planning. Scot., 1871–1940. Father of the Canadian Planning Movement.

AFFLECK, Raymond Tait, visual arts. Penticton, B.C., 1922–89. Architect; designed Place Ville Marie, Place Bonaventure.

AGAR, Carlyle Clare, exploration and discovery. Lion's Head, Ont., 1901–68. Revolutionized helicopter maneuvers for high-altitude landing and takeoff in inaccessible places; instrumental in building B.C.'s Palisade Lake Dam.

AGLUKARK, Susan, performing arts. Arviat, NWT, 1966. Singer/songwriter; first Inuit recording artist. *Unsung Heroes; This Child.*

AIRD, John Black, politics. Toronto, Ont., 1923–95. Liberal senator; Ontario lieutenant-governor 1980–85.

AISLIN (b. Christopher Terry Mosher), visual arts. Ottawa, Ont., 1942. *Montreal Gazette* cartoonist; sports caricaturist.

AITKEN, William Maxwell (Lord Beaverbrook), literary arts. Maple, Ont., 1879–1964. Publisher; newspaper magnate; British Conservative cabinet minister.

AKEEAKTASHUK, visual arts. Hudson Bay, Ont., 1898–1954. Sculptor; first important Inuit carver.

ALBANI, Emma (b. Louise Cecile Emma Lajeunesse), performing arts. Chambly, Que., 1847–1930. Opera singer; grand diva excelled in Wagnerian opera, popular in Britain and US.

ALCOCK, John Alfred, science. Scot., 1938. Expert in laser and plasma physics; winner of Herzberg medal in 1975.

ALEXANDER, Lincoln MacCauley, politics. Toronto, Ont., 1922. First Black in Parliament; Ont. lieutenant-governor 1985–91.

ALGIE, Wallace Lloyd, military. Alton, Ont., 1891–1918. Victoria Cross recipient, WWI, Cambrai, France, 1918. Lieutenant, 20th Bn, 1st Central Ontario Regiment.

ALLAN, Sir Hugh, business. Scot., 1810–82. Railway promoter; suspected of electoral bribery for soliciting favours in Pacific Scandal (1873).

ALLAN, Ted (b. Allan Herman), performing arts. Montreal, Que., 1916–95. Author; screenwriter. *Lies My Father Told Me; Bethune: The Making of a Hero.*

ALLEMANG, John Cameron, literary arts. Toronto, Ont., 1951. Reporter, columnist, food writer. *The Importance of Lunch.*

ALLEN, John F. (Jack), science. Winnipeg, Man., 1908. Co-discoverer of superfluidity in liquid helium.

ALLEN, Sir Montagu, sports. Montreal, Que., 1860–1951. Financier and sportsman who donated Allen Cup in 1908 for senior amateur competition in Canada.

ALLEN, Ralph, literary arts. Winnipeg, Man., 1913–66. Influential *Maclean's* magazine editor (1946–60).

ALMOND, Paul, performing arts. Montreal, Que., 1931. Film director. *Act of the Heart.*

ALTMAN, Sidney, science. Montreal, Que., 1939. Microbiologist; 1989 Nobel Prize in chemistry for role in research into chemical cell reactions.

AMIEL, Barbara, media. Eng., 1940s. Journalist; conservative political and social columnist.

AMOS, Beth (b. Bessie Rymer), performing arts. St. Catharines, Ont., 1915–95. Actor. *Jake and the Kid; Miracle at Indian Creek; Canadian Bacon.*

ANDERSON, Doris Hilda, literary arts. Toronto, Ont., 1921. Writer; feminist; editor of *Chatelaine* magazine1958–77.

ANDERSON, Frank Ross, sports. Edmonton, Alta, 1938–80. International chess master; won gold medals in Amsterdam (1954) and in Munich (1958).

ANDERSON, Pamela Denise, performing arts. Ladysmith, B.C., 1967. Voluptuous actress who has starred in *Baywatch, Barb Wire.*

ANDERSON, Reid Bryce, performing arts. New Westminster, B.C., 1949. Dancer; ballet director of National Ballet of British Columbia; later National Ballet of Canada.

ANDRÉ, Brother (b. Alfred Bissette), religion. St Gregoire d'Iberville, Lower Canada, 1845–1937. Mystic; built Montreal's St Joseph's Oratory.

ANGILIK, Paul Apak, performing arts. Hall Beach, NWT, 1954–98. Documentary filmmaker of Inuit life; adventurer; contributor to Inuit Broadcasting Corporation.

ANKA, Paul Albert, performing arts. Ottawa, Ont., 1941. Singer/songwriter; composed more than 400 songs. "My Way."

APPLEBAUM, Louis, performing arts. Toronto, Ont., 1918–2000. Composer; writer of opera, concerts, film scores.

APPLEYARD, Peter, performing arts. Eng., 1928. Jazz musician; vibraphonist; TV personality. "Swing Fever."

APPS, Charles Joseph Sylvanus (Syl), sports. Paris, Ont., 1915–98. Hockey player; Toronto Maple Leafs (1936–48); 3-time all-star; pole vault contender in 1936 Olympics; 1937 Canadian Athlete of the Year.

AQUIN, Hubert, literary arts. Montreal, Que., 1929–77. Novelist; modernist writer. *Neige Noire.*

ARBOUR, Louise, law. Montreal, Que., 1947. Judge for Supreme Court of Ontario; appointed to Supreme Court of Canada in 1999. From 1996–99 was chief prosecutor for UN's international war crimes tribunal.

ARCAND, Denys, performing arts. Deschambault, Que., 1941. Film director. *Decline of the American Empire; The Barbarian Invasions.*

ARCHAMBAULT, Louis, visual arts. Montreal, Que., 1915–2003. Sculptor; his work is in many museum collections.

ARCHER, Violet, performing arts. Montreal, Que., 1913–2000. Internationally recognized classical music composer, inspired by Canadian folk music. *Prairie Profiles.*

ARCHIBALD, William Munroe, exploration and discovery. Truro, N.S., 1876–1949. Nicknamed "Canada's Flying Businessman," Archibald was the first person to fly into the B.C. interior to locate mining opportunities in remote areas.

ARDEN, Elizabeth (b. Florence Nightingale Graham), business. Woodbridge, Ont., 1884–1966. Founder of the Elizabeth Arden cosmetics empire, Arden was a pioneer in mass advertising and built the business from a small shop in New York City in 1914 to a vast chain of spas and beauty salons.

ARDEN, Jann (b. Jann Arden Richards), performing arts. Calgary, Alta, 1962. Juno-award winning pop singer, songwriter. *Happy?; Time for Mercy.*

ARMSTRONG, Neil J., exploration and discovery. Alvinston, Ont., 1920–94. First helicopter pilot/geologist in North America; in the 1960s he was first to make contact with Inuit of the Barren Lands by flying into their territory. He pioneered the use of electromagnetic systems to detect mineral conductors in earth from a helicopter, and invented the hover sight, which is used universally as an inexpensive method of airborne surveying.

ARTHUR, Eric Ross, visual arts. New Zealand, 1898–1982. Architectural conservancy advocate; writer. *Toronto: No Mean City; The Barn: A Vanishing Landmark in North America.*

ASPER, Israel Harold, business. Minnedosa, Man., 1932–2003. Financier; founder Global-TV; columnist; author.

ATHANS, George S. Jr., sports. Kelowna, B.C., 1952. Three-time world water ski champion.

ATKIN, Harvey, performing arts. Toronto, Ont., 1942. Versatile character actor portrayed Desk Sergeant Ronald Coleman on the long-running TV program *Cagney & Lacey;* also in films including *Atlantic City* and *Meatballs.*

ATKINSON, Joseph, media. Newcastle, Ont., 1865–1948. Journalist; built *Toronto Star* into nation's largest newspaper.

ATWOOD, Margaret Eleanor, literary arts. Ottawa, Ont., 1939. Prolific and award-winning novelist with international following. *The Handmaid's Tale; Alias Grace* (winner of 1996 Giller Prize); *The Blind Assassin* (Booker Prize, 2000).

AUBERT de GASPE, Philippe-Ignace François, literary arts. Quebec City, Que., 1814–41. Novelist; wrote first French-Cdn novel. *L'influence d'un livre* (1837).

AUBERT, Rosemary, literary arts. USA. Novelist, poet, biographer, crime writer; winner of the 1995 Arthur Ellis Award for her short story "The Midnight Boat to Palermo"; also author of Ellis Portal mystery series: *Free Reign; Feast of Stephen.*

AUDETTE, Julien Joseph, science. Radville, Sask., 1914–86. First Canadian to break 300,000 ft (9144 m) in a sailplane, only Canadian to hold all eight competitive soaring awards. His "Audette Project" was a data-collection program that connected climatological information with nonpowered aviation.

AUF DER MAUR, Nick, journalism. Montreal, Que., 1942–98. Long-time columnist for *Montreal Gazette;* co-wrote biography of Brian Mulroney: *The Boy from Baie Comeau.*

AUGUSTINE, Joseph M., exploration and discovery. Big Cove, Nfld, 1911. Native leader and historian who, in 1972, discovered a trove of ancient artifacts dating back 2000 years, near Red Bank, N.B., on the Miramichi River, subsequently named the Augustine Mound.

AUGUSTYN, Frank Joseph, performing arts. Hamilton, Ont., 1953. Former principal dancer, National Ballet of Canada; director, Ottawa Ballet.

AUSTIN, John Alexander McDonald, business. Renfrew, Ont., 1912–84. Co-founder, with brother Charles, of Austin Airways; he pioneered air service to remote communities in the Hudson Bay and James Bay regions. Former director of Air Industries and Transport Association.

AVERY, Oswald, science. Halifax, N.S., 1877–1955. First person to show agent responsible for transferring genetic information was DNA, not a protein as previously thought.

AXELRAD, Arthur Aaron, medicine. Montreal, Que., 1923. Histologist; won international acclaim for his research into leukemia and hemapaiesis, specializing in blood cell differentiation. Head of University of Toronto's anatomy department 1966–85.

AXWORTHY, Norman Lloyd, politics. North Battleford, Sask., 1939. Liberal minister of external affairs; defense.

AYKROYD, Daniel Edward (Dan), performing arts. Ottawa, Ont., 1952. Actor/comedian. *Saturday Night Live; Ghostbusters; Blues Brothers.*

BACHLE, Leo, visual arts. Toronto, Ont., 1923–2003. In 1942 Bachle originated the Johnny Canuck comic books, "Canada's answer to Nazi oppression." Later became a stand-up comic under the name Les Barker.

BACHMAN, Randy, performing arts. Winnipeg, Man., 1946. Rock musician; guitarist for Guess Who, Bachman-Turner Overdrive. Released a retrospective of Canadian guitarist Lenny Breau. *American Woman.*

BADAY, Lida, business. Hamilton, Ont., 1957. Fashion designer of women's clothing; her label is sold across Canada and the US.

BAETZ, Reuben, politics. Chelsey, Ont., 1923–96. Executive director of Canadian Council on Social Development; proponent of national unemployment insurance program.

BAFFIN, William, exploration and discovery. Eng., 1584–1622. Made two Arctic voyages in search of the Northwest Passage; first to conclude Hudson Bay did not lead westward; explored Baffin Island.

BAGSHAW, Elizabeth Catherine, medicine. Victoria County, Ont., 1881–1982. Pioneering woman doctor who, from 1932–66, was medical director of Canada's first (illegal) birth control clinic in Hamilton, Ont., responding to women's financial needs during Depression years.

BAILEY, Brian, business. Galahad, Alta, 1958. Women's sportswear designer; launched label with own name in 1988, later under Iscariot Design; active fashion business promoter.

BAILEY, Donovan, sports. Jamaica, 1967. Track star who won 100 m race at world record time, 9.84, at 1996 Olympics in Atlanta.

BAIN, Conrad, performing arts. Lethbridge, Alta, 1923. Actor who appeared most famously as "Mr. Drummond" on American sitcom *Different Strokes*, also on soaps *The Edge of Night* and *Search for Tomorrow*, and on film. *I Never Sang for My Father.*

BAIRD, Elizabeth Carol, literary arts. Stratford, Ont., 1939. Food writer with *Canadian Living Magazine* and the *Toronto Star*; author of several cookbooks. *Classic Canadian Cooking; Elizabeth Baird's Favourites.*

BAKER, Carroll, performing arts. Bridgewater, N.S., 1949. Singer; country music star.

BAKER, Edmund Albert, education. Collins Bay, Ont., 1893–1968. Founder of the Canadian National Institute for the Blind in 1918; from 1920–62 he was the CNIB's general secretary and managing director. In 1951 be became the first president of the World Council for the Welfare of the Blind.

BALCHEN, Bernt, invention. Norway, 1899–1973. Pilot/engineer who piloted Raoul Amundsen's North Pole expedition; developer of world's northernmost airbase on west coast of Greenland; designed the first commercial air route between Scandinavia and Canada; mapped remote areas of Canada's north.

BALDWIN, Robert, politics. York, Ont., 1804–58. Proponent of responsible government; co-premier (with LaFontaine) of Upper Canada.

BALFOUR, St. Clair, business. Hamilton, Ont., 1910–2002. Grandson of Southam Press's founder, Balfour became president of Southam Press in 1961; chairman of Southam Inc. 1975–85. A noted philanthropist and fundraiser for the University of Toronto, he established the Southam Fellowships Program (later the Canadian Journalism Fellowships) in 1962.

BALLARD, Harold Edwin, sports. Toronto, Ont., 1903–90. Sports capitalist; irascible owner of Toronto Maple Leafs, Hamilton Tiger Cats.

BANKS, Thomas (Tommy), performing arts. Calgary, Alta, 1936. Internationally recognized jazz pianist and conductor who performs with trio members Bob Miller and Tom Doran; appointed to the Senate in 2000.

BANTING, Sir Frederick Grant, medicine. Alliston, Ont., 1891–1941. Medical researcher; co-discoverer of insulin; Nobel Prize for medicine, 1923.

BARBEAU, Charles Marius, ethnology. St-Marie-de-Beauce, Que., 1883–1969. Eminent folklorist.

BARFOOT, Joan Louise, literary arts. Owen Sound, Ont., 1947. Novelist. *Dancing in the Dark; Family News; Charlotte and Claudia Keeping in Touch.*

BARKER, William George (Billy), military. Dauphin, Man., 1894–1930. Victoria Cross recipient, WWI, Fôret de Mormal, France, 1918. Major, 201 Squadron, Royal Air Force.

BARLOW, Maude Victoria, politics. Toronto, Ont., 1947. Political/human rights activist, author. Chair, Council of Canadians.

BARR, Murray Llewellyn, medicine. Belmont, Ont., 1908–95. Anatomist; developed chromosome analysis to diagnose genetic disorders.

BARR, Robert, literary arts. Scot., 1850–1912. Early Canadian crime writer. *The Measure of the Rule; The Girl in the Case.*

BARRIS, Alexander Paul, media. USA, 1922–2004. Journalist; CBC television host of *The Barris Beat* and *Barris and Company,* and an original panellist on *Front Page Challenge. Hollywood According to Hollywood.*

BARRON, Colin Fraser, military. Scot., 1893–59. Victoria Cross recipient, WWI, Battle of Passchendaele, France, 1917. Corporal, 3rd Bn, 1st Central Ontario Regiment.

BARRY, James (b. Miranda Stewart), medicine. Eng., 1795–1865. In 1857 appointed inspector general of military hospitals in Province of Canada; as a woman disguised as a man, was the first woman doctor to work in Canada.

BARTLEMAN, James Karl, politics. Orillia, Ont., 1939. In 2002 became Ontario's first aboriginal lieutenant-governor; previously high commissioner in South Africa and Australia; foreign policy advisor to Prime Minister Jean Chrétien 1994–98.

BASINSKI, Zbigniew Stanislaw, science. Poland, 1928. Outstanding metal physics researcher.

BASSETT, John White Hughes, media. Ottawa, Ont., 1915–98. Media executive; sports entrepreneur; president of Baton Broadcasting.

BASSETT-SEGUSO, Carling Kathrin, sports. Toronto, Ont., 1967. Top-ranked Canadian tennis player. In 1982, '83, '86 winner of closed Canadian championship.

BATA, Sonja Ingrid, public service. Switz., 1926. Founder of the Bata Shoe Museum in Toronto; wife of shoe retailing entrepreneur Thomas Bata.

BATA, Thomas John, business. Czech., 1914. Industrialist; chairman of footwear giant Bata Shoes.

BATEMAN, Robert McLellan, visual arts. Toronto, Ont., 1930. Painter; major international wildlife artist.

BATTLE, Helen Irene, science. London, Ont., 1903–94. World-renowned zoologist; one of the first zoologists to work in the laboratory, specializing in marine biology and using histology and physiology in her research.

BAUER, David William (Father), sports. Kitchener, Ont., 1925–88. Hockey coach; father of Cdn Olympic hockey.

BAUMANN, Alexander (Sasha), sports. Czech., 1964. Swimmer; gold medals in 200 m, 400 m individual medley, 1984 Olympics; 1984 top male athlete.

BAZALGETTE, Ian Willoughby, military. Calgary, Alta, 1918–44. Victoria Cross recipient, WWII, Trossy St. Maximum, France, 1944. Squadron leader, 635 Squadron, RAF Volunteer Reserve.

BEARDY, Quentin Pickering Jackson, visual arts. Island Lake, Man., 1944–84. Graphic stylist using Cree legends.

BEATTY, Henry Perrin, politics. Toronto, Ont., 1950. President of CBC, 1995–98; former PC cabinet minister.

BECK, Sir Adam, business. Baden, Canada W, 1857–1925. Hydro commissioner; built Ontario Hydro.

BECKER, Abigail, military. Frontenac Cty, UC, 1831–1905. Heroine; saved men shipwrecked on Lake Erie.

BECKWITH, John, literary arts/performing arts. Victoria, B.C., 1927. Composer; writer; critic. *The Shivaree.*

BEDARD, Myriam, sports. Loretteville, Que., 1969. Biathlete; two gold medals, biathlon, '94 Olympics.

BEDDOES, Dick, media. Daysland, Alta, 1926–91. Colourful sportswriter, broadcaster, hockey commentator with the *Vancouver Sun, Globe and Mail, Edmonton Bulletin;* broadcaster on CFRB radio in Toronto. *Pal Hal,* a profile of Harold Ballard.

BEECROFT, Norma Marian, performing arts. Oshawa, Ont., 1934. Composer; avant-garde musician. "From Dreams of Brass."

BEERS, William George, medicine/sports. Montreal, Que., 1843–1900. Popularized lacrosse; dean, Canada's first dental college.

BEGIN, Monique, politics. Italy, 1936. First Quebec woman in Commons; health minister.

BEIQUE, Pierre, performing arts. Pointe aux Trembles, Que., 1910–2003. In 1939 became managing director of the Société des Concertes symphoniques de Montréal, the forerunner of the Orchestre symphonique de Montréal.

BELANGER, Michel, business. Lévis, Que., 1929–97. President of Quebec's National Bank; 1991–92 was co-chairman of Belanger-Campeau Commission, which examined constitutional concerns in Quebec.

BELIVEAU, Jean Arthur, sports. Trois-Rivières, Que., 1931. Hockey player; stylish Montreal Canadiens centre, 1953–71; 507 goals.

BELL, Alexander Graham, invention. Scot., 1847–1922. Invented telephone; worked on iron lung, phonograph, seawater desalination.

BELL, George Maxwell (Max), business. Regina, Sask., 1912–72. Industrialist; principal, FP Publications, and sportsman.

BELL, Marilyn, sports. Toronto, Ont., 1937. First person to swim Lake Ontario (1954).

BELL, Robert Edward, science. Ladner, B.C., 1918–92. Nuclear physicist; discovered proton radioactivity.

BELLEW, Edward Donald, military. India, 1882–1974. Victoria Cross recipient, WWI, Second Battle of Ypres, France, 1915. Lieutenant, 7th Canadian Infantry Bn, British Columbia Regiment.

BELLOW, Saul, literary arts. Lachine, Que., 1915. Nobel Prize for Literature. *Herzog.*

BELZBERG, Samuel, business. Calgary, Alta, 1928. Financier; developed real estate financing in W Canada; founder, First City Trust.

BENMERGUI, Ralph, performing arts. Morocco, 1955. CBC radio and television personality; host of television programs *Friday Night!;* CBC's *Midday;* frequent host for CBC radio's *This Morning.*

BENNETT, Richard Bedford, first Viscount, politics. Hopewell Hill, N.B., 1870–1947. Prime minister of Canada 1930–35.

BENNETT, William Andrew Cecil (W.A.C.), politics. Hastings, N.B., 1900–79. Social Credit premier of B.C. 1952–72.

BENNETT, William Richards, politics. Kelowna, B.C., 1932. Social Credit premier of B.C., 1975–86.

BENOIT, Jehane, media. Montreal, Que., 1904–87. Cookbook writer; television host; authority on Cdn/Québécois cuisine. *Enjoying the Art of Canadian Cooking.*

BENT, Philip Eric, military. Halifax, N.S., 1891–1917. Victoria Cross recipient, WWI, Battle of Passchendaele, France, 1917. Lieutenant colonel, 9th Bn, Leicestershire Regiment.

BENY, Roloff (b. Wilfred Roy), visual arts. Medicine Hat, Alta, 1924–84. Photographer; lavish travel books. *India.*

BERBICK, Trevor, sports. Jamaica, 1952. Boxer; Canadian heavyweight champion (1978–85); WBC world heavyweight champion (1986).

BERCZY, William (b. Johann Albrecht Ulrich Moll), visual arts. Germany, 1744–1813. Painter, architect; most famous for his portraits of the native leader Joseph Brant. Also designed church decorations for Christ Church Montreal, in 1903.

BERESFORD-HOWE, Constance Elizabeth, literary arts. Montreal, Que., 1922. Novelist. *Night Studies.*

BERGER, Thomas Rodney, politics. Victoria, B.C., 1933. Jurist; proponent of aboriginal rights; commissioner, Mackenzie Valley Pipeline Inquiry.

BERLIN, Boris, performing arts. Russia, 1907–2001. Taught many of Canada's leading pianists at Toronto's Royal Conservatory of Music; author and co-author of major pedagogical works. *Basics of Ear Training.*

BERNARDI, Mario, performing arts. Kirkland Lake, Ont., 1930. Conductor, Calgary Philharmonic.

BERNIER, Sylvie, sports. Quebec City, Que., 1964. Diver; gold medal, 3 m springboard,1984 Olympics.

BERTON, Pierre, literary arts. Whitehorse, YT, 1920. Popular historian; author and media personality. *The Last Spike.*

BESRE, Jean, performing arts. Sherbrooke, Que., 1936–2001. Beloved Quebec television and stage actor; starred in popular TV series *Jamais deux sans toi* and *La P'tite Semaine;* also performed in children's programs and wrote musical comedy *Madeleine de Verchères.*

BESSETTE, Gerard, literary arts. Ste-Anne-de-Sabrevois, Que., 1920. Novelist, poet, literary critic. *Mes romans et moi.*

BEST, Charles Herbert, medicine. USA, 1899–1978. Physiologist; co-discoverer of insulin.

BETHUNE, Henry Norman, medicine. Gravenhurst, Ont., 1890–1939. Surgeon; hero in China, where he died helping revolutionary army.

BEY, Salome, performing arts. USA, c.1938. Singer, songwriter, actress. Noted for jazz, blues, spirituals. Wrote and starred in *Indigo,* a history of blues. *Shimmytime.*

BIDDLE, Charles, performing arts. USA, 1926–2003. Jazz bassist who owned legendary Montreal jazz club Biddles; instrumental in the organization of the Montreal Jazz Festival.

BIG BEAR, politics. Ft. Carlton, Sask., 1825–88. Cree leader; opposed treaties on grounds they would destroy Cree way of life.

BIGELOW, Dr. Wilfred Gordon, medicine. Brandon, Man., 1913. Surgeon; developed first cardiac pacemaker.

BILLES, Alfred Jackson, business. Toronto, Ont., 1902–95. Co-founder in 1922 of Canada-wide chain Canadian Tire Corporation.

BILLES, John William, business. Toronto, Ont., 1896–1956. Original founder of Canadian Tire chain of hardware stores.

BINNS, Patrick George, politics. Weyburn, Sask., 1948. PC premier of P.E.I., 1996.

BIRDSELL, Sandra, literary arts. Hamiota, Man., 1942. Novelist who weaves domestic and feminist themes into her work. *The Missing Child; The Chrome Suite.*

BIRKS, Henry, business. Montreal, Que., 1840–1928. Silversmith who founded national jewelry chain Henry Birks and Sons, opening his first store in 1879 in Montreal.

BIRNEY, Alfred Earle, literary arts. Calgary, Alta, 1904–95. Narrative poet and professor. *David and Other Poems.*

BISHOP, William Avery (Billy), military. Owen Sound, Ont., 1894–1956. Victoria Cross recipient, WWI, Cambrai, France, 1917. Captain, 60 Squadron, Royal Flying Corps; downed 72 enemy planes.

BISSELL, Keith, performing arts. Meaford, Ont., 1912–92. Composer of choral, vocal, organ, orchestral and chamber music; folksong arrangements for piano and voice; commissioned by Lois Marshall, Charles Peaker and others.

BISSOONDATH, Neil Devindra, literary arts. Trinidad, 1955. Novelist, short story writer. *A Casual Brutality.*

BITOVE, John, business. Toronto, Ont., 1928. Founder of Bitove Corp., food service and hospitality company that has influenced Canadian food catering in hospitals, airlines and railway companies.

BJORSON, Rosella Marie, business. Lethbridge, Alta, 1947. First woman pilot in Canada to fly a commercial flight (Transair); first female flight officer in North America; in 1990 became first female flight captain in Canada (Canadian Airlines).

BLACK, Arthur, media. Toronto, Ont., 1943. Syndicated journalist and broadcaster; host of CBC Radio's *Basic Black,* a program incorporating humour, interviews and music. *Wit and Wisdom of Arthur Black.*

BLACK, Conrad Moffat, business. Montreal, Que., 1944. Press baron; owner of Hollinger Inc. newspaper empire.

BLACK, Davidson, medicine. Toronto, Ont., 1884–1934. China-based anatomist, scholar and anthropologist; identified Peking Man, an ancient human species of *Homo erectus.*

BLAIS, Marie-Claire, literary arts. Quebec City, Que., 1939. Influential novelist. *Une Saison dans la vie d'Emmanuel.*

BLAISE, Clark Lee, literary arts. USA, 1940. Writer; explorer of the displaced person. *Resident Alien.*

BLAKE, Hector "Toe," sports. Victoria Mines, Ont., 1912–95. Hockey player; coached Montreal Canadiens to eight Stanley Cups, 1955–68.

BLAKENEY, Allan Emrys, politics. Bridgewater, N.S., 1925. NDP premier of Saskatchewan 1971–82.

BLISS, John William Michael, politics. Leamington, Ont., 1941. Author, history commentator. *Right Honorable Men: The Descent of Canadian Politics from Macdonald to Mulroney.*

BLOHM, Hans Ludwig, visual arts. Germany, 1927. Photographer; among his photography books, *The Beauty of the Maritimes.*

BLONDIN-ANDREWS, Ethel, politics. Fort Norman, NWT, 1951. In 1988, first native woman elected to Parliament, for Western Arctic (Lib).

BLUMENFELD, Hans, city planning. Germany, 1892–1988. Urban planner; author. *The Modern Metropolis.*

BLYTHE, Dominic, performing arts. Eng., 1947. Actor with Stratford Festival, Ont.

BOBACK, Molly Lamb, visual arts. Vancouver, B.C., 1922. As the only woman war artist assigned during World War II, she documented the Canadian Women's Corp; also a writer and broadcaster.

BOCHNER, Lloyd, performing arts. Toronto, Ont., 1924. Character actor who has appeared in TV series *Dynasty* and *Santa Barbara* and in movies. *Naked Gun 2½.*

BODOGH, Marilyn, sports. Toronto, Ont., 1955. Curler; two-time world champion (skip) in women's curling; member of Team Canada.

BOGGS, Jean Sutherland, visual arts. Peru, 1922. Art curator; National Gallery curator, 1966–76.

BOLDT, Arnie, sports. Osler, Sask., 1957. One-legged high jumper holds disabled world record (2.08 m).

BOLT, Carol, literary arts. Winnipeg, Man., 1941. Playwright; socially conscious writer. *One Night Stand.*

BOMBARDIER, Joseph Armand, invention. Valcourt, Que., 1908–64. Inventor; developer of snowmobiles.

BONDAR, Roberta Lynn, science. Sault Ste Marie, Ont., 1945. Astronaut; first Canadian woman in space.

BONISTEEL, Roy, media. Ameliasburg, Ont., 1930. Host of CBC television's *Man Alive* series 1967–89; early career as a radio producer for church organizations. *In Search of Man Alive.*

BORDEN, Sir Robert Laird, politics. Grand Pré, N.S., 1854–1937. Canada's prime minister throughout WWI (1911–20).

BORDUAS, Paul-Emile, visual arts. St-Hilaire, Que., 1905–60. Painter; founded Automatistes, a group of avant-garde French Canadian artists. *L'etoile noire.*

BORSOS, Phillip, performing arts. Tasmania, 1954–95. Filmmaker. *The Grey Fox* (winner of Best Picture and Best Director, 1982 Genie Awards); *Bethune.*

BOSSY, Michael, sports. Montreal, Que., 1957. Hockey player; NY Islanders winger; nine 50-goal seasons.

BOTSFORD, Sara, performing arts. Dobie, Ont., 1952. Stage, film and TV actress. *Bay Boy; E.N.G.*

BOTTERELL, Edmund Henry, science. Vancouver, B.C., 1906–97. Neurosurgeon who initiated program into spinal chord injury research; during WWII devoted to rehabilitation of veterans.

BOUCHARD, Lucien, politics. St-Coeur-de-Marie, Que., 1938. Founder and leader of Bloc Québécois; leader of Parti Québécois; premier of Quebec, 1996–2001.

BOUCHER, Gaetan, sports. Charlesbourg, Que., 1958. Speedskater; two gold medals (1000 m,1500 m) and a bronze medal (500 m) 1984 Winter Olympics.

BOUEY, Gerald Keith, business. Axford, Sask., 1920–2004. Governor of Bank of Canada 1973–87.

BOURASSA, Henri, politics. Montreal, Que., 1868–1952. Federalist; founded *Le Devoir* newspaper.

BOURASSA, Jocelyne, sports. Shawinigan-Sud, Que., 1947. Golf champion, winner of many awards, including La Canadienne 1973 LPGA event; Golf Personality of the Year, Golf Canada, 1972.

BOURASSA, Robert, politics. Montreal, Que., 1933–96. Quebec premier 1970–76, 1985–93.

BOURGAULT, Pierre, politics. East-Angus, Que., 1934–2003. Journalist, politician; president of Rassemblement pour l'indépendance nationale (RIN), which merged with PQ in 1968. Later advisor to Jacques Parizeau. Journalist with *Le Journal de Montréal. Moi, je m'en souviens.*

BOURGEOYS, Marguerite, religion. France, 1620–1700. Religious educator; canonized, 1982.

BOURGET, Ignace, religion. Lauzon, Que., 1799–1885. Catholic bishop of Montreal; avid ultra-Montanist opposed secular Quebec.

BOURKE, Rowland Richard Louis, military. Eng., 1885–1958. Victoria Cross recipient, WWI, Ostend, Belgium, 1918. Lieutenant, Royal Naval Volunteer Reserve.

BOURNE, Shae-Lynn, sports. Chatham, Ont., 1976. Ice dancing; with Victor Kraatz won Canadian title, 1993–96; third in World Championships, 1996.

BOURQUE, James, politics. Wandering River, Alta, 1935–96. Aboriginal activist appointed to Privy Council, 1992. Co-director of policy for Royal Commission on Aboriginal Peoples, 1994.

BOURQUE, Raymond, sports. Montreal, Que., 1960. Hockey player; Boston Bruins defenceman; four-time Norris Trophy winner.

BOWELL, Sir Mackenzie, politics. Eng., 1823–1917. Canada's fifth prime minister (Cons.), 1894–96.

BOWER, John William (Johnny), sports. Prince Albert, Sask., 1924. Hockey player. Long-time goalkeeper for New York Rangers, Toronto Maple Leafs; led Leafs to four Stanley Cup wins.

BOWERING, George Harry, literary arts. Penticton, B.C., 1935. Prolific poet and prose writer. "Burning Water."

BOWMAN, Scotty, sports. Montreal, Que., 1933. Hockey coach; won nine Stanley Cups; five with Montreal.

BOYD, Liona, performing arts. Eng., 1950. Acclaimed classical guitarist. *The Guitar–Liona Boyd.*

BOYLE, Harry J., media. St. Augustine, Ont., 1915. Producer; media executive; novelist. Joined CBC in 1942, working as co-producer and in executive positions; in 1968 joined the CRTC. *The Canadian Novel; The Luck of the Irish.*

BOYLE, Joseph Whiteside "Klondike Joe," exploration and discovery. Toronto, Ont., 1867–1923. Adventurer; mining entrepreneur; national hero in Romania.

BOYLE, Willard S., invention. Amherst, N.S., 1924. Physicist who co-invented the charge-coupled device for camcorders and telescopes.

BRACKEN, John, politics. Ellisville, Ont., 1883–1969. Cons. Manitoba premier 1922–42.

BRADFORD, Robert William, visual arts/business. Toronto, Ont., 1923. Aviation artist and historian; co-founder of National Aviation Museum in Ottawa, Ont.

BRAITHWAITE, Max, literary arts. Nokomis, Sask., 1911–95. Prairie novelist acclaimed for autobiographical novel, *Why Shoot the Teacher?*

BRAKHAGE, James Stanley (Stan), performing arts. USA, 1933–2003. Award-winning cinematographer noted for his avant-garde methods. *Dog Star Man; Stan's Window.*

BRAND, Oscar, performing arts. Winnipeg, Man., 1920. Folksinger; recorded 80 albums; author of folk song collections. *Squid Jiggin' Ground.*

BRANT, Joseph (b. Thayendanegea), politics/religion. USA, 1742–1807. Mohawk leader; British loyalist during American Revolution; translated Bible into Mohawk.

BRANT, Mary "Molly," politics. USA, c.1736–96. Sister of Joseph Brant; influential leader of Six Nations women's federation; selected chiefs for Mohawk Confederacy; staunch Loyalist.

BRASSARD, Jean-Luc, sports. Valleyfield, Que., 1972. Skier; gold medal moguls 1994 Olympics.

BRASSEUR, Isabelle, sports. Kingsbury, Que., 1970. Skater; with Lloyd Eisler won 1993 pairs world title, two Olympic bronze medals (1992).

BRAULT, Jacques, literary arts. Montreal, Que., 1933. Poet; playwright; novelist. *Agonie.*

BRAUN, Eric, performing arts. Windsor, Ont., 1934–2001. Internationally renowned baritone opera singer; his repertoire spanned classical and modern works, with a special emphasis on Schubert, Wagner and Schumann.

BREAU, Lenny, performing arts. USA, 1941–84. Guitarist, singer, composer of jazz, country, folk and pop; aired on CBC radio in 1940s and '50s.

BRÉBEUF, Jean de, religion. France, 1593–1649. Jesuit martyr; missionary at Sainte Marie among the Hurons.

BRERETON, Alexander Picton, military. Oak River, Man., 1892–1976. Victoria Cross recipient, WWI, Amiens, France, 1918. Corporal, 8th Bn, Manitoba Regiment.

BRILL, Debbie, sports. Mission, B.C., 1953. High jumper; originated "Brill bend" jumping style.

BRILLANT, Jean, military. Assametquaghan, Que., 1890–1918. Victoria Cross recipient, WWI, Méharicourt, France, 1918. Lieutenant, 22nd Bn, Canadien Français.

BRITTAIN, Donald, visual arts. Ottawa, Ont., 1928–89. Documentary filmmaker. *On Guard for Thee.*

BROADBENT, John Edward (Ed), politics. Oshawa, Ont., 1936. National leader, NDP 1975–89.

BROADFOOT, Barry, literary arts. Winnipeg, Man., 1926–2003. Journalist; author of oral history books including *Ten Lost Years* and *Coming Home from the War.* Also his autobiography, *My Ordinary Years.*

BROADFOOT, Dave, performing arts. Toronto, Ont., 1925. Comedian; Sergeant Renfrew character on *Royal Canadian Air Farce.*

BROCK, Sir Isaac, military. Eng., 1769–1812. Soldier; War of 1812 hero; died at Queenston Heights.

BROCKHOUSE, Bertram Neville, science. Lethbridge, Alta, 1918–2003. Pioneered the use of thermal neutrons to study aspects of behaviour of condensed matter systems at atomic level. Won 1994 Nobel Prize for physics.

BROCKINGTON, Leonard Walter, business. Wales, 1888–1966. First chairman of the CBC 1936–39; also expert labour arbitrator, representing clients including the US government, the Toronto Transit Commission and the Seafarers Union. Special assistant to Prime Minister Mackenzie King 1939–42.

BRONFMAN, Charles Rosner, business. Montreal, Que., 1931. Industrialist; chairman, Cemp Investments Ltd; former owner, Montreal Expos.

BRONFMAN, Edgar M., business. Montreal, Que., 1929. Industrialist; CEO, Seagram's Ltd; president, World Jewish Congress.

BRONFMAN, Samuel, business. Brandon, Man., 1891–1971. Capitalist; distiller (Seagram Co. Ltd) and philanthropist.

BROOKS, Marilyn, business. USA, 1932. Fashion designer launched innovative Unicorn boutique in Toronto, Ont., in 1963; founder of Marilyn Brooks boutique chain.

BROSSARD, Nicole, literary arts. Montreal, Que., 1943. Formalist poet and novelist. "Mecanique jongleuse suivi de masculin grammaticale."

BROWN, George, media/politics. Scot., 1818–80. Journalist; founded *Toronto Globe* (1844); as reformer, played major role in Confederation.

BROWN, Harry, military. Gananoque, Ont., 1898–1917. Victoria Cross recipient, WWI, Battle of Hill 70, France, 1917. Private, 10th Bn, Alberta Regiment.

BROWN, John George "Kootenai," exploration and discovery. Ire., 1839–1916. Adventurer; army official; prospector; whisky trader; established Waterton Lakes Natl Park.

BROWN, Rosemary, politics. Jamaica, 1930–2003. Activist; head, Ontario Human Rights Comm.; former NDP leadership candidate.

BROWNING, Kurt, sports. Rocky Mountain House, Alta, 1966. World figure skating champion, 1989–91, 1993.

BRUHN, Erik Belton Evers, performing arts. Denmark, 1928–86. Dancer; choreographer; guiding figure for National Ballet.

BRULE, Etienne, exploration and discovery. France, 1592–1633. Explorer; first known European to reach Lake Superior.

BRZOZOWICZ, Czelaw Peter, engineering. Poland, 1911–97. Structural engineer consulted on Toronto's original subway line, Niagara Falls Skylon Tower and CN Tower in Toronto.

BUCHAN, John, first Baron Tweedsmuir, literary arts. Scot., 1875–1940. Thriller novelist, wrote *The Thirty-Nine Steps*; governor-general, 1935–40.

BUCHANAN, John MacLennan, politics. Sydney, N.S., 1931. Conservative premier of N.S., 1978–90.

BUCK, Tim, politics. Eng., 1891–1973. Radical politician; led Canadian Communist Party, 1929–61.

BUCKE, Richard Maurice, medicine. Eng., 1837–1902. Physician; writer; advocate for the mentally ill; spiritual writer. *Cosmic Consciousness.*

BUCZYNSKI, Walter, performing arts. Toronto, Ont., 1933. Pianist and composer of orchestral, chamber, vocal and piano music; soloist internationally in 1960s and 1970s. *Songs of War; Resurrection II.*

BUJOLD, Geneviève, performing arts. Montreal, Que., 1942. Actress; international star. *Dead Ringers.*

BULL, Gerald Vincent, invention. North Bay, Ont., 1928–90. Inventor; weapons designer; murdered mysteriously.

BURKA, Petra, sports. Holland, 1946. Figure skater; women's world champion, 1965.

BURNARD, Bonnie, literary arts. Petrolia, Ont., 1945. Novelist; her *A Good House* won the 1999 Giller Prize. *Women of Influence,* short stories.

BURNS, Tommy (b. Noah Brusso), sports. Hanover, Ont., 1881–1955. Boxer; world heavyweight champion, 1906–08.

BURR, Raymond William Stacy, performing arts. New Westminster, B.C., 1917–93. Actor; TV's Perry Mason, 1957–66, 1985–93.

BURROUGHS, Jackie, performing arts. Eng., 1942. Actress; versatile performer; Hetty in *Road to Avonlea.*

BUSH, John Hamilton (Jack), visual arts. Toronto, Ont., 1909–77. Abstract artist. "Bridge Passage."

BUSHNELL, Ernest Leslie, media. Lindsay, Ont., 1900–87. Started Canada's first radio advertising agency; VP of CBC 1945–58; founder of CJOH-TV in Ottawa, an affiliate of CTV.

BUTALA, Sharon Annette, literary arts. Nipawin, Sask., 1940. Novelist, short story writer, playwright. *Coming Attractions; The Fourth Archangel.*

BUTCHART, Robert Pim, business. Owen Sound, Ont., 1856–1943. In 1888 founded Owen Sound Portland Cement Co.; later turned quarries in Victoria, B.C., into famed Butchart Gardens.

BY, John, military. Eng., 1779–1836. Engineer; built Rideau Canal, Quebec fortifications.

BYNG, Julian Hedworth George, first Viscount, military. Eng., 1862–1935. Soldier; governor-general, 1921–26.

CABOT, John (b. Giovanni Caboto), exploration and discovery. Italy, c.1450–99. First N American landing since the Vikings.

CABOT, Sebastian, performing arts. Eng., 1918–76. Portly, bearded character actor in film and television. *The Captain's Paradise; The Beachcombers; Family Affair.*

CAIN, Larry, sports. Toronto, Ont., 1963. Canoeist; gold (500 m) and silver (1000 m) medals, 1984 Olympics.

CAIRNS, Hugh, military. Eng., 1896–1918. Victoria Cross recipient, WWI, Valenciennes, France, 1918. Sergeant, 46th South Saskatchewan Bn, Saskatchewan Regiment.

CALDER, Frank Arthur, politics. Nass Harbour, B.C., 1915. Native politician; Nishga leader; B.C. MLA.

CALDWELL, Zoe, performing arts. Australia, 1933. Actor, director. *The Prime of Miss Jean Brodie.*

CALLAGHAN, Barry, literary arts. Toronto, Ont., 1937. Founder of *Exile: A Literary Quarterly*; novelist, journalist; son of Morley Callaghan.

CALLAGHAN, Morley Edward, literary arts. Toronto, Ont., 1903–90. Novelist; memoirist. *The Loved and the Lost.*

CALLBECK, Catherine, politics. Central Bedeque, P.E.I., 1939. First woman premier in Canada (Lib.), P.E.I., 1993–96.

CALLWOOD, June, public service. Chatham, Ont., 1924. Journalist; civil libertarian, AIDS activist.

CALVERT, Lorne Albert, politics. Moose Jaw, Sask., 1952. NDP premier of Saskatchewan 2001–; formerly minister of social services.

CAMERON, Elspeth MacGregor, literary arts. Toronto, Ont., 1943. Biographer. *Robertson Davies: An Appreciation; Hugh MacLennan: A Writer's Life; Irving Layton: A Portrait.*

CAMERON, James, performing arts. Kapuskasing, Ont., 1954. Hollywood-based director of action movies including *Terminator* series, *Aliens, True Lies, Titanic.*

CAMERON, James Munro, literary arts. Eng., 1910. Philosopher; essayist; poet. "Images of Authority."

CAMERON, Michelle, sports. Calgary, Alta, 1962. Gold medallist in synchronized swimming with Carolyn Waldo, 1988 Olympics.

CAMERON, Silver Donald, literary arts. Toronto, Ont., 1937. Novelist, critic, editor, playwright. *Dragon Lady; Wind, Whales and Whisky: A Cape Breton Voyage.*

CAMERON, Thomas Wright Moir, medicine. Scot., 1894–1947. Parasitologist; pioneered study of parasitic worms.

CAMP, Dalton Kingsley, politics. Woodstock, N.B., 1920–2002. PC consultant; newspaper columnist.

CAMPBELL, Sir Alexander, politics. Eng., 1822–92. Tory leader; Father of Confederation.

CAMPBELL, Avril Phaedra (Kim), politics. Port Alberni, B.C., 1947. First woman prime minister of Canada, June 1993–December 1993.

CAMPBELL, Cassie, sports. Brampton, Ont., 1973. Captain of women's gold-medal winning hockey game in 2002 Salt Lake City Olympics, playing defense.

CAMPBELL, Clarence, sports. Fleming, Sask., 1905–84. Sports administrator; headed NHL, 1946–77.

CAMPBELL, Douglas, performing arts. Scot., 1922. Actor at Stratford Festival, Ont. Co-founder of Canadian Players.

CAMPBELL, Frederick William, military. Mount Forest, Ont., 1867–1915. Victoria Cross recipient, WWI, Battle of Givenchy, France, 1915. Lieutenant, 1st Bn, Western Ontario Regiment.

CAMPBELL, Gordon, politics. Vancouver, B.C., 1948. Liberal premier of British Columbia 2001 –; formerly mayor of Vancouver.

CAMPBELL, Neve, performing arts. Guelph, Ont., 1973. Actress/dancer; appeared in Canadian TV series *Catwalk;* US TV series *Party of 5;* and films *The Craft* and *Scream.*

CAMPBELL, Nicholas, performing arts. Toronto, Ont., 1952. Versatile actor, screenwriter, director; star of CBC's *DaVinci's Inquest;* also film *The Omen;* and TV production of *Come Back Little Sheba.*

CAMPBELL, Norman Kenneth, performing arts. USA, 1924–2004. Music producer; innovative developer of ballet and musicals.

CAMPEAU, Robert, business. Sudbury, Ont., 1923. Financier; exemplar of 1980s expansionist business mania; developer; retail store magnate.

CANDY, John Franklin, performing arts. Toronto, Ont., 1950–94. Actor; comedian; bearish *SCTV* regular (Johnny LaRue, William B.). *Uncle Buck; Planes, Trains and Automobiles.*

CAPLAN, Elinor, politics. Toronto, Ont., 1944. Liberal MP; former chairman of management board, has held various portfolios in provincial government, including minister of citizenship and immigration.

CAPLAN, Gerald Lewis, politics. Toronto, Ont., 1938. National director of federal NDP in 1982, campaign director in 1984. Advisor to Stephen Lewis; co-chair of Task Force on Broadcasting Policy in 1985; chairman of Ontario Royal Commission on Education in 1993.

CARDINAL, Douglas Joseph, visual arts. Red Deer, Alta, 1934. Métis architect; Canadian Museum of Civilization.

CARDINAL, Tantoo, performing arts. Fort McMurray, Alta, 1951. Native actress who has appeared in films *Big Bear, Smoke Signals, Black Robe* and CBC's *North of 60.*

CARELESS, James Maurice Stockford, literary arts. Toronto, Ont., 1919. Historian; has written extensively on the effect of cities expanding into the hinterland. *Canada: A Story of Challenge; Brown of the Globe.*

CARIOU, Len, performing arts. St Boniface, Man., 1939. Theatre director and actor; associated with Manitoba Theatre Centre; Stratford Festival, Ont.; and in England and US.

CARLE, Gilles, visual arts. Maniwaki, Que., 1929. Film director. *La Vrai Nature de Bernadette.*

CARLETON, Sir Guy, first Baron Dorchester, politics. Ire., 1724–1808. Quebec governor, 1768–78, 1785–95; supporter of French traditions.

CARMAN, William Bliss, literary arts. Fredericton, N.B., 1861–1929. Poet; journalist. "The Pipes of Pan."

CARMICHAEL, Franklin, visual arts. Orillia, Ont., 1890–1945. Group of Seven founding member.

CARNEGIE, Herb, sports. Toronto, Ont., 1919. Outstanding hockey player, winner of four MVP awards with Black Aces, a semipro team with Quebec Senior Hockey League, during the 1940s and '50s; Carnegie, whose parents were Jamaican, was barred from NHL.

CARNEY, Patricia, politics. China, 1935. PC minister of energy, mines and resources and international trade; entered Senate in 1990.

CARR, Emily, visual arts. Victoria, B.C., 1871–1945. Painter of NW coastal Indians and nature.

CARR, Shirley, politics. Niagara Falls, Ont. First woman to lead CUPE, Canada's largest union. President Emeritus, Canadian Labour Congress.

CARR, William Keir, military. Grand Bank, Nfld, 1923. Known as the "Father of the Canadian Air Force" for his work in consolidating military aviation after the unification of the armed forces.

CARREY, James (Jim), performing arts. Jackson's Point, Ont., 1962. Comedic actor. *Ace Ventura; The Mask; Batman Forever.*

CARRICK, William Henesey, performing arts. Toronto, Ont., 1920–2002. Wildlife filmmaker who worked extensively with the NFB and Ducks Unlimited. His light-aircraft flights with geese led to his consultative role in film *Fly Away Home.* World in a Marsh.

CARRIER, Roch, literary arts. Beauce, Que., 1937. Novelist; playwright. *La Guerre, Yes Sir!*

CARSON, John Elmer (Jack), performing arts. Carman, Man., 1910–63. Square-jawed film actor. *Mildred Pierce.*

CARTER, Cardinal Emmett, religion. Montreal, Que., 1912–2003. Toronto cardinal; instrumental in obtaining full funding for Roman Catholic schools in Ontario.

CARTER, Wilf, performing arts. Port Hilford, N.S., 1904–96. Singer; father of Canadian country music.

CARTIER, Sir Georges-Etienne, politics. St Antoine, UC, 1814–73. Father of Confederation; joint premier of United Canada, 1857–62.

CARTIER, Jacques, exploration and discovery. France, 1491–1557. Credited with European discovery of Canada; first explorer of St. Lawrence River.

CARVER, Brent, performing arts. Cranbrook, B.C., 1951. Actor at Ontario's Stratford Festival (*Hamlet*); television (CBC's *Street Legal*); in musical comedy and on film (*The Wars*).

CARVER, Humphrey Stephen Mumford, politics. Eng., 1902–95. Key figure in Central Mortgage and Housing Corporation 1950s–60s; formed Co-operative Commonwealth Federation, forerunner of NDP.

CASAVANT, Joseph, business. Saint-Hyacinthe, Que., 1807–74. Blacksmith who became Canada's first organ maker; he built 17 organs before his death. His sons took over the business, naming it Casavant Frères.

CASGRAIN, Thérèse, politics. Montreal, Que., 1896–1981. Won Quebec women the right to vote (1940) and hold provincial office; leader of Quebec's CCF party in 1951.

CASSON, Alfred Joseph (A.J.), visual arts. Toronto, Ont., 1898–1992. Member, Group of Seven. *Country Store.*

CATHERWOOD, Ethel, sports. Haldimand Cty, Ont., 1909–87. High jumper; gold in high jump, 1928 Olympics.

CAVOUKIAN, Artin and Lucie, visual arts. Egypt, Armenia, 1915–95, 1923–95. Clientele of photographer Artin with wife Lucie included world leaders.

CHALMERS, Floyd Sherman, public service. USA, 1898–1993. Instituted Floyd S. Chalmers Foundation funding for arts in Canada.

CHAMBERLAIN, Douglas Thomas, performing arts. Toronto, Ont., 1933. Character actor; roles in classics, comedy and light opera, associated with Ontario's Stratford Festival; *Spring Thaw* revue; also at Charlottetown Festival and Vancouver Playhouse Theatre.

CHAMPLAIN, Samuel de, exploration and discovery. France, 1567–1635. Explorer; important cartographer/geographer; "Father of New France."

CHANG, Simon, business. China, 1950. Fashion designer; also branched into fragrances, accessories, uniforms for restaurants and salon design.

CHANG, Thomas Ming Sui, medicine/science. China, 1933. Physiologist; expert on artificial cells and organs.

CHANT, Donald Alfred, science. Toronto, Ont., 1928. Pioneer in environmental movement in the 1960s, specializing in pesticides, pollution, wildlife preservation and ecosystems. Chairman of Ontario Waste Management, 1980.

CHAPMAN, John Herbert, science. London, Ont., 1921–79. Physicist; lead role in Canada's satellite program.

CHAPUT-ROLLAND, Solange, media. Montreal, Que., 1919–2001. Writer; broadcaster; Québécoise federalist.

CHAREST, Jean J., politics. Sherbrooke, Que., 1958. Led PC party after '93 federal electoral debacle; elected PC premier of Quebec 2003.

CHARLEBOIS, Robert, performing arts. Montreal, Que., 1945. Singer/songwriter. "Solidaritude."

CHARLEVOIX, Pierre François Xavier de, literary arts. France, 1682–1761. Historian; wrote first complete history of New France.

CHAYKIN, Maury, performing arts. USA, 1949. Prolific actor has appeared in *Jacob Two-Two Meets the Hooded Fang; Dances with Wolves.*

CHEE CHEE, Benjamin (b. Kenneth Thomas Benjamin), visual arts. Temagami, Ont., 1944–77. Ojibwa artist; block-stamped abstract and animal, bird images; noted for use of movement and humour.

CHERRY, Don, sports. Kingston, Ont., 1934. Hockey coach; commentator; feisty nationalist.

CHEVALIER, Leo, business. Montreal, Que., 1934–2000. Fashion designer of lines sold internationally.

CHING, Julia, academia. China, 1934–2001. Leading scholar in Chinese history and religion, specializing in neo-Confucian philosophy. *Probing China's Soul.*

CHIPMAN, Ward, law. Saint John, N.B., 1787–1851. Jurist; chief justice of N.B.; noted abolitionist.

CHIRAEFF, Ludmilla, performing arts. Latvia, 1924. Choreographer; founder, Les Grands Ballets Canadiennes.

CHISHOLM, George Brock, medicine. Oakville, Ont., 1896–1971. Psychiatrist; early opponent of pollution, nuclear arms; first head of World Health Org.

CHONG, Rae Dawn, performing arts. Vancouver, B.C., 1961. Film actress. *Quest for Fire.*

CHONG, Thomas (Tommy), performing arts. Edmonton, Alta, 1938. Actor; half of Cheech and Chong comedy team. *Cheech and Chong's Nice Dreams.*

CHOUART DES GROSEILLIERS, Medard, exploration and discovery. France, 1618–90. Explorer; fur trader; with Radisson opened western fur trade.

CHOUINARD, Josée, sports. Rosemont, Que., 1969. Three-time Canadian figure skating champion.

CHRÉTIEN, Joseph Jacques Jean, politics. Shawinigan, Que., 1934. Prime minister of Canada, Liberal party, 1993–2003; won three consecutive majorities.

CHRETIEN, Raymond, politics. Shawinigan, Que., 1942. Canadian ambassador to the United States, France; nephew of Prime Minister Jean Chrétien.

CHRISTENSEN, Hayden, performing arts. Vancouver, B.C., 1981. Actor portrayed the young Anakin Skywalker in *Star Wars* series. *Higher Ground.*

CHRISTIE, Robert Wallace, performing arts. Toronto, Ont., 1920–96. Played at Ontario's Stratford Festival; Old Vic in London, England; famous for portrayal of John A. Macdonald.

CHRISTIE, William Mellis, business. Scot., 1829–1900. Biscuit manufacturer; Christie Biscuits founder.

CHUVALO, George, sports. Toronto, Ont., 1937. Boxer; fought three world champions; never knocked down. Anti-drug crusader.

CLAIR, Frank, sports. USA, 1917. Football coach; 174 wins (Ottawa Rough Riders) tops CFL coaches. Also coached Toronto Argonauts to 1950, 1952 Grey Cups.

CLANCY, Francis Michael "King," sports. Ottawa, Ont., 1903–86. Hockey player; defenceman, Ottawa Senators, Toronto Maple Leafs; lively raconteur.

CLARK, Charles Joseph (Joe), politics. High River, Alta, 1939. Prime minister of Canada 1979–80. Leader of federal Progressive Conservative Party, 1998–2003.

CLARK, Greg, literary arts. Toronto, Ont., 1892–1977. Journalist and humorist, winner of Leacock Award for Humour.

CLARK, Karl Adolf, invention. Georgetown, Ont., 1888–1966. Discovered hot-water recovery process used in oil extraction from tar sands, crucial to growth of industry.

CLARK, Susan, performing arts. Sarnia, Ont., 1940. Actress who has appeared in Hollywood movies, television. *Murder by Decree; Coogan's Bluff; Webster.*

CLARK, Wayne, business. Drumheller, Alta, 1949. Canadian fashion designer noted for his dramatic evening wear and high-quality sportswear.

CLARK-KENNEDY, William Hew, military. Scot., 1880–1961. Victoria Cross recipient, WWI, Fresnes-Rouvray Line, France, 1918. Lieutenant colonel, 24th Bn, Quebec Regiment, Victoria's Rifles.

CLARKE, Austin Chesterfield, literary arts. Barbados, 1934. Novelist, short story writer. *The Origin of Waves; The Polished Hoe* won the 2002 Giller Prize, 2003 Commonwealth Writers Prize.

CLARKE, Larry Denman, business. Eng., 1925. Founder of SPAR Aerospace, a major contributor to the development of the Canadarm, used for manoeuvring objects while in orbit.

CLARKE, Lionel Beaumaurice, military. Waterdown, Ont., 1892–1916. Victoria Cross recipient, WWI, the Somme, France, 1916. Corporal, 2nd Bn, Eastern Ontario Regiment.

CLARKSON, Adrienne Louise, media/politics. Hong Kong, 1939. Broadcaster; long-time CBC host. *Take Thirty.* Appointed governor-general of Canada, 1999.

CLAYTON-THOMAS, David, performing arts. Eng., 1941. Singer; member, Blood, Sweat and Tears. *Spinning Wheel.*

COCHRANE, Tom, performing arts. Lynn Lake, Man., 1953. Singer, songwriter, guitarist. Led Toronto-based quintet, Tom Cochrane and Red Rider, formed in 1976. *Breaking Curfew.* Went solo in 1991 with *Mad, Mad World.* "Life is a Highway."

COCKBURN, Bruce, performing arts. Ottawa, Ont., 1945 Singer/songwriter; politically conscious performer. *You've Never Seen Everything.*

COCKBURN, Hampden Zane Churchill, military. Toronto, Ont., 1867–1913. Victoria Cross recipient, Boer War, South Africa, 1900. Lieutenant, Royal Canadian Dragoons.

COE-JONES, Dawn, sports. Lake Cowichan, B.C., 1961. Golfer; leading pro; 1993 LPGA title.

COHEN, Leonard, literary arts/performing arts. Montreal, Que., 1934. Poet, lyricist, singer. *Flowers for Hitler; I'm Your Man.*

COHEN, Matt, literary arts. Kingston, Ont., 1942–2000. Short story writer, novelist, translator. *The Colour of War; Living on Water; Freud: The Paris Notebooks.*

COHEN, Morris (Moishe) Abraham "Two-Gun," military. Eng., 1889–1970. China hand; confidant of Sun Yat-sen; general in Chinese army.

COHEN, Samuel Nathan, literary arts. Sydney, N.S., 1923–71. Critic; Canada's first established drama critic.

COHON, George, business. USA, 1937. CEO, Cdn McDonald's restaurants; philanthropist.

COLDWELL, Major James William, politics. Eng., 1888–1974. CCF founder; leader, 1942–60.

COLE, Holly, performing arts. Halifax, N.S., 1963. Jazz/pop singer with distinctive contralto voice; founder of the Holly Cole Trio. *Don't Smoke in Bed; Christmas Blues; Dear Dark Heart.*

COLE, Jack, business. Toronto, Ont., 1920–97. With brother Carl started Coles chain of bookstores in Toronto, which later became national; created Coles Notes, study booklets for students, in 1947.

COLEMAN, Kathleen Blake (Kit), media. Toronto, Ont., 1864–1915. First woman war correspondent.

COLICOS, John, performing arts. Toronto, Ont., 1928–2000. Stage actor; regular at Ontario's Stratford Festival.

COLLENETTE, David M., politics. Eng., 1946. Liberal MP; has been minister of transportation, national defense and veteran affairs.

COLLIP, James Bertram, medicine. Belleville, Ont., 1892–1965. Biochemist; co-discoverer of insulin.

COLOMBO, John Robert, literary arts. Kitchener, Ont., 1936. Anthologist; prolific compiler of reference books. *Colombo's Canadian Quotations.*

COLVILLE, Alexander, visual arts. Toronto, Ont., 1920. Realistic painter; designed centennial coins.

COMBE, Robert Grierson, military. Scot., 1880–1917. Victoria Cross recipient, WWI, Acheville, France, 1917. Lieutenant, 27th (City of Winnipeg) Bn, Manitoba Regiment.

COMFORT, Charles Fraser, visual arts. Scot., 1900–94. Artist, graphic designer; created murals for Toronto Stock Exchange; director of National Gallery of Canada 1960–65.

CONACHER, Lionel Pretoria, sports. Toronto, Ont., 1901–54. Canada's Athlete of the Half-Century (1900–1950).

CONIBEAR, Kenneth Wilfred, literary arts. Orrville, Ont., 1907–2002. Novelist, outdoorsman, lecturer; Conibear managed Grey Owl's lecture tour of the UK in 1937. His memoir: *Arctic Adventures with the Lady Greenbelly.*

CONNOR, Ralph (b. Charles William Gordon), literary arts. West Indian Lands, Glengarry County, Canada West 1860–1937. Popular novelist, preacher of "red-blooded" Christianity. *The Sky Pilot.*

CONNORS, Charles Thomas "Stompin' Tom," performing arts. Saint John, N.B., 1936. Country singer; nationalist performer. *Across This Land with Stompin' Tom.*

COOK, George Ramsay, literary arts. Alameda, Sask., 1931. Prolific historian. *Canada: A Modern Study; The Maple Leaf Forever.*

COOK, James, exploration and discovery. Eng., 1728–79. Navigator; explored Newfoundland and Northwest coasts.

COOK, Myrtle, sports. Toronto, Ont., 1902–85. Member of the women's track and field team in the 1928 Amsterdam Olympics, setting world record in 100 m race during Olympic trials; sports journalist for the *Montreal Star*; active on Olympic committees throughout career.

COOKE, Jack Kent, business. Hamilton, Ont., 1912–97. Capitalist; flamboyant owner of newspapers, radio stations, sports teams (Washington Redskins; L.A. Lakers; L.A. Kings).

COOMBS, Ernest Arthur (Ernie), performing arts. USA, 1927–2001. Children's entertainer; CBC's *Mr. Dressup.*

COON COME, Matthew, politics. Mistassini, Que., 1956. National Chief of the Assembly of First Nations 2000–2003.

COOP, Jane Austin, performing arts. Saint John, N.B., 1950. Classical pianist; has appeared with both national and international orchestras; Beethoven specialist.

COPP, Harold, science. Toronto, Ont., 1915–98. Physiologist; discovered calcitonon, hormone that regulates calcium in blood.

COPPINS, Frederick George, military. Eng., 1889–1963. Victoria Cross recipient, WWI, Hackett Woods (near Amiens), France, 1918. Corporal, 8th Bn, Manitoba Regiment.

COPPS, Sheila Maureen, politics. Hamilton, Ont., 1952. Liberal deputy prime minister (first woman to hold the post) to Jean Chrétien 1993–1997; left politics 2004.

CORBEIL, Carole, literary arts. Montreal, Que., 1952–2000. Award-winning journalist and novelist wrote *Voice-Over*, which won City of Toronto Book Award in 1993, and *In the Wings.*

CORBETT, Edward Annand, education. Truro, N.S., 1887–1964. Internationally recognized as a pioneer in adult education. From 1936–51 he was director of Canadian Association for Adult Education; organized the Banff School of Fine Arts and was first director 1933–36; developed the CBC's Farm Radio Forum.

CORBETT, Percy Ellwood, education. Tyne Valley, P.E.I., 1892–1983. Legal educator, activist against injustice; one of the world's leading experts on international law. *Law and Society in the Relations of States; The Growth of World Law.*

CORMIER, Ernest, visual arts. Montreal, Que., 1885–1980. Architect; designed University of Montreal.

CORNISH, Judith, business. Toronto, Ont., 1958. With partner Joyce Gunhouse designer of Comrags fashion design label.

CORRIGAL, Jim, sports. Barrie, Ont., 1946. Football player. Lineman with Toronto Argonauts 1970–81; four-time CFL all-star.

COSENS, Aubrey, military. Latchford, Ont., 1921–45. Victoria Cross recipient, WWII, Mooshof, Holland, 1945. Sergeant, Queen's Own Rifles of Canada.

COSENTINO, Frank, sports. Hamilton, Ont., 1937. Football player; CFL quarterback, 1960–69; sports history writer; professor, physical education.

COSTAIN, Thomas Bertram, literary arts. Brantford, Ont., 1885–1965. Historical novelist. *High Towers.*

COUGHTRY, Graham, visual arts. St Lambert, Que., 1931–99. Abstract figurative painter; exhibited in New York's Guggenheim Museum, Museum of Modern Art, as well as across Canada.

COULTHARD, Jean, performing arts. Vancouver, B.C., 1908–2000. Composer. "The Pines of Emily Carr."

COUPLAND, Douglas Campbell, literary arts. Germany. 1961. Novelist; humorist. *Generation X; Microserfs.*

COURNOYEA, Nellie J., politics. Aklavik, NWT, 1940. First woman aboriginal leader of Northwest Territories.

COWAN, Garry, sports. Kitchener, Ont., 1938. Golfer; twice US amateur champion (1966, 1971).

COXETER, Harold Scott Macdonald "H.S.M.," science. Eng., 1907–2003. Mathematician dubbed as the "world's greatest geometer," Coxeter specialized in dimensional analogy, a process of stretching geometric shapes into higher dimensions, a geometric concept known as "Coxeter groups."

CRANSTON, Toller, sports. Hamilton, Ont., 1949. Skater; brought innovation and artistry to men's figure skating.

CRAWLEY, Frank Radford "Budge," visual arts. Ottawa, Ont., 1911–87. Film producer. *The Rowdyman.*

CREAN, Patrick Victor, performing arts. Eng., 1910–2003. Stage fighting expert; after a career in England staged fights at Ontario's Stratford Festival from 1963–83.

CREIGHTON, Donald Grant, literary arts. Toronto, Ont., 1902–79. Historian; developed literary side of history.

CREIGHTON, Douglas, media. Toronto, Ont., 1928–2004. Co-founder of the *Toronto Sun* tabloid in 1971, which later expanded to Edmonton, Calgary and Ottawa.

CREIGHTON, Mary Helen, performing arts. Dartmouth, N.S., 1899–1989. Folk music expert specializing in English, French, Gaelic, Mi'kmaq and Nova Scotian music; associated with National Museum of Canada.

CREMAZIE, Claude Joseph Olivier "Octave," literary arts. Quebec City, Que., 1827–79. Father of French Canadian poetry. "Le Drapeau de Carillon."

CREMO, Lee, performing arts. Cape Breton, N.S., 1939–99. Six-time winner of Maritime Old-Time Fiddling Contest; mix of Irish, Scottish, Mi'kmaq music; winner of Canadian title at Alberta Tar Sands Competition.

CREWSON, Wendy, performing arts. Hamilton, Ont., 1956. Actress in TV and film, starred in *At the End of the Day: The Sue Rodriguez Story.* Also, *I'll Never Get to Heaven; Getting Married in Buffalo Jump.*

CROAK, John Bernard, military. Little Bay, Nfld, 1892–1918. Victoria Cross recipient, Amiens, France, 1918. Private, 13th Bn, Quebec Regiment.

CROLL, David Arnold, politics. Russia, 1900–91. Liberal MLA in 1934; first Jewish Cabinet minister (1955).

CROMBIE, David Edward, politics. Toronto, Ont., 1936. Civic reformer; Toronto mayor 1973–78.

CRONENBERG, David, visual arts. Toronto, Ont., 1943. Film director; inventive horror, science fiction filmmaker. *Videodrome, Crash.*

CRONYN, Hume (b. Hume Blake), performing arts. London, Ont., 1911–2003. Stage, film actor; character roles. *Cocoon; The Moon and Sixpence.*

CROSBIE, John Carnell, politics. St John's, Nfld, 1931. PC minister of fisheries and oceans; international trade; justice.

CROTHERS, William, sports. Markham, Ont., 1940. Runner; silver medal (800 m), 1964 Olympics.

CROW, John William, business. Eng., 1937. Economist; governor of Bank of Canada, 1987–94.

CROWFOOT, military. Belly R, Alta, 1830–90. Blackfoot chief, diplomat.

CRUIKSHANK, Robert Edward, military. Winnipeg, Man., 1881–1961. Only WWI Victoria Cross recipient awarded for service outside of Europe. WWI, Jordan, Palestine, 1918. Private, Egyptian Expeditionary Force, London Regiment (London Scottish), British Army.

CUDDY, James Gordon (Jim), performing arts. Toronto, Ont., 1955. Lead singer for rock group Blue Rodeo. *Palace of Gold.*

CUMMINGS, Burton, performing arts. Winnipeg, Man., 1947. Rock singer; lead singer, The Guess Who; later solo artist. *My Own Way to Rock.*

CUNARD, Sir Samuel, business. Halifax, N.S., 1787–1865. Ship owner; founded Cunard Line forerunner.

CURNOE, Gregory Richard, visual arts. London, Ont., 1936–92. Fine artist whose paintings often incorporated written words; also created collages, drawings, prints.

CURRIE, Sir Arthur William, military. Strathroy, Ont., 1875–1933. Commander, Canadian corps, WWI.

CURRIE, David Vivian, military. Sutherland, Sask., 1912–86. Victoria Cross recipient, WWII, Battle of Falaise, Normandy, France, 1944. Major, 29th Canadian Armoured Reconnaissance Regiment, South Alberta Regiment.

CURRIE, Philip, science. Toronto, Ont., 1948. Curator of dinosaurs for Alberta's Royal Tyrrel Museum in Drumheller and world leader in paleontology; recently discovered a feathered dinosaur that proved birds evolved from dinosaurs.

CURTOLA, Robert Allen (Bobby), performing arts. Thunder Bay, Ont., 1944. Singer; early teen idol. "Fortune Teller."

CYR, Louis, sports. Napierville, Que., 1863–1912. World's strongest man, 1880–1990.

D

DAFOE, Allan Roy, medicine. Madoc, Ont., 1883–1943. Small-town physician who delivered the Dionne quintuplets, May 28, 1934; later faced accusations of exploiting the sisters.

DAFOE, John Wesley, media. Combermere, Ont., 1866–1944. Journalist; influential editor, *Winnipeg Free Press.*

DAIGLE, Sylvie, sports. Sherbrooke, Que., 1962. Won gold in 1988 Calgary Olympics in short-track speed skating, as well as silver and bronze medals; five-time world champion.

DAIR, Carl, visual arts. Welland, Ont., 1912–67. Internationally recognized designer, typographer; created Cartier, first modern Canadian typeface. *Design with Type.*

DALE, Cynthia, performing arts. Toronto, Ont., 1961. Actress known for roles in TV series *Street Legal; Taking the Falls;* and for numerous roles at Ontario's Stratford Festival.

DANBY, Kenneth Edison (Ken), visual arts. Sault Ste Marie, Ont., 1940. Painter using realism technique for landscapes, sports figures.

DANCE, Helen Oakley, performing arts. Toronto, Ont., 1913–2001. Record producer, jazz and blues historian and journalist, Dance was a contemporary of jazz greats such as Duke Ellington; also civil-rights supporter.

DANKO, Rick, performing arts. Simcoe, Ont., 1943–99. Founder and vocal/bass member of folk, blues, rock group The Band, subject of director Martin Scorcese's film *The Last Waltz.*

DAUDELIN, Charles, visual arts. Granby, Que., 1920–2001. Abstract artist, sculptor whose spiritually themed works are displayed in Canada and France. Designed awards for France-Canada and Jutra prizes.

DAUDELIN, Robert, performing arts. West Shefford, Que., 1939. Film administrator; writer; producer; director. Founder of film criticism magazine *Objectif;* International Film Festival in Montreal; director of Cinémathèque québécoise.

DAVEY, Keith, politics. Toronto, Ont., 1926. Long-time Liberal Party strategist.

DAVIES, Robertson William, literary arts. Thamesville, Ont., 1913–95. Novelist; playwright; essayist. *The Deptford Trilogy; The Diary of Samuel Marchbanks.*

DAVIS, Andrew, performing arts. Eng., 1944. Conductor of Toronto Symphony Orchestra 1975–88; participated in 1978 TSO visit to People's Republic of China.

DAVIS, Donald, performing arts. Newmarket, Ont., 1928–98. Distinguished Shakespearean actor, played Ontario's Stratford Festival; also appeared in TV roles: *Mission Impossible.* Co-founder of Toronto's Crest Theatre.

DAVIS, Fred, media. Toronto, Ont., 1921–96. Broadcaster and host of long-running CBC panel show *Front Page Challenge* (1957–95).

DAVIS, Victor, sports. Guelph, Ont., 1964–89. Swimmer; three medals 1984 Olympics; gold in 200 m breaststroke.

DAVIS, Warren, performing arts. Peterborough, Ont., 1926–95. CBC newsman. *The National; This Hour Has Seven Days.*

DAVIS, William Grenville, politics. Brampton, Ont., 1929. PC premier of Ontario, 1971–85.

DAWSON, George Mercer, science. Pictou, N.S., 1849–1901. Geologist; surveyed much of northern and western Canada.

DAWSON, Sir John William, science. Pictou, N.S., 1820–99. Geologist; made McGill a leading university; founded Royal Society of Canada.

DAY, James, sports. Thornhill, Ont., 1946. Equestrian; team gold medal, 1968 Olympics.

DAY, Stockwell, politics. Barrie, Ont., 1950. Former provincial treasurer for Alberta; Canadian Reform Alliance Conservative Party leader, 2000–02.

DE CARLO, Yvonne (b. Peggy Yvonne Middleton), performing arts. Vancouver, B.C., 1924. Actress; film/TV star. *The Munsters.*

DE LA ROCHE, Mazo (b. Maisie Roche), literary arts. Newmarket, Ont., 1879–1961. Prolific popular novelist. *Jalna.*

de VILLIERS, Priscilla, politics. S. Africa, 1942. Activist and founder of CAVEAT, Canadians Against Violence Everywhere Advocating Its Termination.

DEL GRANDE, Louis, performing arts. USA, 1942. Actor, producer, writer. Starred in CBC TV series *Seeing Things.*

DENNYS, Louise, literary arts. Egypt, 1948. Partner of Lester & Orpen Dennys publishing house, then vice president and publisher at Knopf Canada and Random House.

DEPOE, Norman Reade, media. USA, 1917–80. CBC's Ottawa correspondent in the 1960s; instrumental in the development of the CBC in the 1950s.

DESCHENES, Jules, law. Montreal, Que., 1923–2000. Jurist; Que. chief justice; chairman, Inquiry of War Criminals in Canada.

DESJARDINS, Alphonse, business. Lévis, Que., 1854–1920. Banker; established first Caisse populaire (credit union) in 1900.

DESMARAIS, Paul, business. Sudbury, Ont., 1927. Industrialist; chairman of Power Corp., controlling trust, insurance and paper companies.

DESMOND, Trudy, performing arts. USA, 1946–99. Ballad and jazz singer, appeared in 1970 revue *Spring Thaw. My One and Only Love,* a tribute to Gershwin.

DEWAR, Marion, politics. Montreal, Que., 1928. Mayor, Ottawa, 1978–85; NDP MP.

DEWDNEY, Christopher, literary arts. London, Ont., 1951. Eclectic poet. *The Immaculate Perception: The Recent Artifacts from the Institute of Applied Fiction.*

DEWHURST, Colleen, performing arts. Montreal, Que., 1926–91. Actress who cultivated an earth-mother persona; noted for TV and film roles and performances in Albee and O'Neill plays. *Annie Hall; Murphy Brown.*

DE WIND, Edmund, military. Ire., 1883–1918. Victoria Cross recipient, WWI, Race Course Redoubt (Grougie, France), 1918. 2nd Lieutenant, 15th Bn, The Royal Irish Rifles, British Army.

DeWOLF, Harry George, military. Bedford, N.S., 1903–2000. Most decorated officer in Canadian Armed Forces; at helm of HMS *Haida* during Allied invasion of Normandy.

DHALIWAL, Herb, politics. India, 1952. Liberal MP in Chrétien government, minister of fisheries and oceans.

DIAMOND, Abel Joseph (Jack), visual arts. South Africa, 1932. Leading architect; designed Toronto's central YMCA; York University (Toronto) Student Centre; Jerusalem City Hall; Burns Building, Calgary.

DIAMOND, Billy, politics/business. Waskaganish, Que., 1949. Cree chief who successfully negotiated for native rights during James Bay hydroelectric project in Quebec; founder of Cree-owned airline Air Creebec.

DICKENS, Francis Jeffrey, military. Eng., 1844–86. Policeman; son of novelist Charles Dickens; inspector in NWMP.

DICKINS, Clennell Haggerston "Punch," exploration and discovery. Portage la Prairie, Man., 1899–1995. Adventurer. First to fly length of Mackenzie River and above Arctic Circle.

DICKINSON, Peter Allgood Rastall, visual arts. Eng., 1925–61. International-style architect responsible for postwar development: Benvenuto Apartments, Prudential Building (Toronto); CIBC, Windsor Plaza (Montreal).

DICKSON, Robert George Brian, law. Yorkton, Sask., 1916–98. Chief justice of Canada, 1984–90.

DIEFENBAKER, John George, politics. Neustadt, Ont., 1895–1979. PC Prime minister of Canada 1957–63.

DINESON, Thomas, military. Denmark, 1892–1974. Victoria Cross recipient, WWI, Parvillers, France, 1918. Private, 42nd Bn, Quebec Regiment.

DION, Celine, performing arts. Montreal, Que., 1968. Popular Quebec chanteuse. "My Heart Will Go On."

DION, Stéphane, politics. Quebec City, Que., 1955. Political scientist; Liberal minister of intergovernmental affairs in Chrétien government.

DIONNE, Marcel, sports. Drummondville, Que., 1951. Hockey player; centre; 731 goals, third all-time.

DIONNE sisters, medicine. Corbeil, Ont., 1934. Annette, Émilie (d. 1954), Yvonne (d. 2001), Cecile and Marie (d. 1970), identical quintuplets born to poor rural family, became tourist attraction through government exploitation.

DMYTRYK, Edward, visual arts. Grand Forks, B.C., 1908–99. Film director; film noir specialist. One of Hollywood Ten during McCarthy era. *Detour.*

DOBBS, Kildare Robert Eric, literary arts. India, 1923. Short story writer, essayist. *Coastal Canada; Historic Canada.*

DOER, Gary, politics. Winnipeg, Man., 1948. NDP premier of Manitoba, elected in 1999.

DOHERTY, Denny, performing arts. Halifax, N.S., 1941. Pop singer; founding member, The Mamas and the Papas.

DONKIN, Eric Albert, performing arts. Eng., 1930–98. Classical actor who played 26 seasons at Ontario's Stratford Festival.

DONOHUE, Jack, sports. USA, 1931–2003. Basketball coach who brought Canadian teams to the top six in the world during his 18-year career, including a gold medal win at the 1982 World University Games in Edmonton.

DOOHAN, James Montgomery, performing arts. Vancouver, B.C., 1920. Actor; played Scotty (Lt. Commander Montgomery Scott) in *Star Trek* series.

DOSANJH, Ujjah, politics. India, 1947. NDP premier of B.C. 2000–01.

DOUGHTY, Sir Arthur George, archivist. Eng., 1860–1936. Established Public Archives of Canada.

DOUGLAS, Campbell Mellis, military. Quebec City, LC, 1840–1909. Victoria Cross recipient, Andaman Islands Expedition, 1867. Assistant surgeon, 2nd Bn, 24th Regiment (later South Wales Borderers).

DOUGLAS, Sir James, politics. British Guiana, 1803–77. Administrator; governor of B.C., 1858–64.

DOUGLAS, Robert John Wilson, science. Southampton, Ont., 1920. Geologist; famous for geographical survey of structure of Rockies and foothills of southern Alberta.

DOUGLAS, Thomas Clement (Tommy), politics. Scot., 1904–86. Eloquent socialist; Sask. premier, 1944–61; NDP federal leader, 1961–71.

DOYLE, Richard (Dic) James, media. Toronto, Ont., 1923–2003. Editor of the *Globe and Mail* from 1963–83, Doyle transformed the paper from a PC party mouthpiece to a more independent voice; appointed to the Senate in 1985.

DRABINSKY, Garth Howard, performing arts. Toronto, Ont., 1948. Impresario; Cineplex founder, theatrical producer.

DRAPEAU, Jean, politics. Montreal, Que., 1916–99. Montreal mayor for 29 years; brought city Expo 67, 1976 Olympics, Montreal Expos.

DRESSLER, Marie (b. Leila von Koerber), performing arts. Cobourg, Ont., 1869–1934. Actress who specialized in character roles. *Min and Bill.*

DRYDEN, Kenneth Wayne, sports. Hamilton, Ont., 1947. Hockey goaltender; six-time all-star for Montreal; became president and general manager of the Toronto Maple Leafs in 1997. Also lawyer and writer. *The Game.* Elected Member of Parliament (Lib.) for York Centre in 2004 election.

DUCKWORTH, Henry Edmison, science. Brandon, Man., 1915. With associates constructed highly accurate mass spectrometers for determination of atomic masses.

DUDEK, Louis, literary arts. Montreal, Que., 1918–2001. Poet, professor and literary critic, Dudek co-founded with Irving Layton and Raymond Souster Contact Press, which published major Canadian poets in the 1950s and '60s. *Surface of Time.*

DUGUID, Don, sports. Winnipeg, Man., 1935. Curler; Canadian and world champion, 1970, 1971.

DUMONT, Fernand, politics. Montmorency, Que., 1927–97. Quebec sovereigntist named deputy minister of cultural development for PQ in 1976; drafter of Bill 101, French Language Charter.

DUMONT, Gabriel, military. Red River, Sask., 1837–1906. Métis leader; guerrilla leader in NW Rebellion.

DUNBAR, Isobel Moira, science. Scot., 1918–99. Member of the Arctic section of the Defense Research Board; specialized in the study of sea ice and its relationship to climate. *Arctic Canada from the Air.*

DUNN, Alexander Roberts, military. York, Upper Canada, 1833–68. First Canadian-born soldier to receive the Victoria Cross, Charge of the Light Brigade, Crimean War, 1854. Lieutenant, 11th Hussars, Prince Albert's Own, British Army.

DUNNING, George, performing arts. Toronto, Ont., 1920. Animator and director; creator of Beatles *Yellow Submarine* film animation.

DUPLESSIS, Maurice Le Noblet, politics. Trois-Rivières, Que., 1890–1959. Powerful premier of Quebec, 1936–39, 1944–59.

DURBIN, Deanna (b. Edna Mae Durbin), performing arts. Winnipeg, Man., 1921. Actress; singer; teenage movie star. *3 Smart Girls.*

DURELLE, Yvon, sports. Baie Ste Anne, Que., 1929. Canadian middleweight boxing title 1953; light heavyweight 1953–54; British empire light heavyweight champion 1957.

DURHAM, John George Lambton, first Earl of, politics. Eng., 1792–1840. Statesman; "Radical Jack" urged union of English and French Canada.

DURNAN, William Arnold (Bill), sports. Toronto, Ont., 1915–72. Hockey goaltender; six-time Vezina Trophy winner for Montreal Canadiens.

DUTOIT, Charles Edouard, performing arts. Switz., 1936. Conductor of Montreal Symphony Orchestra.

DWAN, Allan, visual arts. Toronto, Ont., 1885–1981. Film director from silent era, made more than 200 Hollywood films. *Sands of Iwo Jima.*

EATON, Cyrus Stephen, business. Pugwash, N.S., 1883–1979. Financier; promoter of international peace.

EATON, Fredrik Stefan, business. Toronto, Ont., 1938. Retailer; former chairman, T. Eaton Co.

EATON, Timothy, business. Ire., 1834–1907. Retailer; innovative founder of T. Eaton Co. in 1867.

EDWARDS, Henrietta, public service. Montreal, Que., 1849–1931. In 1875 published first women's magazine in Canada, *Women's Work in Canada*; with Lady Aberdeen co-established the National Council of Women and the Victorian Order of Nurses.

EDWARDS, Robert Chambers (Bob), media. Scot., 1864–1922. Journalist; published satirical *Calgary Eye Opener.*

EGGLETON, Arthur C., politics. Toronto, Ont., 1943. Liberal MP; mayor of Toronto 1980–91 (Toronto's longest-serving mayor).

EGOYAN, Atom, visual arts. Egypt, 1960. Film director; guitarist; playwright. *The Sweet Hereafter.*

EISLER, Lloyd, sports. Seaforth, Ont., 1963. Figure skater; with Isabelle Brasseur won world pairs title, 1993; Olympic bronze medals.

ELDER, Jim, sports. Toronto, Ont., 1934. Equestrian; team gold medal, 1968 Olympics.

ELGAARD, Ray, sports. Edmonton, Alta, 1959. Football player; Sask. Roughriders star wide receiver.

ELGIN, James Bruce, eighth Earl of, politics. Eng., 1811–63. Governor-general, 1847–54.

ELLIOTT, David James, performing arts. Milton, Ont., 1960. A member of the Young Company at Stratford Festival in Ontario; cast as Nick Del Gado in CBC drama *Street Legal*; has appeared on American TV programs. *The Untouchables.*

ELVIN-LEWIS, Memory, science. Vancouver, B.C., 1933. Ethnobotanist who, with husband Walter Lewis, is a leading world expert on airborne and allergenic pollens, as well as the medicinal uses of tropical plants.

EMERY, Victor, sports. Montreal, Que., 1933. Bobsledder; piloted 1964 Olympic gold medal team.

EMSLIE, Robert Daniel, sports. Guelph, Ont., 1859–1943. Major league baseball pitcher; won 32 games for Baltimore Orioles in 1884; umpire in National League, strove to improve working conditions and umpires' image.

ENGEL, Howard, literary arts. Toronto, Ont., 1931. Mystery writer. *Murder Sees the Light.*

ENGEL, Marian, literary arts. Toronto, Ont., 1933–85. Novelist. *Bear.*

ERASMUS, Georges Henry, politics. Ft Rae, NWT, 1948. Dene leader; vice chief, Assembly of First Nations, 1983–85; elected national chief in 1985.

ERICKSON, Arthur Charles, visual arts. Vancouver, B.C., 1924. Architect; Simon Fraser University (Burnaby, B.C.).

ESPOSITO, Phillip Anthony (Phil), sports. Sault Ste Marie, Ont., 1942. Hockey player; Boston, Chicago, New York Rangers centre; 717 goals, fourth all-time.

ESTEY, Willard Zebedee "Bud," law. Saskatoon, Sask., 1919–2002. Supreme Court justice, 1977–88; headed several royal commissions.

ETROG, Sorel, visual arts. Romania, 1933. Sculptor of monumental works; designer. "Ritual Head."

EVANGELISTA, Linda, media. St Catharines, Ont., 1965. International top model.

EVANS, Gil, performing arts. Toronto, Ont., 1912–88. Composer, arranger, pianist. Played free jazz, rock and funk. Gil Evans Orchestra.

EVANS, James, education. Eng., 1801–46. English Methodist missionary, invented Cree syllabic writing system. *Cree Syllabic Hymn Book.*

EVANSHEN, Terrance Anthony (Terry), sports. Montreal, Que., 1944. Football player; outstanding CFL receiver.

EVES, Ernie, politics. Windsor, Ont., 1946. PC premier of Ontario 2002–03, replacing Mike Harris; from 1995–2001, deputy premier and minister of finance.

EYTON, Trevor, business. Quebec City, Que., 1934. Executive; president, Brascan Ltd; many corporate boards.

FACKENHEIM, Emil Ludwig, literary arts. Germany, 1916–2003. Philosopher; author of works on religion and the Holocaust. *Quest for Past and Future.*

FAIRCLOUGH, Ellen Louks, politics. Hamilton, Ont., 1905. First woman Cabinet minister (1957).

FAIRFIELD, Robert, visual arts. St Catharines, Ont., 1918–95. Designed Stratford Festival Theatre, Ont.; Ontario pavilion at Expo 67.

FAIRLEY, Barker, visual arts. Eng., 1887–1986. Critic; Goethe scholar; portrait painter.

FAITH, Percy, performing arts. Toronto, Ont., 1908–76. Bandleader; top music arranger. "Canadian Sunset."

FALK, Gathie, visual arts. Alexander, Man., 1928. Multimedia artist, specializes in performance art, watercolour, drawings. Work shown at National Gallery of Canada.

FALONEY, Bernie, sports. USA, 1932. Football player; long-time star QB for Edmonton, Hamilton.

FARQUHARSON, Ray, medicine. Claude, Ont., 1897–1965. Doctor who discovered Farquharson phenomenon, a hormone-related theory in secretion activity; his 1958 Farquharson Report led to the formation of the Medical Research Council in 1960.

FAVREAU, Marc, performing arts. Montreal, Que., 1929. Actor; author. Portrayed the hapless, naïve clown Sol, performed on TV and in theatre. *Sol et Gobelet.*

FEINBERG, Rabbi Abraham (b. Abraham Nisselevicz, aka Anthony Frome), politics. USA, 1899–1986. Peace activist; champion of radical causes.

FEORE, Colm, performing arts. USA, 1958. Actor; played Glenn Gould in *Thirty-two Short Films About Glenn Gould.* Roles at Stratford Festival, Ont.; starred in CBC miniseries *Trudeau.*

FERGUSON, Don, performing arts. Montreal, Que., 1946. Actor, writer, director of CBC documentaries; on team of CBC's *Royal Canadian Air Farce.*

FERGUSON, Ivan Graeme, invention. Toronto, Ont., 1929. Inventor; developed IMAX and OMNIMAX film systems.

FERGUSON, James Francis, performing arts. Ire., 1940–97. Founder, with George Millar, of the Irish Rovers, a singing group that popularized Irish pub music.

FERGUSON, Max "Rawhide," media. Eng., 1924. Broadcaster; popular host of CBC radio's *Rawhide.*

FERGUSON, Maynard, performing arts. Verdun, Que., 1928. Jazz trumpeter; versatile stylist made 50 albums.

FERRON, Jacques, literary arts/politics. Louiseville, Que., 1921–85. Playwright, *Contes du pays incertain*; Rhinoceros Party founder.

FESSENDEN, Reginald Aubrey, invention. Milton-Est, Canada E, 1866–1932. Inventor; transmitted world's first radio broadcast (1906).

FIELDING, Joy, literary arts. Toronto, Ont., 1945. Novelist, journalist, scriptwriter. *Tell Me No Stories.*

FILION, Herve, sports. Angers, Que., 1940. Harness driver; all-time leader in victories; 12,000+.

FILMON, Gary Albert, politics. Winnipeg, Man., 1942. PC Manitoba premier, 1988–1999.

FINDLEY, Timothy, literary arts. Toronto, Ont., 1930–2002. Novelist/playwright. *The Wars; The Piano Man's Daughter.*

FISHER, Ruby, sports. Eng., 1908–2001. Winner of the Canadian Open women's tennis doubles championship 1938 and 1948; gold medal in the 1985 World Masters Games.

FITZ-JONES, Philip Chester, science. Vancouver, B.C., 1920. Researched structure and chemical nature of bacterial spores.

FITZGERALD, Lionel LeMoine, visual arts. Winnipeg, Man., 1890–1956. Impressionist turned to abstracts. "Doc Snider's House."

FLAVELLE, Sir Joseph Wesley, business. Peterborough, Ont., 1858–1939. Financier; executive for Canada Packers, Bank of Commerce, National Trust.

FLEMING, Sir Sandford, invention. Scot., 1827–1915. Engineer; developed standard time; designed Canada's first postage stamp; built railways.

FLOWERDEW, Gordon Muriel, military. Eng., 1885–1918. Victoria Cross recipient, WWI, Race Course Redoubt (Grougie, France), 1918. Lieutenant, Lord Strathcona's Horse.

FOLEY, Dave, performing arts. Toronto, Ont., 1963. Actor; role of Dave Nelson in TV series *News Radio;* member of comedy troupe Kids in the Hall.

FOLLOWS, Megan, performing arts. Toronto, Ont., 1969. Actor who portrayed Anne of Green Gables in CBC TV series *Silver Bullet.*

FONTAINE, Larry Phillip (Phil), politics. Fort Alexander Reserve, Man., 1944. Elected national chief of Assembly of First Nations, 2003.

FONYO, Stephen Charles (Steve), sports. Montreal, Que., 1965. Handicapped runner; "Journey for Lives" raised funds for cancer research, 1985.

FOOTE, John Weir, military. Madoc, Ont., 1904–88. Victoria Cross recipient, WWII, Dieppe, France, 1942. Hon. Captain, Canadian Chaplain's Service.

FORBES, Kenneth, visual arts. Toronto, Ont., 1892–1980. War artist, portrait painter (John Diefenbaker); works displayed in Canadian War Museum.

FORD, Glenn (b. Gwyllyn Samuel Newton Ford), performing arts. Quebec City, Que., 1916. Noted American actor of the 1940s and '50s. *Gilda; Teahouse of the August Moon.*

FORRESTER, Helen, literary arts. Eng., 1919. Novelist. Wrote semi-autobiographical Liverpool series: *Twopence to Cross the Mersey; Liverpool Miss; By the Waters of Liverpool; Lime Street at Two.*

FORRESTER, Maureen, performing arts. Montreal, Que., 1930. Operatic contralto; Canada's prima diva.

FORSEY, Eugene Alfred, politics. Grand Bank, Nfld, 1904–91. Intellectual; commentator on public affairs; social radical; strong federalist.

FORTIER, L. Yves, politics. Quebec City, Que., 1935. Canadian ambassador to the United Nations, 1988–92; pres. of UN Security Council 1989.

FOSTER, David Walter, performing arts. Victoria, B.C., 1949. Musician; produced many major acts (Chicago, Barbra Streisand); 12 Grammy awards.

FOSTER, Sir George Eulas, politics. Carleton, N.B., 1847–1931. Statesman; central in Cdn political life; acting PM during Borden's illness (1920).

FOTHERINGHAM, Allan, media. Hearne, Sask., 1932. Journalist; political columnist.

FOULIS, Robert, invention. Scot., 1796–1866. Civil engineer, inventor, artist who invented the steam fog horn; developed New Brunswick's first iron foundry in Saint John.

FOWKE, Edith Margaret, literary arts. Lumsden, Sask., 1913–96. Music ethnologist, published traditional Canadian folksongs. *Penguin Book of Canadian Folksongs; Sally Go Round the Sun.*

FOX, Michael James (J.), performing arts. Edmonton, Alta, 1961. Actor; diminutive leading man in film, television. *Back to the Future; Family Ties.*

FOX, Terrance Stanley (Terry), sports. Winnipeg, Man., 1958–81. Began "Marathon of Hope" cross-Canada run to raise funds for cancer research; Lou Marsh Trophy as Canada's top athlete, 1980.

FRANCA, Celia (b. Celia Franks), performing arts. Eng., 1921. Choreographer; founder of National Ballet of Canada.

FRANCK, Albert Jacques, visual arts. Holland, 1899–1973. Painter especially noted for his depiction of old houses and back lanes in the old city of Toronto.

FRANCKS, Don Harvey, performing arts. Burnaby, B.C., 1932. Veteran actor, jazz musician, appeared in revue *Spring Thaw.* Also TV and film roles. *The Man From U.N.C.L.E.; Finian's Rainbow.*

FRANKLIN, Sir John, exploration and discovery. Eng., 1786–1847. Bold, doomed Arctic explorer.

FRANKLIN, Ursula Martius, science. Germany, 1921. Physicist and educator; specialist in field of archeometry, which relates materials analysis with archeology; advocate for Science for Peace.

FRANKS, Wilbur Rounding, invention. Weston, Ont., 1901–86. Inventor; devised pressure suit for airplane pilots.

FRAPPIER, Armand, science. Valleyfield, Que., 1904–91. Influential microbiologist.

FRASER, Anna, sports. Ottawa, Ont., 1963. Free-style skier; World Cup Aerial Champion (1986).

FRASER, Brendan, performing arts. USA, 1968. Comedic actor who has appeared in films *George of the Jungle, Airheads* and *Dudley Do-Right.*

FRASER, John Anderson, literary arts. Montreal, Que., 1944. Author; former editor of *Saturday Night* magazine; master of Massey College, Toronto. *The Chinese: A Portrait of a People.*

FRASER, Simon, exploration and discovery. USA, 1776–1862. First white man to explore Fraser River.

FRASER, Sylvia Lois, literary arts. Hamilton, Ont., 1935. Novelist. *Pandora; Berlin Solstice; My Father's House; The Emperor's Virgin.*

FRECHETTE, Sylvie, sports. Laval, Que., 1967. Received post-event gold medal in synchronized swimming, 1992 Olympics.

FREEDMAN, Harry, performing arts. Poland, 1922. Composer of chamber, symphonic, instrumental music; also wrote scores for stage and film (*The Pyx*). *Encounter.*

FRENCH, David, literary arts. Coley's Point, Nfld, 1939. Playwright. *Salt-Water Moon; Jitters; Leaving Home.*

FREUND, Kurt, medicine. Czech., 1914–96. Psychiatrist; noted researcher into human sexuality.

FROBISHER, Sir Martin, exploration and discovery. Eng., 1539–94. Mariner; discovered Frobisher Bay.

FRONTENAC ET PALLUAU (Louis de Buade) Comte de, politics. France, 1622–98. Governor-general, New France, 1672–82, 1689–98.

FROST, Leslie Miscampbell, politics. Orillia, Ont., 1895–1973. PC premier of Ontario, 1949–61.

FRUM, Barbara Ruth, media. USA, 1937–92. Broadcaster; interviewer. *As It Happens; The Journal.*

FRUM, David, literary arts. Toronto, Ont., 1960. Journalist of "new right."

FRYE, Herman Northrop, literary arts. Sherbrooke, Que., 1912–91. Canada's most influential literary critic. *Anatomy of Criticism.*

FULFORD, Robert Marshall Blount, media. Ottawa, Ont., 1932. Journalist; former editor, *Saturday Night;* columnist.

FULTON, E. Davie, politics. Kamloops, B.C., 1916–2000. Justice minister in John Diefenbaker's government, beginning 1957; became B.C. Supreme Court judge 1973–81.

FUNG, Donna Lori, sports. Vancouver, B.C., 1963. Rhythmic gymnast; gold medal, 1984 Olympics.

FURST, Judith, performing arts. New Westminster, B.C., 1943. Opera singer; internationally renowned diva.

FURTADO, Nelly, performing arts. Victoria, B.C., 1978. Singer of popular music including folk, hip-hop, bossa nova and reggae, and a Grammy Award winner. *Whoa, Nelly!*

GABEREAU, Vicki Frances, media. Vancouver, B.C., 1946. Broadcaster, author. Host of CBC radio's *Gabereau,* 1988–97. Host of TV talk show on CTV.

GABRIEL, Tony, sports. Hamilton, Ont., 1948. Football player; CFL tight end; held record 138 straight games with receptions until 1995.

GAGNON, André, performing arts. Saint-Pacôme-de-Kamouraska, Que., 1942. Pianist; composer. "Le Saint-Laurent."

GAGNON, André Phillipe, performing arts. Loretteville, Que., 1961. Comedian, impressionist, gives one-man shows.

GAGNON, Charles, visual arts. Montreal, Que., 1934–2003. An abstract painter, photographer, filmmaker and sculptor; his film *The Eighth Day* was created for the Christian Pavilion at Expo 67 in Montreal, a statement against the war in Vietnam.

GAGNON, Marc, sports. Chicoutimi, Que., 1975. Four-time gold medal winner in Salt Lake City 2002 Olympics for men's speed skating and men's relay team; achieved a record-breaking total of five gold medals in three Olympic seasons. Also a four-time world champion short-track speed skater.

GALBRAITH, John Kenneth, business/literary arts. Iona Station, Ont., 1908. Economist; author; influential intellectual. *The Affluent Society.*

GALDIKAS, Biruté, science. Germany, 1946. Anthropologist; world's foremost expert on the physical anthropology of orangutans.

GALLANT, Mavis Leslie, literary arts. Montreal, Que., 1922. Author of more than 100 short stories. "A Fairly Good Time."

GALLEY, Harry A., invention. Montreal, Que., 1903–95. Inco employee; designer of first mass-produced stainless steel sink.

GALLIVAN, Danny, sports. Montreal, Que., 1917–93. Hockey announcer; voice of the Montreal Canadiens.

GALT, Alexander Tilloch, politics. Eng., 1817–93. Railway promoter; proposed union of all British colonies.

GARBER, Victor, performing arts. London, Ont., 1949. Character actor in Hollywood, formerly led folk band The Sugar Shoppe. Roles include Jesus in *Godspell;* also appeared in films *Titanic* and *First Wives Club.*

GARNEAU, François Xavier, literary arts. Quebec City, Que., 1809–66. Writer; early historian. *Histoire du Canada.*

GARNEAU, Hector de Saint Denys, literary arts. Montreal, Que., 1912–43. Poet. "Regards et jeux dans l'espace."

GARNEAU, Marc, science. Quebec City, Que., 1949. First Canadian astronaut (1984) to achieve liftoff.

GARNER, Hugh, literary arts. Eng., 1913–79. Working class novelist. *Cabbagetown.*

GASCON, Jean, performing arts. Montreal, Que., 1921–88. Actor; director; influential man of the theatre; headed Ontario's Stratford Festival, Natl Arts Centre.

GAYFORD, Thomas Franklin, sports. Toronto, Ont., 1928. Equestrian; won gold medal Prix des Nations in 1968 Olympics.

GEDGE, Pauline, literary arts. New Zealand, 1945. Novelist. *Scroll of Saqqara; The Twelfth Transforming; The Covenant.*

GEHRY, Frank, visual arts. Toronto, Ont., 1929. Internationally recognized architect. Guggenheim Museum, Bilbao, Spain; Art and Teaching Museum, University of Minnesota.

GELBER, Arthur Ellis, public service. Toronto, Ont., 1915–98. Philanthropist who was prominent on arts boards, including National Arts Centre, National Ballet of Canada and the Ontario Arts Council.

GELINAS, Gratien, performing arts. St Tite, Que., 1909–99. Actor, director, playwright; crucial to modern Quebec theatre.

GEOFFRION, Joseph André Bernard "Boom Boom," sports. Montreal, Que., 1931. Hockey player; right-winger, Montreal Canadiens (1950–64), noted for strength and speed.

GEORGE, Dan (Teswahno), performing arts. Burrard Reserve, B.C., 1899–1981. Actor; helped redefine image of Aboriginal peoples in media. *Little Big Man.*

GERUSSI, Bruno, performing arts. Medicine Hat, Alta, 1928–95. Actor; regular on *The Beachcombers.*

GESNER, Abraham, invention. Cornwallis, N.S., 1797–1864. Inventor of kerosene oil.

GETTY, Donald Ross, politics/sports. Montreal, Que., 1933. Edmonton Eskimos quarterback; PC premier of Alberta, 1985–92.

GHERMEZIAN, Jacob, business. Azerbaijan, 1902–2000. Founder of Triple Five Corp., he built the West Edmonton Mall in Alberta, the world's largest mall; also developed the Mall of America in Bloomington, Minnesota.

GHIZ, Joseph Atallah, politics. Charlottetown, P.E.I., 1945–97. Liberal premier of P.E.I. 1986–93. Avid supporter of Meech Lake Accord and Charlottetown Accord.

GIAUQUE, William Francis, science. Niagara Falls, Ont., 1895–1982. Chemist who won 1949 Nobel Prize in chemistry for studies of properties of substances at temperatures near absolute zero.

GIBSON, George "Mooney," sports. London, Ont., 1880–1967. Baseball player; pro catcher, 1905–18.

GIBSON, Graeme C., literary arts. London, Ont., 1934. Novelist. *Five Legs; Perpetual Motion.*

GILLIS, Margie, performing arts. Montreal, Que., 1953. Dancer, choreographer; depicts social and political themes; an internationally acclaimed soloist, she has toured with Les Grands Ballet Canadiens, and introduced modern dance to China after the revolution. *Mercy.*

GILMOUR, Clyde, media. Calgary, Alta, 1912–97. Journalist; arts radio broadcaster. *Gilmour's Albums.*

GIMBY, Bobbie (b. Robert Stead), performing arts. Cabri, Sask., 1918–98. Trumpeter, songwriter. Appeared in CBC radio series *The Happy Gang.* Composed "CA-NA-DA" in 1967 for centennial celebrations.

GISBORNE, Frederick Newton, invention. Eng., 1824–92. Inventor; developed undersea telegraph cable (1852).

GIVENS, Philip, politics. Toronto, Ont., 1922–95. Mayor of Toronto 1964–66; responsible for acquisition of Henry Moore's *The Archer* sculpture at Toronto's New City Hall.

GOLDSCHMIDT, Nicholas "Niki," performing arts. Czech., 1908–2004. Conductor, pianist, singer and teacher who founded the Canadian Opera Company and the Vancouver Intl Festival; organized Bach Intl Competition.

GOLDSMITH, Robert, literary arts. St Andrews, N.B., 1794–1861. First Canadian-born poet to write in English: *The Rising Village* described Acadian experience.

GOMBERG, Richard Daniel "Tooker," activism. Montreal, Que., 1955–2004. Colourful social activist and environmentalist dedicated to recycling and inner-city cycling; staged many flamboyant protests.

GOMEZ, Avelino, sports. Cuba, 1928–80. Jockey; over 4,000 career wins, including four Queen's Plates.

GOOD, Herman James, military. South Bathurst, N.B., 1887–1969. Victoria Cross recipient, WWI, Hangard Wood, France, 1918. Corporal, 13th Bn, Quebec Regiment.

GOODERHAM, William, business. Eng., 1790–1881. With nephew James built Canada West's largest distillery, in 1859; Gooderham and Worts eventually had interests in distilleries, railways, transportation and retailing.

GOODIS, Jerry, business. Toronto, Ont., 1929–2002. A singer with the Canadian folk group The Travellers in the 1950s, Goodis wrote a Canadian version of "This Land Is Your Land," originally by Woody Guthrie; co-founded the advertising firm Goodis Goldberg Soren.

GOODMAN, Henry George, business. USA, 1907–97. Philanthropist, volunteer and lawyer who helped initiate, and served as president of, the Jewish Children's Aid Society in Toronto.

GOODYEAR, Scott, sports. Toronto, Ont., 1959. Indy car driver; winner of Canadian Racing Drivers Association Driver of the Year award; first Canadian to win oval race.

GORDON, Charles William, literary arts. Glengarry Cty, Canada W, 1860–1937. Presbyterian minister who wrote western-style novels, *The Sky Pilot, The Prospector,* as well as *Glengarry School Days.*

GORDON, Donald, business. Scot., 1901–69. Executive; controversial head of CNR, 1950–66.

GORDON, Walter Lockhart, politics. Toronto, Ont., 1906–87. Economic nationalist; inspired creation of Committee for an Independent Canada.

GORMAN, Charles, sports. Saint John, N.B., 1897–1940. Speed skater; held seven world records.

GOTLIEB, Allan Ezra, politics. Winnipeg, Man., 1928. Career public servant; Canadian ambassador to US 1981–89.

GOTLIEB, Calvin Carl "King," education. Toronto, Ont., 1921. Pioneer in computer education; co-founder of the Computing and Data Processing Association of Canada. *Social Issues in Computing* (co-author); *Economics of Computers.*

GOTLIEB, Phyllis Fay, literary arts. Toronto, Ont., 1926. Poet, science fiction writer. *Heart of Red Iron; The Kingdom of the Cats.*

GOUGEON, Hélène Carroll, media. Ottawa, Ont., 1924–2000. Veteran journalist on radio, TV and in print; culinary expertise led to her *The Original Canadian Cookbook.* Also wrote for *Weekend, Toronto Star, Ottawa Journal.*

GOUIN, Sir Jean-Lomer, politics. Canada E, 1861–1929. Liberal premier of Quebec, 1905–20.

GOULD, Glenn Herbert, performing arts. Toronto, Ont., 1932–82. Classical pianist; his recording of Bach's *Goldberg Variations* stands out in brilliant, eccentric career.

GOULET, Robert Gerard, performing arts. USA, 1933. Singer/actor, noted for romantic male leads. *South Pacific; Camelot.*

GOUZENKO, Igor Sergeievich, military. USSR, 1919–82. Spy; defector exposed Soviet espionage network.

GOVIER, Katherine Mary, literary arts. Edmonton, Alta, 1948. Novelist, short story writer. *Random Descent; Angel Walk.*

GOWAN, Elsie Park, literary arts. Scot., 1905–99. Internationally recognized playwright for radio and stage. *Beeches from Bond Street; The Building of Canada.*

GOWDY, Barbara, literary arts. Windsor, Ont., 1950. Novelist. *Mister Sandman; The White Bone; The Romantic.*

GOY, Luba, performing arts. Germany, 1946. Comedian on *Royal Canadian Air Farce*; impersonations include Sheila Copps, Pamela Wallin.

GRAHAM, William (Bill) Carvel, politics. Montreal, Que., 1939. Appointed minister of foreign affairs 2002 in Chrétien government.

GRANT, Charles, law. Toronto, Ont., 1902–80. Activist; fought anti-Semitism, racism, bigotry.

GRANT, George Parkin, literary arts. Toronto, Ont., 1918–88. Philosopher; influential pessimistic thinker and nationalist. *Lament for a Nation.*

GRAY, George R., sports. Canada W, 1865–1933. Shot putter; world record holder during 1880s.

GRAY, Herbert Eser, politics. Windsor, Ont., 1931. Liberal Party stalwart; has served as government leader; solicitor general; deputy prime minister for Jean Chrétien 1997–2000.

GRAY, James Henry, literary arts. Whitemouth, Man., 1906–98. Social historian whose works reflected Western Canadian society. *The Winter Years,* a story about the Depression; *The Boy From Winnipeg.*

GRAY, Robert Hampton, military. Trail, B.C., 1917–1945. Victoria Cross recipient, WWII, Honshu, Japan, 1945. Lieutenant, Royal Canadian Naval Volunteer Reserve.

GREALIS, Walter, performing arts. Toronto, Ont., 1929–2004. Pioneer Canadian music promoter; founder in 1964 of *RPI* magazine, which introduced the Gold Leaf Awards, precursor to the Juno Awards.

GREEN, Tom, performing arts. Pembroke, Ont., 1971. Satirical "shock" comedian, stages outrageous publicity stunts. *The Tom Green Show.*

GREENAWAY, Keith Rogers, invention. Woodville, Ont., 1916. Co-inventor of the RCAF Twilight Computer, which is used worldwide for high-latitude navigation; also developed the Earth Convergency Grid, which used gyro-steering techniques.

GREENE, Graham, performing arts. Six Nations Reserve, Ont., 1952. Film/TV actor. *Dances with Wolves.*

GREENE, Lorne Hyman, performing arts. Ottawa, Ont., 1915–87. Actor; Ben Cartwright on TV's *Bonanza* (1959–73) for 14 years.

GREENE, Nancy Catherine, sports. Ottawa, Ont., 1943. Skier; World Cup winner, 1967, 1968; gold and silver slalom medals.

GREENOUGH, Gail, sports. Edmonton, Alta, 1960. Equestrian; 1986 world champion, individual show jumping.

GREENSPAN, Edward Leonard, law. Niagara Falls, Ont., 1944. Distinguished criminal lawyer.

GREGG, Milton Fowler, military. Mountain Dale, N.B., 1892–1978. Victoria Cross recipient, WWI, Cambrai, France, 1918. Lieutenant, Royal Canadian Regiment.

GRENFELL, Sir Wilfred Thomason, medicine. Eng., 1865–1940. Medical missionary; builder of hospitals in Nfld.

GRETZKY, Wayne, sports. Brantford, Ont., 1961. Hockey player; all-time leading NHL scorer (894 goals).

GREY, Deborah C., politics. Vancouver, B.C., 1952. Canadian Alliance MP; deputy parliamentary leader; co-founder of Reform Party. Grey was the first elected Reform Party member of Parliament in 1993.

GREY OWL (b. Archibald Stansfield Belaney), literary arts. Eng., 1888–1938. Writer; conservationist who identified with Aboriginal peoples. *Pilgrims of the Wild.*

GRIERSON, John, visual arts. Scot., 1898–1972. Documentary filmmaker; creator of National Film Board.

GRIFFITH, Linda, performing arts. Toronto, Ont., 1953. Film, TV and stage actress. *Maggie and Pierre.*

GRIMES, Roger D., politics. Grand Falls, Nfld, 1950. Liberal premier of Nova Scotia 2001–; formerly minister of education.

GROSS, Paul, performing arts. Calgary, Alta, 1959. Actor, playwright; starred in TV series *Due South.*

GROSSMAN, Daniel Williams, performing arts. USA, 1942. Founder of the Danny Grossman Dance Co.; specializes in contemporary dance, set to jazz, rock music. *Higher; Nobody's Business.*

GROSSMAN, Lawrence S. (Larry), politics. Toronto, Ont., 1943–97. High-profile minister in Bill Davis's Ontario PC government, ran unsuccessfully as Tory leader against David Peterson in 1975.

GROULX, Lionel Adolphe, religion. Vaudreuil, Que., 1878–1967. Historian; Quebec religious nationalist.

GROVE, Frederick Philip, literary arts. Prussia, 1879–1948. Author; teacher. *In Search of Myself* (winner of 1946 Governor General's Award); *Settlers of the Marsh.*

GUERIN, Gertrude Ettershank (Klaw Law We Leth), politics. Mission Reserve, N. Vancouver, B.C.. A Musqueam chief, considered to be the first native woman to hold such a high-ranking position.

GUILLET, Dr. James Edwin, invention. Toronto, Ont., 1927. Inventor of biodegradable plastics.

GUNHOUSE, Joyce, business. Toronto, Ont., 1961. With partner Judith Cornish designer of Comrags fashion design label.

GUSTAFSON, Ralph Barker, literary arts. Lime Ridge, Que., 1909–95. Founder of League of Canadian Poets. Governor General's Award, 1974. *Fire and Stone.*

GWYN, Richard, media. Eng., 1934. Long-time journalist with the *Toronto Star;* freelance journalist and political commentator. *The 49th Paradox: Canada in North America.*

GWYN, Sandra (Alexandra) Jean Fraser, literary arts. St John's, Nfld, 1935–2000. Governor General's Award, 1984. *The Private Capital; Tapestry of War.*

GWYNNE, Horace "Lefty," sports. Toronto, Ont., 1912–2001. Boxer; bantamweight gold medal, 1932 Olympics.

GZOWSKI, Sir Casimir Stanislaus, exploration and discovery. Russia, 1813–98. Engineer; built roads, bridges and railroads.

GZOWSKI, Peter, media. Toronto, Ont., 1934–2002. Broadcaster; author; long-time CBC Radio host. *Morningside.*

HACKNER, Allan, sports. Nipigon, Ont., 1954. Curler; Canadian and world champion, 1982, 1985.

HADFIELD, Chris Austin, science. Sarnia, Ont., 1959. Astronaut, first Canadian mission specialist on space shuttle, 1996.

HAIG, Don, performing arts. Winnipeg, Man., 1933–2002. Co-founder of the Canadian Film Editors Guild and active in the CBC and National Film Board, Haig was instrumental in the development of the Canadian film industry.

HAILEY, Arthur, literary arts. Eng., 1920. Writer; produced string of best-sellers. *Airport.*

HAIM, Corey, performing arts. Toronto, Ont., 1972. Actor, producer. *Demolition High; Life 101.*

HALDER, Walter (Wally), sports. Toronto, Ont., 1925–94. Leading goal scorer on Canada's gold medallist team at 1948 Olympic Winter Games.

HALIBURTON, Thomas Chandler, literary arts. Windsor, N.S., 1796–1865. Writer; social satirist. *The Clockmaker.*

HALL, Emmett Matthew, public service. Saint-Columban, Que., 1898–1995. Chief Justice of Saskatchewan; co-author of Ontario's 1966 Hall-Dennis education report.

HALL, Frederick William, military. Ire., 1885–1915. Victoria Cross recipient, WWI, Second Battle of Ypres, France, 1915. Company sergeant-major, 8th Bn, Manitoba Regiment.

HALL, Glenn Henry, sports. Humboldt, Sask., 1931. Hockey goaltender; 11-time all-star; record 502 consecutive games.

HALL, Monty, performing arts. Winnipeg, Man., 1925. Long-time TV host of *Let's Make a Deal* TV game show.

HALL, William Edward, military. Horton Bluffs, N.S., 1827–1904. First black soldier to receive the Victoria Cross, Indian Mutiny, 1857. Able seaman, Royal Navy.

HALPERT, Herbert, literary arts. USA, 1911–2000. Newfoundland folklorist and academic; author of *Folktales of Newfoundland; Christmas Mumming in Newfoundland: Folklore and History.*

HAMEL, Theophile, visual arts. Ste-Foy, LC, 1817–70. Painted life-like official portraits.

HAMILTON, Barbara, performing arts. Toronto, Ont., 1926–96. Veteran screen and stage actor. *Anne of Green Gables; Crazy for You.*

HAMM, John F., politics. New Glasgow, N.S., 1938. PC premier of Nova Scotia, 1999–.

HAMPSON, Sharon, performing arts. Toronto, Ont., 1943. Member of children's musical entertainment group Sharon, Lois and Bram; live and on TV. *The Elephant Show.*

HANLAN, Edward (Ned), sports. Toronto, Ont., 1855–1908. World champion oarsman, 1880–84.

HANNA, Robert Hill, military. Ire., 1887–1967. Victoria Cross recipient, WWI, Battle of Hill 70, France, 1917. Company sergeant-major, 29th Bn, British Columbia Regiment.

HANSEN, Rick, sports. Port Alberni, B.C., 1957. Wheelchair athlete; "Man in Motion" tour raised $20M for medical research.

HANSON, Melvin "Fritzie," sports. USA, 1912. Football player; led Winnipeg to first western Grey Cup (1935).

HARCOURT, Michael Franklin, politics. Edmonton, Alta, 1943. NDP Premier of B.C. 1991–96.

HARDY, Hagood, performing arts. USA, 1937–97. Pop/jazz pianist and composer; Juno award-winner. "The Homecoming"; scores for *Anne of Green Gables, Road to Avonlea.*

HARE, Frederick Kenneth, science. Eng., 1919–2002. Environmentalist; expert on climate change, greenhouse effect.

HARNOY, Ofra, performing arts. Israel, 1965. International virtuoso cellist.

HARPER, Elijah, politics. Red Sucker L, Man., 1949. MLA in Manitoba legislature who blocked passage of Meech Lake Accord.

HARPER, J. Russell, visual arts. Caledonia, Ont., 1914–83. Art historian; pioneered study of art history.

HARPER, Stephen, politics. Toronto, Ont., 1959. Elected leader of the Canadian Alliance party in 2002; in 2004 became leader of fledgling Conservative Party of Canada. Former president of National Citizens Coalition.

HARRINGTON, Michael Francis, performing arts. St John's, Nfld, 1916–99. Supporter of an independent Newfoundland prior to 1949 confederation, Harrington hosted popular 1940s Newfoundland radio program *The Barrelman;* co-edited complete National Convention debates.

HARRINGTON, Rex Howard, performing arts. Peterborough, Ont., 1962. Internationally recognized ballet dancer; principal with National Ballet of Canada.

HARRINGTON, Richard, visual arts. Germany, 1911. Photographer whose stark portraits of a starving Inuit population in the late 1940s brought world attention to the grim situation caused partly by the disappearance of the caribou. *The Inuit: Life as It Was; Richard Harrington's Yukon.*

HARRIS, Christie, literary arts. USA, 1907–2002. Expert in West Coast Haida culture, Harris interpreted Haida legends on radio, in classrooms and in literary works. *Raven's Cry; Once Upon a Totem.*

HARRIS, Lawren Stewart, visual arts. Brantford, Ont., 1885–1970. Founder of Group of Seven; noted for stark landscapes. *Above Lake Superior.*

HARRIS, Micheal Deane, politics. Toronto, Ont., 1945. PC premier of Ontario 1995–2002.

HARRIS, Mike, sports. Georgetown, Ont., 1967. Skip of the silver-medal-winning curling team during the 1998 winter Olympics in Nagano, Japan.

HARRIS, Wayne, sports. USA, 1938. Football player; outstanding Calgary Stampeders linebacker.

HARRON, Donald (Don), performing arts. Toronto, Ont., 1924. Actor; comedian; host of *Morningside* 1977–8; appeared in *Spring Thaw* revue; well known for his Charlie Farquharson character.

HART, Corey Mitchell, performing arts. Montreal, Que., 1962. Pop singer; teen heartthrob. *Boy in the Box.*

HART, Evelyn Anne, performing arts. Toronto, Ont., 1956. Prima ballerina, Royal Winnipeg Ballet.

HART, Julia, literary arts. Fredericton, N.B., 1797–1867. Novelist whose *St. Ursula's Convent* written in 1824 was the first work of fiction by a Canadian-born writer to be published in Canada.

HARTMAN, Grace, business. Toronto, Ont., 1918–1993. Labour leader; first woman to head Canadian Union of Public Employees (1975–83).

HARVEY, Douglas N. (Doug), sports. Montreal, Que., 1924–90. Hockey player; Montreal Canadiens defenceman; won seven Norris Trophies.

HARVEY, Frederick Maurice Watson, military. Ire., 1888–1980. Victoria Cross recipient, WWI, Guyencourt, France, 1917. Lieutenant, Lord Strathcona's Horse.

HARVIE, Eric Lafferty, business/philanthropy. Orillia, Ont., 1892–1975. Founder of mining companies Western Leaseholds and Western Minerals; initiated the Glenbow Foundation and Heritage Park in Calgary; also a founding officer of the Canada Council.

HARWOOD, Vanessa Clare, performing arts. Eng., 1947. National Ballet soloist.

HATFIELD, Richard Bennett, politics. Woodstock, N.B., 1931–91. PC premier of N.B., 1970–87.

HAWKINS, Ronald "Rompin' Ronnie," performing arts. USA, 1935. Pop/country singer; pioneer of Canadian rock. "Mary Lou."

HAWLEY, Sanford Desmond (Sandy), sports. Oshawa, Ont., 1949. Jockey; winner of more than 6,000 races.

HAYDEN, Melissa (b. Mildred Herman), performing arts. Toronto, Ont., 1923. Virtuoso with New York City Ballet.

HEALEY, Jeff, performing arts. Toronto, Ont., 1966. Blind vocalist and guitarist, rock, blues music; Jeff Healey Trio. "Angel Eyes"; "See the Light."

HEARNE, Samuel, exploration and discovery. Eng., 1745–92. Explorer; *A Journey from Prince of Wales's Fort in Hudson's Bay to the Northern Ocean* is one of the great travel narratives.

HEATH, John Geoffrey (Jeff), sports. Ft William, Ont., 1915–75. Baseball player; hit .293 in 14-year career.

HEBB, Donald Olding, science. Chester, N.S., 1904–85. Psychologist; developmental work showed importance of environmental stimulation.

HÉBERT, Anne, literary arts. Ste-Catherine-de-Fossambault, Que., 1916–2000. Novelist. *Kamouraska.*

HÉBERT, Louis-Philippe, visual arts. Megantic, Que., 1850–1917. Commemorative sculptor of many public monuments. *Queen Victoria.*

HEDDLE, Kathleen, sports. Vancouver, B.C., 1965. With Marnie McBean won women's double sculls rowing medals: two golds in 1992 at Barcelona Olympics; one gold, one bronze in 1996 Olympics at Atlanta.

HEES, George Harris, politics. Toronto, Ont., 1910–96. PC Cabinet minister for John Diefenbaker and Brian Mulroney.

HEGGTVEIT, Anne, sports. Ottawa, Ont., 1939. Skier; Canada's first Olympic gold medal in skiing; women's slalom, 1960.

HELLSTROM, Sheila Anne (Brig-Gen.), military. Bridgewater, N.S., 1935. Soldier; first Cdn woman general.

HELWIG, David Gordon, literary arts. Toronto, Ont., 1938. Poet; novelist. "Figures in a Landscape."

HEMSWORTH, Albert Wade, performing arts. Brantford, Ont., 1916–2002. Folksinger, banjo and guitar player; Hemsworth's songs were featured on NFB documentaries and sung by contemporary artists such as Kate and Anna McGarrigle. "Foolish You"; "The Blackfly Song."

HENLEY, Garney, sports. USA, 1935. Football player for Hamilton Tiger Cats; CFL's most versatile player.

HENNING, Douglas, performing arts. Ft Garry, Man., 1947–2000. Magician; co-founder, Natural Law Party.

HENRY, Martha, performing arts. USA, 1938. TV/film actress; Ont. Stratford Festival regular. *The Wars.*

HENSON, Josiah, politics. USA, 1789–1883. Black leader; escaped slave; model for *Uncle Tom's Cabin.*

HENSTRIDGE, Natasha, performing arts. Springdale, Nfld, 1974. Model turned actress; appeared in *Species* movie series; also films *Dog Park* and *The Whole Nine Yards.*

HEPBURN, Doug, sports. Vancouver, B.C., 1926. Weight lifter; world heavyweight title, 1953.

HEPBURN, Mitchell Frederick, politics. St Thomas, Ont., 1896–1953. Liberal Ontario premier, 1934–42.

HEPPNER, Ben, performing arts. Murrayville, B.C., 1956. Tenor opera singer, Metropolitan debut in 1991.

HERBERT, Paul, performing arts. Thetford Mines, Que., 1924. Actor; screenwriter; director.

HERIOT, George, visual arts. Scot., 1759–1839. Watercolourist. *Lake St Charles Near Quebec.*

HEROUX, Denis, visual arts. Montreal, Que., 1940. Film producer. *Atlantic City.*

HERZBERG, Gerhard, medicine. Germany, 1904–99. Physicist; molecular analyst; Nobel Prize, chemistry, 1971.

HEWITT, Angela Mary, performing arts. Ottawa, Ont., 1958. Internationally renowned classical pianist; Bach specialist. Winner of 1985 International Bach Competition in Toronto, Ont.

HEWITT, Foster William, sports. Toronto, Ont., 1903–85. Hockey announcer; voice of Toronto Maple Leafs.

HIBBERT, Curtis, sports. Mississauga, Ont., 1966. Gymnast; won five gold medals in 1990 Commonwealth Games.

HIGHWAY, Tomson, literary arts. Brochet, Man., 1951. Playwright; novelist. *Dry Lips Oughta Move to Kapuskasing.*

HILL, Arthur, performing arts. Melfort, Sask., 1922. Stage and film performer. *The Ugly American.*

HILL, Dan Jr, performing arts. Toronto, Ont., 1954. Ballad singer and composer. "Sometimes When We Touch."

HILL, Daniel Grafton Sr, politics. USA, 1923–2003. Reformer; human rights; black history activist and writer.

HILL, James Jerome, business. Rockwood, Ont., 1838–1916. In 1890 consolidated vast railway holdings into the Great Northern Railway Co.; also integral in the building of the Canadian Pacific Railway.

HILLER, Arthur Garfin, visual arts. Edmonton, Alta, 1923. Filmmaker/director. *Love Story.*

HILLIARD, Anna Marion, medicine. Morrisburg, Ont., 1902–58. In 1947 helped develop the Pap test to detect cervical cancer; facilitated its initiation at Women's College Hospital in Toronto in 1948. Wrote *A Woman Doctor Looks at Love and Life.*

HILLIER, James, invention. Brantford, Ont., 1915. Inventor; pioneered electron microscopes.

HIRSCH, John Stephen, performing arts. Hungary, 1930–89. Stage director; founded Manitoba Theatre Centre; headed Ont.'s Stratford Festival, CBC TV drama.

HITSCHMANOVA, Lotta, politics. Czech., 1909–80. Activist; founding director, Unitarian Service Committee of Canada development agency.

HNATYSHYN, Ramon John, politics. Saskatoon, Sask., 1934–2002. Governor general of Canada 1990–95.

HOBSON, Frederick "Hobbie," military. Eng., 1875–1917. Victoria Cross recipient, WWI, Battle of Hill 70, Lens, France. Sergeant, 20th Bn, 1st Central Ontario Regiment.

HODGINS, Jack Stanley, literary arts. Comox, B.C., 1938. Novelist. *The Resurrection of Joseph Bourne.*

HODGSON, George Ritchie, sports. Montreal, Que., 1893–1983. Swimmer; first Canadian Olympic gold medals in swimming; 400 m, 1500 m freestyle in 1912.

HOEY, Charles Ferguson, military. Duncan, B.C., 1914–44. Victoria Cross recipient, WWII, Ngakyedauk Pass, Burma, 1944. Major, 1st Bn, Lincolnshire Regiment, British Army.

HOFFMAN, Abigail (Abbie), sports. Toronto, Ont., 1947. Sports feminist; director of Sport Canada.

HOFFMEISTER, Bertram Meryl, military. Vancouver, B.C., 1907–99. Canadian general in WWII, considered brilliant battle strategist, later chairman of lumber conglomerate MacMillan Bloedel.

HOGG-PRIESTLY, Helen Battles, science. USA, 1905–93. Astronomer; star clusters expert; asteroid named for her.

HOHL, Elmer, sports. Wellesley, Ont., 1919–87. Horseshoe pitcher; world champion, 1965–87.

HOLGATE, Edwin, visual arts. Allandale, Ont., 1892–1977. Group of Seven artist, noted for portraiture; member of Royal Canadian Academy of Arts.

HOLLAND, Edward James Gibson, military. Ottawa, Ont., 1878–1948. Victoria Cross recipient, Boer War, South Africa, 1900. Sergeant, Royal Canadian Dragoons.

HOLLINGSHEAD, Gregory Albert Frank, literary arts. Toronto, Ont., 1947. Governor General's Award for fiction, 1995, *The Roaring Girl.*

HOLMAN, Derek, performing arts. Eng., 1931. Composer, organist, choir director; led the Canadian Children's Opera Chorus 1975–85; wrote theatrical and liturgical choral music. *Doctor Canon's Cure; The Invisible Reality.*

HOLMES, Thomas William, military. Montreal, Que., 1898–1950. Victoria Cross recipient, WWI, Battle of Passchendaele, 1917. Private, 4th Canadian Mounted Rifles, 2nd Central Ontario Regiment.

HOMME, Robert, performing arts. USA, 1919–2000. Portrayed the Friendly Giant on long-running CBC children's program of same name.

HONEY, Samuel Lewis, military. Conn, Ont., 1894–1918. Victoria Cross recipient, WWI, Bourlon Wood, France, 1918. Lieutenant, 78th Bn, Manitoba Regiment.

HOOD, Hugh John Blagdon, literary arts. Toronto, Ont., 1928. Novelist; essayist. *The Swing in the Garden.*

HORNELL, David Ernest, military. Mimico, Ont., 1910–44. Victoria Cross recipient, WWII, Faroe Islands, 1944. Flight lieutenant, 162 Squadron, RCAF.

HORTON, Miles Gilbert "Tim," sports. Cochrane, Ont., 1930–74. Toronto Maple Leaf hockey player, five Stanley Cup wins; founder of national doughnut chain.

HOSPITAL, Janette Turner, literary arts. Australia, 1942. Winner of the Seal First Novel Award, 1982, *The Ivory Swing. Isobars.*

HOUSSER, Yvonne McKague, visual arts. Toronto, Ont., 1898–1996. Group of Seven-influenced paintings: National Art Gallery; Art Gallery of Ontario; McMichael Gallery.

HOUSTON, Heather, sports. Thunder Bay, Ont., 1959. Curler; skip of 1989 world championship team; Canadian championships 1988, 1989.

HOUSTON, James Archibald, literary/visual arts. Toronto, Ont., 1921. In the 1950s became a major buyer and supporter of Inuit art. *White Dawn; Confessions of an Igloo Dweller.*

HOWARD, Russ, sports. Penetanguishene, Ont., 1955. Curler; Canadian and world champion, 1987, 1993.

HOWE, Clarence Decatur (C.D.), business/politics. USA, 1886–1960. Foremost grain elevator builder of his day, Howe was a Liberal minister of transport; helped create Trans-Canada Airlines, forerunner of Air Canada.

HOWE, Gordon (Gordie), sports. Floral, Sask., 1928. Hockey player; Detroit Red Wings great; 801 NHL goals.

HOWE, Joseph, politics. Halifax, N.S., 1804–73. Led fight against Nova Scotia entry into Confederation; later joined cabinet.

HUBEL, David Hunter, science. Windsor, Ont., 1926. Winner of 1981 Nobel Prize in medicine and physiology for research in processing the visual system.

HUGGINS, Charles Brenton, science. Halifax, N.S., 1901–97. Won Nobel Prize for medicine in 1966 for discoveries concerning hormonal treatment of prostate cancer.

HUGHES, Monica, literary arts. Eng., 1925–2003. A popular writer of children's fiction, Hughes was widely acclaimed for her science fiction themes in titles including *Hunter in the Dark, Blaine's Way* and *The Seven Magpies.*

HULL, Robert Marvin, sports. Pte Anne, Ont., 1939. Hockey player; "Golden Jet," left winger for Chicago and Winnipeg; 610 NHL goals.

HUMPHREY, Jack Weldon, visual arts. Saint John, N.B., 1901–67. Internationally recognized painter; his water-colours of landscapes and people were inspired by cubist and expressionist influences.

HUMPHREY, John Peters, public service. Hampton, N.B., 1905–95. Principal author of the Universal Declaration of Human Rights; founder of the Canadian Human Rights Foundation and Amnesty International (Can.).

HUNGERFORD, George William, sports. Vancouver, B.C., 1944. Rower; gold medal, coxless pairs, 1964 Olympics.

HUNTER, Thomas James (Tommy), performing arts. London, Ont., 1937. Country singer; *Tommy Hunter Show* on CBC, 1965–92.

HUNTSMAN, Archibald Gowanlock, science. Tintern, Ont., 1883–1973. Biologist; pioneered fisheries science.

HUOT, Juliette, performing arts. Tétraultville, Que., 1912–2001. Quebec television, theatre and film actress, beloved for matriarchal roles. *Les Plouffes; Jamais deux sans toi.*

HURTIG, Melvyn (Mel), literary arts. Edmonton, Alta, 1932. Publisher; Canadian nationalist. *The Canadian Encyclopedia.*

HUSTON, Walter (b. Walter Houghston), performing arts. Toronto, Ont., 1884–1960. Versatile actor. *Treasure of the Sierra Madre; Dodsworth.*

HUTCHESON, Bellenden Seymour, military. USA, 1883–1954. Victoria Cross recipient, WWI, Quéant Drocourt Support Line, France, 1918. Captain, Canadian Army Medical Corp.

HUTCHISON, William Bruce, literary arts. Prescott, Ont., 1901–92. Political historian; biogapher of W.L. Mackenzie King, *The Incredible Canadian.*

HUTT, William Ian deWitt, performing arts. Toronto, Ont., 1920. Stage actor; distinguished career at Ontario's Stratford Festival.

HYLAND, Francis, performing arts. Regina, Sask., c.1932–2004. Actor with Stratford Festival, Ont.

IBERVILLE, Pierre Le Moyne, Sieur d', military. Montreal, Que., 1661–1706. Soldier; daring, often cruel, adventurer.

IDE, Thomas Ranald (Ran), media. Ottawa, Ont., 1919–96. Appointed in 1966 to set up TVOntario, an innovative education network.

IGALI, Baraladei Daniel, sports. Nigeria, 1974. Won gold medal in 2000 Sydney Olympics in freestyle wrestling.

IGNATIEFF, George, politics. Russia, 1913–89. Diplomat; expert in East-West relations; UN ambassador.

IGNATIEFF, Michael, literary arts/media. Toronto, Ont., 1947. Writer; broadcaster, academic. *The Russian Album.*

IMLACH, George "Punch," sports. Toronto, Ont., 1918–87. Hockey coach and manager; during 11 seasons with Toronto Maple Leafs won four Stanley Cups.

INNIS, Harold Adams, politics. Otterville, Ont., 1894–1952. Political economist; communications theorist. *Empire and Communications.*

IRELAND, John, performing arts. Vancouver, B.C., 1914–92. Actor; often played a heavy. *Red River*

IRONSIDE, Michael, performing arts. Toronto, Ont., 1950. Character actor, specializes in thugs; has appeared in films *Top Gun; Highlander II.* Also on TV's *ER* series.

IRVIN, Dick Sr, sports. Limestone Ridge, Ont., 1892–1957. Hockey executive; innovative coach/mgr of Montreal Canadiens, Toronto Maple Leafs.

IRVING, Kenneth Colin (K.C.), business. Buctouche, N.B., 1899–1992. Industrialist; founder of N.B. business empire, from oil to broadcasting.

IRWIN, Mary (b. May Campbell), performing arts. Whitby, Ont., 1862–1938. Broadway, vaudeville star; famous for first screen kiss in film *The Kiss*, in 1896. Sang "After the Ball."

ISELER, Elmer Walter, performing arts. Port Colborne, Ont., 1927–98. Choral conductor who founded Festival Singers of Canada; from 1964 to 1997 conductor of the Toronto Mendelssohn Choir; also founded the Elmer Iseler Singers.

ISRAEL, Werner, science. Germany, 1931. Physicist; pioneered study of black holes, gravitation.

ISSAJENKO, Angella (Taylor), sports. Jamaica, 1958. Sprinter; many medals in 100 m races.

JACKS, Terry, performing arts. Winnipeg, Man., 1944. Singer; founding member, the Poppy Family.

JACKSON, Alexander Young (A.Y.), visual arts. Montreal, Que., 1882–1974. Painter; landscape artist; member, Group of Seven. *Barns.*

JACKSON, Donald, sports. Oshawa, Ont., 1940. Figure skater; men's world champion, 1962.

JACKSON, Roger, sports. Toronto, Ont., 1942. Rower; gold medal, coxless pairs, 1964 Olympics.

JACKSON, Russell Stanley (Russ), sports. Hamilton, Ont., 1936. Football player; Ottawa quarterback; 3-time Schenley Award winner as CFL top player.

JACKSON, Tom, performing arts. Winnipeg, Man. Native actor and singer, has appeared on CBC's *North of 60, Medicine River, The Diviners.*

JACOBI, Lou, performing arts. Toronto, Ont., 1913. Character actor; has appeared in *Spring Thaw* revue; on Broadway; and in film *(Irma la Douce).*

JACOBS, "Indian" Jack, sports. USA, 1920–74. Football player; fiery quarterback for Winnipeg Blue Bombers; helped popularize CFL.

JACOBS, Jane, literary arts. USA, 1916. Urban critic; major urban thinker. *Systems of Survival.*

JACQUES, Elliott, science. Toronto, Ont., 1917–2003. Psychologist and social scientist whose Jacques' Stratified Systems Theory studied employee patterns in the workplace; he also coined the term "midlife crisis."

JAMES, Colin, performing arts. Regina, Sask., 1964. Songwriter, guitarist; plays blues, pop, swing. *Hook, Line & Single; Colin James.*

JAMES, Gerry, sports. Regina, Sask., 1934. Football/hockey player; rare pro double; Winnipeg Blue Bombers, Toronto Maple Leafs.

JANES, Percy Maxwell, literary arts. St John's, Nfld, 1922–99. Newfoundland writer whose gritty works depicted the reality of life on the island. *House of Hate.*

JARVIS, Graham, performing arts. Toronto, Ont., 1930–2003. Character actor best known for his role as Charlie Haggers in the 1970s sitcom *Mary Hartman, Mary Hartman;* appeared widely on television and film. *M*A*S*H; 7th Heaven.*

JELINEK, Otto John, sports/politics. Czech., 1940. PC minister; with sister Maria won world pairs figure skating title (1972).

JENKINS, Ferguson Arthur, sports. Chatham, Ont., 1943. Baseball pitcher; only Canadian in Hall of Fame, 284 career wins.

JENNESS, Diamond, literary arts. New Zealand, 1886–1969. Anthropologist; author; expert on native Canadians. *The People of the Twilight.*

JENNINGS, Peter Charles, media. Toronto, Ont., 1938. Broadcaster; anchorman, *ABC Evening News.*

JEROME, Harry Winston, sports. Prince Albert, Sask., 1940–82. Sprinter; one-time world record holder in 100 m.

JEWISON, Norman Frederick, visual arts. Toronto, Ont., 1926. Film director; founded Canadian Film Centre in Toronto. *In the Heat of the Night.*

JOHANSSON, Herman Smith "Chief Jackrabbit," sports. Norway, 1875–1986. Skier; popularizer of cross-country skiing.

JOHNS, Dr. Harold Elford, medicine. China, 1915–98. Physician; developed cobalt bomb for treating cancer.

JOHNSON, Ben, sports. Jamaica, 1961. Sprinter; stripped of 100 m world record time gold medal in 1988 Olympics for using banned drug.

JOHNSON, Daniel, politics. Montreal, Que., 1944. Liberal opposition leader in Quebec 1994–98.

JOHNSON, Edward, performing arts. Guelph, Ont., 1878–1959. Opera singer, performed at Metropolitan Opera in New York; later chairman of board of Royal Conservatory of Music in Toronto.

JOHNSON, Emily Pauline "Tekahionwake," literary arts. Six Nations Reserve, UC, 1861–1913. Her poetry celebrated Canada and her native heritage. "Flint and Feather."

JOHNSTON, Francis Hans (Franz), visual arts. Toronto, Ont., 1888–1949. Early Group of Seven member. *Batchawana Falls.*

JOHNSTON, Lynn, visual arts. Collingwood, Ont., 1947. Cartoonist; creator, "For Better or For Worse."

JOHNSTON, Rita Margaret, politics. Melville, Sask., 1935. First woman premier in Canada (B.C.) in 1991, succeeded Bill Vander Zalm.

JOLIAT, Aurèle, sports. Ottawa, Ont., 1908–86. Hockey player; left winger for Montreal Canadiens.

JOLLIET, Louis, exploration and discovery. Quebec City, Que., 1645–1700. Co-discoverer of the Mississippi R.

JONAS, George, literary arts. Hungary, 1935. Poet, writer, scriptwriter. Wrote script for CBC's *The Scales of Justice.* Also book about convicted murderer Peter Demeter: *By Persons Unknown: The Strange Death of Christine Demeter.*

JONES KONIHOWSKI, Diane, sports. Vancouver, B.C., 1951. Canadian pentathlon record holder.

JONES, Oliver Theophilus, performing arts. Montreal, Que., 1934. Internationally acclaimed jazz pianist famous for his lively keyboard style. *Just 88; From Lust to Lively.*

JONES, Richard, public service. USA, 1905–2001. Founder of the Canadian Council of Christians and Jews in 1948; initiator of national Brotherhood Week, in response to the horrors of the then recent Holocaust in Europe.

JORY, Victor, performing arts. Yukon, 1902–82. Actor; Hollywood villain. *Huckleberry Finn.*

JUCKES, Gordon, sports. Watrous, Sask., 1914–95. Hockey and Sports Hall of Fame member, established national team program.

JULIEN, Pauline, performing arts. Trois-Rivières, Que., 1928–98. Quebec singer, political activist, separatist and feminist, Julien embodied the spirit of Quebec through songs of her own composition as well as those of Kurt Weill, Bertolt Brecht and Gilles Vigneault.

JULIETTE (b. Juliette Augustina Sysak), performing arts. Winnipeg, Man., 1927. Singer; early TV star; own show, 1954–66.

JUNEAU, Pierre, business. Verdun, Que., 1922. Broadcast executive; headed CRTC, 1968–75.

JUTRA, Claude, visual arts. Montreal, Que., 1930–87. Film director. *Mon Oncle Antoine.*

K

KAEBLE, Joseph, military. St. Moise, Que., 1893–1926. Victoria Cross recipient, WWI, Neuville-Vitasse, France, 1918. Corporal, 22nd Bn, Canadien Francais.

KAIN, Karen, performing arts. Hamilton, Ont., 1951. Internationally celebrated prima ballerina, National Ballet of Canada.

KALVAK, Helen, visual arts. Victoria I., NWT, 1901–84. Inuit artist; over 300 prints portray the life of the Copper Inuit, frequent spiritual themes. *Kidnapper.*

KANE, Lori, sports. Charlottetown, P.E.I., 1964. Golfer; member of Canadian International Team 1989–92; member of Commonwealth Team in 1991; 1992 Canadian World Amateur Team; 1997, Canadian Athlete of the Year.

KANE, Paul, visual arts. Ire., 1810–71. Painter of the Canadian West and native peoples.

KAREDA, Urjo, performing arts. Estonia, 1944–2002. Artistic director of Toronto's Tarragon Theatre for 20 years; past director of Stratford Festival in Ontario; theatre and opera critic for the *Toronto Star* and the *Globe and Mail.*

KARPIS, Alvin (b. Albin Karpowicz). Montreal, Que., 1908–79. Barker Gang member; US Public Enemy No. 1.

KARSH, Malak, visual arts. Armenia, 1915–2001. Nature and landscape photographer famous for his image of a log jam on the Ottawa River that graced Canada's $1 bill prior to the introduction of the loonie; initiated Ottawa's annual Tulip Festival.

KARSH, Yousuf, visual arts. Armenia, 1908–2002. Photographer; portraitist of the famous, e.g., Churchill; Albert Einstein.

KAYFETZ, Benjamin Kershon, public service. Toronto, Ont., 1919–2002. Director of community relations for the Canadian Jewish Congress for nearly forty years; lobbyist for anti-discrimination legislation through Canada's human rights code.

KEDROVA, Lila Howard, performing arts. Russia, 1920–2000. Actress noted for role as Madame Hortense in film *Zorba the Greek,* also appeared in *High Wind in Jamaica.*

KEELER, Ruby (b. Ethel Keeler), performing arts. Halifax, N.S., 1909–93. Actress; dancer. *42nd Street.*

KEITH, Vicki, sports. Winnipeg, Man., 1961. Swam all five Great Lakes in 1988.

KELESI, Helen Mersi, sports. Victoria, B.C., 1969. Tennis player; Canadian women's championship 1987–90.

KELLY, Leonard "Red," sports. Simcoe, Ont., 1927. Hockey player; star defenceman with Detroit and Toronto; two-time Liberal MP.

KELLY, Milton Terrence (M.T.), literary arts. Toronto, Ont., 1947. Poet, playwright, novelist. *A Dream Like Mine.*

KELSO, John Joseph, politics. Ire., 1864–1935. Reformer; founded Toronto Humane Society, Children's Aid.

KENOJUAK Ashevak, visual arts. Baffin Island, NWT, 1927. Artist noted for bird graphics.

KEON, David Michael, sports. Noranda, Que., 1940. Hockey player with Toronto Maple Leafs 1960–75. Team Canada member 1977. Winner of Conn Smythe trophy, 1967.

KERR, George Fraser, military. Toronto, Ont., 1894–1929. Victoria Cross recipient, WWI, Bourlon Wood, France, 1918. Lieutenant, 3rd Bn, 1st Central Ontario Regiment.

KERR, John Chipman, military. Fox River, N.S., 1887–1963. Victoria Cross recipient, WWI, the Somme, France, 1916. Private, 49th Canadian Infantry Bn, Alberta Regiment.

KERR, Robert Allan, performing arts. Calgary, Alta, 1918–2003. Host of CBC's national classical music program *Off the Record* 1960–96, Kerr had an encyclopedic knowledge, especially in the field of organ music.

KHANJIAN, Arsinée, performing arts. Lebanon, 1958. Film and theatre actress, wife of film director Atom Egoyan. *Next of Kin; Exotica.*

KHORANA, Har Gobind, science. India, 1922. Chemist; Nobel Prize in medicine (1968) for DNA research.

KIDD, Bruce, sports. Ottawa, Ont., 1943. Runner; many wins at various distances; outstanding athlete in Canada, 1961 and 1962.

KIDDER, Margot, performing arts. Yellowknife, NWT, 1948. Actress; Hollywood star. *Superman.*

KIERANS, Eric William, politics. Montreal, Que., 1914–2004. Economist; outspoken nationalist.

KILBOURN, William, literary arts. Toronto, Ont., 1926–95. Writer; historian; biographer of C.D. Howe.

KILLAM, Isaac Walton, business. Yarmouth, N.S., 1885–1955. Industrialist; built business empire; known for philanthropy.

KING, Allan Winton, visual arts. Vancouver, B.C., 1930. Documentary filmmaker;. *Warrendale.*

KING, Charmion, performing arts. Toronto, Ont., 1925. Film, radio, TV and stage actress who has appeared at Ontario's Stratford Festival. *Who Has Seen the Wind; Wind at My Back.*

KING, Thomas, literary arts. USA, 1943. Aboriginal writer, novelist. Creator of "Dead Dog Café" on CBC radio programs *Morningside* and *This Morning. Medicine River; Green Grass, Running Water.*

KING, William Lyon Mackenzie, politics. Kitchener, Ont., 1874–1950. Lib. prime minister of Canada (1921–6; 1926–30; 1935–48).

KINROSS, Cecil John, military. Eng., 1896–1957. Victoria Cross recipient, WWI, Battle of Passchendaele, France, 1917. Private, 49th Bn, Alberta Regiment.

KINSELLA, William Patrick (W.P.), literary arts. Edmonton, Alta, 1935. Writer; known for poetic baseball fiction. *Shoeless Joe.*

KIRCK, Harvey (b. Harvey Krick), media. New Liskeard, Ont., 1928–2002. Anchor and co-anchor, with Lloyd Robertson, of CTV's national news desk; the gruff Kirck also appeared on *Canada A.M.* and *Inside Canada. Nobody Calls Me Mr. Kirck.*

KIRKE, Sir David, exploration and discovery. France, 1597–1654. First governor of Nfld, 1637.

KLEIN, Abraham Moses (A.M.), literary arts. Ukraine, 1909–72. Poet of Jewish themes. "Portrait of the Poet as Landscape."

KLEIN, George John, invention. Hamilton, Ont., 1904–92. Productive inventor: wind tunnels, gearing systems, Canadarm gear design.

KLEIN, Ralph Philip, politics. Calgary, Alta, 1942. PC premier of Alberta, 1992–

KNEEBONE, Tom, performing arts. NZ, 1932–2003. Comic actor who played extensively at Ontario's Stratford and Shaw theatres, and at London's Old Vic and on Broadway. Appeared with Dinah Christie in the revue *Oh Coward!*

KNIGHT, Arthur George, military. Eng., 1886–1918. Victoria Cross recipient, WWI, Villers-les-Cagnicourt, France, 1918. Sergeant, 10th Bn, Alberta Regiment.

KNOTT, Elsie Marie, politics. Curve Lake, Ont., 1922–95. First native woman in Canada to be elected chief, at Ojibwa reserve near Peterborough, Ont.

KNOWLES, Stanley Howard, politics. USA, 1908–97. A founder of the New Democratic Party; represented Winnipeg North Centre riding 1942–81. Admired for his support of old-age pensions; president of Canadian Labour Congress 1958–62.

KNUDSON, George, sports. Winnipeg, Man., 1937–89. Golfer; Canada's top pro; 12 PGA tour victories.

KOFFLER, Murray Bernard, business. Toronto, Ont., 1924. Entrepreneur; made Shopper's Drug Mart Canada's largest pharmacy chain.

KOFFMAN, Morris (Moe), performing arts. Toronto, Ont., 1928–2001. Jazz flautist. "Swinging Shepherd Blues."

KOGAWA, Joy Nozomi, literary arts. Vancouver, B.C., 1935. Writer. *Obasan; Itsuka.*

KONOWAL, Filip, military. Russia, 1887–1959. Victoria Cross recipient, WWI, Battle of Hill 70, Lens, France, 1917. Corporal, 47th Bn, British Columbia Regiment.

KOTCHEFF, William Theodore (Ted), visual arts. Toronto, Ont., 1931. Film director. *The Apprenticeship of Duddy Kravitz.*

KRAATZ, Victor, sports. Germany, 1971. Ice dancing; with Shae-Lynn Bourne won Canadian title, 1993–96; third in World Championships, 1996.

KRALL, Diana, performing arts. Nanaimo, B.C., 1964. Jazz vocalist. *When I Look Into Your Eyes.*

KREBS, Charles J., science. USA, 1936. Zoologist specializing in animal ecology; his Krebs Effect, or Fence Effect, explains the effect fencing has on animal populations. *The Experimental Analysis of Distribution and Abundance.*

KREINER, Kathy, sports. Timmins, Ont., 1957. Skier; gold medal, giant slalom, 1976 Olympics.

KREVER, Horace, law. Montreal, Que., 1929. Judge who led Royal Commission of Inquiry on the Blood System in Canada, 1993–97.

KRIEGHOFF, Cornelius David, visual arts. Holland, 1815–72. Created paintings of Quebec life. *The Habitant Farm.*

KROL, Joseph "Joe King," sports. Hamilton, Ont., 1919. Football player; Toronto Argos star; top athlete, 1946.

KUDELKA, James, performing arts. Newmarket, Ont., 1955. Artistic director for the National Ballet of Canada; also choreographer, dancer. Critically acclaimed work with classical and modern influences. *Spring Awakening.*

KUERTI, Anton Emil, performing arts. Austria, 1938. Leading pianist; composer; Beethoven specialist.

KURELEK, William (Wasyl), visual arts. Whitfield, Alta, 1927–77. Symbolist religious painter.

KUWABARA, Bruce, visual arts. Hamilton, Ont., 1949. Partner with Toronto-based architecture firm Kuwabara Payne McKenna Blumberg; award-winning designer of Kitchener, Ont., City Hall; Canadian embassy, Berlin, Germany.

L

LA SALLE, Rene Robert Cavelier, Sieur de, exploration and discovery. France, 1643–87. Became commandant of Fort Frontenac in present-day Kingston, Ont., 1673.

LA VERENDRYE, Pierre Gaultier de Varennes, Sieur de, exploration and discovery. Trois-Rivières, Que., 1685–1749. Explorer of W Canada.

LABATT, John Kinder, business. Ire., 1803–66. In 1855 became owner of a small brewery in London, Ont., the origin of the giant brewery empire.

LAFLEUR, Guy Damien, sports. Thurso, Que., 1951. Hockey player; Canadiens star right winger; 560 goals.

LAFONTAINE, Sir Louis Hippolyte, politics. Boucherville, LC, 1807–64. In effect, Canada's first PM, 1848–51.

LALONDE, Donny, sports. Kitchener, Ont., 1960. Boxer; WBC light heavyweight champion (1987–88).

LALONDE, Edouard Charles, sports. Cornwall, Ont., 1887–1970. In 1950 named as one of Canada's outstanding lacrosse players of the half century; played NHL Montreal Canadiens, scoring 124 goals in 98 games 1913–18.

LALONDE, Marc, politics. Île-Perrot, Que., 1929. Pierre Trudeau's principle secretary 1968–72; held various portfolios until retirement in 1984.

LAMBERT, Natalie, sports. Montreal, Que., 1963. Speed skater; short-track title, 500 m, 1993.

LAMBERTS, Heath, performing arts. Toronto, Ont., 1941. Actor at Stratford Festival, Ont. *Glengarry Glen Ross; Cyrano de Bergerac.*

LAMER, Antonio, law. Montreal, Que., 1933. Chief justice of the Supreme Court 1990–99.

LAMPMAN, Archibald, literary arts. Morpeth, Canada W, 1861–99. Nature poet. "Lyrics of Earth."

LANCASTER, Ron, sports. USA, 1938. Football player; coach; quarterback set 30 CFL records.

LANCTOT, Françoise, performing arts. Montreal, Que., 1947. Actress, film director; winner of Etrog for *La vrai nature du Bernadette. The Apprenticeship of Duddy Kravitz.*

LANDRY, G. Yves, business. Thetford Mines, Que., 1938–98. Died while chairman, president and CEO of Chrysler Canada; co-chairman of Automotive Advisory Committee to the Minister of Industry Canada.

LANDRY, Jean-Bernard, politics. Saint-Jacques, Montcalm Co., Que., 1937. Parti Québécois premier of Quebec 2001–2003; former deputy premier and minister of finance.

LANG, Kathryn Dawn (k.d.), performing arts. Consort, Alta, 1961. Country-torch singer; vegetarian activist. *Shadowlands.*

LANGFORD, Sam, sports. Weymouth Falls, N.S., 1886–1956. Boxer; great fighter; denied title shot.

LANOIS, Daniel, performing arts. Hamilton, Ont., 1953. Singer; producer of Peter Gabriel's "Sledgehammer" and with Brian Eno U2's *Joshua Tree.*

LANTOS, Robert, visual arts. Hungary, 1949. Film producer; CEO, Alliance Communications. *Black Robe.*

LAPIERRE, Laurier L., media. Megantic, Que., 1929. TV personality, author; co-host, *This Hour Has Seven Days.*

LAPOINTE, Louise Marguerite Renaude, media. Disraeli, Que., 1912–2002. First French Canadian woman to be appointed Speaker of the Senate, 1974–79; journalist with Montreal's *La Presse.* Member of the Group of 78, which called upon Canada to aid the world's poor in 1982.

LASKIN, Bora, law. Ft William, Ont., 1912–84. Chief justice of Canada, 1973–84.

LASTMAN, Melvin Douglas (Mel), politics. Toronto, Ont., 1933. Mayor of the amalgamated City of Toronto 1997–2003; formerly long-time mayor of North York, a satellite "city" of the former Metropolitan Toronto.

LAU, Evelyn, literary arts. Vancouver, B.C., 1971. Poet, novelist, short story writer, used own experiences to portray the lives of street kids. *Runaway: Diary of a Street Kid; You Are Not Who You Claim; Oedipal Dreams.*

LAUMANN, Silken, sports. Toronto, Ont., 1964. Rower; braved broken leg for bronze medal in 1992 Olympics; Athlete of the Year 1991, 1992.

LAURE, Carole (b. Carol Champagne), performing arts. Montreal, Que., 1949. Actress; screen star. *Maria Chapdelaine.*

LAURENCE, Jean Margaret, literary arts. Neepawa, Man., 1926–87. Writer; created fictional setting of Manawaka. *The Diviners; The Stone Angel.*

LAURENDEAU, Joseph-Edmond-André, politics. Montreal, Que., 1912–68. Co-chairman of Royal Commission on Bilingualism and Biculturalism 1963–68; editor of Montreal's *Le Devoir* 1958–68.

LAURIER, Sir Wilfrid, politics. St-Lin, Canada E, 1841–1919. Canada's first French-speaking prime minister (1896–1911).

LAURIN, Camille, politics. Charlemagne, Que., 1922–99. Drafted Bill 101, Quebec's French Language Charter; joined Quebec National Assembly in 1970, member of Parti Québécois.

LAVAL, François de, religion. France, 1623–1708. First bishop of Quebec (1674–88).

LAVALLÉE, Calixa, performing arts. Verchères, Canada E, 1842–1891. Composer of "O Canada."

LAVIGNE, Avril, performing arts. Napanee, Ont., 1984. Outspoken skater/punk rock singer/songwriter; she reached instant fame with her videos *Sk8ter Boi* and *I'm With You,* and album *Let Go.*

LAW, Andrew Bonar, politics. Rexton, N.B., 1858–1923. Prime Minister of Britain 1922–23; signed Treaty of Versailles on behalf of Great Britain in 1919.

LAWRENCE, Florence, performing arts. Hamilton, Ont., 1890–1938. Film and vaudeville actress; first to use publicity stunt to launch career. *Daniel Boone; Resurrection.*

LAYTON, Irving Peter, literary arts. Romania, 1912. Prolific, flamboyant poet. "A Red Carpet for the Sun."

LEARNMONTH, Okill Massey, military. Quebec City, Que., 1894–1917. Victoria Cross recipient, WWI, Battle of Hill 70, Lens, France, 1917. Major, 2nd Bn, Eastern Ontario Regiment.

LE CAINE, Hugh, performing arts/science. Port Arthur, Ont., 1914–77. Physicist; composer; designed the sackbut, the first musical synthesizer.

LEACOCK, Stephen Butler, literary arts. Eng., 1869–1944. Humorist. *Sunshine Sketches of a Little Town.*

LEBLANC, Romeo, politics. Memramcook, N.B., 1927. Governor-general of Canada 1994–99; former Liberal MP.

LEBLOND, Charles Philippe, science. France, 1910. Anatomist; pioneer in cell biology.

LECAVALIER, René, media. Montreal, Que., 1918. In 1952 called first televised hockey game on TV on Radio-Canada; remained as commentator for *La Soirée du hockey* till 1985.

LECLERC, Felix, performing arts. La Tuque, Que., 1914–88. Singer/songwriter; influential chansonnier and Quebec nationalist.

LEE, Dennis Beynon, literary arts. Toronto, Ont., 1939. Poet, children's writer. *Alligator Pie; Garbage Delight.*

LEE, Geddy, performing arts. Toronto, Ont., 1953. Singer/songwriter; lead singer for pop group Rush. *Moving Pictures.*

LEE-GARTNER, Kerrin, sports. Trail, B.C., 1966. Skier; gold medal, women's downhill, 1992 Olympics.

LEGER, Gabrielle Carmel, politics. Montreal, Que., 1916–98. Wife of the late governor-general Jules Leger; acted for her husband when he suffered a stroke shortly after taking office.

LEGER, Jules, politics. St-Anicet, Que., 1913–80. Canada's governor general, 1974–79.

LEGER, Paul-Émile, religion. Valleyfield, Que., 1904–91. Cardinal; eloquent, compassionate religious leader; became missionary in Africa.

LEMELIN, Roger, literary arts. Quebec City, Que., 1919–92. Writer; creator of the popular Plouffe family.

LEMIEUX, Jean-Paul, visual arts. Quebec City, Que., 1904–90. Landscape painter. *Le Visiteur du Soir; Lazare.*

LEMIEUX, Mario, sports. Montreal, Que., 1965. Hockey player; Pittsburgh Penguins centre, one of two players to average two points per game.

LEMIEUX, Raymond Urgel, medicine. La Biche, Alta, 1920. Scientist with National Research Council, solved riddle of synthesis of sucrose; pioneer in blood-typing serum.

LENNOX, Edward James, visual arts. Toronto, Ont., 1854–1933. Architect of "Richardson Romanesque" style. Toronto's Old City Hall, Casa Loma; powerhouse at Niagara Falls, Ont.

LEONARD, Stanley, sports. Vancouver, B.C., 1915. Golfer; won many Canadian titles; three US tour wins.

LEPAGE, Robert, performing arts. Quebec City, Que., 1957. Actor, screenwriter, director; former artistic director of Ottawa's National Arts Centre; Théâtre francais. *Secret War Tour.*

LESAGE, Jean, politics. Montreal, Que., 1912–80. Liberal premier of Quebec, 1960–66.

LETHEREN, Carol Anne, sports. Toronto, Ont., 1942–2001. Chief executive of Canadian Olympic Association.

LEUSZLER, Winnifred Roach, sports. Port Credit, Ont., 1926–2003. First Canadian to swim the English Channel, in 1951. Leuszler also placed third in the 1954 Lake Ontario swim won by Marilyn Bell.

LEVESQUE, Georges-Henri, politics. Roberval, Que., 1902–2000. Dominican priest, founded Faculty of Social Sciences at Laval University; major figure in Quebec's Quiet Revolution.

LEVESQUE, Jean-Louis, business. Nouvelle, Que., 1911–1994. Financier; co-founder of Levesque Beaubien Inc., Quebec's largest brokerage house.

LEVESQUE, René, politics. New Carlisle, Que., 1922–87. Led Parti Québécois; Quebec premier 1976–85.

LEVY, Eugene, performing arts. Hamilton, Ont., 1946. Actor; comedian; *SCTV* regular (Earl Camembert, Bobby Bitman).

LEWIS, David, politics. Russia, 1909–81. Federal NDP leader, 1971–75; eloquent speaker.

LEWIS, Lennox, sports. Eng., 1965. Boxer; super heavyweight gold medal, 1988 Olympics.

LEWIS, Stephen Henry, politics. Ottawa, Ont., 1937. Ont. NDP leader; Cdn UN ambassador.

LEWIS, Walter, science. Ottawa, Ont., 1930. Ethnobotanist who, with wife, Memory Elvin-Lewis, is a leading world expert on airborne and allergenic pollens, as well as the medicinal uses of tropical plants.

LEWIS, Wilfrid Bennett, science. Eng., 1908–87. Physicist; prime role in developing CANDU reactor.

LEYRAC, Monique, performing arts. Montreal, Que., 1928. Actress; popular Quebec chanteuse.

LIGHTFOOT, Gordon Meredith, performing arts. Orillia, Ont., 1938. Singer/songwriter; popular vocalist with many hits. "Canadian Railroad Trilogy."

LILIENSTEIN, Lois, performing arts. USA, 1936. Member of children's musical entertainment group Sharon, Lois and Bram; live and on TV. *The Elephant Show.*

LILLIE, Beatrice Gladys, performing arts. Toronto, Ont., 1894–1989. Stage comedienne. *Auntie Mame.*

LINDER, Cec, performing arts. Poland, 1921–92. Television, stage and film character actor. *Goldfinger; A Touch of Class; The Edge of Night.*

LINDROS, Eric, sports. London, Ont., 1973. Hockey player; centre for Philadelphia Flyers; winner of Hart Trophy, 1995.

LINDSAY, Robert Blake Theodore (Ted), sports. Renfrew, Ont., 1925. Hockey player; left winger 17 seasons with Detroit and Chicago.

LINKLETTER, Art (b. Arthur Brown), performing arts. Moose Jaw, Sask., 1912. Radio/TV host. *People Are Funny; Kids Say the Darndest Things.*

LISMER, Arthur, visual arts. Eng., 1885–1969. Painter; Group of Seven founding member. *September Gale.*

LITTLE, Jean, literary arts. Taiwan, 1932. Popular writer of children's literature, poetry; blends themes of alienation and troubled relationships. *From Anna; Mama's Going to Buy You a Mockingbird; His Banner Over Me.*

LITTLE, Richard Carruthers (Rich), performing arts. Ottawa, Ont., 1938. Impersonator; night club and television performer.

LIVESAY, Dorothy, literary arts. Winnipeg, Man., 1909–96. Poet; sensitive feminist writer. *Poems for People.*

LOATES, Glen Martin, visual arts. Toronto, Ont., 1945. Wildlife artist; painter and naturalist.

LOCKHART, Gene, performing arts. London, Ont., 1891–1957. Character actor appeared in *Miracle on 34th Street, Carousel* and on Broadway. Father of actress June Lockhart.

LOGAN, Sir William Edmond, science. Montreal, Que., 1798–1875. Geologist; first head of Geological Survey of Canada; first to map Laurentian Shield.

LOMBARDI, Johnny, business. Toronto, Ont., 1915–2002. Pioneer broadcaster whose CHIN Radio in Toronto, Ont., became first multicultural broadcasting voice in Ontario.

LOMBARDO, Gaetano Alberto "Guy," performing arts. London, Ont., 1902–77. Bandleader; his Royal Canadians most popular band in N America; 300 million records sold. Also won 1946 International World Cup in speed boating; US champion 1946–49; Canadian title in 1955, 1956.

LONGBOAT, Thomas Charles, sports. Brantford, Ont., 1887–1949. Runner; set record in 1907 Boston Marathon.

LONGDEN, John (Johnny), sports. Eng., 1910–2003. Jockey; first N American with 4,000 winners (career: 6,032).

LORD, Bernard, politics. Moncton, N.B., 1965. PC premier of N.B., elected in 1999.

LORTIE, Louis, performing arts. Montreal, Que., 1959. Pianist; five-time winner of Canadian Music Competition, 1968–72, 1990 Juno for Best Classical Album.

LOUGHEED, Edgar Peter, politics. Calgary, Alta, 1928. PC premier of Alberta, 1971–85; played strong role in federal politics.

LOVELL, Jocelyn, sports. Eng., 1950. Canada's leading cyclist 1970–83; winner of 1000 m silver medal in 1978 world championships; paralyzed in training accident 1983.

LOWRY, (Clarence) Malcolm, literary arts. Eng., 1909–57. British novelist whose powerful novels reflected his turbulent life; lived in B.C. 1937–54. *Under the Volcano.*

LUBA (b. Luba Kowalchyk), performing arts. Montreal, Que., 1958. Pop singer-songwriter. "Between the Earth and Sky"; "All or Nothing."

LUCAS, Clarence, performing arts. Six Nations Reserve, Brantford, Ont., 1866–1947. Internationally recognized composer, conductor for voice, piano, chamber and orchestral music.

LUND, Alan, performing arts. Toronto, Ont., 1927–92. Dancer/choreographer. With wife Blanche Harris performed as an Astaire/Rogers-style dancing team; Stratford Festival, Charlottetown Festival.

LUNDSTROM, Linda, business. Red Lake, Ont., 1951. Founder of fashion business with boutiques across North America; her signature LaParka has long been her Canadian culture statement, as are her all-Canadian-made clothes.

LYALL, Graham Thomson, military. Eng., 1892–1941. Victoria Cross recipient, WWI, Cambrai, France, 1918. Lieutenant, 102nd Bn, 2nd Central Ontario Regiment.

M

MACDONALD, Donald Stovel, politics. Ottawa, Ont., 1932. In 1975 became finance minister for federal Liberals, introducing Wage and Price Controls; in 1982 became chairman of the Royal Commission on Economic Union and Development Prospects for Canada; high commissioner to UK 1988–91.

MacDONALD, Finlay, politics. Sydney, N.S., 1923–2002. Nova Scotia PC senator and broadcasting executive (founding director of CTV); backroom politician for Robert Stanfield and prime ministers Joe Clark and Brian Mulroney.

MacDONALD, Flora Isabel, politics. Sydney, N.S., 1926. First woman to hold senior Cabinet post; external affairs in Clark govt (1979).

MacDONALD, James Edward Hervey (J.E.H.), visual arts. Eng., 1874–1932. Landscape painter; Group of Seven founder. *Mist Fantasy.*

MacDONALD, James Williamson Galloway (Jock), visual arts. Scot., 1897–1960. Early abstract painter; member, Painters Eleven.

MACDONALD, Sir John Alexander, politics. Scot., 1815–91. Canada's first official prime minister.

MacDONALD, Norm, performing arts. Quebec City, Que., 1963. Comedian and impersonator; starred in the TV program *The Norm Show. The People vs. Larry Flynt.*

MacDOUGALL, Fraser, media. Stratford, Ont., 1907–2000. Longtime journalism figure; Ottawa bureau chief for Canadian Press; active on Ontario Press Council; chairman of Michener journalism awards.

MacDOWELL, Thain Wendell, military. Lachute, Que., 1890–1960. Victoria Cross recipient, Vimy Ridge, France, 1917. Captain, 38th Bn, Eastern Ontario Regiment.

MacEACHEN, Allan Joseph, politics. Inverness, N.S., 1921. Liberal MP, portfolios in finance, external affairs; deputy MP in Trudeau government.

MacEWEN, Gwendolyn, literary arts. Toronto, Ont., 1941–87. Poet. *The Shadow-Maker.*

McGREGOR, John, military. Scot., 1888–1952. Victoria Cross recipient, WWI, Cambrai, France, 1918. Captain, 2nd Canadian Mounted Rifles, 1st Canadian Regiment.

MacGREGOR, Roy, literary arts. Whitney, Ont., 1948. Novelist, columnist. *Home Game; The Last Season.*

MacGUIGAN, Mark Rudolph, politics. Charlottetown, P.E.I., 1931–98. Liberal politician who served with Pierre Trudeau, ran unsuccessfully for leader in 1984, later appointed judge of the Federal Court of Appeal. Founding member of the Canadian Civil Liberties Association.

MacISAAC, Ashley, performing arts. Antigonish, N.S., 1975. Eclectic musician who blends pop music with traditional Celtic sound. *How Are You Today?; Fine Thank You Very Much.*

MacKAY, James William (Jim), performing arts. Beaverton, Ont., 1916–2002. Pioneer film animator who began his career with the National Film Board in 1942. With George Dunning founded Graphic Associates, producing some of Canada's first TV commercials; in the 1950s founded Film Design Ltd., contributing to *Sesame Street,* among others.

MacKAY, Peter, politics. New Glasgow, N.S., 1966. Elected federal PC leader 2003, lost to Stephen Harper for leadership of new Conservative Party 2004.

MACKENZIE, Alexander, politics. Scot., 1822–1892. Canada's second prime minister (Lib), 1873–78.

MacKENZIE, Sir Alexander, exploration and discovery. Scot., 1764–1820. Charted MacKenzie R. (1789); crossed from L. Athabasca to Pacific Ocean (1793).

MacKENZIE, Maj.-Gen. Lewis W., military. Truro, N.S., 1940. Soldier; led UN soldiers from 33 nations (incl. Canada) in opening Sarajevo airport for delivery of humanitarian aid during Bosnian civil war.

MacKENZIE, William Lyon, politics. Scot., 1795–1861. Led 1837 rebellion for reform in Upper Canada; Toronto's first mayor.

MacLEAN, John Angus, politics. Lewes, P.E.I., 1914–2000. Premier P.E.I. 1979–81; instigator of equalization payments for troubled Atlantic fisheries.

MACLEAN, John Bayne, media. Crieff, Ont., 1862–1950. Founder of *Maclean's* magazine in 1905; also of *Financial Post, Chatelaine.*

MacLEAN, Steven Glenwood, science. Ottawa, Ont., 1954. Laser physicist who trained with NASA's astronaut program, specializes with NASA's robotics branch.

MacLENNAN, John Hugh, literary arts. Glace Bay, N.S., 1907–90. Novelist. *The Watch That Ends the Night; Barometer Rising.*

MacLEOD, Alistair, literary arts. North Battleford, Sask., 1936. Short story writer, novelist; his Cape Breton saga, *No Great Mischief,* won the Trillium Book Award. *Island: The Collected Stories.*

MacLEOD, John James Rickard, medicine. Scot., 1876–1935. Medical researcher, co-winner with Drs. Banting and Best of Nobel Prize in 1923 for discovery of insulin.

MacMILLAN, Sir Ernest Campbell, performing arts. Mimico, Ont., 1893–1973. Renowned conductor, composer, arranger; championed Canadian works.

MacMILLAN, Harvey Reginald (H.R.), business. Newmarket, Ont., 1885–1976. Industrialist; established forerunner of logging giant MacMillan Bloedel.

MacMILLAN, Margaret Olwen, literary arts. Toronto, Ont., 1943. Historian; author of award-winning *Paris 1919: Six Months That Changed the World.* Also *Women of the Raj.*

MacNAUGHTON, Andrew George Latta, military. Moosomin, NWT, 1887–1966. Soldier; led Cdn army in WWII; endorsed Dieppe raid; diplomat; UN Atomic Energy Assn.

MacNEIL, Rita, performing arts. Big Pond, N.S., 1944. Cape Breton country singer; star of CBC's *Rita MacNeil Show.*

MacNEIL, Robert Breckenridge Ware, media. Toronto, Ont., 1932. TV host, newscaster, reporter, co-hosted public television series in USA, *MacNeil-Lehrer Newshour.*

MacNUTT, Walter, performing arts. Charlottetown, P.E.I., 1910–96. Composer of orchestral, chamber, choral, vocal, and keyboard music; noted for compositions for Anglo-Catholic service.

MACPHAIL, Agnes Campbell, politics. Proton Twp, Ont., 1890–1954. Only woman MP in 1921 (first women's vote); founded Elizabeth Fry Society.

MacPHERSON, Cluny, invention. St John's, Nfld, 1879–1966. Invented the gas helmet.

MacPHERSON, Duncan, visual arts. Toronto, Ont., 1925–93. Long-time *Toronto Star* cartoonist.

MAGEE, Helen Gagan, journalism. Toronto, Ont., 1908–98. Author and food writer for the Toronto *Globe and Mail* and former *Telegram.*

MAGNUSSEN, Karen Diane, sports. North Vancouver, B.C., 1952. Figure skater; world champion, 1973.

MAHONEY, John Keefer, military. New Westminster, B.C., 1911–90. Victoria Cross recipient, WWII, River Melfa, Italy, 1944. Major, Westminster Regiment (Motor).

MAHOVLICH, Francis William, sports. Timmins, Ont., 1938. Toronto Maple Leaf hockey player, 1957–68; winner of Calder Trophy, 1958; in 1998 appointed to the Senate.

MAILLET, Antonine, literary arts. Buctouche, N.B., 1929. Novelist of Acadian life. Winner of France's La Prix Goncourt *La Sagouine.*

MAISONNEUVE, Paul de Chomedey, Sieur de, politics. France, 1612–76. Founder of Montreal, 1642.

MAITLAND, (Herbert) Alan, performing arts. Lilburn, Ont., 1920–99. Long-running CBC radio host noted for his rich, resonant voice; appeared on *Maitland Manor, Read to Me* and from 1974–93 on *As It Happens.*

MAK, Tak Wah, medicine. China, 1946. Research led him to discover the T-cell receptor, crucial to understanding the human immune system.

MANDEL, Howie, performing arts. Toronto, Ont., 1955. Manic comic and TV actor. *St Elsewhere.*

MANGUEL, Alberto Adrian, literary arts. Argentina, 1948. Critic, anthologist, novelist.

MANKIEWICZ, Francis, performing arts. China, 1944–93. Celebrated director noted for his powerful films *Les bons débarras* and *Les Portes Tourantes.* Also directed many CBC dramas.

MANLEY, Elizabeth, sports. Belleville, Ont., 1965. Figure skater; silver medal, 1988 Olympics.

MANLEY, John, politics. Ottawa, Ont., 1950. Liberal MP; Cabinet portfolios have included foreign affairs, industry and finance.

MANNERS, David (b. Rauff de Ryther Duan Acklom), performing arts. Halifax, N.S., 1900–98. Actor; novelist. Manners was a leading Hollywood actor of the 1930s, appearing in films such as *Journey's End; Dracula; The Mummy* and *Jalna.* Wrote novels: *Convenient Season; Under Running Laughter.*

MANNING, Ernest Charles, politics. Carnduff, Sask., 1908–96. Alberta's Social Credit premier 1943–68; father of Reform Party leader Preston Manning.

MANNING, Ernest Preston, politics. Edmonton, Alta, 1942. Led Reform Party to breakthrough in 1993 federal election; leader to 2000.

MANNING, Thomas Henry, exploration and discovery. Eng., 1911–98. Mapmaker who charted vast territories of the Arctic; also biologist and naturalist focusing on Arctic environment.

MANNIS, Harry, media. Toronto, Ont., 1920–2003. Veteran CBC announcer noted for his impeccable delivery; radio announcer for Toronto news program *What's New?* and later hosted TV programs *Themes and Variations* and *Anthology.*

MANSBRIDGE, Peter, media. Eng., 1948. Broadcaster; anchorman, CBC's *The National.*

MANSOURI, Lotfallah (Lotfi), performing arts. Iran, 1929. Former general director of Canadian Opera Company; creator of "surtitles," English translations of librettos screened above stage.

MARCHAND, Leonard Stephen, politics. Vernon, B.C., 1933. Native politician; first native federal cabinet minister.

MARCHILDON, Philip Edward, sports. Penetanguishene, Ont., 1913–97. Baseball player who began his career with Philadelphia Athletics in 1940; won 68 major league games before retirement in 1950.

MARCUS, Rudolph A., science. Montreal, Que., 1923. Winner of 1992 Nobel Prize in chemistry for work on electron transfer reactions in chemical systems.

MARGISON, Richard, performing arts. Victoria, B.C., 1953. Tenor opera singer whose repertoire includes Verdi, Puccini and Bizet; international reputation.

MARIE-VICTORIN, Frère, science. Kingsley Falls, Que., 1885–1944. Distinguished botanist, author of *Croquis laurentiens; Les filicinée de Québec.*

MARK, J. Carson, science. Lindsay, Ont., 1913–97. Head of theoretical division of Los Alamos Scientific Library, influence in creation of hydrogen bomb.

MARQUETTE, Jacques, exploration and discovery. France, 1637–75. Jesuit priest explored North America with Louis Jolliet; served at Sault Ste Marie, 1666.

MARSHALL, Donald, law. Sydney, N.S., 1953. Acquitted of murder after serving 11 years in prison.

MARSHALL, Lois Catherine, performing arts. Toronto, Ont., 1924–97. Soprano, career began with Sir Ernest MacMillan's Bach's *St Matthew's Passion* with Mendelssohn Choir and Toronto Symphony; Toronto Arts Award for Music, 1989.

MARSHALL, Phyllis, performing arts. Barrie, Ont., 1921–96. Jazz singer; pioneer among black Canadian performers; performed with Cab Calloway, Percy Faith; 1949–52 on CBC radio's *Blues for Friday.*

MARTIN, Andrea, performing arts. USA, 1947. Stage, television and film actor particularly well known for comic roles in *SCTV* series.

MARTIN, Clara Brett, law. Toronto, Ont., 1874–1923. First woman lawyer in British Empire.

MARTIN, Paul Edgar Philippe, politics. Windsor, Ont., 1938. Replaced Jean Chrétien as prime minister in 2003. Liberal minister of finance 1993–2002.

MARTIN, Paul Joseph James, politics. Ottawa, Ont., 1903–92. Long-time Liberal Cabinet minister.

MARTIN, Peter, literary arts. Ottawa, Ont., 1934–2003. Founder with his wife, Carol, of the Readers Club of Canada, publishing Canadian authors' books under the Peter Martin Associates imprint.

MARTINI, Paul, sports. Weston, Ont., 1960. Figure skater; world pairs champion (with Barbara Underhill), 1984.

MASON, Roger Burford, literary arts. Eng., 1943–98. Editor and writer, short stories: *The Beaver Picture & Other Stories;* biography of John Evans, who devised a Cree alphabet (*Travels in the Shining Island*); and a biography of artist Franz Johnson.

MASSE, Marcel, politics. St-Jean-de-Matha, Que., 1936. Leader of Union Nationale 1966–70; later minister of communications; national defense in PC federal government.

MASSEY, Charles Vincent, politics. Toronto, Ont., 1887–1967. First Canadian-born governor general, 1952–59.

MASSEY, Hart Almerrin, business. Haldemand Twp, Ont., 1823–96. Capitalist; developed Massey-Ferguson Ltd.

MASSEY, Raymond Hart, performing arts. Toronto, Ont., 1896–1983. Craggy-faced stage, film and TV actor; played Dr. Gillespie in 1960s *Dr. Kildare* TV series. *Prisoner of Zenda; Fire Over England.*

ASSON, Henri Leopold, visual arts. Belgium, 1907–96. Paintings of city and landscapes in the 1940s; National Gallery.

MAXWELL, Lois (b. Lois Ruth Hooker), performing arts. Kitchener, Ont., 1927. Actress, columnist. Played character Moneypenny in James Bond movie series from 1963–83. Former columnist for *Toronto Sun.*

MAYER, Louis B. (Burt) (b. Eliezer Maéyer), performing arts. Russia, 1885–1957. Grew up in Saint John, N.B.; with Samuel Goldwyn formed MGM movie studio in 1924; co-founded the Academy of Motion Picture Arts and Sciences in 1927.

McBEAN, Marnie, sports. Toronto, Ont., 1968. With Kathleen Heddle won women's double sculls rowing medals: two gold in 1992 Barcelona Olympics; one gold, one bronze in 1996 Olympics in Atlanta.

McBRIDE, Robert Bruce (Bob), performing arts. Toronto, Ont., 1946–98. Juno-award-winning lead singer of the 1970s rock band Lighthouse.

McCAIN, H. Harrison, business. Florenceville, N.B., 1927–2004. Industrialist; turned potato-processing plant into international firm.

McCALLUM, John, politics. Montreal, Que., 1950. Appointed minister of defense in 2002 in Chrétien government.

McCARTHY, Doris, visual arts. Calgary, Alta, 1910. Artist, calligrapher, more than 90 solo exhibitions.

McCLELLAND, John Gordon (Jack), literary arts. Toronto, Ont., 1922–2004. Publisher; his McClelland & Stewart nurtured Canadian writing; over 5,000 Canadian titles.

McCLUNG, Nellie Letitia, law. Chatsworth, Ont., 1873–1951. Reformer; fought for women's suffrage.

McCONNELL, Robert Murray Gordon, performing arts. London, Ont., 1935. Jazz musician; founded Boss Brass, major big band.

McCOY, Elijah, invention. Colchester, Ont., 1844–92. Son of American slaves, McCoy invented a lubrication process for steam engines in 1872; the "real McCoy" refers to his oiling device for machinery. Also invented the ironing board and lawn sprinkler.

McCRAE, John, literary arts. Guelph, Ont., 1872–1918. Poet/physician who wrote "In Flanders Fields."

McCULLOCH, Bruce Ian, performing arts. Edmonton, Alta, 1961. Versatile comedic actor and founding member of Kids in the Hall comedy troupe; director; writer. *Dog Park; Stealing Harvard.*

McCURDY, Edward Potts, performing arts. USA, 1919–2000. Folk singer, played in Ontario's Mariposa Folk Festival; specialized in Maritime music.

McCURDY, Howard Douglas, politics. London, Ont., 1932. Black activist; also biologist.

McCURDY, John Alexander Douglas, exploration and discovery. Baddeck, N.S., 1886–1961. Pilot; first airplane flight in British Empire in Silver Dart (1909).

McDERMOTT, Dennis, business. Eng., 1922–2003. Labour leader; former president, Canadian Labour Congress.

McDONALD, Bruce, performing arts. Kingston, Ont., 1959. Film director. *Roadkill; Highway 61; Dance Me Outside.*

McDONALD, Kevin Hamilton, performing arts. Montreal, Que., 1961. Comedian who began his career with the comedy troupe Kids in the Hall with CBC. He has appeared widely on Canadian and US TV and film. *The Martin Short Show; Friends.*

McDONOUGH, Pat, business. Ire., 1935. Successful Canadian fashion designer; formerly designed costumes for Diana Rigg in British TV series *The Avengers* and for Princess Diana.

McDOUGALL, Barbara Jean, politics. Toronto, Ont., 1937. PC external affairs minister 1991–93; political commentator and journalist.

McFARLANE, Leslie (Franklin W. Dixon), literary arts. Ottawa, Ont., 1903–77. Author of *Hardy Boys* adventure series.

McFARLENE, Todd, literary arts. Calgary, Alta, 1961. Creator of cult comic book *Spawn;* the first issue in 1992 was best-selling independent comic at 1.7 million copies sold.

McGARRIGLE, Anna and Kate, performing arts. Montreal, Que., 1944, 1946. Songwriters/singers. "Love Over and Over."

McGEE, Thomas D'Arcy, politics. Ire., 1825–68. Eloquent proponent of Confederation; assassinated 1868.

McGIBBON, Pauline Emily, politics. Sarnia, Ont., 1910–2002. Cda's first woman lieutenant-governor (Ont., 1974–80).

McINTOSH, John, invention. USA, 1777–1845. Inventor; developer of McIntosh apple.

McKELLAR, Don, performing arts. Toronto, Ont., 1963. Filmmaker, screenwriter, actor. *Thirty-Two Short Films About Glenn Gould; Last Night.*

McKENNA, Frank Joseph, politics. Apolaqui, N.B., 1948. Liberal premier of N.B. 1987–97.

McKENNA, Patrick Ivan Peter, performing arts. Hamilton, Ont., 1960. Comic actor played Harold on *Red Green Show.* Also on drama series *Traders.*

McKENNITT, Loreena, performing arts. Morden, Man., 1957. Singer; harpist; Celtic music repertoire.

McKENZIE, Hugh, military. Eng., 1885–1917. Victoria Cross recipient, WWI, Battle of Passchendaele, France, 1917. Lieutenant, 7th Company, Canadian Machine Gun Corps.

McKENZIE, Robert Tait, visual arts. Almonte, Ont., 1867–1938. Sculptor, orthopedic surgeon; designer of war memorials, sculptures.

McKEAN, George Burdon, military. Scot., 1883–1982. Victoria Cross recipient, WWI, Gavrelle Sector, France, 1917. Lieutenant, 14th Bn, Royal Montreal Regiment.

McKINNEY, Louise, politics. Frankville, Ont., 1868–1931. First woman in Commonwealth to serve as an MLA (Alberta, 1917), the first year women could vote and run for office.

McKINNEY, Mark, performing arts. Ottawa, Ont., 1959. Member of the Kids in the Hall comedy troupe.

McKINNON, Catherine, performing arts. Saint John, N.B., 1944. Singer, actress.

McKOY, Mark, sports. Guyana, 1961. Hurdler; gold medal, 110 m hurdles, 1992 Olympics.

McLACHLAN, Beverly, public service. Pincher Creek, Alta, 1943. Former B.C. Chief Justice of Supreme Court; in January 2000 became Chief Justice of Supreme Court of Canada.

McLACHLAN, Sara, performing arts. Halifax, N.S., 1968. Singer-songwriter of pop music. *Surfacing.*

McLAREN, Norman, visual arts. Scot., 1914–87. Filmmaker; innovative NFB animator. *Pas de deux.*

McLARNIN, Jimmy, sports. Ire., 1907. Boxer; world welterweight champion, 1933–35.

McLAUCHLAN, Murray Edward, performing arts. Scot., 1948. Country performer; *Swingin' on a Star,* CBC radio (1990), seven-time Juno award winner.

McLAUGHLIN, Audrey, politics. Dutton, Ont., 1936. NDP national leader 1989–95. First woman to lead a national party.

McLAUGHLIN, Col. Robert Samuel, business. Enniskillen, Ont., 1871–1972. Industrialist; founded firm that became General Motors of Canada.

McLEAN, Grant, performing arts. Yorkton, Sask., 1921–2002. Director of production and acting commissioner at the National Film Board 1941–67, McLean was a pioneer of the cinema verité genre. *Target Berlin; The People Between; Labyrinth,* which was created for Expo 67.

McLEAN, Stuart, media. Montreal, Que., 1948. Broadcaster on CBC radio's *Morningside; Vinyl Café;* author of *Welcome Home: Travels in Small Town Canada.*

McLEOD, Alan Arnett "Bus," military. Stonewall, Man., 1899–1918. Victoria Cross recipient, WWI, Albert, France, 1918. Second lieutenant, 2 Squadron, Royal Flying Corps.

McLUHAN, Herbert Marshall, media. Edmonton, Alta, 1911–80. Media theorist; developed theory about "hot" and "cool" media. *The Gutenburg Galaxy.*

McMURTRY, Roland Roy, politics. Toronto, Ont., 1932. Chief Justice of Ontario Court of Justice.

McNAUGHTON, Andrew George Latta, military. Moosomin, NWT, 1887–1966. Army officer, scientist; as chief of general staff of Armed Forces 1929–35 began modernization of nonpermanent militia; 1935–39 president of National Research Council of Canada.

McNAUGHTON, Duncan Anderson, sports. Cornwall, Ont., 1910–98. High jumper; 1932 Olympic high jump gold medal.

McNEIL, Bill, media. Glace Bay, N.S., 1924–2003. Radio host with the CBC; he hosted *Assignments* and *Fresh Air,* and adapted his series of social history books for television: *Voice of the Pioneer.*

McPHERSON, Aimee Semple, religion. Ingersoll, Ont., 1890–1944. Controversial evangelist.

McPHERSON, Donald, sports. Windsor, Ont., 1945. World professional champion figure skater, 1965.

McTAGGART, David, environment. Vancouver, B.C., 1932–2001. Co-founder of environmental protectionist organization Greenpeace International. McTaggart came to prominence when protesting French nuclear testing in 1972 in Polynesia; the French rammed his boat and testing was postponed.

MEAGHER, Blanche Margaret, public service. Halifax, N.S., 1911–99. Canada's first woman ambassador beginning in 1942, Meagher was posted in various locations: Mexico, Israel, Sweden, Uganda and London.

MEHTA, Deepa, performing arts. India, 1950. Award-winning film director, producer and screenwriter. *Sam and Me; Camilla Fire.*

MEIGHEN, Arthur, politics. Anderson, Ont., 1874–1960. Succeeded Sir Robert Borden as prime minister of Canada.

MEIGS, Mary, visual/literary/performing arts. USA, 1917–2002. Painter, illustrator and writer.

MEILLEUR, Marie Louise Febronie Chasse, Kamouraska, Que., 1880–1998. Recognized in 1997 as the world's oldest person, lived in rural Ontario for most of her life.

MERCER, Ruby, performing arts. USA, 1906–99. Former opera singer who debuted at New York's Metropolitan Opera in 1936, Mercer was instrumental in the development of Canadian opera.

MERCREDI, Ovide William, politics. Grand Rapids, Man., 1946. National chief of the Assembly of First Nations, 1991–2000.

MERRIL, Judith, literary arts. USA, 1923–97. Science fiction writer, novelist, editor, short story writer, critic. *Survival Ship and Other Stories; Daughters of the Earth and Other Stories.*

MERRIFIELD, William, military. Eng., 1890–1943. Victoria Cross recipient, WWI, Abancourt, France, 1918. Sergeant, 4th Bn, 1st Central Ontario Regiment.

MERRITT, Charles Cecil Ingersoll, military. Vancouver, B.C., 1908–2000. Victoria Cross recipient, WWII, Dieppe, France, 1942. Lieutenant colonel, South Saskatchewan Regiment.

MESSER, Donald Charles Frederick (Don), performing arts. Tweedside, N.B., 1909–73. Bandleader; popular performer of traditional fiddle and dance music. *Don Messer's Jubilee.*

METCALF, John Wesley, literary arts. Eng., 1938. Essayist, short story writer, editor and publisher. *Going Down Slow; Private Parts: A Memoir; Adult Entertainment.*

METCALF, William Henry, military. USA, 1885–1968. Victoria Cross recipient, WWI, Arras, France, 1918. Lance-corporal, 16th Bn, Manitoba Regiment.

MICHAELS, Lorne (b. Lorne Lipowitz), media. Toronto, Ont., 1945. TV producer; founding producer, *Saturday Night Live.*

MICHENER, Daniel Roland, politics. Lacombe, Alta, 1900–91. Governor general of Canada, 1967–74.

MIKITA, Stan (b. Stanislaus Gvoth), sports. Czech., 1940. Hockey player; centre with Chicago Blackhawks (1959–80); first Czech to play in NHL.

MILLAR, Ian D., sports. Halifax, N.S., 1947. Eight-time Canadian show-jumping champion, Cdn Athlete of the Year, 1987, 1989.

MILNE, David Brown, visual arts. Paisley, Ont., 1882–1953. Versatile painter. *Raspberry Jam.*

MILNE, William Johnstone, military. Scot., 1892–1917. Victoria Cross recipient, WWI, Vimy Ridge, France, 1917. Private, 16th Bn, Manitoba Regiment.

MILNER, Brenda, science. Eng., 1915. Neuropsychologist; ground-breaking brain researcher.

MINER, Harry Garnet Bedford, military. Cedar Springs, Ont., 1891–1918. Victoria Cross recipient, WWI, Demuin, France, 1918. Corporal, 13th Bn, 2nd Central Ontario Regiment.

MINER, John Thomas (Jack), science. USA, 1865–1944. Conservationist; pioneered bird sanctuaries, migratory banding.

MIRVISH, Edwin (Ed) (b. Yehudi Mirvish), business. USA, 1914. Entrepreneur; retailer (Honest Ed's) and theatre owner in Toronto, Ont.

MISTRY, Rohinton, literary arts. India, 1952. Novelist, short story writer. *Such a Long Journey; A Fine Balance* (Giller Prize, 1995).

MITCHELL, Coulson Norman, military. Winnipeg, Man., 1889–1978. Victoria Cross recipient, WWI, Canal de L'Escaut, France, 1918. Captain, 1st Tunneling Company, 4th Canadian Engineers.

MITCHELL, Joni (b. Roberta Joan Anderson), performing arts. Ft Macleod, Alta, 1943. Singer/songwriter; influential lyricist. *Court and Spark.*

MITCHELL, Ray, sports. Peace River, Alta, 1931. Bowler; winner of 1972 Canadian and world 10-pin championship.

MITCHELL, William Ormond (W.O.), literary arts. Weyburn, Sask., 1914–98. Prairie novelist. *Who Has Seen the Wind?*

MOCHRIE, Colin Andrew, performing arts. Scot., 1957. Popular comedian who has appeared on American improv show *Whose Line Is It, Anyway?* as well as CBC's *This Hour Has 22 Minutes.*

MOLSON, John, business. Eng., 1764–1836. Founded Molson brewery; built railroads.

MONK, Lorraine, visual arts. Montreal, Que. Head of the Still Photography division of the National Film Board; first director of the Canadian Museum of Contemporary Photography in Ottawa. *A Year in the Land; The Female Eye.*

MONTCALM, Louis-Joseph de, Marquis de Montcalm, military. France, 1712–59. Soldier; French commander in Seven Years War; died on Plains of Abraham.

MONTGOMERY, Lucy Maud, literary arts. Clifton, P.E.I., 1874–1942. Writer; creator of *Anne of Green Gables.*

MONTGOMERY, Robert Douglas, performing arts. Bradford, Ont., 1908–66. Movie actor, played Laurie in 1933 version of *Little Women* opposite Katharine Hepburn.

MOODIE, Susanna, literary arts. Eng., 1803–85. Writer; pioneer author of *Roughing It in the Bush.*

MOORE, Brian, literary arts. N Ire., 1921–99. Prolific novelist; winner of two Governor General's Awards. *The Luck of Ginger Coffey; Black Robe.*

MOORE, Dora Mavor, performing arts. Scot., 1888–1979. Actress appeared in Canada and US; founded Village Players in 1938 in Toronto, Ont.; toured schools. *Spring Thaw.*

MOORE, Gregory William, sports. Vancouver, B.C., 1975–99. Four time winner of Championship Auto Racing Teams (CART) circuit; died in Marlboro 500 race in California.

MOORE, James Mavor, literary arts. Toronto, Ont., 1919. TV producer; librettist; columnist; critic.

MOORES, Frank Duff, politics. Carbonear, Nfld, 1933. PC premier of Newfoundland, 1972–79.

MORANIS, Rick, performing arts. Toronto, Ont., 1953. Comedian; actor; *SCTV* regular. *Ghostbusters.*

MORAWETZ, Oskar, performing arts. Czech., 1917. Composer. *From the Diary of Anne Frank.*

MORENZ, Howarth Williams (Howie), sports. Mitchell, Ont., 1902–37. Hockey player, centre; Canada's player of half century (CP), 1950; died of on-ice injuries.

MORGAN, Henry, business. Scot., 1819–93. In 1852 Morgan founded a dry goods store in Montreal, which by 1950 became the national chain Henry Morgan & Co.; merged with Hudson's Bay Company in 1960.

MORGAN, John, performing arts. Wales. Comedian who appeared on CBC's *Royal Canadian Air Farce,* roles include Jock McBile and Mike from Canmore.

MORGENTALER, Henry, medicine. Poland, 1923. Physician; challenge of abortion laws led to Supreme Court ruling them unconstitutional.

MORISSETTE, Alanis Nadine, performing arts. Ottawa, Ont., 1974. Singer-songwriter. Juno award winner 1996 for *Jagged Little Pill* (Best Album) and Female Vocalist of the Year; Grammy Award winner, 1996.

MORIYAMA, Raymond, visual arts. Vancouver, B.C., 1929. Architect; Ontario Science Centre.

MORRICE, James Wilson (J.W.), visual arts. Montreal, Que., 1864–1924. Artist; early modernist. *The Ice Bridge.*

MORRIS, Alwyn, sports. Montreal, Que., 1957. With Hugh Fisher won gold medal in 1000 m and bronze in 500 m kayak doubles at 1984 Olympics.

MORRIS, Joseph (Joe), politics. Eng., 1913–96. Former president of Canadian Labour Congress; chairman of International Labour Organization.

MORRISON, Bram, performing arts. Toronto, Ont., 1940. Member of children's musical entertainment group Sharon, Lois and Bram; live and on TV. *The Elephant Show.*

MORRISSEAU, Norval, visual arts. Sand Point Reserve, Ont., 1932. Ojibwa artist originated pictographic style.

MORSE, Barry, performing arts. Eng., 1918. Stage/film/TV actor; regular on *The Fugitive.*

MORTON, William Lewis (W.L.), literary arts. Gladstone, Man., 1908–80. Historian. *Manitoba: A History.*

MOSS, Carrie-Anne, performing arts. Vancouver, B.C., 1967. Model turned film and television actress. *Matrix; Models Inc; Dark Justice; F/X The Series.*

MOWAT, Claire Angel, literary arts. Toronto, Ont., 1933. Graphic artist, fiction writer, wife of writer Farley Mowat. *The Girl From Away; The Outport People; The French Isles.*

MOWAT, Farley McGill, literary arts. Belleville, Ont., 1921. Controversial, popular naturalist writer. *A Whale for the Killing.*

MOWAT, Sir Oliver, politics. Kingston, UC, 1820–1903. Ontario premier, 1872–96; lieutenant governor, 1897–1903.

MULLIN, George Harry, military. USA, 1892–1963. Victoria Cross recipient, WWI, Battle of Passchendaele, France, 1917. Sergeant, Princess Patricia's Canadian Light Infantry, Eastern Ontario Regiment.

MULRONEY, Brian Martin, politics. Baie Comeau, Que., 1939. PC prime minister of Canada 1984–93.

MUNDELL, Robert, business. Kingston, Ont., 1932. Winner of 1999 Nobel Prize for economics for 1960s study of exchange rates and their relationship to monetary policy.

MUNK, Peter, business. Hungary, 1927. Capitalist; CEO, American Barrick Resources gold mining company.

MUNRO, Alice, literary arts. Wingham, Ont., 1931. Short story writer. Winner of 1998 Giller prize for *The Love of a Good Woman. Lives of Girls and Women.*

MUNSCH, Robert, literary arts. USA, 1945. Children's writer. *The Paper Bag Princess; Love You Forever.*

MURPHY, Emily Cowan, law. Cookstown, Ont., 1868–1933. Legal reformer; first woman magistrate in British Empire; fought for women's rights.

MURPHY, Rex, media. Carbonear, Nfld, 1947. CBC news journalist with acerbic style. *Cross Country Checkup.*

MURRAY, Anne, performing arts. Springhill, N.S., 1945. Singer; Canada's most successful performer; many Junos and Grammys. "Snowbird."

MURRAY, George Henry, politics. Grand Narrows, N.S., 1861–1929. Lib. premier of N.S., 1896–1923.

MURRAY, John Wilson, law. Scot., 1840–1906. Detective; pioneered scientific crime detection.

MURRAY, Margaret Teresa "Ma," media. USA, 1888–1982. Journalist; pungent editorialist in own magazines.

MURRAY, Robert George Everitt, science. Eng., 1919. With Philip Fitz-Jones, researched structure and chemical nature of bacterial spores.

MUSGRAVE, Susan, literary arts. USA, 1951. Poet, novelist, children's writer. *The Embalmer's Art: Poems; The Charcoal Burners.*

MUSTARD, James Fraser, medicine. Toronto, Ont., 1927. Physician; medical humanitarian; found connection between aspirin and blood clotting.

MUSTARD, William, medicine. Clinton, Ont., 1914–87. Physician; beloved children's surgeon developed operations for blue babies, polio victims.

MYERS, Barton, visual arts. USA, 1934. Architect. Seagram Museum in Waterloo, Ont.; U of Toronto's Woodsworth College; UCLA Northwest Commons and Housing.

MYERS, Mike, performing arts. Toronto, Ont., 1963. Comic actor has appeared in movies *Austin Powers; It's a Dog's Life; Wayne's World;* also appeared on TV late-night show *Saturday Night Live.*

MYLES, Alannah, performing arts. Toronto, Ont., 1958. Pop singer/composer of hard rock, ballads. "Lover of Mine"; *Black Velvet; Al-Lan-Nah.*

MYNARSKI, Andrew Charles, military. Winnipeg, Man., 1916–1944. Victoria Cross recipient, WWII, Cambrai, France, 1944. Warrant Officer II, 419 Squadron, RCAF.

NAISMITH, James A., sports. Almonte, Que., 1861–1939. Physician; invented basketball in 1891.

NAKAMURA, Kazuo, visual arts. Vancouver, B.C., 1926–2002. Abstract artist, member of Painters Eleven with such luminaries as William Ronald and Harold Town, noted for his subdued style. *Reflections; Block Structure.*

NAMARO, James (Jimmy), performing arts. USA, 1913–98. A member of the CBC's *Happy Gang,* the longest-running program on the radio network; also led his own jazz band.

NANOGAK, Agnes, visual arts. Baillie I., NWT, 1925. Inuit artist whose prints depict Inuit myths and legends, operating out of Holman I. artist co-op. Illustrated *Tales from the Igloo.*

NASH, Cyril Knowlton, media. Toronto, Ont., 1927. Broadcaster; former anchorman, CBC national news.

NATTRASS, Susan Marie, sports. Medicine Hat, Alta, 1950. Shooter; six women's world trapshooting titles.

NAULT, Fernand (b. Fernand-Noel Boissonneault), performing arts. Montreal, Que., 1921. Dancer; choreographer, Les Grands Ballets Canadiens.

NELLIGAN, Émile, literary arts. Montreal, Que., 1879–1941. Romantic poet. "Romance du Vin."

NELLIGAN, Kate, performing arts. London, Ont., 1951. Actor; appears on both stage and film. *Eleni.*

NEMETZ, Nathaniel "Sonny," law. Winnipeg, Man., 1913–97. Chief Justice of British Columbia 1979–88; leading judicial administrator in B.C..

NEVILLE, John, performing arts. Eng., 1925. Actor, director. Stratford Festival, Ont.; director of Stratford's The Young Company.

NEWMAN, Peter Charles, media. Austria, 1929. Journalist; popular historian. *The Canadian Establishment, Maclean's* editor, 1971–82.

NEWTON, Margaret, science. Montreal, Que., 1887–1971. Plant pathologist; first scientist to research rust in wheat.

NICHOL, Barrie Phillip (bp), literary arts. Vancouver, B.C., 1944–88. Concrete and sound poet, novelist. *Journeying and Returns; Love: A Book of Remembrance.*

NICHOL, Dave, business. Chatham, Ont., 1940. Made Loblaws stores market leader with President's Choice label.

NICHOLAS, Cynthia (Cindy), sports. Toronto, Ont., 1957. Marathon swimmer; first woman to swim English Channel both ways.

NICKERSON, William Henry Snyder, military. Saint John, N.B., 1875–1954. Victoria Cross recipient, Boer War, South Africa, 1900. Lieutenant, Royal Army Medical Corps, British Army.

NICOL, Eric, media. Kingston, Ont., 1919. Humour columnist. "Girdle Me a Globe."

NIELSEN, Erik Hersholt, politics. Regina, Sask., 1924. PC MP elected in Yukon 1957, served as deputy prime minister in Mulroney government.

NIELSEN, Leslie, performing arts. Regina, Sask., 1926. Deadpan film/TV comedian. *Naked Gun.*

NORQUAY, John, politics. St Andrews, Man., 1841–89. Manitoba premier of mixed European and native ancestry, 1878–87.

NORTHCOTT, Ronald Charles, sports. Innisfail, Alta, 1935. Curler; skipped three Brier and world champion rinks.

NOTMAN, William, visual arts. Scot., 1826–91. Innovative Montreal-based portrait photographer who sent his studio photographers across Canada and the US to record social landscape, recording the growth and character of the continent.

NOWLAN, Alden, literary arts. Windsor, N.S., 1933–83. Poet. "Bread, Wine and Salt."

NUNNEY, Claude Joseph Patrick, military. Eng., 1892–1918. Victoria Cross recipient, WWI, Drocourt-Quéant Line, France, 1918. Private, 38th Bn, Eastern Ontario Regiment.

OAKS, Sir Harry, business, USA, 1874–1943. Oaks made his fortune through gold mine near Swastika, Ont., became North America's second-largest gold mine; retired to the Bahamas; victim of unsolved murder.

O'BRIEN, Mary, public service. Scot., 1926–98. Midwife, philosopher; founding member of the Feminist Party of Canada; wrote *The Politics of Reproduction; Reproducing the World.*

ODJIG, Daphne, visual arts. Manitoulin Island, Ont., 1919. Blends western and native styles. *The Indian in Transition.*

OH, Sandra, performing arts. Nepean, Ont., 1971. Korean-Canadian actress appeared in TV version of *The Diary of Evelyn Lau;* also stage production of *Oleanna.*

O'HARA, Catherine, performing arts. Toronto, Ont., 1954. Actor; comedian; *SCTV* regular (Lola Heatherton).

OKALIK, Paul, politics. Pangnirtung, NWT, 1964. First premier of 19-member Legislative Assembly for Nunavit in the Eastern Arctic, created in 1999.

O'KELLY, Christopher Patrick, military. Winnipeg, Man., 1895–1923. Victoria Cross recipient, WWI, Battle of Passchendaele, France, 1917. Captain, 52nd Bn, Manitoba Regiment.

OLCOTT, Sidney, performing arts. Toronto, Ont., 1873–1949. Director of Hollywood silent films, pioneered locations shots, westerns. *Ben Hur.*

O'LEARY, Michael John, military. Ire., 1889–1961. Victoria Cross recipient, WWI, Cuinchy, France, 1915. Lance-corporal, 1st Bn, Irish Guards.

OLIPHANT, Betty, performing arts. Eng., 1918–2004. Founded National Ballet School.

OLSEN, Horace "Bud," politics. Iddesleigh, Alta, 1925–2002. Liberal Cabinet minister during Trudeau years; lieutenant governor of Alberta 1996–2000; noted parliamentarian.

ONDAATJE, Christopher, business/literary arts. Sri Lanka, 1933. Financier; author. *Leopard in the Afternoon.*

ONDAATJE, Michael, literary arts. Sri Lanka, 1943. Poet; editor; novelist. *The English Patient* (Booker Prize); 2000 Giller Prize for *Anil's Ghost.*

O'NEILL, James Edward "Tip," sports. Canada W, 1859–1918. Baseball player; batted .326 in 10-year career.

OONARK, Jessie, visual arts. Back River, NWT, 1906–85. Inuit artist who employed brilliant colours to depict both traditional images and Christian themes in her drawings and wall hangings.

ORBINSKI, James, medicine. Eng., 1960. President, International Council, for Doctors Without Borders; accepted 1999 Nobel Peace Prize on behalf of the international organization.

ORONHYATEKHA (Peter Martin), business. Six Nations Reserve, Ont., 1841–1907. First native Canadian to receive a degree from a Canadian university; founder of the Independent Order of Foresters, a fraternal life insurance organization.

O'ROURKE, Michael James, military. Ire., 1878–1957. Victoria Cross recipient, WWI, Battle of Hill 70, Lens, France, 1917. Private, 7th Bn, British Columbia Regiment.

ORR, Robert Gordon (Bobby), sports. Parry Sound, Ont., 1948. Hockey player; spectacular offensive defenceman; won eight consecutive Norris trophies.

ORSER, Brian Ernest, sports. Belleville, Ont., 1961. Figure skater; 1987 world champion, twice Olympic silver medallist (1984, 1988).

ORTON, George W., sports. Strathroy, Ont., 1873–1958. Runner; Canada's first Olympic gold medallist, winning for USA in 1900 (2500 m steeplechase).

OSBORN, John Robert, military. USA, 1899–1941. Victoria Cross recipient, WWII, Mount Butler, Hong Kong, 1941. Company Sergeant-Major, 1st Bn, Winnipeg Grenadiers.

OSGOODE, William, law. Eng., 1754–1824. First chief justice of Upper Canada; played key role in development of Canadian legislation.

OSLER, Sir William, medicine. Bond Head, UC, 1849–1919. Physician; renowned medical educator; author of authoritative textbooks.

OSTANEK, Walter, performing arts. Duparket, Que., 1935. "King of Polka"; popular piano accordionist with more than 60 polka recordings and multiple Grammy awards.

OTTENBRITE, Anne, sports. Whitby, Ont., 1966. Swimmer; gold medal, 200 m, 1984 Olympics.

OUIMET, Joseph Alphonse, media. Montreal, Que., 1908–88. TV executive; designed first Canadian TV receiver; CBC president, 1958–67.

PACE, Kate, sports. North Bay, Ont., 1969. Skier; World Cup downhill champion, 1993.

PACHTER, Charles, visual arts. Toronto, Ont., 1942. Painter famous for flag series; 1973 acrylic sketch titled *Queen on Moose.*

PAGE, Patricia Kathleen, (P.K.), literary arts. Eng., 1916. Poet; novelist; artist. "The Metal and the Flower."

PANNETON, Philippe (Ringuet), literary arts. Trois-Rivières, Que., 1895–1960. Man of letters; acclaimed Quebec writer. *Trente Arpents.*

PAPINEAU, Louis Joseph, politics. Montreal, Que., 1786–1871. Led political reform movement in Lower Canada.

PARENT, Etienne, politics. Beauport, UC, 1802–74. Editor of *La Gazette de Québec* and *Le Canadien;* early advocate for French-Canadian nationalism, later lectured at Institut Canadien to promote business and industry, education reform and political economy.

PARIS, Erna, literary arts. Toronto, Ont., 1938. Writer. *The Garden and the Gun; End of Days.*

PARIZEAU, Jacques, politics. Montreal, Que., 1930. Leader, Parti Québécois 1987–95.

PARKER, Cecilia, performing arts. Fort William, Ont., 1905–93. Famous for playing Andy Hardy's older sister in the *Andy Hardy* film series; also appeared in Hollywood westerns and action films of the 1930s.

PARKER, Jackie, sports. USA, 1932. Football player; coach; Edmonton Eskimos star quarterback; named CFL outstanding player three times.

PARKER, Jon Kimura, performing arts. Vancouver, B.C., 1959. Concert pianist, performed for Queen, prime ministers, and at Carnegie Hall.

PARKIN, John Burnett, visual arts. Toronto, Ont., 1911–75. Partnered with John Cresswell Parkin (no relation) to build major public buildings, including hospitals, schools, airports. Largest firm in Canada in the 1950s and '60s. Union Station (Ottawa); IBM head office (Toronto).

PARROT, Jean-Claude, business. Montreal, Que., 1936. Labour leader; head of militant postal union.

PARRY, Sir William Edward, exploration and discovery. Eng., 1790–1855. Parry's explorations into the Arctic led to the discovery of the North Pole and the charting of the Northwest Passage.

PARTRIDGE, Edward Alexander, business. Canada W, 1862–1931. Farm reformer; visionary in grain industry who fought monopolies, started growers' cooperative.

PASSAGLIA, Lui, sports. Vancouver, B.C., 1954. Football player; kicker with B.C. Lions; CFL's all-time scoring leader.

PATRICK, Lester, sports. Drummondville, Que., 1883–1960. Hockey executive; NHL builder.

PATTISON, James Allen, business. Saskatoon, Sask., 1928. Industrialist; developed car dealership into business empire; chairman, Expo 86.

PATTISON, John George, military. Eng., 1875–1917. Victoria Cross recipient, WWI, Vimy Ridge, France, 1917. Private, Alberta Regiment.

PAUL, Robert, sports. Toronto, Ont., 1937. Figure skater; with Barbara Wagner, won four pairs titles, 1960 Olympic gold.

PAYETTE, Julie, science. Montreal, Que., 1963. Astronaut and mission specialist on crew of STS-96 *Discovery*, a 10-day logistics and resupply mission that launched in May 1999.

PAYETTE, Lise, media/politics. Montreal, Que., 1931. Broadcaster, writer, politician; her radio show with Radio-Canada, *Place Aux Femmes*, aired in the 1960s; Parti Québécois MNA 1976–80.

PEAKER, Charles, performing arts. Eng., 1899–1978. Organist, choirmaster, writer. Foremost concert organist in Canada. Edited *Organ Music of Canada*.

PEARKES, George Randolph, military. Eng., 1888–1984. Victoria Cross recipient, WWI, Battle of Passchendaele, France, 1917. Major, 5th Canadian Mounted Rifles Bn, Quebec Regiment.

PEARSON, Lester Bowles, politics. Newtonbrook, Ont., 1897–1972. Lib. prime minister of Canada 1963–1968; awarded Nobel Peace Prize in 1957.

PECK, Cyrus Wesley, military. Hopewell Hill, N.B., 1871–1956. Victoria Cross recipient, WWI, Cagnicourt, France, 1918. Lieutenant colonel, 16th Bn, Manitoba Regiment.

PECKFORD, Alfred Brian, politics. Whitbourne, Nfld, 1942. PC premier of Nfld, 1979–89.

PEEL, Paul, visual arts. London, Ont., 1860–92. Painter famous for *After the Bath*, which depicts two children warming themselves before a fireplace. *The Tired Model; Good News, Toronto.*

PELADEAU, Pierre, media. Outremont, Que., 1925–97. Publisher; head of newspaper giant Quebecor.

PELLAN, Alfred, visual arts. Quebec City, Que., 1906–88. Painter; cubist and surrealist artist.

PELLATT, Sir Henry Mill, military. Kingston, Canada W, 1860–1939. Soldier; builder of eccentric Toronto mansion, Casa Loma.

PELLETIER, David, sports. Sayabec, Que., 1974. With Jamie Salé won gold medal in pairs figure skating at 2002 Salt Lake City Winter Olympics; the award was presented after controversy over prior judging that placed Russian team at top with Salé and Pelletier first winning silver.

PELLETIER, Gerard, politics. Victoriaville, Que., 1919–97. Chief editor for *La Presse* (1961–65); federal deputy minister for Montreal riding of Hochelaga 1965–75. Later ambassador for Canada in Paris and for United Nations.

PENFIELD, Wilder Groves Dr, medicine. USA, 1891–1976. Neurologist; writer; pioneered mapping of brain functions; founded Montreal Neurological Inst.

PENNELL, Nicholas, performing arts. Eng., 1938–95. Former actor at Stratford Festival; starred in British TV series *The Forsyte Saga*.

PENNER, Fredrick Ralph, performing arts. Winnipeg, Man., 1946. Popular children's entertainer; host of CBC TV's *Fred Penner's Place;* former national spokesperson for UNICEF. *Moonlight Express.*

PENTLAND, Barbara Lally, performing arts. Winnipeg, Man., 1912–2000. Celebrated avant-garde composer; noted for anti-tonal style. *Concerto for Piano and String Orchestra.*

PEPIN, Jean-Luc, politics. Drummondville, Que., 1924–95. Longtime Liberal cabinet minister; served on Anti-Inflation Board, co-chairman of 1977 unity task force.

PEPIN, Marcel, politics. Montreal, Que., 1926–2000. Became president of Confederation of National Trade unions in 1965; responsible for uniting public service unions in Quebec and instigator of illegal Common Front Strike of 1972; later head of World Confederation of Labour.

PERCIVAL, Lloyd, sports. Toronto, Ont., 1913–74. Sports enthusiast; in 1941 founded CBC Radio Sports College; founder of Fitness Institute and coach to many successful athletes.

PERCY, Karen, sports. Edmonton, Alta, 1966. Skier; won two bronze medals, 1988 Olympics.

PERRAULT, Jean-Pierre, performing arts. Montreal, Que., 1947–2002. Montreal-based dancer and choreographer with signature style of complex lighting and staging techniques. Founder of Fondation Jean-Pierre Perrault.

PERRAULT, Pierre, visual arts. Montreal, Que., 1927. Filmmaker; realist director. *L'Acadie, L'Acadie.*

PETERS, Frederick Thornton, military. Charlottetown, P.E.I., 1889–1942. Victoria Cross recipient, WWII, Oran Harbour, Algeria, 1942. Captain, Royal Navy.

PETERSON, Eric, performing arts. Indian Head, Sask., 1946. Actor. *Billy Bishop Goes to War;* CBC's *Street Legal* series.

PETERSON, Oscar Emmanuel, performing arts. Montreal, Que., 1925. Jazz pianist/composer. As leader of the Oscar Peterson Trio, he has recorded more than 100 albums. *Canadiana Suite; Night Train.*

PETRIE, Daniel, performing arts. Glace Bay, N.S., 1920. Film director, won Genie award for *Bay Boy; A Raisin in the Sun.*

PETTIGREW, Pierre, politics. Quebec City, Que., 1951. Liberal MP; minister of international trade; strong federalist voice against Quebec separatism.

PEZER, Vera, sports. Melfort, Sask., 1939. Curler; Canadian women's champion, 1971–73.

PFLUG, Christiane, visual arts. Germany, 1936–72. Painter of melancholy landscapes and domestic scenes. *Cottingham School After the Rain; Kitchen Door with Esther.*

PHILLIPS, Robin, performing arts. Eng., 1942. Director, Ontario's Stratford Festival, 1975–80, 1986–87.

PICKERSGILL, John Whitney, politics. Wyecombe, Ont., 1905–97. Public servant, politician and historian who advised prime ministers Mackenzie King and Louis St. Laurent on policy; became president of Canadian Transport Commission in 1967. Wrote *My Years With Louis St. Laurent.*

PICKFORD, Mary (b. Gladys Smith), performing arts. Toronto, Ont., 1893–1979. Actress; "America's Sweetheart" was early movie star. *Sparrows.*

PIDGEON, Walter, performing arts. E Saint John, N.B., 1897–1984. Leading man. *Mrs. Miniver.*

PINSENT, Gordon Edward, performing arts. Grand Falls, Nfld, 1930. Versatile actor. *The Rowdyman; Due South.*

PINSENT, Leah, performing arts. Toronto, Ont., 1964. Actress, daughter of Gordon Pinsent. Has appeared on film (*The Bay Boy*) and TV (*More Tears; Made in Canada*).

PITSEOLAK Ashoona, visual arts. NWT, 1904–83. Artist of Inuit myth and legend.

PITSEOLAK, Peter, visual arts. NWT, 1902–73. Photographer; recorded passing of traditional Inuit life.

PLAMONDON, Antoine, visual arts. Lorette, Que., 1804–95. Portraitist and religious painter.

PLAMONDON, Luc, performing arts. St Raymond-de-Portneuf, Que., 1945. Lyricist; wrote rock opera *Starmania;* collaborated with Britain's Tim Rice; has written songs for Céline Dion.

PLANTE, Jacques, sports. Mt Carmel, Que., 1929–86. Hockey goaltender; seven-time Vezina winner; originated face mask.

PLAUNT, Alan Butterworth, media. Ottawa, Ont., 1904–41. With Graham Spry founded the Canadian Radio League in 1930, an association that promoted public broadcasting. The CRL was a precursor to the CBC; Plaunt sat on the first board of governors.

PLAUT, Rabbi Gunther, religion. Germany, 1912. Rabbi (Toronto's Holy Blossom Temple); author; advocate of modern secular Judaism. Wrote *The Torah: A Modern Commentary; The Man Who Would Be Messiah,* a novel.

PLUMMER, Arthur Christopher Orme, performing arts. Toronto, Ont., 1929. Stage and film star. *The Sound of Music.*

POCKLINGTON, Peter H., business. Regina, Sask., 1941. Entrepreneur; former owner of Edmonton Oilers hockey team.

POCOCK, Nancy Meek, philanthropy. USA, 1911–98. Quaker and pacifist, an antiwar and refugee advocate; won the Medal of Friendship from Socialist Republic of Vietnam.

PODBORSKI, Steve, sports. Toronto, Ont., 1957. Skier; world downhill champion, 1982.

POITRAS, Jean-Claude, business. Montreal, Que., 1949. Designer of couture-quality fashion under own label; founder of Fashion Société Design collections.

POLANYI, John Charles, science. Germany, 1929. Chemist; Nobel Prize (1986) for work on infrared chemiluminescence.

POLLEY, Sarah, performing arts. Toronto, Ont., 1979. Actress; *The Road to Avonlea; The Sweet Hereafter.*

POLLOCK, Sam, sports. Montreal, Que., 1925. Hockey executive; built Montreal Canadiens dynasty.

POLLOCK, Sharon, literary arts. Fredericton, N.B., 1936. Playwright; writer of conscience. *Blood Relations.*

PONTIAC, military. USA, c.1720–69. Ottawa Indian chief who formed alliance with various Indian federations to attack English, including a fort at Point Pelee, Ont.; in 1765 key signer of peace treaties with the English.

PORTER, Anna Maria, literary arts. Hungary. Publisher, author. CEO and director of Key Porter Books; mystery writer. *The Bookfair Murders; Mortal Sins.*

POST, Sandra, sports. Oakville, Ont., 1943. Golfer; Canada's first woman touring professional.

POTTS, Jerry (b. Ky-yo-Kosi), military. USA, 1840–96. Native scout; Blackfoot became NWMP special constable.

POTVIN, Dennis, sports. Ottawa, Ont., 1953. Hockey player; as defenceman with New York Islanders (1973–88) all-time leader in goals and assists.

POWELL, Marion, medicine. Toronto, Ont., 1923–97. Former president of Planned Parenthood in Toronto; a pioneer in introducing birth control information in the 1960s.

POWLESS, Alex Ross, sports. Six Nations Reserve, Ont., 1926–2003. Lacrosse champion whose team, the Peterborough Timbermen, won four Mann Cups; he also coached his son Gaylord Powless, champion lacrosse player.

POWLESS, Gaylord Ross, sports. Brantford, Ont., 1946–2001. Award-winning lacrosse player who led the Oshawa Green Gaels to seven successive championships; winner of 1964 Tom Longboat native athlete award.

PRATLEY, Gerald Arthur, performing arts. Eng., 1923. Film critic; founder of Ontario Film Institute in 1968; CBC's first film critic 1948–75. *Pratley at the Movies.*

PRATT, Edwin James (E.J.), literary arts. Western Bay, Nfld, 1883–1964. Leading pre-WWII poet. "Newfoundland Verse."

PRATT, John Christopher, visual arts. St John's, Nfld, 1935. Artist; developed style of "conceptual realism."

PRATT, Mary, visual arts. Fredericton, N.B., 1935. Artist; her paintings portray kitchen imagery and domestic themes. Illustrated Cynthia Wine's *Across the Table: An Indulgent Look at Food in Canada.*

PREVOST, André, performing arts. Hawkesbury, Ont., 1934–2001. Quebec-based composer whose humanistic works included *Terre des Hommes (Man and His World); Cantate pour cordes* and *Choréographie,* which was inspired by the 1972 assassination of Olympic athletes in Munich.

PRIESTLEY, Jason Bradford, performing arts. Vancouver, B.C., 1969. Popular actor. *Beverly Hills, 90210.*

PURDY, Alfred Wellington, literary arts. Wooler, Ont., 1918–2000. Working-class poet. "The Cariboo Horses."

QUARRINGTON, Paul Lewis, literary arts. Toronto, Ont., 1953. Author; won 1989 Governor General's Award for Fiction (*Whale Music*). *Home Game.*

QUILICO, Louis, performing arts. Montreal, Que., 1925–2000. Operatic baritone; appeared with most major companies.

R

RADDAL, Thomas Head, literary arts. Eng., 1903–94. Governor General's Award-winning historical novelist. *Pied Piper of Dipper Creek and Other Tales; His Majesty's Yankees.*

RADISSON, Pierre Esprit, exploration and discovery. France, 1636–1710. Explorer; fur trader; important in early history of Hudson's Bay Co. as guide and advisor.

RAE, John, exploration and discovery. Orkney, 1813–93. Explorer who found evidence of Sir John Franklin's fated expedition in the Canadian north; surveyor for the Hudson's Bay Company, charting northern regions and western Canada.

RAE, Robert Keith (Bob), politics. Ottawa, Ont., 1948. NDP premier of Ontario 1990–95.

RAFFI (b. Raffi Cavoukian), performing arts. Egypt, 1948. Singer; children's entertainer. *Baby Beluga.*

RAIN, Douglas, performing arts. Winnipeg, Man., 1928. Actor; has played more than 30 seasons with Ontario's Stratford Festival; voice of Hal the Computer in the films *2001* and *2002.*

RANKIN, John Morris, performing arts. Mabou, N.S., 1959–2000. Head of musical group The Rankin Family, later The Rankins, Cape Breton musicians instrumental in popular revival of East Coast Celtic tradition.

RASKY, Harry, performing arts. Toronto, Ont., 1928. Noted documentary filmmaker. *The Dispossessed: The War Against the Indians.*

RASMINSKY, Louis, business. Montreal, Que., 1908–98. Governor, Bank of Canada, 1961–72.

RAYFIELD, Walter Leigh, military. Eng., 1881–1949. Victoria Cross recipient, WWI, Arras, France, 1918. Private, 7th Bn, British Columbia Regiment.

RAYNER, Gordon, visual arts. Toronto, Ont., 1935. Realist, abstract painter, landscapes and cityscapes; northern Ontario landscapes. *Magnetawan No. 2.*

READ, Ken, sports. USA, 1955. Canadian skier; winner of five World Cup downhill victories (1975–80).

READE, Herbert Taylor, military. Perth, Upper Canada, 1828–97. Victoria Cross recipient, Indian Mutiny, 1857. Surgeon, 61st Regiment (later the Gloucestershire Regiment).

REANEY, James Crerar, literary arts. Easthope, Ont., 1926. Playwright; poet; critic. "A Suit of Nettles."

REBICK, Judy, politics. USA, 1945. Former head, Natl Action Committee on Status of Women.

REED, George Robert, sports. USA, 1939. Football player; running back with Sask. Roughriders; 44 CFL records.

REEVES, Keanu, performing arts. Lebanon, 1965. Actor. *Bill and Ted's Excellent Adventure; My Own Private Idaho.*

REGAN, Gerald Augustine, politics. Windsor, N.S., 1928. Liberal premier of N.S., 1970–78.

REICHMANN, Paul, business. Austria, 1930. Developer; philanthropist; with brothers Albert and Ralph, built Olympia & York into world's largest real estate developers in 1980s.

REID, Daphne Kate, performing arts. Eng., 1930–93. Primarily stage actress; Ontario Stratford Festival mainstay.

REID, Fiona, performing arts. Eng., 1951. Dramatic and comedic actor. CBC's *King of Kensington* series; Stratford Festival, Ont.

REID, William Ronald (Bill), visual arts. Victoria, B.C., 1920–98. Noted artist who promoted Northwest Coast native carving; also a sculptor whose works appear in major galleries and buildings.

REITMAN, Ivan, visual arts. Czech., 1946. Film director; producer; went from exploitation movies to blockbusters. *Ghostbusters.*

RENNIE, Callum Keith, performing arts. Eng., 1960. Actor noted for role as Stanley Raymond Kowalski in CBC Mountie comedy/drama *Due South;* also appeared in movies *My Life as a Dog; Hard Core Logo;* and in TV series *The X-Files.*

RENO, Ginette, performing arts. Montreal, Que., 1946. Popular chanteuse of sentimental ballads. "Tu vivras toujours dans mon coeur"; "A ma manière."

RICCI, Nino Pio, literary arts. Leamington, Ont., 1959. Novelist, recipient of Governor General's Award for Fiction, 1990, for *Lives of the Saints.*

RICHARD, Joseph Henry Maurice "The Rocket," sports. Montreal, Que., 1921–2000. Hockey player; legendary right winger; hockey's first 50-goal, 500-goal scorer.

RICHARDS, David Adams, literary arts. Newcastle, N.B., 1950. Author of fiction, stage and screen plays, and poetry; co-winner of 2000 Giller Prize for *Mercy Among the Children.*

RICHARDSON, Arthur Herbert Lindsay, military. Eng., 1873–1923. Victoria Cross recipient, Boer War, South Africa, 1900. Sergeant, Lord Strathcona's Horse.

RICHARDSON, Ernie, sports. Stoughton, Sask., 1931. Curler; skipped four Brier and world title rinks.

RICHARDSON, James Armstrong, business. Kingston, Ont., 1885–1939. Financier; founded family grain business and investment house.

RICHARDSON, James Cleland, military. Scot., 1895–1916. Victoria Cross recipient, WWI, the Somme, France, 1916. Piper, 16th Bn, Manitoba Regiment.

RICHLER, Mordecai, literary arts. Montreal, Que., 1931–2001. Novelist; essayist; acerbic comic writer. *The Adventures of Duddy Kravitz; St Urbain's Horseman.* Winner of 1997 Giller Prize for *Barney's Version.*

RICKER, William Edwin, science. Waterdown, Ont., 1908–2001. Creator of the Ricker Curve, an internationally recognized formula for helping fishermen to increase their catch by calculating supply as affected by rate of fishing and spawning success.

RICKETTS, Thomas, military. Middle Arm, White Bay, Nfld, 1901–67. Victoria Cross recipient, WWI, Ledeghem, Belgium, 1918. Private, 1st Bn, Royal Newfoundland Regiment.

RIDOUT, Godfrey, performing arts. Toronto, Ont., 1918–84. Composer of chamber, symphonic and religious choral works.

RIEL, Louis, politics. St Boniface, Man., 1844–85. Métis leader; led North West Rebellion, 1870 and 1885; hanged for treason. Recognized as a founder of Manitoba in 1992.

RIOPELLE, Jean-Paul, visual arts. Montreal, Que., 1923–2002. Acclaimed painter, sculptor. *Autriche.*

RITCHIE, Albert Edgar, politics. Andover, N.B., 1916–2002. Ambassador to the US 1966–69, during the Johnson and Nixon administrations; key advisor to Pierre Trudeau during the October Crisis of 1970.

RITCHIE, Charles Stewart Almon, politics. Halifax, N.S., 1906–95. Diplomat post–WWII; author. *The Siren Years.*

RITTER, Erika, literary arts. Regina, Sask., 1948. Playwright, essayist, broadcaster. *The Visitor From Charleston; Automatic Pilot; Urban Scrawl.*

ROBARTS, John Parmenter, politics. Banff, Alta, 1917–82. PC premier of Ontario, 1961–71.

ROBERSTON, Jaime Robbie, performing arts. Toronto, Ont., 1944. Singer, songwriter, played with Ronnie Hawkins and the Band; wrote scores for films including *Raging Bull, King of Comedy.*

ROBERTS, Sir Charles George Douglas, literary arts. Douglas, N.B., 1860–1943. Poet; animal story writer. *Eyes of the Wilderness.*

ROBERTSON, Heather Margaret, literary arts. Winnipeg, Man., 1942. Novelist, critic. *More Than a Rose: Prime Ministers, Wives and Other Women.*

ROBERTSON, James Peter, military. Pictou, N.S., 1883–1917. Victoria Cross recipient, WWI, Battle of Passchendaele, France, 1917. Private, 27th Bn, Manitoba Regiment.

ROBERTSON, Lloyd, media. Stratford, Ont., 1934. Broadcaster; chief anchor, CTV news.

ROBICHAUD, Louis Joseph, politics. St-Antoine, N.B., 1925. Liberal premier of N.B., 1960–70.

ROBILLARD, Lucienne, politics. Montreal, Que., 1945. Liberal MP active in Quebec referendum debate; president of treasury board; formerly minister of citizenship and immigration.

ROBINETTE, John Josiah (J.J.), law. Toronto, Ont., 1906–96. Lawyer; prominent in criminal and constitutional law.

ROBINSON, Svend J., politics. USA, 1952. NDP MP, British Columbia; social activist, gay rights.

ROBLIN, Dufferin (Duff), politics. Winnipeg, Man., 1917. PC premier of Manitoba, 1958–67.

ROBLIN, Sir Rodmond Palen, politics. Sophiasburg, Canada W, 1853–1937. PC premier of Manitoba, 1900–15.

ROCK, Allan Michael, politics. Ottawa, Ont., 1947. Liberal MP made minister of justice and attorney general in 1993, introduced major changes in Young Offender's Act and gun control legislation; minister of health in Chrétien government.

RODRIGUEZ, Sue, public service. Winnipeg, Man., 1959–94. Lou Gehrig's disease victim who championed right to die.

ROGERS, Edward S. (Ted), business. Toronto, Ont., 1933. Cable TV executive; runs Canada's largest cable system; 1994 takeover of Maclean Hunter.

ROGERS, Edward Samuel, invention. Toronto, Ont., 1900–39. Radio inventor; perfected alternating current radio tube, revolutionizing the industry.

ROGERS, Shelagh, media. Ottawa, Ont., 1956. CBC Radio personality. Host of CBC's *This Morning; Take Five With Shelagh Rogers; Sounds Like Canada.*

ROGERS, Stan, performing arts. Hamilton, Ont., 1949–83. Folk singer/songwriter. "Between the Breaks."

ROLPH, John, medicine. Eng., 1793–1870. Physician; ran medical school; constitutional reformer.

ROMAN, Stephen Boleslav, business. Slovakia, 1921–88. Industrialist; founded Denison Mines Ltd.

ROMANOW, Roy John, politics. Saskatoon, Sask., 1939. NDP premier of Sask, 1991–2001; head of Commission on the Future of Health Care in Canada 2002.

RONALD, William (b. William Smith), visual arts. Stratford, Ont., 1926–98. Abstract artist; host, CBC Radio's *As It Happens.*

ROOKE, Leon, literary arts. USA, 1934. Short story writer, novelist, playwright. *Krokodile; Shakespeare's Dog; How I Saved the Province; A Bit of White Cloth.*

ROSE, Fred (b. Fred Rosenburg), politics. Poland, 1907–83. Only Canadian Communist MP (1945); jailed as spy.

ROSENFELD, Fanny "Bobbie," sports. Russia, 1905–69. Track star; Canada's female athlete of half century.

ROSS, Anne Glass, medicine. Ukraine, 1911–98. Executive director of Winnipeg's Mount Carmel community health clinic, the first of its kind in Canada; birth control advocate. *Pregnant and Alone; Clinic with a Heart.*

ROSS, James Sinclair, literary arts. Shellbrook, Sask., 1908–96. Novelist. *As for Me and My House.*

ROSS, Sir James Clark, exploration and discovery. Eng., 1800–62. With Sir William Edward Parry searched for North Pole; discovered magnetic pole on Boothia Peninsula in 1831.

ROSS, Malcolm, literary arts. Fredericton, N.B., 1911–2002. With Jack McClelland initiated the New Canadian Library paperback series under the McClelland & Stewart imprint. Author of *Our Sense of Identity: The Arts in Canada; The Impossible Sum of Our Traditions.*

ROTHSTEIN, Aser, science. Vancouver, B.C., 1918. Physiologist; introduced radioisotopes in biology.

ROULEAU, Joseph, performing arts. Matane, Que., 1929. Operatic bass; internationally famous singer.

ROUX, Jean-Louis, performing arts/politics. Montreal, Que., 1923. Actor, playwright; was rejected as proposed lieutenant governor of Quebec in 1997 due to youthful support of Nazi regime during WWII; appointed head of Canada Council in 1998.

ROY, Gabrielle, literary arts. St Boniface, Man., 1909–83. Popular novelist. *The Tin Flute.*

ROY, Patrick, sports. Quebec City, Que., 1965. Hockey player with Montreal Canadiens, Colorado Avalanche; youngest ever to win Conn Smythe trophy.

ROZEMA, Patricia, politics. Kingston, Ont., 1958. Filmmaker. *I've Heard the Mermaids Singing, White Room.*

RUBENSTEIN, Louis, sports. Montreal, Que., 1861–1931. Canadian figure skating champion 1883–89; in 1890 won unofficial world title in Russia; also cyclist, bowler.

RUBES, Jan, performing arts. Czech., 1920. Singer; actor; operatic bass; TV host; film actor.

RUBINEK, Saul, performing arts. Toronto, Ont., 1948. Versatile character player. *The Quarrel.*

RUBINSKY, Yuri, business. Lebanon, 1952–96. Founder of Banff Publishing Workshop; co-director of SoftQuad Inc.; software designer.

RULE, Jane Vance, literary arts. USA, 1931. Novelist, short story writer. *Desert of the Heart; After the Fire; Contract with the World.*

RUSSELL, Loris Shano, science. USA, 1904–1998. Paleontologist; suggested dinosaurs might be warm-blooded.

RUTHERFORD, Ann, performing arts. Toronto, Ont., 1920. Actress who appeared as Andy Hardy's girlfriend, Polly Benedict, in 12 Hardy films. *Secret Life of Walter Mitty.*

RUTHERFORD, Charles Smith, military. Colborne, Ont., 1892–1989. Victoria Cross recipient, WWI, Monchy, France, 1918. Lieutenant, 5th Canadian Mounted Rifles Bn, Quebec Regiment.

RUTHERFORD, Ernest (Rutherford of Nelson), science. NZ, 1871–1937. Pioneer in nuclear physics; much of his seminal work done at McGill University.

RYAN, Claude, politics. Montreal, Que., 1925–2004. Editor of *Le Devoir* 1965–78; supporter of Quiet Revolution in Quebec. In 1978 became leader of Quebec Liberal party, losing to René Lévesque in 1982.

RYAN, Pat, sports. Winnipeg, Man., 1955. Curler; skip of world championship team in 1989; Canadian championship 1988, 1989.

RYAN, Thomas F. (Tommy), business. Guelph, Ont., 1872–1961. Entrepreneur; invented five-pin bowling (1909).

RYERSON, Adolphus Egerton, politics. Norfolk County, UC, 1803–82. Leading figure in 19th-century politics and education.

RYGA, George, literary arts. Deep Creek, Alta, 1932–87. Playwright, novelist. *Ecstasy of Rita Joe; Night Desk.*

SABIA, Laura Louise, public service. Pembroke, Ont., 1916–96. Headed Royal Commission on the Status of Women in 1960s; became president of National Action Committee on the Status of Women 1973.

SAFDIE, Moshe, visual arts. Israel, 1938. Architect; Habitat, National Gallery of Canada.

SAFER, Morley, media. Toronto, Ont., 1931. Broadcaster; co-host, *60 Minutes*, since 1971.

SAINTE-MARIE, Buffy, performing arts. Craven, Sask., 1941. Native singer. "Soldier Blue."

SALABERRY, Charles Michel D'Irumberry de, military. Beauport, Que., 1778–1829. Soldier; repelled American force in Battle of Chateauguay (1813).

SALÉ, Jamie, sports. Calgary, Alta, 1977. With David Pelletier won gold medal in pairs figure skating at 2002 Salt Lake City Winter Olympics; the award was given after controversy over prior judging that placed Russian team at top with Salé and Pelletier first winning silver.

SALTZMAN, Harry, performing arts. Saint John, N.B., 1915–94. Co-producer of James Bond films. *The Man With the Golden Gun; The Ipcress File.*

SALUTIN, Rick, literary arts. Toronto, Ont., 1942. Playwright, columnist; commentator. *Marginal Notes; Challenges to the Mainstream; Globe and Mail* columnist.

SARLOS, Andrew, business. Hungary, 1931–97. Financial trader with Toronto Stock Exchange. Realized $22-million profit from Hiram-Walker–Consumer's Gas merger.

SAUL, John Ralston, literary arts. Ottawa, Ont., 1947. Novelist, essayist. *The Paradise Eater; Voltaire's Bastards: The Dictatorship of Reason in the West.*

SAUNDERS, Sir Charles Edward, science. London, Ont., 1867–1937. Agriculturalist; introduced Marquis wheat to W Canada.

SAUVE, Jeanne Mathilde, politics. Prud'homme, Sask., 1922–93. Governor-general, 1984–89.

SAVAGE, John, politics. Wales, 1932–2003. Liberal premier of N.S., 1993–97; as a medical doctor he treated HIV patients in Africa, as well as running a free clinic for a disadvantaged community outside of Halifax.

SAWCHUK, Terrence Gordon, sports. Winnipeg, Man., 1929–70. Hockey goaltender; held record for shutouts (103).

SAWYER, Robert, literary arts. Ottawa, Ont., 1960. Science fiction writer, winner of US Nebula award, awards in Japan, France, Spain. *Flashforward; Factoring Humanity.*

SCHAEFER, Carl Fellman, visual arts. Hanover, Ont., 1903–95. Painter of rural Ontario landscapes, director of Ontario College of Art.

SCHAFER, Raymond Murray, performing arts. Sarnia, Ont., 1933. Composer of contemporary music, first recipient of Glenn Gould Award in 1987.

SCHALLY, Andrew Victor, science. Poland, 1926. Winner of 1977 Nobel Prize in medicine and physiology, for research into understanding peptide hormones in the brain.

SCHAWLOW, Arthur, science. USA, 1921–99. Canadian-educated scientist, winner of 1964 Nobel Prize for physics with Charles Hand Townes, co-patented the laser.

SCHLESINGER, Joe, media. Austria, 1928. Journalist; long-time CBC foreign correspondent.

SCHMIRLER, Sandra Marie, sports. Biggar, Sask., 1963–2000. Skip of the gold-medal-winning curling team at the 1998 Winter Olympics in Nagano, Japan.

SCHNARRE, Monika, performing arts. Toronto, Ont., 1971. Won 1986 Face of the 1980s modeling award; acting career includes role on *The Bold and the Beautiful.*

SCHOLES, Myron, economics. Timmins, Ont., 1941. Stanford University-based co-winner (with Harvard academic Robert Merton) of Nobel Prize for economics, for developing a mathematical formula for estimating values in the worldwide market of derivatives, known as the Black-Scholes formula.

SCHREYER, Edward Richard, politics. Beausejour, Man., 1935. NDP premier of Man., 1969–77; governor general of Canada, 1979–84.

SCHULTZ, Albert, performing arts. Port Hope, Ont., 1963. Stage, film and TV actor, co-founder of Toronto's Soulpepper Theatre Co. Has performed at Ontario's Stratford Festival, Edmonton's Citadel Theatre, and appeared on CBC drama *Street Legal.*

SCHULTZ, Erik, performing arts. Hamilton, Ont., 1952–2002. An internationally renowned trumpeter, Schultz specialized in Baroque music and toured with organist Jan Overduin; with his father established the IBS label, which recorded music of new Canadian artists.

SCOTT, Barbara Ann, sports. Ottawa, Ont., 1928. Figure skater; women's world champion, 1947–48; Olympic gold medal, 1948.

SCOTT, Duncan Campbell, literary arts. Ottawa, Ont., 1862–1947. Poet. "New World Lyrics and Ballads."

SCOTT, Francis (Frank) Reginald, literary arts. Quebec City, Que., 1899–1985. Poet. *Collected Poems.*

SCOTT, Jack, performing arts. Windsor, Ont., 1936. Singer; 1950s rockabilly star. "My True Love."

SCRIMGER, Francis Alexander Caron, military. Montreal, Que., 1881–1937. Victoria Cross recipient, WWI, Second Battle of Ypres, France, 1915. Captain, 14th Bn, Royal Montreal Regiment.

SCRIVEN, Joseph Medlicott, religion. Ire., 1819–86. Hymn writer. "What a Friend We Have in Jesus."

SEAGRAM, Joseph Emm, business. Fishers Mills, Ont., 1841–1919. Founder of world's largest distillery for spirits and wine-making; active as race horse owner; PC MP in Waterloo, Ont.

SECORD, Laura, military. USA, 1775–1868. Heroine; warned British of American attack (1813).

SEGAL, Hugh, politics. Montreal, Que., 1950. Back-room PC advisor to Robert Stanfield, William Davis and Brian Mulroney.

SELKIRK, George, sports. Huntsville, Ont., 1899–1987. Baseball player; outfielder on several NY Yankee championship teams; replaced Babe Ruth in 1934.

SELKIRK, Thomas Douglas, fifth Earl of, exploration and discovery. Scot., 1771–1820. Colonizer; established Red River settlement in Manitoba.

SELYE, Hans, medicine. Austria, 1907–82. Endocrinologist; author; pioneer in stress research. *The Stress of Life.*

SENNETT, Mack (b. Mikail Sinnott), visual arts. Danville, Que., 1880–1960. Producer; silent comedy pioneer; Keystone Kops.

SERVICE, Robert William, literary arts. Eng., 1874–1958. Poet of the Yukon. "Songs of a Sourdough."

SETON, Ernest Thompson, literary arts. Eng., 1860–1946. Naturalist; writer. *Wild Animals I Have Known.*

SEYMOUR, Lynn (b. Lynn Springbett), performing arts. Wainwright, Alta, 1939. Celebrated ballet dancer who performed with Sadler's Wells and the Royal Ballet in London, Eng., also the National Ballet of Canada.

SHADBOLT, John Leonard (Jack), visual arts. Eng., 1909–98. B.C. artist noted for nature and native Canadian influenced work.

SHANKLAND, Robert, military. Scot., 1887–1968. Victoria Cross recipient, WWI, Battle of Passchendaele, France, 1917. Lieutenant, 43rd Cameron Highlands Bn, Manitoba Regiment.

SHANNON, Kathleen, performing arts. Vancouver, B.C., 1935–98. Founder of National Film Board's Studio D in 1974, which provided female filmmakers an opportunity to create documentaries with a feminist perspective. *If You Love This Planet; Not a Love Story.*

SHARP, Mitchell, politics. Winnipeg, Man., 1911–2004. From 1942 to 1978 Liberal Party luminary; personal advisor to Prime Minister Jean Chrétien.

SHARPE, Isadore Nathaniel, business. Toronto, Ont., 1931. Opened first Four Seasons Hotel in Toronto in 1961 on Jarvis Street, now a worldwide chain of luxury hotels.

SHATNER, William, performing arts. Montreal, Que., 1931. Actor; Capt. Kirk on TV/movies *Star Trek.*

SHATTO, Dick, sports. USA, 1936–2003. Star running back for the CFL, Shatto played with the Toronto Argonauts for 12 seasons; established 15 records during his career.

SHAVER, Helen, performing arts. St Thomas, Ont., 1951. Actress appeared in *The Amityville Horror; Bethune: the Making of a Hero.*

SHEARER, Douglas, performing arts. Westmount, Que., 1899–1971. Sound recording technician, 40 years with MGM; won 12 Academy Awards; brother of actress Norma Shearer. *The Great Caruso; The Big House.*

SHEARER, Norma, performing arts. Edmonton, Alta, 1900–83. Actress; Hollywood star. *Romeo and Juliet.*

SHEBIB, Donald, visual arts. Toronto, Ont., 1939. Acclaimed filmmaker: *Goin' Down the Road; Heartaches.*

SHIELDS, Carol, literary arts. USA, 1935–2003. Writer; won 1993 Booker and Pulitzer prizes for *The Stone Diaries.*

SHORE, Eddie, sports. Ft Qu'Apelle, Sask., 1902–85. Hockey player; Boston defenceman; four-time Hart Trophy winner.

SHORE, Howard, performing arts. Toronto, Ont., 1946. Composer; has written scores for all but one of director David Cronenberg's films; three-time Oscar winner for scoring *The Lord of the Rings* trilogy.

SHORT, Martin, performing arts. Toronto, Ont., 1951. Comedian; TV/film star; *SCTV*'s Ed Grimley. *3 Amigos.*

SHULMAN, Dr. Morton, business/medicine. Toronto, Ont., 1925–2000. Investor; physician; author; stock promoter; introduced anti-Parkinson's disease drug into Canada.

SHUSTER, Frank, performing arts. Toronto, Ont., 1918–2002. Comedian; straighter half of Wayne and Shuster team.

SHUSTER, Joe, visual arts. Toronto, Ont., 1914–92. Cartoonist; co-creator of Superman.

SIBERRY, Jane, performing arts. Ottawa, Ont., 1955. Singer, songwriter, guitarist. Contemporary folk style. *Jane Siberry; No Borders Here.*

SIFTON, Sir Clifford, politics. Arva, Canada W, 1861–1929. Promoted immigration to settle western Canada.

SIFTON, Ellis Welwood, military. Wallacetown, Ont., 1891–1917. Victoria Cross recipient, WWI, Vimy Ridge, France, 1917. Lance-sergeant, 18th Bn, Western Ontario Regiment.

SILVERHEELS, Harold Jay Smith, performing arts. Six Nations Reserve, Ont., 1919–80. Actor; played Tonto in *Lone Ranger.*

SIMARD, René, performing arts. Chicoutimi, Que., 1961. Quebec pop singer began as boy soprano turned international pop star. *The René Simard Show* on CBC.

SIMCOE, Elizabeth Posthuma, literary arts. Eng., 1766–1850. Wife of John Graves Simcoe, first governor of Upper Canada; her diary and watercolours of Upper Canada provide a unique picture of life in the colony.

SIMCOE, John Graves, politics. Eng., 1752–1806. Upper Canada's first lieutenant governor, 1792–96.

SIMPSON, Allan John, public service. Ottawa, Ont., 1939–98. Co-founder of Canadians with Disabilities and the Canadian Association of Independent Living Centres; created first Pan-Am Wheelchair Games and Canadian Wheelchair Sports Association. Lobbied to have disabled included in Charter of Rights and Freedoms.

SIMPSON, Sir George, business. Scot., 1787–1860. Financier; governor, Hudson's Bay Co., 1820–60.

SINCLAIR, Gordon Allan, media. Toronto, Ont., 1900–84. Journalist; feisty commentator; long-time *Front Page Challenge* panelist.

SITTLER, Darryl Glen, sports. St Jacob's, Ont., 1950. Hockey player; with Toronto Maple Leafs set NHL record 10 points in one game.

SKRESLET, Laurie Grant, exploration and discovery. Calgary, Alta, 1949. In 1982 became first Canadian to conquer Mount Everest with the Canadian Mount Everest Expedition.

SLADE, Bernard (b. Bernard Slade Newbound), performing arts. St Catharines, Ont., 1930. Sitcom pilot writer for *The Flying Nun; The Partridge Family; Bridget Loves Bernie.* Wrote screenplay for *Same Time Next Year.*

SLOCUM, Joshua, literary arts. Wilmot Twp, N.S., 1844–1909. Sailor; wrote classic *Sailing Alone Around the World.*

SMALLWOOD, Joseph Roberts (Joey), politics. Gambo, Nfld, 1900–92. Led Newfoundland into Confederation, 1949; premier 1949–72.

SMART, Elizabeth, literary arts. Ottawa, Ont., 1913–86. Novelist. *By Grand Central Station I Sat Down and Wept.*

SMELLIE, Elizabeth Lawrie, medicine. Port Arthur, Ont., 1884–1968. Nurse; builder, Victorian Order of Nurses.

SMITH, Alexis, performing arts. Penticton, B.C., 1921–93. Film and television actress appeared in *Marcus Welby; Rhapsody in Blue; Of Human Bondage.*

SMITH, Byron, exploration and discovery. Winnipeg, Man., 1960. Leader of AGF Everest 2000 expedition, reached summit May 21, 2000, with team members Tim Rippel and Brad Wrobleski.

SMITH, Donald Graham, sports. Edmonton, Alta, 1958. Swimmer; six gold medals, 1978 Commonwealth Games.

SMITH, Ernest Alvia "Smokey," military. New Westminster, B.C., 1914. First Canadian private to win the Victoria Cross; last living Canadian recipient, WWII, Italian front, 1944. Private, Seaforth Highlanders of Canada.

SMITH, Lois Irene, performing arts. Vancouver, B.C., 1929. National Ballet's first prima ballerina.

SMITH, Michael, science. Eng., 1932–2000. Biochemist; 1993 Nobel Prize winner in chemistry.

SMITH, Michael, sports. Kenora, Ont., 1967. Decathlete; silver medal, 1991 world championships.

SMITH, Stephen Richard (Steve), performing arts. Toronto, Ont., 1945. Comedian who stars in *Red Green Show;* also plays stand-up comedy.

SMITH, Wilfred Cantwell, literary arts. Toronto, Ont., 1916–2000. Founder of McGill University's Islamic Institute; co-founder of Harvard's Center for Study of World Religions. *Islam in Modern History.*

SMITS, Sonja, performing arts. Sudbury, Ont., 1958. Star of CBC series *Street Legal;* CBC's *The Diviners.* Appeared in stage production of *Nothing Sacred.*

SMYTHE, Constantine Falkland Cary (Conn), sports. Toronto, Ont., 1895–1980. Hockey executive; owner of Toronto Maple Leafs, 1930–61.

SNIDERMAN, Sam, business. Toronto, Ont., 1920. Retailer; established Sam the Record Man; 130 stores.

SNOW, Clarence Eugene "Hank," performing arts. Liverpool, N.S., 1914–2000. Country music singer. "I'm Movin' On."

SNOW, Michael James Aleck, visual arts. Toronto, Ont., 1929. Painter; sculptor; filmmaker; photographer.

SOBEY, Frank, business. Lyons Brook, N.S., 1902–85. Industrialist; turned family grocery business into a major industry.

SOMERS, Harry Stewart, performing arts. Toronto, Ont., 1925–99. Composer of opera, orchestral, vocal and ballet music, acclaimed for operas *Louis Riel* and *The Fool;* commissioned by Yehudi Menuhin to write *Music for Solo Violin.*

SOPINKA, John, law/sports. Broderick, Sask., 1933–97. Supreme Court justice; former CFL player.

SOUSTER, Raymond Holmes, literary arts. Toronto, Ont., 1921. Poet; editor. "The Colour of the Times."

SOUTHAM, William, media. Montreal, Que., 1843–1932. Publisher; founded Southam newspaper dynasty.

SPALL, Robert, military. Eng., 1890–1918. Victoria Cross recipient, WWI, Parvillers, France, 1918. Sergeant, Princess Patricia's Canadian Light Infantry, Eastern Ontario Regiment.

SPARLING, Gordon, performing arts. Toronto, Ont., 1900–94. Pioneer director, writer and producer of about 200 films; responsible for Canadian Cameo Series 1932–55, which brought Canada to international attention. Supervised newsreels during WWII, later worked with NFB.

SPICER, Keith, media. Toronto, Ont., 1934. Civil servant; chairman, Canadian Radio-Television and Telecommunications Commission.

SPOHR, Arnold, performing arts. Rhein, Sask., 1927. Ballet teacher; led Royal Winnipeg Ballet to world fame.

SPRY, Graham, media. St, Thomas, Ont., 1900–83. Journalist and political organizer who, with Alan Plaunt, co-founded the Canadian Radio League in 1930, which promoted public broadcasting. The organization was a precursor of the CBC.

ST. LAURENT, Louis Stephen, politics. Compton, Que., 1882–1973. Lib. prime minister of Canada 1948–57; one of the architects of NATO.

STAEBLER, Edna, media. Kitchener, Ont., 1906. Journalist, cookbook writer, specializing in Mennonite cuisine. *Food That Really Schmecks; Whatever Happened to Maggie?*

STANFIELD, Robert Lorne, politics. Truro, N.S., 1914–2003. PC premier of N.S., 1956–67; as federal PC leader, lost three elections to Trudeau.

STANLEY, George Frances Gillman, literary arts. Westmount, Que., 1907–2002. Historian; proposed basic design of Maple Leaf flag in 1965.

STAROWICZ, Marc, performing arts. Eng., 1946. Longtime CBC luminary; producer of radio and television documentaries and current affairs programming. *Life & Times; The Journal; As It Happens;* and *Canada: A People's History.*

STARYK, Steven, performing arts. Toronto, Ont., 1932. Violinist; virtuoso performer and teacher.

STEACIE, Edgar William Richard, science. Montreal, Que., 1900–62. Chemist; authority on free radical kinetics.

STEELE, Sir Samuel Benfield, military. Purbrook, Canada W, 1849–1919. NWMP and WWI officer.

STEFANSSON, Vilhjalmur, exploration and discovery. Arnes, Man., 1879–1962. Controversial Arctic explorer. Wrote *My Life with the Eskimo; The Friendly Arctic.*

STEINBERG, David (b. Duddy Steinberg), performing arts. St Boniface, Man., 1942. Stand-up comic; talk show host.

STEINBERG, Samuel, business. Hungary, 1905–78. Retailer; turned family grocery into supermarket empire.

STEPHENSON, Sir William Samuel, military. Winnipeg, Man., 1896–1989. Spy; "Intrepid," head of British counterespionage during WWII; invented wire photos.

STERN, Bonnie Susan, business. Toronto, Ont., 1947. Food commentator and cookbook editor; founder of Bonnie Stern Cooking Schools; host of WTN TV show *Bonnie Stern Entertains. Simply Heart Smart Cooking.*

STEWART, Walter Douglas, literary arts. Toronto, Ont., 1931. Journalist, editor, social commentator; noted for acerbic wit. Author of *Shrug; Trudeau in Power; Towers of Gold, Feet of Clay;* and *True Blue, a History of United Empire Loyalists.*

STOJKO, Elvis, sports. Newmarket, Ont., 1972. Figure skater; two-time Olympic silver medallist; three-time world champion.

STOWE, Emily Howard, medicine. Norwich, UC, 1831–1903. Physician; first Canadian woman to practise medicine; had to obtain degree in US.

STRACHAN, Harcus, military. Scot., 1883–1982. Victoria Cross recipient, WWI, Battle of Cambrai, France, 1917. Lieutenant, Fort Garry Horse.

STRACHAN, John, religion. Scot., 1778–1867. Anglican bishop; strove to keep Upper Canada British.

STRATAS, Teresa (b. Anastasia Stratakis), performing arts. Toronto, Ont., 1938. Opera soprano; diva with strong stage presence.

STRATHCONA, Sir Donald Alexander Smith, first Baron, politics. Scot., 1820–1914. Politician, businessman, diplomat; drove the Last Spike.

STRATTON, Dorothy (b. Dorothy Ruth Hoogstratten), performing arts. Vancouver, B.C., 1960–80. Playboy model; murdered by estranged husband. Her story was told in film *Star 80,* starring Mariel Hemingway.

STREIT, Marlene Stewart, sports. Cereal, Alta, 1934. Golfer; won many international titles. Canadian Athlete of the Year, 1951, 1956.

STRONACH, Belinda, politics. Newmarket, Ont., 1966. Former president and CEO of Magna Intl; ran unsuccessfully for leadership of the Conservative Party, 2004.

STRONACH, Frank, business. Austria, 1954. Industrialist; chairman, Magna Intl; built machine company into global enterprise.

STRONG, Lori, sports. Toronto, Ont., 1972. Gymnast; winner of four gold medals at 1990 Commonwealth Games.

STRONG, Maurice Frederick, business. Oak Lake, Man., 1929. Headed Canadian International Development Agency; secretary-general of UN Conference in the Human Environment; head of Petro-Canada and Ontario Hydro; Canadian Ambassador to the UN.

SULLIVAN, Kevin Roderick, performing arts. Toronto, Ont., 1955. Producer; launched popular *Road to Avonlea* TV series. *Anne of Green Gables.*

SUNG, Alfred (b. Sung Wang Moon), business. Toronto, Ont., 1948. Fashion designer; top designer of the 1980s.

SURIN, Bruny, sports. Haiti, 1967. Sprinter; world 100 m outdoor champion, 1993.

SUTHERLAND, Donald, performing arts. Saint John, N.B., 1934. Versatile actor of Hollywood and Canadian films. *Murder by Decree; Don't Look Now.*

SUTHERLAND, Kiefer, performing arts. Eng., 1964. Actor. *Bay Boy; Stand By Me; Flatliners; A Few Good Men.*

SUZUKI, David Takayoshi, media/science. Vancouver, B.C., 1936. Geneticist; promoter of environmental causes; columnist; host of CBC's *The Nature of Things.*

SWAN, Anna Haining, performing arts. Mill Brook, N.S., 1846–88. Giantess, at 7 ft. 6 in., 352 lbs; was P.T. Barnum star.

SWAN, Susan, literary arts. Midland, Ont., 1945. Novelist. *Women of the World; The Last of the Golden Girls.*

SWINTON, George, performing arts. Austria, 1917–2002. Artist, art historian. Leading expert on Inuit art. *Sculpture of the Eskimo.*

SYDOR, Alison, sports. Vancouver, B.C., 1966. Champion mountain biker; won 1996 Olympics silver award, three-time World MTB champion, 1994, 1995, 1996.

SZNAJDER, Andrew, sports. Toronto, Ont., 1968. Four-time Canadian singles tennis champ.

TAIT, James Edward, military. Scot., 1886–1918. Victoria Cross recipient, WWI, Amiens, France, 1918. Lieutenant, 18th Bn, Manitoba Regiment.

TALBOT, Thomas, politics. Ire., 1771–1853. Personal secretary to John Graves Simcoe, then lieutenant governor of Upper Canada; fostered creation of Talbot Trail, the first transport artery to be built across southwestern Ontario.

TALON, Jean-Baptiste, politics. France, 1625–94. Governor; as intendant, sought to diversify economy of New France with minerals, timber, farming.

TANNER, Elaine, sports. Vancouver, B.C., 1951. Canada's best woman swimmer by age 15; world records in individual medley and butterfly; won silver and bronze medals in 1968 Olympics.

TASCHEREAU, Louis-Alexandre, politics. Quebec City, Que., 1867–1952. Liberal premier of Quebec, 1920–36; anti-nationalist leader.

TAUBE, Henry, science. Neudorf, Sask., 1915. Nobel Prize winner in 1983 in chemistry for research into electron transfer reactions, especially in metal complexes.

TAYLOR, Fred "Cyclone," sports. Tara, Ont., 1883–1979. Hockey's first great star.

TAYLOR, Kenneth Douglas, politics. Calgary, Alta, 1934. Diplomat; engineering freedom for six US hostages in Iran made him an instant celebrity in 1980.

TAYLOR, Richard Edward, science. Medicine Hat, Alta, 1929. Physicist; nuclear accelerator pioneer; 1990 Nobel Prize in physics.

TAYLOR, Ronald, medicine/sports. Toronto, Ont., 1937. Major league relief pitcher (1962–72) and sports medicine pioneer.

TECUMSEH, military. USA, 1768–1813. Chief of Shawnee Indians, ally of Britain and Canada during the War of 1812.

TEMPLETON, Charles Bradley, media. Toronto, Ont., 1915–2001. Author, broadcaster, playwright, evangelist, journalist; wrote controversial *Act of God.*

TENNANT, Veronica, performing arts. Eng., 1947. Prima ballerina, National Ballet of Canada.

TEWKSBURY, Mark, sports. Calgary, Alta, 1968. Swimmer; gold medal, 100 m backstroke, 1992 Olympics.

THERIAULT, Yves, literary arts. Quebec City, Que., 1915–83. Novelist, dramatist. *Contes pour un homme seul; Agaguk.*

THICKE, Alan (b. Alan Jeffery), performing arts. Kirkland Lake, Ont., 1948. Actor and talk show host, host of TV game show *Pictionary,* formerly host of talk show *Thicke of the Night.*

THIRSK, Robert Brent (Bob), science. New Westminster, B.C., 1953. In 1996 flew a 17-day journey on space shuttle *Columbia,* conducting experiments on space sickness and researching other areas.

THOM, Linda, sports. Hamilton, Ont., 1943. Shooter; gold medal, women's sports pistol, 1984 Olympics.

THOM, Ronald James, visual arts. Penticton, B.C., 1923. Architect; Shaw Festival Theatre, Toronto Zoo.

THOMAS, Dave, performing arts. Toronto, Ont., 1953. Comedic actor noted for roles on *SCTV* portrayed with Rick Moranis; one of the McKenzie Brothers in *Strange Brew.*

THOMPSON, David, exploration and discovery. Eng., 1770–1857. Charted Columbia River.

THOMPSON, Sir John Sparrow David, politics. Halifax, N.S., 1845–94. Canada's fourth prime minister, 1892–94 (Cons.); largely responsible for establishment of the Criminal Code.

THOMPSON, Scott, performing arts. North Bay, Ont., 1959. Founding member of Kids in the Hall comedy troupe; has appeared in films *Millennium* and *Popcorn* and the TV series *The Larry Sanders Show.*

THOMSON, Andrew, science. Dobbington, Ont., 1893–1974. Co-founder of World Meteorological Organization; established weather-forecasting centres across Canada.

THOMSON, David Kenneth Roy, business. Toronto, Ont., 1923. Businessman; art collector; chairman, Thomson Newspapers Ltd.

THOMSON, Roy Herbert (R.H.), performing arts. Toronto, Ont., 1947. Stage and television actor. *Charlie Grant's War; Cry from the Heart; Ticket to Heaven.*

THOMSON, Roy (Lord Thomson of Fleet), media. Toronto, Ont., 1894–1976. Publisher; owned major newspapers in English-speaking world.

THOMSON, Thomas John (Tom), visual arts. Claremont, Ont., 1877–1917. Influential painter. *Autumn Foliage.*

THORBURN, Clifford Charles Devlin, sports. Victoria, B.C., 1948. Snooker player; world champion, 1980.

TILLY, Jennifer, performing arts. USA, 1959. Actress, appeared in Woody Allen's *Bullets Over Broadway.*

TILLY, Margaret (Meg), performing arts. Texada Is., B.C., 1960. Actress appeared in *The Body Snatchers, The Big Chill.*

TILSTON, Frederick Albert, military. Toronto, Ont., 1906–92. Victoria Cross recipient, WWII, Hochwald Forest, Germany, 1945. Major, Essex-Scottish Regiment.

TIMMINS, Noah Anthony, business. Mattawa, Ont., 1867–1936. Mining developer; developed North America's largest gold mine; town named for him.

TINTNER, Georg, performing arts. Vienna, 1917–99. Conductor of Nova Scotia Symphony Orchestra 1987–94; noted for recordings of Anton Bruckner.

TOBIN, Brian Vincent, politics. Stephenville, Nfld, 1954. Began "cod war" with Spain while serving as Liberal minister of fisheries and oceans, 1995; premier of Nfld, 1996–2001.

TOPHAM, Frederick George, military. Toronto, Ont., 1917–74. Victoria Cross recipient, WWII, Rhine, Germany, 1945. Corporal, 1st Canadian Parachute Bn.

TORGOV, Morley Edward, literary arts. Sault Ste Marie, Ont., 1927. Story writer. *The Abramsky Variations; The Outside Chance of Maximilian Glick.*

TORY, Henry Marshall, education. Pt Shoreham, N.S., 1864–1947. University founder: UBC, Carleton.

TOTH, Jerry (Jaroslav), performing arts. Windsor, Ont., 1929–99. Saxophonist, clarinetist, arranger, conductor and producer, Member of Boss Brass ensemble for 20 years.

TOWN, Harold Barling, visual arts. Toronto, Ont., 1924–90. Influential painter, sculptor, writer.

TOWNSEND, Eleanor, performing arts. Goderich, Ont., 1944–98. Fiddling champion who was first woman to win North American Fiddle Championship at Shelburne, Ont.; member of both Canada's and US Fiddling Halls of Fame.

TRACY, Paul, sports. Scarborough, Ont., 1968. Auto racer; winner of three Indy titles in 1993.

TRAILL, Catharine Parr, literary arts. Eng., 1802–99. Writer. *The Backwoods of Canada.*

TRAVERS, Mary (La Bolduc), performing arts. Newport, Que., 1894–1941. Singer, songwriter, fiddler whose songs in colloquial French about common people's concerns were widely recorded and hugely popular.

TREBEK, Alex, performing arts. Sudbury, Ont., 1940. TV host of *Jeopardy* quiz show.

TREMBLAY, Gilles, performing arts. Arvida, Que., 1932. Composer of soundtrack for Quebec pavilion for Expo 67 (*Sonorisation du Pavillon du Québec*); composer for major Canadian orchestras. *Kékoba; Les Vépres de la Vierge.*

TREMBLAY, Jean-Claude, sports. Bagotville, Ont., 1939–94. Star defenceman for Montreal Canadiens in 1960s.

TREMBLAY, Michel, literary arts. Montreal, Que., 1942. Playwright; novelist. *Le Vrai Monde.*

TRIQUET, Paul, military. Cabano, Que., 1910–80. Victoria Cross recipient, WWII, Casa Berardi, Italy, 1943. Captain, Le Royal 22e Régiment.

TROIANO, Dominic, performing arts. Italy, 1946. Rock guitarist collaborated with the Mandalas, The Guess Who; wrote for CBC TV. *Night Heat; Diamonds.*

TROUT, Jennie Kidd, medicine. Scot., 1841–1921. First woman in Canada licensed to practise medicine; established Ontario Medical College for Women in Kingston, Ont.

TRUDEAU, Pierre Elliott, politics. Montreal, Que., 1919–2000. Prime minister of Canada 1968–79, 1980–84.

TRYGGVASON, Bjarni V., science. Iceland, 1945. Astronaut who flew aboard the *Discovery* in 1997 for 11 days to test Canadian-made equipment at zero gravity.

TSUI, Lap-Chee, medicine. China, 1950. Molecular geneticist who, in 1989, found gene that causes cystic fibrosis and developed the Cystic Fibrosis Transmembrane Regulator principle.

TUBMAN, Harriet Ross (b. Araminta Ross), public service. USA, 1820–1913. Former slave who was instrumental in freeing slaves via the Underground Railroad; escaped persecution in St. Catharines, Ont.

TULK, Robert Raymond, literary arts. Deer Lake, Nfld, 1938–2001. Author of humorous *Newfie Jokes* series; its eight editions were published 1969–91.

TULVING, Endel, medicine. Estonia, 1927. Cognitive psychologist; world authority on human memory function.

TUPPER, Sir Charles, politics. Amherst, N.S., 1821–1915. Appointed as Canada's sixth prime minister, 1896.

TURCOTTE, Ron, sports. Drummond, N.B., 1941. Jockey; long-time leading jockey rode Secretariat to Triple Crown (1973).

TURNBULL, Wallace, invention. Saint John, N.B., 1870–1954. Inventor of variable pitch propeller in 1927, contributed to improved flying safety.

TURNER, John Napier, politics. Eng., 1929. Prime minister of Canada June 1984–July 1984.

TURNER, Richard Ernest William, military. Quebec City, Que., 1871–1961. Victoria Cross recipient, Boer War, 1900. Lieutenant, Royal Canadian Dragoons.

TUROFSKY, Riki, performing arts. Toronto, Ont., 1944. Debuted in 1972 at New York City Opera in *Carmen;* host of CBC's *Summer Festival* in 1978; *Festival Today* in 1984.

TWAIN, Shania (b. Eileen Regina Edwards), performing arts. Windsor, Ont., 1965. Winner of Country Music of the Year Award (US) 1995. *The Woman in Me.*

TYRRELL, Joseph Burr, science. Weston, Canada W, 1858–1957. Geologist; discovered S Alberta dinosaur beds.

TYSON, Ian Dawson, performing arts. Victoria, B.C., 1933. Singer/songwriter; half of Ian and Sylvia. "Four Strong Winds."

TYSON, Sylvia Fricker, performing arts. Chatham, Ont., 1940. Singer; half of Ian and Sylvia. "You Were on My Mind."

U

UCHIDA, Irene Ayako, medicine. Vancouver, B.C., 1917. Cytogeneticist who is world expert on Down Syndrome and other diseases caused by chromosomal abnormalities.

UNDERHILL, Barbara Ann, sports. Pembroke, Ont., 1963. Figure skater; world pairs champion (with Paul Martini), 1984.

UNDERHILL, Frank Hawkins, literary arts. Stouffville, Ont., 1889–1971. Historian and political critic who contributed often to the *Canadian Forum,* he was first president of the League for Social Reconstruction.

UNGER, James, visual arts. Eng., 1937. Cartoonist; creator of popular "Herman" cartoon strip.

URQUHART, Jane, literary arts. Little Long Lac, Que., 1949. Novelist, short story writer. *The Whirlpool; Away; The Underpainter.*

UTECK, Lawrence (Larry), sports. Thornhill, Ont., 1952–2002. Star CFL defensive back who played with B.C., Toronto, Ottawa and Montreal teams; later successfully coached St. Mary's Huskies in Halifax; served as deputy mayor of Halifax. Died of Lou Gehrig's disease.

V

VAILLANCOURT, Armand J. R., visual arts. Black L., Que., 1932. Sculpts in aid of social activism.

VALDY (b. Vladimir Horsdal), performing arts. Ottawa, Ont., 1946. Country-folk singer-songwriter, guitarist. "Rock and Roll Song"; *Valdy; Notes from Places.*

VALLIERES, Pierre, politics. Montreal, Que., 1938–98. Journalist and former leader of Front de Libération de Québec (FLQ); author of *White Niggers of America,* which compared Québécois with American Blacks; fell out with FLQ after murder of labour minister Pierre Laporte.

VAN, Billy (b. Billy Van Evera), performing arts. Toronto, Ont., 1934–2003. Veteran comic actor, appeared on CBC television shows *Nightcap* and *The Hilarious House of Frightenstein;* TVO's *Bits and Bytes;* as well as *The Sonny & Cher Comedy Hour* and *The Bobby Vinton Show.*

VAN HERK, Aritha, literary arts. Wetaskiwin, Alta, 1954. Novelist. *Judith; No Fixed Address; Places Far from Ellesmere.*

VAN HORNE, Sir William Cornelius, business. USA, 1843–1915. Driving force behind Canadian Pacific Railroad.

VAN VOGT, Alfred Elton (A.E.), literary arts. Winnipeg, Man., 1912–2000. Writer; science fiction standout. *Slan.*

VANCOUVER, George, exploration and discovery. Eng., 1757–98. Navigator; surveyor of B.C. coastline.

VANDER ZALM, William Nick, politics. Holland, 1934. Social Credit premier of B.C. 1986–91, proponent of free trade.

VANDERBURG, Helen, sports. Calgary, Alta, 1959. Synchronized swimmer; dominated sport in 1979.

VANDERHAEGHE, Guy Clarence, literary arts. Esterhazy, Sask., 1951. Novelist, won 1982 Governor General's Award for *Man Descending. My Present Age; Homesick; The Englishman's Boy* (Governor General's Award)*; The Last Crossing.*

VANIER, Georges Phileas, politics. Montreal, Que., 1888–1967. Governor-general, 1959–67.

VANIER, Jean, public service. Switz., 1928. Spiritual leader; man of great moral conviction established homes for handicapped around the world.

VANNELLI, Gino, performing arts. Montreal, Que., 1954. Pop singer. *Brother to Brother; Nightwalker.*

VARLEY, Frederick Horsman (F.H.), visual arts. Eng., 1881–1969. Member, Group of Seven. *Vera.*

VASSANJI, M. G., literary arts. Kenya, 1950. Physicist; novelist. Winner of 1994 Giller Prize for *The Book of Secrets;* 2003 Giller Prize for *The In-Between Life of Vikram Lall.*

VEREGIN, Peter Vasilevich, religion. Russia, 1859–1924. Charismatic Doukhobor leader.

VERNON, John, performing arts. Montreal, Que., 1931. TV and film actor. *Wojeck.*

VEZINA, Georges, sports. Chicoutimi, Que., 1887–1926. Hockey goalie; NHL trophy named for him.

VICKERS, Jonathan Stewart (Jon), performing arts. Prince Albert, Sask., 1926. Tenor; operatic star; Wagner specialist.

VICKREY, William, economics. Victoria, B.C., 1914–96. Winner of Nobel Prize in economics in 1996. Worked with United Nations on tax issues in African countries.

VIGNEAULT, Gilles, performing arts. Natashquan, Que., 1928. Beloved poet and cultural icon of Québécois. "Mon Pays."

VILLENEUVE, Gilles, sports. St-Jean, Que., 1950–82. Auto racer; won six Grand Prix titles. Died in crash while attempting to qualify for Belgium Grand Prix.

VILLENEUVE, Jacques, sports. St-Jean, Que., 1971. Winner of Indianapolis 500 in 1995; Lou Marsh trophy for Canadian Athlete of the Year, 1995.

VINCENT, Anthony Gustave, public service. Eng., 1939. Canadian ambassador to Peru when, in December 1996, Tupac Amaru guerrillas stormed Japanese ambassador's residence in Lima, taking 575 hostages. Vincent attempted negotiations with leader Nestor Cerpa.

VOYER, Bernard, sports. Rimouski, Que., 1953. Mountain climber who has reached the tallest summit on every continent on earth, including Antarctica's Mount Vinson, Mount Everest and Mount Kilimanjaro.

W

WAGNER, Barbara Aileen, sports. Toronto, Ont., 1938. Figure skater; with Robert Paul won four pairs titles and 1960 Olympic gold.

WALDO, Carolyn, sports. Montreal, Que., 1964. Synchronized swimmer; two gold medals, 1988 Olympics.

WALKER, Larry, sports. Maple Ridge, B.C., 1966. Baseball player; star outfielder for Montreal Expos, Colorado Rockies. NL MVP, 1997. NL batting champion, 1998.

WALLIN, Pamela, media. Wadena, Sask., 1953. Longtime CBC journalist and independent news magazine host. In 2002 appointed Canadian consul general for New York City.

WALLS, Earl, sports. Puce, Ont., 1928–96. Canadian heavyweight boxing champion, 1952.

WALSH, Richard "Hock," performing arts. Toronto, Ont., 1948–2000. Co-founder in 1969 with brother Donnie of Downchild Blues Band; inspiration for Dan Aykroyd and John Belushi in movie *The Blues Brothers.*

WALTERS, Angus, exploration and discovery. Lunenburg, N.S., 1882–1968. *Bluenose* captain; skipper of celebrated schooner.

WALTERS, Eric, literary arts. Toronto, Ont., 1957. Popular writer of young people's adventure books. *Tiger by the Tail; Trapped in Ice.*

WARD, Maxwell William, business. Edmonton, Alta, 1921. Capitalist; charter flights pioneer; founded Wardair.

WARNER, Jack L., performing arts. London, Ont., 1892–1978. Head of production at Warner Brothers in 1927; launched talkies with *The Jazz Singer,* starring Al Jolson.

WARREN, Earl (b. Earl Warren Segal), media. Regina, Sask., 1933–2002. Popular host of Toronto's CFRB radio program *House of Warren* from 1996–83. Also hosted *The Earl Warren Show.*

WASHINGTON, Jackie, performing arts. Hamilton, Ont., 1919. Jazz/blues musician and actor who originally sang with the Four Washington Brothers and has retained a thriving career with hit albums. *Midnight Choo Choo; Where Old Friends Meet.*

WATKINS, Melville Henry, business. Toronto, Ont., 1932. Economist; founded left-wing Waffle Movement.

WATSON, Harold Percival "Whipper," sports. Saskatoon, Sask., 1923–2002. Left winger hockey player who won four Stanley Cups with the Toronto Maple Leafs between 1947 and 1951 and with the Detroit Red Wings in 1943.

WATSON, Hilda Pauline, politics. Kuest, Sask., 1922–96. Leader of the Yukon Territorial Progressive Conservatives, 1978. First woman to lead a political party in Canada.

WATSON, Homer Ransford, visual arts. Doon, Canada W, 1855–1936. Landscape painter. *The Pioneer Mill.*

WATSON, John, literary arts. Scot., 1847–1939. Philosopher; metaphysician. "Kant and His English Critics."

WATSON, Ken, sports. Minnedosa, Man., 1904–86. Curler; three-time Brier winner; curling teacher.

WATSON, Patrick, media. Toronto, Ont., 1929. TV host; actor; writer; producer. *This Hour Has Seven Days.*

WATSON, Sheila Doherty, literary arts. New Westminster, B.C., 1909–98. Author of *Double Hook,* considered to be the first modern Canadian novel; also *Deep Hollow Creek.*

WATSON, William "Whipper Billy," sports. Toronto, Ont., 1917–1990. Wrestler; twice world pro champion.

WAXMAN, Albert Samuel (Al), performing arts. Toronto, Ont., 1935–2001. Movie and TV performer. *King of Kensington.*

WAYNE, John Louis (Johnny), performing arts. Toronto, Ont., 1918–90. Comedian; wilder half of Wayne and Shuster comedy team.

WEBSTER, Donald Colin "Ben," invention. Montreal, Que., 1928–97. Founder of high-tech Helix Investments (Canada), credited with introduction of the fastening material Velcro.

WEBSTER, John Edgar (Jack), media. Scot., 1918–99. Broadcaster; journalist on *Vancouver Sun.* Noted for outspoken opinions.

WEINZWEIG, John Jacob, performing arts. Toronto, Ont., 1913. Influential composer using 12-tone technique. "Red Far of Corn."

WEIR, Michael Richard, sports. Sarnia, Ont., 1970. Winner of 2000 World Golf Championship and American Express Championship; 1999 PGA Air Canada Championship.

WEIR, Robert Stanley, literary arts. Hamilton, Ont., 1856–1926. Jurist; author; wrote English lyrics of national anthem, "O Canada."

WELLS, Clyde Kirby, politics. Buchans Junction, Nfld, 1937. Newfoundland premier 1989–96.

WELSH, Kenneth, politics. Edmonton, Alta, 1942. Versatile actor noted for roles in *Empire Inc.; And Then You Die; The Tar Sands.*

WESTON, Hilary M., politics. Ire., 1942. Appointed lieutenant governor of Ontario in 1997, wife of grocery magnate Galen Weston.

WESTON, W. Galen Gordon, business. Eng., 1940. Industrialist; Canadian head for George Weston Ltd.

WESTON, Willard Garfield, business. Toronto, Ont., 1893–1978. Industrialist; pioneer in food retailing.

WHEELER, Anne, visual arts. Edmonton, Alta, 1946. Filmmaker. *A Change of Heart; Bye Bye Blues.*

WHEELER, Lucille, sports. Montreal, Que., 1935. Skier; first N American to win world title, downhill and slalom (1958).

WHITE, Bob, business. Ire., 1935. Labour leader; first head of Canadian Auto Workers' Union.

WHITFIELD, Simon, sports. Victoria, B.C., 1975. Gold medallist for triathlon in 2000 Sydney Olympics; 1998, 1999 Canadian champion.

WHITTON, Charlotte Elizabeth, politics. Renfrew, Ont., 1896–1975. Reformer; outspoken Ottawa mayor.

WIEBE, Rudy Henry, literary arts. Speedwell, Sask., 1934. Mennonite novelist. *The Temptations of Big Bear.*

WILLAN, James Healey, performing arts. Eng., 1880–1968. Classical composer and musician. "O Lord, Our Governour" sung at Queen Elizabeth II's coronation in Westminster Abbey.

WILLIAMS, Daffyd (Dave) Rhys, science. Saskatoon, Sask., 1954. Astronaut, flew on 16-day Spacelab flight aboard Space Shuttle Columbia in 1998; coordinator of Canadian Astronaut Program Space Unit Life Simulation (CAPSULS) project.

WILLIAMS, Daniel, politics. St. John's, Nfld, 1950. Elected PC premier of Newfoundland and Labrador, 2003. Co-founder of Nfld and Lab.'s first cable company, Cable Atlantic.

WILLIAMS, Percy Alfred, sports. Vancouver, B.C., 1908–82. Sprinter; Olympic gold in 100 m and 200 m, 1928.

WILSON, Bertha, law. Scot., 1923. First woman named to Supreme Court of Canada (1982).

WILSON, Cairine Reay, politics. Montreal, Que., 1885–1962. Canada's first woman senator, 1930 (Lib.).

WILSON, Sir Daniel, educator. Scot., 1816–92. Darwinian opposed idea of natural selection; energetic administrator, author, scholar.

WILSON, Ethel Davis, literary arts. S Africa, 1888–1980. B.C. novelist. *Swamp Angel.*

WILSON, John Tuzo, science. Ottawa, Ont., 1908–93. Geophysicist; pioneered plate tectonics theory.

WILSON, Lois Miriam, religion. Winnipeg, Man., 1927. First woman president of Canadian Council of Churches, in 1976; first woman Moderator of United Church of Canada in 1980. Peace advocate and active in antipoverty initiatives.

WILSON, Michael Holcombe, politics. Toronto, Ont., 1937. PC minister of industry, science and technology; international trade; finance minister (1984–91).

WISEMAN, Adele, literary arts. Winnipeg, Man., 1928–92. Novelist, poet. *The Sacrifice; Crackpot.*

WISEMAN, Joseph, performing arts. Montreal, Que., 1918. Actor; title role in James Bond movie *Dr. No.*

WOLFE, James, military. Eng., 1727–59. Soldier; took Quebec for British; died on Plains of Abraham.

WONG, Celia Jan, media. Montreal, Que., 1952. *Globe and Mail* correspondent in China, 1988–94. *Red China Blues.*

WOOD, Elizabeth Wyn, visual arts. Orillia, Ont., 1903–66. Sculptor; fountains and panels for Rainbow Bridge Gardens, monument to King George VI, Niagara Falls.

WOOD, Sharon Adele, exploration and discovery. Halifax, N.S., 1957. First woman from the Western Hemisphere to successfully climb Mount Everest as a member of the Canadian Everest Light Expedition in 1986.

WOODCOCK, George, literary arts. Winnipeg, Man., 1912–95. Historian; journalist; activist. *Anarchism.*

WOODSWORTH, James Shaver, politics. Etobicoke, Ont., 1874–1942. Founder Cooperative Commonwealth Federation (later NDP).

WRAY, Fay, performing arts. Medicine Hat, Alta, 1910–2004. Famous as screaming heroine in *King Kong.*

WRIGHT, Eric Stanley, literary arts. Eng., 1929. Mystery writer. *A Sensitive Case; Final Cut.*

WRIGHT, Michelle, performing arts. Merlin, Ont., 1960. Country songstress. "Now and Then."

WRIGHT, Richard B., literary arts. Midland, Ont., 1937. Award-winning novelist; *The Age of Longing; Clara Callan* (winner of the 2001 Giller Prize and 2001 Governor General's Award).

YANOFSKY, Abe (b. Daniel Abraham), sports. Poland, 1925–2000. First chess grandmaster in Commonwealth; child prodigy in 1939 Chess Olympics in Buenos Aires; active in Winnipeg city council.

YANOVSKY, Zal, performing arts. Toronto, Ont., 1944–2002. Singer; member of folk-rock group The Lovin' Spoonful.

YOST, Elwy, performing arts. Toronto, Ont., 1925. Affable and knowledgeable host of TVOntario's popular *Saturday Night at the Movies.*

YOUNG, John Francis, military. Eng., 1893–1929. Victoria Cross recipient, WWI, Dury-Arras Sector, France, 1918. Private, 87th Bn, Quebec Regiment, Canadian Grenadier Guards.

YOUNG, Neil Percival, performing arts. Toronto, Ont., 1945. Singer/songwriter; seminal rocker. *After the Gold Rush.*

YOUNG, Scott Alexander, literary arts. Glenboro, Man., 1918. Novelist, short story writer, children's writer, biographer. *The Boys of Saturday Night; Power Play.*

YOUVILLE, Marie Marguerite d', religion. Varennes, Que., 1701–71. First Canadian to be beatified by Pope; founded Grey Nuns.

ZEIDLER, Eberhard Heinrich, visual arts. Germany, 1936. Award-winning architect of Toronto Eaton Centre, Toronto's Queen's Quay Terminal, Ontario Place.

ZENGEL, Raphael Louis, military. Faribault, Man., 1894–1977. Victoria Cross recipient, WWI, Warvillers, France, 1918. Sergeant, 5th Bn, Saskatchewan Regiment.

ZERAFA, Boris, visual arts. Egypt, 1933–2002. Architect who designed both Canadian and global landmarks, including Toronto's Lothian Mews, Royal Bank Plaza and Hazelton Lanes; Montreal's Bank of Paris; and King Abdul Aziz University in Saudi Arabia.

ZNAIMER, Moses, business. Toronto, Ont., 1942. TV executive; founder of CITY-TV, Much Music.

ZOLF, Larry, media. Winnipeg, Man., 1934. Broadcaster; journalist; writer. CBC's *Fifth Estate.*

ZUCKERMAN, Mortimer, business. Montreal, Que., 1937. Financier; developer, magazine publisher.

CANADIAN IDENTITY

Basic Canadian identification includes birth certificates and driver's licences, plus passports or permanent resident cards for use outside Canada's borders. These documents are necessary to prove identity (including citizenship) or establish eligibility for social benefits.

■ Birth certificate

A birth certificate is the document that establishes legal identity. Individuals should be registered at birth; the Canadian certificate that is issued is necessary to obtain health cards, Social Insurance Numbers and passports. Foreign birth certificates are also a starting point for establishing identity or eligibility in Canada.

If you need to register a birth or replace a lost Canadian birth certificate, contact the Vital Statistics department of your provincial government.

■ Canadian Passports

The best of proof of citizenship when you are travelling outside Canada is a valid passport. It is the only proof that is accepted in all countries. While passports are not required for entry into the U.S., many Canadians have been stopped for failure to have photo identification and proof of citizenship. In the aftermath of September 11, 2001, valid and trusted identification has become even more important. Passports can also be useful when cashing travellers' cheques or completing legal transactions in the U.S., and a passport is essential if the U.S. is only one stop in a multi-destination tour.

Any Canadian citizen may obtain a passport. It is valid for five years; it cannot be renewed or extended. Make sure that you will be home before the expiry date. (Some countries will not allow entry unless the passport is valid long after you plan to return home.) Many countries require a visa in addition to a passport. Always check with your travel agent, the Department of Foreign Affairs or that country's representative in Canada (listed in "Nations of the World") before you leave home, to ensure you have all of the required documentation.

How do you get a passport? Application forms are available at post offices and passport offices across the country. The form requires information about birth, citizenship, marital status and residence, in addition to two copies of a photo, which must conform to requirements relating to size and type of shot. Passport photos can be obtained at many photo supply stores as well as other outlets. They can be in black and white or colour. Family snapshots are not suitable.

The completed form must be witnessed by a "guarantor": someone who has known you for at least two years and can attest to the truth of the information submitted. A guarantor must come from a recognized profession such as engineering, medicine or clergy or be in a senior administrative position in an academic or financial institution.

A passport is a valuable document. To ensure your passport is safe, consider locking it up when away from home—many hotels offer safe places for valuables. If you carry your passport with you, check for it and other valuables at least once a day. You have a better chance of retracing your steps to find a misplaced passport (or reporting a stolen credit card before too much damage is done) if it has been missing for less than 24 hours.

While it is your responsibility to protect your passport and other valuables during your trip, the nearest Canadian diplomatic or consular mission can help **if your passport is lost or stolen.** The loss must also be reported to the local police. (The same applies if your passport is lost or stolen at home. The police must be notified as well as the nearest passport office.)

Canada's Department of Foreign Affairs and International Trade (DFAIT) maintains a network of 250 offices, embassies, high commissions, consulates, honorary consuls and development offices in over 180 countries. (Australian diplomatic officers provide services where Canada does not have a presence.) For a list of Canadian representation abroad, consult the country-by-country listings in "Nations of the World." The offices are also listed in a government booklet entitled *Bon Voyage, But....*

Should you become ill, incapacitated or a victim of crime (or arrested), local consular staff can provide assistance. In addition, **emergency consular services** can be obtained by calling collect to (613) 996-8885, or 1-800-267-6788 within Canada or the U.S.

■ The Permanent Resident Card

Also known as the Maple Leaf Card or the PR card, this is a new, wallet-sized plastic card for people who have completed the immigration process and have Permanent Resident status, but are not Canadian citizens. It replaces the IMM 1000 as the document to be presented by permanent residents who are re-entering Canada on a commercial carrier (plane, boat, train or bus) as of December 31, 2003.

As of June 28, 2002, new permanent residents began receiving the card. As of October 15, 2002, current permanent residents may apply for one. For more information about this new piece of identification, visit www.cic.gc.ca or contact your local Citizenship and Immigration office.

■ Pre-trip Planning

Make sure that you have proper identification before you leave, plus any required visas. Take out-of-country medical insurance and enough medication or other medical appliances you may require. It may be difficult to obtain them elsewhere—"common" items can be hard to find in some places. In addition, DFAIT suggests that detailed travel plan information should be left with family or friends in Canada.

Check to see if DFAIT has issued any Travel Advisories. Call 1-800-575-2500 or visit the government's web site at www.voyage.gc.ca. Travel advisories can cover anything from the local political situation to an outbreak of Yellow Fever.

If you are travelling by air or crossing into the U.S., give yourself extra time to clear security checks. Ensure that you can answer detailed questions about your belongings and provide quick access to everything. There will be random, thorough checks. No sharp objects of any kind will be allowed in aircraft cabins, and casual joking about threats will be taken seriously.

Social Insurance Number (SIN)

*S*ocial Insurance Numbers are issued by Human Resources Development Canada (HRDC). The nine-digit number is a file number that identifies you for taxation, premiums (and payments) for pensions and employment insurance. Your SIN will be requested once you've been hired for a job—your employer will use it to report earnings to the government.

How do you get a SIN? Apply for one at a Human Resources Centre (check the blue pages in your telephone book for the closest office) or by mail. You can obtain the form by downloading it from HRDC's web site (www.hrdc-drhc.gc.ca).

You must complete the application with your name, date of birth, place of birth and your mother's and father's birth names. You must also provide the original (or a certified copy) of the document(s) that prove your identity and your status in Canada. If you are a Canadian citizen born in Canada, a birth certificate or passport is acceptable; in Quebec and Newfoundland, a baptismal certificate is also acceptable. If you are a Canadian citizen born outside the country, a Certificate of Canadian Citizenship or a valid passport is required. A Permanent Resident can use the new Permanent Resident card (see above).

If the name you now use is different from the one on original documents, you must also supply evidence that your name was legally changed.

If the card is lost or stolen, notify the local HRDC office. The staff will advise you of the steps needed to protect yourself from SIN fraud. (This usually takes the form of someone else applying for government benefits under your name. SIN fraud includes: knowingly applying for more than one SIN; using someone else's number to obtain financial benefits or establish an identity; loaning or selling a SIN or card to another party; or manufacturing a card.)

Your SIN is not intended to be a piece of identification and there is no need to supply the number for purposes other than employment or financial transactions such as investments. Store the card in a secure place rather than carrying it with you.

Canadian Postal Rates

(effective January 12, 2004)

		Within Canada	To the USA (airmail)	International
Lettermail and postcards (letter size max. 245 mm x 150 mm x 5 mm)	0–30 g	$0.49[1]	$0.80	$1.40
	31–50 g	$0.80[1]	$0.98	$1.96
Non-standard and oversize items (max. 380 mm x 270 mm x 20 mm)	0–100 g	$0.98	$1.60	$3.20
	101–200 g	$1.60	$2.80	$5.60
	201–500 g	$2.40	$5.60	$11.20
Registered mail		$6.00 plus applicable postage[2]	$11.00 plus applicable postage[2]	$11.00 plus applicable postage[2]

Note: GST is applicable to all postal charges. Other services for parcels, bulk mailings or expedited delivery are also available.
(1) Surcharges apply if mail is not coded. (2) Postage varies by size and weight of mail item.

■ What's the best way to address an envelope?

A wide variety of packages and styles of address make it through Canada Post's system, however there are ways to ensure that your mail is handled most efficiently. While the computerized systems can read a range of addresses—including handwriting—the system's preferred style is as follows:

Line 1: name of the recipient
Line 2: title, floor number, attention line
Line 3: If business, company name
Line 4: unit number (if applicable):
street number and name
If post office box, information should appear above municipality name
Line 5: municipality, province postal code

While the system can read upper and lower case, upper case is preferred, with an aligned left margin. Address lines should be less than 40 characters long. The first three elements of the postal code should be separated from the final three by a space, never a hyphen.

The return address should be formatted the same way, in the upper left corner (or on the back at the top). If on the front, it should be clearly separated from the destination address and preferably be smaller than the destination address.

Characters should be larger than 2 mm and smaller than 5 mm (10 to 12 point).

When addressing mail to the United States, the U.S. Postal Service prefers the use of the two-character state symbol rather than having the name of the state spelled out. The ZIP code should come two spaces after the state code and appear on the same line. The final line should be USA. When addressing international mail, the name of the country should be spelled out in full (e.g., GREAT BRITAIN) and should appear on the last line of the address, below any other municipality, city name or code information.

■ Province and Territory Symbols

The two-character symbols have been designated by Canada Post in order to make mailing more efficient. The codes for Canada's ten provinces and three territories are:

Newfoundland & Labrador (changed from NF as of Oct. 21, 2002)	NL
Prince Edward Island	PE
Nova Scotia	NS
New Brunswick	NB
Quebec	QC
Ontario	ON
Manitoba	MB
Saskatchewan	SK
Alberta	AB
British Columbia	BC
Yukon Territory	YT
Northwest Territories	NT
Nunavut	NU

Source: *Canada Post*

Temperature Equivalents

(Celsius and Fahrenheit)

°C	°F	°C	°F	°C	°F	°C	°F	°C	°F
-50	-58	-30	-22	-10	14	10	50	30	86
-49	-56.2	-29	-20.2	-9	15.8	11	51.8	31	87.8
-48	-54.4	-28	-18.4	-8	17.6	12	53.6	32	89.6
-47	-52.6	-27	-16.6	-7	19.4	13	55.4	33	91.4
-46	-50.8	-26	-14.8	-6	21.2	14	57.2	34	93.2
-45	-49	-25	-13	-5	23	15	59	35	95
-44	-47.2	-24	-11.2	-4	24.8	16	60.8	36	96.8
-43	-45.4	-23	-9.4	-3	26.6	17	62.6	37	98.6
-42	-43.6	-22	-7.6	-2	28.4	18	64.4	38	100.4
-41	-41.8	-21	-5.8	-1	30.2	19	66.2	39	102.2
-40	-40	-20	-4	0	32	20	68	40	104
-39	-38.2	-19	-2.2	1	33.8	21	69.8	41	105.8
-38	-36.4	-18	-0.4	2	35.6	22	71.6	42	107.6
-37	-34.6	-17	1.4	3	37.4	23	73.4	43	109.4
-36	-32.8	-16	3.2	4	39.2	24	75.2	44	111.2
-35	-31	-15	5	5	41	25	77	45	113
-34	-29.2	-14	6.8	6	42.8	26	78.8	50	122
-33	-27.4	-13	8.6	7	44.6	27	80.6	100	212
-32	-25.6	-12	10.4	8	46.4	28	82.4	150	302
-31	-23.8	-11	12.2	9	48.2	29	84.2	200	392

Household Measures, Metric Equivalents

Volume

Imperial	Metric	Imperial	Metric	Imperial	Metric
1/4 tsp	1 mL	1/4 cup	50 mL	4 cups	1 L
1/2 tsp	2 mL	1/3 cup	75 mL	5 cups	1.25 L
3/4 tsp	4 mL	1/2 cup	125 mL	6 cups	1.5 L
1 tsp	5 mL	2/3 cup	150 mL	7 cups	1.75 L
2 tsp	10 mL	3/4 cup	175 mL	8 cups	2 L
1 tbsp (3 tsp)	15 mL	1 cup	250 mL		

Weight

Imperial	Metric	Imperial	Metric	Imperial	Metric
1 oz	25 g	1/2 lb	250 g	1 3/4 lb	875 g
2 oz	50 g	2/3 lb	350 g	2.2 lb	1 kg
3 oz	75 g	3/4 lb	375 g	3 lb	1.5 kg
1/4 lb	125 g	1 lb	500 g	5 lb	2.2 kg
1/3 lb	175 g	1 1/2 lb	750 g	10 lb	4.5 kg

Oven Temperatures

Imperial (°F)	Metric (°C)	Imperial (°F)	Metric (°C)	Imperial (°F)	Metric (°C)
250	120	350	180	450	230
275	135	375	190	475	245
300	150	400	200	500	260
325	160	425	220		

*Equivalents listed here are not exact, but may be used as a guideline.

Canadian Imperial and Metric Measures

Name	Abbrev.	Equivalent in Related Units	Metric Equivalent
■ Length			
inch	in.	—	2.54 cm
foot	ft.	12 in.	30.48 cm
yard	yd.	3 ft.; 36 in.	0.91 m
mile	mi.	1 760 yd.; 5 280 ft.	1.609 km
■ Mass (Weight)			
grain	gr.	—	0.06 g
dram	dr.	27.343 gr.	1.77 g
ounce	oz.	16 dr.	28.35 g
pound	lb.	16 oz.	0.453 kg
hundredweight			
(short)	cwt.	100 lb.	45.36 kg
(long)	cwt.	112 lb.	50.80 kg
ton (short)	—	2 000 lb.	0.907 t
ton (long)	—	2 240 lb.	1.016 t
■ Volume and Capacity			
fluid dram	fl. dr.	0.22 cu. in.	3.55 cm^3
fluid ounce	fl. oz.	8 fl. dr.; 1.7 cu. in.	28.41 cm^3
pint	pt.	20 fl. oz.; 34.7 cu. in.	568.3 cm^3
quart	qt.	2 pt.; 69.4 cu. in.	1.14 dm^3
gallon	gal.	4 qt.; 277 cu. in.	4.55 dm^3
peck	pk.	2 gal.; 555 cu. in.	9.09 dm^3
bushel	bu.	4 pk.; 2 219 cu. in.	36.37 dm^3
barrel (oil)	bbl	35 gal.	0.159 m^3
cubic foot	ft.^{3}	1 728 in.^{3}	0.028 m^3
cubic yard	yd.^{3}	27 ft.^{3}	0.765 m^3
■ Area			
square foot	ft.^{2}	144 sq. in.	0.09 m^2
square yard	yd.^{2}	9 sq. ft.	0.836 m^2
acre	—	4 840 sq. yd.	4 047 m^2
square mile	sq. mi.	640 acres	2.590 km^2

Source: *Gage Canadian Dictionary*

Roman Numerals

I	1	VII	7	XX	20	C	100	$\overline{V}$	5 000
II	2	VIII	8	XXX	30	CC	200	$\overline{X}$	10 000
III	3	IX	9	XL	40	CD	400	$\overline{L}$	50 000
IV	4	X	10	L	50	D	500	$\overline{C}$	100 000
V	5	XI	11	LX	60	CM	900	$\overline{D}$	500 000
VI	6	XIX	19	XC	90	M	1 000	$\overline{M}$	1 000 000

Canada's Food Guide To Healthy Eating[1]

Canada's Food Guide, revised in November of 1992, recognizes that the amount of food each Canadian needs every day from the four food groups and other foods depends on age, body size, activity level, whether the individual is male or female, and if the individual is pregnant or breast-feeding. That's why the Food Guide gives a range of possible servings for each food group—young children can choose the lower number of recommended servings from a particular group, while male teenagers can go to the higher number. Most other people can choose servings somewhere in between.

Canada's Food Guide recommends, every day:

- 5 to 12 servings from the grain products group. An example of one serving would be one slice of bread; 30 g of cold cereal or 175 mL of hot cereal. Two servings would be a bagel, pita or bun; or 250 mL of rice or pasta.

- 5 to 10 servings of vegetables and fruit. One serving would be one medium size vegetable or fruit; 125 mL of fresh, frozen or canned vegetables or fruit; 250 mL of salad; or 125 mL of juice.

- 2 to 3 servings of meat or alternatives. One serving would be 50-100 g of meat, poultry or fish; 1-2 eggs; 125-250 mL of beans; 100 g of tofu; or 30 mL of peanut butter.

- Recommended servings of milk products vary according to age: 2-3 servings for children aged 4-9; 3-4 servings for young people aged 10-16; 2-4 servings for adults; and 3-4 servings for pregnant or breast-feeding women. Examples of one serving would be 250 mL of milk, 50 g of cheese or 175 g of yogurt.

Taste and enjoyment can also come from other foods and beverages that are not part of the four food groups. Some of these foods are higher in fat or calories, so it is recommended that these foods be used in moderation. The important things to remember are: enjoy a variety of foods from each group every day and choose lower-fat foods more often.

Source: *Health and Welfare Canada*

(1) For people four years and over.

Functions of Nutrients

Calcium aids in the formation and maintenance of strong bones and teeth; promotes healthy nerve function and normal blood clotting.

Carbohydrate supplies energy; assists in the utilization of fats.

Fat supplies energy; aids in the absorption of fat-soluble vitamins.

Fibre provides undigestible bulk, which encourages the normal elimination of body wastes.

Folacin (folic acid) aids red blood cell formation.

Iodine aids in function of the thyroid gland.

Iron combines with protein to form hemoglobin, the red blood cell constituent that transports oxygen and carbon dioxide.

Magnesium aids in formation and maintenance of strong bones and teeth; aids in energy metabolism and tissue formation.

Phosphorus aids in formation and maintenance of strong bones and teeth.

Protein builds and repairs body tissues; builds antibodies, the blood components that fight infection.

Riboflavin (vitamin B_2) maintains healthy skin and eyes; maintains a normal nervous system; releases energy to body cells during metabolism.

Thiamin (vitamin B_1) releases energy from carbohydrate; aids normal growth and appetite.

Vitamin A aids normal bone and tooth development; promotes good night vision; maintains the health of skin and membranes.

Vitamin B_{12} (cobalamin) aids in red blood cell formation; maintains healthy nerve and gastrointestinal tissues.

Vitamin C (ascorbic acid) maintains healthy teeth and gums; maintains strong vessel walls.

Vitamin E (tocopherol) protects the fat in body tissues from oxidation.

Zinc aids in energy and metabolism and tissue formation.

Source: *Canada's Food Guide Handbook*

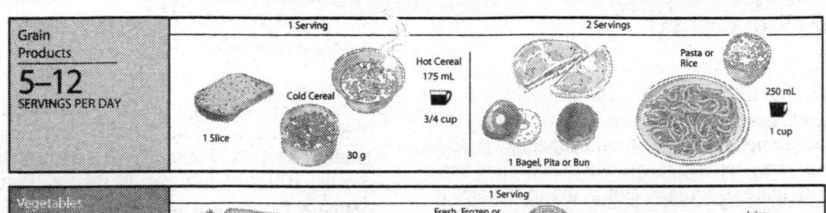

Grain
Products
5–12
SERVINGS PER DAY

1 Serving
1 Slice
Cold Cereal
Hot Cereal
175 mL
3/4 cup
30 g

2 Servings
1 Bagel, Pita or Bun
Pasta or
Rice
250 mL
1 cup

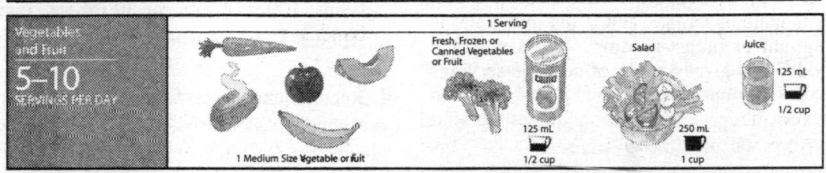

Vegetables
and Fruit
5–10
SERVINGS PER DAY

1 Serving
1 Medium Size Vegetable or Fruit
Fresh, Frozen or
Canned Vegetables
or Fruit
125 mL
1/2 cup
Salad
250 mL
1 cup
Juice
125 mL
1/2 cup

Milk
Products
SERVINGS PER DAY
Children 4–9 years: 2–3
Youth 10–16 years: 3–4
Adults: 2–4
Pregnant and Breast-feeding
Women 3–4

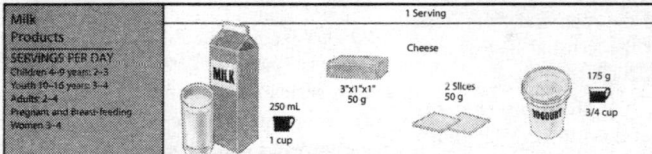

1 Serving
MILK
250 mL
1 cup
Cheese
3"x1"x1"
50 g
2 Slices
50 g
175 g
YOGURT
3/4 cup

Other Foods

Taste and enjoyment can also come from other foods and beverages that are not part of the 4 food groups. Some of these foods are higher in fat or calories, so use these foods in moderation.

Meat and
Alternatives
2–3
SERVINGS PER DAY

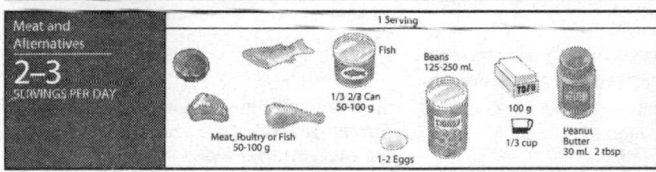

1 Serving
Meat, Poultry or Fish
50–100 g
Fish
1/3 2/3 Can
50–100 g
1–2 Eggs
Beans
125–250 mL
TOFU
100 g
Peanut
Butter
1/3 cup 30 mL 2 tbsp

Different People Need Different Amounts of Food

The amount of food you need every day from the 4 food groups and other foods depends on your age, body size, activity level, whether you are male or female and if you are pregnant or breast-feeding. That is why the Food Guide gives a lower and higher number of servings for each food group. For example, young children can choose the lower number of servings, while male teenagers can go to the higher number. Most other people can choose servings somewhere in between.

Consult Canada's Physical Activity Guide to Healthy Active Living to help you build physical activity into your daily life.

Enjoy eating well, being active and feeling good about yourself. That's **VITALIT**

© Minister of Public Works and Government Services Canada, 1997
Cat. No. H39-252/1992E   ISBN 0-662-19648-1
No changes permitted. Reprint permission not required.

October 1, 2003–September 30, 2004

Names in **Bold** face indicate Canadian-born or a strong link to Canada

ARNOLD, James, 72. Toronto-born original first tenor of The Four Lads, a pop group whose romantic ballads gained them fame in the 1950s. "Standing on the Corner"; "The Mockingbird." June 15, 2004.

ASPER, Israel Harold (Izzy), 71. Media tycoon who founded CanWest Global Communications Corp., a multinational newspaper and television station empire. The original CanWest was considerably strengthened when Asper bought the *National Post* from Conrad Black and the Global Television Network. October 7, 2003.

BARRIS, Alex, 81. A prolific writer for newspapers and television, the US-born Barris was a reporter for the *Globe and Mail* and the *Toronto Telegram.* He later hosted CBC programs including *The Barris Beat* and *Barris and Company,* and appeared on *Front Page Challenge. Oscar Peterson: A Musical Biography.* January 16, 2004.

BATES, Sir Alan, 69. Veteran British film and stage actor who debuted opposite Laurence Olivier in *The Entertainer.* Other roles: *Look Back in Anger, Georgy Girl, Women in Love, Gosford Park* and, most recently, *The Statement.* December 27, 2003.

BERMAN, Joseph, 81. Co-founder, with Jack Kamin and A. E. Diamond, of Cadillac Fairview; by the 1970s, Cadillac Fairview was Toronto's largest landlord. Berman, a generous philanthropist, once suggested a "wealth tax," which would enable rich taxpayers to subsidize the poor. December 10, 2003.

BERNSTEIN, Elmer, 82. A prolific film composer of diverse musical genres, Bernstein provided the scores for at least 200 films, including *To Kill a Mockingbird, The Magnificent Seven, The Great Escape* and *Birdman of Alcatraz.* August 18, 2004.

BERRY, Jan, 62. Surf-style pop singer who, with Dean Torrence, formed the pop group Jan and Dean; their first big hit, "Surf City," was co-written by Berry and Beach Boy Brian Wilson. "Drag City"; "Dead Man's Curve." March 26, 2004.

BLAKE, Mervyn "Butch," 95. A noted character actor who appeared in 42 consecutive seasons at Ontario's Stratford Festival, Blake acted in every one of Shakespeare's plays; he toured with the Canadian Players, played at the Stratford Memorial Theatre in Britain and also worked in television and film. October 9, 2003.

BOUEY, Gerald Keith, 83. Governor of the Bank of Canada 1973-87, Bouey served during a series of economic crises; his tenure saw record interest rates, a low Canadian dollar, and wage and price controls. February 6, 2004.

BRANDO, Marlon, 80. Legendary Hollywood actor whose early career roles firmly established his reputation: Stanley Kowalski in *A Streetcar Named Desire;* Terry Malloy in *On the Waterfront;* and Fletcher Christian in *Mutiny on the Bounty.* His later film successes included *Last Tango in Paris* and, most memorably, mafia leader Vito Corleone in *The Godfather.* A firm advocate of Native American rights, Brando never conformed to the Hollywood stereotype. He lived reclusively in latter years, beset by personal problems and growing debt. July 1, 2004.

BROADFOOT, Barry, 77. Originally a journalist, Broadfoot wrote several oral history books, including *Ten Lost Years,* a chronicle of Canada's Depression era, and *Coming Home From the War,* which related the experiences of servicemen who had returned to Canada after WWII. *My Ordinary Years* (autobiography). November 28, 2003.

BROCKHOUSE, Bertram Neville, 85. Co-winner, with Clifford Shull, of the 1994 Nobel Prize for physics for his research into techniques of measuring the atomic structure of matter; he was the only Canadian to receive the prize who was born in Canada, had a Canadian education, and conducted his research in this country. October 13, 2003.

CAHILL, James, 84. Once convicted of the murder of a Belfast policeman, Cahill became an instigator of the provisional IRA's violent agenda in 1972 after the Bloody Sunday debacle; he later professed a peaceful solution as a means of reconciliation. July 23, 2004.

CAMPBELL, Moran, 78. Inventor of the Venturi oxygen mask, which revolutionized the treatment of respiratory diseases; he was also founder of the Michael G. DeGroote School of Medicine at McMaster University in Hamilton, Ont. April 12, 2004.

CAMPBELL, Norman Kenneth, 80. A veteran CBC radio and television producer, Campbell was studio director of one of the first CBC TV programs, *Let's See*, a variety show. After a stint in Hollywood, he returned to Canada to produce a huge range of programs, from sitcoms to ballets and Gilbert and Sullivan productions. April 12, 2004.

CAPELING-ALAKIJA, Sharon, 59. Executive coordinator of the United Nations Volunteers and organizer of the 2001 International Year of the Volunteer; she was previously director of the UN Development Fund for Women and the UN's Development Program's Office of Evaluation and Strategic Planning. November 4, 2003.

CARNEY, Arthur (Art) William Matthew, 85. American comic actor who portrayed the hapless Ed Norton, the sewer-worker neighbour of Ralph Kramden, played by Jackie Gleason, in the long-running 1950s sitcom *The Honeymooners*. He made a comeback in movies including *Harry and Tonto* and *Last Action Hero*. November 9, 2003.

CARTIER-BRESSON, Henri, 95. World-renowned French photographer whose dramatic images depicted many of the past century's major events, from the actions of French Resistance fighters to the funeral of Mahatma Gandhi. Cartier-Bresson's photos appeared in magazines including *Life, Vogue* and *Harper's Bazaar*. August 4, 2004.

CHAREST, Micheline, 51. Founder, with her husband, Ronald Weinberg, of Cinar

Corp., an award-winning animation production company that was responsible for hit cartoon projects such as *Arthur* and *Caillou*. Cinar was accused of tax fraud and offshore investment scandals, but Charest had recently begun rebuilding her career when she died due to complications from cosmetic surgery. April 13, 2004.

CHARLES, Ray (b. Ray Charles Robinson), 73. Legendary pianist, saxophonist and singer, Charles, who became blind at age 7, began his career at 15 after an impoverished life in rural Georgia and rose to huge success in an array of musical genres: country, big band, jazz, blues and soul. He had a cameo appearance in the film *The Blues Brothers*. "Hit the Road Jack"; "Georgia on My Mind." June 10, 2004.

CHILD, Julia, 91. One of the first celebrity chefs, Julia Child is credited with introducing French cuisine to the American kitchen. Her groundbreaking cookbook, *Mastering the Art of French Cooking*, published in 1961, was a precursor to her public television career; *The French Chef* was the first of several shows that she hosted with her trademark easygoing style. Child also co-founded the American Institute of Wine and Food. *Julia Child's Kitchen*. August 13, 2004.

CLOUTIER, Suzanne, 76. Quebec stage and film actress who appeared internationally; she played Desdemona opposite Orson Welles in the film version of *Othello* and appeared with one-time husband Peter Ustinov in *No Sign of the Dove. Moulin Rouge; Doctor in the House*. December 2, 2003.

COADE, Jessie Amelia, 92. Nicknamed "Mess Deck Annie," Coade, a reporter, interviewed sailors during WWII for her column in the *Halifax Mail*, titled "Messdeck News." She also chronicled the lives of ordinary people in her postwar radio program, *Ship to Shore*. October 19, 2003.

COOK, Alistair, 95. Author, television presenter and foreign correspondent, Cook began his career with the BBC in Britain. Since 1964 he broadcast *Letter From America* for BBC's Radio 4, when he settled in the US; his final broadcast was in February 2004. Cook also hosted the PBS series *Masterpiece Theatre.* March 30, 2004.

CORELLI, Rae, 77. Corelli began his career working as a journalist, for the Canadian Press, the *Kingston Whig-Standard* and the *Toronto Star;* he became a newscaster for Global TV in 1977, and wrote for and eventually became national editor of *Maclean's* magazine. April 2, 2004.

CRAIN, Jeanne, 78. American Hollywood actress who starred in a variety of romantic movies; at one time she rivalled Betty Grable as a pinup girl for soldiers serving overseas in WWII. She is best known for her controversial role in Elia Kazan's *Pinky,* in which she played a black nurse masquerading as a white woman. December 14, 2003.

CREAN, Patrick Victor "Paddy," 93. Dubbed the grand master of stage fighting, the internationally renowned Crean began his career in England; he later immigrated to Canada and served as fight director at Ontario's Stratford Festival from 1963-83. December 22, 2003.

CREIGHTON, Douglas, 75. Founder, as publisher, with editor Peter Worthington, in 1971 of the *Toronto Sun* tabloid in the wake of the demise of the *Toronto Telegram;* his notoriously right-of-centre but highly successful paper eventually expanded to *Sun* papers in Edmonton, Calgary and Ottawa. January 7, 2004.

CRICK, Dr. Francis Harry Compton, 88. British-born co-discoverer, with American Dr. James Watson, of the structure of DNA, in 1953, at Cambridge University. He jointly won the 1962 Nobel Prize for medicine with Watson and fellow researcher Dr. Maurice Wilkins. *What Mad Pursuit.* July 28, 2004.

CROSS, Alexander "Sandy," 89. Alberta cattle rancher who donated 4800 acres (1942 hectares) of his wilderness farmland to the Alberta government as a wildlife sanctuary, ensuring the land would be safe from encroaching development. December 13, 2003.

CUESTA, Henry, 71. US-born clarinettist who played with Benny Goodman and Bobby Hackett in Toronto and subsequently with the Lawrence Welk Orchestra; he also appeared with Mel Torme and Bobby Vinton, and conducted the Jimmy Dorsey Orchestra. December 17, 2003.

CUNNINGHAM, Agnes, 95. Founder with husband, Gordon Friesen, in 1962, of *Broadside,* a periodical featuring folk songs and later protest movement information. The periodical helped launch the careers of folk singers Bob Dylan, Janis Ian, Tom Paxton and Phil Ochs. June 29, 2004.

DIJK, Rudi Martinus van, 71. Born in the Netherlands, van Dijk was a prolific composer, often commissioned by the CBC. Among his compositions: *The Shadowmaker,* based on text by the late poet Gwendolyn MacEwen; and *Kreitens Passion,* which was based on the story of pianist Karlrobert Kreiten, who was executed by the Nazis in 1943. November 29, 2003.

DION, Adhémar, 80. Father of internationally renowned singer Celine Dion; an accomplished accordion player, Dion is credited with nurturing the career of Celine, the youngest of his fourteen children. November 30, 2003.

DONOGHUE, Lynn, 50. Artist whose large colourful canvases are exhibited in galleries worldwide; her works included portraits and installations. *The Last Supper; Mirror Image; Reliquary.* November 22, 2003.

DOWLING, Doris, 81. American film noir actress whose first film, *Lost Weekend,* launched her career; she also played in Orson Welles's *Othello* and films scripted by crime writer Raymond Chandler, and appeared in many Italian films. June 18, 2004.

DUNNE, John Gregory, 71. Writer and screenwriter who reached fame with books *True Confessions* and *The Red White and Blue,* among others, as well as screenplays co-written with his wife, novelist Joan Didion: *A Star is Born* (1976) and *Up Close and Personal.* Dunne was the brother of novelist Dominick Dunne. December 30, 2003.

ELTON, Harry, 74. Toronto-born Elton was an executive producer at Granada Television in Britain; he commissioned the early episodes of *Coronation Street* and brought the show to Canada when he later joined the CBC. He was host of the CBC's *Cross-Country Check-Up* and *Mostly Music.* May 16, 2004.

FIA, Albert, 89. Creator of the Black Brant rocketship, a sub-orbital rocket originally designed to track the northern lights, also used to launch planetary telescopes and cosmic-ray detectors; the rocket was first launched in Churchill, Manitoba, in 1962, when Fia was associated with the Winnipeg-based Bristol Aerospace. June 7, 2004.

FOREST, Don, 83. Mountain-climber whose late-in-life pastime led him to three records: at 59 the first person to have climbed all 54 Rocky Mountain peaks that exceed 11,000 feet; at 71 the oldest person to conquer Mount Logan; at 73 the first man to top all 18 of the highest peaks in the BC Interior. November 27, 2003.

FRAME, Janet, 79. New Zealand novelist, short story writer and poet, whose haunting writings on the human psyche were attributed to her early institutionalizations for misdiagnosed schizophrenia. *The Lagoon and Other Stories; Wrestling with the Angel* (autobiography). January 28, 2004.

GAUDETTE, Barry, 56. Forensics scientist who became an expert witness across North America for his innovative use of hair and fibre analysis; he is credited with introducing DNA technology to the RCMP. October 1, 2003.

GELBER, Sylva Malka, 93. Director of the women's bureau for the federal Department of Labour from 1969-76, Gelber was a strong advocate of equal pay legislation, maternity leave and women's pension benefits, as well as universal medicare. December 9, 2003.

GIBSON, Althea, 76. US tennis champion who during the years 1956-58 led her sport; she was the first black player to win Wimbledon, in 1957. Against the odds of a poverty-stricken childhood in Harlem, she surpassed racial barriers and eventually won 11 Grand Slam titles, five in singles, five in doubles and one in mixed doubles. November 28, 2003.

GIBSON, Ernest Henry James, 102. Last living member of the Royal North-West Mounted Police, which he joined in 1918, two years prior to the force joining the Dominion Police to form the Royal Canadian Mounted Police. January 20, 2004.

GLASSCO, Bill, 69. In 1971, with his then-wife Jane Gordon, co-founded Toronto's Tarragon Theatre, which showcased Canadian playwriting talent. In 1985 he became artistic director of CentreStage, which later merged with the Toronto Free Theatre to become CanStage, and also directed Stratford and Shaw Festival productions. In 1999 he co-founded the Montreal Young Company. September 14, 2004.

GOLD, Joe, 82. Founder of Gold's Gym, in 1965; Gold later sold the innovative gym, which boasted custom-built equipment, and later founded World Gym, which has been franchised across the world. July 11, 2004.

GOLDSCHMIDT, Nicholas "Niki," 95. A conductor, pianist, singer and teacher, the Czechoslovakia-born Goldschmidt was a founder of the Canadian Opera Company, the Vancouver International Festival and Guelph Spring Festival; he also organized the Bach International Competition, Festival Canada at the National Arts Centre and the Benjamin Britten Festival in Toronto. February 8, 2004.

GOMBERG, Richard Daniel "Tooker," 48. A social activist and environmentalist, Gomberg earned a national profile for his colourful protests against politicians and corporations, as well as his dedication to recycling, composting and inner-city cycling. March 3, 2004.

GOSNELL, Lawrence McCullum (Larry), 80. A documentary filmmaker whose work was instrumental in the birth of Canada's environmental movement, Gosnell started out with the NFB but made his mark with the anti-pollution documentary *Air of Death* in 1967 and *One Way to Quit,* a graphic anti-smoking documentary made in 1972. March 23, 2004.

GRAHAM, Barbara Aldwynne, 67. Technical director of the Canadian Figure Skating Association (Skate Canada) 1972-91, Graham was a formidable force within the skating world. She enabled coach Doug Leigh to build his Orillia, Ont., skating school into an international destination for aspiring skaters. May 8, 2004.

GRAY, Spalding, 62. A writer and performance artist, Gray was master of the monologue; among his works were *Swimming to Cambodia, Monster in a Box* and *Life Interrupted,* and a semi-autobiographical novel, *Impossible Vacation.* After battling lifelong depression and suffering from a debilitating car accident in 2001, Gray committed suicide by jumping off the Staten Island ferry; his body was found March 8. January 10, 2004.

GREALIS, Walter, 74. An early promoter of Canadian pop music, Grealis persuaded the country's radio DJs to increase their Canadian content. In 1964 he founded *RPI* magazine, which in 1964 introduced the Gold Leaf Awards ceremony, precursor to the Juno Awards, named after CRTC chairman Pierre Juneau. January 20, 2004.

HART, Stu, 88. Patriarch of the Hart wrestling dynasty, Hart founded Stampede Wrestling, a forerunner to World Wrestling Entertainment, in 1948, in Calgary. The family wrestling tradition was carried on by sons Bret and Owen, the latter dying during a stunt on a pay-per-view TV program. October 16, 2003.

HARVEY, Denis Martin, 74. As editor of Montreal's *Gazette,* Harvey disobeyed the War Measures Act during the October Crisis of 1970 by publishing the manifesto of the Front de Libération du Québec, with details of the kidnapped and murdered Quebec cabinet minister Pierre Laporte and photos of the kidnapped British trade commissioner, James Cross. He later became chief news editor of CBC Television News. December 7, 2003.

HATFIELD, Robert Lee (Bobby), 63. With Bill Medley was a member of the 1960s Righteous Brothers rock duo, with hits such as "You've Lost That Lovin' Feeling" and "Unchained Melody." After a brief break-up in the late sixties, the duo reunited to perform in Las Vegas and across America. November 5, 2003.

HEMMINGS, David, 62. British actor best known for his leading role in Michelangelo Antonioni's 1960s classic *Blow Up,* opposite Vanessa Redgrave; he also appeared in films including *Gladiator, Gangs of New York* and, most recently, *Last Orders.* In latter years he was active as a TV and film director. December 3, 2003.

HILL, James, 73. Award-winning illustrator whose career peaked in the 1950s and '60s. He created covers for magazines including *Maclean's, Saturday Evening Post* and *Playboy,* and was an accomplished portrait painter (Pierre Trudeau, Pope John Paul II). February 3, 2004.

HOLLIDAY, Clifford, 105. Born in Plumas, Man., Holliday was a bugle boy at Vimy Ridge, the last surviving Canadian of the bloody battle, and also a witness to the battle of Hill 60. He was a recipient of the French Legion of Honour and the John McCrae Medallion. May 4, 2004.

HOUSE, Eric, 83. Stage and television actor whose career began during the post-WWI period at Hart House Theatre at the University of Toronto. He went on to act in major theatres across Canada, in London's West End and across the US. Appeared in CBC productions including *Seeing Things* and *A Gift to Last.* March 21, 2004.

HYLAND, Frances, 77. One of Canada's leading Shakespearean actors, Hyland was a mainstay at Ontario's Stratford Theatre for almost 35 years. She appeared on stages in London, Eng., and New York, and also had television roles in *The Twilight Zone, Alfred Hitchcock Presents* and *Road to Avonlea.* July 11, 2004.

IRWIN, Samuel MacDonald, 76. With his brother Arnold turned the family toy company, founded by his father, Samuel B. Irwin, in 1926, into a multimillion-dollar concern, based in Toronto. Irwin Toys manufactured the Hula Hoop, Slinky and Frisbee. The company was sold in 2000, but the family bought it back when it went bankrupt, returning it to financial health. December 24, 2003.

JONES, Elvin (Ray), 76. One of the world's top jazz percussionists, Jones, a rhythmic drummer, joined jazz great John Coltrane's quartet in 1960; he also played with Charlie Parker, Miles Davis and Duke Ellington. *A Love Supreme* (Coltrane album). May 18, 2004.

JULIANA Louise Emma Marie Wilhelmina, 94. Queen of the Netherlands, 1948-80. A popular queen with a marked social conscience, Juliana chose exile in Ottawa when German troops were invading western Europe during WWII; in gratitude for Canada's hospitality, she arranged for an annual delivery of tulips to Ottawa. March 20, 2004.

KASH, Eugene, 91. A violinist who was formerly a soloist with the Toronto Symphony Orchestra and music director of the National Film Board, Kash, who was married to contralto Maureen Forrester, was also a producer for the CBC and BBC and former conductor for the Ottawa Philharmonic. March 6, 2004.

KAYE, M. M. (b. Mary [Molly] Margaret Kaye), 95. Born to a British civil servant in Simla, northern India, Kaye wrote the epic novel *Far Pavilions,* which portrayed the turbulent times of colonial India in the first half of the twentieth century; Kaye also authored detective stories, including *Death Walks in Kashmir* and *Berlin.* January 29, 2004.

KEESHAN, Bob, 76. As Captain Kangaroo, Keeshan entertained children on his TV program, which ran from 1955-85, first with CBS and later on public broadcasting. Keeshan, who early on adopted a grandfatherly look with his walrus moustache, mop of hair and multipocketed jacket, took his young viewers through his Treasure House and introduced the characters of Mr. Green Jeans, Mr. Moose and Bunny Rabbit through skits and songs. January 23, 2004.

KIERANS, Eric William, 90. Independent and passionate politician who worked with

Premier Jean Lesage in the 1960s to achieve the Quiet Revolution in Quebec; as a cabinet minister under Pierre Trudeau he objected to the implementation of the War Measures Act during the 1970 October Crisis. From 1983-94 he joined PC national president Dalton Camp and Stephen Lewis, former leader of Ontario's NDP, on Peter Gzowski's national radio program *Morningside.* May 10, 2004.

KING, Alan (b. Irwin Alan Kniberg), 76. American actor, producer and stand-up comedian who appeared frequently on *The Ed Sullivan Show* as well as films *Bonfire of the Vanities, Casino* and *Rush Hour 2.* His brand of humour was a mix of hilarity and hostility; the suburbs were a favourite butt of his jokes. May 12, 2004.

KLEIN, Estelle, 74. Artistic director of the Mariposa Folk Festival 1964-80, Klein built up the originally Orilllia, Ont.-based festival to a major force in the folk music genre, which featured artists such as Joan Baez, Joni Mitchell and Gordon Lightfoot, and evolved into a workshop and craft venue. June 17, 2004.

KLEIN, Lothar Karl, 71. Prolific avant-garde composer of orchestral and vocal music, which was performed by such luminaries as Sir Andrew Davis, conductor laureate of the Toronto Symphony Orchestra, and contralto Maureen Forrester. *The Philosopher in the Kitchen.* January 3, 2004.

KNEEBONE, Tom, 71. A comic actor who played extensively at Ontario's Stratford and Shaw theatres, as well as at London's Old Vic and on Broadway, Kneebone was best known for his collaboration with Dinah Christie in revues such as *Oh Coward!* Latterly he and Christie entertained the elderly through their Smile Theatre Company. He appeared in the movie *The Luck of Ginger Coffey.* November 15, 2003.

KNOWLES, Robert Gordon, 83. Long-time national supervisor of farm and fisheries broadcasts for the CBC, beginning in 1950; he initiated programs such as *Country Calendar, Country Magazine* and *Summer Fallow.* In the 1940s he oversaw the Farm Radio Forum, an adult-education broadcast that encouraged interactive participation among viewers. November 5, 2003.

KYDD, Frances Shand, 68. The mother of Princess Diana and daughter of Lady Ruth Fermoy, lady in waiting to the late Queen Mother, Kydd was first married to British aristocrat Edward John Spencer; the failure of the marriage created a deep rift between Kydd and her famous daughter. June 3, 2004.

LAFOND, André, 59. From 1989-2002, Lafond was Montreal's film commissioner, promoting the Quebec film industry to the United States; during his 13 years in office he brought more than 50 American film shoots to Montreal. He was formerly associated with the NFB's Paris office. October 22, 2003.

LANGE, Hope, 70. An American stage, film and television actress, Lange debuted with co-star Marilyn Monroe in the film *Bus Stop;* she was renowned for her role in the torrid movie drama *Peyton Place,* and starred in the 1960s TV series *The Ghost & Mrs. Muir.* December 19, 2003.

LAUDER, Estée (b. Josephine Esther Mentzer), 97. Founder of the Estée Lauder cosmetics company, which also manufactures the Clinique, Aramis and Prescriptives lines, Lauder originally developed family cosmetic recipes in her modest home laboratory in the 1930s; eventually her company made the Fortune 500 list. April 24, 2004.

LAWRENCE, Ronald Douglas, 82. Naturalist and co-founder of the Haliburton Forest's Wolf Centre in Ontario, Lawrence published several books including *The Poison Makers, In Praise of Wolves* and *The Green Trees Beyond,* an autobiography. November 27, 2003.

LEUSZLER, Winnifred Francis Roach, 78. The first Canadian to swim the English Channel, on August 16, 1951. Leuszler's achievement was eclipsed by Marilyn Bell's 1954 swim across Lake Ontario (Leuszler placed third in that swim), and Leuszler faded into obscurity. May 1, 2004.

LEVIN, Bernard, 75. Controversial but erudite British journalist and broadcaster who worked primarily with the *Times of London* and the *Sunday Times,* as well as other major British newspapers, in the capacity of theatre critic, columnist and feature writer. Levin also conducted interviews on the BBC's *That Was the Week that Was.* August 7, 2004.

LEWIS, Raymond Gray, 94. The first Canadian-born black athlete to receive an Olympic medal, Lewis won the bronze as a member of Canada's 4 x 400 metre relay in 1932 at the Los Angeles games. His autobiography, *Shadow Running,* chronicles both his sporting life and his long-time job as a porter for the CPR. November 14, 2003.

LINEHAN, Brian, 58. Celebrity interviewer who began his career with Toronto's CITY-TV in 1973; he displayed a depth of knowledge in his *City Lights* program. After leaving CITY in 1988 he went on to host *Linehan,* which was carried on WIC television stations. September 3, 2004.

MAGNUSON, Keith, 56. Former Chicago Blackhawk defenceman died in a car crash near Bolton, Ont., in a vehicle driven by former Maple Leafs captain, Rob Ramage, who was subsequently charged with impaired driving. The two had just attended the funeral of NHL Alumni Association chairman Keith McCreary. December 15, 2003.

MANCHESTER, William, 82. American biographer and historian who gained renown through works including *Portrait of a President: John F. Kennedy in Profile; The Death of a President;* and *American Caesar: Douglas MacArthur, 1880-1964.* He left unfinished a trilogy on the life of Winston Churchill. June 1, 2004.

MARKANDAYA, Kamala, 79. India-born novelist whose works reflected conflicted Indian society in the mid-twentieth century as traditional customs and hardscrabble livelihoods were interrupted by colonialism and eventually Indian independence. *Nectar in a Sieve; Some Inner Fury.* May 16, 2004.

MAYEROVITCH, Harry, 94. Montreal architect and artist designed the city's Jewish Public Library, City Centre, synagogues and private residences. A prolific artist of sculptures, paintings, etchings and other works, his work has appeared in the National Gallery of Canada. April 16, 2004.

McCAIN, Harrison, 76. Founder, in 1957, with brother Wallace, of McCain Foods, the Florenceville, NB-based empire that began as a producer of frozen French fried potatoes; after a rift with Wallace over succession issues in the 1990s, McCain expanded into the juice and frozen pizza markets. March 19, 2004.

McCLELLAND, John G. (Jack). 81. From 1951-88, McClelland was publisher of McClelland & Stewart, a family business founded in 1906, and was instrumental in the development and success of Canada's major writers, including Farley Mowat, Pierre Berton, Margaret Laurence and Margaret Atwood. McClelland's colourful personality and penchant for outrageous publicity stunts were legendary. June 14, 2004.

McLEOD, Barbara, 70. Spirited host of the CBC's *The Barbara McLeod Show,* a noon-hour chat program that ran from 1977-84; she also appeared on various CBC productions. November 3, 2003.

McMICHAEL, Robert, 82. A professional photographer by trade, McMichael and his wife, Signe, donated their vast collection of Group of Seven artwork to the Ontario government in 1965, along with their spacious log home, to serve as a gallery, on their property in Kleinburg, Ont. November 18, 2003.

MILLER, Ann (b. Johnnie Lucille Ann Collier), 80. Although rarely a leading lady, Miller was a popular tap-dancer in movies of the 1940s and '50s, in films such as *Easter Parade, Kiss Me Kate* and *On the Town.* She made a comeback in 1979 teaming with Mickey Rooney in the Broadway hit *Sugar Babies,* and appeared on TV programs including *The Ed Sullivan Show* and *Laugh-In.* January 22, 2004.

MILLER, Robert, 84. An ordained United Church minister, Miller was secretary to the Student Christian Movement and a prominent lecturer at Canadian universities in the 1950s. He initiated the SCM Book Store in Toronto and later founded the eclectic Bob Miller

Book Room near the University of Toronto. December 11, 2003.

MOLINARI, Guido, 70. An abstract painter and art professor at Concordia University in Montreal, Molinari was renowned for his bold, colourful canvasses of geometric shapes. He became a controversial figure, both for his avant-garde style and his tendency toward aesthetic differences with other artists. February 22, 2004.

MURPHY, Nellie, 54. A Newfoundland-born woman who survived a brutal attack by her husband in 1990; shocked that she could not participate in her husband's parole hearings, she went on to champion crime victims' rights to present victim-impact statements in court and to allow them to participate in parole hearings. November 28, 2003.

MYDANS, Carl, 97. Mydans was a staff photographer for *Life* magazine from 1936-72, which coincided with *Life's* span as a weekly publication. He was especially revered for his dramatic photos of war scenes, as well as capturing images of sharecroppers during the Depression. *More Than Meets the Eye* (memoir). August 16, 2004.

NORMAN, Moe, 75. A golfer considered by many as the world's best ball striker, Norman was a two-time Canadian amateur champion, won 13 career Canadian Tour titles and seven Canadian Senior Championships, and played twice in the Masters tournament. He was noted for his unusual swing and unerring accuracy. September 4, 2004.

NEWTON, Helmut (b. Helmut Neustaedter), 83. German-born fashion photographer whose stark black-and-white images of women, often in erotic poses, drew fame and controversy. He photographed celebrities including Naomi Campbell, Paloma Picasso and Claudia Schiffer for advertising layouts and leading fashion magazines. He died when he lost control of his car in Los Angeles. *A World Without Men; Work.* January 23, 2004.

OBERMAN, Sheldon "Obie," 54. An award-winning writer of children's books, Oberman based many of his stories on memories of his boyhood in Winnipeg's Jewish community.

He also wrote songs for Fred Penner. *The Always Prayer Shawl; Island of the Minotaur.* March 26, 2004.

OFFORD, Dr. David (Dan), 71. Child psychiatrist, researcher, clinician and teacher, Offord was the founder of the Canadian Centre for Studies of Children at Risk (renamed the Offord Centre for Child Studies) in Hamilton, Ont., where students from around the world could learn how to treat children suffering from psychiatric ailments. April 10, 2004.

OKE, John Beverley, 75. Born in Sault Ste. Marie, Ont., Oke, a prominent astronomer, was a professor at the California Institute of Technology for 34 years; his early work, building an electro-spectrum spanner, led him to develop a means to analyze the light and intensity of distant stars, and to gauge their temperature. March 2, 2004.

OLIPHANT, Nancy Elizabeth (Betty), 85. English-born ballet dancer who trained dancers for the National Ballet of Canada from its inauguration in 1951, and in 1959 founded, with Celia Franca, the Toronto-based National Ballet School. Oliphant also served a stint as associate artistic director of the National Ballet of Canada. *Miss O: My Life in Dance.* July 12, 2004.

ONLEY, Tony, 75. Creator of watercolour landscapes and prints, Onley was renowned for his depictions of the British Columbia coastline and Arctic regions; although he was sometimes scorned by the avant-garde, the proceeds from his popular art enabled him to donate works to fund-raisers. Onley died when his floatplane crashed into the Fraser River; he was the sole occupant. February 29, 2004.

ORBAN, William, 81. Scientist and athlete whose 5BX (five basic exercises) fitness plan of the 1950s was a huge success and spawned the Participaction national fitness program of the 1970s. Also developed the Physical Energetics System of Equations (PESE) to assess people's potential fitness abilities. October 18, 2003.

ORRELL, John Overton, 68. An English professor specializing in Elizabethan and Jacobean literature, Orrell became the chief academic advisor for the reconstructed Globe Theatre in London, England, which was completed in 1997. *The Quest for Shakespeare's Globe; The Human Stage: English Theatre Design 1567-1640.* September 16, 2003.

PAAR, Jack Harold, 85. In 1957 replaced Steve Allen on NBC's *The Tonight Show;* during his 1957-62 term he established himself as the prototype for late-night talk shows to come. He was replaced in 1962 with Johnny Carson, and retired from TV in 1965. January 27, 2004.

POPLE, Sir John, 78. Winner, with Walter Kohn, of the 1988 Nobel Prize for chemistry. Pople was an expert in quantum chemistry and provided chemists with methods to calculate the bonding of atoms in molecules. He worked with Ottawa's National Research Council 1956-57. March 15, 2004.

PORTILLO, Jose Lopez, 83. President of Mexico 1976-82, Portillo became hugely unpopular when his government borrowed against anticipated oil revenues in the wake of the 1981 collapse of world oil prices; his tenure was marred by charges of nepotism and corruption. February 17, 2004.

POSTMAN, Neil, 72. A professor at New York University and media critic whose 1984 book, *Amusing Ourselves to Death: Public Discourse in the Age of Show Business,* took aim at television's tendency to diminish life's seriousness. His *The Disappearance of Childhood,* in 1994, explored the medium's effect on the minds of children. Founder of the NYU's Steinhardt School of Education's program in media ecology in 1971. October 5, 2003.

POULIOT, Jean, 81. Businessman and television innovator who for 20 years owned Montreal's CFCF-TV station, and later founded Quatre Saisons Television Network, whose focus audience was young, cosmopolitan viewers who preferred the network's nightly movie specials and glitzier programming to the less-compelling fare previously on offer. August 7, 2004.

RAMONE, Johnny (b. John Cummings), 55. Guitarist; co-founder of the punk rock group the Ramones, in 1974, with Joey, Dee Dee and Tommy (the last surviving member). Although the band never hit the Top 40, it epitomized and influenced the punk movement of the late '70s and '80s. "I Wanna Be Sedated"; "Blitzkrieg Bop." September 15, 2004.

RANDALL, Tony (b. Leonard Rosenberg), 84. American actor best known for his role as the fastidious Felix Unger in the television rendition of Neil Simon's *The Odd Couple*, playing opposite Jack Klugman. He also appeared on film, notably as the foil in Doris Day/Rock Hudson movies. *Pillow Talk; Lover Come Back.* May 17, 2004.

RANTISI, Dr. Abdul Aziz, 57. General leader of the Palestinian Hamas movement, assassinated by the Israeli Air Force with a helicopter-driven rocket. He succeeded Sheik Ahmed Yassin, who was assassinated by the Israelis in March 2004. April 17, 2004.

REAGAN, Ronald, 93. Reagan, the fortieth president of the US, began his career as a Hollywood movie and TV star in the 1940s and '50s, then was elected as Republican governor of California in 1966. He served two full terms as president from 1980-89, leading a conservative, anti-Communist government. His relationship with Russian president Mikhail Gorbachev led to the fall of the Berlin Wall in 1989; he also co-established the US free-trade pact with Brian Mulroney in 1988. His career was marred by the Iran-contra scandal in which top US officials were accused of selling arms to Iraq, and by an assassination attempt by John Hinkley in 1981. Died after a 10-year battle with Alzheimer's. June 5, 2004.

KUBLER-ROSS, Elisabeth, 78. A world-renowned expert on death and dying, Kubler-Ross defined the five stages of grief as denial, anger, bargaining, depression and acceptance. Author of more than 20 books, the Swiss-born Kubler-Ross moved to the US in 1958. *On Death and Dying.* August 24, 2004.

RYAN, Claude, 79. From 1978-82 the highly respected Ryan led the Quebec Liberal party and was instrumental in the Liberal victory in the 1980 Quebec referendum. He and Pierre Trudeau disagreed over the nature of Quebec federalism; Ryan insisted Quebec should retain its unique character while still being part of Canada. In earlier years, Ryan was national secretary of Action Catholique Canadienne, a layperson association that opposed domination of the clergy in the church; as publisher and editor of Montreal's *Le Devoir* from 1962-78, he was a prolific editorial and feature writer. February 9, 2004.

SANFORD, Isabel, 86. Sanford played the role of Louise Jefferson in the sitcom *All in the Family,* starting in 1971, and starred in the spin-off, *The Jeffersons,* until 1985. The first black woman to win an Emmy for a comedy series, Sanford also portrayed the disapproving maid in the film *Guess Who's Coming to Dinner.* July 9, 2004.

SCAVULLO, Francesco, 82. American fashion photographer famous for his images of celebrities. Noted for his provocative *Cosmopolitan* magazine covers, he also shot covers for *People, Newsweek, Rolling Stone* and *Vogue. Scavullo on Beauty.* January 6, 2004.

SCOTT, Archbishop Edward (Ted), 85. The Anglican Church of Canada primate 1971-86, Scott led a controversial career, speaking out publicly in support of same-sex marriage, women's ordination, the continued abolition of capital punishment, as well as social responsibility among corporations and governments. He was moderator of the World Council of Churches from 1975-83. Died as a result of a motor vehicle accident. June 21, 2004.

SEVIGNY, Joseph Pierre Albert, 87. An associate minister of defense in the Pearson government in the 1960s, Sevigny was accused by the John Diefenbaker-led PCs in 1966 of having an affair with a supposed German spy, Gerda Munsinger, although investigations led to the fact she was a prostitute. Sevigny's political life was ruined, but he went on to teach finance at Montreal's Concordia University. March 20, 2004.

SHARP, Mitchell William, 92. Sharp entered politics in 1963 when he became minister of trade and commerce under the Pearson

Liberal government; he later was minister of finance, secretary for external affairs, president of the Privy Council and government house leader 1963-76, under both Pearson and Pierre Trudeau. During his tenure in external affairs he supported Pearson's dismissal of French President Charles de Gaulle after his famous 1967 "vive le Québec libre" speech; he also supported Canada's recognition of China. From 1993-2000 he served as Jean Chrétien's key advisor for $1 a year; Sharp was also an accomplished pianist and played with the Toronto Symphony in 1973. March 19, 2004.

SHOEMAKER, Bill, 72. American jockey whose 8,883 Thoroughbred wins during his 40-year career were surpassed only by Laffit Pincay; in 1986, at 54, he became the oldest jockey to win the Kentucky Derby. He also rode the Canadian champion horse, Northern Dancer. Shoemaker was paralyzed in a car accident in 1991, but continued to train horses from his wheelchair. October 12, 2003.

SHULMAN, Milton, 90. Toronto-born longstanding drama critic for Britain's *Evening Standard* (1953-91) and *Daily Express* (1948-58). An outspoken critic who once gave away the culprit in an Agatha Christie whodunit to force the closure of the play, Shulman was also a novelist, non-fiction and children's book writer. *Marilyn, Hitler and Me* (memoir). May 21, 2004.

SMITH, Sid James, 78. One-time captain of the Toronto Maple Leafs, Smith saw his team win three Stanley Cups and was a two-time winner of the Lady Byng Trophy. For eight seasons, he was the Leafs' top scorer, and at his retirement was only fourth after Gordie Howe, Rocket Richard and Ted Lindsay. April 29, 2004.

SNODGRASS, Carrie, 57. Blond, sultry-voiced actress best known for her role in the film *Diary of a Mad Housewife*, Snodgrass was once a partner of Canadian pop singer Neil Young, with whom she had a son. She appeared extensively on television and film. *Pale Rider; Murphy's Law; Blue Sky*. April 1, 2004.

SNYDER, Dan, 25. A forward with the NHL's Atlanta Thrashers, Snyder died in a car crash when the driver, fellow Thrasher Dany Heatley, lost control of his Ferrari, in Atlanta, Georgia. October 5, 2003.

STANFIELD, Robert Lorne, 89. Stanfield was premier of Nova Scotia 1956-67, then became federal PC leader, succeeding John Diefenbaker, and remained in office until Joe Clark replaced him in 1976. During his tenure as NS premier he was credited with his innovations in health and education, but despite the respect he earned from his peers for his intelligence and excellent management qualities, his federal career was stymied by the emergence of Pierre Trudeau, whose charismatic style overshadowed Stanfield's staid political persona. December 16, 2003.

STEWART, Walter Douglas, 73. An irascible newspaperman, Stewart had a blunt, no-nonsense approach. He began his career with the *Toronto Telegram,* worked with *Maclean's* magazine from 1968 to 1977, eventually becoming managing editor. Stewart also appeared as a host on CBC Radio's *As It Happens.* Author of several books: *Shrug: Trudeau in Power; But Not in Canada; Towers of Gold, Feet of Clay: the Canadian Banks; The Golden Fleece: Why the Stock Market Costs You Money; Right Church: Wrong Pew* (a thriller). September 15, 2004.

SUTHERLAND, Paul, 73. Creator of the children's series *Tales of the Riverbank,* which introduced the character Hammy the Hamster, as well as other live animal characters; he originally sold the hugely popular series to the BBC, and it aired on CBC beginning 1963. May 15, 2004.

TAYLOR, Nathan (Nat) Aaron, 98. Film industry veteran who invented (and coined the term) the cineplex theatre. He began modestly in 1957 with the two-theatre Elgin in Ottawa, and by 1973 had opened, with partner Garth Drabinsky, the 18-theatre complex in Toronto's Eaton Centre, which led to the partners' founding of the Odeon-Cineplex cinema chain. He produced several Canadian movies and was founder of the International art-house cinema in Toronto in the 1940s. March 1, 2004.

THULIN, Ingrid, 77. Considered one of Sweden's greatest actresses, Thulin starred in several Ingmar Bergman films, including *Wild Strawberries, The Brink of Life* and *Cries and Whispers.* January 7, 2004.

TURGEON, Serge, 58. A Québécois TV and stage actor, and radio and television journalist, Turgeon was also instrumental in obtaining pensions for self-employed actors while leader of the Union des Artistes; he was a fervent supporter of the use of Québécois voices in the dubbing of English-language films. *Rue des pignons.* May 18, 2004.

USTINOV, Sir Peter, 82. British-born actor whose larger-than-life persona endeared him to audiences throughout his career. An actor, playwright, director and novelist, he appeared extensively on film (*Spartacus, Topkapi, Quo Vadis, Billy Budd,* among them) and in 1979 played Ontario's Stratford Festival. For 35 years Ustinov was a goodwill ambassador for UNICEF. March 28, 2004.

WADDINGTON, Miriam, 86. Leading Canadian poet, authored collections including *The Price of Gold, Green World, The Visitants* and *The Last Landscape.* Lines from Waddington's "Jacques Cartier in Toronto" appear on Canada's new $100 bill, issued in March 2004. March 3, 2004.

WADE, Michael, 59. An actor, playwright and singer, Wade was founder, in 1984, of the Newfoundland Shakespeare Company; he appeared in film and television productions, including *The Boys of St. Vincent, Gullage's* and *John and the Missus.* Among his plays: *The Fig Tree* and *Last Dance at the Avalon* (musical). May 22, 2004.

WELLS, Daryl Frederick, 81. From 1956-86, Wells was a commentator of Thoroughbred racing, announcing from the Ontario Jockey Club; he was famous for his colourful delivery and the excitement he brought to his broadcasting. December 12, 2003.

WILLIS, Austin, 86. Actor best known as host of the 1970s CBC TV show *This Is the Law;* earlier in his career, he appeared on stage in London's West End, on Broadway and in Canadian theatre. His film credits include *The Mouse that Roared* with Peter Sellers and the James Bond film, *Goldfinger.* April 4, 2004.

WINFIELD, Paul, 63. American actor who appeared opposite Diahann Carroll in the television series *Julia.* He also starred in miniseries including *King,* in which he portrayed Martin Luther King Jr.; *Roots: The Next Generation;* and *Scarlett.* He was host of A&E's *City Confidential* at the time of his death. March 7, 2004.

WINSTON, Helene, 81. Actress best known for her role as Gladys Knight, the mother of Al Waxman's character in the CBC's 1970s hit series *The King of Kensington.* Winston also performed at Ontario's Stratford Festival, on Broadway and in Los Angeles. Her television credits include *The Mary Tyler Moore Show* and *Sanford and Son,* and she also published poetry: *From Sleeping Libido to Geriatric Erotica.* March 23, 2004.

WRAY, (Vina) Fay, 96. The Alberta-born actress Fay Wray is best known for her signature movie, the 1933 thriller *King Kong,* whose pioneering special effects were epitomized by the giant gorilla carrying a screaming Wray to the top of the Empire State Building. From 1925-58 she made 77 movies and later appeared in *The Pride of the Family,* a fifties sitcom. *The Vampire Bat; Thunderbolt; The Wedding March.* August 8, 2004.

YASSIN, Sheik Ahmed, 67. Founder and spiritual leader of the Palestinian Islam Hamas movement, Yassin, nearly blind and a quadraplegic, was assassinated by an Israeli missile, allegedly on the orders of Israeli prime minister Ariel Sharon, while leaving a mosque at dawn. Yassin was imprisoned by the Israelis for many years until his release in 1994. March 22, 2004.

ZINK, Lubor, 83. Controversial, outspoken critic of socialism and an expert on East European history, the Czech-born Zink was a columnist from 1961-93, first for the *Toronto Telegram* and later the *Toronto Sun.* He began his newspaper career as editor of the *Brandon Sun.* November 3, 2003.

Index

H

NOTES

CALENDARS AND HOLIDAYS

2005

JANUARY
S	M	T	W	T	F	S
						1
2	3	4	5	6	7	8
9	10	11	12	13	14	15
16	17	18	19	20	21	22
23	24	25	26	27	28	29
30	31					

FEBRUARY
S	M	T	W	T	F	S
		1	2	3	4	5
6	7	8	9	10	11	12
13	14	15	16	17	18	19
20	21	22	23	24	25	26
27	28					

MARCH
S	M	T	W	T	F	S
		1	2	3	4	5
6	7	8	9	10	11	12
13	14	15	16	17	18	19
20	21	22	23	24	25	26
27	28	29	30	31		

APRIL
S	M	T	W	T	F	S
					1	2
3	4	5	6	7	8	9
10	11	12	13	14	15	16
17	18	19	20	21	22	23
24	25	26	27	28	29	30

MAY
S	M	T	W	T	F	S
1	2	3	4	5	6	7
8	9	10	11	12	13	14
15	16	17	18	19	20	21
22	23	24	25	26	27	28
29	30	31				

JUNE
S	M	T	W	T	F	S
			1	2	3	4
5	6	7	8	9	10	11
12	13	14	15	16	17	18
19	20	21	22	23	24	25
26	27	28	29	30		

JULY
S	M	T	W	T	F	S
					1	2
3	4	5	6	7	8	9
10	11	12	13	14	15	16
17	18	19	20	21	22	23
24	25	26	27	28	29	30
31						

AUGUST
S	M	T	W	T	F	S
	1	2	3	4	5	6
7	8	9	10	11	12	13
14	15	16	17	18	19	20
21	22	23	24	25	26	27
28	29	30	31			

SEPTEMBER
S	M	T	W	T	F	S
				1	2	3
4	5	6	7	8	9	10
11	12	13	14	15	16	17
18	19	20	21	22	23	24
25	26	27	28	29	30	

OCTOBER
S	M	T	W	T	F	S
						1
2	3	4	5	6	7	8
9	10	11	12	13	14	15
16	17	18	19	20	21	22
23	24	25	26	27	28	29
30	31					

NOVEMBER
S	M	T	W	T	F	S
		1	2	3	4	5
6	7	8	9	10	11	12
13	14	15	16	17	18	19
20	21	22	23	24	25	26
27	28	29	30			

DECEMBER
S	M	T	W	T	F	S
				1	2	3
4	5	6	7	8	9	10
11	12	13	14	15	16	17
18	19	20	21	22	23	24
25	26	27	28	29	30	31

Holidays and Holy Days, 2005

Chinese New Year: Feb. 9
Christian Holy Days: New Year's Day: Jan. 1; Good Friday: Mar. 25; Easter Sunday: Mar. 27; Christmas Day: Dec. 25
Islamic Holy Days: These are subject to the sighting of the moon. The key days are: Nuzulul Qur'an; Eidul Fitri; Eidul Adha; Islamic New Year; Ashoora; Maulid Nabi; Isra'and Miraj; First Day of Ramadhan.
Jewish Holy Days: (all begin at sundown on the evening before the date given): Purim: Mar. 25; Passover: Apr. 24; Shavuot: June 13; Rosh Hashanah: Oct. 4; Yom Kippur: Oct. 13; Sukkot: Oct. 18; Hanukkah: Dec. 26.
Government, bank and other holidays: New Year's Day: January 1; Good Friday: Mar. 25; Easter Monday: Mar. 28; Victoria Day: May 23; Canada Day: July 1; Civic Holiday: Aug. 1; Labour Day: Sept. 5; Thanksgiving: Oct. 10; Remembrance Day: Nov. 11; Boxing Day: Dec. 26

2004

JANUARY

S	M	T	W	T	F	S
				1	2	3
4	5	6	7	8	9	10
11	12	13	14	15	16	17
18	19	20	21	22	23	24
25	26	27	28	29	30	31

FEBRUARY

S	M	T	W	T	F	S
1	2	3	4	5	6	7
8	9	10	11	12	13	14
15	16	17	18	19	20	21
22	23	24	25	26	27	28
29						

MARCH

S	M	T	W	T	F	S
	1	2	3	4	5	6
7	8	9	10	11	12	13
14	15	16	17	18	19	20
21	22	23	24	25	26	27
28	29	30	31			

APRIL

S	M	T	W	T	F	S
				1	2	3
4	5	6	7	8	9	10
11	12	13	14	15	16	17
18	19	20	21	22	23	24
25	26	27	28	29	30	

MAY

S	M	T	W	T	F	S
						1
2	3	4	5	6	7	8
9	10	11	12	13	14	15
16	17	18	19	20	21	22
23	24	25	26	27	28	29
30	31					

JUNE

S	M	T	W	T	F	S
		1	2	3	4	5
6	7	8	9	10	11	12
13	14	15	16	17	18	19
20	21	22	23	24	25	26
27	28	29	30			

JULY

S	M	T	W	T	F	S
				1	2	3
4	5	6	7	8	9	10
11	12	13	14	15	16	17
18	19	20	21	22	23	24
25	26	27	28	29	30	31

AUGUST

S	M	T	W	T	F	S
1	2	3	4	5	6	7
8	9	10	11	12	13	14
15	16	17	18	19	20	21
22	23	24	25	26	27	28
29	30	31				

SEPTEMBER

S	M	T	W	T	F	S
			1	2	3	4
5	6	7	8	9	10	11
12	13	14	15	16	17	18
19	20	21	22	23	24	25
26	27	28	29	30		

OCTOBER

S	M	T	W	T	F	S
					1	2
3	4	5	6	7	8	9
10	11	12	13	14	15	16
17	18	19	20	21	22	23
24	25	26	27	28	29	30
31						

NOVEMBER

S	M	T	W	T	F	S
	1	2	3	4	5	6
7	8	9	10	11	12	13
14	15	16	17	18	19	20
21	22	23	24	25	26	27
28	29	30				

DECEMBER

S	M	T	W	T	F	S
			1	2	3	4
5	6	7	8	9	10	11
12	13	14	15	16	17	18
19	20	21	22	23	24	25
26	27	28	29	30	31	

2006

JANUARY

S	M	T	W	T	F	S
1	2	3	4	5	6	7
8	9	10	11	12	13	14
15	16	17	18	19	20	21
22	23	24	25	26	27	28
29	30	31				

FEBRUARY

S	M	T	W	T	F	S
			1	2	3	4
5	6	7	8	9	10	11
12	13	14	15	16	17	18
19	20	21	22	23	24	25
26	27	28				

MARCH

S	M	T	W	T	F	S
			1	2	3	4
5	6	7	8	9	10	11
12	13	14	15	16	17	18
19	20	21	22	23	24	25
26	27	28	29	30	31	

APRIL

S	M	T	W	T	F	S
						1
2	3	4	5	6	7	8
9	10	11	12	13	14	15
16	17	18	19	20	21	22
23	24	25	26	27	28	29
30						

MAY

S	M	T	W	T	F	S
	1	2	3	4	5	6
7	8	9	10	11	12	13
14	15	16	17	18	19	20
21	22	23	24	25	26	27
28	29	30	31			

JUNE

S	M	T	W	T	F	S
				1	2	3
4	5	6	7	8	9	10
11	12	13	14	15	16	17
18	19	20	21	22	23	24
25	26	27	28	29	30	

JULY

S	M	T	W	T	F	S
						1
2	3	4	5	6	7	8
9	10	11	12	13	14	15
16	17	18	19	20	21	22
23	24	25	26	27	28	29
30	31					

AUGUST

S	M	T	W	T	F	S
		1	2	3	4	5
6	7	8	9	10	11	12
13	14	15	16	17	18	19
20	21	22	23	24	25	26
27	28	29	30	31		

SEPTEMBER

S	M	T	W	T	F	S
					1	2
3	4	5	6	7	8	9
10	11	12	13	14	15	16
17	18	19	20	21	22	23
24	25	26	27	28	29	30

OCTOBER

S	M	T	W	T	F	S
1	2	3	4	5	6	7
8	9	10	11	12	13	14
15	16	17	18	19	20	21
22	23	24	25	26	27	28
29	30	31				

NOVEMBER

S	M	T	W	T	F	S
			1	2	3	4
5	6	7	8	9	10	11
12	13	14	15	16	17	18
19	20	21	22	23	24	25
26	27	28	29	30		

DECEMBER

S	M	T	W	T	F	S
					1	2
3	4	5	6	7	8	9
10	11	12	13	14	15	16
17	18	19	20	21	22	23
24	25	26	27	28	29	30
31						